JAMES H.
Pickering

University of Houston

JEFFREY D.
Hoeper

Arkansas State University

Macmillan Publishing Co., Inc.
New York
Collier Macmillan Publishers
London

Macmillan Publishing Co., Inc.
866 Third Avenue, New York, New York 10022

Collier Macmillan Canada, Ltd.

Library of Congress Cataloging in Publication Data
Main entry under title:

Literature.

Includes index.
1. Literature—Collections.   I. Pickering,
James H.   II. Hoeper, Jeffrey D.
PN6014.L558   808'.0427   81-5990
ISBN 0-02-395430-2   AACR2

Printing: 2 3 4 5 6 7 8   Year: 2 3 4 5 6 7 8

ACKNOWLEDGMENTS

House of Anansi Press Limited. MARGARET ATWOOD, "The Settlers," copyright © Margaret Atwood 1966, from *The Circle Game* (Toronto, House of Anansi Press).

April-Blackwood Music, Inc. JAMES TAYLOR, "Fire and Rain." Copyright © 1969, 1970 by Blackwood Music, Inc. and Country Road Music, Inc. Used by permission. All rights reserved.

Atheneum Publishers, Inc. ANTHONY HECHT, "More Light! More Light!" from *The Hard House*. Copyright © 1961 by Anthony Hecht. Reprinted by permission of Atheneum Publishers, Inc. James Merrill, "Urban Convalescence" from *Water Street: Poems by James Merrill*. Copyright © 1960 by James Merrill. Reprinted by permission of Atheneum Publishers, Inc. W. S. MERWIN, "Leviathan" from *Green With Beasts* (copyright 1955, 1956 by W. S. Merwin) in *The First Four Books of Poems*. Copyright © 1975 by W. S. Merwin. Reprinted by permission of Atheneum Publishers, Inc.

ATV Music Corp. JOHN LENNON and PAUL MCCARTNEY, "Eleanor Rigby." Copyright © 1966 by Northern Songs Ltd. All rights for the U.S.A., Mexico and the Philippines controlled by Maclen Music, Inc., c/o ATV Music Corp. Used by permission. All rights reserved.

Margaret Avison. MARGARET AVISON, "September Street" from *Winter Sun* by Margaret Avison (Toronto: University of Toronto Press, 1960). Reprinted by permission of the author.

The Bodley Head. GUY DE MAUPASSANT, "The Necklace" from *Boule de Suif and Other Short Stories* by Guy de Maupassant, translated by Marjorie Laurie. Reprinted by permission of The Bodley Head.

Jonathan Clowes Ltd. ARTHUR CONAN DOYLE, "The Adventure of the Speckled Band." Reprinted by permission of Jonathan Clowes Ltd.

Combine Music Corporation. KRIS KRISTOFFERSON, "Me and Bobby McGee" from *The Songs of Kris Kristofferson* by Kristofferson and Foster. Lyrics of "Me and Bobby McGee" by Kris Kristofferson. Reprinted by permission of Combine Music Corporation. All rights reserved.

Continental Total Media Project, Inc. LEONARD COHEN, "Suzanne." Words by Leonard Cohen. Reprinted by permission of Continental Total Media Project, Inc. All rights reserved.

Curtis Brown Ltd. DORIS LESSING, "Wine" from *The Habit of Loving* by Doris Lessing. Copyright © 1957 by Doris Lessing. Reprinted by permission of Curtis Brown Ltd. ROBERT GRAVES, "The Naked and the Nude" from *5 Pens in Hand* by Robert Graves (New York: Doubleday & Company, Inc., 1958). Reprinted by permission of Curtis Brown Ltd.

Jonathan Cape Ltd. HENRY REED, "Naming of Parts" from *A Map of Verona* by Henry Reed. Reprinted by permission of the author.

Chappell Music Company. TOM JONES and HARVEY SCHMIDT, "Try to Remember." Copyright © 1960 by Tom Jones and Harvey Schmidt. Chappell & Co., Inc., owner of publication and allied rights throughout the world. International copyright secured. All rights reserved. Used by permission.

Corinth Books. IMAMU AMIRI BARAKA (LeRoi Jones), "For Hettie." Copyright by Corinth Books. Reprinted by permission of Corinth Books.

Dodd, Mead & Company, Inc. GEORGE BERNARD SHAW, *Mrs. Warren's Profession* by Bernard Shaw. Copyright 1898, 1913, 1926, 1930, 1933, 1941, George Bernard Shaw. Copyright 1905, Brentano's. Copyright 1957, The Public Trustee as Executor of the Estate of George Bernard Shaw. © 1970, The Trustees of the British Museum, The Governors and Guardians of the National Gallery of Ireland and Royal Academy of Dramatic Art. Reprinted by permission of Dodd, Mead & Company, Inc. and The Society of Authors for the Estate of George Bernard Shaw.

Doubleday & Company, Inc. JOSEPH CONRAD, "Heart of Darkness" from *Youth*. Canadian rights to reprint "Heart of Darkness" from *Youth* by Joseph Conrad by permission of Withers, London, and the Trustees of the Joseph Conrad Estate. JOHN BARTH, "Lost in the Funhouse" from *Lost in the Funhouse*. Copyright © 1967 by John Barth. Reprinted by permission of Doubleday & Company, Inc. RUDYARD KIPLING, "Recessional," "Mandalay," and "Gunga Din" from *Rudyard Kipling's Verse: Definitive Edition*. Reprinted by permission of Doubleday & Company, Inc. and The National Trust (Great Britain). THEODORE ROETHKE, "Dolor," copyright 1943 by Modern Poetry Association, Inc.; "The Waking," copyright 1948 by Theodore Roethke; "Elegy for Jane: My Student, Thrown by a Horse," copyright 1950 by Theodore Roethke; and "I Knew a Woman," copyright 1954 by Theodore Roethke, all from *The Collected Poems of Theodore Roethke*. Reprinted by permission of Doubleday & Company, Inc.

Farrar, Straus & Giroux, Inc. SHIRLEY JACKSON, "The Lottery" from *The Lottery* by Shirley Jackson. Copyright 1948, 1949 by Shirley Jackson. Copyright renewed © 1976, 1977 by Lawrence Hyman, Barry Hyman, Mrs. Sarah Webster and Mrs. Joanne Schnurer. "The Lottery" originally appeared in *The New Yorker*. Reprinted by permission of Farrar, Straus & Giroux, Inc. BERNARD

Gentle Into That Good Night." Copyright 1939, 1946 by New Directions Publishing Corporation. Copyright 1952 by Dylan Thomas. Canadian rights to reprint these four poems by Dylan Thomas by permission of J. M. Dent & Sons, Ltd., London. DENISE LEVERTOV, "At the Edge" from *Collected Earlier Poems 1940–1960* by Denise Levertov. Copyright © 1959 by Denise Levertov. Reprinted by permission of New Directions. GARY SNYDER, "A Walk" and "Looking at Pictures to Be Put Away" from *The Back Country* by Gary Snyder. Copyright © 1960, 1968 by Gary Snyder. Reprinted by permission of New Directions.

W. W. Norton & Company, Inc. ADRIENNE RICH, "Storm Warnings," "Living in Sin," and "The Knight" all from *Poems, Selected and New* by Adrienne Rich. Copyright © 1975, 1973, 1971, 1969, 1966 by W. W. Norton & Company, Inc. Copyright © 1967, 1963, 1962, 1961, 1960, 1959, 1958, 1957, 1956, 1955, 1954, 1953, 1952, 1951 by Adrienne Rich. Reprinted with permission of W. W. Norton & Company, Inc. Harold Ober Associates. SHERWOOD ANDERSON, "I Want to Know Why" from *The Triumph of the Egg* by Sherwood Anderson, published by B. W. Huebsch. Reprinted by permission of Harold Ober Associates. LANGSTON HUGHES, "Theme for English B" from *Montage of a Dream Deferred* by Langston Hughes, published 1951 by Henry Holt & Co. Copyright 1951 by Langston Hughes, renewed. Reprinted by permission of Harold Ober Associates.

Oxford University Press. LEO TOLSTOY, "The Death of Ivan Ilych" from *Ivan Ilych, Hadj Murad and Other Stories* by Leo Tolstoy, translated from the Russian by Louise and Aylmer Maude (1935) and published by Oxford University Press, London. GERARD MANLEY HOPKINS, four poems from *The Poems of Gerard Manley Hopkins*, 4th ed. (1967): "Pied Beauty," "The Windhover," "Spring and Fall," and "Thou art indeed just, Lord." All five poems from *The Poems of Gerard Manley Hopkins*, 4th Edition (1967) published by Oxford University Press. RICHARD EBERHART, "The Groundhog" from *Collected Poems 1930–1976* by Richard Eberhart. Copyright © 1976 by Richard Eberhart. Reprinted by permission of Oxford University Press, Inc. Canadian rights to reprint "The Groundhog" by Richard Eberhart by permission of the author and Chatto & Windus, Ltd.

The Putnam Publishing Group. JEAN ANOUILH, *Becket or the Honor of God,* translated by Lucienne Hill. Copyright © 1960 by Jean Anouilh and Lucienne Hill. Reprinted by permission of Coward, McCann and Geohegan, Inc. from *Becket or the Honor of God* by Jean Anouilh. Canadian rights to reprint *Becket or the Honor of God* by Jean Anouilh, translated by Lucienne Hill, by permission of Jan Van Loewen, London.

Random House, Inc. KATHERINE MANSFIELD, "The Fly" from *The Short Stories of Katherine Mansfield* by Katherine Mansfield. Reprinted by permission of Alfred A. Knopf, Inc. WILLIAM FAULKNER, "A Rose for Emily" from *Collected Stories of William Faulkner* by William Faulkner. Reprinted by permission of Random House. Canadian rights to reprint "A Rose for Emily" by William Faulkner by permission of Chatto & Windus Ltd., London. ALBERT CAMUS, "The Guest" from *Exile and the Kingdom* by Albert Camus, translated by Justin O'Brien. Canadian rights to reprint "The Guest" by Albert Camus by permission of Hamish Hamilton Ltd., London. JOHN UPDIKE, "A&P" from *Pigeon Feathers and Other Stories* by John Updike. Reprinted by permission of Alfred A. Knopf. Canadian rights to reprint "A&P" by John Updike by permission of Andre Deutsch Ltd., London. WALLACE STEVENS, five poems from *The Collected Poems of Wallace Stevens*, "Disillusionment of Ten O'Clock," "Peter Quince at the Clavier," "Anecdote of the Jar," "The Snow Man," and "The Emperor of Ice Cream." Reprinted by permission of Alfred A. Knopf. ROBINSON JEFFERS, "Fawn's Foster-Mother" and "Hurt Hawks" both from *The Selected Poetry of Robinson Jeffers.* Copyright 1928, renewed 1956. Reprinted by permission of Random House. JOHN CROWE RANSOM, four poems from *Selected Poems*, Third Edition, Revised and Enlarged: "Bells for John Whiteside's Daughter," copyright 1924 by Alfred A. Knopf, renewed 1952 by John Crowe Ransom; "Winter Remembered" and "Piazza Piece," both copyright 1927 by Alfred A. Knopf, renewed 1955 by John Crowe Ransom; "Two in August." All four poems by John Crowe Ransom reprinted by permission of Alfred A. Knopf. LANGSTON HUGHES, "The Negro Speaks of Rivers" and "Dream Variation" from *Selected Poems of Langston Hughes.* Copyright 1926, renewed 1954 by Langston Hughes. Reprinted by permission of Alfred A. Knopf. "Soledad" from *The Weary Blues* by Langston Hughes. Copyright 1926, renewed 1954 by Langston Hughes. Reprinted by permission of Alfred A. Knopf. W. H. AUDEN, "Look Stranger," "Musee des Beaux Arts," "Lay your sleeping head, my love," and "The Unknown Citizen," all from *W. H. Auden: Collected Poems* by W. H. Auden, edited by Edward Mendelson. Reprinted by permission of Random House. Canadian rights to reprint these four poems by W. H. Auden by permission of Faber and Faber, London. STEPHEN SPENDER, "An Elementary Classroom in a Slum" from *Collected Poems 1928–1953* by Stephen Spender, compiled by Miriam Waddington. Reprinted by permission of Random House. Canadian rights to reprint "An Elementary Classroom in a Slum" by Stephen Spender by permission of Faber and Faber, London. KARL SHAPIRO, "Drug Store" copyright 1941, renewed 1969 by Karl Shapiro, and "Auto Wreck" copyright 1942, renewed 1970 by Karl Shapiro, both reprinted from Poems 1940–1953 by Karl Shapiro by permission of Random House. W. D. SNODGRASS, "April Inventory" from *Heart's Needle* by W. D. Snodgrass. Reprinted by permission of Alfred A. Knopf. EUGENE O'NEILL, "Desire Under the Elms" from *The Plays of Eugene O'Neill.* Copyright 1924, renewed 1952 by Eugene O'Neill. Reprinted by permission of Random House.

Schocken Books. FRANZ KAFKA, "A Hunger Artist" from *The Penal Colony* by Franz Kafka. Copyright © 1948, renewed © 1975 by Schocken Books Inc. Reprinted by permission of Schocken Books, Inc.

Charles Scribner's Sons, a Division of The Scribner Book Companies, Inc. ERNEST HEMINGWAY, "Hills Like White Elephants" from *The Short Stories of Ernest Hemingway* by Ernest Hemingway. Copyright 1938 by Ernest Hemingway; renewal copyright © 1966 by Mary Hemingway. Reprinted by permission of Charles Scribner's Sons. EDWIN ARLINGTON ROBINSON, "Richard Cory" and "Reuben bright" both from *The Children of the Night* by Edwin Arlington Robinson. Copyright 1897 by Charles Scribner's Sons.

Shanks, Davis & Remer (Law Offices). JUDY COLLINS, "My Father." Words and music by Judy Collins. Copyright © 1968 by Rocky Mountain National Park Music Co., Inc. Reprinted by permission. All rights reserved.

Silkie Music Publishers. RICHARD FARINA, "Birmingham Sunday." Words and music by Richard Farina. Copyright © 1964 (unpub.), 1972, 1979 by Silkie Music Publishers, a Division of Vanguard Recording Society, Inc. Used by permission. All rights reserved.

Paul Simon. PAUL SIMON, "Dangling Conversation." Copyright © 1966 by Paul Simon. Used by permission.

Siquomb Publishing Corp. JONI MITCHELL, "Both Sides Now." Words and music by Joni Mitchell. Copyright © 1967 Siquomb Publishing Corp. Used by permission. All rights reserved.

Society of Authors, London. WALTER DE LA MARE, "The Listeners." Reprinted by permission of The Society of Authors and the Literary Trustees of Walter de la Mare.

The Vanguard Press. JOYCE CAROL OATES, "In the Region of Ice" from *The Wheel of Love* by Joyce Carol Oates. Reprinted by permission of The Vanguard Press.

Viking Penguin, Inc. JAMES JOYCE, "Araby" from *Dubliners* by James Joyce. Copyright © 1967 by the Estate of James Joyce. Reprinted by permission of Viking Penguin Inc. D. H. LAWRENCE, "The Rocking-Horse Winner" from *The Complete Short Stories of D. H. Lawrence*, Vol. III. Copyright 1934 by Frieda Lawrence, copyright © renewed 1962 by Angelo Ravagli and C. M. Weekley, Executors of the Estate of Frieda Lawrence Ravagli. Reprinted by permission of Viking Penguin Inc. "Gloire de Dijon" and "A Youth Mowing" from *The Complete Poems of D. H. Lawrence* by D. H. Lawrence. Copyright © 1964, 1971 by Angelo Ravagli and C. M. Weekley, Executors of the Estate of Frieda Lawrence Ravagli. Reprinted by permission of Viking Penguin Inc.

Diane Wakoski. DIANE WAKOSKI, "I Lay Next to You All Night, Trying, Awake, to Understand the Watering Places of the Moon" from *Motorcycle Betrayal Poems* by Diane Wakoski. Reprinted by permission of the author.

Warner Brothers Music, Inc. GORDON LIGHTFOOT, "Early Morning Rain." Copyright © 1964 by Warner Brothers, Inc. All rights reserved. Used by permission. BOB DYLAN, "Mr. Tambourine Man." Lyrics by Bob Dylan. All rights reserved. Used by permission.

A. Watkins, Inc. KAY BOYLE, "Astronomer's Wife" from *The White Horses of Vienna and Other Stories* by Kay Boyle. Reprinted by permission of A. Watkins, Inc.

A. P. Watt Ltd., ROBERT GRAVES, "Friday Night" from *Collected Poems* by Robert Graves. Reprinted by permission of A. P. Watt Ltd.

Wesleyan University Press. JAMES DICKEY, "A Dog Sleeping on My Feet" from *James Dickey: Poems 1957–1967.* Copyright © 1962 by James Dickey. Reprinted from *James Dickey: Poems 1957–1967* by permission of Wesleyan University Press. "A Dog Sleeping on My Feet" first appeared in *Poetry.* LOUIS SIMPSON, "Summer Storm" from *A Dream of Governors* by Louis Simpson. Copyright © 1949 by Louis Simpson. Reprinted from *A Dream of Governors* by permission of Wesleyan University Press. "American Poetry" and "On the Lawn at the Villa" from *At the End of the Open Road* by Louis Simpson. Copyright © 1963 by Louis Simpson. Reprinted from *At the End of the Open Road* by permission of Wesleyan University Press. JAMES WRIGHT, "A Blessing" copyright © 1961 by James Wright. Reprinted from *The Branch Will Not Break* by permission of Wesleyan University Press. "A Blessing" first appeared in *Poetry.*

PREFACE

Literature is a comprehensive text-anthology of fiction, poetry, and drama designed to introduce students to the formal study of literature within a flexible format that allows for a wide variety of course structures. Each of *Literature's* three sections is prefaced by a discussion of the basic elements that go into the making of a story, a poem, or a play, and the way in which such elements relate to each other and to the work as a whole. The intention is to provide both a method of literary analysis and a useful critical vocabulary that can be transferred from one text to another. Rightly pursued, such an approach will encourage students to sharpen and clarify their responses to literature and equip them to articulate those responses.

The literary texts themselves—40 stories, 362 poems, and 11 plays—have been selected on the basis of their representativeness, their historical importance, and their literary merit. Though the selections within each section are arranged chronologically, the instructor is, of course, free to incorporate them into his or her own syllabus as preferences and circumstances dictate. We have also provided a glossary of literary terms to acquaint students with the meaning of terms used most frequently in literary criticism. The page numbers following the terms in the glossary refer the reader to pertinent discussion in the text.

Houston, Texas December, 1980
Jonesboro, Arkansas

JAMES H. PICKERING
JEFFREY D. HOEPER

CONTENTS

�✷✷✷✷

I   FICTION

3 Stories   68

II POETRY

III DRAMA

INTRODUCTION

❧❧❧❧❧❧❧❧

Reading and Studying Literature

Our impulse to read literature is a universal one, answering a number of psychological needs that all of us, in certain moods and on certain occasions, share. Such needs, to be sure, vary greatly from individual to individual, for they are, in turn, the products of our separate tastes, experiences, and educations. They also vary *within* each of us; they shift and alter as we change and grow. Certain books that are "right" for us at one stage of life seem "wrong" or irrelevant later on. *The Wizard of Oz* and *Treasure Island* thrill us as children. While we may and do reread these classics in adulthood and find new pleasure in them, we are likely to find the quality of the experience quite different from the one remembered. Our reading tastes will also vary from one day to the next, depending upon our current moods and intellectual and aesthetic needs. More than one professor of English, for example, has been known to teach Shakespeare or Melville by day, only to turn in the evening to the latest spy novel by John Le Carré. There is nothing particularly unusual in such a contrast for one may have many purposes in reading. Four of these purposes come at once to mind.

WHY WE READ

Reading for Escape

All of the works already mentioned—*The Wizard of Oz, Treasure Island*, the plays of William Shakespeare, and the novels and short stories of Herman Melville—offer exciting narratives that can be read uncritically simply because they allow us to escape the problems and responsibilities of our everyday lives and to participate, however briefly, in a world of experience that differs radically from our own. The average student is most likely to think of vicarious reading

1

in terms of the spy or detective story or the science fiction or historical novel—any kind of fiction that is read for the fun of it. But many works of literature, classics as well as pulps, survive precisely because they succeed in temporarily detaching us from time and place and transporting us to some imaginary world that we otherwise would never know. Although some people tend to regard such a motive as adolescent or even anti-intellectual, the fact remains that literature flourishes, in part at least, because of the escape it affords our imaginations.

Reading to Learn

Literature offers the reader "knowledge" in the form of information. Part of our interest in works as different as Joseph Conrad's "Heart of Darkness," Geoffrey Chaucer's "The Miller's Tale," or Anton Chekhov's *The Cherry Orchard* lies in the fact that in reading them we gain a good deal of information about colonial Africa, medieval England, or Czarist Russia—information that is all the more fascinating because it is part of the author's re-created world. Literature read in this way serves as a social document, giving us insight into the laws, customs, institutions, attitudes, and values of the time and place in which it was written or in which it is set.

When you think about it, there is scarcely a story, a poem, a play we read that doesn't offer us some new piece of information that broadens our knowledge of the world. Not all of this "knowledge" is particularly valuable; and much of it will be forgotten quickly. Some of it may, in fact, turn out to be misleading or even false—but history books, too, may be in error, and the errors in both sorts of literature at least teach us about the preconceptions of the times when such errors found their way into history and fiction.

Reading to Confront Experience

One of the most compelling aspects of literature is its relationship to human experience. Reading is an act of engagement and participation. It is also, simultaneously, an act of clarification and discovery. Literature allows us the chance to overcome, as perhaps no other medium can, the limitations of our own subjectivity and those limitations imposed by sex, age, social and economic condition, and the times in which we live. Literary characters offer us immediate access to a wide range of human experiences we otherwise might never know. As readers we observe these characters' public lives, while also becoming privy to their innermost thoughts, feelings, and motivations. So intimate is this access that psychologists have traditionally found imaginative literature a rich source for case studies to illustrate theories of personality and behavior.

The relationship between literature and experience, however, is highly reciprocal. Just as literature allows us to participate in the experiences of others, so too it has the power to alter our attitudes and expectations. To know why we identify with one character and not another may tell us about the kind of person we are or aspire to be. If we are sensitive and perceptive readers, we can learn from these encounters to enrich the quality and alter the direction of our lives, though the extent of such learning is impossible to predict and will vary from one reader to the next. One mark of a "great" work of literature is its ability to affect nearly every reader, and this affective power of fiction, drama, and poetry helps to explain the survival of those works we regard as "classics." Joseph Conrad's "Heart of Darkness," William Shakespeare's *Othello*, and the poems of Robert Frost, for example, survive as "classics" because they have offered generations of readers the opportunity to clarify and modify their views of life, and also because they shed light on the complexity and ambiguity of human existence.

Reading for Aesthetic Pleasure

We also read for the sheer aesthetic pleasure of observing good craftsmanship. And if, as the poet John Keats insisted, "A thing of beauty is a joy forever," then well-ordered and well-chosen words are certainly one form of immortality. Whatever its other uses, a poem, a play, or a novel is a self-contained work of art, with a describable structure and style. Sensitive and experienced readers will respond to unified stylistic effects, though they may not be initially conscious of exactly what they are responding to, or why. When that response is a positive one, we speak of our sense of pleasure or delight, in much the same way that we respond to a painting, a piece of sculpture, or a musical composition. If we push our inquiry further and try to analyze our response, we begin to move in the direction of literary criticism.

LITERARY CRITICISM

Contrary to rumor, literary criticism is not always an exercise in human ingenuity that professors of English engage in for its own sake. Neither is the word *criticism* to be confused with the kind of petty faultfinding we sometimes encounter in caustic book reviews. Literary criticism is nothing more or less than an attempt to clarify, explain, and evaluate our experience with a given literary work. It allows us to raise and then answer, however tentatively, certain basic questions about an author's achievement and about the ways in which he or she achieved it. Is also allows us to form some judgments about the relative merit or quality of the work as a whole. Literary criticism is a method of learning about literature, and the more we learn about how to approach a story, poem, or play, the greater our appreciation of a truly great work becomes, and greater still the sense of pleasure and enjoyment we can derive from it.

Literary criticism is the inevitable by-product of the reading process itself, for if we take that experience seriously, then criticism of some sort becomes inevitable. The only question is whether the judgments we form will be sensible ones. Literary criticism begins the moment we close our book and start to reflect on what we have just read. At that moment, to be sure, we have a choice. If we have been engaged in light reading, say in a detective story, where our interest and curiosity are satisfied once the solution to the crime is revealed and the criminal apprehended, we may simply put the book aside without a second thought and turn to weightier matters. Such an act, in itself, is a judgment. But if our reading has moved us intellectually or emotionally, we may find ourselves pausing to explore or explain our responses. If, in turn, we choose to organize and define those responses and to communicate them to someone else—to a parent, a roommate, or a close friend—we have in that moment become a literary critic.

The nature of literary criticism and the role of the critic have been simplified in this example for the sake of making a point; however, the illustration is a perfectly valid one. Criticism is the act of reflecting on, organizing, and then articulating, usually on paper, our response to a given literary work. Such an activity does not, however, take place in a vacuum. Like all organized fields of academic study, the study of literature rests on at least three key assumptions that critics and readers must be willing to accept. Literary criticism, first of all, presupposes that a piece of literature contains relationships and patterns of meaning that the reader-critic can discover and share. Without such prior agreement, of course, there can be no criticism, for by definition there would be nothing worthy of communication. Second, literary criticism presupposes the ability of the reader-turned-critic to translate his experience of the work into intellectual terms that can be communicated to and understood by others. Third, literary criticism presupposes that the critic's experience of the work, once organized and articulated, will be generally compatible with the experience of other readers. This is not to imply that critics and other readers will always see eye to eye, for of course they don't and never will. It *is* to say that to be valid and valuable the critic's reading of a work must accord, at least in a general way, with what other intelligent readers over a reasonable period of time are willing to agree on and accept.

To move from this general consideration of the function of literary criticism to the ways in which it can profitably be applied to the study of a given work of fiction, poetry, or drama is our task in the pages that follow. The approach we have chosen in this book is an *analytical* one that attempts to increase the understanding and appreciation of literature by introducing students to the typical devices, or *elements,* that comprise a story, a poem, or a play and to the way in which these elements relate to each other and to the work as a whole. Such an approach has much to recommend it to the student coming to the formal study of literature for the first time.

To begin with, the analytical approach provides a critical vocabulary of such key terms as *point of view, character, image, scene,* and *protagonist.* Such a set of generally agreed-upon definitions is essential if we are to discuss a work intelligently. Without the appropriate vocabulary we cannot organize our responses to a work or share them. A common vocabulary allows us to move our discussion from one literary work to another—it allows us to discuss *literature,* not just individual and isolated literary works. The theory and vocabulary of the elements of literature, along with their application to literary analysis, are neither remote nor arcane. They are the working tools of authors, critics, and intelligent readers. Their great virtue is the common gound they provide for discussing, describing, studying, and ultimately appreciating a literary work.

A second advantage of the analytical approach follows from the first. In order to identify and describe the various elements in a text and their interrelationship, we must ask and then attempt to answer certain basic questions about the text itself: What is the story's point of view and how does it influence our knowledge of the characters? What are the central images of the poem and how do they relate to one another? How do each of the play's scenes contribute to our understanding of the protagonist? Such questions and their answers help us not only to determine what the work says and means but also to form value judgments about how effectively (or ineffectively) the author has used his or her material.

The elements of literature presented and discussed in the sections that follow constitute a modest catalog. Each relates to one or more of the three major genres: fiction, poetry, and drama. Although the elements have no particular order of importance—some are more significant in one work than in another, without affecting the relative merit of the works themselves—they do offer a logical sequence for their examination. Some elements are more obvious than others; a discussion of fiction, for example, may begin conveniently with those elements that create a fictional story (*plot, character,* and *setting*), followed by those that govern an author's interpretation and handling of the story (*point of view, theme, symbol* and *allegory,* and *style* and *tone*).

The analytical method, it should be noted, is just one of a number of approaches taken by critics in their exploration and study of literature. It is true that by focusing our attention exclusively on the literary work we run the risk of minimizing, or ignoring altogether, many other factors that might otherwise contribute to our understanding. With the analytical method, for example, we tend to overlook the author's intention in writing the work, the relationship between the work and the author's life and experience, or the even broader relationship between the work and the historical culture in which it was written and to which it was originally directed. The analytical method also touches only indirectly the vital relationship of literature to human experience in general and to the reader's own experience in particular. All of these subjects are tempting adjuncts to literary study and in the fullness of time deserve to be raised and explored. The beginner, however, must resist the temptation, at least temporarily, and give priority to literary analysis, for before we can profitably turn to the larger implications of a literary work, that work itself must be understood.

I

FICTION

1

※※※※※※※

What Is Fiction?

When we speak of *fiction*, most of us are referring to the short story and the novel—the two genres that have dominated Western literary culture since the late eighteenth century. Broadly defined, however, the word *fiction* refers to any narrative, in prose or in verse, that is wholly or in part the product of the imagination. As such, plays and narrative poems (poems that tell a story) can be classified as fiction, as can folktales, parables, fables, legends, allegories, satires, and romances—all of which contain certain fictional elements. When we talk about fiction in this sense, then, we are not talking about fiction as a genre (the short story and the novel) but about a way of treating subject matter; we are, that is, making a statement about the relationship between real life and the life depicted in literature.

The precise relationship between fiction and life has been debated extensively among critics and authors since classical times. Such a distinction can at times be troublesome, as for example when we recognize that some works we refer to as fiction describe a real time and place and contain information about events and people that historians can document as authentic. Most modern critics agree, however, that whatever its apparent factual content or *verisimilitude*, fiction is finally to be regarded as a structured imitation of life and is not to be confused with a literal transcription of life itself. Fiction organizes and refines the raw material of fact to emphasize and clarify what is most significant in life. The world of fiction is a re-created world apart, a world of the possible or the probable, rather than the actual. It is governed by its own rules and internal completeness. To the extent that we find such a world credible or believable, it is because that world has been made to be consistent and coherent in character and event. Consider the relationship between Daniel Defoe's ship-wrecked hero and his real-life original, Alexander Selkirk:

The "Truth" of *Robinson Crusoe* is the acceptability of the things we are told, their acceptability in the interest of the effects of the narrative, not their correspondence with any actual facts involving Alexander Selkirk or another. . . . That is "true" or "internally necessary" which completes or accords with the rest of the experience, which cooperates to arouse our ordered response. . . . .

—From *Principles of Literary Criticism*, I. A. Richards [1928]

The writer of fiction, however, may deliberately choose not to deal with the world of our everyday experience at all. His chosen manner of treatment may be symbolic or allegorical rather than realistic; the tone may be comic, or satiric, or ironic, rather than serious. The writer of fiction, in short, is free to exercise tremendous freedom in his choice of subject matter and the fictional elements at his disposal, and he is free to invent, select, and arrange those elements so as to achieve any one of a number of desired effects. In every instance, the writer's success depends on how well he or she has succeeded in unifying the story and controlling its impact; it does not depend on how closely or faithfully life is mirrored or copied. To quote Henry James, "The only obligation to which in advance we [as readers] may hold a novel, without incurring the accusation of being arbitrary is that it be interesting. . . . We must grant the artist his subject, his idea, his *donnée:* our criticism is applied only to what he makes of it."[1]

---

[1] Henry James, "The Art of Fiction," *The Art of Fiction and Other Essays by Henry James* (New York: Oxford University Press, 1948), pp. 8, 14.

2

✿✿✿✿✿✿✿

The Elements of Fiction

PLOT

"Story" Versus Plot

"Let us define plot," E. M. Forster wrote:

We have defined a story as a narrative of events arranged in their time-sequence. A plot is also a narrative of events, the emphasis falling on causality. "The king died, and then the queen died of grief" is a plot. The time-sequence is preserved, but the sense of causality overshadows it. Or again, "The queen died, no one knew why, until it was discovered that it was through grief at the death of the king." This is a plot with mystery in it, a form capable of high development. It suspends the time-sequence, it moves as far away from the story as its limitations will allow. Consider the death of the queen. If it is in a story we say: "And then?" If it is in a plot we ask: "Why?" That is the fundamental difference between these two aspects of the novel. A plot cannot be told to a gaping audience of cavemen or to a tyrannical sultan or to their modern descendant the movie-public. They can only be kept awake by "And then— and then—" they can only supply curiosity. But a plot demands intelligence and memory also.[2]

Forster's remarks help us to understand the essential nature of fictional plot. The incidents of a plot, he reminds us, however lifelike and "real" they may seem to the reader, are not to be confused with the kind of random and indeterminate incidents that punctuate our everyday experience. In ordinary life we live through a sequence of events of varying duration linked only by the temporal order of their occurrence. At the same time events that will

---

[2] E. M. Forster, *Aspects of the Novel and Related Writings* (New York: Harcourt Brace and Company, 1927), pp. 130–131.

ultimately concern us, but of whose very existence we are not aware, are taking place elsewhere. If some of these events have a greater magnitude and significance than others, and if a logical and necessary relationship does indeed exist between them, such facts are usually only apparent upon subsequent reflection—a process that, as Forster notes, calls upon both "intelligence and memory."

The creator of a fictional plot deliberately makes such an overview of experience possible. The term *plot* implies just such an overview; it implies the controlling intelligence of an author who has winnowed the raw facts and incidents at his disposal and then arranged them to suggest or expose their causal relationship. In Forster's example, the moment that grief is established as the motive for the death of the queen, two apparently disparate and merely coincidental events become linked together as cause and effect. At that very same moment the author has also radically altered the existing relationship between the reader-onlooker and the events themselves. While they remained apparently unrelated, the death of the king and the subsequent death of the queen were events capable of arousing little more than curiosity. However, once an appeal has been made to the "intelligence and memory" of the reader, through establishing a causal relationship, passive curiosity gives way to active participation and involvement. What was once just a story—a direct, unedited rendering of experience—has been rearranged and translated into a potentially interesting and exciting plot.

The Elements of Plot

When we refer to the plot of a work of fiction, then, we are referring to the *deliberately arranged sequence of interrelated events* that constitute the basic narrative structure of a novel or a short story. Events of any kind, of course, inevitably involve people, and for this reason it is virtually impossible to discuss plot in isolation from character. Character and plot are, in fact, intimately and reciprocally related, especially in modern fiction. In "The Art of Fiction" Henry James asks, "What is character but the determination of incident? What is incident but the illustration of character?" In the sense that James intended it, a major function of plot can be said to be the representation of characters in action, though as we will see the action involved can be internal and psychological as well as external and physical.

In order for a plot to begin, some kind of catalyst is necessary. An existing equilibrium or stasis must be broken that will generate a sequence of events, provide direction to the plot, and focus the attention of the reader. Most plots originate in some significant *conflict.* The conflict may be either external, when the *protagonist* (also referred to as the *hero*[3] or the *focal character*) is pitted against some object outside himself, or internal, in which case the issue to be resolved is one within the protagonist's psyche or personality. External conflict may reflect a basic opposition between man and nature (such as in Jack London's famous short story "To Build a Fire" or Ernest Hemingway's *The Old Man and the Sea*) or between man and society (as in Richard Wright's "The Man Who Was Almost a Man"). It may also take the form of an opposition between man and man (between the protagonist and a human adversary, the *antagonist*),

---

[3] In general, *protagonist* is a better term than *hero;* the latter implies a set of admirable and positive qualities that many protagonists do not have.

as for example in most detective fiction, in which the sleuth is asked to match wits and sometimes muscle with an archcriminal. Internal conflict, on the other hand, is confined to the protagonist. In this case, the opposition is between two or more elements within the protagonist's own character, as in Joseph Conrad's "Heart of Darkness," when Kurtz struggles (and fails) to subdue the savage instincts concealed beneath his civilized English veneer.

Most plots, it should be noted, contain more than one conflict. In "Heart of Darkness," for example, while the basic conflict takes place within Kurtz, its resolution depends on Captain Marlow's determined efforts to forge his way upriver into the very heart of the dark continent and rescue the man whose life and motives have become his fascination (that is, to pit himself against his hostile natural environment and the barriers imposed by the trading company's ineptness). In some cases, however, these multiple conflicts are presented in a way that makes it extremely difficult to say with absolute certainty which one is the most decisive. It should be noted as well that the conflict of a story may exist prior to the formal initiation of the plot itself, rather than be explicitly dramatized or presented in an early scene or chapter. Some conflicts, in fact, are never made explicit and must be inferred by the reader from what the characters do or say as the plot unfolds (as, for example, in Ernest Hemingway's "Hills Like White Elephants"). Conflict, then, is the basic opposition, or tension, that sets the plot of a novel or short story in motion; it engages the reader, builds the suspense or mystery of the work, and arouses expectation for the events that are to follow.

The plot of the traditional short story is often conceived of as moving through five distinct sections or stages, which can be diagrammed roughly as follows:

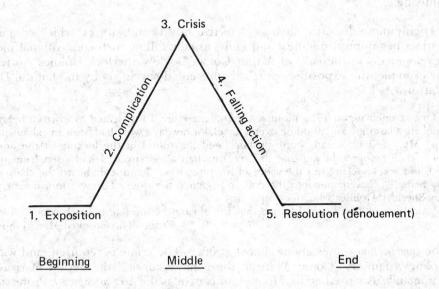

In some novels this five-stage structure is repeated in many of the individual chapters, while the novel as a whole builds on a series of increasing conflicts and crises. Such a structure is found both in such classics of fiction as Flaubert's *Madame Bovary* and in the adventure thrillers of Alistair MacLean.

EXPOSITION: The exposition is the beginning section in which the author provides the necessary background information, sets the scene, establishes the situation, and dates the action. It may also introduce the characters and the conflict, or the potential for conflict. The exposition may be accomplished in a single sentence or paragraph, or, in the case of some novels, occupy an entire chapter or more. Some plots require more exposition than others. A historical novel set in a foreign country several centuries ago obviously needs to provide the reader with more background information than a novel with a contemporary setting.

COMPLICATION: The complication, which is sometimes referred to as the rising action, breaks the existing equilibrium and introduces the characters and the underlying or inciting conflict (if they have not already been introduced by the exposition). The conflict is then developed gradually and intensified.

CRISIS: The crisis (also referred to as the climax) is that moment at which the plot reaches its point of greatest emotional intensity; it is the turning point of the plot, directly precipitating its resolution.

FALLING ACTION: Once the crisis, or turning point, has been reached, the tension subsides and the plot moves toward its appointed conclusion.

RESOLUTION: The final section of the plot is its resolution; it records the outcome of the conflict and establishes some new equilibrium or stability (however tentative and momentary). The resolution is also referred to as the *conclusion* or the *dénouement*, the latter a French word meaning "unknotting" or "untying."

Highly plotted works, such as detective novels and stories, which contain distinct beginnings, middles, and ends, usually follow such conventional plot development. In the case of Arthur Conan Doyle's Sherlock Holmes stories, for example, the exposition is usually presented succinctly by the faithful Dr. Watson:

> One summer night, a few months after my marriage, I was seated by my own hearth smoking a last pipe and nodding over a novel, for my day's work had been an exhausting one. My wife had already gone upstairs, and the sound of the locking of the door some time before told me that the servants had also retired. I had risen from my seat and was knocking out the ashes of my pipe, when I suddenly heard the clang of the bell. . . . I went out into the hall and opened the door. To my astonishment, it was Sherlock Holmes who stood upon my step.
> "Ah, Watson," said he, "I hoped that I might not be too late to catch you."
> —From "The Crooked Man" [1893]

The *complication* comes about almost at once. The crime is reported, and with Holmes's famous "Come, Watson, the game is afoot," the period of rising action and suspense begins. Holmes, of course, is the *hero-protagonist;* Professor Moriarty, or some other suitably sinister villain like Dr. Grimesby Roylott ("The Adventure of the Speckled Band"), is the *antagonist.* For a time at least, the conflict of will and intellect seems almost even. Once Holmes solves the crime or mystery, the *crisis,* or climax, has been reached. The suspense and tension drop away, and the plot enters into the *falling action,* which is devoted to

Holmes's detailed explanation of his method of detection. The *resolution* is short and belongs either to Watson ("A few words may suffice to tell the little that remains"—"The Final Problem") or to Holmes:

"And that's the story of the Musgrave Ritual, Watson. They have the crown down at Hurlstone—though they had some legal bother, and a considerable sum to pay before they were allowed to retain it. I am sure that if you mentioned my name they would be happy to show it to you. Of the woman nothing was ever heard, and the probability is that she got away out of England, and carried herself, and the memory of her crime, to some land beyond the seas."

—From "The Musgrave Ritual" [1893]

Although the terms *exposition, complication, crisis, falling action* and *resolution* are helpful in understanding the relationship among the parts of some kinds of narrative, all plots, unfortunately, do not lend themselves to such neat and exact formulations. Even when they do, it is not unusual for critics and readers to disagree among themselves about the precise nature of the conflict—whether, for example, the protagonist is more in conflict with society than he is with himself—or about where the major crisis, or turning point, of the narrative actually occurs. Nor is there any special reason that the crisis should occur at or near the middle of the plot. It can, in fact, occur at any moment. In James Joyce's "Araby," and in a number of the other companion stories in *Dubliners*, the crisis—in the form of a sudden illumination that Joyce called an epiphany—occurs at the very end of the story, and the falling action and the resolution are dispensed with altogether. Exposition and complication can also be omitted in favor of a plot that begins *in medias res* ("in the midst of things"). In much modern and contemporary fiction the plot consists of a "slice of life" into which we enter on the eve of crisis, and the reader is left to infer beginnings and antecedents—including the precise nature of the conflict—from what he or she is subsequently able to learn.

This is the case in such famous Hemingway short stories as "Hills Like White Elephants" and "A Clean, Well-Lighted Place," in which the author chooses to eliminate not only the traditional beginning, but also the ending in order to focus our attention on a more limited moment of time, the middle, which takes the form of a single, self-contained episode. Both stories are lightly plotted: there is very little description and almost no action. Rather, the reader overhears a continuous dialogue between two characters—a nameless man and woman in the first story, an older waiter and a younger one in the second. Conflict and complication in each case are neither shown nor prepared for, but only revealed; the situation and the "story" are to be understood and completed through the active participation of the reader. Such stories are sometimes referred to as "plotless" in order to suggest that the author's emphasis and interest have been shifted elsewhere, most frequently to character or idea.

Understanding the plot on a schematic level becomes even more difficult when dealing with works, usually novels, that have more than one plot. Many novels contain one or more *subplots* that reinforce by contrast or parallel the main plot. Some novels even contain a double plot, as in Thackeray's *Vanity Fair*, where we are asked to follow the careers of both the selfish adventuress Becky Sharp and the innocent, good-hearted Amelia Sedley. As Amelia's fortunes sink, Becky's rise; then follows a reversal in which Amelia's rise is paralleled by Becky's slow but inevitable decline.

Selectivity

In deciding how much plot to include in a given work, how much emphasis to give individual episodes, and how these episodes are to be related to one another, the author's selectivity comes fully into play. In general, the shorter the narrative, the greater the degree of selectivity that will be required. The very economy of the short story, for example, limits the amount of plot that can be included, a limitation of treatment that usually can be avoided in the longer novel. But no matter how much space there is at the writer's disposal, it is not possible to tell the reader everything that "happened" to the characters. (James Joyce once contemplated writing a short story recording everything that happened during a single day in the lives of Stephen Dedalus and Leopold Bloom. The result was *Ulysses,* which grew to 767 pages and even then covered only twenty-one and a half hours.) In constructing the plot, the author will of necessity be forced to select those incidents that are most relevant to the story to be told. Those incidents that are the most significant will be emphasized and expanded into full-fledged dramatic scenes by using such devices as description, dialogue, and action. Other incidents will be given relatively less emphasis through deliberate subordination. In the latter case, the author may shorten the dramatic elements of the scene or eliminate them altogether in favor of summary—in favor of telling, rather than showing. All these episodes, major or minor, need not advance the plot in precisely the same way or at the same pace, although the reader does have the right to expect that each will contribute in some way to a completed story.

The Ordering of Plot

The customary way of ordering the several episodes in a plot is to present them chronologically, that is, to approximate the order of their occurrence in time. Chronological plotting can be handled in a variety of ways. It can be tightly controlled, as in the conventional five-stage detective story sketched previously. This is also the method in many historical novels, in which the separate episodes are linked closely and visibly in a firm cause/effect relationship, to give the impression of historical verisimilitude—"the way it was." Each episode logically and inevitably unfolds from the one that preceded it, thereby generating a momentum that drives the plot forward toward its appointed resolution.

Chronological plot structure can also be loose, relaxed, and episodic. In Henry Fielding's *Tom Jones* and Mark Twain's *Huckleberry Finn,* the plots are composed of a series of separate and largely self-contained *episodes,* resembling so many beads on a string. The unifying element is the protagonist, as he wanders into and out of a series of adventures that, in their totality, initiate him to life and provide his moral education.

A third type of chronologically arranged plot is encountered in psychological novels, such as James Joyce's *Ulysses,* Virginia Woolf's *To the Lighthouse,* and William Faulkner's *The Sound and the Fury,* in which the reader's attention is centered on the protagonist's unfolding state of mind as it wrestles with some internal conflict or problem. Here the interest is in the passage of "psychological time," which, in these three novels, is presented through a technique called *stream of consciousness.* Reflecting the twentieth-century interest in psychology, stream of consciousness attempts to give the illusion of overhearing the actual workings of a human mind by recording the continuous and apparently random flow of ideas, feelings, sensations, associations, and perceptions as they register on the protagonist's consciousness. The technique is difficult to sustain; and its effectiveness has been much debated among literary critics, in part because of the burden that it imposes on the reader's patience and perceptiveness.

Finally, it is important to recognize that, even within plots which are mainly chronological, the temporal sequence is often deliberately broken and the chronological parts rearranged for the sake of emphasis and effect. Recall the two Hemingway stories cited here in which we encounter the characters in the middle of their "story" and must infer what has happened up to "now." In this case and in others, although the main direction of the plot may be chronological and forward, the author is under no obligation to begin at the beginning. Hemingway has us begin in the middle of things; other authors may begin at the end and then, having intrigued and captured us, work backward to the beginning and then forward again to the middle. In still other cases, the chronology of plot may shift backward and forward in time, as for example in William Faulkner's "A Rose for Emily," where the author deliberately sets aside the chronological ordering of events and their cause/effect relationship in order to establish an atmosphere of unreality, build suspense and mystery, and underscore Emily Grierson's own attempt to deny the passage of time itself.

Perhaps the most frequently and conventionally used device for interrupting the flow of a chronologically ordered plot is the *flashback*, a summary or fully dramatized episode framed by the author in such a way as to make it clear that the events being discussed or dramatized took place at some earlier period of time. Flashbacks are often crucial to our understanding of the story, for they introduce us to information that would otherwise be unavailable and thus increase our knowledge and understanding of present events.

The key point to remember about plot is that it is open to infinite variety. An author is under no obligation whatsoever to make his plot conform to any scheme or pattern but his own. The only requirement that the writer of fiction dares not shirk is that the plot be interesting.[4]

Evaluating Plot

Having studied a given story or novel to see how the author has arranged and made use of the elements of plot, we should be ready to evaluate his or her success. The customary test of a plot's effectiveness is its unity: the degree to which each episode and the place it occupies in the narrative structure of the work bear in some necessary and logical (or psychological) way upon the resolution of the initial conflict. In the process one can also raise questions

---

[4] It is worth remembering that the conventions of plot are not merely a matter of tradition, as John Barth makes clear in the following passage from his short story "Lost in the Funhouse":

> While there is no reason to regard this pattern as an absolute necessity, like many other conventions it became conventional because great numbers of people over many years learned by trial and error that it was effective; one ought not to forsake it, therefore, unless one wishes to forsake as well the effect of drama or has clear cause to feel that deliberate violation of the "normal" pattern can better . . . effect that effect.

John Barth, "Lost in the Funhouse," *Lost in the Funhouse: Fiction for Print, Tape, Live Voice* (New York: Doubleday & Company, Inc., 1968), p. 95. In this particular instance, it should be noted, Barth calls attention to convention as a means of emphasizing his own deviations from "the 'normal' pattern."

about the plausibility of a given episode or, for that matter, about the plausibility of the plot as a whole—that is, whether the events and their resolution are guilty of violating our sense of the probable or possible. The violation of plausibility—which is, in turn, a violation of the basic intelligence of the reader—is a quality we often associate with popular commercial fiction, in which a happy ending seems to be grafted on a plot for the sake of convenience and propriety, when everything that preceded pointed in the opposite direction.

One frequently used test of plausibility involves the author's use of *chance* (events that occur without apparent cause or sufficient preparation) and *coincidence* (the accidental occurrence of two events that have a certain correspondence). Although chance and coincidence do occur in real life, their use in literature becomes suspect if they seem to be merely an artificial device for arranging events or imposing a resolution. Such events tend to mar or even destroy a plot's plausibility and unity.

Analyzing Plot

In approaching a work of fiction for the first time, we can analyze the plot by attempting to answer such questions as the following:

1. What is the conflict (or conflicts) on which the plot turns? Is it external, internal, or some combination of the two?
2. What are the chief episodes or incidents that make up the plot? Is its development strictly chronological, or is the chronology rearranged in some way?
3. Compare the plot's beginning and end. What essential changes have taken place?
4. Describe the plot in terms of its exposition, complication, crisis, falling action, and resolution.
5. Is the plot unified? Do the individual episodes logically relate to one another?
6. Is the ending appropriate to and consistent with the rest of the plot?
7. Is the plot plausible? What role, if any, do chance and coincidence play?

CHARACTER

The relationship between plot and character is a vital and necessary one. Without character, there would be no plot and, hence, no story. For most readers of fiction the primary attraction lies in the characters, in the endlessly fascinating collection of men and women whose experiences and adventures in life form the basis of the plots of the novels and stories in which they appear. Few of us reach literary maturity without having our favorites—Tom Jones and Parson Adams, Rip Van Winkle and Ichabod Crane, Heathcliff, Jane Eyre, Hester Prynne, Captain Ahab, Becky Sharp, Mr. Micawber and David Copperfield, Tom Sawyer and Huckleberry Finn, Sherlock Holmes and Dr. Watson, Nick Carraway and Jay Gatsby, Marlow and Kurtz; the list goes on and on. Fiction presents us with an almost endless variety of memorable human beings, some who delight and amuse us, others who puzzle, intrigue, or terrify us. We can sympathize, or even empathize, with some of these characters in their open enjoyment of life, in their doubts and sorrows, in their loneliness and endless search for value and meaning. Other characters only appall us with their greed, their burning hatred and desire for revenge, or their ability to manipulate others coldly for selfish ends.

Part of the fascination with the characters of fiction is that we come to know them so well, perhaps at times too well. In real life we come to know people for the most part only on the basis of externals—on the basis of what they say and what they do; the essential complexity of their inner lives can be inferred only after years of close acquaintance, if at all. Fiction, on the other hand, often provides us with direct and immediate access to that inner life— to the intellectual, emotional, and moral complexities of human personality that lie beneath the surface. And even when the author withholds that access, he usually provides sufficient information to allow us to make judgments about the internal makeup of the men and women to whom we are introduced. In either case, however, the ability to make such judgments—the ability to interpret correctly the evidence the author provides—is always crucial to our understanding.

When we speak of character in terms of literary analysis, we are concerned essentially with three separate but closely connected activities. We are concerned, first of all, with being able to establish the personalities of the characters themselves and to identify their intellectual, emotional, and moral qualities. Second, we are concerned with the techniques an author uses to create, develop, and present characters to the reader. Third, we are concerned with whether the characters so presented are credible and convincing. In evaluating the success of characterization, the third issue is a particularly crucial one, for although plot can carry a work of fiction to a point, it is a rare work whose final value and importance are not somehow intimately connected with just how convincingly the author has managed to portray the characters. Naturally, such an evaluation can only take place within the context of the novel or short story as a whole, which inevitably links character to the other elements of fiction.

Characters in Fiction

The term *character* applies to any individual in a literary work. For purposes of analysis, characters in fiction are customarily described by their relationship to plot, by the degree of development they are given by the author, and by whether or not they undergo significant character change.

The major, or central, character of the plot is the protagonist; his opponent, the character against whom the protagonist struggles or contends is the antagonist. The protagonist is usually easy enough to identify: he or she is the essential character without whom there would be no plot in the first place. It is the protagonist's fate (the conflict or problem being wrestled with) on which the attention of the reader is focused. The terms *protagonist* and *antagonist* do not, however, imply a judgment about the moral worth of either, for many protagonists and antagonists (like their counterparts in real life) embody a complex mixture of both positive and negative qualities. For this reason they are more suitable terms than *hero, heroine,* or *villain,* which connote a degree of moral absoluteness that major characters in great fictional works, as opposed, say, to popular melodrama, simply do not exhibit.

Very often the title of the work identifies the protagonist: *King Oedipus, Othello, Tom Jones,* "Rip Van Winkle," *Don Juan, The Deerslayer, Madame Bovary, Hedda*

Gabler, Sister Carrie, "The Darling," "A Rose for Emily," *Herzog,* and *Becket* are examples. But titles can be deceptive. It can be argued that the protagonist of Herman Melville's "Bartleby the Scrivener" is not the enigmatic copyist, but rather the amiable and benevolent lawyer who is asked to cope with a bizarre individual whom he can finally neither understand nor reach.

The antagonist can be somewhat more difficult to identify, especially if he is not a human being, as with Herman Melville's great white whale in *Moby-Dick* or the marlin that challenges the courage and endurance of the old fisherman Santiago in Ernest Hemingway's *The Old Man and the Sea.* In fact, as was intimated earlier, the antagonist may not be a living creature at all, but rather the hostile social or natural environment with which the protagonist is forced to contend. The protagonist may not always manage to compete successfully with and defeat the antagonist, either; often, as in the case of Samuel L. Clemens' (Mark Twain's) "The Notorious Jumping Frog of Cavaleras County" and Stephen Crane's "The Blue Hotel," just the opposite is true.

To describe the relative degree to which fictional characters are developed by their creators, E. M. Forster distinguishes between what he calls *flat* and *round characters. Flat characters* are those who embody or represent a single characteristic, trait, or idea, or at most a very limited number of such qualities. Flat characters are also referred to as *type characters,* as *one-dimensional characters,* or, when they are distorted to create humor, as *caricatures.* "The really flat character," Forster notes, "can be expressed in one sentence such as 'I never will desert Mr. Micawber.' There is Mrs. Micawber—she says she won't desert Mr. Micawber; she doesn't, and there she is. Or: 'I must conceal, even by subterfuges, the poverty of my master's house.' There is Caleb Balderstone in [Sir Walter Scott's] *The Bride of Lammermoor.*"[5] Fiction is full of such individuals, and they are almost always immediately recognizable—by their incompleteness, by the oddity of their appearance, by their mannerisms, by the recurring words they utter. For this reason, as is the case in many of Dickens' novels, they often serve as convenient vehicles for humor and satire. These characters and their deeds are always predictable and never vary; for as Forster notes, they are not changed by circumstance.

Flat characters are usually minor actors in the novels and stories in which they appear, but not always so. For example, Montresor and Fortunato are the protagonist and antagonist, respectively, in Edgar Allan Poe's "The Cask of Amontillado." Yet they are both flat characters: Montresor, who leads the unsuspecting Fortunato to be walled up in his family crypt, embodies nothing but cold-blooded revenge. And Fortunato, who is dressed in the cap and motley of the jester, complete with bells, is quite literally a fool. Flat characters have much in common with the kind of *stock characters* who appear again and again in certain types of literary works: e.g., the rich uncle of domestic comedy, the hard-boiled private eye of the detective story, the female confidante of the romance, and the mustachioed villain of old-fashioned drama.

Round characters are just the opposite. They embody a number of qualities and traits, and are complex multidimensional characters of considerable intellectual and emotional depth who have the capacity to grow and change. Major characters in fiction are usually round characters, and it is with the very complexity of such characters that most of us become engrossed and fascinated. The terms *round* and *flat* do not automatically imply value judgments. Each kind

---

[5] Forster, op. cit., p. 104.

of character has its uses in literature—witness Poe's successful use of flat characters to dramatize the theme of revenge in "The Cask of Amontillado." Even
when they are minor characters, as they usually are, flat characters often are
convenient devices to draw out and help us to understand the personalities
of characters who are more fully realized. Finally, round characters are not
necessarily more alive or more convincing than flat ones. If they are, it is
because the author has succeeded in making them so.

Characters in fiction can also be distinguished on the basis of whether they
demonstrate the capacity to develop or change as the result of their experiences.
Dynamic characters exhibit a capacity to change; *static characters* do not. As might
be expected, the degree and rate of character change varies widely, even among
dynamic characters. In some works, the development is so subtle that it may
go almost unnoticed; in others, it is sufficiently drastic and profound to cause
a total reorganization of the character's personality or system of values. Change
in character may come slowly and incrementally over many pages and chapters,
or it may take place with a dramatic suddenness that surprises, and even overwhelms, the character. With characters who fully qualify as dynamic, such
change can be expected to alter subsequent behavior in some significant way.

Dynamic characters include the protagonists in most novels, which by virtue
of their very size and scope provide excellent vehicles for illustrating the process
of change. So-called initiation novels, such as *David Copperfield, Huckleberry Finn,*
and *The Great Gatsby,* are examples. In each case the author has arranged the
events of the plot so that they reveal the slow and painful maturing of the
young protagonist coming into contact with the world of adult experience.
But short stories can illustrate character change, as in the case of Hawthorne's
young country rustic Robin Molineux in "My Kinsman, Major Molineux," who
journeys to colonial Boston in search of his kinsman only to undergo an ordeal
that leaves him on the threshold of maturity. What that maturity consists of,
Hawthorne refuses to say, but there can be little doubt that by the story's
conclusion Robin has passed into and through a significant emotional and
spiritual crisis.

Static characters leave the plot as they entered it, largely untouched by the
events that have taken place. Although static characters tend to be minor ones,
because the author's principal focus is elsewhere, this is not always the case.
Olenka, the protagonist of Anton Chekhov's "The Darling" is a static character
whose essential qualities are submissiveness and blind devotion. Without opinions, personality, or inner resources of her own, she passes through a series
of relationships which leave her character essentially unchanged. But protagonists like Olenka are comparatively rare; for the most part, an author creates
static characters as *foils* to emphasize and set off by contrast the development
taking place in others.

Methods of Characterization

In presenting and establishing character, an author has two basic methods
or techniques at his disposal. One method is *telling,* which relies on exposition
and direct commentary by the author. In telling—a method preferred by many
older fiction writers—the guiding hand of the author is very much in evidence.
We learn primarily from what the author calls to our attention. The other
method is the indirect, dramatic method of *showing,* which involves the author's
stepping aside, as it were, to allow the characters to reveal themselves directly

through their dialogue and their actions. With showing, much of the burden of character analysis is shifted to the reader, who is required to infer character on the basis of the evidence provided in the narrative. Telling and showing are not mutually exclusive, however. Most authors employ a combination of the two, even when the exposition, as in the case of most of Hemingway's stories, is limited to several lines of descriptive detail establishing the scene.

Most modern authors prefer showing to telling, but neither method is neces-sarily better or more fruitful than the other. As with so many other choices that the writer of fiction must make, the choice of a method of characterization depends on a number of different circumstances. These include the author's temperament, the particular literary conventions of the period in which he or she is writing, the size and scope of the work, the degree of distance and objectivity the author wishes to establish between himself and the characters, the author's literary and philosophical beliefs about how a sense of reality can best be captured and conveyed to the reader, and, of course, the kind of story the author wishes to tell. All these factors heavily influence the technique of characterization; collectively they determine why and how the author does what he does. And all these factors are worthy of consideration in the course of literary discussion and analysis.

Direct methods of revealing character—characterization by telling—include the following methods.

1. CHARACTERIZATION THROUGH THE USE OF NAMES. Names are often used to provide essential clues that aid in characterization. Some characters are given names that suggest their dominant or controlling traits, as, for example, Edward Murdstone (in Dickens' *David Copperfield*) and Roger Chillingsworth (in Hawthorne's *The Scarlet Letter*). Both men are the cold-hearted villains their names suggest. Other characters are given names that reinforce (or sometimes are in contrast to) their physical appearance, much in the way that Ichabod Crane, the gangling schoolmaster in Irving's "The Legend of Sleepy Hollow," resembles his long-legged namesake. Names can also contain literary or histori-cal allusions that aid in characterization by means of association. The name "Ethan Brand," referring to the wandering lime burner who gives his name to Hawthorne's short story, contains an allusion to the mark or brand of Cain, a legacy of guilt that the outcast Brand shares with his Biblical counterpart. One must also, however, be alert to names used ironically which characterize through inversion. Such is the case with the foolish Fortunato of Poe's "The Cask of Amontillado," who surely must rank with the most *un*fortunate of men.

2. CHARACTERIZATION THROUGH APPEARANCE. Although in real life most of us are aware that appearances are often deceiving, in the world of fiction details of appearance (what a character wears and how he looks) often provide essential clues to character. Take, for example, the second paragraph of "My Kinsman, Major Molineux," in which Hawthorne introduces his protagonist to the reader:

He was a youth of barely eighteen years, evidently country-bred, and now, as it should seem, upon his first visit to town. He was clad in a coarse gray coat, well worn, but in excellent repair; his under garments were durably constructed of leather, and fitted tight to a pair of serviceable and well-shaped limbs; his stockings of blue yarn were the incontrovertible work of a mother or a sister; and on his head was a three-cornered hat, which in its better days had perhaps sheltered the graver brow of the lad's father. Under his left arm was a heavy cudgel formed of an oak sapling, and retaining a part of the hardened root; and his equipment was completed by a wallet, not so abundantly stocked as to incommode the vigorous shoulders on which it hung. Brown, curly hair, well-shaped features, and bright, cheerful eyes were nature's gifts, and worth all that art could have done for his adornment.

—From "My Kinsman, Major Molineux," Nathaniel Hawthorne [1832]

The several details in the paragraph tell us a good deal about Robin's character and basic situation. We learn that he is a "country-bred" youth nearing the end of a long journey, as his nearly empty wallet suggests. His clothes confirm that he is relatively poor. Yet Robin is clearly no runaway or rebel, for his clothes though "well worn" are "in excellent repair," and the references to his stockings and hat suggest that a loving and caring family has helped prepare him for his journey. The impression thus conveyed by the total paragraph, and underscored by its final sentence describing Robin's physical appearance, is of a decent young man on the threshold of adulthood who is making his first journey into the world. The only disquieting note—a clever bit of foreshadowing—is the reference to the heavy oak cudgel that Robin has brought with him. He later will brandish it at strangers in an attempt to assert his authority and in the process reveal just how inadequately prepared he is to cope with the strange urban world in which he finds himself.

As in Hawthorne's story, details of dress and physical appearance should be scrutinized closely for what they may reveal about character. Details of dress may offer clues to background, occupation, economic and social status, and perhaps, as with Robin Molineux, even a clue to the character's degree of self-respect. Details of physical appearance can help to identify a character's age and the general state of his physical and emotional health and well-being: whether the character is strong or weak, happy or sad, calm or agitated. Appearance can be used in other ways as well, particularly with minor characters who are flat and static. By common agreement, certain physical attributes have become identified over a period of time with certain kinds of inner psychological states. For example, characters who are tall and thin are often associated with intellectual or aesthetic types who are withdrawn and introspective. Arthur Dimmesdale and Roger Chillingsworth, the two major male characters in *The Scarlet Letter*, share these traits, as does the pallid recluse Roderick Usher, in Poe's "The Fall of the House of Usher." Portly or fat characters, on the other hand, suggest an opposite kind of personality, one characterized by a degree of laziness, self-indulgence, and congeniality, as in the case of Fielding's Parson Adams or Dickens' Tony Weller. Such convenient and economical shortcuts to characterization are perfectly permissible, of course, as long as they result in characters who are in their own way convincing.

3. CHARACTERIZATION BY THE AUTHOR. In the most customary form of telling, the author interrupts the narrative and reveals directly, through a series of editorial comments, the nature and personality of the characters, including the thoughts and feelings that enter and pass through the characters' minds. By so doing the author asserts and retains full control over characterization. The author not only directs our attention to a given character, but tells us exactly what our attitude toward that character ought to be. Nothing is left to the reader's imagination. Unless the author is being ironic—and there is always that possibility—we can do little more than assent and allow our concep-

tion of character to be formed on the basis of what the author has told us.
Consider the following passages:

In that same village . . . there lived . . . a simple good-natured fellow by the name
of Rip Van Winkle. . . . I have observed that he was a simple good-natured man; he
was, moreover, a kind neighbor and an obedient henpecked husband. Indeed, to the
latter circumstance might be owing that meekness of spirit which gained him such
universal popularity. . . . The great error in Rip's composition was an insuperable
aversion to all kinds of profitable labor. . . . In a word, Rip was ready to attend to
anybody's business but his own; but as to doing family duty and keeping his farm in
order, he found it impossible.
                                  —From "Rip Van Winkle," Washington Irving [1819]

It was one of the secret opinions, such as we all have, of Peter Brench that his
main success in life would have consisted in his never having committed himself about
the work, as it was called, of his friend Morgan Mallow. This was a subject on which
it was, to the best of his belief, impossible with veracity to quote him, and it was
nowhere on record that he had, in the connexion, on any occasion and in any embarrassment, either lied or spoken the truth. Such a triumph has its honour even for a man
of other triumphs—a man who had reached fifty, who had escaped marriage, who had
lived within his means, who had been in love with Mrs. Mallow for years without breathing it, and who, last not least, had judged himself once for all. He had so judged
himself in fact that he felt an extreme and general humility to be his proper portion;
yet there was nothing that made him think so well of his parts as the course he had
steered so often through the shallows just mentioned.
                                   —From "The Tree of Knowledge," Henry James [1900]

There was a woman who was beautiful, who started with all the advantages, yet
she had no luck. She married for love, and the love turned to dust. She had bonny
children, yet she felt they had been thrust upon her, and she could not love them.
They looked at her coldly, as if they were finding fault with her. And hurriedly she
felt she must cover up some fault in herself. Yet what it was that she must cover up
she never knew. Nevertheless, when her children were present, she always felt the
centre of her heart go hard. This troubled her, and in her manner she was all the
more gentle and anxious for her children, as if she loved them very much. Only she
herself knew that at the centre of her heart was a hard little place that could not feel
love, no, not for anybody.
                             —From "The Rocking-Horse Winner," D. H. Lawrence [1932]

In each of the preceding examples, the general orientation of the character's
personality has been fixed by the author once and for all—the author provides
us with a given and then proceeds to construct a plot that illustrates such
characters in action.

By contrast, there are essentially two methods of indirect characterization
by showing: characterization through dialogue (what characters say) and characterization through action (what characters do). Unlike the direct methods of
characterization already discussed, showing involves the gradual rather than
the immediate establishment of character. Such a process requires rather than
excludes the active participation of the reader and in so doing calls upon
what Forster called "intelligence and memory."

4. CHARACTERIZATION THROUGH DIALOGUE. Real life is quite literally filled
with talk. People are forever talking about themselves and between themselves,
communicating bits and pieces of information. Not all of this information is
important or even particularly interesting; much of it smacks of the kind of
inconsequential small talk we expect at a cocktail party; it tells us relatively

little about the personality of the speaker, except, perhaps, whether he or
she is at ease in social situations. Some light fiction reproduces dialogue as
it might occur in reality, but the best authors trim everything that is inconsequential. What remains is weighty and substantial and carries with it the force
of the speaker's attitudes, values, and beliefs. We pay attention to such talk
because it is interesting and, if we are attempting to understand the speaker,
because it may consciously or unconsciously serve to reveal his innermost
character and personality.

The task of establishing character through dialogue is not a simple one.
Some characters are careful and guarded in what they say: they speak only
by indirection, and we must infer from their words what they actually mean.
Others are open and candid; they tell us, or appear to tell us, exactly what is
on their minds. Some characters are given to chronic exaggeration and overstatement; others to understatement and subtlety.

It is a rare work of fiction whose author does not employ dialogue in some
way to reveal, establish, and reinforce character. For this reason the reader
must be prepared to analyze dialogue in a number of different ways: for (a)
what is being said, (b) the identity of the speaker, (c) the occasion, (d) the
identity of the person or persons the speaker is addressing, (e) the quality of
the exchange, and (f) the speaker's tone of voice, stress, dialect, and vocabulary.

a. *What is being said.* To begin with, the reader must pay close attention to
   the substance of the dialogue itself. Is it small talk, or is the subject an
   important one in the developing action of the plot? In terms of characterization, if the speaker insists on talking only about himself or only on a single
   subject, we may conclude that we have either an egotist or a bore. If the
   speaker talks only about others, we may have merely a gossip and busybody.
b. *The identity of the speaker.* Obviously, on balance, what the protagonist says
   must be considered to be potentially more important (and hence revealing)
   than what minor characters say, although the conversation of a minor character often provides crucial information and can also shed important light
   on the personalities of the other characters and on his or her own as well.
c. *The occasion.* In real life, conversations that take place in private at night
   are usually more serious and, hence, more revealing than conversations
   that take place in public during the day. Talk in the bedroom, for example,
   is usually more significant than talk in the street or at the supermarket.
   On the whole, this is probably also true in fiction as well, but the reader
   should always consider the likelihood that seemingly idle talk on the street
   or at the supermarket has been included by the author because it is somehow
   important to the story being told.
d. *The identity of the person or persons the speaker is addressing.* Dialogue between
   friends is usually more candid and open, and thus more significant, than
   dialogue between strangers. The necessary degree of intimacy is usually
   established by the author in setting a scene or through the dialogue itself.
   When a character addresses no one in particular, or when others are not
   present, his speech is called a *monologue,* although, strictly speaking, monologues occur more frequently in drama than in fiction.[6]

---

[6] A specialized form of monologue is the stream-of-consciousness technique, in which the author
enters the mind or consciousness of his character and directly expresses unfolding thoughts
and emotions. Stream of consciousness implies a recognition that speech is inadequate to communicate inner psychological life.

e. *The quality of the exchange.* The way a conversation ebbs and flows is important, too. When there is real give-and-take to a discussion, the characters can be presumed to be open-minded. Where there is none, one or more of the characters are presumably opinionated, doctrinaire or close-minded. Where there is a certain degree of evasiveness in the responses, a character may be secretive and have something to hide.

f. *The speaker's tone of voice, stress, dialect, and vocabulary.* The speaker's tone of voice (either stated or implied) may reveal his attitude toward himself (whether, for example, he is confident and at ease or self-conscious and shy) and his attitude toward those with whom he is speaking. His attitude to others may, for example, be either warm and friendly or cold, detached, and even hostile. Moreover, the reader must also be alert to suggestions of irony in the speaker's voice, which would suggest that what is being said is quite the opposite from what is actually meant. Finally, dialect, stress, and word choice all provide important clues to character: they may reflect the character's origin, education, occupation, or social class.

In evaluating what a given character says about himself and others, one always faces (in the absence of clarifying comments by the author) the problem of the character's reliability and trustworthiness. Both deliberate deception and unconscious self-deception always lurk as distinct possibilities in fictional characters, as in real people. Although determining the reliability and veracity of characters can be difficult, most authors provide clues. When one character is contradicted in whole or in part by another, the accumulated evidence on both sides must be carefully weighed and examined. One can also test reliability by looking at the character's subsequent conduct or behavior to see if what he does somehow contradicts what he says. Finally, there is always the appeal to the subsequent events of the plot itself to see whether those events tend to support or contradict the character's statements. Any number of fictional plots turn, in fact, on the failure of one character to understand the personalities of others. The badly frightened Swede in Stephen Crane's "The Blue Hotel," for example, is so steeped in the folklore of the frontier West that he convinces himself that his companions are conspiring to rob or to murder him, a misapprehension that triggers a chain of violent events that costs the Swede his life.

5. CHARACTERIZATION THROUGH ACTION. Character and action, as we have noted, are often regarded as two sides of the same coin. To quote Henry James again: "What is character but the determination of incident? What is incident but the illustration of character?" James' premise is a widely shared one: behavior is a logical and necessary extension of psychology and personality. Inner reality can be measured through external event. What a given character *is* is revealed by what that character *does*. In short, the single most important and definitive method of revealing character is through action.

To establish character on the basis of action, it is necessary to scrutinize the several events of the plot for what they seem to reveal about the characters, about their unconscious emotional and psychological states as well as about their conscious attitudes and values. Some actions, of course, are inherently more meaningful in this respect than others. A gesture or a facial expression usually carries with it less significance than some larger and overt act. But this is not always the case. Very often it is the small and involuntary action, by very virtue of its spontaneous and unconscious quality, that tells us more about a character's inner life than a larger, premeditated act reflecting decision and choice. In either case, whether the action is large or small, conscious or unconscious, it is necessary to identify the common pattern of behavior of which each separate action is a part. One helpful way of doing so is on the basis of *motive,* the attempt to trace certain effects back to their underlying causes. If we are successful in doing so, if a consistent pattern of motivation appears, then it is fairly safe to assume that we have made some important discoveries about the character. To be sure, we must always allow for the gratuitous or motiveless act—we must not, that is, assume that for every action there is immediate or adequate preparation.

Robin Molineux's responses to the events that befall him provide a good example of character revealed through action. Robin's adventure is a journey of moral and psychological initiation, a rite of passage from youth to adulthood, innocence to maturity, and ignorance to knowledge. Ironically, the provincial capital that Robin enters is on the brink of a political revolution whose first victim is none other than the very kinsman whom Robin is seeking. For all his self-proclaimed "shrewdness," Robin and his cudgel are no match for the disorienting world of the city, whose crooked and narrow streets are incomprehensible to all but the initiated. Robin is not among the knowing. His country ways and naive-because-untested expectation leave him open and vulnerable to the world of the city, a world filled with danger, hostility, temptation, and elemental human violence. Through one event after another, including a meeting with a group of conspirators whose password Robin can neither understand nor return, Robin's ignorance, inadequacy, and lack of preparation are exposed. Taken together, the events of the plot, and Robin's response to them, reveal his essential character and prepare him for the climax of the story; his smug self-confidence is undermined while his confusion, anxiety, doubt, and sense of his own helplessness increase.

Evaluating Character

Having identified, on the basis of the evidence presented by the author, the essential nature and personality of the characters in the work, we must also be prepared to evaluate how successful the author has been in their creation. Although it is unreasonable to expect that the characters of fiction will necessarily be close approximations of the kind of people that we know—for part of the joy of fiction is having the opportunity to meet new people—we can expect the author's creations to be convincing and credible on their own terms. If they are not, such characters can be counted as relative failures, for our interest in them will surely flag.

What we chiefly require in the behavior of fictional characters, however, is *consistency.* Characterization implies a kind of unspoken contract between author and reader; and the reader has the right to expect that a character, once established, will not then behave in ways contrary to his or her nature. The principle of consistency by no means implies that characters in fiction cannot undergo development and change, for, as we have noted, the plots of many works are organized precisely upon just such a possibility. Rather, when a character undergoes change, such change should be well motivated by events and consistent in some basic and identifiable way with the nature of the character. Thus, in seeking to test for consistency, we most frequently ask ourselves whether the motive for a particular action or series of actions is adequate, justified, and probable, given what we know about that character. If the question can be answered in the affirmative, even in the context of behavior that at first glance seems puzzling or confusing, the principle of consistency has not been violated.

Analyzing Character

1. Who is the protagonist of the work and who (or what) is the antagonist? Describe the major traits and qualities of each.
2. What is the function of the work's minor characters?
3. Identify the characters in terms of whether they are flat and round, dynamic or static.
4. What methods does the author employ to establish and reveal the characters? Are the methods primarily of showing or of telling?
5. Are the actions of the characters properly motivated and consistent?
6. Are the characters of the work finally credible and interesting?

SETTING

Fiction can be defined as character in action at a certain time and place. The first two elements of this equation, *character* and *action,* have already been discussed. Now we turn our attention to *setting,* a term that, in its broadest sense, encompasses both the physical locale that frames the action *and* the time of day or year, the climatic conditions, and the historical period during which the action takes place. At its most basic, setting helps the reader visualize the action of the work, and thus adds credibility and an air of authenticity to the characters. It helps, in other words, to create and sustain the illusion of life, to provide what we call *verisimilitude.* There are, however, many different kinds of setting in fiction and they function in a variety of ways.

Some settings are relatively unimportant. They serve as little more than incidental and decorative backdrops, not unlike the wood and canvas sets we have grown accustomed to expect in modern situation comedies, which have little or no necessary relationship to either the plot or the characters. Some settings, on the other hand, are intimately and necessarily connected with the meaning and unity of the total work. It is with these that as critics we must be chiefly concerned. "Scene," remarks British author Elizabeth Bowen, "is only justified in the novel where it can be shown, or at least felt, to act upon action and character; in fact, where it has dramatic use."[7] Ms. Bowen may overstate her point since any setting can be justified as long as it is appropriate, but her basic argument is a valid one. The most important fictional settings are those that are "dramatic," those that are organic and essential parts of the work as a whole.

In order to understand the purpose and function of setting, the reader must pay particular attention to the descriptive passages in which the details of setting are introduced. Generally speaking, unless such passages are intended merely as local color, the greater the attention given to them, the greater their importance in the total work. In most short stories and in many novels, setting is established at or near the beginning of the work as a means of orienting the reader and framing the action that is to follow. Where the empha-

[7] Elizabeth Bowen, *Pictures and Conversations* (New York: Alfred A. Knopf, 1975), p. 178.

sis on setting in such passages is slight, as it is, for example, in most of Hemingway's short stories, or where the setting once established is then referred to again only incidentally, if at all, one can assume that setting as such is subordinate to the author's other concerns and purposes. If, on the other hand, the emphasis on the setting in early passages is substantial, and if similar references to the setting recur periodically as a kind of echoing refrain, one can reasonably assume that the setting is designed to serve some larger function in relation to the work as a whole.

The quality of the language by which the author projects the setting provides another clue as to his or her intention. When that intention is to invest the setting with a photographic vividness that appeals essentially to the reader's eye, the details of the setting will be rendered through language that is concrete and denotative. The author will pile specific detail on top of specific detail in an attempt to provide the illusion of a stable external reality. On the other hand, the author may want us to "feel" rather than simply "see" the setting, as is the case when setting is to be used as a means of creating atmosphere. In that case the appeal will be to the reader's imagination and emotions through language that is connotative, emotionally heightened, and suggestive. The author will, that is, manipulate the poetic qualities of language to elicit from the reader the desired and appropriate response. Often the author will want the reader to *both* see and feel the setting and will use the resources of language to bring about both effects simultaneously.

The Functions of Setting

Setting in fiction is called on to perform a number of desired functions. Setting may serve (1) to provide background for the action; (2) as an antagonist; (3) as a means of creating appropriate atmosphere; (4) as a means of revealing character; and (5) as a means of reinforcing theme. These functions must not, however, be thought of as mutually exclusive. In many works of fiction, setting can and does perform a number of different functions simultaneously.

1. SETTING AS BACKGROUND FOR ACTION. To quote Elizabeth Bowen once more: "Nothing can happen nowhere." For this reason, if for no other, fiction requires a setting or background of some kind, even if it only resembles the stage set of a daytime television soap opera. Sometimes this background is extensive and highly developed, as in many historical novels where setting—in the form of costume, manners, events, and institutions, all peculiar to a certain time and place—is rendered in minute detail to give a sense of "life as it was." In other cases, as in many modern short stories, setting is so slight that it can be dispensed with in a single sentence or must be inferred altogether from dialogue and action. When we speak of setting as background, then, we have in mind a kind of setting that exists largely for its own sake, without any clear relationship to action or characters, or at best a relationship that is only tangential and slight.

To see whether setting acts as an essential element in the fiction, or whether it exists merely as a decorative and functionless background, we need to ask ourselves this: Could the work in question be set in another time and another place without doing it essential damage? If the answer is yes, then the setting can be said to serve as a decorative background whose function is largely irrelevant to the purpose of the work as a whole.

2. SETTING AS ANTAGONIST. Often, the forces of nature function as a causal agent or antagonist, helping to establish conflict and to determine the outcome of events. The Yukon wilderness with which Jack London's nameless tenderfoot tries unsuccessfully to contend in his famous story "To Build a Fire" is one example of a setting that functions as antagonist; the "tumultuous" and "snarling" sea in Stephen Crane's "The Open Boat" is another. Perhaps the most famous example of setting as an agent that shapes and determines the lives and fate of those who come within its presence is Hardy's menacing Egdon Heath in *The Return of the Native.* The overpowering "titanic" personality of the Heath is established immediately, in the first chapter ("A Face on Which Time Makes but Little Impression"), well before the reader is introduced to the characters or the plot:

The most thorough-going ascetic could feel that he had a natural right to wander on Egdon: he was keeping within the line of legitimate indulgence when he laid himself open to influences such as these. Colors and beauties so far subdued were, at least, the birthright of all. Only in summer days of highest feather did its mood touch the level of gaity. Intensity was more usually reached by way of the solemn than by way of the brilliant, and such a sort of intensity was often arrived at during winter darkness, tempests, and mists. Then Egdon was aroused to reciprocity; for the storm was its lover, and the wind its friend. Then it became the home of strange phantoms; and it was found to be the hitherto unrecognized original of those wild regions of obscurity which are vaguely felt to be compassing us about in midnight dreams of flight and disaster, and are never thought of after the dream till revived by scenes like this.
—From *The Return of the Native,* Thomas Hardy [1878]

Egdon Heath, as Hardy makes clear, is no mere neutral backdrop to action, but a sinister, almost human (or even superhuman) force, intimately connected with the lives of its inhabitants. Hardy speaks of the "influences" of the Heath and personifies its qualities ("the storm was its lover, and the wind its friend") to suggest a dominating presence whose influence is inescapable. As one well-known critic has correctly observed, "This dynamic use of scene to determine the lives of the characters . . . is technically the most interesting thing in the book."[8] And one might add, it is the most impressive as well.

3. SETTING AS A MEANS OF CREATING APPROPRIATE ATMOSPHERE. Thomas Hardy's Egdon Heath serves his novel not only as a causative agent but as a means of establishing atmosphere. Hardy, of course, is not alone. Many authors manipulate their settings as a means of arousing the reader's expectations and establishing an appropriate state of mind for events to come. No author is more adept in this respect than Edgar Allan Poe. In the following passage from "The Fall of the House of Usher," the narrator first enters Roderick Usher's room. Notice how Poe not only provides the details of setting, but tells the reader just how to respond to them:

The room in which I found myself was very large and lofty. The windows were long, narrow, and pointed, and at so vast a distance from the black oaken floor as to be altogether inaccessible from within. Feeble gleams of encrimsoned light made their way through the trellissed panes, and served to render sufficiently distinct the more

[8] Edward Wagenknecht, *Cavalcade of the English Novel* (New York: Henry Holt and Company, 1943), p. 361.

prominent objects around; the eye, however, struggled in vain to reach the remoter angles of the chamber, or the recesses of the vaulted and fretted ceiling. Dark draperies hung upon the walls. The general furniture was profuse, comfortless, antique, and tattered. Many books and musical instruments lay scattered about, but failed to give any vitality to the scene. I felt that I breathed an atmosphere of sorrow. An air of stern, deep and irredeemable gloom hung over and pervaded all.

—From "The Fall of the House of Usher," Edgar Allan Poe [1839]

The room, which Poe skillfully makes us both see and feel, is as "inaccessible" and "gloomy" as its owner and as such establishes an appropriate mood that anticipates and foreshadows our eventual meeting with Roderick himself.

4. SETTING AS A MEANS OF REVEALING CHARACTER. Very often the way in which a character perceives the setting, and the way he or she reacts to it, will tell the reader more about the character and his state of mind than it will about the setting itself. This is particularly true of works in which the author carefully controls the point of view. In "My Kinsman, Major Molineux," for example, there is no indication that the outlandishly attired conspirators, who move easily through Boston's streets, are confused in the slightest by the city. Yet Robin Molineux, Hawthorne's young protagonist, most certainly is. For Robin the city is scarcely real; he is "almost ready to believe that a spell was on him." The dark "crooked and narrow" streets seem to lead nowhere, and the disorienting moonlight, so perfect for the carrying out of clandestine activities, serves only to make "the forms of distant objects" fade away "with almost ghostly indistinctness, just as his eye appeared to grasp them." As Hawthorne presents it, the urban landscape mirrors perfectly Robin's growing sense of isolation, loneliness, frustration, and confusion.

An author can also clarify and reveal character by deliberately making setting a metaphoric or symbolic extension of character. Roderick Usher's "inaccessible" room is a perfect representation of its owner-occupant. So, too, with the entire house. As Poe's nameless narrator rides toward the House of Usher, he notes its "insufferable gloom," its "vacant eye-like windows," the "minute fungi . . . hanging in fine tangled web-work from the eaves," its advanced state of decay, and, finally, the "barely perceptible fissure" extending the full length of the house "until it became lost in the sullen waters of the tarn." As the reader soon discovers, Roderick Usher and his house are mirror images of one another. Roderick is as remote and gloomy as the house itself: his eyes, like the windows, are vacant and lifeless; his hair has the same gossamer consistency as the fungi growing from the eaves; and there is within him the same perceptible and fatal fissure. As the action of the story proceeds to make clear, Roderick and his house are in an advanced state of internal disintegration. Setting and character are one; the house objectifies, and in this way serves to clarify, its master. It is only fitting, therefore, that at Roderick's death the melancholy House of Usher should collapse into the "deep and dank tarn."

5. SETTING AS A MEANS OF REINFORCING THEME. Setting can also be used as a means of reinforcing and clarifying the themes of a novel or short story. In Hardy's *The Return of the Native,* for example, Egdon Heath not only serves as an antagonist and as a means of creating and sustaining atmosphere, but also as a way of illustrating Hardy's vision of the role of blind causality in an unfriendly universe. Stephen Crane, who shared much of Hardy's belief in

naturalism, utilizes setting in a similar way in his story "The Blue Hotel."
The setting of Crane's story is introduced in the very first sentences:

The Palace Hotel at Fort Romper was painted a light blue, a shade that is on the
legs of a kind of heron, causing the bird to declare its position against any background.
The Palace Hotel, then, was always screaming and howling in a way that made the
dazzling winter landscape of Nebraska seem only a grey swampish hush. It stood alone
on the prairie, and when the snow was falling the town two hundred yards away was
not visible.

—From "The Blue Hotel," Stephen Crane [1898]

The reader subsequently discovers that this setting has direct thematic relevance to Crane's conception of the relationship between man and nature, as
the author-narrator makes clear:

We picture the world as thick with conquering and elate humanity, but here, with the
bugles of the tempest pealing, it was hard to imagine a peopled earth. One viewed
the existence of man then as a marvel, and conceded a glamour of wonder to these
lice which were caused to cling to a whirling, fire-smitten, ice-locked, disease-stricken,
space-lost bulb. The conceit of man was explained by this storm to be the very engine
of life. One was a coxcomb not to die in it.

In a fundamentally indifferent universe, a man's survival (and, ironically, at
times his destruction) depends on a capacity for self-assertion, much in the
way that the blue hotel asserts its lonely presence against the stark, inhospitable
Nebraska landscape.

A Note on Setting in Time

In most of the preceding examples we have emphasized the physical aspects
of setting at the expense of the temporal ones. But the time of day, time of
year, or period in history at which a given event or series of events occurs
can also contribute importantly to setting, as in the case of historical novels.
The fact that the events of Hawthorn's "My Kinsman, Major Molineux" take
place at night is a highly relevant part of the setting, for darkness is traditionally
an appropriate cover for deeds of conspiracy and violence. In Poe's "The
Cask of Amontillado," the action takes place not only in the evening, but
"during the supreme madness of the carnival season" in the dark crypts beneath
Montresor's palazzo. Poe could scarcely have conjured up a more effective
setting in which to dramatize the way insanity emerges from beneath the surface
of apparent respectability to consummate its single-minded desire for vengeance. Many of the most climactic moments of fiction, in fact, seem to take
place at night (note, for example, the scaffold scene in *The Scarlet Letter*) as if
to suggest that it is after the rest of the world is asleep that we stand most
ready to reveal the essential truths about ourselves to the world.

In much the same way, certain seasons of the year lend themselves more
to certain kinds of events than to others. Poe's narrator arrives at the House
of Usher on "a dull, dark, and soundless day in the autumn of the year," a
period we normally associate with the coming of winter and of death. Winter
also is an appropriate setting for the action of Crane's "The Blue Hotel,"
for the howling storm which swirls around the hotel is perfectly in keeping
with the physical violence that soon overtakes and destroys the Swede. Authors

will often use the cycle of the year and the cycle of the day to establish settings precisely *because* of the traditional association with the successive cycles in human life: spring-morning-youth; summer-noon-maturity; fall-evening-old age; winter-night-death.

Analyzing Setting

1. What is the work's setting in space and time?
2. How does the author go about establishing setting? Does the author want the reader to see *or* feel the setting; or does the author want the reader both to see *and* feel it? What details of the setting does the author isolate and describe?
3. Is the setting important? If so, what is its function? Is it used to reveal, reinforce, or influence character, plot, or theme?
4. Is the setting an appropriate one?

POINT OF VIEW

A story must have a plot, characters, and a setting. It must also have a storyteller: a narrative voice, real or implied, that presents the story to the reader. When we talk about narrative voice, we are talking about *point of view,* the method of narration that determines the position, or angle of vision, from which the story is told. The nature of the relationship between the narrator and the story, the teller and the tale, is always crucial to the art of fiction. It governs the reader's access to the story and determines just how much he can know at any given moment about what is taking place. So crucial is point of view that, once having been chosen, it will color and shape the way in which everything else is presented and perceived, including plot, character, and setting. Alter or change the point of view, and you alter and change the story.

The choice of point of view is the choice of who is to tell the story, who talks to the reader. It may be a narrator outside the work (*omniscient* point of view); a narrator inside the work, telling the story from a *limited omniscient* or *first-person* point of view; or apparently no one (*dramatic* point of view). As we will see in the subsequent discussion, these four basic points of view, and their variations, involve at the extreme a choice between omniscient point of view and dramatic point of view—a choice that involves, among other things, the distance that the author wishes to maintain between the reader and the story and the extent to which the author is willing to involve the reader in its interpretation. As the author moves away from omniscience along this spectrum of choices, he progressively surrenders the ability to see into the minds of his characters. However, the question of point of view, perhaps to a greater degree than any element of fiction that we have examined so far, is as complex and complicated as it is important; the selected categories summarized here only begin to account for the possibilities that readers will encounter in their adventures with fiction.

Commonly Used Points of View

1. OMNISCIENT POINT OF VIEW. With the *omniscient point of view* (sometimes also referred to as *panoramic, shifting,* or *multiple point of view*), an "all-knowing"

narrator firmly imposes himself between the reader and the story, and retains full and complete control over the narrative. The omniscient narrator is not a character in the story and is not at all involved in the plot. From a vantage point outside the story, the narrator is free to tell us much or little, to dramatize or summarize, to interpret, speculate, philosophize, moralize or judge. He or she can tell us directly what the characters are like and why they behave as they do; record their words and conversations and dramatize their actions; or enter their minds to explore directly their innermost thoughts and feelings. The narrator can move the reader from one event to the next, being just as explicit (or evasive) as he wishes about their significance and meaning; he can skip backward and forward in time, now dramatizing, now summarizing as he chooses. When the omniscient narrator speaks to us in his own voice, there is a natural temptation to identify that voice with the author's. Sometimes such an identification is warranted; at other times it may not be, for the voice that tells the story and speaks to the reader, although it may seem to reflect the author's beliefs and values, is as much the author's creation as any of the characters in the story.

Omniscient narration frequently occurs in eighteenth- and nineteenth-century novels—Fielding's *Tom Jones* and Thackeray's *Vanity Fair* are good examples. In the latter, the narrator frankly assumes the role of puppeteer, "the Manager of the Performance," in a manner that may seem offensive and condescending to modern readers who are used to more realistic treatment:

> But my kind reader will please to remember that this history has "Vanity Fair" for a title, and that Vanity Fair is a very vain, wicked, foolish place, full of all sorts of humbugs and falsenesses and pretensions. And while the moralist, who is holding forth on the cover (an accurate protrait of your humble servant), professes to wear neither gown nor bands, but only the very same long-eared livery in which his congregation is arrayed; yet, look you, one is bound to speak the truth as far as one knows it, whether one mounts a cap and bells or a shovel-hat; and a deal of disagreeable matter must come out in the course of such an undertaking.
> —From *Vanity Fair,* William Makepeace Thackeray [1848]

In our own discussions, we have seen the commentary of the omniscient narrator in Crane's "The Blue Hotel," where men are compared to lice clinging to "a whirling, fire-smitten, ice-locked, disease-stricken, space-lost bulb." In Hawthorne's "My Kinsman, Major Molineux," an omniscient narrator introduces the story with a lengthy paragraph of historical "remarks . . . as a preface to the following adventures" and then suggests that "The reader, in order to avoid a long and dry detail of colonial affairs . . . dispense with an account of the train of circumstances that had caused much temporary inflammation of the popular mind." Though the story that follows is narrated principally from Robin's point of view, the omniscient narrator is ever in the wings. At the story's climactic moment, he breaks in to record the reaction of the moon to Robin's catharsis: "The Man in the Moon heard the far bellow. 'Oho,' quoth he, 'the old earth is frolicsome to-night.' "

A more typical example of the omniscient point of view is found in the following passage from Hardy's *The Mayor of Casterbridge*. It occurs at the very beginning of the seventh chapter as Elizabeth-Jane and her mother arrive at the Three Mariners Inn:

Elizabeth-Jane and her mother had arrived some twenty minutes earlier. Outside the house they had stood and considered whether even this homely place, though recommended as moderate, might not be too serious in its prices for their light pockets. Finally, however, they had found courage to enter, and duly met Stannidge the landlord; a silent man, who drew and carried frothing measures to this room and to that, shoulder to shoulder with his waiting-maids—a stately slowness, however, entering into his ministrations by contrast with theirs, as became one whose service was somewhat optional. It would have been altogether optional but for the orders of the landlady, a person who sat in the bar, corporeally motionless, but with a flitting eye and quick ear, with which she observed and heard through the open door and hatchway the pressing needs of customers whom her husband overlooked though close at hand. Elizabeth and her mother were passively accepted as sojourners, and shown to a small bedroom under one of the gables, where they sat down.

—From *The Mayor of Casterbridge*, Thomas Hardy [1886]

In a single paragraph the narrator summarizes the action, provides details of setting, and reveals the state of mind of four characters, in turn.

Some critics draw a distinction between omniscient methods that permit their narrators to comment freely in their own voices, using "I" or the editorial "we," (*editorial* omniscience) and those that present the thoughts and actions of characters without such overt editorial intrusions (*neutral* or *impartial* omniscience). Crane and Thackeray in the examples cited are clearly among the former; Hardy, at least in the passage here, is among the latter.

Although there is an observable direction in modern literature away from using omniscience—in part because of an intellectual temperament that tends to distrust, and even deny, absolutes, certainties, and all-knowing attitudes—twentieth-century authors continue to debate its value and to exploit its advantages. Like so many of the critical choices that the writer of fiction is called on to make, however, the choice of point of view is finally a matter of appropriateness. The omniscient point of view, while inappropriate to a Hemingway story, is certainly very appropriate to large, panoramic novels like Tolstoy's national epic *War and Peace,* in which an omniscient mode of narration is used to suggest the complexity and scope of Russian life itself.

The great advantage of the omniscient point of view, then, is the flexibility it gives its "all-knowing" narrator, who can direct the reader's attention and control the sources of information. As we move away from omniscient telling in the direction of dramatic showing, the narrator progressively surrenders these advantages. In choosing to move inside the framework of the work to merge his or her identity with that of one of the characters (limited omniscient or first-person point of view) or to give up all identity (dramatic point of view), the narrator restricts the channels through which information can be transmitted to the reader; as a result, the reader is involved more and more directly in the task of interpretation.

2. LIMITED OMNISCIENT POINT OF VIEW. With a *limited omniscient* (sometimes referred to as *third-person* or *selective omniscient*) *point of view,* the narrator limits his ability to penetrate the minds of characters by selecting a single character to act as the center of revelation. What the reader knows and sees of events is always restricted to what this focal character can know or see. This point of view differs significantly from the first-person point of view, which we will discuss later. At times the reader may be given direct access to this focal charac-

ter's own "voice" and thoughts, insofar as these are reproduced through dialogue or presented dramatically through monologue or stream of consciousness. On all other occasions, the reader's access is indirect: it is the narrator's
voice, somewhere on the sidelines, that tells the story and transmits the action,
characterization, description, analysis, and other informing details upon which
the reader's understanding and interpretation depend. Although the focal character is a visible presence within the story in a way that a fully omniscient
narrator is not, at any moment that character is only as available and accessible
to the reader as the narrator will permit.

The character chosen as narrative center, and often referred to through
the use of a third-person pronoun as *he* or *she*, may be the protagonist or
may be some other major character, as is Charles Marlow in Conrad's "Heart
of Darkness." Often, however, the assignment is given to a minor character
who functions in the role of an onlooker, watching and speculating from the
periphery of the story and only minimally involved, if at all, in its action.
Once chosen, it is this character's mind and eyes that become the story's angle
of vision and the point of entry for the reader. Henry James aptly refers to
this character in his critical essays and prefaces as "the reflector" or "mirroring
consciousness," for it is through the prism of his or her conscious mind that
the story is filtered and reflected.

The advantages of the limited omniscient point of view are the tightness
of focus and control that it provides and the intensity of treatment that it
makes possible. These advantages explain why the limited omniscient point
of view is so admirably suited to the short story, whose restricted scope can
accommodate full omniscience only with great difficulty. The limited omniscient
point of view predominates in Hawthorne's "My Kinsman, Major Molineux,"
as seen, for example, in the previously-quoted passage describing Robin's physical appearance and clothing. It is used with good effect as well in another of
Hawthorne's famous tales, "Young Goodman Brown," in which the author is
interested in the way in which the conviction of sin can totally influence and
distort an individual's outlook. In order to chronicle Goodman Brown's progressive disillusionment with the world, climaxed by his conviction that his
fellow townspeople, and even his wife Faith, are numbered among the Devil's
disciples, the narrator positions himself at Goodman's shoulder and reveals
the world as it takes shape before Goodman's innocent eyes. Whether or not
Goodman Brown's night in the forest is dream or reality finally makes no
difference; Goodman is convinced beyond redemption that the Devil is correct:
that "Evil is the nature of mankind." Goodman's naïve and untested faith is
destroyed; his vision of life is darkened; and he goes to his grave a gloomy,
distrustful, and lonely man. The limited omniscient point of view serves Hawthorne's purposes well, for it is Brown's personal vision of the way that things
appear to be—rather than the way that things actually *are*—that is at the center
of Hawthorne's story.

The limited omniscient point of view also works particularly well as a means
of creating and sustaining *irony*, because it can exploit the disparity between
what the focal character thinks he or she knows and the true state of affairs.
Henry James, whose novels and stories make heavy use of a third-person "reflector" in the form of a "finely aware and richly responsible" character who
prides himself on these traits, is an excellent case in point. In "The Tree of
Knowledge," for example, a story that, as its title suggests, turns on "knowledge" and "knowing," the reflector is the middle-aged bachelor Peter Brench,

who had dedicated his life to making sure that Mrs. Mallow and her son Lancelot are kept ignorant of the "Master's" lack of artistic talent. Brench, James tells us, is an individual who "had judged himself once for all": "It was one of the secret opinions . . . of Peter Brench that his main success in life would have consisted in his never having committed himself about the work, as it was called, of his friend Morgan Mallow." As it turns out, Peter Brench's heroic gesture has been an unnecessary one, for Mrs. Mallow and Lancelot know only too well that the Master's talent is impoverished. For years they have successfully kept from Brench the very knowledge he would keep from *them.* The irony of the situation is made possible by James' ability to narrate the story from Peter Brench's point of view while slowly revealing to the reader the exact degree of Peter's false assumptions.

3. FIRST-PERSON POINT OF VIEW. The use of first-person point of view places still another restriction on the voice that tells the story. As already noted, the movement from full to limited omniscience essentially involves the narrator's decision to limit his omniscience to what can be known by a single character. First-person point of view goes one step further by having that focal character address the reader directly, without an intermediary. This character refers to himself or herself as "I" in the story and addresses the reader as "you," either explicitly or by implication.

The first-person point of view thus combines the advantages and restrictions of limited omniscience with his own. As with limited omniscience, first-person narration is tightly controlled and limited in its access to information. The first-person narrator, like his limited omniscient counterpart, while free to speculate, can only report information that falls within his own first-hand knowledge of the world or what he comes to learn second hand from others.[9] First-person narratives, however, are necessarily subjective. The only thoughts and feelings that first-person narrators experience directly are their own, and authors sometimes explore and exploit this subjectivity by allowing their narrators' thoughts and feelings—their perceptions of the world—to become colored by unwitting prejudices and biases. The implications of this uncorrected subjectivity are crucially important, for it means that the reader can never expect to see characters and events as they actually are but only as they *appear* to be to the mediating consciousness of the "I"-narrator who stands between the reader and the work. For this reason it is always necessary to pay particular attention to the character that fills that role—to his or her personality; built-in biases, values, and beliefs; and degree of awareness and perceptivity—in order to measure his reliability as a narrator.[10] In this respect, of course, first-person point of view closely resembles the perspective from which each of us views our own life and times.

[9] Some authors get around this limitation by introducing letters, diaries, and journals into their narratives, thus giving the narrator (and the reader) direct and immediate access to the thoughts and feelings of others. Samuel Richardson's *Pamela* (1740) and *Clarissa* (1748) and Bram Stoker's *Dracula* (1897) are good examples of the use of this device and as a result are sometimes referred to as epistolary novels. The problem with works that rely heavily on such written documentation is mainly one of credibility: are men and women, caught up in adventures of one sort or another, willing and able to sit down to compose their thoughts and feelings on paper? Pamela, for example, writes six letters on her wedding day!

[10] It is also true, of course, that the *author's* biases can and often do color the writing. In first-person point of view, these biases may be an intentional element in the plot. In other points of view, they may be unintentional, but equally important.

Like the protagonist-narrator, we can *see* everything that falls within our line of vision, but we can only *know* the content of our own mind, and we must be constantly alert to the influences, large and small, that shape and possibly distort our outlook on the world.

First-person point of view has its advantages, however, not the least of which is the marvelous sense of immediacy, credibility, and psychological realism that autobiographical storytelling always carries with it. "Call me Ishmael," begins Herman Melville's *Moby-Dick;* the reader is at once addressed in a conversational tone as a friend worthy of confidence by one who is about to tell us directly in his own person about his adventures in pursuit of a white whale. Ishmael's invitation to share with the reader his own unedited experiences is a seductive one. If the appeal is accepted—and there is little reason, at least initially, why it should not be—the reader and his sympathies are at once engaged on behalf of the narrator and his story, and the illusion is created that subsequent participation and discovery will be joint. No other point of view is more effective in its capacity for eliciting the reader's direct intellectual and emotional involvement in the teller and the tale.

First-person narrators are usually identified and differentiated on the basis of their degree of involvement with the events of the plot. They may be protagonists, like Mark Twain's Huckleberry Finn, who tell the stories of their own lives and adventures. In such works, the protagonist-narrator is always firmly in control of the content, pace, and method of presentation. Certain events will be fully or partially dramatized as the protagonist witnessed them; others will be transmitted to the reader indirectly through the use of summary and comment. Protagonist-narrators, not surprisingly, tend to dominate their works to the disadvantage of other characters, and by continually calling attention to their own presence, and to their own thoughts and feelings, fully characterize themselves in the process. To the extent that such characters are perceptive and intelligent and able to make sense of the events in which they participate, their stories frequently, like Huckleberry Finn's, illustrate their growth and maturation. Where such sensitivity and intelligence are lacking, the protagonist-narrator becomes at once a ready-made subject for irony.

Protagonist-narrators may narrate events ostensibly as they take place, as in Daniel Defoe's *Robinson Crusoe,* or in leisurely retrospect, with the narrator looking backward over a period of time on adventures that have already been concluded, as Pip does in Charles Dickens' *Great Expectations.* In retrospective views, the extent to which the narrator has managed in the interim to achieve appropriate distance and objectivity can be an issue, as well. The unnamed protagonist-narrator of James Joyce's "Araby," for example, looking backward at his own boyish romanticism has clearly not reached such a position. In calling himself "a creature driven and derided by vanity," he is clearly judging himself too harshly for an act that an older, and a presumably wiser, adult would be willing to excuse as part of the inevitable process of growing up. In addition, to the extent that life-endangering situations are at stake, protagonist-narration offers little real suspense over the eventual outcome; that the protagonist is able to tell his or her story means that, at the very least, as with Melville's Ishmael, "I only am escaped alone to tell thee."

A particularly good example of the way in which protagonist-narrators are established as the narrative authority of their works is found in the opening lines of Mark Twain's *Huckleberry Finn:*

You don't know about me, without you have read a book by the name of *The Adventures of Tom Sawyer*, but that ain't no matter. That book was made by Mr. Mark Twain, and he told the truth, mainly. There was things which he stretched, but mainly he told the truth. That is nothing. I never seen anybody but lied, one time or another, without it was Aunt Polly, or the widow, or maybe Mary. Aunt Polly—Tom's Aunt Polly, she is—and Mary, and the Widow Douglas, is all told about in that book—which is mostly a true book; with some stretchers, as I said before.

    —From *The Adventures of Huckleberry Finn,* Mark Twain [1885]

In this brief passage, Huck succeeds in achieving a number of important things on behalf of his creator. We are introduced to the protagonist, or, rather, he introduces himself to us, and in a way that makes him at once credible and convincing. This is achieved in part by Huck's declaration of his own candor and honesty, but partly too by the slightly ungrammatical backwoods idiom in which he speaks, a "voice" that strikes us as highly appropriate for a largely self-educated rural youth raised in Mark Twain's nineteenth-century Missouri. Huck's speech is a very important part of his characterization; and Mark Twain has clearly succeeded—where other authors often fail—in creating characters who "talk like they ought to." By alluding specifically to the author, "Mr. Mark Twain," Huck also creates the illusion—so necessary with first-person narrative—that author and character are distinct and separate; in this case, that Huck, in effect, has an identity of his own, quite apart from the man who wrote *The Adventures of Tom Sawyer.* (The intelligent reader, in his role as critic, will naturally see such as assertion for the convention that it is.)

What Huck says and the confidential and intimate way in which he says it are of course deliberately calculated to engage the reader's sympathy and trust. And what better way to engage the reader than by generously allowing that while Mark Twain "mainly . . . told the truth" in *Tom Sawyer,* there were some "stretchers" because "I never seen anybody but lied, one time or another." The implication and invitation are clear: If, as Huck assures us, *The Adventures of Tom Sawyer* is "mostly a true book," we can count on the veracity of the present work, for Huckleberry Finn, who knows a "stetcher" when he sees one, will be in charge. The opening paragraph thus serves Mark Twain's purposes well: it establishes immediacy and intimacy because it purports to be a firsthand account of experience without the intervention or analysis of an outside narrator; and it marks the beginning of a growing acquaintance with Huckleberry Finn, a character who invites our belief because of his self-proclaimed awareness and sensitivity where matters of truth are concerned.

Not all protagonist-narrators tell their own stories. Sometimes the protagonist-narrator is charged with the responsibility of telling someone else's story, as Nick Carraway, the protagonist of F. Scott Fitzgerald's *The Great Gatsby,* is charged with the responsibility of telling Jay Gatsby's. Because the narrative focus is shifted elsewhere, the characterization of such narrators will be less fully developed than that of a Huckleberry Finn. In the end, however, the purpose of Fitzgerald and Mark Twain is very much the same: to record the impact of the story upon the growth and maturation of the narrator.

The first-person narrator is frequently not the protagonist at all, but rather a character whose role in the plot is clearly secondary. He or she may, in fact, have almost no visible role in the plot and exist primarily as a convenient device for transmitting the narrative to the reader. Such is the case with the narrators of Poe's "The Fall of the House of Usher" and Conrad's "Heart of Darkness." Narrators of this type will be, at best, only partially characterized and may remain little more than disembodied voices distinguishable only by the fact that they address the reader in the first person. Such narrators do, however, enjoy certain definite advantages. Often they have greater freedom of movement than the protagonist-narrator. From their positions at the periphery of the action they may move among the other characters with relative ease, using them as sources to acquire helpful information. Minor characters serving as first-person narrators very often appear in the role of *confidant,* as genial and sympathetic personalities in whose wisdom and judgment (or presumed neutrality) others seem willing, or even desperate, to confide. Such is the lot of Nick Carraway, who tells the reader on the very first page of the novel that "I'm inclined to reserve all judgments, a habit that has opened up many curious natures to me and also made me the victim of not a few veteran bores." Likewise, the indefatigable Dr. Watson is the *foil* to whom Holmes can explain in meticulous detail his method of detection, thus building and heightening the suspense while allowing Holmes to keep his readers in the dark until the last about the problem-solving going on in his mind.

In their relationship to the other characters and to the action of the plot, first-person narrators may be either interested and involved or disinterested and detached. In either case, however, they are always subject to hidden biases and prejudices in their telling of the story. Minor characters serving as narrators, no less than major ones, must be watched constantly, especially if the reader has reason to suspect that they may be other than totally reliable guides to the truth of what they report.

4. STREAM OF CONSCIOUSNESS. We have already described *stream of consciousness* as the technique of characterization that renders *from the inside* the conscious or unconscious content of the human mind and the myriad of thoughts, perceptions, feelings, and associations that ebb and flow there. To the extent that an author chooses to locate the center of narrative authority exclusively inside the mind of a single character and to record external reality, including speech and action, only as it registers its impression upon that mind, stream of consciousness can also be used as a variation of first-person point of view. An excellent example is offered by the opening passage of William Faulkner's *The Sound and the Fury:*

Through the fence, between the curling flower spaces, I could see them hitting. They were coming toward where the flag was and I went along the fence. Luster was hunting in the grass by the flower tree. They took the flag out, and they were hitting. Then they put the flag back and they went to the table, and he hit and the other hit. Then they went on, and I went along the fence. Luster came away from the flower tree and we went along the fence and they stopped and we stopped and I looked through the fence while Luster was hunting in the grass.
—From *The Sound and the Fury,* William Faulkner [1929]

The speaker is Benjy Compson, the thirty-three-year-old idiot whose point of view dominates the first section of Faulkner's novel. But the voice that addresses the reader is not Benjy's speaking voice. Rather we are being made privy to the pattern of thought and sensation unfolding within Benjy's infantile mind as he stands in the Compson garden watching golfers through the fence.

Stream-of-consciousness used as first-person point of view is of course difficult to sustain over an extended period of time because of the heavy demands it makes on the author and reader alike. Not only does it fasten the story's angle of vision exclusively to the *inside* of a single mind, whose patterns of conscious and unconscious thoughts and feelings are frequently illogical and hard to follow, but, theoretically at least, it also effectively prevents the author from providing stage directions and clarifying comments and from asserting other forms of direct managerial control over the development of the narrative. To avoid these difficulties, and still take full advantage of the possibilities of stream-of-consciousness narration, authors will typically utilize either the omniscient or limited omniscient point of view, which, as already noted, allows the necessary external control while making it possible to explore the content of the mind of one or more of the characters. This is the case with such well-known works as Virginia Woolf's *To the Lighthouse* and James Joyce's *The Portrait of the Artist as a Young Man,* which make extensive use of the stream-of-consciousness technique.

5. DRAMATIC POINT OF VIEW. In the dramatic, or objective, point of view the story is told ostensibly by no one. The narrator, who to this point in our discussion has been a visible, mediating authority standing between the reader and the work, now disappears completely and the story is allowed to present itself dramatically through action and dialogue. With the disappearance of the narrator, telling is replaced by showing, and the illusion is created that the reader is a direct and immediate witness to an unfolding drama.[11] Without a narrator to serve as mentor and guide, the reader is left largely on his own. There is no way of entering the minds of the characters; no evaluative comments are offered; the reader is not told directly how to respond, either intellectually or emotionally, to the events or the characters. The reader is permitted to view the work only in its externals, from the outside. Although the author may supply certain descriptive details, particularly at the beginning of the work, the reader is called on to shoulder much of the responsibility for analysis and interpretation. He or she must deduce the circumstances of the action, past and present, and how and why the characters think and feel as they do on the basis of their overt behavior and conversation.

In its relation to the reader, dramatic point of view is often compared to the perspective from which we observe a film or a stage play. As with dramatic point of view, the viewer, sitting in the audience, has no way of penetrating the minds of the characters and is left to infer their mental or emotional states from the dialogue (or monologue) and the action. The plot unfolds in scenes before the viewer, whose angle of vision is fixed by the seat in which he or she sits; there is no one at the viewer's shoulder, or at the foot or the side of the stage, to provide additional information and to say where, in particular, his wandering eyes should focus. To be sure, this analogy, although helpful, is by no means perfect. The writer of fiction, whose medium is language, selects and arranges language within the confines of a printed page and exercises far greater control than either the filmmaker or dramatist in focusing the reader's attention and, through the quality of the words themselves, manipulating the reader's response.

[11] The words *ostensibly* and *illusion* are used advisedly here, for a narrative voice is almost always present somewhere in the story, if only to provide a few brief sentences of description or stage direction. In truth, the narrator never totally disappears in a work of fiction, and the task of the critic is to know where and when he makes his presence felt.

The dramatic point of view appeals to many modern and contemporary writers because of the impersonal and objective way it presents experience and because of the vivid sense of the actual that it creates. Ernest Hemingway is its leading exemplar. The dramatic mode dominates Hemingway's short stories and novels where it is used to illustrate and reinforce the Hemingway "code," with its emphasis on psychological and emotional detachment and self-control.

The following passage of dramatic narration occurs at the beginning of Hemingway's short story "Hills Like White Elephants."

The Hills across the valley of the Ebro were long and white. On this side there was no shade and no trees and the station was between two lines of rails in the sun. Close against the side of the station there was the warm shadow of the building and a curtain, made of strings of bamboo beads, hung across the open door into the bar, to keep out flies. The American and the girl with him sat at a table in the shade, outside the building. It was very hot and the express from Barcelona would come in forty minutes. It stopped at this junction for two minutes and went on to Madrid.

"What should we drink?" the girl asked. She had taken off her hat and put it on the table.

"It's pretty hot," the man said.

"Let's drink beer."

"Dos cervezas," the man said into the curtain.

"Big ones?" a woman asked from the doorway.

"Yes. Two big ones."

The woman brought two glasses of beer and two felt pads. She put the felt pads and the beer glasses on the table and looked at the man and the girl. The girl was looking off at the line of hills. They were white in the sun and the country was brown and dry.

"They look like white elephants," she said.

"I've never seen one," the man drank his beer.

"No, you wouldn't have."

—From "Hills Like White Elephants," Ernest Hemingway [1927]

The action unfolds dramatically. The concrete, factual details are introduced without comment; and the action and the characters are allowed to present themselves directly to the reader without benefit of an intervening narrator. The effect is one of pure showing. What we are shown are two Americans, a man and a woman, sitting at a table next to a railroad station, waiting for the train from Barcelona. The weather is hot, they order two beers, and begin a casual, listless conversation which gradually reveals the situation (the girl's pregnancy), the tension that exists between them (he wants her to have an abortion; she does not), and the basic, underlying differences in attitudes and sensibilities (his selfishness and callousness, her sensitivity and imagination) that now threaten their entire relationship. The differences in sensibilities are first clearly signalled by her imaginative observation that the hills in the distance "look like white elephants," his indifferent response ("I've never seen one"), and the cynicism of her curt reply ("No, you wouldn't have"). Hemingway's story, telescoped into the forty minutes it takes for the train to arrive, unfolds slowly, inexorably, almost artlessly, through the medium of flat, unemotional dialogue. The story we witness and assemble largely by ourselves is one of two unhappy people caught up in a conflict which, given the differences in their respective characters and personalities, will not yield a clear-cut or satisfactory resolution.

Reliable and Unreliable Narrators

In analyzing the point of view of a given work of fiction, the reader is often forced to confront the question of the relative trustworthiness or reliability of the narrator. With omniscient point of view, the question of reliability is usually not a troublesome one, for when the narrator is placed outside the work and aids directly in its analysis and interpretation, his reliability can be largely assumed. Much the same thing is true with the dramatic point of view, where there is no apparent narrator present. When, however, the narrative voice is positioned inside the work and belongs to a character who is directly involved in the action, the question of the narrator's reliability often becomes pertinent indeed.

Reliability, it should be understood, is not a matter of whether the reader happens to agree with the narrator's views or opinions. We can choose to agree or not with such views, but our agreement or lack thereof will not fundamentally affect how we view and understand the work. Reliability refers to something far more serious, for an unreliable narrator who is allowed to go undetected and uncorrected can distort our understanding of the author's own intention, attitudes, and meaning.

Often, of course, an unreliable narrator is a stylistic device used by the author to make an obvious thematic point. For example, in Richard Wright's "The Man Who Was Almost a Man," Dave's equation of a gun with manliness underscores the false and corrupting values of the society in which he lives. In such a case, the author usually provides somewhere a clear indication of the narrator's unreliability, for the failure to do so will result in ambiguity if not downright unintelligibility.

The question of reliability becomes most complex, however, with perfectly honest and well-intentioned narrators who make every effort to tell the truth of things insofar as they are able to perceive it. Sincerity and good intentions are one thing; reliability is another. Such narrators may prove to be unreliable because they are ignorant or because they commit an error in judgment by drawing the wrong conclusions from the facts available. They may also prove to be unreliable because they are victims of their own self-deception. Whatever the cause, once the reader begins to suspect that the narrator is unreliable, a note of ambiguity or irony is introduced into the work.

To overcome this problem, the reader must first be able to identify the narrator and perceive his unreliability; and having done so the reader must be able to supply, on his own, an alternative perspective which will allow him to view the work correctly. Sometimes the necessary correction can be made by analyzing and attempting to understand the intellectual and moral qualities of the narrator or by studying carefully what the other characters have to say about him or her. Winterbourne, the first-person narrator of Henry James' short novel *Daisy Miller*, is a case in point. A Europeanized American, Winterbourne errs in judging the moral character of his fellow-countryman because he has "lived too long in foreign parts." His outlook has become corrupted by his Old World view of human nature, and he is unable to understand, much less appreciate, the genuine innocence and spontaneity of a young American girl who simply does in Rome as she would do at home in Schenectady. Winterbourne confuses manners with morality; as a result the impression of Daisy that the reader receives from him for much of the story is a misleading one. Only by understanding Winterbourne, and what he has become, can the reader correct his opinion of Daisy Miller and see her for the radical, if foolish, innocent that she is. James' fiction is filled with misguided and misguiding narrators like Winterbourne, and his example has been followed by many modern and contemporary writers who use the fallible narrator as a device for the deliberate creation of irony.

Winterbourne, like Peter Brench in "The Tree of Knowledge," largely corrects his own reliability as a narrator by coming to see the extent to which he has been blinded by his own biases and false assumptions. Other narrators never reach such self-knowledge, and our problem as readers is further compounded when we are unable to establish reliability or unreliability conclusively by studying their characters or by studying the evidence offered by others. On such occasions the reader will have to look to the other norms within the work, to the implied or expressed values that help to determine its meaning and theme, or to the vision of life it offers. Where such norms can be said to be different from those the narrator presents or affirms, that narrator is likely to be a fallible and unreliable one.

Unfortunately, authors writing fiction do not have textbook definitions in front of them. If they did, and if they followed them, the task of analyzing point of view would be greatly simplified. The essential problem with point of view, as we noted earlier, is that the separate categories we have outlined often do not occur in a pure and undiluted form. *Moby-Dick* begins with Ishmael telling his own story in the first person. Toward the middle of the book, Ishmael disappears from sight and Ahab emerges to dominate the story. At that point, the narrative structure takes on the qualities of a Shakespearean play, complete with stage directions. In Melville's case, the violation of consistency can hardly be construed a weakness, and what is true of *Moby-Dick* is true, to a greater or lesser extent, of many other works of fiction as well.

Analyzing Point of View

1. What is the point of view; who talks to the reader? Is the point of view consistent throughout the work or does it shift in some way?
2. Where does the narrator stand in relation to the work? Where does the reader stand?
3. To what sources of knowledge or information does the point of view give the reader access? What sources of knowledge or information does it serve to conceal?
4. If the work is told from the point of view of one of the characters, is the narrator reliable? Does his or her personality, character, or intellect affect an ability to interpret the events or the other characters correctly?
5. Given the author's purposes, is the chosen point of view an appropriate and effective one?
6. How would the work be different if told from another point of view?

THEME

Theme is one of those critical terms that mean very different things to different people. To some, who think of literature mainly as a vehicle for teaching, preaching, propagating a favorite idea, or encouraging some form of correct conduct, theme may mean the moral or lesson that can be extracted from the work, as with one of Aesop's fables or Parson Weems' famous (and, sadly, apocryphal) story about George Washington and the cherry tree. Theme is also used sometimes to refer to the basic issue, problem, or subject with which the work is concerned: for example, "the nature of man," "the discovery of truth," or "the brotherhood of man." In this sense, a number of the stories included in this anthology—Sherwood Anderson's "I Want to Know Why," James Joyce's "Araby," Katherine Anne Porter's "The Grave," and John Updike's "A&P"—may all be said to deal in common with the theme of initiation, the rite of passage into the world of adulthood. Or, we may speak of theme as a familiar pattern or motif that occurs again and again in literature, say the journey theme found in works as different and similar as John Barth's "Lost in the Funhouse," Joseph Conrad's "Heart of Darkness," Nathaniel Hawthorne's "My Kinsman, Major Molineux," and Flannery O'Connor's "The Artificial Nigger."

When we speak of theme in connection with the critical analysis of a literary work, however, we usually have a broader and more inclusive definition in mind. In literature, the theme is the central idea or statement about life that unifies and controls the total work. By this definition, then, the theme is not the issue, or problem, or subject with which the work deals, as violence is the subject of Stephen Crane's "The Blue Hotel." Rather, the theme is the comment or statement the author makes about that subject as it necessarily and inevitably emerges from the interplay of the various elements of the work.

Theme in literature, whether it takes the form of a brief and meaningful insight or a comprehensive vision of life, is the author's way of communicating and sharing ideas, perceptions, and feelings with his readers or, as is so often the case, of probing and exploring with them the puzzling questions of human existence, most of which do not yield neat, tidy, and universally acceptable answers. Although we cannot, as critics, judge a work solely on the basis of the quality of the ideas presented (or on their degree of complexity or sophistication), it is nevertheless true that one of the marks of a great work of literature—a work that we generally regard as a "classic"—is the significance of its theme; an author's ability to construct a work whose various elements work together to yield a significant theme is an important test of the quality of that author's mind and art.

"What does it mean?" "What is the author trying to say?" "What *is* the theme of the work?" These are the questions that students are often most eager and impatient to discuss. Why, then, one may properly ask, did we not begin our discussion of fiction by discussing theme? Why delay its introduction until after having considered plot, character, setting, and point of view?

We have done so for a reason that has a great deal to do not only with the nature of theme, but with the nature of fiction itself. We have organized our discussion to illustrate the fact that a work of fiction consists of a number of crucial elements *in addition* to theme; that the identification and understanding of these other elements—particularly the interaction of character and incident—can be as important to the story as theme, or more so; and that any discussion of the theme must be prepared to take those other elements into account. Theme does not exist as an intellectual abstraction that an author superimposes on the work like icing on a cake although, at times, there is a temptation to treat it as such; the theme is organically and necessarily related to the work's total structure and texture. This is the point made by Flannery

O'Connor, one of America's most important twentieth-century writers of fiction, using one of her typically homely metaphors:

People talk about the theme of a story as if the theme were like a string that a sack of chicken feed is tied with. They think that if you can pick out the theme, the way you pick the right thread in the chicken-feed sack, you can rip the story open and feed the chickens. But this is not the way meaning works in fiction. . . . The meaning of a story has to be embodied in it, has to be made concrete in it. A story is a way to say something that can't be said any other way, and it takes every word in the story to say what the meaning is.

—From "Writing Short Stories," Flannery O'Connor [1969]

Theme in fiction is discoverable to the extent that we are willing as critics to subject its various elements—its "every word"—to the process of analysis and interpretation.

Three more important points about theme in fiction need to be made. First of all, theme may be less prominent and less fully developed in some works of fiction than in others. This is especially true in the case of detective, gothic, and adventure fiction, where the author wants primarily to entertain by producing mystification, inducing chills and nightmare, or engaging the reader in a series of exciting, fast-moving incidents.

Such works may not have a demonstrable theme at all, at least in the sense in which we have defined the term. To identify the theme of a detective story with the idea that "crime doesn't pay" is not only to confuse theme with moral, but in all probability to misinterpret where the author has chosen to place the work's emphasis. One must, however, be careful. Many works of humor and satire—for example, short stories like Samuel L. Clemens' "The Notorious Jumping Frog of Calaveras County" and novels like Sinclair Lewis's *Babbitt*—while they make us smile, and perhaps laugh, do have thematic content and offer the reader significant, and in Lewis's case serious, insights into modern and contemporary life. Much the same thing is often true of gothic fiction, where, in the hands of genuine artists like Poe, Faulkner, and Carlos Fuentes, melodrama and terror are used not for their own sake but to probe the recesses of the human soul.

Second, it is entirely possible that intelligent readers and critics will differ, at times radically, on just what the theme of a given work is. It is on the basis of such disagreements that the reputations of literary critics are frequently made, or discredited. Critical disagreements often occur when the elements of the work are arranged in a way that yields two or more acceptable, yet mutually exclusive, statements. A case in point is "Young Goodman Brown," Hawthorne's story of a young Puritan who leaves his wife of three months (appropriately named Faith) and embarks on a nighttime journey into the forest to keep a prearranged appointment with the Devil. As he makes his way through the woods, first alone and then in the company of a stranger (presumably the Devil) who resembles his own father, Goodman Brown becomes increasingly convinced that his fellow townspeople, and finally even Faith, are members of the Devil's unholy communion. The story climaxes in a lurid rite of initiation, in which Goodman Brown cries out: "My Faith is gone! . . . There is no good on earth, and sin is but a name. Come Devil! for to thee is the world given."

In the aftermath, Brown's faith is destroyed; he shrinks from the bosom of his wife and goes to his grave convinced that "Evil is the nature of mankind." The final theme of the story, however, is anything but clear. Hawthorne's tale is made deliberately ambiguous through the use of a limited omniscient point of view: the narrator refuses to commit himself as to whether what Goodman Brown thinks he sees is really happening or whether it is merely the figment of Brown's distorted imagination.

As a result, the story has been analyzed by its various critics to yield a multitude of possible themes, all of them plausibly rooted in the facts of the story as the critics have interpreted those facts. Some have accepted Goodman Brown's own interpretation as the definitive statement of Hawthorne's theme; others have argued that Hawthorne is attempting to illustrate the failure of belief and the effects of moral scepticism. The story has also been variously interpreted as an attack on the hypocrisy of Puritan society, as an attack on Calvinistic theology, and as a psychoanalytic study of arrested sexual development that has nothing at all to do with the question of religious faith. Nor does Hawthorne's story stand alone as an example of protracted (and, one might add, finally inconclusive) literary debates.

Third, and last, the theme of a given work need not be in accord with the reader's particular beliefs and values. On those grounds many of us would surely object to a reading of Hawthorne's story that determined its theme to be the assertion that mankind is inherently evil and goodness is an illusion. To be sure, we are under no obligation as readers to accept a story's theme as it is presented to us, especially if we believe that it violates the truth of our own experience and that of others. But we must remember that although literature is full of ideas that may strike us, at least initially, as unpleasant, controversial, or simply wrong-headed, literary sophistication and plain common sense should warn us against dismissing them out of hand. Stories such as Hawthorne's survive, in part at least, because of the fresh and startling ideas and insights they offer. Such ideas and insights have the power to liberate our minds and our imaginations and to cause us to reflect critically about our own values, beliefs, and assumptions. At the very least, before rejecting an author's ideas, we owe it to the author and to ourselves to make certain that we understand why we reject them.

An author's ideas, as they are embodied in the theme, may be *unconvincing* on still other, more important, grounds. An author's theme may be unconvincing because the work itself fails to substantiate that theme, that is, because the interplay of the elements of the story as we experience and analyze them may not support or justify the theme that the author apparently wanted us to draw from it. Thus, if the reader can sometimes fail to do full justice to an author, an author may, on occasion, fail equally to do full justice to his reader.

Identifying Theme

When we attempt to identify the theme of a work of fiction we are attempting to formulate in our own words the statement about life or human experience that is made by the total work. The task is often far from easy because it necessarily involves us in the analysis of a number of elements in their relation to one another and to the work as a whole. Part of the value of attempting to identify theme is that it forces us to bring together and to understand the various aspects of the work; in this process we may notice things we had previously ignored or undervalued. We will be successful in the task to the extent that we are willing to be open-minded and objective and resist the temptation to pay attention to *some* rather than *all* the elements of the work, or, what is worse, to read into them what simply is not there. The identification of theme, then, is a way to validate our understanding, to focus our response, and to make the work finally and fully our own.

The ideas that constitute a work's theme may be relatively commonplace ones that easily fall within the framework of our own experience. They may also be fairly complex and abstract—somewhat hard to understand and put into words—either because we have not encountered them before or because they relate to concepts that are in themselves inherently difficult. Some themes are topical in nature (that is, they involve ideas that are valid only in relation to a specific time and place, or to a specific set of circumstances); others are universal in their application. On some occasions the theme may be explicitly stated by one of the characters (who serves as a spokesman for the author) or by the author in the guise of an omniscient narrator. Even though such explicit statements must be taken seriously into account, a degree of caution is also necessary—for, as we know, characters and narrators alike can be unreliable and misleading. In many cases, however, theme is not stated but rather implied by the work's total rendering of experience; it is only gradually revealed through the treatment of character and incident and by the development of the story. This is particularly true of works in which theme is tied to the revelation of character and takes the form of a statement about that character and/ or what the fate of that character may imply about people or life in general.

Because different kinds of works will yield different themes in different ways, there is no one correct approach to identifying theme. The following suggestions and comments, however, may prove helpful:

1. *It is important in considering theme to avoid confusing it with the work's subject or situation.* Theme is the abstract, generalized statement or comment that the work makes about a concrete subject or situation. It is also true that unless we are first successful in establishing the subject, or establishing the work's basic situation, we are unlikely to be able to establish its theme. Begin then with the subject or situation; once that is identified, we are in a position to formulate a thematic statement about the work.

    Take the case of Hawthorne's "My Kinsman, Major Molineux." Its subject, young Robin Molineux, is easily enough identified. We will then want to ask ourselves a series of questions about what happens to Robin in the course of the story. What visible changes take place in his situation, in his character, or in both? What does he discover and learn as the result of his experiences? To what extent does Robin represent a kind of everyman figure whose urban adventures have symbolic or allegorical implications? Now we are in a position to propose a theme for the story and, having done so, to defend our thesis in the form of a critical analysis that will relate all the significant aspects of the story—especially character, event, and point of view—in support of our interpretation.

2. *We must be as certain as we can that our statement of theme does the work full justice.* There is always the danger of either understating the theme by failing to discover its total significance or of overstating and enlarging it beyond what the elements of the story can be shown to support, and thus making the work appear more universally applicable than it is. The danger of the

latter is probably greater than the danger of the former. Authors, like all intelligent people, know that universal, all-embracing statements about life are frequently refuted by the experiences of individuals, and they will usually restrict their claims accordingly. They know that there are very few generalizations about experience that will hold true under every circumstance. Authors also know that most of the really important questions about human existence do not yield easy, formulistic answers. As readers we must be careful not to credit literary works with solutions and answers where such issues and questions are only being explored or where only tentative answers are being proposed.

On the other hand, there is a danger of not seeing the full thematic significance of a work. We fail to grasp a work's total implications by being inattentive in our reading. If we ignore the final two pages of Fitzgerald's *The Great Gatsby,* or skim them in the belief that all is said and done, then we might be tempted to say that the theme of the novel is the danger of founding one's idealism on false gods, as Gatsby does in his belief that he can recapture the past by regaining Daisy Buchanan. At one level, at least, it is certainly true that this is the novel's theme; it is the author's implied comment on the situation that we have watched unfold through Nick Carraway's eyes. But in those final two pages Fitzgerald deliberately gives his theme (and his book) a much wider implication by deliberately equating Gatsby's dream with the American continent, "the last and greatest of all human dreams." In this way, the theme of *The Great Gatsby* becomes Fitzgerald's statement about the failure of the American Dream itself.

3. We defined theme as a "statement about life that unifies and controls the total work"; thus, *the test of any theme that we may propose is whether it is fully and completely supported by the work's other elements.* If our statement of the theme leaves certain elements or details unexplained, or if those elements and details fail to confirm our statement, then unless the work itself is flawed, chances are we have been only partially successful in our identification.

4. The title that an author gives the work often suggests a particular focus or emphasis for the reader's attention. Frequently, the title of a work serves to identify the work's protagonist or essential character ("The Darling," "A Hunger Artist," "A Rose for Emily," "King of the Bingo Game"). Titles may also provide clues about theme. Joseph Conrad's "Heart of Darkness" refers not only to the uncharted center of Africa, the "dark" continent, but to the capacity for evil or corruption that exists in the human heart, a title relevant to both the plot situation and the theme of Conrad's story. As usual, however, titles can be as deceptive or misleading in their relation to theme as to anything else. The title of Charles Dickens' novel *Great Expectations,* for example, is clearly ironic, for Pip can reach maturity only *after* he renounces his "great expectations" and the false assumptions and values upon which they are based.

5. As readers get more and more involved with literary study they want to know more about the life and personalities of the authors they read. Biographical and autobiographical explorations are helpful and illuminating—as are the personal statements an author makes about his or her life and work in prefaces, letters, journals, notebooks, and critical writings—and they can tell us a great deal about the author, the times in which he lived and wrote, and the relationship between the author and the work. They can also tell us something about the author's *intentions.* Although there is

a great and natural temptation to take the author at his word (for what is that word, really, but a type of expert testimony?), conclusions about theme that are erected on the author's own statement need careful evaluation. Authors, especially when writing in retrospect, are often as fallible as the rest of us in explaining motive, and in some cases may be the least reliable of guides as to what their work finally means. D. H. Lawrence is certainly correct in this respect, when he reminds us in his *Studies in Classic American Literature* (1923), "Never trust the artist. Trust the tale."

Analyzing Theme

1. Does the work have a theme? Is it stated or implied?
2. What generalization(s) or statement(s) about life or human experience does the work make?
3. What elements of the work contribute most heavily to the formulation of the theme?
4. Does the theme emerge organically and naturally, or does the author seem to force the theme upon the work?
5. What is the value or significance of the work's theme? Is it topical or universal in its application?

SYMBOL AND ALLEGORY

A symbol, according to Webster's Dictionary, is "something that stands for or suggests something else by reason of relationship, association, convention, or accidental resemblance . . . a visible sign of something invisible." Symbols, in this sense, are with us all the time, for there are few words or objects that do not evoke, at least in certain contexts, a wide range of associated meanings and feelings. For example, the word *home* (as opposed to *house*) conjures up feelings of warmth and security and personal associations of family, friends, and neighborhood, while the American flag suggests country and patriotism. Human beings by virtue of their capacity for language are symbol-making creatures. As Melville's Ishmael muses in the famous "Doubloon" chapter of *Moby-Dick:* "And some certain significance lurks in all things, else all things are little worth, and the round world itself but an empty cipher, except to sell by the cartload, as they do hills about Boston, to fill up some morass in the Milky Way."

Most of our daily symbol-making and symbol-reading is unconscious and accidental, the inescapable product of our experience as human beings. In literature, however, symbols—in the form of words, images, objects, settings, events and characters—are often used deliberately to suggest and reinforce meaning, to provide enrichment by enlarging and clarifying the experience of the work, and to help to organize and unify the whole. William York Tindall likens a literary symbol to "a metaphor one half of which remains unstated and indefinite."[12] The analogy is a good one. Although symbols exist first as something literal and concrete within the work itself, they also have the capacity to call to mind a range of invisible and abstract associations, both intellectual and emotional, that transcend the literal and concrete and extend their mean-

[12] William York Tindall, *The Literary Symbol* (New York: Columbia University Press, 1955), p. 12.

ing. A literary symbol brings together what is material and concrete within the work (the visible half of Tindall's metaphor) with its series of associations (that "which remains unstated and indefinite"); by fusing them, however briefly, in the reader's imagination, new layers and dimensions of meaning, suggestiveness, and significance are added.

The identification and understanding of literary symbols require a great deal from the reader. They demand awareness and intelligence: an ability to detect when the emphasis an author places on certain elements within the work can be legitimately said to carry those elements to larger, symbolic levels, and when the author means to imply nothing beyond what is literally stated. They also make demands on the reader's maturity and sophistication, for only when we are sufficiently experienced with the world will the literal and concrete strike an appropriate symbolic chord. If, that is to say, we have not had the occasion to think much or think deeply about life and experience it is not likely that we will be able to detect, much less understand, the larger hidden meanings to which symbols point. As Tindall observes, "What the reader gets from a symbol depends not only upon what the author has put into it but upon the reader's sensitivity and his consequent apprehension of what is there."[13]

However, there are dangers as well. Although the author's use of symbol may be unconscious, ours is an age in which the conscious and deliberate use of symbolism defines much of our literary art, as the criticism of the past forty years amply bears witness. There is, consequently, a tendency among students of literature, especially beginning students, to forget that all art contains a mixture of both the literal and the symbolic and to engage in a form of indiscriminate "symbol hunting" that either unearths symbols and symbolic meanings where none are intended or pushes the interpretation of legitimate symbols beyond what is reasonable and proper. Both temptations must be avoided.

It is perfectly true, of course, that the meaning of any symbol is, by definition, indefinite and open-ended, and that a given symbol will evoke a slightly different response in different readers, no matter how discriminating. Yet there is an acceptable range of possible readings for any symbol beyond which we must not stray. We are always limited in our interpretation of symbols by the total context of the work in which they occur and by the way in which the author has established and arranged its other elements; and we are not free to impose— from the outside—our own personal and idiosyncratic meanings simply because they appeal to us. Finally, in working with symbols we must be careful to avoid the danger of becoming so preoccupied with the larger significance of meaning that we forget the literal importance of the concrete thing being symbolized. Moby Dick, for all he may be said to represent to Ahab, Ishmael, Starbuck, Flask, Stubb, Herman Melville, and finally to the reader, is still a whale, a living, breathing mammal of the deep that is capable of inflicting crushing damage on those who pursue him too closely.

Types of Symbols

Symbols are often classified as being traditional, original, or private, depending on the source of the associations that provide their meanings.

---

[13] *Ibid.*, p. 17.

1. TRADITIONAL SYMBOLS. *Traditional symbols* are those whose associations are the common property of a society or a culture and are so widely recognized and accepted that they can be said to be almost universal. The symbolic associations that generally accompany the forest and the sea, the moon and the sun, night and day, the colors black, white and red, and the seasons of the year are examples of traditional symbols. They are so much a part of our culture that we take their significance pretty much for granted. A special kind of traditional symbol is the *archetype*, a term that derives from anthropologist James G. Frazer's famous study of myth and ritual *The Golden Bough* (1890–1915) and the depth psychology of Carl Jung. (Jung holds that certain symbols are so deeply rooted in the repeated and shared experiences of our common ancestors—he refers to them as the "collective unconsciousness" of the human race—as to evoke an immediate and strong, if unconscious, response in any reader.) Conrad's use of blackness in "Heart of Darkness," with its obvious overtones of mystery, evil, and Satanism, is an example of an archetypal symbol. Stories which focus on the initiation of the young—for example, Sherwood Anderson's "I Want to Know Why," James Joyce's "Araby," Flannery O'Connor's "The Artificial Nigger," and Katherine Anne Porter's "The Grave"—all carry with them archetypal overtones; Frazer discovered that such rites of passage exist everywhere in the cultural patterns of the past and continue to exert a powerful influence on the patterns of our own behavior.

2. ORIGINAL SYMBOLS. *Original symbols* are those whose associations are neither immediate nor traditional; instead, they derive their meaning, largely if not exclusively, from the context of the work in which they are used. Melville's white whale is an original symbol, for while whales are often associated in the popular imagination with brute strength and cunning, Moby Dick assumes his larger, metaphysical significance (for Ahab he is the pasteboard mask behind which lurks the pent-up malignity of the universe) only within the contextual limits of Melville's novel. Outside that novel, a whale is just a whale.

3. PRIVATE SYMBOLS. *Private symbols* restrict the source of their meaning even more than original symbols. Just as all of us have certain objects in our lives that call to mind a variety of private associations (the way a family heirloom does), certain authors employ symbols that are the products of their own peculiar and idiosyncratic systems of philosophy or belief, as is the case with a number of the symbols found in the poetry of William Blake and William Butler Yeats. Private symbols, by virtue of their source, are esoteric and largely unintelligible, except to those whom the author or the author's critics and interpreters have succeeded in educating. Fortunately, most of the symbols that the average reader encounters are either traditional or original. The presence of traditional symbols, it should be noted, does not mean that we are free to ignore the framing context of the work and to impose from the outside one pattern or another as we see fit. Traditional symbols, for all their accompanying associations, must always be established by the context of the work and find their significance inside the work, not beyond it.

Uses of Symbols

Symbols operating at the level of individual words and combinations of words called images are crucial to the art of poetry, and for their discussion the reader is referred to the discussion of poetry that follows. In this section, we will briefly consider how writers of fiction employ symbols in conjunction with setting, plot, and character.

SETTING AND SYMBOL. In a number of the examples used in the preceding section on setting—Hardy's Egdon Heath, Crane's snow-surrounded blue hotel, Roderick Usher's house, and the city streets through which Robin Molineux roams in search of his kinsman—we noted how the details of setting are used functionally to extend, clarify, and reinforce the author's larger intention and meaning. We also called attention to the ways in which authors employ the seasons of the year and the time of day because of the traditional associations these have for the reader. These identifications are not arbitrary ones, for in each of the works cited the author deliberately calls attention to the setting, not once but on several occasions, in a way that suggests that it is integrally related to his larger purposes. In the case of Hardy and Crane, it is to call attention to the thematic implications of the work; in the case of Poe and Hawthorne, it is to help reveal the personalities of their characters. Setting in fiction that goes beyond mere backdrop is often used in such symbolic ways. Symbolic settings are particularly useful to authors when they frame and encompass the events of plot and thus provide the work as a whole with an overarching pattern of unity.

PLOT AND SYMBOL. Single events of plot, large or small, or plots in their entirety often function symbolically. *Moby-Dick* is literally filled with examples of the former, and in each of the cases cited here, Melville deliberately calls the reader's attention to the event by setting it off in a brief, appropriately titled chapter that forces the reader to consider its larger significance. In Chapter XXX ("The Pipe"), Ahab hurls his pipe into the sea ("This thing is meant for sereneness, to send up mild white vapors among mild white hairs, not among iron-grey locks like mine. I'll smoke no more—"), an act that suggests Ahab's lack of inner tranquility and his growing social isolation from the members of his crew. In confirmation of this interpretation, the alert reader will recall two earlier scenes in the Spouter-Inn at New Bedford, where Ishmael and his new-found friend, the giant harpooner Queequeg, share a pipe together in celebration of the ancient ritual of friendship and solidarity. Later in the novel (Chapter CXVIII, "The Quadrant"), as the *Pequod* approaches its appointed rendezvous with the great while whale, Ahab seizes the ship's quadrant and smashes it ("no longer will I guide my earthly way by thee") a symbolic gesture signaling the monomaniacal captain's arrogant assertion of his own power and omnipotence; from that moment onward, the destiny of ship and crew is to be squarely in his own hands.

In both examples, Melville encourages his reader to seek larger significance and meaning in what might otherwise be overlooked as small and apparently insignificant actions. And in both examples, our ability to interpret these actions correctly—to see their symbolic importance—increases our understanding of Captain Ahab. In most instances, however, the author will not be so obliging. Although it is certainly true that even the most commonplace action or event— even to the level of a gesture, if it is a spontaneous and unconscious one— can carry symbolic meaning, it is often difficult, at least upon first reading, to tell for certain whether symbolism is involved. Its symbolic character may not become clear until we have finished the work and look backward to see how the individual parts of the plot relate to the whole. In Hawthorne's "My Kinsman, Major Molineux," for example, it may not be clear until the end of the story that each of the separate incidents that punctuate Robin's journey in search of his kinsman form a chain of symbolic events that are an integral part of his ritual of initiation.

When the entire sequence of events that constitutes a plot falls into a symbolic pattern, as in "My Kinsman, Major Molineux," the events are often archetypal. Such a plot, that is, conforms to basic patterns of human behavior so deeply rooted in our experience that they recur ritualistically, time and time again, in the events of myth, folklore, and narrative literature. In fiction, perhaps the most frequently encountered archetypal pattern is the journey or *quest*, in which young men and women undergo a series of trials and ordeals that finally confirms their coming of age and new-found maturity.

CHARACTER AND SYMBOL. Symbolism is frequently employed as a way of deepening our understanding of character. Some characters are given symbolic names to suggest underlying moral, intellectual, or emotional qualities. The name "Robin Molineux," for example, suggests springtime, youth, and innocence, while the name "Roger Chillingsworth" (Hester Prynne's husband in *The Scarlet Letter*) suggests cold intellectuality and lack of human warmth, in keeping with his demonic character. The objects assigned to characters function in the same way: the heavy oak cudgel that Robin carries with him into the city is a symbol of his youthful aggressiveness; Miranda's attraction to the carved wedding ring which her brother has discovered in the grave in Katherine Anne Porter's story symbolizes her vague intimation of the role in life she is destined to play; the gun which Dave covets in Richard Wright's "The Man Who Was Almost a Man" is a symbol of the masculine independence which is not yet his; Ahab's ivory leg, the badge of his first encounter with Moby Dick, serves to objectify the psychic wound that gnaws at him from within; and the house in which Emily Grierson has lived so long in William Faulkner's "A Rose for Emily" functions as an analog to Emily herself, "lifting its stubborn and coquettish decay" alone and apart.

But while the personalities of major characters are often revealed and clarified through the use of symbols rooted in the language that describes them, their very complexity as human beings usually prevents their being defined by a single symbol. This is not true of minor characters, especially those who are flat and one-dimensional and are "constructed round a single idea or quality."[14] Fiction is filled with such individuals. The girl in James Joyce's "Araby," significantly known only as "Mangan's sister," in whose service and religious-like adoration the narrator visits the bazaar, symbolizes the mystery, enchantment, and "otherness" that typifies and objectifies a young boy's first love. In Conrad's "Heart of Darkness" the Director of Companies, the Lawyer, and the Accountant who sit on the deck of the *Nellie* in the "brooding gloom" of evening listening to Marlow recount his journey in search of Kurtz symbolize the type of men who are incapable of appreciating or understanding the moral complexity of experience. Self-satisfied, complacent men, who have become successful by mastering the practical affairs of the world, they are "too dull even to know [that they, too,] are being assaulted by the powers of darkness." And, finally, there is Old Man Warner in Shirley Jackson's "The Lottery," who as

---

[14] Forster, *loc. cit.*, pp. 103–104.

a participant in the lottery on seventy-six previous occasions and as its chief defender ("There's always been a lottery") symbolizes blind subservience to an established ritual that has long since ceased to have a rational purpose.

Symbolism thus enhances fiction by holding "the parts of a literary work together in the service of the whole"[15] in such a way as to help readers organize and enlarge their experience of the work. This is not to say that a work of fiction containing symbolism is inherently better than or superior to one that does not. Nor is it to say that the use of symbolism in and of itself can make a given work successful. It is to say that symbolism, when employed as an integral and organic part of the language and structure of a work of fiction, can stimulate and release the imagination—which is, after all, one of the chief goals of any form of art.

Allegory

Allegory is a technique for expanding the meaning of a literary work by having the characters, and sometimes the setting and the events, represent certain abstract ideas, qualities, or concepts—usually moral, religious, or political in nature. Unlike symbolism,[16] the abstractions of allegory are fixed and definite and tend to take the form of simple and specific ideas that, once identified, can be readily understood. Because they remain constant, they also are easily remembered. In their purest form, works of allegory operate consistently and simultaneously at two separate but parallel levels of meaning: one located inside the work itself, at the concrete surface level of plot and character; the other, outside the work, at the level of the particular ideas or qualities to which these internal elements point. Such works function best when these two levels reinforce and complement each other: we read the work as narrative, but are also aware of the ideas that lie beyond the concrete representations. Allegories tend to break down when the author's focus and emphasis shifts in the direction of the abstract, when we have reason to suspect that the characters, for example, exist only for the sake of the ideas they represent. At such times our interest in the narrative inevitably falls away and we tend to read the work for the message or thesis it promotes.

In the most famous sustained prose allegory in the English language, John Bunyan's *The Pilgrim's Progress* (published in two parts, in 1678 and 1684), the didactic impulse always latent within allegory is very clear. *Pilgrim's Progress* is a moral and religious allegory of the Christian soul in search of salvation. It tells the story of an individual, appropriately named "Christian," who, warned by the Evangelist to leave his home in the City of Destruction, sets off with his pack (containing his load of worldly sins) to seek the Celestial City (heaven). His road, however, is a long and difficult one, and at every turn Christian meets individuals and obstacles whose names and personalities (or characteristics) embody the ideals, virtues, and vices for which they stand: Mr. Worldly Wiseman (who dwells in the town of Carnal-Policy), Mistrust, Timorous, Faithful (who tells about his own encounters with Pliable, Discontent, Shame, and Talkative), Giant Despair (who holds Christian prisoner for a time in Doubting

---

[15] Tindall, op. cit., p. 16.
[16] Allegory and symbolism are not antithetical; in fact, allegory can be said to be a simplified form of symbolism. Allegory, like symbolism, functions as a type of metaphor, but in the case of allegory, the two halves of the metaphor are stated and definite.

Castle), the Slough of Despond, the Valley of the Shadow of Death, Hill Difficulty, and so on.

Although such works of pure allegory as Bunyan's *Pilgrim's Progress* and Edmund Spenser's *The Faerie Queene* are relatively rare, many works make extended
use of allegory (Jonathan Swift's *Gulliver's Travels,* Nathaniel Hawthorne's *The
Scarlet Letter,* William Golding's *The Lord of the Flies,* and George Orwell's *Animal
Farm*), and many more make occasional use of allegory, not infrequently combined with symbolism. As a fictional mode of presentation, however, allegory
is unquestionably out of favor among modern and contemporary authors and
critics, for reasons that have to do with the nature of allegory itself. First of
all, the didacticism of allegory and its tendency toward a simplified, if not
simplistic, view of life is suspect in a world where there is very little common
agreement about truth and the validity of certain once universally respected
ideas and ideals. Second, the way allegory presents character is simply not in
keeping with the modern conception of fictional characterization. In allegory
the characters, and the ideas and ideals those characters embody, are presented
as a given. The modern author, on the other hand, prefers to build characters
and to develop and reveal their personalities gradually, in stages, throughout
the course of the work. And, finally, twentieth-century critics tends to be intoler-
ant of any literary work whose meaning is not totally contained within the
structure of the work.

Several of the stories included in this anthology either contain clear instances
of the use of allegory or lend themselves to allegorical readings. Franz Kafka's
"A Hunger Artist," for example, has been interpreted as an allegory treating
the plight of the artist in the modern world. An allegorical reading has also
been suggested for Hawthorne's "My Kinsman, Major Molineux." Read as a
historical and political allegory of America's coming of age and maturation
as a young and independent nation, Robin can be said to represent colonial
America and his kinsman, the British colonial authority that must be displaced
and overthrown. Both Robin and colonial America share a number of common
characteristics: both have rural, agrarian origins; both are young and strong,
yet insecure and self-conscious because untested and inexperienced in the
ways of the world; both are pious and proud (even arrogant) and given to
aggressive behavior; and both have a reputation, deserved or not, for native
"shrewdness." Just as Robin learns that he can "rise in the world without
the help of [his] . . . . kinsman, Major Molineux," so colonial America realizes
that it can achieve its destiny as a mature and independent nation without
the paternalistic control of Great Britain. In each of the preceding examples,
an allegorical interpretation does seem to "work," in the sense that it allows
us to organize the elements of the story around a central illuminating idea.
Nevertheless, it would be a mistake to press such readings too far. To read
these works *exclusively* as allegories is to oversimplify the internal dynamics of
each story and to distort the author's vision.

Although most modern writers prefer symbolism to allegory as a technique
for enlarging the meaning of their works, allegory continues to make an occasional appearance in modern and contemporary fiction, particularly among
such writers as C. S. Lewis, George Orwell, and William Golding, whose works
are underscored by a strong philosophical, political, or religious vision. The
names of many of the fictional creations of Flannery O'Connor, who confessed
that she felt "more of a kinship with Hawthorne than with any other American
writer," openly hint that they exemplify the kind of abstractions we associate

with allegory (Joy Hopewell, Mrs. Freeman, Manley Pointer, Grandmother Godhigh, Mrs. Chestny, Mr. Head, Mrs. Cope, Mr. Cheatam, Mr. Greenleaf, Mrs. May). When authors like Flannery O'Connor do employ allegorical names, they usually take care not to allow the names to carry the full burden of characterization. O'Connor's characters are far more complex individuals than the single qualities of their names suggest.

Analyzing Symbol and Allegory

1. What symbols or patterns of symbolism (or allegory) are present in the work? Are the symbols traditional, original or private?
2. What aspects of the work (e.g., theme, setting, plot, characterization) does the symbolism (allegory) serve to explain, clarify, or reinforce?
3. Does the author's use of symbolism (allegory) seem contrived or forced in any way, or does it arise naturally out of the interplay of the story's major elements?

STYLE AND TONE

Style

The distinctive quality of literature that sets it apart from all other forms of artistic expression is its reliance on language. Using words is the writer's craft. They are the writer's means of recovering and objectifying experience; and they are his or her means of presenting, shaping, and controlling subject matter. Language is also the means by which the writer controls and influences the reader: in responding to literature we are always responding *to* and *through* the author's words. The literary critic must pay close attention to those words; not only because they convey the sum and substance of the author's message— the story he wishes to tell—but because they provide important clues to the author's emotional and psychological life, beliefs, and attitudes and to the way in which he perceives and experiences himself and the world around him.

When we talk about an author's words and the characteristic ways he uses the resources of language to achieve certain effects, we are talking about *style*. In its most general sense, style consists of *diction* (the individual words an author chooses) and *syntax* (the arrangement of those words into phrases, clauses, and sentences), as well as such devices as rhythm and sound, allusion, ambiguity, irony, paradox, and figurative language. The latter elements of style are crucial to the art of poetry; and they are discussed more fully under that heading. We will touch on them here in order to establish that the language of fiction, no less than the language of poetry and drama, is distinguished by the author's ability to make full and effective use of the language at his or her command.

Each writer's style is unique. "Every writer," British critic David Lodge notes in his *Language of Fiction*, "displays his own unique 'signature' in the way he uses language, something which all his works, however diverse, have in common, and which distinguishes them from the work of any other writer. . . ."[17]

---

[17] David Lodge, *Language of Fiction: Essays in Criticism and Verbal Analysis of the English Novel* (London: Routledge and Kegan Paul, 1966), p. 50.

One test of the distinctiveness of an author's style is its ability to resist paraphrase. The test is relatively simple. Take a passage from any well-regarded
work and rephrase it. Although the underlying ideas may remain the same,
the words themselves will probably register a quite different effect upon you.
Much the same dilemma is faced by the translator, who attempts to reproduce
faithfully the stylistic qualities of an author's poetry or prose. The words may
have translatable equivalents, but what they often lack in translation are the
emotional qualities and nuances of their originals. "We are conscious, reading
him in a language not his own," Henry James observed, of an attempt to
translate Turgenev from the Russian, "of not being reached by his personal
tone, his individual accent." The reason, of course, takes us back to the very
medium of the writer. That medium, Lodge observes, "differs from the media
of most other arts—pigment, stone, musical notes, etc.—in that it is never
virgin: words come to the writer already violated by other men, impressed
with meanings derived from the world of common experience."[18] In the case
of Ivan Turgenev, that experience, the product of a certain man living at a
certain time and place, goes far toward explaining the origin of those distinctive
elements of style that apparently eluded his translator.

By examining the style of a work of fiction we are seeking as critics to accomplish a number of objectives. First of all, we are seeking to isolate and identify
those distinctive traits that comprise the author's "signature." Second, we are
interested in understanding the effects produced by particular stylistic devices
and techniques and how these effects influence our response to the work's
other elements—particularly character, incident, setting, and theme—and to
the work as a whole. Third, we are attempting, by way of evaluation, to arrive
at a judgment based on a consideration of just how effectively the author
has managed to integrate form and content. This examination is an attempt
to measure just how well an author has succeeded in a given work with the
style he or she has chosen. It is not intended to demonstrate, or even imply,
the inherent superiority of one author's style—or one kind of style—over another, although comparisons can, of course, be made.

Elements of Style

The following are some basic elements of style that we examine in order
to characterize an author's writing.

DICTION. Although words are usually meaningful only in the context of other
words, stylistic analysis begins with the attempt to identify and understand
the type and quality of the individual words that comprise an author's basic
vocabulary. When used in connection with characterization, words are the vehicles by which a character's ideas, attitudes, and values are expressed. Words
convey the details of outer appearance and inner state of mind. In dialogue
they reflect the speaker's intelligence and sophistication, general level of conscious awareness, and socioeconomic, geographical, and educational background. When used to describe incidents, words help to convey the narrator's
(or author's) attitude toward those events and the characters involved in them.
When used to describe setting, words help to create and sustain an appropriate
atmosphere.

[18] *Ibid.*, p. 47.

The analysis of diction includes the following considerations: the *denotative* (or dictionary) meaning of words, as opposed to their *connotative* meaning (the ideas associated with or suggested by them); their degree of concreteness or abstractness; their degree of allusiveness; the *parts of speech* they represent; their length and construction; the *level of usage* they reflect (standard or nonstandard; formal, informal, or colloquial); the *imagery* (details of sensory experience) they contain; the *figurative devices* (simile, metaphor, personification) they embody; their *rhythm* and *sound patterns* (alliteration, assonance, consonance, onomatopeia). In studying diction, we also need to pay close attention to the use of *repetition:* the way key words recur in a given passage or series of passages in such a way as to call special attention to themselves.

SYNTAX. When we examine style at the level of syntax, we are attempting to analyze the ways the author arranges words into phrases, clauses, and finally whole sentences to achieve particular effects. Although syntax is determined partly by the lexical content (or meaning) of the words and partly by the basic grammatical structure of the language, every writer enjoys considerable freedom to shape and control the syntactic elements of style. In looking at an author's syntax we want to know how the words have been arranged and particularly how they deviate from the normal and expected.

Although one can study syntactic units smaller than the sentence—for example, individual phrases that call attention to themselves by their length, construction, and placement—syntax is probably most easily approached and analyzed in sentences. Such an approach mirrors most closely the writing process itself, for sentences are the major units of thought, and it is on the crafting of sentences that most authors concentrate their creative energies. Sentences can be examined in terms of their length—whether they are short, spare, and economical or long and involved; in terms of their form—whether they are simple, compound, or complex; and in terms of their construction—whether they are *loose* (sentences that follow the normal subject-verb-object pattern, stating their main idea near the beginning in the form of an independent clause), *periodic* (sentences that deliberately withhold or suspend the completion of the main idea until the end of the sentence), or *balanced* (sentences in which two similar or antithetical ideas are balanced).

Each type of sentence will have a slightly different effect on the reader. Long, complicated sentences slow down and retard the pace of a narrative, whereas short, simple sentences hasten it. Loose sentences, because they follow the normal, predictable patterns of speech, tend to appear more natural and less contrived than either periodic or balanced sentences, particularly when they are used in the creation of dialogue. Moreover, the deliberate arrangement of words within individual sentences or groups of sentences can result in patterns of rhythm and sound (pleasant or unpleasant) that establish or reinforce feeling and emotion. Although an author will usually vary the kinds of sentences used in order to avoid monotony (unless monotony is intended), certain syntactic patterns will dominate and become characteristic of that author's style.

Stylistic Analysis

Because stylistic analysis is generally carried out by isolating and examining one or more representative passages from a given work, the following examples may prove illustrative.

I was born in the year 1632, in the City of York, of a good family, tho' not of that country, my father being a foreigner of Bremen, who settled first at Hull. He got a good estate by merchandise, and leaving off his trade, lived afterward at York, from whence he had married my mother, whose relations were named *Robinson,* a very good family in that country, and from whom I was called *Robinson Kreutznaer;* but by the usual corruption of words in England, we are now called, nay, we call our selves, and write our name *Crusoe,* and so my companions always call'd me.

—From *The Life and Adventures of Robinson Crusoe,* Daniel Defoe [1719]

Stylistic Analysis: In this first paragraph of the novel, the narrator (Robinson Crusoe) is intent on establishing his voice and identity as a real person with a family history. It is composed of two loose, fairly intricate sentences (one in some editions) in which the main clause is followed by a series of phrases and clauses that add concrete and denotative facts and detail, by way of additional information. The single exception to this emphasis on fact is the repetition of the judgemental adjective *good* ("good family," "good estate," "good family"), which is intended to lend an impression of stability and respectability to an otherwise neutral description, whose details are irrelevant to the story that Defoe wants to tell.

The style is simple and straightforward, much as you would expect from someone trying to persuade us that he is a real person worthy of belief. Note, for example, how Crusoe scrupulously catches himself in mid-sentence in order to set the record straight: "we are now called, nay, we call ourselves." The reader is being skillfully imposed upon by the author's calculated use of language: once we are willing to believe in the fundamental honesty and sincerity of the narrator—a man who pays close attention to facts and who obviously lacks verbal pretension—we are likely to accept pretty much at face value the authenticity of the exciting adventures that are to follow.

During the whole of a dull, dark, and soundless day in the autumn of the year, when the clouds hung oppressively low in the heavens, I had been passing alone, on horseback, through a singularly dreary tract of country; and at length found myself, as the shades of evening drew on, within view of the melancholy House of Usher. I know not how it was—but, with the first glimpse of the building, a sense of insufferable gloom pervaded my spirit. I say insufferable; for the feeling was unrelieved by any of that half-pleasurable, because poetic, sentiment with which the mind usually receives even the sternest natural images of the desolate or terrible.

—From "The Fall of the House of Usher," Edgar Allan Poe [1839]

Stylistic Analysis: In this first paragraph of the story, the unnamed narrator, Roderick Usher's boyhood acquaintance, first approaches the melancholy and decaying house. Poe's obvious intent is to establish, from the outset, the appropriate setting and atmosphere for the story—one that will simultaneously arrest the reader's attention and evoke an appropriate emotional response. The opening sentence, surely one of the most famous in all of American literature, is a long, periodic one, in which a series of rhythmic phrases and clauses are deliberately arranged to suspend, until the very end, and so prepare the way for, the object of the narrator's search. Within the sentence, Poe carefully intensifies his visual details with adjectives and adverbs and reinforces their effect through the use of alliteration and onomatopeia. The second and third sentences, which record the narrator's response to the scene, continue to invite the reader to respond in the same way. Poe's emotion-charged prose is clearly excessive (note the use of such words as "oppressively," "dreary," "melancholy," "insufferable," "half-pleasurable," "sternest," "desolate," and "terrible"), yet its very excess effectively establishes the mood that is to dominate and surround the story from beginning to end.

I was pretty tired, and the first thing I knowed, I was asleep. When I woke up I didn't know where I was, for a minute, I set up and looked around, a little scared. Then I remembered. The river looked miles and miles across. The moon was so bright I could a counted the drift logs that went a slipping along, black and still, hundred of yards out from shore. Everything was dead quiet, and it looked late, and *smelt* late. You know what I mean—I don't know the words to put it in.

—From *The Adventures of Huckleberry Finn*, Mark Twain [1885]

Stylistic Analysis: When Ernest Hemingway wrote in his *Green Hills of Africa* (1935) that "All modern American literature comes from one book by Mark Twain called *Huckleberry Finn,*" he was referring to the realism of Mark Twain's style, which differs so markedly from the heavy, formal, "literary" prose of writers like Poe. The defining qualities of Mark Twain's style—which does, clearly, look ahead to the twentieth century—are very much in evidence in this passage. Huck Finn is speaking in a voice and manner appropriate to a largely self-educated rural adolescent. Note his informal, colloquial language, with its small grammatical flaws, his simple, uncomplicated, relaxed sentences, and the sparse, yet vivid, imagery he uses to describe the moonlit river—all of which convey the impression of something real, honestly reported. His final confession of inadequacy, although hardly necessary, is perfectly in keeping with a character who constantly refuses to falsify his experience of the world.

When the short days of winter came dusk fell before we had well eaten our dinner. When we met in the street the houses had grown sombre. The space of sky above us was the color of ever-changing violet and towards it the lamps of the street lifted their feeble lanterns. The cold air stung us and we played till our bodies glowed. Our shouts echoed in the silent street. The career of our play brought us through the dark muddy lanes behind the houses where we ran the gauntlet of the rough tribes from the cottages, to the back doors of the dark dripping gardens where odors arose from the ashpits, to the dark odorous stables where a coachman smoothed and combed the horse or shook music from the buckled harness. When we returned to the street light from the kitchen windows had filled the areas. If my uncle was seen turning the corner we hid in the shadow until we had seen him safely housed. Or if Mangan's sister came out on the doorstep to call her brother in to his tea we watched her from our shadow peer up and down the street. We waited to see whether she would remain or go in and, if she remained, we left our shadow and walked up to Mangan's steps resignedly. She was waiting for us, her figure defined by the light from the half-opened door. Her brother always teased her before he obeyed and I stood by the railings looking at her. Her dress swung as she moved her body and the soft rope of her hair tossed from side to side.

—From "Araby," James Joyce [1914]

Stylistic Analysis: Joyce's "Araby" is a love story, told, retrospectively, by an older, and presumably wiser, adult looking backwards on a bittersweet moment of adolescence. In the third paragraph of the story, Joyce describes the Dublin neighborhood (North Richmond Street) that makes up the boy's physical world. The details he uses are less important for their concrete, denotative qualities, however, than for the way they capture and reflect the boy's own subjective appreciation of life and its sensual pleasures. What Joyce provides is a series of rich, lyrical, and evocative images which appeal to the eye, to the touch, to the ear, and to the nose, as well as kinetic images which convey a sense of life in motion—images that are made all the more alive and poetic because they seem to spring from the crowded associations of memory. Joyce also employs a number of the devices we normally expect to find in poetry: personification, metaphor, and distinctive patterns of rhythm and sound. Note, for example, the final sentence describing "Mangan's sister," upon whom the focus of the passage finally and fittingly comes to rest, where the swinging of her dress and the tossing metaphoric "rope" of her hair are emphasized by swishing alliterative "s" sounds that are used to suggest the hypnotic and sensual appeal she exercises on the imagination of a young man caught up in the infatuation of first love.

The girl stood up and walked to the end of the station. Across, on the other side, were fields of grain and trees along the banks of the Ebro. Far away, beyond the river, were mountains. The shadow of a cloud moved across the field of grain and she saw the river through the trees.

"And we could have all this," she said. "And we could have everything and every day we make it more impossible."

"What did you say?"

"I said we could have everything."

"We can have everything."

"No, we can't."

"We can have the whole world."

"No, we can't."

"We can go everywhere."

"No, we can't. It isn't ours any more."

"It's ours."

"No, it isn't. And once they take it away, you never get it back."

"But they haven't taken it away."

"We'll wait and see."

"Come on back in the shade," he said. "You mustn't feel that way."

"I don't feel any way," the girl said. "I just know things."

—From "Hills Like White Elephants," Ernest Hemingway [1927]

Stylistic Analysis: The passage perfectly illustrates the famous Hemingway style—economical and terse. It is characterized by short, simple sentences and active verbs; by an informal, commonplace vocabulary of short, denotative words; the absence of unnecessary adjectives and adverbs; and by a concentration on particular concrete images that record the surface level of experience. Descriptive details of setting are sparse though important—in this case they juxtapose the sensuous fertility across the river with the hot, sterile foreground where the conversation between the two characters takes place. Such details, however, are clearly subordinate to the dialogue, which carries the narrative movement of the story and explores and illuminates the attitudes and temperaments of the character-participants. The objective point of view places the burden of interpretation on the reader, who must pay close attention to what is being said in order to identify correctly the verbal nuances and overtones that define both character and conflict.

The dialogue itself is difficult to follow. It is random, indirect, and inexplicit, for Hemingway's characters, aware as they are that to expose oneself openly is to risk psychic injury, tend to approach each other obliquely, their real thoughts and emotions hidden and held tightly in check. In this passage, the girl senses, though she cannot or will not articulate the fact, that it is not the matter of her pregnancy—or the "awfully simple operation" he proposes— that jeopardizes their relationship, but rather his failure to understand that human relationships themselves inevitably curtail and limit one's freedom. Her inability to communicate this message and his failure to understand it—the failure of dialogue, if you will—thus serves to underscore and explain both the differences in their attitudes and personalities and the size of the barrier existing between them.

Ambrose was "at that awkward age." His voice came out high-pitched as a child's if he let himself get carried away; to be on the safe side, therefore, he moved and spoke with *deliberate calm* and *adult gravity*. Talking soberly of unimportant or irrelevant matters and listening consciously to the sound of your own voice are useful habits for maintaining control in this difficult interval. *En route* to Ocean City he sat in the back seat of the family car with his brother Peter, age fifteen, and Magda G_____, age fourteen, a pretty girl and exquisite young lady, who lived not far from them on B_____ Street in the town of D_____, Maryland. Initials, blanks, or both were often substituted for proper names in nineteenth-century fiction to enhance the illusion of reality. It is as if the author felt it necessary to delete the names for reasons of tact or legal liability. Interestingly, as with other aspects of realism, it is an *illusion* that is being enhanced, by purely artificial means.

        —From "Lost in the Funhouse," John Barth [1967]

Stylistic Analysis: "A different way to come to terms with the discrepancy between art and the Real Thing," John Barth has said, "is to *affirm* the artificial element in art (you can't get rid of it anyhow), and make the artifice part of your point instead of working for higher and higher fi with a lot of literary woofers and tweeters."[19] And one way to "*affirm* the artificial element in art," he might have added, is by making the reader an equally self-conscious party to the artifice, by letting him in on the game, and then forcing him to participate in the act of creation and discovery. Such statements help to explain the playful, self-conscious quality of Barth's own fiction; they also help to explain Barth's choice of subject matter and narrative technique, and his choice of style as well. Barth's funhouse is a metaphor both for fiction and fiction-making and for the potentialities of the self, and the author openly invites the reader to participate in Ambrose's story, even to the extent of inviting him to choose which of the multiple versions of the plot is, finally, the correct one. Barth's style—with its long, complex, and convoluted sentences, its abstract diction, its rapid changes in point of view, its resort to pun, parody, allusion, and other forms of verbal wordplay, and its use of such visual devices as italics, blank spaces, quotation marks, dashes, and diagrams—is designed to "make the artifice part of" the "point" and to solicit our active involvement as intelli-

---

[19] John Barth, "John Barth: An Interview," *Wisconsin Studies in Contemporary Literature,* VI: 6 (Winter–Spring 1965).

gent readers. What Barth says and the way he says it invite us to think about fiction and fiction-making even as they create frustration by losing us, along with Ambrose, in the labyrinthine funhouse of the story.

The preceding examples illustrate how style can be used to serve characterization (Defoe, Mark Twain, Joyce and Hemingway), the creation of setting and atmosphere (Poe and Joyce), and the reinforcement of theme (Hemingway and Barth). They also illustrate the dynamic, changing nature of the language of fiction itself. In comparing the style of Poe to the style of Hemingway, for example, we can see a movement toward less formality and more concrete diction, as well as simpler syntax; the differences reflect the modern tendency toward realism in fiction. Generalizations about style can be dangerous, however, as the passage by John Barth makes clear. Style is a highly personal and sometimes a highly idiosyncratic matter, open to endless opportunities for innovation and experimentation. Although some fictional styles are easier to read and understand than others, and although all readers sooner or later come to express stylistic preferences, there is, finally, no one style that is best or most appropriate. The critic's job is not to state preferences but to render judgments: to try to understand the distinctive elements that comprise an author's style, the various effects that those elements create, and the way in which they serve to reveal and reinforce the other elements of the work.

Tone

All of us are familiar with the term *tone* as it is used to characterize the special qualities of accent, inflection, and duration in a speaker's voice. From early childhood on we learn to identify and respond to these elements of speech. For example, a mother can tell her child to "Come here!" in a manner that is angry, threatening, concerned, amused, sympathetic, or affectionate, simply by altering her tone of voice. In each case, the mother's meaning is the same—she wants her child to come. However, the relationship she creates with her auditor (the child) will differ dramatically according to her tone. Tone, then, is a means of creating a relationship or conveying an attitude. The particular qualities of a speaking voice are unavailable to a writer in creating tone, but to a certain extent rhythm and punctuation can substitute for a speaker's accent and inflection, while word order and word choice can influence tone as easily in prose as in speech.

Just as the tone of the mother's voice communicates her attitude of anger or concern, so tone in fiction is frequently a guide to an author's attitude toward the subject or audience. For example, one recognizes at once the friendly, informal, and folksy tone of Huck Finn's introduction to his adventures:

You don't know about me, without you have read a book by the name of *The Adventures of Tom Sawyer*, but that ain't no matter.

Huck wants to make us his friends, so he writes just as he would speak, without striving for grammatical perfection. As soon as he realizes that we might be put off by the sense of self-importance in his allusion to *The Adventures of Tom Sawyer*, he reassures us that it "ain't no matter" if we have failed to read the book. The tone and content of the sentence combine to indicate that Huck wants us to like him and that he wants to like us.

In contrast, in Mark Twain's preface to *Huckleberry Finn* his tone is threatening at the same time that it is ironic and humorous:

NOTICE

Persons attempting to find a motive in this narrative will be prosecuted; persons attempting to find a moral in it will be banished; persons attempting to find a plot in it will be shot.

BY ORDER OF THE AUTHOR
Per G. G., CHIEF OF ORDNANCE

We are not accustomed to such threats from authors, and our first reaction might be shock—after that, perhaps confusion. Why should Mark Twain make threats that are obviously exaggerated and impossible to carry out? Why, indeed, except to attract our attention to the novel's motive, moral, and plot. We may be amused by the author's obvious antipathy to literary critics and literary criticism, but we may also feel slightly goaded, a bit more eager to look for a motive, moral, and plot anywhere we damned well please! And after a moment we may recognize that Mark Twain's purpose in including this notice must have been to obtain just such a reaction; he forbids us to examine his book's literary meaning in order to suggest ironically that it does have serious literary purposes. Thus, although Huck's tone has accurately reflected his attitude toward the reader, it is doubtful that the same is true of Mark Twain's "Notice." His tone is ironic and he means just the opposite of what he says.

As these examples indicate, an author's tone is linked closely to intention and meaning; the tone must be inferred from a close and careful study of the various elements within the work, including plot, character, setting, point of view, and style.[20]

No matter how hard an author tries to mask his attitudes and feelings, and to hide his presence within the work, perhaps by taking refuge somewhere behind the narrative voice that tells the story, the author's tone can be inferred by the choices he makes in the process of ordering and presenting his material: by what is included and emphasized and what, by contrast, is omitted. In such choices lie what Wayne Booth refers to as "the implicit evaluation which the author manages to convey behind his explicit presentation."[21] The literary critic learns to look at such choices carefully—at the characters, incidents, setting, and details depicted; at the issues and problems that are raised and explored; at the style the author has employed; at every decision, in short, that the author has made—in order to infer from them the underlying attitudes and tone that color and control the work as a whole. The task is not at all an easy one, and for this reason tone is perhaps the most difficult and elusive of all the literary elements we have thus far discussed.

---

[20] It should be noted that the author-speaker who determines the tone of the work and to whom the reader responds may or may not be, and often is not, the historical author who wrote the work. The concept of the "implied author" and "the intricate relationship of the so-called real author with his various official versions of himself" are explored in Wayne C. Booth's *The Rhetoric of Fiction* (Chicago: University of Chicago Press, 1961). The distinction is, however, at times a difficult one, and for that reason can be left for more advanced literary study.

[21] *Ibid.*, p. 74.

IRONY. When Huckleberry Finn steps forward to introduce himself, he is both frank and open, and there is little reason to believe that he means anything other than what he says. The same thing, however, is not always true of Mark Twain himself, who is far more circumspect and cautious and prefers to adopt a posture of detachment and objectivity. Authors like Mark Twain recognize that life is not always simple or straightforward; that the affairs of men are full of surprises, ambiguities, contradictions, and complexities; and that appearances can and often do deceive. In order to reflect the puzzling, problematic nature of experience, such authors choose to approach their subjects indirectly, through the use of irony. They use techniques to create within a work two separate and contrasting levels of experience and a "disparity of understanding" between then.

The three types of irony that occur most frequently in literature are *verbal irony* (in which there is a contrast between what a speaker literally says and what he or she means); *irony of situation* (in which an event or situation turns out to be the reverse of what is expected or appropriate); and *dramatic irony* (in which the state of affairs known to the reader or the audience is the reverse of what its participants suppose it to be).

Verbal irony is easily enough recognized in speech because of the intonation of the speaker's voice. For example, when Mark Anthony refers to Brutus in Shakespeare's *Julius Caesar* as "an honorable man," few members of the audience are likely to misunderstand the irony in his statement. When used in fiction, however, verbal irony is sometimes more difficult to identify because it is conveyed exclusively through the author's style, through the words on the printed page. Sometimes the author helps the reader by means of repetition, as Hawthorne does in "My Kinsman, Major Molineux," where Robin, the uninitiated youth from the country, prides himself on his native "shrewdness." Shrewd, at least in the ways of the city, Robin is most certainly not.

Irony of situation, on the other hand, results from the careful manipulation of plot, point of view, setting and atmosphere. Robin's prolonged and frustrating search for his kinsman, for example, is rendered ironic by the fact that his arrival in Boston coincides exactly with a revolutionary plot whose chief object is the very individual who Robin believes will help him to rise in the world. Robin Molineux is but one in a long line of fictional characters whose expectations are altered or reversed by the events that overtake them. The situational irony in Hawthorne's story is sustained not only by the plot, but by the point of view, which reveals the true state of things only gradually both to Robin and the reader. In Shirley Jackson's "The Lottery," irony of situation is established by the ostensibly gay and lighthearted atmosphere and festive scene on the June morning on which the story opens and by Jackson's use of a detached and matter-of-fact dramatic point of view:

The morning of June 27th was clear and sunny, with the fresh warmth of a full-summer day; the flowers were blossoming profusely and the grass was richly green. The people of the village began to gather in the square, between the post office and the bank, around ten o'clock; in some towns there were so many people that the lottery took two days and had to be started on June 26th, but in this village, where there were only about three hundred people, the whole lottery took less than two hours, so it could begin at ten o'clock in the morning and still be through in time to allow the villagers to get home for noon dinner.

—From "The Lottery," Shirley Jackson [1948]

Only as the events of the morning unfold does the reader come to grasp the underlying horror of ritualistic violence that the villagers are about to perpetrate on one of their own.

Dramatic irony, like irony of situation, depends on the use of plot, character, and point of view. An omniscient narrator, for example, will sometimes reveal information to the reader that his characters do not yet know; this allows the narrator (and the reader) to judge the subsequent actions of those characters and to anticipate the likely outcome of events. Dramatic irony can also be established by means of characters whose innocence and naïveté cause them to misperceive or misinterpret events whose significance is perfectly clear to the reader. The plots of such works frequently turn on the matter of knowing or not knowing, as in Henry James' "The Tree of Knowledge," and result in outcomes that are either comic or tragic in their final implication.

As critics Robert Scholes and Robert Kellogg note, there are "In any example of narrative art . . . broadly speaking, three points of view—those of the characters, the narrator, and the audience." When any of the three "perceives more—or less—than another, irony must be either actually or potentially present."[22] In any work of fiction, it is crucially important that we are able to determine if and how that potential has been exploited; to overlook or misinterpret the presence of irony can only lead to a misinterpretation of the author's attitudes and tone and the way he would have us approach and judge the work.

Analyzing Style and Tone

1. Describe the author's diction. Is the language concrete or abstract, formal or informal, literal or figurative? What parts of speech occur most often?
2. What use does the author make of imagery; figurative devices (simile, metaphor, personification); patterns of rhythm and sound (alliteration, assonance, consonance, onomatopoeia); repetition; allusion?
3. Are the sentences predominantly long or short; simple, compound, or complex; loose, periodic, or balanced?
4. Describe the author's tone. Is it, for example, sympathetic, detached, condescending, serious, humorous, or ironic? How is the tone established and revealed?
5. What kind(s) of irony does the author use: verbal irony, irony of situation, dramatic irony? What purpose(s) does the irony serve?
6. What are the distinctive characteristics of the author's style? In what ways is the style appropriate to the work's subject and theme?

[22] Robert Scholes and Robert Kellogg, *The Nature of Narrative* (New York: Oxford University Press, 1966). p. 240.

3

Stories

Nathaniel Hawthorne *1804–1864*

MY KINSMAN, MAJOR MOLINEUX

After the kings of Great Britain had assumed the right of appointing the colonial governors, the measures of the latter seldom met with the ready and general approbation which had been paid to those of their predecessors, under the original charters. The people looked with most jealous scrutiny to the exercise of power which did not emanate from themselves, and they usually rewarded their rulers with slender gratitude for the compliances by which, in softening their instructions from beyond the sea, they had incurred the reprehension of those who gave them. The annals of Massachusetts Bay will inform us, that of six governors in the space of about forty years from the surrender of the old charter, under James II., two were imprisoned by a popular insurrection; a third, as Hutchinson inclines to believe,[1] was driven from the province by the whizzing of a musket-ball; a fourth, in the opinion of the same historian, was hastened to his grave by continual bickerings with the House of Representatives; and the remaining two, as well as their successors, till the Revolution, were favored with few and brief intervals of peaceful sway. The inferior members of the court party, in times of high political excitement, led scarcely a more desirable life. These remarks may serve as a preface to the following adventures, which chanced upon a summer night, not far from a hundred years ago.[2] The reader, in order to avoid a long and dry detail of colonial

---

[1] Thomas Hutchinson (1711–1780), royal governor of Massachusetts from 1771 to 1774, and author of the *History of the Colony and Province of Massachusetts Bay*, published in three parts between 1764 and 1828.
[2] Hawthorne's story was first published in 1832.

affairs, is requested to dispense with an account of the train of circumstances that had caused much temporary inflammation of the popular mind.

It was near nine o'clock of a moonlight evening, when a boat crossed the ferry with a single passenger, who had obtained his conveyance at that unusual hour by the promise of an extra fare. While he stood on the landing-place, searching in either pocket for the means of fulfilling his agreement, the ferryman lifted a lantern, by the aid of which, and the newly risen moon, he took a very accurate survey of the stranger's figure. He was a youth of barely eighteen years, evidently country-bred, and now, as it should seem, upon his first visit to town. He was clad in a coarse gray coat, well worn, but in excellent repair; his under garments were durably constructed of leather, and fitted tight to a pair of serviceable and well-shaped limbs; his stockings of blue yarn were the incontrovertible work of a mother or a sister; and on his head was a three-cornered hat, which in its better days had perhaps sheltered the graver brow of the lad's father. Under his left arm was a heavy cudgel formed of an oak sapling, and retaining a part of the hardened root; and his equipment was completed by a wallet, not so abundantly stocked as to incommode the vigorous shoulders on which it hung. Brown, curly hair, well-shaped features, and bright, cheerful eyes were nature's gifts, and worth all that art could have done for his adornment.

The youth, one of whose names was Robin, finally drew from his pocket the half of a little province bill of five shillings, which, in the depreciation in the sort of currency, did but satisfy the ferryman's demand, with the surplus of a sexangular piece of parchment, valued at three pence. He then walked forward into the town, with as light a step as if his day's journey had not already exceeded thirty miles, and with as eager an eye as if he were entering London city, instead of the little metropolis of a New England colony. Before Robin had proceeded far, however, it occurred to him that he knew not whither to direct his steps; so he paused, and looked up and down the narrow street, scrutinizing the small and mean wooden buildings that were scattered on either side.

"This low hovel cannot be my kinsman's dwelling," thought he, "nor yonder old house, where the moonlight enters at the broken casement; and truly I see none hereabouts that might be worthy of him. It would have been wise to inquire my way of the ferryman, and doubtless he would have gone with me, and earned a shilling from the Major for his pains. But the next man I meet will do as well."

He resumed his walk, and was glad to perceive that the street now became wider, and the houses more respectable in their appearance. He soon discerned a figure moving on moderately in advance, and hastened his steps to overtake it. As Robin drew nigh, he saw that the passenger was a man in years, with a full periwig of gray hair, a wide-skirted coat of dark cloth, and silk stockings rolled above his knees. He carried a long and polished cane, which he struck down perpendicularly before him at every step; and at regular intervals he uttered two successive hems, of a peculiarly solemn and sepulchral intonation. Having made these observations, Robin laid hold of the skirt of the old man's coat, just when the light from the open door and windows of a barber's shop fell upon both their figures.

"Good evening to you, honored sir," said he, making a low bow, and still retaining his hold of the skirt. "I pray you tell me whereabouts is the dwelling of my kinsman, Major Molineux."

The youth's question was uttered very loudly; and one of the barbers, whose razor was descending on a well-soaped chin, and another who was dressing a Ramillies wig,[3] left their occupations, and came to the door. The citizen, in the mean time, turned a long-favored countenance upon Robin, and answered him in a tone of excessive anger and annoyance. His two sepulchral hems, however, broke into the very centre of his rebuke, with most singular effect, like a thought of the cold grave obtruding among wrathful passions.

"Let go my garment, fellow! I tell you, I know not the man you speak of. What! I have authority, I have—hem, hem—authority; and if this be the respect you show for your betters, your feet shall be brought acquainted with the stocks by daylight, tomorrow morning!"

Robin released the old man's skirt, and hastened away, pursued by an ill-mannered roar of laughter from the barber's shop. He was at first considerably surprised by the result of his question, but, being a shrewd youth, soon thought himself able to account for the mystery.

"This is some country representative," was his conclusion, "who has never seen the inside of my kinsman's door, and lacks the breeding to answer a stranger civilly. The man is old, or verily—I might be tempted to turn back and smite him on the nose. Ah, Robin, Robin! even the barber's boys laugh at you for choosing such a guide! You will be wiser in time, friend Robin."

He now became entangled in a succession of crooked and narrow streets, which crossed each other, and meandered at no great distance from the water-side. The smell of tar was obvious to his nostrils, the masts of vessels pierced the moonlight above the tops of the buildings, and the numerous signs, which Robin paused to read, informed him that he was near the centre of business. But the streets were empty, the shops were closed, and lights were visible only in the second stories of a few dwelling-houses. At length, on the corner of a narrow lane, through which he was passing, he beheld the broad countenance of a British hero swinging before the door of an inn, whence proceeded the voices of many guests. The casement of one of the lower windows was thrown back, and a very thin curtain permitted Robin to distinguish a party at supper, round a well-furnished table. The fragrance of the good cheer steamed forth into the outer air, and the youth could not fail to recollect that the last remnant of his travelling stock of provision had yielded to his morning appetite, and that noon had found and left him dinnerless.

"Oh, that a parchment three-penny might give me a right to sit down at yonder table!" said Robin, with a sigh. "But the Major will make me welcome to the best of his victuals; so I will even step boldly in, and inquire my way to his dwelling."

He entered the tavern, and was guided by the murmur of voices and the fumes of tobacco to the public-room. It was a long and low apartment, with oaken walls, grown dark in the continual smoke, and a floor which was thickly sanded, but of no immaculate purity. A number of persons—the larger part of whom appeared to be mariners, or in some way connected with the sea—occupied the wooden benches, or leather-bottomed chairs, conversing on various matters, and occasionally lending their attention to some topic of general interest. Three or four little groups were draining as many bowls of punch, which the West India trade had long since made a familiar drink in the colony.

---

[3] A type of wig with a long tail named after Ramillies in Belgium, site of a British military victory.

Others, who had the appearance of men who lived by regular and laborious handicraft, preferred the insulated bliss of an unshared potation, and became more taciturn under its influence. Nearly all, in short, evinced a predilection for the Good Creature in some of its various shapes, for this is a vice to which, as Fast Day[4] sermons of a hundred years ago will testify, we have a long hereditary claim. The only guests to whom Robin's sympathies inclined him were two or three sheepish countrymen, who were using the inn somewhat after the fashion of a Turkish caravansary;[5] they had gotten themselves into the darkest corner of the room, and heedless of the Nicotian[6] atmosphere, were supping on the bread of their own ovens, and the bacon cured in their own chimney-smoke. But though Robin felt a sort of brotherhood with these strangers, his eyes were attracted from them to a person who stood near the door, holding whispered conversation with a group of ill-dressed associates. His features were separately striking almost to grotesqueness, and the whole face left a deep impression on the memory. The forehead bulged out into a double prominence, with a vale between; the nose came boldly forth in an irregular curve, and its bridge was of more than a finger's breadth; the eyebrows were deep and shaggy, and the eyes glowed beneath them like fire in a cave.

While Robin deliberated of whom to inquire respecting his kinsman's dwelling, he was accosted by the innkeeper, a little man in a stained white apron, who had come to pay his professional welcome to the stranger. Being in the second generation from a French Protestant,[7] he seemed to have inherited the courtesy of his parent nation; but no variety of circumstances was ever known to change his voice from the one shrill note in which he now addressed Robin.

"From the country, I presume, sir?" said he, with a profound bow. "Beg leave to congratulate you on your arrival, and trust you intend a long stay with us. Fine town here, sir, beautiful buildings, and much that may interest a stranger. May I hope for the honor of your commands in respect to supper?"

"The man sees a family likeness! the rogue has guessed that I am related to the Major!" thought Robin, who had hitherto experienced little superfluous civility.

All eyes were now turned on the country lad, standing at the door, in his worn three-cornered hat, gray coat, leather breeches, and blue yarn stockings leaning on an oaken cudgel, and bearing a wallet on his back.

Robin replied to the courteous innkeeper, with such an assumption of confidence as befitted the Major's relative. "My honest friend," he said, "I shall make it a point to patronize your house on some occasion, when"—here he could not help lowering his voice—"when I may have more than a parchment three-pence in my pocket. My present business," continued he, speaking with lofty confidence, "is merely to inquire my way to the dwelling of my kinsman, Major Molineux."

There was a sudden and general movement in the room, which Robin interpreted as expressing the eagerness of each individual to become his guide. But the innkeeper turned his eyes to a written paper on the wall, which he

[4] A day set aside each spring throughout New England for public fasting, prayer, and sermonizing.
[5] An inn in eastern countries where caravans lodge for the night.
[6] Tobacco smoke, in reference to Jean Nicot, a diplomat on assignment to Spain, who introduced the use of tobacco to France in 1560.
[7] Many French Protestants or Huguenots fled France to America after their freedom to worship was revoked with the Edict of Nantes in 1685.

read, or seemed to read, with occasional recurrences to the young man's figure.

"What have we here?" said he, breaking his speech into little dry fragments.
" 'Left the house of the subscriber, bounden servant;[8] Hezekiah Mudge,—had
on, when he went away, gray coat, leather breeches, master's third-best hat.
One pound currency reward to whosoever shall lodge him in any jail of the
province.' Better trudge, boy; beter trudge!"

Robin had begun to draw his hand towards the lighter end of the oak cudgel,
but a strange hostility in every countenance induced him to relinquish his
purpose of breaking the courteous innkeeper's head. As he turned to leave
the room, he encountered a sneering glance from the bold-featured personage
whom he had before noticed; and no sooner was he beyond the door, than
he heard a general laugh, in which the innkeeper's voice might be distinguished,
like the dropping of small stones into a kettle.

"Now, is it not strange," thought Robin, with his usual shrewdness,—"is it
not strange that the confession of an empty pocket should outweigh the name
of my kinsman, Major Molineux? Oh, if I had one of those grinning rascals
in the woods, where I and my oak sapling grew up together, I would teach
him that my arm is heavy though my purse be light!"

On turning the corner of the narrow lane, Robin found himself in a spacious
street, with an unbroken line of lofty houses on each side, and a steepled
building at the upper end, whence the ringing of a bell announced the hour
of nine. The light of the moon, and the lamps from the numerous shop-windows, discovered people promenading on the pavement, and amongst them
Robin hoped to recognize his hitherto inscrutable relative. The result of his
former inquiries made him unwilling to hazard another, in a scene of such
publicity, and he determined to walk slowly and silently up the street, thrusting
his face close to that of every elderly gentleman, in search of the Major's
lineaments. In his progress, Robin encountered many gay and gallant figures.
Embroidered garments of showy colors, enormous periwigs, gold-laced hats,
and silver-hilted swords glided past him and dazzled his optics. Travelled
youths, imitators of the European fine gentlemen of the period, trod jauntily
along, half dancing to the fashionable tunes which they hummed, and making
poor Robin ashamed of his quiet and natural gait. At length, after many pauses
to examine the gorgeous display of goods in the shop-windows, and after
suffering some rebukes for the impertinence of his scrutiny into people's faces,
the Major's kinsman found himself near the steepled building, still unsuccessful
in his search. As yet, however, he had seen only one side of the thronged
street; so Robin crossed, and continued the same sort of inquisition down
the opposite pavement, with stronger hopes than the philosopher seeking an
honest man, but with no better fortune. He had arrived about midway towards
the lower end, from which his course began, when he overheard the approach
of some one who struck down a cane on the flag-stones at every step, uttering,
at regular intervals, two sepulchral hems.

"Mercy on us!" quoth Robin, recognizing the sound.

Turning a corner, which chanced to be close at his right hand, he hastened
to pursue his researches in some other part of the town. His patience now
was wearing low, and he seemed to feel more fatigue from his rambles since
he crossed the ferry, than from his journey of several days on the other side.

---

[8] Indentured servants were bound over to their master's service for a period of years—often in
return for having their passages to the colonies paid.

Hunger also pleaded loudly within him, and Robin began to balance the propriety of demanding, violently, and with lifted cudgel, the necessary guidance from the first solitary passenger whom he should meet. While a resolution to this effect was gaining strength, he entered a street of mean appearance, on either side of which a row of ill-built houses was straggling towards the harbor. The moonlight fell upon no passenger along the whole extent, but in the third domicile which Robin passed there was a half-opened door, and his keen glance detected a woman's garment within.

"My luck may be better here," said he to himself.

Accordingly, he approached the door, and beheld it shut closer as he did so; yet an open space remained, sufficing for the fair occupant to observe the stranger, without a corresponding display on her part. All that Robin could discern was a strip of scarlet petticoat, and the occasional sparkle of an eye, as if the moonbeams were trembling on some bright thing.

"Pretty mistress," for I may call her so with a good conscience, thought the shrewd youth, since I know nothing to the contrary,—"my sweet pretty mistress, will you be kind enough to tell me whereabouts I must seek the dwelling of my kinsman, Major Molineux?"

Robin's voice was plaintive and winning, and the female, seeing nothing to be shunned in the handsome country youth, thrust open the door, and came forth into the moonlight. She was a dainty little figure, with a white neck, round arms, and a slender waist, at the extremity of which her scarlet petticoat jutted out over a hoop, as if she were standing in a balloon. Moreover, her face was oval and pretty, her hair dark beneath the little cap, and her bright eyes possessed a sly freedom, which triumphed over those of Robin.

"Major Molineux dwells here," said this fair woman.

Now, her voice was the sweetest Robin had heard that night, the airy counterpart of a stream of melted silver; yet he could not help doubting whether that sweet voice spoke Gospel truth. He looked up and down the mean street, and then surveyed the house before which they stood. It was a small, dark edifice of two stories, the second of which projected over the lower floor, and the front apartment had the aspect of a shop for petty commodities.

"Now, truly, I am in luck," replied Robin, cunningly, "and so indeed is my kinsman, the Major, in having so pretty a housekeeper. But I prithee trouble him to step to the door; I will deliver him a message from his friends in the country, and then go back to my lodgings at the inn."

"Nay, the Major has been abed this hour or more," said the lady of the scarlet petticoat; "and it would be to little purpose to disturb him to-night, seeing his evening draught was of the strongest. But he is a kind-hearted man, and it would be as much as my life's worth to let a kinsman of his turn away from the door. You are the good old gentleman's very picture, and I could swear that was his rainy-weather hat. Also he has garments very much resembling those leather small-clothes. But come in, I pray, for I bid you hearty welcome in his name."

So saying, the fair and hospitable dame took our hero by the hand; and the touch was light, and the force was gentleness, and though Robin read in her eyes what he did not hear in her words, yet the slender-waisted woman in the scarlet petticoat proved stronger than the athletic country youth. She had drawn his half-willing footsteps nearly to the threshold, when the opening of a door in the neighborhood startled the Major's housekeeper, and, leaving the Major's kinsman, she vanished speedily into her own domicile. A heavy yawn preceded the appearance of a man, who, like the Moonshine of Pyramus and Thisbe, carried a lantern,[9] needlessly aiding his sister luminary in the heavens. As he walked sleepily up the street, he turned his broad, dull face on Robin, and displayed a long staff, spiked at the end.

"Home, vagabond, home!" said the watchman, in accents that seemed to fall asleep as soon as they were uttered. "Home, or we'll set you in the stocks by peep of day!"

"This is the second hint of the kind," thought Robin. "I wish they would end my difficulties, by setting me there to-night."

Nevertheless, the youth felt an instinctive antipathy towards the guardian of midnight order, which at first prevented him from asking his usual question. But just when the man was about to vanish behind the corner, Robin resolved not to lose the opportunity, and shouted lustily after him,—

"I say, friend! will you guide me to the house of my kinsman, Major Molineux?"

The watchman made no reply, but turned the corner and was gone; yet Robin seemed to hear the sound of drowsy laughter stealing along the solitary street. At that moment, also, a pleasant titter saluted him from the open window above his head; he looked up, and caught the sparkle of a saucy eye; a round arm beckoned to him, and next he heard light footsteps descending the staircase within. But Robin, being of the household of a New England clergyman, was a good youth, as well as a shrewd one; so he resisted temptation, and fled away.

He now roamed desperately, and at random, through the town, almost ready to believe that a spell was on him, like that by which a wizard of his country had once kept three pursuers wandering, a whole winter night, within twenty paces of the cottage which they sought. The streets lay before him, strange and desolate, and the lights were extinguished in almost every house. Twice, however, little parties of men, among whom Robin distinguished individuals in outlandish attire, came hurrying along; but, though on both occasions they paused to address him, such intercourse did not at all enlighten his perplexity. They did but utter a few words in some language of which Robin knew nothing, and perceiving his inability to answer, bestowed a curse upon him in plain English and hastened away. Finally, the lad determined to knock at the door of every mansion that might appear worthy to be occupied by his kinsman, trusting that perseverance would overcome the fatality that had hitherto thwarted him. Firm in this resolve, he was passing beneath the walls of a church, which formed the corner of two streets, when, as he turned into the shade of its steeple, he encountered a bulky stranger, muffled in a cloak. The man was proceeding with the speed of earnest business, but Robin planted himself full before him, holding the oak cudgel with both hands across his body as a bar to further passage.

"Halt, honest man, and answer me a question," said he, very resolutely. "Tell me, this instant, whereabouts is the dwelling of my kinsman, Major Molineux!"

"Keep your tongue between your teeth, fool, and let me pass!" said a deep,

---

[9] An allusion to the comic play presented by the tradesmen in *A Midsummer Night's Dream* (1600) by William Shakespeare (1564–1616) in which a character named Moonshine appears with lantern in hand.

gruff voice, which Robin partly remembered. "Let me pass, I say, or I'll strike you to the earth!"

"No, no, neighbor!" cried Robin, flourishing his cudgel, and then thrusting its larger end close to the man's muffled face. "No, no, I'm not the fool you take me for, nor do you pass till I have an answer to my question. Whereabouts is the dwelling of my kinsman, Major Molineux?"

The stranger, instead of attempting to force his passage, stepped back into the moonlight, unmuffled his face, and stared full into that of Robin.

"Watch here an hour, and Major Molineux will pass by," said he.

Robin gazed with dismay and astonishment on the unprecedented physiognomy of the speaker. The forehead with its double prominence, the broad hooked nose, the shaggy eyebrows, and fiery eyes were those which he had noticed at the inn, but the man's complexion had undergone a singular, or, more properly, a twofold change. One side of the face blazed an intense red, while the other was black as midnight, the division line being in the broad bridge of the nose; and a mouth which seemed to extend from ear to ear was black or red; in contrast to the color of the cheek. The effect was as if two individual devils, a fiend of fire and a fiend of darkness, had united themselves to form this infernal visage. The stranger grinned in Robin's face, muffled his party-colored features, and was out of sight in a moment.

"Strange things we travellers see!" ejaculated Robin.

He seated himself, however, upon the steps of the church-door, resolving to wait the appointed time for his kinsman. A few moments were consumed in philosophical speculations upon the species of man who had just left him; but having settled this point shrewdly, rationally, and satisfactorily, he was compelled to look elsewhere for his amusement. And first he threw his eyes along the street. It was of more respectable appearance than most of those into which he had wandered; and the moon, creating, like the imaginative power, a beautiful strangeness in familiar objects, gave something of romance to a scene that might not have possessed it in the light of day. The irregular and often quaint architecture of the houses, some of whose roofs were broken into numerous little peaks, while others ascended, steep and narrow, into a single point, and others again were square; the pure snow-white of some of their complexions, the aged darkness of others, and the thousand sparklings, reflected from bright substances in the walls of many; these matters engaged Robin's attention for a while, and then began to grow wearisome. Next he endeavored to define the forms of distant objects, starting away, with almost ghostly indistinctness, just as his eye appeared to grasp them; and finally he took a minute survey of an edifice which stood on the opposite side of the street, directly in front of the church-door, where he was stationed. It was a large, square mansion, distinguished from its neighbors by a balcony, which rested on tall pillars, and by an elaborate Gothic window, communicating therewith.

"Perhaps this is the very house I have been seeking," thought Robin.

Then he strove to speed away the time, by listening to a murmur which swept continually along the street, yet was scarcely audible, except to an unaccustomed ear like his; it was a low, dull, dreamy sound, compounded of many noises, each of which was at too great a distance to be separately heard. Robin marvelled at this snore of a sleeping town, and marvelled more whenever its continuity was broken by now and then a distant shout, apparently loud where

it originated. But altogether it was a sleep-inspiring sound, and, to shake off
its drowsy influence, Robin arose, and climbed a window-frame, that he might
view the interior of the church. There the moonbeams came trembling in,
and fell down upon the deserted pews, and extended along the quiet aisles.
A fainter yet more awful radiance was hovering around the pulpit, and one
solitary ray had dared to rest upon the open page of the great Bible. Had
nature, in that deep hour, become a worshipper in the house which man had
builded? Or was that heavenly light the visible sanctity of the place,—visible
because no earthly and impure feet were within the walls? The scene made
Robin's heart shiver with a sensation of loneliness stronger than he had ever
felt in the remotest depths of his native woods; so he turned away and sat
down again before the door. There were graves around the church, and now
an uneasy thought obtruded into Robin's breast. What if the object of his
search, which had been so often and so strangely thwarted, were all the time
mouldering in his shroud? What if his kinsman should glide through yonder
gate, and nod and smile to him in dimly passing by?

"Oh that any breathing thing were here with me!" said Robin.

Recalling his thoughts from this uncomfortable track, he sent them over
forest, hill, and stream, and attempted to imagine how that evening of ambiguity
and weariness had been spent by his father's household. He pictured them
assembled at the door, beneath the tree, the great old tree, which had been
spared for its huge twisted trunk and venerable shade, when a thousand leafy
brethren fell. There, at the going down of the summer sun, it was his father's
custom to perform domestic worship, that the neighbors might come and join
with him like brothers of the family, and that the wayfaring man might pause
to drink at that fountain, and keep his heart pure by freshening the memory
of home. Robin distinguished the seat of every individual of the little audience;
he saw the good man in the midst, holding the Scriptures in the golden light
that fell from the western clouds; he beheld him close the book and all rise
up to pray. He heard the old thanksgivings for daily mercies, the old supplica-
tions for their continuance, to which he had so often listened in weariness,
but which were now among his dear remembrances. He perceived the slight
inequality of his father's voice when he came to speak of the absent one; he
noted how his mother turned her face to the broad and knotted trunk; how
his elder brother scorned, because the beard was rough upon his upper lip,
to permit his features to be moved; how the younger sister drew down a low
hanging branch before her eyes; and how the little one of all, whose sports
had hitherto broken the decorum of the scene, understood the prayer for
her playmate, and burst into clamorous grief. Then he saw them go in at the
door; and when Robin would have entered also, the latch tinkled into its place,
and he was excluded from his home.

"Am I here, or there?" cried Robin, starting; for all at once, when his thoughts
had become visible and audible in a dream, the long, wide, solitary street
shone out before him.

He aroused himself, and endeavored to fix his attention steadily upon the
large edifice which he had surveyed before. But still his mind kept vibrating
between fancy and reality; by turns, the pillars of the balcony lengthened into
the tall, bare stems of pines, dwindled down to human figures, settled again
into their true shape and size, and then commenced a new succession of
changes. For a single moment, when he deemed himself awake, he could have
sworn that a visage—one which he seemed to remember, yet could not abso-

lutely name as his kinsman's—was looking towards him from the Gothic window.
A deeper sleep wrestled with and nearly overcame him, but fled at the sound
of footsteps along the opposite pavement. Robin rubbed his eyes, discerned
a man passing at the foot of the balcony, and addressed him in a loud, peevish,
and lamentable cry.

"Hallo, friend! must I wait here all night for my kinsman, Major Molineux?"

The sleeping echoes awoke, and answered the voice; and the passenger,
barely able to discern a figure sitting in the oblique shade of the steeple,
traversed the street to obtain a nearer view. He was himself a gentleman in
his prime, of open, intelligent, cheerful, and altogether prepossessing countenance. Perceiving a country youth, apparently homeless and without friends,
he accosted him in a tone of real kindness, which had become strange to
Robin's ears.

"Well, my good lad, why are you sitting here?" inquired he. "Can I be of
service to you in any way?"

"I am afraid not, sir," replied Robin, despondingly; "yet I shall take it kindly,
if you'll answer me a single question. I've been searching, half the night, for
one Major Molineux; now, sir, is there really such a person in these parts, or
am I dreaming?"

"Major Molineux! The name is not altogether strange to me," said the gentleman, smiling. "Have you any objection to telling me the nature of your business
with him?"

Then Robin briefly related that his father was a clergyman, settled on a
small salary, at a long distance back in the country, and that he and Major
Molineux were brothers' children. The Major, having inherited riches, and
acquired civil and military rank, had visited his cousin, in great pomp, a year
or two before; had manifested much interest in Robin and an elder brother,
and, being childless himself, had thrown out hints respecting the future establishment of one of them in life. The elder brother was destined to succeed
to the farm which his father cultivated in the interval of sacred duties; it was
therefore determined that Robin should profit by his kinsman's generous intentions, especially as he seemed to be rather the favorite, and was thought to
possess other necessary endowments.

"For I have the name of being a shrewd youth," observed Robin, in this
part of his story.

"I doubt not you deserve it," replied his new friend, good-naturedly; "but
pray proceed."

"Well, sir, being nearly eighteen years old, and well grown, as you see,"
continued Robin, drawing himself up to his full height, "I thought it high
time to begin the world. So my mother and sister put me in handsome trim,
and my father gave me half the remnant of his last year's salary, and five
days ago I started for this place, to pay the Major a visit. But, would you
believe it, sir! I crossed the ferry a little after dark, and have yet found nobody
that would show me the way to his dwelling; only, an hour or two since, I
was told to wait here, and Major Molineux would pass by."

"Can you describe the man who told you this?" inquired the gentleman.

"Oh, he was a very ill-favored fellow, sir," replied Robin, "with two great
bumps on his forehead, a hook nose, fiery eyes; and, what struck me as the
strangest, his face was of two different colors. Do you happen to know such
a man, sir?"

"Not intimately," answered the stranger, "but I chanced to meet him a little time previous to your stopping me. I believe you may trust his word, and that the Major will very shortly pass through this street. In the mean time, as I have a singular curiosity to witness your meeting, I will sit down here upon the steps and bear you company."

He seated himself accordingly, and soon engaged his companion in animated discourse. It was but of brief continuance, however, for a noise of shouting, which had long been remotely audible, drew so much nearer that Robin inquired its cause.

"What may be the meaning of this uproar?" asked he. "Truly, if your town be always as noisy, I shall find little sleep while I am an inhabitant."

"Why, indeed, friend Robin, there do appear to be three or four riotous fellows abroad to-night," replied the gentleman. "You must not expect all the stillness of your native woods here in our streets. But the watch will shortly be at the heels of these lads and"—

"Ay, and set them in the stocks by peep of day," interrupted Robin, recollecting his own encounter with the drowsy lantern-bearer. "But, dear sir, if I may trust my ears, an army of watchmen would never make head against such a multitude of rioters. There were at least a thousand voices went up to make that one shout."

"May not a man have several voices, Robin, as well as two complexions?" said his friend.

"Perhaps a man may; but Heaven forbid that a woman should!" responded the shrewd youth, thinking of the seductive tones of the Major's housekeeper.

The sounds of a trumpet in some neighboring street now became so evident and continual, that Robin's curiosity was strongly excited. In addition to the shouts, he heard frequent bursts from many instruments of discord, and a wild and confused laughter filled up the intervals. Robin rose from the steps, and looked wistfully towards a point whither people seemed to be hastening.

"Surely some prodigious merry-making is going on," exclaimed he. "I have laughed very little since I left home, sir, and should be sorry to lose an opportunity. Shall we step round the corner by that darkish house, and take our share of the fun?"

"Sit down again, sit down, good Robin," replied the gentleman, laying his hand on the skirt of the gray coat. "You forget that we must wait here for your kinsman; and there is reason to believe that he will pass by, in the course of a very few moments."

The near approach of the uproar had now disturbed the neighborhood; windows flew open on all sides; and many heads, in the attire of the pillow, and confused by sleep suddenly broken, were protruded to the gaze of whoever had leisure to observe them. Eager voices hailed each other from house to house, all demanding the explanation, which not a soul could give. Half-dressed men hurried towards the unknown commotion, stumbling as they went over the stone steps that thrust themselves into the narrow foot-walk. The shouts, the laughter, and the tuneless bray, the antipodes of music, came onwards with increasing din, till scattered individuals, and then denser bodies, began to appear round a corner at the distance of a hundred yards.

"Will you recognize your kinsman, if he passes in this crowd?" inquired the gentleman.

"Indeed, I can't warrant it, sir; but I'll take my stand here, and keep a bright lookout," answered Robin, descending to the outer edge of the pavement.

A mighty stream of people now emptied into the street, and came rolling slowly towards the church. A single horseman wheeled the corner in the midst of them, and close behind him came a band of fearful wind-instruments, sending forth a fresher discord now that no intervening buildings kept it from the ear. Then a redder light disturbed the moonbeams, and a dense multitude of torches shone along the street, concealing, by their glare, whatever object they illuminated. The single horseman, clad in a military dress, and bearing a drawn sword, rode onward as the leader, and, by his fierce and variegated countenance, appeared like war personified; the red of one cheek was an emblem of fire and sword; the blackness of the other betokened the mourning that attends them. In his train were wild figures in the Indian dress, and many fantastic shapes without a model, giving the whole march a visionary air, as if a dream had broken forth from some feverish brain, and were sweeping visibly through the midnight streets. A mass of people, inactive, except as applauding spectators, hemmed the procession in; and several women ran along the sidewalk, piercing the confusion of heavier sounds with their shrill voices of mirth or terror.

"The double-faced fellow has his eye upon me," muttered Robin, with an indefinite but an uncomfortable idea that he was himself to bear a part in the pageantry.

The leader turned himself in the saddle, and fixed his glance full upon the country youth, as the steed went slowly by. When Robin had freed his eyes from those fiery ones, the musicians were passing before him, and the torches were close at hand; but the unsteady brightness of the latter formed a veil which he could not penetrate. The rattling of wheels over the stones sometimes found its way to his ear, and confused traces of a human form appeared at intervals, and then melted into the vivid light. A moment more, and the leader thundered a command to halt: the trumpets vomited a horrid breath, and then held their peace; the shouts and laughter of the people died away, and there remained only a universal hum, allied to silence. Right before Robin's eyes was an uncovered cart. There the torches blazed the brightest, there the moon shone out like day, and there, in tar-and-feathery dignity, sat his kinsman, Major Molineux!

He was an elderly man, of large and majestic person, and strong, square features, betokening a steady soul; but steady as it was, his enemies had found means to shake it. His face was pale as death, and far more ghastly; the broad forehead was contracted in his agony, so that his eyebrows formed one grizzled line; his eyes were red and wild, and the foam hung white upon his quivering lip. His whole frame was agitated by a quick and continual tremor, which his pride strove to quell, even in those circumstances of overwhelming humiliation. But perhaps the bitterest pang of all was when his eyes met those of Robin; for he evidently knew him on the instant, as the youth stood witnessing the foul disgrace of a head grown gray in honor. They stared at each other in silence, and Robin's knees shook, and his hair bristled, with a mixture of pity and terror. Soon, however, a bewildering excitement began to seize upon his mind; the preceding adventures of the night, the unexpected appearance of the crowd, the torches, the confused din and the hush that followed, the spectre of his kinsman reviled by that great multitude,—all this, and more than all, a perception of tremendous ridicule in the whole scene, affected him with a sort of mental inebriety. At that moment a voice of sluggish merriment saluted Robin's ears; he turned instinctively, and just behind the corner of the church stood the lantern-bearer, rubbing his eyes, and drowsily enjoying the lad's

amazement. Then he heard a peal of laughter like the ringing of silvery bells;
a woman twitched his arm, a saucy eye met his, and he saw the lady of the
scarlet petticoat. A sharp, dry cachinnation appealed to his memory, and, standing on tiptoe in the crowd, with his white apron over his head, he beheld
the courteous little innkeeper. And lastly, there sailed over the heads of the
multitude a great, broad laugh, broken in the midst by two sepulchral hems;
thus, "Haw, haw, haw,—hem, hem,—haw, haw, haw, haw!"

The sound proceeded from the balcony of the opposite edifice, and thither
Robin turned his eyes. In front of the Gothic window stood the old citizen,
wrapped in a wide gown, his gray periwig exchanged for a nightcap, which
was thrust back from his forehead, and his silk stockings hanging about his
legs. He supported himself on his polished cane in a fit of convulsive merriment,
which manifested itself on his solemn old features like a funny inscription
on a tombstone. Then Robin seemed to hear the voices of the barbers, of
the guests of the inn, and of all who had made sport of him that night. The
contagion was spreading among the multitude, when all at once, it seized
upon Robin, and he sent forth a shout of laughter that echoed through the
street,—every man shook his sides, every man emptied his lungs, but Robin's
shout was the loudest there. The cloud-spirits peeped from their silvery islands,
as the congregated mirth went roaring up the sky! The Man in the Moon
heard the far bellow. "Oho," quoth he, "the old earth is frolicsome to-night!"

When there was a momentary calm in that tempestuous sea of sound, the
leader gave the sign, the procession resumed its march. On they went, like
fiends that throng in mockery around some dead potentate, mighty no more,
but majestic still in his agony. On they went, in counterfeited pomp, in senseless
uproar, in frenzied merriment, trampling all on an old man's heart. On swept
the tumult, and left a silent street behind.

"Well, Robin, are you dreaming?" inquired the gentleman, laying his hand
on the youth's shoulder.

Robin started, and withdrew his arm from the stone post to which he had
instinctively clung, as the living stream rolled by him. His cheek was somewhat
pale, and his eye not quite as lively as in the earlier part of the evening.

"Will you be kind enough to show me the way to the ferry?" said he, after
a moment's pause.

"You have, then, adopted a new subject of inquiry?" observed his companion,
with a smile.

"Why, yes, sir," replied Robin, rather dryly. "Thanks to you, and to my
other friends, I have at last met my kinsman, and he will scarce desire to see
my face again. I begin to grow weary of a town life, sir. Will you show me
the way to the ferry?"

"No, my good friend Robin,—not to-night, at least," said the gentleman.
"Some few days hence, if you wish it, I will speed you on your journey. Or,
if you prefer to remain with us, perhaps, as you are a shrewd youth, you
may rise in the world without the help of your kinsman, Major Molineux."

[1832]

Edgar Allan Poe   *1809–1849*

THE FALL OF THE HOUSE OF USHER

Son cœur est un luth suspendu;
Sitôt qu'on le touche il résonne.
De Béranger[1]

Rod is house

During the whole of a dull, dark, and soundless day in the autumn of the year, when the clouds hung oppressively low in the heavens, I had been passing alone, on horseback, through a singularly dreary tract of country; and at length found myself, as the shades of the evening drew on, within view of the melancholy House of Usher. I know not how it was—but, with the first glimpse of the building, a sense of insufferable gloom pervaded my spirit. I say insufferable; for the feeling was unrelieved by any of that half-pleasurable, because poetic, sentiment, with which the mind usually receives even the sternest natural images of the desolate or terrible. I looked upon the scene before me—upon the mere house, and the simple landscape features of the domain—upon the bleak walls—upon the vacant eye-like windows—upon a few rank sedges—and upon a few white trunks of decayed trees—with an utter depression of soul which I can compare to no earthly sensation more properly than to the after-dream of the reveller upon opium—the bitter lapse into everyday life—the hideous dropping off of the veil. There was an iciness, a sinking, a sickening of the heart—an unredeemed dreariness of thought which no goading of the imagination could torture into aught of the sublime. What was it—I paused to think—what was it that so unnerved me in the contemplation of the House of Usher? It was a mystery all insoluble; nor could I grapple with the shadowy fancies that crowded upon me as I pondered. I was forced to fall back upon the unsatisfactory conclusion, that while, beyond doubt, there *are* combinations of very simple natural objects which have the power of thus affecting us, still the analysis of this power lies among considerations beyond our depth. It was possible, I reflected, that a mere different arrangement of the particulars of the scene, of the details of the picture, would be sufficient to modify, or perhaps to annihilate its capacity for sorrowful impression; and, acting upon this idea, I reined my horse to the precipitous brink of a black and lurid tarn[2] that lay in unruffled lustre by the dwelling, and gazed down—but with a shudder even more thrilling than before—upon the remodelled and inverted images of the gray sedge, and the ghastly tree-stems, and the vacant and eye-like windows.

Nevertheless, in this manison of gloom I now proposed to myself a sojourn of some weeks. Its proprietor, Roderick Usher, had been one of my boon companions in boyhood; but many years had elapsed since our last meeting. A letter, however, had lately reached me in a distant part of the country—a letter from him—which, in its wildly importunate nature, had admitted of no other than a personal reply. The MS. gave evidence of nervous agitation. The writer spoke of acute bodily illness—of a mental disorder which oppressed

---

[1] Lines from a poem by Pierre-Jean de Béranger (1780–1857): "His heart is a suspended lute;/ Whenever one touches it, it responds."
[2] A small mountain lake or pond.

him—and of an earnest desire to see me, as his best, and indeed his only personal friend, with a view of attempting, by the cheerfulness of my society, some alleviation of his malady. It was the manner in which all this, and much more, was said—it was the apparent *heart* that went with his request—which allowed me no room for hesitation; and I accordingly obeyed forthwith what I still considered a very singular summons.

Although, as boys, we had been even intimate associates, yet I really knew little of my friend. His reserve had been always excessive and habitual. I was aware, however, that his very ancient family had been noted, time out of mind, for a peculiar sensibility of temperament, displaying itself, through long ages, in many works of exalted art, and manifested, of late, in repeated deeds of munificent yet unobtrusive charity, as well as in a passionate devotion to the intricacies, perhaps even more than to the orthodox and easily recognizable beauties, of musical science. I had learned, too, the very remarkable fact, that the stem of the Usher race, all time-honoured as it was, had put forth, at no period, any enduring branch; in other words, that the entire family lay in the direct line of descent, and had always, with very trifling and very temporary variation, so lain. It was this deficiency, I considered, while running over in thought the perfect keeping of the character of the premises with the accredited character of the people, and while speculating upon the possible influence which the one, in the long lapse of centuries, might have exercised upon the other—it was this deficiency, perhaps, of collateral issue, and the consequent undeviating transmission, from sire to son, of the patrimony with the name, which had, at length, so identified the two as to merge the original title of the estate in the quaint and equivocal appellation of the "House of Usher"— an appellation which seemed to include, in the minds of the peasantry who used it, both the family and the family mansion.

I have said that the sole effect of my somewhat childish experiment—that of looking down within the tarn—had been to deepen the first singular impression. There can be no doubt that the consciousness of the rapid increase of my superstition—for why should I not so term it?—served mainly to accelerate the increase itself. Such, I have long known, is the paradoxical law of all sentiments having terror as a basis. And it might have been for this reason only, that, when I again uplifted my eyes to the house itself, from its image in the pool, there grew in my mind a strange fancy—a fancy so ridiculous, indeed, that I but mention it to show the vivid force of the sensations which oppressed me. I had so worked upon my imagination as really to believe that about the whole mansion and domain there hung an atmosphere peculiar to themselves and their immediate vicinity—an atmosphere which had no affinity with the air of heaven, but which had reeked up from the decayed trees, and the gray wall, and the silent tarn—a pestilent and mystic vapour, dull, sluggish, faintly discernible, and leaden-hued.

Shaking off from my spirit what *must* have been a dream, I scanned more narrowly the real aspect of the building. Its principal feature seemed to be that of an excessive antiquity. The discoloration of ages had been great. Minute fungi overspread the whole exterior, hanging in a fine tangled web-work from the eaves. Yet all this was apart from any extraordinary dilapidation. No portion of the masonry had fallen; and there appeared to be a wild inconsistency between its still perfect adaptation of parts, and the crumbling condition of the individual stones. In this there was much that reminded me of the specious totality of old wood-work which has rotted for long years in some neglected vault, with no disturbance from the breath of the external air. Beyond this indication of extensive decay, however, the fabric gave little token of instability. Perhaps the eye of a scrutinizing observer might have discovered a barely perceptible fissure, which, extending from the roof of the building in front, made its way down the wall in a zigzag direction, until it became lost in the sullen waters of the tarn.   *CRACK*

Noticing these things, I rode over a short causeway to the house. A servant in waiting took my horse, and I entered the Gothic archway of the hall. A valet, of stealthy step, thence conducted me, in silence, through many dark and intricate passages in my progress to the *studio* of his master. Much that I encountered on the way contributed, I know not how, to heighten the vague sentiments of which I have already spoken. While the objects around me— while the carvings of the ceilings, the sombre tapestries of the walls, the ebon blackness of the floors, and the phantasmagoric armorial trophies which rattled as I strode, were but matters to which, or to such as which, I had been accustomed from my infancy—while I hesitated not to acknowledge how familiar was all this—I still wondered to find how unfamiliar were the fancies which ordinary images were stirring up. On one of the staircases, I met the physician of the family. His countenance, I thought, wore a mingled expression of low cunning and perplexity. He accosted me with trepidation and passed on. The valet now threw open a door and ushered me into the presence of his master.

The room in which I found myself was very large and lofty. The windows were long, narrow, and pointed, and at so vast a distance from the black oaken floor as to be altogether inaccessible from within. Feeble gleams of encrimsoned light made their way through the trellised panes, and served to render sufficiently distinct the more prominent objects around; the eye, however, struggled in vain to reach the remoter angles of the chamber, or the recesses of the vaulted and fretted ceiling. Dark draperies hung upon the walls. The general furniture was profuse, comfortless, antique, and tattered. Many books and musical instruments lay scattered about, but failed to give any vitality to the scene. I felt that I breathed an atmosphere of sorrow. An air of stern, deep, and irredeemable gloom hung over and pervaded all.

Upon my entrance, Usher arose from a sofa on which he had been lying at full length, and greeted me with a vivacious warmth which had much in it, I at first thought, of an overdone cordiality—of the constrained effort of the *ennuyé*[3] man of the world. A glance, however, at his countenance, convinced me of his perfect sincerity. We sat down; and for some moments, while he spoke not, I gazed upon him with a feeling half of pity, half of awe. Surely, man had never before so terribly altered, in so brief a period, as had Roderick Usher! It was with difficulty that I could bring myself to admit the identity of the wan being before me with the companion of my early boyhood. Yet the character of his face had been at all times remarkable. A cadaverousness of complexion; an eye large, liquid, and luminous beyond comparison; lips somewhat thin and very pallid, but of a surpassingly beautiful curve; a nose of a delicate Hebrew model, but with a breadth of nostril unusual in similar formations; a finely moulded chin, speaking, in its want of prominence, of a want of moral energy; hair of a more than web-like softness and tenuity; these features, with an inordinate expansion above the regions of the temple, made up altogether a countenance not easily to be forgotten. And now in the mere

[3] Bored.

Rod's face to house exterior

exaggeration of the prevailing character of these features, and of the expression they were wont to convey, lay so much of change that I doubted to whom I spoke. The now ghastly pallor of the skin, and the now miraculous lustre of the eye, above all things startled and even awed me. The silken hair, too, had been suffered to grow all unheeded, and as, in its wild gossamer texture, it floated rather than fell about the face, I could not, even with effort, connect its Arabesque[4] expression with any idea of simple humanity.

In the manner of my friend I was at once struck with an incoherence—an inconsistency; and I soon found this to arise from a series of feeble and futile struggles to overcome an habitual trepidancy—an excessive nervous agitation. For something of this nature I had indeed been prepared, no less by his letter, than by reminiscences of certain boyish traits, and by conclusions deduced from his peculiar physical conformation and temperament. His action was alternately vivacious and sullen. His voice varied rapidly from a tremulous indecision (when the animal spirits seemed utterly in abeyance) to that species of energetic concision—that abrupt, weighty, unhurried, and hollow-sounding enunciation—that leaden, self-balanced and perfectly modulated guttural utterance, which may be observed in the lost drunkard, or the irreclaimable eater of opium, during the periods of his most intense excitement.

It was thus that he spoke of the object of my visit, of his earnest desire to see me, and of the solace he expected me to afford him. He entered, at some length, into what he conceived to be the nature of his malady. It was, he said, a constitutional and a family evil, and one for which he despaired to find a remedy—a mere nervous affection, he immediately added, which would undoubtedly soon pass off. It displayed itself in a host of unnatural sensations. Some of these, as he detailed them, interested and bewildered me; although, perhaps, the terms, and the general manner of the narration had their weight. He suffered much from a morbid acuteness of the senses; the most insipid food was alone endurable; he could wear only garments of certain texture; the odours of all flowers were oppressive; his eyes were tortured by even a faint light; and there were but peculiar sounds, and these from stringed instruments, which did not inspire him with horror.

To an anomalous species of terror I found him a bounden slave. "I shall perish," said he, "I *must* perish in this deplorable folly. Thus, thus, and not otherwise, shall I be lost. I dread the events of the future, not in themselves, but in their results. I shudder at the thought of any, even the most trivial, incident, which may operate upon this intolerable agitation of soul. I have, indeed, no abhorrence of danger, except in its absolute effect—in terror. In this unnerved—in this pitiable condition—I feel that the period will sooner or later arrive when I must abandon life and reason together, in some struggle with the grim phantasm, FEAR."

I learned, moreover, at intervals, and through broken and equivocal hints, another singular feature of his mental condition. He was enchained by certain superstitious impressions in regard to the dwelling which he tenanted, and whence, for many years, he had never ventured forth—in regard to an influence whose supposititious force was conveyed in terms too shadowy here to be re-stated—an influence which some peculiarities in the mere form and substance of his family mansion, had, by dint of long sufferance, he said, obtained over his spirit—an effect which the *physique* of the gray walls and turrets, and of

---

[4] Strange or exotic.

the dim tarn into which they all looked down, had, at length, brought about upon the *morale* of his existence.

He admitted, however, although with hesitation, that much of the peculiar gloom which thus afflicted him could be traced to a more natural and far more palpable origin—to the severe and long-continued illness—indeed to the evidently approaching dissolution—of a tenderly beloved sister—his sole companion for long years—his last and only relative on earth. "Her decease," he said, with a bitterness which I can never forget, "would leave him (him the hopeless and the frail) the last of the ancient race of the Ushers." While he spoke, the lady Madeline (for so was she called) passed slowly through a remote portion of the apartment, and, without having noticed my presence, disappeared. I regarded her with an utter astonishment not unmingled with dread—and yet I found it impossible to account for such feelings. A sensation of stupor oppressed me, as my eyes followed her retreating steps. When a door, at length, closed upon her, my glance sought instinctively and eagerly the countenance of the brother—but he had buried his face in his hands, and I could only perceive that a far more than ordinary wanness had overspread the emaciated fingers through which trickled many passionate tears.

The disease of the lady Madeline had long baffled the skill of her physicians. A settled apathy, a gradual wasting away of the person, and frequent although transient affections of a partially cataleptical character,[5] were the unusual diagnosis. Hitherto she had steadily borne up against the pressure of her malady, and had not betaken herself finally to bed; but, on the closing in of the evening of my arrival at the house, she succumbed (as her brother told me at night with inexpressible agitation) to the prostrating power of the destroyer; and I learned that the glimpse I had obtained of her person would thus probably be the last I should obtain—that the lady, at least while living, would be seen by me no more.

For several days ensuing, her name was unmentioned by either Usher or myself: and during this period I was busied in earnest endeavours to alleviate the melancholy of my friend. We painted and read together; or I listened, as if in a dream, to the wild improvisations of his speaking guitar. And thus, as a closer and still closer intimacy admitted me more unreservedly into the recesses of his spirit, the more bitterly did I perceive the futility of all attempt at cheering a mind from which darkness, as if an inherent positive quality, poured forth upon all objects of the moral and physical universe, in one unceasing radiation of gloom.

I shall ever bear about me a memory of the many solemn hours I thus spent alone with the master of the House of Usher. Yet I should fail in any attempt to convey an idea of the exact character of the studies, or of the occupations, in which he involved me, or led me the way. An excited and highly distempered ideality threw a sulphureous lustre over all. His long improvised dirges will ring forever in my ears. Among other things, I hold painfully in mind a certain singular perversion and amplification of the wild air of the last waltz of Von Weber.[6] From the paintings over which his elaborate fancy brooded, and which grew, touch by touch, into vaguenesses at which I shud-

---

[5] Catalepsy is an illness characterized by a trance-like state in which the person loses the will or desire to move.

[6] Karl Maria von Weber (17986–1826), a famous composer of German operas. "The Last Waltz of Von Weber" was, however, the work of Karl Gottlieb Reissiger (1798–1859).

dered the more thrillingly, because I shuddered knowing not why;—from these
paintings (vivid as their images now are before me) I would in vain endeavour
to educe more than a small portion which should lie within the compass of
merely written words. By the utter simplicity, by the nakedness of his designs,
he arrested and overawed attention. If ever mortal painted an idea, that mortal
was Roderick Usher. For me at least—in the circumstances then surrounding
me—there arose out of the pure abstractions which the hypochondriac contrived to throw upon his canvas, an intensity of intolerable awe, no shadow
of which felt I ever yet in the contemplation of the certainly glowing yet too
concrete reveries of Fuseli.[7]

One of the phantasmagoric conceptions of my friend, partaking not so rigidly
of the spirit of abstraction, may be shadowed forth, although feebly, in words.
A small picture presented the interior of an immensely long and rectangular
vault or tunnel, with low walls, smooth, white, and without interruption or
device. Certain accessory points of the design served well to convey the idea
that this excavation lay at an exceeding depth below the surface of the earth.
No outlet was observed in any portion of its vast extent, and no torch, or
other artificial source of light was discernible; yet a flood of intense rays rolled
throughout, and bathed the whole in a ghastly and inappropriate splendour.

I have just spoken of that morbid condition of the auditory nerve which
rendered all music intolerable to the sufferer, with the exception of certain
effects of stringed instruments. It was, perhaps, the narrow limits to which
he thus confined himself upon the guitar, which gave birth, in great measure,
to the fantastic character of his performances. But the fervid *facility* of his
impromptus could not be so accounted for. They must have been, and were,
in the notes, as well as in the words of his wild fantasias (for he not unfrequently
accompanied himself with rhymed verbal improvisations), the result of that
intense mental collectedness and concentration to which I have previously
alluded as observable only in particular moments of the highest artificial excitement. The words of one of these rhapsodies I have easily remembered. I was,
perhaps, the more forcibly impressed with it, as he gave it, because, in the
under or mystic current of its meaning, I fancied that I perceived, and for
the first time, a full consciousness on the part of Usher, of the tottering of
his lofty reason upon her throne. The verses, which were entitled "The Haunted
Palace,"[8] ran very nearly, if not accurately, thus:

I

In the greenest of our valleys,
  By good angels tenanted,
Once a fair and stately palace—
  Radiant palace—reared its head.
In the monarch Thought's dominion—
  It stood there!
Never seraph spread a pinion
  Over fabric half so fair.

[7] Henry Fuseli (1741–1825), a Swiss-born English painter, was noted for his wildly romantic impres-
sionism.
[8] Poe published the poen in the *American Museum* in April of 1839, some five months before the
story itself appeared in *Burton's Gentleman's Magazine.*

II

Banners yellow, glorious, golden,
  On its roof did float and flow;
(This—all this—was in the olden
  Time long ago)
And every gentle air that dallied,
  In that sweet day,
Along the ramparts plumed and pallid,
  A winged odour went away.

III

Wanderers in that happy valley
  Through two luminous windows saw
Spirits moving musically
  To a lute's well-tunèd law,
Round about a throne, where sitting
  (Porphyrogene![9])
In state his glory well befitting,
  The ruler of the realm was seen.

IV

And all with pearl and ruby glowing
  Was the fair palace door,
Through which came flowing, flowing, flowing
  And sparkling evermore,
A troop of Echoes whose sweet duty
  Was but to sing,
In voices of surpassing beauty,
  The wit and wisdom of their king.

V

But evil things, in robes of sorrow,
  Assailed the monarch's high estate;
(Ah, let us mourn, for never morrow
  Shall dawn upon him, desolate!)
And, round about his home, the glory
  That blushed and bloomed
Is but a dim-remembered story
  Of the old time entombed.

Madeline 7 gone
House

VI

And travellers now within that valley,
  Through the red-litten windows, see
Vast forms that move fantastically
  To a discordant melody;
While, like a rapid ghastly river,
  Through the pale door,
A hideous throng rush out forever,
  And laugh—but smile no more.

[9] Of royal birth.

I well remember that suggestions arising from this ballad, led us into a train of thought wherein there became manifest an opinion of Usher's which I mention not so much on account of its novelty, (for other men* have thought thus,) as on account of the pertinacity with which he maintained it. This opinion, in its general form, was that of the sentience of all vegetable things. But, in his disordered fancy, the idea had assumed a more daring character, and trespassed, under certain conditions, upon the kingdom of inorganization. I lack words to express the full extent, or the earnest *abandon* of his persuasion. The belief, however, was connected (as I have previously hinted) with the gray stones of the home of his forefathers. The conditions of the sentience had been here, he imagined, fulfilled in the method of collocation of these stones—in order of their arrangement, as well as in that of the many *fungi* which overspread them, and of the decayed trees which stood around—above all, in the long undisturbed endurance of this arrangement, and in its reduplication in the still waters of the tarn. Its evidence—the evidence of the sentience— was to be seen, he said, (and I here started as he spoke,) in the gradual yet certain condensation of an atmosphere of their own about the waters and the walls. The result was discoverable, he added, in that silent, yet importunate and terrible influence which for centuries had moulded the destinies of his family, and which made *him* what I now saw him—what he was. Such opinions need no comment, and I will make none.

Our books—the books which, for years, had formed no small portion of the mental existence of the invalid—were, as might be supposed, in strict keeping with this character of phantasm. We pored together over such works as the Ververt et Chartreuse of Gresset; the Belphegor of Machiavelli; the Heaven and Hell of Swedenborg; the Subterranean Voyage of Nicholas Klimm by Holberg; the Chiromancy of Robert Flud, of Jean d'Indaginé, and of De la Chambre; the Journey into the Blue Distance of Tieck; and the City of the Sun of Campanella. One favourite volume was a small octavo edition of the *Directorium Inquisitorum,* by the Dominican Eymeric de Gironne; and there were passages in Pomponius Mela, about the old African Satyrs and Ægipans, over which Usher would sit dreaming for hours. His chief delight, however, was found in the perusal of an exceedingly rare and curious book in quarto Gothic—the manual of a forgotten church—the *Vigiliæ Mortuorum secundum Chorum Ecclesiæ Maguntinæ.*[10]

---

* Watson, Dr. Percival, Spallanzani, and especially the Bishop of Landaff.—See "Chemical Essays," vol. v. [Poe's note]
  The allusions are, specifically, to Richard Watson (1737–1819), the Bishop of Landaff, a British chemist; James Gates Percival (1795–1856), an American doctor and poet; and Lazzaro Spallanzani (1729–1799), an Italian professor of natural history.

[10] The titles and authors which compose Roderick Usher's library are real: *Vairvert* and *Chartreuse* are light-hearted, anti-religious poems by Jean-Baptiste-Louis Gresset (1709–1777); *Belphegor* is a novel by Niccolò Machiavelli (1469–1527), in which a demon visits the earth to argue that women are man's damnation; *Heaven and Hell* by the Swedish mystic and scientist Emanuel Swedenborg (1688–1772) deals with the spiritual continuity of man and matter. The *Subterranean Voyage* by the Danish dramatist, novelist, and historian Ludwig Holberg (1684–1754) is an account of a voyage into the underworld; while chiromancy, or palm-reading, is the subject of books by English physician and pseudo-scientist Robert Flud (1574–1637) and two Frenchmen, Jean d'Indaginé (16th century) and Maria Cireau de la Chambre (1594–1669). The *Journey into the Blue Distance* by the German writer Ludwig Tieck (1773–1853) and the *City of the Sun* by Italian writer Tommaso Campanella (1568–1639) both deal with voyages to other worlds. Nicholas Eymeric de Gironne (1320–1399) served as Inquisitor-General of Castile and his book, *Directorium Inquisitorium,* is an account of the procedures to be used for torturing heretics. Pomponius Mela

I could not help thinking of the wild ritual of this work, and of its probable influence upon the hypochondriac, when, one evening, having informed me abruptly that the lady Madeline was no more, he stated his intention of preserving her corpse for a fortnight, (previously to its final interment,) in one of the numerous vaults within the main walls of the building. The worldly reason, however, assigned for this singular proceeding, was one which I did not feel at liberty to dispute. The brother had been led to his resolution (so he told me) by consideration of the unusual character of the malady of the deceased, of certain obtrusive and eager inquiries on the part of her medical men, and of the remote and exposed situation of the burial-ground of the family. I will not deny that when I called to mind the sinister countenance of the person whom I met upon the staircase, on the day of my arrival at the house, I had no desire to oppose what I regarded as at best but a harmless, and by no means an unnatural, precaution.[11]

At the request of Usher, I personally aided him in the arrangements for the temporary entombment. The body having been encoffined, we two alone bore it to its rest. The vault in which we placed it (and which had been so long unopened that our torches, half smothered in its oppressive atmosphere, gave us little opportunity for investigation) was small, damp, and entirely without means of admission for light; lying, at great depth, immediately beneath that portion of the building in which was my own sleeping apartment. It had been used, apparently, in remote feudal times, for the worst purposes of a dungeon-keep, and, in later days, as a place of deposit for powder, or some other highly combustible substance, as a portion of its floor, and the whole interior of a long archway through which we reached it, were carefully sheathed with copper. The door, of massive iron, had been, also, similarly protected. Its immense weight caused an unusually sharp grating sound, as it moved upon its hinges.

Having deposited our mournful burden upon trestles within this region of horror, we partially turned aside the yet unscrewed lid of the coffin, and looked upon the face of the tenant. A striking similitude between the brother and sister now first arrested my attention; and Usher, divining, perhaps, my thoughts, murmured out some few words from which I learned that the deceased and himself had been twins, and that sympathies of a scarcely intelligible nature had always existed between them. Our glances, however, rested not long upon the dead—for we could not regard her unawed. The disease which had thus entombed the lady in the maturity of youth, had left, as usual in all maladies of a strictly cataleptical character, the mockery of a faint blush upon the bosom and the face, and that suspiciously lingering smile upon the lip which is so terrible in death. We replaced and screwed down the lid, and, having secured the door of iron, made our way, with toil, into the scarcely less gloomy apartments of the upper portion of the house.

And now, some days of bitter grief having elapsed, an observable change came over the features of the mental disorder of my friend. His ordinary manner had vanished. His ordinary occupations were neglected or forgotten. He

---

was a first-century Roman whose books of geography depicted the fabulously strange satyrs and aegipans (goat-men) of Africa. The last title, *The Vigils of the Dead according to the Choir of the Church of Mayence,* was printed at Basel in Switzerland about 1500.

[11] The allusion is to the all-too-common contemporary practice of stealing fresh corpses and selling them to medical students and physicians for use in dissection and experimentation.

roamed from chamber to chamber with hurried, unequal, and objectless step. The pallor of his countenance had assumed, if possible, a more ghastly hue— but the luminousness of his eye had utterly gone out. The once occasional huskiness of his tone was heard no more; and a tremulous quaver, as if of extreme terror, habitually characterized his utterance. There were times, indeed, when I thought his unceasingly agitated mind was labouring with some oppressive secret, to divulge which he struggled for the necessary courage. At times, again, I was obliged to resolve all into the mere inexplicable vagaries of madness, for I beheld him gazing upon vacancy for long hours, in an attitude of the profoundest attention, as if listening to some imaginary sound. It was no wonder that his condition terrified—that it infected me. I felt creeping upon me, by slow yet certain degrees, the wild influences of his own fantastic yet impressive superstitions.

It was, especially, upon retiring to bed late in the night of the seventh or eighth day after the placing of the lady Madeline within the donjon, that I experienced the full power of such feelings. Sleep came not near my couch— while the hours waned and waned away. I struggled to reason off the nervousness which had dominion over me. I endeavoured to believe that much, if not all of what I felt, was due to the bewildering influence of the gloomy furniture of the room—of the dark and tattered draperies, which, tortured into motion by the breath of a rising tempest, swayed fitfully to and fro upon the walls, and rustled uneasily about the decorations of the bed. But my efforts were fruitless. An irrepressible tremor gradually pervaded my frame; and, at length, there sat upon my very heart an incubus[12] of utterly causeless alarm. Shaking this off with a gasp and a struggle, I uplifted myself upon the pillows, and, peering earnestly within the intense darkness of the chamber, hearkened— I know not why, except that an instinctive spirit prompted me—to certain low and indefinite sounds which came, through the pauses of the storm, at long intervals, I knew not whence. Overpowered by an intense sentiment of horror, unaccountable yet unendurable, I threw on my clothes with haste (for I felt that I should sleep no more during the night), and endeavoured to arouse myself from the pitiable condition into which I had fallen, by pacing rapidly to and fro through the apartment.

I had taken but few turns in this manner, when a light step on an adjoining staircase arrested my attention. I presently recognised it as that of Usher. In an instant afterward he rapped, with a gentle touch, at my door, and entered, bearing a lamp. His countenance was, as usual, cadaverously wan—but, moreover, there was a species of mad hilarity in his eyes—an evidently restrained *hysteria* in his whole demeanour. His air appalled me—but anything was preferable to the solitude which I had so long endured, and I even welcomed his presence as a relief.

"And you have not seen it?" he said abruptly, after having stared about him for some moments in silence—"you have not then seen it?—but, stay! you shall." Thus speaking, and having carefully shaded his lamp, he hurried to one of the casements, and threw it freely open to the storm.

The impetuous fury of the entering gust nearly lifted us from our feet. It was, indeed, a tempestuous yet sternly beautiful night, and one wildly singular in its terror and its beauty. A whirlwind had apparently collected its force in our vicinity; for there were frequent and violent alterations in the direction

---

[12] A demon or evil spirit.

of the wind; and the exceeding density of the clouds (which hung so low as to press upon the turrets of the house) did not prevent our perceiving the life-like velocity with which they flew careering from all points against each other, without passing away into the distance. I say that even their exceeding density did not prevent our perceiving this—yet we had no glimpse of the moon or stars—nor was there any flashing forth of the lightning. But the under surfaces of the huge masses of agitated vapour, as well as all terrestrial objects immediately around us, were glowing in the unnatural light of a faintly luminous and distinctly visible gaseous exhalation which hung about and en-shrouded the mansion.

"You must not—you shall not behold this!" said I, shudderingly, to Usher, as I led him, with a gentle violence, from the window to a seat. "These appear-ances, which bewilder you, are merely electrical phenomena not uncommon—or it may be that they have their ghastly origin in the rank miasma of the tarn. Let us close this casement;—the air is chilling and dangerous to your frame. Here is one of your favourite romances. I will read, and you shall listen;—and so we will pass away this terrible night together."

The antique volume which I had taken up was the "Mad Trist" of Sir Laun-celot Canning[13]; but I had called it a favourite of Usher's more in sad jest than in earnest; for, in truth, there is little in its uncouth and unimaginative prolixity which could have had interest for the lofty and spiritual ideality of my friend. It was, however, the only book immediately at hand; and I indulged a vague hope that the excitement which now agitated the hypochondriac, might find relief (for the history of mental disorder is full of similar anomalies) even in the extremeness of the folly which I should read. Could I have judged, indeed, by the wild overstrained air of vivacity with which he hearkened, or apparently hearkened, to the words of the tale, I might well have congratulated myself upon the success of my design.

I had arrived at that well-known portion of the story where Ethelred, the hero of the Trist, having sought in vain for peaceable admission into the dwell-ing of the hermit, proceeds to make good an entrance by force. Here, it will be remembered, the words of the narrative run thus:

"And Ethelred, who was by nature of a doughty heart, and who was now mighty withal, on account of the powerfulness of the wine which he had drunken, waited no longer to hold parley with the hermit, who, in sooth, was of an obstinate and maliceful turn, but, feeling the rain upon his shoulders, and fearing the rising of the tempest, uplifted his mace outright, and, with blows, made quickly room in the plankings of the door for his gauntleted hand; and now pulling therewith sturdily, he so cracked, and ripped, and tore all asunder, that the noise of the dry and hollow-sounding wood alarumed and reverberated throughout the forest."

At the termination of this sentence I started, and for a moment, paused; for it appeared to me (although I at once concluded that my excited fancy had deceived me)—it appeared to me that, from some very remote portion of the mansion, there came, indistinctly, to my ears, what might have been, in its exact similarity of character, the echo (but a stifled and dull one certainly) of the very cracking and ripping sound which Sir Launcelot had so particularly described. It was, beyond doubt, the coincidence alone which had arrested my attention; for, amid the rattling of the sashes of the casements, and the

[13] A title of Poe's own invention.

ordinary commingled noises of the still increasing storm, the sound, in itself, had nothing, surely, which should have interested or disturbed me. I continued the story:

"But the good champion Ethelred, now entering within the door, was sore enraged and amazed to perceive no signal of the maliceful hermit; but, in the stead thereof, a dragon of a scaly and prodigious demeanour, and of a fiery tongue, which sat in guard before a palace of gold, with a floor of silver; and upon the wall there hung a shield of shining brass with this legend enwritten—

> Who entereth herein, a conqueror hath bin;
> Who slayeth the dragon, the shield he shall win;

And Ethelred uplifted his mace, and struck upon the head of the dragon, which fell before him, and gave up his pesty breath, with a shriek so horrid and harsh, and withal so piercing, that Ethelred had fain to close his ears with his hands against the dreadful noise of it, the like whereof was never before heard."

Here again I paused abruptly, and now with a feeling of wild amazement—for there could be no doubt whatever that, in this instance, I did actually hear (although from what direction it proceeded I found it impossible to say) a low and apparently distant, but harsh, protracted, and most unusual screaming or grating sound—the exact counterpart of what my fancy had already conjured up for the dragon's unnatural shriek as described by the romancer.

Oppressed, as I certainly was, upon the occurrence of the second and most extraordinary coincidence, by a thousand conflicting sensations, in which wonder and extreme terror were predominant, I still retained sufficient presence of mind to avoid exciting, by any observation, the sensitive nervousness of my companion. I was by no means certain that he had noticed the sounds in question; although, assuredly, a strange alteration had, during the last few minutes, taken place in his demeanour. From a position fronting my own, he had gradually brought round his chair, so as to sit with his face to the door of the chamber; and thus I could but partially perceive his features, although I saw that his lips trembled as if he were murmuring inaudibly. His head had dropped upon his breast—yet I knew that he was not asleep, from the wide and rigid opening of the eye as I caught a glance of it in profile. The motion of his body, too, was at variance with this idea—for he rocked from side to side with a gentle yet constant and uniform sway. Having rapidly taken notice of all this, I resumed the narrative of Sir Launcelot, which thus proceeded:

"And now, the champion, having escaped from the terrible fury of the dragon, bethinking himself of the brazen shield, and of the breaking up of the enchantment which was upon it, removed the carcass from out of the way before him, and approached valorously over the silver pavement of the castle to where the shield was upon the wall; which in sooth tarried not for his full coming, but fell down at his feet upon the silver floor, with a mighty great and terrible ringing sound."

No sooner had these syllables passed my lips, than—as if a shield of brass had indeed, at the moment, fallen heavily upon a floor of silver—I became aware of a distinct, hollow, metallic, and clangorous, yet apparently muffled reverberation. Completely unnerved, I leaped to my feet; but the measured rocking movement of Usher was undisturbed. I rushed to the chair in which he sat. His eyes were bent fixedly before him, and throughout his whole countenance there reigned a stony rigidity. But, as I placed my hand upon his shoulder, there came a strong shudder over his whole person; a sickly smile quivered about his lips; and I saw that he spoke in a low, hurried, and gibbering murmur, as if unconscious of my presence. Bending closely over him, I at length drank in the hideous import of his words.

"Not hear it?—yes, I hear it, and *have* heard it. Long—long—long—many minutes, many hours, many days, have I heard it—yet I dared not—oh, pity me, miserable wretch that I am!—I dared not—I *dared* not speak! *We have put her living in the tomb!* Said I not that my senses were acute? I *now* tell you that I heard her first feeble movements in the hollow coffin. I heard them—many, many days ago—yet I dared not—*I dared not speak!* And now—to-night—Ethelred—ha! ha!—the breaking of the hermit's door, and the death-cry of the dragon, and the clangour of the shield!—say, rather, the rending of her coffin, and the grating of the iron hinges of her prison, and her struggles within the coppered archway of the vault! Oh whither shall I fly? Will she not be here anon? Is she not hurrying to upbraid me for my haste? Have I not heard her footstep on the stair? Do I not distinguish that heavy and horrible beating of her heart? MADMAN!" here he sprang furiously to his feet, and shrieked out his syllables, as if in the effort he were giving up his soul—"MADMAN! I TELL YOU THAT SHE NOW STANDS WITHOUT THE DOOR!"

As if in the superhuman energy of his utterance there had been found the potency of a spell—the huge antique panels to which the speaker pointed, threw slowly back, upon the instant, their ponderous and ebony jaws. It was the work of the rushing gust—but then without those doors there DID stand the lofty and enshrouded figure of the lady Madeline of Usher. There was blood upon her white robes, and the evidence of some bitter struggle upon every portion of her emaciated frame. For a moment she remained trembling and reeling to and fro upon the threshold, then, with a low moaning cry, fell heavily inward upon the person of her brother, and in her violent and now final death-agonies, bore him to the floor a corpse, and a victim to the terrors he had anticipated.

From that chamber, and from that mansion, I fled aghast. The storm was still abroad in all its wrath as I found myself crossing the old causeway. Suddenly there shot along the path a wild light, and I turned to see whence a gleam so unusual could have issued; for the vast house and its shadows were alone behind me. The radiance was that of the full, setting, and blood-red moon which now shone vividly through that once barely-discernible fissure of which I have before spoken as extending from the roof of the building, in a zigzag direction, to the base. While I gazed, this fissure rapidly widened—there came a fierce breath of the whirlwind—the entire orb of the satellite burst at once upon my sight—my brain reeled as I saw the mighty walls rushing asunder—there was a long tumultuous shouting sound like the voice of a thousand waters—and the deep and dank tarn at my feet closed sullenly and silently over the fragments of the "HOUSE OF USHER."

[1839]

Ivan Turgenev *1818–1883*

THE COUNTRY DOCTOR*

One autumn, on the way back from an outlying property, I caught a heavy chill. Luckily I was in the local market-town, at the inn, when the fever came on. I sent for the doctor. After half an hour he appeared, a shortish, thinnish man, with black hair. He prescribed the usual sudorific, ordered a mustard-plaster to be applied, deftly tucked my five-rouble[1] note away up his sleeve— meanwhile coughing loudly, it is true, and averting his gaze—and was on the point of going home, when somehow or other he got talking and stayed on. I was oppressed by my fever; I foresaw a sleepless night and was glad to have the chance of a talk with the good man. We had tea served. My friend the doctor let himself go. The little fellow was no fool. He had a lively and rather amusing way of expressing himself. It's strange how things happen in life: you live with someone for a long time, you are on the best of terms, yet you never once speak to them frankly and from the heart; with someone else, you've hardly even got acquainted—and there you are: as if at confession, one or other of you is blurting out all his most intimate secrets. I do not know what I did to deserve the confidence of my new friend—anyway, for no particular reason, he got going, as they say, and told me a rather remarkable story, which I will relate here for the benefit of my courteous reader. I will try to express myself in the doctor's own words.

"You don't happen to know," he began, in a voice that had grown suddenly faint and trembling (such is the effect of unadulterated "birch" snuff), "you don't happen to know our local judge, Pavel Lukich Mylov? You don't? . . . Well, it doesn't matter." He cleared his throat and wiped his eyes. "Anyway, this is the story. Let me see, now—to be exact, it was in Lent, at the time of the thaw. I was sitting at the judge's, playing Preference.[2] Our judge is a capital fellow and a great hand at Preference. Suddenly"—this was a word that the doctor often used—"a message comes that someone is asking for me. I say, 'What does he want?' 'He's brought a note'—doubtless from a patient. 'Give me the note,' I say. Yes: It's from a patient. . . . Well, all right—you know, it's our daily bread. . . . The note is from a land-owner's widow; she says: 'My daughter is dying, for God's sake come, I've sent horses to fetch you.' Well, that's all right . . . but the lady lives twenty versts[3] from town, and night's upon us, and the roads are in such a state, my word! and the lady herself is not so well off as she was; two silver roubles is the most you can expect, and even that is doubtful. Perhaps all that I shall get out of it will be a piece of linen and a little flour. . . . However, duty first, you know: someone's dying. At once I pass my hand to Councillor Kalliopin and return home. I see a small cart standing outside my porch; real peasant's horses—enormous pot bellies, and woolly hair as thick as felt; and a coachman sitting bareheaded, as a sign of respect. Well, my friend, I think, it's plain that *your* masters don't eat off gold plate. . . . You, sir, may well smile, but I tell you: we are poor men in our profession and we have to notice all these things. . . . If the coach-

* Translated by Charles and Natasha Hepburn.
[1] The rouble (or ruble) is the basic Russian monetary unit.
[2] A card game resembling bridge.   [3] A verst equals about two-thirds of a mile.

94

man sits up like a prince and doesn't take off his cap, if he sniggers at you in his beard and toys with his whip—you can rely on a couple of five-rouble notes. But this turn-out here is a very different pair of shoes. Well, I think, it can't be helped: duty first. I grab the essential medicines, and off I go. Believe me, it was all we could do to get there. The road was hellish: streams, snow, mud, ravines, then, suddenly, a burst dam. Chaos! At last I'm there. A little house with a thatched roof. The windows are lit up: they must be waiting for me. A dignified little old lady in a cap comes to meet me. 'Save her,' she says, 'she is dying.' I say: 'Pray calm yourself. . . . Where is the patient?' 'Here, please come this way.' I see a small, clean room, an oil-lamp in the corner, on the bed a girl of about twenty, unconscious, heat fairly blazing from her, breathing heavily: a high fever. There are two other girls there, too, her sisters—badly scared, and in tears. 'Yesterday,' they say, 'she was perfectly well and had a good appetite; this morning she complained of a headache, then suddenly in the evening she became like this.' I repeat again, 'Pray calm yourselves'—it's part of the doctor's job, you know—and I set to work. I bleed her, I order mustard-plasters, I prescribe a mixture. Meanwhile I look at her. I look and look; my goodness, never have I seen such a face before . . . an absolute beauty! I feel so sorry for the girl, it fairly tears me to pieces. Such lovely features, such eyes. . . . At last, thank God, she gets more comfortable; she begins to sweat, partly recovers consciousness; looks round, smiles, passes her hand over her face. . . . The sisters bend over her and ask: 'What's the matter?' 'Nothing,' she says, and turns her head away. . . . I look—she's dropped off to sleep. 'Well,' I say, 'now we must leave the patient in peace.' We all tiptoe out; only the maid stays behind in case of emergencies. In the sitting-room the samovar's[4] on the table and a bottle of rum beside it: in our job we can't get along without it. They gave me tea; they ask me to stay the night. I accepted: where else could I go at that hour! The old lady keeps up a steady groaning. 'What's the matter?' I ask. 'She'll live; calm yourself and go to bed: it's two o-clock.' 'You'll have me woken up if anything happens?' 'Of course I will.' The old lady retired and the girls went to their room; a bed was put up for me in the drawing-room. I lay down—but couldn't get to sleep, strangely enough. You'd have thought that I'd worried my head enough already. I couldn't get my patient out of my head. Finally I could stand it no longer and all of a sudden I got up; I thought I'd just go and see how she was. Her bedroom adjoined the drawing-room. Well, I got up, and quietly opened the door, and my heart was fairly beating away. I saw the maid asleep, with her mouth open, snoring away like an animal, and the patient lying with her face towards me, her arms moving restlessly, poor girl! I went up to her . . . and suddenly she opened her eyes and stared at me. 'Who are you?' I felt awkward. 'Don't be afraid,' I said; 'I am the doctor; I've come to see how you feel.' 'You're the doctor?' 'Yes, I am . . . your mother sent for me from town; we've bled you, and now, please, you must rest, and in two days, with God's help, we shall have you up and about.' 'Oh yes, yes, doctor, don't let me die . . . please, please.' 'Good Heavens, whatever next!' But, I thought to myself, the fever is on her again; I felt her pulse: yes, I was right. She looked at me—and suddenly she took me by the hand. 'I'll tell you why I don't want to die, I'll tell you . . . now that we're alone: only not a word, please . . . listen. . . .' I bent over her; her lips moved

[4] An urn used to boil water.

right against my ear, her hair touched my cheek—I admit, my head went round in circles—and she began to whisper. . . . I didn't understand a word. . . . Oh, of course, she must be delirious. She whispered and whispered, but so quickly, as if in a foreign language, and when she had done she shuddered, dropped her head on the pillow and raised a finger at me. 'Listen, doctor, not a word.' . . . Somehow or other I calmed her, gave her a drink, woke the maid and went out."

The doctor took another violent pinch of snuff and sat stock-still for a moment.

"Anyhow," he continued, "next day, contrary to my expectations, the patient was no better. I thought and thought and suddenly decided to stay on, although I had other patients waiting for me. . . . You know, one shouldn't neglect them: it's bad for one's practice. But, in the first place, the girl was really desperately ill; and secondly, to tell the truth, I felt myself strongly attracted to her. Besides, I liked the whole family. Although they were very hard up, they were extraordinarily cultivated people. . . . The father had been a scholar, a writer; he died a poor man, of course, but he'd managed to give his children an excellent education; he left them a lot of books, too. Whether it was because I put my whole heart into looking after the patient, or whether there were other reasons, anyway, I'd go so far as to say that they came to love me in that house like one of the family. . . . Meanwhile the thaw got worse and worse: communications were completely broken, I could hardly even get medicines sent out from town. . . . The girl got no better . . . day after day, day after day . . . but then . . . well . . ." The doctor paused. "The truth is that I don't know how to explain to you . . ." He took another pinch of snuff, sneezed, and swallowed a gulp of tea. . . . "I'll tell you straight out, my patient . . . how shall I put it? . . . fell in love with me, I suppose . . . or rather, she wasn't exactly in love . . . but anyway . . . it's certainly . . ." The doctor looked down and blushed.

"No," he continued with some animation, " 'Love' is the wrong word. One must see oneself at one's own worth, after all. She was a cultivated, intelligent, well-read girl, and I, well, I'd even forgotten my Latin, more or less completely. My figure, too"—and the doctor looked at himself with a smile—"is nothing to boast about, I think. But God didn't make me a fool either: I don't call white black; I've got a mind that works at times. For instance, I understood very well that what Alexandra Andreyevna—that was her name—felt towards me was not love, but affection, so to speak, regard, or what not. Although she herself probably misread her feelings towards me, her condition was such, as you can imagine . . . Anyhow," added the doctor, who had uttered all these disjointed statements without drawing breath, and with obvious embarrassment, "I think I've let my tongue run away with me . . . and the result is that you won't understand what happened . . . so I'll tell you the story in its proper order."

He finished his glass of tea and resumed in a calmer voice.

"This is how it was. My patient continued to get worse and worse. You, my good sir, are not a doctor; you have no idea of what goes on inside a doctor's head, especially in his early days, when it dawns on him that a patient's illness is defeating him. All his self-assurance vanishes into thin air. I can't tell you how scared he gets. It seems to him that he's forgotten everything he ever knew, that his patient has no confidence in him, that other people

are beginning to notice that he's out of his depth, and don't want to describe
the patient's symptoms, that they are looking at him strangely, and whispering
. . . oh, it's terrible! He feels there must be some way of treating the case if
only it could be found. Perhaps this is it? He tries—no, wrong after all. He
leaves no time for the treatment to take its proper effect. . . . He snatches
first at one method, then at another. He takes up his book of prescriptions
. . . here it is, he thinks, this is it! To be quite honest, sometimes he opens
the book at random: this, he thinks, must be the hand of fate. . . . Meanwhile
there is someone dying; someone whom another doctor would have saved. I
must have another opinion, you think; I won't take the whole responsibility
myself. But what a fool you look on such occasions! Well, as time goes on,
you get used to it, you say to yourself: never mind. The patient has died—
it's not your fault; you only followed the rules. But what disturbs you still
more is this: when other people have blind confidence in yourself, and all
the time you know that you're helpless. It was exactly such confidence that
all Alexandra Andreyevna's family felt towards me: they no longer even thought
of her as in danger. And I, on my side, was assuring them that there was
nothing to worry about, but really my heart was in my boots. To make things
even worse, the thaw became so bad that the coachman spent whole days
fetching medicines. Meanwhile I never left the patient's room; I simply couldn't
tear myself away. I told her all sorts of funny stories; I played cards with
her; I spent the nights at her bedside. The old lady would thank me with
tears in her eyes; but I thought to myself: I don't deserve your gratitude. I
confess to you frankly—there is no reason why I should conceal it now—I
was in love with my patient. And Alexandra Andreyevna grew fonder and
fonder of me: she would allow no one into her room except me. We would
get talking; she would ask me where I studied, what sort of life I led, and
about my parents and my friends. And I felt that we shouldn't be talking,
but to stop her, stop her really firmly, was more than I could do. I would
bury my head in my hands: what are you doing, scoundrel? . . . And then
she would take my hand and hold it, look at me for a long, long time, turn
away, sigh and say: 'How good you are!' Her hands were so feverish, her
eyes so big and languid. 'Yes,' she would say, 'You're a good, kind man. You're
not like our neighbours . . . you're quite, quite different. . . . To think that
I never knew you until now!' 'Alexandra Andreyevna, calm yourself,' I'd say.
'Believe me, I appreciate it; I don't know what I've done to . . . only calm
yourself, for Heaven's sake, calm yourself . . . everything will be all right;
you'll get quite well again.' By the way, I must tell you," added the doctor,
leaning forward and lifting his eyebrows, "they had little to do with their neighbours, because the smaller people weren't up to them, and they were too
proud to get to know the richer ones. I tell you, it was an extraordinarily
cultivated family; so that, for me, it was quite flattering. Alexandra would only
take her medicine from my hands . . . the poor girl would lift herself up,
with my help, swallow the medicine and gaze at me . . . and my heart would
fairly turn over. But all the time she was getting worse and worse: she will
die, I thought, she will surely die. Believe me or not, I would gladly have
lain in the coffin instead of her; but there were her mother and sisters watching
me, looking into my eyes, and I could feel their confidence on the wane. 'Well,
how is she?' 'Nothing to worry about, nothing at all'—but what did I mean,
'nothing at all'? My head was in a daze. There I was, one night, alone, as

usual, sitting at the bedside. The maid was sitting in the room too, snoring for all she was worth . . . well, one couldn't find fault with the poor girl, she too was quite exhausted. Alexandra had been feeling very bad the whole evening; the fever gave her no rest. Right up to midnight she had been tossing away; at last she seemed to fall asleep; at any rate she stopped moving and lay still. The oil-lamp was burning in the corner in front of the icon.[5] I sat there, my head dropped forward, you know, and I too dozed off. Suddenly it was as if someone had given me a push in the ribs; I looked around . . . God Almighty! Alexandra was staring at me wide-eyed . . . her lips parted, her cheeks aflame. 'What is it?' 'Doctor, am I going to die?' 'For Heaven's sake!' 'No, please, doctor, please, don't tell me that I'm going to live . . . don't tell me that . . . if only you knew . . . listen, for God's sake don't try to hide my condition from me.' I noticed how quickly she was breathing. 'If I can know for sure that I am going to die . . . then I can tell you everything I have to say.' 'Alexandra Andreyevna, for mercy's sake!' 'Listen, I haven't slept a wink, I've been looking and looking at you . . . for God's sake . . . I trust you, you're kind, you're honest, I implore you by everything that's holy on earth—tell me the truth! If only you knew how much it matters to me. . . . Doctor, tell me, for God's sake, am I in danger?' 'What *can* I tell you, Alexandra Andreyevna?' 'For God's sake, I beseech you to tell me.' 'Alexandra Andreyevna, I can't hide the truth from you—you *are* in danger, but God is merciful . . .' 'I'm going to die, I'm going to die . . .' And it was as if she was overjoyed at the thought, her face lit up so; I was fairly terrified. 'Never fear, never fear, death has no terror for me.' All of a sudden she raised herself on one elbow. 'Now . . . well, now I can tell you that I'm grateful to you from all my heart; that you're good and kind; that I love you.' . . . I looked at her like a man possessed; I can tell you, I had quite a creepy feeling. . . . 'Listen to me. I love you.' 'Alexandra Andreyevna, what have I done to deserve this?' 'No, no, you don't understand me, my dear one . . .' And suddenly she reached out, took my head in her hands and kissed me. Believe me or not, it was all I could do not to cry out loud. . . . I fell on my knees and hid my head in the pillow. She said nothing; her fingers trembled on my hair; I could hear her crying. I began to comfort her, to assure her. . . . I really don't know what I said to her. 'You'll wake the maid . . . believe me when I say . . . how grateful I am . . . and calm yourself.' 'Don't . . . don't,' she kept repeating. 'Never mind any of them, let them wake, let them come—it doesn't signify: I'm dying anyway. . . . Why are you so shy and timid? Lift your head . . . Or can it be that you don't love me, that I was mistaken? . . . If that is so, please forgive me.' 'What are you saying? . . . I love you, Alexandra Andreyevna.' She gazed at me, straight in the eyes, and opened her arms. 'Then, put your arms around me.' . . . I tell you honestly: I don't understand how I got through that night without going out of my mind. I knew that my patient was killing herself; I saw that she was half delirious; I also understood that if she had not believed herself on the point of death, she would never have given me a thought; but, say what you like, there must be something appalling about dying at twenty-five without ever having loved; that was the thought that tormented her, that was why, in despair, she seized on me. Now do you see it all? She still held me tightly in her arms. 'Have

[5] A traditional religious painting.

pity on me, Alexandra Andreyevna, have pity on us both,' I said, 'Why?' she answered, 'what is there to pity? Don't you understand that I've got to die?' She kept on repeating this phrase. 'If I knew that I was going to live and turn into a well-brought-up young lady again, I should be ashamed, yes, ashamed . . . but, as it is? . . .' 'And who told you that you were going to die?' 'Oh, no, enough of that, you can't deceive me, you don't know how to lie, just look at yourself.' 'You will live, Alexandra Andreyevna; I will cure you; we will ask your mother for her blessing . . . nothing will part us; we shall be happy.' 'No, no, I have your word that I must die . . . you promised me . . . you told me I must . . .' It was a bitter moment for me, bitter for many reasons. You know, sometimes small things can happen: they amount to nothing, but they hurt all the same. It occurred to her to ask me my name, my Christian name, I mean. Of course it would be my ill-luck to be called Trifon.[6] Yes, sir; Trifon, Trifon Ivanich. In the house, all the family called me doctor. Well, there was nothing for it, so I answered: 'Trifon.' She screwed her eyes up, shook her head and whispered something in French—oh, it was something unflattering, and she laughed unkindly, too. Well, like this, I spent almost the whole night with her. At dawn I went out, like one possessed; it was midday when I returned to her room, after taking tea. God Almighty! You couldn't recognize her: I've seen prettier sights laid out in the coffin. Upon my word, I don't know to this day, I simply don't know how I stood the ordeal. For three days and three nights my patient's life still flickered on . . . and what nights they were! What things she told me! . . . On the last night of the three—just fancy—I was sitting beside her, praying now for one thing only: O, God, take her quickly, and take me as well . . . when suddenly the old lady, her mother, burst into the room. . . . I had already told her the day before that there was little hope, that things were bad, and that it would be as well to send for the priest. As soon as she saw her mother, the sick girl said: 'I'm glad that you've come . . . look at us, we love each other, we are pledged to each other.' 'What's she saying, doctor, what's she saying?' I went pale as death. 'She's delirious,' I said, 'it's the fever.' But then, from Alexandra: 'Enough of that, just now you spoke to me quite differently and accepted my ring. . . . Why pretend? My mother is kind, she will forgive, she will understand, but I am dying—why should I lie? Give me your hand.' I jumped up and ran from the room. Of course, the old lady guessed the whole story.

"Anyway, I won't attempt to bore you further, and, what's more, to tell you the truth, it hurts me to remember. The following day my patient passed away. May God rest her soul!" added the doctor hurriedly, with a sigh. "Before she died, she asked that everyone should go out and leave me alone with her. 'Forgive me,' she said. 'Perhaps I've acted wrongly towards you . . . it's my illness . . . but, believe me, I've never loved anyone more than you . . . don't forget me . . . treasure my ring. . . .'"

The doctor turned away; I seized him by the hand.

"Och!" he said, "let's talk about something else, or perhaps you'd like a little game of Preference for low stakes? You know, in our profession we should never give way to such exalted sentiments. In our profession all we should think about is how to stop the children from yelling and the wife from nagging.

---

[6] "Trifon" is roughly the equivalent of "Cuthbert." (Translators' note)

For, since then, I have gone in for holy matrimony, as they call it . . . with a vengeance . . . . I married a merchant's daughter: seven thousand roubles dowry. Her name is Akulina; it's on a par with Trifon. A spiteful hag, I must say, but luckily she sleeps all day. . . . . What about that game of Preference?"

We got down to Preference for copeck[7] stakes. Trifon Ivanich won two and a half roubles from me—and went home late, very pleased with his victory.

[1852]

---

[7] There are a hundred copecks (or kopecks) in a rouble (or ruble).

Herman Melville *1819–1891*

BENITO CERENO

In the year 1799, Captain Amasa Delano,[1] of Duxbury, in Massachusetts, commanding a large sealer and general trader, lay at anchor with a valuable cargo, in the harbour of St. Maria—a small, desert, uninhabited island toward the southern extremity of the long coast of Chile. There he had touched for water.

On the second day, not long after dawn, while lying in his berth, his mate came below, informing him that a strange sail was coming into the bay. Ships were then not so plenty in those waters as now. He rose, dressed, and went on deck.

The morning was one peculiar to that coast. Everything was mute and calm; everything gray. The sea, though undulated into long roods of swells, seemed fixed, and was sleeked at the surface like waved lead that has cooled and set in the smelter's mould. The sky seemed a gray surtout.[2] Flights of troubled gray fowl, kith and kin with flights of troubled gray vapours among which they were mixed, skimmed low and fitfully over the waters, as swallows over meadows before storms. Shadows present, foreshadowing deeper shadows to come.

To Captain Delano's surprise, the stranger, viewed through the glass, showed no colours; though to do so upon entering a haven, however uninhabited in its shores, where but a single other ship might be lying, was the custom among peaceful seamen of all nations. Considering the lawlessness and loneliness of the spot, and the sort of stories, at that day, associated with those seas, Captain Delano's surprise might have deepened into some uneasiness had he not been a person of a singularly undistrustful good-nature, not liable, except on extraordinary and repeated incentives, and hardly then, to indulge in personal alarms, any way involving the imputation of malign evil in man. Whether, in view of what humanity is capable, such a trait implies, along with a benevolent heart, more than ordinary quickness and accuracy of intellectual perception, may be left to the wise to determine.

But whatever misgivings might have obtruded on first seeing the stranger, would almost, in any seaman's mind, have been dissipated by observing that the ship, in navigating into the harbour, was drawing too near the land; a sunken reef making out off her bow. This seemed to prove her a stranger, indeed, not only to the sealer, but the island; consequently, she could be no wonted[3] freebooter on that ocean. With no small interest, Captain Delano continued to watch her—a proceeding not much facilitated by the vapours partly mantling the hull, through which the far matin light from her cabin streamed equivocally enough; much like the sun—by this time hemisphered on the rim of the horizon, and, apparently, in company with the strange ship entering the harbour—which, wimpled by the same low, creeping clouds,

---

[1] Melville's story is based on the real-life adventures of Amasa Delano (1763–1823) as recounted in the eighteenth chapter of his *Narrative of Voyages and Travels in the Northern and Southern Hemispheres* (Boston, 1817).
[2] A long overcoat.   [3] Known.

showed not unlike a Lima[4] intriguante's[5] one sinister eye peering across the
Plaza from the Indian loop-hole of her dusk *saya-y-manta.*[6]

It might have been but a deception of the vapors, but the longer the stranger
was watched the more singular appeared her maneuvers. Ere long it seemed
hard to decide whether she meant to come in or no—what she wanted, or
what she was about. The wind, which had breezed up a little during the night,
was now extremely light and baffling, which the more increased the apparent
uncertainty of her movements.

Surmising, at last, that it might be a ship in distress, Captain Delano ordered
his whale-boat to be dropped, and, much to the wary opposition of his mate,
prepared to board her, and, at the least, pilot her in. On the night previous,
a fishing-party of the seamen had gone a long distance to some detached
rocks out of sight from the sealer, and, an hour or two before daybreak, had
returned, having met with no small success. Presuming that the stranger might
have been long off soundings, the good captain put several baskets of fish,
for presents, into his boat, and so pulled away. From her continuing too near
the sunken reef, deeming her in danger, calling to his men, he made all haste
to apprise those on board of their situation. But, some time ere the boat
came up, the wind, light though it was, having shifted, had headed the vessel
off, as well as partly broken the vapours from about her.

Upon gaining a less remote view, the ship, when made signally visible on
the verge of the leaden-hued swells, with the shreds of fog here and there
raggedly furring her, appeared like a whitewashed monastery after a thunderstorm, seen perched upon some dun cliff among the Pyrenees.[7] But it was
no purely fanciful resemblance which now, for a moment, almost led Captain
Delano to think that nothing less than a ship-load of monks was before him.
Peering over the bulwarks were what really seemed, in the hazy distance,
throngs of dark cowls; while, fitfully revealed through the open port-holes,
other dark moving figures were dimly descried, as of Black Friars[8] pacing the
cloisters.

Upon a still nigher approach, this appearance was modified, and the true
character of the vessel was plain—a Spanish merchantman of the first class,
carrying Negro slaves, amongst other valuable freight, from one colonial port
to another. A very large, and, in its time, a very fine vessel, such as in those
days were at intervals encountered along that main; sometimes superseded
Acapulco[9] treasure-ships, or retired frigates of the Spanish king's navy, which,
like superannuated Italian palaces, still, under a decline of masters, preserved
signs of former state.

As the whale-boat drew more and more nigh, the cause of the peculiar pipe-
clayed[10] aspect of the stranger was seen in the slovenly neglect pervading
her. The spars, ropes, and great part of the bulwarks, looked woolly, from
long unacquaintance with the scraper, tar, and the brush. Her keel seemed
laid, her ribs put together, and she launched, from Ezekiel's Valley of Dry
Bones.[11]

In the present business in which she was engaged, the ship's general model

---

[4] The capital city of Peru.   [5] A female intriguer.
[6] A hooded robe that can be drawn closely about the face.
[7] The mountain range on the border between France and Spain.
[8] Dominican monks.   [9] A Mexican seaport.   [10] Whitened.   [11] See Ezekiel 37:1.

and rig appeared to have undergone no material change from their original warlike and Froissart pattern.[12] However, no guns were seen.

The tops were large, and were railed about with what had once been octagonal net-work, all now in sad disrepair. These tops hung overhead like three ruinous aviaries, in one of which was seen perched, on a rattlin,[13] a white noddy,[14] a strange fowl, so called from its lethargic, somnambulistic character, being frequently caught by hand at sea. Battered and mouldy, the castellated forecastle seemed some ancient turret, long ago taken by assault, and then left to decay. Toward the stern, two high-raised quarter-galleries—the balustrades here and there covered with dry, tindery sea-moss—opening out from the unoccupied state-cabin, whose dead-lights,[15] for all the mild weather, were hermetically closed and caulked—these tenantless balconies hung over the sea as if it were the grand Venetian canal. But the principal relic of faded grandeur was the ample oval of the shield-like stern-piece, intricately carved with the arms of Castile and Leon,[16] medallioned about by groups of mythological or symbolical devices; uppermost and central of which was a dark satyr in a mask, holding his foot on the prostrate neck of a writhing figure, likewise masked.

Whether the ship had a figure-head, or only a plain beak, was not quite certain, owing to canvas wrapped about that part, either to protect it while undergoing a refurbishing, or else decently to hide its decay. Rudely painted or chalked, as in a sailor freak, along the forward side of a sort of pedestal below the canvas, was the sentence, "*Seguid vuestro jefe*" (follow your leader); while upon the tarnished head-boards, near by, appeared, in stately capitals, once gilt, the ship's name, "*SAN DOMINICK,*" each letter streakingly corroded with tricklings of copper-spike rust; while, like mourning weeds, dark festoons of sea-grass slimily swept to and fro over the name, with every hearse-like roll of the hull.

As, at last, the boat was hooked from the bow along toward the gangway amidship, its keel, while yet some inches separated from the hull, harshly grated as on a sunken coral reef. It proved a huge bunch of conglobated[17] barnacles adhering below the water to the side like a wen[18]—a token of baffling airs and long calms passed somewhere in those seas.

Climbing the side, the visitor was at once surrounded by a clamorous throng of whites and blacks, but the latter outnumbering the former more than could have been expected, Negro transportation-ship as the stranger in port was. But, in one language, and as with one voice, all poured out a common tale of suffering; in which the negresses, of whom there were not a few, exceeded the others in their dolorous vehemence. The scurvy, together with the fever, had swept off a great part of their number, more especially the Spaniards. Off Cape Horn[19] they had narrowly escaped shipwreck; then, for days together, they had lain tranced without wind; their provisions were low; their water next to none; their lips that moment were baked.

While Captain Delano was thus made the mark of all eager tongues, his one eager glance took in all faces, with every other object about him.

[12] Jean Froissart (1337–1416?) was a medieval French poet and historian who chronicled the Hundred Years' War; in this context, "Froissart pattern" refers to an ancient ship.
[13] Ropes forming the rungs of a ladder.   [14] A small gull-like bird.   [15] Shutters.
[16] Two ancient Spanish principalities.   [17] Ball-shaped.   [18] Cyst.
[19] The cape at the tip of South America.

Always upon first boarding a large and populous ship at sea, especially a foreign one, with a nondescript crew such as Lascars or Manilla men,[20] the impression varies in a peculiar way from that produced by first entering a strange house with strange inmates in a strange land. Both house and ship— the one by its walls and blinds, the other by its high bulwarks like ramparts— hoard from view their interiors till the last moment; but in the case of the ship there is this addition: that the living spectacle it contains, upon its sudden and complete disclosure, has, in contrast with the blank ocean which zones it, something of the effect of enchantment. The ship seems unreal; these strange costumes, gestures, and faces, but a shadowy tableau just emerged from the deep, which directly must receive back what it gave.

Perhaps it was some such influence, as above is attempted to be described, which, in Captain Delano's mind, heightened whatever, upon a staid scrutiny, might have seemed unusual; especially the conspicuous figures of four elderly grizzled Negroes, their heads like black, doddered[21] willow-tops, who, in venerable contrast to the tumult below them, were couched, sphinx-like, one on the starboard cat-head,[22] another on the larboard,[23] and the remaining pair face to face on the opposite bulwarks above the main-chains.[24] They each had bits of unstranded old junk[25] in their hands, and, with a sort of stoical self-content, were picking the junk into oakum,[26] a small heap of which lay by their sides. They accompanied the task with a continuous, low, monotonous chant; droning and druling away like so many gray-headed bagpipers playing a funeral march.

The quarter-deck rose into an ample elevated poop,[27] upon the forward verge of which, lifted, like the oakum-pickers, some eight feet above the general throng, sat along in a row, separated by regular spaces, the cross-legged figures of six other blacks; each with a rusty hatchet in his hand, which, with a bit of brick and a rag, he was engaged like a scullion,[28] in scouring; while between each two was a small stack of hatchets, their rusted edges turned forward awaiting a like operation. Though occasionally the four oakum-pickers would briefly address some person or persons in the crowd below, yet the six hatchet-polishers neither spoke to others, nor breathed a whisper among themselves, but sat intent upon their task, except at intervals, when, with the peculiar love in negroes of uniting industry with pastime, two and two they sideways clashed their hatchets together, like cymbals, with a barbarous din. All six, unlike the generality, had the raw aspect of unsophisticated Africans.

But that first comprehensive glance which took in those ten figures, with scores less conspicuous, rested but an instant upon them, as, impatient of the hubbub of voices, the visitor turned in quest of whomsoever it might be that commanded the ship.

But as if not unwilling to let nature make known her own case among his suffering charge, or else in despair of restraining it for the time, the Spanish captain, a gentlemanly, reserved-looking, and rather young man to a stranger's eye, dressed with singular richness, but bearing plain traces of recent sleepless cares and disquietudes, stood passively by, leaning against the mainmast, at one moment casting a dreary, spiritless look upon his excited people, at the

---

[20] East Indian and Philippine sailors.   [21] Infirm or feeble.
[22] A beam projecting from the ship's bow used to raise and secure the anchor.
[23] The port side.   [24] Chains secured to the mainmast.   [25] Old rope.
[26] Fibers used for caulking the seams of wooden ships.   [27] The deck nearest the stern.
[28] Menial kitchen servant.

next an unhappy glance toward his visitor. By his side stood a black of small stature, in whose rude face, as occasionally, like a shepherd's dog, he mutely turned it up into the Spaniard's, sorrow and affection were equally blended.

Struggling through the throng, the American advanced to the Spaniard, assuring him of his sympathies, and offering to render whatever assistance might be in his power. To which the Spaniard returned for the present but grave and ceremonious acknowledgments, his national formality dusked,[29] by the saturnine[30] mood of ill-health.

But losing no time in mere compliments, Captain Delano, returning to the gangway, had his basket of fish brought up; and as the wind still continued light, so that some hours at least must elapse ere the ship could be brought to the anchorage, he bade his men return to the sealer, and fetch back as much water as the whale-boat could carry, with whatever soft bread the steward might have, all the remaining pumpkins on board, with a box of sugar, and a dozen of his private bottles of cider.

Not many minutes after the boat's pushing off, to the vexation of all, the wind entirely died away, and the tide turning, began drifting back the ship helplessly seaward. But trusting this would not last long, Captain Delano sought, with good hopes, to cheer up the strangers, feeling no small satisfaction that, with persons in their condition, he could—thanks to his frequent voyages along the Spanish main—converse with some freedom in their native tongue.

While left alone with them, he was not long in observing some things tending to heighten his first impressions; but surprise was lost in pity, both for the Spaniards and blacks, alike evidently reduced from scarcity of water and provisions; while long-continued suffering seemed to have brought out the less good-natured qualities of the Negroes, besides, at the same time, impairing the Spaniard's authority over them. But, under the circumstances, precisely this condition of things was to have been anticipated. In armies, navies, cities, or families, in nature herself, nothing more relaxes good order than misery. Still, Captain Delano was not without the idea, that had Benito Cereno been a man of greater energy, misrule would hardly have come to the present pass. But the debility, constitutional or induced by hardships, bodily and mental, of the Spanish captain, was too obvious to be overlooked. A prey to settled dejection, as if long mocked with hope he would not now indulge it, even when it had ceased to be a mock, the prospect of that day, or evening at furthest, lying at anchor, with plenty of water for his people, and a brother captain to counsel and befriend, seemed in no perceptible degree to encourage him. His mind appeared unstrung, if not still more seriously affected. Shut up in these oaken walls, chained to one dull round of command, whose unconditionality cloyed him, like some hypochondriac abbot he moved slowly about, at times suddenly pausing, starting, or staring, biting his lip, biting his finger-nail, flushing, paling, twitching his beard, with other symptoms of an absent or moody mind. This distempered spirit was lodged, as before hinted, in as distempered a frame. He was rather tall, but seemed never to have been robust, and now with nervous suffering was almost worn to a skeleton. A tendency to some pulmonary complaint appeared to have been lately confirmed. His voice was like that of one with lungs half gone—hoarsely suppressed, a husky whisper. No wonder that, as in this state he tottered about, his private servant apprehensively followed him. Sometimes the Negro gave his master his arm,

[29] Darkened.   [30] Gloomy, taciturn.

or took his handkerchief out of his pocket for him; performing these and similar offices with that affectionate zeal which transmutes into something filial or fraternal acts in themselves but menial; and which has gained for the Negro the repute of making the most pleasing body-servant in the world; one, too, whom a master need be on no stiffly superior terms with, but may treat with familiar trust; less a servant than a devoted companion.

Marking the noisy indocility of the blacks in general, as well as what seemed the sullen inefficiency of the whites, it was not without humane satisfaction that Captain Delano witnessed the steady good conduct of Babo.

But the good conduct of Babo, hardly more than the ill-behaviour of others, seemed to withdraw the half-lunatic Don Benito from his cloudy languor. Not that such precisely was the impression made by the Spaniard on the mind of his visitor. The Spaniard's individual unrest was, for the present, but noted as a conspicuous feature in the ship's general affliction. Still, Captain Delano was not a little concerned at what he could not help taking for the time to be Don Benito's unfriendly indifference toward himself. The Spaniard's manner, too, conveyed a sort of sour and gloomy disdain, which he seemed at no pains to disguise. But this the American in charity ascribed to the harassing effects of sickness, since, in former instances, he had noted that there are peculiar natures on whom prolonged physical suffering seems to cancel every social instinct of kindness; as if, forced to black bread themselves, they deemed it but equity that each person coming nigh them should, indirectly, by some slight or affront, be made to partake of their fare.

But ere long Captain Delano bethought him that, indulgent as he was at the first, in judging the Spaniard, he might not, after all, have exercised charity enough. At bottom it was Don Benito's reserve which displeased him; but the same reserve was shown toward all but his faithful personal attendant. Even the formal reports which, according to sea-usage, were, at stated times, made to him by some petty underling, either a white, mulatto, or black, he hardly had patience enough to listen to, without betraying contemptuous aversion. His manner upon such occasions was, in its degree, not unlike that which might be supposed to have been his imperial countryman's, Charles V,[31] just previous to the anchoritish retirement of that monarch from the throne.

This splenetic disrelish of his place was evinced in almost every function pertaining to it. Proud as he was moody, he condescended to no personal mandate. Whatever special orders were necessary, their delivery was delegated to his body-servant, who in turn transferred them to their ultimate destination, through runners, alert Spanish boys or slave-boys, like pages or pilot-fish[32] within easy call continually hovering round Don Benito. So that to have beheld this undemonstrative invalid gliding about, apathetic and mute, no landsman could have dreamed that in him was lodged a dictatorship beyond which, while at sea, there was no earthly appeal.

Thus, the Spaniard, regarded in his reserve, seemed the involuntary victim of mental disorder. But, in fact, his reserve might, in some degree, have proceeded from design. If so, then here was evinced the unhealthy climax of that icy though conscientious policy, more or less adopted by all commanders of large ships, which, except in signal emergencies, obliterates alike the manifes-

[31] Charles V (1500–1558), King of Spain, who in 1556 sought religious ("anchoritish") seclusion in a monastery.
[32] A small fish often accompanying sharks.

tation of sway with every trace of sociality; transforming the man into a block, or rather into a loaded cannon, which, until there is call for thunder, has nothing to say.

Viewing him in this light, it seemed but a natural token of the perverse habit induced by a long course of such hard self-restraint, that, notwithstanding the present condition of his ship, the Spaniard should still persist in a demeanour, which, however harmless, or, it may be, appropriate, in a well-appointed vessel, such as the *San Dominick* might have been at the outset of the voyage, was anything but judicious now. But the Spaniard, perhaps, thought that it was with captains as with gods: reserve, under all events, must still be their cue. But probably this appearance of slumbering dominion might have been but an attempted disguise to conscious imbecility—not deep policy, but shallow device. But be all this as it might, whether Don Benito's manner was designed or not, the more Captain Delano noted its pervading reserve, the less he felt uneasiness at any particular manifestation of that reserve toward himself.

Neither were his thoughts taken up by the captain alone. Wonted to the quiet orderliness of the sealer's comfortable family of a crew, the noisy confusion of the *San Dominick*'s suffering host repeatedly challenged his eye. Some prominent breaches, not only of discipline but of decency, were observed. These Captain Delano could not but ascribe, in the main, to the absence of those subordinate deck-officers to whom, along with higher duties, is entrusted what may be styled the police department of a populous ship. True, the old oakum-pickers appeared at times to act the part of monitorial constables to their countrymen, the blacks; but though occasionally succeeding in allaying trifling outbreaks now and then between man and man, they could do little or nothing toward establishing general quiet. The *San Dominick* was in the condition of a transatlantic emigrant ship, among whose multitude of living freight are some individuals, doubtless, as little troublesome as crates and bales; but the friendly remonstrances of such with their ruder companions are of not so much avail as the unfriendly arm of the mate. What the *San Dominick* wanted was, what the emigrant ship has, stern superior officers. But on these decks not so much as a fourth mate was to be seen.

The visitor's curiosity was roused to learn the particulars of those mishaps which had brought about such absenteeism, with its consequences; because, though deriving some inkling of the voyage from the wails which at the first moment had greeted him, yet of the details no clear understanding had been had. The best account would, doubtless, be given by the captain. Yet at first the visitor was loth to ask it, unwilling to provoke some distant rebuff. But plucking up courage, he at last accosted Don Benito, renewing the expression of his benevolent interest, adding, that did he (Captain Delano) but know the particulars of the ship's misfortunes, he would, perhaps, be better able in the end to relieve them. Would Don Benito favour him with the whole story.

Don Benito faltered; then, like some somnambulist suddenly interfered with, vacantly stared at his visitor, and ended by looking down on the deck. He maintained this posture so long, that Captain Delano, almost equally disconcerted, and involuntarily almost as rude, turned suddenly from him, walking forward to accost one of the Spanish seamen for the desired information. But he had hardly gone five paces, when, with a sort of eagerness, Don Benito invited him back, regretting his momentary absence of mind, and professing readiness to gratify him.

While most part of the story was being given, the two captains stood on the after part of the main-deck, a privileged spot, no one being near but the servant.

"It is now a hundred, and ninety days," began the Spaniard, in his husky whisper, "that this ship, well officered and well manned, with several cabin passengers—some fifty Spaniards in all—sailed from Buenos Aires[33] bound to Lima, with a general cargo, hardware, Paraguay tea and the like—and," pointing forward, "that parcel of Negroes, now not more than a hundred and fifty, as you see, but then numbering over three hundred souls. Off Cape Horn we had heavy gales. In one moment, by night, three of my best officers, with fifteen sailors, were lost, with the main-yard; the spar snapping under them in the slings,[34] as they sought, with heavers,[35] to beat down the icy sail. To lighten the hull, the heavier sacks of maté[36] were thrown into the sea, with most of the water-pipes[37] lashed on deck at the time. And this last necessity it was, combined with the prolonged detentions afterward experienced, which eventually brought about our chief causes of suffering. When——"

Here there was a sudden fainting attack of his cough, brought on, no doubt, by his mental distress. His servant sustained him, and drawing a cordial from his pocket placed it to his lips. He a little revived. But unwilling to leave him unsupported while yet imperfectly restored, the black with one arm still encircled his master, at the same time keeping his eye fixed on his face, as if to watch for the first sign of complete restoration, or relapse, as the event might prove.

The Spaniard proceeded, but brokenly and obscurely, as one in a dream.

—"Oh, my God! rather than pass through what I have, with joy I would have hailed the most terrible gales; but——"

His cough returned and with increased violence; this subsiding, with reddened lips and closed eyes he fell heavily against his supporter.

"His mind wanders. He was thinking of the plague that followed the gales" plaintively sighed the servant; "my poor, poor master!" wringing one hand, and with the other wiping the mouth. "But be patient, señor," again turning to Captain Delano, "these fits do not last long; master will soon be himself."

Don Benito reviving, went on; but as this portion of the story was very brokenly delivered, the substance only will here be set down.

It appeared that after the ship had been many days tossed in storms off the Cape, the scurvy[38] broke out, carrying off numbers of the whites and blacks. When at last they had worked round into the Pacific, their spars and sails were so damaged, and so inadequately handled by the surviving mariners, most of whom were become invalids, that, unable to lay her northerly course by the wind, which was powerful, the unmanageable ship, for successive days and nights, was blown northwestward, where the breeze suddenly deserted her, in unknown waters, to sultry calms. The absence of the water-pipes now proved as fatal to life as before their presence had menaced it. Induced, or at least aggravated, by the more than scanty allowance of water, a malignant fever followed the scurvy; with the excessive heat of the lengthened calm, making such short work of it as to sweep away, as by billows, whole families

---

[33] Capital of Argentina and a seaport.   [34] Ropes or chains supporting the yardarms.
[35] Short bars used as levers for twisting ropes.
[36] Another name for Paraguay tea, a South American drink containing large amounts of caffeine.
[37] Casks of water.   [38] Disease caused by a deficiency of vitamin C.

of the Africans, and a yet larger number, proportionably, of the Spaniards, including, by a luckless fatality, every remaining officer on board. Consequently, in the smart west winds eventually following the calm, the already rent sails, having to be simply dropped, not furled, at need, had been gradually reduced to the beggars' rags they were now. To procure substitutes for his lost sailors, as well as supplies of water and sails, the captain, at the earliest opportunity, had made for Baldivia, the southernmost civilised port of Chili and South America; but upon nearing the coast the thick weather had prevented him from so much as sighting that harbour. Since which period, almost without a crew, and almost without canvas, and almost without water, and, at intervals, giving its added dead to the sea, the *San Dominick* had been battledored[39] about by contrary winds, inveigled by currents, or grown weedy in calms. Like a man lost in woods, more than once she had doubled upon her own track.

"But throughout these calamities," huskily continued Don Benito, painfully turning in the half-embrace of his servant, "I have to thank those Negroes you see, who, though to your inexperienced eyes appearing unruly, have, indeed, conducted themselves with less of restlessness than even their owner could have thought possible under such circumstances."

Here he again fell faintly back. Again his mind wandered; but he rallied, and less obscurely proceeded.

"Yes, their owner was quite right in assuring me that no fetters would be needed with his blacks; so that while, as in wont in this transportation, these Negroes have always remained upon deck—not thrust below, as in the Guinea-men[40]—they have, also, from the beginning, been freely permitted to range within given bounds at their pleasure."

Once more the faintness returned—his mind roved—but, recovering, he resumed.

"But it is Babo here to whom, under God, I owe not only my own preservation, but likewise to him, chiefly, the merit is due, of pacifying his more ignorant brethren, when at intervals tempted to murmurings."

"Ah, master," sighed the black, bowing his face, "don't speak of me; Babo is nothing; what Babo has done was but duty."

"Faithful fellow!" cried Captain Delano. "Don Benito, I envy you such a friend; slave I cannot call him."

As master and man stood before him, the black upholding the white, Captain Delano could not but bethink him of the beauty of that relationship which could present such a spectacle of fidelity on the one hand and confidence on the other. The scene was heightened by the contrast in dress, denoting their relative positions. The Spaniard wore a loose Chile jacket of dark velvet; white small-clothes and stockings, and silver buckles at the knee and instep; a high-crowned sombrero, of fine grass; a slender sword, silver mounted, hung from a knot in his sash—the last being an almost invariable adjunct, more for utility than ornament, of a South American gentleman's dress to this hour. Excepting when his occasional nervous contortions brought about disarray, there was a certain precision in his attire curiously at variance with the unsightly disorder around; especially in the belittered ghetto, forward of the mainmast, wholly occupied by the blacks.

The servant wore nothing but wide trousers, apparently, from their coarseness and patches, made out of some old topsail; they were clean, and confined

---

[39] Batted or knocked about.   [40] West African slave ships.

at the waist by a bit of unstranded rope, which, with his composed, deprecatory air at times, made him look something like a begging friar of St. Francis.[41]

However unsuitable for the time and place, at least in the blunt-thinking American's eyes, and however strangely surviving in the midst of all his afflictions, the toilet of Don Benito might not, in fashion at least, have gone beyond the style of the day among South Americans of his class. Though on the present voyage sailing from Buenos Aires, he had avowed himself a native and resident of Chile, whose inhabitants had not so generally adopted the plain coat and once plebeian pantaloons; but, with a becoming modification, adhered to their provincial costume, picturesque as any in the world. Still, relatively to the pale history of the voyage, and his own pale face, there seemed something so incongruous in the Spaniard's apparel, as almost to suggest the image of an invalid courtier tottering about London streets in the time of the plague.

The portion of the narrative which, perhaps, most excited interest, as well as some surprise, considering the latitudes in question, was the long calms spoken of, and more particularly the ship's so long drifting about. Without communicating the opinion, of course, the American could not but impute at least part of the detentions both to clumsy seamanship and faulty navigation. Eyeing Don Benito's small, yellow hands, he easily inferred that the young captain had not got into command at the hawse-hole,[42] but the cabin window; and if so, why wonder at incompetence, in youth, sickness, and gentility united?

But drowning criticism in compassion, after a fresh repetition of his sympathies, Captain Delano, having heard out his story, not only engaged, as in the first place, to see Don Benito and his people supplied in their immediate bodily needs, but, also, now further promised to assist him in procuring a large permanent supply of water, as well as some sails and rigging; and, though it would involve no small embarrassment to himself, yet he would spare three of his best seamen for temporary deck officers; so that without delay the ship might proceed to Concepcion,[43] there fully to refit for Lima, her destined port.

Such generosity was not without its effect, even upon the invalid. His face lighted up; eager and hectic, he met the honest glance of his visitor. With gratitude he seemed overcome.

"This excitement is bad for master," whispered the servant, taking his arm, and with soothing words gently drawing him aside.

When Don Benito returned, the American was pained to observe that his hopefulness, like the sudden kindling in his cheek, was but febrile and transient.

Ere long, with a joyless mien, looking up toward the poop, the host invited his guest to accompany him there, for the benefit of what little breath of wind might be stirring.

As, during the telling of the story, Captain Delano had once or twice started at the occasional cymballing of the hatchet-polishers, wondering why such an interruption should be allowed, especially in that part of the ship, and in the ears of an invalid; and moreover, as the hatchets had anything but an attractive look, and the handlers of them still less so, it was, therefore, to tell the truth, not without some lurking reluctance, or even shrinking, it may be, that Captain

---

[41] Members of the religious order founded by St. Francis of Assissi in 1209—often called the "grey friars."

[42] Opening in a ship's bow through which the anchor cable (hawser) is passed.

[43] Seaport in west-central Chile.

Delano, with apparent complaisance, acquiesced in his host's invitation. The more so, since, with an untimely caprice of punctilio, rendered distressing by his cadaverous aspect, Don Benito, with Castilian[44] bows, solemnly insisted upon his guest's preceding him up the ladder leading to the elevation; where, one on each side of the last step, sat for armorial supporters and sentries two of the ominous file. Gingerly enough stepped good Captain Delano between them, and in the instant of leaving them behind, like one running the gauntlet, he felt an apprehensive twitch in the calves of his legs.

But when, facing about, he saw the whole file, like so many organ-grinders, still stupidly intent on their work, unmindful of everything besides, he could not but smile at his late fidgety panic.

Presently, while standing with his host, looking forward upon the decks below, he was struck by one of those instances of insubordination previously alluded to. Three black boys, with two Spanish boys, were sitting together on the hatches, scraping a rude wooden platter, in which some scanty mess had recently been cooked. Suddenly, one of the black boys, enraged at a word dropped by one of his white companions, seized a knife, and, though called to forbear by one of the oakum-pickers, struck the lad over the head, inflicting a gash from which blood flowed.

In amazement, Captain Delano inquired what this meant. To which the pale Don Benito dully muttered, that it was merely the sport of the lad.

"Pretty serious sport, truly," rejoined Captain Delano. "Had such a thing happened on board the *Bachelor's Delight,* instant punishment would have followed."

At these words the Spaniard turned upon the American one of his sudden, staring, half-lunatic looks; then, relapsing into his torpor, answered, "Doubtless, doubtless, señor."

Is it, thought Captain Delano, that this hapless man is one of those paper captains I've known, who by policy wink at what by power they cannot put down? I know no sadder sight than a commander who has little of command but the name.

"I should think, Don Benito," he now said, glancing toward the oakum-picker who had sought to interfere with the boys, "that you would find it advantageous to keep all your blacks employed, especially the younger ones, no matter at what useless task, and no matter what happens to the ship. Why, even with my little band, I find such a course indispensable. I once kept a crew on my quarter-deck thrumming[45] mats for my cabin, when, for three days, I had given up my ship—mats, men, and all—for a speedy loss, owing to the violence of a gale, in which we could do nothing but helplessly drive before it."

"Doubtless, doubtless," muttered Don Benito.

"But," continued Captain Delano, again glancing upon the oakum-pickers and then at the hatchet-polishers, near by, "I see you keep some, at least, of your host employed."

"Yes," was again the vacant response.

"Those old men there, shaking their pows[46] from their pulpits," continued Captain Delano, pointing to the oakum-pickers, "seem to act the part of old

[44] Courtly.
[45] Sewing short pieces or ends of rope into the mats to make them thick and strengthen them against chafing.
[46] Heads.

dominies[47] to the rest, little heeded as their admonitions are at times. Is this voluntary on their part, Don Benito, or have you appointed them shepherds to your flock of black sheep?"

"What posts they fill, I appointed them," rejoined the Spaniard, in an acrid tone, as if resenting some supposed satiric reflection.

"And these others, these Ashantee,[48] conjurers here," continued Captain Delano, rather uneasily eyeing the brandished steel of the hatchet-polishers, where, in spots, it had been brought to a shine, "this seems a curious business they are at, Don Benito?"

"In the gales we met," answered the Spaniard, "what of our general cargo was not thrown overboard was much damaged by the brine. Since coming the calm weather, I have had several cases of knives and hatchets daily brought up for overhauling and cleaning."

"A prudent idea, Don Benito. You are part owner of ship and cargo, I presume; but none of the slaves, perhaps?"

"I am owner of all you see," impatiently returned Don Benito, "except the main company of blacks, who belonged to my late friend, Alexandro Aranda."

As he mentioned this name, his air was heart-broken; his knees shook; his servant supported him.

Thinking he divined the cause of such unusual emotion, to confirm his surmise, Captain Delano, after a pause, said: "And may I ask, Don Benito, whether—since a while ago you spoke of some cabin passengers—the friend, whose loss so afflicts you at the outset of the voyage accompanied his blacks?"

"Yes."

"But died of the fever?"

"Died of the fever. Oh, could I but——"

Again quivering, the Spaniard paused.

"Pardon me," said Captain Delano lowly, "but I think that, by a sympathetic experience, I conjecture, Don Benito, what it is that gives the keener edge to your grief. It was once my hard fortune to lose, at sea, a dear friend, my own brother, then supercargo.[49] Assured of the welfare of his spirit, its departure I could have borne like a man; but the honest eye, that honest hand—both of which had so often met mine—and that warm heart; all, all—like scraps to the dogs—to throw all to the sharks! It was then I vowed never to have for fellow-voyager a man I loved, unless, unbeknown to him, I had provided every requisite, in case of a fatality, for embalming his mortal part for interment on shore. Were your friend's remains now on board this ship, Don Benito, not thus strangely would the mention of his name affect you."

"On board this ship?" echoed the Spaniard. Then, with horrified gestures, as directed against some spectre, he unconsciously fell into the ready arms of his attendant, who, with a silent appeal toward Captain Delano, seemed beseeching him not again to broach a theme so unspeakably distressing to his master.

This poor fellow now, thought the pained American, is the victim of that sad superstition which associates goblins with the deserted body of man, as ghosts with an abandoned house. How unlike are we made! What to me, in like case, would have been a solemn satisfaction, the bare suggestion, even, terrifies the Spaniard into this trance. Poor Alexandro Aranda! what would

---

[47] Dutch clergymen.   [48] Natives of western Africa (now Ghana).
[49] Merchant officer in charge of the cargo.

you say could you here see your friend—who, on former voyages, when you, for months, were left behind, has, I dare say, often longed, and longed, for one peep at you—now transported with terror at the least thought of having you any way nigh him.

At this moment, with a dreary graveyard toll, betokening a flaw, the ship's forecastle bell, smote by one of the grizzled oakum-pickers, proclaimed ten o'clock through the leaden calm; when Captain Delano's attention was caught by the moving figure of a gigantic black, emerging from the general crowd below, and slowly advancing toward the elevated poop. An iron collar was about his neck, from which depended a chain, thrice wound round his body; the terminating links padlocked together at a broad band of iron, his girdle.

"How like a mute Atufal moves," murmured the servant.

The black mounted the steps of the poop, and, like a brave prisoner, brought up to receive sentence, stood in unquailing muteness before Don Benito, now recovered from his attack.

At the first glimpse of his approach, Don Benito had started, a resentful shadow swept over his face; and, as with the sudden memory of bootless[50] rage, his white lips glued together.

This is some mulish mutineer, thought Captain Delano, surveying, not without a mixture of admiration, the colossal form of the Negro.

"See, he waits your question, master," said the servant.

Thus reminded, Don Benito, nervously averting his glance, as if shunning, by anticipation, some rebellious response, in a disconcerted voice, thus spoke:

"Atufal, will you ask my pardon now?"

The black was silent.

"Again, master," murmured the servant, with bitter upbraiding eyeing his countryman, "again, master; he will bend to master yet."

"Answer," said Don Benito, still averting his glance, "say but the one word, *pardon*, and your chains shall be off."

Upon this, the black, slowly raising both arms, let them lifelessly fall, his links clanking, his head bowed; as much as to say, "No, I am content."

"Go," said Don Benito, with inkept and unknown emotion.

Deliberately as he had come, the black obeyed.

"Excuse me, Don Benito," said Captain Delano, "but this scene surprises me; what means it, pray?"

"It means that that Negro alone, of all the band, has given me peculiar cause of offence. I have put him in chains; I——"

Here he paused; his hand to his head, as if there were a swimming there, or a sudden bewilderment of memory had come over him; but meeting his servant's kindly glance seemed reassured, and proceeded:

"I could not scourge such a form. But I told him he must ask my pardon. As yet he has not. At my command, every two hours he stands before me."

"And how long has this been?"

"Some sixty days."

"And obedient in all else? And respectful?"

"Yes,"

"Upon my conscience, then," exclaimed Captain Delano impulsively, "he has a royal spirit in him, this fellow."

[50] Without help or remedy.

"He may have some right to it," bitterly returned Don Benito, "he says he was king in his own land."

"Yes," said the servant, entering a word, "those slits in Atufal's ears once held wedges of gold; but poor Babo here, in his own land, was only a poor slave; a black man's slave was Babo, who now is the white's."

Somewhat annoyed by these conversational familiarities, Captain Delano turned curiously upon the attendant, then glanced inquiringly at his master; but, as if long wonted to these little informalities, neither master nor man seemed to understand him.

"What, pray, was Atufal's offence, Don Benito?" asked Captain Delano; "if it was not something very serious, take a fool's advice, and, in view of his general docility, as well as in some natural respect for his spirit, remit him his penalty."

"No, no, master never will do that," here murmured the servant to himself, "proud Atufal must first ask master's pardon. The slave there carries the padlock, but master here carries the key."

His attention thus directed, Captain Delano now noticed for the first time, that, suspended by a slender silken cord from Don Benito's neck, hung a key. At once, from the servant's muttered syllables, divining the key's purpose, he smiled and said:—"So, Don Benito—padlock and key—significant symbols, truly."

Biting his lip, Don Benito faltered.

Though the remark of Captain Delano, a man of such native simplicity as to be incapable of satire or irony, had been dropped in playful allusion to the Spaniard's singularly evidenced lordship over the black; yet the hypochondriac seemed some way to have taken it as a malicious reflection upon his confessed inability thus far to break down, at least, on a verbal summons, the entrenched will of the slave. Deploring this supposed misconception, yet despairing of correcting it, Captain Delano shifted the subject; but finding his companion more than ever withdrawn, as if still sourly digesting the lees of the presumed affront above mentioned, by and by Captain Delano likewise became less talkative, oppressed, against his own will, by what seemed the secret vindictiveness of the morbidly sensitive Spaniard. But the good sailor, himself of a quite contrary disposition, refrained, on his part, alike from the appearance as from the feeling of resentment, and if silent, was only so from contagion.

Presently the Spaniard, assisted by his servant, somewhat discourteously crossed over from his guest; a procedure which, sensibly enough, might have been allowed to pass for idle caprice of ill-humour, had not master and man, lingering round the corner of the elevated skylight, begun whispering together in low voices. This was unpleasing. And more; the moody air of the Spaniard, which at times had not been without a sort of valetudinarian stateliness, now seemed anything but dignified; while the menial familiarity of the servant lost its original charm of simple-hearted attachment.

In his embarrassment, the visitor turned his face to the other side of the ship. By so doing, his glance accidentally fell on a young Spanish sailor, a coil of rope in his hand, just stepped from the deck to the first round of the mizzen-rigging.[51] Perhaps the man would not have been particularly noticed, were it not that, during his ascent to one of the yards, he, with a sort of

---

[51] Rigging attached to the rear mast.

covert intentness, kept his eye fixed on Captain Delano, from whom, presently, it passed, as if by a natural sequence, to the two whispers.

His own attention thus redirected to that quarter, Captain Delano gave a slight start. From something in Don Benito's manner just then, it seemed as if the visitor had, at least partly, been the subject of the withdrawn consultation going on—a conjecture as little agreeable to the guest as it was little flattering to the host.

The singular alternations of courtesy and ill-breeding in the Spanish captain were unaccountable, except on one of two suppositions—innocent lunacy, or wicked imposture.

But the first idea, though it might naturally have occurred to an indifferent observer, and, in some respect, had not hitherto been wholly a stranger to Captain Delano's mind, yet, now that, in an incipient way, he began to regard the stranger's conduct something in the light of an intentional affront, of course the idea of lunacy was virtually vacated. But if not a lunatic, what then? Under the circumstances, would a gentleman, nay, any honest boor, act the part now acted by his host? The man was an impostor. Some low-born adventurer, masquerading as an oceanic grandee;[52] yet so ignorant of the first requisites of mere gentlemanhood as to be betrayed into the present remarkable indecorum. That strange ceremoniousness, too, at other times evinced, seemed not uncharacteristic of one playing a part above his real level. Benito Cereno—Don Benito Cereno—a sounding name. One, too, at that period, not unknown, in the surname, to supercargoes and sea-captains trading along the Spanish Main, as belonging to one of the most enterprising and extensive mercantile families in all those provinces; several members of it having titles; a sort of Castilian Rothschild,[53] with a noble brother, or cousin, in every great trading town of South America. The alleged Don Benito was in early manhood, about twenty-nine or thirty. To assume a sort of roving cadetship[54] in the maritime affairs of such a house, what more likely scheme for a young knave of talent and spirit? But the Spaniard was a pale invalid. Never mind. For even to the degree of simulating mortal disease, the craft of some tricksters had been known to attain. To think that, under the aspect of infantile weakness, the most savage energies might be couched—those velvets of the Spaniard but the silky paw to his fangs.

From no train of thought did these fancies come; not from within, but from without; suddenly, too, and in one throng, like hoar frost; yet as soon to vanish as the mild sun of Captain Delano's good-nature regained its meridian.

Glancing over once more toward his host—whose side-face, revealed above the skylight, was now turned toward him—he was struck by the profile, whose clearness of cut was refined by the thinness, incident to ill-health, as well as ennobled about the chin by the beard. Away with suspicion. He was a true off-shoot of a true hidalgo[55] Cereno.

Relieved by these and other better thoughts, the visitor, lightly humming a tune, now began indifferently pacing the poop, so as not to betray to Don Benito that he had at all mistrusted incivility, much less duplicity; for such mistrust would yet be proved illusory, and by the event; though, for the present, the circumstance which had provoked that distrust remained unexplained. But when that little mystery should have been cleared up, Captain Delano thought

---

[52] A person of rank or nobility.
[53] The Rothschilds were (and are today) a famous European banking family.
[54] Apprenticeship.   [55] Nobleman.

he might extremely regret it, did he allow Don Benito to become aware that he had indulged in ungenerous surmises. In short, to the Spaniard's black-letter[56] text, it was best, for a while, to leave open margins.[57]

Presently, his pale face twitching and overcast, the Spaniard, still supported by his attendant, moved over toward his guest, when, with even more than his usual embarrassment, and a strange sort of intriguing intonation in his husky whisper, the following conversation began:—

"Señor, may I ask how long you have lain at this isle?"

"Oh, but a day or two, Don Benito."

"And from what port are you last?"

"Canton."[58]

"And there, señor, you exchanged your seal-skins for teas and silks, I think you said?"

"Yes. Silks, mostly."

"And the balance you took in specie,[59] perhaps?"

Captain Delano, fidgeting a little, answered:

"Yes; some silver; not a very great deal, though."

"Ah—well. May I ask how many men have you, señor?"

Captain Delano slightly started, but answered:

"About five-and-twenty, all told."

"And at present, señor, all on board, I suppose?"

"All on board, Don Benito," replied the captain, now with satisfaction.

"And will be to-night, señor?"

At this last question, following so many pertinacious ones, for the soul of him Captain Delano could not but look very earnestly at the questioner, who, instead of meeting the glance, with every token of craven discomposure dropped his eyes to the deck; presenting an unworthy contrast to his servant, who, just then, was kneeling at his feet, adjusting a loose shoe-buckle; his disengaged face meantime, with humble curiosity, turned openly up into his master's downcast one.

The Spaniard, still with a guilty shuffle, repeated his question:

"And—and will be to-night, señor?"

"Yes, for aught I know," returned Captain Delano—"but nay," rallying himself into fearless truth, "some of them talked of going off on another fishing party about midnight."

"Your ships generally go—go more or less armed, I believe, señor?"

"Oh, a six-pounder or two, in case of emergency," was the intrepidly indifferent reply, "with a small stock of muskets, sealing-spears, and cutlasses, you know."

As he thus responded, Captain Delano again glanced at Don Benito, but the latter's eyes were averted; while abruptly and awkwardly shifting the subject, he made some peevish allusion to the calm, and then, without apology, once more, with his attendant, withdrew to the opposite bulwarks, where the whispering was resumed.

At this moment, and ere Captain Delano could cast a cool thought upon what had just passed, the young Spanish sailor, before mentioned, was seen descending from the rigging. In act of stooping over to spring in-board to the deck, his voluminous, unconfined frock, or shirt, of coarse woollen, much

[56] Text printed in heavy, ornate, gothic typeface.   [57] Without comment.
[58] A city in China.   [59] Gold or silver currency.

spotted with tar, opened out far down the chest, revealing a soiled undergarment of what seemed the finest linen, edged, about the neck, with a narrow blue ribbon, sadly faded and worn. At this moment the young sailor's eye was again fixed on the whisperers, and Captain Delano thought he observed a lurking significance in it, as if silent signs, of some Freemason[60] sort, had that instant been interchanged.

This once more impelled his own glance in the direction of Don Benito, and, as before, he could not but infer that himself formed the subject of the conference. He paused. The sound of the hatchet-polishing fell on his ears. He cast another swift side-look at the two. They had the air of conspirators. In connection with the late questionings, and the incident of the young sailor, these things now begat such return of involuntary suspicion, that the singular guilelessness of the American could not endure it. Plucking up a gay and humorous expression, he crossed over to the two rapidly, saying: "Ha, Don Benito, your black here seems high in your trust; a sort of privy-counsellor,[61] in fact."

Upon this, the servant looked up with a good-natured grin, but the master started as from a venomous bite. It was a moment or two before the Spaniard sufficiently recovered himself to reply; which he did, at last, with cold constraint: "Yes, señor, I have trust in Babo."

Here Babo, changing his previous grin of mere animal humour into an intelligent smile, not ungratefully eyed his master.

Finding that the Spaniard now stood silent and reserved, as if involuntarily, or purposely giving hint that his guest's proximity was inconvenient just then, Captain Delano, unwilling to appear uncivil even to incivility itself, made some trivial remark and moved off; again and again turning over in his mind the mysterious demeanour of Don Benito Cereno.

He had descended from the poop, and, wrapped in thought, was passing near a dark hatchway, leading down into the steerage,[62] when, perceiving motion there, he looked to see what moved. The same instant there was a sparkle in the shadowly hatchway, and he saw one of the Spanish sailors, prowling there, hurriedly placing his hand in the bosom of his frock, as if hiding something. Before the man could have been certain who it was that was passing, he slunk below out of sight. But enough was seen of him to make it sure that he was the same young sailor before noticed in the rigging.

What was that which so sparkled? thought Captain Delano. It was no lamp—no match—no live coal. Could it have been a jewel? But how come sailors with jewels?—or with silk-trimmed under-shirts either? Has he been robbing the trunks of the dead cabin passengers? But if so, he would hardly wear one of the stolen articles on board ship here. Ah, ah—if, now, that was, indeed, a secret sign I saw passing between this suspicious fellow and his captain a while since; if I could only be certain that, in my uneasiness, my senses did not deceive me, then——

Here, passing from one suspicious thing to another, his mind revolved the strange questions put to him concerning his ship.

By a curious coincidence, as each point was recalled, the black wizards of Ashantee would strike up with their hatchets, as in ominous comment on the

---

[60] A secret fraternal society which, in Melville's time, exercised a measure of political influence as well and which had become controversial as a result.
[61] A highly placed or highly regarded adviser.   [62] A ship's cabin area.

white stranger's thoughts. Pressed by such enigmas and portents, it would have been almost against nature, had not, even into the least distrustful heart, some ugly misgivings obtruded.

Observing the ship, now helplessly fallen into a current, with enchanted sails, drifting with increased rapidity seaward; and noting that, from a lately intercepted projection of the land, the sealer was hidden, the stout mariner began to quake at thoughts which he barely durst confess to himself. Above all, he began to feel a ghostly dread of Don Benito. And yet, when he roused himself, dilated his chest, felt himself strong on his legs, and coolly considered it—what did all these phantoms amount to?

Had the Spaniard any sinister scheme, it must have reference not so much to him (Captain Delano) as to his ship (the *Bachelor's Delight*). Hence the present drifting away of the one ship from the other, instead of favouring any such possible scheme, was, for the time, at least, opposed to it. Clearly any suspicion, combining such contradictions, must needs be delusive. Besides, was it not absurd to think of a vessel in distress—a vessel by sickness almost dismanned of her crew—a vessel whose inmates were parched for water—was it not a thousand times absurd that such a craft should, at present, be of a piratical character; or her commander, either for himself or those under him, cherish any desire but for speedy relief and refreshment? But then, might not general distress, and thirst in particular, be affected? And might not that same undiminished Spanish crew, alleged to have perished off to a remnant, be at that very moment lurking in the hold? On heart-broken pretence of entreating a cup of cold water, fiends in human form had got into lonely dwellings, nor retired until a dark deed had been done. And among the Malay[63] pirates, it was no unusual thing to lure ships after them into their treacherous harbours, or entice boarders from a declared enemy at sea, by the spectacle of thinly manned or vacant decks, beneath which prowled a hundred spears with yellow arms ready to upthrust them through the mats. Not that Captain Delano had entirely credited such things. He had heard of them—and now, as stories, they recurred. The present destination of the ship was the anchorage. There she would be near his own vessel. Upon gaining that vicinity, might not the *San Dominick*, like a slumbering volcano, suddenly let loose energies now hid?

He recalled the Spaniard's manner while telling his story. There was a gloomy hesitancy and subterfuge about it. It was just the manner of one making up his tale for evil purposes as he goes. But if that story was not true, what was the truth? That the ship had unlawfully come into the Spaniard's possession? But in many of its details, especially in reference to the more calamitous parts, such as the fatalities among the seamen, the consequent prolonged beating about, the past sufferings from obstinate calms, and still continued suffering from thirst; in all these points, as well as others, Don Benito's story had corroborated not only the wailing ejaculations of the indiscriminate multitude, white and black, but likewise—what seemed impossible to be counterfeit—by the very expression and play of every human feature, which Captain Delano saw. If Don Benito's story was, throughout, an invention, then every soul on board, down to the youngest Negress, was his carefully drilled recruit in the plot: an incredible inference. And yet, if there was ground for mistrusting his veracity, that inference was a legitimate one.

But those questions of the Spaniard. There, indeed, one might pause. Did

[63] Malaysian.

they not seem put with much the same object with which the burglar or assassin, by day-time, reconnoitres the walls of a house? But, with ill purposes, to solicit such information openly of the chief person endangered, and so, in effect, setting him on his guard; how unlikely a procedure was that. Absurd, then, to suppose that those questions had been prompted by evil designs. Thus, the same conduct, which, in this instance, had raised the alarm, served to dispel it. In short, scarce any suspicion or uneasiness, however apparently reasonable at the time, which was not now, with equal apparent reason, dismissed.

At last he began to laugh at his former forebodings; and laugh at the strange ship for, in its aspect, some way siding with them, as it were; and laugh, too, at the odd-looking blacks, particularly those old scissors-grinders, the Ashantees; and those bedridden old knitting women, the oakum-pickers; and almost at the dark Spaniard himself, the central hobgoblin of all.

For the rest, whatever in a serious way seemed enigmatical, was now good-naturedly explained away by the thought that, for the most part, the poor invalid scarcely knew what he was about; either sulking in black vapours, or putting idle questions without sense or object. Evidently, for the present, the man was not fit to be entrusted with the ship. On some benevolent plea withdrawing the command from him, Captain Delano would yet have to send her to Conception, in charge of his second mate, a worthy person and good navigator—a plan not more convenient for the *San Dominick* than for Don Benito; for, relieved from all anxiety, keeping wholly to his cabin, the sick man, under the good nursing of his servant, would, probably, by the end of the passage, be in a measure restored to health, and with that he should also be restored to authority.

Such were the American's thoughts. They were tranquillizing. There was a difference between the idea of Don Benito's darkly preordaining Captain Delano's fate, and Captain Delano's lightly arranging Don Benito's. Nevertheless, it was not without something of relief that the good seaman presently perceived his whale-boat in the distance. Its absence had been prolonged by unexpected detention at the sealer's side, as well as its returning trip lengthened by the continual recession of the goal.

The advancing speck was observed by the blacks. Their shouts attracted the attention of Don Benito, who, with a return of courtesy, approaching Captain Delano, expressed satisfaction at the coming of some supplies, slight and temporary as they must necessarily prove.

Captain Delano responded; but while doing so, his attention was drawn to something passing on the deck below: among the crowd climbing the landward bulwarks, anxiously watching the coming boat, two blacks, to all appearances accidentally incommoded by one of the sailors, violently pushed him aside, which the sailor some way resenting, they dashed him to the deck, despite the earnest cries of the oakum-pickers.

"Don Benito," said Captain Delano quickly, "do you see what is going on there? Look!"

But, seized by his cough, the Spaniard staggered, with both hands to his face, on the point of falling. Captain Delano would have supported him, but the servant was more alert, who, with one hand sustaining his master, with the other applied the cordial.[64] Don Benito restored, the black withdrew his

---

[64] Some sort of stimulant.

support, slipping aside a little, but dutifully remaining within call of a whisper. Such discretion was here evinced as quite wiped away, in the visitor's eyes, any blemish of impropriety which might have attached to the attendant from the indecorous conferences before mentioned; showing, too, that if the servant were to blame, it might be more the master's fault than his own, since, when left to himself, he could conduct thus well.

His glance called away from the spectacle of disorder to the more pleasing one before him, Captain Delano could not avoid again congratulating his host upon possessing such a servant, who, though perhaps a little too forward now and then, must upon the whole be invaluable to one in the invalid's situation.

"Tell me, Don Benito," he added, with a smile—"I should like to have your man here, myself—what will you take for him? Would fifty doubloons[65] be any object?"

"Master wouldn't part with Babo for a thousand doubloons," murmured the black, overhearing the offer, and taking it in earnest, and, with the strange vanity of a faithful slave, appreciated by his master, scorning to hear so paltry a valuation put upon him by a stranger. But Don Benito, apparently hardly yet completely restored, and again interrupted by his cough, made but some broken reply.

Soon his physical distress became so great, affecting his mind, too, apparently, that, as if to screen the sad spectacle, the servant gently conducted his master below.

Left to himself, the American, to while away the time till his boat should arrive, would have pleasantly accosted some one of the few Spanish seamen he saw; but recalling something that Don Benito had said touching their ill conduct, he refrained; as a shipmaster indisposed to countenance cowardice or unfaithfulness in seamen.

While, with these thoughts, standing with eye directed forward toward that handful of sailors, suddenly he thought that one or two of them returned the glance and with a sort of meaning. He rubbed his eyes, and looked again; but again seemed to see the same thing. Under a new form, but more obscure than any previous one, the old suspicions recurred, but, in the absence of Don Benito, with less of panic than before. Despite the bad account given of the sailors, Captain Delano resolved forthwith to accost one of them. Descending the poop, he made his way through the blacks, his movement drawing a queer cry from the oakum-pickers, prompted by whom, the Negroes, twitching each other aside, divided before him; but, as if curious to see what was the object of this deliberate visit to their ghetto, closing in behind, in tolerable order, followed the white stranger up. His progress thus proclaimed as by mounted kings-at-arms,[66] and escorted as by a Caffre[67] guard of honour, Captain Delano, assuming a good-humoured, off-handed air, continued to advance; now and then saying a blithe word to the Negroes, and his eye curiously surveying the white faces, here and there sparsely mixed in with the blacks, like stray white pawns venturously involved in the ranks of the chessmen opposed.

While thinking which of them to select for his purpose, he chanced to observe a sailor seated on the deck engaged in tarring the strap of a large block, a circle of blacks squatted round him inquisitively eyeing the process.

The mean employment of the man was in contrast with something superior

[65] Spanish gold coins.   [66] High ranking English heraldic officers.
[67] Kaffir: A member of the Bantu tribe of South Africa noted for their height.

in his figure. His hand, black with continually thrusting it into the tar-pot held for him by a Negro, seemed not naturally allied to his face, a face which would have been a very fine one but for its haggardness. Whether this haggardness had aught to do with criminality, could not be determined; since, as intense heat and cold, though unlike, produce like sensations, so innocence and guilt, when, through casual association with mental pain, stamping any visible impress, use one seal—a hacked one.

Not again that this reflection occurred to Captain Delano at the time, charitable man as he was. Rather another idea. Because observing so singular a haggardness combined with a dark eye, averted as in trouble and shame, and then again recalling Don Benito's confessed ill opinion of his crew, insensibly he was operated upon by certain general notions which, while disconnecting pain and abashment from virtue, invariably link them with vice.

If, indeed, there be any wickedness on board this ship, thought Captain Delano, be sure that man there has fouled his hand in it, even as now he fouls it in the pitch. I don't like to accost him. I will speak to this other, this old Jack here on the windlass.[68]

He advanced to an old Barcelona tar,[69] in ragged red breeches and dirty night-cap, cheeks trenched and bronzed, whiskers dense as thorn hedges. Seated between two sleepy-looking Africans, this mariner, like his younger shipmate, was employed upon some rigging—splicing a cable—the sleepy-looking blacks performing the inferior function of holding the outer parts of the ropes for him.

Upon Captain Delano's approach, the man at once hung his head below its previous level; the one necessary for business. It appeared as if he desired to be thought absorbed, with more than common fidelity, in his task. Being addressed, he glanced up, but with what seemed a furtive, diffident air, which sat strangely enough on his weather-beaten visage, much as if a grizzly bear, instead of growling and biting, should simper and cast sheep's eyes. He was asked several questions concerning the voyage—questions purposely referring to several particulars in Don Benito's narrative, not previously corroborated by those impulsive cries greeting the visitor on first coming on board. The questions were briefly answered, confirming all that remained to be confirmed of the story. The Negroes about the windlass joined in with the old sailor; but, as they became talkative, he by degrees became mute, and at length quite glum, seemed morosely unwilling to answer more questions, and yet, all the while, this ursine[70] air was somehow mixed with his sheepish one.

Despairing of getting into unembarrassed talk with such a centaur,[71] Captain Delano, after glancing round for a more promising countenance, but seeing none, spoke pleasantly to the blacks to make way for him; and so, amid various grins and grimaces, returned to the poop, feeling a little strange at first, he could hardly tell why, but upon the whole with regained confidence in Benito Cereno.

How plainly, thought he, did that old whiskerando[72] yonder betray a consciousness of ill desert. No doubt, when he saw me coming, he dreaded lest I, apprised by his captain of the crew's general misbehaviour, came with sharp words for him, and so down with his head. And yet—and yet, now that I

[68] A cylindrical device used for winding rope.   [69] A sailor from Barcelona, Spain.
[70] Bear-like.   [71] A race of monsters from Greek mythology, half-man and half-horse.
[72] Someone heavily bearded.

think of it, that very old fellow, if I err not, was one of those who seemed so earnestly eyeing me here a while since. Ah, these currents spin one's head round almost as much as they do the ship. Ha, there now's a pleasant sort of sunny sight; quite sociable, too.

His attention had been drawn to a slumbering Negress, partly disclosed through the lacework of some rigging, lying, with youthful limbs carelessly disposed, under the lee of the bulwarks, like a doe in the shade of a woodland rock. Sprawling at her lapped breasts was her wide-awake fawn, stark naked, its black little body half lifted from the deck, crosswise with its dam's'; its hands, like two paws, clambering upon her; its mouth and nose ineffectually rooting to get at the mark; and meantime giving a vexatious half-grunt, blending with the composed snore of the Negress.

The uncommon vigour of the child at length roused the mother. She started up, at a distance facing Captain Delano. But as if not at all concerned at the attitude in which she had been caught, delightedly she caught the child up, with maternal transports, covering it with kisses.

There's naked nature, now; pure tenderness and love, thought Captain Delano, well pleased.

This incident prompted him to remark the other Negresses more particularly than before. He was gratified with their manners: like most uncivilised women, they seemed at once tender of heart and tough of constitution; equally ready to die for their infants or fight for them. Unsophisticated as leopardesses; loving as doves. Ah! thought Captain Delano, these, perhaps, are some of the very women whom Ledyard saw in Africa,[73] and gave such a noble account of.

These natural sights somehow insensibly deepened his confidence and ease. At last he looked to see how his boat was getting on; but it was still pretty remote. He turned to see if Don Benito had returned; but he had not.

To change the scene, as well as to please himself with a leisurely observation of the coming boat, stepping over into the mizzen-chains, he clambered his way into the starboard quarter-gallery—one of those abandoned Venetian-looking water-balconies previously mentioned—retreats cut off from the deck. As his foot pressed the half-damp, half-dry sea-mosses matting the place, and a chance phantom cat's-paw[74]—an islet of breeze, unheralded, unfollowed—as this ghostly cat's-paw came fanning his cheek; as his glance fell upon the row of small, round dead-lights—all closed like coppered eyes of the coffined— and the state-cabin door, once connecting with the gallery, even as the dead-lights had once looked out upon it, but now caulked fast like a sarcophagus lid; and to a purple-black, tarred-over panel, threshold, and post; and he bethought him of the time, when that state-cabin and this state-balcony had heard the voices of the Spanish king's officers, and the forms of the Lima viceroy's[75] daughters had perhaps leaned where he stood—as these and other images flitted through his mind, as the cat's-paw through the calm, gradually he felt rising a dreamy inquietude, like that of one who alone on the prairie feels unrest from the repose of the noon.

He leaned against the carved balustrade, again looking off toward his boat; but found his eye falling upon the ribbon grass, trailing along the ship's water-line, straight as a border of green box; and parterres[76] of seaweed, broad

---

[73] John Ledyard (1751–1789), an American who wrote an account of his travels in Africa.
[74] A light breeze that ruffles the surface of the water.   [75] A colonial governor's.
[76] Patterned gardens.

ovals and crescents, floating nigh and far, with what seemed long formal alleys between, crossing the terraces of swells, and sweeping round as if leading to the grottoes below. And overhanging all was the balustrade by his arm, which, partly stained with pitch and partly embossed with moss, seemed the charred ruin of some summer-house in a grand garden long running to waste.

Trying to break one charm, he was but becharmed anew. Though upon the wide sea, he seemed in some far inland country; prisoner in some deserted château, left to stare at empty grounds, and peer out at vague roads, where never wagon or wayfarer passed.

But these enchantments were a little disenchanted as his eye fell on the corroded main-chains. Of an ancient style, massy and rusty in link, shackle, and bolt, they seemed even more fit for the ship's present business than the one for which she had been built.

Presently he thought something moved nigh the chains. He rubbed his eyes, and looked hard. Groves of rigging were about the chains; and there, peering from behind a great stay, like an Indian from behind a hemlock, a Spanish sailor, a marlin-spike[77] in his hand, was seen, who made what seemed an imperfect gesture toward the balcony, but immediately, as if alarmed by some advancing step along the deck within, vanished into the recesses of the hempen forest, like a poacher.

What meant this? Something the man had sought to communicate, unbeknown to anyone, even to his captain. Did the secret involve aught unfavorable to his captain? Were those previous misgivings of Captain Delano's about to be verified? Or, in his haunted mood at the moment, had some random, unintentional motion of the man, while busy with the stay, as if repairing it, been mistaken for a significant beckoning?

Not unbewildered, again he gazed off for his boat. But it was temporarily hidden by a rocky spur of the isle. As with some eagerness he bent forward, watching for the first shooting view of its beak, the balustrade gave way before him like charcoal. Had he not clutched an outreaching rope he would have fallen into the sea. The crash, though feeble, and the fall, though hollow, of the rotten fragments, must have been overheard. He glanced up. With sober curiosity peering down upon him was one of the old oakum-pickers, slipped from his perch to an outside boom[78]; while below the old Negro, and, invisible to him, reconnoitring from a port-hole like a fox from the mouth of its den, crouched the Spanish sailor again. From something suddenly suggested by the man's air, the mad idea now darted into Captain Delano's mind, that Don Benito's plea of indisposition, in withdrawing below, was but a pretence: that he was engaged there maturing his plot, of which the sailor, by some means gaining an inkling, had a mind to warn the stranger against; incited, it may be, by gratitude for a kind word on first boarding the ship. Was it from foreseeing some possible interference like this, that Don Benito had, beforehand, given such a bad character of his sailors, while praising the Negroes; though, indeed, the former seemed as docile as the latter the contrary? The whites, too, by nature, were the shrewder race. A man with some evil design, would he not be likely to speak well of that stupidity which was blind to his depravity, and malign that intelligence from which it might not be hidden? Not unlikely, perhaps. But if the whites had dark secrets concerning Don Benito, could then Don Benito be any way in complicity with the blacks? But they were

---

[77] A spike used to separate the strands of a rope in splicing.   [78] A long spar.

too stupid. Besides, who ever heard of a white so far a renegade as to apostatise from his very species almost, by leaguing in against it with Negroes? These difficulties recalled former ones. Lost in their mazes, Captain Delano, who had now regained the deck, was uneasily advancing along it, when he observed a new face; an aged sailor seated cross-legged near the main hatchway. His skin was shrunk up with wrinkles like a pelican's empty pouch; his hair frosted; his countenance grave and composed. His hands were full of ropes, which he was working into a large knot. Some blacks were about him obligingly dipping the strands for him, here and there, as the exigencies of the operation demanded.

Captain Delano crossed over to him, and stood in silence surveying the knot; his mind, by a not uncongenial transition, passing from its own entanglements to those of the hemp. For intricacy, such a knot he had never seen in an American ship, nor indeed any other. The old man looked like an Egyptian priest, making Gordian knots[79] for the temple of Ammon.[80] The knot seemed a combination of double-bowline-knot, treble-crown-knot, back-handed-well-knot, knot-in-and-out-knot, and jamming-knot.

At last, puzzled to comprehend the meaning of such a knot, Captain Delano addressed the knotter:—

"What are you knotting there, my man?"

"The knot," was the brief reply, without looking up.

"So it seems; but what is it for?"

"For someone else to undo," muttered back the old man, plying his fingers harder than ever, the knot being now nearly completed.

While Captain Delano stood watching him, suddenly the old man threw the knot toward him, saying in broken English—the first heard in the ship—something to this effect: "Undo it, cut it, quick." It was said lowly, but with such condensation of rapidity that the long, slow words in Spanish, which had preceded and followed, almost operated as covers to the brief English between.

For a moment, knot in hand, and knot in head, Captain Delano stood mute; while, without further heeding him, the old man was now intent upon other ropes. Presently there was a slight stir behind Captain Delano. Turning, he saw the chained Negro, Atufal, standing quietly there. The next moment the old sailor rose, muttering, and, followed by his subordinate Negroes, removed to the forward part of the ship, where in the crowd he disappeared.

An elderly Negro, in a clout[81] like an infant's, and with a pepper-and-salt head, and a kind of attorney air, now approached Captain Delano. In tolerable Spanish, and with a good-natured, knowing wink, he informed him that the old knotter was simple-witted, but harmless; often playing his odd tricks. The Negro concluded by begging the knot, for of course the stranger would not care to be troubled with it. Unconsciously, it was handed to him. With a sort of *congé*,[82] the Negro received it, and, turning his back, ferreted into it like a detective custom-house officer after smuggled laces. Soon, with some African word, equivalent to pshaw, he tossed the knot overboard.

[79] In Greek mythology a carefully tied, intricate knot. According to legend the person who could loosen the knot of King Gordius, father of Midas, would become ruler of all Asia. It remained tied until Alexander the Great cut the knot with his sword and declared that he had fulfilled the prophecy.

[80] A god of ancient Egypt.   [81] Clothing (loincloth).   [82] Ceremonious bow.

All this is very queer now, thought Captain Delano, with a qualmish sort of emotion; but, as one feeling incipient sea-sickness, he strove, by ignoring the symptoms, to get rid of the malady. Once more he looked off for his boat. To his delight, it was now again in view, leaving the rocky spur astern.

The sensation here experienced, after at first relieving his uneasiness, with unforeseen efficacy soon began to remove it. The less distant sight of that well-known boat—showing it, not as before, half blended with the haze, but with outline defined, so that its individuality, like a man's, was manifest; that boat, *Rover* by name, which, though now in strange seas, had often pressed the beach of Captain Delano's home, and, brought to its threshold for repairs, had familiarly lain there, as a Newfoundland dog; the sight of that household boat evoked a thousand trustful associations, which, contrasted with previous suspicions, filled him not only with lightsome confidence, but somehow with half-humorous self-reproaches at his former lack of it.

"What, I, Amasa Delano—Jack of the Beach, as they called me when a lad—I, Amasa; the same that, duck-satchel[83] in hand, used to paddle along the water-side to the school-house made from the old hulk—I, little Jack of the Beach, that used to go berrying with cousin Nat and the rest; I to be murdered here at the ends of the earth, on board a haunted pirate-ship by a horrible Spaniard? Too nonsensical to think of! Who would murder Amasa Delano? His conscience is clean. There is someone above. Fie, fie, Jack of the Beach! you are a child indeed; a child of the second childhood, old boy; you are beginning to dote and drule,[84] I'm afraid."

Light of heart and foot, he stepped aft, and there was met by Don Benito's servant, who, with a pleasing expression, responsive to his own present feelings, informed him that his master had recovered from the effects of his coughing fit, and had just ordered him to go present his compliments to his good guest, Don Amasa, and say that he (Don Benito) would soon have the happiness to rejoin him.

There now, do you mark that? again thought Captain Delano, walking the poop. What a donkey I was. This kind gentleman who here sends me his kind compliments, he, but ten minutes ago, dark-lantern in hand, was dodging round some old grindstone in the hold, sharpening a hatchet for me, I thought. Well, well; these long calms have a morbid effect on the mind, I've often heard, though I never believed it before. Ha! glancing toward the boat; there's *Rover;* good dog; a white bone in her mouth.[85] A pretty big bone though, seems to me.—What? Yes, she has fallen afoul of the bubbling tide-rip[86] there. It sets her the other way, too, for the time. Patience.

It was now about noon, though, from the grayness of everything, it seemed to be getting toward dusk.

The calm was confirmed. In the far distance, away from the influence of land, the leaden ocean seemed laid out and leaded up, its course finished, soul gone, defunct. But the current from landward, where the ship was, increased; silently sweeping her further and further toward the tranced waters beyond.

Still, from his knowledge of those latitudes, cherishing hopes of a breeze, and a fair and fresh one, at any moment, Captain Delano, despite present prospects, buoyantly counted upon bringing the *San Dominick* safely to anchor

---

[83] Satchel made of a heavy durable cotton fabric.   [84] To grow feeble or senile.
[85] Delano is referring to the white foam beneath the whale boat's bow.   [86] Current of water.

ere night. The distance swept over was nothing; since, with a good wind, ten minutes' sailing would retrace more than sixty minutes' drifting. Meantime, one moment turning to mark *Rover* fighting the tide-rip, and the next to see Don Benito approaching, he continued walking the poop.

Gradually he felt a vexation arising from the delay of his boat; this soon merged into uneasiness; and at last—his eye falling continually, as from a stage-box into the pit, upon the strange crowd before and below him, and, by and by, recognizing there the face—now composed to indifference—of the Spanish sailor who had seemed to beckon from the main-chains—something of his old trepidations returned.

Ah, thought he—gravely enough—this is like the ague:[87] because it went off, it follows not that it won't come back.

Though ashamed of the relapse, he could not altogether subdue it; and so, exerting his good-nature to the utmost, insensible he came to a compromise.

Yes, this is a strange craft; a strange history, too, and strange folks on board. But—nothing more.

By way of keeping his mind out of mischief till the boat should arrive, he tried to occupy it with turning over and over, in a purely speculative sort of way, some lesser peculiarities of the captain and crew. Among others, four curious points recurred:—

First, the affair of the Spanish lad assailed with a knife by the slave-boy; an act winked at by Don Benito. Second, the tyranny in Don Benito's treatment of Atufal, the black; as if a child should lead a bull of the Nile by the ring in his nose. Third, the trampling of the sailor by the two Negroes; a piece of insolence passed over without so much as a reprimand. Fourth, the cringing submission to their master of all the ship's underlings, mostly blacks; as if by the least inadvertence they feared to draw down his despotic displeasure.

Coupling these points, they seemed somewhat contradictory. But what then, thought Captain Delano, glancing toward his now nearing boat—what then? Why, Don Benito is a very capricious commander. But he is not the first of the sort I have seen; though it's true he rather exceeds any other. But as a nation—continued he in his reveries—these Spaniards are all an odd set; the very word Spaniard has a curious, conspirator, Guy-Fawkish[88] twang to it. And yet, I dare say, Spaniards in the main are as good folks as any in Duxbury, Massachusetts. Ah, good! At last *Rover* has come.

As, with its welcome freight, the boat touched the side, the oakum-pickers, with venerable gestures, sought to restrain the blacks, who, at the sight of three gurried[89] water-casks in its bottom, and a pile of wilted pumpkins in its bow, hung over the bulwarks in disorderly raptures.

Don Benito, with his servant, now appeared; his coming, perhaps, hastened by hearing the noise. Of him Captain Delano sought permission to serve out the water, so that all might share alike, and none injure themselves by unfair excess. But sensible, and, on Don Benito's account, kind as this offer was, it was received with what seemed impatience; as if aware that he lacked energy as a commander, Don Benito, with the true jealousy of weakness, resented as an affront any interference. So, at least, Captain Delano inferred.

[87] A chill or fit of shivering.
[88] Guy Fawkes (1570–1606) attempted to blow up the British Parliament in the famous "Gunpowder Plot" of 1605.
[89] Spattered with fish offal.

In another moment the casks were being hoisted in, when some of the eager Negroes accidentally jostled Captain Delano, where he stood by the gangway; so that, unmindful of Don Benito, yielding to the impulse of the moment, with good-natured authority he bade the blacks stand back; to enforce his words making use of a half-mirthful, half-menacing gesture. Instantly the blacks paused, just where they were, each Negro and Negress suspended in his or her posture, exactly as the word had found them—for a few seconds continuing so—while, as between the responsive posts of a telegraph, an unknown syllable ran from man to man among the perched oakum-pickers. While the visitor's attention was fixed by this scene, suddenly the hatchet-polishers half rose, and a rapid cry came from Don Benito.

Thinking that at the signal of the Spaniard he was about to be massacred, Captain Delano would have sprung for his boat, but paused, as the oakum-pickers, dropping down into the crowd with earnest exclamations, forced every white and every Negro back, at the same moment, with gestures friendly and familiar, almost jocose, bidding him, in substance, not be a fool. Simultaneously the hatchet-polishers resumed their seats, quietly as so many tailors, and at once, as if nothing had happened, the work of hoisting in the casks was resumed, whites and blacks singing at the tackle.

Captain Delano glanced toward Don Benito. As he saw his meagre form in the act of recovering itself from reclining in the servant's arms, into which the agitated invalid had fallen, he could not but marvel at the panic by which himself had been surprised, on the darting supposition that such a commander, who, upon a legitimate occasion, so trivial, too, as it now appeared, could lose all self-command, was, with energetic iniquity, going to bring about his murder.

The casks being on deck, Captain Delano was handed a number of jars and cups by one of the steward's aids, who, in the name of his captain, entreated him to do as he had proposed—dole out the water. He complied, with republican impartiality as to this republican element, which always seeks one level, serving the oldest white no better than the youngest black; excepting, indeed, poor Don Benito, whose condition, if not rank, demanded an extra allowance. To him, in the first place, Captain Delano presented a fair pitcher of the fluid; but, thirsting as he was for it, the Spaniard quaffed not a drop until after several grave bows and salutes. A reciprocation of courtesies which the sight-loving Africans hailed with clapping of hands.

Two of the less wilted pumpkins being reserved for the cabin table, the residue were minced up on the spot for the general regalement. But the soft bread, sugar, and bottled cider, Captain Delano would have given the whites alone, and in chief Don Benito; but the latter objected; which disinterestedness not a little pleased the American; and so mouthfuls all around were given alike to whites and blacks; excepting one bottle of cider, which Babo insisted upon setting aside for his master.

Here it may be observed that as on the first visit of the boat, the American had not permitted his men to board the ship, neither did he now; being unwilling to add to the confusion of the decks.

Not uninfluenced by the peculiar good-humor at present prevailing, and for the time oblivious of any but benevolent thoughts, Captain Delano, who, from recent indications, counted upon a breeze within an hour or two at furthest, dispatched the boat back to the sealer, with orders for all the hands that could be spared immediately to set about rafting casks to the watering-place

and filling them. Likewise he bade word be carried to his chief officer, that
if, against present expectation, the ship was not brought to anchor by sunset,
he need be under no concern; for as there was to be a full moon that night,
he (Captain Delano) would remain on board ready to play the pilot, come
the wind soon or late.

As the two captains stood together, observing the departing boat—the servant, as it happened, having just spied a spot on his master's velvet sleeve,
and silently engaged rubbing it out—the American expressed his regrets that
the *San Dominick* had no boats; none, at least, but the unseaworthy old hulk
of the long-boat, which, warped as a camel's skeleton in the desert, and almost
as bleached, lay pot-wise inverted amidships, one side a little tipped, furnishing
a subterraneous sort of den for family groups of the blacks, mostly women
and small children; who, squatting on old mats below, or perched above in
the dark dome, on the elevated seats, were descried, some distance within,
like a social circle of bats, sheltering in some friendly cave; at intervals, ebon
flights of naked boys and girls, three or four years old, darting in and out of
the den's mouth.

"Had you three or four boats now, Don Benito," said Captain Delano, "I
think that, by tugging at the oars, your Negroes here might help along matters
some. Did you sail from port without boats, Don Benito?"

"They were stove[90] in the gales, señor."

"That was bad. Many men, too, you lost then. Boats and men. Those must
have been hard gales, Don Benito."

"Past all speech," cringed the Spaniard.

"Tell me, Don Benito," continued his companion with increased interest,
"tell me, were these gales immediately off the pitch[91] of Cape Horn?"

"Cape Horn?—who spoke of Cape Horn?"

"Yourself did, when giving me an account of your voyage," answered Captain
Delano, with almost equal astonishment at this eating of his own words, even
as he ever seemed eating his own heart, on the part of the Spaniard. "You
yourself, Don Benito, spoke of Cape Horn," he emphatically repeated.

The Spaniard turned, in a sort of stooping posture, pausing an instant, as
one about to make a plunging exchange of elements, as from air to water.

At this moment a messenger-boy, a white, hurried by, in the regular performance of his function carrying the last expired half-hour forward to the forecastle, from the cabin time-piece, to have it struck at the ship's large bell.

"Master," said the servant, discontinuing his work on the coat sleeve, and
addressing the rapt Spaniard with a sort of timid apprehensiveness, as one
charged with a duty, the discharge of which, it was foreseen, would prove
irksome to the very person who had imposed it, and for whose benefit it was
intended, "master told me never mind where he was, or how engaged, always
to remind him, to a minute, when shaving-time comes. Miguel has gone to
strike the half-hour afternoon. It is *now,* master. Will master go into the
cuddy?"[92]

"Ah—yes," answered the Spaniard, starting, as from dreams into realities;
then turning upon Captain Delano, he said that ere long he would resume
the conversation.

"Then if master means to talk more to Don Amasa," said the servant, "why

---

[90] Smashed in.   [91] The end or tip.   [92] A small cabin.

not let Don Amasa sit by master in the cuddy, and master can talk, and Don Amasa can listen, while Babo here lathers and strops."[93]

"Yes," said Captain Delano, not unpleased with this sociable plan, "yes, Don Benito, unless you had rather not, I will go with you."

"Be it so, señor."

As the three passed aft, the American could not but think it another strange instance of his host's capriciousness, this being shaved with such uncommon punctuality in the middle of the day. But he deemed it more than likely that the servant's anxious fidelity had something to do with the matter; inasmuch as the timely interruption served to rally his master from the mood which had evidently been coming upon him.

The place called the cuddy was a light deck-cabin formed by the poop, a sort of attic to the large cabin below. Part of it had formerly been the quarters of the officers; but since their death all the partitionings had been thrown down, and the whole interior converted into one spacious and airy marine hall; for absence of fine furniture and picturesque disarray of odd appurtenances, somewhat answering to the wide, cluttered hall of some eccentric bachelor-squire in the country, who hangs his shooting-jacket and tobacco-pouch on deer antlers, and keeps his fishing-rod, tongs, and walking-stick in the same corner.

The similitude was heightened, if not originally suggested, by glimpses of the surrounding sea; since, in one aspect, the country and the ocean seem cousins-german.[94]

The floor of the cuddy was matted. Overhead, four or five old muskets were stuck into horizontal holes along the beams. On one side was a claw-footed old table lashed to the deck; a thumbed missal[95] on it, and over it a small, meagre crucifix attached to the bulkhead.[96] Under the table lay a dented cutlass or two, with a hacked harpoon, among some melancholy old rigging, like a heap of poor friars' girdles.[97] There were also two long, sharp-ribbed settees[98] of Malacca cane, black with age, and uncomfortable to look at as inquisitors' racks, with a large misshapen arm-chair, which, furnished with a rude barber's crotch[99] at the back, working with a screw, seemed some grotesque engine of torment. A flag locker was in one corner, open, exposing various coloured bunting, some rolled up, others half unrolled, still others tumbled. Opposite was a cumbrous washstand, of black mahogany, all of one block, with a pedestal, like a font, and over it a railed shelf, containing combs, brushes, and other implements of the toilet. A torn hammock of stained grass swung near; the sheets tossed, and the pillow wrinkled up like a brow, as if whoever slept here slept but illy, with alternate visitations of sad thoughts and bad dreams.

The further extremity of the cuddy, overhanging the ship's stern, was pierced with three openings, windows or port-holes, according as men or cannon might peer, socially or unsocially, out of them. At present neither men nor cannon were seen, though huge ring-bolts and other rusty iron fixtures of the woodwork hinted of twenty-four-pounders.

Glancing toward the hammock as he entered, Captain Delano said, "You sleep here, Don Benito?"

---

[93] Sharpens the blade of a razor with a piece of leather (a strop).   [94] First cousins.
[95] A prayer book.   [96] Upright partition dividing a ship into compartments.   [97] Rope belts.
[98] A couch or bench with a backrest.   [99] Headrest.

"Yes, señor, since we got into mild weather."

"This seems a sort of dormitory, sitting-room, sailloft, chapel, armoury, and private closet all together, Don Benito," added Captain Delano, looking round.

"Yes, señor; events have not been favourable to much order in my arrangements."

Here the servant, napkin on arm, made a motion as if waiting his master's good pleasure. Don Benito signified his readiness, when, seating him in the Malacca arm-chair, and for the guest's convenience drawing opposite one of the settees, the servant commenced operations by throwing back his master's collar and loosening his cravat.[100]

There is something in the Negro which, in a peculiar way, fits him for avocations about one's person. Most Negroes are natural valets and hair-dressers; taking to the comb and brush congenially as to the castanets, and flourishing them apparently with almost equal satisfaction. There is, too, a smooth tact about them in this employment, with a marvellous, noiseless, gliding briskness, not ungraceful in its way, singularly pleasing to behold, and still more so to be the manipulated subject of. And above all is the great gift of good-humour. Not the mere grin or laugh is here meant. Those were unsuitable. But a certain easy cheerfulness, harmonious in every glance and gesture; as though God had set the whole Negro to some pleasant tune.

When to this is added the docility arising from the unaspiring contentment of a limited mind, and that susceptibility of blind attachment sometimes inhering in indisputable inferiors, one readily perceives why those hypochondriacs, Johnson and Byron—it may be, something like the hypochondriac Benito Cereno—took to their hearts, almost to the exclusion of the entire white race, their serving-men, the Negroes, Barber and Fletcher.[101] But if there be that in the Negro which exempts him from the inflicted sourness of the morbid or cynical mind, how, in his most prepossessing aspects, must he appear to a benevolent one? When at ease with respect to exterior things, Captain Delano's nature was not only benign, but familiarly and humorously so. At home, he had often taken rare satisfaction in sitting in his door, watching some free man of colour at his work or play. If on a voyage he chanced to have a black sailor, invariably he was on chatty and half-gamesome terms with him. In fact, like most men of a good, blithe heart, Captain Delano took to Negroes, not philanthropically, but genially, just as other men to Newfoundland dogs.

Hitherto, the circumstances in which he found the *San Dominick* had repressed the tendency. But in the cuddy, relieved from his former uneasiness, and, for various reasons, more sociably inclined than at any previous period of the day, and seeing the colored servant, napkin on arm, so debonnaire about his master, in a business so familiar as that of shaving, too, all his old weakness for Negroes returned.

Among other things, he was amused with an odd instance of the African love of bright colours and fine shows, in the black's informally taking from the flag-locker a great piece of bunting of all hues, and lavishly tucking it under his master's chin for an apron.

The mode of shaving among the Spaniards is a little different from what it is with other nations. They have a basin, specifically called a barber's basin,

[100] Scarf.
[101] Francis Barber, the servant to English man of letters Samuel Johnson (1709–1784) and William Fletcher, the valet of English poet George Gordon, Lord Byron (1788–1824); Barber was black, Fletcher white.

which on one side is scooped out, so as accurately to receive the chin, against which it is closely held in lathering; which is done, not with a brush, but with soap dipped in the water of the basin and rubbed on the face.

In the present instance salt-water was used for lack of better; and the parts lathered were only the upper lip, and low down under the throat, all the rest being cultivated beard.

The preliminaries being somewhat novel to Captain Delano, he sat curiously eyeing them, so that no conversation took place, nor, for the present, did Don Benito appear disposed to renew any.

Setting down his basin, the Negro searched among the razors, as for the sharpest, and having found it, gave it an additional edge by expertly stropping it on the firm, smooth, oily skin of his open palm; he then made a gesture as if to begin, but midway stood suspended for an instant, one hand elevating the razor, the other professionally dabbling among the bubbling suds on the Spaniard's lank neck. Not unaffected by the close sight of the gleaming steel, Don Benito nervously shuddered; his usual ghastliness was heightened by the lather, which lather, again, was intensified in its hue by the contrasting sootiness of the Negro's body. Altogether the scene was somewhat peculiar, at least to Captain Delano, nor, as he saw the two thus postured, could he resist the vagary, that in the black he saw a headsman, and in the white a man at the block. But this was one of those antic conceits, appearing and vanishing in a breath, from which, perhaps, the best regulated mind is not always free.

Meantime the agitation of the Spaniard had a little loosened the bunting from around him, so that one broad fold swept curtain-like over the chair-arm to the floor, revealing, amid a profusion of armorial bars and ground-colours—black, blue and yellow—a closed castle in a blood-red field diagonal with a lion rampant in a white.

"The castle and the lion," exclaimed Captain Delano—"why, Don Benito, this is the flag of Spain you use here. It's well it's only I, and not the king, that sees this," he added, with a smile, "but"—turning toward the black—"it's all one, I suppose, so the colours be gay"; which playful remark did not fail somewhat to tickle the Negro.

"Now, master," he said, readjusting the flag, and pressing the head gently further back into the crotch of the chair; "now, master," and the steel glanced nigh the throat.

Again Don Benito faintly shuddered.

"You must not shake so, master. See, Don Amasa, master always shakes when I shave him. And yet master knows I never yet have drawn blood, though it's true, if master will shake so, I may some of these times. Now, master," he continued. "And now, Don Amasa, please go on with your talk about the gale, and all that; master can hear, and, between times, master can answer."

"Ah yes, these gales," said Captain Delano; "but the more I think of your voyage, Don Benito, the more I wonder, not at the gales, terrible as they must have been, but at the disastrous interval following them. For here, by your account, have you been these two months and more getting from Cape Horn to St. Maria,[102] a distance which I myself, with a good wind, have sailed in a few days. True, you had calms, and long ones, but to be becalmed for two months, that is, at least, unusual. Why, Don Benito, had almost any other

[102] One of the Galapagos Islands.

gentleman told me such a story, I should have been half disposed to a little incredulity."

Here an involuntary expression came over the Spaniard, similar to that just before on the deck, and whether it was the start he gave, or a sudden gawky roll of the hull in the calm, or a momentary unsteadiness of the servant's hand, however it was, just then the razor drew blood, spots of which stained the creamy lather under the throat: immediately the black barber drew back his steel, and, remaining in his professional attitude, back to Captain Delano, and face to Don Benito, held up the trickling razor, saying, with a sort of half-humorous sorrow, "See, master—you shook so—here's Babo's first blood."

No sword drawn before James the First of England,[103] no assassination in that timid king's presence, could have produced a more terrified aspect than was now presented by Don Benito.

Poor fellow, thought Captain Delano, so nervous he can't even bear the sight of barber's blood; and this unstrung, sick man, is it credible that I should have imagined he meant to spill all my blood, who can't endure the sight of one little drop of his own? Surely, Amasa Delano, you have been beside yourself this day. Tell it not when you get home, sappy Amasa. Well, well, he looks like a murderer, doesn't he? More like as if himself were to be done for. Well, well, this day's experience shall be a good lesson.

Meantime, while these things were running though the honest seaman's mind, the servant had taken the napkin from his arm, and to Don Benito had said: "But answer Don Amasa, please, master, while I wipe this ugly stuff off the razor, and strop it again."

As he said the words, his face was turned half round, so as to be alike visible to the Spaniard and the American, and seemed, by its expression, to hint, that he was desirous, by getting his master to go on with the conversation, considerately to withdraw his attention from the recent annoying accident. As if glad to snatch the offered relief, Don Benito resumed, rehearsing to Captain Delano, that not only were the calms of unusual duration, but the ship had fallen in with obstinate currents; and other things he added, some of which were but repetitions of former statements, to explain how it came to pass that the passage from Cape Horn to St. Maria had been so exceedingly long; now and then mingling with his words incidental praises, less qualified than before, to the blacks, for their general good conduct. These particulars were not given consecutively, the servant, at convenient times, using his razor, and so, between the intervals of shaving, the story and panegyric[104] went on with more than usual huskiness.

To Captain Delano's imagination, now again not wholly at rest, there was something so hollow in the Spaniard's manner, with apparently some reciprocal hollowness in the servant's dusky comment of silence, that the idea flashed across him, that possibly master and man, for some unknown purpose, were acting out, both in word and deed, nay, to the very tremor of Don Benito's limbs, some juggling play before him. Neither did the suspicion of collusion lack apparent support, from the fact of those whispered conferences before mentioned. But then, what could be the object of enacting this play of the barber before him? At last, regarding the notion as a whimsy, insensibly suggested, perhaps, by the theatrical aspect of Don Benito in his harlequin ensign,[105] Captain Delano speedily banished it.

[103] James I (1566–1625) reigned as King of England from 1603 to 1625.   [104] Elaborate praise.
[105] Colored flag.

The shaving over, the servant bestirred himself with a small bottle of scented waters, pouring a few drops on the head, and then diligently rubbing; the vehemence of the exercise causing the muscles of his face to twitch rather strangely.

His next operation was with comb, scissors, and brush; going round and round, smoothing a curl here, clipping an unruly whisker-hair there, giving a graceful sweep to the temple-lock, with other impromptu touches evincing the hand of a master; while, like any resigned gentleman in barber's hands, Don Benito bore all, much less uneasily, at least, than he had done the razoring; indeed, he sat so pale and rigid now, that the Negro seemed a Nubian[106] sculptor finishing off a white statue-head.

All being over at last, the standard of Spain removed, tumbled up, and tossed back into the flag-locker, the Negro's warm breath blowing away any stray hair which might have lodged down his master's neck; collar and cravat readjusted; a speck of lint whisked off the velvet lapel; all this being done; backing off a little space, and pausing with an expression of subdued self-complacency, the servant for a moment surveyed his master, as, in toilet at least, the creature of his own tasteful hands.

Captain Delano playfully complimented him upon his achievement; at the same time congratulating Don Benito.

But neither sweet waters, nor shampooing, nor fidelity, nor sociality, delighted the Spaniard. Seeing him relapsing into forbidding gloom, and still remaining seated, Captain Delano, thinking that his presence was undesired just then, withdrew, on pretence of seeing whether, as he had prophesied, any signs of a breeze were visible.

Walking forward to the mainmast, he stood a while thinking over the scene, and not without some undefined misgivings, when he heard a noise near the cuddy, and turning, saw the Negro, his hand to his cheek. Advancing, Captain Delano perceived that the cheek was bleeding. He was about to ask the cause, when the Negro's wailing soliloquy enlightened him.

"Ah, when will master get better from his sickness; only the sour heart that sour sickness breeds made him serve Babo so; cutting Babo with the razor, because, only by accident, Babo had given master one little scratch; and for the first time in so many a day, too. Ah, ah, ah," holding his hand to his face.

Is it possible, thought Captain Delano; was it to wreak in private his Spanish spite against this poor friend of his, that Don Benito, by his sullen manner, impelled me to withdraw? Ah, this slavery breeds ugly passions in man.—Poor fellow!

He was about to speak in sympathy to the Negro, but with a timid reluctance he now re-entered the cuddy.

Presently master and man came forth; Don Benito leaning on his servant as if nothing had happened.

But a sort of love-quarrel, after all, thought Captain Delano.

He accosted Don Benito, and they slowly walked together. They had gone but a few paces, when the steward—a tall, rajah-looking[107] mulatto,[108] orientally set off with a pagoda turban formed by three or four Madras[109] handkerchiefs

---

[106] A native of Nubia in eastern Africa. [107] Resembling an Indian prince.
[108] A person of mixed black and white parentage.
[109] Brightly colored silk or cotton cloth originally produced in Madras, India.

wound about his head, tier on tier—approaching with a salaam,[110] announced lunch in the cabin.

On their way thither, the two captains were preceded by the mulatto, who, turning round as he advanced, with continual smiles and bows, ushered them on, a display of elegance which quite completed the insignificance of the small bare-headed Babo, who, as if not unconscious of inferiority, eyed askance the graceful steward. But in part, Captain Delano imputed his jealous watchfulness to that peculiar feeling which the full-blooded African entertains for the adulterated one. As for the steward, his manner, if not bespeaking much dignity of self-respect, yet evidenced his extreme desire to please; which is doubly meritorious, as at once Christian and Chesterfieldian.[111]

Captain Delano observed with interest that while the complexion of the mulatto was hybrid, his physiognomy was European—classically so.

"Don Benito," whispered he, "I am glad to see this usher-of-the-golden-rod[112] of yours; the sight refutes an ugly remark once made to me by a Barbados[113] planter; that when a mulatto has a regular European face, look out for him; he is a devil. But see, your steward here has features more regular than King George's of England;[114] and yet there he nods, and bows, and smiles; a king, indeed—the king of kind hearts and polite fellows. What a pleasant voice he has, too!"

"He has, señor."

"But tell me, has he not, so far as you have known him, always proved a good, worthy fellow?" said Captain Delano, pausing, while with a final genuflection the steward disappeared into the cabin; "come, for the reason just mentioned, I am curious to know."

"Francesco is a good man," a sort of sluggishly responded Don Benito, like a phlegmatic[115] appreciator, who would neither find fault nor flatter.

"Ah, I thought so. For it were strange, indeed, and not very creditable to us white-skins, if a little of our blood mixed with the African's should, far from improving the latter's quality, have the sad effect of pouring vitriolic acid into black broth; improving the hue, perhaps, but not the wholesomeness."

"Doubtless, doubtless, señor, but"—glancing at Babo—"not to speak of Negroes, your planter's remark I have heard applied to the Spanish and Indian intermixtures in our provinces. But I know nothing about the matter," he listlessly added.

And here they entered the cabin.

The lunch was a frugal one. Some of Captain Delano's fresh fish and pumpkins, biscuit and salt beef, the reserved bottle of cider, and the *San Dominick*'s last bottle of Canary.[116]

As they entered, Francesco, with two or three colored aids, was hovering over the table giving the last adjustments. Upon perceiving their master they withdrew, Francesco making a smiling *congé,* and the Spaniard, without condescending to notice it, fastidiously remarking to his companion that he relished not superfluous attendance.

[110] A Moslem ceremonial greeting.
[111] In the tradition of good manners and graceful deportment identified with Philip Dormer Stanhope, Lord Chesterfield (1694–1773).
[112] An attendant who ceremoniously precedes persons of rank with a rod or scepter in hand.
[113] An island in the West Indies.
[114] George III (1738–1820), the reigning British monarch.   [115] Without emotion, sluggish.
[116] Wine from the Canary Islands, a Spanish possession off the coast of Africa.

Without companions, host and guest sat down, like a childless married couple, at opposite ends of the table, Don Benito waving Captain Delano to his place, and, weak as he was, insisting upon that gentleman being seated before himself.

The Negro placed a rug under Don Benito's feet, and a cushion behind his back, and then stood behind, not his master's chair, but Captain Delano's. At first, this a little surprised the latter. But it was soon evident that, in taking his position, the black was still true to his master; since by facing him he could the more readily anticipate his slightest want.

"This is an uncommonly intelligent fellow of yours, Don Benito," whispered Captain Delano across the table.

"You say true, señor."

During the repast, the guest again reverted to parts of Don Benito's story, begging further particulars here and there. He inquired how it was that the scurvy and fever should have committed such wholesale havoc upon the whites, while destroying less than half of the blacks. As if this question reproduced the whole scene of plague before the Spaniard's eyes, miserably reminding him of his solitude in a cabin where before he had had so many friends and officers round him, his hand shook, his face became hueless, broken words escaped; but directly the sane memory of the past seemed replaced by insane terrors of the present. With starting eyes he stared before him at vacancy. For nothing was to be seen but the hand of his servant pushing the Canary over toward him. At length a few sips served partially to restore him. He made random reference to the different constitution of races, enabling one to offer more resistance to certain maladies than another. The thought was new to his companion.

Presently Captain Delano, intending to say something to his host concerning the pecuniary part of the business he had undertaken for him, especially—since he was strictly accountable to his owners—with reference to the new suit of sails, and other things of that sort; and naturally preferring to conduct such affairs in private, was desirous that the servant should withdraw; imagining that Don Benito for a few minutes could dispense with his attendance. He, however, waited a while; thinking that, as the conversation proceeded, Don Benito, without being prompted, would perceive the propriety of the step.

But it was otherwise. At last catching his host's eye, Captain Delano, with a slight backward gesture of his thumb, whispered, "Don Benito, pardon me, but there is an interference with the full expression of what I have to say to you."

Upon this the Spaniard changed countenance; which was imputed to his resenting the hint, as in some way a reflection upon his servant. After a moment's pause, he assured his guest that the black's remaining with them could be of no disservice; because since losing his officers he had made Babo (whose original office, it now appeared, had been captain of the slaves) not only his constant attendant and companion, but in all things his confidant.

After this, nothing more could be said; though, indeed, Captain Delano could hardly avoid some little tinge of irritation upon being left ungratified in so inconsiderable a wish, by one, too, for whom he intended such solid services. But it is only his querulousness, thought he; and so filling his glass he proceeded to business.

The price of the sails and other matters was fixed upon. But while this was being done, the American observed that, though his original offer of assistance had been hailed with hectic animation, yet now when it was reduced to a business transaction, indifference and apathy were betrayed. Don Benito, in fact, appeared to submit to hearing the details more out of regard to common propriety than from any impression that weighty benefit to himself and his voyage was involved.

Soon, his manner became still more reserved. The effort was vain to seek to draw him into social talk. Gnawed by his splenetic[117] mood, he sat twitching his beard, while to little purpose the hand of his servant, mute as that on the wall, slowly pushed over the Canary.

Lunch being over, they sat down on the cushioned transom;[118] the servant placing a pillow behind his master. The long continuance of the calm had now affected the atmosphere. Don Benito sighed heavily, as if for breath.

"Why not adjourn to the cuddy," said Captain Delano; "there is more air there." But the host sat silent and motionless.

Meantime his servant knelt before him, with a large fan of feathers. And Francesco, coming in on tiptoes, handed the Negro a little cup of aromatic waters, with which at intervals he chafed his master's brow; smoothing the hair along the temples as a nurse does a child's. He spoke no word. He only rested his eye on his master's, as if, amid all Don Benito's distress, a little to refresh his spirit by the silent sight of fidelity.

Presently the ship's bell sounded two o'clock; and through the cabin windows a slight rippling of the sea was discerned; and from the desired direction.

"There," exclaimed Captain Delano, "I told you so, Don Benito, look!"

He had risen to his feet, speaking in a very animated tone, with a view the more to rouse his companion. But though the crimson curtain of the stern window near him that moment fluttered against his pale cheek, Don Benito seemed to have even less welcome for the breeze than the calm.

Poor fellow, thought Captain Delano, bitter experience has taught him that one ripple does not make a wind, any more than one swallow a summer. But he is mistaken for once. I will get his ship in for him, and prove it.

Briefly alluding to his weak condition, he urged his host to remain quietly where he was, since he (Captain Delano) would with pleasure take upon himself the responsibility of making the best use of the wind.

Upon gaining the deck, Captain Delano started at the unexpected figure of Atufal, monumentally fixed at the threshold, like one of those sculptured porters of black marble guarding the porches of Egyptian tombs.

But this time the start was, perhaps, purely physical. Atufal's presence, singularly attesting docility even in sullenness, was contrasted with that of the hatchet-polishers, who in patience evinced their industry; while both spectacles showed, that lax as Don Benito's general authority might be, still, whenever he chose to exert it, no man so savage or colossal but must, more or less, bow.

Snatching a trumpet which hung from the bulwarks, with a free step Captain Delano advanced to the forward edge of the poop, issuing his orders in his best Spanish. The few sailors and many negroes, all equally pleased, obediently set about heading the ship toward the harbour.

While giving some directions about setting a lower stun'-sail,[119] suddenly Captain Delano heard a voice faithfully repeating his orders. Turning, he saw Babo, now for the time acting, under the pilot, his original part of captain of the slaves. This assistance proved valuable. Tattered sails and warped yards

---

[117] Ill-humored, irritable.   [118] A ship's crossbeam.   [119] Sail used in fair weather.

were soon brought into some trim. And no brace or halyard was pulled but to the blithe songs of the inspired Negroes.

Good fellows, thought Captain Delano, a little training would make fine sailors of them. Why, see, the very women pull and sing too. These must be some of those Ashantee Negresses that make such capital soldiers, I've heard. But who's at the helm? I must have a good hand there.

He went to see.

The *San Dominick* steered with a cumbrous tiller, with large horizontal pulleys attached. At each pulley-end stood a subordinate black, and between them, at the tiller-head, the responsible post, a Spanish seaman, whose countenance evinced his due share in the general hopefulness and confidence at the coming of the breeze.

He proved the same man who had behaved with so shamefaced an air on the windlass.

"Ah—it is you, my man," exclaimed Captain Delano—"well, no more sheep's-eyes now;—look straight forward and keep the ship so. Good hand, I trust? And want to get into the harbour, don't you?"

The man assented with an inward chuckle, grasping the tiller-head firmly. Upon this, unperceived by the American, the two blacks eyed the sailor intently.

Finding all right at the helm, the pilot went forward to the forecastle,[120] to see how matters stood there.

The ship now had way enough to breast the current. With the approach of evening, the breeze would be sure to freshen.

Having done all that was needed for the present, Captain Delano, giving his last orders to the sailors, turned aft to report affairs to Don Benito in the cabin; perhaps additionally incited to rejoin him by the hope of snatching a moment's private chat while the servant was engaged upon deck.

From opposite sides, there were, beneath the poop, two approaches to the cabin; one further forward than the other, and consequently communicating with a longer passage. Marking the servant still above, Captain Delano, taking the nighest entrance—the one last named, and at whose porch Atufal still stood—hurried on his way, till, arrived at the cabin threshold, he paused an instant, a little to recover from his eagerness. Then, with the words of his intended business upon his lips, he entered. As he advanced toward the seated Spaniard, he heard another footstep, keeping time with his. From the opposite door, a salver in hand, the servant was likewise advancing.

"Confound the faithful fellow," thought Captain Delano; "what a vexatious coincidence."

Possibly the vexation might have been something different, were it not for the brisk confidence inspired by the breeze. But even as it was, he felt a slight twinge, from a sudden indefinite association in his mind of Babo with Atufal.

"Don Benito," said he "I give you joy; the breeze will hold, and will increase. By the way, your tall man and time-piece, Atufal, stands without. By your order, of course?"

Don Benito recoiled, as if at some bland satirical touch, delivered with such adroit garnish of apparent good breeding as to present no handle for retort.

He is like one flayed alive, thought Captain Delano; where may one touch him without causing a shrink?

---

[120] The crew's quarters toward the bow.

The servant moved before his master, adjusting a cushion; recalled to civility, the Spaniard stiffly replied: "You are right. The slave appears where you saw him, according to my command; which is, that if at the given hour I am below, he must take his stand and abide my coming."

"Ah now, pardon me, but that is treating the poor fellow like an ex-king indeed. Ah, Don Benito," smiling, "for all the licence you permit in some things, I fear lest, at bottom, you are a bitter hard master."

Again Don Benito shrank; and this time, as the good sailor thought, from a genuine twinge of his conscience.

Again conversation became constrained. In vain Captain Delano called attention to the now perceptible motion of the keel gently cleaving the sea; with lack-lustre eyes, Don Benito returned words few and reserved.

By and by, the wind having steadily risen, and still blowing right into the harbour, bore the *San Dominick* swiftly on. Rounding a point of land, the sealer at distance came into open view.

Meantime Captain Delano had again repaired to the deck, remaining there some time. Having at last altered the ship's course, so as to give the reef a wide berth, he returned for a few moments below.

I will cheer up my poor friend this time, thought he.

"Better and better, Don Benito," he cried as he blithely re-entered: "there will soon be an end to your cares, at least for a while. For when, after a long, sad voyage, you know, the anchor drops into the haven, all its vast weight seems lifted from the captain's heart. We are getting on famously, Don Benito. My ship is in sight. Look through this side-light here; there she is; all a-taunt-o![121] The *Bachelor's Delight*, my good friend. Ah, how this wind braces one up. Come, you must take a cup of coffee with me this evening. My old steward will give you as fine a cup as ever any sultan tasted. What say you, Don Benito, will you?"

At first, the Spaniard glanced feverishly up, casting a longing look toward the sealer, while with mute concern his servant gazed into his face. Suddenly the old ague and coldness returned, and dropping back to his cushions he was silent.

"You do not answer. Come, all day you have been my host; would you have hospitality all on one side?"

"I cannot go," was the response.

"What? it will not fatigue you. The ships will lie together as near as they can, without swinging foul. It will be little more than stepping from deck to deck; which is but as from room to room. Come, come, you must not refuse me."

"I cannot go," decisively and repulsively repeated Don Benito.

Renouncing all but the last appearance of courtesy, with a sort of cadaverous sullenness, and biting his thin nails to the quick, he glanced, almost glared, at his guest, as if impatient that a stranger's presence should interfere with the full indulgence of his morbid hour. Meantime the sound of the parted waters came more and more gurglingly and merrily in at the windows; as reproaching him for his dark spleen; as telling him that, sulk as he might, and go mad with it, nature cared not a jot; since, whose fault was it, pray?

But the foul mood was now at its depth, as the fair wind at its height.

There was something in the man so far beyond any mere unsociality or

[121] Fully rigged.

sourness previously evinced, that even the forbearing good-nature of his guest could no longer endure it. Wholly at a loss to account for such demeanour, and deeming sickness with eccentricity, however extreme, no adequate excuse, well satisfied, too, that nothing in his own conduct could justify it, Captain Delano's pride began to be roused. Himself became reserved. But all seemed one to the Spaniard. Quitting him, therefore, Captain Delano once more went to the deck.

The ship was now within less than two miles of the sealer. The whale-boat was seen darting over the interval.

To be brief, the two vessels, thanks to the pilot's skill, ere long in neighbourly style lay anchored together.

Before returning to his own vessel, Captain Delano had intended communicating to Don Benito the smaller details of the proposed services to be rendered. But, as it was, unwilling anew to subject himself to rebuffs, he resolved, now that he had seen the *San Dominick* safely moored, immediately to quit her, without further allusion to hospitality or business. Indefinitely postponing his ulterior plans, he would regulate his future actions according to future circumstances. His boat was ready to receive him; but his host still tarried below. Well, thought Captain Delano, if he has little breeding, the more need to show mine. He descended to the cabin to bid a ceremonious, and, it may be, tacitly rebukeful adieu. But to his great satisfaction, Don Benito, as if he began to feel the weight of that treatment with which his slighted guest had, not indecorously, retaliated upon him, now supported by his servant, rose to his feet, and grasping Captain Delano's hand, stood tremulous; too much agitated to speak. But the good augury hence drawn was suddenly dashed, by his resuming all his previous reserve, with augmented gloom, as, with half-averted eyes, he silently reseated himself on his cushions. With a corresponding return of his own chilled feelings, Captain Delano bowed and withdrew.

He was hardly midway in the narrow corridor, dim as a tunnel, leading from the cabin to the stairs, when a sound, as of the tolling for execution in some jail-yard, fell on his ears. It was the echo of the ship's flawed bell, striking the hour, drearily reverberated in this subterranean vault. Instantly, by a fatality not to be withstood, his mind, responsive to the portent, swarmed with superstitious suspicions. He paused. In images far swifter than these sentences, the minutest details of all his former distrusts swept through him.

Hitherto, credulous good-nature had been too ready to furnish excuses for reasonable fears. Why was the Spaniard, so superfluously punctilious at times, now heedless of common propriety in not accompanying to the side his departing guest? Did indisposition forbid? Indisposition had not forbidden more irksome exertion that day. His last equivocal demeanour recurred. He had risen to his feet, grasped his guest's hand, motioned toward his hat; then, in an instant, all was eclipsed in sinister muteness and gloom. Did this imply one brief, repentant relenting at the final moment, from some iniquitous plot, followed by remorseless return to it? His last glance seemed to express a calamitous, yet acquiescent farewell to Captain Delano forever. Why decline the invitation to visit the sealer that evening? Or was the Spaniard less hardened than the Jew, who refrained not from supping at the board of him whom the same night he meant to betray?[122] What imported all those day-long enigmas and contradictions, except they were intended to mystify, preliminary to some

---

[122] An allusion to Judas Iscariot, who ate with Jesus before betraying Him to Roman authorities.

stealthy blow? Atufal, the pretended rebel, but punctual shadow, that moment lurked by the threshold without. He seemed a sentry, and more. Who, by his own confession, had stationed him there? Was the Negro now lying in wait?

The Spaniard behind—his creature before: to rush from darkness to light was the involuntary choice.

The next moment, with clenched jaw and hand, he passed Atufal, and stood unharmed in the light. As he saw his trim ship lying peacefully at anchor, and almost within ordinary call; as he saw his household boat, with familiar faces in it, patiently rising and falling on the short waves by the *San Dominick*'s side; and then, glancing about the decks where he stood, saw the oakum-pickers still gravely plying their fingers; and heard the low, buzzing whistle and industrious hum of the hatchet-polishers, still bestirring themselves over their endless occupation; and more than all, as he saw the benign aspect of nature, taking her innocent repose in the evening; the screened sun in the quiet camp of the west shining out like the mild light from Abraham's[123] tent; as charmed eye and ear took in all these, with the chained figure of the black, clenched jaw and hand relaxed. Once again he smiled at the phantoms which had mocked him, and felt something like a tinge of remorse, that, by harbouring them even for a moment, he should, by implication, have betrayed an atheist doubt of the ever-watchful Providence above.

There was a few minutes' delay, while, in obedience to his orders, the boat was being hooked along to the gangway. During this interval, a sort of saddened satisfaction stole over Captain Delano, at thinking of the kindly offices he had that day discharged for a stranger. Ah, thought he, after good actions one's conscience is never ungrateful, however much so the benefited party may be.

Presently, his foot, in the first act of descent into the boat, pressed the first round of the side-ladder, his face presented inward upon the deck. In the same moment, he heard his name courteously sounded; and, to his pleased surprise, saw Don Benito advancing—an unwonted energy in his air, as if, at the last moment, intent upon making amends for his recent discourtesy. With instinctive good feeling, Captain Delano, withdrawing his foot, turned and reciprocally advanced. As he did so, the Spaniard's nervous eagerness increased, but his vital energy failed; so that, the better to support him, the servant, placing his master's hand on his naked shoulder, and gently holding it there, formed himself into a sort of crutch.

When the two captains met, the Spaniard again fervently took the hand of the American, at the same time casting an earnest glance into his eyes, but, as before, too much overcome to speak.

I have done him wrong, self-reproachfully thought Captain Delano; his apparent coldness has deceived me; in no instance has he meant to offend.

Meantime, as if fearful that the continuance of the scene might too much unstring his master, the servant seemed anxious to terminate it. And so, still presenting himself as a crutch, and walking between the two captains, he advanced with them toward the gangway; while still, as if full of kindly contrition, Don Benito would not let go the hand of Captain Delano, but retained it in his, across the black's body.

Soon they were standing by the side, looking over into the boat, whose crew turned up their curious eyes. Waiting a moment for the Spaniard to

[123] The Old Testament patriarch of Genesis.

relinquish his hold, the now embarrassed Captain Delano lifted his foot, to overstep the threshold of the open gangway; but still Don Benito would not let go his hand. And yet, with an agitated tone, he said, "I can go no further; here I must bid you adieu. Adieu, my dear, dear Don Amasa. Go-go!" suddenly tearing his hand loose, "go, and God guard you better than me, my best friend."

Not unaffected, Captain Delano would now have lingered; but catching the meekly admonitory eye of the servant, with a hasty farewell he descended into his boat, followed by the continual adieus of Don Benito, standing rooted in the gangway.

Seating himself in the stern, Captain Delano, making a last salute, ordered the boat shoved off. The crew had their oars on end. The bowsmen pushed the boat a sufficient distance for the oars to be lengthwise dropped. The instant that was done, Don Benito sprang over the bulwarks, falling at the feet of Captain Delano; at the same time calling toward his ship, but in tones so frenzied, that none in the boat could understand him. But, as if not equally obtuse, three sailors, from three different and distant parts of the ship, splashed into the sea, swimming after their captain, as if intent upon his rescue.

The dismayed officer of the boat eagerly asked what this meant. To which, Captain Delano, turning a disdainful smile upon the unaccountable Spaniard, answered that, for his part, he neither knew nor cared; but it seemed as if Don Benito had taken it into his head to produce the impression among his people that the boat wanted to kidnap him. "Or else—give way for your lives," he wildly added, starting at a clattering hubbub in the ship, above which rang the tocsin[124] of the hatchet-polishers; and seizing Don Benito by the throat he added, "this plotting pirate means murder!" Here, in apparent verification of the words, the servant, a dagger in his hand, was seen on the rail overhead, poised, in the act of leaping, as if with desperate fidelity to befriend his master to the last; while, seemingly to aid the black, the three white sailors were trying to clamber into the hampered bow. Meantime, the whole host of negroes, as if inflamed at the sight of their jeopardised captain, impended in one sooty avalanche over the bulwarks.

All this, with what preceded, and what followed, occurred with such involutions of rapidity, that past, present, and future seemed one.

Seeing the Negro coming, Captain Delano had flung the Spaniard aside, almost in the very act of clutching him, and, by the unconscious recoil, shifting his place, with arms thrown up, so promptly grappled the servant in his descent, that with dagger presented at Captain Delano's heart, the black seemed of purpose to have leaped there as to his mark. But the weapon was wrenched away, and the assailant dashed down into the bottom of the boat, which now, with disentangled oars, began to speed through the sea.

At this juncture, the left hand of Captain Delano, on one side, again clutched the half-reclined Don Benito, heedless that he was in a speechless faint, while his right foot, on the other side, ground the prostrate Negro; and his right arm pressed for added speed on the after-oar, his eye bent forward, encouraging his men to their utmost.

But here, the officer of the boat, who had at last succeeded in beating off the towing sailors, and was now, with face turned aft, assisting the bowsman at his oar, suddenly called to Captain Delano, to see what the black was about;

[124] Alarm.

while a Portuguese oarsman shouted to him to give heed to what the Spaniard was saying.

Glancing down at his feet, Captain Delano saw the freed hand of the servant aiming with a second dagger—a small one, before concealed in his wool—with this he was snakishly writhing up from the boat's bottom, at the heart of his master, his countenance lividly vindictive, expressing the centred purpose of his soul; while the Spaniard, half choked, was vainly shrinking away, with husky words, incoherent to all but the Portuguese.

That moment, across the long-benighted mind of Captain Delano, a flash of revelation swept, illuminating, in unanticipated clearness, his host's whole mysterious demeanour, with every enigmatic event of the day, as well as the entire past voyage of the *San Dominick.* He smote Babo's hand down, but his own heart smote him harder. With infinite pity he withdrew his hold from Don Benito. Not Captain Delano, but Don Benito, the black, in leaping into the boat, had intended to stab.

Both the black's hands were held, as, glancing up toward the *San Dominick,* Captain Delano, now with scales dropped from his eyes, saw the Negroes, not in misrule, not in tumult, not as if frantically concerned for Don Benito, but with mask torn away, flourishing hatchets and knives, in ferocious piratical revolt. Like delirious black dervishes,[125] the six Ashantees danced on the poop. Prevented by their foes from springing into the water, the Spanish boys were hurrying up to the topmost spars, while such of the few Spanish sailors, not already in the sea, less alert, were descried; helplessly mixed in, on deck, with the blacks.

Meantime Captain Delano hailed his own vessel, ordering the ports up, and the guns run out. But by this time the cable of the *San Dominick* had been cut; and the fag-end, in lashing out, whipped away the canvas shroud about the beak, suddenly revealing, as the bleached hull swung round toward the open ocean, death for the figure-head, in a human skeleton; chalky comment on the chalked words below, *"Follow your leader."*

At the sight, Don Benito, covering his face, wailed out: "Tis he, Aranda! my murdered, unburied friend!"

Upon reaching the sealer, calling for ropes, Captain Delano bound the Negro, who made no resistance, and had him hoisted to the deck. He would then have assisted the now almost helpless Don Benito up the side; but Don Benito, wan as he was, refused to move, or be moved, until the Negro should have been first put below out of view. When, presently assured that it was done, he no more shrank from the ascent.

The boat was immediately dispatched back to pick up the three swimming sailors. Meantime, the guns were in readiness, though, owing to the *San Dominick* having glided somewhat astern of the sealer, only the aftermost one could be brought to bear. With this, they fired six times; thinking to cripple the fugitive ship by bringing down her spars. But only a few inconsiderable ropes were shot away. Soon the ship was beyond the gun's range, steering broad out of the bay; the blacks thickly clustering round the bowsprit, one moment with taunting cries toward the whites, the next with upthrown gestures hailing the now dusky moors of ocean—cawing crows escaped from the hand of the fowler.

[125] Moslem holymen noted for their whirling dances.

The first impulse was to slip the cables and give chase. But, upon second thoughts, to pursue with whale-boat and yawl seemed more promising.

Upon inquiring of Don Benito what firearms they had on board the *San Dominick*, Captain Delano was answered that they had none that could be used; because, in the earlier stages of the mutiny, a cabin passenger, since dead, had secretly put out of order the locks of what few muskets there were. But with all his remaining strength, Don Benito entreated the American not to give chase, either with ship or boat; for the Negroes had already proved themselves such desperadoes, that, in case of a present assault, nothing but a total massacre of the whites could be looked for. But, regarding this warning as coming from one whose spirit had been crushed by misery, the American did not give up his design.

The boats were got ready and armed. Captain Delano ordered his men into them. He was going himself when Don Benito grasped his arm.

"What! have you saved my life, señor, and are you now going to throw away your own?"

The officers also, for reasons connected with their interests and those of the voyage, and a duty owing to the owners, strongly objected against their commander's going. Weighing their remonstrances a moment, Captain Delano felt bound to remain; appointing his chief mate—an athletic and resolute man, who had been a privateer's-man—to head the party. The more to encourage the sailors, they were told, that the Spanish captain considered his ship good as lost; that she and her cargo, including some gold and silver, were worth more than a thousand doubloons. Take her, and no small part should be theirs. The sailors replied with a shout.

The fugitives had now almost gained an offing.[126] It was nearly night; but the moon was rising. After hard, prolonged pulling, the boats came up on the ship's quarters, at a suitable distance laying upon their oars to discharge their muskets. Having no bullets to return, the Negroes sent their yells. But, upon the second volley, Indian-like, they hurtled their hatchets. One took off a sailor's fingers. Another struck the whale-boat's bow, cutting off the rope there, and remaining stuck in the gunwale like a woodman's axe. Snatching it, quivering from its lodgment, the mate hurled it back. The returned gauntlet now stuck in the ship's broken quarter-gallery, and so remained.

The Negroes giving too hot a reception, the whites kept a more respectful distance. Hovering now just out of reach of the hurtling hatchets, they, with a view to the close encounter which must soon come, sought to decoy the blacks into entirely disarming themselves of their most murderous weapons in a hand-to-hand fight, by foolishly flinging them, as missiles, short of the mark, into the sea. But, ere long, perceiving the stratagem, the Negroes desisted, though not before many of them had to replace their lost hatchets with handspikes; an exchange which, as counted upon, proved, in the end, favourable to the assailants.

Meantime, with a strong wind, the ship still clove the water; the boats alternately falling behind, and pulling up, to discharge fresh volleys.

The fire was mostly directed toward the stern, since there, chiefly, the Negroes, at present, were clustering. But to kill or maim the Negroes was not the object. To take them, with the ship, was the object. To do it, the ship

---

[126] Deep water.

must be boarded; which could not be done by boats while she was sailing so fast.

A thought now struck the mate. Observing the Spanish boys still aloft, high as they could get, he called to them to descend to the yards, and cut adrift the sails. It was done. About this time, owing to causes hereafter to be shown, two Spaniards, in the dress of sailors, and conspicuously showing themselves, were killed; not by volleys, but by deliberate marksman's shots; while, as it afterward appeared, by one of the general discharges, Atufal, the black, and the Spaniard at the helm likewise were killed. What now with the loss of the sails, and loss of leaders, the ship became unmanageable to the Negroes.

With creaking masts, she came heavily round to the wind; the prow slowly swinging into view of the boats, its skeleton gleaming in the horizontal moonlight, and casting a gigantic ribbed shadow upon the water. One extended arm of the ghost seemed beckoning the whites to avenge it.

"Follow your leader!" cried the mate; and, one on each bow, the boats boarded. Sealing-spears and cutlasses crossed hatchets and handspikes. Huddled upon the long-boat amidships, the Negresses raised a wailing chant, whose chorus was the clash of the steel.

For a time, the attack wavered; the Negroes wedging themselves to beat it back; the half-repelled sailors, as yet unable to gain a footing, fighting as troopers in the saddle, one leg sideways flung over the bulwarks, and one without, plying their cutlasses like carters' whips. But in vain. They were almost overborne, when, rallying themselves into a squad as one man, with a huzza, they sprang inboard, where, entangled, they involuntarily separated again. For a few breaths' space, there was a vague, muffled, inner sound, as of submerged sword-fish rushing hither and thither through shoals of black-fish. Soon, in a reunited band, and joined by the Spanish seamen, the whites came to the surface, irresistibly driving the Negroes toward the stern. But a barricade of casks and sacks, from side to side, had been thrown up by the mainmast. Here the Negroes faced about, and though scorning peace or truce, yet fain would have had respite. But, without pause, overleaping the barrier, the unflagging sailors again closed. Exhausted, the blacks now fought in despair. Their red tongues lolled, wolf-like, from their black mouths. But the pale sailors' teeth were set; not a word was spoken; and, in five minutes more, the ship was won.

Nearly a score of the Negroes were killed. Exclusive of those by the balls, many were mangled; their wounds—mostly inflicted by the long-edged sealing-spears[127]—resembling those shaven ones of the English at Prestonpans,[128] made by the poled scythes[129] of the Highlanders. On the other side, none were killed, though several were wounded; some severely, including the mate. The surviving Negroes were temporarily secured, and the ship, towed back into the harbour at midnight, once more lay anchored.

Omitting the incidents and arrangements ensuing, suffice it that, after two days spent in refitting, the ships sailed in company for Concepcion, in Chile, and thence for Lima, in Peru; where, before the vice-regal courts, the whole affair, from the beginning, underwent investigation.

[127] Spears used in the killing of seals.
[128] Site in Scotland of Bonnie Prince Charlie's victory over the English in the short–lived uprising of 1745.
[129] Poles with scythes fastened to their tops.

Though, midway on the passage, the ill-fated Spaniard, relaxed from constraint, showed some signs of regaining health with free-will; yet, agreeably to his own foreboding, shortly before arriving at Lima, he relapsed, finally becoming so reduced as to be carried ashore in arms. Hearing of his story and plight, one of the many religious institutions of the City of Kings opened an hospitable refuge to him, where both physician and priest were his nurses, and a member of the order volunteered to be his one special guardian and consoler, by night and by day.

The following extracts, translated from one of the official Spanish documents, will, it is hoped, shed light on the preceding narrative, as well as, in the first place, reveal the true port of departure and true history of the *San Dominick's* voyage, down to the time of her touching at the island of St. Maria.

But, ere the extracts come, it may be well to preface them with a remark.

The document selected, from among many others, for partial translation, contains the deposition of Benito Cereno; the first taken in the case. Some disclosures therein were, at the time, held dubious for both learned and natural reasons. The tribunal inclined to the opinion that the deponent, not undisturbed in his mind by recent events, raved of some things which could never have happened. But subsequent depositions of the surviving sailors, bearing out the revelations of their captain in several of the strangest particulars, gave credence to the rest. So that the tribunal, in its final decision, rested its capital sentences upon statements which, had they lacked confirmation, it would have deemed it but duty to reject.

I, DON JOSÉ DE ABOS AND PADILLA, His Majesty's Notary for the Royal Revenue, and Register of this Province, and Notary Public of the Holy Crusade of this Bishopric, etc.

Do certify and declare, as much as is requisite in law, that, in the criminal cause commenced the twenty-fourth of the month of September, in the year seventeen hundred and ninety-nine, against the Negroes of the ship *San Dominick,* the following declaration before me was made:—

Declaration of the first witness, DON BENITO CERENO.

The same day, and month, and year, His Honour, Doctor Juan Martinez de Rozas, Councillor of the Royal Audience of this Kingdom, and learned in the law of this Intendency,[130] ordered the captain of the ship *San Dominick,* Don Benito Cereno, to appear; which he did in his litter,[131] attended by the monk Infelez; of whom he received the oath, which he took by God, our Lord, and a sign of the Cross; under which he promised to tell the truth of whatever he should know and should be asked;—and being interrogated agreeably to the tenor of the act commencing the process, he said, that on the twentieth of May last, he set sail with his ship from the port of Valparaiso,[132] bound to that of Callao;[133] loaded with the produce of the country besides thirty cases of hardware and one hundred and sixty blacks, of both sexes, mostly belonging to Don Alexandro Aranda, gentleman, of the city of Mendoza;[134] that the crew of the ship consisted of thirty-six men, besides the persons who went as passengers; that the Negroes were in part as follows:—

[130] A district in Spanish America under the charge or direction of an official called an intendent.
[131] Stretcher.   [132] A seaport in Chile.   [133] The principal seaport of Peru.
[134] A city in west-central Argentina.

[*Here, in the original, follows a list of some fifty names, descriptions, and ages, compiled from certain recovered documents of Aranda's, and also from recollections of the deponent, from which portions only are extracted.*][135]

—One, from about eighteen to nineteen years, named José, and this was the man that waited upon his master, Don Alexandro, and who speaks well the Spanish, having served him four or five years; * * * a mulatto, named Francesco, the cabin steward, of a good person and voice, having sung in the Valparaiso churches, native of the province of Buenos Aires, aged about thirty-five years. * * * A smart Negro, named Dago, who had been for many years a gravedigger among the Spaniards, aged forty-six years. * * * Four old Negroes, born in Africa, from sixty to seventy, but sound, caulkers by trade, whose names are as follows:—the first was named Muri, and he was killed (as was also his son named Diamelo); the second, Nacta; the third, Yola, likewise killed; the fourth, Ghofan; and six full-grown Negroes, aged from thirty to forty-five, all raw, and born among the Ashantees—Matiluqui, Yan, Lecbe, Mapenda, Yambaio, Akim; four of whom were killed; * * * a powerful Negro named Atufal, who being supposed to have been a chief in Africa, his owner set great store by him. * * * And a small Negro of Senegal,[136] but some years among the Spaniards, aged about thirty, which Negro's name was Babo; * * * that he does not remember the names of the others, but that still expecting the residue of Don Alexandro's papers will be found, will then take due account of them all, and remit to the court; * * * and thirty-nine women and children of all ages.

[*The catalogue over, the deposition goes on:*]

* * * That all the Negroes slept upon deck, as is customary in this navigation, and none wore fetters, because the owner, his friend Aranda, told him that they were all tractable; * * * that on the seventh day after leaving port, at three o'clock in the morning, all the Spaniards being asleep except the two officers on the watch, who were the boatswain,[137] Juan Robles, and the carpenter, Juan Bautista Gayete, and the helmsman and his boy, the Negroes revolted suddenly, wounded dangerously the boatswain and the carpenter, and successively killed eighteen men of those who were sleeping upon deck, some with handspikes and hatchets, and others by throwing them alive overboard, after tying them; that of the Spaniards upon deck, they left about seven, as he thinks, alive and tied, to maneuvre the ship, and three or four more, who hid themselves, remained also alive. Although in the act of revolt the Negroes made themselves masters of the hatchway, six or seven wounded went through it to the cockpit;[138] without any hindrance on their part; that during the act of revolt, the mate and another person, whose name he does not recollect, attempted to come up through the hatchway, but being quickly wounded, were obliged to return to the cabin; that the deponent resolved at break of day to come up the companion-way, where the Negro Babo was, being the ringleader, and Atufal, who assisted him, and having spoken to them, exhorted them to cease committing such atrocities, asking them, at the same time, what they wanted and intended to do, offering, himself, to obey their commands; that notwithstanding this, they threw, in his presence, three men, alive and tied,

---

[135] The brackets and editorial marks are Melville's own.
[136] At the time of the story a province of French West Africa.
[137] A petty officer in charge of a ship's deck crew.   [138] Quarters for a ship's junior officers.

overboard; that they told the deponent to come up, and that they would not kill him; which having done, the Negro Babo asked him whether there were in these seas any Negro countries where they might be carried, and he answered them, No; that the Negro Babo afterward told him to carry them to Senegal, or to the neighbouring islands of St. Nicholas; and he answered, that this was impossible, on account of the great distance, the necessity involved of rounding Cape Horn, the bad condition of the vessel, the want of provisions, sails, and water; but that the Negro Babo replied to him he must carry them in any way; that they would do and conform themselves to everything the deponent should require as to eating and drinking; that after a long conference, being absolutely compelled to please them, for they threatened to kill all the whites if they were not, at all events, carried to Senegal, he told them that what was most wanting for the voyage was water; that they would go near the coast to take it, and thence they would proceed on their course; that the Negro Babo agreed to it; and the deponent steered toward the intermediate ports, hoping to meet some Spanish or foreign vessel that would save them; that within ten or eleven days they saw the land, and continued their course by it in the vicinity of Nasca,[139] that the deponent observed that the Negroes were now restless and mutinous, because he did not effect the taking in of water, the Negro Babo having required, with threats, that it should be done, without fail, the following day; he told him he saw plainly that the coast was steep, and the rivers designated in the maps were not to be found, with other reasons suitable to the circumstances; that the best way would be to go to the island of Santa Maria, where they might water easily, it being a solitary island, as the foreigners did; that the deponent did not go to Pisco,[140] that was near, nor make any other port of the coast, because the Negro Babo had intimated to him several times, that he would kill all the whites the very moment he should perceive any city, town, or settlement of any kind on the shores to which they should be carried: that having determined to go to the island of Santa Maria, as the deponent had planned, for the purpose of trying whether, on the passage or near the island itself, they could find any vessel that should favour them, or whether he could escape from it in a boat to the neighboring coast of Arruco,[141] to adopt the necessary means he immediately changed his course, steering for the island; that the Negroes Babo and Atufal held daily conferences, in which they discussed what was necessary for their design of returning to Senegal, whether they were to kill all the Spaniards, and particularly the deponent; that eight days after parting with the coast of Nasca, the deponent being on the watch a little after daybreak, and soon after the Negroes had their meeting, the Negro Babo came to the place where the deponent was, and told him that he had determined to kill his master, Don Alexandro Aranda, both because he and his companions could not otherwise be sure of their liberty, and that to keep the seamen in subjection, he wanted to prepare a warning of what road they should be made to take did they or any of them oppose him; and that, by means of the death of Don Alexandro, that warning would best be given; but, that what this last meant, the deponent did not at the time comprehend, nor could not, further than that the death of Don Alexandro was intended; and moreover the Negro Babo proposed to the deponent to call the mate Raneds, who was sleeping in the cabin, before the thing was done, for fear, as the deponent understood it, that the mate,

---

[139] A city in Peru.　　[140] A seaport town in Peru.　　[141] Arauco: a town in west-central Chile.

who was a good navigator, should be killed with Don Alexandro and the rest; that the deponent, who was the friend, from youth, of Don Alexandro, prayed and conjured, but all was useless; for the Negro Babo answered him that the thing could not be prevented, and that all the Spaniards risked their death if they should attempt to frustrate his will in this matter, or any other; that, in this conflict, the deponent called the mate, Raneds, who was forced to go apart, and immediately the Negro Babo commanded the Ashantee Matiluqui and the Ashantee Lecbe to go and commit the murder; that those two went down with hatchets to the berth of Don Alexandro; that, yet half alive and mangled, they dragged him on deck; that they were going to throw him overboard in that state, but the Negro Babo stopped them, bidding the murder be completed on the deck before him, which was done, when, by his orders, the body was carried below, forward; that nothing more was seen of it by the deponent for three days; * * * that Don Alonzo Sidonia, an old man, long resident at Valparaiso, and lately appointed to a civil office in Peru, whither he had taken passage, was at the time sleeping in the berth opposite Don Alexandro's; that awakening at his cries, surprised by them, and at the sight of the Negroes with their bloody hatchets in their hands, he threw himself into the sea through a window which was near him, and was drowned, without it being in the power of the deponent to assist or take him up; * * * that a short time after killing Aranda, they brought upon deck his german-cousin, of middle-age, Don Francisco Masa, of Mendoza, and the young Don Joaquin, Marques de Aramboalaza, then lately from Spain, with his Spanish servant Ponce, and the three young clerks of Aranda, José Mozairi, Lorenzo Bargas, and Hermenegildo Gandix, all of Cadiz; that Don Joaquin and Hermenegildo Gandix, the Negro Babo, for purposes hereafter to appear, preserved alive; but Don Francisco Masa José Mozairi, and Lorenzo Bargas, with Ponce the servant, besides the boatswain, Juan Robles, the boatswain's mates, Manual Viscaya and Roderigo Hurta, and four of the sailors, the Negro Babo ordered to be thrown alive into the sea, although they made no resistance, nor begged for anything else but mercy; that the boatswain, Juan Robles, who knew how to swim, kept the longest above water, making acts of contrition, and, in the last words he uttered, charged this deponent to cause mass to be said for his soul to our Lady of Succour: * * * that, during the three days which followed, the deponent, uncertain what fate had befallen the remains of Don Alexandro, frequently asked the Negro Babo where they were, and, if still on board, whether they were to be preserved for interment ashore, entreating him so to order it; that the Negro Babo answered nothing till the fourth day, when at sunrise, the deponent coming on deck, the Negro Babo showed him a skeleton, which had been substituted for the ship's proper figure-head—the image of Christopher Colon,[142] the discoverer of the New World; that the Negro Babo asked him whose skeleton that was, and whether, from its whiteness, he should not think it a white's; that, upon discovering his face, the Negro Babo, coming close, said words to this effect: "Keep faith with the blacks from here to Senegal, or you shall in spirit, as now in body, follow your leader," pointing to the prow; * * * that the same morning the Negro Babo took by succession each Spaniard forward, and asked him whose skeleton that was, and whether, from its whiteness, he should not think it a white's; that each Spaniard covered his face; that then to each the Negro Babo repeated the words in the first

[142] Christopher Columbus.

place said to the deponent; * * * that they (the Spaniards), being then assembled aft, the Negro Babo harangued them, saying that he had now done all; that the deponent (as navigator for the Negroes) might pursue his course, warning him and all of them that they should, soul and body, go the way of Don Alexandro, if he saw them (the Spaniards) speak or plot anything against them (the Negroes)—a threat which was repeated every day; that, before the events last mentioned, they had tied the cook to throw him overboard, for it is not known what thing they heard him speak, but finally the Negro Babo spared his life, at the request of the deponent; that a few days after, the deponent, endeavouring not to omit any means to preserve the lives of the remaining whites, spoke to the Negroes peace and tranquillity, and agreed to draw up a paper, signed by the deponent and the sailors who could write, as also by the Negro Babo, for himself and all the blacks, in which the deponent obliged himself to carry them to Senegal, and they not to kill any more, and he formally to make over to them the ship, with the cargo, with which they were for that time satisfied and quieted. * * * But the next day, the more surely to guard against the sailors' escape, the Negro Babo commanded all the boats to be destroyed but the long-boat, which was unseaworthy, and another, a cutter in good condition, which knowing it would yet be wanted for towing the water-casks, he had it lowered down into the hold.

[*Various particulars of the prolonged and perplexed navigation ensuing here follow, with incidents of a calamitous calm, from which portion one passage is extracted, to wit:*]

—That on the fifth day of the calm, all on board suffering much from the heat, and want of water, and five having died in fits, and mad, the Negroes became irritable, and for a chance gesture, which they deemed suspicious— though it was harmless—made by the mate, Raneds, to the deponent in the act of handing a quadrant,[143] they killed him; but that for this they afterward were sorry, the mate being the only remaining navigator on board, except the deponent.

—That omitting other events, which daily happened, and which can only serve uselessly to recall past misfortunes and conflicts, after seventy-three days' navigation, reckoned from the time they sailed from Nasca, during which they navigated under a scanty allowance of water, and were afflicted with the calms beforementioned, they at last arrived at the island of Santa Maria, on the seventeenth of the month of August, at about six o'clock in the afternoon, at which hour they cast anchor very near the American ship, *Bachelor's Delight,* which lay in the same bay, commanded by the generous Captain Amasa Delano; but at six o'clock in the morning, they had already descried the port, and the Negroes became uneasy, as soon as at distance they saw the ship, not having expected to see one there; that the Negro Babo pacified them, assuring them that no fear need be had; that straightway he ordered the figure on the bow to be covered with canvas, as for repairs, and had the decks a little set in order; that for a time the Negro Babo and the Negro Atufal conferred; that the Negro Atufal was for sailing away, but the Negro Babo would not, and, by himself, cast about what to do; that at last he came to the deponent, proposing to him to say and do all that the deponent declares to have said and done to the American captain; * * * that the Negro Babo warned him

---

[143] An instrument for measuring latitude.

that if he varied in the least, or uttered any word, or gave any look that should give the least intimation of the past events or present state, he would instantly kill him, with all his companions, showing a dagger, which he carried hid, saying something which, as he understood it, meant that that dagger would be alert as his eye; that the Negro Babo then announced the plan to all his companions, which pleased them; that he then, the better to disguise the truth, devised many expedients, in some of them uniting deceit and defence; that of this sort was the device of the six Ashantees before-named, who were his bravos;[144] that them he stationed on the break of the poop, as if to clean certain hatchets (in cases, which were part of the cargo), but in reality to use them, and distribute them at need, and at a given word he told them; that, among other devices, was the device of presenting Atufal, his right-hand man, as chained, though in a moment the chains could be dropped; that in every particular he informed the deponent what part he was expected to enact in every device, and what story he was to tell on every occasion, always threatening him with instant death if he varied in the least; that, conscious that many of the Negroes would be turbulent, the Negro Babo appointed the four aged Negroes, who were caulkers, to keep what domestic order they could on the decks; that again and again he harangued the Spaniards and his companions, informing them of his intent, and of his devices, and of the invented story that this deponent was to tell; charging them lest any of them varied from that story; that these arrangements were made and matured during the interval of two or three hours, between their first sighting the ship and the arrival on board of Captain Amasa Delano; that this happened about half-past seven o'clock in the morning, Captain Amasa Delano coming in his boat, and all gladly receiving him; that the deponent, as well as he could force himself, acting then the part of principal owner, and a free captain of the ship, told Captain Amasa Delano, when called upon, that he came from Buenos Aires, bound to Lima, with three hundred Negroes; that off Cape Horn, and in a subsequent fever, many Negroes had died; that also, by similar casualties, all the sea-officers and the greatest part of the crew had died.

[*And so the deposition goes on, circumstantially recounting the fictitious story dictated to the deponent by Babo, and through the deponent imposed upon Captain Delano; and also recounting the friendly offers of Captain Delano, with other things, but all of which is here omitted. After the fictitious story, etc., the deposition proceeds:*]

—that the generous Captain Amasa Delano remained on board all the day, till he left the ship anchored at six o'clock in the evening, deponent speaking to him always of his pretended misfortunes, under the forementioned principles, without having had it in his power to tell a single word, or give him the least hint, that he might know the truth and state of things; because the Negro Babo, performing the office of an officious servant with all the appearance of submission of the humble slave, did not leave the deponent one moment; that this was in order to observe the deponent's actions and words, for the Negro Babo understands well the Spanish; and besides, there were thereabout some others who were constantly on the watch, and likewise understood the Spanish; * * * that upon one occasion, while deponent was standing on the deck conversing with Amasa Delano, by a secret sign the Negro Babo drew him (the deponent) aside, the act appearing as if originating with the deponent;

---

[144] Hired assassins.

that then, he being drawn aside, the Negro Babo proposed to him to gain from Amasa Delano full particulars about his ship, and crew, and arms; that the deponent asked "For what?" that the Negro Babo answered he might conceive; that, grieved at the prospect of what might overtake the generous Captain Amasa Delano, the deponent at first refused to ask the desired questions, and used every argument to induce the Negro Babo to give up this new design; that the Negro Babo showed the point of his dagger; that, after the information had been obtained, the Negro Babo again drew him aside, telling him that that very night he (the deponent) would be captain of two ships, instead of one, for that, great part of the American's ship's crew being to be absent fishing, the six Ashantees, without anyone else, would easily take it; that at this time he said other things to the same purpose; that no entreaties availed; that, before Amasa Delano's coming on board, no hint had been given touching the capture of the American ship: that to prevent this project the deponent was powerless; * * * —that in some things his memory is confused, he cannot distinctly recall every event; * * * —that as soon as they had cast anchor at six of the clock in the evening, as has before been stated, the American captain took leave, to return to his vessel; that upon a sudden impulse, which the deponent believes to have come from God and his angels, he, after the farewell had been said, followed the generous Captain Amasa Delano as far as the gunwale,[145] where he stayed, under pretence of taking leave, until Amasa Delano should have been seated in his boat; that on shoving off, the deponent sprang from the gunwale into the boat, and fell into it, he knows not how, God guarding him; that——

[*Here, in the original, follows the account of what further happened at the escape, and how the* San Dominick *was retaken, and of the passage to the coast; including in the recital many expressions of "eternal gratitude" to the "generous Captain Amasa Delano." The deposition then proceeds with recapitulatory remarks, and a partial renumeration of the negroes, making record of their individual part in the past events, with a view to furnishing, according to command of the court, the data whereon to found the criminal sentences to be pronounced. From this portion is the following:*]

—That he believes that all the Negroes, though not in the first place knowing to the design of revolt, when it was accomplished, approved it. * * * That the Negro, José, eighteen years old, and in the personal service of Don Alexandro, was the one who communicated the information to the Negro Babo, about the state of things in the cabin, before the revolt; that this is known, because, in the preceding midnight, he used to come from his berth, which was under his master's, in the cabin, to the deck where the ringleader and his associates were, and had secret conversations with the Negro Babo, in which he was several times seen by the mate; that, one night, the mate drove him away twice; * * * that this same Negro José was the one who, without being commanded to do so by the Negro Babo, as Lecbe and Matiluqui were, stabbed his master, Don Alexandro, after he had been dragged half-lifeless to the deck; * * * that the mulatto steward, Francesco, was of the first band of revolters, that he was, in all things, the creature and tool of the Negro Babo; that, to make his court, he, just before a repast in the cabin, proposed, to the Negro Babo, poisoning a dish for the generous Captain Amasa Delano; this is known and believed, because the Negroes have said it; but that the Negro Babo,

---

[145] Upper part of a ship's side.

having another design, forbade Francesco; * * * that the Ashantee Lecbe was one of the worst of them; for that, on the day the ship was retaken, he assisted in the defence of her, with a hatchet in each hand, with one of which he wounded, in the breast, the chief mate of Amasa Delano, in the first act of boarding; this all knew; that, in sight of the deponent, Lecbe struck, with a hatchet, Don Francisco Masa, when, by the Negro Babo's orders, he was carrying him to throw him overboard, alive, besides participating in the murder, before mentioned, of Don Alexandro Aranda, and others of the cabin passengers; that, owing to the fury with which the Ashantees fought in the engagement with the boats, but this Lecbe and Yan survived; that Yan was bad as Lecbe; that Yan was the man who, by Babo's command, willingly prepared the skeleton of Don Alexandro, in a way the Negroes afterward told the deponent, but which he, so long as reason is left him, can never divulge; that Yan and Lecbe were the two who, in a calm by night, riveted the skeleton to the bow; this also the negroes told him; that the Negro Babo was he who traced the inscription below it; that the Negro Babo was the plotter from first to last; he ordered every murder, and was the helm and keel of the revolt; that Atufal was his lieutenant in all; but Atufal, with his own hand, committed no murder; nor did the Negro Babo; * * * that Atufal was shot, being killed in the fight with the boats, ere boarding; * * * that the Negresses, of age, were knowing to the revolt, and testified themselves satisfied at the death of their master, Don Alexandro; that, had the Negroes not restrained them, they would have tortured to death, instead of simply killing, the Spaniards slain by command of the Negro Babo; that the Negresses used their utmost influence to have the deponent made away with; that, in the various acts of murder, they sang songs and danced—not gaily, but solemnly; and before the engagement with the boats, as well as during the action, they sang melancholy songs to the Negroes, and that this melancholy tone was more inflaming than a different one would have been, and was so intended; that all this is believed, because the Negroes have said it.

—That of the thirty-six men of the crew, exclusive of the passengers (all of whom are now dead), which the deponent had knowledge of, six only remained alive, with four cabin-boys and ship-boys, not included with the crew; * * * —that the Negroes broke an arm of one of the cabin-boys and gave him strokes with hatchets.

[*Then follow various random disclosures referring to various periods of time. The following are extracted:*]

—That during the presence of Captain Amasa Delano on board, some attempts were made by the sailors, and one by Hermenegildo Gandix, to convey hints to him of the true state of affairs; but that these attempts were ineffectual, owing to fear of incurring death, and, furthermore, owing to the devices which offered contradictions to the true state of affairs, as well as owing to the generosity and piety of Amasa Delano incapable of sounding such wickedness; * * * that Luys Galgo, a sailor about sixty years of age, and formerly of the king's navy, was one of those who sought to convey tokens to Captain Amasa Delano; but his intent, though undiscovered, being suspected, he was, on a pretence, made to retire out of sight, and at last into the hold, and there was made away with. This the Negroes have since said; * * * that one of the ship-boys feeling, from Captain Amasa Delano's presence, some hopes of release, and not having enough prudence, dropped some chance word respecting his expectations, which being overheard and understood by a slave-boy with whom he was eating at the time, the latter struck him on the head with a knife, inflicting a bad wound, but of which the boy is now healing; that likewise, not long before the ship was brought to anchor, one of the seamen, steering at the time, endangered himself by letting the blacks remark some expression in his countenance, arising from a cause similar to the above; but this sailor, by his heedful after conduct, escaped; * * * that these statements are made to show the court that from the beginning to the end of the revolt, it was impossible for the deponent and his men to act otherwise than they did; * * * —that the third clerk, Hermenegildo Gandix, who before had been forced to live among the seamen, wearing a seaman's habit, and in all respects appearing to be one for the time, he, Gandix, was killed by a musket-ball fired through mistake from the boats before boarding; having in his fright run up the mizzen-rigging, calling to the boats—"don't board," lest upon their boarding the Negroes should kill him; that this inducing the Americans to believe he some way favoured the cause of the Negroes, they fired two balls at him, so that he fell wounded from the rigging, and was drowned in the sea; * * * —that the young Don Joaquin, Marques de Aramboalaza, like Hermenegildo Gandix, the third clerk, was degraded to the office and appearance of a common seaman; that upon one occasion when Don Joaquin shrank, the Negro Babo commanded the Ashantee Lecbe to take tar and heat it, and pour it upon Don Joaquin's hands; * * * —that Don Joaquin was killed owing to another mistake of the Americans, but one impossible to be avoided, as upon the approach of the boats, Don Joaquin, with a hatchet tied edge out and upright to his hand, was made by the Negroes to appear on the bulwarks; whereupon, seen with arms in his hands and in a questionable attitude, he was shot for a renegade seaman; * * * —that on the person of Don Joaquin was found secreted a jewel, which, by papers that were discovered, proved to have been meant for the shrine of our Lady of Mercy in Lima; a votive offering, beforehand prepared and guarded, to attest his gratitude, when he should have landed in Peru, his last destination, for the safe conclusion of his entire voyage from Spain; * * * —that the jewel, with the other effects of the late Don Joaquin, is in the custody of the brethren of the Hospital de Sacerdotes, awaiting the disposition of the honourable court; * * * —that, owing to the condition of the deponent, as well as the haste in which the boats departed for the attack, the Americans were not forewarned that there were, among the apparent crew, a passenger and one of the clerks disguised by the Negro Babo; * * * —that, besides the Negroes killed in the action, some were killed after the capture and re-anchoring at night, when shackled to the ring-bolts on deck; that these deaths were committed by the sailors, ere they could be prevented. That so soon as informed of it, Captain Amasa Delano used all his authority, and, in particular with his own hand, struck down Martinez Gola, who, having found a razor in the pocket of an old jacket of his, which one of the shackled negroes had on, was aiming it at the negro's throat; that the noble Captain Amasa Delano also wrenched from the hand of Bartholomew Barlo a dagger, secreted at the time of the massacre of the whites, with which he was in the act of stabbing a shackled Negro, who, the same day, with another Negro, had thrown him down and jumped upon him; * * * —that, for all the events, befalling through so long a time, during which the ship was in the hands of the Negro Babo, he cannot here give account; but that, what he has said is the most substantial of what occurs to him at present, and is the truth under the oath which he has taken; which declaration he affirmed and ratified, after hearing it read to him.

He said that he is twenty-nine years of age, and broken in body and mind; that when finally dismissed by the court, he shall not return home to Chile, but betake himself to the monastery on Mount Agonia without; and signed with his honour, and crossed himself, and for the time, departed as he came, in his litter, with the monk Infelez, to the Hospital de Sacerdotes.

BENITO CERENO.

DOCTOR ROZAS.

If the Deposition have served as the key to fit into the lock of the complications which precede it, then, as a vault whose door has been flung back, the *San Dominick*'s hull lies open to-day.

Hitherto the nature of this narrative, besides rendering the intricacies in the beginning unavoidable, has more or less required that many things, instead of being set down in the order of occurrence, should be retrospectively, or irregularly given; this last is the case with the following passages, which will conclude the account:—

During the long, mild voyage to Lima, there was, as before hinted, a period during which the sufferer a little recovered his health, or, at least in some degree, his tranquility. Ere the decided relapse which came, the two captains had many cordial conversations—their fraternal unreserve in singular contrast with former withdrawments.

Again and again it was repeated, how hard it had been to enact the part forced on the Spaniard by Babo.

"Ah, my dear friend," Don Benito once said, "at those very times when you thought me so morose and ungrateful, nay, when, as you now admit, you half thought me plotting your murder, at those very times my heart was frozen; I could not look at you, thinking of what, both on board this ship and your own, hung, from other hands, over my kind benefactor. And as God lives, Don Amasa, I know not whether desire for my own safety alone could have nerved me to that leap into your boat, had it not been for the thought that, did you, unenlightened, return to your ship, you, my best friend, with all who might be with you, stolen upon, that night, in your hammocks, would never in this world have wakened again. Do but think how you walked this deck, how you sat in this cabin, every inch of ground mined into honeycombs under you. Had I dropped the least hint, made the least advance toward an understanding between us, death, explosive death—yours as mine—would have ended the scene."

"True, true," cried Captain Delano, starting, "you have saved my life, Don Benito, more than I yours; saved, it, too, against my knowledge and will."

"Nay, my friend," rejoined the Spaniard, courteous even to the point of religion, "God charmed your life, but you saved mine. To think of some things you did—those smilings and chattings, rash pointings and gesturings. For less than these, they slew my mate, Raneds; but you had the Prince of Heaven's safe-conduct through all ambuscades."

"Yes, all is owing to Providence, I know: but the temper of my mind that morning was more than commonly pleasant, while the sight of so much suffering, more apparent than real, added to my good-nature, compassion, and charity, happily interweaving the three. Had it been otherwise, doubtless, as you hint, some of my interferences might have ended unhappily enough. Besides, those feelings I spoke of enabled me to get the better of momentary distrust, at times when acuteness might have cost me my life, without saving another's. Only at the end did my suspicions get the better of me, and you know how wide of the mark they then proved."

"Wide, indeed," said Don Benito sadly; "you were with me all day; stood with me, sat with me, talked with me, looked at me, ate with me, drank with me; and yet, your last act was to clutch for a monster, not only an innocent man, but the most pitiable of all men. To such degree may malign machinations and deceptions impose. So far may even the best man err, in judging the conduct of one with the recesses of whose condition he is not acquainted. But you were forced to it; and you were in time undeceived. Would that, in both respects, it was so ever, and with all men."

"You generalise, Don Benito; and mournfully enough. But the past is past; why moralise upon it? Forget it. See, yon bright sun has forgotten it all, and the blue sea, and the blue sky; these have turned over new leaves."

"Because they have no memory," he dejectedly replied; "because they are not human."

"But these mild Trades[146] that now fan your cheek, do they not come with a human-like healing to you? Warm friends, steadfast friends are the Trades."

"With their steadfastness they but waft me to my tomb, señor," was the foreboding response.

"You are saved," cried Captain Delano, more and more astonished and pained; "you are saved: what has cast such a shadow upon you?"

"The Negro."

There was silence, while the moody man sat, slowly and unconsciously gathering his mantle about him, as if it were a pall.

There was no more conversation that day.

But if the Spaniard's melancholy sometimes ended in muteness upon topics like the above, there were others upon which he never spoke at all; on which, indeed, all his old reserves were piled. Pass over the worst, and, only to elucidate, let an item or two of these be cited. The dress, so precise and costly, worn by him on the day whose events have been narrated, had not willingly been put on. And that silver-mounted sword, apparent symbol of despotic command, was not, indeed, a sword, but the ghost of one. The scabbard, artificially stiffened, was empty.

As for the black—whose brain, not body, had schemed and led the revolt, with the plot—his slight frame, inadequate to that which it held, had at once yielded to the superior muscular strength of his captor, in the boat. Seeing all was over, he uttered no sound, and could not be forced to. His aspect seemed to say, since I cannot do deeds, I will not speak words. Put in irons in the hold, with the rest, he was carried to Lima. During the passage, Don Benito did not visit him. Nor then, nor at any time after, would he look at him. Before the tribunal he refused. When pressed by the judges he fainted. On the testimony of sailors alone rested the legal identity of Babo.

Some months after, dragged to the gibbet at the tail of a mule, the black met his voiceless end. The body was burned to ashes; but for many days the

---

[146] Trade winds.

head, that hive of subtlety, fixed on a pole in the Plaza, met, unabashed, the gaze of the whites; and across the Plaza looked toward St. Bartholomew's church, in whose vaults slept then, as now, the recovered bones of Aranda: and across the Rimac bridge looked toward the monastery, on Mount Agonia without; where, three months after being dismissed by the court, Benito Cereno, borne on the bier, did, indeed, follow his leader.

[1855]

Samuel L. Clemens (Mark Twain) *1835–1910*

THE NOTORIOUS JUMPING FROG
OF CALAVERAS COUNTY

In compliance with the request of a friend of mine, who wrote me from the East, I called on good-natured, garrulous old Simon Wheeler, and inquired after my friend's friend, Leonidas W. Smiley, as requested to do, and I hereunto append the result. I have a lurking suspicion that *Leonidas W.* Smiley is a myth; that my friend never knew such a personage; and that he only conjectured that if I asked old Wheeler about him, it would remind him of his infamous *Jim* Smiley, and he would go to work and bore me to death with some exasperating reminiscence of him as long and as tedious as it should be useless to me. If that was the design, it succeeded.

I found Simon Wheeler dozing comfortably by the bar-room stove of the dilapidated tavern in the decayed mining camp of Angel's,[1] and I noticed that he was fat and bald-headed, and had an expression of winning gentleness and simplicity upon his tranquil countenance. He roused up, and gave me good day. I told him that a friend of mine had commissioned me to make some inquiries about a cherished companion of his boyhood named *Leonidas W.* Smiley—*Rev. Leonidas W.* Smiley, a young minister of the Gospel, who he had heard was at one time a resident of Angel's Camp. I added that if Mr. Wheeler could tell me anything about this Rev. Leonidas W. Smiley, I would feel under many obligations to him.

Simon Wheeler backed me into a corner and blockaded me there with his chair, and then sat down and reeled off the monotonous narrative which follows this paragraph. He never smiled, he never frowned, he never changed his voice from the gentle-flowing key to which he tuned his initial sentence, he never betrayed the slightest suspicion of enthusiasm; but all through the interminable narrative there ran a vein of impressive earnestness and sincerity, which showed me plainly that, so far from his imagining that there was anything ridiculous or funny about his story, he regarded it as a really important matter, and admired its two heroes as men of transcendent genius in *finesse.* I let him go on in his own way, and never interrupted him once.

"Rev. Leonidas W. H'm, Reverend Le—well, there was a feller here once by the name of *Jim* Smiley, in the winter of '49—or maybe it was the spring of '50—I don't recollect exactly, somehow, though what makes me think it was one or the other is because I remember the big flume[2] warn't finished when he first come to the camp; but anyway, he was the curiousest man about always betting on anything that turned up you ever see, if he could get anybody to bet on the other side; and if he couldn't he'd change sides. Any way that suited the other man would suit *him*—any way just so's he got a bet, *he* was satisfied. But still he was lucky, uncommon lucky; he most always come out winner. He was always ready and laying for a chance; there couldn't be no solit'ry thing mentioned but that feller'd offer to bet on it, and take ary side you please, as I was just telling you. If there was a horse-race, you'd find

---

[1] An early mining camp in Calaveras County, California, northeast of San Francisco.
[2] A slanting wooden trough through which water is directed during the placer mining of gold.

him flush or you'd find him busted at the end of it; if there was a dog-fight, he'd bet on it; if there was a cat-fight, he'd bet on it; if there was a chicken-fight, he'd bet on it; why, if there was two birds setting on a fence, he would bet you which one would fly first; or if there was a camp-meeting, he would be there reg'lar to bet on Parson Walker, which he judged to be the best exhorter about here, and so he was too, and a good man. If he even see a straddle-bug start to go anywheres, he would bet you how long it would take him to get to—to wherever he was going to, and if you took him up, he would foller that straddle-bug to Mexico but what he would find out where he was bound for and how long he was on the road. Lots of the boys here has seen that Smiley, and can tell you about him. Why, it never made no difference to *him*—he'd bet on *any* thing—the dangdest feller. Parson Walker's wife laid very sick once, for a good while, and it seemed as if they warn't going to save her; but one morning he come in, and Smiley up and asked him how she was, and he said she was considerable better—thank the Lord for his inf'nite mercy—and coming on so smart that with the blessing of Prov'dence she'd get well yet; and Smiley, before he thought, says, 'Well, I'll resk two-and-a-half she don't anyway.'

"Thish-yer Smiley had a mare—the boys called her the fifteen-minute nag, but that was only in fun, you know, because of course she was faster than that—and he used to win money on that horse, for all she was so slow and always had the asthma, or the distemper, or the consumption, or something of that kind. They used to give her two or three hundred yards' start, and then pass her under way; but always at the fag end of the race she'd get excited and desperate like, and come cavorting and straddling up, and scattering her legs around limber, sometimes in the air, and sometimes out to one side among the fences, and kicking up m-o-r-e dust and raising m-o-r-e racket with her coughing and sneezing and blowing her nose—and *always* fetch up at the stand just about a neck ahead, as near as you could cipher it down.

"And he had a little small bull-pup, that to look at him you'd think he warn't worth a cent but to set around and look ornery and lay for a chance to steal something. But as soon as money was up on him he was a different dog; his under-jaw'd begin to stick out like the fo'castle of a steamboat, and his teeth would uncover and shine like the furnaces. And a dog might tackle him and bully-rag him, and bite him, and throw him over his shoulder two or three times, and Andrew Jackson[3]—which was the name of the pup—Andrew Jackson would never let on but what *he* was satisfied, and hadn't expected nothing else—and the bets being doubled and doubled on the other side all the time, till the money was all up; and then all of a sudden he would grab that other dog jest by the j'int of his hind leg and freeze to it—not chaw, you understand, but only just grip and hang on till they throwed up the sponge, if it was a year. Smiley always come out winner on that pup, till he harnessed a dog once that didn't have no hind legs, because they'd been sawed off in a circular saw, and when the thing had gone along far enough, and the money was all up, and he come to make a snatch for his pet holt, he see in a minute how he'd been imposed on, and how the other dog had him in the door, so to speak, and he 'peared surprised, and then he looked sorter discouraged-like, and didn't try no more to win the fight, and so he got shucked out bad. He give Smiley a look, as much as to say his heart was broke, and it was *his*

---

[3] Andrew Jackson (1767–1845), the seventh President of the U.S.

fault, for putting up a dog that hadn't no hind legs for him to take holt of, which was his main dependence in a fight, and then he limped off a piece and laid down and died. It was a good pup, was that Andrew Jackson, and would have made a name for hisself if he'd live, for the stuff was in him and he had genius—I know it, because he hadn't no opportunities to speak of, and it don't stand to reason that a dog could make such a fight as he could under them circumstances if he hadn't no talent. It always makes me feel sorry when I think of that last fight of his'n, and the way it turned out.

"Well, thish-yer Smiley had rat-tarriers, and chicken cocks, and tomcats and all them kind of things, till you couldn't rest, and you couldn't fetch nothing for him to bet on but he'd match you. He ketched a frog one day, and took him home, and said he cal'lated to educate him; and so he never done nothing for three months but set in his back yard and learn that frog to jump. And you bet you he *did* learn him, too. He'd give him a little punch behind, and the next minute you'd see that frog whirling in the air like a doughnut—see him turn one summerset, or maybe a couple, if he got a good start, and come down flat-footed and all right, like a cat. He got him up so in the matter of ketching flies, and kep' him in practice so constant, that he'd nail a fly every time as fur as he could see him. Smiley said all a frog wanted was education, and he could do 'most anything—and I believe him. Why, I've seen him set Dan'l Webster[4] down here on this floor—Dan'l Webster was the name of the frog—and sing out, 'Flies, Dan'l, flies!' and quicker'n you could wink he'd spring straight up and snake a fly off'n the counter there, and flop down on the floor ag'in as solid as a gob of mud, and fall to scratching the side of his head with his hind foot as indifferent as if he hadn't no idea he'd been doin' any more'n any frog might do. You never see a frog so modest and straight-for'ard as he was, for all he was so gifted. And when it come to fair and square jumping on a dead level, he could get over more ground at one straddle than any animal of his breed you ever see. Jumping on a dead level was his strong suit, you understand; and when it come to that, Smiley would ante up money on him as long as he had a red.[5] Smiley was monstrous proud of his frog, and well he might be, for fellers that had traveled and been everywheres all said he laid over any frog that every *they* see.

"Well, Smiley kep' the beast in a little lattice box, and he used to fetch him down-town sometimes and lay for a bet. One day a feller—a stranger in the camp, he was—come acrost him with his box, and says:

" 'What might it be that you've got in the box?'

"And Smiley says, sorter indifferent-like, 'It might be a parrot, or it might be a canary, maybe, but it ain't—it's only just a frog.'

"And the feller took it, and looked at it careful, and turned it round this way and that, and says, 'H'm—so 'tis. Well, what's *he* good for?'

" 'Well,' Smiley says, easy and careless, 'he's good enough for *one* thing, I should judge—he can outjump any frog in Calaveras County.'

"The feller took the box again, and took another long, particular look, and give it back to Smiley, and says, very deliberate, 'Well,' he says, 'I don't see no p'ints about that frog that's any better'n any other frog.'

" 'Maybe you don't,' Smiley says. 'Maybe you understand frogs and maybe you don't understand 'em; maybe you've had experience, and maybe you ain't

[4] Daniel Webster (1782–1852), the U.S. Senator from Massachusetts.
[5] A "red cent," or penny.

only a amature, as it were. Anyways, I've got *my* opinion, and I'll resk forty dollars that he can outjump any frog in Calaveras County.'

"And the feller studied a minute, and then says, kinder sadlike, 'Well, I'm only a stranger here, and I ain't got no frog; but if I had a frog, I'd bet you.'

"And then Smiley says, 'That's all right—that's all right—if you'll hold my box a minute, I'll go and get you a frog.' And so the feller took the box, and put up his forty dollars along with Smiley's, and set down to wait.

"So he set there a good while thinking and thinking to himself, and then he got the frog out and prized his mouth open and took a teaspoon and filled him full of quail-shot—filled him pretty near up to his chin—and set him on the floor. Smiley he went to the swamp and slopped around in the mud for a long time, and finally he fetched a frog, and fetched him in, and give him to this feller, and says:

"'Now, if you're ready, set him alongside of Dan'l, with his fore paws just even with Dan'l's, and I'll give the word.' Then he says, 'One—two—three—git!' and him and the feller touched up the frogs from behind, and the new frog hopped off lively, but Dan'l give a heave, and hysted up his shoulders—so—like a Frenchman, but it warn't no use—he couldn't budge; he was planted as solid as a church, and he couldn't no more stir than if he was anchored out. Smiley was a good deal surprised, and he was disgusted too, but he didn't have no idea what the matter was, of course.

"The feller took the money and started away; and when he was going out at the door, he sorter jerked his thumb over his shoulder—so—at Dan'l, and says again, very deliberate, 'Well,' he says, "*I* don't see no p'ints about that frog that's any better'n any other frog.'

"Smiley he stood scratching his head and looking down at Dan'l a long time, and at last he says, 'I do wonder what in the nation that frog throw'd off for—I wonder if there ain't something the matter with him—he 'pears to look mighty baggy, somehow.' And he ketched Dan'l by the nap of the neck, and hefted him, and says, 'Why blame my cats if he don't weigh five pound!' and turned him upside down and he belched out a double handful of shot. And then he see how it was, and he was the maddest man—he set the frog down and took out after that feller, but he never ketched him. And—"

[Here Simon Wheeler heard his name called from the front yard, and got up to see what was wanted.] And turning to me as he moved away, he said: "Just set where you are, stranger, and rest easy—I ain't going to be gone a second."

But, by your leave, I did not think that a continuation of the history of the enterprising vagabond *Jim* Smiley would be likely to afford me much information concerning the Rev. *Leonidas W.* Smiley, and so I started away.

At the door I met the sociable Wheeler returning, and he buttonholed me and recommenced:

"Well, thish-yer Smiley had a yaller one-eyed cow that didn't have no tail, only just a short stump like a bannanner, and—"

However, lacking both time and inclination, I did not wait to hear about the afflicted cow, but took my leave.

[1865]

Guy de Maupassant *1850–1893*

THE NECKLACE

She was one of those pretty and charming girls who are sometimes, as if by a mistake of destiny, born in a family of clerks. She had no dowry, no expectations, no means of being known, understood, loved, wedded by any rich and distinguished man; and she let herself be married to a little clerk at the Ministry of Public Instruction.

She dressed plainly because she could not dress well, but she was as unhappy as though she had really fallen from her proper station, since with women there is neither caste nor rank: and beauty, grace, and charm act instead of family and birth. Natural fineness, instinct for what is elegant, suppleness of wit, are the sole heirarchy, and make from women of the people the equals of the very greatest ladies.

She suffered ceaselessly, feeling herself born for all the delicacies and all the luxuries. She suffered from the poverty of her dwelling, from the wretched look of the walls, from the worn-out chairs, from the ugliness of the curtains. All those things, of which another woman of her rank would never even have been conscious, tortured her and made her angry. The sight of the little Breton peasant[1] who did her humble housework aroused in her regrets which were despairing, and distracted dreams. She thought of the silent antechambers hung with Oriental tapestry, lit by tall bronze candelabra, and of the two great footmen in knee breeches who sleep in the big armchairs, made drowsy by the heavy warmth of the hot-air stove. She thought of the long *salons*[2] fitted up with ancient silk, of the delicate furniture carrying priceless curiosities, and of the coquettish perfumed boudoirs made for talks at five o'clock with intimate friends, with men famous and sought after, whom all women envy and whose attention they all desire.

When she sat down to dinner, before the round table covered with a tablecloth three days old, opposite her husband, who uncovered the soup tureen and declared with an enchanted air, "Ah, the good *pot-au-feu!*[3] I don't know anything better than that," she thought of dainty dinners, of shining silverware, of tapestry which peopled the walls with ancient personages and with strange birds flying in the midst of a fairy forest; and she thought of delicious dishes served on marvelous plates, and of the whispered gallantries which you listen to with a sphinxlike smile, while you are eating the pink flesh of a trout or the wings of a quail.

She had no dresses, no jewels, nothing. And she loved nothing but that; she felt made for that. She would so have liked to please, to be envied, to be charming, to be sought after.

She had a friend, a former schoolmate at the convent, who was rich, and whom she did not like to go and see any more, because she suffered so much when she came back.

But one evening, her husband returned home with a triumphant air, and holding a large envelope in his hand.

---

[1] A native of Brittany, a region (historically a province) in northwest France.
[2] Drawing rooms.   [3] Stew.

"There," said he. "Here is something for you."

She tore the paper sharply, and drew out a printed card which bore these words:

"The Minister of Public Instruction and Mme. Georges Ramponneau request the honor of M. and Mme. Loisel's company at the palace of the Ministry on Monday evening, January eighteenth."

Instead of being delighted, as her husband hoped, she threw the invitation on the table with disdain, murmuring:

"What do you want me to do with that?"

"But, my dear, I thought you would be glad. You never go out, and this is such a fine opportunity. I had awful trouble to get it. Everyone wants to go; it is very select, and they are not giving many invitations to clerks. The whole official world will be there."

She looked at him with an irritated glance, and said, impatiently:

"And what do you want me to put on my back?"

He had not thought of that; he stammered:

"Why, the dress you go to the theater in. It looks very well, to me."

He stopped, distracted, seeing his wife was crying. Two great tears descended slowly from the corners of her eyes toward the corners of her mouth. He stuttered:

"What's the matter? What's the matter?"

But, by violent effort, she had conquered her grief, and she replied, with a calm voice, while she wiped her wet cheeks:

"Nothing. Only I have no dress and therefore I can't go to this ball. Give your card to some colleague whose wife is better equipped than I."

He was in despair. He resumed:

"Come, let us see, Mathilde. How much would it cost, a suitable dress, which you could use on other occasions. Something very simple?"

She reflected several seconds, making her calculations and wondering also what sum she could ask without drawing on herself an immediate refusal and a frightened exclamation from the economical clerk.

Finally, she replied, hesitatingly:

"I don't know exactly, but I think I could manage it with four hundred francs."

He had grown a little pale, because he was laying aside just that amount to buy a gun and treat himself to a little shooting next summer on the plain of Nanterre,[4] with several friends who went to shoot larks down there, of a Sunday.

But he said:

"All right. I will give you four hundred francs. And try to have a pretty dress."

The day of the ball drew near, and Mme. Loisel seemed sad, uneasy, anxious. Her dress was ready, however. Her husband said to her one evening:

"What is the matter? Come, you've been so queer these last three days."

And she answered:

"It annoys me not to have a single jewel, not a single stone, nothing to put on. I shall look like distress. I should almost rather not go at all."

He resumed:

---

[4] A town west of Paris.

"You might wear natural flowers. It's very stylish at this time of the year. For ten francs you can get two or three magnificent roses."

She was not convinced.

"No; there's nothing more humiliating than to look poor among other women who are rich."

But her husband cried:

"How stupid you are! Go look up your friend Mme. Forestier, and ask her to lend you some jewels. You're quite thick enough with her to do that."

She uttered a cry of joy:

"It's true. I never thought of it."

The next day she went to her friend and told of her distress.

Mme. Forestier went to a wardrobe with a glass door, took out a large jewel-box, brought it back, opened it, and said to Mme. Loisel:

"Choose, my dear."

She saw first of all some bracelets, then a pearl necklace, then a Venetian cross, gold and precious stones of admirable workmanship. She tried on the ornaments before the glass, hesitated, could not make up her mind to part with them, to give them back. She kept asking:

"Haven't you any more?"

"Why, yes. Look. I don't know what you like."

All of a sudden she discovered, in a black satin box, a superb necklace of diamonds, and her heart began to beat with an immoderate desire. Her hands trembled as she took it. She fastened it around her throat, outside her high-necked dress, and remained lost in ecstasy at the sight of herself.

Then she asked, hesitating, filled with anguish:

"Can you lend me that, only that?"

"Why, yes, certainly."

She sprang upon the neck of her friend, kissed her passionately, then fled with her treasure.

The day of the ball arrived. Mme. Loisel made a great success. She was prettier than them all, elegant, gracious, smiling, and crazy with joy. All the men looked at her, asked her name, endeavored to be introduced. All the attachés of the Cabinet wanted to waltz with her. She was remarked by the minister himself.

She danced with intoxication, with passion, made drunk by pleasure, forgetting all, in the triumph of her beauty, in the glory of her success, in a sort of cloud of happiness composed of all this homage, of all this admiration, of all these awakened desires, and of that sense of complete victory which is so sweet to a woman's heart.

She went away about four o'clock in the morning. Her husband had been sleeping since midnight, in a little deserted anteroom, with three other gentlemen whose wives were having a very good time. He threw over her shoulders the wraps which he had brought, modest wraps of common life, whose poverty contrasted with the elegance of the ball dress. She felt this, and wanted to escape so as not to be remarked by the other women, who were enveloping themselves in costly furs.

Loisel held her back.

"Wait a bit. You will catch cold outside. I will go and call a cab."

But she did not listen to him, and rapidly descended the stairs. When they were in the street they did not find a carriage; and they began to look for one, shouting after the cabmen whom they saw passing by at a distance.

They went down toward the Seine[5] in despair, shivering with cold. At last they found on the quay one of those ancient noctambulant coupés[6] which, exactly as if they were ashamed to show their misery during the day, are never seen round Paris until after nightfall.

It took them to their door in the Rue des Martyrs, and once more, sadly, they climbed up homeward. All was ended, for her. And as to him, he reflected that he must be at the Ministry at ten o'clock.

She removed the wraps which covered her shoulders, before the glass, so as once more to see herself in all her glory. But suddenly she uttered a cry. She no longer had the necklace around her neck!

Her husband, already half undressed, demanded:

"What is the matter with you?"

She turned madly towards him:

"I have—I have—I've lost Mme. Forestier's necklace."

He stood up, distracted.

"What!—how?—impossible!"

And they looked in the folds of her dress, in the folds of her cloak, in her pockets, everywhere. They did not find it.

He asked:

"You're sure you had it on when you left the ball?"

"Yes, I felt it in the vestibule of the palace."

"But if you had lost it in the street we should have heard it fall. It must be in the cab."

"Yes. Probably. Did you take his number?"

"No. And you, didn't you notice it?"

"No."

They looked, thunderstruck, at one another. At last Loisel put on his clothes.

"I shall go back on foot," said he, "over the whole route which we have taken to see if I can find it."

And he went out. She sat waiting on a chair in her ball dress, without strength to go to bed, overwhelmed, without fire, without a thought.

Her husband came back about seven o'clock. He had found nothing.

He went to Police Headquarters, to the newspaper offices, to offer a reward; he went to the cab companies—everywhere, in fact, whither he was urged by the least suspicion of hope.

She waited all day, in the same condition of mad fear before this terrible calamity.

Loisel returned at night with a hollow, pale face; he had discovered nothing.

"You must write to your friend," said he, "that you have broken the clasp of her necklace and that you are having it mended. That will give us time to turn round."

She wrote at his dictation.

At the end of a week they had lost all hope.

And Loisel, who had aged five years, declared:

"We must consider how to replace that ornament."

The next day they took the box which had contained it, and they went to the jeweler whose name was found within. He consulted his books.

"It was not I, madame, who sold that necklace; I must simply have furnished the case."

<hr>

[5] The river that flows through Paris.   [6] A closed four-wheeled carriage.

Then they went from jeweler to jeweler, searching for a necklace like the other, consulting their memories, sick both of them with chagrin and anguish.

They found, in a shop at the Palais Royal,[7] a string of diamonds which seemed to them exactly like the one they looked for. It was worth forty thousand francs. They could have it for thirty-six.

So they begged the jeweler not to sell it for three days yet. And they made a bargain that he should buy it back for thirty-four thousand francs, in case they found the other one before the end of February.

Loisel possessed eighteen thousand francs which his father had left him. He would borrow the rest.

He did borrow, asking a thousand francs of one, five hundred of another, five louis[8] here, three louis there. He gave notes, took up ruinous obligations, dealt with usurers and all the race of lenders. He compromised all the rest of his life, risked his signature without even knowing if he could meet it; and, frightened by the pains yet to come, by the black misery which was about to fall upon him, by the prospect of all the physical privation and of all the moral tortures which he was to suffer, he went to get the new necklace, putting down upon the merchant's counter thirty-six thousand francs.

When Mme. Loisel took back the necklace, Mme. Forestier said to her, with a chilly manner:

"You should have returned it sooner; I might have needed it."

She did not open the case, as her friend had so much feared. If she had detected the substitution, what would she have thought, what would she have said? Would she not have taken Mme. Loisel for a thief?

Mme. Loisel now knew the horrible existence of the needy. She took her part, moreover, all of a sudden, with heroism. That dreadful debt must be paid. She would pay it. They dismissed their servant; they changed their lodgings; they rented a garret under the roof.

She came to know what heavy housework meant and the odious cares of the kitchen. She washed the dishes, using her rosy nails on the greasy pots and pans. She washed the dirty linen, the shirts, and the dishcloths, which she dried upon a line; she carried the slops down to the street every morning, and carried up the water, stopping for breath at every landing. And, dressed like a woman of the people, she went to the fruiterer, the grocer, the butcher, her basket on her arm, bargaining, insulted, defending her miserable money sou by sou.[9]

Each month they had to meet some notes, renew others, obtain more time.

Her husband worked in the evening making a fair copy of some tradesman's accounts, and late at night he often copied manuscript for five sous a page.

And this life lasted for ten years.

At the end of ten years, they had paid everything, everything, with the rates of usury, and the accumulations of the compound interest.

Mme. Loisel looked old now. She had become the woman of impoverished households—strong and hard and rough. With frowsy hair, skirts askew, and red hands, she talked loud while washing the floor with great swishes of water. But sometimes, when her husband was at the office, she sat down near the

---

[7] At the time the story was written the shops in the vicinity of the Palais Royal included many of the most famous jewellers in Paris.

[8] A French coin worth twenty francs.

[9] A small French coin worth one-twentieth of a franc.

window, and she thought of that gay evening of long ago, of that ball where she had been so beautiful and so fêted.

What would have happened if she had not lost that necklace? Who knows? Who knows? How life is strange and changeful! How little a thing is needed for us to be lost or to be saved!

But, one Sunday, having gone to take a walk in the Champs Elysées[10] to refresh herself from the labor of the week, she suddenly perceived a woman who was leading a child. It was Mme. Forestier, still young, still beautiful, still charming.

Mme. Loisel felt moved. Was she going to speak to her? Yes, certainly. And now that she had paid, she was going to tell her all about it. Why not?

She went up.

"Good-day, Jeanne."

The other, astonished to be familiarly addressed by this plain goodwife, did not recognize her at all, and stammered:

"But—madam!—I do not know—You must be mistaken."

"No. I am Mathilde Loisel."

Her friend uttered a cry.

"Oh, my poor Mathilde! How you are changed!"

"Yes, I have had days hard enough, since I have seen you, days wretched enough—and that because of you!"

"Of me! How so?"

"Do you remember that diamond necklace which you lent me to wear at the ministerial ball?"

"Yes. Well?"

"Well, I lost it."

"What do you mean? You brought it back."

"I brought you back another just like it. And for this we have been ten years paying. You can understand that it was not easy for us, us who had nothing. At last it is ended, and I am very glad."

Mme. Forestier had stopped.

"You say that you bought a necklace of diamonds to replace mine?"

"Yes. You never noticed it, then! They were very like."

And she smiled with a joy which was proud and naïve at once.

Mme. Forestier, strongly moved, took her two hands.

"Oh, my poor Mathilde! Why, my necklace was paste. It was worth at most five hundred francs!"

[1884]

---

[10] Paris' most famous avenue, lined with trees and gardens.

Leo Tolstoy   *1828–1910*

THE DEATH OF IVAN ILYCH*

I

During an interval in the Melvinski trial in the large building of the Law Courts the members and public prosecutor met in Ivan Egorovich Shebek's private room, where the conversation turned on the celebrated Krasovski case. Fedor Vasilievich warmly maintained that it was not subject to their jurisdiction, Ivan Egorovich maintained the contrary, while Peter Ivanovich, not having entered into the discussion at the start, took no part in it but looked through the *Gazette* which had just been handed in.

"Gentlemen," he said, "Ivan Ilych has died!"

"You don't say so!"

"Here, read it yourself," replied Peter Ivanovich, handing Fedor Vasilievich the paper still damp from the press. Surrounded by a black border were the words: "Praskovya Fedorovna Golovina, with profound sorrow, informs relatives and friends of the demise of her beloved husband Ivan Ilych Golovin, Member of the Court of Justice, which occurred on February the 4th of this year 1882. The funeral will take place on Friday at one o'clock in the afternoon."

Ivan Ilych had been a colleague of the gentlemen present and was liked by them all. He had been ill for some weeks with an illness said to be incurable. His post had been kept open for him, but there had been conjectures that in case of his death Alexeev might receive his appointment, and that either Vinnikov or Shtabel would succeed Alexeev. So on receiving the news of Ivan Ilych's death the first thought of each of the gentlemen in that private room was of the changes and promotions it might occasion among themselves or their acquaintances.

"I shall be sure to get Shtabel's place or Vinnikov's," thought Fedor Vasilievich. "I was promised that long ago, and the promotion means an extra eight hundred rubles a year for me besides the allowance."

"Now I must apply for my brother-in-law's transfer from Kaluga," thought Peter Ivanovich. "My wife will be very glad, and then she won't be able to say that I never do anything for her relations."

"I thought he would never leave his bed again," said Peter Ivanovich aloud. "It's very sad."

"But what really was the matter with him?"

"The doctors couldn't say—at least they could, but each of them said something different. When last I saw him I thought he was getting better."

"And I haven't been to see him since the holidays. I always meant to go."

"Had he any property?"

"I think his wife had a little—but something quite trifling."

"We shall have to go to see her, but they live so terribly far away."

"Far away from you, you mean. Everything's far away from your place."

"You see, he never can forgive my living on the other side of the river," said Peter Ivanovich, smiling at Shebek. Then, still talking of the distances between different parts of the city, they returned to the Court.

* *Translated by Louise and Aylmer Maude.*

Besides considerations as to the possible transfers and promotions likely to result from Ivan Ilych's death, the mere fact of the death of a near acquaintance aroused, as usual, in all who heard of it the complacent feeling that, "it is he who is dead and not I."

Each one thought or felt, "Well, he's dead but I'm alive!" But the more intimate of Ivan Ilych's acquaintances, his so-called friends, could not help thinking also that they would now have to fulfil the very tiresome demands of propriety by attending the funeral service and paying a visit of condolence to the widow.

Fedor Vasilievich and Peter Ivanovich had been his nearest acquaintances. Peter Ivanovich had studied law with Ivan Ilych and had considered himself to be under obligations to him.

Having told his wife at dinner-time of Ivan Ilych's death, and of his conjecture that it might be possible to get her brother transferred to their circuit, Peter Ivanovich sacrificed his usual nap, put on his evening clothes, and drove to Ivan Ilych's house.

At the entrance stood a carriage and two cabs. Leaning against the wall in the hall downstairs near the cloak-stand was a coffin lid covered with cloth of gold, ornamented with gold cord and tassels, that had been polished up with metal powder. Two ladies in black were taking off their fur cloaks. Peter Ivanovich recognized one of them as Ivan Ilych's sister, but the other was a stranger to him. His colleague Schwartz was just coming downstairs, but on seeing Peter Ivanovich enter he stopped and winked at him, as if to say: "Ivan Ilych has made a mess of things—not like you and me."

Schwartz's face with his Piccadilly whiskers, and his slim figure in evening dress, had as usual an air of elegant solemnity which contrasted with the playfulness of his character and had a special piquancy here, or so it seemed to Peter Ivanovich.

Peter Ivanovich allowed the ladies to precede him and slowly followed them upstairs. Schwartz did not come down but remained where he was, and Peter Ivanovich understood that he wanted to arrange where they should play bridge that evening. The ladies went upstairs to the widow's room, and Schwartz with seriously compressed lips but a playful look in his eyes, indicated by a twist of his eyebrows the room to the right where the body lay.

Peter Ivanovich, like everyone else on such occasions, entered feeling uncertain what he would have to do. All he knew was that at such times it is always safe to cross oneself. But he was not quite sure whether one should make obeisances while doing so. He therefore adopted a middle course. On entering the room he began crossing himself and made a slight movement resembling a bow. At the same time, as far as the motion of his head and arm allowed, he surveyed the room. Two young men—apparently nephews, one of whom was a high-school pupil—were leaving the room, crossing themselves as they did so. An old woman was standing motionless, and a lady with strangely arched eyebrows was saying something to her in a whisper. A vigorous, resolute Church Reader, in a frock-coat, was reading something in a loud voice with an expression that precluded any contradiction. The butler's assistant, Gerasim, stepping lightly in front of Peter Ivanovich, was strewing something on the floor. Noticing this, Peter Ivanovich was immediately aware of a faint odour of a decomposing body.

The last time he had called on Ivan Ilych, Peter Ivanovich had seen Gerasim in the study. Ivan Ilych had been particularly fond of him and he was performing the duty of a sick nurse.

Peter Ivanovich continued to make the sign of the cross slightly inclining his head in an intermediate direction between the coffin, the Reader, and the icons[1] on the table in a corner of the room. Afterwards, when it seemed to him that this movement of his arm in crossing himself had gone on too long, he stopped and began to look at the corpse.

The dead man lay, as dead men always lie, in a specially heavy way, his rigid limbs sunk in the soft cushions of the coffin, with the head forever bowed on the pillow. His yellow waxen brow with bald patches over his sunken temples was thrust up in the way peculiar to the dead, the protruding nose seeming to press on the upper lip. He was much changed and had grown even thinner since Peter Ivanovich had last seen him, but, as is always the case with the dead, his face was handsomer and above all more dignified than when he was alive. The expression on the face said that what was necessary had been accomplished, and accomplished rightly. Besides this there was in that expression a reproach and a warning to the living. This warning seemed to Peter Ivanovich out of place, or at least not applicable to him. He felt a certain discomfort and so he hurriedly crossed himself once more and turned and went out of the door—too hurriedly and too regardless of propriety, as he himself was aware.

Schwartz was waiting for him in the adjoining room with legs spread wide apart and both hands toying with his top hat behind his back. The mere sight of that playful, well-groomed, and elegant figure refreshed Peter Ivanovich. He felt that Schwartz was above all these happenings and would not surrender to any depressing influences. His very look said that this incident of a church service for Ivan Ilych could not be a sufficient reason for infringing the order of the session—in other words, that it would certainly not prevent his unwrapping a new pack of cards and shuffling them that evening while a footman placed four fresh candles on the table: in fact, that there was no reason for supposing that this incident would hinder their spending the evening agreeably. Indeed he said this in a whisper as Peter Ivanovich passed him, proposing that they should meet for a game at Fedor Vasilievich's. But apparently Peter Ivanovich was not destined to play bridge that evening. Praskovya Fedorovna (a short, fat woman who despite all efforts to the contrary had continued to broaden steadily from her shoulders downwards and who had the same extraordinarily arched eyebrows as the lady who had been standing by the coffin), dressed all in black, her head covered with lace, came out of her own room with some other ladies, conducted them to the room where the dead body lay, and said: "The service will begin immediately. Please go in."

Schwartz, making an indefinite bow, stood still, evidently neither accepting nor declining this invitation. Praskovya Fedorovna recognizing Peter Ivanovich, sighed, went close up to him, took his hand, and said: "I know you were a true friend to Ivan Ilych . . ." and looked at him awaiting some suitable response. And Peter Ivanovich knew that, just as it had been the right thing to cross himself in that room, so what he had to do here was to press her hand, sigh, and say, "Believe me. . . ." So he did all this and as he did it felt that the desired result had been achieved: that both he and she were touched.

[1] Traditional religious paintings.

"Come with me. I want to speak to you before it begins," said the widow. "Give me your arm."

Peter Ivanovich gave her his arm and they went to the inner rooms, passing Schwartz who winked at Peter Ivanovich compassionately.

"That does for our bridge! Don't object if we find another player. Perhaps you can cut in when you do escape," said his playful look.

Peter Ivanovich sighed still more deeply and despondently, and Praskovya Fedorovna pressed his arm gratefully. When they reached the drawing-room, upholstered in pink cretonne[2] and lighted by a dim lamp, they sat down at the table—she on a sofa and Peter Ivanovich on a low pouffe,[3] the springs of which yielded spasmodically under his weight. Praskovya Fedorovna had been on the point of warning him to take another seat, but felt that such a warning was out of keeping with her present condition and so changed her mind. As he sat down on the pouffe Peter Ivanovich recalled how Ivan Ilych had arranged this room and had consulted him regarding this pink cretonne with green leaves. The whole room was full of furniture and knick-knacks, and on her way to the sofa the lace of the widow's black shawl caught on the carved edge of the table. Peter Ivanovich rose to detach it, and the springs of the pouffe, relieved of his weight, rose also and gave him a push. The widow began detaching her shawl herself, and Peter Ivanovich again sat down, suppressing the rebellious springs of the pouffe under him. But the widow had not quite freed herself and Peter Ivanovich got up again, and again the pouffe rebelled and even creaked. When this was all over she took out a clean cambric handkerchief and began to weep. The episode with the shawl and the struggle with the pouffe had cooled Peter Ivanovich's emotions and he sat there with a sullen look on his face. This awkward situation was interrupted by Sokolov, Ivan Ilych's butler, who came to report that the plot in the cemetery that Praskovya Fedorovna had chosen would cost two hundred rubles. She stopped weeping and, looking at Peter Ivanovich with the air of a victim, remarked in French that it was very hard for her. Peter Ivanovich made a silent gesture signifying his full conviction that it must indeed be so.

"Please smoke," she said in a magnanimous yet crushed voice, and turned to discuss with Sokolov the price of the plot for the grave.

Peter Ivanovich while lighting his cigarette heard her inquiring very circumstantially into the prices of different plots in the cemetery and finally decide which she would take. When that was done she gave instructions about engaging the choir. Sokolov then left the room.

"I look after everything myself," she told Peter Ivanovich, shifting the albums that lay on the table; and noticing that the table was endangered by his cigarette-ash, she immediately passed him an ashtray, saying as she did so: "I consider it an affectation to say that my grief prevents my attending to practical affairs. On the contrary, if anything can—I won't say console me, but—distract me, it is seeing to everything concerning him." She again took out her handkerchief as if preparing to cry, but suddenly, as if mastering her feeling, she shook herself and began to speak calmly. "But there is something I want to talk to you about."

Peter Ivanovich bowed, keeping control of the springs of the pouffe, which immediately began quivering under him.

"He suffered terribly the last few days."

---

[2] Heavy cotton or linen fabric.   [3] A rounded ottoman.

"Did he?" said Peter Ivanovich.

"Oh, terribly! He screamed unceasingly, not for minutes but for hours. For the last three days he screamed incessantly. It was unendurable. I cannot understand how I bore it; you could hear him three rooms off. Oh, what I have suffered!"

"Is it possible that he was conscious all that time?" asked Peter Ivanovich.

"Yes," she whispered. "To the last moment. He took leave of us a quarter of an hour before he died, and asked us to take Volodya away."

The thought of the sufferings of this man he had known so intimately, first as a merry little boy, then as a school-mate, and later as a grown-up colleague, suddenly struck Peter Ivanovich with horror, despite an unpleasant consciousness of his own and this woman's dissimulation. He again saw that brow, and that nose pressing down on the lip, and felt afraid for himself.

"Three days of frightful suffering and then death! Why, that might suddenly, at any time, happen to me," he thought, and for a moment felt terrified. But— he did not himself know how—the customary reflection at once occurred to him that this had happened to Ivan Ilych and not to him, and that it should not and could not happen to him, and that to think that it could would be yielding to depression which he ought not to do, as Schwartz's expression plainly showed. After which reflection Peter Ivanovich felt reassured, and began to ask with interest about the details of Ivan Ilych's death, as though death was an accident natural to Ivan Ilych but certainly not to himself.

After many details of the really dreadful physical sufferings Ivan Ilych had endured (which details he learnt only from the effect those sufferings had produced on Praskovya Fedorovna's nerves) the widow apparently found it necessary to get to business.

"Oh, Peter Ivanovich, how hard it is! How terribly, terribly hard!" and she again began to weep.

Peter Ivanovich sighed and waited for her to finish blowing her nose. When she had done so he said, "Believe me . . . ," and she again began talking and brought out what was evidently her chief concern with him—namely, to question him as to how she could obtain a grant of money from the government on the occasion of her husband's death. She made it appear that she was asking Peter Ivanovich's advice about her pension, but he soon saw that she already knew about that to the minutest detail, more even than he did himself. She knew how much could be got out of the government in consequence of her husband's death, but wanted to find out whether she could not possibly extract something more. Peter Ivanovich tried to think of some means of doing so, but after reflecting for a while and, out of propriety, condemning the government for it niggardliness, he said he thought that nothing more could be got. Then she sighed and evidently began to devise means of getting rid of her visitor. Noticing this, he put out his cigarette, rose, pressed her hand, and went out into the anteroom.

In the dining-room where the clock stood that Ivan Ilych had liked so much and had bought at an antique shop, Peter Ivanovich met a priest and a few acquaintances who had come to attend the service, and he recognized Ivan Ilych's daughter, a handsome young woman. She was in black and her slim figure appeared slimmer than ever. She had a gloomy, determined, almost angry expression, and bowed to Peter Ivanovich as though he were in some way to blame. Behind her, with the same offended look, stood a wealthy young man, an examining magistrate, whom Peter Ivanovich also knew and who was her fiancé, as he had heard. He bowed mournfully to them and was about to pass into the death-chamber, when from under the stairs appeared the figure of Ivan Ilych's schoolboy son, who was extremely like his father. He seemed a little Ivan Ilych, such as Peter Ivanovich remembered when they studied law together. His tear-stained eyes had in them the look that is seen in the eyes of boys of thirteen or fourteen who are not pure-minded. When he saw Peter Ivanovich he scowled morosely and shamefacedly. Peter Ivanovich nodded to him and entered the death-chamber. The service began: candles, groans, incense, tears, and sobs. Peter Ivanovich stood looking gloomily down at his feet. He did not look once at the dead man, did not yield to any depressing influence, and was one of the first to leave the room. There was no one in the anteroom, but Gerasim darted out of the dead man's room, rummaged with his strong hands among the fur coats to find Peter Ivanovich's and helped him on with it.

"Well, friend Gerasim," said Peter Ivanovich, so as to say something. "It's a sad affair, isn't it?"

"It's God's will. We shall all come to it some day," said Gerasim, displaying his teeth—the even, white teeth of a healthy peasant—and, like a man in the thick of urgent work, he briskly opened the front door, called the coachman, helped Peter Ivanovich into the sledge,[4] and sprang back to the porch as if in readiness for what he had to do next.

Peter Ivanovich found the fresh air particularly pleasant after the smell of incense, the dead body, and carbolic acid.

"Where to, sir?" asked the coachman.

"It's not too late even now. . . . I'll call round on Fedor Vasilievich."

He accordingly drove there and found them just finishing the first rubber, so that it was quite convenient for him to cut in.

II

Ivan Ilych's life had been most simple and most ordinary and therefore most terrible.

He had been a member of the Court of Justice, and died at the age of forty-five. His father had been an official who after serving in various ministries and departments in Petersburg had made the sort of career which brings men to positions from which by reason of their long service they cannot be dismissed, though they are obviously unfit to hold any responsible position, and for whom therefore posts are specially created, which though fictitious carry salaries of from six to ten thousand rubles that are not fictitious, and in receipt of which they live on to a great age.

Such was the Privy Councillor and superfluous member of various superfluous institutions, Ilya Epimovich Golovin.

He had three sons, of whom Ivan Ilych was the second. The eldest son was following in his father's footsteps only in another department, and was already approaching that stage in the service at which a similar sinecure would be reached. The third son was a failure. He had ruined his prospects in a number of positions and was now serving in the railway department. His father and brothers, and still more their wives, not merely disliked meeting him, but avoided remembering his existence unless compelled to do so. His sister had married Baron Greff, a Petersburg official of her father's type. Ivan Ilych

---

[4] A low, sled-like vehicle on runners, drawn by horses.

was *le phénix de la famille*[5] as people said. He was neither as cold and formal as his elder brother nor as wild as the younger, but was a happy mean between them—an intelligent, polished, lively and agreeable man. He had studied with his younger brother at the School of Law, but the latter had failed to complete the course and was expelled when he was in the fifth class. Ivan Ilych finished the course well. Even when he was at the School of Law he was just what he remained for the rest of his life: a capable, cheerful, good-natured, and sociable man, though strict in the fulfilment of what he considered to be his duty: and he considered his duty to be what was so considered by those in authority. Neither as a boy nor as a man was he a toady, but from early youth was by nature attracted to people of high station as a fly is drawn to the light, assimilating their ways and views of life and establishing friendly relations with them. All the enthusiasms of childhood and youth passed without leaving much trace on him; he succumbed to sensuality, to vanity, and latterly among the highest classes to liberalism, but always within limits which his instinct unfailingly indicated to him as correct.

At school he had done things which had formerly seemed to him very horrid and made him feel disgusted with himself when he did them; but when later on he saw that such actions were done by people of good position and that they did not regard them as wrong, he was able not exactly to regard them as right, but to forget about them entirely or not be at all troubled at remembering them.

Having graduated from the School of Law and qualified for the tenth rank of the civil service, and having received money from his father for his equipment, Ivan Ilych ordered himself clothes at Scharmer's, the fashionable tailor, hung a medallion inscribed *respice finem*[6] on his watch-chain, took leave of his professor and the prince who was patron of the school, had a farewell dinner with his comrades at Donon's first-class restaurant, and with his new and fashionable portmanteau, linen, clothes, shaving and other toilet appliances, and a travelling rug, all purchased at the best shops, he was off for one of the provinces where, through his father's influence, he had been attached to the Governor as an official for special service.

In the province Ivan Ilych soon arranged as easy and agreeable a position for himself as he had had at the School of Law. He performed his official tasks, made his career, and at the same time amused himself pleasantly and decorously. Occasionally he paid official visits to country districts, where he behaved with dignity both to his superiors and inferiors, and performed the duties entrusted to him, which related chiefly to the sectarians,[7] with an exactness and incorruptible honesty of which he could not but feel proud.

In official matters, despite his youth and taste for frivolous gaiety, he was exceedingly reserved, punctilious, and even severe; but in society he was often amusing and witty, and always good-natured, correct in his matter, and *bon enfant*,[8] as the governor and his wife—with whom he was like one of the family—used to say of him.

In the province he had an affair with a lady who made advances to the elegant young lawyer, and there was also a milliner; and there were carousals with aides-de-camp who visited the district, and after-supper visits to a certain

[5] The pheonix [e.g. rare bird] of the family.   [6] A Latin motto: "Regard the end."
[7] A religious sect which had broken with the Russian Orthodox Church in the seventeenth century and whose activities were legally restricted.
[8] A good child.

outlying street of doubtful reputation; and there was too some obsequiousness to his chief and even to his chief's wife, but all this was done with such a tone of good breeding that no hard names could be applied to it. It all came under the heading of the French saying: *"Il faut que jeunesse se passe."*[9] It was all done with clean hands, in clean linen, with French phrases, and above all among people of the best society and consequently with the approval of people of rank.

So Ivan Ilych served for five years and then came a change in his official life. The new and reformed judicial institutions were introduced, and new men were needed. Ivan Ilych became such a new man. He was offered the post of Examining Magistrate, and he accepted it though the post was in another province and obliged him to give up the connexions he had formed and to make new ones. His friends met to give him a send-off; they had a group-photograph taken and presented him with a silver cigarette-case, and he set off to his new post.

As examining magistrate Ivan Ilych was just as *comme il faut*[10] and decorous a man, inspiring general respect and capable of separating his official duties from his private life, as he had been when acting as an official on special service. His duties now as examining magistrate were far more interesting and attractive than before. In his former position it had been pleasant to wear an undress uniform made by Scharmer, and to pass through the crowd of petitioners and officials who were timorously awaiting an audience with the governor, and who envied him as with free and easy gait he went straight into his chief's private room to have a cup of tea and a cigarette with him. But not many people had then been directly dependent on him—only police officials and the sectarians when he went on special missions—and he liked to treat them politely, almost as comrades, as if he were letting them feel that he who had the power to crush them was treating them in this simple, friendly way. There were then but few such people. But now, as an examining magistrate, Ivan Ilych felt that everyone without exception, even the most important and self-satisfied, was in his power, and that he need only write a few words on a sheet of paper with a certain heading, and this or that important, self-satisfied person would be brought before him in the role of an accused person or a witness, and if he did not choose to allow him to sit down, would have to stand before him and answer his questions. Ivan Ilych never abused his power; he tried on the contrary to soften its expression, but the conscious-ness of it and of the possibility of softening its effect, supplied the chief interest and attraction of his office. In his work itself, especially in his examinations, he very soon acquired a method of eliminating all considerations irrelevant to the legal aspect of the case, and reducing even the most complicated case to a form in which it would be presented on paper only in its externals, com-pletely excluding his personal opinion of the matter, while above all observing every prescribed formality. The work was new and Ivan Ilych was one of the first men to apply the new Code of 1864.[11]

On taking up the post of examining magistrate in a new town, he made new acquaintances and connexions, placed himself on a new footing, and as-sumed a somewhat different tone. He took up an attitude of rather dignified

[9] Youth must have its fling. (Translators' note)   [10] Proper.
[11] The emancipation of the serfs in 1861 was followed by a thorough all-round reform of judicial proceedings. (Translators' note)

aloofness towards the provincial authorities, but picked out the best circle of legal gentlemen and wealthy gentry living in the town and assumed a tone of slight dissatisfaction with the government, of moderate liberalism, and of enlightened citizenship. At the same time, without at all altering the elegance of his toilet, he ceased shaving his chin and allowed his beard to grow as it pleased.

Ivan Ilych settled down very pleasantly in this new town. The society there, which inclined towards opposition to the Governor, was friendly, his salary was larger, and he began to play *vint* [a form of bridge], which he found added not a little to the pleasure of life, for he had a capacity for cards, played good-humoredly, and calculated rapidly and astutely, so that he usually won.

After living there for two years he met his future wife, Praskovya Fedorovna Mikhel, who was the most attractive, clever, and brilliant girl of the set in which he moved, and among other amusements and relaxations from his labours as examining magistrate, Ivan Ilych established light and playful relations with her.

While he had been an official on special service he had been accustomed to dance, but now as an examining magistrate it was exceptional for him to do so. If he danced now, he did it as if to show that though he served under the reformed order of things, and had reached the fifth official rank, yet when it came to dancing he could do it better than most people. So at the end of an evening he sometimes danced with Praskovya Fedorovna, and it was chiefly during these dances that he captivated her. She fell in love with him. Ivan Ilych had at first no definite intention of marrying, but when the girl fell in love with him he said to himself: "Really, why shouldn't I marry?"

Praskovya Fedorovna came of a good family, was not bad looking, and had some little property. Ivan Ilych might have aspired to a more brilliant match, but even this was good. He had his salary, and she, he hoped, would have an equal income. She was well connected, and was a sweet, pretty, and thoroughly correct young woman. To say that Ivan Ilych married because he fell in love with Praskovya Fedorovna and found that she sympathized with his views of life would be as incorrect as to say that he married because his social circle approved of the match. He was swayed by both these considerations: the marriage gave him personal satisfaction, and at the same time it was considered the right thing by the most highly placed of his associates.

So Ivan Ilych got married.

The preparations for marriage and the beginning of married life, with its conjugal caresses, the new furniture, new crockery, and new linen, were very pleasant until his wife became pregnant—so that Ivan Ilych had begun to think that marriage would not impair the easy, agreeable, gay and always decorous character of his life, approved of by society and regarded by himself as natural, but would even improve it. But from the first months of his wife's pregnancy, something new, unpleasant, depressing, and unseemly, and from which there was no way of escape, unexpectedly showed itself.

His wife, without any reason—*de gaieté de cœur*[12] as Ivan Ilych expressed it to himself—began to disturb the pleasure and propriety of their life. She began to be jealous without any cause, expected him to devote his whole attention to her, found fault with everything, and made coarse and ill-mannered scenes.

At first Ivan Ilych hoped to escape from the unpleasantness of this state of

[12] Out of wantonness.

affairs by the same easy and decorous relation to life that had served him
heretofore: he tried to ignore his wife's disagreeable moods, continued to
live in his usual easy and pleasant way, invited friends to his house for a game
of cards, and also tried going out to his club or spending his evenings with
friends. But one day his wife began upbraiding him so vigorously, using such
coarse words, and continued to abuse him every time he did not fulfil her
demands, so resolutely and with such evident determination not to give way
till he submitted—that is, till he stayed at home and was bored just as she
was—that he became alarmed. He now realized that matrimony—at any rate
with Praskovya Fedorovna—was not always conducive to the pleasures and
amenities of life but on the contrary often infringed both comfort and propriety,
and that he must therefore entrench himself against such infringement. And
Ivan Ilych began to seek for means of doing so. His official duties were the
one thing that imposed upon Praskovya Fedorovna, and by means of his official
work and the duties attached to it he began struggling with his wife to secure
his own independence.

With the birth of their child, the attempts to feed it and the various failures
in doing so, and with the real and imaginary illnesses of mother and child,
in which Ivan Ilych's sympathy was demanded but about which he understood
nothing, the need of securing for himself an existence outside his family life
became still more imperative.

As his wife grew more irritable and exacting and Ivan Ilych transferred the
centre of gravity of his life more and more to his official work, so did he
grow to like his work better and became more ambitious than before.

Very soon, within a year of his wedding, Ivan Ilych had realized that marriage,
though it may add some comforts to life, was in fact a very intricate and difficult
affair towards which in order to perform one's duty, that is, to lead a decorous
life approved of by society, one must adopt a definite attitude just as towards
one's official duties.

And Ivan Ilych evolved such an attitude toward married life. He only required
of it those conveniences—dinner at home, housewife, and bed—which it could
give him, and above all that propriety of external forms required by public
opinion. For the rest he looked for light-hearted pleasure and propriety, and
was very thankful when he found them, but if he met with antagonism and
querulousness he at once retired into his separate fenced-off world of official
duties, where he found satisfaction.

Ivan Ilych was esteemed a good official, and after three years was made
Assistant Public Prosecutor. His new duties, their importance, the possibility
of indicting and imprisoning anyone he chose, the publicity his speeches received, and the success he had in all these things, made his work still more
attractive.

More children came. His wife became more and more querulous and ill-
tempered, but the attitude Ivan Ilych had adopted towards his home life rendered him almost impervious to her grumbling.

After seven years' service in that town he was transferred to another province
as Public Prosecutor. They moved, but were short of money and his wife did
not like the place they moved to. Though the salary was higher the cost of
living was greater, besides which two of their children died and family life
became still more unpleasant for him.

Praskovya Fedorovna blamed her husband for every inconvenience they encountered in their new home. Most of the conversations between husband

and wife, especially as to the children's education, led to topics which recalled former disputes, and those disputes were apt to flare up again at any moment. There remained only those rare periods of amorousness which still came to them at times but did not last long. These were islets at which they anchored for a while and then again set out upon that ocean of veiled hostility which showed itself in their aloofness from one another. This aloofness might have grieved Ivan Ilych had he considered that it ought not to exist, but he now regarded the position as normal, and even made it the goal at which he aimed in family life. His aim was to free himself more and more from those unpleasantnesses and to give them a semblance of harmlessness and propriety. He attained this by spending less and less time with his family, and when obliged to be at home he tried to safeguard his position by the presence of outsiders. The chief thing however was that he had his official duties. The whole interest of his life now centered in the official world and that interest absorbed him. The consciousness of his power, being able to ruin anybody he wished to ruin, the importance, even the external dignity of his entry into court, or meetings with subordinates, his success with superiors and inferiors, and above all his masterly handling of cases, of which he was conscious—all this gave him pleasure and filled his life, together with chats with his colleagues, dinners, and bridge. So that on the whole Ivan Ilych's life continued to flow as he considered it should do—pleasantly and properly.

So things continued for another seven years. His eldest daughter was already sixteen, another child had died, and only one son was left, a schoolboy and a subject of dissension. Ivan Ilych wanted to put him in the School of Law, but to spite him Praskovya Fedorovna entered him at the High School. The daughter had been educated at home and had turned out well: the boy did not learn badly either.

III

So Ivan Ilych lived for seventeen years after his marriage. He was already a Public Prosecutor of long standing, and had declined several proposed transfers while awaiting a more desirable post, when an unanticipated and unpleasant occurrence quite upset the peaceful course of his life. He was expecting to be offered the post of presiding judge in a University town, but Happe somehow came to the front and obtained the appointment instead. Ivan Ilych became irritable, reproached Happe, and quarrelled both with him and with his immediate superiors—who became colder to him and again passed him over when other appointments were made.

This was in 1880, the hardest year of Ivan Ilych's life. It was then that it became evident on the one hand that his salary was insufficient for them to live on, and on the other that he had been forgotten, and not only this, but that what was for him the greatest and most cruel injustice appeared to others a quite ordinary occurrence. Even his father did not consider it was his duty to help him. Ivan Ilych felt himself abandoned by everyone, and that they regarded his position with a salary of 3,500 roubles [about £350] as quite normal and even fortunate. He alone knew that with the consciousness of the injustices done him, with his wife's incessant nagging, and with the debts he had contracted by living beyond his means, his position was far from normal.

In order to save money that summer he obtained leave of absence and went with his wife to live in the country at her brother's place.

In the country, without his work, he experienced *ennui* for the first time in his life, and not only *ennui* but intolerable depression, and he decided that it was impossible to go on living like that, and that it was necessary to take energetic measures.

Having passed a sleepless night pacing up and down the veranda, he decided to go to Petersburg[13] and bestir himself, in order to punish those who had failed to appreciate him and to get transferred to another ministry.

Next day, despite many protests from his wife and her brother, he started for Petersburg with the sole object of obtaining a post with a salary of five thousand rubles a year. He was no longer bent on any particular department, or tendency, or kind of activity. All he now wanted was an appointment to another post with a salary of five thousand rubles, either in the administration, in the banks, with the railways, in one of the Empress Marya's Institutions,[14] or even in the customs—but it had to carry with it a salary of five thousand rubles and be in a ministry other than that in which they had failed to appreciate him.

And this quest of Ivan Ilych's was crowned with remarkable and unexpected success. At Kursk an acquaintance of his, F. I. Ilyin, got into the first-class carriage, sat down beside Ivan Ilych, and told him of a telegram just received by the Governor of Kursk announcing that a change was about to take place in the ministry: Peter Ivanovich was to be superseded by Ivan Semenovich.

The proposed change, apart from its significance for Russia, had a special significance for Ivan Ilych, because by bringing forward a new man, Peter Petrovich, and consequently his friend Zachar Ivanovich, it was highly favourable for Ivan Ilych, since Zachar Ivanovich was a friend and colleague of his.

In Moscow this news was confirmed, and on reaching Petersburg Ivan Ilych found Zachar Ivanovich and received a definite promise of an appointment in his former department of Justice.

A week later he telegraphed his wife: "Zachar in Miller's place. I shall receive appointment on presentation of report."

Thanks to this change of personnel, Ivan Ilych had unexpectedly obtained an appointment in his former ministry which placed him two stages above his former colleagues besides giving him five thousand rubles salary and three thousand five hundred rubles for expenses connected with his removal. All his ill humour towards his former enemies and the whole department vanished, and Ivan Ilych was completely happy.

He returned to the country more cheerful and contented than he had been for a long time. Praskovya Fedorovna also cheered up and a truce was arranged between them. Ivan Ilych told of how he had been fêted by everybody in Petersburg, how all those who had been his enemies were put to shame and now fawned on him, how envious they were of his appointment, and how much everybody in Petersburg had liked him.

Praskovya Fedorovna listened to all this and appeared to believe it. She did not contradict anything, but only made plans for their life in the town to which they were going. Ivan Ilych saw with delight that these plans were his plans, that he and his wife agreed, and that, after a stumble, his life was regaining its due and natural character of pleasant lightheartedness and decorum.

Ivan Ilych had come back for a short time only, for he had to take up his new duties on the 10th of September. Moreover, he needed time to settle

[13] St. Petersburg, the Imperial capital of Russia. Renamed Lenningrad in 1924.
[14] Charities founded by Empress Marya Feodorovna (1759–1828), the wife of Czar Paul I.

into the new place, to move all his belongings from the province, and to buy and order many additional things: in a word, to make such arrangements as he had resolved on, which were almost exactly what Praskovya Fedorovna too had decided on.

Now that everything had happened so fortunately, and that he and his wife were at one in their aims and moreover saw so little of one another, they got on together better than they had done since the first years of marriage. Ivan Ilych had thought of taking his family away with him at once, but the insistence of his wife's brother and her sister-in-law, who had suddenly become particularly amiable and friendly to him and his family, induced him to depart alone.

So he departed, and the cheerful state of mind induced by his success and by the harmony between his wife and himself, the one intensifying the other, did not leave him. He found a delightful house, just the thing both he and his wife had dreamt of. Spacious, lofty reception rooms in the old style, a convenient and dignified study, rooms for his wife and daughter, a study for his son—it might have been specially built for them. Ivan Ilych himself superintended the arrangements, chose the wallpapers, supplemented the furniture (preferably with antiques which he considered particularly *comme il faut*), and supervised the upholstering. Everything progressed and progressed and approached the ideal he had set himself: even when things were only half completed they exceeded his expectations. He saw what a refined and elegant character, free from vulgarity, it would all have when it was ready. On falling asleep he pictured to himself how the reception-room would look. Looking at the yet unfinished drawing-room he could see the fireplace, the screen, the what-not, the little chairs dotted here and there, the dishes and plates on the walls, and the bronzes, as they would be when everything was in place. He was pleased by the thought of how his wife and daughter, who shared his taste in this matter, would be impressed by it. They were certainly not expecting as much. He had been particularly successful in finding, and buying cheaply, antiques which gave a particularly aristocratic character to the whole place. But in his letters he intentionally understated everything in order to be able to surprise them. All this so absorbed him that his new duties—though he liked his official work—interested him less than he expected. Sometimes he even had moments of absent-mindedness during the Court Sessions, and would consider whether he should have straight or curved cornices for his curtains. He was so interested in it all that he often did things himself, rearranging the furniture, or rehanging the curtains. Once when mounting a step-ladder to show the upholsterer, who did not understand, how he wanted the hangings draped, he made a false step and slipped, but being a strong and agile man he clung on and only knocked his side against the knob of the window frame. The bruised place was painful but the pain soon passed, and he felt particularly bright and well just then. He wrote: "I feel fifteen years younger." He thought he would have everything ready by September, but it dragged on till mid-October. But the result was charming not only in his eyes but to everyone who saw it.

In reality it was just what is usually seen in the houses of people of moderate means who want to appear rich, and therefore succeed only in resembling others like themselves: there were damasks, dark wood, plants, rugs, and dull and polished bronzes—all the things people of a certain class have in order to resemble other people of that class. His house was so like the others that

it would never have been noticed, but to him it all seemed to be quite exceptional. He was very happy when he met his family at the station and brought
them to the newly furnished house all lit up, where a footman in a white tie
opened the door into the hall decorated with plants, and when they went on
into the drawing-room and the study uttering exclamations of delight. He
conducted them everywhere, drank in their praises eagerly, and beamed with
pleasure. At tea that evening, when Praskovya Fedorovna among other things
asked him about his fall, he laughed, and showed them how he had gone
flying and had frightened the upholsterer.

"It's a good thing I'm a bit of an athlete. Another man might have been
killed, but I merely knocked myself, just here; it hurts when it's touched, but
it's passing off already—it's only a bruise."

So they began living in their new home—in which, as always happens, when
they got thoroughly settled in they found they were just one room short—
and with the increased income, which as always was just a little (some five
hundred rubles) too little, but it was all very nice.

Things went particularly well at first, before everything was finally arranged
and while something had still to be done: this thing bought, that thing ordered,
another thing moved, and something else adjusted. Though there were some
disputes between husband and wife, they were both so well satisfied and had
so much to do that it all passed off without any serious quarrels. When nothing
was left to arrange it became rather dull and something seemed to be lacking,
but they were then making acquaintances, forming habits, and life was growing
fuller.

Ivan Ilych spent his mornings at the law court and came home to dinner,
and at first he was generally in a good humour, though he occasionally became
irritable just on account of his house. (Every spot on the tablecloth or the
upholstery, and every broken window-blind string, irritated him. He had devoted so much trouble to arranging it all that every disturbance of it distressed
him.) But on the whole his life ran its course as he believed life should do:
easily, pleasantly, and decorously.

He got up at nine, drank his coffee, read the paper, and then put on his
undress uniform and went to the law courts. There the harness in which he
worked had already been stretched to fit him and he donned it without a
hitch: petitioners, inquiries at the chancery, the chancery itself, and the sittings
public and administrative. In all this the thing was to exclude everything fresh
and vital, which always disturbs the regular course of official business, and
to admit only official relations with people, and then only on official grounds.
A man would come, for instance, wanting some information. Ivan Ilych, as
one in whose sphere the matter did not lie, would have nothing to do with
him: but if the man had some business with him in his official capacity, something that could be expressed on officially stamped paper, he would do everything, positively everything he could within the limits of such relations, and
in doing so would maintain the semblance of friendly human relations, that
is, would observe the courtesies of life. As soon as the official relations ended,
so did everything else. Ivan Ilych possessed this capacity to separate his real
life from the official side of affairs and not mix the two, in the highest degree,
and by long practice and natural aptitude had brought it to such a pitch that
sometimes, in the manner of a virtuoso, he would even allow himself to let
the human and official relations mingle. He let himself do this just because

he felt that he could at any time he chose resume the strictly official attitude again and drop the human relation. And he did it all easily, pleasantly, correctly, and even artistically. In the intervals between the sessions he smoked, drank tea, chatted a little about politics, a little about general topics, a little about cards, but most of all about official appointments. Tired, but with the feelings of a virtuoso—one of the first violins who had played his part in an orchestra with precision—he would return home to find that his wife and daughter had been out paying calls, or had a visitor, and that his son had been to school, had done his homework with his tutor, and was duly learning what is taught at High Schools. Everything was as it should be. After dinner, if they had no visitors, Ivan Ilych sometimes read a book that was being much discussed at the time, and in the evening settled down to work, that is, read official papers, compared the depositions of witnesses, and noted paragraphs of the Code applying to them. This was neither dull nor amusing. It was dull when he might have been playing bridge, but if no bridge was available it was at any rate better than doing nothing or sitting with his wife. Ivan Ilych's chief pleasure was giving little dinners to which he invited men and women of good social position, and just as his drawing-room resembled all other drawing-rooms so did his enjoyable little parties resemble all other such parties.

Once they even gave a dance. Ivan Ilych enjoyed it and everything went off well, except that it led to a violent quarrel with his wife about the cakes and sweets. Praskovya Fedorovna had made her own plans, but Ivan Ilych insisted on getting everything from an expensive confectioner and ordered too many cakes, and the quarrel occurred because some of those cakes were left over and the confectioner's bill came to forty-five rubles. It was a great and disagreeable quarrel. Praskovya Fedorovna called him "a fool and an imbecile," and he clutched at his head and made angry allusions to divorce.

But the dance itself had been enjoyable. The best people were there, and Ivan Ilych had danced with Princess Trufonova, a sister of the distinguished founder of the Society "Bear my Burden."

The pleasures connected with his work were pleasures of ambition; his social pleasures were those of vanity; but Ivan Ilych's greatest pleasure was playing bridge. He acknowledged that whatever disagreeable incident happened in his life, the pleasure that beamed like a ray of light above everything else was to sit down to bridge with good players, not noisy partners, and of course to four-handed bridge (with five players it was annoying to have to stand out, though one pretended not to mind), to play a clever and serious game (when the cards allowed it) and then to have supper and drink a glass of wine. After a game of bridge, especially if he had won a little (to win a large sum was unpleasant), Ivan Ilych went to bed in specially good humour.

So they lived. They formed a circle of acquaintances among the best people and were visited by people of importance and by young folk. In their views as to their acquaintances, husband and wife and daughter were entirely agreed, and tacitly and unanimously kept at arm's length and shook off the various shabby friends and relations who, with much show of affection, gushed into the drawing-room with its Japanese plates on the walls. Soon these shabby friends ceased to obtrude themselves and only the best people remained in the Golovins' set.

Young men made up to Lisa, and Petrischhev, an examining magistrate and Dmitri Ivanovich Petrischev's son and sole heir, began to be so attentive to her that Ivan Ilych had already spoken to Praskovya Fedorovna about it, and considered whether they should not arrange a party for them, or get up some private theatricals.

So they lived, and all went well, without change, and life flowed pleasantly.

IV

They were all in good health. It could not be called ill health if Ivan Ilych sometimes said that he had a queer taste in his mouth and felt some discomfort in his left side.

But this discomfort increased and, though not exactly painful, grew into a sense of pressure in his side accompanied by ill humour. And his irritability became worse and worse and began to mar the agreeable, easy, and correct life that had established itself in the Golovin family. Quarrels between husband and wife became more and more frequent, and soon the ease and amenity disappeared and even the decorum was barely maintained. Scenes again became frequent, and very few of those islets remained on which husband and wife could meet without an explosion. Praskovya Fedorovna now had good reason to say that her husband's temper was trying. With characteristic exaggeration she said he had always had a dreadful temper, and that it had needed all her good nature to put up with it for twenty years. It was true that now the quarrels were started by him. His bursts of temper always came just before dinner, often just as he began to eat his soup. Sometimes he noticed that a plate or dish was chipped, or the food was not right, or his son put his elbow on the table, or his daughter's hair was not done as he liked it, and for all this he blamed Praskovya Fedorovna. At first she retorted and said disagreeable things to him, but once or twice he fell into such a rage at the beginning of dinner that she realized it was due to some physical derangement brought on by taking food, and so she restrained herself and did not answer, but only hurried to get the dinner over. She regarded this self-restraint as highly praiseworthy. Having come to the conclusion that her husband had a dreadful temper and made her life miserable, she began to feel sorry for herself, and the more she pitied herself the more she hated her husband. She began to wish he would die; yet she did not want him to die because then his salary would cease. And this irritated her against him still more. She considered herself dreadfully unhappy just because not even his death could save her, and though she concealed her exasperation, that hidden exasperation of hers increased his irritation also.

After one scene in which Ivan Ilych had been particularly unfair and after which he had said in explanation that he certainly was irritable but that it was due to his not being well, she said that if he was ill it should be attended to, and insisted on his going to see a celebrated doctor.

He went. Everything took place as he had expected and as it always does. There was the usual waiting and the important air assumed by the doctor, with which he was so familiar (resembling that which he himself assumed in court), and the sounding and listening, and the questions which called for answers that were foregone conclusions and were evidently unnecessary, and the look of importance which implied that "if only you put yourself in our hands we will arrange everything—we know indubitably how it has to be done, always in the same way for everybody alike." It was all just as it was in the law courts. The doctor put on just the same air towards him as he himself put on towards an accused person.

The doctor said that so-and-so indicated that there was so-and-so inside the patient, but if the investigation of so-and-so did not confirm this, then he must assume that and that. If he assumed that and that, then . . . and so on. To Ivan Ilych only one question was important: was his case serious or not? But the doctor ignored that inappropriate question. From his point of view it was not the one under consideration, the real question was to decide between a floating kidney, chronic catarrh, or appendicitis. It was not a question of Ivan Ilych's life or death, but one between a floating kidney and appendicitis. And that question the doctor solved brilliantly, as it seemed to Ivan Ilych, in favour of the appendix, with the reservation that should an examination of the urine give fresh indications the matter would be reconsidered. All this was just what Ivan Ilych had himself brilliantly accomplished a thousand times in dealing with men on trial. The doctor summed up just as brilliantly, looking over his spectacles triumphantly and even gaily at the accused. From the doctor's summing up Ivan Ilych concluded that things were bad, but that for the doctor, and perhaps for everybody else, it was a matter of indifference, though for him it was bad. And this conclusion struck him painfully, arousing in him a great feeling of pity for himself and of bitterness towards the doctor's indifference to a matter of such importance.

He said nothing of this, but rose, placed the doctor's fee on the table, and remarked with a sigh: "We sick people probably often put inappropriate questions. But tell me, in general, is this complaint dangerous, or not? . . ."

The doctor looked at him sternly over his spectacles with one eye, as if to say: "Prisoner, if you will not keep to the questions put to you, I shall be obliged to have you removed from the court."

"I have already told you what I consider necessary and proper. The analysis may show something more." And the doctor bowed.

Ivan Ilych went out slowly, seated himself disconsolately on his sledge, and drove home. All the way home he was going over what the doctor had said, trying to translate those complicated, obscure, scientific phrases into plain language and find in them an answer to the question: "Is my condition bad? Is it very bad? Or is there as yet nothing much wrong?" And it seemed to him that the meaning of what the doctor had said was that it was very bad. Everything in the streets seemed depressing. The cabmen, the houses, the passers-by, and the shops, were dismal. His ache, this dull gnawing ache that never ceased for a moment, seemed to have acquired a new and more serious significance from the doctor's dubious remarks. Ivan Ilych now watched it with a new and oppressive feeling.

He reached home and began to tell his wife about it. She listened, but in the middle of his account his daughter came in with her hat on, ready to go out with her mother. She sat down reluctantly to listen to this tedious story, but could not stand it long, and her mother too did not hear him to the end.

"Well, I am very glad," she said. "Mind now to take your medicine regularly. Give me the prescription and I'll send Gerasim to the chemist's." And she went to get ready to go out.

While she was in the room Ivan Ilych had hardly taken time to breathe, but he sighed deeply when she left it.

"Well," he thought, "perhaps it isn't so bad after all."

He began taking his medicine and following the doctor's directions, which had been altered after the examination of the urine. But then it happened that there was a contradiction between the indications drawn from the examination of the urine and the symptoms that showed themselves. It turned out that what was happening differed from what the doctor had told him, and that he had either forgotten, or blundered, or hidden something from him. He could not, however, be blamed for that, and Ivan Ilych still obeyed his orders implicitly and at first derived some comfort from doing so.

From the time of his visit to the doctor, Ivan Ilych's chief occupation was the exact fulfilment of the doctor's instructions regarding hygiene and the taking of medicine, and the observation of his pain and his excretions. His chief interests came to be people's ailments and people's health. When sickness, deaths, or recoveries, were mentioned in his presence, especially when the illness resembled his own, he listened with agitation which he tried to hide, asked questions, and applied what he heard to his own case.

The pain did not grow less, but Ivan Ilych made efforts to force himself to think that he was better. And he could do this so long as nothing agitated him. But as soon as he had any unpleasantness with his wife, any lack of success in his official work, or held bad cards at bridge, he was at once acutely sensible of his disease. He had formerly borne such mischances, hoping soon to adjust what was wrong, to master it and attain success, or make a grand slam. But now every mischance upset him and plunged him into despair. He would say to himself: "There now, just as I was beginning to get better and the medicine had begun to take effect, comes this accursed misfortune, or unpleasantness . . ." And he was furious with the mishap, or with the people who were causing the unpleasantness and killing him, for he felt that this fury was killing him but could not restrain it. One would have thought that it should have been clear to him that this exasperation with circumstances and people aggravated his illness, and that he ought therefore to ignore unpleasant occurrences. But he drew the very opposite conclusion: he said that he needed peace, and he watched for everything that might disturb it and became irritable at the slightest infringement of it. His condition was rendered worse by the fact that he read medical books and consulted doctors. The progress of his disease was so gradual that he could deceive himself when comparing one day with another—the difference was so slight. But when he consulted the doctors it seemed to him that he was getting worse, and even very rapidly. Yet despite this he was continually consulting them.

That month he went to see another celebrity, who told him almost the same as the first had done but put his questions rather differently, and the interview with this celebrity only increased Ivan Ilych's doubts and fears. A friend of a friend of his, a very good doctor, diagnosed his illness again quite differently from the others, and though he predicted recovery, his questions and suppositions bewildered Ivan Ilych still more and increased his doubts. A homeopathist[15] diagnosed the disease in yet another way, and prescribed medicine which Ivan Ilych took secretly for a week. But after a week, not feeling any improvement and having lost confidence both in the former doctor's treatment and in this one's, he became still more despondent. One day a lady acquaintance mentioned a cure effected by a wonder-working icon. Ivan Ilych caught himself listening attentively and beginning to believe that it had occurred. This incident alarmed him. "Has my mind really weakened to such an extent?" he asked himself. "Nonsense! It's all rubbish. I mustn't give way

---

[15] A medical practitioner who treated disease with drugs.

to nervous fears but having chosen a doctor must keep strictly to his treatment. That is what I will do. Now it's all settled. I won't think about it, but will follow the treatment seriously till summer, and then we shall see. From now there must be no more of this wavering!" This was easy to say but impossible to carry out. The pain in his side oppressed him and seemed to grow worse and more incessant, while the taste in his mouth grew stranger and stranger. It seemed to him that his breath had a disgusting smell, and he was conscious of a loss of appetite and strength. There was no deceiving himself: something terrible, new, and more important than anything before in his life, was taking place within him of which he alone was aware. Those about him did not understand or would not understand it, but thought everything in the world was going on as usual. That tormented Ivan Ilych more than anything. He saw that his household, especially his wife and daughter who were in a perfect whirl of visiting, did not understand anything of it and were annoyed that he was so depressed and exacting, as if he were to blame for it. Though they tried to disguise it he saw that he was an obstacle in their path, and that his wife had adopted a definite line in regard to his illness and kept to it regardless of anything he said or did. Her attitude was this: "You know," she would say to her friends, "Ivan Ilych can't do as other people do, and keep to the treatment prescribed for him. One day he'll take his drops and keep strictly to his diet and go to bed in good time, but the next day unless I watch him he'll suddenly forget his medicine, eat sturgeon—which is forbidden—and sit up playing cards until one o'clock in the morning."

"Oh, come, when was that?" Ivan Ilych would ask in vexation. "Only once at Peter Ivanovich's."

"And yesterday with Shebek."

"Well, even if I hadn't stayed up, this pain would have kept me awake."

"Be that as it may you'll never get well like that, but will always make us wretched."

Praskovya Fedorovna's attitude to Ivan Ilych's illness, as she expressed it both to others and to him, was that it was his own fault and was another of the annoyances he caused her. Ivan Ilych felt that this opinion escaped her involuntarily—but that did not make it easier for him.

At the law courts too, Ivan Ilych noticed, or thought he noticed, a strange attitude towards himself. It sometimes seemed to him that people were watching him inquisitively as a man whose place might soon be vacant. Then again, his friends would suddenly begin to chaff him in a friendly way about his low spirits, as if the awful, horrible, and unheard-of thing that was going on within him, incessantly gnawing at him and irresistibly drawing him away, was a very agreeable subject for jests. Schwartz in particular irritated him by his jocularity, vivacity, and *savoir-faire*, which reminded him of what he himself had been ten years ago.

Friends came to make up a set and they sat down to cards. They dealt, bending the new cards to soften them, and he sorted the diamonds in his hand and found he had seven. His partner said "No trumps" and supported him with two diamonds. What more could be wished for? It ought to be jolly and lively. They would make a grand slam. But suddenly Ivan Ilych was conscious of that gnawing pain, that taste in his mouth, and it seemed ridiculous that in such circumstances he should be pleased to make a grand slam.

He looked at his partner Mikhail Mikhaylovich, who rapped the table with his strong hand and instead of snatching up the tricks pushed the cards courteously and indulgently towards Ivan Ilych that he might have the pleasure of gathering them up without the trouble of stretching out his hand for them. "Does he think I am too weak to stretch out my arm?" thought Ivan Ilych, and forgetting what he was doing he over-trumped his partner, missing the grand slam by three tricks. And what was most awful of all was that he saw how upset Mikhail Mikhaylovich was about it but did not himself care. And it was dreadful to realize why he did not care.

They all saw that he was suffering, and said: "We can stop if you are tired. Take a rest." Lie down? No, he was not at all tired, and he finished the rubber. All were gloomy and silent. Ivan Ilych felt that he had diffused this gloom over them and could not dispel it. They had supper and went away, and Ivan Ilych was left alone with the consciousness that his life was poisoned and was poisoning the lives of others, and that this poison did not weaken but penetrated more and more deeply into his whole being.

With this consciousness, and with physical pain besides the terror, he must go to bed, often to lie awake the greater part of the night. Next morning he had to get up again, dress, go to the law courts, speak, and write; or if he did not go out, spend at home those twenty-four hours a day each of which was a torture. And he had to live thus all alone on the brink of an abyss, with no one who understood or pitied him.

V

So one month passed and then another. Just before the New Year his brother-in-law came to town and stayed at their house. Ivan Ilych was at the law courts and Praskovya Fedorovna had gone shopping. When Ivan Ilych came home and entered his study he found his brother-in-law there—a healthy, florid man—unpacking his portmanteau himself. He raised his head on hearing Ivan Ilych's footsteps and looked up at him for a moment without a word. That stare told Ivan Ilych everything. His brother-in-law opened his mouth to utter an exclamation of surprise but checked himself, and that action confirmed all.

"I have changed, eh?"

"Yes, there is a change."

And after that, try as he would to get his brother-in-law to return to the subject of his looks, the latter would say nothing about it. Praskovya Fedorovna came home and her brother went out to her. Ivan Ilych locked the door and began to examine himself in the glass, first full face, then in profile. He took up a portrait of himself taken with his wife, and compared it with what he saw in the glass. The change in him was immense. Then he bared his arms to the elbow, looked at them, drew the sleeves down again, sat down on an ottoman, and grew blacker than night.

"No, no, this won't do!" he said to himself, and jumped up, went to the table, took up some law papers and began to read them, but could not continue. He unlocked the door and went into the reception-room. The door leading to the drawing-room was shut. He approached it on tiptoe and listened.

"No, you are exaggerating!" Praskovya Fedorovna was saying.

"Exaggerating! Don't you see it? Why, he's a dead man! Look at his eyes—there's no light in them. But what is it that is wrong with him?"

"No one knows. Nikolaevich [that was another doctor] said something, but I don't know what. And Leschetitsky [this was the celebrated specialist] said quite the contrary . . ."

Ivan Ilych walked away, went to his own room, lay down, and began musing:

"The kidney, a floating kidney." He recalled all the doctors had told him of how it detached itself and swayed about. And by an effort of imagination he tried to catch that kidney and arrest it and support it. So little was needed for this, it seemed to him. "No, I'll go to see Peter Ivanovich again." [That was the friend whose friend was a doctor.] He rang, ordered the carriage, and got ready to go.

"Where are you going, Jean?" asked his wife, with a specially sad and exceptionally kind look.

This exceptionally kind look irritated him. He looked morosely at her.

"I must go to see Peter Ivanovich."

He went to see Peter Ivanovich, and together they went to see his friend, the doctor. He was in, and Ivan Ilych had a long talk with him.

Reviewing the anatomical and psychological details of what in the doctor's opinion was going on inside him, he understood it all.

There was something, a small thing, in the vermiform appendix. It might all come right. Only stimulate the energy of the organ and check the activity of another, then absorption would take place and everything would come right. He got home rather late for dinner, ate his dinner, and conversed cheerfully, but could not for a long time bring himself to go back to work in his room. At last, however, he went to his study and did what was necessary, but the consciousness that he had put something aside—an important, intimate matter which he would revert to when his work was done—never left him. When he had finished his work he remembered that this intimate matter was the thought of his vermiform appendix. But he did not give himself up to it, and went to the drawing-room for tea. There were callers there, including the examining magistrate who was a desirable match for his daughter, and they were conversing, playing the piano and singing. Ivan Ilych, as Praskovya Fedorovna remarked, spent that evening more cheerfully than usual, but he never for a moment forgot that he had postponed the important matter of the appendix. At eleven o'clock he said good-night and went to his bedroom. Since his illness he had slept in a small room next to his study. He undressed and took up a novel by Zola,[16] but instead of reading it he fell into thought, and in his imagination that desired improvement in the vermiform appendix occurred. There was the absorption and evacuation and the reestablishment of normal activity. "Yes, that's it!" he said to himself. "One need only assist nature, that's all." He remembered his medicine, rose, took it, and lay down on his back watching for the beneficient action of the medicine and for it to lessen the pain. "I need only take it regularly and avoid all injurious influences. I am already feeling better, much better." He began touching his side: it was not painful to the touch. "There, I really don't feel it. It's much better already." He put out the light and turned on his side . . . "The appendix is getting better, absorption is occurring." Suddenly he felt the old, familiar, dull, gnawing pain, stubborn and serious. There was the same familiar loathsome taste in his mouth. His heart sank and he felt dazed. "My God! My God!" he muttered. "Again, again! And it will never cease." And suddenly the matter presented itself in a quite different aspect. "Vermiform appendix! Kidney!" he said to himself. "It's not a question of appendix or kidney, but of life and . . . death. Yes, life was there and now it is going, going and I cannot stop it. Yes. Why deceive myself? Isn't it obvious to everyone but me that I'm dying, and that it's only

---

[16] Émile Zola (1840–1902), the French novelist; "father" of the naturalistic novel.

a question of weeks, days . . . it may happen this moment. There was light and now there is darkness. I was here and now I'm going there! Where?" A chill came over him, his breathing ceased, and he felt only the throbbing of his heart.

"When I am not, what will there be? There will be nothing. Then where shall I be when I am no more? Can this be dying? No, I don't want to!" He jumped up and tried to light the candle, felt for it with trembling hands, dropped candle and candlestick on the floor, and fell back on his pillow.

"What's the use? It makes no difference," he said to himself, staring with wide-open eyes into the darkness. "Death. Yes, death. And none of them know or wish to know it, and they have no pity for me. Now they are playing." (He heard through the door the distant sound of a song and its accompaniment.) "It's all the same to them, but they will die too! Fools! I first, and they later, but it will be the same for them. And now they are merry . . . the beasts!"

Anger choked him and he was agonizingly, unbearably miserable. "It is impossible that all men have been doomed to suffer this awful horror!" He raised himself.

"Something must be wrong. I must calm myself—must think it all over from the beginning." And he again began thinking. "Yes, the beginning of my illness: I knocked my side, but I was still quite well that day and the next. It hurt a little, then rather more. I saw the doctors, then followed despondency and anguish, more doctors, and I drew nearer to the abyss. My strength grew less and I kept coming nearer and nearer, and now I have wasted away and there is no light in my eyes. I think of the appendix—but this is death! I think of mending the appendix, and all the while here is death! Can it really be death?" Again terror seized him and he gasped for breath. He leant down and began feeling for the matches, pressing with his elbow on the stand beside the bed. It was in his way and hurt him, he grew furious with it, pressed on it still harder, and upset it. Breathless and in despair he fell on his back, expecting death to come immediately.

Meanwhile the visitors were leaving. Praskovya Fedorovna was seeing them off. She heard something fall and came in.

"What has happened?"

"Nothing. I knocked it over accidentally."

She went out and returned with a candle. He lay there panting heavily, like a man who has run a thousand yards, and stared upwards at her with a fixed look.

"What is it, Jean?"

"No . . . o . . . thing. I upset it." ("Why speak of it? She won't understand," he thought.)

And in truth she did not understand. She picked up the stand, lit the candle, and hurried away to see another visitor off. When she came back he still lay on his back, looking upwards.

"What is it? Do you feel worse?"

"Yes."

She shook her head and sat down.

"Do you know, Jean, I think we must ask Leshchetitsky to come and see you here."

This meant calling in the famous specialist, regardless of expense. He smiled malignantly and said "No." She remained a little longer and then went up to him and kissed his forehead.

While she was kissing him he hated her from the bottom of his soul and with difficulty refrained from pushing her away.

"Good-night. Please God you'll sleep."

"Yes."

VI

Ivan Ilych saw that he was dying, and he was in continual despair.

In the depth of his heart he knew he was dying, but not only was he not accustomed to the thought, he simply did not and could not grasp it.

The syllogism he had learnt from Kiezewetter's Logic:[17] "Caius is a man, men are mortal, therefore Caius is mortal," had always seemed to him correct as applied to Caius, but certainly not as applied to himself. That Caius—man in the abstract—was mortal, was perfectly correct, but he was not Caius, not an abstract man, but a creature quite quite separate from all others. He had been little Vanya, with a mamma and a papa, with Mitya and Volodya, with the toys, a coachman and a nurse, afterwards with Katenka and with all the joys, griefs, and delights of childhood, boyhood, and youth. What did Caius know of the smell of that striped leather ball Vanya had been so fond of? Had Caius kissed his mother's hand like that, and did the silk of her dress rustle so for Caius? Had he rioted like that at school when the pastry was bad? Had Caius been in love like that? Could Caius preside at a session as he did? "Caius really was mortal, and it was right for him to die; but for me, little Vanya, Ivan Ilych, with all my thoughts and emotions, it's altogether a different matter. It cannot be that I ought to die. That would be too terrible."

Such was his feeling.

"If I had to die like Caius I should have known it was so. An inner voice would have told me so, but there was nothing of the sort in me and I and all my friends felt that our case was quite different from that of Caius. And now here it is!" he said to himself. "It can't be. It's impossible! But here it is. How is this? How is one to understand it?"

He could not understand it, and tried to drive this false, incorrect, morbid thought away and to replace it by other proper and healthy thoughts. But that thought, and not the thought only but the reality itself, seemed to come and confront him.

And to replace that thought he called up a succession of others, hoping to find in them some support. He tried to get back into the former current of thoughts that had once screened the thought of death from him. But strange to say, all that had formerly shut off, hidden, and destroyed, his consciousness of death, no longer had that effect. Ivan Ilych now spent most of his time in attempting to re-establish that old current. He would say to himself: "I will take up my duties again—after all I used to live by them." And banishing all doubts he would go to the law courts, enter into conversation with his colleagues, and sit carelessly as was his wont, scanning the crowd with a thoughtful look and leaning both his emaciated arms on the arms of his oak chair; bending over as usual to a colleague and drawing his papers nearer he would interchange whispers with him, and then suddenly raising his eyes and sitting erect would pronounce certain words and open the proceedings. But suddenly in the midst of those proceedings the pain in his side, regardless of the stage the proceedings

---

[17] Karl Kiezewetter (1766–1819), the German philosopher who authored a widely used text on logic (1796).

had reached, would begin its own gnawing work. Ivan Ilych would turn his attention to it and try to drive the thought of it away, but without success. *It* would come and stand before him and look at him, and he would be petrified and the light would die out of his eyes, and he would again begin asking himself whether *It* alone was true. And his colleagues and subordinates would see with surprise and distress that he, the brilliant and subtle judge, was becoming confused and making mistakes. He would shake himself, try to pull himself together, manage somehow to bring the sitting to a close, and return home with the sorrowful consciousness that his judicial labours could not as formerly hide from him what he wanted them to hide, and could not deliver him from *It.* And what was worst of all was that *It* drew his attention to itself not in order to make him take some action but only that he should look at *It*, look it straight in the face: look at it and without doing anything, suffer inexpressibly.

And to save himself from this condition Ivan Ilych looked for consolations—new screens—and new screens were found and for a while seemed to save him, but then they immediately fell to pieces or rather became transparent, as if *It* penetrated them and nothing could veil *It.*

In these latter days he would go into the drawing-room he had arranged—that drawing-room where he had fallen and for the sake of which (how bitterly ridiculous it seemed) he had sacrificed his life—for he knew that his illness originated with that knock. He would enter and see that something had scratched the polished table. He would look for the cause of this and find that it was the bronze ornamentation of an album, that had got bent. He would take up the expensive album which he had lovingly arranged, and feel vexed with his daughter and her friends for their untidiness—for the album was torn here and there and some of the photographs turned upside down. He would put it carefully in order and bend the ornamentation back into position. Then it would occur to him to place all those things in another corner of the room, near the plants. He would call the footman, but his daughter or wife would come to help him. They would not agree, and his wife would contradict him, and he would dispute and grow angry. But that was all right, for then he did not think about *It. It* was invisible.

But then, when he was moving something himself, his wife would say: "Let the servants do it. You will hurt yourself again." And suddenly *It* would flash through the screen and he would see it. It was just a flash, and he hoped it would disappear, but he would involuntarily pay attention to his side. "It sits there as before, gnawing just the same!" And he could no longer forget *It,* but could distinctly see it looking at him from behind the flowers. "What is it all for?"

"It really is so! I lost my life over that curtain as I might have done when storming a fort. Is that possible? How terrible and how stupid. It can't be true! It can't, but it is."

He would go to his study, lie down, and again be alone with *It:* face to face with *It.* And nothing could be done with *It* except to look at it and shudder.

VII

How it happened it is impossible to say because it came about step by step, unnoticed, but in the third month of Ivan Ilych's illness, his wife, his daughter, his son, his acquaintances, the doctors, the servants, and above all he himself, were aware that the whole interest he had for other people was whether he would soon vacate his place, and at last release the living from the discomfort caused by his presence and be himself released from his sufferings.

He slept less and less. He was given opium and hypodermic injections or morphine, but this did not relieve him. The dull depression he experienced in a somnolent condition at first gave him a little relief, but only as something new, afterwards it became as distressing as the pain itself or even more so.

Special foods were prepared for him by the doctors' orders, but all those foods became increasingly distasteful and disgusting to him.

For his excretions also special arrangements had to be made, and this was a torment to him every time—a torment from the uncleanliness, the unseemliness, and the smell, and from knowing that another person had to take part in it.

But just through this most unpleasant matter Ivan Ilych obtained comfort. Gerasim, the butler's young assistant, always came in to carry the things out. Gerasim was a clean, fresh peasant lad, grown stout on town food and always cheerful and bright. At first the sight of him, in his clean Russian peasant costume, engaged on that disgusting task embarrassed Ivan Ilych.

Once when he got up from the commode too weak to draw up his trousers, he dropped into a soft armchair and looked with horror at his bare, enfeebled thighs with the muscles so sharply marked on them.

Gerasim with a firm light tread, his heavy boots emitting a pleasant smell of tar and fresh winter air, came in wearing a clean Hessian apron, the sleeves of his print shirt tucked up over his strong bare young arms and refraining from looking at his sick master out of consideration for his feelings, and restraining the joy of life that beamed from his face, he went up to the commode.

"Gerasim!" said Ivan Ilych in a weak voice.

Gerasim started, evidently afraid he might have committed some blunder, and with a rapid movement turned his fresh, kind, simple young face which just showed the first downy signs of a beard.

"Yes, sir?"

"That must be very unpleasant for you. You must forgive me. I am helpless."

"Oh, why, sir," and Gerasim's eyes beamed and he showed his glistening white teeth, "what's a little trouble? It's a case of illness with you, sir."

And his deft strong hands did their accustomed task, and he went out of the room stepping lightly. Five minutes later he as lightly returned.

Ivan Ilych was still sitting in the same position in the armchair.

"Gerasim," he said when the latter had replaced the freshly-washed utensil. "Please come here and help me." Gerasim went up to him. "Life me up. It is hard for me to get up, and I have sent Dmitri away."

Gerasim went up to him, grasped his master with his strong arms deftly but gently, in the same way that he stepped—lifted him, supported him with one hand, and with the other drew up his trousers and would have set him down again, but Ivan Ilych asked to be led to the sofa. Gerasim, without an effort and without apparent pressure, led him, almost lifting him, to the sofa and placed him on it.

"Thank you. How easily and well you do it all!"

Gerasim smiled again and turned to leave the room. But Ivan Ilych felt his presence such a comfort that he did not want to let him go.

"One thing more, please move up that chair. No, the other one—under my feet. It is easier for me when my feet are raised."

Gerasim brought the chair, set it down gently in place, and raised Ivan Ilych's legs on to it. It seemed to Ivan Ilych that he felt better while Gerasim was holding up his legs.

"It's better when my legs are higher," he said. "Place that cushion under them."

Gerasim did so. He again lifted the legs and placed them, and again Ivan Ilych felt better while Gerasim held his legs. When he set them down Ivan Ilych fancied he felt worse.

"Gerasim," he said. "Are you busy now?"

"Not at all, sir," said Gerasim, who had learnt from the townfolk how to speak to gentlefolk.

"What have you still to do?"

"What have I to do? I've done everything except chopping the logs for tomorrow."

"Then hold my legs up a bit higher, can you?"

"Of course I can. Why not?" And Gerasim raised his master's legs higher and Ivan Ilych thought that in that position he did not feel any pain at all.

"And how about the logs?"

"Don't trouble about that, sir. There's plenty of time."

Ivan Ilych told Gerasim to sit down and hold his legs, and began to talk to him. And strange to say it seemed to him that he felt better while Gerasim held his legs up.

After that Ivan Ilych would sometimes call Gerasim and get him to hold his legs on his shoulders, and he liked talking to him. Gerasim did it all easily, willingly, simply, and with a good nature that touched Ivan Ilych. Health, strength, and vitality in other people were offensive to him, but Gerasim's strength and vitality did not mortify but soothed him.

What tormented Ivan Ilych most was the deception, the lie, which for some reason they all accepted, that he was not dying but was simply ill, and that he only need keep quiet and undergo a treatment and then something very good would result. He however knew that do what they would nothing would come of it, only still more agonizing suffering and death. This deception tortured him—their not wishing to admit what they all knew and what he knew, but wanting to lie to him concerning his terrible condition, and wishing and forcing him to participate in that lie. Those lies—lies enacted over him on the eve of his death and destined to degrade this awful, solemn act to the level of their visitings, their curtains, their sturgeon for dinner—were a terrible agony for Ivan Ilych. And strangely enough, many times when they were going through their antics over him he had been within a hairbreadth of calling out to them: "Stop lying! You know and I know that I am dying. Then at least stop lying about it!" But he had never had the spirit to do it. The awful terrible act of his dying was, he could see, reduced by those about him to the level of a casual, unpleasant, and almost indecorous incident (as if someone entered a drawing-room diffusing an unpleasant odor) and this was done by that very decorum which he had served all his life long. He saw that no one felt for him, because no one even wished to grasp his position. Only Gerasim recognized it and pitied him. And so Ivan Ilych felt at ease only with him. He felt comforted when Gerasim supported his legs (sometimes all night long) and refused to go to bed, saying: "Don't you worry, Ivan Ilych. I'll get sleep enough later on," or when he suddenly became familiar and exclaimed: "If you weren't sick it would be another matter, but as it is, why should I grudge a little trouble?" Gerasim alone did not lie; everything showed that he alone understood the facts of the case and did not consider it necessary to disguise them, but simply felt sorry for his emaciated and enfeebled master. Once when Ivan Ilych was sending him away he even said straight out: "We shall all of us die, so why should I grudge a little trouble?"—expressing the fact that he did not think his work burdensome, because he was doing it for a dying man and hoped someone would do the same for him when his time came.

Apart from this lying, or because of it, what most tormented Ivan Ilych was that no one pitied him as he wished to be pitied. At certain moments after prolonged suffering he wished most of all (though he would have been ashamed to confess it) for someone to pity him as a sick child is pitied. He longed to be petted and comforted. He knew he was an important functionary, that he had a beard turning grey, and that therefore what he longed for was impossible, but still he longed for it. And in Gerasim's attitude toward him there was something akin to what he wished for, and so that attitude comforted him. Ivan Ilych wanted to be petted and cried over, and then his colleague Shebek would come, and instead of weeping and being petted, Ivan Ilych would assume a serious, severe, and profound air, and by force of habit would express his opinon on a decision of the Court of Cassation[18] and would stubbornly insist on that view. This falsity around him and within him did more than anything else to poison his last days.

VIII

It was morning. He knew it was morning because Gerasim had gone, and Peter the footman had come and put out the candles, drawn back one of the curtains, and began quietly to tidy up. Whether it was morning or evening, Friday or Sunday, made no difference, it was all just the same: the gnawing, unmitigated, agonizing pain, never ceasing for an instant, the consciousness of life inexorably waning but not yet extinguished, the approach of that ever dreaded and hateful Death which was the only reality, and always the same falsity. What were days, weeks, hours, in such a case?

"Will you have some tea, sir?"

"He wants things to be regular, and wishes the gentlefolk to drink tea in the morning," thought Ivan Ilych, and only said "No."

"Wouldn't you like to move onto the sofa, sir?"

"He wants to tidy up the room, and I'm in the way. I am uncleanliness and disorder," he thought, and said only:

"No, leave me alone."

The man went on bustling about. Ivan Ilych stretched out his hand. Peter came up, ready to help.

"What is it, sir?"

"My watch."

Peter took the watch which was close at hand and gave it to his master.

"Half-past eight. Are they up?"

"No sir, except Vladimir Ivanich" (the son) "who has gone to school. Praskovya Fedorovna ordered me to wake her if you asked for her. Shall I do so?"

"No, there's no need to." "Perhaps I'd better have some tea," he thought, and added aloud: "Yes, bring me some tea."

---

[18] The court of high appeals.

Peter went out. Left alone Ivan Ilych dreaded being left alone. "How can I keep him here? Oh yes, my medicine." "Peter, give me my medicine." "Why not? Perhaps it may still do me some good." He took a spoonful and swallowed it. "No, it won't help. It's all tomfoolery, all deception," he decided as soon as he became aware of the familiar, sickly, hopeless taste. "No, I can't believe in it any longer. But the pain, why this pain? If it would only cease just for a moment!" And he moaned. Peter turned towards him. "It's all right. Go and fetch me some tea."

Peter went out. Left alone Ivan Ilych groaned not so much with pain, terrible though that was, as from mental anguish. Always and for ever the same, always these endless days and nights. If only it would come quicker! If only *what* would come quicker? Death, darkness? . . . No, no! Anything rather than death!

When Peter returned with the tea on a tray, Ivan Ilych stared at him for a time in perplexity, not realizing who and what he was. Peter was disconcerted by that look and his embarrassment brought Ivan Ilych to himself.

"Oh, tea! All right, put it down. Only help me to wash and put on a clean shirt."

And Ivan Ilych began to wash. With pauses for rest, he washed his hands and then his face, cleaned his teeth, brushed his hair, and looked in the glass. He was terrified by what he saw, especially by the limp way in which his hair clung to his pallid forehead.

While his shirt was being changed he knew that he would be still more frightened at the sight of his body, so he avoided looking at it. Finally he was ready. He drew on a dressing-gown, wrapped himself in a plaid, and sat down in the armchair to take his tea. For a moment he felt refreshed, but as soon as he began to drink the tea he was again aware of the same taste, and the pain also returned. He finished it with an effort, and then lay down stretching out his legs, and dismissed Peter.

Always the same. Now a spark of hope flashes up, then a sea of despair rages, and always pain; always pain, always despair, and always the same. When alone he had a dreadful and distressing desire to call someone, but he knew beforehand that with others present it would be still worse. "Another dose of morphine—to lose consciousness. I will tell him, the doctor, that he must think of something else. It's impossible, impossible, to go on like this."

An hour and another pass like that. But now there is a ring at the door bell. Perhaps it's the doctor? It is. He comes in fresh, hearty, plump, and cheerful, with that look on his face that seems to say: "There now, you're in a panic about something, but we'll arrange it all for you directly!" The doctor knows this expression is out of place here, but he has put it on once for all and can't take it off—like a man who has put on a frock-coat in the morning to pay a round of calls.

The doctor rubs his hands vigorously and reassuringly.

"Brr! How cold it is! There's such a sharp frost; just let me warm myself!" he says, as if it were only a matter of waiting till he was warm, and then he would put everything right.

"Well now, how are you?"

Ivan Ilych feels that the doctor would like to say: "Well, how are our affairs?" but that even he feels that this would not do, and says instead: "What sort of a night have you had?"

Ivan Ilych looks at him as much as to say: "Are you really never ashamed of lying?" But the doctor does not wish to understand this question, and Ivan

Ilych says: "Just as terrible as ever. The pain never leaves me and never subsides. If only something . . ."

"Yes, you sick people are always like that. . . . There, now I think I am warm enough. Even Praskovya Fedorovna, who is so particular, could find no fault with my temperature. Well, now I can say good-morning," and the doctor presses his patient's hand.

Then, dropping his former playfulness, he begins with a most serious face to examine the patient, feeling his pulse and taking his temperature, and then begins the sounding and auscultation.

Ivan Ilych knows quite well and definitely that all this is nonsense and pure deception, but when the doctor, getting down on his knee, leans over him, putting his ear first higher then lower, and performs various gymnastic movements over him with a significant expression on his face, Ivan Ilych submits to it all as he used to submit to the speeches of the lawyers, though he knew very well that they were all lying and why they were lying.

The doctor, kneeling on the sofa, is still sounding him when Praskovya Fedorovna's silk dress rustles at the door and she is heard scolding Peter for not having let her know of the doctor's arrival.

She comes in, kisses her husband, and at once proceeds to prove that she has been up a long time already, and only owing to a misunderstanding failed to be there when the doctor arrived.

Ivan Ilych looks at her, scans her all over, sets against her the whiteness and plumpness and cleanness of her hands and neck, the gloss of her hair, and the sparkle of her vivacious eyes. He hates her with his whole soul. And the thrill of hatred he feels for her makes him suffer from her touch.

Her attitude towards him and his disease is still the same. Just as the doctor had adopted a certain relation to his patient which he could not abandon, so had she formed one towards him—that he was not doing something he ought to do and was himself to blame, and that she reproached him lovingly for this—and she could not now change that attitude.

"You see he doesn't listen to me and doesn't take his medicine at the proper time. And above all he lies in a position that is no doubt bad for him—with his legs up."

She described how he made Gerasim hold his legs up.

The doctor smiled with a contemptuous affability that said: "What's to be done? These sick people do have foolish fancies of that kind, but we must forgive them."

When the examination was over the doctor looked at his watch, and then Praskovya Fedorovna announced to Ivan Ilych that it was of course as he pleased, but she had sent to-day for a celebrated specialist who would examine him and have a consultation with Michael Danilovich (their regular doctor).

"Please don't raise any objections. I am doing this for my own sake," she said ironically, letting it be felt that she was doing it all for his sake and only said this to leave him no right to refuse. He remained silent, knitting his brows. He felt that he was so surrounded and involved in a mesh of falsity that it was hard to unravel anything.

Everything she did for him was entirely for her own sake, and she told him she was doing for herself what she actually was doing for herself, as if that was so incredible that he must understand the opposite.

At half-past eleven the celebrated specialist arrived. Again the sounding began and the significant conversations in his presence and in another room, about the kidneys and the appendix, and the questions and answers, with such an air of importance that again, instead of the real question of life and death which now alone confronted him, the question arose of the kindey and appendix which were not behaving as they ought to and would now be attacked by Michael Danilovich and the specialist and forced to amend their ways.

The celebrated specialist took leave of him with a serious though not hopeless look, and in reply to the timid question Ivan Ilych, with eyes glistening with fear and hope, put to him as to whether there was a chance of recovery, said that he could not vouch for it but there was a possibility. The look of hope with which Ivan Ilych watched the doctor out was so pathetic that Praskovya Fedorovna, seeing it, even wept as she left the room to hand the doctor his fee.

The gleam of hope kindled by the doctor's encouragement did not last long. The same room, the same pictures, curtains, wall-paper, medicine bottles, were all there, and the same aching suffering body, and Ivan Ilych began to moan. They gave him a subcutaneous injection and he sank into oblivion.

It was twilight when he came to. They brought his dinner and he swallowed some beef tea with difficulty, and then everything was the same again and night was coming on.

After dinner, at seven o'clock, Praskovya Fedorovna came into the room in evening dress, her full bosom pushed up by her corset, and with traces of powder on her face. She had reminded him in the morning that they were going to the theatre. Sarah Bernhardt[19] was visiting the town and they had a box, which he had insisted on their taking. Now he had forgotten about it and her toilet offended him, but he concealed his vexation when he remembered that he had himself insisted on their securing a box and going because it would be an instructive and aesthetic pleasure for the children.

Praskovya Fedorovna came in, self-satisfied but yet with a rather guilty air. She sat down and asked how he was but, as he saw, only for the sake of asking and not in order to learn about it, knowing that there was nothing to learn—and then went on to what she really wanted to say: that she would not on any account have gone but that the box had been taken and Helen and their daughter were going, as well as Petrishchev (the examining magistrate, their daughter's fiancé) and that it was out of the question to let them go alone; but that she would have much preferred to sit with him for a while; and he must be sure to follow the doctor's orders while she was away.

"Oh, and Fedor Petrovich" (the fiancé) "would like to come in. May he? And Lisa?"

"All right."

Their daughter came in in full evening dress, her fresh young flesh exposed (making a show of that very flesh which in his own case caused so much suffering), strong, healthy, evidently in love, and impatient with illness, suffering, and death, because they interfered with her happiness.

Fedor Petrovich came in too, in evening dress, his hair curled à la Capoul,[20] a tight stiff collar round his long sinewy neck, an enormous white shirt-front and narrow black trousers tightly stretched over his strong thighs. He had one white glove tightly drawn on, and was holding his opera hat in his hand.

[19] Sarah Bernhardt (1844–1923), the famous French actress; she appeared in St. Petersburg in 1882.

[20] A popular contemporary hair style named after the French tenor Victor Capoul (1839–1924).

Following him the schoolboy crept in unnoticed, in a new uniform, poor little fellow, and wearing gloves. Terribly dark shadows showed under his eyes, the meaning of which Ivan Ilych knew well.

His son had always seemed pathetic to him, and now it was dreadful to see the boy's frightened look of pity. It seemed to Ivan Ilych that Vasya was the only one besides Gerasim who understood and pitied him.

They all sat down and again asked how he was. A silence followed. Lisa asked her mother about the opera-glasses, and there was an altercation between mother and daughter as to who had taken them and where they had been put. This occasioned some unpleasantness.

Fedor Petrovich inquired of Ivan Ilych whether he had ever seen Sarah Bernhardt. Ivan Ilych did not at first catch the question, but then replied: "No, have you seen her before?"

"Yes, in *Adrienne Lecouvreur*."[21]

Praskovya Fedorovna mentioned some rôles in which Sarah Bernhardt was particularly good. Her daughter disagreed. Conversation sprang up as to the elegance and realism of her acting—the sort of conversation that is always repeated and is always the same.

In the midst of the conversation Fedor Petrovich glanced at Ivan Ilych and became silent. The others also looked at him and grew silent. Ivan Ilych was staring with glittering eyes straight before him, evidently indignant with them. This had to be rectified, but it was impossible to do so. The silence had to be broken, but for a time no one dared to break it and they all became afraid that the conventional deception would suddenly become obvious and the truth become plain to all. Lisa was the first to pluck up courage and break that silence, but by trying to hide what everybody was feeling, she betrayed it.

"Well, if we are going it's time to start," she said, looking at her watch, a present from her father, and with a faint and significant smile at Fedor Petrovich relating to something known only to them. She got up with a rustle of her dress.

They all rose, said good-night, and went away.

When they had gone it seemed to Ivan Ilych that he felt better; the falsity had gone with them. But the pain remained—that same pain and that same fear that made everything monotonously alike, nothing harder and nothing easier. Everything was worse.

Again minute followed minute and hour followed hour. Everything remained the same and there was no cessation. And the inevitable end of it all became more and more terrible.

"Yes, send Gerasim here," he replied to a question Peter asked.

IX

His wife returned late at night. She came in on tiptoe, but he heard her, opened his eyes, and made haste to close them again. She wished to send Gerasim away and to sit with him herself, but he opened his eyes and said: "No, go away."

"Are you in great pain?"

"Always the same."

"Take some opium."

He agreed and took some. She went away.

[21] The play written by French dramatist Eugène Scribe (1791–1861).

Till about three in the morning he was in a state of stupified misery. It seemed to him that he and his pain were being thrust into a narrow, deep black sack, but though they were pushed further and further in they could not be pushed to the bottom. And this, terrible enough in itself, was accompanied by suffering. He was frightened yet wanted to fall through the sack, he struggled but yet co-operated. And suddenly he broke through, fell, and regained consciousness. Gerasim was sitting at the foot of the bed dozing quietly and patiently, while he himself lay with his emaciated stockinged legs resting on Gerasim's shoulders; the same shaded candle was there and the same unceasing pain.

"Go away, Gerasim," he whispered.

"It's all right, sir. I'll stay a while."

"No. Go away."

He removed his legs from Gerasim's shoulders, turned sideways onto his arm, and felt sorry for himself. He only waited till Gerasim had gone into the next room and then restrained himself no longer but wept like a child. He wept on account of his helplessness, his terrible loneliness, the cruelty of man, the cruelty of God, and the absence of God.

"Why hast Thou done all this? Why hast Thou brought me here? Why, why dost Thou torment me so terribly?"

He did not expect an answer and yet wept because there was no answer and could be none. The pain again grew more acute, but he did not stir and did not call. He said to himself: "Go on! Strike me! But what is it for? What have I done to Thee? What is it for?"

Then he grew quiet and not only ceased weeping but even held his breath and became all attention. It was as though he were listening not to an audible voice but to the voice of his soul, to the current of thoughts arising within him.

"What is it you want?" was the first clear conception capable of expression in words, that he heard.

"What do you want? What do you want?" he repeated to himself.

"What do I want? To live and not to suffer," he answered.

And again he listened with such concentrated attention that even his pain did not distract him.

"To live? How?" asked his inner voice.

"Why, to live as I used to—well and pleasantly."

"As you lived before, well and pleasantly?" the voice repeated.

And in imagination he began to recall the best moments of his pleasant life. But strange to say none of those best moments of his pleasant life now seemed at all what they had then seemed—none of them except the first recollections of childhood. There, in childhood, there had been something really pleasant with which it would be possible to live if it could return. But the child who had experienced that happiness existed no longer, it was like a reminiscence of somebody else.

As soon as the period began which had produced the present Ivan Ilych, all that had then seemed joys now melted before his sight and turned into something trivial and often nasty.

And the further he departed from childhood and the nearer he came to the present the more worthless and doubtful were the joys. This began with the School of Law. A little that was really good was still found there—there was light-heartedness, friendship, and hope. But in the upper classes there had already been fewer of such good moments. Then during the first years of his official career, when he was in the service of the Governor, some pleasant moments again occurred: they were the memories of love for a woman. Then all became confused and there was still less of what was good; later on again there was still less that was good, and the further he went the less there was. His marriage, a mere accident, then the disenchantment that followed it, his wife's bad breath and the sensuality and hypocrisy: then that deadly official life and those preoccupations about money, a year of it, and two, and ten, and twenty, and always the same thing. And the longer it lasted the more deadly it became. "It is as if I had been going downhill while I imagined I was going up. And that is really what it was. I was going up in public opinion, but to the same extent life was ebbing away from me. And now it is all done and there is only death."

"Then what does it mean? Why? It can't be that life is so senseless and horrible. But if it really has been so horrible and senseless, why must I die and die in agony? There is something wrong!"

"Maybe I did not live as I ought to have done," it suddenly occurred to him. "But how could that be, when I did everything properly?" he replied, and immediately dismissed from his mind this, the sole solution of all the riddles of life and death, as something quite impossible.

"Then what do you want now? To live? Live how? Live as you lived in the law courts when the usher proclaimed 'The Judge is coming!' The judge is coming, the judge!" he repeated to himself. "Here he is, the judge. But I am not guilty!" he exclaimed angrily. "What is it for?" And he ceased crying, but turning his face to the wall continued to ponder on the same question: Why, and for what purpose, is there all this horror? But however much he pondered he found no answer. And whenever the thought occurred to him, as it often did, that it all resulted from his not having lived as he ought to have done, he at once recalled the correctness of his whole life and dismissed so strange an idea.

x

Another fortnight passed. Ivan Ilych now no longer left his sofa. He would not lie in bed but lay on the sofa, facing the wall nearly all the time. He suffered ever the same unceasing agonies and in his loneliness pondered always on the same insoluble question: "What is this? Can it be that it is Death?" And the inner voice answered: "Yes, it is Death."

"Why these sufferings?" And the voice answered, "For no reason—they just are so." Beyond and besides this there was nothing.

From the very beginning of his illness, ever since he had first been to see the doctor, Ivan Ilych's life had been divided between two contrary and alternating moods: now it was despair and the expectation of this uncomprehended and terrible death, and now hope and an intently interested observation of the functioning of his organs. Now before his eyes there was only a kidney or an intestine that temporarily evaded its duty, and now only that incomprehensible and dreadful death from which it was impossible to escape.

These two states of mind had alternated from the very beginning of his illness, but the further it progressed the more doubtful and fantastic became the conception of the kidney, and the more real the sense of impending death.

He had but to call to mind what he had been three months before and what he was now, to call to mind with what regularity he had been going downhill, for every possibility of hope to be shattered.

Latterly during that loneliness in which he found himself as he lay facing the back of the sofa, a loneliness in the midst of a populous town and surrounded by numerous acquaintances and relations but that yet could not have been more complete anywhere—either at the bottom of the sea or under the earth—during that terrible loneliness Ivan Ilych had lived only in memories of the past. Pictures of his past rose before him one after another. They always began with what was nearest in time and then went back to what was most remote—to his childhood—and rested there. If he thought of the stewed prunes that had been offered him that day, his mind went back to the raw shrivelled French plums of his childhood, their peculiar flavour and the flow of saliva when he sucked their stones, and along with the memory of that taste came a whole series of memories of those days: his nurse, his brother, and their toys. "No, I mustn't think of that. . . . It is too painful," Ivan Ilych said to himself, and brought himself back to the present—to the button on the back of the sofa and the creases in its morocco. "Morocco is expensive, but it does not wear well: there had been a quarrel about it. It was a different kind of quarrel and a different kind of morocco that time when we tore father's portfolio and were punished, and mamma brought us some tarts. . . ." And again his thought dwelt on his childhood, and again it was painful and he tried to banish them and fix his mind on something else.

Then again together with that chain of memories another series passed through his mind—of how his illness had progressed and grown worse. There also the further back he looked the more life there had been. There had been more of what was good in life and more of life itself. The two merged together. "Just as the pain went on getting worse and worse so my life grew worse and worse," he thought. "There is one bright spot there at the back, at the beginning of life, and afterwards all becomes blacker and blacker and proceeds more and more rapidly—in inverse ratio to the square of the distance from death," thought Ivan Ilych. And the example of a stone falling downwards with increasing velocity entered his mind. Life, a series of increasing sufferings, flies further and further towards its end—the most terrible suffering. "I am flying. . . ." He shuddered, shifted himself, and tried to resist, but was already aware that resistance was impossible, and again with eyes weary of gazing but unable to cease seeing what was before them, he stared at the back of the sofa and waited—awaiting that dreadful fall and shock and destruction.

"Resistance is impossible!" he said to himself. "If I could only understand what it is all for! But that too is impossible. An explanation would be possible if it could be said that I have not lived as I ought to. But it is impossible to say that," and he remembered all the legality, correctitude, and propriety of his life. "That at any rate can certainly not be admitted," he thought, and his lips smiled ironically as if someone could see that smile and be taken in by it. "There is no explanation! Agony, death. . . . What for?"

XI

Another two weeks went by in this way and during that fortnight an event occured that Ivan Ilych and his wife had desired. Petrishchev formally proposed. It happened in the evening. The next day Praskovya Fedorovna came into her husband's room considering how best to inform him of it, but that very night there had been a fresh change for the worse in his condition. She found him still lying on the sofa but in a different position. He lay on his back, groaning and staring fixedly straight in front of him.

She began to remind him of his medicines, but he turned his eyes towards her with such a look that she did not finish what she was saying; so great an animosity, to her in particular, did that look express.

"For Christ's sake let me die in peace!" he said.

She would have gone away, but just then their daughter came in and went up to say good morning. He looked at her as he had done at his wife, and in reply to her inquiry about his health said dryly that he would soon free them all of himself. They were both silent and after sitting with him for a while went away.

"Is it our fault?" Lisa said to her mother. "It's as if we were to blame! I am sorry for papa, but why should we be tortured?"

The doctor came at his usual time. Ivan Ilych answered "Yes" and "No," never taking his angry eyes from him, and at last said: "You know you can do nothing for me, so leave me alone."

"We can ease your sufferings."

"You can't even do that. Let me be."

The doctor went into the drawing-room and told Praskovya Fedorovna that the case was very serious and that the only resource left was opium to allay her husband's sufferings, which must be terrible.

It was true, as the doctor said, that Ivan Ilych's physical sufferings were terrible, but worse than the physical sufferings were his mental sufferings which were his chief torture.

His mental sufferings were due to the fact that that night, as he looked at Gerasim's sleepy, good-natured face with its prominent cheek-bones, the question suddenly occurred to him: "What if my whole life has really been wrong?"

It occurred to him that what had appeared perfectly impossible before, namely that he had not spent his life as he should have done, might after all be true. It occurred to him that his scarcely perceptible attempts to struggle against what was considered good by the most highly placed people, those scarcely noticeable impulses which he had immediately suppressed, might have been the real thing, and all the rest false. And his professional duties and the whole arrangement of his life and of his family, and all his social and official interests, might all have been false. He tried to defend all those things to himself and suddenly felt the weakness of what he was defending. There was nothing to defend.

"But if that is so," he said to himself, "and I am leaving this life with the consciousness that I have lost all that was given me and it is impossible to rectify it—what then?"

He lay on his back and began to pass his life in review in quite a new way. In the morning when he saw first his footman, then his wife, then his daughter, and then the doctor, their every word and movement confirmed to him the awful truth that had been revealed to him during the night. In them he saw himself—all that for which he had lived—and saw clearly that it was not real at all, but a terrible and huge deception which had hidden both life and death. This consciousness intensified his physical suffering tenfold. He groaned and tossed about, and pulled at his clothing which choked and stifled him. And he hated them on that account.

He was given a large dose of opium and became unconscious, but at noon his sufferings began again. He drove everybody away and tossed from side to side.

His wife came to him and said:

"Jean, my dear, do this for me. It can't do any harm and often helps. Healthy people often do it."

He opened his eyes wide.

"What? Take communion? Why? It's unnecessary! However. . . ."

She began to cry.

"Yes, do, my dear. I'll send for our priest. He is such a nice man."

"All right. Very well," he muttered.

When the priest came and heard his confession, Ivan Ilych was softened and seemed to feel a relief from his doubts and consequently from his sufferings, and for a moment there came a ray of hope. He again began to think of the vermiform appendix and the possibility of correcting it. He received the sacrament with tears in his eyes.

When they laid him down again afterwards he felt a moment's ease, and the hope that he might live awoke in him again. He began to think of the operation that had been suggested to him. "To live! I want to live!" he said to himself.

His wife came in to congratulate him after his communion, and when uttering the usual conventional words she added:

"You feel better, don't you?"

Without looking at her he said "Yes."

Her dress, her figure, the expression of her face, the tone of her voice, all revealed the same thing. "This is wrong, it is not as it should be. All you have lived for and still live for is falsehood and deception, hiding life and death from you." And as soon as he admitted that thought, his hatred and his agonizing physical suffering again sprang up, and with that suffering a consciousness of the unavoidable, approaching end. And to this was added a new sensation of grinding shooting pain and a feeling of suffocation.

The expression of his face when he uttered that "yes" was dreadful. Having uttered it, he looked her straight in the eyes, turned on his face with a rapidity extraordinary in his weak state and shouted:

"Go away! Go away and leave me alone!"

XII

From that moment the screaming began that continued for three days, and was so terrible that one could not hear it through two closed doors without horror. At the moment he answered his wife he realized that he was lost, that there was no return, that the end had come, the very end, and his doubts were still unsolved and remained doubts.

"Oh! Oh! Oh!" he cried in various intonations. He had begun by screaming "I won't!" and continued screaming on the letter "o."

For three whole days, during which time did not exist for him, he struggled in that black sack into which he was being thrust by an invisible, resistless force. He struggled as a man condemned to death struggles in the hands of the executioner, knowing that he cannot save himself. And every moment he felt that despite all his efforts he was drawing nearer and nearer to what terrified him. He felt that his agony was due to his being thrust into that black hole and still more to his not being able to get right into it. He was hindered from getting into it by his conviction that his life had been a good one. That very justification of his life held him fast and prevented his moving forward, and it caused him most torment of all.

Suddenly some force struck him in the chest and side, making it still harder to breathe, and he fell through the hole and there at the bottom was a light. What had happened to him was like the sensation one sometimes experiences in a railway carriage when one thinks one is going backwards while one is really going forwards and suddenly becomes aware of the real direction.

"Yes, it was all not the right thing," he said to himself, "but that's no matter. It can be done. But what *is* the right thing?" he asked himself, and suddenly grew quiet.

This occurred at the end of the third day, two hours before his death. Just then his schoolboy son had crept softly in and gone up to the bedside. The dying man was still screaming desperately and waving his arms. His hand fell on the boy's head, and the boy caught it, pressed it to his lips, and began to cry.

At that very moment Ivan Ilych fell through and caught sight of the light, and it was revealed to him that though his life had not been what it should have been, this could still be rectified. He asked himself, "What *is* the right thing?" and grew still, listening. Then he felt that someone was kissing his hand. He opened his eyes, looked at his son, and felt sorry for him. His wife came up to him and he glanced at her. She was gazing at him open-mouthed, with undried tears on her nose and cheek and a despairing look on her face. He felt sorry for her too.

"Yes, I am making them wretched," he thought. "They are sorry, but it will be better for them when I die." He wished to say this but had not the strength to utter it. "Besides, why speak? I must act," he thought. With a look at his wife he indicated his son and said: "Take him away . . . sorry for him . . . sorry for you too. . . ." He tried to add, "forgive me," but said "forego" and waved his hand, knowing that He whose understanding mattered would understand.

And suddenly it grew clear to him that what had been oppressing him and would not leave him was all dropping away at once from two sides, from ten sides, and from all sides. He was sorry for them, he must act so as not to hurt them: release them and free himself from these sufferings. "How good and how simple!" he thought. "And the pain?" he asked himself. "What has become of it? Where are you, pain?"

He turned his attention to it.

"Yes, here it is. Well, what of it? Let the pain be."

"And death . . . where is it?"

He sought his former accustomed fear of death and did not find it. "Where is it? What death?" There was no fear because there was no death.

In place of death there was light.

"So that's what it is!" he suddenly exclaimed aloud. "What joy!"

To him all this happened in a single instant, and the meaning of that instant did not change. For those present his agony continued for another two hours. Something rattled in his throat, his emaciated body twitched, then the gasping and rattle became less and less frequent.

"It is finished!" said someone near him.

He heard these words and repeated them in his soul.

"Death is finished," he said to himself. "It is no more!"

He drew in a breath, stopped in the midst of a sigh, stretched out, and died.

[1886]

Arthur Conan Doyle   *1859–1930*

THE ADVENTURE OF THE SPECKLED BAND

In glancing over my notes of the seventy odd cases in which I have during the last eight years studied the methods of my friend Sherlock Holmes, I find many tragic, some comic, a large number merely strange, but none commonplace; for, working as he did rather for the love of his art than for the acquirement of wealth, he refused to associate himself with any investigation which did not tend towards the unusual, and even the fantastic. Of all these varied cases, however, I cannot recall any which presented more singular features than that which was associated with the well-known Surrey family of the Roylotts of Stoke Moran. The events in question occurred in the early days of my association with Holmes, when we were sharing rooms as bachelors, in Baker Street. It is possible that I might have placed them upon record before, but a promise of secrecy was made at the time, from which I have only been freed during the last month by the untimely death of the lady to whom the pledge was given. It is perhaps as well that the facts should now come to light, for I have reasons to know there are widespread rumours as to the death of Dr. Grimesby Roylott which tend to make the matter even more terrible than the truth.

It was early in April, in the year '83, that I woke one morning to find Sherlock Holmes standing, fully dressed, by the side of my bed. He was a late riser as a rule, and, as the clock on the mantelpiece showed me that it was only a quarter past seven, I blinked up at him in some surprise, and perhaps just a little resentment, for I was myself regular in my habits.

"Very sorry to knock you up, Watson," said he, "but it's the common lot this morning. Mrs. Hudson has been knocked up, she retorted upon me, and I on you."

"What is it, then? A fire?"

"No, a client. It seems that a young lady has arrived in a considerable state of excitement, who insists upon seeing me. She is waiting now in the sitting-room. Now, when young ladies wander about the metropolis at this hour of the morning, and knock sleepy people up out of their beds, I presume that it is something very pressing which they have to communicate. Should it prove to be an interesting case, you would, I am sure, wish to follow it from the outset. I thought at any rate that I should call you, and give you the chance."

"My dear fellow, I would not miss it for anything."

I had no keener pleasure than in following Holmes in his professional investigations, and in admiring the rapid deductions, as swift as intuitions, and yet always founded on a logical basis, with which he unravelled the problems which were submitted to him. I rapidly threw on my clothes, and was ready in a few minutes to accompany my friend down to the sitting-room. A lady dressed in black and heavily veiled, who had been sitting in the window, rose as we entered.

"Good morning, madam," said Holmes cheerily. "My name is Sherlock Holmes. This is my intimate friend and associate, Dr. Watson, before whom you can speak as freely as before myself. Ha, I am glad to see that Mrs. Hudson has had the good sense to light the fire. Pray draw up to it, and I shall order you a cup of hot coffee, for I observe that you are shivering."

"It is not cold which makes me shiver," said the woman in a low voice, changing her seat as requested.

"What then?"

"It is fear, Mr. Holmes. It is terror." She raised her veil as she spoke, and we could see that she was indeed in a pitiable state of agitation, her face all drawn and grey, with restless, frightened eyes, like those of some hunted animal. Her features and figure were those of a woman of thirty, but her hair was shot with premature grey, and her expression was weary and haggard. Sherlock Holmes ran her over with one of his quick, all-comprehensive glances.

"You must not fear," said he soothingly, bending forward and patting her forearm. "We shall soon set matters right, I have no doubt. You have come in by train this morning, I see."

"You know me, then?"

"No, but I observe the second half of a return ticket in the palm of your left glove. You must have started early, and yet you had a good drive in a dog-cart, along heavy roads, before you reached the station."

The lady gave a violent start, and stared in bewilderment at my companion.

"There is no mystery, my dear madam," said he, smiling. "The left arm of your jacket is spattered with mud in no less than seven places. The marks are perfectly fresh. There is no vehicle save a dog-cart which throws up mud in that way, and then only when you sit on the left-hand side of the driver."

"Whatever your reasons may be, you are perfectly correct," said she. "I started from home before six, reached Leatherhead at twenty past, and came in by the first train to Waterloo.[1] Sir, I can stand this strain no longer, I shall go mad if it continues. I have no one to turn to—none, save only one, who cares for me, and he, poor fellow, can be of little aid. I have heard of you, Mr. Holmes; I have heard of you from Mrs. Farintosh, whom you helped in the hour of her sore need. It was from her that I had your address. Oh, sir, do you not think you could help me too, and at least throw a little light through the dense darkness which surrounds me? At present it is out of my power to reward you for your services, but in a month or two I shall be married, with the control of my own income, and then at least you shall not find me ungrateful."

Holmes turned to his desk, and unlocking it, drew out a small case-book which he consulted.

"Farintosh," said he. "Ah, yes, I recall the case; it was concerned with an opal tiara. I think it was before your time, Watson. I can only say, madam, that I shall be happy to devote the same care to your case as I did to that of your friend. As to reward, my profession is its reward; but you are at liberty to defray whatever expenses I may be put to, at the time which suits you best. And now I beg that you will lay before us everything that may help us in forming an opinion upon the matter."

"Alas!" replied our visitor. "The very horror of my situation lies in the fact that my fears are so vague, and my suspicions depend so entirely upon small points, which might seem trivial to another, that even he to whom of all others I have a right to look for help and advice looks upon all that I tell him about it as the fancies of a nervous woman. He does not say so, but I

---

[1] Waterloo Station, London.

can read it from his soothing answers and averted eyes. But I have heard, Mr. Holmes, that you can see deeply into the manifold wickedness of the human heart. You may advise me how to walk amid the dangers which encompass me."

"I am all attention, madam."

"My name is Helen Stoner, and I am living with my stepfather, who is the last survivor of one of the oldest Saxon families in England, the Roylotts of Stoke Moran, on the western border of Surrey."

Holmes nodded his head. "The name is familiar to me," said he.

"The family was at one time among the richest in England, and the estate extended over the borders into Berkshire in the north, and Hampshire in the west. In the last century, however, four successive heirs were of a dissolute and wasteful disposition, and the family ruin was eventually completed by a gambler, in the days of the Regency.[2] Nothing was left save a few acres of ground and the two-hundred-year-old house, which is itself crushed under a heavy mortgage. The last squire dragged out his existence there, living the horrible life of an aristocratic pauper; but his only son, my stepfather, seeing that he must adapt himself to the new conditions, obtained an advance from a relative, which enabled him to take a medical degree, and went out to Calcutta, where, by his professional skill and his force of character, he established a large practice. In a fit of anger, however, caused by some robberies which had been perpetrated in the house, he beat his native butler to death, and narrowly escaped a capital sentence. As it was, he suffered a long term of imprisonment, and afterwards returned to England a morose and disappointed man.

"When Dr. Roylott was in India he married my mother, Mrs. Stoner, the young widow of Major-General Stoner, of the Bengal Artillery. My sister Julia and I were twins, and we were only two years old at the time of my mother's re-marriage. She had a considerable sum of money, not less than a thousand a year, and this she bequeathed to Dr. Roylott entirely whilst we resided with him, with a provision that a certain annual sum should be allowed to each of us in the event of our marriage. Shortly after our return to England my mother died—she was killed eight years ago in a railway accident near Crewe. Dr. Roylott then abandoned his attempts to establish himself in practice in London, and took us to live with him in the ancestral house at Stoke Moran. The money which my mother had left was enough for all our wants, and there seemed no obstacle to our happiness.

"But a terrible change came over our stepfather about this time. Instead of making friends and exchanging visits with our neighbours, who had at first been overjoyed to see a Roylott of Stoke Moran back in the old family seat, he shut himself up in his house, and seldom came out save to indulge in ferocious quarrels with whoever might cross his path. Violence of temper approaching to mania has been hereditary in the men of the family, and in my stepfather's case it had, I believe, been intensified by his long residence in the tropics. A series of disgraceful brawls took place, two of which ended in the police-court, until at last he became the terror of the village, and the folks would fly at his approach, for he is a man of immense strength, and absolutely uncontrollable in his anger.

---

[2] 1811–1820, the years of George III's incapacity, when the government was run by the Prince of Wales, later George IV.

"Last week he hurled the local blacksmith over a parapet into a stream and it was only by paying over all the money that I could gather together that I was able to avert another public exposure. He had no friends at all save the wandering gipsies, and he would give these vagabonds leave to encamp upon the few acres of bramble-covered land which represent the family estate, and would accept in return the hospitality of their tents, wandering away with them sometimes for weeks on end. He has a passion also for Indian animals, which are sent over to him by a correspondent, and he has at this moment a cheetah and a baboon, which wander freely over his grounds, and are feared by the villagers almost as much as their master.

"You can imagine from what I say that my poor sister Julia and I had no great pleasure in our lives. No servant would stay with us, and for a long time we did all the work of the house. She was but thirty at the time of her death, and yet her hair had already begun to whiten, even as mine has."

"Your sister is dead, then?"

"She died just two years ago, and it is of her death that I wish to speak to you. You can understand that, living the life which I have described, we were little likely to see anyone of our own age and position. We had, however, an aunt, my mother's maiden sister, Miss Honoria Westphail, who lives near Harrow, and we were occasionally allowed to pay short visits at this lady's house. Julia went there at Christmas two years ago, and met there a half-pay Major of Marines, to whom she became engaged. My stepfather learned of the engagement when my sister returned, and offered no objection to the marriage; but within a fortnight of the day which had been fixed for the wedding, the terrible event occurred which has deprived me of my only companion."

Sherlock Holmes had been leaning back in his chair with his eyes closed, and his head sunk in a cushion, but he half opened his lids now, and glanced across at his visitor.

"Pray be precise as to details," said he.

"It is easy for me to be so, for every event of that dreadful time is seared into my memory. The manor house is, as I have already said, very old, and only one wing is now inhabited. The bedrooms in this wing are on the ground floor, the sitting-rooms being in the central block of the buildings. Of these bedrooms, the first is Dr. Roylott's, the second my sister's, and the third my own. There is no communication between them, but they all open out into the same corridor. Do I make myself plain?"

"Perfectly so."

"The windows of the three rooms open out upon the lawn. That fatal night Dr. Roylott had gone to his room early, though we knew that he had not retired to rest, for my sister was troubled by the smell of the strong Indian cigars which it was his custom to smoke. She left her room, therefore, and came into mine, where she sat for some time, chatting about her approaching wedding. At eleven o'clock she rose to leave me, but she paused at the door and looked back.

" 'Tell me, Helen,' said she, 'have you ever heard anyone whistle in the dead of the night?'

" 'Never,' said I.

" 'I suppose that you could not possibly whistle yourself in your sleep?'

" 'Certainly not. But why?'

" 'Because during the last few nights I have always, about three in the morning, heard a low clear whistle. I am a light sleeper, and it has awakened me.

I cannot tell where it came from—perhaps from the next room, perhaps from the lawn. I thought that I would just ask you whether you had heard it.'

" 'No, I have not. It must be those wretched gipsies in the plantation.'

" 'Very likely. And yet if it were on the lawn I wonder that you did not hear it also.'

" 'Ah, but I sleep more heavily than you.'

" 'Well, it is of no great consequence, at any rate,' she smiled back at me, closed my door, and a few moments later I heard her key turn in the lock."

"Indeed," said Holmes. "Was it your custom always to lock yourselves in at night?"

"Always."

"And why?"

"I think that I mentioned to you that the Doctor kept a cheetah and a baboon. We had no feeling of security unless our doors were locked."

"Quite so. Pray proceed with your statement."

"I could not sleep that night. A vague feeling of impending misfortune impressed me. My sister and I, you will recollect, were twins, and you know how subtle are the links which bind two souls which are so closely allied. It was a wild night. The wind was howling outside, and the rain was beating and splashing against the windows. Suddenly, amidst all the hubbub of the gale, there burst forth the wild scream of a terrified woman. I knew that it was my sister's voice. I sprang from my bed, wrapped a shawl round me, and rushed into the corridor. As I opened my door I seemed to hear a low whistle, such as my sister described, and a few moments later a clanging sound, as if a mass of metal had fallen. As I ran down the passage my sister's door was unlocked, and revolved slowly upon its hinges. I stared at it horror-stricken, not knowing what was about to issue from it. By the light of the corridor lamp I saw my sister appear at the opening, her face blanched with terror, her hands groping for help, her whole figure swaying to and fro like that of a drunkard. I ran to her and threw my arms round her, but at that moment her knees seemed to give way and she fell to the ground. She writhed as one who is in terrible pain, and her limbs were dreadfully convulsed. At first I thought that she had not recognized me, but as I bent over her she suddenly shrieked out in a voice which I shall never forget, 'O, my God! Helen! It was the band! The speckled band!' There was something else which she would fain have said, and she stabbed with her finger into the air in the direction of the Doctor's room, but a fresh convulsion seized her and choked her words. I rushed out, calling loudly for my stepfather, and I met him hastening from his room in his dressing-gown. When he reached my sister's side she was unconscious, and though he poured brandy down her throat, and sent for medical aid from the village, all efforts were in vain, for she slowly sank and died without having recovered her consciousness. Such was the dreadful end of my beloved sister."

"One moment," said Holmes; "are you sure about this whistle and metallic sound? Could you swear to it?"

"That was what the county coroner asked me at the inquiry. It is my strong impression that I heard it, and yet among the crash of the gale, and the creaking of an old house, I may possibly have been deceived."

"Was your sister dressed?"

"No, she was in her nightdress. In her right hand was found the charred stump of a match, and in her left a matchbox."

"Showing that she had struck a light and looked about her when the alarm took place. That is important. And what conclusions did the coroner come to?"

"He investigated the case with great care, for Dr. Roylott's conduct had long been notorious in the county, but he was unable to find any satisfactory cause of death. My evidence showed that the door had been fastened upon the inner side, and the windows were blocked by oldfashioned shutters with broad iron bars, which were secured every night. The walls were carefully sounded, and were shown to be quite solid all round, and the flooring was also thoroughly examined, with the same result. The chimney is wide, but is bared up by four large staples. It is certain, therefore, that my sister was quite alone when she met her end. Besides, there were no marks of any violence upon her."

"How about poison?"

"The doctors examined her for it, but without success."

"What do you think that this unfortunate lady died of, then?"

"It is my belief that she died of pure fear and nervous shock, though what it was which frightened her I cannot imagine."

"Were there gipsies in the plantation at the time?"

"Yes, there are nearly always some there."

"Ah, and what did you gather from this allusion to a band—a speckled band?"

"Sometimes I have thought that it was merely the wild talk of delirium, sometimes that it may have referred to some band of people, perhaps to these very gipsies in the plantation. I do not know whether the spotted handkerchiefs which so many of them wear over their heads might have suggested the strange adjective which she used."

Holmes shook his head like a man who is far from being satisfied.

"These are very deep waters," said he; "pray go on with your narrative."

"Two years have passed since then, and my life has been until lately lonelier than ever. A month ago, however, a dear friend, whom I have known for many years, has done me the honour to ask my hand in marriage. His name is Armitage—Percy Armitage—the second son of Mr. Armitage, of Crane Water, near Reading. My stepfather has offered no opposition to the match, and we are to be married in the course of the spring. Two days ago some repairs were started in the west wing of the building, and my bedroom wall has been pierced, so that I have had to move into the chamber in which my sister died, and to sleep in the very bed in which she slept. Imagine, then, my thrill of terror when last night, as I lay awake, thinking over her terrible fate, I suddenly heard in the silence of the night the low whistle which had been the herald of her own death. I sprang up and lit the lamp, but nothing was to be seen in the room. I was too shaken to go to bed again, however, so I dressed, and as soon as it was daylight I slipped down, got a dog-cart at the Crown Inn, which is opposite, and drove to Leatherhead, from whence I have come on this morning, with the one object of seeing you and asking your advice."

"You have done wisely," said my friend. "But have you told me all?"

"Yes, all."

"Miss Stoner, you have not. You are screening your stepfather."

"Why, what do you mean?"

For answer Holmes pushed back the frill of black lace which fringed the hand that lay upon our visitor's knee. Five little livid spots, the marks of four fingers and a thumb, were printed upon the white wrist.

"You have been cruelly used," said Holmes.

The lady coloured deeply, and covered over her injured wrist. "He is a hard man," she said, "and perhaps he hardly knows his own strength."

There was a long silence, during which Holmes leaned his chin upon his hands and stared into the crackling fire.

"This is a very deep business," he said at last. "There are a thousand details which I should desire to know before I decide upon our course of action. Yet we have not a moment to lose. If we were to come to Stoke Moran to-day, would it be possible for us to see over these rooms without the knowledge of your stepfather?"

"As it happens, he spoke of coming into town to-day upon some most important business. It is probable that he will be away all day, and that there would be nothing to disturb you. We have a housekeeper now, but she is old and foolish, and I could easily get her out of the way."

"Excellent. You are not averse to this trip, Watson?"

"By no means."

"Then we shall both come. What are you going to do yourself?"

"I have one or two things which I would wish to do now that I am in town. But I shall return by the twelve o'clock train, so as to be there in time for your coming."

"And you may expect us early in the afternoon. I have myself some small business matters to attend to. Will you not wait and breakfast?"

"No, I must go. My heart is lightened already since I have confided my trouble to you. I shall look forward to seeing you again this afternoon." She dropped her thick black veil over her face, and glided from the room.

"And what do you think of it all, Watson?" asked Sherlock Holmes, leaning back in his chair.

"It seems to me to be a most dark and sinister business."

"Dark enough and sinister enough."

"Yet if the lady is correct in saying that the flooring and walls are sound, and that the door, window, and chimney are impassable, then her sister must have been undoubtedly alone when she met her mysterious end."

"What becomes, then, of these nocturnal whistles, and what of the very peculiar words of the dying woman?"

"I cannot think."

"When you combine the ideas of whistles at night, the presence of a band of gipsies who are on intimate terms with this old doctor, the fact that we have every reason to believe that the doctor has an interest in preventing his stepdaughter's marriage, the dying allusion to a band, and finally, the fact that Miss Helen Stoner heard a metallic clang, which might have been caused by one of those metal bars which secured the shutters falling back into their place, I think there is good ground to think that the mystery may be cleared along those lines."

"But what, then, did the gipsies do?"

"I cannot imagine."

"I see many objections to any such a theory."

"And so do I. It is precisely for that reason that we are going to Stoke Moran this day. I want to see whether the objections are fatal, or if they may be explained away. But what, in the name of the devil!"

The ejaculation had been drawn from my companion by the fact that our door had been suddenly dashed open, and that a huge man framed himself in the aperture. His costume was a peculiar mixture of the professional and of the agricultural, having a black top-hat, a long frock-coat, and a pair of high gaiters, with a hunting-crop swinging in his hand. So tall was he that his hat actually brushed the cross-bar of the doorway, and his breadth seemed to span it across from side to side. A large face, seared with a thousand wrinkles, burned yellow with the sun, and marked with every evil passion, was turned from one to the other of us, while his deep-set, bile-shot eyes, and the high thin fleshless nose, gave him somewhat the resemblance to a fierce old bird of prey.

"Which of you is Holmes?" asked this apparition.

"My name, sir, but you have the advantage of me," said my companion quietly.

"I am Dr. Grimesby Roylott, of Stoke Moran."

"Indeed, Doctor," said Holmes blandly. "Pray take a seat."

"I will do nothing of the kind. My stepdaughter has been here. I have traced her. What has she been saying to you?"

"It is a little cold for the time of the year," said Holmes.

"What has she been saying to you?" screamed the old man furiously.

"But I have heard that the crocuses promise well," continued my companion imperturbably.

"Ha! You put me off, do you?" said our new visitor, taking a step forward, and shaking his hunting-crop. "I know you, you scoundrel! I have heard of you before. You are Holmes the meddler."

My friend smiled.

"Holmes the busybody!"

His smile broadened.

"Holmes the Scotland Yard jack-in-office."

Holmes chuckled heartily. "Your conversation is most entertaining," said he. "When you go out close the door, for there is a decided draught."

"I will go when I have had my say. Don't you dare to meddle with my affairs. I know that Miss Stoner has been here—I traced her! I am a dangerous man to fall foul of! See here." He stepped swiftly forward, seized the poker, and bent it into a curve with his huge brown hands.

"See that you keep yourself out of my grip," he snarled, and hurling the twisted poker into the fireplace, he strode out of the room.

"He seems a very amiable person," said Holmes, laughing. "I am not quite so bulky, but if he had remained I might have shown him that my grip was not much more feeble than his own." As he spoke he picked up the steel poker, and with a sudden effort straightened it out again.

"Fancy his having the insolence to confound me with the official detective force! This incident gives zest to our investigation, however, and I only trust that our little friend will not suffer from her imprudence in allowing this brute to trace her. And now, Watson, we shall order breakfast, and afterwards I shall walk down to Doctors' Commons,[3] where I hope to get some data which may help us in this matter."

---

[3] Holmes is obviously speaking in a general sense of the will office, for in 1874—nine years previous to the time of the story—the will office was moved from "Doctor's Common" (the College of Doctors of Civil Law) to Somerset House, its present location.

It was nearly one o'clock when Sherlock Holmes returned from his excursion. He held in his hand a sheet of blue paper, scrawled over with notes and figures.

"I have seen the will of the deceased wife," said he. "To determine its exact meaning I have been obliged to work out the present prices of the investments with which it is concerned. The total income, which at the time of the wife's death was little short of £1,100, is now through the fall in agricultural prices not more than £750. Each daughter can claim an income of £250, in case of marriage. It is evident, therefore, that if both girls had married this beauty would have had a mere pittance, while even one of them would cripple him to a serious extent. My morning's work has not been wasted, since it has proved that he has the very strongest motives for standing in the way of anything of the sort. And now, Watson, this is too serious for dawdling, especially as the old man is aware that we are interesting ourselves in his affairs, so if you are ready we shall call a cab and drive to Waterloo. I should be very much obliged if you would slip your revolver into your pocket. An Eley's No. 2 is an excellent argument with gentlemen who can twist steel pokers into knots. That and a toothbrush are, I think, all that we need."

At Waterloo we were fortunate in catching a train for Leatherhead, where we hired a trap at the station inn, and drove for four or five miles through the lovely Surrey lanes. It was a perfect day, with a bright sun and a few fleecy clouds in the heavens. The trees and wayside hedges were just throwing out their first green shoots, and the air was full of the pleasant smell of the moist earth. To me at least there was a strange contrast between the sweet promise of the spring and this sinister quest upon which we were engaged. My companion sat in front of the trap, his arms folded, his hat pulled down over his eyes, and his chin sunk upon his breast, buried in the deepest thought. Suddenly, however, he started, tapped me on the shoulder, and pointed over the meadows.

"Look there!" said he.

A heavily timbered park stretched up in a gentle slope, thickening into a grove at the highest point. From amidst the branches there jutted out the gray gables and high roof-tree of a very old mansion.

"Stoke Moran?" said he.

"Yes, sir, that be the house of Dr. Grimesby Roylott," remarked the driver.

"There is some building going on there," said Holmes; "that is where we are going."

"There's the village," said the driver, pointing to a cluster of roofs some distance to the left; "but if you want to get to the house, you'll find it shorter to go over this stile, and so by the footpath over the fields. There it is, where the lady is walking."

"And the lady, I fancy, is Miss Stoner," observed Holmes, shading his eyes. "Yes, I think we had better do as you suggest."

We got off, paid our fare, and the trap rattled back on its way to Leatherhead.

"I thought it as well," said Holmes, as we climbed the stile, "that this fellow should think we had come here as architects, or on some definite business. It may stop his gossip. Good afternoon, Miss Stoner. You see that we have been as good as our word."

Our client of the morning had hurried forward to meet us with a face which spoke her joy. "I have been waiting so eagerly for you," she cried, shaking hands with us warmly. "All has turned out splendidly. Dr. Roylott has gone to town, and it is unlikely that he will be back before evening."

"We have had the pleasure of making the Doctor's acquaintance," said Holmes, and in a few words he sketched out what had occurred. Miss Stoner turned white to the lips as she listened.

"Good heavens!" she cried, "he has followed me, then."

"So it appears."

"He is so cunning that I never know when I am safe from him. What will he say when he returns?"

"He must guard himself, for he may find that there is someone more cunning than himself upon his track. You must lock yourself from him to-night. If he is violent, we shall take you away to your aunt's at Harrow. Now, we must make the best use of our time, so kindly take us at once to the rooms which we are to examine."

The building was of grey, lichen-blotched stone, with a high central portion, and two curving wings, like the claws of a crab, thrown out on each side. In one of these wings the windows were broken, and blocked with wooden boards, while the roof was partly caved in, a picture of ruin. The central portion was in little better repair, but the right-hand block was comparatively modern, and the blinds in the windows, with the blue smoke curling up from the chimneys, showed that this was where the family resided. Some scaffolding had been erected against the end wall, and the stonework had been broken into, but there were no signs of any workmen at the moment of our visit. Holmes walked slowly up and down the ill-trimmed lawn, and examined with deep attention the outsides of the windows.

"This, I take it, belongs to the room in which you used to sleep, the centre one to your sister's, and the one next to the main building to Dr. Roylott's chamber?"

"Exactly so. But I am now sleeping in the middle one."

"Pending the alterations, as I understand. By the way, there does not seem to be any very pressing need for repairs at that end wall."

"There were none. I believe that it was an excuse to move me from my room."

"Ah! that is suggestive. Now, on the other side of this narrow wing runs the corridor from which these three rooms open. There are windows in it, of course?"

"Yes, but very small ones. Too narrow for anyone to pass through."

"As you both locked your doors at night, your rooms were unapproachable from that side. Now, would you have the kindness to go into your room, and to bar your shutters."

Miss Stoner did so, and Holmes, after a careful examination through the open window, endeavoured in every way to force the shutter open, but without success. There was no slit through which a knife could be passed to raise the bar. Then with his lens he tested the hinges, but they were of solid iron, built firmly into the massive masonry. "Hum!" said he, scratching his chin in some perplexity, "my theory certainly presents some difficulties. No one could pass these shutters if they were bolted. Well, we shall see if the inside throws any light upon the matter."

A small side-door led into the whitewashed corridor from which the three bedrooms opened. Holmes refused to examine the third chamber, so we passed at once to the second, that in which Miss Stoner was now sleeping, and in which her sister had met her fate. It was a homely little room, with a low ceiling and a gaping fireplace, after the fashion of old country houses. A brown chest of drawers stood in one corner, a narrow white-counterpaned bed in another, and a dressing-table on the left-hand side of the window. These articles, with two small wickerwork chairs, made up all the furniture in the room, save for a square of Wilton carpet in the centre. The boards round and the panelling of the walls were brown, wormeaten oak, so old and discoloured that it may have dated from the original building of the house. Holmes drew one of the chairs into a corner and sat silent, while his eyes travelled round and round and up and down, taking in every detail of the apartment.

"Where does that bell communicate with?" he asked at last, pointing to a thick bell-rope which hung down beside the bed, the tassel actually lying upon the pillow.

"It goes to the housekeeper's room."

"It looks newer than the other things?"

"Yes, it was only put there a couple of years ago."

"Your sister asked for it, I suppose?"

"No, I never heard of her using it. We used always to get what we wanted for ourselves."

"Indeed, it seemed unnecessary to put so nice a bell-pull there. You will excuse me for a few minutes while I satisfy myself as to this floor." He threw himself down upon his face with his lens in his hand, and crawled swiftly backwards and forwards, examining minutely the cracks between the boards. Then he did the same with the woodwork with which the chamber was panelled. Finally he walked over to the bed and spent some time in staring at it, and in running his eye up and down the wall. Finally he took the bell-rope in his hand and gave it a brisk tug.

"Why, it's a dummy," said he.

"Won't it ring?"

"No, it is not even attached to a wire. This is very interesting. You can see now that it is fastened to a hook just above where the little opening of the ventilator is."

"How very absurd! I never noticed that before."

"Very strange!" muttered Holmes, pulling at the rope. "There are one or two very singular points about this room. For example, what a fool a builder must be to open a ventilator in another room, when, with the same trouble, he might have communicated with the outside air!"

"That is also quite modern," said the lady.

"Done about the same time as the bell-rope," remarked Holmes.

"Yes, there were several little changes carried out about that time."

"They seem to have been of a most interesting character—dummy bell-ropes, and ventilators which do not ventilate. With your permission, Miss Stoner, we shall now carry our researches into the inner apartment."

Dr. Grimesby Roylott's chamber was larger than that of his stepdaughter, but was as plainly furnished. A camp bed, a small wooden shelf full of books, mostly of a technical character, an arm-chair beside the bed, a plain wooden chair against the wall, a round table, and a large iron safe were the principal things which met the eye. Holmes walked slowly round and examined each and all of them with the keenest interest.

"What's in here?" he asked, tapping the safe.

"My stepfather's business papers."

"Oh! you have seen inside, then?"

"Only once, some years ago. I remember that it was full of papers."

"There isn't a cat in it, for example?"

"No. What a strange idea!"

"Well, look at this!" He took up a small saucer of milk which stood on the top of it.

"No; we don't keep a cat. But there is a cheetah and a baboon."

"Ah, yes, of course! Well, a cheetah is just a big cat, and yet a saucer of milk does not go very far in satisfying its wants, I daresay. There is one point which I should wish to determine." He squatted down in front of the wooden chair, and examined the seat of it with the greatest attention.

"Thank you. That is quite settled," said he, rising and putting his lens in his pocket. "Hullo! here is something interesting!"

The object which had caught his eye was a small dog lash hung on one corner of the bed. The lash, however, was curled upon itself, and tied so as to make a loop of whipcord.

"What do you make of that, Watson?"

"It's a common enough lash. But I don't know why it should be tied."

"That is not quite so common, is it? Ah, me! it's a wicked world, and when a clever man turns his brain to crime it is the worst of all. I think that I have seen enough now, Miss Stoner, and, with your permission, we shall walk out upon the lawn."

I had never seen my friend's face so grim, or his brow so dark, as it was when we turned from the scene of this investigation. We had walked several times up and down the lawn, neither Miss Stoner nor myself liking to break in upon his thoughts before he roused himself from his reverie.

"It is very essential, Miss Stoner," said he, "that you should absolutely follow my advice in every respect."

"I shall most certainly do so."

"The matter is too serious for any hesitation. Your life may depend upon your compliance."

"I assure you that I am in your hands."

"In the first place, both my friend and I must spend the night in your room."

Both Miss Stoner and I gazed at him in astonishment.

"Yes, it must be so. Let me explain. I believe that that is the village inn over there?"

"Yes, that is the 'Crown.'"

"Very good. Your windows would be visible from there?"

"Certainly."

"You must confine yourself to your room, on pretence of a headache, when your stepfather comes back. Then when you hear him retire for the night, you must open the shutters of your window, undo the hasp, put your lamp there as a signal to us, and then withdraw with everything which you are likely to want into the room which you used to occupy. I have no doubt that, in spite of the repairs, you could manage there for one night."

"Oh, yes, easily."

"The rest you will leave in our hands."

"But what will you do?"

"We shall spend the night in your room, and we shall investigate the cause of this noise which has disturbed you."

"I believe, Mr. Holmes, that you have already made up your mind," said Miss Stoner, laying her hand upon my companion's sleeve.

"Perhaps I have."

"Then for pity's sake tell me what was the cause of my sister's death."

"I should prefer to have clearer proofs before I speak."

"You can at least tell me whether my own thought is correct, and if she died from some sudden fright."

"No, I do not think so. I think that there was probably some more tangible cause. And now, Miss Stoner, we must leave you, for if Dr. Roylott returned and saw us, our journey would be in vain. Good-bye, and be brave, for if you will do what I have told you, you may rest assured that we shall soon drive away the dangers that threaten you."

Sherlock Holmes and I had no difficulty in engaging a bedroom and sitting-room at the Crown Inn. They were on the upper floor, and from our window we could command a view of the avenue gate, and of the inhabited wing of Stoke Moran Manor House. At dusk we saw Dr. Grimesby Roylott drive past, his huge form looming up beside the little figure of the lad who drove him. The boy had some slight difficulty in undoing the heavy iron gates, and we heard the hoarse roar of the Doctor's voice, and saw the fury with which he shook his clenched fists at him. The trap drove on, and a few minutes later we saw a sudden light spring up among the trees as the lamp was lit in one of the sitting rooms.

"Do you know, Watson," said Holmes, as we sat together in the gathering darkness, "I have really some scruples as to taking you to-night. There is a distinct element of danger."

"Can I be of assistance?"

"Your presence might be invaluable."

"Then I shall certainly come."

"It is very kind of you."

"You speak of danger. You have evidently seen more in these rooms than was visible to me."

"No, but I fancy that I may have deduced a little more. I imagine that you saw all that I did."

"I saw nothing remarkable save the bell-rope, and what purpose that could answer I confess is more than I can imagine."

"You saw the ventilator, too?"

"Yes, but I do not think that it is such a very unusual thing to have a small opening between two rooms. It was so small that a rat could hardly pass through."

"I knew that we should find a ventilator before ever we came to Stoke Moran."

"My dear Holmes!"

"Oh, yes, I did. You remember in her statement she said that her sister could smell Dr. Roylott's cigar. Now, of course that suggests at once that there must be a communication between the two rooms. It could only be a small one, or it would have been remarked upon at the coroner's inquiry. I deduced a ventilator."

"But what harm can there be in that?"

"Well, there is at least a curious coincidence of dates. A ventilator is made, a cord is hung, and a lady who sleeps in the bed dies. Does not that strike you?"

"I cannot as yet see any connection."

"Did you observe anything very peculiar about that bed?"

"No."

"It was clamped to the floor. Did you ever see a bed fastened like that before?"

"I cannot say that I have."

"The lady could not move her bed. It must always be in the same relative position to the ventilator and to the rope—for so we may call it, since it was clearly never meant for a bell-pull."

"Holmes," I cried. "I seem to see dimly what you are hitting at. We are only just in time to prevent some subtle and horrible crime."

"Subtle enough and horrible enough. When a doctor does go wrong he is the first of criminals. He has nerve and he has knowledge. Palmer and Pritchard[4] were among the heads of their profession. This man strikes even deeper, but I think, Watson, that we shall be able to strike deeper still. But we shall have horrors enough before the night is over: for goodness' sake let us have a quiet pipe, and turn our minds for a few hours to something more cheerful."

About nine o'clock the light among the trees was extinguished, and all was dark in the direction of the Manor House. Two hours passed slowly away, and then, suddenly, just at the stroke of eleven, a single bright light shone out right in front of us.

"That is our signal," said Holmes, springing to his feet; "it comes from the middle window."

As we passed out he exchanged a few words with the landlord, explaining that we were going on a late visit to an acquaintance, and that it was possible that we might spend the night there. A moment later we were out on the dark road, a chill wind blowing in our faces, and one yellow light twinkling in front of us through the gloom to guide us on our sombre errand.

There was little difficulty in entering the grounds, for unrepaired breaches gaped in the old park wall. Making our way among the trees, we reached the lawn, crossed it, and were about to enter through the window, when out from a clump of laurel bushes there darted what seemed to be a hideous and distorted child, who threw itself on the grass with writhing limbs, and then ran swiftly across the lawn into the darkness.

"My God!" I whispered, "did you see it?"

Holmes was for the moment as startled as I. His hand closed like a vice upon my wrist in his agitation. Then he broke into a low laugh, and put his lips to my ear.

"It is a nice household," he murmured, "that is the baboon."

I had forgotten the strange pets which the Doctor affected. There was a cheetah, too; perhaps we might find it upon our shoulders at any moment. I confess that I felt easier in my mind when, after following Holmes' example and slipping off my shoes, I found myself inside the bedroom. My companion noiselessly closed the shutters, moved the lamp onto the table, and cast his eyes round the room. All was as we had seen it in the day-time. Then creeping up to me and making a trumpet of his hand, he whispered into my ear again so gently that it was all that I could do to distinguish the words:

"The least sound would be fatal to our plans."

I nodded to show that I had heard.

[4] Two doctors executed for murder in 1856 and 1865, respectively.

"We must sit without a light. He would see it through the ventilator."

I nodded again.

"Do not go to sleep; your very life may depend upon it. Have your pistol ready in case we should need it. I will sit on the side of the bed, and you in that chair."

I took out my revolver and laid it on the corner of the table.

Holmes had brought up a long thin cane, and this he placed upon the bed beside him. By it he laid the box of matches and the stump of candle. Then he turned down the lamp and we were left in darkness.

How shall I ever forget that dreadful vigil? I could not hear a sound, not even the drawing of a breath, and yet I knew that my companion sat open-eyed, within a few feet of me, in the same state of nervous tension in which I was myself. The shutters cut off the least ray of light, and we waited in absolute darkness. From outside came the occasional cry of a night-bird, and once at our very window a long drawn, cat-like whine, which told us that the cheetah was indeed at liberty. Far away we could hear the deep tones of the parish clock, which boomed out every quarter of an hour. How long they seemed, those quarters! Twelve o'clock, and one, and two, and three, and still we sat waiting silently for whatever might befall.

Suddenly there was the momentary gleam of a light up in the direction of the ventilator, which vanished immediately, but was succeeded by a strong smell of burning oil and heated metal. Someone in the next room had lit a dark lantern. I heard a gentle sound of movement, and then all was silent once more, though the smell grew stronger. For half an hour I sat with straining ears. Then suddenly another sound became audible—a very gentle, soothing sound, like that of a small jet of steam escaping continually from a kettle. The instant that we heard it, Holmes sprang from the bed, struck a match, and lashed furiously with his cane at the bell-pull.

"You see it, Watson?" he yelled. "You see it?"

But I saw nothing. At the moment when Holmes struck the light I heard a low, clear whistle, but the sudden glare flashing into my weary eyes made it impossible for me to tell what it was at which my friend lashed so savagely. I could, however, see that his face was deadly pale, and filled with horror and loathing.

He had ceased to strike, and was gazing up at the ventilator, when suddenly there broke from the silence of the night the most horrible cry to which I have ever listened. It swelled up louder and louder, a hoarse yell of pain and fear and anger all mingled in the one dreadful shriek. They say that away down in the village, and even in the distant parsonage, that cry raised the sleepers from their beds. It struck cold to our hearts, and I stood gazing at Holmes, and he at me, until the last echoes of it had died away into the silence from which it rose.

"What can it mean?" I gasped.

"It means that it is all over," Holmes answered. "And perhaps, after all, it is for the best. Take your pistol, and we shall enter Dr. Roylott's room."

With a grave face he lit the lamp, and led the way down the corridor. Twice he struck at the chamber door without any reply from within. Then he turned the handle and entered, I at his heels, with the cocked pistol in my hand.

It was a singular sight which met our eyes. On the table stood a dark lantern with the shutter half open, throwing a brilliant beam of light upon the iron safe, the door of which was ajar. Beside this table, on the wooden chair, sat

Dr. Grimesby Roylott, clad in a long grey dressing-gown, his bare ankles protruding beneath, and his feet thrust into red heelless Turkish slippers. Across
his lap lay the short stock with the long lash which we had noticed during
the day. His chin was cocked upwards, and his eyes were fixed in a dreadful
rigid stare at the corner of the ceiling. Round his brow he had a peculiar
yellow band, with brownish speckles, which seemed to be bound tightly round
his head. As we entered he made neither sound nor motion.

"The band! the speckled band!" whispered Holmes.

I took a step forward. In an instant his strange head-gear began to move,
and there reared itself from among his hair the squat diamond-shaped head
and puffed neck of a loathsome serpent.

"It is a swamp adder!" cried Holmes—"the deadliest snake in India. He
has died within ten seconds of being bitten. Violence does, in truth, recoil
upon the violent, and the schemer falls into the pit which he digs for another.
Let us thrust this creature back into its den, and we can then remove Miss
Stoner to some place of shelter, and let the county police know what has
happened."

As he spoke he drew the dog whip swiftly from the dead man's lap, and
throwing the noose round the reptile's neck, he drew it from its horrid perch,
and, carrying it at arm's length, threw it into the iron safe, which he closed
upon it.

Such are the true facts of the death of Dr. Grimesby Roylott, of Stoke Moran.
It is not necessary that I should prolong a narrative which has already run
to too great a length, by telling how we broke the sad news to the terrified
girl, how we conveyed her by the morning train to the care of her good aunt
at Harrow, of how the slow process of official inquiry came to the conclusion
that the Doctor met his fate while indiscreetly playing with a dangerous pet.
The little which I had yet to learn of the case was told me by Sherlock Holmes
as we travelled back next day.

"I had," said he, "come to an entirely erroneous conclusion, which shows,
my dear Watson, how dangerous it always is to reason from insufficient data.
The presence of the gipsies, and the use of the word 'band,' which was used
by the poor girl, no doubt, to explain the appearance which she had caught
a horrid glimpse of by the light of her match, were sufficient to put me upon
an entirely wrong scent. I can only claim the merit that I instantly reconsidered
my position when, however, it became clear to me that whatever danger threatened an occupant of the room could not come either from the window or
the door. My attention was speedily drawn, as I have already remarked to
you, to this ventilator, and to the bell-rope which hung down to the bed.
The discovery that this was a dummy, and that the bed was clamped to the
floor, instantly gave rise to the suspicion that the rope was there as a bridge
for something passing through the hole, and coming to the bed. The idea of
a snake instantly occurred to me, and when I coupled it with my knowledge
that the Doctor was furnished with a supply of creatures from India, I felt
that I was probably on the right track. The idea of using a form of poison
which could not possibly be discovered by any chemical test was just such a
one as would occur to a clever and ruthless man who had had an Eastern
training. The rapidity with which such a poison would take effect would also,
from his point of view, be an advantage. It would be a sharp-eyed coroner
indeed who could distinguish the two little dark punctures which would show

where the poison fangs had done their work. Then I thought of the whistle. Of course, he must recall the snake before the morning light revealed it to the victim. He had trained it, probably by the use of the milk which we saw, to return to him when summoned. He would put it through the ventilator at the hour that he thought best, with the certainty that it would crawl down the rope, and land on the bed. It might or might not bite the occupant, perhaps she might escape every night for a week, but sooner or later she must fall a victim.

"I had come to these conclusions before ever I had entered his room. An inspection of his chair showed me that he had been in the habit of standing on it, which, or course, would be necessary in order that he should reach the ventilator. The sight of the safe, the saucer of milk, and the loop of whipcord were enough to finally dispel any doubts which may have remained. The metallic clang heard by Miss Stoner was obviously caused by her father hastily closing the door of his safe upon its terrible occupant. Having once made up my mind, you know the steps which I took in order to put the matter to the proof. I heard the creature hiss, as I have no doubt that you did also, and I instantly lit the light and attacked it."

"With the result of driving it through the ventilator."

"And also with the result of causing it to turn upon its master at the other side. Some of the blows of my cane came home, and roused its snakish temper, so that it flew upon the first person it saw. In this way I am no doubt indirectly responsible for Dr. Grimesby Roylott's death, and I cannot say that it is likely to weigh very heavily upon my conscience."

[1892]

Charlotte Perkins Gilman   *1860–1935*

THE YELLOW WALL-PAPER

It is very seldom that mere ordinary people like John and myself secure ancestral halls for the summer.

A colonial mansion, a hereditary estate, I would say a haunted house, and reach the height of romantic felicity—but that would be asking too much of fate!

Still I will proudly declare that there is something queer about it.

Else, why should it be let so cheaply? And why have stood so long untenanted?

John laughs at me, of course, but one expects that in marriage.

John is practical in the extreme. He has no patience with faith, an intense horror of superstition, and he scoffs openly at any talk of things not to be felt and seen and put down in figures.

John is a physician, and *perhaps*—(I would not say it to a living soul, of course, but this is dead paper and a great relief to my mind—) *perhaps* that is one reason I do not get well faster.

You see he does not believe I am sick!

And what can one do?

If a physician of high standing, and one's own husband, assures friends and relatives that there is really nothing the matter with one but temporary nervous depression—a slight hysterical tendency—what is one to do?

My brother is also a physician, and also of high standing, and he says the same thing.

So I take phosphates or phosphites—whichever it is, and tonics, and journeys, and air, and exercise, and am absolutely forbidden to "work" until I am well again.

Personally, I disagree with their ideas.

Personally, I believe that congenial work, with excitement and change, would do me good.

But what is one to do?

I did write for a while in spite of them; but it *does* exhaust me a good deal—having to be so sly about it, or else meet with heavy opposition.

I sometimes fancy that in my condition if I had less opposition and more society and stimulus—but John says the very worst thing I can do is to think about my condition, and I confess it always makes me feel bad.

So I will let it alone and talk about the house.

The most beautiful place! It is quite alone, standing well back from the road, quite three miles from the village. It makes me think of English places that you read about, for there are hedges and walls and gates that lock, and lots of separate little houses for the gardeners and people.

There is a *delicious* garden! I never saw such a garden—large and shady, full of box-bordered paths, and lined with long grape-covered arbors with seats under them.

There were greenhouses, too, but they are all broken now.

There was some legal trouble, I believe, something about the heirs and coheirs; anyhow, the place has been empty for years.

That spoils my ghostliness, I am afraid, but I don't care—there is something strange about the house—I can feel it.

I even said so to John one moonlight evening, but he said what I felt was a *draught,* and shut the window.

I get unreasonably angry with John sometimes. I'm sure I never used to be so sensitive. I think it is due to this nervous condition.

But John says if I feel so, I shall neglect proper self-control; so I take pains to control myself—before him, at least, and that makes me very tired.

I don't like our room a bit. I wanted one downstairs that opened on the piazza and had roses all over the window, and such pretty old-fashioned chintz hangings! but John would not hear of it.

He said there was only one window and not room for two beds, and no near room for him if he took another.

He is very careful and loving, and hardly lets me stir without special direction.

I have a schedule prescription for each hour in the day; he takes all care from me, and so I feel basely ungrateful not to value it more.

He said we came here solely on my account, that I was to have perfect rest and all the air I could get. "Your exercise depends on your strength, my dear." said he, "and your food somewhat on your appetite; but air you can absorb all the time." So we took the nursery at the top of the house.

It is a big, airy room, the whole floor nearly, with windows that look all ways, and air and sunshine galore. It was nursery first and then playroom and gymnasium, I should judge; for the windows are barred for little children, and there are rings and things in the walls.

The paint and paper look as if a boys' school had used it. It is stripped off—the paper—in great patches all around the head of my bed, about as far as I can reach, and in a great place on the other side of the room low down. I never saw a worse paper in my life.

One of those sprawling flamboyant patterns committing every artistic sin.

It is dull enough to confuse the eye in following, pronounced enough to constantly irritate and provoke study, and when you follow the lame uncertain curves for a little distance they suddenly commit suicide—plunge off at outrageous angles, destroy themselves in unheard of contradictions.

The color is repellent, almost revolting; a smouldering unclean yellow, strangely faded by the slow-turning sunlight.

It is a dull yet lurid orange in some places, a sickly sulphur tint in others.

No wonder the children hated it! I should hate it myself if I had to live in this room long.

There comes John, and I must put this away,—he hates to have me write a word.

*

We have been here two weeks, and I haven't felt like writing before, since that first day.

I am sitting by the window now, up in this atrocious nursery, and there is nothing to hinder my writing as much as I please, save lack of strength.

John is away all day, and even some nights when his cases are serious.

I am glad my case is not serious!

But these nervous troubles are dreadfully depressing.

John does not know how much I really suffer. He knows there is no *reason* to suffer, and that satisfies him.

Of course it is only nervousness. It does weigh on me so not to do my duty in any way!

I meant to be such a help to John, such a real rest and comfort, and here I am a comparative burden already!

Nobody would believe what an effort it is to do what little I am able,—to dress and entertain, and order things.

It is fortunate Mary is so good with the baby. Such a dear baby!

And yet I *cannot* be with him, it makes me so nervous.

I suppose John never was nervous in his life. He laughs at me so about this wall-paper!

At first he meant to repaper the room, but afterwards he said that I was letting it get the better of me, and that nothing was worse for a nervous patient than to give way to such fancies.

He said that after the wall-paper was changed it would be the heavy bedstead, and then the barred windows, and then that gate at the head of the stairs, and so on.

"You know the place is doing you good," he said, "and really, dear, I don't care to renovate the house just for a three months' rental."

"Then do let us go downstairs," I said, "there are such pretty rooms there."

Then he took me in his arms and called me, a blessed little goose, and said he would go down cellar, if I wished, and have it whitewashed into the bargain.

But he is right enough about the beds and windows and things.

It is an airy and comfortable room as any one need wish, and, of course, I would not be so silly as to make him uncomfortable just for a whim.

I'm really getting quite fond of the big room, all but that horrid paper.

Out of one window I can see the garden, those mysterious deep-shaded arbors, the riotous old-fashioned flowers, and bushes and gnarly trees.

Out of another I get a lovely view of the bay and a little private wharf belonging to the estate. There is a beautiful shaded lane that runs down there from the house. I always fancy I see people walking in these numerous paths and arbors, but John has cautioned me not to give way to fancy in the least. He says that with my imaginative power and habit of story-making, a nervous weakness like mine is sure to lead to all manner of excited fancies, and that I ought to use my will and good sense to check the tendency. So I try.

I think sometimes that if I were only well enough to write a little it would relieve the press of ideas and rest me.

But I find I get pretty tired when I try.

It is so discouraging not to have any advice and companionship about my work. When I get really well, John says we will ask Cousin Henry and Julia down for a long visit; but he says he would as soon put fireworks in my pillow-case as to let me have those stimulating people about now.

I wish I could get well faster.

But I must not think about that. This paper looks to me as if it *knew* what a vicious influence it had!

There is a recurrent spot where the pattern lolls like a broken neck and two bulbous eyes stare at you upside down.

I get positively angry with the impertinence of it and the everlastingness. Up and down and sideways they crawl, and those absurd, unblinking eyes are everywhere. There is one place where two breadths didn't match, and the eyes go all up and down the line, one a little higher than the other.

I never saw so much expression in an inanimate thing before, and we all know how much expression they have! I used to lie awake as a child and get more entertainment and terror out of blank walls and plain furniture than most children could find in a toy-store.

I remember what a kindly wink the knobs of our big, old bureau used to have, and there was one chair that always seemed like a strong friend.

I used to feel that if any of the other things looked too fierce I could always hop into that chair and be safe.

The furniture in this room is no worse than inharmonious, however, for we had to bring it all from downstairs. I suppose when this was used as a playroom they had to take the nursery things out, and no wonder! I never saw such ravages as the children have made here.

The wall-paper, as I said before, is torn off in spots, and it sticketh closer than a brother—they must have had perseverance as well as hatred.

Then the floor is scratched and gouged and splintered, the plaster itself is dug out here and there, and this great heavy bed which is all we found in the room, looks as if it had been through the wars.

But I don't mind it a bit—only the paper.

There comes John's sister. Such a dear girl as she is, and so careful of me! I must not let her find me writing. *(how women are)*

She is a perfect and enthusiastic housekeeper, and hopes for no better profession. I verily believe she thinks it is the writing which made me sick!

But I can write when she is out, and see her a long way off from these windows.

There is one that commands the road, a lovely shaded winding road, and one that just looks off over the country. A lovely country, too, full of great elms and velvet meadows.

This wall-paper has a kind of subpattern in a different shade, a particularly irritating one, for you can only see it in certain lights, and not clearly then.

But in the places where it isn't faded and where the sun is just so—I can see a strange, provoking, formless sort of figure, that seems to skulk about behind that silly and conspicuous front design. *She sees herself as trapped in her life conflict*

There's sister on the stairs!

*

Well, the Fourth of July is over! The people are all gone and I am tired out. John thought it might do me good to see a little company, so we just had mother and Nellie and the children down for a week.

Of course I didn't do a thing. Jennie sees to everything now.

But it tired me all the same.

John says if I don't pick up faster he shall send me to Weir Mitchel[1] in the fall.

But I don't want to go there at all. I had a friend who was in his hands once, and she says he is just like John and my brother, only more so!

Besides, it is such an undertaking to go so far.

I don't feel as if it was worth while to turn my hand over for anything, and I'm getting dreadfully fretful and querulous.

---

[1] Silas Weir Mitchell (1829–1914), the Philadelphia neurologist-psychologist who introduced "rest cure" for nervous diseases. His medical books include *Diseases of the Nervous System, Especially of Woman* (1881).

I cry at nothing, and cry most of the time.

Of course I don't when John is here, or anybody else, but when I am alone.

And I am alone a good deal just now. John is kept in town very often by serious cases, and Jennie is good and lets me alone when I want her to.

So I walk a little in the garden or down that lovely lane, sit on the porch under the roses, and lie down up here a good deal.

I'm getting really fond of the room in spite of the wall-paper. Perhaps *because* of the wall-paper.

It dwells in my mind so!

I lie here on this great immovable bed—it is nailed down, I believe—and follow that pattern about by the hour. It is as good as gymnastics, I assure you. I start, we'll say, at the bottom, down in the corner over there where it has not been touched, and I determine for the thousandth time that I *will* follow that pointless pattern to some sort of a conclusion. *She tries to resolve conflict*

I know a little of the principle of design, and I know this thing was not arranged on any laws of radiation, or alternation, or repetition, or symmetry, or anything else that I ever heard of.

It is repeated, of course, by the breadths, but not otherwise.

Looked at in one way each breadth stands alone, the bloated curves and flourishes—a kind of "debased Romanesque" with *delirium tremens*[2] go waddling up and down in isolated columns of fatuity.

But, on the other hand, they connect diagonally, and the sprawling outlines run off in great slanting waves of optic horror, like a lot of wallowing seaweeds in full chase.

The whole thing goes horizontally, too, at least it seems so, and I exhaust myself in trying to distinguish the order of its going in that direction.

They have used a horizontal breadth for a frieze, and that adds wonderfully to the confusion.

There is one end of the room where it is almost intact, and there, when the crosslights fade and the low sun shines directly upon it, I can almost fancy radiation after all,—the interminable grotesques seems to form around a common centre and rush off in headlong plunges of equal distraction.

It makes me tired to follow it. I will take a nap I guess.

*

I don't know why I should write this.

I don't want to.

I don't feel able.

And I know John would think it absurd. But I *must* say what I feel and think in some way—it is such a relief!

But the effort is getting to be greater than the relief.

Half the time now I am awfully lazy, and lie down ever so much.

John says I mustn't lose my strength, and has me take cod liver oil and lots of tonics and things, to say nothing of ale and wine and rare meat.

Dear John! He loves me very dearly, and hates to have me sick. I tried to have a real earnest reasonable talk with him the other day, and tell him how I wish he would let me go and make a visit to Cousin Henry and Julia.

But he said I wasn't able to go, nor able to stand it after I got there; and

---

[2] Mental disorientation caused by excessive use of alcohol and characterized by physical tremors.

I did not make out a very good case for myself, for I was crying before I had finished.

It is getting to be a great effort for me to think straight. Just this nervous weakness I suppose.

And dear John gathered me up in his arms, and just carried me upstairs and laid me on the bed, and sat by me and read to me till it tired my head.

He said I was his darling and his comfort and all he had, and that I must take care of myself for his sake, and keep well.

He says no one but myself can help me out of it, that I must use my will and self-control and not let any silly fancies run away with me.

There's one comfort, the baby is well and happy, and does not have to occupy this nursery with the horrid wall-paper.

If we had not used it, that blessed child would have! What a fortunate escape! Why, I wouldn't have a child of mine, an impressionable little thing, live in such a room for worlds.

I never thought of it before, but it is lucky that John kept me here after all, I can stand it so much easier than a baby, you see.

Of course I never mention it to them any more—I am too wise,—but I keep watch of it all the same.

There are things in that paper that nobody knows but me, or ever will.

Behind that outside pattern the dim shapes get clearer every day.

It is always the same shape, only very numerous.

And it is like a woman stooping down and creeping about behind that pattern. I don't like it a bit. I wonder—I begin to think—I wish John would take me away from here!

*

It is so hard to talk with John about my case, because he is so wise, and because he loves me so.

But I tried it last night.

It was moonlight. The moon shines in all around just as the sun does.

I hate to see it sometimes, it creeps so slowly, and always comes in by one window or another.

John was asleep and I hated to waken him, so I kept still and watched the moonlight on that undulating wall-paper til I felt creepy.

The faint figure behind seemed to shake the pattern, just as if she wanted to get out.

I got up softly and went to feel and see if the paper *did* move, and when I came back John was awake.

"What is it, little girl?" he said. "Don't go walking about like that—you'll get cold."

I thought it was a good time to talk, so I told him that I really was not gaining here, and that I wished he would take me away.

"Why, darling!" said he, "our lease will be up in three weeks, and I can't see how to leave before.

"The repairs are not done at home, and I cannot possibly leave town just now. Of course if you were in any danger, I could and would, but you really are better, dear, whether you can see it or not. I am a doctor, dear, and I know. You are gaining flesh and color, your appetite is better, I feel really much easier about you."

"I don't weigh a bit more," said I, "nor as much; and my appetite may be

better in the evening when you are here, but it is worse in the morning when
you are away!"

"Bless her little heart!" said he with a big hug, "she shall be as sick as she
pleases! But now let's improve the shining hours by going to sleep, and talk
about it in the morning!"

"And you won't go away?" I asked gloomily.

"Why, how can I, dear? It is only three weeks more and then we will take
a nice little trip of a few days while Jennie is getting the house ready. Really
dear you are better!"

"Better in body perhaps—" I began, and stopped short, for he sat up straight
and looked at me with such a stern, reproachful look that I could not say
another word. *Choices— he doesn't Allow her*

"My darling," said he, "I beg of you, for my sake and for our child's sake,
as well as for your own, that you will never for one instant let that idea enter
your mind! There is nothing so dangerous, so fascinating, to a temperament
like yours. It is a false and foolish fancy. Can you not trust me as a physician
when I tell you so?"

So of course I said no more on that score, and we went to sleep before
long. He thought I was asleep first, but I wasn't, and lay there for hours trying
to decide whether that front pattern and the back pattern really did move
together or separately. *Choice*

*

On a pattern like this, by daylight, there is a lack of sequence, a defiance
of law, that is a constant irritant to a normal mind.

The color is hideous enough, and unreliable enough, and infuriating enough,
but the pattern is torturing.

You think you have mastered it, but just as you get well underway in following,
it turns a back-somersault and there you are. It slaps you in the face, knocks
you down, and tramples upon you. It is like a bad dream.

The outside pattern is a florid arabesque, reminding one of a fungus. If
you can imagine a toadstool in joints, an interminable string of toadstools,
budding and sprouting in endless convolutions—why, that is something like
it.

That is, sometimes!

There is one marked peculiarity about this paper, a thing nobody seems
to notice but myself, and that is that it changes as the light changes.

When the sun shoots in through the east windows—I always watch for that
first long, straight ray—it changes so quickly that I never can quite believe
it.

That is why I watch it always.

By moonlight—the moon shines in all night when there is a moon—I wouldn't
know it was the same paper.

At night in any kind of light, in twilight, candlelight, lamplight, and worst
of all by moonlight, it becomes bars! The outside pattern I mean, and the
woman behind it is as plain as can be.

I didn't realize for a long time what the thing was that showed behind,
that dim sub-pattern, but now I am quite sure it is a woman.

By daylight she is subdued, quiet. I fancy it is the pattern that keeps her
so still. It is so puzzling. It keeps me quiet by the hour.

I lie down ever so much now. John says it is good for me, and to sleep all I can.

Indeed he started the habit by making me lie down for an hour after each meal.

It is a very bad habit I am convinced, for you see I don't sleep.

And that cultivates deceit, for I don't tell them I'm awake—O no!

The fact is I am getting a little afraid of John.

He seems very queer sometimes, and even Jennie has an inexplicable look.

It strikes me occasionally, just as a scientific hypothesis,—that perhaps it is the paper!

I have watched John when he did not know I was looking, and come into the room suddenly on the most innocent excuses, and I've caught him several times *looking at the paper!* And Jennie too. I caught Jennie with her hand on it once.

She didn't know I was in the room, and when I asked her in a quiet, a very quiet voice, with the most restrained manner possible, what she was doing with the paper—she turned around as if she had been caught stealing, and looked quite angry—asked me why I should frighten her so!

Then she said that the paper stained everything it touched, that she had found yellow smooches on all my clothes and John's, and she wished we would be more careful!

Did not that sound innocent? But I know she was studying that pattern, and I am determined that nobody shall find it out but myself!

*

Life is very much more exciting now than it used to be. You see I have something more to expect, to look forward to, to watch. I really do eat better, and am more quiet than I was.

John is so pleased to see me improve! He laughed a little the other day, and said I seemed to be flourishing in spite of my wall-paper.

I turned it off with a laugh. I had no intention of telling him it was *because* of the wall-paper—he would make fun of me. He might even want to take me away.

I don't want to leave now until I have found it out. There is a week more, and I think that will be enough.

Close to decision— finding herself

*

I'm feeling ever so much better! I don't sleep much at night, for it is so interesting to watch developments; but I sleep a good deal in the daytime.

In the daytime it is tiresome and perplexing.

There are always new shoots on the fungus, and new shades of yellow all over it. I cannot keep count of them, though I have tried conscientiously.

It is the strangest yellow, that wallpaper! It makes me think of all the yellow things I ever saw—not beautiful ones like buttercups, but old foul, bad yellow things.

But there is something else about that paper—the smell! I noticed it the moment we came into the room, but with so much air and sun it was not bad. Now we have had a week of fog and rain, and whether the windows are open or not, the smell is here.

It creeps all over the house.

I find it hovering in the dining-room, skulking in the parlor, hiding in the hall, lying in wait for me on the stairs.

It gets into my hair.

Even when I go to ride, if I turn my head suddenly and surprise it—there is that smell!

Such a peculiar odor, too! I have spent hours in trying to analyze it, to find what it smelled like.

It is not bad—at first, and very gentle, but quite the subtlest, most enduring odor I ever met.

In this damp weather it is awful, I wake up in the night and find it hanging over me.

It used to disturb me at first. I thought seriously of burning the house—to reach the smell.

But now I am used to it. The only thing I can think of that it is like is the *color* of the paper! A yellow smell.

There is a very funny mark on this wall, low down, near the mopboard. A streak that runs round the room. It goes behind every piece of furniture, except the bed, a long, straight, even *smooch,* as if it had been rubbed over and over.

I wonder how it was done and who did it, and what they did it for. Round and round and round—round and round and round!—it makes me dizzy!

*

I really have discovered something at last.

Through watching so much at night when it changes so, I have finally found out.   *She can be independent.*

The front pattern *does* move—and no wonder! The woman behind shakes it!

Sometimes I think there are a great many women behind, and sometimes only one, and she crawls around fast, and her crawling shakes it all over.

Then in the very bright spots she keeps still, and in the very shady spots she just takes hold of the bars and shakes them hard.

And she is all the time trying to climb through. But nobody could climb through that pattern—it strangles so; I think that is why it has so many heads.

They get through, and then the pattern strangles them off and turns them upside down, and makes their eyes white!

If those heads were covered or taken off it would not be half so bad.

*

I think that woman gets out in the daytime!

And I'll tell you why—privately—I've seen her!

I can see her out of every one of my windows!

It is the same woman, I know, for she is always creeping, and most women do not creep by daylight.

I see her in that long shaded lane, creeping up and down. I see her in those dark grape arbors, creeping all around the garden.

I see her on that long road under the trees, creeping along, and when a carriage comes she hides under the blackberry vines.

I don't blame her a bit. It must be very humiliating to be caught creeping by daylight!

I always lock the door when I creep by daylight. I can't do it at night, for I know John would suspect something at once.

And John is so queer now, that I don't want to irritate him. I wish he would take another room! Besides, I don't want anybody to get that woman out at night but myself.

I often wonder if I could see her out of all the windows at once.

But, turn as fast as I can, I can only see out of one at one time.

And though I always see her, she *may* be able to creep faster than I can turn!

I have watched her sometimes away off in the open country, creeping as fast as a cloud shadow in a high wind.

*

If only that top pattern could be gotten off from the under one! I mean to try it, little by little.

I have found out another funny thing, but I shan't tell it this time! It does not do to trust people too much.

There are only two more days to get this paper off, and I believe John is beginning to notice. I don't like the look in his eyes.

And I heard him ask Jennie a lot of professional questions about me. She had a very good report to give.

She said I slept a good deal in the daytime.

John knows I don't sleep very well at night, for all I'm so quiet!

He asked me all sorts of questions, too, and pretended to be very loving and kind.

As if I couldn't see through him!

Still, I don't wonder he acts so, sleeping under this paper for three months.

It only interests me, but I feel sure John and Jennie are secretly affected by it.

*

Hurrah! This is the last day, but it is enough. John to stay in town over night, and won't be out until this evening.

Jennie wanted to sleep with me—the sly thing! but I told her I should undoubtedly rest better for a night all alone.

That was clever, for really I wasn't alone a bit! As soon as it was moonlight and that poor thing began to crawl and shake the pattern, I got up and ran to help her.

I pulled and she shook, I shook and she pulled, and before morning we had peeled off yards of that paper.

A strip about as high as my head and half around the room.

And then when the sun came and that awful pattern began to laugh at me, I declared I would finish it to-day!

We go away to-morrow, and they are moving all my furniture down again to leave things as they were before.

Jennie looked at the wall in amazement, but I told her merrily that I did it out of pure spite at the vicious thing.

She laughed and said she wouldn't mind doing it herself, but I must not get tired.

How she betrayed herself that time!

But I am here, and no person touches this paper but me,—not *alive!*

She tried to get me out of the room—it was too patent! But I said it was so quiet and empty and clean now that I believed I would lie down again and sleep all I could; and not to wake me even for dinner—I would call when I woke.

So now she is gone, and the servants are gone, and the things are gone, and there is nothing left but that great bedstead nailed down, with the canvas mattress we found on it.

We shall sleep downstairs to-night, and take the boat home to-morrow.

I quite enjoy the room, now it is bare again.

How those children did tear about here!

This bedstead is fairly gnawed!

But I must get to work.

I have locked the door and thrown the key down into the front path.

I don't want to go out, and I don't want to have anybody come in, till John comes.

I want to astonish him.

I've got a rope up here that even Jennie did not find. If that woman does get out, and tries to get away. I can tie her!

But I forgot I could not reach far without anything to stand on!

This bed will *not* move!

I tried to lift and push it until I was lame, and then I got so angry I bit off a little piece at one corner—but it hurt my teeth.

Then I peeled off all the paper I could reach standing on the floor. It sticks horribly and the pattern just enjoys it! All those strangled heads and bulbous eyes and waddling fungus growths just shriek with derision!

I am getting angry enough to do something desperate. To jump out of the window would be admirable exercise, but the bars are too strong even to try.

Besides I wouldn't do it. Of course not. I know well enough that a step like that is improper and might be misconstrued.

I don't like to *look* out of the windows even—there are so many of those creeping women, and they creep so fast.

I wonder if they all come out of that wall-paper as I did?

But I am securely fastened now by my well-hidden rope—you don't get *me* out in the road there!

I suppose I shall have to get back behind the pattern when it comes night, and that is hard!

It is so pleasant to be out in this great room and creep around as I please!

I don't want to go outside. I won't, even if Jennie asks me to.

For outside you have to creep on the ground, and everything is green instead of yellow.

But here I can creep smoothly on the floor, and my shoulder just fits in that long smooch around the wall, so I cannot lose my way.

Why there's John at the door!

It is no use, young man, you can't open it!

How he does call and pound!

Now he's crying for an axe.

It would be a shame to break down that beautiful door!

"John dear!" said I in the gentlest voice, "the key is down by the front steps, under a plaintain leaf!"

That silenced him for a few moments.

Then he said—very quietly indeed, "Open the door, my darling!"

"I can't," said I. "The key is down by the front door under a plaintain leaf!"

And then I said it again, several times, very gently and slowly, and said it so often that he had to go and see, and he got it of course, and came in. He stopped short by the door.

"What is the matter?" he cried. "For God's sake, what are you doing!"

I kept on creeping just the same, but I looked at him over my shoulder.

"I've got out at last," said I, "in spite of you and Jane? And I've pulled off most of the paper, so you can't put me back!"

Now why should that man have fainted? But he did, and right across my path by the wall, so that I had to creep over him every time!

[1892]

She loses it!
Will never turn
back to her
previous life —

her

Stephen Crane   *1871–1900*

THE BLUE HOTEL

I

The Palace Hotel at Fort Romper was painted a light blue, a shade that is on the legs of a kind of heron, causing the bird to declare its position against any background. The Palace Hotel, then, was always screaming and howling in a way that made the dazzling winter landscape of Nebraska seem only a grey swampish hush. It stood alone on the prairie, and when the snow was falling the town two hundred yards away was not visible. But when the traveller alighted at the railway station he was obliged to pass the Palace Hotel before he could come upon the company of low clapboard houses which composed Fort Romper, and it was not to be thought that any traveller could pass the Palace Hotel without looking at it. Pat Scully, the proprietor, had proved himself a master of strategy when he chose his paints. It is true that on clear days, when the great transcontinental expresses, long lines of swaying Pullmans, swept through Fort Romper, passengers were overcome at the sight, and the cult that knows the brown-reds and the subdivisions of the dark greens of the East expressed shame, pity, horror, in a laugh. But to the citizens of this prairie town and to the people who would naturally stop there, Pat Scully had performed a feat. With this opulence and splendour, these creeds, classes, egotisms, that streamed through Romper on the rails day after day, they had no colour in common.

As if the displayed delights of such a blue hotel were not sufficiently enticing, it was Scully's habit to go every morning and evening to meet the leisurely trains that stopped at Romper and work his seductions upon any man that he might see wavering, gripsack in hand.

One morning, when a snow-crusted engine dragged its long string of freight cars and its one passenger coach to the station. Scully performed the marvel of catching three men. One was a shaky and quick-eyed Swede, with a great shining cheap valise; one was a tall bronzed cowboy, who was on his way to a ranch near the Dakota line; one was a little silent man from the East, who didn't look it, and didn't announce it. Scully practically made them prisoners. He was so nimble and merry and kindly that each probably felt it would be the height of brutality to try to escape. They trudged off over the creaking board sidewalks in the wake of the eager little Irishman. He wore a heavy fur cap squeezed tightly down on his head. It caused his two red ears to stick out stiffly, as if they were made of tin.

At last, Scully, elaborately, with boisterous hospitality, conducted them through the portals of the blue hotel. The room which they entered was small. It seemed to be merely a proper temple for an enormous stove, which, in the centre, was humming with godlike violence. At various points on its surface the iron had become luminous and glowed yellow from the heat. Beside the stove Scully's son Johnnie was playing High-Five[1] with an old farmer who had whiskers both grey and sandy. They were quarrelling. Frequently the old farmer turned his face toward a box of sawdust—coloured brown from tobacco

---

[1] A popular card game, the forerunner of modern contract bridge; also called Cinch or Pedro.

juice—that was behind the stove, and spat with an air of great impatience and irritation. With a loud flourish of words Scully destroyed the game of cards, and bustled his son upstairs with part of the baggage of the new guests. He himself conducted them to three basins of the coldest water in the world. The cowboy and the Easterner burnished themselves fiery red with this water, until it seemed to be some kind of metal-polish. The Swede, however, merely dipped his fingers gingerly and with trepidation. It was notable that throughout this series of small ceremonies the three travellers were made to feel that Scully was very benevolent. He was conferring great favours upon them. He handed the towel from one to another with an air of philanthropic impulse.

Afterward they went to the first room, and, sitting about the stove, listened to Scully's officious clamour at his daughters, who were preparing the midday meal. They reflected in the silence of experienced men who tread carefully amid new people. Nevertheless, the old farmer, stationary, invincible in his chair near the warmest part of the stove, turned his face from the sawdust-box frequently and addressed a glowing commonplace to the strangers. Usually he was answered in short but adequate sentences by either the cowboy or the Easterner. The Swede said nothing. He seemed to be occupied in making furtive estimates of each man in the room. One might have thought that he had the sense of silly suspicion which comes to guilt. He resembled a badly frightened man. *Falsely sizes up men as killers*

Later, at dinner, he spoke a little, addressing his conversation entirely to Scully. He volunteered that he had come from New York, where for ten years he had worked as a tailor. These facts seemed to strike Scully as fascinating, and afterward he volunteered that he had lived at Romper for fourteen years. The Swede asked about the crops and the price of labour. He seemed barely to listen to Scully's extended replies. His eyes continued to rove from man to man. *Paranoyia*

Finally, with a laugh and a wink, he said that some of these Western communities were very dangerous; and after his statement he straightened his legs under the table, tilted his head, and laughed again, loudly. It was plain that the demonstration had no meaning to the others. They looked at him wondering and in silence.

II

AS THE MEN trooped heavily back into the front room, the two little windows presented views of a turmoiling sea of snow. The huge arms of the wind were making attempts—mighty, circular, futile—to embrace the flakes as they sped. A gate-post like a still man with a blanched face stood aghast amid this profligate fury. In a hearty voice Scully announced the presence of a blizzard. The guests of the blue hotel, lighting their pipes, assented with grunts of lazy masculine contentment. No island of the sea could be exempt in the degree of this little room with its humming stove. Johnnie, son of Scully, in a tone which defined his opinion of his ability as a card-player, challenged the old farmer of both grey and sandy whiskers to a game of High-Five. The farmer agreed with a contemptuous and bitter scoff. They sat close to the stove, and squared their knees under a wide board. The cowboy and the Easterner watched the game with interest. The Swede remained near the window, aloof, but with a counte-nance that showed signs of an inexplicable excitement. *Mind gets carried*

The play of Johnnie and the grey-beard was suddenly ended by another quarrel. The old man arose while casting a look of heated scorn at his adversary.

He slowly buttoned his coat, and then stalked with fabulous dignity from the room. In the discreet silence of all other men the Swede laughed. His laughter rang somehow childish. Men by this time had begun to look at him askance, as if they wished to inquire what ailed him.

A new game was formed jocosely. The cowboy volunteered to become the partner of Johnnie, and they all then turned to ask the Swede to throw in his lot with the little Easterner. He asked some questions about the game, and, learning that it wore many names, and that he had played it when it was under an alias, he accepted the invitation. He strode toward the men nervously, as if he expected to be assaulted. Finally, seated, he gazed from face to face and laughed shrilly. This laugh was so strange that the Easterner looked up quickly, the cowboy sat intent and with his mouth open, and Johnnie paused, holding the cards with still fingers.

Afterward there was a short silence. Then Johnnie said, "Well, let's get at it. Come on now!" They pulled their chairs forward until their knees were bunched under the board. They began to play, and their interest in the game caused the others to forget the manner of the Swede.

The cowboy was a board-whacker. Each time that he held superior cards he whanged them, one by one, with exceeding force, down upon the improvised table, and took the tricks with a glowing air of prowess and pride that sent thrills of indignation into the hearts of his opponents. A game with a board-whacker in it is sure to become intense. The countenances of the Easterner and the Swede were miserable whenever the cowboy thundered down his aces and kings, while Johnnie, his eyes gleaming with joy, chuckled and chuckled.

Because of the absorbing play none considered the strange ways of the Swede. They paid strict heed to the game. Finally, during a lull caused by a new deal, the Swede suddenly addressed Johnnie: "I suppose there have been a good many men killed in this room." The jaws of the others dropped and they looked at him.

"What in hell are you talking about?" said Johnnie.

The Swede laughed again his blatant laugh, full of a kind of false courage and defiance. "Oh, you know what I mean all right," he answered.

"I'm a liar if I do!" Johnnie protested. The card was halted, and the men stared at the Swede. Johnnie evidently felt that as the son of the proprietor he should make a direct inquiry. "Now, what might you be drivin' at, mister?" he asked. The Swede winked at him. It was a wink full of cunning. His fingers shook on the edge of the board. "Oh, maybe you think I have been to nowheres. Maybe you think I'm a tenderfoot?"

"I don't know nothin' about you," answered Johnnie, "and I don't give a damn where you've been. All I got to say is that I don't know what you're driving at. There hain't never been nobody killed in this room."

The cowboy, who had been steadily gazing at the Swede, then spoke: "What's wrong with you, mister?"

Apparently it seemed to the Swede that he was formidably menaced. He shivered and turned white near the corners of his mouth. He sent an appealing glance in the direction of the little Easterner. During these moments he did not forget to wear his air of advanced pot-valour.[2] "They say they don't know what I mean," he remarked mockingly to the Easterner.

[2] Drunken bravado.

The latter answered after prolonged and cautious reflection. "I don't understand you," he said, impassively.

The Swede made a movement then which announced that he thought he had encountered treachery from the only quarter where he had expected sympathy, if not help. "Oh, I see you are all against me. I see——"

The cowboy was in a state of deep stupefaction. "Say," he cried, as he tumbled the deck violently down upon the board, "say, what are you gittin' at, hey?"

The Swede sprang up with the celerity of a man escaping from a snake on the floor. "I don't want to fight!" he shouted. "I don't want to fight!"

The cowboy stretched his long legs indolently and deliberately. His hands were in his pockets. He spat into the sawdust-box. "Well, who the hell thought you did?" he inquired.

The Swede backed rapidly toward a corner of the room. His hands were out protectingly in front of his chest, but he was making an obvious struggle to control his fright. "Gentlemen," he quavered, "I suppose I am going to be killed before I can leave this house! I suppose I am going to be killed before I can leave this house!" In his eyes was the dying-swan look. Through the windows could be seen the snow turning blue in the shadow of dusk. The wind tore at the house, and some loose thing beat regularly against the clapboards like a spirit tapping.

A door opened, and Scully himself entered. He paused in surprise as he noted the tragic attitude of the Swede. Then he said, "What's the matter here?"

The Swede answered him swiftly and eagerly: "These men are going to kill me."

"Kill you!" ejaculated Scully. "Kill you! What are you talkin'?"

The Swede made the gesture of a martyr.

Scully wheeled sternly upon his son. "What is this, Johnnie?"

The lad had grown sullen. "Damned if I know," he answered. "I can't make no sense to it." He began to shuffle the cards, fluttering them together with an angry snap. "He says a good many men have been killed in this room, or something like that. And he says he's goin' to be killed here too. I don't know what ails him. He's crazy, I shouldn't wonder."

Scully then looked for explanation to the cowboy, but the cowboy simply shrugged his shoulders.

"Kill you?" said Scully again to the Swede. "Kill you? Man, you're off your nut."

"Oh, I know," burst out the Swede. "I know what will happen. Yes, I'm crazy—yes. Yes, of course, I'm crazy—yes. But I know one thing—" There was a sort of sweat of misery and terror upon his face. "I know I won't get out of here alive."

The cowboy drew a deep breath, as if his mind was passing into the last stages of dissolution. "Well, I'm doggoned," he whispered to himself.

Scully wheeled suddenly and faced his son. "You've been troublin' this man!"

Johnnie's voice was loud with its burden of grievance. "Why, good Gawd, I ain't done nothin' to 'im."

The Swede broke in. "Gentlemen, do not disturb yourselves. I will leave this house. I will go away, because"—he accused them dramatically with his glance—"because I do not want to be killed."

Scully was furious with his son. "Will you tell me what is the matter, you young divil? What's the matter, anyhow? Speak out!"

"Blame it!" cried Johnnie in despair, "don't I tell you I don't know? He— he says we want to kill him, and that's all I know. I can't tell what ails him."

The Swede continued to repeat: "Never mind, Mr. Scully; never mind. I will leave this house. I will go away, because I do not wish to be killed. Yes, of course, I am crazy—yes. But I know one thing! I will go away. I will leave this house. Never mind, Mr. Scully; never mind. I will go away."

"You will not go 'way," said Scully. "You will not go 'way until I hear the reason of this business. If anybody has troubled you I will take care of him. This is my house. You are under my roof, and I will not allow any peaceable man to be troubled here." He cast a terrible eye upon Johnnie, the cowboy, and the Easterner.

"Never mind, Mr. Scully; never mind. I will go away. I do not wish to be killed." The Swede moved toward the door which opened upon the stairs. It was evidently his intention to go at once for his baggage.

"No, no," shouted Scully peremptorily; but the white-faced man slid by him and disappeared. "Now," said Scully severely, "what does this mane?"

Johnnie and the cowboy cried together: "Why, we didn't do nothin' to 'im!"

Scully's eyes were cold. "No," he said, "you didn't?"

Johnnie swore a deep oath. "Why, this is the wildest loon I ever see. We didn't do nothin' at all. We were just sittin' here playin' cards, and he——"

The father suddenly spoke to the Easterner. "Mr. Blanc," he asked, "what has these boys been doin'?"

The Easterner reflected again. "I didn't see anything wrong at all," he said at last, slowly.

Scully began to howl. "But what does it mane?" He stared ferociously at his son. "I have a mind to lather you for this, me boy."

Johnnie was frantic. "Well, what have I done?" he bawled at his father.

III

"I THINK you are tongue-tied," said Scully finally to his son, the cowboy, and the Easterner; and at the end of this scornful sentence he left the room.

Upstairs the Swede was swifly fastening the straps of his great valise. Once his back happened to be half turned toward the door, and, hearing a noise there, he wheeled and sprang up, uttering a loud cry. Scully's wrinkled visage showed grimly in the light of the small lamp he carried. This yellow effulgence, streaming upward, coloured only his prominent features, and left his eyes, for instance, in mysterious shadow. He resembled a murderer.

"Man! man!" he exclaimed, "have you gone daffy?"

"Oh, no! Oh, no!" rejoined the other. "There are people in this world who know pretty nearly as much as you do—understand?"

For a moment they stood gazing at each other. Upon the Swede's deathly pale cheeks were two spots brightly crimson and sharply edged, as if they had been carefully painted. Scully placed the light on the table and sat himself on the edge of the bed. He spoke ruminatively. "By cracky, I never heard of such a thing in my life. It's a complete muddle. I can't, for the soul of me, think how you ever got this idea into your head." Presently he lifted his eyes and asked: "And did you sure think they were going to kill you?"

The Swede scanned the old man as if he wished to see into his mind. "I did," he said at last. He obviously suspected that this answer might precipitate an outbreak. As he pulled on a strap his whole arm shook, the elbow wavering like a bit of paper.

Scully banged his hand impressively on the footboard of the bed. "Why, man, we're goin' to have a line of ilictric street-cars in this town next spring."

" 'A line of electric street-cars,' " repeated the Swede, stupidly.

"And," said Scully, "there's a new railroad goin' to be built down from Broken Arm to here. Not to mintion the four churches and the smashin' big brick schoolhouse. Then there's the big factory, too. Why, in two years Romper'll be a met-tro-*pol*-is."

Having finished the preparation of his baggage, the Swede straightened himself. "Mr. Scully," he said, with sudden hardihood, "how much do I owe you?"

"You don't owe my anythin'," said the old man, angrily.

"Yes, I do," retorted the Swede. He took seventy-five cents from his pocket and tendered it to Scully; but the latter snapped his fingers in disdainful refusal. However, it happened that they both stood gazing in a strange fashion at three silver pieces on the Swede's open palm.

"I'll not take your money," said Scully at last. "Not after what's been goin' on here." Then a plan seemed to strike him. "Here," he cried, picking up his lamp and moving toward the door. "Here! Come with me a minute."

"No," said the Swede, in overwhelming alarm.

"Yes," urged the old man. "Come on! I want you to come and see a picter— just across the hall—in my room."

The Swede must have concluded that his hour was come. His jaw dropped and his teeth showed like a dead man's. He ultimately followed Scully across the corridor, but he had the step of one hung in chains.

Scully flashed the light high on the wall of his own chamber. There was revealed a ridiculous photograph of a little girl. She was leaning against a balustrade of gorgeous decoration, and the formidable bang to her hair was prominent. The figure was as graceful as an upright sled-stake, and, withal, it was of the hue of lead. "There," said Scully, tenderly, "that's the picter of my little girl that died. Her name was Carrie. She had the purtiest hair you ever saw! I was that fond of her, she——"

Turning then, he saw that the Swede was not contemplating the picture at all, but, instead, was keeping keen watch on the gloom in the rear.

"Look, man!" cried Scully, heartily. "That's the picter of my little gal that died. Her name was Carrie. And then here's the picter of my oldest boy, Michael. He's a lawyer in Lincoln, an' doin' well. I gave that boy a grand eddication, and I'm glad for it now. He's a fine boy. Look at 'im now. Ain't he bold as blazes, him there in Lincoln, an honoured an' respicted gintleman! An honoured and respicted gintleman," concluded Scully with a flourish. And, so saying, he smote the Swede jovially on the back.

The Swede faintly smiled.

"Now," said the old man, "there's only one more thing." He dropped suddenly to the floor and thrust his head beneath the bed. The Swede could hear his muffled voice. "I'd keep it under me piller if it wasn't for that boy Johnnie. Then there's the old woman—— Where is it now? I never put it twice in the same place. Ah, now come out with you!"

Presently he backed clumsily from under the bed, dragging with him an old coat rolled into a bundle. "I've fetched him," he muttered. Kneeling on the floor, he unrolled the coat and extracted from its heart a large yellow-brown whisky-bottle.

His first maneuver was to hold the bottle up to the light. Reassured, apparently, that nobody had been tampering with it, he thrust it with a generous movement toward the Swede.

The weak-kneed Swede was about to eagerly clutch this element of strength, but he suddenly jerked his hand away and cast a look of horror upon Scully.

"Drink," said the old man affectionately. He had risen to his feet, and now stood facing the Swede.

There was a silence. Then again Scully said: "Drink!"

The Swede laughed wildly. He grabbed the bottle, put it to his mouth; and as his lips curled absurdly around the opening and his throat worked, he kept his glance, burning with hatred, upon the old man's face.

Knows he's being killed

IV

AFTER the departure of Scully the three men, with the card-board still upon their knees, preserved for a long time an astounded silence. Then Johnnie said: "That's the dod-dangedest Swede I ever see."

"He ain't no Swede," said the cowboy, scornfully.

"Well, what is he then?" cried Johnnie. "What is he then?"

"It's my opinion," replied the cowboy deliberately, "he's some kind of a Dutchman." It was a venerable custom of the country to entitle as Swedes all light-haired men who spoke with a heavy tongue. In consequence the idea of the cowboy was not without its daring. "Yes, sir," he repeated. "It's my opinion this feller is some kind of a Dutchman."

"Well, he says he's a Swede, anyhow," muttered Johnnie, sulkily. He turned to the Easterner: "What do you think, Mr. Blanc?"

"Oh, I don't know," replied the Easterner.

"Well, what do you think makes him act that way?" asked the cowboy.

"Why, he's frightened." The Easterner knocked his pipe against a rim of the stove. "He's clear frightened out of his boots."

"What at?" cried Johnnie and the cowboy together.

The Easterner reflected over his answer.

"What at?" cried the others again.

"Oh, I don't know, but it seems to me this man has been reading dime novels, and he thinks he's right out in the middle of it—the shootin' and stabbin' and all."

"But," said the cowboy, deeply scandalized, "this ain't Wyoming, ner none of them places. This is Nebrasker."

"Yes," added Johnnie, "an' why don't he wait till he gits *out West*?"

The travelled Easterner laughed. "It isn't different there even—not in these days. But he thinks he's right in the middle of hell."

Johnnie and the cowboy mused long.

"It's awful funny," remarked Johnnie at last.

"Yes," said the cowboy. "This is a queer game. I hope we don't git snowed in, because then we'd have to stand this here man bein' around with us all the time. That wouldn't be no good."

"I wish pop would throw him out," said Johnnie.

Presently they heard a loud stamping on the stairs, accompanied by ringing jokes in the voice of old Scully, and laughter, evidently from the Swede. The men around the stove stared vacantly at each other. "Gosh!" said the cowboy. The door flew open, and old Scully, flushed and anecdotal, came into the room. He was jabbering at the Swede, who followed him, laughing bravely. It was the entry of two roisterers from a banquet hall.

"Come now," said Scully sharply to the three seated men, "move up and give us a chance at the stove." The cowboy and the Easterner obediently sidled their chairs to make room for the new-comers. Johnnie, however, simply arranged himself in a more indolent attitude, and then remained motionless.

"Come! Git over, there," said Scully.

"Plenty of room on the other side of the stove," said Johnnie.

"Do you think we want to sit in the draught?" roared the father.

But the Swede here interposed with a grandeur of confidence. "No, no. Let the boy sit where he likes," he cried in a bullying voice to the father.

"All right! All right!" said Scully, deferentially. The cowboy and the Easterner exchanged glances of wonder.

The five chairs were formed in a crescent about one side of the stove. The Swede began to talk; he talked arrogantly, profanely, angrily. Johnnie, the cowboy, and the Easterner maintained a morose silence, while old Scully appeared to be receptive and eager, breaking in constantly with sympathetic ejaculations.

Finally the Swede announced that he was thirsty. He moved in his chair, and said that he would go for a drink of water.

"I'll git it for you," cried Scully at once.

"No," said the Swede, contemptuously. "I'll get it for myself." He arose and stalked with the air of an owner off into the executive parts of the hotel.

As soon as the Swede was out of hearing Scully sprang to his feet and whispered intensely to the others: "Upstairs he thought I was tryin' to poison 'im.''

"Say," said Johnnie, "this makes me sick. Why don't you throw 'im out in the snow?"

"Why, he's all right now," declared Scully. "It was only that he was from the East, and he thought this was a tough place. That's all. He's all right now."

The cowboy looked with admiration upon the Easterner. "You were straight," he said. "You were on to that there Dutchman."

"Well," said Johnnie to his father, "he may be all right now, but I don't see it. Other time he was scared, but now he's too fresh."

Scully's speech was always a combination of Irish brogue and idiom, Western twang and idiom, and scraps of curiously formal diction taken from the story-books and newspapers. He now hurled a strange mass of language at the head of his son. "What do I keep? What do I keep? What do I keep?" he demanded, in a voice of thunder. He slapped his knee impressively, to indicate that he himself was going to make reply, and that all should heed. "I keep a hotel," he shouted. "A hotel, do you mind? A guest under my roof has sacred privileges. He is to be intimidated by none. Not one word shall he hear that would prijudice him in favour of goin' away. I'll not have it. There's no place in this here town where they can say they iver took in a guest of mine because he was afraid to stay here." He wheeled suddenly upon the cowboy and the Easterner. "Am I right?"

"Yes, Mr. Scully," said the cowboy, "I think you're right."

"Yes, Mr. Scully," said the Easterner, "I think you're right."

V

AT SIX-O'CLOCK SUPPER, the Swede fizzed like a fire-wheel. He sometimes seemed on the point of bursting into riotous song, and in all his madness he was encouraged by old Scully. The Easterner was encased in reserve; the cowboy sat in wide-mouthed amazement, forgetting to eat, while Johnnie wrathily demolished great plates of food. The daughters of the house, when they were obliged to replenish the biscuits, approached as warily as Indians, and, having succeeded in their purpose, fled with ill-concealed trepidation. The Swede domineered the whole feast, and he gave it the appearance of a cruel bacchanal. He seemed to have grown suddenly taller; he gazed, brutally disdainful, into every face. His voice rang through the room. Once when he jabbed out harpoon-fashion with his fork to pinion a biscuit, the weapon nearly impaled the hand of the Easterner, which had been stretched quietly out for the same biscuit.

After supper, as the men filed toward the other room, the Swede smote Scully ruthlessly on the shoulder. "Well, old boy, that was a good, square meal." Johnnie looked hopefully at his father; he knew that shoulder was tender from an old fall; and, indeed, it appeared for a moment as if Scully was going to flame out over the matter, but in the end he smiled a sickly smile and remained silent. The others understood from his manner that he was admitting his responsibility for the Swede's new view-point.

Johnnie, however, addressed his parent in an aside. "Why don't you license somebody to kick you downstairs?" Scully scowled darkly by way of reply.

When they were gathered about the stove, the Swede insisted on another game of High-Five. Scully gently deprecated the plan at first, but the Swede turned a wolfish glare upon him. The old man subsided, and the Swede canvassed the others. In his tone there was always a great threat. The cowboy and the Easterner both remarked indifferently that they would play. Scully said that he would presently have to go to meet the 6.58 train, and so the Swede turned menacingly upon Johnnie. For a moment their glances crossed like blades, and then Johnnie smiled and said, "Yes, I'll play."

They formed a square, with the little board on their knees. The Easterner and the Swede were again partners. As the play went on, it was noticeable that the cowboy was not board-whacking as usual. Meanwhile, Scully, near the lamp, had put on his spectacles and, with an appearance curiously like an old priest, was reading a newspaper. In time he went out to meet the 6.58 train, and, despite his precautions, a gust of polar wind whirled into the room as he opened the door. Besides scattering the cards, it chilled the players to the marrow. The Swede cursed frightfully. When Scully returned, his entrance disturbed a cosy and friendly scene. The Swede again cursed. But presently they were once more intent, their heads bent forward and their hands moving swiftly. The Swede had adopted the fashion of board-whacking.

Scully took up his paper and for a long time remained immersed in matters which were extraordinarily remote from him. The lamp burned badly, and once he stopped to adjust the wick. The newspaper, as he turned from page to page, rustled with a slow and comfortable sound. Then suddenly he heard three terrible words: "You are cheatin'!"

Such scenes often prove that there can be little of dramatic import in environment. Any room can present a tragic front; any room can be comic. This little den was now hideous as a torture-chamber. The new faces of the men themselves had changed it upon the instant. The Swede held a huge fist in front of Johnnie's face, while the latter looked steadily over it into the blazing orbs of his accuser. The Easterner had grown pallid; the cowboy's jaw had dropped in that expression of bovine amazement which was one of his important mannerisms. After the three words, the first sound in the room was made by

Scully's paper as it floated forgotten to his feet. His spectacles had also fallen from his nose, but by a clutch he had saved them in air. His hand, grasping the spectacles, now remained poised awkwardly and near his shoulder. He stared at the card-players.

Probably the silence was while a second elapsed. Then, if the floor had been suddenly twitched out from under the men they could not have moved quicker. The five had projected themselves headlong toward a common point. It happened that Johnnie, in rising to hurl himself upon the Swede, had stumbled slightly because of his curiously instinctive care for the cards and the board. The loss of the moment allowed time for the arrival of Scully, and also allowed the cowboy time to give the Swede a great push which sent him staggering back. The men found tongue together, and hoarse shouts of rage, appeal, or fear burst from every throat. The cowboy pushed and jostled feverishly at the Swede, and the Easterner and Scully clung wildly to Johnnie; but through the smoky air, above the swaying bodies of the peace-compellers, the eyes of the two warriors ever sought each other in glances of challenge that were at once hot and steely.

Of course the board had been overturned, and now the whole company of cards was scattered over the floor, where the boots of the men trampled the fat and painted kings and queens as they gazed with their silly eyes at the war that was waging above them.

Scully's voice was dominating the yells. "Stop now! Stop, I say! Stop, now—"

Johnnie, as he struggled to burst through the rank formed by Scully and the Easterner, was crying, "Well, he says I cheated! He says I cheated! I won't allow no man to say I cheated! If he says I cheated, he's a —— ——!"

The cowboy was telling the Swede, "Quit, now! Quit, d'ye hear——"

The screams of the Swede never ceased: "He did cheat! I saw him! I saw him——"

As for the Easterner, he was importuning in a voice that was not heeded: "Wait a moment, can't you? Oh, wait a moment. What's the good of a fight over a game of cards? Wait a moment——"

In this tumult no complete sentences were clear. "Cheat"—"Quit"—"He says"—these fragments pierced the uproar and rang out sharply. It was remarkable that, whereas Scully undoubtedly made the most noise, he was the least heard of any of the riotous band.

Then suddenly there was a great cessation. It was as if each man had paused for breath; and although the room was still lighted with the anger of men, it could be seen that there was no danger of immediate conflict, and at once Johnnie, shouldering his way forward, almost succeeded in confronting the Swede. "What did you say I cheated for? What did you say I cheated for? I don't cheat, and I won't let no man say I do!"

The Swede said, "I saw you! I saw you!"

"Well," cried Johnnie, "I'll fight any man what says I cheat!"

"No, you won't," said the cowboy. "Not here."

"Ah, be still, can't you?" said Scully, coming between them.

The quiet was sufficient to allow the Easterner's voice to be heard. He was repeating, "Oh, wait a moment, can't you? What's the good of a fight over a game of cards? Wait a moment!"

Johnnie, his red face appearing above his father's shoulder, hailed the Swede again. "Did you say I cheated?"

The Swede showed his teeth. "Yes."

"Then," said Johnnie, "we must fight."

"Yes, fight," roared the Swede. He was like a demoniac. "Yes, fight! I'll show you what kind of a man I am! I'll show you who you want to fight! Maybe you think I can't fight! Maybe you think I can't! I'll show you, you skin, you card-sharp! Yes, you cheated! You cheated! You cheated!"

"Well, let's go at it, then, mister," said Johnnie, coolly.

The cowboy's brow was beaded with sweat from his efforts in intercepting all sorts of raids. He turned in despair to Scully. "What are you goin' to do now?"

A change had come over the Celtic visage of the old man. He now seemed all eagerness; he eyes glowed.

"We'll let them fight," he answered, stalwartly. "I can't put up with it any longer. I've stood this damned Swede till I'm sick. We'll let them fight."

VI

THE MEN prepared to go out of doors. The Easterner was so nervous that he had great difficulty in getting his arms into the sleeves of his new leather coat. As the cowboy drew his fur cap down over his ears his hands trembled. In fact, Johnnie and old Scully were the only ones who displayed no agitation. These preliminaries were conducted without words.

Scully threw open the door. "Well, come on," he said. Instantly a terrific wind caused the flame of the lamp to struggle at its wick, while a puff of black smoke sprang from the chimney-top. The stove was in mid-current of the blast, and its voice swelled to equal the roar of the storm. Some of the scarred and bedabbled cards were caught up from the floor and dashed helplessly against the farther wall. The men lowered their heads and plunged into the tempest as into a sea.

No snow was falling, but great whirls and clouds of flakes, swept up from the ground by the frantic winds, were streaming southward with the speed of bullets. The covered land was blue with the sheen of an unearthly satin, and there was no other hue save where, at the low, black railway station—which seemed incredibly distant—one light gleamed like a tiny jewel. As the men floundered into a thigh-deep drift, it was known that the Swede was bawling out something. Scully went to him, put a hand on his shoulder, and projected an ear. "What's that you say?" he shouted.

"I say," bawled the Swede again, "I won't stand much show against this gang. I know you'll all pitch on me."

Scully smote him reproachfully on the arm. "Tut, man!" he yelled. The wind tore the words from Scully's lips and scattered them far alee.

"You are all a gang of——" boomed the Swede, but the storm also seized the remainder of this sentence.

Immediately turning their backs upon the wind, the men had swung around a corner to the sheltered side of the hotel. It was the function of the little house to preserve here, amid this great devastation of snow, an irregular V-shape of heavily encrusted grass, which crackled beneath the feet. One could imagine the great drifts piled against the windward side. When the party reached the comparative peace of this spot it was found that the Swede was still bellowing.

"Oh, I know what kind of a thing this is! I know you'll all pitch on me. I can't lick you all!"

Scully turned upon him panther-fashion. "You'll not have to whip all of

us. You'll have to whip my son Johnnie. An' the man what troubles you durin'
that time will have me to dale with."

The arrangements were swiftly made. The two men faced each other, obedient to the harsh commands of Scully, whose face, in the subtly luminous gloom,
could be seen set in the austere impersonal lines that are pictured on the
countenances of the Roman veterans. The Easterner's teeth were chattering,
and he was hopping up and down like a mechanical toy. The cowboy stood
rock-like.

The contestants had not stripped off any clothing. Each was in his ordinary
attire. Their fists were up, and they eyed each other in a calm that had the
elements of leonine cruelty in it.

During this pause, the Easterner's mind, like a film, took lasting impressions
of three men—the iron-nerved master of the ceremony; the Swede, pale, motionless, terrible; and Johnnie, serene yet ferocious, brutish yet heroic. The
entire prelude had in it a tragedy greater than the tragedy of action, and
this aspect was accentuated by the long, mellow cry of the blizzard, as it sped
the tumbling and wailing flakes into the black abyss of the south.

"Now!" said Scully.

The two combatants leaped forward and crashed together like bullocks. There
was heard the cushioned sound of blows, and of a curse squeezing out from
between the tight teeth of one.

As for the spectators, the Easterner's pent-up breath exploded from him
with a pop of relief, absolute relief from the tension of the preliminaries.
The cowboy bounded into the air with a yowl. Scully was immovable as from
supreme amazement and fear at the fury of the fight which he himself had
permitted and arranged.

For a time the encounter in the darkness was such a perplexity of flying
arms that it presented no more detail than would a swiftly revolving wheel.
Occasionally a face, as if illumined by a flash of light, would shine out, ghastly
and marked with pink spots. A moment later, the men might have been known
as shadows, if it were not for the involuntary utterance of oaths that came
from them in whispers.

Suddenly a holocaust of warlike desire caught the cowboy, and he bolted
forward with the speed of a broncho. "Go it, Johnnie! go it! Kill him! Kill
him!"

Scully confronted him. "Kape back," he said; and by his glance the cowboy
could tell that this man was Johnnie's father.

To the Easterner there was a monotony of unchangeable fighting that was
an abomination. This confused mingling was eternal to his sense, which was
concentrated in a longing for the end, the priceless end. Once the fighters
lurched near him, and as he scrambled hastily backward he heard them breathe
like men on the rack.

"Kill him, Johnnie! Kill him! Kill him! Kill him!" The cowboy's face was
contorted like one of those agony masks in museums.

"Keep still," said Scully, icily.

Then there was a sudden loud grunt, incomplete, cut short, and Johnnie's
body swung away from Swede and fell with sickening heaviness to the grass.
The cowboy was barely in time to prevent the mad Swede from flinging himself
upon his prone adversary. "No, you don't," said the cowboy, interposing an
arm. "Wait a second."

Scully was at his son's side. "Johnnie! Johnnie, me boy!" His voice had a quality of melancholy tenderness. "Johnnie! Can you go on with it?" He looked anxiously down into the bloody, pulpy face of his son.

There was a moment of silence, and then Johnnie answered in his ordinary voice, "Yes, I—it—yes."

Assisted by his father he struggled to his feet. "Wait a bit now till you git your wind," said the old man.

A few paces away the cowboy was lecturing the Swede. "No, you don't! Wait a second!"

The Easterner was plucking at Scully's sleeve. "Oh, this is enough," he pleaded. "This is enough! Let it go as it stands. This is enough!"

"Bill," said Scully, "git out of the road." The cowboy stepped aside. "Now." The combatants were actuated by a new caution as they advanced toward collision. They glared at each other, and then the Swede aimed a lightning blow that carried with it his entire weight. Johnnie was evidently half stupid from weakness, but he miraculously dodged, and his fist sent the over-balanced Swede sprawling.

The cowboy, Scully, and the Easterner burst into a cheer that was like a chorus of triumphant soldiery, but before its conclusion the Swede had scuffed agilely to his feet and come in berserk abandon at his foe. There was another perplexity of flying arms, and Johnnie's body again swung away and fell, even as a bundle might fall from a roof. The Swede instantly staggered to a little wind-waved tree and leaned upon it, breathing like an engine, while his savage and flamelit eyes roamed from face to face as the men bent over Johnnie. There was a splendour of isolation in his situation at this time which the Easterner felt once when, lifting his eyes from the man on the ground, he beheld that mysterious and lonely figure, waiting.

"Are you any good yet, Johnnie?" asked Scully in a broken voice.

The son gasped and opened his eyes languidly. After a moment he answered, "No—I ain't—any good—any—more." Then, from shame and bodily ill, he began to weep, the tears furrowing down through the blood-stains on his face. "He was too—too—too heavy for me."

Scully straightened and addressed the waiting figure.

"Stranger," he said, evenly, "it's all up with our side." Then his voice changed into that vibrant huskiness which is commonly the tone of the most simple and deadly announcements. "Johnnie is whipped."

Without replying, the victor moved off on the route to the front door of the hotel.

The cowboy was formulating new and unspellable blasphemies. The Easterner was startled to find that they were out in a wind that seemed to come direct from the shadowed arctic floes. He heard again the wail of the snow as it was flung to its grave in the south. He knew now that all this time the cold had been sinking into him deeper and deeper, and he wondered that he had not perished. He felt indifferent to the condition of the vanquished man.

"Johnnie, can you walk?" asked Scully.

"Did I hurt—hurt him any?" asked the son.

"Can you walk, boy? Can you walk?"

Johnnie's voice was suddenly strong. There was a robust impatience in it. "I asked you whether I hurt him any!"

"Yes, yes, Johnnie," answered the cowboy, consolingly; "he's hurt a good deal."

They raised him from the ground, and as soon as he was on his feet he went tottering off, rebuffing all attempts at assistance. When the party rounded the corner they were fairly blinded by the pelting of the snow. It burned their faces like fire. The cowboy carried Johnnie through the drift to the door. As they entered, some cards again rose from the floor and beat against the wall.

The Easterner rushed to the stove. He was so profoundly chilled that he almost dared to embrace the glowing iron. The Swede was not in the room. Johnnie sank into a chair and, folding his arms on his knees, buried his face in them. Scully, warming one foot and then the other at a rim of the stove, muttered to himself with Celtic mournfulness. The cowboy had removed his fur cap, and with a dazed and rueful air he was running one hand through his tousled locks. From overhead they could hear the creaking of boards, as the Swede tramped here and there in his room.

The sad quiet was broken by the sudden flinging open of a door that led toward the kitchen. It was instantly followed by an inrush of women. They precipitated themselves upon Johnnie amid a chorus of lamentation. Before they carried their prey off to the kitchen, there to be bathed and harangued with that mixture of sympathy and abuse which is a feat of their sex, the mother straightened herself and fixed old Scully with an eye of stern reproach, "Shame be upon you, Patrick Scully!" she cried. "Your own son, too. Shame be upon you!"

"There, now! Be quiet, now!" said the old man, weakly.

"Shame be upon you, Patrick Scully!" The girls, rallying to this slogan, sniffed disdainfully in the direction of those trembling accomplices, the cowboy and the Easterner. Presently they bore Johnnie away, and left the three men to dismal reflection.

VII

"I'D LIKE to fight this here Dutchman myself," said the cowboy, breaking a long silence.

Scully wagged his head sadly. "No, that wouldn't do. It wouldn't be right. It wouldn't be right."

"Well, why wouldn't it?" argued the cowboy. "I don't see no harm in it."

"No," answered Scully, with mournful heroism. "It wouldn't be right. It was Johnnie's fight, and now we mustn't whip the man just because he whipped Johnnie."

"Yes, that's true enough," said the cowboy; "but—he better not get fresh with me, because I couldn't stand no more of it."

"You'll not say a word to him," commanded Scully, and even then they heard the tread of the Swede on the stairs. His entrance was made theatric. He swept the door back with a bang and swaggered to the middle of the room. No one looked at him. "Well," he cried, insolently, at Scully, "I s'pose you'll tell me now how much I owe you?"

The old man remained stolid. "You don't owe me nothin'."

"Huh!" said the Swede, "huh! Don't owe 'im nothin'."

The cowboy addressed the Swede. "Stranger, I don't see how you come to be so gay around here."

Old Scully was instantly alert. "Stop!" he shouted, holding his hand forth, fingers upward. "Bill, you shut up!"

The cowboy spat carelessly into the sawdust-box. "I didn't say a word, did I?" he asked.

"Mr. Scully," called the Swede, "how much do I owe you?" It was seen that he was attired for departure, and that he had his valise in his hand.

"You don't owe me nothin'," repeated Scully in the same imperturbable way.

"Huh!" said the Swede. "I guess you're right. I guess if it was any way at all, you'd owe me somethin'. That's what I guess." He turned to the cowboy. " 'Kill him! Kill him! Kill him!' " he mimicked, and then guffawed victoriously. " 'Kill him!' " He was convulsed with ironical humour.

But he might have been jeering the dead. The three men were immovable and silent, staring with glassy eyes at the stove.

The Swede opened the door and passed into the storm, giving one derisive glance backward at the still group.

As soon as the door was closed, Scully and the cowboy leaped to their feet and began to curse. They trampled to and fro, waving their arms and smashing into the air with their fists. "Oh, but that was a hard minute!" wailed Scully. "That was a hard minute! Him there leerin' and scoffin'! One bang at his nose was worth forty dollars to me that minute! How did you stand it, Bill?"

"How did I stand it?" cried the cowboy in a quivering voice. "How did I stand it? Oh!"

The old man burst into sudden brogue. "I'd loike to take that Swade," he wailed, "and hould 'im down on a shtone flure and bate 'im to a jelly wid a shtick!"

The cowboy groaned in sympathy. "I'd like to git him by the neck and ha-ammer him"—he brought his hand down on a chair with a noise like a pistol-shot—"hammer that there Dutchman until he couldn't tell himself from a dead coyote!"

"I'd bate 'im until he——"

"I'd show *him* some things——"

And then together they raised a yearning, fanatic cry—"Oh-o-oh! if we only could——"

"Yes!"

"Yes!"

"And then I'd——"

"O-o-oh!"

VIII

The Swede, tightly gripping his valise, tacked across the face of the storm as if he carried sails. He was following a line of little naked, gasping trees which, he knew, must mark the way of the road. His face, fresh from the pounding of Johnnie's fists, felt more pleasure than pain in the wind and the driving snow. A number of square shapes loomed upon him finally, and he knew them as the houses of the main body of the town. He found a street and made travel along it, leaning heavily upon the wind whenever, at a corner, a terrific blast caught him.

He might have been in a deserted village. We picture the world as thick with conquering and elate humanity, but here, with the bugles of the tempest pealing, it was hard to imagine a peopled earth. One viewed the existence of man then as a marvel, and conceded a glamour of wonder to these lice which were caused to cling to a whirling, fire-smitten, ice-locked, disease-stricken, space-lost bulb. The conceit of man was explained by this storm to be the very engine of life. One was a coxcomb not to die in it. However, the Swede found a saloon.

In front of it an indomitable red light was burning, and the snowflakes were made blood-colour as they flew through the circumscribed territory of the lamp's shining. The Swede pushed open the door of the saloon and entered. A sanded expanse was before him, and at the end of it four men sat about a table drinking. Down one side of the room extended a radiant bar, and its guardian was leaning upon his elbows listening to the talk of the men at the table. The Swede dropped his valise upon the floor and, smiling fraternally upon the barkeeper, said, "Gimme some whisky, will you?" The man placed a bottle, a whisky-glass, and a glass of ice-thick water upon the bar. The Swede poured himself an abnormal portion of whisky and drank it in three gulps. "Pretty bad night," remarked the bartender, indifferently. He was making the pretension of blindness which is usually a distinction of his class; but it could have been seen that he was furtively studying the half-erased blood-stains on the face of the Swede. "Bad night," he said again.

"Oh, it's good enough for me," replied the Swede, hardily, as he poured himself some more whisky. The barkeeper took his coin and manœuvred it through its reception by the highly nickelled cash-machine. A bell rang; a card labelled "20 cts." had appeared.

"No," continued the Swede, "this isn't too bad weather. It's good enough for me."

"So?" murmured the barkeeper, languidly.

The copious drams made the Swede's eyes swim, and he breathed a trifle heavier. "Yes, I like this weather. I like it. It suits me." It was apparently his design to impart a deep significance to these words.

"So?" murmured the bartender again. He turned to gaze dreamily at the scroll-like birds and bird-like scrolls which had been drawn with soap upon the mirrors in back of the bar.

"Well, I guess I'll take another drink," said the Swede, presently. "Have something?"

"No, thanks; I'm not drinkin'," answered the bartender. Afterward he asked, "How did you hurt your face?"

The Swede immediately began to boast loudly. "Why, in a fight. I thumped the soul out of a man down here at Scully's hotel."

The interest of the four men at the table was at last aroused.

"Who was it?" said one.

"Johnnie Scully," blustered the Swede. "Son of the man what runs it. He will be pretty near dead for some weeks, I can tell you. I made a nice thing of him, I did. He couldn't get up. They carried him in the house. Have a drink?"

Instantly the men in some subtle way encased themselves in reserve. "No, thanks," said one. The group was of curious formation. Two were prominent local business men; one was the district attorney; and one was a professional gambler of the kind known as "square." But a scrutiny of the group would not have enabled an observer to pick the gambler from the men of more reputable pursuits. He was, in fact, a man so delicate in manner, when among people of fair class, and so judicious in his choice of victims, that in the strictly masculine part of the town's life he had come to be explicitly trusted and admired. People called him a thoroughbred. The fear and contempt with which his craft was regarded were undoubtedly the reason why his quiet dignity shone conspicuous above the quiet dignity of men who might be merely hatters, billiard-markers, or grocery clerks. Beyond an occasional unwary traveller who came by rail, this gambler was supposed to prey solely upon reckless and senile farmers, who, when flush with good crops, drove into town in all the pride and confidence of an absolutely invulnerable stupidity. Hearing at times in circuitous fashion of the despoilment of such a farmer, the important men of Romper invariably laughed in contempt of the victim, and if they thought of the wolf at all, it was with a kind of pride at the knowledge that he would never dare think of attacking their wisdom and courage. Besides, it was popular that this gambler had a real wife and two real children in a neat cottage in a suburb, where he led an exemplary home life; and when any one even suggested a discrepancy in his character, the crowd immediately vociferated descriptions of this virtuous family circle. Then men who led exemplary home lives, and men who did not lead exemplary home lives, all subsided in a bunch, remarking that there was nothing more to be said.

However, when a restriction was placed upon him—as, for instance, when a strong clique of members of the new Pollywog Club refused to permit him, even as a spectator, to appear in the rooms of the organization—the candour and gentleness with which he accepted the judgment disarmed many of his foes and made his friends more desperately partisan. He invariably distinguished between himself and a respectable Romper man so quickly and frankly that his manner actually appeared to be a continual broadcast compliment.

And one must not forget to declare the fundamental fact of his entire position in Romper. It is irrefutable that in all affairs outside his business, in all matters that occur eternally and commonly between man and man, this thieving card-player was so generous, so just, so moral, that, in a contest, he could have put to flight the consciences of nine tenths of the citizens of Romper.

And so it happened that he was seated in this saloon with the two prominent local merchants and the district attorney.

The Swede continued to drink raw whisky, meanwhile babbling at the bar-keeper and trying to induce him to indulge in potations. "Come on. Have a drink. Come on. What—no? Well, have a little one, then. By gawd, I've whipped a man to-night, and I want to celebrate. I whipped him good, too. Gentlemen," the Swede cried to the men at the table, "have a drink?"

"Ssh!" said the barkeeper.

The group at the table, although furtively attentive, had been pretending to be deep in talk, but now a man lifted his eyes toward the Swede and said, shortly, "Thanks. We don't want any more."

At this reply the Swede ruffled out his chest like a rooster. "Well," he exploded, "it seems I can't get anybody to drink with me in this town. Seems so, don't it? Well!"

"Ssh!" said the barkeeper.

"Say," snarled the Swede, "don't you try to shut me up. I won't have it. I'm a gentleman, and I want people to drink with me. And I want 'em to drink with me now. *Now*—do you understand?" He rapped the bar with his knuckles.

Years of experience had calloused the bartender. He merely grew sulky. "I hear you," he answered.

"Well," cried the Swede, "listen hard then. See those men over there? Well, they're going to drink with me, and don't you forget it. Now you watch."

"Hi!" yelled the barkeeper, "this won't do!"

"Why won't it?" demanded the Swede. He stalked over to the table, and by chance laid his hand upon the shoulder of the gambler. "How about this?" he asked wrathfully. "I asked you to drink with me."

The gambler simply twisted his head and spoke over his shoulder. "My friend, I don't know you."

"Oh, hell!" answered the Swede, "come and have a drink."

"Now, my boy," advised the gambler, kindly, "take your hand off my shoulder and go 'way and mind your own business." He was a little, slim man, and it seemed strange to hear him use this tone of heroic patronage to the burly Swede. The other men at the table said nothing.

"What! You won't drink with me, you little dude? I'll make you, then! I'll make you!" The Swede had grasped the gambler frenziedly at the throat, and was dragging him from his chair. The other men sprang up. The barkeeper dashed around the corner of his bar. There was a great tumult, and then was seen a long blade in the hand of the gambler. It shot forward, and a human body, this citadel of virtue, wisdom, power, was pierced as easily as if it had been a melon. The Swede fell with a cry of supreme astonishment.

The prominent merchants and the district attorney must have at once tumbled out of the place backward. The bartender found himself hanging limply to the arm of a chair and gazing into the eyes of a murderer.

"Henry," said the latter, as he wiped his knife on one of the towels that hung beneath the bar rail, "you tell 'em where to find me. I'll be home, waiting for 'em." Then he vanished. A moment afterward the barkeeper was in the street dinning through the storm for help and, moreover, companionship.

The corpse of the Swede, alone in the saloon, had its eyes fixed upon a dreadful legend that dwelt atop of the cash-machine: "This registers the amount of your purchase."

IX

MONTHS LATER, the cowboy was frying pork over the stove of a little ranch near the Dakota line, when there was a quick thud of hoofs outside, and presently the Easterner entered with the letters and the papers.

"Well," said the Easterner at once, "the chap that killed the Swede has got three years. Wasn't much, was it?"

"He has? Three years?" The cowboy poised his pan of pork, while he ruminated upon the news. "Three years. That ain't much."

"No. It was a light sentence," replied the Easterner as he unbuckled his spurs. "Seems there was a good deal of sympathy for him in Romper."

"If the bartender had been any good," observed the cowboy, thoughtfully, "he would have gone in and cracked that there Dutchman on the head with a bottle in the beginnin' of it and stopped all this here murderin'."

"Yes, a thousand things might have happened," said the Easterner, tartly.

The cowboy returned his pan of pork to the fire, but his philosophy continued. "It's funny, ain't it? If he hadn't said Johnnie was cheatin' he'd be alive this minute. He was an awful fool. Game played for fun, too. Not for money. I believe he was crazy."

"I feel sorry for that gambler," said the Easterner.

"Oh, so do I," said the cowboy. "He don't deserve none of it for killin' who he did."

"The Swede might not have been killed if everything had been square."

"Might not have been killed?" exclaimed the cowboy. "Everythin' square? Why, when he said that Johnnie was cheatin' and acted like such a jackass? And then in the saloon he fairly walked up to git hurt?" With these arguments the cowboy browbeat the Easterner and reduced him to rage.

"You're a fool!" cried the Easterner, viciously. "You're a bigger jackass than the Swede by a million majority. Now let me tell you one thing. Let me tell you something. Listen! Johnnie *was* cheating!"

" 'Johnnie,' " said the cowboy, blankly. There was a minute of silence, and then he said, robustly, "Why, no. The game was only for fun."

"Fun or not," said the Easterner, "Johnnie was cheating. I saw him. I know it. I saw him. And I refused to stand up and be a man. I let the Swede fight it out alone. And you—you were simply puffing around the place wanting to fight. And then old Scully himself! We are all in it! This poor gambler isn't even a noun. He is kind of an adverb. Every sin is the result of a collaboration. We, five of us, have collaborated in the murder of this Swede. Usually there are from a dozen to forty women really involved in every murder, but in this case it seems to be only five men—you, I, Johnnie, old Scully; and that fool of an unfortunate gambler came merely as a culmination, the apex of a human movement, and gets all the punishment."

The cowboy, injured and rebellious, cried out blindly into this fog of mysterious theory: "Well, I didn't do anythin', did I?"

[1898]

Anton Chekhov   1860–1904

THE DARLING*

Olenka, the daughter of the retired collegiate assessor, Plemyanniakov, was sitting in her back porch, lost in thought. It was hot, the flies were persistent and teasing, and it was pleasant to reflect that it would soon be evening. Dark rainclouds were gathering from the east, and bringing from time to time a breath of moisture in the air.

Kukin, who was the manager of an open-air theatre called the Tivoli, and who lived in the lodge, was standing in the middle of the garden looking at the sky.

"Again!" he observed despairingly. "It's going to rain again! Rain every day, as though to spite me. I might as well hang myself! It's ruin! Fearful losses every day."

He flung up his hands, and went on, addressing Olenka:

"There! that's the life we lead, Olga Semyonovna. It's enough to make one cry. One works and does one's utmost; one wears oneself out, getting no sleep at night, and racks one's brain what to do for the best. And then what happens? To begin with, one's public is ignorant, boorish. I give them the very best operetta, a dainty masque, first rate music-hall artists. But do you suppose that's what they want! They don't understand anything of that sort. They want a clown; what they ask for is vulgarity. And then look at the weather! Almost every evening it rains. It started on the tenth of May, and it's kept it up all May and June. It's simply awful! The public doesn't come, but I've to pay the rent just the same, and pay the artists."

The next evening the clouds would gather again, and Kukin would say with an hysterical laugh:

"Well, rain away, then! Flood the garden, drown me! Damn my luck in this world and the next! Let the artists have me up! Send me to prison!—to Siberia!—the scaffold! Ha, ha, ha!"

And next day the same thing.

Olenka listened to Kukin with silent gravity, and sometimes tears came into her eyes. In the end his misfortunes touched her; she grew to love him. He was a small thin man, with a yellow face, and curls combed forward on his forehead. He spoke in a thin tenor; as he talked his mouth worked on one side, and there was always an expression of despair on his face; yet he aroused a deep and genuine affection in her. She was always fond of some one, and could not exist without loving. In earlier days she had loved her papa, who now sat in a darkened room, breathing with difficulty; she had loved her aunt who used to come every other year from Bryansk;[1] and before that, when she was at school, she had loved her French master. She was a gentle, soft-hearted, compassionate girl, with mild, tender eyes and very good health. At the sight of her full rosy cheeks, her soft white neck with a little dark mole on it, and the kind, naïve smile, which came into her face when she listened to anything pleasant, men thought, "Yes, not half bad," and smiled too, while

---

* Translated by Constance Garnett
[1] A city southwest of Moscow.

lady visitors could not refrain from seizing her hand in the middle of a conversation, exclaiming in a gush of delight, "You darling!"

The house in which she had lived from her birth upwards, and which was left her in her father's will, was at the extreme end of the town, not far from the Tivoli. In the evenings and at night she could hear the band playing, and the crackling and banging of fireworks, and it seemed to her that it was Kukin struggling with his destiny, storming the entrenchments of his chief foe, the indifferent public; there was a sweet thrill at her heart, she had no desire to sleep, and when he returned home at daybreak, she tapped softly at her bedroom window, and showing him only her face and one shoulder through the curtain, she gave him a friendly smile. . . .

He proposed to her, and they were married. And when he had a closer view of her neck and her plump, fine shoulders, he threw up his hands, and said:

"You darling!"

He was happy, but as it rained on the day and night of his wedding, his face still retained an expression of despair.

They got on very well together. She used to sit in his office, to look after things in the Tivoli, to put down the accounts and pay the wages. And her rosy cheeks, her sweet, naïve, radiant smile, were to be seen now at the office window, now in the refreshment bar or behind the scenes of the theatre. And already she used to say to her acquaintances that the theatre was the chief and most important thing in life, and that it was only through the drama that one could derive true enjoyment and become cultivated and humane.

"But do you suppose the public understands that?" she used to say. "What they want is a clown. Yesterday we gave 'Faust Inside Out,' and almost all the boxes were empty; but if Vanitchka and I had been producing some vulgar thing, I assure you the theatre would have been packed. Tomorrow Vanitchka and I are doing 'Orpheus in Hell.'[2] Do come."

And what Kukin said about the theatre and the actors she repeated. Like him she despised the public for their ignorance and their indifference to art; she took part in the rehearsals, she corrected the actors, she kept an eye on the behaviour of the musicians, and when there was an unfavourable notice in the local paper, she shed tears, and then went to the editor's office to set things right.

The actors were fond of her and used to call her "Vanitchka and I," and "the darling"; she was sorry for them and used to lend them small sums of money, and if they deceived her, she used to shed a few tears in private, but did not complain to her husband.

They got on well in the winter too. They took the theatre in the town for the whole winter, and let it for short terms to a Little Russian company, or to a conjurer, or to a local dramatic society. Olenka grew stouter, and was always beaming with satisfaction, while Kukin grew thinner and yellower, and continually complained of their terrible losses, although he had not done badly all the winter. He used to cough at night, and she used to give him hot raspberry tea or lime-flower water, to rub him with eau-de-Cologne and to wrap him in her warm shawls.

"You're such a sweet pet!" she used to say with perfect sincerity, stroking his hair. "You're such a pretty dear!"

---

[2] Two nineteenth-century plays, the first a "travesty" (1888), the second a musical (1858).

Towards Lent he went to Moscow to collect a new troupe, and without him she could not sleep, but sat all night at her window, looking at the stars, and she compared herself with the hens, who are awake all night and uneasy when the cock is not in the hen-house. Kukin was detained in Moscow, and wrote that he would be back at Easter, adding some instructions about the Tivoli. But on the Sunday before Easter, late in the evening, came a sudden ominous knock at the gate; some one was hammering on the gate as though on a barrel—boom, boom, boom! The drowsy cook went flopping with her bare feet through the puddles, as she ran to open the gate.

"Please open," said some one outside in a thick bass. "There is a telegram for you."

Olenka had received telegrams from her husband before, but this time for some reason she felt numb with terror. With shaking hands she opened the telegram and read as follows:

"Ivan Petrovitch died suddenly to-day. Awaiting immate instructions fufuneral Tuesday."

That was how it was written in the telegram—"fufuneral," and the utterly incomprehensible word "immate." It was signed by the stage manager of the operatic company.

"My darling!" sobbed Olenka. "Vanitchka, my precious, my darling! Why did I ever meet you! Why did I know you and love you! Your poor heartbroken Olenka is all alone without you!"

Kukin's funeral took place on Tuesday in Moscow, Olenka returned home on Wednesday, and as soon as she got indoors she threw herself on her bed and sobbed so loudly that it could be heard next door, and in the street.

"Poor darling!" the neighbours said, as they crossed themselves. "Olga Semyonovna, poor darling! How she does take on!"

Three months later Olenka was coming home from mass, melancholy and in deep mourning. It happened that one of her neighbours, Vassily Andreitch Pustovalov, returning home from church, walked back beside her. He was the manager at Babakayev's, the timber merchant's. He wore a straw hat, a white waistcoat, and a gold watch-chain, and looked more like a country gentleman than a man in trade.

"Everything happens as it is ordained, Olga Semyonovna," he said gravely, with a sympathetic note in his voice; "and if any of our dear ones die, it must be because it is the will of God, so we ought to have fortitude and bear it submissively."

After seeing Olenka to her gate, he said good-bye and went on. All day afterwards she heard his sedately dignified voice, and whenever she shut her eyes she saw his dark beard. She liked him very much. And apparently she had made an impression on him, too, for not long afterwards an elderly lady, with whom she was only slightly acquainted, came to drink coffee with her, and as soon as she was seated at table began to talk about Pustovalov, saying that he was an excellent man whom one could thoroughly depend upon, and that any girl would be glad to marry him. Three days later Pustovalov came himself. He did not stay long, only about ten minutes, and he did not say much, but when he left, Olenka loved him—loved him so much that she lay awake all night in a perfect fever, and in the morning she sent for the elderly lady. The match was quickly arranged, and then came the wedding.

Pustovalov and Olenka got on very well together when they were married.

Usually he sat in the office till dinner-time, then he went out on business, while Olenka took his place, and sat in the office till evening, making up accounts and booking orders.

"Timber gets dearer every year; the price rises twenty per cent," she would say to her customers and friends. "Only fancy we used to sell local timber, and now Vassitchka always has to go for wood to the Mogilev district.[3] And the freight!" she would add, covering her cheeks with her hands in horror. "The freight!"

It seemed to her that she had been in the timber trade for ages and ages, and that the most important and necessary thing in life was timber; and there was something intimate and touching to her in the very sound of words such as "baulk," "post," "beam," "pole," "scantling," "batten," "lath," "plank," etc.

At night when she was asleep she dreamed of perfect mountains of planks and boards, and long strings of wagons, carting timber somewhere far away. She dreamed that a whole regiment of six-inch beams forty feet high, standing on end, was marching upon the timber-yard; that logs, beams, and boards knocked together with the resounding crash of dry wood, kept falling and getting up again, piling themselves on each other. Olenka cried out in her sleep, and Pustovalov said to her tenderly: "Olenka, what's the matter, darling? Cross yourself!"

Her husband's ideas were hers. If he thought the room was too hot, or that business was slack, she thought the same. Her husband did not care for entertainments, and on holidays he stayed at home. She did likewise.

"You are always at home or in the office," her friends said to her. "You should go to the theatre, darling, or to the circus."

"Vassitchka and I have no time to go to theatres," she would answer sedately. "We have no time for nonsense. What's the use of these theatres?"

On Saturdays Pustovalov and she used to go to the evening service; on holidays to early mass, and they walked side by side with softened faces as they came home from church. There was a pleasant fragrance about them both, and her silk dress rustled agreeably. At home they drank tea, with fancy bread and jams of various kinds, and afterwards they ate pie. Every day at twelve o'clock there was a savoury smell of beet-root soup and of mutton or duck in their yard, and on fast-days of fish, and no one could pass the gate without feeling hungry. In the office the samovar[4] was always boiling, and customers were regaled with tea and cracknels.[5] Once a week the couple went to the baths and returned side by side, both red in the face.

"Yes, we have nothing to complain of, thank God," Olenka used to say to her acquaintances. "I wish every one were as well off as Vassitchka and I."

When Pustovalov went away to buy wood in the Mogilev district, she missed him dreadfully, lay awake and cried. A young veterinary surgeon in the army, called Smirnin, to whom they had let their lodge, used sometimes to come in in the evening. He used to talk to her and play cards with her, and this entertained her in her husband's absence. She was particularly interested in what he told her of his home life. He was married and had a little boy, but was separated from his wife because she had been unfaithful to him, and now

---

[3] A city on the Dnieper River west of Moscow.
[4] An urn used to boil water.   [5] Hard brittle biscuits.

he hated her and used to send her forty roubles a month for the maintenance of their son. And hearing of all this, Olenka sighed and shook her head. She was sorry for him.

"Well, God keep you," she used to say to him at parting, as she lighted him down the stairs with a candle. "Thank you for coming to cheer me up, and may the Mother of God give you health."

And she always expressed herself with the same sedateness and dignity, the same reasonableness, in imitation of her husband. As the veterinary surgeon was disappearing behind the door below, she would say,

"You know, Vladimir Platonitch, you'd better make it up with your wife. You should forgive her for the sake of your son. You may be sure the little fellow understands."

And when Pustovalov came back, she told him in a low voice about the veterinary surgeon and his unhappy home life, and both sighed and shook their heads and talked about the boy, who, no doubt, missed his father, and by some strange connection of ideas, they went up to the holy ikons,[6] bowed to the ground before them and prayed that God would give them children.

And so the Pustovalovs lived for six years quietly and peaceably in love and complete harmony.

But behold! one winter day after drinking hot tea in the office, Vassily Andreitch went out into the yard without his cap on to see about sending off some timber, caught cold and was taken ill. He had the best doctors, but he grew worse and died after four months' illness. And Olenka was a widow once more.

"I've nobody, now you've left me, my darling," she sobbed, after her husband's funeral. "How can I live without you, in wretchedness and misery! Pity me, good people, all alone in the world!"

She went about dressed in black with long "weepers,"[7] and gave up wearing hat and gloves for good. She hardly ever went out, except to church, or to her husband's grave, and led the life of a nun. It was not till six months later that she took off the weepers and opened the shutters of the windows. She was sometimes seen in the mornings, going with her cook to market for provisions, but what went on in her house and how she lived now could only be surmised. People guessed, from seeing her drinking tea in her garden with the veterinary surgeon, who read the newspaper aloud to her, and from the fact that, meeting a lady she knew at the post-office, she said to her:

"There is no proper veterinary inspection in our town, and that's the cause of all sorts of epidemics. One is always hearing of people's getting infection from the milk supply, or catching diseases from horses and cows. The health of domestic animals ought to be as well cared for as the health of human beings."

She repeated the veterinary surgeon's words, and was of the same opinion as he about everything. It was evident that she could not live a year without some attachment, and had found new happiness in the lodge. In any one else this would have been censured, but no one could think ill of Olenka; everything she did was so natural. Neither she nor the veterinary surgeon said anything to other people of the change in their relations, and tried, indeed, to conceal it, but without success, for Olenka could not keep a secret. When he had visitors, men serving in his regiment, and she poured out tea or served

---

[6] Religious images.   [7] Mourning bands.

the supper, she would begin talking of the cattle plague, of the foot and mouth disease, and of the municipal slaughter-houses. He was dreadfully embarrassed, and when the guests had gone, he would seize her by the hand and hiss angrily:

"I've asked you before not to talk about what you don't understand. When we veterinary surgeons are talking among ourselves, please don't put your word in. It's really annoying."

And she would look at him with astonishment and dismay, and ask him in alarm: "But, Voloditchka, what *am* I to talk about?"

And with tears in her eyes she would embrace him, begging him not to be angry, and they were both happy.

But this happiness did not last long. The veterinary surgeon departed, departed for ever with his regiment, when it was transferred to a distant place— to Siberia, it may be. And Olenka was left alone.

Now she was absolutely alone. Her father had long been dead, and his armchair lay in the attic, covered with dust and lame of one leg. She got thinner and plainer, and when people met her in the street they did not look at her as they used to, and did not smile to her; evidently her best years were over and left behind, and now a new sort of life had begun for her, which did not bear thinking about. In the evening Olenka sat in the porch, and heard the band playing and the fireworks popping in the Tivoli, but now the sound stirred no response. She looked into her yard without interest, thought of nothing, wished for nothing, and afterwards, when night came on she went to bed and dreamed of her empty yard. She ate and drank as it were unwillingly.

And what was worst of all, she had no opinions of any sort. She saw the objects about her and understood what she saw, but could not form any opinion about them, and did not know what to talk about. And how awful it is not to have any opinions! One sees a bottle, for instance, or the rain, or a peasant driving in his cart, but what the bottle is for, or the rain, or the peasant, and what is the meaning of it, one can't say, and could not even for a thousand roubles. When she had Kukin, or Pustovalov, or the veterinary surgeon, Olenka could explain everything, and give her opinion about anything you like, but now there was the same emptiness in her brain and in her heart as there was in her yard outside. And it was as harsh and as bitter as wormwood in the mouth.

Little by little the town grew in all directions. The road became a street, and where the Tivoli and the timber-yard had been, there were new turnings and houses. How rapidly time passes! Olenka's house grew dingy, the roof got rusty, the shed sank on one side, and the whole yard was overgrown with docks and stinging-nettles.[8] Olenka herself had grown plain and elderly; in summer she sat in the porch, and her soul, as before, was empty and dreary and full of bitterness. In winter she sat at her window and looked at the snow. When she caught the scent of spring, or heard the chime of the church bells, a sudden rush of memories from the past came over her, there was a tender ache in her heart, and her eyes brimmed over with tears; but this was only for a minute, and then came emptiness again and the sense of the futility of life. The black kitten, Briska, rubbed against her and purred softly, but Olenka was not touched by these feline caresses. That was not what she needed. She wanted a love that would absorb her whole being, her whole soul and reason—

[8] Weedy and prickly plants.

that would give her ideas and an object in life, and would warm her old blood. And she would shake the kitten off her skirt and say with vexation:

"Get along; I don't want you!"

And so it was, day after day and year after year, and no joy, and no opinions. Whatever Mavra, the cook, said she accepted.

One hot July day, towards evening, just as the cattle were being driven away, and the whole yard was full of dust, some one suddenly knocked at the gate. Olenka went to open it herself and was dumbfounded when she looked out: she saw Smirnin, the veterinary surgeon, grey-headed, and dressed as a civilian. She suddenly remembered everything. She could not help crying and letting her head fall on his breast without uttering a word, and in the violence of her feeling she did not notice how they both walked into the house and sat down to tea.

"My dear Vladimir Platonitch! What fate has brought you?" she muttered, trembling with joy.

"I want to settle here for good, Olga Semyonovna," he told her. "I have resigned my post, and have come to settle down and try my luck on my own account. Besides, it's time for my boy to go to school. He's a big boy. I am reconciled with my wife, you know."

"Where is she?" asked Olenka.

"She's at the hotel with the boy, and I'm looking for lodgings."

"Good gracious, my dear soul! Lodgings? Why not have my house? Why shouldn't that suit you? Why, my goodness, I wouldn't take any rent!" cried Olenka in a flutter, beginning to cry again. "You live here, and the lodge will do nicely for me. Oh dear! how glad I am!"

Next day the roof was painted and the walls were whitewashed, and Olenka, with her arms akimbo, walked about the yard giving directions. Her face was beaming with her old smile, and she was brisk and alert as though she had waked from a long sleep. The veterinary's wife arrived—a thin, plain lady, with short hair and a peevish expression. With her was her little Sasha, a boy of ten, small for his age, blue-eyed, chubby, with dimples in his cheeks. And scarcely had the boy walked into the yard when he ran after the cat, and at once there was the sound of his gay joyous laugh.

"Is that your puss, auntie?" he asked Olenka. "When she has little ones, do give us a kitten. Mamma is awfully afraid of mice."

Olenka talked to him, and gave him tea. Her heart warmed and there was a sweet ache in her bosom, as though the boy had been her own child. And when he sat at the table in the evening, going over his lessons, she looked at him with deep tenderness and pity as she murmured to herself:

"You pretty pet! . . . my precious! . . . Such a fair little thing, and so clever."

" 'An island is a piece of land which is entirely surrounded by water,' " he read aloud.

"An island is a piece of land," she repeated, and this was the first opinion to which she gave utterance with positive conviction after so many years of silence and dearth of ideas.

Now she had opinions of her own, and at supper she talked to Sasha's parents, saying how difficult the lessons were at the high schools, but that yet the high-school was better than a commercial one, since with a high-school education all careers were open to one, such as being a doctor or an engineer.

Sasha began going to the high school. His mother departed to Harkov to her sister's and did not return; his father used to go off every day to inspect cattle, and would often be away from home for three days together, and it seemed to Olenka as though Sasha was entirely abandoned, that he was not wanted at home, that he was being starved, and she carried him off to her lodge and gave him a little room there.

And for six months Sasha had lived in the lodge with her. Every morning Olenka came into his bedroom and found him fast asleep, sleeping noiselessly with his hand under his cheek. She was sorry to wake him.

"Sashenka," she would say mournfully, "get up, darling. It's time for school."

He would get up, dress and say his prayers, and then sit down to breakfast, drink three glasses of tea, and eat two large cracknels and half a buttered roll. All this time he was hardly awake and a little ill-humoured in consequence.

"You don't quite know your fable, Sashenka," Olenka would say, looking at him as though he were about to set off on a long journey. "What a lot of trouble I have with you! You must work and do your best, darling, and obey your teachers."

"Oh, do leave me alone!" Sasha would say.

Then he would go down the street to school, a little figure, wearing a big cap and carrying a satchel on his shoulder. Olenka would follow him noiselessly.

"Sashenka!" she would call after him, and she would pop into his hand a date or a caramel. When he reached the street where the school was, he would feel ashamed of being followed by a tall, stout woman; he would turn round and say:

"You'd better go home, auntie. I can go the rest of the way alone."

She would stand still and look after him fixedly till he had disappeared at the school-gate.

Ah, how she loved him! Of her former attachments not one had been so deep; never had her soul surrendered to any feeling so spontaneously, so disinterestedly, and so joyously as now that her maternal instincts were aroused. For this little boy with the dimple in his cheek and the big school cap, she would have given her whole life, she would have given it with joy and tears of tenderness. Why? Who can tell why?

When she had seen the last of Sasha, she returned home, contented and serene, brimming over with love; her face, which had grown younger during the last six months, smiled and beamed; people meeting her looked at her with pleasure.

"Good-morning, Olga Semyonovna, darling. How are you, darling?"

"The lessons at the high school are very difficult now," she would relate at the market. "It's too much; in the first class yesterday they gave him a fable to learn by heart, and a Latin translation and a problem. You know it's too much for a little chap."

And she would begin talking about the teachers, the lessons, and the school books, saying just what Sasha said.

At three o'clock they had dinner together: in the evening they learned their lessons together and cried. When she put him to bed, she would stay a long time making the Cross over him and murmuring a prayer; then she would go to bed and dream of that far-away misty future when Sasha would finish his studies and become a doctor or an engineer, would have a big house of his own with horses and a carriage, would get married and have children. . . . She would fall asleep still thinking of the same thing, and tears would run down her cheeks from her closed eyes, while the black cat lay purring beside her: "Mrr, mrr, mrr."

Suddenly there would come a loud knock at the gate.

Olenka would wake up breathless with alarm, her heart throbbing. Half a minute later would come another knock.

"It must be a telegram from Harkov," she would think, beginning to tremble from head to foot. "Sasha's mother is sending for him from Harkov. . . . Oh, mercy on us!"

She was in despair. Her head, her hands, and her feet would turn chill, and she would feel that she was the most unhappy woman in the world. But another minute would pass, voices would be heard: it would turn out to be the veterinary surgeon coming home from the club.

"Well, thank God!" she would think.

And gradually the load in her heart would pass off, and she would feel at ease. She would go back to bed thinking of Sasha, who lay sound asleep in the next room, sometimes crying out in his sleep:

"I'll give it you! Get away! Shut up!"

[1899]

Joseph Conrad   *1857–1924*

HEART OF DARKNESS

The *Nellie*, a cruising yawl, swung to her anchor without a flutter of the sails, and was at rest. The flood had made, the wind was nearly calm, and being bound down the river, the only thing for it was to come to and wait for the turn of the tide.

The sea-reach of the Thames stretched before us like the beginning of an interminable waterway. In the offing the sea and the sky were welded together without a joint, and in the luminous space the tanned sails of the barges drifting up with the tide seemed to stand still in red clusters of canvas sharply peaked, with gleams of varnished spirits. A haze rested on the low shores that ran out to sea in vanishing flatness. The air was dark above Gravesend,[1] and farther back still seemed condensed into a mournful gloom, brooding motionless over the biggest, and the greatest, town on earth.

The Director of Companies was our captain and our host. We four affectionately watched his back as he stood in the bows looking to seaward. On the whole river there was nothing that looked half so nautical. He resembled a pilot, which to a seaman is trustworthiness personified. It was difficult to realize his work was not out there in the luminous estuary, but behind him, within the brooding gloom.

Between us there was, as I have already said somewhere, the bond of the sea. Besides holding our hearts together through long periods of separation, it had the effect of making us tolerant of each other's yarns—and even convictions. The Lawyer—the best of old fellows—had, because of his many years and many virtues, the only cushion on deck, and was lying on the only rug. The Accountant had brought out already a box of dominoes, and was toying architecturally with the bones. Marlow sat cross-legged right aft, leaning against the mizzen-mast. He had sunken cheeks, a yellow complexion, a straight back, an ascetic aspect, and, with his arms dropped, the palms of hands outwards, resembled an idol. The director, satisfied the anchor had good hold, made his way aft and sat down amongst us. We exchanged a few words lazily. Afterwards there was silence on board the yacht. For some reason or other we did not begin that game of dominoes. We felt meditative, and fit for nothing but placid staring. The day was ending in a serenity of still and exquisite brilliance. The water shone pacifically; the sky, without a speck, was a benign immensity of unstained light; the very mist on the Essex marshes was like a gauzy and radiant fabric, hung from the wooded rises inland, and draping the low shores in diaphanous folds. Only the gloom to the west, brooding over the upper reaches, became more sombre every minute, as if angered by the approach of the sun.

And at last, in its curved and imperceptible fall, the sun sank low, and from glowing white changed to a dull red without rays and without heat, as if about to go out suddenly, stricken to death by the touch of that gloom brooding over a crowd of men.

Forthwith a change came over the waters, and the serenity became less bril-

[1] A city on the Thames River, 26 miles east of London.

liant but more profound. The old river in its broad reach rested unruffled at the decline of day, after ages of good service done to the race that peopled its banks, spread out in the tranquil dignity of a waterway leading to the uttermost ends of the earth. We looked at the venerable stream not in the vivid flush of a short day that comes and departs for ever, but in the august light of abiding memories. And indeed nothing is easier for a man who has, as the phrase goes, "followed the sea" with reverence and affection, than to evoke the great spirit of the past upon the lower reaches of the Thames. The tidal current runs to and fro in its unceasing service, crowded with memories of men and ships it had borne to the rest of home or to the battles of the sea. It had known and served all the men of whom the nation is proud, from Sir Francis Drake to Sir John Franklin,[2] knights all, titled and untitled—the great knights-errant of the sea. It had borne all the ships whose names are like jewels flashing in the night of time, from the *Golden Hind* returning with her round flanks full of treasure, to be visited by the Queen's Highness and thus pass out of the gigantic tale, to the *Erebus* and *Terror*, bound on other conquests—and that never returned. It had known the ships and the men. They had sailed from Deptford, from Greenwich, from Erith[3]—the adventurers and the settlers; kings' ships and the ships of men on 'Change;[4] captains, admirals, the dark "interlopers"[5] of the Eastern trade, and the commissioned "generals" of East India fleets. Hunters for gold or pursuers of fame, they all had gone out on that stream, bearing the sword, and often the torch, messengers of the might within the land, bearers of a spark from the sacred fire. What greatness had not floated on the ebb of that river into the mystery of an unknown earth! . . . The dreams of men, the seed of commonwealths, the germs of empires.

The sun set; the dusk fell on the stream, and lights began to appear along the shore. The Chapman lighthouse, a three-legged thing erect on a mudflat, shone strongly. Lights of ships moved in the fairway—a great stir of lights going up and going down. And father west on the upper reaches the place of the monstrous town was still marked ominously on the sky, a brooding gloom in sunshine, a lurid glare under the stars.

"And this also," said Marlow suddenly, "has been one of the dark places of the earth."

He was the only man of us who still "followed the sea." The worst that could be said of him was that he did not represent his class. He was a seaman, but he was a wanderer, too, while most seamen lead, if one may so express it, a sedentary life. Their minds are of the stay-at-home order, and their home is always with them—the ship; and so is their country—the sea. One ship is very much like another, and the sea is always the same. In the immutability of their surroundings the foreign shores, the foreign faces, the changing immensity of life, glide past, veiled not by a sense of mystery but by a slightly disdainful ignorance; for there is nothing mysterious to a seaman unless it be the sea itself, which is the mistress of his existence and as inscrutable as Destiny. For the rest, after his hours of work, a casual stroll or a casual spree on shore

---

[2] Sir Francis Drake (1540–1596) was knighted aboard the *Golden Hind* by Queen Elizabeth I, following his circumnavigation of the globe, 1577–1580. Sir John Franklin (1786–1847), the Arctic explorer, perished, together with the crews of the *Erebus* and *Terror*, while searching for the Northwest Passage.
[3] Three ports on the Thames River.   [4] The Exchange: the London financial district.
[5] "Interlopers" refers to ships that illegally competed with trading monopolies like the East India Company.

suffices to unfold for him the secret of a whole continent, and generally he finds the secret not worth knowing. The yarns of seamen have a direct simplicity, the whole meaning of which lies within the shell of a cracked nut. But Marlow was not typical (if his propensity to spin yarns be excepted), and to him the meaning of an episode was not inside like a kernel but outside, enveloping the tale which brought it out only as a glow brings out a haze, in the likeness of one of these misty halos that sometimes are made visible by the spectral illumination of moonshine.

His remark did not seem at all surprising. It was just like Marlow. It was accepted in silence. No one took the trouble to grunt even; and presently he said, very slow—

"I was thinking of very old times, when the Romans first came here, nineteen hundred years ago—the other day. . . . Light came out of this river since— you say Knights? Yes; but it is like a running blaze on a plain, like a flash of lightning in the clouds. We live in the flicker—may it last as long as the old earth keeps rolling! But darkness was here yesterday. Imagine the feelings of a commander of a fine—what d'ye call 'em?—trireme[6] in the Mediterranean, ordered suddenly to the north; run overland across the Gauls[7] in a hurry; put in charge of one of these craft the legionaries—a wonderful lot of handy men they must have been, too—used to build, apparently by the hundred, in a month or two, if we may believe what we read. Imagine him here—the very end of the world, a sea the colour of lead, a sky the colour of smoke, a kind of ship about as rigid as a concertina—and going up this river with stores, or orders, or what you like. Sand-banks, marshes, forests, savages,—precious little to eat fit for a civilized man, nothing but Thames water to drink. No Falernian wine[8] here, no going ashore. Here and there a military camp lost in a wilderness, like a needle in a bundle of hay—cold, fog, tempests, disease, exile, and death,—death skulking in the air, in the water, in the bush. They must have been dying like flies here. Oh, yes—he did it. Did it very well, too, no doubt, and without thinking much about it either, except afterwards to brag of what he had gone through in his time, perhaps. They were men enough to face the darkness. And perhaps he was cheered by keeping his eye on a chance of promotion to the fleet at Ravenna[9] by-and-by, if he had good friends in Rome and survived the awful climate. Or think of a decent young citizen in a toga—perhaps too much dice, you know—coming out here in the train of some prefect, or tax-gatherer, or trader even, to mend his fortunes. Land in a swamp, march through the woods, and in some inland post feel the savagery, the utter savagery, had closed round him,—all that mysterious life of the wilderness that stirs in the forest, in the jungles, in the hearts of wild men. There's no initiation either into such mysteries. He has to live in the midst of the incomprehensible, which is also detestable. And it has a fascination, too, that goes to work upon him. The fascination of the abomination—you know, imagine the growing regrets, the longing to escape, the powerless disgust, the surrender, the hate."

He paused.

[6] A Roman galley.
[7] Gaul occupied an area now embraced by France, Belgium, and the western part of Germany; the Gauls were finally conquered by Julius Ceasar and his Roman legions between 58 and 51 B.C.
[8] A famous Roman wine.
[9] An Adriatic seaport in northern Italy that served as a base of operations for the Roman fleet.

"Mind," he began again, lifting one arm from the elbow, the palm of the hand outwards, so that, with his legs folded before him, he had the pose of a Buddha preaching in European clothes and without a lotusflower—"Mind, none of us would feel exactly like this. What saves us is efficiency—the devotion to efficiency. But these chaps were not much account, really. They were no colonists; their administration was merely a squeeze, and nothing more, I suspect. They were conquerors, and for that you want only brute force—nothing to boast of, when you have it, since your strength is just an accident arising from the weakness of others. They grabbed what they could get for the sake of what was to be got. It was just robbery with violence, aggravated murder on a great scale, and men going at it blind—as is very proper for those who tackle a darkness. The conquest of the earth, which mostly means the taking it away from those who have a different complexion or slightly flatter noses than ourselves, is not a pretty thing when you look into it too much. What redeems it is the idea only. An idea at the back of it; not a sentimental pretence but an idea; and an unselfish belief in the idea—something you can set up, and bow down before, and offer a sacrifice to. . . ."

He broke off. Flames glided in the river, small green flames, red flames, white flames, pursuing, overtaking, joining, crossing each other—then separating slowly or hastily. The traffic of the great city went on in the deepening night upon the sleepless river. We looked on, waiting patiently—there was nothing else to do till the end of the flood; but it was only after a long silence, when he said, in a hesitating voice, "I suppose you fellows remember I did once turn fresh-water sailor for a bit," that we knew we were fated, before the ebb began to run, to hear about one of Marlow's inconclusive experiences.

"I don't want to bother you much with what happened to me personally," he began, showing in this remark the weakness of many tellers of tales who seem so often unaware of what their audience would best like to hear; "yet to understand the effect of it on me you ought to know how I got out there, what I saw, how I went up that river to the place where I first met the poor chap. It was the farthest point of navigation and the culminating point of my experience. It seemed somehow to throw a kind of light on everything about me—and into my thoughts. It was sombre enough, too—and pitiful—not extraordinary in any way—not very clear either. No, not very clear. And yet it seemed to throw a kind of light.

"I had then, as you remember, just returned to London after a lot of Indian Ocean, Pacific, China Seas—a regular dose of the East—six years or so, and I was loafing about, hindering you fellows in your work and invading your homes, just as though I had got a heavenly mission to civilize you. It was very fine for a time, but after a bit I did get tired of resting. Then I began to look for a ship—I should think the hardest work on earth. But the ships wouldn't even look at me. And I got tired of that game, too.

"Now when I was a little chap I had a passion for maps. I would look for hours at South America, or Africa, or Australia, and lose myself in all the glories of exploration. At that time there were many blank spaces on the earth, and when I saw one that looked particularly inviting on a map (but they all look that) I would put my finger on it and say, When I grow up I will go there. The North Pole was one of these places, I remember. Well, I haven't been there yet, and shall not try now. The glamour's off. Other places were scattered about the Equator, and in every sort of latitude all over the two hemispheres. I have been in some of them, and . . . well, we won't talk about that. But there was one yet—the biggest, the most blank, so to speak—that I had a hankering after.[10]

"True, by this time it was not a blank space any more. It had got filled since my boyhood with rivers and lakes and names. It had ceased to be a blank space of delightful mystery—a white patch for a boy to dream gloriously over. It had become a place of darkness. But there was in it one river especially, a mighty big river, that you could see on the map, resembling an immense snake uncoiled, with its head in the sea, its body at rest curving afar over a vast country, and its tail lost in the depths of the land. And as I looked at the map of it in a shop-window, it fascinated me as a snake would a bird—a silly little bird. Then I remembered there was a big concern, a Company for trade on that river. Dash it all! I thought to myself, they can't trade without using some kind of craft on that lot of fresh water—steamboats! Why shouldn't I try to get charge of one? I went on along Fleet Street,[11] but could not shake off the idea. The snake had charmed me.

"You understand it was a Continental concern, that Trading society; but I have a lot of relations living on the Continent, because it's cheap and not so nasty as it looks, they say.

"I am sorry to own I began to worry them. This was already a fresh departure for me. I was not used to get things that way, you know. I always went my own road and on my own legs where I had a mind to go. I wouldn't have believed it of myself; but, then—you see—I felt somehow I must get there by hook or by crook. So I worried them. The men said 'My dear fellow,' and did nothing. Then—would you believe it?—I tried the women. I, Charle Marlow, set the women to work—to get a job. Heavens! Well, you see, the notion drove me. I had an aunt, a dear enthusiastic soul. She wrote: 'It will be delightful. I am ready to do anything, anything for you. It is a glorious idea. I know the wife of a very high personage in the Administration, and also a man who has lots of influence with,' etc., etc. She was determined to make no end of fuss to get me appointed skipper of a river steamboat, if such was my fancy.

"I got my appointment—of course; and I got it very quick. It appears the Company had received news that one of their captains had been killed in a scuffle with the natives. This was my chance, and it made me the more anxious to go. It was only months and months afterwards, when I made the attempt to recover what was left of the body, that I heard the original quarrel arose from a misunderstanding about some hens. Yes, two black hens. Fresleven— that was the fellow's name, a Dane—thought himself wronged somehow in the bargain, so he went ashore and started to hammer the chief of the village with a stick. Oh, it didn't surprise me in the least to hear this, and at the same time to be told that Fresleven was the gentlest, quietest creature that ever walked on two legs. No doubt he was; but he had been a couple of years already out there engaged in the noble cause, you know, and he probably felt the need at last of asserting his self-respect in some way. Therefore he whacked the old nigger mercilessly, while a big crowd of his people watched him, thunderstruck, till some man—I was told the chief's son—in desperation

---

[10] The Congo Free State (now Zaire) was established by Leopold II of Belgium in 1885, and remained his personal domain which he economically exploited to his own advantage until his death in 1908 by granting concessions to overseas trading companies.

[11] A major street in London's business district.

at hearing the old chap yell, made a tentative jab with a spear at the white man—and of course it went quite easy between the shoulderblades. Then the whole population cleared into the forest, expecting all kinds of calamities to happen, while, on the other hand, the steamer Fresleven commanded left also in a bad panic, in charge of the engineer, I believe. Afterwards nobody seemed to trouble much about Fresleven's remains, till I got out and stepped into his shoes. I couldn't let it rest, though; but when an opportunity offered at last to meet my predecessor, the grass growing through his ribs was tall enough to hid his bones. They were all there. The supernatural being had not been touched after he fell. And the village was deserted, the huts gaped black, rotting, all askew within the fallen enclosures. A calamity had come to it, sure enough. The people had vanished. Mad terror had scattered them, men, women, and children, through the bush, and they had never returned. What became of the hens I don't know either. I should think the cause of progress got them, anyhow. However, through this glorious affair I got my appointment, before I had fairly begun to hope for it.

"I flew around like mad to get ready, and before forty-eight hours I was crossing the Channel to show myself to my employers, and sign the contract. In a very few hours I arrived in a city that always makes me think of a whited sepulchre.[12] Prejudice no doubt. I had no difficulty in finding the Company's offices. It was the biggest thing in the town, and everybody I met was full of it. They were going to run an over-sea empire, and make no end of coin by trade.

"A narrow and deserted street in deep shadow, high houses, innumerable windows with venetian blinds, a dead silence, grass sprouting between the stones, imposing carriage archways right and left, immense double doors standing ponderously ajar. I slipped through one of these cracks, went up a swept and ungarnished staircase, as arid as a desert, and opened the first door I came to. Two women, one fat and the other slim, sat on straw-bottomed chairs, knitting black wool. The slim one got up and walked straight at me—still knitting with down-cast eyes—and only just as I began to think of getting out of her way, as you would a somnambulist, stood still, and looked up. Her dress was as plain as an umbrella-cover, and she turned round without a word and preceded me into a waiting-room. I gave my name, and looked about. Deal table in the middle, plain chairs all round the walls, on one end a large shining map, marked with all the colours of a rainbow. There was a vast amount of red—good to see at any time, because one knows that some real work is done in there, a deuce of a lot of blue, a little green, smears of orange, and, on the East Coast, a purple patch, to show where the jolly pioneers of progress drink the jolly lager-beer.[13] However, I wasn't going into any of these. I was going into the yellow. Dead in the centre. And the river was there—fascinating—deadly—like a snake. Ough! A door opened, a white-haired secretarial head, but wearing a compassionate expression, appeared, and a skinny forefinger beckoned me into the sanctuary. Its light was dim, and a heavy writing-desk squatted in the middle. From behind that structure came out an impression of pale plumpness in a frock-coat. The great man himself. He was five feet six, I should judge, and had his grip on the handle-end of

[12] Brussels, Belgium.
[13] A map of Africa, with separate colors for each colonial power: red, Great Britain; blue, France; green, Italy; orange, Portugal; purple, Germany; yellow, Belgium.

ever so many millions. He shook hands, I fancy, murmured vaguely, was satisfied with my French. *Bon voyage.*

"In about forty-five seconds I found myself again in the waiting-room with the compassionate secretary, who, full of desolation and sympathy, made me sign some document. I believe I undertook amongst other things not to disclose any trade secrets. Well, I am not going to.

"I began to feel slightly uneasy. You know I am not used to such ceremonies, and there was something ominous in the atmosphere. It was just as though I had been let into some conspiracy—I don't know—something not quite right; and I was glad to get out. In the outer room the two women knitted black wool feverishly. People were arriving, and the younger one was walking back and forth introducing them. The old one sat on her chair. Her flat cloth slippers were propped up on a foot-warmer, and a cat reposed on her lap. She wore a starched white affair on her head, had a wart on one cheek, and silver-rimmed spectacles hung on the tip of her nose. She glanced at me above the glasses. The swift and indifferent placidity of that look troubled me. Two youths with foolish and cheery countenances were being piloted over, and she threw at them the same quick glance of unconcerned wisdom. She seemed to know all about them and about me, too. An eerie feeling came over me. She seemed uncanny and fateful. Often far away there I thought of these two, guarding the door of Darkness, knitting black wool as for a warm pall, one introducing, introducing continuously to the unknown, the other scrutinizing the cheery and foolish faces with unconcerned old eyes. *Ave!* Old knitter of black wool. *Morituri te salutant.*[14] Not many of those she looked at ever saw her again— not half, by a long way.

"There was yet a visit to the doctor. 'A simple formality,' assured me the secretary, with an air of taking an immense part in all my sorrows. Accordingly a young chap wearing his hat over the left eyebrow, some clerk I suppose,— there must have been clerks in the business, though the house was as still as a house in a city of the dead—came from somewhere up-stairs, and led me forth. He was shabby and careless, with inkstains on the sleeves of his jacket, and his cravat was large and billowy, under a chin shaped like the toe of an old boot. It was a little too early for the doctor, so I proposed a drink, and thereupon he developed a vein of joviality. As we sat over our vermouths he glorified the Company's business, and by-and-by I expressed casually my surprise at him not going out there. He became very cool and collected all at once. 'I am not such a fool as I look, quoth Plato to his disciples,' he said sententiously, emptied his glass with great resolution, and we rose.

"The old doctor felt my pulse, evidently thinking of something else the while. 'Good, good for there,' he mumbled, and then with a certain eagerness asked me whether I would let him measure my head. Rather surprised, I said Yes, when he produced a thing like calipers and got the dimensions back and front and every way, taking notes carefully. He was an unshaven little man in a threadbare coat like a gaberdine with his feet in slippers, and I thought him a harmless fool. "I always ask leave, in the interests of science, to measure the crania of those going back out there,' he said. 'And when they come back, too?' I asked. 'Oh, I never see them,' he remarked; 'and, moreover, the changes take place inside, you know.' He smiled, as if at some

---

[14] "Hail! . . . Those who are about to die salute you." The salute of Roman gladiators entering the arena.

quiet joke. 'So you are going out there. Famous. Interesting, too.' He gave me a searching glance, and made another note. 'Ever any madness in your family?' he asked, in a matter-of-fact tone. I felt very annoyed. 'Is that question in the interests of science, too?' 'It would be,' he said, without taking notice of my irritation, 'interesting for science to watch the mental changes of individuals, on the spot, but . . .' 'Are you an alienist?[15] I interrupted. 'Every doctor should be—a little,' answered that original, imperturbably. 'I have a little theory which you Messieurs who go out there must help me to prove. This is my share in the advantages my country shall reap from the possession of such a magnificent dependency. The mere wealth I leave to others. Pardon my questions, but you are the first Englishman coming under my observation . . .' I hastened to assure him I was not in the least typical. 'If I were,' said I, 'I wouldn't be talking like this with you.' 'What you say is rather profound, and probably erroneous,' he said, with a laugh. 'Avoid irritation more than exposure to the sun. Adieu. How do you English say, eh? Goodbye. Ah! Goodbye. Adieu. In the tropics one must before everything keep calm.' . . . He lifted a warning forefinger. . . . '*Du calme, du calme. Adieu.*'[16]

"One thing more remained to do—say good-bye to my excellent aunt. I found her triumphant. I had a cup of tea—the last decent cup of tea for many days—and in a room that most soothingly looked just as you would expect a lady's drawing-room to look, we had a long quiet chat by the fireside. In the course of these confidences it became quite plain to me I had been represented to the wife of the high dignitary, and goodness knows how many more people besides, as an exceptional and gifted creature—a piece of good fortune for the Company—a man you don't get hold of every day. Good heavens! and I was going to take charge of a two-penny-half-penny river-steamboat with a penny whistle attached! It appeared, however, I was also one of the Workers, with a capital—you know. Something like an emissary of light, something like a lower sort of apostle. There had been a lot of such rot let loose in print and talk just about that time, and the excellent woman, living right in the rush of all that humbug, got carried off her feet. She talked about 'weaning those ignorant millions from their horrid ways,' till, upon my word, she made me quite uncomfortable. I ventured to hint that the Company was run for profit.

" 'You forget, dear Charlie, that the labourer is worthy of his hire,' she said, brightly. It's queer how out of touch with truth women are. They live in a world of their own, and there had never been anything like it, and never can be. It is too beautiful altogether, and if they were to set it up it would go to pieces before the first sunset. Some confounded fact we men have been living contentedly with ever since the day of creation would start up and knock the whole thing over.

"After this I got embraced, told to wear flannel, be sure to write often, and so on—and I left. In the street—I don't know why—a queer feeling came to me that I was an impostor. Odd thing that I, who used to clear out for any part of the world at twenty-four hours' notice, with less thought than most men give to the crossing of a street, had a moment—I won't say of hesitation, but of startled pause, before this commonplace affair. The best way I can explain it to you is by saying that, for a second or two, I felt as

---

[15] A doctor specializing in diseases of the mind.
[16] "Keep calm, keep calm. Goodbye."

though, instead of going to the centre of a continent, I were about to set off for the centre of the earth.

"I left in a French steamer, and she called in every blamed port they have out there, for, as far as I could see, the sole purpose of landing soldiers and custom-house officers. I watched the coast. Watching a coast as it slips by the ship is like thinking about an enigma. There it is before you—smiling, frowning, inviting, grand, mean, insipid, or savage, and always mute with an air of whispering, Come and find out. This one was almost featureless, as if still in the making, with an aspect of monotonous grimness. The edge of a colossal jungle, so dark-green as to be almost black, fringed with white surf, ran straight, like a ruled line, far, far away along a blue sea whose glitter was blurred by a creeping mist. The sun was fierce, the land seemed to glisten and drip with steam. Here and there grayish-whitish specks showed up clustered inside the white surf, with a flag flying above them perhaps. Settlements some centuries old, and still no bigger than pinheads on the untouched expanse of their background. We pounded along, stopped, landed soldiers; went on, landed custom-house clerks to levy toll in what looked like a God-forsaken wilderness, with a tin shed and a flag-pole lost in it; landed more soldiers— to take care of the custom-house clerks, presumably. Some, I heard, got drowned in the surf; but whether they did or not, nobody seemed particularly to care. They were just flung out there, and on we went. Every day the coast looked the same, as though we had not moved; but we passed various places— trading places—with names like Gran' Bassam, Little Popo; names that seemed to belong to some sordid farce acted in front of a sinister back-cloth. The idleness of a passenger, my isolation amongst all these men with whom I had no point of contact, the oily and languid sea, the uniform sombreness of the coast, seemed to keep me away from the truth of things, within the toil of a mournful and senseless delusion. The voice of the surf heard now and then was a positive pleasure, like the speech of a brother. It was something natural, that had its reason, that had a meaning. Now and then a boat from the shore gave one a momentary contact with reality. It was paddled by black fellows. You could see from afar the white of their eyeballs glistening. They shouted, sang; their bodies streamed with perspiration; they had faces like grotesque masks—these chaps; but they had bone, muscle, a wild vitality, an intense energy of movement, that was as natural and true as the surf along their coast. They wanted no excuse for being there. They were a great comfort to look at. For a time I would feel I belonged still to a world of straight-forward facts; but the feeling would not last long. Something would turn up to scare it away. Once, I remember, we came upon a man-of-war anchored off the coast. There wasn't even a shed there, and she was shelling the bush. It appears the French had one of their wars going on thereabouts. Her ensign dropped limp like a rag; the muzzles of the long six-inch guns stuck out all over the low hull; the greasy, slimy swell swung her up lazily and let her down, swaying her thin masts. In the empty immensity of earth, sky, and water, there she was, incomprehensible, firing into a continent. Pop, would go one of the six-inch guns; a small flame would dart and vanish, a little white smoke would disappear, a tiny projectile would give a feeble screech—and nothing happened. Nothing could happen. There was a touch of insanity in the proceeding, a sense of lugubrious drollery in the sight; and it was not dissipated by somebody on board assuring me earnestly there was a camp of natives—he called them enemies!—hidden out of sight somewhere.

"We gave her letters (I heard the men in that lonely ship were dying of fever at the rate of three a-day) and went on. We called at some more places with farcical names, where the merry dance of death and trade goes on in a still and earthy atmosphere as of an overheated catacomb; all along the formless coast bordered by dangerous surf, as if Nature herself had tried to ward off intruders; in and out of rivers, streams of death in life, whose banks were rotting into mud, whose waters, thickened into slime, invaded the contorted mangroves, that seemed to writhe at us in the extremity of an impotent despair. Nowhere did we stop long enough to get a particularized impression, but the general sense of vague and oppressive wonder grew upon me. [It was like a weary pilgrimage amongst hints for nightmares.]

"It was upward of thirty days before I saw the mouth of the big river.[17] We anchored off the seat of the government. But my work would not begin till some two hundred miles farther on. So as soon as I could I made a start for a place thirty miles higher up.

"I had my passage on a little sea-going steamer. Her captain was a Swede, and knowing me for a seaman, invited me on the bridge. He was a young man, lean, fair, and morose, with lanky hair and a shuffling gait. As we left the miserable little wharf, he tossed his head contemptuously at the shore. 'Been living there?' he asked. I said, 'Yes.' 'Fine lot these government chaps—are they not?' he went on, speaking English with great precision and considerable bitterness. 'It is funny what some people will do for a few francs a-month. I wonder what becomes of that kind when it goes up country?' I said to him I expected to see that soon. 'So-o-o!' he exlaimed. He shuffled athwart, keeping one eye ahead viligantly. 'Don't be too sure," he continued. 'The other day I took up a man who hanged himself on the road. He was a Swede, too.' 'Hanged himself! Why, in God's name?' I cried. He kept on looking out watchfully. 'Who knows? The sun too much for him, or the country perhaps.'

"At last we opened a reach. A rocky cliff appeared, mounds of turned-up earth by the shore, houses on a hill, others with iron roofs, amongst a waste of excavations, or hanging to the declivity. A continuous noise of the rapids above hovered over this scene of inhabited devastation. A lot of people, mostly black and naked, moved about like ants. A jetty projected into the river. A blinding sunlight drowned all this at times in a sudden recrudescence of glare. 'There's your Company's station,' said the Swede, pointing to three wooden barrack-like structures on the rocky slope. 'I will send your things up. Four boxes did you say? So. Farewell.'

"I came upon a boiler wallowing in the grass, then found a path leading up the hill. It turned aside for the boulders, and also for an undersized railway-truck lying there on its back with its wheels in the air. One was off. The thing looked as dead as the carcass of some animal. I came upon more pieces of decaying machinery, a stack of rusty nails. To the left a clump of trees made a shady spot, where dark things seemed to stir feebly. I blinked, the path was steep. A horn tooted to the right, and I saw the black people run. A heavy and dull detonation shook the ground, a puff of smoke came out of the cliff, and that was all. No change appeared on the face of the rock. They were building a railway. The cliff was not in the way or anything; but this objectless blasting was all the work going on.

"A slight clinking behind me made me turn my head. Six black men advanced

---

[17] The Congo.

in a file, toiling up the path. They walked erect and slow, balancing small baskets full of earth on their heads, and the clink kept time with their footsteps. Black rags were wound round their loins, and the short ends, behind waggled to and fro like tails. I could see every rib, the joints of their limbs were like knots in a rope; each had an iron collar on his neck, and all were connected together with a chain whose bights swung between them, rhythmically clinking. Another report from the cliff made me think suddenly of that ship of war I had seen firing into a continent. It was the same kind of ominous voice; but these men could by no stretch of imagination be called enemies. They were called criminals, and the out-raged law, like the bursting shells, had come to them, an insoluble mystery from the sea. All their meagre breasts panted together, the violently dilated nostrils quivered, the eyes stared stonily up-hill. They passed me within six inches, without a glance, with that complete, death-like indifference of unhappy savages. Behind this raw matter one of the re-claimed, the product of the new forces at work, strolled despondently, carrying a rifle by its middle. He had a uniform jacket with one button off, and seeing a white man on the path, hoisted his weapon to his shoulder with alacrity. This was simple prudence, white men being so much alike at a distance that he could not tell who I might be. He was speedily reassured, and with a large, white, rascally grin, and a glance at his charge, seemed to take me into partner-ship in his exalted trust. After all, I also was a part of the great cause of these high and just proceedings.

"Instead of going up, I turned and descended to the left. My idea was to let that chain-gang get out of sight before I climbed the hill. You know I am not particularly tender; I've had to strike and to fend off. I've had to resist and attack sometimes—that's only one way of resisting—without counting the exact cost, according to the demands of such sort of life as I had blundered into. I've seen the devil of violence, and the devil of greed, and the devil of hot desire; but, by all the stars! these were strong, lusty, red-eyed devils, that swayed and drove men—men, I tell you. But as I stood on this hillside, I foresaw that in the blinding sunshine of that land I would become acquainted with a flabby, pretending, weak-eyed devil of a rapacious and pitiless folly. How insidious he could be, too, I was only to find out several months later and a thousand miles farther. For a moment I stood appalled, as though by a warning. Finally I descended the hill, obliquely, towards the trees I had seen.

"I avoided a vast artificial hole somebody had been digging on the slope, the purpose of which I found it impossible to divine. It wasn't a quarry or a sandpit, anyhow. It was just a hole. It might have been connected with the philanthropic desire of giving the criminals something to do. I don't know. Then I nearly fell into a very narrow ravine, almost no more than a scar in the hillside. I discovered that a lot of imported drainage-pipes for the settlement had been tumbled in there. There wasn't one that was not broken. It was a wanton smash-up. As last I got under the trees. My purpose was to stroll into the shade for a moment; but no sooner within than it seemed to me I had stepped into the gloomy circle of some Inferno. The rapids were near, and an uninterrupted, uniform, headlong, rushing noise filled the mournful stillness of the grove, where not a breath stirred, not a leaf moved, with a mysterious sound—as though the tearing pace of the launched earth had suddenly become audible.

"Black shapes crouched, lay, sat between the trees leaning against the trunks, clinging to the earth, half coming out, half effaced within the dim light, in all the attitudes of pain, abandonment, and despair. Another mine on the cliff went off, followed by a slight shudder of the soil under my feet. The work was going on. The work! And this was the place where some of the helpers had withdrawn to die.

"They were dying slowly—it was very clear. They were not enemies, they were not criminals, they were nothing earthly now,—nothing but the black shadows of disease and starvation, lying confusedly in the greenish gloom. Brought from all the recesses of the coast in all the legality of time contracts, lost in uncongenial surroundings, fed on unfamiliar food, they sickened, became inefficient, and were then allowed to crawl away and rest. These moribund shapes were free as air—and nearly as thin. I began to distinguish the gleam of the eyes under the trees. Then, glancing down, I saw a face near my hand. The black bones reclined at full length with one shoulder against the tree, and slowly the eyelids rose and the sunken eyes looked up at me, enormous and vacant, a kind of blind, white flicker in the depths of the orbs, which died out slowly. The man seemed young—almost a boy—but you know with them it's hard to tell. I found nothing else to do but to offer him one of my good Swede's ship's biscuits I had in my pocket. The fingers closed slowly on it and held—there was no other movement and no other glance. He had tied a bit of white worsted round his neck—Why? Where did he get it? Was it a badge—an ornament—a charm—a propitiatory act? Was there any idea at all connected with it? It looked startling round his black neck, this bit of white thread from beyond the seas.

"Near the same tree two more bundles of acute angles sat with their legs drawn up. One, with his chin propped on his knees, started at nothing, in an intolerable and appalling manner: his brother phantom rested its forehead, as if overcome with a great weariness; and all about others were scattered in every pose of contorted collapse, as in some picture of a massacre or a pestilence. While I stood horror-struck, one of these creatures rose to his hands and knees, and went off on all-fours towards the river to drink. He lapped out of his hand, then sat up in the sunlight, crossing his shins in front of him, and after a time let his woolly head fall on his breastbone.

"I didn't want any more loitering in the shade, and I made haste towards the station. When near the buildings I met a white man, in such an unexpected elegance of get-up that in the first moment I took him for a sort of vision. I saw a high starched collar, white cuffs, a light alpaca jacket, snowy trousers, a clear necktie, and varnished boots. No hat. Hair parted, brushed, oiled, under a green-lined parasol held in a big white hand. He was amazing, and had a penholder behind his ear.

"I shook hands with this miracle, and I learned he was the Company's chief accountant, and that all the book-keeping was done at this station. He had come out for a moment, he said, 'to get a breath of fresh air.' The expression sounded wonderfully odd, with with its suggestion of sedentary desk-life. I wouldn't have mentioned the fellow to you at all, only it was from his lips that I first heard the name of the man who is so indissolubly connected with the memories of that time. Moreover, I respected the fellow. Yes; I respected his collars, his vast cuffs, his brushed hair. His appearance was certainly that of a hairdresser's dummy; but in the great demoralization of the land he kept up his appearance. That's backbone. His starched collars and got-up shirt-fronts were achievements of character. He had been out nearly three years;

and, later, I could not help asking him how he managed to sport such linen. He had just the faintest blush, and said modestly, 'I've been teaching one of the native women about the station. It was difficult. She had a distaste for the work.' Thus this man had verily accomplished something. And he was devoted to his books, which were in apple-pie order.

"Everything else in the station was in a muddle,—heads, things, buildings. Strings of dusty niggers with splay feet arrived and departed; a stream of manufactured goods, rubbishy cottons, beads, and brass-wire set into the depths of darkness, and in return came a precious trickle of ivory.

"I had to wait in the station for ten days—an eternity. I lived in a hut in the yard, but to be out of the chaos I would sometimes get into the accountant's office. It was built of horizontal planks, and so badly put together that, as he bent over his high desk, he was barred from neck to heels with narrow strips of sunlight. There was no need to open the big shutter to see. It was hot there, too; big flies buzzed fiendishly, and did not sting, but stabbed. I sat generally on the floor, while of faultless appearance (and even slightly scented), perching on a high stool, he wrote, he wrote. Sometimes he stood up for exercise. When a trucklebed with a sick man (some invalid agent from upcountry) was put in there, he exhibited a gentle annoyance. "The groans of this sick person,' he said, 'distract my attention. And without that it is extremely difficult to guard against clerical errors in this climate.'

'One day he remarked, without lifting his head, 'In the interior you will no doubt meet Mr. Kurtz.' On my asking who Mr. Kurtz was, he said he was a first-class agent; and seeing my disappointment at this information, he added slowly, laying down his pen, 'He is a very remarkable person.' Further questions elicited from him that Kurtz was at present in charge of a trading post, a very important one, in the true ivory-country, at 'the very bottom of there. Sends in as much ivory as all the others put together . . .' He began to write again. The sick man was too ill to groan. The flies buzzed in a great peace.

"Suddenly there was a growing murmur of voices and a great tramping of feet. A caravan had come in. A violent babble of uncouth sounds burst out on the other side of the planks. All the carriers were speaking together, and in the midst of the uproar the lamentable voice of the chief agent was heard 'giving it up' tearfully for the twentieth time that day. . . . He rose slowly. "What a frightful row,' he said. He crossed the room gently to look at the sick man, and returning, said to me, 'He does not hear.' 'What! Dead?' I asked, startled. 'No, not yet,' he answered, with great composure. Then, alluding with a toss of the head to the tumult in the station-yard. "When one has got to make correct entries, one comes to hate those savages—hate them to the death.' He remained thoughtful for a moment. 'When you see Mr. Kurtz,' he went on, 'tell him from me that everything here'—he glanced at the desk—'is very satisfactory. I don't like to write to him—with those messengers of ours you never know who may get hold of your letter—at that Central Station.' He stared at me for a moment with his mild, bulging eyes. 'Oh, he will go far, very far,' he began again. 'He will be a somebody in the Administration before long. They, above—the Council in Europe, you know—mean him to be.'

"He turned to his work. The noise outside had ceased, and presently in going out I stopped at the door. In the steady buzz of flies the homeward-bound agent was lying flushed and insensible; the other, bent over his books,

was making correct entries of perfectly correct transactions; and fifty feet below
the doorstep I could see the still tree-tops of the grove of death.

"Next day I left that station at last, with a caravan of sixty men, for a two-
hundred-mile tramp.

"No use telling you much about that. Paths, paths, everywhere; a stamped-
in network of paths spreading over the empty land, through long grass, through
burnt grass, through thickets, down and up chilly ravines, up and down stony
hills ablaze with heat; and a solitude, a solitude, nobody not a hut. The population had cleared out a long time ago. Well, if a lot of mysterious niggers
armed with all kinds of fearful weapons suddenly took to travelling on the
road between Deal and Gravesend, catching the yokels right and left to carry
heavy loads for them, I fancy every farm and cottage thereabouts would get
empty very soon. Only here the dwellings were gone, too. Still I passed through
several abandoned villages. There's something pathetically childish in the ruins
of grass walls. Day after day, with the stamp and shuffle of sixty pair of bare
feet behind me, each pair under a 60 lb. load. Camp, cook, sleep, strike camp,
march. Now and then a carrier dead in harness, at rest in the long grass near
the path, with an empty water-gourd and his long staff lying by his side. A
great silence around and above. Perhaps on some quiet night the tremor of
far-off drums, sinking, swelling, a tremor vast, faint; a sound weird, appealing,
suggestive, and wild—and perhaps with as profound a meaning as the sound
of bells in a Christian country. Once a white man in an unbuttoned uniform,
camping on the path with an armed escort of lank Zanzibaris,[18] very hospitable
and festive—not to say drunk. Was looking after the upkeep of the road he
declared. Can't say I saw any road or any upkeep, unless the body of a middle-
aged negro, with a bullet-hole in the forehead, upon which I absolutely stumbled three miles farther on, may be considered as a permanent improvement.
I had a white companion, too, not a bad chap, but rather too fleshy and with
the exasperating habit of fainting on the hot hillsides, miles away from the
least bit of shade and water. Annoying, you know, to hold your own coat
like a parasol over a man's head while he is coming-to. I couldn't help asking
him once what he meant by coming there at all. 'To make money, of course.
What do you think?' he said, scornfully. Then he got fever, and had to be
carried in a hammock slung under a pole. As he weighted sixteen stone.[19] I
had no end of rows with the carriers. They jibbed, ran away, sneaked off with
their loads in the night—quite a mutiny. So, one evening, I made a speech
in English with gestures, not one of which was lost to the sixty pairs of eyes
before me, and the next morning I started the hammock off in front all right.
An hour afterwards I came upon the whole concern wrecked in a bush—man,
hammock, groans, blankets, horrors. The heavy pole had skinned his poor
nose. He was very anxious for me to kill somebody, but there wasn't the shadow
of a carrier near. I remember the old doctor,—'It would be interesting for
science to watch the mental changes of individuals, on the spot.' I felt I was
becoming scientifically interesting. However, all that is to no purpose. On
the fifteenth day I came in sight of the big river again, and hobbled into the
Central Station. It was on a back water surrounded by scrub and forest, with

---

[18] Natives of Zanzibar, an island off the east coast of Africa, employed as mercenaries.
[19] A *stone* is an official British unit of weight: one stone equals 14 pounds; sixteen stones equal
224 pounds.

a pretty border of smelly mud on one side, and on the three others enclosed by a crazy fence of rushes. A neglected gap was all the gate it had, and the first glance at the place was enough to let you see the flabby devil was running that show. White men with long staves in their hands appeared languidly from amongst the buildings, strolling up to take a look at me, and then retired out of sight somewhere. One of them, a stout, excitable chap with black moustaches, informed me with great volubility and many digressions, as soon as I told him who I was, that my steamer was at the bottom of the river. I was thunderstruck. What, how, why? Oh, it was 'all right.' The 'manager himself' was there. All quite correct. 'Everybody had behaved splendidly! splendidly!'— 'you must,' he said in agitation, 'go and see the general manager at once. He is waiting!'

"I did not see the real significance of that wreck at once. I fancy I see it now, but I am not sure—not at all. Certainly the affair was too stupid—when I think of it—to be altogether natural. Still . . . But at the moment it presented itself simply as a confounded nuisance. The steamer was sunk. They had started two days before in a sudden hurry up the river with the manager on board, in charge of some volunteer skipper, and before they had been out three hours they tore the bottom out of her on stones, and she sank near the south bank. I asked myself what I was to do there, now my boat was lost. As a matter of fact, I had plenty to do in fishing my command out of the river. I had to set about it the very next day. That, and the repairs when I brought the pieces to the station, took some months.

"My first interview with the manager was curious. He did not ask me to sit down after my twenty-mile walk that morning. He was commonplace in complexion, in feature, in manners, and in voice. He was of middle size and of ordinary build. His eyes, of the usual blue, were perhaps remarkably cold, and he certainly could make his glance fall on one as trenchant and heavy as an axe. But even at these times the rest of his person seemed to disclaim the intention. Otherwise there was only an indefinable, faint expression of his lips, something stealthy—a smile—not a smile—I remember it, but I can't explain. It was unconscious, this smile was, though just after he had said something it got intensified for an instant. It came at the end of his speeches like a seal applied on the words to make the meaning of the commonest phrase appear absolutely inscrutable. He was a common trader, from his youth up employed in these parts—nothing more. He was obeyed, yet he inspired neither love nor fear, nor even respect. He inspired uneasiness. That was it! Uneasiness. Not a definite mistrust—just uneasiness—nothing more. You have no idea how effective such a . . . a . . . faculty can be. He had no genius for organizing, for initiative, or for order even. That was evident in such things as the deplorable state of the station. He had no learning, and no intelligence. His position had come to him—why? Perhaps because he was never ill . . . He had served three terms of three years out there . . . Because triumphant health in the general rout of constitutions is a kind of power in itself. When he went home on leave he rioted on a large scale—pompously. Jack ashore[20]—with a difference—in externals only. This one could gather from his casual talk. He originated nothing, he could keep the routine going—that's all. But he was great. He was great by this little thing that it was impossible to tell what could control such a man. He never gave that secret away. Perhaps there was nothing within

---

[20] A sailor on leave.

him. Such a suspicion made one pause—for out there there were no external checks. Once when various tropical diseases had laid low almost every 'agent' in the station, he was heard to say, 'Men who come out here should have no entrails.' He sealed the utterance with that smile of his, as though it had been a door opening into a darkness he had in his keeping. You fancied you had seen things—but the seal was on. When annoyed at meal-times by the constant quarrels of the white men about precedence, he ordered an immense round table to be made, for which a special house had to be built. This was the station's mess-room. Where he sat was the first place—the rest were nowhere. One felt this to be his unalterable conviction. He was neither civil nor uncivil. He was quiet. He allowed his 'boy'—an overfed young negro from the coast— to treat the white men, under his very eyes, with provoking insolence.

"He began to speak as soon as he saw me. I had been very long on the road. He could not wait. Had to start without me. The up-river stations had to be relieved. There had been so many delays already that he did not know who was dead and who was alive, and how they got on—and so on, and so on. He paid no attention to my explanations, and, playing with a stick of sealing-wax, repeated several times that the situation was 'very grave, very grave.' There were rumours that a very important station was in jeopardy, and its chief, Mr. Kurtz, was ill. Hoped it was not true. Mr. Kurtz was . . . I felt weary and irritable. Hang Kurtz, I thought. I interrupted him by saying I had heard of Mr. Kurtz on the coast. 'Ah! So they talk of him down there,' he murmured to himself. Then he began again, assuring me Mr. Kurtz was the best agent he had, an exceptional man, of the greatest importance to the Company; therefore I could understand his anxiety. He was, he said, 'very, very uneasy.' Certainly he fidgeted on his chair a good deal, exclaimed, 'Ah, Mr. Kurtz!' broke the stick of sealing-wax and seemed dumbfounded by the accident. Next thing he wanted to know 'how long it would take to' . . . I interrupted him again. Being hungry, you know, and kept on my feet, too, I was getting savage. 'How could I tell?' I said. 'I hadn't even seen the wreck yet—some months, no doubt.' All this talk seemed to me so futile. 'Some months,' he said. 'Well, let us say three months before we can make a start. Yes. That ought to do the affair.' I flung out of his hut (he lived all alone in a clay hut with a sort of verandah) muttering to myself my opinion of him. He was a chattering idiot. Afterwards I took it back when it was borne in upon me startlingly with that extreme nicety he had estimated the time requisite for the 'affair.'

"I went to work the next day, turning, so to speak, my back on that station. In that way only it seemed to me I could keep my hold on the redeeming facts of life. Still, one must look about sometimes; and then I saw this station, these men strolling aimlessly about in the sunshine of the yard. I asked myself sometimes what it all meant. They wandered here and there with their absurd long staves in their hands, like a lot of faithless pilgrims bewitched inside a rotten fence. The word 'ivory' rang in the air, was whispered, was sighed. You would think they were praying to it. A taint of imbecile rapacity blew through it all, like a whiff from some corpse. By Jove! I've never seen anything so unreal in my life. And outside, the silent wilderness surrounding this cleared speck on the earth struck me as something great and invincible, like evil or truth, waiting patiently for the passing away of this fantastic invasion.

"Oh, these months! Well, never mind. Various things happened. One evening a grass shed full of calico, cotton prints, beads, and I don't know what else, burst into a blaze so suddenly that you would have thought the earth had opened to let an avenging fire consume all that trash. I was smoking my pipe quietly by my dismantled steamer, and saw them all cutting capers in the light, with their arms lifted high, when the stout man with moustaches came tearing down to the river, a tin pail in his hand, assured me that everybody was 'behaving splendidly, splendidly,' dipped about a quart of water and tore back again. I noticed there was a hole in the bottom of his pail.

"I strolled up. There was no hurry. You see the thing had gone off like a box of matches. It had been hopeless from the very first. The flame had leaped high, driven everybody back, lighted up everything—and collapsed. The shed was already a heap of embers glowing fiercely. A nigger was being beaten near by. They said he had caused the fire in some way; be that as it may, he was screeching most horribly. I saw him, later, for several days, sitting in a bit of shade looking very sick and trying to recover himself: afterwards he arose and went out—and the wilderness without a sound took him into its bosom again. As I approached the glow from the dark I found myself at the back of two men, talking. I heard the name of Kurtz pronounced, then the words, 'take advantage of this unfortunate accident.' One of the men was the manager. I wished him a good evening. 'Did you ever see anything like it— eh? it is incredible,' he said, and walked off. The other man remained. He was a first-class agent, young, gentlemanly, a bit reserved, with a forked little beard and a hooked nose. He was stand-offish with the other agents, and they on their side said he was the manager's spy upon them. As to me, I had hardly ever spoken to him before. We got into talk, and by-and-by we strolled away from the hissing ruins. Then he asked me to his room, which was in the main building of the station. He struck a match, and I perceived that this young aristocrat had not only a silver-mounted dressing-case but also a whole candle all to himself. Just at that time the manager was the only man supposed to have any right to candles. Native mats covered the clay walls; a collection of spears, assegais,[21] shields, knives, was hung up in trophies. The business intrusted to this fellow was the making of bricks—so I had been informed; but there wasn't a fragment of a brick anywhere in the station, and he had been there more than a year—waiting. It seems he could not make bricks without something, I don't know what—straw maybe. Anyways, it could not be found there, and as it was not likely to be sent from Europe, it did not appear clear to me what he was waiting for. An act of special creation perhaps. However, they were all waiting—all the sixteen or twenty pilgrims of them—for something; and upon my word it did not seem an uncongenial occupation, from the way they took it, though the only thing that ever came to them was disease—as far as I could see. They beguiled the time by backbiting and intriguing against each other in a foolish kind of way. There was an air of plotting about this station, but nothing came of it, of course. It was as unreal as everything else—as the philanthropic pretence of the whole concern, as their talk, as their government, as their show of work. The only real feeling was a desire to get appointed to a trading-post where ivory was to be had, so that they could earn percentages. They intrigued and slandered and hated each other only on that account,—but as to effectually lifting a little finger— oh, no. By heavens! there is something after all in the world allowing one man to steal a horse while another must not look at a halter. Steal a horse

---

[21] Slender throwing spears made of hard wood.

straight out. Very well. He has done it. Perhaps he can ride. But there is a way of looking at a halter that would provoke the most charitable of saints into a kick.

"I had no idea why he wanted to be sociable, but as we chatted in there it suddenly occurred to me the fellow was trying to get at something—in fact, pumping me. He alluded constantly to Europe, to the people I was supposed to know there—putting leading questions as to my acquaintances in the sepulchral city, and so on. His little eyes glittered like mica discs—with curiosity—though he tried to keep up a bit of superciliousness. At first I was astonished, but very soon I became awfully curious to see what he would find out from me. I couldn't possibly imagine what I had in me to make it worth his while. It was very pretty to see how he baffled himself, for in truth my body was full only of chills, and my head had nothing in it but that wretched steamboat business. It was evident he took me for a perfectly shameless prevaricator. At last he got angry, and, to conceal a movement of furious annoyance, he yawned. I rose. Then I noticed a small sketch in oils, on a panel, representing a woman, draped and blindfolded, carrying a lighted torch. The background was sombre—almost black. The movement of the woman was stately, and the effect of the torch-light on the face was sinister.

"It arrested me, and he stood by civilly, holding an empty half-pint champagne bottle (medical comforts) with the candle stuck in it. To my question he said Mr. Kurtz had painted this—in this very station more than a year ago—while waiting for means to go to his trading-post. 'Tell me, pray,' said I, 'who is this Mr. Kurtz?'

"The chief of the Inner Station,' he answered in a short tone, looking away. 'Much obliged,' I said, laughing. 'And you are the brickmaker of the Central Station. Everyone knows that.' He was silent for a while. 'He is a prodigy,' he said at last. 'He is an emissary of pity, and science, and progress, and devil knows what else. We want,' he began to declaim suddenly, 'for the guidance of the cause intrusted to us by Europe, so to speak, higher intelligence, wide sympathies, a singleness of purpose.' 'Who says that?' I asked. 'Lots of them,' he replied. 'Some even write that; and so *he* comes here, a special being, as you ought to know.' 'Why ought I to know?' I interrupted, really surprised. He paid no attention. 'Yes. To-day he is chief of the best station, next year he will be assistant-manager, two years more and . . . but I daresay you know what he will be in two years' time. You are of the new gang—the gang of virtue. The same people who sent him specially also recommended you. Oh, don't say no. I've my own eyes to trust.' Light dawned upon me. My dear aunt's influential acquaintances were producing an unexpected effect upon that young man. I nearly burst into a laugh. 'Do you read the Company's confidential correspondence?' I asked. He hadn't a word to say. It was great fun. 'When Mr. Kurtz,' I continued, severely, 'is General Manger, you won't have the opportunity.'

"He blew the candle out suddenly, and we went outside. The moon had risen. Black figures strolled about listlessly, pouring water on the glow, whence proceeded a sound of hissing; steam ascended in the moonlight, the beaten nigger groaned somewhere. 'What a row the brute makes!' said the indefatigable man with the moustaches, appearing near us. 'Serve him right. Transgression—punishment—bang! Pitiless, pitiless. That's the only way. This will prevent all conflagrations for the future. I was just telling the manager . . .' He noticed my companion, and became crestfallen all at once. 'Not in bed yet,' he said, with a kind of servile heartiness; 'it's so natural. Ha! Danger—agitation.' He vanished. I went on to the river-side and the other followed me. I heard a scathing murmur at my ear. 'Heap of muffs—go to.' The pilgrims could be seen in knots gesticulating, discussing. Several had still their staves in their hands. I verily believe they took these sticks to bed with them. Beyond the fence the forest stood up spectrally in the moonlight, and through the dim stir, through the faint sounds of that lamentable courtyard, the silence of the land went home to one's very heart—its mystery, its greatness, the amazing reality of its concealed life. The hurt nigger moaned feebly somewhere near by, and then fetched a deep sigh that made me mend my pace away from there. I felt a hand introducing itself under my arm. 'My dear sir,' said the fellow. 'I don't want to be misunderstood, and especially by you, who will see Mr. Kurtz long before I can have that pleasure. I wouldn't like him to get a false idea of my disposition. . . .'

"I let him run on, this papier-maché Mephistopheles, and it seemed to me that if I tried I could poke my forefinger through him, and would find nothing inside but a little loose dirt, maybe. He, don't you see, had been planning to be assistant-manager by-and-by under the present man, and I could see that the coming of that Kurtz had upset them both not a little. He talked precipitately, and I did not try to stop him. I had my shoulders against the wreck of my steamer, hauled up on the slope like a carcass of some big river animal. The smell of mud, of primeval mud, by Jove! was in my nostrils, the high stillness of primeval forest was before my eyes; there were shiny patches on the black creek. The moon had spread over everything a thin layer of silver—over the rank grass, over the mud, upon the wall of matted vegetation standing higher than the wall of a temple, over the great river I could see through a sombre gap glittering, glittering, as it flowed broadly by without a murmur. All this was great, expectant, mute, while the man jabbered about himself. I wondered whether the stillness on the face of the immensity looking at us two were meant as an appeal or as a menace. What were we who had strayed in here? Could we handle that dumb thing, or would it handle us? I felt how big, how confoundly big, was that thing that couldn't talk, and perhaps was deaf as well. What was in there? I could see a little ivory coming out from there, and I had heard Mr. Kurtz was in there. I had heard enough about it, too—God knows! Yet somehow it didn't bring any image with it—no more than if I had been told an angel or a fiend was in there. I believed it in the same way one of you might believe there are inhabitants in the planet Mars. I knew once a Scotch sailmaker who was certain, dead sure, there were people in Mars. If you asked him for some idea how they looked and behaved, he would get shy and mutter something about 'walking on all-fours.' If you as much as smiled, he would—though a man of sixty—offer to fight you. I would not have gone so far as to fight for Kurtz, but I went for him near enough to a lie. You know I hate, detest, and can't bear a lie, not because I am straighter than the rest of us, but simply because it appals me. There is a taint of death, a flavour of mortality in lies—which is exactly what I hate and detest in the world—what I want to forget. It makes me miserable and sick, like biting something rotten would do. Temperament, I suppose. Well, I went near enough to it by letting the young fool there believe anything he liked to imagine as to my influence in Europe. I became in an instant as much of a pretence as the rest of the bewitched pilgrims. This simply because I had a notion it somehow would be of help to that Kurtz whom at the time I did not see—you understand. He was just a word for me. I did not see the man in the name any more than you do. Do you see him? Do you see the story? Do you see anything? It seems to me I am trying to tell you a dream—making a vain attempt, because no relation of a dream can convey the dream-sensation, that commingling of absurdity, surprise, and bewilderment in a tremor of struggling revolt, that notion of being captured by the incredible which is of the very essence of dreams. . . ."

He was silent for a while.

". . . No, it is impossible; it is impossible to convey the life-sensation of any given epoch of one's existence—that which makes its truth, its meaning— its subtle and penetrating essence. It is impossible. We live, as we dream— alone. . . ."

He paused again as if reflecting, then added—

"Of course in this you fellows see more than I could then. You see me now, whom you know. . . ."

It had become so pitch dark that we listeners could hardly see one another. For a long time already he, sitting apart, had been no more to us than a voice. There was not a word from anybody. The others might have been asleep, but I was awake. I listened, I listened on the watch for the sentence, for the word, that would give me the clue to the faint uneasiness inspired by this narrative that seemed to shape itself without human lips in the heavy night-air of the river.

". . . Yes—I let him run on," Marlow began again, "and think what he pleased about the powers that were behind me. I did! And there was nothing behind me! There was nothing but that wretched, old, mangled steamboat I was leaning against, while he talked fluently about 'the necessity for every man to get on.' 'And when one comes out here, you conceive, it is not to gaze at the moon.' Mr. Kurtz was a 'universal genius,' but even a genius would find it easier to work with 'adequate tools—intelligent men.' He did not make bricks—why, there was a physical impossibility in the way—as I was well aware; and if he did secretarial work for the manager, it was because 'no sensible man rejects wantonly the confidence of his superiors.' Did I see it? I saw it. What more did I want? What I really wanted was rivets, by heaven! Rivets. To get on with the work—to stop the hole. Rivets I wanted. There were cases of them down at the coast—cases—piled up—burst—split! You kicked a loose rivet at every second step in that station yard on the hillside. Rivets had rolled into the grove of death. You could fill your pockets with rivets for the trouble of stooping down—and there wasn't one rivet to be found where it was wanted. We had plates that would do, but nothing to fasten them with. And every week the messenger, a lone negro, letter-bag on shoulder and staff in hand, left our station for the coast. And several times a week a coast caravan came in with trade goods—ghastly glazed calico that made you shudder only to look at it, glass beads value about a penny a quart, confounded spotted cotton handkerchiefs. An no rivets. Three carriers could have brought all that was wanted to see that steamboat afloat.

"He was becoming confidential now, but I fancy my unresponsive attitude must have exasperated him at last, for he judged it necessary to inform me he feared neither God nor the devil, let alone any mere man. I said I could see that very well, but what I wanted was a certain quantity of rivets—and rivets were what really Mr. Kurtz wanted, if he had only known it. Now letters went to the coast every week. . . . 'My dear sir,' he cried, 'I write from dictation.'

I demanded rivets. There was a way—for an intelligent man. He changed his manner; became very cold, and suddenly began to talk about a hippopotamus; wondered whether sleeping on board the steamer (I stuck to my salvage night and day) I wasn't disturbed. There was an old hippo that had the bad habit of getting out on the bank and roaming at night over the station grounds. The pilgrims used to turn out in a body and empty every rifle they could lay hands on at him. Some even had sat up o' nights for him. All this energy was wasted, though. 'That animal has a charmed life,' he said; 'but you can say this only of brutes in this country. No man—you apprehend me?—no man here bears a charmed life.' He stood there for a moment in the moonlight with his delicate hooked nose set a little askew, and his mica eyes glittering without a wink, then, with a curt Good-night, he strode off. I could see he was disturbed and considerably puzzled, which made me feel more hopeful than I had been for days. It was a great comfort to turn from that chap to my influential friend, the battered, twisted, ruined, tin-pot steamboat. I clambered on board. She rang under my feet like an empty Huntley & Palmer biscuit-tin kicked along a gutter; she was nothing so solid in make, and rather less pretty in shape, but I had expended enough hard work on her to make me love her. No influential friend would have served me better. She had given me a chance to come out a bit—to find out what I could do. No, I don't like work. I had rather laze about and think of all the fine things that can be done. I don't like work—no man does—but I like what is in the work,—the chance to find yourself. Your own reality—for yourself, not for others—what no other man can ever know. They can only see the mere show, and never can tell what it really means.

"I was not surprised to see somebody sitting aft, on the deck, with his legs dangling over the mud. You see I rather chummed with the few mechanics there were in that station, whom the other pilgrims naturally despised—on account of their imperfect manners, I suppose. This was the foreman—a boiler-maker by trade—a good worker. He was a lank, bony, yellow-faced man, with big intense eyes. His aspect was worried, and his head was as bald as the palm of my hand; but his hair in falling seemed to have stuck to his chin, and had prospered in the new locality, for his beard hung down to his waist. He was a widower with six young children (he had left them in charge of a sister of his to come out there), and the passion of his life was pigeon-flying. He was an enthusiast and a connoisseur. He would rave about pigeons. After work hours he used sometimes to come over from his hut for a talk about his children and his pigeons; at work, when he had to crawl in the mud under the bottom of the steamboat, he would tie up that beard of his in a kind of white serviette[22] he brought for the purpose. It had loops to go over his ears. In the evening he could be seen squatted on the bank rinsing that wrapper in the creek with great care, then spreading it solemnly on a bush to dry.

"I slapped him on the back and shouted 'We shall have rivets!' He scrambled to his feet exclaiming 'No! Rivets!' as though he couldn't believe his ears. Then in a low voice, 'You . . . eh?' I don't know why we behaved like lunatics. I put my finger to the side of my nose and nodded mysteriously. 'Good for you!' he cried, snapped his fingers above his head, lifting one foot. I tried a jig. We capered on the iron deck. A frightful clatter came out of that hulk,

---

[22] A napkin.

and the virgin forest on the other bank of the creek sent it back in a thundering roll upon the sleeping station. It must have made some of the pilgrims sit up in their hovels. A dark figure obscured the lighted doorway of the manager's hut, vanished, then, a second or so after, the doorway itself vanished, too. We stopped, and the silence driven away by the stamping of our feet flowed back again from the recesses of the land. The great wall of vegetation, an exuberant and entangled mass of trunks, branches, leaves, boughs, festoons, motionless in the moonlight, was like a rioting invasion of soundless life, a rolling wave of plants, piled up, crested, ready to topple over the creek, to sweep every little man of us out of his little existence. And it moved not. A deadened burst of mighty splashes and snorts reached us from afar, as though an ichthyosaurus,[23] had been taking a bath of glitter in the great river. 'After all,' said the boiler-maker in a reasonable tone, 'why shouldn't we get the rivets?' Why not, indeed! I did not know of any reason why we shouldn't. 'They'll come in three weeks,' I said, confidently.

"But they didn't. Instead of rivets there came an invasion, an infliction, a visitation. It came in sections during the next three weeks, each section headed by a donkey carrying a white man in new clothes and tan shoes, bowing from that elevation right and left to the impressed pilgrims. A quarrelsome band of footsore sulky niggers trod on the heels of the donkey; a lot of tents, camp-stools, tin boxes, white cases, brown bales would be shot down in the courtyard, and the air of mystery would deepen a little over the muddle over the station. Five such instalments came, with their absurd air or disorderly flight with the loot of innumerable outfit shops and provision stores, that, one would think, they were lugging, after a raid, into the wilderness for equitable division. It was an inextricable mess of things decent in themselves but that human folly made look like spoils of thieving.

"This devoted band called itself the Eldorado Exploring Expedition, and I believe they were sworn to secrecy. Their talk, however, was the talk of sordid buccaneers: it was reckless without hardihood, greedy without audacity, and cruel without courage; there was not an atom of foresight or of serious intention in the whole batch of them, and they did not seem aware these things are wanted for the work of the world. To tear treasure out of the bowels of the land was their desire, with no more moral purpose at the back of it than there is in burglars breaking into a safe. Who paid the expenses of the noble enterprise I don't know; but the uncle of our manager was leader of that lot.

"In exterior he resembled a butcher in a poor neighbourhood, and his eyes had a look of sleepy cunning. He carried his fat paunch with ostentation on his short legs, and during the time his gang infested the station spoke to no one but his nephew. You could see these two roaming about all day long with their heads together in an everlasting confab.

"I had given up worrying myself about the rivets. One's capacity for that kind of folly is more limited than you would suppose. I said Hang!—and let things slide. I had plenty of time for meditation, and now and then I would give some thought to Kurtz. I wasn't very interested in him. No. Still, I was curious to see whether this man, who had come out equipped with moral ideas of some sort, would climb to the top after all and how he would set about his work when there."

[23] An extinct marine dinosaur.

"One evening as I was lying flat on the deck of my steamboat, I heard voices approaching—and there were the nephew and the uncle strolling along the bank. I laid my head on my arm again, and had nearly lost myself in a doze, when somebody said in my ear, as it were: 'I am as harmless as a little child, but I don't like to be dictated to. Am I the manager—or am I not? I was ordered to send him there. It's incredible.' . . . . I became aware that the two were standing on the shore alongside the forepart of the steamboat, just below my head. I did not move; it did not occur to me to move: I was sleepy. 'It *is* unpleasant,' grunted the uncle. 'He has asked the Administration to be sent there,' said the other, 'with the idea of showing what he could do; and I was instructed accordingly. Look at the influence that man must have. Is it not frightful?' They both agreed it was frightful, then made several bizarre remarks: 'Make rain and fine weather—one man—the Council—by the nose'— bits of absurd sentences that got the better of my drowsiness, so that I had pretty near the whole of my wits about me when the uncle said, 'The climate may do away with this difficulty for you. Is he alone there?' 'Yes,' answered the manager; 'he sent his assistant down the river with a note to me in these terms: "Clear this poor devil out of the country, and don't bother sending more of that sort. I had rather be alone than have the kind of men you can dispose of with me." It was more than a year ago. Can you imagine such impudence!' 'Anything since then?' asked the other, hoarsely. 'Ivory,' jerked the nephew; 'lots of it—prime sort—lots—most annoying, from him.' 'And with that?' questioned the heavy rumble. 'Invoice,' was the reply fired out, so to speak. Then silence. They had been talking about Kurtz.

"I was broad awake by this time, but, lying perfectly at ease, remained still, having no inducement to change my position. 'How did that ivory come all this way?' growled the elder man, who seemed very vexed. The other explained that it had come with a fleet of canoes in charge of an English half-caste clerk Kurtz had with him; that Kurtz had apparently intended to return himself, the station being by that time bare of goods and stores, but after coming three hundred miles, had suddenly decided to go back, which he started to do alone in a small dugout with four paddlers, leaving the half-caste to continue down the river with the ivory. The two fellows there seemed astounded at anybody attempting such a thing. They were at a loss for an adequate motive. As to me, I seemd to see Kurtz for the first time. It was a distinct glimpse: the dugout, four paddling savages, and the lone white man turning his back suddenly on the headquarters, on relief, on thoughts of home—perhaps; setting his face towards the depths of the wilderness, towards his empty and desolate station. I did not know the motive. Perhaps he was just simply a fine fellow who stuck to his work for its own sake. His name, you understand, had not been pronounced once. He was 'that man.' The half-caste, who, as far as I could see, had conducted a difficult trip with great prudence and pluck, was invariably alluded to as 'that scoundrel.' The 'scoundrel' had reported that the 'man' had been very ill—had recovered imperfectly. . . . The two below me moved away then a few paces, and strolled back and forth at some little distance. I heard: 'Military post—doctor—two hundred miles—quite alone now—unavoidable, delays—nine months—no news—strange rumours.' They approached again, just as the manager was saying, 'No one, as far as I know, unless a species of wandering trader—a pestilential fellow, snapping ivory from the natives.' Who was it they were talking about now? I gathered in snatches that this was some man supposed to be in Kurtz's district, and of whom the manger did not approve. 'We will not be free from unfair competition till one of these fellows is hanged for an example,' he said. 'Certainly,' grunted the other; 'get him hanged! Why not? Anything—anything can be done in this country. That's what I say; nobody here, you understand, *here*, can endanger your position. And why? You stand the climate—you outlast them all. The danger is in Europe; but there before I left I took care to——' They moved off and whispered, then their voices rose again. 'The extraordinary series of delays is not my fault. I did my best.' The fat man sighed. 'Very sad.' 'And the pestiferous absurdity of his talk,' continued the other; 'he bothered me enough when he was here. "Each station should be like a beacon on the road towards better things, a centre for trade of course, but also for humanizing, improving, instructing." Conceive you—that ass! And he wants to be manager! No, it's——' Here he got choked by excessive indignation, and I lifted my head the least bit. I was surprised to see how near they were—right under me. I could have spat upon their hats. They were looking on the ground, absorbed in thought. The manager was switching his leg with a slender twig: his sagacious relative lifted his head. 'You have been well since you came out this time?' he asked. The other gave a start. 'Who? I? Oh! Like a charm—like a charm. But the rest—oh, my goodness! All sick. They die so quick, too, that I haven't the time to send them out of the country—it's incredible!' 'H'm. Just so,' grunted the uncle. 'Ah! my boy, trust to this—I say, trust to this.' I saw him extend his short flipper of an arm for a gesture that took in the forest, the creek, the mud, the river,—seemed to beckon with a dishonouring flourish before the sunlit face of the land a treacherous appeal to the lurking death, to the hidden evil, to the profound darkness of its heart. It was so startling that I leaped to my feet and looked back at the edge of the forest, as though I had expected an answer of some sort to that black display of confidence. You know the foolish notions that come to one sometimes. The high stillness confronted these two figures with its ominous patience, waiting for the passing away of a fantastic invasion.

"They swore aloud together—out of sheer fright, I believe—then pretending not to know anything of my existence, turned back to the station. The sun was low; and leaning forward side by side, they seemed to be tugging painfully uphill their two ridiculous shadows of unequal length, that trailed behind them slowly over the tall grass without bending a single blade.

"In a few days the Eldorado Expedition went into the patient wilderness, that closed upon it as the sea closes over a diver. Long afterwards the news came that all the donkeys were dead. I know nothing as to the fate of the less valuable animals. They, no doubt, like the rest of us, found what they deserved. I did not inquire. I was then rather excited at the prospect of meeting Kurtz very soon. When I say very soon I mean it comparatively. It was just two months from the day we left the creek when we came to the bank below Kurtz's station.

"Going up that river was like travelling back to the earliest beginnings of the world, when vegetation rioted on the earth and the big trees were kings. An empty stream, a great silence, an impenetrable forest. The air was warm, thick, heavy, sluggish. There was no joy in the brilliance of sunshine. The long stretches of the waterway ran on, deserted, into the gloom of overowed distances. On silvery sandbanks hippos and alligators sunned the side by side. The broadening waters flowed through a mob of wooded you lost your way on that river as you would in a desert, and butted all day long against shoals, trying to find the channel, till you thought yourself bewitched and cut off for ever from everything you had known once—somewhere—far away—in another existence perhaps. There were moments when one's past came back to one, as it will sometimes when you have not a moment to spare to yourself; but it came in the shape of an unrestful and noisy dream, remembered with wonder amongst the overwhelming realities of this strange world of plants, and water, and silence. And this stillness of life did not in the least resemble a peace. It was the stillness of an implacable force brooding over an inscrutable intention. It looked at you with a vengeful aspect. I got used to it afterwards; I did not see it any more; I had no time. I had to keep guessing at the channel; I had to discern, mostly by inspiration, the signs of hidden banks; I watched for sunken stones; I was learning to clap my teeth smartly before my heart flew out, when I shaved by a fluke some infernal sly old snag that would have ripped the life out of the tin-pot steamboat and drowned all the pilgrims; I had to keep a look-out for the signs of dead wood we could cut up in the night for next day's steaming. When you have to attend to things of that sort, to the mere incidents of the surface, the reality—the reality, I tell you—fades. The inner truth is hidden—luckily, luckily. But I felt it all the same; I felt often its mysterious stillness watching me at my monkey tricks, just as it watches you fellows performing on your respective tight-ropes for—what is it? half-a-crown a tumble——"

"Try to be civil, Marlow," growled a voice, and I knew there was at least one listener awake besides myself.

"I beg your pardon. I forgot the heartache which makes up the rest of the price. And indeed what does the price matter, if the trick be well done? You do your tricks very well. And I didn't do badly either, since I managed not to sink that steamboat on my first trip. It's a wonder to me yet. Imagine a blindfolded man set to drive a van over a bad road. I sweated and shivered over that business considerably, I can tell you. After all, for a seaman, to scrape the bottom of the thing that's supposed to float all the time under his care is the unpardonable sin. No one may know of it, but you never forget the thump—eh? A blow on the very heart. You remember it, you dream of it, you wake up at night and think of it—years after—and go hot and cold all over. I don't pretend to say that steamboat floated all the time. More than once she had to wade for a bit, with twenty cannibals splashing around and pushing. We had enlisted some of these chaps on the way for a crew. Fine fellows—cannibals—in their place. They were men one could work with, and I am grateful to them. And, after all, they did not eat each other before my face: they had brought along a provision of hippo-meat which went rotten, and made the mystery of the wilderness stink in my nostrils. Phoo! I can sniff it now. I had the manager on board and three or four pilgrims with their staves—all complete. Sometimes we came upon a station close by the bank, clinging to the skirts of the unknown, and the white men rushing out of a tumbledown hovel, with great gestures of joy and surprise and welcome, seemed very strange—had the appearance of being held there captive by a spell. The word ivory would ring in the air for a while—and on we went again into the silence, along empty reaches, round the still bends, between the high walls of our winding way, reverberating in hollow claps the ponderous beat of the stern-wheel. Trees, trees, millions of trees, massive, immense, running up high; and at their foot, hugging the bank against the stream, crept the little begrimed steamboat, like a sluggish beetle crawling on the floor of a lofty portico. It made you feel very small, very lost, and yet it was not altogether depressing, that feeling. After all, if you were small, the grimy beetle crawled on—which was just what you wanted it to do. Where the pilgrims imagined it crawled to I don't know. To some place where they expected to get something, I bet! For me it crawled towards Kurtz—exclusively; but when the steam-pipes started leaking we crawled very slow. The reaches opened before us and closed behind, as if the forest had stepped leisurely across the water to bar the way for our return. We penetrated deeper and deeper into the heart of darkness. It was very quiet there. At night sometimes the roll of drums behind the curtain of trees would run up the river and remain sustained faintly, as if hovering in the air high over our heads, till the first break of day. Whether it meant war, peace, or prayer we could not tell. The dawns were heralded by the descent of a chill stillness; the wood-cutters slept, their fires burned low; the snapping of a twig would make you start. We were wanderers on prehistoric earth, on an earth that wore the aspect of an unknown planet. We could have fancied ourselves the first of men taking possession of an accursed inheritance, to be subdued at the cost of profound anguish and of excessive toil. But suddenly, as we struggled round a bend, there would be a glimpse of rush walls, of peaked grass-roofs, a burst of yells, a whirl of black limbs, a mass of hands clapping, of feet stamping, of bodies swaying, of eyes rolling, under the droop of heavy and motionless foliage. The steamer toiled along slowly on the edge of a black and incomprehensible frenzy. The prehistoric man was cursing us, praying to us, welcoming us—who could tell? We were cut off from the comprehension of our surroundings; we glided past like phantoms, wondering and secretly appalled, as sane men would be before an enthusiastic outbreak in a madhouse. We could not understand because we were too far and could not remember, because we were travelling in the night of first ages, of those ages that are gone, leaving hardly a sign—and no memories.

"The earth seemed unearthly. We are accustomed to look upon the shackled form of a conquered monster, but there—there you could look at a thing monstrous and free. It was unearthly, and the men were—— No, they were not inhuman. Well, you know, that was the worst of it—this suspicion of their not being inhuman. It would come slowly to one. They howled and leaped, and spun, and made horrid faces; but what thrilled you was just the thought of their humanity—like yours—the thought of your remote kinship with this wild and passionate uproar. Ugly. Yes, it was ugly enough; but if you were man enough you would admit to yourself that there was in you just the faintest trace of a response to the terrible frankness of that noise, a dim suspicion of there being a meaning in it which you—you so remote from the night of first ages—could comprehend. And why not? The mind of man is capable of anything—because everything is in it, all the past as well as all the future. What was there after all? Joy, fear, sorrow, devotion, valour, rage—who can tell?—but truth—truth stripped of its cloak of time. Let the fool gape and shudder—the man knows, and can look on without a wink. But he must at least be as much of a man as these on the shore. He must meet that truth with his own true stuff—with his own inborn strength. Principles won't do. Acquisitions, clothes, pretty rags—rags that would fly off at the first good shake. No; you want a deliberate belief. An appeal to me in this fiendish row—is there? Very well; I hear; I admit, but I have a voice, too, and for good or evil mine is the speech that cannot be silenced. Of course, a fool, what with sheer fright and fine sentiments, is always safe. Who's that grunting? You wonder I didn't go ashore for a howl and a dance? Well, no—I didn't. Fine sentiments, you say? Fine sentiments, be hanged! I had not time. I had to mess about with white-lead and strips of woollen blanket helping to put bandages on those leaky steampipes—I tell you. I had to watch the steering, and circumvent those snags, and get the tin-pot along by hook or by crook. There was surface-truth enough in these things to save a wiser man. And between whiles I had to look after the savage who was fireman. He was an improved specimen; he could fire up a vertical boiler. He was there below me, and, upon my word, to look at him was as edifying as seeing a dog in a parody of breeches and a feather hat, walking on his hind-legs. A few months of training had done for that really fine chap. He squinted at the steam-gauge and at the water-gauge with an evident effort of intrepidity—and he had filed teeth, too, the poor devil, and the wool of his pate shaved into queer patterns, and three ornamental scars on each of his cheeks. He ought to have been clapping his hands and stamping his feet on the bank, instead of which he was hard at work, a thrall to strange witchcraft, full of improving knowledge. He was useful because he had been instructed; and what he knew was this—that should the water in that transparent thing disappear, the evil spirit inside the boiler would get angry through the greatness of his thirst, and take a terrible vengeance. So he sweated and fired up and watched the glass fearfully (with an impromptu charm, made of rags, tied to his arm, and a piece of polished bone, as big as a watch, stuck flatways through his lower lip), while the wooded banks slipped past us slowly, the short noise was left behind, the interminable miles of silence—and we crept on, towards Kurtz. But the snags were thick, the water was treacherous and shallow, the boiler seemed indeed to have a sulky devil in it, and thus neither that fireman nor I had any time to peer into our creepy thoughts.

"Some fifty miles below the Inner Station we came upon a hut of reeds, an inclined and melancholy pole, with the unrecognizable tatters of what had been a flag of some sort flying from it, and a neatly stacked wood-pile. This was unexpected. We came to the bank, and on the stack of firewood found a flat piece of board with some faded pencil-writing on it. When deciphered it said: 'Wood for you. Hurry up. Approach cautiously.' There was a signature, but it was illegible—not Kurtz—a much longer word. Hurry up. Where? Up the river? 'Approach cautiously.' We had not done so. But the warning could not have been meant for the place where it could be only found after approach. Something was wrong above. But what—and how much? That was the question. We commented adversely upon the imbecility of that telegraphic style. The bush around said nothing, and would not let us look very far, either. A torn curtain of red twill hung in the doorway of the hut, and flapped sadly in our faces. The dwelling was dismantled; but we could see a white man had lived there not very long ago. There remained a rude table—a plank on two posts; a heap of rubbish reposed in a dark corner, and by the door I picked up a book. It had lost its covers, and the pages had been thumbed into a state of extremely dirty softness; but the back had been lovingly stitched afresh with white cotton thread, which looked clean yet. It was an extraordinary find. Its title was, *An Inquiry into some Points of Seamanship,* by a man Tower, Towson—some such name—Master in his Majesty's Navy. The matter looked dreary reading enough, with illustrative diagrams and repulsive tables of figures, and the copy was sixty years old. I handled this amazing antiquity with the greatest possible tenderness, lest it should dissolve in my hands. Within, Towson or Towser was inquiring earnestly into the breaking strain of ships' chains and tackle, and other such matters. Not a very enthralling book; but at the first glance you could see there a singleness of intention, an honest concern for the right way of going to work, which made these humble pages, thought out so many years ago, luminous with another than a professional light. The simple old sailor, with his talk of chains and purchases,[24] made me forget the jungle and the pilgrims in a delicious sensation of having come upon something unmistakably real. Such a book being there was wonderful enough; but still more astounding were the notes pencilled in the margin, and plainly referring to the text. I couldn't believe my eyes! They were in cipher! Yes, it looked like cipher. Fancy a man lugging with him a book of that description into this nowhere and studying it—and making notes—in cipher at that! It was an extravagant mystery.

"I had been dimly aware for some time of a worrying noise, and when I lifted my eyes I saw the wood-pile was gone, and the manager, aided by all the pilgrims, was shouting at me from the river-side. I slipped the book into my pocket. I assure you to leave off reading was like tearing myself away from the shelter of an old and solid friendship.

"I started the lame engine ahead. 'It must be this miserable trader—this intruder,' exclaimed the manager, looking back malevolently at the place we had left. 'He must be English,' I said. 'It will not save him from getting into trouble if he is not careful,' muttered the manager darkly. I observed with assumed innocence that no man was safe from trouble in this world.

"The current was more rapid now, the steamer seemed at her last gasp, the stern-wheel flopped languidly, and I caught myself listening on tiptoe for the next beat of the boat, for in sober truth I expected the wretched thing to give up every moment. It was like watching the last flickers of a life. But still we crawled. Sometimes I would pick out a tree a little way ahead to measure our progress towards Kurtz by, but I lost it invariably before we got abreast. To keep the eyes so long on one thing was too much for human patience. The manager displayed a beautiful resignation. I fretted and fumed and took to arguing with myself whether or no I would talk openly with Kurtz; but before I could come to any conclusion it occurred to me that my speech or my silence, indeed any action of mine, would be a mere futility. What did it matter what any one knew or ignored? What did it matter who was manager? One gets sometimes such a flash of insight. The essentials of this affair lay deep under the surface, beyond my reach, and beyond my power of meddling.

"Towards the evening of the second day we judged ourselves about eight miles from Kurtz's station. I wanted to push on; but the manager looked grave, and told me the navigation up there was so dangerous that it would be advisable, the sun being very low already, to wait where we were till next morning. Moreover, he pointed out that if the warning to approach cautiously were to be followed, we must approach in daylight—not at dusk, or in the dark. This was sensible enough. Eight miles meant nearly three hours' steaming for us, and I could also see suspicious ripples at the upper end of the reach. Nevertheless, I was annoyed beyond expression at the delay, and most unreasonably, too, since one night more could not matter much after so many months. As we had plenty of wood, and caution was the word, I brought up in the middle

[24] Nautical devices for applying leverage.

of the stream. The reach was narrow, straight, with high sides like a railway cutting. The dusk came gliding into it long before the sun had set. The current ran smooth and swift, but a dumb immobility sat on the banks. The living trees, lashed together by the creepers and every living bush of the undergrowth, might have been changed into stone, even to the slenderest twig, to the lightest leaf. It was not sleep—it seemed unnatural, like a state of trance. Not the faintest sound of any kind could be heard. You looked on amazed, and began to suspect yourself of being deaf—then the night came suddenly, and struck you blind as well. About three in the morning some large fish leaped, and the loud splash made me jump as though a gun had been fired. When the sun rose there was a white fog, very warm and clammy, and more blinding than the night. It did not shift or drive; it was just there, standing all round you like something solid. At eight or nine, perhaps, it lifted as a shutter lifts. We had a glimpse of the towering multitude of trees, of the immense matted jungle, with the blazing little ball of the sun hanging over it—all perfectly still—and then the white shutter came down again, smoothly, as if sliding in greased grooves. I ordered the chain, which we had begun to heave in, to be paid out again. Before it stopped running with a muffled rattle, a cry, a very loud cry, as of infinite desolation, soared slowly in the opaque air. It ceased. A complaining clamour, modulated in savage discords, filled our ears. The sheer unexpectedness of it made my hair stir under my cap. I don't know how it struck the others; to me it seemed as though the mist itself had screamed, so suddenly, and apparently from all sides at once, did this tumultuous and mournful uproar arise. It culminated in a hurried outbreak of almost intolerably excessive shrieking, which stopped short, leaving us stiffened in a variety of silly attitudes, and obstinately listening to the nearly as appalling and excessive silence. 'Good God! What is the meaning——' stammered at my elbow one of the pilgrims,—a little fat man, with sandy hair and red whiskers, who wore sidespring boots, and pink pyjamas tucked into his socks. Two others remained open-mouthed a whole minute, then dashed into the little cabin, to rush out incontinently and stand darting scared glances, with Winchesters[25] at 'ready' in their hands. What we could see was just the steamer we were on, her outlines blurred as though she had been on the point of dissolving, and a misty strip of water, perhaps two feet broad, around her—and that was all. The rest of the world was nowhere, as far as our eyes and ears were concerned. Just no-where. Gone, disappeared; swept off without leaving a whisper or a shadow behind.

"I went forward, and ordered the chain to be hauled in short, so as to be ready to trip the anchor and move the steamboat at once if necessary. 'Will they attack?' whispered an awed voice. 'We will be all butchered in this fog,' murmured another. The faces twitched with the strain, the hands trembled slightly, the eyes forgot to wink. It was very curious to see the contrast of expressions of the white men and of the black fellows of our crew, who were as much strangers to that part of the river as we, though their homes were only eight hundred miles away. The whites, of course greatly discomposed, had besides a curious look of being painfully shocked by such an outrageous row. The others had an alert, naturally interested expression; but their faces were essentially quiet, even those of the one or two who grinned as they hauled at the chain. Several exchanged short, grunting phrases, which seemed to settle

[25] A type of American-made rifle.

the matter to their satisfaction. Their headman, a young, broad-chested black, severely draped in dark-blue fringed cloths, with fierce nostrils and his hair all done up artfully in oily ringlets, stood near me. 'Aha!' I said, just for good fellowship's sake. 'Catch 'im,' he snapped, with a bloodshot widening of his eyes and a flash of sharp teeth—'catch 'im. Give 'im to us.' 'To you, eh?' I asked; 'what would you do with them?' 'Eat 'im!' he said, curtly, and, leaning his elbow on the rail, looked out into the fog in a dignified and profoundly pensive attitude. I would no doubt have been properly horrified, had it not occurred to me that he and his chaps must be very hungry: that they must have been growing increasingly hungry for at least this month past. They had been engaged for six months (I don't think a single one of them had any clear idea of time, as we at the end of countless ages have. They still belonged to the beginnings of time—had no inherited experience to teach them as it were), and of course, as long as there was a piece of paper written over in accordance with some farcical law or other made down the river, it didn't enter anybody's head to trouble how they would live. Certainly they had brought with them some rotten hippo-meat, which couldn't have lasted very long, anyway, even if the pilgrims hadn't, in the midst of a shocking hullabaloo, thrown a considerable quantity of it overboard. It looked like a high-handed proceeding; but it was really a case of legitimate self-defence. You can't breathe dead hippo waking, sleeping, and eating, and at the same time keep your precarious grip on existence. Besides that, they had given them every week three pieces of brass wire, each about nine inches long; and the theory was they were to buy their provisions with that currency in river-side villages. You can see how *that* worked. There were either no villages, or the people were hostile, or the director, who like the rest of us fed out of tins, with an occasional old he-goat thrown in, didn't want to stop the steamer for some more or less recondite reason. So, unless they swallowed the wire itself, or made loops of it to snare the fishes with, I don't see what good their extravagant salary could be to them. I must say it was paid with a regularity worthy of a large and honourable trading company. For the rest, the only thing to eat—though it didn't look eatable in the least—I saw in their possession was a few lumps of some stuff like half-cooked dough, of a dirty lavender colour, they kept wrapped in leaves, and now and then swallowed a piece of, but so small that it seemed done more for the looks of the thing than for any serious purpose of sustenance. Why in the name of all the gnawing devils of hunger they didn't go for us— they were thirty to five—and have a good tuck-in[26] for once, amazes me now when I think of it. They were big powerful men, with not much capacity to weigh the consequences, with courage, with strength, even yet, though their skins were no longer glossy and their muscles no longer hard. And I saw that something restraining, one of those human secrets that baffle probability, had come into play there. I looked at them with a swift quickening of interest— not because it occurred to me I might be eaten by them before very long, though I own to you that just then I perceived—in a new light, as it were— how unwholesome the pilgrims looked, and I hoped, yes, I positively hoped, that my aspect was not so—what shall I say?—so—unappetizing: a touch of fantastic vanity which fitted well with the dream-sensation that pervaded all my days at that time. Perhaps I had a little fever, too. One can't live with one's finger everlasting on one's pulse. I had often 'a little fever,' or a little

---

[26] British slang for a hearty meal.

touch of other things—the playful paw-strokes of the wilderness, the preliminary trifling before the more serious onslaught which came in due course. Yes; I looked at them as you would on any human being, with a curiosity of their impulses, motives, capacities, weaknesses, when brought to the test of an inexorable physical necessity. Restraint! What possible restraint? Was it superstition, disgust, patience, fear—or some kind of primitive honour? No fear can stand up to hunger, no patience can wear it out, disgust simply does not exist where hunger is; and as to superstition, beliefs, and what you may call principles, they are less than chaff in a breeze. Don't you know that devilry of lingering starvation, its exasperating torment, its black thoughts, its sombre and brooding ferocity? Well, I do. It takes a man all his inborn strength to fight hunger properly. It's really easier to face bereavement, dishonour, and the perdition of one's soul—than this kind of prolonged hunger. Sad, but true. And these chaps, too, had no earthly reason for any kind of scruple. Restraint! I would just as soon have expected restraint from a hyena prowling amongst the corpses of a battlefield. But there was the fact facing me—the fact dazzling, to be seen, like the foam on the depths of the sea, like a ripple on an unfathomable enigma, a mystery greater—when I thought of it—than the curious, inexplicable note of desperate grief in this savage clamour that had swept by us on the river-bank, behind the blind whiteness of the fog.

"Two pilgrims were quarrelling in hurried whispers as to which bank. 'Left.' 'No, no; how can you? Right, right, of course.' 'It is very serious,' said the manager's voice behind me; 'I would be desolated if anything should happen to Mr. Kurtz before we came up.' I looked at him, and had not the slightest doubt he was sincere. He was just the kind of man who would wish to preserve appearances. That was his restraint. But when he muttered something about going on at once, I did not even take the trouble to answer him. I knew, and he knew, that it was impossible. Were we to let go our hold of the bottom, we would be absolutely in the air—in space. We wouldn't be able to tell where we were going to—whether up or down stream, or across—till we fetched against one bank or the other,—and then we wouldn't know at first which it was. Of course I made no move. I had no mind for a smash-up. You couldn't imagine a more deadly place for a shipwreck. Whether drowned at once or not, we were sure to perish speedily in one way or another. 'I authorize you to take all the risks,' he said, after a short silence. 'I refuse to take any,' I said, shortly; which was just the answer he expected, though its tone might have surprised him. 'Well, I must defer to your judgment. You are captain,' he said, with marked civility. I turned my shoulder to him in sign of my appreciation, and looked into the fog. How long would it last? It was the most hopeless look-out. The approach to this Kurtz grubbing for ivory in the wretched bush was beset by as many dangers as though he had been an enchanted princess sleeping in a fabulous castle. 'Will they attack, do you think?' asked the manager, in a confidential tone.

"I did not think they would attack, for several obvious reasons. The thick fog was one. If they left the bank in their canoes they would get lost in it, as we would be if we attempted to move. Still, I had also judged the jungle of both banks quite impenetrable—and yet eyes were in it, eyes that had seen us. The river-side bushes were certainly very thick; but the undergrowth behind was evidently penetrable. However, during the short lift I had seen no canoes anywhere in the reach—certainly not abreast of the steamer. But what made the idea of attack inconceivable to me was the nature of the noise—of the cries we had heard. They had not the fierce character boding of immediate hostile intention. Unexpected, wild, and violent as they had been, they had given me an irresistible impression of sorrow. The glimpse of the steamboat had for some reason filled those savages with unrestrained grief. The danger, if any, I expounded, was from our proximity to a great human passion let loose. Even extreme grief may ultimately vent itself in violence—but more generally takes the form of apathy. . . .

"You should have seen the pilgrims stare! They had no heart to grin, or even to revile me: but I believe they thought me gone mad—with fright, maybe. I delivered a regular lecture. My dear boys, it was no good bothering. Keep a look-out? Well, you may guess I watched the fog for the signs of lifting as a cat watches a mouse; but for anything else our eyes were of no more use to us than if we had been buried miles deep in a heap of cotton-wool. It felt like it, too—choking, warm, stifling. Besides, all I said, though it sounded extravagant, was absolutely true to fact. What we afterwards alluded to as an attack was really an attempt at repulse. The action was very far from being aggressive—it was not even defensive, in the usual sense: it was undertaken under the stress of desperation, and in its essence was purely protective.

"It developed itself, I should say, two hours after the fog lifted, and its commencement was at a spot, roughly speaking, about a mile and a half below Kurtz's station. We had just floundered and flopped round a bend, when I saw an islet, a mere grassy hummock of bright green, in the middle of the stream. It was the only thing of the kind; but as we opened the reach more, I perceived it was the head of a long sandbank, or rather of a chain of shallow patches stretching down the middle of the river. They were discoloured, just awash, and the whole lot was seen just under the water, exactly as a man's backbone is seen running down the middle of his back under the skin. Now, as far as I did see, I could go to the right or to the left of this. I didn't know either channel, of course. The banks looked pretty well alike, the depth appeared the same; but as I had been informed the station was on the west side, I naturally headed for the western passage.

"No sooner had we fairly entered it than I became aware it was much narrower than I had supposed. To the left of us there was the long uninterrupted shoal, and to the right a high, steep bank heavily overgrown with bushes. Above the bush the trees stood in serried ranks. The twigs overhung the current thickly, and from distance to distance a large limb of some tree projected rigidly over the stream. It was then well on in the afternoon, the face of the forest was gloomy, and a broad strip of shadow had already fallen on the water. In this shadow we steamed up—very slowly, as you may imagine. I sheered her well inshore—the water being deepest near the bank, as the sounding-pole informed me.

"One of my hungry and forebearing friends was sounding[27] in the bows just below me. This steamboat was exactly like a decked scow. On the deck, there were two little teak-wood houses, with doors and windows. The boiler was in the fore-end, and the machinery right astern. Over the whole there was a light roof, supported on stanchions. The funnel projected through that roof, and in front of the funnel a small cabin built of light planks served for a pilot-house. It contained a couch, two camp-stools, a loaded Martini-Henry[28]

---

[27] Measuring the depth of the water.
[28] A rifle named after its Swiss and Scotch inventors.

leaning in one corner, a tiny table, and the steering-wheel. It had a wide door in front and a broad shutter at each side. All these were always thrown open, of course. I spent my days perched up there on the extreme fore-end of that roof, before the door. At night I slept, or tried to, on the couch. An athletic black belonging to some coast tribe, and educated by my poor predecessor, was the helmsman. He sported a pair of brass earrings, wore a blue cloth wrapper from the waist to the ankles, and thought all the world of himself. He was the most unstable kind of fool I had ever seen. He steered with no end of a swagger while you were by; but if he lost sight of you, he became instantly the prey of an abject funk, and would let that cripple of a steamboat get the upper hand of him in a minute.

"I was looking down at the sounding-pole, and feeling much annoyed to see at each try a little more of it stick out of that river, when I saw my poleman give up the business suddenly, and stretch himself flat on the deck, without even taking the trouble to haul his pole in. He kept hold on it though, and it trailed in the water. At the same time the fireman, whom I could also see below me, sat down abruptly before his furnace and ducked his head. I was amazed. Then I had to look at the river mighty quick, because there was a snag in the fairway. Sticks, little sticks, were flying about—thick: they were whizzing before my nose, dropping below me, striking behind me against my pilot-house. All this time the river, the shore, the woods, were very quiet— perfectly quiet. I could only hear the heavy splashing thump of the stern-wheel and the patter of these things. We cleared the snag clumsily. Arrows, by Jove! We were being shot at! I stepped in quickly to close the shutter on the land-side. That fool-helmsman, his hands on the spokes, was lifting his knees high, stamping his feet, champing his mouth, like a reined-in horse. Confound him! And we were staggering within ten feet of the bank. I had to lean right out to swing the heavy shutter, and I saw a face amongst the leaves on the level with my own, looking at me very fierce and steady; and then suddenly, as though a veil had been removed from my eyes, I made out, deep in the tangled gloom, naked breasts, arms, legs, glaring eyes,—the bush was swarming with human limbs in movement, glistening, of bronze colour. The twigs shook, swayed, and rustled, the arrows flew out of them, and then the shutter came to. 'Steer her straight,' I said to the helmsman. He held his head rigid, face forward; but his eyes rolled, he kept on, lifting and setting down his feet gently, his mouth foamed a little. 'Keep quiet!' I said in a fury. I might just as well have ordered a tree not to sway in the wind. I darted out. Below me there was a great scuffle of feet on the iron deck; confused exclamations; a voice screamed, 'Can you turn back?' I caught sight of a V-shaped ripple on the water ahead. What? Another snag! A fusillade burst out under my feet. The pilgrims had opened with their Winchesters and were simply squirting lead into that bush. A deuce of a lot of smoke came up and drove slowly forward. I swore at it. Now I couldn't see the ripple or the snag either. I stood in the doorway, peering, and the arrows came in swarms. They might have been poisoned, but they looked as though they wouldn't kill a cat. The bush began to howl. Our wood-cutters raised a warlike whoop; the report of a rifle just at my back deafened me. I glanced over my shoulder, and the pilot-house was yet full of noise and smoke when I made a dash at the wheel. The fool-nigger had dropped everything, to throw the shutter open and let off that Martini-Henry. He stood before the wide opening, glaring, and I yelled at him to come back, while I straightened the sudden twist out of that steamboat. There was no room to turn even if I had wanted to, the snag was somewhere very near ahead in that confounded smoke, there was no time to lose, so I just crowded her into the bank—right into the bank, where I knew the water was deep.

"We tore slowly along the overhanging bushes in a whirl of broken twigs and flying leaves. The fusillade below stopped short, as I had foreseen it would when the squirts got empty. I threw my head back to a glinting whizz that traversed the pilot-house, in at one shutter-hole and out at the other. Looking past that mad helmsman, who was shaking the empty rifle and yelling at the shore, I saw vague forms of men running bent double, leaping, gliding, distinct, incomplete, evanescent. Something big appeared in the air before the shutter, the rifle went overboard, and the man stepped back swiftly, looked at me over his shoulder in an extraordinary, profound, familiar manner, and fell upon my feet. The side of his head hit the wheel twice, and the end of what appeared a long cane clattered round and knocked over a little camp-stool. It looked as though after wrenching that thing from somebody ashore he had lost his balance in the effort. The thin smoke had blown away, we were clear of the snag, and looking ahead I could see that in another hundred yards or so I would be free to sheer off, away from the bank; but my feet felt so very warm and wet that I had to look down. The man had rolled on his back and stared straight up at me; both his hands clutched that cane. It was the shaft of a spear that, either thrown or lunged through the opening, had caught him in the side just below the ribs; the blade had gone in out of sight, after making a frightful gash; my shoes were full; a pool of blood lay very still, gleaming dark-red under the wheel; his eyes shone with an amazing lustre. The fusillade burst out again. He looked at me anxiously, gripping the spear like something precious, with an air of being afraid I would try to take it away from him. I had to make an effort to free my eyes from his gaze and attend to the steering. With one hand I felt above my head for the line of the steam whistle, and jerked out screech after screech hurriedly. The tumult of angry and warlike yells was checked instantly, and then from the depths of the woods went out such a tremulous and prolonged wail of mournful fear and utter despair as may be imagined to follow the flight of the last hope from the earth. There was a great commotion in the bush; the shower of arrows stopped, a few dropping shots rang out sharply—then silence, in which the languid beat of the stern-wheel came plainly to my ears. I put the helm hard a-star-board at the moment when the pilgrim in pink pyjamas, very hot and agitated, appeared in the doorway. 'The manager sends me——' he began in an official tone, and stopped short. 'Good God!' he said, glaring at the wounded man.

"We two whites stood over him, and his lustrous and inquiring glance enveloped us both. I declare it looked as though he would presently put to us some question in an understandable language; but he died without uttering a sound, without moving a limb, without twitching a muscle. Only in the very last moment, as though in response to some sign we could not see, to some whisper we could not hear, he frowned heavily, and that frown gave to his black death-mask an inconceivably sombre, brooding, and menacing expression. The lustre of inquiring glance faded swiftly into vacant glassiness. 'Can you steer?' I asked the agent eagerly. He looked very dubious; but I made a grab at his arm, and he understood at once I meant him to steer whether or no. I tell you the truth, I was morbidly anxious to change my shoes and socks.

'He is dead,' murmured the fellow, immensely impressed. 'No doubt about
it,' said I, tugging like mad at the shoe-laces. 'And by the way, I suppose
Mr. Kurtz is dead as well by this time.'

"For the moment that was the dominant thought. There was a sense of
extreme disappointment, as though I had found out I had been striving after
something altogether without a substance. I couldn't have been more digusted
if I had travelled all this way for the sole purpose of talking with Mr. Kurtz.
Talking with. . . . I flung one shoe overboard, and became aware that that
was exactly what I had been looking forward to—a talk with Kurtz. I made
the strange discovery that I had never imagined him as doing, you know, but
as discoursing. I didn't say to myself, 'Now I will never see him,' or 'Now I
will never shake him by the hand,' but, 'now I will never hear him.' The man
presented himself as a voice. Not of course that I did not connect him with
some sort of action. Hadn't I been told in all the tones of jealousy and admiration that he had collected, bartered, swindled, or stolen more ivory than all
the other agents together? That was not the point. The point was in his being
a gifted creature, and that of all his gifts the one that stood out preëminently,
that carried with it a sense of real presence, was his ability to talk, his words—
the gift of expression, the bewildering, the illuminating, the most exalted and
the most contemptible, the pulsating stream of light, or the deceitful flow
from the heart of an impenetrable darkness.

"The other shoe went flying unto the devil-god of that river. I thought,
By Jove! it's all over. We are too late; he has vanished—the gift has vanished,
by means of some spear, arrow, or club. I will never hear that chap speak
after all,—and my sorrow had a startling extravagance of emotion, even such
as I had noticed in the howling sorrow of these savages in the bush. I couldn't
have felt more of lonely desolation somehow, had I been robbed of a belief
or had missed my destiny in life. . . . Why do you sigh in this beastly way,
somebody? Absurd? Well, absurd. Good Lord! mustn't a man ever—— Here,
give me some tobacco.". . .

There was a pause of profound stillness, then a match flared, and Marlow's
lean face appeared, worn, hollow, with downward folds and dropped eyelids,
with an aspect of concentrated attention; and as he took vigorous draws at
his pipe, it seemed to retreat and advance out of the night in the regular
flicker of the tiny flame. The match went out.

"Absurd!" he cried. "This is the worst of trying to tell. . . . Here you all
are, each moored with two good addresses, like a hulk with two anchors, a
butcher round one corner, a policeman round another, excellent appetites,
and temperature normal—you hear—normal from year's end to year's end.
And you say, Absurd! Absurd be—exploded! Absurd! My dear boys, what
can you expect from a man who out of sheer nervousness had just flung overboard a pair of new shoes! Now I think of it, it is amazing I did not shed
tears. I am, upon the whole, proud of my fortitude. I was cut to the quick at
the idea of having lost the inestimable privilege of listening to the gifted Kurtz.
Of course I was wrong. The privilege was waiting for me. Oh, yes, I heard
more than enough. And I was right, too. A voice. He was very little more
than a voice. And I heard—him—it—this voice—other voices—all of them were
so little more than voices—and the memory of that time itself lingers around
me, impalpable, like a dying vibration of one immense jabber, silly, atrocious,
sordid, savage, or simply mean, without any kind of sense. Voices, voices—
even the girl herself—now——"

He was silent for a long time.

"I laid the ghost of his gifts at last with a lie," he began, suddenly. "Girl! What? Did I mention a girl? Oh, she is out of it—completely. They—the women I mean—are out of it—should be out of it. We must help them to stay in that beautiful world of their own, lest ours get worse. Oh, she had to be out of it. You should have heard the disinterred body of Mr. Kurtz saying, 'My Intended.' You would have perceived directly then how completely she was out of it. And the lofty frontal bone of Mr. Kurtz! They say the hair goes on growing sometimes, but this—ah—specimen, was impressively bald. The wilderness had patted him on the head, and, behold, it was like a ball—an ivory ball; it had caressed him, and—lo!—he had withered; it had taken him, loved him, embraced him, got into his veins, consumed his flesh, and sealed his soul to its own by the inconceivable ceremonies of some devilish initiation. He was its spoiled and pampered favourite. Ivory? I should think so. Heaps of it, stacks of it. The old mud shanty was bursting with it. You would think there was not a single tusk left either above or below the ground in the whole country. 'Mostly fossil,' the manager had remarked, disparagingly. It was no more fossil than I am; but they call it fossil when it is dug up. It appears these niggers do bury the tusks sometimes—but evidently they couldn't bury this parcel deep enough to save the gifted Mr. Kurtz from his fate. We filled the steamboat with it, and had to pile a lot on the deck. Thus he could see and enjoy as long as he could see, because the appreciation of this favour had remained with him to the last. You should have heard him say, 'My ivory.' Oh yes, I heard him. 'My Intended, my ivory, my station, my river, my——' everything belonged to him. It made me hold my breath in expectation of hearing the wilderness burst into a prodigious peal of laughter that would shake the fixed stars in their places. Everything belonged to him—but that was a trifle. The thing was to know what he belonged to, how many powers of darkness claimed him for their own. That was the reflection that made you creepy all over. It was impossible—it was not good for one either—trying to imagine. He had taken a high seat amongst the devils of the land—I mean literally. You can't understand. How could you?—with solid pavement under your feet, surrounded by kind neighbours ready to cheer you or to fall on you, stepping delicately between the butcher and the policeman, in the holy terror of scandal and gallows and lunatic asylums—how can you imagine what particular region of the first ages a man's untrammelled feet may take him into by the way of solitude—utter solitude without a policeman—by the way of silence—utter silence, where no warning voice of a kind neighbour can be heard whispering of public opinion? These little things make all the great difference. When they are gone you must fall back upon your own innate strength, upon your own capacity for faithfulness. Of course you may be too much of a fool to go wrong—too dull even to know you are being assaulted by the powers of darkness. I take it, no fool ever made a bargain for his soul with the devil: the fool is too much of a fool, or the devil too much of a devil—I don't know which. Or you may be such a thunderingly exalted creature as to be altogether deaf and blind to anything but heavenly sights and sounds. Then the earth for you is only a standing place—and whether to be like this is your loss or your gain I won't pretend to say. But most of us are neither one nor the other. The earth for us is a place to live in, where we must put up with sights, with sounds, with smells, too, by Jove!—breathe dead hippo, so to speak, and not be contaminated. And there, don't you see? your strength comes in, the faith in your ability for the digging of unostentatious holes to bury the stuff in—your power of devotion, not to yourself, but to an obscure, back-breaking business. And that's difficult enough. Mind, I am not trying to excuse or even explain—I am trying to account to myself for—for—Mr. Kurtz—for the shade of Mr. Kurtz. This initiated wraith from the back of Nowhere honoured me with its amazing confidence before it vanished altogether. This was because it could speak English to me. The original Kurtz had been educated partly in England, and—as he was good enough to say himself—his sympathies were in the right place. His mother was half-English, his father was half-French. All Europe contributed to the making of Kurtz; and by-and-by I learned that, most appropriately, the International Society for the Suppression of Savage Customs had intrusted him with the making of a report, for its future guidance. And he had written it, too. I've seen it. I've read it. It was eloquent, vibrating with eloquence, but too high-strung, I think. Seventeen pages of close writing he had found time for! But this must have been before his—let us say—nerves, went wrong, and caused him to preside at certain midnight dances ending with unspeakable rites, which—as far as I reluctantly gathered from what I heard at various times—were offered up to him—do you understand?—to Mr. Kurtz himself. But it was a beautiful piece of writing. The opening paragraph, however, in the light of later informa- tion, strikes me now as ominous. He began with the argument that we whites, from the point of development we had arrived at, 'must necessarily appear to them [savages] in the nature of supernatural beings—we approach them with the might as of a deity,' and so on, and so on. 'By the simple exercise of our will we can exert a power for good practically unbounded,' etc. etc. From that point he soared and took me with him. The peroration was magnifi- cent, though difficult to remember, you know. It gave me the notion of an exotic Immensity ruled by an august Benevolence. It made me tingle with enthusiasm. This was the unbounded power of eloquence—of words—of burn- ing noble words. There were no practical hints to interrupt the magic current of phrases, unless a kind of note at the foot of the last page, scrawled evidently much later, in an unsteady hand, may be regarded as the exposition of a method. It was very simple, and at the end of that moving appeal to every altruistic sentiment it blazed at you, luminous and terrifying, like a flash of lightning in a serene sky: 'Exterminate all the brutes!' The curious part was that he had apparently forgotten all about that valuable postscriptum, because, later on, when he in a sense came to himself, he repeatedly entreated me to take good care of 'my pamphlet' (he called it), as it was sure to have in the future a good influence upon his career. I had full information about all these things, and, besides, as it turned out, I was to have the care of his memory. I've done enough for it to give me the indisputable right to lay it, if I choose, for an everlasting rest in the dust-bin of progress, amongst all the sweepings and, figuratively speaking, all the dead cats of civilization. But then, you see, I can't choose. He won't be forgotten. Whatever he was, he was not common. He had the power to charm or frighten rudimentary souls into an aggravated witch-dance in his honour; he could also fill the small souls of the pilgrims with bitter misgivings: he had one devoted friend at least, and he had conquered one soul in the world that was neither rudimentary nor tainted with self-seeking. No; I can't forget him, though I am not prepared to affirm the fellow was exactly worth the life we lost in getting to him. I missed my late helmsman awfully,—I missed him even while his body was still lying in the pilot-house.

Perhaps you will think it passing strange this regret for a savage who was no more account than a grain of sand in a black Sahara. Well, don't you see, he had done something, he had steered; for months I had him at my back—a help—an instrument. It was a kind of partnership. He steered for me—I had to look after him, I worried about his deficiencies, and thus a subtle bond had been created, of which I only became aware when it was suddenly broken. And the intimate profundity of that look he gave me when he received his hurt remains to this day in my memory—like a claim of distant kinship affirmed in a supreme moment.

"Poor fool! If he had only left that shutter alone. He had no restraint, no restraint—just like Kurtz—a tree swayed by the wind. As soon as I had put on a dry pair of slippers, I dragged him out, after first jerking the spear out of his side, which operation I confess I performed with my eyes shut tight. His heels leaped together over the little door-step; his shoulders were pressed to my breast; I hugged him from behind desperately. Oh! he was heavy, heavy; heavier than any man on earth, I should imagine. Then without more ado I tipped him overboard. The current snatched him as though he had been a wisp of grass, and I saw the body roll over twice before I lost sight of it for ever. All the pilgrims and the manager were then congregated on the awning-deck about the pilot-house, chattering at each other like a flock of excited magpies, and there was a scandalized murmur at my heartless promptitude. What they wanted to keep that body hanging about for I can't guess. Embalm it, maybe. But I had also heard another, and a very ominous, murmur on the deck below. My friends the wood-cutters were likewise scandalized, and with a better show of reason—though I admit that the reason itself was quite inadmissible. Oh, quite! I had made up my mind that if my late helmsman was to be eaten, the fishes alone should have him. He had been a very second-rate helmsman while alive, but now he was dead he might have become a first-class temptation, and possibly cause some startling trouble. Besides, I was anxious to take the wheel, the man in pink pyjamas showing himself a hopeless duffer at the business.

"This I did directly the simple funeral was over. We were going half-speed, keeping right in the middle of the stream, and I listened to the talk about me. They had given up Kurtz, they had given up the station; Kurtz was dead, and the station had been burnt—and so on—and so on. The red-haired pilgrim was beside himself with the thought that at least this poor Kurtz had been properly avenged. 'Say! We must have made a glorious slaughter of them in the bush. Eh? What do you think? Say?' He positively danced, the bloodthirsty little gingery beggar.[29] And he had nearly fainted when he saw the wounded man! I could not help saying, 'You made a glorious lot of smoke, anyhow.' I had seen, from the way the tops of the bushes rustled and flew, that almost all the shots had gone too high. You can't hit anything unless you take aim and fire from the shoulder; but these chaps fired from the hip with their eyes shut. The retreat, I maintained—and I was right—was caused by the screeching of the steamwhistle. Upon this they forgot Kurtz, and began to howl at me with indignant protests.

"The manager stood by the wheel murmuring confidentially about the necessity of getting well away down the river before dark at all events, when I saw in the distance a clearing on the river-side and the outlines of some sort of

---

[29] British slang for a sandy-haired rogue.

building. 'What's this?' I asked. He clapped his hands in wonder. 'The station!'
he cried. I edged in at once, still going half-speed.

"Through my glasses I saw the slope of a hill interspersed with rare trees
and perfectly free from undergrowth. A long decaying building on the summit
was half buried in the high grass; the large holes in the peaked roof gaped
black from afar; the jungle and the woods made a background. There was
no enclosure or fence of any kind; but there had been one apparently, for
near the house half-a-dozen slim posts remained in a row, roughly trimmed,
and with their upper ends ornamented with round carved balls. The rails, or
whatever there had been between, had disappeared. Of course the forest surrounded all that. The river-bank was clear, and on the water-side I saw a
white man under a hat like a cart-wheel beckoning persistently with his whole
arm. Examining the edge of the forest above and below, I was almost certain
I could see movements—human forms gliding here and there. I steamed past
prudently, then stopped the engines and let her drift down. The man on the
shore began to shout, urging us to land. 'We have been attacked,' screamed
the manager. 'I know—I know. It's all right,' yelled back the other, as cheerful
as you please. 'Come along. It's all right. I am glad.'

"His aspect reminded me of something I had seen—something funny I had
seen somewhere. As I manœuvred to get alongside, I was asking myself, 'What
does this fellow look like?' Suddenly I got it. He looked like a harlequin.[30]
His clothes had been made of some stuff that was brown holland probably,
but it was covered with patches all over, with bright patches, blue, red, and
yellow,—patches on the back, patches on the front, patches on elbows, on
knees; coloured binding around his jacket, scarlet edging at the bottom of
his trousers; and the sunshine made him look extremely gay and wonderfully
neat withal, because you could see how beautifully all this patching had been
done. A beardless, boyish face, very fair, no features to speak of, nose peeling,
little blue eyes, smiles and frowns chasing each other over that open countenance like sunshine and shadow on a wind-swept plain. 'Look out, captain!'
he cried; 'there's a snag lodged in here last night.' What! Another snag? I
confess I swore shamefully. I had nearly holed my cripple, to finish off that
charming trip. The harlequin on the bank turned his little pug-nose up to
me. 'You English?' he asked, all smiles. 'Are you?' I shouted from the wheel.
The smiles vanished, and he shook his head as if sorry for my disappointment.
Then he brightened up. 'Never mind!' he cried, encouragingly. 'Are we in
time?' I asked. 'He is up there,' he replied, with a toss of the head up the
hill, and becoming gloomy all of a sudden. His face was like the autumn sky,
overcast one moment and bright the next.

"When the manager, escorted by the pilgrims, all of them armed to the
teeth, had gone to the house this chap came on board. 'I say, I don't like
this. These natives are in the bush,' I said. He assured me earnestly it was
all right. 'They are simple people,' he added; 'well, I am glad you came. It
took me all my time to keep them off.' 'But you said it was all right,' I cried.
'Oh, they meant no harm,' he said; and as I stared he corrected himself, 'Not
exactly.' Then vivaciously, 'My faith, your pilot-house wants a clean up!' In
the next breath he advised me to keep enough steam on the boiler to blow
the whistle in case of any trouble. 'One good screech will do more for you
than all your rifles. They are simple people,' he repeated. He rattled away at

[30] A character in comedy and pantomime wearing a mask and parti-colored tights.

such a rate he quite overwhelmed me. He seemed to be trying to make up for lots of silence, and actually hinted, laughing, that such was the case. 'Don't you talk with Mr. Kurtz?' I said. 'You don't talk with that man—you listen to him,' he exclaimed with severe exaltation. 'But now——' He waved his arm, and in the twinkling of an eye was in the uttermost depths of despondency. In a moment he came up again with a jump, possessed himself of both my hands, shook them continuously, while he gabbled: 'Brother sailor . . . honour . . . pleasure . . . delight . . . introduce myself . . . Russian . . . son of an arch-priest . . . Government of Tambov . . . What? Tobacco! English tobacco; the excellent English tobacco! Now, that's brotherly. Smoke? Where's a sailor that does not smoke?'

"The pipe soothed him, and gradually I made out he had run away from school, had gone to sea in a Russian ship; ran away again; served some time in English ships; was now reconciled with the arch-priest. He made a point of that. 'But when one is young one must see things, gather experience, ideas; enlarge the mind.' 'Here!' I interrupted. 'You can never tell! Here I met Mr. Kurtz,' he said, youthfully solemn and reproachful. I held my tongue after that. It appears he had persuaded a Dutch trading-house on the coast to fit him out with stores and goods, and had started for the interior with a light heart, and no more idea of what would happen to him than a baby. He had been wandering about that river for nearly two years alone, cut off from everybody and everything. 'I am not so young as I look. I am twenty-five,' he said. 'At first old Van Shuyten would tell me to go to the devil,' he narrated with keen enjoyment; 'but I stuck to him, and talked and talked, till at last he got afraid I would talk the hind-leg off his favourite dog, so he gave me some cheap things and a few guns, and told me he hoped he would never see my face again. Good old Dutchman, Van Shuyten. I've sent him one small lot of ivory a year ago, so that he can't call me a little thief when I get back. I hope he got it. And for the rest I don't care. I had some wood stacked for you. That was my old house. Did you see?'

"I gave him Towson's book. He made as though he would kiss me, but restrained himself. 'The only book I had left, and I thought I had lost it,' he said, looking at it ecstatically. 'So many accidents happen to a man going about alone, you know. Canoes get upset sometimes—and sometimes you've got to clear out so quick when the people get angry.' He thumbed the pages. 'You made notes in Russian?' I asked. He nodded. 'I thought they were written in cipher,' I said. He laughed, then became serious. 'I had lots of trouble to keep these people off,' he said. 'Did they want to kill you?' I asked. 'Oh, no!' he cried, and checked himself. 'Why did they attack us?' I pursued. He hesitated, then said shamefacedly, 'They don't want him to go.' 'Don't they?' I said, curiously. He nodded a nod full of mystery and wisdom. 'I tell you,' he cried, 'this man has enlarged my mind.' He opened his arms wide, staring at me with his little blue eyes that were perfectly round."

III

"I looked at him, lost in astonishment. There he was before me, in motley, as though he had absconded from a troupe of mimes, enthusiastic, fabulous. His very existence was improbable, inexplicable, and altogether bewildering. He was an insoluble problem. It was inconceivable how he had existed, how he had succeeded in getting so far, how he had managed to remain—why he did not instantly disappear. 'I went a little farther,' he said, 'then still a little farther—till I had gone so far that I don't know how I'll ever get back. Never mind. Plenty time. I can manage. You take Kurtz away quick—quick—I tell you.' The glamour of youth enveloped his particoloured rags, his destitution, his loneliness, the essential desolation of his futile wanderings. For months— for years—his life hadn't been worth a day's purchase; and there he was gallantly, thoughtlessly alive, to all appearance indestructible solely by the virtue of his few years and of his unreflecting audacity. I was seduced into something like admiration—like envy. Glamour urged him on, glamour kept him unscathed. He surely wanted nothing from the wilderness but space to breathe in and to push on through. His need was to exist, and to move onwards at the greatest possible risk, and with a maximum of privation. If the absolutely pure, uncalculating, unpractical spirit of adventure had ever ruled a human being, it ruled this be-patched youth. I almost envied him the possession of this modest and clear flame. It seemed to have consumed all thought of self so completely, that even while he was talking to you, you forgot that it was he—the man before your eyes—who had gone through these things. I did not envy him his devotion to Kurtz, though. He had not meditated over it. It came to him, and he accepted it with a sort of eager fatalism. I must say that to me it appeared about the most dangerous thing in every way he had come upon so far.

"They had come together unavoidably, like two ships becalmed near each other, and lay rubbing sides at last. I suppose Kurtz wanted an audience, because on a certain occasion, when encamped in the forest, they had talked all night, or more probably Kurtz had talked. 'We talked of everything,' he said, quite transported at the recollection. 'I forgot there was such a thing as sleep. The night did not seem to last an hour. Everything! Everything! . . . Of love, too.' 'Ah, he talked to you of love!' I said, much amused. 'It isn't what you think,' he cried, almost passionately. 'It was in general. He made me see things—things.'

"He threw his arms up. We were on deck at the time, and the headman of my wood-cutters, lounging near by, turned upon him his heavy and glittering eyes. I looked around, and I don't know why, but I assure you that never, never before, did this land, this river, this jungle, the very arch of this blazing sky, appear to me so hopeless and so dark, so impenetrable to human thought, so pitiless to human weakness. 'And, ever since, you have been with him, of course?' I said.

"On the contrary. It appears their intercourse had been very much broken by various causes. He had, as he informed me proudly, managed to nurse Kurtz through two illnesses (he alluded to it as you would to some risky feat), but as a rule Kurtz wandered alone, far in the depths of the forest. 'Very often coming to this station, I had to wait days and days before he would turn up,' he said. 'Ah, it was worth waiting for!—sometimes.' 'What was he doing? exploring or what?' I asked. 'Oh, yes, of course;' he had discovered lots of villages, a lake, too—he did not know exactly in what direction; it was dangerous to inquire too much—but mostly his expeditions had been for ivory. 'But he had no goods to trade with by that time,' I objected. 'There's a good lot of cartridges left even yet,' he answered, looking away. 'To speak plainly, he raided the country,' I said. He nodded. 'Not alone, surely!' He muttered something about the villages round that lake. 'Kurtz got the tribe to follow him, did he?' I suggested. He fidgeted a little. 'They adored him,' he said. The tone of these words was so extraordinary that I looked at him searchingly.

It was curious to see his mingled eagerness and reluctance to speak of Kurtz. The man filled his life, occupied his thoughts, swayed his emotions. 'What can you expect?' he burst out; 'he came to them with thunder and lightning, you know—and they had never seen anything like it—and very terrible. He could be very terrible. You can't judge Mr. Kurtz as you would an ordinary man. No, no, no! Now—just to give you an idea—I don't mind telling you, he wanted to shoot me, too, one day—but I don't judge him.' 'Shoot you!' I cried. 'What for?' 'Well, I had a small lot of ivory the chief of that village near my house gave me. You see I used to shoot game for them. Well, he wanted it, and wouldn't hear reason. He declared he would shoot me unless I gave him the ivory and then cleared out of the country, because he could do so, and had a fancy for it, and there was nothing on earth to prevent him killing whom he jolly well pleased. And it was true, too. I gave him the ivory. What did I care! But I didn't clear out. No, no. I couldn't leave him. I had to be careful, of course, till we got friendly again for a time. He had his second illness then. Afterwards I had to keep out of the way; but I didn't mind. He was living for the most part in those villages on the lake. When he came down to the river, sometimes he would take to me, and sometimes it was better for me to be careful. This man suffered too much. He hated all this, and somehow he couldn't get away. When I had a chance I begged him to try and leave while there was time; I offered to go back with him. And he would say yes, and then he would remain; go off on another ivory hunt; disappear for weeks; forget himself amongst these people—forget himself—you know.' 'Why! he's mad,' I said. He protested indignantly. Mr. Kurtz couldn't be mad. If I had heard him talk, only two days ago, I wouldn't dare hint at such a thing. . . . I had taken up my binoculars while we talked, and was looking at the shore, sweeping the limit of the forest at each side and at the back of the house. The consciousness of there being people in that bush, so silent, so quiet—as silent and quiet as the ruined house on the hill—made me uneasy. There was no sign on the face of nature of this amazing tale that was not so much told as suggested to me in desolate exclamations, completed by shrugs, in interrupted phrases, in hints ending in deep sighs. The woods were unmoved, like a mask—heavy, like the closed door of a prison—they looked with their air of hidden knowledge, of patient expectation, of unapproachable silence. The Russian was explaining to me that it was only lately that Mr. Kurtz had come down to the river, bringing along with him all the fighting men of that lake tribe. He had been absent for several months—getting himself adored, I suppose—and had come down unexpectedly, with the intention to all appearance of making a raid either across the river or down stream. Evidently the appetite for more ivory had got the better of the—what shall I say?—less material aspirations. However he had got much worse suddenly. 'I heard he was lying helpless, and so I came up—took my chance,' said the Russian. 'Oh, he is bad, very bad.' I directed my glass to the house. There were no signs of life, but there was the ruined roof, the long mud wall peeping above the grass, with three little square window-holes, no two of the same size; all this brought within reach of my hand, as it were. And then I made a brusque movement, and one of the remaining posts of that vanished fence leaped up in the field of my glass. You remember I told you I had been struck at the distance by certain attempts at ornamentation, rather remarkable in the ruinous aspect of the place. Now I had suddenly a nearer view, and its first result was to make me throw my head back as if before a blow. Then I went carefully from post to post with my glass, and I saw my mistake. These round knobs were not ornamental but symbolic; they were expressive and puzzling, striking and disturbing—food for thought and also for the vultures if there had been any looking down from the sky; but at all events for such ants as were industrious enough to ascend the pole. They would have been even more impressive, those heads on the stakes, if their faces had not been turned to the house. Only one, the first I had made out, was facing my way. I was not so shocked as you may think. The start back I had given was really nothing but a movement of surprise. I had expected to see a knob of wood there, you know. I returned deliberately to the first I had seen—and there it was, black, dried, sunken, with closed eyelids,—a head that seemed to sleep at the top of that pole, and, with the shrunken dry lips showing a narrow white line of the teeth, was smiling, too, smiling continuously at some endless and jocose dream of that eternal slumber.

"I am not disclosing any trade secrets. In fact, the manager said afterwards that Mr. Kurtz's methods had ruined the district. I have no opinion on that point, but I want you clearly to understand that there was nothing exactly profitable in these heads being there. They only showed that Mr. Kurtz lacked restraint in the gratification of his various lusts, that there was something wanting in him—some small matter which, when the pressing need arose, could not be found under his magnificent eloquence. Whether he knew of this deficiency himself I can't say. I think the knowledge came to him at last—only at the very last. But the wilderness had found him out early, and had taken on him a terrible vengeance for the fantastic invasion. I think it had whispered to him things about himself which he did not know, things of which he had no conception till he took counsel with this great solitude—and the whisper had proved irresistibly fascinating. It echoed loudly within him because he was hollow at the core. . . . I put down the glass, and the head that had appeared near enough to be spoken to seemed at once to have leaped away from me into inaccessible distance.

"The admirer of Mr. Kurtz was a bit crestfallen. In a hurried, indistinct voice he began to assure me he had not dared to take these—say, symbols— down. He was not afraid of the natives; they would not stir till Mr. Kurtz gave the word. His ascendancy was extraordinary. The camps of these people surrounded the place, and the chiefs came every day to see him. They would crawl. . . . 'I don't want to know anything of the ceremonies used when approaching Mr. Kurtz,' I shouted. Curious, this feeling that came over me that such details would be more intolerable than those heads drying on the stakes under Mr. Kurtz's windows. After all, that was only a savage sight, while I seemed at one bound to have been transported into some lightless region of subtle horrors, where pure, uncomplicated savagery was a positive relief, being something that had a right to exist—obviously—in the sunshine. The young man looked at me with surprise. I suppose it did not occur to him that Mr. Kurtz was no idol of mine. He forgot I hadn't heard any of these splendid monologues on, what was it? on love, justice, conduct of life—or what not. If it had come to crawling before Mr. Kurtz, he crawled as much as the veriest savage of them all. I had no idea of the conditions, he said: these heads were the heads of rebels. I shocked him excessively by laughing. Rebels! What would be the next definition I was to hear? There had been enemies, criminals, workers—and these were rebels. Those rebellious heads looked very subdued to me on their sticks. 'You don't know how such a life tries a man like Kurtz,' cried Kurtz's last disciple. 'Well, and you?' I said. 'I! I! I am a simple man. I have no great thoughts. I want nothing from anybody. How can you compare me to? . . .' His feelings were too much for speech, and suddenly he broke down. 'I don't understand,' he groaned. 'I've been doing my best to keep him alive, and that's enough. I had no hand in all this. I have no abilities. There hasn't been a drop of medicine or a mouthful of invalid food for months here. He was shamefully abandoned. A man like this, with such ideas. Shamefully! Shamefully! I—I—haven't slept for the last ten nights. . .'

"His voice lost itself in the calm of the evening. The long shadows of the forest had slipped down hill while we talked, had gone far beyond the ruined hovel, beyond the symbolic row of stakes. All this was in the gloom, while we down there were yet in the sunshine, and the stretch of the river abreast of the clearing glittered in a still and dazzling splendour, with a murky and overshadowed bend above and below. Not a living soul was seen on the shore. The bushes did not rustle.

"Suddenly round the corner of the house a group of men appeared, as though they had come up from the ground. They waded waist-deep in the grass, in a compact body, bearing an improvised stretcher in their midst. Instantly, in the emptiness of the landscape, a cry arose whose shrillness pierced the still air like a sharp arrow flying straight to the very heart of the land; and, as if by enchantment, streams of human beings—of naked human beings—with spears in their hands, with bows, with shields, with wild glances and savage movements, were poured into the clearing by the dark-faced and pensive forest. The bushes shook, the grass swayed for a time, and then everything stood still in attentive immobility.

"'Now, if he does not say the right thing to them we are all done for,' said the Russian at my elbow. The knot of men with the stretcher had stopped, too, halfway to the steamer, as if petrified. I saw the man on the stretcher sit up, lank and with an uplifted arm, above the shoulders of the bearers. 'Let us hope that the man who can talk so well of love in general will find some particular reason to spare us this time,' I said. I resented bitterly the absurd danger of our situation, as if to be at the mercy of that atrocious phantom had been a dishonouring necessity. I could not hear a sound, but through my glasses I saw the thin arm extended commandingly, the lower jaw moving, the eyes of that apparition shining darkly far in its bony head that nodded with grotesque jerks. Kurtz—Kurtz—that means short in German don't it? Well, the name was as true as everything else in his life—and death. He looked at least seven feet long. His covering had fallen off, and his body emerged from it pitiful and appalling as from a winding-sheet. I could see the cage of his ribs all astir, the bones of his arm waving. It was as though an animated image of death carved out of old ivory had been shaking its hand with menaces at a motionless crowd of men made of dark and glittering bronze. I saw him open his mouth wide—it gave him a weirdly voracious aspect, as though he had wanted to swallow all the air, all the earth, all the men before him. A deep voice reached me faintly. He must have been shouting. He fell back suddenly. The stretcher shook as the bearers staggered forward again, and almost at the same time I noticed that the crowd of savages was vanishing without any perceptible movement of retreat, as if the forest that had ejected these beings so suddenly had drawn them in again as the breath is drawn in a long aspiration.

"Some of the pilgrims behind the stretcher carried his arms—two shot-guns, a heavy rifle, and a light revolver-carbine—the thunderbolts of that pitiful Jupiter. The manager bent over him murmuring as he walked beside his head. They laid him down in one of the little cabins—just a room for a bedplace and a camp-stool or two, you know. We had brought his belated correspondence, and a lot of torn envelopes and open letters littered his bed. His hand roamed feebly amongst these papers. I was struck by the fire of his eyes and the composed languor of his expression. It was not so much the exhaustion of disease. He did not seem in pain. This shadow looked satiated and calm, as though for the moment it had had its fill of all the emotions.

"He rustled one of the letters, and looking straight in my face said, 'I am glad.' Somebody had been writing to him about me. These special recommendations were turning up again. The volume of tone he emitted without effort, almost without the trouble of moving his lips, amazed me. A voice! a voice! It was grave, profound, vibrating, while the man did not seem capable of a whisper. However, he had enough strength in him—factitious no doubt—to very nearly make an end of us, as you shall hear directly.

"The manager appeared silently in the doorway; I stepped out at once and he drew the curtain after me. The Russian, eyed curiously by the pilgrims, was staring at the shore. I followed the direction of his glance.

"Dark human shapes could be made out in the distance, flitting indistinctly against the gloomy border of the forest, and near the river two bronze figures, leaning on tall spears, stood in the sunlight under fantastic head-dresses of spotted skins, warlike and still in statuesque repose. And from right to left along the lighted shore moved a wild and gorgeous apparition of a woman.

"She walked with measured steps, draped in striped and fringed cloths, treading the earth proudly,with a slight jingle and flash of barbarous ornaments. She carried her head high; her hair was done in the shape of a helmet; she had brass leggings to the knee, brass wire gauntlets to the elbow, a crimson spot on her tawny cheek, innumerable necklaces of glass beads on her neck; bizarre things, charms, gifts of witch-men, that hung about her, glittered and trembled at every step. She must have had the value of several elephant tusks upon her. She was savage and superb, wild-eyed and magnificent; there was something ominous and stately in her deliberate progress. And in the hush that had fallen suddenly upon the whole sorrowful land, the immense wilderness, the colossal body of the fecund and mysterious life seemed to look at her, pensive, as though it had been looking at the image of its own tenebrous and passionate soul.

"She came abreast of the steamer, stood still, and faced us. Her long shadow fell to the water's edge. Her face had a tragic and fierce aspect of wild sorrow and of dumb pain mingled with the fear of some struggling, half-shaped resolve. She stood looking at us without a stir, and like the wilderness itself, with an air of brooding over an inscrutable purpose. A whole minute passed, and then she made a step forward. There was a low jingle, a glint of yellow metal, a sway of fringed draperies, and she stopped as if her heart had failed her. The young fellow by my side growled. The pilgrims murmured at my back. She looked at us all as if her life had depended upon the unswerving steadiness of her glance. Suddenly she opened her bared arms and threw them up rigid above her head, as though in an uncontrollable desire to touch the sky, and at the same time the swift shadows darted out on the earth, swept around on the river, gathering the steamer into a shadowy embrace. A formidable silence hung over the scene.

"She turned away slowly, walked on, following the bank, and passed into the bushes to the left. Once only her eyes gleamed back at us in the dusk of the thickets before she disappeared.

" 'If she had offered to come aboard I really think I would have tried to shoot her,' said the man of patches, nervously. 'I had been risking my life every day for the last fortnight to keep her out of the house. She got in one day and kicked up a row about those miserable rags I picked up in the storeroom to mend my clothes with. I wasn't decent. At least it must have been that, for she talked like a fury to Kurtz for an hour, pointing at me now and then. I don't understand the dialect of this tribe. Luckily for me, I fancy Kurtz felt too ill that day to care, or there would have been mischief. I don't understand. . . . No—it's too much for me. Ah, well, it's all over now.'

"At this moment I heard Kurtz's deep voice behind the curtain: 'Save me!—save the ivory, you mean. Don't tell me. Save *me!* Why, I've had to save you. You are interrupting my plans now. Sick! Sick! Not so sick as you would like to believe. Never mind. I'll carry my ideas out yet—I will return. I'll show you what can be done. You with your little peddling notions—you are interfering with me. I will return. I. . . .'

"The manager came out. He did me the honour to take me under the arm and lead me aside. 'He is very low, very low,' he said. He considered it necessary to sigh, but neglected to be consistently sorrowful. 'We have done all we could for him—haven't we? But there is no disguising the fact, Mr. Kurtz has done more harm than good to the Company. He did not see the time was not ripe for vigorous action. Cautiously, cautiously—that's my principle. We must be cautious yet. The district is closed to us for a time. Deplorable! Upon the whole, the trade will suffer. I don't deny there is a remarkable quantity of ivory—mostly fossil. We must save it, at all events—but look how precarious the position is—and why? Because the method is unsound.' 'Do you,' said I, looking at the shore, 'call it "unsound method?" ' 'Without doubt,' he exclaimed hotly. 'Don't you?' . . . 'No method at all,' I murmured after a while. 'Exactly,' he exulted. 'I anticipated this. Shows a complete want of judgment. It is my duty to point it out in the proper quarter.' 'Oh,' said I, 'that fellow—what's his name?—the brickmaker, will make a readable report for you.' He appeared confounded for a moment. It seemed to me I had never breathed an atmosphere so vile, and I turned mentally to Kurtz for relief—positively for relief. 'Nevertheless I think Mr. Kurtz is a remarkable man,' I said with emphasis. He started, dropped on me a cold heavy glance, said very quietly, 'he *was*,' and turned his back on me. My hour of favour was over; I found myself lumped along with Kurtz as a partisan of methods for which the time was not ripe: I was unsound! Ah! but it was something to have at least a choice of nightmares.

"I had turned to the wilderness really, not to Mr. Kurtz, who, I was ready to admit, was as good as buried. And for a moment it seemed to me as if I also were buried in a vast grave full of unspeakable secrets. I felt an intolerable weight oppressing my breast, the smell of the damp earth, the unseen presence of victorious corruption, the darkness of an impenetrable night. . . . The Russian tapped me on the shoulder. I heard him mumbling and stammering something about 'brother seaman—couldn't conceal—knowledge of matters that would affect Mr. Kurtz's reputation.' I waited. For him evidently Mr. Kurtz was not in his grave; I suspect that for him Mr. Kurtz was one of the immortals. 'Well!' said I at last, 'speak out. As it happens, I am Mr. Kurtz's friend—in a way.'

"He stated with a good deal of formality that had we not been 'of the same profession,' he would have kept the matter to himself without regard to consequences. 'He suspected there was an active ill will towards him on the part of these white men that——' 'You are right,' I said, remembering a certain conversation I had overheard. 'The manager thinks you ought to be hanged.' He showed a concern at this intelligence which amused me at first. 'I had better get out of the way quietly,' he said, earnestly. 'I can do no more for Kurtz now, and they would soon find some excuse. What's to stop them? There's a military post three hundred miles from here.' 'Well, upon my word,' said I, 'perhaps you had better go if you have any friends amongst the savages near by.' 'Plenty,' he said. 'They are simple people—and I want nothing, you know.' He stood biting his lip, then: 'I don't want any harm to happen to these whites here, but of course I was thinking of Mr. Kurtz's reputation—but you are a brother seaman and——' 'All right,' said I, after a time. 'Mr. Kurtz's reputation is safe with me.' I did not know how truly I spoke.

"He informed me, lowering his voice, that it was Kurtz who had ordered the attack to be made on the steamer. 'He hated sometimes the idea of being taken away—and then again. . . . But I don't understand these matters. I am a simple man. He thought it would scare you away—that you would give it up, thinking him dead. I could not stop him. Oh, I had an awful time of it this last month.' 'Very well,' I said. 'He is all right now.' 'Ye-e-es,' he muttered, not very convinced apparently. 'Thanks,' said I; 'I shall keep my eyes open.' 'But quiet—eh?' he urged, anxiously. 'It would be awful for his reputation if anybody here——' I promised a complete discretion with great gravity. 'I have a canoe and three black fellows waiting not very far. I am off. Could you give me a few Martini-Henry cartridges?' I could, and did, with proper secrecy. He helped himself, with a wink at me, to a handful of my tobacco. 'Between sailors—you know—good English tobacco.' At the door of the pilot-house he turned round—'I say, haven't you a pair of shoes you could spare?' He raised one leg. 'Look.' The soles were tied with knotted strings sandal-wise under his bare feet. I rooted out an old pair, at which he looked with admiration before tucking it under his left arm. One of his pockets (bright red) was bulging with cartridges, from the other (dark blue) peeped 'Towson's Inquiry,' etc., etc. He seemed to think himself excellently well equipped for a renewed encounter with the wilderness. 'Ah! I'll never, never meet such a man again. You ought to have hear him recite poetry—his own, too, it was, he told me. Poetry!' He rolled his eyes at the recollection of these delights. 'Oh, he enlarged my mind!' 'Goodbye,' said I. He shook hands and vanished in the night. Sometimes I ask myself whether I had ever really seen him—whether it was possible to meet such a phenomenon! . . .

"When I woke up shortly after midnight his warning came to my mind with its hint of danger that seemed, in the starred darkness, real enough to make me get up for the purpose of having a look round. On the hill a big fire burned, illuminating fitfully a crooked corner of the station-house. One of the agents with a picket of a few of our blacks, armed for the purpose, was keeping guard over the ivory; but deep within the forest, red gleams that wavered, that seemed to sink and rise from the ground amongst confused columnar shapes of intense blackness, showed the exact position of the camp where Mr. Kurtz's adorers were keeping their uneasy vigil. The monotonous beating of a big drum filled the air with muffled shocks and a lingering vibration. A steady droning sound of many men chanting each to himself some weird incantation came out from the black, flat wall of the woods as the humming of bees comes out of a hive, and had a strange narcotic effect upon my half-awake senses. I believe I dozed off leaning over the rail, till an abrupt burst of yells, an overwhelming outbreak of a pent-up and mysterious frenzy, woke me up in a bewildered wonder. It was cut short all at once, and the low droning went on with an effect of audible and soothing silence. I glanced casually into the little cabin. A light was burning within, but Mr. Kurtz was not there.

"I think I would have raised an outcry if I had believed my eyes. But I didn't believe them at first—the thing seem so impossible. The fact is I was completely unnerved by a sheer blank fright, pure abstract terror, unconnected with any distinct shape of physical danger. What made this emotion so overpowering was—how shall I define it?—the moral shock I received, as if something altogether monstrous, intolerable to thought and odious to the soul, had been thrust upon me unexpectedly. This lasted of course the merest fraction of a second, and then the usual sense of commonplace, deadly danger, the possibility of a sudden onslaught and massacre, or something of the kind, which I saw impending, was positively welcome and composing. It pacified me, in fact, so much, that I did not raise an alarm.

"There was an agent buttoned up inside an ulster and sleeping on a chair on deck within three feet of me. The yells had not awakened him; he snored very slightly; I left him to his slumbers and leaped ashore. I did not betray Mr. Kurtz—it was ordered I should never betray him—it was written I should be loyal to the nightmare of my choice. I was anxious to deal with this shadow by myself alone,—and to this day I don't know why I was so jealous of sharing with any one the peculiar blackness of that experience.

"As soon as I got on the bank I saw a trail—a broad trail through the grass. I remember the exultation with which I said to myself, 'He can't walk—he is crawling on all-fours—I've got him.' The grass was wet with dew. I strode rapidly with clenched fists. I fancy I had some vague notion of falling upon him and giving him a drubbing. I don't know. I had some imbecile thoughts. The knitting old woman with the cat obtruded herself upon my memory as a most improper person to be sitting at the other end of such an affair. I saw a row of pilgrims squirting lead in the air out of Winchesters held to the hip. I thought I would never get back to the steamer, and imagined myself living alone and unarmed in the woods to an advanced age. Such silly things—you know. And I remember I confounded the beat of the drum with the beating of my heart, and was pleased at its calm regularity.

"I kept to the track though—then stopped to listen. The night was very clear; a dark blue space, sparkling with dew and starlight, in which black things stood very still. I thought I could see a kind of motion ahead of me. I was strangely cocksure of everything that night. I actually left the track and ran in a wide semicircle (I verily believe chuckling to myself) so as to get in front of that stir, of that motion I had seen—if indeed I had seen anything. I was circumventing Kurtz as though it had been a boyish game.

"I came upon him, and, if he had not heard me coming, I would have fallen over him, too, but he got up in time. He rose, unsteady, long, pale, indistinct, like a vapour exhaled by the earth, and swayed slightly, misty and silent before me; while at my back the fires loomed between the trees, and the murmur of many voices issued from the forest. I had cut him off cleverly; but when actually confronting him I seemed to come to my senses. I saw the danger in its right proportion. It was by no means over yet. Suppose he began to shout? Though

he could hardly stand, there was still plenty of vigour in his voice. 'Go away—
hide yourself,' he said, in that profound tone. It was very awful. I glanced
back. We were within thirty yards from the nearest fire. A black figure stood
up, strode on long black legs, waving long black arms, across the glow. It
had horns—antelope horns, I think—on its head. Some sorcerer, some witch-
man, no doubt: it looked fiend-like enough. 'Do you know what you are doing?'
I whispered. 'Perfectly,' he answered, raising his voice for that single word:
it sounded to me far off and yet loud, like a hail through a speaking-trumpet.
If he makes a row we are lost, I thought to myself. This clearly was not a
case for fisticuffs, even apart from the very natural aversion I had to beat
that Shadow—this wandering and tormented thing. 'You will be lost,' I said—
'utterly lost.' One gets sometimes such a flash of inspiration, you know. I
did say the right thing, though indeed he could not have been more irretrievably
lost than he was at this very moment, when the foundations of our intimacy
were being laid—to endure—to endure—even to the end—even beyond.

" 'I had immense plans,' he muttered irresolutely. 'Yes,' said I; 'but if you
try to shout I'll smash your head with——' There was not a stick or a stone
near. 'I will throttle you for good,' I corrected myself. 'I was on the threshold
of great things,' he pleaded, in a voice of longing, with a wistfulness of tone
that made my blood run cold. 'And now for this stupid scoundrel—' 'Your
success in Europe is assured in any case,' I affirmed, steadily. I did not want
to have the throttling of him, you understand—and indeed it would have been
very little use for any practical pupose. I tried to break the spell—the heavy,
mute spell of the wilderness—that seemed to draw him to its pitiless breast
by the awakening of forgotten and brutal instincts, by the memory of gratified
and monstrous passions. This alone, I was convinced, had driven him out to
the edge of the forest, to the bush, towards the gleam of fires, the throb of
drums, the drone of weird incantations; this alone had beguiled his unlawful
soul beyond the bounds of permitted aspirations. And, don't you see, the
terror of the position was not in being knocked on the head—though I had
a very lively sense of that danger, too—but in this, that I had to deal with a
being to whom I could not appeal in the name of anything high or low. I
had, even like the niggers, to invoke him—himself—his own exalted and incredible degradation. There was nothing either above or below him, and I knew
it. He had kicked himself loose of the earth. Confound the man! he had kicked
the very earth to pieces. He was alone, and I before him did not know whether
I stood on the ground or floated in the air. I've been telling you what we
said—repeating the phrases we pronounced—but what's the good? They were
common everyday words—the familiar, vague sounds exchanged on every waking day of life. But what of that? They had behind them, to my mind, the
terrific suggestiveness of words heard in dreams, of phrases spoken in nightmares. Soul! If anybody had ever struggled with a soul, I am the man. And I
wasn't arguing with a lunatic either. Believe me or not, his intelligence was
perfectly clear—concentrated, it is true, upon himself with horrible intensity,
yet clear; and therein was my only chance—barring, of course, the killing him
there and then, which wasn't so good, on account of unavoidable noise. But
his soul was mad. Being alone in the wilderness, it had looked within itself,
and, by heavens! I tell you, it had gone mad. I had—for my sins, I suppose—
to go through the ordeal of looking into it myself. No eloquence could have
been so withering to one's belief in mankind as his final burst of sincerity.
He struggled with himself, too. I saw it,—I heard it. I saw the inconceivable

mystery of a soul that knew no restraint, no faith, and no fear, yet struggling blindly with itself. I kept my head pretty well; but when I had him at last stretched on the couch, I wiped my forehead, while my legs shook under me as though I had carried half a ton on my back down that hill. And yet I had only supported him, his bony arm clasped round my neck—and he was not much heavier than a child.

"When next day we left at noon, the crowd, of whose presence behind the curtain of trees I had been acutely conscious all the time, flowed out of the woods again, filled the clearing, covered the slope with a mass of naked, breathing, quivering, bronze bodies. I steamed up a bit, then swung downstream, and two thousand eyes followed the evolutions of the splashing, thumping, fierce river-demon beating the water with its terrible tail and breathing black smoke into the air. In front of the first rank, along the river, three men, plastered with bright red earth from head to foot, strutted to and fro restlessly. When we came abreast again, they faced the river, stamped their feet, nodded their horned heads, swayed their scarlet bodies; they shook towards the fierce river-demon a bunch of black feathers, a mangy skin with a pendent tail—something that looked like a dried gourd; they shouted periodically together strings of amazing words that resembled no sounds of human language; and the deep murmurs of the crowd, interrupted suddenly, were like the responses of some satanic litany.

"We had carried Kurtz into the pilot-house: there was more air there. Lying on the couch, he stared through the open shutter. There was an eddy in the mass of human bodies, and the woman with helmeted head and tawny cheeks rushed out to the very brink of the stream. She put out her hands, shouted something, and all that wild mob took up the shout in a roaring chorus of articulated, rapid breathless utterance.

" 'Do you understand this?' I asked.

"He kept on looking out past me with fiery, longing eyes, with a mingled expression of wistfulness and hate. He made no answer, but I saw a smile, a smile of indefinable meaning, appear on his colourless lips that a moment after twitched convulsively. 'Do I not?' he said slowly, gasping, as if the words had been torn out of him by a supernatural power.

"I pulled the string of the whistle, and I did this because I saw the pilgrims on deck getting out their rifles with an air of anticipating a jolly lark. At the sudden screech there was a movement of abject terror through that wedged mass of bodies. 'Don't! don't you frighten them away,' cried someone on deck disconsolately. I pulled the string time after time. They broke and ran, they leaped, they crouched, they swerved, they dodged the flying terror of the sound. The three red chaps had fallen flat, face down on the shore, as though they had been shot dead. Only the barbarous and superb woman did not so much as flinch, and stretched tragically her bare arms after us over the sombre and glittering river.

"And then that imbecile crowd down on the deck started their little fun, and I could see nothing more for smoke.

"The brown current ran swiftly out of the heart of darkness, bearing us down toward the sea with twice the speed of our upward progress; and Kurtz's life was running swiftly, too, ebbing, ebbing out of his heart into the sea of inexorable time. The manager was very placid, he had no vital anxieties now, he took us both in with a comprehensive and satisfied glance: the 'affair' had come off as well as could be wished. I saw the time approaching when I would be left alone of the party of 'unsound method.' The pilgrims looked upon me with disfavour. I was, so to speak, numbered with the dead. It is strange how I accepted this unforeseen partnership, this choice of nightmares forced upon me in the tenebrous land invaded by these mean and greedy phantoms.

"Kurtz discoursed. A voice! a voice! It rang deep to the very last. It survived his strength to hide in the magnificent folds of eloquence the barren darkness of his heart. Oh, he struggled! he struggled! The wastes of his weary brain were haunted by shadowy images now—images of wealth and fame revolving obsequiously round his unextinguishable gift of noble and lofty expression. My Intended, my station, my career, my ideas—these were the subjects for the occasional utterances of elevated sentiments. The shade of the original Kurtz frequented the bedside of the hollow sham, whose fate it was to be buried presently in the mould of primeval earth. But both the diabolic love and the unearthly hate of the mysteries it had penetrated fought for the posses- sion of that soul satiated with primitive emotions, avid of lying fame, of sham distinction, of all the appearances of success and power.

"Sometimes he was contemptibly childish. He desired to have kings meet him at railway-stations on his return from some ghastly Nowhere, where he intended to accomplish great things. 'You show them you have in you something that is really profitable, and then there will be no limits to the recognition of your ability,' he would say. 'Of course you must take care of the motives— right motives—always.' The long reaches that were like one and the same reach, monotonous bends that were exactly alike, slipped past the steamer with their multitude of secular[31] trees looking patiently after this grimy fragment of another world, the forerunner of change, of conquest, of trade, of massacres, of blessings. I looked ahead—piloting. 'Close the shuttter,' said Kurtz suddenly one day; 'I can't bear to look at this.' I did so. There was a silence. 'Oh, but I will wring your heart yet!' he cried at the invisible wilderness.

"We broke down—as I had expected—and had to lie up for repairs at the head of an island. This delay was the first thing that shook Kurtz's confidence. One morning he gave me a packet of papers and a photograph—the lot tied together with a shoe-string. 'Keep this for me,' he said. 'This noxious fool' (meaning the manager) 'is capable of prying into my boxes when I am not looking.' In the afternoon I saw him. He was lying on his back with closed eyes, and I withdrew quietly, but I heard him mutter, 'Live rightly, die, die . . .' I listened. There was nothing more. Was he rehearsing some speech in his sleep, or was it a fragment of a phrase from some newspaper article? He had been writing for the papers and meant to do so again, 'for the furthering of my ideas. It's a duty.'

"His was an impenetrable darkness. I looked at him as you peer down at a man who is lying at the bottom of a precipice where the sun never shines. But I had not much time to give him, because I was helping the engine-driver to take to pieces the leaky cylinders, to straighten a bent connecting-rod, and in other such matters. I lived in an infernal mess of rust, filings, nuts, bolts, spanners, hammers, ratchet-drills—things I abominate, because I don't get on with them. I tended the little forge we fortunately had aboard; I toiled wearily in a wretched scrap-heap—unless I had the shakes too bad to stand.

"One evening coming in with a candle I was startled to hear him say a

---

[31] Centuries old.

little tremulously, 'I am lying here in the dark waiting for death.' The light was within a foot of his eyes. I forced myself to murmur, 'Oh, nonsense!' and stood over him as if transfixed.

"Anything approaching the change that came over his features I have never seen before, and hope never to see again. Oh, I wasn't touched. I was fascinated. It was as though a veil had been rent. I saw on that ivory face the expression of sombre pride, of ruthless power, of craven terror—of an intense and hopeless despair. Did he live his life again in every detail of desire, temptation, and surrender during that supreme moment of complete knowledge? He cried in a whisper at some image, at some vision—he cried out twice, a cry that was no more than a breath—

" 'The horror! The horror!'

"I blew the candle out and left the cabin. The pilgrims were dining in the mess-room, and I took my place opposite the manager, who lifted his eyes to give me a questioning glance, which I successfully ignored. He leaned back, serene, with that peculiar smile of his sealing the unexpressed depths of his meanness. A continuous shower of small flies streamed upon the lamp, upon the cloth, upon our hands and faces. Suddenly the manager's boy put his insolent black head in the doorway, and said in a tone of scathing contempt—

" 'Mistah Kurtz—he dead.'

"All the pilgrims rushed out to see. I remained, and went on with my dinner. I believe I was considered brutally callous. However, I did not eat much. There was a lamp in there—light, don't you know—and outside it was so beastly, beastly dark. I went no more near the remarkable man who had pronounced a judgment upon the adventures of his soul on this earth. The voice was gone. What else had been there? But I am of course aware that next day the pilgrims buried something in a muddy hole.

"And then they very nearly buried me.

"However, as you see, I did not go to join Kurtz there and then. I did not. I remained to dream the nightmare out to the end, and to show my loyalty to Kurtz once more. Destiny. My destiny! Droll thing life is—that mysterious arrangement of merciless logic for a futile purpose. The most you can hope from it is some knowledge of yourself—that comes too late—a crop of unextinguishable regrets. I have wrestled with death. It is the most unexciting contest you can imagine. It takes place in an impalpable grayness, with nothing underfoot, with nothing around, without spectators, without clamour, without glory, without the great desire of victory, without the great fear of defeat, in a sickly atmosphere of tepid scepticism, without much belief in your own right, and still less in that of your adversary. If such is the form of ultimate wisdom, then life is a greater riddle than some of us think it to be. I was within a hair's-breadth of the last opportunity for pronouncement, and I found with humiliation that probably I would have nothing to say. This is the reason why I affirm that Kurtz was a remarkable man. He had something to say. He said it. Since I had peeped over the edge myself, I understand better the meaning of his stare, that could not see the flame of the candle, but was wide enough to embrace the whole universe, piercing enough to penetrate all the hearts that beat in the darkness. He had summed up—he had judged. 'The horror!' He was a remarkable man. After all, this was the expression of some sort of belief; it had candour, it had conviction, it had a vibrating note of revolt in its whisper, it had the appalling face of a glimpsed truth—the strange commingling of desire and hate. And it is not my own extremity I remember best—a vision of grayness without form filled with physical pain, and a careless contempt for the evanescence of all things—even of this pain itself. No! It is his extremity that I seem to have lived through. True, he had made that last stride, he had stepped over the edge, while I had been permitted to draw back my hesitating foot. And perhaps in this is the whole difference; perhaps all the wisdom, and all truth, and all sincerity, are just compressed into that inappreciable moment of time in which we step over the threshold of the invisible. Perhaps! I like to think my summing-up would not have been a word of careless contempt. Better his cry—much better. It was an affirmation, a moral victory paid for by innumerable defeats, by abominable terrors, by abominable satisfactions. But it was a victory! That is why I have remained loyal to Kurtz to the last, and even beyond, when a long time after I heard once more, not his own voice, but the echo of his magnificent eloquence thrown to me from a soul as translucently pure as a cliff of crystal.

"No, they did not bury me, though there is a period of time which I remember mistily, with a shuddering wonder, like a passage through some inconceivable world that had no hope in it and no desire. I found myself back in the sepulchral city resenting the sight of people hurrying through the streets to filch a little money from each other, to devour their infamous cookery, to gulp their unwholesome beer, to dream their insignificant and silly dreams. They trespassed upon my thoughts. They were intruders whose knowledge of life was to me an irritating pretence, because I felt so sure they could not possibly know the things I knew. Their bearing, which was simply the bearing of commonplace individuals going about their business in the assurance of perfect safety, was offensive to me like the outrageous flauntings of folly in the face of a danger it is unable to comprehend. I had no particular desire to enlighten them, but I had some difficulty in restraining myself from laughing in their faces, so full of stupid importance. I daresay I was not very well at that time. I tottered about the streets—there were various affairs to settle—grinning bitterly at perfectly respectable persons. I admit my behaviour was inexcusable, but then my temperature was seldom normal in these days. My dear aunt's endeavours to 'nurse up my strength' seemed altogether beside the mark. It was not my strength that wanted nursing, it was my imagination that wanted soothing. I kept the bundle of papers given me by Kurtz, not knowing exactly what to do with it. His mother had died lately, watched over, as I was told, by his Intended. A clean-shaved man, with an official manner and wearing goldrimmed spectacles, called on me one day and made inquiries, at first circuitous, afterwards suavely pressing, about what he was pleased to denominate certain 'documents.' I was not surprised, because I had had two rows with the manager on the subject out there. I had refused to give up the smallest scrap out of that package, and I took the same attitude with the spectacled man. He became darkly menacing at last, and with much heat argued that the Company had the right to every bit of information about its 'territories.' And said he, 'Mr. Kurtz's knowledge of unexplored regions must have been necessarily extensive and peculiar—owing to his great abilities and to the deplorable circumstances in which he had been placed: therefore——' I assured him Mr. Kurtz's knowledge, however extensive, did not bear upon the problems of commerce or administration. He invoked then the name of science. 'It would be an incalculable loss if,' etc., etc. I offered him the report on the 'Suppression of Savage Customs,' with the postscriptum torn off. He took it up eagerly, but ended by sniffing at it with an air of contempt. 'This is not what we had a right to expect,' he remarked. 'Expect nothing else,' I said. 'There are only private letters.' He withdrew upon some threat of legal proceedings, and I saw him no more; but another fellow, calling himself Kurtz's cousin, appeared two days later, and was anxious to hear all the details about his dear relative's last moments. Incidentally he gave me to understand that Kurtz had been essentially a great musician. 'There was the making of an immense success,' said the man, who was an organist, I believe, with lank gray hair flowing over a greasy coat-collar. I had no reason to doubt his statement; and to this day I am unable to say what was Kurtz's profession, whether he ever had any—which was the greatest of his talents. I had taken him for a painter who wrote for the papers, or else for a journalist who could paint—but even the cousin (who took snuff during the interview) could not tell me what he had been—exactly. He was a universal genius—on that point I agreed with the old chap, who thereupon blew his nose noisily into a large cotton handkerchief and withdrew in senile agitation, bearing off some family letters and memoranda without importance. Ultimately a journalist anxious to know something of the fate of his 'dear colleague' turned up. This visitor informed me Kurtz's proper sphere ought to have been politics 'on the popular side.' He had furry straight eyebrows, bristly hair cropped short, an eye-glass on a broad ribbon, and, becoming expansive, confessed his opinion that Kurtz really couldn't write a bit—'but heavens! how that man could talk. He electrified large meetings. He had faith—don't you see?—he had the faith. He could get himself to believe anything—anything. He would have been a splendid leader of an extreme party.' 'What party?' I asked. 'Any party,' answered the other. 'He was an—an—extremist.' Did I not think so? I assented. Did I know, he asked, with a sudden flash of curiosity, 'what it was that had induced him to go out there?' 'Yes,' said I, and forthwith handed him the famous Report for publication, if he thought fit. He glanced through it hurriedly, mumbling all the time, judged 'it would do,' and took himself off with this plunder.

"Thus I was left at last with a slim packet of letters and the girl's portrait. She struck me as beautiful—I mean she had a beautiful expression. I know that the sunlight can be made to lie, too, yet one felt that no manipulation of light and pose could have conveyed the delicate shade of truthfulness upon those features. She seemed ready to listen without mental reservation, without suspicion, without a thought for herself. I concluded I would go and give her back her portrait and those letters myself. Curiosity? Yes; and also some other feeling perhaps. All that had been Kurtz's had passed out of my hands: his soul, his body, his station, his plans, his ivory, his career. There remained only his memory and his Intended—and I wanted to give that up, too, to the past, in a way—to surrender personally all that remained of him with me to that oblivion which is the last word of our common fate. I don't defend myself. I had no clear perception of what it was I really wanted. Perhaps it was an impulse of unconscious loyalty, or the fulfilment of one of these ironic necessities that lurk in the facts of human existence. I don't know. I can't tell. But I went.

"I thought his memory was like the other memories of the dead that accumulate in every man's life—a vague impress on the brain of shadows that had fallen on it in their swift and final passage; but before the high and ponderous door, between the tall houses of a street as still and decorous as a well-kept alley in a cemetery, I had a vision of him on the stretcher, opening his mouth voraciously, as if to devour all the earth with all its mankind. He lived then before me; he lived as much as he had ever lived—a shadow insatiable of splendid appearances, of frightful realities; a shadow darker than the shadow of the night, and draped nobly in the folds of a gorgeous eloquence. The vision seemed to enter the house with me—the stretcher, the phantom-bearers, the wild crowd of obedient worshippers, the gloom of the forests, the glitter of the reach between the murky bends, the beat of the drum, regular and muffled like the beating of a heart—the heart of a conquering darkness. It was a moment of triumph for the wilderness, an invading and vengeful rush which, it seemed to me, I would have to keep back alone for the salvation of another soul. And the memory of what I had heard him say afar there, with the horned shapes stirring at my back, in the glow of fires, within the patient woods, those broken phrases came back to me, were heard again in their ominous and terrifying simplicity. I remembered his abject pleading, his abject threats, the colossal scale of his vile desires, the meanness, the torment, the tempestuous anguish of his soul. And later on I seemed to see his collected languid manner, when he said one day, 'This lot of ivory now is really mine. The Company did not pay for it. I collected it myself at a very great personal risk. I am afraid they will try to claim it as theirs though. H'm. It is a difficult case. What do you think I ought to do—resist? Eh? I want no more than justice.' . . . He wanted no more than justice—no more than justice. I rang the bell before a mahogany door on the first floor, and while I waited he seemed to stare at me out of the glassy panel—stare with that wide and immense stare embracing, condemning, loathing all the universe. I seemed to hear the whispered cry, 'The horror! The horror!'

"The dusk was falling. I had to wait in a lofty drawing-room with three long windows from floor to ceiling that were like three luminous and bedraped columns. The bent gilt legs and backs of the furniture shone in indistinct curves. The tall marble fireplace had a cold and monumental whiteness. A grand piano stood massively in a corner; with dark gleams on the flat surfaces like a sombre and polished sarcophagus. A high door opened—closed. I rose.

"She came forward, all in black, with a pale head, floating towards me in the dusk. She was in mourning. It was more than a year since his death, more than a year since the news came; she seemed as though she would remember and mourn for ever. She took both my hands in hers and murmured. 'I had heard you were coming.' I noticed she was not very young—I mean not girlish. She had a mature capacity for fidelity, for belief, for suffering. The room seemed to have grown darker, as if all the sad light of the cloudy evening had taken refuge on her forehead. This fair hair, this pale visage, this pure brow, seemed surrounded by an ashy halo from which the dark eyes looked out at me. Their glance was guileless, profound, confident, and trustful. She carried her sorrowful head as though she were proud of that sorrow, as though she would say, I—I alone know how to mourn for him as he deserves. But while we were still shaking hands, such a look of awful desolation came upon her face that I perceived she was one of those creatures that are not the playthings of Time. For her he had died only yesterday. And, by Jove! the impression was so powerful that for me, too, he seemed to have died only yesterday—nay, this very minute. I saw her and him in the same instant of time—his death and her sorrow—I saw her sorrow in the very moment of his death. Do you understand? I saw them together—I heard them together. She had said, with a deep catch of the breath, 'I have survived' while my strained ears seemed to hear distinctly, mingled with her tone of despairing regret, the summing up whisper of his eternal condemnation. I asked myself what I was doing there, with a sensation of panic in my heart as though I had blundered into a place of cruel and absurd mysteries not fit for a human being to behold. She motioned me to a chair. We sat down. I laid the packet gently on the little table, and she put her hand over it. . . . 'You knew him well,' she murmured, after a moment of mourning silence.

" 'Intimacy grows quickly out there,' I said. 'I knew him as well as it is possible for one man to know another.'

" 'And you admired him,' she said. 'It was impossible to know him and not to admire him. Was it?'

" 'He was a remarkable man,' I said, unsteadily. Then before the appealing fixity of her gaze, that seemed to watch for more words on my lips, I went on. 'It was impossible not to——'

" 'Love him,' she finished eagerly, silencing me into an appalled dumbness. 'How true! how true! But when you think that no one knew him so well as I! I had all his noble confidence. I knew him best.'

" 'You knew him best,' I repeated. And perhaps she did. But with every word spoken the room was growing darker, and only her forehead, smooth and white, remained illumined by the unextinguishable light of belief and love.

" 'You were his friend,' she went on. 'His friend,' she repeated, a little louder. 'You must have been, if he had given you this, and sent you to me. I feel I can speak to you—and oh! I must speak. I want you—you who have heard his last words—to know I have been worthy of him. . . . It is not pride. . . . Yes! I am proud to know I understood him better than any one on earth—he told me so himself. And since his mother died I have had no one—no one—to—to——'

"I listened. The darkness deepened. I was not even sure whether he had given me the right bundle. I rather suspect he wanted me to take care of another batch of his papers which, after his death, I saw the manager examining under the lamp. And the girl talked, easing her pain in the certitude of my sympathy; she talked as thirsty men drink. I had heard that her engagement with Kurtz had been disapproved by her people. He wasn't rich enough or something. And indeed I don't know whether he had not been a pauper all his life. He had given me some reason to infer that it was his impatience of comparative poverty that drove him out there.

" '. . . Who was not his friend who had heard him speak once?' she was saying. 'He drew men towards him by what was best in them.' She looked at me with intensity. 'It is the gift of the great,' she went on, and the sound of her low voice seemed to have the accompaniment of all the other sounds, full of mystery, desolation, and sorrow, I had ever heard—the ripple of the river, the soughing of the trees swayed by the wind, the murmurs of the crowds, the faint ring of incomprehensible words cried from afar, the whisper of a voice speaking from beyond the threshold of an eternal darkness. 'But you have heard him! You know!' she cried.

" 'Yes, I know,' I said with something like despair in my heart, but bowing my head before the faith that was in her, before that great and saving illusion that shone with an unearthly glow in the darkness, in the triumphant darkness from which I could not have defended her—from which I could not even defend myself.

" 'What a loss to me—to us!'—she corrected herself with beautiful generosity; then added in a murmur, 'To the world.' By the last gleams of twilight I could see the glitter of her eyes, full of tears—of tears that would not fall.

" 'I have been very happy—very fortunate—very proud,' she went on. 'Too fortunate. Too happy for a little while. And now I am unhappy for—for life.'

"She stood up; her fair hair seemed to catch all the remaining light in a glimmer of gold. I rose, too.

" 'And of all this,' she went on, mournfully, 'of all his promise, and of all his greatness, of his generous mind, of his noble heart, nothing remains— nothing but a memory. You and I——'

" 'We shall always remember him,' I said, hastily.

" 'No!' she cried. 'It is impossible that all this should be lost—that such a life should be sacrificed to leave nothing—but sorrow. You know what vast plans he had. I knew of them, too—I could not perhaps understand—but others knew of them. Something must remain. His words, at least, have not died.'

" 'His words will remain,' I said.

" 'And his example,' she whispered to herself. 'Men looked up to him—his goodness shone in every act. His example——'

" 'True,' I said; 'his example, too. Yes, his example. I forgot that.'

" 'But I do not. I cannot—I cannot believe—not yet. I cannot believe that I shall never see him again, that nobody will see him again, never, never, never.'

"She put out her arms as if after a retreating figure, stretching them black and with clasped pale hands across the fading and narrow sheen of the window. Never see him! I saw him clearly enough then. I shall see this eloquent phantom as long as I live, and I shall see her, too, a tragic and familiar Shade, resembling in this gesture another one, tragic also, and bedecked with powerless charms, stretching bare brown arms over the glitter of the infernal stream, the stream of darkness. She said suddenly very low, 'He died as he lived.'

" 'His end,' said I, with dull anger stirring in me, 'was in every way worthy of his life.'

" 'And I was not with him,' she murmured. My anger subsided before a feeling of infinite pity.

" 'Everything that could be done——' I mumbled.

" 'Ah, but I believed in him more than any one on earth—more than his own mother, more than—himself. He needed me! Me! I would have treasured every sigh, every word, every sign, every glance.'

"I felt like a chill grip on my chest. 'Don't,' I said, in a muffled voice.

" 'Forgive me. I—I—have mourned so long in silence—in silence. . . . You were with him—to the last? I think of his loneliness. Nobody near to understand him as I would have understood. Perhaps no one to hear. . . .'

" 'To the very end,' I said, shakily. 'I heard his very last words.. . .' I stopped in a fright.

" 'Repeat them,' she murmured in a heart-broken tone. 'I want—I want— something—something—to—to live with.'

"I was on the point of crying at her, 'Don't you hear them?' The dusk was repeating them in a persistent whisper all around us, in a whisper that seemed to swell menacingly like the first whisper of a rising wind. 'The horror! the horror!'

" 'His last word—to live with,' she insisted. 'Don't you understand I loved him—I loved him—I loved him!'

"I pulled myself together and spoke slowly.

" 'The last word he pronounced was—your name.'

"I heard a light sigh and then my heart stood still, stopped dead short by an exulting and terrible cry, by the cry of inconceivable triumph and of unspeakable pain. 'I knew it—I was sure!' . . . She knew. She was sure. I heard her weeping; she had hidden her face in her hands. It seemed to me that the house would collapse before I could escape, that the heavens would fall upon my head. But nothing happened. The heavens do not fall for such a trifle. Would they have fallen, I wonder, if I had rendered Kurtz that justice which was his due? Hadn't he said he wanted only justice? But I couldn't. I could not tell her. It would have been too dark—too dark altogether. . . ."

Marlow ceased, and sat apart, indistinct and silent, in the pose of a meditating Buddha. Nobody moved for a time. "We have lost the first of the ebb," said the Director, suddenly. I raised my head. The offing was barred by a black bank of clouds, and the tranquil waterway leading to the uttermost ends of the earth flowed sombre under an overcast sky—seemed to lead into the heart of an immense darkness.

[1899]

Henry James   *1843–1916*

THE TREE OF KNOWLEDGE

I

It was one of the secret opinions, such as we all have, of Peter Brench that his main success in life would have consisted in his never having committed himself about the work, as it was called, of his friend Morgan Mallow. This was a subject on which it was, to the best of his belief, impossible with veracity to quote him, and it was nowhere on record that he had, in the connexion, on any occasion and in any embarrassment, either lied or spoken the truth. Such a triumph had its honour even for a man of other triumphs—a man who had reached fifty, who had escaped marriage, who had lived within his means, who had been in love with Mrs. Mallow for years without breathing it, and who, last not least, had judged himself once for all. He had so judged himself in fact that he felt an extreme and general humility to be his proper portion; yet there was nothing that made him think so well of his parts as the course he had steered so often through the shallows just mentioned. It became thus a real wonder that the friends in whom he had most confidence were just those with whom he had most reserves. He couldn't tell Mrs. Mallow— or at least he supposed, excellent man, he couldn't—that she was the one beautiful reason he had never married; any more than he could tell her husband that the sight of the multiplied marbles in that gentleman's studio was an affliction of which even time had never blunted the edge. His victory, however, as I have intimated, in regard to these productions, was not simply in his not having let it out that he deplored them; it was, remarkably, in his not having kept it in by anything else.

The whole situation, among these good people, was verily a marvel, and there was probably not such another for a long way from the spot that engages us—the point at which the soft declivity of Hampstead[1] began at that time to confess in broken accents to Saint John's Wood. He despised Mallow's statues and adored Mallow's wife, and yet was distinctly fond of Mallow, to whom, in turn, he was equally dear. Mrs. Mallow rejoiced in the statues—though she preferred, when pressed, the busts; and if she was visibly attached to Peter Brench it was because of his affection for Morgan. Each loved the other moreover for the love borne in each case to Lancelot, whom the Mallows respectively cherished as their only child and whom the friend of their fireside identified as the third—but decidedly the handsomest—of his godsons. Already in the old years it had come to that—that no one, for such a relation, could possibly have occurred to any of them, even to the baby itself, but Peter. There was luckily a certain independence, of the pecuniary sort, all round: the Master could never otherwise have spent his solemn *Wanderjahre*[2] in Florence and Rome, and continued by the Thames as well as by the Arno and the Tiber to add unpurchased group to group and model, for what was too apt to prove in the event mere love, fancy-heads of celebrities either too busy or too buried— too much of the age or too little of it—to sit. Neither could Peter, lounging

[1] A fashionable residential district in northwest London.
[2] A year spent wandering or traveling.

in almost daily, have found time to keep the whole complicated tradition so alive by his presence. He was massive but mild, the depositary of these mysteries—large and loose and ruddy and curly, with deep tones, deep eyes, deep pockets, to say nothing of the habit of long pipes, soft hats and brownish greyish weather-faded clothes, apparently always the same.

He had "written," it was known, but had never spoken, never spoken in particular of that; and he had the air (since, as was believed, he continued to write) of keeping it up in order to have something more—as if he hadn't at the worst enough—to be silent about. Whatever his air, at any rate, Peter's occasional unmentioned prose and verse were quite truly the result of an impulse to maintain the purity of his taste by establishing still more firmly the right relation of fame to feebleness. The little green door of his domain was in a garden-wall on which the discoloured stucco made patches, and in the small detached villa behind it everything was old, the furniture, the servants, the books, the prints, the immemorial habits and the new improvements. The Mallows, at Carrara[3] Lodge, were within ten minutes, and the studio there was on their little land, to which they had added, in their happy faith, for building it. This was the good fortune, if it was not the ill, of her having brought him in marriage a portion that put them in a manner at their ease and enabled them thus, on their side, to keep it up. And they did keep it up—they always had—the infatuated sculptor and his wife, for whom nature had refined on the impossible by relieving them of the sense of the difficult. Morgan had at all events everything of the sculptor but the spirit of Phidias[4]— the brown velvet, the becoming *beretto*, the "plastic" presence, the fine fingers, the beautiful accent in Italian and the old Italian factotum. He seemed to make up for everything when he addressed Egidio with the "tu" and waved him to turn one of the rotary pedestals of which the place was full. They were tremendous Italians at Carrara Lodge, and the secret of the part played by this fact in Peter's life was in a large degree that it gave him, sturdy Briton as he was, just the amount of "going abroad" he could bear. The Mallows were all his Italy, but it was in a measure for Italy he liked them. His one worry was that Lance—to which they had shortened his godson—was, in spite of a public school, perhaps a shade too Italian. Morgan meanwhile looked like somebody's flattering idea of somebody's own person as expressed in the great room provided at the Uffizzi[5] Museum for the general illustration of that idea by eminent hands. The Master's sole regret that he hadn't been born rather to the brush than to the chisel sprang from his wish that he might have contributed to that collection.

It appeared with time at any rate to be to the brush that Lance had been born; for Mrs. Mallow, one day when the boy was turning twenty, broke it to their friend, who shared, to the last delicate morsel, their problems and pains, that it seemed as if nothing would really do but that he should embrace the career. It had been impossible longer to remain blind to the fact that he was gaining no glory at Cambridge, where Brench's own college had for a year tempered its tone to him as for Brench's own sake. Therefore why renew the vain form of preparing him for the impossible? The impossible—it had become clear—was that he should be anything but an artist.

---

[3] A famous type of marble, quarried at Carrara, Italy.
[4] The great fifth century B.C. Greek sculptor, famous for his marble statues.
[5] The famous art museum in Florence, Italy.

"Oh dear, dear!" said poor Peter.

"Don't you believe in it?" asked Mrs. Mallow, who still, at more than forty, had her violet velvet eyes, her creamy satin skin and her silken chestnut hair.

"Believe in what?"

"Why in Lance's passion."

"I don't know what you mean by 'believing in it.' I've never been unaware, certainly, of his disposition, from his earliest time, to daub and draw; but I confess I've hoped it would burn out."

"But why should it," she sweetly smiled, "with his wonderful heredity? Passion is passion—though of course indeed *you,* dear Peter, know nothing of that. Has the Master's ever burned out?"

Peter looked off a little and, in his familiar formless way, kept up for a moment a sound between a smothered whistle and a subdued hum. "Do you think he's going to be another Master?"

She seemed scarce prepared to go that length, yet she had on the whole a marvellous trust. "I know what you mean by that. Will it be a career to incur the jealousies and provoke the machinations that have been at times almost too much for his father? Well—say it may be, since nothing but clap-trap, in these dreadful days, *can,* it would seem, make its way, and since, with the curse of refinement and distinction, one may easily find one's self begging one's bread. Put it at the worst—say he *has* the misfortune to wing his flight further than the vulgar taste of his stupid countrymen can follow. Think, all the same, of the happiness—the same the Master has had. He'll *know.*"

Peter looked rueful. "Ah but *what* will he know?"

"Quiet joy!" cried Mrs. Mallow, quite impatient and turning away.

II

He had of course before long to meet the boy himself on it and to hear that practically everything was settled. Lance was not to go up again, but to go instead to Paris where, since the die was cast, he would find the best advantages. Peter had always felt he must be taken as he was, but had never perhaps found him so much of that pattern as on this occasion. "You chuck Cambridge then altogether? Doesn't that seem rather a pity?"

Lance would have been like his father, to his friend's sense, had he had less humour, and like his mother had he had more beauty. Yet it was a good middle way for Peter that, in the modern manner, he was, to the eye, rather the young stock-broker than the young artist. The youth reasoned that it was a question of time—there was such a mill to go through, such an awful lot to learn. He had talked with fellows and had judged. "One has got, to-day," he said, "don't you see? to know."

His interlocutor, at this, gave a groan. "Oh hang it, *don't* know!"

Lance wondered. "'Don't'? Then what's the use—?"

"The use of what?"

"Why of anything. Don't you think I've talent?"

Peter smoked away for a little in silence; then went on: "It isn't knowledge, it's ignorance that—as we've been beautifully told—is bliss."

"Don't you think I've talent?" Lance repeated.

Peter, with his trick of queer kind demonstrations, passed his arm round his godson and held him a moment. "How do I know?"

"Oh," said the boy, "if it's your own ignorance you're defending—!"

Again, for a pause, on the sofa, his godfather smoked. "It isn't. I've the misfortune to be omniscient."

"Oh well," Lance laughed again, "if you know *too* much—!"

"That's what I do, and it's why I'm so wretched."

Lance's gaiety grew. "Wretched? Come, I say!"

"But I forgot," his companion went on—"you're not to know about that. It would indeed for you too make the too much. Only I'll tell you what I'll do." And Peter got up from the sofa. "If you'll go up again I'll pay your way at Cambridge."

Lance stared, a little rueful in spite of being still more amused. "Oh Peter! You disapprove so of Paris?"

"Well, I'm afraid of it."

"Ah I see!"

"No, you don't see—yet. But you will—that is you would. And you mustn't." The young man thought more gravely. "But one's innocence, already—!"

"Is considerably damaged? Ah that won't matter," Peter persisted—"we'll patch it up here."

"Here? Then you want me to stay at home?"

Peter almost confessed to it. "Well, we're so right—we four together—just as we are. We're so safe. Come, don't spoil it."

The boy, who had turned to gravity, turned from this, on the real pressure in his friend's tone, to consternation. "Then what's a fellow to be?"

"My particular care. Come, old man"—and Peter now fairly pleaded—"*I'll* look out for you."

Lance, who had remained on the sofa with his legs out and his hands in his pockets, watched him with eyes that showed suspicion. Then he got up. "You think there's something the matter with me—that I can't make a success."

"Well, what do you call a success?"

Lance thought again. "Why the best sort, I suppose, is to please one's self. Isn't that the sort that, in spite of cabals and things, is—in his own peculiar line—the Master's?"

There were so much too many things in this question to be answered at once that they practically checked the discussion, which became particularly difficult in the light of such renewed proof that, though the young man's innocence might, in the course of his studies, as he contended, somewhat have shrunken, the finer essence of it still remained. That was indeed exactly what Peter had assumed and what above all he desired; yet perversely enough it gave him a chill. The boy believed in the cabals and things, believed in the peculiar line, believed, to be brief, in the Master. What happened a month or two later wasn't that he went up again at the expense of his godfather, but that a fortnight after he had got settled in Paris this personage sent him fifty pounds.

He had meanwhile at home, this personage, made up his mind to the worst; and what that might be had never yet grown quite so vivid to him as when, on his presenting himself one Sunday night, as he never failed to do, for supper, the mistress of Carrara Lodge met him with an appeal as to—of all things in the world—the wealth of the Canadians. She was earnest, she was even excited. "Are many of them *really* rich?"

He had to confess he knew nothing about them, but he often thought afterwards of that evening. The room in which they sat was adorned with sundry specimens of the Master's genius, which had the merit of being, as Mrs. Mallow herself frequently suggested, of an unusually convenient size. They were indeed of dimensions not customary in the products of the chisel, and they had the singularity that, if the objects and features intended to be small looked too large, the objects and features intended to be large looked too small. The Master's idea, either in respect to this matter or to any other, had in almost any case, even after years, remained undiscoverable to Peter Brench. The creations that so failed to reveal it stood about on pedestals and brackets, on tables and shelves, a little staring white population, heroic, idyllic, allegoric, mythic, symbolic, in which "scale" had so strayed and lost itself that the public square and the chimney-piece seemed to have changed places, the monumental being all diminutive and the diminutive all monumental; branches at any rate, markedly, of a family in which stature was rather oddly irrespective of function, age and sex. They formed, like the Mallows themselves, poor Brench's own family—having at least to such a degree the note of familiarity. The occasion was one of those he had long ago learnt to know and to name—short flickers of the faint flame, soft gusts of a kinder air. Twice a year regularly the Master believed in his fortune, in addition to believing all the year round in his genius. This time it was to be made by a bereaved couple from Toronto, who had given him the handsomest order for a tomb to three lost children, each of whom they desired to see, in the composition, emblematically and characteristically represented.

Such was naturally the moral of Mrs. Mallow's question: if their wealth was to be assumed, it was clear, from the nature of their admiration, as well as from mysterious hints thrown out (they were a little odd!) as to other possibilites of the same mortuary sort, that their further patronage might be; and not less evident that should the Master become at all known in those climes nothing would be more inevitable than a run of Canadian custom. Peter had been present before at runs of custom, colonial and domestic—present at each of those of which the aggregation had left so few gaps in the marble company round him; but it was his habit never at these junctures to prick the bubble in advance. The fond illusion, while it lasted, eased the wound of elections never won, the long ache of medals and diplomas carried off, on every chance, by every one but the Master; it moreover lighted the lamp that would glimmer through the next eclipse. They lived, however, after all—as it was always beautiful to see—at a height scarce susceptible of ups and downs. They strained a point at times charmingly, strained it to admit that the public was here and there not too bad to buy; but they would have been nowhere without their attitude that the Master was always too good to sell. They were at all events deliciously formed, Peter often said to himself, for their fate; the Master had a vanity, his wife had a loyalty, of which success, depriving these things of innocence, would have diminished the merit and the grace. Any one could be charming under a charm, and as he looked about him at a world of prosperity more void of proportion even than the Master's museum he wondered if he knew another pair that so completely escaped vulgarity.

"What a pity Lance isn't with us to rejoice!" Mrs. Mallow on this occasion sighed at supper.

"We'll drink to the health of the absent," her husband replied, filling his friend's glass and his own and giving a drop to their companion; "but we must hope he's preparing himself for a happiness much less like this of ours this evening—excusable as I grant it to be!—than like the comfort we have always (whatever has happened or has not happened) been able to trust our-selves to enjoy. The comfort," the Master explained, leaning back in the pleas-ant lamplight and firelight, holding up his glass and looking round at his marble family, quartered more or less, a monstrous brood, in every room—"the com-fort of art in itself!"

Peter looked a little shyly at his wine. "Well—I don't care what you may call it when a fellow doesn't—but Lance must learn to *sell*, you know. I drink to his acquisition of the secret of a base popularity!"

"Oh yes, *he* must sell," the boy's mother, who was still more, however, this seemed to give out, the Master's wife, rather artlessly allowed.

"Ah," the sculptor after a moment confidently pronounced, "Lance *will*. Don't be afraid. He'll have learnt."

"Which is exactly what Peter," Mrs. Mallow gaily returned—"why in the world were you so perverse, Peter?—wouldn't when he told him hear of."

Peter, when this lady looked at him with accusatory affection—a grace on her part not infrequent—could never find a word; but the Master, who was always all amenity and tact, helped him out now as he had often helped him before. "That's his old idea, you know—on which we've so often differed: his theory that the artist should be all impulse and instinct. *I* go in of course for a certain amount of school. Not too much—but a due proportion. There's where his protest came in," he continued to explain to his wife, "as against what *might*, don't you see? be in question for Lance."

"Ah well"—and Mrs. Mallow turned the violet eyes across the table at the subject of this discourse—"he's sure to have meant of course nothing but good. Only what wouldn't have prevented him, if Lance *had* taken his advice, from being in effect horribly cruel."

They had a sociable way of talking of him to his face as if he had been in the clay or—at most—in the plaster, and the Master was unfailingly generous. He might have been waving Egidio to make him revolve. "Ah but poor Peter wasn't so wrong as to what it may after all come to that he *will* learn."

"Oh but nothing artistically bad," she urged—still, for poor Peter, arch and dewy.

"Why just the little French tricks," said the Master: on which their friend had to pretend to admit, when pressed by Mrs. Mallow, that these æsthetic vices had been the objects of his dread.

III

"I know now," Lance said to him the next year, "why you were so much against it." He had come back supposedly for a mere interval and was looking about him at Carrara Lodge, where indeed he had already on two or three occasions since his expatriation briefly reappeared. This had the air of a longer holiday. "Something rather awful has happened to me. It *isn't* so very good to know."

"I'm bound to say high spirits don't show in your face," Peter was rather ruefully forced to confess. "Still, are you very sure you do know?"

"Well, I at least know about as much as I can bear." These remarks were exchanged in Peter's den, and the young man, smoking cigarettes, stood before the fire with his back against the mantel. Something of his bloom seemed really to have left him.

Poor Peter wondered. "You're clear then as to what in particular I wanted you not to go for?"

"In particular?" Lance thought. "It seems to me that in particular there can have been only one thing."

They stood for a little sounding each other. "Are you quite sure?"

"Quite sure I'm a beastly duffer? Quite—by this time."

"Oh!"—and Peter turned away as if almost with relief.

"It's *that* that isn't pleasant to find out."

"Oh I don't care for 'that,' " said Peter, presently coming round again. "I mean I personally don't."

"Yet I hope you can understand a little that I myself should!"

"Well, what do you mean by it?" Peter sceptically asked.

And on this Lance had to explain—how the upshot of his studies in Paris had inexorably proved a more deep doubt of his means. These studies had so waked him up that a new light was in his eyes; but what the new light did was really to show him too much. "Do you know what's the matter with me? I'm too horribly intelligent. Paris was really the last place for me. I've learnt what I can't do."

Poor Peter stared—it was a staggerer; but even after they had had, on the subject, a longish talk in which the boy brought out to the full the hard truth of his lesson, his friend betrayed less pleasure than usually breaks into a face to the happy tune of "I told you so!" Poor Peter himself made now indeed so little a point of having told him so that Lance broke ground in a different place a day or two after. "What was it then that—before I went—you were afraid I should find out?" This, however, Peter refused to tell him—on the ground that if he hadn't yet guessed perhaps he never would, and that in any case nothing at all for either of them was to be gained by giving the thing a name. Lance eyed him on this an instant with the bold curiosity of youth—with the air indeed of having in his mind two or three names, of which one or other would be right. Peter nevertheless, turning his back again, offered no encouragement, and when they parted afresh it was with some show of impatience on the side of the boy. Accordingly on their next encounter Peter saw at a glance that he had now, in the interval, divined and that, to sound his note, he was only waiting till they should find themselves alone. This he had soon arranged and he then broke straight out. "Do you know your conundrum has been keeping me awake? But in the watches of the night the answer came over me—so that, upon my honour, I quite laughed out. Had you been supposing I had to go to Paris to learn *that?*" Even now, to see him still so sublimely on his guard, Peter's young friend had to laugh afresh. "You won't give a sign till you're sure? Beautiful old Peter!" But Lance at last produced it. "Why, hang it, the truth about the Master."

It made between them for some minutes a lively passage, full of wonder for each at the wonder of the other. "Then how long have you understood—"

"The true value of his work? I understood it," Lance recalled, "as soon as I began to understand anything. But I didn't begin fully to do that, I admit, till I got *là-bas*."[6]

"Dear, dear!"—Peter gasped with retrospective dread.

"But for what have you taken me? I'm a hopeless muff—that I *had* to have rubbed in. But I'm not such a muff as the Master!" Lance declared.

"Then why did you never tell me—?"

"That I hadn't, after all"—the boy took him up—"remained such an idiot?

---

[6] Over there.

Just because I never dreamed *you* knew. But I beg your pardon. I only wanted to spare you. And what I don't now understand is how the deuce then for so long you've managed to keep bottled."

Peter produced his explanation, but only after some delay and with a gravity not void of embarrassment. "It was for your mother."

"Oh!" said Lance.

"And that's the great thing now—since the murder *is* out. I want a promise from you. I mean"—and Peter almost feverishly followed it up—"a vow from you, solemn and such as you owe me here on the spot, that you'll sacrifice anything rather than let her ever guess—"

"That *I've* guessed?"—Lance took it in. "I see." He evidently after a moment had taken in much. "But what is it you've in mind that I may have a chance to sacrifice?"

"Oh one has always something."

Lance looked at him hard. "Do you mean that *you've* had—?" The look he received back, however, so put the question by that he found soon enough another. "Are you really sure my mother doesn't know?"

Peter, after renewed reflexion, was really sure. "If she does she's too wonderful."

"But aren't we all too wonderful?"

"Yes," Peter granted—"but in different ways. The thing's so desperately important because your father's little public consists only, as you know then," Peter developed—"well, of how many?"

"First of all," the Master's son risked, "of himself. And last of all too. I don't quite see of whom else."

Peter had an approach to impatience. "Of your mother, I say—*always.*"

Lance cast it all up. "You absolutely feel that?"

"Absolutely."

"Well then with yourself that makes three."

"Oh *me!*"—and Peter, with a wag of his kind old head, modestly excused himself. "The number's at any rate small enough for any individual dropping out to be too dreadfully missed. Therefore, to put it in a nutshell, take care, my boy—that's all—that *you're* not!"

"I've got to keep on humbugging?" Lance wailed.

"It's just to warn you of the danger of your failing of that that I've seized this opportunity."

"And what do you regard in particular," the young man asked, "as the danger?"

"Why this certainty: that the moment your mother, who feels so strongly, should suspect your secret—well," said Peter desperately, "the fat would be on the fire."

Lance for a moment seemed to stare at the blaze. "She'd throw me over?"

"She'd throw *him* over."

"And come round to us?"

Peter, before he answered, turned away. "Come round to *you.*" But he had said enough to indicate—and, as he evidently trusted, to avert—the horrid contingency.

IV

Within six months again, none the less, his fear was on more occasions than one all before him. Lance had returned to Paris for another trial; then had reappeared at home and had had, with his father, for the first time in his life, one of the scenes that strike sparks. He described it with much expression to Peter, touching whom (since they had never done so before) it was the sign of a new reserve on the part of the pair at Carrara Lodge that they at present failed, on a matter of intimate interest, to open themselves—if not in joy then in sorrow—to their good friend. This produced perhaps practically between the parties a shade of alienation and a slight intermission of commerce—marked mainly indeed by the fact that to talk at his ease with his old playmate Lance had in general to come to see him. The closest if not quite the gayest relation they had yet known together was thus ushered in. The difficulty for poor Lance was a tension at home—begotten by the fact that his father wished him to be at least the sort of success he himself had been. He hadn't "chucked" Paris—though nothing appeared more vivid to him than that Paris had chucked him: he would go back again because of the fascination of trying, in seeing, in sounding the depths—in learning one's lesson, briefly, even if the lesson were simply that of one's impotence in the presence of one's larger vision. But what did the Master, all aloft in his senseless fluency, know of impotence, and what vision—to be called such—had he in all his blind life ever had? Lance, heated and indignant, frankly appealed to his godparent on this score.

His father, it appeared, had come down on him for having, after so long, nothing to show, and hoped that on his next return this deficiency would be repaired. *The* thing, the Master complacently set forth was—for any artist, however inferior to himself—at least to "do" something. "What can you do? That's all I ask!" *He* had certainly done enough, and there was no mistake about what he had to show. Lance had tears in his eyes when it came thus to letting his old friend know how great the strain might be on the "sacrifice" asked of him. It wasn't so easy to continue humbugging—as from son to parent— after feeling one's self despised for not grovelling in mediocrity. Yet a noble duplicity was what, as they intimately faced the situation, Peter went on requiring; and it was still for a time what his young friend, bitter and sore, managed loyally to comfort him with. Fifty pounds more than once again, it was true, rewarded both in London and in Paris the young friend's loyalty; none the less sensibly, doubtless, at the moment, that the money was a direct advance on a decent sum for which Peter had long since privately prearranged an ultimate function. Whether by these arts or others, at all events, Lance's just resentment was kept for a season—but only for a season—at bay. The day arrived when he warned his companion that he could hold out—or hold in— no longer. Carrara Lodge had had to listen to another lecture delivered from a great height—an infliction really heavier at last than, without striking back or in some way letting the Master have the truth, flesh and blood could bear.

"And what I don't see is," Lance observed with a certain irritated eye for what was after all, if it came to that, owing to himself too; "what I don't see is, upon my honour, how *you*, as things are going, can keep the game up."

"Oh the game for me is only to hold my tongue," said placid Peter. "And I have my reason."

"Still my mother?"

Peter showed a queer face as he had often shown it before—that is by turning it straight away. "What will you have? I haven't ceased to like her."

"She's beautiful—she's a dear of course," Lance allowed; "but what is she to you, after all, and what is it to you that, as to anything whatever, she should or she shouldn't?"

Peter, who had turned red, hung fire a little. "Well—it's all simply what I make of it."

There was now, however, in his young friend a strange, an adopted insistence. "What are you after all to *her?*"

"Oh nothing. But that's another matter."

"She cares only for my father," said Lance the Parisian.

"Naturally—and that's just why."

"Why you've wished to spare her?"

"Because she cares so tremendously much."

Lance took a turn about the room, but with his eyes still on his host. "How awfully—always—you must have liked her!"

"Awfully. Always," said Peter Brench.

The young man continued for a moment to muse—then stopped again in front of him. "Do you know how much she cares?" Their eyes met on it, but Peter, as if his own found something new in Lance's, appeared to hesistate, for the first time in an age, to say he did know. "*I've* only just found out," said Lance. "She came to my room last night, after being present, in silence and only with her eyes on me, at what I had had to take from him: she came—and she was with me an extraordinary hour."

He had paused again and they had again for a while sounded each other. Then something—and it made him suddenly turn pale—came to Peter. "She *does* know?"

"She does know. She let it all out to me—so as to demand of me no more than 'that,' as she said, of which she herself had been capable. She has always, always known," said Lance without pity.

Peter was silent a long time; during which his companion might have heard him gently breathe, and on touching him might have felt within him the vibration of a long low sound suppressed. By the time he spoke at last he had taken everything in. "Then I do see how tremendously much."

"Isn't it wonderful?" Lance asked.

"Wonderful," Peter mused.

"So that if your original effort to keep me from Paris was to keep me from knowledge—!" Lance exclaimed as if with a sufficient indication of this futility.

It might have been at the futility Peter appeared for a little to gaze. "I think it must have been—without my quite at the time knowing it—to keep *me!*" he replied at last as he turned away.

[1900]

James Joyce   *1882–1941*

ARABY

North Richmond Street, being blind, was a quiet street except at the hour when the Christian Brothers' School[1] set the boys free. An uninhabited house of two storeys stood at the blind end, detached from its neighbours in a square ground. The other houses of the street, conscious of decent lives within them, gazed at one another with brown imperturbable faces.

The former tenant of our house, a priest, had died in the back drawing-room. Air, musty from having been long enclosed, hung in all the rooms, and the waste room behind the kitchen was littered with old useless papers. Among these I found a few paper-covered books, the pages of which were curled and damp: *The Abbot,* by Walter Scott, *The Devout Communicant* and *The Memoirs of Vidocq.*[2] I liked the last best because its leaves were yellow. The wild garden behind the house contained a central apple-tree and a few straggling bushes under one of which I found the late tenant's rusty bicycle-pump. He had been a very charitable priest; in his will he had left all his money to institutions and the furniture of his house to his sister.

When the short days of winter came dusk fell before we had well eaten our dinners. When we met in the street the houses had grown sombre. The space of sky above us was the colour of ever-changing violet and towards it the lamps of the street lifted their feeble lanterns. The cold air stung us and we played till our bodies glowed. Our shouts echoed in the silent street. The career of our play brought us through the dark muddy lanes behind the houses where we ran the gauntlet of the rough tribes from the cottages, to the back doors of the dark dripping gardens where odours arose from the ashpits, to the dark odorous stables where a coachman smoothed and combed the horse or shook music from the buckled harness. When we returned to the street light from the kitchen windows had filled the areas. If my uncle was seen turning the corner we hid in the shadow until we had seen him safely housed. Or if Mangan's sister came out on the doorstep to call her brother in to his tea we watched her from our shadow peer up and down the street. We waited to see whether she would remain or go in and, if she remained, we left our shadow and walked up to Mangan's steps resignedly. She was waiting for us, her figure defined by the light from the half-opened door. Her brother always teased her before he obeyed and I stood by the railings looking at her. Her dress swung as she moved her body and the soft rope of her hair tossed from side to side.

Every morning I lay on the floor in the front parlour watching her door. The blind was pulled down to within an inch of the sash so that I could not be seen. When she came out on the doorstep my heart leaped. I ran to the hall, seized my books and followed her. I kept her brown figure always in my eye and, when we came near the point at which our ways diverged, I quick-

---

[1] A famous Catholic day school in Dublin.

[2] *The Abbot* (1820) by Sir Walter Scott (1771–1832) is an historical romance about Mary Queen of Scots; *The Devout Communicant* (1813) is a Catholic guide to "pious meditations" by Friar Pacificus Baker (1695–1774); *The Memoirs of Vidocq* (1829) traces the career of François-Jules Vidocq (1775–1857), a French criminal-turned-detective.

ened my pace and passed her. This happened morning after morning. I had never spoken to her, except for a few casual words, and yet her name was like a summons to all my foolish blood.

Her image accompanied me even in places the most hostile to romance. On Saturday evenings when my aunt went marketing I had to go to carry some of the parcels. We walked through the flaring streets, jostled by drunken men and bargaining women, amid the curses of labourers, the shrill litanies of shop-boys who stood on guard by the barrels of pigs' cheeks, the nasal chanting of street-singers, who sang a *come-all-you*[3] about O'Donovan Rossa,[4] or a ballad about the troubles in our native land. These noises converged in a single sensation of life for me: I imagined that I bore my chalice safely through a throng of foes. Her name sprang to my lips at moments in strange prayers and praises which I myself did not understand. My eyes were often full of tears (I could not tell why) and at times a flood from my heart seemed to pour itself out into my bosom. I thought little of the future. I did not know whether I would ever speak to her or not or, if I spoke to her, how I could tell her of my confused adoration. But my body was like a harp and her words and gestures were like fingers running upon the wires.

One evening I went into the back drawing-room in which the priest had died. It was a dark rainy evening and there was no sound in the house. Through one of the broken panes I heard the rain impinge upon the earth, the fine incessant needles of water playing in the sodden beds. Some distant lamp or lighted window gleamed below me. I was thankful that I could see so little. All my senses seemed to desire to veil themselves and, feeling that I was about to slip from them, I pressed the palms of my hands together until they trembled, murmuring: *"O love! O love!"* many times.

At last she spoke to me. When she addressed the first words to me I was so confused that I did not know what to answer. She asked me was I going to *Araby*. I forgot whether I answered yes or no. It would be a splendid bazaar, she said she would love to go.

"And why can't you?" I asked.

While she spoke she turned a silver bracelet round and round her wrist. She could not go, she said, because there would be a retreat that week in her convent. Her brother and two other boys were fighting for their caps and I was alone at the railings. She held one of the spikes, bowing her head towards me. The light from the lamp opposite our door caught the white curve of her neck, lit up her hair that rested there and, falling, lit up the hand upon the railing. It fell over one side of her dress and caught the white border of a petticoat, just visible as she stood at ease.

"It's well for you," she said.

"If I go," I said, "I will bring you something."

What innumerable follies laid waste my waking and sleeping thoughts after that evening! I wished to annihilate the tedious intervening days. I chafed against the work of school. At night in my bedroom and by day in the classroom her image came between me and the page I strove to read. The syllables of the word *Araby* were called to me through the silence in which my soul luxuriated and cast an Eastern enchantment over me. I asked for leave to go to the

---

[3] One of any number of popular street songs on a topical subject beginning "Come all you . . . ."

[4] Refers to Jeremiah O'Donovan (1831–1915), a leader in Ireland's struggle for independence, whose activities earned him the nickname "Dynamite Rossa."

bazaar on Saturday night. My aunt was surprised and hoped it was not some Freemason[5] affair. I answered few questions in class. I watched my master's face pass from amiability to sternness; he hoped I was not beginning to idle. I could not call my wandering thoughts together. I had hardly any patience with the serious work of life which, now that it stood between me and my desire, seemed to me child's play, ugly monotonous child's play.

On Saturday morning I reminded my uncle that I wished to go to the bazaar in the evening. He was fussing at the hallstand, looking for the hat-brush, and answered me curtly:

"Yes, boy, I know."

As he was in the hall I could not go into the front parlour and lie at the window. I left the house in bad humour and walked slowly towards the school. The air was pitilessly raw and already my heart misgave me.

When I came home to dinner my uncle had not yet been home. Still it was early. I sat staring at the clock for some time and, when its ticking began to irritate me, I left the room. I mounted the staircase and gained the upper part of the house. The high cold empty gloomy rooms liberated me and I went from room to room singing. From the front window I saw my companions playing below in the street. Their cries reached me weakened and indistinct and, leaning my forehead against the cool glass, I looked over at the dark house where she lived. I may have stood there for an hour, seeing nothing but the brown-clad figure cast by my imagination, touched discreetly by the lamplight at the curved neck, at the hand upon the railings and at the border below the dress.

When I came downstairs again I found Mrs. Mercer sitting at the fire. She was an old garrulous woman, a pawnbroker's widow, who collected used stamps for some pious purpose. I had to endure the gossip of the tea-table. The meal was prolonged beyond an hour and still my uncle did not come. Mrs. Mercer stood up to go: she was sorry she couldn't wait any longer, but it was after eight o'clock and she did not like to be out late, as the night air was bad for her. When she had gone I began to walk up and down the room, clenching my fists. My aunt said:

"I'm afraid you may put off your bazaar for this night of Our Lord."

At nine o'clock I heard my uncle's latchkey in the halldoor. I heard him talking to himself and heard the hallstand rocking when it had received the weight of his overcoat. I could interpret these signs. When he was midway through his dinner I asked him to give me the money to go to the bazaar. He had forgotten.

"The people are in bed and after their first sleep now," he said.

I did not smile. My aunt said to him energetically:

"Can't you give him the money and let him go? You've kept him late enough as it is."

My uncle said he was very sorry he had forgotten. He said he believed in the old saying: "All work and no play makes Jack a dull boy." He asked me where I was going and, when I had told him a second time he asked me did I know *The Arab's Farewell to his Steed.*[6] When I left the kitchen he was about to recite the opening lines of the piece to my aunt.

I held a florin[7] tightly in my hand as I strode down Buckingham Street

---

[5] A Protestant fraternal organization.
[6] A poem by the English poet-novelist Caroline Norton (1808–1877).
[7] Two shillings; a shilling was until recently one-twentieth of a British pound.

towards the station. The sight of the streets thronged with buyers and glaring with gas recalled to me the purpose of my journey. I took my seat in a third-class carriage of a deserted train. After an intolerable delay the train moved out of the station slowly. It crept onward among ruinous houses and over the twinkling river. At Westland Row Station a crowd of people pressed to the carriage doors; but the porters moved them back, saying that it was a special train for the bazaar. I remained alone in the bare carriage. In a few minutes the train drew up beside an improvised wooden platform. I passed out on to the road and saw by the lighted dial of a clock that it was ten minutes to ten. In front of me was a large building which displayed the magical name.

I could not find any sixpenny entrance and, fearing that the bazaar would be closed, I passed in quickly through a turnstile, handing a shilling to a weary-looking man. I found myself in a big hall girdled at half its height by a gallery. Nearly all the stalls were closed and the greater part of the hall was in darkness. I recognised a silence like that which pervades a church after a service. I walked into the centre of the bazaar timidly. A few people were gathered about the stalls which were still open. Before a curtain, over which the words *Café Chantant*[8] were written in coloured lamps, two men were counting money on a salver. I listened to the fall of the coins.

Remembering with difficulty why I had come I went over to one of the stalls and examined porcelain vases and flowered tea-sets. At the door of the stall a young lady was talking and laughing with two young gentlemen. I remarked their English accents and listened vaguely to their conversation.

"O, I never said such a thing!"

"O, but you did!"

"O, but I didn't!"

"Didn't she say that?"

"Yes. I heard her."

"O, there's a . . . fib!"

Observing me the young lady came over and asked me did I wish to buy anything. The tone of her voice was not encouraging; she seemed to have spoken to me out of a sense of duty. I looked humbly at the great jars that stood like eastern guards at either side of the dark entrance to the stall and murmured:

"No, thank you."

The young lady changed the position of one of the vases and went back to the two young men. They began to talk of the same subject. Once or twice the young lady glanced at me over her shoulder.

I lingered before her stall, though I knew my stay was useless, to make my interest in her wares seem the more real. Then I turned away slowly and walked down the middle of the bazaar. I allowed the two pennies to fall against the sixpence in my pocket. I heard a voice call from one end of the gallery that the light was out. The upper part of the hall was now completely dark.

Gazing up into the darkness I saw myself as a creature driven and derided by vanity; and my eyes burned with anguish and anger.

[1914]

---

[8] Concert coffee house.

Sherwood Anderson   *1876–1941*

I WANT TO KNOW WHY

We got up at four in the morning, that first day in the east. On the evening before we had climbed off a freight train at the edge of town, and with the true instinct of Kentucky boys had found our way across town and to the race track and the stables at once. Then we knew we were all right. Hanley Turner right away found a nigger we knew. It was Bildad Johnson who in the winter works at Ed Becker's livery barn in our home town, Beckersville. Bildad is a good cook as almost all our niggers are and of course he, like everyone in our part of Kentucky who is anyone at all, likes the horses. In the spring Bildad begins to scratch around. A nigger from our country can flatter and wheedle anyone into letting him do most anything he wants. Bildad wheedles the stable men and the trainers from the horse farms in our country around Lexington. The trainers come into town in the evening to stand around and talk and maybe get into a poker game. Bildad gets in with them. He is always doing little favors and telling about things to eat, chicken browned in a pan, and how is the best way to cook sweet potatoes and corn bread. It makes your mouth water to hear him.

When the racing season comes on and the horses go to the races and there is all the talk on the streets in the evenings about the new colts, and everyone says when they are going over to Lexington or to the spring meeting at Churchill Downs or to Latonia,[1] and the horsemen that have been down to New Orleans or maybe at the winter meeting at Havana in Cuba come home to spend a week before they start out again, at such a time when everything talked about in Beckersville is just horses and nothing else and the outfits start out and horse racing is in every breath of air you breathe, Bildad shows up with a job as cook for some outfit. Often when I think about it, his always going all season to the races and working in the livery barn in the winter where horses are and where men like to come and talk about horses, I wish I was a nigger. It's a foolish thing to say, but that's the way I am about being around horses, just crazy. I can't help it.

Well, I must tell you about what we did and let you in on what I'm talking about. Four of us boys from Beckersville, all whites and sons of men who live in Beckersville regular, made up our minds we were going to the races, not just to Lexington or Louisville, I don't mean, but to the big eastern track we were always hearing our Beckersville men talk about, to Saratoga. We were all pretty young then. I was just turned fifteen and I was the oldest of the four. It was my scheme. I admit that and I talked the others into trying it. There was Hanley Turner and Henry Rieback and Tom Tumberton and myself. I had thirty-seven dollars I had earned during the winter working nights and Saturdays in Enoch Myer's grocery. Henry Rieback had eleven dollars and the others, Hanley and Tom had only a dollar or two each. We fixed it all up and laid low until the Kentucky spring meetings were over and some of

---

[1] Keeneland at Lexington, Churchill Downs at Louisville, and Latonia at Florence are three famous Kentucky race tracks. Saratoga, referred to later, is a race track located at Saratoga Springs, New York.

our men, the sportiest ones, the ones we envied the most, had cut out—then we cut out too.

I won't tell you the trouble we had beating our way on freights and all. We went through Cleveland and Buffalo and other cities and saw Niagara Falls. We bought things there, souvenirs and spoons and cards and shells with pictures of the falls on them for our sisters and mothers, but thought we had better not send any of the things home. We didn't want to put the folks on our trail and maybe be nabbed.

We got into Saratoga as I said at night and went to the track. Bildad fed us up. He showed us a place to sleep in hay over a shed and promised to keep still. Niggers are all right about things like that. They won't squeal on you. Often a white man you might meet, when you had run away from home like that, might appear to be all right and give you a quarter or a half dollar or something, and then go right and give you away. White men will do that, but not a nigger. You can trust them. They are squarer with kids. I don't know why.

At the Saratoga meeting that year there were a lot of men from home. Dave Williams and Arthur Mulford and Jerry Myers and others. Then there was a lot from Louisville and Lexington Henry Rieback knew but I didn't. They were professional gamblers and Henry Rieback's father is one too. He is what is called a sheet writer and goes away most of the year to tracks. In the winter when he is home in Beckersville he don't stay there much but goes away to cities and deals faro. He is a nice man and generous, is always sending Henry presents, a bicycle and a gold watch and a boy scout suit of clothes and things like that.

My own father is a lawyer. He's all right, but don't make much money and can't buy me things and anyway I'm getting so old now I don't expect it. He never said nothing to me against Henry, but Hanley Turner and Tom Tumberton's fathers did. They said to their boys that money so come by is no good and they didn't want their boys brought up to hear gambler's talk and be thinking about such things and maybe embrace them.

That's all right and I guess the men know what they are talking about, but I don't see what it's got to do with Henry or with horses either. That's what I'm writing this story about. I'm puzzled. I'm getting to be a man and want to think straight and be O. K., and there's something I saw at the race meeting at the eastern tract I can't figure out.

I can't help it, I'm crazy about thoroughbred horses. I've always been that way. When I was ten years old and saw I was growing to be big and couldn't be a rider I was so sorry I nearly died. Harry Hellinfinger in Beckersville, whose father is Postmaster, is grown up and too lazy to work, but likes to stand around in the street and get up jokes on boys like sending them to a hardware store for a gimlet to bore square holes and other jokes like that. He played one on me. He told me that if I would eat a half a cigar I would be stunted and not grow any more and maybe could be a rider. I did it. When father wasn't looking I took a cigar out of his pocket and gagged it down some way. It made me awful sick and the doctor had to be sent for, and then it did no good. I kept right on growing. It was a joke. When I told what I had done and why most fathers would have whipped me but mine didn't.

Well, I didn't get stunted and didn't die. It serves Harry Hellinfinger right. Then I made up my mind I would like to be a stable boy, but had to give that up too. Mostly niggers do that work and I knew father wouldn't let me go into it. No use to ask him.

If you've never been crazy about thoroughbreds it's because you've never been around where they are much and don't know any better. They're beautiful. There isn't anything so lovely and clean and full of spunk and honest and everything as some race horses. On the big horse farms that are all around our town Beckersville there are tracks and the horses run in the early morning. More than a thousand times I've got out of bed before daylight and walked two or three miles to the tracks. Mother wouldn't of let me go but father always says, "Let him alone." So I got some bread out of the bread box and some butter and jam, gobbled it and lit out.

At the tracks you sit on the fence with men, whites and niggers, and they chew tobacco and talk, and then the colts are brought out. It's early and the grass is covered with shiny dew and in another field a man is plowing and they are frying things in a shed where the track niggers sleep, and you know how a nigger can giggle and laugh and say things that make you laugh. A white man can't do it and some niggers can't but a track nigger can every time.

And so the colts are brought out and some are just galloped by stable boys, but almost every morning on a big track owned by a rich man who lives maybe in New York, there are always, nearly every morning, a few colts and some of the old race horses and geldings and mares that are cut loose.

It brings a lump up into my throat when a horse runs. I don't mean all horses but some. I can pick them nearly every time. It's in my blood like in the blood of race track niggers and trainers. Even when they just go slop-jogging along with a little nigger on their backs I can tell a winner. If my throat hurts and it's hard for me to swallow, that's him. He'll run like Sam Hill when you let him out. If he don't win every time it'll be a wonder and because they've got him in a pocket behind another or he was pulled or got off bad at the post or something. If I wanted to be a gambler like Henry Rieback's father I could get rich. I know I could and Henry says so too. All I would have to do is to wait 'til that hurt comes when I see a horse and then bet every cent. That's what I would do if I wanted to be a gambler, but I don't.

When you're at the tracks in the morning—not the race tracks but the training tracks around Beckersville—you don't see a horse, the kind I've been talking about, very often, but it's nice anyway. Any thoroughbred, that is sired right and out of a good mare and trained by a man that knows how, can run. If he couldn't what would he be there for and not pulling a plow?

Well, out of the stables they come and the boys are on their backs and it's lovely to be there. You hunch down on top of the fence and itch inside you. Over in the sheds the niggers giggle and sing. Bacon is being fried and coffee made. Everything smells lovely. Nothing smells better than coffee and manure and horses and niggers and bacon frying and pipes being smoked out of doors on a morning like that. It just gets you, that's what it does.

But about Saratoga. We was there six days and not a soul from home seen us and everything came off just as we wanted it to, fine weather and horses and races and all. We beat our way home and Bildad gave us a basket with fried chicken and bread and other eatables in, and I had eighteen dollars when we got back to Beckersville. Mother jawed and cried but Pop didn't say much. I told everything we done except one thing. I did and saw that alone. That's what I'm writing about. It got me upset. I think about it at night. Here it is.

At Saratoga we laid up nights in the hay in the shed Bildad had showed us and ate with the niggers early and at night when the race people had all gone away. The men from home stayed mostly in the grandstand and betting field, and didn't come out around the places where the horses are kept except to the paddocks just before a race when the horses are saddled. At Saratoga they don't have paddocks under an open shed as at Lexington and Churchill Downs and other tracks down in our country, but saddle the horses right out in an open place under trees on a lawn as smooth and nice as Banker Bohon's front yard here in Beckersville. It's lovely. The horses are sweaty and nervous and shine and the men come out and smoke cigars and look at them and the trainers are there and the owners, and your heart thumps so you can hardly breathe.

Then the bugle blows for post and the boys that ride come running out with their silk clothes on and you run to get a place by the fence with the niggers.

I always am wanting to be a trainer or owner, and at the risk of being seen and caught and sent home I went to the paddocks before every race. The other boys didn't but I did.

We got to Saratoga on a Friday and on Wednesday the next week the big Mullford Handicap was to be run. Middlestride was in it and Sunstreak. The weather was fine and the track fast. I couldn't sleep the night before.

What had happened was that both these horses are the kind it makes my throat hurt to see. Middlestride is long and looks awkward and is a gelding. He belongs to Joe Thompson, a little owner from home who only has a half dozen horses. The Mullford Handicap is for a mile and Middlestride can't untrack fast. He goes away slow and is always way back at the half, then he begins to run and if the race is a mile and a quarter he'll just eat up everything and get there.

Sunstreak is different. He is a stallion and nervous and belongs on the biggest farm we've got in our country, the Van Riddle place that belongs to Mr. Van Riddle of New York. Sunstreak is like a girl you think about sometimes but never see. He is hard all over and lovely too. When you look at his head you want to kiss him. He is trained by Jerry Tillford who knows me and has been good to me lots of times, lets me walk into a horse's stall to look at him close and other things. There isn't anything as sweet as that horse. He stands at the post quiet and not letting on, but he is just burning up inside. Then when the barrier goes up he is off like his name, Sunstreak. It makes you ache to see him. It hurts you. He just lays down and runs like a bird dog. There can't anything I ever see run like him except Middlestride when he gets untracked and stretches himself.

Gee! I ached to see that race and those two horses run, ached and dreaded it too. I didn't want to see either of our horses beaten. We had never sent a pair like that to the races before. Old men in Beckersville said so and the niggers said so. It was a fact.

Before the race I went over to the paddocks to see. I looked a last look at Middlestride, who isn't such a much standing in a paddock that way, then I went to see Sunstreak.

It was his day. I knew when I see him. I forgot all about being seen myself and walked right up. All the men from Beckersville were there and no one noticed me except Jerry Tillford. He saw me and something happened. I'll tell you about that.

I was standing looking at that horse and aching. In some way, I can't tell how, I knew just how Sunstreak felt inside. He was quiet and letting the niggers rub his legs and Mr. Van Riddle himself put the saddle on, but he was just a raging torrent inside. He was like the water in the river at Niagara Falls just before its goes plunk down. That horse wasn't thinking about running. He don't have to think about that. He was just thinking about holding himself back 'til the time for the running came. I knew that. I could just in a way see right inside him. He was going to do some awful running and I knew it. He wasn't bragging or letting on much or prancing or making a fuss, but just waiting. I knew it and Jerry Tillford his trainer knew. I looked up and then that man and I looked into each other's eyes. Something happened to me. I guessed I loved the man as much as I did the horse because he knew what I knew. Seemed to me there wasn't anything in the world but that man and the horse and me. I cried and Jerry Tillford had a shine in his eyes. Then I came away to the fence to wait for the race. The horse was better than me, or steadier, and now I know better than Jerry. He was the quietest and he had to do the running.

Sunstreak ran first of course and he busted the world's record for a mile. I've seen that if I never see anything more. Everything came out just as I expected. Middlestride got left at the post and was way back and closed up to be second, just as I knew he would. He'll get a world's record too some day. They can't skin the Beckersville country on horses.

I watched the race calm because I knew what would happen. I was sure. Hanley Turner and Henry Rieback and Tom Tumberton were all more excited than me.

A funny thing had happened to me. I was thinking about Jerry Tillford the trainer and how happy he was all through the race. I liked him that afternoon even more than I ever liked my own father. I almost forgot the horses thinking that way about him. It was because of what I had seen in his eyes as he stood in the paddocks beside Sunstreak before the race started. I knew he had been watching and working with Sunstreak since the horse was a baby colt, had taught him to run and be patient and when to let himself out and not to quit, never. I knew that for him it was like a mother seeing her child do something brave or wonderful. It was the first time I ever felt for a man like that.

After the race that night I cut out from Tom and Hanley and Henry. I wanted to be by myself and I wanted to be near Jerry Tillford if I could work it. Here is what happened.

The track in Saratoga is near the edge of town. It is all polished up and trees around, the evergreen kind, and grass and everything painted and nice. If you go past the track you get to a hard road made of asphalt for automobiles, and if you go along this for a few miles there is a road turns off to a little rummy-looking farm house set in a yard.

That night after the race I went along that road because I had seen Jerry and some other men go that way in an automobile. I didn't expect to find them. I walked for a ways and then sat down by a fence to think. It was the direction they went in. I wanted to be as near Jerry as I could. I felt close to him. Pretty soon I went up the side road—I don't know why—and came to the rummy farm house. I was just lonesome to see Jerry, like wanting to see your father at night when you are a young kid. Just then an automobile came along and turned in. Jerry was in it and Henry Rieback's father, and Arthur Bedford from home, and Dave Williams and two other men I didn't know. They got out of the car and went into the house, all but Henry Rieback's father who quarreled with them and said he wouldn't go. It was only about nine o'clock, but they were all drunk and the rummy looking farm house was a place for bad women to stay in. That's what it was. I crept up along a fence and looked through a window and saw.

It's what give me the fantods. I can't make it out. The women in the house were all ugly mean-looking women, not nice to look at or be near. They were homely too, except one who was tall and looked a little like the gelding Middlestride, but not clean like him, but with a hard ugly mouth. She had red hair. I saw everything plain. I got up by an old rose bush by an open window and looked. The women had on loose dresses and sat around in chairs. The men came in and some sat on the women's laps. The place smelled rotten and there was rotten talk, the kind a kid hears around a livery stable in a town like Beckersville in the winter but don't ever expect to hear talked when there are women around. It was rotten. A nigger wouldn't go into such a place.

I looked at Jerry Tillford. I've told you how I had been feeling about him on account of his knowing what was going on inside of Sunstreak in the minute before he went to the post for the race in which he made a world's record.

Jerry bragged in that bad woman house as I know Sunstreak wouldn't never have bragged. He said that he made that horse, that it was him that won the race and made the record. He lied and bragged like a fool. I never heard such silly talk.

And then, what do you suppose he did! He looked at the woman in there, the one that was lean and hard-mouthed and looked a little like the gelding Middlestride, but not clean like him, and his eyes began to shine just as they did when he looked at me and at Sunstreak in the paddocks at the track in the afternoon. I stood there by the window—gee!—but I wished I hadn't gone away from the tracks, but had stayed with the boys and the niggers and the horses. The tall rotten looking woman was between us just as Sunstreak was in the paddocks in the afternoon.

Then, all of a sudden, I began to hate that man. I wanted to scream and rush in the room and kill him. I never had such a feeling before. I was so mad clean through that I cried and my fists were doubled up so my finger nails cut my hands.

And Jerry's eyes kept shining and he waved back and forth, and then he went and kissed that woman and I crept away and went back to the tracks and to bed and didn't sleep hardly any, and then next day I got the other kids to start home with me and never told them anything I seen.

I been thinking about it ever since. I can't make it out. Spring has come again and I'm nearly sixteen and go to the tracks mornings same as always, and I see Sunstreak and Middlestride and a new colt named Strident I'll bet will lay them all out, but no one thinks so but me and two or three niggers.

But things are different. At the tracks the air don't taste as good or smell as good. It's because a man like Jerry Tillford, who knows what he does, could see a horse like Sunstreak run, and kiss a woman like that the same day. I can't make it out. Darn him, what did he want to do like that for? I keep thinking about it and it spoils looking at horses and smelling things and hearing niggers laugh and everything. Sometimes I'm so mad about it I want to fight someone. It gives me the fantods. What did he do it for? I want to know why.

[1919]

Franz Kafka *1883–1924*

A HUNGER ARTIST*

During these last decades the interest in professional fasting has markedly diminished. It used to pay very well to stage such great performances under one's own management, but today that is quite impossible. We live in a different world now. At one time the whole town took a lively interest in the hunger artist; from day to day of his fast the excitement mounted; everybody wanted to see him at least once a day; there were people who bought season tickets for the last few days and sat from morning till night in front of his small barred cage; even in the nighttime there were visiting hours, when the whole effect was heightened by torch flares; on fine days the cage was set out in the open air, and then it was the children's special treat to see the hunger artist; for their elders he was often just a joke that happened to be in fashion, but the children stood openmouthed, holding each other's hands for greater security, marveling at him as he sat there pallid in black tights, with his ribs sticking out so prominently, not even on a seat but down among straw on the ground, sometimes giving a courteous nod, answering questions with a constrained smile, or perhaps stretching an arm through the bars so that one might feel how thin it was, and then again withdrawing deep into himself, paying no attention to anyone or anything, not even to the all-important striking of the clock that was the only piece of furniture in his cage, but merely staring into vacancy with half-shut eyes, now and then taking a sip from a tiny glass of water to moisten his lips.

Besides casual onlookers there were also relays of permanent watchers selected by the public, usually butchers, strangely enough, and it was their task to watch the hunger artist day and night, three of them at a time, in case he should have some secret recourse to nourishment. This was nothing but a formality, instituted to reassure the masses, for the initiates knew well enough that during his fast the artist would never in any circumstances, not even under the forcible compulsion, swallow the smallest morsel of food; the honor of his profession forbade it. Not every watcher, of course, was capable of understanding this, there were often groups of night watchers who were very lax in carrying out their duties and deliberately huddled together in a retired corner to play cards with great absorption, obviously intending to give the hunger artist the chance of a little refreshment, which they supposed he could draw from some private hoard. Nothing annoyed the artist more than such watchers; they made him miserable; they made his fast seem unendurable; sometimes he mastered his feebleness sufficiently to sing during their watch for as long as he could keep going, to show them how unjust their suspicions were. But that was of little use; they only wondered at his cleverness in being able to fill his mouth even while singing. Much more to his taste were the watchers who sat close up to the bars, who were not content with the dim night lighting of the hall but focused him in the full glare of the electric pocket torch given them by the impresario. The harsh light did not trouble him at all, in any case he could never sleep properly, and he could always drowse a

* Translated by Willa & Edwin Muir

little, whatever the light, at any hour, even when the hall was thronged with noisy onlookers. He was quite happy at the prospect of spending a sleepless night with such watchers; he was ready to exchange jokes with them, to tell them stories out of his nomadic life, anything at all to keep them awake and demonstrate to them again that he had no eatables in his cage and that he was fasting as not one of them could fast. But his happiest moment was when the morning came and an enormous breakfast was brought them, at his expense, on which they flung themselves with the keen appetite of healthy men after a weary night of wakefulness. Of course there were people who argued that this breakfast was an unfair attempt to bribe the watchers, but that was going rather too far, and when they were invited to take on a night's vigil without a breakfast, merely for the sake of the cause, they made themselves scarce, although they stuck stubbornly to their suspicions.

Such suspicions, anyhow, were a necessary accompaniment to the profession of fasting. No one could possibly watch the hunger artist continuously, day and night, and so no one could produce first-hand evidence that the fast had really been rigorous and continuous; only the artist himself could know that, he was therefore bound to be the sole completely satisfied spectator of his own fast. Yet for other reasons he was never satisfied; it was not perhaps mere fasting that had brought him to such skeleton thinness that many people had regretfully to keep away from his exhibitions, because the sight of him was too much for them, perhaps it was dissatisfaction with himself that had worn him down. For he alone knew, what no other initiate knew, how easy it was to fast. It was the easiest thing in the world. He made no secret of this, yet people did not believe him, at the best they set him down as modest, most of them, however, thought he was out for publicity or else was some kind of cheat who found it easy to fast because he had discovered a way of making it easy, and then had the impudence to admit the fact, more or less. He had to put up with all that, and in the course of time had got used to it, but his inner dissatisfaction always rankled, and never yet, after any term of fasting—this must be granted to his credit—had he left the cage of his own free will. The longest period of fasting was fixed by his impresario at forty days, beyond that term he was not allowed to go, not even in great cities, and there was good reason for it, too. Experience had proved that for about forty days the interest of the public could be stimulated by a steadily increasing pressure of advertisement, but after that the town began to lose interest, sympathetic support began notably to fall off; there were of course local variations as between one town and another or one country and another, but as a general rule forty days marked the limit. So on the fortieth day the flower-bedecked cage was opened, enthusiastic spectators filled the hall, a military band played, two doctors entered the cage to measure the results of the fast, which were announced through a megaphone, and finally two young ladies appeared, blissful at having been selected for the honor, to help the hunger artist down the few steps leading to a small table on which was spread a carefully chosen invalid repast. And at this very moment the artist always turned stubborn. True, he would entrust his bony arms to the outstretched helping hands of the ladies bending over him, but stand up he would not. Why stop fasting at this particular moment, after forty days of it? He had held out for a long time, an illimitably long time; why stop now, when he was in his best fasting form, or rather, not yet quite in his best fasting form? Why should he be cheated of the fame he would get for fasting longer, for being not only the record hunger artist of all time, which presumably he was already, but for beating his own record by a performance beyond human imagination, since he felt that there were no limits to his capacity for fasting? His public pretended to admire him so much, why should it have so little patience with him; if he could endure fasting longer, why shouldn't the public endure it? Besides, he was tired, he was comfortable sitting in the straw, and now he was supposed to lift himself to his full height and go down to a meal the very thought of which gave him a nausea that only the presence of the ladies kept him from betraying, and even that with an effort. And he looked up into the eyes of the ladies who were apparently so friendly and in reality so cruel, and shook his head, which felt too heavy on its strengthless neck. But then there happened yet again what always happened. The impresario came forward, without a word—for the band made speech impossible—lifted his arms in the air above the artist, as if inviting Heaven to look down upon its creature here in the straw, this suffering martyr, which indeed he was, although in quite another sense; grasped him around the emaciated waist, with exaggerated caution, so that the frail condition he was in might be appreciated; and committed him to the care of the blenching ladies, not without secretly giving him a shaking so that his legs and body tottered and swayed. The artist now submitted completely; his head lolled on his breast as if it had landed there by chance; his body was hollowed out; his legs in a spasm of self-preservation clung close to each other at the knees, yet scraped on the ground as if it were not really solid ground, as if they were only trying to find solid ground; and the whole weight of his body, a featherweight after all, relapsed onto one of the ladies, who, looking around for help and panting a little—this post of honor was not at all what she had expected it to be—first stretched her neck as far as she could to keep her face at least free from contact with the artist, then finding this impossible, and her more fortunate companion not coming to her aid but merely holding extended in her own trembling hand the little bunch of knucklebones that was the artist's, to the great delight of the spectators burst into tears and had to be replaced by an attendant who had long been stationed in readiness. Then came the food, a little of which the impresario managed to get between the artist's lips, while he sat in a kind of half-fainting trance, to the accompaniment of cheerful patter designed to distract the public's attention from the artist's condition; after that, a toast was drunk to the public, supposedly prompted by a whisper from the artist in the impresario's ear; the band confirmed it with a mighty flourish, the spectators melted away, and no one had any cause to be dissatisfied with the proceedings, no one except the hunger artist himself, he only, as always.

So he lived for many years, with small regular intervals of recuperation, in visible glory, honored by the world, yet in spite of that troubled in spirit, and all the more troubled because no one would take his trouble seriously. What comfort could he possibly need? What more could he possibly wish for? And if some good-natured person, feeling sorry for him, tried to console him by pointing out that his melancholy was probably caused by fasting, it could happen, especially when he had been fasting for some time, that he reacted with an outburst of fury and to the general alarm began to shake the bars of his cage like a wild animal. Yet the impresario had a way of punishing these outbreaks which he rather enjoyed putting into operation. He would apologize publicly for the artist's behavior, which was only to be excused, he admitted, because of the irritability caused by fasting; a condition hardly to be understood by well-fed people; then by natural transition he went on to mention the artist's equally incomprehensible boast that he could fast for much longer than he was doing; he praised the high ambition, the good will, the great self-denial undoubtedly implicit in such a statement; and then quite simply countered it by bringing out photographs, which were also on sale to the public, showing the artist on the fortieth day of a fast lying in bed almost dead from exhaustion. This perversion of the truth, familiar to the artist though it was, always unnerved him afresh and proved too much for him. What was a consequence of the premature ending of his fast was here presented as the cause of it! To fight against this lack of understanding, against a whole world of nonunderstanding, was impossible. Time and again in good faith he stood by the bars listening to the impresario, but as soon as the photographs appeared he always let go and sank with a groan back onto his straw, and the reassured public could once more come close and gaze at him.

A few years later when the witnesses of such scenes called them to mind, they often failed to understand themselves at all. For meanwhile the aforementioned change in public interest had set in; it seemed to happen almost overnight; there may have been profound causes for it, but who was going to bother about that; at any rate the pampered hunger artist suddenly found himself deserted one fine day by the amusement-seekers, who went streaming past him to other more-favored attractions. For the last time the impresario hurried him over half Europe to discover whether the old interest might still survive here and there; all in vain; everywhere, as if by secret agreement, a positive revulsion from professional fasting was in evidence. Of course it could not really have sprung up so suddenly as all that, and many premonitory symptoms which had not been sufficiently remarked or suppressed during the rush and glitter of success now came retrospectively to mind, but it was now too late to take any countermeasures. Fasting would surely come into fashion again at some future date, yet that was no comfort for those living in the present. What, then, was the hunger artist to do? He had been applauded by thousands in his time and could hardly come down to showing himself in a street booth at village fairs, and as for adopting another profession, he was not only too old for that but too fanatically devoted to fasting. So he took leave of the impresario, his partner in an unparalleled career, and hired himself to a large circus; in order to spare his own feelings he avoided reading the conditions of his contract.

A large circus with its enormous traffic in replacing and recruiting men, animals, and apparatus can always find a use for people at any time, even for a hunger artist, provided of course that he does not ask too much, and in this particular case anyhow it was not only the artist who was taken on but his famous and long-known name as well, indeed considering the peculiar nature of his performance, which was not impaired by advancing age, it could not be objected that here was an artist past his prime, no longer at the height of his professional skill, seeking a refuge in some quiet corner of a circus; on the contrary, the hunger artist averred that he could fast as well as ever, which was entirely credible, he even alleged that if he were allowed to fast as he liked, and this was at once promised him without more ado, he could astound the world by establishing a record never yet achieved, a statement that certainly provoked a smile among the other professionals, since it left out of account the change in public opinion, which the hunger artist in his zeal conveniently forgot.

He had not, however, actually lost his sense of the real situation and took it as a matter of course that he and his cage should be stationed, not in the middle of the ring as a main attraction, but outside, near the animal cages, on a site that was after all easily accessible. Large and gaily painted placards made a frame for the cage and announced what was to be seen inside it. When the public came thronging out in the intervals to see the animals, they could hardly avoid passing the hunger artist's cage and stopping there for a moment, perhaps they might even have stayed longer had not those pressing behind them in the narrow gangway, who did not understand why they should be held up on their way toward the excitements of the menagerie, made it impossible for anyone to stand gazing quietly for any length of time. And that was the reason why the hunger artist, who had of course been looking forward to these visiting hours as the main achievement of his life, began instead to shrink from them. At first he could hardly wait for the intervals; it was exhilarating to watch the crowds come streaming his way, until only too soon—not even the most obstinate self-deception, clung to almost consciously, could hold out against the fact—the conviction was borne in upon him that these people, most of them, to judge from their actions, again and again, without exception, were all on their way to the menagerie. And the first sight of them from the distance remained the best. For when they reached his cage he was at once deafened by the storm of shouting and abuse that arose from the two contending factions, which renewed themselves continuously, of those who wanted to stop and stare at him—he soon began to dislike them more than the others—not out of real interest but only out of obstinate self-assertiveness, and those who wanted to go straight on to the animals. When the first great rush was past, the stragglers came along, and these, whom nothing could have prevented from stopping to look at him as long as they had breath, raced past with long strides, hardly even glancing at him, in their haste to get to the menagerie in time. And all too rarely did it happen that he had a stroke of luck, when some father of a family fetched up before him with his children, pointed a finger at the hunger artist, and explained at length what the phenomenon meant, telling stories of earlier years when he himself had watched similar but much more thrilling performances, and the children, still rather uncomprehending, since neither inside nor outside school had they been sufficiently prepared for this lesson—what did they care about fasting?— yet showed by the brightness of their intent eyes that new and better times might be coming. Perhaps, said the hunger artist to himself many a time, things would be a little better if his cage were set not quite so near the menag- erie. That made it too easy for people to make their choice, to say nothing of what he suffered from the stench of the menagerie, the animals' restlessness by night, the carrying past of raw lumps of flesh for the beasts of prey, the roaring at feeding times, which depressed him continually. But he did not dare to lodge a complaint with the management; after all, he had the animals to thank for the troops of people who passed his cage, among whom there might always be one here and there to take an interest in him, and who could tell where they might seclude him if he called attention to his existence and thereby to the fact that, strictly speaking, he was only an impediment on the way to the menagerie.

A small impediment, to be sure, one that grew steadily less. People grew familiar with the strange idea that they could be expected, in times like these, to take an interest in a hunger artist, and with this familiarity the verdict went out against him. He might fast as much as he could, and he did so; but nothing could save him now, people passed him by. Just try to explain to anyone the art of fasting! Anyone who has no feeling for it cannot be made to understand it. The fine placards grew dirty and illegible, they were torn down; the little notice board telling the number of fast days achieved, which at first was changed carefully every day, had long stayed at the same figure, for after the first few weeks even this small task seemed pointless to the staff; and so the artist simply fasted on and on, as he had once dreamed of doing, and it was no trouble to him, just as he had always foretold, but no one counted the days, no one, not even the artist himself, knew what records he was already breaking, and his heart grew heavy. And when once in a while some leisurely passer-by stopped, made merry over the old figure on the board, and spoke of swindling, that was in its way the stupidest lie ever invented by indifference and inborn malice, since it was not the hunger artist who was cheating, he was working honestly, but the world was cheating him of his reward.

Many more days went by, however, and that too came to an end. An overseer's eye fell on the cage one day and he asked the attendants why this perfectly good cage should be left standing there unused with dirty straw inside it; nobody knew, until one man, helped out by the notice board, remembered about the hunger artist. They poked into the straw with sticks and found him in it. "Are you still fasting?" asked the overseer, "when on earth do you mean to stop?" "Forgive me, everybody," whispered the hunger artist; only the overseer, who had his ear to the bars, understood him. "Of course," said the overseer, and tapped his forehead with a finger to let the attendants know what state the man was in, "we forgive you." "I always wanted you to admire my fasting," said the hunger artist. "We do admire it," said the overseer, affably. "But you shouldn't admire it," said the hunger artist. "Well then we don't admire it," said the overseer, "but why shouldn't we admire it?" "Because I have to fast, I can't help it," said the hunger artist. "What a fellow you are," said the overseer, "and why can't you help it?" "Because," said the hunger artist, lifting his head a little and speaking, with his lips pursed, as if for a kiss, right into the overseer's ear, so that no syllable might be lost, "because I couldn't find the food I liked. If I had found it, believe me, I should have made no fuss and stuffed myself like you or anyone else." These were his last words, but in his dimming eyes remained the firm though no longer proud persuasion that he was still continuing to fast.

"Well, clear this out now!" said the overseer, and they buried the hunger artist, straw and all. Into the cage they put a young panther. Even the most insensitive felt it refreshing to see this wild creature leaping around the cage that had so long been dreary. The panther was all right. The food he liked was brought him without hesitation by the attendants; he seemed not even to miss his freedom; his noble body, furnished almost to the bursting point with all that it needed, seemed to carry freedom around with it too; somewhere in his jaws it seemed to lurk; and the joy of life streamed with such ardent passion from his throat that for the onlookers it was not easy to stand the shock of it. But they braced themselves, crowded around the cage, and did not want ever to move away.

[1922]

Katherine Mansfield   *1888–1923*

THE FLY

"Y'are very snug in here," piped old Mr. Woodifield, and he peered out of the great, green leather armchair by his friend the boss's desk as a baby peers out of its pram. His talk was over; it was time for him to be off. But he did not want to go. Since he had retired, since his . . . stroke, the wife and the girls kept him boxed up in the house every day of the week except Tuesday. On Tuesday he was dressed up and brushed and allowed to cut back to the City for the day. Though what he did there the wife and girls couldn't imagine. Made a nuisance of himself to his friends, they supposed. . . . Well, perhaps so. All the same, we cling to our last pleasures as the tree clings to its last leaves. So there sat old Woodifield, smoking a cigar and staring almost greedily at the boss, who rolled in his office chair, stout, rosy, five years older than he, and still going strong, still at the helm. It did one good to see him.

Wistfully, admiringly, the old voice added, "It's snug in here, upon my word!"

"Yes, it's comfortable enough," agreed the boss, and he flipped the *Financial Times* with a paper-knife. As a matter of fact he was proud of his room; he liked to have it admired, especially by old Woodifield. It gave him a feeling of deep, solid satisfaction to be planted there in the midst of it in full view of that frail old figure in the muffler.

"I've had it done up lately," he explained, as he had explained for the past— how many?—weeks. "New carpet," and he pointed to the bright red carpet with a pattern of large white rings. "New furniture," and he nodded towards the massive bookcase and the table with legs like twisted treacle. "Electric heating!" He waved almost exultantly towards the five transparent, pearly sausages glowing so softly in the tilted copper pan.

But he did not draw old Woodifield's attention to the photograph over the table of a grave-looking boy in uniform standing in one of those spectral photographers' parks with photographers' storm-clouds behind him. It was not new. It had been there for over six years.

"There was something I wanted to tell you," said old Woodifield, and his eyes grew dim remembering. "Now what was it? I had it in my mind when I started out this morning." His hands began to tremble, and patches of red showed above his beard.

Poor old chap, he's on his last pins, thought the boss. And, feeling kindly, he winked at the old man, and said jokingly, "I tell you what. I've got a little drop of something here that'll do you good before you go out into the cold again. It's beautiful stuff. It wouldn't hurt a child." He took a key off his watch-chain, unlocked a cupboard below his desk, and drew forth a dark, squat bottle. "That's the medicine," said he. "And the man from whom I got it told me on the strict Q.T. it came from the cellars at Windsor Cassel."[1]

Old Woodifield's mouth fell open at the sight. He couldn't have looked more surprised if the boss had produced a rabbit.

"It's whisky, ain't it?" he piped, feebly.

---

[1] Windsor Castle, west of London; the residence of the British royal family.

The boss turned the bottle and lovingly showed him the label. Whisky it was.

"D'you know," said he, peering up at the boss wonderingly, "they won't let me touch it at home." And he looked as though he was going to cry.

"Ah, that's where we know a bit more than the ladies," cried the boss, swooping across for two tumblers that stood on the table with the water-bottle, and pouring a generous finger into each. "Drink it down. It'll do you good. And don't put any water with it. It's sacrilege to tamper with stuff like this. Ah!" He tossed off his, pulled out his handkerchief, hastily wiped his moustaches, and cocked an eye at old Woodifield, who was rolling his in his chaps.

The old man swallowed, was silent a moment, and then said faintly, "It's nutty!"

But it warmed him; it crept into his chill old brain—he remembered.

"That was it," he said, heaving himself out of his chair. "I thought you'd like to know. The girls were in Belgium last week having a look at poor Reggie's grave,[2] and they happened to come across your boy's. They're quite near each other, it seems."

Old Woodifield paused, but the boss made no reply. Only a quiver in his eyelids showed that he heard.

"The girls were delighted with the way the place is kept," piped the old voice. "Beautifully looked after. Couldn't be better if they were at home. You've not been across, have yer?"

"No, no!" For various reasons the boss had not been across.

"There's miles of it," quavered old Woodifield, "and it's all as neat as a garden. Flowers growing on all the graves. Nice broad paths." It was plain from his voice how much he liked a nice broad path.

The pause came again. Then the old man brightened wonderfully.

"D'you know what the hotel made the girls pay for a pot of jam?" he piped. "Ten francs! Robbery, I call it. It was a little pot, so Gertrude says, no bigger than a half-crown. And she hadn't taken more than a spoonful when they charged her ten francs. Gertrude brought the pot away with her to teach 'em a lesson. Quite right, too; it's trading on our feelings. They think because we're over there having a look around we're ready to pay anything. That's what it is." And he turned towards the door.

"Quite right, quite right!" cried the boss, though what was quite right he hadn't the least idea. He came round by his desk, followed the shuffling footsteps to the door, and saw the old fellow out. Woodifield was gone.

For a long moment the boss stayed, staring at nothing, while the grey-haired office messenger, watching him, dodged in and out of his cubbyhole like a dog that expects to be taken for a run. Then: "I'll see nobody for half an hour, Macey," said the boss. "Understand? Nobody at all."

"Very good, sir."

The door shut, the firm heavy steps recrossed the bright carpet, the fat body plumped down in the spring chair, and leaning forward, the boss covered his face with his hands. He wanted, he intended, he had arranged to weep. . . .

It had been a terrible shock to him when old Woodifield sprang that remark upon him about the boy's grave. It was exactly as though the earth had opened and he had seen the boy lying there with Woodifield's girls staring down at him. For it was strange. Although over six years had passed away, the boss

[2] The reference is to one of a number of World War I British military cemeteries in Belgium.

never thought of the boy except as lying unchanged, unblemished in his uniform, asleep for ever. "My son!" groaned the boss. But no tears came yet. In the past, in the first months and even years after the boy's death, he had only to say those words to be overcome by such grief that nothing short of a violent fit of weeping could relieve him. Time, he had declared then, he had told everybody, could make no difference. Other men perhaps might recover, might live their loss down, but not he. How was it possible? His boy was an only son. Ever since his birth the boss had worked at building up this business for him; it had no other meaning if it was not for the boy. Life itself had come to have no other meaning. How on earth could he have slaved, denied himself, kept going all those years without the promise for ever before him of the boy's stepping into his shoes and carrying on where he left off?

And that promise had been so near being fulfilled. The boy had been in the office learning the ropes for a year before the war. Every morning they had started off together; they had come back by the same train. And what congratulations he had received as the boy's father! No wonder; he had taken to it marvellously. As to his popularity with the staff, every man jack of them down to old Macey couldn't make enough of the boy. And he wasn't in the least spoilt. No, he was just his bright, natural self, with the right word for everybody, with that boyish look and his habit of saying, "Simply splendid!"

But all that was over and done with as though it never had been. The day had come when Macey had handed him the telegram that brought the whole place crashing about his head. "Deeply regret to inform you . . ." And he had left the office a broken man, with his life in ruins.

Six years ago, six years . . . How quickly time passed! It might have happened yesterday. The boss took his hands from his face; he was puzzled. Something seemed to be wrong with him. He wasn't feeling as he wanted to feel. He decided to get up and have a look at the boy's photograph. But it wasn't a favorite photograph of his; the expression was unnatural. It was cold, even sternlooking. The boy had never looked like that.

At that moment the boss noticed that a fly had fallen into his broad inkpot, and was trying feebly but desperately to clamber out again. Help! help! said those struggling legs. But the sides of the inkpot were wet and slippery; it fell back again and began to swim. The boss took up a pen, picked the fly out of the ink, and shook it on to a piece of blotting-paper. For a fraction of a second it lay still on the dark patch that oozed round it. Then the front legs waved, took hold, and, pulling its small sodden body up it began the immense task of cleaning the ink from its wings. Over and under, over and under, went a leg along a wing, as the stone goes over and under the scythe. Then there was a pause, while the fly, seeming to stand on the tips of its toes, tried to expand first one wing and then the other. It succeeded at last, and, sitting down, it began, like a minute cat, to clean its face. Now one could imagine that the little front legs rubbed against each other lightly, joyfully. The horrible danger was over; it had escaped; it was ready for life again.

But just then the boss had an idea. He plunged his pen back into the ink, leaned his thick wrist on the blotting paper, and as the fly tried its wings down came a great heavy blot. What would it make of that? What indeed! The little beggar seemed absolutely cowed, stunned, and afraid to move because of what would happen next. But then, as if painfully, it dragged itself forward. The front legs waved, caught hold, and, more slowly this time, the task began from the beginning.

He's a plucky little devil, thought the boss, and he felt a real admiration for the fly's courage. That was the way to tackle things; that was the right spirit. Never say die; it was only a question of . . . But the fly had again finished its laborious task, and the boss had just time to refill his pen, to shake fair and square on the new-cleaned body yet another dark drop. What about it this time? A painful moment of suspense followed. But behold, the front legs were again waving; the boss felt a rush of relief. He leaned over the fly and said to it tenderly, "You artful little b . . ." And he actually had the brilliant notion of breathing on it to help the drying process. All the same, there was something timid and weak about its efforts now, and the boss decided that this time should be the last, as he dipped the pen into the inkpot.

It was. The last blot on the soaked blotting-paper, and the draggled fly lay in it and did not stir. The back legs were stuck to the body; the front legs were not to be seen.

"Come on," said the boss. "Look sharp!" And he stirred it with his pen— in vain. Nothing happened or was likely to happen. The fly was dead.

The boss lifted the corpse on the end of the paper-knife and flung it into the waste-paper basket. But such a grinding feeling of wretchedness seized him that he felt positively frightened. He started forward and pressed the bell for Macey.

"Bring me some fresh blotting-paper," he said, sternly, "and look sharp about it." And while the old dog padded away he fell to wondering what it was he had been thinking about before. What was it? It was . . . He took out his handkerchief and passed it inside his collar. For the life of him he could not remember.

[1922]

Ernest Hemingway *1898–1961*

HILLS LIKE WHITE ELEPHANTS

The hills across the valley of the Ebro were long and white. On this side there was no shade and no trees and the station was between two lines of rails in the sun. Close against the side of the station there was the warm shadow of the building and a curtain, made of strings of bamboo beads, hung across the open door into the bar, to keep out flies. The American and the girl with him sat at a table in the shade, outside the building. It was very hot and the express from Barcelona would come in forty minutes. It stopped at this junction for two minutes and went on to Madrid.[1]

"What should we drink?" the girl asked. She had taken off her hat and put it on the table.

"It's pretty hot," the man said.

"Let's drink beer."

"Dos cervezas," the man said into the curtain.

"Big ones?" a woman asked from the doorway.

"Yes. Two big ones."

The woman brought two glasses of beer and two felt pads. She put the felt pads and the beer glasses on the table and looked at the man and the girl. The girl was looking off at the line of hills. They were white in the sun and the country was brown and dry.

"They look like white elephants," she said.

"I've never seen one," the man drank his beer.

"No, you wouldn't have."

"I might have," the man said. "Just because you say I wouldn't have doesn't prove anything."

The girl looked at the bead curtain. "They've painted something on it," she said. "What does it say?"

"Anis del Toro. It's a drink."

"Could we try it?"

The man called "Listen" through the curtain. The woman came out from the bar.

"Four reales."[2]

"We want two Anis del Toro."

"With water?"

"Do you want it with water?"

"I don't know," the girl said. "Is it good with water?"

"It's all right."

"You want them with water?" asked the woman.

"Yes, with water."

"It tastes like licorice," the girl said and put the glass down.

"That's the way with everything."

"Yes," said the girl. "Everything tastes of licorice. Especially all the things you've waited so long for, like absinthe."

---

[1] The references to the Ebro River and the cities of Barcelona and Madrid identify the setting as Spain.
[2] Spanish coins.

"Oh, cut it out."

"You started it," the girl said. "I was being amused. I was having a fine time."

"Well, let's try and have a fine time."

"All right. I was trying. I said the mountains looked like white elephants. Wasn't that bright?"

"That was bright."

"I wanted to try this new drink. That's all we do, isn't it—look at things and try new drinks?"

"I guess so."

The girl looked across at the hills.

"They're lovely hills," she said. "They don't really look like white elephants. I just meant the coloring of their skin through the trees."

"Should we have another drink?"

"All right."

The warm wind blew the bead curtain against the table.

"The beer's nice and cool," the man said.

"It's lovely," the girl said.

"It's really an awfully simple operation, Jig," the man said. "It's not really an operation at all."

The girl looked at the ground the table legs rested on.

"I know you wouldn't mind it, Jig. It's really not anything. It's just to let the air in."

The girl did not say anything.

"I'll go with you and I'll stay with you all the time. They just let the air in and then it's all perfectly natural."

"Then what will we do afterward?"

"We'll be fine afterward. Just like we were before."

"What makes you think so?"

"That's the only thing that bothers us. It's the only thing that's made us unhappy."

The girl looked at the bead curtain, put her hand out and took hold of two of the strings of beads.

"And you think then we'll be all right and be happy."

"I know we will. You don't have to be afraid. I've known lots of people that have done it."

"So have I," said the girl. "And afterward they were all so happy."

"Well," the man said, "if you don't want to you don't have to. I wouldn't have you do it if you didn't want to. But I know it's perfectly simple."

"And you really want to?"

"I think it's the best thing to do. But I don't want you to do it if you don't really want to."

"And if I do it you'll be happy and things will be like they were and you'll love me?"

"I love you now. You know I love you."

"I know. But if I do it, then it will be nice again if I say things are like white elephants, and you'll like it?"

"I'll love it. I love it now but I just can't think about it. You know how I get when I worry."

"If I do it you won't ever worry?"

"I won't worry about that because it's perfectly simple."

"Then I'll do it. Because I don't care about me."

"What do you mean?"

"I don't care about me."

"Well, I care about you."

"Oh, yes. But I don't care about me. And I'll do it and then everything will be fine."

"I don't want you to do it if you feel that way."

The girl stood up and walked to the end of the station. Across, on the other side, were fields of grain and trees along the banks of the Ebro. Far away, beyond the river, were mountains. The shadow of a cloud moved across the field of grain and she saw the river through the trees.

"And we could have all this," she said. "And we could have everything and every day we make it more impossible."

"What did you say?"

"I said we could have everything."

"We can have everything."

"No, we can't."

"We can have the whole world."

"No, we can't."

"We can go everywhere."

"No, we can't. It isn't ours any more."

"It's ours."

"No, it isn't. And once they take it away, you never get it back."

"But they haven't taken it away."

"We'll wait and see."

"Come on back in the shade," he said. "You mustn't feel that way."

"I don't feel any way," the girl said. "I just know things."

"I don't want you to do anything that you don't want to do——"

"Nor that isn't good for me," she said. "I know. Could we have another beer?"

"All right. But you've got to realize——"

"I realize," the girl said. "Can't we maybe stop talking?"

They sat down at the table and the girl looked across at the hills on the dry side of the valley and the man looked at her and at the table.

"You've got to realize," he said, "that I don't want you to do it if you don't want to. I'm perfectly willing to go through with it if means anything to you."

"Doesn't it mean anything to you? We could get along."

"Of course it does. But I don't want anybody but you. I don't want any one else. And I know it's perfectly simple."

"Yes, you know it's perfectly simple."

"It's all right for you to say that, but I do know it."

"Would you do something for me now?"

"I'd do anything for you."

"Would you please please please please please please please stop talking?"

He did not say anything but looked at the bags against the wall of the station. There were labels on them from all the hotels where they had spent nights.

"But I don't want you to," he said, "I don't care anything about it."

"I'll scream," the girl said.

The woman came out through the curtains with two glasses of beer and put them down on the damp felt pads. "The train comes in five minutes," she said.

"What did she say?" asked the girl.

"That the train is coming in five minutes."

The girl smiled brightly at the woman, to thank her.

"I'd better take the bags over to the other side of the station," the man said. She smiled at him.

"All right. Then come back and we'll finish the beer."

He picked up the two heavy bags and carried them around the station to the other tracks. He looked up the tracks but could not see the train. Coming back, he walked through the barroom, where people waiting for the train were drinking. He drank an Anis at the bar and looked at the people. They were all waiting reasonably for the train. He went out through the bead curtain. She was sitting at the table and smiled at him.

"Do you feel better?" he asked.

"I feel fine," she said. "There's nothing wrong with me. I feel fine."

[1927]

William Faulkner 1897–1962

A ROSE FOR EMILY

Emily is house (handwritten)

I

When Miss Emily Grierson died, our whole town went to her funeral: the men through a sort of respectful affection for a fallen monument, the women mostly out of curiosity to see the inside of her house, which no one save an old manservant—a combined gardener and cook—had seen in at least ten years.

Emily big (handwritten)

It was a big, squarish frame house that had once been white, decorated with cupolas and spires and scrolled balconies in the heavily lightsome style of the seventies, set on what had once been our most select street. But garages and cotton gins had encroached and obliterated even the august names of that neighborhood; only Miss Emily's house was left, lifting its stubborn and coquettish decay above the cotton wagons and the gasoline pumps—an eyesore among eyesores. And now Miss Emily had gone to join the representatives of those august names where they lay in the cedar-bemused cemetery among the ranked and anonymous graves of Union and Confederate soldiers who fell at the battle of Jefferson.

Emily is house (handwritten)

Alive, Miss Emily had been a tradition, a duty, and a care; a sort of hereditary obligation upon the town, dating from that day in 1894 when Colonel Sartoris, the mayor—he who fathered the edict that no Negro woman should appear on the streets without an apron—remitted her taxes, the dispensation dating from the death of her father on into perpetuity. Not that Miss Emily would have accepted charity. Colonel Sartoris invented an involved tale to the effect that Miss Emily's father had loaned money to the town, which the town, as a matter of business, preferred this way of repaying. Only a man of Colonel Sartoris' generation and thought could have invented it, and only a woman could have believed it.

When the next generation, with its more modern ideas, became mayors and aldermen, this arrangement created some little dissatisfaction. On the first of the year they mailed her a tax notice. February came, and there was no reply. They wrote her a formal letter, asking her to call at the sheriff's office at her convenience. A week later the mayor wrote her himself, offering to call or to send his car for her, and received in reply a note on paper of an archaic shape, in a thin, flowing calligraphy in faded ink, to the effect that she no longer went out at all. The tax notice was also enclosed, without comment.

They called a special meeting of the Board of Aldermen. A deputation waited upon her, knocked at the door through which no visitor had passed since she ceased giving china-painting lessons eight or ten years earlier. They were admitted by the old Negro into a dim hall from which a stairway mounted into still more shadow. It smelled of dust and disuse—a close, dank smell. The Negro led them into the parlor. It was furnished in heavy, leather-covered furniture. When the Negro opened the blinds of one window, they could see that the leather was cracked; and when they sat down, a faint dust rose sluggishly about their thighs, spinning with slow motes in the single sun-ray. On a tarnished gilt easel before the fireplace stood a crayon portrait of Miss Emily's father.

They rose when she entered—a small, fat woman in black, with a thin gold chain descending to her waist and vanishing into her belt, leaning on an ebony cane with a tarnished gold head. Her skeleton was small and spare; perhaps that was why what would have been merely plumpness in another was obesity in her. She looked bloated, like a body long submerged in motionless water, and of that pallid hue. Her eyes, lost in the fatty ridges of her face, looked like two small pieces of coal pressed into a lump of dough as they moved from one face to another while the visitors stated their errand.

She did not ask them to sit. She just stood in the door and listened quietly until the spokesman came to a stumbling halt. Then they could hear the invisible watch ticking at the end of the gold chain.

Her voice was dry and cold. "I have no taxes in Jefferson. Colonel Sartoris explained it to me. Perhaps one of you can gain access to the city records and satisfy yourselves."

"But we have. We are the city authorities, Miss Emily. Didn't you get a notice from the sheriff, signed by him?"

"I received a paper, yes," Miss Emily said. "Perhaps he considers himself the sheriff . . . I have no taxes in Jefferson."

"But there is nothing on the books to show that, you see. We must go by the—"

"See Colonel Sartoris. I have no taxes in Jefferson."

"But, Miss Emily—"

"See Colonel Sartoris." (Colonel Sartoris had been dead almost ten years.) "I have no taxes in Jefferson. Tobe!" The Negro appeared. "Show these gentlemen out."

II

So she vanquished them, horse and foot, just as she had vanquished their fathers thirty years before about the smell. That was two years after her father's death and a short time after her sweetheart—the one we believed would marry her—had deserted her. After her father's death she went out very little; after her sweetheart went away, people hardly saw her at all. A few of the ladies had the temerity to call, but were not received, and the only sign of life about the place was the Negro man—a young man then—going in and out with a market basket.

"Just as if a man—any man—could keep a kitchen properly," the ladies said; so they were not surprised when the smell developed. It was another link between the gross, teeming world and the high and mighty Griersons.

A neighbor, a woman, complained to the mayor, Judge Stevens, eighty years old.

"But what will you have me do about it, madam?" he said.

"Why, send her word to stop it," the woman said. "Isn't there a law?"

"I'm sure that won't be necessary," Judge Stevens said. "It's probably just a snake or a rat that nigger of hers killed in the yard. I'll speak to him about it."

The next day he received two more complaints, one from a man who came in diffident deprecation. "We really must do something about it, Judge. I'd be the last one in the world to bother Miss Emily, but we've got to do something." That night the Board of Aldermen met—three graybeards and one younger man, a member of the rising generation.

"It's simple enough," he said. "Send her word to have her place cleaned up. Give her a certain time to do it in, and if she don't . . ."

"Dammit, sir," Judge Stevens said, "will you accuse a lady to her face of smelling bad?"

So the next night, after midnight, four men crossed Miss Emily's lawn and slunk about the house like burglars, sniffing along the base of the brickwork and at the cellar openings while one of them performed a regular sowing motion with his hand out of a sack slung from his shoulder. They broke open the cellar door and sprinkled lime there, and in all the outbuildings. As they recrossed the lawn, a window that had been dark was lighted and Miss Emily sat in it, the light behind her, and her upright torso motionless as that of an idol. They crept quietly across the lawn and into the shadow of the locusts that lined the street. After a week or two the smell went away.

That was when people had begun to feel really sorry for her. People in our town, remembering how old lady Wyatt, her great-aunt, had gone completely crazy at last, believed that the Griersons held themselves a little too high for what they really were. None of the young men were quite good enough for Miss Emily and such. We had long thought of them as a tableau, Miss Emily a slender figure in white in the background, her father a spraddled silhouette in the foreground, his back to her and clutching a horsewhip, the two of them framed by the back-flung front door. So when she got to be thirty and was still single, we were not pleased exactly, but vindicated; even with insanity in the family she wouldn't have turned down all of her chances if they had really materialized.

When her father died, it got about that the house was all that was left to her; and in a way, people were glad. At last they could pity Miss Emily. Being left alone, and a pauper, she had become humanized. Now she too would know the old thrill and the old despair of a penny more or less.

The day after his death all the ladies prepared to call at the house and offer condolence and aid, as is our custom. Miss Emily met them at the door, dressed as usual and with no trace of grief on her face. She told them that her father was not dead. She did that for three days, with the ministers calling on her, and the doctors, trying to persuade her to let them dispose of the body. Just as they were about to resort to law and force, she broke down, and they buried her father quickly.

We did not say she was crazy then. We believed she had to do that. We remembered all the young men her father had driven away, and we knew that with nothing left, she would have to cling to that which had robbed her, as people will.

III

She was sick for a long time. When we saw her again, her hair was cut short, making her look like a girl, with a vague resemblance to those angels in colored church windows—sort of tragic and serene.

The town had just let the contracts for paving the sidewalks, and in the summer after her father's death they began the work. The construction company came with niggers and mules and machinery, and a foreman named Homer Barron, a Yankee—a big, dark, ready man, with a big voice and eyes lighter than his face. The little boys would follow in groups to hear him cuss the niggers, and the niggers singing in time to the rise and fall of picks. Pretty soon he knew everybody in town. Whenever you heard a lot of laughing anywhere about the square, Homer Barron would be in the center of the group. Presently we began to see him and Miss Emily on Sunday afternoons driving in the yellow-wheeled buggy and the matched team of bays from the livery stable.

At first we were glad that Miss Emily would have an interest, because the ladies all said, "Of course a Grierson would not think seriously of a Northerner, a day laborer." But there were still others, older people, who said that even grief could not cause a real lady to forget *noblesse oblige*—without calling it *noblesse oblige*. They just said, "Poor Emily. Her kinsfolk should come to her." She had some kin in Alabama; but years ago her father had fallen out with them over the estate of old lady Wyatt, the crazy woman, and there was no communication between the two families. They had not even been represented at the funeral.

And as soon as the old people said, "Poor Emily," the whispering began. "Do you suppose it's really so?" they said to one another. "Of course it is. What else could . . ." This behind their hands; rustling of craned silk and satin behind jalousies closed upon the sun of Sunday afternoon as the thin, swift clop-clop-clop of the matched team passed: "Poor Emily."

She carried her head high enough—even when we believed that she was fallen. It was as if she demanded more than ever the recognition of her dignity as the last Grierson; as if it had wanted that touch of earthiness to reaffirm her imperviousness. Like when she bought the rat poison, the arsenic. That was over a year after they had begun to say "Poor Emily," and while the two female cousins were visiting her.

"I want some poison," she said to the druggist. She was over thirty then, still a slight woman, though thinner than usual, with cold, haughty black eyes in a face the flesh of which was strained across the temples and about the eyesockets as you imagine a lighthouse-keeper's face ought to look. "I want some poison," she said.

"Yes, Miss Emily. What kind? For rats and such? I'd recom—"

"I want the best you have. I don't care what kind."

The druggist named several. "They'll kill anything up to an elephant. But what you want is—"

"Arsenic," Miss Emily said. "Is that a good one?"

"Is . . . arsenic? Yes, ma'am. But what you want—"

"I want arsenic."

The druggist looked down at her. She looked back at him, erect, her face like a strained flag. "Why, of course," the druggist said. "If that's what you want. But the law requires you to tell what you are going to use it for."

Miss Emily just stared at him, her head tilted back in order to look him eye for eye, until he looked away and went and got the arsenic and wrapped it up. The Negro delivery boy brought her the package; the druggist didn't come back. When she opened the package at home there was written on the box, under the skull and bones: "For rats."

IV

So the next day we all said, "She will kill herself"; and we said it would be the best thing. When she had first begun to be seen with Homer Barron, we had said, "She will marry him." Then we said, "She will persuade him yet," because Homer himself had remarked—he liked men, and it was known that he drank with the younger men in the Elks' Club—that he was not a marrying man. Later we said, "Poor Emily" behind the jalousies as they passed on Sunday afternoon in the glittering buggy, Miss Emily with her head high and Homer Barron with his hat cocked and a cigar in his teeth, reins and whip in a yellow glove.

Then some of the ladies began to say that it was a disgrace to the town and a bad example to the young people. The men did not want to interfere, but at last the ladies forced the Baptist minister—Miss Emily's people were Episcopal—to call upon her. He would never divulge what happened during that interview, but he refused to go back again. The next Sunday they again drove about the streets, and the following day the minister's wife wrote to Miss Emily's relations in Alabama.

So she had blood-kin under her roof again and we sat back to watch developments. At first nothing happened. Then we were sure that they were to be married. We learned that Miss Emily had been to the jeweler's and ordered a man's toilet set in silver, with the letters H. B. on each piece. Two days later we learned that she had bought a complete outfit of men's clothing, including a nightshirt, and we said, "They are married." We were really glad. We were glad because the two female cousins were even more Grierson than Miss Emily had ever been.

So we were not surprised when Homer Barron—the streets had been finished some time since—was gone. We were a little disappointed that there was not a public blowing-off, but we believed that he had gone on to prepare for Miss Emily's coming, or to give her a chance to get rid of the cousins. (By that time it was a cabal, and we were all Miss Emily's allies to help circumvent the cousins.) Sure enough, after another week they departed. And, as we had expected all along, within three days Homer Barron was back in town. A neighbor saw the Negro man admit him at the kitchen door at dusk one evening.

And that was the last we saw of Homer Barron. And of Miss Emily for some time. The Negro man went in and out with the market basket, but the front door remained closed. Now and then we would see her at a window for a moment, as the men did that night when they sprinkled the lime, but for almost six months she did not appear on the streets. Then we knew that this was to be expected too; as if that quality of her father which had thwarted her woman's life so many times had been too virulent and too furious to die.

When we next saw Miss Emily, she had grown fat and her hair was turning gray. During the next few years it grew grayer and grayer until it attained an even pepper-and-salt iron-gray, when it ceased turning. Up to the day of her death at seventy-four it was still that vigorous iron-gray, like the hair of an active man.

From that time on her front door remained closed, save for a period of six or seven years, when she was about forty, during which she gave lessons in china-painting. She fitted up a studio in one of the downstairs rooms, where the daughters and granddaughters of Colonel Sartoris' contemporaries were sent to her with the same regularity and in the same spirit that they were sent to church on Sundays with a twenty-five cent piece for the collection plate. Meanwhile her taxes had been remitted.

Then the newer generation became the backbone and the spirit of the town, and the painting pupils grew up and fell away and did not send their children to her with boxes of color and tedious brushes and pictures cut from the ladies' magazines. The front door closed upon the last one and remained closed for good. When the town got free postal delivery, Miss Emily alone refused to let them fasten the metal numbers above her door and attach a mailbox to it. She would not listen to them.

Daily, monthly, yearly we watched the Negro grow grayer and more stooped, going in and out with the market basket. Each December we sent her a tax notice, which would be returned by the post office a week later, unclaimed. Now and then we would see her in one of the downstairs windows—she had evidently shut up the top floor of the house—like the carven torso of an idol in a niche, looking or not looking at us, we could never tell which. Thus she passed from generation to generation—dear, inescapable, impervious, tranquil, and perverse.

And so she died. Fell ill in the house filled with dust and shadows, with only a doddering Negro man to wait on her. We did not even know she was sick; we had long since given up trying to get any information from the Negro. He talked to no one, probably not even to her, for his voice had grown harsh and rusty, as if from disuse.

She died in one of the downstairs rooms, in a heavy walnut bed with a curtain, her gray head propped on a pillow yellow and moldy with age and lack of sunlight.

v

The Negro met the first of the ladies at the front door and let them in, with their hushed, sibilant voices and their quick, curious glances, and then he disappeared. He walked right through the house and out the back and was not seen again.

The two female cousins came at once. They held the funeral on the second day, with the town coming to look at Miss Emily beneath a mass of bought flowers, with the crayon face of her father musing profoundly above the bier and the ladies sibilant and macabre; and the very old men—some in their brushed Confederate uniforms—on the porch and the lawn, talking of Miss Emily as if she had been a contemporary of theirs, believing that they had danced with her and courted her perhaps, confusing time with its mathematical progression, as the old do, to whom all the past is not a diminishing road but, instead, a huge meadow which no winter ever quite touches, divided from them now by the narrow bottle-neck of the most recent decade of years.

Already we knew that there was one room in that region above stairs which no one had seen in forty years, and which would have to be forced. They waited until Miss Emily was decently in the ground before they opened it.

The violence of breaking down the door seemed to fill this room with pervading dust. A thin, acrid pall as of the tomb seemed to lie everywhere upon this room decked and furnished as for a bridal: upon the valance curtains of faded rose color, upon the rose-shaded lights, upon the dressing table, upon the delicate array of crystal and the man's toilet things backed with tarnished silver, silver so tarnished that the monogram was obscured. Among them lay a collar and tie, as if they had just been removed, which, lifted, left upon the surface a pale crescent in the dust. Upon a chair hung the suit, carefully folded; beneath it the two mute shoes and the discarded socks.

The man himself lay in the bed.

For a long while we just stood there, looking down at the profound and fleshless grin. The body had apparently once lain in the attitude of an embrace, but now the long sleep that outlasts love, that conquers even the grimace of love, had cuckolded him. What was left of him, rotten beneath what was left of the nightshirt, had become inextricable from the bed in which he lay; and upon him and upon the pillow beside him lay that even coating of the patient and biding dust.

Then we noticed that in the second pillow was the indentation of a head. One of us lifted something from it, and leaning forward, that faint and invisible dust dry and acrid in the nostrils, we saw a long strand of iron-gray hair.

[1930]

D. H. Lawrence   *1885–1930*

THE ROCKING-HORSE WINNER

There was a woman who was beautiful, who started with all the advantages, yet she had no luck. She married for love, and the love turned to dust. She had bonny children, yet she felt they had been thrust upon her, and she could not love them. They looked at her coldly, as if they were finding fault with her. And hurriedly she felt she must cover up some fault in herself. Yet what it was that she must cover up she never knew. Nevertheless, when her children were present, she always felt the centre of her heart go hard. This troubled her, and in her manner she was all the more gentle and anxious for her children, as if she loved them very much. Only she herself knew that at the centre of her heart was a hard little place that could not feel love, no, not for anybody. Everybody else said of her: "She is such a good mother. She adores her children." Only she herself, and her children themselves, knew it was not so. They read it in each other's eyes.

There were a boy and two little girls. They lived in a pleasant house, with a garden, and they had discreet servants, and felt themselves superior to anyone in the neighbourhood.

Although they lived in style, they felt always an anxiety in the house. There was never enough money. The mother had a small income, and the father had a small income, but not nearly enough for the social position which they had to keep up. The father went into town to some office. But though he had good prospects, these prospects never materialized. There was always the grinding sense of the shortage of money, though the style was always kept up.

At last the mother said: "I will see if *I* can't make something." But she did not know where to begin. She racked her brains, and tried this thing and the other, but could not find anything successful. The failure made deep lines come into her face. Her children were growing up, they would have to go to school. There must be more money, there must be more money. The father, who was always very handsome and expensive in his tastes, seemed as if he never *would* be able to do anything worth doing. And the mother, who had a great belief in herself, did not succeed any better, and her tastes were just as expensive.

And so the house came to be haunted by the unspoken phrase: *There must be more money! There must be more money!* The children could hear it all the time, though nobody said it aloud. They heard it at Christmas, when the expensive and splendid toys filled the nursery. Behind the shining modern rocking-horse, behind the smart doll's house, a voice would start whispering: "There *must* be more money! There *must* be more money!" And the children would stop playing, to listen for a moment. They would look into each other's eyes, to see if they had all heard. And each one saw in the eyes of the other two that they too had heard. "There *must* be more money! There *must* be more money!"

It came whispering from the springs of the still-swaying rocking-horse, and even the horse, bending his wooden, champing head, heard it. The big doll, sitting so pink and smirking in her new pram, could hear it quite plainly, and seemed to be smirking all the more self-consciously because of it. The foolish puppy, too, that took the place of the teddybear, he was looking so extraordinarily foolish for no other reason but that he heard the secret whisper all over the house: "There *must* be more money!"

Yet nobody ever said it aloud. The whisper was everywhere, and therefore no one spoke it. Just as no one ever says: "We are breathing!" in spite of the fact that breath is coming and going all the time.

"Mother," said the boy Paul one day, "why don't we keep a car of our own? Why do we always use uncle's, or else a taxi?"

"Because we're the poor members of the family," said the mother.

"But why *are* we, mother?"

"Well—I suppose," she said slowly and bitterly, "it's because your father has no luck."

The boy was silent for some time.

"Is luck money, mother?" he asked, rather timidly.

"No, Paul. Not quite. It's what causes you to have money."

"Oh!" said Paul vaguely. "I thought when Uncle Oscar said *filthy lucker*, it meant money."

"*Filthy lucre* does mean money," said the mother. "But it's lucre, not luck."

"Oh!" said the boy. "Then what *is* luck, mother?"

"It's what causes you to have money. If you're lucky you have money. That's why it's better to be born lucky than rich. If you're rich, you may lose your money. But if you're lucky, you will always get more money."

"Oh! Will you? And is father not lucky?"

"Very unlucky, I should say," she said bitterly.

The boy watched her with unsure eyes.

"Why?" he asked.

"I don't know. Nobody ever knows why one person is lucky and another unlucky."

"Don't they? Nobody at all? Does *nobody* know?"

"Perhaps God. But He never tells."

"He ought to, then. And aren't you lucky either, mother?"

"I can't be, if I married an unlucky husband."

"But by yourself, aren't you?"

"I used to think I was, before I married. Now I think I am very unlucky indeed."

"Why?"

"Well—never mind! Perhaps I'm not really," she said.

The child looked at her to see if she meant it. But he saw, by the lines of her mouth, that she was only trying to hide something from him.

"Well, anyhow," he said stoutly, "I'm a lucky person."

"Why?" said his mother, with a sudden laugh.

He stared at her. He didn't even know why he had said it.

"God told me," he asserted, brazening it out.

"I hope He did, dear!" she said, again with a laugh, but rather bitter.

"He did, mother!"

"Excellent!" said the mother, using one of her husband's exclamations.

The boy saw she did not believe him; or rather, that she paid no attention to his assertion. This angered him somewhere, and made him want to compel her attention.

He went off by himself, vaguely, in a childish way, seeking for the clue to 'luck.' Absorbed, taking no heed of other people, he went about with a sort of stealth, seeking inwardly for luck. He wanted luck, he wanted it, he wanted it. When the two girls were playing dolls in the nursery, he would sit on his big rocking-horse, charging madly into space, with a frenzy that made the little girls peer at him uneasily. Wildly the horse careered, the waving dark hair of the boy tossed, his eyes had a strange glare in them. The little girls dared not speak to him.

When he had ridden to the end of his mad little journey, he climbed down and stood in front of his rocking-horse, staring fixedly into its lower face. Its red mouth was slightly open, its big eye was wide and glassy-bright.

"Now!" he would silently command the snorting steed. "Now, take me to where there is luck! Now take me!"

And he would slash the horse on the neck with the little whip he had asked Uncle Oscar for. He *knew* the horse could take him to where there was luck, if only he forced it. So he would mount again and start on his furious ride, hoping at last to get there. He knew he could get there.

"You'll break your horse, Paul!" said the nurse.

"He's always riding like that! I wish he'd leave off!" said his elder sister Joan.

But he only glared down on them in silence. Nurse gave him up. She could make nothing of him. Anyhow, he was growing beyond her.

One day his mother and his Uncle Oscar came in when he was on one of his furious rides. He did not speak to them.

"Hallo, you young jockey! Riding a winner?" said his uncle.

"Aren't you growing too big for a rocking-horse? You're not a very little boy any longer, you know," said his mother.

But Paul only gave a blue glare from his big, rather close-set eyes. He would speak to nobody when he was in full tilt. His mother watched him with an anxious expression on her face.

At last he suddenly stopped forcing his horse into the mechanical gallop and slid down.

"Well, I got there!" he announced fiercely, his blue eyes still flaring, and his sturdy long legs straddling apart.

"Where did you get to?" asked his mother.

"Where I wanted to go," he flared back at her.

"That's right, son!" said Uncle Oscar. "Don't you stop till you get there. What's the horse's name?"

"He doesn't have a name," said the boy.

"Gets on without all right?" asked the uncle.

"Well, he has different names. He was called Sansovino last week."

"Sansovino, eh? Won the Ascot.[1] How did you know this name?"

"He always talks about horse-races with Bassett," said Joan.

The uncle was delighted to find that his small nephew was posted with all the racing news. Bassett, the young gardener, who had been wounded in the left foot in the war and had got his present job through Oscar Cresswell, whose batman he had been, was a perfect blade of the 'turf.' He lived in the racing events, and the small boy lived with him.

Oscar Cresswell got it all from Bassett.

"Master Paul comes and asks me, so I can't do more than tell him, sir," said Bassett, his face terribly serious, as if he were speaking of religious matters.

[1] The famous horse race run at the Ascot Heath racetrack near Ascot, England.

"And does he ever put anything on a horse he fancies?"

"Well—I don't want to give him away—he's a young sport, a fine sport, sir. Would you mind asking him himself? He sort of takes a pleasure in it, and perhaps he'd feel I was giving him away, sir, if you don't mind."

Bassett was serious as a church.

The uncle went back to his nephew and took him off for a ride in the car.

"Say, Paul, old man, do you ever put anything on a horse?" the uncle asked.

The boy watched the handsome man closely.

"Why, do you think I oughtn't to?" he parried.

"Not a bit of it! I thought perhaps you might give me a tip for the Lincoln."[2]

The car sped on into the country, going down to Uncle Oscar's place in Hampshire.

"Honour bright?" said the nephew.

"Honour bright, son!" said the uncle.

"Well, then, Daffodil."

"Daffodil! I doubt it, sonny. What about Mirza?"

"I only know the winner," said the boy. "That's Daffodil."

"Daffodil, eh?"

There was a pause. Daffodil was an obscure horse comparatively.

"Uncle!"

"Yes, son?"

"You won't let it go any further, will you? I promised Bassett."

"Bassett be damned, old man! What's he got to do with it?"

"We're partners. We've been partners from the first. Uncle, he lent me my first five shillings, which I lost. I promised him, honour bright, it was only between me and him; only you gave me that ten-shilling note I started winning with, so I thought you were lucky. You won't let it go any further, will you?"

The boy gazed at his uncle from those big, hot, blue eyes, set rather close together. The uncle stirred and laughed uneasily.

"Right you are, son! I'll keep your tip private. Daffodil, eh? How much are you putting on him?"

"All except twenty pounds," said the boy. "I keep that in reserve."

The uncle thought it a good joke.

"You keep twenty pounds in reserve, do you, you young romancer? What are you betting then?"

"I'm betting three hundred," said the boy gravely. "But it's between you and me, Uncle Oscar! Honour bright?"

The uncle burst into a roar of laughter.

"It's between you and me all right, you young Nat Gould,"[3] he said, laughing. "But where's your three hundred?"

"Bassett keeps it for me. We're partners."

"You are, are you! And what is Bassett putting on Daffodil?"

"He won't go quite as high as I do, I expect. Perhaps he'll go a hundred and fifty."

"What, pennies?" laughed the uncle.

"Pounds," said the child, with a surprised look at his uncle. "Bassett keeps a bigger reserve than I do."

[2] The Lincolnshire Handicap run at Lincoln Downs.

[3] Nathaniel Gould (1857–1919), a well-known writer who used horse racing as the subject for his journalism and fiction.

Between wonder and amusement Uncle Oscar was silent. He pursued the matter no further, but he determined to take his nephew with him to the Lincoln races.

"Now, son," he said, "I'm putting twenty on Mirza, and I'll put five on for you on any horse you fancy. What's your pick?"

"Daffodil, uncle."

"No, not the fiver on Daffodil!"

"I should if it was my own fiver," said the child.

"Good! Good! Right you are! A fiver for me and a fiver for you on Daffodil."

The child had never been to a racemeeting before, and his eyes were blue fire. He pursed his mouth tight and watched. A Frenchman just in front had put his money on Lancelot. Wild with excitement, he flayed his arms up and down, yelling *"Lancelot! Lancelot!"* in his French accent.

Daffodil came in first, Lancelot second, Mirza third. The child, flushed and with eyes blazing, was curiously serene. His uncle brought him four five-pound notes, four to one.

"What am I to do with these?" he cried, waving them before the boy's eyes.

"I suppose we'll talk to Bassett," said the boy. "I expect I have fifteen hundred now; and twenty in reserve; and this twenty."

His uncle studied him for some moments.

"Look here, son!" he said. "You're not serious about Bassett and that fifteen hundred, are you?"

"Yes, I am. But it's between you and me, uncle. Honour bright?"

"Honour bright all right, son! But I must talk to Bassett."

"If you'd like to be a partner, uncle, with Bassett and me, we could all be partners. Only, you'd have to promise, honour bright, uncle, not to let it go beyond us three. Bassett and I are lucky, and you must be lucky, because it was your ten shillings I started winning with. . . ."

Uncle Oscar took both Bassett and Paul into Richmond Park for an afternoon, and there they talked.

"It's like this, you see, sir," Bassett said. "Master Paul would get me talking about racing events, spinning yarns, you know, sir. And he was always keen on knowing if I'd made or if I'd lost. It's about a year since, now, that I put five shillings on Blush of Dawn for him: and we lost. Then the luck turned, with that ten shillings he had from you: that we put on Singhalese. And since that time, it's been pretty steady, all things considering. What do you say, Master Paul?"

"We're all right when we're sure," said Paul. "It's when we're not quite sure that we go down."

"Oh, but we're careful then," said Bassett.

"But when are you *sure?*" smiled Uncle Oscar.

"It's Master Paul, sir," said Bassett in a secret, religious voice. "It's as if he had it from heaven. Like Daffodil, now, for the Lincoln. That was as sure as eggs."

"Did you put anything on Daffodil?" asked Oscar Cresswell.

"Yes, sir. I made my bit."

"And my nephew?"

Bassett was obstinately silent, looking at Paul.

"I made twelve hundred, didn't I, Bassett? I told uncle I was putting three hundred on Daffodil."

"That's right," said Bassett, nodding.

"But where's the money?" asked the uncle.

"I keep it safe locked up, sir. Master Paul he can have it any minute he likes to ask for it."

"What, fifteen hundred pounds?"

"And twenty! And *forty,* that is, with the twenty he made on the course."

"It's amazing!" said the uncle.

"If Master Paul offers you to be partners, sir, I would, if I were you: if you'll excuse me," said Bassett.

Oscar Cresswell thought about it.

"I'll see the money," he said.

They drove home again, and, sure enough, Bassett came round to the garden-house with fifteen hundred pounds in notes. The twenty pounds reserve was left with Joe Glee, in the Turf Commission deposit.

"You see, it's all right, uncle, when I'm *sure!* Then we go strong, for all we're worth. Don't we, Bassett?"

"We do that, Master Paul."

"And when are you sure?" said the uncle, laughing.

"Oh, well, sometimes I'm *absolutely* sure, like about Daffodil," said the boy; "and sometimes I have an idea; and sometimes I haven't even an idea, have I, Bassett? Then we're careful, because we mostly go down."

"You do, do you! And when you're sure, like about Daffodil, what makes you sure, sonny?"

"Oh, well, I don't know," said the boy uneasily. "I'm sure, you know, uncle; that's all."

"It's as if he had it from heaven, sir," Bassett reiterated.

"I should say so!" said the uncle.

But he became a partner. And when the Leger[4] was coming on Paul was "sure" about Lively Spark, which was a quite inconsiderable horse. The boy insisted on putting a thousand on the horse, Bassett went for five hundred, and Oscar Cresswell two hundred. Lively Spark came in first, and the betting had been ten to one against him. Paul had made ten thousand.

"You see," he said, "I was absolutely sure of him."

Even Oscar Cresswell had cleared two thousand.

"Look here, son," he said, "this sort of thing makes me nervous."

"It needn't, uncle! Perhaps I shan't be sure again for a long time."

"But what are you going to do with your money?" asked the uncle.

"Of course," said the boy, "I started it for mother. She said she had no luck, because father is unlucky, so I thought if *I* was lucky, it might stop whispering."

"What might stop whispering?"

"Our house. I *hate* our house for whispering."

"What does it whisper?"

"Why—why"—the boy fidgeted—"why, I don't know. But it's always short of money, you know, uncle."

"I know it, son, I know it."

"You know people send mother writs,[5] don't you uncle?"

"I'm afraid I do," said the uncle.

---

[4] The St. Leger Stakes run at Doncaster.   [5] Presumably, dunning letters from creditors.

"And then the house whispers, like people laughing at you behind your back. It's awful, that is! I thought if I was lucky————"

"You might stop it," added the uncle.

The boy watched him with big blue eyes, that had an uncanny cold fire in them, and he said never a word.

"Well, then!" said the uncle. "What are we doing?"

"I shouldn't like mother to know I was lucky," said the boy.

"Why not, son?"

"She'd stop me."

"I don't think she would."

"Oh!"—and the boy writhed in an odd way—"I *don't* want her to know, uncle."

"All right, son! We'll manage it without her knowing."

They managed it very easily. Paul, at the other's suggestion, handed over five thousand pounds to his uncle, who deposited it with the family lawyer, who was then to inform Paul's mother that a relative had put five thousand pounds into his hands, which sum was to be paid out a thousand pounds at a time, on the mother's birthday, for the next five years.

"So she'll have a birthday present of a thousand pounds for five successive years," said Uncle Oscar. "I hope it won't make it all the harder for her later."

Paul's mother had her birthday in November. The house had been 'whispering' worse than ever lately, and, even in spite of his luck, Paul could not bear up against it. He was very anxious to see the effect of the birthday letter, telling his mother about the thousand pounds.

When there were no visitors, Paul now took his meals with his parents, as he was beyond the nursery control. His mother went into town nearly every day. She had discovered that she had an odd knack of sketching furs and dress materials, so she worked secretly in the studio of a friend who was the chief 'artist' for the leading drapers. She drew the figures of ladies in furs and ladies in silk and sequins for the newspaper advertisements. This young woman artist earned several thousand pounds a year, but Paul's mother only made several hundreds, and she was again dissatisfied. She so wanted to be first in something, and she did not succeed, even in making sketches for drapery advertisements.

She was down to breakfast on the morning of her birthday. Paul watched her face as she read her letters. He knew the lawyer's letter. As his mother read it, her face hardened and became more expressionless. Then a cold, determined look came on her mouth. She hid the letter under the pile of others, and said not a word about it.

"Didn't you have anything nice in the post for your birthday, mother?" said Paul.

"Quite moderately nice," she said, her voice cold and absent.

She went away to town without saying more.

But in the afternoon Uncle Oscar appeared. He said Paul's mother had had a long interview with the lawyer, asking if the whole five thousand could not be advanced at once, as she was in debt.

"What do you think, uncle?" asked the boy.

"I leave it to you, son."

"Oh, let her have it, then! We can get some more with the other," said the boy.

"A bird in the hand is worth two in the bush, laddie!" said Uncle Oscar.

"But I'm sure to *know* for the Grand National; or the Lincolnshire; or else the Derby.[6] I'm sure to know for *one* of them," said Paul.

So Uncle Oscar signed the agreement, and Paul's mother touched the whole five thousand. Then something very curious happened. The voices in the house suddenly went mad, like a chorus of frogs on a spring evening. There were certain new furnishings, and Paul had a tutor. He was *really* going to Eton, his father's school, in the following autumn. There were flowers in the winter, and a blossoming of the luxury Paul's mother had been used to. And yet the voices in the house, behind the sprays of mimosa and almond-blossom, and from under the piles of iridescent cushions, simply trilled and screamed in a sort of ecstasy: "There *must* be more money! Oh-h-h; there *must* be more money. Oh, now, now-w! Now-w-w—there *must* be more money!—more than ever! More than ever!"

It frightened Paul terribly. He studied away at his Latin and Greek with his tutor. But his intense hours were spent with Bassett. The Grand National had gone by: he had not 'known,' and had lost a hundred pounds. Summer was at hand. He was in agony for the Lincoln. But even for the Lincoln he didn't 'know,' and he lost fifty pounds. He became wild-eyed and strange, as if something were going to explode in him.

"Let it alone, son! Don't you bother about it!" urged Uncle Oscar. But it was as if the boy couldn't really hear what his uncle was saying.

"I've got to know for the Derby! I've got to know for the Derby!" the child reiterated, his big blue eyes with a sort of madness.

His mother noticed how overwrought he was.

"You'd better go to the seaside. Wouldn't you like to go now to the seaside, instead of waiting? I think you'd better," she said, looking down at him anxiously, her heart curiously heavy because of him.

But the child lifted his uncanny blue eyes.

"I couldn't possibly go before the Derby, mother!" he said. "I couldn't possibly!"

"Why not?" she said, her voice becoming heavy when she was opposed. "Why not? You can still go from the seaside to see the Derby with your Uncle Oscar, if that's what you wish. No need for you to wait here. Besides, I think you care too much about these races. It's a bad sign. My family has been a gambling family, and you won't know till you grow up how much damage it has done. But it has done damage. I shall have to send Bassett away, and ask Uncle Oscar not to talk racing to you, unless you promise to be reasonable about it: go away to the seaside and forget it. You're all nerves!"

"I'll do what you like, mother, so long as you don't send me away till after the Derby," the boy said.

"Send you away from where? Just from this house?"

"Yes," he said, gazing at her.

"Why, you curious child, what makes you care about this house so much, suddenly? I never knew you loved it."

He gazed at her without speaking. He had a secret within a secret, something he had not divulged, even to Bassett or to his Uncle Oscar.

But his mother, after standing undecided and a little bit sullen for some moments, said:

---

[6] Well-known British horse races: the Grand National run at Aintree, the Lincolnshire run at Lincoln Downs, and the Derby run at Epsom Downs.

"Very well, then! Don't go to the seaside till after the Derby, if you don't wish it. But promise me you won't let your nerves go to pieces. Promise you won't think so much about horse-racing and *events*, as you call them!"

"Oh no," said the boy casually. "I won't think much about them, mother. You needn't worry. I wouldn't worry, mother, if I were you."

"If you were me and I were you," said his mother, "I wonder what we *should* do!"

"But you know you needn't worry, mother, don't you?" the boy repeated.

"I should be awfully glad to know it," she said wearily.

"Oh, well, you *can*, you know. I mean, you *ought* to know you needn't worry," he insisted.

"Ought I? Then I'll see about it," she said.

Paul's secret of secrets was his wooden horse, that which had no name. Since he was emancipated from a nurse and a nursery-governess, he had had his rocking-horse removed to his own bedroom at the top of the house.

"Surely you're too big for a rocking-horse!" his mother had remonstrated.

"Well, you see, mother, till I can have a *real* horse, I like to have *some* sort of animal about," had been his quaint answer.

"Do you feel he keeps you company?" she laughed.

"Oh yes! He's very good, he always keeps me company, when I'm there," said Paul.

So the horse, rather shabby, stood in an arrested prance in the boy's bedroom.

The Derby was drawing near, and the boy grew more and more tense. He hardly heard what was spoken to him, he was very frail, and his eyes were really uncanny. His mother had sudden strange seizures of uneasiness about him. Sometimes, for half an hour, she would feel a sudden anxiety about him that was almost anguish. She wanted to rush to him at once, and know he was safe.

Two nights before the Derby, she was at a big party in town, when one of her rushes of anxiety about her boy, her firstborn, gripped her heart till she could hardly speak. She fought with the feeling, might and main, for she believed in common sense. But it was too strong. She had to leave the dance and go downstairs to telephone to the country. The children's nursery-governess was terribly surprised and startled at being rung up in the night.

"Are the children all right, Miss Wilmot?"

"Oh yes, they are quite all right."

"Master Paul? Is he all right?"

"He went up to bed as right as a trivet. Shall I run up and look at him?"

"No," said Paul's mother reluctantly. "No! Don't trouble. It's all right. Don't sit up. We shall be home fairly soon." She did not want her son's privacy intruded upon.

"Very good," said the governess.

It was about one o'clock when Paul's mother and father drove up to their house. All was still. Paul's mother went to her room and slipped off her white fur cloak. She had told her maid not to wait up for her. She heard her husband downstairs, mixing a whisky and soda.

And then, because of the strange anxiety at her heart, she stole upstairs to her son's room. Noiselessly she went along the upper corridor. Was there a faint noise? What was it?

She stood, with arrested muscles, outside his door, listening. There was a strange, heavy, and yet not loud noise. Her heart stood still. It was a soundless noise, yet rushing and powerful. Something huge, in violent, hushed motion. What was it? What in God's name was it? She ought to know. She felt that she knew the noise. She knew what it was.

Yet she could not place it. She couldn't say what it was. And on and on it went, like a madness.

Softly, frozen with anxiety and fear, she turned the door-handle.

The room was dark. Yet in the space near the window, she heard and saw something plunging to and fro. She gazed in fear and amazement.

Then suddenly she switched on the light, and saw her son, in his green pyjamas, madly surging on the rocking-horse. The blaze of light suddenly lit him up, as he urged the wooden horse, and lit her up, as she stood, blonde, in her dress of pale green and crystal, in the doorway.

"Paul!" she cried. "Whatever are you doing?"

"It's Malabar!" he screamed in a powerful, strange voice. "It's Malabar!"

His eyes blazed at her for one strange and senseless second, as he ceased urging his wooden horse. Then he fell with a crash to the ground, and she, all her tormented motherhood flooding upon her, rushed to gather him up.

But he was unconscious, and unconscious he remained, with some brain-fever. He talked and tossed, and his mother sat stonily by his side.

"Malabar! It's Malabar! Bassett, Bassett, I *know!* it's Malabar!"

So the child cried, trying to get up and urge the rocking-horse that gave him his inspiration.

"What does he mean by Malabar?" asked the heart-frozen mother.

"I don't know," said the father stonily.

"What does he mean by Malabar?" she asked her brother Oscar.

"It's one of the horses running for the Derby," was the answer.

And, in spite of himself, Oscar Cresswell spoke to Bassett, and himself put a thousand on Malabar: at fourteen to one.

The third day of the illness was critical: they were waiting for a change. The boy, with his rather long, curly hair, was tossing ceaselessly on the pillow. He neither slept nor regained consciousness, and his eyes were like blue stones. His mother sat, feeling her heart had gone, turned actually into a stone.

In the evening, Oscar Cresswell did not come, but Bassett sent a message, saying could he come up for one moment, just one moment? Paul's mother was very angry at the intrusion, but on second thoughts she agreed. The boy was the same. Perhaps Bassett might bring him to consciousness.

The gardener, a shortish fellow with a little brown moustache and sharp little brown eyes, tiptoed into the room, touched his imaginary cap to Paul's mother, and stole to the bedside, staring with glittering, smallish eyes at the tossing, dying child.

"Master Paul!" he whispered. "Master Paul! Malabar came in first all right, a clean win. I did as you told me. You've made over seventy thousand pounds, you have; you've got over eighty thousand. Malabar came in all right, Master Paul."

"Malabar! Malabar! Did I say Malabar, mother? Did I say Malabar? Do you think I'm lucky, mother? I knew Malabar, didn't I? Over eighty thousand pounds! I call that lucky, don't you, mother? Over eighty thousand pounds! I knew, didn't I know I knew? Malabar came in all right. If I ride my horse till I'm sure, then I tell you, Bassett, you can go as high as you like. Did you go for all you were worth, Bassett?"

"I went a thousand on it, Master Paul."

"I never told you, mother, that if I can ride my horse, and *get there,* then I'm absolutely sure—oh, absolutely! Mother, did I ever tell you? I *am* lucky!"

"No, you never did," said his mother.

But the boy died in the night.

And even as he lay dead, his mother heard her brother's voice saying to her: "My God, Hester, you're eighty-odd thousand to the good, and a poor devil of a son to the bad. But, poor devil, poor devil, he's best gone out of a life where he rides his rocking-horse to find a winner."

[1932]

Kay Boyle   1903–

ASTRONOMER'S WIFE

There is an evil moment on awakening when all things seem to pause. But for women, they only falter and may be set in action by a single move: a lifted hand and the pendulum will swing, or the voice raised and through every room the pulse takes up its beating. The astronomer's wife felt the interval gaping and at once filled it to the brim. She fetched up her gentle voice and sent it warily down the stairs for coffee, swung her feet out upon the oval mat, and hailed the morning with her bare arms' quivering flesh drawn taunt in rhythmic exercise: left, left, left my wife and fourteen children, right, right, right in the middle of the dusty road.

The day would proceed from this, beat by beat, without reflection, like every other day. The astronomer was still asleep, or feigning it, and she, once out of bed, had come into her own possession. Although scarcely ever out of sight of the impenetrable silence of his brow, she would be absent from him all the day in being clean, busy, kind. He was a man of other things, a dreamer. At times he lay still for hours, at others he sat upon the roof behind his telescope, or wandered down the pathway to the road and out across the mountains. This day, like any other, would go on from the removal of the spot left there from dinner on the astronomer's vest to the severe thrashing of the mayonnaise for lunch. That man might be each time the new arching wave, and woman the undertow that sucked him back, were things she had been told by his silence were so.

In spite of the earliness of the hour, the girl had heard her mistress's voice and was coming up the stairs. At the threshold of the bedroom she paused, and said: "Madame, the plumber is here."

The astronomer's wife put on her white and scarlet smock very quickly and buttoned it at the neck. Then she stepped carefully around the motionless spread of water in the hall.

"Tell him to come right up," she said. She laid her hands on the bannisters and stood looking down the wooden stairway. "Ah, I am Mrs. Ames," she said softly as she saw him mounting. "I am Mrs. Ames," she said softly, softly down the flight of stairs. "I am Mrs. Ames," spoken soft as a willow weeping. "The professor is still sleeping. Just step this way."

The plumber himself looked up and saw Mrs. Ames with her voice hushed, speaking to him. She was a youngish woman, but this she had forgotten. The mystery and silence of her husband's mind lay like a chiding finger on her lips. Her eyes were gray, for the light had been extinguished in them. The strange dim halo of her yellow hair was still uncombed and sideways on her head.

For all of his heavy boots, the plumber quieted the sound of his feet, and together they went down the hall, picking their way around the still lake of water that spread as far as the landing and lay docile there. The plumber was a tough, hardy man; but he took off his hat when he spoke to her and looked her fully, almost insolently in the eye.

"Does it come from the wash-basin," he said, "or from the other . . . ?"

"Oh, from the other," said Mrs. Ames without hesitation.

373

In this place the villas were scattered out few and primitive, and although beauty lay without there was no reflection of her face within. Here all was awkward and unfit; a sense of wrestling with uncouth forces gave everything an austere countenance. Even the plumber, dealing as does a woman with matters under hand, was grave and stately. The mountains round about seemed to have cast them into the shadow of great dignity.

Mrs. Ames began speaking of their arrival that summer in the little villa, mourning each event as it followed on the other.

"Then, just before going to bed last night," she said, "I noticed something was unusual."

The plumber cast down a folded square of sackcloth on the brimming floor and laid his leather apron on it. Then he stepped boldly onto the heart of the island it shaped and looked long into the overflowing bowl.

"The water should be stopped from the meter in the garden," he said at last.

"Oh, I did that," said Mrs. Ames, "the very first thing last night. I turned it off at once, in my nightgown, as soon as I saw what was happening. But all this had already run in."

The plumber looked for a moment at her red kid slippers. She was standing just at the edge of the clear, pure-seeming tide.

"It's no doubt the soil lines," he said severely. "It may be that something has stopped them, but my opinion is that the water seals aren't working. That's the trouble often enough in such cases. If you had a valve you wouldn't be caught like this."

Mrs. Ames did not know how to meet this rebuke. She stood, swaying a little, looking into the plumber's blue relentless eye.

"I'm sorry—I'm sorry that my husband," she said, "is still—resting and cannot go into this with you. I'm sure it must be very interesting. . . ."

"You'll probably have to have the traps sealed," said the plumber grimly, and at the sound of this Mrs. Ames' hand flew in dismay to the side of her face. The plumber made no move, but the set of his mouth as he looked at her seemed to soften. "Anyway, I'll have a look from the garden end," he said.

"Oh, do," said the astronomer's wife in relief. Here was a man who spoke of action and object as simply as women did! But however hushed her voice had been, it carried clearly to Professor Ames who lay, dreaming and solitary, upon his bed. He heard their footsteps come down the hall, pause, and skip across the pool of overflow.

"Katherine!" said the astronomer in a ringing tone. "There's a problem worthy of your mettle!"

Mrs. Ames did not turn her head, but led the plumber swiftly down the stairs. When the sun in the garden struck her face, he saw there was a wave of color in it, but this may have been anything but shame.

"You see how it is," said the plumber, as if leading her mind away. "The drains run from these houses right down the hill, big enough for a man to stand upright in them, and clean as a whistle too." There they stood in the garden with the vegetation flowering in disorder all about. The plumber looked at the astronomer's wife. "They come out at the torrent[1] on the other side of the forest beyond there," he said.

[1] Stream.

But the words the astronomer had spoken still sounded in her in despair. The mind of man, she knew, made steep and sprightly flights, pursued illusion, took foothold in the nameless things that cannot pass between the thumb and finger. But whenever the astronomer gave voice to the thoughts that soared within him, she returned in gratitude to the long expanses of his silence. Desert-like they stretched behind and before the articulation of his scorn.

Life, life is an open sea, she sought to explain it in sorrow, and to survive women cling to the floating débris on the tide. But the plumber had suddenly fallen upon his knees in the grass and had crooked his fingers through the ring of the drains' trap-door. When she looked down she saw that he was looking up into her face, and she saw too that his hair was as light as gold.

"Perhaps Mr. Ames," he said rather bitterly, "would like to come down with me and have a look around?"

"Down?" said Mrs. Ames in wonder.

"Into the drains," said the plumber brutally. "They're a study for a man who likes to know what's what."

"Oh, Mr. Ames," said Mrs. Ames in confusion. "He's still—still in bed, you see."

The plumber lifted his strong, weathered face and looked curiously at her. Surely it seemed to him strange for a man to linger in bed, with the sun pouring yellow as wine all over the place. The astronomer's wife saw his lean cheeks, his high, rugged bones, and the deep seams in his brow. His flesh was as firm and clean as wood, stained richly tan with the climate's rigor. His fingers were blunt, but comprehensible to her, gripped in the ring and holding the iron door wide. The backs of his hands were bound round and round with ripe blue veins of blood.

"At any rate," said the astronomer's wife, and the thought of it moved her lips to smile a little, "Mr. Ames would never go down there alive. He likes going up," she said. And she, in her turn, pointed, but impudently, towards the heavens. "On the roof. Or on the mountains. He's been up on the tops of them many times."

"It's matter of habit," said the plumber, and suddenly he went down the trap. Mrs. Ames saw a bright little piece of his hair still shining, like a star, long after the rest of him had gone. Out of the depths, his voice, hollow and dark with foreboding, returned to her. "I think something has stopped the elbow," was what he said.

This was speech that touched her flesh and bone and made her wonder. When her husband spoke of height, having no sense of it, she could not picture it nor hear. Depth or magic passed her by unless a name were given. But madness in a daily shape, as elbow stopped, she saw clearly and well. She sat down on the grasses, bewildered that it should be a man who had spoken to her so.

She saw the weeds springing up, and she did not move to tear them up from life. She sat powerless, her senses veiled, with no action taking shape beneath her hands. In this way some men sat for hours on end, she knew, tracking a single thought back to its origin. The mind of man could balance and divide, weed out, destroy. She sat on the full, burdened grasses, seeking to think, and dimly waiting for the plumber to return.

Whereas her husband had always gone up, as the dead go, she knew now that there were others who went down, like the corporeal being of the dead. That men were then divided into two bodies now seemed clear to Mrs. Ames.

This knowledge stunned her with its simplicity and took the uneasy motion from her limbs. She could not stir, but sat facing the mountains' rocky flanks, and harking in silence to lucidity. Her husband was the mind, this other man the meat, of all mankind.

After a little, the plumber emerged from the earth: first the light top of his head, then the burnt brow, and then the blue eyes fringed with whitest lash. He braced his thick hands flat on the pavings of the garden-path and swung himself completely from the pit.

"It's the soil lines," he said pleasantly. "The gases," he said as he looked down upon her lifted face, "are backing up the drains."

"What in the world are we going to do?" said the astronomer's wife softly. There was a young and strange delight in putting questions to which true answers would be given. Everything the astronomer had ever said to her was a continuous query to which there could be no response. _conflict_

"Ah, come, now," said the plumber, looking down and smiling. "There's a remedy for every ill, you know. Sometimes it may be that," he said as if speaking to a child, "or sometimes the other thing. But there's always a help for everything a-miss."

Things come out of herbs and make you young again, he might have been saying to her; or the first good rain will quench any drought; or time of itself will put a broken bone together.

"I'm going to follow the ground pipe out right to the torrent," the plumber was saying. "The trouble's between here and there and I'll find it on the way. There's nothing at all that can't be done over for the caring," he was saying, and his eyes were fastened on her face in insolence, or gentleness, or love.

He's helping her again what she lost

The astronomer's wife stood up, fixed a pin in her hair, and turned around towards the kitchen. Even while she was calling the servant's name, the plumber began speaking again.

"I once had a cow that lost her cud," the plumber was saying. The girl came out on the kitchen-step and Mrs. Ames stood smiling at her in the sun.

"The trouble is very serious, very serious," she said across the garden. "When Mr. Ames gets up, please tell him I've gone down."

She pointed briefly to the open door in the pathway, and the plumber hoisted his kit on his arm and put out his hand to help her down.

"But I made her another in no time," he was saying, "out of flowers and things and what-not."

"Oh," said the astronomer's wife in wonder as she stepped into the heart of the earth. She took his arm, knowing that what he said was true.

[1936]

He'll help her

Eudora Welty   *1909–*

PETRIFIED MAN

"Reach in my purse and git me a cigarette without no powder in it if you kin, Mrs. Fletcher, honey," said Leota to her ten o'clock shampoo-and-set customer. "I don't like no perfumed cigarettes."

Mrs. Fletcher gladly reached over to the lavender shelf under the lavender-framed mirror, shook a hair net loose from the clasp of the patent-leather bag, and slapped her hand down quickly on a powder puff which burst out when the purse was opened.

"Why, look at the peanuts, Leota!" said Mrs. Fletcher in her marvelling voice.

"Honey, them goobers has been in my purse a week if they's been in it a day. Mrs. Pike bought them peanuts."

"Who's Mrs. Pike?" asked Mrs. Fletcher, settling back. Hidden in this den of curling fluid and henna packs, separated by a lavender swing-door from the other customers, who were being gratified in other booths, she could give her curiosity its freedom. She looked expectantly at the black part in Leota's yellow curls as she bent to light the cigarette.

"Mrs. Pike is this lady from New Orleans," said Leota, puffing, and pressing into Mrs. Fletcher's scalp with strong red-nailed fingers. "A friend, not a customer. You see, like maybe I told you last time, me and Fred and Sal and Joe all had us a fuss, so Sal and Joe up and moved out, so we didn't do a thing but rent out their room. So we rented it to Mrs. Pike. And Mr. Pike." She flicked an ash into the basket of dirty towels. "Mrs. Pike is a very decided blonde. *She* bought me the peanuts."

"She must be cute," said Mrs. Fletcher.

"Honey, 'cute' ain't the word for what she is. I'm tellin' you, Mrs. Pike is attractive. She has her a good time. She's got a sharp eye out, Mrs. Pike has."

She dashed the comb through the air, and paused dramatically as a cloud of Mrs. Fletcher's hennaed hair floated out of the lavender teeth like a small storm-cloud.

"Hair fallin'."

"Aw, Leota."

"Uh-huh, commencin' to fall out," said Leota, combing again, and letting fall another cloud.

"Is it any dandruff in it?" Mrs. Fletcher was frowning, her hair-line eyebrows diving down toward her nose, and her wrinkled, beady-lashed eyelids batting with concentration.

"Nope." She combed again. "Just fallin' out."

"Bet it was that last perm'nent you gave me that did it," Mrs. Fletcher said cruelly. "Remember you cooked me fourteen minutes."

"You had fourteen minutes comin' to you," said Leota with finality.

"Bound to be somethin'," persisted Mrs. Fletcher. "Dandruff, dandruff. I couldn't of caught a thing like that from Mr. Fletcher, could I?"

"Well," Leota answered at last, "you know what I heard in here yestiddy, one of Thelma's ladies was settin' over yonder in Thelma's booth gittin' a machineless, and I don't mean to insist or insinuate or anything, Mrs. Fletcher,

but Thelma's lady just happ'med to throw out—I forgotten what she was talkin'
about at the time—that you was p-r-e-g., and lots of times that'll make your
hair do awful funny, fall out and God knows what all. It just ain't our fault,
is the way I look at it."

There was a pause. The women stared at each other in the mirror.

"Who was it?" demanded Mrs. Fletcher.

"Honey, I really couldn't say," said Leota. "Not that you look it."

"Where's Thelma? I'll get it out of her," said Mrs. Fletcher.

"Now, honey, I wouldn't go and git mad over a little thing like that," Leota
said, combing hastily, as though to hold Mrs. Fletcher down by the hair. "I'm
sure it was somebody didn't mean no harm in the world. How far gone are
you?"

"Just wait," said Mrs. Fletcher, and shrieked for Thelma, who came in and
took a drag from Leota's cigarette.

"Thelma, honey, throw your mind back to yestiddy if you kin," said Leota,
drenching Mrs. Fletcher's hair with a thick fluid and catching the overflow in
a cold wet towel at her neck.

"Well, I got my lady half wound for a spiral," said Thelma doubtfully.

"This won't take but a minute," said Leota. "Who is it you got in there,
old Horse Face? Just cast your mind back and try to remember who your
lady was yestiddy who happ'm to mention that my customer was pregnant,
that's all. She's dead to know."

Thelma drooped her blood-red lips and looked over Mrs. Fletcher's head
into the mirror. "Why, honey, I ain't got the faintest," she breathed. "I really
don't recollect the faintest. But I'm sure she meant no harm. I declare, I forgot
my hair finally got combed and thought it was a stranger behind me."

"Was it that Mrs. Hutchinson?" Mrs. Fletcher was tensely polite.

"Mrs. Hutchinson? Oh, Mrs. Hutchinson." Thelma batted her eyes. "Naw,
precious, she come on Thursday and didn't ev'm mention your name. I doubt
if she ev'm knows you're on the way."

"Thelma!" cried Leota staunchly.

"All I know is, whoever it is 'll be sorry some day. Why, I just barely knew
it myself!" cried Mrs. Fletcher. "Just let her wait!"

"Why? What're you gonna do to her?"

It was a child's voice, and the women looked down. A little boy was making
tents with aluminum wave pinchers on the floor under the sink.

"Billy Boy, hon, mustn't bother nice ladies," Leota smiled. She slapped
him brightly and behind her back waved Thelma out of the booth. "Ain't
Billy Boy a sight? Only three years old and already just nuts about the beauty-
parlor business."

"I never saw him here before," said Mrs. Fletcher, still unmollified.

"He ain't been here before, that's how come," said Leota. "He belongs to
Mrs. Pike. She got her a job but it was Fay's Millinery. He oughtn't to try on
those ladies' hats, they come down over his eyes like I don't know what. They
just git to look ridiculous, that's what, an' of course he's gonna put 'em on:
hats. They tole Mrs. Pike they didn't appreciate him hangin' around there.
Here, he couldn't hurt a thing."

"Well! I don't like children that much," said Mrs. Fletcher.

"Well!" said Leota moodily.

"Well! I'm almost tempted not to have this one," said Mrs. Fletcher. "That

Mrs. Hutchinson! Just looks straight through you when she sees you on the street and then spits at you behind your back."

"Mr. Fletcher would beat you on the head if you didn't have it now," said Leota reasonably. "After going this far."

Mrs. Fletcher sat up straight. "Mr. Fletcher can't do a thing with me."

"He can't!" Leota winked at herself in the mirror.

"No, siree, he can't. If he so much as raises his voice against me, he knows good and well I'll have one of my sick headaches, and then I'm just not fit to live with. And if I really look that pregnant already—"

"Well, now, honey, I just want you to know—I habm't told any of my ladies and I ain't goin' to tell 'em—even that you're losin' your hair. You just get you one of those Stork-a-Lure dresses and stop worryin'. What people don't know don't hurt nobody, as Mrs. Pike says."

"Did you tell Mrs. Pike?" asked Mrs. Fletcher sulkily.

"Well, Mrs. Fletcher, look, you ain't ever goin' to lay eyes on Mrs. Pike or her lay eyes on you, so what diffunce does it make in the long run?"

"I knew it!" Mrs. Fletcher deliberately nodded her head so as to destroy a ringlet Leota was working on behind her ear. "Mrs. Pike!"

Leota sighed. "I reckon I might as well tell you. It wasn't any more Thelma's lady tole me you was pregnant than a bat."

"Not Mrs. Hutchinson?"

"Naw, Lord! It was Mrs. Pike."

"Mrs. Pike!" Mrs. Fletcher could only sputter and let curling fluid roll into her ear. "How could Mrs. Pike possibly know I was pregnant or otherwise, when she doesn't even know me? The nerve of some people!"

"Well, here's how it was. Remember Sunday?"

"Yes," said Mrs. Fletcher.

"Sunday, Mrs. Pike an' me was all by ourself. Mr. Pike and Fred had gone over to Eagle Lake, saying' they was goin' to catch 'em some fish, but they didn't a course. So we was settin' in Mrs. Pike's car, it's a 1939 Dodge—"

"1939, eh," said Mrs. Fletcher.

"—An' we was gettin' us a Jax beer apiece—that's the beer that Mrs. Pike says is made right in N.O., so she won't drink no other kind. So I seen you drive up to the drugstore an' run in for just a secont, leavin' I reckon Mr. Fletcher in the car, an' come runnin' out with looked like a perscription. So I says to Mrs. Pike, just to be makin' talk, 'Right yonder's Mrs. Fletcher, and I reckon that's Mr. Fletcher—she's one of my regular customers,' I says."

"I had on a figured print," said Mrs. Fletcher tentatively.

"You sure did," agreed Leota. "So Mrs. Pike, she give you a good look— she's very observant, a good judge of character, cute as a minute, you know— and she says, 'I bet you another Jax that lady's three months on the way.'"

"What gall!" said Mrs. Fletcher. "Mrs. Pike!"

"Mrs. Pike ain't goin' to bite you," said Leota. "Mrs. Pike is a lovely girl, you'd be crazy about her, Mrs. Fletcher. But she can't sit still a minute. We went to the travellin' freak show yestiddy after work. I got through early— nine o'clock. In the vacant store next door. What, you ain't been?"

"No, I despise freaks," declared Mrs. Fletcher.

"Aw. Well, honey, talkin' about bein' pregnant an' all, you ought to see those twins in a bottle, you really owe it to yourself."

"What twins?" asked Mrs. Fletcher out of the side of her mouth.

"Well, honey, they got these two twins in a bottle, see? Born joined plumb together—dead a course." Leota dropped her voice into a soft lyrical hum. "They was about this long—pardon—must of been full time, all right, wouldn't you say?—an' they had these two heads an' two faces an' four arms an' four legs, all kind of joined *here.* See, this face looked this-a-way, and the other face looked that-a-way, over their shoulder, see. Kinda pathetic."

"Glah!" said Mrs. Fletcher disapprovingly.

"Well, ugly? Honey, I mean to tell you—their parents was first cousins and all like that. Billy Boy, git me a fresh towel from off Teeny's stack—this 'n's wringin' wet—an' quit ticklin' my ankles with that curler. I declare! He don't miss nothin'."

"Me and Mr. Fletcher aren't one speck of kin, or he could never of had me," said Mrs. Fletcher placidly.

"Of course not!" protested Leota. "Neither is me an' Fred, not that we know of. Well, honey, what Mrs. Pike liked was the pygmies. They've got these pygmies down there, too, an' Mrs. Pike was just wild about 'em. You know, the teeniniest men in the universe? Well, honey, they can just rest back on their little bohunkus an' roll around an' you can't hardly tell if they're sittin' or standin'. That'll give you some idea. They're about forty-two years old. Just suppose it was your husband!"

"Well, Mr. Fletcher is five foot nine and one half," said Mrs. Fletcher quickly.

"Fred's five foot ten," said Leota, "but I tell him he's still a shrimp, account of I'm so tall." She made a deep wave over Mrs. Fletcher's other temple with the comb. "Well, these pygmies are a kind of a dark brown, Mrs. Fletcher. Not bad-lookin' for what they are, you know."

"I wouldn't care for them," said Mrs. Fletcher. "What does that Mrs. Pike see in them?"

"Aw, I don't know," said Leota. "She's just cute, that's all. But they got this man, this petrified man, that ever'thing ever since he was nine years old, when it goes through his digestion, see, somehow Mrs. Pike says it goes to his joints and has been turning to stone."

"How awful!" said Mrs. Fletcher.

"He's forty-two too. That looks like a bad age."

"Who said so, that Mrs. Pike? I bet she's forty-two," said Mrs. Fletcher.

"Naw," said Leota, "Mrs. Pike's thirty-three, born in January, an Aquarian. He could move his head—like this. A course his head and mind ain't a joint, so to speak, and I guess his stomach ain't, either—not yet, anyways. But see— his food, he eats it, and it goes down, see, and then he digests it"—Leota rose on her toes for an instant—"and it goes out to his joints and before you can say 'Jack Robinson,' it's stone—pure stone. He's turning to stone. How'd you like to be married to a guy like that? All he can do, he came move his head just a quarter of an inch. A course he *looks* just *terrible.*"

"I should think he would," said Mrs. Fletcher frostily. "Mr. Fletcher takes bending exercises every night of the world. I make him."

"All Fred does is lay around the house like a rug. I wouldn't be surprised if he woke up some day and couldn't move. The petrified man just sat there moving his quarter of an inch though," said Leota reminiscently.

"Did Mrs. Pike like the petrified man?" asked Mrs. Fletcher.

"Not as much as she did the others," said Leota deprecatingly. "And then she likes a man to be a good dresser, and all that."

"Is Mr. Pike a good dresser?" asked Mrs. Fletcher sceptically.

"Oh, well, yeah," said Leota, "but he's twelve or fourteen years older'n her. She ast Lady Evangeline about him."

"Who's Lady Evangeline?" asked Mrs. Fletcher.

"Well, it's this mind reader they got in the freak show," said Leota. "Was real good. Lady Evangeline is her name, and if I had another dollar I wouldn't do a thing but have my other palm read. She had what Mrs. Pike said was the 'sixth mind' but she had the worst manicure I ever saw on a living person."

"What did she tell Mrs. Pike?" asked Mrs. Fletcher.

"She told her Mr. Pike was as true to her as he could be and besides, would come into some money."

"Humph!" said Mrs. Fletcher. "What does he do?"

"I can't tell," said Leota, "because he don't work. Lady Evangeline didn't tell me enough about my nature or anything. And I would like to go back and find out some more about this boy. Used to go with this boy until he got married to this girl. Oh, shoot, that was about three and a half years ago, when you was still goin' to the Robert E. Lee Beauty Shop in Jackson. He married her for her money. Another fortune-teller tole me that at the time. So I'm not in love with him any more, anyway, besides being married to Fred, but Mrs. Pike thought, just for the hell of it, see, to ask Lady Evangeline was he happy."

"Does Mrs. Pike know everything about you already?" asked Mrs. Fletcher unbelievingly. "Mercy!"

"Oh, yeah, I tole her ever'thing about ever'thing, from now on back to I don't know when—to when I first started goin' out," said Leota. "So I ast Lady Evangeline for one of my questions, was he happily married, and she says, just like she was glad I ask her, 'Honey,' she says, 'naw, he idn't. You write down this day, March 8, 1941,' she says, 'and mock it down: three years from today him and her won't be occupyin' the same bed.' There it is, up on the wall with them other dates—see, Mrs. Fletcher? And she says, 'Child, you ought to be glad you didn't git him, because he's so mercenary.' So I'm glad I married Fred. He sure ain't mercenary, money don't mean a thing to him. But I sure would like to go back and have my other palm read."

"Did Mrs. Pike believe in what the fortuneteller said?" asked Mrs. Fletcher in a superior tone of voice.

"Lord, yes, she's from New Orleans. Ever'body in New Orleans believes ever'thing spooky. One of 'em in New Orleans before it was raided says to Mrs. Pike one summer she was goin' to go from State to State and meet some grey-headed men, and, sure enough, she says she went on a beautician convention up to Chicago. . . ."

"Oh!" said Mrs. Fletcher. "Oh, is Mrs. Pike a beautician too?"

"Sure she is," protested Leota. "She's a beautician. I'm goin' to git her in here if I can. Before she married. But it don't leave you. She says sure enough, there was three men who was a very large part of making her trip what it was, and they all three had grey in their hair and they went in six States. Got Christmas cards from 'em. Billy Boy, go see if Thelma's got any dry cotton. Look how Mrs. Fletcher's a-drippin'."

"Where did Mrs. Pike meet Mr. Pike?" asked Mrs. Fletcher primly.

"On another train," said Leota.

"I met Mr. Fletcher, or rather he met me, in a rental library," said Mrs. Fletcher with dignity, as she watched the net come down over her head.

"Honey, me an' Fred, we met in a rumble seat eight months ago and we was practically on what you might call the way to the altar inside of half an hour," said Leota in a guttural voice, and bit a bobby pin open. "Course it don't last. Mrs. Pike says nothin' like that ever lasts."

"Mr. Fletcher and myself are as much in love as the day we married," said Mrs. Fletcher belligerently as Leota stuffed cotton into her ears.

"Mrs. Pike says it don't last," repeated Leota in a louder voice. "Now go git under the dryer. You can turn yourself on, can't you? I'll be back to comb you out. Durin' lunch I promised to give Mrs. Pike a facial. You know—free. Her bein' in the business, so to speak."

"I bet she needs one," said Mrs. Fletcher, letting the swing-door fly back against Leota. "Oh, pardon me."

A week later, on time for her appointment, Mrs. Fletcher sank heavily into Leota's chair after first removing a drug-store rental book, called *Life Is Like That,* from the seat. She stared in a discouraged way into the mirror.

"You can tell it when I'm sitting down, all right," she said.

Leota seemed preoccupied and stood shaking out a lavender cloth. She began to pin it around Mrs. Fletcher's neck in silence.

"I said you sure can tell it when I'm sitting straight on and coming at you this way," Mrs. Fletcher said.

"Why, honey, naw you can't," said Leota gloomily. "Why, I'd never know. If somebody was to come up to me on the street and say, 'Mrs. Fletcher is pregnant!' I'd say, 'Heck, she don't look it to me.' "

"If a certain party hadn't found it out and spread it around, it wouldn't be too late even now," said Mrs. Fletcher frostily, but Leota was almost choking her with the cloth, pinning it so tight, and she couldn't speak clearly. She paddled her hands in the air until Leota wearily loosened her.

"Listen, honey, you're just a virgin compared to Mrs. Montjoy," Leota was going on, still absent-minded. She bent Mrs. Fletcher back in the chair and, sighing, tossed liquid from a teacup on to her head and dug both hands into her scalp. "You know Mrs. Montjoy—her husband's that premature-grey-headed fella?"

"She's in the Trojan Garden Club, is all I know," said Mrs. Fletcher.

"Well, honey," said Leota, but in a weary voice, "she come in here not the week before and not the day before she had her baby—she come in here the very selfsame day, I mean to tell you. Child, we was all plumb scared to death. There she was! Come for her shampoo an' set. Why, Mrs. Fletcher, in an hour an' twenty minutes she was layin' up there in the Babtist Hospital with a seb'm-pound son. It was that close a shave. I declare, if I hadn't been so tired I would of drank up a bottle of gin that night."

"What gall," said Mrs. Fletcher. "I never knew her at all well."

"See, her husband was waitin' outside in the car, and her bags was all packed an' in the back seat, an' she was all ready, 'cept she wanted her shampoo an' set. An' havin' one pain right after another. Her husband kep' comin' in here, scared-like, but couldn't do nothin' with her a course. She yelled bloody murder, too, but she always yelled her head off when I give her a perm'nent."

"She must of been crazy," said Mrs. Fletcher. "How did she look?"

"Shoot!" said Leota.

"Well, I can guess," said Mrs. Fletcher. "Awful."

"Just wanted to look pretty while she was havin' her baby, is all," said Leota airily. "Course, we was glad to give the lady what she was after—that's our motto—but I bet a hour later she wasn't payin' no mind to them little end curls. I bet she wasn't thinkin' about she ought to have on a net. It wouldn't of done her no good if she had."

"No, I don't suppose it would," said Mrs. Fletcher.

"Yeah man! She was a-yellin'. Just like when I give her perm'nent."

"Her husband ought to make her behave. Don't it seem that way to you?" asked Mrs. Fletcher. "He ought to put his foot down."

"Ha," said Leota. "A lot he could do. Maybe some women is soft."

"Oh, you mistake me, I don't mean for her to get soft—far from it! Women have to stand up for themselves, or there's just no telling. But now you take me—I ask Mr. Fletcher's advice now and then, and he appreciates it, especially on something important, like is it time for a permanent—not that I've told him about the baby. He says, 'Why, dear, go ahead!' Just ask their *advice.*"

"Huh! If I ever ast Fred's advice we'd be floatin' down the Yazoo River on a houseboat or somethin' by this time," said Leota. "I'm sick of Fred. I told him to go over to Vicksburg."

"Is he going?" demanded Mrs. Fletcher.

"Sure. See, the fortune-teller—I went back and had my other palm read, since we've got to rent the room agin—said my lover was goin' to work in Vicksburg, so I don't know who she could mean, unless she meant Fred. And Fred ain't workin' here—that much is so."

"Is he going to work in Vicksburg?" asked Mrs. Fletcher. "And—"

"Sure. Lady Evangeline said so. Said the future is going to be brighter than the present. He don't want to go, but I ain't gonna put up with nothin' like that. Lays around the house an' bulls—did bull—with that good-for-nothin' Mr. Pike. He says if he goes who'll cook, but I says I never get to eat anyway— not meals. Billy Boy, take Mrs. Grover that *Screen Secrets* and leg it."

Mrs. Fletcher heard stamping feet go out the door.

"Is that that Mrs. Pike's little boy here again?" she asked, sitting up gingerly.

"Yeah, that's still him." Leota stuck out her tongue.

Mrs. Fletcher could hardly believe her eyes. "Well! How's Mrs. Pike, your attractive new friend with the sharp eyes who spreads it around town that perfect strangers are pregnant?" she asked in a sweetened tone.

"Oh, Mizziz Pike." Leota combed Mrs. Fletcher's hair with heavy strokes.

"You act like you're tired," said Mrs. Fletcher.

"Tired? Feel like it's four o'clock in the afternoon already," said Leota. "I ain't told you the awful luck we had, me and Fred? It's the worst thing you ever heard of. Maybe *you* think Mrs. Pike's got sharp eyes. Shoot, there's a limit! Well, you know, we rented out our room to this Mr. and Mrs. Pike from New Orleans when Sal an' Joe Fentress got mad at us 'cause they drank up some home-brew we had in the closet—Sal an' Joe did. So, a week ago Sat'day Mr. and Mrs. Pike moved in. Well, I kinda fixed up the room, you know—put a sofa pillow on the couch and picked some ragged robbins and put in a vase, but they never did say they appreciated it. Anyway, then I put some old magazines on the table."

"I think that was lovely," said Mrs. Fletcher.

"Wait. So, come night 'fore last, Fred and this Mr. Pike, who Fred just took up with, was back from they said they was fishin', bein' as neither one of 'em has got a job to his name, and we was all settin' around in their room. So Mrs. Pike was settin' there, readin' a old *Startling G-Man Tales* that was mine, mind you, I'd bought it myself, and all of a sudden she jumps!—into the air—you'd 'a' thought she'd set on a spider—an' says, 'Canfield'—ain't that silly, that's Mr. Pike—'Canfield, my God A'mighty,' she says, 'honey,' she says, 'we're rich, and you won't have to work.' Not that he turned one hand anyway. Well, me and Fred rushes over to her, and Mr. Pike, too, and there she sets, pointin' her finger at a photo in my copy of *Startling G-Man.* 'See that man!' yells Mrs. Pike. 'Remember him, Canfield?' 'Never forget a face,' says Mr. Pike. 'It's Mr. Petrie, that we stayed with him in the apartment next to ours in Toulouse Street in N.O. for six weeks. Mr. Petrie.' 'Well,' says Mrs. Pike, like she can't hold out one secont longer, 'Mr. Petrie is wanted for five hundred dollars cash, for rapin' four women in California, and I know where he is.' "

"Mercy!" said Mrs. Fletcher. "Where was he?"

At some time Leota had washed her hair and now she yanked her up by the back locks and sat her up.

"Know where he was?"

"I certainly don't," Mrs. Fletcher said. Her scalp hurt all over.

Leota flung a towel around the top of her customer's head. "Nowhere else but in that freak show! I saw him just as plain as Mrs. Pike. *He* was the petrified man!"

"Who would ever have thought that!" cried Mrs. Fletcher sympathetically.

"So Mr. Pike says, 'Well whatta you know about that,' an' he looks real hard at the photo and whistles. And she starts dancin' and singin' about her good luck. She meant our bad luck! I made a point of tellin' that fortune-teller the next time I saw her. I said, 'Listen, that magazine was layin' around the house for a month, and there was the freak show runnin' night an' day, not two steps away from my own beauty palor, with Mr. Petrie just settin' there waitin'. An' it had to be Mr. and Mrs. Pike, almost perfect strangers.' "

"What gall," said Mrs. Fletcher. She was only sitting there, wrapped in a turban, but she did not mind.

"Fortune-tellers don't care. And Mrs. Pike, she goes around actin' like she thinks she was Mrs. God," said Leota. "So they're goin' to leave tomorrow, Mr. and Mrs. Pike. And in the meantime I got to keep that mean, bad little ole kid here, gettin' under my feet ever' minute of the day an' talkin' back too."

"Have they gotten the five hundred dollars' reward already?" asked Mrs. Fletcher.

"Well," said Leota, "at first Mr. Pike didn't want to do anything about it. Can you feature that? Said he kinda liked that ole bird and said he was real nice to 'em, lent 'em money or somethin'. But Mrs. Pike simply tole him he could just go to hell, and I can see her point. She says, 'You ain't worked a lick in six months, and here I make five hundred dollars in two seconts, and what thanks do I get for it? You go to hell, Canfield,' she says. So," Leota went on in a despondent voice, "they called up the cops and they caught the ole bird, all right, right there in the freak show where I saw him with my own eyes, thinkin' he was petrified. He's the one. Did it under his real name— Mr. Petrie. Four women in California, all in the month of August. So Mrs. Pike gits five hundred dollars. And my magazine, and right next door to my beauty parlor. I cried all night, but Fred said it wasn't a bit of use and to go to sleep, because the whole thing was just a sort of coincidence—you know: can't do nothin' about it. He says it put him clean out of the notion of goin' to Vicksburg for a few days till we rent out the room agin—no tellin' who we'll git this time."

"But can you imagine anybody knowing this old man, that's raped four women?" persisted Mrs. Fletcher, and she shuddered audibly. "Did Mrs. Pike *speak* to him when she met him in the freak show?"

Leota had begun to comb Mrs. Fletcher's hair. "I says to her, I says, 'I didn't notice you fallin' on his neck when he was the petrified man—don't tell me you didn't recognize your fine friend?' And she says, 'I didn't recognize him with that white powder all over his face. He just looked familiar.' Mrs. Pike says, 'and lots of people look familiar.' But she says that ole petrified man did put her in mind of somebody. She wondered who it was! Kep' her awake, which man she'd ever knew it reminded her of. So when she seen the photo, it all come to her. Like a flash. Mr. Petrie. The way he'd turn his head and look at her when she took him in his breakfast."

"Took him in his breakfast!" shrieked Mrs. Fletcher. "Listen—don't tell me. I'd 'a' felt something."

"Four women. I guess those women didn't have the faintest notion at the time they'd be worth a hunderd an' twenty-five bucks a piece some day to Mrs. Pike. We ast her how old the fella was then, an' she says he musta had one foot in the grave, at least. Can you beat it?"

"Not really petrified at all, of course," said Mrs. Fletcher meditatively. She drew herself up. "I'd 'a' felt something," she said proudly.

"Shoot! I did feel somethin'," said Leota. "I tole Fred when I got home I felt so funny. I said, 'Fred, that ole petrified man sure did leave me with a funny feelin'.' He says, 'Funny-haha or funny-peculiar?' and I says, 'Funny-peculiar.' " She pointed her comb into the air emphatically.

"I'll bet you did," said Mrs. Fletcher.

They both heard a crackling noise.

Leota screamed, "Billy Boy! What you doin' in my purse?"

"Aw, I'm just eatin' these ole stale peanuts up," said Billy Boy.

"You come here to me!" screamed Leota, recklessly flinging down the comb, which scattered a whole ashtray full of bobby pins and knocked down a row of Coca-Cola bottles. "This is the last straw!"

"I caught him! I caught him!" giggled Mrs. Fletcher. "I'll hold him on my lap. You bad, bad boy, you! I guess I better learn how to spank little old bad boys," she said.

Leota's eleven o'clock customer pushed open the swing-door upon Leota paddling him heartily with the brush, while he gave angry but belittling screams which penetrated beyond the booth and filled the whole curious beauty parlor. From everywhere ladies began to gather round to watch the paddling. Billy Boy kicked both Leota and Mrs. Fletcher as hard as he could, Mrs. Fletcher with her new fixed smile.

Billy Boy stomped through the group of wildhaired ladies and went out the door, but flung back the words, "If you're so smart, why ain't you rich?"

[1939]

Richard Wright *1908–1960*

THE MAN WHO WAS ALMOST A MAN

Dave struck out across the fields, looking homeward through paling light. Whut's the use talkin wid em niggers in the field? Anyhow, his mother was putting supper on the table. Them niggers can't understan nothing. One of these days he was going to get a gun and practice shooting, then they couldn't talk to him as though he were a little boy. He slowed, looking at the ground. Shucks, Ah ain scareda them even ef they are biggern me! Aw, Ah know whut Ahma do. Ahm going by ol Joe's sto n git that Sears Roebuck catlog n look at them guns. Mebbe Ma will lemme buy one when she gits mah pay from ol man Hawkins. Ahma beg her t gimme some money. Ahm ol ernough to hava gun. Ahm seventeen. Almost a man. He strode, feeling his long loose-jointed limbs. Shucks, a man oughta hava little gun aftah he done worked hard all day.

He came in sight of Joe's store. A yellow lantern glowed on the front porch. He mounted steps and went through the screen door, hearing it bang behind him. There was a strong smell of coal oil and mackerel fish. He felt very confident until he saw fat Joe walk in through the rear door, then his courage began to ooze.

"Howdy, Dave! Whutcha want?"

"How yuh, Mistah Joe? Aw, Ah don wanna buy nothing. Ah jus wanted t see ef yuhd lemme look at tha catlog erwhile."

"Sure! You wanna see it here?"

"Nawsuh. Ah wans t take it home wid me. Ah'll bring it back termorrow when Ah come in from the fiels."

"You plannin on buying something?"

"Yessuh."

"Your ma lettin you have your own money now?"

"Shucks. Mistah Joe, Ahm gittin t be a man like anybody else!"

Joe laughed and wiped his greasy white face with a red bandanna.

"Whut you plannin on buyin?"

Dave looked at the floor, scratched his head, scratched his thigh, and smiled. Then he looked up shyly.

"Ah'll tell yuh, Mistah Joe, ef yuh promise yuh won't tell."

"I promise."

"Waal, Ahma buy a gun."

"A gun? Whut you want with a gun?"

"Ah wanna keep it."

"You ain't nothing but a boy. You don't need a gun."

"Aw, lemme have the catlog, Mistah Joe. Ah'll bring it back."

Joe walked through the rear door. Dave was elated. He looked around at barrels of sugar and flour. He heard Joe coming back. He craned his neck to see if he were bringing the book. Yeah, he's got it. Gawddog, he's got it!

"Here, but be sure you bring it back. It's the only one I got."

"Sho, Mistah Joe."

"Say, if you wanna buy a gun, why don't you buy one from me? I gotta gun to sell."

"Will it shoot?"

"Sure it'll shoot."

"Whut kind is it?"

"Oh, it's kinda old . . . a left-hand Wheeler. A pistol. A big one."

"Is it got bullets in it?"

"It's loaded."

"Kin Ah see it?"

"Where's your money?"

"Whut yuh wan fer it?"

"I'll let you have it for two dollars."

"Just two dollahs? Shuck, Ah could buy tha when Ah git mah pay."

"I'll have it here when you want it."

"Awright, suh. Ah be in fer it."

He went through the door, hearing it slam again behind him. Ahma git some money from Ma n buy me a gun! Only two dollahs! He tucked the thick catalogue under his arm and hurried.

"Where yuh been, boy?" His mother held a steaming dish of black-eyed peas.

"Aw, Ma, Ah jus stopped down the road t talk wid the boys."

"Yuh know bettah t keep suppah waitin."

He sat down, resting the catalogue on the edge of the table.

"Yuh git up from there and git to the well n wash yosef! Ah ain feedin no hogs in mah house!"

She grabbed his shoulder and pushed him. He stumbled out of the room, then came back to get the catalogue.

"Whut this?"

"Aw, Ma, it's jusa catlog."

"Who yuh git it from?"

"From Joe, down at the sto."

"Waal, thas good. We kin use it in the outhouse."

"Naw, Ma." He grabbed for it. "Gimme ma catlog, Ma."

She held onto it and glared at him.

"Quit hollerin at me! Whut's wrong wid yuh? Yuh crazy?"

"But Ma, please. It ain mine! It's Joe's! He tol me t bring it back t im termorrow."

She gave up the book. He stumbled down the back steps, hugging the thick book under his arm. When he had splashed water on his face and hands, he groped back to the kitchen and fumbled in a corner for the towel. He bumped into a chair; it clattered to the floor. The catalogue sprawled at his feet. When he had dried his eyes he snatched up the book and held it again under his arm. His mother stood watching him.

"Now, ef yuh gonna act a fool over that ol book, Ah'll take it n burn it up."

"Nah, Ma, please."

"Waal, set down n be still!"

He sat down and drew the oil lamp close. He thumbed page after page, unaware of the food his mother set on the table. His father came in. Then his smaller brother.

"Whutcha got there, Dave?" his father asked.

"Jusa catlog," he answered, not looking up.

"Yeah, here they is!" His eyes glowed at blue-and-black revolvers. He glanced up, feeling sudden guilt. His father was watching him. He eased the book under the table and rested it on his knees. After the blessing was asked, he ate. He scooped up peas and swallowed fat meat without chewing. Buttermilk helped to wash it down. He did not want to mention money before his father. He would do much better by cornering his mother when she was alone. He looked at his father uneasily out of the edge of his eye.

"Boy, how come yuh don quit foolin wid tha book n eat yo suppah?"

"Yessuh."

"How you n ol man Hawkins gitten erlong?"

"Suh?"

"Can't yuh hear? Why don yuh lissen? Ah ast yu how wuz yuh n ol man Hawkins gittin erlong?"

"Oh, swell, Pa. Ah plows mo lan than anybody over there."

"Waal, yuh oughta keep yo mind on whut yuh doin."

"Yessuh."

He poured his plate full of molasses and sopped it up slowly with a chunk of cornbread. When his father and brother had left the kitchen, he still sat and looked again at the guns in the catalogue, longing to muster courage enough to present his case to his mother. Lawd, ef Ah only had tha pretty one! He could almost feel the slickness of the weapon with his fingers. If he had a gun like that he would polish it and keep it shining so it would never rust. N Ah'd keep it loaded, by Gawd!

"Ma?" His voice was hesitant.

"Hunh?"

"Ol man Hawkins give yuh mah money yit?"

"Yeah, but ain no use yuh thinking bout throwin nona it erway. Ahm keepin tha money sos yuh kin have cloes t go to school this winter."

He rose and went to her side with the open catalogue in his palms. She was washing dishes, her head bent low over a pan. Shyly he raised the book. When he spoke, his voice was husky, faint.

"Ma, Gawd knows Ah wans one of these."

"One of whut?" she asked, not raising her eyes.

"One of these," he said again, not daring even to point. She glanced up at the page, then at him with wide eyes.

"Nigger, is yuh gone plumb crazy?"

"Aw, Ma—"

"Git outta here! Don yuh talk t me bout no gun! Yuh a fool!"

"Ma, Ah kin buy one fer two dollahs."

"Not ef Ah knows it, yuh ain!"

"But yuh promised me one—"

"Ah don care whut Ah promised! Yuh ain nothing but a boy yit!"

"Ma, ef yuh lemme buy one Ah'll *never* ast yuh fer nothing no mo."

"Ah tol yuh t git outta here! Yuh ain gonna toucha penny of tha money fer no gun! Thas how come Ah has Mistah Hawkins t pay yo wages t me, cause Ah knows yuh ain got no sense."

"But, Ma, we needa gun. Pa ain got no gun. We needa gun in the house. Yuh kin never tell whut might happen."

"Now don yuh try to maka fool outta me, boy! Ef we did hava gun, yuh wouldn't have it!"

He laid the catalogue down and slipped his arm around her waist.

"Aw, Ma, Ah done worked hard alla summer n ain ast yuh fer nothin, is Ah, now?"

"Thas whut yuh spose t do!"

"But Ma, Ah wans a gun. Yuh kin lemme have two dollahs outta mah money. Please, Ma. I kin give it to Pa . . . Please, Ma! Ah loves yuh, Ma."

When she spoke her voice came soft and low.

"Whut yu wan wida gun, Dave? Yuh don need no gun. Yuh'll git in trouble. N ef yo pa jus thought Ah let yuh have money t buy a gun he'd hava fit."

"Ah'll hide it, Ma. It ain but two dollahs."

"Lawd, chil, whut's wrong wid yuh?"

"Ain nothin wrong, Ma. Ahm almos a man now. Ah wans a gun."

"Who gonna sell yuh a gun?"

"Ol Joe at the sto."

"N it don cos but two dollahs?"

"Thas all, Ma. Jus two dollahs. Please, Ma."

She was stacking the plates away; her hands moved slowly, reflectively. Dave kept an anxious silence. Finally, she turned to him.

"Ah'll let yuh git tha gun ef yuh promise me one thing."

"Whut's tha, Ma?"

"Yuh bring it straight back t me, yuh hear? It be fer Pa."

"Yessum! Lemme go now, Ma."

She stooped, turned slightly to one side, raised the hem of her dress, rolled down the top of her stocking, and came up with a slender wad of bills.

"Here," she said. "Lawd knows yuh don need no gun. But yer pa does. Yuh bring it right back t me, yuh hear? Ahma put it up. Now ef yuh don, Ahma have yuh pa lick yuh so hard yuh won fergit it."

"Yessum."

He took the money, ran down the steps, and across the yard.

"Dave! Yuuuuuh Daaaaave!"

He heard, but he was not going to stop now. "Naw, Lawd!"

The first movement he made the following morning was to reach under his pillow for the gun. In the gray light of dawn he held it loosely, feeling a sense of power. Could kill a man with a gun like this. Kill anybody, black or white. And if he were holding his gun in his hand, nobody could run over him; they would have to respect him. It was a big gun, with a long barrel and a heavy handle. He raised and lowered it in his hand, marveling at its weight.

He had not come straight home with it as his mother had asked; instead he had stayed out in the fields, holding the weapon in his hand, aiming it now and then at some imaginary foe. But he had not fired it; he had been afraid that his father might hear. Also he was not sure he knew how to fire it.

To avoid surrendering the pistol he had not come into the house until he knew that they were all asleep. When his mother had tiptoed to his bedside late that night and demanded the gun, he had first played possum; then he had told her that the gun was hidden outdoors, that he would bring it to her in the morning. Now he lay turning it slowly in his hands. He broke it, took out the cartridges, felt them, and then put them back.

He slid out of bed, got a long strip of old flannel from a trunk, wrapped the gun in it, and tied it to his naked thigh while it was still loaded. He did not go in to breakfast. Even though it was not yet daylight, he started for Jim Hawkins' plantation. Just as the sun was rising he reached the barns where the mules and plows were kept.

"Hey! That you Dave?"

He turned. Jim Hawkins stood eying him suspiciously.

"What're yuh doing here so early?"

"Ah didn't know Ah wuz gittin up so early, Mistah Hawkins. Ah wuz fixin t hitch up ol Jenny n take her t the fiels."

"Good. Since you're so early, how about plowing that stretch down by the woods?"

"Suits me, Mistah Hawkins."

"O.K. Go to it!"

He hitched Jenny to a plow and started across the fields. Hot dog! This was just what he wanted. If he could get down by the woods, he could shoot his gun and nobody would hear. He walked behind the plow, hearing the traces creaking, feeling the gun tied tight to his thigh.

When he reached the woods, he plowed two whole rows before he decided to take out the gun. Finally, he stopped, looked in all directions, then untied the gun and held it in his hand. He turned to the mule and smiled.

"Know whut this is, Jenny? Naw, yuh wouldn know! Yuhs jusa ol mule! Anyhow, this is a gun, n it kin shoot, by Gawd!"

He held the gun at arm's length. Whut t hell, Ahma shoot this thing! He looked at Jenny again.

"Lissen here, Jenny! When Ah pull this ol trigger, Ah don wan yuh t run n acka fool now!"

Jenny stood with head down, her short ears pricked straight. Dave walked off about twenty feet, held the gun far out from him at arm's length, and turned his head. Hell, he told himself, Ah ain afraid. The gun felt loose in his fingers; he waved it wildly for a moment. Then he shut his eyes and tightened his forefinger. Bloom! A report half deafened him and he thought his right hand was torn from his arm. He heard Jenny whinnying and galloping over the field, and he found himself on his knees, squeezing his fingers hard between his legs. His hand was numb, he jammed it into his mouth, trying to warm it, trying to stop the pain. The gun lay at his feet. He did not quite know what had happened. He stood up and stared at the gun as though it were a living thing. He gritted his teeth and kicked the gun. Yuh almos broke mah arm! He turned to look for Jenny; she was far over the fields, tossing her head and kicking wildly.

"Hol on there, ol mule!"

When he caught up with her she stood trembling, walling her big white eyes at him. The plow was far away; the traces had broken. Then Dave stopped short, looking, not believing. Jenny was bleeding. Her left side was red and wet with blood. He went closer. Lawd, have mercy! Wondah did Ah shoot this mule? He grabbed for Jenny's mane. She flinched, snorted, whirled, tossing her head.

"Hol on now! Hol on."

Then he saw the hole in Jenny's side, right between the ribs. It was round, wet, red. A crimson stream streaked down the front leg, flowing fast. Good Gawd! Ah wuzn't shootin at tha mule. He felt panic. He knew he had to stop that blood, or Jenny would bleed to death. He had never seen so much blood in all his life. He chased the mule for half a mile, trying to catch her. Finally she stopped, breathing hard, stumpy tail half arched. He caught her mane and led her back to where the plow and gun lay. Then he stooped and grabbed handfuls of damp black earth and tried to plug the bullet hole. Jenny shuddered, whinnied, and broke from him.

"Hol on! Hol on now!"

He tried to plug it again, but blood came anyhow. His fingers were hot and sticky. He rubbed dirt into his palms, trying to dry them. Then again he attempted to plug the bullet hole, but Jenny shied away, kicking her heels high. He stood helpless. He had to do something. He ran at Jenny; she dodged him. He watched a red stream of blood flow down Jenny's leg and form a bright pool at her feet.

"Jenny . . . Jenny," he called weakly.

His lips trembled. She's bleeding t death! He looked in the direction of home, wanting to go back, wanting to get help. But he saw the pistol lying in the damp black clay. He had a queer feeling that if he only did something, this would not be; Jenny would not be there bleeding to death.

When he went to her this time, she did not move. She stood with sleepy, dreamy eyes; and when he touched her she gave a low-pitched whinny and knelt to the ground, her front knees slopping in blood.

"Jenny . . . Jenny . . ." he whispered.

For a long time she held her neck erect; then her head sank, slowly. Her ribs swelled with a mighty heave and she went over.

Dave's stomach felt empty, very empty. He picked up the gun and held it gingerly between his thumb and forefinger. He buried it at the foot of a tree. He took a stick and tried to cover the pool of blood with dirt—but what was the use? There was Jenny lying with her mouth open and her eyes walled and glassy. He could not tell Jim Hawkins he had shot his mule. But he had to tell something. Yeah, Ah'll tell em Jenny started gittin wil n fell on the joint of the plow. . . . But that would hardly happen to a mule. He walked across the field slowly, head down.

It was sunset. Two of Jim Hawkins' men were over near the edge of the woods digging a hole in which to bury Jenny. Dave was surrounded by a knot of people, all of whom were looking down at the dead mule.

"I don't see how in the world it happened," said Jim Hawkins for the tenth time.

The crowd parted and Dave's mother, father, and small brother pushed into the center.

"Where Dave?" his mother called.

"There he is," said Jim Hawkins.

His mother grabbed him.

"Whut happened, Dave? Whut yuh done?"

"Nothin."

"C mon, boy, talk," his father said.

Dave took a deep breath and told the story he knew nobody believed.

"Waal," he drawled. "Ah brung ol Jenny down here sos Ah could do mah plowin. Ah plowed bout two rows, just like yuh see." He stopped and pointed at the long rows of upturned earth. "Then somethin musta been wrong wid ol Jenny. She wouldn ack right a-tall. She started snortin n kickin her heels. Ah tried t hol her, but she pulled erway, rearin n goin in. Then when the point of the plow was stickin up in the air, she swung erroun n twisted herself back on it . . . She stuck herself n started t bleed. N fo Ah could do anything, she wuz dead."

"Did you ever hear of anything like that in all your life?" asked Jim Hawkins.

There were white and black standing in the crowd. They murmured. Dave's mother came close to him and looked hard into his face. "Tell the truth, Dave," she said.

"Looks like a bullet hole to me," said one man.

"Dave, whut yuh do wid the gun?" his mother asked.

The crowd surged in, looking at him. He jammed his hands into his pockets, shook his head slowly from left to right, and backed away. His eyes were wide and painful.

"Did he hava gun?" asked Jim Hawkins.

"By Gawd, Ah tol yuh tha wuz a gun wound," said a man, slapping his thigh.

His father caught his shoulders and shook him till his teeth rattled.

"Tell whut happened, yuh rascal! Tell whut . . ."

Dave looked at Jenny's stiff legs and began to cry.

"Whut yuh do wid tha gun?" his mother asked.

"Whut wuz he doin wida gun?" his father asked.

"Come on and tell the truth," said Hawkins. "Ain't nobody going to hurt you . . ."

His mother crowded close to him.

"Did yuh shoot tha mule, Dave?"

Dave cried, seeing blurred white and black faces.

"Ahh ddinn gggo tt sshooot hher . . . Ah ssswear ffo Gawd Ahh ddin. . . . Ah wuz a-trying to sssee ef the old gggun would sshoot—"

"Where yuh git the gun from?" his father asked.

"Ah got it from Joe, at the sto."

"Where yuh git the money?"

"Ma give it t me."

"He kept worryin me, Bob. Ah had t. Ah tol im t bring the gun right back t me . . . It was fer yuh, the gun."

"But how yuh happen to shoot that mule?" asked Jim Hawkins.

"Ah wuzn shootin at the mule, Mistah Hawkins. The gun jumped when Ah pulled the trigger . . . N fo Ah knowed anythin Jenny was there a-bleedin."

Somebody in the crowd laughed. Jim Hawkins walked close to Dave and looked into his face.

"Well, looks like you have bought you a mule, Dave."

"Ah swear fo Gawd, Ah didn go t kill the mule, Mistah Hawkins!"

"But you killed her!"

All the crowd was laughing now. They stood on tiptoe and poked heads over one another's shoulders.

"Well, boy, looks like yuh done bought a dead mule! Hahaha!"

"Ain tha ershame."

"Hohohohoho."

Dave stood, head down, twisting his feet in the dirt.

"Well, you needn't worry about it, Bob," said Jim Hawkins to Dave's father. "Just let the boy keep on working and pay me two dollars a month."

"What yuh wan fer yo mule, Mistah Hawkins?"

Jim Hawkins screwed up his eyes.

"Fifty dollars."

"Whut yuh do wid tha gun?" Dave's father demanded.

David said nothing.

"Yuh wan me t take a tree n beat yuh till yuh talk!"

"Nawsuh!"

"What yuh do wid it?"

"Ah throwed it erway."

"Where?"

"Ah . . . Ah throwed it in the creek."

"Waal, c mon home. N firs thing in the mawnin git to tha creek n fin tha gun."

"Yessuh."

"Whut yuh pay fer it?"

"Two dollahs."

"Take tha gun n git yo money back n carry it t Mistah Hawkins, yuh hear? N don fergit Ahma lam you black bottom good fer this! Now march yosef on home, suh!"

Dave turned and walked slowly. He heard people laughing. Dave glared, his eyes welling with tears. Hot anger bubbled in him. Then he swallowed and stumbled on.

That night Dave did not sleep. He was glad that he had gotten out of killing the mule so easily, but he was hurt. Something hot seemed to turn over inside him each time he remembered how they had laughed. He tossed on his bed, feeling his hard pillow. *N Pa says he's gonna beat me . . .* He remembered other beatings, and his back quivered. *Naw, naw, Ah sho don wan im t beat me tha way no mo. Dam em all! Nobody ever gave him anything. All he did was work. They treat me like a mule, n then they beat me.* He gritted his teeth. *N Ma had t tell on me.*

Well, if he had to, he would take old man Hawkins that two dollars. But that meant selling the gun. And he wanted to keep that gun. Fifty dollars for a dead mule.

He turned over, thinking how he had fired the gun. He had an itch to fire it again. *Ef other men kin shoota gun, by Gawd, Ah kin!* He was still, listening. *Mebbe they all sleepin now.* The house was still. He heard the soft breathing of his brother. *Yes, now!* He would go down and get that gun and see if he could fire it! He eased out of bed and slipped into overalls.

The moon was bright. He ran almost all the way to the edge of the woods. He stumbled over the ground, looking for the spot where he had buried the gun. *Yeah, here it is.* Like a hungry dog scratching for a bone, he pawed it up. He puffed his black cheeks and blew dirt from the trigger and barrel. He broke it and found four cartridges unshot. He looked around; the fields were filled with silence and moonlight. He clutched the gun stiff and hard in his fingers. But, as soon as he wanted to pull the trigger, he shut his eyes and turned his head. *Naw, Ah can't shoot wid mah eyes closed n mah head turned.* With effort he held his eyes open; then he squeezed. *Blooooom!* He was stiff, not breathing. The gun was still in his hands. Dammit, he'd done it! He fired again, *Blooooom!* He smiled. *Bloooom! Blooooom! Click, click.* There! It was empty. If anybody could shoot a gun, he could. He put the gun into his hip pocket and started across the fields.

When he reached the top of a ridge he stood straight and proud in the moonlight, looking at Jim Hawkins' big white house, feeling the gun sagging in his pocket. Lawd, ef Ah had just one mo bullet Ah'd taka shot at tha house. Ah'd like t scare ol man Hawkins jusa little . . . Jusa enough t let im know Dave Saunders is a man.

To his left the road curved, running to the tracks of the Illinois Central. He jerked his head, listening. From far off came a faint *hoooof-hoooof; hoooof-hoooof; hoooof-hoooof.* . . . He stood rigid. Two dollahs a mont. Les see now . . . Tha means it'll take bout two years. Shucks! Ah'll be dam!

He started down the road, toward the tracks. Yeah, here she comes! He stood beside the track and held himself stiffly. Here she comes, erroun the ben . . . C mon, yuh slow poke! C mon! He had his hand on his gun; something quivered in his stomach. Then the train thundered past, the gray and brown box cars rumbling and clinking. He gripped the gun tightly; then he jerked his hand out of his pocket. Ah betcha Bill wouldn't do it! Ah betcha . . . The cars slid past, steel grinding upon steel. Ahm ridin yuh ternight, so hep me Gawd! He was hot all over. He hesitated just a moment; then he grabbed, pulled atop of a car, and lay flat. He felt his pocket; the gun was still there. Ahead the long rails were glinting in the moonlight, stretching away, away to somewhere, somewhere where he could be a man . . .

[1940]

Jorge Luis Borges   *1899–*

THE GARDEN OF FORKING PATHS*

On page 22 of Liddell Hart's *History of World War I* you will read that an attack against the Serre-Montauban line by thirteen British divisions (supported by 1,400 artillery pieces), planned for the 24th of July, 1916, had to be postponed until the morning of the 29th. The torrential rains, Captain Liddell Hart comments, caused this delay, an insignificant one, to be sure.[1]

The following statement, dictated, reread and signed by Dr. Yu Tsun, former professor of English at the *Hochschule* at Tsingtao,[2] throws an unsuspected light over the whole affair. The first two pages of the document are missing.

". . . and I hung up the receiver. Immediately afterwards, I recognized the voice that had answered in German. It was that of Captain Richard Madden. Madden's presence in Viktor Runeberg's apartment meant the end of our anxieties and—but this seemed, *or should have seemed,* very secondary to me—also the end of our lives. It meant that Runeberg had been arrested or murdered.† Before the sun set on that day, I would encounter the same fate. Madden was implacable. Or rather, he was obliged to be so. An Irishman at the service of England, a man accused of laxity and perhaps of treason, how could he fail to seize and be thankful for such a miraculous opportunity: the discovery, capture, maybe even the death of two agents of the German Reich? I went up to my room; absurdly I locked the door and threw myself on my back on the narrow iron cot. Through the window I saw the familiar roofs and the cloud-shaded six o'clock sun. It seemed incredible to me that that day without premonitions or symbols should be the one of my inexorable death. In spite of my dead father, in spite of having been a child in a symmetrical garden of Hai Feng, was I—now—going to die? Then I reflected that everything happens to a man precisely, precisely *now.* Centuries of centuries and only in the present do things happen; countless men in the air, on the face of the earth and the sea, and all that really is happening is happening to me . . . The almost intolerable recollection of Madden's horselike face banished these wanderings. In the midst of my hatred and terror (it means nothing to me now to speak of terror, now that I have mocked Richard Madden, now that my throat yearns for the noose) it occurred to me that that tumultuous and doubtless happy warrior did not suspect that I possessed the Secret. The name of the exact location of the new British artillery park on the River Ancre.[3] A bird streaked across the gray sky and blindly I translated it into an airplane and that airplane into many (against the French sky) annihilating the artillery station with vertical bombs. If only my mouth, before a bullet shattered it, could cry out that secret name so it could be heard in Germany . . . My human voice was very weak.

---

* Translated by Donald A. Yates

[1] Hart is describing the Battle of the Somme, fought in northern France in July of 1916. See also Note 18.

[2] A port and manufacturing city in northern China.

† An hypothesis both hateful and odd. The Prussian spy Hans Rabener, alias Viktor Runeberg, attacked with drawn automatic the bearer of the warrant for his arrest, Captain Richard Madden. The latter, in self-defense, inflicted the wound which brought about Runeberg's death. (Note supplied by Borges' "Editor.")

[3] A tributary of the Somme River.

How might I make it carry to the ear of the Chief? To the ear of that sick and hateful man who knew nothing of Runeberg and me save that we were in Staffordshire[4] and who was waiting in vain for our report in his arid office in Berlin, endlessly examining newpapers . . . I said out loud: *I must flee.* I sat up noiselessly, in useless perfection of silence, as if Madden were already lying in wait for me. Something—perhaps the mere vain ostentation of proving my resources were nil—made me look through my pockets. I found what I knew I would find. The American watch, the nickel chain and the square coin, the key ring with the incriminating useless keys to Runeberg's apartment, the notebook, a letter which I resolved to destroy immediately (and which I did not destroy), a crown, two shillings and a few pence, the red and blue pencil, the handkerchief, the revolver with one bullet. Absurdly, I took it in my hand and weighed it in order to inspire courage within myself. Vaguely I thought that a pistol report can be heard at a great distance. In ten minutes my plan was perfected. The telephone book listed the name of the only person capable of transmitting the message; he lived in a suburb of Fenton,[5] less than a half hour's train ride away.

I am a cowardly man. I say it now, now that I have carried to its end a plan whose perilous nature no one can deny. I know its execution was terrible. I didn't do it for Germany, no. I care nothing for a barbarous country which imposed upon me the abjection of being a spy. Besides, I know of a man from England—a modest man—who for me is no less great than Goethe.[6] I talked with him for scarcely an hour, but during that hour he was Goethe . . . I did it because I sensed that the Chief somehow feared people of my race—for the innumerable ancestors who merge within me. I wanted to prove to him that a yellow man could save his armies. Besides, I had to flee from Captain Madden. His hands and his voice could call at my door at any moment. I dressed silently, bade farewell to myself in the mirror, went downstairs, scrutinized the peaceful street and went out. The station was not far from my home, but I judged it wise to take a cab. I argued that in this way I ran less risk of being recognized; the fact is that in the deserted street I felt myself visible and vulnerable, infinitely so. I remember that I told the cab driver to stop a short distance before the main entrance. I got out with voluntary, almost painful slowness; I was going to the village of Ashgrove[7] but I bought a ticket for a more distant station. The train left within a very few minutes, at eight-fifty. I hurried; the next one would leave at nine-thirty. There was hardly a soul on the platform. I went through the coaches; I remember a few farmers, a woman dressed in mourning, a young boy who was reading with fervor the *Annals* of Tacitus,[8] a wounded and happy soldier. The coaches jerked forward at last. A man whom I recognized ran in vain to the end of the platform. It was Captain Richard Madden. Shattered, trembling, I shrank into the far corner of the seat, away from the dreaded window.

From this broken state I passed into an almost abject felicity. I told myself that the duel had already begun and that I had won the first encounter by frustrating, even if for forty minutes, even if by a stroke of fate, the attack of

---

[4] A county in the English midlands.   [5] A town near Newcastle in Staffordshire.
[6] Johann Wolfgang von Goethe (1749–1832), whose contributions to German literature, philosophy, and science made him the intellectual giant of his age.
[7] Unidentified.
[8] The *Annals* by the Roman historian Tacitus (c. 55–120 A.D.) trace the history of the empire from Augustus to Nero.

my adversary. I argued that this slightest of victories foreshadowed a total victory. I argued (no less fallaciously) that my cowardly felicity proved that I was a man capable of carrying out the adventure successfully. From this weakness I took strength that did not abandon me. I foresee that man will resign himself each day to more atrocious undertakings; soon there will be no one but warriors and brigands; I give them this counsel: *The author of an atrocious undertaking ought to imagine that he has already accomplished it, ought to impose upon himself a future as irrevocable as the past.* Thus I proceeded as my eyes of a man already dead registered the elapsing of that day, which was perhaps the last, and the diffusion of the night. The train ran gently along, amid ash trees. It stopped, almost in the middle of the fields. No one announced the name of the station. "Ashgrove?" I asked a few lads on the platform. "Ashgrove," they replied. I got off.

A lamp enlightened the platform but the faces of the boys were in shadow. One questioned me, "Are you going to Dr. Stephen Albert's house?" Without waiting for my answer, another said, "The house is a long way from here, but you won't get lost if you take this road to the left and at every crossroads turn again to your left." I tossed them a coin (my last), descended a few stone steps and started down the solitary road. It went downhill, slowly. It was of elemental earth; overhead the banches were tangled; the low, full moon seemed to accompany me.

For an instant, I thought that Richard Madden in some way had penetrated my desperate plan. Very quickly, I understood that that was impossible. The instructions to turn always to the left reminded me that such was the common procedure for discovering the central point of certain labyrinths. I have some understanding of labyrinths: not for nothing am I the great grandson of that Ts'ui Pên who was governor of Yunnan[9] and who renounced wordly power in order to write a novel that might be even more populous than the *Hung Lu Meng*[10] and to construct a labyrinth in which all men would become lost. Thirteen years he dedicated to these heterogeneous tasks, but the hand of a stranger murdered him—and his novel was incoherent and no one found the labyrinth. Beneath English trees I meditated on that lost maze: I imagined it inviolate and perfect at the secret crest of a mountain; I imagined it erased by rice fields or beneath the water; I imagined it infinite, no longer composed of octagonal kiosks and returning paths, but of rivers and provinces and kingdoms . . . I thought of a labyrinth of labyrinths, of one sinuous spreading labyrinth that would encompass the past and the future and in some way involve the stars. Absorbed in these illusory images, I forgot my destiny of one pursued. I felt myself to be, for an unknown period of time, an abstract perceiver of the world. The vague, living countryside, the moon, the remains of the day worked on me, as well as the slope of the road which eliminated any possibility of weariness. The afternoon was intimate, infinite. The road descended and forked among the now confused meadows. A high-pitched, almost syllabic music approached and receded in the shifting of the wind, dimmed by leaves and distance. I thought that a man can be an enemy of other men, of the moments of other men, but not of a country: not of fireflies, words, gardens, streams of water, sunsets. Thus I arrived before a tall, rusty gate. Between

[9] A province in southwest China.
[10] *The Hung Lu Meng* (1754) by Tsao Hseuh-Chin (1719–1764) with its 421 characters is considered one of the greatest Chinese novels.

the iron bars I made out a poplar grove and a pavilion. I understood suddenly two things, the first trivial, the second almost unbelievable: the music came from the pavilion, and the music was Chinese. For precisely that reason I had openly accepted it without paying it any heed. I do not remember whether there was a bell or whether I knocked with my hand. The sparkling of the music continued.

From the rear of the house within a lantern approached: a lantern that the trees sometimes striped and sometimes eclipsed, a paper lantern that had the form of a drum and the color of the moon. A tall man bore it. I didn't see his face for the light blinded me. He opened the door and said slowly, in my own language: "I see that the pious Hsi P'êng persists in correcting my solitude. You no doubt wish to see the garden?"

I recognized the name of one of our consuls and I replied, disconcerted, "The garden?"

"The garden of forking paths."

Something stirred in my memory and I uttered with incomprehensible certainty, "The garden of my ancestor Ts'ui Pên,"

"Your ancestor? Your illustrious ancestor? Come in."

The damp path zigzagged like those of my childhood. We came to a library of Eastern and Western books. I recognized bound in yellow silk several volumes of the Lost Encyclopedia, edited by the Third Emperor of the Luminous Dynasty but never printed. The record on the phonograph revolved next to a bronze phoenix. I also recall a *famille rose*[11] vase and another, many centuries older, of that shade of blue which our craftsmen copied from the potters of Persia . . .

Stephen Albert observed me with a smile. He was, as I have said, very tall, sharp-featured, with gray eyes and a gray beard. He told me that he had been a missionary in Tientsin[12] before aspiring to become a Sinologist."

We sat down—I on a long, low divan, he with his back to the window and a tall circular clock. I calculated that my pursuer, Richard Madden, could not arrive for at least an hour. My irrevocable determination could wait.

"An astounding fate, that of Ts'ui Pên," Stephen Albert said. "Governor of his native province, learned in astronomy, in astrology and in the tireless interpretation of the canonical books, chess player, famous poet and calligrapher—he abandoned all this in order to compose a book and a maze. He renounced the pleasures of both tyranny and justice, of his populous couch, of his banquets and even of erudition—all to close himself up for thirteen years in the Pavilion of the Limpid Solitude. When he died, his heirs found nothing save chaotic manuscripts. His family, as you may be aware, wished to condemn them to the fire; but his executor—a Taoist or Buddhist monk[13]— insisted on their publication."

"We descendants of Ts'ui Pên," I replied, "continue to curse that monk. Their publication was senseless. The book is an indeterminate heap of contradictory drafts. I examimined it once: in the third chapter the hero dies, in the fourth he is alive. As for the other undertaking of Ts'ui Pên, his labyrinth . . ."

"Here is Ts'ui Pên's labyrinth," he said, indicating a tall lacquered desk.

---

[11] A type of Chinese porcelain.   [12] Like Tsingtao, a port city in northern China.
[13] China's two major religious orders.

"An ivory labyrinth!" I exclaimed. "A minimum labyrinth."

"A labyrinth of symbols," he corrected. "An invisible labyrinth of time. To me, a barbarous Englishman, has been entrusted the revelation of this diaphanous mystery. After more than a hundred years, the details are irretrievable; but it is not hard to conjecture what happened. Ts'ui Pên must have said once: *I am withdrawing to write a book.* And another time: *I am withdrawing to construct a labyrinth.* Every one imagined two works; to no one did it occur that the book and the maze were one and the same thing. The Pavilion of the Limpid Solitude stood in the center of a garden that was perhaps intricate; that circumstance could have suggested to the heirs a physical labyrinth. Hs'ui Pên died; no one in the vast territories that were his came upon the labyrinth; the confusion of the novel suggested to me that *it* was the maze. Two circumstances gave me the correct solution of the problem. One: the curious legend that Ts'ui Pên had planned to create a labyrinth which would be strictly infinite. The other: a fragment of a letter I discovered."

Albert rose. He turned his back on me for a moment; he opened a drawer of the black and gold desk. He faced me and in his hands he held a sheet of paper that had once been crimson, but was now pink and tenuous and cross-sectioned. The fame of Ts'ui Pên as a calligrapher had been justly won. I read, uncomprehendingly and with fervor, these words written with a minute brush by a man of my blood: *I leave to the various futures (not to all) my garden of forking paths.* Wordlessly, I returned the sheet. Albert continued:

"Before unearthing this letter, I had questioned myself about the ways in which a book can be infinite. I could think of nothing other than a cyclic volume, a circular one. A book whose last page was identical with the first, a book which had the possibility of continuing indefinitely. I remembered too that night which is at the middle of the Thousand and One Nights[14] when Scheherazade (through a magical oversight of the copyist) begins to relate word for word the story of the Thousand and One Nights establishing the risk of coming once again to the night when she must repeat it, and thus on to infinity. I imagined as well a Platonic,[15] hereditary work, transmitted from father to son, in which each new individual adds a chapter or corrects with pious care the pages of his elders. These conjectures diverted me; but none seemed to correspond, not even remotely, to the contradictory chapters of Ts'ui Pên. In the midst of this perplexity, I received from Oxford the manuscript you have examined. I lingered, naturally, on the sentence: *I leave to the various futures (not to all) my garden of forking paths.* Almost instantly, I understood: 'the garden of forking paths' was the chaotic novel; the phrase 'the various futures (not to all)' suggested to me the forking in time, not in space. A broad rereading of the work confirmed the theory. In all fictional works, each time a man is confronted with several alternatives, he chooses one and eliminates the others; in the fiction of Ts'ui Pên, he chooses—simultaneously—all of them. *He creates,* in this way, diverse futures, diverse times which themselves also proliferate and fork. Here, then, is the explanation of the novel's contradictions. Fang, let us say, has a secret; a stranger calls at his door; Fang resolves to kill him. Naturally, there are several possible outcomes: Fang can kill the intruder, the

---

[14] The series of fascinating stories ("The Arabian Nights") that Scheherazade told the sultan in order to prolong her life.

[15] Characteristic of the Greek philosopher Plato (427?–347 B.C.).

intruder can kill Fang, they both can escape, they both can die, and so forth. In the work of Ts'ui Pên, all possible outcomes occur; each one is the point of departure for other forkings. Sometimes, the paths of this labyrinth converge: for example, you arrive at this house, but in one of the possible pasts you are my enemy, in another, my friend. If you will resign yourself to my incurable pronunciation, we shall read a few pages."

His face, within the vivid circle of the lamplight, was unquestionably that of an old man, but with something unalterable about it, even immortal. He read with slow precision two versions of the same epic chapter. In the first, an army marches to a battle across a lonely mountain; the horror of the rocks and shadows makes the men undervalue their lives and they gain an easy victory. In the second, the same army traverses a palace where a great festival is taking place; the resplendent battle seems to them a continuation of the celebration and they win the victory. I listened with proper veneration to these ancient narratives, perhaps less admirable in themselves than the fact that they had been created by my blood and were being restored to me by a man of a remote empire, in the course of a desperate adventure, on a Western isle. I remember the last words, repeated in each version like a secret commandment: *Thus fought the heroes, tranquil their admirable hearts, violent their swords, resigned to kill and to die.*

From that moment on, I felt about me and within my dark body an invisible, intangible swarming. Not the swarming of the divergent, parallel and finally coalescent armies, but a more inaccessible, more intimate agitation that they in some manner prefigured. Stephen Albert continued:

"I don't believe that your illustrious ancestor played idly with these variations. I don't consider it credible that he would sacrifice thirteen years to the infinite execution of a rhetorical experiment. In your country, the novel is a subsidiary form of literature; in Ts'ui Pên's time it was a despicable form. Ts'ui Pên was a brilliant novelist, but he was also a man of letters who doubtless did not consider himself a mere novelist. The testimony of his contemporaries proclaims—and his life fully confirms—his metaphysical and mystical interests. Philosophic controversy usurps a good part of the novel. I know that of all problems, none disturbed him so greatly nor worked upon him so much as the abysmal problem of time. Now then, the latter is the only problem that does not figure in the pages of the *Garden*. He does not even use the word that signifies *time*. How do you explain this voluntary omission?"

I proposed several solutions—all unsatisfactory. We discussed them. Finally, Stephen Albert said to me:

"In a riddle whose answer is chess, what is the only prohibited word?"

I thought a moment and replied, "The word *chess*."

"Precisely," said Albert. "*The Garden of Forking Paths* is an enormous riddle, or parable, whose theme is time; this recondite cause prohibits its mention. To omit a word always, to resort to inept metaphors and obvious periphrases, is perhaps the most emphatic way of stressing it. That is the tortuous method preferred, in each of the meanderings of his indefatigable novel, by the oblique Ts'ui Pên. I have compared hundreds of manuscripts, I have corrected the errors that the negligence of the copyists has introduced, I have guessed the plan of this chaos, I have re-established—I believe I have re-established—the primordial organization, I have translated the entire work: it is clear to me that not once does he employ the word 'time.' The explanation is obvious: *The Garden of Forking Paths* is an incomplete, but not false, image of the universe as Ts'ui Pên conceived it. In contrast to Newton and Schopenhauer,[16] your ancestor did not believe in a uniform, absolute time. He believed in an infinite series of times, in a growing, dizzying net of divergent, convergent and parallel times. This network of times which approached one another, forked, broke off, or were unaware of one another for centuries, embraces *all* possibilities of time. We do not exist in the majority of these times; in some you exist, and not I; in others I, and not you; in others, both of us. In the present one, which a favorable fate has granted me, you have arrived at my house; in another, while crossing the garden, you found me dead; in still another, I utter these same words, but I am a mistake, a ghost."

"In every one," I pronounced, not without a tremble to my voice, "I am grateful to you and revere you for your re-creation of the garden of Ts'ui Pên."

"Not in all," he murmured with a smile. "Time forks perpetually toward innumerable futures. In one of them I am your enemy."

Once again I felt the swarming sensation of which I have spoken. It seemed to me that the humid garden that surrounded the house was infinitely saturated with invisible persons. Those persons were Albert and I, secret, busy and multiform in other dimensions of time. I raised my eyes and the tenuous nightmare dissolved. In the yellow and black garden there was only one man; but this man was as strong as a statue . . . this man was approaching along the path and he was Captain Richard Madden.

"The future already exists," I replied, "but I am your friend. Could I see the letter again?"

Albert rose. Standing tall, he opened the drawer of the tall desk; for the moment his back was to me. I had readied the revolver. I fired with extreme caution. Albert fell uncomplainingly, immediately. I swear his death was instantaneous—a lightning stroke.

The rest is unreal, insigificant. Madden broke in, arrested me. I have been condemned to the gallows. I have won out abominably; I have communicated to Berlin the secret name of the city they must attack. They bombed it yesterday; I read it in the same papers that offered to England the mystery of the learned Sinologist Stephen Albert who was murdered by a stranger, one Yu Tsun. The Chief had deciphered this mystery. He knew my problem was to indicate (through the uproar of the war) the city called Albert,[17] and that I had found no other means to do so than to kill a man of that name. He does not know (no one can know) my innumerable contrition and weariness.

[1941]

---

[16] Sir Isaac Newton (1642–1727), the English scientist, astronomer, and mathematician, and Arthur Schopenhauer (1788–1860), the German philosopher.
[17] A French town on the River Ancre.

Katherine Anne Porter   *1890–1980*

THE GRAVE

The grandfather, dead for more than thirty years, had been twice disturbed in his long repose by the constancy and possessiveness of his widow. She removed his bones first to Louisiana and then to Texas as if she had set out to find her own burial place, knowing well she would never return to the places she had left. In Texas she set up a small cemetery in a corner of her first farm, and as the family connection grew, and oddments of relations came over from Kentucky to settle, it contained at last about twenty graves. After the grandmother's death, part of her land was to be sold for the benefit of certain of her children, and the cemetery happened to lie in the part set aside for sale. It was necessary to take up the bodies and bury them again in the family plot in the big new public cemetery, where the grandmother had been buried. At last her husband was to lie beside her for eternity, as she had planned.

The family cemetery had been a pleasant small neglected garden of tangled rose bushes and ragged cedar trees and cypress, the simple flat stones rising out of uncropped sweet-smelling wild grass. The graves were lying open and empty one burning day when Miranda and her brother Paul, who often went together to hunt rabbits and doves, propped their twenty-two Winchester rifles carefully against the rail fence, climbed over and explored among the graves. She was nine years old and he was twelve.

They peered into the pits all shaped alike with such purposeful accuracy, and looking at each other with pleased adventurous eyes, they said in solemn tones: "These were graves!" trying by words to shape a special, suitable emotion in their minds, but they felt nothing except an agreeable thrill of wonder: they were seeing a new sight, doing something they had not done before. In them both there was also a small disappointment at the entire commonplaceness of the actual spectacle. Even if it had once contained a coffin for years upon years, when the coffin was gone a grave was just a hole in the ground. Miranda leaped into the pit that had held her grandfather's bones. Scratching around aimlessly and pleasurably as any young animal, she scooped up a lump of earth and weighed it in her palm. It had a pleasantly sweet, corrupt smell, being mixed with cedar needles and small leaves, and as the crumbs fell apart, she saw a silver dove no larger than a hazel nut, with spread wings and a neat fan-shaped tail. The breast had a deep round hollow in it. Turning it up to the fierce sunlight, she saw that the inside of the hollow was cut in little whorls. She scrambled out, over the pile of loose earth that had fallen back into one end of the grave, calling to Paul that she had found something, he must guess what . . . His head appeared smiling over the rim of another grave. He waved a closed hand at her. "I've got something too!" They ran to compare treasures, making a game of it, so many guesses each, all wrong, and a final showdown with opened palms. Paul had found a thin wide gold ring carved with intricate flowers and leaves. Miranda was smitten at the sight of the ring and wished to have it. Paul seemed more impressed by the dove. They made a trade, with some little bickering. After he had got the dove in his hand, Paul said, "Don't you know what this is? This is a screw head for a *coffin!* . . . I'll bet nobody else in the world has one like this!"

Miranda glanced at it without covetousness. She had the gold ring on her thumb; it fitted perfectly. "Maybe we ought to go now," she said, "maybe one of the niggers 'll see us and tell somebody." They knew the land had been sold, the cemetery was no longer theirs, and they felt like trespassers. They climbed back over the fence, slung their rifles loosely under their arms— they had been shooting at targets with various kinds of firearms since they were seven years old—and set out to look for the rabbits and doves or whatever small game might happen along. On these expeditions Miranda always followed at Paul's heels along the path, obeying instructions about handling her gun when going through fences; learning how to stand it up properly so it would not slip and fire unexpectedly; how to wait her time for a shot and not just bang away in the air without looking, spoiling shots for Paul, who really could hit things if given a chance. Now and then, in her excitement at seeing birds whizz up suddenly before her face, or a rabbit leap across her very toes, she lost her head, and almost without sighting she flung her rifle up and pulled the trigger. She hardly ever hit any sort of mark. She had no proper sense of hunting at all. Her brother would be often completely disgusted with her. "You don't care whether you get your bird or not," he said. "That's no way to hunt." Miranda could not understand his indignation. She had seen him smash his hat and yell with fury when he had missed his aim. "What I like about shooting," said Miranda, with exasperating inconsequence, "is pulling the trigger and hearing the noise."

"Then, by golly," said Paul, "whyn't you go back to the range and shoot at bulls-eyes?"

"I'd just as soon," said Miranda, "only like this, we walk around more."

"Well, you just stay behind and stop spoiling my shots," said Paul, who, when he made a kill, wanted to be certain he had made it. Miranda, who alone brought down a bird once in twenty rounds, always claimed as her own any game they got when they fired at the same moment. It was tiresome and unfair and her brother was sick of it.

"Now, the first dove we see, or the first rabbit, is mine," he told her. "And the next will be yours. Remember that and don't get smarty."

"What about snakes?" asked Miranda idly. "Can I have the first snake?"

Waving her thumb gently and watching her gold ring glitter, Miranda lost interest in shooting. She was wearing her summer roughing outfit: dark blue overalls, a light blue shirt, a hired-man's straw hat, and thick brown sandals. Her brother had the same outfit except his was a sober hickory-nut color. Ordinarily Miranda preferred her overalls to any other dress, though it was making rather a scandal in the countryside, for the year was 1903, and in the back country the law of female decorum had teeth in it. Her father had been criticized for letting his girls dress like boys and go careering around astride barebacked horses. Big sister Maria, the really independent and fearless one, in spite of her rather affected ways, rode at a dead run with only a rope knotted around her horse's nose. It was said the motherless family was running down, with the Grandmother no longer there to hold it together. It was known that she had discriminated against her son Harry in her will, and that he was in straits about money. Some of his old neighbors reflected with vicious satisfaction that now he would probably not be so stiffnecked, nor have any more high-stepping horses either. Miranda knew this, though she could not say how. She had met along the road old women of the kind who smoked corn-cob pipes, who had treated her grandmother with most sincere respect. They slanted their gummy old eyes side-ways at the granddaughter and said, "Ain't you ashamed of yoself, Missy? It's aginst the Scriptures to dress like that. Whut yo Pappy thinkin about?" Miranda, with her powerful social sense, which was like a fine set of antennae radiating from every pore of her skin, would feel ashamed because she knew well it was rude and ill-bred to shock anybody, even bad-tempered old crones, though she had faith in her father's judgment and was perfectly comfortable in the clothes. Her father had said, "They're just what you need, and they'll save your dresses for school . . ." This sounded quite simple and natural to her. She had been brought up in rigorous economy. Wastefulness was vulgar. It was also a sin. These were truths; she had heard them repeated many times and never once disputed.

Now the ring, shining with the serene purity of fine gold on her rather grubby thumb, turned her feelings against her overalls and sockless feet, toes sticking through the thick brown leather straps. She wanted to go back to the farmhouse, take a good cold bath, dust herself with plenty of Maria's violet talcum powder—provided Maria was not present to object, of course—put on the thinnest, most becoming dress she owned, with a big sash, and sit in a wicker chair under the trees . . . These things were not all she wanted, of course; she had vague stirrings of desire for luxury and a grand way of living which could not take precise form in her imagination but were founded on family legend of past wealth and leisure. These immediate comforts were what she could have, and she wanted them at once. She lagged rather far behind Paul, and once she thought of just turning back without a word and going home. She stopped, thinking that Paul would never do that to her, and so she would have to tell him. When a rabbit leaped, she let Paul have it without dispute. He killed it with one shot.

When she came up with him, he was already kneeling, examining the wound, the rabbit trailing from his hands. "Right through the head," he said complacently, as if he had aimed for it. He took out his sharp, competent bowie knife and started to skin the body. He did it very cleanly and quickly. Uncle Jimbilly knew how to prepare the skins so that Miranda always had fur coats for her dolls, for though she never cared much for her dolls she liked seeing them in fur coats. The children knelt facing each other over the dead animal. Miranda watched admiringly while her brother stripped the skin away as if he were taking off a glove. The flayed flesh emerged dark scarlet, sleek, firm; Miranda with thumb and finger felt the long fine muscles with the silvery flat strips binding them to the joints. Brother lifted the oddly bloated belly. "Look," he said, in a low amazed voice. "It was going to have young ones."

Very carefully he slit the thin flesh from the center ribs to the flanks, and a scarlet bag appeared. He slit again and pulled the bag open, and there lay a bundle a tiny rabbits, each wrapped in a thin scarlet veil. The brother pulled these off and there they were, dark gray, their sleek wet down lying in minute even ripples, like a baby's head just washed, their unbelievably small delicate ears folded close, their little blind faces almost featureless.

Miranda said, "Oh, I want to *see*," under her breath. She looked and looked— excited but not frightened, for she was accustomed to the sight of animals killed in hunting—filled with pity and astonishment and a kind of shocked delight in the wonderful little creatures for their own sakes, they were so pretty.

She touched one of them ever so carefully, "Ah, there's blood running over them," she said and began to tremble without knowing why. Yet she wanted most deeply to see and to know. Having seen, she felt at once as if she had known all along. The very memory of her former ignorance faded, she had always known just this. No one had ever told her anything outright, she had been rather unobservant of the animal life around her because she was so accustomed to animals. They seemed simply disorderly and unaccountably rude in their habits, but altogether natural and not very interesting. Her brother had spoken as if he had known about everything all along. He may have seen all this before. He had never said a word to her, but she knew now a part at least of what he knew. She understood a little of the secret, formless intuitions in her own mind and body, which had been clearing up, taking form, so gradually and so steadily she had not realized that she was learning what she had to know. Paul said cautiously, as if he were talking about something forbidden: "They were just about ready to be born." His voice dropped on the last word. "I know," said Miranda, "like kittens. I know, like babies." She was quietly and terribly agitated, standing again with her rifle under her arm, looking down at the bloody heap. "I don't want the skin," she said, "I won't have it." Paul buried the young rabbits again in their mother's body, wrapped the skin around her, carried her to a clump of sage bushes, and hid her away. He came out again at once and said to Miranda, with an eager friendliness, a confidential tone quite unusual in him, as if he were taking her into an important secret on equal terms: "Listen now. Now you listen to me, and don't ever forget. Don't you ever tell a living soul that you saw this. Don't tell a soul. Don't tell Dad because I'll get into trouble. He'll say I'm leading you into things you ought not to do. He's always saying that. So now don't you go and forget and blab out sometime the way you're always doing . . . Now, that's a secret. Don't you tell."

Miranda never told, she did not wish to tell anybody. She thought about the whole worrisome affair with confused unhappiness for a few days. Then it sank quietly into her mind and was heaped over by accumulated thousands of impressions, for nearly twenty years. One day she was picking her path among the puddles and crushed refuse of a market street in a strange city of a strange country, when without warning, plain and clear in its true colors as if she looked through a frame upon a scene that had not stirred nor changed since the moment it happened, the episode of that far-off day leaped from its burial place before her mind's eye. She was so reasonlessly horrified she halted suddenly staring, the scene before her eyes dimmed by the vision back of them. An Indian vendor had held up before her a tray of dyed sugar sweets, in the shapes of all kinds of small creatures: birds, baby chicks, baby rabbits, lambs, baby pigs. They were in gay colors and smelled of vanilla, maybe. . . . It was a very hot day and the smell in the market, with its piles of raw flesh and wilting flowers, was like the mingled sweetness and corruption she had smelled that other day in the empty cemetery at home: the day she had remembered always until now vaguely as the time she and her brother had found treasure in the opened graves. Instantly upon this thought the dreadful vision faded, and she saw clearly her brother, whose childhood face she had forgotten, standing again in the blazing sunshine, again twelve years old, a pleased sober smile in his eyes, turning the silver dove over and over in his hands.

[1944]

Ralph Ellison   *1914–*

KING OF THE BINGO GAME

The Woman in front of him was eating roasted peanuts that smelled so good that he could barely contain his hunger. He could not even sleep and wished they'd hurry and begin the bingo game. There, on his right, two fellows were drinking wine out of a bottle wrapped in a paper bag, and he could hear soft gurgling in the dark. His stomach gave a low, gnawing growl. "If this was down South," he thought, "all I'd have to do is lean over and say, 'Lady, gimme a few of those peanuts, please ma'am,' and she'd pass me the bag and never think nothing of it." Or he could ask the fellows for a drink in the same way. Folks down South stuck together that way; they didn't even have to know you. But up here it was different. Ask somebody for something, and they'd think you were crazy. Well, I ain't crazy. I'm just broke, 'cause I got no birth certificate to get a job, and Laura 'bout to die 'cause we got no money for a doctor. But I ain't crazy. And yet a pinpoint of doubt was focused in his mind as he glanced toward the screen and saw the hero stealthily entering a dark room and sending the beam of a flashlight along a wall of bookcases. This is where he finds the trapdoor, he remembered. The man would pass abruptly through the wall and find the girl tied to a bed, her legs and arms spread wide, and her clothing torn to rags. He laughed softly to himself. He had seen the picture three times, and this was one of the best scenes.

On his right the fellow whispered wide-eyed to his companion, "Man, look ayonder!"

"Damn!"

"Wouldn't I like to have her tied up like that . . ."

"Hey! That fool's letting her loose!"

"Aw, man, he loves her."

"Love or no love!"

The man moved impatiently beside him, and he tried to involve himself in the scene. But Laura was on his mind. Tiring quickly of watching the picture he looked back to where the white beam filtered from the projection room above the balcony. It started small and grew large, specks of dust dancing in its whiteness as it reached the screen. It was strange how the beam always landed right on the screeen and didn't mess up and fall somewhere else. But they had it all fixed. Everything was fixed. Now suppose when they showed that girl with her dress torn the girl started taking off the rest of her clothes, and when the guy came in he didn't untie her but kept her there and went to taking off his own clothes? *That* would be something to see. If a picture got out of hand like that those guys up there would go nuts. Yeah, and there'd be so many folks in here you couldn't find a seat for nine months! A strange sensation played over his skin. He shuddered. Yesterday he'd seen a bedbug on a woman's neck as they walked out into the bright street. But exploring his thigh through a hole in his pocket he found only goose pimples and old scars.

The bottle gurgled again. He closed his eyes. Now a dreamy music was accompanying the film and train whistles were sounding in the distance, and he was a boy again walking along a railroad trestle down South, and seeing the train coming, and running back as fast as he could go, and hearing the whistle blowing, and getting off the trestle to solid ground just in time, with the earth trembling beneath his feet, and feeling relieved as he ran down the cinder-strewn embankment onto the highway, and looking back and seeing with terror that the train had left the track and was following him right down the middle of the street, and all the white people laughing as he ran screaming . . .

"Wake up there, buddy! What the hell do you mean hollering like that? Can't you see we trying to enjoy this here picture?"

He stared at the man with gratitude.

"I'm sorry, old man," he said. "I musta been dreaming."

"Well, here, have a drink. And don't be making no noise like that, damn!"

His hands trembled as he tilted his head. It was not wine, but whiskey. Cold rye whiskey. He took a deep swoller, decided it was better not to take another, and handed the bottle back to its owner.

"Thanks, old man," he said.

Now he felt the cold whiskey breaking a warm path straight through the middle of him, growing hotter and sharper as it moved. He had not eaten all day, and it made him light-headed. The smell of the peanuts stabbed him like a knife, and he got up and found a seat in the middle aisle. But no sooner did he sit than he saw a row of intense-faced young girls, and got up again, thinking, "You chicks musta been Lindy-hopping somewhere." He found a seat several rows ahead as the lights came on, and he saw the screen disappear behind a heavy red and gold curtain; then the curtain rising, and the man with the microphone and a uniformed attendant coming on the stage.

He felt for his bingo cards, smiling. The guy at the door wouldn't like it if he knew about his having *five* cards. Well, not everyone played the bingo game; and even with five cards he didn't have much of a chance. For Laura, though, he had to have faith. He studied the cards, each with its different numerals, punching the free center hole in each and spreading them neatly across his lap; and when the lights faded he sat slouched in his seat so that he could look from his cards to the bingo wheel with but a quick shifting of his eyes.

Ahead, at the end of the darkness, the man with the microphone was pressing a button attached to a long cord and spinning the bingo wheel and calling out the number each time the wheel came to rest. And each time the voice rang out his finger raced over the cards for the number. With five cards he had to move fast. He became nervous; there were too many cards, and the man went too fast with his grating voice. Perhaps he should just select one and throw the others away. But he was afraid. He became warm. Wonder how much Laura's doctor would cost? Damn that, watch the cards! And with despair he heard the man call three in a row which he missed on all five cards. This way he'd never win . . .

When he saw the row of holes punched across the third card, he sat paralyzed and heard the man call three more numbers before he stumbled forward, screaming.

"Bingo! Bingo!"

"Let that fool up there," someone called.

"Get up there, man!"

He stumbled down the aisle and up the steps to the stage into a light so sharp and bright that for a moment it blinded him, and he felt that he had moved into the spell of some strange, mysterious power. Yet it was as familiar as the sun, and he knew it was the perfectly familiar bingo.

The man with the microphone was saying something to the audience as he held out his card. A cold light flashed from the man's finger as the card left his hand. His knees trembled. The man stepped closer, checking the card against the numbers chalked on the board. Suppose he had made a mistake? The pomade on the man's hair made him feel faint, and he backed away. But the man was checking the card over the microphone now, and he had to stay. He stood tense, listening.

"Under the O, forty-four," the man chanted. "Under the I, seven. Under the G, three. Under the B, ninety-six. Under the N, thirteen!"

His breath came easier as the man smiled at the audience.

"Yessir, ladies and gentlemen, he's one of the chosen people!"

The audience rippled with laughter and applause.

"Step right up to the front of the stage."

He moved slowly forward, wishing that the light was not so bright.

"To win to-night's jackpot of $36.90 the wheel must stop between the double zero, understand?"

He nodded, knowing the ritual from the many days and nights he had watched the winners march across the stage to press the button that controlled the spinning wheel and receive the prizes. And now he followed the instructions as though he'd crossed the slippery stage a million prize-winning times.

The man was making some kind of a joke, and he nodded vacantly. So tense had he become that he felt a sudden desire to cry and shook it away. He felt vaguely that his whole life was determined by the bingo wheel; not only that which would happen now that he was at last before it, but all that had gone before, since his birth, and his mother's birth and the birth of his father. It had always been there, even though he had not been aware of it, handing out the unlucky cards and numbers of his days. The feeling persisted, and he started quickly away. I better get down from here before I make a fool of myself, he thought.

"Here, boy," the man called. "You haven't started yet."

Someone laughed as he went hesitantly back.

"Are you all reet?"

He grinned at the man's jive talk, but no words would come, and he knew it was not a convincing grin. For suddenly he knew that he stood on the slippery brink of some terrible embarrassment.

"Where are you from, boy?" the man asked.

"Down South."

"He's from down South, ladies and gentlemen," the man said. "Where from? Speak right into the mike."

"Rocky Mont," he said. "Rock' Mont, North Car'lina."

"So you decided to come down off that mountain to the U.S.," the man laughed. He felt that the man was making a fool of him, but then something cold was placed in his hand, and the lights were no longer behind him.

Standing before the wheel he felt alone, but that was somehow right, and he remembered his plan. He would give the wheel a short quick twirl. Just a touch of the button. He had watched it many times, and always it came close to double zero when it was short and quick. He steeled himself; the fear had left, and he felt a profound sense of promise, as though he were about to be repaid for all the things he'd suffered all his life. Trembling, he pressed the button. There was a whirl of lights, and in a second he realized with finality that though he wanted to, he could not stop. It was as though he held a high-powered line in his naked hand. His nerves tightened. As the wheel increased its speed it seemed to draw him more and more into its power, as though it held his fate; and with it came a deep need to submit, to whirl, to lose himself in its swirl of color. He could not stop it now. So let it be.

The button rested snugly in his palm where the man had placed it. And now he became aware of the man beside him, advising him through the microphone, while behind the shadowy audience hummed with noisy voices. He shifted his feet. There was still that feeling of helplessness within him, making part of him desire to turn back, even now that the jackpot was right in his hand. He squeezed the button until his fist ached. Then, like the sudden shriek of a subway whistle, a doubt tore through his head. Suppose he did not spin the wheel long enough? What could he do, and how could he tell? And then he knew, even as he wondered, that as long as he pressed the button, he could control the jackpot. He and only he could determine whether or not it was to be his. Not even the man with the microphone could do anything about it now. He felt drunk. Then, as though he had come down from a high hill into a valley of people, he heard the audience yelling.

"Come down from there, you jerk!"

"Let somebody else have a chance . . ."

"Old Jack thinks he done found the end of the rainbow . . ."

The last voice was not unfriendly, and he turned and smiled dreamily into the yelling mouths. Then he turned his back squarely on them.

"Don't take too long, boy," a voice said.

He nodded. They were yelling behind him. Those folks did not understand what had happened to him. They had been playing the bingo game day in and night out for years, trying to win rent money or hamburger change. But not one of those wise guys had discovered this wonderful thing. He watched the wheel whirling past the numbers and experienced a burst of exaltation: That is God! This is the really truly God! He said it aloud, "This is God!"

He said it with such absolute conviction that he feared he would fall fainting into the footlights. But the crowd yelled so loud that they could not hear. Those fools, he thought. I'm here trying to tell them the most wonderful secret in the world, and they're yelling like they gone crazy. A hand fell upon his shoulder.

"You'll have to make a choice now, boy. You've taken too long."

He brushed the hand violently away.

"Leave me alone, man. I know what I'm doing!"

The man looked surprised and held on to the microphone for support. And because he did not wish to hurt the man's feelings he smiled, realizing with a sudden pang that there was no way of explaining to the man just why he had to stand there pressing the button forever.

"Come here," he called tiredly.

The man approached, rolling the heavy microphone across the stage.

"Anybody can play this bingo game, right?" he said.

"Sure, but . . ."

He smiled, feeling inclined to be patient with this slick looking white man with his blue shirt and his sharp gabardine suit.

"That's what I thought," he said. "Anybody can win the jackpot as long as they get the lucky number, right?"

"That's the rule, but after all . . ."

"That's what I thought," he said. "And the big prize goes to the man who knows how to win it?"

The man nodded speechlessly.

"Well then, go on over there and watch me win like I want to. I ain't going to hurt nobody," he said, "and I'll show you how to win. I mean to show the whole world how it's got to be done."

And because he understood, he smiled again to let the man know that he held nothing against him for being white and impatient. Then he refused to see the man any longer and stood pressing the button, the voices of the crowd reaching him like sounds in distant streets. Let them yell. All the Negroes down there were just ashamed because he was black like them. He smiled inwardly, knowing how it was. Most of the time he was ashamed of what Negroes did himself. Well, let them be ashamed for something this time. Like him. He was like a long thin black wire that was being stretched and wound upon the bingo wheel; wound until he wanted to scream; wound, but this time himself controlling the winding and the sadness and the shame, and because he did, Laura would be all right. Suddenly the lights flickered. He staggered backwards. Had something gone wrong? All this noise. Didn't they know that although he controlled the wheel, it also controlled him, and unless he pressed the button forever and forever and ever it would stop, leaving him high and dry, dry and high on this hard high slippery hill and Laura dead? There was only one chance; he had to do whatever the wheel demanded. And gripping the button in despair, he discovered with surprise that it imparted a nervous energy. His spine tingled. He felt a certain power.

Now he faced the raging crowd with defiance, its screams penetrating his eardrums like trumpets shrieking from a juke-box. The vague faces glowing in the bingo lights gave him a sense of himself that he had never known before. He was running the show, by God! They had to react to him, for he was their luck. This is *me*, he thought. Let the bastards yell. Then someone was laughing inside him, and he realized that somehow he had forgotten his own name. It was a sad, lost feeling to lose your name, and a crazy thing to do. That name had been given him by the white man who had owned his grandfather a long lost time ago down South. But maybe those wise guys knew his name.

"Who am I?" he screamed.

"Hurry up and bingo, you jerk!"

They didn't know either, he thought sadly. They didn't even know their own names, they were all poor nameless bastards. Well, he didn't need that old name; he was reborn. For as long as he pressed the button he was The-man-who-pressed-the-button-who-held-the-prize-who-was-the-King-of-Bingo. That was the way it was, and he'd have to press the button even if nobody understood, even though Laura did not understand.

"Live!" he shouted.

The audience quieted like the dying of a huge fan.

"Live, Laura, baby. I got holt of it now, sugar. Live!"

He screamed it, tears streaming down his face. "I got nobody but YOU!"

The screams tore from his very guts. He felt as though the rush of blood to this head would burst out in baseball seams of small red droplets, like a head beaten by police clubs. Bending over he saw a trickle of blood splashing the toe of his shoe. With his free hand he searched his head. It was his nose. God, suppose something has gone wrong? He felt that the whole audience had somehow entered him and was stamping its feet in his stomach and he was unable to throw them out. They wanted the prize, that was it. They wanted the secret for themselves. But they'd never get it; he would keep the bingo wheel whirling forever, and Laura would be safe in the wheel. But would she? It had to be, because if she were not safe the wheel would cease to turn; it could not go on. He had to get away, *vomit* all, and his mind formed an image of himself running with Laura in his arms down the tracks of the subway just ahead of an A train, running desperately *vomit* with people screaming for him to come out but knowing no way of leaving the tracks because to stop would bring the train crushing down upon him and to attempt to leave across the other tracks would mean to run into a hot third rail as high as his waist which threw blue sparks that blinded his eyes until he could hardly see.

He heard singing and the audience was clapping its hands.

> Shoot the liquor to him, Jim, boy!
> Clap-clap-clap
> Well a-calla the cop
> He's blowing his top!
> Shoot the liquor to him, Jim, boy!

Bitter anger grew within him at the singing. They think I'm crazy. Well let 'em laugh. I'll do what I got to do.

He was standing in an attitude of intense listening when he saw that they were watching something on the stage behind him. He felt weak. But when he turned he saw no one. If only his thumb did not ache so. Now they were applauding. And for a moment he thought that the wheel had stopped. But that was impossible, his thumb still pressed the button. They he saw them. Two men in uniform beckoned from the end of the stage. They were coming toward him, walking in step, slowly, like a tap-dance team returning for a third encore. But their shoulders shot forward, and he backed away, looking wildly about. There was nothing to fight them with. He had only the long black cord which led to a plug somewhere back stage, and he couldn't use that because it operated the bingo wheel. He backed slowly, fixing the men with his eyes as his lips stretched over his teeth in a tight, fixed grin; moved toward the end of the stage and realizing that he couldn't go much further, for suddenly the cord became taut and he couldn't afford to break the cord. But he had to do something. The audience was howling. Suddenly he stopped dead, seeing the men halt, their legs lifted as in an interrupted step of a slow-motion dance. There was nothing to do but run in the other direction and he dashed forward, slipping and sliding. The men fell back, surprised. He struck out violently going past.

"Grab him!"

He ran, but all too quickly the cord tightened, resistingly, and he turned and ran back again. This time he slipped them, and discovered by running in a circle before the wheel he could keep the cord from tightening. But this way he had to flail his arms to keep the men away. Why couldn't they leave a man alone? He ran, circling.

"Ring, down the curtain," someone yelled. But they couldn't do that. If they did the wheel flashing from the projection room would be cut off. But they had him before he could tell them so, trying to pry open his fist, and he was wrestling and trying to bring his knees into the fight and holding on to the button, for it was his life. And now he was down, seeing a foot coming down, crushing his wrist cruelly, down, as he saw the wheel whirling serenely above.

"I can't give it up," he screamed. Then quietly, in a confidential tone, "Boys, I really can't give it up."

It landed hard against his head. And in the blank moment they had it away from him, completely now. He fought them trying to pull him up from the stage as he watched the wheel spin slowly to a stop. Without surprise he saw it rest at double-zero.

"You see," he pointed bitterly.

"Sure, boy, sure, it's O. K.," one of the men said smiling.

And seeing the man bow his head to someone he could not see, he felt very, very happy; he would receive what all the winners received.

But as he warmed in the justice of the man's tight smile he did not see the man's slow wink, nor see the bow-legged man behind him step clear of the swiftly descending curtain and set himself for a blow. He only felt the dull pain exploding in his skull, and he knew even as it slipped out of him that his luck had run out on the stage.

[1944]

Shirley Jackson *1919–1965*

THE LOTTERY

The morning of June 27th was clear and sunny, with the fresh warmth of a full-summer day; the flowers were blossoming profusely and the grass was richly green. The people of the village began to gather in the square, between the post office and the bank, around ten o'clock; in some towns there were so many people that the lottery took two days and had to be started on June 26th, but in this village, where there were only about three hundred people, the whole lottery took less than two hours, so it could begin at ten o'clock in the morning and still be through in time to allow the villagers to get home for noon dinner.

The children assembled first, of course. School was recently over for the summer, and the feeling of liberty sat uneasily on most of them; they tended to gather together quietly for a while before they broke into boisterous play, and their talk was still of the classroom and the teacher, of books and repri-mands. Bobby Martin had already stuffed his pockets full of stones, and the other boys soon followed his example, selecting the smoothest and roundest stones; Bobby and Harry Jones and Dickie Delacroix—the villagers pronounced this name "Dellacroy"—eventually made a great pile of stones in one corner of the square and guarded it against the raids of the other boys. The girls stood aside, talking among themselves, looking over their shoulders at the boys, and the very small children rolled in the dust or clung to the hands of their older brothers or sisters.

Soon the men began to gather, surveying their own children, speaking of planting and rain, tractors and taxes. They stood together, away from the pile of stones in the corner, and their jokes were quiet and they smiled rather than laughed. The women, wearing faded house dresses and sweaters, came shortly after their menfolk. They greeted one another and exchanged bits of gossip as they went to join their husbands. Soon the women, standing by their husbands, began to call to their children, and the children came reluc-tantly, having to be called four or five times. Bobby Martin ducked under his mother's grasping hand and ran, laughing, back to the pile of stones. His father spoke up sharply, and Bobby came quickly and took his place between his father and his oldest brother.

The lottery was conducted—as were the square dances, the teenage club, the Halloween program—by Mr. Summers, who had time and energy to devote to civic activities. He was a round-faced, jovial man and he ran the coal business, and people were sorry for him, because he had no children and his wife was a scold. When he arrived in the square, carrying the black wooden box, there was a murmur of conversation among the villagers, and he waved and called, "Little late today, folks." The postmaster, Mr. Graves, followed him, carrying a three-legged stool, and the stool was put in the center of the square and Mr. Summers set the black box down on it. The villagers kept their distance, leaving a space between themselves and the stool, and when Mr. Summers said, "Some of you fellows want to give me a hand?" there was a hesitation before two men, Mr. Martin and his oldest son, Baxter, came forward to hold the box steady on the stool while Mr. Summers stirred up the papers inside it.

The original paraphernalia for the lottery had been lost long ago, and the black box now resting on the stool had been put into use even before Old Man Warner, the oldest man in town, was born. Mr. Summers spoke frequently to the villagers about making a new box, but no one liked to upset even as much tradition as was represented by the black box. There was a story that the present box had been made with some pieces of the box which had preceded it, the one that had been constructed when the first people settled down to make a village here. Every year, after the lottery, Mr. Summers began talking again about a new box, but every year the subject was allowed to fade off without anything's being done. The black box grew shabbier each year; by now it was no longer completely black but splintered badly along one side to show the original wood color, and in some places faded or stained.

Mr. Martin and his oldest son, Baxter, held the black box securely on the stool until Mr. Summers had stirred the papers thoroughly with his hand. Because so much of the ritual had been forgotten or discarded, Mr. Summers had been successful in having slips of paper substituted for the chips of wood that had been used for generations. Chips of wood, Mr. Summers had argued, had been all very well when the village was tiny, but now that the population was more than three hundred and likely to keep on growing, it was necessary to use something that would fit more easily into the black box. The night before the lottery, Mr. Summers and Mr. Graves made up the slips of paper and put them in the box, and it was then taken to the safe of Mr. Summers's coal company and locked up until Mr. Summers was ready to take it to the square next morning. The rest of the year, the box was put away, sometimes one place, sometimes another; it had spent one year in Mr. Graves's barn and another year underfoot in the post office, and sometimes it was set on a shelf in the Martin grocery and left there.

There was a great deal of fussing to be done before Mr. Summers declared the lottery open. There were the lists to make up—of heads of families, heads of households in each family, members of each household in each family. There was the proper swearing-in of Mr. Summers by the postmaster, as the official of the lottery; at one time, some people remembered, there had been a recital of some sort, performed by the official of the lottery, a perfunctory, tuneless chant that had been rattled off duly each year; some people believed that the official of the lottery used to stand just so when he said or sang it, others believed that he was supposed to walk among the people, but years and years ago this part of the ritual had been allowed to lapse. There had been, also, a ritual salute, which the official of the lottery had had to use in addressing each person who came up to draw from the box, but this also had changed with time, until now it was felt necessary only for the official to speak to each person approaching. Mr. Summers was very good at all this; in his clean white shirt and blue jeans, with one hand resting carelessly on the black box, he seemed very proper and important as he talked interminably to Mr. Graves and the Martins.

Just as Mr. Summers finally left off talking and turned to the assembled villagers, Mrs. Hutchinson came hurriedly along the path to the square, her sweater thrown over her shoulders, and slid into place in the back of the crowd. "Clean forgot what day it was," she said to Mrs. Delacroix, who stood next to her, and they both laughed softly. "Thought my old man was out back stacking wood," Mrs. Hutchinson went on, "and then I looked out the window and the kids was gone, and then I remembered it was the twenty-seventh and came a-running." She dried her hands on her apron, and Mrs. Delacroix said, "You're in time, though. They're still talking away up there."

Mrs. Hutchinson craned her neck to see through the crowd and found her husband and children standing near the front. She tapped Mrs. Delacroix on the arm as a farewell and began to make her way through the crowd. The people separated good-humoredly to let her through; two or three people said, in voices just loud enough to be heard across the crowd, "Here comes your Missus, Hutchinson," and "Bill, she made it after all." Mrs. Hutchinson reached her husband, and Mr. Summers, who had been waiting, said cheerfully, "Thought we were going to have to get on without you, Tessie." Mrs. Hutchinson said, grinning, "Wouldn't have me leave m'dishes in the sink, now, would you, Joe?" and soft laughter ran through the crowd as the people stirred back into position after Mrs. Hutchinson's arrival.

"Well, now," Mr. Summers said soberly, "guess we better get started, get this over with, so's we can go back to work. Anybody ain't here?"

"Dunbar," several people said. "Dunbar, Dunbar."

Mr. Summers consulted his list. "Clyde Dunbar," he said. "That's right. He's broke his leg, hasn't he? Who's drawing for him?"

"Me, I guess," a woman said, and Mr. Summers turned to look at her. "Wife draws for her husband," Mr. Summers said. "Don't you have a grown boy to do it for you, Janey?" Although Mr. Summers and everyone else in the village knew the answer perfectly well, it was the business of the official of the lottery to ask such questions formally. Mr. Summers waited with an expression of polite interest while Mrs. Dunbar answered.

"Horace's not but sixteen yet," Mrs. Dunbar said regretfully. "Guess I gotta fill in for the old man this year."

"Right," Mr. Summers said. He made a note on the list he was holding. Then he asked, "Watson boy drawing this year?"

A tall boy in the crowd raised his hand. "Here," he said. "I'm drawing for m'mother and me." He blinked his eyes nervously and ducked his head as several voices in the crowd said things like "Good fellow, Jack," and "Glad to see your mother's got a man to do it."

"Well," Mr. Summers said, "guess that's everyone. Old Man Warner make it?"

"Here," a voice said, and Mr. Summers nodded.

A sudden hush fell on the crowd as Mr. Summers cleared his throat and looked at the list. "All ready?" he called. "Now, I'll read the names—heads of families first—and the men come up and take a paper out of the box. Keep the paper folded in your hand without looking at it until everyone has had a turn. Everything clear?"

The people had done it so many times that they only half listened to the directions; most of them were quiet, wetting their lips, not looking around. Then Mr. Summers raised one hand high and said, "Adams." A man disengaged himself from the crowd and came forward. "Hi, Steve," Mr. Summers said, and Mr. Adams said, "Hi, Joe." They grinned at one another humorlessly and nervously. Then Mr. Adams reached into the black box and took out a folded paper. He held it firmly by one corner as he turned and went hastily back to his place in the crowd, where he stood a little apart from his family, not looking down at his hand.

"Allen," Mr. Summers said. "Anderson. . . . Bentham."

"Seems like there's no time at all between lotteries any more," Mrs. Delacroix said to Mrs. Graves in the back row. "Seems like we got through with the last one only last week."

"Time sure goes fast," Mrs. Graves said.

"Clark. . . . Delacroix."

"There goes my old man," Mrs. Delacroix said. She held her breath while her husband went forward.

"Dunbar," Mr. Summers said, and Mrs. Dunbar went steadily to the box while one of the women said, "Go on, Janey," and another said, "There she goes."

"We're next," Mrs. Graves said. She watched while Mr. Graves came around from the side of the box, greeted Mr. Summers gravely, and selected a slip of paper from the box. By now, all through the crowd there were men holding the small folded papers in their large hands, turning them over and over nervously. Mrs. Dunbar and her two sons stood together, Mrs. Dunbar holding the slip of paper.

"Harburt. . . . Hutchinson."

"Get up there, Bill," Mrs. Hutchinson said, and the people near her laughed.

"Jones."

"They do say," Mr. Adams said to Old Man Warner, who stood next to him, "that over in the north village they're talking of giving up the lottery."

Old Man Warner snorted. "Pack of crazy fools," he said. "Listening to the young folks, nothing's good enough for *them.* Next thing you know, they'll be wanting to go back to living in caves, nobody work any more, live *that* way for a while. Used to be a saying about 'Lottery in June, corn be heavy soon.' First thing you know, we'd all be eating stewed chickweed and acorns. There's *always* been a lottery," he added petulantly. "Bad enough to see young Joe Summers up there joking with everybody."

"Some places have already quit lotteries," Mrs. Adams said.

"Nothing but trouble in *that,*" Old Man Warner said stoutly. "Pack of young fools."

"Martin." And Bobby Martin watched his father go forward. "Overdyke. . . . Percy."

"I wish they'd hurry," Mrs. Dunbar said to her older son. "I wish they'd hurry."

"They're almost through," her son said.

"You get ready to run tell Dad," Mrs. Dunbar said.

Mr. Summers called his own name and then stepped forward precisely and selected a slip from the box. Then he called, "Warner."

"Seventy-seventh year I been in the lottery," Old Man Warner said as he went through the crowd. "Seventy-seventh time."

"Watson." The tall boy came awkwardly through the crowd. Someone said, "Don't be nervous, Jack," and Mr. Summers said, "Take your time, son."

"Zanini."

After that, there was a long pause, a breathless pause, until Mr. Summers, holding his slip of paper in the air, said, "All right, fellows." For a minute, no one moved, and then all the slips of paper were opened. Suddenly, all the women began to speak at once, saying, "Who is it?," "Who's got it?," "Is it the Dunbars?," "Is it the Watsons?" Then the voices began to say, "It's Hutchinson. It's Bill," "Bill Hutchinson's got it."

"Go tell your father," Mrs. Dunbar said to her older son.

People began to look around to see the Hutchinsons. Bill Hutchinson was standing quiet, staring down at the paper in his hand. Suddenly, Tessie Hutchinson shouted to Mr. Summers, "You didn't give him time enough to take any paper he wanted. I saw you. It wasn't fair!"

"Be a good sport, Tessie," Mrs. Delacroix called, and Mrs. Graves said, "All of us took the same chance."

"Shut up, Tessie," Bill Hutchinson said.

"Well, everyone," Mr. Summers said, "that was done pretty fast, and now we've got to be hurrying a little more to get done in time." He consulted his next list. "Bill," he said, "you draw for the Hutchinson family. You got any other households in the Hutchinsons?"

"There's Don and Eva," Mrs. Hutchinson yelled. "Make *them* take their chance!"

"Daughters draw with their husbands' families, Tessie," Mr. Summers said gently. "You know that as well as anyone else."

"It wasn't *fair*," Tessie said.

"I guess not, Joe," Bill Hutchinson said regretfully. "My daughter draws with her husband's family, that's only fair. And I've got no other family except the kids."

"Then, as far as drawing for families is concerned, it's you," Mr. Summers said in explanation, "and as far as drawing for households is concerned, that's you, too. Right?"

"Right," Bill Hutchinson said.

"How many kids, Bill?" Mr. Summers asked formally.

"Three," Bill Hutchinson said. "There's Bill, Jr., and Nancy, and little Dave. And Tessie and me."

"All right, then," Mr. Summers said. "Harry, you got their tickets back?"

Mr. Graves nodded and held up the slips of paper. "Put them in the box, then," Mr. Summers directed. "Take Bill's and put it in."

"I think we ought to start over," Mrs. Hutchinson said, as quietly as she could. "I tell you it wasn't *fair*. You didn't give him time enough to choose. *Everybody* saw that."

Mr. Graves had selected the five slips and put them in the box, and he dropped all the papers but those onto the ground, where the breeze caught them and lifted them off.

"Listen, everybody," Mrs. Hutchinson was saying to the people around her.

"Ready, Bill?" Mr. Summers asked, and Bill Hutchinson, with one quick glance around at his wife and children, nodded.

"Remember," Mr. Summers said, "take the slips and keep them folded until each person has taken one. Harry, you help little Dave." Mr. Graves took the hand of the little boy, who came willingly with him up to the box. "Take a paper out of the box, Davy," Mr. Summers said. Davy put his hand into the box and laughed. "Take just *one* paper," Mr. Summers said. "Harry, you hold it for him." Mr. Graves took the child's hand and removed the folded paper from the tight fist and held it while little Dave stood next to him and looked up at him wonderingly.

"Nancy next," Mr. Summers said. Nancy was twelve, and her school friends breathed heavily as she went forward, switching her skirt, and took a slip daintily from the box. "Bill, Jr.," Mr. Summers said, and Billy, his face red and his feet overlarge, nearly knocked the box over as he got a paper out. "Tessie," Mr. Summers said. She hesitated for a minute, looking around defiantly, and then set her lips and went up to the box. She snatched a paper out and held it behind her.

"Bill," Mr. Summers said, and Bill Hutchinson reached into the box and felt around, bringing his hand out at last with the slip of paper in it.

The crowd was quiet. A girl whispered, "I hope it's not Nancy," and the sound of the whisper reached the edges of the crowd.

"It's not the way it used to be," Old Man Warner said clearly. "People ain't the way they used to be."

"All right," Mr. Summers said. "Open the papers. Harry, you open little Dave's."

Mr. Graves opened the slip of paper and there was a general sigh through the crowd as he held it up and everyone could see that it was blank. Nancy and Bill, Jr., opened theirs at the same time, and both beamed and laughed, turning around to the crowd and holding their slips of paper above their heads.

"Tessie," Mr. Summers said. There was a pause, and then Mr. Summers looked at Bill Hutchinson, and Bill unfolded his paper and showed it. It was blank.

"It's Tessie," Mr. Summers said, and his voice was hushed. "Show us her paper, Bill."

Bill Hutchinson went over to his wife and forced the slip of paper out of her hand. It had a black spot on it, the black spot Mr. Summers had made the night before with the heavy pencil in the coal-company office. Bill Hutchinson held it up, and there was a stir in the crowd.

"All right, folks," Mr. Summers said. "Let's finish quickly."

Although the villagers had forgotten the ritual and lost the original black box, they still remembered to use stones. The pile of stones the boys had made earlier was ready; there were stones on the ground with the blowing scraps of paper that had come out of the box. Mrs. Delacroix selected a stone so large she had to pick it up with both hands and turned to Mrs. Dunbar. "Come on," she said. "Hurry up."

Mrs. Dunbar had small stones in both hands, and she said, gasping for breath, "I can't run at all. You'll have to go ahead and I'll catch up with you."

The children had stones already, and someone gave little Davy Hutchinson a few pebbles.

Tessie Hutchinson was in the center of a cleared space by now, and she held her hands out desperately as the villagers moved in on her. "It isn't fair," she said. A stone hit her on the side of the head.

Old Man Warner was saying, "Come on, come on, everyone." Steve Adams was in the front of the crowd of villagers, with Mrs. Graves beside him.

"It isn't fair, it isn't right," Mrs. Hutchinson screamed, and then they were upon her.

[1948]

Ray Bradbury   *1920–*

AUGUST 2002: NIGHT MEETING

Before going on up into the blue hills, Tomás Gomez stopped for gasoline at the lonely station.

"Kind of alone out here, aren't you, Pop?" said Tomás.

The old man wiped off the windshield of the small truck. "Not bad."

"How do you like Mars, Pop?"

"Fine. Always something new. I made up my mind when I came here last year I wouldn't expect nothing, nor ask nothing, nor be surprised at nothing. We've got to forget Earth and how things were. We've got to look at what we're in here, and how *different* it is. I get a hell of a lot of fun out of just the weather here. It's *Martian* weather. Hot as hell daytimes, cold as hell nights. I get a big kick out of the different flowers and different rain. I came to Mars to retire and I wanted to retire in a place where everything is different. An old man needs to have things different. Young people don't want to talk to him, other old people bore hell out of him. So I thought the best thing for me is a place so different that all you got to do is open your eyes and you're entertained. I got this gas station. If business picks up too much, I'll move on back to some other old highway that's not so busy, where I can earn just enough to live on and still have time to feel the *different* things here."

"You got the right idea, Pop," said Tomás, his brown hands idly on the wheel. He was feeling good. He had been working in one of the new colonies for ten days straight and now he had two days off and was on his way to a party.

"I'm not surprised at anything any more," said the old man. "I'm just looking. I'm just experiencing. If you can't take Mars for what she is, you might as well go back to Earth. Everything's crazy up here, the soil, the air, the canals, the natives (I never saw any yet, but I hear they're around), the clocks. Even my clock acts funny. Even *time* is crazy up here. Sometimes I feel I'm here all by myself, no one else on the whole damn planet. I'd take bets on it. Sometimes I feel about eight years old, my body squeezed up and everything else tall. Jesus, it's just the place for an old man. Keeps me alert and keeps me happy. You know what Mars is? It's like a thing I got for Christmas seventy years ago—don't know if you ever had one—they called them kaleidoscopes, bits of crystal and cloth and beads and pretty junk. You held it up to the sunlight and looked in through at it, and it took your breath away. All the patterns! Well, that's Mars. Enjoy it. Don't ask it to be nothing else but what it is. Jesus, you know that highway right there, built by the Martians, is over sixteen centuries old and still in good condition? That's one dollar and fifty cents, thanks and good night."

Tomás drove off down the ancient highway, laughing quietly.

It was a long road going into darkness and hills and he held to the wheel, now and again reaching into his lunch bucket and taking out a piece of candy. He had been driving steadily for an hour, with no other car on the road, no light, just the road going under, the hum, the roar, and Mars out there, so quiet. Mars was always quiet, but quieter tonight than any other. The deserts and empty seas swung by him, and the mountains against the stars.

There was a smell of Time in the air tonight. He smiled and turned the fancy in his mind. There was a thought. What did Time smell like? Like dust and clocks and people. And if you wondered what Time sounded like it sounded like water running in a dark cave and voices crying and dirt dropping down upon hollow box lids, and rain. And, going further, what did Time *look* like? Time looked like snow dropping silently into a black room or it looked like a silent film in an ancient theater, one hundred billion faces falling like those New Year balloons, down and down into nothing. That was how Time smelled and looked and sounded. And tonight—Tomás shoved a hand into the wind outside the truck—tonight you could almost *touch* Time.

He drove the truck between hills of Time. His neck prickled and he sat up, watching ahead.

He pulled into a little dead Martian town, stopped the engine, and let the silence come in around him. He sat, not breathing, looking out at the white buildings in the moonlight. Uninhabited for centuries. Perfect, faultless, in ruins, yes, but perfect, nevertheless.

He started the engine and drove on another mile or more before stopping again, climbing out, carrying his lunch bucket, and walking to a little promontory where he could look back at that dusty city. He opened his thermos and poured himself a cup of coffee. A night bird flew by. He felt very good, very much at peace.

Perhaps five minutes later there was a sound. Off in the hills, where the ancient highway curved, there was a motion, a dim light, and then a murmur.

Tomás turned slowly with the coffee cup in his hand.

And out of the hills came a strange thing.

It was a machine like a jade-green insect, a praying mantis, delicately rushing through the cold air, indistinct, countless green diamonds winking over its body, and red jewels that glittered with multifaceted eyes. Its six legs fell upon the ancient highway with the sounds of a sparse rain which dwindled away, and from the back of the machine a Martian with melted gold for eyes looked down at Tomás as if he were looking into a well.

Tomás raised his hand and thought Hello! automatically but did not move his lips, for this *was* a Martian. But Tomás had swum in blue rivers on Earth, with strangers passing on the road, and eaten in strange houses with strange people, and his weapon had always been his smile. He did not carry a gun. And he did not feel the need of one now, even with the little fear that gathered about his heart at this moment.

The Martian's hands were empty too. For a moment they looked across the cool air at each other.

It was Tomás who moved first.

"Hello!" he called.

"Hello!" called the Martian in his own language.

They did not understand each other.

"Did you say hello?" they both asked.

"What did you say?" they said, each in a different tongue.

They scowled.

"Who are you?" said Tomás in English.

"What are you doing here?" In Martian; the stranger's lips moved.

"Where are you going?" they said, and looked bewildered.

"I'm Tomás Gomez."

"I'm Muhe Ca."

Neither understood, but they tapped their chests with the words and then it became clear.

And then the Martian laughed. "Wait!" Tomás felt his head touched, but no hand had touched him. "There!" said the Martian in English. "That is better!"

"You learned my language, so quick!"

"Nothing at all!"

They looked, embarrassed with a new silence, at the steaming coffee he had in one hand.

"Something different?" said the Martian, eying him and the coffee, referring to them both, perhaps.

"May I offer you a drink?" said Tomás.

"Please."

The Martian slid down from his machine.

A second cup was produced and filled, steaming. Tomás held it out.

Their hands met and—like mist—fell through each other.

"Jesus Christ!" cried Tomás, and dropped the cup.

"Name of the Gods!" said the Martian in his own tongue.

"Did you see what happened?" they both whispered.

They were very cold and terrified.

The Martian bent to touch the cup but could not touch it.

"Jesus!" said Tomás.

"Indeed." The Martian tried again and again to get hold of the cup, but could not. He stood up and thought for a moment, then took a knife from his belt. "Hey!" cried Tomás. "You misunderstand, catch!" said the Martian, and tossed it. Tomás cupped his hands. The knife fell through his flesh. It hit the ground. Tomás bent to pick it up but could not touch it, and he recoiled, shivering.

Now he looked at the Martian against the sky.

"The stars!" he said.

"The stars!" said the Martian, looking, in turn, at Tomás.

The stars were white and sharp beyond the flesh of the Martian, and they were sewn into his flesh like scintillas swallowed into the thin, phosphorescent membrane of a gelatinous sea fish. You could see stars flickering like violet eyes in the Martian's stomach and chest, and through his wrists, like jewelry.

"I can see through you!" said Tomás.

"And I through you!" said the Martian, stepping back.

Tomás felt of his own body and, feeling the warmth, was reassured. *I am real*, he thought.

The Martian touched his own nose and lips. "*I* have flesh," he said, half aloud. "*I* am alive."

Tomás stared at the stranger. "And if *I* am real, then you must be dead."

"No, you!"

"A ghost!"

"A phantom!"

They pointed at each other, with starlight burning in their limbs like daggers and icicles and fireflies, and then fell to judging their limbs again, each finding himself intact, hot, excited, stunned, awed, and the other, ah yes, that other over there, unreal, a ghostly prism flashing the accumulated light of distant worlds.

I'm drunk, thought Tomás. I won't tell anyone of this tomorrow, no, no.

They stood there on the ancient highway, neither of them moving.

"Where are you from?" asked the Martian at last.

"Earth."

"What is that?"

"There." Tomás nodded to the sky.

"When?"

"We landed over a year ago, remember?"

"No."

"And all of you were dead, all but a few. You're rare, don't you *know* that?"

"That's not true."

"Yes. Dead. I saw the bodies. Black, in the rooms, in the houses, dead. Thousands of them."

"That's ridiculous. We're *alive!*"

"Mister, you're invaded, only you don't know it. You must have escaped."

"I haven't escaped; there was nothing to escape. What do you mean? I'm on my way to a festival now at the canal, near the Eniall Mountains. I was there last night. Don't you see the city there?" The Martian pointed.

Tomás looked and saw the ruins. "Why, that city's been dead thousands of years."

The Martian laughed. "Dead. I slept there yesterday!"

"And I was in it a week ago and the week before that, and I just drove through it now, and it's a heap. See the broken pillars?"

"Broken? Why, I see them perfectly. The moonlight helps. And the pillars are upright."

"There's dust in the streets," said Tomás.

"The streets are clean!"

"The canals are empty right there."

"The canals are full of lavender wine!"

"It's dead."

"It's alive!" protested the Martian, laughing more now. "Oh, you're quite wrong. See all the carnival lights? There are beautiful boats as slim as women, beautiful women as slim as boats, women the color of sand, women with fire flowers in their hands. I can see them, small, running in the streets there. That's where I'm going now, to the festival; we'll float on the waters all night long; we'll sing, we'll drink, we'll make love. Can't you *see* it?"

"Mister, that city is dead as a dried lizard. Ask any of our party. Me, I'm on my way to Green City tonight; that's the new colony we just raised over near Illinois Highway. You're mixed up. We brought in a million board feet of Oregon lumber and a couple dozen tons of good steel nails and hammered together two of the nicest little villages you ever saw. Tonight we're warming one of them. A couple rockets are coming in from Earth, bringing our wives and girl friends. There'll be barn dances and whisky——"

The Martian was now disquieted. "You say it is over *that* way?"

"There are the rockets." Tomás walked him to the edge of the hill and pointed down. "See?"

"No."

"Damn it, there they *are!* Those long silver things."

"No."

Now Tomás laughed. "You're blind!"

"I see very well. You are the one who does not see."

"But you see the new *town*, don't you?"

"I see nothing but an ocean, and water at low tide."

"Mister, that water's been evaporated for forty centuries."

"Ah, now, now, that *is* enough."

"It's true, I tell you."

The Martian grew very serious. "Tell me again. You do not see the city the way I describe it? The pillars very white, the boats very slender, the festival lights—oh, I see them *clearly!* And listen! I can hear them singing. It's no space away at all."

Tomás listened and shook his head. "No."

"And I, on the other hand," said the Martian, "cannot see what you describe. Well."

Again they were cold. An ice was in their flesh.

"Can it be . . .?"

"What?"

"You say 'from the sky'?"

"Earth."

"Earth, a name, nothing," said the Martian. *"But . . .* as I came up the pass an hour ago . . ." He touched the back of his neck. "I felt . . ."

"Cold?"

"Yes."

"And now?"

"Cold again. Oddly. There was a thing to the light, to the hills, the road," said the Martian. "I felt the strangeness, the road, the light, and for a moment I felt as if I were the last man alive on this world. . . ."

"So did I!" said Tomás, and it was like talking to an old and dear friend, confiding, growing warm with the topic.

The Martian closed his eyes and opened them again. "This can only mean one thing. It has to do with Time. Yes. You are a figment of the Past!"

"No, you are from the Past," said the Earth Man, having had time to think of it now.

"You are so *certain.* How can you prove who is from the Past, who from the Future? What year is it?"

"Two thousand and one!"

"What does that mean to *me?*"

Tomás considered and shrugged. "Nothing."

"It is as if I told you that it is the year 4462853 s.e.c. It is nothing and more than nothing! Where is the clock to show us how the stars stand?"

"But the ruins prove it! They prove that *I* am the Future, *I* am alive, *you* are dead!"

"Everything in me denies this. My heart beats, my stomach hungers, my mouth thirsts. No, no, not dead, but alive, either of us. More alive than anything else. Caught between is more like it. Two strangers passing in the night, that is it. Two strangers passing. Ruins, you say?"

"Yes. You're afraid?"

"Who wants to see the Future, who *ever* does? A man can face the Past, but to think—the pillars *crumbled,* you say? And the sea empty, and the canals dry, and the maidens dead, and the flowers withered?" The Martian was silent, but then he looked on ahead. "But there they *are*. I *see* them. Isn't that enough for me? They wait for me now, no matter *what* you say."

And for Tomás the rockets, far away, waiting for *him*, and the town and the women from Earth. "We can never agree," he said.

"Let us agree to disagree," said the Martian. "What does it matter who is Past or Future, if we are both alive, for what follows will follow, tomorrow or in ten thousand years. How do you know that those temples are not the temples of your own civilization one hundred centuries from now, tumbled and broken? You do not know. Then don't ask. But the night is very short. There go the festival fires in the sky, and the birds."

Tomás put out his hand. The Martian did likewise in imitation.

Their hands did not touch; they melted through each other.

"Will we meet again?"

"Who knows? Perhaps some other night."

"I'd like to go with you to that festival."

"And I wish I might come to your new town, to see this ship you speak of, to see these men, to hear all that has happened."

"Good-by," said Tomás.

"Good night."

The Martian rode his green metal vehicle quietly away into the hills. The Earth Man turned his truck and drove it silently in the opposite direction.

"Good lord, what a dream that was," sighed Tomás, his hands on the wheel, thinking of the rockets, the women, the raw whisky, the Virginia reels, the party.

How strange a vision was that, thought the Martian, rushing on, thinking of the festival, the canals, the boats, the women with golden eyes, and the songs.

The night was dark. The moons had gone down. Starlight twinkled on the empty highway where now there was not a sound, no car, no person, nothing. And it remained that way all the rest of the cool dark night.

[1950]

Bernard Malamud *1914–*

THE MAGIC BARREL

Not long ago there lived in uptown New York, in a small, almost meager room, though crowded with books, Leo Finkle, a rabbinical student in the Yeshivah University. Finkle, after six years of study, was to be ordained in June and had been advised by an acquaintance that he might find it easier to win himself a congregation if he were married. Since he had no present prospects of marriage, after two tormented days of turning it over in his mind, he called in Pinye Salzman, a marriage broker whose two-line advertisement he had read in the *Forward*.[1]

The matchmaker appeared one night out of the dark fourth-floor hallway of the graystone rooming house where Finkle lived, grasping a black, strapped portfolio that had been worn thin with use. Salzman, who had been long in the business, was of slight but dignified build, wearing an old hat, and overcoat too short and tight for him. He smelled frankly of fish, which he loved to eat, and although he was missing a few teeth, his presence was not displeasing, because of an amiable manner curiously contrasted with mournful eyes. His voice, his lips, his wisp of beard, his bony fingers were animated, but give him a moment of repose and his mild blue eyes revealed a depth of sadness, a characteristic that put Leo a little at ease although the situation, for him, was inherently tense.

He at once informed Salzman why he had asked him to come, explaining that his home was in Cleveland, and that but for his parents, who had married comparatively late in life, he was alone in the world. He had for six years devoted himself almost entirely to his studies, as a result of which, understandably, he had found himself without time for a social life and the company of young women. Therefore he thought it the better part of trial and error—of embarrassing fumbling—to call in an experienced person to advise him on these matters. He remarked in passing that the function of the marriage broker was ancient and honorable, highly approved in the Jewish community, because it made practical the necessary without hindering joy. Moreover, his own parents had been brought together by a matchmaker. They had made, if not a financially profitable marriage—since neither had possessed any worldly goods to speak of—at least a successful one in the sense of their everlasting devotion to each other. Salzman listened in embarrassed surprise, sensing a sort of apology. Later, however, he experienced a glow of pride in his work, an emotion that had left him years ago, and he heartily approved of Finkle.

The two went to their business. Leo had led Salzman to the only clear place in the room, a table near a window that overlooked the lamp-lit city. He seated himself at the matchmaker's side but facing him, attempting by an act of will to suppress the unpleasant tickle in his throat. Salzman eagerly unstrapped his portfolio and removed a loose rubber band from a thin packet of much-handled cards. As he flipped through them, a gesture and sound that physically hurt Leo, the student pretended not to see and gazed steadfastly out the window. Although it was still February, winter was on its last legs, signs of which

---

[1] The *Jewish Daily Forward*, a Yiddish-language newspaper.

he had for the first time in years begun to notice. He now observed the round white moon, moving high in the sky through a cloud menagerie, and watched with half-open mouth as it penetrated a huge hen, and dropped out of her like an egg laying itself. Salzman, though pretending through eyeglasses he had just slipped on, to be engaged in scanning the writing on the cards, stole occasional glances at the young man's distinguished face, noting with pleasure the long, severe scholar's nose, brown eyes heavy with learning, sensitive yet ascetic lips, and a certain, almost hollow quality of the dark cheeks. He gazed around at shelves upon shelves of books and let out a soft, contented sigh.

When Leo's eyes fell upon the cards, he counted six spread out in Salzman's hand.

"So few?" he asked in disappointment.

"You wouldn't believe me how much cards I got in my office," Salzman replied. "The drawers are already filled to the top, so I keep them now in a barrel, but is every girl good for a new rabbi?"

Leo blushed at this, regretting all he had revealed of himself in a curriculum vitae[2] he had sent to Salzman. He had thought it best to acquaint him with his strict standards and specifications, but in having done so, felt he had told the marriage broker more than was absolutely necessary.

He hesitantly inquired, "Do you keep photographs of your clients on file?"

"First comes family, amount of dowry, also what kind promises," Salzman replied, unbuttoning his tight coat and settling himself in the chair. "After comes pictures, rabbi."

"Call me Mr. Finkle. I'm not yet a rabbi."

Salzman said he would, but instead called him doctor, which he changed to rabbi when Leo was not listening too attentively.

Salzman adjusted his horn-rimmed spectacles, gently cleared his throat and read in an eager voice the contents of the top card:

"Sophie P. Twenty four years. Widow one year. No children. Educated high school and two years college. Father promises eight thousand dollars. Has wonderful wholesale business. Also real estate. On the mother's side comes teachers, also one actor. Well known on Second Avenue."

Leo gazed up in surprise. "Did you say a widow?"

"A widow don't mean spoiled, rabbi. She lived with her husband maybe four months. He was a sick boy she made a mistake to marry him."

"Marrying a widow has never entered my mind."

"This is because you have no experience. A widow, especially if she is young and healthy like this girl, is a wonderful person to marry. She will be thankful to you the rest of her life. Believe me, if I was looking now for a bride, I would marry a widow."

Leo reflected, then shook his head.

Salzman hunched his shoulders in an almost imperceptible gesture of disappointment. He placed the card down on the wooden table and began to read another:

"Lily H. High school teacher. Regular. Not a substitute. Has savings and new Dodge car. Lived in Paris one year. Father is successful dentist thirty-five years. Interested in professional man. Well Americanized family. Wonderful opportunity."

---

[2] A resumé of one's career.

"I knew her personally," said Salzman. "I wish you could see this girl. She is a doll. Also very intelligent. All day you could talk to her about books and theyater and what not. She also knows current events."

"I don't believe you mentioned her age?"

"Her age?" Salzman said, raising his brows. "Her age is thirty-two years."

Leo said after a while, "I'm afraid that seems a little too old."

Salzman let out a laugh. "So how old are you, rabbi?"

"Twenty-seven."

"So what is the difference, tell me, between twenty-seven and thirty-two? My own wife is seven years older than me. So what did I suffer—Nothing. If Rothschild's a daughter wants to marry you, would you say on account of her age, no?"

"Yes," Leo said dryly.

Salzman shook off the no in the yes. "Five years don't mean a thing. I give you my word that when you will live with her for one week you will forget her age. What does it mean five years—that she lived more and knows more than somebody who is younger? On this girl, God bless her, years are not wasted. Each one that it comes makes better the bargain."

"What subject does she teach in high school?"

"Languages. If you heard the way she speaks French, you will think it is music. I am in the business twenty-five years, and I recommend her with my whole heart. Believe me, I know what I'm talking, rabbi."

"What's on the next card?" Leo said abruptly.

Salzman reluctantly turned up the third card:

"Ruth K. Nineteen years. Honor student. Father offers thirteen thousand cash to the right bridegroom. He is a medical doctor. Stomach specialist with marvelous practice. Brother in law owns own garment business. Particular people."

Salzman looked as if he had read his trump card.

"Did you say nineteen?" Leo asked with interest.

"On the dot."

"Is she attractive?" He blushed. "Pretty?"

Salzman kissed his finger tips. "A little doll. On this I give you my word. Let me call the father tonight and you will see what means pretty."

But Leo was troubled. "You're sure she's that young?"

"This I am positive. The father will show you the birth certificate."

"Are you positive there isn't something wrong with her?" Leo insisted.

"Who says there is wrong?"

"I don't understand why an American girl her age should go to a marriage broker."

A smile spread over Salzman's face.

"So for the same reason you went, she comes."

Leo flushed. "I am pressed for time."

Salzman, realizing he had been tactless, quickly explained. "The father came, not her. He wants she should have the best, so he looks around himself. When we will locate the right boy he will introduce him and encourage. This makes a better marriage than if a young girl without experience takes for herself. I don't have to tell you this."

"But don't you think this young girl believes in love?" Leo spoke uneasily.

Salzman was about to guffaw but caught himself and said soberly, "Love comes with the right person, not before."

Leo parted dry lips but did not speak. Noticing that Salzman had snatched a glance at the next card, he cleverly asked, "How is her health?"

"Perfect," Salzman said, breathing with difficulty. "Of course, she is a little lame on her right foot from an auto accident that it happened to her when she was twelve years, but nobody notices on account she is so brilliant and also beautiful."

Leo got up heavily and went to the window. He felt curiously bitter and upbraided himself for having called in the marriage broker. Finally, he shook his head.

"Why not?" Salzman persisted, the pitch of his voice rising.

"Because I detest stomach specialists."

"So what do you care what is his business? After you marry her do you need him? Who says he must come every Friday night in your house?"

Ashamed of the way the talk was going, Leo dismissed Salzman, who went home with heavy, melancholy eyes.

Though he had felt only relief at the marriage broker's departure, Leo was in low spirits the next day. He explained it as arising from Salzman's failure to produce a suitable bride for him. He did not care for his type of clientele. But when Leo found himself hesitating whether to seek out another matchmaker, one more polished than Pinye, he wondered if it could be—his protestations to the contrary, and although he honored his father and mother—that he did not, in essence, care for the matchmaking institution? This thought he quickly put out of mind yet found himself still upset. All day he ran around in the woods—missed an important appointment, forgot to give out his laundry, walked out of a Broadway cafeteria without paying and had to run back with the ticket in his hand; had even not recognized his landlady in the street when she passed with a friend and courteously called out, "A good evening to you, Doctor Finkle." By nightfall, however, he had regained sufficient calm to sink his nose into a book and there found peace from his thoughts.

Almost at once there came a knock on the door. Before Leo could say enter, Salzman, commercial cupid, was standing in the room. His face was gray and meager, his expression hungry, and he looked as if he would expire on his feet. Yet the marriage broker managed, by some trick of the muscles, to display a broad smile.

"So good evening. I am invited?"

Leo nodded, disturbed to see him again, yet unwilling to ask the man to leave.

Beaming still, Salzman laid his portfolio on the table. "Rabbi, I got for you tonight good news."

"I've asked you not to call me rabbi. I'm still a student."

"Your worries are finished. I have for you a first-class bride."

"Leave me in peace concerning this subject." Leo pretended lack of interest.

"The world will dance at your wedding."

"Please, Mr. Salzman, no more."

"But first must come back my strength," Salzman said weakly. He fumbled with the portfolio straps and took out of the leather case an oily paper bag, from which he extracted a hard, seeded roll and a small, smoked white fish. With a quick motion of his hand he stripped the fish out of its skin and began ravenously to chew. "All day in a rush," he muttered.

Leo watched him eat.

"A slice of tomato you have maybe?" Salzman hesitantly inquired.

"No."

The marriage broker shut his eyes and ate. When he had finished he carefully cleaned up the crumbs and rolled up the remains of the fish, in the paper bag. His spectacled eyes roamed the room until he discovered, amid some piles of books, a one-burner gas stove. Lifting his hat he humbly asked, "A glass of tea you got, rabbi?"

Conscience-stricken, Leo rose and brewed the tea. He served it with a chunk of lemon and two cubes of lump sugar, delighting Salzman.

After he had drunk his tea, Salzman's strength and good spirits were restored.

"So tell me, rabbi," he said amiably, "you considered some more the three clients I mentioned yesterday?"

"There was no need to consider."

"Why not?"

"None of them suits me."

"What then suits you?"

Leo let it pass because he could give only a confused answer.

Without waiting for a reply, Salzman asked, "You remember this girl I talked to you—the high school teacher?"

"Age thirty-two?"

But, surprisingly, Salzman's face lit in a smile. "Age twenty-nine."

Leo shot him a look. "Reduced from thirty-two?"

"A mistake," Salzman avowed. "I talked today with the dentist. He took me to his safety deposit box and showed me the birth certificate. She was twenty-nine years last August. They made her a party in the mountains where she went for her vacation. When her father spoke to me the first time I forgot to write the age and I told you thirty-two, but now I remember this was a different client, a widow."

"The same one you told me about? I thought she was twenty-four?"

"A different. Am I responsible that the world is filled with widows?"

"No, but I'm not interested in them, nor for that matter, in school teachers."

Salzman pulled his clasped hands to his breast. Looking at the ceiling he devoutly exclaimed, "Yiddishe kinder,[3] what can I say to somebody that he is not interested in high school teachers? So what then you are interested?"

Leo flushed but controlled himself.

"In what else will you be interested," Salzman went on, "if you not interested in this fine girl that she speaks four languages and has personally in the bank ten thousand dollars? Also her father guarantees further twelve thousand. Also she has a new car, wonderful clothes, talks on all subjects, and she will give you a first-class home and children. How near do we come in our life to paradise?"

"If she's so wonderful, why wasn't she married ten years ago?"

"Why?" said Salzman with a heavy laugh. "—Why? Because she is *partikiler.* This is why. She wants the *best.*"

Leo was silent, amused at how he had entangled himself. But Salzman had aroused his interest in Lily H., and he began seriously to consider calling on her. When the marriage broker observed how intently Leo's mind was at work on the facts he had supplied, he felt certain they would soon come to an agreement.

[3] "Yiddish children."

Late Saturday afternoon, conscious of Salzman, Leo Finkle walked with Lily Hirschorn along Riverside Drive. He walked briskly and erectly, wearing with distinction the black fedora he had that morning taken with trepidation out of the dusty hat box on his closet shelf, and the heavy black Saturday coat he had thoroughly whisked clean. Leo also owned a walking stick, a present from a distant relative, but quickly put temptation aside and did not use it. Lily, petite and not unpretty, had on something signifying the approach of spring. She was au courant,[4] animatedly, with all sorts of subjects, and he weighed her words and found her surprisingly sound—score another for Salzman, whom he uneasily sensed to be somewhere around, hiding perhaps high in a tree along the street, flashing the lady signals with a pocket mirror; or perhaps a cloven-hoofed Pan,[5] piping nuptial ditties as he danced his invisible way before them, strewing wild buds on the walk and purple grapes in their path, symbolizing fruit of a union, though there was of course still none.

Lily startled Leo by remarking, "I was thinking of Mr. Salzman, a curious figure, wouldn't you say?"

Not certain what to answer, he nodded.

She bravely went on, blushing, "I for one am grateful for his introducing us. Aren't you?"

He courteously replied, "I am."

"I mean," she said with a little laugh—and it was all in good taste, or at least gave the effect of being not in bad—"do you mind that we came together so?"

He was not displeased with her honesty, recognizing that she meant to set the relationship aright, and understanding that it took a certain amount of experience in life, and courage, to want to do it quite that way. One had to have some sort of past to make that kind of beginning.

He said that he did not mind. Salzman's function was traditional and honorable—valuable for what it might achieve, which, he pointed out, was frequently nothing.

Lily agreed with a sigh. They walked on for a while and she said after a long silence, again with a nervous laugh, "Would you mind if I asked you something a little bit personal? Frankly, I find the subject fascinating." Although Leo shrugged, she went on half embarrassedly, "How was it that you came to your calling? I mean was it a sudden passionate inspiration?"

Leo, after a time, slowly replied, "I was always interested in the Law."

"You saw revealed in it the presence of the Highest?"

He nodded and changed the subject. "I understand that you spent a little time in Paris, Miss Hirschorn?"

"Oh, did Mr. Salzman tell you, Rabbi Finkle?" Leo winced but she went on, "It was ages ago and almost forgotten. I remember I had to return for my sister's wedding."

And Lily would not be put off. "When," she asked in a trembly voice, "did you become enamored of God?"

He stared at her. Then it came to him that she was talking not about Leo Finkle, but of a total stranger, some mystical figure, perhaps even passionate prophet that Salzman had dreamed up for her—no relation to the living or dead. Leo trembled with rage and weakness. The trickster had obviously sold her a bill of goods, just as he had him, who'd expected to become acquainted

---

[4] Up-to-date.   [5] The goat-like Greek god of forests, fields, and flocks.

with a young lady of twenty-nine, only to behold, the moment he laid eyes upon her strained and anxious face, a woman past thirty-five and aging rapidly. Only his self control had kept him this long in her presence.

"I am not," he said gravely, "a talented religious person," and in seeking words to go on, found himself possessed by shame and fear. "I think," he said in a strained manner, "that I came to God not because I loved Him, but because I did not."

This confession he spoke harshly because its unexpectedness shook him.

Lily wilted. Leo saw a profusion of loaves of bread go flying like ducks high over his head, not unlike the winged loaves by which he had counted himself to sleep last night. Mercifully, then, it snowed, which he would not put past Salzman's machinations.

He was infuriated with the marriage broker and swore he would throw him out of the room the minute he reappeared. But Salzman did not come that night, and when Leo's anger had subsided, an unaccountable despair grew in its place. At first he thought this was caused by his disappointment in Lily, but before long it became evident that he had involved himself with Salzman without a true knowledge of his own intent. He gradually realized—with an emptiness that seized him with six hands—that he had called in the broker to find him a bride because he was incapable of doing it himself. This terrifying insight he had derived as a result of his meeting and conversation with Lily Hirschorn. Her probing questions had somehow irritated him into revealing— to himself more than her—the true nature of his relationship to God, and from that it had come upon him, with shocking force, that apart from his parents, he had never loved anyone. Or perhaps it went the other way, that he did not love God so well as he might, because he had not loved man. It seemed to Leo that his whole life stood starkly revealed and he saw himself for the first time as he truly was—unloved and loveless. This bitter but somehow not fully unexpected revelation brought him to a point of panic, controlled only by extraordinary effort. He covered his face with his hands and cried.

The week that followed was the worst of his life. He did not eat and lost weight. His beard darkened and grew ragged. He stopped attending seminars and almost never opened a book. He seriously considered leaving the Yeshivah, although he was deeply troubled at the thought of the loss of all his years of study—saw them like pages torn from a book, strewn over the city—and at the devastating effect of this decision upon his parents. But he had lived without knowledge of himself, and never in the Five Books,[6] and all the Commentaries— mea culpa[7]—had the truth been revealed to him. He did not know where to turn, and in all this desolating loneliness there was no *to whom*, although he often thought of Lily but not once could bring himself to go downstairs and make the call. He became touchy and irritable, especially with his landlady, who asked him all manner of personal questions; on the other hand, sensing his own disagreeableness, he waylaid her on the stairs and apologized abjectly, until mortified, she ran from him. Out of this, however, he drew the consolation that he was a Jew and that a Jew suffered. But gradually, as the long and terrible week drew to a close, he regained his composure and some idea of purpose in life: to go on as planned. Although he was imperfect, the ideal was not. As for his quest of a bride, the thought of continuing afflicted him

[6] The first five books of the Old Testament, the Pentateuch. [7] Through my own fault.

with anxiety and heartburn, yet perhaps with this new knowledge of himself
he would be more successful than in the past. Perhaps love would now come
to him and a bride to that love. And for this sanctified seeking who needed
Salzman?

The marriage broker, a skeleton with haunted eyes, returned that very night.
He looked, withal, the picture of frustrated expectancy—as if he had steadfastly
waited the week at Miss Lily Hirschorn's side for a telephone call that never
came.

Casually coughing, Salzman came immediately to the point: "So how did
you like her?"

Leo's anger rose and he could not refrain from chiding the matchmaker:
"Why did you lie to me, Salzman?"

Salzman's pale face went dead white, the world had snowed on him.

"Did you not state that she was twenty-nine?" Leo insisted.

"I give you my word—"

"She was thirty-five, if a day. *At least* thirty-five."

"Of this don't be too sure. Her father told me—"

"Never mind. The worst of it was that you lied to her."

"How did I lie to her, tell me?"

"You told her things about me that weren't true. You made me out to be
more, consequently less than I am. She had in mind a totally different person,
a sort of semimystical Wonder Rabbi."

"All I said, you was a religious man."

"I can imagine."

Salzman sighed. "This is my weakness that I have," he confessed. "My wife
says to me I shouldn't be a salesman, but when I have two fine people that
they would be wonderful to be married, I am so happy that I talk too much."
He smiled wanly. "This is why Salzman is a poor man."

Leo's anger left him. "Well, Salzman, I'm afraid that's all."

The marriage broker fastened hungry eyes on him.

"You don't want any more a bride?"

"I do," said Leo, "but I have decided to seek her in a different way. I am
no longer interested in an arranged marriage. To be frank, I now admit the
necessity of premarital love. That is, I want to be in love with the one I marry."

"Love?" said Salzman, astounded. After a moment he remarked, "For us,
our love is our life, not for the ladies. In the ghetto they—"

"I know, I know," said Leo. "I've thought of it often. Love, I have said to
myself, should be a by-product of living and worship rather than its own end.
Yet for myself I find it necessary to establish the level of my need and fulfill
it."

Salzman shrugged but answered, "Listen, rabbi, if you want love, this I can
find for you also. I have such beautiful clients that you will love them the
minute your eyes will see them."

Leo smiled unhappily. "I'm afraid you don't understand."

But Salzman hastily unstrapped his portfolio and withdrew a manila packet
from it.

"Pictures," he said, quickly laying the envelope on the table.

Leo called after him to take the pictures away, but as if on the wings of
the wind, Salzman had disappeared.

March came. Leo had returned to his regular routine. Although he felt not
quite himself yet—lacked energy—he was making plans for a more active social

life. Of course it would cost something, but he was an expert in cutting corners; and when there were no corners left he would make circles rounder. All the while Salzman's pictures had lain on the table, gathering dust. Occasionally as Leo sat studying, or enjoying a cup of tea, his eyes fell on the manila envelope, but he never opened it.

The days went by and no social life to speak of developed with a member of the opposite sex—it was difficult, given the circumstances of his situation. One morning Leo toiled up the stairs to his room and stared out the window at the city. Although the day was bright his view of it was dark. For some time he watched the people in the street below hurrying along and then turned with a heavy heart to his little room. On the table was the packet. With a sudden relentless gesture he tore it open. For a half-hour he stood by the table in a state of excitement, examining the photographs of the ladies Salzman had included. Finally, with a deep sigh he put them down. There were six, of varying degrees of attractiveness, but look at them long enough and they all became Lily Hirschorn: all past their prime, all starved behind bright smiles, not a true personality in the lot. Life, despite their frantic yoohooings, had passed them by; they were pictures in a brief case that stank of fish. After a while, however, as Leo attempted to return the photographs into the envelope, he found in it another, a snapshot of the type taken by a machine for a quarter. He gazed at it a moment and let out a cry.

Her face deeply moved him. Why, he could at first not say. It gave him the impression of youth—spring flowers, yet age—a sense of having been used to the bone, wasted; this came from the eyes, which were hauntingly familiar, yet absolutely strange. He had a vivid impression that he had met her before, but try as he might he could not place her although he could almost recall her name, as if he had read it in her own handwriting. No, this couldn't be; he would have remembered her. It was not, he affirmed, that she had an extraordinary beauty—no, though her face was attractive enough; it was that *something* about her moved him. Feature for feature, even some of the ladies of the photographs could do better; but she leaped forth to his heart—had *lived,* or wanted to—more than just wanted, perhaps regretted how she had lived— had somehow deeply suffered: it could be seen in the depths of those reluctant eyes, and from the way the light enclosed and shone from her, and within her, opening realms of possibility: this was her own. Her he desired. His head ached and eyes narrowed with the intensity of his gazing, then as if an obscure fog had blown up in the mind, he experienced fear of her and was aware that he had received an impression, somehow, of evil. He shuddered, saying softly, it is thus with us all. Leo brewed some tea in a small pot and sat sipping it without sugar, to calm himself. But before he had finished drinking, again with excitement he examined the face and found it good: good for Leo Finkle. Only such a one could understand him and help him seek whatever he was seeking. She might, perhaps, love him. How she had happened to be among the discards in Salzman's barrel he could never guess, but he knew he must urgently go find her.

Leo rushed downstairs, grabbed up the Bronx telephone book, and searched for Salzman's home address. He was not listed, nor was his office. Neither was he in the Manhattan book. But Leo remembered having written down the address on a slip of paper after he had read Salzman's advertisement in the "personals" column of the *Forward.* He ran up to his room and tore through his papers, without luck. It was exasperating. Just when he needed the matchmaker he was nowhere to be found. Fortunately Leo remembered to look in his wallet. There on a card he found his name written and a Bronx address. No phone number was listed, the reason—Leo now recalled—he had originally communicated with Salzman by letter. He got on his coat, put a hat on over his skull cap and hurried to the subway station. All the way to the far end of the Bronx he sat on the edge of his seat. He was more than once tempted to take out the picture and see if the girl's face was as he remembered it, but he refrained, allowing the snapshot to remain in his inside coat pocket, content to have her so close. When the train pulled into the station he was waiting at the door and bolted out. He quickly located the street Salzman had advertised.

The building he sought was less than a block from the subway, but it was not an office building, nor even a loft, nor a store in which one could rent office space. It was a very old tenement house. Leo found Salzman's name in pencil on a soiled tag under the bell and climbed three dark flights to his apartment. When he knocked, the door was opened by a thin, asthmatic, gray-haired woman, in felt slippers.

"Yes?" she said, expecting nothing. She listened without listening. He could have sworn he had seen her, too, before but knew it was an illusion.

"Salzman—does he live here? Pinye Salzman," he said, "the matchmaker?"

She stared at him a long minute. "Of course."

He felt embarrassed. "Is he in?"

"No." Her mouth, though left open, offered nothing more.

"The matter is urgent. Can you tell me where his office is?"

"In the air." She pointed upward.

"You mean he has no office?" Leo asked.

"In his socks."

He peered into the apartment. It was sunless and dingy, one large room divided by a half-open curtain, beyond which he could see a sagging metal bed. The near side of a room was crowded with rickety chairs, old bureaus, a three-legged table, racks of cooking utensils, and all the apparatus of a kitchen. But there was no sign of Salzman or his magic barrel, probably also a figment of the imagination. An odor of frying fish made Leo weak to the knees.

"Where is he?" he insisted. "I've got to see your husband."

At length she answered, "So who knows where he is? Every time he thinks a new thought he runs to a different place. Go home, he will find you."

"Tell him Leo Finkle."

She gave no sign she had heard.

He walked downstairs, depressed.

But Salzman, breathless, stood waiting at his door.

Leo was astounded and overjoyed. "How did you get here before me?"

"I rushed."

"Come inside."

They entered. Leo fixed tea, and a sardine sandwich for Salzman. As they were drinking he reached behind him for the packet of pictures and handed them to the marriage broker.

Salzman put down his glass and said expectantly, "You find somebody you like?"

"Not among these."

The marriage broker turned away.

"Here is the one I want." Leo held forth the snapshot.

Salzman slipped on his glasses and took the picture into his trembling hand. He turned ghastly and let out a groan.

"What's the matter?" cried Leo.

"Excuse me. Was an accident this picture. She isn't for you."

Salzman frantically shoved the manila packet into his portfolio. He thrust the snapshot into his pocket and fled down the stairs.

Leo, after momentary paralysis, gave chase and cornered the marriage broker in the vestibule. The landlady made hysterical outcries but neither of them listened.

"Give me back the picture, Salzman."

"No." The pain in his eyes was terrible.

"Tell me who she is then."

"This I can't tell you. Excuse me."

He made to depart, but Leo, forgetting himself, seized the matchmaker by his tight coat and shook him frenziedly.

"Please," sighed Salzman. *"Please."*

Leo ashamedly let him go. "Tell me who she is," he begged. "It's very important for me to know."

"She is not for you. She is a wild one—wild, without shame. This is not a bride for a rabbi."

"What do you mean wild?"

"Like an animal. Like a dog. For her to be poor was a sin. This is why to me she is dead now."

"In God's name, what do you mean?"

"Her I can't introduce to you," Salzman cried.

"Why are you so excited?"

"Why, he asks," Salzman said, bursting into tears. "This is my baby, my Stella, she should burn in hell."

Leo hurried up to bed and hid under the covers. Under the covers he thought his life through. Although he soon fell asleep he could not sleep her out of his mind. He woke, beating his breast. Though he prayed to be rid of her, his prayers went unanswered. Through days of torment he endlessly struggled not to love her; fearing success, he escaped it. He then concluded to convert her to goodness, himself to God. The idea alternately nauseated and exalted him.

He perhaps did not know that he had come to a final decision until he encountered Salzman in a Broadway cafeteria. He was sitting alone at a rear table, sucking the bony remains of a fish. The marriage broker appeared haggard, and transparent to the point of vanishing.

Salzman looked up at first without recognizing him. Leo had grown a pointed beard and his eyes were weighted with wisdom.

"Salzman," he said, "love has at last come to my heart."

"Who can love from a picture?" mocked the marriage broker.

"It is not impossible."

"If you can love her, then you can love anybody. Let me show you some new clients that they just sent me their photographs. One is a little doll."

"Just her I want," Leo murmured.

"Don't be a fool, doctor. Don't bother with her."

"Put me in touch with her, Salzman," Leo said humbly. "Perhaps I can be of service."

Salzman had stopped eating and Leo understood with emotion that it was now arranged.

Leaving the cafeteria, he was, however, afflicted by a tormenting suspicion that Salzman had planned it all to happen this way.

Leo was informed by letter that she would meet him on a certain corner, and she was there one spring night, waiting under a street lamp. He appeared, carrying a small bouquet of violets and rosebuds. Stella stood by the lamp post, smoking. She wore white with red shoes, which fitted his expectations, although in a troubled moment he had imagined the dress red, and only the shoes white. She waited uneasily and shyly. From afar he saw that her eyes—clearly her father's—were filled with desperate innocence. He pictured in her, his own redemption. Violins and lit candles revolved in the sky. Leo ran forward with flowers outthrust.

Around the corner, Salzman, leaning against a wall, chanted prayers for the dead.

[1954]

Flannery O'Connor *1925–1964*

THE ARTIFICIAL NIGGER

Mr. Head awakened to discover that the room was full of moonlight. He sat up and stared at the floor boards—the color of silver—and then at the ticking on his pillow, which might have been brocade, and after a second, he saw half of the moon five feet away in his shaving mirror, paused as if it were waiting for his permission to enter. It rolled forward and cast a dignifying light on everything. The straight chair against the wall looked stiff and attentive as if it were awaiting an order and Mr. Head's trousers, hanging to the back of it, had an almost noble air, like the garment some great man had just flung to his servant; but the face on the moon was a grave one. It gazed across the room and out the window where it floated over the horse stall and appeared to contemplate itself with the look of a young man who sees his old age before him.

Mr. Head could have said to it that age was a choice blessing and that only with years does a man enter into that calm understanding of life that makes him a suitable guide for the young. This, at least, had been his own experience.

He sat up and grasped the iron posts at the foot of his bed and raised himself until he could see the face on the alarm clock which sat on an overturned bucket beside the chair. The hour was two in the morning. The alarm on the clock did not work but he was not dependent on any mechanical means to awaken him. Sixty years had not dulled his responses; his physical reactions, like his moral ones, were guided by his will and strong character, and these could be seen plainly in his features. He had a long tube-like face with a long rounded open jaw and a long depressed nose. His eyes were alert but quiet, and in the miraculous moonlight they had a look of composure and of ancient wisdom as if they belonged to one of the great guides of men. He might have been Vergil summoned in the middle of the night to go to Dante, or better, Raphael, awakened by a blast of God's light to fly to the side of Tobias.[1] The only dark spot in the room was Nelson's pallet, underneath the shadow of the window.

Nelson was hunched over on his side, his knees under his chin and his heels under his bottom. His new suit and hat were in the boxes that they had been sent in and these were on the floor at the foot of the pallet where he could get his hands on them as soon as he woke up. The slop jar, out of the shadow and made snow-white in the moonlight, appeared to stand guard over him like a small personal angel. Mr. Head lay back down, feeling entirely confident that he could carry out the moral mission of the coming day. He meant to be up before Nelson and to have the breakfast cooking by the time he awakened. The boy was always irked when Mr. Head was the first up. They would have to leave the house at four to get to the railroad junction by five-

---

[1] In the *Divine Comedy* (1321) by Italian poet Dante Alighieri (1265–1321), the Roman poet Vergil (70–19 B.C.) served as guide during Dante's voyage through Hell and Purgatory. The archangel Raphael serves a similar function in the Book of Tobit, an apocryphal book of the Old Testament, where he guides Tobit on his journey to recover ten talents of silver.

thirty. The train was to stop for them at five forty-five and they had to be there on time for this train was stopping merely to accommodate them.

This would be the boy's first trip to the city though he claimed it would be his second because he had been born there. Mr. Head had tried to point out to him that when he was born he didn't have the intelligence to determine his whereabouts but this had made no impression on the child at all and he continued to insist that this was to be his second trip. It would be Mr. Head's third trip. Nelson had said, "I will've already been there twict and I ain't but ten."

Mr. Head had contradicted him.

"If you ain't been there in fifteen years, how you know you'll be able to find your way about?" Nelson had asked. "How you know it hasn't changed some?"

"Have you ever," Mr. Head had asked, "seen me lost?"

Nelson certainly had not but he was a child who was never satisfied until he had given an impudent answer and he replied, "It's nowhere around here to get lost at."

"The day is going to come," Mr. Head prophesied, "when you'll find you ain't as smart as you think you are." He had been thinking about this trip for several months but it was for the most part in moral terms that he conceived it. It was to be a lesson that the boy would never forget. He was to find out from it that he had no cause for pride merely because he had been born in a city. He was to find out that the city is not a great place. Mr. Head meant him to see everything there is to see in a city so that he would be content to stay at home for the rest of his life. He fell asleep thinking how the boy would at last find out that he was not as smart as he thought he was.

He was awakened at three-thirty by the smell of fatback[2] frying and he leaped off his cot. The pallet was empty and the clothes boxes had been thrown open. He put on his trousers and ran into the other room. The boy had a corn pone on cooking and had fried the meat. He was sitting in the half-dark at the table, drinking cold coffee out of a can. He had on his new suit and his new gray hat pulled low over his eyes. It was too big for him but they had ordered it a size large because they expected his head to grow. He didn't say anything but his entire figure suggested satisfaction at having arisen before Mr. Head.

Mr. Head went to the stove and brought the meat to the table in the skillet. "It's no hurry," he said. "You'll get there soon enough and it's no guarantee you'll like it when you do neither," and he sat down across from the boy whose hat teetered back slowly to reveal a fiercely expressionless face, very much the same shape as the old man's. They were grandfather and grandson but they looked enough alike to be brothers and brothers not too far apart in age, for Mr. Head had a youthful expression by daylight, while the boy's look was ancient, as if he knew everything already and would be pleased to forget it.

Mr. Head had once had a wife and daughter and when the wife died, the daughter ran away and returned after an interval with Nelson. Then one morning, without getting out of bed, she died and left Mr. Head with sole care of the year-old child. He had made the mistake of telling Nelson that he had

[2] A strip of fat from the back of a hog.

been born in Atlanta. If he hadn't told him that, Nelson couldn't have insisted that this was going to be his second trip.

"You may not like it a bit," Mr. Head continued. "It'll be full of niggers."

The boy made a face as if he could handle a nigger.

"All right," Mr. Head said. "You ain't ever seen a nigger."

"You wasn't up very early," Nelson said.

"You ain't ever seen a nigger," Mr. Head repeated. "There hasn't been a nigger in this county since we run that one out twelve years ago and that was before you were born." He looked at the boy as if he were daring him to say he had ever seen a Negro.

"How you know I never saw a nigger when I lived there before?" Nelson asked. "I probably saw a lot of niggers."

"If you seen one you didn't know what he was," Mr. Head said, completely exasperated. "A six-month-old child don't know a nigger from anybody else."

"I reckon I'll know a nigger if I see one," the boy said and got up and straightened his slick sharply creased gray hat and went outside to the privy.

They reached the junction some time before the train was due to arrive and stood about two feet from the first set of tracks. Mr. Head carried a paper sack with some biscuits and a can of sardines in it for their lunch. A coarse-looking orange-colored sun coming up behind the east range of mountains was making the sky a dull red behind them, but in front of them it was still gray and they faced a gray transparent moon, hardly stronger than a thumbprint and completely without light. A small tin switch box and a black fuel tank were all there was to mark the place as a junction; the tracks were double and did not converge again until they were hidden behind the bends at either end of the clearing. Trains passing appeared to emerge from a tunnel of trees and, hit for a second by the cold sky, vanished terrified into the woods again. Mr. Head had had to make special arrangements with the ticket agent to have this train stop and he was secretly afraid it would not, in which case, he knew Nelson would say, "I never thought no train was going to stop for you." Under the useless morning moon the tracks looked white and fragile. Both the old man and the child stared ahead as if they were awaiting an apparition.

Then suddenly, before Mr. Head could make up his mind to turn back, there was a deep warning bleat and the train appeared, gliding very slowly, almost silently around the bend of trees about two hundred yards down the track, with one yellow front light shining. Mr. Head was still not certain it would stop and he felt it would make an even bigger idiot of him if it went by slowly. Both he and Nelson, however, were prepared to ignore the train if it passed them.

The engine charged by, filling their noses with the smell of hot metal and then the second coach came to a stop exactly where they were standing. A conductor with the face of an ancient bloated bulldog was on the step as if he expected them, though he did not look as if it mattered one way or the other to him if they got on or not. "To the right," he said.

Their entry took only a fraction of a second and the train was already speeding on as they entered the quiet car. Most of the travelers were still sleeping, some with their heads hanging off the chair arms, some stretched across two seats, and some sprawled out with their feet in the aisle. Mr. Head saw two unoccupied seats and pushed Nelson toward them. "Get in there by the win-der," he said in his normal voice which was very loud at this hour of the morning. "Nobody cares if you sit there because it's nobody in it. Sit right there."

"I heard you," the boy muttered. "It's no use in you yelling," and he sat down and turned his head to the glass. There he saw a pale ghost-like face scowling at him beneath the brim of a pale ghost-like hat. His grandfather, looking quickly too, saw a different ghost, pale but grinning, under a black hat.

Mr. Head sat down and settled himself and took out his ticket and started reading aloud everything that was printed on it. People began to stir. Several woke up and stared at him. "Take off your hat," he said to Nelson and took off his own and put it on his knee. He had a small amount of white hair that had turned tobacco-colored over the years and this lay flat across the back of his head. The front of his head was bald and creased. Nelson took off his hat and put it on his knee and they waited for the conductor to come ask for their tickets.

The man across the aisle from them was spread out over two seats, his feet propped on the window and his head jutting into the aisle. He had on a light blue suit and a yellow shirt unbuttoned at the neck. His eyes had just opened and Mr. Head was ready to introduce himself when the conductor came up from behind and growled, "Tickets."

When the conductor had gone, Mr. Head gave Nelson the return half of his ticket and said, "Now put that in your pocket and don't lose it or you'll have to stay in the city."

"Maybe I will," Nelson said as if this were a reasonable suggestion.

Mr. Head ignored him. "First time this boy has ever been on a train," he explained to the man across the aisle, who was sitting up now on the edge of his seat with both feet on the floor.

Nelson jerked his hat on again and turned angrily to the window.

"He's never seen anything before," Mr. Head continued. "Ignorant as the day he was born, but I mean for him to get his fill once and for all."

The boy leaned forward, across his grandfather and toward the stranger. "I was born in the city," he said. "I was born there. This is my second trip." He said it in a high positive voice but the man across the aisle didn't look as if he understood. There were heavy purple circles under his eyes.

Mr. Head reached across the aisle and tapped him on the arm. "The thing to do with a boy," he said sagely, "is to show him all it is to show. Don't hold nothing back."

"Yeah," the man said. He gazed down at his swollen feet and lifted the left one about ten inches from the floor. After a minute he put it down and lifted the other. All through the car people began to get up and move about and yawn and stretch. Separate voices could be heard here and there and then a general hum. Suddenly Mr. Head's serene expression changed. His mouth almost closed and a light, fierce and cautious both, came into his eyes. He was looking down the length of the car. Without turning, he caught Nelson by the arm and pulled him forward. "Look," he said.

A huge coffee-colored man was coming slowly forward. He had on a light suit and yellow satin tie with a ruby pin in it. One of his hands rested on his stomach which rode majestically under his buttoned coat, and in the other he held the head of a black walking stick that he picked up and set down with a deliberate outward motion each time he took a step. He was proceeding very slowly, his large brown eyes gazing over the heads of the passengers. He had a small white mustache and white crinkly hair. Behind him there were two young women, both coffee-colored, one in a yellow dress and one in a green. Their progress was kept at the rate of his and they chatted in low throaty voices as they followed him.

Mr. Head's grip was tightened insistently on Nelson's arm. As the procession passed them, the light from a sapphire ring on the brown hand that picked up the cane reflected in Mr. Head's eye, but he did not look up nor did the tremendous man look at him. The group proceeded up the rest of the aisle and out of the car. Mr. Head's grip on Nelson's arm loosened. "What was that?" he asked.

"A man," the boy said and gave him an indignant look as if he were tired of having his intelligence insulted.

"What kind of a man?" Mr. Head persisted, his voice expressionless.

"A fat man," Nelson said. He was beginning to feel that he had better be cautious.

"You don't know what kind?" Mr. Head said in a final tone.

"An old man," the boy said and had a sudden foreboding that he was not going to enjoy the day.

"That was a nigger," Mr. Head said and sat back.

Nelson jumped up on the seat and stood looking backward to the end of the car but the Negro had gone.

"I'd of thought you'd know a nigger since you seen so many when you was in the city on your first visit," Mr. Head continued. "That's his first nigger," he said to the man across the aisle.

The boy slid down into the seat. "You said they were black," he said in an angry voice. "You never said they were tan. How do you expect me to know anything when you don't tell me right?"

"You're just ignorant is all," Mr. Head said and he got up and moved over in the vacant seat by the man across the aisle.

Nelson turned backward again and looked where the Negro had disappeared. He felt that the Negro had deliberately walked down the aisle in order to make a fool of him and he hated him with a fierce raw flesh hate; and also, he understood now why his grandfather disliked them. He looked toward the window and the face there seemed to suggest that he might be inadequate to the day's exactions. He wondered if he would even recognize the city when they came to it.

After he had told several stories, Mr. Head realized that the man he was talking to was asleep and he got up and suggested to Nelson that they walk over the train and see the parts of it. He particularly wanted the boy to see the toilet so they went first to the men's room and examined the plumbing. Mr. Head demonstrated the ice-water cooler as if he had invented it and showed Nelson the bowl with the single spigot where the travelers brushed their teeth. They went through several cars and came to the diner.

This was the most elegant car in the train. It was painted a rich egg-yellow and had a wine-colored carpet on the floor. There were wide windows over the tables and great spaces of the rolling view were caught in miniature in the sides of the coffee pots and in the glasses. Three very black Negroes in white suits and aprons were running up and down the aisle, swinging trays and bowing and bending over the travelers eating breakfast. One of them rushed up to Mr. Head and Nelson and said, holding up two fingers, "Space for two!" but Mr. Head replied in a loud voice, "We eaten before we left!"

The waiter wore large brown spectacles that increased the size of his eye whites. "Stan' aside then please," he said with an airy wave of the arm as if he were brushing aside flies.

Neither Nelson nor Mr. Head moved a fraction of an inch. "Look," Mr. Head said.

The near corner of the diner, containing two tables, was set off from the rest by a saffron-colored curtain. One table was set but empty but at the other, facing them, his back to the drape, sat the tremendous Negro. He was speaking in a soft voice to the two women while he buttered a muffin. He had a heavy sad face and his neck bulged over his white collar on either side. "They rope them off," Mr. Head explained. Then he said, "Let's go see the kitchen," and they walked the length of the diner but the black waiter was coming fast behind them.

"Passengers are not allowed in the kitchen!" he said in a haughty voice. "Passengers are NOT allowed in the kitchen!"

Mr. Head stopped where he was and turned. "And there's good reason for that," he shouted into the Negro's chest, "because the cockroaches would run the passengers out!"

All the travelers laughed and Mr. Head and Nelson walked out, grinning. Mr. Head was known at home for his quick wit and Nelson felt a sudden keen pride in him. He realized the old man would be his only support in the strange place they were approaching. He would be entirely alone in the world if he were ever lost from his grandfather. A terrible excitement shook him and he wanted to take hold of Mr. Head's coat and hold on like a child.

As they went back to their seats they could see through the passing windows that the countryside was becoming speckled with small houses and shacks and that a highway ran alongside the train. Cars sped by on it, very small and fast. Nelson felt that there was less breath in the air than there had been thirty minutes ago. The man across the aisle had left and there was no one near for Mr. Head to hold a conversation with so he looked out the window, through his own reflection, and read aloud the names of the buildings they were passing. "The Dixie Chemical Corp!" he announced. "Southern Maid Flour! Dixie Doors! Southern Belle Cotton Products! Patty's Peanut Butter! Southern Mammy Cane Syrup!"

"Hush up!" Nelson hissed.

All over the car people were beginning to get up and take their luggage off the overhead racks. Women were putting on their coats and hats. The conductor stuck his head in the car and snarled, "Firstopppppmry," and Nelson lunged out of his sitting position, trembling. Mr. Head pushed him down by the shoulder.

"Keep your seat," he said in dignified tones. "The first stop is on the edge of town. The second stop is at the main railroad station." He had come by this knowledge on his first trip when he had got off at the first stop and had had to pay a man fifteen cents to take him into the heart of town. Nelson sat back down, very pale. For the first time in his life, he understood that his grandfather was indispensable to him.

The train stopped and let off a few passengers and glided on as if it had never ceased moving. Outside, behind rows of brown rickety houses, a line of blue buildings stood up, and beyond them a pale rosy-gray sky faded away to nothing. The train moved into the railroad yard. Looking down, Nelson saw lines and lines of silver tracks multiplying and criss-crossing. Then before he could start counting them, the face in the window started out at him, gray but distinct, and he looked the other way. The train was in the station. Both he and Mr. Head jumped up and ran to the door. Neither noticed that they had left the paper sack with the lunch in it on the seat.

They walked stiffly through the small station and came out of a heavy door into the squall of traffic. Crowds were hurrying to work. Nelson didn't know where to look. Mr. Head leaned against the side of the building and glared in front of him.

Finally Nelson said, "Well, how do you see what all it is to see?"

Mr. Head didn't answer. Then as if the sight of people passing had given him the clue, he said, "You walk," and started off down the street. Nelson followed, steadying his hat. So many sights and sounds were flooding in on him that for the first block he hardly knew what he was seeing. At the second corner, Mr. Head turned and looked behind him at the station they had left, a putty-colored terminal with a concrete dome on top. He thought that if he could keep the dome always in sight, he would be able to get back in the afternoon to catch the train again.

As they walked along, Nelson began to distinguish details and take note of the store windows, jammed with every kind of equipment—hardware, drygoods, chicken feed, liquor. They passed one that Mr. Head called his particular attention to where you walked in and sat on a chair with your feet upon two rests and let a Negro polish your shoes. They walked slowly and stopped and stood at the entrances so he could see what went on in each place but they did not go into any of them. Mr. Head was determined not to go into any city store because on his first trip here, he had got lost in a large one and had found his way out only after many people had insulted him.

They came in the middle of the next block to a store that had a weighing machine in front of it and they both in turn stepped up on it and put in a penny and received a ticket. Mr. Head's ticket said, "You weigh 120 pounds. You are upright and brave and all your friends admire you." He put the ticket in his pocket, surprised that the machine should have got his character correct but his weight wrong, for he had weighed on a grain scale not long before and knew he weighed 110. Nelson's ticket said, "You weigh 98 pounds. You have a great destiny ahead of you but beware of dark women." Nelson did not know any women and he weighed only 68 pounds but Mr. Head pointed out that the machine had probably printed the number upsidedown, meaning the 9 for a 6.

They walked on and at the end of five blocks the dome of the terminal sank out of sight and Mr. Head turned to the left. Nelson could have stood in front of every store window for an hour if there had not been another more interesting one next to it. Suddenly he said, "I was born here!" Mr. Head turned and looked at him with horror. There was a sweaty brightness about his face. "This is where I come from!" he said.

Mr. Head was appalled. He saw the moment had come for drastic action. "Lemme show you one thing you ain't seen yet," he said and took him to the corner where there was a sewer entrance. "Squat down," he said, "and stick your head in there," and he held the back of the boy's coat while he got down and put his head in the sewer. He drew it back quickly, hearing a gurgling in the depths under the sidewalk. Then Mr. Head explained the sewer system, how the entire city was underlined with it, how it contained all the drainage and was full of rats and how a man could slide into it and be sucked along down endless pitchblack tunnels. At any minute any man in the city might be sucked into the sewer and never heard from again. He described it so well that Nelson was for some seconds shaken. He connected the sewer passages with the entrance to hell and understood for the first time how the world was put together in its lower parts. He drew away from the curb.

Then he said, "Yes, but you can stay away from the holes," and his face took on that stubborn look that was so exasperating to his grandfather. "This is where I come from!" he said.

Mr. Head was dismayed but he only muttered, "You'll get your fill," and they walked on. At the end of two more blocks he turned to the left, feeling that he was circling the dome; and he was correct for in a half-hour they passed in front of the railroad station again. At first Nelson did not notice that he was seeing the same stores twice but when they passed the one where you put your feet on the rests while the Negro polished your shoes, he perceived that they were walking in a circle.

"We done been here!" he shouted. "I don't believe you know where you're at!"

"The direction just slipped my mind for a minute," Mr. Head said and they turned down a different street. He still did not intend to let the dome get too far away and after two blocks in their new direction, he turned to the left. This street contained two- and three-story wooden dwellings. Anyone passing on the sidewalk could see into the rooms and Mr. Head, glancing through one window, saw a woman lying on an iron bed, looking out, with a sheet pulled over her. Her knowing expression shook him. A fierce-looking boy on a bicycle came driving down out of nowhere and he had to jump to the side to keep from being hit. "It's nothing to them if they knock you down," he said. "You better keep closer to me."

They walked on for some time on streets like this before he remembered to turn again. The houses they were passing now were all unpainted and the wood in them looked rotten; the street between was narrower. Nelson saw a colored man. Then another. Then another. "Niggers live in these houses," he observed.

"Well come on and we'll go somewheres else," Mr. Head said. "We didn't come to look at niggers," and they turned down another street but they continued to see Negroes everywhere. Nelson's skin began to prickle and they stepped along at a faster pace in order to leave the neighborhood as soon as possible. There were colored men in their undershirts standing in the doors and colored women rocking on the sagging porches. Colored children played in the gutters and stopped what they were doing to look at them. Before long they began to pass rows of stores with colored customers in them but they didn't pause at the entrances of these. Black eyes in black faces were watching them from every direction. "Yes," Mr. Head said, "there is where you were born—right here with all these niggers."

Nelson scowled. "I think you done got us lost," he said.

Mr. Head swung around sharply and looked for the dome. It was nowhere in sight. "I ain't got us lost either," he said. "You're just tired of walking."

"I ain't tired, I'm hungry," Nelson said. "Give me a biscuit."

They discovered then that they had lost the lunch.

"You were the one holding the sack," Nelson said. "I would have kepaholt of it."

"If you want to direct this trip, I'll go on by myself and leave you right here," Mr. Head said and was pleased to see the boy turn white. However, he realized they were lost and drifting farther every minute from the station. He was hungry himself and beginning to be thirsty and since they had been in the colored neighborhood, they had both begun to sweat. Nelson had on his shoes and he was unaccustomed to them. The concrete sidewalks were very hard. They both wanted to find a place to sit down but this was impossible and they kept on walking, the boy muttering under his breath, "First you lost the sack and then you lost the way," and Mr. Head growling from time to time, "Anybody wants to be from this nigger heaven can be from it!"

By now the sun was well forward in the sky. The odor of dinners cooking drifted out to them. The Negroes were all at their doors to see them pass. "Whyn't you ast one of these niggers the way?" Nelson said. "You got us lost."

"This is where you were born," Mr. Head said. "You can ast one yourself if you want to."

Nelson was afraid of the colored men and he didn't want to be laughed at by the colored children. Up ahead he saw a large colored woman leaning in a doorway that opened onto the sidewalk. Her hair stood straight out from her head for about four inches all around and she was resting on bare brown feet that turned pink at the sides. She had on a pink dress that showed her exact shape. As they came abreast of her, she lazily lifted one hand to her head and her fingers disappeared into her hair.

Nelson stopped. He felt his breath drawn up by the woman's dark eyes. "How do you get back to town?" he said in a voice that did not sound like his own.

After a minute she said, "You in town now," in a rich low tone that made Nelson feel as if a cool spray had been turned on him.

"How do you get back to the train?" he said in the same reed-like voice.

"You can catch you a car," she said.

He understood she was making fun of him but he was too paralyzed even to scowl. He stood drinking in every detail of her. His eyes traveled up from her great knees to her forehead and then made a triangular path from the glistening sweat on her neck down and across her tremendous bosom and over her bare arm back to where her fingers lay hidden in her hair. He suddenly wanted her to reach down and pick him up and draw him against her and then he wanted to feel her breath on his face. He wanted to look down and down into her eyes while she held him tighter and tighter. He had never had such a feeling before. He felt as if he were reeling down through a pitchblack tunnel.

"You can go a block down yonder and catch you a car take you to the railroad station, Sugarpie," she said.

Nelson would have collapsed at her feet if Mr. Head had not pulled him roughly away. "You act like you don't have any sense!" the old man growled.

They hurried down the street and Nelson did not look back at the woman. He pushed his hat sharply forward over his face which was already burning with shame. The sneering ghost he had seen in the train window and all the foreboding feelings he had on the way returned to him and he remembered that his ticket from the scale had said to beware of dark women and that his grandfather's had said he was upright and brave. He took hold of the old man's hand, a sign of dependence that he seldom showed.

They headed down the street toward the car tracks where a long yellow rattling trolley was coming. Mr. Head had never boarded a streetcar and he let that one pass. Nelson was silent. From time to time his mouth trembled slightly but his grandfather, occupied with his own problems, paid him no attention. They stood on the corner and neither looked at the Negroes who were passing, going about their business just as if they had been white, except that most of them stopped and eyed Mr. Head and Nelson. It occurred to Mr. Head that since the streetcar ran on tracks, they could simply follow the tracks. He gave Nelson a slight push and explained that they would follow the tracks on into the railroad station, walking, and they set off.

Presently to their great relief they began to see white people again and Nelson sat down on the sidewalk against the wall of a building. "I got to rest myself some," he said. "You lost the sack and the direction. You can just wait on me to rest myself."

"There's the tracks in front of us," Mr. Head said. "All we got to do is keep them in sight and you could have remembered the sack as good as me. This is where you were born. This is your old home town. This is your second trip. You ought to know how to do," and he squatted down and continued in this vein but the boy, easing his burning feet out of his shoes, did not answer.

"And standing there grinning like a chim-pan-zee while a nigger woman gives you directions. Great Gawd!" Mr. Head said.

"I never said I was nothing but born here," the boy said in a shaky voice. "I never said I would or wouldn't like it. I never said I wanted to come. I only said I was born here and I never had nothing to do with that. I want to go home. I never wanted to come in the first place. It was all your big idea. How you know you ain't following the tracks in the wrong direction?"

This last had occurred to Mr. Head too. "All these people are white," he said.

"We ain't passed here before," Nelson said. This was a neighborhood of brick buildings that might have been lived in or might not. A few empty automobiles were parked along the curb and there was an occasional passerby. The heat of the pavement came up through Nelson's thin suit. His eyelids began to droop, and after a few minutes his head tilted forward. His shoulders twitched once or twice and then he fell over on his side and lay sprawled in an exhausted fit of sleep.

Mr. Head watched him silently. He was very tired himself but they could not both sleep at the same time and he could not have slept anyway because he did not know where he was. In a few minutes Nelson would wake up, refreshed by his sleep and very cocky, and would begin complaining that he had lost the sack and the way. You'd have a mighty sorry time if I wasn't here, Mr. Head thought; and then another idea occurred to him. He looked at the sprawled figure for several minutes; presently he stood up. He justified what he was going to do on the grounds that it is sometimes necessary to teach a child a lesson he won't forget, particularly when the child is always reasserting his position with some new impudence. He walked without a sound to the corner about twenty feet away and sat down on a covered garbage can in the alley where he could look out and watch Nelson wake up alone.

The boy was dozing fitfully, half conscious of vague noises and black forms moving up from some dark part of him into the light. His face worked in his sleep and he had pulled his knees up under his chin. The sun shed a dull dry light on the narrow street; everything looked like exactly what it was. After a while Mr. Head, hunched like an old monkey on the garbage can lid, decided that if Nelson didn't wake up soon, he would make a loud noise by bamming his foot against the can. He looked at his watch and discovered that it was two o'clock. Their train left at six and the possibility of missing it was too awful for him to think of. He kicked his foot backwards on the can and a hollow boom reverberated in the alley.

Nelson shot up onto his feet with a shout. He looked where his grandfather should have been and stared. He seemed to whirl several times and then, picking up his feet and throwing his head back, he dashed down the street like a wild maddened pony. Mr. Head jumped off the can and galloped after but the child was almost out of sight. He saw a streak of gray disappearing diagonally a block ahead. He ran as fast as he could, looking both ways down every intersection, but without sight of him again. Then as he passed the third intersection, completely winded, he saw about half a block down the street a scene that stopped him altogether. He crouched behind a trash box to watch and get his bearings.

Nelson was sitting with both legs spread out and by his side lay an elderly woman, screaming. Groceries were scattered about the sidewalk. A crowd of women had already gathered to see justice done and Mr. Head distinctly heard the old woman on the pavement shout, "You've broken my ankle and your daddy'll pay for it! Every nickel! Police! Police!" Several of the women were plucking at Nelson's shoulder but the boy seemed too dazed to get up.

Something forced Mr. Head from behind the trash box and forward, but only at a creeping pace. He had never in his life been accosted by a policeman. The women were milling around Nelson as if they might suddenly all dive on him at once and tear him to pieces, and the old woman continued to scream that her ankle was broken and to call for an officer. Mr. Head came on so slowly that he could have been taking a backward step after each forward one, but when he was about ten feet away, Nelson saw him and sprang. The child caught him around the hips and clung panting against him.

The women all turned on Mr. Head. The injured one sat up and shouted, "You sir! You'll pay every penny of my doctor's bill that your boy has caused. He's a juve-nile delinquent! Where is an officer? Somebody take this man's name and address!"

Mr. Head was trying to detach Nelson's fingers from the flesh in the back of his legs. The old man's head had lowered itself into his collar like a turtle's; his eyes were glazed with fear and caution.

"Your boy has broken my ankle!" the old woman shouted. "Police!"

Mr. Head sensed the approach of the policeman from behind. He stared straight ahead at the women who were massed in their fury like a solid wall to block his escape. "This is not my boy," he said. "I never seen him before."

He felt Nelson's fingers fall out of his flesh.

The women dropped back, staring at him with horror, as if they were so repulsed by a man who would deny his own image and likeness that they could not bear to lay hands on him. Mr. Head walked on, through a space they silently cleared, and left Nelson behind. Ahead of him he saw nothing but a hollow tunnel that had once been the street.

The boy remained standing where he was, his neck craned forward and his hands hanging by his sides. His hat was jammed on his head so that there were no longer any creases in it. The injured woman got up and shook her fist at him and the others gave him pitying looks, but he didn't notice any of them. There was no policeman in sight.

In a minute he began to move mechanically, making no effort to catch up with his grandfather but merely following at about twenty paces. They walked on for five blocks in this way. Mr. Head's shoulders were sagging and his neck hung forward at such an angle that it was not visible from behind. He was afraid to turn his head. Finally he cut a short hopeful glance over his shoulder. Twenty feet behind him, he saw two small eyes piercing into his back like pitchfork prongs.

The boy was not of a forgiving nature but this was the first time he had ever had anything to forgive. Mr. Head had never disgraced himself before. After two more blocks, he turned and called over his shoulder in a high desperately gay voice. "Let's us go get us a Co' Cola somewheres!"

Nelson, with a dignity he had never shown before, turned and stood with his back to his grandfather.

Mr. Head began to feel the depth of his denial. His face as they walked on became all hollows and bare ridges. He saw nothing they were passing but he perceived that they had lost the car tracks. There was no dome to be seen anywhere and the afternoon was advancing. He knew that if dark overtook them in the city, they would be beaten and robbed. The speed of God's justice was only what he expected for himself, but he could not stand to think that his sins would be visited upon Nelson and that even now, he was leading the boy to his doom.

They continued to walk on block after block through an endless section of small brick houses until Mr. Head almost fell over a water spigot sticking up about six inches off the edge of a grass plot. He had not had a drink of water since early morning but he felt he did not deserve it now. Then he thought that Nelson would be thirsty and they would both drink and be brought together. He squatted down and put his mouth to the nozzle and turned a cold stream of water into his throat. Then he called out in the high desperate voice, "Come on and getcher some water!"

This time the child stared through him for nearly sixty seconds. Mr. Head got up and walked on as if he had drunk poison. Nelson, though he had not had water since some he had drunk out of a paper cup on the train, passed by the spigot, disdaining to drink where his grandfather had. When Mr. Head realized this, he lost all hope. His face in the waning afternoon light looked ravaged and abandoned. He could feel the boy's steady hate, traveling at an even pace behind him and he knew that (if by some miracle they escaped being murdered in the city) it would continue just that way for the rest of his life. He knew that now he was wandering into a black strange place where nothing was like it had ever been before, a long old age without respect and an end that would be welcome because it would be the end.

As for Nelson, his mind had frozen around his grandfather's treachery as if he were trying to preserve it intact to present at the final judgment. He walked without looking to one side or the other, but every now and then his mouth would twitch and this was when he felt, from some remote place inside himself, a black mysterious form reach up as if it would melt his frozen vision in one hot grasp.

The sun dropped down behind a row of houses and hardly noticing, they passed into an elegant suburban section where mansions were set back from the road by lawns with birdbaths on them. Here everything was entirely de-

serted. For blocks they didn't pass even a dog. The big white houses were
like partially submerged icebergs in the distance. There were no sidewalks,
only drives, and these wound around and around in endless ridiculous circles.
Nelson made no move to come nearer to Mr. Head. The old man felt that if
he saw a sewer entrance he would drop down into it and let himself be carried
away; and he could imagine the boy standing by, watching with only a slight
interest, while he disappeared.

A loud bark jarred him to attention and he looked up to see a fat man
approaching with two bulldogs. He waved both arms like someone shipwrecked
on a desert island. "I'm lost!" he called. "I'm lost and can't find my way
and me and this boy have got to catch this train and I can't find the station.
Oh Gawd I'm lost! Oh hep me Gawd I'm lost!"

The man, who was bald-headed and had on golf knickers, asked him what
train he was trying to catch and Mr. Head began to get out his tickets, trembling
so violently he could hardly hold them. Nelson had come up to within fifteen
feet and stood watching.

"Well," the fat man said, giving him back the tickets, "you won't have time
to get back to town to make this but you can catch it at the suburb stop.
That's three blocks from here," and he began explaining how to get there.

Mr. Head stared as if he were slowly returning from the dead and when
the man had finished and gone off with the dogs jumping at his heels, he
turned to Nelson and said breathlessly, "We're going to get home!"

The child was standing about ten feet away, his face bloodless under the
gray hat. His eyes were triumphantly cold. There was no light in them, no
feeling, no interest. He was merely there, a small figure, waiting. Home was
nothing to him.

Mr. Head turned slowly. He felt he knew now what time would be like without
seasons and what heat would be like without light and what man would be
like without salvation. He didn't care if he never made the train and if it had
not been for what suddenly caught his attention, like a cry out of the gathering
dusk, he might have forgotten there was a station to go to.

He had not walked five hundred yards down the road when he saw, within
reach of him, the plaster figure of a Negro sitting bent over on a low yellow
brick fence that curved around a wide lawn. The Negro was about Nelson's
size and he was pitched forward at an unsteady angle because the putty that
held him to the wall had cracked. One of his eyes was entirely white and he
held a piece of brown watermelon.

Mr. Head stood looking at him silently until Nelson stopped at a little distance. Then as the two of them stood there, Mr. Head breathed, "An artificial
nigger!"

It was not possible to tell if the artificial Negro were meant to be young
or old; he looked too miserable to be either. He was meant to look happy
because his mouth was stretched up at the corners but the chipped eye and
the angle he was cocked at gave him a wild look of misery instead.

"An artificial nigger!" Nelson repeated in Mr. Head's exact tone.

The two of them stood there with their necks forward at almost the same
angle and their shoulders curved in almost exactly the same way and their
hands trembling identically in their pockets. Mr. Head looked like an ancient
child and Nelson like a miniature old man. They stood gazing at the artificial
Negro as if they were faced with some great mystery, some monument to
another's victory that brought them together in their common defeat. They

could both feel it dissolving their differences like an action of mercy. Mr. Head had never known before what mercy felt like because he had been too good to deserve any, but he felt he knew now. He looked at Nelson and understood that he must say something to the child to show that he was still wise and in the look the boy returned he saw a hungry need for that assurance. Nelson's eyes seemed to implore him to explain once and for all the mystery of existence.

Mr. Head opened his lips to make a lofty statement and heard himself say, "They ain't got enough real ones here. They got to have an artificial one."

After a second, the boy nodded with a strange shivering about his mouth, and said, "Let's go home before we get ourselves lost again."

Their train glided into the suburb stop just as they reached the station and they boarded it together, and ten minutes before it was due to arrive at the junction, they went to the door and stood ready to jump off if it did not stop; but it did, just as the moon, restored to its full splendor, sprang from a cloud and flooded the clearing with light. As they stepped off, the sage grass was shivering gently in shades of silver and the clinkers under their feet glittered with a fresh black light. The treetops, fencing the junction like the protecting walls of a garden, were darker than the sky which was hung with gigantic white clouds illuminated like lanterns.

Mr. Head stood very still and felt the action of mercy touch him again but this time he knew that there were no words in the world that could name it. He understood that it grew out of agony, which is not denied to any man and which is given in strange ways to children. He understood it was all a man could carry into death to give his Maker and he suddenly burned with shame that he had so little of it to take with him. He stood appalled, judging himself with the thoroughness of God, while the action of mercy covered his pride like a flame and consumed it. He had never thought himself a great sinner before but he saw now that his true depravity had been hidden from him lest it cause him despair. He realized that he was forgiven for sins from the beginning of time, when he had conceived in his own heart the sin of Adam, until the present, when he had denied poor Nelson. He saw that no sin was too monstrous for him to claim as his own, and since God loved in proportion as He forgave, he felt ready at that instant to enter Paradise.

Nelson, composing his expression under the shadow of his hat brim, watched him with a mixture of fatigue and suspicion, but as the train glided past them and disappeared like a frightened serpent into the woods, even his face lightened and he muttered, "I'm glad I've went once, but I'll never go back again!"

[1955]

Albert Camus   *1913–1960*

THE GUEST*

The schoolmaster was watching the two men climb toward him. One was on horseback, the other on foot. They had not yet tackled the abrupt rise leading to the schoolhouse built on the hillside. They were toiling onward, making slow progress in the snow, among the stones, on the vast expanse of the high, deserted plateau.[1] From time to time the horse stumbled. Without hearing anything yet, he could see the breath issuing from the horse's nostrils. One of the men, at least, knew the region. They were following the trail although it had disappeared days ago under a layer of dirty white snow. The schoolmaster calculated that it would take them half an hour to get onto the hill. It was cold; he went back into the school to get a sweater.

He crossed the empty, frigid classroom. On the blackboard the four rivers of France, drawn with four different colored chalks, had been flowing toward their estuaries for the past three days. Snow had suddenly fallen in mid-October after eight months of drought without the transition of rain, and the twenty pupils, more or less, who lived in the villages scattered over the plateau had stopped coming. With fair weather they would return. Daru now heated only the single room that was his lodging, adjoining the classroom and giving also onto the plateau to the east. Like the class windows, his window looked to the south too. On that side the school was a few kilometers from the point where the plateau began to slope toward the south. In clear weather could be seen the purple mass of the mountain range where the gap opened onto the desert.

Somewhat warmed, Daru returned to the window from which he had first seen the two men. They were no longer visible. Hence they must have tackled the rise. The sky was not so dark, for the snow had stopped falling during the night. The morning had opened with a dirty light which had scarcely become brighter as the ceiling of clouds lifted. At two in the afternoon it seemed as if the day were merely beginning. But still this was better than those three days when the thick snow was falling amidst unbroken darkness with little gusts of wind that rattled the double door of the classroom. Then Daru had spent long hours in his room, leaving it only to go to the shed and feed the chickens or get some coal. Fortunately the delivery truck from Tadjid, the nearest village to the north, had brought his supplies two days before the blizzard. It would return in forty-eight hours.

Besides, he had enough to resist a siege, for the little room was cluttered with bags of wheat that the administration left as a stock to distribute to those of his pupils whose families had suffered from the drought. Actually they had all been victims because they were all poor. Every day Daru would distribute a ration to the children. They had missed it, he knew, during these bad days. Possibly one of the fathers or big brothers would come this afternoon and he could supply them with grain. It was just a matter of carrying them over to the next harvest. Now shiploads of wheat were arriving from France and

* Translated by Justin O'Brien
[1] The setting of the story is northern Algeria during the period of unrest which finally led to open rebellion against French rule and which ended with Algerian independence in 1962.

451

the worst was over. But it would be hard to forget that poverty, that army of ragged ghosts wandering in the sunlight, the plateaus burned to a cinder month after month, the earth shriveled up little by little, literally scorched, every stone bursting into dust under one's foot. The sheep had died then by thousands and even a few men, here and there, sometimes without anyone's knowing.

In contrast with such poverty, he who lived almost like a monk in his remote schoolhouse, nonetheless satisfied with the little he had and with the rough life, had felt like a lord with his whitewashed walls, his narrow couch, his unpainted shelves, his well, and his weekly provision of water and food. And suddenly this snow, without warning, without the foretaste of rain. This is the way the region was, cruel to live in, even without men—who didn't help matters either. But Daru had been born here. Everywhere else, he felt exiled.

He stepped out onto the terrace in front of the schoolhouse. The two men were now halfway up the slope. He recognized the horseman as Balducci, the old gendarme[2] he had known for a long time. Balducci was holding on the end of a rope an Arab who was walking behind him with hands bound and head lowered. The gendarme waved a greeting to which Daru did not reply, lost as he was in contemplation of the Arab dressed in a faded blue jellaba,[3] his feet in sandals but covered with socks of heavy raw wool, his head surmounted by a narrow, short *chèche*.[4] They were approaching. Balducci was holding back his horse in order not to hurt the Arab, and the group was advancing slowly.

Within earshot, Balducci shouted: "One hour to do the three kilometers from El Ameur!" Daru did not answer. Short and square in his thick sweater, he watched them climb. Not once had the Arab raised his head. "Hello," said Daru when they got up onto the terrace. "Come in and warm up." Balducci painfully got down from his horse without letting go the rope. From under his bristling mustache he smiled at the schoolmaster. His little dark eyes, deep-set under a tanned forehead, and his mouth surrounded with wrinkles made him look attentive and studious. Daru took the bridle, led the horse to the shed, and came back to the two men, who were now waiting for him in the school. He led them into his room. "I am going to heat up the classroom," he said. "We'll be more comfortable there." When he entered the room again, Balducci was on the couch. He had undone the rope tying him to the Arab, who had squatted near the stove. His hands still bound, the *chèche* pushed back on his head, he was looking toward the window. At first Daru noticed only his huge lips, fat, smooth, almost Negroid; yet his nose was straight, his eyes were dark and full of fever. The *chèche* revealed an obstinate forehead and, under the weathered skin now rather discolored by the cold, the whole face had a restless and rebellious look that struck Daru when the Arab, turning his face toward him, looked him straight in the eyes. "Go into the other room," said the schoolmaster, "and I'll make you some mint tea." "Thanks," Balducci said. "What a chore! How I long for retirement." And addressing his prisoner in Arabic: "Come on, you." The Arab got up and, slowly, holding his bound wrists in front of him, went into the classroom.

With the tea, Daru brought a chair. But Balducci was already enthroned on the nearest pupil's desk and the Arab had squatted against the teacher's platform facing the stove, which stood between the desk and the window.

---

[2] A military policeman.   [3] A hooded cloak.   [4] A scarf or sash which serves as a turban.

When he held out the glass of tea to the prisoner, Daru hesitated at the sight of his bound hands. "He might perhaps be untied." "Sure," said Balducci. "That was for the trip." He started to get to his feet. But Daru, setting the glass on the floor, had knelt beside the Arab. Without saying anything, the Arab watched him with his feverish eyes. Once his hands were free, he rubbed his swollen wrists against each other, took the glass of tea, and sucked up the burning liquid in swift little sips.

"Good," said Daru. "And where are you headed?"

Balducci withdrew his mustache from the tea. "Here, son."

"Odd pupils! And you're spending the night?"

"No. I'm going back to El Ameur. And you will deliver this fellow to Tinguit. He is expected at police headquarters."

Balducci was looking at Daru with a friendly little smile.

"What's this story?" asked the schoolmaster. "Are you pulling my leg?"

"No, son. Those are the orders."

"The orders? I'm not . . ." Daru hesitated, not wanting to hurt the old Corsican.[5] "I mean, that's not my job."

"What! What's the meaning of that? In wartime people do all kinds of jobs."

"Then I'll wait for the declaration of war!"

Balducci nodded.

"O.K. But the orders exist and they concern you too. Things are brewing, it appears. There is talk of a forthcoming revolt. We are mobilized, in a way."

Daru still had his obstinate look.

"Listen, son," Balducci said. "I like you and you must understand. There's only a dozen of us at El Ameur to patrol throughout the whole territory of a small department and I must get back in a hurry. I was told to hand this guy over to you and return without delay. He couldn't be kept there. His village was beginning to stir; they wanted to take him back. You must take him to Tinguit tomorrow before the day is over. Twenty kilometers shouldn't faze a husky fellow like you. After that, all will be over. You'll come back to your pupils and your comfortable life."

Behind the wall the horse could be heard snorting and pawing the earth. Daru was looking out the window. Decidedly, the weather was clearing and the light was increasing over the snowy plateau. When all the snow was melted, the sun would take over again and once more would burn the fields of stone. For days, still, the unchanging sky would shed its dry light on the solitary expanse where nothing had any connection with man.

"After all," he said, turning toward Balducci, "what did he do?" And, before the gendarme had opened his mouth, he asked: "Does he speak French?"

"No, not a word. We had been looking for him for a month, but they were hiding him. He killed his cousin."

"Is he against us?"

"I don't think so. But you can never be sure."

"Why did he kill?"

"A family squabble, I think. One owed the other grain, it seems. It's not at all clear. In short, he killed his cousin with a billhook.[6] You know, like a sheep, *kreezk!*"

Balducci made the gesture of drawing a blade across his throat and the

---

[5] A native of Corsica, a French island in the Mediterranean.
[6] A cutting or pruning tool with a hooked point.

Arab, his attention attracted, watched him with a sort of anxiety. Daru felt a sudden wrath against the man, against all men with their rotten spite, their tireless hates, their blood lust.

But the kettle was singing on the stove. He served Balducci more tea, hesitated, then served the Arab again, who, a second time, drank avidly. His raised arms made the jellaba fall open and the schoolmaster saw his thin, muscular chest.

"Thanks, kid," Balducci said. "And now, I'm off."

He got up and went toward the Arab, taking a small rope from his pocket.

"What are you doing?" Daru asked dryly.

Balducci, disconcerted, showed him the rope.

"Don't bother."

The old gendarme hesitated. "It's up to you. Of course, you are armed?"

"I have my shotgun."

"Where?"

"In the trunk."

"You ought to have it near your bed."

"Why? I have nothing to fear."

"You're crazy, son. If there's an uprising, no one is safe, we're all in the same boat."

"I'll defend myself. I'll have time to see them coming."

Balducci began to laugh, then suddenly the mustache covered the white teeth.

"You'll have time? O.K. That's just what I was saying. You have always been a little cracked. That's why I like you, my son was like that."

At the same time he took out his revolver and put it on the desk.

"Keep it; I don't need two weapons from here to El Ameur."

The revolver shone against the black paint of the table. When the gendarme turned toward him, the schoolmaster caught the smell of leather and horseflesh.

"Listen, Balducci," Daru said suddenly, "every bit of this disgusts me, and first of all your fellow here. But I won't hand him over. Fight, yes, if I have to. But not that."

The old gendarme stood in front of him and looked at him severely.

"You're being a fool," he said slowly. "I don't like it either. You don't get used to putting a rope on a man even after years of it, and you're even ashamed—yes, ashamed. But you can't let them have their way."

"I won't hand him over," Daru said again.

"It's an order, son, and I repeat it."

"That's right. Repeat to them what I've said to you: I won't hand him over."

Balducci made a visible effort to reflect. He looked at the Arab and at Daru. At last he decided.

"No, I won't tell them anything. If you want to drop us, go ahead; I'll not denounce you. I have an order to deliver the prisoner and I'm doing so. And now you'll just sign this paper for me."

"There's no need. I'll not deny that you left him with me."

"Don't be mean with me. I know you'll tell the truth. You're from hereabouts and you are a man. But you must sign, that's the rule."

Daru opened his drawer, took out a little square bottle of purple ink, the red wooden penholder with the "sergeant-major" pen he used for making models of penmanship, and signed. The gendarme carefully folded the paper and put it into his wallet. Then he moved toward the door.

"I'll see you off," Daru said.

"No," said Balducci. "There's no use being polite. You insulted me."

He looked at the Arab, motionless in the same spot, sniffed peevishly, and turned away toward the door. "Good-by, son," he said. The door shut behind him. Balducci appeared suddenly outside the window and then disappeared. His footsteps were muffled by the snow. The horse stirred on the other side of the wall and several chickens fluttered in fright. A moment later Balducci reappeared outside the window leading the horse by the bridle. He walked toward the little rise without turning around and disappeared from sight with the horse following him. A big stone could be heard bouncing down. Daru walked back toward the prisoner, who, without stirring, never took his eyes off him. "Wait," the schoolmaster said in Arabic and went toward the bedroom. As he was going through the door, he had a second thought, went to the desk, took the revolver, and stuck it in his pocket. Then, without looking back, he went into his room.

For some time he lay on his couch watching the sky gradually close over, listening to the silence. It was this silence that had seemed painful to him during the first days here, after the war. He had requested a post in the little town at the base of the foothills separating the upper plateaus from the desert. There, rocky walls, green and black to the north, pink and lavender to the south, marked the frontier of eternal summer. He had been named to a post farther north, on the plateau itself. In the beginning, the solitude and the silence had been hard for him on these wastelands peopled only by stones. Occasionally, furrows suggested civilization, but they had been dug to uncover a certain kind of stone good for building. The only plowing here was to harvest rocks. Elsewhere a thin layer of soil accumulated in the hollows would be scraped out to enrich paltry village gardens. This is the way it was: bare rock covered three quarters of the region. Towns sprang up, flourished, then disappeared; men came by, loved one another or fought bitterly, then died. No one in this desert, neither he nor his guest, mattered. And yet, outside this desert neither of them, Daru knew, could have really lived.

When he got up, no noise came from the classroom. He was amazed at the unmixed joy he derived from the mere thought that the Arab might have fled and that he would be alone with no decision to make. But the prisoner was there. He had merely stretched out between the stove and the desk. With eyes open, he was staring at the ceiling. In that position, his thick lips were particularly noticeable, giving him a pouting look. "Come," said Daru. The Arab got up and followed him. In the bedroom, the schoolmaster pointed to a chair near the table under the window. The Arab sat down without taking his eyes off Daru.

"Are you hungry?"

"Yes," the prisoner said.

Daru set the table for two. He took flour and oil, shaped a cake in the frying-pan, and lighted the little stove that functioned on bottled gas. While the cake was cooking, he went out to the shed to get cheese, eggs, dates, and condensed milk. When the cake was done he set it on the window sill to cool, heated some condensed milk diluted with water, and beat up the eggs into an omelette. In one of his motions he knocked against the revolver stuck in his right pocket. He set the bowl down, went into the classroom, and put the revolver back in his desk drawer. When he came back to the room, night was falling. He put on the light and served the Arab. "Eat," he said. The

Arab took a piece of the cake, lifted it eagerly to his mouth, and stopped short.

"And you?" he asked.

"After you. I'll eat too."

The thick lips opened slightly. The Arab hesitated, then bit into the cake determinedly.

The meal over, the Arab looked at the schoolmaster. "Are you the judge?"

"No, I'm simply keeping you until tomorrow."

"Why do you eat with me?"

"I'm hungry."

The Arab fell silent. Daru got up and went out. He brought back a folding bed from the shed, set it up between the table and the stove, perpendicular to his own bed. From a large suitcase which, upright in a corner, served as a shelf for papers, he took two blankets and arranged them on the camp bed. Then he stopped, felt useless, and sat down on his bed. There was nothing more to do or to get ready. He had to look at this man. He looked at him, therefore, trying to imagine his face bursting with rage. He couldn't do so. He could see nothing but the dark yet shining eyes and the animal mouth.

"Why did you kill him?" he asked in a voice whose hostile tone surprised him.

The Arab looked away.

"He ran away. I ran after him."

He raised his eyes to Daru again and they were full of a sort of woeful interrogation. "Now what will they do to me?"

"Are you afraid?"

He stiffened, turning his eyes away.

"Are you sorry?"

The Arab stared at him openmouthed. Obviously he did not understand. Daru's annoyance was growing. At the same time he felt awkward and self-conscious with his big body wedged between the two beds.

"Lie down there," he said impatiently. "That's your bed."

The Arab didn't move. He called to Daru:

"Tell me!"

The schoolmaster looked at him.

"Is the gendarme coming back tomorrow?"

"I don't know."

"Are you coming with us?"

"I don't know. Why?"

The prisoner got up and stretched out on top of the blankets, his feet toward the window. The light from the electric bulb shone straight into his eyes and he closed them at once.

"Why?" Daru repeated, standing beside the bed.

The Arab opened his eyes under the blinding light and looked at him, trying not to blink.

"Come with us," he said.

In the middle of the night, Daru was still not asleep. He had gone to bed after undressing completely; he generally slept naked. But when he suddenly realized that he had nothing on, he hesitated. He felt vulnerable and the temptation came to him to put his clothes back on. Then he shrugged his shoulders; after all, he wasn't a child, and, if need be, he could break his adversary in two. From his bed he could observe him, lying on his back, still motionless with his eyes closed under the harsh light. When Daru turned out the light, the darkness seemed to coagulate all of a sudden. Little by little, the night came back to life in the window where the starless sky was stirring gently. The schoolmaster soon made out the body lying at his feet. The Arab still did not move, but his eyes seemed open. A faint wind was prowling around the schoolhouse. Perhaps it would drive away the clouds and the sun would reappear.

During the night the wind increased. The hens fluttered a little and then were silent. The Arab turned over on his side with his back to Daru, who thought he heard him moan. Then he listened for his guest's breathing, become heavier and more regular. He listened to that breath so close to him and mused without being able to go to sleep. In this room where he had been sleeping alone for a year, this presence bothered him. But it bothered him also by imposing on him a sort of brotherhood he knew well but refused to accept in the present circumstances. Men who share the same rooms, soldiers or prisoners, develop a strange alliance as if, having cast off their armor with their clothing, they fraternized every evening, over and above their differences, in the ancient community of dream and fatigue. But Daru shook himself; he didn't like such musings, and it was essential to sleep.

A little later, however, when the Arab stirred slightly, the schoolmaster was still not asleep. When the prisoner made a second move, he stiffened, on the alert. The Arab was lifting himself slowly on his arms with almost the motion of a sleepwalker. Seated upright in bed, he waited motionless without turning his head toward Daru, as if he were listening attentively. Daru did not stir; it had just occurred to him that the revolver was still in the drawer of his desk. It was better to act at once. Yet he continued to observe the prisoner, who, with the same slithery motion, put his feet on the ground, waited again, then began to stand up slowly. Daru was about to call out to him when the Arab began to walk, in a quite natural but extraordinarily silent way. He was heading toward the door at the end of the room that opened into the shed. He lifted the latch with precaution and went out, pushing the door behind him but without shutting it. Daru had not stirred. "He is running away," he merely thought. "Good riddance!" Yet he listened attentively. The hens were not fluttering; the guest must be on the plateau. A faint sound of water reached him, and he didn't know what it was until the Arab again stood framed in the doorway, closed the door carefully, and came back to bed without a sound. Then Daru turned his back on him and fell asleep. Still later he seemed, from the depths of his sleep, to hear furtive steps around the schoolhouse. "I'm dreaming! I'm dreaming!" he repeated to himself. And he went on sleeping.

When he awoke, the sky was clear; the loose window let in a cold, pure air. The Arab was asleep, hunched up under the blankets now, his mouth open, utterly relaxed. But when Daru shook him, he started dreadfully, staring at Daru with wild eyes as if he had never seen him and such a frightened expression that the schoolmaster stepped back. "Don't be afraid. It's me. You must eat." The Arab nodded his head and said yes. Calm had returned to his face, but his expression was vacant and listless.

The coffee was ready. They drank it seated together on the folding bed as they munched their pieces of the cake. Then Daru led the Arab under the shed and showed him the faucet where he washed. He went back into the

room, folded the blankets and the bed, made his own bed and put the room
in order. Then he went through the classroom and out onto the terrace. The
sun was already rising in the blue sky; a soft, bright light was bathing the
deserted plateau. On the ridge the snow was melting in spots. The stones
were about to reappear. Crouched on the edge of the plateau, the schoolmaster
looked at the deserted expanse. He thought of Balducci. He had hurt him,
for he had sent him off in a way as if he didn't want to be associated with
him. He could still hear the gendarme's farewell and, without knowing why,
he felt strangely empty and vulnerable. At that moment, from the other side
of the schoolhouse, the prisoner coughed. Daru listened to him almost despite
himself and then, furious, threw a pebble that whistled through the air before
sinking into the snow. The man's stupid crime revolted him, but to hand him
over was contrary to honor. Merely thinking of it made him smart with humiliation. And he cursed at one and the same time his own people who had sent
him this Arab and the Arab too who had dared to kill and not managed to
get away. Daru got up, walked in a circle on the terrace, waited motionless,
and then went back into the schoolhouse.

The Arab, leaning over the cement floor of the shed, was washing his teeth
with two fingers. Daru looked at him and said: "Come." He went back into
the room ahead of the prisoner. He slipped a hunting-jacket on over his sweater
and put on walking shoes. Standing, he waited until the Arab had put on his
chèche and sandals. They went into the classroom and the schoolmaster pointed
to the exit, saying: "Go ahead." The fellow didn't budge. "I'm coming," said
Daru. The Arab went out. Daru went back into the room and made a package
of pieces of rusk, dates, and sugar. In the classroom, before going out, he
hesitated a second in front of his desk, then crossed the threshold and locked
the door. "That's the way," he said. He started toward the east, followed by
the prisoner. But, a short distance from the schoolhouse, he thought he heard
a slight sound behind them. He retraced his steps and examined the surroundings of the house; there was no one there. The Arab watched him without
seeming to understand. "Come on," said Daru.

They walked for an hour and rested beside a sharp peak of limestone. The
snow was melting faster and faster and the sun was drinking up the puddles
at once, rapidly cleaning the plateau, which gradually dried and vibrated like
the air itself. When they resumed walking, the ground rang under their feet.
From time to time a bird rent the space in front of them with a joyful cry.
Daru breathed in deeply the fresh morning light. He felt a sort of rapture
before the vast familiar expanse, now almost entirely yellow under its dome
of blue sky. They walked an hour more, descending toward the south. They
reached a level height made up of crumbly rocks. From there on, the plateau
sloped down, eastward, toward a low plain where there were a few spindly
trees and, to the south, toward outcroppings of rock that gave the landscape
a chaotic look.

Daru surveyed the two directions. There was nothing but the sky on the
horizon. Not a man could be seen. He turned toward the Arab, who was looking
at him blankly. Daru held out the package to him. "Take it," he said. "There
are dates, bread, and sugar. You can hold out for two days. Here are a thousand
francs too." The Arab took the package and the money but kept his full hands
at chest level as if he didn't know what to do with what was being given him.
"Now look," the schoolmaster said as he pointed in the direction of the east,
"there's the way to Tinguit. You have a two-hour walk. At Tinguit you'll find

the administration and the police. They are expecting you." The Arab looked toward the east, still holding the package and the money against his chest. Daru took his elbow and turned him rather roughly toward the south. At the foot of the height on which they stood could be seen a faint path. "That's the trail across the plateau. In a day's walk from here you'll find pasturelands and the first nomads. They'll take you in and shelter you according to their law." The Arab had now turned toward Daru and a sort of panic was visible in his expression. "Listen," he said. Daru shook his head: "No, be quiet. Now I'm leaving you." He turned his back on him, took two long steps in the direction of the school, looked hesitantly at the motionless Arab, and started off again. For a few minutes he heard nothing but his own step resounding on the cold ground and did not turn his head. A moment later, however, he turned around. The Arab was still there on the edge of the hill, his arms hanging now, and he was looking at the schoolmaster. Daru felt something rise in his throat. But he swore with impatience, waved vaguely, and started off again. He had already gone some distance when he again stopped and looked. There was no longer anyone on the hill.

Daru hesitated. The sun was now rather high in the sky and was beginning to beat down on his head. The schoolmaster retraced his steps, at first somewhat uncertainly, then with decision. When he reached the little hill, he was bathed in sweat. He climbed it as fast as he could and stopped, out of breath, at the top. The rock-fields to the south stood out sharply against the blue sky, but on the plain to the east a steamy heat was already rising. And in that slight haze, Daru, with heavy heart, made out the Arab walking slowly on the road to prison.

A little later, standing before the window of the classroom, the schoolmaster was watching the clear light bathing the whole surface of the plateau, but he hardly saw it. Behind him on the blackboard, among the winding French rivers, sprawled the clumsily chalked-up words he had just read: "You handed over our brother. You will pay for this." Daru looked at the sky, the plateau, and, beyond, the invisible lands stretching all the way to the sea. In this vast landscape he had loved so much, he was alone.

[1957]

Doris Lessing   *1919–*

WINE

A man and woman walked towards the boulevard from a little hotel in a side street.

The trees were still leafless, black, cold; but the fine twigs were swelling towards spring, so that looking upward it was with an expectation of the first glimmering greenness. Yet everything was calm, and the sky was a calm, classic blue.

The couple drifted slowly along. Effort, after days of laziness, seemed impossible; and almost at once they turned into a cafe and sank down, as if exhausted, in the glass-walled space that was thrust forward into the street.

The place was empty. People were seeking the midday meal in the restaurants. Not all: that morning crowds had been demonstrating, a procession had just passed, and its straggling end could still be seen. The sounds of violence, shouted slogans and singing, no longer absorbed the din of Paris traffic; but it was these sounds that had roused the couple from sleep.

A waiter leaned at the door, looking after the crowds, and he reluctantly took an order for coffee.

The man yawned; the woman caught the infection; and they laughed with an affectation of guilt and exchanged glances before their eyes, without regret, parted. When the coffee came, it remained untouched. Neither spoke. After some time the woman yawned again; and this time the man turned and looked at her critically, and she looked back. Desire asleep, they looked. This remained: that while everything which drove them slept, they accepted from each other a sad irony; they could look at each other without illusion, steady-eyed.

And then, inevitably, the sadness deepened in her till she consciously resisted it; and into him came the flicker of cruelty.

"Your nose needs powdering," he said.

"You need a whipping boy."

But always he refused to feel sad. She shrugged, and, leaving him to it, turned to look out. So did he. At the far end of the boulevard there was a faint agitation, like stirred ants, and she heard him mutter, "Yes, and it still goes on. . . ."

Mocking, she said, "Nothing changes, everything always the same. . . ."

But he had flushed. "I remember," he began, in a different voice. He stopped, and she did not press him, for he was gazing at the distant demonstrators with a bitterly nostalgic face.

Outside drifted the lovers, the married couples, the students, the old people. There the stark trees; there the blue, quiet sky. In a month the trees would be vivid green; the sun would pour down heat; the people would be brown, laughing, bare-limbed. No, no, she said to herself, at this vision of activity. Better the static sadness. And, all at once, unhappiness welled up in her, catching her throat, and she was back fifteen years in another country. She stood in blazing tropical moonlight, stretching her arms to a landscape that offered her nothing but silence; and then she was running down a path where small stones glinted sharp underfoot, till at last she fell spent in a swath of glistening grass. Fifteen years.

460

It was at this moment that the man turned abruptly and called the waiter and ordered wine.

"What," she said humorously, "already?"

"Why not?"

For the moment she loved him completely and maternally, till she suppressed the counterfeit and watched him wait, fidgeting, for the wine, pour it, and then set the two glasses before them beside the still-brimming coffee cups. But she was again remembering that night, envying the girl ecstatic with moonlight, who ran crazily through the trees in an unsharable desire for—but what was the point.

"What are you thinking of?" he asked, still a little cruel.

"Ohhh," she protested humorously.

"That's the trouble, that's the trouble." He lifted his glass, glanced at her, and set it down. "Don't you want to drink?"

"Not yet."

He left his glass untouched and began to smoke.

These movements demanded some kind of gesture—something slight, even casual, but still an acknowledgement of the separateness of those two people in each of them; the one seen, perhaps, as a soft-staring never-closing eye, observing, always observing, with a tired compassion; the other, a shape of violence that struggled on in the cycle of desire and rest, creation and achievement.

He gave it to her. Again their eyes met in the grave irony, before he turned away, flicking his fingers irritably against the table; and she turned also, to note the black branches where the sap was tingling.

"I remember," he began; and again she said, in protest, "Ohhh!"

He checked himself. "Darling," he said dryly, "you're the only woman I've ever loved." They laughed.

"It must have been this street. Perhaps this cafe—only they change so. When I went back yesterday to see the place where I came every summer, it was a *pâtisserie*,[1] and the woman had forgotten me. There was a whole crowd of us—we used to go around together—and I met a girl here, I think, for the first time. There were recognized places for contacts; people coming from Vienna or Prague, or wherever it was, knew the places—it couldn't be this cafe, unless they've smartened it up. We didn't have the money for all this leather and chromium."

"Well, go on."

"I keep remembering her, for some reason. Haven't thought of her for years. She was about sixteen, I suppose. Very pretty—no, you're quite wrong. We used to study together. She used to bring her books to my room. I liked her, but I had my own girl, only she was studying something else, I forget what." He paused again, and again his face was twisted with nostalgia, and involuntarily she glanced over her shoulder down the street. The procession had completely disappeared; not even the sounds of singing and shouting remained.

"I remember her because . . ." And after a preoccupied silence: "Perhaps it is always the fate of the virgin who comes and offers herself, naked, to be refused."

---

[1] A bakery specializing in pastry.

"What!" she exclaimed, startled. Also, anger stirred in her. She noted it, and sighed. "Go on."

"I never made love to her. We studied together all that summer. Then, one weekend, we all went off in a bunch. None of us had any money, of course, and we used to stand on the pavements and beg lifts, and meet up again in some village. I was with my own girl, but that night we were helping the farmer get in his fruit, in payment for using his barn to sleep in, and I found this girl Marie was beside me. It was moonlight, a lovely night, and we were all singing and making love. I kissed her, but that was all. That night she came to me. I was sleeping up in the loft with another lad. He was asleep. I sent her back down to the others. They were all together down in the hay. I told her she was too young. But she was no younger than my own girl." He stopped; and after all these years his face was rueful and puzzled. "I don't know," he said. "I don't know why I sent her back." Then he laughed. "Not that it matters, I suppose."

"Shameless hussy," she said. The anger was strong now. "You had kissed her, hadn't you?"

He shrugged. "But we were all playing the fool. It was a glorious night—gathering apples, the farmer shouting and swearing at us because we were making love more than working, and singing and drinking wine. Besides, it was that time: the youth movement. We regarded faithfulness and jealousy and all that sort of thing as remnants of bourgeois morality." He laughed again, rather painfully. "I kissed her. There she was, beside me, and she knew my girl was with me that weekend."

"You kissed her," she said accusingly.

He fingered the stem of his wine glass, looking over at her and grinning. "Yes, darling," he almost crooned at her. "I kissed her."

She snapped over into anger. "There's a girl all ready for love. You make use of her for working. Then you kiss her. You know quite well . . ."

"What do I know quite well?"

"It was a cruel thing to do."

"I was a kid myself. . . ."

"Doesn't matter." She noted, with discomfort, that she was almost crying. "Working with her! Working with a girl of sixteen, all summer!"

"But we all studied very seriously. She was a doctor afterwards, in Vienna. She managed to get out when the Nazis came in, but . . ."

She said impatiently, "Then you kiss her, on *that* night. Imagine her, waiting till the others were asleep, then she climbed up the ladder to the loft, terrified the other man might wake up, then she stood watching you sleep, and she slowly took off her dress and . . ."

"Oh, I wasn't asleep. I pretended to be. She came up dressed. Shorts and sweater—our girls didn't wear dresses and lipstick—more bourgeois morality. I watched her strip. The loft was full of moonlight. She put her hand over my mouth and came down beside me." Again, his face was filled with rueful amazement. "God knows, I can't understand it myself. She was a beautiful creature. I don't know why I remember it. It's been coming into my mind the last few days." After a pause, slowly twirling the wine glass: "I've been a failure in many things, but not with . . ." He quickly lifted her hand, kissed it, and said sincerely: "I don't know why I remember it now, when . . ." Their eyes met, and they sighed.

She said slowly, her hand lying in his: "And so you turned her away."

He laughed. "Next morning she wouldn't speak to me. She started a love affair with my best friend—a man who'd been beside me that night in the loft, as a matter of fact. She hated my guts, and I suppose she was right."

"Think of her. Think of her at that moment. She picked up her clothes, hardly daring to look at you. . . ."

"As a matter of fact, she was furious. She called me all the names she could think of; I had to keep telling her to shut up, she'd wake the whole crowd."

"She climbed down the ladder and dressed again, in the dark. Then she went out of the barn, unable to go back to the others. She went into the orchard. It was still brilliant moonlight. Everything was silent and deserted, and she remembered how you'd all been singing and laughing and making love. She went to the tree where you'd kissed her. The moon was shining on the apples. She'll never forget it, never, never!"

He looked at her curiously. The tears were pouring down her face.

"It's terrible," she said. "Terrible. Nothing could ever make up to her for that. Nothing, as long as she lived. Just when everything was most perfect, all her life, she'd suddenly remember that night, standing alone, not a soul anywhere, miles of damned empty moonlight. . . ."

He looked at her shrewdly. Then, with a sort of humorous, deprecating grimace, he bent over and kissed her and said: "Darling, it's not my fault; it just isn't my fault."

"No," she said.

He put the wine glass into her hands; and she lifted it, looked at the small crimson globule of warming liquid, and drank with him.

[1957]

Alain Robbe-Grillet *1922–*

THE SECRET ROOM*

The first thing to be seen is a red stain, of a deep, dark, shiny red, with almost black shadows. It is in the form of an irregular rosette, sharply outlined, extending in several directions in wide outflows of unequal length, dividing and dwindling afterward into single sinuous streaks. The whole stands out against a smooth, pale surface, round in shape, at once dull and pearly, a hemisphere joined by gentle curves to an expanse of the same pale color—white darkened by the shadowy quality of the place: a dungeon, a sunken room, or a cathedral—glowing with a diffused brilliance in the semidarkness.

Farther back, the space is filled with cylindrical trunks of columns, repeated with progressive vagueness in their retreat toward the beginning of a vast stone stairway, turning slightly as it rises, growing narrower and narrower as it approaches the high vaults where it disappears.

The whole setting is empty, stairway and colonnades. Alone, in the foreground, the stretched-out body gleams feebly, marked with the red stain—a white body whose full, supple flesh can be sensed, fragile, no doubt, and vulnerable. Alongside the bloody hemisphere another identical round form, this one intact, is seen at almost the same angle of view; but the haloed point at its summit, of darker tint, is in this case quite recognizable, whereas the other one is entirely destroyed, or at least covered by the wound.

In the background, near the top of the stairway, a black silhouette is seen fleeing, a man wrapped in a long, floating cape, ascending the last steps without turning around, his deed accomplished. A thin smoke rises in twisting scrolls from a sort of incense burner placed on a high stand of ironwork with a silvery glint. Nearby lies the milkwhite body, with wide streaks of blood running from the left breast, along the flank and on the hip.

It is a fully rounded woman's body, but not heavy, completely nude, lying on its back, the bust raised up somewhat by thick cushions thrown down on the floor, which is covered with Oriental rugs. The waist is very narrow, the neck long and thin, curved to one side, the head thrown back into a darker area where, even so, the facial features may be discerned, the partly opened mouth, the wide-staring eyes, shining with a fixed brilliance, and the mass of long, black hair spread out in a complicated wavy disorder over a heavily folded cloth, of velvet perhaps, on which also rest the arm and shoulder.

It is a uniformly colored velvet of dark purple, or which seems so in this lighting. But purple, brown, blue also seem to dominate in the colors of the cushions—only a small portion of which is hidden beneath the velvet cloth, and which protrude noticeably, lower down, beneath the bust and waist—as well as in the Oriental patterns of the rugs on the floor. Farther on, these same colors are picked up again in the stone of the paving and the columns, the vaulted archways, the stairs, and the less discernible surfaces that disappear into the farthest reaches of the room.

The dimensions of this room are difficult to determine exactly; the body of the young sacrificial victim seems at first glance to occupy a substantial portion of it, but the vast size of the stairway leading down to it would imply

* *Translated by Bruce Morrissette.*

rather that this is not the whole room, whose considerable space must in reality extend all around, right and left, as it does toward the faraway browns and blues among the columns standing in line, in every direction, perhaps toward other sofas, thick carpets, piles of cushions and fabrics, other tortured bodies, other incense burners.

It is also difficult to say where the light comes from. No clue, on the columns or on the floor, suggests the direction of the rays. Nor is any window or torch visible. The milkwhite body itself seems to light the scene, with its full breasts, the curve of its thighs, the rounded belly, the full buttocks, the stretched-out legs, widely spread, and the black tuft of the exposed sex, provocative, proffered, useless now.

The man has already moved several steps back. He is now on the first steps of the stairs, ready to go up. The bottom steps are wide and deep, like the steps leading up to some great building, a temple or theater; they grow smaller as they ascend, and at the same time describe a wide, helical curve, so gradually that the stairway has not yet made a half-turn by the time it disappears near the top of the vaults, reduced then to a steep, narrow flight of steps without handrail, vaguely outlined, moreover, in the thickening darkness beyond.

But the man does not look in this direction, where his movement nonetheless carries him; his left foot on the second step and his right foot already touching the third, with his knee bent, he has turned around to look at the spectacle for one last time. The long, floating cape thrown hastily over his shoulders, clasped in one hand at his waist, has been whirled around by the rapid circular motion that has just caused his head and chest to turn in the opposite direction, and a corner of the cloth remains suspended in the air as if blown by a gust of wind; this corner, twisting around upon itself in the form of a loose S, reveals the red silk lining with its gold embroidery.

The man's features are impassive, but tense, as if in expectation—or perhaps fear—of some sudden event, or surveying with one last glance the total immobility of the scene. Though he is looking backward, his whole body is turned forward, as if he were continuing up the stairs. His right arm—not the one holding the edge of the cape—is bent sharply toward the left, toward a point in space where the balustrade should be, if this stairway had one, an interrupted gesture, almost incomprehensible, unless it arose from an instinctive movement to grasp the absent support.

As to the direction of his glance, it is certainly aimed at the body of the victim lying on the cushions, its extended members stretched out in the form of a cross, its bust raised up, its head thrown back. But the face is perhaps hidden from the man's eyes by one of the columns, standing at the foot of the stairs. The young woman's right hand touches the floor just at the foot of this column. The fragile wrist is encircled by an iron bracelet. The arm is almost in darkness, only the hand receiving enough light to make the thin, outspread fingers clearly visible against the circular protrusion at the base of the stone column. A black metal chain running around the column passes through a ring affixed to the bracelet, binding the wrist tightly to the column.

At the top of the arm a rounded shoulder, raised up by the cushions, also stands out well lighted, as well as the neck, the throat, and the other shoulder, the armpit with its soft hair, the left arm likewise pulled back with its wrist bound in the same manner to the base of another column, in the extreme foreground; here the iron bracelet and the chain are fully displayed, represented with perfect clarity down to the slightest details.

The same is true, still in the foreground but at the other side, for a similar chain, but not quite as thick, wound directly around the ankle, running twice around the column and terminating in a heavy iron ring embedded in the floor. About a yard further back, or perhaps slightly farther, the right foot is identically chained. But it is the left foot, and its chain that are most minutely depicted.

The foot is small, delicate, finely modeled. In several places the chain has broken the skin, causing noticeable if not extensive depressions in the flesh. The chain links are oval, thick, the size of an eye. The ring in the floor resembles those used to attach horses; it lies almost touching the stone pavement to which it is riveted by a massive iron peg. A few inches away is the edge of a rug; it is grossly wrinkled at this point, doubtless as a result of the convulsive, but necessarily very restricted movements of the victim attempting to struggle.

The man is still standing about a yard away, half leaning over her. He looks at her face, seen upside down, her dark eyes made larger by their surrounding eye shadow, her mouth wide open as if screaming. The man's posture allows his face to be seen only in a vague profile, but one senses in it a violent exaltation, despite the rigid attitude, the silence, the immobility. His back is slightly arched. His left hand, the only one visible, holds up at some distance from the body a piece of cloth, some dark-colored piece of clothing, which drags on the carpet, and which must be the long cape with its gold-embroidered lining.

This immense silhouette hides most of the bare flesh over which the red stain, spreading from the globe of the breast, runs in long rivulets that branch out, growing narrower, upon the pale background of the bust and the flank. One thread has reached the armpit and runs in an almost straight line along the arm; others have run down toward the waist and traced out, along one side of the belly, the hip, the top of the thigh, a more random network already starting to congeal. Three or four tiny veins have reached the hollow between the legs, meeting in a sinuous line, touching the point of the V formed by the outspread legs, and disappearing into the black tuft.

Look, now the flesh is still intact: the black tuft and the white belly, the soft curve of the hips, the narrow waist, and, higher up, the pearly breasts rising and falling in time with the rapid breathing, whose rhythm grows more accelerated. The man, close to her, one knee on the floor, leans farther over. The head, with its long, curly hair, which alone is free to move somewhat, turns from side to side, struggling; finally the woman's mouth twists open, while the flesh is torn open, the blood spurts out over the tender skin, stretched tight, the carefully shadowed eyes grow abnormally larger, the mouth opens wider, the head twists violently, one last time, from right to left, then more gently, to fall back finally and become still, amid the mass of black hair spread out on the velvet.

At the very top of the stone stairway, this little door has opened, allowing a yellowish but sustained shaft of light to enter, against which stands out the dark silhouette of the man wrapped in his long cloak. He has but to climb a few more steps to reach the threshold.

Afterward, the whole setting is empty, the enormous room with its purple shadows and its stone columns proliferating in all directions, the monumental staircase with no handrail that twists upward, growing narrower and vaguer as it rises into the darkness, toward the top of the vaults where it disappears.

Near the body, whose wound has stiffened, whose brilliance is already growing dim, the thin smoke from the incense burner traces complicated scrolls in the still air: first a coil turned horizontally to the left, which then straightens out and rises slightly, then returns to the axis of its point of origin, which it crosses as it moves to the right, then turns back in the first direction, only to wind back again, thus forming an irregular sinusoidal curve, more and more flattened out, and rising vertically, toward the top of the canvas.

[1962]

Alice Munro *1931–*

THE OFFICE

The solution to my life occurred to me one evening while I was ironing a shirt. It was simple but audacious. I went into the living room where my husband was watching television and I said, "I think I ought to have an office."

It sounded fantastic, even to me. What do I want an office for? I have a house; it is pleasant and roomy and has a view of the sea; it provides appropriate places for eating and sleeping, and having baths and conversations with one's friends. Also I have a garden; there is no lack of space.

No. But here comes the disclosure which is not easy for me: I am a writer. That does not sound right. Too presumptuous; phony, or at least unconvincing. Try again. I write. Is that better? I *try* to write. That makes it worse. Hypocritical humility. Well then?

It doesn't matter. However I put it, the words create their space of silence, the delicate moment of exposure. But people are kind, the silence is quickly absorbed by the solicitude of friendly voices, crying variously, how wonderful, and good for *you*, and well, that *is* intriguing. And what do you write, they inquire with spirit. Fiction, I reply, bearing my humiliation by this time with ease, even a suggestion of flippancy, which was not always mine, and again, again, the perceptible circles of dismay are smoothed out by such ready and tactful voices—which have however exhausted their stock of consolatory phrases, and can say only, *"Ah!"*

So this is what I want an office for (I said to my husband): to write in. I was at once aware that it sounded like a finicky requirement, a piece of rare self-indulgence. To write, as everyone knows, you need a typewriter, or at least a pencil, some paper, a table and chair; I have all these things in a corner of my bedroom. But now I want an office as well.

And I was not even sure that I was going to write in it, if we come down to that. Maybe I would sit and stare at the wall; even that prospect was not unpleasant to me. It was really the sound of the word "office" that I liked, its sound of dignity and peace. And purposefulness and importance. But I did not care to mention this to my husband, so I launched instead into a high-flown explanation which went, as I remember, like this:

A house is all right for a man to work in. He brings his work into the house, a place is cleared for it; the house rearranges itself as best it can around him. Everybody recognizes that his work *exists*. He is not expected to answer the telephone, to find things that are lost, to see why the children are crying, or feed the cat. He can shut his door. Imagine (I said) a mother shutting her door, and the children knowing she is behind it; why, the very thought of it is outrageous to them. A woman who sits staring into space, into a country that is not her husband's or her children's is likewise known to be an offence against nature. So a house is not the same for a woman. She is not someone who walks into the house, to make use of it, and will walk out again. She *is* the house; there is no separation possible.

(And this is true, though as usual when arguing for something I am afraid I do not deserve, I put it in too emphatic and emotional terms. At certain times, perhaps on long spring evenings, still rainy and sad, with the cold bulbs in bloom and a light too mild for promise drifting over the sea, I have opened the windows and felt the house shrink into wood and plaster and those humble elements of which is it made, and the life in it subside, leaving me exposed, empty-handed, but feeling a fierce and lawless quiver of freedom, of loneliness too harsh and perfect for me now to bear. Then I know how the rest of the time I am sheltered and encumbered, how insistently I am warmed and bound.)

"Go ahead, if you can find one cheap enough," is all my husband had to say to this. He is not like me, he does not really want explanations. That the heart of another person is a closed book, is something you will hear him say frequently, and without regret.

Even then I did not think it was something that could be accomplished. Perhaps at bottom it seemed to me too improper a wish to be granted. I could almost more easily have wished for a mink coat, for a diamond necklace; these are things women do obtain. The children, learning of my plans, greeted them with the most dashing skepticism and unconcern. Nevertheless I went down to the shopping centre which is two blocks from where I live; there I had noticed for several months, and without thinking how they could pertain to me, a couple of For Rent signs in the upstairs windows of a building that housed a drugstore and a beauty parlour. As I went up the stairs I had a feeling of complete unreality; surely renting was a complicated business, in the case of offices; you did not simply knock on the door of the vacant premises and wait to be admitted; it would have to be done through channels. Also, they would want too much money.

As it turned out, I did not even have to knock. A woman came out of one of the empty offices, dragging a vacuum cleaner, and pushing it with her foot, towards the open door across the hall, which evidently led to an apartment in the rear of the building. She and her husband lived in this apartment; their name was Malley; and it was indeed they who owned the building and rented out the offices. The rooms she had just been vacuuming were, she told me, fitted out for a dentist's office, and so would not interest me, but she would show me the other place. She invited me into her apartment while she put away the vacuum and got her key. Her husband, she said with a sigh I could not interpret, was not at home.

Mrs. Malley was a black-haired, delicate-looking woman, perhaps in her early forties, slatternly but still faintly appealing, with such arbitrary touches of femininity as the thin line of bright lipstick, the pink feather slippers on obviously tender and swollen feet. She had the swaying passivity, the air of exhaustion and muted apprehension, that speaks of a life spent in close attention on a man who is by turns vigorous, crotchety and dependent. How much of this I saw at first, how much decided on later is of course impossible to tell. But I did think that she would have no children, the stress of her life, whatever it was, did not allow it, and in this I was not mistaken.

The room where I waited was evidently a combination living room and office. The first things I noticed were models of ships—galleons, clippers, Queen Marys—sitting on the tables, the window sills, the television. Where there were no ships there were potted plants and a clutter of what are sometimes called "masculine" ornaments—china deer heads, bronze horses, huge ashtrays of heavy, veined, shiny material. On the walls were framed photographs and what might have been diplomas. One photo showed a poodle and a bulldog, dressed in masculine and feminine clothing, and assuming with dismal embarrassment a pose of affection. Written across it was "Old Friends." But the room was really dominated by a portrait, with its own light and a gilded frame; it was of a good-looking, fair-haired man in middle age, sitting behind a desk, wearing a business suit and looking pre-eminently prosperous, rosy and agreeable. Here again, it is probably hindsight on my part that points out that in the portrait there is evident also some uneasiness, some lack of faith the man has in this role, a tendency he has to spread himself too bountifully and insistently, which for all anyone knows may lead to disaster.

Never mind the Malleys. As soon as I saw that office, I wanted it. It was larger than I needed, being divided in such a way that it would be suitable for a doctor's office. (We had a chiropractor in here but he left, says Mrs. Malley in her regretful but uninformative way.) The walls were cold and bare, white with a little grey, to cut the glare for the eyes. Since there were no doctors in evidence, nor had been, as Mrs. Malley freely told me, for some time, I offered twenty-five dollars a month. She said she would have to speak to her husband.

The next time I came my offer was agreed upon, and I met Mr. Malley in the flesh. I explained, as I had already done to his wife, that I did not want to make use of my office during regular business hours, but during the weekends and sometimes in the evening. He asked me what I would use it for, and I told him, not without wondering first whether I ought to say I did stenography.

He absorbed the information with good humour, "Ah, you're a writer."

"Well yes. I write."

"Then we'll do our best to see you're comfortable here," he said expansively. "I'm a great man for hobbies myself. All these ship-models, I do them in my spare time, they're a blessing for the nerves. People need an occupation for their nerves. I daresay you're the same."

"Something the same," I said, resolutely agreeable, even relieved that he saw my behaviour in this hazy and tolerant light. At least he did not ask me, as I half-expected, who was looking after the children, and did my husband approve? Ten years, maybe fifteen, had greatly softened, spread and defeated the man in the picture. His hips and thighs had now a startling accumulation of fat, causing him to move with a sigh, a cushiony settling of flesh, a ponderous matriarchal discomfort. His hair and eyes had faded, his features blurred, and the affable, predatory expression had collapsed into one of troubling humility and chronic mistrust. I did not look at him. I had not planned, in taking an office, to take on the responsibility of knowing any more human beings.

On the weekend I moved in, without the help of my family, who would have been kind. I brought my typewriter and a card table and chair, also a little wooden table on which I set a hot plate, a kettle, a jar of instant coffee, a spoon and a yellow mug. That was all. I brooded with satisfaction on the bareness of my walls, the cheap dignity of my essential furnishings, the remarkable lack of things to dust, wash or polish.

The sight was not so pleasing to Mr. Malley. He knocked on my door soon after I was settled and said that he wanted to explain a few things to me—about unscrewing the light in the outer room, which I would not need, about the radiator and how to work the awning outside the window. He looked around at everything with gloom and mystification and said it was an awfully uncomfortable place for a lady.

"Its perfectly all right for me," I said, not as discouragingly as I would have liked to, because I always have a tendency to placate people whom I dislike for no good reason, or simply do not want to know. I make elaborate offerings of courtesy sometimes, in the foolish hope that they will go away and leave me alone.

"What you want is a nice easy chair to sit in, while you're waiting for inspiration to hit. I've got a chair down in the basement, all kinds of stuff down there since my mother passed on last year. There's a bit of carpet rolled up in a corner down there, it isn't doing anybody any good. We could get this place fixed up so's it'd be a lot more homelike for you."

But really, I said, but really I like it as it is.

"If you wanted to run up some curtains, I'd pay you for the material. Place needs a touch of colour, I'm afraid you'll get morbid sitting in here."

Oh, no, I said, and laughed, I'm sure I won't.

"It'd be a different story if you was a man. A woman wants things a bit cosier."

So I got up and went to the window and looked down into the empty Sunday street through the slats of the Venetian blind, to avoid the accusing vulnerability of his fat face and I tried out a cold voice that is to be heard frequently in my thoughts but has great difficulty getting out of my cowardly mouth. "Mr. Malley, please don't bother me about this any more. I said it suits me. I have everything I want. Thanks for showing me about the light."

The effect was devastating enough to shame me. "I certainly wouldn't dream of bothering you," he said, with precision of speech and aloof sadness. "I merely made these suggestions for your comfort. Had I realized I was in your way, I would of left some time ago." When he had gone I felt better, even a little exhilarated at my victory though still ashamed of how easy it had been. I told myself that he would have had to be discouraged sooner or later, it was better to have it over with at the beginning.

The following weekend he knocked on my door. His expression of humility was exaggerated, almost enough so to seem mocking, yet in another sense it was real and I felt unsure of myself.

"I won't take up a minute of your time," he said. "I never meant to be a nuisance. I just wanted to tell you I'm sorry I offended you last time and I apologize. Here's a little present if you will accept."

He was carrying a plant whose name I did not know; it had thick, glossy leaves and grew out of a pot wrapped lavishly in pink and silver foil.

"There," he said, arranging this plant in a corner of my room. "I don't want any bad feelings with you and me. I'll take the blame. And I thought, maybe she won't accept furnishings, but what's the matter with a nice little plant, that'll brighten things up for you."

It was not possible for me, at this moment, to tell him that I did not want a plant. I hate house plants. He told me how to take care of it, how often to water it and so on; I thanked him. There was nothing else I could do, and I had the unpleasant feeling that beneath his offering of apologies and gifts he was well aware of this and in some way gratified by it. He kept on talking, using the words *bad feelings, offended, apologize*. I tried once to interrupt, with the idea of explaining that I had made provision for an area in my life where good feelings, or bad, did not enter in, that between him and me, in fact, it was not necessary that there be any feelings at all; but this struck me as a hopeless task. How could I confront, in the open, this craving for intimacy? Besides, the plant in its shiny paper had confused me.

"How's the writing progressing?" he said, with an air of putting all our unfortunate differences behind him.

"Oh, about as usual."

"Well if you ever run out of things to write about, I got a barrelful." Pause. "But I guess I'm just eatin' into your time here," he said with a kind of painful buoyancy. This was a test, and I did not pass it. I smiled, my eyes held by that magnificent plant; I said it was all right.

"I was just thinking about the fellow was in here before you. Chiropractor. You could of wrote a book about him."

I assumed a listening position, my hands no longer hovering over the keys. If cowardice and insincerity are big vices of mine, curiosity is certainly another.

"He had a good practice built up here. The only trouble was, he gave more adjustments than was listed in the book of chiropractory. Oh, he was adjusting right and left. I came in here after he moved out, and what do you think I found? Soundproofing! This whole room was soundproofed, to enable him to make his adjustments without disturbing anybody. This very room you're sitting writing your stories in.

"First we knew of it was a lady knocked on my door one day, wanted me to provide her with a passkey to his office. He'd locked his door against her.

"I guess he just got tired of treating her particular case. I guess he figured he'd been knocking away at it long enough. Lady well on in years, you know, and him just a young man. He had a nice young wife too and a couple of the prettiest children you ever would want to see. Filthy some of the things that go on in this world."

It took me some time to realize that he told this story not simply as a piece of gossip, but as something a writer would be particularly interested to hear. Writing and lewdness had a vague delicious connection in his mind. Even this notion, however, seemed so wistful, so infantile, that it struck me as a waste of energy to attack it. I knew now I must avoid hurting him for my own sake, not for his. It had been a great mistake to think that a little roughness would settle things.

The next present was a teapot. I insisted that I drank only coffee and told him to give it to his wife. He said that tea was better for the nerves and that he had known right away I was a nervous person, like himself. The teapot was covered with gilt and roses and I knew that it was not cheap, in spite of its extreme hideousness. I kept it on my table. I also continued to care for the plant, which thrived obscenely in the corner of my room. I could not decide what else to do. He bought me a wastebasket, a fancy one with Chinese mandarins on all eight sides; he got a foam rubber cushion for my chair. I despised myself for submitting to this blackmail. I did not even really pity him; it was just that I could not turn away, I could not turn away from that obsequious hunger. And he knew himself my tolerance was bought; in a way he must have hated me for it.

When he lingered in my office now he told me stories of himself. It occurred to me that he was revealing his life to me in the hope that I would write it down. Of course he had probably revealed it to plenty of people for no particular reason, but in my case there seemed to be a special, even desperate necessity. His life was a series of calamities, as people's lives often are; he had been let down by people he had trusted, refused help by those he had depended on, betrayed by the very friends to whom he had given kindness and material help. Other people, mere strangers and passersby, had taken time to torment him gratuitously, in novel and inventive ways. On occasion, his very life had been threatened. Moreover his wife was a difficulty, her health being poor and her temperament unstable; what was he to do? You see how it is, he said, lifting his hands, but I live. He looked to me to say yes.

I took to coming up the stairs on tiptoe, trying to turn my key without making a noise; this was foolish of course because I could not muffle my typewriter. I actually considered writing in longhand, and wished repeatedly for the evil chiropractor's soundproofing. I told my husband my problem and he said it was not a problem at all. Tell him you're busy, he said. As a matter of fact I did tell him; every time he came to my door, always armed with a little gift or an errand, he asked me how I was and I said that today I was busy. Ah, then, he said, as he eased himself through the door, he would not keep me a minute. And all the time, as I have said, he knew what was going on in my mind, how I weakly longed to be rid of him. He knew but could not afford to care.

One evening after I had gone home I discovered that I had left at the office a letter I had intended to post, and so I went back to get it. I saw from the street that the light was on in the room where I worked. Then I saw him bending over the card table. Of course, he came in at night and read what I had written! He heard me at the door, and when I came in he was picking up my wastebasket, saying he thought he would just tidy things up for me. He went out at once. I did not say anything, but found myself trembling with anger and gratification. To have found a just cause was a wonder, an unbearable relief.

Next time he came to my door I had locked it on the inside. I knew his step, his chummy cajoling knock. I continued typing loudly, but not uninterruptedly, so he would know I heard. He called my name, as if I was playing a trick; I bit my lips together not to answer. Unreasonably as ever, guilt assailed me but I typed on. That day I saw the earth was dry around the roots of the plant; I let it alone.

I was not prepared for what happened next. I found a note taped to my door, which said that Mr. Malley would be obliged if I would step into his office. I went at once to get it over with. He sat at his desk surrounded by obscure evidences of his authority; he looked at me from a distance, as one who was now compelled to see me in a new and sadly unfavourable light; the embarrassment which he showed seemed not for himself, but me. He started off by saying, with a rather stagey reluctance, that he had known of course when he took me in that I was a writer.

"I didn't let that worry me, though I have heard things about writers and artists and that type of person that didn't strike me as very encouraging. You know the sort of thing I mean."

This was something new; I could not think what it might lead to.

"Now you came to me and said, Mr. Malley, I want a place to write in. I believed you. I gave it to you. I didn't ask any questions. That's the kind of person I am. But you know the more I think about it, well, the more I am inclined to wonder."

"Wonder what?" I said.

"And your own attitude, that hasn't helped to put my mind at ease. Locking yourself in and refusing to answer your door. That's not a normal way for a

person to behave. Not if they got nothing to hide. No more than it's normal
for a young woman, says she has a husband and kids, to spend her time rattling
away on a typewriter.''

"But I don't think that—''

He lifted his hand, a forgiving gesture. "Now all I ask is, that you be open
and aboveboard with me, I think I deserve that much, and if you are using
that office for any other purpose, or at any other times than you let on, and
having your friends or whoever they are up to see you—''

"I don't know what you mean.''

"And another thing, you claim to be a writer. Well I read quite a bit of
material, and I never have seen your name in print. Now maybe you write
under some other name?''

"No,'' I said.

"Well I don't doubt there are writers whose names I haven't heard,'' he
said genially. "We'll let that pass. Just you give me your word of honour there
won't be any more deceptions, or any carryings-on, et cetera, in that office
you occupy—''

My anger was delayed somehow, blocked off by a stupid incredulity. I only
knew enough to get up and walk down the hall, his voice trailing after me,
and lock the door. I thought—I must go. But after I had sat down in my
own room, my work in front of me, I thought again how much I liked this
room, how well I worked in it, and I decided not to be forced out. After all,
I felt, the struggle between us had reached a deadlock. I could refuse to open
the door, refuse to look at his notes, refuse to speak to him when we met.
My rent was paid in advance and if I left now it was unlikely that I would
get any refund. I resolved not to care. I had been taking my manuscript home
every night, to prevent his reading it, and now it seemed that even this precaution was beneath me. What did it matter if he read it, any more than if the
mice scampered over it in the dark? Several times after this I found notes
on my door. I intended not to read them, but I always did. His accusations
grew more specific. He had heard voices in my room. My behaviour was disturbing his wife when she tried to take her afternoon nap. (I never came in the
afternoons, except on weekends.) He had found a whisky bottle in the garbage.

I wondered a good deal about that chiropractor. It was not comfortable to
see how the legends of Mr. Malley's life were built up.

As the notes grew more virulent our personal encounters ceased. Once or
twice I saw his stooped, sweatered back disappearing as I came into the hall.
Gradually our relationship passed into something that was entirely fantasy.
He accused me now, by note, of being intimate with people from *Numero Cinq.*
This was a coffee-house in the neighbourhood, which I imagine he invoked
for symbolic purposes. I felt that nothing much more would happen now,
the notes would go on, their contents becoming possibly more grotesque and
so less likely to affect me.

He knocked on my door on a Sunday morning, about eleven o'clock. I had
just come in and taken my coat off and put my kettle on the hot plate.

This time it was another face, remote and transfigured, that shone with
the cold light of intense joy at discovering the proofs of sin.

"I wonder,'' he said with emotion, "if you would mind following me down
the hall?''

I followed him. The light was on in the washroom. This washroom was
mine and no one else used it, but he had not given me a key for it and it

was always open. He stopped in front of it, pushed back the door and stood with his eyes cast down, expelling his breath discreetly.

"Now who done that?" he said, in a voice of pure sorrow.

The walls above the toilet and above the washbasin were covered with drawings and comments of the sort you see sometimes in public washrooms on the beach, and in town hall lavatories in the little decaying towns where I grew up. They were done with a lipstick, as they usually are. Someone must have got up here the night before, I thought, possibly some of the gang who always loafed and cruised around the shopping centre on Saturday nights.

"It should have been locked," I said, coolly and firmly as if thus to remove myself from the scene. "It's quite a mess."

"It sure is. It's pretty filthy language, in my book. Maybe it's just a joke to your friends, but it isn't to me. Not to mention the art work. That's a nice thing to see when you open a door on your own premises in the morning."

I said, "I believe lipstick will wash off."

"I'm just glad I didn't have my wife see a thing like this. Upsets a woman that's had a nice bringing up. Now why don't you ask your friends up here to have a party with their pails and brushes? I'd like to have a look at the people with that kind of a sense of humour."

I turned to walk away and he moved heavily in front of me.

"I don't think there's any question how these decorations found their way onto my walls."

"If you're trying to say I had anything to do with it," I said, quite flatly and wearily, "you must be crazy."

"How did they get there then? Whose lavatory is this? Eh, whose?"

"There isn't any key to it. Anybody can come up here and walk in. Maybe some kids off the street came up here and did it last night after I went home, how do I know?"

"It's a shame the way the kids gets blamed for everything, when it's the elders that corrupts them. That's a thing you might do some thinking about, you know. There's laws. Obscenity laws. Applies to this sort of thing and literature too as I believe."

This is the first time I ever remember taking deep breaths, consciously, for purposes of self-control. I really wanted to murder him. I remember how soft and loathsome his face looked, with the eyes almost closed, nostrils extended to the soothing odour of righteousness, the odour of triumph. If this stupid thing had not happened, he would never have won. But he had. Perhaps he saw something in my face that unnerved him, even in this victorious moment, for he drew back to the wall, and began to say that actually, as a matter of fact, he had not really felt it was the sort of thing I personally would do, more the sort of thing that perhaps certain friends of mine—I got into my own room, shut the door.

The kettle was making a fearful noise, having almost boiled dry. I snatched it off the hot plate, pulled out the plug and stood for a moment choking on rage. This spasm passed and I did what I had to do. I put my typewriter and paper on the chair and folded the card table. I screwed the top tightly on the instant coffee and put it and the yellow mug and the teaspoon into the bag in which I had brought them; it was still lying folded on the shelf. I wished childishly to take some vengeance on the potted plant, which sat in the corner with the flowery teapot, the wastebasket, the cushion, and—I forgot—a little plastic pencil sharpener behind it.

When I was taking things down to the car Mrs. Malley came. I had seen little of her since the first day. She did not seem upset, but practical and resigned.

"He is lying down," she said. "He is not himself."

She carried the bag with the coffee and the mug in it. She was so still I felt my anger leave me, to be replaced by an absorbing depression.

I have not yet found another office. I think that I will try again some day, but not yet. I have to wait at least until that picture fades that I see so clearly in my mind, though I never saw it in reality—Mr. Malley with his rags and brushes and a pail of soapy water, scrubbing in his clumsy way, his deliberately clumsy way, at the toilet walls, stooping with difficulty, breathing sorrowfully, arranging in his mind the bizarre but somehow never quite satisfactory narrative of yet another betrayal of trust. While I arrange words, and think it is my right to be rid of him.

[1962]

John Updike   *1932–*

A & P

In walks these three girls in nothing but bathing suits. I'm in the third check-out slot, with my back to the door, so I don't see them until they're over by the bread. The one that caught my eye first was the one in the plaid green two-piece. She was a chunky kid, with a good tan and a sweet broad soft-looking can with those two crescents of white just under it, where the sun never seems to hit, at the top of the backs of her legs. I stood there with my hand on a box of HiHo crackers trying to remember if I rang it up or not. I ring it up again and the customer starts giving me hell. She's one of these cash-register-watchers, a witch about fifty with rouge on her cheekbones and no eyebrows, and I know it made her day to trip me up. She'd been watching cash registers for fifty years and probably never seen a mistake before.

By the time I got her feathers smoothed and her goodies into a bag—she gives me a little snort in passing, if she'd been born at the right time they would have burned her over in Salem—by the time I get her on her way the girls had circled around the bread and were coming back, without a pushcart, back my way along the counters, in the aisle between the checkouts and the Special bins. They didn't even have shoes on. There was this chunky one, with the two-piece—it was bright green and the seams on the bra were still sharp and her belly was still pretty pale so I guessed she just got it (the suit)—there was this one, with one of those chubby berry-faces, the lips all bunched together under her nose, this one, and a tall one, with black hair that hadn't quite frizzed right, and one of these sunburns right across under the eyes, and a chin that was too long—you know, the kind of girl other girls think is very "striking" and "attractive" but never quite makes it, as they very well know, which is why they like her so much—and then the third one, that wasn't quite so tall. She was the queen. She kind of led them, the other two peeking around and making their shoulders round. She didn't look around, not this queen, she just walked straight on slowly, on these long white prima-donna legs. She came down a little hard on her heels, as if she didn't walk in her bare feet that much, putting down her heels and then letting the weight move along to her toes as if she was testing the floor with every step, putting a little deliberate extra action into it. You never know for sure how girls' minds work (do you really think it's a mind in there or just a little buzz like a bee in a glass jar?) but you got the idea she had talked the other two into coming in here with her, and now she was showing them how to do it, walk slow and hold yourself straight.

She had on a kind of dirty-pink—beige maybe, I don't know—bathing suit with a little nubble all over it and, what got me, the straps were down. They were off her shoulders looped loose around the cool tops of her arms, and I guess as a result the suit had slipped a little on her, so all around the top of the cloth there was this shining rim. If it hadn't been there you wouldn't have known there could have been anything whiter than those shoulders. With the straps pushed off, there was nothing between the top of the suit and the top of her head except just *her*, this clean bare plane of the top of her chest down from the shoulder bones like a dented sheet of metal tilted in the light. I mean, it was more than pretty.

She had sort of oaky hair that the sun and salt had bleached, done up in a bun that was unravelling, and a kind of prim face. Walking into the A & P with your straps down, I suppose it's the only kind of face you *can* have. She held her head so high her neck, coming up out of those white shoulders, looked kind of stretched, but I didn't mind. The longer her neck was, the more of her there was.

She must have felt in the corner of her eye me and over my shoulder Stokesie in the second slot watching, but she didn't tip. Not this queen. She kept her eyes moving across the racks, and stopped, and turned so slow it made my stomach rub the inside of my apron, and buzzed to the other two, who kind of huddled against her for relief, and then they all three of them went up the cat-and-dog-food-breakfast-cereal-macaroni-rice-raisins-seasonings-spreads-spaghetti-soft-drinks-crackers-and-cookies aisle. From the third slot I look straight up this aisle to the meat counter, and I watched them all the way. The fat one with the tan sort of fumbled with the cookies, but on second thought she put the package back. The sheep pushing their carts down the aisle—the girls were walking against the usual traffic (not that we have one-way signs or anything)—were pretty hilarious. You could see them, when Queenie's white shoulders dawned on them, kind of jerk, or hop, or hiccup, but their eyes snapped back to their own baskets and on they pushed. I bet you could set off dynamite in an A & P and the people would by and large keep reaching and checking oatmeal off their lists and muttering "Let me see, there was a third thing, began with A, asparagus, no, ah, yes, applesauce!" or whatever it is they do mutter. But there was no doubt, this jiggled them. A few houseslaves in pin curlers even looked around after pushing their carts past to make sure what they had seen was correct.

You know, it's one thing to have a girl in a bathing suit down on the beach, where what with the glare nobody can look at each other much anyway, and another thing in the cool of the A & P, under the fluorescent lights, against all those stacked packages, with her feet paddling along naked over our checkerboard green-and-cream rubber-tile floor.

"Oh Daddy," Stokesie said beside me. "I feel so faint."

"Darling," I said. "Hold me tight." Stokesie's married, with two babies chalked up on his fuselage already, but as far as I can tell that's the only difference. He's twenty-two, and I was nineteen this April.

"Is it done?" he asks, the responsible married man finding his voice. I forgot to say he thinks he's going to be manager some sunny day, maybe in 1990 when it's called the Great Alexandrov and Petrooshki Tea Company or something.

What he meant was, our town is five miles from a beach, with a big summer colony out on the Point, but we're right in the middle of town, and the women generally put on a shirt or shorts or something before they get out of the car into the street. And anyway these are usually women with six children and varicose veins mapping their legs and nobody, including them, could care less. As I say, we're right in the middle of town, and if you stand at our front doors you can see two banks and the Congregational church and the newspaper store and three real-estate offices and about twenty-seven old free-loaders tearing up Central Street because the sewer broke again. It's not as if we're on the Cape; we're north of Boston and there's people in this town haven't seen the ocean for twenty years.

The girls had reached the meat counter and were asking McMahon something. He pointed, they pointed, and they shuffled out of sight behind a pyramid of Diet Delight peaches. All that was left for us to see was old McMahon patting his mouth and looking after them sizing up their joints. Poor kids, I began to feel sorry for them, they couldn't help it.

.   .   .

Now here comes the sad part of the story, at least my family says it's sad, but I don't think it's so sad myself. The store's pretty empty, it being Thursday afternoon, so there was nothing much to do except lean on the register and wait for the girls to show up again. The whole store was like a pinball machine and I didn't know which tunnel they'd come out of. After a while they come around out of the far aisle, around the light bulbs, records at discount of the Caribbean Six or Tony Martin Sings or some such gunk you wonder they waste the wax on, sixpacks of candy bars, and plastic toys done up in cellophane that fall apart when a kid looks at them anyway. Around they come, Queenie still leading the way, and holding a little gray jar in her hand. Slots Three through Seven are unmanned and I could see her wondering between Stokes and me, but Stokesie with his usual luck draws an old party in baggy gray pants who stumbles up with four giant cans of pineapple juice (what do these bums *do* with all that pineapple juice? I've often asked myself) so the girls come to me. Queenie puts down the jar and I take it into my fingers icy cold. Kingfish Fancy Herring Snacks in Pure Sour Cream: 49¢. Now her hands are empty, not a ring or a bracelet, bare as God made them, and I wonder where the money's coming from. Still with that prim look she lifts a folded dollar bill out of the hollow at the center of her nubbled pink top. The jar went heavy in my hand. Really, I thought that was so cute.

Then everybody's luck begins to run out. Lengel comes in from haggling with a truck full of cabbages on the lot and is about to scuttle into that door marked MANAGER behind which he hides all day when the girls touch his eye. Lengel's pretty dreary, teaches Sunday school and the rest, but he doesn't miss that much. He comes over and says, "Girls, this isn't the beach."

Queenie blushes, though maybe it's just a brush of sunburn I was noticing for the first time, now that she was so close. "My mother asked me to pick up a jar of herring snacks." Her voice kind of startled me, the way voices do when you see the people first, coming out so flat and dumb yet kind of tony, too, the way it ticked over "pick up" and "snacks." All of a sudden I slid right down her voice into her living room. Her father and the other men were standing around in ice-cream coats and bow ties and the women were in sandals picking up herring snacks on toothpicks off a big glass plate and they were all holding drinks the color of water with olives and sprigs of mint in them. When my parents have somebody over they get lemonade and if it's a real racy affair Schlitz in tall glasses with "They'll Do It Every Time" cartoons stencilled on.

"That's all right," Lengel said. "But this isn't the beach." His repeating this struck me as funny, as if it had just occurred to him, and he had been thinking all these years the A & P was a great big dune and he was the head lifeguard. He didn't like my smiling—as I say he doesn't miss much—but he concentrates on giving the girls that sad Sunday-school-superintendent stare.

Queenie's blush is no sunburn now, and the plump one in plaid, that I liked better from the back—a really sweet can—pipes up, "We weren't doing any shopping. We just came in for the one thing."

"That makes no difference," Lengel tells her, and I could see from the way his eyes went that he hadn't noticed she was wearing a two-piece before. "We want you decently dressed when you come in here."

"We *are* decent," Queenie says suddenly, her lower lip pushing, getting sore now that she remembers her place, a place from which the crowd that runs the A & P must look pretty crummy. Fancy Herring Snacks flashed in her very blue eyes.

"Girls, I don't want to argue with you. After this come in here with your shoulders covered. It's our policy." He turns his back. That's policy for you. Policy is what the kingpins want. What the others want is juvenile delinquency.

All this while, the customers had been showing up with their carts but, you know, sheep, seeing a scene, they had all bunched up on Stokesie, who shook open a paper bag as gently as peeling a peach, not wanting to miss a word. I could feel in the silence everybody getting nervous, most of all Lengel, who asks me, "Sammy, have you rung up their purchase?"

I thought and said "No" but it wasn't about that I was thinking. I go through the punches, 4, 9, GROC, TOT—it's more complicated than you think, and after you do it often enough, it begins to make a little song, that you hear words to, in my case "Hello (*bing*) there, you (*gung*) hap-py *pee*-pul (*splat*)!"—the *splat* being the drawer flying out. I uncrease the bill, tenderly as you may imagine, it just having come from between the two smoothest scoops of vanilla I had ever known were there, and pass a half and a penny into her narrow pink palm, and nestle the herrings in a bag and twist its neck and hand it over, all the time thinking.

The girls, and who'd blame them, are in a hurry to get out, so I say "I quit" to Lengel quick enough for them to hear, hoping they'll stop and watch me, their unsuspected hero. They keep right on going, into the electric eye; the door flies open and they flicker across the lot to their car, Queenie and Plaid and Big Tall Goony-Goony (not that as raw material she was so bad), leaving me with Lengel and a kink in his eyebrow.

"Did you say something, Sammy?"

"I said I quit."

"I thought you did."

"You didn't have to embarrass them."

"It was they who were embarrassing us."

I started to say something that came out "Fiddle-de-doo." It's a saying of my grandmother's, and I know she would have been pleased.

"I don't think you know what you're saying," Lengel said.

"I know you don't," I said. "But I do." I pull the bow at the back of my apron and start shrugging it off my shoulders. A couple customers that had been heading for my slot begin to knock against each other, like scared pigs in a chute.

Lengel sighs and begins to look very patient and old and gray. He's been a friend of my parents for years. "Sammy, you don't want to do this to your Mom and Dad," he tells me. It's true, I don't. But it seems to me that once you begin a gesture it's fatal not to go through with it. I fold the apron, "Sammy" stitched in red on the pocket, and put it on the counter, and drop the bow tie on top of it. The bow tie is theirs, if you've ever wondered. "You'll feel this for the rest of your life," Lengel says, and I know that's true, too, but remembering how he made that pretty girl blush makes me so scrunchy inside I punch the No Sale tab and the machine whirs "pee-pul" and the drawer splats out. One advantage to this scene taking place in summer, I can follow this up with a clean exit, there's no fumbling around getting your coat and galoshes, I just saunter into the electric eye in my white shirt that my mother ironed the night before, and the door heaves itself open, and outside the sunshine is skating around on the asphalt.

I looked around for my girls, but they're gone, of course. There wasn't anybody but some young married screaming with her children about some candy they didn't get by the door of a powder-blue Falcon station wagon. Looking back in the big windows, over the bags of peat moss and aluminum lawn furniture stacked on the pavement, I could see Lengel in my place in the slot, checking the sheep through. His face was dark gray and his back stiff, as if he'd just had an injection of iron, and my stomach kind of fell as I felt how hard the world was going to be to me hereafter.

[1962]

Joyce Carol Oates 1938–

IN THE REGION OF ICE

Sister Irene was a tall, deft woman in her early thirties. What one could see of her face made a striking impression—serious, hard gray eyes, a long slender nose, a face waxen with thought. Seen at the right time, from the right angle, she was almost handsome. In her past teaching positions she had drawn a little upon the fact of her being young and brilliant and also a nun, but she was beginning to grow out of that.

This was a new university and an entirely new world. She had heard—of course it was true—that the Jesuit[1] administration of this school had hired her at the last moment to save money and to head off the appointment of a man of dubious religious commitment. She had prayed for the necessary energy to get her through this first semester. She had no trouble with teaching itself; once she stood before a classroom she felt herself capable of anything. It was the world immediately outside the classroom that confused and alarmed her, though she let none of this show—the cynicism and her colleagues, the indifference of many of the students, and, above all, the looks she got that told her nothing much would be expected of her because she was a nun. This took energy, strength. At times she had the idea that she was on trial and that the excuses she made to herself about her discomfort were only the common excuses made by guilty people. But in front of a class she had no time to worry about herself or the conflicts in her mind. She became, once and for all, a figure existing only for the benefit of others, an instrument by which facts were communicated.

About two weeks after the semester began, Sister Irene noticed a new student in her class. He was slight and fair-haired, and his face was blank, but not blank by accident, blank on purpose, suppressed and restricted into a dumbness that looked hysterical. She was prepared for him before he raised his hand, and when she saw his arm jerk, as if he had at last lost control of it, she nodded to him without hesitation.

"Sister, how can this be reconciled with Shakespeare's vision in *Hamlet?* How can these opposing views be in the same mind?"

Students glanced at him, mildly surprised. He did not belong in the class, and this was mysterious, but his manner was urgent and blind.

"There is no need to reconcile opposing views," Sister Irene said, leaning forward against the podium. "In one play Shakespeare suggests one vision, in another play another; the plays are not simultaneous creations, and even if they were, we never demand a logical—"

"We must demand a logical consistency," the young man said. "The idea of education is itself predicated upon consistency, order, sanity—"

He had interrupted her, and she hardened her face against him—for his sake, not her own, since she did not really care. But he noticed nothing. "Please see me after class," she said.

After class the young man hurried up to her.

"Sister Irene, I hope you didn't mind my visiting today. I'd heard some

---

[1] The Jesuits, members of the Society of Jesus, are a Catholic religious order noted for their work in education. They operate a number of American colleges and universities.

things, interesting things," he said. He stared at her, and something in her face allowed him to smile. "I . . . could we talk in your office? Do you have time?"

They walked down to her office. Sister Irene sat at her desk, and the young man sat facing her; for a moment they were self-conscious and silent.

"Well, I suppose you know—I'm a Jew," he said.

Sister Irene stared at him. "Yes?" she said.

"What am I doing at a Catholic university, huh?" He grinned. "That's what you want to know."

She made a vague movement of her hand to show that she had no thoughts on this, nothing at all, but he seemed not to catch it. He was sitting on the edge of the straight-backed chair. She saw that he was young but did not really look young. There were harsh lines on either side of his mouth, as if he had misused that youthful mouth somehow. His skin was almost as pale as hers, his eyes were dark and not quite in focus. He looked at her and through her and around her, as his voice surrounded them both. His voice was a little shrill at times.

"Listen, I did the right thing today—visiting your class! God, what a lucky accident it was; some jerk mentioned you, said you were a good teacher—I thought, what a laugh! These people know about good teachers here? But yes, listen, yes, I'm not kidding—you are good. I mean that."

Sister Irene frowned. "I don't quite understand what all this means."

He smiled and waved aside her formality, as if he knew better. "Listen, I got my B.A. at Columbia, then I came back here to this crappy city. I mean, I did it on purpose, I wanted to come back. I wanted to. I have my reasons for doing things. I'm on a three-thousand-dollar fellowship," he said, and waited for that to impress her. "You know, I could have gone almost anywhere with that fellowship, and I came back home here—my home's in the city—and enrolled here. This was last year. This is my second year. I'm working on a thesis, I mean I was, my master's thesis—but the hell with that. What I want to ask you is this: Can I enroll in your class, is it too late? We have to get special permission if we're late."

Sister Irene felt something nudging her, some uneasiness in him that was pleading with her not to be offended by his abrupt, familiar manner. He seemed to be promising another self, a better self, as if his fair, childish, almost cherubic face were doing tricks to distract her from what his words said.

"Are you in English studies?" she asked.

"I was in history. Listen," he said, and his mouth did something odd, drawing itself down into a smile that made the lines about it deepen like knives, "listen, they kicked me out."

He sat back, watching her. He crossed his legs. He took out a package of cigarettes and offered her one. Sister Irene shook her head, staring at his hands. They were small and stubby and might have belonged to a ten-year-old, and the nails were a strange near-violet color. It took him awhile to extract a cigarette.

"Yeah, kicked me out. What do you think of that?"

"I don't understand."

"My master's thesis was coming along beautifully, and then this bastard—I mean, excuse me, this professor, I won't pollute your office with his name— he started making criticisms, he said some things were unacceptable, he—" The boy leaned forward and hunched his narrow shoulders in a parody of secrecy. "We had an argument. I told him some frank things, things only a broad-minded person could hear about himself. That takes courage, right? He didn't have it! He kicked me out of the master's program, so now I'm coming into English. Literature is greater than history; European history is one big pile of garbage. Sky-high. Filth and rotting corpses, right? Aristotle says that poetry is higher than history;[2] he's right; in your class today I suddenly realized that this is my field, Shakespeare, only Shakespeare is—"

Sister Irene guessed that he was going to say that only Shakespeare was equal to him, and she caught the moment of recognition and hesitation, the half-raised arm, the keen, frowning forehead, the narrowed eyes; then he thought better of it and did not end the sentence. "The students in your class are mainly negligible, I can tell you that. You're new here, and I've been here a year—I would have finished my studies last year but my father got sick, he was hospitalized, I couldn't take exams and it was a mess—but I'll make it through English in one year or drop dead. I can do it, I can do anything. I'll take six courses at once—" He broke off, breathless. Sister Irene tried to smile. "All right then, it's settled? You'll let me in? Have I missed anything so far?"

He had no idea of the rudeness of his question. Sister Irene, feeling suddenly exhausted, said, "I'll give you a syllabus of the course."

"Fine! Wonderful!"

He got to his feet eagerly. He looked through the schedule, muttering to himself, making favorable noises. It struck Sister Irene that she was making a mistake to let him in. There were these moments when one had to make an intelligent decision. . . . But she was sympathetic with him, yes. She was sympathetic with something about him.

She found out his name the next day: Allen Weinstein.

After this she came to her Shakespeare class with a sense of excitement. It became clear to her at once that Weinstein was the most intelligent student in the class. Until he had enrolled, she had not understood what was lacking, a mind that could appreciate her own. Within a week his jagged, protean mind had alienated the other students, and though he sat in the center of the class, he seemed totally alone, encased by a miniature world of his own. When he spoke of the "frenetic humanism of the High Renaissance," Sister Irene dreaded the raised eyebrows and mocking smiles of the other students, who no longer bothered to look at Weinstein. She wanted to defend him, but she never did, because there was something rude and dismal about his knowledge; he used it like a weapon, talking passionately of Nietzsche and Goethe and Freud[3] until Sister Irene would be forced to close discussion.

In meditation, alone, she often thought of him. When she tried to talk about him to a young nun, Sister Carlotta, everything sounded gross. "But no, he's an excellent student," she insisted. "I'm very grateful to have him in class. It's just that . . . he thinks ideas are real." Sister Carlotta, who loved literature also, had been forced to teach grade-school arithmetic for the last four years. That might have been why she said, a little sharply, "You don't think ideas are real?"

[2] An allusion to the *Poetics* by the Greek philosopher Aristotle (384–322 B.C.).

[3] Friedrich Nietzche (1844–1900), the German philosopher and poet; Johann Wolfgang von Goethe (1749–1832), the German poet, novelist, and playwright; and Sigmund Freud (1856–1939), the Austrian physician who pioneered the field of psychoanalysis.

Sister Irene acquiesced with a smile, but of course she did not think so: only reality is real.

When Weinstein did not show up for class on the day the first paper was due, Sister Irene's heart sank, and the sensation was somehow a familiar one. She began her lecture and kept waiting for the door to open and for him to hurry noisily back to his seat, grinning an apology toward her—but nothing happened.

If she had been deceived by him, she made herself think angrily, it was as a teacher and not as a woman. He had promised her nothing.

Weinstein appeared the next day near the steps of the liberal arts building. She heard someone running behind her, a breathless exclamation: "Sister Irene!" She turned and saw him, panting and grinning in embarrassment. He wore a dark-blue suit with a necktie, and he looked, despite his childish face, like a little old man; there was something oddly precarious and fragile about him. "Sister Irene, I owe you an apology, right?" He raised his eyebrows and smiled a sad, forlorn, yet irritatingly conspiratorial smile. "The first paper— not in on time, and I know what your rules are. . . . You won't accept late papers, I know—that's good discipline, I'll do that when I teach too. But, unavoidably, I was unable to come to school yesterday. There are many— many—" He gulped for breath, and Sister Irene had the startling sense of seeing the real Weinstein stare out at her, a terrified prisoner behind the confident voice. "There are many complications in family life. Perhaps you are unaware—I mean—"

She did not like him, but she felt this sympathy, something tugging and nagging at her the way her parents had competed for her love so many years before. They had been whining, weak people, and out of their wet need for affection, the girl she had been (her name was Yvonne) had emerged stronger than either of them, contemptuous of tears because she had seen so many. But Weinstein was different; he was not simply weak—perhaps he was not weak at all—but his strength was confused and hysterical. She felt her customary rigidity as a teacher begin to falter. "You may turn your paper in today if you have it," she said, frowning.

Weinstein's mouth jerked into an incredulous grin. "Wonderful! Marvelous!" he said. "You are very understanding, Sister Irene, I must say. I must say . . . I didn't expect, really . . ." He was fumbling in a shabby old briefcase for the paper. Sister Irene waited. She was prepared for another of his excuses, certain that he did not have the paper, when he suddenly straightened up and handed her something. "Here! I took the liberty of writing thirty pages instead of just fifteen," he said. He was obviously quite excited; his cheeks were mottled pink and white. "You may disagree violently with my interpreta- tion—I expect you to, in fact I'm counting on it—but let me warn you, I have the exact proof, right here in the play itself!" He was thumping at a book, his voice growing louder and shriller. Sister Irene, startled, wanted to put her hand over his mouth and soothe him.

"Look," he said breathlessly, "may I talk with you? I have a class now I hate, I loathe, I can't bear to sit through! Can I talk with you instead?"

Because she was nervous, she stared at the title page of the paper: " 'Erotic Melodies in *Romeo and Juliet*' by Allen Weinstein, Jr."

"All right?" he said. "Can we walk around here? Is it all right? I've been anxious to talk with you about some things you said in class."

She was reluctant, but he seemed not to notice. They walked slowly along the shaded campus paths. Weinstein did all the talking, of course, and Sister Irene recognized nothing in his cascade of words that she had mentioned in class. "The humanist must be committed to the totality of life," he said passionately. "This is the failing one finds everywhere in the academic world! I found it in New York and I found it here and I'm no ingénu,[4] I don't go around with my mouth hanging open—I'm experienced, look, I've been to Europe, I've lived in Rome! I went everywhere in Europe except Germany, I don't talk about Germany . . . Sister Irene, think of the significant men in the last century, the men who've changed the world! Jews, right? Marx, Freud, Einstein![5] Not that I believe Marx, Marx is a madman . . . and Freud, no, my sympathies are with spiritual humanism. I believe that the Jewish race is the exclusive . . . the exclusive, what's the word, the exclusive means by which humanism will be extended. . . . Humanism begins by excluding the Jew, and now," he said with a high, surprised laugh, "the Jew will perfect it. After the Nazis, only the Jew is authorized to understand humanism, its limitations and its possibilities. So, I say that the humanist is committed to life in its totality and not just to his profession! The religious person is totally religious, he is his religion! What else? I recognize in you a humanist and a religious person—"

But he did not seem to be talking to her or even looking at her.

"Here, read this," he said. "I wrote it last night." It was a long free-verse poem, typed on a typewriter whose ribbon was worn out.

"There's this trouble with my father, a wonderful man, a lovely man, but his health—his strength is fading, do you see? What must it be to him to see his son growing up? I mean, I'm a man now, he's getting old, weak, his health is bad—it's hell, right? I sympathize with him. I'd do anything for him, I'd cut open my veins, anything for a father—right? That's why I wasn't in school yesterday," he said, and his voice dropped for the last sentence, as if he had been dragged back to earth by a fact.

Sister Irene tried to read the poem, then pretended to read it. A jumble of words dealing with "life" and "death" and "darkness" and "love." "What do you think?" Weinstein said nervously, trying to read it over her shoulder and crowding against her.

"It's very . . . passionate," Sister Irene said.

This was the right comment; he took the poem back from her in silence, his face flushed with excitement. "Here, at this school, I have few people to talk with. I haven't shown anyone else that poem." He looked at her with his dark, intense eyes, and Sister Irene felt them focus upon her. She was terrified at what he was trying to do—he was trying to force her into a human relationship.

"Thank you for your paper," she said, turning away.

When he came the next day, ten minutes late, he was haughty and disdainful. He had nothing to say and sat with his arms folded. Sister Irene took back with her to the convent a feeling of betrayal and confusion. She had been hurt. It was absurd, and yet— She spent too much time thinking about him, as if he were somehow a kind of crystallization of her own loneliness; but she had no right to think so much of him. She did not want to think of him

---

[4] Someone who is naïve.

[5] Karl Marx (1818–1883), the German philosopher and political theorist and Albert Einstein (1879–1955), the German physicist, like Sigmund Freud, were Jewish.

or of her loneliness. But Weinstein did so much more than think of his predicament: he embodied it, he acted it out, and that was perhaps why he fascinated her. It was as if he were doing a dance for her, a dance of shame and agony and delight, and so long as he did it, she was safe. She felt embarrassment for him, but also anxiety; she wanted to protect him. When the dean of the graduate school questioned her about Weinstein's work, she insisted that he was an "excellent" student, though she knew the dean had not wanted to hear that.

She prayed for guidance, she spent hours on her devotions, she was closer to her vocation than she had been for some years. Life at the convent became tinged with unreality, a misty distortion that took its tone from the glowering skies of the city at night, identical smokestacks ranged against the clouds and giving to the sky the excrement of the populated and successful earth. This city was not her city, this world was not her world. She felt no pride in knowing this, it was a fact. The little convent was not like an island in the center of this noisy world, but rather a kind of hole or crevice the world did not bother with, something of no interest. The convent's rhythm of life had nothing to do with the world's rhythm, it did not violate or alarm it in any way. Sister Irene tried to draw together the fragments of her life and synthesize them somehow in her vocation as a nun: she was a nun, she was recognized as a nun and had given herself happily to that life, she had a name, a place, she had dedicated her superior intelligence to the Church, she worked without pay and without expecting gratitude, she had given up pride, she did not think of herself but only of her work and her vocation, she did not think of anything external to these, she saturated herself daily in the knowledge that she was involved in the mystery of Christianity.

A daily terror attended this knowledge, however, for she sensed herself being drawn by that student, that Jewish boy, into a relationship she was not ready for. She wanted to cry out in fear that she was being forced into the role of a Christian, and what did that mean? What could her studies tell her? What could the other nuns tell her? She was alone, no one could help; he was making her into a Christian, and to her that was a mystery, a thing of terror, something others slipped on the way they slipped on their clothes, casually and thoughtlessly, but to her a magnificent and terrifying wonder.

For days she carried Weinstein's paper, marked A, around with her; he did not come to class. One day she checked with the graduate office and was told that Weinstein had called in to say his father was ill and that he would not be able to attend classes for a while. "He's strange, I remember him," the secretary said. "He missed all his exams last spring and made a lot of trouble. He was in and out of here every day."

So there was no more of Weinstein for a while, and Sister Irene stopped expecting him to hurry into class. Then, one morning, she found a letter from him in her mailbox.

He had printed it in black ink, very carefully, as if he had not trusted handwriting. The return address was in bold letters that, like his voice, tried to grab onto her: Birchcrest Manor. Somewhere north of the city. "Dear Sister Irene," the block letters said, "I am doing well here and have time for reading and relaxing. The Manor is delightful. My doctor here is an excellent, intelligent man who has time for me, unlike my former doctor. If you have time, you might drop in on my father, who worries about me too much, I think, and explain to him what my condition is. He doesn't seem to understand. I feel about this new life the way that boy, what's his name, in *Measure for Measure*,[6] feels about the prospects of a different life; you remember what he says to his sister when she visits him in prison, how he is looking forward to an escape into another world. Perhaps you could *explain* this to my father and he would stop worrying." The letter ended with the father's name and address, in letters that were just a little too big. Sister Irene, walking slowly down the corridor as she read the letter, felt her eyes cloud over with tears. She was cold with fear, it was something she had never experienced before. She knew what Weinstein was trying to tell her, and the desperation of his attempt made it all the more pathetic; he did not deserve this, why did God allow him to suffer so?

She read through Claudio's speech to his sister, in *Measure for Measure*:

> Ay, but to die, and go we know not where;
> To lie in cold obstruction and to rot;
> This sensible warm motion to become
> A kneaded clod; and the delighted spirit
> To bathe in fiery floods, or to reside
> In thrilling region of thick-ribbed ice,
> To be imprison'd in the viewless winds
> And blown with restless violence round about
> The pendent world; or to be worse than worst
> Of those that lawless and incertain thought
> Imagines howling! 'Tis too horrible!
> The weariest and most loathed worldly life
> That age, ache, penury, and imprisonment
> Can lay on nature is a paradise
> To what we fear of death.

Sister Irene called the father's number that day. "Allen Weinstein residence, who may I say is calling?" a woman said, bored. "May I speak to Mr. Weinstein? It's urgent—about his son," Sister Irene said. There was a pause at the other end. "You want to talk to his mother, maybe?" the woman said. "His mother? Yes, his mother, then. Please. It's very important."

She talked with this strange, unsuspected woman, a disembodied voice that suggested absolutely no face, and insisted upon going over that afternoon. The woman was nervous, but Sister Irene, who was a university professor, after all, knew enough to hide her own nervousness. She kept waiting for the woman to say, "Yes, Allen has mentioned you . . ." but nothing happened.

She persuaded Sister Carlotta to ride over with her. This urgency of hers was something they were all amazed by. They hadn't suspected that the set of her gray eyes could change to this blurred, distracted alarm, this sense of mission that seemed to have come to her from nowhere. Sister Irene drove across the city in the late afternoon traffic, with the high whining noises from residential streets where trees were being sawed down in pieces. She understood now the secret, sweet wildness that Christ must have felt, giving himself for man, dying for the billions of men who would never know of him and never understand the sacrifice. For the first time she approached the realization of that great act. In her troubled mind the city traffic was jumbled and yet oddly

[6] *Measure for Measure*, like the two plays previously mentioned, is the work of William Shakespeare (1564–1616).

coherent, an image of the world that was always out of joint with what was happening in it, its inner history struggling with its external spectacle. This sacrifice of Christ's, so mysterious and legendary now, almost lost in time— it was that by which Christ transcended both God and man at one moment, more than man because of his fate to do what no other man could do, and more than God because no god could suffer as he did. She felt a flicker of something close to madness.

She drove nervously, uncertainly, afraid of missing the street and afraid of finding it too, for while one part of her rushed forward to confront these people who had betrayed their son, another part of her would have liked nothing so much as to be waiting as usual for the summons to dinner, safe in her room. . . . When she found the street and turned onto it, she was in a state of breathless excitement. Here lawns were bright green and marred with only a few leaves, magically clean, and the houses were enormous and pompous, a mixture of styles: ranch houses, colonial houses, French country houses, white-bricked wonders with curving glass and clumps of birch trees somehow encircled by white concrete. Sister Irene stared as if she had blundered into another world. This was a kind of heaven, and she was too shabby for it.

The Weinstein's house was the strangest one of all: it looked like a small Alpine lodge, with an inverted-V-shaped front entrance. Sister Irene drove up to the black-topped driveway and let the car slow to a stop; she told Sister Carlotta she would not be long.

At the door she was met by Weinstein's mother, a small, nervous woman with hands like her son's. "Come in, come in," the woman said. She had once been beautiful, that was clear, but now in missing beauty she was not handsome or even attractive but looked ruined and perplexed, the misshapen swelling of her white-blond professionally set hair like a cap lifting up from her surprised face. "He'll be right in. Allen?" she called, "our visitor is here." They went into the living room. There was a grand piano at one end and an organ at the other. In between were scatterings of brilliant modern furniture in conversational groups, and several puffed-up white rugs on the polished floor. Sister Irene could not stop shivering.

"Professor, it's so strange, but let me say when the phone rang I had a feeling—I had a feeling," the woman said, with damp eyes. Sister Irene sat, and the woman hovered about her. "Should I call you Professor? We don't . . . you know . . . we don't understand the technicalities that go with—Allen, my son, wanted to go here to the Catholic school; I told my husband why not? Why fight? It's the thing these days, they do anything they want for knowledge. And he had to come home, you know. He couldn't take care of himself in New York, that was the beginning of the trouble. . . . Should I call you Professor?"

"You can call me Sister Irene."

"Sister Irene?" the woman said, touching her throat in awe, as if something intimate and unexpected had happened.

Then Weinstein's father appeared, hurrying. He took long, impatient strides. Sister Irene stared at him and in that instant doubted everything—he was in his fifties, a tall, sharply handsome man, heavy but not fat, holding his shoulders back with what looked like an effort, but holding them back just the same. He wore a dark suit and his face was flushed, as if he had run a long distance.

"Now," he said, coming to Sister Irene and with a precise wave of his hand motioning his wife off, "now, let's straighten this out. A lot of confusion over that kid, eh?" He pulled a chair over, scraping it across a rug and pulling one corner over, so that its brown underside was exposed. "I came home early just for this, Libby phoned me. Sister, you got a letter from him, right?"

The wife looked at Sister Irene over her husband's head as if trying somehow to coach her, knowing that this man was so loud and impatient that no one could remember anything in his presence.

"A letter—yes—today—"

"He says what in it? You got the letter, eh? Can I see it?"

She gave it to him and wanted to explain, but he silenced her with a flick of his hand. He read through the letter so quickly that Sister Irene thought perhaps he was trying to impress her with his skill at reading. "So?" he said, raising his eyes, smiling, "so what is this? He's happy out there, he says. He doesn't communicate with us any more, but he writes to you and says he's happy—what's that? I mean, what the hell is that?"

"But he isn't happy. He wants to come home," Sister Irene said. It was so important that she make him understand that she could not trust her voice; goaded by this man, it might suddenly turn shrill, as his son's did. "Someone must read their letters before they're mailed, so he tried to tell me something by making an allusion to—"

"What?"

"—an allusion to a play, so that I would know. He may be thinking suicide, he must be very unhappy—"

She ran out of breath. Weinstein's mother had begun to cry, but the father was shaking his head jerkily back and forth. "Forgive me, Sister, but it's a lot of crap, he needs the hospital, he needs help—right? It costs me fifty a day out there, and they've got the best place in the state, I figure it's worth it. He needs help, that kid, what do I care if he's unhappy? He's unbalanced!" he said angrily. "You want us to get him out again? We argued with the judge for two hours to get him in, an acquaintance of mine. Look, he can't control himself—he was smashing things here, he was hysterical. They need help, lady, and you do something about it fast! You do something! We made up our minds to do something and we did it! This letter—what the hell is this letter? He never talked like that to us!"

"But he means the opposite of what he says—"

"Then he's crazy! I'm the first to admit it." He was perspiring, and his face had darkened. "I've got no pride left this late. He's a little bastard, you want to know? He calls me names, he's filthy, got a filthy mouth—that's being smart, huh? They give him a big scholarship for his filthy mouth? I went to college too, and I got out and knew something, and I for Christs's sake did something with it; my wife is an intelligent woman, a learned woman, would you guess she does book reviews for the little newspaper out here? Intelligent isn't crazy—crazy isn't intelligent. Maybe for you at the school he writes nice papers and gets an A, but out here, around the house, he can't control himself, and we got him committed!"

"But—"

"We're fixing him up, don't worry about it!" He turned to his wife. "Libby, get out of here, I mean it. I'm sorry, but get out of here, you're making a fool of yourself, go stand in the kitchen or something, you and the goddamn maid can cry on each other's shoulders. That one in the kitchen is nuts too, they're all nuts. Sister," he said, his voice lowering, "I thank you immensely for coming out here. This is wonderful, your interest in my son. And I see

Weinstein: the name was to become disembodied from the figure, as time went on. The semester passed, the autumn drizzle turned into snow, Sister Irene rode to school in the morning and left in the afternoon, four days a week, anonymous in her black winter cloak, quiet and stunned. University teaching was an anonymous task, each day dissociated from the rest, with no necessary sense of unity among the teachers: they came and went separately and might for a year just miss a colleague who left his office five minutes before they arrived, and it did not matter.

She heard of Weinstein's death, his suicide by drowning, from the English Department secretary, a handsome white-haired woman who kept a transistor radio on her desk. Sister Irene was not surprised; she had been thinking of him as dead for months. "They identified him by some special television way they have now," the secretary said. "They're shipping the body back. It was up in Quebec. . . ."

Sister Irene could feel a part of herself drifting off, lured by the plains of white snow to the north, the quiet, the emptiness, the sweep of the Great Lakes up to the silence of Canada. But she called that part of herself back. She could only be one person in her lifetime. That was the ugly truth, she thought, that she could not really regret Weinstein's suffering and death; she had only one life and had already given it to someone else. He had come too late to her. Fifteen years ago, perhaps, but not now.

She was only one person, she thought, walking down the corridor in a dream. Was she safe in this single person, or was she trapped? She had only one identity. She could make only one choice. What she had done or hadn't done was the result of that choice, and how was she guilty? If she could have felt guilt, she thought, she might at least have been able to feel something.

[1965]

Yukio Mishima   *1925–1970*

PATRIOTISM*

On the twenty-eighth day of February, 1936 (on the third day, that is, of
the February 26 Incident),[1] Lieutenant Shinji Takeyama of the Konoe Transport
Battalion—profoundly disturbed by the knowledge that his closest colleagues
had been with the mutineers from the beginning, and indignant at the imminent
prospect of Imperial troops attacking Imperial troops—took his officer's sword
and ceremonially disemboweled himself in the eight-mat room of his private
residence in the sixth block of Aoba-chō, in Yotsuya Ward. His wife, Reiko,
followed him, stabbing herself to death. The lieutenant's farewell note consisted
of one sentence: "Long live the Imperial Forces." His wife's, after apologies
for her unfilial conduct in thus preceding her parents to the grave, concluded:
"The day which, for a soldier's wife, had to come, has come. . . ." The last
moments of this heroic and dedicated couple were such as to make the gods
themselves weep. The lieutenant's age, it should be noted, was thirty-one,
his wife's twenty-three; and it was not half a year since the celebration of
their marriage.

II

Those who saw the bride and bridegroom in the commemorative photograph—perhaps no less than those actually present at the lieutenant's wedding—had exclaimed in wonder at the bearing of this handsome couple. The
lieutenant, majestic in military uniform, stood protectively beside his bride,
his right hand resting upon his sword, his officer's cap held at his left side.
His expression was severe, and his dark brows and wide-gazing eyes well conveyed the clear integrity of youth. For the beauty of the bride in her white
over-robe no comparisons were adequate. In the eyes, round beneath soft
brows, in the slender, finely shaped nose, and in the full lips, there was both
sensuousness and refinement. One hand, emerging shyly from a sleeve of the
over-robe, held a fan, and the tips of the fingers, clustering delicately, were
like the bud of a moonflower.

After the suicide, people would take out this photograph and examine it,
and sadly reflect that too often there was a curse on these seemingly flawless
unions. Perhaps it was no more than imagination, but looking at the picture
after the tragedy it almost seemed as if the two young people before the gold-
lacquered screen were gazing, each with equal clarity, at the deaths which
lay before them.

Thanks to the good offices of their go-between, Lieutenant General Ozeki,
they had been able to set themselves up in a new home at Aoba-chō in Yotsuya.
"New home" is perhaps misleading. It was an old three-room rented house
backing onto a small garden. As neither the six- nor the four-and-a-half mat
room downstairs was favored by the sun, they used the upstairs eight-mat

---

* *Translated by Geoffrey W. Sargent*
[1] The coup against the government was led by young right-wing military officers. The rebels
briefly occupied the heart of Tokyo, murdered several officials, including Admiral Saito, the
Lord Keeper of the Privy Seal and a close adviser to the Emperor (referred to below), and was
finally put down with the surrender of the rebels on February 29th. A purge of the military
followed.

room as both bedroom and guest room. There was no maid, so Reiko was left alone to guard the house in her husband's absence.

The honeymoon trip was dispensed with on the grounds that these were times of national emergency. The two of them had spent the first night of their marriage at this house. Before going to bed, Shinji, sitting erect on the floor with his sword laid before him, had bestowed upon his wife a soldierly lecture. A woman who had become the wife of a soldier should know and resolutely accept that her husband's death might come at any moment. It could be tomorrow. It could be the day after. But, no matter when it came—he asked—was she steadfast in her resolve to accept it? Reiko rose to her feet, pulled open a drawer of the cabinet, and took out what was the most prized of her new possessions, the dagger her mother had given her. Returning to her place, she laid the dagger without a word on the mat before her, just as her husband had laid his sword. A silent understanding was achieved at once, and the lieutenant never again sought to test his wife's resolve.

In the first months of her marriage Reiko's beauty grew daily more radiant, shining serene like the moon after rain.

As both were possessed of young, vigorous bodies, their relationship was passionate. Nor was this merely a matter of the night. On more than one occasion, returning home straight from maneuvers, and begrudging even the time it took to remove his mud-splashed uniform, the lieutenant had pushed his wife to the floor almost as soon as he had entered the house. Reiko was equally ardent in her response. For a little more or a little less than a month, from the first night of their marriage Reiko knew happiness, and the lieutenant, seeing this, was happy too.

Reiko's body was white and pure, and her swelling breasts conveyed a firm and chaste refusal; but, upon consent, those breasts were lavish with their intimate, welcoming warmth. Even in bed these two were frighteningly and awesomely serious. In the very midst of wild, intoxicating passions, their hearts were sober and serious.

By day the lieutenant would think of his wife in the brief rest periods between training; and all day long, at home, Reiko would recall the image of her husband. Even when apart, however, they had only to look at the wedding photograph for their happiness to be once more confirmed. Reiko felt not the slightest surprise that a man who had been a complete stranger until a few months ago should now have become the sun about which her whole world revolved.

All these things had a moral basis, and were in accordance with the Education Rescript's injunction that "husband and wife should be harmonious." Not once did Reiko contradict her husband, nor did the lieutenant ever find reason to scold his wife. On the god shelf below the stairway, alongside the tablet from the Great Ise Shrine, were set photographs of their Imperial Majesties, and regularly every morning, before leaving for duty, the lieutenant would stand with his wife at this hallowed place and together they would bow their heads low. The offering water was renewed each morning, and the sacred sprig of *sasaki* was always green and fresh. Their lives were lived beneath the solemn protection of the gods and were filled with an intense happiness which set every fiber in their bodies trembling.

III

Although Lord Privy Seal Saitō's house was in their neighborhood, neither of them heard any noise of gunfire on the morning of February 26. It was a

bugle, sounding muster in the dim, snowy dawn, when the ten-minute tragedy
had already ended, which first disrupted the lieutenant's slumbers. Leaping
at once from his bed, and without speaking a word, the lieutenant donned
his uniform, buckled on the sword held ready for him by his wife, and hurried
swiftly out into the snow-covered streets of the still darkened morning. He
did not return until the evening of the twenty-eighth.

Later, from the radio news, Reiko learned the full extent of this sudden,
eruption of violence. Her life throughout the subsequent two days was lived
alone, in complete tranquillity, and behind locked doors.

In the lieutenant's face, as he hurried silently out into the snowy morning,
Reiko had read the determination to die. If her husband did not return, her
own decision was made: she too would die. Quietly she attended to the disposition of her personal possesions. She chose her sets of visiting kimonos as
keepsakes for friends of her schooldays, and she wrote a name and address
on the stiff paper wrapping in which each was folded. Constantly admonished
by her husband never to think of the morrow, Reiko had not even kept a
diary and was now denied the pleasure of assiduously rereading her record
of the happiness of the past few months and consigning each page to the
fire as she did so. Ranged across the top of the radio were a small china
dog, a rabbit, a squirrel, a bear, and a fox. There were also a small vase and
a water pitcher. These comprised Reiko's one and only collection. But it would
hardly do, she imagined, to give such things as keepsakes. Nor again would
it be quite proper to ask specifically for them to be included in the coffin. It
seemed to Reiko, as these thoughts passed through her mind, that the expressions on the small animals' faces grew even more lost and forlorn.

Reiko took the squirrel in her hand and looked at it. And then, her thoughts
turning to a realm far beyond these child-like affections, she gazed up into
the distance at the great sunlike principle which her husband embodied. She
was ready, and happy, to be hurtled along to her destruction in that gleaming
sun chariot—but now, for these moments of solitude, she allowed herself to
luxuriate in this innocent attachment of trifles. The time when she had genuinely
loved these things, however, was long past. Now she merely loved the memory
of having once loved them, and their place in her heart had been filled by
more intense passions, by a more frenzied happiness. . . . For Reiko had never,
even to herself, thought of those soaring joys of the flesh as a mere pleasure.
The February cold, and the icy touch of the china squirrel, had numbed Reiko's
slender fingers; yet, even so, in her lower limbs, beneath the ordered repetition
of the pattern which crossed the skirt of her trim *meisen* kimono, she could
feel now, as she thought of the lieutenant's powerful arms reaching out toward
her, a hot moistness of the flesh which defied the snows.

She was not in the least afraid of the death hovering in her mind. Waiting
alone at home, Reiko firmly believed that everything her husband was feeling
or thinking now, his anguish and distress, was leading her—just as surely as
the power in his flesh—to a welcome death. She felt as if her body could
melt away with ease and be transformed to the merest fraction of her husband's
thought.

Listening to the frequent announcements on the radio, she heard the names
of several of her husband's colleagues mentioned among those of the insur-
gents. This was news of death. She followed the developments closely, wondering anxiously, as the situation became daily more irrevocable, why no Imperial
ordinance was sent down, and watching what had at first been taken as a

movement to restore the nation's honor come gradually to be branded with the infamous name of mutiny. There was no communication from the regiment. At any moment, it seemed, fighting might commence in the city streets, where the remains of the snow still lay.

Toward sundown on the twenty-eighth Reiko was startled by a furious pounding on the front door. She hurried downstairs. As she pulled with fumbling fingers at the bolt, the shape dimly outlined beyond the frosted-glass panel made no sound, but she knew it was her husband. Reiko had never known the bolt on the sliding door to be stiff. Still it resisted. The door just would not open.

In a moment, almost before she knew she had succeeded, the lieutenant was standing before her on the cement floor inside the porch, muffled in a khaki greatcoat, his top boots heavy with slush from the street. Closing the door behind him, he returned the bolt once more to its socket. With what significance, Reiko did not understand.

"Welcome home."

Reiko bowed deeply, but her husband made no response. As he had already unfastened his sword and was about to remove his greatcoat, Reiko moved around behind to assist. The coat, which was cold and damp and had lost the odor of horse dung it normally exuded when exposed to the sun, weighed heavily upon her arm. Draping it across a hanger, and cradling the sword and leather belt in her sleeves, she waited while her husband removed his top boots and then followed behind him into the "living room." This was the six-mat room downstairs.

Seen in the clear light from the lamp, her husband's face, covered with a heavy growth of bristle, was almost unrecognizably wasted and thin. The cheeks were hollow, their luster and resilience gone. In his normal good spirits he would have changed into old clothes as soon as he was home and have pressed her to get supper at once, but now he sat before the table still in his uniform, his head drooping dejectedly. Reiko refrained from asking whether she should prepare the supper.

After an interval the lieutenant spoke.

"I knew nothing. They hadn't asked me to join. Perhaps out of consideration, because I was newly married. Kanō, and Homma too, and Yamaguchi."

Reiko recalled momentarily the faces of high-spirited young officers, friends of her husband, who had come to the house occasionally as guests.

"There may be an Imperial ordinance sent down tomorrow. They'll be posted as rebels, I imagine. I shall be in command of a unit with orders to attack them. . . . I can't do it. It's impossible to do a thing like that."

He spoke again.

"They've taken me off guard duty, and I have permission to return home for one night. Tomorrow morning, without question, I must leave to join the attack. I can't do it, Reiko."

Reiko sat erect with lowered eyes. She understood clearly that her husband had spoken of his death. The lieutenant was resolved. Each word, being rooted in death, emerged sharply and with powerful significance against this dark, unmovable background. Although the lieutenant was speaking of his dilemma, already there was no room in his mind for vacillation.

However, there was a clarity, like the clarity of a stream fed from melting snows, in the silence which rested between them. Sitting in his own home after the long two-day ordeal, and looking across at the face of his beautiful

wife, the lieutenant was for the first time experiencing true peace of mind.
For he had at once known, though she said nothing, that his wife divined
the resolve which lay beneath his words.

"Well, then . . ." The lieutenant's eyes opened wide. Despite his exhaustion
they were strong and clear, and now for the first time they looked straight
into the eyes of his wife. "To-night I shall cut my stomach."

Reiko did not flinch.

Her round eyes showed tension, as taut as the clang of a bell.

"I am ready," she said. "I ask permission to accompany you."

The lieutenant felt almost mesmerized by the strength in those eyes. His
words flowed swiftly and easily, like the utterances of a man in delirium, and
it was beyond his understanding how permission in a matter of such weight
could be expressed so casually.

"Good. We'll go together. But I want you as a witness, first, for my own
suicide. Agreed?"

When this was said a sudden release of abundant happiness welled up in
both their hearts. Reiko was deeply affected by the greatness of her husband's
trust in her. It was vital for the lieutenant, whatever else might happen, that
there should be no irregularity in his death. For that reason there had to be
a witness. The fact that he had chosen his wife for this was the first mark of
his trust. The second, and even greater mark, was that though he had pledged
that they should die together he did not intend to kill his wife first—he had
deferred her death to a time when he would no longer be there to verify it.
If the lieutenant had been a suspicious husband, he would doubtless, as in
the usual suicide pact, have chosen to kill his wife first.

When Reiko said, "I ask permission to accompany you," the lieutenant felt
these words to be the final fruit of the education which he had himself given
his wife, starting on the first night of their marriage, and which had schooled
her, when the moment came, to say what had to be said without a shadow
of hesitation. This flattered the lieutenant's opinion of himself as a self-reliant
man. He was not so romantic or conceited as to imagine that the words were
spoken spontaneously, out of love for her husband.

With happiness welling almost too abundantly in their hearts, they could
not help smiling at each other. Reiko felt as if she had returned to her wedding
night.

Before her eyes was neither pain nor death. She seemed to see only a free
and limitless expanse opening out into vast distances.

"The water is hot. Will you take your bath now?"

"Ah yes, of course."

"And supper . . . ?"

The words were delivered in such level, domestic tones that the lieutenant
came near to thinking, for the fraction of a second, that everything had been
a hallucination.

"I don't think we'll need supper. But perhaps you could warm some sake?"

"As you wish."

As Reiko rose and took a *tanzen* gown from the cabinet for after the bath,
she purposely directed her husband's attention to the opened drawer. The
lieutenant rose, crossed to the cabinet, and looked inside. From the ordered
array of paper wrappings he read, one by one, the addresses of the keepsakes.
There was no grief in the lieutenant's response to this demonstration of heroic
resolve. His heart was filled with tenderness. Like a husband who is proudly

shown the childish purchases of a young wife, the lieutenant, overwhelmed by affection, lovingly embraced his wife from behind and implanted a kiss upon her neck.

Reiko felt the roughness of the lieutenant's unshaven skin against her neck. This sensation, more than being just a thing of this world, was for Reiko almost the world itself, but now—with the feeling that it was soon to be lost forever—it had freshness beyond all her experience. Each moment had its own vital strength, and the senses in every corner of her body were reawakened. Accepting her husband's caresses from behind, Reiko raised herself on the tips of her toes, letting the vitality seep through her entire body.

"First the bath, and then, after some sake . . . lay out the bedding upstairs, will you?"

The lieutenant whispered the words into his wife's ear. Reiko silently nodded.

Flinging off his uniform, the lieutenant went to the bath. To faint background noises of slopping water Reiko tended the charcoal brazier in the living room and began the preparations for warming the sake.

Taking the *tanzen,* a sash, and some underclothes, she went to the bathroom to ask how the water was. In the midst of a coiling cloud of steam the lieutenant was sitting cross-legged on the floor, shaving, and she could dimly discern the rippling movements of the muscles on his damp, powerful back as they responded to the movement of his arms.

There was nothing to suggest a time of any special significance. Reiko, going busily about her tasks, was preparing side dishes from odds and ends in stock. Her hands did not tremble. If anything, she managed even more efficiently and smoothly than usual. From time to time, it is true, there was a strange throbbing deep within her breast. Like distant lightning, it had a moment of sharp intensity and then vanished without trace. Apart from that, nothing was in any way out of the ordinary.

The lieutenant, shaving in the bathroom, felt his warmed body miraculously healed at last of the desperate tiredness of the days of indecision and filled—in spite of the death which lay ahead—with pleasurable anticipation. The sound of his wife going about her work came to him faintly. A healthy physical craving, submerged for two days, reasserted itself.

The lieutenant was confident there had been no impurity in that joy they had experienced when resolving upon death. They had both sensed at that moment—though not, of course, in any clear and conscious way—that those permissible pleasures which they shared in private were once more beneath the protection of Righteousness and Divine Power, and of a complete and unassailable morality. On looking into each other's eyes and discovering there an honorable death, they had felt themselves safe once more behind steel walls which none could destroy, encased in an impenetrable armor of Beauty and Truth. Thus, so far from seeing any inconsistency or conflict between the urges of his flesh and the sincerity of his patriotism, the lieutenant was even able to regard the two as parts of the same thing.

Thrusting his face close to the dark, cracked, misted wall mirror, the lieutenant shaved himself with great care. This would be his death face. There must be no unsightly blemishes. The clean-shaven face gleamed once more with a youthful luster, seeming to brighten the darkness of the mirror. There was a certain elegance, he even felt, in the association of death with this radiantly healthy face.

Just as it looked now, this would become his death face! Already, in fact, it had half departed from the lieutenant's personal possession and had become the bust above a dead soldier's memorial. As an experiment he closed his eyes tight. Everything was wrapped in blackness, and he was no longer a living, seeing creature.

Returning from the bath, the traces of the shave glowing faintly blue beneath his smooth cheeks, he seated himself beside the now well-kindled charcoal brazier. Busy though Reiko was, he noticed, she had found time lightly to touch up her face. Her cheeks were gay and her lips moist. There was no shadow of sadness to be seen. Truly, the lieutenant felt, as he saw this mark of his young wife's passionate nature, he had chosen the wife he ought to have chosen.

As soon as the lieutenant had drained his sake cup he offered it to Reiko. Reiko had never before tasted sake, but she accepted without hesitation and sipped timidly.

"Come here," the lieutenant said.

Reiko moved to her husband's side and was embraced as she leaned backward across his lap. Her breast was in violent commotion, as if sadness, joy, and the potent sake were mingling and reacting within her. The lieutenant looked down into his wife's face. It was the last face he would see in this world, the last face he would see of his wife. The lieutenant scrutinized the face minutely, with the eyes of a traveler bidding farewell to splendid vistas which he will never revisit. It was a face he could not tire of looking at—the features regular yet not cold, the lips lightly closed with a soft strength. The lieutenant kissed those lips, unthinkingly. And suddenly, though there was not the slightest distortion of the face into the unsightliness of sobbing, he noticed that tears were welling slowly from beneath the long lashes of the closed eyes and brimming over into a glistening stream.

When, a little later, the lieutenant urged that they should move to the upstairs bedroom, his wife replied that she would follow after taking a bath. Climbing the stairs alone to the bedroom, where the air was already warmed by the gas heater, the lieutenant lay down on the bedding with arms outstretched and legs apart. Even the time at which he lay waiting for his wife to join him was no later and no earlier than usual.

He folded his hands beneath his head and gazed at the dark boards of the ceiling in the dimness beyond the range of the standard lamp. Was it death he was now waiting for? Or a wild ecstasy of the senses? The two seemed to overlap, almost as if the object of this bodily desire was death itself. But, however that might be, it was certain that never before had the lieutenant tasted such total freedom.

There was the sound of a car outside the window. He could hear the screech of its tires skidding in the snow piled at the side of the street. The sound of its horn re-echoed from near-by walls. . . . Listening to these noises he had the feeling that this house rose like a solitary island in the ocean of a society going as restlessly about its business as ever. All around, vastly and untidily, stretched the country for which he grieved. He was to give his life for it. But would that great country, with which he was prepared to remonstrate to the extent of destroying himself, take the slightest heed of his death? He did not know; and it did not matter. His was a battlefield without glory, a battlefield where none could display deeds of valor: it was the front line of the spirit.

Reiko's footsteps sounded on the stairway. The steep stairs in this old house creaked badly. There were fond memories in that creaking, and many a time, while waiting in bed, the lieutenant had listened to its welcome sound. At the thought that he would hear it no more he listened with intense concentration, striving for every corner of every moment of this precious time to be filled with the sound of those soft footfalls on the creaking stairway. The moments seemed transformed to jewels, sparkling with inner light.

Reiko wore a Nagoya sash about the waist of her *yukata*, but as the lieutenant reached toward it, its redness sobered by the dimness of the light, Reiko's hand moved to his assistance and the sash fell away, slithering swiftly to the floor. As she stood before him, still in her *yukata*, the lieutenant inserted his hands through the side slits beneath each sleeve, intending to embrace her as she was; but at the touch of his finger tips upon the warm naked flesh, and as the armpits closed gently about his hands, his whole body was suddenly aflame.

In a few moments the two lay naked before the glowing gas heater.

Neither spoke the thought, but their hearts, their bodies, and their pounding breasts blazed with the knowledge that this was the very last time. It was as if the words "The Last Time" were spelled out, in invisible brushstrokes, across every inch of their bodies.

The lieutenant drew his wife close and kissed her vehemently. As their tongues explored each other's mouths, reaching out into the smooth, moist interior, they felt as if the still-unknown agonies of death had tempered their senses to the keenness of red-hot steel. The agonies they could not yet feel, the distant pains of death, had refined their awareness of pleasure.

"This is the last time I shall see your body," said the lieutenant. "Let me look at it closely." And, tilting the shade on the lampstand to one side, he directed the rays along the full length of Reiko's outstretched form.

Reiko lay still with her eyes closed. The light from the low lamp clearly revealed the majestic sweep of her white flesh. The lieutenant, not without a touch of egocentricity, rejoiced that he would never see this beauty crumble in death.

At his leisure, the lieutenant allowed the unforgettable spectacle to engrave itself upon his mind. With one hand he fondled the hair, with the other he softly stroked the magnificent face, implanting kisses here and there where his eyes lingered. The quiet coldness of the high, tapering forehead, the closed eyes with their long lashes beneath faintly etched brows, the set of the finely shaped nose, the gleam of teeth glimpsed between full, regular lips, the soft cheeks and the small, wise chin . . . these things conjured up in the lieutenant's mind the vision of a truly radiant death face, and again and again he pressed his lips tight against the white throat—where Reiko's own hand was soon to strike—and the throat reddened faintly beneath his kisses. Returning to the mouth he laid his lips against it with the gentlest of pressures, and moved them rhythmically over Reiko's with the light rolling motion of a small boat. If he closed his eyes, the world became a rocking cradle.

Wherever the lieutenant's eyes moved his lips faithfully followed. The high, swelling breasts, surmounted by nipples like the buds of a wild cherry, hardened as the lieutenant's lips closed about them. The arms flowed smoothly downward from each side of the breast, tapering toward the wrists, yet losing nothing of their roundness or symmetry, and at their tips were those delicate fingers which had held the fan at the wedding ceremony. One by one, as the lieutenant kissed them, the fingers withdrew behind their neighbor as if in shame. . . . The natural hollow curving between the bosom and the stomach carried in its lines a suggestion not only of softness but of resilient strength, and while it gave forewarning of the rich curves spreading outward from here to the hips it had, in itself, an appearance only of restraint and proper discipline. The whiteness and richness of the stomach and hips was like milk brimming in a great bowl, and the sharply shadowed dip of the navel could have been the fresh impress of a raindrop, fallen there that very moment. Where the shadows gathered more thickly, hair clustered, gentle and sensitive, and as the agitation mounted in the now no longer passive body there hung over this region a scent like the smoldering of fragrant blossoms, growing steadily more pervasive.

At length, in a tremulous voice, Reiko spoke.

"Show me. . . . Let me look too, for the last time."

Never before had he heard from his wife's lips so strong and unequivocal a request. It was as if something which her modesty had wished to keep hidden to the end had suddenly burst its bonds of constraint. The lieutenant obediently lay back and surrendered himself to his wife. Lithely she raised her white, trembling body, and—burning with an innocent desire to return to her husband what he had done for her—placed two white fingers on the lieutenant's eyes, which gazed fixedly up at her, and gently stroked them shut.

Suddenly overwhelmed by tenderness, her cheeks flushed by a dizzying uprush of emotion, Reiko threw her arms about the lieutenant's close-cropped head. The bristly hairs rubbed painfully against her breast, the prominent nose was cold as it dug into her flesh, and his breath was hot. Relaxing her embrace, she gazed down at her husband's masculine face. The severe brows, the closed eyes, the splendid bridge of the nose, the shapely lips drawn firmly together . . . the blue, clean-shaven cheeks reflecting the light and gleaming smoothly. Reiko kissed each of these. She kissed the broad nape of the neck, the strong, erect shoulders, the powerful chest with its twin circles like shields and its russet nipples. In the armpits, deeply shadowed by the ample flesh of the shoulders and chest, a sweet and melancholy odor emanated from the growth of hair, and in the sweetness of this odor was contained, somehow, the essence of young death. The lieutenant's naked skin glowed like a field of barley, and everywhere the muscles showed in sharp relief, converging on the lower abdomen about the small, unassuming navel. Gazing at the youthful, firm stomach, modestly covered by a vigorous growth of hair, Reiko thought of it as it was soon to be, cruelly cut by the sword, and she laid her head upon it, sobbing in pity, and bathed it with kisses.

At the touch of his wife's tears upon his stomach the lieutenant felt ready to endure with courage the cruelest agonies of his suicide.

What ecstasies they experienced after these tender exchanges may well be imagined. The lieutenant raised himself and enfolded his wife in a powerful embrace, her body now limp with exhaustion after her grief and tears. Passionately they held their faces close, rubbing cheek against cheek. Reiko's body was trembling. Their breasts, moist with sweat, were tightly joined, and every inch of the young and beautiful bodies had become so much one with the other that it seemed impossible there should ever again be a separation. Reiko cried out. From the heights they plunged into the abyss, and from the abyss they took wing and soared once more to dizzying heights. The lieutenant panted like the regimental standard-bearer on a route march. . . . As one cycle ended, almost immediately a new wave of passion would be generated, and together—

with no trace of fatigue—they would climb again in a single breathless movement to the very summit.

IV

When the lieutenant at last turned away, it was not from weariness. For one thing, he was anxious not to undermine the considerable strength he would need in carrying out his suicide. For another, he would have been sorry to mar the sweetness of these last memories by over-indulgence.

Since the lieutenant had clearly desisted, Reiko too, with her usual compliance, followed his example. The two lay naked on their backs, with fingers interlaced, staring fixedly at the dark ceiling. The room was warm from the heater, and even when the sweat had ceased to pour from their bodies they felt no cold. Outside, in the hushed night, the sounds of passing traffic had ceased. Even the noises of the trains and streetcars around Yotsuya station did not penetrate this far. After echoing through the region bounded by the moat, they were lost in the heavily wooded park fronting the broad driveway before Akasaka Palace. It was hard to believe in the tension gripping this whole quarter, where the two factions of the bitterly divided Imperial Army now confronted each other, poised for battle.

Savoring the warmth glowing within themselves, they lay still and recalled the ecstasies they had just known. Each moment of the experience was relived. They remembered the taste of kisses which had never wearied, the touch of naked flesh, episode after episode of dizzying bliss. But already, from the dark boards of the ceiling, the face of death was peering down. These joys had been final, and their bodies would never know them again. Not that joy of this intensity—and the same thought had occurred to them both—was ever likely to be reexperienced, even if they should live on to old age.

The feel of their fingers intertwined—this too would soon be lost. Even the wood-grain patterns they now gazed at on the dark ceiling boards would be taken from them. They could feel death edging in, nearer and nearer. There could be no hesitation now. They must have the courage to reach out to death themselves, and to seize it.

"Well, let's make our preparations," said the lieutenant. The note of determination in the words was unmistakable, but at the same time Reiko had never heard her husband's voice so warm and tender.

After they had risen, a variety of tasks awaited them.

The lieutenant, who had never once before helped with the bedding, now cheerfully slid back the door of the closet, lifted the mattress across the room by himself, and stowed it away inside.

Reiko turned off the gas heater and put away the lamp standard. During the lieutenant's absence she had arranged this room carefully, sweeping and dusting it to a fresh cleanness, and now—if one overlooked the rosewood table drawn into one corner—the eight-mat room gave all the appearance of a reception room ready to welcome an important guest.

"We've seen some drinking here, haven't we? With Kanō and Homma and Noguchi . . ."

"Yes, they were great drinkers, all of them."

"We'll be meeting them before long, in the other world. They'll tease us, I imagine, when they find I've brought you with me."

Descending the stairs, the lieutenant turned to look back into this calm, clean room, now brightly illuminated by the ceiling lamp. There floated across his mind the faces of the young officers who had drunk there, and laughed, and innocently bragged. He had never dreamed then that he would one day cut open his stomach in this room.

In the two rooms downstairs husband and wife busied themselves smoothly and serenely with their respective preparations. The lieutenant went to the toilet, and then to the bathroom to wash. Meanwhile Reiko folded away her husband's padded robe, placed his uniform tunic, his trousers, and a newly cut bleached loincloth in the bathroom, and set out sheets of paper on the living-room table for the farewell notes. Then she removed the lid from the writing box and began rubbing ink from the ink tablet. She had already decided upon the wording of her own note.

Reiko's fingers pressed hard upon the cold gilt letters of the ink tablet, and the water in the shallow well at once darkened, as if a black cloud had spread across it. She stopped thinking that this repeated action, this pressure from her fingers, this rise and fall of faint sound, was all and solely for death. It was a routine domestic task, a simple paring away of time until death should finally stand before her. But somehow, in the increasingly smooth motion of the tablet rubbing on the stone, and in the scent from the thickening ink, there was unspeakable darkness.

Neat in his uniform, which he now wore next to his skin, the lieutenant emerged from the bathroom. Without a word he seated himself at the table, bolt upright, took a brush in his hand, and stared undecidedly at the paper before him.

Reiko took a white silk kimono with her and entered the bathroom. When she reappeared in the living room, clad in the white kimono and with her face lightly made up, the farewell note lay completed on the table beneath the lamp. The thick black brushstrokes said simply:

"Long Live the Imperial Forces—Army Lieutenant Takeyama Shinji."

While Reiko sat opposite him writing her own note, the lieutenant gazed in silence, intensely serious, at the controlled movement of his wife's pale fingers as they manipulated the brush.

With their respective notes in their hands—the lieutenant's sword strapped to his side, Reiko's small dagger thrust into the sash of her white kimono— the two of them stood before the god shelf and silently prayed. Then they put out all the downstairs lights. As he mounted the stairs the lieutenant turned his head and gazed back at the striking, white-clad figure of his wife, climbing behind him, with lowered eyes, from the darkness beneath.

The farewell notes were laid side by side in the alcove of the upstairs room. They wondered whether they ought not to remove the hanging scroll, but since it had been written by their go-between, Lieutenant General Ozeki, and consisted, moreover, of two Chinese characters signifying "Sincerity," they left it where it was. Even if it were to become stained with splashes of blood, they felt that the lieutenant general would understand.

The lieutenant, sitting erect with his back to the alcove, laid his sword on the floor before him.

Reiko sat facing him, a mat's width away. With the rest of her so severely white the touch of rouge on her lips seemed remarkably seductive.

Across the dividing mat they gazed intently into each other's eyes. The lieutenant's sword lay before his knees. Seeing it, Reiko recalled their first night and was overwhelmed with sadness. The lieutenant spoke, in a hoarse voice:

"As I have no second to help me I shall cut deep. It may look unpleasant, but please do not panic. Death of any sort is a fearful thing to watch. You must not be discouraged by what you see. Is that all right?"

"Yes."

Reiko nodded deeply.

Looking at the slender white figure of his wife the lieutenant experienced a bizarre excitement. What he was about to perform was an act in his public capacity as a soldier, something he had never previously shown his wife. It called for a resolution equal to the courage to enter battle; it was a death of no less degree and quality than death in the front line. It was his conduct on the battlefield that he was now to display.

Momentarily the thought led the lieutenant to a strange fantasy. A lonely death on the battlefield, a death beneath the eyes of his beautiful wife . . . in the sensation that he was now to die in these two dimensions, realizing an impossible union of them both, there was sweetness beyond words. This must be the very pinnacle of good fortune, he thought. To have every moment of his death observed by those beautiful eyes—it was like being borne to death on a gentle, fragrant breeze. There was some special favor here. He did not understand precisely what it was, but it was a domain unknown to others: a dispensation granted to no one else had been permitted to himself. In the radiant, bridelike figure of his white-robed wife the lieutenant seemed to see a vision of all those things he had loved and for which he was to lay down his life—the Imperial Household, the Nation, the Army Flag. All these, no less than the wife who sat before him, were presences observing him closely with clear and never-faltering eyes.

Reiko too was gazing intently at her husband, so soon to die, and she thought that never in this world had she seen anything so beautiful. The lieutenant always looked well in uniform, but now, as he contemplated death with severe brows and firmly closed lips, he revealed what was perhaps masculine beauty at its most superb.

"It's time to go," the lieutenant said at last.

Reiko bent her body low to the mat in a deep bow. She could not raise her face. She did not wish to spoil her make-up with tears, but the tears could not be held back.

When at length she looked up she saw hazily through the tears that her husband had wound a white bandage around the blade of his now unsheathed sword, leaving five or six inches of naked steel showing at the point.

Resting the sword in its cloth wrapping on the mat before him, the lieutenant rose from his knees, resettled himself cross-legged, and unfastened the hooks of his uniform collar. His eyes no longer saw his wife. Slowly, one by one, he undid the flat brass buttons. The dusky brown chest was revealed, and then the stomach. He unclasped his belt and undid the buttons of his trousers. The pure whiteness of the thickly coiled loincloth showed itself. The lieutenant pushed the cloth down with both hands, further to ease his stomach, and then reached for the white-bandaged blade of his sword. With his left hand he massaged his abdomen, glancing downward as he did so.

To reassure himself on the sharpness of his sword's cutting edge the lieutenant folded back the left trouser flap, exposing a little of his thigh, and lightly drew the blade across the skin. Blood welled up in the wound at once, and several streaks of red trickled downward, glistening in the strong light.

It was the first time Reiko had ever seen her husband's blood, and she felt

a violent throbbing in her chest. She looked at her husband's face. The lieutenant was looking at the blood with calm appraisal. For a moment—though thinking at the time that it was hollow comfort—Reiko experienced a sense of relief.

The lieutenant's eyes fixed his wife with an intense, hawk-like stare. Moving
the sword around to his front, he raised himself slightly on his hips and let
the upper half of his body lean over the sword point. That he was mustering
his whole strength was apparent from the angry tension of the uniform at
his shoulders. The lieutenant aimed to strike deep into the left of his stomach.
His sharp cry pierced the silence of the room.

Despite the effort he had himself put into the blow, the lieutenant had the
impression that someone else had struck the side of his stomach agonizingly
with a thick rod of iron. For a second or so his head reeled and he had no
idea what had happened. The five or six inches of naked point had vanished
completely into his flesh, and the white bandage, gripped in his clenched fist,
pressed directly into his stomach.

He returned to consciousness. The blade had certainly pierced the wall of
the stomach, he thought. His breathing was difficult, his chest thumped violently, and in some far deep region, which he could hardly believe was a part
of himself, a fearful and excruciating pain came welling up as if the ground
had split open to disgorge a boiling stream of molten rock. The pain came
suddenly nearer, with terrifying speed. The lieutenant bit his lower lip and
stifled an instinctive moan.

Was this *seppuku?*—he was thinking. It was a sensation of utter chaos, as if
the sky had fallen on his head and the world was reeling drunkenly. His will
power and courage, which had seemed so robust before he had made the
incision, had now dwindled to something like a single hairlike thread of steel,
and he was assailed by the uneasy feeling that he must advance along this
thread, clinging to it with desperation. His clenched fist had grown moist.
Looking down, he saw that both his hand and the cloth about the blade were
drenched in blood. His loincloth too was dyed a deep red. It struck him as
incredible that, amidst this terrible agony, things which could be seen could
still be seen, and existing things existed still.

The moment the lieutenant thrust the sword into his left side and she saw
the deathly pallor fall across his face, like an abruptly lowered curtain, Reiko
had to struggle to prevent herself from rushing to his side. Whatever happened,
she must watch. She must be a witness. That was the duty her husband had
laid upon her. Opposite her, a mat's space away, she could clearly see her
husband biting his lip to stifle the pain. The pain was there, with absolute
certainty, before her eyes. And Reiko had no means of rescuing him from it.

The sweat glistened on her husband's forehead. The lieutenant closed his
eyes, and then opened them again, as if experimenting. The eyes had lost
their luster, and seemed innocent and empty like the eyes of a small animal.

The agony before Reiko's eyes burned as strong as the summer sun, utterly
remote from the grief which seemed to be tearing herself apart within. The
pain grew steadily in stature, stretching upward. Reiko felt that her husband
had already become a man in a separate world, a man whose whole being
had been resolved into pain, a prisoner in a cage of pain where no hand
could reach out to him. But Reiko felt no pain at all. Her grief was not pain.
As she thought about this, Reiko began to feel as if someone had raised a
cruel wall of glass high between herself and her husband.

Ever since her marriage her husband's existence had been her own existence, and every breath of his had been a breath drawn by herself. But now, while her husband's existence in pain was a vivid reality, Reiko could find in this grief of hers no certain proof at all of her own existence.

With only his right hand on the sword the lieutenant began to cut sideways across his stomach. But as the blade became entangled with the entrails it was pushed constantly outward by their soft resilience; and the lieutenant realized that it would be necessary, as he cut, to use both hands to keep the point pressed deep into his stomach. He pulled the blade across. It did not cut as easily as he had expected. He directed the strength of his whole body into his right hand and pulled again. There was a cut of three or four inches.

The pain spread slowly outward from the inner depths until the whole stomach reverberated. It was like the wild clanging of a bell. Or like a thousand bells which jangled simultaneously at every breath he breathed and every throb of his pulse, rocking his whole being. The lieutenant could no longer stop himself from moaning. But by now the blade had cut its way through to below the navel, and when he noticed this he felt a sense of satisfaction, and a renewal of courage.

The volume of blood had steadily increased, and now it spurted from the wound as if propelled by the beat of the pulse. The mat before the lieutenant was drenched red with splattered blood, and more blood overflowed onto it from pools which gathered in the folds of the lieutenant's khaki trousers. A spot, like a bird, came flying across to Reiko and settled on the lap of her white silk kimono.

By the time the lieutenant had at last drawn the sword across to the right side of his stomach, the blade was already cutting shallow and had revealed its naked tip, slippery with blood and grease. But, suddenly stricken by a fit of vomiting, the lieutenant cried out hoarsely. The vomiting made the pain fiercer still, and the stomach, which had thus far remained firm and compact, now abruptly heaved, opening wide its wound, and the entrails burst through, as if the wound too were vomiting. Seemingly ignorant of their master's suffering, the entrails gave an impression of robust health and almost disagreeable vitality as they slipped smoothly out and spilled over into the crotch. The lieutenant's head drooped, his shoulders heaved, his eyes opened to narrow slits, and a thin trickle of saliva dribbled from his mouth. The gold markings on his epaulettes caught the light and glinted.

Blood was scattered everywhere. The lieutenant was soaked in it to his knees, and he saw now in a crumpled and listless posture, one hand on the floor. A raw smell filled the room. The lieutenant, his head drooping, retched repeatedly, and the movement showed vividly in his shoulders. The blade of the sword, now pushed back by the entrails and exposed to its tip, was still in the lieutenant's right hand.

It would be difficult to imagine a more heroic sight than that of the lieutenant at this moment, as he mustered his strength and flung back his head. The movement was performed with sudden violence, and the back of his head struck with a sharp crack against the alcove pillar. Reiko had been sitting until now with her face lowered, gazing in fascination at the tide of blood advancing toward her knees, but the sound took her by surprise and she looked up.

The lieutenant's face was not the face of a living man. The eyes were hollow, the skin parched, the once so lustrous cheeks and lips the color of dried mud. The right hand alone was moving. Laboriously gripping the sword, it hovered shakily in the air like the hand of a marionette and strove to direct the point at the base of the lieutenant's throat. Reiko watched her husband make this last, most heart-rending, futile exertion. Glistening with blood and grease, the point was thrust at the throat again and again. And each time it missed its aim. The strength to guide it was no longer there. The straying point struck the collar and the collar badges. Although its hooks had been unfastened, the stiff military collar had closed together again and was protecting the throat.

Reiko could bear the sight no longer. She tried to go to her husband's help, but she could not stand. She moved through the blood on her knees, and her white skirts grew deep red. Moving to the rear of her husband, she helped no more than by loosening the collar. The quivering blade at last contacted the naked flesh of the throat. At that moment Reiko's impression was that she herself had propelled her husband forward; but that was not the case. It was a movement planned by the lieutenant himself, his last exertion of strength. Abruptly he threw his body at the blade, and the blade pierced his neck, emerging at the nape. There was a tremendous spurt of blood and the lieutenant lay still, cold blue-tinged steel protruding from his neck at the back.

V

Slowly, her socks slippery with blood, Reiko descended the stairway. The upstairs room was now completely still.

Switching on the ground-floor lights, she checked the gas jet and the main gas plug and poured water over the smoldering, half-buried charcoal in the brazier. She stood before the upright mirror in the four-and-a-half mat room and held up her skirts. The bloodstains made it seem as if a bold, vivid pattern was printed across the lower half of her white kimono. When she sat down before the mirror, she was conscious of the dampness and coldness of her husband's blood in the region of her thighs, and she shivered. Then, for a long while, she lingered over her toilet preparations. She applied the rouge generously to her cheeks, and her lips too she painted heavily. This was no longer make-up to please her husband. It was make-up for the world which she would leave behind, and there was a touch of the magnificent and the spectacular in her brushwork. When she rose, the mat before the mirror was wet with blood. Reiko was not concerned about this.

Returning from the toilet, Reiko stood finally on the cement of the porchway. When her husband had bolted the door here last night it had been in preparation for death. For a while she stood immersed in the consideration of a simple problem. Should she now leave the bolt drawn? If she were to lock the door, it could be that the neighbors might not notice their suicide for several days. Reiko did not relish the thought of their two corpses putrefying before discovery. After all, it seemed, it would be best to leave it open. . . . She released the bolt, and also drew open the frosted-glass door a fraction. . . . At once a chill wind blew in. There was no sign of anyone in the midnight streets, and stars glittered ice-cold through the trees in the large house opposite.

Leaving the door as it was, Reiko mounted the stairs. She had walked here and there for some time and her socks were no longer slippery. About halfway up, her nostrils were already assailed by a peculiar smell.

The lieutenant was lying on his face in a sea of blood. The point protruding from his neck seemed to have grown even more prominent than before. Reiko walked heedlessly across the blood. Sitting beside the lieutenant's corpse, she stared intently at the face, which lay on one cheek on the mat. The eyes were opened wide, as if the lieutenant's attention had been attracted by something. She raised the head, folding it in her sleeve, wiped the blood from the lips, and bestowed a last kiss.

Then she rose and took from the closet a new white blanket and a waist cord. To prevent any derangement of her skirts, she wrapped the blanket around her waist and bound it there firmly with the cord.

Reiko sat herself on a spot about one foot distant from the lieutenant's body. Drawing the dagger from her sash, she examined its dully gleaming blade intently, and held it to her tongue. The taste of the polished steel was slightly sweet.

Reiko did not linger. When she thought how the pain which had previously opened such a gulf between herself and her dying husband was now to become a part of her own experience, she saw before her only the joy of herself entering a realm her husband had already made his own. In her husband's agonized face there had been something inexplicable which she was seeing for the first time. Now she would solve that riddle. Reiko sensed that at last she too would be able to taste the true bitterness and sweetness of that great moral principle in which her husband believed. What had until now been tasted only faintly through her husband's example she was about to savor directly with her own tongue.

Reiko rested the point of the blade against the base of her throat. She thrust hard. The wound was only shallow. Her head blazed, and her hands shook uncontrollably. She gave the blade a strong pull sideways. A warm substance flooded into her mouth, and everything before her eyes reddened, in a vision of spouting blood. She gathered her strength and plunged the point of the blade deep into her throat.[2]

[1966]

---

[2] Editors' afterword: On November 25, 1970, Yukio Mishima committed hara-kiri in protest against the "spinelessness" of the Japanese military.

John Barth   *1930–*

LOST IN THE FUNHOUSE

For whom is the funhouse fun? Perhaps for lovers. For Ambrose it is *a place of fear and confusion.* He has come to the seashore with his family for the holiday, *the occasion of their visit is Independence Day, the most important secular holdiay of the United States of America.* A single straight underline is the manuscript mark for italic type, *which in turn* is the printed equivalent to oral emphasis of words and phrases as well as the customary type for titles of complete works, not to mention. Italics are also employed, in fiction stories especially, for "outside," intrusive, or artificial voices, such as radio announcements, the texts of telegrams and newspaper articles, et cetera. They should be used *sparingly.* If passages originally in roman type are italicized by someone repeating them, it's customary to acknowledge the fact. *Italics mine.*

Ambrose was "at that awkward age." His voice came out high-pitched as a child's if he let himself get carried away; to be on the safe side, therefore, he moved and spoke with *deliberate calm* and *adult gravity.* Talking soberly of unimportant or irrelevant matters and listening consciously to the sound of your own voice are useful habits for maintaining control in this difficult interval. *En route* to Ocean City he sat in the back seat of the family car with his brother Peter, age fifteen, and Magda G——, age fourteen, a pretty girl an exquisite young lady, who lived not far from them on B—— Street in the town of D——, Maryland. Initials, blanks, or both were often substituted for proper names in nineteenth-century fiction to enhance the illusion of reality. It is as if the author felt it necessary to delete the names for reasons of tact or legal liability. Interestingly, as with other aspects of realism, it is an *illusion* that is being enhanced, by purely artificial means. Is it likely, does it violate the principle of verisimilitude, that a thirteen-year-old boy could make such a sophisticated observation? A girl of fourteen is *the psychological coeval* of a boy of fifteen or sixteen; a thirteen-year-old boy, therefore, even one precocious in some other respects, might be three years *her emotional junior.*

Thrice a year—on Memorial, Independence, and Labor Days—the family visits Ocean City for the afternoon and evening. When Ambrose and Peter's father was their age, the excursion was made by train, as mentioned in the novel *The 42nd Parallel* by John Dos Passos. Many families from the same neighborhood used to travel together, with dependent relatives and often with Negro servants; schoolfuls of children swarmed through the railway cars; everyone shared everyone else's Maryland fried chicken, Virginia ham, deviled eggs, potato salad, beaten biscuits, iced tea. Nowadays (that is, in 19—, the year of our story) the journey is made by automobile—more comfortably and quickly though without the extra fun though without the *camaraderie* of a general excursion. It's all part of the deterioration of American life, their father declares; Uncle Karl supposes that when the boys take *their* families to Ocean City for the holidays they'll fly in Autogiros. Their mother, sitting in the middle of the front seat like Magda in the second, only with her arms on the seat-back behind the men's shoulders, wouldn't want the good old days back again, the steaming trains and stuffy long dresses; on the other hand she can do without Autogiros, too, if she has to become a grandmother to fly in them.

Description of physical appearance and mannerisms is one of several standard methods of characterization used by writers of fiction. It is also important to "keep the senses operating"; when a detail from one of the five senses, say visual, is "crossed" with a detail from another, say auditory, the reader's imagination is oriented to the scene, perhaps unconsciously. This procedure may be compared to the way surveyors and navigators determine their positions by two or more compass bearings, a process known as triangulation. The brown hair on Abrose's mother's forearms gleamed in the sun like. Though right-handed, she took her arm from the seat-back to press the dashboard cigar lighter for Uncle Karl. When the glass bead in its handle glowed red, the lighter was ready for use. The smell of Uncle Karl's cigar smoke reminded one of. The fragrance of the ocean came strong to the picnic ground where they always stopped for lunch, two miles inland from Ocean City. Having to pause for a full hour almost within sound of the breakers was difficult for Peter and Ambrose when they were younger; even at their present age it was not easy to keep their anticipation, *stimulated by the briny spume*, from turning into short temper. The Irish author James Joyce, in his unusual novel entitled *Ulysses*, now available in this country, uses the adjectives *snot-green* and *scrotum-tightening* to describe the sea. Visual, auditory, tactile, olfactory, gustatory. Peter and Ambrose's father, while steering their black 1936 LaSalle sedan with one hand, could with the other remove the first cigarette from a white pack of Lucky Strikes and, more remarkably, light it with a match forefingered from its book and thumbed against the flint paper without being detached. The matchbook cover merely advertised U.S. War Bonds and Stamps. A fine metaphor, simile, or other figure of speech, in addition to its obvious "first-order" relevance to the thing it describes, will be seen upon reflection to have a second order of significance: it may be drawn from the *milieu* of the action, for example, or be particularly appropriate to the sensibility of the narrator, even hinting to the reader things of which the narrative is unaware; or it may cast further and subtler lights upon the thing it describes, sometimes ironically qualifying the more evident sense of the comparison.

To say that Ambrose's and Peter's mother was *pretty* is to accomplish nothing; the reader may acknowledge the proposition, but his imagination is not engaged. Besides, Magda was also pretty, yet in an altogether different way. Although she lived on B_____ Street she had very good manners and did better than average in school. Her figure was very well developed for her age. Her right hand lay casually on the plush upholstery of the seat, very near Ambrose's left leg, on which his own hand rested. The space between their legs, between her right and his left leg, was out of the line of sight of anyone sitting on the other side of Magda, as well as anyone glancing into the rearview mirror. Uncle Karl's face resembled Peter's—rather, vice versa. Both had dark hair and eyes, short husky statures, deep voices. Magda's left hand was probably in a similar position on her left side. The boy's father is difficult to describe; no particular feature of his appearance or manner stood out. He wore glasses and was principal of a T_____ County grade school. Uncle Karl was a masonry contractor.

Although Peter must have known as well as Ambrose that the latter, because of his position in the car, would be the first to see the electrical towers of the power plant at V_____, the halfway point of their trip, he leaned forward and slightly through the center of the car and pretended to be looking for them through the flat pinewoods and tuckahoe creeks[1] along the highway. For as long as the boys could remember, "looking for the Towers" had been a feature of the first half of their excursions to Ocean City, "looking for the standpipe" of the second. Though the game was childish, their mother preserved the tradition of rewarding the first to see the Towers with a candy-bar or piece of fruit. She insisted now that Magda play the game; the prize, she said, was "something hard to get nowadays." Ambrose decided not to join in; he sat far back in his seat. Magda, like Peter, leaned forward. Two sets of straps were discernible through the shoulders of her sun dress; the inside right one, a brassiere-strap, was fastened or shortened with a small safety pin. The right armpit of her dress, presumably the left as well, was damp with perspiration. The simple strategy for being first to espy the Towers, which Ambrose had understood by the age of four, was to sit on the right-hand side of the car. Whoever sat there, however, had also to put up with the worst of the sun, and so Ambrose, without mentioning the matter, chose sometimes one and sometimes the other. Not impossibly Peter had never caught on to the trick, or thought that his brother hadn't simply because Ambrose on occasion preferred shade to a Baby Ruth or tangerine.

The shade-sun situation didn't apply to the front seat, owing to the windshield; if anything the driver got more sun, since the person on the passenger side not only was shaded below by the door and dashboard but might swing down his sunvisor all the way too.

"Is that them?" Magda asked. Ambrose's mother teased the boys for letting Magda win, insinuating that "somebody [had] a girlfriend." Peter and Ambrose's father reached a long thin arm across their mother to butt his cigarette in the dashboard ashtray, under the lighter. The prize this time for seeing the Towers first was a banana. Their mother bestowed it after chiding their father for wasting a half-smoked cigarette when everything was so scarce. Magda, to take the prize, moved her hand from so near Ambrose's that he could have touched it as though accidentally. She offered to share the prize, things like that were hard to find; but everyone insisted it was hers alone. Ambrose's mother sang an iambic trimeter couplet from a popular song, femininely rhymed:

> "What's good is in the Army;
> What's left will never harm me."

Uncle Karl tapped his cigar ash out the ventilator window; some particles were sucked by the slipstream back into the car through the rear window on the passenger side. Magda demonstrated her ability to hold a banana in one hand and peel it with her teeth. She still sat forward; Ambrose pushed his glasses back onto the bridge of his nose with his left hand, which he then negligently let fall to the seat cushion immediately behind her. He even permitted the single hair, gold, on the second joint of his thumb to brush the fabric of her skirt. Should she have sat back at that instant, his hand would have been caught under her.

Plush upholstery prickles uncomfortably through gabardine slacks in the July sun. The function of the *beginning* of a story is to introduce the principal

[1] Creeks bordered by a distinctive type of leafy plant.

characters, establish their initial relationships, set the scene for the main action, expose the background of the situation if necessary, plant motifs and fore-shadowings where appropriate, and initiate the first complication or whatever of the "rising action." Actually, if one imagines a story called "The Funhouse," or "Lost in the Funhouse," the details of the drive to Ocean City don't seem especially relevant. The *beginning* should recount the events between Ambrose's first sight of the funhouse early in the afternoon and his entering it with Magda and Peter in the evening. The *middle* would narrate all relevant events from the time he goes in to the time he loses his way; middles have the double and contradictory function of delaying the climax while at the same time prepar-ing the reader for it and fetching him to it. Then the *ending* would tell what Ambrose does while he's lost, how he finally finds his way out, and what every-body makes of the experience. So far there's been no real dialogue, very little sensory detail, and nothing in the way of a *theme.* And a long time has gone by already without anything happening; it makes a person wonder. We haven't reached Ocean City yet: we will never get out of the funhouse.

The more closely an author identifies with the narrator, literally or metaphori-cally, the less advisable it is, as a rule, to use the first-person narrative viewpoint. Once three years previously the young people *aforementioned* played Niggers and Masters in the backyard; when it was Ambrose's turn to be Master and theirs to be Niggers Peter had to go serve his evening papers; Ambrose was afraid to punish Magda alone, but she led him to the whitewashed Torture Chamber between the woodshed and the privy in the Slaves Quarters; there she knelt sweating among bamboo rakes and dusty Mason jars, pleadingly embraced his knees, and while bees droned in the lattice as if on an ordinary summer afternoon, purchased clemency at a surprising price set by herself. Doubtless she remembered nothing of this event; Ambrose on the other hand seemed unable to forget the least detail of his life. He even recalled how, standing beside himself with awed impersonality in the reeky heat, he'd stared the while at an empty cigar box in which Uncle Karl kept stone-cutting chisels: beneath the words *El Producto,* a laureled, loose-toga'd lady regarded the sea from a marble bench; beside her, forgotten or not yet turned to, was a five-stringed lyre. Her chin reposed on the back of her right hand; her left depended negligently from the bench-arm. The lower half of scene and lady was peeled away; the words EXAMINED BY _____ were inked there into the wood. Nowadays cigar boxes are made of pasteboard. Ambrose wondered what Magda would have done. Ambrose wondered what Magda would do when she sat back on his hand as he resolved she should. Be angry. Make a teasing joke of it. Give no sign at all. For a long time she leaned forward, playing cow-poker with Peter against Uncle Karl and Mother and watching for the first sign of Ocean City. At nearly the same instant, picnic ground and Ocean City standpipe hove into view; an Amoco filling station on their side of the road cost Mother and Uncle Karl fifty cows and the game; Magda bounced back, clapping her right hand on Mother's right arm; Ambrose moved clear "in the nick of time."

At this rate our hero, at this rate our protagonist will remain in the funhouse forever. Narrative ordinarily consists of alternating dramatization and summa-rization. One symptom of nervous tension, paradoxically, is repeated and vio-lent yawning; neither Peter nor Magda nor Uncle Karl nor Mother reacted in this manner. Although they were no longer small children, Peter and Am-brose were each given a dollar to spend on boardwalk amusements in addition to what money of their own they'd brought along. Magda too, though she protested she had ample spending money. The boys' mother made a little scene out of distributing the bills; she pretended that her sons and Magda were small children and cautioned them not to spend the sum too quickly or in one place. Magda promised with a merry laugh and, having both hands free, took the bill with her left. Peter laughed also and pledged in a falsetto to be a good boy. His imitation of a child was not clever. The boy's father was tall and thin, balding, fair-complexioned. Assertions of that sort are not effective; the reader may acknowledge the proposition, but. We should be much farther along than we are; something has gone wrong; not much of this preliminary rambling seems relevant. Yet everyone begins in the same place; how is it that most go along without difficulty but a few lose their way?

"Stay out from under the boardwalk," Uncle Karl growled from the side of his mouth. The boys' mother pushed his shoulder *in mock annoyance.* They were all standing before Fat May the Laughing Lady who advertised the funhouse. Larger than life, Fat May mechanically shook, rocked on her heels, slapped her thighs while recorded laughter—uproarious, female—came amplified from a hidden loudspeaker. It chuckled, wheezed, wept; tried in vain to catch its breath; tittered, groaned, exploded raucous and anew. You couldn't hear it without laughing yourself, no matter how you felt. Father came back from talking to a Coast-Guardsman on duty and reported that the surf was spoiled with crude oil from tankers recently torpedoed offshore. Lumps of it, difficult to remove, made tarry tidelines on the beach and stuck on swimmers. Many bathed in the surf nevertheless and came out speckled; others paid to use a municipal pool and only sunbathed on the beach. We would do the latter. We would do the latter. We would do the latter.

Under the boardwalk, matchbook covers, grainy other things. What is the story's theme? Ambrose is ill. He perspires in the dark passages; candied apples-on-a-stick, delicious-looking, disappointing to eat. Funhouses need men's and ladies' rooms at intervals. Others perhaps have also vomited in corners and corridors; may even have had bowel movements liable to be stepped in in the dark. The word *fuck* suggests suction and/or and/or flatulence. Mother and Father; grandmothers and grandfathers on both sides; great-grandmothers and great-grandfathers on four sides, et cetera. Count a generation as thirty years: in approximately the year when Lord Baltimore was granted charter to the province of Maryland by Charles I, five hundred twelve women—English, Welsh, Bavarian, Swiss—of every class and character, received into themselves the penises the intromittent organs of five hundred twelve men, ditto, in every circumstance and posture, to conceive the five hundred twelve ancestors of the two hundred fifty-six ancestors of the et cetera et cetera et cetera et cetera et cetera et cetera et cetera of the author, of the narrator, of this story, *Lost in the Funhouse.* In alleyways, ditches, canopy beds, pinewoods, bridal suites, ship's cabins, coach-and-fours, coaches-and-four, sultry toolsheds; on the cold sand under boardwalks, littered with *El Producto* cigar butts, treasured with Lucky Strike cigarette stubs, Coca-Cola caps, gritty turds, cardboard lollipop sticks, matchbook covers warning that A Slip of the Lip Can Sink a Ship.[2] The shluppish whisper, continuous as seawash round the globe, tidelike falls and rises with the circuit of dawn and dusk.

Magda's teeth. She *was* left-handed. Perspiration. They've gone all the way,

---

[2] One of many World War II slogans designed to make Americans cautious about sharing information that might be of value to the enemy.

through, Magda and Peter, they've been waiting for hours with Mother and Uncle Karl while Father searches for his lost son; they draw french-fried potatoes from a paper cup and shake their heads. They've named the children they'll one day have and bring to Ocean City on holidays. Can spermatozoa properly be thought of as male animalcules when there are no female spermatozoa? They grope through hot, dark windings, past Love's Tunnel's fearsome obstacles. Some perhaps lose their way.

Peter suggested then and there that they do the funhouse; he had been through it before, so had Magda, Ambrose hadn't and suggested, his voice cracking on account of Fat May's laughter, that they swim first. All were chuckling, couldn't help it; Ambrose's and Peter's father came up grinning like a lunatic with two boxes of syrup-coated popcorn, one for Mother, one for Magda; the men were to help themselves. Ambrose walked on Magda's right; being by nature left-handed, she carried the box in her left hand. Up front the situation was reversed.

"What are you limping for?" Magda inquired of Ambrose. He supposed in a husky tone that his foot had gone to sleep in the car. Her teeth flashed. "Pins and needles?" It was the honeysuckle on the lattice of the former privy that drew the bees. Imagine being stung there. How long is this going to take?

The adults decided to forgo the pool; but Uncle Karl insisted they change into swimsuits and do the beach. "He wants to watch the pretty girls," Peter teased, and ducked behind Magda from Uncle Karl's pretended wrath. "You've got all the pretty girls you need right here," Magda declared, and Mother said: "Now that's the gospel truth." Magda scolded Peter, who reached over her shoulder to sneak some popcorn. "Your brother and father aren't getting any." Uncle Karl wondered if they were going to have fireworks that night, what with the shortages. It wasn't the shortages, Mr. M_____ replied; Ocean City had fireworks from pre-war. But it was too risky on account of the enemy submarines, some people thought.

"Don't seem like Fourth of July without fireworks," said Uncle Karl. The inverted tag in dialogue writing is still considered permissible with proper names or epithets, but sounds old-fashioned with personal pronouns. "We'll have 'em again soon enough," predicted the boys' father. Their mother declared she could do without fireworks: they reminded her too much of the real thing. Their father said all the more reason to shoot off a few now and again. Uncle Karl asked *rhetorically* who needed reminding, just look at people's hair and skin.

"The oil, yes," said Mrs. M_____.

Ambrose had a pain in his stomach and so didn't swim but enjoyed watching the others. He and his father burned red easily. Magda's figure was exceedingly well developed for her age. She too declined to swim, and got mad, and became angry when Peter attempted to drag her into the pool. She always swam, he insisted; what did she mean not swim? Why did a person come to Ocean City?

"Maybe I want to lay here with Ambrose," Magda teased.

Nobody likes a pedant.

"Aha," said Mother. Peter grabbed Magda by one ankle and ordered Ambrose to grab the other. She squealed and rolled over on the beach blanket. Ambrose pretended to help hold her back. Her tan was darker than even Mother's and Peter's. "Help out, Uncle Karl!" Peter cried. Uncle Karl went to seize the other ankle. Inside the top of her swimsuit, however, you could see the line where the sunburn ended and, when she hunched her shoulders and squealed again, one nipple's auburn edge. Mother made them behave themselves. "*You should certainly know,*" she said to Uncle Karl. Archly. "That when a lady says she doesn't feel like swimming, a gentleman doesn't ask questions." Uncle Karl said excuse *him;* Mother winked at Magda; Ambrose blushed; stupid Peter kept saying "Phooey on *feel like!*" and tugging at Magda's ankle; then even he got the point, and cannonballed with a holler into the pool.

"I swear," Magda said, in mock *in feigned* exasperation.

The diving would make a suitable literary symbol. To go off the high board you had to wait in a line along the poolside and up the ladder. Fellows tickled girls and goosed one another and shouted to the ones at the top to hurry up, or razzed them for bellyfloppers. Once on the springboard some took a great while posing or clowning or deciding on a dive or getting up their nerve; others ran right off. Especially among the younger fellows the idea was to strike the funniest pose or do the craziest stunt as you fell, a thing that got harder to do as you kept on and kept on. But whether you hollered *Geronimo!* or *Sieg heil!*,[3] held your nose or "rode a bicycle," pretended to be shot or did a perfect jacknife or changed your mind halfway down and ended up with nothing, it was over in two seconds, after all that wait. Spring, pose, splash. Spring, neat-o, splash. Spring, aw fooey, splash.

The grown-ups had gone on; Ambrose wanted to converse with Magda; she was remarkably well developed for her age; it was said that that came from rubbing with a turkish towel, and there were other theories. Ambrose could think of nothing to say except how good a diver Peter was, who was showing off for her benefit. You could pretty well tell by looking at their bathing suits and arm muscles how far along the different fellows were. Ambrose was glad he hadn't gone in swimming, the cold water shrank you up so. Magda pretended to be uninterested in the diving; she probably weighed as much as he did. If you knew your way around in the funhouse like your own bedroom, you could wait until a girl came along and then slip away without every getting caught, even if her boyfriend was right with her. She'd think *he* did it! It would be better to be the boyfriend, and act outraged, and tear the funhouse apart.

Not act; *be.*

"He's a master diver," Ambrose said. In feigned admiration. "You really have to slave away at it to get that good." What would it matter anyhow if he asked her right out whether she remembered, even teased her with it as Peter would have?

There's no point in going farther; this isn't getting anybody anywhere; they haven't even come to the funhouse yet. Ambrose is off the track, in some new or old part of the place that's not supposed to be used; he strayed into it by some one-in-a-million chance, like the time the roller-coaster car left the tracks in the nineteen-teens against all the laws of physics and sailed over the boardwalk in the dark. And they can't locate him because they don't know where to look. Even the designer and operator have forgotten this other part, that winds around on itself like a whelk shell. That winds around the right part like the snakes on Mercury's caduceus.[4] Some people, perhaps don't "hit

---

[3] "Geronimo!" was the battle cry used by American paratroopers, reportedly in reference to the famous Indian chief; "Sieg Heil!"—"Hail to Victory!"—was the traditional Nazi salute.

[4] The symbolic staff carried by the Roman god Mercury, the messenger god, bearing two entwined snakes crowned by a pair of wings.

their stride" until their twenties, when the growing-up business is over and women appreciate other things besides wisecracks and teasing and strutting. Peter didn't have one-tenth the imagination *he* had, not one-tenth. Peter did this naming-their-children thing as a joke, making up names like Aloysius and Murgatroyd, but Ambrose knew *exactly* how it would feel to be married and have children of your own, and be a loving husband and father, and go comfortably to work in the mornings and to bed with your wife at night, and wake up with her there. With a breeze coming through the sash and birds and mockingbirds singing in the Chinese-cigar trees. His eyes watered, there aren't enough ways to say that. He would be quite famous in his line of work. Whether Magda was his wife or not, one evening when he was wise-lined and gray at the temples he'd smile gravely, at a fashionable dinner party, and remind her of his youthful passion. The time they went with his family to Ocean City; the *erotic fantasies* he used to have about her. How long ago it seemed, and childish! Yet tender, too, *n'est-ce pas?*[5] Would she have imagined that the world-famous whatever remembered how many strings were on the lyre on the bench beside the girl on the label of the cigar box he'd stared at in the toolshed at age ten while she, age eleven. Even then he had felt *wise beyond his years;* he'd stroked her hair and said in his deepest voice and correctest English, as to a dear child: "I shall never forget this moment."

But though he had breathed heavily, groaned as if ecstatic, what he'd really felt throughout was an odd detachment, as though someone else were Master. Strive as he might to be transported, he heard his mind take notes upon the scene: *This is what they call* passion. *I am experiencing it.* Many of the digger machines were out of order in the penny arcades and could not be repaired or replaced for the duration. Moreover, the prizes, made now in USA, were less interesting than formerly, pasteboard items for the most part, and some of the machines wouldn't work on white pennies.[6] The gypsy fortune-teller machine might have provided a foreshadowing of the climax of this story if Ambrose had operated it. It was even dilapidateder than most: the silver coating was worn off the brown metal handles, the glass windows around the dummy were cracked and taped, her kerchiefs and silks long-faded. If a man lived by himself, he could take a department-store mannequin with flexible joints and modify her in certain ways. *However:* by the time he was that old he'd have a real woman. There was a machine that stamped your name around a white-metal coin with a star in the middle: *A_____.* His son would be the second, and when the lad reached thirteen or so he would put a strong arm around his shoulder and tell him calmly: "It is perfectly normal. We have all been through it. It will not last forever." Nobody knew how to be what they were right. He'd smoke a pipe, teach his son how to fish and softcrab, assure him he needn't worry about himself. Magda would certainly give, Magda would certainly yield a great deal of milk, although guilty of occasional solecisms. It don't taste so bad. Suppose the lights came on now!

The day wore on. You think you're yourself, but there are other persons in you. Ambrose gets hard when Ambrose doesn't want to, *and obversely.* Ambrose watches them disagree; Ambrose watches him watch. In the funhouse mirror-room you can't see yourself go on forever, because no matter how you stand,

---

[5] A rhetorical question, meaning "Isn't that right?" or "Don't you agree?"

[6] In 1943 the government minted zinc-coated steel pennies in an effort to conserve copper needed for the war effort.

your head gets in the way. Even if you had a glass periscope, the image of your eye would cover up the thing you really wanted to see. The police will come; there'll be a story in the papers. That must be where it happened. Unless he can find a surprise exit, an unofficial backdoor or escape hatch opening on an alley, say, and then stroll up to the family in front of the funhouse and ask where everybody's been; *he's* been out of the place for ages. That's just where it happened, in that last lighted room: Peter and Magda found the right exit; he found one that you weren't supposed to find and strayed off into the works somewhere. In a perfect funhouse you'd be able to go only one way, like the divers off the highboard; getting lost would be impossible; the doors and halls would work like minnow traps or the valves in veins.

On account of German U-boats,[7] Ocean City was "browned out": streetlights were shaded on the seaward side; shop-windows and boardwalk amusement places were kept dim, not to silhouette tankers and Liberty-ships[8] for torpedoing. In a short story about Ocean City, Maryland, during World War II, the author could make use of the image of sailors on leave in the penny arcades and shooting galleries, sighting through the crosshairs of toy machine guns at swastika'd subs, while out in the black Atlantic a U-boat skipper squints through his periscope at real ships outlined by the glow of penny arcades. After dinner the family strolled back to the amusement end of the boardwalk. The boys' father had burnt as red as always and was masked with Noxzema, a minstrel in reverse. The grown-ups stood at the end of the boardwalk where the Hurricane of '33 had cut an inlet from ocean to Assawoman Bay.

"Pronounced with a long *o*," Uncle Karl reminded Magda with a wink. His shirt sleeves were rolled up; Mother punched his brown biceps with the arrowed heart on it and said his mind was naughty. Fat May's laugh came suddenly from the funhouse, as if she'd just got the joke; the family laughed too at the coincidence. Ambrose went under the boardwalk to search for out-of-town matchbook covers with the aid of his pocket flashlight; he looked out from the edge of the North American continent and wondered how far their laughter carried over the water. Spies in rubber rafts; survivors in lifeboats. If the joke had been beyond his understanding, he could have said: *"The laughter was over his head."* And let the reader see the serious wordplay on second reading.

He turned the flashlight on and then off at once even before the woman whooped. He sprang away, heart athud, dropping the light. What had the man grunted? Perspiration drenched and chilled him by the time he scrambled up to the family. "See anything?" his father asked. His voice wouldn't come; he shrugged and violenty brushed sand from his pants legs.

"Let's ride the old flying horses!" Magda cried. I'll never be an author. It's been forever already, everybody's gone home, Ocean City's deserted, the ghost-crabs are tickling across the beach and down the littered cold streets. And the empty halls of clapboard hotels and abandoned funhouses. A tidal wave; an enemy air raid; a monster-crab swelling like an island from the sea. *The inhabitants fled in terror.* Magda clung to his trouser leg; he alone knew the maze's secret. "He gave his life that we might live," said Uncle Karl with a scowl of pain, as he. The fellow's hands had been tattooed; the woman's legs, the woman's fat white legs had. *An astonishing coincidence.* He yearned to tell Peter. He wanted to throw up for excitement. They hadn't even chased him. He wished he were dead.

---

[7] Submarines.   [8] The name given to mass-produced cargo ships.

One possible ending would be to have Ambrose come across another lost person in the dark. They'd match their wits together against the funhouse, struggle like Ulysses[9] past obstacle after obstacle, help and encourage each other. Or a girl. By the time they found the exit they'd be closest friends, sweethearts if it were a girl; they'd know each other's inmost souls, be bound together *by the cement of shared adventure;* then they'd emerge into the light and it would turn out that his friend was a Negro. A blind girl. President Roosevelt's son. Ambrose's former archenemy.

Shortly after the mirror room he'd groped along a musty corridor, his heart already misgiving him at the absence of phosphorescent arrows and other signs. He'd found a crack of light—not a door, it turned out, but a seam between the plyboard wall panels—and squinting up to it, espied a small old man, *in appearance not unlike* the photographs at home of Ambrose's late grandfather, nodding upon a stool beneath a bare, speckled bulb. A crude panel of toggle- and knife-switches hung beside the open fuse box near his head; elsewhere in the little room were wooden levers and ropes belayed to boat cleats. At the time, Ambrose wasn't lost enough to rap or call; later he couldn't find that crack. Now it seemed to him that he'd possibly dozed off for a few minutes somewhere along the way; certainly he was exhausted from the afternoon's sunshine and the evening's problems; he couldn't be sure he hadn't dreamed part or all of the sight. Had an old black wall fan droned like bees and shimmied two flypaper streamers? Had the funhouse operator—gentle, somewhat sad and tired-appearing, in expression not unlike the photographs at home of Ambrose's late Uncle Konrad—murmured in his sleep? Is there really such a person as Ambrose, or is he a figment of the author's imagination? Was it Assawoman Bay or Sinepuxent? Are there other errors of fact in this fiction? Was there another sound besides the little slap of thigh on ham, like water sucking at the chine-boards of a skiff?

When you're lost, the smartest thing to do is stay put till you're found, hollering if necessary. But to holler guarantees humiliation as well as rescue; keeping silent permits some saving of face—you can act surprised at the fuss when your rescuers find you and swear you weren't lost, if they do. What's more you might find your own way yet, *however belatedly.*

"Don't tell me your foot's still aleep!" Magda exclaimed as the three young people walked from the inlet to the area set aside for ferris wheels, carrousels, and other carnival rides, they having decided in favor of the vast and ancient merry-go-round instead of the funhouse. What a sentence, everything was wrong from the outset. People don't know what to make of him, he doesn't know what to make of himself, he's only thirteen, *athletically and socially inept,* not astonishingly bright, but there are antennae; he has . . . some sort of receivers in his head; things speak to him, he understands more than he should, the world winks at him through its objects, grabs grinning at his coat. Everybody else is in on some secret he doesn't know; they've forgotten to tell him. Through simple *procrastination* his mother put off his baptism until this year. Everyone else had it done as a baby; he'd assumed the same of himself, as had his mother, so she claimed, until it was time for him to join Grace Methodist-Protestant and the oversight came out. He was mortified, but pitched sleepless through his private catechizing, intimidated by the ancient mysteries, a thirteen year old would never say that, resolved to experience conversion like St.

[9] The Roman name of Odysseus, the hero of Homer's *Odyssey.*

Augustine.[10] When the water touched his brow and Adam's sin left him, he contrived by a strain like defecation to bring tears into his eyes—but felt nothing. There was some simple, radical difference about him; he hoped it was genius, feared it was madness, devoted himself to amiability and inconspicuousness. Alone on the seawall near his house he was seized by the terrifying transports he'd thought to find in toolshed, in Communion-cup. The grass was alive! The town, the river, himself, were not imaginary; time roared in his ears like wind; the world was *going on!* This part ought to be dramatized. The Irish author James Joyce once wrote. Ambrose M_____ is going to scream.

There is no *texture of rendered sensory detail,* for one thing. The faded distorting mirrors beside Fat May; the impossibility of choosing a mount when one had but a single ride on the great carrousel; the *vertigo attendant on his recognition* that Ocean City was worn out, the place of fathers and grandfathers, strawboatered men and parasoled ladies survived by their amusements. Money spent, the three paused at Peter's insistence beside Fat May to watch the girls get their skirts blown up. The object was to tease Magda, who said: "I swear, Peter M_____, you've got a one-track mind! Amby and me aren't *interested* in such things." In the tumbling-barrel, too, just inside the Devil's-mouth entrance to the funhouse, the girls were upended and their boyfriends and others could see up their dresses if they cared to. Which was the whole point, Ambrose realized. Of the entire funhouse! If you looked around, you noticed that almost all the people on the boardwalk were paired off into couples except the small children; in a way, that was the whole point of Ocean City! If you had X-ray eyes and could see everything going on at that instant under the boardwalk and in all the hotel rooms and cars and alleyways, you'd realize that all that normally *showed,* like restaurants and dance halls and clothing and test-your-strength machines, was merely preparation and intermission. Fat May screamed.

Because he watched the goings-on from the corner of his eye, it was Ambrose who spied the half-dollar on the boardwalk near the tumbling-barrel. Losers weepers. The first time he'd heard some people moving through a corridor not far away, just after he'd lost sight of the crack of light, he'd decided not to call to them, for fear they'd guess he was scared and poke fun; it sounded like roughnecks; he'd hoped they'd come by and he could follow in the dark without their knowing. Another time he'd heard just one person, unless he imagined it, bumping along as if on the other side of the plywood; perhaps Peter coming back for him, or Father, or Magda lost too. Or the owner and operator of the funhouse. He'd called out once, as though merrily: "Anybody know where the heck we are?" But the query was too stiff, his voice cracked, when the sounds stopped he was terrified: maybe it was a queer who waited for fellows to get lost, or a longhaired filthy monster that lived in some cranny of the funhouse. He stood rigid for hours it seemed like, scarcely respiring. His future was shockingly clear, in outline. He tried holding his breath to the point of unconsciousness. There ought to be a button you could push to end your life absolutely without pain; disappear in a flick, like turning out a light. He would push it instantly! He despised Uncle Karl. But he despised his father too, for not being what he was supposed to be. Perhaps his father hated *his* father, and so on, and his son would hate him, and so on. Instantly!

[10] St. Augustine's (354–430) conversion to Christianity in 386 was inspired by his reading of the writings of St. Ambrose (340?–397). St. Ambrose was Bishop of Milan and the friend and adviser of three Roman emperors.

Naturally he didn't have nerve enough to ask Magda to go through the funhouse with him. With incredible nerve and to everyone's surprise he invited Magda, quietly and politely, to go through the funhouse with him. "I warn you, I've never been through it before," he added, *laughing easily;* "but I reckon we can manage somehow. The important thing to remember, after all, is that it's meant to be a *fun*house; that is, a place of amusement. If people really got lost or injured or too badly frightened in it, the owner'd go out of business. There'd even be lawsuits. No character in a work of fiction can make a speech this long without interruption or acknowledgment from the other characters."

Mother teased Uncle Karl: "Three's a crowd, I always heard." But actually Ambrose was relieved that Peter now had a quarter too. Nothing was what it looked like. Every instant, under the surface of the Atlantic Ocean, millions of living animals devoured one another. Pilots were falling in flames over Europe; women were being forcibly raped in the South Pacific. His father should have taken him aside and said: "There is a simple secret to getting through the funhouse, as simple as being first to see the Towers. Here it is. Peter does not know it; neither does your Uncle Karl. You and I are different. Not surprisingly, you've often wished you weren't. Don't think I haven't noticed how unhappy your childhood has been! But you'll understand, when I tell you, why it had to be kept secret until now. And you won't regret not being like your brother and your uncle. *On the contrary!*" If you knew all the stories behind all the people on the boardwalk, you'd see that *nothing* was what it looked like. Husbands and wives often hated each other; parents didn't necessarily love their children; et cetera. A child took things for granted because he had nothing to compare his life to and everybody acted as if things were as they should be. Therefore each saw himself as the hero of the story, when the truth might turn out to be that he's the villain, or the coward. And there wasn't one thing you could do about it!

Hunchbacks, fat ladies, fools—that no one chose what he was was unbearable. In the movies he'd meet a beautiful young girl in the funhouse; they'd have hairs-breadth escapes from real dangers; he'd do and say the right things; she also; in the end they'd be lovers; their dialogue lines would match up; he'd be perfectly at ease; she'd not only like him well enough, she'd think he was *marvelous;* she'd lie awake thinking about *him,* instead of vice versa— the way *his* face looked in different lights and how he stood and exactly what he'd said—and yet that would be only one small episode in his wonderful life, among many many others. Not a *turning point* at all. What had happened in the toolshed was nothing. He hated, he loathed his parents! One reason for not writing a lost-in-the-funhouse story is that either everybody's felt what Ambrose feels, in which case it goes without saying, or else no normal person feels such things, in which case Ambrose is a freak. "Is anything more tiresome, in fiction, than the problems of sensitive adolescents?" And it's all too long and rambling, as if the author. For all a person knows the first time through, the end could be just around any corner; perhaps, *not impossibly* it's been within reach any number of times. On the other hand he may be scarcely past the start, with everything yet to get through, an intolerable idea.

Fill in: His father's raised eyebrows when he announced his decision to do the funhouse with Magda. Ambrose understands now, but didn't then, that his father was wondering whether he knew what the funhouse was *for*—especially since he didn't object, as he should have, when Peter decided to come along too. The ticket-woman, witchlike, mortifying him when inadvertently he gave her his name-coin instead of the half-dollar, then unkindly calling Magda's attention to the birthmark on his temple: "Watch out for him, girlie, he's a marked man!" She wasn't even cruel, he understood, only vulgar and insensitive. Somewhere in the world there was a young woman with such splendid understanding that she'd see him entire, like a poem or story, and find his words so valuable after all that when he confessed his apprehensions she would explain why they were in fact the very things that made him precious to her . . . and to Western Civilization! There was no such girl, the simple truth being. Violent yawns as they approached the mouth. Whispered advice from an old-timer on a bench near the barrel: "Go crabwise and ye'll get an eyeful without upsetting!" Composure vanished at the first pitch: Peter hollered joyously, Magda tumbled, shrieked, clutched her skirt; Ambrose scrambled crabwise, tight-lipped with terror, was soon out, watched his dropped name-coin slide among the couples. Shame-faced he saw that to get through expeditiously was not the point; Peter feigned assistance in order to trip Magda up, shouted "I see Christmas!" when her legs went flying. The old man, his latest betrayer, cracked approval. A dim hall then of black-thread cobwebs and recorded gibber: he took Magda's elbow to steady her against revolving discs set in the slanted floor to throw your feet out from under, and explained to her in a calm, deep voice his theory that each phase of the funhouse was triggered either automatically, by a series of photoelectric devices, or else manually by operators stationed at peepholes. But he lost his voice thrice as the discs unbalanced him; Magda was anyhow squealing; but at one point she clutched him about the waist to keep from falling, and her right cheek pressed for a moment against his belt-buckle. Heroically he drew her up, it was his chance to clutch her close as if for support and say: "I love you." He even put an arm lightly about the small of her back before a sailor-and-girl pitched into them from behind, sorely treading his left big toe and knocking Magda asprawl with them. The sailor's girl was a string-haired hussy with a loud laugh and light blue drawers; Ambrose realized that he wouldn't have said "I love you" anyhow, and was smitten with self-contempt. How much better it would be to be that common sailor! A wiry little Seaman 3rd, the fellow squeezed a girl to each side and stumbled hilarious into the mirror room, closer to Magda in thirty seconds than Ambrose had got in thirteen years. She giggled at something the fellow said to Peter; she drew her hair from her eyes with a movement so womanly it struck Ambrose's heart; Peter's smacking her backside then seemed particularly coarse. But Magda made a pleased indignant face and cried, "All right for *you*, mister!" and pursued Peter into the maze without a backward glance. The sailor followed after, leisurely, drawing his girl against his hip; Ambrose understood not only that they were all so relieved to be rid of his burdensome company that they didn't even notice his absence, but that he himself shared their relief. Stepping from the treacherous passage at last into the mirror-maze, he saw once again, more clearly than ever, how readily he deceived himself into supposing he was a person. He even foresaw, wincing at his dreadful self-knowledge, that he would repeat the deception, at ever-rarer intervals, all his wretched life, so fearful were the alternatives. Fame, madness, suicide; perhaps all three. It's not believable that so young a boy could articulate that reflection, and in fiction the merely true must always yield to the plausible. Moreover, the symbolism is in places heavy-footed. Yet Ambrose M____ understood, as few adults do, that the famous loneliness of the great was no popular myth but a general truth—furthermore, that it was as much cause as effect.

All the preceding except the last few sentences is exposition that should've been done earlier or interspersed with the present action instead of lumped together. No reader would put up with so much with such *prolixity*. It's interesting that Ambrose's father, though presumably an intelligent man (as indicated by his role as grade-school principal), neither encouraged nor discouraged his sons at all in any way—as if he either didn't care about them or cared all right but didn't know how to act. If this fact should contribute to one of them's becoming a celebrated but wretchedly unhappy scientist, was it a good thing or not? He too might someday face the question; it would be useful to know whether it had tortured his father for years, for example, or never once crossed his mind.

In the maze two important things happened. First, our hero found a name-coin someone else had lost or discarded: *AMBROSE,* suggestive of the famous lightship[11] and of his late grandfather's favorite dessert,[12] which his mother used to prepare on special occasions out of coconut, oranges, grapes, and what else. Second, as he wondered at the endless replication of his image in the mirrors, second, as he *lost himself in the reflection* that the necessity for an observer makes perfect observation impossible, better make him eighteen at least, yet that would render other things unlikely, he heard Peter and Magda chuckling somewhere together in the maze. "Here!" "No, here!" they shouted to each other; Peter said, "Where's Amby?" Magda murmured. "Amb?" Peter called. In a pleased, friendly voice. He didn't reply. The truth was, his brother was a *happy-go-lucky youngster* who'd've been better off with a regular brother of his own, but who seldom complained of his lot and was generally cordial. Ambrose's throat ached; there aren't enough different ways to say that. He stood quietly while the two young people giggled and thumped through the glittering maze, hurrah'd their discovery of its exit, cried out in joyful alarm at what next beset them. Then he set his mouth and followed after, as he supposed, took a wrong turn, strayed into the pass *wherein he lingers yet.*

The action of conventional dramatic narrative may be represented by a diagram called Freitag's Triangle:[13]

or more accurately by a variant of that diagram:

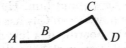

in which *AB* represents the exposition, *B* the introduction of conflict, *BC* the "rising action," complication, or development of the conflict, *C* the climax, or turn of the action, *CD* the dénouement, or resolution of the conflict. While

---

[11] The Ambrose lightship, protecting the entrance to New York harbor.

[12] Ambrosia, a dessert made from oranges and shredded coconut.

[13] Named after German critic and novelist Gustav Freytag (1816–1895) who described the conventions of dramatic plot.

there is no reason to regard this pattern as an absolute necessity, like many other conventions it became conventional because great numbers of people over many years learned by trial and error that it was effective; one ought not to forsake it, therefore, unless one wishes to forsake as well the effect of drama or has clear cause to feel that deliberate violation of the "normal" pattern can better can better effect that effect. This can't go on much longer; it can go on forever. He died telling stories to himself in the dark; years later, when that vast unsuspected area of the funhouse came to light, the first expedition found his skeleton in one of its labyrinthine corridors and mistook it for part of the entertainment. He died of starvation telling himself stories in the dark; but unbeknownst unbeknownst to him, an assistant operator of the funhouse, happening to overhear him, crouched just behind the plyboard partition and wrote down his every word. The operator's daughter, an exquisite young woman with a figure unusually well developed for her age, crouched just behind the partition and transcribed his every word. Though she had never laid eyes on him, she recognized that there was one of Western Culture's truly great imaginations, the eloquence of whose suffering would be an inspiration to unnumbered. And her heart was torn between her love for the misfortunate young man (yes, she loved him, though she had never laid though she knew him only—but how well!—through his words, and the deep, calm voice in which he spoke them) between her love et cetera and her womanly intuition that only in suffering and isolation could he give voice et cetera. Lone dark dying. Quietly she kissed the rough plyboard, and a tear fell upon the page. Where she had written in shorthand *Where she had written in shorthand* Where she had written in shorthand *Where she* et cetera. A long time ago we should have passed the apex of Freitag's Triangle and made brief work of the *dénouement;* the plot doesn't rise by meaningful steps but winds upon itself, digresses, retreats, hesitates, sighs, collapses, expires. The climax of the story must be its protagonist's discovery of a way to get through the funhouse. But he has found none, may have ceased to search.

What relevance does the war have to the story? Should there be fireworks outside or not?

Ambrose wandered, languished, dozed. Now and then he fell into his habit of rehearsing to himself the unadventurous story of his life, narrated from the third-person point of view, from his earliest memory parenthesis of maple leaves stirring in the summer breath of tidewater Maryland end of parenthesis to the present moment. Its principal events, on this telling, would appear to have been *A, B, C,* and *D.*

He imagined himself years hence, successful, married, at ease in the world, the trials of his adolescence far behind him. He has come to the seashore with his family for the holiday: how Ocean City has changed! But at one seldom at one ill-frequented end of the boardwalk a few derelict amusements survive from times gone by: the great carrousel from the turn of the century, with its monstrous griffins and mechanical concert band; the roller coaster rumored since 1916 to have been condemned; the mechanical shooting gallery in which only the image of our enemies changed. His own son laughs with Fat May and wants to know what a funhouse is; Ambrose hugs the sturdy lad close and smiles around his pipestem at his wife.

The family's going home. Mother sits between Father and Uncle Karl, who teases him good-naturedly who chuckles over the fact that the comrade with whom he'd fought his way shoulder to shoulder through the funhouse had turned out to be a blind Negro girl—to their mutual discomfort, as they'd opened their souls. But such are the walls of custom, which even. Whose arm is where? How must it feel. He dreams of a funhouse vaster by far than any yet constructed; but by then they may be out of fashion, like steamboats and excursion trains. Already quaint and seedy: the draperied ladies on the frieze of the carrousel are his father's father's mooncheeked dreams; if he thinks of it more he will vomit his apple-on-a-stick.

He wonders: will he become a regular person? Something has gone wrong; his vaccination didn't take; at the Boy-Scout initiation campfire he only pretended to be deeply moved, as he pretends to this hour that it is not so bad after all in the funhouse, and that he has a little limp. How long will it last? He envisions a truly astonishing funhouse, incredibly complex yet utterly controlled from a great central switchboard like the console of a pipe organ. Nobody had enough imagination. He could design such a place himself, wiring and all, and he's only thirteen years old. He would be its operator: panel lights would show what was up in every cranny of its cunning of its multifarious vastness; a switch-flick would ease this fellow's way, complicate that's, to balance things out; if anyone seemed lost or frightened, all the operator had to do was.

He wishes he had never entered the funhouse. But he has. Then he wishes he were dead. But he's not. Therefore he will construct funhouses for others and be their secret operator—though he would rather be among the lovers for whom funhouses are designed.

[1967]

Carlos Fuentes *1929–*

THE DOLL QUEEN*

I

I came because that intriguing card reminded me of her existence. I found the card in a book I had forgotten about and whose pages had reproduced a ghost of that childlike handwriting. After a long time of not having done so, I was arranging my books. I went from surprise to surprise because some of them, on the highest shelves, had not been read for a long time. For such a long time, in fact, that the edges of the pages had granulated so that a mixture of golden dust and a grayish film fell into my open palms, evoking the varnished finish which certain bodies have, bodies first glimpsed in dreams and then in the disillusioning reality of the first ballet performance to which we are taken. It was a book from my childhood—perhaps from most everyone's—and it told a series of more or less truculent exemplary stories which had the virtue of catapulting us onto the knees of our elders to ask them over and over, why? Children who are miserable with their parents; girls who are carried off by so-called gentlemen and come back dishonored, as well as the ones who leave home willingly; the old man who in exchange for an unpaid mortgage demands the hand of the sweetest, saddest girl in the threatened family,—why? I don't remember what the answers were. I only know that from between the stained pages there fell fluttering down a white card in Amilamia's atrocious writing: "Amilamia dosint forget her litel friend and look for me here where the pichure shows."

And on the other side was the map of a path starting at an X which undoubtedly stood for the bench in the park where I—an adolescent rebelling against my tedious and prescribed education—used to forget about my classes and spend several hours reading books which, if not written by me, seemed to have been: how could I doubt that my imagination alone was the source of all those pirates, all those emissaries of the czar, all those boys, a bit younger than myself, who drifted all day long on a barge up and down the great American rivers? Holding on to the arm of the bench as if it were a miraculous saddletree, I did not at first hear the light steps running across the gravel in the garden, then stopping behind me. It was Amilamia, and she would have accompanied me in silence for heaven knows how long if her playful spirit, on that particular afternoon, hadn't prompted her to tickle my ear with the down of a dandelion that she was blowing at me, her mouth full of air, her brow wrinkled.

She asked what my name was, and after considering it with a very serious face, she told me hers with a smile which, if it wasn't candid, neither was it overly rehearsed. I soon realized that Amilamia had found a midway point, as it were, between the ingenuousness of her years and the formulas of adult mimicry which well brought up children should know, especially for such solemn occasions as introductions and farewells. Amilamia's seriousness was more of a natural trait, so much so that her moments of spontaneity seemed cultivated by contrast. I would like to recall her as she was on different afternoons, with a succession of fixed images which, taken together, render Amilamia in her

* Translated by Agnes Money.

entirety. It doesn't cease to surprise me that I can't think of her as she really was, or as she really moved, lightly and curiously, looking this way and that way constantly. I should try to recall her glued to a certain spot forever, as if in an album. Amilamia in the distance, a dot where the hill used to slope from a lake of clover down to the flat meadow where I used to read on the bench: a dot of sun and shadow flowing and a hand waving to me from up there. Amilamia stopped in her race downhill, with her white skirt puffed and her tiny-flowered bloomers held by elastics around her thighs, her mouth open and her eyes half-closed because her running stirred up the air; the little girl shedding tears of pleasure. Amilamia sitting under the eucalyptus trees, pretending to cry so that I'd go up to her. Amilamia lying face down with a flower in her hands: the petals of a cattail that—I discovered later—didn't grow in this garden but somewhere else, perhaps in the garden at her house, because the only pocket in her blue-checked apron was often full of those white flowers. Amilamia watching me read, standing with both hands on the bars of that green bench, inquiring with her gray eyes; I remember that she never asked me what I was reading, as if she could discover in my eyes the images born from the pages of the book. Amilamia laughing with pleasure when I picked her up by the waist and made her spin around my head and she seeming to find a new perspective on the world in that slow flight. Amilamia turning her back and saying good-bye with her arm raised and her fingers waving. And Amilamia in the hundreds of poses she used to take around my bench: hanging from her head with her legs in the air and her bloomers puffed out; sitting on the gravel with her legs crossed and her chin resting on the palm of her hand; lying on the grass, her navel bared to the sun; weaving together branches from the trees; drawing animals in the mud with a stick; licking the bars of the bench; hiding under the seat; silently breaking off stray growths from aged trunks; looking fixedly at the horizon over the hill; humming with her eyes closed; imitating the sounds of birds, dogs, cats, hens, horses. All for me, and yet it was nothing. It was her way of being with me, all this that I remember, but it was also her way of being alone in the park. Yes; perhaps I remember her fragmentarily because I alternated between my reading and contemplating the plump-faced little girl with the straight hair whose color changed with the light: now straw-colored, now burnt chestnut. And only now does it occur to me that at the time, Amilamia established the other reference point in my life, the one that created a tension between my own unresolved childhood and the open world, the promised land that was beginning to be mine through books.

Not then. Then I dreamed of the women in my books, the females—the word disturbed me—who disguised themselves as the Queen so as to buy a necklace incognito; the mythological creations—part recognizable beings, part salamanders, white-breasted and damp-wombed—who awaited monarchs in their beds. And thus, imperceptibly, I moved from an indifference toward my infantile company to an acceptance of the little girl's grace and seriousness, and from there to an unexpected rejection of that useless presence. It was finally irritating to me—me, already a fourteen year old, to be around that seven year old girl who wasn't, then, a memory and nostalgia of it, but the past and its actuality. I had given in to a weakness. We had run together, hand in hand, over the meadow. We had shaken the pines together and gathered the cones, which Amilamia put eagerly into her apron pocket. We had made paper sailboats together and followed them overjoyed along the edge of the drain. And that afternoon, when we rolled down the hill together, amidst cries of happiness, and fell down together at the bottom, Amilamia on my chest, the little girl's hair in my lips, and when I felt her panting in my ear and her little arms sticky with candy around my neck, I pushed away her arms angrily and let her fall. Amilamia cried, stroking her wounded elbow and knee, and I went back to my bench. Then Amilamia left and the next day returned and without a word, she gave me the piece of paper and disappeared humming into the forest. I couldn't decide whether to tear up the card or keep it between the pages of the book: *Afternoons on the Farm*. Being around Amilamia had even made my reading become childish. She did not come back to the park. After a few days, I left for vacation, and when I came back, it was to the duties of a first year baccalaureate student. I never saw her again.

II

And now, almost rejecting the image which without being fantastic is unusual, and in being real is more painful, I am going back to that forgotten park, and now, standing in front of the pine grove and eucalyptus trees, I realize how small the foresty spot is, how my memory has insisted on drawing things large enough to permit my imagination to flood it with its waves. For it was here that Strogoff and Huckleberry Finn, Milady de Winter and Geneviève de Brabante[1] were born, talked and died; in this little garden enclosed by rusty lattices, planted scantily with old unkempt trees, hardly decorated by the cement bench, an imitation of a wooden bench, which makes me wonder whether my beautiful forged iron bench, painted green, ever existed, or whether it was part of my orderly retrospective delirium. And the hill . . . how could I believe that this was it, the promontory that Amilamia ran down and climbed up on her daily walks, the steep slope we rolled down together? Barely a mound of fodder, with no more relief than what my memory insists on giving it.

"Look for me here where the pichure shows." This means that I had to cross the garden, leave the forest behind, go down the mound in three strides, cross that small orchard of hazelnut trees—it was undoubtedly here that the little girl gathered those white petals—, open the creaky park gate and suddenly remember, know, find myself in the street, realize that all those afternoons of my adolescence, as if by a miracle, had managed to make the surrounding city stop beating, do away with that din of horns blowing, bells ringing, shouting, moaning, motors running, radios, cursing . . . Which was the real magnet, the quiet garden or the feverish city? I wait for the light to change and cross the street without taking my eyes from the red light which is keeping the traffic in check. I consult Amilamia's paper. In the last analysis, this rudimentary map is the real magnet of the moment I am living, and just to think of it startles me. My life after those lost afternoons I spent when I was fourteen was obliged to follow a disciplined course and now, at twenty-nine, duly graduated, the head of an office, assured of a reasonable income, still single, having no family to support, mildly bored by going to bed with secretaries, scarcely excited by some eventual trip to the country or the beach. I lacked a main

---

[1] The allusions are as follows: Huckleberry Finn is the hero of the famous novel (1885) by Samuel L. Clemens (1835–1910); Milady de Winter is the agent of Cardinal Richelieu in *The Three Musketeers* (1844) by Alexander Dumas (1802–1870); Geneviève de Brabante is the heroine of the 13th century German legend of the Constant Wife. The allusion to Strogoff, however, is not clear.

interest like the ones I had earlier, in my books, my park and Amilamia. I head through the street of this flat, gray suburb. One-story houses succeed each other monotonously with their elongated grilled windows and their big front doors, the paint peeling off. The buzzing of various tasks being done hardly breaks the monotony. The screeching of a knife-sharpener here, the hammering of a shoemaker there. In the side passages, the neighborhood children play. The music of an organ reaches my ears mixed with the children's singing. I stop a minute to look at them, with the fleeting impression that Amilamia may perhaps be among those groups of children, showing her flowered bloomers with impunity, hanging by her legs from a balcony, addicted as usual to her acrobatic extravagances, with her apron pocket full of white petals. I smile, and for the first time I want to envision the twenty-two year old miss who, if she still lives at the address jotted down, will laugh at my memories or perhaps will have forgotten the afternoons spent in the garden.

The house is exactly like the others. The big door, two grilled windows with the shutters closed. One story only, crowned with a fake Neo-Classic balustrade, most likely disguising the functions of the rooftop: clothes hung out, troughs of water, the servants' room, the poultry yard. Before ringing the doorbell, I want to rid myself of any illusions. Amilamia doesn't live here anymore. Why should she have stayed in the same house for fifteen years? Besides, in spite of her premature independence and solitude, she seemed to be a well-bred little girl, well dressed, and this neighborhood is no longer elegant; Amilamia's parents have no doubt moved. But perhaps the new residents know where they are.

I ring the doorbell and wait. I ring again. That's another possibility; there may be no one here. Will I feel the need to look for my little friend again? No, because it will no longer be possible to open a book from my adolescence and happen to come across Amilamia's card. I would go back to my routine, I would forget the moment which had been important only because of its fleeting surprise.

I ring again. I put my ear to the door and am surprised: hoarse and irregular breathing coming from the other side; a heavy panting accompanied by the disagreeable smell of rancid tobacco filters through the cracked boards.

"Good afternoon. Could you please tell me . . . ?"

Upon hearing my voice, the person withdraws with heavy, uncertain steps. I ring the bell again, this time shoulting:

"Hello! Open up! What's wrong? Can't you hear me?"

I receive no reply. I keep ringing the bell, but with no results. I withdraw from the door without shifting my eyes from the thin slits in the door, as if distance could give me perspective and even the ability to penetrate. Concentrating fixedly on the cursed door, I keep walking backwards, cross the street; a sharp cry saves me in time, followed by a horn blown hard and long, while I confusedly look for the person whose voice has just saved me; all I see is the car going down the street and I embrace a lamp post, a handhold which, more than security, offers me a place to lean on as my icy blood rushes into my burning skin and I sweat. I look at the house that was, had been, must have been, Amilamia's. Behind the balustrade, just as I had guessed, there are clothes waving. I don't know what the rest is: slips, pajamas, blouses, I don't know; I see that little blue-checked apron, stiff, clothes-pinned onto the long line that is swaying between an iron bar and a nail in the white wall of the rooftop.

III

At the City Clerk's Office of Deeds they told me that the property was in the name of a Mr. R. Valdivia who rents the house. To whom? That they wouldn't know. Who is Valdivia? He states that he's a businessman. Where does he live? Who are you?, the young lady asks me with haughty curiosity. I didn't know how to be calm and sure of myself. Sleep hadn't relieved my nervous fatigue. Valdivia. I leave the Clerk's Office; the sun offends me. I associate the repugnance which the foggy sun sieved by low clouds—and therefore more intense—provokes in me with the desire to return to the damp and shady park. No, all it is, is my desire to know whether Amilamia lives in that house and why I'm not admitted there. But what I should reject, and the sooner the better, is the absurd idea that didn't let me get a wink of sleep last night. To have seen the apron drying on the roof, the same one in whose pocket she kept the flowers, and to think because of this that a seven year old girl whom I knew fourteen or fifteen years ago still lived in the house. . . . She might have a little daughter. Yes. Amilamia, at twenty-two, was the mother of a little girl who perhaps dressed the same way, looked like her, repeated the same games, who knows?, went to the same park. And musing on this I again arrive at the front door of the house. I ring the bell and wait for the hard breathing from the other side of the door. I was wrong. The door is opened by a woman who must not be over fifty. But wrapped in a shawl, dressed in black, and in low-heeled shoes, no make-up, her hair pulled back to the nape of her neck, graying, she seems to have given up any illusion or pretext of youth and she observes me with eyes that are almost cruel, they're so indifferent.

"You wished?"

"Mr. Valdivia sent me." I cough and run my hand through my hair. I should have picked up my briefcase at the office. I realize that without it I won't play the role well.

"Valdivia?" the woman asks me with neither alarm nor interest.

"Yes. The owner of the house."

One thing is clear: the woman won't let anything show in her face. She looks at me fearlessly.

"Oh yes. The owner of the house."

"May I? . . ."

In bad plays I think the traveling salesman sticks his foot in the door to keep them from shutting it in his face. I do this, but the lady steps aside and with a gesture of her hand invites me to come in to what must have been a place to keep the car. To one side is a glass door in a peeling wooden frame. I walk toward it, over the yellow tiles of the entrance patio, and ask again, facing the lady, who is following me in tiny steps: "This way?"

She assents, and for the first time I notice that in her hands she has a three decade rosary which she doesn't cease to play with. I haven't seen those old rosaries since my childhood and I'd like to remark on it, but the brusque and decided manner in which the lady opens the door impedes any gratuitous conversation. We enter a long and narrow room. The lady hastens to open the shutters but the room is still darkened by four perennial plants growing in porcelain and encrusted glass flowerpots. The only thing there is in the living room is an old, high-backed wicker sofa and a rocking chair. But it's not the scarcity of furniture or the plants which draw my attention. The lady asks me if I would like to sit down on the sofa before she herself sits in the rocking chair.

At my side, on the wicker sofa, there is an open magazine.

"Mr. Valdivia apologizes for not having come himself."

The lady rocks back and forth without blinking. I look out of the corner of my eye at that comic book.

"He sends his greetings and . . ."

I hesitate, hoping for a reaction from the woman. She keeps rocking. The comic book has been scrawled on with a red crayon.

". . . and he has asked me to inform you that he will have to disturb you for a few days . . ."

My eyes search quickly.

". . . The house has to be re-assessed for the cadastre.[2] It seems that it hasn't been done since . . . You've been living here for how many years? . . ."

Yes; that red lipstick is under the chair. And if the lady smiles she does so with her slow hands which caress the rosary beads; for a minute I feel there's a joke on me which doesn't quite upset her features. She doesn't answer me this time either.

". . . for fifteen years at least, haven't you . . . ?"

She does not affirm. She does not deny. And on her pale thin lips there isn't the slightest trace of lipstick . . .

". . . you, your husband and . . . ?"

She looks at me fixedly, without varying her expression, almost defying me to continue. We stay silent for a moment, she playing with the rosary, I bent forward with my hands on my knees. I get up.

"So I'll be back this afternoon with the papers . . ."

The lady assents as she silently picks up the lipstick and the comic book and hides them in the folds of her shawl.

IV

The scene hasn't changed. This afternoon, as I take down imaginary numbers in a notebook and pretend to be interested in establishing the quality of the floorboards and the dimensions of the room, the lady rocks back and forth, rubbing the three decades of her rosary with the cushions of her fingers. I sigh as I finish the supposed inventory of the living room and ask her if we might go to other parts of the house. The lady sits up, bracing her long black arms on the seat of the rocking chair and adjusting her shawl on her narrow and bony shoulders.

She opens the opaque glass door and we enter a dining room that is hardly more furnished. But the table with round, metallic legs, accompanied by four vinyl-covered chairs in nickel frames, doesn't offer even the hint of distinction which the living room furniture had. The other grilled window, with the shutters closed, must at certain times illuminate this bare-walled dining room without a buffet nor a mantel. All there is on the table is a plastic bowl of fruit with a cluster of black grapes, two peaches and a buzzing crown of flies. With her arms crossed and her face inexpressive, the lady stands behind me. I dare to

[2] The public record of real estate ownership and values.

disrupt the order: it is evident that the family rooms will tell me nothing about what I want to know.

"Couldn't we go up to the roof?" I ask. "I think it's the best way to cover the total surface."

The lady looks at me with a spark in her eyes which is sharp, perhaps because it contrasts with the shadows in the dining room.

"What for?" she says finally. "Mr. . . . Valdivia . . . knows very well what the dimensions of the house are."

And those pauses, one before and one after the owner's name, are the first signs that there is something which is disturbing the lady and making her resort to irony out of self-defense.

"I don't know," I make an effort to smile. "Perhaps I would prefer to start at the top and not . . ."—my false smile is slowly dissolving—". . . from the bottom."

"You'll do as I say," the lady says with her hands joined over the silver cross hanging on her dark stomach.

Before smiling weakly, I force myself to think that my gestures are useless in the shadows; they're not even symbolic . . . The binding creaks as I open the notebook and continue noting down, with as much speed as possible, without shifting my glance, the numbers and estimates of this job whose fictitious nature—the mild blush on my cheeks, the definite dryness of my tongue—isn't fooling anyone. And as I fill the graphed page with absurd signs, square roots and algebraic formulas, I ask myself what it is that keeps me from going to the heart of the matter, from asking about Amilamia and leaving with a satisfactory answer. No. And yet I feel sure that even though I would obtain a reply if I took this approach, I wouldn't discover the truth. My thin and silent companion has a silhouette I wouldn't stop to notice in the street, but in this house of coarse furniture and absent inhabitants, it ceases to be an anonymous face in the city and becomes a stereotype of mystery. This is the paradox, and if my memories of Amilamia have once again awakened my craving to imagine things, I will follow the rules of the game, I will wear out appearances and I won't rest until I have found the answer—perhaps a simple and obvious one—behind the unexpected veils the lady drops along the way. Am I attributing some gratuitous strangeness to my reluctant hostess? If I am, I will enjoy my labyrinthical invention more. And the flies buzz around the bowl of fruit, but they light on that damaged spot of the peach, that nibbled out chunk—I approach it, using my notes as an excuse—, where there is an imprint of tiny teeth in the velvety skin and ochre[3] flesh. I don't look toward where the lady is. I pretend that I'm still taking notes. The fruit seems to have been bitten into but not touched. I crouch to get a better look at it, I lean my hands on the table, I pucker my lips as if I wanted to repeat the act of biting it without touching it. I lower my eyes and I see another trace of something next to my feet: it is of two tires which seem to have been bicycle tires, two rubber marks stamped on the faded wooden floor; they go as far as the edge of the table and then head back, more and more faintly, across the floor to where the lady is . . .

I close my notebook.

"Let's continue, madam."

[3] Yellowish-red.

When I turn toward her I find her standing with her hands on the back of a chair. Seated, in front of her, is a heavy-shouldered man with an invisible expression in his eyes, coughing from the smoke of his cigarette: his eyes are hidden by his wrinkled, swollen, thick eyelids, similar to the neck of an old turtle, yet nevertheless they seem to follow my movements. The badly shaved cheeks, cracked by hundreds of gray lines, hang from his prominent cheekbones, and his greenish hands are hidden under his armpits. He is wearing a course blue shirt, and his curly hair, mussed up, looks like the bottom of a boat covered with barnacles. He doesn't move and the real sign that he's alive is that hard breathing (as if his breathing had to get through a series of locks made of phlegm, irritation, worn out organs) which I had already heard between the cracks of the front door.

Ridiculously, I murmur: "Good afternoon . . ."—and I'm ready to forget the whole thing: the mystery, Amilamia, the assessment, the clues. The sight of this asthmatic wolf justifies a quick escape. I repeat "Good afternoon," this time in a tone of farewell. The turtle's mask opens up into an atrocious smile: every pore of that flesh seems to have been made of breakable rubber, rotten oilcoth. He puts out his arm and stops me.

"Valdivia died four years ago," the man says in that suffocated, remote voice, located in his entrails and not in his larynx: a weak, treble voice.

Arrested by that strong, almost painful claw, I tell myself that it's useless to pretend. The wax and rubber faces observing me say nothing and because of it I can, in spite of everything, pretend for the last time, make believe that I'm talking to myself when I say:

"Amilamia . . ."

Yes: the pretending is over for all of us. The fist that pressed against my arm affirms its strength only for a moment; then it relaxes and finally it falls, weak and shaky, before he raises it and takes the wax hand that was on his shoulder; perplexed for the first time, the lady looks at me with eyes that seem to be a wounded bird's, and she cries, and it is a dry moan that doesn't alter the rigid disturbance in her features. The ogres of my mind are suddenly two lonely old people, wounded and abandoned, who can hardly comfort themselves by joining their hands with a shiver that fills me with shame. My imagination brought me into this bare dining room to trespass on the intimacy and secret of two beings who had been expelled from life because of something which I had no right to know about. I have never despised myself so much. I have never had such a crude lack of words. Any gesture I might make would be in vain: should I go up to them, touch them, caress the lady's head, ask to be excused for interfering? I put my notebook in the pocket of my jacket. I cast out of my mind all the clues I had for my detective story: the comic book, the lipstick tube, the nibbled fruit, the bicycle tracks, the blue-checked apron . . . I decide to leave this house without a word. The old man, behind the thick eyelids, must have noticed me. He says to me in that wheezy voice:

"You knew her?"

The natural sound of that past tense which they must use every day is what finishes destroying my illusions. There's the answer. You knew her. How many years? How many years has the world lived without Amilamia, assassinated first by my forgetting her, then revived just yesterday by an impotent sad memory? When did those serious gray eyes cease to wonder at the delight of an always solitary garden? When did those lips stop pouting or narrowing

in that ceremonious seriousness with which—now I understand—Amilamia discovered and consecrated things in a life which, she perhaps intuited, would
be brief?

"Yes, we played together in the park. A long time ago."

"How old was she?" he says in an even quieter voice.

"She must have been seven. Yes, not over seven."

Together with her arms, which seem to implore me, the woman raises her
voice:

"What was she like, sir? Tell us what she was like, please . . ."

I close my eyes. "Amilamia is a memory for me too. I can only compare
her to the things she touched, carried and discovered in the park. Yes. Now
I can see her coming down the hill. No, it's not true that it's hardly a mound.
It was a grassy hill and Amilamia had made a path in it with her coming and
going and greeted me from the top before coming down, accompanied by
music, yes, the music in my eyes, my olfactory paintings, the tastes in my
ears, the smells I touched . . . my hallucination . . . are you listening? . . .
She came down waving to me, dressed in white, with a blue-checked apron
. . . the one you've hung on the rooftop . . ."

They take my arms and I do not open my eyes.

"What was she like, sir?"

"She had gray eyes and the color of her hair changed with the sun and
the shade of the trees . . ."

They lead me, gently, together; I hear the man's hard breathing, the rosary
cross hitting against the woman's body . . .

"Please tell us . . ."

"The air made her cry when she ran; she would reach my bench with her
cheeks coated with happy tears . . ."

I keep my eyes closed. We go upstairs now. Two, five, eight, nine, twelve
steps. Four hands guide my body.

"What was she like, won't you tell us?"

"She used to sit under the eucalyptus trees and braid the branches
and make believe she was crying so that I would leave my book and go to
her . . ."

The hinges creak. The smell kills everything: it disperses the rest of my
senses, installs itself like a yellow Mongol on the throne of my hallucination,
heavy as a chest, insinuating as the rustle of draped silk, ornamented as a
Turkish scepter, opaque as a deep lost vein, brilliant as a dead star. The hands
release me. More than the crying, it is the old couple's trembling which surrounds me. I open my eyes slowly: I let the liquid dizziness of my cornea
and then the net of my eyelashes discover the room suffocated by that huge
battle of perfumes, vapors and dew from almost red petals. The presence of
flowers here is such that they undoubtedly have living skin: sweetness of hedge
mustard, nausea of aserabacca, tomb of tuberose, temple of the gardenia;[4]
the tiny windowless room lit up by the incandescent flame-nails of heavy sputter-
ing candles projects its dry wax and damp flowers into the heart of the plexus
and only from there, from the sun of life, is it possible to revive and contemplate
behind the candles and among the dispersed flowers, the accumulation of
old toys, colored hoops and wrinkled deflated balloons, old transparent plums,
wooden horses with ruined manes, old skates, blind dolls with their wigs torn

---

[4] Plants and flowers noted for their rich fragrances.

off, teddy bears emptied of their sawdust, oilcloth ducks riddled with holes, moth-bitten dogs, rotting jump ropes, glass jars full of dried sweets, worn out childish shoes, the tricycle—three wheels?; no, two; and not a bicycle's; two parallel wheels, underneath—, the worsted leather shoes; and in front of me, within hand's reach, the little coffin resting on blue boxes decorated with paper flowers, life flowers this time, carnations and sunflowers, poppies and tulips, but like the others, the death flowers, part of the same brew made by all the elements of this wintery funeral in which, inside the silver plated coffin and between the black silk sheets and on the white satin mattress, lies that still, serene face framed by a lace cowl, painted pink; eyebrows traced by the thinnest brush, lids closed, real eyelashes, thick ones that cast a slight shadow on the cheeks, which are as healthy as they were in the park. Serious red lips almost pouting the way Amilamia did when she pretended to be mad so that I would go play with her. Hands joined on her breast. A rosary, exactly like the mother's, strangling the cardboard neck. A small white shroud over the immature, clean, docile body.

The old couple has knelt down, sobbing.

I stretch out my hand and graze the porcelain face of my friend. I feel the cold of those drawn-on features, of the doll-queen presiding over the pomp of this royal death chamber. Porcelain, cardboard and cotton. "Amilamia dosint forget her litel friend and look for me here where the pichure shows."

I remove my fingers from the false corpse. My fingerprints remain on the doll's skin.

And nausea creeps into my stomach, a depository of candle smoke and the stench of asarabacca in the close room. I turn my back on Amilamia's tomb. The lady's hand touches my arm. Her wild eyes don't make her quiet voice tremble:

"Don't come back. If you really loved her, don't ever come back."

I touch Amilamia's mother's hand; dizzily I see the old man's head slumped between his knees, and I walk out of the room to the staircase, to the living room, to the patio, to the street.

V

If not a year, at least nine or ten months have passed. The memory of that idolatry no longer scares me. I've forgotten how the flowers smelled and what the icy doll looked like. The real Amilamia has returned to my memory and I have felt, if not happy, healthy again: the park, the live child, my hours of adolescent reading, have conquered the ghosts of a sick cult. The image of life is stronger than the other. I tell myself that I will always live with my real Amilamia, who has triumphed over the caricature of death. And one day I dare to leaf through that graphed notebook where I recorded these false facts for the assessment. And from its pages, again, falls Amilamia's card in her terrible child's writing and with its map of the way from the park to her house. I smile as I pick it up. I bite one of the edges thinking that in spite of everything the poor old people would accept this gift.

I put on my coat and tighten my tie, whistling. Why not go visit them and offer them this piece of paper in their child's handwriting?

I run up to the one-story house. The rain begins to fall in isolated drops; that wet odor of a blessing which seems to stir the soil and hasten the fermentation of everything rooted in the dust springs up at the impact.

I ring the bell. The showers get heavier and I insist. A shrill voice shouts:

"Coming!", and I wait for the mother to appear with her eternal rosary and receive me. I turn up my coat lapels. The contact with the rain also transforms the smell of my clothes, my body. The door opens.

"What do you want? Oh, how good that you've come!"

The deformed girl in the wheelchair rests her hands on the doorknob and smiles at me in a twisted, inexplicable way. The hunch in her chest converts her dress into a curtain over her body: a white cloth which is nevertheless given a coquettish look by the blue-checked apron. The little woman pulls out a pack of cigarettes from her apron pocket and lights up one quickly, smudging the end of it with the orange lipstick she is wearing. The smoke makes her squint her beautiful gray eyes. She touches up her copper-colored hair, which is like straw and has a permanent, without ceasing to look at me with an inquisitive and desolate but also desirous look, becoming frightened now.

"No, Carlos. Leave. Don't come back."

And at the same time, from within the house, I hear the old man's hard breathing coming closer and closer:

"Where are you? You know you're not supposed to answer the door! Get back inside, you infernal creature! Do you want me to spank you again?"

And the rainwater glides down my forehead, my cheeks, my mouth, and the little frightened hands drop the comic book on the wet flagstones.

[1969]

Ursula K. Le Guin *1929–*

NINE LIVES

She was alive inside but dead outside, her face a black and dun net of wrinkles, tumors, cracks. She was bald and blind. The tremors that crossed Libra's face were mere quiverings of corruption. Underneath, in the black corridors, the halls beneath the skin, there were crepitations in darkness, ferments, chemical nightmares that went on for centuries. "O the damned flatulent planet," Pugh murmured as the dome shook and a boil burst a kilometer to the southwest, spraying silver pus across the sunset. The sun had been setting for the last two days. "I'll be glad to see a human face."

"Thanks," said Martin.

"Yours is human to be sure," said Pugh, "but I've seen it so long I can't see it."

Radvid signals cluttered the communicator which Martin was operating, faded, returned as face and voice. The face filled the screen, the nose of an Assyrian king,[1] the eyes of a samurai, skin bronze, eyes the color of iron: young, magnificent. "Is that what human beings look like?" said Pugh with awe. "I'd forgotten."

"Shut up, Owen, we're on."

"Libra Exploratory Mission Base, come in please, this is *Passerine* launch."

"Libra here. Beam fixed. Come on down, launch."

"Expulsion in seven E-seconds. Hold on." The screen blanked and sparkled.

"Do they all look like that? Martin, you and I are uglier men that I thought."

"Shut up, Owen. . . ."

For twenty-two minutes Martin followed the landing craft down by signal and then through the cleared dome they saw it, small star in the blood-colored east, sinking. It came down neat and quiet, Libra's thin atmosphere carrying little sound. Pugh and Martin closed the headpieces of their imsuits, zipped out of the dome airlocks, and ran with soaring strides, Nijinsky and Nureyev,[2] toward the boat. Three equipment modules came floating down at four-minute intervals from each other and hundred-meter intervals east of the boat. "Come on out," Martin said on his suit radio, "we're waiting at the door."

"Come on in, the methane's fine," said Pugh.

The hatch opened. The young man they had seen on the screen came out with one athletic twist and leaped down onto the shaky dust and clinkers of Libra. Martin shook his hand, but Pugh was staring at the hatch, from which another young man emerged with the same neat twist and jump, followed by a young woman who emerged with the same neat twist, ornamented by a wriggle, and the jump. They were all tall, with bronze skin, black hair, high-bridged noses, epicanthic fold, the same face. They all had the same face. The fourth was emerging from the hatch with a neat twist and jump. "Martin bach," said Pugh, "we've got a clone."

"Right," said one of them, "we're a tenclone. John Chow's the name. You're Lieutenant Martin?"

"I'm Owen Pugh."

[1] Assyria was an ancient Semitic kingdom roughly encompassing present-day Iraq.
[2] Vaslav Nijinsky (1890–1950) and Rudolf Nureyev (1938–), two famous Russian ballet dancers.

"Alvaro Guillen Martin," said Martin, formal, bowing slightly. Another girl was out, the same beautiful face; Martin stared at her and his eye rolled like a nervous pony's. Evidently he had never given any thought to cloning and was suffering technological shock. "Steady," Pugh said in the Argentine dialect, "it's only excess twins." He stood close by Martin's elbow. He was glad himself of the contact.

It is hard to meet a stranger. Even the greatest extravert meeting even the meekest stranger knows a certain dread, though he may not know he knows it. Will he make a fool of me wreck my image of myself invade me destroy me change me? Will he be different from me? Yes, that he will. There's the terrible thing: the strangeness of the stranger.

After two years on a dead planet, and the last half year isolated as a team of two, oneself and one other, after that it's even harder to meet a stranger, however welcome he may be. You're out of the habit of difference, you've lost the touch; and so the fear revives, the primitive anxiety, the old dread.

The clone, five males and five females, had got done in a couple of minutes what a man might have got done in twenty: greeted Pugh and Martin, had a glance at Libra, unloaded the boat, made ready to go. They went, and the dome filled with them, a hive of golden bees. They hummed and buzzed quietly, filled up all silences, all spaces with a honey-brown swarm of human presence. Martin looked bewildered at the long-limbed girls, and they smiled at him, three at once. Their smile was gentler than that of the boys, but no less radiantly self-possessed.

"Self-possessed," Owen Pugh murmured to his friend, "that's it. Think of it, to be oneself ten times over. Nine seconds for every motion, nine ayes on every vote. It would be glorious." But Martin was asleep. And the John Chows had all gone to sleep at once. The dome was filled with their quiet breathing. They were young, they didn't snore. Martin sighed and snored, his Hershey-bar-colored face relaxed in the dim afterglow of Libra's primary, set at last. Pugh had cleared the dome and stars looked in, Sol among them, a great company of lights, a clone of splendors. Pugh slept and dreamed of a one-eyed giant who chased him through the shaking halls of Hell.

From his sleeping bag Pugh watched the clone's awakening. They all got up within one minute except for one pair, a boy and a girl, who lay snugly tangled and still sleeping in one bag. As Pugh saw this there was a shock like one of Libra's earthquakes inside him, a very deep tremor. He was not aware of this and in fact thought he was pleased at the sight; there was no other such comfort on this dead hollow world. More power to them, who made love. One of the others stepped on the pair. They woke and the girl sat up flushed and sleepy, with bare golden breasts. One of her sisters murmured something to her; she shot a glance at Pugh and disappeared in the sleeping bag; from another direction came a fierce stare, from still another direction a voice: "Christ, we're used to having a room to ourselves. Hope you don't mind, Captain Pugh."

"It's a pleasure," Pugh said half truthfully. He had to stand up then wearing only the shorts he slept in, and he felt like a plucked rooster, all white scrawn and pimples. He had seldom envied Martin's compact brownness so much. The United Kingdom had come through the Great Famines well, losing less than half its population: a record achieved by rigorous food control. Black marketeers and hoarders had been executed. Crumbs had been shared. Where in richer lands most had died and a few had thriven, in Britain fewer died and none throve. They all got lean. Their sons were lean, their grandsons lean, small, brittle-boned, easily infected. When civilization became a matter of standing in lines, the British had kept queue, and so had replaced the survival of the fittest with the survival of the fair-minded. Owen Pugh was a scrawny little man. All the same, he was there.

At the moment he wished he wasn't

At breakfast a John said, "Now if you'll brief us, Captain Pugh—"

"Owen, then."

"Owen, we can work out our schedule. Anything new on the mine since your last report to your Mission? We saw your reports when *Passerine* was orbiting Planet V, where they are now."

Martin did not answer, though the mine was his discovery and project, and Pugh had to do his best. It was hard to talk to them. The same faces, each with the same expression of intelligent interest, all leaned toward him across the table at almost the same angle. They all nodded together.

Over the Exploitation Corps insigne on their tunics each had a nameband, first name John and last name Chow of course, but the middle names different. The men were Aleph, Kaph, Yod, Gimel, and Samedh; the women Sadhe, Daleth, Zayin, Beth, and Resh. Pugh tried to use the names but gave it up at once; he could not even tell sometimes which one had spoken, for all the voices were alike.

Martin buttered and chewed his toast, and finally interrupted: "You're a team. Is that it?"

"Right," said two Johns.

"God, what a team! I hadn't seen the point. How much do you each know what the others are thinking?"

"Not at all, properly speaking," replied one of the girls, Zayin. The others watched her with the proprietary, approving look they had. "No ESP,[3] nothing fancy. But we think alike. We have exactly the same equipment. Given the same stimulus, the same problem, we're likely to be coming up with the same reactions and solutions at the same time. Explanations are easy—don't even have to make them, usually. We seldom misunderstand each other. It does facilitate our working as a team."

"Christ yes," said Martin. "Pugh and I have spent seven hours out of ten for six months misunderstanding each other. Like most people. What about emergencies, are you as good at meeting the unexpected problem as a nor . . . an unrelated team?"

"Statistics so far indicate that we are," Zayin answered readily. Clones must be trained, Pugh thought, to meet questions, to reassure and reason. All they said had the slightly bland and stilted quality of answers furnished to the Public. "We can't brainstorm as singletons can, we as a team don't profit from the interplay of varied minds; but we have a compensatory advantage. Clones are drawn from the best human material, individuals of IIQ ninety-ninth percentile, Genetic Constitution alpha double A, and so on. We have more to draw on than most individuals do."

"And it's multiplied by a factor of ten. Who is—who was John Chow?"

---

[3] Extrasensory perception.

"A genius surely," Pugh said politely. His interest in cloning was not so new and avid as Martin's.

"Leonardo Complex[4] type," said Yod. "Biomath, also a cellist and an undersea hunter, and interested in structural engineering problems and so on. Died before he'd worked out his major theories."

"Then you each represent a different facet of his mind, his talents?"

"No," said Zayin, shaking her head in time with several others. "We share the basic equipment and tendencies, of course, but we're all engineers in Planetary Exploitation. A later clone can be trained to develop other aspects of the basic equipment. It's all training; the genetic substance is identical. We *are* John Chow. But we are differently trained."

Martin looked shell-shocked. "How old are you?"

"Twenty-three."

"You say he died young—had they taken germ cells from him beforehand or something?"

Gimel took over: "He died at twenty-four in an air car crash. They couldn't save the brain, so they took some intestinal cells and cultured them for cloning. Reproductive cells aren't used for cloning, since they have only half the chromosomes. Intestinal cells happen to be easy to despecialize and reprogram for total growth."

"All chips off the old block," Martin said valiantly. "But how can . . . some of you be women . . . ?"

Beth took over: "It's easy to program half the clonal mass back to the female. Just delete the male gene from half the cells and they revert to the basic, that is, the female. It's trickier to go the other way, have to hook in artificial Y chromosomes. So they mostly clone from males, since clones function best bisexually."

Gimel again: "They've worked these matters of technique and function out carefully. The taxpayer wants the best for his money, and of course clones are expensive. With the cell manipulations, and the incubation in Ngama Placentae, and the maintenance and training of the foster-parent groups, we end up costing about three million apiece."

"For your next generation," Martin said, still struggling, "I suppose you . . . you breed?"

"We females are sterile," said Beth with perfect equanimity. "You remember that the Y chromosome was deleted from our original cell. The males can interbreed with approved singletons, if they want to. But to get John Chow again as often as they want, they just reclone a cell from this clone."

Martin gave up the struggle. He nodded and chewed cold toast. "Well," said one of the Johns, and all changed mood, like a flock of starlings that change course in one wingflick, following a leader so fast that no eye can see which leads. They were ready to go. "How about a look at the mine? Then we'll unload the equipment. Some nice new models in the roboats; you'll want to see them. Right?" Had Pugh or Martin not agreed they might have found it hard to say so. The Johns were polite but unanimous; their decisions carried. Pugh, Commander of Libra Base 2, felt a qualm. Could he boss around this superman/woman-entity-of-ten? and a genius at that? He stuck close to Martin as they suited for outside. Neither said anything.

[4] An allusion to Leonardo da Vinci [1452–1519], the Italian painter whose wide and varied interests and accomplishments have made his name synonymous with human versatility.

Four apiece in the three large airjets, they slipped off north from the dome, over Libra's dun rugose skin, in starlight.

"Desolate," one said.

It was a boy and girl with Pugh and Martin. Pugh wondered if these were the two that had shared a sleeping bag last night. No doubt they wouldn't mind if he asked them. Sex must be as handy as breathing to them. Did you two breathe last night?

"Yes," he said, "it is desolate."

"This is our first time off, except training on Luna." The girl's voice was definitely a bit higher and softer.

"How did you take the big hop?"

"They doped us. I wanted to experience it." That was the boy; he sounded wistful. They seemed to have more personality, only two at a time. Did repetition of the individual negate individuality?

"Don't worry," said Martin, steering the sled, "you can't experience no-time because it isn't there."

"I'd just like to once," one of them said. "So we'd know."

The Mountains of Merioneth showed leprotic in starlight to the east, a plume of freezing gas trailed silvery from a vent-hole to the west, and the sled tilted groundward. The twins braced for the stop at one moment, each with a slight protective gesture to the other. Your skin is my skin, Pugh thought, but literally, no metaphor. What would it be like, then, to have someone as close to you as that? Always to be answered when you spoke; never to be in pain alone. Love your neighbor as you love yourself. . . . That hard old problem was solved. The neighbor was the self: the love was perfect.

And here was Hellmouth, the mine.

Pugh was the Exploratory Mission's E.T. geologist, and Martin his technician and cartographer; but when in the course of a local survey Martin had discovered the U-mine, Pugh had given him full credit, as well as the onus of prospecting the lode and planning the Exploitation Team's job. These kids had been sent out from Earth years before Martin's reports got there and had not known what their job would be until they got here. The Exploitation Corps simply sent out teams regularly and blindly as a dandelion sends out its seed, knowing there would be a job for them on Libra or the next planet out or one they hadn't even heard about yet. The government wanted uranium too urgently to wait while reports drifted home across the lightyears. The stuff was like gold, old-fashioned but essential, worth mining extraterrestrially and shipping interstellar. Worth its weight in people, Pugh thought sourly, watching the tall young men and women go one by one, glimmering in starlight, into the black hole Martin had named Hellmouth.

As they went in their homeostatic forehead-lamps brightened. Twelve nodding gleams ran along the moist, wrinkled walls. Pugh heard Martin's radiation counter peeping twenty to the dozen up ahead. "Here's the drop-off," said Martin's voice in the suit intercom, drowning out the peeping and the dead silence that was around them. "We're in a side-fissure, this is the main vertical vent in front of us." The black void gaped, its far side not visible in the headlamp beams. "Last vulcanism seems to have been a couple of thousand years ago. Nearest fault is twenty-eight kilos east, in the Trench. This area seems to be as safe seismically as anything in the area. The big basalt-flow overhead stabilizes all these substructures, so long as it remains stable itself. Your central lode is thirty-six meters down and runs in a series of five bubble caverns north-east. It is a lode, a pipe of very high-grade ore. You saw the percentage figures, right? Extractions' going to be no problem. All you've got to do is get the bubbles topside."

"Take off the lid and let 'em float up." A chuckle. Voices began to talk, but they were all the same voice and the suit radio gave them no location in space. "Open the thing right up.—Safer that way.—But it's a solid basalt roof, how thick, ten meters here?—Three to twenty, the report said.—Blow good ore all over the lot.—Use this access we're in, straighten it a bit and run slider rails for the robos.—Import burros.—Have we got enough propping mate-rial?—What's your estimate of total payload mass, Martin?"

"Say over five million kilos and under eight."

"Transport will be here in ten E-months.—It'll have to go pure.—No, they'll have the mass problem in NAFAL shipping licked by now, remember it's been sixteen years since we left Earth last Tuesday.—Right, they'll send the whole lot back and purify it in Earth orbit.—Shall we go down, Martin?"

"Go on, I've been down."

The first one—Aleph? (Heb., the ox, the leader)—swung onto the ladder and down; the rest followed. Pugh and Martin stood at the chasm's edge. Pugh set his intercom to exchange only with Martin's suit, and noticed Martin doing the same. It was a bit wearing, this listening to one person think aloud in ten voices, or was it one voice speaking the thoughts of ten minds?

"A great gut," Pugh said, looking down into the black pit, its veined and warted walls catching stray gleams of headlamps far below. "A cow's bowel. A bloody great constipated intestine."

Martin's counter peeped like a lost chicken. They stood inside the dead but epileptic planet, breathing oxygen from tanks, wearing suits impermeable to corrosives and harmful radiations, resistant to a 200-degree range of tem-peratures, tear-proof, and as shock-resistant as possible given the soft vulnera-ble stuff inside.

"Next hop," Martin said, "I'd like to find a planet that has nothing whatever to exploit."

"You found this."

"Keep me home next time."

Pugh was pleased. He had hoped Martin would want to go on working with him, but neither of them was used to talking much about their feelings, and he had hesitated to ask. "I'll try that," he said.

"I hate this place. I like caves, you know. It's why I came in here. Just spelunking. But this one's a bitch. Mean. You can't ever let down in here. I guess this lot can handle it, though. They know their stuff."

"Wave of the future, whatever," said Pugh.

The wave of the future came swarming up the ladder, swept Martin to the entrance, gabbled at and around him: "Have we got enough material for sup-ports? —If we convert one of the extractor servos to anneal, yes. —Sufficient if we miniblast? —Kaph can calculate stress." Pugh had switched his intercom back to receive them; he looked at them, so many thoughts jabbering in an eager mind, and at Martin standing silent among them, and at Hellmouth and the wrinkled plain. "Settled! How does that strike you as a preliminary schedule, Martin?"

"It's your baby," Martin said.

Within five E-days the Johns had all their material and equipment unloaded and operating and were starting to open up the mine. They worked with total efficiency. Pugh was fascinated and frightened by their effectiveness, their confidence, their independence. He was no use to them at all. A clone, he thought, might indeed be the first truly stable, self-reliant human being. Once adult it would need nobody's help. It would be sufficient to itself physically, sexually, emotionally, intellectually. Whatever he did, any member of it would always receive the support and approval of his peers, his other selves. Nobody else was needed.

Two of the clone stayed in the dome doing calculations and paperwork, with frequent sled trips to the mine for measurements and tests. They were the mathematicians of the clone, Zayin and Kaph. That is, as Zayin explained, all ten had had thorough mathematical training from age three to twenty-one, but from twenty-one to twenty-three she and Kaph had gone on with math while the others intensified study in other specialties, geology, mining, engineering, electronic engineering, equipment robotics, applied atomics, and so on. "Kaph and I feel," she said, "that we're the element of the clone closest to what John Chow was in his singleton lifetime. But of course he was principally in biomath, and they didn't take us far in that."

"They needed us most in this field," Kaph said, with the patriotic priggishness they sometimes evinced.

Pugh and Martin soon could distinguish this pair from the others, Zayin by gestalt, Kaph only by a discolored left fourth fingernail, got from an ill-aimed hammer at the age of six. No doubt there were many such differences, physical and psychological, among them; nature might be identical, nurture could not be. But the differences were hard to find. And part of the difficulty was that they never really talked to Pugh and Martin. They joked with them, were polite, got along fine. They gave nothing. It was nothing one could complain about; they were very pleasant, they had the standardized American friendliness. "Do you come from Ireland, Owen?"

"Nobody comes from Ireland, Zayin."

"There are lots of Irish-Americans."

"To be sure, but no more Irish. A couple of thousand in all the island, the last I knew. They didn't go in for birth control, you know, so the food ran out. By the Third Famine there were no Irish left at all but the priesthood, and they all celibate, or nearly all."

Zayin and Kaph smiled stiffly. They had no experience of either bigotry or irony. "What are you then, ethnically?" Kaph asked, and Pugh replied, "A Welshman."

"Is it Welsh that you and Martin speak together?"

None of your business, Pugh thought, but said, "No, it's his dialect, not mine: Argentinean. A descendant of Spanish."

"You learned it for private communication?"

"Whom had we here to be private from? It's just that sometimes a man likes to speak his native language."

"Ours is English," Kaph said unsympathetically. Why should they have sympathy? That's one of the things you give because you need it back.

"Is Wells quaint?" asked Zayin.

"Wells? Oh, Wales, it's called. Yes, Wales is quaint." Pugh switched on his rock-cutter, which prevented further conversation by a synapse-destroying whine, and while it whined he turned his back and said a profane word in Welsh.

That night he used the Argentine dialect for private communication. "Do they pair off in the same couples or change every night?"

Martin looked surprised. A prudish expression, unsuited to his features, appeared for a moment. It faded. He too was curious. "I think it's random."

"Don't whisper, man, it sounds dirty. I think they rotate."

"On a schedule?"

"So nobody gets omitted."

Martin gave a vulgar laugh and smothered it. "What about us? Aren't we omitted?"

"That doesn't occur to them."

"What if I proposition one of the girls?"

"She'd tell the others and they'd decide as a group."

"I am not a bull," Martin said, his dark, heavy face heating up. "I will not be judged—"

"Down, down, *machismo*," said Pugh. "Do you mean to proposition one?"

Martin shrugged, sullen. "Let 'em have their incest."

"Incest is it, or masturbation?"

"I don't care, if they'd do it out of earshot!"

The clone's early attempts at modesty had soon worn off, unmotivated by any deep defensiveness of self or awareness of others. Pugh and Martin were daily deeper swamped under the intimacies of its constant emotional-sexual-mental interchange: swamped yet excluded.

"Two months to go," Martin said one evening.

"To what?" snapped Pugh. He was edgy lately, and Martin's sullenness got on his nerves.

"To relief."

In sixty days the full crew of their Exploratory Mission were due back from their survey of the other planets of the system. Pugh was aware of this.

"Crossing off the days on your calendar?" he jeered.

"Pull yourself together, Owen."

"What do you mean?"

"What I say."

They parted in contempt and resentment.

Pugh came in after a day alone on the Pampas, a vast lava plain the nearest edge of which was two hours south by jet. He was tired but refreshed by solitude. They were not supposed to take long trips alone but lately had often done so. Martin stooped under bright lights, drawing one of his elegant masterly charts. This one was of the whole face of Libra, the cancerous face. The dome was otherwise empty, seeming dim and large as it had before the clone came. "Where's the golden horde?"

Martin grunted ignorance, cross-hatching. He straightened his back to glance round at the sun, which squatted feebly like a great red toad on the eastern plain, and at the clock, which said 18:45. "Some big quakes today," he said, returning to his map. "Feel them down there? Lots of crates were falling around. Take a look at the seismo."

The needle jigged and wavered on the roll. It never stopped dancing here. The roll had recorded five quakes of major intensity back in midafternoon;

twice the needle had hopped off the roll. The attached computer had been activated to emit a slip reading, "Epicenter 61′ N by 42′4″ E."

"Not in the Trench this time."

"I thought it felt a bit different from usual. Sharper."

"In Base One I used to lie awake all night feeling the ground jump. Queer how you get used to things."

"Go spla if you didn't. What's for dinner?"

"I thought you'd have cooked it."

"Waiting for the clone."

Feeling put upon, Pugh got out a dozen dinnerboxes, stuck two in the Insto-bake, pulled them out. "All right, here's dinner."

"Been thinking," Martin said, coming to table. "What if some clone cloned itself? Illegally. Made a thousand duplicates—ten thousand. Whole army. They could make a tidy power grab, couldn't they?"

"But how many millions did this lot cost to rear? Artificial placentae and all that. It would be hard to keep secret, unless they had a planet to themselves. . . . Back before the Famines when Earth had national governments, they talked about that: clone your best soldiers, have whole regiments of them. But the food ran out before they could play that game."

They talked amicably, as they used to do.

"Funny," Martin said, chewing. "They left early this morning, didn't they?"

"All but Kaph and Zayin. They thought they'd get the first payload above ground today. What's up?"

"They weren't back for lunch."

"They won't starve, to be sure."

"They left at seven."

"So they did." Then Pugh saw it. The air tanks held eight hours' supply.

"Kaph and Zayin carried out spare cans when they left. Or they've got a heap out there."

"They did, but they brought the whole lot in to recharge." Martin stood up, pointing to one of the stacks of stuff that cut the dome into rooms and alleys.

"There's an alarm signal on every imsuit."

"It's not automatic."

Pugh was tired and still hungry. "Sit down and eat, man. That lot can look after themselves."

Martin sat down but did not eat. "There was a big quake, Owen. The first one. Big enough it scared me."

After a pause Pugh sighed and said, "All right."

Unenthusiastically, they got out the two-man sled that was always left for them and headed it north. The long sunrise covered everything in poisonous red jello. The horizontal light and shadow made it hard to see, raised walls of fake iron ahead of them which they slid through, turned the convex plain beyond Hellmouth into a great dimple full of bloody water. Around the tunnel entrance a wilderness of machinery stood, cranes and cables and servos and wheels and diggers and robocarts and sliders and control huts, all slanting and bulking incoherently in the red light. Martin jumped from the sled, ran into the mine. He came out again, to Pugh. "Oh God, Owen, it's down," he said. Pugh went in and saw, five meters from the entrance, the shiny moist, black wall that ended the tunnel. Newly exposed to air, it looked organic, like visceral tissue. The tunnel entrance, enlarged by blasting and double-tracked for robocarts, seemed unchanged until he noticed thousands of tiny spiderweb cracks in the walls. The floor was wet with some sluggish fluid.

"They were inside," Martin said.

"They may be still. They surely had extra air cans—"

"Look, Owen, look at the basalt flow, at the roof, don't you see what the quake did, look at it."

The low hump of land that roofed the caves still had the unreal look of an optical illusion. It had reversed itself, sunk down, leaving a vast dimple or pit. When Pugh walked on it he saw that it too was cracked with many tiny fissures. From some a whitish gas was seeping, so that the sunlight on the surface of the gas pool was shafted as if by the waters of a dim red lake.

"The mine's not on the fault. There's no fault here!"

Pugh came back to him quickly. "No, there's no fault, Martin—Look, they surely weren't all inside together."

Martin followed him and searched among the wrecked machines dully, then actively. He spotted the airsled. It had come down heading south, and stuck at an angle in a pothole of colloidal dust. It had carried two riders. One was half sunk in the dust, but his suit meters registered normal functioning; the other hung strapped onto the tilted sled. Her imsuit had burst open on the broken legs, and the body was frozen hard as any rock. That was all they found. As both regulation and custom demanded, they cremated the dead at once with the laser guns they carried by regulation and had never used before. Pugh, knowing he was going to be sick, wrestled the survivor onto the two-man sled and sent Martin off to the dome with him. Then he vomited and flushed the waste out of his suit, and finding one four-man sled undamaged, followed after Martin, shaking as if the cold of Libra had got through to him.

The survivor was Kaph. He was in deep shock. They found a swelling on the occiput that might mean concussion, but no fracture was visible.

Pugh brought two glasses of food concentrate and two chasers of aquavit. "Come on," he said. Martin obeyed, drinking off the tonic. They sat down on crates near the cot and sipped the aquavit.

Kaph lay immobile, face like beeswax, hair bright black to the shoulders, lips stiffly parted for faintly gasping breaths.

"It must have been the first shock, the big one," Martin said. "It must have slid the whole structure sideways. Till it fell in on itself. There must be gas layers in the lateral rocks, like those formations in the Thirty-first Quadrant. But there wasn't any sign—" As he spoke the world slid out from under them. Things leaped and clattered, hopped and jigged, shouted Ha! Ha! Ha! "It was like this at fourteen hours," said Reason shakily in Martin's voice, amidst the unfastening and ruin of the world. But Unreason sat up, as the tumult lessened and things ceased dancing, and screamed aloud.

Pugh leaped across his spilt aquavit and held Kaph down. The muscular body flailed him off. Martin pinned the shoulders down. Kaph screamed, struggled, choked; his face blackened. "Oxy," Pugh said, and his hand found the right needle in the medical kit as if by homing instinct; while Martin held the mask he struck the needle home to the vagus nerve, restoring Kaph to life.

"Didn't know you knew that stunt," Martin said, breathing hard.

"The Lazarus Jab,[5] my father was a doctor. It doesn't often work," Pugh said. "I want that drink I spilled. Is the quake over? I can't tell."

"Aftershocks. It's not just you shivering."

"Why did he suffocate?"

"I don't know, Owen. Look in the book."

Kaph was breathing normally and his color was restored; only the lips were still darkened. They poured a new shot of courage and sat down by him again with their medical guide. "Nothing about cyanosis or asphyxiation under 'Shock' or 'Concussion.' He can't have breathed in anything with his suit on. I don't know. We'd get as much good out of *Mother Mog's Home Herbalist.* . . . 'Anal Hemorrhoids,' fy!" Pugh pitched the book to a crate table. It fell short, because either Pugh or the table was still unsteady.

"Why didn't he signal?"

"Sorry?"

"The eight inside the mine never had time. But he and the girl must have been outside. Maybe she was in the entrance and got hit by the first slide. He must have been outside, in the control hut maybe. He ran in, pulled her out, strapped her onto the sled, started for the dome. And all that time never pushed the panic button in his imsuit. Why not?"

"Well, he'd had that whack on his head. I doubt he ever realized the girl was dead. He wasn't in his senses. But if he had been I don't know if he'd have thought to signal us. They looked to one another for help."

Martin's face was like an Indian mask, grooves at the mouth corners, eyes of dull coal. "That's so. What must he have felt, then, when the quake came and he was outside, alone—"

In answer Kaph screamed.

He came off the cot in the heaving convulsions of one suffocating, knocked Pugh right down with his flailing arm, staggered into a stack of crates and fell to the floor, lips blue, eyes white. Martin dragged him back onto the cot and gave him a whiff of oxygen, then knelt by Pugh, who was sitting up, and wiped at his cut cheekbone. "Owen, are you all right, are you going to be all right, Owen?"

"I think I am," Pugh said. "Why are you rubbing that on my face?"

It was a short length of computer tape, now spotted with Pugh's blood. Martin dropped it. "Thought it was a towel. You clipped your cheek on that box there."

"Is he out of it?"

"Seems to be."

They stared down at Kaph lying stiff, he teeth a white line inside dark parted lips.

"Like epilepsy. Brain damage maybe?"

"What about shooting him full of meprobamate?"

Pugh shook his head. "I don't know what's in that shot I already gave him for shock. Don't want to overdose him."

"Maybe he'll sleep it off now."

"I'd like to myself. Between him and the earthquake I can't seem to keep on my feet."

[5] An allusion to Lazarus, the brother of Mary and Martha, whom Jesus raised from the dead (John 11:1–44).

"You got a nasty crack there. Go on, I'll sit up a while."

Pugh cleaned his cut cheek and pulled off his shirt, then paused.

"Is there anything we ought to have done—have tried to do—"

"They're all dead," Martin said heavily, gently.

Pugh lay down on top of his sleeping bag and one instant later was wakened by a hideous, sucking, struggling noise. He staggered up, found the needle, tried three times to jab it in correctly and failed, began to massage over Kaph's heart. "Mouth-to-mouth," he said, and Martin obeyed. Presently Kaph drew a harsh breath, his heartbeat steadied, his rigid muscles began to relax.

"How long did I sleep?"

"Half an hour."

They stood up sweating. The ground shuddered, the fabric of the dome sagged and swayed. Libra was dancing her awful polka again, her *Totentanz*.[6] The sun, though rising, seemed to have grown larger and redder; gas and dust must have been stirred up in the feeble atmosphere.

"What's wrong with him, Owen?"

"I think he's dying with them."

"Them—But they're all dead, I tell you."

"Nine of them. They're all dead, they were crushed or suffocated. They were all him, he is all of them. They died, and now he's dying their deaths one by one."

"Oh, pity of God," said Martin.

The next time was much the same. The fifth time was worse, for Kaph fought and raved, trying to speak but getting no words out, as if his mouth were stopped with rocks or clay. After that the attacks grew weaker, but so did he. The eight seizure came at about four-thirty; Pugh and Martin worked till five-thirty doing all they could to keep life in the body that slid without protest into death. They kept him, but Martin said, "The next will finish him." And it did; but Pugh breathed his own breath into the inert lungs, until he himself passed out.

He woke. The dome was opaqued and no light on. He listened and heard the breathing of two sleeping men. He slept, and nothing woke him till hunger did.

The sun was well up over the dark plains, and the planet had stopped dancing. Kaph lay asleep. Pugh and Martin drank tea and looked at him with proprietary triumph.

When he woke Martin went to him: "How do you feel, old man?" There was no answer. Pugh took Martin's place and looked into the brown, dull eyes that gazed toward but not into his own. Like Martin he quickly turned away. He heated food concentrate and brought it to Kaph. "Come on, drink."

He could see the muscles in Kaph's throat tighten. "Let me die," the young man said.

"You're not dying."

Kaph spoke with clarity and precision: "I am nine-tenths dead. There is not enough of me left alive."

That precision convinced Pugh, and he fought the conviction. "No," he said, peremptory. "They are dead. The others. Your brothers and sisters. You're not them, you're alive. You are John Chow. Your life is in your own hands."

The young man lay still, looking into a darkness that was not there.

---

[6] Dance of death.

Martin and Pugh took turns taking the Exploitation hauler and a spare set of robos over to Hellmouth to salvage equipment and protect it from Libra's sinister atmosphere, for the value of the stuff was, literally, astronomical. It was slow work for one man at a time, but they were unwilling to leave Kaph by himself. The one left in the dome did paperwork, while Kaph sat or lay and stared into his darkness and never spoke. The days went by, silent.

The radio spat and spoke: the Mission calling from the ship. "We'll be down on Libra in five weeks, Owen. Thirty-four E-days nine hours I make it as of now. How's tricks in the old dome?"

"Not good, chief. The Exploit team were killed, all but one of them, in the mine. Earthquake. Six days ago."

The radio crackled and sang starsong. Sixteen seconds' lag each way; the ship was out around Planet II now. "Killed, all but one? You and Martin were unhurt?"

"We're all right, chief."

Thirty-two seconds.

"*Passerine* left an Exploit team out here with us. I may put them on the Hellmouth project then, instead of the Quadrant Seven project. We'll settle that when we come down. In any case you and Martin will be relieved at Dome Two. Hold tight. Anything else?"

"Nothing else."

Thirty-two seconds.

"Right then. So long, Owen."

Kaph had heard all this, and later on Pugh said to him, "The chief may ask you to stay here with the other Exploit team. You know the ropes here." Knowing the exigencies of Far Out life, he wanted to warn the young man. Kaph made no answer. Since he had said, "There is not enough of me left alive," he had not spoken a word.

"Owen," Martin said on suit intercom, "he's spla. Insane. Psycho."

"He's doing very well for a man who's died nine times."

"Well? Like a turned-off android is well? The only emotion he has left is hate. Look at his eyes."

"That's not hate, Martin. Listen, it's true that he has, in a sense, been dead. I cannot imagine what he feels. But it's not hatred. He can't even see us. It's too dark."

"Throats have been cut in the dark. He hates us because we're not Aleph and Yod and Zayin."

"Maybe. But I think he's alone. He doesn't see us or hear us, that's the truth. He never had to see anyone else before. He never was alone before. He had himself to see, talk with, live with, nine other selves all his life. He doesn't know how you go it alone. He must learn. Give him time."

Martin shook his heavy head. "Spla," he said. "Just remember when you're alone with him that he could break your neck one-handed."

"He could do that," said Pugh, a short, soft-voiced man with a scarred cheekbone; he smiled. They were just outside the dome airlock, programming one of the servos to repair a damaged hauler. They could see Kaph sitting inside the great half-egg of the dome like a fly in amber.

"Hand me the insert pack there. What makes you think he'll get any better?"

"He has a strong personality, to be sure."

"Strong? Crippled. Nine-tenths dead, as he put it."

"But he's not dead. He's a live man: John Kaph Chow. He had a jolly queer upbringing, but after all every boy has got to break free of his family. He will do it."

"I can't see it."

"Think a bit, Martin bach. What's this cloning for? To repair the human race. We're in a bad way. Look at me. My IIQ and GC are half this John Chow's. Yet they wanted me so badly for the Far Out Service that when I volunteered they took me and fitted me out with an artificial lung and corrected my myopia. Now if there were enough good sound lads about would they be taking one-lunged short-sighted Welshmen?"

"Didn't know you had an artifical lung."

"I do then. Not tin, you know. Human, grown in a tank from a bit of some-body; cloned, if you like. That's how they make replacement organs, the same general idea as cloning, but bits and pieces instead of whole people. It's my own lung now, whatever. But what I am saying is this, there are too many like me these days and not enough like John Chow. They're trying to raise the level of the human genetic pool, which is a mucky little puddle since the population crash. So then if a man is cloned, he's a strong and clever man. It's only logic, to be sure."

Martin grunted; the servo began to hum.

Kaph had been eating little; he had trouble swallowing his food, choking on it, so that he would give up trying after a few bites. He had lost eight or ten kilos. After three weeks or so, however, his appetite began to pick up, and one day he began to look through the clone's possessions, the sleeping bags, kits, papers which Pugh had stacked neatly in a far angle of a packing-crate alley. He sorted, destroyed a heap of papers and oddments, made a small packet of what remained, then relapsed into his walking coma.

Two days later he spoke. Pugh was trying to correct a flutter in the tape-player and failing; Martin had the jet out, checking their maps of the Pampas. "Hell and damnation!" Pugh said, and Kaph said in a toneless voice, "Do you want me to do that?"

Pugh jumped, controlled himself, and gave the machine to Kaph. The young man took it apart, put it back together, and left it on the table.

"Put on a tape," Pugh said with careful casualness, busy at another table.

Kaph put on the topmost tape, a chorale. He lay down on his cot. The sound of a hundred human voices singing together filled the dome. He lay still, his face blank.

In the next days he took over several routine jobs, unasked. He undertook nothing that wanted initiative, and if asked to do anything he made no response at all.

"He's doing well," Pugh said in the dialect of Argentina.

"He's not. He's turning himself into a machine. Does what he's programmed to do, no reaction to anything else. He's worse off than when he didn't function at all. He's not human any more."

Pugh sighed. "Well, good night," he said in English. "Good night, Kaph."

"Good night," Martin said; Kaph did not.

Next morning at breakfast Kaph reached across Martin's plate for the toast. "Why don't you ask for it?" Martin said with the geniality of repressed exaspera-tion. "I can pass it."

"I can reach it," Kaph said in his flat voice.

"Yes, but look. Asking to pass things, saying good night or hello, they're not important, but all the same when somebody says something a person ought to answer. . . ."

The young man looked indifferently in Martin's direction; his eyes still did not seem to see clear through to the person he looked toward. "Why should I answer?"

"Because somebody has said something to you."

"Why?"

Martin shrugged and laughed. Pugh jumped up and turned on the rock-cutter.

Later on he said, "Lay off that, please, Martin."

"Manners are essential in small isolated crews, some kind of manners, whatever you work out together. He's been taught that, everybody in Far Out knows it. Why does he deliberately flout it?"

"Do you tell yourself good night?"

"So?"

"Don't you see Kaph's never known anyone but himself?"

Martin brooded and then broke out. "Then by God this cloning business is all wrong. It won't do. What are a lot of duplicate geniuses going to do for us when they don't even know we exist?"

Pugh nodded. "It might be wiser to separate the clones and bring them up with others. But they make such a grand team this way."

"Do they? I don't know. If this lot had been ten average inefficient E.T. engineers, would they all have got killed? What if, when the quake came and things started caving in, what if all those kids ran the same way, farther into the mine, maybe, to save the one who was farthest in? Even Kaph was outside and went in. . . . It's hypothetical. But I keep thinking, out of ten ordinary confused guys, more might have got out."

"I don't know. It's true that identical twins tend to die at about the same time, even when they have never seen each other. Identity and death, it is very strange. . . ."

The days went on, the red sun crawled across the dark sky, Kaph did not speak when spoken to, Pugh and Martin snapped at each other more frequently each day. Pugh complained of Martin's snoring. Offended, Martin moved his cot clear across the dome and also ceased speaking to Pugh for some while. Pugh whistled Welsh dirges until Martin complained, and then Pugh stopped speaking for a while.

The day before the Mission ship was due, Martin announced he was going over to Merioneth.

"I thought at least you'd be giving me a hand with the computer to finish the rock analyses," Pugh said, aggrieved.

"Kaph can do that. I want one more look at the Trench. Have fun," Martin added in dialect, and laughed, and left.

"What is that language?"

"Argentinean. I told you that once, didn't I?"

"I don't know." After a while the young man added, "I have forgotten a lot of things, I think."

"It wasn't important, to be sure," Pugh said gently, realizing all at once how important this conversation was. "Will you give me a hand running the computer, Kaph?"

He nodded.

Pugh had left a lot of loose ends, and the job took them all day. Kaph was a good co-worker, quick and systematic, much more so than Pugh himself. His flat voice, now that he was talking again, got on the nerves; but it didn't matter, there was only this one day left to get through and then the ship would come, the old crew, comrades and friends.

During tea break Kaph said, "What will happen if the Explore ship crashes?"

"They'd be killed."

"To you, I mean."

"To us? We'd radio SOS signals and live on half rations till the rescue cruiser from Area Three Base came. Four and a half E-years away it is. We have life support here for three men for, let's see, maybe between four and five years. A bit tight, it would be."

"Would they send a cruiser for three men?"

"They would."

Kaph said no more.

"Enough cheerful speculations," Pugh said cheerfully, rising to get back to work. He slipped sideways and the chair avoided his hand; he did a sort of half-pirouette and fetched up hard against the dome hide. "My goodness," he said, reverting to his native idiom, "what is it?"

"Quake," said Kaph.

The teacups bounced on the table with a plastic cackle, a litter of papers slid off a box, the skin of the dome swelled and sagged. Underfoot there was a huge noise, half sound, half shaking, a subsonic boom.

Kaph sat unmoved. An earthquake does not frighten a man who died in an earthquake.

Pugh, white-faced, wiry black hair sticking out, a frightened man, said, "Martin is in the Trench."

"What trench?"

"The big fault line. The epicenter for the local quakes. Look at the seismograph." Pugh struggled with the stuck door of a still-jittering locker.

"Where are you going?"

"After him."

"Martin took the jet. Sleds aren't safe to use during quakes. They go out of control."

"For God's sake man, shut up."

Kaph stood up, speaking in a flat voice as usual. "It's unnecessary to go out after him now. It's taking an unnecessary risk."

"If his alarm goes off, radio me," Pugh said, shut the head-piece of his suit, and ran to the lock. As he went out Libra picked up her ragged skirts and danced a belly dance from under his feet clear to the red horizon.

Inside the dome, Kaph saw the sled go up, tremble like a meteor in the dull red daylight, and vanish to the northeast. The hide of the dome quivered, the earth coughed. A vent south of the dome belched up a slow-flowing bile of black gas.

A bell shrilled and a red light flashed on the central control board. The sight under the light read Suit 2 and scribbled under that, A. G. M. Kaph did not turn the signal off. He tried to radio Martin, then Pugh, but got no reply from either.

When the aftershocks decreased he went back to work and finished up Pugh's job. It took him about two hours. Every half hour he tried to contact Suit 1 and got no reply, then Suit 2 and got no reply. The red light had stopped flashing after an hour.

It was dinnertime. Kaph cooked dinner for one and ate it. He lay down on his cot.

The aftershocks had ceased except for faint rolling tremors at long intervals. The sun hung in the west, oblate, pale red, immense. It did not sink visibly. There was no sound at all.

Kaph got up and began to walk about the messy, half-packed-up, over-crowded, empty dome. The silence continued. He went to the player and put on the first tape that came to hand. It was pure music, electronic, without harmonies, without voices. It ended. The silence continued.

Pugh's uniform tunic, one button missing, hung over a stack of rock samples. Kaph stared at it a while.

The silence continued.

The child's dream: There is no one else alive in the world but me. In all the world.

Low, north of the dome, a meteor flickered.

Kaph's mouth opened as if he were trying to say something, but no sound came. He went hastily to the north wall and peered out into the gelatinous red light.

The little star came in and sank. Two figures blurred the airlock. Kaph stood close beside the lock as they came in. Martin's imsuit was covered with some kind of dust so that he looked raddled and warty like the surface of Libra. Pugh had him by the arm.

"Is he hurt?"

Pugh shucked his suit, helped Martin peel off his. "Shaken up," he said, curt.

"A piece of cliff fell onto the jet," Martin said, sitting down at the table and waving his arms. "Not while I was in it though. I was parked, see, and poking about that carbon-dust area when I felt things humping. So I went out onto a nice bit of early igneous I'd noticed from above, good footing and out from under the cliffs. Then I saw this bit of the planet fall off onto the flyer, quite a sight it was, and after a while it occurred to me the spare aircans were in the flyer, so I leaned on the panic button. But I didn't get any radio reception, that's always happening here during quakes, so I didn't know if the signal was getting through either. And things went on jumping around and pieces of the cliff coming off. Little rocks flying around, and so dusty you couldn't see a meter ahead. I was really beginning to wonder what I'd do for breathing in the small hours, you know, when I saw old Owen buzzing up the Trench in all that dust and junk like a big ugly bat—"

"Want to eat?" said Pugh.

"Of course I want to eat. How'd you come through the quake here, Kaph? No damage? It wasn't a big one actually, was it, what's the seismo say? My trouble was I was in the middle of it. Old Epicenter Alvaro. Felt like Richter[7] fifteen there—total destruction of planet—"

"Sit down," Pugh said. "Eat."

After Martin had eaten a little his spate of talk ran dry. He very soon went

[7] The Richter scale, developed in 1935 by American seismologist Charles F. Richter, measures in numbers the strength of earthquakes.

off to his cot, still in the remote angle where he had removed it when Pugh complained of his snoring. "Good night, you one-lunged Welshman," he said across the dome.

"Good night."

There was no more out of Martin. Pugh opaqued the dome, turned the lamp down to a yellow glow less than a candle's light, and sat doing nothing, saying nothing, withdrawn.

The silence continued.

"I finished the computations."

Pugh nodded thanks.

"The signal from Martin came through, but I couldn't contact you or him."

Pugh said with effort, "I should not have gone. He had two hours of air left even with only one can. He might have been heading home when I left. This way we were all out of touch with one another. I was scared."

The silence came back, punctuated now by Martin's long, soft snores.

"Do you love Martin?"

Pugh looked up with angry eyes: "Martin is my friend. We've worked together, he's good man." He stopped. After a while he said, "Yes, I love him. Why did you ask that?"

Kaph said nothing, but he looked at the other man. His face was changed, as if he were glimpsing something he had not seen before; his voice too was changed. "How can you . . . How do you . . ."

But Pugh could not tell him. "I don't know," he said, "it's practice, partly. I don't know. We're each of us alone, to be sure. What can you do but hold your hand out in the dark?"

Kaph's strange gaze dropped, burned out by its own intensity.

"I'm tired," Pugh said. "That was ugly, looking for him in all that black dust and muck, and mouths opening and shutting in the ground. . . . I'm going to bed. The ship will be transmitting to us by six or so." He stood up and stretched.

"It's a clone," Kaph said. "The other Exploit Team they're bringing with them."

"Is it then?"

"A twelveclone. They came out with us on the *Passerine.*"

Kaph sat in the small yellow aura of the lamp seeming to look past it at what he feared: the new clone, the multiple self of which he was not part. A lost piece of a broken set, a fragment, inexpert at solitude, not knowing even how you go about giving love to another individual, now he must face the absolute, closed self-sufficiency of the clone of twelve; that was a lot to ask of the poor fellow, to be sure. Pugh put a hand on his shoulder in passing. "The chief won't ask you to stay here with a clone. You can go home. Or since you're Far Out maybe you'll come on farther out with us. We could use you. No hurry deciding. You'll make out all right."

Pugh's quiet voice trailed off. He stood unbuttoning his coat, stooped a little with fatigue. Kaph looked at him and saw the thing he had never seen before, saw him: Owen Pugh, the other, the stranger who held his hand out in the dark.

"Good night," Pugh mumbled, crawling into his sleeping bag and half asleep already, so that he did not hear Kaph reply after a pause, repeating, across darkness, benediction.

[1969]

II

POETRY

4

❧❧❧❧❧❧

What Is Poetry?

What is poetry? One modern poet, perhaps a little vexed by this question, replied that poetry, unlike prose, is a form of writing in which few lines run to the edge of the page. Although this half-facetious response may have been intended to force the questioner to formulate his own definition of poetry, it also expresses how difficult it is to distinguish between poetry and prose on any grounds other than their appearance on the printed page. All imaginative literature—whether poetry, prose, or drama—is primarily concerned with human feelings and attitudes. This is why literature is one of the humanities. And nearly all great literature tries to recreate human experiences that involve the reader emotionally and intellectually. What then makes poetry unique and important? What *is* poetry?

The question is not a new one, and answers to it do not come easily. Samuel Johnson, the great eighteenth-century lexicographer and critic, reflecting the frustration that many must feel in responding to the question, replied with his usual directness: "Why, Sir, it is much easier to say what it is not. We all know what light is; but it is not easy to *tell* what it is." For more than two thousand years, in fact, poets, philosophers, and literary critics have struggled in the telling without shedding much light. Nevertheless, a brief survey of some of their answers will help both to clarify the issues involved and to illustrate the major stages in the development and history of poetry.

POETRY AS ELEVATED OR LOFTY EXPRESSION

Although Aristotle in his *Poetics* (4th century B.C.) clearly linked mankind's enjoyment of poetry with our innate love of imitation and our sense of harmony and rhythm, he concluded that the reader's pleasure is largely governed by the relationship between the subject of the poem and the way in which that

557

subject is treated. He noted, for example, that epic poems and romances, which depict men and women as more heroic than they are in reality, seem more effective when their diction is lofty but still clear. Unfortunately, many of Aristotle's followers transformed this observation into a rigid dictum that all serious poetry must be written in what is called the high style, a style characterized by rhetorical devices, inverted syntax, unfamiliar terms, and (to quote Aristotle) "everything remote from the ordinary."[1] The Aristotelian formula persisted unchallenged for centuries, and a good deal of inferior poetry was written in an effort to comply with it—some of the worst of it in direct imitation of the compound epithets found in Homer's poetry. Poets who fancied Homer's "wine-dark" sea and "rosy-fingered" dawn have given us in imitation such lame phrases as "sky-topp'd" hills, "daily-climbing" flocks, and "leaf-shaking" fear.

THE DIDACTIC PURPOSE OF POETRY

The first English refinement of Aristotelian, or classical, theory came in the fifteenth and sixteenth centuries when, as a result of the Reformation emphasis on the morally useful and didactic, poetry came to be viewed as "an art of imitation . . . with this end, to teach and delight."[2] Thus, many poems of the late medieval period and early Renaissance were accompanied by didactic commentaries in verse designed to force the poem's moral value explicitly upon the attention of its readers. Even so sensuous a poem as Ovid's *Metamorphoses*, which attempts to explain most natural phenomena in terms of the vicissitudes of love, was described in 1565 as a work that gives, for the trouble one takes in reading it,

> double recompense with pleasure and with gain:
> With pleasure through variety and strangeness of the things,
> With gain for good instruction which the understanding brings.
> —From *The XV Books Entytuled Ovid's Metamorphosis*,
> tr. Arthur Golding [1565]

This idea that poetry should instruct even as it entertains anticipates the kind of literature known as allegory, in which such English Renaissance writers as Edmund Spenser excelled and in which all the characters in a story (and sometimes its events and its setting, as well) represent abstract qualities. For example, in the first book of Spenser's *Faerie Queene* (1590), the Red Cross Knight, in addition to being the hero in the romantic episodes, also represents holiness and the Anglican church; his enemies, Duessa (a wicked enchantress) and Archimago (an evil wizard) stand for duplicity and hypocrisy, as well as the Roman Catholic church and the Pope. Similarly, the Faerie Queene is Elizabeth I of England; Duessa, her enemy, is Queen Mary of Scotland. Thanks to Spenser's allegory, the *Faerie Queene* (see p. 676) can be read for its romantic adventures, its moral philosophy, its political commentary, its poetic beauty, or all four at once.

The concept of poetry as instruction did not, of course, originate in medieval England, nor did it disappear when poetry began to be viewed as a means of communicating pleasure rather than philosophy. Centuries earlier, the Ro-

---

[1] John Warrington, trans., *The Poetics* (London: J. M. Dent and Sons, 1963), p. 38.
[2] Sir Philip Sidney, *Apology for Poetry* (1583).

man poet Horace had already pronounced that poetry should be *utile et dulce*—"useful and sweet." And even as late as the nineteenth century, Percy Bysshe Shelley argued that "poets are the unacknowledged legislators of the world," in the sense that ideas first expressed by poets often become adopted by society as a whole. Yet, even by Shelley's time, this theory of poetry had been generally discredited, and few today would argue that didacticism is a central, or even a desirable, purpose of poetry. Most of us prefer to get our philosophy and our morality from other sources.

THE METAPHORIC AND METAPHYSICAL PURPOSES OF POETRY

In the last decade of the reign of Queen Elizabeth I, thanks to the influence of William Shakespeare and Christopher Marlowe, poetry was again redefined. In *A Midsummer Night's Dream*, Shakespeare argued that

> The poet's eye, in a fine frenzy rolling,
> Doth glance from heaven to earth, from earth to heaven;
> And, as imagination bodies forth
> The forms of things unknown, the poet's pen
> Turns them to shapes, and gives to airy nothing
> A local habitation and a name.
> —From *A Midsummer Night's Dream*,
> William Shakespeare [ca. 1595]

Literally, these lines describe the poet, pen in hand, in the act of composition. His eyes dart from the sky to his immediate surroundings as he struggles to put his thoughts into words. But when Shakespeare writes "the poet's eye," he also means to suggest "the poet's imagination"—thus, he is drawing an implied comparison between the movements of the eye and those of the imagination. Shakespeare is saying that, by definition, a poet is one who *sees* relationships, in this case relationships between earth and heaven and between mundane events and their philosophical implications. Many Elizabethan and Jacobean poets came to define their craft in just this way, so that Shakepeare's image of the poet's eye is a good example of imaginative Renaissance poetry and of what is meant by the term *metaphysical verse*. Although this phrase, coined from the suffix *meta* (meaning "beyond") and the root *physics*, has traditionally been used to describe the philosophical concerns and elaborate images in the work of such seventeenth-century poets as John Donne, George Herbert, Edmund Waller, and Andrew Marvell, it really refers to any elaborate or far-fetched comparison, especially one with philosophical implications.

Of all the poets who employ the metaphysical comparison (or *conceit*), none is more famous than John Donne. In "A Valediction: Forbidding Mourning" he develops a series of elaborate comparisons to demonstrate the difference between true spiritual lovers and the passions of ordinary men and women:

A VALEDICTION: FORBIDDING MOURNING

> As virtuous men pass mildly away,
> And whisper to their souls, to go,
> Whilst some of their sad friends do say,
> The breath goes now, and some say, no;

So let us melt, and make no noise,
　　No tear-floods, nor sigh-tempests move,
'Twere profanation of our joys
　　To tell the laity our love.

Moving of th' earth brings harms and fears,
　　Men reckon what it did and meant,
But trepidation of the spheres,
　　Though greater far, is innocent.

Dull sublunary lovers' love
　　(Whose soul is sense) cannot admit
Absence, because it doth remove
　　Those things which elemented it.

But we by a love, so much refined
　　That our selves know not what it is,
Inter-assured of the mind,
　　Care less, eyes, lips, and hands to miss.

Our two souls therefore, which are one,
　　Though I must go, endure not yet
A breach, but an expansion
　　Like gold to airy thinness beat.

If they be two, they are two so
　　As stiff twin compasses are two,
Thy soul, the fixt foot, makes no show
　　To move, but doth, if th' other do.

And though it in the center sit,
　　Yet when the other far doth roam,
It leans, and hearkens after it,
　　And grows erect, as that comes home.

Such wilt thou be to me, who must
　　Like th' other foot, obliquely run;
Thy firmness makes my circle just,
　　And makes me end, where I begun.
　　　　　　　　　　　　—John Donne [1633]

Donne's intention in writing the poem just before his trip to the Continent in 1612 was to explain to his wife that their impending separation should be a mild and peaceful one. It is characteristic of the metaphysical style that each comparison, each metaphor or simile, leads to others. In this case, "melting" leads Donne to think of the transformation of ice to water, suggesting that perhaps his wife will "dissolve in tears" at their parting. In the second stanza, Donne goes on to forbid such conventional displays of sorrow—"tear-floods" and "sigh-tempests"—because " 'Twere profanation of our joys/ To tell the laity our love." In other words, he is saying that any public display of sorrow at their parting will only draw attention to their relationship and thereby cheapen it. No longer will it have the ennobling quality of a religious ceremony (as implied by the words "profanation" and "laity"); instead it will resemble a common carnal love.

Donne's poem continues with a series of similarly striking metaphysical analogies (including, with the phrase "trepidation of the spheres," an allusion to the Ptolemaic system of astronomy) until it reaches an apparent paradox. Although he has begun the poem with the idea of a pious and gentle separation, he decides that there will be no final separation at all, only an attenuation, or stretching. This thought leads him to conclude the poem with two arresting metaphors in which he likens the relationship with his wife first to "gold to airy thinness beat" (sixth stanza) and then to the two legs of a drawing compass (seventh to ninth stanzas).

Donne's conception of parting—and this is the key point—changes in the course of the poem. Although he starts out explaining to his wife how she should react to their separation, he ends up by explaining to himself—and to all of us—how the constancy and purity of their love will keep them together. The kind of delightful discovery that Donne makes is precisely what renders his poetry, and that of many other poets, so exciting. If Donne had only repeated his initial metaphor in a series of ingenious but essentially unchanging comparisons, there would be very little point in reading past the first stanza. But in the process of writing, Donne's thoughts crystallize. As readers, we discover, through his changing metaphors and similes, the significance of his love— and of any spiritual love. It was precisely for this reason that Samuel Johnson, after expressing a number of reservations, ultimately praised the metaphysical conception of poetry: "If they [the metaphysical poets] frequently threw away their wit upon false conceits, they likewise sometimes struck out unexpected truths; if their conceits were far-fetched, they were often worth the carriage. To write on their plan it was at least necessary to read and think."[3]

POETRY AS CONCENTRATED PROSE

Dr. Johnson's rather restrained appreciation of metaphysical poetry helps to identify him as one of the characteristic spokesmen of the eighteenth century during which poetry once again was redefined. No longer was poetry to be viewed as a form of pleasant instruction, as it had been in the medieval period, or startlingly metaphoric, as it had been in the Renaissance. Rather it was to be smooth, witty, and gracious, in keeping with the century's ideal of decorum and restraint. Alexander Pope, the greatest poet of the period, best defined the new ideal in his *Essay on Criticism* (1711):

> True wit is Nature to advantage dress'd;
> What oft was thought but ne'er so well expressed.

The emphasis here is on craft rather than creativity. Not surprisingly, many of the best poets of the age once again turned their attention to translation. John Dryden, for example, translated Virgil's *Aeneid* into English, and Pope spent some thirteen years working on translations of Homer's *Illiad* and *Odyssey*. When not engaged in translating the classics, eighteenth-century poets were inclined to imitate them. Pope's two most famous poems, *The Rape of the Lock* and *The Dunciad,* are both mock epics, and the century was full of ambitious but ill-advised attempts to imitate classical forms of poetry. Because of this

[3] G. B. Hill, ed., "Cowley" in *Lives of the English Poets* (Oxford: Clarendon Press, 1905), I, 20.

emphasis on the translation and imitation of established classics, the eighteenth century is often called the neoclassical period.

As a result of the eighteenth-century taste for wit and grace in expression, most poets abandoned the elaborate rhetorical effects—"the fine frenzies"—common in medieval and Renaissance poetry. Instead, they sought to compress their thoughts, to waste no words, to create poetry that was as neatly trimmed as the formal gardens they loved to pace while composing it. The principal achievement of their poetic style was the closed couplet, an example of which is the one by Pope just quoted. We will have more to say later about the closed couplet; for the moment it will suffice to note how supremely self-sufficient those two lines by Pope are. The first line is a metaphoric definition of wit, whereas the second line explains and modifies, even as it complements and balances, the first. Also note that the words employed are common ones—the ordinary, everyday language of men—and that the syntax follows a normal and expected pattern instead of reflecting the poet's traditional right to rearrange the standard word order of prose to meet the requirements of verse. These lines, in short, realize the eighteenth-century ideal that all language "must be genteel and neat—no pains taken."[4]

In reality, of course, this "new" conception of poetry was no more revolutionary than the didactic and metaphysical views discussed earlier. Donne's "A Valediction: Forbidding Mourning," for example, differs from prose in the number and range of its comparisons, but not its syntax. The sentences of the poem fall into the standard grammatical patterns of prose; and Donne shuns conventional poetic language in favor of a rather startling comparison between true lovers and a compass. The neoclassical poets, however, went well beyond Donne in seeking to make smoothness in diction and meter the measure of their verse. They held that poetry should be to prose as diamonds are to coal: the structure much the same, with a great difference in brilliance, weight, strength, the clarity. This view was endorsed by every major poet from Dryden to Wordsworth. To be sure, on many aspects of their craft these poets were in violent disagreement, but they could, nevertheless, all agree in principle with Wordsworth's assertion in the "Preface" to *Lyrical Ballads* (1802) that the poet's goal should be to write "as far as was possible in a selection of language really used by men."

POETRY AS A VENT FOR EMOTIONS

No sooner had the eighteenth century developed the theory that poetry is nothing more than a crafted and refined version of standard language than the nineteenth century—an age of rebellion in literature as in politics—announced a new and partially contradictory definition. Indeed, only a few pages after advocating that poetry should be written in the "language really used by men," Wordsworth unexpectedly endorsed the idea that "poetry is the spontaneous overflow of powerful feelings." Wordsworth, who was obviously a transitional poet, does not appear to have sensed any contradiction in expecting *uncommon* feelings to be expressed in *common* language. He also went on to deny that the emotional content of poetry demanded tear-floods, sigh-tem-

---

[4] Anthony à Wood, ca. 1675. From *Life and Times of Anthony à Wood,* collected from his diaries and other papers by Andrew Clark (Oxford: Oxford University Press, 1889–1900), II, p. 332.

pests, or any of the nymphs, fawns, and fairies traditionally used by poets, ranging from Ovid to Shakespeare, in an effort to give "to airy nothing a local habitation and a name."

Wordsworth's insistence on the poetic value of the language actually used by ordinary men was at heart anti-Romantic and not characteristic of the nineteenth century, for the word *Romantic* (used frequently to describe the poets of the early nineteenth century) recalls the language and feelings of the medieval romance or *romans*. Romance returns us to a world of high adventure, noble actions, archaic language, chivalry, courtliness, knights, dragons, and beautiful maidens. All of the poets in the generation after Wordsworth believed with Lord Byron that poetry is "the lava of imagination whose eruption prevents an earthquake" and that there is a "poetic" way of thinking that differs dramatically from prosaic thinking. It is typified by energy, emotion, excitement, and audacity.

In many respects, of course, the Romantic definition of poetry was a return to the Renaissance ideal of highly metaphoric language, for Romantic poets filled their lines with vibrant imagery. Indeed, such Romantic poets as John Keats and Thomas Hood consciously imitated the Elizabethans. Hood, in fact, was the author of the most successful of the many attempts to conclude Christopher Marlowe's unfinished verse tale *Hero and Leander,* while Keats imitated the Elizabethans less in plot than in attitude, an attitude that is expressed well in his enthusiastic response to reading a translation of Homer by the sixteenth-century poet George Chapman:

ON FIRST LOOKING INTO CHAPMAN'S HOMER

> Much have I travell'd in the realms of gold,
> And many goodly states and kingdoms seen:
> Round many western islands have I been
> Which bards in fealty to Apollo hold.
> Oft of one wide expanse had I been told
> That deep-browed Homer ruled as his demesne;
> Yet did I never breathe its pure serene
> Till I heard Chapman speak out loud and bold:
> Then felt I like some watcher of the skies
> When a new planet swims into his ken;
> Or like stout Cortez when with eagle eyes
> He stared at the Pacific—and all his men
> Looked at each other with a wild surmise—
> Silent, upon a peak in Darien.
>
> —John Keats [1816]

This sonnet develops an analogy between Keats's pleasure in discovering a new imaginative world in Homer's poetry and the pleasure of an explorer like Cortez in sighting the Pacific Ocean from a mountain in Darien, a region in eastern Panama.[5] The similarity between Keats's bold comparison and Donne's metaphysical conceit is clear: Keats's images, like Donne's, range from earth to heaven and from mind to matter. Keats compares reading with traveling and the poet's "golden" words with the Indies' golden realms. The real curiosity

---

[5] Actually, Balboa first stood on this mountain, as Keats was doubtless well aware. The sound of Cortez's name and the romantic associations that name conjures up explain and justify the historical inaccuracy.

in this poem, however, is Keats's sudden and brief change of imagery in the ninth and tenth lines, when he switches from his geographic metaphor to an astronomical one. He compares the pleasures of reading Homer to the sudden delight an astronomer might feel in discovering a new planet. Such an assertion makes the point that poetry can provide all the pleasure of an intellectual discovery and by doing so underscores the preoccupation of the romantic poets with transcendental "ideas" and the life of the mind. These poets were influenced by the eighteenth-century empirical philosophers—particularly Bishop Berkeley, who argued in *The Principles of Human Knowledge* "that all the choir of heaven, the furniture of the earth,—in a word all those bodies which compose the mighty frame of the world,—have not any subsistence without a mind." According to this view, nothing is certain to exist unless it can be perceived by the mind using the physical senses. Hence, thoughts are more "real" than objects, and poetry, because it is a form of concentrated thinking, is an important and justifiable philosophic pursuit.

The Romantic's definition required that poetry be both emotional and introspective. To quote Keats again:

Poetry should surprise by a fine excess and not by singularity. It should strike the reader as a wording of his own highest thoughts and appear almost as a remembrance. Its touches of beauty should never be halfway. The rise, the progress, the setting of imagery should, like the sun, come natural to him.

—John Keats's letter to John Taylor, Feb. 27, 1818

To be sure, there are inaccuracies in this as in other definitions of poetry. Instead of being a fiery record of evanescent thoughts, most Romantic poems, like those written in other periods, were meticulously crafted and repeatedly revised. Byron, for example, had implied that his poetry was tossed off in a feverish passion; in fact, all the original manuscripts of his poetry show signs of careful rewriting, and the same is true of the other Romantic poets.

POETRY AS AN ORGANIC STRUCTURE

Early in the twentieth century, poets again redefined their art through new experiments with structure, content, and style. Walt Whitman and Gerard Manley Hopkins, writing in the last third of the nineteenth century in America and in England, respectively, had shaken poetry free from its dependence on fixed patterns of rhyme and meter. To these men, rhyme and meter were only two of the techniques useful in creating pleasing patterns of sound. Their *free verse* substituted balanced and parallel phrases for syllabic counting and replaced the rhyming words at the end of each line with other musical effects (alliteration, assonance, and dissonance) that were not new to English poetry but attained greater prominence in free verse. The experimentation in poetic structure that took place during the first half of the twentieth century has led to many successes. Free verse is particularly effective when, as in the following poem by e. e. cummings, it uses the poem's structure on the printed page as a guide to its rhythms:

"BUFFALO BILL'S"

Buffalo Bill's[6]
defunct
    who used to
    ride a watersmooth-silver
              stallion
and break onetwothreefourfive pigeonsjustlikethat
                         Jesus
he was a handsome man
               and what i want to know is
how do you like your blueeyed boy
Mister Death

                    —e. e. cummings [1923]

Other modern writers contributed to the redefinition of poetry by insisting that it need not be confined to "romantic" subjects and that the range of human experience treated by poetry should be broadened to include "restless nights in one-night cheap hotels" and all the other trivial, humiliating, or inane aspects of modern life. In "The Love Song of J. Alfred Prufrock" (1917), from which we have just quoted, T. S. Eliot took the position that poets, like all the rest of us, must live in a world made trivial by "a hundred indecisions" and that the Romantic poet's visions of hearing "mermaids singing, each to each," are only *dreams*. The Romantic poet, Eliot insists, is more like Polonius than Prince Hamlet:

> Full of high sentence, but a bit obtuse;
> At times, indeed, almost ridiculous—
> Almost, at times, the Fool.

Eliot's use of mundane, realistic events in this poem had been foreshadowed in the nineteenth century by realism and naturalism in fiction and by the work of George Meredith in verse. Meredith's *Modern Love* (1862) was the first attempt in poetry to treat love, an inherently "romantic" subject, in a strictly realistic and antiromantic fashion by laying bare the emotional and psychological implications of ordinary and sometimes trivial interactions between a husband and wife. One stanza from the fifty that comprise the poem may serve to illustrate the modern temper:

> By this he knew she wept with waking eyes:
> That, at his hand's light quiver by her head,
> The strange low sobs that shook their common bed,
> Were called into her with a sharp surprise,
> And strangle mute, like little gaping snakes,
> Dreadfully venomous to him. She lay
> Stone-still, and the long darkness flowed away
> With muffled pulses. Then, as midnight makes
> Her giant heart of Memory and Tears
> Drink the pale drug of silence, and so beat
> Sleep's heavy measure, they from head to feet

---

[6] The nickname of William F. Cody (1846–1917), a famous American Indian fighter and frontier scout and an impressario of the wild west show.

Were moveless, looking through their dead black years
By vain regret scrawled over the blank wall.
Like sculptured effigies they might be seen
Upon their marriage-tomb, the sword between;
Each wishing for the sword that severs all.
                —From *Modern Love,* George Meredith [1862]

The situation here is quite unlike anything written before in English verse. There is no love, just as there is no conversation, between the two unhappy people—the scant distance between them in bed cannot be spanned because of an immense, and as yet unspoken, distance in spirit. This stanza records the husband's realization that their marriage is dying. His wife has been weeping silently in bed, and when he reaches over to comfort her, she stiffens, betraying her repugnance. On the surface, the incident appears ordinary and perhaps even insignificant, but Meredith analyzes the meaning of the action through a poetic rhetoric that is terse, difficult, and occasionally obscure. The husband's attitude is revealed in imagery dominated by death. Snakes, venoms, midnight drugs, dead years, sculptured effigies, and marriage-tombs all play a part in transforming the narrator's discovery of his wife's tears into an acute death-wish. The significance of the wife's sobbing is to be found almost entirely in the poisonous thoughts that those tears seed and water in her husband's mind.

The difficulties we may experience on our first quick reading of *Modern Love* are the results of another general characteristic of modern poetry: its terse language and tight structure. An analogy can be drawn between the construction of the poem and organic growth; each word in the poem, like each cell in a plant, should perform a specific function in the life of the whole. The poem itself is the natural outgrowth of the idea that gave it birth. Although such a view of poetry was vigorously expressed by Coleridge in his *Biographia Literaria* (1817) and later by Ralph Waldo Emerson, only in the twentieth century has it been greeted with general acceptance. Archibald MacLeish, speaking for his contemporaries, has written that

A poem should be palpable and mute
As a globed fruit
                .   .   .
A poem should not mean
But be.
                —From "Ars Poetica."
                Archibald MacLeish [1926]

The increased emphasis on imagery and symbolism implied by this view adds to each line of poetry a greater richness and density; however, it also complicates the critic's task of understanding the author's purpose and clarifying his achievement.

Taken as a whole, then, the poetry of the twentieth century demands more of its readers than it has in the past. According to Allan Tate, an important contemporary poet and critic, the reader must give to the poem "the fullest cooperation of his intellectual resources, all his knowledge of the world, and all the persistence and alertness that he now thinks of giving to scientific studies."[7] Tate encourages us "to look upon language as a field of study,

[7] Allen Tate, "Understanding Modern Poetry," *Essays of Four Decades* (Chicago: Swallow Press, 1968), p. 163.

not as an impressionistic debauch."[8] The analytical approach to literary criticism, which we adopt in this text, is an outgrowth of this modern attitude that language and literature are academic disciplines and that poetry can be both read and studied.

In the preceding pages we have surveyed the changing historical consensus about the nature and purpose of poetry. Each generation of poets has contributed something to our understanding of the genre, but no generation has had the whole answer; and it is unrealistic to expect that such an answer will ever be forthcoming. If we stand outside the historical spectrum, we can see how one view dominates an age only to give way to another. So long as poetry remains a vital form of human expression, we can expect that its techniques and purposes will continue to change.

What *is* poetry? We ask again. Although we may be unable to answer this question for all time, we *can* summarize those elements in the definition of poetry that have remained nearly constant throughout the ages.

Poetry, like all literature, attempts to communicate an author's emotional and philosophical responses to his or her own existence and to the surrounding world. It is an expression of what is thought and felt, rather than what is known as fact. It depends on observation, just as science does, but poetry draws comparisons between phenomena that science might find distant and unrelated. When Keats wishes to share his emotions upon first reading Chapman's translation of Homer's poetry, he finds an apt metaphor in the conquistador's silent wonder at the vast Pacific Ocean. When Meredith wishes to describe the emotional impact of a wife's stifled sobs, he conjures up venomous snakes. Such comparisons require a bold leap of the imagination in both the poet and his audience. When they are effective, they reproduce emotions in the reader similar to those actually experienced by the author. Thus, poetry is fundamentally metaphoric and is capable of communicating in very few words thoughts and emotions of great complexity.

Prose literature, of course, is capable of achieving everything suggested in the preceding paragraph. As a result of modern experiments with free verse and the increasing literary artistry of short story writers and novelists, the distinctions between poetry and prose are often slight. Hence, all of the techniques of poetry can, on occasion, be properly considered in the critical explication of fiction and drama. However, poetry ordinarily does differ from prose in several significant regards. First, it provides an accepted format (in ballads, odes, and sonnets) for the publication of short but independent pieces of narration, description, or reflection. Second, "poetic license" permits verse to depart on occasion from the standard rules of logic and grammar governing ordinary prose. Third, poetry tends to make more use than prose of symbolism, imagery, and figures of speech. And finally, poetry relies more heavily than prose on the sound and rhythm of speech and hence usually employs both rhyme and meter.

The formal patterns of meter and rhyme, which continue to dominate poetry despite modern experiments with free verse, place obvious restrictions on the poet's choice of words. The poet must write carefully and reflectively in order to find words that not only fulfill the demands of meter and rhyme, but also express the meaning in a manner that complements the imagery and tone of

[8] Ibid., p. 168.

the rest of the poem. This careful use of language is the most significant difference between ordinary prose and poetry. The ordinary prose writer neatly builds an argument using words the way a mason builds a house using bricks; the poet is a craftsman who creates a fieldstone hearth—each stone or each word is turned over, examined, and often laid aside until it can be placed where its shape, weight, and color will contribute to the strength and beauty of the whole. Prose, according to Samuel Taylor Coleridge, is "words in their best order," and poetry is "the best words in their best order."

Very little of the verse of any age comes up to the high standards set in the previous paragraph. Even great poets write relatively few great poems, and our disappointment in the inferior works of notable poets is greater than it is in the secondary works of great novelists. This, too, points out a difference between prose and poetry. Mediocre prose is often enjoyable in much the same way that a walk in the city can be enjoyable even though it is not so fresh and invigorating as a hike through the wilderness. But prose is still linguistic walking, and poetry is linguistic riding. Either the rider *or* his mount will have control over the rhythm, the pace, and the direction of the journey. When the horse is in command—that is, when the meter and rhyme govern and control the poet—the ride will be uneven, misdirected, unintelligible, and sometimes fearsome. When the rider is in control—that is, when the poet fully controls the meter and rhyme—and gait will be swift, smooth, graceful, and elegant, like Buffalo Bill's ride on his "watersmooth-silver stallion."

In the preceding paragraphs we have compared the poet with an artisan and an equestrian. Both comparisons convey something about the essential quality of poetry, but perhaps they emphasize too strongly the skill of the poet and not strongly enough the skills that are necessary in an appreciative reader. Poetry shares with all other forms of literature the fact that it is a form of communication between the author and the reader. It depends as much on the good will, intelligence, and experience of the latter as on the genius of the former. Robert Frost once said that writing free verse is like playing tennis with the net down. Regardless of whether we agree with Frost's implied criticism of free verse, his remark underscores the fact that poetry is a game played according to established rules between poet and form and also between poet and reader. In order to play the game, in order to understand poetry, one must first learn the rules.

5

❧❧❧❧❧❧

Poetic Diction

THE MEANING OF WORDS

Words are the building blocks of poetry. By the time students enter college, they have heard at least 100 million words in school; spoken 30 million words in school and out; and read, in spite of television, some 10 million words. During the years of formal schooling language is so ingrained in us that we cannot imagine an existence without words; our most private thoughts often take the form of an inner dialogue and even our dreams incorporate words. In short, we become so sophisticated in language, and at such an early age, that we seldom realize the complexity of the language we read, speak, and hear.

Our understanding of language, whether as auditors or as readers, depends almost entirely on two factors: our knowledge of the meaning of individual words and our recognition of various cues (syntax, punctuation, and structure in reading; syntax, emphasis, and vocal pauses in listening) directing our attention to the relationships among the words.[1] Our first concern is with the meaning of individual words, but it will soon become clear that meaning is largely determined by context and by the interrelationships of words in a sentence. Several of the elements of poetry, however, are occasionally independent of context: specifically, denotation, connotation, and allusion. Each word in a language is distinguished from every other word by its unique combination of denotations and connotations; there are no perfect synonyms. Poetry is

---

[1] Literary critics have not sufficiently emphasized the fact that poetry gives—through rhythm, rhyme, and verse form—more cues about meaning than prose. This was even more obvious in the Middle Ages than it is now. Our elaborate gradations of punctuation are relatively recent inventions; medieval scribes used only the slash and the period. Consequently, medieval manuscripts are much easier to read in verse than in prose and, perhaps as a result, verse was often preferred for any composition of lasting value.

the form of writing that takes greatest advantage of the personalities of words; it welcomes their eccentricities. Therefore, no word in great poetry can be moved or replaced without changing and perhaps harming the whole. An understanding of the meaning of individual words, therefore, is the first step in understanding poetry.

Denotation

"When I use a word," Humpty Dumpty said in rather a scornful tone, "it means just what I choose it to mean—neither more nor less."

"The question is," said Alice, "whether you *can* make words mean so many different things."

"The question is," said Humpty Dumpty, "which is to be Master—that's all."

Alice was too much puzzled to say anything, so after a minute Humpty Dumpty began again. "They've a temper, some of them—particularly verbs, they're the proudest—adjectives you can do anything with, but not verbs—however, *I* can manage the whole lot of them! Impenetrability! That's what *I* say!"

—From *Through the Looking Glass,* Lewis Carroll [1871]

As is often the case, Lewis Carroll's humor is far from absurd. In fact, the quotation points to an interesting paradox about words. A word is only an accurate tool of communication if it conveys the same idea to both the speaker and the listener; yet the meanings of words continually change and, despite the existence of dictionaries, can only be said to mean what people *think* they mean. New words are continually entering the language and old words dropping out or changing their implications. Furthermore, the same word can mean different things to different people or different things in different contexts. If, for example, we say of someone, "He's a bit red," we may mean that he is embarrassed, sunburned, or attracted to Communism, depending on the context. Similarly, if a man living in the fifteenth century introduced a woman as John Smith's "mistress," he would have been praising her as an honest wife of noble blood; today, he might be disparaging her lack of a marriage license. (The word *mistress* is derived from the same root as *master* and was long represented by the abbreviation *Mrs.* Paradoxically, the abbreviation now has a meaning incompatible with that of the word it represents.) And if we object to using words that carry the clutter of variant definitions based on history, location, and context . . . well, we can turn to *new* words, freshly minted to meet their creators' needs. Lewis Carroll was remarkably adept at coining such words. We are indebted to him for the *boojum* (which is now the name of a species of tree found in southern California), the *snark* (now used as the trade name of a small sailboat), and the Cheshire Cat's smile. To Joseph Heller, we owe the expression *Catch-22,* and to Harriet Beecher Stowe, we owe *Uncle Tom.* The military's fondness for acronyms has produced *radar* (radio detection and ranging) and *snafu* (situation normal all fouled up).[2] The list goes on.

The various meanings of the words we have been discussing so far are all denotative—that is, they are listed as definitions in nearly any good dictionary. Most of us, when asked the meaning of any particular word, reply with a single,

[2] Not all acronyms are felicitous or dignified. Richard Nixon's ill-fated Committee to Re-elect the President was known as CREEP, and the device used by NASA to blow up misguided missiles is called EGADS (Electronic Ground Automatic Destruct System.)

rather loose, definition. But we know that nearly every word has many definitions and that its denotation in a particular instance will depend largely on the context. These multiple meanings make the whole issue of a word's denotation much more complex and much less clear-cut than it may seem at first. It is an indication of the complexity of this issue that the most authoritative dictionary in the language, *The Oxford English Dictionary* (1933), is 16,464 pages long. In it one finds, for example, more than eighteen pages, with three columns of print to the page, defining the verb *set*, which is capable of taking on 154 separate senses with nearly a thousand minor subdivisions of meaning.

The first task in understanding a poem is to understand thoroughly each word in it. Often, the best clues to the meaning of an unfamiliar word are to be found within the poem itself. Suppose, for example, that one wishes to know the meaning of "heal-all" in the following sonnet by Robert Frost:

DESIGN

I found a dimpled spider, fat and white,
On a white heal-all, holding up a moth
Like a piece of rigid satin cloth—
Assorted characters of death and blight
Mixed ready to begin the morning right,
Like the ingredients of a witches' broth—
A snow-drop spider, a flower like a froth,
And dead wings carried like a paper kite.
What had that flower to do with being white,
The wayside blue and innocent heal-all?
What brought the kindred spider to that height,
Then steered the white moth thither in the night?
What but the design of darkness to appall?—
If design govern in a thing so small.
—Robert Frost [1936]

A dictionary only tells us that a "heal-all" is either a panacea of some kind or one of a number of plants (*Rhodiola rosea, Valeriana officinalis, Prunella vulgaris,* and *Collinsonia canadensis*) that are thought to have medicinal value. This, although accurate, is no real help. If we don't know what a "heal-all" is in the first place, we certainly aren't going to know anything about a *Rhodiola rosea* or any of the other species listed. If we turn to a book on horticulture for help, we will learn where these plants grow, how large they get, how many stamens and pistils the flower have, and so on. We may even find pictures of each of the four plants, but without referring to the poem we won't learn anything telling us which of the four Frost meant or what emotions he hoped to evoke in the reader through the name. In comparison, look at the mass of information about the word contained in the poem itself. We know that a heal-all is a blue flower (lines nine and ten) of substantial height and size (large enough to support a fat spider and tall enough so that Frost is surprised to see the spider on it). We know that it grows by the wayside and that it is innocent; if it doesn't heal everything, as its name suggests, it is not ordinarily poisonous either. But the particular heal-all in the poem is unusual and almost an object of horror. It is blighted and white, a deformed member of its species. Thus, Frost sees its frothlike flowers as a fitting element in a witches' brew— and a fitting element in a poem that raises the possibility of malevolent destiny.

In the course of the poem, Frost has defined what he means by a heal-all.

He has told us about the flower and, more importantly, he has told us about himself and the destiny he thinks governs existence. We learn what the word means and also what it symbolizes for Frost. The risk involved in defining a word from its context is, of course, that we are often unable to differentiate between the general denotative meaning of the word and its special symbolism for the poet. For this reason it is wise to check any definitions derived from context with those given in the dictionary.

Any ample dictionary will answer most of the needs of the student-critic; but one should keep in mind that the meaning of words changes with time, and dictionaries of only one volume seldom trace historical change. As a result of the civil rights movement of the 1960s, for example, the verb *discriminate* has come to mean "to make a decision based on prejudice." In the *Oxford English Dictionary*, however, the history of the word reveals that prior to about 1880 the verb meant only "to distinguish, differentiate, or exercise discernment." According to these early meanings of the word, an intelligent person should always be discriminating; today, we hope to avoid discriminating. Such changes in language are so common that we can expect to find some archaism in virtually every poem written before the beginning of the eighteenth century.

Connotation

As we have seen, denotation refers to the dictionary meaning of a word. Connotation, on the other hand, is determined by the ideas associated with or suggested by the word. Denotation is the meaning a word gives *to* a sentence; connotation is the verbal coloring a word takes on *from* those sentences in which it is commonly used. When a word like *discriminate* is uniformly employed in a narrow set of circumstances (in this case, involving some form of prejudice), its connotations may eventually be incorporated into the definition of the word itself. This is the principal process by which the definitions of words change. Thus, a word's connotations may be compared to the living, growing bark of a tree, and its denotations, like the rings in the tree's core, are the permanent record of its past growth. To change the simile slightly, the denotations of a word are visible, like a tree's branches and leaves; the connotations are the roots, which go deeply into the subsoil of our experience creating invisible ties between contexts and associations and drawing up nourishment for a continuing growth above ground.

Many words have multiple and even conflicting connotations. In the sonnet by Frost on page 571 the spider, the moth, and the flower are all white. Most of the time we associate the adjective *white* with innocence, purity, and cleanliness. A young bride is customarily married in a white gown and angels are depicted wearing white robes. In other contexts, however, this color can also signify pallor, illness, blight, or even death. Frost is probably drawing on both sets of connotations in his poem. The white moth fluttering toward its destruction in the darkness is harmless and innocent; the white flower that attracts it is blighted and unusual; and the fat white spider is a ghastly object of poison and death. Frost expects us to react—perhaps even shudder—at this departure from the normal and expected. Indeed, Frost's own attitude changes. In the last six lines he moves from questioning to despair—("What had . . . ? What brought . . . ? What but . . . ?")—as his conviction grows that such an evil distortion of "whiteness" can only be brought about by "the design of darkness to appall."

A word's connotations, like its denotations, may change over time; indeed, even the connotations of an *idea* may change with time. In "A Valediction: Forbidding Mourning" (1663), John Donne compares the separation of lovers with death:

> As virtuous men pass mildly away,
>   And whisper to their souls, to go,
> Whilst some of their sad friends do say,
>   The breath goes now, and some say, no:
>
> So let us melt, and make no noise,
>   No tear-floods, nor sigh-tempests move,
> T'were profanation of our joys
>   To tell the laity our love.

To a modern reader, love would seem least of all like death, but Donne sees the separation of lovers and the death of a saintly man as similar changes in state, from earthly to spiritual. At the same time, Donne is also playing with the connotations of *dying*. He is, no doubt, well aware that the verb *to die*, when used by Renaissance poets in discussing sexual love, inevitably refers to sexual exhaustion. He immediately reinforces these erotic implications in the fifth line, when he chooses the verb *melt* instead of *part*, because the former may suggest the "melting looks" of lovers and the "melting ecstasies" of passion. Thus, Donne's superficial piety in referring to the passing of virtuous men is undercut by erotic connotations. Most modern readers become aware of such connotations only through the labors of literary historians.

Perhaps a more dramatic example of change in a word's connotations occurs in Samuel Taylor Coleridge's "Sonnet to the Reverend W. L. Bowles" (1796). Coleridge claims that the verses of Reverend Bowles were capable of soothing a tumultuous mind:

> As the great Spirit erst with plastic sweep
> Mov'd on the darkness of the unform'd deep.

Coleridge here uses *plastic* to mean "having the power of molding or shaping formless material"—a meaning of the word that the dictionary still lists. He is not referring to the ubiquitous plastic that we associate with cheap merchandise and that was then still an alchemist's dream. Instead of implying artificiality, *plastic* then connoted superhuman power.

The connotations of *white, melt, die*, and *plastic* all result from the common uses of the words, but all words have different sounds, and the connotations associated with these sounds may also influence poetic meaning. Thus, when Donne writes, "As virtuous men pass mildly away, . . . So let us melt, and make no noise," part of the emotional effect is caused by the soft sounds of "mild," "melt," and the implied background of murmurs. Similarly, in *Don Juan* Byron exaggerates the sappy tra-la-la of lovely *l* sounds before satirically blasting the effect with the summarizing word "bland" in the following lines:

> When amatory poets sing their loves
> In liquid lines mellifluously bland,
> . . . .
> They little think what mischief is in hand.

As these examples indicate, our sensitivity to connotations of sound is generally reinforced by alliteration, consonance, or assonance—musical devices that will be discussed more fully later.

Allusion

When the English peasants marched against London in their ill-fated revolt of 1381, it is said that they rallied their spirits by chanting this brief ditty:

> When Adam dalf°   °*delved, farmed*
> And Eve span°   °*spun (yarn)*
> Who was then the gentleman?

The peasants wanted to throw off their serfdom and assume the rights of free-born citizens. Their argument, at least in the chant, depended on a Biblical allusion: in Genesis, when God created mankind, he made Adam and Eve, not nobles and serfs—how then is serfdom justified?

A literary allusion is a brief reference to a person, place, phrase, or event drawn from history or literature. Allusions are effective not because of the meaning of the words themselves but because of the associations or connotations that allusive words carry for the informed reader. The use of allusion allows poets to reinforce an argument by illustration, to compress complex ideas into brief phrases, and to suggest thoughts they may not wish to state directly. In the case at hand, the peasants' allusive chant allowed them to request their freedom without putting it in the form of rebellious demand and to support their position with the authority of the Bible.

Names, as in the example just cited, are the most common forms of allusion and the easiest to identify. As another example of names used allusively, let us look again at the stanza from Lord Byron's *Don Juan* that we started to quote earlier:

> When amatory poets sing their loves
>   In liquid lines mellifluously bland,
> And pair their rhymes as Venus yokes her doves,
>   They little think what mischief is in hand;
> The greater their success the worse it proves,
>   As Ovid's verse may give to understand;
> Even Petrarch's self, if judged with due severity,
>   Is the Platonic pimp of all posterity.
>   —From *Don Juan,* Lord Byron [1821]

Byron uses four allusions in eight lines. The first is almost self-explanatory: a poet's rhymes are paired in the same way as the doves that draw Venus's chariot through the heavens are yoked into pairs. The allusion is intended less to send the reader stumbling off to consult his copy of Ovid's *Metamorphoses* than to imitate the similes of love poetry. Byron then goes on to argue that the more successful poets are in writing about love, the worse it is for public morality, "As Ovid's verse may give to understand." Although Byron only expects from his reader the general knowledge that Ovid is renowned as the most seductive of all love poets, he may also be alluding to the rumor that Ovid was banished from Rome because his verse had tempted the daughter of Emperor Caesar Augustus to turn from the path of virtue. The reference to Petrarch in line seven assumes that the reader will know that this fourteenth-century Italian poet (who wrote 227 sonnets about his unrequited love for Laura living and another 90 about his love for Laura dead) inspired most subsequent sonnet cycles. Elizabethan poets like Wyatt and Surrey used Petrarch's sonnets as models in their own attempts to seduce the maidens of their day. A final allusion is contained in the expression *Platonic love,* but this term is so commonly used for "spiritual love" that it is now less allusive than denotative and serves to emphasize that allusion, like denotation and connotation, is one of the factors in determining the meaning of words.

Allusion through literary name-dropping is generally less effective than allusion through quotation or imitation of an author's works. Historically important and well-stated words have an emotional impact that transcends their denotative meaning. A literary allusion that is created through quotation draws on our reaction to the quoted work, the circumstances under which the work was written, and the whole range of our attitudes toward the author. We respond with patriotism to the idealism of the *Declaration of Independence* ("We hold these truths to be self-evident . . ."); with mystical piety to the Gospel according to St. John ("In the beginning was the Word, and the Word was with God, and the Word was God"); and with a shiver to the opening of Edgar Allan Poe's "The Raven" ("Once upon a midnight dreary . . ."). When Keats wrote of "deep-browed Homer" (see p. 563), he was imitating Homer's penchant for such epithets as his often repeated "rosy-fingered Dawn." When Coleridge, in his sonnet to Reverend Bowles, compared the calming of his mind to the calming of waves after the great Spirit "Mov'd on the darkness of the unform'd deep," he was alluding to Genesis, Chapter 1, verse 2:

And the earth was without form, and void; and darkness was upon the face of the deep. And the Spirit of God moved upon the face of the waters.

Such examples of allusion all refer to *famous* people, events, or words, because an allusion is only effective if it is understood and appreciated by the reader. But poets themselves often gain considerable notoriety as public figures, so that allusions to events in their personal lives come to be widely understood. For instance, when Byron writes in the first canto of *Don Juan,*

> 'Tis pity learned virgins ever wed
>   With persons of no sort of education.
> Or gentlemen, who, though well born and bred,
>   Grow tired of scientific conversation:
> I don't choose to say much on this head.
>   I'm a plain man, and in a single station,
> But—Oh! ye lords of ladies intellectual,
> Inform us truly, have they nor hen-peck'd you all?
>   —From *Don Juan,* Lord Byron [1819]

the irony in the stanza may elude us if we fail to recognize that Byron's wife Annabella had been a "learned virgin," that he often called her the "Princess of Parallelograms" and "a walking calculation," and that their separation proceedings provided scandal enough to delight gossips throughout England *and* Europe. Similarly, when Laurence Sterne, the eighteenth-century novelist and clergyman, was married, he wryly made reference to this event in his personal life by taking as his keynote for the following day's sermon this passage from Luke 5:5: "We have toiled all the night and taken nothing."

Repetition

Thus far, we have been examining elements in the meaning of words that are nearly independent of their context in a poem. It is the poetic context, however, that now requires attention because context alone allows us to distinguish among the competing possibilities offered by a word's denotations and connotations. A word will rarely mean exactly the same thing in two different contexts, even within the same poem.

The repetition of a word or phrase in itself tends to change the emphasis and to make prominent what otherwise might be overlooked. This is Robert Frost's intention in repeating the last line in the final stanza of the well-known poem "Stopping by Woods on a Snowy Evening":

STOPPING BY WOODS ON A SNOWY EVENING

Whose woods these are I think I know.
His house is in the village though;
He will not see me stopping here
To watch his woods fill up with snow.

My little horse must think it queer
To stop without a farmhouse near
Between the woods and frozen lake
The darkest evening of the year.

He gives his harness bells a shake
To ask if there is some mistake.
The only other sound's the sweep
Of easy wind and downy flake.

The woods are lovely, dark and deep,
But I have promises to keep,
And miles to go before I sleep,
And miles to go before I sleep.
—Robert Frost [1923]

At first we are inclined to take the last line literally: the narrator must not linger because his trip home is a long one, and presumably he is already late. But, when repeated, the line attains an emphasis that makes this literal interpretation unsatisfactory. We may then ask ourselves a number of questions: What "promises" might go unkept because of this sojourn in the woods? What have the dark woods to do with "sleep?" And, finally, what kind of sleep is the poet talking about? The literal interpretation of the lines seems too mundane to accept the emphasis that Frost's repetition creates, and we are tempted to look for additional meaning. The "promises to keep" may be the whole burden of life's obligations, while the dark woods may be a bittersweet symbol of escape from these responsibilities into fantasy, fairyland, or premature death. And the final word "sleep," when repeated, assumes a greater finality, for death *is* an eternal sleep. In this case, therefore, the simple repetition of a line may encourage us to change our interpretation of the entire poem, affecting both its denotation and symbolism.

Frost achieves a different transformation of meaning by repeating the word "white" in the first three lines of his sonnet "Design":

> I found a dimpled spider, fat and white,
> On a white heal-all, holding up a moth
> Like a white piece of rigid satin cloth—

By repeating the word "white" he focuses our attention on it. Nothing obliged Frost to repeat himself; adjectives like *pallid, bleached, sallow, wan, hoary,* and *pale* are roughly synonymous and could have introduced the variety in style and imagery that ordinarily is desirable in a poem. But each of these alternatives suggests a slightly different shade of white and each carries a slightly different connotation. Only by repeating the *same* word can Frost make the point that the colors are identical. The blighted flower has perfectly concealed the hideous albino spider, and the single white flower in a field of blue has, presumably, enticed the moth into the trap. The incident is remarkable because of its improbability and suggests to the poet that this eerie nighttime rendezvous may have been foreordained. The repetition of "white," a color associated with both innocence and death, builds in the reader a foreboding of evil design, a bleak and blighted destiny in which even the purest of colors can serve the purposes of darkness.

In stanzaic poetry and ballads, repetition is often introduced in the form of a *refrain,* or chorus. The refrain generally occurs at the close of a stanza, where it helps to establish meter, influence mood, or add emphasis. A refrain may be identical in each stanza or it may vary in subtle but important ways during the course of the poem. An example of the effective use of a refrain is found in Rudyard Kipling's "Recessional":

RECESSIONAL

> God of our fathers, known of old,
>   Lord of our far-flung battle-line,
> Beneath whose awful Hand we hold
>   Dominion over palm and pine—
> Lord God of Hosts, be with us yet,
> Lest we forget—lest we forget!
>
> The tumult and the shouting dies;
>   The captains and the kings depart:
> Still stands Thine ancient sacrifice,
>   An humble and a contrite heart.
> Lord God of Hosts, be with us yet,
> Lest we forget—lest we forget!
>
> Far-called, our navies melt away:
>   On dune and headland sinks the fire:
> Lo, all our pomp of yesterday
>   Is one with Nineveh and Tyre![3]
> Judge of nations, spare us yet,
> Lest we forget—lest we forget!

---

[3] Nineveh and Tyre: Prosperous Old Testament cities destroyed by God because of their impiety.

If, drunk with sight of power, we loose
    Wild tongues that have not Thee in awe,
Such boastings as the Gentiles[4] use,
    Or lesser breeds without the Law—
Lord God of Hosts, be with us yet,
Lest we forget—lest we forget!

For heathen heart that puts her trust
    In reeking tube and iron shard,
All valiant dust that builds on dust,
    And guarding, calls not Thee to guard,
For frantic boast and foolish word—
Thy mercy on Thy people, Lord!
        —Rudyard Kipling [1897]

A recessional is a hymn sung at the end of a religious service to signal the stately withdrawal of the clergy and choir from the altar to the vestry. Kipling's "Recessional," however, was not intended as a contribution to Anglican liturgy. It was written at the end of the festivities commemorating Queen Victoria's Diamond Jubilee, in her sixtieth year on the throne of England, and it reflects Kipling's emotions as he contemplates the end of an era. In 1897 Great Britain still governed an extensive empire, but her colonial power had already been challenged by the Sepoy rebellion in India and the Boer War in South Africa. Kipling was born in India and had sympathy for the native population, even though he endorsed the ideals of English colonial government. As we will see in this section and the next (on ambiguity), Kipling's poem expresses the complexity of his attitudes and, in doing so, draws on many of the literary devices we have discussed here. Behind the celebration of the Diamond Jubilee—behind even Kipling's expression of faith in God—we sense in the poem a prophetic lament for the decline of a once glorious empire.

Three of the poem's five stanzas contain an identical two-line refrain:

Lord God of Hosts, be with us yet,
Lest we forget—lest we forget!

The contribution of this refrain to the meaning of the poem depends in part on its literary allusions, in part on the meaning of the words themselves, and in part on repetition. The phrase "Lord God of Hosts" or "Lord of Hosts" occurs frequently in the Bible, especially in the passages describing the destruction of Nineveh by heathen hordes and God's subsequent warnings against impiety. Apart from these Biblical allusions, Kipling's two-line refrain combines both a prayer and a warning: a prayer for God's continuing presence in the hearts of Englishmen and an implicit warning about the consequences of neglecting Him. The repetition of "lest we forget" in the second line of the refrain makes this warning all the more solemn; and by repeating the entire refrain three times, Kipling increases the religious implications (*three* is a number with mystical overtones). Thus, the refrain and the repetition within it not only add an air of solemnity and piety to the mood of the poem, but also underscore the slight differences in the refrain of the third stanza and the radical differences in the last stanza. As it happens, these stanzas present us

[4] Gentiles: Any persons who are not Jewish. Here used to mean anyone who does not believe in the true faith as, for example, the inhabitants of Nineveh and Tyre.

with important clues to the meaning of the poem, clues best discussed in the context of *ambiguity*.

Ambiguity

The use of a word or phrase in such a way as to give it two or more competing meanings is called *ambiguity*. In many instances, ambiguity is both a stylistic flaw and an annoyance because it creates confusion. In fact, the famous "Charge of the Light Brigade," immortalized in verse by Alfred Lord Tennyson (p. 782), would never have taken place were it not for an ambiguity in Lord Raglan's orders to the commander in the field, Lord Lucan: "Lord Raglan wishes the cavalry to advance rapidly to the front, and try to prevent the enemy carrying away the guns." Unfortunately, as Tennyson pointed out, there were cannon to the right of them, cannon to the left of them, and cannon straight ahead. When the baffled Lord Lucan asked *which* guns were meant, the officer who had delivered the order frowned, pointed vaguely into the valley, and said sharply, "There, my Lord, is your enemy. There are your guns." With more courage than common sense, the Light Brigade charged the most distant guns—into the pages of history. As a result of ambiguity in the initial orders, of the 673 horsemen who entered the valley, only 195 returned.

The ambiguity in Lord Raglan's order was a result of imprecise wording. Other forms of ambiguity involve a play on the dual meanings of a particular word or a particular syntactic structure. As an example of the former, let us say that you are driving a friend home for the first time. As you approach an intersection, you ask, "Which way? Left?"

"Right!" your companion replies.

No exercise of logic can tell you whether the word *Right* here means "That is correct, turn left!" or "No! Turn right!" Only more information can clarify your friend's meaning.

Most cases of ambiguity involve a similar play on the meanings of a particular word, but it is also possible to have syntactic ambiguity—that is, ambiguity caused by the ordering of words. For example, there is a story that when Pyrrhus, the king of Epirus, consulted the oracle at Delphi before going into battle, he was encouraged by the prophesy that "Pyrrhus the Romans shall conquer," which he interpreted as meaning that he, Pyrrhus, would prove victorious. The Romans, however, were also encouraged because the sentence seemed to them equivalent to "The Romans shall conquer Pyrrhus." The actual battle demonstrated that the ambiguity of the oracle was appropriate. Although Pyrrhus won the field, he did so at such a cost that he was recorded as saying, "Another such victory, and we are lost." This battle, by the way, gave rise to the phrase *Pyrrhic victory*, which in itself incorporates the paradox (a form of ambiguity) of an undesirable victory.

As the preceding example illustrates, ambiguity can be used by a careful writer to increase the subtlety, impact, and concision of an expression. It can conceal truths that are only superficially contradictory (as in the oracle's prophesy), display an honest ambivalence, expand poetic meaning, or create humor or shock.

Ambivalence and expanded meaning are both revealed in Kipling's "Recessional." Here the ambiguity is not created by a single word with contradictory meanings, but rather by the dual interpretations that the poem as a whole invites. Each stanza is appropriate to the occasion of Victoria's Diamond Jubilee, at the end of which the captains and the kings depart, the naval vessels return to their normal duties, the celebratory bonfires die into embers, and the satisfied masses boast of the national might. But at the same time each stanza can also be interpreted as a comment on the future of the empire, and it is this prophetic element that makes the poem so memorable.

This duality of meaning is not forced on us until the third stanza. If by the lines, "Far-called, our navies melt away;/ On dune and headland sinks the fire," Kipling is referring to the dispersal of ships after the naval display on the Thames and to the fading of bonfires, then surely he is exaggerating when he says, "Lo, all our pomp of yesterday/ Is one with Nineveh and Tyre." The end of a celebration is scarcely like the annihilation of two cities and their civilizations. And surely his prayer, "Judge of Nations, spare us yet,/ Lest we forget—lest we forget!" is nonsensical because nothing about the close of the Jubilee directly suggests the fall of the British empire.

In order to make sense of the stanza we must interpret it *figuratively*, paying as much attention to connotation as to denotation. It is true that the bonfires of the Jubilee were set on England's "dune and headland," but these words are equally applicable to the extremities of the empire—Egypt, India, and Africa. In discussions of empires a "fire" or conflagration may be used to describe a minor uprising, such as the Indian Mutiny of 1857, the first Boer War in 1881, or the British defeat at Khartoum in 1885. All of these well-publicized "fires" along the outskirts of the British empire occurred during the years preceding Victoria's Diamond Jubilee. Furthermore, in primitive regions, the campfire is the symbol of civilization, which staves off encroaching savagery. The sinking fire, when accompanied by allusions to the fall of Nineveh and Tyre, thus suggests unrest and upheaval along the fringes of the empire. The same suggestion is included in the preceding line, "Far-called, our navies melt away"—especially because melting (as with ice) is ordinarily an irreversible process. By implication, the strength of a navy that melts away is permanently diminished. Furthermore, "far-called" is not quite the same as "widely deployed." Kipling's term suggests that the navy has been called into action rather than merely reassigned to simple peace-keeping missions.

After Kipling has drawn our attention to his intentional ambiguity in this third stanza, we may turn with renewed interest to the earlier stanzas. If we pursue Kipling's allusions to Nineveh and Tyre by reading in the Bible Chapters 26–28 of Ezekiel and Chapters 1–3 of Nahum, we discover that Nineveh, like England, had "multiplied [her] merchants above the stars of heaven" and that her "crowned are as the locusts, and [her] captains as the great grasshoppers, which camp in the hedges in the cold day, but when the sun ariseth they flee away." Suddenly Kipling's simple statement that "the captains and the kings depart" takes on ominous connotations. No longer is this just a reference to their return to other duties after the Diamond Jubilee; now it has become a prophesy of their unreliability during future upheavals in the empire.

Similarly, the expression "Lord God of Hosts" becomes ambiguous as the poem progresses and as we begin to track down Kipling's Biblical allusions. In the first stanza it seems obvious that God is on England's side. He is, after all, "Lord of our far-flung battle-line." His "Hosts" are the hordes of British "tommies" and loyal Indian sepoys who have long and successfully defended the empire. But again, after reading the Bible, we discover that the "Lord of Hosts" destroys Tyre by raising up in revolt "the terrible of nations." Like England, Tyre had been a great sea power but eventually had begun to boast,

"I am a God, and I sit in the midst of the seas." These boasts, like those Kipling admonishes in the fourth and fifth stanzas, were made by men "drunk with sight of power" who put their trust in "reeking tube and iron shard" (guns and bullets) instead of in God. Their fate was to be swallowed up by the "lesser breeds without the law" and this is exactly what Kipling fears will happen to England. Thus, in commemorating Queen Victoria's Diamond Jubilee, Kipling has written what he fears may prove to be the empire's dirge. He is obviously ambivalent—torn between his pride in the "far-flung battle-line" and his shame in the "reeking tube and iron shard" that maintain it. This ambivalence laps at his consciousness like the waves of a rising tide through the repetitions of the word "lest," meaning "for fear that . . . for fear that!" Eventually his fears predominate and he bursts out with the concluding prayer:

> For frantic boast and foolish word—
> Thy mercy on thy people, Lord!

Puns and Paradoxes

THE PUN. An ambiguous statement that is intended to be humorous is called a *pun*. Puns almost invariably attain their effect by using one of the thousands of word pairs in English (called homonyms) that are identical in sound and spelling but different in meaning. If, for example, a woman tells us that she knows nothing of labor, she has either never borne children or never held down a job, depending on whether she is using *labor* to mean "the pains and efforts of childbirth" or "employment." When such word play is risqué or sexually suggestive, it is called *double entendre* (a French phrase meaning "to understand in two ways").

Shakespeare uses *double entendre* with exuberance in the final couplet of Sonnet CXLIII:

CXLIII

Lo, as a careful housewife runs to catch
One of her feathered creatures broke away,
Sets down her babe, and makes all swift dispatch
In pursuit of the thing she would have stay;
Whilst her neglected child holds her in chase,
Cries to catch her whose busy care is bent
To follow that which flies before her face,
Not prizing her poor infant's discontent:
So runn'st thou after that which flies from thee,
Whilst I thy babe chase thee afar behind;
But if thou catch thy hope, turn back to me,
And play the mother's part, kiss me, be kind;
So will I pray that thou mayst have thy "Will,"
If thou turn back and my loud crying still.
    —William Shakespeare [ca. 1600]

If we have read Shakespeare's other sonnets (particularly, numbers CXXXIII, CXXXIV, CXLII, and CXLIV), we know that this one is addressed to the famous "woman colour'd ill," with whom he is in love; we also know that she is in love with Shakespeare's friend, "a man right fair." The first twelve lines of the poem carefully prepare us for the concluding couplet. The dark lady is compared with a housewife who chases after a "feathered" creature (presumably a cock or hen, but possibly also a fashionable, "feathered" courtier),[5] while her "neglected child" (Shakespeare) chases after her. Thus, the phrase "have thy 'Will' " may mean:

> So I will pray that thou mayst catch thy cock,
> If thou turn back and my loud crying still.

But the original phrase "have thy will," when applied to relations between the sexes, may also mean to "satisfy one's lust"; and finally, to "have thy 'Will' " may mean—rather shockingly—that "Will" Shakespeare is prepared to tolerate his mistress's sexual infidelities so long as she returns to him afterward. In effect, Shakespeare has created a *triple entendre!*

THE PARADOX. Just as a pun is a form of ambiguity that plays on words, a *paradox* plays on *ideas*. When Mark Twain wrote, for example, that soap and education are less sudden than a massacre but more deadly in the long run, he was using a paradox. He expected his readers to recognize that, although the analogy is literally untrue, it would pass for truth with anyone who has seen the anguish of a schoolboy forced to wash or sit still. The paradox turns on the difference between physical death and the "deadly fear" of soap or the "deadly boredom" of school, and it alludes to the death of imagination that sometimes results from the "civilizing" influence of soap and education. Thus, a paradox is a statement that is true in some sense, even though at first it appears self-contradictory and absurd. When a paradox is expressed in only two words (living death, wise fool, etc.) it is called an *oxymoron.*

Paradoxes are used in poetry for at least three reasons. First, they invariably startle the reader. They are unexpected and, initially, inexplicable. Next, paradoxes involve the reader in an effort at understanding. And finally, if that effort is successful, each paradox delights the reader with a personal sense of discovery. Like allegory and metaphor, a paradox requires the reader to participate intellectually in the creation of literary meaning. Without this active participation, the paradoxes are simply incomprehensible.

In the sonnet "Design" (p. 571) Frost builds toward a paradox by lulling us into complacency with his fluid and unanswerable rhetorical questions:

> What had that flower to do with being white,
> The wayside blue and innocent heal-all?
> What brought the kindred spider to that height,
> Then steered the white moth thither in the night?

Then, just as we are beginning to reassure ourselves that such incidents are the result of pure happenstance, Frost startles us by suggesting a paradoxical solution:

> What but design of darkness to appall?—
> If design govern in a thing so small.

---

[5] The phrase *"feathered creatures"* is, therefore, *ambiguous* and can serve as one more example of that rhetorical device.

According to Frost, the odd congruence of whites in the poem is the "design of darkness." At first, perhaps, our intellects rebel against the paradox that darkness controls these three white objects—it is, after all, a little nonsensical. But Frost's intention is to hint at the possibility that malevolence lurks beneath the otherwise orderly surface of the natural world. By creating the paradox of a darkness that transforms the purest of whites into "assorted characters of death and blight," he makes us question our faith in the eventual triumph of good over evil.

In general, a paradox involves a contradiction between the physical or material meaning of words and their spiritual, emotional, or supernatural connotation, as in the case of Frost's poem. Such contradictory connotations also govern the lighthearted paradox by Twain, for soap and education are emotionally, but not physically, painful. Because paradoxes are capable of playing on the contrasts between earthly and spiritual truths, they are particularly common in religious revelations. In the ancient *Upanishads* of India (the chief theological documents of Hinduism), we learn, for instance, that "the gods love the obscure and hate the obvious." And the *Katha Upanishad* contains a number of paradoxes that raise questions about the interrelationship among mind, matter, and reality:

> If the slayer thinks he slays,
> If the slain thinks he is slain,
> Both these do not understand:
> He slays not, is not slain.
> —From the *Katha Upanishad*
> [700–600 B.C.]

Similarly, Taoism, a Chinese religion that dates back more than 2,000 years, teaches that

> One may know the world without going out of doors.
> One may see the Way of Heaven without looking through the windows.
> The further one goes, the less one knows.
> Therefore the sage knows without going about,
> Understands without seeing,
> And accomplishes without any action.
> —From *The Way of Lao-tzu* [600–200 B.C.]

Later, in the Gospel according to St. John, 11:25–6, we find Jesus saying,

> I am the resurrection, and the life: he that believeth in me, though he were dead, yet shall he live:
> And whosoever liveth and believeth in me shall never die.
> —From *the New Testament* [first century A.D.]

In each case the paradox is initially disconcerting, or at least difficult to understand; however, each ultimately extends to us the principal consolation of religion: the faith in an existence that is more permanent and more attractive than the nasty, brutish, and short life allotted to ordinary man.

Pure paradoxes, involving wholly contradictory ideas, are relatively uncommon in poetry. However, *incongruity*, a similar rhetorical device, is plentiful. A word, a phrase, or an idea is said to be incongruous when it is out of keeping, inconsistent, or inappropriate in its particular surroundings. As was the case

with ambiguity, incongruity is sometimes a stylistic flaw—a sign of sloppy thinking or imprecise writing—but when used carefully, it can subtly change the
meaning of the surrounding words. When Byron wrote about amatory poets
who "sing their loves/ In liquid lines mellifluously bland," he relied on the
incongruity of the word "bland" to indicate his satiric disapproval of most
love poetry. Byron knew very well that bland writing, like bland food, is usually
dull or tasteless—the very opposite of the spicy passion one would expect to
find in love poetry. This startling word choice hits us like a slap in the face
when we have been expecting a gentle goodnight kiss. It creates a paradox
in tone.

Irony

The term *irony* refers to a contrast or discrepancy between appearance and
reality. This discrepancy can take on a number of different forms.

In *dramatic irony* the state of affairs known to the audience (or reader) is
the reverse of what its participants suppose it to be. This is the form of irony
used in *Oedipus Rex*. When the action of the play begins, Oedipus believes
that, by fleeing his homeland as a youth, he has evaded the prophesy that he
will murder his father and marry his mother. The audience knows, however,
that he has already committed these crimes. (The audience's knowledge derives
in part from the fact that Sophocles was writing about a widely known Theban
legend and in part from the prophecies made by the oracle Teiresias early
in the play.) Thus, the tragic impact of *Oedipus Rex* depends largely on our
fascination with the plight of a man who is unaware of his own past, unable
to avoid his own destiny, and driven remorselessly toward his fate by his very
efforts to avoid it.

In *situational irony* a set of circumstances turns out to be the reverse of what
is appropriate or expected. Richard Cory, the "hero" of Edwin Arlington Robinson's poem of 1897 by that name, is widely envied and admired because of
his wealth, his charm, and his apparently agreeable life. Everything about him
leads the "people on the pavement"—and the reader as well—to assume that
he must be happy. He is "a gentleman from sole to crown," "clean favored,"
"quietly arrayed," and "richer than a king." In a world polarized between
rich and poor, beautiful and plain, dignified and common, "them" and "us,"
Richard Cory seems without question to be "one of them," until the last lines
of the poem show us otherwise:

RICHARD CORY

Whenever Richard Cory went down town,
We people on the pavement looked at him:
He was a gentleman from sole to crown,
Clean favored, and imperially slim.

And he was always quietly arrayed,
And he was always human when he talked;
But still he fluttered pulses when he said;
"Good-morning," and he glittered when he walked.

And he was rich—yes, richer than a king—
And admirably schooled in every grace:
In fine, we thought that he was everything
To make us wish that we were in his place.

So on we worked, and waited for the light,
And went without the meat, and cursed the bread;
And Richard Cory, one calm summer night,
Went home and put a bullet through his head.
    —Edwin Arlington Robinson [1897]

Henry David Thoreau once wrote that "the mass of men lead lives of quiet desperation." Ironically, Richard Cory's suicide proves that he was "one of us."

The most common form of irony, *verbal irony*, involves a contrast between what is literally said and what is actually meant. Lord Byron wittily uses this figure of speech to satirize religion in explaining that a series of consumptive attacks have made him pious—presumably because of the usual fear of dying unrepentant:

The first attack at once proved the Divinity
 (But that I never doubted, nor the Devil);
The next, the Virgin's mystical virginity
 The third, the usual Origin of Evil;
The fourth at once established the whole Trinity
 On so uncontrovertible a level
That I devoutly wished the three were four,
On purpose to believe so much the more.
    —From *Don Juan,* Lord Byron [1823]

Verbal irony always requires the reader to detect the discrepancy between the denotative meaning of the words and the author's intention in using them—in this case, between Byron's *claim* that he wished the three persons of the Trinity were four and his *purpose* in satirizing death-bed piety and Christian credulity in general. Thus, verbal irony is the riskiest of all poetic devices because there is always the possibility that the author's intentions will go unrecognized. In 1702, for example, Daniel Defoe, who was himself a Puritan "dissenter," anonymously wrote an essay called "The Shortest Way with the Dissenters," in which he tried to satirize the excessive zeal of his Anglican opponents by ironically contending that Puritan ministers should be hanged and all members of their congregations banished. To his surprise, no one perceived the irony: the Anglican establishment fully endorsed his proposals. Public unrest followed, the government intervened, and Defoe was fined, pilloried, and imprisoned—all because his irony was misunderstood.

Jonathan Swift, Defoe's contemporary, escaped a similar misunderstanding by making his ironic exaggerations so extreme that no one could take them seriously. In 1729, when he wanted to draw the attention of the Anglican government to the plight of starving Catholic children, he published *A Modest Proposal for Preventing the Children of Poor People in Ireland from Being a Burden to Their Parents or Country, and for Making Them Beneficial to the Public.* In this pamphlet he suggested that they be fattened, slaughtered, and sold as a delicacy like veal:

A child will make two dishes at an entertainment for friends; and when the family dines alone, the fore or hind quarter will make a reasonable dish, and seasoned with a little pepper or salt will be very good boiled on the fourth day, especially in winter.
    —From *A Modest Proposal,* Jonathan Swift [1729]

In using such overstatement to ridicule the government's disregard of the sufferings of the Irish Catholics, Swift hoped to force a change in policy. Just as a surgeon's blade cuts so that it may cure, Swift's language is corrosive so that it may be corrective. Writing such as this, which holds up persons, ideas, or things to varying degrees of ridicule or contempt in order to bring about some desirable change, is known as *satire*.

Swift, Defoe, and Byron all sought to underscore and identify their ironies through comic *overstatement* (sometimes called *hyperbole*). Each hoped that the reader would perceive the exaggeration and therefore interpret the text as meaning the opposite of what it appeared to say. Swift really recommended Christian charity, not infanticide; Defoe really endorsed Christian tolerance, not narrow bigotry; and Byron really advocated Deism or agnosticism, not Christian credulity. The risk of misunderstanding an author's irony is particularly great when we ourselves have strong prejudices. Byron was so well aware of the potential ambiguity of irony that he probably considered it a form of protection. If accused of atheism and heresy for his comments on the Trinity, he could always claim he was merely satirizing death-bed repentances.

The other principal means by which poets signal irony is *understatement*—as when J. Alfred Prufrock, the protagonist of T. S. Eliot's famous poem, sadly reflects in a moment of self-disparagement that he has "measured out [his] life with coffee spoons." Just as overstatement is too emphatic, too exuberant, or too harsh, an understatement is too mild or too reserved. In both cases the reader's attention is arrested and his sensitivity to potential irony heightened because the poet's words are inappropriate and literally unbelievable.

Understated irony is often sarcastic. Unlike satire, *sarcasm* (from the Greek word *sarkazein* meaning "to tear flesh") is intended to hurt, not heal. Prufrock's bitter reflections about his life are often sarcastic. For a more modern and clearer example of sarcasm, consider Sir Winston Churchill's characterization of his political rival, Clement Atlee (Prime Minister of England, 1949–1951): "a very modest man—and with reason." Sarcasm, however, is not always so understated. Oscar Wilde, the nineteenth-century English novelist and dramatist, for example, was obviously exaggerating when he sarcastically claimed that "there are two ways of disliking poetry: one way is to dislike it, the other is to read Pope."

Although we have suggested that both overstatement and understatement often signal irony, it is wise to remember that they are not invariably ironic. Overstatement is especially susceptible to use and abuse in everyday speech by those who hope to be vivacious and enthusiastic. It is the linguistic equivalent of a facile smile. Thus, we sometimes exclaim, "How time flies!" when we mean, "it's getting late"; or, when we meet someone for the first time, we may say, "I'm delighted to meet you!" when we mean only, "Hello." Sometimes poets also overstate the truth as a means of showing enthusiasm; but, they, of course, find fresh and original ways of revitalizing tired hyperbolic formulas. Andrew Marvell expresses the idea of time flying by writing in "To His Coy Mistress" (1681),

> But ever at my back I hear
> Time's winged chariot hurrying near.

And Dr. Faustus, in Christopher Marlowe's play of that name, greets Helen of Troy, not with a lame "pleased to meet you," but with a rhetorical question that combines metonymy and overstatement in an expression of sheer rapture:

> Was this the face that launched a thousand ships,
> And burnt the topless towers of Ilium?

Indeed, it may be that exuberance and a delight in words are the fundamental qualities of poetry. Poetry, it has been said, is what is lost in translation. The poet's use of ambiguity, irony, puns, and paradoxes depends almost entirely on the fact that certain words have multiple meanings. A skilled poet is almost by definition sensitive to the specific denotations and connotations of each word at his or her command. A poet knows that any change in word choice is a change in poetic meaning; that any attempt to translate, paraphrase, or summarize a poem is also an attempt to rewrite it—an act that inevitably damages its essence. Even the gentlest touch can be destructive. One cannot, even in admiration, stretch out the wings of the monarch butterfly without brushing the gold from their tips.

But if, in criticism as in entomology, we murder to dissect, what we murder through literary criticism is imperishable. After we have learned all we can from dissection, we have only to turn away from the battered specimen on the critic's pages—we have only to turn back to the poem itself—in order to find our monarch butterfly both alive and made more beautiful by understanding.

IMAGERY

Every word which is used to express a moral or intellectual fact, if traced to its root, is found to be borrowed from some material appearance. "Right" means "straight"; "wrong" means "twisted." "Spirit" primarily means "wind"; "transgression," the "crossing of a line"; "supercilious," the "raising of an eyebrow."
—From "Nature," Ralph Waldo Emerson [1836]

Words that describe a "material appearance" are referred to as *images*. Of course images may take a variety of forms. We see our reflected image in a mirror, and we find a representational image of Liberty in New York harbor. But when we speak of images in literature we mean primarily mental images— words that evoke our memories of events and objects. Poetic language pours out to us, like the plenteous and varied fruits of a cornucopia, a rich, sweet, and nourishing series of mental images that recall sensory experiences.

We commonly think of an image as something seen, and indeed most imagery *is* visual. Thus, Emerson traces the words "right" and "wrong" to their visual roots in objects that are either "straight" or "twisted"; similarly, an offense against the law, a "transgression" (from the Latin *trans,* meaning "across," plus *gradi,* meaning "to step"), recalls the observable action of "crossing a line"; and a haughty or "supercilious" attitude describes the facial expression of someone—perhaps an aristocrat—"raising an eyebrow" in scorn.

Yet Emerson also shows us that not all imagery is primarily visual, for the word "spirit" once meant "wind." We cannot *see* the wind, although we may see its results as it scatters dead leaves along the ground. The wind is more often felt than seen. Like most other words for emotional, intellectual, or philosophic concepts, the word "spirit" probably evolved out of a comparison—in this case between the sensory experience of breathing ("catching one's wind") and the abstract concept of vitality. This effort to make an abstract concept understandable through the use of sensory imagery is characteristic of nearly all poetic comparisons; but before examining the many uses of imagery, we ought to understand why imagery is essential to poetry and what forms it may take.

As Emerson's examples indicate, even the most abstract words often contain a tacit appeal to the senses. Everything we know about the world and about life is a result of what we have seen, heard, smelled, tasted, touched, and felt internally. Our senses provide the link between our minds and external reality. Sensations alone create for us the familiar world of men and women, mountains and valleys, lakes and rivers, physical pleasure and physical pain. So, too, with poetry. Poems without imagery are like a people without vision or hearing. Both exist in darkness and in silence, struggling for understanding in a world of inexpressible abstractions.

One of the achievements of mankind, of course, is the development of languages and systems of thought that allow us to intellectualize our experiences. When we read a poem we are actually declaring ourselves independent of the sensations of the moment. We call forth from our memories various sensual experiences or images. We rearrange those memories in the patterns suggested by the poet—patterns that often do not correspond with any of our actual experiences. In so doing, we participate in vicarious experiences. Images, therefore, are the windows through which we see (or imagine) how other men and women live, and love, and die. They enable us to make discoveries about ourselves and about the world in which we live.

To some extent, as Emerson reminds us, all words create images. The most abstract terms, as well as the most precise verbal pictures, require us to find meaning *in the words* by recollecting, however vaguely, experiences of our own in which we have read, heard, or used those words. Words such as *dragonfly, hollow,* and *heft* summon up fairly specific sensual responses based on sight, sound, and muscular exertion. We see mentally the bulbous eyes, the quivering wings, and the slim, hovering body of the dragonfly. We hear mentally the "hollow" sound of a voice in an empty room. We feel mentally a muscular play in the forearm and shoulder at the "heft" of a nine-iron, a favorite tennis racquet, or a crammed suitcase. But if we replace these imagistic words with scientific or generic terms—if, that is, *dragonfly* becomes *insect, hollow* becomes *void,* and *heft* becomes *specific gravity*—suddenly our mental images are deflated, like limp balloons, because the new terms are mere abstractions divorced from physical sensation.

A good poet always uses an exact image—an image with its own spicy taste, aroma, and appearance—in preference to the trite and overly general words or combinations of words served up like a tasteless pasta in sentimental verse. The difference between concrete, original imagery and imprecise, overworked banality can be illustrated by comparing the first stanza of George Meredith's *Modern Love* with three stanzas on the same subject (the discovery of infidelity) in "Lady Byron's Reply to Lord Byron's 'Fare Thee Well'":

By this he knew she wept with waking eyes:
That, at his hand's light quiver by her head,
The strange low sobs that shook their common bed,
Were called into her with a sharp surprise,
And strangled mute, like little gaping snakes,
Dreadfully venomous to him. She lay
Stone-still, and the long darkness flowed away
With muffled pulses. Then, as midnight makes

Her giant heart of Memory and Tears
Drink the pale drug of silence, and so beat
Sleep's heavy measure, they from head to feet
Were moveless, looking through their dead black years,
By vain regret scrawled over the blank wall.
Like sculptured effigies, they might be seen
Upon their marriage-tomb, the sword between;
Each wishing for the sword that severs all.
    —From *Modern Love,* George Meredith [1862]

Yes, farewell, farewell forever,
    Thou thyself hast fix'd our doom,
Bade hope's sweetest blossoms wither,
    Never more for me to bloom.

. . .

Wrapt in dreams of joy abiding
    On thy breast my head hath lain,
In thy love and truth confiding,
    Bliss I cannot know again.

When thy heart by me "glanc'd over"
    First displayed the guilty stain,
Would these eyes had closed forever,
    Ne'er to weep thy crimes again.
    —From "Lady Byron's Reply,"
    Anonymous

Both poets describe their feelings of betrayal, but "Lady Byron's" hack work is entirely devoid of real action and imagery. It is made up of sentimental commonplaces. Each line from "Yes, farewell, farewell forever" to "Ne'er to weep thy crimes again" deserves, and most likely gets, nothing more than an exasperated groan from readers who recognize that this "poet" has nothing to say, nothing to describe, no actions to represent, no knowledge of the world, and no understanding of poetic style beyond that which allows her to pull at the "throbbing heart-strings" of the most lachrymose and imperceptive readers.

In contrast, Meredith's poetry is packed with specific sense experiences. It is true that throughout the stanza the unhappy marriage partners lie almost motionless. But Meredith allows us to see the wife as she weeps with "waking eyes," to watch her reaction at "his hand's light quiver by her head," to hear and feel "the strange low sobs that shook their common bed," and perhaps even to taste the bitterness of "the pale drug of silence." Furthermore, a series of vivid phrases builds a sense of muscular tension: the wife's sobs were *"strangled mute";* she *"lay stone still";* together they looked back on "dead black years,/ By vain regret *scrawled* over the blank wall."

Even the greatest poets rarely find ways to call into play as many different senses as Meredith has in this stanza. Only the sense of smell is missing; and, as if to make up for the deficiency, Meredith manages to work an image of smell into his second stanza, where the wife's beauty sickens the husband, "as at breath of poison flowers." No doubt this exhaustive catalogue of sensuous imagery is intentional. Meredith's purpose is to show that the subtle change in the relationship between the former lovers has uprooted their lives and left them unable to engage in any human experience without seeing it anew and finding in it signs of their own emotional decay.

Thus, Meredith makes a thematic point by showing that every sensation the couple feels is altered by their present unhappiness. The use of poetic imagery does far more than simply add vigor to his writing; and what is true of Meredith's poem is true of poetry in general. Poets often choose their imagery according to some *principle of selection* and develop it with some meaningful pattern in mind. In Meredith's case, the principle of selection is an attempt to register the fact that all of the husband's senses have been altered by the discovery of his wife's infidelity. A second principle of selection is at work in Meredith's preoccupation throughout the poem with images of death. The first stanza alone makes reference to snakes, venoms, pale drugs, dead black years, sculptured effigies, and marriage tombs. At no point in the stanza does Meredith *tell* us that he is describing the death of love; however, his images allow us to determine that this must be his theme—that the wife's slight stiffening at her husband's touch is a sign of marital *rigor mortis*.

We should also be aware of the *pattern of development* in the imagery of the stanza. Initially, the focus is on the woman's waking eyes and the quivering hand beside her head. Then Meredith expands our vision to take in the bed, the surrounding darkness, and finally midnight's "giant heart of Memory and Tears." The effect is like that achieved by "zooming out" while filming a movie. It puts the marriage partners at the center of a universe that resonates "with muffled pulses" to their sufferings. Having established this broad perspective, Meredith uses imagery that closes in again—first to the memories scrawled across the blank walls and then to the marriage-tomb and the imaginary sword between the man and wife. This cyclical pattern in the development of the imagery is one of several devices Meredith uses to make each stanza a self-contained and satisfying "sonnet."[6] It contributes to our impression that *Modern Love* is an autobiographical series of journal entries written at discrete and circumspect moments as a real marriage decays. This poetic illusion, derived in large part from the pattern in the development of Meredith's imagery, makes *Modern Love* seem contemporary and realistic to each new generation of readers. It is one of the major stylistic features of the poem.

On rare occasions the principle of selection or pattern of development in imagery is more than simply a stylistic feature. It may provide a key to the entire poem or even to the poet's entire personality. In the poetry of Percy Bysshe Shelley, for example, we find repeated images involving sunsets, the wind and waves, moonlight, fountains, veiled women, and shadows. The very fact that Shelley returns so frequently to the same images suggests that he is giving voice to a philosophical preoccupation—namely, that the reality of life lies beneath its surface features and that everything we think to be real is the product of unseen forces. As a result, Shelley's images are all indirect: the colors of the sunset proceed from the unseen sun; the waves are driven by the unseen wind, and the wind itself is caused by unknown forces; moonlight is reflected indirectly from the sun; fountains pulse as a result of unseen pressures; veils conceal feminine beauty; and shadows are indirect images. In each image there is a veil of some kind that conceals the true source of beauty, for Shelley was a strong believer in Platonic idealism.[7]

---

[6] The stanza is not technically a sonnet because it is formed entirely of quatrains and contains sixteen lines to the sonnet's fourteen. Nevertheless, critics from Swinburne to Trevelyan have recognized the independence of each stanza by using the term *sonnet*.

[7] In Plato's allegory of the cave in *The Republic*, human beings are chained in such a way that they see only shadows cast on the wall of the cave and hear voices echoing from that wall. Naturally, they mistake the shadows and echoes for reality.

We have seen that images make writing tangible, and we have seen that the manipulation of imagery is implicit in creative thought. The more exact and evocative the imagery in a poem, the more interested and entertained the reader will remain. Imagery is as indispensable to an exciting poem as action and emotion are to an exciting life. Furthermore, the poet's choice and arrangement of images may provide important clues to thematic and artistic purposes in philosophical poetry. Shelley's belief in the Platonic ideal of intellectual beauty was abstract in the extreme, and it was a continual challenge to his poetic capabilities to find a way to write about the themes that interested him without allowing his poetry to degenerate into images the reader would be unable to comprehend intellectually or emotionally.

Even themes less abstract than Shelley's are necessarily difficult to express imagistically. Although Meredith examines the effect on the human spirit of disappointments in love, he finds no direct way to tell us that this is his theme. Indeed, the human spirit is itself an abstraction, and Emerson's brief indication that the word *spirit* originated as a metaphor is enough to remind us that comparison is the principal technique used by poets to render the abstract in images. Poetic comparisons—more often than any other devices in the arsenal of figurative language—are the keys to a work's philosophical or ethical implications. They allow abstract ideas to be expressed in terms of sensory images that, in turn, find counterparts in the reader's imagination.

COMPARISONS

Prominent among the twelve "good rules" by which King Charles I of England sought to live was his proscription, "Make no comparisons!" It is suspected that his disdain for comparisons grew out of his belief in the divine and *incomparable* status of kings; this egotism so grated on his subjects that Oliver Cromwell, after comparing the king with other "traitors," ordered him executed in 1649. Since then, the right to draw comparisons—even invidious ones—has been one of the most cherished prerogatives of a free people, for it allows us to acquire new information, helps us to reach rational decisions, enables us to express abstract ideas imagistically, and provides us with endless opportunities for entertainment and the exercise of imagination.

We compare politicians before voting and products before purchasing as a means of collecting information and arriving at a decision. Poetic comparisons (*simile, metaphor, implied comparison, metonymy, personification, apostrophe, animism,* and *juxtaposition*) are more entertaining than those of everyday life, but the usefulness of comparison in influencing decisions remains virtually unchanged. John Donne, for example, in wooing a young woman compares the act of love with the predations of a flea:

THE FLEA

MARK but this flea, and mark in this,
How little that, which thou deny'st me, is;
Me it sucked first, and now sucks thee,
And in this flea our two bloods mingled be;
Confess it. This cannot be said
A sin, or shame, or loss of maidenhead,

Yet this enjoys, before it woo,
And pampered swells with one blood made of two,
And this, alas! is more than we would do.[8]

Oh stay, three lives in one flea spare,
Where we almost, nay more than married are.
This flea is you and I, and this
Our marriage bed and marriage temple is;
Though parents grudge, and you, we are met,
And cloistered in these living walls of jet.
Though use° make you apt° to kill me,   *custom / inclined*
Let not to that, self-murder added be,
And sacrilege, three sins in killing three.

Cruel and sudden, hast thou since
Purpled thy nail in blood of innocence?
Wherein could this flea guilty be,
Except in that drop, which it sucked from thee?
Yet thou triumph'st, and say'st that thou
Find'st not thyself nor me the weaker now;
'Tis true; then learn how false fears be:
Just so much honor, when thou yield'st to me,
Will waste, as this flea's death took life from thee.
                                        —John Donne [1633]

In developing this analogy at such length—Donne is creating an *extended comparison.* He uses the flea as one argument to illustrate that the physical relationship he desires is not in itself a significant event: a very similar union has already taken place within the flea without "sin, nor shame, nor loss of maidenhead." Thus, in "The Flea," as in shopping or voting, a comparison identifies and illustrates some of the issues involved in making a decision.

Most poetry, however, is not directly intended to influence conduct or decisions. John Donne's comparison of true lovers to the twin legs of a geometric compass (see p. 559) is a good example of an illuminating comparison that has few implications for conduct; that analogy merely allows Donne to reassure his wife that distance can do nothing to separate them for, as Donne observes, "Thy firmness [as the fixed foot] makes my circle just,/ And makes me end, where I begun."

Whether used to influence conduct or to define abstract ideas through specific images, poetic comparisons may take on a variety of forms. This variety is well represented by the five comparisons in the first two stanzas of Donne's "Valediction: Forbidding Mourning":

As virtuous men pass mildly away,
   And whisper to their souls, to go,
Whilst some of their sad friends do say,
   The breath goes now, and some say, no:

[8] I.e., and this swelling (suggesting pregnancy) is more than we would wish to do.

> So let us melt, and make no noise,
>   No tear-floods, nor sigh-tempests move,
> 'Twere profanation of our joys
>   To tell the laity our love.

The first of the comparisons runs through four and one-half lines and says, in essence, "Let us be just as calm in separating as virtuous men are in dying." Comparisons such as this, which formally develop a similarity between two things using *as, as when, like, than,* or other equivalent constructions, are known as *similes* (similes assert similarity). However, when a poet insists that two terms are identical instead of merely similar he creates a *metaphor*. In Donne's lines here, the hyphenated terms ("tear-floods" and "sigh-tempests"), although exaggerations, are good examples of metaphors; it is, however, more common to find a slightly fuller statement of the metaphor, using a form of the verb "to be," as in Shakespeare's assertion that "All the world's a stage." Both similes and metaphors are common in everyday speech. We say somebody is "sharp as a tack" or "as slow as molasses"; a brand-new car may be either a "lemon" or a "peach." Such similes and metaphors may once have been original and exciting, but they have become overused. Indeed, a shiny new comparison, like the latest model from Detroit, may emerge from the factory with a built-in obsolescence. Even though the comparison may originally have been a very good one, constant repetition may eventually cause us to react with insensitivity, indifference, or even hostility. The better the metaphor is, the more miles are put on it and the more rapidly it is worn out. Good poets, like all good writers, know this and as a result seek constantly to manufacture new analogies.

All similes and metaphors contain two parts, or terms. The *principal* or *primary term* is the one that conveys the literal statement made in the poem. In Donne's metaphors of "tear-floods" and "sign-tempests," the literal statement concerns tears and sighs—hence, these are his principal terms. The *secondary term* in a metaphor is used figuratively to add color, connotations, and specificity to the more abstract primary term. Thus, Donne's "floods" and "tempests" are his secondary terms. Some literary critics call the primary term in a metaphor its *tenor* and the secondary term its *vehicle*.

An analogy in which one or both of these terms is implied but not stated may properly be called a metaphor, but we prefer the term *implied comparison* as being clearer and more accurate. When, for example, Donne writes, " 'Twere profanation of our joys/ To tell the laity our love," he is using one form of implied comparison. What he means is that their love is holy and spiritual like a secret religious ceremony, but only the primary term of the simile ("our love") is actually expressed. The idea that this love is analogous to a religious rite is implicit in the connotations of "profanation" and "laity," but this is left unstated.

On rare occasions, both terms in a comparison may be implied, as in Donne's phrase, "So let us melt." Here he is comparing the separation of spiritual lovers with the gentle natural process that transforms ice to water; however, he relies on the reader to reconstruct mentally this comparison from the single clue he provides in the verb "melt."

While metaphors, similes, and implied comparisons are useful to poets primarily because they offer a mechanism for stating abstract truths through specific images, they also contribute intellectual stimulation, emotional connotations, and conciseness. In the two stanzas just examined, Donne has been struggling to put into words his conception of the relationship between himself and his lover and of how their separation can best reveal the depth of their love. Donne wisely avoids any generalized statement of his intentions, choosing instead to express himself entirely through images of a dying man, of melting, of floods and tempests, and of clergy and laity. In addition to making his writing vivid and concrete, these images are intellectually stimulating, imaginative, and even a little audacious. The gist of Donne's argument is that true love is not wholly physical. It is capable of going through a change in state from physical to spiritual (as the soul does in death), or from fixed to formless (as hard ice becomes fluid water). By confronting, in the beginning, the hyperbolic fear that separation foreshadows death, Donne is able to transform that fear into a religious consolation in which the secret joys of the lovers become sacramental experiences. In one bold and inherently sacrilegious sentence, Donne manages to tie together an awesome image of human mortality, a fundamental law of physics, the stormy forces of nature, and the powerful attraction of love. All of this imagery is permeated with emotional overtones (sorrow, resignation, fear, piety) that might have been lost in any direct statement about spiritual love, self-restraint, and patience. Finally, Donne's comparisons allow him to express all of this in only fifty-five words. Comparisons, in short, give to poetry both conciseness and density. They link the human senses and the human psychology without acknowledging the stages in logic and analysis that underlie this union.

Several other forms of implied comparison may occasionally be encountered in poetry. In *synecdoche,* a part of something is used to suggest the *whole* thing. George Meredith includes synecdoche when he uses the phrase "she wept with waking eyes" (p. 588). Obviously the woman is awake—not just her "waking eyes." In *metonymy* (meaning "change of name"), something associated with an object or idea replaces what is actually meant. Shakespeare uses metonymy when he writes that "the poet's pen/ . . . gives to airy nothing/ A local habitation and a name," since the poet, and not his pen, is clearly responsible for imaginative creation. Both synecdoche and metonymy are frequently found in slang. A "redneck" is a working man whose neck has been toughened by years in the wind and sun; an "old hand" means an experienced workman; and the "heavy" in a movie is a villain whose enormous size and aggressive behavior have become conventional.

The distinction between metonymy and synecdoche is not always clear, as we can see by reconsidering the first stanza of Rudyard Kipling's "Recessional":

> God of our fathers, known of old,
> Lord of our far-flung battle-line,
> Beneath whose awful Hand we hold
> Dominion over palm and pine—
> Lord God of Hosts, be with us yet,
> Lest we forget—lest we forget!

Is the "far-flung battle-line" to be taken as a part of the British empire (and is it, therefore, synecdoche), or is it a product of that empire (and thus metonymy)? Are the "palm and pine," which suggest the huge expanse of an empire ranging from the Middle East to Canada, the partial elements of the empire or are they allied and suggestive objects? Obviously, metonymy and synecdoche overlap in these images, and the most sensible decision is to use one word, metonymy, for both rhetorical devices.

An idea, object, or animal that is portrayed as having human traits is said to be personified. Storms, for example, have been traditionally personified by being given women's names. *Personification,* then, constitutes a form of implied comparison and allows the poet to describe with energy and vitality what might otherwise have remained inanimate or lackluster. Thus, John Milton in "Lycidas" uses personification in writing, "Under the opening eyelids of the Morn/ We drove a-field," when he really means that they drove out at daybreak. Similarly, Chaucer personifies the sunset in writing, "the brighte sonne lost his hewe;/ For th' orisonte hath reft the sonne his lyght," when he actually means what he says in the next line, "This is as muche to seye as it was night!" And George Meredith in the stanza quoted on p. 588 personifies midnight when he writes, "midnight makes/ Her giant heart of Memory and Tears/ Drink the pale drug of silence."

Personification is not always effective, as the third of these examples illustrates. The crucial test here, as with other rhetorical devices, is whether conciseness, specificity, meaning, and clarity are increased or decreased by the personification. In each of our examples, what is gained in vividness through personification is threatened by verbosity or exaggeration. Chaucer, however, makes fun of his own rhetorical excesses, while Milton's image of "the opening eyelids of Morn" effectively unites the emotional associations of daybreak, physical awakening, and dawning understanding. Chaucer's rhetoric is neither defensible nor intended to be so; it is comic. Milton's comparison, on the other hand, is appealing because it is imagistic and thoughtful. Meredith's imagery in this instance is simply baffling, however. We cannot be certain whether "Her giant heart" refers to Meredith's wife's heart or to midnight's heart. If it is midnight's, in what sense does midnight have a heart? Why should this heart be composed of "Memory and Tears"? Why should these nouns be capitalized? How can midnight be said to "beat/ Sleep's heavy measure"? And, finally, how can a "heart" be said to "drink"? But if it is the wife who is sleeping, does she wake up again when she looks back through her dead black years, wishing "for the sword that severs all"? Such ambiguities weaken Meredith's verse and demonstrate that personification is often facile and ridiculous.

Apostrophe, a limited form of personification, occurs when a poet or one of his characters addresses a speech to someone absent or something nonhuman. Although apostrophe is often ineffective in poetry, Geoffrey Chaucer uses it throughout his humorous "Complaint to His Empty Purse" (1399), which begins:

> To you, my purse, and to non other wight°   *person*
> Complayne I, for ye be my lady dere!

and Shakespeare uses apostrophe during King Lear's ragings on the heath:

> Blow, winds, and crack your cheeks! Rage! Blow!
> You cataracts and hurricanoes, spout
> Till you have drench'd our steeples, drown'd the cocks!°.   *weathervanes*
> You sulph'rous and thought-executing fires,
> Vaunt-couriers° of oak-cleaving thunderbolts,   *fore-runners*
> Singe my white head! And thou, all-shaking thunder,

> Strike flat the thick rotundity o' th' world!
> Crack nature's mold, all germens° spill at once   *germs, seeds*
> that makes ingrateful man!
> —From *King Lear*, William Shakespeare [1605]

However, Chaucer's address to his purse is but a playful piece of foolishness and Lear's address to the storm is but a symptom of his madness. In neither case does the poet expect us to see any utility in talking to wallets and winds. If apostrophe were *always* used ironically, as in both of these examples, or comically, as in Robert Burns' poems "To a Mouse" and "To a Louse," then inept poets would undoubtedly have developed some other means of debauching the English language. As things are, however, too many second-rate poems are packed with silly and sentimental apostrophes to Truth, Beauty, Love, and a host of other capitalized abstractions. Weak poets, having worked themselves or their characters up to a stage of violent emotions, often degenerate into what John Ruskin called the "pathetic fallacy" of facile and unimaginative personification. The trite and insipid tribute of Anna Laetitia Barbauld to "Life" is a typical example of the worst form of apostrophe:

> Life! We've been long together,
> Through pleasant and through cloudy weather;
> 'Tis hard to part when friends are dear—
> Perhaps 'twill cost a sigh, a tear.
> —From "Life," Anna Laetitia Barbauld [1811]

Excessive personification or apostrophe is not the only way to ruin a poem, but it may be the most reliable.

A poet may also describe an idea or inanimate object as though it were living, without attributing human traits to it. Before the development of the motion picture, this device could be called animation, but because that term is now best confined to cartoons, we will use the term *animism* for poetic comparisons that give life to inanimate objects. Carl Sandburg employs animism to good effect in his brief poem "Fog":

> FOG
>
> The fog comes
> on little cat feet
>
> It sits looking
> over harbor and city
> on silent haunches
> and then moves on.
> —Carl Sandburg
> [1916]

Similarly, Robert Burns uses an animistic simile when he compares the high spirits of love with the appearance of a newly sprung rose:

> O, my luve is like a red red rose
> That's newly sprung in June
> O, my luve is like the melodie
> That's sweetly played in tune.
> —From "A Red, Red Rose,"
> Robert Burns [1796]

Of course, Burns is also comparing the woman he loves (as well as the emotion of love) with a red rose—young, fresh, fragrant, and beautiful. All depends on whether "my luve" is taken as meaning "my feeling when in love" or "my loved one." In the former, a feeling or idea is animated by comparison with the rose; in the later, the appearance and personality of the maiden are described. Because both interpretations are compatible, this pleasant ambiguity is best left unresolved; however, we should at least mention that the second reading suggests yet another form of comparison. This technique of speaking about a person in terms that are more applicable to a plant, animal, or machine is just the opposite of personification, and yet, oddly, it has no commonly accepted name other than simile or metaphor. T. S. Eliot used this form of comparison in "The Love Song of J. Alfred Prufrock" (1917) to add to the narrator's scorn for his own insignificance:

> I should have been a pair of ragged claws
> Scuttling across the floors of silent seas.

Theodore Roethke, in his "Elegy to Jane," described the "sidelong pickerel smile" of one of his former students, whom he also compared to a wren, a sparrow, and a skittery pigeon. And early blues musicians, whose roots were in the soil of the Mississippi Delta, compared themselves to a variety of country creatures in such songs as "The Bull Frog Blues" (Willie Harris), "The Crawling Kingsnake Blues" (John Lee Hooker), and "The Milk Cow's Calf Blues" (Robert Johnson) in describing their passions and sorrows.

One final form of implied comparison is created through *juxtaposition*. In juxtaposition, two items are merely placed side by side. The author makes no overt comparison between these items and draws no inferences. The reader is free to make of them what he or she will. An impressive example of juxtaposition occurs in Henry Reed's post-World War II poem entitled "Lessons of the War: Naming of Parts." Each of the five stanzas in the poem describes some stage in the military exercise of breaking down and naming the parts of an army rifle; and then, in juxtaposition to this, Reed "names" some of the parts of springtime. The first stanza is representative of the technique followed throughout the poem:

> Today we have naming of parts. Yesterday,
> We had daily cleaning. And tomorrow morning,
> We shall have what to do after firing. But today,
> Today we have naming of the parts. Japonica
> Glistens like coral in all of the neighboring gardens,
>   and today we have naming of parts.
>   —From "Lessons of War: Naming of Parts,"
> Henry Reed [1947]

The first four sentences of the stanza are mechanical, denotative, and dull, whereas the first clause in the next sentence ("Japonica/ Glistens like coral in all of the neighboring gardens") is naturalistic, figurative, imagistic, and appreciative. We see the author's mind at play just as it had been at rather dull work in the preceding lines. We see him transform himself from a military automaton to a sensually aware human being. We see him in an act of mental rebellion against a numbing, mechanical, and inhumane routine. At the same time that his hands and arms go through the rituals of slaughter, his eyes and intellect follow the processes of natural rebirth. From a strictly logical point of view, the two parts of Reed's stanza are incompatible, but he unites them by his repetition of the final phrase, "today we have naming of parts." And in that repetition Reed is implicitly asserting his ability to metamorphose his army experiences in a triumph of human feeling over inhumane behavior.

Juxtaposition is rarely used with as great a dramatic effect as in "Naming of Parts," but it is frequently important in creating the impression of fate or inevitability. When Edwin Arlington Robinson wrote that "Richard Cory, one calm summer night,/ Went home and put a bullet through his head," he was juxtaposing the calm, warm weather and the cold, irrational action in order to prod us into pondering possible reasons for Richard Cory's death. And when Robert Frost found "a dimpled spider, fat and white,/ On a white heal-all, holding up a moth," the juxtaposition of those symbols of death, blight, and innocence became ominous and potentially fateful.

SYMBOL AND ALLEGORY

As we noted in our earlier discussion of fiction, a symbol is something that stands for something else, and an allegory is a narrative that uses a system of implied comparisons—often including symbols—to develop two or more simultaneous levels of meaning. Both devices occur naturally in literature to expand the suggestiveness and significance of writing.

A symbol may be *private* (its meaning known only to one person), *original* (its meaning defined by its context in a particular work), or *traditional* (its meaning defined by our common culture and heritage). At its most complex, a symbol may be all three as, for example, in this extract from "The Whale," a poem that occurs in the ninth chapter of Herman Melville's *Moby Dick:*

THE WHALE

The ribs and terrors in the whale,
   Arched over me a dismal gloom,
While all God's sun-lit waves rolled by,
   And left me deepening down to doom.

I saw the opening maw° of hell,   *jaws*
   With endless pains and sorrows there;
Which none but they that feel can tell—
   Oh, I was plunging to despair.

In black distress, I called my God,
   When I could scarce believe him mine,
He bowed his ear to my complaints—
   No more the whale did me confine.

With speed he flew to my relief,
   As on a radiant dolphin borne;
Awful, yet bright, as lightning shone
   The face of my Deliverer God.

My song for ever shall record
   That terrible, that joyful hour;
I give the glory to my God,
   His all the mercy and the power.
           —Herman Melville [1851]

Here, and throughout *Moby Dick,* the whale is a private symbol, in the sense that it emerges from Melville's own whaling experiences. Melville once wrote, "If, at my death my executors (or more properly, my creditors) find any precious manuscripts in my desk, then I prospectively ascribe all the honor and glory to whaling; for a whale-ship was my Yale and Harvard." But actual experience with whales may have been responsible for only part of the private symbolism in the poem. The battle with the whale may also have served as a metaphor for confrontation with Melville's own despair and may also reflect the "dismal gloom" of his failure to make a living as a bank clerk, a teacher, a surveyor, a seaman, and finally an author. At the time that he completed *Moby Dick,* Melville was in debt to his publisher and to his friends, and he saw little hope of attaining solvency.

No one, of course, can truly gauge the extent to which a poem symbolizes an author's personal turmoil, but there can be no doubt that the whale in *Moby Dick* is an original, powerful, and fully developed symbol within the novel. Even in this brief poem it is clear that the whale is an object of horror, a force of evil, and an embodiment of the darkest spiritual despair. These symbolic associations arise out of the poem itself and require of the reader only a sensitivity to the meaning of words.

The poem, however, also suggest the traditional *parable* (an instructive moral story) of Jonah, who was thrown to the whale because of a lack of faith in God, confined to the whale's belly in black distress, and finally resurrected after calling upon God for assistance. In this sense, the whale is an *archetype* (a basic and repeated element of plot, character, or theme) that symbolizes separation from God and even death; its symbolic associations are traditional— that is, common to all readers who share the Judeo-Christian heritage.

Symbols are not, however, always this complex. In one sense, symbolism is the most common of all linguistic devices. After all, a word is nothing but a sound that symbolizes a particular image or concept. No word has meaning unless our human ability to symbolize makes it so. There is no necessary connection, for example, between the word *dog* and the familiar four-legged animal we associate with that word; after all, people of other nations have developed the same symbolic associations with other sounds: *chien* in French, *hund* in German, *canis* in Latin, and so on.

Even literary symbols are often quite simple. Winter, for example, often is a symbol of old age, spring of youth, summer of maturity, and autumn of decline. Similarly, a lamb may be a symbol of innocence, a lion of courage, a fire of vitality, and a rock of firmness. In each case, an implied comparison is drawn between a vivid image and an abstract quality.

The one-to-one correspondences set up by these symbols are akin to those established in simple *allegories* like the medieval morality play, *Everyman.* The hero, Everyman, is accompanied on his journey to the grave by characters whose actions and even names symbolize his Good-Deeds, Five Wits, Strength, Discretion, Beauty, and Knowledge. *Everyman* is known as an allegory because its simple symbols are systematically used to emphasize the moral point that only our good deeds are of lasting value both in life and after death. The systems of symbols used in allegories often tend toward didacticism and overt moral instruction. Such blatancy is a major reason why allegory is no longer a popular literary mode.

It is incorrect, however, to say that allegory no longer has a place in literature. Just as symbolism is a universal element of language, allegory is a universal element of fictional narration. Any literary (as opposed to journalistic) presentation of characters or events invariably prompts the reader to inquire, "What does it mean? What is the author's point?" And such questions represent the first step toward uncovering an allegorical purpose. Graham Hough, an important contemporary scholar, has developed a useful example of the process:

We read some report of, say, treachery, sexual misadventure, and violence in the newspapers, and it is there only to record the fact that such events took place. We read of the same sequence of events in a novel or a short story, and we can hardly escape the feeling that it is there to say something to us about human passions and motives in general. From there it is only a step to seeing the characters as types of Treachery, Violence and Lust. . . .[9]

If the actions of fictional characters are highly idiosyncratic and suggest no universal traits of humanity, we will probably be reluctant to identify them as allegorical "types"; but if the thematic element in the story is strong— that is, if the story seems to be making a general comment about humanity— it must to some extent suggest allegorical possibilities.

The problem facing the student of literature is not, then, whether a given story, poem, or play includes symbolism and allegory, but whether these nearly universal elements of literature are so important in the specific work that they need to be isolated, discussed, and evaluated. We can best resolve this problem by answering two questions. First, does the author put unusual emphasis on a particular image or series of images? Second, does the poem or story fail to make literal sense *unless* we interpret the images symbolically or allegorically? An affirmative answer to either or both questions should make us suspect that the author may be using images as symbols—perhaps, but not necessarily, in an allegory.

Discussions of symbolic or allegorical meanings in literature should always be very cautious. Because all words are in some sense symbolic and because every theme is in some sense allegorical, inexperienced critics (and even some experienced ones) are too easily tempted to "read things into" the works they study. Even at its best, symbol hunting is an attempt at mind reading. We can all easily identify the images an author uses, but we often get into trouble when we begin to speculate about what the author intended in choosing them. Unless we can find strong evidence in the poem to support our symbolic interpretations, there is a very high probability that the only mind we are capable of reading is our own. When an author thinks his use of symbols is important, we can be quite confident that he will hint at their meaning in one or more places. When no authorial interpretation (or even acknowledgment) of the symbols can be found, the wise critic will think carefully before insisting on a symbolic interpretation. Like Hawthorne's Ethan Brand, who looked throughout the world for signs of the Unpardonable Sin—before finding it in himself— we may find that the symbolic meanings we seek in the works of others exist only in the smithy of our own souls.

Perhaps the best known of all forced symbolic interpretations is the one once given by religious authorities to the "Song of Solomon" in the Old Testament. For centuries ecclesiastical scholars saw the entire poem as an allegory in which the Lord is portrayed as a love-stricken shepherd and His church

---

[9] *An Essay on Criticism* (London: Duckworth, 1966), p. 121.

as a beautiful Shulamite maiden. Thus, the following four verses are alleged, in the gloss of the King James version of the Bible, to be "a further description of the graces of the church":

1. How beautiful are thy feet with shoes, O prince's daughter! the joints of thy thighs are like jewels, the work of the hands of a cunning workman.

2. Thy navel is like a round goblet, which wanteth not liquor: thy belly is like a heap of wheat set about with lillies.

3. Thy two breasts are like two young roes that are twins.

4. Thy neck is as a tower of ivory; thine eyes like the fishpools in Heshbon, by the gate of Bath-rabbim: thy nose is as the tower of Lebanon which looketh toward Damascus.

—From "The Song of Solomon," Chapter 7

Clearly, this passage creates difficulties for very strait-laced and pious readers. If the entire Bible is a direct revelation of the word of God, what is the purpose of this tantalizing description of how a maiden's thighs, navel, and breasts have proven her to be most "fair and pleasant . . . for delights"? Why should God want to take up our time with what on the surface appears to build toward censurable heavy breathing? To many religious readers, a symbolic interpretation seemed like the only escape from biblical pornography. To them, the first verse was not really about the juncture of a maiden's thighs, but rather about the beauties of Holy Mother Church. In truth, even an atheistic reader might find some comfort in an interpretation that allows an escape from the apparent fact that in the fourth verse the shepherd compliments his lover upon having a nose like the tower of Lebanon. But nothing in the poem itself gives much support to a symbolic or an allegorical reading. Evidently the "Song of Solomon" is just what it appears to be, a beautiful and imagistic love poem. And it is reassuring to note that, after nearly two millennia of distorted allegorical approaches, Biblical scholars now hold that "the poem may be interpreted literally," while they cautiously and ambiguously observe that it is yet another question "whether the allegorical interpretation . . . is admissible."[10]

If we are to draw any lessons from the "Song of Solomon," they should certainly include the following points: (1) That vivid imagery in poetry is an end in itself and need not imply a symbolic purpose; (2) that symbolic and allegorical interpretations of imagery are always possible but not always defensible; and (3) that it is better to say nothing about a few true symbols than to find false ones everywhere. Many stones are best left unturned. While one in a million may conceal a glittering treasure, the rest are homes for vipers.

THE PLAIN SENSE OF POETRY

As I. A. Richards noted almost half a century ago in his seminal book *Practical Criticism* (1929), the chief problem faced by the student of poetry is "the difficulty of making out [the poem's] plain sense." In the preceding pages we have identified some of the sources of this difficulty by demonstrating that poets

---

[10] George J. Spurrell and Rev. Charles H. H. Wright, "Books of the Bible and the Apocrypha," in *The Holy Bible: Authorized King James Version* (Philadelphia: The Judson Press, 1936), Part III, p. 35.

often use unfamiliar denotations, connotations, or allusions and may change the meaning of words through repetition, ambiguity, puns, paradoxes, and irony. Furthermore, poetic comparisons, although often vivid and delightful, may also be suggestive, symbolic, or ambiguous. Finally, poetry is, as a general rule, much more densely packed with meaning than prose. The author of a sonnet has, after all, only fourteen lines in which to make a point—a restriction that requires him either to confine himself to a very minor point or to make every word count. A sonnetlike density is traditionally expected in poetry, even when the actual length of the poem is not limited by any formal strictures. In spite of these difficulties, the simple prose meaning of most poetry can be determined by using common sense and our accumulated knowledge of how poetry works. By following seven relatively simple steps, the risk of misapprehending the plain sense of poetry can be reduced.

LIST DENOTATIONS AND CONNOTATIONS. As we have already shown, many words have multiple meanings, and poets often intentionally play on this multiplicity. We need to be cautious, of course, about assuming that an author is always—or even generally—toying with multiple denotations. In poetry, as in prose, an author normally intends to make a clear and forceful point, and ambiguity, by its very nature, must always interfere with the clarity of a statement. But even if the poet avoids ambiguity, he or she is almost certainly cognizant of the connotations of each word and may use them to modify the meaning. Thus, in studying a poem for the first time, the reader should look up in the dictionary any difficult or unfamiliar words and jot down their definitions and connotations. Let us see how we can apply this first recommendation to the analysis of the following well-known lyric:

UPON JULIA'S CLOTHES

Whenas in silks my Julia goes
Then, then (methinks) how sweetly flows
That liquefaction of her clothes.

Next, when I cast mine eyes and see
That brave vibration each way free;
O how that glittering taketh me!
　　　　　　　　　—Robert Herrick [1648]

Like most poetry written in an age and in circumstances quite distant from our own, these six lines present several problems in denotation. After more than three hundred years, we have naturally changed some of the ways in which we use words, and Herrick's vocabulary, although not archaic, is uncommon and distinctive. To be on the safe side, we might look up a half-dozen words with the following results:

> *whenas:* whenever
> *goes:* moves about, leaves
> *methinks:* it seems to me
> *liquefaction:* fluidity
> *cast:* turn, direct, throw
> *brave:* finely dressed, courageous

In moving from denotation to connotation, we find more to interest a literary critic:

silks: Silken clothing is thin, expensive, lustrous, and sensuous. Although Herrick is presumably referring to a silken dress, "silks" may also connote silk stockings or a silk nightgown. Thus, the connotations of the word are luxuriant and slightly sensual.

my Julia: The use of the possessive adjective "my" suggests that Julia may be Herrick's possession, his mistress—both confirming and compounding the sensuous connotations of "silks."

goes: This is a curious word choice. Clearly, when Julia "goes," she is walking. Perhaps Herrick thought that walking was too common an activity and perhaps, too, he was trying to be precise, for a woman in a long, full skirt may seem to glide about—or "go"—without seeming to walk at all. Possibly Herrick wanted to suggest that Julia was leaving, "going away." If so, "whenas" reminds us that this is something that she does frequently, and we may be tempted to assume that Herrick is describing her as she leaves after a lovers' tryst. Certainly, "goes" was in part dictated by Herrick's need for a word to rhyme with "flows" and "clothes."

liquefaction: Here sound connotations come into play. The word itself is equivalent to "liquid action," but it rolls off the tongue more smoothly and thus is most appropriate.

cast mine eyes: The phrase is vigorous and active. Because Herrick had been watching Julia in the first three lines, these words must mean something more than that he simply continued to look at her. If indeed Julia had been leaving in the first sentence, then in "casting" his eyes, Herrick is probably turning his head to watch her receding figure. The phrase shows Herrick's strong attraction to Julia.

brave: We have already had something to say about the denotations of the adjective "brave." Undoubtedly, Herrick is using the archaic definition, "finely attired"; however, that was a secondary definition even in Herrick's day, and therefore the connotations of "boldness" and "courage" cannot be escaped.

vibration: In the twentieth century we are apt to associate this word with very rapid oscillations—especially with the vibrations of automobiles, trains, and planes moving at high speed. In the seventeenth century, however, the word was most often used to describe the slow swing of a pendulum. In this poem, therefore, "that brave vibration each way free" suggests the gentle side-to-side swishing of a woman's skirts. And, in fact, the bravado and freedom of these oscillations may indicate that Julia's swaying motion is a trifle wanton.

ANALYZE SYNTAX. If the meaning of a particular sentence is unclear, analyze its syntax by identifying the subject, the verb, the object, and the function of the major clauses. We have just as much right to expect syntactic clarity in verse as in prose, and no poet who habitually disregards the rules of English grammar can attain the respect of literate readers unless his or her verse has remarkable compensatory elements. Of course, good poets sometimes, by design, use syntax ambiguously to suggest competing interpretations (remember the Delphic oracle's, "Pyrrhus the Romans shall conquer"?); however, this possibility merely underscores the need to understand fully the syntactic relationships among words.

Herrick's brief poem "Upon Julia's Clothes" is constructed of two parallel sentences. Each consists of a subordinate clause followed by an exclamation. Because the two sentences are similar in so many respects, the slight differences between them are all the more pronounced. The first sentence is introspective ("methinks") and intransitive ("how sweetly flows/ That liquefaction of her clothes"). In contrast, the second sentence is active ("I cast mine eyes") and transitive ("O how that glittering taketh me"). In the first sentence, Herrick is a reflective observer; in the second, he is acting and being acted upon. The two sentences combine to show that he is prey to a passion that intensifies as he watches the rustling of his mistress's clothing. Even in the choice of his syntactic subjects, we find him moving from water ("liquefaction") to fire ("glittering") and thus from tranquility to excitement.

IDENTIFY THE FIGURES OF SPEECH. By definition, figurative language is not meant to be taken literally. Poetic language deviates from ordinary language to point the way toward meaningful emotional truths. When Herrick exclaims, "Then, then (methinks) how sweetly flows/ That liquefaction of her clothes," he certainly does not mean that Julia's dress dribbles down into a soggy pool at her feet—although that is the image we may get if we try to interpret his lines literally. Actually, Herrick is drawing an implied comparison between the soft, shiny movements of Julia's silken dress and the gentle, rippling flow of a stream.

This is the only figure of speech used in Herrick's brief poem, and we should not ordinarily expect to find more in such short poetic passages. Figures of speech are like distilled liquors: the first dram or two elevates the spirits, but successive draughts befuddle and bewilder the brain. (They may also leave an unfortunate aftertaste.) Whenever an author *does* use numerous figures of speech, it becomes absolutely essential to identify the various types being used (whether allusion, ambiguity, irony, paradox, pun, or one of the various forms of comparison), and it is often useful as well to recast those figures, at least temporarily, into language that is not poetic. Allusions, ironies, paradoxes, and puns should be explained; metaphors and implied comparisons should be rewritten as similes; and symbols should be identified. To do so without greatly distorting the poem, we must be sensitive to the connotations of words and to the uses of ambiguity.

PARAPHRASE THE POEM. The purpose of a paraphrase is to help us understand the prose sense of a poem by changing the poetic language of difficult passages into language that we can easily comprehend. This process is the most direct means of making sure that we understand what a poem says—quite apart from how well it is said.

Having enumerated denotations and connotations, analyzed syntax, and identified figures of speech, it should not be difficult to write down a full prose statement of the poem's content. Thus, "Upon Julia's Clothes" might be paraphrased in the following manner:

Whenever my Julia walks in silks, then (it seems to me) that the sounds made by the movement of her clothing are as lovely as the rippling of a stream. Next, when I look at the glamorous vibrations of her skirts, O how their glittering attracts me!

Any paraphrase, as long as it is reasonable, helps us to check our understanding of a poem's literal meaning by expressing it in slightly different words. The process itself, however, is fraught with risks. We may be tempted to substitute our own prose statement for the poem itself, which may obscure our appreciation of the poem's style and feeling. Or, we may persuade ourselves that the poem means exactly what we say it means and nothing else—a conclusion that glosses over the questionable decisions about denotation and connotation that must be made in attempting to paraphrase any poem. We might, for example, be tempted to change a few words in our paraphrase of "Upon Julia's Clothes" and as a result come to interpret the poem more sensuously:

Whenever my mistress Julia comes toward me dressed in silks, then (it seems to me) that her clothes flow about her body as smoothly and beautifully as water in a stream. Next, when I turn my eyes and see the saucy and free swing in her walk as she passes, O how the glittering of her skirts enamours me!

It would be difficult to determine a rational reason for preferring one of these paraphrases over the other. The first moves from the *sound* of Julia's dress to the *sight* of it, whereas the second implies that Herrick watches Julia as she walks by—admiring her figure from front and rear. The first paraphrase is a little too staid; the second a little too steamy. The poem itself contains something of both; it manages to be suggestive without the slightest trace of immorality. This elusiveness is, of course, exactly what makes poetry more interesting than common prose. Stripping the nuances from a poem is like skimming the cream from milk: it takes away the richness and taste. In each case, all that remains is a thin, watery, and almost denatured product. The language of poetry is *not* static or technical or purely denotative; it is rich and complex, and no paraphrase can fully do it justice. Yet, the risks of leaving the poem's prose meaning unstated are even greater, for then the ambiguities of poetic diction may entice the reader into believing that his or her own preoccupations and fantasies are somehow mirrored in each line. If anything, the temptation to read something into the poem that its actual content will not justify implies a greater disrespect for the written word than the opposite risk of relying too heavily on the paraphrase. The latter may be nothing more than a shadow of the true poetic substance, but the former is too often the product of an overstimulated imagination, having no relationship whatsoever to the poem.

VISUALIZE AND SUMMARIZE THE IMAGERY AND ACTIONS. The preceding steps have all been analytical. They require us to look up definitions, to examine verbal structures, to reword sentences: to act, to think, and to write. In doing so, however, we have omitted what is certainly the most important process of all: to enjoy. When we relax and allow the poet's imagery to carry us into the world of imagination, we are most in harmony with the true poetic impulse. But more than that, visualizing the events in the poem and attempting to recreate imaginatively everything that the poet describes can often be indispensable to careful critical judgment. Careless writers sometimes juxtapose incongruous and even ludicrous images because they themselves fail to see clearly what they ask their readers to envision: for example, "March roared in like a lion and crawled out like a baby." Here the conventional analogies have been preserved—probably without any expectation that we will actually visualize this lion transformed into a puling infant. The use of such incongruous comparisons is called *mixed metaphor*.

Once we have tried to visualize everything that the poet describes for us, we will find it easier to summarize the action and circumstances in the poem. In so doing, we will generally wish to identify the speaker (who may or may not be the poet himself), the setting, and the circumstances. A summary of "Upon Julia's Clothes" will not add much to our understanding of the poem because the poem itself is so short and uncomplicated. However, Frost's sonnet "Design," which is only slightly longer, can snap into focus if we first visualize it and then summarize our vision in something like the following manner:

The poet, on a morning walk along a roadside, sees a white moth within the grasp of a white spider perched on a white and blighted wildflower. This strange and incongruous combination leads him to reflect about the role of fate in the events of the world.

A line-by-line paraphrase of "Design" might isolate and clarify problems in the interpretation of specific words and phrases, but it would also equal or exceed the length of the original fourteen-line poem. A simple three-line summary, such as the one proposed here, has an advantage: it allows us to think of the poem as a totality—to get a single image of it—and that image, if well formed, can serve as a starting point for further explanation, analysis, and understanding.

EVALUATE THE POEM'S TONE. The tone of a poem is created by the author's overall attitude toward his subject or audience. It helps to determine the choice of words and rhetorical devices. Thus, when we wish to evaluate a poem's tone, we do so by examining the emotional effects of its words, images, and figures of speech (particularly overstatement, understatement, irony, paradox, and ambiguity). In any collection of poetry, we will find some poems in which the tone is obvious; others in which it is complex; and still others in which it changes as the poet develops his or her thoughts.

In many cases, the author's tone is unmistakable. "Upon Julia's Clothes," for example, clearly reflects Herrick's passionate preoccupation with Julia. His attitude is expressed directly by his exclamations, "how sweetly flows/ That liquefaction of her clothes" and "O how that glittering taketh me!" And it is expressed indirectly by the fact that the poet's excitement is stimulated so easily. We recognize that he must indeed be deeply in love if so small a thing as the rustle of Julia's skirts drives him to poetic expression. Herrick's tone, then, is enraptured, loving, and excited.

The analysis of tone becomes more difficult when the author uses irony, paradox, or ambiguity because conflicting meanings and, hence, conflicting attitudes toward the subject are implied by those devices. When, for example, Byron writes that a serious illness made him so devoutly religious that he wished the three persons of the Trinity were four "On purpose to believe so much the more," we will wholly misunderstand his tone and meaning unless we recognize that he is being ironic. The literal sense of the words is at odds with their real intention, and Byron's tone is sceptical, instead of pious, and playful, instead of serious.

The determination of tone becomes even more complex when, as in the case of Frost's "Design," the poet's attitude seems to change as he reflects more and more deeply on the significance of the events he describes. The first eight lines of Frost's poem are largely descriptive. The tone is observing, meticulous, and perhaps a little eerie. We see the flower, the moth, and the spider close up, as if through a magnifying glass; and the preoccupation with death and blight, along with the analogy to a witches' broth, is chilling. The next six lines present three rhetorical questions and a final conditional clause. Here Frost begins to inquire into the meaning of what he has just described. The first two questions merely underscore the unusual combination of events that brought together the blighted flower, the albino spider, and the innocent white moth. Frost's tone is inquisitive and concerned, but still fairly neutral and objective. In the last question, the tone suddenly becomes fearful. What else, Frost asks, can this incident be "but the design of darkness to appall?" Then Frost moves in a direction that at first appears reassuring when he doubts, almost as an afterthought, "If design govern in a thing so small." Yet the line also opens up the unsettling possibility that there is no design at all and the world is governed by chance. If there is any reassurance in these thoughts, that reassurance ought to be thoroughly undermined by the fearful realization that the scene *has* seemed fated. The designs of darkness *have* seemed to operate—even at the insignificant level of the moth, the spider, and the innocent heal-all! This sobering and somewhat horrifying possibility ultimately summarizes the direction toward which the poem—both in tone and in meaning—has been driving all along.

IDENTIFY THE THEME. A literary *theme*, as we use the term in this text, is the central idea or insight that unifies and controls the total work. It is the main point an author wishes to make about his subject. As such, identifying a poem's theme involves two steps: finding the poem's subject and formulating the poet's main statement about that subject.

It is easy to determine the subject of most poems: often it is named or suggested by the title, and, of course, it is the focus of the whole poem. Herrick's title, "Upon Julia's Clothes," clearly names his subject—although we might add that the only significance of the clothes is that Julia is wearing them. At heart, the poem is an expression of Herrick's love for Julia. And this more general statement of the subject carries us far toward understanding the poem's theme, which—broadly stated—is that everything associated with the woman one loves becomes as beautiful and enchanting as she is.

The title of Frost's sonnet, "Design," reflects both the poem's subject and its theme. The subject is the possibility of design in the convergence of the white flower, the white moth, and the white spider. The theme—as nearly as one can state what Frost leaves only as a question—is that perhaps the designs of darkness control even the trivial and insignificant events in nature.

Stating a poem's theme in one sentence can be useful in summarizing its purpose and importance, but it is also a coarse and misleading approach to poetry. If Herrick or Frost had wished to develop only those themes that we have assigned to their poems, then they could easily have stated their purposes more directly. In the case of Herrick's poem, we have probably looked too hard for the significance of his simple imagistic description. Herrick himself probably realized that a poem of six lines cannot state abstract truths without sounding pompous and grandiose. A brief description may suggest those truths, but it ought not insist on them. The scope of Herrick's poem is wisely confined to the movement of Julia's clothes; it does not actually describe her clothing nor does it describe her person, for these subjects, presumably, would require a much more lavish treatment. The poem does not mention Herrick's love for Julia, nor does it assert Julia's beauty—everything, therefore, that we have said about the poem's theme is deduced without any direct support from a text that is imagistic rather than judgmental or argumentative.

6

❧❧❧❧❧❧

Versification

RHYTHM AND METER

If you hold a conch shell to your ear, you will seem to hear within it the rhythmic rush and retreat of the sea surf. Although children find deep fascination and mystery in this audible reminder of the ocean, science explains away that magic meter as an echo of the blood throbbing in the listener's inner ear. But in this case, as indeed in many others, the scientific explanation does less to erase our wonder than to transpose it and intellectualize it. The rhythm of the conch—the crashing of the sea—is also in the beat of our blood, the core of our very being. We are, it seems, rhythm-making creatures. When we listen to the monotone ticking of a wristwatch, we hear it as a rhythmic tic-tock. The rattle of a moving train is heard as a rhythmic clickety-clack. We hear the drumming of a horse's hooves as clip-clop. We make something rhythmic out of even the most dull and invariable experiences.

This affection for rhythm has never been fully explained, but it is probably the result of the natural rhythms of human life. In addition to the systolic and diastolic beat of the heart, there are similar rhythms in our breathing, in our movements as bipeds, and in a great variety of our habitual activities. Generations of farmers, pressing one ear to a cow's churning and drum-tight belly, have rhythmically squeezed her milk into a pail. Generations of farm men have raised and dropped a hoe or slung and recoiled a scythe. Generations of farm women have rhythmically kneaded dough or scrubbed at a washboard. Generations of children have grown up loving chants, nursery rhymes, and jingles.

It should come as no surprise then that both prose and poetry are rhythmic. According to the nineteenth-century French poet Charles Baudelaire, "rhythm and rhyme answer in man to the immortal needs of monotony, symmetry, and surprise." Furthermore, strong emotions tend to find memorable expres-

609

sion through strong rhythms. This is obviously true of music, dance, and poetry; but it can also be true of prose. Julius Caesar's pride in conquering Gaul shone through the rhythms of his message to the Roman senate, "Veni, vidi, vici!" ("I *came*, I *saw*, I *conquered!*") Patrick Henry's belief in the cause of American independence was passionately expressed through the strong patterns in his speech to the Virginia Convention on March 23, 1775:

The gentlemen may cry, Peace, Peace! but there is no peace. The war is actually begun! The next gale that sweeps from the north shall bring to our ears the clash of resounding arms! . . . Is life so dear or peace so sweet as to be purchased at the price of chains and slavery? Forbid it, Almighty God. I know not what course others may take, but as for me, give me liberty or give me death!

Abraham Lincoln's firm belief in the need for reconciliation following the Civil War was beautifully embodied in the cadence of his second inaugural address of 1865:

With malice toward none, with charity for all, with firmness in the right as God gives us to see the right, let us bind up the Nation's wounds.

As we have just seen, poets have no monopoly on meter; it is also true that the correct use of meter does not make a poet, any more than the correct use of grammar makes a novelist or the correct use of chewing tobacco makes a baseball player. As Ralph Waldo Emerson observed in 1844, "it is not meters, but a meter-making argument that makes a poem—a thought so passionate and alive that like the spirit of a plant or an animal it has an architecture of its own and adorns nature with a new thing." Just as our hearts beat vigorously at moments of violent emotion, so, too, our words begin to beat more forcefully while we express those emotions—and the rhythms of poetic words often re-create in a careful reader the same sense of breathless excitement that possessed the poet.

Although we respond as readily to the rhythms of prose as poetry and although, to quote Shelley, "the distinction between poets and prose writers is a vulgar error," the fact remains that most poetry (and little prose) is cast into formal metrical patterns. Perhaps the reasons for this, as we have already suggested, is that the metrical patterns of verse help to create a more direct relationship to natural human rhythms than is possible in prose. When the alternating accents of iambic verse are read aloud, they almost inevitably match the 72 beats per minute of our pulse. Moreover, when we speak aloud, our words are naturally grouped in response to our breathing. After giving voice to eight or ten syllables, most speakers must pause for another breath. English verse makes the speaker's breathing easier by being written in lines of roughly equal length. The two most common measures in our language, tetrameter and pentameter, normally contain eight and ten syllables, respectively. Lines longer than pentameter are uncommon because they can be difficult to recite. Shorter lines, like trimeter which has six syllables, by encouraging rapid breathing, give the illusion of haste or excitement. Thus, verse itself is both a response to human physiology and an influence on it. Like a natural force, verse sets up a pattern of expectations that we recognize intuitively and to which we respond both physically and emotionally. The study of metrics allows us to name and to analyze the prevailing rhythms of most poems.

Meter is basically a system for helping the reader reproduce the rhythm intended by the author. The word *meter* comes from the Greek "metron," meaning "measure." These words, *meter* and *measure,* are used interchangeably in describing poetic rhythms. The units with which we measure verse are the syllable, the foot, the line, and sometimes the stanza and the canto. A *syllable,* which is the smallest unit in metrics, is any word or part of a word produced in speech by a single pulse of breath. It is a simple link in the chain of sounds. Between sixty and eighty percent of the words in English poetry are monosyllables—words like *root, tree, leaf, fruit, man, child, boy, girl, a, an,* and *the.* The remaining words are polysyllabic and are divided by dictionaries into their individual links of sound: *re-main-ing, pol-y-syl-lab-ic, di-vi-ded,* etc. The basic rhythmic unit in verse is called a *foot* and is composed of an established number of stressed (emphasized) and unstressed syllables. An established number of feet makes up a *line* and an established number of lines often makes up a *stanza.* The number of lines or stanzas in a *canto* is rarely fixed in advance.

Scansion

The process by which we discover the dominant rhythm in a poem is called *scansion.* The basic steps in scanning a poem are quite simple and entail (1) finding the average number of syllables in a typical line, (2) marking the stressed or accented syllables in each line and (3) identifying the prevailing foot and the number of feet per line. It should be noted that the entire process focuses on the number of syllables and stresses in a given line of poetry. For this reason, English verse is said to be written in syllabic-stress meters.

Now let us go through each step in scansion for a representative poem, "On First Looking into Chapman's Homer" by John Keats:

ON FIRST LOOKING INTO CHAPMAN'S HOMER

1 Much have I travell'd in the realms of gold
2 And many goodly states and kingdoms seen,
3 Round many western islands have I been
4 Which bards in fealty to Apollo hold.
5 Oft of one wide expanse had I been told
6 That deep-browed Homer ruled as his demesne:
7 Yet did I never breathe its pure serene
8 Till I heard Chapman speak out loud and bold.
9 Then felt I like some watcher of the skies
10 When a new planet swims into his ken;
11 Or like stout Cortez when with eagle eyes
12 He stared at the Pacific—and all his men
13 Look'd at each other with a wild surmise—
14 Silent upon a peak in Darien.

—John Keats [1816]

1. Inspection of the poem shows that the average line contains ten syllables, but lines 4, 6, 12, and 14 present minor problems in syllabification. The word "fealty" in line four is usually divided into three syllables, "fe/al/ty," but because this would give the line a total of eleven, we may feel more comfortable eliding "fe/al" into one syllable which sounds like the word *feel.* There are, in fact, an unusual number of words in our language that are divided differently on different occasions: for example, *unusual* (un-use-yul, un-use-u-al), *our* (are,

ow-er), *different* (diff-er-ent, diff-rent), *occasions* (o-cay-zhuns, o-cay-zhi-ens). Moreover, the syllabification of certain words has changed over the centuries—notably in the pronunciation of the *ed* forms of verbs: *bathed* was once *bath-ed, in-spired* was once *in-spi-red, changed* was once *chang-ed,* and even now *aged* may be pronounced *age-ed.* Archaic forms are, of course, common in medieval verse, but they are sometimes deliberately used in more contemporary poetry where the unanticipated accents are generally marked *(changéd).* Keats, however, so often required his readers to pronounce the final *ed* of verbs that in the first line of "On First Looking into Chapman's Homer," he used the contraction "travell'd" to show that the end of the verb was *not* to be sounded.

Alternate pronunciations and archaisms are only two of the problems of syllabification. Many of us are unfamiliar with the pronunciation of some words used in poetry. In line 6, for example, the word "demesne" appears to have three syllables, but we learn from the dictionary that it may be pronounced to rhyme with "serene," in line 7:

$$de \cdot mesne \text{ (di-man', -en'), n . . . . 3.any territory or domain.}$$

Thus, line 6, like most of the others, contains the expected ten syllables. In line 14 we might again turn to a dictionary to reassure ourselves that "Darien" does indeed have the three syllables (Da/ri/en) required by the meter.

No reading of line 12, however, can produce any fewer than eleven syllables, and therefore we are forced to describe that one line as slightly irregular. The expectation of ten syllables should be *only* an expectation. Slight variations are normal and even desirable when they serve some rhythmic function. But in order to discuss a poem's rhythm, we must learn to identify the pattern of stressed and unstressed syllables.

2. The problem of determining where the stresses fall in poetry is more complex than counting the syllables, but with a good ear and the guidance of a few simple rules, most readers can produce satisfactory results.

The first rule is that a poem's meter cannot change the normal pronunciation of a polysyllabic word. In all words of two syllables or more, the permissible accentuation is defined by the dictionary.[1] Thus, in lines 3 and 4, for example, we can immediately mark several stressed syllables. The dictionary tells us that the accent falls on the middle syllable of "A·pól·lo" and on the first syllables of "mán·y," "wés·tern," "ís·lands," and "feál·ty." If we place a straight line over the accented syllables, the preliminary scansion of the lines looks like this:

> Round mány wéstern íslands have I been
> Which bards in feálty to Apóllo hold.

The second rule is that monosyllabic words have no inherent stress; they take on stresses to fit the metrical pattern of the poem and the rhetorical rhythm of a particular sentence. In other words, monosyllables may be either stressed or unstressed. In general, however, the emphasis should fall where it would in a normal prose reading of the lines; and in normal English prose, stressed

---

[1] One should note, however, that not all dictionaries mark the secondary accents in polysyllabic words, and sometimes the same word can be pronounced in different ways. E.g., *ínfinitive* and *infínitive.*

and unstressed syllables tend to alternate. When we read Keats's lines aloud we find that weak, but still noticeable, stresses fall on "have" and "been," while more pronounced emphasis is placed on "bards" and "hold." If we now mark each of these as an accented syllable and mark the remaining unaccented syllables with a cup (˘), we will have produced a complete metrical picture of the lines:

> Round many western islands have I been
> Which bards in fealty to Apollo hold.

3. Having scanned the lines, we now need only name the specific meter being used. In the syllabic-stress system there are only five commonly used feet: iambic, anapestic, trochaic, dactylic, and spondaic.

TABLE OF METRICAL FEET

Name	Example
Dactyl	"Much have I
Trochee	travell'd
Anapest	in the realms
iamb	of gold."
Spondee	John Keats.

Of these, the iamb is by far the most popular and versatile. It is the principal foot used in such narrative and dramatic verse as Chaucer's *Canterbury Tales,* Shakespeare's plays, Milton's *Paradise Lost,* Wordsworth's *Prelude,* Byron's *Don Juan,* and most other substantial poems written in English. The iambic foot is equally popular in lyric verse and is predominant in ballads and obligatory in sonnets. It is, therefore, used in Keats's sonnet, "On First Looking into Chapman's Homer," and the two lines that we have just scanned can be shown to have five iambic feet to the line:

> Round man/y wes/tern is/lands have/ I been
> Which bards/ in feal/ty to/ Apol/lo hold.

We use a vertical slash (/) to mark the divisions between the feet. These divisions are helpful in counting the feet, but they do not signal pauses in speech; they may fall either between words or between the syllables of a word.

In critical analysis we generally replace the wordy and awkward phrase "five feet to the line" with the term *pentameter.* The technical term for each of the possible lines in English poetry is provided in the following table:

> *monometer:* one foot per line
> *dimeter:* two feet per line
> *trimeter:* three feet per line

> *tetrameter:* four feet per line
> *pentameter:* five feet per line
> *hexameter:* six feet per line
> *heptameter:* seven feet per line
> *octameter:* eight feet per line

Of these, pentameter and tetrameter are the most commonly used.

Once chosen, the dominant metrical foot normally remains fixed throughout a given poem. Thus, for example, iambic rhythm prevails in Donne's "A Valediction: Forbidding Mourning" (p. 559), whereas trochaic rhythm prevails in Poe's "The Raven" (p. 618) and anapestic rhythm dominates his "Annabel Lee" (p. 620). Although the principal metrical foot almost invariably remains unchanged throughout a poem, the length of the lines often varies according to a pre-established pattern. "A Valediction: Forbidding Mourning" is tetrameter throughout, but the odd-numbered lines in "The Raven" are trochaic octameter, and the even-numbered lines lack one syllable in the final foot (*catalectic* trochaic octameter). In "Annabel Lee" tetrameter alternates with trimeter.

Thus, in choosing iambic pentameter for "Chapman's Homer," Keats commits himself to creating the possibility of a scansion that includes five metrical feet in each line, and he has to work within the expectation that each line will follow an iambic rhythm. We use the words *possibility* and *expectation* because the metrical pattern of a poem is not intended to be a straitjacket that restricts all movement and permits scant room to breathe. Rather, the pattern should be cut like a well-tailored dress that, like Julia's silks, complements both the shape and the movement of the human form it adorns. Deviations from the expected metrical pattern create surprise, emphasis, and often delight.

Anapestic, dactylic, trochaic, and spondaic feet are all used more frequently to provide variety in iambic verse than to set the rhythm of an entire poem. As the examples in our Table of Metrical Feet show, each of these (except the spondee) is used in the first line of Keats's sonnet:

>   *dactyl*   *trochee*   *anapest*   *iamb*
> Much have Ĭ/ trăvell'd/ ĭn thĕ reālms/ ŏf gōld . . .

Keats's first line is, therefore, highly irregular, and two questions now confront us: What purposes are served by variations from an established meter? And how do different rhythms affect our emotional response to poetry?

A partial answer to the first question was proposed by Samuel Johnson when he wrote, in his "Life of Dryden" (1781), that "the essence of verse is regularity and its ornament is variety." This implies that a poem should be regular enough to establish a pattern and varied enough to banish monotony. It is a corollary to the familiar rule endorsing moderation in all things, and in recent years it has become almost commonplace to condemn poets whose meters are too regular. In a fine example of logical inconsistency, however, Johnson went on to defend Alexander Pope from detractors who charged that the monotonous regularity of his heroic couplets (pairs of rhymed iambic pentameter lines) diminished their power by "glutting the ear with unvaried sweetness." To this Johnson replied, "I suspect this objection to be the cant of those who judge by principles rather than perception: and who would even themselves have less pleasure in his words, if he had tried to relieve attention by studied discords, or affected to break his lines and vary his pauses."

There is, then, little value in any attempt to state a general principle about regularity and variety in meter. Such esthetic judgments can only be made within the context of a particular poem's meaning. What *can* be said, however, is that rhythm and any deviations from rhythm should contribute to the overall effect sought in the poem. "What is wanted is neither a dead mechanical beat nor a jumble of patternless incoherence, but the rich expressiveness of a verse that is alive with the tension of living speech."[2]

"The tension of living speech" is an apt expression for the effect of metrical variation in "On First Looking into Chapman's Homer." If we look again at its first line, we see that, although it has ten syllables and can conceivably be read as iambic pentameter,

Mŭch HĀVE/ Ĭ TR̄A/vell'd ĪN/ thĕ RĒALMS/ ŏf GŌLD,

such a reading distorts the rhythms of living speech. But if we read the line naturally,

MŪCH hăve Ĭ/ TR̄Avell'd/ ĭn thĕ RĒALMS/ ŏf GŌLD,

we find neither a metrical pattern—indeed, each foot is different—nor the five feet we expect in pentameter. Clearly, Keats is creating a tension between living speech and our expectations of a sonnet. The line has fewer accents and more unstressed syllables than we expect; and because unstressed syllables roll rapidly from the tongue, the pace of the line is more rapid than in standard iambic pentameter.[3] Furthermore, Keats has arranged the unstressed syllables so that nearly all of them pour forth in two rolling clusters. Thus, the poem begins with a sense of surprise and breathless excitement. As we continue reading, we learn that this tone is exactly right for the story Keats has to tell. Reading Chapman's translation of Homer was a new and exciting experience for Keats. It showed him that poetry could unexpectedly "speak out loud and bold"; it did not need to be an effeminate concoction of unvaried sweetness. The rhythm in the first line of the sonnet helps to capture and communicate Keats's emotions.

One line in a sonnet is, of course, insufficient to set the tone for the rest of the poem, but the rhythm of this first line is repeated again and again. The dactyl-trochee combination, which helps to make these first syllables forceful and rugged, occurs at the beginning of lines 5, 7, 9, 13, and 14:

1 Mūch hăve Ĭ/ trāvell'd/ . . .

5 Ōft ŏf ŏne/ wīde ĕx/panse . . .

7 Yēt dĭd Ĭ/ nĕvĕr/ . . .

9 Thēn fĕlt Ĭ/ līke sŏme/ . . .

13 Lōok'd ăt eăch/ ōthĕr/ . . .

14 Sīlĕnt ŭp/on̄ ă/ . . .

---

[2] Cleanth Brooks and Robert Penn Warren, *Understanding Poetry*, 4th ed. (New York: Holt, Rhinehart, and Winston, 1976), p. 503.

[3] This can be stated as a general principle of metrics: unaccented syllables in anapests and dactyls accelerate the pace of narration; heavily accented syllables in spondees slow the pace.

The tension between regular iambic pentameter and Keats's startling irregularity is especially noticeable in the final verses, both because these lines occur at the poem's climax and because two irregular patterns occur in immediate succession. Keats achieves a perfect blending of sound and sense when he says of Cortez:

> 12   He stared/ at the Pa/cific//—and all/ his men
>
> 13   Look'd at each/ other// with a wild/ surmise—
>
> 14   Silent// upon/ a peak/ in Da/rien.

In describing the metrical effects in this combination of lines, we will find it useful to define three more terms: *end-stopped verse, enjambment,* and the *caesura.* An end-stopped line, like line 13 in Keats's sonnet, is simply one that concludes with a pause. A strongly end-stopped verse ends with some mark of punctuation—a comma, semicolon, colon, dash, question mark, exclamation point, or period. The punctuation tells the reader to pause for breath and emphasis. Although a lightly end-stopped verse may have no formal punctuation, it must still mark a pause between phrases or clauses. Lines one, three, five, seven, and eleven are all lightly end-stopped. *Enjambment* (or "striding over"), as in line 12 of Keats's sonnet, is the running on of one line into the next without a grammatical pause. End-stopping tends to reinforce the metrical structure of a poem, whereas enjambment tends to minimize the difference between the sound of verse and that of prose. A *caesura* (marked with a double slash, //) is a pause that occurs near the middle of most verses. This pause may be indicated by punctuation, as in line 12; or it may fall between phrases, as in line 13. If a line has an even number of feet, the caesura tends to bisect it, as in line 13. One advantage of iambic pentameter is that its five accents can never be divided evenly. This ensures a certain amount of variety in even the most regular pentameters and opens up the possibility of a caesural pause as late as the fourth foot or as early as the first (line 14).

How do end-stopping, enjambment, and the caesural pause contribute to the impact of Keats's poem? It is quite apparent that a dramatic pause is signaled by the dash at the end of line 13. The effect of this pause is to emphasize the "wild surmise" and to encourage us to determine *what* is surmised. These men have discovered an entirely new ocean and are briefly struck dumb with wonder. They pause, just as Keats's punctuation forces us to pause. The content of these lines is in absolute harmony with their end-stopped rhythm.

The contribution of the enjambment from line 12 to 13 is also important, but it is atypical of the general effect of that device. If we examine Keats's poem as a whole, we find that exactly half of the lines are run-on or very lightly end-stopped. Thus, the poem has the typographical appearance of verse, but because strongly end-stopped lines are avoided, it has a fluid movement resembling that of melodious prose. In this respect, Keats's style is unusually mature for a poet who had not yet reached the age of legal majority. Most other great poets from Chaucer and Shakespeare to Byron and Wordsworth passed through a period of strong end-stopping before evolving at last to a more flexible style. But the enjambment at line 12 is grammatical only. In prose we do not ordinarily pause between a subject and verb. We use but one breath to say, "and all his men looked at each other." But when these words are put into a sonnet and scanned as on this page, a substantial pause before "Look'd" is almost obligatory for several reasons. In the first place most readers of poetry inevitably pause slightly at the end of a line of verse—even when such a pause is not syntactic. The end-line pause is one of our expectations in verse. Furthermore, in this particular case, the last syllable of line 12 ("men") is accented, as is the first syllable of line 13 ("Look'd"). As we mentioned before, strong accents in juxtaposition always slow the pace of poetry, here augmenting the natural end-line pause. And finally, it makes dramatic sense to pause before "Look'd." The pause helps to create suspense and emphasis. It informs us that this is a penetrating look, a look of rapture and astonishment. Hence, the grammatical enjambment between lines 12 and 13 is offset by a combination of poetic effects, and once again we have "verse that is alive with the tension of living speech."

The caesural pauses in lines 12 and 13 merit no special analysis—the one in line 12 is plainly grammatical and the one in line 13 falls at the exact midpoint of the line and between two prepositional phrases, each of which independently modifies the verb. We might, however, be tempted to omit the caesura we placed after the first foot in line 14,

$$\text{Sīlĕnt// ŭpōn/ ă pēak/ ĭn Dā/r\bar{i}en.}$$

It certainly could not be placed later in the line because it would then either divide words within a prepositional phrase or separate two phrases closely linked both in logic and in grammar. And in placing a caesura after "Silent," we disrupt the rhythm of the dactyl-trochee combination that has characterized the poem. But if we wish to protect that rhythm, we must omit the caesura altogether and scan the line in a way that produces an unusual monosyllabic foot:

$$\text{Sīlĕnt ŭp/ōn ă/ pēak/ ĭn Dā/r\bar{i}en.}[4]$$

Of the two options, the former is clearly preferable. It is closer to regular iambic pentameter; it includes the expected caesura at a grammatically acceptable place; and, most importantly, it helps the sound of the poem to echo its sense. A momentary silence *should* follow the word—as if in recognition of its meaning.

In summary, the goal of a metrical analysis is to clarify how the rhythm of language contributes to its poetic meaning. In order to assist in this process, the full scansion of a poem or passage should identify the underlying metrical pattern; analyze the important deviations from that pattern; and consider the effects of end-stopping, enjambment, and placement of the caesura. An analysis of rhythmic effects that is not based on scansion is likely to be imprecise and unintelligible; however, scansion that does not include analysis and interpretation is mechanical and meaningless.

The iambic pentameter of Keats's sonnet on "Chapman's Homer," although the most common of English meters, is by no means the only possible rhythm. Nor is the syllabic-stress system the only possible approach to writing and

---

[4] Note that the placement of the caesura marks the only audible difference in the two possibilities in scansion. It makes no difference in the rhythm whether the feet are scanned as a trochee and four iambs or as a dactyl, a trochee, a monosyllable, and two iambs. Both scansions should be read in precisely the same manner.

scanning verse. Before closing our discussion of rhythm and meter it is, therefore, expedient to survey the variety of poetic meters, the limitations of syllabic-
stress scansion, and the other possible systems of scanning English verse.

VARIETY OF METERS. While trochees, anapests, and dactyls are most frequently used to provide variety within an iambic rhythm, each can also establish
the underlying meter of a poem, and each creates a very different rhythmic
effect. The rhythm of a poem does not, of course, dictate its tone. Rhythm
is at best a contributing factor that can be used by able poets to complement
the mood created through the denotations and connotations of words. There
are, however, differences among the four basic meters of English poetry, and
these differences can easily be heard, even though their effects cannot be perfectly described.

The *trochee* (travell'd) is the mirror image of the iamb and is perhaps even
more common than the iamb in everyday speech. The plurals of many monosyllabic words become trochaic (*fishes, houses, axes,* etc.) and a great many two-
syllable words are natural trochees (*poet, water, able,* etc.).

Trochaic and iambic meters do not differ greatly in their effects. In fact,
trochaic pentameter can be described as iambic pentameter with a defective
first foot and an extra syllable at the end.

$$\text{trochaic} \quad {-}\,|\,{\smile}\,{-}\,|\,{\smile}\,{-}\,|\,{\smile}\,{-}\,|\,{\smile}\,{-}\,{\smile}$$
$$\text{iambic} \quad {\smile}\,{-}\,|\,{\smile}\,{-}\,|\,{\smile}\,{-}\,|\,{\smile}\,{-}\,|\,{\smile}\,{-}$$

Because the first syllable in a trochaic line is accented, poems in this meter
often sound assertive and vigorous. But the use of trochees makes end rhyme
difficult because rhyme words are usually stressed. Thus, some poems that
start out with a trochaic rhythm end up iambic, as in the catalectic (meaning
"incomplete") trochaic octameter of Swinburne's "The Sunbows":

Spray of/ song that/ sings in/ April,// light of/ love that/ laughs through/ May

Live and/ die and/ live for/ever:// nought of/ all things/ far less/ fair

Keeps a/ surer/ life than/ these that//seem to/ pass like/ fire a/way.
                    —From "The Sunbows," Algernon Charles Swinburne [1884]

Incantations are often trochaic, possibly because the strong accents that begin
each trochaic line complement a chanting rhythm:

Double/, double// toil and/ trouble;

Fire/ burn and// cauldron/ bubble.
                    —From *Macbeth,*
                    William Shakespeare [c. 1607]

Very probably, this affinity for the supernatural in trochaic rhythms guided
Edgar Allan Poe in choosing the meter for "The Raven" (1845):

Once up/on a/ midnight/ dreary,// while I/ pondered/ weak and/ weary,

Over/ many a/ quaint and/ curious// volume/ of for/gotten/ lore—

A *dactyl* (Mŭch hăve Ĭ) is a trochee with an extra unstressed syllable. Because unstressed syllables are pronounced easily, poems in dactylic meter move with a rapid, waltzing beat (dum-dee-dee, dum-dee-dee). The dactylic dimeter of the following stanza from Ralph Hodgson's "Eve" provides a good example of the lyrical but unsettling possibilities in the rhythm:

> Pīctŭre thăt/ ōrchărd sprīte;
> Ēve, wĭth hĕr/ bōdў whĭte,
> Sūpplĕ ănd/ smōoth tŏ hĕr
> Thīn fĭngĕr/ tīps;
> Wōndĕrĭng,/ līstĕnĭng
> Līstĕnĭng,/ wōndĕrĭng,
> Ēve wĭth ă/ bĕrrў
> Hālf-wāy/ tŏ hĕr līps.
> —From "Eve,"
> Ralph Hodgson [1913]

Alfred Tennyson took advantage of the strength and speed of dactyls to imitate the drumming of galloping horses in his famous "Charge of the Light Brigade":

> Hālf ă lēague,/ hālf ă lēague
> Hālf ă lēague/ ōnwărd,
> Āll ĭn thĕ/ Vāllĕy ŏf/ Dēath
> Rōde thĕ sĭx/ hūndrĕd
> "Fōrwărd thĕ/ Līght Brĭgade!
> Chārge fŏr thĕ/ gūns!" hĕ sāid:
> Īntŏ thĕ/ Vāllĕy ŏf/ Dēath
> Rōde thĕ sĭx/ hūndrĕd.
> —From "The Charge of the Light Brigade,"
> Alfred, Lord Tennyson [1854]

And Longfellow used the unfamiliar sound of the dactylic line to accentuate the primitive, pagan mood at the beginning of "Evangeline" (1847):

> Thīs ĭs thĕ/ fōrĕst prĭm/ēvăl.// Thĕ/ mūrmŭrĭng/ pīnĕs ănd thĕ/ hēmlŏcks/ . . .
> Stānd lĭke/ Drūĭds ŏf/ ōld.

The *anapest* (ĭn thĕ rēalms), like the dactyl, is a rapid meter, but in proceeding from unstressed syllables to stressed ones, it also parallels the iamb. Hence, it has none of the strangeness of the dactyl or trochee. It works well in rapidly paced poems:

> Thĕ Āssўr/ĭ-ăn cāme/ dŏwn// lĭke thĕ wŏlf/ ŏn thĕ fŏld,
> Ănd hĭs cō/hŏrts wĕre glēam/ĭng ĭn pūr/plĕ ănd gŏld;

Ǎnd thě shēen/ ǒf thěir spēars// wǎs līke stǎrs/ ǒn thě sēa,

Whěn thě Blūe/ wǎve rōlls night/lў ǒn dēep/ Gǎlǐlēe.
—From "The Destruction of Sennacherib,"
Lord Byron [1815]

And it also pleases in very mellifluous ones:

Ǐt wǎs mān/ў ǎnd mān/ў ǎ yēar/ ǎgo,

Ǐn ǎ king/dǒm bў/ thě sēa,

Thǎt ǎ māid/ěn thěre līved// whǒm yǒu/ mǎy knōw

Bў thě nāme// ǒf Ǎn/nǎběl Lēe;
—From "Annabel Lee," Edgar Allan Poe [1849]

Someone once argued that a long poem in anapests, like a long ride on a roller coaster, is apt to cause nausea, but there can be little doubt that this rolling meter is exquisitely suited to many brief pieces.

The *spondee* (John Keats) is never the dominant meter in a whole poem, but one or two spondees will tend to dominate a line. This is well illustrated in Alexander Pope's lines on the role of sound and rhythm in poetry:

True ease in writing comes from art, not chance,
As those move easiest who have learned to dance.
'Tis not enough no harshness gives offense,
The sound must seem an echo to the sense:
Soft is the strain when Zepher gently blows,
And the smooth stream in smoother numbers flows;
Bǔt whěn/ lǒud sūr/gěs lāsh// thě sōund/ǐng shōre,

Thě hōarse,/ rōugh vērse// shǒuld līke/ thě tōr/rěnt rōar;

Whěn Ā/jǎx strīves// sǒme rōck's/ vǎst wēight/ tǒ thrōw,

Thě līne/ tōo/ lābǒrs,/ ǎnd thě wōrds/ mōve slōw.
—From "An Essay on Criticism," Alexander Pope [1711]

There is at least one spondee in each of the last four lines, and each time a spondee occurs three stressed syllables line up in front of us like hard blocks of granite that our voices must surmount. Stressed syllables require more effort from the speaker and they take longer to pronounce than unstressed syllables. As a result, spondees always slow down the pace of a poem. They can be especially useful when an author wishes to express anger or violence, as in King Lear's line:

Blōw, wīnds,/ ǎnd crāck/ yǒur chēeks!// Rāge! Blōw!

In addition to the four principal rhythms (iambic, trochaic, anapestic, and dactylic) and that of the slow spondee, there are a great many feet with unpronounceable Greek names that pop up occasionally to vary the dominant rhythm of a poem: *pyrrhic* (˘ ˘), *bacchius* (˘ − −), *antibacchius* (− − ˘), *amphimacer* (− ˘ −), *amphibrach* (˘ − ˘), and so on. Although there is no need to remember these names, their existence demonstrates that, within the framework of a dominant rhythm, a poet may proceed almost as he pleases. He has what is called the "poetic license" to take liberties with meter, syntax, and even diction, *providing* the result is a more forceful, unified, and distinctive poem.

THE LIMITATIONS OF SYLLABIC STRESS SCANSION. The rules of scansion are loose, and nearly every line of verse can be marked in a number of ways. We have, for example, scanned King Lear's line as two spondees and two iambs:

> Blow, winds,/ and crack/ your cheeks!// Rage! Blow!

But because the line occurs in a passage that is predominantly iambic pentameter, we might choose to give it the required five feet by marking with a caret (ʌ) the pauses that would naturally fall at the exclamation points:

> Blow, winds,/ and crack/ your cheeks!// Rage ̂/ Blow ̂

Similarly, we have scanned the first line of "On First Looking into Chapman's Homer" as a dactyl, trochee, anapest, and iamb.

> Much have I/ travell'd// in the realms/ of gold.

It could also be a trochee, iamb, pyrrhic, and two iambs:

> Much have/ I tra/vell'd in/ the realms/ of gold.

Such changes in scansion are cosmetic only and indicate no significant difference in the way each line *should be* read.

There is, however, considerable room for actual changes in the way a line *can* be read. Different readers rarely use stresses and pauses in precisely the same places, as anyone can testify after hearing one of Hamlet's soliloquies spoken by actors so different as Laurence Olivier, Richard Burton, and Richard Chamberlain. Sometimes we do not agree on the syllables that should be stressed or on the relative amount of stress on each. Scansion is, after all, a system of simplifying and visually presenting the complex rhythm in a line. It is not an exact science. Even if a precise system were possible, it would be too complicated to be useful in pointing out the simple, recurring rhythms of poetry. There must be a certain amount of ambiguity in the scansion of any poem.

Although we must accept the limitations of our system and recognize that there will rarely be only one "right" way of scanning a poem, yet we must also recognize that this loosely constructed system is of considerable usefulness to both poets and readers. Because syllabic-stress meters are common in English poetry and their scansion is well understood, poets can confidently expect that readers will pick up most of the clues to rhythm that the meter conveys and therefore will read the lines with an emphasis closely approximating what was intended. Conversely, readers can easily determine a poem's underlying meter and then decide how they wish to read each line. The decisions made should be based, where possible, on the poem's content, its prose emphases, and its basic meter. The commonly accepted terminology of scansion allows us to explain more easily the decisions about the rhythm that we have made and how these decisions reflect and reinforce the meaning of the poem. Finally, the prevalence of syllabic-stress meters allows great poets to create a tension between the rhythm of ordinary speech and the heartbeat of the poetic line. The discovery of new possibilities in poetic rhythm in a poem like "Chapman's Homer" is one of the pleasures of travel in the realms of gold.

ALTERNATE SYSTEMS OF SCANSION. The syllabic stress system of metrics slowly came to dominate English poetry between the twelfth and sixteenth centuries because it proved better suited to the evolving English language than any of the competing systems: *accentual-alliterative meters, purely syllabic meters, quantitative meters,* and *free verse.* Nonetheless, each of these has left its mark on English poetry.

Alliterative, accentual, or *strong-stress* verse was the metrical system native to our Anglo-Saxon forebears. An impressive amount of alliterative poetry survived the Middle Ages, but only two poems in this meter are encountered frequently enough to be mentioned here. *Beowulf,* the earliest surviving poem in a European language, was composed about A.D. 725; it describes the epic adventures of Beowulf in defeating the male monster Grendel and then Grendel's dam before Beowulf himself succumbs to a fire-breathing dragon. The poem is written in Old English, which is so different from modern English that it must be learned just like a foreign language. Each line in the poem has a variable number of unaccented syllables and four strong stresses, three of which are usually emphasized by alliteration. The line is bisected by a caesural pause.

The same alliterative meter is used in the Middle English Arthurian romance, *Sir Gawain and the Green Knight.* The following lines, which describe Gawain's sufferings during his winter quest for the Green Knight, provide an example of the original appearance of the meter. Note where the accents are in the following lines:

> For werre wrathed hym not so much,// that wynter was wors,
>
> When the colde cler water// from the clouds schadde,
>
> And fries er hit falle mygth// to the fale erthe.
>
> Ner slayn wyth the slete// he sleped in his yrnes
>
> Mo nyghtes then innoghe// in naked rokkes,
>
> Ther as claterande fro the crest// the colde borne rennes,
>
> And henged heghe// over his hede in hard ysse-ikkles.[5]
>
> —From *Sir Gawain and the Green Knight,* anonymous [ca. 1375]

Of the poems considered in this text, "Eve" (p. 619) is perhaps more easily classified as strong-stress dimeter than as dactylic dimeter. Each line has only two strong stresses, while the number of unstressed syllables varies from two to four. "Fog," by Carl Sandburg, is also best classified as strong-stress dimeter. Each line has two major stresses that are surrounded, in no particular pattern,

---

[5] Translation: For fighting troubled him not so much, that winter was worse,/ When the cold clear water from the clouds fell,/ And froze ere it might fall to the faded earth./ Near slain with sleet he slept in his irons (armor)/ More nights than enough in naked rocks,/ There where clattering from the crest the cold stream ran,/ And hung high over his head in hard icicles.

by weakly stressed or unstressed syllables. In general, the strong-stress system requires alliteration if it is to sound poetic, and the required alliteration is too limiting and too repetitive to appeal to most modern poets. When strong-stress verse is used without alliteration, as in Sandburg's "Fog," it has the appearance and sound of free verse.

Purely *syllabic meters* represent another alternative to the syllabic-stress system. Some modern languages, notably French, make little use of stress in speech. Each syllable is given roughly the same weight. As a result, French poetry is based almost entirely on syllable count.

After the French-speaking Normans conquered the Saxons at Hastings in 1066, our modern English language began to emerge as a hybrid between Old English and Old French; at the same time, modern syllabic-stress meters began to emerge, as the alliterative tradition of Old English poetry met with the syllabic tradition of French verse.

In the absence of other musical devices (rhyme, alliteration, etc.), *syllabic verse* is often indistinguishable from prose, as we see in the following "stanza" from Thom Gunn's "Vox Humana":

> Being without quality
> I appear to you at first
> as an unkempt smudge, a blur,
> an indefinite haze, mere-
> ly pricking the eyes, almost
> nothing. Yet you perceive me.
> —From "Vox Humana,"
> Thom Gunn [1957]

Although these lines can be defended on the basis that their formlessness is in harmony with the poem's theme that our own human spirit is difficult to define, they are still open to the criticism that anyone with the mental capacity to count on his fingers can write as poetically as this. Under the circumstances, it is no surprise that few English poems are written in purely syllabic verse.

A third alternative to syllabic-stress verse is made possible by the differences in the amount of time it takes to pronounce various syllables. The word *truths,* for example, takes longer to say than *lies*—even though each is monosyllabic. *Quantitative meter* is based on the length (in units of time) of various syllables, instead of on the relative degree of their stress.

Greek and Latin poetry was based on quantitative metrics, and therefore the few English poems in quantitative verse have usually been written by poets who were heavily influenced by the classics. During the late sixteenth century, at the height of the English revival of Greek and Latin learning, such poets as Spenser and Sidney experimented briefly with quantity in verse before concluding that most English syllables take up about the same amount of time in pronunciation and that few readers are able to perceive the slight differences that do exist.

It is, however, possible to demonstrate some quantitative differences in English pronunciation. The first line of the following couplet reads much more rapidly than the second, even though both have an identical number of syllables.:

> By slight syllables we show
> Those truths whose worth you now know.

But there is a great difference between this theoretical possibility and its application in fluent poetry. The most that can be said is that quantitative factors sometimes play a secondary role in the impact of normal syllabic-stress verse. When, for example, Alexander Pope wrote about the effects of sound in poetry, he skillfully used lengthy vowel sounds (ow, oar, ough, ur) to slow down the movement of his lines:

> But when loud surges lash the sounding shore.

> The hoarse, rough verse should like the torrent roar.

Free verse, the final alternative to syllabic-stress meter, is not a meter at all. In free verse, no formal patterns of metrical feet, quantitative feet, or syllable count are sought, and the verse is "free" to develop in any manner that fits the poem and contributes to the overall rhythm of the words. The only real distinctions between the free verse and the rhythmical prose of Thomas Paine or Abraham Lincoln are that (1) free verse uses variable line length as a unit in rhythm, (2) free verse may use rhyme more frequently than would be acceptable in prose, and (3) free verse is less restrained than prose by the rules of logic and grammar.

In Elizabeth Bishop's "Sandpiper," for example, the number of syllables per line ranges from 6 to 13, the number of stresses ranges from three to six, and the metrical pattern remains irregular throughout the poem:

SANDPIPER

The roaring alongside he takes for granted,
and that every so often the world is bound to shake.
He runs, he runs to the south, finical, awkward,
in a state of controlled panic, a student of Blake.

The beach hisses like fat. On his left, a sheet
of interrupting water comes and goes
and glazes over his dark and brittle feet.
He runs, he runs straight through it, watching his toes.

—Watching, rather, the spaces of sand between them,
where (no detail too small) the Atlantic drains
rapidly backwards and downwards. As he runs,
he stares at the dragging grains.

The world is a mist. And then the world is
minute and vast and clear. The tide
is higher or lower. He couldn't tell you which.
His beak is focussed; he is preoccupied.

looking for something, something, something.
Poor bird, he is obsessed!
The millions of grains are black, white, tan, and gray,
mixed with quartz grains, rose and amethyst.
                                        —Elizabeth Bishop [1947]

It would be inaccurate, however, to say that Bishop's free verse lacks form. The poem is broken up into four-line units, or stanzas, in which the second line always rhymes with the fourth. Thus, the poem has the visual appearance and sound of verse, while its rhythm remains as hectic and irregular as the darting motion of the sandpiper itself. The poem begins with two flowing and forceful lines describing the surf; then it continues with brief, erratic, and repetitious phrases that help to characterize the bird's mindless panic: "He runs, he runs . . . watching . . . watching . . . he runs, he stares . . . focussed . . . preoccupied,/ looking for something, something, something./ Poor bird, he is obsessed!" The central portion of the poem is a descriptive tour de force, but it shows only the bleak and monotonous aspects of the sandpiper's existence. In the final lines, however, the point of view shifts. After being told *about* a bird "looking for something, something, something," we now see *with* him that the millions of grains of sand that slip through his toes are "black, white, tan, and gray,/ mixed with quartz grains, rose and amethyst." The existence that had seemed so futile and repetitious a moment earlier is now varied, and even beautiful. The endless patterns of sliding sand, like those in a child's kaleidoscope, offer their own delightful rewards. And suddenly, too, the poem achieves an unexpected unity. We may at first have chuckled at Bishop's description of the sandpiper as "finical, awkward,/ in a state of controlled panic, a student of Blake." The implied comparison makes fun of the often fanatical followers of the famous Romantic poet, William Blake, whose preoccupation with his own visionary experiences was so great that his wife once complained, "I have very little of Mr. Blake's company. He is always in Paradise." But by the end of the poem we learn to view the sandpiper and all "students of Blake" more sympathetically. Certainly they see something the rest of us do not; and perhaps in their preoccupation they see many things more closely, more clearly, and more perceptively than we.

Free verse is no longer experimental or even new. Although it is an established and popular alternative to syllabic-stress meters, it does not appear that free verse will ever entirely supplant conventional metrics, for there are many advantages to meter. In the first place, poets use meter because it is traditional. It allies them with Chaucer, Shakespeare, Milton, Wordsworth, Byron, Tennyson, Frost, and scores of other distinguished literary men and women. A poem that breaks with this long tradition risks an unsympathetic response from an audience that is accustomed to meter in poetry. Second, the use of meter demonstrates that the author took at least some care in writing, and this implies that he or she considered the content of the poem important. Few authors are likely to bother versifying ideas they think are trivial. (It is true, of course, that prose and free verse may be every bit as carefully crafted as metrical poetry, but the latter signals its importance through its form.) Third, a regular rhythm is inherently musical. It lays down a beat that appeals to us not only in poetry, but also in the sonatas of Beethoven and the songs of The Beach Boys. Fourth, regular rhythms arise out of strong emotions and enhance them in an auditor. They seem to be tied in with the rhythms of our human body. And fifth, meter creates an opportunity for interaction between the sound and sense of language. The tension between the expected and the actual rhythm of a particular line makes it easier for a poet to establish a tone—to speed up the rhythm where the illusion of speed, excitement, or fluidity is wanted, and to slow it down where the content demands emphasis and sobriety. Meter, then, is useful, but it cannot make an otherwise weak poem strong. Meter is only one of many ingredients in verse, although it is a catalytic ingredient, as Coleridge noted in comparing it to yeast, "worthless or disagreeable by itself, but giving vivacity and spirit to the liquor with which it is proportionally combined." Dame Edith Sitwell may have been even closer to the truth, however, when she argued that rhythm is "to the world of sound, what light is to the world of sight."[6] It is, finally, the rhythm of a poem, and not its meter, that should be the focus of commentary.

RHYME AND OTHER MANIPULATIONS OF SOUND

Two words *rhyme* when they end with the same sound. In *perfect rhyme*, the final vowel and any succeeding consonant sounds are identical, and the preceding consonant sounds are different. Although words in perfect rhyme may be similar in spelling, they need not be. Thus, *ripe* and *tripe* rhyme to the eye and to the ear, but *rhyme* and *sublime* or *enough* and *snuff* rely entirely on aural similarity.

Rhyme is the most unnatural, the most noticeable, the most controversial, and possibly the most common of all poetic devices. Almost as soon as critics began to examine the elements of poetry, they also began to bicker about the merits of rhyme. Milton, for example, claimed, in 1668, that rhyme is "the invention of a barbarous age" and appeals only to "vulgar readers," to which Edward Young added the observation, a century later (1759), that rhyme, "in epic poetry is a sore disease, in the tragic absolute death. . . . but our lesser poetry stands in need of a toleration for it; it raises that, but sinks the great, as spangles adorn children, but expose men." Interestingly enough, it is harder to find defenders of rhyme, although John Dryden, writing in 1664, felt that the device has so many advantages "that it were lost time to name them," and in 1702, Edward Bysshe called rhyme "the chief ornament of versification in any of the modern languages." On the whole, rhyme's detractors seem to make a more vigorous and impassioned argument; yet the great majority of all anthologized poetry in every period (including our own) is rhymed. Evidently, rhyme adds something to exceptional poetry. The question is, what?

Rhyme contributes to the effect of poetry in several ways.

1. It rings an audible end to each line. This is important because the rhythm of iambic verse is so similar to that of prose that without the aid of rhyme the sense of hearing poetry can easily be lost. Rhyme helps us to recognize aurally where one line ends and the next begins and thus reinforces the rhythmic pattern of the poem.

2. Rhyme makes words memorable. Of course, it cannot in itself make words *worthy* of being remembered; the content of the poem must do that. But rhyme has always been used to make things *easier* to remember. Wandering medieval minstrels, whose livelihood depended on their ability to delight a crowd with the lengthy adventures of Sir Gawain or King Arthur, used a tale's rhyming pattern as a prod to memory in the same way that we still use rhyming chants in daily life ("Thirty days hath September").

3. Rhyme is pleasing because it is inherently musical. Verse appeals to small children long before they understand the full meaning of the words they chant, and rhyme is almost always used in popular songs.

4. Rhyme can be used to affect the pace and tone of poetry, as well. In the following stanza from "The Rime of the Ancient Mariner," for example,

[6] *Taken Care Of* (London: Hutchinson, 1965), p. 123.

Coleridge uses the first four rhyme words ("prow," "blow," "shadow," and "foe") at the eighth, sixteenth, twenty-first, and twenty-fourth syllables to enhance the illusion of a chasing (and gaining!) storm:

> With sloping masts and dipping prow,
> As who pursued with yell and blow
> Still treads the shadow of his foe,
> And forward bends his head,
> The ship drove fast, loud roared the blast,
> And southward aye we fled.
> —From "The Rime of the Ancient Mariner,"
> Samuel Taylor Coleridge [1798]

5. Well-managed rhymes are a sign of skill. Much of the fun in reading a poem like Byron's *Don Juan* is to observe how the poet wriggles out of the tight spots created by words that seem impossible to rhyme. When, for example, he ends the first line of the following quatrain with "annuities," we may think him trapped, only to find him scamper gleefully through the rhyme without the slightest apparent strain:

> 'Tis said that persons living on annuities
> Are longer lived than others,—God knows why,
> Unless to plague the grantors,—yet so true it is,
> That some, I really think, do never die.
> —From *Don Juan*, Lord Byron [1819]

Conversely, poorly managed rhymes are a sign of clumsiness, as Pope made clear in his "Essay on Criticism":

> Where'er you find 'the cooling western breeze,"
> In the next line it 'whispers through the trees';
> If crystal streams 'with pleasing murmurs creep,'
> The reader's threatened (not in vain) with 'sleep.'
> —From "Essay on Criticism,"
> Alexander Pope [1711]

6. Because worn rhymes are so tiring and because interesting ones are difficult to find, a good rhyme facilitates witticism. Rhyme used in comic or satiric poetry tends to sharpen a well-honed phrase, as, for example, in the "Epitaph Intended for his Wife," attributed to John Dryden:

> Here lies my wife: here let her lie!
> Now she's at rest, and so am I.

and in Hilaire Belloc's sardonic "Lines for a Christmas Card":

> May all my enemies go to Hell.
> Noel, Noel, Noel, Noel.

One has only to rewrite these lines without rhyme (substituting *dwell* for Dryden's "lie" and *Amen* for Belloc's "Noel") to recognize that, with the change of words, the humor is lost.

In summary, rhyme in poetry is like salt in cooking. It adds almost nothing to nutrition, but it appeals to our taste. A poem that is unseasoned by rhyme may be as dull as a saltless diet, whereas too much rhyme, like too much salt, may spoil the dish.

Rhyme ordinarily falls on an accented syllable at the end of a line, in which case it is called *masculine end rhyme.* In *feminine (or double) rhyme,* the final two syllables in a line rhyme, and the final syllable is unaccented. In *triple rhyme,* three syllables rhyme. Both double and triple rhyme are generally used to create a comic effect. In the following stanza, lines one, three, and five are masculine end rhymes, lines four and six are feminine end rhymes, and lines seven and eight are triple rhymes.

> 'Tis pity learned virgins ever wed
>   With persons of no sort of education,
> Or gentlemen, who, though well born and bred,
>   Grow tired of scientific conversation:
> I don't choose to say much on this head,
>   I'm a plain man, and in a simple station,
> But—Oh! ye lords of ladies intellectual,
> Inform us truly have they not hen-peck'd you all?
>   —From *Don Juan,* Lord Byron [1819]

Not all rhymes fall at the end of a line. *Internal rhyme* occurs within a line of poetry. Often the word preceding the caesura rhymes with the last word in the line, as in Poe's "The Raven":

> Once upon a midnight *dreary,* while I pondered weak and *weary*

But internal rhyme may occur anywhere within a line or even between lines:

> And the silken, sad, *uncertain* rustling of each purple *curtain*
>   *Thrilled* me—*filled* me with fantastic terrors never felt before
> So that now, to still the *beating* of my heart I stood *repeating*
>   " 'Tis some visiter *entreating* entrance at my chamber door."
>   —From "The Raven," Edgar Allan Poe [1845]

In *imperfect rhyme* the sound of two words is similar but it is not as close as is required in *true* or *perfect rhyme.* In the lines just quoted, "silken" and "uncertain" are imperfect rhymes, as are "filled," "felt," and "still." Ogden Nash combines imperfect rhyme with an ingenious play on words in the following anecdote on a happy marriage:

> I believe a little incompatibility is
> the spice of life, particularly if he has
> income and she is pattable.

Imperfectly rhymed words generally contain identical vowels or identical consonants, but not both. Imperfect rhyme is also referred to as approximate rhyme, or as half-rhyme, near rhyme, oblique rhyme, off-rhyme, or slant rhyme.

False rhyme pairs the sounds of accented with unaccented syllables. In the lines we quoted from "The Rime of the Ancient Mariner," "shadow" is a false internal rhyme with "his foe:"

> With sloping masts and dipping prow,
> As who pursued with yell and blow
> Still treads the *shadow* of *his foe* . . .

And at the same time, "prow" and "blow" are known as *visual rhymes*. These words—and such others as "rough-bough" and "love-prove"—rhyme to the eye, but not to the ear. Their spellings are similar, but their pronunciations are different.

Finally, *repetition* is occasionally used as an alternative to true rhyme. It provides the recurrence of sound expected in rhyme, but not the difference in meaning and initial consonants that makes rhyme delightful.

Modern poets have, on the whole, set themselves apart from much traditional poetry by replacing true rhymes with one or more of the alternatives, and so retaining some sense of music without rhyme's characteristic chime. Let us examine how W. H. Auden uses rhyme in describing the surf-washed shore of an island:

LOOK, STRANGER

> Look, stranger, at this island now
> The leaping light for your delight discovers,
> Stand stable here
> And silent be,
> That through the channels of the ear
> May wander like a river
> The swaying sound of the sea.
>
> Here at the small field's ending pause
> Where the chalk wall falls to the foam, and its tall ledges
> Oppose the pluck
> And knock of the tide,
> And the shingle scrambles after the suck-
> ing surf, and the gull lodges
> A moment on its sheer side.
>
> Far off like floating seeds the ships
> Diverge on urgent voluntary errands;
> And the full view
> Indeed may enter
> And move in memory as now these clouds do,
> That pass the harbor mirror
> And all the summer through the water saunter.
>
> —W. H. Auden [1936]

Although the words are musical, the poem is not arranged in any of the easily recognizable patterns of verse. The meter is loosely based on the strong-stress system, and the rhyme scheme is unconventional. The first line in each stanza is unrhymed. The second and sixth lines are imperfect rhymes. The third line rhymes perfectly with the fifth, as does the fourth line with the seventh. We can simplify our description of the rhyme scheme in "Look, Stranger" (or any other poem) by representing each new rhyme sound by a different letter of the alphabet, with capital letters reserved for perfect rhymes and lower-case letters for imperfect, false, or visual rhymes, and by representing unrhymed lines with an X. Thus, each of Auden's stanzas rhymes according to the scheme XaBCBaC. Identifying the *rhyme scheme* in this way is an important stage in cataloguing the manipulations of rhythm and rhyme within a specific poem. Although some critics prefer to ignore the various forms of partial rhyme, the system we have outlined allows us to indicate the subtle presence of imperfect, false, and visual rhymes without unduly complicating our representation of the total rhyme pattern. The rhyme schemes of most poems, of course, can be fully described using only the capital letters and the X for unrhymed lines.

Schematizing the rhyme in this way leads us to two important observations about the effect of Auden's verse. First, although six out of these seven lines rhyme, each of the first four lines ends with a different and unrelated sound. (In the first stanza the actual words are "now," "discovers," "here," and "be.") This means that each stanza is more than half complete before Auden begins to give it the sound of rhyming verse. Second, Auden never establishes a strong and repeated interval between rhymes. In most poetry, the rhymes recur predictably—every ten syllables in Pope's iambic pentameter couplets (p. 620), every twelve syllables in the anapestic tetrameter couplets of Byron's "The Destruction of Sennacherib" (p. 619), and so on. Almost immediately, we subconsciously pick up the rhyme pattern and begin to *expect* rhymes at the proper intervals. Auden makes it difficult for us to have any such expectations because he varies the interval between his rhymes. "Here" (line 3) is separated by 12 syllables from its rhyming partner "ear" (line 5), while "be" (line four) is separated by 22 syllables from "sea" (line 7) and "discovers" (line two) is separated by 23 syllables from its approximate rhyme with "river" (line 6). Although the second and third stanzas follow the same rhyme scheme, the number of syllables separating the rhyme words may vary because lines of strong-stress meter often differ in number of syllables. "Look, Stranger" is in fact rhyme-dense (for example, it has a total of six rhyming words in the 49 syllables of the first stanza, whereas a comparable number of rhymes in Pope's iambic pentameter would require sixty syllables). But we scarcely even perceive the rhyme in reading Auden's verse, whereas it is unmistakable in Pope's.

By declining to use a conventional, repetitive rhyme scheme, Auden willingly risks alienating those readers who feel his writing is "just not poetry" in order to capture that subtle sense of beauty and harmony that is the poem's theme. Auden is, indeed, attempting to describe the chalk cliffs, the surf-driven pebbles (or shingle), the perched gull, the urgent ships, and the drifting clouds, but he is even more interested in the process by which he and presumably all of us take such scenes of natural beauty to heart until "the full view/ Indeed may enter/ And move in memory as now these clouds do." Auden, no doubt, knows that a poet cannot hope to match the visual representation of the seaside in a photograph, a painter's landscape, or a film. But he knows as well that these visual media are not as effective as words in conveying the effects of rhythmic and natural movement on a human observer. Thus, his description of the setting is filled with activity: the "leaping light," "the pluck and knock of the tide," the "sucking surf," and even the memory of the whole scene that, like the drifting clouds, will "all the summer through the water saunter." And yet the actions he describes are not the purposeful and goal-oriented actions of hectic human life; they are sedate, rhythmic, and inherent in nature.

Even the ships, which Auden knows "diverge on urgent voluntary errands," appear to him from the cliffs "like floating seeds."

What Auden wants, then, is not the methodical chime of repeated rhyme and not the businesslike stolidity of prose, but a more natural harmony that "through the channels of the ear/ May wander like a river" recreating "the swaying sound of the sea." Auden's idiosyncratic use of rhyme is but one of the musical devices that help him to do so. The similarity of vowel or consonant sounds, which we call *imperfect rhyme* when it occurs at the ends of lines, may also occur within lines where it is known more specifically as *alliteration, assonance,* or *consonance.*

Alliteration is the repetition in two or more nearby words of initial consonant sounds ("Where the chalk wall *f*alls to the *f*oam," line 9). *Assonance* is the repetition in two or more nearby words of similar vowel sounds ("ch*a*lk w*a*ll f*a*lls"), And *consonance* is the repetition in two or more nearby words of similar consonant sounds preceded by different accented vowels ("cha*lk*," "plu*ck*," "kno*ck*"). Each of these devices is melodious—although less so than rhyme itself. For this reason, each is particularly appropriate in developing Auden's description of a natural and harmonious setting. Virtually every line reverberates with the subtle music of one or more of these three devices, and in some lines several musical effects are interwoven. Take, for example, the second stanza. The *aw* sound in "small" is repeated in "pause," and then in the next line this assonance is compounded by consonance and internal rhyme in the series "chalk wall falls." the *f* of "falls" alliterates with "foam," and the *all* sound is picked up again in "tall." In the third line, the *p*'s of "oppose" are reiterated in "pluck." (This hybrid of consonance and alliteration is one of many musical effects in verse with no formal name.) The fourth line has consonance ("pluck/ knock"); the fifth has alliteration and assonance, which carry over into the sixth ("*s*hingle *s*crambles after the *s*uck-/ ing *s*urf" and "*s*ucking *s*urf and the g*u*ll"); and the seventh line combines alliteration ("*s*heer *s*ide") with the repetition of the *m* sounds in "*m*o*m*ent." This high concentration of musical effects is repeated in both of the other stanzas.

As if all this were not enough, Auden also uses the emotional overtones of the various vowels and consonants to further heighten the beauty of his description. In general, those vowels that are produced through pursed and rounded lips tend to be soothing and *euphonious*—although sometimes somber. We say "Oooh," "Ahh," and "Oh" in spontaneous expressions of pleasure and surprise. Conversely, those vowels that are produced with widely stretched lips tend to convey excitement, astonishment, or fright. Scared women "SHRIEEEK" and unhappy children "whine" and "wail." Such grating and unpleasant sounds are said to be *cacophonous*. Consonants, too, tend to divide into euphonious and cacophonous groups. Among the former we should list the liquid sounds of *r* and *l,* the nasal sounds of *m* and *n,* and such gentle sounds as *f, v, th,* and *sh.* Auden uses these soft consonants in "Look, Stranger" when he is decribing the static appearance of the ships,

> Far off like floating seeds the ships,
>
> Diverge on urgent voluntary errands;

He also uses them to reinforce the idea that the very harmony of the scene makes it memorable:

And the full view

Indeed may enter

And move in memory as now these clouds do.

Other consonants, called explosives—*p, b, d, k, t,* and hard *g*—create harsh, cacophonous effects. Auden uses these in his second stanza to describe the crash of the surf against the shore:

. . . its tall ledges

Oppose the pluck

And knock of the tide,

And the shingle scrambles after the suck-

ing surf and the gull lodges

A moment on its sheer side.

In fact, in "Look, Stranger" the meaning of the words may be less important than their rhythm and sound. To be sure, Auden describes the setting clearly, but it is a scene that, in one form or another, has been experienced by all. We are impressed not so much by what Auden has to say, as by the way he says it.

In our analysis of Auden's poem perhaps we have emphasized too heavily the emotional overtones implicit in verbal sounds. If we examine any significant number of successful poems, we will find examples of harsh sounds used to create beauty or smooth sounds used with force and vigor. Few poets have ever been more conscious of the effects of sound than Pope in his lines on sound and sense in poetry (p. 620). It is indeed easy to applaud the liquid consonants (*f, r, n, m, th*) and melodious vowels ("s*o*ft," "bl*o*ws," "sm*oo*th") in his couplet on the sound of smooth verse:

Soft is the strain when Zepher gently blows,
And the smooth stream in smoother numbers flows.

In the next couplet, the sibilants (*s, sh*) and guttural vowels ("h*o*arse, r*o*u*gh* *verse*") help to complement the stormy theme:

But when loud surges lash the sounding shore
The hoarse, rough verse should like the torrent roar.

And in the third couplet, a series of awkward consonantal combinations ("A*j*a*x st*rives some roc*k's* va*st* *w*eight") helps to slow the pace of the labored lines:

When Ajax strives some rock's vast weight to throw,
The line too labors, and the verse moves slow.

Yet Pope's lines also show us the dangers of generalization about the emotional effects of vowel and consonant sounds. The "hoarse, rough verse" in the second couplet is packed with liquid and nasal consonants, "whe*n l*oud surges *l*ash the sou*nd*ing *sh*ore," and the same is true in the third couplet where "*the l*ine too *l*abors, a*nd the ve*rse *m*o*v*es s*l*ow." In these lines the liquid sounds have little moderating effect on the prevailing harshness of the verse. Obviously, the meaning of words can be more important than their sound in determining emotional connotations. Softness of vowels and consonants cannot make "foulness" fair or "murder" musical. With the exception of a few truly *onomatopoetic* words—for example, words like *moo, hiss,* and *clang,* whose sounds suggest their meanings—it is doubtful that the sounds of individual words often echo their senses. When "loud surges lash the sounding shore" in Pope's verse, the words *sound* harsh and forceful because of their denotations. And although the *l* and *s*-alliteration may in fact be pleasing to the ear, it does less to create a liquid beauty than to increase our sense of harshness by emphasizing the important words.

In the final analysis, the manipulations of sound that we have examined in this section are characteristic of all good writing. Authors base their word choice in large part on what "sounds" best. Theoretically, then, every piece of prose or poetry could be examined for the effect of sound on sense, but the problem is that our techniques of analysis are coarse and many of the decisions that authors make are complex, delicate, and even subconscious. We are like chemists struggling to determine a molecular weight using a physician's scale. In such circumstances one must concentrate on the macroscopic, cumulative effect of many microscopic interactions, for it is out of such interactions that the sounds of poetry are created.

7

❧❧❧❧❧❧❧

Structure and Form in Poetry

Nearly all writing combines the narrative, dramatic, descriptive, and expository modes of expression. We rarely find any of these in a pure form in literature because an author's goal of creating interest and variety ordinarily requires that the modes be mixed. For the purpose of illustration, however, we can compose examples of how the same situation might be treated in each of the four modes:

Narrative: The boys crossed the street and entered the store.
Dramatic: "Look! There's a candy store."
"Let's cross over and buy some."
Descriptive: On one side of the street stood the two boys, jingling the coins in their pockets; on the other side were the large-paned windows of the store front, advertising in antique letters: DAN'S OLD-FASHIONED CANDIES.
Expository: The boys wanted to cross the street to buy some candy.

A narrative approach concentrates on action. In its pure form, it uses only nouns and transitive verbs, but such writing usually lacks appeal to the senses and to the intellect. As a result, narration does not necessarily predominate in narrative poetry; rather, the impulse to tell a story remains uppermost in the narrative poet's mind as he or she interweaves narration, description, dialogue, and explanation.

The principal forms of narrative poetry are the *epic*, which tells the book-length adventures of the founders of a nation or a culture (for example, *The Iliad, Paradise Lost*); the *romance*, which often resembles the epic in length and adventurousness but puts greater emphasis on love and supernatural events (*The Odyssey*, Tennyson's *Idylls of the King*); the *poetic tale* or short story in verse (Chaucer's *Miller's Tale*, Burns' *Tam o' Shanter*); and the ballad, a short narrative song (see p. 638). The structure of narrative poetry closely resembles that of

634

fiction, proceeding from an exposition of the setting, circumstances, and characters, through a period of complication (rising action), to a crisis and subsequent resolution.

The dramatic approach focuses on dialogue. Action and setting are conveyed through the spoken comments of the characters rather than through direct authorial description. Because poetry makes use of the aural qualities of language, most plays written before the twentieth century were composed in verse. Verse is, however, an artificial form of speech, and therefore twentieth-century realistic drama has mainly been written in prose, although the continuing popularity of musicals serves to remind us that poetic effects do appeal to theatrical audiences.

The *dramatic monologue*, which is the chief format for dramatic poetry, is a fairly long speech by a fictional narrator that is usually addressed to a second, silent character. During such monologues as Robert Browning's "My Last Duchess" or Tennyson's "Ulysses," the narrator reveals both his character and his motives at some crucial moment in his life. Because a monologue is basically reflective, the structure of a dramatic monologue rarely follows that of the conventional short story. It is likely to be digressive, argumentative, and analytic rather than strictly narrative.

A poem that is primarily descriptive or expository is called a *lyric*. Lyric poems range widely in subject, theme, and scope of treatment, but they are alike in their preoccupation with ideas, emotions, and the poet's state of mind. Although a narrative element is sometimes present, the lyric poet never concentrates on the story.

Many of the poems in this anthology are lyrics, and by briefly examining a few of them, we can only begin to suggest the dozens of possible structures for lyric verse. A description may, for example, move from nearby objects to far-off ones, as in the second and third stanzas of Auden's "Look, Stranger" (p. 629). Or description may be followed by inquiry and analysis, as in Frost's "Design" (p. 571). Frequently a specific incident leads up to a more general conclusion, as when Shakespeare (see p. 581) describes the emotions of an infant crawling after its mother as a symbol of his own passion for his mistress. The presentation may be chronological, like Herrick's in "Upon Julia's Clothes" (p. 602); may increase in emotional intensity, like Kipling's "Recessional" (p. 577); or may be analogical, like Donne's "A Valediction: Forbidding Mourning" (p. 559). In addition, descriptions can conceivably be organized according to the various senses or emotions evoked, and an argument can use comparison and contrast, order of importance, or parallelism to give structure to the whole. No exhaustive list of organizational structures is either possible or desirable.

In each of its formats—narrative, dramatic, and lyric—poetry varies more in length and content than either fiction or drama. Hence, the only useful generalizations about poetic structure are the broad ones that every element in a well-structured poem should have an identifiable function, and that the poem itself should build to a unified effect or series of effects.

STANDARD VERSE FORMS

In prose fiction, form is almost entirely subservient to meaning, but in poetry the verse form provides guidelines to the development of ideas. Verse is, as we argued earlier, a game played between the poet and his form. As in other games, the rules are essentially arbitrary. Why must a baseball cross the plate to be called a strike? What practical purpose is served by hitting a tennis ball over a mesh net and into a rectangular court? Why cannot a pawn move backward or a bishop sideways? Why must a sonnet have just 14 lines? The answer in each case is that the rules of the game help to provide a structure within which we can act and a standard against which we can measure our skills and the skills of others. A poet is challenged by his verse form to write as well as he can within certain restrictions. These restrictions do make the writing more difficult, but they also add to the achievement; and by forcing the poet to experiment with different means of expressing thoughts, they often help to better define what the poet really wants to say and how it can best be said.

Blank Verse

As we have seen, verse can be either rhymed or unrhymed. Unrhymed iambic pentameter is called blank verse. English blank verse was first written in 1557 by Henry Howard, the Earl of Surrey, in his translation of Virgil's *Aeneid*. It was then adopted for use in drama by Sackville and Norton in *Gorboduc* (1565); however, not until Marlowe and Shakespeare took up the line in the 1580s did its strength, sonority, and variety become evident, as illustrated in Shakespeare's famous characterization of Julius Caesar:

> Why, man he doth bestride the narrow world
> Like a colossus, and we petty men
> Walk under his huge legs and peep about
> To find ourselves dishonorable graves
> —From *Julius Caesar,*
> William Shakespeare [c. 1600]

In 1664 Milton extended the uses of blank verse to the epic in his *Paradise Lost*. Although little blank verse was written in the eighteenth century, it has been used extensively since.

Stanzaic Verse

Although blank verse is normally organized, like prose, into paragraphs of variable length, rhymed verse is usually cast into units called stanzas. Often, the meter, rhyme scheme, and number of lines are identical in each stanza of a given poem (as in Donne's "The Flea," p. 591). Occasionally, particularly in odes, the structure may vary from stanza to stanza, but no poem really deserves to be called stanzaic unless it regularly uses rhyme or a refrain. Individual stanzas must contain at least two lines and rarely exceed nine.

A *couplet*, formed of a single pair of rhymed lines, is the smallest possible stanzaic unit. When many of the couplets in a poem express a complete thought in two rhetorically balanced lines (as in Pope's lines on sound and sense, p. 620), the poet is said to use the *closed couplet*. The mere use of closed couplets does not, however, constitute a stanzaic structure. Pope's couplets are not visually separate from one another, nor are they always syntactically separate. Individual sentences frequently carry over into a third or fourth line. These run-on verses limit the utility of the couplet as an element of logical structure, and as a result Pope uses paragraphs instead of stanzas as his organizational units.

A few poems, however, are cast into stanzaic couplets, among them Stephen Vincent Benét's "The Mountain Whippoorwill: Or, How Hill-Billy Jim Won the Great Fiddler's Prize":

> Up in the mountains, it's lonesome all the time
> (Sof' win' slewin' thru' the sweet-potato vine.)
>
> Up in the mountains, it's lonesome for a child,
> (Whippoorwills a-callin' when the sap runs wild.)
>
> Up in the mountains, mountains in the fog,
> Everythin's as lazy as an old houn' dog.
>
> Born in the mountains, never raised a pet,
> Don't want nuthin' an' never got it yet.
>
> Born in the mountains, lonesome-born,
> Raised runnin' ragged thru' the cockleburrs and corn.
>
> Never knew my pappy, mebbe never should.
> Think he was a fiddle made of mountain laurel-wood.
>
> Never had a mammy to teach me pretty-please.
> Think she was a whippoorwill, a-skitin' thru' the trees.
>
> Never had a brother nor a whole pair of pants,
> But when I start to fiddle, why, yuh got to start to dance!
>
> *Listen to my fiddle—Kingdom Come—Kingdom Come!*
> *Hear the frogs a-chunkin' "Jug o' rum, Jug o' rum!"*
> *Hear that mountain whippoorwill be lonesome in the air,*
> *An' I'll tell yuh how I travelled to the Essex County Fair.*
> —From "The Mountain Whippoorwill,"
> Stephen Vincent Benét (1925)

In addition to the use of stanzaic couplets, Benét's poem is unusual in at least two ways. Each line of its accentual tetrameter is bisected by a caesura into units of two feet apiece *(dipodic meter)*. Therefore, each couplet could easily be recast as four lines of accentual dimeter. Second, Benét does not commit himself to using stanzaic couplets throughout the remaining hundred lines of the poem. The quoted segment concludes with a quatrain, and Benét later abandons all stanzaic structure. Thus, for substantial segments of the poem, Benét has not overcome the limitations of stanzaic couplets; instead he has freely altered the structure of his poem in adapting to those limitations.

If couplets have rarely been used as independent stanzas, they have nevertheless been popular as complete poems. Most two-line poems are *epigrams*. An epigram is a concentrated witticism that can be written in either verse or prose— although the couplet is the dominant choice. Whatever its form, an epigram must be short, sharp, and swift—as startling as a wasp and as quick to sting. Both Belloc's "Lines for a Christmas Card" and Dryden's "Epitaph on His Wife" (p. 627) are epigrammatic. For a third example of an epigram, consider Coleridge's definition of the form:

What is an epigram? A dwarfish whole;
Its body brevity, and wit its soul.

Many epigrams are buried within longer poems. All of Pope's poems are packed with this form of wit (for example, the first two lines on sound and sense, p. 620); and the final couplets in many of the stanzas in Byron's *Don Juan* are epigrammatic (see pp. 574 and 575), as are the concluding couplets of many of Shakespeare's sonnets.

A three-line stanza is called a *tercet* or *triplet*, if all three lines rhyme together. Herrick's "Upon Julia's Clothes" (p. 602) is an example of a poem using this stanza. *Terza rima*, a form of three-line stanza popularized by the thirteenth-century Italian poet Dante, establishes an interlocking rhyme scheme in the following pattern: ABA BCB CDC, etc. The closing stanza is either a quatrain or a couplet. The most famous English poems in this stanza are Shelley's "Ode to the West Wind," Robert Browning's "The Statue and the Bust," and William Morris's "The Defence of Guenevere."

A unit of four lines, a *quatrain*, is the most common stanzaic form in English poetry. Although many different rhyme schemes have been used in quatrains, the most often used is *crossed rhyme*, in which the first line rhymes with the third and the second with the fourth, ABAB. Usually the first and third lines are tetrameter, the second and fourth trimeter. This is the pattern of Donne's "Valediction: Forbidding Mourning" (p. 559), Wordsworth's "She Dwelt Among the Untrodden Ways" and Poe's "Annabel Lee."

An iambic pentameter quatrain in which the first two lines rhyme with the last (AAXA) is known as a *rubais* because it was popularized in the *Rubáiyát of Omar Khayyám* (1859) by Edward FitzGerald. The stanza is particularly useful in epigrams because it is similar to a closed couplet, although it develops its point in four lines instead of just two. The first two lines in the quatrain are metrically identical to a closed couplet, but the next two lines, instead of developing a separate idea, extend and complement the first two. Thus, the entire quatrain is like a single couplet in which each line has twenty syllables and the first line has an internal rhyme:

> *Couplet 1* — Come, fill the Cup, and in the fire of Spring
> Your Winter-garment of Repentance fling:
> The Bird of Time has but a little way
> *Couplet 2* — To flutter—and the Bird is on the Wing.
> —From *The Rubáiyát of Omar Khayyám*,
> Edward FitzGerald (1859)

In short, the *rubais* combines the unity and wit of a couplet with the freedom and scope of a quatrain.

Other quatrains use rhyme schemes based on a single rhyme (AAAA), a pair of couplets (AABB), or an "envelope" (ABBA), but the most important quatrain of all is the stanza used in traditional folk ballads—a stanza composed of alternating lines of iambic tetrameter and iambic trimeter rhyming (XAXA).

A *ballad* is a short narrative poem telling of a single dramatic incident. The *traditional ballad* is part of our oral heritage, and one basic story may evolve into dozens of variant forms as it is recited or sung at different times to different audiences. "Bonny Barbara Allan" is certainly one of the most widely known and frequently altered of all ballads. It has gone through so many different versions over the years that one critic has observed wryly, "Barbara Allan's ninety-two progeny are something of a record achievement, certainly for a lady who, according to the ballad, scorned her lover. One is thankful that she did not encourage him!"[1]

BARBARA ALLAN

In Scarlet Town, where I was born,
   There was a fair maid dwelling,
Made every youth cry well-a-way!
   Her name was Barbara Allan.

All in the merry month of May,
   When green buds they were swelling,
Young Jemmy Grove on his death-bed lay,
   For love of Barbara Allan.

O slowly, slowly rose she up,
   To the place where he was lying,
And when she drew the curtain by,
   "Young man, I think you're dying."

"O 'tis I'm sick, and very, very sick,
   And 'tis a' for Barbara Allan;"
"O the better for me ye's never be,
   Tho your heart's blood were spilling."

"O dinna ye mind, young man," said she,
   "When ye was in the tavern drinking,
That ye made the healths go round and round
   And slighted Barbara Allan?"

He turned his face unto the wall,
   And death was with him dealing:
"Adieu, adieu, my dear friends all,
   And be kind to Barbara Allan!"

And slowly, slowly rose she up,
   And slowly, slowly left him,
And sighing said she could not stay,
   Since death of life had reft him.

She had not gone a mile but two,
   When she heard the dead-bell knelling,
And every toll that the dead-bell gave
   Cried, "Woe to Barbara Allan!"

"O mother, mother, make my bed!
   O make it soft and narrow!
Since my love died for me today,
   I'll die for him tomorrow."

                —Anonymous

---

[1] Arthur Kyle Davis, Jr., *Traditional Ballads of Virginia.* (Cambridge, Mass.: Harvard University Press, 1929), p. 302.

Because traditional ballads (also referred to as *folk* or *popular ballads*) were composed for an oral presentation before an audience, they tell simple, direct stories using dialogue, repetition, and refrains in an effort to capture the interest and attention of an audience that may, after all, be hearing the story for the first time. Ballads tend to be objective, abrupt, and concise. The first few lines catch our interest with a question or a tense situation. Thereafter, the characters spring to life, acting and speaking with relatively little external commentary by the author. Some ballads use the refrain for the purpose of advancing or commenting on the narrative. The themes of ballads are those of continuing popular interest: unhappy love, feats of war or bravado, shipwrecks, murder, and domestic quarrels.

After the end of the Middle Ages and after the development of the printing press, concern for originality in composition naturally increased, and the circulation and communal creation of folk ballads declined. The ballad stanza has, however, remained popular, particularly in the former slave states of the South, where Negro spirituals and blues evolved with the same format and vitality as in the traditional ballad. Furthermore, professional poets and songwriters ranging from Rudyard Kipling (*Barrack-Room Ballads*) to Bob Dylan ("The Ballad of the Thin Man," etc.) have composed delightful literary ballads that prove both the adaptability and the continuing popularity of the form.

Stanzas of five lines, or *quintets,* are infrequently found in English poetry and none of the many possible rhyme schemes has emerged as particularly prevalent. It says something about the unpopularity of this stanza that the best-known of the poems that employ it are such slight lyrics as Robert Herrick's "The Night-Piece, to Julia" (rhyming AABBA) and Edmund Waller's "Go, Lovely Rose" (rhyming ABABB). The two poems together total only forty lines.

The most common six-line stanza is the *Shakespearean sestet,* the pattern Shakespeare always used for the last six lines (or sestet) in his sonnets. It is composed of a crossed rhyme quatrain followed by a couplet (ABABCC), all in iambic pentameter. Shakespeare first used this sestet in his innovative and popular erotic tale, *Venus and Adonis* (1593), in which his handling of the stanza is light, humorous, and witty; he normally describes the action in the quatrain and cleverly summarizes it or introduces a new and incongruous image in the succeeding, epigrammatic couplet. In the following lines Venus has just seen Adonis and courted him with breathless, burning phrases:

> With this she seizeth on his sweating palm,
> The precedent of pith and livelihood,
> And, trembling in her passion, calls it balm,
> Earth's sovereign salve to do a goddess good.
> > Being so enrag'd, desire doth lend her force
> > Courageously to pluck him from his horse.
>
> Over one arm the lusty courser's rein,
> Under the other was the tender boy,
> Who blush'd and pouted in a dull disdain,
> With leaden appetite, unapt to toy;
> > She red and hot as coals of glowing fire,
> > He red for shame, but frosty in desire.
> > > —From *Venus and Adonis,*
> > > William Shakespeare [1593]

Here, the concluding couplets emphasize the comic reversal of roles in the poem: Venus manfully plucks Adonis from his horse in the first stanza, and in the second she is flushed with dissolute passion while Adonis blushes in virginal shame.

The *septet*, or seven-line stanza, is normally cast into the pattern known as *rhyme royal* because it was used in the only long poem written by an English-speaking king, *The King's Quhair* by James I of Scotland (c. 1425). The rhyme scheme differs from that of the Shakespearean sestet by the addition of another B-rhyme at the end of the quatrain (ABABBCC); the line remains iambic pentameter.

Rhyme royal was first used in English poetry by Chaucer, who felt that the stanza was appropriate for the themes of "The Prioress's Tale," *Troilus and Criseyde,* and other serious poems. When Shakespeare came to write the "graver labour" that he had promised in the dedication to *Venus and Adonis,* he chose to use rhyme royal, and the result was the tragic and melodramatic *Rape of Lucrece* (1594]. There is, however, nothing necessarily serious about poems written in this stanza. If anything, its closely packed rhymes and paired couplets may be most appropriate in witty verse, as in W. H. Auden's rambling and comic "Letter to Lord Byron."

The most important eight-line stanza is *ottava rima,* which is like a stretched Shakespearean sestet: eight lines of iambic pentameter rhyming (ABABABCC). Lord Byron stamped this stanza with the witty, satiric, and exuberant characteristics of his own personality by using it in his epic comedy, *Don Juan,* from which we have already quoted (see pp. 574 and 575).

Of all stanzaic patterns, the most intricate is the nine-line *Spenserian stanza.* First used by Edmund Spenser in *The Faerie Queene* (1590), this stanza is made up of eight lines of iambic pentameter rhyming ABABBCBC and a final C-rhyme of iambic hexameter (called an Alexandrine). The stanza has often been praised for its majesty and effectiveness in poems with serious themes. To a large extent, this praise is only a recognition that Spenser made majestic and effective use of the stanza in *The Faerie Queene.* Because the stanza inevitably recalls Spenser's poem, later poets have generally used it to create a Spenserian sense of romance, morality, and heroism. So, too, *ottava rima* connotes Byron's witty hedonism, and the Shakespearean sestet connotes the light eroticism of *Venus and Adonis.* The impact of each form on the tone and mood of poetry is often less a product of the stanza itself, than of one unforgettable use of the stanza. Unlike most other stanzas, however, the Spenserian is capable of great variety. Depending on how the poet breaks up his or her thoughts, the stanza can either produce the sound of two couplets (ABA <u>BB</u> CB <u>CC</u>), of a modified *terza rima* (<u>ABA</u> BB <u>CBC</u> C), or of many variations of couplets, tercets, quatrains, and quintets. Spenser frequently molds his stanza into two clear quatrains and a final stark Alexandrine, as in the following description of a knight who has lost his honor and his chastity in a luxurious "Bower of Bliss":

> His warlike armes, the idle instruments
> Of sleeping praise, were hong upon a tree,
> And his brave shield, full of old moniments,
> Was fowly ra'st, that none the signes might see;
> Ne for them, ne for honour cared hee,
> Ne ought, that did to his advancement tend,
> But in lewd loves, and wastefull luxuree,

His dayes, his goods, his bodie he did spend:
O horrible enchantment, that him so did blend.
—From *The Faerie Queene*, Book II, Canto XII,
Edmund Spenser (1590)

By avoiding a monotonous pattern, poets using Spenserian stanzas can vary
the effect of their rhymes in much the same way that musicians create variations
of a melody. This variety of sound patterns may explain why the Spenserian
is the only complex stanza that has been repeatedly used in long poems. In
addition to *The Faerie Queene*, it is the stanza of Robert Burns's *Cotter's Saturday
Night*, Shelley's *Adonais*, Keats's *Eve of St. Agnes*, and Byron's *Childe Harold*.

The Spenserian is the longest of the well-known stanzas, and it includes in
itself many of the lyrical possibilities of shorter stanzas. As such it reconfirms
a number of general observations about the nature and function of stanzaic
verse itself. First, stanzaic verse gives the poet an opportunity to impose something akin to the order and structure of prose (for stanzas have many of the
virtues of paragraphs) without unduly restricting or sacrificing internally the
peculiar expressiveness of poetry. Second, the type of stanza the poet chooses
is important. Certain stanzaic patterns inevitably carry with them traditional
associations which neither poet nor reader can ignore. The heroic couplet,
for example, is unavoidably associated with Pope's satiric wit, in much the
same way that ottava rima calls to mind Byron's riqué and exuberant humor.
Finally, the less dense the rhymes in a particular stanza, the more frequently
it is used in developing serious plots and themes; conversely, the more dense
the rhyme, the less serious the subject matter and the greater the probability
of a witty, satiric, or comic treatment.

Not all stanzaic poems are constructed out of regular and repeating structural
units. *Odes* are particularly likely to be idiosyncratic, with each stanza differing
from others in the same poem both in rhyme scheme and in length of line.
This freedom is limited only by a common understanding that an ode must
be a long lyric poem that is serious and dignified in subject, tone, and style.
It strives to create a mood of meditative sublimity. Some of the more notable
free-form odes in English include Wordsworth's "Intimations of Immortality,"
Coleridge's "Dejection," Shelley's "Ode to the West Wind," and Allen Tate's
"Ode to the Confederate Dead."

Historically, odes were not always as free in form as they usually are today.
In ancient Greece they were strictly organized choral songs that sometimes
were written to signal the division between scenes in a play and at other times
to celebrate an event or individual. These *Pindaric odes*, named after the Greek
poet Pindar (518–438 B.C.), develop through sequences of three different stanzas: *strophe, antistrophe,* and *epode*. The metrical pattern of each strophe remains
the same throughout the ode, as does the pattern of each antistrophe and
epode. Originally, the strophe was sung and danced by one half of the chorus,
after which antistrophe was performed by the other half of the chorus using
the same steps of the strophe in reverse. The epode was then performed by
the combined chorus. Regular Pindaric odes are quite uncommon in English,
the best known being Thomas Gray's "The Bard" and "The Progress of Poetry."

Horatian odes, patterned after those of the Roman poet Horace (65–8 B.C.),
retain one stanzaic structure throughout—that is, they are regular stanzaic

poems dealing with lofty, lyrical subjects. Some of the better-known Horatian odes are Andrew Marvell's "An Horatian Ode upon Cromwell's Return from Ireland" and Keats's "To Autumn" and "Ode on a Grecian Urn."

Fixed Poetic Forms

The stanzaic patterns we have described are only one way in which poets attempt to create a recognizable tune analogous to a song-writer's melody. The other way is to use one of the fixed poetic forms—the haiku, sonnet, ballade, villanelle, rondeau, sestina, limerick, and so on. Of these, the haiku, the limerick, and the sonnet have achieved a significant place in English poetry; however, all are alike in two respects: all are brief, and all create their moods through the combined effects of a fixed verse pattern and the traditional connotations associated with that pattern. The haiku, for example, is generally associated with brief suggestive images, the limerick with light humor, and the sonnet with love.

A *haiku* is a form of poetry that originated in Japan during the thirteenth century. It consists of three lines of five, seven, and five syllables, respectively. Because of the brevity of the form there is little room for anything more than the presentation of a single concentrated image or emotion. Thus, haiku poems, like these examples by Moritake and Basho, tend to be allusive and suggestive:

THE FALLING FLOWER	LIGHTNING IN THE SKY
What I thought to be	Lightning in the sky!
Flowers soaring to their boughs	In the deeper dark is heard
Were bright butterflies.	A night-heron's cry.
—Moritake [1452–1540]	—Matsuo Basho [1644–1694]

The influence of the Japanese haiku on the twentieth-century Imagist movement has been profound and is reflected in such familiar anthology pieces as Ezra Pound's "In a Station of the Metro" and William Carlos Williams' "Red Wheelbarrow."

A *limerick* is a form of light verse that is often scratched on the tiles of public rest rooms. Its five lines rhyme AABBA. The A-rhymed lines are in anapestic trimeter; the others are in dimeter. Surprisingly, many authors of good repute have tried their hand at this little form—among them Edward Lear (who wrote over two hundred limericks), Robert Louis Stevenson, Rudyard Kipling, and Oliver Wendell Holmes. The following pun attributed to Holmes on the name "Henry Ward Beecher" helps to create one of the best of the printable limericks:

> The Reverend Henry Ward Beecher
> Called a hen a most elegant creature.
>   The hen, pleased with that,
>   Laid an egg in his hat.
> And thus did the hen reward Beecher.
>   —Anonymous

In comparison with the haiku and the limerick, the *sonnet* is a more distinguished and inspiring form. Indeed, poets often become so enamoured of the "little song" (the literal meaning of *sonnet*) that some have written nothing

else and a few—including William Wordsworth and Dante Gabriel Rossetti—
have composed rapturous sonnets on sonnetry.

Technically, a sonnet is a lyric poem of fourteen iambic pentameter lines,
usually following one of two established models: the Italian form or the English
form. The *Italian sonnet* (or *Petrarchan sonnet,* named after the Italian Renaissance
poet Petrarch) consists of an eight-line octave, rhyming ABBAABBA, followed
by a six-line sestet, rhyming variously CDECDE, CDCDCD, etc. Normally, the
octave presents a situation or issue, and the sestet explores or resolves it.
Both "On First Looking into Chapman's Homer" (p. 563) and "Design" (p.
571) are Petrarchan sonnets. Keats's octave relates what he had heard about
Homer before reading his poetry, while the sestet examines Keats's emotions
after discovering the beauties of Homer through Chapman's translation. Frost
uses his octave to describe the three objects he encounters on his morning
walk, whereas his sestet raises questions about their origin and meaning.

The *English sonnet* (or *Shakespearean sonnet*) consists of three quatrains and a
concluding couplet, rhyming ABAB CDCD EFEF GG. A variant of the English
sonnet, the *Spenserian sonnet,* links its quatrains by employing the rhyme scheme
ABAB BCBC CDCD EE. Although the English sonnet may describe an issue
and its resolution using the same octave-sestet structure as in the Italian form,
the three quatrains of the Shakespearean sonnet often present three successive
images, actions, or arguments, which are then summed up in a final, epigrammatic couplet. A typical Shakespearean sonnet (number CXLIII) is quoted
on page 581. Note that in this case the sonnet does take the form of an octave,
presenting a hypothesis ("as a careful housewife"), and a sestet, presenting a
conclusion ("So runn'st thou"). But the sonnet also breaks into three quatrains
and a couplet. The first quatrain describes a housewife in pursuit of a stray
cock or hen; the second tells how her neglected child chases after her; and
the third explains that Shakespeare is in a situation like that of the child,
whereas his mistress (who is presumably running after another man) is like
the housewife. Finally, the concluding couplet summarizes and resolves the
situation with a pun on William Shakespeare's first name:

> So I will pray that thou mayst have thy "Will,"
> If thou turn back and my loud crying still.

The sonnet became popular in England during the sixteenth century largely
because of translations and imitations of Petrarch's passionate cycle of sonnets
addressed to his mistress Laura. Similar sonnet sequences were written by
Sir Philip Sidney (*Astrophel and Stella,* 1580), Samuel Daniel (*Delia,* 1592), Michael
Drayton (*Idea,* 1593), Edmund Spenser (*Amoretti* and *Epithalamion,* 1595), and
William Shakespeare (*Sonnets,* 1609). This deluge of amorous sonnets helped
to establish the belief that the sonnet itself must always deal with love—a
presumption that is still widespread. As early as 1631, Milton challenged this
popular notion by writing sonnets of personal reflection, moral criticism, and
political comment. The sonnets by Shakespeare, Keats, and Frost, quoted earlier in this text, demonstrate that Milton was correct and that the sonnet can
be used in themes ranging from Shakespeare's illicit sexual proposal to Keats's
rapturous literary appreciation to Frost's somber metaphysical brooding. It
is this adaptability that makes the sonnet so much more important in literary
history than other fixed forms, such as the haiku and the limerick.

VISUAL FORMS

All verse makes some appeal to the eye. We see where the lines begin and end, and from that information we can often tell something about the poetic emphasis and meaning. For some poets, however, this limited visual element is not enough. William Blake, for example, printed his poems himself so that he would be sure that both the calligraphy and the marginal illustrations would contribute to the overall effect. Thus, when we read the poems from his *Songs of Innocence* (1789) and *Songs of Experience* (1794), we must at the very least remember that the words only convey part of his intention. Few other poets have shared Blake's broad interests in both literature and graphic art, but many have experimented with three methods of expanding poetic meaning through visual form.

Typographical Analogies

Throughout history writers have underscored the content of their work by manipulating the way that words appear on the page. Capital letters convey urgency and loudness: STOP! HELP! COME HERE! Lower-case letters, particularly in names, suggest humility or timidity (but paradoxically also attract attention): *e.e. cummings, archie and mehitabel,* and so on. Additional letters or spaces in a line can suggest stuttering *(c-c-cold),* reverberation *(shockkk),* delay *(s l o w l y),* and distance *(l o n g).* Conversely, deleted letters or spaces indicate speed *(quickasawink)* and compactness *(huddld).* Misspellings, like *X-mass* and *Amerikkka,* make a visual statement by reminding us respectively of the cross borne by Christ and of the role played by the Ku Klux Klan during certain periods of American history. Futhermore, certain typesetting techniques allow the appearance of words to mirror their meanings: over, under, cramped, or tailing. e. e. cummings popularized the use of typographical analogies in modern poetry (see "Buffalo Bill's," p. 565). Although these devices sometimes become contrived and gimmicky, other contemporary poets such as Robert Duncan, Allen Ginsberg, and Howard Nemerov have occasionally introduced tricks of typography into their poems.

Picture Poems

By careful word choice and clever typesetting, poets can sometimes create a visual image of the object or idea they are describing. Although picture poems have never been numerous, they are by no means new. One finds them in ancient Greek literature, as well as in the recent movement toward *concretism* (the concern with a poem's visual appearance rather than with its words). In most cases, visual poems tend to be frivolous, as in Lewis Carroll's *Alice in Wonderland,* where the tale the Mouse tells Alice takes the form of a long, serpentine "tail" that wanders down half a page. The ingenious seventeenth-century poet George Herbert proved, however, that visual effects are not always frivolous. He formed his religious meditation on the altar of the human heart into the shape of an altar in the following poem:

THE ALTAR

A   broken   ALTAR,   Lord,   thy   servant   rears,
Made   of   a   heart,   and   cemented   with   tears:
    Whose   parts   are   as   thy   hand   did   frame;
    No   workman's   tool   hath   touched   the   same.
          A   HEART   alone
          Is   such   a   stone,
          As   nothing   but
          Thy   power   doth   cut.
          Wherefore   each   part
          Of   my   hard   heart
          Meets   in   this   frame,
          To   praise   thy   Name:
    That,   if   I   chance   to   hold   my   peace,
    These   stones   to   praise   thee   may   not   cease.
O   let   thy   blessed   SACRIFICE   be   mine,
And   sanctify   this   ALTAR   to   be   thine.
            —George Herbert [1633]

Acrostics

An acrostic is a poem in which certain letters (ordinarily the first in each line) spell out a word when read from top to bottom or bottom to top. The best-known acrostics in English literature are those by John Davies in praise of Queen Elizabeth I. Every poem in his volume of *Hymns of Astraea* (1599) spells out the words *Elizabetha Regina*—Elizabeth, the Queen.

TO THE SPRING

E   arth now is green and heaven is blue,
L   ively spring which makes all new,
I   olly spring, doth enter;
S   weet young sun-beams do subdue
A   ngry, aged winter.
B   lasts are mild and seas are calm,
E   very meadow flows with balm,
T   he earth wears all her riches;
H   armonious birds sing such a psalm
A   s ear and heart bewitches.

R   eserve, sweet spring, this nymph of ours
E   ternal garlands of thy flowers;
G   reen garlands never wasting;
I   n her shall last our fair spring
N   ow and forever flourishing
A   s long as heaven is lasting.
            —John Davies [1599]

All of these visual effects may occasionally play a useful role in good poetry, but they are more often signs of weakness—superficial and relatively easy techniques used by poets who are content to be ingenious. In the final analysis, the words of poetry and the energy, intellect, and feeling communicated by those words are of far more importance to truly great writing than even the most meticulous adherence to the external requirements of verse form.

8

❧❧❧❧❧❧

Analyzing and Evaluating Poetry

In the preceding pages we have introduced and discussed the formal elements of poetry. An essential problem remains, a problem faced by any reader coming upon a new poem for the very first time: namely, how best to isolate and identify the chief elements of the poem for the purposes of analysis, understanding, and evaluation. There is, to be sure, no one "right" or "best" way to proceed, for individual poems vary greatly not only in their external formal characteristics, but in the way they handle and manipulate their internal elements as well. But the would-be critic must begin somewhere, and we will suggest here a series of questions that can be asked of any poem.

Before listing the questions, we should, however, add a few words of caution. First, poems differ greatly in their emphases. Not all of the questions that follow will be equally applicable to the analysis of every poem; therefore, the reader needs to follow to some extent his or her intuition in order to understand what makes a particular poem vital and appealing. Second, although analysis of an author's success in manipulating the elements of poetry can add to an appreciation and understanding of any poem, the reader should not assume that poems that *require* extensive explication to be understood are necessarily better than those that do not. Explication is one means—and generally the most important means—of coming to understand why an author has written what he or she has. Some poems require much explication and some little. But great poetry should be a pleasure to read, not a punishment. We can expect this pleasure to grow as analysis and mature reflection increase our understanding, but the enjoyment of poetry is, and should remain, visceral as well as intellectual.

Questions to Ask and Answer

First, read the poem carefully (aloud at least once), making sure that you understand the *denotative meaning* of each word. (Be sure to use both your dictionary and the editor's notes, if any.)

1. Does the poet manipulate the meanings of words using any of the following devices: *connotation, allusion, repetition, ambiguity, punning, paradox, irony?* How does the use of these devices add to the resonance and significance of the denotative meaning?

2. Examine the poem's *imagery.* Are any images repeated or otherwise emphasized? Does the imagery in the poem develop according to a logical pattern? Can you determine why the poet uses the images that he or she does?

3. What forms of poetic comparison (*metaphor, simile,* etc.) are used and what do they add to the poem's imagery and meaning?

4. Does the poem make use of *symbol* or *allegory?*

5. Who is the speaker? What kind of person does he or she seem to be? To whom is he speaking and what are his point of view and his relation to the subject? What is the general mood or *tone* of the poem? Is it consistent throughout, or is there a shift?

6. What is the situation or occasion of the poem? What is the setting in time and space?

7. *Paraphrase* and *summarize* the poem. What is the poem's *theme,* argument, or central idea and how is it developed? (Be alert to repeated images, the stanzaic pattern, rhetorical devices, etc.)

8. What is the *meter* and *rhyme scheme* of the poem? What other significant repetitions of sounds (*alliteration, assonance, consonance*) occur in the poem? How do they contribute to the effect of the poem? What is the form of the poem (*sonnet, ode, lyric, dramatic monologue,* etc.)? Are the meter, rhyme scheme, and form appropriate?

9. *Criticize* and *evaluate.* How well do you think the poet has achieved a total integration of his materials? What is *your* reaction to the poem? Do you like the poem? If so, why? If not, why not?

Poems

EARLY POPULAR SONGS AND BALLADS[1]

"O WESTERN WIND"

O western° wind, when wilt thou blow   *I.e., spring*
  That the small rain down can rain?
Christ, that my love were in my arms
  And I in my bed again!

LORD RANDAL

"O where hae ye been, Lord Randal, my son?
O where hae ye been, my handsome young man?"
"I hae been to the wild wood; mother, make my bed soon,
For I'm weary wi' hunting, and fain wald lie down."

[1] The five anonymous poems that follow originated in England during the Middle Ages and, in a variety of versions, became part of our oral heritage in poetry. The sixth poem is a nineteenth-century American ballad that evolved from oral traditions similar to those in medieval England. In each case we have selected the version of the poem that seems to us to have the greatest poetic value.

5   "Where gat ye your dinner, Lord Randal, my son?
    Where gat ye your dinner, my handsome young man?"
    "I dined wi' my true-love; mother, make my bed soon,
    For I'm weary wi' hunting, and fain wald lie down."

    "What gat ye to your dinner, Lord Randal, my son?
10 What gat ye to your dinner, my handsome young man?"
    "I gat eels boiled in broo;° mother, make my bed soon,   broth
    For I'm weary wi' hunting, and fain wald lie down."

    "What became of your bloodhounds, Lord Randal, my son?
    What became of your bloodhounds, my handsome young man?"
15 "O they swelled and they died; mother, make my bed soon,
    For I'm weary wi' hunting, and fain wald lie down."

    "O I fear ye are poisoned, Lord Randal, my son!
    O I fear ye are poisoned, my handsome young man!"
    "O yes! I am poisoned; mother, make my bed soon,
20 For I'm sick at the heart, and I fain wald lie down."

GET UP AND BAR THE DOOR

It fell about the Martinmas time,°   Nov. 11
    And a gay time it was then,
When our good wife got puddings to make,
    And she's boiled them in the pan.

5   The wind sae cauld° blew south and north,   So cold
    And blew into the floor;
Quoth our goodman to our goodwife,
    "Gae° out and bar the door."   Go

"My hand is in my hussyfskap,°   housework
10   Goodman, as ye may see;
An° it shoud nae be barred this hundred year,   If
    It's no be° barred for° me."   not going to be / by

They made a paction° tween them twa,°   pact / two
    They made it firm and sure,
15 That the first word whaeer° shoud speak,   whoever
    Shoud rise and bar the door.

Then by there came two gentlemen,
    At twelve o'clock at night,
And they could neither see house nor hall,
20   Nor coal nor candle-light.

"Now whether is this a rich man's house,
    Or whether is it a poor?"
But neer a word wad ane° o them speak,   either
    For barring of the door.

25 And first they ate the white puddings,
And then they ate the black;
Tho muckle° thought the goodwife to hersel,   *much*
Yet neer a word she spake.

Then said the one unto the other,
30 "Here, man, tak ye my knife;
Do ye tak aff the auld man's beard,
And I'll kiss the goodwife."

"But there 's nae water in the house,
And what shall we do than?"
35 "What ails ye at the pudding-broo,°   *broth of the pudding*
That boils into the pan?"

O up then started our goodman,
An angry man was he:
"Will ye kiss my wife before my een,
40 And scad° me wi pudding-bree?"   *scald*

Then up and started our goodwife,
Gied three skips on the floor:
"Goodman, you've spoken the foremost word,
Get up and bar the door."

SIR PATRICK SPENS

The king sits in Dumferling town,
Drinking the blude-reid° wine: *blood-red*
"O whar will I get guid° sailor,   *good*
To sail this ship of mine?"

5 Up and spak an eldern° knicht,   *elderly*
Sat at the king's richt knee:
"Sir Patrick Spens is the best sailor
That sails upon the sea."

The king has written a braid° letter   *broad*
10 And signed it wi' his hand,
And sent it to Sir Patrick Spens,
Was walking on the sand.

The first line that Sir Patrick read,
A loud lauch° lauched he;   *laugh*
15 The next line that Sir Patrick read,
The tear blinded his ee.°   *eye*

"O wha° is this has done this deed,   *who*
This ill deed done to me,
To send me out this time o' the year,
20 To sail upon the sea?

"Mak haste, mak haste, my mirry men all,
  Our guid ship sails the morn."
"O say na° sae,° my master dear,   *not / so*
  For I fear a deadly storm.

25   Late, late yestre'en I saw the new moon
  Wi' the auld moon in her arm,
And I fear, I fear, my dear master,
  That we will come to harm."

O our Scots nobles were richt° laith°   *right / loath*
30   To weet° their cork-heeled shoon,°   *wet / shoes*
Bot lang° or° a' the play were played   *long / ere*
  Their hats they swam aboon.°   *above*

O lang, lang may their ladies sit,
  Wi' their fans into their hand,
35   Or ere they see Sir Patrick Spens
  Come sailing to the land.

O lang, lang may the ladies stand
  Wi' their gold kems° in their hair,   *combs*
Waiting for their ain° dear lords,   *own*
40   For they'll see them na mair.

Half o'er,° half o'er to Aberdour   *over*
  It's fifty fadom° deep,   *fathoms*
And there lies guid Sir Patrick Spens
  Wi' the Scots lords at his feet.

THE THREE RAVENS

There were three ravens sat on a tree,
  Down a down, hay down, hay down
There were three ravens sat on a tree,
  With a down
5   There were three ravens sat on a tree,
They were as black as they might be.
  With a down derry, derry, derry, down, down.[1]

The one of them said to his mate,
"Where shall we our breakfast take?"

10   "Down in yonder green field,
There lies a knight slain under his shield.

"His hounds they lie down at his feet,
So well they can their master keep.

---

[1] In each subsequent stanza of the poem the pattern of lines is the same as in this one, with lines 2, 4 and 6 serving as unchanging refrains.

<table>
<tr><td>15</td><td></td></tr>
</table>

"His hawks they fly so eagerly,
There's no fowl dare him come nigh."

Down there comes a fallow° doe,   *brownish-yellow*
As great with young as she might go.

She lift up his bloody head
And kissed his wounds that were so red.

She got him up upon her back
And carried him to earthen lake.°   *grave*

She buried him before the prime;°   *break of day*
She was dead herself ere even-song time.° *dusk*

God send every gentleman
Such hawks, such hounds, and such a leman.° *lover*

FRANKIE AND JOHNNY

Frankie and Johnny were lovers,
    Lordy, how they could love,
Swore to be true to each other,
    True as the stars up above,
        He was her man, but he done her wrong.

Frankie went down to the corner,
    To buy her a bucket of beer,
Frankie says "Mister Bartender,
    Has my lovin' Johnny been here?
        He is my man, but he's doing me wrong."

"I don't want to cause you no trouble
    Don't want to tell you no lie,
I saw your Johnny half-an-hour ago
    Making love to Nelly Bly.
        He is your man, but he's doing you wrong."

Frankie went down to the hotel
    Looked over the transom so high,
There she saw her lovin' Johnny
    Making love to Nelly Bly.
        He was her man; he was doing her wrong.

Frankie threw back her kimono,
    Pulled out her big forty-four;
Rooty-toot-toot: three times she shot
    Right through that hotel door,
        She shot her man, who was doing her wrong.

"Roll me over gently,
   Roll me over slow,
Roll me over on my right side,
   'Cause these bullets hurt me so,
30   I was your man, but I done you wrong."

Bring all your rubber-tired hearses
   Bring all your rubber-tired hacks,
They're carrying poor Johnny to the burying ground
   And they ain't gonna bring him back,
35   He was her man, but he done her wrong.

Frankie says to the sheriff,
   "What are they going to do?"
The sheriff he said to Frankie,
   "It's the 'lectric chair for you.
40   He was your man, and he done you wrong."

"Put me in that dungeon,
   Put me in that cell,
Put me where the northeast wind
   Blows from the southeast corner of hell,
45   I shot my man, 'cause he done me wrong."
                                        [19th century]

❧ MEDIEVAL POETRY ❧

Geoffrey Chaucer *1342?–1400*

THE CANTERBURY TALES

FROM *"General Prologue"*

	Whan that Aprille with his shoures sote°	sweet
	The droghte of Marche hath perced to the rote,	
	And bathed every veyne in swich licour,	
	Of which vertu° engendered is the flour;°	power / flower
5	Whan Zephirus° eek° with his swete breeth	the west wind / also
	Inspired hath in every holt° and heeth°	woods / heath
	The tendre croppes, and the yonge sonne	
	Hath in the Ram his halfe cours y-ronne,¹	
	And smale fowles maken melodye,	
10	That slepen al the night with open yë;°	eye
	(So priketh° hem nature in hir corages):°	pricks / hearts
	Than longen folk to goon on pilgrimages	
	(And palmers° for to seken straunge strondes)°	pilgrims / lands
	To ferne halwes, couthe in sondry londes;²	
15	And specially, from every shires ende	
	Of Engelond, to Caunterbury³ they wende,°	go
	The holy blisful martir for to seke,	
	That hem hath holpen,° whan that they were	helped
	seke.°	sick
	Bifel° that, in that seson on a day,	It happened
20	In Southwerk at the Tabard⁴ as I lay	
	Redy to wenden° on my pilgrimage	go
	To Caunterbury with ful devout corage,	
	At night was come in-to that hostelrye°	inn
	Wel nyne and twenty in a companye,	
25	Of sondry folk, by aventure° y-falle	chance
	In felawshipe, and pilgrims were they alle,	
	That toward Caunterbury wolden° ryde;	wished to
	The chambres and the stables weren wyde,	
	And wel we weren esed atte beste.⁵	
30	And shortly, whan the sonne was to reste,	

---

¹ The sun is young because it is only half-way through the Ram, or Aries (March 21 to April 20), the first sign in the medieval zodiac.
² I.e., to foreign shrines well-known in sundry lands.
³ Canterbury, a cathedral city in England, where St. Thomas à Becket became a martyr ("the holy blisful martir," line 17) in 1170.
⁴ The Tabard, an inn in Southwark, then a suburb of London.
⁵ I.e., accommodated in the best manner.

So hadde I spoken with hem everichon,°   *every one*
That I was of hir felawshipe anon,°   *at once*
And made forward° erly for to ryse,   *a pact*
To take our wey, ther as I yow devyse.°   *describe*
35   But natheles, whyl I have tyme and space,
Er that I ferther in this tale pace,
Me thinketh it acordaunt° to resoun,   *according*
To telle yow al the condicioun
Of ech of hem, so as it semed me,
40   And whiche they weren, and of what degree;°   *status*
And eek in what array° that they were inne: *clothing*

MILLER

545   The Miller was a stout carl,° for the nones   *churl,*
Ful big he was of braun, and eek of bones;
That proved° wel, for over-al ther° he cam,   *was proven / wherever*
At wrastling he wolde have alwey the ram.¹
He was short-sholdred, brood,° a thikke   *broad*
        knarre,°   *head*
550   Ther nas no dore that he nolde° heve of harre,°   *could not / off hinge*
Or breke it, at a renning,° with his heed.   *running*
His berd° as any sowe or fox was reed,   *beard*
And ther-to brood, as though it were a spade.
Up-on the cop° right of his nose he hade   *top*
555   A werte,° and ther-on stood a tuft of heres,°   *wart / hairs*
Reed as the bristles of a sowes eres;°   *ears*
His nose-thirles° blake° were and wyde.   *nostrils / black*
A swerd and bokeler° bar° he by his syde;   *shield / bore*
His mouth as greet was as a greet forneys.°   *furnace*
560   He was a janglere° and a goliardeys,°   *loudmouth / lewd joker*
And that was most of sinne and harlotryes.°   *ribaldry*
Wel coude he stelen corn, and tollen thryes;²
And yet he hadde a thombe of gold,³ pardee.°   *by God*
A whyt cote° and a blew hood wered° he.   *coat / wore*
565   A baggepype wel coude he blowe and sowne,
And ther-with-al he broghte us out of towne.

REEVE

The Reve° was a sclendre colerik man,   *overseer*
His berd was shave as ny° as ever he can.   *close*
His heer was by his eres round y-shorn.
590   His top was dokked° lyk a preest biforn.   *cut short, tonsured*
Ful longe were his legges, and ful lene,
Y-lyk° a staf, ther was no calf y-sene.°   *like / visible*
Wel coude he kepe° a gerner° and a binne,°   *guard / granary / chest*

¹ The ram, first prize in medieval wrestling matches.
² I.e., take thrice his proper fee for grinding corn.
³ Proverbially, "an honest miller has a thumb of gold."

Ther was noon auditour coude on him winne.°   *get the better of him*
595 Wel wiste° he, by the droghte, and by the reyn,   *knew*
The yelding of his seed, and of his greyn.
His lordes sheep, his neet,° his dayerye,   *cattle*
His swyn, his hors, his stoor,° and his pultyre,   *stock*
600 Was hoolly in this reves governing,
And by his covenaunt° yaf° the rekening,   *agreement / gave*
Sin that his lord was twenty yeer of age;
Ther coude no man bringe him in arrerage.°   *arrears*
Ther nas baillif, ne herde,° ne other hyne.°   *herdsman / farmhand*
That he ne knew his sleighte and his covyne,°   *deceit*
605 They were adrad° of him, as of the deeth.°   *afraid / the plague*
His woning° was ful fair up-on an heeth,   *dwelling*
With grene treës shadwed was his place.
He coude bettre than his lord purchace.
Ful riche he was astored prively,°   *stocked secretly*
610 His lord wel coude he plesen subtilly,
To yeve° and lene° him of his owne good,°   *give / lend / goods*
And have a thank, and yet a cote and hood.
In youthe he lerned hadde a good mister;°   *occupation*
He was a wel good wrighte,° a carpenter.   *workman*
615 This reve sat up-on a full good stot,°   *horse*
That was al pomely° grey, and highte° Scot.   *dappled / named*
A long surcote° of pers° up-on he hade,   *overcoat / blue*
And by his syde he bar a rusty blade.
Of Northfolk was this reve, of which I telle,
620 Bisyde a toun men clepen Baldeswelle.
Tukked[1] he was, as is a frere, aboute,
And ever he rood the hindreste of our route.

THE MILLER'S PROLOGUE

Here folwen the wordes bitween the Host and the Millere.

Whan that the Knight had thus his tale y-told,
3110 In al the route° nas ther yong ne old   *company*
That he ne seyde it was a noble storie,
And worthy for to drawn to memorie;
And namely the gentils° everichoon.   *well bred folks*
Our Hoste lough and swoor, "so moot° I goon,°   *might/go (walk)*
3115 This gooth aright; unbokeled is the male;°   *pack*
Lat see now who shal telle another tale:
For trewely, the game is wel bigonne.
Now telleth ye, sir Monk, if that ye conne,°   *can*
Sumwhat, to quyte° with the Knightes tale."   *requite*
3120 The Miller, that for-dronken° was al pale,   *because of drink*

[1] He wore his cloak tucked up.

	So that unnethe° up-on his hors he sat,	scarcely
	He nolde avalen° neither hood ne hat,	take off
	Ne abyde no man for his curteisye,	
	But in Pilates vois[1] he gan to crye,	
3125	And swoor by armes and by blood and bones,	
	"I can° a noble tale for the nones,	know
	With which I wol now quyte the Knightes tale."	
	Our Hoste saugh° that he was dronke of ale,	saw
	And seyde: "abyd, Robin, my leve° brother,	dear
3130	Som bettre man shal telle us first another:	
	Abyd, and lat us werken thriftily."°	sensibly
	"By goddes soul," quod he, "that wol nat I;	
	For I wol speke, or elles go my wey."	
	Our Hoste answerde: "tel on, a devel wey!°	in the devil's name
3135	Thou art a fool, thy wit is overcome."	
	"Now herkneth,"° quod the Miller, "alle and some!	listen
	But first I make a protestacioun	
	That I am dronke, I knowe it by my soun;	
	And therfore, if that I misspeke or seye,	
3140	Wyte° it the ale of Southwerk, I yow preye;	think
	For I wol telle a legende and a lyf	
	Bothe of a Carpenter, and of his wyf,	
	How that a clerk hath set the wrightes cappe."[2]	
	The Reve answerde and seyde, "stint thy clappe,°	chatter
3145	Lat be thy lewed dronken harlotrye.	
	It is a sinne and eek a greet folye	
	To apeiren° any man, or him diffame,	injure
	And eek to bringen wyves in swich fame.	
	Thou mayst y-nogh of othere thinges seyn."	
3150	This dronken Miller spak ful sone ageyn,	
	And seyde, "leve brother Osewold,	
	Who hath no wyf, he is no cokewold.°	cuckold
	But I sey nat therfore that thou art oon;	
	Ther been ful gode wyves many oon,	
3155	And ever a thousand gode ayeyns° oon badde,	against
	That knowestow wel thy-self, but-if° thou madde.°	unless / are mad
	Why artow angry with my tale now?	
	I have a wyf, pardee,° as well as thou,	by god
	Yet nolde° I, for the oxen in my plogh,	would not
3160	Taken up-on me more than y-nogh,	
	As demen° of my-self that I were oon;	deeming
	I wol beleve wel that I am noon.	
	An housbond shal nat been inquisitif	
	Of goddes privetee,° nor of his wyf.	private matters
3165	So° he may finde goddes foyson° there,	so long as / plenty
	Of the remenant nedeth nat enquere."°	inquire
	What sholde I more seyn, but this Millere	

[1] In the medieval mystery plays Pontius Pilate, the governor of Judea when Christ was crucified, spoke loudly and harshly.

[2] I.e., how a clerk got the better of the carpenter.

He nolde his wordes for no man forbere,
But tolde his cherles tale in his manere;
3170 Me thinketh that I shal reherce° it here.   *retell*
And ther-fore every gentil wight° I preye,   *genteel person*
For goddes love, demeth nat° that I seye   *do not think*
Of evel entente, but that I moot reherce
Hir tales alle, be they bettre or werse,
3175 Or elles falsen° som of my matere.   *falsify*
And therfore, who-so list it nat y-here,
Turne over the leef, and chese another tale;
For he shal finde y-nowe, grete and smale,
Of storial° thing that toucheth gentillesse,   *historical*
3180 And eek moralitee and holinesse;
Blameth nat me if that ye chese amis.
The Miller is a cherl, ye knowe wel this;
So was the Reve, and othere many mo,
And harlotrye they tolden bothe two.
3185 Avyseth yow° and putte me out of blame;   *be advised*
And eek men shal nat make ernest of game.

Here endeth the prologe.

THE MILLERES TALE

Here biginneth the Millere his tale.

Whylom° ther was dwellinge at Oxenford   *once*
A riche gnof,° that gestes° heeld to bord,°   *knave / guests / board*
And of his craft he was a Carpenter.
3190 With him ther was dwellinge a povre° scoler,   *poor*
Had lerned art, but al his fantasye
Was turned for to lerne astrologye,
And coude a certeyn of conclusiouns
To demen by interrogaciouns,[1]
3195 If that men axed° him in certain houres,   *asked*
Whan that men sholde have droghte or elles
    shoures,
Or if men axed him what sholde bifalle
Of every thing, I may nat rekene hem alle.
  This clerk was cleped° hende° Nicholas;   *named / courteous*
3200 Of derne° love he coude° and of solas;°   *secret / knew / pleasure*
And ther-to he was sleigh and ful privee,°   *secretive*
And lyk a mayden meke for to see.
A chambre hadde he in that hostelrye
Allone, with-outen any companye,
3205 Ful fetisly° y-dight° with herbes swote,°   *fitly / furnished / sweet*
And he him-self as swete as is the rote

---

[1] I.e., and knew how to reach a certain number of conclusions through interrogations.

Of licorys, or any cetewale.°   setwall (a spice)
His Almageste² and bokes grete and smale,
His astrelabie,° longinge for° his art,   astrolabe / belonging to
3210   His augrim-stones° layen faire a-part   counting stones
On shelves couched° at his beddes heed: placed
His presse° y-covered with a falding° reed.   cupboard / woolen cloth
And al above ther lay a gay sautrye,³
On which he made a nightes melodye
3215   So swetely, that al the chambre rong;
And *Angelus ad virginem*⁴ he song;
And after that he song the kinges note,°   tune
Ful often blessed was his mery throte.
And thus this swete clerk his tyme spente
3220   After his freendes finding° and his rente.°   presents / regular income
   This Carpenter had wedded newe° a wyf   recently
Which that he lovede more than his lyf;
Of eightetene yeer she was of age.
Jalous he was, and heeld hir narwe° in cage,   closely
3225   For she was wilde and yong, and he was old,
And demed him-self ben lyk a cokewold.°   cuckold
He new nat Catoun,⁵ for his wit was rude,
That bad° man sholde wedde his similitude.   bade
Men sholde wedden after° hir estaat,°   according to / state
3230   For youthe and elde° is often at debaat.   old age
But sith that he was fallen in the snare,
He moste endure, as other folk, his care.
   Fair was this yonge wyf, and ther-with-al
As any wesele° hir body gent° and smal.   weasel / graceful
3235   A ceynt° she werede barred° al of silk,   belt / striped
A barmclooth° eek as whyt as morne milk   apron
Up-on hir lendes,° ful of many a gore.°   loins / pleat
Whyt was hir smok° and brouded° al bifore   smock / embroidered
And eek bihinde, on hir coler° aboute,   collar
3240   Of col-blak silk, with-inne and eek with-oute.
The tapes° of hir whyte voluper°   ribbons / cap
Were of the same suyte of° hir coler;   material as
Hir filet° brood° of silk, and set ful hye: headband / broad
And sikerly° she hadde a likerous° yë.   certainly / lecherous
3245   Ful smale° y-pulled° were hir browes two,   finely / plucked
And tho were bent, and blake as any sloo.°   sloe (a plum)
She was ful more blisful on to see
Than is the newe pere-jonette° tree;   pear
And softer than the wolle is of a wether.°   sheep
3250   And by hir girdel heeng a purs of lether
Tasseld with silk, and perled° with latoun.°   studded / brass
In al this world, to seken up and doun,

---

² A treatise on astrology.   ³ A psaltery, an ancient stringed instrument.
⁴ "The Angel to the Virgin"
⁵ Dionysius Cato (fourth-century A.D. Roman author) in whose *Distichs* occurs the maxim cited
by the Miller.

There nis no man so wys, that coude thenche°   think of
So gay a popelote,° or swich° a wenche.   doll / such
3255 Ful brighter was the shyning of hir hewe°   complexion
Than in the tour° the noble° y-forged newe.   tower / gold coin
But of hir song, it was as loude and yerne°   lively
As any swalwe° sittinge on a berne.   swallow
Ther-to she coude skippe and make game,
3260 As any kide or calf folwinge his dame.
Hir mouth was swete as bragot° or the meeth,°   bragget / mead
Or hord of apples leyd in hey or heeth.°   heather
Winsinge° she was, as is a joly colt,   skittish
Long as a mast, and upright as a bolt.°   arrow
3265 A brooch she baar up-on hir lowe coler,
As brood as is the bos° of a bocler.°   boss/shield
Hir shoes were laced on hir legges hye;
She was a prymerole,° a pigges-nye°   primrose / sweetie
For any lord to leggen° in his bedde,   lay
3270 Or yet for any good yeman° to wedde.   yeoman
    Now sire, and eft° sire, so bifel the cas,   again
That on a day this hende Nicholas
Fil° with this yonge wyf to rage° and pleye,   happened / romp
Whyl that hir housbond was at Oseneye,[6]
3275 As clerkes ben ful subtile and ful queynte;°   clever
And prively he caughte hir by the queynte,°   crotch
And seyde, "y-wis,° but if ich° have my wille,   truly / I
For derne° love of thee, lemman,° I spille."°   secret / lover / die
And heeld hir harde by the haunche-bones,°   hip bones
3280 And seyde, "lemman, love me al at-ones,°   at once
Or I wol dyen, also° god me save!"   so
And she sprong as a colt doth in the trave,[7]
And with hir heed she wryed° faste awey,   wriggled
And seyde, "I wol nat kisse thee, by my fey,
3285 Why, lat be," quod she, "lat be, Nicholas,
Or I wol crye out harrow° and allas.   help
Do wey° your handes for your curteisye!"   take away
    This Nicholas gan mercy for to crye,
And spak so faire, and profred hir° so faste,   propositioned her
3290 That she hir love him graunted atte laste,
And swoor hir ooth, by seint Thomas of Kent,[8]
That she wol been at his comandement,
Whan that she may hir leyser° wel espye.   leisure
"Myn housbond is so ful of jalousye,
3295 That but ye wayte wel and been privee,°   secretive
I woot right wel I nam but deed," quod she.
"Ye moste been ful derne, as in this cas."
    "Nay ther-of care thee noght," quod Nicholas,
"A clerk had litherly° biset° his whyle,°   ill / used / time
3300 But-if he coude a carpenter bigyle."

---

[6] Oseney, near Oxford.   [7] A frame used in shoeing a restive horse.
[8] St. Thomas à Becket, who was slain in Canterbury Cathedral in Kent in 1170.

And thus they been acorded and y-sworn
To wayte a tyme, as I have told biforn.
Whan Nicholas had doon thus everydeel,
And thakked° hir aboute the lendes° weel,   stroked / loins
3305 He kist hir swete, and taketh his sautrye,
And pleyeth faste, and maketh melodye.
Than fil° it thus, that to the parish-chirche,   befell
Cristes owne werkes for to wirche,
This gode wyf wente on an haliday;°   holy day
3310 Hir forheed shoon as bright as any day,
So was it wasshen whan she leet° hir werk.   left
    Now was ther of that chirche a parish-clerk,
The which that was y-cleped° Absolon.   called
Crul° was his heer, and as the gold it shoon,   curly
3315 And strouted° as a fanne large and brode;   spread out
Ful streight and even lay his joly shode.°   part
His rode° was reed, his eyen greye as goos;°   complexion / goose
With Powles window corven on his shoos,⁹
In hoses° rede he wente fetisly.°   stockings / fashionably
3320 Y-clad he was ful smal° and proprely,   finely
Al in a kirtel° of a light wachet;°   tunic / blue
Ful faire and thikke been the poyntes° set.   laces
And ther-up-on he hadde a gay surplys°   surplice
As whyt as is the blosme up-on the rys.°   bough
3325 A mery child he was, so god me save,
Wel coude he laten° blood and clippe and shave,   let
And make a chartre° of lond or acquitaunce.   title
In twenty manere coude he trippe and daunce
After the scole of Oxenforde tho,
3330 And with his legges casten° to and fro,   leap
And pleyen songes on a small rubible;°   fiddle
Ther-to he song som-tyme a loud quinible;°   falsetto
And as wel coude he pleye on his giterne.°   guitar
In al the toun nas brewhous ne taverne
3335 That he ne visited with his solas,°   entertainment
Ther any gaylard° tappestere° was.   flirtateous / barmaid
But sooth to seyn, he was somdel squaymous°   squeamish
Of farting, and of speche daungerous.°   fastidious
    This Absolon, that jolif was and gay,
3340 Gooth with a sencer° on the haliday,   censer
Sensinge the wyves of the parish faste;
And many a lovely look on hem he caste,
And namely on this carpenteres wyf.
To loke on hir him thoughte a mery lyf,
3345 She was so propre and swete and likerous.°   voluptuous
I dar wel seyn, if she had been a mous,
And he a cat, he wolde hir hente° anon.   seize
    This parish-clerk, this joly Absolon,

⁹ Absalon's fashionable shoes were latticed like the windows of St. Paul's Cathedral in London.

Hath in his herte swich a love-longinge,
3350 That of no wyf ne took he noon offringe;
For curteisye, he seyde, he wolde noon.
The mone, whan it was night, ful brighte shoon,
And Absolon his giterne hath y-take,
For paramours, he thoghte for to wake.
3355 And forth he gooth, jolif and amorous,
Till he cam to the carpenteres hous
A litel after cokkes hadde y-crowe;
And dressed him up by a shot-windowe°   *shuttered window*
That was up-on the carpenteres wal.
3360 He singeth in his vois gentil and smal,
"Now, dere lady, if thy wille be,
I preye yow that ye wol rewe° on me,"   *have pity*
Ful wel acordaunt° to his giterninge.°   *pitched / guitar-playing*
This carpenter awook, and herde him singe,
3365 And spak un-to his wyf, and seyde anon,
"What! Alison! herestow nat Absolon
That chaunteth thus under our boures° wal?"   *bedroom*
And she answerde hir housbond ther-with-al,
"Yis, god wot, John, I here it every-del."
3370   This passeth forth; what wol ye bet° than wel?   *better*
Fro day to day this joly Absolon
So woweth° hir, that him is wo bigon.   *woos*
He waketh al the night and al the day;
He kempte° hise lokkes brode, and made him   *combed*
      gay;
3375 He woweth hir by menes° and brocage,°   *go-betweens / mediation*
And swoor he wolde been hir owne page;
He singeth, brokkinge° as a nightingale;   *quavering*
He sente hir piment,° meeth,° and spyced ale,   *spiced wine / mead*
And wafres,° pyping hote out of the glede;°   *pastries / coals*
3380 And for she was of toune, he profred mede.°   *payment*
For som folk wol ben wonnen for richesse,
And som for strokes, and som for gentillesse.
    Somtyme, to shewe his lightnesse and
      maistrye,°   *virtuosity*
He pleyeth Herodes on a scaffold hye.[10]
3385 But what availleth him as in this cas?
She loveth so this hende Nicholas,
That Absolon may blowe the bukkes horn,[11]
He ne hadde for his labour but a scorn;
And thus she maketh Absolon hir ape,
3390 And al his ernest turneth til a jape.°   *joke*
Ful sooth is this proverbe, it is no lye,
Men seyn right thus, "alwey the nye slye
Maketh the ferre leve to be looth."[12]
For though that Absolon be wood° or wrooth,°   *mad/wrathful*

---

[10] He acted the part of Herod in a nativity play staged on a high platform.
[11] I.e., Absolon will go unrewarded.
[12] "Always the nigh, sly man makes the far-away lover loathed."

3395   By-cause that he fer was from hir sighte,
        This nye° Nicholas stood in his lighte.   *nearby*
            Now bere thee wel, thou hende Nicholas!
        For Absolon may waille and singe "allas."
        And so bifel it on a Saterday,
3400   This carpenter was goon til° Osenay;   *to*
        And hende Nicholas and Alisoun
        Acorded been to this conclusioun,
        That Nicholas shal shapen him a wyle
        This sely° jalous housbond to bigyle;   *naïve*
3405   And if so be the game wente aright,
        She sholde slepen in his arm al night,
        For this was his desyr and hir also.
        And right anon, with-outen wordes mo,
        This Nicholas no lenger wolde tarie,
3410   But doth ful softe un-to his chambre carie
        Bothe mete and drinke for a day or tweye,°   *two*
        And to hir housbonde bad hir for to seye,
        If that he axed after Nicholas,
        She sholde seye she niste° where he was,   *knew not*
3415   Of al that day she saugh him nat with yë;
        She trowed° that he was in maladye,   *believed*
        For, for no cry, hir mayde coude him calle;
        He nolde answere, for no-thing that mighte falle.
            This passeth forth al thilke° Saterday,   *that*
3420   That Nicholas stille in his chambre lay,
        And eet and sleep, or dide what him leste,°   *pleased*
        Til Sonday, that the sonne gooth to reste.
            This sely carpenter hath greet merveyle
        Of Nicholas, or what thing mighte him eyle,°   *ail*
3425   And seyde, "I am adrad,° by seint Thomas,   *afraid*
        It stondeth nat aright with Nicholas.
        God shilde° that he deyde sodeynly!   *forbid*
        This world is now ful tikel,° sikerly;   *unstable*
        I saugh to-day a cors° y-born to chirche   *corpse*
3430   That now, on Monday last, I saugh him wirche.°   *work*
            Go up," quod he un-to his knave anoon,
        "Clepe° at his dore, or knokke with a stoon,   *call*
        Loke how it is, and tel me boldely."
            This knave gooth him up ful sturdily,
3435   And at the chambre-dore, whyl that he stood,
        He cryde and knokked as that he were wood:°   *insane*
        "What! how! what do ye, maister Nicholay?
        How may ye slepen al the longe day?"
            But al for noght, he herde nat a word;
3440   An hole he fond, ful lowe up-on a bord,
        Ther as° the cat was wont in for to crepe;   *where*
        And at that hole he looked in ful depe,
        And at the laste he hadde of him a sighte.
        This Nicholas sat gaping over up-righte,

3445	As he had kyked° on the newe mone.	*gazed*
	Adoun he gooth, and tolde his maister sone	
	In what array he saugh this ilke man.	
	This carpenter to blessen him bigan,	
	And seyde, "help us, seinte Frideswyde!¹³	
3450	A man woot° litel what him shal bityde.	*knows*
	This man is falle, with his astromye,	
	In som woodnesse° or in som agonye;	*madness*
	I thoghte ay wel how that it sholde be!	
	Men sholde nat knowe of goddes privetee.°	*secrets*
3455	Ye, blessed be alwey a lewed° man,	*ignorant*
	That noght but only his bileve° can!°	*faith / knows*
	So ferde° another clerk with astromye;	*fared*
	He walked in the feeldes for to prye	
	Up-on the sterres, what ther sholde bifalle,	
3460	Til he was in a marle-pit y-falle;	
	He saugh nat that. But yet, by seint Thomas,	
	Me reweth° sore° of hende Nicholas.	*sorrow / greatly*
	He shal be rated of° his studying,	*berated for*
	If that I may, by Jesus, hevene king!	
3465	Get me a staf, that I may underspore,°	*pry up*
	Whyl that thou, Robin, hevest up the dore.	
	He shal out of his studying, as I gesse"—	
	And to the chambre-dore he gan him dresse.°	*address*
	His knave was a strong carl° for the nones,°	*fellow / task*
3470	And by the haspe he haf° it up atones,°	*heaved / at once*
	In-to the floor the dore fil anon.	
	This Nicholas sat ay as stille as stoon,	
	And ever gaped upward in-to the eir.	
	This carpenter wende° he were in despeir,	*thought*
3475	And hente° him by the sholdres mightily,	*grasped*
	And shook him harde, and cryde spitously,°	*harshly*
	"What! Nicholay! what, how! what! loke adoun!	
	Awake, and thenk on Cristes passioun;	
	I crouche° thee from elves and fro wightes!"°	*exorcise / creatures*
3480	Ther-with the night-spel seyde he anon-rightes°	*immediately*
	On foure halves° of the hous aboute,	*sides*
	And on the threshfold of the dore withoute:—	
	"Jesu Crist, and sëynt Benedight,°	*St. Benedict*
	Blesse this hous from every wikked wight,	
3485	For nightes verye,¹⁴ the white *paternoster!*°	*Lord's prayer*
	Where wentestow, seynt Petres soster?°	*sister*
	And atte laste this hende Nicholas	
	Gan for to syke° sore, and seyde, "allas!	*sigh*
	Shal al the world be lost eftsones° now?"	*again*
3490	This carpenter answerde, "what seystow?	

---

¹³ The patron saint of Oxford.
¹⁴ Possibly a contraction of *venerye* meaning "hanky-panky," or else a variant of *werye* meaning "worry"—hence, *for night's worry.*

What! thenk on god, as we don, men that
    swinke."°   *work*
    This Nicholas answerde, "fecche me drinke;
And after wol I speke in privetee
Of certeyn thing that toucheth me and thee;
3495 I wol telle it non other man, certeyn."
    This carpenter goth doun, and comth ageyn,
And broghte of mighty ale a large quart;
And whan that each of hem had dronke his part,
This Nicholas his dore faste shette,
3500 And doun the carpenter by him he sette.
    He seyde, "John, myn hoste lief° and dere,   *beloved*
Thou shalt up-on thy trouthe° swere me here,   *word of honor*
That to no wight thou shalt this conseil° wreye;°   *advice / betray*
For it is Cristes conseil that I seye,
3505 And if thou telle it man,° thou are forlore,°   *to anyone / lost*
For this vengaunce thou shalt han° therfore,   *have*
That if thou wreye me, thou shalt be wood!"
"Nay, Crist forbede it, for his holy blood!"
Quod tho° this sely man, "I nam no labbe,°   *then / blabber*
3510 Ne, though I seye, I name nat lief° to gabbe.   *likely*
Sey what thou wolt, I shal it never telle
To child ne wyf, by him that harwed° helle!"[15]   *harrowed*
"Now John," quod Nicholas, "I wol nat lye;
I have y-founde in myn astrologye,
3515 As I have loked in the mone bright,
That now, a Monday next, at quarter-night,°   *nearly dawn*
Shal falle a reyn and that so wilde and wood,
That half so greet was never Noës° flood.   *Noah's*
This world," he seyde, "in lasse than in an hour
3520 Shal al be dreynt,° so hidous is the shour;   *drowned*
Thus shal mankynde drenche° and lese° hir lyf."   *drown / lose*
    This carpenter answerde, "allas, my wyf!
And shal she drenche? allas! myn Alisoun!"
For sorwe of this he fil almost adoun,
3525 And seyde, "is ther no remedie in this cas?"
    "Why, yis, for gode," quod hende Nicholas,
"If thou wolt werken after lore° and reed;°   *learning / advice*
Thou mayst nat werken after thyn owene heed.°   *head*
For thus seith Salomon, that was ful trewe,
3530 'Work al by conseil, and thou shalt nat rewe.'°   *repent*
And if thou werken wolt by good conseil,
I undertake, with-outen mast and seyl,°   *sail*
Yet shal I saven hir and thee and me.
Hastow nat herd how saved was Noë,
3535 Whan that our lord had warned him biforn
That al the world with water sholde be lorn?"°   *lost*

---

[15] Many Christians believe that Christ descended into Hell between his crucifixion and his resurrection to bring the just out of Limbo.

"Yis," quod this carpenter, "ful yore ago."
"Hastow nat herd," quod Nicholas, "also
The sorwe of Noë with his felawshipe,
3540 Er that he mighte gete his wyf to shipe?
Him had be lever,° I dar wel undertake,   *more happy*
At thilke tyme, than alle hise wetheres° blake,   *rams*
That she hadde had a ship hir-self allone.
And ther-fore, wostou° what is best to done?   *do you know*
3545 This asketh haste, and of an hastif° thing   *urgent*
Men may nat preche or maken tarying.

Anon go gete us faste in-to this in°   *inn*
A kneding-trogh, or elles a kimelin,°   *tub*
For ech of us, but loke that they be large,
3550 In whiche we mowe° swimme° as in a barge,   *may / float*
And han ther-inne vitaille° suffisant   *victuals*
But for a day; fy on the remenant!
The water shal aslake° and goon away   *abate*
Aboute pryme° up-on the nexte day.   *daybreak*
3555 But Robin may nat wite° of this, thy knave,   *know*
Ne eek° thy mayde Gille I may nat save;   *also*
Axe nat why, for though thou aske me,
I wol nat tellen goddes privetee.
Suffiseth thee, but if° thy wittes madde,°   *unless / go mad*
3560 To han° as greet° a grace as Noë hadde.   *have / great*
Thy wyf shal I wel saven, out of doute,
Go now thy wey, and speed thee heeraboute.

But whan thou hast, for hir and thee and me,
Y-geten us thise kneding-tubbes three,
3565 Than shaltow hange hem in the roof ful hye,
That no man of our purveyaunce° spye.   *preparations*
And whan thou thus hast doon as I have seyd,
And hast our vitaille faire in hem y-leyd,
And eek an ax, to smyte the corde atwo
3570 When that the water comth, that we may go,
And broke an hole an heigh,° up-on the gable,   *on high*
Unto the gardin-ward,° over the stable,   *garden-side*
That we may frely passen forth our way
Whan that the grete shour is goon away—
3575 Than shaltow swimme as myrie, I undertake,
As doth the whyte doke° after hir drake.   *duck*
Than wol I clepe, 'how! Alison! how! John!
Be myrie, for the flood wol passe anon.'
And thou wolt seyn, 'hayl, maister Nicholay!
3580 Good morwe, I se thee wel, for it is day.'
And than shul we be lordes al our lyf
Of al the world, as Noë and his wyf.

But of o thyng I warne thee ful right,
Be wel avysed, on that ilke night
3585 That we ben entred in-to shippes bord,
That noon of us ne speke nat a word,

Ne clepe, ne crye, but been in his preyere;
For it is goddes owne heste dere.°   *dear behest*
   Thy wyf and thou mote hange fer a-twinne,°   *apart*
3590 For that bitwixe yow shal be no sinne
No more in looking than ther shal in dede;
This ordinance is seyd, go, god thee spede!
Tomorwe at night, whan men ben alle aslepe,
In-to our kneding-tubbes wol we crepe,
3595 And sitten ther, abyding goddes grace.
Go now thy wey, I have no lenger space
To make of this no lenger sermoning.
Men seyn thus, 'send the wyse, and sey no-thing;'[16]
Thou art so wys, it nedeth thee nat teche;
3600 Go, save our lyf, and that I thee biseche."
   This sely carpenter goth forth his wey.
Ful ofte he seith "allas" and "weylawey,"
And to his wyf he tolde his privetee;°   *secret*
And she was war,° and knew it bet° than he,   *aware / better*
3605 What al this queynte cast° was for to seye.   *device*
But nathelees she ferde° as she wolde deye,   *pretended*
And seyde, "allas! go forth thy wey anon,
Help us to scape,° or we ben lost echon;°   *escape / each one*
I am thy trewe verray wedded wyf;
3610 Go, dere spouse, and help to save our lyf."
   Lo! which a greet thyng is affeccioun!°   *emotion*
Men may dye of imaginacioun,
So depe may impressioun be take.
This sely carpenter biginneth quake;
3615 Him thinketh verraily that he may see
Noës flood come walwing° as the see   *tumbling*
To drenchen Alisoun, his hony dere.
He wepeth, weyleth, maketh sory chere,
He syketh with ful many a sory swogh.°   *sound*
3620 He gooth and geteth him a kneding-trogh,
And after that a tubbe and a kimelin,
And prively he sente hem to his in,°   *house*
And heng hem in the roof in privetee.
His owne hand he made laddres three,
3625 To climben by the ronges and the stalkes°   *uprights*
Un-to the tubbes hanginge in the balkes,°   *beams*
And hem vitailled,° bothe trogh and tubbe,   *stocked*
With breed and chese, and good ale in a jubbe,°   *jug*
Suffysinge right y-nogh as for a day.
3630 But er° that he had maad al this array,°   *before / arrangements*
He sente his knave, and eek his wenche also,
Up-on his nede° to London for to go.   *need or business*
And on the Monday, whan it drow to night,
He shette his dore with-oute candel-light,

---

[16] "A word to the wise is enough."

3635	And dressed° al thing as it sholde be,	set up
	And shortly, up they clomben alle three;	
	They sitten stille wel a furlong-way.[17]	
	"Now, *Pater-noster*, clom!"° seyde Nicholay,	clam up
	And "clom," quod John, and "clom," seyde Alisoun.	
3640	This carpenter seyde his devocioun,°	prayers
	And stille he sit, and biddeth his preyere,	
	Awaytinge on the reyn, if he it here.	
	The dede sleep, for wery bisinesse,	
	Fil° on this carpenter right, as I gesse,	Fell
3645	Aboute corfew-tyme,° or litel more;	curfew time (dusk)
	For travail° of his goost° he groneth sore,	suffering / spirit
	And eft° he routeth,° for his heed mislay.	later / snores
	Doun of the laddre stalketh Nicholay.	
	And Alisoun, ful softe adoun she spedde;	
3650	With-outen wordes mo, they goon to bedde	
	Ther-as the carpenter is wont to lye.	
	Ther was the revel and the melodye;	
	And thus lyth Alison and Nicholas,	
	In bisinesse of mirthe and of solas,°	pleasure
3655	Til that the belle of laudes° gan to ringe,	lauds (before dawn)
	And freres in the chauncel° gonne singe.	chancel
	This parish-clerk, this amorous Absolon,	
	That is for love alwey so wo bigon,	
	Up-on the Monday was at Oseneye	
3660	With companye, him to disporte and pleye,	
	And axed up-on cas° a cloisterer	chance
	Ful prively after John the carpenter;	
	And he drough him a-part out of the chirche,	
	And seyde, "I noot,° I saugh him here nat wirche	know not
3665	Sin Saterday; I trow that he be went	
	For timber, ther our abbot hath him sent;	
	For he is wont for timber for to go,	
	And dwellen at the grange° a day or two;	farm
	Or elles he is at his house, certeyn;	
3670	Wher that he be, I can nat sothly° seyn."	truthfully
	This Absolon ful joly was and light,	
	And thoghte, "now is tyme wake° al night;	to wake
	For sikirly° I saugh him nat stiringe	certainly
	Aboute his dore sin day bigan to springe.	
3675	So moot I thryve, I shal, at cokkes crowe,	
	Ful prively knokken at his windowe	
	That stant ful lowe up-on his boures wal.°	bedroom wall
	To Alison now wol I tellen al	
	My love-longing, for yet I shal nat misse	
3680	That at the leste wey I shal hir kisse.	

[17] The time it takes to walk a furlong (⅛ mile).

Som maner confort shal I have, parfay,°　　　　　　*in faith*
My mouth hath icched° al this longe day;　　　　　*itched*
That is a signe of kissing atte leste.
Al night me mette° eek, I was at a feste.　　　　　*dreamed*
3685　Therfor I wol gon slepe an houre or tweye.
And al the night than wol I wake and pleye."
　　　Whan that the firste cok hath crowe, anon
Up rist° this joly lover Absolon,　　　　　　　　*rised*
And him arrayeth gay, at point-devys.°　　　　　*meticulously*
3690　But first he cheweth greyn[18] and lycorys,
To smellen swete, er he had kembd° his heer.　　　*combed*
Under his tonge a trewe love° he beer,　　　　　*a four-leafed herb*
For ther-by wende° he to ben gracious.°　　　　*supposed / attractive*
He rometh to the carpenteres hous,
3695　And stille he stant under the shot-windowe;
Un-to his brest it raughte,° it was so lowe;　　　*reached*
And softe he cogheth with a semi-soun°—　　　　*low voice*
"What do ye, honey-comb, swete Alisoun?
My faire brid, my swete cinamome,°　　　　　　*cinnamon*
3700　Awaketh, lemman myn,° and speketh to me!　　*my love*
Wel litel thenken ye up-on my wo,
That for your love I swete° ther I go.　　　　　*sweat*
No wonder is thogh that I swelte° and swete;　　*swelter*
I moorne as doth a lamb after the tete.°　　　　*teat*
3705　Y-wis, lemman, I have swich love-longinge,
That lyk a turtel° trewe is my moorninge;　　　*turtledove*
I may nat ete na more than a mayde."
　　　"Go fro the window, Jakke fool," she sayde,
"As help me god, it wol nat be 'com ba° me,'　　*kiss*
3710　I love another, and elles I were to blame,
Wel bet than thee, by Jesu, Absolon!
Go forth thy wey, or I wol caste a ston,
And lat me slepe, a twenty devel wey!"
　　　"Allas," quod Absolon, "and weylawey!
3715　That trewe love was ever so yvel° biset!　　　*evilly*
Than kisse me, sin° it may be no bet,　　　　　*since*
For Jesus love and for the love of me."
　　　"Wiltow than go thy wey ther-with?" quod she.
　　　"Ye, certes, lemman," quod this Absolon.
3720　"Thanne make thee redy," quod she, "I come
　　　anon;"
And un-to Nicholas she seyde stille,°　　　　　*softly*
"Now hust,° and thou shalt laughen al thy fille."　*hush*
This Absolon doun sette him on his knees,
And seyde, "I am a lord at all degrees;°　　　　*accounts*
3725　For after this I hope ther cometh more!
Lemman, thy grace, and swete brid, thyn ore!"
　　　The window she undoth, and that in haste,
"Have do," quod she, "com of, and speed thee
　　　faste,

[18] Grain of Paradise, a spice.

Lest that our neighebores thee espye."

3730   This Absolon gan wype his mouth ful drye;

Derk was the night as pich, or as the cole,

And at the window out she putte hir hole,

And Absolon, him fil no bet no wers,

But with his mouth he kiste hir naked ers°   *ass*

3735 Ful savoury,° er he was war° of this.   *savorily / aware*

    Abak he sterte,° and thoghte it was amis,   *started*

For wel he wiste a womman hath no berd;

He felte a thing al rough and long y-herd,°   *haired*

And seyde, "fy! allas! what have I do?"

3740   "Tehee!" quod she, and clapte the window to;

And Absolon goth forth a sory pas.°   *at a sad pace*

    "A berd, a berd!" quod hende Nicholas.

"By goddes *corpus*,° this goth faire and weel!"   *body*

This sely Absolon herde every deel,°   *bit*

3745 And on his lippe he gan for anger byte;

And to him-self he seyde, "I shal thee quyte!"°   *requite*

    Who rubbeth now, who froteth° now his lippes   *scrubs*

With dust, with sond, with straw, with clooth, with chippes,

But Absolon, that seith ful ofte, "allas!

3750 My soule bitake° I un-to Sathanas,°   *commend / Satan*

But me wer lever° than al this toun," quod he,   *more eager*

"Of this despyt awroken° for to be!   *avenged*

Allas!" quod he, "allas! I ne hadde y-bleynt!"[19]

His hote love was cold and al y-queynt;°   *quenched*

3755 For fro that tyme that he had kiste hir ers,

Of paramours he sette° nat a kers,°   *cared / cress*

For he was heled° of his maladye;   *healed*

Ful ofte paramours he gan deffye,

And weep as dooth a child that is y-bete.°   *beaten*

3760 A softe paas° he wente over the strete   *quietly*

Un-til a smith men cleped daun° Gerveys,   *master*

That in his forge smithed plough-harneys,°   *plough fittings*

He sharpeth shaar° and culter° bisily.   *plowshare / coulter*

This Absolon knokketh al esily,°   *softly*

3765 And seyde, "undo, Gerveys, and that anon."

    "What, who artow?" "It am I, Absolon."

"What, Absolon! for Cristes swete tree,°   *cross*

Why ryse ye so rathe,° ey, *ben'cite!*°   *early / bless me*

What eyleth yow? som gay gerl, god it woot,

3770 Hath broght yow thus up-on the viritoot;

By sëynt Note,[20] ye woot wel what I mene."

    This Absolon ne roghte° nat a bene°   *cared / bean*

Of al his pley, no word agayn he yaf;

He hadde more tow on his distaf[21]

---

[19] I.e., Alas, that I had not turned aside!

[20] St. Neot who lived during the ninth century A.D.

[21] More tow on his distaff—hence, more on his mind.

3775 Than Gerveys knew, and seyde, "freend so dere,
That hote culter° in the chimenee here,   *hot iron plow-blade*
As lene° it me, I have ther-with to done,   *Please loan*
And I wol bringe it thee agayn ful sone."
Gerveys answered, "certes, were it gold,
3780 Or in a poke nobles° alle untold,   *coins in a poke (bag)*
Thou sholdest have, as I am trewe smith;
Ey, Cristes foo! what wol ye do ther-with?"
"Ther-of," quod Absolon, "be as be may;
I shal wel telle it thee to-morwe day"—
3785 And caughte the culter by the colde stele.
Ful softe out at the dore he gan to stele,
And wente un-to the carpenteres wal.
He cogheth first, and knokketh ther-with-al
Upon the windowe, right as he dide er.
3790 This Alison answerde, "Who is ther
That knokketh so? I warante° it a theef."   *bet*
"Why, nay," quod he, "god woot, my swete
leef,°   *beloved*
I am thyn Absolon, my dereling!
Of gold," quod he, "I have thee broght a ring;
3795 My moder yaf it me, so god me save,
Ful fyn it is, and ther-to wel y-grave;°   *engraved*
This wol I yeve thee, if thou me kisse!"
This Nicholas was risen for to pisse,
And thoghte he wolde amenden° al the jape,°   *improve / joke*
3800 He sholde kisse his ers er that he scape.
And up the windowe dide he hastily,
And out his ers he putteth prively
Over the buttok, to the haunche-bon;°   *thigh-bone*
And ther-with spak this clerk, this Absolon,
3805 "Spek, swete brid, I noot nat wher thou art."
This Nicholas anon leet flee° a fart,   *fly*
As greet as it had been a thonder-dent,°   *thunderclap*
That with the strook he was almost y-blent;°   *blinded*
And he was redy with his iren hoot,
3810 And Nicholas amidde the ers he smoot.°   *smote*
Of gooth° the skin an hande-brede° aboute,   *off goes / handsbreadth*
The hote culter brende so his toute,°   *rump*
And for the smert he wende for° to dye.   *hoped*
As he were wood,° for wo he gan to crye—   *out of his mind*
3815 "Help! water! water! help, for goddes herte!"
This carpenter out of his slomber sterte,
And herde oon cryen "water" as he were wood,
And thoghte, "Allas! now comth Nowélis flood!"
He sit him up with-outen wordes mo,
3820 And with his ax he smoot the corde a-two,
And doun goth al; he fond neither to selle,
Ne breed ne ale, til he cam to the selle

Up-on the floor;[22] and ther aswowne° he lay.   *unconscious*
  Up sterte hir Alison, and Nicholay,
3825 And cryden "out" and "harrow" in the strete.
The neighebores, bothe smale and grete,
In ronnen, for to gauren° on this man,   *stare*
That yet aswowne he lay, bothe pale and wan;
For with the fal he brosten° hadde his arm;   *broken*
3830 But stonde he moste un-to his owne harm.
For whan he spak, he was anon° bore doun°   *at once / borne down*
With hende Nicholas and Alisoun.
They tolden every man that he was wood,
He was agast so of "Nowélis flood"
3835 Thurgh fantasye, that of his vanitee
He hadde y-boght him kneding-tubbes three.
And hadde hem hanged in the roof above;
And that he preyed hem, for goddes love,
To sitten in the roof, *par companye.*°   *for company*
3840   The folk gan laughen at his fantasye;
In-to the roof they kyken° and they gape,   *gaze*
And turned al his harm un-to a jape.
For what so that this carpenter answerde,
It was for noght, no man his reson herde;
3845 With othes° grete he was so sworn adoun,   *oaths, curses*
That he was holden wood in al the toun;
For every clerk anon-right heeld with other.
They seyde, "the man is wood, my leve brother;"
And every wight gan laughen of this stryf.°   *strife*
3850   Thus swyved° was the carpenteres wyf,   *seduced*
For al his keping and his jalousye;
And Absolon hath kist hir nether° yë;   *bottom*
And Nicholas is scalded in the toute.°   *rump*
This tale is doon, and god save al the route!°   *company*

[c. 1390]

---

[22] He found time to sell neither bread nor ale until he hit the floor.

❧ RENAISSANCE POETRY ❧

John Skelton   *1460–1529*

TO MISTRESS MARGARET HUSSEY

Merry Margaret,
As midsummer flower,
Gentle as falcon
Or hawk of the tower.
5 With solace and gladness,
Much mirth and no madness,
All good and no badness,
So joyously,
So maidenly,
10 So womanly
Her demeaning
In every thing—
Far, far passing
That I can endite,[1]
15 Or suffice to write
Of Merry Margaret,
As midsummer flower,
Gentle as falcon,

Or hawk of the tower;
20 As patient and still
And as full of good will,
As fair Isaphill.[2]
Coriander,[3]
Sweet pomander,[4]
25 Good Cassander;[5]
Steadfast of thought,
Well made, well wrought;
Far may be sought,
Ere that ye can find,
30 So courteous, so kind,
As merry Margaret,
This midsummer flower: .
Gentle as falcon
Or hawk of the tower.

[1523]

Sir Thomas Wyatt   *1503–1542*

"THEY FLEE FROM ME,
THAT SOMETIME DID ME SEEK"

They flee from me, that sometime did me seek,
With naked foot, stalking in my chamber.
I have seen them gentle, tame, and meek;
That now are wild, and do not remember
5   That sometime they put themselves in danger
To take bread at my hand: and now they range,
Busily seeking, with a continual change.

[1] Say.
[2] Hypsipyle, Queen of Lemnos (an island in the Aegean Sea), was praised in Boccaccio's *Of Famous Women* for her kindness to her father and children.
[3] An aromatic, medicinal herb.   [4] A perfumed ball.
[5] Cassandra, whose prophesies were always accurate but never believed.

Thanked be fortune! it hath been otherwise
 Twenty times better! But once, in special,
10 In thin array, after a pleasant guise,
 When her loose gown from her shoulders did fall,
 And she me caught in her arms long and small,
  Therewithal sweetly did me kiss;
  And softly said, "Dear heart! how like you this?"

15 It was no dream! I lay broad waking!
 But all is turned, thorough my gentleness,
Into a strange fashion of forsaking;
 And I have leave to go, of her goodness!
 And she also, to use newfangleness!
20 But since that I so kindely am served,
  I would fain know what she hath deserved?

        [posthumous, 1557]

"WHOSO LIST TO HUNT, I KNOW WHERE IS AN HIND"[1]

Whoso list° to hunt, I know where is an hind!   *wishes*
 But as for me, helas! I may no more!
 The vain travail hath wearied me so sore,
I am of them that furthest come behind!
5 Yet may I, by no means, my wearied mind
 Draw from the deer! but as she fleeth afore,
 Fainting I follow. I leave off therefore,
Since in a net I seek to hold the wind!
Who list her hunt, I put him out of doubt,
10 As well as I, may spend his time in vain!
 And graven with diamonds, in letters plain,
There is written, her fair neck round about,
 'Noli me tangere![2] *for CÆSAR's I am;*
And wild for to hold, though I seem tame.'

        [posthumous, 1557]

"MY GALLEY, CHARGÈD WITH FORGETFULNESS"

My galley, chargèd with forgetfulness,
 Through sharp seas, in winter nights, doth pass
 'Tween rock and rock; and eke° mine enemy, alas, *also*
That is my lord, steereth with cruelness.
5 And, every oar, a thought in readiness,
 As though that death were light in such a case.
 An endless wind doth tear the sail apace,

[1] Adapted from Petrarch, *Rime,* sonnet 190.
[2] "Touch me not!" Wyatt's sonnet is thought to refer to the situation of Anne Boleyn (1507–1536) in whom Wyatt took an interest both before and after her liaison with Henry VIII (1491–1547).

Of forcèd sighs, and trusty fearfulness.
A rain of tears, a cloud of dark disdain,
10   Hath done the wearied cords great hinderance,
Wreathèd with error, and eke with ignorance.
The stars be hid, that led me to this pain.
Drownèd in reason, that should me comfort;[1]
And I remain, despairing of the port.

                      [posthumous, 1557]

Edmund Spenser   *1552–1599*

THE FAERIE QUEENE

FROM *Book 1, Canto 1*

A Gentle Knight was pricking° on the plaine,	*spurring*
Y cladd in mightie armes and silver shielde,	
Wherein old dints of deepe wounds did remaine,	
The cruell markes of many a bloudy fielde;	
5 Yet armes till that time did he never wield:	
His angry steede did chide his foming bitt,	
As much disdayning to the curbe to yield:	
Full jolly° knight he seemd, and faire did sitt,	*handsome*
As one for knightly giusts° and fierce encounters fitt.	*jousts*

But on his brest a bloudie Crosse he bore,	
The deare remembrance of his dying Lord,	
For whose sweete sake that glorious badge he wore,	
And dead as living ever him ador'd:	
Upon his shield the like was also scor'd,	
15 For soveraine° hope, which in his helpe he had:	*powerful*
Right faithful true he was in deede and word,	
But of his cheere° did seeme too solemne sad;	*expression*
Yet nothing did he dread, but ever was ydrad.°	*dreaded*

Upon a great adventure he was bond,°	*bound*
20 That greatest *Gloriana* to him gave,	
That greatest Glorious Queene of *Faerie* lond,	
To winne him worship, and her grace to have,	
Which of all earthly things he most did crave;	
And ever as he rode, his hart did earne°	*yearn*
25 To prove his puissance° in battell brave	*might*
Upon his foe, and his new force to learne;	
Upon his foe, a Dragon horrible and stearne.	

---

[1] Some versions of the poem read "consort" for "comfort."

A lovely Ladie rode him faire beside,
 Upon a lowly Asse more white then snow,
30 Yet she much whiter, but the same did hide
  Under a vele,° that wimpled° was full low, *veil / folded*
 And over all a blacke stole she did throw,
 As one that inly mournd: so was she sad,
 And heavie sat upon her palfrey° slow: *a gentle horse*
35 Seemed in heart some hidden care she had,
And by her in a line° a milke white lambe she lad.° *leash / led*

So pure an innocent, as that same lambe,
 She was in life and every vertuous lore,
 And by descent from Royall lynage came
40 Of ancient Kings and Queenes, that had of yore
 Their scepters stretcht from East to Westerne shore,
 And all the world in their subjection held;
 Till that infernal feend with foule uprore
 Forwasted° all their land, and them expeld: *destroyed*
45 Whom to avenge, she had this Knight from far
  compeld.° *summoned*

Behind her farre away a Dwarfe did lag,
 That lasie seemd in being ever last,
 Or wearièd with bearing of her bag
 Of needments at his backe. Thus as they past,
50 The day with cloudes was suddeine overcast,
 And angry *Jove* an hideous storme of raine
 Did poure into his Lemans lap° so fast, *lover's lap (earth)*
 That every wight° to shrowd° it did constrain, *creature / shelter*
And this faire couple eke° to shroud themselves were *also*
  fain.° *eager*

55 Enforst° to seeke some covert° nigh at hand, *Forced / cover*
 A shadie grove not far away they spide,
 That promist ayde the tempest to withstand:
 Whose loftie trees yclad with sommers pride,
 Did spred so broad, that heavens light did hide,
60 Not perceable° with power of any starre: *pierceable*
 And all within were pathes and alleies wide,
 With footing worne, and leading inward farre:
Faire harbour that them seems; so in they entred arre.

And foorth they passe, with pleasure forward led,
65 Joying to heare the birdes sweete harmony,
 Which therein shrouded from the tempest dred,
 Seemd in their song to scorne the cruell sky.
 Much can° they prayse the trees so straight and hy, *did*
 The sayling Pine, the Cedar proud and tall,
70 The vine-prop Elme, the Poplar never dry,
 The builder Oake, sole king of forrests all,
The Aspine good for staves, the Cypresse funerall.

      The Laurell, meed° of mightie Conquerors   reward
         And Poets sage, the Firre that weepeth still,°   always
75   The Willow worne of forlorne Paramours,
      The Eugh° obedient to the benders will,   yew
      The Birch for shaftes, the Sallow° for the mill,   goat willow
      The Mirrhe sweete bleeding in the bitter wound,[1]
      The warlike Beech, the Ash for nothing ill,
80   The fruitfull Olive, and the Platane° round,   plane tree
      The carver Holme,° the Maple seeldom inward sound.   holm oak

      Led with delight, they thus beguile the way,
         Untill the blustring storme is overblowne;
      When weening° to returne, whence they did stray,   thinking
85   They cannot finde that path, which first was showne,
      But wander too and fro in wayes unknowne,
      Furthest from end then, when they neerest weene,°   think themselves
      That makes them doubt, their wits be not their owne:
      So many pathes, so many turnings seene,
90   That which of them to take, in diverse doubt they been.

      At last resolving forward still to fare,
         Till that some end they finde or° in or out,   either
      That path they take, that beaten seemd most bare,
      And like to lead the labyrinth about;°   without
95   Which when by tract° they hunted had throughout,   lapse of time
      At length it brought them to a hollow cave,
      Amid the thickest woods. The Champion stout
      Eftsoones° dismounted from his courser brave,   Then
      And to the Dwarfe a while his needlesse spere he gave.

100   Be well aware, quoth then that Ladie milde,
         Least suddaine mischiefe ye too rash provoke:
      The danger hid, the place unknowne and wilde,
      Breedes dreadfull doubts: Oft fire is without smoke,
      And perill without show: therefore your stroke
105   Sir knight with-hold, till further triall made.
      Ah Ladie (said he) shame were to revoke
      The forward footing for° an hidden shade: on account of
      Vertue gives her selfe light, through darkenesse for to
            wade.

      Yea but (quoth she) the perill of this place
110   I better wot° then you, though now too late   know
      To wish you backe returne with foule disgrace,
      Yet wisedome warnes, whilest foot is in the gate,
      To stay the steppe, ere forcèd to retrate.°   retreat
      This is the wandring wood, this *Errours den,*
115   A monster vile, whom God and man does hate:
      Therefore I read° beware. Fly fly (quoth then   advise
      The fearefull Dwarfe:) this is no place for living men.

---

[1] Myrrh is obtained from cuts ("wounds") in the tree's bark.

But full of fire and greedy hardiment,
  The youthfull knight could not for ought be staide,
120 But forth unto the darksome hole he went,
  And lookèd in: his glistring armor made
  A litle glooming light, much like a shade,
  By which he saw the ugly monster plaine,
  Halfe like a serpent horribly displaide,
125 But th'other halfe did womans shape retaine,
Most lothsom, filthie, foule, and full of vile disdaine.

And as she lay upon the durtie ground,
  Her huge long taile her den all overspred,
  Yet was in knots and many boughtes° upwound,   *coils*
130 Pointed with mortall sting. Of her there bred
  A thousand yong ones, which she dayly fed,
  Sucking upon her poisonous dugs, eachone
  Of sundry shapes, yet all ill favorèd:
  Soone as that uncouth° light upon them shone,   *unfamiliar*
135 Into her mouth they crept, and suddain all were gone.

Their dam upstart, out of her den effraide,°   *frightened*
  And rushed forth, hurling her hideous taile
  About her cursèd head, whose folds displaid
  Were stretcht now forth at length without entraile.°   *windings*
140 She lookt about, and seeing one in mayle
  Armèd to point,° sought back to turne againe;   *to the teeth*
  For light she hated as the deadly bale,°   *harm*
  Ay° wont in desert darknesse to remaine,   *Always*
Where plaine none might her see, nor she see any
    plaine.

145 Which when the valiant Elfe° perceiv'd, he lept   *fairy knight*
  As Lyon fierce upon the flying pray,
  And with his trenchand° blade her boldly kept   *sharp*
  From turning backe, and forcèd her to stay:
  Therewith enrag'd she loudly gan to bray,
150 And turning fierce, her speckled taile advaunst,
  Threatning her angry sting, him to dismay:
  Who nought aghast, his mightie hand enhaunst:°   *lifted*
The stroke down from her head unto her shoulder
    glaunst.°   *glanced*

Much daunted with that dint,° her sence was dazd,   *stroke*
155 Yet kindling rage, her selfe she gathered round,
  And all attonce her beastly body raizd
  With doubled forces high above the ground:
  Tho° wrapping up her wrethèd sterne° arownd,   *Then / tail*
  Lept fierce upon his shield, and her huge traine°   *tail*
160 All suddenly about his body wound,
  That hand or foot to stirre he strove in vaine:
God helpe the man so wrapt in *Errours* endlesse traine.°   *course*

His Lady sad to see his sore constraint,
   Cride out, Now now Sir knight, shew what ye bee,
165   Add faith unto your force, and be not faint:
   Strangle her, else she sure will strangle thee.
   That when he heard, in great perplexitie,
   His gall did grate for griefe° and high disdaine,   *wrath*
   And knitting all his force got one hand free,
170   Wherewith he grypt her gorge with so great paine,
That soone to loose her wicked bands did her constraine.

Therewith she spewd out of her filthy maw°   *gut*
   A floud of poyson horrible and blacke,
   Full of great lumpes of flesh and gobbets° raw,   *fragments*
175   Which stunck so vildly,° that it forst him slacke   *vilely*
   His grasping hold, and from her turne him backe:
   Her vomit full of bookes and papers was,
   With loathly frogs and toades, which eyes did lacke,
   And creeping sought way in the weedy gras:
180 Her filthy parbreake° all the place defilèd has.   *vomit*

As when old father *Nilus* gins to swell
   With timely pride above the *Aegyptian* vale,
   His fattie° waves do fertile slime outwell,   *greasy*
   And overflow each plaine and lowly dale:
185 But when his later spring° gins to avale,°   *flood / abate*
   Huge heapes of mudd he leaves, wherein there
      breed
   Ten thousand kindes of creatures, partly male
   And partly female of his fruitfull seed;
Such ugly monstrous shapes elsewhere may no man
      reed.°   *see*

190 The same so sore annoyèd has the knight,
   That welnigh chokèd with the deadly stinke,
   His forces faile, ne° can no longer fight.   *nor*
   Whose corage when the feend perceiv'd to shrinke,
   She pourèd forth out of her hellish sinke
195 Her fruitfull cursèd spawne of serpents small,
   Deformèd monsters, fowle, and blacke as inke,
   Which swarming all about his legs did crall,
And him encombred sore, but could not hurt at all.

As gentle Shepheard in sweete even-tide,
200 When ruddy *Phœbus* gins to welke° in west,   *sink*
   High on an hill, his flocke to vewen° wide,   *view*
   Markes which do byte their hasty supper best;
   A cloud of combrous gnattes do him molest,
   All striving to infixe their feeble stings,
205 That from their noyance° he no where can rest,   *annoyance*
   But with his clownish hands their tender wings
He brusheth oft, and oft doth mar their murmurings.

Thus ill bestedd,° and fearefull more of shame,   *situated*
Then of the certaine perill he stood in,
210 Halfe furious° unto his foe he came,   *mad*
Resolv'd in minde all suddenly to win,
Or soone to lose, before he once would lin;°   *cease*
And strooke at her with more than manly force,
That from her body full of filthie sin
215 He raft° her hatefull head without remorse;   *cut off*
A streame of cole bloud forth gushed from her corse.°   *corpse*

Her scattred brood, soone as their Parent deare
They saw so rudely falling to the ground,
Groning full deadly, all with troublous feare,
220 Gathred themselves about her body round,
Weening their wonted entrance to have found
At her wide mouth: but being there withstood
They flockèd all about her bleeding wound,
And suckèd up their dying mothers blood,
225 Making her death their life, and eke her hurt their
good.

That detestàble sight him much amazde,
To see th'unkindly Impes° of heaven accurst,   *young demons*
Devoure their dam;° on whom while so he gazd,   *mother*
Having all satisfide their bloudy thurst,
230 Their bellies swolne he saw with fulnesse burst,
And bowels gushing forth: well worthy end
Of such as drunke her life, the which them nurst;
Now needeth him no lenger labour spend,
His foes have slaine themselves, with whom he should
contend.

235 His Ladie seeing all, that chaunst, from farre
Approcht in hast to greet his victorie,
And said, Faire knight, borne under happy starre,
Who see your vanquisht foes before you lye;
Well worthy be you of that Armorie,°   *coat of arms*
240 Wherein ye have great glory wonne this day,
And proov'd your strength on a strong enimie,
Your first adventure: many such I pray,
And henceforth ever wish, that like succeed it may.

(1590]

"ONE DAY I WROTE HER NAME UPON THE STRAND"

One day I wrote her name upon the strand,°   *beach*
But came the waves and washed it away:
Again I wrote it with a second hand,
But came the tide and made my pains his prey.

5   "Vain man," said she, "that doest in vain assay,
           A mortal thing so to immortalize,
           For I myself shall like to this decay,
           And eek° my name be wiped out likewise."   *also*
       "Not so," quod° I, "let baser things devise   *said*
10   To die in dust, but you shall live by fame:
           My verse your virtues rare shall eternize,
           And in the heavens write your glorious name.
       Where whenas death shall all the world subdue,
           Our love shall live, and later life renew."

                                                    [1595]

Sir Walter Ralegh   *1552–1618*

[THE NYMPH'S REPLY TO THE SHEPHERD][1]

           If all the world and love were young,
           And truth in every shepherd's tongue,
           These pretty pleasures might me move
           To live with thee and be thy love.

5   Time drives flocks from field to fold;
           When rivers rage and rocks grow cold;
           And Philomel[2] becometh dumb;
           The rest complain of cares to come.

           The flowers do fade, and wanton fields
10   To wayward winter reckoning yields:
           A honey tongue, a heart of gall,
           Is fancy's spring, but sorrow's fall.

           Thy gowns, thy shoes, thy beds of roses,
           Thy cap, thy kirtle,° and thy posies,   *dress*
15   Soon break, soon wither, soon forgotten:
           In folly ripe, in reason rotten.

           Thy belt of straw and ivy-buds,
           Thy coral clasps and amber studs,—
           All these in me no means can move
20   To come to thee and be thy love.

---

[1] This poem was written in answer to Christopher Marlowe's "The Passionate Shepherd to His Love" (1599).
[2] One of the myths in Ovid's *Metamorphoses* (c. 8 A.D.) relates that Philomel's tongue was cut out by her brother-in-law Tereus, who wished to silence her complaints and keep her from revealing that he had raped her.

But could youth last, and love still breed,
Had joys no date, nor age no need,
Then these delights my mind might move
25   To live with thee and be thy love.

[1600]

"WHAT IS OUR LIFE? A PLAY OF PASSION"

What is our life? A play of passion,
Our mirth the music of division;°   *variation*
Our mothers' wombs the tiring-houses° be   *dressing rooms*
Where we are dressed for this short comedy;
5   Heaven the judicious, sharp spectator is
That sits and marks still who doth act amiss;
Our graves that hide us from the searching sun
Are like drawn curtains when the play is done:
Thus march we, playing, to our latest° rest,   *last*
10   Only we die in earnest, that's no jest.

[1612]

EPITAPH

Even such is time, that takes in trust
Our youth, our joys, our all we have,
And pays us but with earth and dust;
   Who in the dark and silent grave,
5   When we have wandered all our ways,
Shuts up the story of our days;
But from this earth, this grave, this dust,
My God shall raise me up, I trust.

[posthumous, 1628]

Sir Philip Sidney   *1554–1586*

"LEAVE ME, O LOVE, WHICH REACHEST BUT TO DUST"

Leave me, O love, which reachest but to dust,
And thou, my mind, aspire to higher things!
Grow rich in that which never taketh rust:
Whatever fades, but fading pleasure brings.
5   Draw in thy beams, and humble all thy might

To that sweet yoke where lasting freedoms be;
Which breaks the clouds and opens forth the light
That doth both shine and give us sight to see.
O take fast hold! let that light be thy guide
10   In this small course which birth draws out to death,
And think how evil becometh him to slide
Who seeketh heaven, and comes of heavenly breath.
   Then farewell, world! thy uttermost I see:
   Eternal Love, maintain thy life in me!
                        [posthumous, 1598]

"THOU BLIND MAN'S MARK"

Thou blind man's mark, thou fool's self-chosen snare,
Fond fancy's scum, and dregs of scattered thought;
Band of all evils, cradle of causeless care;
Thou web of will, whose end is never wrought;
5   Desire, desire! I have too dearly bought,
With price of mangled mind, thy worthless ware;
Too long, too long, asleep thou hast me brought,
Who should my mind to higher things prepare.
But yet in vain thou hast my ruin sought;
10   In vain thou madest me to vain things aspire;
In vain thou kindlest all thy smoky fire;
For virtue hath this better lesson taught,—
Within myself to seek my only hire,
Desiring nought but how to kill desire.
                        [posthumous, 1598]

Chidiock Tichborne   *1558?–1586*

ON THE EVE OF HIS EXECUTION[1]

My prime of youth is but a frost of cares,
  My feast of joy is but a dish of pain,
My crop of corn° is but a field of tares,°   *wheat / weeds*
  And all my good is but vain hope of gain;
5   The day is past, and yet I saw no sun,
    And now I live, and now my life is done.

[1] On September 20, 1586, Tichborne was hanged and then "disemboweled before life was extinct"
for participating in a plot to murder Queen Elizabeth I.

My tale was heard and yet it was not told,
  My fruit is fallen, yet my leaves are green,
My youth is spent and yet I am not old,
10   I saw the world and yet I was not seen;
    My thread is cut and yet it is not spun,
    And now I live, and now my life is done.

I sought my death and found it in my womb,
  I looked for life and saw it was a shade,
15 I trod the earth and knew it was my tomb,
  And now I die, and now I was but made;
    My glass is full, and now my glass is run,
    And now I live, and now my life is done.

[1586]

Michael Drayton   *1563–1631*

"SINCE THERE'S NO HELP, COME LET US KISS AND PART"

Since there's no help, come let us kiss and part;
Nay, I have done, you get no more of me;
And I am glad, yea, glad with all my heart,
That thus so cleanly I myself can free.
5 Shake hands for ever, cancel all our vows,
And when we meet at any time again,
Be it not seen in either of our brows
That we one jot of former love retain.
Now at the last gasp of love's latest breath,
10 When, his pulse failing, passion speechless lies,
When faith is kneeling by his bed of death,
And innocence is closing up his eyes,
  —Now if thou wouldst, when all have given him over,
  From death to life thou might'st him yet recover.

[1619]

Christopher Marlowe *1564–1593*

THE PASSIONATE SHEPHERD TO HIS LOVE

Come live with me and be my love;
And we will all the pleasures prove°   *test*
That hills and valleys, dales and fields,
Or woods or steepy mountain yields.

5   And we will sit upon the rocks,
And see the shepherds feed their flocks
By shallow rivers, to whose falls
Melodious birds sing madrigals.°   *songs*

And I will make thee beds of roses
10   And a thousand fragrant posies;
A cap of flowers, and a kirtle°   *dress*
Embroidered all with leaves of myrtle.

A gown made of the finest wool
Which from our pretty lambs we pull;
15   Fair-linèd slippers for the cold,
With buckles of the purest gold.

A belt of straw and ivy-buds
With coral clasps and amber studs:
And if these pleasures may thee move,
20   Come live with me and be my love.

The shepherd swains shall dance and sing
For thy delight each May morning:
If these delights thy mind may move,
Then live with me and be my love.
                    [posthumous, 1599]

William Shakespeare *1564–1616*

SPRING

[*A Song at the End of* Love's Labor's Lost]

When daisies pied,° and violets blue,   *many-colored*
   And lady-smocks all silver white,
And cuckoo-buds, of yellow hue,
   Do paint the meadows with delight,

5   The cuckoo then on ev'ry tree
    Mocks married men, for thus sings he;
                Cuckoo!
    Cuckoo! cuckoo!—O word of fear,
    Unpleasing to a married ear!

10 When shepherds pipe on oaten straws,°   *reed pipes*
        And merry larks are ploughmen's clocks,
    When turtles tread° and rooks and daws,   *turtledoves mate*
        And maidens bleach their summer smocks;
    The cuckoo then on every tree
15 Mocks married men, for thus sings he;
                Cuckoo!
    Cuckoo! Cuckoo!—O word of fear,
    Unpleasing to a married ear!
                            [1594]

WINTER

[*A Song at the End of* Love's Labor's Lost]

    When icicles hang by the wall,
        And Dick the shepherd blows his nail,
    And Tom bears logs into the hall,
        And milk comes frozen home in pail;
5   When blood is nipt, and ways be foul,
    Then nightly sings the staring owl,
                Tu-whoo!
    Tu-whit! tu-whoo! a merry note,
    While greasy Joan doth keel° the pot.   *stir*

10 When all aloud the wind doth blow,
        And coughing drowns the parson's saw,°   *proverb*
    And birds sit brooding in the snow,
        And Marian's nose looks red and raw;
    When roasted crabs° hiss in the bowl,   *crabapples*
15 Then nightly sings the staring owl,
                Tu-whoo!
    Tu-whit! tu-whoo! a merry note,
    While greasy Joan doth keel the pot.
                            [1594]

"WHO IS SYLVIA?"

[*A Song from* The Two Gentlemen of Verona]

    "Who is Silvia? What is she,
        That all our swains° commend her?"   *gallants*
    Holy, fair, and wise is she;
        The Heavens such grace did lend her,
5   That she might admiréd be.

"Is she kind as she is fair?
    For beauty lives with kindness."
Love doth to her eyes repair,
    To help him of his blindness;[1]
10   And, being helped, inhabits there.

Then to Sylvia let us sing,
    That Sylvia is excelling;
She excels each mortal thing
    Upon the dull earth dwelling;
15   To her let us garlands bring.

                                                            [1594]

"IF I PROFANE WITH MY UNWORTHIEST HAND"

[*A Sonnet from* Romeo and Juliet]

ROMEO. *(To Juliet)* If I profane with my unworthiest hand
    This holy shrine,° the gentle sin is this;   *i.e., Juliet's hand*
    My lips, two blushing pilgrims,° ready stand   *travelers to a shrine*
    To smooth that rough touch with a tender kiss.
5   JULIET. Good pilgrim, you do wrong your hand too
            much,
    Which mannerly° devotion shows in this;   *well bred*
    For saints have hands that pilgrims' hands do
            touch,
    And palm to palm is holy palmer's° kiss.   *pilgrim's*
    ROMEO. Have not saints lips, and holy palmers too?
10 JULIET. Ay, pilgrim, lips that they must use in prayer.
    ROMEO. O! then, dear saint, let lips do what hands do;
    They pray. Grant thou, lest faith turn to despair.
    JULIET. Saints do not move, though grant for
            prayer's sake.
    ROMEO. Then move not, while my prayers' effect I take.
                        [*Kisses her*]
                                                            [1596]

SONNET XVIII

Shall I compare thee to a summer's day?
Thou art more lovely and more temperate:
Rough winds do shake the darling buds of May,
And summer's lease hath all too short a date:
5   Sometime too hot the eye of heaven shines,
And often is his gold complexion dimmed;
And every fair° from fair sometime declines,   *fair woman*
By chance, or nature's changing course, untrimmed;°   *stripped of trimmings*

---

[1] Cupid, the infant god of love, is usually depicted as blind.

But thy eternal summer shall not fade,
Nor lose possession of that fair thou owest;°   *ownest*
Nor shall death brag thou wander'st in his
    shade,
When in eternal lines to time thou growest:
So long as men can breathe, or eyes can see,
So long lives this, and this gives life to thee.

                                  [1609]

SONNET XXIX

When in disgrace with fortune and men's eyes,
I all alone beweep my outcast state,
And trouble deaf heaven with my bootless° cries,   *futile*
And look upon myself, and curse my fate,
5   Wishing me like to one more rich in hope,
Featured like him, like him with friends possessed,
Desiring this man's art, and that man's scope,
With what I most enjoy contented least;
Yet in these thoughts myself almost despising,
10 Haply I think on thee—and then my state
(Like to the lark at break of day arising
From sullen earth) sings hymns at heaven's gate;
For thy sweet love remembered, such wealth brings,
That then I scorn to change my state with kings.

                                  [1609]

SONNET LV

Not marble, nor the gilded monuments
Of princes, shall outlive this powerful rhyme;
But you shall shine more bright in these contents
Than unswept stone, besmeared with sluttish time.
5   When wasteful war shall statues overturn,
And broils root out the works of masonry;
Nor Mars his sword[1] nor war's quick fire shall burn
The living record of your memory.
'Gainst death and all-oblivious enmity
10 Shall you pace forth; your praise shall still find
    room,
Even in the eyes of all posterity
That wear this world out to the ending doom.°   *Judgment Day*
So till the judgment that yourself arise,
You live in this, and dwell in lovers' eyes.

                                  [1609]

---

[1] Mars' sword. Mars is the Roman god of war.

SONNET LXV

Since brass, nor stone, nor earth, nor boundless sea,
But sad mortality o'er-sways their power,
How with this rage shall beauty hold a plea,°   *defense in law*
Whose action° is no stronger than a flower?   *legal action*
5   O how shall summer's honey breath hold out
Against the wreckful siege of battering days,
When rocks impregnable are not so stout,
Nor gates of steel so strong, but time decays?
O fearful meditation! where, alack!
10 Shall time's best jewel from time's chest lie hid?
Or what strong hand can hold his swift foot back?
Or who his spoil of beauty can forbid?
O none, unless this miracle have might,
That in black ink my love may still shine bright.

[1609]

SONNET LXXIII

That time of year thou may'st in me behold
When yellow leaves, or none, or few, do hang
Upon those boughs which shake against the cold,
Bare ruined choirs, where late the sweet birds sang.
5   In me thou seest the twilight of such day,
As after sunset fadeth in the west,
Which by and by black night doth take away,
Death's second self, that seals up all in rest.
In me thou seest the glowing of such fire,
10 That on the ashes of his youth doth lie,
As the death-bed whereon it must expire,
Consumed with that which it was nourished by.
This thou perceiv'st, which makes thy love more strong,
To love that well which thou must leave ere long.

[1609]

SONNET CXVI

Let me not to the marriage of true minds
Admit impediments.[1] Love is not love
Which alters when it alteration finds,
Or bends with the remover to remove:
5   O no! it is an ever-fixèd mark,
That looks on tempests, and is never shaken;
It is the star to every wandering bark,°   *ship*
Whose worth's unknown, although his height° be taken.   *altitude*

[1] Hindrances. Shakespeare is alluding to the words used in the Anglican marriage service.

Love's not time's fool, though rosy lips and cheeks
10 Within his bending sickle's compass° come;   *reach*
Love alters not with his brief hours and weeks,
But bears° it out even to the edge of doom.   *lasts*
If this be error, and upon me proved,
I never writ, nor no man ever loved.

[1609]

SONNET CXXIX

The expense° of spirit in a waste° of shame   *draining / wasteland*
Is lust in action; and till action, lust
Is perjured, murderous, bloody, full of blame,
Savage, extreme, rude, cruel, not to trust;
5 Enjoyed no sooner, but despisèd straight;
Past reason hunted; and no sooner had,
Past reason hated, as a swallowed bait,
On purpose laid to make the taker mad:
Mad in pursuit, and in possession so;
10 Had, having, and in quest to have, extreme;
A bliss in proof,°—and proved, a very woe;   *the act (of coition)*
Before, a joy proposed; behind, a dream:
All this the world well knows; yet none
   knows well
To shun the heaven that leads men to this hell.

[1609]

SONNET CXXX

My mistress' eyes are nothing like the sun;
Coral is far more red than her lips' red:
If snow be white, why then her breasts are dun;°   *dull brown*
If hairs be wires, black wires grow on her head.
5 I have seen roses damasked,° red and white,   *blush-colored*
But no such roses see I in her cheeks;
And in some perfumes is there more delight
Than in the breath that from my mistress reeks.
I love to hear her speak,—yet well I know
10 That music hath a far more pleasing sound;
I grant I never saw a goddess go,°—   *walk*
My mistress, when she walks, treads on the ground;
And yet, by heaven, I think my love as rare
As any she bely'd° with false compare.   *proved false*

[1609]

SONNET CXLVI

Poor soul, the centre of my sinful earth,
Fooled by¹ these rebel powers that thee
    array,°   *dress*
Why dost thou pine within, and suffer dearth,
Painting thy outward walls so costly gay?
5   Why so large cost, having so short a lease,
Dost thou upon thy fading mansion spend?
Shall worms, inheritors of this excess,
Eat up thy charge? Is this thy body's end?
Then, soul, live thou upon thy servant's loss,
10 And let that° pine to aggravate° thy store;   *the body / increase*
Buy terms° divine in selling hours of dross;°   *periods of time / refuse*
Within be fed, without be rich no more:
So shall thou feed on death, that feeds on
    men,
And, death once dead, there's no more dying
    then.
                            [1609]

"FEAR NO MORE THE HEAT O' TH' SUN"

[*A Song in* Cymbeline]

Fear no more the heat o' th' sun,
    Nor the furious winter's rages;
Thou thy worldly task hast done,
    Home art gone, and ta'en thy wages:
5   Golden lads and girls all must,
As chimney-sweepers, come to dust.

Fear no more the frown o' th' great,
    Thou art past the tyrant's stroke;
Care no more to clothe and eat,
    To thee the reed is as the oak.
10 The sceptre, learning, physic, must
All follow this, and come to dust.

Fear no more the lightning-flash,
    Nor th' all-dreaded thunder stone;²
Fear not slander, censure rash,
15   Thou hast finished joy and moan.
All lovers young, all lovers must
Consign° to thee, and come to dust.   *deliver (themselves)*

---

¹ "Fooled by" is an emendation; the first edition repeats the last three words of line 1.
² Falling stones were believed to cause the sound of thunder.

No exorciser harm thee!
Nor no witchcraft charm thee!
20   Ghost unlaid forbear thee!
Nothing ill come near thee!
Quiet consummation have,
And renownèd be thy grave!

[1610]

Thomas Campion   *1567–1620*

MY SWEETEST LESBIA[1]

My sweetest Lesbia, let us live and love.
And, though the sager sort our deeds reprove,
Let us not weigh them. Heaven's great lamps do dive
Into their west, and straight again revive.
5   But soon as once set is our little light,
Then must we sleep one ever-during° night.   *everlasting*

If all would lead their lives in love like me,
Then bloody swords and armor should not be.
No drum nor trumpet peaceful sleeps should move,
10   Unless alarm came from the camp of Love.
But fools do live and waste their little light,
And seek with pain their ever-during night.

When timely death my life and fortune ends,
Let not my hearse be vexed with mourning friends.
15   But let all lovers, rich in triumph, come
And with sweet pastimes grace my happy tomb.
And, Lesbia, close up thou my little light,
And crown with love my ever-during night.

[1601]

WHEN TO HER LUTE CORINNA SINGS

When to her lute Corinna sings,
Her voice revives the leaden strings,
And doth in highest notes appear
As any challenged echo clear.
5   But when she doth of mourning speak,
Even with her sighs the strings do break.

[1] The Roman poet Catullus (87–c. 54 B.C.), whom Campion imitated in this poem, often addressed his poetry to Lesbia. The name has no connection with the word *Lesbian*, which was originally used to describe the homosexual followers of the Greek poetess Sappho (c. 600 B.C.) on the island of Lesbos in the Aegean Sea.

And as her lute doth live or die.
Led by her passion, so must I.
For when of pleasure she doth sing,
My thoughts enjoy a sudden spring;
But if she doth of sorrow speak,
Even from my heart the strings do break.

[1601]

❧ SEVENTEENTH CENTURY POETRY ❧

John Donne   *1572–1631*

THE GOOD MORROW

I wonder by my troth, what thou and I
   Did, till we loved? Were we not weaned till then,
But sucked on country pleasures, childishly?
   Or snorted we in the seven sleepers' den?[1]
5   'Twas so; but this,° all pleasures fancies be.   *except for love*
   If ever any beauty I did see,
Which I desired, and got, 'twas but a dream of thee.

And now good morrow to our waking souls,
   Which watch not one another out of fear;
10   For love, all love of other sights controls,
   And makes one little room, an everywhere.
Let sea-discoverers to new worlds have gone,
Let maps to others, worlds on worlds have shown,
Let us possess one world; each hath one, and is one.

15   My face in thine eye, thine in mine appears,
   And true plain hearts do in the faces rest;
Where can we find two better hemispheres
   Without sharp° north, without declining west?   *cold*
Whatever dies, was not mixed equally;[2]
20   If our two loves be one, or, thou and I
Love so alike that none do slacken, none can die.
              [posthumous, 1633]

SONG

Go, and catch a falling star,
   Get with child a mandrake root,[1]
Tell me where all past years are,
   Or who cleft the Devil's foot.

---

[1] Seven young Christians supposedly slept for 187 years after being walled up in a cave in 249 A.D. during the reign of the Roman emperor Decius.
[2] In medieval philosophy death was a result of an imperfect mixture of elements; when the elements are perfectly balanced, immortality should be possible.
[1] The root of the mandrake resembles a human torso and legs.

5 Teach me to hear mermaids singing,
   Or to keep off envy's stinging,
            And find,
            What wind
   Serves to advance an honest mind.

10 If thou be'st born to strange sights,
      Things invisible to see,
   Ride ten thousand days and nights,
      Till age snow white hairs on thee.
   Thou, when thou return'st, wilt tell me
15 All strange wonders, that befell thee,
            And swear,
            No where
   Lives a woman true and fair.

   If thou find'st one, let me know,
20   Such a pilgrimage were sweet;
   Yet do not, I would not go,
      Through at next door we might meet.
   Though she were true when you met her,
   And last, till you write your letter,
25   Yet she
            Will be
   False, ere I come, to two or three.

                          [posthumous, 1633]

Handwritten margin note: Theme—Can't trust a woman / Conceit—comparing unusual things to trusty women

THE SUN RISING

   Busy old fool, unruly sun,
      Why dost thou thus,
   Through windows, and through curtains call on us?
   Must to thy motions lovers' seasons run?
5   Saucy pedantic wretch, go chide
      Late school-boys, and sour prentices.°   *apprentices*
   Go tell court-huntsmen, that the King will ride.
      Call country ants to harvest offices;
   Love, all alike, no season knows, nor clime,
10 Nor hours, days, months, which are the rags of time.

   Thy beams, so reverend, and strong
      Why shouldst thou think?
   I could eclipse and cloud them with a wink,
   But that I would not lose her sight so long:
15   If her eyes have not blinded thine,
      Look, and tomorrow late, tell me,
   Whether both the Indias[1] of spice and mine

---

[1] The East Indies were noted for spices; the West Indies for gold and silver mines.

Be where thou left'st them, or lie here with me.
  Ask for those kings whom thou saw'st yesterday,
20   And thou shalt hear, All here in one bed lay.

    She is all states, and all princes, I,
      Nothing else is.
  Princes do but play us; compared to this,
  All honor's mimic;° all wealth alchemy.[2]   *mimicry*
25   Thou sun art half as happy as we,
      In that the world's contracted thus;
    Thine age asks ease, and since thy duties be
    To warm the world, that's done in warming us.
  Shine here to us, and thou art everywhere;
30   This bed thy center is, these walls, thy sphere.

[posthumous, 1633]

THE CANONIZATION

For God's sake hold your tongue, and let me love,
  Or chide my palsy, or my gout,
My five grey hairs, or ruined fortunes flout;
With wealth your state, your mind with arts
    improve,
5   Take you a course,° get you a place,°   *direction / appointment*
  Observe His Honor or his Grace,
Or the king's real or his stamped face°   *i.e., on a coin*
  Contemplate; what you will, approve,°   *try out*
    So you will let me love.

10 Alas, alas! who's injured by my love?
  What merchant's ships have my sighs drowned?
Who says my tears have overflowed his ground?
When did my colds a forward spring remove?
  When did the heats, which my veins fill,
15   Add one more to the plaguy bill?[1]
Soldiers find wars, and lawyers find out still
  Litigious men, which quarrels move,
    Though she and I do love.

Call us what you will, we are made such by love;
20   Call her one, me another fly;
We are tapers too, and at our own cost die;
And we in us find th' eagle and the dove;

[2] The pseudo-science of turning base metal into gold—hence, in this context, "fraudulent" or "phoney."
[1] Deaths from the plague were recorded in a weekly bill or list.

The phoenix riddle hath more wit
  By us, we two being one, are it:[2]
25 So to one neutral thing both sexes fit.
  We die and rise the same, and prove
    Mysterious by this love.

We can die by it, if not live by love.
  And if unfit for tomb and hearse
30 Our legend be, it will be fit for verse;
And if no piece of chronicle we prove,
  We'll build in sonnets pretty rooms.
  As well a well-wrought urn becomes
The greatest ashes, as half-acre tombs;
35   And by these hymns all shall approve°   *certify*
    Us canonized for love:

And thus invoke° us: "You whom reverend love *pray to*
  Made one another's hermitage;
You to whom love was peace, that now is rage,
40 Who did the whole world's soul contract, and
      drove
  Into the glasses° of your eyes,   *reflecting surfaces*
  (So made such mirrors, and such spies,
That they did all to you epitomize)[3]
  Countries, towns, courts: beg from above
    A pattern of your love."[4]
                        [posthumous, 1633]

THE RELIQUE

When my grave is broke up again
Some second guest to entertain,
(For graves have learned that woman-head,° *female trait*
To be to more than one a bed)
5   And he that digs it, spies
A bracelet of bright hair about the bone,
  Will he not let us alone,
And think that there a loving couple lies?

---

[2] The mythological phoenix lights its own funeral pyre, is consumed by the fire, and then is resurrected from its own ashes. Donne's lovers repeat this cycle through their desire, gratification, sexual exhaustion, and renewed desire.

[3] Donne's lovers see reflected in each other's eyes not only themselves, but also (more figuratively than literally) a background of countries, towns, and courts; therefore they have found in each other an epitome of the whole world.

[4] I.e., Donne and his mistress, as saints of love, should beg God to send to earth a model of their love.

Who thought that this device might be some way
10   To make their souls, at the last busy day,
Meet at this grave, and make a little stay?

    If this fall in a time, or land,
    Where mis-devotion° doth command,   *idolatry*
    Then he that digs us up, will bring
15   Us to the bishop, and the king,
        To make us reliques; then
Thou shalt be a Mary Magdalen, and I
    A something else thereby;
All women shall adore us, and some men;
20 And since at such time miracles are sought,
I would have that age by this paper taught
What miracles we harmless lovers wrought.

    First we loved well and faithfully,
    Yet knew not what we loved, nor why;
25   Diff'rence of sex no more we knew,
    Than our guardian angels do;
        Coming and going we
Perchance might kiss, but not between those meals;
    Our hands ne'er touched the seals,
30 Which Nature, injured by late law, set free:
These miracles we did; but now, alas!
All measure and all language I should pass,
Should I tell what a miracle she was.

                           [posthumous, 1633]

"DEATH BE NOT PROUD"

Death, be not proud, though some have called thee
Mighty and dreadful, for thou art not so;
For those, whom thou think'st thou dost overthrow,
Die not, poor death; nor yet canst thou kill me.
5 From rest and sleep, which but thy picture° be,   *image, representation*
Much pleasure; then from thee much more must flow:
And soonest our best men with thee do go,
Rest of their bones, and soul's delivery.
Thou art slave to fate, chance, kings, and desperate
    men,
10 And dost with poison, war, and sickness dwell,
And poppy° or charms can make us sleep as well,   *opium*
And better than thy stroke. Why swell'st thou then?
One short sleep past, we wake eternally;
And death shall be no more; death, thou shalt die.

                           [posthumous, 1633]

"BATTER MY HEART, THREE-PERSONED GOD"

Batter my heart, three-personed God; for you
As yet but knock, breathe, shine, and seek to mend;
That I may rise and stand, o'erthrow me and bend
Your force, to break, blow, burn, and make me new,
5   I, like an usurped° town to another due,   *seized*
Labor to admit you, but oh, to no end;
Reason, your viceroy° in me, me should defend,   *deputy*
But is captived, and proves weak or untrue;
Yet dearly I love you, and would be loved fain,°   *gladly*
10   But am betrothed unto your enemy:
Divorce me, untie, or break that knot again,
Take me to you, imprison me; for I,
Except you enthrall me, never shall be free;
Nor ever chaste, except you ravish me.

[posthumous, 1633]

Ben Jonson   *1572–1637*

SONG: TO CELIA

Drink to me only with thine eyes,
   And I will pledge° with mine;   *toast you*
Or leave a kiss but in the cup,
   And I'll not look for wine.
5   The thirst, that from the soul doth rise,
   Doth ask a drink divine:
But might I of Jove's nectar sup,
   I would not change for thine.

I sent thee, late, a rosy wreath,
10   Not so much honoring thee,
As giving it a hope, that there
   It could not withered be.
But thou thereon did'st only breathe,
   And sent'st it back to me:
15   Since when, it grows, and smells, I swear,
   Not of itself, but thee.

[1616]

"IT IS NOT GROWING LIKE A TREE"[1]

It is not growing like a tree
In bulk, doth make man better be;
Or standing long an oak, three hundred year,
To fall a log, at last, dry, bald, and sere:
5   A lily of a day,
Is fairer far in May,
Although it fall, and die that night;
It was the plant and flower of light.
In small proportions we just beauties see:
10   And in short measures life may perfect be.

[posthumous, 1640]

Robert Herrick *1591–1674*

TO THE VIRGINS, TO MAKE MUCH OF TIME

Gather ye rosebuds while ye may,
    Old Time is still a-flying:
And this same flower that smiles today
    Tomorrow will be dying.

5   The glorious lamp of heaven, the sun,
    The higher he's a-getting,
The sooner will his race be run,
    And nearer he's to setting.

That age is best which is the first,
10   When youth and blood are warmer;
But being spent, the worse, and worst
    Times still succeed the former.

Then be not coy, but use your time,
    And while ye may, go marry:
15 For having lost but once your prime,
    You may for ever tarry.

[1648]

---

[1] From his poem entitled "To the Immortal Memory and Friendship of that Noble Pair, Sir Lucius Cary and Sir H. Morison."

DELIGHT IN DISORDER

A sweet disorder in the dress
Kindles in clothes a wantonness:
A lawn° about the shoulders thrown   *fine linen shawl*
Into a fine distraction:
5   An erring lace, which here and there
Enthrals the crimson stomacher:[1]
A cuff neglectful, and thereby
Ribbands° to flow confusedly: *Ribbons*
A winning wave, deserving note,
10 In the tempestuous petticoat:
A careless shoe-string, in whose tie
I see a wild civility:
Do more bewitch me than when art
Is too precise in every part.
                                    [1648]

THE NIGHT-PIECE: TO JULIA

Her eyes the glow-worm° lend thee,   *larva of the firefly*
The shooting stars attend thee;
    And the elves also,
    Whose little eyes glow
5   Like the sparks of fire, befriend thee.

No Will-o'-the-wisp° mislight thee,   *swamp fire*
Nor snake or slow-worm° bite thee;   *lizard*
    But on, on thy way,
    Not making a stay,
10 Since ghost there's none to affright thee.

Let not the dark thee cumber:°   *encumber*
What though the moon does slumber?
    The stars of the night
    Will lend thee their light
15 Like tapers clear without number.

Then, Julia, let me woo thee,
Thus, thus to come unto me;
    And when I shall meet
    Thy silv'ry feet,
20 My soul I'll pour into thee.
                                    [1648]

---

[1] A separate piece of cloth held in place by laces and covering a woman's bosom.

TO DAFFODILS

Fair daffodils, we weep to see
  You haste away so soon;
As yet the early-rising sun
  Has not attained his noon.
5   Stay, stay
  Until the hasting day
      Has run
  But to the evensong;
And, having prayed together, we
10   Will go with you along.

We have short time to stay, as you,
  We have as short a spring;
As quick a growth to meet decay,
  As you, or anything.
15   We die
  As your hours do, and dry
      Away
  Like to the summer's rain;
Or as the pearls of morning's dew,
  Ne'er to be found again.

[1648]

TO DAISIES, NOT TO SHUT SO SOON

Shut not so soon; the dull-eyed
    night
  Has not as yet begun
To make a seizure on the light,
  Or to seal up the sun.

5 No marigolds yet closèd are,
  No shadows great appear;
Nor doth the early shepherd's star
  Shine like a spangle here.

   Stay but till my Julia close
10   Her life-begetting eye,
  And let the whole world then dispose
    Itself to live or die.

[1648]

George Herbert *1593–1633*

THE PULLEY

  When God at first made man,
Having a glass of blessings standing by—
"Let us," said He, "pour on him all we can;
Let the world's riches, which dispersèd lie,
5   Contract into a span."°   *a handspan*

  So strength first made a way,
Then beauty flowed, then wisdom, honor, pleasure:
When almost all was out, God made a stay,
Perceiving that, alone of all his treasure,
10   Rest in the bottom lay.

"For if I should," said He,
"Bestow this jewel also on my creature,
He would adore my gifts instead of me,
And rest in nature, not the God of nature;
15   So both should losers be.

"Yet let him keep the rest,
But keep them with repining restlessness;
Let him be rich and weary, that at least,
If goodness lead him not, yet weariness
20   May toss him to my breast.

[1633]

LOVE

Love bade me welcome; yet my soul drew back,
          Guilty of dust and sin.
But quick-eyed Love, observing me grow slack
          From my first entrance in,
5   Drew nearer to me, sweetly questioning
          If I lacked anything.
"A guest," I answered, "worthy to be here:"
          Love said, "You shall be he."
"I, the unkind, ungrateful? Ah, my dear,
10   I cannot look on thee."
Love took my hand and smiling did reply,
          "Who made the eyes but I?"
"Truth, Lord; but I have marred them: let my shame
          Go where it doth deserve."
15 "And know you not," says Love, "who bore the blame?"
          "My dear, then I will serve."
"You must sit down," says Love, "and taste my meat."
          So I did sit and eat.

[1633]

Edmund Waller   *1606–1687*

GO, LOVELY ROSE

Go lovely Rose—
Tell her that wastes her time and me,
That now she knows,
When I resemble° her to thee,   *compare*
5   How sweet and fair she seems to be.

Tell her that's young,

And shuns to have her graces spied,
   That hadst thou sprung
In deserts where no men abide,
10   Thou must have uncommended died.

   Small is the worth
Of beauty from the light retired:
   Bid her come forth,
Suffer herself to be desired,
15   And not blush so to be admired.

   Then die—that she
The common fate of all things rare
   May read in thee;
How small a part of time they share
20   That are so wondrous sweet and fair!
[1645]

ON A GIRDLE

That which her slender waist confined
Shall now my joyful temples bind;
No monarch but would give his crown,
His arms might do what this had done.

5   It was my heaven's extremest sphere,
The pale° which held that lovely deer: *encircling fence*
My joy, my grief, my hope, my love,
Did all within this circle move.

A narrow compass! and yet there
10   Dwelt all that's good, and all that's fair!
Give me but what this ribband° bound,   *ribbon*
Take all the rest the sun goes round!
[1686]

John Milton *1608–1674*

PARADISE LOST

FROM *Book 1*

Of man's first disobedience and the fruit[1]
Of that forbidden tree, whose mortal taste

[1] I.e., the forbidden apple, but also the result (or "fruit") of Adam and Eve's disobedience.

Brought death into the world and all our woe,
With loss of Eden, till one greater Man°   *Christ*
5   Restore us and regain the blissful seat,
Sing heavenly Muse, that on the secret top
Of Oreb, or of Sinai,[2] didst inspire
That shepherd, who first taught the chosen seed,
In the beginning how the heavens and earth
10 Rose out of Chaos; or if Sion hill[3]
Delight thee more, and Siloa's brook that flowed
Fast by the oracle of God; I thence
Invoke thy aid to my advent'rous song,
That with no middle flight intends to soar
15 Above th' Aonian mount,[4] while it pursues
Things unattempted yet in prose or rhyme.
     And chiefly thou, O Spirit,° that dost prefer   *the Holy Spirit*
Before all temples th' upright heart and pure,
Instruct me, for thou know'st; thou from the first
20 Wast present, and with mighty wings outspread
Dove-like sat'st brooding on the vast abyss,
And mad'st it pregnant:[5] what in me is dark
Illumine, what is low raise and support;
That to the height of this great argument°   *theme*
25 I may assert eternal Providence,
And justify the ways of God to men.
     Say first, for heaven hides nothing from thy view,
Nor the deep tract of hell; say first, what cause
Moved our grand parents in that happy state,
30 Favored of heaven so highly, to fall off
From their Creator, and transgress his will
For one restraint, lords of the world besides?
Who first seduced them to that foul revolt?
Th' infernal serpent; he it was, whose guile,
35 Stirred up with envy and revenge, deceived
The mother of mankind, what time° his pride   *when*
Had cast him out from heaven, with all his host
Of rebel angels, by whose aid aspiring
To set himself in glory above his peers,
40 He trusted to have equalled the Most High,
If he opposed; and with ambitious aim
Against the throne and monarchy of God
Raised impious war in heaven and battle proud,
With vain attempt. Him the Almighty Power
45 Hurled headlong flaming from th' ethereal sky,
With hideous ruin and combustion, down
To bottomless perdition, there to dwell
In adamantine° chains and penal fire,   *unbreakable*
Who durst° defy th' Omnipotent to arms.   *dared to*

[2] Both are names for Mt. Sinai where Moses heard the word of God.
[3] Zion hill and Siloam brook are near the temple (the "oracle of God") in Jerusalem.
[4] Mt. Helicon, home of the Muses.
[5] An allusion to Genesis 1:2.

50 Nine times the space that measures day and night
To mortal men, he with his horrid crew
Lay vanquished, rolling in the fiery gulf,
Confounded though immortal: but his doom
Reserved him to more wrath; for now the thought
55 Both of lost happiness and lasting pain
Torments him; round he throws his baleful eyes,
That witnessed huge affliction and dismay,
Mixed with obdurate pride and steadfast hate.
At once, as far as angels ken,° he views   *vision*
60 The dismal situation waste and wild;
A dungeon horrible, on all sides round,
As one great furnace, flamed; yet from those flames
No light, but rather darkness visible
Served only to discover sights of woe,
65 Regions of sorrow, doleful shades, where peace
And rest can never dwell, hope never comes,
That comes to all; but torture without end
Still urges, and a fiery deluge, fed
With ever-burning sulphur unconsumed.
70 Such place eternal justice had prepared
For those rebellious; here their prison ordained
In utter darkness, and their portion set
As far removed from God and light of heaven,
As from the center thrice to th' utmost pole.
75 O how unlike the place from whence they fell!
There the companions of his fall, o'erwhelmed
With floods and whirlwinds of tempestuous fire,
He soon discerns, and welt'ring° by his side   *wallowing*
One next himself in power, and next in crime,
80 Long after known in Palestine, and named
Beëlzebub:[6] To whom th' arch-enemy,
And thence in heaven called Satan, with bold words
Breaking the horrid silence, thus began:
    "If thou beest he—But O how fallen! how
        changed
85 From him, who in the happy realms of light,°   *heaven*
Clothed with transcendent brightness, didst outshine
Myriads, though bright! if he, whom mutual league,
United thoughts and counsels, equal hope
And hazard in the glorious enterprize,
90 Joined with me once, now misery hath joined
In equal ruin: into what pit thou seest
From what height fallen; so much the stronger
        proved
He with his thunder. And till then who knew
The force of those dire arms? Yet not for those,
95 Nor what the potent victor in his rage
Can else inflict, do I repent, or change,

---

[6] A sun god worshipped in ancient Palestine—here Satan's lieutenant.

Though changed in outward luster, that fixed mind,
And high disdain from sense of injured merit,
That with the Mightiest raised me to contend,
100 And to the fierce contention brought along
Innumerable force of spirits armed,
That durst dislike his reign; and, me preferring,
His utmost power with adverse power opposed
In dubious battle on the plains of heaven,
105 And shook his throne. What though the field be
      lost?
All is not lost; th' unconquerable will,
And study° of revenge, immortal hate   *pursuit*
And courage never to submit or yield,
And what is else not to be overcome;
110 That glory never shall his wrath or might
Extort from me. To bow and sue for grace
With suppliant knee, and deify his power,
Who from the terror of this arm so late
Doubted° his empire, that were low indeed;   *Feared for*
115 That were an ignominy and shame beneath
This downfall; since, by fate, the strength of gods
And this empyreal° substance cannot fail;   *heavenly*
Since through experience of this great event,
In arms not worse, in foresight much advanced,
120 We may with more successful hope resolve
To wage by force or guile eternal war,
Irreconcileable to our grand foe,
Who now triumphs, and in th' excess of joy
Sole reigning holds the tyranny of heaven."

                                                        [1667]

"WHEN I CONSIDER HOW MY LIGHT IS SPENT"

When I consider how my light is spent[1]
   Ere half my days, in this dark world and wide,
   And that one talent° which is death to hide,   *i.e., writing*
   Lodged with me useless, though my soul more bent
5 To serve therewith my maker, and present
   My true account, lest he returning chide.
   "Doth God exact day-labor, light denied?"
   I fondly° ask; but patience, to prevent   *foolishly*
That murmur, soon replies, "God doth not need
10   Either man's work, or his own gifts; who best
   Bear his mild yoke, they serve him best: his state
Is kingly; thousands at his bidding speed,
   And post o'er land and ocean without rest;
   They also serve who only stand and wait."

                                                        [1673]

[1] Milton gradually lost his vision between 1644 and 1652.

ON THE LATE MASSACRE IN PIEDMONT.[1]

Avenge, O Lord, thy slaughtered saints, whose bones
    Lie scattered on the Alpine mountains cold;
    Even them who kept thy truth so pure of old,
    When all our fathers worshipped stocks and
        stones,°   *graven images*
5   Forget not: in thy book record their groans
    Who were thy sheep, and in their ancient fold
    Slain by the bloody Piemontese that rolled
    Mother with infant down the rocks. Their moans
The vales° redoubled to the hills, and they   *valleys*
10   To Heaven. Their martyred blood and ashes sow
    O'er all the Italian fields, where still doth sway
The triple tyrant;° that from these may grow   *the Pope*
    A hundred fold, who having learned thy way
    Early may fly the Babylonian woe.[2]

                                   [1673]

Sir John Suckling   *1609–1642*

WHY SO PALE AND WAN?

Why so pale and wan, fond lover?
    Prithee, why so pale?
Will, when looking well can't move her,
    Looking ill prevail?
5   Prithee, why so pale?

Why so dull and mute, young sinner?
    Prithee, why so mute?
Will, when speaking well can't win her,
    Saying nothing do 't?
10   Prithee, why so mute?

Quit, quit for shame? This will not move;
    This cannot take her.
If of herself she will not love,
    Nothing can make her:
15   The devil take her!

                                   [1638]

---

[1] On April 24, 1655, the Protestants living in the Alpine villages of the Piedmont (northern Italy and southern France) were slaughtered by the Catholic soldiers of neighboring Savoy.
[2] Milton and other puritans often associated the Catholic Church with the "whore of Babylon" (Revelations 17).

THE CONSTANT LOVER

Out upon it! I have loved
   Three whole days together!
And am like to love three more,
   If it prove fair weather.

5   Time shall moult away his wings
   Ere he shall discover
In the whole wide world again
   Such a constant lover.

But the spite° on 't is, no praise   *chagrin*
10   Is due at all to me:
Love with me had made no stays,
   Had it any been but she.

Had it any been but she,
   And that very face,
15 There had been at least ere this
   A dozen dozen in her place.
               [1659]

Richard Lovelace   *1618–1657*

TO LUCASTA, GOING TO THE WARS

Tell me not, sweet, I am unkind,
   That from the nunnery
Of thy chaste breast and quiet mind
   To war and arms I fly.

5 True, a new mistress now I chase,
   The first foe in the field;
And with a stronger faith embrace
   A sword, a horse, a shield.

Yet this inconstancy is such
10   As thou too shalt adore;
I could not love thee, dear, so much,
   Loved I not honor more.
             [1649]

TO ALTHEA, FROM PRISON

When Love with unconfinèd wings
   Hovers within my gates,
And my divine Althea brings
   To whisper at the grates;

5   When I lie tangled in her hair
      And fettered to her eye,
The birds that wanton in the air
      Know no such liberty.

When flowing cups run swiftly round
10   With no allaying Thames,[1]
Our careless heads with roses bound,
      Our hearts with loyal flames;
When thirsty grief in wine we steep,
      When healths and draughts go free—
15 Fishes that tipple in the deep
      Know no such liberty.

When, like committed° linnets,° I   *caged / songbirds*
      With shriller throat shall sing
The sweetness, mercy, majesty,
20   And glories of my King;
When I shall voice aloud how good
      He is, how great should be,
Enlargèd winds, that curl the flood,
      Know no such liberty.

25 Stone walls do not a prison make,
      Nor iron bars a cage;
Minds innocent and quiet take
      That for an hermitage;
If I have freedom in my love
30   And in my soul am free,
Angels alone, that soar above,
      Enjoy such liberty.

               [1649]

TO AMARANTHA, THAT SHE
WOULD DISHEVEL HER HAIR

Amarantha sweet and fair,
Ah, braid no more that shining hair!
As my curious hand or eye
Hovering round thee, let it fly!

Let it fly as unconfined
As its calm ravisher the wind,
Who hath left his darling, th' East,
To wanton o'er that spicy nest.

Every tress must be confest,
But neatly tangled at the best;
Like a clew° of golden thread
Most excellently ravellèd.

Do not then wind up that light
In ribbands, and o'ercloud in night,
Like the Sun in 's early ray;
But shake your head, and scatter day!
               [1649]

[1] I.e., undiluted with water.

See, 'tis broke! Within this grove,
The bower and the walks of love,
Weary lie we down and rest
And fan each other's panting breast.

Here we'll strip and cool our fire
In cream below, in milk-baths higher;
And when all wells are drawn dry,
I'll drink a tear out of thine eye,

Which our very joys shall leave,
That sorrows thus we can deceive;
Or our very sorrows weep,
That joys so ripe so little keep.

[1649]

Andrew Marvell   *1621–1678*

TO HIS COY MISTRESS

— unwilling girl
— he tries to
"put the moves
on her"

Had we but world enough, and time,
This coyness, lady, were no crime
We would sit down and think which way
To walk, and pass our long love's day.
5   Thou by the Indian Ganges' side
Shouldst rubies find: I by the tide
Of Humber[1] would complain. I would
Love you ten years before the Flood,
And you should, if you please, refuse

flatters her
slow language

10 Till the conversion of the Jews.[2]
My vegetable love should grow
Vaster than empires, and more slow;
An hundred years should go to praise
Thine eyes and on thy forehead gaze;
15 Two hundred to adore each breast,
But thirty thousand to the rest;
An age at least to every part,
And the last age should show your heart.
For, lady, you deserve this state,[3]
20 Nor would I love at lower rate.

dangers + threats

    But at my back I always hear
Time's wingèd chariot hurrying near;
And yonder all before us lie
Deserts of vast eternity.
25 Thy beauty shall no more be found,
Nor, in thy marble vault, shall sound

[1] The Humber River flowing past Hull, a city in the North of England, where Marvell lived.
[2] According to traditional Christian beliefs, this is to take place just before the Last Judgment.
[3] Stateliness.

*trying
to scale
her—
death*

(My echoing song: then worms shall try
That long preserved virginity,
)And your quaint honor turn to dust,
30 And into ashes all my lust:
The grave's a fine and private place,
But none, I think, do there embrace.
Now therefore, while the youthful hue
Sits on thy skin like morning dew,
35 And while thy willing soul transpires
At every pore with instant fires,[4]

*okay let's
get to it*

Now let us sport us while we may,
And now, like amorous birds of prey,
Rather at once our time devour

*what
to do
about
it*

40 Than languish in his slow-chapt[5] power.
Let us roll all our strength and all
Our sweetness up into one ball,
And tear our pleasures with rough strife
Thorough the iron gates of life:
45 Thus, though we cannot make our sun
Stand still, yet we will make him run.

                    [posthumous, 1681]

THE DEFINITION OF LOVE

My love is of a birth as rare
As 'tis, for object, strange and high;
It was begotten by despair,
Upon impossibility.

5 Magnanimous despair alone
Could show me so divine a thing,
Where feeble hope could ne'er have flown,
But vainly flapped its tinsel wing.

And yet I quickly might arrive
10 Where my extended soul is fixed;[1]
But fate does iron wedges drive,
And always crowds itself betwixt.

For fate with jealous eye does see
Two perfect loves, nor lets them close,[2]
15 Their union would her ruin be,
And her tyrannic power depose.

---

[4] I.e., while your willing soul reveals itself through your blushes ("instant fires").
[5] Slow-jawed—hence, slowly destroying.
[1] Marvell imagines his soul extending out and fixed upon his mistress.   [2] Come together.

And therefore her decrees of steel
Us as the distant poles have placed,
(Though Love's whole world on us doth wheel)
20   Not by themselves to be embraced,

Unless the giddy heaven fall,
And earth some new convulsion tear,
And, us to join, the world should all
Be cramped into a planisphere.[3]

25   As lines, so loves oblique may well
Themselves in every angle greet:[4]
But ours, so truly parallel,
Though infinite, can never meet.

Therefore the love which us doth bind,
30   But fate so enviously debars,
Is the conjunction of the mind,
And opposition of the stars.

                  [posthumous, *1681*]

John Dryden   *1631–1700*

ALEXANDER'S FEAST

or, The Power of Music;
An Ode in Honour of St. Cecilia's Day

'Twas at the royal feast for Persia won
    By Philip's warlike son:[1]
    Aloft in awful state
    The godlike hero sate
5   On his imperial throne:
His valiant peers were placed around;
Their brows with roses and with myrtles bound:
    (So should desert in arms be crowned.)
The lovely Thais, by his side,
10   Sat like a blooming Eastern bride
In flower of youth and beauty's pride.

---

[3] A sphere flattened so that the north and south poles touch.
[4] Oblique or non-parallel lines eventually intersect, just as imperfect, sinful lovers do.
[1] Alexander the Great (356–323 B.C.), son of King Philip II of Macedonia, defeated the Persian Emperor Darius III and occupied his capital city in 331 B.C.

Happy, happy, happy pair!
None but the brave,
None but the brave,
15   None but the brave deserves the fair.

CHORUS

Happy, happy, happy pair!
None but the brave,
None but the brave,
None but the brave deserves the fair.

II

20   Timotheus, placed on high
         Amid the tuneful choir,
         With flying fingers touched the lyre:
The trembling notes ascend the sky,
25   And heavenly joys inspire.
The song began from Jove,[2]
Who left his blissful seats above,
(Such is the power of mighty love.)
A dragon's fiery form belied the god:
Sublime on radiant spires° he rode,   *shining coils*
30   When he to fair Olympia pressed;
         And while he sought her snowy breast:
Then, round her slender waist he curled,
And stamped an image of himself, a sovereign of the
         world.
The listening crowd admire° the lofty sound;   *marvel at*
35 "A present deity," they shout around;
"A present deity," the vaulted roofs rebound:
         With ravished ears
         The monarch hears,
         Assumes the god,
40   Affects to nod,
And seems to shake the spheres.[3]

CHORUS

With ravished ears
The monarch hears,
Assumes the god,
45   *Affects to nod,*
And seems to shake the spheres.

III

The praise of Bacchus[4] then the sweet musician sung,
Of Bacchus ever fair and ever young:

[2] Here and in the subsequent lines Timotheus relates the mythological account of Alexander's birth. Supposedly, Jove in the form of a dragon mated with Alexander's mother, Olympias.
[3] The nods of Jove were thought to cause earthquakes ("shake the spheres").
[4] The Roman name of the god of wine (Dionysos in Greek).

"The jolly god in triumph comes;
50   Sound the trumpets; beat the drums;
                Flushed with a purple grace
                He shows his honest face:
     Now give the hautboys° breath; he comes, he comes.   *oboes*
                Bacchus, ever fair and young.
55   Drinking joys did first ordain;
                Bacchus' blessings are a treasure,
                Drinking is the soldier's pleasure:
                   Rich the treasure,
                   Sweet the pleasure,
60   Sweet is pleasure after pain."

                                   CHORUS
                    Bacchus' blessings are a treasure,
                    Drinking is the soldier's pleasure:
                       Rich the treasure,
                       Sweet the pleasure,
65   *Sweet is pleasure after pain.*

                                     IV
          Soothed with the sound, the king grew vain;
                Fought all his battles o'er again;
          And thrice he routed all his foes; and thrice he slew
                         the slain.
                The master[5] saw the madness rise;
70   His glowing cheeks, his ardent eyes;
          And, while he heaven and earth defied,
          Changed his hand and checked his pride.
                He chose a mournful Muse,
                   Soft pity to infuse:
75   He sung Darius great and good,
                   By too severe a fate,
          Fallen, fallen, fallen, fallen,
                   Fallen from his high estate,
                      And weltering in his blood;
80   Deserted, at his utmost need,
          By those his former bounty fed;
          On the bare earth exposed he lies,
          With not a friend to close his eyes.
          With downcast looks the joyless victor sate,
85   Revolving in his altered soul
                The various turns of chance below;
                And, now and then, a sigh he stole;
                And tears began to flow.

[5] Timotheus.

CHORUS

Revolving in his altered soul
90   *The various turns of chance below;*
And, now and then, a sigh he stole;
And tears began to flow.

V

The mighty master smiled, to see
That love was in the next degree:
95 'Twas but a kindred sound to move,
For pity melts the mind to love.
    Softly sweet, in Lydian measures,[6]
    Soon he soothed his soul to pleasures.
    "War," he sung, "is toil and trouble;
100   Honor but an empty bubble.
      Never ending, still beginning,
    Fighting still, and still destroying,
      If the world be worth thy winning,
    Think, O think it worth enjoying.
105   Lovely Thais sits beside thee,
    Take the good the gods provide thee."
The many rend the skies with loud applause;
So Love was crowned, but Music won the cause.
The prince, unable to conceal his pain,
110   Gazed on the fair
      Who caused his care,
    And sighed and looked, sighed and looked,
Sighed and looked, and sighed again:
At length, with love and wine at once oppressed,
115 The vanquished victor sunk upon her breast.

CHORUS

The prince, unable to conceal his pain,
    Gazed on the fair
    Who caused his care,
    And sighed and looked, sighed and looked,
120 *Sighed and looked, and sighed again:*
At length, with love and wine at once oppressed,
The vanquished victor sunk upon her breast.

VI

Now strike the golden lyre again:
A louder yet, and yet a louder strain.
125 Break his bands of sleep asunder,
And rouse him, like a rattling peal of thunder.
    Hark, hark, the horrid sound
      Has raised up his head:
      As awaked from the dead,
130   And amazed, he stares around.

---

[6] Soft and voluptuous melodies.

"Revenge, revenge!" Timotheus cries,
    "See the Furies[7] arise!
    See the snakes that they rear,
    How they hiss in their hair,
135   And the sparkles that flash from their eyes!
    Behold a ghastly band,
    Each a torch in his hand!
Those are Grecian ghosts that in battle were slain,
    And unburied remain
140   Inglorious on the plain:
    Give the vengeance due
    To the valiant crew.
Behold how they toss their torches on high,
    How they point to the Persian abodes,
145 And glittering temples of their hostile gods!"
The princes applaud with a furious joy;
And the king seized a flambeau° with zeal to destroy;   *torch*
    Thais led the way,
    To light him to his prey,
150 And, like another Helen, fired another Troy.[8]

CHORUS

And the king seized a flambeau with zeal to destroy;
    Thais led the way,
    To light him to his prey,
And, like another Helen, fired another Troy.

VII

155   Thus, long ago,
    Ere heaving bellows learned to blow,
    While organs yet were mute;
    Timotheus, to his breathing flute,
    And sounding lyre,
160 Could swell the soul to rage or kindle soft desire.
    At last, divine Cecilia[9] came,
    Inventress of the vocal frame,°   *organ*
The sweet enthusiast, from her sacred store,
    Enlarged the former narrow bounds,
165   And added length[10] to solemn sounds,
With nature's mother wit and arts unknown before.
    Let old Timotheus yield the prize,
    Or both divide the crown;
    He raised a mortal to the skies;
170   She drew an angel down.[11]

---

[7] The snaky-haired female spirits of revenge.
[8] Having married Menelaus (a Greek king), Helen eloped with Paris (a Trojan prince), providing the cause for the wars celebrated by the poet Homer that ultimately led to the burning of Troy.
[9] The patron saint of music.   [10] I.e., lengthy, sustained notes from the organ.
[11] The beauty of St. Cecilia's music was said to have drawn an angel down to earth, thinking that such beautiful music could only have come from heaven.

GRAND CHORUS

At last, divine Cecilia came,
Inventress of the vocal frame;
The sweet enthusiast, from her sacred store,
Enlarged the former narrow bounds,
175 *And added length to solemn sounds,*
With nature's mother wit and arts unknown before.
Let old Timotheus yield the prize,
Or both divide the crown;
He raised a mortal to the skies;
180 *She drew an angel down.*

[1697]

❧ EIGHTEENTH CENTURY POETRY ❧

Jonathan Swift   *1667–1745*

A DESCRIPTION OF THE MORNING

Now hardly here and there a hackney-coach°   *carriage for hire*
Appearing, showed the ruddy morn's approach.
Now Betty from her master's bed had flown,
And softly stole to discompose her own;
5 The slip-shod 'prentice from his master's door
Had pared° the dirt and sprinkled° round the floor.   *diminished / moistened*
Now Moll had whirled her mop with dext'rous airs,
Prepared to scrub the entry and the stairs.
The youth with broomy stumps began to trace°   *search for old nails*
10 The kennel-edge,° where wheels had worn the place.   *gutter*
The small-coal man° was heard with cadence deep,   *charcoal vendor*
Till drowned in shriller notes of chimney-sweep:
Duns° at his lordship's gate began to meet;   *bill collectors*
And brickdust Moll had screamed through half
    the street.[1]
15 The turnkey now his flock returning sees,
Duly let out a-nights to steal for fees:[2]
The watchful bailiffs take their silent stands,
And schoolboys lag with satchels in their hands.

                           [1709]

John Gay   *1685–1732*

MY OWN EPITAPH

Life is a jest; and all things show it.
I thought so once; but now I know it.
                [1720]

---

[1] Moll sells brick dust for use as a scouring powder.
[2] The jailer lets his prisoners out to steal during the night and then collects a fee from them as they return in the morning.

THE MAN AND THE FLEA

Whether on earth, in air, or main,°   *open sea*
Sure every thing alive is vain!
  Does not the hawk all fowls survey,
As destined only for his prey?
5 And do not tyrants, prouder things,
Think men were born for slaves to kings?
  When the crab views the pearly strands,°   *beaches*
Or Tagus,[1] bright with golden sands,
Or crawls beside the coral grove,
10 And hears the ocean roll above;
"Nature is too profuse," says he,
"Who gave all these to pleasure me!"
  When bord'ring pinks and roses bloom,
And every garden breaths perfume,
15 When peaches glow with sunny dyes,
Like Laura's cheek, when blushes rise;
When with huge figs the branches bend;
When clusters from the vine depend;
The snail looks round on flower and tree,
20 And cries, "All these were made for me!"

  "What dignity's in human nature,"
Says Man, the most conceited creature,
As from a cliff he cast his eye,
And viewed the sea and arched sky!
25 The sun was sunk beneath the main,
The moon, and all the starry train
Hung the vast vault of heaven. The Man
His contemplation thus began.
  "When I behold this glorious show,
30 And the wide watry world below,
The scaly people of the main,
The beasts that range the wood or plain,
The winged inhabitants of air,
The day, the night, the various year,
35 And know all these by heaven designed
As gifts to pleasure human kind,
I cannot raise my worth too high;
Of what vast consequence am I!"
  "Not of th' importance you suppose,"
40 Replies a Flea upon his nose:
"Be humble, learn thyself to scan;°   *analyze*
Know, pride was never made for man.
'Tis vanity that swells thy mind.
What, heaven and earth for thee designed!
45 For thee! Made only for our need;
That more important Fleas might feed."

[1727]

[1] The Tagus River flows through central Spain and Portugal to the Atlantic.

Alexander Pope   *1688–1744*

AN ESSAY ON CRITICISM

FROM *Part 2*

A little learning is a dangerous thing;
Drink deep, or taste not the Pierian spring.[1]
There shallow draughts intoxicate the brain,
And drinking largely sobers us again.
Fired at first sight with what the Muse imparts,
220 In fearless youth we tempt the heights of arts,
While from the bounded level of our mind,
Short views we take, nor see the lengths behind,
But more advanced, behold with strange surprise
New, distant scenes of endless science° rise!   *knowledge*
225 So pleased at first, the towering Alps we try,
Mount o'er the vales, and seem to tread the sky;
The eternal snows appear already past,
And the first clouds and mountains seem the last:
But those attained, we tremble to survey
230 The growing labors of the lengthened way,
The increasing prospect tires our wandering eyes,
Hills peep o'er hills, and Alps on Alps arise!
. . . .

True ease in writing comes from art, not chance,
As those move easiest who have learned to dance.
'Tis not enough no harshness gives offence,
365 The sound must seem an echo to the sense.
Soft is the strain when Zephyr° gently blows,   *the west wind*
And the smooth stream in smoother numbers flows;
But when loud surges lash the sounding shore,
The hoarse, rough verse should like the torrent roar.
370 When Ajax[2] strives, some rock's vast weight to throw,
The line too labours, and the words move slow;
Not so, when swift Camilla[3] scours the plain,
Flies o'er the unbending corn, and skims along the
main.
Hear how Timotheus'[4] varied lays surprise,
375 And bid alternate passions fall and rise!
While, at each change, the son of Libyan Jove[5]
Now burns with glory, and then melts with love;
Now his fierce eyes with sparkling fury glow;
Now sighs steal out, and tears begin to flow:
380 Persians and Greeks like turns° of nature° found,   *changes / mood*
And the world's victor stood subdued by sound!

[1] A spring sacred to the Muses.   [2] A hero in the *Iliad* celebrated for his strength.
[3] A heroine in the *Aeneid.*   [4] See "Alexander's Feast," p. 714.   [5] Alexander the Great.

The power of music all our hearts allow,
And what Timotheus was, is Dryden now.

[1711]

AN ESSAY ON MAN

FROM *Epistle II*

I. Know then thyself, presume not God to scan;°   *scrutinize*
The proper study of mankind is Man.
Placed on this isthmus of a middle state,
A being darkly wise, and rudely° great;   *crudely*
5   With too much knowledge for the Sceptic side,
With too much weakness for the Stoic's pride,
He hangs between; in doubt to act, or rest,
In doubt to deem himself a god, or beast;
In doubt his mind or body to prefer,
10 Born but to die, and reasoning but to err;
Alike in ignorance, his reason such,
Whether he thinks too little, or too much:
Chaos of thought and passion, all confused;
Still by himself abused, or disabused;
15 Created half to rise, and half to fall;
Great lord of all things, yet a prey to all;
Sole judge of truth, in endless error hurled:
The glory, jest, and riddle of the world!

[1733]

Thomas Gray   *1716–1771*

ELEGY WRITTEN IN A COUNTRY CHURCHYARD

The curfew tolls the knell of parting day,
   The lowing herd wind slowly o'er the lea,°   *meadow*
The plowman homeward plods his weary way,
   And leaves the world to darkness and to me.

5 Now fades the glimmering landscape on the sight,
   And all the air a solemn stillness holds,
Save where the beetle wheels his droning flight,
   And drowsy tinklings lull the distant folds;

Save that from yonder ivy-mantled tower
    The moping owl does to the moon complain
Of such as, wand'ring near her secret bower,
    Molest her ancient solitary reign.

Beneath those rugged elms, the yew-tree's shade,
    Where heaves the turf in many a mould'ring heap,
Each in his narrow cell for ever laid,
    The rude° forefathers of the hamlet sleep.   *rugged*

The breezy call of incense-breathing Morn,
    The swallow twitt'ring from the straw-built shed,
The cock's shrill clarion, or the echoing horn,
    No more shall rouse them from their lowly bed.

For them no more the blazing hearth shall burn,
    Or busy housewife ply her evening care:
No children run to lisp their sire's return,
    Or climb his knees the envied kiss to share.

Oft did the harvest to their sickle yield,
    Their furrow oft the stubborn glebe° has broke: *field*
How jocund did they drive their team afield!
    How bowed the woods beneath their sturdy stroke!

Let not Ambition mock their useful toil,
    Their homely joys, and destiny obscure;
Nor Grandeur hear with a disdainful smile
    The short and simple annals of the poor.

The boast of heraldry, the pomp of power,
    And all that beauty, all that wealth e'er gave,
Awaits alike th' inevitable hour:
    The paths of glory lead but to the grave.

Nor you, ye proud, impute to these the fault,
    If Memory o'er their tomb no trophies° rise,   *monuments*
Where through the long-drawn aisle and fretted° vault   *decorated*
    The pealing anthem swells the note of praise.

Can storied urn or animated° bust   *lifelike*
    Back to its mansion call the fleeting breath?
Can Honor's voice provoke° the silent dust,   *arouse*
    Or Flatt'ry soothe the dull cold ear of death?

Perhaps in this neglected spot is laid
    Some heart once pregnant with celestial fire;
Hands, that the rod of empire might have swayed,
    Or waked to ecstasy the living lyre.

But Knowledge to their eyes her ample page
    Rich with the spoils of time did ne'er unroll;
50 Chill Penury° repressed their noble rage,   *poverty*
    And froze the genial current of the soul.

Full many a gem of purest ray serene
    The dark unfathomed caves of ocean bear:
55 Full many a flower is born to blush unseen,
    And waste its sweetness on the desert air.

Some village Hampden[1] that with dauntless breast
    The little tyrant of his fields withstood,
Some mute inglorious Milton here may rest,
60   Some Cromwell guiltless of his country's blood.

Th' applause of list'ning senates to command,
    The threats of pain and ruin to despise,
To scatter plenty o'er a smiling land,
    And read their history in a nation's eyes,

65 Their lot forbade; nor circumscribed alone
    Their growing virtues, but their crimes confined;
Forbade to wade through slaughter to a throne.
    And shut the gates of mercy on mankind,

The struggling pangs of conscious truth to hide,
70   To quench the blushes of ingenuous shame,
Or heap the shrine of Luxury and Pride
    With incense kindled at the Muse's flame.

Far from the madding° crowd's ignoble strife   *raving*
    Their sober wishes never learned to stray;
75 Along the cool sequestered vale of life
    They kept the noiseless tenor of their way.

Yet even these bones from insult to protect
    Some frail memorial still erected nigh,
With uncouth rhymes and shapeless sculpture decked,°   *decorated*
80   Implores the passing tribute of a sigh.

Their name, their years, spelt by th' unlettered muse,
    The place of fame and elegy supply:
And many a holy text around she strews,
    That teach the rustic moralist to die.

---

[1] John Hampden (1594–1643), a member of the English House of Commons, forcefully opposed Charles I. John Milton (1608–1674), the author of *Paradise Lost,* wrote vigorously against the divine right of kings to rule and became Cromwell's spokesman. Oliver Cromwell (1599–1658) led the forces that deposed Charles I; he subsequently became the puritan dictator of England.

85 For who, to dumb Forgetfulness a prey,
        This pleasing anxious being e'er resigned,
    Left the warm precincts of the cheerful day,
        Nor cast one longing lingering look behind?

    On some fond breast the parting soul relies,
90   Some pious drops the closing eye requires;
    E'en from the tomb the voice of Nature cries,
        E'en in our ashes live their wonted fires.

    For thee, who, mindful of th' unhonored dead,
        Dost in these lines their artless tale relate;
95 If chance, by lonely contemplation led,
        Some kindred spirit shall inquire thy fate,

    Haply some hoary-headed° swain may say,   *gray-haired*
        "Oft have we seen him at the peep of dawn
    Brushing with hasty steps the dews away
100   To meet the sun upon the upland lawn.

    "There at the foot of yonder nodding beech
        That wreathes its old fantastic roots so high,
    His listless length at noontide would he stretch,
        And pore upon the brook that babbles by.

105 "Hard by yon wood, now smiling as in scorn,
        Mutt'ring his wayward fancies he would rove,
    Now drooping, woeful wan, like one forlorn,
        Or crazed with care, or crossed in hopeless love.

    "One morn I missed him on the customed hill,
110   Along the heath and near his fav'rite tree;
    Another came; nor yet beside the rill,
        Nor up the lawn, nor at the wood was he;

    "The next with dirges due in sad array
        Slow through the church-way path we saw him borne.
115 Approach and read (for thou canst read) the lay
        Graved on the stone beneath yon agèd thorn:"

The Epitaph

Here rests his head upon the lap of Earth
    A youth to Fortune and to Fame unknown.
Fair Science° frowned not on his humble birth,   *knowledge*
120 *And Melancholy marked him for her own.*

Large was his bounty, and his soul sincere,
    Heaven did a recompense as largely send:
He gave to Mis'ry all he had, a tear,
    He gained from Heaven ('twas all he wished) a friend.

125 *No farther seek his merits to disclose,*
    Or draw his frailties from their dread abode
(There they alike in trembling hope repose),
    The bosom of his Father and his God.

[1751]

William Blake   *1757–1827*

FROM *Songs of Innocence*

THE LITTLE BLACK BOY

My mother bore me in the southern wild,
    And I am black, but O, my soul is white!
White as an angel is the English child,
    But I am black, as if bereaved° of light.   *robbed*

5 My mother taught me underneath a tree,
    And, sitting down before the heat of day,
She took me on her lap and kissèd me,
    And, pointing to the east, began to say:

"Look at the rising sun: there God does live,
10   And gives his light, and gives his heat away,
And flowers and trees and beasts and men receive
    Comfort in morning, joy in the noonday.

"And we are put on earth a little space,
    That we may learn to bear the beams of love;
15 And these black bodies and this sunburnt face
    Are but a cloud, and like a shady grove.

"For when our souls have learned the heat to bear,
    The cloud will vanish, we shall hear his voice,
Saying, 'Come out from the grove, my love and care,
20   And round my golden tent like lambs rejoice.'"

Thus did my mother say, and kissèd me,
    And thus I say to little English boy.
When I from black and he from white cloud free,
    And round the tent of God like lambs we joy,

25 I'll shade him from the heat till he can bear
    To lean in joy upon our Father's knee;
And then I'll stand and stroke his silver hair,
    And be like him, and he will then love me.

[1789]

THE CHIMNEY SWEEPER

[handwritten: Persona— Orphan Chimney sweep / Childlike rhyme / Sacrifice]

When my mother died I was very young,
And my father sold me while yet my tongue
Could scarcely cry " 'weep! 'weep! 'weep! 'weep!"
So your chimneys I sweep and in soot I sleep.

[handwritten: Persona tries to make best of everything / Optimistic]

There's little Tom Dacre, who cried when his head
That curled like a lamb's back, was shaved, so I said,
"Hush, Tom! never mind it, for when your head's bare,
You know that the soot cannot spoil your white hair."

And so he was quiet, and that very night,
As Tom was a-sleeping he had such a sight!
10 That thousands of sweepers, Dick, Joe, Ned, and Jack,
Were all of them locked up in coffins of black;

And by came an angel who had a bright key,
And he opened the coffins and set them all free;
15 Then down a green plain, leaping, laughing they run,
And wash in a river and shine in the sun;

Then naked and white, all their bags left behind,
They rise upon clouds and sport in the wind.
And the angel told Tom, if he'd be a good boy,
20 He'd have God for his father and never want joy.

And so Tom awoke; and we rose in the dark
And got with our bags and our brushes to work.
Tho' the morning was cold, Tom was happy and warm;
So if all do their duty, they need not fear harm.

[1789]

[handwritten: Child is innocent]

FROM *Songs of Experience*

THE CHIMNEY SWEEPER

[handwritten: observer / Irony]

A little black thing among the snow:
Crying weep, weep, in notes of woe!
Where are thy father and mother? Say?
They are both gone up to the church to pray.

5 Because I was happy upon the heath,
And smiled among the winter's snow:
They clothed me in the clothes of death,
And taught me to sing the notes of woe.

And because I am happy, and dance and sing,
10 They think they have done me no injury:
And are gone to praise God and his priest and king
Who make up a heaven of our misery.

[1794]

Eng. is religious but look at conditions'.

THE SICK ROSE

O Rose thou art sick.
The invisible worm,
That flies in the night
In the howling storm:

5 Has found out thy bed
Of crimson joy:
And his dark secret love
Does thy life destroy.

[1794]

THE TYGER

Tyger, Tyger, burning bright
In the forests of the night,
What immortal hand or eye
Could frame thy fearful symmetry?

5 In what distant deeps or skies
Burnt the fire of thine eyes?
On what wings dare he aspire?
What the hand dare seize the fire?

And what shoulder and what art
10 Could twist the sinews of thy heart?
And, when thy heart began to beat,
What dread hand and what dread feet?

What the hammer? What the chain?
In what furnace was thy brain?
15 What the anvil? What dread grasp
Dare its deadly terrors clasp?

When the stars threw down their spears,
And watered heaven with their tears,
Did He smile his work to see?
20 Did He who made the lamb make thee?

Tyger, Tyger, burning bright
In the forests of the night,
What immortal hand or eye?
Dare frame thy fearful symmetry?

[1794]

LONDON

I wander thro' each chartered street,
Near where the chartered° Thames does flow.   *bound*
And mark in every face I meet
Marks of weakness, marks of woe.

5   In every cry of every man,
In every infant's cry of fear,
In every voice: in every ban,
The mind-forged manacles I hear.

How the chimney-sweeper's cry
10   Every blackning church appalls,
And the hapless soldier's sigh,
Runs in blood down palace walls.

But most thro' midnight streets I hear
How the youthful harlot's curse
15   Blasts the new-born infant's tear
And blights with plagues the marriage hearse.

[1794]

A POISON TREE

I was angry with my friend:
I told my wrath, my wrath did
    end.
I was angry with my foe:
I told it not, my wrath did grow.

5   And I watered it in fears,
Night and morning with my tears;
And I sunnèd it with smiles,
And with soft deceitful wiles.

And it grew both day and night,
10   Till it bore an apple bright.
And my foe beheld it shine,
And he knew that it was mine,

And into my garden stole,
When the night had veiled the
    pole;
15   In the morning glad I see
My foe outstretched beneath the
    tree.

[1794]

Robert Burns   *1759–1796*

TO A MOUSE, ON TURNING HER UP IN HER NEST
WITH THE PLOUGH, NOVEMBER, 1785

Wee, sleekit,° cow'rin', tim'rous beastie,   *sleek*
O what a panic's in thy breastie!

Thou need na start awa sae hasty,
     Wi' bickering brattle!°   *scamper*
5 I wad be laith to rin an' chase thee
     Wi' murd'ring pattle!

I'm truly sorry man's dominion
Has broken Nature's social union,
An' justifies that ill opinion
10   Which makes thee startle
At me, thy poor earth-born companion,
     An' fellow-mortal!

I doubt na, whiles,° but thou may thieve;   *at times*
What then? poor beastie, thou maun live!
15 A daimen-icker° in a thrave°   *odd ear / thousand*
     'S a sma' request:
I'll get a blessin' wi' the lave,°   *remnant*
     And never miss 't!

Thy wee bit housie, too, in ruin!
20 Its silly wa's° the win's are strewin'!   *walls*
An' naething, now, to big° a new ane,   *build*
     O' foggage° green!   *foliage*
An' bleak December's winds ensuin',
     Baith snell° an' keen!   *bitter*

25 Thou saw the fields laid bare and waste.
An' weary winter comin' fast,
An' cozie here, beneath the blast,
     Thou thought to dwell,
Till crash! the cruel coulter° past   *plow*
30   Out-thro' thy cell.

That wee bit heap o' leaves an' stibble
Has cost thee mony a weary nibble!
Now thou's turn'd out, for a' thy trouble,
     But° house or hald,°   *Without / hold*
35 To thole° the winter's sleety dribble,   *suffer*
     An' cranreuch° cauld!   *frozen dew*

But, Mousie, thou art no thy lane,°   *not alone*
In proving foresight may be vain:
The best laid schemes o' mice an' men
40   Gang aft a-gley,°   *awry*
An' lea'e us nought but grief an' pain
     For promis'd joy.

Still thou art blest compar'd wi' me!
The present only toucheth thee:
45 But oh! I backward cast my e'e
     On prospects drear!
An' forward tho' I canna see,
     I guess an' fear!
                [1786]

TAM O' SHANTER

When chapman billies° leave the street,	*fellow peddlers*
And drouthy° neibors° neibors meet,	*thirsty / neighbors*
As market-days are wearing late,	
An' folk begin to tak the gate;	
5 While we sit bousing at the nappy,°	*ale*
An' getting fou° and unco° happy,	*drunk / very*
We think na on the lang Scots miles,	
The mosses, waters, slaps,° and styles,°	*gates / steps over walls*
That lie between us and our hame,	
10 Where sits our sulky sullen dame,	
Gathering her brows like gathering storm,	
Nursing her wrath to keep it warm.	
This truth fand honest Tam o' Shanter,	
As he frae Ayr[1] ae night did canter—	
15 (Auld Ayr, wham ne'er a town surpasses	
For honest men and bonnie lasses).	
O Tam! hadst thou but been sae wise	
As ta'en thy ain wife Kate's advice!	
She tauld thee weel thou was a skellum,°	*bum*
20 A bletherin', blusterin', drunken blellum,°	*babbler*
That frae November till October,	
Ae market-day thou was na sober;	
That ilka° melder° wi' the miller	*each / load of grain*
Thou sat as lang as thou had siller;°	*silver*
25 That every naig° was ca'd° a shoe on,	*nag / hammered*
The smith and thee gat roarin' fou on;	
That at the Lord's house, even on Sunday,	
Thou drank wi' Kirkton Jean till Monday.	
She prophesied that, late or soon,	
30 Thou would be found deep drown'd in Doon;[2]	
Or catch'd wi' warlocks in the mirk	
By Alloway's auld haunted kirk.	
Ah, gentle dames! it gars me greet°	*makes me weep*
To think how mony counsels sweet,	
35 How mony lengthen'd sage advices,	
The husband frae the wife despises!	
But to our tale: Ae market night,	
Tam had got planted unco right,	
Fast by an ingle,° bleezing° finely,	*fireplace / blazing*
40 Wi' reaming swats,° that drank divinely;	*foaming ale*
And at his elbow, Souter° Johnny,	*Cobbler*
His ancient, trusty, drouthy crony;	
Tam lo'ed him like a very brither;	
They had been fou for weeks thegither.	
45 The night drave on wi' sangs and clatter.	
And aye the ale was growing better:	

---

[1] A county seat in southwestern Scotland.
[2] The River Doon that flows by Alloway church ("kirk").

The landlady and Tam grew gracious,
Wi' favours secret, sweet, and precious;
The souter tauld his queerest stories;
50 The landlord's laugh was ready chorus:
The storm without might rair and rustle,
Tam did na mind the storm a whistle.
   Care, mad to see a man sae happy,
E'en drown'd himsel amang the nappy.
55 As bees flee hame wi' lades° o' treasure,   *loads*
The minutes wing'd their way wi' pleasure;
Kings may be blest, but Tam was glorious,
O'er a' the ills o' life victorious!
   But pleasures are like poppies spread—
60 You seize the flow'r, its bloom is shed;
Or like the snow falls in the river—
A moment white, then melts for ever;
Or like the borealis³ race,
That flit ere you can point their place;
65 Or like the rainbow's lovely form
Evanishing amid the storm.
Nae man can tether time nor tide;
The hour approaches Tam maun° ride;   *must*
That hour, o' night's black arch the key-stane,
70 That dreary hour, he mounts his beast in;
And sic a night he taks the road in,
As ne'er poor sinner was abroad in.
   The wind blew as 'twad blawn its last;
The rattling show'rs rose on the blast;
75 The speedy gleams the darkness swallow'd;
Loud, deep, and lang, the thunder bellow'd:
That night, a child might understand,
The Deil had business on his hand.
   Weel mounted on his gray mare, Meg,
80 A better never lifted leg,
Tam skelpit° on thro' dub° and mire,   *hurried / puddle*
Despising wind, and rain, and fire;
Whiles holding fast his gude blue bonnet;
Whiles crooning o'er some auld Scots sonnet;
85 Whiles glow'ring round wi' prudent cares,
Lest bogles° catch him unawares.   *goblins*
Kirk-Alloway was drawing nigh,
Whare ghaists and houlets° nightly cry.   *owls*
   By this time he was cross the ford,
90 Where in the snaw the chapman smoor'd;°   *peddler smothered*
And past the birks° and meikle stane,°   *birches / huge stone*
Where drunken Charlie brak's neck-bane;
And thro' the whins,° and by the cairn,°   *shrubs / heap of stones*
Where hunters fand the murder'd bairn;°   *child*

---

³ Northern lights.

95   And near the thorn, aboon the well,
       Where Mungo's mither hang'd hersel.
       Before him Doon pours all his floods;
       The doubling storm roars thro' the woods;
       The lightnings flash from pole to pole;
100   Near and more near the thunders roll:
       When, glimmering thro' the groaning trees,
       Kirk-Alloway seem'd in a bleeze;
       Thro' ilka bore° the beams were glancing;   *chink*
       And loud resounded mirth and dancing.
105   Inspiring bold John Barleycorn![4]
       What dangers thou canst make us scorn!
       Wi' tippenny,° we fear nae evil;   *twopenny ale*
       Wi' usquebae,° we'll face the devil!   *whisky*
       The swats sae ream'd in Tammie's noddle,
110   Fair play, he car'd na deils a boddle![5]
       But Maggie stood right sair° astonish'd,   *sore (= very)*
       Till, by the heel and hand admonish'd,
       She ventur'd forward on the light;
       And, vow! Tam saw an unco° sight!   *strange*
115   Warlocks and witches in a dance!
       Nae cotillon brent new frae° France,   *brand new from*
       But hornpipes, jigs, strathspeys,[6] and reels,
       Put life and mettle in their heels.
       A winnock-bunker° in the east,   *window seat*
120   There sat auld Nick, in shape o' beast—
       A touzie tyke,° black, grim, and large!   *shaggy cur*
       To gie them music was his charge:
       He screw'd the pipes and gart them skirl.[7]
       Till roof and rafters a' did dirl.°   *vibrate*
125   Coffins stood round like open presses,
       That shaw'd the dead in their last dresses:
       And by some devilish cantraip° sleight   *magic*
       Each in its cauld hand held a light,
       By which heroic Tam was able
130   To note upon the haly table
       A murderer's banes in gibbet-airns;°   *gallows chains*
       Twa span-lang,° wee, unchristen'd bairns;   *span-long (about 9″)*
       A thief new-cutted frae the rape—
       Wi' his last gasp his gab° did gape;   *mouth*
135   Five tomahawks, wi' blude red rusted;
       Five scymitars, wi' murder crusted;
       A garter, which a babe had strangled;
       A knife, a father's throat had mangled,
       Whom his ain son o' life bereft—
140   The gray hairs yet stack to the heft;
       Wi' mair of horrible and awfu',
       Which even to name wad be unlawfu'.

---

[4] A personification of ale.   [5] In truth, he cared not a bit for devils!
[6] A lively Scottish dance for couples.   [7] He twisted the bagpipes and made them shriek.

As Tammie glowr'd, amaz'd, and curious,
The mirth and fun grew fast and furious:
145 The piper loud and louder blew;
The dancers quick and quicker flew;
They reel'd, they set, they cross'd, they cleekit,°   *linked arms*
Till ilka carlin° swat and reekit,   *hag*
And coost her duddies to the wark,[8]
150 And linkit at it in her sark!°   *slip*
    Now Tam, O Tam! had thae been queans,°   *maidens*
A' plump and strapping in their teens;
Their sarks, instead o' creeshie flannen,°   *greasy flannel*
Been snaw-white seventeen hunder linen!°   *very fine linen*
155 Thir breeks° o' mine, my only pair,   *these breeches*
That ance were plush, o' gude blue hair,
I wad hae gi'en them off my hurdies,°   *hips*
For ae blink o' the bonnie burdies!
    But wither'd beldams, auld and droll,
160 Rigwoodie° hags wad spean° a foal,   *boney / wean (by fright)*
Louping° and flinging on a crummock,°   *leaping / crooked staff*
I wonder didna turn thy stomach.
    But Tam kent° what was what fu' brawlie°   *knew / well*
There was ae winsome wench and walie°   *voluptuous*
165 That night enlisted in the core,
Lang after kent° on Carrick shore!   *known*
(For mony a beast to dead she shot,
And perish'd mony a bonnie boat,
And shook baith meikle corn and bear,°   *barley*
170 And kept the country-side in fear.)
Her cutty sark,° o' Paisley harn,°   *short slip / yarn*
That while a lassie she had worn,
In longitude tho' sorely scanty,
It was her best, and she was vauntie.°   *vain*
175 Ah! little kent thy reverend grannie
That sark she coft° for her wee Nannie   *bought*
Wi' twa pund Scots ('twas a' her riches)
Wad ever grac'd a dance of witches!
    But here my muse her wing maun cour;°   *curb*
180 Sic flights are far beyond her pow'r—
To sing how Nannie lap and flang,
(A souple jade she was, and strang);
And how Tam stood, like ane bewitch'd,
And thought his very een enrich'd;
185 Even Satan glowr'd, and fidg'd fu' fain,°   *fidgeted very eagerly*
And hotch'd° and blew wi' might and main: *hitched*
Till first ae caper, syne° anither,   *then*
Tam tint° his reason a' thegither,   *lost*
And roars out 'Weel done, Cutty-sark!'
190 And in an instant all was dark!

---

[8] And cast off her duds (clothes) for the sake of the work.

And scarcely had he Maggie rallied,
When out the hellish legion sallied.
　　As bees bizz out wi' angry fyke°   *fuss*
When plundering herds assail their byke,°   *hive*
195　As open pussie's mortal foes
When pop! she starts before their nose,
As eager runs the market-crowd,
When 'Catch the thief!' resounds aloud.
So Maggie runs; the witches follow,
200　Wi' mony an eldritch° skriech and hollow.   *frightful*
　　Ah, Tam! ah, Tam! thou'll get thy fairin'!
In hell they'll roast thee like a herrin'!
In vain thy Kate awaits thy comin'!
Kate soon will be a woefu' woman!
205　Now do thy speedy utmost, Meg,
And win the key-stane o' the brig:°   *bridge*
There at them thou thy tail may toss,
A running stream they darena cross.
But ere the key-stane she could make,
210　The fient° a tail she had to shake!   *devil a bit of*
For Nannie, far before the rest,
Hard upon noble Maggie prest,
And flew at Tam wi' furious ettle,°   *design*
But little wist she Maggie's mettle!
215　Ae spring brought off her master hale,
But left behind her ain gray tail:
The carlin claught° her by the rump,   *clutched*
And left poor Maggie scarce a stump.
　　Now, wha this tale o' truth shall read,
220　Each man and mother's son, take heed;
Whene'er to drink you are inclin'd,
Or cutty-sarks run in your mind,
Think! ye may buy the joys o'er dear,
Remember Tam o' Shanter's mare.

                                                                    [1791]

MY LOVE IS LIKE A RED RED ROSE

My love is like a red red rose
　That's newly sprung in June:
My love is like the melodie
　That's sweetly play'd in tune.

5　So fair art thou, my bonnie lass,
　　So deep in love am I:
And I will love thee still, my
　　dear,
　Till a' the seas gang dry.

Till a' the seas gang dry, my dear,
10　And the rocks melt wi' the sun:
And I will love thee still, my
　dear,
　　While the sands o' life shall run.

And fare thee weel, my only love,
　And fare thee weel awhile!
15　And I will come again, my love,
　Tho' it were ten thousand mile.

                                                                    [1794]

SCOTS WHA HAE

Robert Bruce's Address to his Army, Before the Battle of Bannockburn[1]

Scots, wha hae° wi' Wallace[2] bled,   *who have*
Scots, wham° Bruce has aften led,   *whom*
Welcome to your gory bed,
    Or to victorie.

5   Now's the day, and now's the hour;
See the front o' battle lour!°   *threaten*
See approach proud Edward's power—
    Chains and slaverie!

Wha will be a traitor knave?
10   Wha can fill a coward's grave?
Wha sae base as be a slave?
    Let him turn and flee!

Wha for Scotland's King and law
Freedom's sword will strongly draw,
15   Freeman stand, or freeman fa'?°   *fall*
    Let him follow me!

By oppression's woes and pains!
By your sons in servile chains!
We will drain our dearest veins,
20   But they shall be free!

Lay the proud usurpers low!
Tyrants fall in every foe!
Liberty's in every blow!
    Let us do or die!

                            [1794]

FOR A' THAT AND A' THAT

Is there, for honest poverty,
    That hings his head, and a' that;
The coward-slave, we pass him by,
    We dare be poor for a' that!
5   For a' that, and a' that,
        Our toils obscure, and a' that,
    The rank is but the guinea's stamp,
    The man's the gowd° for a' that.   *gold*

---

[1] As a result of the battle of Bannockburn (1314) the English armies of King Edward II were driven out of Scotland and Robert the Bruce became the Scottish king.
[2] Sir William Wallace (1272?–1306) was a Scottish national hero.

What though on hamely fare we dine,
   Wear hoddin-grey,° and a' that;   *coarse, undyed wool*
Gie fools their silks, and knaves their wine,
   A man's a man for a' that.
     For a' that, and a' that,
       Their tinsel show, and a' that;
       The honest man, tho' e'er sae poor,
       Is king o' men for a' that.

Ye see yon birkie,° ca'd a lord,   *young fellow*
   Wha struts, and stares, and a' that;
Tho' hundreds worship at his word,
   He's but a coof° for a' that.   *numbskull*
     For a' that, and a' that,
       His ribband, star,° and a' that,   *star of knighthood*
     The man of independent mind,
       He looks and laughs at a' that.

A prince can mak a belted knight,
   A marquis, duke, and a' that;
But an honest man's aboon° his might,   *above*
   Guid faith, he mauna fa'° that!   *mustn't claim*
     For a' that, and a' that,
       Their dignities, and a' that,
       The pith o' sense, and pride o' worth,
       Are higher rank than a' that.

Then let us pray that come it may,
   As come it will for a' that,
That sense and worth, o'er a' the earth,
   Shall bear the gree,° and a' that.   *prize*
     For a' that and a' that,
       It's coming yet, for a' that,
       That man to man, the warld o'er,
       Shall brothers be for a' that.
               [1795]

❧ NINETEENTH CENTURY POETRY ❧

William Wordsworth   *1770–1850*

LINES

Composed a Few Miles Above Tintern Abbey
On Revisiting the Banks of the Wye During a Tour. July 13, 1798

Five years have passed; five summers, with the length
Of five long winters! and again I hear
These waters, rolling from their mountain-springs
With a soft inland murmur. —Once again
5   Do I behold these steep and lofty cliffs,
That on a wild secluded scene impress
Thoughts of more deep seclusion; and connect
The landscape with the quiet of the sky.
The day is come when I again repose
10 Here, under this dark sycamore, and view
These plots of cottage-ground, these orchard-tufts,
Which at this season, with their unripe fruits,
Are clad in one green hue, and lose themselves
'Mid groves and copses. Once again I see
15 These hedge-rows, hardly hedge-rows, little lines
Of sportive wood run wild: these pastoral farms,
Green to the very door; and wreaths of smoke
Sent up, in silence, from among the trees!
With some uncertain notice, as might seem
20 Of vagrant dwellers in the houseless woods,
Or of some hermit's cave, where by his fire
The hermit sits alone.   These beauteous forms,
Through a long absence, have not been to me
As is a landscape to a blind man's eye:
25 But oft, in lonely rooms, and 'mid the din
Of towns and cities, I have owed to them
In hours of weariness, sensations sweet,
Felt in the blood, and felt along the heart;
And passing even into my purer mind,
30 With tranquil restoration:°—feelings too   *recollection*
Of unremembered pleasure: such, perhaps,
As have no slight or trivial influence
On that best portion of a good man's life,
His little, nameless, unremembered, acts

739

35 Of kindness and of love. Nor less, I trust,
To them I may have owed another gift,
Of aspect more sublime; that blessed mood
In which the burthen of the mystery,
In which the heavy and the weary weight
40 Of all this unintelligible world,
Is lightened:—that serene and blessed mood,
In which the affections gently lead us on,—
Until, the breath of this corporeal frame
And even the motion of our human blood
45 Almost suspended, we are laid asleep
In body, and become a living soul:
While with an eye made quiet by the power
Of harmony, and the deep power of joy,
We see into the life of things.
                                        If this
50 Be but a vain belief, yet, oh! how oft—
In darkness and amid the many shapes
Of joyless daylight; when the fretful stir
Unprofitable, and the fever of the world,
Have hung upon the beatings of my heart—
55 How oft, in spirit, have I turned to thee,
O sylvan Wye! thou wanderer through the woods,
How often has my spirit turned to thee!

    And now, with gleams of half-extinguished thought,
With many recognitions dim and faint,
60 And somewhat of a sad perplexity,
The picture of the mind revives again:
While here I stand, not only with the sense
Of present pleasure, but with pleasing thoughts
That in this moment there is life and food
65 For future years. And so I dare to hope,
Though changed, no doubt, from what I was when
        first
I came along these hills; when like a roe°   a small deer
I bounded o'er the mountains, by the sides
Of the deep rivers, and the lonely streams,
70 Wherever nature led: more like a man
Flying from something that he dreads than one
Who sought the thing he loved. For nature then
(The coarser pleasures of my boyish days,
And their glad animal movements all gone by)
75 To me was all in all.—I cannot paint
What then I was. The sounding cataract°   waterfall
Haunted me like a passion: the tall rock,
The mountain, and the deep and gloomy wood,
Their colors and their forms, were then to me
80 An appetite; a feeling and a love,
That had no need of a remoter charm,
By thought supplied, nor any interest

Unborrowed from the eye.—That time is past,
And all its aching joys are now no more,
85   And all its dizzy raptures. Not for this
Faint I, nor mourn nor murmur; other gifts
Have followed; for such loss, I would believe,
Abundant recompense. For I have learned
To look on nature, not as in the hour
90   Of thoughtless youth; but hearing oftentimes
The still, sad music of humanity,
Nor harsh nor grating, though of ample power
To chasten and subdue. And I have felt
A presence that disturbs me with the joy
95   Of elevated thoughts; a sense sublime
Of something far more deeply interfused,
Whose dwelling is the light of setting suns,
And the round ocean and the living air,
And the blue sky, and in the mind of man:
100   A motion and a spirit, that impels
All thinking things, all objects of all thought,
And rolls through all things. Therefore am I still
A lover of the meadows and the woods,
And mountains; and of all that we behold
105   From this green earth; of all the mighty world
Of eye, and ear,—both what they half create,
And what perceive; well pleased to recognize
In nature and the language of the sense
The anchor of my purest thoughts, the nurse,
110   The guide, the guardian of my heart, and soul
Of all my moral being.
                      Nor perchance,
If I were not thus taught, should I the more
Suffer my genial spirits° to decay: *creative powers*
For thou art with me here upon the banks
115   Of this fair river; thou my dearest Friend,°   *his sister Dorothy*
My dear, dear Friend; and in thy voice I catch
The language of my former heart, and read
My former pleasures in the shooting lights
Of thy wild eyes. Oh! yet a little while
120   May I behold in thee what I was once,
My dear, dear Sister! and this prayer I make,
Knowing that Nature never did betray
The heart that loved her; 'tis her privilege,
Through all the years of this our life, to lead
125   From joy to joy: for she can so inform
The mind that is within us, so impress
With quietness and beauty, and so feed
With lofty thoughts, that neither evil tongues,
Rash judgments, nor the sneers of selfish men,
130   Nor greetings where no kindness is, nor all
The dreary intercourse of daily life,
Shall e'er prevail against us, or disturb

Our cheerful faith, that all which we behold
Is full of blessings. Therefore let the moon
135   Shine on thee in thy solitary walk;
And let the misty mountain-winds be free
To blow against thee: and, in after years,
When these wild ecstasies shall be matured
Into a sober pleasure; when thy mind
140   Shall be a mansion for all lovely forms,
Thy memory be as a dwelling-place
For all sweet sounds and harmonies; oh! then,
If solitude, or fear, or pain, or grief,
Should be thy portion, with what healing thoughts
145   Of tender joy wilt thou remember me,
And these my exhortations! Nor, perchance—
If I should be where I no more can hear
Thy voice, nor catch from thy wild eyes these gleams
Of past existence—wilt thou then forget
150   That on the banks of this delightful stream
We stood together; and that I, so long
A worshipper of Nature, hither came
Unwearied in that service: rather say
With warmer love—oh! with far deeper zeal
155   Of holier love. Nor wilt thou then forget,
That after many wanderings, many years
Of absence, these steep woods and lofty cliffs,
And this green pastoral landscape, were to me
More dear, both for themselves and for thy sake!

[1798]

irony—
Dot went
insane.

"SHE DWELT AMONG THE UNTRODDEN WAYS"

She dwelt among the untrodden ways
    Beside the springs of Dove,
A maid whom there were none to praise
    And very few to love:

5   A violet by a mossy stone
    Half hidden from the eye!
Fair as a star, when only one
    Is shining in the sky.

She lived unknown, and few could know
10   When Lucy ceased to be;
But she is in her grave, and oh,
    The difference to me!

[1800]

"I WANDERED LONELY AS A CLOUD"

I wandered lonely as a cloud
   That floats on high o'er vales and hills,
When all at once I saw a crowd,
   A host, of golden daffodils;
5   Beside the lake, beneath the trees,
Fluttering and dancing in the breeze.

Continuous as the stars that shine
   And twinkle on the Milky Way,
They stretched in never-ending line
10   Along the margin of a bay:
Ten thousand saw I at a glance,
Tossing their heads in sprightly dance.

The waves beside them danced, but they
   Out-did the sparkling waves in glee:
15   A poet could not but be gay,
   In such a jocund company:
I gazed—and gazed—but little thought
What wealth the show to me had brought:

For oft, when on my couch I lie
20   In vacant or in pensive mood,
They flash upon that inward eye
   Which is the bliss of solitude;
And then my heart with pleasure fills,
And dances with the daffodils.
                     [1807]

MY HEART LEAPS UP

My heart leaps up when I behold
   A rainbow in the sky:
So was it when my life began;
So is it now I am a man;
5   So be it when I shall grow old,
   Or let me die!
The Child is father of the Man;
And I could wish my days to be
Bound each to each by natural piety.
                     [1807]

"SHE WAS A PHANTOM OF DELIGHT"

She was a phantom of delight
When first she gleamed upon my sight;

A lovely apparition, sent
To be a moment's ornament;
Her eyes as stars of twilight fair;
Like twilight's, too, her dusky hair;
But all things else about her drawn
From May-time and the cheerful dawn;
A dancing shape, an image gay,
To haunt, to startle, and waylay.

I saw her upon nearer view,
A spirit, yet a woman too!
Her household motions light and free,
And steps of virgin liberty;
A countenance in which did meet
Sweet records, promises as sweet;
A creature not too bright or good
For human nature's daily food;
For transient sorrows, simple wiles,
Praise, blame, love, kisses, tears, and smiles.

And now I see with eye serene
The very pulse of the machine;
A being breathing thoughtful breath,
A traveller between life and death;
The reason firm, the temperate will,
Endurance, foresight, strength, and skill;
A perfect woman, nobly planned,
To warn, to comfort, and command;
And yet a spirit still, and bright
With something of angelic light.

                                                [1807]

THE SOLITARY REAPER

Behold her, single in the field,
Yon solitary Highland Lass!
Reaping and singing by herself;
Stop here, or gently pass!
Alone she cuts and binds the grain,
And sings a melancholy strain;
O listen! for the vale profound
Is overflowing with the sound.

No nightingale did ever chaunt
More welcome notes to weary bands
Of travellers in some shady haunt,
Among Arabian sands:
A voice so thrilling ne'er was heard
In spring-time from the cuckoo-bird,

15   Breaking the silence of the seas
        Among the farthest Hebrides.[1]

        Will no one tell me what she sings?—
        Perhaps the plaintive numbers flow
        For old, unhappy, far-off things,
20   And battles long ago:
        Or is it some more humble lay,
        Familiar matter of today?
        Some natural sorrow, loss, or pain,
        That has been, and may be again?

25   Whate'er the theme, the maiden sang
        As if her song could have no ending;
        I saw her singing at her work,
        And o'er the sickle bending:—
        I listened, motionless and still;
30   And, as I mounted up the hill,
        The music in my heart I bore,
        Long after it was heard no more.

                             [1807]

COMPOSED UPON WESTMINSTER BRIDGE, SEPTEMBER 3, 1802

    Earth has not anything to show more fair:
        Dull would he be of soul who could pass by
        A sight so touching in its majesty:
    This city now doth like a garment wear
5   The beauty of the morning; silent, bare,
        Ships, towers, domes, theaters, and temples lie
        Open unto the fields, and to the sky;
    All bright and glittering in the smokeless air.
    Never did sun more beautifully steep
10   In his first splendor, valley, rock, or hill;
    Ne'er saw I, never felt, a calm so deep!
        The river glideth at his own sweet will:
    Dear God! the very houses seem asleep;
        And all that mighty heart is lying still!

                             [1807]

"THE WORLD IS TOO MUCH WITH US"

    The world is too much with us; late and soon,
        Getting and spending, we lay waste our powers:
        Little we see in Nature that is ours;

[1] A group of islands west of Scotland.

We have given our hearts away, a sordid boon:
5   This sea that bares her bosom to the moon;
      The winds that will be howling at all hours,
      And are up-gathered now like sleeping flowers;
    For this, for everything, we are out of tune;
    It moves us not.—Great God! I'd rather be
10   A pagan suckled in a creed outworn;
    So might I, standing on this pleasant lea,°   *meadow*
      Have glimpses that would make me less forlorn;
    Have sight of Proteus[1] rising from the sea;
      Or hear old Triton[2] blow his wreathèd horn.

[1807]

Samuel Taylor Coleridge   *1772–1834*

KUBLA KHAN

Theme:
Two Sides of
Creation

MAN-MADE

    In Xanadu did Kubla Khan
      A stately pleasure-dome decree:
    Where Alph, the sacred river, ran
    Through caverns measureless to man
5   Down to a sunless sea.
    So twice five miles of fertile ground
    With walls and towers were girdled round:
    And there were gardens bright with sinuous rills
    Where blossomed many an incense-bearing tree;
10   And here were forests ancient as the hills,
    Enfolding sunny spots of greenery.

    But O, that deep romantic chasm which slanted
    Down the green hill athwart a cedarn cover!°   *across a cedar woods*
    A savage place! as holy and enchanted
15   As e'er beneath a waning moon was haunted
    By woman wailing for her demon-lover!
    And from this chasm, with ceaseless turmoil
        seething
    As if this earth in fast thick pants were
        breathing,
    A mighty fountain momently° was forced;   *every moment*
20   Amid whose swift half-intermitted burst
    Huge fragments vaulted like rebounding hail,
    Or chaffy grain beneath the thresher's flail:

–paradise
–fantastic images
Supernatural images
Savage in middle of paradise

[1] A Greek sea god capable of changing shapes at will.
[2] A Greek sea god often depicted with a conch-shell trumpet.

And 'mid these dancing rocks at once and ever
It flung up momently the sacred river.
25   Five miles meandering with a mazy motion
Through wood and dale the sacred river ran,
Then reached the caverns measureless to man,
And sank in tumult to a lifeless ocean:
And 'mid this tumult Kubla heard from far
30   Ancestral voices prophesying war!
         The shadow of the dome of pleasure
             Floated midway on the waves;
         Where was heard the mingled measure
             From the fountain and the caves.
35   It was a miracle of rare device,
A sunny pleasure-dome with caves of ice!

         A damsel with a dulcimer
             In a vision once I saw:
         It was an Abyssinian maid,
40   And on her dulcimer she played,
         Singing of Mount Abora.
         Could I revive within me,
             Her symphony and song,
To such a deep delight 'twould win me,
45   That with music loud and long,
I would build that dome in air,
That sunny dome! those caves of ice!
And all who heard should see them there,
And all should cry, Beware! Beware!
50   His flashing eyes, his floating hair!
Weave a circle round him thrice,
         And close your eyes with holy dread,
             For he on honey-dew hath fed,
And drunk the milk of Paradise.

[1816]

WORK WITHOUT HOPE

All Nature seems at work. Slugs leave their lair—
The bees are stirring—birds are on the wing—
And Winter, slumbering in the open air,
Wears on his smiling face a dream of Spring!
5   And I, the while, the sole unbusy thing,
Nor honey make, nor pair, nor build, nor sing.

Yet well I ken° the banks where amaranths[1] blow,   know
Have traced the fount whence streams of nectar flow.
Bloom, O ye amaranths! bloom for whom ye may,
10   For me ye bloom not! Glide, rich streams, away!

[1] Mythical ever-blooming flowers.

With lips unbrightened, wreathless brow, I stroll:
And would you learn the spells that drowse my soul?
Work without hope draws nectar in a sieve,
And hope without an object cannot live.

[1828]

ON DONNE'S POETRY

With Donne, whose muse on dromedary° trots,   *camel*
Wreathe iron pokers into truelove knots;
Rhyme's sturdy cripple, fancy's maze and clue,
Wit's forge and fire-blast, meaning's press and screw.

[posthumous, 1836]

Walter Savage Landor   *1775–1864*

PAST RUINED ILION

Past ruined Ilion Helen lives,
    Alcestis rises from the shades;[1]
Verse calls them forth; 'tis verse that gives
    Immortal youth to mortal maids.

5   Soon shall oblivion's deepening veil
    Hide all the peopled hills you see,
The gay, the proud, while lovers hail
    These many summers you and me.

[1831]

ON HIS SEVENTY-FIFTH BIRTHDAY

I strove with none, for none was worth my strife.
Nature I loved and, next to nature, art:
I warmed both hands before the fire of life;
It sinks, and I am ready to depart.

[1853]

---

[1] Helen brought about the destruction of Troy (Ilion). Alcestis died to save her husband, but was rescued from the underworld by Hercules.

Leigh Hunt   *1784–1859*

RONDEAU

Jenny kissed me when we met,
 Jumping from the chair she sat in;
Time, you thief, who love to get
 Sweets into your list, put that in!
Say I'm weary, say I'm sad,
 Say that health and wealth have missed me,
Say I'm growing old, but add,
  Jenny kissed me.

         [1838]

George Gordon, Lord Byron   *1788–1824*

THE DESTRUCTION OF SENNACHERIB[1]

The Assyrian came down like the wolf on the fold,
And his cohorts were gleaming in purple and gold;
And the sheen of their spears was like stars on the sea,
When the blue wave rolls nightly on deep Galilee.

Like the leaves of the forest when summer is green,
That host with their banners at sunset were seen:
Like the leaves of the forest when autumn hath blown,
That host on the morrow lay withered and strown.

For the Angel of Death spread his wings on the blast,
And breathed in the face of the foe as he passed;
And the eyes of the sleepers waxed deadly and chill,
And their hearts but once heaved, and for ever grew still!

And there lay the steed with his nostril all wide,
But through it there rolled not the breath of his pride;
And the foam of his gasping lay white on the turf,
And cold as the spray of the rock-beating surf.

And there lay the rider distorted and pale,
With the dew on his brow and the rust on his mail;
And the tents were all silent, the banners alone,
The lances unlifted, the trumpet unblown.

[1] King of Assyria. See II Kings 19.

And the widows of Ashur° are loud in their wail,   *Assyria*
And the idols are broke in the temple of Baal;°   *a sun god*
And the might of the Gentile,° unsmote by the sword,   *non-Jew*
Hath melted like snow in the glance of the Lord!

[1815]

DON JUAN

Fragment on the back of the Poet's MS. of Canto 1.

I would to heaven that I were so much clay,
    As I am blood, bone, marrow, passion, feeling—
Because at least the past were passed away—
    And for the future—(but I write this reeling,
5 Having got drunk exceedingly today.
    So that I seem to stand upon the ceiling)
I say—the future is a serious matter—
And so—for God's sake—hock° and soda-water!   *a white wine*

FROM *Canto 1*

CCXVIII

What is the end of Fame? 'tis but to fill
    A certain portion of uncertain paper:
Some liken it to climbing up a hill,
    Whose summit, like all hills, is lost in vapor;
5 For this men write, speak, preach, and heroes kill,
        And bards burn what they call their "midnight
            taper,"
To have, when the original is dust,
A name, a wretched picture, and worse bust.

[1819]

FROM *Canto 2*

CLXXIX

Man, being reasonable, must get drunk;
    The best of life is but intoxication:
Glory, the grape, love, gold, in these are sunk
    The hopes of all men, and of every nation;
5 Without their sap, how branchless were the trunk
    Of life's strange tree, so fruitful on occasion:
But to return—Get very drunk: and when
You wake with headache, you shall see what then.

. . . .

CXCVI

An infant when it gazes on a light,
    A child the moment when it drains the breast,

A devotee when soars the Host° in sight,   *Eucharist*
    An Arab with a stranger for a guest,
5 A sailor when the prize has struck° in fight,   *surrendered*
    A miser filling his most hoarded chest,
Feel rapture; but not such true joy are reaping
    As they who watch o'er what they love while sleeping.

CXCVII

For there it lies so tranquil, so beloved,
10   All that it hath of life with us is living;
So gentle, stirless, helpless, and unmoved,
    And all unconscious of the joy 'tis giving;
All it hath felt, inflicted, passed, and proved,
    Hushed into depths beyond the watcher's diving;
15 There lies the thing we love with all its errors
And all its charms, like death without its terrors.

                    [1819]

FROM *Canto 3*

V

'Tis melancholy, and a fearful sign
    Of human frailty, folly, also crime,
That love and marriage rarely can combine,
    Although they both are born in the same clime;
5 Marriage from love, like vinegar from wine—
    A sad, sour, sober beverage—by time
Is sharpened from its high celestial flavor
Down to a very homely household savor.

VI

There's something of antipathy, as 'twere,
10   Between their present and their future state;
A kind of flattery that's hardly fair
    Is used until the truth arrives too late—
Yet what can people do, except despair?
    The same things change their names at such a rate;
15 For instance—passion in a lover's glorious,
But in a husband is pronounced uxorious.°   *too fond*

VII

Men grow ashamed of being so very fond;
    They sometimes also get a little tired
(But that, of course, is rare), and then despond:
20   The same things cannot always be admired,
Yet 'tis "so nominated in the bond,"[1]
    That both are tied till one shall have expired.
Sad thought! to lose the spouse that was adorning
Our days, and put one's servants into mourning.

---

[1] The bond of marriage. See Shakespeare's *The Merchant of Venice*, Act 4, Scene 1.

VIII

25 There's doubtless something in domestic doings
    Which forms, in fact, true love's antithesis;
    Romances paint at full length people's wooings,
    But only give a bust of marriages;
    For no one cares for matrimonial cooings,
30   There's nothing wrong in a connubial° kiss: *marital*
    Think you, if Laura had been Petrarch's wife,
    He would have written sonnets all his life?[2]

IX

    All tragedies are finished by a death,
    All comedies are ended by a marriage;
35 The future states of both are left to faith,
    For authors fear description might disparage
    The worlds to come of both, or fall beneath,
    And then both worlds would punish their miscarriage;
    So leaving each their priest and prayer-book ready,
40 They say no more of Death or of the Lady.

                . . . .

LXXXVIII

    But words are things, and a small drop of ink,
    Falling like dew, upon a thought, produces
    That which makes thousands, perhaps millions, think;
    'Tis strange, the shortest letter which man uses
5   Instead of speech, may form a lasting link
    Of ages; to what straits old Time reduces
    Frail man, when paper—even a rag like this,
    Survives himself, his tomb, and all that's his.

                                            [1821]

FROM *Canto II*

I

    When Bishop Berkeley[1] said "there was no matter"
    And proved it—'twas no matter what he said:
    They say his system 'tis in vain to batter,
    Too subtle for the airiest human head;
5   And yet who can believe it? I would shatter
    Gladly all matters down to stone or lead,
    Or adamant, to find the world a spirit,
    And wear my head, denying that I wear it.

[2] The Italian poet Petrarch (1304–1374) wrote a famous cycle of sonnets to Laura. In his manuscript Byron gave a more risqué twist to these lines:
    Had Petrarch's passion led to Petrarch's wedding,
    How many sonnets had ensued the bedding?
[1] Bishop George Berkeley (1685–1753) was an Irish philosopher who argued that physical objects exist only in the mind of the perceiver and in the mind of God.

FROM *Canto 14*

I

If from great nature's or our own abyss
    Of thought we could but snatch a certainty,
Perhaps mankind might find the path they miss—
    But then 'twould spoil much good philosophy.
One system eats another up, and this
    Much as old Saturn ate his progeny;[1]
For when his pious consort gave him stones
In lieu of sons, of these he made no bones.

II

But System doth reverse the Titan's breakfast,
    And eats her parents, albeit the digestion
Is difficult: Pray tell me, can you make fast,
    After due search, your faith to any question?
Look back o'er ages, ere unto the stake fast
    You bind yourself, and call some mode the best one.
Nothing more true than *not* to trust your senses;
And yet what are your other evidences?

III

For me, I know nought; nothing I deny,
    Admit, reject, contemn;° and what know *you*,   *scorn*
Except perhaps that you were born to die?
    And both may after all turn out untrue.
An age may come, Font° of Eternity,   *beginning*
    When nothing shall be either old or new.
Death, so called, is a thing which makes men weep,
And yet a third of life is passed in sleep.

IV

A sleep without dreams, after a rough day
    Of toil, is what we covet most; and yet
How clay shrinks back from more quiescent clay!
    The very Suicide that pays his debt
At once without instalments (an old way
    Of paying debts, which creditors regret)
Lets out impatiently his rushing breath,
Less from disgust of life than dread of death.

[1823]

---

[1] Saturn is the Roman name for Cronus, a Titan who was warned that he would be destroyed by his own children. Therefore he ate each of his offspring at birth until one, Zeus, was concealed from him and later forced his father to vomit forth the other gods.

SO, WE'LL GO NO MORE A-ROVING

So, we'll go no more a-roving
　　So late into the night,
Though the heart be still as loving,
　　And the moon be still as bright.

5　　For the sword outwears its sheath,
　　And the soul wears out the breast,
And the heart must pause to breathe,
　　And love itself have rest.

Though the night was made for loving,
10　　And the day returns too soon,
Yet we'll go no more a-roving
　　By the light of the moon.

　　　　　　　　　　　　　　[posthumous, *1836*]

Percy Bysshe Shelley　*1792–1822*

MONT BLANC[1]

Lines Written in the Vale of Chamouni

I

The everlasting universe of things
Flows through the mind, and rolls its rapid waves,
Now dark, now glittering, now reflecting gloom,
Now lending splendor, where from secret springs
5　The source of human thought its tribute brings
Of waters,—with a sound but half its own,
Such as a feeble brook will oft assume
In the wild woods, among the mountains lone,
Where waterfalls around it leap forever,
10　Where woods and winds contend, and a vast river
Over its rocks ceaselessly bursts and raves.

---

[1] "The poem was composed under the immediate impression of the deep and powerful feelings excited by the objects which it attempts to describe; and, as an undisciplined overflowing of the soul, rests its claim to approbation on an attempt to imitate the untamable wildness and inaccessible solemnity from which those feelings sprang." [Shelley's note.]

　The "objects" were Mont Blanc (the highest mountain in Europe) and the river Arve that descends from the mountain's inaccessible glaciers through the valley of Chamonix in southeastern France.

II

Thus thou, Ravine of Arve—dark, deep Ravine—
Thou many-colored, many-voicèd vale,
Over whose pines, and crags, and caverns sail
15 Fast cloud-shadows, and sunbeams! awful scene,
Where Power in likeness of the Arve comes down
From the ice-gulfs that grid his secret throne
Bursting through these dark mountains like the flame
Of lightning through the tempest! thou dost lie,—
20 Thy giant brood of pines around thee clinging,
Children of elder time, in whose devotion
The chainless winds still come and ever came
To drink their odors, and their mighty swinging
To hear—an old and solemn harmony;
25 Thine earthly rainbows stretched across the sweep
Of the ethereal waterfall, whose veil
Robes some unsculptured image; the strange sleep
Which when the voices of the desert fail
Wraps all in its own deep eternity;
30 Thy caverns echoing to the Arve's commotion—
A loud, lone sound no other sound can tame.
Thou art pervaded with that ceaseless motion,
Thou art the path of that unresting sound,
Dizzy Ravine! and when I gaze on thee,
35 I seem as in a trance sublime and strange
To muse on my own separate fantasy,
My own, my human mind, which passively
Now renders and receives fast influencings,
Holding an unremitting interchange
40 With the clear universe of things around;
One legion of wild thoughts, whose wandering wings
Now float above thy darkness, and now rest,
Where that or thou art no unbidden guest,
In the still cave of the witch Poesy,
45 Seeking among the shadows that pass by—
Ghosts of all things that are—some shade of thee,
Some phantom, some faint image; till the breast
From which they fled recalls them, thou art there!

III

Some say that gleams of a remoter world
50 Visit the soul in sleep,—that death is slumber,
And that its shapes the busy thoughts outnumber
Of those who wake and live. I look on high;
Has some unknown Omnipotence unfurled
The veil of life and death? or do I lie
55 In dream, and does the mightier world of sleep
Spread far around and inaccessibly
Its circles? For the very spirit fails,
Driven like a homeless cloud from steep to steep
That vanishes among the viewless gales!

60   Far, far above, piercing the infinite sky,
     Mont Blanc appears,—still, snowy and serene—
     Its subject mountains their unearthly forms
     Pile around it, ice and rock; broad vales between
     Of frozen floods, unfathomable deeps,
65   Blue as the overhanging heaven, that spread
     And wind among the accumulated steeps;
     A desert peopled by the storms alone,
     Save when the eagle brings some hunter's bone,
     And the wolf tracks her there. How hideously
70   Its shapes are heaped around! rude, bare and high,
     Ghastly, and scarred, and riven.—Is this the scene
     Where the old Earthquake-dæmon taught her young
     Ruin? Were these their toys? or did a sea
     Of fire envelop once this silent snow?
75   None can reply—all seems eternal now.
     The wilderness has a mysterious tongue
     Which teaches awful doubt, or faith so mild,
     So solemn, so serene, that man may be
     But for such faith with Nature reconciled;[2]
80   Thou hast a voice, great Mountain, to repeal
     Large codes of fraud and woe;[3] not understood
     By all, but which the wise, and great, and good,
     Interpret, or make felt, or deeply feel.

                          IV
     The fields, the lakes, the forests and the streams,
85   Ocean, and all the living things that dwell
     Within the dædal° earth; lightning, and rain,   *varied*
     Earthquake, and fiery flood, and hurricane,
     The torpor of the year when feeble dreams
     Visit the hidden buds or dreamless sleep
90   Holds every future leaf and flower, the bound
     With which from that detested trance they leap,
     The works and ways of man, their death and birth,
     And that of him and all that his may be,—
     All things that move and breathe with toil and sound
95   Are born and die, revolve, subside and swell;
     Power dwells apart in its tranquillity,
     Remote, serene, and inaccessible;—
     And *this,* the naked countenance of earth
     On which I gaze, even these primeval mountains,
100 Teach the adverting° minds. The glaciers creep,   *observing*
     Like snakes that watch their prey, from their far fountains,
     Slow rolling on; there many a precipice

---

[2] The wilderness teaches either scepticism about the existence of God or (less acceptable to Shelley)
a simple, Wordsworthian faith "that all which we behold / Is full of blessings" (*Tintern Abbey,*
lines 133–134).
[3] The "voice" of the mountain contradicts the commonly held social and religious codes.

Frost and the sun in scorn of mortal power
Have piled—dome, pyramid and pinnacle,
105 A city of death, distinct with many a tower
And wall impregnable of beaming ice;
Yet not a city, but a flood of ruin
Is there, that from the boundaries of the sky
Rolls its perpetual stream; vast pines are strewing
110 Its destined path, or in the mangled soil
Branchless and shattered stand; the rocks, drawn down
From yon remotest waste, have overthrown
The limits of the dead and living world,
Never to be reclaimed. The dwelling-place
115 Of insects, beasts and birds, becomes its spoil,
Their food and their retreat forever gone;
So much of life and joy is lost. The race
Of man flies far in dread; his work and dwelling
Vanish, like smoke before the tempest's stream,
120 And their place is not known. Below, vast caves
Shine in the rushing torrents' restless gleam,
Which from those secret chasms in tumult welling
Meet in the vale; and one majestic river,
The breath and blood of distant lands, forever
125 Rolls its loud waters to the ocean waves,
Breathes its swift vapors to the circling air.

v

Mont Blanc yet gleams on high: the power is there,
The still and solemn power of many sights
And many sounds, and much of life and death.
130 In the calm darkness of the moonless nights,
In the lone glare of day, the snows descend
Upon that mountain; none beholds them there,
Nor when the flakes burn in the sinking sun,
Or the star-beams dart through them; winds contend
135 Silently there, and heap the snow, with breath
Rapid and strong, but silently! Its home
The voiceless lightning in these solitudes
Keeps innocently, and like vapor broods
Other the snow. The secret strength of things,
140 Which governs thought, and to the infinite dome
Of heaven is as a law, inhabits thee!
And what were thou, and earth, and stars, and sea,
If to the human mind's imaginings
Silence and solitude were vacancy?[4]

[1817]

___

[4] Shelley concludes by asking what importance the silent and solitary power of Mont Blanc would
have if the human mind were incapable of imagination.

OZYMANDIAS[1]

I met a traveller from an antique land
Who said: "Two vast and trunkless legs of stone
Stand in the desert. Near them, on the sand,
Half sunk, a shattered visage lies, whose frown,
And wrinkled lip, and sneer of cold command,
Tell that its sculptor well those passions read
Which yet survive, stamped on these lifeless things,
The hand that mocked them and the heart that fed.[2]
And on the pedestal these words appear—
'My name is Ozymandias, king of kings:
Look on my works, ye mighty, and despair!'
Nothing beside remains. Round the decay
Of that colossal wreck, boundless and bare
The lone and level sands stretch far away."

[1818]

ODE TO THE WEST WIND[1]

I

O wild west wind, thou breath of autumn's being,
Thou, from whose unseen presence the leaves dead
Are driven, like ghosts from an enchanter fleeing,

Yellow, and black, and pale, and hectic red
Pestilence-stricken multitudes: O thou,
Who chariotest to their dark wintry bed

The wingèd seeds, where they lie cold and low,
Each like a corpse within its grave, until
Thine azure sister of the spring shall blow

Her clarion o'er the dreaming earth, and fill
(Driving sweet buds like flocks to feed in air)
With living hues and odors plain and hill:

Wild Spirit, which art moving everywhere;
Destroyer and preserver; hear, oh, hear!

[1] The Greek name for Ramses II, a king of Egypt in the thirteenth century B.C.
[2] "Hand" and "heart" are the direct objects of the verb "survive." The sneering passions shown in the sculpture have outlived the hand of the artist and the heart of Ozymandias.
[1] "This poem was conceived and chiefly written in a wood that skirts the Arno, near Florence, and on a day when that tempestuous wind, whose temperature is at once mild and animating, was collecting the vapors which pour down the autumnal rains. They began, as I foresaw, at sunset with a violent tempest of hail and rain, attended by that magnificent thunder and lightning peculiar to the Cisalpine regions.

"The phenomenon alluded to at the conclusion of the third stanza is well known to naturalists. The vegetation at the bottom of the sea, of rivers, and of lakes, sympathizes with that of the land in the change of seasons, and is consequently influenced by the winds which announce it." [Shelley's note.]

II

15 Thou on whose stream, mid the steep sky's commotion,
   Loose clouds like earth's decaying leaves are shed,
   Shook from the tangled boughs of heaven and ocean,

   Angels of rain and lightning: there are spread
   On the blue surface of thine airy surge,
20 Like the bright hair uplifted from the head

   Of some fierce Mænad,[2] even from the dim verge
   Of the horizon to the zenith's height,
   The locks of the approaching storm. Thou dirge

   Of the dying year, to which this closing night
25 Will be the dome of a vast sepulchre,
   Vaulted with all thy congregated might

   Of vapors, from whose solid atmosphere
   Black rain, and fire, and hail will burst: oh, hear!

[handwritten margin: Wind moves clouds (storm) opens heavens]
[handwritten margin: ending of world?]
[handwritten margin: to westwind — Storm will bring revolution in Eng]

III

   Thou who didst waken from his summer dreams
30 The blue Mediterranean, where he lay,
   Lulled by the coil of his crystalline streams,

   Beside a pumice isle[3] in Baiæ's bay,[4]
   And saw in sleep old palaces and towers
   Quivering within the wave's intenser day,

35 All overgrown with azure moss and flowers
   So sweet the sense faints picturing them! Thou
   For whose path the Atlantic's level powers

   Cleave themselves into chasms, while far below
   The sea-blooms and the oozy woods which wear
40 The sapless foliage of the ocean know

   Thy voice, and suddenly grow gray with fear,
   And tremble and despoil themselves: oh, hear!

[handwritten margin: Wind is moving / ocean around]
[handwritten margin: Ocean has a dream / Abandoned palaces / —Aristocracy]

IV

   If I were a dead leaf thou mightest bear;
   If I were a swift cloud to fly with thee;
45 A wave to pant beneath thy power, and share

   The impulse of thy strength, only less free
   Than thou, O uncontrollable! If even
   I were as in my boyhood, and could be

---

[2] A frenzied female follower of Bacchus, the Greek god of wine.
[3] An island of volcanic stone.   [4] Near Naples.

[handwritten margin notes: "could cloud, wants to be part of nature" / "Despair" / "Wishes he could be a leaf, a cloud"]

The comrade of thy wanderings over heaven,
50   As then, when to outstrip thy skyey speed
Scarce seemed a vision; I would ne'er have striven

As thus with thee in prayer in my sore need.
Oh, lift me as a wave, a leaf, a cloud!
I fall upon the thorns of life! I bleed!

55   A heavy weight of hours has chained and bowed
One too like thee: tameless, and swift, and proud.

V

Make me thy lyre, even as the forest is:
What if my leaves are falling like its own!
The tumult of thy mighty harmonies

60   Will take from both a deep, autumnal tone,
Sweet though in sadness. Be thou, Spirit fierce,
My spirit! Be thou me, impetuous one!

Drive my dead thoughts over the universe
Like withered leaves to quicken a new birth!
65   And, by the incantation of this verse,

[handwritten margin notes: "Heal people w/ his words" / "Optimistic" / "There is eternal life"]

Scatter, as from an unextinguished hearth
Ashes and sparks, my words among mankind!
Be through my lips to unawakened earth

The trumpet of a prophecy! O Wind,
70   If winter comes, can spring be far behind?

[1820]

TO ——

Music, when soft voices die,
Vibrates in the memory;
Odors, when sweet violets sicken,
Live within the sense they quicken.

5   Rose leaves, when the rose is dead,
Are heaped for the belovèd's bed;
And so thy thoughts, when thou art gone,
Love itself shall slumber on.

[posthumous, 1824]

John Clare   *1793–1864*

I AM

Written in Northampton County Asylum

I am: yet what I am none cares or knows,
  My friends forsake me like a memory lost;
I am the self-consumer of my woes,
  They rise and vanish in oblivious host,
5 Like shades in love and death's oblivion lost;
And yet I am, and live with shadows tost.

Into the nothingness of scorn and noise,
  Into the living sea of waking dreams,
Where there is neither sense of life nor joys,
10 But the vast shipwreck of my life's esteems;
And e'en the dearest—that I loved the best—
Are strange—nay, rather stranger than the rest.

I long for scenes where man has never trod;
  A place where woman never smiled or wept;
15 There to abide with my Creator, God,
  And sleep as I in childhood sweetly slept:
Untroubling and untroubled where I lie;
The grass below—above the vaulted sky.

                           [1848]

William Cullen Bryant   *1794–1878*

TO A WATERFOWL

Whither, midst falling dew,
  While glow the heavens with the last steps of day,
Far, through their rosy depths, dost thou pursue
  Thy solitary way?

5 Vainly the fowler's eye
Might mark thy distant flight to do thee wrong,
As, darkly painted on the crimson sky,
  Thy figure floats along.

Seek'st thou the plashy° brink   *marshy*
10   Of weedy lake, or marge of river wide,
Or where the rocking billows rise and sink
On the chafed ocean-side?

There is a Power whose care
Teaches thy way along that pathless coast—
15   The desert and illimitable air—
Lone wandering, but not lost.

All day thy wings have fanned,
At that far height, the cold, thin atmosphere,
Yet stoop not, weary, to the welcome land,
20   Though the dark night is near.

And soon that toil shall end;
Soon shalt thou find a summer home, and rest,
And scream among thy fellows; reeds shall bend,
Soon, o'er thy sheltered nest.

25   Thou'rt gone, the abyss of heaven
Hath swallowed up thy form; yet, on my heart
Deeply has sunk the lesson thou hast given,
And shall not soon depart.

He who, from zone to zone,
30   Guides through the boundless sky thy certain flight,
In the long way that I must tread alone,
Will lead my steps aright.

[1818]

John Keats   *1795–1821*

ODE TO A NIGHTINGALE

I

My heart aches, and a drowsy numbness pains
My sense, as though of hemlock I had drunk,
Or emptied some dull opiate to the drains
One minute past, and Lethe-wards[1] had sunk:
5   'T is not through envy of thy happy lot,
But being too happy in thine happiness,—
That thou, light-wingèd Dryad[2] of the trees,
In some melodious plot

[1] Toward Lethe, the river of forgetfulness in the Underworld.   [2] Wood nymph.

Of beechen green, and shadows numberless,
10   Singest of summer in full-throated ease.

II

O for a draught of vintage! that hath been
    Cooled a long age in the deep-delved earth,
Tasting of Flora³ and the country-green,
    Dance, and Provençal song,⁴ and sunburnt mirth!   *wants to fade into drunkenness*
15 O for a beaker full of the warm South,
    Full of the true, the blushful Hippocrene,⁵
        With beaded bubbles winking at the brim,
            And purple-stainèd mouth;
    That I might drink, and leave the world unseen,
20   And with thee fade away into the forest dim:

III

Fade far away, dissolve, and quite forget
    What thou among the leaves hast never known,
The weariness, the fever, and the fret
    Here, where men sit and hear each other groan;
25 Where palsy shakes a few, sad, last gray hairs,
    Where youth grows pale, and spectre-thin, and dies;
        Where but to think is to be full of sorrow
            And leaden-eyed despairs,
    Where Beauty cannot keep her lustrous eyes,
30   Or new Love pine at them beyond tomorrow.

IV

Away! away! for I will fly to thee,
    Not charioted by Bacchus and his pards,⁶
But on the viewless wings of Poesy,
    Though the dull brain perplexes and retards:
35 Already with thee! tender is the night,
    And haply the Queen-Moon is on her throne,
        Clustered around by all her starry Fays;°   *fairies*
            But here there is no light,
    Save what from heaven is with the breezes blown
40   Through verdurous glooms and winding mossy
            ways.   *mystic experience*

V

I cannot see what flowers are at my feet,
    Nor what soft incense hangs upon the boughs,   *smells sweet smelling flowers*
But, in embalmèd° darkness, guess each sweet
    Wherewith the seasonable month endows

---

³ The goddess of flowers.
⁴ The medieval troubadors of Provence in southern France were famous for their songs.
⁵ A mythological fountain whose waters bring poetic inspiration.
⁶ Bacchus, the god of wine, rode in a chariot drawn by leopards.

45   The grass, the thicket, and the fruit-tree wild;
      White hawthorn, and the pastoral eglantine;
      Fast fading violets covered up in leaves;
        And mid-May's eldest child,
      The coming musk-rose, full of dewy wine,
50   The murmurous haunt of flies on summer eves.

VI

    Darkling[7] I listen; and, for many a time
    I have been half in love with easeful Death,
    Called him soft names in many a musèd rhyme,
      To take into the air my quiet breath;
55   Now more than ever seems it rich to die,
      To cease upon the midnight with no pain,
        While thou art pouring forth thy soul abroad
          In such an ecstasy!
    Still wouldst thou sing, and I have ears in vain—
60   To thy high requiem become a sod.

VII

    Thou wast not born for death, immortal Bird!
    No hungry generations tread thee down;
    The voice I hear this passing night was heard
      In ancient days by emperor and clown:
65   Perhaps the self-same song that found a path
      Through the sad heart of Ruth,[8] when, sick for home,
        She stood in tears amid the alien corn;
          The same that oft-times hath
    Charmed magic casements, opening on the foam
70   Of perilous seas, in faery lands forlorn.

VIII

    Forlorn! the very word is like a bell
    To toll me back from thee to my sole self!
    Adieu! the fancy cannot cheat so well
      As she is famed to do, deceiving elf.
75   Adieu! adieu! thy plaintive anthem fades
      Past the near meadows, over the still stream,
        Up the hill-side; and now 't is buried deep
          In the next valley-glades:
    Was it a vision, or a waking dream?
80   Fled is that music:—do I wake or sleep?

                              [1819]

[handwritten: bird flies away]

---

[7] In the dark.   [8] A young widow in the Bible, Ruth 2.

ODE ON A GRECIAN URN

I

Thou still unravished bride of quietness,
   Thou foster-child of Silence and slow Time,
Sylvan historian, who canst thus express
   A flowery tale more sweetly than our rhyme:
What leaf-fringed legend haunts about thy shape
    Of deities or mortals, or of both,
      In Tempe[1] or the dales of Arcady?[2]
   What men or gods are these? What maidens loth?
What mad pursuit? What struggle to escape?
    What pipes and timbrels? What wild ecstasy?

II

Heard melodies are sweet, but those unheard
   Are sweeter; therefore, ye soft pipes, play on;
Not to the sensual ear, but, more endeared
   Pipe to the spirit ditties of no tone:
Fair youth, beneath the trees, thou canst not leave
   Thy song, nor ever can those trees be bare;
    Bold lover, never, never canst thou kiss,
Though winning near the goal—yet, do not grieve;
    She cannot fade, though thou hast not thy bliss,
   For ever wilt thou love, and she be fair!

III

Ah, happy, happy boughs! that cannot shed
   Your leaves, nor ever bid the spring adieu;
And, happy melodist, unwearièd,
   For ever piping songs for ever new;
More happy love! more happy, happy love!
   For ever warm and still to be enjoyed,
    For ever panting, and for ever young;
All breathing human passion far above,
   That leaves a heart high-sorrowful and cloyed,
    A burning forehead, and a parching tongue.

IV

Who are these coming to the sacrifice?
   To what green altar, O mysterious priest,
Lead'st thou that heifer lowing at the skies,
   And all her silken flanks with garlands drest?
What little town by river or sea shore,
   Or mountain-built with peaceful citadel,
    Is emptied of this folk, this pious morn?
And, little town, thy streets for evermore
   Will silent be; and not a soul to tell
    Why thou art desolate, can e'er return.

[1] A valley in Greece famous for its beauty.
[2] Arcadia, a region in ancient Greece, often used to represent the perfect pastoral environment.

V

O Attic shape! Fair attitude! with brede°   ornamentation
  Of marble men and maidens overwrought,
With forest branches and the trodden weed;
  Thou, silent form, dost tease us out of thought
45 As doth eternity: Cold pastoral!
  When old age shall this generation waste,
    Thou shalt remain, in midst of other woe
  Than ours, a friend to man, to whom thou say'st,
"Beauty is truth, truth beauty,"—that is all
50   Ye know on earth, and all ye need to know.

[1820]

TO AUTUMN

I

Season of mists and mellow fruitfulness,
  Close bosom-friend of the maturing sun;
Conspiring with him how to load and bless
  With fruit the vines that round the thatch-eaves run;
5 To bend with apples the mossed cottage-trees,
  And fill all fruit with ripeness to the core;
    To swell the gourd, and plump the hazel shells
  With a sweet kernel; to set budding more,
And still more, later flowers for the bees,
10 Until they think warm days will never cease,
    For summer has o'er-brimmed their clammy cells.

II

Who hath not seen thee oft amid thy store?
  Sometimes whoever seeks abroad may find
Thee sitting careless on a granary floor,
15   Thy hair soft-lifted by the winnowing wind;
Or on a half-reaped furrow sound asleep,
  Drowsed with the fume of poppies, while thy hook
    Spares the next swath and all its twinèd flowers:
And sometimes like a gleaner thou dost keep
20   Steady thy laden head across a brook;
  Or by a cider-press, with patient look,
    Thou watchest the last oozings hours by hours.

III

Where are the songs of spring? Ay, where are they?
  Think not of them, thou hast thy music too,—
25 While barred clouds bloom the soft-dying day,
  And touch the stubble-plains with rosy hue;
Then in a wailful choir the small gnats mourn

Among the river swallows,° borne aloft   *willows*
Or sinking as the light wind lives or dies;
30   And full-grown lambs loud bleat from hilly bourn;°   *territory*
Hedge-crickets sing; and now with treble soft
The redbreast whistles from a garden-croft,°   *a garden plot*
And gathering swallows twitter in the skies.

[1820]

LA BELLE DAME SANS MERCI[1]

"O what can ail thee, knight-at-arms,
Alone and palely loitering?
The sedge° is withered from the lake,   *coarse, clumped grass*
And no birds sing.

5   "O what can ail thee, knight-at-arms,
So haggard and so woe-begone?
The squirrel's granary is full,
And the harvest's done.

"I see a lily on thy brow
10   With anguish moist and fever dew;
And on thy cheek a fading rose
Fast withereth too."

"I met a lady in the meads,°   *meadows*
Full beautiful—a faery's child,
15   Her hair was long, her foot was light,
And her eyes were wild.

"I made a garland for her head,
And bracelets too, and fragrant zone;°   *girdle (belt)*
She looked at me as she did love,
20   And made sweet moan.

"I set her on my pacing steed
And nothing else saw all day long,
For sideways would she lean, and sing
A faery's song.

25   "She found me roots of relish sweet,
And honey wild and manna[2] dew,
And sure in language strange she said,
'I love thee true!'

---

[1] The title, which means "The Beautiful Lady Without Mercy," is borrowed from a medieval French poem by Alain Chartier.
[2] Miraculous and sustaining. See the Bible, Exodus 16:14–36.

"She took me to her elfin grot,
 And there she wept and sighed full sore;
30 And there I shut her wild, wild eyes
 With kisses four.

"And there she lullèd me asleep,
 And there I dreamed—Ah! woe betide!
35 The latest dream I ever dreamed
 On the cold hill's side.

"I saw pale kings and princes too,
 Pale warriors, death-pale were they all;
Who cried—'La belle dame sans merci
40 Hath thee in thrall!'

"I saw their starved lips in the gloam°   *twilight*
 With horrid warning gapèd wide,
And I awoke and found me here
 On the cold hill's side.

45 "And this is why I sojourn here
 Alone and palely loitering,
Though the sedge is withered from the lake,
 And no birds sing."

[1820]

ODE ON MELANCHOLY

I

No, no! go not to Lethe,[1] neither twist
 Wolf's-bane, tight-rooted, for its poisonous wine;
Nor suffer thy pale forehead to be kissed
 By nightshade, ruby grape of Proserpine,[2]
5 Make not your rosary of yew-berries,
 Nor let the beetle, or the death-moth be
 Your mournful Psyche, nor the downy owl
A partner in your sorrow's mysteries;
 For shade to shade will come too drowsily,
10 And drown the wakeful anguish of the soul.

II

But when the melancholy fit shall fall
 Sudden from heaven like a weeping cloud,
That fosters the droop-headed flowers all,
 And hides the green hills in an April shroud;

[1] The river of forgetfulness in the Underworld.
[2] In Roman mythology Proserpine is the queen of the Underworld. Wolf'sbane (line 2) and nightshade (line 4) are poisonous plants. Yew-berries (line 5), the beetle (line 6), and the death-moth (line 6) are all associated with death. Psyche (line 7), or the butterfly, personifies the soul in Greek mythology.

15 Then glut thy sorrow on a morning rose,
  Or on the rainbow of the salt-sand wave,
  Or on the wealth of globèd peonies;
 Or if thy mistress some rich anger shows,
  Emprison her soft hand, and let her rave,
20 And feed deep, deep upon her peerless eyes.

III

 She dwells with Beauty—Beauty that must die;
  And Joy, whose hand is ever at his lips
 Bidding adieu; and aching Pleasure nigh,
  Turning to poison while the bee-mouth sips:
25 Aye, in the very temple of Delight
  Veiled Melancholy has her sovran shrine,
   Though seen of none save him whose strenuous tongue
 Can burst Joy's grape against his palate fine;
 His soul shall taste the sadness of her might,
30 And be among her cloudy trophies hung.

[1820]

"BRIGHT STAR, WOULD I WERE AS STEADFAST THOU ART!"

 Bright star, would I were steadfast as thou art!
  Not in lone splendor hung aloft the night,
 And watching, with eternal lids apart,
  Like Nature's patient sleepless Eremite,°   *hermit*
5 The moving waters at their priestlike task
  Of pure ablution° round earth's human shores *washing, purifying*
 Or gazing on the new soft fallen mask
  Of snow upon the mountains and the moors:
 No—yet still steadfast, still unchangeable,
10 Pillowed upon my fair love's ripening breast,
 To feel for ever its soft fall and swell,
  Awake for ever in a sweet unrest,
 Still, still to hear her tender-taken breath,
 And so live ever—or else swoon to death.

[posthumous, 1838]

SONNET

"IF BY DULL RHYMES OUR ENGLISH MUST BE CHAINED"

 If by dull rhymes our English must be chained,
  And, like Andromeda,[1] the sonnet sweet

---

[1] Chained to a rock as a sacrifice to a sea monster, Andromeda in Greek mythology was saved at the last moment by Perseus.

Fettered, in spite of pained loveliness;
Let us find out, if we must be constrained,
5   Sandals more interwoven and complete
To fit the naked foot of poesy;
Let us inspect the lyre, and weigh the stress
Of every chord, and see what may be gained
By ear industrious, and attention meet;
10   Misers of sound and syllable, no less
Than Midas² of his coinage, let us be
Jealous of dead leaves in the bay-wreath crown:
So, if we may not let the Muse be free,
She will be bound with garlands of her own.

[posthumous, 1848]

"WHEN I HAVE FEARS THAT I MAY CEASE TO BE"

When I have fears that I may cease to be
Before my pen has gleaned my teeming brain,
Before high pilèd books, in charactry,°   *letters*
Hold like rich garners° the full-ripened grain;   *granaries*
5   When I behold, upon the night's starred face,
Huge cloudy symbols of a high romance,
And think that I may never live to trace
Their shadows, with the magic hand of chance;
And when I feel, fair creature of an hour!
10   That I shall never look upon thee more,
Never have relish in the faery power
Of unreflecting love;—then on the shore
Of the wide world I stand alone, and think
Till love and fame to nothingness do sink.

[posthumous, 1848]

Ralph Waldo Emerson   *1803–1882*

THE RHODORA:

On Being Asked, Whence Is the Flower?

In May, when sea-winds pierced our solitudes,
I found the fresh Rhodora in the woods,
Spreading its leafless blooms in a damp nook,
To please the desert and the sluggish brook.
5   The purple petals, fallen in the pool,

---

² The miserly King Midas is a character in Greek mythology who was granted his wish that everything
he touched should turn to gold.

Made the black water with their beauty gay;
Here might the red-bird come his plumes to cool,
And court the flower that cheapens his array.
Rhodora! if the sages ask thee why
10 This charm is wasted on the earth and sky,
Tell them, dear, that if eyes were made for seeing,
Then Beauty is its own excuse for being:
Why thou wert there, O rival of the rose!
I never thought to ask, I never knew:
15 But, in my simple ignorance, suppose
The self-same Power that brought me there brought you.

[1839]

EACH AND ALL

Little thinks, in the field, yon red-cloaked clown[1]
Of thee from the hill-top looking down;
The heifer that lows in the upland farm,
Far-heard, lows not thine ear to charm;
5 The sexton, tolling his bell at noon,
Deems not that great Napoleon
Stops his horse, and lists with delight,
Whilst his files sweep round yon Alpine height;
Nor knowest thou what argument
10 Thy life to thy neighbor's creed has lent.
All are needed by each one;
Nothing is fair or good alone.
I thought the sparrow's note from heaven,
Singing at dawn on the alder bough;
15 I brought him home, in his nest, at even;
He sings the song, but it cheers not now,
For I did not bring home the river and sky;—
He sang to my ear,—they sang to my eye.
The delicate shells lay on the shore;
20 The bubbles of the latest wave
Fresh pearls to their enamel gave,
And the bellowing of the savage sea
Greeted their safe escape to me.
I wiped away the weeds and foam,
25 I fetched my sea-born treasures home;
But the poor, unsightly, noisome things
Had left their beauty on the shore
With the sun and the sand and the wild uproar.
The lover watched his graceful maid,
30 As 'mid the virgin train she strayed,
Nor knew her beauty's best attire
Was woven still by the snow-white choir.
At last she came to his hermitage,

---

[1] A farmer or peasant.

Like the bird from the woodlands to the cage;—
35 The gay enchantment was undone,
A gentle wife, but fairy none.
Then I said, "I covet truth;
Beauty is unripe childhood's cheat;
I leave it behind with the games of youth:"—
40 As I spoke, beneath my feet
The ground-pine curled its pretty wreath,
Running over the club-moss burrs;
I inhaled the violet's breath;
Around me stood the oaks and firs;
45 Pine-cones and acorns lay on the ground;
Over me soared the eternal sky,
Full of light and of deity;
Again I saw, again I heard,
The rolling river, the morning bird;—
50 Beauty through my senses stole;
I yielded myself to the perfect whole.

[1839]

THE SNOW-STORM

Announced by all the trumpets of the sky,
Arrives the snow, and, driving o'er the fields,
Seems nowhere to alight: the whited air
Hides hills and woods, the river, and the heaven,
5 And veils the farm-house at the garden's end.
The sled and traveller stopped, the courier's feet
Delayed, all friends shut out, the housemates sit
Around the radiant fireplace, enclosed
In a tumultuous privacy of storm.

10 Come see the north wind's masonry.
Out of an unseen quarry evermore
Furnished with tile, the fierce artificer
Curves his white bastions with projected roof
Round every windward stake, or tree, or door.
15 Speeding, the myriad-handed, his wild work
So fanciful, so savage, nought cares he
For number or proportion. Mockingly,
On coop or kennel he hangs Parian[1] wreaths;
A swan-like form invests the hidden thorn;
20 Fills up the farmer's lane from wall to wall,
Maugre° the farmer's sighs; and at the gate   *Despite*
A tapering turret overtops the work.
And when his hours are numbered, and the world
Is all his own, retiring, as he were not,

---

[1] A famous type of white marble from the Greek islands of Paros.

25   Leaves, when the sun appears, astonished Art
        To mimic in slow structures, stone by stone,
        Built in an age, the mad wind's night-work,
        The frolic architecture of the snow.

                          [1841]

DAYS

    Daughters of Time, the hypocritic Days,
    Muffled and dumb like barefoot dervishes,[1]
    And marching single in an endless file,
    Bring diadems° and fagots° in their hands.   *crowns / bundles of sticks*
5   To each they offer gifts after his will,
    Bread, kingdoms, stars, and sky that holds
      them all.
    I, in my pleached garden,[2] watched the pomp,
    Forgot my morning wishes, hastily
    Took a few herbs and apples, and the Day
10   Turned and departed silent. I, too late,
    Under her solemn fillet° saw the scorn.   *headband*

                          [1857]

BRAHMA[1]

    If the red slayer think he slays,
      Or if the slain think he is slain,
    They know not well the subtle ways
      I keep, and pass, and turn again.

5   Far or forgot to me is near;
      Shadow and sunlight are the same;
    The vanished gods to me appear;
      And one to me are shame and fame.

    They reckon ill who leave me out;
      When me they fly, I am the wings;
10   I am the doubter and the doubt,
      And I the hymn the Brahmin sings.

    The strong gods pine for my abode,
      And pine in vain the sacred Seven;[2]
    But thou, meek lover of the good!
15   Find me, and turn thy back on heaven.

                          [1857]

---

[1] Moslem ascetics who achieve ecstasy by performing whirling dances.
[2] A type of formal garden in which the trees and bushes have been interlaced.
[1] The supreme god of Hinduism.   [2] The highest saints of Hinduism.

Elizabeth Barrett Browning *1806–1861*

"HOW DO I LOVE THEE?
LET ME COUNT THE WAYS"

How do I love thee? Let me count the ways.
I love thee to the depth and breadth and height
My soul can reach, when feeling out of sight
For the ends of Being and ideal Grace.
I love thee to the level of every day's
Most quiet need, by sun and candlelight.
I love thee freely, as men strive for right;
I love thee purely, as they turn from praise.
I love thee with the passion put to use
In my old griefs, and with my childhood's faith.
I love thee with a love I seemed to lose
With my lost saints—I love thee with the breath,
Smiles, tears, of all my life!—and, if God choose,
I shall but love thee better after death.

[1850]

Henry Wadsworth Longfellow *1807–1882*

MEZZO CAMMIN[1]

Written at Boppard on the Rhine, August 25, 1842
Just Before Leaving for Home

Half of my life is gone, and I have let
The years slip from me and have not fulfilled
The aspiration of my youth, to build
Some tower of song with lofty parapet.
Not indolence, nor pleasure, nor the fret
Of restless passions that would not be stilled,
But sorrow, and a care that almost killed,[2]
Kept me from what I may accomplish yet;

---

[1] The title (meaning "midway along the journey") is taken from the first line of Dante's *Divine Comedy* (completed in 1321); when he wrote this poem in 1842 at age 35, Longfellow had reached the midpoint of the Biblical "three-score years and ten."
[2] The poet's first wife had died in 1835.

Though, half-way up the hill, I see the Past
10   Lying beneath me with its sounds and sights,—
A city in the twilight dim and vast,
     With smoking roofs, soft bells, and gleaming lights,—
And hear above me on the autumnal blast
     The cataract of Death far thundering from the heights.

               [1845]

SNOW-FLAKES

Out of the bosom of the Air,
    Out of the cloud-folds of her garments shaken,
Over the woodlands brown and bare,
    Over the harvest-fields forsaken,
5   Silent, and soft, and slow
       Descends the snow.

Even as our cloudy fancies take
    Suddenly shape in some divine expression,
Even as the troubled heart doth make
10   In the white countenance confession,
       The troubled sky reveals
       The grief it feels.

This is the poem of the air,
    Slowly in silent syllables recorded;
15 This is the secret of despair
    Long in its cloudy bosom hoarded,
       Now whispered and revealed
       To wood and field.

               [1863]

CHAUCER

An old man in a lodge within a park;
    The chamber walls depicted all around
    With portraitures of huntsman, hawk, and hound,
    And the hurt deer. He listeneth to the lark,
5 Whose song comes with the sunshine through the dark
    Of painted glass in leaden lattice bound;
    He listened and he laugheth at the sound,
    Then writeth in a book like any clerk.°   *scholar*
He is the poet of the dawn, who wrote
10   The Canterbury Tales, and his old age
    Made beautiful with song; and as I read
I hear the crowing cock, I hear the note
    Of lark and linnet, and from every page
    Rise odors of ploughed field or flowery mead.

               [1875]

THE TIDE RISES, THE TIDE FALLS

The tide rises, the tide falls,
The twilight darkens, the curlew° calls;   *shore bird*
Along the sea-sands damp and brown
The traveller hastens toward the town,
5   And the tide rises, the tide falls.

Darkness settles on roofs and walls,
But the sea, the sea in the darkness calls;
The little waves, with their soft, white hands,
Efface the footprints in the sands,
10   And the tide rises, the tide falls.

The morning breaks; the steeds in their stalls
Stamp and neigh, as the hostler° calls;   *stableman*
The day returns, but nevermore
Returns the traveller to the shore.
15   And the tide rises, the tide falls.

[1880]

Edgar Allan Poe *1809–1849*

TO HELEN

Helen, thy beauty is to me
   Like those Nicéan[1] barks of yore,
That gently, o'er a perfumed sea,
   The weary, way-worn wanderer bore
   To his own native shore.

On desperate seas long wont to roam,
   Thy hyacinth[2] hair, thy classic face,
Thy Naiad[3] airs have brought me home
   To the glory that was Greece
5 And the grandeur that was Rome.

Lo! in yon brilliant window-niche
   How statue-like I see thee stand,
   The agate lamp within thy hand!
Ah, Psyche[4] from the regions which
10   Are Holy Land!

[1831]

---

[1] The allusion is unclear.   [2] Curly or wavy.
[3] Nymphs of Greek mythology associated with lakes, rivers, and fountains.
[4] The Greek word for "soul," personified in Greek mythology as a beautiful maiden loved by Cupid.

ANNABEL LEE

It was many and many a year ago.
    In a kingdom by the sea.
That a maiden there lived whom you may know
    By the name of Annabel Lee;—
5 And this maiden she lived with no other thought
    Than to love and be loved by me.

She was a child and *I* was a child,
    In this kingdom by the sea,
But we loved with a love that was more than love—
10   I and my Annabel Lee—
With a love that the wingèd seraphs° of Heaven   angels
    Coveted her and me.

And this was the reason that, long ago,
    In this kingdom by the sea,
15 A wind blew out of a cloud by night
    Chilling my Annabel Lee;
So that her highborn kinsmen came
    And bore her away from me,
To shut her up in a sepulchre
20   In this kingdom by the sea.

The angels, not half so happy in Heaven,
    Went envying her and me:—
Yes! that was the reason (as all men know,
    In this kingdom by the sea)
25 That the wind came out of the cloud, chilling
    And killing my Annabel Lee.

But our love it was stronger by far than the love
    Of those who were older than we—
    Of many far wiser than we—
30 And neither the angels in Heaven above
    Nor the demons down under the sea.
Can ever dissever my soul from the soul
    Of the beautiful Annabel Lee:—

For the moon never beams without bringing me dreams
35   Of the beautiful Annabel Lee;
And the stars never rise but I see the bright eyes
    Of the beautiful Annabel Lee;
And so, all the night-tide, I lie down by the side
Of my darling, my darling, my life and my bride,
40   In her sepulchre there by the sea—
    In her tomb by the side of the sea.

[1849]

Edward FitzGerald *1809–1883*

FROM THE RUBÁIYÁT OF OMAR KHAYYÁM[1]

Come, fill the Cup, and in the fire of Spring
Your Winter-garment of Repentance fling:
   The Bird of Time has but a little way
To flutter—and the Bird is on the Wing.

5   Whether at Naishápúr or Babylon,
Whether the Cup with sweet or bitter run,
   The Wine of Life keeps oozing drop by drop,
The Leaves of Life keep falling one by one.

A Book of Verses underneath the Bough,
10 A Jug of wine, a Loaf of Bread—and Thou
   Beside me singing in the Wilderness—
Oh, Wilderness were Paradise enow!

Some for the Glories of This World; and some
Sigh for the Prophet's Paradise to come;
15   Ah, take the Cash, and let the Credit go,
Nor heed the rumble of a distant Drum!

The Worldly Hope men set their Hearts upon
Turns Ashes—or it prospers; and anon,
   Like Snow upon the Desert's dusty Face,
20 Lighting a little hour or two—is gone.

Why, all the Saints and Sages who discussed
Of the Two Worlds so wisely—they are thrust
   Like foolish Prophets forth; their Words to Scorn
Are scattered, and their Mouths are stopt with Dust.

25 Myself when young did eagerly frequent
Doctor and Saint, and heard great argument
   About it and about: but evermore
Came out by the same Door where in I went.

With them the seed of Wisdom did I sow,
30 And with mine own hand wrought to make it grow;
   And this was all the Harvest that I reaped—
"I came like Water, and like Wind I go."

---

[1] The 17 quatrains reprinted here are selected from the 97 quatrains in FitzGerald's fourth edition of the *Rubáiyát*. Each quatrain (or *rubais*) is an independent poem—though occasionally (as in lines 21–32 and 37–44) a series of *rubais* may develop related ideas.

Perplext no more with Human or Divine,
Tomorrow's tangle to the winds resign,
    And lose your fingers in the tresses of
35   The Cypress-slender Minister of Wine.

You know, my Friends, with what a brave Carouse
I made a Second Marriage in my house;
    Divorced old barren Reason from my Bed,
40   And took the Daughter of the Vine to Spouse

For "Is" and "Is-not" though with Rule and Line
And "Up-and-down" by Logic I define,
    Of all that one should care to fathom, I
Was never deep in anything but—Wine.

45   O threats of Hell and Hopes of Paradise!
One thing at least is certain—*This* Life flies;
    One thing is certain and the rest is Lies;
The Flower that once was blown for ever dies.

But helpless Pieces of the Game He plays
50   Upon this Chequer-board of Nights and Days;
    Hither and thither moves, and checks, and slays,
And one by one back in the Closet lays.

The Moving Finger writes; and, having writ,
Moves on: nor all your Piety nor Wit
55   Shall lure it back to cancel half a Line,
Nor all your Tears wash out a Word of it.

Yesterday *This* Day's Madness did prepare;
Tomorrow's Silence, Triumph, or Despair:
    Drink! for you know not whence you came, nor why:
60   Drink! for you know not why you go, nor where.

And much as Wine has played the Infidel,
And robbed me of my Robe of Honor—Well,
    I wonder often what the Vintners buy
One half so precious as the stuff they sell.

65   Ah Love! could you and I with Him conspire
To grasp this sorry Scheme of Things entire,
    Would not we shatter it to bits—and then
Remould it nearer to the Heart's Desire!

[1859]

Alfred, Lord Tennyson   *1809–1892*

ULYSSES[1]

It little profits that an idle king,
By this still hearth, among these barren crags,
Matched with an aged wife, I mete° and dole°   *allot / give sparingly*
Unequal laws unto a savage race,
5   That hoard, and sleep, and feed, and know not me.
I cannot rest from travel: I will drink
Life to the lees:° all times I have enjoyed   *dregs*
Greatly, have suffered greatly, both with those
That loved me, and alone; on shore, and when
10   Thro' scudding drifts° the rainy Hyades°   *spray / a constellation*
Vexed the dim sea. I am become a name;
For always roaming with a hungry heart
Much have I seen and known: cities of men
And manners, climates, councils, governments,
15   Myself not least, but honored of them all;
And drunk delight of battle with my peers,
Far on the ringing plains of windy Troy.
I am a part of all that I have met;
Yet all experience is an arch wherethro'
20   Gleams that untravelled world, whose margin fades
For ever and for ever when I move.
How dull it is to pause, to make an end,
To rust unburnished, not to shine in use!
As tho' to breathe were life. Life piled on life
25   Were all too little, and of one to me
Little remains: but every hour is saved
From that eternal silence, something more,
A bringer of new things; and vile it were
For some three suns° to store and hoard myself,   *years*
30   And this gray spirit yearning in desire
To follow knowledge like a sinking star,
Beyond the utmost bound of human thought.
     This is my son, mine own Telemachus,
To whom I leave the sceptre and the isle—
35   Well-loved of me, discerning to fulfil
This labor, by slow prudence to make mild
A rugged people, and thro' soft degees
Subdue them to the useful and the good.
Most blameless is he, centered in the sphere
40   Of common duties, decent not to fail
In offices of tenderness, and pay
Meet adoration to my household gods,
When I am gone. He works his work, I mine.

---

[1] The poem takes place after Ulysses' return from the Trojan War and after he has had time to
grow bored with peace, Penelope, and politics. Ulysses is, of course, the Roman name for Odysseus, the hero of Homer's *Odyssey*.

There lies the port; the vessel puffs her sail:
45 There gloom the dark broad seas. My mariners,
Souls that have toiled, and wrought, and thought with me—
That ever with a frolic welcome took
The thunder and the sunshine, and opposed
Free hearts, free foreheads—you and I are old;
50 Old age hath yet his honor and his toil;
Death closes all; but something ere the end,
Some work of noble note, may yet be done,
Not unbecoming men that strove with Gods.
The lights begin to twinkle from the rocks:
55 The long day wanes: the slow moon climbs: the deep
Moans round with many voices. Come, my friends,
'T is not too late to seek a newer world.
Push off, and sitting well in order smite
The sounding furrows; for my purpose holds
60 To sail beyond the sunset, and the baths
Of all the western stars, until I die.
It may be that the gulfs will wash us down:
It may be we shall touch the Happy Isles,°   *Elysium or Paradise*
And see the great Achilles,° whom we knew.   *a Greek hero*
65 Tho' much is taken, much abides; and tho'
We are not now that strength which in old days
Moved earth and heaven, that which we are, we are:
One equal temper of heroic hearts,
Made weak by time and fate, but strong in will
70 To strive, to seek, to find, and not to yield.

[1842]

BREAK, BREAK, BREAK

Break, break, break,
On thy cold gray stones, O Sea!
And I would that my tongue could utter
The thoughts that arise in me.

5   O well for the fisherman's boy,
That he shouts with his sister at play!
O well for the sailor lad,
That he sings in his boat on the bay!

And the stately ships go on
10 To their haven under the hill;
But O for the touch of a vanished hand,
And the sound of a voice that is still!

Break, break, break,
At the foot of thy crags, O Sea!
15 But the tender grace of a day that is dead
Will never come back to me.

[1842]

THE EAGLE: A FRAGMENT

He clasps the crag with crooked hands;
Close to the sun in lonely lands,
Ringed with the azure world, he stands.

The wrinkled sea beneath him crawls:
5   He watches from his mountain walls,
And like a thunderbolt he falls.

[1851]

THE CHARGE OF THE LIGHT BRIGADE

Half a league, half a league,
  Half a league onward,
All in the valley of Death
  Rode the six hundred.
5 "Forward, the Light Brigade!
Charge for the guns!" he said:
Into the valley of Death
  Rode the six hundred.

"Forward, the Light Brigade!"
10 Was there a man dismayed?
Not tho' the soldier knew
  Some one had blundered:
Theirs not to make reply,
Theirs not to reason why,
15 Theirs but to do and die:
Into the valley of Death
  Rode the six hundred.

Cannon to right of them,
Cannon to left of them,
20 Cannon in front of them
  Volleyed and thundered;
Stormed at with shot and shell,
Boldly they rode and well,
Into the jaws of Death,
25 Into the mouth of Hell
  Rode the six hundred.

Flashed all their sabres bare,
Flashed as they turned in air

Sabring the gunners there,
30 Charging an army, while
  All the world wondered:
Plunged in the battery-smoke
Right thro' the line they broke;
Cossack and Russian
35 Reeled from the sabre-stroke
  Shattered and sundered.
Then they rode back, but not
  Not the six hundred.

Cannon to right of them,
40 Cannon to left of them,
Cannon behind them
  Volleyed and thundered;
Stormed at with shot and shell,
While horse and hero fell,
45 They that had fought so well
Came thro' the jaws of Death,
Back from the mouth of Hell,
All that was left of them,
  Left of six hundred.

When can their glory fade?
50 O the wild charge they made!
  All the world wondered.
Honor the charge they made!
Honor the Light Brigade,
55 Noble six hundred!

[1854]

FLOWER IN THE CRANNIED WALL

Flower in the crannied wall,
I pluck you out of the crannies,
I hold you here, root and all, in my hand.
Little flower—but *if* I could understand
5   What you are, root and all, and all in all,
I should know what God and man is.

[1869]

CROSSING THE BAR

Sunset and evening star,
And one clear call for me!
And may there be no moaning of the bar,[1]
When I put out to sea,

5   But such a tide as moving seems asleep,
Too full for sound and foam,
When that which drew from out the boundless deep
Turns again home.

Twilight and evening bell,
10   And after that the dark!
And may there be no sadness of farewell,
When I embark;

For tho' from out our bourne° of Time and Place   *limits*
The flood may bear me far,
15   I hope to see my Pilot face to face
When I have crossed the bar.

[1889]

Robert Browning   *1812–1889*

PORPHYRIA'S LOVER

The rain set early in to-night,
The sullen wind was soon awake,
It tore the elm-tops down for spite,
And did its worst to vex the lake:
5   I listened with heart fit to break;

---

[1] The sound of surf washing over a very shallow sand bar at the mouth of a river.

When glided in Porphyria; straight
   She shut the cold out and the storm,
And kneeled and made the cheerless grate
   Blaze up, and all the cottage warm;
10   Which done, she rose, and from her form
Withdrew the dripping cloak and shawl,
   And laid her soiled gloves by, untied
Her hat, and let the damp hair fall,
   And, last, she sat down by my side
15   And called me. When no voice replied,
She put my arm about her waist,
   And made her smooth white shoulder bare,
And all her yellow hair displaced,
   And, stooping, made my cheek lie there,
20   And spread, o'er all, her yellow hair,
Murmuring how she loved me—she
   Too weak, for all her heart's endeavor,
To set its struggling passion free
   From pride, and vainer ties dissever,
25   And give herself to me forever.
But passion sometimes would prevail,
   Nor could tonight's gay feast restrain
A sudden thought of one so pale
   For love of her, and all in vain:
30   So, she was come through wind and rain.
Be sure I looked up at her eyes
   Happy and proud; at last I knew
Porphyria worshipped me; surprise
   Made my heart swell, and still it grew
35   While I debated what to do.
That moment she was mine, mine, fair,
   Perfectly pure and good: I found
A thing to do, and all her hair
   In one long yellow string I wound
40   Three times her little throat around,
And strangled her. No pain felt she;
   I am quite sure she felt no pain.
As a shut bud that holds a bee,
   I warily oped her lids: again
45   Laughed the blue eyes without a stain.
And I untightened next the tress
   About her neck; her cheek once more
Blushed bright beneath my burning kiss:
   I propped her head up as before,
50   Only, this time my shoulder bore
Her head, which droops upon it still:
   The smiling rosy little head,
So glad it has its utmost will,
   That all it scorned at once is fled,
55   And I, its love, am gained instead!

Porphyria's love: she guessed not how
Her darling one wish would be heard.
And thus we sit together now,
And all night long we have not stirred,
And yet God has not said a word!

[1836]

MY LAST DUCHESS[1]

Ferrara

That's my last Duchess painted on the wall,
Looking as if she were alive. I call
That piece a wonder, now: Frà Pandolf's hands
Worked busily a day, and there she stands.
Will 't please you sit and look at her? I said
"Frà Pandolf" by design: for never read
Strangers like you that pictured countenance,
The depth and passion of its earnest glance,
But to myself they turned (since none puts by
The curtain I have drawn for you, but I)
And seemed as they would ask me, if they durst,
How such a glance came there; so, not the first
Are you to turn and ask thus. Sir, 't was not
Her husband's presence only, called that spot
Of joy into the Duchess' check: perhaps
Frà Pandolf chanced to say "Her mantle laps
Over my lady's wrist too much," or "Paint
Must never hope to reproduce the faint
Half-flush that dies along her throat:" such stuff
Was courtesy, she thought, and cause enough
For calling up that spot of joy. She had
A heart—how shall I say?—too soon made glad,
Too easily impressed; she liked whate'er
She looked on, and her looks went everywhere.
Sir, 't was all one! My favor at her breast,
The dropping of the daylight in the West,
The bough of cherries some officious fool
Broke in the orchard for her, the white mule
She rode with round the terrace—all and each
Would draw from her alike the approving speech,
Or blush, at least. She thanked men,—good! but thanked
Somehow—I know not how—as if she ranked
My gift of a nine-hundred-years-old name
With anybody's gift. Who'd stoop to blame

---

[1] In 1564 Alphonso II, Duke of Ferrara, actually did negotiate a second marriage after the death (under suspicious circumstances) of his first wife, Lucrezia, at the age of seventeen.

35   This sort of trifling? Even had you skill
In speech—(which I have not)—to make your will
Quite clear to such an one, and say, "Just this
Or that in you disgusts me; here you miss,
Or there exceed the mark"—and if she let
40   Herself be lessoned so, nor plainly set
Her wits to yours, forsooth, and made excuse,
—E'en then would be some stooping; and I choose
Never to stoop. Oh sir, she smiled, no doubt,
Whene'er I passed her; but who passed without
45   Much the same smile? This grew; I gave commands;
Then all smiles stopped together. There she stands
As if alive. Will 't please you rise? We'll meet
The company below, then. I repeat,
The Count your master's known munificence
50   Is ample warrant that no just pretence
Of mine for dowry will be disallowed;
Though his fair daughter's self, as I avowed
At starting, is my object. Nay, we'll go
Together down, sir. Notice Neptune, though,
55   Taming a sea-horse, thought a rarity,
Which Claus of Innsbruck cast in bronze for me?

[1842]

MEETING AT NIGHT

The gray sea and the long black land;
And the low yellow half-moon large and low:
And the startled little waves that leap
In fiery ringlets from their sleep,
5   As I gain the cove with pushing prow,
And quench its speed i' the slushy sand.

Then a mile of warm sea-scented beach;
Three fields to cross till a farm appears;
A tap at the pane, the quick sharp scratch
10   And blue spurt of a lighted match,
And a voice less loud, through joys and fears,
Than the two hearts beating each to each!

[1845]

PARTING AT MORNING

Round the cape of a sudden came the sea,
And the sun looked over the mountain's rim:
And straight was a path of gold for him,°   *the sun*
And the need of a world of men for me.

[1845]

SOLILOQUY OF THE SPANISH CLOISTER

I

Gr-rr—there go, my heart's abhorrence!
    Water your damned flower-pots, do!
If hate killed men, Brother Lawrence,
    God's blood, would not mine kill you!
5   What? your myrtle-bush wants trimming?
    Oh, that rose has prior claims—
Needs its leaden vase filled brimming?
    Hell dry you up with its flames!

II

At the meal we sit together:
10   *Salve tibi!*° I must hear   *Hail to thee!*
Wise talk of the kind of weather,
    Sort of season, time of year:
Not a plenteous cork-crop: scarcely
    Dare we hope oak-galls,[1] *I doubt:*
15   *What's the Latin name for "parsley"?*
    What's the Greek name for Swine's Snout?

III

Whew! We'll have our platter burnished,
    Laid with care on our own shelf!
With a fire-new spoon we're furnished,
20   And a goblet for ourself,
Rinsed like something sacrificial
    Ere 'tis fit to touch our chaps°—   *lips*
Marked with L. for our initial!
    (He-he! There his lily snaps!)

IV

25   *Saint,* forsooth! While brown Dolores
    Squats outside the Covent bank
With Sanchicha, telling stories,
    Steeping tresses in the tank,
Blue-black, lustrous, thick like horsehairs,
30   —Can't I see his dead eye glow,
Bright as 'twere a Barbary corsair's?°   *pirate's*
    (That is, if he'd let it show!)

V

When he finishes refection,°   *refreshment*
    Knife and fork he never lays
35   Cross-wise, to my recollection,
    As do I, in Jesu's praise.

[1] Diseased oak shoots, used in tanning.

I the Trinity illustrate,
    Drinking watered orange-pulp—
In three sips the Arian[2] frustrate;
40   While he drains his at one gulp.

VI

Oh, those melons? If he's able
    We're to have a feast! so nice!
One goes to the Abbot's table,
    All of us get each a slice.
45 How go on your flowers? None double?
    Not one fruit-sort can you spy?
Strange!—And I, too, at such trouble,
    Keep them close-nipped on the sly!

VII

There's a great text in Galatians,[3]
50   Once you trip on it, entails
Twenty-nine distinct damnations,
    One sure, if another fails:
If I trip him just a-dying,
    Sure of heaven as sure can be,
55 Spin him round and send him flying
    Off to hell, a Manichee?[4]

VIII

Or, my scrofulous° French novel   *degenerate*
    On grey paper with blunt type!
Simply glance at it, you grovel
60   Hand and foot in Belial's gripe:°   *the Devil's grip*
If I double down its pages
    At the woeful sixteenth print,
When he gathers his greengages,°   *plums*
    Ope a sieve and slip it in't?

IX

65 Or, there's Satan!—one might venture
    Pledge one's soul to him, yet leave
Such a flaw in the indenture
    As he'd miss till, past retrieve,
Blasted lay that rose-acacia
70 We're so proud of! *Hy, Zy, Hine* . . .
'St, there's Vespers!° *Plena gratiâ*   *evening prayers*
Ave, Virgo![5] Gr-r-r—you swine!

[1842]

---

[2] The Arian heresy (after Arius, 256–336 A.D.) was to deny the doctrine of the Trinity.
[3] See the Bible, Galatians 5:15–23.
[4] A follower of Manes, a third-century Persian philosopher who held that the world was governed by contending principles of light and darkness.
[5] Hail Virgin, full of grace.

Walt Whitman   *1819–1892*

OUT OF THE CRADLE ENDLESSLY ROCKING

Out of the cradle endlessly rocking,
Out of the mocking-bird's throat, the musical shuttle,
Out of the Ninth-month midnight,
Over the sterile sands and the fields beyond, where the child leaving
    his bed wandered alone, bareheaded, barefoot,
5   Down from the showered halo,
Up from the mystic play of shadows twining and twisting as if they were
    alive,
Out from the patches of briers and blackberries,
From the memories of the bird that chanted to me,
From your memories sad brother, from the fitful risings and fallings I
    heard,
10   From under that yellow half-moon late-risen and swollen as if with tears,
From those beginning notes of yearning and love there in the mist,
From the thousand responses of my heart never to cease,
From the myriad thence-aroused words,
From the word stronger and more delicious than any,
15   From such as now they start the scene revisiting,
As a flock, twittering, rising, or overhead passing,
Borne hither, ere all eludes me, hurriedly,
A man, yet by these tears a little boy again,
Throwing myself on the sand, confronting the waves,
20   I, chanter of pains and joys, uniter of here and hereafter,
Taking all hints to use them, but swiftly leaping beyond them,
A reminiscence sing.

Once Paumanok,[1]
When the lilac-scent was in the air and Fifth-month grass was growing,
25   Up this seashore in some briers,
Two feathered guests from Alabama, two together,
And their nest, and four light-green eggs spotted with brown,
And every day the he-bird to and fro near at hand,
And every day the she-bird crouched on her nest, silent, with bright
    eyes,
30   And every day I, a curious boy, never too close, never disturbing them,
Cautiously peering, absorbing, translating.

Shine! shine! shine!
Pour down your warmth, great sun!
While we bask, we two together.

35   *Two together!*
Winds blow south, or winds blow north,

---

[1] The Indian name for Long Island.

Day come white, or night come black,
Home, or rivers and mountains from home,
Singing all time, minding no time,
40   *While we two keep together.*

Till of a sudden,
May-be killed, unknown to her mate,
One forenoon the she-bird crouched not on the nest,
Nor returned that afternoon, nor the next,
45   Nor ever appeared again.

And thenceforward all summer in the sound of the sea,
And at night under the full of the moon in calmer weather,

Over the hoarse surging of the sea,
Or flitting from brier to brier by day,
50   I saw, I heard at intervals the remaining one, the he-bird,
The solitary guest from Alabama.

Blow! blow! blow!
Blow up sea-winds along Paumanok's shore;
I wait and I wait till you blow my mate to me.

55   Yes, when the stars glistened,
All night long on the prong of a moss-scalloped stake,
Down almost amid the slapping waves,
Sat the lone singer wonderful causing tears.

He called on his mate,
60   He poured forth the meanings which I of all men know.

Yes my brother I know,
The rest might not, but I have treasured every note,
For more than once dimly down to the beach gliding,
Silent, avoiding the moonbeams, blending myself with the shadows,
65   Recalling now the obscure shapes, the echoes, the sounds and sights
        after their sorts,
The white arms out in the breakers tirelessly tossing,
I, with bare feet, a child, the wind wafting my hair,
Listened long and long.

Listened to keep, to sing, now translating the notes,
70   Following you my brother.

Soothe! soothe! soothe!
Close on its wave soothes the wave behind,
And again another behind embracing and lapping, every one close,
But my love soothes not me, not me.

75   *Low hangs the moon, it rose late,*
It is lagging—O I think it is heavy with love, with love.

O madly the sea pushes upon the land,
With love, with love.

O night! do I not see my love fluttering out among the breakers?
80   *What is that little black thing I see there in the white?*

Loud! loud! loud!
Loud I call to you, my love?

High and clear I shoot my voice over the waves,
Surely you must know who is here, is here,
85   *You must know who I am, my love.*

Low-hanging moon!
What is that dusky spot in your brown yellow?
O it is the shape, the shape of my mate!
O moon do not keep her from me any longer.

90   *Land! land! O land!*
Whichever way I turn, O I think you could give me my mate back again if you
    only would,
For I am almost sure I see her dimly whichever way I look.

O rising stars!
Perhaps the one I want so much will rise, will rise with some of you.

95   *O throat! O trembling throat!*
Sound clearer through the atmosphere!
Pierce the woods, the earth,
Somewhere listening to catch you must be the one I want.

Shake out carols!
100   *Solitary here, the night's carols!*
Carols of lonesome love! death's carols!
Carols under that lagging, yellow, waning moon!
O under that moon where she droops almost down into the sea!
O reckless despairing carols.

105   *But soft! sink low!*
Soft! let me just murmur,
And do you wait a moment you husky-noised sea,
For somewhere I believe I heard my mate responding to me,
So faint, I must be still, be still to listen,
110   *But not altogether still, for then she might not come immediately to me.*

Hither my love!
Here I am! here!
With this just-sustained note I announce myself to you,
This gentle call is for you my love, for you.
115   *Do not be decoyed elsewhere,*
That is the whistle of the wind, it is not my voice,

That is the fluttering, the fluttering of the spray,
Those are the shadows of leaves.

O darkness! O in vain!
120 *O I am very sick and sorrowful.*

O brown halo in the sky near the moon, drooping upon the sea!
O troubled reflection in the sea!
O throat! O throbbing heart!
And I singing uselessly, uselessly all the night.

125 *O past! O happy life! O songs of joy!*
In the air, in the woods, over fields,
Loved! loved! loved! loved! loved!
But my mate no more, no more with me!
We two together no more.

130 The aria sinking,
All else continuing, the stars shining,
The winds blowing, the notes of the bird continuous echoing,
With angry moans the fierce old mother incessantly moaning,
On the sands of Paumanok's shore gray and rustling,
135 The yellow half-moon enlarged, sagging down, drooping, the face of the
    sea almost touching,
The boy ecstatic, with his bare feet the waves, with his hair the atmosphere
    dallying,
The love in the heart long pent, now loose, now at last tumultuously burst-
    ing,
The aria's meaning, the ears, the soul, swiftly depositing,
The strange tears down the cheeks coursing,
140 The colloquy there, the trio, each uttering,
The undertone, the savage old mother incessantly crying,
To the boy's soul's questions sullenly timing, some drowned secret
    hissing,
To the outsetting bard.

Demon or bird! (said the boy's soul,)
145 Is it indeed toward your mate you sing? or is it really to me?
For I, that was a child, my tongue's use sleeping, now I have heard you,
Now in a moment I know what I am for, I awake,
And already a thousand singers, a thousand songs, clearer, louder and
    more sorrowful than yours,
A thousand warbling echoes have started to life within me, never to die.

150 O you singer solitary, singing by yourself, projecting me,
O solitary me listening, never more shall I cease perpetuating you,
Never more shall I escape, never more the reverberations,
Never more the cries of unsatisfied love be absent from me,
Never again leave me to be the peaceful child I was before what there in
    the night,

155 By the sea under the yellow and sagging moon,
The messenger there aroused, the fire, the sweet hell within,
The unknown want, the destiny of me.

O give me the clue! (it lurks in the night here somewhere,)
O if I am to have so much, let me have more!

160 A word then, (for I will conquer it,)
The word final, superior to all,
Subtle, sent up—what is it?—I listen;
Are you whispering it, and have been all the time, you seawaves?
Is that it from your liquid rims and wet sands?

165 Whereto answering, the sea,
Delaying not, hurrying not,
Whispered me through the night, and very plainly before daybreak,
Lisped to me the low and delicious word death,
And again death, death, death, death,
170 Hissing melodious, neither like the bird nor like my aroused child's heart,
But edging near as privately for me rustling at my feet,
Creeping thence steadily up to my ears and laving me softly all over,
Death, death, death, death, death.

Which I do not forget,
175 But fuse the song of my dusky demon and brother,
That he sang to me in the moonlight on Paumanok's gray beach,
With the thousand responsive songs at random,
My own songs awaked from that hour,
And with them the key, the word up from the waves,
180 The word of the sweetest song and all songs,
That strong and delicious word which, creeping to my feet,
(Or like some old crone rocking the cradle, swathed in sweet garments,
    bending aside,)
The sea whispered me.

[1859]

WHEN I HEARD THE LEARNED ASTRONOMER

When I heard the learned astronomer,
When the proofs, the figures, were ranged in columns before me,
When I was shown the charts and diagrams, to add, divide,
    and measure them,
When I sitting heard the astronomer where he lectured with much
    applause in the lecture-room,
5 How soon unaccountable I became tired and sick,
Till rising and gliding out I wandered off by myself,
In the mystical moist night-air, and from time to time,
Looked up in perfect silence at the stars.

[1865]

A NOISELESS PATIENT SPIDER

A noiseless patient spider,
I marked where on a little promontory it stood isolated,
Marked how to explore the vacant vast surrounding,
It launched forth filament, filament, filament, out of itself,
5   Ever unreeling them, ever tirelessly speeding them.

And you O my soul where you stand,
Surrounded, detached, in measureless oceans of space,
Ceaselessly musing, venturing, throwing, seeking the spheres to connect
    them,
Till the bridge you will need be formed, till the ductile anchor hold,
10   Till the gossamer thread you fling catch somewhere, O my soul.

                                                              [1868]

CAVALRY CROSSING A FORD

A line in long array where they wind betwixt green islands,
They take a serpentine course, their arms flash in the sun—hark to the
    musical clank,
Behold the silvery river; in it the splashing horses loitering stop to drink,
Behold the brown-faced men, each group, each person a picture, the
    negligent rest on the saddles,
5   Some emerge on the opposite bank, others are just entering the ford—
    while,
Scarlet and blue and snowy white,
The guidon flags flutter gayly in the wind.

                                                              [1871]

Matthew Arnold   *1822–1888*

DOVER BEACH

The sea is calm to-night.
The tide is full, the moon lies fair
Upon the straits;—on the French coast the light
Gleams and is gone; the cliffs of England stand,
5   Glimmering and vast, out in the tranquil bay.
Come to the window, sweet is the night-air!
Only, from the long line of spray
Where the sea meets the moon-blanched sand,
Listen! you hear the grating roar
10   Of pebbles which the waves draw back, and fling,
At their return, up the high strand,°   *shore*

Begin, and cease, and then again begin,
With tremulous cadence slow, and bring
The eternal note of sadness in.

15 Sophocles long ago
Heard it on the Aegæan, and it brought
Into his mind the turbid ebb and flow
Of human misery; we
Find also in the sound a thought,
20 Hearing it by this distant northern sea.

The sea of faith
Was once, too, at the full, and round earth's shore
Lay like the folds of a bright girdle furled.
But now I only hear
25 Its melancholy, long, withdrawing roar,
Retreating, to the breath
Of the night-wind, down the vast edges drear
And naked shingles° of the world.   *gravelly beaches*

Ah, love, let us be true
30 To one another! for the world, which seems
To lie before us like a land of dreams,
So various, so beautiful, so new,
Hath really neither joy, nor love, nor light,
Nor certitude, nor peace, nor help for pain;
35 And we are here as on a darkling° plain   *darkening*
Swept with confused alarms of struggle and flight,
Where ignorant armies clash by night.

[1867]

George Meredith   *1828–1909*

FROM MODERN LOVE[1]

II

It ended, and the morrow brought the task.
Her eyes were guilty gates, that let him in
By shutting all too zealous for their sin:

[1] This series of fifty sonnet-like poems provides a fictionalized account of the disintegration of Meredith's own marriage. In 1858 his wife, the daughter of the English poet and novelist, Thomas Love Peacock, left him to live with a painter. The first poem in the series (p. 565) describes the poet's initial realization of a problem in his marriage. The four poems given here recount his suffering from this knowledge on the following day (II), his memories of the happier period when their love was young (XVI), his reflections by the sea on the death of love (XLIII), and his final analysis of the flaws in his marriage (L).

Each sucked a secret, and each wore a mask.
5   But, oh, the bitter taste her beauty had!
He sickened as at breath of poison-flowers:
A languid humor stole among the hours,
And if their smiles encountered, he went mad,
And raged deep inward, till the light was brown
10 Before his vision, and the world, forgot,
Looked wicked as some old dull murder-spot.
A star with lurid beams, she seemed to crown
The pit of infamy: and then again
He fainted on his vengefulness, and strove
15 To ape the magnanimity of love,
And smote himself, a shuddering heap of pain.

XVI

In our old shipwrecked days there was an hour,
When in the firelight steadily aglow,
Joined slackly, we beheld the red chasm grow
Among the clicking coals. Our library-bower
5   That eve was left to us: and hushed we sat
As lovers to whom Time is whispering.
From sudden-opened doors we heard them sing:
The nodding elders mixed good wine with chat.
Well knew we that Life's greatest treasure lay
10 With us, and of it was our talk. "Ah, yes!
Love dies!" I said: I never thought it less.
She yearned to me that sentence to unsay.
Then when the fire domed blackening, I found
Her cheek was salt against my kiss, and swift
15 Up the sharp scale of sobs her breast did lift:—
Now am I haunted by that taste! that sound!

XLIII

Mark where the pressing wind shoots javelin-like
Its skeleton shadow on broad-backed wave!
Here is a fitting spot to dig Love's grave;
Here where the ponderous breakers plunge and strike,
5   And dart their hissing tongues high up the sand:
In hearing of the ocean, and in sight
Of those ribbed wind-streaks running into white.
If I the death of Love had deeply planned,
I never could have made it half so sure,
10 As by the unblest kisses which upbraid
The full-waked sense; or failing that, degrade!
'Tis morning: but no morning can restore
What we have forfeited. I see no sin:
The wrong is mixed. In tragic life, God wot,
15 No villain need be! Passions spin the plot:
We are betrayed by what is false within.

L

Thus piteously Love closed what he begat:
The union of this ever-diverse pair!
These two were rapid falcons in a snare,
Condemned to do the flitting of the bat.
5   Lovers beneath the singing sky of May,
They wandered once; clear as the dew on flowers:
But they fed not on the advancing hours:
Their hearts held cravings for the buried day.
Then each applied to each that fatal knife,
10   Deep questioning, which probes to endless dole.
Ah, what a dusty answer gets the soul
When hot for certainties in this our life!—
In tragic hints here see what evermore
Moves dark as yonder midnight ocean's force,
15   Thundering like ramping hosts of warrior horse,
To throw that faint thin line upon the shore!

[1862]

Emily Dickinson *1830–1886*

"SUCCESS IS COUNTED SWEETEST"

Success is counted sweetest
By those who ne'er succeed.
To comprehend a nectar
Requires sorest need.

5   Not one of all the purple Host
Who took the Flag today
Can tell the definition
So clear of Victory

As he defeated—dying—
10   On whose forbidden ear
The distant strains of triumph
Burst agonized and clear!

[1878]

"I TASTE A LIQUOR NEVER BREWED"

I taste a liquor never brewed—
From Tankards scooped in Pearl—
Not all the Vats upon the Rhine
Yield such an Alcohol!

5   Inebriate of Air—am I—
    And Debauchee of Dew—
    Reeling—thro endless summer days—
    From inns of Molten Blue—

    When "Landlords" turn the drunken Bee
10 Out of the Foxglove's door—
    When Butterflies—renounce their "drams"—
    I shall but drink the more!

    Till Seraphs° swing their snowy Hats—   *angels*
    And Saints—to windows run—
15 To see the little Tippler
    Leaning against the—Sun—

                                               [1861]

"THE SOUL SELECTS HER OWN SOCIETY"

    The Soul selects her own Society—
    Then—shuts the Door—
    To her divine Majority—
    Present no more—

5   Unmoved—she notes the Chariots—pausing—
    At her low Gate—
    Unmoved—an Emperor be kneeling
    Upon her Mat—

    I've known her—from an ample nation—
10 Choose One—
    Then—close the Valves of her attention—
    Like Stone—

                              [posthumous, 1890]

"A BIRD CAME DOWN THE WALK"

    A Bird came down the Walk—
    He did not know I saw—
    He bit an Angleworm in halves
    And ate the fellow, raw,

5   And then he drank a Dew
    From a convenient Grass—
    And then hopped sidewise to the Wall
    To let a Beetle pass—

    He glanced with rapid eyes
10 That hurried all around—
    They looked like frightened Beads, I thought—
    He stirred his Velvet Head

Like one in danger, Cautious,
I offered him a Crumb
15 And he unrolled his feathers
And rowed him softer home—

Than Oars divide the Ocean,
Too silver for a seam—
Or Butterflies, off Banks of Noon
20 Leap, plashless as they swim.

[posthumous, 1891]

"AFTER GREAT PAIN, A FORMAL FEELING COMES"

After great pain, a formal feeling comes—
The Nerves sit ceremonious, like Tombs—
The stiff Heart questions was it He, that bore,
And Yesterday, or Centuries before?

5 The Feet, mechanical, go round—
Of Ground, or Air, or Ought—
A Wooden way
Regardless grown,
A Quartz contentment, like a stone—

10 This is the Hour of Lead—
Remembered, if outlived,
As Freezing persons, recollect the Snow—
First—Chill—then Stupor—then the letting go—

[posthumous, 1929]

"I HEARD A FLY BUZZ—WHEN I DIED"

I heard a Fly buzz—when I died—
The Stillness in the Room
Was like the Stillness in the Air—
Between the Heaves of Storm—

5 The Eyes around—had wrung them dry—
And Breaths were gathering firm
For that last Onset—when the King
Be witnessed—in the Room—

I willed my Keepsakes—Signed away
10 What portion of me be
Assignable—and then it was
There interposed a Fly—

With Blue—uncertain stumbling Buzz—
Between the light—and me—
15   And then the Windows failed—and then
I could not see to see—

[posthumous, 1896]

"I LIKE TO SEE IT LAP THE MILES"

I like to see it lap the Miles—
And lick the Valleys up—
And stop to feed itself at Tanks—
And then—prodigious step

5   Around a Pile of Mountains—
And supercilious peer
In Shanties—by the sides of Roads—
And then a Quarry pare

To fit its Ribs
10   And crawl between
Complaining all the while
In horrid—hooting stanza—
Then chase itself down Hill—

And neigh like Boanerges[1]—
15   Then—punctual as a Star
Stop—docile and omnipotent
At its own stable door—

[posthumous, 1891]

"BECAUSE I COULD NOT STOP FOR DEATH"

Because I could not stop for Death—
He kindly stopped for me—
The Carriage held but just Ourselves—
And Immortality.

5   We slowly drove—He knew no haste
And I had put away
My labor and my leisure too,
For His Civility—

We passed the School, where Children strove
10   At Recess—in the Ring—
We passed the Fields of Gazing Grain—
We passed the Setting Sun—

Or rather—He passed Us—
The Dews drew quivering and chill—
15   For only Gossamer, my Gown—
My Tippet°—only Tulle°—   *shawl / silk gauze*

We paused before a House that seemed
A Swelling of the Ground—
The Roof was scarcely visible—
20   The Cornice—in the Ground—

[1] A loud preacher or orator, from two Hebrew words meaning "sons of thunder."

Since then—'tis Centuries—and yet
Feels shorter than the Day
I first surmised the Horses' Heads
Were toward Eternity—
[posthumous, 1890]

"A NARROW FELLOW IN THE GRASS"

A narrow Fellow in the Grass
Occasionally rides—
You may have met Him—did you not
His notice sudden is—

5 The Grass divides as with a Comb—
A spotted shaft is seen—
And then it closes at your feet
And opens further on—

He likes a Boggy Acre
10 A Floor too cool for Corn—
Yet when a Boy, a Barefoot—
I more than once at Noon
Have passed, I thought, a Whip lash
Unbraiding in the Sun
15 When stooping to secure it
It wrinkled, and was gone—

Several of Nature's People
I know, and they know me—
I feel for them a transport
20 Of cordiality—

But never met this Fellow
Attended, or alone
Without a tighter breathing
And Zero at the Bone—
[1866]

"I NEVER SAW A MOOR"

I never saw a Moor—
I never saw the Sea—
Yet know I how the Heather looks
And what a Billow be.

5 I never spoke with God
Nor visited in Heaven—
Yet certain am I of the spot
As if the Checks were given—
[posthumous, 1890]

"APPARENTLY WITH NO SURPRISE"

Apparently with no surprise
To any happy Flower
The Frost beheads it at its play—
In accidental power—
The blonde Assassin passes on—
The Sun proceeds unmoved
To measure off another Day
For an Approving God.

[posthumous, 1890]

"MY LIFE CLOSED TWICE BEFORE ITS CLOSE"

My life closed twice before its close—
It yet remains to see
If Immortality unveil
A third event to me

So huge, so hopeless to conceive
As these that twice befell.
Parting is all we know of heaven,
And all we need of hell.

[posthumous, 1896]

Christina Rossetti *1830–1894*

IN AN ARTIST'S STUDIO

One face looks out from all his canvases,
  One selfsame figure sits or walks or leans:
  We found her hidden just behind those screens,
That mirror gave back all her loveliness.
A queen in opal or in ruby dress,
  A nameless girl in freshest summer-greens,
  A saint, an angel—every canvas means
The same one meaning, neither more nor less.
He feeds upon her face by day and night,
  And she with true kind eyes looks back on him,
Fair as the moon and joyful as the light:
  Not wan with waiting, not with sorrow dim;
Not as she is, but was when hope shone bright;
  Not as she is, but as she fills his dream.

[1861]

A BIRTHDAY

My heart is like a singing bird
  Whose nest is in a watered shoot:
My heart is like an apple-tree
  Whose boughs are bent with thickset fruit;
5 My heart is like a rainbow shell
    That paddles in a halcyon° sea;   *calm*
My heart is gladder than all these
  Because my love is come to me.

Raise me a dais° of silk and down;   *throne*
10   Hang it with vair° and purple dyes;   *fur*
Carve it in doves and pomegranates,
  And peacocks with a hundred eyes;
Work it in gold and silver grapes,
  In leaves and silver fleurs-de-lys;°   *lily-shaped emblems*
15 Because the birthday of my life
  Is come, my love is come to me.

                [1862]

Lewis Carroll   *1832–1898*

JABBERWOCKY[1]

'T was brillig, and the slithy toves
  Did gyre and gimble in the wabe;
All mimsy were the borogoves,
  And the mome raths outgrabe.

5 "Beware the Jabberwock, my son!
    The jaws that bite, the claws that catch!
Beware the Jubjub bird, and shun
  The frumious Bandersnatch!"

He took his vorpal sword in hand:
10   Long time the manxome foe he sought—
So rested he by the Tumtum tree,
  And stood awhile in thought.

And as in uffish thought he stood,
  The Jabberwock, with eyes of flame,
15 Came whiffling through the tulgey wood,
  And burbled as it came!

---

[1] From *Through the Looking Glass.* In Chapter 6 Humpty Dumpty attempts to explain the poem.

One, two! One, two! And through and through
    The vorpal blade went snicker-snack!
He left it dead, and with its head
20   He went galumphing back.

"And hast thou slain the Jabberwock?
    Come to my arms, my beamish boy!
O frabjous day! Callooh! Callay!"
    He chortled in his joy.

25   'T was brillig, and the slithy toves
    Did gyre and gimble in the wabe;
All mimsy were the borogoves,
    And the mome raths outgrabe.

[1872]

William Morris   *1834–1896*

THE HAYSTACK IN THE FLOODS

Had she come all the way for this,
To part at last without a kiss?
Yea, had she borne the dirt and rain
That her own eyes might see him slain
5   Beside the haystack in the floods?

Along the dripping leafless woods,
The stirrup touching either shoe,
She rode astride as troopers do;
With kirtle kilted to her knee,°   *with skirt tucked up*
10   To which the mud splashed wretchedly;
And the wet dripped from every tree
Upon her head and heavy hair,
And on her eyelids broad and fair;
The tears and rain ran down her face.
15   By fits and starts they rode apace,
And very often was his place
Far off from her; he had to ride
Ahead, to see what might betide
When the roads crossed; and sometimes,
        when
20   There rose a murmuring from his men,
Had to turn back with promises;
Ah me! she had but little ease;

And often for pure doubt and dread
She sobbed, made giddy in the head
25   By the swift riding; while, for cold,
Her slender fingers scarce could hold
The wet reins; yea, and scarcely, too,
She felt the foot within her shoe
Against the stirrup: all for this,
30   To part at last without a kiss
Beside the haystack in the floods.

For when they neared that old soaked hay,
They saw across the only way
That Judas, Godmar, and the three
35   Red running lions dismally
Grinned from his pennon, under which
In one straight line along the ditch,
They counted thirty heads.
                            So then,
While Robert turned round to his men,
40   She saw at once the wretched end,
And, stooping down, tried hard to rend
Her coif° the wrong way from her head,   *hood*
And hid her eyes; while Robert said:
"Nay, love, 'tis scarcely two to one,
45   At Poictiers[1] where we made them run
So fast—why, sweet my love, good cheer.
The Gascon frontier[2] is so near,
Nought after this."

                    But, "O," she said,
"My God! my God! I have to tread
50   The long way back without you; then
The court at Paris; those six men;°   *the judges*
The gratings of the Chatelet;°   *a prison*
The swift Seine on some rainy day
Like this, and people standing by,
55   And laughing, while my weak hands try
To recollect how strong men swim.[3]
All this, or else a life with him,
For which I should be damned at last.
Would God that this next hour were past!"

60   He answered not, but cried his cry,
"St. George for Marny!" cheerily;

[1] At the Battle of Poitiers (France, 1356), in which Robert presumably took part, a small English force defeated a much larger French army.
[2] Gascony, now a region in southwestern France, was controlled by England in 1356.
[3] In witch trials, women were thrown into a body of water: if they drowned, they were judged innocent of witchcraft; if they floated, they were thought to be enchantresses and burned at the stake.

And laid his hand upon her rein.
Alas! no man of all his train
Gave back that cheery cry again;
65 And, while for rage his thumb beat fast
Upon his sword-hilts, some one cast
About his neck a kerchief long,
And bound him.

                          Then they went along
70 To Godmar; who said: "Now, Jehane,
Your lover's life is on the wane
So fast, that, if this very hour
You yield not as my paramour,
He will not see the rain leave off—
75 Nay, keep your tongue from gibe and scoff,
Sir Robert, or I slay you now."

She laid her hand upon her brow,
Then gazed upon the palm, as though
She thought her forehead bled, and—"No!"
She said, and turned her head away,
80 As there were nothing else to say,
And everything were settled: red
Grew Godmar's face from chin to head:
"Jehane, on yonder hill there stands
My castle, guarding well my lands:
85 What hinders me from taking you,
And doing that I list to do
To your fair wilful body, while
Your knight lies dead?"

                          A wicked smile
Wrinkled her face, her lips grew thin,
90 A long way out she thrust her chin:
"You know that I should strangle you
While you were sleeping; or bite through
Your throat, by God's help—ah!" she said,
"Lord Jesus, pity your poor maid!
95 For in such wise they hem me in,
I cannot choose but sin and sin,
Whatever happens: yet I think
They could not make me eat or drink,
And so should I just reach my rest."
100 "Nay, if you do not my behest,
O Jehane! though I love you well,"
Said Godmar, "would I fail to tell
All that I know?" "Foul lies," she said.
"Eh? lies my Jehane? by God's head,
105 At Paris folks would deem them true!
Do you know, Jehane, they cry for you:
'Jehane the brown! Jehane the brown!
Give us Jehane to burn or drown!'—

Eh—gag me Robert!—sweet my friend,
110 This were indeed a piteous end
For those long fingers, and long feet,
And long neck, and smooth shoulders sweet,
An end that few men would forget
That saw it—So, an hour yet:
115 Consider, Jehane, which to take
Of life or death!"
                              So, scarce awake,
Dismounting, did she leave that place,
And totter some yards: with her face
Turned upward to the sky she lay,
120 Her head on a wet heap of hay,
And fell asleep: and while she slept,
And did not dream, the minutes crept
Round to the twelve again; but she,
Being waked at last, sighed quietly,
125 And strangely childlike came, and said:
"I will not." Straightway Godmar's head,
As though it hung on strong wires, turned
Most sharply round, and his face burned.

For Robert—both his eyes were dry,
130 He could not weep, but gloomily
He seemed to watch the rain; yea, too,
His lips were firm; he tried once more
To touch her lips; she reached out, sore
And vain desire so tortured them,
135 The poor grey lips, and now the hem
Of his sleeve brushed them.
                              With a start
Up Godmar rose, thrust them apart;
From Robert's throat he loosed the bands
Of silk and mail; with empty hands
140 Held out, she stood and gazed, and saw
The long bright blade without a flaw
Glide out from Godmar's sheath, his hand
In Robert's hair; she saw him bend
Back Robert's head; she saw him send
145 The thin steel down; the blow told well,
Right backward the knight Robert fell,
And moaned as dogs do, being half dead,
Unwitting, as I deem: so then
Godmar turned grinning to his men,
150 Who ran, some five or six, and beat
His head to pieces at their feet.

Then Godmar turned again and said:
"So, Jehane, the first fitte° is read!   *canto*
Take note, my lady, that your way
155 Lies backward to the Chatelet!"

She shook her head and gazed awhile
At her cold hands with a rueful smile,
As though this thing had made her mad.

This was the parting that they had
160   Beside the haystack in the floods.

[1858]

Algernon Charles Swinburne   *1837–1909*

[CHORUS FROM ATALANTA IN CALYDON]

When the hounds of spring are on winter's traces,
    The mother of months[1] in meadow or plain
Fills the shadows and windy places
    With lisp of leaves and ripple of rain;
5   And the brown bright nightingale amorous
Is half assuaged for Itylus,
For the Thracian ships and the foreign faces,
    The tongueless vigil, and all the pain.[2]

Come with bows bent and with emptying of quivers,
10   Maiden most perfect, lady of light,
With a noise of winds and many rivers,
    With a clamor of waters, and with might;
Bind on my sandals, O thou most fleet,
Over the splendor and speed of thy feet;
15   For the faint east quickens, the wan west shivers,
    Round the feet of the day and the feet of the night.

Where shall we find her, how shall we sing to her,
    Fold our hands round her knees, and cling?
O that man's heart were as fire and could spring to her,
20   Fire, or the strength of the streams that spring!
For the stars and the winds are unto her
As raiment,° as sons of the harp-player;   *clothing*
For the risen stars and the fallen cling to her,
    And the southwest-wind and the west-wind sing.

---

[1] The poem is addressed to Artemis, the Greek goddess of wild animals and the moon—hence, "the mother of months."

[2] In Greek mythology Zeus transformed the suffering Philomela into a nightingale. Before this, Philomela had been raped and had her tongue cut out by her brother-in-law Tereus, a Thracian. In vengeance Philomela's sister, Procne, had slaughtered her own son, Itylus, and fed him in a stew to her husband.

25   For winter's rains and ruins are over,
        And all the season of snows and sins;
     The days dividing lover and lover,
        The light that loses, the night that wins;
     The time remembered is grief forgotten,
30   And frosts are slain and flowers begotten,
     And in green underwood and cover
        Blossom by blossom the spring begins.

     The full streams feed on flower of rushes,
        Ripe grasses trammel a travelling foot,
35   The faint fresh flame of the young year flushes
        From leaf to flower and flower to fruit;
     And fruit and leaf are as gold and fire,
     And the oat° is heard above the lyre,   *flute*
     And the hoofèd heel of a satyr crushes
40   The chestnut-husk at the chestnut-root.

     And Pan[3] by noon and Bacchus[4] by night,
        Fleeter of foot than the fleet-foot kid,°   *young goat*
     Follows with dancing and fills with delight
        The Mænad and the Bassarid;[5]
45   And soft as lips that laugh and hide
     The laughing leaves of the trees divide.
     And screen from seeing and leave in sight
        The god pursuing, the maiden hid.

     The ivy falls with the Bacchanal's hair
50   Over her eyebrows hiding her eyes;
     The wild vine slipping down leaves bare
        Her bright breast shortening into sighs;
     The wild vine slips with the weight of its leaves,
     But the berried ivy catches and cleaves
55   To the limbs that glitter, the feet that scare
        The wolf that follows, the fawn that flies.
                    [1865]

THE SUNBOWS[1]

Spray of song that springs in April, light of love that laughs through May,
Live and die and live for ever: nought of all things far less fair
Keeps a surer life than these that seem to pass like fire away.
    In the souls they live which are but all the brighter that they were;
5   In the hearts that kindle, thinking what delight of old was there.

---

[3] A Greek pastoral god fond of music and dancing.   [4] The Greek god of wine and revelry.
[5] Maenad, Bassarid, and Bacchanal (1. 49) are all names for the female followers of Bacchus.
[1] Rainbows from sea spray.

Wind that shapes and lifts and shifts them bids perpetual memory play
Over dreams, and in and out of deeds and thoughts, which seem to wear
Light that leaps and runs and revels through the springing flames of spray.

Dawn is wild upon the waters where we drink of dawn today:
10 Wide, from wave to wave rekindling in rebound through radiant air,
Flash the fires unwoven, and woven again, of wind that works in play,—
Working wonders more than heart may note, or sight may wellnigh dare,
Wefts[2] of rarer light than colors rain from heaven, though this be rare.
Arch on arch unbuilt in building, reared and ruined ray by ray,
15 Breaks and brightens, laughs and lessens,—even till eyes may hardly bear
Light that leaps and runs and revels through the springing flames of spray.

Year on year sheds light and music, rolled and flashed from bay to bay
Round the summer capes of time and winter headlands keen and bare,
Whence the soul keeps watch, and bids her vassal memory watch and
        pray,
20 If perchance the dawn may quicken,[3] or perchance the midnight spare.
Silence quells not music, darkness takes not sunlight in her snare:
Shall not joys endure that perish? Yea, saith dawn, though night say nay:
Life on life goes out; but very life enkindles everywhere
Light that leaps and runs and revels through the springing flames of spray.

25 Friend, were life no more than this is, well would yet the living fare.
All aflower and all afire and all flung heavenward, who shall say
Such a flash of life were worthless? This is worth a world of care,—
Light that leaps and runs and revels through the springing flames of spray.

[1884]

---

[2] Woven substances.   [3] Come to life.

❧ MODERN POETRY ❧

Thomas Hardy   *1840–1928*

HAP

If but some vengeful god would call to me
From up the sky, and laugh: "Thou suffering thing,
Know that thy sorrow is my ecstasy,
That thy love's loss is my hate's profiting!"

5 Then would I bear it, clench myself, and die,
Steeled by the sense of ire unmerited;
Half-eased in that a Powerfuller than I
Had willed and meted me the tears I shed.

But not so. How arrives it joy lies slain,
10 And why unblooms the best hope ever sown?
—Crass Casualty obstructs the sun and rain,
And dicing Time for gladness casts a moan. . . .
These purblind Doomsters had as readily strown
Blisses about my pilgrimage as pain.

[1898]

NEUTRAL TONES

We stood by a pond that winter day,
And the sun was white, as though chidden of God,
And a few leaves lay on the starving sod;
    —They had fallen from an ash, and were gray.

5 Your eyes on me were as eyes that rove
Over tedious riddles of years ago;
And some words played between us to and fro
    On which lost the more by our love.

The smile on your mouth was the deadest thing
10 Alive enough to have strength to die;
And a grin of bitterness swept thereby
    Like an ominous bird a-wing. . . .

Since then, keen lessons that love deceives,
And wrings with wrong, have shaped to me
15 Your face, and the God-curst sun, and a tree,
    And a pond edged with grayish leaves.

[1898]

THE DARKLING[1] THRUSH

I leant upon a coppice gate[2]
     When Frost was spectre-gray,
And Winter's dregs made desolate
     The weakening eye of day.
5   The tangled bine-stems[3] scored the sky
     Like strings of broken lyres,
And all mankind that haunted nigh
     Had sought their household fires.

The land's sharp features seemed to be
10   The Century's corpse[4] outleant,
His crypt the cloudy canopy,
     The wind his death-lament.
The ancient pulse of germ and birth
     Was shrunken hard and dry,
15   And every spirit upon earth
     Seemed fervorless as I.

At once a voice arose among
     The bleak twigs overhead
In a full-hearted evensong
20   Of joy illimited;
An aged thrush, frail, gaunt, and small,
     In blast-beruffled plume,
Had chosen thus to fling his soul
     Upon the growing gloom.

25   So little cause for carolings
     Of such ecstatic sound
Was written on terrestrial things
     Afar or nigh around,
That I could think there trembled through
30   His happy good-night air
Some blessed Hope, whereof he knew
     And I was unaware.

                                        [1902]

THE MAN HE KILLED

"Had he and I but met
     By some old ancient inn,
We should have sat us down to wet
     Right many a nipperkin![1]

[1] In the dark.   [2] The gate to a small thicket.   [3] Twining stems of shrubbery.
[4] The poem was composed on December 31, 1900.   [1] Half-pint of beer or ale.

5   "But ranged as infantry,
         And staring face to face,
    I shot at him as he at me,
         And killed him in his place.

         "I shot him dead because—
10   Because he was my foe,
    Just so: my foe of course he was;
         That's clear enough; although

         "He thought he'd 'list, perhaps,
         Off-hand like—just as I—
15   Was out of work—had sold his traps—
         No other reason why.

         "Yes; quaint and curious war is!
         You shoot a fellow down
    You'd treat if met where any bar is,
20   Or help to half-a-crown."

                         [1902]

THE CONVERGENCE OF THE TWAIN

(Lines on the loss of the 'Titanic'[1])

I

    In a solitude of the sea
    Deep from human vanity,
And the Pride of Life that planned her, stilly couches she.

II

    Steel chambers, late the pyres
5   Of her salamandrine[2] fires,
Cold currents thrid,° and turn to rhythmic tidal lyres.   *thread*

III

    Over the mirrors meant
    To glass the opulent
The sea-worm crawls—grotesque, slimed, dumb, indifferent.

IV

10   Jewels in joy designed
    To ravish the sensuous mind
Lie lightless, all their sparkles bleared and black and blind.

---

[1] The "unsinkable" luxury liner that sank with enormous loss of life after striking an iceberg on April 15, 1912.
[2] An allusion to mythological reptiles supposed to be able to live in fire or, possibly, an allusion to the elemental spirit living in fire in the natural philosophy of Paracelsus (c. 1493–1541).

V

Dim moon-eyed fishes near
Gaze at the gilded gear
15   And query: "What does this vaingloriousness down here?" . . .

VI

Well: while was fashioning
This creature of cleaving wing,
The Immanent Will that stirs and urges everything

VII

Prepared a sinister mate
20   For her—so gaily great—
A Shape of Ice, for the time far and dissociate.

VIII

And as the smart ship grew
In stature, grace, and hue,
In shadowy silent distance grew the Iceberg too.

IX

25   Alien they seemed to be:
No mortal eye could see
The intimate welding of their later history,

X

Or sign that they were bent
By paths coincident
30   On being anon twin halves of one august event,

XI

Till the Spinner of the Years
Said "Now!" And each one hears,
And consummation comes, and jars two hemispheres.

[1912]

CHANNEL FIRING[1]

That night your great guns, unawares,
Shook all our coffins as we lay,
And broke the chancel[2] window-squares,
We thought it was the Judgment-day

5   And sat upright. While drearisome
Arose the howl of wakened hounds:
The mouse let fall the altar-crumb,
The worms drew back into the mounds,

---

[1] The title refers to gunnery practice in the English Channel shortly before the commencement of World War I.
[2] The part of a church around the altar.

The glebe cow[3] drooled. Till God called, "No;
10 It's gunnery practice out at sea
Just as before you went below;
The world is as it used to be:

"All nations striving strong to make
Red war yet redder. Mad as hatters
15 They do no more for Christès sake
Than you who are helpless in such matters.

"That this is not the judgment-hour
For some of them's a blessed thing,
For if it were they'd have to scour
20 Hell's floor for so much threatening. . . .

"Ha, ha. It will be warmer when
I blow the trumpet (if indeed
I ever do; for you are men,
And rest eternal sorely need)."

25 So down we lay again. "I wonder,
Will the world ever saner be,"
Said one, "than when He sent us under
In our indifferent century!"

And many a skeleton shook his head.
30 "Instead of preaching forty year,"
My neighbour Parson Thirdly said,
"I wish I had stuck to pipes and beer."

Again the guns disturbed the hour,
Roaring their readiness to avenge,
35 As far inland as Stourton Tower,[4]
And Camelot, and starlit Stonehenge.

[1914]

Gerard Manley Hopkins   *1844–1889*

GOD'S GRANDEUR

The world is charged with the grandeur of God.
It will flame out, like shining from shook foil;°   *gold foil*
It gathers to a greatness, like the ooze of oil

---

[3] The cow of the parsonage.
[4] Stourton Tower commemorates King Alfred's victory over the invading Danes in 879. Camelot was the location of King Arthur's court (supposedly in the sixth century A.D.). The massive stones at Stonehenge were used in the mysterious Druidic rites of prehistoric England.

Crushed. Why do men then now not reck° his rod?   *take heed of*
5 Generations have trod, have trod, have trod;
    And all is seared with trade; bleared, smeared with toil;
    And wears man's smudge and shares man's smell: the soil
Is bare now, nor can foot feel, being shod.

And for all this, nature is never spent;
10   There lives the dearest freshness deep down things;
    And though the last lights off the black West went
        Oh, morning, at the brown brink eastward, springs—
Because the Holy Ghost over the bent
        World broods with warm breast and with ah! bright
            wings.
                                             [posthumous, 1918]

PIED BEAUTY

Glory be to God for dappled things—
    For skies of couple-color as a brinded° cow;   *spotted*
        For rose-moles all in stipple° upon trout that swim;   *dots*
Fresh-firecoal chestnut-falls; finches' wings;
5   Landscape plotted and pieced—fold, fallow, and plough;
        And áll trádes, their gear and tackle and trim.°   *equipment*

All things counter, original, spare, strange;
    Whatever is fickle, freckled (who knows how?)
        With swift, slow; sweet, sour; adazzle, dim;
10 He fathers-forth whose beauty is past change:
                    Praise him.
                                             [posthumous, 1918]

THE WINDHOVER:[1]

To Christ our Lord

I caught this morning morning's minion,° kingdom of   *favorite*
    daylight's dauphin,° dapple°-dawn-drawn Falcon, in   *heir / mottled*
        his riding
Of the rolling level underneath him steady air, and
        striding
High there, how he rung° upon the rein of a wimpling°   *circled / rippling*
        wing
5 In his ecstasy! then off, off forth on swing,
    As a skate's heel sweeps smooth on a bow-bend: the
        hurl and gliding
    Rebuffed the big wind. My heart in hiding
Stirred for a bird,—the achieve of, the mastery of the
        thing!

[1] The sparrowhawk, which seems to hover in a headwind.

Brute beauty and valor and act, oh, air, pride, plume, here
10   Buckle! AND the fire that breaks from thee then, a billion
Times told lovelier, more dangerous, O my chevalier!

No wonder of it: shéer plód makes plough down sillion[2]
Shine, and blue-bleak embers, ah my dear,
Fall, gall° themselves, and gash gold-vermilion.   *chafe*
[posthumous, 1918]

SPRING AND FALL:

To a Young Child

Márgarét, áre you gríeving
Over Goldengrove unleaving?
Leáves, líke the things of man, you
With your fresh thoughts care for, can you?
5   Áh! ás the heart grows older
It will come to such sights colder
By and by, nor spare a sigh
Though worlds of wanwood leafmeal[1] lie;
And yet you *will* weep and know why.
10   Now no matter, child, the name:
Sórrow's spríngs áre the same.
Nor mouth had, no nor mind, expressed
What heart heard of, ghost° guessed: *spirit*
It ís the blight man was born for,
15   It is Margaret you mourn for.
[posthumous, 1918]

"THOU ART INDEED JUST, LORD"

*Justus quidem tu es, Domine, si disputem tecum; verumtamen
justa loquar ad te: Quare via impiorum prosperatur? &c.*[1]

Thou art indeed just, Lord, if I contend
With thee; but, sir, so what I plead is just.
Why do sinners' ways prosper? and why must
Disappointment all I endeavor end?

5   Wert thou my enemy, O thou my friend,
How wouldst thou worse, I wonder, than thou dost
Defeat, thwart me? Oh, the sots and thralls° of lust   *prisoners*
Do in spare hours more thrive than I that spend,

---

[2] An archaic word meaning "a ridge between furrows."
[1] Hopkins has created the words *wanwood* and *leafmeal*. *Leafmeal* is probably a noun meaning "a
mulch of leaves." *Wanwood* would then be an adjective meaning "dark-woods."
[1] From the Bible, Jeremiah 12:1. Hopkins translates the Latin in the first three lines of the poem.

10   Sir, life upon thy cause. See, banks and brakes°   *thickets*
Now, leavèd how thick! lacèd they are again
With fretty chervil,° look, and fresh wind shakes   *lacy parsley*

Them; birds build—but not I build; no, but strain,
Time's eunuch, and not breed one work that wakes.
Mine, O thou lord of life, send my roots rain.

[posthumous, 1918]

A. E. Housman   *1859–1936*

"WHEN I WAS ONE-AND-TWENTY"

When I was one-and-twenty
  I heard a wise man say,
"Give crowns and pounds and guineas
  But not your heart away;
5   Give pearls away and rubies
  But keep your fancy free."
But I was one-and-twenty,
  No use to talk to me.

When I was one-and-twenty
10   I heard him say again,
"The heart out of the bosom
  Was never given in vain;
'Tis paid with sighs a plenty
  And sold for endless rue."
15   And I am two-and-twenty,
  And oh, 'tis true, 'tis true.

[1896]

"WITH RUE MY HEART IS LADEN"

With rue my heart is laden
  For golden friends I had,
For many a rose-lipt maiden
  And many a lightfoot lad.

5   By brooks too broad for leaping
  The lightfoot boys are laid;
The rose-lipt girls are sleeping
  In fields where roses fade.

[1896]

TO AN ATHLETE DYING YOUNG

The time you won your town the race
We chaired you through the market-place;
Man and boy stood cheering by,
And home we brought you shoulder-high.

5   Today, the road all runners come,
Shoulder-high we bring you home,
And set you at your threshold down,
Townsman of a stiller town.

Smart lad, to slip betimes away
10 From fields where glory does not stay
And early though the laurel grows
It withers quicker than the rose.

Eyes the shady night has shut
Cannot see the record cut,
15 And silence sounds no worse than cheers
After earth has stopped the ears:

Now you will not swell the rout
Of lads that wore their honors out,
Runners whom renown outran
20 And the name died before the man.

So set, before its echoes fade,
The fleet foot on the sill of shade,
And hold to the low lintel up
The still-defended challenge-cup.

25 And round that early-laurelled head
Will flock to gaze the strengthless dead,
And find unwithered on its curls
The garland briefer than a girl's.

[1896]

"TERENCE, THIS IS STUPID STUFF"

"Terence, this[1] is stupid stuff:
You eat your victuals fast enough;
There can't be much amiss, 'tis clear,
To see the rate you drink your beer.
5 But oh, good Lord, the verse you make,
It gives a chap the belly-ache.
The cow, the old cow, she is dead;
It sleeps well, the hornèd head:
We poor lads, 'tis our turn now
10 To hear such tunes as killed the cow.
Pretty friendship 'tis to rhyme
Your friends to death before their time
Moping melancholy mad:
Come, pipe a tune to dance to, lad."

15 Why, if 'tis dancing you would be,
There's brisker pipes than poetry.
Say, for what were hop-yards meant,
Or why was Burton built on Trent?[2]

---

[1] This poetry.   [2] Burton-on-Trent is an English city famous for its breweries.

Oh many a peer of England brews
Livelier liquor than the Muse,
And malt does more than Milton can
To justify God's ways to man.[3]
Ale, man, ale's the stuff to drink
For fellows whom it hurts to think:
Look into the pewter pot
To see the world as the world's not.
And faith, 'tis pleasant till 'tis past:
The mischief is that 'twill not last.
Oh I have been to Ludlow[4] fair
And left my necktie God knows where,
And carried halfway home, or near,
Pints and quarts of Ludlow beer:
Then the world seemed none so bad,
And I myself a sterling lad;
And down in lovely muck I've lain,
Happy till I woke again.
Then I saw the morning sky:
Heigho, the tale was all a lie;
The world, it was the old world yet,
I was I, my things were wet,
And nothing now remained to do
But begin the game anew.

Therefore, since the world has still
Much good, but much less good than ill,
And while the sun and moon endure
Luck's a chance, but trouble's sure,
I'd face it as a wise man would,
And train for ill and not for good.
'Tis true, the stuff I bring for sale
Is not so brisk a brew as ale:
Out of a stem that scored[5] the hand
I wrung it in a weary land.
But take it: if the smack is sour,
The better for the embittered hour;
It should do good to heart and head
When your soul is in my soul's stead;
And I will friend you, if I may,
In the dark and cloudy day.

There was a king reigned in the East:
There, when kings will sit to feast,
They get their fill before they think
With poisoned meat and poisoned drink.
He gathered all that springs to birth
From the many-venomed earth;

---

[3] An allusion to the opening of Milton's *Paradise Lost* (1667).
[4] A town in Shropshire.   [5] Cut.

65 First a little, thence to more,
He sampled all her killing store;
And easy, smiling, seasoned sound,
Sate the king when healths went round.
They put arsenic in his meat
70 And stared aghast to watch him eat;
They poured strychnine in his cup
And shook to see him drink it up:
They shook, they stared as white's their shirt:
Them it was their poison hurt.
75 —I tell the tale that I heard told.
Mithridates,[6] he died old.

[1896]

ON WENLOCK EDGE

On Wenlock Edge[1] the wood's in trouble;
His forest fleece the Wrekin[2] heaves;
The gale, it plies the saplings double,
And thick on Severn[3] snow the leaves.

5 'Twould blow like this through holt and hanger[4]
When Uricon[5] the city stood:
'Tis the old wind in the old anger,
But then it threshed another wood.

Then, 'twas before my time, the Roman
10 At yonder heaving hill would stare:
The blood that warms an English yeoman,
The thoughts that hurt him, they were there.

There, like the wind through woods in riot,
Through him the gale of life blew high;
15 The tree of man was never quiet:
Then 'twas the Roman, now 'tis I.

The gale, it plies the saplings double,
It blows so hard, 'twill soon be gone:
Today the Roman and his trouble
20 Are ashes under Uricon.

[1896]

---

[6] In his *Natural History* the Roman writer Pliny (23–79 A.D.) tells this story of Mithradates VI, King of Pontus (c. 133 B.C.–63 B.C.).
[1] Ridge. [2] Wrekin Hill. [3] The Severn River. [4] Woods and shed.
[5] A Roman city once located near Shrewsbury, England.

LOVELIEST OF TREES

Loveliest of trees, the cherry now
Is hung with bloom along the bough,
And stands about the woodland ride
Wearing white for Eastertide.

5   Now, of my threescore years and ten,
Twenty will not come again,
And take from seventy springs a score,
It only leaves me fifty more.

And since to look at things in bloom
10 Fifty springs are little room,
About the woodlands I will go
To see the cherry hung with snow.

                                        [1896]

IS MY TEAM PLOWING

"Is my team ploughing,
    That I was used to drive
And hear the harness jingle
    When I was man alive?"

5   Ay, the horses trample,
    The harness jingles now;
No change though you lie under
    The land you used to plough.

"Is football playing
10   Along the river shore,
With lads to chase the leather,
    Now I stand up no more?"

Ay, the ball is flying,
    The lads play heart and soul;
15 The goal stands up, the keeper
    Stands up to keep the goal.

"Is my girl happy,
    That I thought hard to leave,
And has she tired of weeping
20   As she lies down at eve?"

Ay, she lies down lightly,
    She lies not down to weep:
Your girl is well contented.
    Be still, my lad, and sleep.

25 "Is my friend hearty,
    Now I am thin and pine,
And has he found to sleep in
    A better bed than mine?"

Yes, lad, I lie easy,
30   I lie as lads would choose;
I cheer a dead man's sweetheart,
    Never ask me whose.

                                        [1896]

EIGHT O'CLOCK

He stood, and heard the steeple
    Sprinkle the quarters on the morning town.
One, two, three, four, to market-place and people
    It tossed them down.

5   Strapped, noosed, nighing his hour,
           He stood and counted them and cursed his luck;
        And then the clock collected in the tower
           Its strength, and struck.

                                    [1922]

Rudyard Kipling   *1865–1936*

MANDALAY[1]

By the old Moulmein Pagoda, lookin' lazy at the sea,
There's a Burma girl a-settin', and I know she thinks o' me;
For the wind is in the palm-trees, and the temple-bells they
    say:
"Come you back, you British soldier; come you back to
    Mandalay!"
5   Come you back to Mandalay,
           Where the old Flotilla lay:
           Can't you 'ear their paddles chunkin' from Rangoon[2] to
             Mandalay?
           On the road to Mandalay,
           Where the flyin'-fishes play,
10   An' the dawn comes up like thunder outer China
            'crost the Bay!

'Er petticoat was yaller an' 'er little cap was green,
An' 'er name was Supi-yaw-lat—jes' the same as Theebaw's[3]
    Queen,
An' I seed her first a-smokin' of a whackin' white cheroot,°   *cigar*
An' a-wastin' Christian kisses on an 'eathen idol's foot:
15   Bloomin' idol made o' mud—
           Wot they called the Great Gawd Budd—
           Plucky lot she cared for idols when I kissed 'er
             where she stud!
           On the road to Mandalay . . .

When the mist was on the rice-fields an' the sun was
    droppin' slow,
20   She'd git 'er little banjo an' she'd sing *"Kulla-lo-lo!"*

---

[1] A city in Burma.   [2] The capital of Burma.
[3] Theebaw was king of Upper Burma from 1878 to 1885.

With 'er arm upon my shoulder an' 'er cheek again my cheek
We useter watch the steamers an' the *hathis*° pilin' teak.   *elephants*
     Elephints a-pilin' teak
     In the sludgy, squdgy creek,
25   Where the silence 'ung that 'eavy you was 'arf afraid to
       speak!
     On the road to Mandalay . . .

But that's all shove be'ind me—long ago an' fur away,
An' there ain't no 'buses runnin' from the Bank to Mandalay;
An' I'm learnin' 'ere in London what the ten-year soldier
   tells:
30 "If you've 'eard the East a-callin', you won't never 'eed
  naught else."
     No! you won't 'eed nothin' else
     But them spicy garlic smells,
     An' the sunshine an' the palm-trees an' the tinkly
      temple-bells;
     On the road to Mandalay . . .

35 I am sick o' wastin' leather on these gritty pavin'-stones,
An' the blasted English drizzle wakes the fever in my bones;
Tho' I walks with fifty 'ousemaids outer Chelsea to the
   Strand,
An' they talks a lot o' lovin', but wot do they understand?
     Beefy face an' grubby 'and—
40   Law! wot do they understand?
     I've a neater, sweeter maiden in a cleaner, greener
      land!
     On the road to Mandalay . . .

Ship me somewheres east of Suez, where the best is like the
   worst,
Where there aren't no Ten Commandments an' a man can
   raise a thirst;
45 For the temple-bells are callin', an' it's there that I would
  be—
By the old Moulmein Pagoda, looking lazy at the sea;
     On the road to Mandalay,
     Where the old Flotilla lay,
     With our sick beneath the awnings when we went to
      Mandalay!
50   O the road to Mandalay,
     Where the flyin'-fishes play,
     An' the dawn comes up like thunder outer China
      'crost the Bay!

                          [1890]

GUNGA DIN

You may talk o' gin and beer
When you're quartered safe out 'ere,
An' you're sent to penny-fights an' Aldershot it;
But when it comes to slaughter
5   You will do your work on water,
An' you'll lick the bloomin' boots of 'im that's got it.
Now in Injia's sunny clime,
Where I used to spend my time
A-servin' of 'Er Majesty the Queen,
10 Of all them blackfaced crew
The finest man I knew
Was our regimental bhisti,° Gunga Din.   *water bearer*
         He was "Din! Din! Din!
   "You limpin' lump o' brick-dust, Gunga Din!
15   "Hi! Slippy *hitherao!*
         "Water, get it! *Panee lao,*°   *Bring water swiftly*
   "You squidgy-nosed old idol, Gunga Din."

The uniform 'e wore
Was nothin' much before,
20 An' rather less than 'arf o' that be'ind,
For a piece o' twisty rag
An' a goatskin water-bag
Was all the field-equipment 'e could find.
When the sweatin' troop-train lay
25 In a sidin' through the day,
Where the 'eat would make your bloomin' eyebrows
        crawl,
We shouted "Harry By!"°   *O brother*
Till our throats were bricky-dry,
Then we wopped 'im 'cause 'e couldn't serve us all.
30   It was "Din! Din! Din!
   "You 'eathen, where the mischief 'ave you been?
        "You put some *juldee*° in it   *haste*
        "Or I'll *marrow*° you this minute   *clobber*
   "If you don't fill up my helmet, Gunga Din!"

35 'E would dot an' carry one
Till the longest day was done;
An' 'e didn't seem to know the use o' fear.
If we charged or broke or cut,
You could bet your bloomin' nut,
40 'E'd be waitin' fifty paces right flank rear.
With 'is mussick° on 'is back,   *water-skin*
'E would skip with our attack,
An' watch us till the bugles made "Retire,"
An' for all 'is dirty 'ide
45 'E was white, clear white, inside
When 'e went to tend the wounded under fire!

It was "Din! Din! Din!"
With the bullets kickin' dust-spots on the green.
When the cartridges ran out,
50   You could hear the front-ranks shout,
"Hi! ammunition-mules an' Gunga Din!"

I shan't forgit the night
When I dropped be'ind the fight
With a bullet where my belt-plate should 'a' been.
55   I was chokin' mad with thirst,
An' the man that spied me first
Was our good old grinnin', gruntin' Gunga Din.
'E lifted up my 'ead,
An' he plugged me where I bled,
60   An' 'e guv me 'arf-a-pint o' water green.
It was crawlin' and it stunk,
But of all the drinks I've drunk,
I'm gratefullest to one from Gunga Din.
It was "Din! Din! Din!
65   " 'Ere's a beggar with a bullet through 'is spleen;
" 'E's chawin' up the ground,
"An' 'e's kickin' all around:
"For Gawd's sake git the water, Gunga Din!"

'E carried me away
70   To where a dooli° lay,   *stretcher*
An' a bullet come an' drilled the beggar clean.
'E put me safe inside,
An' just before 'e died,
"I 'ope you liked your drink," sez Gunga Din.
75   So I'll meet 'im later on
At the place where 'e is gone—
Where it's always double drill and no canteen.
'E'll be squattin' on the coals
Givin' drink to poor damned souls,
80   An' I'll get a swig in hell from Gunga Din!
Yes, Din! Din! Din!
You Lazarushian-leather Gunga Din!
Though I've belted you and flayed you,
By the livin' Gawd that made you,
85   You're a better man than I am, Gunga Din!

[1890]

William Butler Yeats   *1865–1939*

THE LAKE ISLE OF INNISFREE

I will arise and go now, and go to Innisfree,
And a small cabin build there, of clay and wattles° made: *woven limbs*
Nine bean-rows will I have there, a hive for the honeybee,
And live alone in the bee-loud glade.

5   And I shall have some peace there, for peace comes
     dropping slow,
Dropping from the veils of the morning to where the cricket
     sings;
There midnight's all a glimmer, and noon a purple glow,
And evening full of the linnet's° wings.   *a songbird*

I will arise and go now, for always night and day
10   I hear lake water lapping with low sounds by the shore;
While I stand on the roadway, or on the pavements grey,
I hear it in the deep heart's core.

[1892]

NO SECOND TROY

Why should I blame her[1] that she filled my days
With misery, or that she would of late
Have taught to ignorant men most violent ways,
Or hurled the little streets upon the great,
5   Had they but courage equal to desire?
What could have made her peaceful with a mind
That nobleness made simple as a fire,
With beauty like a tightened bow, a kind
That is not natural in an age like this,
10   Being high and solitary and most stern?
Why, what could she have done, being what she is?
Was there another Troy for her to burn?

[1910]

THE WILD SWANS AT COOLE[2]

The trees are in their autumn beauty,
The woodland paths are dry,
Under the October twilight the water
Mirrors a still sky;

---

[1] The unnamed woman in this poem is Maud Gonne, an Irish nationalist and revolutionary, who is here compared with Helen of Troy, the woman indirectly responsible for the destruction of Troy in the classical Greek legend.

[2] Between 1897 and 1916 (when this poem was written), Yeats had often been a guest at Coole Park, his friend Lady Gregory's country estate.

5 Upon the brimming water among the stones
   Are nine-and-fifty swans.

   The nineteenth autumn has come upon me
   Since I first made my count;
   I saw, before I had well finished,
10 All suddenly mount
   And scatter wheeling in great broken rings
   Upon their clamorous wings.

   I have looked upon those brilliant creatures,
   And now my heart is sore.
15 All's changed since I, hearing at twilight,
   The first time on this shore,
   The bell-beat of their wings above my head,
   Trod with a lighter tread.

   Unwearied still, lover by lover,
20 They paddle in the cold
   Companionable streams or climb the air;
   Their hearts have not grown old;
   Passion or conquest, wander where they will,
   Attend upon them still.

25 But now they drift on the still water,
   Mysterious, beautiful;
   Among what rushes will they build,
   By what lake's edge or pool
   Delight men's eyes when I awake some day
30 To find they have flown away?

                                                    [1917]

THE SECOND COMING[1]

   Turning and turning in the widening gyre[2]
   The falcon cannot hear the falconer;
   Things fall apart; the center cannot hold;
   Mere anarchy is loosed upon the world,
5 The blood-dimmed tide is loosed, and everywhere
   The ceremony of innocence is drowned;
   The best lack all conviction, while the worst
   Are full of passionate intensity.

   Surely some revelation is at hand;
10 Surely the Second Coming is at hand.
   The Second Coming! Hardly are those words out

[1] The title alludes to the Second Coming of Christ predicted in Matthew 24, but also symbolizes
the end of one age and the commencement of another.
[2] The widening spiral flown by the falcon takes it so far out that it no longer hears its master.
Yeats uses the gyre or spiral as a symbol of extension and dissolution in the cycle of our civilization.

When a vast image out of *Spiritus Mundi*[3]
Troubles my sight: somewhere in sands of the desert
A shape with lion body and the head of a man,[4]
15   A gaze blank and pitiless as the sun,
Is moving its slow thighs, while all about it
Reel shadows of the indignant desert birds.
The darkness drops again; but now I know
That twenty centuries of stony sleep
20   Were vexed to nightmare by a rocking cradle,[5]
And what rough beast, its hour come round at last,
Slouches toward Bethlehem to be born?

                                        [1921]

LEDA AND THE SWAN[1]

A sudden blow: the great wings beating still
Above the staggering girl, her thighs caressed
By the dark webs, her nape caught in his bill,
He holds her helpless breast upon his breast.

5   How can those terrified vague fingers push
The feathered glory from her loosening thighs?
And how can body, laid in that white rush,
But feel the strange heart beating where it lies?

A shudder in the loins engenders there
10   The broken wall, the burning roof and tower
And Agamemnon dead.
                        Being so caught up,
So mastered by the brute blood of the air,
Did she put on his knowledge with his power
Before the indifferent beak could let her drop?

                                        [1924]

SAILING TO BYZANTIUM

I

That is no country for old men. The young
In one another's arms, birds in the trees
—Those dying generations—at their song,
The salmon-falls, the mackerel-crowded seas,
5   Fish, flesh, or fowl, commend all summer long

---

[3] The spirit of the world, a form of universal subconscious serving as a storehouse of images.
[4] A Sphinx-like creature.
[5] Yeats's idea is, perhaps, that the rocking of Christ's cradle produced, after twenty centuries, the awakening Sphinx.
[1] In Greek mythology Leda was raped by Zeus in the form of a swan; she subsequently gave birth to Helen, who caused the destruction of Troy, and Clytemnestra, who murdered her husband Agamemnon upon his return from Troy.

Whatever is begotten, born, and dies.
Caught in that sensual music all neglect
Monuments of unageing intellect.

                              II

10 An aged man is but a paltry thing,
A tattered coat upon a stick, unless
Soul clap its hands and sing, and louder sing
For every tatter in its mortal dress,
Nor is there singing school but studying
Monuments of its own magnificence;
15 And therefore I have sailed the seas and come
To the holy city of Byzantium.[1]

                              III

O sages standing in God's holy fire
As in the gold mosaic of a wall,
Come from the holy fire, perne in a gyre,[2]
20 And be the singing-masters of my soul.
Consume my heart away; sick with desire
And fastened to a dying animal
It knows not what it is; and gather me
Into the artifice of eternity.

                              IV

25 Once out of nature I shall never take
My bodily form from any natural thing,
But such a form as Grecian goldsmiths make
Of hammered gold and gold enamelling
To keep a drowsy Emperor awake;
30 Or set upon a golden bough to sing
To lords and ladies of Byzantium
Of what is past, or passing, or to come.

                                              [1927]

CRAZY JANE TALKS WITH THE BISHOP

I met the Bishop on the road
And much said he and I.
"Those breasts are flat and fallen now,
Those veins must soon be dry;
5 Live in a heavenly mansion,
Not in some foul sty."

[1] Yeats contrasts the sensuality and mortality of the modern world with the permanence and artifice found in medieval Byzantium (the site of modern Istanbul, Turkey). In *A Vision* (1937) he wrote: "I think that in early Byzantium, maybe never before or since in recorded history, religious, aesthetic and practical life were one, that architect and artificer . . . spoke to the multitude and the few alike. The painter, the mosaic worker, the worker in gold and silver, the illuminator of sacred books, were almost impersonal, almost perhaps without the consciousness of individual design, absorbed in their subject-matter and that the vision of a whole people."
[2] Spiral down.

"Fair and foul are near of kin,
And fair needs foul," I cried.
"My friends are gone, but that's a truth
10 Nor grave nor bed denied,
Learned in bodily lowliness
And in the heart's pride.

"A woman can be proud and stiff
When on love intent;
15 But Love has pitched his mansion in
The place of excrement;
For nothing can be sole or whole
That has not been rent."

[1932]

Ernest Dowson   *1867–1900*

VITAE SUMMA BREVIS SPEM NOS VETAT
INCOHARE LONGAM[1]

They are not long, the weeping and the laughter,
Love and desire and hate:
I think they have no portion in us after
We pass the gate.

5 They are not long, the days of wine and roses:
Out of a misty dream
Our path emerges for a while, then closes
Within a dream.

[1896]

NON SUM QUALIS ERAM BONAE
SUB REGNO CYNARAE[2]

Last night, ah, yesternight, betwixt her lips and mine
There fell thy shadow, Cynara! thy breath was shed
Upon my soul between the kisses and the wine;
And I was desolate and sick of an old passion,
5 Yea, I was desolate and bowed my head:
I have been faithful to thee, Cynara! in my fashion.

[1] A line by the Roman poet Horace (65–8 B.C.) meaning, "The brevity of life prevents us from entertaining far-reaching expectations."
[2] A line by the Roman poet Horace (65–8 B.C.) meaning, "I am not as I was under the reign of kind Cynara."

All night upon mine heart I felt her warm heart beat,
Night-long within mine arms in love and sleep she lay;
Surely the kisses of her bought red mouth were sweet;
10   But I was desolate and sick of an old passion,
    When I awoke and found the dawn was gray:
I have been faithful to thee, Cynara! in my fashion.

I have forgot much, Cynara! gone with the wind,
Flung roses, roses riotously with the throng,
15   Dancing, to put thy pale, lost lilies out of mind;
But I was desolate and sick of an old passion,
    Yea, all the time, because the dance was long:
I have been faithful to thee, Cynara! in my fashion.

I cried for madder music and for stronger wine,
20   But when the feast is finished and the lamps expire,
Then falls thy shadow, Cynara! the night is thine;
And I am desolate and sick of an old passion,
    Yea hungry for the lips of my desire:
I have been faithful to thee, Cynara! in my fashion.

[1896]

Edwin Arlington Robinson   1869–1935

REUBEN BRIGHT

Because he was a butcher and thereby
Did earn an honest living (and did right),
I would not have you think that Reuben Bright
Was any more a brute than you or I;
5   For when they told him that his wife must die,
He stared at them, and shook with grief and fright,
And cried like a great baby half that night,
And made the women cry to see him cry.

And after she was dead, and he had paid
10   The singers and the sexton and the rest,
He packed a lot of things that she had made
Most mournfully away in an old chest
Of hers, and put some chopped-up cedar boughs
In with them, and tore down the slaughter-house.

[1897]

THE MILL

The miller's wife had waited long,
   The tea was cold, the fire was dead;
And there might yet be nothing wrong
   In how he went and what he said:
5 "There are no millers any more,"
   Was all that she had heard him say;
And he had lingered at the door
   So long that it seemed yesterday.

Sick with a fear that had no form
10   She knew that she was there at last;
And in the mill there was a warm
   And mealy fragrance of the past.
What else there was would only seem
   To say again what he had meant;
15 And what was hanging from a beam
   Would not have heeded where she went.

And if she thought it followed her,
   She may have reasoned in the dark
That one way of the few there were
20   Would hide her and would leave no mark:
Black water, smooth above the weir°   *dam*
   Like starry velvet in the night,
Though ruffled once, would soon appear
   The same as ever to the sight.

                                [1920]

MR. FLOOD'S PARTY

Old Eben Flood, climbing alone one night
Over the hill between the town below
And the forsaken upland hermitage
That held as much as he should ever know
5 On earth again of home, paused warily.
The road was his with not a native near;
And Eben, having leisure, said aloud,
For no man else in Tillbury Town to hear:

"Well, Mr. Flood, we have the harvest moon
10 Again, and we may not have many more;
The bird is on the wing, the poet says,[1]
And you and I have said it here before.
Drink to the bird." He raised up to the light

[1] The poet is Edward FitzGerald (1809–1883) in his "The Rubaiyat of Omar Khayyám" (1859).
See p. 778.

The jug that he had gone so far to fill,
15   And answered huskily: "Well, Mr. Flood,
Since you propose it, I believe I will."

Alone, as if enduring to the end
A valiant armor of scarred hopes outworn,
He stood there in the middle of the road
20   Like Roland's ghost winding a silent horn.[2]
Below him, in the town among the trees,
Where friends of other days had honored him,
A phantom salutation of the dead
Rang thinly till old Eben's eyes were dim.

25   Then, as a mother lays her sleeping child
Down tenderly, fearing it may awake,
He set the jug down slowly at his feet
With trembling care, knowing that most things break;
And only when assured that on firm earth
30   It stood, as the uncertain lives of men
Assuredly did not, he paced away,
And with his hand extended paused again:

"Well, Mr. Flood, we have not met like this
In a long time; and many a change has come
35   To both of us, I fear, since last it was
We had a drop together. Welcome home!"
Convivially returning with himself,
Again he raised the jug up to the light;
And with an acquiescent quaver said:
40   "Well, Mr. Flood, if you insist, I might.

"Only a very little, Mr. Flood—
For auld lang syne. No more, sir; that will do."
So, for the time, apparently it did,
And Eben evidently thought so too;
45   For soon amid the silver loneliness
Of night he lifted up his voice and sang,
Secure, with only two moons listening,
Until the whole harmonious landscape rang—

"For auld lang syne." The weary throat gave out,
50   The last word wavered, and the song was done.
He raised again the jug regretfully
And shook his head, and was again alone.
There was not much that was ahead of him,
And there was nothing in the town below—
55   Where strangers would have shut the many doors
That many friends had opened long ago.

                                                        [1920]

[2] Roland is the hero of the twelfth-century French romance *The Song of Roland*, who fought valiantly
against the Saracens (Spanish Moslems), at Roncesvalles (778) and, overwhelmed at last, sounded
his horn to summon help from Charlemagne, and died.

NEW ENGLAND

Here where the wind is always north-north-east
And children learn to walk on frozen toes,
Wonder begets an envy of all those
Who boil elsewhere with such a lyric yeast
5   Of love that you will hear them at a feast
Where demons would appeal for some repose,
Still clamoring where the chalice overflows
And crying wildest who have drunk the least.

Passion is here a soilure of the wits,
10   We're told, and Love a cross for them to bear;
Joy shivers in the corner where she knits
And Conscience always has the rocking-chair,
Cheerful as when she tortured into fits
The first cat that was ever killed by Care.

                                        [1923]

Paul Laurence Dunbar   *1872–1906*

SYMPATHY

I know what the caged bird feels, alas!
   When the sun is bright on the upland slopes;
When the wind stirs soft through the springing grass,
And the river flows like a stream of glass;
5   When the first bird sings and the first bud opes,
And the faint perfume from its chalice steals—
I know what the caged bird feels!

I know why the caged bird beats his wing
   Till its blood is red on the cruel bars;
10   For he must fly back to his perch and cling
When he fain would be on the bough a-swing;
   And a pain still throbs in the old, old scars
And they pulse again with a keener sting—
I know why he beats his wing!

15   I know why the caged bird sings, ah me,
   When his wing is bruised and his bosom sore,—
When he beats his bars and he would be free;
It is not a carol of joy or glee,
   But a prayer that he sends from his heart's deep core,
20   But a plea, that upward to Heaven he flings—
I know why the caged bird sings!

                                        [1899]

Ralph Hodgson   *1872–1962*

EVE

Eve, with her basket, was
Deep in the bells and grass,
Wading in bells and grass
Up to her knees,
5 Picking a dish of sweet
Berries and plums to eat,
Down in the bells and grass
Under the trees.

Mute as a mouse in a
10 Corner the cobra lay,
Curled round a bough of the
Cinnamon tall. . . .
Now to get even and
Humble proud Heaven and
15 Now was the moment or
Never at all.

"Eva!" Each syllable
Light as a flower fell,
"Eva!" he whispered the
20 Wondering maid,
Soft as a bubble sung
Out of a linnet's[1] lung,
Soft and most silverly
"Eva!" he said.

25 Picture that orchard sprite,
Eve, with her body white,
Supple and smooth to her
Slim finger tips,
Wondering, listening,
30 Listening, wondering,
Eve with a berry
Half-way to her lips.

Oh had our simple Eve
Seen through the make-believe!
35 Had she but known the
Pretender he was!
Out of the boughs he came,
Whispering still her name,
Tumbling in twenty rings
40 Into the grass.

Here was the strangest pair
In the world anywhere,
Eve in the bells and grass
Kneeling, and he
45 Telling his story low. . . .
Singing birds saw them go
Down the dark path to
The Blasphemous Tree.

Oh what a clatter when
50 Titmouse[2] and Jenny Wren
Saw him successful and
Taking his leave!
How the birds rated him,
How they all hated him!
55 How they all pitied
Poor motherless Eve!

Picture her crying
Outside in the lane,
Eve, with no dish of sweet
60 Berries and plums to eat,
Haunting the gate of the
Orchard in vain. . . .
Picture the lewd delight
Under the hill tonight—
65 "Eva!" the toast goes round,
"Eva!" again.

[1913]

---

[1] A small songbird.   [2] A chickadee.

Walter de la Mare   *1873–1956*

THE LISTENERS

"Is there anybody there?" said the Traveler,
  Knocking on the moonlit door;
And his horse in the silence champed the grasses
  Of the forest's ferny floor.
5 And a bird flew up out of the turret,
  Above the Traveler's head:
And he smote upon the door again a second time;
  "Is there anybody there?" he said.
But no one descended to the Traveler;
10 No head from the leaf-fringed sill
Leaned over and looked into his gray eyes,
  Where he stood perplexed and still.
But only a host of phantom listeners
  That dwelt in the lone house then
15 Stood listening in the quiet of the moonlight
  To that voice from the world of men:
Stood thronging the faint moonbeams on the dark stair
  That goes down to the empty hall,
Hearkening in an air stirred and shaken
20 By the lonely Traveler's call.
And he felt in his heart their strangeness,
  Their stillness answering his cry,
While his horse moved, cropping the dark turf,
  'Neath the starred and leafy sky;
25 For he suddenly smote on the door, even
  Louder, and lifted his head:—
"Tell them I came, and no one answered,
  That I kept my word," he said.
Never the least stir made the listeners,
30 Though every word he spake
Fell echoing through the shadowiness of the still house
  From the one man left awake:
Aye, they heard his foot upon the stirrup,
  And the sound of iron on stone,
35 And how the silence surged softly backward,
  When the plunging hoofs were gone.

[1912]

Amy Lowell *1874–1925*

PATTERNS

I walk down the garden paths,
And all the daffodils
Are blowing, and the bright blue squills.
I walk down the patterned garden-paths
5 In my stiff, brocaded gown.
With my powdered hair and jewelled fan,
I too am a rare
Pattern. As I wander down
The garden paths.

10 My dress is richly figured,
And the train
Makes a pink and silver stain
On the gravel, and the thrift
Of the borders.
15 Just a plate of current fashion,
Tripping by in high-heeled, ribboned shoes.
Not a softness anywhere about me,
Only whalebone and brocade.
And I sink on a seat in the shade
20 Of a lime tree. For my passion
Wars against the stiff brocade.
The daffodils and squills
Flutter in the breeze
As they please.
25 And I weep;
For the lime-tree is in blossom
And one small flower has dropped upon my bosom.

And the plashing of waterdrops
In the marble fountain
30 Comes down the garden-paths.
The dripping never stops.
Underneath my stiffened gown
Is the softness of a woman bathing in a marble basin,
A basin in the midst of hedges grown
35 So thick, she cannot see her lover hiding,
But she guesses he is near,
And the sliding of the water
Seems the stroking of a dear
Hand upon her.
40 What is Summer in a fine brocaded gown!
I should like to see it lying in a heap upon the ground.
All the pink and silver crumpled up on the ground.

I would be the pink and silver as I ran along the paths,
And he would stumble after,
45 Bewildered by my laughter.
I should see the sun flashing from his sword-hilt and the buckles
    on his shoes.
I would choose
To lead him in a maze along the patterned paths,
A bright and laughing maze for my heavy-booted lover.
50 Till he caught me in the shade,
And the buttons of his waistcoat bruised my body as he clasped me,
Aching, melting, unafraid.
With the shadows of the leaves and the sundrops
And the plopping of the waterdrops,
55 All about us in the open afternoon—
I am very like to swoon
With the weight of this brocade,
For the sun sifts through the shade.

Underneath the fallen blossom
60 In my bosom,
Is a letter I have hid.
It was brought to me this morning by a rider from the Duke.
"Madam, we regret to inform you that Lord Hartwell
Died in action Thursday se'nnight."[1]
65 As I read it in the white, morning sunlight,
The letters squirmed like snakes.
"Any answer, Madam?" said my footman.
"No," I told him.
"See that the messenger takes some refreshment.
70 No, no answer."
And I walked into the garden,
Up and down the patterned paths,
In my stiff, correct brocade.
The blue and yellow flowers stood up proudly in the sun,
75 Each one.
I stood upright too,
Held rigid to the pattern
By the stiffness of my gown.
Up and down I walked,
80 Up and down.

In a month he would have been my husband.
In a month, here, underneath this lime,
We would have broken the pattern;
He for me, and I for him,
85 He as Colonel, I as Lady,
On this shady seat.
He had a whim
That sunlight carried blessing.

[1] Seven days and nights, a week.

And I answered, "It shall be as you have said."
90   Now he is dead.

In Summer and in Winter I shall walk
Up and down
The patterned garden-paths
In my stiff, brocaded gown.
95   The squills and daffodils
Will give place to pillared roses, and to asters, and to snow.
I shall go
Up and down,
In my gown.
100 Gorgeously arrayed,
Boned and stayed.
And the softness of my body will be guarded from embrace
By each button, hook, and lace.
For the man who should loose me is dead,
105 Fighting with the Duke in Flanders,
In a pattern called a war.
Christ! What are patterns *for*?

[1915]

Robert Frost   *1874–1963*

THE ROAD NOT TAKEN

Two roads diverged in a yellow wood,
And sorry I could not travel both
And be one traveler, long I stood
And looked down one as far as I could
5   To where it bent in the undergrowth;

Then took the other, as just as fair,
And having perhaps the better claim,
Because it was grassy and wanted wear;
Though as for that the passing there
10   Had worn them really about the same,

And both that morning equally lay
In leaves no step had trodden black.
Oh, I kept the first for another day!
Yet knowing how way leads on to way,
15   I doubted if I should ever come back.

I shall be telling this with a sigh
Somewhere ages and ages hence:
Two roads diverged in a wood, and I—
I took the one less traveled by,
And that has made all the difference.

[1915]

BIRCHES

When I see birches bend to left and right
Across the lines of straighter darker trees,
I like to think some boy's been swinging them.
But swinging doesn't bend them down to stay
As ice-storms do. Often you must have seen them
Loaded with ice a sunny winter morning
After a rain. They click upon themselves
As the breeze rises, and turn many-colored
As the stir cracks and crazes their enamel.
Soon the sun's warmth makes them shed crystal shells
Shattering and avalanching on the snow-crust—
Such heaps of broken glass to sweep away
You'd think the inner dome of heaven had fallen.
They are dragged to the withered bracken° by the load,   *coarse ferns*
And they seem not to break; though once they are bowed
So low for long, they never right themselves:
You may see their trunks arching in the woods
Years afterwards, trailing their leaves on the ground
Like girls on hands and knees that throw their hair
Before them over their heads to dry in the sun.
But I was going to say when Truth broke in
With all her matter-of-fact about the ice-storm
I should prefer to have some boy bend them
As he went out and in to fetch the cows—
Some boy too far from town to learn baseball,
Whose only play was what he found himself,
Summer or winter, and could play alone.
One by one he subdued his father's trees
By riding them down over and over again
Until he took the stiffness out of them,
And not one but hung limp, not one was left
For him to conquer. He learned all there was
To learn about not launching out too soon
And so not carrying the tree away
Clear to the ground. He always kept his poise
To the top branches, climbing carefully
With the same pains you use to fill a cup
Up to the brim, and even above the brim.
Then he flung outward, feet first, with a swish,
Kicking his way down through the air to the ground.

So was I once myself a swinger of birches.
And so I dream of going back to be.
It's when I'm weary of considerations,
And life is too much like a pathless wood
45 Where your face burns and tickles with the cobwebs
Broken across it, and one eye is weeping
From a twig's having lashed across it open.
I'd like to get away from earth awhile
And then come back to it and begin over.
50 May no fate willfully misunderstand me
And half grant what I wish and snatch me away
Not to return. Earth's the right place for love:
I don't know where it's likely to go better.
I'd like to go by climbing a birch tree,
55 And climb black branches up a snow-white trunk
Toward heaven, till the tree could bear no more,
But dipped its top and set me down again.
That would be good both going and coming back.
One could do worse than be a swinger of birches.

                                                                    [1915]

DUST OF SNOW

The way a crow   5   Has given my heart
Shook down on me   A change of mood
The dust of snow   And saved some part
From a hemlock tree   Of a day I had rued.

                                                                    [1920]

FIRE AND ICE

Some say the world will end in fire,
Some say in ice.
From what I've tasted of desire
I hold with those who favor fire.
5 But if it had to perish twice,
I think I know enough of hate
To say that for destruction ice
Is also great
And would suffice.

                                                                    [1920]

NOTHING GOLD CAN STAY

Nature's first green is gold,
Her hardest hue to hold.
Her early leaf's a flower;
But only so an hour.

5   Then leaf subsides to leaf.
So Eden sank to grief,
So dawn goes down to day.
Nothing gold can stay.

[1923]

THE NEED OF BEING VERSED IN COUNTRY THINGS

The house had gone to bring again
To the midnight sky a sunset glow.
Now the chimney was all of the house that stood,
Like a pistil after the petals go.

5   The barn opposed across the way,
That would have joined the house in flame
Had it been the will of the wind, was left
To bear forsaken the place's name.

No more it opened with all one end
10   For teams that came by the stony road
To drum on the floor with scurrying hoofs
And brush the mow with the summer load.

The birds that came to it through the air
At broken windows flew out and in,
15   Their murmur more like the sigh we sigh
From too much dwelling on what has been.

Yet for them the lilac renewed its leaf,
And the aged elm, though touched with fire;
And the dry pump flung up an awkward arm;
20   And the fence post carried a strand of wire.

For them there was really nothing sad.
But though they rejoiced in the nest they kept,
One had to be versed in country things
Not to believe the phoebes wept.

[1923]

ACQUAINTED WITH THE NIGHT

I have been one acquainted with the night.
I have walked out in rain—and back in rain.
I have outwalked the furthest city light.

I have looked down the saddest city lane.
5   I have passed by the watchman on his beat
And dropped my eyes, unwilling to explain.

I have stood still and stopped the sound of feet
When far away an interrupted cry
Came over houses from another street,

10 But not to call me back or say good-by;
And further still at an unearthly height,
One luminary clock against the sky

Proclaimed the time was neither wrong nor right.
I have been one acquainted with the night.

[1928]

NEITHER OUT FAR NOR IN DEEP

The people along the sand
All turn and look one way.
They turn their back on the land.
They look at the sea all day.

5 As long as it takes to pass
A ship keeps raising its hull;
The wetter ground like glass
Reflects a standing gull.

The land may vary more;
10 But wherever the truth may be—
The water comes ashore,
And the people look at the sea.

They cannot look out far.
They cannot look in deep.
15 But when was that ever a bar
To any watch they keep?

[1934]

DESERT PLACES

Snow falling and night falling fast, oh, fast
In a field I looked into going past,
And the ground almost covered smooth in snow,
But a few weeds and stubble showing last.

5 The woods around it have it—it is theirs.
All animals are smothered in their lairs.
I am too absent-spirited to count;
The loneliness includes me unaware.

And lonely as it is that loneliness
10 Will be more lonely ere it will be less—
A blanker whiteness of benighted[1] snow
With no expression, nothing to express.

They cannot scare me with their empty spaces
Between stars—on stars where no human race is.
15 I have it in me so much nearer home
To scare myself with my own desert places.

[1934]

[1] Overtaken by darkness or night.

TWO TRAMPS IN MUD TIME

Out of the mud two strangers came
And caught me splitting wood in the yard.
And one of them put me off my aim
By hailing cheerily 'Hit them hard!'
5   I knew pretty well why he dropped behind
And let the other go on a way.
I knew pretty well what he had in mind:
He wanted to take my job for pay.

Good blocks of oak it was I split,
10   As large around as the chopping block;
And every piece I squarely hit
Fell splinterless as a cloven rock.
The blows that a life of self-control
Spares to strike for the common good
15   That day, giving a loose to my soul,
I spent on the unimportant wood.

The sun was warm but the wind was chill.
You know how it is with an April day
When the sun is out and the wind is still,
20   You're one month on in the middle of May.
But if you so much as dare to speak,
A cloud comes over the sunlit arch,
A wind comes off a frozen peak,
And you're two months back in the middle of March.

25   A bluebird comes tenderly up to alight
And turns to the wind to unruffle a plume
His song so pitched as not to excite
A single flower as yet to bloom.
It is snowing a flake: and he half knew
30   Winter was only playing possum.
Except in color he isn't blue,
But he wouldn't advise a thing to blossom.

The water for which we may have to look
In summertime with a witching-wand,
35   In every wheelrut's now a brook,
In every print of a hoof a pond.
Be glad of water, but don't forget
The lurking frost in the earth beneath
That will steal forth after the sun is set
40   And show on the water its crystal teeth.

The time when most I loved my task
These two must make me love it more
By coming with what they came to ask.
You'd think I never had felt before

45 The weight of an ax-head poised aloft,
The grip on earth of outspread feet.
The life of muscles rocking soft
And smooth and moist in vernal heat.

Out of the woods two hulking tramps
50 (From sleeping God knows where last night,
But not long since in the lumber camps).
They thought all chopping was theirs of right.
Men of the woods and lumberjacks,
They judged me by their appropriate tool.
55 Except as a fellow handled an ax,
They had no way of knowing a fool.

Nothing on either side was said.
They knew they had but to stay their stay
And all their logic would fill my head:
60 As that I had no right to play
With what was another man's work for gain.
My right might be love but theirs was need.
And where the two exist in twain
Theirs was the better right—agreed.

65 But yield who will to their separation,
My object in living is to unite
My avocation and my vocation
As my two eyes make one in sight.
Only where love and need are one,
70 And the work is play for mortal stakes,
Is the deed ever really done
For Heaven and the future's sakes.

[1936]

DEPARTMENTAL

An ant on the tablecloth
Ran into a dormant moth
Of many times his size.
He showed not the least surprise.
5 His business wasn't with such.
He gave it scarcely a touch,
And was off on his duty run.
Yet if he encountered one
Of the hive's enquiry squad
10 Whose work is to find out God
And the nature of time and space,
He would put him onto the case.
Ants are a curious race;
One crossing with hurried tread
15 The body of one of their dead
Isn't given a moment's arrest—
Seems not even impressed.
But he no doubt reports to any
With whom he crosses antennae,
20 And they no doubt report
To the higher up at court.
Then word goes forth in Formic:[1]
'Death's come to Jerry McCormic,
Our selfless forager Jerry.
25 Will the special Janizary[2]
Whose office it is to bury

---

[1] A type of acid found in ants—here used as a name for the language of ants.
[2] Literally, a soldier in an elite corps of Turkish troops.

The dead of the commissary
Go bring him home to his people.
Lay him in state on a sepal.

30   Wrap him for shroud in a petal.
Embalm him with ichor[3] of nettle.

This is the word of your Queen.'
And presently on the scene
Appears a solemn mortician;

35   And taking formal position

With feelers calmly atwiddle,
Seizes the dead by the middle,
And heaving him high in air,
Carries him out of there.

40   No one stands round to stare.
It is nobody else's affair.

It couldn't be called ungentle.
But how thoroughly departmental.

[1936]

THE GIFT OUTRIGHT[1]

The land was ours before we were the land's.
She was our land more than a hundred years
Before we were her people. She was ours
In Massachusetts, in Virginia,

5   But we were England's, still colonials,
Possessing what we still were unpossessed by,
Possessed by what we now no more possessed.
Something we were withholding made us weak
Until we found out that it was ourselves

10   We were withholding from our land of living,
And forthwith found salvation in surrender.
Such as we were we gave ourselves outright
(The deed of gift was many deeds of war)
To the land vaguely realizing westward,

15   But still unstoried, artless, unenhanced,
Such as she was, such as she would become.

[1942]

Carl Sandburg   *1878–1967*

CHICAGO

Hog Butcher for the World,
Tool Maker, Stacker of Wheat,
Player with Railroads and the Nation's Freight Handler;
Stormy, husky, brawling,

5   City of the Big Shoulders:

---

[3] The fluid flowing in the veins of the Greek gods.
[1] Frost read this poem at the inauguration of John F. Kennedy in January 1961.

They tell me you are wicked and I believe them, for I have seen
   your painted women under the gas lamps luring the farm boys.
And they tell me you are crooked and I answer: Yes, it is true I
   have seen the gunman kill and go free to kill again.
And they tell me you are brutal and my reply is: On the faces of
   women and children I have seen the marks of wanton hunger.
And having answered so I turn once more to those who sneer at this
   my city, and I give them back the sneer and say to them:
10   Come and show me another city with lifted head singing so proud
   to be alive and coarse and strong and cunning.
Flinging magnetic curses amid the toil of piling job on job, here is a tall
   bold slugger set vivid against the little soft cities;
Fierce as a dog with tongue lapping for action, cunning as a savage
   pitted against the wilderness,
      Bareheaded,
      Shoveling,
15   Wrecking,
      Planning,
      Building, breaking, rebuilding,
Under the smoke, dust all over his mouth, laughing with white teeth,
Under the terrible burden of destiny laughing as a young man
   laughs,
20   Laughing even as an ignorant fighter laughs who has never lost a
   battle,
Bragging and laughing that under his wrist is the pulse, and under his
   ribs the heart of the people,
      Laughing!
Laughing the stormy, husky, brawling laughter of Youth, half-naked,
   sweating, proud to be Hog Butcher, Tool Maker, Stacker of
   Wheat, Player with railroads and Freight Handler to the Nation.

                                         [1914]

COOL TOMBS

When Abraham Lincoln was shoveled into the tombs, he forgot the
   copperheads and the assassin[1] . . . in the dust, in the cool tombs.

And Ulysses Grant lost all thought of con men and Wall Street, cash
   and collateral turned ashes . . . in the dust, in the cool tombs.[2]

Pocahontas'[3] body, lovely as a poplar, sweet as a red haw[4] in
   November or a pawpaw[5] in May, did she wonder? does she
   remember? . . . in the dust, in the cool tombs?

[1] The Copperheads were supporters of the Confederacy who lived in the North; Lincoln's "assassin"
was the actor John Wilkes Booth (1838–1865).
[2] Ulysses S. Grant's (1822–1885) term as President (1869–1877) was stained by disclosures of
corruption.
[3] Pocahontas (1595?–1617), the daughter of the Indian chief Powhatan, who is reputed to have
saved the life of Captain John Smith.
[4] Hawthorn, a tree or shrub with reddish fruit.
[5] A tropical tree with edible, orange-fleshed fruit.

Take any streetful of people buying clothes and groceries, cheering a hero
or throwing confetti and blowing tin horns . . . tell me if the lovers
are losers . . . tell me if any get more than the lovers . . . in the
dust . . . in the cool tombs.

[1918]

Wallace Stevens 1879–1955

DISILLUSIONMENT OF TEN O'CLOCK

The houses are haunted
By white night-gowns.
None are green,
Or purple with green rings,
5 Or green with yellow rings,
Or yellow with blue rings.
None of them are strange,
With socks of lace
And beaded ceintures.° *sashes or belts*
10 People are not going
To dream of baboons and periwinkles.° *edible snails*
Only, here and there, an old sailor,
Drunk and asleep in his boots,
Catches tigers
15 In red weather.

[1915]

PETER QUINCE AT THE CLAVIER[1]

I

Just as my fingers on these keys
Make music, so the selfsame sounds
On my spirit make a music, too.

Music is feeling, then, not sound;
5 And thus it is that what I feel,
Here in this room, desiring you,

Thinking of your blue-shadowed silk,
Is music. It is like the strain
Waked in the elders by Susanna.[2]

---

[1] A keyboard; presumably the keyboard of a harmonium or reed organ. *Harmonium* (1923) was
the title of Stevens' first volume of collected poems.
[2] The virtuous wife in "The History of Susanna" in the Old Testament Apocrypha, falsely accused
of adultery by two Hebrew elders whose advances she had rejected. Their charge was exposed
by Daniel who had the two men put to death.

10 Of a green evening, clear and warm,
She bathed in her still garden, while
The red-eyed elders watching, felt

The basses of their beings throb
In witching chords, and their thin blood
15 Pulse pizzicati[3] of Hosanna.[4]

II
In the green water, clear and warm,
Susanna lay.
She searched
The touch of springs,
20 And found
Concealed imaginings.
She sighed,
For so much melody.

Upon the bank, she stood
25 In the cool
Of spent emotions.
She felt, among the leaves,
The dew
Of old devotions.

30 She walked upon the grass,
Still quavering.
The winds were like her maids,
On timid feet,
Fetching her woven scarves,
35 Yet wavering.

A breath upon her hand
Muted the night,
She turned—
A cymbal crashed,
40 And roaring horns.

III
Soon, with a noise like tambourines,
Came her attendant Byzantines.[5]

They wondered why Susanna cried
Against the elders by her side;

45 And as they whispered, the refrain
Was like a willow swept by rain.

Anon, their lamps' uplifted flame
Revealed Susanna and her shame.

[3] Musical notes produced by plucking a stringed instrument.
[4] An exclamation of praise or adoration to God.
[5] Natives of the Greek city of Byzantium, now Istanbul in Turkey.

And then, the simpering Byzantines
50 Fled, with a noise like tambourines.

IV
Beauty is momentary in the mind—
The fitful tracing of a portal;
But in the flesh it is immortal.

The body dies; the body's beauty lives.
55 So evenings die, in their green going,
A wave, interminably flowing.
So gardens die, their meek breath scenting
The cowl of winter, done repenting.
So maidens die, to the auroral°   dawn
60 Celebration of a maiden's choral.

Susanna's music touched the bawdy strings
Of those white elders; but, escaping,
Left only Death's ironic scraping.
Now, in its immortality, it plays
65 On the clear viol of her memory,
And makes a constant sacrament of praise.

[1915]

ANECDOTE OF THE JAR

I placed a jar in Tennessee,
And round it was, upon a hill.
It made the slovenly wilderness
Surround that hill.

5 The wilderness rose up to it,
And sprawled around, no longer wild.
The jar was round upon the ground
And tall and of a port in air.

It took dominion everywhere.
10 The jar was gray and bare.
It did not give of bird or bush,
Like nothing else in Tennessee.

[1919]

THE SNOW MAN

One must have a mind of winter
To regard the frost and the boughs
Of the pine-trees crusted with snow;

And have been cold a long time
5 To behold the junipers shagged with ice,
The spruces rough in the distant glitter

Of the January sun; and not to think
Of any misery in the sound of the wind,
In the sound of a few leaves,

10 Which is the sound of the land
Full of the same wind
That is blowing in the same bare place

For the listener, who listens in the snow,
And, nothing himself, beholds
15 Nothing that is not there and the nothing that is
the ultimate romantic ideal
[1921]

THE EMPEROR OF ICE-CREAM

Call the roller of big cigars,
The muscular one, and bid him whip
In kitchen cups concupiscent curds.
Let the wenches dawdle in such dress
5 As they are used to wear, and let the boys
Bring flowers in last month's newspapers.
Let be be finale of seem.
The only emperor is the emperor of ice-cream.

Take from the dresser of deal,°   *pine*
10 Lacking the three glass knobs, that sheet
On which she embroidered fantails once
And spread it so as to cover her face.
If her horny feet protrude, they come
To show how cold she is, and dumb.
15 Let the lamp affix its beam.
The only emperor is the emperor of ice-cream.
[1922]

William Carlos Williams   *1883–1963*

QUEEN-ANN'S-LACE

Her body is not so white as
anemone petals nor so smooth—nor
so remote a thing. It is a field
of the wild carrot[1] taking
5 the field by force; the grass
does not raise above it.

[1] Queen Anne's Lace, or wild carrot, is a plant with numerous tiny white blossoms clustered around a single purple one, or mole.

Here is no question of whiteness,
white as can be, with a purple mole
at the center of each flower.
Each flower is a hand's span
of her whiteness. Wherever
his hand has lain there is
a tiny purple blemish. Each part
is a blossom under his touch
to which the fibres of her being
stem one by one, each to its end,
until the whole field is a
white desire, empty, a single stem,
a cluster, flower by flower,
a pious wish to whiteness gone over—
or nothing.

[1921]

THE RED WHEELBARROW

so much depends
upon

a red wheel
barrow

glazed with rain
water

beside the white
chickens.

[1923]

THE DANCE

In Breughel's great picture, The Kermess,[1]
the dancers go round, they go round and
around, the squeal and the blare and the
tweedle of bagpipes, a bugle and fiddles
tipping their bellies (round as the thick-
sided glasses whose wash they impound)
their hips and their bellies off balance
to turn them. Kicking and rolling about
the Fair Grounds, swinging their butts, those
shanks must be sound to bear up under such
rollicking measures, prance as they dance
in Breughel's great picture, The Kermess.

[1940]

---

[1] The picture by Flemish painter Peter Breughel (c. 1525–1569) depicts the annual outdoor festival or fair (the kermess) celebrated in the Low Countries (the Netherlands, Belgium, and Luxembourg).

THE NIGHT RIDER

Scoured like a conch[1]   an even mood
or the moon's shell   10   warm with summer dwindling,
I ride from my love   relic of heat:
through the damp night.   Ruin dearly bought

5   there are lights   smoothed to a round
     through the trees,   carved by the sand
     falling leaves,   15   the pulse a remembered pulse
     the air and the blood   of full-tide gone

                                                              [1946]

LANDSCAPE WITH THE FALL OF ICARUS[1]

According to Brueghel   10   the edge of the sea
when Icarus fell   concerned
it was spring   with itself

a farmer was ploughing   sweating in the sun
5   his field   that melted
     the whole pageantry   15   the wings' wax

of the year was   unsignificantly
awake tingling   off the coast
near   there was

               a splash quite unnoticed
          20   this was
               Icarus drowning
                              [1960]

D. H. Lawrence   *1885–1930*

GLOIRE DE DIJON[1]

When she rises in the morning
I linger to watch her;
She spreads the bath-cloth underneath the window

[1] A large spiral seashell.
[1] The title of a painting by Peter Breughel (c. 1525–1569). It depicts the myth of icarus, a young Greek, who, in escaping with his father from the island of Crete by means of wings held together by wax, flew too near the sun; the wax melted and Icarus fell to his death in the sea.
[1] Literally, "glory of Dijon," a city of France—also a variety of rose.

And the sunbeams catch her
5 Glistening white on the shoulders,
While down her sides the mellow
Golden shadow glows as
She stoops to the sponge, and her swung breasts
Sway like full-bloom yellow
10 Gloire de Dijon roses.

She drips herself with water, and her shoulders
Glisten as silver, they crumple up
Like wet and falling roses, and I listen
For the sluicing of their rain-dishevelled petals.
15 In the window full of sunlight
Concentrates her golden shadow
Fold on fold, until it glows as
Mellow as the glory roses.

[1917]

A YOUTH MOWING

There are four men mowing down by the Isar,[1]
I can hear the swish of the scythe-strokes, four
Sharp breaths taken: yea, and I
Am sorry for what's in store.

5 The first man out of the four that's mowing
Is mine, I claim him once and for all;
Though it's sorry I am, on his young feet, knowing
None of the trouble he's led to stall.

As he sees me bringing the dinner, he lifts
10 His head as proud as a deer that looks
Shoulder-deep out of the corn; and wipes
His scythe-blade bright, unhooks

The scythe-stone and over the stubble to me.
Lad, thou hast gotten a child in me,
15 Laddie, a man thou'lt ha'e to be,
Yea, though I'm sorry for thee.

[1917]

[1] A river flowing through Austria and Germany.

Ezra Pound *1885–1972*

PORTRAIT D'UNE FEMME[1]

Your mind and you are our Sargasso Sea,[2]
London has swept about you this score years
And bright ships left you this or that in fee:
Ideas, old gossip, oddments of all things,
5   Strange spars of knowledge and dimmed wares of price.
Great minds have sought you—lacking someone else.
You have been second always. Tragical?
No. You preferred it to the usual thing:
One dull man, dulling and uxorious,[3]
10   One average mind—with one thought less, each year.
Oh, you are patient, I have seen you sit
Hours, where something might have floated up.
And now you pay one. Yes, you richly pay.
You are a person of some interest, one comes to you
15   And takes strange gain away:
Trophies fished up; some curious suggestion;
Fact that leads nowhere; and a tale or two,
Pregnant with mandrakes,[4] or with something else
That might prove useful and yet never proves,
20   That never fits a corner or shows use,
Or finds its hour upon the loom of days:
The tarnished, gaudy, wonderful old work;
Idols and ambergris[5] and rare inlays,
These are your riches, your great store; and yet
25   For all this sea-hoard of deciduous things,
Strange woods half sodden, and new brighter stuff:
In the slow float of differing light and deep,
No! there is nothing! In the whole and all,
Nothing that's quite your own.
                    Yet this is you.

                                        [1912]

IN A STATION OF THE METRO°   *The Paris subway*

The apparition of these faces in the crowd;
Petals on a wet, black bough.

                                        [1913]

---

[1] French: "Portrait of a Lady."
[2] A calm, seaweed-choked area in the North Atlantic where it was once believed that ships became entangled and lost.
[3] Excessively submissive (to his wife).
[4] A plant whose roots were once thought to stimulate conception.
[5] A substance found in the intestines of sperm whales used in the making of perfumes.

Robinson Jeffers *1887–1962*

FAWN'S FOSTER-MOTHER

The old woman sits on a bench before the door and quarrels
With her meager pale demoralized daughter.
Once when I passed I found her alone, laughing in the sun
And saying that when she was first married
5   She lived in the old farmhouse up Garapatas Canyon.
(It is empty now, the roof has fallen
But the log walls hang on the stone foundation; the redwoods
Have all been cut down, the oaks are standing;
The place is now more solitary than ever before.)
10   "When I was nursing my second baby
My husband found a day-old fawn hid in a fern-brake
And brought it: I put its mouth to the breast
Rather than let it starve, I had milk enough for three babies.
Hey, how it sucked, the little nuzzler,
15   Digging its little hoofs like quills into my stomach.
I had more joy from that than from the others."
Her face is deformed with age, furrowed like a bad road
With market-wagons, mean cares and decay.
She is thrown up to the surface of things, a cell of dry sky
20   Soon to be shed from the earth's old eyebrows,
I see that once in her spring she lived in the streaming arteries,
The stir of the world, the music of the mountain.

                                               [1928]

HURT HAWKS

I

The broken pillar of the wing jags from the clotted shoulder,
The wing trails like a banner in defeat,
No more to use the sky forever but live with famine
And pain a few days: cat nor coyote
5   Will shorten the week of waiting for death, there is game without
    talons.
He stands under the oak-bush and waits
The lame feet of salvation; at night he remembers freedom
And flies in a dream, the dawns ruin it.
He is strong and pain is worse to the strong, incapacity is worse.
10   The curs of the day come and torment him
At distance, no one but death the redeemer will humble that head,
The intrepid readiness, the terrible eyes.
The wild God of the world is sometimes merciful to those
That ask mercy, not often to the arrogant.
15   You do not know him, you communal people, or you have forgotten him;
Intemperate and savage, the hawk remembers him;

Beautiful and wild, the hawks, and men that are dying, remember
   him.

II

I'd sooner, except the penalties, kill a man than a hawk; but the
   great redtail
Had nothing left but unable misery
20   From the bone too shattered for mending, the wing that trailed
   under his talons when he moved.
We had fed him six weeks, I gave him freedom,
He wandered over the foreland hill and returned in the evening,
   asking for death,
Not like a beggar, still eyed with the old
Implacable arrogance. I gave him the lead gift in the twilight. What fell
   was relaxed,
25   Owl-downy, soft feminine feathers; but what
Soared: the fierce rush: the night-herons by the flooded river cried
   fear at its rising
Before it was quite unsheathed from reality.

[1928]

Marianne Moore   *1887–1972*

POETRY

     I, too, dislike it: there are things that are important beyond
         all this fiddle.
       Reading it, however, with a perfect contempt for it, one
           discovers in
5   it after all, a place for the genuine.
           Hands that can grasp, eyes
            that can dilate, hair that can rise
              if it must, these things are important not because a

     high-sounding interpretation can be put upon them but be-
10   cause they are
       useful. When they become so derivative as to become
           unintelligible,
       the same thing may be said for all of us, that we
         do not admire what
15   we cannot understand: the bat
            holding on upside down or in quest of something to

      eat, elephants pushing, a wild horse taking a roll, a tireless
          wolf under

a tree, the immovable critic twitching his skin like a horse
20   that feels a flea, the base-
ball fan, the statistician—
nor is it valid
to discriminate against "business documents and

school-books"; all these phenomena are important. One
25   must make a distinction
however: when dragged into prominence by half poets,
the result is not poetry,
nor till the poets among us can be
"literalists of
30   the imagination"—above
insolence and triviality and can present

for inspection, "imaginary gardens with real toads in them,"
shall we have
it. In the meantime, if you demand on the one hand,
35   the raw material of poetry in
all its rawness and
that which is on the other hand
genuine, you are interested in poetry.

[1921]

T. S. Eliot   *1888–1965*

THE LOVE SONG OF J. ALFRED PRUFROCK

S'io crédesse che mia risposta fosse
A persona che mai tornasse al mondo,
Questa fiamma staria senza piu scosse.
Ma perciocche giammai di questo fondo
Non torno vivo alcun, s'i'odo il vero,
Senza tema d'infamia ti rispondo.[1]

Let us go then, you and I,   *talking to himself*
When the evening is spread out against the sky
Like a patient etherised upon a table;
Let us go, through certain half-deserted streets,
5   The muttering retreats

---

[1] The statement introducing the confession of the poet Guido da Montefeltro in Dante's *Inferno* (1321), canto xxvii, 61–66: "If I thought that I was speaking/ to someone who would go back to the world,/ this flame would shake no more. / But since nobody has ever gone back alive from this place, if what I hear is true,/ I answer you without fear of infamy."

Of restless nights in one-night cheap hotels
And sawdust restaurants with oyster-shells:
Streets that follow like a tedious argument
Of insidious intent
10   To lead you to an overwhelming question. . . .
Oh, do not ask, "What is it?"
Let us go and make our visit.

     In the room the women come and go
Talking of Michelangelo.[2]

15   The yellow fog that rubs its back upon the window-panes,
The yellow smoke that rubs its muzzle on the window-panes
Licked its tongue into the corners of the evening,
Lingered upon the pools that stand in drains,
Let fall upon its back the soot that falls from chimneys,
20   Slipped by the terrace, made a sudden leap,
And seeing that it was a soft October night,
Curled once about the house, and fell asleep.

     And indeed there will be time
For the yellow smoke that slides along the street,
25   Rubbing its back upon the window-panes;
There will be time, there will be time
To prepare a face to meet the faces that you meet;
There will be time to murder and create,
And time for all the works and days[3] of hands
30   That lift and drop a question on your plate;
Time for you and time for me,
And time yet for a hundred indecisions,
And for a hundred visions and revisions,
Before the taking of a toast and tea.

35   In the room the women come and go
Talking of Michelangelo.

     And indeed there will be time
To wonder, "Do I dare?" and, "Do I dare?"
Time to turn back and descend the stair,
40   With a bald spot in the middle of my hair—
[They will say: "How his hair is growing thin!"]
My morning coat, my collar mounting firmly to the chin,
My necktie rich and modest, but asserted by a simple pin—
[They will say: "But how his arms and legs are thin!"]
45   Do I dare
Disturb the universe?
In a minute there is time
For decisions and revisions which a minute will reverse.

[2] Michelangelo (1474–1564), the most famous artist of the Italian Renaissance.
[3] Possibly an allusion to *Works and Days*, a poem giving practical advise on farming by the Greek poet Hesiod (8th century B.C.).

been to meetings before

50 For I have known them all already, known them all:—
Have known the evenings, mornings, afternoons,
I have measured out my life with coffee spoons;
I know the voices dying with a dying fall[4]
Beneath the music from a farther room.
    So how should I presume?

He knows this life — nothing exciting in life

55 And I have known the eyes already, known them all—
The eyes that fix you in a formulated phrase,
And when I am formulated, sprawling on a pin,
When I am pinned and wriggling on the wall,
Then how should I begin
60 To spit out all the butt-ends of my days and ways?
    And how should I presume?

he is returning *women classify him*

And I have known the arms already, known them all—
Arms that are braceleted and white and bare
[But in the lamplight, downed with light brown hair!]
65 Is it perfume from a dress
That makes me so digress?
Arms that lie along a table, or wrap about a shawl.
    And should I then presume?
    And how should I begin?

Arms of women *astonished at the fact that women have hair*

          . . . . . .

70 Shall I say, I have gone at dusk through narrow streets
And watched the smoke that rises from the pipes
Of lonely men in shirt-sleeves, leaning out of windows?

he doesn't want to be lonely

I should have been a pair of ragged claws
Scuttling across the floors of silent seas.

should have been a crab

          . . . . . .

75 And the afternoon, the evening, sleeps so peacefully!
Smoothed by long fingers,
Asleep . . . tired . . . or it malingers,
Stretched on the floor, here beside you and me.
Should I, after tea and cakes and ices,
80 Have the strength to force the moment to its crisis?
But though I have wept and fasted, wept and prayed,
Though I have seen my head [grown slightly bald] brought in
    upon a platter,[5]
I am no prophet—and here's no great matter;
I have seen the moment of my greatness flicker,
85 And I have seen the eternal Footman hold my coat, and snicker,
And in short, I was afraid.

He's been done wrong. *he's aging* *decides not to go to rooms*

    And would it have been worth it, after all,
After the cups, the marmalade, the tea,
Among the porcelain, among some talk of you and me,

[4] See Shakespeare's *Twelfth Night* (1623), Act 1, Scene 1, 1–4.
[5] An allusion to John the Baptist, the New Testament prophet, whose head was presented to Queen Herodias on a charger. *Matthew* 14:3–11.

90 ⎧Would it have been worth while,
⎨To have bitten off the matter with a smile,
⎩To have squeezed the universe into a ball[6]
⎩To roll it toward some overwhelming question,
To say: "I am Lazarus,[7] come from the dead,
Come back to tell you all, I shall tell you all"—
If one, settling a pillow by her head,
    Should say: "That is not what I meant at all.
    That is not it, at all."

    And would it have been worth it, after all,
100 Would it have been worth while,
After the sunsets and the dooryards and the sprinkled streets,
After the novels, after the teacups, after the skirts that trail along
    the floor—
And this, and so much more?—
It is impossible to say just what I mean!
105 But as if a magic lantern threw the nerves in patterns on a
    screen:
Would it have been worth while
If one, settling a pillow or throwing off a shawl,
And turning toward the window, should say:
    "That is not it at all,
110   That is not what I meant, at all."
      . . . . .

No! I am not Prince Hamlet,[8] nor was meant to be;
Am an attendant lord, one that will do
To swell a progress,[9] start a scene or two,
Advise the prince; no doubt, an easy tool,
115 Deferential, glad to be of use,
Politic, cautious, and meticulous;
Full of high sentence[10] but a bit obtuse;
At times, indeed, almost ridiculous—
Almost, at times, the Fool.

120   I grow old . . .I grow old . . .
I shall wear the bottoms of my trousers rolled.

    Shall I part my hair behind? Do I dare to eat a peach?
I shall wear white flannel trousers, and walk upon the beach.
I have heard the mermaids singing, each to each.

125   I do not think that they will sing to me.

    I have seen them riding seaward on the waves
Combing the white hair of the waves blown back
When the wind blows the water white and black.

[6] See Andrew Marvell's "To His Coy Mistress" (1681), lines 41–42, p. 000.
[7] The man raised by Jesus from the dead, John 11:1–44.
[8] The hero of Shakespeare's tragedy (1603); the "attendant lord" may refer to Polonius, the senten-
tious courtier in the same play.
[9] A formal state journey by a king through his realm.   [10] Sententiousness.

[Handwritten margin annotations: "he wants to ask her what she thinks"; "catalog of typical women's conversations"; "slide projector"; "room seedy part of town"; "Fantasy World – Sea Isolation"; "to cover bald spot"]

We have lingered in the chambers of the sea
By sea-girls wreathed with seaweed red and brown
Till human voices wake us, and we drown.

If he didn't have to stay in fantasy world-he'd be okay.

[1915]

JOURNEY OF THE MAGI[1]

"A cold coming we had of it,
Just the worst time of the year
For a journey, and such a long journey:
The ways deep and the weather sharp,
5 The very dead of winter."
And the camels galled,[2] sore-footed, refractory,
Lying down in the melting snow.
There were times we regretted
The summer palaces on slopes, the terraces,
10 And the silken girls bringing sherbet.
Then the camel men cursing and grumbling
And running away, and wanting their liquor and women,
And the night-fires going out, and the lack of shelters,
And the cities hostile and the towns unfriendly
15 And the villages dirty and charging high prices:
A hard time we had of it.
At the end we preferred to travel all night,
Sleeping in snatches,
With the voices singing in our ears, saying
20 That this was all folly.

Then at dawn we came down to a temperate valley,
Wet, below the snow line, smelling of vegetation;
With a running stream and a water-mill beating the darkness,
And three trees on the low sky,
25 And an old white horse galloped away in the meadow.
Then we came to a tavern with vine-leaves over the lintel,
Six hands at an open door dicing for pieces of silver,
And feet kicking the empty wine-skins.
But there was no information, and so we continued
30 And arrived at evening, not a moment too soon
Finding the place; it was (you may say) satisfactory.

All this was a long time ago, I remember,
And I would do it again, but set down
This set down
35 This: were we led all that way for
Birth or Death? There was a Birth, certainly,
We had evidence and no doubt. I had seen birth and death,

---

[1] The wise men from the East who journeyed to Bethlehem to pay homage to the baby Jesus (*Matthew*, 2:1–12).
[2] Sores caused by the friction of a saddle.

But had thought they were different; this Birth was
Hard and bitter agony for us, like Death, our death.
40   We returned to our places, these Kingdoms,
But no longer at ease here, in the old dispensation,
With an alien people clutching their gods.
I should be glad of another death.

                                                                              [1927]

John Crowe Ransom   *1888–1974*

BELLS FOR JOHN WHITESIDE'S DAUGHTER

There was such speed in her little body,
And such lightness in her footfall,
It is no wonder her brown study
Astonishes us all.

5   Her wars were bruited in our high window.
We looked among orchard trees and beyond
Where she took arms against her shadow,
Or harried unto the pond

The lazy geese, like a snow cloud
10   Dripping their snow on the green grass,
Tricking and stopping, sleepy and proud,
Who cried in goose, Alas,

For the tireless heart within the little
Lady with rod that made them rise
15   From their noon apple-dreams and scuttle
Goose-fashion under the skies!

But now go the bells, and we are ready,
In one house we are sternly stopped
To say we are vexed at her brown study,
20   Lying so primly propped.

                                                                              [1924]

WINTER REMEMBERED

Two evils, monstrous either one apart,
Possessed me, and were long and loath at going:
A cry of Absence, Absence, in the heart,
And in the wood the furious winter blowing.

5 Think not, when fire was bright upon my bricks,
And past the tight boards hardly a wind could enter,
I glowed like them, the simple burning sticks,
Far from my cause, my proper heat and center.

Better to walk forth in the frozen air
10 And wash my wound in the snows; that would be healing;
Because my heart would throb less painful there,
Being caked with cold, and past the smart of feeling.

And where I walked, the murderous winter blast
Would have this body bowed, these eyeballs streaming,
15 And though I think this heart's blood froze not fast
It ran too small to spare one drop for dreaming.

Dear love, these fingers that had known your touch,
And tied our separate forces first together,
Were ten poor idiot fingers not worth much,
20 Ten frozen parsnips hanging in the weather.

[1924]

PIAZZA PIECE

—I am a gentleman in a dustcoat trying
To make you hear. Your ears are soft and small
And listen to an old man not at all,
They want the young men's whispering and sighing.
5 But see the roses on your trellis dying
And hear the spectral singing of the moon;
For I must have my lovely lady soon,
I am a gentleman in a dustcoat trying.

—I am a lady young in beauty waiting
10 Until my truelove comes, and then we kiss.
But what grey man among the vines is this
Whose words are dry and faint as in a dream?
Back from my trellis, Sir, before I scream!
I am a lady young in beauty waiting.

[1925]

TWO IN AUGUST

Two that could not have lived their single lives
As can some husbands and wives
Did something strange: they tensed their vocal chords
And attacked each other with silences and words
5 Like catapulted stones and arrowed knives.

Dawn was not yet; night is for loving or sleeping,
Sweet dreams or safekeeping;
Yet he of the wide brows that were used to laurel
And she, the famed for gentleness, must quarrel,
10   Furious both of them, and scared, and weeping.

How sleepers groan, twitch, wake to such a mood
Is not well understood,
Nor why two entities grown almost one
Should rend and murder trying to get undone,
15   With individual tigers in their blood.

In spring's luxuriant weather had the bridal
Transpired, nor had the growing parts been idle,
Nor was it easily dissolved;
Therefore they tugged but were still intervolved,
20   With pain prodigious. The exploit was suicidal.

She in terror fled from the marriage chamber
Circuiting the dark room like a string of amber
Round and round and back,
And would not light one lamp against the black,
25   And heard the clock that clanged: Remember, Remember.

And he must tread barefooted the dim lawn,
Soon he was up and gone;
High in the trees the night-mastered birds were crying
With fear upon their tongues, no singing nor flying
30   Which are their lovely attitudes by dawn.

Whether those bird-cries were of heaven or hell
There is no way to tell;
In the long ditch of darkness the man walked
Under the hackberry trees where the birds talked
35   With words too sad and strange to syllable.

[1927]

Claude McKay   *1890–1948*

THE HARLEM DANCER

Applauding youths laughed with young prostitutes
And watched her perfect, half-clothed body sway;

Her voice was like the sound of blended flutes
Blown by black players upon a picnic day.
5 She sang and danced on gracefully and calm,
The light gauze hanging loose about her form;
To me she seemed a proudly-swaying palm
Grown lovelier for passing through a storm.
Upon her swarthy neck black shiny curls
10 Luxuriant fell; and tossing coins in praise,
The wine-flushed, bold-eyed boys, and even the girls,
Devoured her shape with eager, passionate gaze;
But looking at her falsely-smiling face,
I knew her self was not in that strange place.

[1922]

Edna St. Vincent Millay *1892–1950*

RECUERDO[1]

We were very tired, we were very merry—
We had gone back and forth all night on the ferry.
It was bare and bright, and smelled like a stable—
But we looked into a fire, we leaned across a table,
5 We lay on a hill-top underneath the moon;
And the whistles kept blowing, and the dawn came soon.

We were very tired, we were very merry—
We had gone back and forth all night on the ferry;
And you ate an apple, and I ate a pear,
10 From a dozen of each we had bought somewhere;
And the sky went wan, and the wind came cold,
And the sun rose dripping, a bucketful of gold.

We were very tired, we were very merry,
We had gone back and forth all night on the ferry.
15 We hailed, "Good morrow, mother!" to a shawl-covered head,
And bought a morning paper, which neither of us read;
And she wept, "God bless you!" for the apples and pears,
And we gave her all our money but our subway fares.

[1919]

[1] Spanish meaning "A Remembrance."

Archibald MacLeish   *1892–*

ARS POETICA[1]

A poem should be palpable and mute
As a globed fruit,

Dumb
As old medallions to the thumb,

5 Silent as the sleeve-worn stone
Of casement ledges where the moss has grown—

A poem should be wordless
As the flight of birds.

                    *

A poem should be motionless in time
10 As the moon climbs,

Leaving, as the moon releases
Twig by twig the night-entangled trees,

Leaving, as the moon behind the winter leaves,
Memory by memory the mind—

15 A poem should be motionless in time
As the moon climbs.

                    *

A poem should be equal to:
Not true.

For all the history of grief
20 An empty doorway and a maple leaf.

For love
The leaning grasses and two lights above the sea—

A poem should not mean
But be.

                                        [1926]

YOU, ANDREW MARVELL[2]

And here face down beneath the sun
And here upon earth's noonward height

---

[1] Latin meaning "The Art of Poetry."
[2] The allusion is to English 17th century poet Andrew Marvell (1621–1678), and specifically to
lines 21–22 of his "To His Coy Mistress" (1681), see p. 712.

To feel the always coming on
The always rising of the night:

5 To feel creep up the curving east
The earthly chill of dusk and slow
Upon those under lands the vast
And ever climbing shadow grow

And strange at Ecbatan[3] the trees
10 Take leaf by leaf the evening strange
The flooding dark about their knees
The mountains over Persia change

And now at Kermanshah the gate
Dark empty and the withered grass
15 And through the twilight now the late
Few travelers in the westward pass

And Baghdad darken and the bridge
Across the silent river gone
And through Arabia the edge
20 Of evening widen and steal on

And deepen on Palmyra's street
The wheel rut in the ruined stone
And Lebanon fade out and Crete
High through the clouds and overblown

25 And over Sicily the air
Still flashing with the landward gulls
And loom and slowly disappear
The sails above the shadowy hulls

And Spain go under and the shore
30 Of Africa the gilded sand
And evening vanish and no more
The low pale light across that land

Nor now the long light on the sea:
And here face downward in the sun
35 To feel how swiftly how secretly
The shadow of the night comes on . . .

[1930]

---

[3] A city in ancient Persia; the cities that follow, Kermanshah in Iran, Baghdad in Iraq, and Palmyra in Syria, are all associated with ancient civilizations.

Wilfred Owen *1893–1918*

DULCE ET DECORUM EST

Bent double, like old beggars under sacks,
Knock-kneed, coughing like hags, we cursed through sludge,
Till on the haunting flares we turned our backs,
And towards our distant rest began to trudge.
5   Men marched asleep. Many had lost their boots,
But limped on, blood-shod. All went lame, all blind;
Drunk with fatigue; deaf even to the hoots
Of gas-shells dropping softly behind.

Gas! GAS! Quick, boys!—An ecstasy of fumbling,
10   Fitting the clumsy helmets just in time,
But someone still was yelling out and stumbling
And floundering like a man in fire or lime.—
Dim through the misty panes and thick green light,
As under a green sea, I saw him drowning.

15   In all my dreams before my helpless sight
He plunges at me, guttering, choking, drowning.

If in some smothering dreams, you too could pace
Behind the wagon that we flung him in,
And watch the white eyes writhing in his face,
20   His hanging face, like a devil's sick of sin;
If you could hear, at every jolt, the blood
Come gargling from the froth-corrupted lungs,
Bitter as the cud
Of vile, incurable sores on innocent tongues,—
25   My friend, you would not tell with such high zest
To children ardent for some desperate glory,
The old Lie: Dulce et decorum est
Pro patria mori.[1]

[posthumous, 1920]

ANTHEM FOR DOOMED YOUTH

What passing-bells for these who die as cattle?
    Only the monstrous anger of the guns.
    Only the stuttering rifles' rapid rattle
Can patter out their hasty orisons°   *prayers*
5   No mockeries for them from prayers or bells,
    Nor any voice of mourning save the choirs,—
The shrill, demented choirs of wailing shells;
    And bulges calling for them from sad shires.

[1] A line by the Roman poet Horace (65–8 B.C.) meaning, "It is sweet and fitting to die for your country."

What candles may be held to speed them all?
10   Not in the hands of boys, but in their eyes
Shall shine the holy glimmers of good-byes.
        The pallor of girls' brows shall be their pall;
Their flowers the tenderness of silent minds,
And each slow dusk a drawing-down of blinds.
                                    [posthumous, 1920]

e. e. cummings   *1894–1962*

"IN JUST-"

in Just-
spring   when the world is mud-
luscious the little
lame balloonman

5   whistles   far   and wee

        and eddieandbill come
        running from marbles and
        piracies and it's
        spring

10   when the world is puddle-wonderful

        the queer
        old balloonman whistles
        far   and   wee
        and bettyandisbel come dancing

15   from hop-scotch and jump-rope and

        it's
        spring
        and
            the

20   goat-footed

        balloonMan   whistles
        far
        and
        wee
                            [1920]

"NOBODY LOSES ALL THE TIME"

nobody loses all the time

i had an uncle named
Sol who was a born failure and
nearly everybody said he should have gone
5   into vaudeville perhaps because my Uncle Sol could
sing McCann He Was A Diver on Xmas Eve like Hell Itself which
may or may not account for the fact that my Uncle

Sol indulged in that possibly most inexcusable
of all to use a highfalootin phrase
10   luxuries that is or to
wit farming and be
it needlessly
added

my Uncle Sol's farm
15   failed because the chickens
ate the vegetables so
my Uncle Sol had a
chicken farm till the
skunks ate the chickens when

20   my Uncle Sol
had a skunk farm but
the skunks caught cold and
died and so
my Uncle Sol imitated the
25   skunks in a subtle manner

or by drowning himself in the watertank
but somebody who'd given my Uncle Sol a Victor
Victrola and records while he lived presented to
him upon the auspicious occasion of his decease a
30   scrumptious not to mention splendiferous funeral with
tall boys in black gloves and flowers and everything and

i remember we all cried like the Missouri
when my Uncle Sol's coffin lurched because
somebody pressed a button
35   (and down went
my Uncle
Sol

and started a worm farm)

[1923]

"NEXT TO OF COURSE GOD AMERICA I"

"next to of course god america i
love you land of the pilgrims' and so forth oh
say can you see by the dawn's early my
country 'tis of centuries come and go
5 and are no more what of it we should worry
in every language even deafanddumb
thy sons acclaim your glorious name by gorry
by jingo by gee by gosh by gum
why talk of beauty what could be more beaut-
10 iful than these heroic happy dead
who rushed like lions to the roaring slaughter
they did not stop to think they died instead
then shall the voice of liberty be mute?"

He spoke. And drank rapidly a glass of water
[1925]

"MY SWEET OLD ETCETERA"

my sweet old etcetera
aunt lucy during the recent

war could and what
is more did tell you just
5 what everybody was fighting

for,
my sister
isabel created hundreds
(and
10 hundreds)of socks not to
mention shirts fleaproof earwarmers

etcetera wristers etcetera, my
mother hoped that

i would die etcetera
15 bravely of course my father used
to become hoarse talking about how it was
a privilege and if only he
could meanwhile my

self etcetera lay quietly
20 in the deep mud et

cetera
(dreaming,
et
  cetera, of
25   Your smile
eyes knees and of your Etcetera)

                       [1926]

"ANYONE LIVED IN A PRETTY HOW TOWN"

anyone lived in a pretty how town
(with up so floating many bells down)
spring summer autumn winter
he sang his didn't he danced his did.

5   Women and men (both little and small)
cared for anyone not at all
they sowed their isn't they reaped their same
sun moon stars rain

children guessed (but only a few
10   and down they forgot as up they grew
autumn winter spring summer)
that noone loved him more by more

when by now and tree by leaf
she laughed his joy she cried his grief
15   bird by snow and stir by still
anyone's any was all to her

someone married their everyones
laughed their cryings and did their dance
(sleep wake hope and then) they
20   said their nevers they slept their dream

stars rain sun moon
(and only the snow can begin to explain
how children are apt to forget to remember
with up so floating many bells down)

25   one day anyone died i guess
(and noone stooped to kiss his face)
busy folk buried them side by side
little by little and was by was

all by all and deep by deep
30   and more by more they dream their sleep
noone and anyone earth by april
wish by spirit and if by yes.

Women and men (both dong and ding)
summer autumn winter spring
35 reaped their sowing and went their came
sun moon stars rain

[1940]

"PITY THIS BUSY MONSTER, MANUNKIND,"

pity this busy monster,manunkind,

not. Progress is a comfortable disease:
your victim(death and life safely beyond)

plays with the bigness of his littleness
5 —electrons deify one razorblade
into a mountainrange;lenses extend

unwish through curving wherewhen till unwish
returns on its unself.
                              A world of made
10 is not a world of born—pity poor flesh

and trees,poor stars and stones,but never this
fine specimen of hypermagical

ultraomnipotence. We doctors know

a hopeless case if—listen:there's a hell
15 of a good universe next door;let's go

[1943]

Robert Graves   *1895–*

THE NAKED AND THE NUDE

For me, the naked and the nude
(By lexicographers[1] construed
As synonyms that should express
The same deficiency of dress
5 Or shelter) stand as wide apart
As love from lies, or truth from art.

---

[1] Those who make dictionaries.

Lovers without reproach will gaze
On bodies naked and ablaze;
The Hippocratic[2] eye will see
10   In nakedness, anatomy;
And naked shines the Goddess when
She mounts her lion among men.

The nude are bold, the nude are sly
To hold each treasonable eye.
15   While draping by a showman's trick
Their dishabille[3] in rhetoric,
They grin a mock-religious grin
Of scorn at those of naked skin.

The naked, therefore, who compete
20   Against the nude may know defeat;
Yet when they both together tread
The briary pastures of the dead,
By Gorgons[4] with long whips pursued,
How naked go the sometime nude!

[1957]

FRIDAY NIGHT

Love, the sole Goddess fit for swearing by,
Concedes us graciously the little lie:
The white lie, the half-lie, the lie corrective
Without which love's exchange might prove defective,
5   Confirming hazardous relationships
By kindly *maquillage*° of Truth's pale lips.   make-up

This little lie was first told, so they say,
On the sixth day (Love's planetary day)
When, meeting her full-bosomed and half dressed,
10   Jove roared out suddenly: "Hell take the rest!
Six hard days of Creation are enough"—
And clasped her to him, meeting no rebuff.

Next day he rested, and she rested too.
The busy little lie between them flew:
15   "If this is not perfection," Love would sigh,
"Perfection is a great, black, thumping lie. . . ."
Endearments, kisses, grunts, and whispered oaths;
But were her thoughts on breakfast, or on clothes?

[1957]

---

[2] Hippocrates (c. 460–377 B.C.) was the Greek physician generally thought to have founded medical science.
[3] State of being undressed.
[4] Hideous, terrifying women of Greek mythology—the mere sight of whom turns men to stone.

Stephen Vincent Benét   *1898–1943*

THE MOUNTAIN WHIPPOORWILL[1]

Or, How Hill-Billy Jim Won the Great Fiddlers' Prize
(A Georgia Romance)

Up in the mountains, it's lonesome all the time,
(Sof' win' slewin' thu' the sweet-potato vine).

Up in the mountains, it's lonesome for a child,
(Whippoorwills a-callin' when the sap runs wild).

5   Up in the mountains, mountains in the fog,
Everythin's as lazy as an old houn' dog.

Born in the mountains, never raised a pet,
Don't want nuthin' an' never got it yet.

Born in the mountains, lonesome-born,
10   Raised runnin' ragged thu' the cockleburrs and corn.

Never knew my pappy, mebbe never should.
Think he was a fiddle made of mountain laurel-wood.

Never had a mammy to teach me pretty-please.
Think she was a whippoorwill, a-skitin' thu' the trees.

15   Never had a brother ner a whole pair of pants,
But when I start to fiddle, why, yuh got to start to dance!

Listen to my fiddle—Kingdom Come—Kingdom Come!
Hear the frogs a-chunkin' "Jug o' rum, Jug o' rum!"
Hear that mountain-whippoorwill be lonesome in the air,
20   *An' I'll tell yuh how I traveled to the Essex County Fair.*

Essex County has a mighty pretty fair,
All the smarty fiddlers from the South come there.

Elbows flyin' as they rosin up the bow
For the First Prize Contest in the Georgia Fiddlers' Show.

25   Old Dan Wheeling, with his whiskers in his ears,
King-pin fiddler for nearly twenty years.

Big Tom Sargent, with his blue wall-eye,[2]
An' Little Jimmy Weezer that can make a fiddle cry.

---

[1] A brownish nocturnal bird native to the eastern United States, whose vigorous cry (*"whip*-or-*weel"*) echoes its name.
[2] An eye that shows more than a normal amount of white.

All sittin' roun', spittin' high an' struttin' proud,
30   *(Listen, little whippoorwill, yuh better bug your eyes!)*
Tun-a-tun-a-tunin' while the jedges told the crowd
Them that got the mostest claps'd win the bestest prize.

Everybody waitin' for the first tweedle-dee,
When in comes a-stumblin'—hill-billy me!

35   Bowed right pretty to the jedges an' the rest,
Took a silver dollar from a hole inside my vest,

Plunked it on the table an' said, "There's my callin' card!
An' anyone that licks me—well, he's got to fiddle hard!"

Old Dan Wheeling, he was laughin' fit to holler,
40   Little Jimmy Weezer said, "There's one dead dollar!"

Big Tom Sargent had a yaller-toothy grin,
But I tucked my little whippoorwill spang[3] underneath my chin,
An' petted it an' tuned it till the jedges said, "Begin!"

Big Tom Sargent was the first in line;
45   He could fiddle all the bugs off a sweet-potato vine.

He could fiddle down a possum from a mile-high tree.
He could fiddle up a whale from the bottom of the sea.

Yuh could hear hands spankin' till they spanked each other raw,
When he finished variations on "Turkey in the Straw."

50   Little Jimmy Weezer was the next to play;
He could fiddle all night, he could fiddle all day.

He could fiddle chills, he could fiddle fever,
He could make a fiddle rustle like a lowland river.

He could make a fiddle croon like a lovin' woman.
55   An' they clapped like thunder when he'd finished strummin'.

Then came the ruck of the bob-tailed fiddlers,
The let's go-easies, the fair-to-middlers.

They got their claps an' they lost their bicker,
An' settled back for some more corn-licker.

60   An' the crowd was tired of their no-count squealing,
When out in the center steps Old Dan Wheeling.

---

[3] Directly, exactly.

He fiddled high and he fiddled low,
(Listen, little whippoorwill; yuh got to spread yore wings!)
He fiddled with a cherrywood bow.
65   *(Old Dan Wheeling's got bee-honey in his strings.)*

He fiddled the wind by the lonesome moon,
He fiddled a most almighty tune.

He started fiddling like a ghost,
He ended fiddling like a host.

70   He fiddled north an' he fiddled south,
He fiddled the heart right out of yore mouth.

He fiddled here an' he fiddled there.
He fiddled salvation everywhere.

When he was finished, the crowd cut loose,
75   *(Whippoorwill, they's rain on yore breast.)*
An' I sat there wonderin', "What's the use?"
(Whippoorwill, fly home to yore nest.)

But I stood up pert an' I took my bow,
An' my fiddle went to my shoulder, so.

80   An'—they wasn't no crowd to get me fazed—
But I was alone where I was raised.

Up in the mountains, so still it makes yuh skeered.
Where God lies sleepin' in his big white beard.

An' I heard the sound of the squirrel in the pine,
85   An' I heard the earth a-breathin' thu' the long night-time.

They've fiddled the rose, an' they've fiddled the thorn,
But they haven't fiddled the mountain-corn.

They've fiddled sinful an' fiddled moral,
But they haven't fiddled the breshwood-laurel.

90   They've fiddled loud, an' they've fiddled still,
But they haven't fiddled the whippoorwill.

I started off with a *dump-diddle-dump,*
(Oh, hell's broke loose in Georgia!)
Skunk-cabbage growin' by the bee-gum stump,
95   *(Whippoorwill, yo're singin' now!)*

Oh, Georgia booze is mighty fine booze,
The best yuh ever poured yuh,
But it eats the soles right offen yore shoes,
For Hell's broke loose in Georgia.

100   My mother was a whippoorwill pert,
        My father, he was lazy,
        But I'm Hell broke loose in a new store shirt
        To fiddle all Georgia crazy.

        Swing yore partners—up an' down the middle!
105   Sashay now—oh, listen to that fiddle!
        Flapjacks flippin' on a red-hot griddle,
        An' hell broke loose,
        Hell broke loose,
        Fire on the mountains—snakes in the grass.
110   Satan's here a-bilin'—oh, Lordy, let him pass!
        Go down Moses, set my people free,
        Pop goes the weasel thu' the old Red Sea!⁴
        Jonah sittin' on a hickory-bough,
        Up jumps a whale⁵—an' where's yore prophet now?
115   Rabbit in the pea-patch, possum in the pot,
        Try an' stop my fiddle, now my fiddle's gettin' hot!
        Whippoorwill, singin' thu' the mountain hush,
        Whippoorwill, shoutin' from the burnin' bush,
        Whippoorwill, cryin' in the stable-door,
120   Sing to-night as yuh never sang before!
        Hell's broke loose like a stompin' mountain-shoat,⁶
        Sing till yuh bust the gold in yore throat!
        Hell's broke loose for forty miles aroun'
        Bound to stop yore music if yuh don't sing it down.
125   Sing on the mountains, little whippoorwill,
        Sing to the valleys, an' slap 'em with a hill,
        For I'm struttin' high as an eagle's quill,
        An' Hell's broke loose,
        Hell's broke loose,
130   Hell's broke loose in Georgia!

        They wasn't a sound when I stopped bowin',
        (Whippoorwill, yuh can sing no more.)
        But, somewhere or other, the dawn was growin',
        (Oh, mountain whippoorwill!)

135   An' I thought, "I've fiddled all night an' lost.
        Yo're a good hill-billy, but yuh've been bossed."

        So I went to congratulate old man Dan,
        —But he put his fiddle into my han'—
        An' then the noise of the crowd began.

                                                            [1925]

---

⁴ Moses, the great Hebrew leader, led his people across the Red Sea by causing its waters to part (*Exodus* 14:21–23).
⁵ The Hebrew prophet who was cast into the sea only to be swallowed by a great fish sent by God to save him (*Jonah* 1:17).
⁶ A young hog.

Hart Crane   *1899–1932*

BLACK TAMBOURINE

The interests of a black man in a cellar
Mark tardy judgment on the world's closed door.
Gnats toss in the shadow of a bottle,
And a roach spans a crevice in the floor.

5   Aesop,[1] driven to pondering, found
Heaven with the tortoise and the hare;
Fox brush and sow ear top his grave
And mingling incantations on the air.

The black man, forlorn in the cellar,
10   Wanders in some mid-kingdom, dark, that lies,
Between his tambourine, stuck on the wall,
And, in Africa, a carcass quick with flies.

                         [1921]

Langston Hughes   *1902–1967*

THE NEGRO SPEAKS OF RIVERS

I've known rivers:
I've known rivers ancient as the world and older than the
    flow of human blood in human veins.

My soul has grown deep like the rivers.

5   I bathed in the Euphrates[2] when dawns were young.
I built my hut near the Congo and it lulled me to sleep.
I looked upon the Nile and raised the pyramids above it.
I heard the singing of the Mississippi when Abe Lincoln
    went down to New Orleans, and I've seen its muddy
10   bosom turn all golden in the sunset.

I've known rivers:
Ancient, dusky rivers.

My soul has grown deep like the rivers.

                         [1921]

---

[1] The sixth-century B.C. slave to whom is attributed the famous collection of beast fables.
[2] The Euphrates, flowing from Turkey into Syria and Iraq, and the Nile, flowing through Egypt,
helped to nurture the ancient Babylonian and Egyptian civilizations. The Congo flows through
central Africa to the Atlantic, while the Mississippi cuts through the heartland of the United
States on its way to New Orleans and the Gulf of Mexico.

SOLEDAD¹

A Cuban Portrait

The shadows
Of too many nights of love
Have fallen beneath your eyes.
Your eyes,
5   So full of pain and passion,
So full of lies.
So full of pain and passion,
Soledad,
So deeply scarred,
10 So still with silent cries.

[1926]

DREAM VARIATION

To fling my arms wide
In some place of the sun,
To whirl and to dance
Till the white day is done.
5   Then rest at cool evening
Beneath a tall tree
While night comes on gently,
    Dark like me—
That is my dream!

10 To fling my arms wide
In the face of the sun,
Dance! Whirl! Whirl!
Till the quick day is done.
Rest at pale evening . . .
15 A tall, slim tree . . .
Night coming tenderly
    Black like me.

[1924]

THEME FOR ENGLISH B

The instructor said,

> *Go home and write*
> *a page tonight.*
> *And let that page come out of you—*
> 5   *Then, it will be true.*

I wonder if it's that simple?
I am twenty-two, colored, born in Winston-Salem.
I went to school there, then Durham,² then here
to this college³ on the hill above Harlem.⁴
10 I am the only colored student in my class.
The steps from the hill lead down into Harlem,
through a park, then I cross St. Nicholas,⁵

¹ *Spanish:* solitude, loneliness.   ² Cities in North Carolina.   ³ Columbia University.
⁴ Traditionally Black section of New York City.   ⁵ Avenue in Harlem.

Eighth Avenue, Seventh, and I come to the Y,
the Harlem Branch Y, where I take the elevator
15   up to my room, sit down, and write this page:

It's not easy to know what is true for you or me
at twenty-two, my age. But I guess I'm what
I feel and see and hear, Harlem, I hear you:
hear you, hear me—we two—you, me, talk on this page,
20   (I hear New York, too.) Me—who?

Well, I like to eat, sleep, drink, and be in love.
I like to work, read, learn, and understand life.
I like a pipe for a Christmas present,
or records—Bessie,⁶ bop, or Bach.⁷
25   I guess being colored doesn't make me *not* like
the same things other folks like who are other races.
So will my page be colored that I write?

Being me, it will not be white.
But it will be
30   a part of you, instructor.
You are white—
yet a part of me, as I am a part of you.
That's American.
Sometimes perhaps you don't want to be a part of me.
35   Nor do I often want to be a part of you.
But we are, that's true!
As I learn from you,
I guess you learn from me—
although you're older—and white—
40   and somewhat more free.

This is my page for English B.

[1949]

Ogden Nash   *1902–1971*

VERY LIKE A WHALE

One thing that literature would be greatly the better for
Would be a more restricted employment by authors of simile and
     metaphor.
Authors of all races, be they Greeks, Romans, Teutons or Celts,

---

⁶ Bessie Smith (1898?–1937), the famous American blues singer.
⁷ Johann Sebastian Bach (1685–1750), the German composer.

Can't seem just to say that anything is the thing it is but have to go out
    of their way to say that it is like something else.
5   What does it mean when we are told
That the Assyrian came down like a wolf on the fold?[1]
In the first place, George Gordon Byron had had enough experience
To know that it probably wasn't just one Assyrian, it was a lot of
    Assyrians.
However, as too many arguments are apt to induce apoplexy and thus
    hinder longevity.
10 We'll let it pass as one Assyrian for the sake of brevity.
Now then, this particular Assyrian, the one whose cohorts were gleaming
    in purple and gold,
Just what does the poet mean when he says he came down like a wolf on
    the fold?
In heaven and earth more than is dreamed of in our philosophy there
    are a great many things.
But I don't imagine that among them there is a wolf with purple and
    gold cohorts or purple and gold anythings.
15 No, no, Lord Byron, before I'll believe that this Assyrian was actually like
    a wolf I must have some kind of proof;
Did he run on all fours and did he have a hairy tail and a big red mouth
    and big white teeth and did he say Woof woof?
Frankly I think it very unlikely, and all you were entitled to say, at the
    very most,
Was that the Assyrian cohorts came down like a lot of Assyrian cohorts
    about to destroy the Hebrew host.
But that wasn't fancy enough for Lord Byron, oh dear me no, he had to
    invent a lot of figures of speech and then interpolate them.
20 With the result that whenever you mention Old Testament soldiers to
    people they say Oh yes, they're the ones that a lot of wolves dressed
    up in gold and purple ate them.
That's the kind of thing that's being done all the time by poets, from
    Homer to Tennyson;
They're always comparing ladies to lilies and veal to venison.
And they always say things like that the snow is a white blanket after a
    winter storm.
Oh it is, is it, all right then, you sleep under a six-inch blanket of snow
    and I'll sleep under a half-inch blanket of unpoetical blanket material
    and we'll see which one keeps warm.
25 And after that maybe you'll begin to comprehend dimly
What I mean by too much metaphor and simile.

[1935]

---

[1] The first line of "The Destruction of Sennacherib" (1815) by Lord Byron (1788–1824); see p.
749. (Assyria was an ancient culture of the Near East.)

A. J. M. Smith   *1902–1980*

BRIGADIER

A Song of French Canada

One Sunday morning soft and fine
Two old campaigners let their nags meander;
One was a Sergeant of the Line,
The other a Brigade Commander.
The General spoke with martial roar,
"Nice weather for this time of year!"
　　And "Right you are," replied Pandore,
　　"Right you are, my Brigadier."

"A Guardsman's is a thankless calling,
Protecting private property,
In summer or when snows are falling,
From malice, rape, or robbery;
While the wife whom I adore
Sleeps alone and knows no cheer."
　　And "Right you are," replied Pandore,
　　"Right you are, my Brigadier."

"I have gathered Glory's laurel
With the rose of Venus[1] twined—
I am Married, and a General;
Yet, by Jesus, I've a mind
To start like Jason[2] for the golden shore
And follow my Star—away from here!"
　　"Ah, right you are," replied Pandore,
　　"Right you are, my Brigadier."

"I remember the good days of my youth
And the old songs that rang
So cheerily. In that time, forsooth,
I had a doting mistress, full of tang . . .
But, ah! the heart—I know not wherefore—
Loves to change its bill of fare."
　　And "Right you are," replied Pandore,
　　"Right you are, my Brigadier."

Now Phoebus[3] neared his journey's end;
Our heroes' shadows fell behind:
Yet still the Sergeant did attend,
And still the General spoke his mind.

---

[1] The Greek goddess of love and beauty.
[2] The Greek hero who led his men, the Argonauts, in search of the fabled golden fleece.
[3] Phoebus Apollo, the Greek god of the sun.

"Observe," he said, "how more and more
Yon orb ensanguines[4] all the sphere."
    And "Right you are," replied Pandore,
    "Right you are, my Brigadier."

They rode in silence for a while:
You only heard the measured tread
Of muffled hoof beats, mile on mile—
But when Aurora[5] rosy red,
40   Unbarred her Eastern door,
The faint refrain still charmed the ear,
    As "Right you are," replied Pandore,
    "Right you are, my Brigadier."

Countee Cullen *1903–1946*

FOR A LADY I KNOW

She even thinks that up in heaven
    Her class lies late and snores,
While poor black cherubs rise at seven
    To do celestial chores.
                                                [1924]

INCIDENT

(For Eric Walrond)

Once riding in old Baltimore,
    Heart-filled, head-filled with glee,
I saw a Baltimorean
    Keep looking straight at me.

5   Now I was eight and very small,
    And he was no whit bigger,
And so I smiled, but he poked out
    His tongue, and called me, "Nigger."

I saw the whole of Baltimore
10   From May until December;
Of all the things that happened there
    That's all that I remember.
                                                [1925]

---

[4] Makes crimson.   [5] The Roman goddess of the dawn.

Richard Eberhart   *1904–*

THE GROUNDHOG

In June, amid the golden fields,
I saw a groundhog lying dead.
Dead lay he; my senses shook,
And mind outshot our naked frailty.
₅ There lowly in the vigorous summer
His form began its senseless change,
And made my senses waver dim
Seeing nature ferocious in him.
Inspecting close his maggots' might
₁₀ And seething cauldron of his being,
Half with loathing, half with a strange love,
I poked him with an angry stick.
The fever arose, became a flame
And Vigour circumscribed the skies,
₁₅ Immense energy in the sun,
And through my frame a sunless trembling.
My stick had done nor good nor harm.
Then stood I silent in the day
Watching the object, as before;
₂₀ And kept my reverence for knowledge
Trying for control, to be still,
To quell the passion of the blood;
Until I had bent down on my knees
Praying for joy in the sight of decay.
₂₅ And so I left; and I returned
In Autumn strict of eye, to see
The sap gone out of the groundhog,
But the bony sodden hulk remained.
But the year had lost its meaning,
₃₀ And in intellectual chains
I lost both love and loathing,
Mured° up in the wall of wisdom.   *walled*
Another summer took the fields again
Massive and burning, full of life,
₃₅ But when I chanced upon the spot
There was only a little hair left,
And bones bleaching in the sunlight
Beautiful as architecture;
I watched them like a geometer,[1]
₄₀ And cut a walking stick from a birch.
It has been three years, now.
There is no sign of the groundhog.
I stood there in the whirling summer,

[1] A specialist in geometry.

My hand capped a withered heart,
45   And thought of China and of Greece,
           Of Alexander in his tent;[2]
           Of Montaigne in his tower,[3]
           Of Saint Theresa in her wild lament.[4]
                                                    [1936]

W. H. Auden   *1907–1973*

MUSÉE DES BEAUX ARTS[1]

About suffering they were never wrong,
The Old Masters: how well they understood
Its human position; how it takes place
While someone else is eating or opening a window or just walking
                                                    dully along;
5   How, when the aged are reverently, passionately waiting
For the miraculous birth, there always must be
Children who did not specially want it to happen, skating
On a pond at the edge of the wood:
They never forgot
10   That even the dreadful martyrdom must run its course
Anyhow in a corner, some untidy spot
Where the dogs go on with their doggy life and the torturer's horse
Scratches its innocent behind on a tree.

In Brueghel's *Icarus*,[2] for instance: how everything turns away
15   Quite leisurely from the disaster; the ploughman may
Have heard the splash, the forsaken cry,
But for him it was not an important failure; the sun shone
As it had to on the white legs disappearing into the green
Water; and the expensive delicate ship that must have seen
20   Something amazing, a boy falling out of the sky,
Had somewhere to get to and sailed calmly on.
                                                    [1940]

---

[2] Alexander the Great (356–323 B.C.), the King of Macedonia and the conqueror of much of the civilized world.
[3] Michel de Montaigne (1533–1592), a French essayist who maintained his study in a tower.
[4] Saint Theresa of Avila (1515–1582), a Spanish nun who became famous for her visions and mysticism.
[1] Museum of Fine Arts.
[2] *Icarus* by the Flemish painter Pieter Brueghel (c. 1520–1569) depicts the fall of Icarus, who in Greek mythology, had flown too close to the sun on man-made wings of feathers and wax.

"LAY YOUR SLEEPING HEAD, MY LOVE"

Lay your sleeping head, my love,
Human on my faithless arm;
Time and fevers burn away
Individual beauty from
5 Thoughtful children, and the grave
Proves the child ephemeral:
But in my arms till break of day
Let the living creature lie,
Mortal, guilty, but to me
10 The entirely beautiful.

Soul and body have no bounds:
To lovers as they lie upon
Her tolerant enchanted slope
In their ordinary swoon,
15 Grave the vision Venus sends
Of supernatural sympathy,
Universal love and hope;
While an abstract insight wakes
Among the glaciers and the rocks
20 The hermit's sensual ecstasy.

Certainty, fidelity
On the stroke of midnight pass
Like vibrations of a bell,
And fashionable madmen raise
25 Their pedantic boring cry:
Every farthing of the cost,
All the dreaded cards foretell,
Shall be paid, but from this night
Not a whisper, not a thought,
30 Not a kiss nor look be lost.

Beauty, midnight, vision dies:
Lets the winds of dawn that blow
Softly round your dreaming head
Such a day of sweetness show
35 Eye and knocking heart may bless,
Find the mortal world enough;
Noons of dryness see you fed
By the involuntary powers,
Nights of insult let you pass
40 Watched by every human love.

[1940]

THE UNKNOWN CITIZEN

(To JS/07/M/378
This Marble Monument
Is Erected by the State)

He was found by the Bureau of Statistics to be
One against whom there was no official complaint,
And all the reports on his conduct agree
That, in the modern sense of an old-fashioned word, he was a saint,
5 For in everything he did he served the Greater Community.
Except for the War till the day he retired
He worked in a factory and never got fired,
But satisfied his employers, Fudge Motors Inc.
Yet he wasn't a scab or odd in his views,
10 For his Union reports that he paid his dues,
(Our report on his Union shows it was sound)
And our Social Psychology workers found
That he was popular with his mates and liked a drink.
The Press are convinced that he bought a paper every day
15 And that his reactions to advertisements were normal in every way.
Policies taken out in his name prove that he was fully insured,
And his Health-card shows he was once in hospital but left it cured.
Both Producers Research and High-Grade Living declare

He was fully sensible to the advantages of the Instalment Plan
20 And had everything necessary to the Modern Man,
A phonograph, a radio, a car and a frigidaire.
Our researchers into Public Opinion are content
That he held the proper opinions for the time of year;
When there was peace, he was for peace; when there was war, he
    went.
25 He was married and added five children to the population,
Which our Eugenist says was the right number for a parent of his
    generation,
And our teachers report that he never interfered with their education.
Was he free? Was he happy? The question is absurd:
Had anything been wrong, we should certainly have heard.

                              [1939]

Theodore Roethke   *1908–1963*

DOLOR

I have known the inexorable sadness of pencils,
Neat in their boxes, dolor of pad and paper-weight,
All the misery of manilla folders and mucilage,
Desolation in immaculate public places,
5 Lonely reception room, lavatory, switchboard,
The unalterable pathos of basin and pitcher,
Ritual of multigraph, paper-clip, comma,
Endless duplication of lives and objects.
And I have seen dust from the walls of institutions,
10 Finer than flour, alive, more dangerous than silica,
Sift, almost invisible, through long afternoons of tedium,
Dropping a fine film on nails and delicate eyebrows,
Glazing the pale hair, the duplicate grey standard faces.

                              [1943]

THE WAKING

I strolled across
An open field;
The sun was out;
Heat was happy.

5 This way! This way!
The wren's throat shimmered,
Either to other,
The blossoms sang.

The stones sang,
10 The little ones did,
And flowers jumped
Like small goats.

A ragged fringe
Of daisies waved;
15 I wasn't alone
In a grove of apples.

Far in the wood
A nestling sighed;
The dew loosened
20   Its morning smells.

I came where the river
Ran over stones:
My ears knew
An early joy.

25   And all the waters
Of all the streams
Sang in my veins
That summer day.
[1953]

ELEGY FOR JANE

My Student, Thrown by a Horse

I remember the neckcurls, limp and damp as tendrils;
And her quick look, a sidelong pickerel smile;
And how, once startled into talk, the light syllables leaped for her,
And she balanced in the delight of her thought,
5   A wren, happy, tail into the wind,
Her song trembling the twigs and small branches.
The shade sang with her;
The leaves, their whispers turned to kissing;
And the mold sang in the bleached valleys under the rose.

10   Oh, when she was sad, she cast herself down into such a pure depth,
Even a father could not find her:
Scraping her cheek against straw;
Stirring the clearest water.

My sparrow, you are not here,
15   Waiting like a fern, making a spiny shadow.
The sides of wet stones cannot console me,
Nor the moss, wound with the last light.

If only I could nudge you from this sleep,
My maimed darling, my skittery pigeon.
20   Over this damp grave I speak the words of my love:
I, with no rights in this matter,
Neither father nor lover.

[1954]

I KNEW A WOMAN

I knew a woman, lovely in her bones,
When small birds sighed, she would sigh back at them;
Ah, when she moved, she moved more ways than one:
The shapes a bright container can contain!

5   Of her choice virtues only gods should speak,
       Or English poets who grew up on Greek
       (I'd have them sing in chorus, cheek to cheek).

       How well her wishes went! She stroked my chin,
       She taught me Turn, and Counter-turn, and Stand;
10   She taught me Touch, that undulant white skin;
       I nibbled meekly from her proffered hand;
       She was the sickle; I, poor I, the rake,
       Coming behind her for her pretty sake
       (But what prodigious mowing we did make).

15   Love likes a gander, and adores a goose:
       Her full lips pursed, the errant note to seize;
       She played it quick, she played it light and loose;
       My eyes, they dazzled at her flowing knees;
       Her several parts could keep a pure repose,
20   Or one hip quiver with a mobile nose
       (She moved in circles, and those circles moved).

       Let seed be grass, and grass turn into hay:
       I'm martyr to a motion not my own;
       What's freedom for? To know eternity.
25   I swear she cast a shadow white as stone.
       But who would count eternity in days?
       These old bones live to learn her wanton ways:
       (I measure time by how a body sways).

                                                      [1958]

A. M. Klein   *1909–1972*

INDIAN RESERVATION: CAUGHNAWAGA[1]

       Where are the braves, the faces like autumn fruit,
       who stared at the child from the coloured frontispiece?
       And the monosyllabic chief who spoke with his throat?
       Where are the tribes, the feathered bestiaries?—
5   Rank Aesop's[2] animals erect and red,
       with fur on their names to make all live things kin—
       Chief Running Deer, Black Bear, Old Buffalo Head?

---

[1] A Canadian reservation near Montreal.
[2] The Greek slave (c. 600 B.C.) who is credited with the famous series of beast fables bearing his name.

Childhood, that wished me Indian, hoped that
one afterschool I'd leave the classroom chalk,
10   the varnish smell, the watered dust of the street,
to join the clean outdoors and the Iroquois[3] track.
Childhood; but always,—as on a calendar,—
there stood that chief, with arms akimbo, waiting
the runaway mascot paddling to his shore.

15   With what strange moccasin stealth that scene is changed!
With French names, without paint, in overalls,
their bronze, like their nobility expunged,—
the men. Beneath their alimentary[4] shawls
sit like black tents their squaws; while for the tourist's
20   brown pennies scattered at the old church door,
the ragged papooses jump, and bite the dust.

Their past is sold in a shop: the beaded shoes,
the sweetgrass basket, the curio Indian,
burnt wood and gaudy cloth and inch-canoes—
25   trophies and scalpings for a traveller's den.
Sometimes, it's true, they dance, but for a bribe;
after a deal don the bedraggled feather
and welcome a white mayor to the tribe.

This is a grassy ghetto, and no home.
30   And these are fauna in a museum kept.
The better hunters have prevailed. The game,
losing its blood, now makes these grounds its crypt.
The animals pale, the shine of the fur is lost,
bleached are their living bones. About them watch
35   as through a mist, the pious prosperous ghosts.

[1948]

Stephen Spender *1909–*

AN ELEMENTARY SCHOOL CLASSROOM IN A SLUM

Far far from gusty waves these children's faces.
Like rootless weeds, the hair torn round their pallor.
The tall girl with her weighed-down head. The paper-
seeming boy, with rat's eyes. The stunted, unlucky heir

---

[3] The federation of Indian tribes who were once a power in upper New York State. Following the American Revolution, when many of the Iroquois supported the British, some of these tribes moved into Canada.
[4] In the sense of supporting.

5 Of twisted bones, reciting a father's gnarled disease,
   His lesson from his desk. At back of the dim class
   One unnoted, sweet and young. His eyes live in a dream
   Of squirrel's game, in tree room, other than this.

   On sour cream walls, donations. Shakespeare's head,
10 Cloudless at dawn, civilized dome riding all cities.
   Belled, flowery, Tyrolese° valley. Open-handed map   *Austrian*
   Awarding the world its world. And yet, for these
   Children, these windows, not this world, are world,
   Where all their future's painted with a fog,
15 A narrow street sealed in with a lead sky,
   Far far from rivers, capes, and stars of words.

   Surely, Shakespeare is wicked, the map a bad example
   With ships and sun and love tempting them to steal—
   For lives that slyly turn in their cramped holes
20 From fog to endless night? On their slag heap, these
       children
   Wear skins peeped through by bones and spectacles of steel
   With mended glass, like bottle bits on stones.
   All of their time and space are foggy slum.
   So blot their maps with slums as big as doom.

25 Unless, governor, teacher, inspector, visitor,
   This map becomes their window and these windows
   That shut upon their lives like catacombs,
   Break O break open till they break the town
   And show the children to green fields, and make their world
30 Run azure on gold sands, and let their tongues
   Run naked into books, the white and green leaves open
   History theirs whose language is the sun.

                                                             [1939]

Elizabeth Bishop *1911–1979*

AT THE FISHHOUSES

Although it is a cold evening,
down by one of the fishhouses
an old man sits netting,
his net, in the gloaming¹ almost invisible

---

¹ Dusk or twilight.

5   a dark purple-brown,
and his shuttle[2] worn and polished.
The air smells so strong of codfish
it makes one's nose run and one's eyes water.
The five fishhouses have steeply peaked roofs
10   and narrow, cleated gangplanks slant up
to storerooms in the gables
for the wheelbarrows to be pushed up and down on.
All is silver: the heavy surface of the sea,
swelling slowly as if considering spilling over,
15   is opaque, but the silver of the benches,
the lobster pots, and masts, scattered
among the wild jagged rocks,
is of an apparent translucence
like the small old buildings with an emerald moss
20   growing on their shoreward walls.
The big fish tubs are completely lined
with layers of beautiful herring scales
and the wheelbarrows are similarly plastered
with creamy iridescent coats of mail,
25   with small iridescent flies crawling on them.
Up on the little slope behind the houses,
set in the sparse bright sprinkle of grass,
is an ancient wooden capstan,[3]
cracked, with two long bleached handles
30   and some melancholy stains, like dried blood,
where the ironwork has rusted.
The old man accepts a Lucky Strike.[4]
He was a friend of my grandfather.
We talk of the decline in the population
35   and of codfish and herring
while he waits for a herring boat to come in.
There are sequins on his vest and on his thumb.
He has scraped the scales, the principal beauty,
from unnumbered fish with that black old knife,
40   the blade of which is almost worn away.

Down at the water's edge, at the place
where they haul up the boats, up the long ramp
descending into the water, thin silver
tree trunks are laid horizontally
45   across the gray stones, down and down
at intervals of four or five feet.

Cold dark deep and absolutely clear,
element bearable to no mortal,
to fish and to seals . . . One seal particularly

---

[2] A device used for weaving.
[3] A vertical drum used in hauling, around which rope or cable is wound.
[4] A brand of cigarettes.

50 I have seen here evening after evening.
He was curious about me. He was interested in music;
like me a believer in total immersion,[5]
so I used to sing him Baptist hymns.
I also sang "A Mighty Fortress Is Our God."
55 He stood up in the water and regarded me
steadily, moving his head a little.
Then he would disappear, then suddenly emerge
almost in the same spot, with a sort of shrug
as if it were against his better judgment.
60 Cold dark deep and absolutely clear,
the clear gray icy water . . . . Back, behind us,
the dignified tall firs begin.
Bluish, associated with their shadows,
a million Christmas trees stand
65 waiting for Christmas. The water seems suspended
above the rounded gray and blue-gray stones.
I have seen it over and over, the same sea, the same,
slightly, indifferently swinging above the stones,
icily free above the stones,
70 above the stones and then the world.
If you should dip your hand in,
your wrist would ache immediately,
your bones would begin to ache and your hand would burn
as if the water were a transmutation of fire
75 that feeds on stones and burns with a dark gray flame.
If you tasted it, it would first taste bitter,
then briny, then surely burn your tongue.
It is like what we imagine knowledge to be:
dark, salt, clear, moving, utterly free,
80 drawn from the cold hard mouth
of the world, derived from the rocky breasts
forever, flowing and drawn, and since
our knowledge is historical, flowing, and flown.

[1955]

Robert Hayden   *1913–1980*

THE BALLAD OF SUE ELLEN WESTERFIELD

(for Clyde)

She grew up in bedeviled southern wilderness,
but had not been a slave, she said,

[5] A form of baptism practiced by the Baptist Church.

because her father wept and set her mother free.
She hardened in perilous rivertowns

5   and after The Surrender,[1]
went as maid upon the tarnished Floating Palaces.[2]
Rivermen reviled her for the rankling cold
sardonic pride
that gave a knife-edge to her comeliness.

10   When she was old, her back still straight,
her hair still glossy black,
she'd talk sometimes
of dangers lived through on the rivers.
But never told of him,

15   whose name she'd vowed she would not speak again
till after Jordan.[3]
Oh, he was nearer nearer now
than wearisome kith and kin.
His blue eyes followed her

20   as she moved about her tasks upon the *Memphis Rose.*
He smiled and joshed, his voice quickening her.
She cursed the circumstance. . . .

The crazing horrors of that summer night,
the swifting flames, he fought his way to her,

25   the savaging panic, and helped her swim to shore.
The steamer like besieged Atlanta blazing,
the cries, the smoke and bellowing flames,
the flamelit thrashing forms in hellmouth water,
and he swimming out to them,

30   leaving her dazed and lost.
A woman screaming under the raddled[4] trees—
Sue Ellen felt it was herself who screamed.
The moaning of the hurt, the terrified—
she held off shuddering despair

35   and went to comfort whom she could.
Wagons torches bells
and whimpering dusk of morning
and blankness lostness nothingness for her
until his arms had lifted her

40   into wild and secret dark.

How long how long was it they wandered,
loving fearing loving,
fugitives whose dangerous only hidingplace
was love?

45   How long was it before she knew

[1] Lee's surrender to Grant at Appomatox Courthouse, April 9, 1865, ending the Civil War.
[2] Steamboats.
[3] Until she has crossed the River Jordan and entered the Promised Land—until, that is, she has died.
[4] Broken.

she could not forfeit what she was,
even for him—could not, even for him,
forswear her pride?
They kissed and said farewell at last.
50   He wept as had her father once.
They kissed and said farewell.
Until her dying-bed,
she cursed the circumstance.

[1962]

Karl Shapiro   *1913–*

DRUG STORE

I do remember an apothecary,
And hereabouts 'a dwells[1]

It baffles the foreigner like an idiom,
And he is right to adopt it as a form
Less serious than the living-room or bar;
        For it disestablishes the cafe,
5   Is a collective, and on basic country.

Not that it praises hygiene and corrupts
The ice-cream parlor and the tobacconist's
Is it a center; but that the attractive symbols
        Watch over puberty and leer
10   Like rubber bottles waiting for sick-use.

Youth comes to jingle nickels and crack wise;
The baseball scores are his, the magazines
Devoted to lust, the jazz, the Coca-Cola,
        The lending-library of love's latest.
15   He is the customer; he is heroized.

And every nook and cranny of the flesh
Is spoken to by packages with wiles.
"Buy me, buy me," they whimper and cajole;
        The hectic range of lipsticks pouts,
20   Revealing the wicked and the simple mouth.

---

[1] The quotation is from William Shakespeare's *Romeo and Juliet* (1597), Act 5, Scene 1.

With scarcely any evasion in their eye
They smoke, undress their girls, exact a stance;
But only for a moment. The clock goes round;
    Crude fellowships are made and lost;
25   They slump on booths like rags, not even drunk.
                      [1942]

AUTO WRECK

Its quick soft silver bell beating, beating,
And down the dark one ruby flare
Pulsing out red light like an artery,
The ambulance at top speed floating down
5   Past beacons and illuminated clocks
Wings in a heavy curve, dips down,
And brakes speed, entering the crowd.
The doors leap open, emptying light;
Stretchers are laid out, the mangled lifted
10   And stowed into the little hospital.
Then the bell, breaking the hush, tolls once,
And the ambulance with its terrible cargo
Rocking, slightly rocking, moves away,
As the doors, an afterthought, are closed.

15   We are deranged, walking among the cops
Who sweep glass and are large and composed.
One is still making notes under the light.
One with a bucket douches ponds of blood
Into the street and gutter.
20   One hangs lanterns on the wrecks that cling,
Empty husks of locusts, to iron poles.

Our throats were tight as tourniquets,
Our feet were bound with splints, but now,
Like convalescents intimate and gauche,
25   We speak through sickly smiles and warn
With the stubborn saw of common sense,
The grim joke and the banal resolution.
The traffic moves around with care,
But we remain, touching a wound
30   That opens to our richest horror.
Already old, the question Who shall die?
Becomes unspoken Who is innocent?
For death in war is done by hands;
Suicide has cause and stillbirth, logic;
35   And cancer, simple as a flower, blooms.
But this invites the occult mind,
Cancels our physics with a sneer,
And spatters all we knew of denouement
Across the expedient and wicked stones.
                      [1942]

Dylan Thomas *1914–1953*

THE FORCE THAT THROUGH THE GREEN FUSE DRIVES THE FLOWER

The force that through the green fuse drives the flower
Drives my green age; that blasts the roots of trees
Is my destroyer.
And I am dumb to tell the crooked rose
5   My youth is bent by the same wintry fever.

The force that drives the water through the rocks
Drives my red blood; that dries the mouthing streams
Turns mine to wax.
And I am dumb to mouth unto my veins
10   How at the mountain spring the same mouth sucks.

The hand that whirls the water in the pool
Stirs the quicksand; that ropes the blowing wind
Hauls my shroud sail.
And I am dumb to tell the hanging man
15   How of my clay is made the hangman's lime.

The lips of time leech to the fountain head;
Love drips and gathers, but the fallen blood
Shall calm her sores.
And I am dumb to tell a weather's wind
20   How time has ticked a heaven round the stars.

And I am dumb to tell the lover's tomb
How at my sheet goes the same crooked worm.

[1933]

FERN HILL[1]

Now as I was young and easy under the apple boughs
About the lilting house and happy as the grass was green,
    The night above the dingle° starry,   *wooded dale*
      Time let me hail and climb
5   Golden in the heydays of his eyes,
And honoured among wagons I was prince of the apple
    towns
And once below a time I lordly had the trees and leaves
      Trail with daisies and barley
    Down the rivers of the windfall light.

---
[1] A farm owned by Thomas's aunt.

900

10   And as I was green and carefree, famous among the barns
       About the happy yard and singing as the farm was home,
             In the sun that is young once only,
                 Time let me play and be
             Golden in the mercy of his means,
15   And green and golden I was huntsman and herdsman, the
         calves
       Sang to my horn, the foxes on the hills barked clear and
         cold,
             And the sabbath rang slowly
             In the pebbles of the holy streams.

       All the sun long it was running, it was lovely, the hay
20   Fields high as the house, the tunes from the chimneys,
         it was air
             And playing, lovely and watery
                 And fire green as grass.
             And nightly under the simple stars
       As I rode to sleep the owls were bearing the farm away,
25   All the moon long I heard, blessed among stables, the
         night-jars°   *nighthawks*
             Flying with the ricks,° and the horses   *haystacks*
                 Flashing into the dark.

       And then to awake, and the farm, like a wanderer white
       With the dew, come back, the cock on his shoulder: it was
         all
30   Shining, it was Adam and maiden,
                 The sky gathered again
             And the sun grew round that very day.
       So it must have been after the birth of the simple light
       In the first, spinning place, the spellbound horses walking
         warm
35   Out of the whinnying green stable
                 On to the fields of praise.

       And honoured among foxes and pheasants by the gay house
       Under the new made clouds and happy as the heart was
         long,
             In the sun born over and over,
40   I ran my heedless ways,
             My wishes raced through the house high hay
       And nothing I cared, at my sky blue trades, that time allows
       In all his tuneful turning so few and such morning songs
             Before the children green and golden
45   Follow him out of grace,

       Nothing I cared, in the lamb white days, that time would
         take me

Up to the swallow thronged loft by the shadow of my hand,
    In the moon that is always rising,
        Nor that riding to sleep
50   I should hear him fly with the high fields
And wake to the farm forever fled from the childless land.
Oh as I was young and easy in the mercy of his means,
    Time held me green and dying
Though I sang in my chains like the sea.

[1946]

IN MY CRAFT OR SULLEN ART

In my craft or sullen art
Exercised in the still night
When only the moon rages
And the lovers lie abed
5   With all their griefs in their arms,
I labour by singing light
Not for ambition or bread
Or the strut and trade of charms
On the ivory stages
10   But for the common wages
Of their most secret heart.

Not for the proud man apart
From the raging moon I write
On these spindrift° pages   *spray from surf*
15   Nor for the towering dead
With their nightingales and psalms
But for the lovers, their arms
Round the griefs of the ages,
Who pay no praise or wages
20   Nor heed my craft or art.

[1946]

DO NOT GO GENTLE INTO THAT GOOD NIGHT

Do not go gentle into that good night,
Old age should burn and rave at close of day;
Rage, rage against the dying of the light.

Though wise men at their end know dark is right,
5   Because their words had forked no lightning they
Do not go gentle into that good night.

Good men, the last wave by, crying how bright
Their frail deeds might have danced in a green bay,
Rage, rage against the dying of the light.

10 Wild men who caught and sang the sun in flight,
And learn, too late, they grieved it on its way,
Do not go gentle into that good night.

Grave men, near death, who see with blinding sight
Blind eyes could blaze like meteors and be gay,
15 Rage, rage against the dying of the light.

And you, my father, there on the sad height,
Curse, bless, me now with your fierce tears, I pray.
Do not go gentle into that good night.
Rage, rage against the dying of the light.

[1952]

Randall Jarrell *1914–1965*

THE DEATH OF THE BALL TURRET GUNNER[1]

From my mother's sleep I fell into the State,
And I hunched in its belly till my wet fur froze.
Six miles from earth, loosed from its dream of life,
I woke to black flak and the nightmare fighters.
When I died they washed me out of the turret with a hose.

[1945]

EIGHTH AIR FORCE

If, in an odd angle of the hutment,°   *encampment*
A puppy laps the water from a can
Of flowers, and the drunk sergeant shaving
Whistles *O Paradiso!*[2]—shall I say that man
5 Is not as men have said: a wolf to man?

The other murderers troop in yawning;
Three of them play Pitch,° one sleeps, and one   *a card game*
Lies counting missions, lies there sweating
Till even his heart beats: One; One; One.
10 *O murderers!* . . . Still, this is how it's done:

[1] "A ball turret was a plexiglass sphere set into the belly of a B-17 or B-24, and inhabited by two .50 caliber machine guns and one man, a short small man." (Jarrell's note)
[2] Aria from Giacomo Meyerbeer's opera *L'Africaine* (1865).

This is a war. . . . But since these play, before they die,
Like puppies with their puppy; since, a man,
I did as these have done, but did not die—
I will content the people as I can
15   And give up these to them: Behold the man![3]

I have suffered, in a dream, because of him,
Many things;[4] for this last savior, man,
I have lied as I lie now. But what is lying?
Men wash their hands, in blood, as best they can:
20   I find no fault in this just man.

[1948]

Henry Reed *1914–*

LESSONS OF WAR: NAMING OF PARTS

Today we have naming of parts. Yesterday,
We had daily cleaning. And tomorrow morning,
We shall have what to do after firing. But today,
Today we have naming of parts. Japonica
5   Glistens like coral in all of the neighboring gardens,
        And today we have naming of parts.

This is the lower sling swivel. And this
Is the upper sling swivel, whose use you will see,
when you are given your slings. And this is the piling swivel,
10   Which in your case you have not got. The branches
Hold in the gardens their silent, eloquent gestures,
        Which in our case we have not got.

This is the safety-catch, which is always released
With an easy flick of the thumb. And please do not let me
15   See anyone using his finger. You can do it quite easy
If you have any strength in your thumb. The blossoms
Are fragile and motionless, never letting anyone see
        Any of them using their finger.

And this you can see is the bolt. The purpose of this
20   Is to open the breech, as you see. We can slide it
Rapidly backwards and forwards: we call this
Easing the spring. And rapidly backwards and forwards
The early bees are assaulting and fumbling the flowers:
        They call it easing the Spring.

[3] See John 19:4–5.   [4] See Matthew 27:19.

25   They call it easing the Spring: it is perfectly easy
      If you have any strength in your thumb: like the bolt,
      And the breech, and the cocking-piece, and the point of balance,
      Which in our case we have not got; and the almond-blossom
      Silent in all of the gardens and the bees going backwards and
         forwards,
30   For today we have naming of parts.

                                       [1947]

Robert Lowell *1917–1977*

FOR THE UNION DEAD

"Relinquunt omnia servare rem publicam."[1]

The old South Boston Aquarium stands
in a Sahara of snow now. Its broken windows are boarded.
The bronze weathervane cod has lost half its scales.
The airy tanks are dry.

5   Once my nose crawled like a snail on the glass;
my hand tingled
to burst the bubbles
drifting from the noses of the cowed, compliant fish.

My hand draws back. I often sigh still
10   for the dark downward and vegetating kingdom
of the fish and reptile. One morning last March,
I pressed against the new barbed and galvanized

fence on the Boston Common. Behind their cage,
yellow dinosaur steamshovels were grunting
15   as they cropped up tons of mush and grass
to gouge their underworld garage.

Parking spaces luxuriate like civic
sandpiles in the heart of Boston.
A girdle of orange, Puritan-pumpkin colored girders
20   braces the tingling Statehouse,

---

[1] *Latin:* "They give up everything to serve the Republic." The headnote is a slightly altered version of the inscription on the monument to Robert Gould Shaw (1837–1863), commander of the first black Northern regiment during the Civil War, who was killed during the attack on Fort Wagner in South Carolina. The monument, erected on the Boston Common (a public park) opposite the Massachusetts State House, is a bronze relief by the sculptor Augustus Saint-Gaudens (1848–1907); it was dedicated in 1897.

shaking over the excavations, as it faces Colonel Shaw
and his bell-cheeked Negro infantry
on St. Gaudens' shaking Civil War relief,
propped by a plank splint against the garage's earthquake.

25   Two months after marching through Boston,
half the regiment was dead;
at the dedication,
William James[2] could almost hear the bronze Negroes breathe.

Their monument sticks like a fishbone
30   in the city's throat.
Its Colonel is as lean
as a compass-needle.

He has an angry wrenlike vigilance,
a greyhound's gentle tautness;
35   he seems to wince at pleasure,
and suffocate for privacy.

He is out of bounds now. He rejoices in man's lovely,
peculiar power to choose life and die—
when he leads his black soldiers to death,
40   he cannot bend his back.

On a thousand small town New England greens,
the old white churches hold their air
of sparse, sincere rebellion; frayed flags
quilt the graveyards of the Grand Army of the Republic.

45   The stone statues of the abstract Union Soldier
grow slimmer and younger each year—
wasp-waisted, they doze over muskets
and muse through their sideburns . . .

Shaw's father wanted no monument
50   except the ditch,
where his son's body was thrown[3]
and lost with his "niggers."

The ditch is nearer.
There are no statues for the last war[4] here;
55   on Boylston Street,[5] a commercial photograph
shows Hiroshima boiling

over a Mosler Safe, the "Rock of Ages"
that survived the blast. Space is nearer.

[2] William James (1842–1910), the Harvard psychologist and philosopher; brother of American
novelist Henry James.
[3] By Confederate soldiers.   [4] World War II.   [5] A street in Boston.

When I crouch to my television set,
60   the drained faces of Negro school-children rise like balloons.

Colonel Shaw
is riding on his bubble,
he waits
for the blessèd break.

65   The Aquarium is gone. Everywhere,
giant finned cars nose forward like fish;
a savage servility
slides by on grease.

[1959]

THE MOUTH OF THE HUDSON[1]

(For Esther Brooks)

A single man stands like a bird-watcher,
and scuffles the pepper and salt snow
from a discarded, gray
Westinghouse Electric cable drum.
5   He cannot discover America by counting
the chains of condemned freight-trains
from thirty states. They jolt and jar
and junk in the siding below him.
He has trouble with his balance.
10   His eyes drop,
and he drifts with the wild ice
ticking seaward down the Hudson,
like the blank sides of a jig-saw puzzle.

The ice ticks seaward like a clock.
15   A Negro toasts
wheat-seeds over the coke-fumes
of a punctured barrel.
Chemical air
sweeps in from New Jersey,
20   and smells of coffee.

Across the river,
ledges of suburban factories tan
in the sulphur-yellow sun
of the unforgivable landscape.

[1964]

[1] The Hudson River flows into New York Bay.

ROBERT FROST[1]

Robert Frost at midnight,[2] the audience gone
to vapor, the great act laid on the shelf in mothballs,
his voice is musical and raw—he writes in the flyleaf:
For Robert from Robert, his friend in the art.
5   "Sometimes I feel too full of myself," I say.
And he, misunderstanding, "When I am low,
I stray away. My son[3] wasn't your kind. The night
we told him Merrill Moore[4] would come to treat him,
he said, 'I'll kill him first.' One of my daughters thought things,
10 thought every male she met was out to make her;
the way she dressed, she couldn't make a whorehouse."
And I, "Sometimes I'm so happy I can't stand myself."
And he, "When I am too full of joy, I think
how little good my health did anyone near me."

                                                        [1969]

Gwendolyn Brooks   *1917–*

WE REAL COOL

The Pool Players.
Seven at the Golden Shovel.

We real cool. We
Left school. We

Lurk late. We
Strike straight. We

5   Sing sin. We
Thin gin. We

Jazz June. We
Die soon.
                [1960]

---

[1] Robert Frost (1874–1963), the American poet.
[2] An allusion to "Frost at Midnight" (1798), a poem by the Romantic poet Samuel Taylor Coleridge
   (1772–1834).
[3] Frost's son, Carol, committed suicide in 1940.
[4] Merrill Moore (1903–1957), a poet-psychiatrist who was a friend of Frost.

THE CHICAGO DEFENDER[1] SENDS A MAN TO LITTLE ROCK

Fall, 1957[2]

In Little Rock the people bear
Babes, and comb and part their hair
And watch the want ads, put repair
To roof and latch. While wheat toast burns
5   A woman waters multiferns.

Time upholds or overturns
The many, tight, and small concerns.

In Little Rock the people sing
Sunday hymns like anything,
10   Through Sunday pomp and polishing.

And after testament and tunes,
Some soften Sunday afternoons
With lemon tea and Lorna Doones.[3]

I forcast
15   And I believe
Come Christmas Little Rock will cleave
To Christmas tree and trifle, weave,
From laugh and tinsel, texture fast.

In Little Rock is baseball; Barcarolle.[4]
20   That hotness in July . . . the uniformed figures raw and implacable
And not intellectual,
Battling the hotness or clawing the suffering dust.
The Open Air Concert, on the special twilight green . . .
When Beethoven is brutal or whispers to lady-like air.
25   Blanket-sitters are solemn, as Johann troubles to lean
To tell them what to mean. . . .

There is love, too, in Little Rock. Soft women softly
Opening themselves in kindness,
Or, pitying one's blindness,
30   Awaiting one's pleasure
In azure
Glory with anguished rose at the root. . . .
To wash away old semi-discomfitures.
They re-teach purple and unsullen blue.

---

[1] A Chicago newspaper.
[2] Little Rock, Arkansas, the scene of racial disturbances in 1957 when the governor of the state tried to prevent court-ordered integration of a city high school.
[3] A brand of cookies.   [4] A Venetian gondolier's song.

35   The wispy soils go. And uncertain
     Half-havings have they clarified to sures.

     In Little Rock they know
     Not answering the telephone is a way of rejecting life,
     That it is our business to be bothered, is our business
40   To cherish bores or boredom, be polite
     To lies and love and many-faceted fuzziness.

     I scratch my head, massage the hate-I-had.
     I blink across my prim and pencilled pad.
     The saga I was sent for is not down.
45   Because there is a puzzle in this town.
     The biggest News I do not dare
     Telegraph to the Editor's chair:
     "They are like people everywhere."

     The angry Editor would reply
50   In hundred harryings of Why.

     And true, they are hurling spittle, rock,
     Garbage and fruit in Little Rock.
     And I saw coiling storm a-writhe
     On bright madonnas. And a scythe
55   Of men harassing brownish girls.
     (The bows and barrettes in the curls
     And braids declined away from joy.)

     I saw a bleeding brownish boy. . . .

     The lariat lynch-wish I deplored.

60   The loveliest lynchee was our Lord.

                                    [1960]

Margaret Avison   *1918–*

SEPTEMBER STREET

Harvest apples lack tartness.
The youngest child stares at the brick school wall.
After the surprising *coup*[1] at a late luncheon meeting

[1] A brilliantly conceived, sudden, and successful move or stratagem.

the young man shifting for green concludes
5 the future makes his bitten thumb the fake.
   A convalescent steps around
wet leaves, resolving on the post-box corner.
   Next time, the young man glimpses,
he will be one of three, not the lone fourth
10   susceptible to elation.
   Yellow. The pride saddens him.
A van grinds past. Somebody with
considerable dash and a strong left hand
plays Annie Laurie[2] on an untuned piano.
15   Granada[3] will not rhyme with Canada.
The home-grown wines have sharpness.
   A scissor-grinder used to come
   about the hour the school let out
   and children knocked down chestnuts.
20   On the yellow porch
one sits, not reading headlines; the old eyes
   read far out into the mild
      air, runes.[4]
See. There: a stray sea-gull.

                                        [1960]

Howard Nemerov   *1920–*

THE VACUUM

The house is so quiet now
the vacuum cleaner sulks in the corner closet,
Its bag limp as a stopped lung, its mouth
Grinning into the floor, maybe at my
5 Slovenly life, my dog-dead youth.

I've lived this way long enough,
But when my old woman died her soul
Went into that vacuum cleaner, and I can't bear
To see the bag swell like a belly, eating the dust
10 And the woolen mice, and begin to howl

---

[2] A traditional Scottish folk song.   [3] Province in southern Spain.
[4] An ancient Scandinavian alphabet, used for magic and divination. Also, any ancient Scandinavian
poem.

Because there is old filth everywhere
She used to crawl, in the corner and under the stair.
I know now how life is cheap as dirt,
And still the hungry, angry heart
15   Hangs on and howls, biting at air.

[1955]

THE GOOSE FISH[1]

On the long shore, lit by the moon
To show them properly alone,
Two lovers suddenly embraced
So that their shadows were as one.
5   The ordinary night was graced
For them by the swift tide of blood
That silently they took at flood,
And for a little time they prized
    Themselves emparadised.

10   Then, as if shaken by stage-fright
Beneath the hard moon's bony light,
They stood together on the sand
Embarrassed in each other's sight
But still conspiring hand in hand,
15   Until they saw, there underfoot,
As though the world had found them out,
The goose fish turning up, though dead,
    His hugely grinning head.

There in the china light he lay,
20   Most ancient and corrupt and grey
They hesitated at his smile,
Wondering what it seemed to say
To lovers who a little while
Before had thought to understand,
25   By violence upon the sand,
The only way that could be known
    To make a world their own.

It was a wide and moony grin
Together peaceful and obscene;
30   They know not what he would express,
So finished a comedian
He might mean failure or success,
But took it for an emblem of
Their sudden, new and guilty love
35   To be observed by, when they kissed,
    That rigid optimist.

[1] The goosefish, or "monkfish," is common to the waters of the North Atlantic.

So he became their patriarch,
Dreadfully mild in the half-dark.
His throat that the sand seemed to choke,
40   His picket teeth, these left their mark
But never did explain the joke
That so amused him, lying there
While the moon went down to disappear
Along the still and tilted track
45   That bears the zodiac.

[1955]

Richard Wilbur   *1921–*

THE DEATH OF A TOAD

A toad the power mower caught,
Chewed and clipped of a leg, with a hobbling hop has got
To the garden verge, and sanctuaried him
Under the cineraria[1] leaves, in the shade
5   Of the ashen heartshaped leaves, in a dim,
Low, and a final glade.

The rare original heartsblood goes,
Spends on the earthen hide, in the folds and wizenings, flows
In the gutters of the banked and staring eyes. He lies
10   As still as if he would return to stone,
And soundlessly attending, dies
Toward some deep monotone,

Toward misted and ebullient seas
And cooling shores, toward lost Amphibia's[2] emperies.[3]
15   Day dwindles, drowning, and at length is gone
In the wide and antique eyes, which still appear
To watch, across the castrate lawn,
The haggard daylight steer.

[1948]

[1] A common plant in gardens.
[2] The class of cold-blooded vertebrates to which toads belong.
[3] Archaic: the domains or kingdoms of an emperor.

MUSEUM PIECE

The good gray guardians of art
Patrol the halls on spongy shoes,
Impartially protective, though
Perhaps suspicious of Toulouse.[1]

5   Here dozes one against the wall,
Disposed upon a funeral chair.
A Degas dancer pirouettes[2]
Upon the parting of his hair.

See how she spins! The grace is
    there,
10 But strain as well is plain to see.
Degas loved the two together:
Beauty joined to energy.

Edgar Degas purchased once
A fine El Greco,[3] which he kept
15 Against the wall beside his bed
To hang his pants on while he slept.

                                    [1948]

THE PARDON

My dog lay dead five days without a grave
In the thick of summer, hid in a clump of pine
And a jungle of grass and honeysuckle-vine.
I who had loved him while he kept alive

5   Went only close enough to where he was
To sniff the heavy honeysuckle-smell
Twined with another odor heavier still
And hear the flies' intolerable buzz.

Well, I was ten and very much afraid.
10   In my kind world the dead were out of range
And I could not forgive the sad or strange
In beast or man. My father took the spade

And buried him. Last night I saw the grass
Slowly divide (it was the same scene
15   But now it glowed a fierce and mortal green)
And saw the dog emerging. I confess

I felt afraid again, but still he came
In the carnal sun, clothed in a hymn of flies,
And death was breeding in his lively eyes.
20   I started in to cry and call his name,

Asking forgiveness of his tongueless head.
. . . I dreamt the past was never past redeeming:
But whether this was false or honest dreaming
I beg death's pardon now. And mourn the dead.

                                    [1950]

---

[1] Henri de Toulouse-Lautrec (1864–1901), a French painter and lithographer.
[2] Edgar Degas (1834–1917), a French painter noted for his pictures of ballet dancers.
[3] El Greco (1548?–1614?), a Spanish painter.

Philip Larkin *1922–*

CHURCH GOING

Once I am sure there's nothing going on
I step inside, letting the door thud shut.
Another church: matting, seats, and stone,
And little books; sprawlings of flowers, cut
For Sunday, brownish now; some brass and stuff
Up at the holy end; the small neat organ;
And a tense, musty, unignorable silence,
Brewed God knows how long. Hatless, I take off
My cycle-clips in awkward reverence,

Move forward, run my hand around the font.
From where I stand, the roof looks almost new—
Cleaned, or restored? Someone would know: I don't.
Mounting the lectern, I peruse a few
Hectoring large-scale verses, and pronounce
"Here endeth" much more loudly than I'd meant.
The echoes snigger briefly. Back at the door
I sign the book, donate an Irish sixpence,
Reflect the place was not worth stopping for.

Yet stop I did: in fact I often do,
And always end much at a loss like this,
Wondering what to look for; wondering, too,
When churches fall completely out of use
What we shall turn them into, if we shall keep
A few cathedrals chronically on show,
Their parchment, plate and pyx[1] in locked cases,
And let the rest rent-free to rain and sheep.
Shall we avoid them as unlucky places?

Or, after dark, will dubious women come
To make their children touch a particular stone;
Pick simples[2] for a cancer; or on some
Advised night see walking a dead one?
Power of some sort or other will go on
In games, in riddles, seemingly at random;
But superstition, like belief, must die,
And what remains when disbelief has gone?
Grass, weedy pavement, brambles, buttress,[3] sky,

[1] A container in which the Communion wafers are kept.
[2] Plants or herbs with real or reputed medicinal powers.
[3] A structure, often of stone, lending support to a wall.

A shape less recognisable each week,
A purpose more obscure. I wonder who
Will be the last, the very last, to seek
40   This place for what it was; one of the crew
That tap and jot and know what rood-lofts[4] were?
Some ruin-bibber,[5] randy[6] for antique,
Or Christmas-addict, counting on a whiff
Of gown-and-bands and organ-pipes and myrrh?[7]
45   Or will he be my representative,

Bored, uninformed, knowing the ghostly silt
Dispersed, yet tending to this cross of ground
Through suburb scrub because it held unspilt
So long and equably what since is found
50   Only in separation—marriage, and birth,
And death, and thoughts of these—for whom was built
This special shell? For, though I've no idea
What this accoutred frowsty[8] barn is worth,
It pleases me to stand in silence here;

55   A serious house on serious earth it is,
In whose blent air all our compulsions meet,
Are recognized, and robed as destinies.
And that much never can be obsolete,
Since someone will forever be surprising
60   A hunger in himself to be more serious,
And gravitating with it to this ground,
Which, he once heard, was proper to grow wise in,
If only that so many dead lie round.

[1955]

SUNNY PRESTATYN[1]

Come to Sunny Prestatyn
Laughed the girl on the poster,
Kneeling up on the sand
In tautened white satin.
5   Behind her, a hunk of coast, a
Hotel with palms
Seemed to expand from her thighs and
Spread breast-lifting arms.

She was slapped up one day in March.
10   A couple of weeks, and her face
Was snaggle-toothed and boss-eyed;
Huge tits and a fissured crotch
Were scored well in, and the space

---

[4] Lofts or galleries within a church.   [5] An habitué of ruins.   [6] Literally, lecherous
[7] Incense.   [8] Musty.   [1] A seaside resort in northern Wales.

Between her legs held scrawls
15   That set her fairly astride
A tuberous cock and balls

Autographed *Titch Thomas,* while
Someone had used a knife
Or something to stab right through
20   The moustached lips of her smile.
She was too good for this life.
Very soon, a great transverse tear
Left only a hand and some blue.
Now *Fight Cancer* is there.

[1964]

James Dickey *1923–*

A DOG SLEEPING ON MY FEET

Being his resting place,
I do not even tense
The muscles of a leg
Or I would seem to be changing.
5   Instead, I turn the page
Of the notebook, carefully not

Remembering what I have written,
For now, with my feet beneath him
Dying like embers,
10   The poem is beginning to move
Up through my pine-prickling legs
Out of the night wood,

Taking hold of the pen by my fingers.
Before me the fox floats lightly,
15   On fire with his holy scent.
All, all are running.
Marvelous is the pursuit,
Like a dazzle of nails through the ankles,

Like a twisting shout through the trees
20   Sent after the flying fox
Through the holes of logs, over streams
Stock-still with the pressure of moonlight.
My killed legs,
My legs of a dead thing, follow,

25   Quick as pins, through the forest,
      And all rushes on into dark
      And ends on the brightness of paper.
      When my hand, which speaks in a daze
      The hypnotized language of beasts,
30   Shall falter, and fail

      Back into the human tongue,
      And the dog gets up and goes out
      To wander the dawning yard,
      I shall crawl to my human bed
35   And lie there smiling at sunrise,
      With the scent of the fox

      Burning my brain like an incense,
      Floating out of the night wood,
      Coming home to my wife and my sons
40   From the dream of an animal,
      Assembling the self I must wake to,
      Sleeping to grow back my legs.

                                               [1962]

Anthony Hecht   *1923–*

"MORE LIGHT! MORE LIGHT!"[1]

For Heinrich Blücher and Hannah Arendt[2]

Composed in the Tower before his execution
These moving verses, and being brought at that time
Painfully to the stake, submitted, declaring thus:
"I implore my God to witness that I have made no crime."

5   Nor was he forsaken of courage, but the death was horrible,
      The sack of gunpowder failing to ignite.
      His legs were blistered sticks on which the black sap
      Bubbled and burst as he howled for the Kindly Light.

[1] Supposedly the final words of Johann Wolfgang von Goethe (1749–1832), a German whose accomplishments as a poet, novelist, playwright, scientist, and philosopher made him one of the intellectual giants of his age.
[2] Hannah Arendt (1906–1975), the author of the classic *Origins of Totalitarianism* (1951), who came to the United States from Germany in 1941 with her husband Heinrich Blücher, a professor of philosophy.

And that was but one, and by no means one of the worst;
10   Permitted at least his pitiful dignity;
And such as were by made prayers in the name of Christ,
That shall judge all men, for his soul's tranquility.

We move now to outside a German wood
Three men are there commanded to dig a hole
15   In which the two Jews are ordered to lie down
And be buried alive by the third, who is a Pole.

Not light from the shrine at Weimar[3] beyond the hill
Nor light from heaven appeared. But he did refuse.
A Lüger[4] settled back deeply in its glove.
20   He was ordered to change places with the Jews.

Much casual death had drained away their souls.
The thick dirt mounted toward the quivering chin.
When only the head was exposed the order came
To dig him out again and to get back in.

25   No light, no light in the blue Polish eye.
When he finished a riding boot packed down the earth.
The Lüger hovered lightly in its glove.
He was shot in the belly and in three hours bled to death.

No prayers or incense rose up in those hours
30   Which grew to be years, and every day came mute
Ghosts from the ovens, sifting through crisp air,
And settled upon his eyes in a black soot.

[1967]

Denise Levertov   *1923–*

AT THE EDGE

How much I should like to begin
a poem with And—presupposing
the hardest said—
the moss cleared off the stone,
5   the letters plain.
How the round moon

[3] A city in Germany, once the home of Goethe; nearby stood Buchenwald, the infamous Nazi concentration camp.
[4] A German make of pistol.

would shine into all the corners
of such a poem and show
the words! Moths and dazzled
10   awakened birds
would freeze in its light!
The lines would be
an outbreak of bells
and I swinging on the rope!

15   Yet, not desiring apocrypha[1]
but true revelation,
what use to pretend the stone discovered,
anything visible?
That poem indeed
20   may not be carved there, may lie
—the quick of mystery—
in animal eyes gazing
from the thicket,
a creature of unknown size,
25   fierce, terrified, having teeth or
no defense, but whom
no And may approach suddenly.

[1959]

Louis Simpson   *1923–*

SUMMER STORM

In that so sudden summer storm they tried
Each bed, couch, closet, carpet, car-seat, table,
Both river banks, five fields, a mountain side,
Covering as much ground as they were able.

5   A lady, coming on them in the dark
In a white fixture, wrote to the newspapers
Complaining of the statues in the park.
By Cupid, but they cut some pretty capers!

The envious oxen in still rings would stand
10   Ruminating. Their sweet incessant plows
I think had changed the contours of the land
And made two modest conies° move their house.   *rabbits*

---

[1] Books of the Bible that are of questionable authority or authenticity as opposed to those which
have the sanction of "true revelation."

God rest them well, and firmly shut the door.
Now they are married Nature breathes once more.

[1949]

AMERICAN POETRY

Whatever it is, it must have
A stomach that can digest
Rubber, coal, uranium, moons, poems.

Like the shark, it contains a shoe.
5   It must swim for miles through the desert
Uttering cries that are almost human.

[1963]

ON THE LAWN AT THE VILLA

On the lawn at the villa—
That's the way to start, eh, reader?
We know where we stand—somewhere expensive—
You and I *imperturbes,*° as Walt would say,[1]   unperturbed
5   Before the diversions of wealth, you and I *engagés.*°   engaged, intrigued

On the lawn at the villa
Sat a manufacturer of explosives,
His wife from Paris,
And a young man named Bruno,

10   And myself, being American,
Willing to talk to these malefactors,
The manufacturer of explosives, and so on,
But somehow superior. By that I mean democratic.
It's complicated, being an American,
15   Having the money and the bad conscience, both at the
        same time.
Perhaps, after all, this is not the right subject for a poem.

We were all sitting there paralyzed
In the hot Tuscan[2] afternoon,
And the bodies of the machine-gun crew were draped over
        the balcony.
20   So we sat there all afternoon.

[1963]

---

[1] An allusion to Walt Whitman (1819–1892), an American poet.
[2] A region in central Italy.

James Merrill   *1926–1980*

AN URBAN CONVALESCENCE

Out for a walk, after a week in bed,
I find them tearing up part of my block
And, chilled through, dazed and lonely, join the dozen
In meek attitudes, watching a huge crane
5   Fumble luxuriously in the filth of years.
Her jaws dribble rubble. An old man
Laughs and curses in her brain,
Bringing to mind the close of *The White Goddess*.[1]

As usual in New York, everything is torn down
10   Before you have had time to care for it.
Head bowed, at the shrine of noise, let me try to recall
What building stood here. Was there a building at all?
I have lived on this same street for a decade.

Wait. Yes. Vaguely a presence rises
15   Some five floors high, of shabby stone
—Or am I confusing it with another one
In another part of town, or of the world?—
And over its lintel into focus vaguely
Misted with blood (my eyes are shut)
20   A single garland sways, stone fruit, stone leaves,
Which years of grit had etched until it thrust
Roots down, even into the poor soil of my seeing.
When did the garland become part of me?
I ask myself, amused almost,
25   Then shiver once from head to toe,

Transfixed by a particular cheap engraving of garlands
Bought for a few francs long ago,
All calligraphic[2] tendril and cross-hatched rondure,[3]
Ten years ago, and crumpled up to stanch
30   Boughs dripping, whose white gestures filled a cab,
And thought of neither then nor since.
Also, to clasp them, the small, red-nailed hand
Of no one I can place. Wait. No. Her name, her features
Lie toppled underneath that year's fashions.
35   The words she must have spoken, setting her face
To fluttering like a veil, I cannot hear now,
Let alone understand.

---

[1] A book published by Robert Graves (1895–   ) in 1948 on the mythological sources of poetry, which theorizes that all true poetry is inspired by a primitive female muse, who is both creative and destructive; the crane is her bird.
[2] Calligraphy is the art of fine penmanship, including the creation of ornamental curved designs.
[3] Gracefully rounded.

So that I am already on the stair,
As it were, of where I lived,
40 When the whole structure shudders at my tread
And soundlessly collapses, filling
The air with motes of stone.
Onto the still erect building next door
Are pressed levels and hues—
45 Pocked rose, streaked greens, brown whites.
Who drained the pousse-café?[4]
Wires and pipes, snapped off at the roots, quiver.

Well, that is what life does. I stare
A moment longer, so. And presently
50 The massive volume of the world
Closes again.

Upon that book I swear
To abide by what it teaches:
Gospels of ugliness and waste,
55 Of towering voids, of soiled gusts,
Of a shrieking to be faced
Full into, eyes astream with cold—

With cold?
All right then. With self-knowledge.

60 Indoors at last, the pages of *Time* are apt
To open, and the illustrated mayor of New York,
Given a glimpse of how and where I work,
To note yet one more house that can be scrapped.

Unwillingly I picture
65 My walls weathering in the general view.
It is not even as though the new
Buildings did very much for architecture.

Suppose they did. The sickness of our time requires
That these as well be blasted in their prime.
70 You would think the simple fact of having lasted
Threatened our cities like mysterious fires.

There are certain phrases which to use in a poem
Is like rubbing silver with quicksilver. Bright
But facile, the glamour deadens overnight.
75 For instance, how 'the sickness of our time'

Enhances, then debases, what I feel.
At my desk I swallow in a glass of water
No longer cordial, scarcely wet, a pill
They had told me not to take until much later.

[4] A liqueur served with coffee as an after-dinner drink.

80   With the result that back into my imagination
      The city glides, like cities seen from the air,
      Mere smoke and sparkle to the passenger
      Having in mind another destination

      Which now is not that honey-slow descent
85   Of the Champs-Elysées,[5] her hand in his,
      But the dull need to make some kind of house
      Out of the life lived, out of the love spent.

                                                    [1962]

W. D. Snodgrass   *1926–*

APRIL INVENTORY

      The green catalpa tree has turned
      All white; the cherry blooms once more.
      In one whole year I haven't learned
      A blessed thing they pay you for.
5   The blossoms snow down in my hair;
      The trees and I will soon be bare.

      The trees have more than I to spare.
      The sleek, expensive girls I teach,
      Younger and pinker every year,
10   Bloom gradually out of reach.
      The pear tree lets its petals drop
      Like dandruff on a tabletop.

      The girls have grown so girlish now
      I have to nudge myself to stare.
15   This year they smile and mind me how
      My teeth are falling with my hair.
      In thirty years I may not get
      Younger, shrewder, or out of debt.

      The tenth time, just a year ago,
20   I made myself a little list
      Of all the things I'd ought to know,
      Then told my parents, analyst,
      And everyone who's trusted me
      I'd be substantial, presently.

[5] A famous boulevard in Paris.

25   I haven't read one book about
     A book or memorized one plot.
     Or found a mind I did not doubt.
     I learned one date. And then forgot.
     And one by one the solid scholars
30   Get the degrees, the jobs, the dollars.

     And smile above their starchy collars.
     I taught my classes Whitehead's[1] notions;
     One lovely girl, a song of Mahler's.[2]
     Lacking a source book and promotions,
35   I taught one child the colors of
     A luna moth and how to love.

     I taught myself to name my name,
     To bark back, loosen love and crying;
     To ease my woman so she came,
40   To ease an old man who was dying.
     I have not learned how often I
     Can win, can love, but choose to die.

     I have not learned there is a lie
     Love shall be blonder, slimmer, younger;
45   That my equivocating eye
     Loves only by my body's hunger;
     That I have forces, true to feel,
     Or that the lovely world is real.

     While scholars speak authority
50   And wear their ulcers on their sleeves,
     My eyes in spectacles shall see
     These trees procure and spend their leaves.
     There is a value underneath
     The gold and silver in my teeth.

55   Though trees turn bare and girls turn wives,
     We shall afford our costly seasons;
     There is a gentleness survives
     That will outspeak and has its reasons.
     There is a loveliness exists,
60   Preserves us; not for specialists.

                  [1957]

---

[1] Alfred North Whitehead (1861–1947), an English philosopher and mathematician.
[2] Gustav Mahler (1860–1911), an Austrian composer and conductor.

W. S. Merwin   *1927–*

LEVIATHAN[1]

This is the black sea-brute bulling through wave-wrack,
Ancient as ocean's shifting hills, who in sea-toils
Travelling, who furrowing the salt acres
Heavily, his wake hoary behind him,[2]
5   Shoulder spouting, the fist of his forehead
Over wastes gray-green crashing, among horses unbroken
From bellowing fields, past bone-wreck of vessels,
Tide-ruin, wash of lost bodies bobbing
No longer sought for, and islands of ice gleaming,
10   Who ravening the rank flood, wave-marshalling,
Overmastering the dark sea-marches, finds home
And harvest. Frightening to foolhardiest
Mariners, his size were difficult to describe:
The hulk of him is like hills heaving,
15   Dark, yet as crags of drift-ice, crowns cracking in thunder,
Like land's self by night black-looming, surf churning and trailing
Along his shores' rushing, shoal-water boding
About the dark of his jaws; and who should moor at his edge
And fare on afoot would find gates of no gardens,
20   But the hill of dark underfoot diving,
Closing overhead, the cold deep, and drowning.
He is called Leviathan, and named for rolling,
First created he was of all creatures,[3]
He has held Jonah[4] three days and nights,
25   He is that curling serpent that in ocean is,[5]
Sea-fright he is, and the shadow under the earth.
Days there are, nonetheless, when he lies
Like an angel, although a lost angel
On the waste's unease, no eye of man moving,
30   Bird hovering, fish flashing, creature whatever
Who after him came to herit earth's emptiness.
Froth at flanks seething soothes to stillness,
Waits; with one eye he watches
Dark of night sinking last, with one eye dayrise
35   As at first over foaming pastures. He makes no cry
Though that light is a breath. The sea curling,
Star-climbed, wind-combed, cumbered with itself still
As at first it was, is the hand not yet contented
Of the Creator. And he waits for the world to begin.

[1956]

[1] Literally, any large creature; usually associated with the whale.
[2] See Job, 41:32.
[3] See Genesis, 1:21.
[4] The Old Testament prophet who was swallowed by a "great fish." See the Book of Jonah.
[5] See Isaiah, 27:1.

James Wright   *1927–*

A BLESSING

Just off the highway to Rochester, Minnesota,
Twilight bounds softly forth on the grass.
And the eyes of those two Indian ponies
Darken with kindness.
5   They have come gladly out of the willows
To welcome my friend and me.
We step over the barbed wire into the pasture
Where they have been grazing all day, alone.
They ripple tensely, they can hardly contain their happiness
10 That we have come.
They bow shyly as wet swans. They love each other.
There is no loneliness like theirs.
At home once more,
They begin munching the young tufts of spring in the darkness.
15 I would like to hold the slenderer one in my arms,
For she has walked over to me
And nuzzled my left hand.
She is black and white.
Her mane falls wild on her forehead,
20 And the light breeze moves me to caress her long ear
That is delicate as the skin over a girl's wrist.
Suddenly I realize
That if I stepped out of my body I would break
Into blossom.

[1963]

Anne Sexton   *1928–1974*

LULLABY

It is a summer evening.
The yellow moths sag
against the locked screens
and the faded curtains
5   suck over the window sills
and from another building
a goat calls in his dreams.

This is the TV parlour
in the best ward at Bedlam[1]
10 The night nurse is passing
out the evening pills.
She walks on two erasers,
padding by us one by one.

---

[1] A lunatic asylum or madhouse; originally the popular name for the Hospital of St. Mary of Bethlehem in London, an early asylum for the insane.

15 My sleeping pill is white.
    It is a splendid pearl;
    it floats me out of myself,
    my stung skin as alien
    as a loose bolt of cloth.
    I will ignore the bed.
20 I am linen on a shelf.

Let the others moan in secret;
let each lost butterfly
go home. Old woollen head,
take me like a yellow moth
25 while the goat calls hush-
a-bye.

[1960]

HER KIND

I have gone out, a possessed witch,
haunting the black air, braver at night;
dreaming evil, I have done my hitch
over the plain houses, light by light:
5 lonely thing, twelve-fingered, out of mind.
A woman like that is not a woman, quite.
I have been her kind.

I have found the warm caves in the woods,
filled them with skillets, carvings, shelves,
10 closets, silks, innumerable goods;
fixed the suppers for the worms and the elves:
whining, rearranging the disaligned.
A woman like that is misunderstood.
I have been her kind.

15 I have ridden in your cart, driver,
waved my nude arms at villages going by,
learning the last bright routes, survivor
where your flames still bite my thigh
and my ribs crack where your wheels wind.
20 A woman like that is not ashamed to die.
I have been her kind.

[1960]

THE TRUTH THE DEAD KNOW

For My Mother, Born March 1902, Died March 1959
and My Father, Born February 1900, Died June 1959

Gone, I say and walk from church,
refusing the stiff procession to the grave,
letting the dead ride alone in the hearse.
It is June. I am tired of being brave.

5 We drive to the Cape.[1] I cultivate
myself where the sun gutters from the sky,
where the sea swings in like an iron gate
and we touch. In another country people die.

---

[1] Cape Cod, Massachusetts.

My darling, the wind falls in like stones
from the whitehearted water and when we touch
we enter touch entirely. No one's alone.
Men kill for this, or for as much.

And what of the dead? They lie without shoes
in their stone boats. They are more like stone
10 than the sea would be if it stopped. They refuse
to be blessed, throat, eye and knucklebone.

[1962]

Thom Gunn   *1929–*

VOX HUMANA[1]

Being without quality
I appear to you at first
as an unkempt smudge, a blur,
an indefinite haze, mere-
5 ly pricking the eyes, almost
nothing. Yet you perceive me.

I have been always most close
when you had least resistance,
falling asleep, or in bars;
10 during the unscheduled hours,
though strangely without
substance,
I hang, there and ominous.

Aha, sooner or later
you will have to name me, and,
15 as you name, I shall focus,
I shall become more precise.
O Master (for you command
in naming me, you prefer)!

I was, for Alexander,[2]
20 the certain victory; I
was hemlock for Socrates;[3]
and, in the dry night, Brutus
waking before Philippi
stopped me, crying out,
"Caesar!"[4]

25 Or if you call me the blur
that in fact I am, you shall
yourself remain blurred, hanging
like smoke indoors. For you bring,
to what you define now, all
30 there is, ever, of future.

[1957]

[1] The human voice.
[2] Alexander the Great (356–323 B.C.) helped through his conquests to spread Greek culture through Egypt and the East.
[3] The Greek philosopher Socrates (c. 470–399 B.C.) engaged in his most important and influential dialogues as a result of his trial, imprisonment, and condemnation for impiety and corrupting the youth of Athens.
[4] In Shakespeare's play, Brutus, who had earlier helped to murder Caesar, sees Caesar's ghost on the night before his defeat at Philippi.

Adrienne Rich   *1929–*

STORM WARNINGS

The glass° *barometer* has been falling all the afternoon,
And knowing better than the instrument
What winds are walking overhead, what zone
Of gray unrest is moving across the land,
5   I leave the book upon a pillowed chair
And walk from window to closed window, watching
Boughs strain against the sky

And think again, as often when the air
Moves inward toward a silent core of waiting,
10   How with a single purpose time has traveled
By secret currents of the undiscerned
Into this polar realm. Weather abroad
And weather in the heart alike come on
Regardless of prediction.

15   Between foreseeing and averting change
Lies all the mastery of elements
Which clocks and weatherglasses cannot alter.
Time in the hand is not control of time,
Nor shattered fragments of an instrument
20   A proof against the wind; the wind will rise,
We can only close the shutters.

I draw the curtains as the sky goes black
And set a match to candles sheathed in glass
Against the keyhole draught, the insistent whine
25   Of weather through the unsealed aperture.
This is our sole defense against the season;
These are the things that we have learned to do
Who live in troubled regions.

[1951]

LIVING IN SIN

She had thought the studio would keep itself;
no dust upon the furniture of love.
Half heresy, to wish the taps less vocal,
the panes relieved of grime. A plate of pears,
5   a piano with a Persian shawl, a cat
stalking the picturesque amusing mouse
had risen at his urging.
Not that at five each separate stair would writhe
under the milkman's tramp; that morning light

930

10   so coldly would delineate the scraps
of last night's cheese and three sepulchral bottles;
that on the kitchen shelf among the saucers
a pair of beetle-eyes would fix her own—
envoy from some village in the moldings . . .
15   Meanwhile, he, with a yawn,
sounded a dozen notes upon the keyboard,
declared it out of tune, shrugged at the mirror,
rubbed at his beard, went out for cigarettes;
while she, jeered by the minor demons,
20   pulled back the sheets and made the bed and found
a towel to dust the table-top,
and let the coffee-pot boil over on the stove.
By evening she was back in love again,
though not so wholly but throughout the night
25   she woke sometimes to feel the daylight coming
like a relentless milkman up the stairs.

[1955]

THE KNIGHT

A knight rides into the noon,
and his helmet points to the sun,
and a thousand splintered suns
are the gaiety of his mail.
5   The soles of his feet glitter
and his palms flash in reply,
and under his crackling banner
he rides like a ship in sail.

A knight rides into the noon,
10   and only his eye is living,
a lump of bitter jelly
set in a metal mask,
betraying rags and tatters
that cling to the flesh beneath
15   and wear his nerves to ribbons
under the radiant casque.

Who will unhorse this rider
and free him from between
the walls of iron, the emblems
20   crushing his chest with their weight?
Will they defeat him gently,
or leave him hurled on the green,
his rags and wounds still hidden
under the great breastplate?

[1957]

Gary Snyder   *1930–*

A WALK

Sunday the only day we don't work:
Mules farting around the meadow,
        Murphy fishing,
The tent flaps in the warm
5   Early sun: I've eaten breakfast and I'll
        take a walk
To Benson Lake.[1] Packed a lunch,
Goodbye. Hopping on creekbed boulders
Up the rock throat three miles
10   Piute Creek—
In steep gorge glacier-slick rattlesnake country
Jump, land by a pool, trout skitter,
The clear sky. Deer tracks.
Bad place by a falls, boulders big as houses,
15   Lunch tied to belt,
I stemmed up a crack and almost fell
But rolled out safe on a ledge
        and ambled on.
Quail chicks freeze underfoot, color of stone
20   Then run cheep! away, hen quail fussing.
Craggy west end of Benson Lake—after edging
Past dark creek pools on a long white slope—
Lookt down in the ice-black lake
        lined with cliff
25   From far above: deep shimmering trout.
A lone duck in a gunsightpass
        steep side hill
Through slide-aspen and talus, to the east end,
Down to grass, wading a wide smooth stream
30   Into camp. At last.
        By the rusty three-year-
Ago left-behind cookstove
Of the old trail crew,
Stoppt and swam and ate my lunch.
              [1968]

LOOKING AT PICTURES TO BE PUT AWAY

Who was this girl
In her white night gown
Clutching a pair of jeans

5 On a foggy redwood deck.
She looks up at me tender.
Calm, surprised,

---

[1] Benson Lake, like Piute Creek (line 10), is located in California's Yosemite National Park.

What will we remember
Bodies thick with food and lovers
After twenty years.

[1968]

Sylvia Plath   *1932–1963*

DADDY

You do not do, you do not do
Any more, black shoe
In which I have lived like a foot
For thirty years, poor and white,
5   Barely daring to breathe or Achoo.

Daddy, I have had to kill you.
You died before I had time——
Marble-heavy, a bag full of God,
Ghastly statue with one grey toe[1]
10   Big as a Frisco[2] seal

And a head in the freakish Atlantic
Where it pours bean green over blue
In the waters off beautiful Nauset.[3]
I used to pray to recover you.
15   Ach, du.[4]

In the German tongue, in the Polish town[5]
Scraped flat by the roller
Of wars, wars, wars.
But the name of the town is common.
20   My Polack friend

Says there are a dozen or two.
So I never could tell where you
Put your foot, your root,
I never could talk to you.
25   The tongue stuck in my jaw.

---

[1] Plath's father's toe turned black as a result of diabetes.
[2] San Francisco.
[3] A beach area at the eastern end of Cape Cod, Massachusetts.
[4] *German:* Ah, you.
[5] The birthplace of Plath's father.

It stuck in a barb wire-snare.
Ich, ich, ich, ich,[6]
I could hardly speak.
I thought every German was you.
30   And the language obscene

An engine, an engine
Chuffing me off like a Jew.
A Jew to Dachau, Auschwitz, Belsen.[7]
I began to talk like a Jew.
35   I think I may well be a Jew.

The snows of the Tyrol,[8] the clear beer of Vienna
Are not very pure or true.
With my gypsy ancestress and my weird luck
And my Taroc pack[9] and my Taroc pack
40   I may be a bit of a Jew.

I have always been scared of *you*,
With your Luftwaffe,[10] your gobbledygoo.
And your neat moustache
And your Aryan[11] eye, bright blue.
45   Panzer-man,[12] panzer-man, O You——

Not God but a swastika
So black no sky could squeak through.
Every woman adores a Fascist,
The boot in the face, the brute
50   Brute heart of a brute like you.

You stand at the blackboard, daddy,
In the picture I have of you,
A cleft in your chin instead of your foot
But no less a devil for that, no not
55   Any less the black man who

Bit my pretty red heart in two.
I was ten when they buried you.
At twenty I tried to die
And get back, back, back to you.
60   I thought even the bones would do.

But they pulled me out of the sack,
And they stuck me together with glue.[13]
And then I knew what to do.

---

[6] *German:* I.   [7] Nazi concentration camps.   [8] Alpine region in western Austria.
[9] A deck of fortune-telling cards.   [10] The German air force.
[11] In Nazi ideology the term was applied to Caucasian gentiles, especially those of Nordic ("eye, bright blue") stock.
[12] Relating to a unit of German armor, usually a tank unit.
[13] An allusion to Plath's attempt at suicide.

I made a model of you,
65   A man in black with a Meinkampf[14] look

And a love of the rack and the screw.
And I said I do, I do.
So daddy, I'm finally through.
The black telephone's off at the root,
70   The voices just can't worm through.

If I've killed one man, I've killed two——
The vampire who said he was you
And drank my blood for a year,
Seven years, if you want to know.
75   Daddy, you can lie back now.

There's a stake in your fat black heart
And the villagers never liked you.
They are dancing and stamping on you.
They always *knew* it was you.
80   Daddy, daddy, you bastard, I'm through.

                     [1963]

Imamu Amiri Baraka (LeRoi Jones)   *1934–*

FOR HETTIE

My wife is left-handed.
which implies a fierce determination. A complete other
worldliness. ITS WEIRD, BABY.
5   The way some folks
are always trying to be
different. A sin & a shame.

But then, she's been a bohemian[1]
all of her life . . . black stockings
10   refusing to take orders. I sit
patiently, trying to tell her
whats right. TAKE THAT DAMM
PENCIL OUTTA THAT HAND. YOU'RE
RITING BACKWARDS. & such. But

---

[14] "My Struggle," Adolph Hitler's (1889–1945) autobiography, in which he set forth his plan for world conquest.
[1] An unconventional person; often applied to artistic individuals who shun conventional behavior.

15   to no avail. & it shows
in her work. Left-handed coffee,
Left-handed eggs; when she comes
in at night . . . it's her left hand
offered for me to kiss. Damm.

20   & now her belly droops over the seat.
They say it's a child. But
I ain't quite so sure.

                    [1961]

Diane Wakoski *1937–*

I LAY NEXT TO YOU ALL NIGHT, TRYING AWAKE TO UNDERSTAND THE WATERING PLACES OF THE MOON

    I lay next to you
all night,
trying,
awake,
5   to understand the watering places
of the moon,
              how my own body
dry and restless
like rootless tumbleweed
10   moves through the night,
through my eyes,
staying awake in bed
while you sleep
allowing my presence
15   but not wanting to touch,
allowing my presence
in the way
the earth
tolerates the moon,
20   allowing its restless pull.

    I lay next to you
all night,
trying,
awake,
25   to understand what dead moon
I am,
why I shine in the sky at all.

But it is a physical function
of presence.

30 The moon
never complains.
The moon knows
it shines
at night
35 moving relentlessly
awake
through the sky
while everyone else sleeps,
while you're away.
40   The metaphor fatigues me.
I am less patient from my sleepless night.
I could carry the moon
across this room,
across the lawn,
45 out through the wet morning streets
through this whole town
and make
references
that would make you
50 as impatient with my life
as I am.

             But my sharp tongue
gleams at me
out of its drawer,
55 a sharpened knife,
and reminds me of the people I've been chiding
for the past few weeks,
telling them to burn
like the sun,
60 telling them to ignore the lack of love in their lives,
telling them to smile and walk past telescopes
photographing their dissatisfactions
like craters on the moon,
telling them to name them and find
65 new landscapes,
while I lie awake
next to you
all night
trying
70 to understand why
the sun's rays leave me so hot and thirsty,
why I am lonely and chilly at night,
why I,
the avid astronomer,
75 allow myself to be confused
and look out of the wrong end of the telescope.

Forgive me
for my restlessness
and my expectations.
80   I am the moon. Diane.
Poets have speculated about me too long.
At last I am circled,
photographed,
and soon to be explored.
85   A dry dusty shell
of something that once lived.
My literary content
is a vanishing species,
like sea otters.
90   Forgive me if I dive into the desert every night
and call out for water.
Forgive me if I dive into the moon, myself,
and cannot escape the pull of your gravity.
Forgive me if I expect you to love me. I mistake you
95   for a poet.
I lay next to you
all night,
trying,
awake,
100   to understand the watering places
of the moon,
knowing there are no Li Pos[1] left
to drunkenly fall into a river
attempting to hold its radiant face
105   all night.
My dry arms
try to gather
water.

[1969]

Margaret Atwood   *1939–*

THE SETTLERS

A second after
the first boat touched the shore,
there was a quick skirmish
brief as a twinge
5   and then the land was settled

[1] Li Po (705–762), a famous Chinese lyric poet. His verse has been translated into English by
Amy Lowell.

(of course there was really
no shore: the water turned
to land by having
objects in it: caught and kept
10 from surge, made
less than immense
by networks of
roads and grids of fences)

and as for us, who drifted
15 picked by the sharks
during so many bluegreen
centuries before they came:
they found us
inland, stranded
20 on a ridge of bedrock,
defining our own island.

From our inarticulate
skeleton (so
intermixed, one
25 carcass),
they postulated wolves.

They dug us down
into the solid granite
where our bones grew flesh again,
30 came up trees and
grass.

Still
we are the salt
seas that uphold these lands.

35 Now horses graze
inside this fence of ribs, and

children run, with green
smiles, (not knowing
where) across
40 the fields of our open hands.

[1966]

❧ CONTEMPORARY SONGS AND BALLADS ❧

Tom Jones   *1940–*

TRY TO REMEMBER

Try to remember the kind of September
When life was slow and, oh, so mellow.
Try to remember the kind of September
When grass was green and grain was yellow.
5   Try to remember the kind of September
When you were a tender and callow fellow.
Try to remember and if you remember,
Then follow. *(Echo)* Follow, follow, follow.

Try to remember when life was so tender
10   That no one wept except the willow.
Try to remember when life was so tender
That dreams were kept beside your pillow.
Try to remember when life was so tender
That love was an ember about to billow.
15   Try to remember and if you remember,
Then follow. *(Echo)* Follow, follow, follow.

Deep in December it's nice to remember
Although you know the snow will follow.
Deep in December it's nice to remember
20   Without a hurt the heart is hollow.
Deep in December, it's nice to remember
The fire of September that made us mellow.
Deep in December our hearts should remember,
And follow. *(Echo)* Follow, follow, follow.

[1960]

Bob Dylan   *1941–*

MISTER TAMBOURINE MAN

Hey, Mister Tambourine Man, play a song for me,
I'm not sleepy and there ain't no place I'm going to.
Hey, Mister Tambourine Man, play a song for me,
In the jingle, jangle morning I'll come followin' you.

I

5 Though I know that evenin's empire has returned into sand
Vanished from my hand,
Left me blindly here to stand
But still no sleepin'.
My weariness amazes me,
10 I'm branded on my feet,
I have no one to meet,
And the ancient empty street's
Too dead for dreamin'.
Chorus

II

Take me on a trip upon your magic swirlin' ship,
15 My senses have been stripped,
My hands can't feel to grip,
My toes too numb to step,
Wait only for my boot heels to be wanderin'.
I'm ready to go anywhere,
20 I'm ready for to fade
Into my own parade.
Cast your dancin' spell my way,
I promise to go under it.
Chorus

III

Though you might hear laughin', spinnin', swingin' madly
through the sun,
25 It's not aimed at anyone,
It's just escapin' on the run,
And but for the sky there are no fences facin'.
And if you hear vague traces
Of skippin' reels of rhyme
30 To your tambourine in time,
It's just a ragged clown behind,
I wouldn't pay it any mind,
It's just a shadow
You're seein' that he's chasin'.
Chrous

IV

35   Take me disappearin' through the smoke rings of my mind
      Down the foggy ruins of time,
      Far past the frozen leaves,
      The haunted, frightened trees
      Out to the windy beach
40   Far from the twisted reach of crazy sorrow.
      Yes, to dance beneath the diamond sky
      With one hand wavin' free,
      Silhouetted by the sea,
      Circled by the circus sands,
45   With memory and fate
      Driven deep beneath the waves.
      Let me forget about today until tomorrow.
      Chorus

                                                            [1964]

Richard Farina   *1937–1966*

BIRMINGHAM SUNDAY[1]

      Come round by my side and I'll sing you a song.
        I'll sing it so softly it'll do no one wrong.
      On Birmingham Sunday the blood ran like wine,
        And the choirs kept singing of Freedom.

5   That cold autumn morning no eyes saw the sun,
        And Addie Mae Collins her number was one.
      At an Old Baptist Church there was no need to run,
        And the choirs kept singing of Freedom.

      The clouds they were grey and the autumn winds blew,
10   And Denise McNair brought the number to two.
      The falcon of death was a creature they knew,
        And the choirs kept singing of Freedom.

      The church it was crowded but no one could see
        That Cynthia Wesley's dark number was three.

---

[1] On September 15, 1963, as Bible school classes were coming to a close at the 16th Street Baptist Church in Birmingham, Alabama, a bomb exploded leveling much of the building and killing four young Negro girls: Carole Robertson, age 14; Cynthia Wesley, age 14; Addie Mae Collins, age 14; and Denise McNair, age 11. The text they had been studying was from Matthew 5:43–44—"Ye have heard that it hath been said, Thou shalt love they neighbor, and hate thine enemy. But I say unto you, Love your enemies, bless them that curse you, do good to them that hate you, and pray for them which despitefully use you, and persecute you."

15   Her prayers and her feelings would shame you and me,
       And the choirs kept singing of Freedom.

     Young Carol Robertson entered the door,
       And the number her killers had given was four.
     She asked for a blessing but asked for no more,
20   And the choirs kept singing of Freedom.

     The men in the forest they once asked of me,
       "How many black berries grow in the Blue Sea?"
     And I asked them right back with a tear in my eye,
       "How many dark ships in the forest?"

25   The Sunday has come, the Sunday has gone,
       And I can't do much more than to sing you a song.
     I'll sing it so softly it'll do no one wrong,
       And the choirs keep singing of Freedom.

                   [1964]

Gordon Lightfoot *1939–*

EARLY MORNING RAIN

    In the early mornin' rain
    With a dollar in my hand.
    With an achin' in my heart
    And my pockets full of sand.
5   I'm a long way from home
    And I miss my loved one so.
    In the early mornin' rain
    And no place to go.

    Out on runway number nine
10   Big seven-o-seven set to go,
    Well I'm standin' on the grass
    Where the cold wind blows.
    Well, the liquor tasted good
    And the women all were fast,
15   Well, there she goes, my friend
    She's rollin' now at last.

    Hear the mighty engines roar,
    See the silver bird on high,
    She's away and westward bound
20   Far above the clouds she'll fly,

Where the mornin' rain don't fall
And the sun always shines,
She'll be flyin' o'er my home
In about three hours time.

25   Well, this old airport's got me down.
It's no earthly good to me,
'Cause I'm stuck here on the ground
As cold and drunk as I can be.
You can't jump a jet plane
30   Like you can a freight train,
So I best be on my way
In the early mornin' rain.

[1964]

Buffy Sainte-Marie   *1941–*

UNTIL IT'S TIME FOR YOU TO GO

You're not a dream
You're not an angel,
You're a man;
I'm not a queen,
5   I'm a woman
Take my hand.
We'll make a space
In the lives
That we planned
10   And here we'll stay
Until it's time
For you to go.

Don't ask why.
Don't ask how.
15   Don't ask forever.
Love me now!

Yes, we're different,
Worlds apart,
We're not the same.
20   We laughed and played
At the start
Like in a game.

You could have stayed
Outside my heart
25   But in you came
And here you'll stay
Until it's time
For you to go.

Don't ask why.
30   Don't ask how.
Don't ask forever.
Love me now!

This love of mine
Had no beginning
35   It has no end.
I was an oak
Now I'm a willow
Now I can bend.
And though I'll never
40   In my life
See you again
Still I'll stay
Until it's time
For you to go.

45   Don't ask why of me,
Don't ask how of me.
Don't ask forever of me.
Love me, love me now!

[1965]

Paul Simon   *1942–*

DANGLING CONVERSATION

It's a still-life water color
Of a now late afternoon
As the sun shines through the curtain lace
And shadows wash the room.

5   And we sit and drink our coffee
Cast in our indifference
Like shells upon a shore
You can hear the ocean roar.

In the dangling conversation
10   And the superficial sighs
The borders of our lives.

And you read your Emily Dickinson
And I my Robert Frost
As we note our place with bookmarkers
15   That measure what we've lost.

Like a poem poorly written
We are verses out of rhythm
Couplets out of rhyme
In syncopated[1] time.

20   And the dangling conversation
And the superficial sighs
Are the borders of our lives.

Yes, we speak the things that matter
With words that must be said
25   Can analysis be worthwhile?
Is the theatre really dead?

---

[1] In music, a tone begun on the last half of a beat and continued through the first half of the following beat—hence, out of rhythm.

And now the room is softly faded
And I only kiss your shadow
I cannot feel your hand
30   You're a stranger now unto me.

Lost in the dangling conversation
And the superficial sighs
In the borders of our lives.

[1966]

Leonard Cohen   *1934–*

SUZANNE

Suzanne takes you down
to her place near the river,
you can hear the boats go by
you can stay the night beside her.
5   And you know that she's half crazy
but that's why you want to be there
and she feeds you tea and oranges
that come all the way from China.
Just when you mean to tell her
10   that you have no gifts to give her,
she gets you on her wave-length
and she lets the river answer
that you've always been her lover.
   And you want to travel with her,
15   you want to travel blind
   and you know that she can trust you
   because you've touched her perfect body
   with your mind.

Jesus was a sailor
20   when he walked upon the water[1]
and he spent a long time watching
from a lonely wooden tower
and when he knew for certain
only drowning men could see him
25   he said All men will be sailors then
until the sea shall free them,

---

[1] See Matthew 14:25–31.

but he himself was broken
long before the sky would open,
forsaken, almost human,
30 he sank beneath your wisdom like a stone.
    And you want to travel with him,
    you want to travel blind
    and you think maybe you'll trust him
    because he touched your perfect body
35   with his mind.

Now Suzanne takes your hand
and she leads you to the river,
she is wearing rags and feathers
from Salvation Army counters,
40 and the sun pours down like honey
on our lady of the harbour,
and she shows you where to look
among the garbage and the flowers.
There are heroes in the seaweed,
45 there are children in the morning,
they are leaning out for love
and they will lean that way forever
while Suzanne holds the mirror.
    And you want to travel with her,
    you want to travel blind
50   and you know that you can trust her
    because she's touched your perfect body
    with her mind.

                   [1966]

John Lennon *1940–1980*
Paul McCartney *1942–*

ELEANOR RIGBY

Ah, look at all the lonely people!
Ah, look at all the lonely people!

Eleanor Rigby
Picks up the rice in the church where a wedding has been,
5 Lives in a dream,
Waits at the window
Wearing the face that she keeps in a jar by the door.
Who is it for?

All the lonely people,
10 Where do they all come from?
All the lonely people,
Where do they all belong?

Father McKenzie,
Writing the words of a sermon that no one will hear,
15 No one comes near
Look at him working,
Darning his socks in the night when there's nobody there.
What does he care?

All the lonely people
20 Where do they all come from?
All the lonely people
Where do they all belong?

Eleanor Rigby
Died in the church and was buried along with her name.
25 Nobody came.
Father McKenzie,
Wiping the dirt from his hands as he walks from the grave,
No one was saved.

All the lonely people,
30 Where do they all come from?

                               [1966]

Joni Mitchell *1943–*

BOTH SIDES NOW

Bows and flows of angel hair,
And ice cream castles in the air,
And feather canyons ev'rywhere,
I've looked at clouds that way.
5 But now they only block the sun,
They rain and snow on ev'ryone.
So many things I would have done,
But clouds got in my way.
I've looked at clouds from both sides now,
10 From up and down and still somehow
It's cloud illusions I recall;
I really don't know clouds
At all.

Moons and Junes and ferris wheels,
15 The dizzy dancing way you feel,
As ev'ry fairy tale comes real,
I've looked at love that way.

But now it's just another show,
You leave 'em laughing when you go.
20 And if you care, don't let them know,
Don't give yourself away.
I've looked at love from both sides now,
From give and take and still somehow
It's love's illusions I recall;
25 I really don't know love
At all.

Tears and fears and feeling proud,
To say "I love you" right out loud,
Dreams and schemes and circus crowds,
30 I've looked at life that way.
But now old friends are acting strange,
They shake their heads, they say I've changed.
But something's lost but something's gained.
In living ev'ry day.
35 I've looked at life from both sides now,
From win and lose and still somehow
It's life's illusions I recall;
I really don't know life
At all.

[1967]

Judy Collins   *1939–*

MY FATHER

My father always promised us
   that we would live in France,
We'd go boating on the Seine
   and I would learn to dance.
5 We lived in Ohio then
   he worked in the mines,
On his streams like boats we knew
   we'd sail, in time.

All my sisters soon were gone
10   to Denver and Cheyenne,
Marrying their grownup dreams,
   the lilacs and the man.
I stayed behind the youngest still,
   only danced alone,
15 The colors of my father's dreams
   faded without a sigh.

And I live in Paris now,
   my children dance and dream
Hearing the ways of a miner's life
20   in words they've never seen.
I sail my memories afar
   like boats across the Seine,
And watch the Paris sun
   set in my father's eyes again.

25 My father always promised us
   that we would live in France,
We'd go boating on the Seine
   and I would learn to dance.
We lived in Ohio then
30   he worked in the mines,
On his streams like boats we knew
   we'd sail, in time.

[1968]

James Taylor *1948–*

FIRE AND RAIN

Just yesterday morning they let me know you were gone—
Susan the plans they made put an end to you.
I walked out this morning and I wrote down this song—
I just can't remember who to send it to.—

CHORUS
5   I've seen fire and I've seen rain
I've seen sunny days that I thought would never end—
I've seen lonely times when I could not find a friend—
But I always thought that I'd see you again.

Won't you look down upon me, Jesus, you've got to help me make a
    stand—
10 You've just got to see me through another day.
My body's aching and my time is at hand—
And I won't make it any other way.
Chorus

Now I'm walking my mind to an easy time my back turned towards
    the sun.
Lord knows when the cold wind blows it'll turn your head around
15 Well, there's hours of time on the telephone line to talk about things
    to come—
Sweet dreams and flying machines in pieces on the ground.
Chorus

[1969]

Kris Kristofferson *1936–*

ME AND BOBBY McGEE

Busted flat in Baton Rouge;
Headin' for the trains,
Feelin' nearly faded as my jeans,
Bobby thumbed a diesel down
5   Just before it rained;
Took us all the way to New Orleans,
I took my harpoon° out of my dirty red bandanna   *harmonica*
And was blowin' sad, while Bobby sang the blues;

With them windshield wipers slappin' time and Bobby clappin' hands
10 We fin'ly sang up every song that driver knew;

Freedom's just another word for nothin' left to lose,
And nothin' ain't worth nothin' but it's free;
Feeling good was easy, Lord, when Bobby sang the blues;
And, Buddy, that was good enough for me;
15 Good enough for me and Bobby McGee.

From the coal mines of Kentucky to the
California sun,
Bobby shared the secret of my soul;
Standin' right beside me, Lord, through
20 Everything I done,
And every night she kept me from the cold;
Then somewhere near Salinas, Lord, I let her slip away
Lookin' for the home I hope she'll find;
And I'd trade all of my tomorrows for a
25 Single yesterday, holdin' Bobby's body next to mine;

Freedom's just another word for nothin' left to lose,
And nothin' is all she left for me;
Feelin' good was easy, Lord, when Bobby sang the blues;
And, Buddy, that was good enough for me;
30 Good enough for me and Bobby McGee.

[1971]

III

DRAMA

10

❧❧❧❧❧❧

What Is Drama?

The word *drama* comes from the Greek verb *dran*, meaning "to perform." When we speak of a drama, we mean a story in dialogue performed by actors, on a stage, before an audience—in other words, a *play*. We also use the term *drama* in a more general sense to refer to the literary genre that encompasses all written plays and to the profession of writing, producing, and performing plays.

Because drama presupposes performance, it is not a purely literary genre. It combines the use of language with representational arts involving scenery, costuming, and the actors' physical appearance. It also makes use of vocal emphasis and tone of voice, along with such nonverbal forms of expression as physical gesture, facial expression, and sometimes music and dance. Thus, a drama only becomes a complete work of art when it is seen on the stage, and the written text of a play is only its skeletal frame—lacking flesh, blood, and a life of its own. This skeletal script is, however, the only permanent part of a play. The rest is ephemeral: it changes to some degree with each night's performance and, to a considerable extent, with each new production. Presentations of Greek tragedy, for example, have ranged from stately, historically accurate productions to loose, avant-garde adaptations. In one production of Euripides' *The Bacchae* (c. 405 B.C.) we watch "larger than life" actors struggle to speak clearly while costumed in oversized masks, padded clothing, and sandals with thick platform soles. And in another production of the same play (renamed *Dionysus in 69*), we find naked women splashing their way through oceans of stage blood, engaging in simulated sex, and writhing through a savage "birth ritual."

Such extremes serve to remind us that the script is the only part of the play over which the author has complete control; the rest is the collaborative creation of many different artists, some of whom may misunderstand and therefore misrepresent what the author intended. Because we can never know exactly

955

how Sophocles, Shakespeare, Molière, and other early dramatists staged their plays, we can never reproduce exactly the work of art they intended. But in reading the words of the play, we *can* share in the imaginative experience that—even more than success on the stage—is responsible for the survival and enduring popularity of great drama. We know, for example, that the plays of Euripides (c. 480–407 B.C.) were not popular with the audience when first presented in ancient Greece. Yet Euripides' plays have survived through the ages, and those of his more popular contemporaries are all but forgotten. Apparently, Euripides' intense, introverted style and penetrating character analyses appealed to the readers who commissioned and preserved manuscripts of his plays. In contrast, the record for the longest continuous run for a single play is held by Agatha Christie's *The Mousetrap*, which, whatever its merit as drama, as of 1979 had been on stage for 27 years and almost 11,000 performances. Christie's play will not, of course, continue its run forever. Someday the show will close, and thereafter its survival will depend on readers. Only if the demand by the play-reading public is sufficient to keep a play in print, and only if the play in its written form appeals to a succession of producers and directors, can we expect that it will truly become a stage classic.

This is precisely what has happened in the case of Euripides, Shakespeare, and other great classic and modern dramatists, whose readers have always outnumbered their viewers. Even today, when the average citizen has an unparalleled opportunity to see outstanding theater on stage, copies of printed scripts continue to be sold in ever-increasing numbers. Although most lovers of the theater insist upon *seeing* great drama performed, they insist equally upon owning, reading, and studying the plays they love.

The reason for this phenomenon is clear enough: when we study drama as literature—that is, when we study the text of the play, apart from its staging—we may not see the entire work intended by the author, but we do see the words exactly as the playwright wrote them, or as they have been translated, without any cutting, rearranging, or rewriting by the director and without the interpretive assistance (or hindrance) of the actors. The written script may be skeletal compared to a stage presentation, but that limitation can help us to concentrate on the play's structure and on those elements of drama that fall directly under the author's control.

DRAMA AND POETRY

As soon as we think of drama as a form of literature, we begin to notice that a play shares many similarities with a long narrative poem. In fact, from the days of ancient Greece through the first half of the nineteenth century, most plays were written in verse. The dramatic works of Aeschylus, Sophocles, Euripides, Aristophanes, Marlowe, Shakespeare, Jonson, Molière, Racine, Corneille, and many others are largely or entirely poetic. Even Ibsen, who probably did more than any other dramatist to make prose acceptable in tragedy, wrote two of his most famous plays, *Brand* (1866) and *Peer Gynt* (1867), in verse.

The reasons for the historical predominance of verse in drama are not difficult to discover. Drama, like poetry, is meant to be heard. As a result, like poetry, it makes use of the aural qualities of rhythm and rhyme. Furthermore, because Greek drama originally grew out of choral songs, it was only natural that the musical elements in the songs should be preserved in the plays; and because Greek drama served as a model for most subsequent generations, verse remained an integral part of most playwriting until a growing preoccupation with realism near the end of the nineteenth century made the contrivance of dialogue in verse both unnecessary and undesirable. Finally, many of the stages used for drama were relatively barren, and the playwright was forced to evoke through poetic language any characteristics of the setting that he wished the audience to envision. Thus, poetic diction, imagery, and techniques of versification became thoroughly integrated into the drama.

One cannot conclude, however, that drama is inevitably a form of poetry. Indeed, in the last century new poetic dramas have rarely been successful on the stage. Popular taste has changed, and audiences now demand realism instead of poetic flourishes. Of course, many of these realistic plays—especially those of Tennessee Williams and Eugene O'Neill—are written in prose which is so imagistic and suggestive that it may be studied as a form of free verse, but even if we confine this discussion to plays more obviously written in verse, we will find some differences between poetry and drama. In the first place, a poem is meant for only one speaker; a play for two or more. Similarly, a poem can be written in virtually any verse form, while a play (in English) is limited by tradition to blank verse, heroic couplets, or prose. Finally, most poems are quite short, while most plays are comparatively long. When we speak of the poetry in Shakespeare's plays, we ordinarily refer to only a few well-known passages: the descriptions of Cleopatra's barge or her death in *Antony and Cleopatra,* Marc Antony's oration in *Julius Caesar,* Portia's speech on mercy in *The Merchant of Venice,* Othello's last words, Hamlet's soliloquies, and so on. Such passages, and others like them, are memorized and anthologized almost as if they were separate poems, while the rest of each play, whether it is truly poetic or not, is read, performed, and analyzed in much the same way as if it were prose. Shakespeare, after all, was human and like other men was apt to put in an occasional dull day at his desk. Take, for example, the following brief scene from *Othello:*

SCENE 2. *A room in the castle. Enter* OTHELLO, IAGO, *and* GENTLEMEN.

> OTHELLO. These letters give, Iago, to the pilot,
> And by him do my duties to the Senate.
> That done, I will be walking on the works.
> Repair there to me.
>> IAGO. Well, my good lord, I'll do 't.
>> OTHELLO. This fortification, gentlemen, shall we see 't?
>> GENTLEMEN. We'll wait upon your lordship.
>> (*Exeunt.*)
>
> —From *Othello,* act 3, scene 2,
> William Shakespeare [1604]

Even if this scene of only six lines served some dramatic function, it would be uninspired writing. Othello's letters to the Senate have no further significance, nor does his inspection of the fortifications. The scene is an encounter of no substance that serves only to waste a little stage time, allowing Cassio to begin the interview with Desdemona that was promised in the preceding scene and that we join in progress in the subsequent one.

The same kind of mechanical drama is even more common in the works

of lesser dramatists. The quantity of true poetry in a play is always slight
when compared with the larger body of dialogue that is necessary to move
the characters around and push the action forward. Indeed, the preponderance
of prosaic and merely competent lines in a play helps to make the poetic
moments stand out more clearly, so that they seem (to quote Shakespeare)
"as the spots of heaven,/ More fiery by the night's blackness."

DRAMA AND FICTION

If we take it as axiomatic that the best of a play approaches the level of
poetry while the bulk of it remains prosaic, then it follows that most drama
is closer to fiction than to poetry. Plays are fictitious both in the literal sense
that their plots are generally untrue and in the figurative sense that they intend
to convey general truths. Like a novel, a play always tells a story. It cannot
be purely lyric, descriptive, or argumentative—although each of these modes
of expression has a place in drama. Instead, a play begins like a typical short
story with an introduction to the characters, the situation, and the setting. It
rapidly develops some conflict among the characters that typically reaches a
crisis in the fourth act and finds its resolution in the fifth. And in presenting
its action, a play manipulates many of the elements found in a short story.
Aristotle, the first theoretician of drama, identified six basic elements in the
genre: setting, character, plot, language, theme, and music. All but the last
are also elements of fiction, and music is no longer requisite or even common
in modern drama.

Despite these similarities, a play clearly differs from a short story and drama
differs from fiction. Some of the main differences between the genres emerge
in the handling of point of view, time, and structure. Unlike a short story,
which can present the action from many different points of view, a play is
obliged to present its story dramatically. The characters speak directly to one
another, and the audience observes their actions without the assistance of a
narrator to fill in background information, draw conclusions, and generally
serve as a guide to the significance of unfolding events.[1] The playwright cannot
pry into the minds of the characters as an omniscient narrator might, and
the audience can have no knowledge of a character's thoughts, emotions, or
past unless these emerge through dialogue, physical action, or the use of soliloquy.

Because of its dramatic point of view, a play takes place in the perpetual
present tense. Where the short story or the novel always implicitly begins,
"Once upon a time . . . ," a play both begins and proceeds with "now . . .
now . . . now!" The audience always knows what the characters *are doing* while
they are onstage, but the playwright has no unobtrusive means of showing
what they *have done* either before the curtain rises or while they are offstage.
The confidant, who is made privy to another's past, and the messenger, who
reports offstage activities, are obvious and sometimes inadequate substitutes
for fictional omniscience. Indeed, the author's desire to supply characters with

---

[1] *Our Town* (1938) by Thornton Wilder, *The Glass Menagerie* (1944) by Tennessee Williams, *After
the Fall* (1964) by Arthur Miller and a number of other modern plays use a narrator to introduce
and control the action, but even in these plays the narrator must eventually step aside and
allow the events to unfold objectively and dramatically.

a past helps us to understand why many plays focus on heroes whose exploits are already known to the audience through history or legend.

Another way of stating the difference between fiction and drama is to observe that a play is structured around a succession of *scenes.* A new scene is needed whenever there is a change of setting or time. (In many French and a few English dramas, a new scene also begins with the entrance or exit of any major character.) The scenes are often then grouped into *acts,* which indicate the major units in the development of the plot. The formal division of plays into acts and scenes represents a major difference between the structure of drama and that of fiction. In the latter, the plot *may* unfold as a chronological series of scenes, but there is nothing to keep an author from reminiscing within a scene. Thus, fiction may present a convoluted series of stories within stories— *The Arabian Nights* provides many examples—but drama is obliged to present only those plots that can be developed continuously and chronologically.[2]

In the following pages, as we examine the influence of the actors, the audience, and the stage, we will discover other ways in which drama differs from poetry and fiction; it should now be clear, however, that the major elements of drama are also the major elements of poetry and fiction. Our present task is not to describe new literary elements, but rather to explain how the special conditions of dramatic presentation influence the playwright's handling of fictional and poetic devices.

THE ACTORS

Because drama is primarily designed for performance, we can expect that the greatest plays will encourage and successfully incorporate the creative potential of the actors. A dramatist writes with the knowledge that his or her lines will be presented on stage in a way that emphasizes tonal implications and fulfills the incidents suggested by the dialogue. But while a professional playwright seeks to encourage the actors to interpret their lines creatively, he may wish to be sure that the larger thematic impact of the play remains unchanged by different acting styles. By writing their plays for specific stage companies, some dramatists are able to retain a greater measure of control over the initial stage production. Not only can these dramatists conceive the play and write the first draft with the strengths and limitations of key actors and actresses already in mind, but they can also supervise the rehearsals and revise the parts of the play that seem ill-suited to the actors. In many cases, therefore, the text of the play that emerges is the result of some form of collaboration between the playwright and the actors.

Because a playwright must assume that the roles in the script will be played by real people, with real idiosyncracies in personality and appearance, there is no need to describe any character's external appearance. The audience can see for itself what Ibsen's Hedda Gabler looks like, and a description of Hedda's appearance, such as one might find in a novel, becomes redundant and unnecessary in the dialogue of a play. Of course, the author's parenthetic stage directions sometimes do include a description of the characters. Hedda, for example, is introduced as

---

[2] There are, to be sure, exceptions, as usual. In *Our Town,* to cite Wilder's play again, the action returns to the past in the last act.

a woman of nine-and-twenty. Her face and figure show refinement and distinction. Her complexion is pale and opaque. Her steel-gray eyes express a cold, unruffled repose. Her hair is of an agreeable medium brown but not particularly abundant. She is dressed in a tasteful, somewhat loose-fitting morning gown.

—From *Hedda Gabler*, act 1, Henrik Ibsen [1890]

But such comments are directed at readers, not viewers. They underscore the fact that a playwright often writes simultaneously for two audiences: one in the theater and the other in the armchair.

In writing for the theater, the dramatist has in the actors a great advantage over the novelist, for the characters in a play *are* real. They live and breathe, stand up and sit down, sigh and smile, enter and exit—all with greater realism than even the most competent novelist can create. The actions and expressions of several characters can be conveyed on stage in a matter of seconds, whereas a novelist might have to devote several pages to a description of the same incidents. As a result, drama has an immediate impact that fiction and poetry can never equal. The illusion of reality in some plays or films is as close as art can ever come to bringing its fictional incidents to life.

But although the playwright is relieved from describing the physical appearance or actions of his characters at length, he *cannot* analyze their personalities and motives directly and concisely. An omniscient inquiry into how and why a character speaks, moves, and thinks as he or she does is both desirable and entertaining in a novel by Dickens, but it is not easy to present through dialogue on a stage. Instead, a dramatist individualizes his characters by giving them distinctive habits or quirks of speech and by allowing them to express their personalities through action. Soon after Hedda Gabler first appears on stage, for example, we see her impatience with any references to her femininity or possible pregnancy:

TESMAN. . . . Auntie, take a good look at Hedda before you go! See how handsome she is!

MISS TESMAN. Oh, my dear boy, there's nothing new in that. Hedda was always lovely. [*She nods and goes toward the right.*]

TESMAN [*following*]. Yes, but have you noticed what splendid condition she is in? How she has filled out on the journey?

HEDDA [*crossing the room*]. Oh, do be quiet!

MISS TESMAN [*who has stopped and turned*]. Filled out?

TESMAN. Of course you don't notice it so much now that she has that dress on. But I, who can see—

HEDDA [*at the glass door, impatient*]. Oh, you can't see anything.

TESMAN. It must be the mountain air in the Tyrol—

HEDDA [*curtly interrupting*]. I am exactly as I was when I started.

TESMAN. So you insist, but I'm quite certain you are not. Don't you agree with me, Auntie?

MISS TESMAN [*who has been gazing at her with folded hands*]. Hedda is lovely—lovely—lovely. [*Goes up to her, takes her head between both hands, draws it downward and kisses her hair.*] God bless and preserve Hedda Tesman—for George's sake.

HEDDA [*gently freeing herself*]. Oh! Let me go.

MISS TESMAN [*in quiet emotion*]. I shall not let a day pass without coming to see you.

TESMAN. No, you won't, will you, Auntie? Eh?

MISS TESMAN. Good-by—good-by! [*She goes out by the hall door.* TESMAN *accompanies her. The door remains half open.* TESMAN *can be heard repeating his message to Aunt Rina and his thanks for the slippers. In the meantime* HEDDA *walks about the room raising her arms and clenching her hands as if in desperation. Then she flings back the curtains from the glass door and stands there looking out.*]

—From *Hedda Gabler*, act 1, Henrik Ibsen [1890]

Even here the superiority of fictional omniscience in describing motives and emotions is obvious. Ibsen's parenthetic stage directions succinctly and unambiguously inform the reader about the attitudes of the characters. Where these describe actions ("She nods and goes toward the right"), there is no problem presenting them on the stage. Where they describe a tone of voice ("HEDDA [at the glass door, impatient]") they can be a challenge to acting skills but are still likely to be understood by the audience. When, however, they indicate a state of mind more than a tone of voice, the reader is apt to fare very much better than the viewer. How, for example, is Miss Tesman's "quiet emotion" to be conveyed in her final comment to Hedda?

Usually, Ibsen avoids vague instructions about an actor's tone of voice and strives instead to bring out his characters' attitudes through their words and actions. Hedda, for example, is frustrated by the timid and retiring role that nineteenth-century women were expected to play. Like many other women of the day, she feels imprisoned by the one-sided decorum imposed by her male-dominated society. To dramatize this, Ibsen never allows her to leave her own constricting household during the play's four acts. Through her conversations with Eilert Lövborg and Judge Brack, we discover that she wishes she could participate in the excitement and dissipations of masculine life, but is hindered by a dread of scandal. Thus, although she tries to satisfy her adventurous urges by manipulating the lives of others—particularly Tesman and Eilert—her repressed passions continually break out. These aspects of her personality are given dramatic form by her actions in the brief scene quoted here. She grows irritated at the allusions to pregnancy, clenches her fists, restlessly paces to and from the windows of the parlor, and a few moments later begins to toy with guns. Using these and other dramatic indications of Hedda's underlying turmoil, Ibsen is able to expose the hidden core of her personality without access to the novelist's omniscient narration.

While writing into the script words and actions that help to define the characters, a playwright must also allow some room for the actors' interpretation and self-expression. In other words, a succesful play will stimulate and inspire the actors to use their talents creatively in presenting the play before an audience. In practice, the meaning of the play and the vital intellectual substance that animates each character should be suggested in the script but not rigidly imposed on it. Thus, Ibsen wisely leaves it unclear whether Hedda truly wishes she were a man or is simply rebelling against the traditionally subdued role of her sex. Part of the pleasure of the theater for habitual playgoers derives from this artistic ambiguity. In successive productions of established classics, those who follow the theater closely are able to see how different actresses and actors interpret their roles and are able to compare those interpretations with perceptions based on a study of the text.

But while a dramatist is required to leave some slack in the characterizations to accommodate the actors' differences in physical appearance as well as their need for creative self-expression, he or she must not allow these freedoms to get out of hand. A play, like most other literary works, ordinarily presents an ethical point or some thematic statement about the world and our place in it that the playwright feels to be both relevant and significant. Because drama is a collaborative art—drawing on the talents of the actors, director, musicians, stagehands, scenic artists, and others—a playwright must learn to sketch theme and plot in simple, vigorous, and bold strokes, to be certain that the "message" will come through to the audience. Good drama implies the successive unfolding of the implications of one overarching idea: Hedda's desire to control a human destiny, Tartuffe's hypocrisy, Othello's jealousy, Oedipus's false pride. In each case the central idea is traced by the course of seemingly inevitable events. It is not in the power of the actors to change the concept of the play, just as it is not in the power of an engineer to change the downhill flow of a river. The natural path may be momentarily blocked, but its ultimate course cannot be stopped or stayed.

A careful and single-minded plot development is but one means by which playwrights sometimes seek to control the influence of the cast on the impact of a play. As already noted, many dramatists have composed their plays with the specific abilities of specific actors in mind in an effort to minimize the risk of parts being misplayed. The parts in Shakespeare's plays, for example, were often carefully tailored to suit his fellow members of the Lord Chamberlain's Men (later the King's Men), a professional acting company with which Shakespeare was associated throughout his career. Thus, we find that while Will Kempe was with the company, Shakespeare wrote into his plays a part for a boisterous and farcical clown; but when Kempe was replaced by Robert Armin, the role of the clown became more subtle and witty. Similarly, Shakespeare could confidently create the demanding roles of Hamlet, Lear, and Othello because he knew that in Richard Burbage the company had an actor capable of playing such diverse parts. One of the many contemporary tributes to Burbage's skill describes him as follows:

> His stature small, but every thought and mood
> Might thoroughly from the face be understood
> And his whole action he could change with ease
> From ancient Lear to youthful Pericles.

Shakespeare himself is said to have specialized in playing old men—the old servant Adam in *As You Like It*, the ghost in *Hamlet*, and so on.

In addition to writing specific roles for specific actors, Shakespeare and other Renaissance playwrights had to write all the female parts in such a way that they could be played by preadolescent boys. (Up until about 1660, acting was considered a profession too depraved for women. Men played all the women's parts, even in ancient Greece and Rome.) Naturally, the nude scenes that now abound in films and on the stage would have been out of the question in Shakespeare's day—for reasons other than moral docorum. Indeed, demonstrations of physical passion are comparatively rare in Shakespearean drama because too much kissing and clutching between characters whom the audience knows full well to be a man and a boy might break down the dramatic illusion and become either ludicrous or offensive. In all of *Othello*, a play about sexual conduct and misconduct, there are only four kisses. Three are mere courtesy kisses given to Desdemona in public by Cassio and Othello after she has survived a fierce storm at sea. The only kiss in private is the one Othello gives the sleeping Desdemona just before he suffocates her. Similarly, the height of the balcony in *Romeo and Juliet* keeps the lovers apart during their most passionate moments, and in *Antony and Cleopatra* there is but one embrace before the death scene.

The influence of the actors on the script of a play is not unique to Shakespearean drama. All playwrights must work within the limitations imposed by the medium. Dramatists are, for example, obviously limited in the number of characters they can use. Even though Aristophanes in *Lysistrata* (411 B.C.) wanted to show the effects of a sex strike by the entire female population of Greece, he actually used only three Athenians and one Spartan in speaking roles—with perhaps a score of nonspeaking women to stand for all the rest. Apart from the fact that only a limited number of actors can fit on a stage, the number of speaking roles in a play must be few enough so that the director can round up (and pay) enough accomplished actors and few enough so that the audience can remember who they all are. By convention, as well as by economic and practical necessity, Greek dramatists limited themselves to three speakers and a chorus. This does not mean that there were only three parts in a play, but rather that only three speaking characters could be on stage at any one time. Because the same actors might play several roles (changing masks and costumes offstage), the number of speaking roles could range anywhere from two to twenty, but the dramatist had at all times to balance the requirements of his story with the practical concerns both of allowing the actors sufficient time to change costume and of matching the physical and vocal demands of the roles to those of the actors available to play them. It would not do, for example, to send an actor playing a husky, deep-voiced king offstage and then to bring him back as a petite princess. The same character would be physically unable to play both parts. These restrictions are less stringent in plays written after the golden age of Greek drama (c. 480–380 B.C.), but accomplished playwrights have always manipulated their plots to allow some doubling up of parts and have always been aware that the stage does not allow them to portray the assembled masses of contending armies. Hence, in the prologue to *Henry the Fifth*, Shakespeare asks the audience to

> Suppose within the girdle of these walls
> Are now confined two mighty monarchies,
> . . . .
> Into a thousand parts divide one man;
> And make imaginary puissance;
> Think, when we talk of horses, that you see them
> Printing their proud hoofs i' th' receiving earth.
> For 'tis your thoughts that now must deck our kings.
> —From *Henry the Fifth*, "Prologue,"
> William Shakespeare [1599]

One final way in which the actors influence the drama deserves mention: plays are sometimes conceived, and often revised, as a result of the advice of the actors and the director. Indeed, contemporary plays normally open "out of town" to allow time for revision before risking an expensive production—and facing the critics—in the heart of New York. A similar process has operated throughout the history of the theater, and Shakespeare's plays, in this sense at least, are probably much the better for having remained unpublished until long experience on the stage had taught the members of his company which lines played well and which were in need of revision.

THE AUDIENCE

A few plays are intended only to be read and therefore are known as *closet dramas* (*Samson Agonistes* by Milton, *Cain* by Byron, and *Prometheus Unbound* by Shelley are notable examples); but most plays make an effort to please an audience massed in a theater. Playwrights who compose for the stage have learned by experience the truth of Samuel Johnson's eighteenth century dictum that

> The drama's laws the drama's patrons give,
> And we who live to please, must please to live.

The goal of a playwright is to fill the theater and to keep on filling it for as long as possible. A play must have popular appeal, and the quest for it naturally influences the choice and treatment of dramatic subjects.

Alexander Dumas (the elder) once claimed that all he needed for success on the stage was "four boards, two actors, and a passion." Dumas knew, as all of us now do, that the ingredients for a popular play (and certainly popular TV) usually include sex and violence—the two principal motives for passionate dialogue. As the tragedian in Tom Stoppard's *Rosencrantz and Guildenstern Are Dead* put it, well-liked plays are of "the blood, love, and rhetoric school"?

> . . . I can do you blood and love without the rhetoric, and I can do you blood and rhetoric without the love, and I can do you all three concurrent or consecutive, but I can't do you love and rhetoric without the blood. Blood is compulsory—they're all blood [in tragedy], you see.
> —From *Rosencrantz and Guildenstern Are Dead*, act 1, Tom Stoppard [1967]

The plots of most plays do in fact focus on one of the violent passions (anger, jealousy, revenge, lust, treachery) or on some form of love (love of woman, love of home, love of country, love of justice). Aristophanes' *Lysistrata*, for example, cleverly combines love of woman, love of country, and simple lust; *Othello* builds on jealousy; and much of the plot of *Hedda Gabler* revolves on Hedda's envy of Thea. Other plays examine the effect of less violent, but still powerful, passions: pride in *King Oedipus*, zealotry in *Tartuffe*, and prudery in *Mrs. Warren's Profession*.

Plays do differ, however, as John Dryden once observed, because of the historical differences in the play-going audience:

> They who have best succeeded on the stage
> Have still conformed their genius to the age.

Greek dramas were presented before huge audiences drawn from all levels of society, from poor to rich and from illiterate to sophisticated. Attendance was viewed as a religious duty. As a result, the tragedies dealt with simple and well-known stories that all members of the audience could understand; but they did have to deal with the play's subject in a way that underscored the necessity of reverence for the gods and their decrees. Elizabethan dramas were also aimed at an audience drawn from all levels of society, but by then the connection of the theater with religion had been severed. Thus, Shakespeare's plays contained enough blood and love to keep the illiterate mob in the pit entertained and enough lofty rhetoric to please the lords and ladies in the box seats, but they did not seek to inculcate any particular religious or philosophic views.

By the late nineteenth century, the price of a theater ticket exceeded the means of the laboring classes, and therefore plays like *Hedda Gabler* (1890) portray the problems and conditions of life in the upper and middle classes. There is occasionally a bit of gentlemanly poverty in the plays of this period, but the degrading and impoverished conditions of factory labor are almost entirely ignored. More recently, the technological revolution of the twentieth century has meant that people can often find their entertainment at home on television or at the local movie theater. Most of the people who attend plays today do so because they want to combine culture with entertainment. As a result, much contemporary drama tends to be intellectual and allusive, as in the witty manipulations of *Hamlet* in Tom Stoppard's *Rosencrantz and Guildenstern Are Dead* (1967) or in the parody of Agatha Christie's *Mousetrap* in Stoppard's *The Real Inspector Hound* (1967).

Even in modern drama, however, the plot usually makes an appeal to mass psychology. The playwright must cling first to those elemental passions and emotions common to all men and only secondarily, if at all, stimulate the qualities of intellect, in which men differ. The audience in a theater is, after all, a crowd and therefore "less intellectual and more emotional than the individuals that compose it. It is less reasonable, less judicious, less disinterested, more credulous, more primitive, more partisan."[3] In a theater, the sophisticated responses of the few are outnumbered by the instinctive responses of the many. As a result, the dramatist writes for a live audience that is spontaneous and unreflective in both its approval and disapproval.

Because most members of the audience can be expected to see the play once and only once, a successful play must be clearly plotted, easy to understand, and both familiar and acceptable in its theme. Playwrights satisfy the tastes of the times, but they rarely guide them. A novel may survive, even if its initial acclaim is slight, so long as those who first read and understand it are able to influence subsequent intellectual and literary thinking. But a play that fails in its first performance is unlikely to be published at all. Even if a few enthusiasts keep it from sinking immediately into oblivion, one costly failure on Broadway is usually sufficient to scare away future producers. The financial risks in producing plays are more clear-cut than those in publishing novels. If a new play proves to be unpopular, the initial costs involved in scenery, costuming, and rehearsal are not recouped, and the debts mount every day that actors play before a half-filled house. In contrast, if a new novel at first seems unpopular, the cost of storing a few thousand copies will scarcely distress the publisher as long as the demand is constant and seems likely to grow. Thus, a play, unlike a novel, must please upon first acquaintance; and if it is to have durable literary value, it must continue to please during successive viewings or readings. The challenge in writing drama is, thus, to be at once popular *and* intellectually stimulating. Comparatively few playwrights have succeeded at being both.

There are a number of good reasons for the frequent failures in the theater.

---

[3] Clayton Hamilton, as quoted by Brander Matthews, *A Study of the Drama* (New York: Houghton Mifflin, 1910), p. 88.

Even if a playwright chooses a popular subject and develops the plot with simplicity and grace, he cannot be confident of pleasing an audience unless the structure of the play is carefully crafted to meet the physical needs of spectators: the duration of scenes and the mixture of dialogue and action, for example, must be adapted to the audience's attention span. A play, like other forms of literature, is principally composed of words, but too much talk and too little action may produce a result about as exciting as a town council meeting. Conversely, actions that remain uninterpreted by dialogue quickly become chaotic. A sword fight on stage may show the physical agility of the actors and the conflict between characters; but if it is continued too long, it threatens to turn the drama into a gladiatorial exhibition, in which most of the interest is drained by the recognition that the swords are wooden, the blood is artificial, and each thrust or parry has been carefully choreographed in advance.

In some ways, of course, the playwright has a tremendous amount of control. Once the theater is darkened and the play begins, the audience is captive: the seats all face the stage, the only well lit part of the theater. When the curtain rises, any lingering conversations are "shushed." The closely packed patrons watch and listen attentively because they have paid to do so, because there is little else they *can* do in a dark theater, and because the seating arrangement makes it difficult to leave before the intermission.

These theatrical conditions directly influence the structure of the play. As much as dramatists may lust after the novelist's right to a leisurely introduction, they must resign themselves to the bald fact that, because no audience can sit still for more than about an hour at a time, the play must be at its intriguing best by the intermission. Similarly, a play that begins at 8:00 P.M. must certainly end by 11:00 P.M., lest all the teenagers with curfews, all the parents with babysitters, and all the young couples with "other things on their minds" leave *en masse* before the final curtain.

THE THEATER

In writing a play, a dramatist is always aware of the physical conditions of the theater. These conditions often govern the actions and settings that can be presented, as well as the way in which the scenes are developed. The size of the theater, the proximity of the audience to the stage, and the characteristics of the stage itself influence the scenery, the costuming, and the actors' methods.

As we will see, the conditions for staging Greek drama were unlike those for Elizabethan drama, Elizabethan unlike neoclassical, and neoclassical unlike modern. Nonetheless, each stage provides an arena within which the words and actions of the performers are observed by an audience of substantial size. It follows that some actions are too minute and others too grand to be staged effectively. In Shakespeare's *Othello,* for example, Desdemona's handkerchief is a vital element in the plot, but this piece of cloth, which is too small to bind Othello's forehead, is also too small to be seen clearly by the most distant members of the audience. Thus, Shakespeare takes care to identify it in the dialogue whenever he introduces it on stage. For example, when Bianca flings the handkerchief back to Cassio in act 4, scene 1, Othello, who is watching from a distance, says, "By heaven, that should be my handkerchief!" And then, to clear up any possible confusion, Iago, who has had a closer vantage point, drives home the identification:

> IAGO. And did you see the handkerchief?
> OTHELLO. Was that mine?
> IAGO. Yours, by this hand. And to see how he prizes the foolish woman your wife! She gave it him, and he hath given it his whore.

Large events can be even more difficult to present on stage. In the second act of *Othello*, Shakespeare wishes to describe the arrival at Cyprus of Cassio, Desdemona, and Othello after they have been separated by a storm at sea. Naturally it is difficult to depict either the turbulent sea or the arrival of the shattered flotilla. Instead Shakespeare introduces three minor characters whose primary function is to help us imagine the setting and events offstage:

SCENE 1. *A seaport in Cyprus. An open place near the wharf.*
Enter MONTANO *and* TWO GENTLEMEN.

MONTANO. What from the cape can you discern at sea?	
FIRST GENTLEMAN. Nothing at all. It is a high-wrought flood.	
I cannot 'twixt the heaven and the main	
Descry° a sail.	*see*
MONTANO. Methinks the wind hath spoke aloud at land,	
A fuller blast ne'er shook our battlements.	
If it hath ruffianed° so upon the sea	*raged*
What ribs of oak, when mountains melt on them,	
Can hold the mortise? What shall we hear of this?	
SECOND GENTLEMAN. A segration° of the Turkish fleet.	*dispersal*
For do but stand upon the foaming shore,	
The chidden billow seems to pelt the clouds;	
The wind-shaked surge, with high and monstrous mane,	
Seems to cast water on the burning bear,°	*a constellation*
And quench the guards of the ever-fixèd pole.	
I never did like molestation° view	*disruption*
On the enchafèd flood.°	*raging sea*
MONTANO. If that the Turkish fleet	
Be not ensheltered and embayed, they are drowned.	
It is impossible to bear it out.	
(*Enter a* THIRD GENTLEMAN.)	
THIRD GENTLEMAN. News, lads! Our wars are done.	
The desperate tempest hath so banged the Turks	
That their designment° halts. A noble ship of Venice	*plan*
Hath seen a grievous wreck and sufferance°	*suffering*
On most part of their fleet.	
MONTANO. How! Is this true?	
THIRD GENTLEMAN. The ship is here put in,	
A Veronesa. Michael Cassio,	
Lieutenant to the warlike Moor Othello,	
Is come on shore, the Moor himself at sea,	
And is in full commission here for Cyprus.	

—From *Othello*, act 2, scene 1, William Shakespeare [1604]

Presumably the first gentleman is standing at one edge of the stage looking into the distance as though out to sea. He shouts back to the others that he sees nothing but enormous waves. The second gentleman, who has recently stood on the shore, gives a fuller and more poetic account of the storm. Then the third gentleman, having just come from the wharf, brings news of the destruction of the Turkish fleet and the arrival of Cassio's ship. Thus, events that Shakespeare would have had difficulty portraying on stage are made vivid and convincing through the dramatic accounts of three different reporters.

Just as the actions in a drama are limited by the size of the stage and its distance from the audience, so, too, the settings are influenced by the practical problems associated with a visual presentation. Some scenes are next to impossible to stage. Act 2 of Lord Byron's *Cain* (1822), for example, opens in "the Abyss of Space" and a stage direction in act 3 (which is set outside of Eden) reads: "The fire upon the altar of Abel kindles into a column of the brightest flame, and ascends to heaven; while a whirlwind throws down the altar of Cain, and scatters the fruits abroad upon the earth."

As a *closet drama*, Byron's play was never intended to be staged, but similar difficulties sometimes present themselves in conventional plays. Shortly after Byron's death, in fact, his poem "Mazeppa" was dramatized. We can only pity the poor director who was asked in one scene to show the hero "strapped to the back of a wild horse, while birds peck at his eyes, lightning destroys a tree on stage, and wolves pursue the horse."

During the late nineteenth century, in response to a demand for greater realism, playwrights began to specify the arrangement of furniture in a room, the number of pictures on the walls, and sometimes even the thickness of the butter on a piece of stage toast. Here is the first stage direction in Ibsen's *Hedda Gabler:*

SCENE: *A spacious, handsome and tastefully furnished drawing room, decorated in dark colors. In the back a wide doorway with curtains drawn back, leading into a smaller room decorated in the same style as the drawing room. In the right-hand wall of the front room a folding door leading out to the hall. In the opposite wall, on the left, a glass door, also with curtains drawn back. Through the panes can be seen part of a veranda outside and trees covered with autumn foliage. An oval table, with a cover on it and surrounded by chairs, stand well forward. In front, by the wall on the right, a wide stove of dark porcelain, a high-backed armchair, a cushioned footrest and two footstools. A settee with a small round table in front of it fills the upper right-hand corner. In front, on the left, a little way from the wall, a sofa. Further back than the glass door a piano. On either side of the doorway at the back a whatnot with terra-cotta and majolica ornaments. Against the back wall of the inner room a sofa, with a table, and one or two chairs. Over the sofa hangs the portrait of a handsome elderly man in a general's uniform. Over the table, a hanging lamp with an opal glass shade. A number of bouquets are arranged about the drawing room in vases and glasses. Others lie upon the tables. The floors in both rooms are covered with thick carpets. Morning light. The sun shines in through the glass door.*
—From *Hedda Gabler*, act 1, Henrik Ibsen [1890]

Clearly, a setting as complex as this cannot be changed for every new scene. As it happens, all of the action in *Hedda Gabler* takes place in the same two rooms. Similarly, the entire action of *King Oedipus* takes place in front of the royal palace at Thebes, that of *Lysistrata* before the Acropolis, and that of *Tartuffe* in Orgon's house. In a fair number of plays, however, the scene changes with every act, and in a few, like *Othello*, it changes for virtually every scene. Yet, even in *Othello*, a stage with half-dozen different acting areas and a few movable props can be made to convey the whole range of settings.

Unlike the novelist or the film maker, the playwright cannot allow the plot to flow freely across unlimited fields of action. If the scenery is to be at all realistic, very few settings can be used unless the playwright is prepared to have the work produced only in the few modern theaters with "revolving stages," on which several realistic sets can be erected and alternately used. Even if the scenery is only suggestive, the playwright is much more limited by his genre than other narrative artists. In general, the action of a play takes place in only one or two locales. These may be quite narrowly and specifically defined in realistic drama (Hedda's drawing room, for example) or broadly conceived in more imaginative works (Venice and Cyprus in *Othello*), but a play that uses too many settings risks confusing the audience and consequently failing in the theater. Shakespeare's *Antony and Cleopatra*, for example, is a poetic masterpiece, but it has rarely been successful on the stage because its forty-two scenes skip bewilderingly around the Roman Empire, and the action spans years rather than days. Ordinarily, it is only through the devices of a film-maker or a novelist that such action can be presented clearly and convincingly.

Thus far, we have been discussing the general effects of any theater on the scenes and actions of drama, but different theaters in different historical periods have had quite different impacts on the drama. A play like *Othello* is written for the intimate Elizabethan stage. The subtle and insinuating facial expressions necessary for a convincing portrayal of Iago's manipulation of Othello would have been lost in the vast amphitheaters of ancient Greece. Similarly, the stark plots and grand rhetoric of Greek tragedy might seem histrionic and ridiculous in the confines of a small modern theater. In order to understand a play, in short, we must know something about the stage for which it was written. In the past, most masterpieces of the drama have been produced in one of four basic theaters: the classical Greek theater, the Elizabethan theater, the neoclassical French theater, and the realistic "box set." Modern drama, however, has moved toward a more flexible theater that can easily be adapted to suit the specific needs of each new play.

The Classical Greek Theater (c. 480–380 B.C.)

Greek Drama grew out of the primitive rituals performed in conjunction with the three annual festivals dedicated to Dionysus (or Bacchus), the god of fertility, regeneration, and wine.[4] Although, in time, such rituals evolved into the drama of Aeschylus, Euripides, Sophocles, and Aristophanes and the uninhibited revels of Dionysus were exchanged for more dignified role playing within a formal theatrical setting, the classic drama of the ancient Greeks retained, however loosely, its original ties with religion. It continued to be performed only three times a year and then in massive doses of four or five plays a day—circumstances that had an important impact on the audience, the content, and the structure of Greek drama.

In the first place, the audience in a Greek theater was enormous. Everyone who wanted to see a play had only a few opportunities each year to do so, and the idea of attending was all the more attractive because of the sporting

---

[4] Indeed, the very names for the three forms of Greek drama—tragedy, comedy, and satyr play—derive from the worship of Dionysus. The word *tragedy* means "goat song," probably referring to the goat-skinned satyrs; the derivation of the term *satyr play* is obvious; and the word comedy comes from *comos*, Greek for "revelry."

element inherent in the prizes awarded for the best tragedies and comedies. The theater of Dionysus at Athens (see Figures 1 and 2), which was used in the first productions of all the great fifth-century Greek plays, probably seated about 17,000. The theater at Epidaurus, built a century later, seated 20,000; and the theater at Ephesus held more than 50,000. Because no existing building was large enough to accommodate so vast a crowd, the plays were performed outdoors in the natural basin formed where two hills met.

During the life of Sophocles (495–406 B.C.) the audience sat on wooden benches that ascended the hillside, more than half encircling an *orchestra* or "dancing place" some 78 feet in diameter. A wooden building called the *skene* (from which we derive the term *scene*) closed off the second half of the amphitheater and served simultaneously as an acoustical wall (reflecting the voices of the actors back into the audience), a scenic background (representing any building central to the action), and a convenient place for the three principal actors to change masks and costumes. The narrow space between the *skene* and the *orchestra* was known as the *proskenion* and served as the main acting area.[5]

The chorus normally remained in the *orchestra*, while the major characters moved from the *proskenion* to the *orchestra* and back again, according to the script. The chorus and any processions entered and exited along the edge of the stands to the far right or left of the *skene*. Although the major characters used these aisles when the plot called for an outside entrance, at times they also emerged from, or retreated into, one of the three doors of the *skene* as if from a temple, palace, or some other building. Action on a balcony or a cliff could be staged on top of the *skene*, and when the gods appeared, as they sometimes did to interfere directly in the affairs of men, they were lowered from the top of the *skene* by a crane. The term *deus ex machina* (meaning "the god from the machine") is sometimes used to describe (and often deride) such divine interventions.

This massive open-air arena naturally imposed special conditions on the plays performed in it. First of all, there was no curtain to rise at the beginning, fall at the end, and separate the various scenes. As a result, the chorus had to march on stage early in the play (the *parados*) and off stage at the end (the *exodos*). The continuous presence of the chorus during the intervening period encouraged a constant setting throughout the play and a close correspondence between the period of time covered by the play and the amount of real time that elapsed during the actual on-stage presence of the chorus. As a result, Greek drama tended to concentrate on a single complex situation.[6] The typical Greek tragedy begins only a matter of hours before its catastrophe is to occur. The characters stand on the brink of disaster, and the playwright swiftly tells us how they got there, using a formal prologue or a series of interviews with messengers, nurses, and other minor characters. In the first

---

[5] There is much confusion over what the Greeks actually meant by the term *proskenion*. Some scholars think that it referred to the wall of the *skene;* others that it referred to a row of columns that supported the roof of a porch extending out from the *skene;* and still others agree with our interpretation. Literally, the word means "before" *(pro-)* "the skene" *(skenion)*. The *proscenium*, in modern stagecraft, is the forward part of the stage between the curtain and the orchestra. The arch from which the curtain hangs is the *proscenium arch.*

[6] The unity of place, time, and action demanded in the neoclassical drama of the seventeenth and eighteenth centuries was an outgrowth of these tendencies. Greek playwrights did not, however, formally require adherence to these three unities.

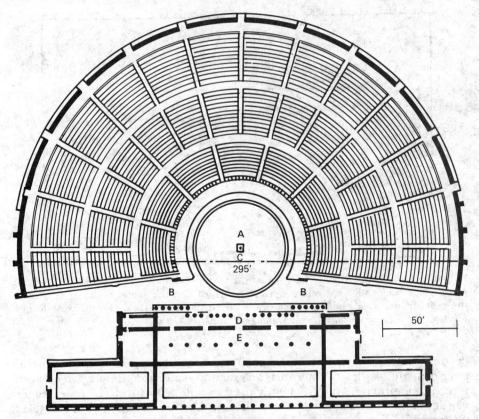

FIGURE 1. Plan of the Theater of Dionysus at Athens. *A. orchestra; B. chorus entrance; C. altar to Dionysus; D. proskenion; E. skene.*

moments of *King Oedipus,* for example, we learn that a plague afflicts Thebes because the murderer of the former king, Laius, has not been punished. Oedipus immediately vows to find the killer and drive him from the land. The remainder of the play works out the consequences of this impetuous vow by revealing that Oedipus himself is the killer, that Laius was his father, and therefore that Laius's wife, Jocasta, is actually Oedipus's mother as well as his wife and the mother of his children.

The four scenes, or *episodes,* during which Oedipus discovers the tragedy of his past are separated from one another not by the fall of a curtain but by a series of choral interludes called odes. Each *ode* (or *stasimon*) was accompanied by music, to which the chorus danced back and forth across the stage in a sober and symbolic fashion. During these odes the chorus was able to provide essential background information, reflect on past actions, or anticipate future ones. Often, too, the responses of the chorus represent those of an ideal audience or provide a lyric respite from the intense emotions of the episodes. In addition these interludes may symbolize the passage of time necessary to send for a character or accomplish some other offstage action.

Because the theater was unenclosed and the plays were performed during the daytime, the action of Greek drama normally also took place during the

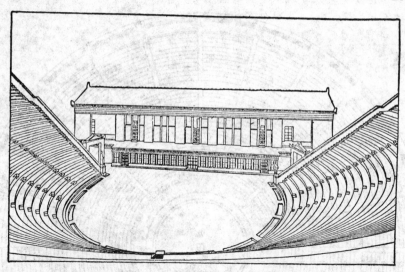

FIGURE 2. A Reconstruction of a Classical Greek Theater. Note the large "dancing place" or *orchestra,* the encircling tiers of benches, and the scene building or *skene* at the rear. In this case the *skene* includes a raised platform stage. (From Ernst Robert Fiechter's *Die Baugeschichtliche Entwicklung des Antiken Theaters.*)

daytime, out-of-doors. However, some events in Greek drama did require an interior setting—Jocasta's suicide is an example—and, accordingly, Greeks were forced to improvise. One frequently used technique was to have a messenger, or some other character, come outside and describe in detail what had taken place within. This is exactly how Sophocles handled the death of Jocasta:

CHORUS. Alas, miserable woman, how did she die?
SECOND MESSENGER. By her own hand. It cannot be as terrible to you as to one that saw it with his eyes, yet so far as words can serve, you shall see it. When she had come into the vestibule, she ran half crazed towards her marriage-bed, clutching at her hair with the fingers of both hands, and once within the chamber dashed the doors together behind her. Then called upon the name of Laius, long since dead, remembering that son who killed the father and upon the mother begot an accursed race. And wailed because of that marriage wherein she had borne a two-fold race—husband by husband, children by her child. Then Oedipus with a shriek burst in and running here and there asked for a sword, asked where he would find the wife that was no wife but a mother who had borne his children and himself. Nobody answered him, we all stood dumb; but supernatural power helped him, for, with a dreadful shriek, as though beckoned, he sprang at the double doors, drove them in, burst the bolts out of their sockets, and ran into the room. There we saw the woman hanging in a swinging halter, and with a terrible cry he loosened the halter from her neck.

—From *King Oedipus,* Sophocles [430 B.C.]

A second possibility was simply to throw open the doors of the *skene* and allow the audience to peer inside. Although this technique later worked in the smaller Elizabethan theater, the size of the Greek theater and the unavoidable obscurity of the interior of the *skene* rendered this approach unsatisfactory. To overcome this obstacle, the Greeks constructed a platform on wheels (the *eccyclema*) that could be rolled out of the *skene* as required, and this device became the accepted convention for portraying an interior scene or tableau.

The size of the Greek theater had still other effects on the nature of Greek drama. The actors wore large masks, padded clothing, and platform sandals in order to increase their stature and expressiveness for the viewers at the rear of the amphitheater. Although those costumes must have significantly restricted mobility and made physical actions awkward, the masks were designed to function like primitive megaphones and improved the carrying power of the actors' voices. As such, it is little wonder that Greek drama came to be made up of words rather than actions. This verbal emphasis complements the Greek dramatist's preoccupation with motive and character rather than plot, for the state of mind and feelings of an individual can only be fully explained and analyzed using words. The pre-eminence of Greek tragedy came about in part because it was a drama of the mind and not the body.

Then, as now, the audience exerted its influence on both the structure and the content of the plays presented. Because Greek audiences remained in the theater all day, lapses of attention, and periods of jostling, munching, joking, and dozing were inevitable. It was nevertheless essential that all the members of the audience understand the key turning points of the action if the play were to succeed at all; as a result, playwrights preferred to present bold, simple stories that were either familiar to the audience (for example, the story of Oedipus) or, in the case of comedy, predicated on a simple, straightforward hypothesis (in *Lysistrata* that sexual denial can put an end to war). Not surprisingly, given the religious traditions associated with drama and the stylization imposed by the use of masks, many tragic plots were drawn from mythology. The comedies, on the other hand, sought a similar ease of understanding by burlesquing contemporary personalities and events.

The Elizabethan Theater (c. 1550–1620)

The decline of the Roman Empire brought an end to the Greek theater, and for nearly a thousand years Europe produced little drama of significant literary merit. It is true that the Catholic church, in about the tenth century, began to encourage the production of plays filled with moral or religious instruction, but these anonymous creations are more important as historical curiosities than as dramatic achievements. As a result, when the rediscovery of Greek and Roman literature first spread through Europe to England, few people had any idea what a theater ought to look like. Plays were put on wherever a stage could be erected or a crowd could gather. Amateur groups performing at a university and professionals performing at an inn found that the courtyard provided a ready-made theater. A fairly large stage could be easily set up at one end, and the audience could watch the play from the surrounding yard or balconies. The balcony immediately above the stage, in turn, could be conveniently used by the actors for playing scenes that called for a hill, a cliff, an upstairs window, or any other high place.

No doubt innkeepers found that an afternoon play stimulated business. Those standing in the courtyard watching the play could take their minds off their aching feet by calling for more beer, and the surrounding bedchambers encouraged other forms of trade—so much so that the municipal officials of London (who were staunch puritans) soon began to regulate the production of plays, denouncing the "evil practices of incontinency in great Inns having chambers

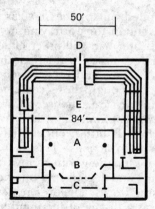

FIGURE 3. Plan of the Fortune Theater, London. *A. front stage; B. back stage; C. inner stage; D. entrance; E. courtyard.*

and secret places adjoining to their open stages and galleries, inveigling and allurement of maidens." As a result of these regulations, several of the theatrical companies decided to build their own playhouses just outside of the city limits. It is hardly surprising that when they did so, beginning in about 1576, they patterned their theaters on the very courtyards to which they had become accustomed.

The existing evidence about the size, shape, and structure of the Elizabethan stage and theater is scanty, but it does allow us to state some facts positively and to make other educated guesses. From a contract for the construction of the Fortune Theater (see Figures 3 and 4) we know that the building was square and relatively small, measuring 80 feet on each side. (The Globe Theater, where Shakespeare's plays were performed, was about the same size, but octagonal.) The pit, or inner yard, of the Fortune measured 55 feet per side, and the stage, which was 43 feet wide, projected halfway (exactly 27½ feet) into the yard. Three galleries were partitioned into "two-penny rooms" and "convenient divisions for gentlemen's rooms"—presumably the equivalent of box seats. When filled to capacity, the theater probably held a crowd of about a thousand, with the common folk pressed elbow to elbow around three sides of the stage.

Because the stage intruded so far into the middle of the audience, most spectators sat or stood within thirty feet of the actors, and even the distant corners of the third balcony were but sixty feet away. As a result, the Elizabethan theater fostered a sense of intimacy utterly foreign to its predecessor. *Asides* and *soliloquies*, which would seem contrived if the actor had to strain visibly to make his stage whisper carry to a distant audience, here seemed natural and unaffected; as a consequence, Elizabethan plays came to be filled with lines intended for the audience alone. In the third act of *Othello*, where Iago comes *downstage*[7] toward the audience with Desdemona's handkerchief in his hand, he is so near the audience that his low reflections are delivered almost conspiratorially into their ears:

[7] The terms *downstage* and *upstage* derive from the period when the stage was raked, or tilted, toward the audience. When actors moved toward the audience they literally moved down the stage, and in moving away they climbed slightly up.

I will in Cassio's lodging lose this napkin,
And let him find it. Trifles light as air
Are to the jealous confirmations strong
As proofs of Holy Writ. This may do something.
The Moor already changes with my poison.
Dangerous conceits are in their natures poisons,
Which at the first are scarce found to distaste,
But with a little act upon the blood
Burn like the mines of sulphur.

—From *Othello*, act 3, scene 3,
William Shakespeare [1604]

When Othello subsequently enters *upstage*, he is some forty to fifty feet away from Iago; consequently, Iago can comment on Othello's visible agitation without fear of being overheard. He sees that, in fact, jealousy does "burn like the mines of sulphur" within Othello's breast, and he addresses the spectators directly: "I did say so. / Look where he comes!"

In addition to intimacy, the Elizabethan stage also had versatility. It contained at least six different acting areas (see Figure 4). The main one was, of course, the 27½- by 43-foot platform. In this large neutral area, characters could meet and interact without raising any question in the minds of Elizabethan audience about the exact setting. In the original text of *Othello*, for example, there are only three directions for setting, and all of them are quite indefinite: two call for the use of an inner chamber and one for an upstairs window. If, for some

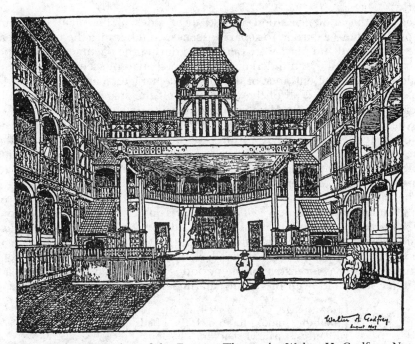

FIGURE 4. A Reconstruction of the Fortune Theater by Walter H. Godfrey. Note the platform stage projecting into the "pit," the curtained inner stage, the two side entrances, the balcony, the "crow's nest," and the three rows of galleries for spectators. (From *Shakespeare's Theatre* by Ashley H. Thorndike.)

reason, a specific setting *was* important, the characters themselves would describe it, as in the seaport scene quoted earlier (p. 967).

An inner stage behind the main platform was used to represent the interior of a council chamber, a bedroom, a tent, a tomb, a throne room, and so on. Act 1, scene 3 of *Othello* requires that this inner stage be screened by curtains that can be drawn to reveal "the Duke and Senators set at a table." Similarly, act 5, scene 2 opens on "Desdemona in bed." Because every other scene in the play calls for each character to enter, speak his lines, and then exit, only these two scenes need to be staged in the curtained inner chamber.

According to the records available to us, a balcony, bounded by two window stages, apparently extended above the inner stage. In act 1, scene 1 of *Othello,* Roderigo and Iago converse in the street before calling up to Brabantio who "appears above, at a window." Similarly, Juliet appears at a window in her first balcony scene. Such stage directions, together with the "convenient windows" called for in the contract for the Fortune Theater, imply that these areas were either shuttered or curtained so that the characters could suddenly "appear." But the balcony must also on occasion have provided a fairly large area in which several characters could meet, as indicated by such stage directions as "Enter Cleopatra and her maids aloft."

Although there may also have been an even higher balcony for the musicians (or for action taking place in a tower or in the crow's nest of a ship), few scenes—none in *Othello*—were staged very far above the crowd assembled in the yard. In fact, the vast majority of the scenes in Elizabethan drama were presented on the main stage, so that the audience was able to see and hear clearly.

Because the audience stood around three sides of the main stage, it was impossible to use a curtain to separate scenes. And because the public theaters were unenclosed and plays were performed during the daytime, it was impossible to throw the stage into darkness during a change of scene. Hence, a scene would start with the entrance of one or more characters, and the locale would remain the same until all of the characters left the stage—or were carted off, if dead ("Exeunt severally; Hamlet dragging in [i.e., offstage] Polonius"). Action in a new locale would then commence with a new set of entrances. Usually the characters would enter from one side door and exit through the other—although in conflicts the entrances were made simultaneously from opposing doors ("Enter Pompey at one door, with drum and trumpet: at another, Caesar, Lepidus, Antony, Maecenas, Agrippa, with soldiers marching").

The different settings in an Elizabethan play were rarely indicated by any change in props or scenery. *Othello* contains fifteen different scenes, and if the suggested stage directions of modern editions are followed, a production would require at least eleven different settings. Obviously, such changes were impossible on an open stage. Indeed, if the list of properties owned by the Fortune Theater is indicative of the period, scenery was used mainly to adorn the inner stage and even there only sparingly. Among the bulkiest were:

> i rock, i cage, i tomb, i Hell mouth.
> i tomb of Guido, i tomb of Dido, i bedstead.
> viii lances, i pair of stairs for Phaeton.
> i golden fleece; ii rackets; i bay tree.
> Iris head, & rainbow; i little altar.
> ii fanes of feathers; Bellendon stable; i tree of golden
>   apples; Tantalus' tree; ix iron targets.

> i copper target, & xvii foils.
> i wheel and frame in the Siege of London.
> i cauldron for the Jew.

For the most part, Elizabethans relied on words rather than props to give a sense of locale.

All of this means that the Elizabethan theater, with its multiple acting areas and its imaginary settings, was well suited to plays with rapidly shifting scenes and continuous action. It gave rise to a form of drama entirely unlike that of ancient Greece. Instead of the play starting a few fictional hours before the crisis (as in *Oedipus*), the Renaissance play starts at the beginning of a story and skips from time to time and place to place until the crisis is reached. Act 1 of *Othello*, for example, begins in Venice on the night of Othello and Desdemona's marriage. Then act 2 skips more than a week ahead to a period when all of the principles arrive in Cyprus, and there the action requires two more nights and a day. Because Elizabethan plays range freely in time and setting, all of the most dramatic moments in a story are presented on stage. Thus, if *King Oedipus* had been written by Shakespeare, the audience might have seen and heard events that Sophocles included only as reminiscences— particularly, the original prophecies of the oracle to Oedipus, Oedipus' flight from Corinth, and his murder of Laius at the place where three roads meet. Scenes of violence, which occur offstage in Greek tragedy (like the death of Jocasta) were physically enacted before the Elizabethan audience. *Othello* includes several sword fights, three murders, and a suicide—all on stage. And this carnage is only moderate by Renaissance standards. (Note that despite its general paucity of props, the Fortune Theater inventoried *seventeen* foils!) The audience standing in the yard demanded action, and the versatile Elizabethan stage made this demand easy to fulfill.

The Neoclassical French Theater (c. 1660–1800)

The early acting companies of France, like those of England, toured the countryside, playing wherever they could. As luck would have it, tennis had been popular in France during the fifteenth century, and many noblemen had erected indoor tennis courts, some of which were transformed during the next two centuries into primitive theaters. A temporary stage would be erected on one half of the court; ordinary folk would stand or sit on wooden benches in the other half, and the nobles would be seated in the galleries overlooking the playing area. It was in such converted quarters that Corneille and Molière, two of the greatest of the neoclassical playwrights, saw their first plays produced.

Thus, early French theaters evolved in a direction that differed radically from their Elizabethan counterparts. The single most significant change was the increased separation of the actors from the audience. Whereas the Elizabethan audience had nearly encircled the actors, the seventeenth-century French audience sat along one side of the stage and looked in on the action, as if peering through an invisible wall (see Figures 5 and 6). This arrangement eventually led to the use of a front curtain to conceal the stage between acts and made possible elaborate changes of scenery.

Because all members of the audience watched the play from a similar vantage point, the setting could be vividly depicted on huge flat canvases, using the devices of perspective developed by the painters of the Italian Renaissance

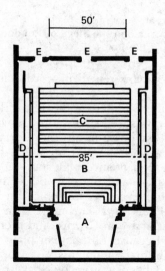

FIGURE 5.   Plan of the Richelieu-Molière Theater, Paris. *A. stage; B. parterre; C. seats; D. galleries; E. entrances.*

(see figure 6). These flats could easily be replaced between acts, providing the opportunity for changes in setting. The curtain concealed the scene before the start of the play, but thereafter any changes in scenery were made mechanically in full view of the audience, as a form of special effect. Molière himself was not beyond using fountains, aerial chariots, the descent of a god in a cloud, or a maiden emerging from a sea shell to bring the crowd to its feet and to delight the king.

It is almost axiomatic in theater that whenever innovations in staging begin to turn drama into spectacle, the quality of the writing in plays declines. However, at least three factors kept seventeenth-century French drama from degenerating into exhibitionistic extravaganzas. First, neoclassical scholars and critics imposed their standards on the age by requiring that every play fulfill the three unities: *unity of time* mandated that the play's action should be confined to a single day; *unity of action* forbade subplots and irrelevant episodes; and *unity of place* required that all of the action take place in a single setting or vicinity. The exclusion of digressions and the limitation on settings greatly constricted the use that French playwrights could make of their curtained stage. Molière's *Tartuffe (1664)*, for example, takes place in fewer than twelve hours, in a single setting that has a simple dinner table as its most elaborate prop. Those plays by Molière that do include spectacular stage effects usually confine them to a prologue or epilogue, so that formal adherence to the unities is preserved.

The simplicity of Molière's settings was encouraged by two physical characteristics of the neoclassical theater: weak lighting and the presence of spectators on the stage itself. French drama was performed indoors, often under artificial light, and the tallow candles then in use burned dimly. As a result, most of the acting took place immediately under the chandeliers and as far downstage (as close to the audience) as possible. Thus, the elaborately painted flats served less as the setting for the play than as a general backdrop to the action, which

FIGURE 6.   A Neoclassical Theater in Strasburg (1655). Note the flat wings representing rows of buildings, the painted backdrop showing the continuation of the street, and the actors at the forefront of the stage beneath the chandeliers. (From *Wiener Szenische Kunst* by Joseph Gregor.)

often took place on the narrow strip or *apron* in front of the *proscenium arch.* The dark interior also presented problems for the fops and dandies who came to the theater as much to be seen as to see the play itself. The box seats were likely to remain in the shadows, and because many of those vain creatures were wealthy patrons, the theater owners accommodated them with seats (sometimes as many as two hundred) on the stage. Naturally, such seating cut down the available acting area and limited the ability of stagehands to move bulky properties around.

As a result of the seating, the lighting, and the neoclassical rules of composition, most of the plays in this period were set in a single place of general resort—a courtyard, a street, a drawing room. The plots developed scenes of emotional intensity, but because decorum and probability were required by unity of action, they rarely erupted into the violent activity that so often left the Elizabethan stage littered with bodies. The drama of the period is witty, intellectual, and refined. Characteristically, it depicts highly idealized and artificial conversations among men and women representing broad human types—classical heroes or gods in tragedy, contemporary scoundrels or buffoons in comedy. It is an intentionally stylized drama based on the premise that fixed rules of structure are necessary in refined literature.

The Development of the Box Set (c. 1830–1920)

In 1642 Oliver Cromwell and his Puritan followers closed down all the play-houses in England, and by the time they were reopened in 1660, the Elizabethan theater was dead. Not surprisingly, given the predilection of Charles II and his court for all things French, the English drama that succeeded the Restoration was heavily influenced by the neoclassical conventions of the French theater—an influence that persisted throughout most of the eighteenth century. In the nineteenth century, however, the situation changed. A series of important technical innovations encouraged dramatists to abandon neoclassicism in favor of a drama characterized by realistic (mimetic) plots performed within equally realistic settings.

The first of these changes was the introduction, between 1820 and 1840, of gas lighting. Not only were gas lights brighter than the candles and oil lamps that had hitherto served, but now all the lights in the house could be controlled from a single instrument panel. For the first time, a director could focus the audience's attention on the lighted stage by leaving the rest of the auditorium in total darkness; this increased control over stage lights allowed playwrights to switch their scenes from day to night without recourse to cumbersome passages of dialogue calling attention to the fact. The improved lighting also allowed the actors to move more or less freely about the setting, instead of forcing them to remain out in front of the proscenium arch. Such maneuverability naturally called greater attention to the setting, which could now become a functional, rather than simply an ornamental, feature of the play. As a consequence, directors began to eliminate the backdrops and the artificial perspective of movable flats.

Soon after 1830, the *box set* was introduced in England. In its ultimate development, the box set is identical to a real room with one wall removed. Even though the audience can peer through this "invisible" fourth wall to eavesdrop on the action taking place within, the actors pretend that the invisible wall exists. Thus, asides directed to the audience can no longer occur and soliloquies must be strictly limited to those emotional moments during which a character might logically be overheard talking to himself. Nineteenth-century producers understandably relished these innovations and some went so far even as to boast in their advertisements of having sets with real ceilings, real doors, and working locks. The description of the set for *Hedda Gabler* is a typical example of the meticulous care with which late nineteenth-century playwrights envisioned the locale of their plays.

At about the same time that candlelight was being replaced by gas, directors also discovered ways to focus spotlights on single characters. This was first achieved by burning small chunks of lime and reflecting the light off of curved mirrors onto the leading man or leading lady (who was then, quite literally, "in the limelight"). Most directors, understandably, became enamored with the technique, and throughout the nineteenth century talented actors and actresses often held to the limelight to the detriment of the play as a whole. A particularly fine speech by Edmund Kean or Sarah Kemble Siddons, for example, might bring the audience to its feet in midscene. And if the applause were long and loud enough, Mr. Kean or Mrs. Siddons would simply recite the speech again as an encore. The inevitable effect of such an emphasis was to encourage dramatists to concentrate on writing good parts for the leading roles without giving equal attention to plot, structure, and theme.

A further development in nineteenth-century stagecraft was the increasing use made of the curtain spanning the proscenium arch. Until about 1875, the curtain was used only to screen the stage before the start of the play; once raised, it did not fall again until the end of the last act. The intention, of course, was to startle and delight the spectators when the curtain first rose on the fanciful world of the theater and then to entertain them by magically transforming that world before their eyes. So long as the scenery was mainly composed of paintings on flats that could be slid off stage mechanically and replaced by others, such changes of scene could occur swiftly and smoothly. But the advent of the realistic box set inevitably brought with it an increasing number of unwieldy props. The stage became cluttered with footstools, sofas, armchairs, end tables, vases, and portraits that stagehands were required to cart off or rearrange during any change of scene. The whole process soon became more frantic than magical and more distracting than entertaining. Furthermore, to effect such changes before the eyes of the audience only served to break down the illusion of reality. In order to sustain the illusion, directors and playwrights began to use the curtain between acts and even between scenes.

This had an immediate and important influence on the text of plays written in the final quarter of the nineteenth century. Before then a scene or an act necessarily began with a set of entrances and concluded with some pretext calling for the characters to exit—usually a variant of "Come! Let's be off to dine [or drink, or dance, or what have you]." The increased use of the curtain freed the dramatist from such constrictions. The emphasis changed from finding a way of getting the characters offstage to finding a way of building dramatic tension and emphasizing basic themes at the end of acts or scenes. The resulting *curtain line* is perhaps the most distinctive feature of modern drama. Ibsen was among the first to employ the curtain line, and in *Hedda Gabler* he honed it to perfection. Each act ends on a note of high drama, but for the purpose of illustration, we will look at the conclusion to the third act:

LÖVBORG. Good-by, Mrs Tesman. And give George Tesman my love. [*He is on the point of going.*]

HEDDA. No, wait! I must give you a memento to take with you. [*She goes to the writing table and opens the drawer and the pistol case, then returns to* LÖVBORG *with one of the pistols.*]

LÖVBORG [*looks at her*]. This? Is this the memento?

HEDDA [*nodding slowly*]. Do you recognize it? It was aimed at you once.

LÖVBORG. You should have used it then.

HEDDA. Take it—and do you use it now.

LÖVBORG [*puts the pistol in his breast pocket*]. Thanks!

HEDDA. And beautifully, Eilert Lövborg. Promise me that!

LÖVBORG. Good-by, Hedda Gabler. [*He goes out by the hall door.*]

[HEDDA *listens for a moment at the door. Then she goes up to the writing table, takes out the packet of manuscript, peeps under the cover, draws a few of the sheets half out and looks at them. Next she goes over and seats herself in the armchair beside the stove, with the packet in her lap. Presently she opens the stove door and then the packet.*]

HEDDA [*throws one of the quires into the fire and whispers to herself*]. Now I am burning your child, Thea! Burning it, curlylocks! [*Throwing one or two more quires into the stove.*] Your child and Eilert Lövborg's. [*Throws the rest in.*] I am burning—I am burning your child.

—From *Hedda Gabler,* act 3, Henrik Ibsen [1890]

With growing horror, we realize not only that Hedda is encouraging Eilert to kill himself, but also that she could have prevented his death by returning the manuscript. She burns the only copy of Eilert's book because she is insanely jealous that Thea, "that pretty little fool" as Hedda thinks of her, should after all have had "her fingers in a man's destiny." The curtain drops just as Hedda reaches her deepest and most chilling insight into her own actions: "I am burning—I am burning your child."

The Modern Theater

Twentieth-century stagecraft has been characterized by flexibility. An improved understanding of the past has allowed us to stage the plays of Sophocles, Shakespeare, Molière, and others with greater fidelity to the original intentions of the author. Furthermore, modern critical principles encourage playwrights and directors to put aside their *a priori* notions about staging and recognize that each play requires and deserves a separate approach. Continuing technical developments in the twentieth century have facilitated this flexibility both through further refinements in lighting and through machinery that can easily manipulate the sets and sometimes even the seating arrangement in the theater.

Although most modern theaters retain the proscenium arch and a clear division between the audience and the actors, many small theaters (especially temporary ones) have experimented with other structures. The most innovative of these have tried to recreate the intimacy and versatility of the Elizabethan stage either in small semicircular amphitheaters or in arena theaters. *Arena staging* or *theater-in-the-round* has emerged as the most distinctive twentieth-century contribution to stagecraft. The audience totally surrounds the stage and is therefore as close to the action of the play as is physically possible. Entrances and exits are made through the aisles normally used by the spectators and in some cases these become secondary acting areas, as well. Inevitably, however, the actors cannot simultaneously face all members of the audience. So long as the play focuses on the conflict between at least two characters, this presents no problem. When the two square off, all members of the audience will have at least a frontal view of one character or a profile of both. When the dramatic interest is focused totally on one character, however, as it is in the final moments of *Othello,* one fourth of the audience is apt to feel frustrated at being unable to see and hear properly his climactic speech. For this reason, arena staging is less successful than other approaches for plays with one dominant role.

Most of the major playhouses in America were built long before arena staging became widely accepted, but they, too, have adapted to the twentieth-century demand for flexibility. Modern set designs have been transformed by a consensus that their primary purpose is to provide three-dimensional areas for acting. The movable flats that were used well into the twentieth century to create perspective in outdoor settings have now been all but eliminated. Playwrights and directors seem to agree that everything depicted on stage should be functional and esthetically pleasing but not necessarily realistic. The sets should draw no attention to themselves or away from the acting. The general trend has been toward a simple, almost architectural stage, with platforms at various levels linked by stairways and ramps. The modern set strives to be suggestive and intellectually stimulating instead of purely pictorial, and this aim is facilitated by modern eletrical lighting, which can actually create moods by "drawing" on the stage with shadows and prismatic colors to transform a single set into a constantly changing environment.

The trends in the modern theater have imposed no new conditions on playwrights; instead, they have been freed from many of the old limitations of the stage. This flexibility is best illustrated by the range of settings used in the classics of modern drama. Eugene O'Neill's *Desire Under the Elms* (1931), for example, takes place in, and immediately outside of, the Cabot farmhouse. O'Neill's own sketches show the exterior of the farmhouse, with various sections of the wall removed as the action shifts from one room to another. In effect, it is a stage with multiple box sets. Arthur Miller's *Death of a Salesman* (1949) also calls for the interior of a house, but in this case all of the walls are invisible and the house itself becomes a large, skeletal structure of various platforms for acting or observing actions. Finally, Tom Stoppard's *Rosencrantz and Guildenstern Are Dead* (1967) is set on a barren stage, "a place without any visible character"; it requires only a platform with two different levels and a few simple properties.

The causes of the modern trend toward flexibility, suggestivity, and simplicity of setting are complex, but certainly television and the movies have had something to do with it. Before films became popular, there had been an ever-increasing trend toward spectacle in the theater. Although crowds once flocked to playhouses to see a theatrical railroad engine steaming along toward the bound heroine or baying bloodhounds pursuing the bleeding hero, they soon found that the movies—through close-ups, cuts, and editing—could present those thrills more realistically while indulging in the additional expensive luxuries of having the train explode or the hero slog through miles of snake-infested swamp. Within a few years, therefore, playhouses ceased to stage spectacular extravaganzas, and drama once again became the verbal and intellectual experience previously enjoyed by the Elizabethans and the Greeks.

II

❦❦❦❦❦❦

The Elements of Drama

For the most part, the elements of drama are identical to those of fiction and poetry. Plays have plots, themes, characters, and settings and make use of the many devices of poetic diction. Thus, many of the steps in the analysis of a play should parallel those used for a poem or a short story. At the same time, however, drama is a different literary genre and it imposes its own constraints on the playwright's use of certain elements of literature. These unique aspects of dramatic writing are our present concern.

Every play unfolds a story through the dialogue and actions of its characters. An understanding of these four elements—story, dialogue, action, and character—is therefore crucial to the appreciation of drama.

DIALOGUE

Tom Stoppard's *Rosencrantz and Guildenstern Are Dead* has no story apart from that already told in *Hamlet;* its principal characters are notable mainly because no one can distinguish between them; and the most significant action in the play is prolonged waiting. Part of the fun of Stoppard's work is that he has nearly stripped drama to its one indispensible element, dialogue.

A theatrical production without dialogue can be a mime or a ballet, but it is never a play. As Stoppard himself might have put it: a play can give you talk and characters without much action. And a play can give you talk and action without strong characters. But a play cannot give you characters and action without talk. It is all talk in drama.

Dramatic dialogue, however, is very different from the kind of dialogue that makes up so much of our ordinary lives. Actual conversation is full of hesitations, pauses, fragments, misunderstandings, and repetitions. The communication itself is often as much a product of inflections, gestures, and facial expressions as it is of the spoken word. It depends so much on innuendo and allusions to previous conversations that an outsider is often unable to determine the exact meaning of a discussion heard out of context. This in fact was Richard Nixon's contention when he protested in July and August 1973 against the release of the transcripts of his conversations about Watergate. The following selection from the Nixon tapes may have been one of the most important moments in the history of the United States presidency; its release shocked the nation and eventually led to Nixon's resignation in August 1974. As we will see, however, it is far from being good drama:

THE SETTING. *March 21, 1973, 10:12 A.M. The Oval Office*
THE PARTICIPANTS. *Richard Nixon and John Dean*
THE SITUATION. *Dean has just reviewed the history of the Watergate cover-up, calling it a "cancer" close to the presidency. Having described the continual demands for hush money by the Watergate burglars, he continues:*

DEAN. . . . It will cost money. It is dangerous. People around here are not pros at this sort of thing. This is the sort of thing Mafia people can do: washing money, getting clean money, and things like that. We just don't know about those things, because we are not criminals and not used to dealing in that business.
NIXON. That's right.
DEAN. It is a tough thing to know how to do.
NIXON. Maybe it takes a gang to do that.
DEAN. That's right. There is a real problem as to whether we could even do it. Plus there is a real problem in raising money. Mitchell has been working on raising some money. He is one of the ones with the most to lose. But there is no denying the fact that the White House, in Ehrlichman, Haldeman, and Dean, are involved in some of the early money decisions.
NIXON. How much money do you need?
DEAN. I would say these people are going to cost a million dollars over the next two years.
NIXON. We could get that. On the money, if you need the money you could get that. You could get a million dollars. You could get it in cash. I know where it could be gotten. It is not easy, but it could be done. But the question is who the hell would handle it? Any ideas on that?
DEAN. That's right. Well, I think that is something that Mitchell ought to be charged with.
NIXON. I would think so too.
DEAN. And get some pros to help him.
        —From *Submission of Recorded Presidential Conversations,* April 30, 1974

It is clear enough that the president and his chief counsel are discussing obstruction of justice, acquiescence in blackmail, and involvement with professional criminals. The very topics of conversation are momentous and appalling. Yet the passage is stylistically weak and grammatically inept. The conversation redundantly returns to the difficulty of raising the money and the need for "pros" to handle the payoffs; and when Dean disgresses into a discussion of the White House involvement, the president brings him back to the point by asking, "How much money do you need?" The sentences are choppy and inelegant, and the participants do not come to a clear decision until many exchanges later. Even then the discussion does not end. It meanders along for at least another hour, with the participants drifting away from the central issue and then darting back to it like minnows chasing a spinner.

In contrast, important conversations in drama slash past trivial details and strike the lure with vigor and directness. A play necessarily packs a story of significance into two or three hours of stage time. As a result, each sentence is hard and muscular—made up of concrete nouns and active verbs. The dialogue continuously and clearly builds toward its point, eliminating irrelevancies and unnecessary repetitions. When trimmed to its dramatic core, a real conversation, like the one between Richard Nixon and John Dean, might well be cut by half.

Dramatic dialogue ordinarily carries with it still another burden: it must include sufficient background information to fix the time, place, and circumstances of the action firmly in the mind of the audience. Nixon and Dean, after all, knew each other well and also knew the circumstances surrounding the issues described in their conversation; the playwright, however, must introduce the characters and provide background information before the audience can really understand what is going on. Although some playwrights prefer to have a narrator set the scene in a formal prologue—as, for example, in Williams's *The Glass Menagerie* or Wilder's *Our Town*—most try to bring out the background information gradually during the play's first act. Ibsen was a master of the gradual introduction, as illustrated in the first few moments of *Hedda Gabler:*

MISS JULIANA TESMAN, *with her bonnet on and carrying a parasol, comes in from the hall, followed by* BERTA, *who carries a bouquet wrapped in paper.* MISS TESMAN *is a comely and pleasant-looking lady of about sixty-five. She is nicely but simply dressed in a gray walking costume.* BERTA *is a middle-aged woman of plain and rather countrified appearance.*

MISS TESMAN [*stops close to the door, listens and says softly*]. Upon my word, I don't believe they are stirring yet!

BERTA [*also softly*]. I told you so, miss. Remember how late the steamboat got in last night. And then, when they got home!—good lord, what a lot the young mistress had to unpack before she could get to bed.

MISS TESMAN. Well, well—let them have their sleep out. But let us see that they get a good breath of the fresh morning air when they do appear. [*She goes to the glass door and throws it open.*]

BERTA [*beside table, at a loss what to do with the bouquet in her hand*]. I declare, there isn't a bit of room left. I think I'll put it down here, miss. [*She places it on the piano.*]

MISS TESMAN. So you've got a new mistress now, my dear Berta. Heaven knows it was a wrench to me to part with you.

BERTA [*on the point of weeping*]. And do you think it wasn't hard for me too, miss? After all the blessed years I've been with you and Miss Rina.

MISS TESMAN. We must make the best of it, Berta. There was nothing else to be done. George can't do without you, you see—he absolutely can't. He has had you to look after him ever since he was a little boy.

BERTA. Ah, but, Miss Julia, I can't help thinking of Miss Rina lying helpless at home there, poor thing. And with only that new girl too! She'll never learn to take proper care of an invalid.

MISS TESMAN. Oh, I shall manage to train her. And of course, you know, I shall take most of it upon myself. You needn't be uneasy about my poor sister, my dear Berta.

BERTA. Well, but there's another thing, miss. I'm so mortally afraid I shan't be able to suit the young mistress.

MISS TESMAN. Oh well—just at first there may be one or two things—

BERTA. Most like she'll be terrible grand in her ways.

MISS TESMAN. Well, you can't wonder at that—General Gabler's daughter! Think of the sort of life she was accustomed to in her father's time. Don't you remember how we used to see her riding down the road along with the general? In that long black habit—and with feathers in her hat?

BERTA. Yes indeed—I remember well enough! But, good lord, I should never have dreamt in those days that she and Master George would make a match of it.

MISS TESMAN. Nor I. But by-the-bye, Berta—while I think of it: in future you mustn't say Master George. You must say Doctor Tesman.

BERTA. Yes, the young mistress spoke of that too—last night—the moment they set foot in the house. Is it true then, miss?

MISS TESMAN. Yes, indeed it is. Only think, Berta—some foreign university has made him a doctor—while he has been abroad, you understand. I hadn't heard a word about it until he told me himself upon the pier.

BERTA. Well, well, he's clever enough for anything, he is. But I didn't think he'd have gone in for doctoring people too.

MISS TESMAN. No, no, it's not that sort of doctor he is. [*Nods significantly.*] But let me tell you, we may have to call him something still grander before long.

BERTA. You don't say so! What can that be, miss?

MISS TESMAN [*smiling*]. H'm—wouldn't you like to know!

—From *Hedda Gabler,* Henrik Ibsen [1890]

Everything in this conversation is natural and unstrained, yet it tells us all that we immediately need to know about the main characters and their relationships with one another. We learn that George Tesman and his new wife have just returned from their honeymoon, that no one had ever dreamt the two would wed, that prior to his marriage George had lived with his two aunts and the maid Berta, and that George had recently been awarded a doctorate by "some foreign university." These few facts give us our bearings and prepare us for the entrance of George and Hedda. They also hint at Hedda's romantic past and George's professorial ambitions, thus preparing us for the entrance of Eilert Lövborg, who is about to compete for George's academic position as he had once competed for Hedda's affections.

But we learn even more. Ibsen is so economical a craftsman that these few lines of dialogue also contribute to the characterization of George, Hedda, and Aunt Julia. We learn, for example, that George is helpless and relies on others to provide him with the comforts of life. When Aunt Julia must choose whether Berta should stay with Aunt Rina or go with George, she decides that her invalid sister is more self-sufficient than her nephew. We also learn that George is not the elegant sort of man one would expect to marry a general's daughter, although his aunts and Berta are genuinely fond of him. Thus, when we first see Tesman on stage we have been prepared, subtly, for his kindly, methodical, sentimental, and slightly incompetent approach to life. Hedda, on the other hand, is a far more formidable character. She is mentioned by Berta and Julia with anxiety. Because Hedda is so "grand in her ways," Berta fears that she "shan't be able to suit the young mistress" and Aunt Julia agrees that "at first there may be one or two things." Aunt Julia's reminiscences about how Hedda used to ride in a long black habit with feathers in her hat prepare us for a woman of aristocratic and romantic disposition. And Hedda's insistence that her husband be called Doctor Tesman hints at her desire for a dignified and proper place in society. These few introductory remarks, then, indicate that Hedda is likely to be emotionally unsuited to a drab life with Tesman and suggest that her romantic predilections may eventually come into conflict with her equally strong desire for propriety. Finally, the lines indirectly characterize Aunt Julia. She is a fussy, meddling, and kindly woman who habitually thinks of others first. She listens carefully to find out if the newlyweds are stirring, throws open the glass door to give them plenty of air, and gives up her own maid to be sure they will be well served. Berta's mistaken assumption that George has become a medical doctor apparently triggers one of the preoccupations of Aunt Julia's prying mind. The allusion to a medical doctor in the context of George's marriage evidently arouses her hope that the household may soon need an obstetrical physician and that George will become a father as well as a doctor of philosophy. She nods significantly and says mysteriously, "we may have to call him something still grander [than doctor] before long."

A third function of the dialogue in this introductory scene is to foreshadow themes of later importance. The oblique allusion to Hedda's possible pregnancy is but one such example. In a more overt and pragmatic way, the opening dialogue and accompanying actions often help to initiate events that are further developed as the play progresses. The bouquet that is in Berta's hand as the play opens carries a card promising a visit from Thea Elvsted, a visit that will develop into a competition between Hedda and Thea for control over Eilert Lövborg. Similarly, Aunt Julia's well-intentioned opening of the glass doors will later irritate Hedda, who prefers a "softer light" and complains, "Oh—there the servant has gone and opened the veranda door and let in a whole flood of sunshine." From that point on, Hedda maliciously seeks opportunities to goad Aunt Julia and to prevent any attempt to create a tight family circle that will include George's aunts. As the play unfolds, the expressed anxieties of Aunt Julia and Berta that "there may be one or two" points of conflict between them and Hedda are amply confirmed.

In summary, the dialogue in Ibsen's plays, as in most other plays, serves many simultaneous functions. It is used to provide necessary factual information, to reminisce, to characterize, to speculate, and to foreshadow. Such dialogue may take the form of discussion (as in the quoted scene), argument, or inquiry. It may accompany and clarify actions or simply reveal attitudes and opinions. In short, good dialogue is a very flexible narrative tool.

Dialogue is not, however, an easy tool to use. A playwright, unlike a novelist, cannot simply halt proceedings to introduce formal character sketches or to set a scene; nor can a playwright exert the same direct control over the "story." A fictional "yarn" is spun out of a voice that the author, as narrator, can fully control. But the dramatist has no voice of his or her own. When the curtain rises, the fabric of the plot must emerge naturally from interwoven and independent threads of conversation.

When we argue that the plot of a play must emerge naturally from its dialogue, we do not mean that the dialogue itself must inevitably be "natural" or "realistic." As the Watergate tapes demonstrate, the real words of real people often seem awkward and unnatural in transcript. But art is not life. We hold art to a higher standard of probability, eloquence, and organization; therefore, nearly all dramatic dialogue is more rhetorical—more poetic, if you will—than real dialogue. Even so, however, there is an enormous range between the dialogue of *Hedda Gabler,* for example, and that of *Othello.* Part of the difference results from the fact that the former is written in prose, the latter in verse; and verse is always much richer than prose in sound, rhythm, and imagery.

There is, however, also the matter of level of style. The language of *Othello* is often lofty and formal; the language of *Hedda Gabler,* by contrast, is colloquial and informal. Listen to the reflections of Othello as he looks upon Desdemona by candlelight before mercilessly slaying her:

If I quench thee, thou flaming minister,
I can thy former light restore,
Should I repent me: but once put out thy light,
Thou cunning'st pattern of excelling nature,
I know not where is that Promethean heat
That can thy light relume. When I have plucked the rose,
I cannot give it vital growth again,
It must needs wither: I'll smell it on the tree.
                              [*Kissing her.*]
Ah, balmy breath, that dost almost persuade
Justice to break her sword! One more, one more.
Be thus when thou art dead, and I will kill thee,
And love thee after.

—From *Othello*, act 5, scene 2,
William Shakespeare [1604]

Even in this moment of aroused emotion Othello's thoughts roll forth in grammatically complete and relatively complex sentences. His fevered and fertile imagination leads him to express himself through a series of poetic devices. First he compares snuffing a candle with snuffing Desdemona's life; then he alludes to the Greek myth of Prometheus, a Titan who originally gave fire to mankind; next he compares the beauty of Desdemona with that of the rose that "must needs wither" when plucked; and finally, after bending to "smell it on the tree," he uses personification in claiming that Desdemona's "balmy breath" could "almost persuade / Justice to break her sword." Plays like *Othello*, which make use of careful syntax and copious poetic devices, are said to be written in the "high" style.

The language of *Hedda Gabler* is, of course, far different. Notice, for example, the casual and conversational tone. Phrases are inserted to capture the flavor of everyday speech ("upon my word," "good lord," "well, well," "I declare"[1]). Grammatical relationships, too, are informal: the dialogue is sprinkled with dashes to indicate incomplete thoughts or sudden changes in direction. And Ibsen makes no attempt to use poetical devices. Playwrights occasionally carry this colloquial, or "low," style even further and use ungrammatical and dialectical speech as a tool of characterization. The back-country accents and diction of the Cabots, for example, help Eugene O'Neill explore crude and elemental passions in *Desire Under the Elms* (1924). Similarly, Stanley Kowalski's inarticulate speech in Tennessee Williams's *A Streetcar Named Desire* (1947) underscores his assertive, uneducated, and violent character. And even in *Othello* Iago's worldly and profane speech helps to identify him as a villain.

Dramatic theory during the classical and neoclassical periods held that tragedy should be written in the high style and that the colloquial, or low, style was appropriate only to comedy. In practice, however, as the plays of Shakespeare amply demonstrate, such a distinction need not be rigidly observed, and in more modern times it has been all but abandoned. Most drama is mixed in style, rising to eloquence or falling to informality according to the inherent demands of the dramatic situation.

---

[1] If these expressions seem too stilted to qualify as "everyday speech," remember that *Hedda Gabler* was written nearly 100 years ago and has been translated into English from the original Norwegian. It is always well to bear such factors in mind when considering the language of a play.

STORY

People come to the theater because they wish to be entertained. Although they may be willing to admire fine writing or to tolerate moral instruction, they demand an engrossing story. An audience is, after all, a crowd, and the principal desire of a crowd is to find out "what happens next." Drama, however, would emphasize story even if it were not demanded by the audience, for the dramatic point of view necessitates a fundamentally chronological development of action. Reminiscences can be, and often are, used to precipitate the action, but once the play has begun, the events on the stage inevitably unfold according to the simple time sequence of a story.

Dramatic actions as they unfold upon the stage do not, of course, simply "happen"; they are premediated and aristically arranged by the playwright to yield a dramatic plot. The ability to understand the story (the "what happens") may satisfy our basic desire as theatergoers to be entertained, but as literary critics we also need to understand not only "what happens" but "why"—a question that invariably forces us to consider the dynamics of plot.

Like a typical short story, the plot of nearly every play contains five structural elements: *exposition, complication, crisis, falling action,* and *resolution.* The principal difference between fictional and dramatic plots is that the latter are more regular in their use of these five elements, as is illustrated in the following paragraphs.

Exposition

The exposition provides essential background information, introduces the cast, begins the characterization, and initiates the action. Some exposition is always provided in the first scene, and all of the essential background material is usually provided by the end of the first act. Sometimes a formal prologue or introduction by a narrator helps to set the scene, but more often there is no sharp division between the exposition and the complication that follows. In fact, most plays begin *in medias res* (in the middle of things), just after some event has taken place that will eventually lead to the crisis.

EXAMPLES OF THE SITUATION AT THE COMMENCEMENT OF DRAMATIC ACTION

King Oedipus. A plague afflicts Thebes because the murderer of King Laius has never been punished.

Othello. Othello and Desdemona have secretly married; and Cassio, rather than Iago, has been made Othello's lieutenant.

Tartuffe. To be nearer to his religious adviser, Orgon has installed Tartuffe in his home.

Hedda Gabler. After their honeymoon, Hedda and George have returned to town, as has Eilert Lövborg, who is seeking to publish a new book. Rumor has it that George's faculty appointment must await the outcome of a competition with Eilert.

The situation at the outset of a play usually gives us important clues to its direction and meaning. We do not, for example, see Oedipus at his moment of early triumph over the Sphinx; instead we first see him as he proudly promises that he will discover Laius's killer just as he once discovered the meaning of the Sphinx's riddle. The play explores the consequences of this rash promise. Similarly, *Othello* does not begin with a scene showing Othello's wedding ceremony, but rather with the conspiracy between Roderigo and Iago, in order to focus the audience's attention immediately on Iago's thirst for revenge.

Complication

This section of the plot introduces and develops the conflict. It commences when one or more of the main characters first become aware of an impending difficulty or when their relationships first begin to change.

EXAMPLES OF INITIAL COMPLICATION

King Oedipus. Tiresias alleges that Oedipus has murdered Laius.

Othello. Iago recognizes that Cassio's courteous attentions to Desdemona can be used to make Othello jealous (act 2, scene 2).

Tartuffe. Orgon reveals his decision that Mariane must marry Tartuffe instead of Valère, whom she loves (act 2, scene 1).

Hedda Gabler. Thea informs Hedda that Eilert Lövborg is in town and that he is still preoccupied by the memory of an unknown woman (act 1).

It is not always possible to identify the precise point at which the complication of the plot begins. The plot of *Othello*, for example, obviously turns on Iago's ability to make Othello suspect Desdemona of infidelity. But how does this suspicion originate? Does it begin as a scheme in Iago's brain when, having seen Cassio take Desdemona by the hand (act 2, scene 2), he whispers slyly, "With as little a web as this will I ensnare as great a fly as Cassio"? Or does it begin somewhat later (act 3, scene 3), when (as Cassio parts from Desdemona) Iago says to Othello, "Ha! I like not that"? Or did Othello's jealousy start as early as act 1, scene 3, when Brabantio exclaimed, "Look to her, Moor, if thou has eyes to see. She has deceived her father, and may thee"? In a sense it begins at each place. It was foreshadowed in act 1, scene 3; first plotted by Iago in act 2, scene 2; and first felt by Othello in act 3, scene 3. From relatively small beginnings, Othello's jealousy grows until it dominates his entire personality. Much of the impact of the play results from the fact that the tragedy that ultimately destroys Othello has its roots in such indefinite beginnings.

In other plays, however, the conflict and its thematic significance are immediately clear. Oedipus' pride and impetuosity are implicit in his very first speech, but they only take on the aspect of tragic flaws when he refuses to check the accuracy of the prophesies reported by Tiresias and rashly concludes that the priest has joined with Creon in conspiring to usurp his throne. Similarly, Orgon's excessive faith in Tartuffe is clear throughout the first act, but only becomes dangerous and destructive when it leads him to break his promise that Valère shall marry Mariane. In both plays, the tensions that dramatically affect the protagonist's subsequent conduct are implicit in the opening scenes.

Crisis

The crisis, or turning point of the play, occurs at the moment of peak emotional intensity and usually involves a decision, a decisive action, or an open conflict between the protagonist and antagonist. It is often called the *obligatory scene* because the audience demands to *see* such moments acted out on stage.

EXAMPLES OF THE CRISIS

King Oedipus. The shepherd's information about Oedipus's birth finally convinces the king that he has murdered his father and married his mother. Meanwhile Jocasta has gone into the palace to kill herself.

Othello. Through the machinations of Iago, Othello sees Desdemona's handkerchief in the hand of Cassio and concludes that she must die for her infidelity (act 4, scene 1).

Tartuffe. While hidden under a table, Orgon hears Tartuffe trying to seduce his wife and finally recognizes Tartuffe's hypocrisy for what it is (act 4, scene 5).

Hedda Gabler. Instead of returning Eilert's manuscript, Hedda encourages him to believe it is lost and gives him a pistol with which to commit suicide. After he has left, she burns the manuscript (act 3).

Just as it is sometimes difficult to determine where the conflict originates, it is sometimes also difficult to determine when the crisis takes place. Once Othello has seen Cassio with Desdemona's handkerchief, he is convinced of her guilt and the tragic conclusion of the play is foreordained. The scene, then, marks an important turning point in the characterization of Othello. But the dramatic tension continues to mount until the confrontation between Othello and Desdemona in her bed chamber (act 5, scene 2). We do not *know* that Othello will actually kill Desdemona until he does so. And only when he does so in spite of Desdemona's moving pleas and his own obvious reluctance, do we recognize the extent to which his jealousy has blinded him. Clearly, this scene, too, is a crisis in the plot and another turning point in the characterization of Othello. A hundred lines further into the scene we find yet another crisis and another turning point when Emilia tells Othello that Desdemona could not have given the handkerchief to Cassio for she, Emilia, had found it and given it to Iago. This revelation is the turning point in Iago's fortunes; it finally shows Othello how mistaken he has been all along. In the few remaining moments of the play, Othello rises again to the dignity and nobility that had first characterized him.

It is a mistake, therefore, in plays like *Othello* always to seek the crisis within a single moment of emotional intensity. Great literature is never bound by formula. Instead, as critics we must learn to look carefully at each moment of high drama in an effort to determine what we can learn from it about the play, its characters, and their relationship to the playwright's overall intention.

Falling Action and Resolution

As the consequences of the crisis accumulate, events develop a momentum of their own. Especially in tragedy, the falling action of the play results from the protagonist's loss of control and a final catastrophe often appears inevitable. The resolution of a comedy, however, frequently includes some unexpected twist in the plot (for example, the intervention of the king or the revelation of the hero's true parents). This twist cuts sharply through all difficulties and allows the play to end on a happy note. In both tragedy and comedy, the resolution brings to an end the conflict that has been implicit (or explicit) since the play's opening scenes. When the curtain falls, the relationships among the characters have once more stabilized.

EXAMPLES OF THE FALLING ACTION AND RESOLUTION

King Oedipus. Oedipus blinds himself in sorrow and then is banished by the new king, Creon.

Othello. After smothering Desdemona, Othello learns of her innocence and slays himself.

Tartuffe: Using a deed that Orgon had foolishly signed, Tartuffe attempts to expel Orgon and his family from their own home. At the last moment, Tartuffe is arrested and imprisoned by order of the king.

Hedda Gabler: After Eilert's death, George and Thea set to work reproducing the lost manuscript. Hedda, whom George has commended to Judge Brack's attention, finds herself in Brack's power when he threatens to reveal information that would involve her in scandal. Rather than become Brack's mistress or tolerate scandal, Hedda shoots herself.

The resolution, or dénouement, merits special attention because it is the author's last chance to get the point across. Thus, it is not surprising that the resolution often contains a clear statement (or restatement) of the theme and a full revelation of character. In the last lines of *Hedda Gabler,* for example, Hedda realizes that Thea will indeed inspire Tesman just as she had Eilert Lövborg, while she, Hedda, can do "nothing in the world to help them." And Othello, in his last lines, begs that, when relating his story, Lodovico and Gratiano will speak

> Of one that loved not wisely but too well,
> Of one not easily jealous, but, being wrought,
> Perplexed in the extreme, of one whose hand,
> Like the base Indian, threw a peal away
> Richer than all his tribe—of one whose subdued eyes,
> Albeit unused to the melting mood,
> Drop tears as fast as the Arabian trees
> Their medicinal gum.
>
> —From *Othello,* act 5, scene 2,
> William Shakespeare [1604]

In the last lines of *Tartuffe,* the officer presents Molière's conception of the ideal man:

We live under a king who is an enemy to fraud, a king whose eyes look into the depths of all hearts, and who cannot be deceived by the most artful imposter. Gifted with a fine discernment, his lofty soul at all times sees things in the right light. He is never betrayed into exaggeration, and his sound judgment never falls into any excess. He confers an everlasting glory upon men of worth; but this zeal does not radiate blindly: his esteem for the sincere does not close his heart to the horror aroused by those who are treacherous.

—From *Tartuffe,* act 5, scene 7, Moliere [1664]

And finally, the chorus pronounces a telling judgment upon Oedipus, as that play closes:

> *Chorus.* Make way for Oedipus. All people said,
>   "That is a fortunate man;"
>   And now what storms are beating on his head!
>   "That is a fortunate man,"
>   Call no man fortunate that is not dead.
>   The dead are free from pain.
>   —From *King Oedipus,* Sophocles [430 B.C.]

In each case the lines are so crucial and so clearly a summary of what the author finds most important that literary critics often use them as keys to unlock the riches of each play.

Although virtually all plays include an exposition, complication, crisis, falling action, and resolution, and all take approximately the same amount of time to perform, they differ drastically in the amount of fictional time covered by the action shown on stage. In plays like *King Oedipus, Tartuffe,* and *Hedda Gabler,* the action begins just a few hours before the crisis. This allows the drama to unfold before the spectators' eyes, much as if they were looking in on real events. But because nearly any plot of significance builds to a crisis that caps a series of events dating back months or years, these *unfolding plots* necessarily make use of reminiscences introduced via the testimony of elderly step-parents, conversations between servants, or other similar strategies. The manipulation of these reminiscences requires considerable ingenuity in order to avoid a sense of obvious contrivance. One alternative is to present the action episodically, skipping weeks, months, or years between scenes as the chief events leading up to the crisis are acted out on stage. *Othello* and most other Elizabethan plays employ such *episodic plots.*

Whether a plot is unfolding or episodic, it ought to be tightly structured and pruned of unnecessary characters, actions, speeches, and scenes. The term *well-made play,* or *"pièce bien faite,"* was coined by Eugène Scribe, a French playwright (1791–1861), to describe such plots—especially when they proceed logically from cause to effect in building toward a climactic scene in which the hero triumphs by revealing some adeptly foreshadowed secret. Although the formula prescribed by Scribe is now out-of-date, the craftsmanship he advocated will never be. It is, and always has been, an unmistakable sign of good drama. The first truly well-made plays were not written by Scribe or Ibsen, but by Aeschylus and Sophocles. And the latter's *King Oedipus* probably conforms more closely than any later drama to the description of the well-made play first given in Aristotle's *Poetics:*

The plot, being an imitation of an action must imitate one action and that a whole, the structural union of the parts being such that, if any one of them is displaced or removed, the whole will be disjointed and disturbed.[2]

CHARACTER

For many of us, an interest in literature is an outgrowth of our interest in people and their personalities. Drama is particularly satisfying in this respect, for plays are inevitably and immediately concerned with the human beings

---

[2] *The Poetics of Aristotle,* 3rd ed., trans. by S. H. Butcher (New York: Macmillan Publishing Company, 1902), p. 35.

who are impersonated by live actors and actresses on the stage. The terms used to describe characters in drama are, for the most part, the same as those used for fiction. In fact, some of these terms were originally borrowed from drama to describe fictional qualities. The *dramatis personae* of a play usually include a *protagonist* and an *antagonist* or an antagonistic force. (The protagonist in a tragedy, however, is often called the *tragic hero.*) Othello and Oedipus are clearly protagonists; Iago is Othello's antagonist; and the will of the gods is the antagonistic force opposing Oedipus. A great many plays also include a *confidant* (*confidante* if female) to whom a major character "confides" his or her most private thoughts and feelings. Emilia, for example, serves as Desdemona's confidante in *Othello,* just as Dorine is Mariane's confidante in *Tartuffe.* A *foil* is a minor figure whose contrasting personality in some way clarifies or enhances that of a major character, as Cléante's moderation serves as a foil for Orgon's zealotry in *Tartuffe* and as Shakespeare's Laertes becomes a foil for Hamlet while both are seeking to revenge their fathers' deaths. A *caricature* is a character with one motive or trait that is carried to a ridiculous extreme. In *Hedda Gabler* George Tesman, who has spent his honeymoon researching a book on "the domestic industries of Brabant during the Middle Ages" is a caricature of the scholarly temperament. And nearly everyone in *Tartuffe* is a caricature of some aspect of seventeenth-century French society.

This terminology underscores the obvious difference between major and minor characters. The parts of the protagonist and antagonist are major, whereas those of the confidant and foil are often (but not always) minor. Because it is only reasonable to assume that most of a playwright's attention will be focused on his major characters, one of our first steps in the analysis of a play should be to identify the characters who have leading roles. The most obvious clue is the number of lines spoken by each character: major characters have many, and minor characters few. But more importantly, major characters are usually individualized and given both complex motives and a past, while minor characters often have no past at all and sometimes represent no more than a common character type. One has said nearly all that need be said about the characters of the messenger and the shepherd in *King Oedipus* as soon as their titles are mentioned. They have few individual traits and serve primarily to convey information to Oedipus and the audience. Similarly, Judge Brack in *Hedda Gabler* is a middle-aged rake whose single motive is to establish a comfortable triangular friendship in which Hedda becomes his mistress while George remains his friend. No such simple statements, however, can accurately describe the personalities of major characters like Oedipus, Othello, and Hedda. In order to understand these individuals, we must look carefully at the various means of characterization used to bring them to life.

Characterizing details in drama come to us from many different sources. We immediately learn something from the *name and physical appearance* of each character—although this information is often unreliable. The characters in *Othello,* for example, so often use the adjective *honest* when they refer to Iago that it seems (ironically) a part of his name, and they mistakenly take his coarse manner and military bearing as signs of simplicity and firmness. A second method of characterization is through an individual's *patterns of action* over the course of the play. Hedda Gabler's pacing, for example, is an indication of her sense of suffocating confinement in her role as a woman. Much characterization, however, is accomplished through dialogue in one of four ways. A character can reveal his or her personality and motives, as Iago often does, through *asides and soliloquies.* There may also be self-revelation in *the way a character speaks* because dialect, word choice, and grammar all provide clues to a person's background and intelligence. Othello's "perfect soul" is partially revealed through his eloquence, while Iago's idiomatic slang marks him as a "profane wretch" (according to Brabantio) in the very first scene of the play. *The way a character responds* to others is also important. Adversity seems at first only to make Othello more self-confident. When swords on both sides are drawn as Brabantio seeks to arrest Othello, the latter averts a crisis with composure: "Good signior, you shall more command with years / Than with your weapons." Yet the violent temper of this eminent soldier eventually surfaces, and he himself recognizes that he is one not easily made jealous or moved to anger, "but, being wrought,/ Perplexed in the extreme." Finally, *what others say about a character* can help us to understand him or her. As we have seen, the conversation between Aunt Julia and Berta is packed with observations, speculations, reminiscences, and judgments about Hedda and Tesman. These characterizing details come at us in fragmentary glimpses during the normal ebb and flow of the conversation. Occasionally, however, an author may provide a more concentrated sketch of a character's actions or personality—usually in the form of such *hidden narration* as the messenger's account of Oedipus' rage after learning his true parentage (see p. 972).

The process of understanding drama is very closely linked to our ability to understand the personalities and motives of the major characters. As we read and study a play, we inevitably raise a host of questions: Why does Iago dedicate himself to tormenting Othello? Why is Othello so susceptible to Iago's manipulations? What makes the lost handkerchief so important to Othello? Why does Desdemona lie about the handkerchief? What stops Othello and Desdemona from talking about their misunderstanding openly and fully? Is Othello thoroughly noble or is his character seriously flawed in some way? These questions, and others like them, are concerned with fundamental character traits and express our expectation that the actions of the characters should be plausible, consistent, and adequately motivated. In attempting to answer them, we continually compare what is said by or about a character with the way in which that character acts on stage, searching for the thread of unity that creates a convincing personality.

At the same time, however, characters who are too consistent generally seem unrealistic. Conventional wisdom tells us that real people are full of surprises and so, in literature, we tend to demand characters who are capable of surprising us in a convincing way. Their motives should be complex and even competing, as Othello's obvious love for Desdemona competes with his injured pride when he thinks that she has been unfaithful to him. Moreover, those characters who most interest us usually undergo a process of growth and change during the course of the play. Othello fascinates us as he sinks from his initial nobility to an all-consuming jealousy, before rising again in the tragic self-knowledge of his last speech. Similarly, Oedipus's blind complacency and self-satisfaction break down as the unfolding events force him to see the criminal actions of his past. At the end of the play, this banished and self-blinded man realizes that, although his eyes once were clear, he has had "neither sight nor knowledge."

We must be careful, however, not to push too far the demand for growth and change in character. Many fine plays, including *Tartuffe* and *Hedda Gabler,* present personalities or dilemmas without even hinting at the possibility of moral improvement or permanent solutions. Apparently Molière felt that a man like Tartuffe can be imprisoned but rarely improved, and that Orgon is as naturally impetuous in desiring Tartuffe's punishment as he had earlier been in praising him. Similarly, *Hedda Gabler* is a bleak study of a fundamentally pathological personality. The value of such drama is not that it creates characters just like our next-door neighbors, but rather that it shows how only slight distortions in personality can destabilize the whole structure of ordinary social relationships.

ACTION

John Wilmot, the Earl of Rochester, once criticized Charles II as a king who "never said a foolish thing / Nor ever did a wise one." Many a dramatist, after seeing his plays poorly acted, must have sympathized with the response of Charles II: "This is very true: for my words are my own, and my actions are my ministers'." The playwright must live with the parallel and sometimes melancholy realization that, while his words are his own, his actions are the actors'. Fortunately for the play-going public, actors are much more successful at putting the words of a play into action than bureaucrats are at implementing those of the head of government.

Although the actions in a play may sometimes be indicated or suggested in the script, they are just as often the inevitable by-products of the performance. When Berta and Aunt Julia are talking in the first scene of *Hedda Gabler* (see p. 986), we should not assume that they face each other motionlessly throughout their conversation. Ibsen himself directs them to perform a few actions—close the front door, open the door to the veranda, put down the bouquet, and so on—but twelve consecutive exchanges take place without a single stage direction. What do these women do with their hands during these exchanges? Do they remain motionless or move about the room? Do they face each other, the audience, or neither? Ibsen doesn't say, but surely some actions must take place—if only an averted glance here and a penetrating look there. Although the lines must be spoken, the director is free to present them as he wishes, and this presentation will affect both the characterization of the speakers and the degree of dramatic emphasis given to their words.

As readers of drama, we may attempt to be our own director, moving the characters about an imaginary stage and endowing them with gestures and expressions suitable to the dialogue. Most of us, however, are content to concentrate on the words in the play and leave the accompanying actions vague, except where they are demanded by the script. In either approach, however, we must be very sensitive to actions implied in the dialogue. This is especially true when we read plays written before the middle of the nineteenth century. Thereafter the techniques of the novel began to infiltrate drama and the playwright's stage directions became more frequent and more detailed. But early playwrights kept their stage directions to an absolute minimum. Here, for example, is part of a scene from Shakespeare's *Othello* as it was published in the famous *First Folio* (1623):

(*Enter* LODOVICO, DESDEMONA, *and* ATTENDANTS)

LODOVICO. Save you worthy General!
OTHELLO. With all my heart, sir.

LODOVICO. The Duke and Senators of Venice greet you.

OTHELLO. I kiss the instrument of their pleasures.

DESDEMONA. And what's the news, good Cousin Lodovico?   5

IAGO: I am very glad to see you, signior.
Welcome to Cyprus.

LODOVICO. I thank you. How does Lieutenant Cassio?

IAGO. Lives, sir.

DESDEMONA. Cousin, there's fall'n between him and my lord   10
An unkind breach, but you shall make all well.

OTHELLO. Are you sure of that?

DESDEMONA. My lord?

OTHELLO. "This fail you not to do, as you will—"

LODOVICO. He did not call, he's busy in the paper.   15
Is there division 'twixt my lord and Cassio?

DESDEMONA. A most unhappy one. I would do much
To atone them, for the love I bear to Cassio.

OTHELLO. Fire and brimstone!

DESDEMONA. My lord?   20

OTHELLO. Are you wise?

DESDEMONA. What, is he angry?

LODOVICO. Maybe the letter moved him,
For, as I think, they do command him home,
Deputing Cassio in his government.   25

DESDEMONA. By my troth, I am glad on 't.

OTHELLO. Indeed!

DESDEMONA. My lord?

OTHELLO. I am glad to see you mad.

DESDEMONA. Why, sweet Othello?   30

OTHELLO. Devil!

DESDEMONA. I have not deserved this.

LODOVICO. My lord, this would not be believed in Venice.
Though I should swear I saw 't. 'Tis very much.
Make her amends, she weeps.   35

OTHELLO. O devil, devil!
If that the earth could teem with a woman's tears,
Each drop she falls would prove a crocodile.
Out of my sight!

DESDEMONA. I will not stay to offend you.   40

LODOVICO. Truly, an obedient lady.
I do beseech your lordship, call her back.

—From *Othello,* act 4, scene 1, William Shakespeare [1604]

The only stage direction is that calling for the entrance of Lodovico, Desdemona, and attendants. But if we read the lines with care, we realize that Lodovico
has brought a letter from Venice that he gives to Othello at line 3, and that
Othello refers to this letter when he says, "I kiss the instrument of their pleasures." Presumably, Othello does kiss the letter, and he must open it before
line 14, when he pretends to be deeply engrossed in his reading. We can
also conclude that Othello slaps Desdemona when he calls her a devil in line
31, for Lodovico later exclaims to Iago, "What, strike his wife!" And we know
that Desdemona must start to leave the stage after saying, "I will not stay to
offend you" (line 40), because Lodovico asks Othello to call her back in line
42.

All of these actions are implicit in the dialogue, and most modern texts of the play formally incorporate them into editorial stage directions. Even so, however, the questions, counterquestions, exclamations, and asides in the rapid exchanges between lines 8 and 31 presume many additional actions and interactions. As readers we may not pause to speculate on the exact nature of this interplay, but we should realize that here, as in all drama, the script itself is only a partial guide to the dramatic action, as any glance at a director's prompt book would quickly prove. Both the formal stage directions and the creative contributions of the actors and director are designed either to emphasize the themes and character traits introduced in the dialogue or to stimulate further dialogue. The relationship between dialogue and dramatic action is like that between a diamond and its setting in a ring: in both cases the latter enhances and emphasizes the value and clarity of the former.

12

The Classifications of Drama

No one denies that *tragedy* and *comedy* are the major subgenres of drama, but the debate over their precise meaning has persisted through at least one hundred generations of philosophers and literary critics. Can this immense investment of intellectual energy have been worthwhile? The ability to classify plays does not help us in any important way to understand what a playwright has done, why he or she has done it, or what makes the play interesting. Yet these are the questions with which we must always deal in order to understand literature. Moreover, making a simple distinction between tragedy and comedy is about as easy as determining whether we more often sorrow or smile in reading or viewing a particular play. It is only when we demand precision in defining the kinds of plot, character, and action that create tragic or comic emotions that the issue becomes complex and irresolvable.

Most playwrights have been indifferent to these matters of classification, preferring simply to write their plays and let others worry about categorizing them. Plato tells us that Socrates once cornered Agathon, a respected tragic playwright, and Aristophanes, the greatest comic playwright, at the end of a party in Athens. In his enthusiasm for philosophy, Socrates began to bend their ears with his theory that the genius of comedy is the same as that of tragedy. Being drowsy and half drunk, both poets agreed, shared another cup of wine, and promptly dozed off, leaving Socrates to peddle his theory elsewhere.

If the responses of Agathon and Aristophanes were universal, we would not need to discuss tragedy and comedy any further. However, some playwrights do write plays according to some theory of the formal principles for each subgenre, and therefore we need to have at least rudimentary knowledge of the theories behind tragedy and comedy.

TRAGEDY

The first, and most influential, literary theorist was Aristotle (
whose famous definition of tragedy remains the cornerstone u|
discussions of the subject must build. Tragedy, Aristotle contended,

is an imitation of an action of high importance, complete and of some amplitude; in language enhanced by distinct and varying beauties; acted not narrated; by means of pity and fear effecting its purgation of these emotions.[1]

This definition puts much of its emphasis on the tragic action, or story, which Aristotle thought should be serious, complex, and tightly structured. Tragedy does not need to show events that have happened, but only those that would happen, given a certain set of circumstances. The events must be arranged in a causal progression, so that no action in the play can be eliminated or displaced without damaging the whole structure. Ideally the plot should include both irony and a disclosure, each evolving naturally out of the story. In *King Oedipus,* for example, the arrival of the messenger is ironic because the news of Polybos's death might be expected to release Oedipus from any fear of murdering his father, but instead it leads directly to the disclosure of his incest and parricide. Thus, the plot interweaves the irony with the fatal disclosure.

The requirement that the action of a tragedy be of "high importance" led Aristotle to demand that the protagonist be nobly born and more admirable than ordinary men. He cannot, however, be morally perfect because the best plots arise when his downfall is the inevitable consequence of some defect in character (or *tragic flaw*). The spectacle of a good man dragged to destruction by a single error arouses in the audience both pity and fear, leading to a *catharsis,* a psychological state through which those emotions are purged; the audience leaves the theater relieved, or even exalted, rather than depressed.

This Aristotelian definition accurately reflects the goal of most Greek, Roman, and neoclassical tragedy, but it is too narrow to include many serious and important plays written during other periods. Richard III, Macbeth, and Hedda Gabler, for example, are certainly *less* virtuous than ordinary men and women; it is debatable whether Romeo, Juliet, Hamlet, and Othello have tragic flaws; and very few of the characters in modern drama are nobly born. A definition of tragedy that excludes most of the work of Shakespeare and all of Ibsen— not to mention that of more recent playwrights—cannot be complete.

A more modern view is that there are at least three variations of the tragic situation or tragic emotion.[2] Some plays ask us to look on the sufferings of the tragic hero as a human sacrifice that is necessary to cleanse society. The fall of Oedipus, for example, is necessary to purge Thebes of hidden crime and to free the city from a plague imposed by the gods. Similarly, Richard III, Iago, and Macbeth can all be viewed as warped personalities who must perish before ordinary and stable social relationships can reassert themselves. As these examples suggest, the plots of sacrificial tragedies take one of two forms. The tragic hero suffers either through the will of the gods (like Oedipus)

---

[1] Aristotle on *The Art of Fiction,* trans. by L. J. Potts (Cambridge, England: Cambridge University Press, 1962), p. 24.

[2] See E. M. W. Tillyard, *Shakespeare's Problem Plays* (Toronto: University of Toronto Press, 1949), pp. 14–17.

through a rejection by society (like Macbeth). And in either form the protagonist may merit his suffering, as Oedipus and Macbeth do, or he may be an
innocent victim of forces beyond his control, as are Romeo and Juliet.

A second tragic pattern arises from the paradox of the fortunate fall. As
plots of this kind unfold, we realize that the hero's destruction is necessary
if he is to rise to a higher level of personal awareness and development. Othello,
for example, must be brought to recognize his responsibility for Desdemona's
death if he is to change from a man who once spoke smugly of his "perfect
soul" into a tragic figure who accepts himself as one who "Like the base Indian,
threw away a pearl / Richer than all his tribe." Oedipus must be blinded
before he can truly see. And King Lear must be stripped of his regal pride
and forced to "hovel . . . with swine and rogues forlorn in short and musty
straw" before he can find his humanity. Tragedies of this second kind reaffirm
our human capacity to learn from our experiences; they extend to us the reassurance that even in defeat we can rise above our limitations to an immortal
grandeur.

A third tragic pattern involves the simple spectacle of sufferings that greatly
exceed normal bounds. The tragic characters struggle helplessly to survive
in an environment weighted against them. Like small insects entangled in a
web, their futile flutterings express their surprise, regret, and bewilderment
at the difference between their own fate and that of other men. Such plays
usually include an inquiry by the characters and the playwright into the purpose
(or futility) of the tragic individual's sufferings and the role of all human suffering in the scheme of the universe. If Tom Stoppard's *Rosencrantz and Guildenstern
Are Dead* is a tragedy at all, it is a tragedy of inexplicable suffering. From the
first scene to the last, the characters question the reasons for their involvement
in the action and the nature of the world into which they are unwillingly cast.
Ultimately their plight becomes a symbol of our plight, and Stoppard persuades
us that the death they experience is not simply a variant of the tragedian's
phoney "deaths for all ages and occasions," but rather, like real death, "the
endless time of never coming back . . . a gap you can't see, and when the
wind blows through it, it makes no sound. . . ."

Should we, however, define *Rosencrantz and Guildenstern Are Dead* as a tragedy?
It is tragic in the sense that the main characters are victims of forces beyond
their control; it is tragic in the sense that the protagonists are destroyed; and,
moreover, it is tragic in the sense that the plot deals with issues of high importance, such as reality, fate, and death. But from start to finish, the dialogue
is hilarious. If comedy has anything to do with humor, then surely this play
qualifies as comic. The situation of Stoppard's characters, and by extension
that of all human beings, is absurd—both macabre and wildly funny. It is
senseless, silly, and sobering, all at the same time. In contemporary theater,
we call this mixture of tragedy and comedy the *theater of the absurd;* its very
existence reminds us that there need be no sharp distinction between the
frowning mask of tragedy and the smiling mask of comedy.

COMEDY

Horace Walpole, the eighteenth-century man of letters, once observed that
"the world is a comedy to those that think, a tragedy to those who feel."
Walpole's comparison is as good a guide as any to the key differences between

these two modes of drama. The tragic hero is closely examined and portrayed as an individual; the comic character is viewed intellectually from a distance and represents a broad human "type"—a young lover, a hypocrite, an elegant fop, and so on. The tragic mode asks us to sympathize with the hero and imagine ourselves in his position; the comic mode suggests that we step back from life and look with amusement on the humorous predicament of others. The subject matter of comedy is often as serious as that of tragedy, but the comic playwright consciously distorts events and personalities in order to remind the audience that the play deals with fantasy and not fact. The plots of comedy are usually convoluted exercises in authorial imagination; the plots of tragedy are sobering relevations of our emotional and psychological core.

A lighthearted but intellectual approach to comedy has prevailed from the very beginning. The extant plays of Aristophanes (called *Old Comedy*) are carefully structured explorations of a bizarre intellectual hypothesis. What would happen, he asks in *Lysistrata* (411 B.C.), if all Greek women refused to participate in sexual relations until the Peloponnesian War was brought to an end? Suppose (in *The Birds*) that one could found an empire in the air and starve the gods by intercepting the smoke from earthly sacrifices. Imagine (in *The Clouds*) that a farmer attends the school of Socrates in hopes of learning how to avoid paying his debts. In each case the idea and background of the situation are presented in the prologue. The merits and deficiencies of the hypothesis are then formally explored in an *agon,* or debate. The application of the debate is then illustrated in a series of episodes that conclude with a final song and a scene of merriment. In addition, each play contains a number of elements that apparently were required by convention: the entrance of a wildly costumed chorus, an elaborately structured song *(parabasis)* in which the playwright lectures the audience and satirizes the society, and a host of meticulous rules ranging from a required form of *agon* to the necessity of reciting the *pignos* or "choking song" in only one breath.

Within this highly structured form, Aristophanes continually sought to satirize the society at large and its most prominent individuals. He repeatedly attacked the Peloponnesian War and decadent innovations in religion, education, and poetry. He created ridiculous caricatures of Socrates, Euripides, Aeschylus, the politicians of Athens, and even the Greek gods. And throughout it all he continually explored and distorted the implications of his initial intellectual hypothesis.

Few modern comedies have been influenced by the Aristophanic tradition because the hypothetical postulate with which Old Comedy begins tends to favor a rather limiting form of social satire. The plays of Aristophanes are so filled with topical and personal allusions that many parts of them are now unintelligible. In order to survive as a literary form, comedy had to begin using plots and characters that could be universally understood and enjoyed.

By the time Aristophanes wrote his last comedy, *Plutus,* in 388 B.C., he had already evolved beyond the conventions of Old Comedy. The *New Comedy* that ensued has proven to be remarkably durable. Even today most comedies continue to follow the same plot structure:

What normally happens is that a young man wants a young woman, that his desire is resisted by some opposition, usually paternal, and that near the end of the play some twist in the plot enables the hero to have his will. . . . The movement of comedy is usually a movement from one kind of society to another. At the beginning of the play the obstructing characters are in charge of the play's society, and the audience recognizes that they are usurpers. At the end of the play the device in the plot that brings the hero and heroine together causes a new society to crystallize around the hero. . . .

The appearance of this new society is frequently signalized by some kind of party or festive ritual, which either appears at the end of the play or is assumed to take place immediately afterward.[3]

Northrop Frye, the critic cited here, has also identified most of the other conventional elements of comedy. He argues that the form appeals most directly to the young men and women in the audience, who identify with the hero and heroine precisely because these protagonists are unindividualized representatives of youth in whom each member of the audience can find his or her own traits. The antagonist who blocks the hero's wishes is either a father or a father-figure and is often made ridiculous by the exaggeration of a single character trait. Molière's Tartuffe and Orgon are typical blocking figures, just as Mariane and Valère are the nondescript protagonists. The plot itself usually overflows with complications that place all of the characters in ticklish situations, and these complications are often resolved by an unexpected twist in the plot, such as the miraculous intervention of the king at the end of *Tartuffe*. At the beginning of *Tartuffe*, hypocrisy dominates the play's society, but by the end a more sensible and honest social structure has emerged that will be celebrated through the marriage of Valère and Mariane.

When the main sources of humor in a play are the ludicrous complications of love, the play is called a *romantic comedy*. When the emphasis is on the ridiculous foibles or characteristics of the blocking figures, it is called a *comedy of humours*. (This term derives from the medieval physiological theory of the "four humours," four identifiable elements believed to determine and control individual temperament and personality; an imbalance was thought to result in a lopsided, eccentric personality who became a natural object for comic treatment.) When the play makes fun of the affectations, manners, and conventions of human behavior, it is called a *comedy of manners*. And when it achieves its effects through buffoonery, horseplay, and crude jokes, it is called a *farce*.

Minute subcategories such as those defined in the preceding paragraph can be compounded almost indefinitely by considering that broad middle ground between tragedy and comedy. The players who performed before the court in *Hamlet* were supposed to be capable of acting "tragedy, comedy, history, pastoral, pastoral-comical, historical-pastoral, tragical-historical, tragical-comical-historical-pastoral, scene individable, or poem unlimited." Shakespeare's mockery of such generic hair splitting is implicit in the exaggerations of the list and in his satire of Polonius, who utters it. Contemporary drama criticism may have moved away from pastoral, historical, and the various hyphenated couplings, but it has developed a myriad of other terms to describe minor classifications of the tone and structure of drama. The most significant of these (*domestic tragedy, melodrama, naturalism, realism, revenge tragedy, thesis play*, etc.) are defined in the glossary appended to this text.

[3] Northrop Frye, *Anatomy of Criticism: Four Essays* (Princeton: Princeton University Press, 1957), p. 163.

13

❧❧❧❧❧❧❧

Analyzing and
Evaluating Drama

Although all plays differ from one another, at times radically, certain fundamental questions can be asked of virtually every play as an aid in identifying
and understanding its major features. As noted in our discussion of drama,
plays inevitably share many elements with both fiction and poetry; as a result,
a number of the questions that follow assume a general familiarity with the
two earlier sections of this book.

QUESTIONS TO ASK AND ANSWER

Plot

1. Describe the plot in terms of its *exposition, complication, crisis, falling action,*
   and *conclusion.* Is the plot unified? Do the individual acts and scenes seem
   logically related to each other? Are there any scenes that seem to be unnecessary?
2. What is the essential problem or conflict on which the plot turns? Where
   does the turning point seem to occur? How is the plot resolved? Does
   the resolution seem to be an appropriate and satisfactory one?
3. Compare the end of the play with its beginning. What are the major changes
   that have taken place?
4. Describe the function of each act and scene. Do certain scenes seem to
   be linked in some way in order to contrast with or reinforce one another?
   Do any of the scenes seem to present a microcosm, condensation, or metaphor of the play as a whole?
5. In what ways does the opening act or scene serve the purpose of exposition,
   and how is this exposition achieved? What important events have taken

place before the play opens? In what ways does the exposition serve to introduce or *foreshadow* the major problems or conflicts of the plot?

6. Does the play contain one or more *subplots?* If so, what is their relationship to the main plot of the play? Are they, for example, intended to reinforce, contrast, or parody the main action?

Character

1. Who is the *protagonist* of the play, and who is the *antagonist?*
2. What is the function of the play's other major characters? What is their relationship to the protagonist and antagonist and to each other?
3. What is the function of the play's minor characters? Is their role mainly one of exposition or interpretation, or are they used as *foils* to oppose, contrast, or caricature certain of the major characters?
4. What methods does the playwright employ to establish and reveal the characters?
5. Are the actions of the characters properly motivated, consistent, and plausible?
6. Do any of the characters serve *symbolic* or *allegorical* functions?
7. To what extent does the playwright rely on the reader's or audience's prior knowledge of one or more of the characters? (Remember that many of the major figures of Greek tragedy were well known in advance to their audiences.)

Dialogue

1. Is the dialogue written in *high style, low style,* or some combination of the two?
2. How does the dialogue of the characters differ? How do such differences serve as an aid in characterization?
3. What stylistic devices contribute most to the play's dialogue? (Consider, for example, the use the playwright makes of patterns of poetic rhythm and sound, repetition, puns or word play, comparison, allusion, imagery, irony, symbolism, etc.)
4. Does the playwright make use of certain key words or phrases that gain a cumulative effect and added significance through repetition in a succession of contexts?

Setting

1. What is the play's setting in time and space?
2. To what extent does the setting functionally serve to aid in characterization, establish and sustain atmosphere, and/or influence plot?
3. What is the relationship of the setting to the play's action? Does it serve to reinforce the action, or is the relationship one of contrast?
4. Does the setting have symbolic overtones?

Theme

1. What is the play's theme or controlling idea?
2. How is the theme presented? Is it explicitly stated by one or more of the

characters or is it merely implied by the action? What specific passages of dialogue or action contribute most clearly to the revelation or presentation of theme? To what extent do such moments occur at or near the ends of acts or scenes as a way of building dramatic tension?
3. What is the value or significance of the play's theme? Is it topical or universal in its application?

Other Aspects of Drama

1. *Title.* Consider the play's title. What clues does it provide, if any, in identifying the playwright's emphasis?
2. *Dramatic conventions.* To what extent does the playwright make use of such dramatic conventions as *asides, soliloquies,* a *chorus,* or the *three unities* of time, place, and action? What function or functions do these conventions serve? To what extent do these conventions reflect the kind of theater in which the play was originally staged?
3. *Actions and stage directions.* Identify the major physical actions of the play and explain their significance.
4. What help, if any, do the author's stage directions provide in helping the reader to understand the play?
5. *Classification.* Is the play a *tragedy,* a *comedy,* or some hybrid of two or more types? (Be prepared to explain your answer by making reference to the discussion in the text.)
6. *Audience appeal.* To what extent is the appeal of the play topical (that is, to what extent does it contain certain elements that reflect the manners, customs, attitudes, and beliefs of the society for which it was originally written)? To what extent is its appeal permanent and universal?

Evaluating the Whole

1. How well do you think the playwright has managed to achieve a total integration of his or her materials?
2. What is *your* reaction to the play? Do you like the play? If so, why? If not, why not?

14

Plays

Sophocles *c. 496–406* B.C.

SOPHOCLES' KING OEDIPUS

Translated by William Butler Yeats

PERSONS IN THE PLAY

OEDIPUS, *King of Thebes* TIRESIAS, *a seer*
JOCASTA, *wife of Oedipus* A PRIEST
ANTIGONE, *daughter of Oedipus* MESSENGERS
ISMENE, *daughter of Oedipus* A HERDSMAN
CREON, *brother-in-law of Oedipus*
CHORUS

SCENE

The Palace of King Oedipus at Thebes

OEDIPUS. Children, descendants of old Cadmus,[1] why do you come before
me, why do you carry the branches of suppliants, while the city smokes
with incense and murmurs with prayer and lamentation? I would not learn
from any mouth but yours, old man, therefore I question you myself. Do
you know of anything that I can do and have not done? How can I, being

---

[1] Cadmus was the legendary founder of ancient Thebes, a city located about 30 miles northwest
of Athens, Greece.

the man I am, being King Oedipus, do other than all I know? I were indeed hard of heart did I not pity such suppliants.

PRIEST. Oedipus, King of my country, we who stand before your door are of all ages, some too young to have walked so many miles, some—priests of Zeus such as I—too old. Among us stand the pick of the young men, and behind in the market-places the people throng, carrying suppliant branches.[2] We all stand here because the city stumbles towards death, hardly able to raise up its head. A blight has fallen upon the fruitful blossoms of the land, a blight upon flock and field and upon the bed of marriage—plague ravages the city. Oedipus, King, not God but foremost of living men, seeing that when you first came to this town of Thebes you freed us from that harsh singer, the riddling Sphinx,[3] we beseech you, all we suppliants, to find some help; whether you find it by your power as a man, or because, being near the Gods, a God has whispered you. Uplift our State; think upon your fame; your coming brought us luck, be lucky to us still; remember that it is better to rule over men than over a waste place, since neither walled town nor ship is anything if it be empty and no man within it.

OEDIPUS. My unhappy children! I know well what need has brought you, what suffering you endure; yet, sufferers though you be, there is not a single one whose suffering is as mine—each mourns himself, but my soul mourns the city, myself, and you. It is not therefore as if you came to arouse a sleeping man. No! Be certain that I have wept many tears and searched hither and thither for some remedy. I have already done the only thing that came into my head for all my search. I have sent the son of Menoeceus, Creon, my own wife's brother, to the Pythian House of Phoebus,[4] to hear if deed or word of mine may yet deliver this town. I am troubled, for he is a long time away—a longer time than should be—but when he comes I shall not be an honest man unless I do whatever the God commands.

PRIEST. You have spoken at the right time. They have just signalled to us that Creon has arrived.

OEDIPUS. O King Apollo, may he bring brighter fortune, for his face is shining!

PRIEST. He brings good news, for he is crowned with bay.

OEDIPUS. We shall know soon. Brother-in-law, Menoeceus' son, what news from the God?

CREON. Good news; for pain turns to pleasure when we have set the crooked straight.

OEDIPUS. But what is the oracle?—so far the news is neither good nor bad.

CREON. If you would hear it with all these about you, I am ready to speak. Or do we go within?

OEDIPUS. Speak before all. The sorrow I endure is less for my own life than these.

CREON. Then, with your leave, I speak. Our lord Phoebus bids us drive out a defiling thing that has been cherished in this land.

---

[2] Before praying for help, the Greeks often laid laurel boughs at the temples of the gods.

[3] The Sphinx, a monster half female and half lion, terrorized Thebes by slaying every traveller who failed to solve her riddle: "What goes on four feet in the morning, two at noon, and three in the evening?" When Oedipus answered "Man" (who crawls in infancy, walks erect in maturity, and leans on a cane in senility), the Sphinx leaped in despair from the side of a cliff.

[4] The priests of Phoebus Apollo (the god of the Sun, prophecy, truth, poetry, and music) were reputed to see into the future, though often expressing their knowledge in ambiguous quotations or riddles. Their golden house was called "Pythian" in honor of Apollo's victory over the serpent Python.

OEDIPUS. By what purification?[5]

CREON. King Laius was our King before you came to pilot us.

OEDIPUS. I know—but not of my own knowledge, for I never saw him.

CREON. He was killed; and the God now bids us revenge it on his murderers, whoever they be.

OEDIPUS. Where shall we come upon their track after all these years? Did he meet his death in house or field, at home or in some foreign land?

CREON. In a foreign land: he was journeying to Delphi.

OEDIPUS. Did no fellow-traveller see the deed? Was there none there who could be questioned?

CREON. All perished but one man who fled in terror and could tell for certain but one thing of all he had seen.

OEDIPUS. One thing might be a clue to many things.

CREON. He said that they were fallen upon by a great troop of robbers.

OEDIPUS. What robbers would be so daring unless bribed from here?

CREON. Such things were indeed guessed at, but Laius once dead no avenger arose. We were amid our troubles.

OEDIPUS. But when royalty had fallen what troubles could have hindered search?

CREON. The riddling Sphinx put those dark things out of our thoughts—we thought of what had come to our own doors.

OEDIPUS. But I will start afresh and make the dark things plain. In doing right by Laius I protect myself, for whoever slew Laius might turn a hand against me. Come, my children, rise up from the altar steps; lift up these suppliant boughs and let all the children of Cadmus be called thither that I may search out everything and find for all happiness or misery as God wills.

PRIEST. May Phoebus, sender of the oracle, come with it and be our saviour and deliverer!

The CHORUS *enter.*

Chorus

What message comes to famous Thebes from the Golden House?
What message of disaster from that sweet-throated Zeus?
What monstrous thing our fathers saw do the seasons bring?
Or what that no man ever saw, what new monstrous thing?
Trembling in every limb I raise my loud importunate cry,
And in a sacred terror wait the Delian God's[6] reply.

Apollo chase the God of Death that leads no shouting men,
Bears no rattling shield and yet consumes this form with pain.

---

[5] In drafting this modernized version of the play, Yeats, who was himself a playwright of considerable reputation, frequently omitted portions of the original text that he found either redundant or dramatically inadvisable. Here, and in subsequent footnotes we have supplied the most significant of the omitted passages using the translation by Richard C. Jebb consulted by Yeats himself. Thus, Jebb's translation continues:

> CREON. By banishing a man, or by bloodshed in quittance of bloodshed, since it is that blood which brings the tempest on our city.
> OEDIPUS. And who is the man whose fate he thus reveals?

[6] Apollo was supposedly born on Delos, an island about 90 miles east-southeast of Athens.

Famine takes what the plague spares, and all the crops are lost;
No new life fills the empty place—ghost flits after ghost
To that God-trodden western shore, as flit benighted birds.
Sorrow speaks to sorrow, but no comfort finds in words.

Hurry him from the land of Thebes with a fair wind behind
Out on to that formless deep where not a man can find
Hold for an anchor-fluke, for all is world-enfolding sea;
Master of the thunder-cloud, set the lightning free,
And add the thunder-stone to that and fling them on his head,
For death is all the fashion now, till even Death be dead.

We call against the pallid face of this God-hated God
The springing heel of Artemis[7] in the hunting sandal shod,
The tousle-headed Maenads,[8] blown torch and drunken sound,
The stately Lysian king[9] himself with golden fillet crowned,
And in his hands the golden bow and the stretched golden string,
And Bacchus' wine-ensanguined face that all the Maenads sing.

OEDIPUS. You are praying, and it may be that your prayer will be answered;
that if you hear my words and do my bidding you may find help out of all
your trouble. This is my proclamation, children of Cadmus. Whoever among
you knows by what man Laius, son of Labdacus, was killed, must tell all
he knows. If he fear for himself and being guilty denounce himself, he shall
be in the less danger, suffering no worse thing than banishment. If on the
other hand there be one that knows that a foreigner did the deed, let him
speak, and I shall give him a reward and my thanks: but if any man keep
silent from fear or to screen a friend, hear all what I will do to that man.
No one in this land shall speak to him, nor offer sacrifice beside him; but
he shall be driven from their homes as if he himself had done the deed.
And in this I am the ally of the Pythian God and of the murdered man,
and I pray that the murderer's life may, should he be so hidden and screened,
drop from him and perish away, whoever he may be, whether he did the
deed with others or by himself alone:[10] and on you I lay it to make—so far
as man may—these words good, for my sake, and for the God's sake, and
for the sake of this land. And even if the God had not spurred us to it, it
were a wrong to leave the guilt unpurged, when one so noble, and he your
King, had perished; and all have sinned that could have searched it out
and did not: and now since it is I who hold the power which he held once,
and have his wife for wife—she who would have borne him heirs had he
but lived—I take up this cause even as I would were it that of my own
father. And if there be any who do not obey me in it, I pray that the Gods
send them neither harvest of the earth nor fruit of the womb; but let them
be wasted by his plague, or by one more dreadful still. But may all be blessed
for ever who hear my words and do my will!

[7] Artemis (or Diana) was a goddess associated with chastity, hunting, and the moon.
[8] The Maenads were female followers of Bacchus (or Dionysus), the god of wine and revelry.
[9] Apollo.
[10] Jebb's translation continues: "And for myself I pray that if, with my privity, he should become
an inmate of my house, I may suffer the same things which even now I called down upon
others."

CHORUS. We do not know the murderer, and it were indeed more fitting that Phoebus, who laid the task upon us, should name the man.

OEDIPUS. No man can make the Gods speak against their will.

CHORUS. Then I will say what seems the next best thing.

OEDIPUS. If there is a third course, show it.

CHORUS. I know that our lord Tiresias is the seer most like to our lord Phoebus, and through him we may unravel all.

OEDIPUS. So I was advised by Creon, and twice already have I sent to bring him.

CHORUS. If we lack his help we have nothing but vague and ancient rumours.

OEDIPUS. What rumours are they? I would examine every story.

CHORUS. Certain wayfarers were said to have killed the King.

OEDIPUS. I know, I know. But who was there that saw it?

CHORUS. If there is such a man, and terror can move him, he will not keep silence when they have told him of your curses.

OEDIPUS. He that such a deed did not terrify will not be terrified because of a word.

CHORUS. But there is one who shall convict him. For the blind prophet comes at last—in whom alone of all men the truth lives.

Enter TIRESIAS, *led by a boy.*

OEDIPUS. Tiresias, mast of all knowledge, whatever may be spoken, whatever is unspeakable, whatever omens of earth and sky reveal, the plague is among us, and from that plague, Great Prophet, protect us and save us. Phoebus in answer to our question says that it will not leave us till we have found the murderers of Laius, and driven them into exile or put them to death. Do you therefore neglect neither the voice of birds, nor any other sort of wisdom, but rescue yourself, rescue the State, rescue me, rescue all that are defiled by the deed. For we are in your hands, and what greater task falls to a man than to help other men with all he knows and has?

TIRESIAS. Aye, and what worse task than to be wise and suffer for it? I know this well; it slipped out of mind, or I would never have come.

OEDIPUS. What now?

TIRESIAS. Let me go home. You will bear your burden to the end more easily, and I bear mine—if you but give me leave for that.

OEDIPUS. Your words are strange and unkind to the State that bred you.

TIRESIAS. I see that you, on your part, keep your lips tight shut, and therefore I have shut mine that I may come to no misfortune.

OEDIPUS. For God's love do not turn away—if you have knowledge. We suppliants implore you on our knees.

TIRESIAS. You are fools—I will bring misfortune neither upon you nor upon myself.

OEDIPUS. What is this? You know all and will say nothing? You are minded to betray me and Thebes?

TIRESIAS. Why do you ask these things? You will not learn them from me.

OEDIPUS. What! Basest of the base! You would enrage the very stones. Will you never speak out? Cannot anything touch you?

TIRESIAS. The future will come of itself though I keep silent.

OEDIPUS. Then seeing that come it must, you had best speak out.

TIRESIAS. I will speak no further. Rage if you have a mind to; bring out all the fierceness that is in your heart.

OEDIPUS. That will I. I will not spare to speak my thoughts. Listen to what I have to say. It seems to me that you have helped to plot the deed; and, short of doing it with your own hands, have done the deed yourself. Had you eyesight I would declare that you alone had done it.

TIRESIAS. So that is what you say? I charge you to obey the decree that you yourself have made, and from this day out to speak neither to these nor to me. You are the defiler of this land.

OEDIPUS. So brazen in your impudence? How do you hope to escape punishment?

TIRESIAS. I have escaped; my strength is in my truth.

OEDIPUS. Who taught you this? You never got it by your art.

TIRESIAS. You, because you have spurred me to speech against my will.

OEDIPUS. What speech? Speak it again that I may learn it better.

TIRESIAS. You are but tempting me—you understood me well enough.

OEDIPUS. No; not so that I can say I know it; speak it again.

TIRESIAS. I say that you are yourself the murderer that you seek.

OEDIPUS. You shall rue it for having spoken twice such outrageous words.

TIRESIAS. Would you that I say more that you may be still angrier?

OEDIPUS. Say what you will. I will not let it move me.

TIRESIAS. I say that you are living with your next of kin in unimagined shame.

OEDIPUS. Do you think you can say such things and never smart for it?

TIRESIAS. Yes, if there be strength in truth.

OEDIPUS. There is; yes—for everyone but you. But not for you that are maimed in ear and in eye and in wit.

TIRESIAS. You are but a poor wretch flinging taunts that in a little while everyone shall fling at you.

OEDIPUS. Night, endless night has covered you up so that you can neither hurt me nor any man that looks upon the sun.

TIRESIAS. Your doom is not to fall by me. Apollo is enough: it is his business to work out your doom.

OEDIPUS. Was it Creon that planned this or you yourself?

TIRESIAS. Creon is not your enemy; you are your own enemy.

OEDIPUS. Power, ability, position, you bear all burdens, and yet what envy you create! Great must that envy be if envy of my power in this town—a power put into my hands unsought—has made trusty Creon, my old friend Creon, secretly long to take that power from me; if he has suborned this scheming juggler, this quack and trickster, this man with eyes for his gains and blindness in his art. Come, come, where did you prove yourself a seer? Why did you say nothing to set the townsmen free when the riddling Sphinx was here? Yet that riddle was not for the first-comer to read; it needed the skill of a seer. And none such had you! Neither found by help of birds, nor straight from any God. No, I came; I silenced her, I the ignorant Oedipus, it was I that found the answer in my mother-wit, untaught by any birds. And it is I that you would pluck out of my place, thinking to stand close to Creon's throne. But you and the plotter of all this shall mourn despite your zeal to purge the land. Were you not an old man, you had already learnt how bold you are and learnt it to your cost.

CHORUS. Both this man's words and yours, Oedipus, have been said in anger.

Such words cannot help us here, nor any but those that teach us to obey the oracle.

TIRESIAS. King though you are, the right to answer when attacked belongs to both alike. I am not subject to you, but to Loxias;[11] and therefore I shall never be Creon's subject. And I tell you, since you have taunted me with blindness, that though you have your sight, you cannot see in what misery you stand, nor where you are living, nor with whom, unknowing what you do—for you do not know the stock you come of—you have been your own kin's enemy be they living or be they dead. And one day a mother's curse and father's curse alike shall drive you from this land in dreadful haste with darkness upon those eyes.[12] Therefore, heap your scorn on Creon and on my message if you have a mind to; for no one of living men shall be crushed as you shall be crushed.

OEDIPUS. Begone this instant! Away, away! Get you from these doors!

TIRESIAS. I had never come but that you sent for me.

OEDIPUS. I did not know you were mad.

TIRESIAS. I may seem mad to you, but your parents thought me sane.

OEDIPUS. My parents! Stop! Who was my father?

TIRESIAS. This day shall you know your birth; and it will ruin you.

OEDIPUS. What dark words you always speak!

TIRESIAS. But are you not most skilful in the unravelling of dark words?

OEDIPUS. You mock me for that which made me great?

TIRESIAS. It was that fortune that undid you.

OEDIPUS. What do I care? For I delivered all this town.

TIRESIAS. Then I will go: boy, lead me out of this.

OEDIPUS. Yes, let him lead you. You take vexation with you.

TIRESIAS. I will go: but first I will do my errand. For frown though you may you cannot destroy me. The man for whom you look, the man you have been threatening in all the proclamations about the death of Laius, the man is here. He seems, so far as looks go, an alien; yet he shall be found a native Theban and shall nowise be glad of that fortune. A blind man, though now he has his sight; a beggar, though now he is most rich; he shall go forth feeling the ground before him with his stick;[13] so you go in and think on that, and if you find I am in fault say that I have no skill in prophecy. [TIRESIAS *is led out by the boy.* OEDIPUS *enters the palace.*]

Chorus

The Delphian rock has spoken out, now must a wicked mind,
Planner of things I dare not speak and of this bloody wrack,
Pray for feet that are as fast as the four hoofs of the wind:
Cloudy Parnassus[14] and the Fates thunder at his back.

---

[11] Another name for Apollo.

[12] Jebb's translation continues: "And what place shall not be harbour to thy shriek, what of all Cithaeron shall not ring with it soon when thou hast learnt the meaning of the nuptials in which, within that house, thou didst find a fatal haven, after a voyage so fair? And a throng of other ills thou guessest not, which shall make thee level with thy true self and with thine own brood."

[13] Jebb's tanslation continues: "And he shall be found at once brother and father of the children with whom he consorts; son and husband of the woman who bore him; heir to his father's bed, shedder of his father's blood."

[14] A mountain near Delphi, sacred to Apollo; hence, through metonymy, another name for Apollo himself.

That sacred crossing-place of lines upon Parnassus' head,
Lines that have run through North and South, and run through
    West and East,
That navel of the world[15] bids all men search the mountain wood,
The solitary cavern, till they have found that infamous beast.

CREON *enters from the house.*

CREON. Fellow-citizens, having heard that King Oedipus accuses me of dreadful things, I come in my indignation. Does he think that he has suffered wrong from me in these present troubles, or anything that could lead to wrong, whether in word or deed? How can I live under blame like that? What life would be worth having if by you here, and by my nearest friends, called a traitor through the town?
CHORUS. He said it in anger, and not from his heart out.
CREON. He said it was I put up the seer to speak those falsehoods.
CHORUS. Such things were said.
CREON. And had he his right mind saying it?
CHORUS. I do not know—I do not know what my masters do.

OEDIPUS *enters.*

OEDIPUS. What brought you here? Have you a face so brazen that you come to my house—you, the proved assassin of its master—the certain robber of my crown? Come, tell me in the face of the Gods what cowardice, or folly, did you discover in me that you plotted this? Did you think that I would not see what you were at till you had crept upon me, or seeing it would not ward it off? What madness to seek a throne, having neither friends nor followers!
CREON. Now, listen, hear my answer, and then you may with knowledge judge between us.
OEDIPUS. You are plausible, but waste words now that I know you.
CREON. Hear what I have to say. I can explain it all.
OEDIPUS. One thing you will not explain away—that you are my enemy.
CREON. You are a fool to imagine that senseless stubbornness sits well upon you.
OEDIPUS. And you to imagine that you can wrong a kinsman and escape the penalty.
CREON. That is justly said, I grant you; but what is this wrong that you complain of?
OEDIPUS. Did you advise, or not, that I should send for that notorious prophet?
CREON. And I am of the same mind still.
OEDIPUS. How long is it, then, since Laius—
CREON. What, what about him?
OEDIPUS. Since Laius was killed by an unknown hand?
CREON. That was many years ago.
OEDIPUS. Was this prophet at his trade in those days?
CREON. Yes; skilled as now and in equal honour.
OEDIPUS. Did he ever speak of me?

---

[15] The "navel of the world" and the "sacred crossing place of lines" is Delphi.

CREON. Never certainly when I was within earshot.

OEDIPUS. And did you enquire into the murder?

CREON. We did enquire but learnt nothing.

OEDIPUS. And why did he not tell out his story then?

CREON. I do not know. When I know nothing I say nothing.

OEDIPUS. This much at least you know and can say out.

CREON. What is that? If I know it I will say it.

OEDIPUS. That if he had not consulted you he would never have said that it was I who killed Laius.

CREON. You know best what he said; but now, question for question.

OEDIPUS. Question your fill—I cannot be proved guilty of that blood.

CREON. Answer me then. Are you not married to my sister?

OEDIPUS. That cannot be denied.

CREON. And do you not rule as she does? And with a like power?

OEDIPUS. I give her all she asks for.

CREON. And am not I the equal of you both?

OEDIPUS. Yes: and that is why you are so false a friend.

CREON. Not so; reason this out as I reason it, and first weigh this: who would prefer to lie awake amid terrors rather than to sleep in peace, granting that his power is equal in both cases? Neither I nor any sober-minded man. You give me what I ask and let me do what I want, but were I King I would have to do things I did not want to do. Is not influence and no trouble with it better than any throne, am I such a fool as to hunger after unprofitable honours? Now all are glad to see me, every one wishes me well, all that want a favour from you ask speech of me—finding in that their hope. Why should I give up these things and take those? No wise mind is treacherous. I am no contriver of plots, and if another took to them he would not come to me for help. And in proof of this go to the Pythian Oracle, and ask if I have truly told what the Gods said: and after that, if you have found that I have plotted with the Soothsayer, take me and kill me; not by the sentence of one mouth only—but of two mouths, yours and my own. But do not condemn me in a corner, upon some fancy and without proof. What right have you to declare a good man bad or a bad good? It is as bad a thing to cast off a true friend as it is for a man to cast away his own life—but you will learn these things with certainty when the time comes; for time alone shows a just man; though a day can show a knave.

CHORUS. King! He has spoken well, he gives himself time to think; a headlong talker does not know what he is saying.

OEDIPUS. The plotter is at his work, and I must counterplot headlong, or he will get his ends and I miss mine.

CREON. What will you do then? Drive me from the land?

OEDIPUS. Not so; I do not desire your banishment—but your death.

CREON. You are not sane.

OEDIPUS. I am sane at least in my own interest.

CREON. You should be in mine also.

OEDIPUS. No, for you are false.

CREON. But if you understand nothing?

OEDIPUS. Yet I must rule.

CREON. Not if you rule badly.

OEDIPUS. Hear him, O Thebes!

CREON. Thebes is for me also, not for you alone.

CHORUS. Cease, princes: I see Jocasta coming out of the house; she comes just in time to quench the quarrel.

JOCASTA *enters.*

JOCASTA. Unhappy men! Why have you made this crazy uproar? Are you not ashamed to quarrel about your own affairs when the whole country is in trouble? Go back into the palace, Oedipus, and you, Creon, to your own house. Stop making all this noise about some petty thing.

CREON. Your husband is about to kill me—or to drive me from the land of my fathers.

OEDIPUS. Yes: for I have convicted him of treachery against me.

CREON. Now may I perish accursed if I have done such a thing!

JOCASTA. For God's love believe it, Oedipus. First, for the sake of his oath, and then for my sake, and for the sake of these people here.

CHORUS [*all*]. King, do what she asks.

OEDIPUS. What would you have me do?

CHORUS. Not to make a dishonourable charge, with no more evidence than rumour, against a friend who has bound himself with an oath.

OEDIPUS. Do you desire my exile or my death?

CHORUS. No, by Helios,[16] by the first of all the Gods, may I die abandoned by Heaven and earth if I have that thought! What breaks my heart is that our public griefs should be increased by your quarrels.

OEDIPUS. Then let him go, though I am doomed thereby to death or to be thrust dishonoured from the land; it is your lips, not his, that move me to compassion; wherever he goes my hatred follows him.

CREON. You are as sullen in yielding as you were vehement in anger, but such natures are their own heaviest burden.

OEDIPUS. Why will you not leave me in peace and begone?

CREON. I will go away; what is your hatred to me? In the eyes of all here I am a just man. [*He goes.*]

CHORUS. Lady, why do you not take your man in to the house?

JOCASTA. I will do so when I have learned what has happened.

CHORUS. The half of it was blind suspicion bred of talk; the rest the wounds left by injustice.

JOCASTA. It was on both sides?

CHORUS. Yes.

JOCASTA. What was it?

CHORUS. Our land is vexed enough. Let the thing alone now that it is over. [*Exit leader of Chorus.*]

JOCASTA. In the name of the Gods, King, what put you in this anger?

OEDIPUS. I will tell you; for I honour you more than these men do. The cause is Creon and his plots against me.

JOCASTA. Speak on, if you can tell clearly how this quarrel arose.

OEDIPUS. He says that I am guilty of the blood of Laius.

JOCASTA. On his own knowledge, or on hearsay?

OEDIPUS. He has made a rascal of a seer his mouthpiece.

JOCASTA. Do not fear that there is truth in what he says. Listen to me, and

---

[16] Apollo.

learn to your comfort that nothing born of woman can know what is to come. I will give you proof of that. An oracle came to Laius once, I will not say from Phoebus, but from his ministers, that he was doomed to die by the hand of his own child sprung from him and me. When his child was but three days old, Laius bound its feet together and had it thrown by sure hands upon a trackless mountain; and when Laius was murdered at the place where three highways meet, it was, or so at least the rumour says, by foreign robbers. So Apollo did not bring it about that the child should kill its father, nor did Laius die in the dreadful way he feared by his child's hand. Yet that was how the message of the seers mapped out the future. Pay no attention to such things. What the God would show he will need no help to show it, but bring it to light himself.

OEDIPUS. What restlessness of soul, lady, has come upon me since I heard you speak, what a tumult of the mind!

JOCASTA. What is this new anxiety? What has startled you?

OEDIPUS. You said that Laius was killed where three highways meet.

JOCASTA. Yes: that was the story.

OEDIPUS. And where is the place?

JOCASTA. In Phocis where the road divides branching off to Delphi and to Daulia.

OEDIPUS. And when did it happen? How many years ago?

JOCASTA. News was published in this town just before you came into power.

OEDIPUS. O Zeus! What have you planned to do unto me?

JOCASTA. He was tall; the silver had just come into his hair; and in shape not greatly unlike to you.

OEDIPUS. Unhappy that I am! It seems that I have laid a dreadful curse upon myself, and did not know it.

JOCASTA. What do you say? I tremble when I look on you, my King.

OEDIPUS. And I have a misgiving that the seer can see indeed. But I will know it all more clearly, if you tell me one thing more.

JOCASTA. Indeed, though I tremble I will answer whatever you ask.

OEDIPUS. Had he but a small troop with him; or did he travel like a great man with many followers?

JOCASTA. There were but five in all—one of them a herald; and there was one carriage with Laius in it.

OEDIPUS. Alas! It is now clear indeed. Who was it brought the news, lady?

JOCASTA. A servant—the one survivor.

OEDIPUS. Is he by chance in the house now?

JOCASTA. No; for when he found you reigning instead of Laius he besought me, his hand clasped in mine, to send him to the fields among the cattle that he might be far from the sight of this town; and I sent him. He was a worthy man for a slave and might have asked a bigger thing.

OEDIPUS. I would have him return to us without delay.

JOCASTA. Oedipus, it is easy. But why do you ask this?

OEDIPUS. I fear that I have said too much, and therefore I would question him.

JOCASTA. He shall come, but I too have a right to know what lies so heavy upon your heart, my King.

OEDIPUS. Yes: and it shall not be kept from you now that my fear has grown so heavy. Nobody is more to me than you, nobody has the same right to learn my good or evil luck. My father was Polybus of Corinth, my mother *mad* the Dorian Merope, and I was held the foremost man in all that town until a thing happened—a thing to startle a man, though not to make him angry as it made me. We were sitting at the table, and a man who had drunk too much cried out that I was not my father's son—and I, though angry, restrained my anger for that day; but the next day went to my father and my mother and questioned them. They were indignant at the taunt and that comforted me—and yet the man's words rankled, for they had spread a rumour through the town. Without consulting my father or my mother I went to Delphi, but Phoebus told me nothing of the thing for which I came, but much of other things—things of sorrow and of terror: that I should *death of father* live in incest with my mother, and beget a brood that men would shudder to look upon; that I should be my father's murderer. Hearing those words I fled out of Corinth, and from that day have but known where it lies when I have found its direction by the stars. I sought where I might escape those infamous things—the doom that was laid upon me. I came in my flight to that very spot where you tell me this king perished. Now, lady, I will tell you the truth. When I had come close up to those three roads, I came upon a herald, and a man like him you have described seated in a carriage. The man who held the reins and the old man himself would not give me *Anger* room, but thought to force me from the path, and I struck the driver in my anger. The old man, seeing what I had done, waited till I was passing him and then struck me upon the head. I paid him back in full, for I knocked him out of the carriage with a blow of my stick. He rolled on his back, and after that I killed them all. If this stranger were indeed Laius, is there a more miserable man in the world than the man before you? Is there a man more hated of Heaven? No stranger, no citizen, may receive him into his house, not a soul may speak to him, and no mouth but my own mouth has laid this curse upon me. Am I not wretched? May I be swept from this world before I have endured this doom!

CHORUS. These things, O King, fill us with terror; yet hope till you speak with him that saw the deed, and have learnt all.

OEDIPUS. Till I have learnt all, I may hope. I await the man that is coming from the pastures.

JOCASTA. What is it that you hope to learn?

OEDIPUS. I will tell you. If his tale agrees with yours, then I am clear.

JOCASTA. What tale of mine?

OEDIPUS. He told you that Laius met his death from robbers; if he keeps to that tale now and speaks of several slayers, I am not the slayer. But if he says one lonely wayfarer, then beyond a doubt the scale dips to me.

JOCASTA. Be certain of this much at least, his first tale was of robbers. He cannot revoke that tale—the city heard it and not I alone. Yet, if he should somewhat change his story, King, at least he cannot make the murder of Laius square with prophecy; for Loxias plainly said of Laius that he would die by the hand of my child. That poor innocent did not kill him, for it died before him. Therefore from this out I would not, for all divination can do, so much as look to my right hand or to my left hand, or fear at all.

OEDIPUS. You have judged well; and yet for all that, send and bring this peasant to me.

JOCASTA. I will send without delay. I will do all that you would have of me— but let us come in to the house. [*They go in to the house.*]

Chorus

For this one thing above all I would be praised as a man,
That in my words and my deeds I have kept those laws in mind
Olympian Zeus, and that high clear Empyrean,[17]
Fashioned, and not some man or people of mankind,
Even those sacred laws nor age nor sleep can blind.

A man becomes a tyrant out of insolence,
He climbs and climbs, until all people call him great,
He seems upon the summit, and God flings him thence;
Yet an ambitious man may lift up a whole State,
And in his death be blessed, in his life fortunate.

And all men honour such; but should a man forget
The holy images, the Delphian Sibyl's trance,[18]
And the world's navel-stone, and not be punished for it
And seem most fortunate, or even blessed perchance,
Why should we honour the Gods, or join the sacred dance?

JOCASTA *enters from the palace.*

JOCASTA. It has come into my head, citizens of Thebes, to visit every altar of
the Gods, a wreath in my hand and a dish of incense. For all manner of
alarms trouble the soul of Oedipus, who instead of weighing new oracles
by old, like a man of sense, is at the mercy of every mouth that speaks
terror. Seeing that my words are nothing to him, I cry to you, Lysian Apollo,
whose altar is the first I meet: I come, a suppliant, bearing symbols of prayer;
O, make us clean, for now we are all afraid, seeing him afraid, even as
they who see the helmsman afraid.

Enter MESSENGER.

MESSENGER. May I learn from you, strangers, where is the home of King Oedi-
pus? Or better still, tell me where he himself is, if you know.
CHORUS. This is his house, and he himself, stranger, is within it, and this
lady is the mother of his children.
MESSENGER. Then I call a blessing upon her, seeing what man she has married.
JOCASTA. May God reward those words with a like blessing, stranger! But what
have you come to seek or to tell?
MESSENGER. Good news for your house, lady, and for your husband.
JOCASTA. What news? From whence have you come?
MESSENGER. From Corinth, and you will rejoice at the message I am about
to give you; yet, maybe, it will grieve you.
JOCASTA. What is it? How can it have this double power?
MESSENGER. The people of Corinth, they say, will take him for king.
JOCASTA. How then? Is old Polybus no longer on the throne?
MESSENGER. No. He is in his tomb.

---

[17] Zeus, the most powerful of the Greek gods, was said to live on Mt. Olympus, the highest mountain
in Greece. The Empyrean is the highest heaven.
[18] The Sibyl, a female soothsayer, fell into a trance while telling fortunes.

JOCASTA. What do you say? Is Polybus dead, old man?

MESSENGER. May I drop dead if it is not the truth.

JOCASTA. Away! Hurry to your master with this news. O oracle of the Gods, where are you now? This is the man whom Oedipus feared and shunned lest he should murder him, and now this man has died a natural death, and not by the hand of Oedipus.

Enter OEDIPUS.

OEDIPUS. Jocasta, dearest wife, why have you called me from the house?

JOCASTA. Listen to this man, and judge to what the oracles of the Gods have come.

OEDIPUS. And he—who may he be? And what news has he?

JOCASTA. He has come from Corinth to tell you that your father, Polybus, is dead.

OEDIPUS. How, stranger? Let me have it from your own mouth.

MESSENGER. If I am to tell the story, the first thing is that he is dead and gone.

OEDIPUS. By some sickness or by treachery?

MESSENGER. A little thing can bring the aged to their rest.

OEDIPUS. Ah! He died, it seems, from sickness?

MESSENGER. Yes; and of old age.

OEDIPUS. Alas! Alas! Why, indeed, my wife, should one look to that Pythian seer, or to the birds that scream above our heads? For they would have it that I was doomed to kill my father. And now he is dead—hid already beneath the earth. And here am I—who had no part in it, unless indeed he died from longing for me. If that were so, I may have caused his death; but Polybus has carried the oracles with him into Hades—the oracles as men have understood them—and they are worth nothing.

JOCASTA. Did I not tell you so, long since?

OEDIPUS. You did, but fear misled me.

JOCASTA. Put this trouble from you.[19]

OEDIPUS. Those bold words would sound better, were not my mother living. But as it is—I have some grounds for fear; yet you have said well.

JOCASTA. Yet your father's death is a sign that all is well.

OEDIPUS. I know that: but I fear because of her who lives.

MESSENGER. Who is this woman who makes you afraid?

OEDIPUS. Merope, old man, the wife of Polybus.

MESSENGER. What is there in her to make you afraid?

OEDIPUS. A dreadful oracle sent from Heaven, stranger.

MESSENGER. Is it a secret, or can you speak it out?

OEDIPUS. Loxias said that I was doomed to marry my own mother, and to shed my father's blood. For that reason I fled from my house in Corinth; and I did right, though there is great comfort in familiar faces.

MESSENGER. Was it indeed for that reason that you went into exile?

---

[19] Jebb's translation continues:

> OEDIPUS. But surely I must needs fear my mother's bed?
> JOCASTA. Nay, what should mortal fear, for whom the decrees of fortune are supreme, and who hath clear foresight of nothing? 'Tis best to live at random, as one may. But fear not thou touching wedlock with thy mother. Many men ere now have so fared in dreams also: but he to whom these things are as nought bears his life most easily.

OEDIPUS. I did not wish, old man, to shed my father's blood.

MESSENGER. King, have I not freed you from that fear?

OEDIPUS. You shall be fittingly rewarded.

MESSENGER. Indeed, to tell the truth, it was for that I came; to bring you home and be the better for it——

OEDIPUS. No! I will never go to my parents' home.

MESSENGER. Oh, my son, it is plain enough, you do not know what you do.

OEDIPUS. How, old man? For God's love, tell me.

MESSENGER. If for these reasons you shrink from going home.

OEDIPUS. I am afraid lest Phoebus has spoken true.

MESSENGER. You are afraid of being made guilty through Merope?

OEDIPUS. That is my constant fear.

MESSENGER. A vain fear.

OEDIPUS. How so, if I was born of that father and mother?

MESSENGER. Because they were nothing to you in blood.

OEDIPUS. What do you say? Was Polybus not my father?

MESSENGER. No more nor less than myself.

OEDIPUS. How can my father be no more to me than you who are nothing to me?

MESSENGER. He did not beget you any more than I.

OEDIPUS. No? Then why did he call me his son?

MESSENGER. He took you as a gift from these hands of mine.

OEDIPUS. How could he love so dearly what came from another's hands?

MESSENGER. He had been childless.

OEDIPUS. If I am not your son, where did you get me?

MESSENGER. In a wooded valley of Cithaeron.

OEDIPUS. What brought you wandering there?

MESSENGER. I was in charge of mountain sheep.

OEDIPUS. A shepherd—a wandering, hired man.

MESSENGER. A hired man who came just in time.

OEDIPUS. Just in time—had it come to that?

MESSENGER. Have not the cords left their marks upon your ankles?

OEDIPUS. Yes, that is an old trouble.

MESSENGER. I took your feet out of the spancel.[20]

OEDIPUS. I have had those marks from the cradle.

MESSENGER. They have given you the name you bear.[21]

OEDIPUS. Tell me, for God's sake, was that deed my mother's or my father's?

MESSENGER. I do not know—he who gave you to me knows more of that than I.

OEDIPUS. What? You had me from another? You did not chance on me yourself?

MESSENGER. No. Another shepherd gave you to me.

OEDIPUS. Who was he? Can you tell me who he was?

MESSENGER. I think that he was said to be of Laius' household.

OEDIPUS. The king who ruled this country long ago?

MESSENGER. The same—the man was herdsman in his service.

OEDIPUS. Is he alive, that I might speak with him?

MESSENGER. You people of this country should know that.

OEDIPUS. Is there any one here present who knows the herd he speaks of?

---

[20] A noose for tethering animals.   [21] Oedipus means "swollen-feet."

Any one who has seen him in the town pastures? The hour has come when all must be made clear.

CHORUS. I think he is the very herd you sent for but now; Jocasta can tell you better than I.

JOCASTA. Why ask about that man? Why think about him? Why waste a thought on what this man has said? What he has said is of no account.

OEDIPUS. What, with a clue like that in my hands and fail to find out my birth?

JOCASTA. For God's sake, if you set any value upon your life, give up this search—my misery is enough.

OEDIPUS. Though I be proved the son of a slave, yes, even of three generations of slaves, you cannot be made base-born.

JOCASTA. Yet, hear me, I implore you. Give up this search.

OEDIPUS. I will not hear of anything but searching the whole thing out.

JOCASTA. I am only thinking of your good—I have advised you for the best.

OEDIPUS. Your advice makes me impatient.

JOCASTA. May you never come to know who you are, unhappy man!

OEDIPUS. Go, some one, bring the herdsman here—and let that woman glory in her noble blood.

JOCASTA. Alas, alas, miserable man! Miserable! That is all that I can call you now or for ever. [*She goes out.*]

CHORUS. Why has the lady gone, Oedipus, in such a transport of despair? Out of this silence will burst a storm of sorrows.

OEDIPUS. Let come what will. However lowly my origin I will discover it. That woman, with all a woman's pride, grows red with shame at my base birth. I think myself the child of Good Luck, and that the years are my foster-brothers. Sometimes they have set me up, and sometimes thrown me down, but he that has Good Luck for mother can suffer no dishonour. That is my origin, nothing can change it, so why should I renounce this search into my birth?

Chorus

> Oedipus' nurse, mountain of many a hidden glen,
> Be honoured among men;
> A famous man, deep-thoughted, and his body strong;
> Be honoured in dance and song.
> Who met in the hidden glen? Who let his fancy run
> Upon nymph of Helicon?[22]
> Lord Pan or Lord Apollo or the mountain Lord
> By the Bacchantes adored?

OEDIPUS. If I, who have never met the man, may venture to say so, I think that the herdsman we await approaches; his venerable age matches with this stranger's, and I recognize as servants of mine those who bring him. But you, if you have seen the man before, will know the man better than I.

---

[22] The Chorus speculates that perhaps Oedipus's mother was a Greek nymph seduced by Pan (a playful god of the fields and forests), or Apollo, or Dionysus (the god of wine and revelry, worshipped by his female followers, the Bacchantes).

CHORUS. Yes, I know the man who is coming; he was indeed in Laius' service, and is still the most trusted of the herdsmen.

OEDIPUS. I ask you first, Corinthian stranger, is this the man you mean?

MESSENGER. He is the very man.

OEDIPUS. Look at me, old man! Answer my questions. Were you once in Laius' service?

HERDSMAN. I was: not a bought slave, but reared up in the house.

OEDIPUS. What was your work—your manner of life?

HERDSMAN. For the best part of my life I have tended flocks.

OEDIPUS. Where, mainly?

HERDSMAN. Cithaeron or its neighbourhood.

OEDIPUS. Do you remember meeting with this man there?

HERDSMAN. What man do you mean?

OEDIPUS. This man. Did you ever meet him?

HERDSMAN. I cannot recall him to mind.

MESSENGER. No wonder in that, master; but I will bring back his memory. He and I lived side by side upon Cithaeron. I had but one flock and he had two. Three full half-years we lived there, from spring to autumn, and every winter I drove my flock to my own fold, while he drove his to the fold of Laius. Is that right? Was it not so?

HERDSMAN. True enough; though it was long ago.

MESSENGER. Come, tell me now—do you remember giving me a boy to rear as my own foster-son?

HERDSMAN. What are you saying? Why do you ask me that?

MESSENGER. Look at that man, my friend, he is the child you gave me.

HERDSMAN. A plague upon you! Cannot you hold your tongue?

OEDIPUS. Do not blame him, old man; your own words are more blameable.

HERDSMAN. And how have I offended, master?

OEDIPUS. In not telling of that boy he asks of.

HERDSMAN. He speaks from ignorance, and does not know what he is saying.

OEDIPUS. If you will not speak with a good grace you shall be made to speak.

HERDSMAN. Do not hurt me for the love of God, I am an old man.

OEDIPUS. Some one there, tie his hands behind his back.

HERDSMAN. Alas! Wherefore! What more would you learn?

OEDIPUS. Did you give this man the child he speaks of?

HERDSMAN. I did: would I had died that day!

OEDIPUS. Well, you may come to that unless you speak the truth.

HERDSMAN. Much more am I lost if I speak it.

OEDIPUS. What! Would the fellow make more delay?

HERDSMAN. No, no. I said before that I gave it to him.

OEDIPUS. Where did you come by it? Your own child, or another?

HERDSMAN. It was not my own child—I had it from another.

OEDIPUS. From any of those here? From what house?

HERDSMAN. Do not ask any more, master; for the love of God do not ask.

OEDIPUS. You are lost if I have to question you again.

HERDSMAN. It was a child from the house of Laius.

OEDIPUS. A slave? Or one of his own race?

HERDSMAN. Alas! I am on the edge of dreadful words.

OEDIPUS. And I of hearing: yet hear I must.

HERDSMAN. It was said to have been his own child. But your lady within can tell you of these things best.

OEDIPUS. How? It was she who gave it to you?

HERDSMAN. Yes, King.

OEDIPUS. To what end?

HERDSMAN. That I should make away with it.

OEDIPUS. Her own child?

HERDSMAN. Yes: from fear of evil prophecies.

OEDIPUS. What prophecies?

HERDSMAN. That he should kill his father.

OEDIPUS. Why, then, did you give him up to this old man?

HERDSMAN. Through pity, master, believing that he would carry him to whatever land he had himself come from—but he saved him for dreadful misery; for if you are what this man says, you are the most miserable of all men.

OEDIPUS. O! O! All brought to pass! All truth! Now, O light, may I look my last upon you, having been found accursed in bloodshed, accursed in marriage, and in my coming into the world accursed! [*He rushes into the palace.*]

Chorus

What can the shadow-like generations of man attain
But build up a dazzling mockery of delight that under their touch
    dissolves again?
Oedipus seemed blessed, but there is no man blessed amongst men.

Oedipus overcame the woman-breasted Fate;[23]
He seemed like a strong tower against Death and first among the
    fortunate;
He sat upon the ancient throne of Thebes, and all men called him
    great.

But, looking for a marriage-bed, he found the bed of his birth,
Tilled the field his father had tilled, cast seed into the same abound-
    ing earth;
Entered through the door that had sent him wailing forth.

Begetter and begot as one! How could that be hid?
What darkness cover up that marriage-bed? Time watches, he is
    eagle-eyed,
And all the works of man are known and every soul is tried.

Would you had never come to Thebes, nor to this house,
Nor riddled with the woman-breasted Fate, beaten off Death and
    succoured us,
That I had never raised this song, heartbroken Oedipus!

SECOND MESSENGER [*coming from the house*]. Friends and kinsmen of this house! What deeds must you look upon, what burden of sorrow bear, if true to race you still love the House of Labdacus. For not Ister nor Phasis[24] could wash this house clean, so many misfortunes have been brought upon it, so many has it brought upon itself, and those misfortunes are always the worst that a man brings upon himself.

---

[23] I.e., the Sphinx, whose riddle Oedipus solved.   [24] Two large rivers.

CHORUS. Great already are the misfortunes of this house, and you bring us a new tale.

SECOND MESSENGER. A short tale in the telling: Jocasta, our Queen, is dead.

CHORUS. Alas, miserable woman, how did she die?

SECOND MESSENGER. By her own hand. It cannot be as terrible to you as to one that saw it with his eyes, yet so far as words can serve, you shall see it. When she had come into the vestibule, she ran half crazed towards her marriage-bed, clutching at her hair with the fingers of both hands, and once within the chamber dashed the doors together behind her. Then called upon the name of Laius, long since dead, remembering that son who killed the father and upon the mother begot an accursed race. And wailed because of that marriage wherein she had borne a two-fold race—husband by husband, children by her child. Then Oedipus with a shriek burst in and running here and there asked for a sword, asked where he would find the wife that was no wife but a mother who had borne his children and himself. Nobody answered him, we all stood dumb; but supernatural power helped him, for, with a dreadful shriek, as though beckoned, he sprang at the double doors, drove them in, burst the bolts out of their sockets, and ran into the room. There we saw the woman hanging in a swinging halter, and with a terrible cry he loosened the halter from her neck. When that unhappiest woman lay stretched upon the ground, we saw another dreadful sight. He dragged the golden brooches from her dress and lifting them struck them upon his eyeballs, crying out, 'You have looked enough upon those you ought never to have looked upon, failed long enough to know those that you should have known; henceforth you shall be dark.' He struck his eyes, not once, but many times, lifting his hands and speaking such or like words. The blood poured down and not with a few slow drops, but all at once over his beard in a dark shower as it were hail. [*The* CHORUS *wails and he steps further on to the stage.*] Such evils have come forth from the deeds of those two and fallen not on one alone but upon husband and wife. They inherited much happiness, much good fortune; but to-day, ruin, shame, death, and loud crying, all evils that can be counted up, all, all are theirs.

CHORUS. Is he any quieter?

SECOND MESSENGER. He cries for someone to unbar the gates and to show to all the men of Thebes his father's murderer, his mother's—the unholy word must not be spoken. It is his purpose to cast himself out of the land that he may not bring all this house under his curse. But he has not the strength to do it. He must be supported and led away. The curtain is parting; you are going to look upon a sight which even those who shudder must pity.

Enter OEDIPUS.

OEDIPUS. Woe, woe is me! Miserable, miserable that I am! Where am I? Where am I going? Where am I cast away? Who hears my words?

CHORUS. Cast away indeed, dreadful to the sight of the eye, dreadful to the ear.

OEDIPUS. Ah, friend, the only friend left to me, friend still faithful to the blind man! I know that you are there; blind though I am, I recognise your voice.

CHORUS. Where did you get the courage to put out your eyes? What unearthly power drove you to that?

OEDIPUS. Apollo, friends, Apollo, but it was my own hand alone, wretched that I am, that quenched these eyes.

CHORUS. You were better dead than blind.

OEDIPUS. No, it is better to be blind. What sight is there that could give me joy? How could I have looked into the face of my father when I came among the dead, aye, or on my miserable mother, since against them both I sinned such things that no halter can punish? And what to me this spectacle, town, statue, wall, and what to me this people, since I, thrice wretched, I, noblest of Theban men, have doomed myself to banishment, doomed myself when I commanded all to thrust out the unclean thing?

CHORUS. It had indeed been better if that herdsman had never taken your feet out of the spancel or brought you back to life.

OEDIPUS. O three roads, O secret glen; O coppice²⁵ and narrow way where three roads met; you that drank up the blood I spilt, the blood that was my own, my father's blood: remember what deeds I wrought for you to look upon, and then, when I had come hither, the new deeds that I wrought. O marriage-bed that gave me birth and after that gave children to your child, creating an incestuous kindred of fathers, brothers, sons, wives, and mothers. Yes, all the shame and the uncleanness that I have wrought among men.

CHORUS. For all my pity I shudder and turn away.

OEDIPUS. Come near, condescend to lay your hands upon a wretched man; listen, do not fear. My plague can touch no man but me. Hide me somewhere out of this land for God's sake, or kill me, or throw me into the sea where you shall never look upon me more.

Enter CREON *and attendants.*

CHORUS. Here Creon comes at a fit moment; you can ask of him what you will, help or counsel, for he is now in your place. He is King.

OEDIPUS. What can I say to him? What can I claim, having been altogether unjust to him.

CREON. I have not come in mockery, Oedipus, nor to reproach you. Lead him in to the house as quickly as you can. Do not let him display his misery before strangers.

OEDIPUS. I must obey, but first, since you have come in so noble a spirit, you will hear me.

CREON. Say what you will.

OEDIPUS. I know that you will give her that lies within such a tomb as befits your own blood, but there is something more, Creon. My sons are men and can take care of themselves, but my daughters, my two unhappy daughters, that have ever eaten at my own table and shared my food, watch over my daughters, Creon. If it is lawful, let me touch them with my hands. Grant it, Prince, grant it, noble heart. I would believe, could I touch them, that I still saw them. [ISMENE *and* ANTIGONE *are led in by attendants.*] But do I hear them sobbing? Has Creon pitied me and sent my children, my darlings? Has he done this?

CREON. Yes, I ordered it, for I know how greatly you have always loved them.

OEDIPUS. Then may you be blessed, and may Heaven be kinder to you than

²⁵ A thicket of small trees.

it has been to me! My children, where are you? Come hither—hither—come
to the hands of him whose mother was your mother; the hands that put
out your father's eyes, eyes once as bright as your own; his who, understanding nothing, seeing nothing, became your father by her that bore him. I
weep when I think of the bitter life that men will make you live, and the
days that are to come. Into what company dare you go, to what festival,
but that you shall return home from it not sharing in the joys, but bathed
in tears? When you are old enough to be married, what man dare face the
reproach that must cling to you and to your children? What misery is there
lacking? Your father killed his father, he begat you at the spring of his own
being, offspring of her that bore him. That is the taunt that would be cast
upon you and on the man that you should marry. That man is not alive;
my children, you must wither away in barrenness. Ah, son of Menoeceus,[26]
listen. Seeing that you are the only father now left to them, for we their
parents are lost, both of us lost, do not let them wander in beggary—are
they not your own kindred?—do not let them sink down into my misery.
No, pity them, seeing them utterly wretched in helpless childhood if you
do not protect them. Show me that you promise, generous man, by touching
me with your hand. [CREON *touches him.*] My children, there is much advice
that I would give you were you but old enough to understand, but all I
can do now is bid you pray that you may live wherever you are let live,
and that your life be happier than your father's.

CREON. Enough of tears. Pass into the house.

OEDIPUS. I will obey, though upon conditions.

CREON. Conditions?

OEDIPUS. Banish me from this country. I know that nothing can destroy me,
for I wait some incredible fate; yet cast me upon Cithaeron, chosen by my
father and my mother for my tomb.

CREON. Only the Gods can say yes or no to that.

OEDIPUS. No, for I am hateful to the Gods.

CREON. If that be so you will get your wish the quicker. They will banish
that which they hate.

OEDIPUS. Are you certain of that?

CREON. I would not say it if I did not mean it.

OEDIPUS. Then it is time to lead me within.

CREON. Come, but let your children go.

OEDIPUS. No, do not take them from me.

CREON. Do not seek to be master; you won the mastery but could not keep
it to the end. [*He leads Oedipus into the palace, followed by Ismene, Antigone, and
attendants.*]

Chorus

Make way for Oedipus. All people said,
"That is a fortunate man";
And now what storms are beating on his head!
"That is a fortunate man,"
Call no man fortunate that is not dead.
The dead are free from pain.

THE END

[C. 429 B.C.]

---

[26] Creon.

Aristophanes *c. 450–385* B.C.

LYSISTRATA

Translated by Douglass Parker

CHARACTERS OF THE PLAY

LYSISTRATA ⎫
KLEONIKE ⎬ *Athenian women*
MYRRHINE ⎭
LAMPITO, *a Spartan woman*
ISMENIA, *a Boiotian girl*
KORINTHIAN GIRL
POLICEWOMAN
KORYPHAIOS OF THE MEN
CHORUS OF OLD MEN *of Athens*
KORYPHAIOS OF THE WOMEN
CHORUS OF OLD WOMEN *of Athens*
COMMISSIONER OF PUBLIC SAFETY

FOUR POLICEMEN
KINESIAS, *Myrrhine's husband*
CHILD *of Kinesias and Myrrhine*
SLAVE
SPARTAN HERALD
SPARTAN AMBASSADOR
FLUTE-PLAYER
ATHENIAN WOMEN
PELOPONNESIAN WOMEN
PELOPONNESIAN MEN
ATHENIAN MEN

SCENE

A street in Athens. In the background, the Akropolis; center, its gateway, the Propylaia. The time is early morning. LYSISTRATA *is discovered alone, pacing back and forth in furious impatience.*

LYSISTRATA.
  Women!
Announce a debauch in honor of Bacchos,
a spree for Pan,[1] some footling fertility fieldday,
and traffic stops—the streets are absolutely clogged
with frantic females banging on tambourines. No urging
for an orgy!
        But *today*—there's not one woman here.
[*Enter* KLEONIKE].
Correction: one. Here comes my next door neighbor.
—Hello, Kleonike.
KLEONIKE.
        Hello to *you*, Lysistrata.
—But what's the fuss? Don't look so barbarous, baby;
knitted brows just aren't your style.
LYSISTRATA.
          It doesn't
matter, Kleonike—I'm on fire right down to the bone.
I'm positively ashamed to be a woman—a member
of a sex which can't even live up to male slanders!

---

[1] Bacchos (or Bacchus) is the Greek god of wine and revelry. Pan, the god of the fields and forests, is usually depicted as a lecherous satyr with the head and torso of a man but the horns and shaggy hindquarters of a goat.

To hear our husbands talk, we're *sly:* deceitful,
always plotting, monsters of intrigue. . . .
KLEONIKE. *Proudly.*]

                                                 That's us!
LYSISTRATA.
And so we agreed to meet today and plot
an intrigue that really deserves the name of monstrous . . .
and WHERE are the women?

                                Slyly asleep at home—
they won't get up for anything!
KLEONIKE.

                                Relax, honey.
They'll be here. You know a woman's way is hard—
mainly the way out of the house: fuss over hubby,
wake the maid up, put the baby down, bathe him,
feed him . . .
LYSISTRATA.

                     Trivia. They have more fundamental busi-
ness to engage in.
KLEONIKE.

                  Incidentally, Lysistrata, just why are
you calling this meeting? Nothing teeny, I trust?
LYSISTRATA.
Immense.
KLEONIKE.

               Hmmm. And pressing?
LYSISTRATA.

                        Unthinkably tense.
KLEONIKE.
Then where IS everybody?
LYSISTRATA.

                     Nothing like that. If it were,
we'd already be in session. Seconding motions.
—No, *this* came to hand some time ago. I've spent
my nights kneading it, mulling it, filing it down. . . .
KLEONIKE.
Too bad. There can't be very much left.
LYSISTRATA.

                        Only this:
the hope and salvation of Hellas lies with the WOMEN!
KLEONIKE.
Lies with the women? Now *there's* a last resort.
LYSISTRATA.
It lies with us to decide affairs of state
and foreign policy.

                The Spartan Question:[2] Peace
or Extirpation?

---

[2] "The Spartan Question" is a reference to the Peloponnesian War (431–404 B.C.) which was
dominating Athenian life at the time this play was written (411 B.C.). The war was fought between
Sparta and Athens, the most powerful of the city-states in Greece (also called Hellas). The
various women in the play gather from all parts of Greece and represent the contending factions
and their allies.

KLEONIKE.
> How *fun!*
>> I cast an Aye for Extirpation

LYSISTRATA.
The Utter Annihilation of every last Boiotian?

KLEONIKE.
AYE!—I mean Nay. Clemency, please, for those
scrumptious eels.[3]

LYSISTRATA.
> And as for Athens . . . I'd rather not put
the thought into words. Just fill in the blanks, if you will.
—To the point: if we can meet and reach agreement
here and now with the girls from Thebes and the Peloponnese,
we'll form an alliance and save the States of Greece!

KLEONIKE.
Us? Be practical. Wisdom from women? There's nothing
cosmic about cosmetics—and Glamor is our only talent.
All we can do is *sit,* primped and painted,
made up and dressed up,

[*Getting carried away in spite of her argument.*]
> ravishing in saffron wrappers,
peekaboo peignoirs, exquisite negligees, those chic,
expensive little slippers that come from the East . . .

LYSISTRATA.
Exactly. You've hit it. I see our way to salvation
in just such ornamentation—in slippers and slips, rouge
and perfumes, negligees and decolletage. . . .

KLEONIKE.
> How so?

LYSISTRATA.
So effectively that not one husband will take up his spear
against another . . .

KLEONIKE.
> Peachy!
>> I'll have that kimono

dyed . . .

LYSISTRATA.
> . . . or shoulder his shield . . .

KLEONIKE.
> . . . squeeze into that

daring negligee . . .

LYSISTRATA.
> . . . or unsheathe his sword!

KLEONIKE.
> . . . and buy those

slippers!

LYSISTRATA.
Well, now. Don't you think the girls should be here?

KLEONIKE.
Be here? Ages ago—they should have flown! [*She stops.*]

---

[3] Eels from Lake Kopais in Boiotia were considered a delicacy.

But no. You'll find out. These are authentic Athenians:
no matter what they do, they do it late.

LYSISTRATA.

But what about the out-of-town delegations? There isn't
a woman here from the Shore; none from Salamis . . .

KLEONIKE.

That's quite a trip. They usually get on board
at sunup. Probably riding at anchor now.

LYSISTRATA.

I thought the girls from Acharnai would be here first.
I'm especially counting on them. And they're not here.

KLEONIKE.

I think Theogenes' wife is under way.
When I went by, she was hoisting her sandals . . . [*Looking off right.*]
                                                                        But look!

Some of the girls are coming!

Women enter from the right. LYSISTRATA *looks off to the left
where more—a ragged lot—are straggling in.*

LYSISTRATA.

                              And more over here!

KLEONIKE.

Where did you find *that* group?

LYSISTRATA.

                              They're from the outskirts.

KLEONIKE.

Well, that's something. If you haven't done anything
else, you've really ruffled up the outskirts.

MYRRHINE *enters guiltily from the right.*

MYRRHINE.

                                        Oh, Lysistrata,
we aren't late, are we?
                    Well, *are* we?
                              Speak to me!

LYSISTRATA.

What is it, Myrrhine? Do you want a medal for tardiness?
Honestly, such behavior, with so much at stake . . .

MYRRHINE.

I'm sorry. I couldn't find my girdle in the dark.
And anyway, we're here now. So tell us all about it,
whatever it is.

KLEONIKE.

                    No, wait a minute. Don't
begin just yet. Let's wait for those girls from Thebes
and the Peloponnese.

LYSISTRATA.

                    Now *there* speaks the proper attitude.

[LAMPITO, *a strapping Spartan woman, enters left, leading
a pretty Boiotian girl* (ISMENIA) *and a huge, steatopygous*[4]
Korinthian.]

    And here's our lovely Spartan.

                                    He*lo*, Lampito
dear. Why darling, you're simply ravishing! Such
a blemishless complexion—so clean, so out-of-doors!
And will you look at that figure—the pink of perfection!

KLEONIKE.
    I'll bet you could strangle a bull.

LAMPITO.
                              I calklate so.
Hit's fitness whut done it, fitness and dancin'. You know
the step?
[*Demonstrating.*]
                Foot it out back'ards an' toe yore twitchet. [*The women crowd around
            Lampito.*]

KLEONIKE.
    What unbelievably beautiful bosoms!

LAMPITO.
                        Shuckins,
whut fer you tweedlin' me up so? I feel like a heifer
come fair-time.

LYSISTRATA. [*Turning to Ismenia.*]
                And who is this young lady here?

LAMPITO.
    Her kin's purt-near the bluebloodiest folk in Thebes—
the First Fam'lies of Boiotia.

LYSISTRATA. [*As they inspect Ismenia.*]
                  Ah, picturesque Boiotia:
her verdant meadows, her fruited plain . . .

KLEONIKE. [*Peering more closely.*]
                        Her sunken
garden where no grass grows. A cultivated country.

LYSISTRATA. [*Gaping at the gawking Korinthian.*]
    And who is *this*—er—little thing?

LAMPITO.
                  She hails
from over by Korinth, but her kinfolk's quality—mighty
big back there.

KLEONIKE. [*On her tour of inspection.*]
                She's mighty big back *here.*

LAMPITO.
    The womenfolk's all assemblied. Who-all's notion
was this-hyer confabulation?

LYSISTRATA.
                Mine.

LAMPITO.
                Git on with the give-out.

---

[4] Big-buttocked.

I'm hankerin' to hear.

MYRRHINE.

                          Me, too! I can't imagine
what could be so important. Tell us about it!

LYSISTRATA.

    Right away.

                    —But first, a question. It's not
an involved one. Answer yes or no. [*A pause.*]

MYRRHINE.

                              Well, ASK it!

LYSISTRATA.

It concerns the fathers of your children—your husbands,
    absent on active service. I know you all have men
    abroad.

                —Wouldn't you like to have them home?

KLEONIKE.

    My husband's been gone for the last five months! Way up
    to Thrace, watchdogging military waste. It's horrible!

MYRRHINE.

    Mine's been posted to Pylos for seven whole months!

LAMPITO.

    My man's no sooner rotated out of the line
    than he's plugged back in. Hain't no discharge in this war!

KLEONIKE.

    And lovers can't be had for love or money,
    not even synthetics. Why, since those beastly Milesians
    revolted and cut off the leather trade, that handy
    do-it-yourself kit's *vanished* from the open market!

LYSISTRATA.

    If I can devise a scheme for ending the war,
    I gather I have your support?

KLEONIKE.

                            You can count on me!
    If you need money, I'll pawn the shift off my back—[*Aside.*] and drink up
    the cash before the sun goes down.

MYRRHINE.

    Me, too! I'm ready to split myself right up
    the middle like a mackerel, and give you half!

LAMPITO.

    Me, too! I'd climb Taygetos Mountain plumb
    to the top to git the leastes' peek at Peace!

LYSISTRATA.

    Very well, I'll tell you. No reason to keep a secret. [*Importantly, as the women
    cluster around her.*]
    We can force our husbands to negotiate Peace,
    Ladies, by exercising steadfast Self-Control—
    By Total Abstinence . . . [*A pause.*]

KLEONIKE.

                          From WHAT?

MYRRHINE.

                                          Yes, what?

LYSISTRATA.

You'll do it?

KLEONIKE.

Of course we'll do it! We'd even *die!*

LYSISTRATA.

Very well,

then here's the program:

Total Abstinence

from SEX! [*The cluster of women dissolves.*]

—Why are you turning away? Where are you going? [*Moving among the women.*]
—What's this? Such stricken expressions! Such gloomy gestures!
—Why so pale?

—Whence these tears?

—What IS this?

Will you do it or won't you?

Cat got your tongue?

KLEONIKE.

Afraid I can't make it. Sorry.

On with the War!

MYRRHINE.

Me neither. Sorry.

On with the War!

LYSISTRATA.

This from

my little mackerel? The girl who was ready, a minute
ago, to split herself right up the middle?

KLEONIKE. [*Breaking in between Lysistrata and Myrrhine.*]
Try something else. Try anything. If you say so,
I'm willing to walk through fire barefoot.

But not

to give up SEX—there's nothing like it, Lysistrata!

LYSISTRATA. [*To Myrrhine.*]
And you?

MYRRHINE.

Me, too! I'll walk through fire.

LYSISTRATA.

Women!

Utter sluts, the entire sex! Will-power,
nil. We're perfect raw material for Tragedy,
the stuff of heroic lays. "Go to bed with a god
and then get rid of the baby"—that sums us up! [*Turning to Lampito.*]
—Oh, Spartan, be a dear. If *you* stick by me,
just you, we still may have a chance to win.
Give me your vote.

LAMPITO.

Hit's right onsettlin' fer gals

to sleep all lonely-like, withouten no humpin'.
But I'm on yore side. We shore need Peace, too.

LYSISTRATA.

You're a darling—the only woman here
worthy of the name!

KLEONIKE.

Well, just suppose we *did,*
as much as possible, abstain from . . . what you said,
you know—not that we *would*—could something like
that bring Peace any sooner?

LYSISTRATA.

Certainly. Here's how it works:
We'll paint, powder, and pluck ourselves to the last
detail, and stay inside, wearing those filmy
tunics that set off everything we *have*—

and then
slink up to the men. They'll snap to attention, go
absolutely *mad* to love us—

but we won't let them. We'll Abstain.
—I imagine they'll conclude a treaty rather quickly.

LAMPITO. [*Nodding.*]
Menelaos he tuck one squint at Helen's bubbies
all nekkid, and plumb throwed up. [*Pause for thought.*]

Throwed up his sword.

KLEONIKE.
Suppose the men just leave us flat?

LYSISTRATA.

In that case,
we'll have to take things into our own hands.

KLEONIKE.
There simply isn't any reasonable facsimile!
—Suppose they take us by force and drag us off
to the bedroom against our wills?

LYSISTRATA.

Hang on to the door.

KLEONIKE.
Suppose they beat us?

LYSISTRATA.

Give in——but be bad sports.
Be nasty about it—they don't enjoy these forced
affairs. So make them suffer.

Don't worry; they'll stop
soon enough. A married man wants harmony—
cooperation, not rape.

KLEONIKE.

Well, I suppose so. . . .
[*Looking from Lysistrata to Lampito.*]
If *both* of you approve this, then so do we.

LAMPITO.
Hain't worried over our menfolk none. We'll bring 'em
round to makin' a fair, straightfor'ard Peace
withouten no nonsense about it. But take this rackety
passel in Athens: I misdoubt no one could make 'em
give over thet blabber of theirn.

LYSISTRATA.

They're our concern.
Don't worry. We'll bring them around.

LAMPITO.
                                        Not likely.
Not long as they got ships kin still sail straight,
an' thet fountain of money up thar in Athene's temple.[5]
LYSISTRATA.
That point is quite well covered:
                                        We're taking over
The Akropolis, including Athene's temple, today.
It's set: Our oldest women have their orders.
They're up there now, pretending to sacrifice, waiting
for us to reach an agreement. As soon as we do,
they seize the Akropolis.
LAMPITO.
                                The way you put them thengs,
I swear I can't see how we kin possibly lose!
LYSISTRATA.
Well, now that it's settled, Lampito, let's not lose
any time. Let's take the Oath to make this binding.
LAMPITO.
Just trot out thet-thar Oath. We'll swear it.
LYSISTRATA.
                                                Excellent.
—Where's a policewoman? [*A huge girl, dressed as a Skythian archer (the Athenian
police) with bow and circular shield, lumbers up and gawks.*]
                                        —What are *you* looking for?
[*Pointing to a spot in front of* the women.] Put your shield down here.
[*The girl obeys.*]
                No, hollow *up!* [*The girl reverses the shield. Lysistrata looks about
                brightly.*]
—Someone give me the entrails. [*A dubious silence.*]
KLEONIKE.
                                Lysistrata, what kind
of an Oath are we supposed to swear?
LYSISTRATA.
                                        The Standard.
Aischylos[6] used it in a play, they say—the one where
you slaughter a sheep and swear on a shield.
KLEONIKE.
                                        Lysistrata,
you *do not* swear an Oath for *Peace* on a *shield!*
LYSISTRATA.
What Oath do you want? [*Exasperated.*]
                                Something bizarre and expensive?
A fancier victim—"Take one white horse and
disembowel"?
KLEONIKE.
White horse: The symbolism's too obscure.

---

[5] The Athenians kept a reserve fund of one thousand silver coins in the back of Athene's temple,
located on a hill called the Akropolis.
[6] Aeschylus (525–456 B.C.) was the earliest of the great Greek playwrights.

LYSISTRATA.

                                                        Then how
do we swear this oath?
KLEONIKE.

                                                   Oh, *I* can tell you
that, if you'll let me.
                              First, we put an enormous
black cup right here—hollow up, of course.
Next, into the cup we slaughter a jar of Thasian
wine, and swear a mighty Oath that we won't . . .
dilute it with water.
LAMPITO. [*To Kleonike.*]
                              Let me corngratulate you—
that were the beatenes' Oath I ever heerd on!
LYSISTRATA. [*Calling inside.*] Bring out a cup and a jug of wine!
[*Two women emerge, the first staggering under the weight of a huge black cup, the
second even more burdened with a tremendous wine jar. Kleonike addresses them.*]
KLEONIKE.

                                                        You darlings!
What a tremendous display of pottery! [*Fingering the cup.*]
                              A girl
could get a glow just *holding* a cup like this! [*She grabs it away from the first
woman, who exits.*]
LYSISTRATA. [*Taking the wine jar from the second serving woman (who exits), she barks
at Kleonike.*] Put that down and help me butcher this boar! [*Kleonike puts
down the cup, over which she and Lysistrata together hold the jar of wine (the "boar").
Lysistrata prays.*]
                              O Mistress Persuasion,
                              O Cup of Devotion,
                              Attend our invocation:
                              Accept this oblation,
                              Grant our petition,
                              Favor our mission.
[*Lysistrata and Kleonike tip up the jar and pour the gurgling wine into the cup. Myrrhine,
Lampito, and the others watch closely.*]
MYRRHINE.
Such an attractive shade of blood. And the spurt—
pure Art!
LAMPITO.
                 Hit shore do smell mighty purty!
[*Lysistrata and Kleonike put down the empty wine jar.*]
KLEONIKE.
Girls, let me be the first [*Launching herself at the cup.*] to take the Oath!
LYSISTRATA. [*Hauling Kleonike back.*]
You'll have to wait your turn like everyone else.
—Lampito, how do we manage with this mob?
                                                   Cumbersome.
—Everyone place her right hand on the cup. [*The women surround the cup
and obey.*]
I need a spokeswoman. One of you to take
the Oath in behalf of the rest. [*The women edge away from Kleonike, who reluctantly
finds herself elected.*]

                    The rite will conclude
with a General Pledge of Assent by all of you, thus
confirming the Oath. Understood? [*Nods from the women. Lysistrata addresses Kleonike.*]

                              Repeat after me:

LYSISTRATA.
  I will withhold all rights of access or entrance
KLEONIKE.
  I will withhold all rights of access or entrance
LYSISTRATA.
  From every husband, lover, or casual acquaintance
KLEONIKE.
  from every husband, lover, or casual acquaintance
LYSISTRATA.
  Who moves in my direction in erection.

                                        —Go on

KLEONIKE.
  who m-moves in my direction in erection.

                                        Ohhhhh!
  —Lysistrata, my knees are shaky. Maybe I'd better . . .
LYSISTRATA.
  I will create, imperforate in cloistered chastity,
KLEONIKE.
  I will create, imperforate in cloistered chastity,
LYSISTRATA.
  A newer, more glamorous, supremely seductive me
KLEONIKE.
  a newer, more glamorous, supremely seductive me
LYSISTRATA.
  And fire my husband's desire with my molten allure—
KLEONIKE.
  and fire my husband's desire with my molten allure—
LYSISTRATA.
  But remain, to his panting advances, icily pure.
KLEONIKE.
  but remain, to his panting advances, icily pure.
LYSISTRATA.
  If he should force me to share the connubial couch,
KLEONIKE.
  If he should force me to share the connubial couch,
LYSISTRATA.
  I refuse to return his stroke with the teeniest twitch.
KLEONIKE.
  I refuse to return his stroke with the teeniest twitch.
LYSISTRATA.
  I will not lift my slippers to touch the thatch
KLEONIKE.
  I will not lift my slippers to touch the thatch
LYSISTRATA.
  Or submit sloping prone in a hangdog crouch.
KLEONIKE.
  or submit sloping prone in a hangdog crouch.

LYSISTRATA.

If I this oath maintain,
may I drink this glorious wine.

KLEONIKE.

If I this oath maintain,
may I drink this glorious wine.

LYSISTRATA.

But if I slip or falter,
let me drink water.

KLEONIKE.

But if I slip or falter,
let me drink water.

LYSISTRATA.

—And now the General Pledge of Assent:

WOMEN.

                                                          A-MEN!

LYSISTRATA.

Good. I'll dedicate the oblation. [*She drinks deeply.*]

KLEONIKE.

                                        Not too much,
darling. You know how anxious we are to become
allies and friends.
                        Not to mention *staying* friends.

[*She pushes Lysistrata away and drinks. As the women take their turns at the cup,*
loud cries and alarums are heard offstage.]

LAMPITO.

What-all's that bodacious ruckus?

LYSISTRATA.

                                        Just what I told you:
It means the women have taken the Akropolis. Athene's
Citadel is ours!
                        It's time for you to go,
Lampito, and set your affairs in order in Sparta. [*Indicating the other women*
in Lampito's group.]
Leave these girls here as hostages.
[*Lampito exits left. Lysistrata turns to the others.*]
                                        Let's hurry inside
the Akropolis and help the others shoot the bolts.

KLEONIKE.

Don't you think the men will send reinforcements
against us as soon as they can?

LYSISTRATA.

                                        So where's the worry?
The men can't burn their way in or frighten us out.
The Gates are ours—they're proof against fire and fear—
and they open only on our conditions.

KLEONIKE.

                                        Yes!
That's the spirit—let's deserve our reputations: [*As the women hurry off into*
the Akropolis.]

UP THE SLUTS!
WAY FOR THE OLD IMPREGNABLES!

The door shuts behind the women, and the stage is empty. A pause, and the CHORUS
OF MEN *shuffles on from the left in two groups, led by their* KORYPHAIOS.[7] *They are
incredibly aged Athenians; though they may acquire spryness later in the play, at this
point they are sheer decrepitude. Their normally shaky progress is impeded by their burdens:
each man not only staggers under a load of wood across his shoulders, but has his hands
full as well—in one, an earthen pot containing fire (which is in constant danger of going
out); in the other, a dried vinewood torch, not yet lit. Their progress toward the Akropolis
is very slow.*

KORYPHAIOS OF MEN. [*To the right guide of the First Semichorus, who is stumbling
along in mild agony.*]
   Forward, Swifty, keep 'em in step! Forget your shoulder.
   I know these logs are green and heavy—but duty, boy, duty!
SWIFTY. [*Somewhat inspired, he quavers into slow song to set a pace for his group.*]
         I'm never surprised. At my age, life
         is just one damned thing after another.
         And yet, I never thought my wife
         was anything more than a home-grown bother.
            But now, dadblast her,
            she's a National Disaster!
FIRST SEMICHORUS OF MEN.

         What a catastrophe—
            MATRIARCHY!
         They've brought Athene's statue[8] to heel,
         they've put the Akropolis under a seal,
         they've copped the whole damned commonweal . . .
         What is there left for them to steal?
KORYPHAIOS OF MEN. [*To the right guide of the Second Semichorus—a slower soul, if
possible, than Swifty.*]
   Now, Chipper, speed's the word. The Akropolis, on the double!
   Once we're there, we'll pile these logs around them, and convene
   a circuit court for a truncated trial. Strictly impartial:
   With a show of hands, we'll light a spark of justice under
   every woman who brewed this scheme. We'll burn them all
   on the first ballot—and the first to go is Ly . . .
[*Pause for thought.*]
                                                       is Ly . . .

[*Remembering and pointing at a spot in the audience.*]
   is Lykon's wife—and there she is, right over there![9]
CHIPPER. [*Taking up the song again.*]
         I won't be twitted, I won't be guyed,
         I'll teach these women not to trouble us!

---

[7] A term for the leader of the chorus.
[8] A wooden statue thought of as the guardian of the city.
[9] "Rhodia, wife of the demagogue Lykon, was a real person, frequently lampooned for her morality.
In a not unusual breaking of the dramatic illusion, her name occurs here as a surprise for the
expected 'Lysistrata.' " (Translator's note.)

Kleomenes the Spartan tried
expropriating our Akropolis[10]
some time ago—
ninety-five years or so—
SECOND SEMICHORUS OF MEN.
but he suffered damaging losses
when he ran across US!
He breathed defiance—and more as well:
No bath for six years—you could tell.
We fished him out of the Citadel
and quelled his spirit—but not his smell.
KORYPHAIOS OF MEN.
That's how I took him. A savage siege:
Seventeen ranks
of shields were massed at that gate, with blanket infantry cover.
I slept like a baby.
So when mere women (who gall the gods
and make Euripides[11] sick) try the same trick, should I
sit idly by?
Then demolish the monument I won at Marathon![12]
FIRST SEMICHORUS OF MEN. [*Singly.*]
—The last lap of our journey!
—I greet it with some dismay.
—The danger doesn't deter me,
—but
it's uphill
—all the way.
—Please, somebody,
—find a jackass
to drag these logs
to the top.
—I ache to join the fracas,
—but
my shoulder's aching
—to stop.
SWIFTY.
Backward there's no turning.
Upward and onward, men!
And keep those firepots burning, or
we make this trip again.
CHORUS OF MEN. [*Blowing into their firepots, which promptly send forth clouds of smoke.*]
With a puff (pfffff). . . .
and a cough (hhhhhh). . . .
The smoke! I'll choke! Turn it off!

---

[10] "Kleomenes' occupation of the Akropolis in 508, high point of his unsuccessful bid to help
establish the Athenian aristocrats, lasted rather less than the six years which the Chorus seems
to remember. The actual time was two days." (Translator's note.)
[11] A Greek playwright (c. 480–407 B.C.).
[12] The site of a famous Greek victory over the Persians in 490 B.C.

SECOND SEMICHORUS OF MEN. [*Singly.*]
      —Damned embers.
               —Should be muzzled.
      —There oughta be a law.
      —They jumped me
               —when I whistled
                        —and then
they gnawed my eyeballs
                   —raw.
      —There's lava in my lashes.
      —My lids are oxidized.
      —My brows are braised.
               —These ashes are
volcanoes
          —in disguise.

CHIPPER.
        This way, men. And remember,
        The Goddess needs our aid.
        So don't be stopped by cinders. Let's
        press on to the stockade!

CHORUS OF MEN. [*Blowing again into their firepots, which erupt as before.*]
        With a huff (hfffff). . . .
        and a chuff (chffff). . . .
        Drat that smoke. Enough is enough!

KORYPHAIOS OF MEN. [*Signalling the Chorus, which has now tottered into position before the Akropolis gate, to stop, and peering into his firepot.*]
Praise be to the gods, it's awake. There's fire in the old fire yet.
—Now the directions. See how they strike you:
                      First, we deposit
these logs at the entrance and light our torches. Next, we crash
the gate. When that doesn't work, we request admission. Politely.
When *that* doesn't work, we burn the damned door down, and smoke
these women into submission,
                That seem acceptable? Good.
Down with the load . . . ouch, that smoke! Sonofabitch!
[*A horrible tangle results as the Chorus attempts to deposit the logs. The Koryphaios turns to the audience.*]
Is there a general in the house? We have a logistical
problem. . . .
[*No answer. He shrugs.*] Same old story. Still at loggerheads over in Samos.[13]
[*With great confusion, the logs are placed somehow.*] That's better. The pressure's
off. I've got my backbone back. [*To his firepot.*]
What, pot? You forgot your part in the plot?
                    Urge that smudge.
to be hot on the dot and scorch my torch.
                  Got it, pot?

---

[13] After the annihilation of the Athenian forces sent to the island of Sicily in 415 B.C., most of the remaining generals were sent to Samos (a Greek island off Asia Minor) in an effort to shore up the allegiance and prepare an attack against those city states that had defected to Sparta.

[*Praying.*]

> Queen Athene, let these strumpets
> crumple before our attack.
> Grant us victory, male supremacy . . .
> and a testimonial plaque.

The men plunge their torches into firepots and arrange themselves purposefully before the gate. Engaged in their preparations, they do not see the sudden entrance, from the right, of the CHORUS OF WOMEN, *led by their* KORYPHAIOS. *These wear long cloaks and carry pitchers of water. They are very old—though not so old as the men—but quite spry. In their turn, they do not perceive the* CHORUS OF MEN.

KORYPHAIOS OF WOMEN. [*Stopping suddenly.*]
  What's this—soot? And smoke as well? I may be all wet,
  but this might mean fire. Things look dark, girls; we'll
  have to dash. [*They move ahead, at a considerably faster pace than the men.*]
FIRST SEMICHORUS OF WOMEN.
[*Singly.*]

Speed! Celerity!	Save our sorority
from arson. Combustion.	And heat exhaustion.
Don't let our sisterhood	shrivel to blisterhood.
Fanned into slag by hoary typhoons.	
By flatulent, nasty, gusty baboons.	
We're late! Run!	
The girls might be done	

[*Tutte.*[14]]

Filling my pitcher	was absolute torture:
The fountains in town	are so *crowded* at dawn,
glutted with masses	of the lower classes
blatting and battering,	shoving, and shattering
jugs. But I juggled	my burden, and wriggled
away to extinguish	the igneous anguish
of neighbor, and sister, and daughter—	
Here's Water!	

SECOND SEMICHORUS OF WOMEN.
[*Singly.*]

Get wind of the news?	The gaffers are loose.
The blowhards are off	with fuel enough
to furnish a bathhouse.	But the finish is pathos:
They're scaling the heights with a horrid proposal.	
They're threatening women with rubbish disposal!	
How ghastly—how gauche![15]	
burned up with the trash!	

[*Tutte.*]

Preserve me, Athene,	from gazing on any
matron or maid	auto-da-fé'd.[16]
Cover with grace	these redeemers of Greece
from battles, insanity,	Man's inhumanity.
Gold-browed goddess,	hither to aid us!

---

[14] All together.   [15] Awkward, graceless.   [16] Burned at the stake.

    Fight as our ally,   join in our sally
        against pyromaniac slaughter—
            Haul Water!
Koryphaios of Women. [*Noticing for the first time the Chorus of Men, still busy at
    their firepots, she cuts off a member of her Chorus who seems about to continue the
    song.*]
    Hold it. What have we here? You don't catch true-blue
    patriots red-handed. These are authentic degenerates,
    male, taken *in flagrante.*[17]
Koryphaios of Men.
            Oops. Female troops. This could be upsetting.
    I didn't expect such a flood of reserves.
Koryphaios of Women.
                            Merely a spearhead.
    If our numbers stun you, watch that yellow streak
    spread. We represent just one percent of one percent of
    This Woman's Army.
Koryphaios of Men.
    Never been confronted with such backtalk. Can't allow
    it. Somebody pick up a log and pulverize that brass.
                            Any volunteers?
[*There are none among the male chorus.*]
Koryphaios of Women.
    Put down the pitchers, girls. If they start waving that lumber,
    we don't want to be encumbered.
Koryphaios of Men.
                Look, men, a few sharp jabs
    will stop that jawing. It never fails.
                        The poet Hipponax
    swears by it.[18] [*Still no volunteers. The Koryphaios of Women advances.*]
Koryphaios of Women.
            Then step right up. Have a jab at me.
    Free shot.
Koryphaios of Men. [*Advancing reluctantly to meet her.*]
            Shut up! I'll peel your pelt. I'll pit your pod.
Koryphaios of Women.
    The name is Stratyllis. I dare you to lay one finger on me.
Koryphaios of Men.
    I'll lay on you with a fistful. Er—any specific threats?
Koryphaios of Women. [*Earnestly.*]
    I'll crop your lungs and reap your bowels, bite by bite,
    and leave no balls on the body for other bitches to
    gnaw.
Koryphaios of Men. [*Retreating hurriedly.*]
    Can't beat Euripides for insight. And I quote:
                            *No creature's found
    so lost to shame as Woman.*
                    Talk about realist playwrights!

---

[17] In the act.
[18] The Greek refers to Boupalos, a sculptor, who was frequently mocked by Hipponax: e.g., "Hold
    my clothes; I'll sock Boupalos in the jaw."

KORYPHAIOS OF WOMEN.
Up with the water, ladies. Pitchers at the ready, place!
KORYPHAIOS OF MEN.
Why the water, you sink of iniquity? More sedition?
KORYPHAIOS OF WOMEN.
Why the fire, you walking boneyard? Self-cremation?
KORYPHAIOS OF MEN.
I brought this fire to ignite a pyre and fricassee your
friends.
KORYPHAIOS OF WOMEN.
I brought this water to douse your pyre. Tit for tat.
KORYPHAIOS OF MEN.
You'll douse my fire? Nonsense!
KORYPHAIOS OF WOMEN.
       You'll see, when the facts soak in.
KORYPHAIOS OF MEN.
I have the torch right here. Perhaps I should barbecue
you.
KORYPHAIOS OF WOMEN.
If you have any soap, I could give you a bath.
KORYPHAIOS OF MEN.
         A bath from those
polluted hands?
KORYPHAIOS OF WOMEN.
    Pure enough for a blushing young bridegroom.
KORYPHAIOS OF MEN.
Enough of that insolent lip.
KORYPHAIOS OF WOMEN.
      It's merely freedom of speech.
KORYPHAIOS OF MEN.
I'll stop that screeching!
KORYPHAIOS OF WOMEN.
     You're helpless outside the jury-box.
KORYPHAIOS OF MEN. [*Urging his men, torches at the ready, into a charge.*]
Burn, fire, burn!
KORYPHAIOS OF WOMEN. [*As the women empty their pitchers over the men.*]
   And cauldron bubble.
KORYPHAIOS OF MEN. [*Like his troops, soaked and routed.*]
       Arrgh!
KORYPHAIOS OF WOMEN.
         Goodness.
What seems to be the trouble? Too hot?
KORYPHAIOS OF MEN.
        Hot, hell! Stop it!
What do you think you're doing?
KORYPHAIOS OF WOMEN.
     If you must know, I'm gardening.
Perhaps you'll bloom.
KORYPHAIOS OF MEN.
     Perhaps I'll fall right off the vine!
I'm withered, frozen, shaking . . .

KORYPHAIOS OF WOMEN.
                    Of course. But, providentially,
you brought along your smudgepot.
                    The sap should rise eventually.
[*Shivering, the Chorus of Men retreats in utter defeat.*]

A COMMISSIONER *of Public Safety enters from the left, followed quite reluctantly by a squad of police—four Skythian archers. He surveys the situation with disapproval.*

COMMISSIONER.
    Fire, eh? Females again—spontaneous combustion
    of lust. Suspected as much.
                    Rubadubdubbing, incessant
    incontinent keening for wine, damnable funeral
    foofaraw for Adonis resounding from roof to roof—
    heard it all before . . .[19] [*Savagely, as the Koryphaios of Men tries to interpose a remark.*]
                    and WHERE?
                    The ASSEMBLY!
    Recall, if you can, the debate on the Sicilian Question:
    That bullbrained demagogue Demostratos (who will rot, I trust)
    rose to propose a naval task force.
                    His wife,
    writhing with religion on a handy roof, bleated
    a dirge:
            "BEREFT! OH WOE OH WOE FOR ADONIS!"
    And so of course Demostratos, taking his cue,
    outblatted her:
            "A DRAFT! ENROLL THE WHOLE OF
        ZAKYNTHOS!"
    His wife, a smidgin stewed, renewed her yowling:
    "OH GNASH YOUR TEETH AND BEAT YOUR
    BREASTS FOR ADONIS!"
    And so of course Demostratos (that god-detested blot,
    that foul-lunged son of an ulcer) gnashed tooth and nail
    and voice, and bashed and rammed his program through.
    And THERE is the Gift of Women:
                    MORAL CHAOS!

KORYPHAIOS OF MEN.
    Save your breath for actual felonies, Commissioner;
    see what's happened to us! Insolence, insults,
    these we pass over, but not lèse-majesté.[20]
                    We're flooded

---

[19] In mythology Adonis was adored by Aphrodite, the goddess of love, but he was killed while hunting a boar after disregarding a warning from Aphrodite. His death was mourned by the Greek women in annual religious festivals. During one of the festivals of Adonis the ill-fated Sicilian expedition was debated in the Athenian assembly. In the following lines the Commissioner recalls the arguments in favor of sending out a naval task force and manning it with troops drafted on the island of Zakynthos.
[20] Treason.

with indignity from those bitches' pitchers—like a bunch
of weak-bladdered brats. Our cloaks are sopped. We'll sue!
COMMISSIONER.
  Useless. Your suit won't hold water. Right's on their side.
For female depravity, gentlemen, WE stand guilty—
we, their teachers, preceptors of prurience, accomplices
before the fact of fornication. We sowed them in sexual
license, and now we reap rebellion.
                                          The proof?
Consider. Off we trip to the goldsmith's to leave
an order:
     "That bangle you fashioned last spring for my wife
  is sprung. She was thrashing around last night, and the prong
  popped out of the bracket. I'll be tied up all day—I'm
  boarding the ferry right now—but my wife'll be home.
  If you get the time, please stop by the house in a bit
  and see if you can't do something—anything—to fit
  a new prong into the bracket of her bangle."
                                          And bang.
Another one ups to a cobbler—young, but no apprentice,
full kit of tools, ready to give his awl—
and delivers this gem:
                    "My wife's new sandals are tight.
  The cinch pinches her pinkie right where she's sensitive.
  Drop in at noon with something to stretch her cinch
  and give it a little play."
                                          And a cinch it is.
Such hanky-panky we have to thank for today's
Utter Anarchy: I, a Commissioner of Public
Safety, duly invested with extraordinary powers
to protect the State in the Present Emergency, have secured
a source of timber to outfit our fleet and solve
the shortage of oarage. I need the money immediately . . .
and WOMEN, no less, have locked me out of the Treasury! [*Pulling himself
together.*]
—Well, no profit in standing around. [*To one of the archers.*]
                                          Bring
the crowbars. I'll jack these women back on their
pedestals!
  —WELL, you slack-jawed jackass? What's the
attraction? Wipe that thirst off your face. I said *crow*bar,
not saloon!—all right, men, all together. Shove those
bars underneath the gate and HEAVE! [*Grabbing up a crowbar.*]
                                          I'll take this side.
And now let's root them out, men, ROOT them out.
One, Two . . .

The gates to the Akropolis burst open suddenly, disclosing LYSISTRATA. *She is perfectly
composed and bears a large spindle. The* COMMISSIONER *and the* POLICE *fall back in
consternation.*

LYSISTRATA.
    Why the moving equipment?
I'm quite well motivated, thank you, and here I am.
Frankly, you don't need crowbars nearly so much as
brains.
COMMISSIONER.
    Brains? O name of infamy! Where's a policemen?
[*He grabs wildly for the First Archer and shoves him toward Lysistrata.*]
    Arrest that woman!
                    Better tie her hands behind her.
LYSISTRATA.
    By Artemis, goddess of the hunt, if he lays a finger
on me, he'll rue the day he joined the force!
[*She jabs the spindle viciously at the First Archer, who leaps, terrified, back to his comrades.*]
COMMISSIONER.
    What's this—retreat? never! Take her on the flank.
[*The First Archer hangs back. The Commissioner grabs the Second Archer.*]
    —Help him.
                    —Will the two of you kindly TIE HER UP?
[*He shoves them toward Lysistrata. Kleonike, carrying a large chamber pot, springs out
of the entrance and advances on the Second Archer.*]
KLEONIKE.
    By Artemis, goddess of the dew, if you so much
as touch her, I'll stomp the shit right out of you!
[*The two Archers run back to their group.*]
COMMISSIONER.
    Shit? Shameless! Where's another policeman? [*He grabs the Third Archer and
propels him toward Kleonike.*]
    Handcuff *her* first. Can't stand a foul-mouthed female.

MYRRHINE, *carrying a large, blazing lamp, appears at the entrance and advances on
the* THIRD ARCHER.

MYRRHINE.
    By Artemis, bringer of light, if you lay a finger
on her, you won't be able to stop the swelling!
[*The Third Archer dodges her swing and runs back to the group.*]
COMMISSIONER.
    Now what? Where's an officer? [*Pushing the Fourth Archer toward Myrrhine.*]
                    Apprehend that woman!
I'll see that *somebody* stays to take the blame!

Ismenia the Boiotian, carrying a huge pair of pincers, appears at the entrance and advances
on the Fourth Archer.

ISMENIA.
    By Artemis, goddess of Tauris, if you go near
that girl, I'll rip the hair right out of your head!
[*The Fourth Archer retreats hurriedly.*]

COMMISSIONER.

  What a colossal mess: Athens' Finest—
  finished! [*Arranging the Archers.*]
          —Now, men, a little *esprit de corps.*[21] Worsted
  by women? Drubbed by drabs?
                                          Never!
                                    Regroup,
  reform that thin red line.
                            Ready?
                              CHARGE!
[*He pushs them ahead of him.*]

LYSISTRATA.

  I warn you. We have four battalions behind us—
  full-armed combat infantrywomen, trained
  from the cradle . . .

COMMISSIONER.

                    Disarm them, Officers! Go for the hands!

LYSISTRATA. [*Calling inside the Akropolis.*]

  MOBILIZE THE RESERVES!
[*A horde of women, armed with household articles, begins to pour from the Akropolis.*]
                      Onward, you ladies from hell!
  Forward, you market militia, you battle-hardened
  bargain hunters, old sales compaigners, grocery
  grenadiers, veterans never bested by an overcharge!
  You troops of the breadline, doughgirls—
                              INTO THE FRAY!
  Show them no mercy!
                    Push!
                        Jostle!
                            Shove!
  Call them nasty names!
                      Don't be ladylike.
[*The women charge and rout the Archers in short order.*]
  Fall back—don't strip the enemy! The day is ours!
[*The women obey, and the Archers run off left. The Commissioner, dazed, is left muttering to himself.*]

COMMISSIONER.

  Gross ineptitude. A sorry day for the Force.

LYSISTRATA.

  Of course. What did you expect? We're not slaves;
  we're freeborn Women, and when we're scorned, we're
  full of fury. Never Underestimate the Power of a Woman.

COMMISSIONER.

  Power? You mean Capacity. I should have remembered
  the proverb: *The lower the tavern, the higher the dudgeon.*

KORYPHAIOS OF MEN.

  Why cast your pearls before swine, Commissioner? I know you're a civil
  servant, but don't overdo it. Have you forgotten the bath

<hr>

[21] Group spirit.

they gave us—in public,
>>> fully dressed,
>>>>>> totally soapless?
Keep rational discourse for *people!*
[*He aims a blow at the Koryphaios of Women, who dodges and raises her pitcher.*]
KORYPHAIOS OF WOMEN.
>>> I might point out that lifting
one's hand against a neighbor is scarcely civilized
behavior—and entails, for the lifter, a black eye.
>>> I'm really peaceful by nature,
compulsively inoffensive—a perfect doll. My ideal is a
well-bred repose that doesn't even stir up dust . . . [*Swinging at the Koryphaios of Men with the pitcher.*]
>>> unless some no-good lowlife
tries to rifle my hive and gets my dander up!
[*The Koryphaios of Men backs hurriedly away, and the Chorus of Men goes into a worried dance.*]
CHORUS OF MEN.
[*Singly.*]
>>> O Zeus, what's the use of this constant abuse?
>>> How do we deal with this female zoo?
>>> Is there no solution to Total Immersion?
>>> What can a poor man DO?
[*Tutti.*]
>>> Query the Adversary!
>>> Ferret out their story!
>>> What end did they have in view,
>>> to seize the city's sanctuary,
>>> snatch its legendary eyrie,[22]
>>> snare an area so very
>>> terribly taboo?
KORYPHAIOS OF MEN. [*To the Commissioner.*]
Scrutinize those women! Scour their depositions—assess their rebuttals!
Masculine honor demands this affair be probed to the bottom!
COMMISSIONER. [*Turning to the women from the Akropolis.*]
All right, you. Kindly inform me, dammit, in your own words:
What possible object could you have had in blockading the Treasury?
LYSISTRATA.
We thought we'd deposit the money in escrow and withdraw you men
from the war.
COMMISSIONER.
>>> The money's the cause of the war?
LYSISTRATA.
>>> And all our internal
disorders—the Body Politic's chronic bellyaches: What
causes Peisandros' frantic rantings, or the raucous cau-
cuses of the Friends of Oligarchy?[23] The chance for graft.
>>> But now, with the money up there,

---

[22] Eagle's nest—hence, the Acropolis, a stronghold on a hill overlooking the rest of Athens.
[23] One of the political clubs in Athens that sought public offices for their members.

they can't upset the City's equilibrium—or lower its
balance.

COMMISSIONER.
And what's your next step?

LYSISTRATA.
                          Stupid question. We'll budget the money.

COMMISSIONER.
You'll budget the money?

LYSISTRATA.
                    Why should you find that so shocking?
We budget the household accounts, and you don't object
at all.

COMMISSIONER.
That's different.

LYSISTRATA.
              Different? How?

COMMISSIONER.
                    The War Effort needs this money!

LYSISTRATA.
Who needs the War Effort?

COMMISSIONER.
                        Every patriot who pulses to save
all that Athens holds near and dear . . .

LYSISTRATA.
                                Oh, *that*. Don't worry.
We'll save you.

COMMISSIONER.
              You will save us?

LYSISTRATA.
                        Who else?

COMMISSIONER.
                        But this is unscrupulous!

LYSISTRATA.
We'll save you. You can't deter us.

COMMISSIONER.
                            Scurrilous!

LYSISTRATA.
                            You seem disturbed.
This makes it difficult. But, still—we'll save you.

COMMISSIONER.
                            Doubtless illegal!

LYSISTRATA.
We deem it a duty. For friendship's sake.

COMMISSIONER.
                        Well, forsake this friend:
I DO NOT WANT TO BE SAVED, DAMMIT!

LYSISTRATA.
                        All the more reason.
It's not only Sparta; now we'll have to save you from
you.

COMMISSIONER.
  Might I ask where you women conceived this concern
  about War and Peace?
LYSISTRATA. [*Loftily.*]
                         We shall explain.
COMMISSIONER. [*Making a fist.*]
                           Hurry up, and you won't
  get hurt.
LYSISTRATA.
           Then *listen*. And do try to keep your hands to
  yourself.
COMMISSIONER. [*Moving threateningly toward her.*]
  I can't. Righteous anger forbids restraint, and decrees . . .
KLEONIKE. [*Brandishing her chamber pot.*]
  Multiple fractures?
COMMISSIONER. [*Retreating.*]
              Keep those croaks for yourself, you old crow!
[*To Lysistrata.*]
  All right, lady, I'm ready. Speak.
LYSISTRATA.
                           I shall proceed:
When the War began, like the prudent, dutiful wives that
we are, we tolerated you men, and endured your actions
   in silence. (Small wonder—
   you wouldn't let us say boo.)
                         You were not precisely the answer
to a matron's prayer—we knew you too well, and found out more.
Too many times, as we sat in the house, we'd hear that
you'd done it again—manhandled another affair of
state with your usual staggering incompetence. Then,
masking our worry with a nervous laugh,
we'd ask you, brightly, "How was the Assembly today, dear? Anything
in the minutes about Peace?" And my husband would give his stock reply.
"What's that to you? Shut up!" And I did.
KLEONIKE. [*Proudly.*]
                             I never shut up!
COMMISSIONER.
  I trust you were shut up. Soundly.
LYSISTRATA.
                         Regardless, *I* shut up.
And then we'd learn that you'd passed another decree,
fouler than the first, and we'd ask again: "Darling, how
did you manage anything so idiotic?" And my
husband, with his customary glare, would tell me to spin
my thread, or else get a clout on the head.
And of course he'd quote from Homer:
                    *Y*e *menne must husband y*e *warre*.[24]

[24] From the *Iliad*, Book 6, line 492.

COMMISSIONER.
  Apt and irrefutably right.
LYSISTRATA.
                    Right, you miserable misfit?
To keep us from giving advice while you fumbled the
City away in the Senate? Right, indeed!
                    But this time was really too much:
Wherever we went, we'd hear you engaged in the same conversation:
"What Athens needs is a Man."
                    "But there isn't a Man in the country."
"You can say that again."
                    There was obviously no time to lose.
We women met in immediate convention and passed a
unanimous resolution: To work in concert for safety and
Peace in Greece. We have valuable advice to impart,
and if you can possibly deign to emulate our silence,
and take your turn as audience, we'll rectify you—
we'll straighten you out and set you right.
COMMISSIONER.
  You'll set *us* right? You go too far. I cannot permit
such a statement to . . .
LYSISTRATA.
                    Shush.
COMMISSIONER.
                    I categorically decline to shush
for some confounded woman, who wears—as a constant
reminder of congenital inferiority, an injunction to
public silence—a veil!
Death before such dishonor!
LYSISTRATA. [*Removing her veil.*]
                    If that's the only obstacle . . .
          I feel you need a new panache,
          so take the veil, my dear Commis-
          sioner, and drape it thus—
                    and SHUSH!
[*As she winds the veil around the startled Commissioner's head, Kleonike and Myrrhine,
with carding-comb and wool-basket, rush forward and assist in transforming him into a
woman.*]
KLEONIKE.
          Accept, I pray, this humble comb.
MYRRHINE.
          Receive this basket of fleece as well.
LYSISTRATA.
          Hike up your skirts, and card your wool,
          and gnaw your beans—and stay at home!
            While we rewrite Homer:
            Y^e WOMEN must WIVE ye warre!
[*To the Chorus of Women, as the Commissioner struggles to remove his new outfit.*]
  Women, weaker vessels, arise!
                    Put down your pitchers.

It's our turn, now. Let's supply our friends with some
moral support.
[*The Chorus of Women dances to the same tune as the Men, but with much more confidence.*]
CHORUS OF WOMEN.
[*Singly.*]

> Oh, yes! I'll dance to bless their success.
> Fatigue won't weaken my will. Or my knees.
> I'm ready to join in any jeopardy.
> > with girls as good as *these!*

[*Tutte.*]

> A tally of their talents
> convinces me they're giants
> of excellence. To commence:
> there's Beauty, Duty, Prudence, Science,
> Self-Reliance, Compliance, Defiance,
> and Love of Athens in balanced alliance
> > with Common Sense!

KORYPHAIOS OF WOMEN. [*To the women from the Akropolis.*]
Autochthonous[25] daughters of Attika, sprung from the
soil that bore your mothers, the spiniest, spikiest
nettles known to man, prove your mettle and attack!
Now is no time to dilute your anger. You're
running ahead of the wind!
LYSISTRATA.

> We'll wait for the wind
from heaven. The gentle breath of Love and his Kyprian
mother[26] will imbue our bodies with desire, and raise a
storm to tense and tauten these blasted men until they
crack. And soon we'll be on every tongue in
Greece—the *Pacifiers.*
COMMISSIONER.

> That's quite
a mouthful. How will you win it?
LYSISTRATA.

> First, we intend to withdraw
that crazy Army of of Occupation from the downtown
shopping section.
KLEONIKE.
Aphrodite be praised!
LYSISTRATA.

> The pottery shop and the grocery stall
are overstocked with soldiers, clanking around like
those maniac Korybants,[27]
armed to the teeth for a battle.
COMMISSIONER.

> A Hero is Always Prepared!

[25] Native.
[26] Aphrodite; Kyprian because she was said to have been born from the sea near Cyprus.
[27] Armed priests of Cybele, the goddess of Nature.

LYSISTRATA.
I suppose he is. But it does look silly to shop for sardines
from behind a shield.
KLEONIKE.
                                   I'll second that. I saw
a cavalry captain buy vegetable soup on horseback. He
carried the whole mess home in his helmet.
                                   And then that fellow from Thrace,
shaking his buckler and spear—a menace straight from the stage.
The saleslady was stiff with fright. He was hogging her ripe figs—free.
COMMISSIONER.
I admit, for the moment, that Hellas' affairs are in one
hell of a snarl. But how can you set them straight?
LYSISTRATA.
                                                Simplicity itself.
COMMISSIONER.
Pray demonstrate.
LYSISTRATA.
            It's rather like yarn. When a hank's in a tangle,
we lift it—*so*—and work out the snarls by winding it up
on spindles, now this way, now that way.
                              That's how we'll wind up the War,
if allowed: We'll work out the snarls by sending Special Commissions—
back and forth, now this way, now that way—to ravel
these tense international kinks.
COMMISSIONER.
            I lost your thread, but I know there's a hitch.
Spruce up the world's disasters with spindles—typically
woolly female logic.
LYSISTRATA.
                 If *you* had a scrap of logic, you'd adopt
our wool as a master plan for Athens.
COMMISSIONER.
                              What course of action
does the wool advise?
LYSISTRATA.
                 Consider the City as fleece, recently
shorn. The first step is Cleansing: Scrub it in a public
bath, and remove all corruption, offal, and sheepdip.
                              Next, to the couch
for Scutching and Plucking: Cudgel the leeches and
similar vermin loose with a club, then pick the prickles
and cockleburs out. As for the clots—those lumps
that clump and cluster in knots and snarls to snag
important posts—you comb these out,
twist off their heads, and discard.
                              Next, to raise the City's
nap, you card the citizens together in a single basket
of common weal and general welfare. Fold in our loyal
Resident Aliens, all Foreigners of proven and tested

friendship, and any Disenfranchised Debtors. Combine
these closely with the rest.
Lastly, cull the colonies settled by our own people:
these are nothing but flocks of wool from the City's
fleece, scattered throughout the world. So gather home
these far-flung flocks, amalgamate them with the others.
                    Then, drawing this blend
of stable fibers into one fine staple, you spin a mighty
bobbin of yarn—and weave, without bias or seam, a
cloak to clothe the City of Athens!

COMMISSIONER.
                              This is too much! The City's
died in the wool, worsted by the distaff side—by women
who bore no share in the War. . . .

LYSISTRATA.
                         None, you hopeless hypocrite?
The quota we bear is double. First, we delivered our
sons to fill out the front lines in Sicily . . .

COMMISSIONER.
                         Don't tax me with that memory.

LYSISTRATA.
Next, the best years of our lives were levied. Top-level
strategy attached our joy, and we sleep alone.
                         But it's not the matrons
like us who matter. I mourn for the virgins, bedded in
single blessedness, with nothing to do but grow old.

COMMISSIONER.
                         Men *have* been known
to age, as well as women.

LYSISTRATA.
                         No, not as well as—better.
A man, an absolute antique, comes back from the war, and he's barely
doddered into town before he's married the veriest nymphet.
But a woman's season is brief; it slips, and she'll have
no husband, but sit out her life groping at omens—and finding no men.

COMMISSIONER.
Lamentable state of affairs. Perhaps we can rectify matters:
[*To the audience.*]
TO EVERY MAN JACK, A CHALLENGE:
                              ARISE!
Provided you can . . .

LYSISTRATA.
Instead, Commissioner, why not simply curl up and *die?*
                    Just buy a coffin; here's the place.
[*Banging him on the head with her spindle.*]
                    I'll knead you a cake for the wake—and *these*
[*Winding the threads from the spindle around him.*]
                    make excellent wreaths. So Rest In Peace.

KLEONIKE. [*Emptying the chamber pot over him.*]
                    Accept these tokens of deepest grief.

MYRRHINE. [*Breaking her lamp over his head.*]
                A final garland for the dear deceased.
LYSISTRATA.
                May I supply any last request?
                Then run along. You're due at the wharf:
                    Charon's[28] anxious to sail—
                    you're holding up the boat for Hell!
COMMISSIONER.
    This is monstrous—maltreatment of a public official—
    maltreatment of ME!
                        I must repair directly
    to the Board of Commissioners, and present my
    colleagues concrete evidence of the sorry specifics of
    this shocking attack!
[*He staggers off left. Lysistrata calls after him.*]
LYSISTRATA.
    You won't haul us into court on a charge of neglecting
    the dead, will you? (How like a man to insist
    on his rights—even his last ones.) Two days between
    death and funeral, that's the rule.
                                    Come back here early
    day after tomorrow, Commissioner:
                            We'll lay you out.
[*Lysistrata and her women re-enter the Akropolis. The Koryphaios of Men advances to address the audience.*]
KORYPHAIOS OF MEN.
    Wake up, Athenians! Preserve your freedom—the time
    is Now! [*To the Chorus of Men.*]
    Strip for action, men. Let's cope with the current mess.
[*The men put off their long mantles, disclosing short tunics underneath, and advance toward the audience.*]
CHORUS OF MEN.
    This trouble may be terminal; it has a loaded odor,
        an ominous aroma of constitutional rot.
    My nose gives a prognosis of radical disorder—
        it's just the first installment of an absolutist plot!
            The Spartans are behind it:
            they must have masterminded
    some morbid local contacts (engineered by Kleisthenes).[29]
            Predictably infected,
            the women straightway acted
    to commandeer the City's cash. They're feverish to freeze
            my be-all,
            my end-all . . .
            my *payroll!*
KORYPHAIOS OF MEN.
    The symptoms are clear. Our birthright's already nibbled. And oh, so

---

[28] The boatman who ferries dead souls across the river Styx.
[29] Kleisthenes was a notoriously effeminate contemporary of Aristophanes'—hence, suspected of being in league with the women.

daintily: WOMEN ticking off troops for improper etiquette.
WOMEN propounding their featherweight views on the fashionable use
and abuse of the shield. And (if any more proof were needed) WOMEN
nagging us to trust the Nice Spartan, and put our heads
in his toothy maw—to make a dessert and call it Peace.
They've woven the City a seamless shroud, bedecked with the legend
DICTATORSHIP.
                            But I won't be hemmed in. I'll use
their weapon against them, and uphold the right by sneakiness
                            With knyf under cloke,
gauntlet in glove, sword in olivebranch, [*Slipping slowly toward the Koryphaios
of Women.*]
                            I'll take up my post
in Statuary Row, beside our honored National Heroes,
the natural foes of tyranny: Harmodios,
                            Aristogeiton,
                                      and Me.[30]

[*Next to her.*]
    Striking an epic pose, so, with the full approval
    of the immortal gods,
                            I'll bash this loathsome hag in the jaw!
[*He does, and runs cackling back to the Men. She shakes a fist after him.*]
KORYPHAIOS OF WOMEN.
    Mama won't know her little boy when he gets home!
[*To the Women, who are eager to launch a full-scale attack.*]
    Let's not be hasty, fellow . . . hags. Cloaks off first.
[*The Women remove their mantles, disclosing tunics very like those of the Men, and advance
toward the audience.*]
CHORUS OF WOMEN.
    We'll address you, citizens, in beneficial, candid,
        patriotic accents, as our breeding says we must,
    since, from the age of seven, Athens graced me with a
        splendid string of civic triumphs to signalize her
            trust:
            I was Relic-Girl quite early,
                then advanced to Maid of Barley;
    in Artemis' "Pageant of the Bear" I played the lead.
            To cap this proud progression,
            I led the whole procession
    at Athene's Celebration, certified and pedigreed
            —that cachet[31]
            so distingué[32]—
            a *Lady!*
KORYPHAIOS OF WOMEN. [*To the audience.*]
    I trust this establishes my qualifications. I may, I take it,
    address the City to its profit? Thank you.
                            I admit to being a woman—
    but don't sell my contribution short on that account.
    It's better than the present panic. And my word is as

---

[30] Statues of the heroes Harmodios and Aristogeiton were carved by the sculptor Kritios.
[31] Official seal.   [32] Distinguished.

good as my bond, because I hold stock in Athens—
stock I paid for in sons.
[*To the Chorus of Men.*]
—But you, you doddering bankrupts, where are your
shares in the State?
[*Slipping slowly toward the Koryphaios of Men.*]
Your grandfathers willed you the Mutual Funds from
    the Persian War—
and where are they?[33]
[*Nearer.*]
            You dipped into capital, then lost interest . . .
and now a pool of your assets won't fill a hole in the ground.
All that remains is one last potential killing—Athens.
Is there any rebuttal?
[*The Koryphaios of Men gestures menacingly. She ducks down, as if to ward off a blow,
and removes a slipper.*]
            Force is a footling resort. I'll take
my very sensible shoe, and paste you in the jaw!
[*She does so, and runs back to the women.*]
CHORUS OF MEN.
            Their native respect for our manhood is small,
            and keeps getting smaller. Let's bottle their gall.
            The man who won't battle has no balls at all!
KORYPHAIOS OF MEN.
All right, men, skin out of the skivvies. Let's give them
a whiff of Man, full strength. No point in muffling
the essential Us. [*The men remove their tunics.*]
CHORUS OF MEN.
            A century back, we soared to the Heights[34]
                and beat down Tyranny there.
            Now's the time to shed our moults
                and fledge our wings once more,
            to rise to the skies in our reborn force,
                and beat back Tyranny here!
KORYPHAIOS OF MEN.
No fancy grappling with these grannies; straightforward strength. The tiniest
toehold, and those nimble, fiddling fingers will have their
foot in the door, and we're done for.
                No amount of know-how can lick
a woman's knack.
            They'll want to build ships . . . next thing we know,
we're all at sea, fending off female boarding parties.

---

[33] "This money originally made up the treasury of the Delian League, an alliance of Greek states
against Persia formed by the Athenian Aristeides in 477; following its transfer, for safety's
sake, from the island of Delos to Athens in 454, it became for all practical purposes Athenian
property, supported by tribute from the Allies. Athens' heavy expenses in Sicily, followed by
the Allies' nonpayment and defection, made this question all too pointed in early 411." (Translator's note.)

[34] The men of the family of Pericles held out in the mountains north of Athens during their
first attempt to overthrow the tyrant Hippias in 513 B.C.

(Artemisia fought us at Salamis. Tell me, has anyone
caught her yet?)
    But we're *really* sunk if they take up horses. Scratch
the Cavalry:
            A woman is an easy rider with a natural seat.
Take her over the jumps bareback, and she'll never slip
her mount. (That's how the Amazons nearly took Athens. On horseback.
Check on Mikon's mural down in the Stoa.)
                                            Anyway,
the solution is obvious. Put every woman in her place—
stick her in the stocks.
        To do this, first snare your woman around the neck.
[*He attempts to demonstrate on the Koryphaios of Women. After a brief tussle, she works
loose and chases him back to the Men.*]

CHORUS OF WOMEN.
            The beast in me's eager and fit for a brawl.
            Just rile me a bit and she'll kick down the wall.
            You'll bawl to your friends that you've no balls at all.

KORYPHAIOS OF WOMEN.
    All right, ladies, strip for action. Let's give them a whiff
    of *Femme Enragée*—piercing and pungent, but not at
    all tart. [*The women remove their tunics.*]

CHORUS OF WOMEN.
            We're angry. The brainless bird who tangles
                with *us* has gummed his last mush.
            In fact, the coot who even heckles
                is being daringly rash.
            So look to your nests, you reclaimed eagles—
                whatever you lay, we'll squash!

KORYPHAIOS OF WOMEN.
    Frankly, you don't faze me. *With* me, I have my friends—
    Lampito from Sparta; that genteel girl from Thebes, Ismenia—
    committed to me forever. *Against* me, *you*—permanently
    out of commission. So do your damnedest.
                                    Pass a law.
    Pass seven. Continue the winning ways that have made
    your name a short and ugly household word.
                                    Like yesterday:
    I was giving a little party, nothing fussy, to honor
    the goddess Hekate. Simply to please my daughters,
    I'd invited a sweet little thing from the neighborhood—flawless pedigree,
        perfect
    taste, a credit to any gathering—a Boiotian eel.
    But she had to decline. Couldn't pass the border. You'd passed a law.
    Not that you care for my party. You'll overwork your right of passage
    till your august body is overturned,
                            and you break your silly neck!
[*She deftly grabs the Koryphaios of Men by the ankle and upsets him. He scuttles back
to the Men, who retire in confusion.*]

LYSISTRATA *emerges from the citadel, obviously distraught.*

KORYPHAIOS OF WOMEN. [*Mock-tragic.*]
   Mistress, queen of this our subtle scheme
   why burst you from the hall with brangled brow?
LYSISTRATA.
   Oh, wickedness of woman! The female mind
   does sap my soul and set my wits a-totter.
KORYPHAIOS OF WOMEN.
   What drear accents are these?
LYSISTRATA.
                                    The merest truth.
KORYPHAIOS OF WOMEN.
   Be nothing loath to tell the tale to friends.
LYSISTRATA.
   'Twere shame to utter, pain to hold unsaid.
KORYPHAIOS OF WOMEN.
   Hide not from me affliction which we share.
LYSISTRATA.
   In briefest compass,
[*Dropping the paratragedy.*]
                           we want to get laid.
KORYPHAIOS OF WOMEN.
                                    By Zeus!
LYSISTRATA.
   No, no, not HIM!
                        Well, that's the way things are.
I've lost my grip on the girls—they're mad for men!
But sly—they slip out in droves.
                                    A minute ago,
I caught one scooping out the little hole
that breaks through just below Pan's grotto.[35]
                                                   One
had jerry-rigged some block-and-tackle business
and was wriggling away on a rope.
                                    Another just flat
deserted.
           Last night I spied one mounting a sparrow,
all set to take off for the nearest bawdyhouse. I hauled
her back by the hair.
                        And excuses, pretexts for overnight
passes? I've heard them all.
                                Here comes one. Watch.
[*To the* FIRST WOMAN, *as she runs out of the Akropolis.*]
   —You, there! What's your hurry?
FIRST WOMAN.
                                    I have to get home.
I've got all this lovely Milesian wool in the house,
and the moths will simply batter it to bits!

---

[35] A cave on the Acropolis.

LYSISTRATA.

I'll bet.

Get back inside.

FIRST WOMAN.

I swear I'll hurry right back!
—Just time enough to spread it out on the couch?

LYSISTRATA.

Your wool will stay unspread. And you'll stay here.

FIRST WOMAN.

Do I have to let my piecework *rot?*

LYSISTRATA.

Possibly.

The SECOND WOMAN *runs on.*

SECOND WOMAN.

Oh dear, oh goodness, what shall I do—my flax!
I left and forgot to peel it!

LYSISTRATA.

Another one.

She suffers from unpeeled flax.

—Get back inside!

SECOND WOMAN.

I'll be right back. I just have to pluck the fibers.

LYSISTRATA.

No. No plucking. You start it, and everyone else
will want to go and do their plucking, too.

The THIRD WOMAN, *swelling conspicuously, hurries on, praying loudly.*

THIRD WOMAN.

*O Goddess of Childbirth, grant that I not deliver
until I get me from out this sacred precinct!*

LYSISTRATA.

What sort of nonsense is *this?*

THIRD WOMAN.

I'm due—any second!

LYSISTRATA.

You weren't pregnant yesterday.

THIRD WOMAN.

Today I am—

a miracle!

Let me go home for a midwife, *please!*
I may not make it!

LYSISTRATA.

[*Restraining her.*]

You can do better than that.

[*Tapping the woman's stomach and receiving a metallic clang.*]

What's this? It's hard.

THIRD WOMAN.

I'm going to have a boy.

LYSISTRATA.
   Not unless he's made of bronze. Let's see.
[*She throws open the Third Woman's cloak, exposing a huge bronze helmet.*]
   Of all the brazen . . . You've stolen the helmet from
  Athene's statue! Pregnant, indeed!
THIRD WOMAN.
                      I am *so* pregnant!
LYSISTRATA.
   Then why the helmet?
THIRD WOMAN.
                  I thought my time might come
  while I was still on forbidden ground. If it did,
  I could climb inside Athene's helmet and have
  my baby there.
             The pigeons do it all the time.
LYSISTRATA.
   Nothing but excuses! [*Taking the helmet.*]
                This is your baby. I'm afraid
  you'll have to stay until we give it a name.
THIRD WOMAN.
   But the Akropolis is *awful.* I can't even sleep! I saw
  the snake that guards the temple.
LYSISTRATA.
                  That snake's a fabrication.
THIRD WOMAN.
   I don't care *what* kind it is—I'm *scared!*
[*The other women, who have emerged from the citadel, crowd around.*]
KLEONIKE.
   And those goddamned holy owls; All night long,
  tu-wit; tu-wu—they're hooting me into my grave!
LYSISTRATA.
   Darlings, let's call a halt to this hocus-pocus.
  You miss your men—now isn't that the trouble?
[*Shamefaced nods from the group.*]
   Don't you think they miss you just as much?
  I can assure you, their nights are every bit
  as hard as yours. So be good girls; endure!
  Persist a few days more, and Victory is ours.
  It's fated: a current prophecy declares that the men
  will go down to defeat before us, provided that *we*
  maintain a United Front. [*Producing a scroll.*]
                I happen to have
  a copy of the prophecy.
KLEONIKE.
               Read it!
LYSISTRATA.
                  Silence, *please:*
[*Reading from the scroll.*]
But when the swallows, in flight from the
  hoopoes, have flocked to a hole

on high, and stoutly eschew their
    accustomed perch on the pole,
yea, then shall Thunderer Zeus to
    their suff'ring establish a stop,
by making the lower the upper . . .

KLEONIKE.
    Then *we'll* be lying on top?

LYSISTRATA.
    But should these swallows, indulging their
        lust for the perch, lose heart,
    dissolve their flocks in winged dissension,
        and singly depart
    the sacred stronghold, breaking the
        bands that bind them together—
    then know them as lewd, the pervertedest
        birds that ever wore feather.

KLEONIKE.
    There's nothing obscure about *that* oracle. Ye gods!

LYSISTRATA.
    Sorely beset as we are, we must not flag
    or falter. So back to the citadel!

[*As the women troop inside.*]
                    And if we fail
that oracle, darlings, our image is absolutely *mud!*

[*She follows them in. A pause, and the Choruses assemble.*]

CHORUS OF MEN.
                I have a simple
                tale to relate you,
                a sterling example
                of masculine virtue:

                The huntsman bold Melanion
                    was once a harried quarry.
            The women in town tracked him down
                  and badgered him to marry.

                Melanion knew the cornered male
                    eventually cohabits.
            Assessing the odds, he took to the woods
                  and lived by trapping rabbits.

                He stuck to the virgin stand, sustained
                    by rabbit meat and hate,
            and never returned, but ever remained
                    an alfresco[36] celibate.

                Melanion is our ideal;
                  his loathing makes us free.
            Our dearest aim is the gemlike flame
                    of his misogyny.[37]

---

[36] Outdoor.   [37] Hatred of women.

OLD MAN.

> Let me kiss that wizened cheek. . . .

OLD WOMAN.
[*Threatening with a fist.*]

> A wish too rash for that withered flesh.

OLD MAN.

> and lay you low with a highflying kick.

[*He tries one and misses.*]
OLD WOMAN.

> Exposing an overgrown underbrush.

OLD MAN.

> A hairy behind, historically, means
>   masculine force: Myronides
> harassed the foe with his mighty mane,
>   and furry Phormion swept the seas
>   of enemy ships, never meeting his match—
>   such was the nature of his thatch.[38]

CHORUS OF WOMEN.

> I offer an anecdote
> for your opinion,
> an adequate antidote
> for your Melanion:
>
> Timon, the noted local grouch,
> put rusticating hermits
> out of style by building his wilds
> inside the city limits
>
> He shooed away society
> with natural battlements:
> his tongue was edged; his shoulder, frigid;
> his beard, a picket fence
>
> When random contacts overtaxed him,
> he didn't stop to pack,
> but loaded curses on the male of the species,
> left town, and never came back.
>
> Timon, you see, was a misanthrope
> in a properly narrow sense:
> his spleen was vented only on men . . .
> *we* were his dearest friends.

OLD WOMAN. [*Making a fist.*]

> Enjoy a chop to that juiceless chin?

OLD MAN. [*Backing away.*]

> I'm jolted already. Thank you, no.

OLD WOMAN.

> Perhaps a trip from a well-turned shin?

---

[38] Myronides, an Athenian general, and Phormion, an Athenian admiral, won important military
battles many years before the action in the play.

[*She tries a kick and misses.*]
OLD MAN.
      Brazenly baring the mantrap below.
OLD WOMAN.
    At least it's *neat*. I'm not too sorry
      to have you see my daintiness.
    My habits are still depilatory;
      age hasn't made me a bristly mess.
        Secure in my smoothness, I'm never in doubt—
          though even down is out.
[*Lysistrata mounts the platform and scans the horizon. When her gaze reaches the left, she stops suddenly.*]
LYSISTRATA.
    Ladies, attention! Battle stations, please!
    And quickly!
[*A general rush of women to the battlements.*]
KLEONIKE.
        What is it?
MYRRHINE.
             What's all the shouting for?
LYSISTRATA.
    A MAN!
[*Consternation.*]
        Yes, it's a man. And he's coming this way!
    Hmm. Seems to have suffered a seizure. Broken out
    with a nasty attack of love.
[*Prayer, aside.*]
                O Aphrodite,
      Mistress all-victorious,
      mysterious, voluptuous,
      you who make the crooked straight . . .
      don't let this happen to US!
KLEONIKE.
    I don't care who he is—*where is he?*
LYSISTRATA. [*Pointing.*]
                Down there—
    just flanking that temple—Demeter the Fruitful.
KLEONIKE.
                      My.

    Definitely a man.
MYRRHINE. [*Craning for a look.*]
        I wonder who it can be?
LYSISTRATA.
    See for yourselves.—Can anyone identify him?
MYRRHINE.
    Oh lord, I can.
          That is my husband—Kinesias.
LYSISTRATA. [*To Myrrhine.*]
    Your duty is clear.
          Pop him on the griddle, twist
    the spit, braize him, baste him, stew him in his own

juice, do him to a turn. Sear him with kisses,
coyness, caresses, *everything*—
                                but stop where Our Oath
begins.
MYRRHINE.
            Relax. I can take care of this.
LYSISTRATA.
                                                    Of course
you can, dear. Still, a little help can't hurt, now
can it? I'll just stay around for a bit
and—er—poke up the fire.
                          —Everyone else inside!

Exit all the women but LYSISTRATA, *on the platform, and* MYRRHINE, *who stands near
the Akropolis entrance, hidden from her husband's view.* KINESIAS *staggers on, in erection
and considerable pain, followed by a male slave who carries a baby boy.*

KINESIAS.
    OUCH!!
            Omigod.
    Hypertension, twinges. . . . I can't hold out much more.
    I'd rather be dismembered.
                            How long, ye gods, how long?
LYSISTRATA.
[*Officially.*]
    WHO GOES THERE?
                    WHO PENETRATES OUR POSITIONS?
KINESIAS.
    Me.
LYSISTRATA.
    —A Man?
KINESIAS.
                Every inch.
LYSISTRATA.
                            Then inch yourself out
    of here. Off Limits to Men.
KINESIAS.
                            This *is* the limit.
    Just who are *you* to throw me out?
LYSISTRATA.
                                The Lookout.
KINESIAS.
    Well, look here, Lookout. I'd like to see Myrrhine.
    How's the outlook?
LYSISTRATA.
                    Unlikely. Bring Myrrhine
    to you? The idea!
                    Just by the by, who are you?
KINESIAS.
    A private citizen. Her husband, Kinesias.

LYSISTRATA.
                                        No!
Meeting you—I'm overcome!
                              Your name, you know,
is not without its fame among us girls.
[*Aside.*]
    —Matter of fact, we have a name for *it*.—
I swear, you're never out of Myrrhine's mouth.
She won't even nibble a quince, or swallow an egg,
without reciting, "Here's to Kinesias!"
KINESIAS.
                                      For god's sake,
will you . . .
LYSISTRATA. [*Sweeping on over his agony.*]
                Word of honor, it's true. Why, when
we discuss our husbands (you know how women are),
Myrrhine refuses to argue. She simply insists:
"Compared with Kinesias, the rest have *nothing!*"
Imagine!
KINESIAS.
Bring her out here!
LYSISTRATA.
                      Really? And what would I
get out of this?
KINESIAS.
              You see my situation. I'll raise
whatever I can. This can all be yours.
LYSISTRATA.
                                      Goodness.
It's really her place. I'll go and get her.
[*She descends from the platform and moves to Myrrhine, out of Kinesias' sight.*]
KINESIAS.
                                    Speed!
—Life is a husk. She left our home, and happiness
went with her. Now pain is the tenant. Oh, to enter
that wifeless house, to sense that awful emptiness,
to eat that tasteless, joyless food—it makes
it hard, I tell you.
                  Harder all the time.
MYRRHINE. [*Still out of his sight, in a voice to be overheard.*]
    Oh, I *do* love him! I'm mad about him! But he
doesn't want my love. Please don't make me see him.
KINESIAS.
Myrrhine darling, why do you *act* this way?
Come down here!
MYRRHINE. [*Appearing at the wall.*]
              Down there? Certainly not!
KINESIAS.
It's me, Myrrhine. I'm begging you. Please come down.
MYRRHINE.
I don't see why you're begging me. You don't need me.

KINESIAS.
  I don't need you? I'm at the end of my rope!
MYRRHINE.
  I'm leaving. [*She turns. Kinesias grabs the boy from the slave.*]
KINESIAS.
              No! Wait! At least you'll have to listen
  to the voice of your child.
  [*To the boy, in a fierce undertone.*]
                          —(Call your mother!)
  [*Silence.*]
                                          . . . to the voice
  of your very own child . . .
                          —(Call your mother, brat!)
CHILD.
  MOMMYMOMMYMOMMY!
KINESIAS.
  Where's your maternal instinct? He hasn't been washed
  or fed for a week. How can you be so pitiless?
MYRRHINE.
  Him I pity. Of all the pitiful excuses
  for a father. . . .
KINESIAS.
              Come down here, dear. For the baby's sake.
MYRRHINE.
  Motherhood! I'll have to come. I've got no choice.
KINESIAS. [*Soliloquizing as she descends.*]
  It may be me, but I'll swear she looks years younger—
  and gentler—her eyes caress me. And then they flash:
  that anger, that verve, that high-and-mighty air!
  She's fire, she's ice—and I'm stuck right in the middle.
MYRRHINE. [*Taking the baby.*]
  Sweet babykins with such a nasty daddy!
  Here, let Mummy kissums. Mummy's little darling.
KINESIAS. [*The injured husband.*]
  You should be ashamed of yourself, letting those women
  lead you around. Why do you DO these things?
  You only make me suffer and hurt your poor,
  sweet self.
MYRRHINE.
              Keep your hands away from me!
KINESIAS.
  But the house, the furniture, everything we own—you're
  letting it go to hell!
MYRRHINE.
              Frankly, I couldn't care less.
KINESIAS.
  But your weaving's unraveled—the loom is full of
  chickens! You couldn't care less about *that*?
MYRRHINE.
                          I certainly couldn't.

Kinesias.

And the holy rites of Aphrodite? Think how long
that's been.
                    Come on, darling, let's go home.
Myrrhine.

I absolutely refuse!
                    Unless you agree to a truce
to stop the war.
Kinesias.
                    Well, then, if that's your decision,
we'll STOP the war!
Myrrhine.
                    Well, then, if that's your decision,
I'll come back—*after* it's done.
                    But, for the present,
I've sworn off.
Kinesias.
            At least lie down for a minute.
We'll talk.
Myrrhine.
            I know what you're up to—NO!
—And yet. . . . I really can't say I don't love you . . .
Kinesias.
                                        You love me?
So what's the trouble? *Lie down.*
Myrrhine.
                            Don't be disgusting.
In front of the baby?
Kinesias.
                    Er . . . no. Heaven Forefend.
[*Taking the baby and pushing it at the slave.*]
—Take this home.
[*The slave obeys.*]
                    —Well, darling, we're rid of the kid . . .
let's go to bed?
Myrrhine.
            Poor dear.
                    But where does one do
this sort of thing?
Kinesias.
                Where? All we need is a little
nook. . . . We'll try Pan's grotto. Excellent spot.
Myrrhine.
[*With a nod at the Akropolis.*]
I'll have to be pure to get back in *there.* How can I
expunge my pollution?
Kinesias.
                    Sponge off in the pool next door.
Myrrhine.
I did swear an Oath. I'm supposed to purjure myself?

KINESIAS.
Bother the Oath. Forget it—I'll take the blame. [*A pause.*]
MYRRHINE.
Now I'll go get us a cot.
KINESIAS.
                              No! Not a cot!
The ground's enough for us.
MYRRHINE.
                              I'll get the cot.
For all your faults, I refuse to put you to bed
in the dirt. [*She exits into the Akropolis.*]
KINESIAS.
                    She certainly loves me. That's nice to know.
MYRRHINE. [*Returning with a rope-tied cot.*]
Here. You hurry to bed while I undress.
[*Kinesias lies down.*]
Gracious me—I forgot. We need a mattress.
KINESIAS.
Who wants a mattress? Not me!
MYRRHINE.
                                        Oh, yes, you do.
It's perfectly squalid on the ropes.
KINESIAS.
                                        Well, give me a kiss
to tide me over.
MYRRHINE.
              Voilà.
[*She pecks at him and leaves.*]
KINESIAS.
                    OoolaLAlala!
—Make it a quick trip, dear.
MYRRHINE.
[*Entering with the mattress, she waves Kinesias off the cot and lays the mattress on it.*]
                              Here we are.
Our mattress. Now hurry to bed while I undress. [*Kinesias lies down again.*]
Gracious me—I forgot. You don't have a pillow.
KINESIAS.
I do *not* need a pillow.
MYRRHINE.
                    I know, but *I* do.
[*She leaves.*]
KINESIAS.
What a lovefeast! Only the table gets laid.
MYRRHINE. [*Returning with a pillow.*]
Rise and shine!
[*Kinesias jumps up. She places the pillow.*]
                    And now I have everything I need.
KINESIAS. [*Lying down again.*]
You certainly do.
                    Come here, my little jewelbox!

MYRRHINE.
Just taking off my bra.
                              Don't break your promise:
no cheating about the Peace.
KINESIAS.
                              I swear to god,
I'll die first!
MYRRHINE.
[*Coming to him.*]
                    Just look. You don't have a blanket.
KINESIAS.
I didn't plan to go camping—I want to make love!
MYRRHINE.
Relax. You'll get your love. I'll be right back. [*She leaves.*]
KINESIAS.
Relax? I'm dying a slow death by dry goods!
MYRRHINE. [*Returning with the blanket.*]
                                                      Get up!

KINESIAS. [*Getting out of bed.*]
I've been up for hours. I was up before I was up.
[*Myrrhine spreads the blanket on the mattress, and he lies down again.*]
MYRRHINE.
I presume you want perfume?
KINESIAS.
                              Positively NO!
MYRRHINE.
Absolutely *yes*—whether you want it or not. [*She leaves.*]
KINESIAS.
Dear Zeus, I don't ask for much—but please let her
    spill it.
MYRRHINE. [*Returning with a bottle.*]
Hold out your hand like a good boy.
                                        Now rub it in.
KINESIAS. [*Obeying and sniffing.*]
This is to quicken desire? Too strong. It grabs
your nose and bawls out: *Try again tomorrow.*
MYRRHINE.
I'm *awful!* I brought you that rancid Rhodian brand. [*She starts off with the
bottle.*]
KINESIAS.
This is just *lovely.* Leave it, woman!
MYRRHINE.
                                          Silly!
[*She leaves.*]
KINESIAS.
God damn the clod who first concocted perfume!
MYRRHINE. [*Returning with another bottle.*]
Here, try this flask.
KINESIAS.
                        Thanks—but you try mine.

Come to bed, you witch—
                              and please stop bringing
    things!
MYRRHINE.
          That is exactly what I'll do.
    There go my shoes.
                        Incidentally, darling, you *will*
    remember to vote for the truce?
KINESIAS.
                                    I'LL THINK IT OVER!
[*Myrrhine runs off for good.*]
    That woman's laid me waste—destroyed me, root
    and branch!
                    I'm scuttled,
                          gutted,
                                up the spout!
              And Myrrhine's gone!
[*In a parody of a tragic kommos.*[39]]
                        Out upon't! But how? But where?
                        Now I have lost the fairest fair,
                        how screw my courage to yet another
                        sticking-place? Aye, there's the rub—
                        And yet, this wagging, wanton babe
                        must soon be laid to rest, or else . . .
                        Ho, Pandar!
                              Pandar!
                                    I'd hire a nurse.
KORYPHAIOS OF MEN.
                        Grievous your bereavement, cruel
                        the slow tabescence[40] of your soul.
                        I bid my liquid pity mingle.

                        Oh, where the soul, and where, alack!
                        the cod to stand the taut attack
                        of swollen prides, the scorching tensions
                        that ravine up the lumbar regions?
                              His morning lay
                              has gone astray.
KINESIAS. [*In agony.*]
                        O Zeus, reduce the throbs, the throes!
KORYPHAIOS OF MEN.
                        I turn my tongue to curse the cause
                        of your affliction—that jade, that slut,
                        that hag, that ogress . . .
KINESIAS.
                                    No! Slight not
                        my light-o'-love, my dove, my sweet!

---

[39] A lyric performed by the actor and chorus together.   [40] Wasting away.

KORYPHAIOS OF MEN.

Sweet!
O Zeus who rul'st the sky,
snatch that slattern up on high,
crack thy winds, unleash thy thunder,
tumble her over, trundle her under,
juggle her from hand to hand;
twirl her ever near the ground—
drop her in a well-aimed fall
on our comrade's tool! That's all.

KINESIAS *exits left.*

A SPARTAN HERALD *enters from the right, holding his cloak together in a futile attempt to conceal his condition.*

HERALD.

This Athens? Where-all kin I find the Council of Elders
or else the Executive Board? I brung some news.

The COMMISSIONER, *swathed in his cloak, enters from the left.*

COMMISSIONER.

And what are you—a man? a signpost? a joint-stock
company?

HERALD.

A herald, sonny, a honest-to-Kastor[41]
herald. I come to chat 'bout thet-there truce.

COMMISSIONER.

. . . carrying a concealed weapon? Pretty underhanded.

HERALD.

[*Twisting to avoid the Commissioner's direct gaze.*]
Hain't done no sech a thang!

COMMISSIONER.

Very well, stand still.
Your cloak's out of crease—hernia? Are the roads that bad?

HERALD.

I swear this feller's plumb tetched in the haid!

COMMISSIONER. [*Throwing open the Spartan's cloak, exposing the phallus.*]
You clown,
you've got an erection!

HERALD. [*Wildly embarrassed.*]
Hain't got no sech a thang!
You stop this-hyer foolishment!

COMMISSIONER.

What *have* you got there, then?

---

[41] The twin gods, Castor and Pollux, were especially revered by the Spartans.

HERALD.
Thet-thur's a Spartan *e*pistle.[42] In code.
COMMISSIONER.

I have the key.

[*Throwing open his cloak.*]
Behold another Spartan *e*pistle. In code.
[*Tiring of teasing.*]
Let's get down to cases. I know the score,
so tell me the truth.

How are things with you in Sparta?

HERALD.
Thangs is up in the air. The whole Alliance
is purt-near 'bout to explode. We-uns'll need barrels,
'stead of women.

COMMISSIONER.
What was the cause of this outburst?
The great god Pan?

HERALD.
Nope. I'll lay 'twere Lampito,
most likely. She begun, and then they was off
and runnin' at the post in a bunch, every last little gal
in Sparta, drivin' their menfolk away from the winner's
circle.

COMMISSIONER.
How are you taking this?

HERALD.
Painful-like.
Everyone's doubled up worse as a midget nursin'
a wick in a midnight wind come moon-dark time.
Cain't even tetch them little old gals on the moosey
without we all agree to a Greece-wide Peace.

COMMISSIONER.
Of course!
A universal female plot—all Hellas
risen in rebellion—I should have known!

Return
to Sparta with this request:

Have them despatch us
A Plenipotentiary Commission, fully empowered
to conclude an armistice. I have full confidence
that I can persuade our Senate to do the same,
without extending myself. The evidence is at hand.

HERALD.
I'm a-flyin', Sir! I hev never heered your equal!

[*Exeunt hurriedly, the Commissioner to the left, the Herald to the right.*]

KORYPHAIOS OF MEN.
The most unnerving work of nature,

---

[42] A rod used in sending coded messages. The original message was written on a strip of paper
spiralled around the rod. Once unwrapped it could only be deciphered if wrapped around an
identical rod.

the pride of applied immortality,
is the common female human.
No fire can match, no beast can best her.
O Unsurmountability,
thy name—worse luck—is Woman.

KORYPHAIOS OF WOMEN.
After such knowledge, why persist
in wearing out this feckless
war between the sexes?
When can I apply for the post
of ally, partner, and general friend?

KORYPHAIOS OF MEN.
I won't be ployed to revise, re-do,
amend, extend, or bring to an end
my irreversible credo:
Misogyny Forever!
—The answer's never.

KORYPHAIOS OF WOMEN.
All right. Whenever you choose.
But, for the present, I refuse
to let you look your absolute worst,
parading around like an unfrocked freak:
I'm coming over and get you dressed.

[*She dresses him in his tunic, an action (like others in this scene) imitated by the members
of the Chorus of Women toward their opposite numbers in the Chorus of Men.*]

KORYPHAIOS OF MEN.
This seems sincere. It's not a trick.
Recalling the rancor with which I stripped,
I'm overlaid with chagrin.

KORYPHAIOS OF WOMEN.
Now you resemble a man,
not some ghastly practical joke.
And if you show me a little respect
(and promise not to kick), I'll extract
the beast in you.

KORYPHAIOS OF MEN. [*Searching himself.*]
                              What beast in me?

KORYPHAIOS OF WOMEN.
That insect. There. The bug that's stuck
in your eye.

KORYPHAIOS OF MEN. [*Playing along dubiously.*]
This gnat?

KORYPHAIOS OF WOMEN.
Yes, nitwit!

KORYPHAIOS OF MEN.
Of course.
That steady, festering agony. . . .
You've put your finger on the source
of all my lousy troubles. Please
roll back the lid and scoop it out.
I'd like to see it.

KORYPHAIOS OF WOMEN.

>All right, I'll do it.

[*Removing the imaginary insect.*]

>Although, of all the impossible cranks. . . .
>Do you sleep in a swamp? Just look at this.
>I've never seen a bigger chigger.

KORYPHAIOS OF MEN.

>Thanks.
>Your kindness touches me deeply. For years,
>that thing's been sinking wells in my eye.
>Now you've unplugged me. Here come the tears.

KORYPHAIOS OF WOMEN.

>I'll dry your tears, though I can't say why.

[*Wiping away the tears.*]

>Of all the irresponsible boys. . . .
>*And* I'll kiss you.

KORYPHAIOS OF MEN.

>Don't you kiss me!

KORYPHAIOS OF WOMEN.

>What made you think you had a choice? [*She kisses him.*]

KORYPHAIOS OF MEN.

All right, damn you, that's enough of that ingrained palaver.
I can't dispute the truth or logic of the pithy old proverb:

>>*Life with women is hell.*
>>*Life without women is hell, too.*

And so we conclude a truce with you, on the following terms:
in future, a mutual moratorium on mischief in all its forms.
Agreed?—Let's make a single chorus and start our song.

[*The two Choruses unite and face the audience.*]

CHORUS OF MEN.

>>We're not about to introduce
>>the standard personal abuse—
>>>the Choral Smear
>>Of Present Persons (usually,
>>in every well-made comedy,
>>>inserted here).
>>Instead, in deed and utterance, we
>>shall now indulge in philanthropy
>>>because we feel
>>that members of the audience
>>endure, in the course of current events,
>>>sufficient hell.
>>Therefore, friends, be rich! Be flush!
>>Apply to us, and borrow cash
>>>in large amounts.
>>The Treasury stands behind us—there—
>>and we can personally take care
>>>of small accounts.
>>Drop up today. Your credit's good.
>>Your loan won't have to be repaid
>>>in full until

the war is over. And then, your debt
is only the money you actually get—
    nothing at all.

CHORUS OF WOMEN.

    Just when we meant to entertain
    some madcap gourmets from out of town
       —such flawless taste!—
    the present unpleasantness intervened,
    and now we fear the feast we planned
       will go to waste.
    The soup is waiting, rich and thick;
    I've sacrificed a suckling pig
       —the *pièce de résistance*[43]—
    whose toothsome cracklings should amaze
    the most fastidious gourmets—
       you, for instance.
    To everybody here, I say
    take potluck at my house today
       with me and mine.
    Bathe and change as fast as you can,
    bring the children, hurry down,
       and walk right in.
    Don't bother to knock. No need at all.
    My house is yours. Liberty Hall.
       What are friends for?
    Act self-possessed when you come over;
    it may help out when you discover
       I've locked the door.

A delegation of Spartans enters from the right, with difficulty. They have removed their cloaks, but hold them before themselves in an effort to conceal their condition.

KORYPHAIOS OF MEN.
  What's this? Behold the Spartan ambassadors,
    dragging their beards,
  pussy-footing along. It appears they've developed
    a hitch in the crotch.
[*Advancing to greet them.*]
  Men of Sparta, I bid you welcome!
                  And now
  to the point: What predicament brings you among us?
SPARTAN.
  We-uns is up a stump. Hain't fit fer chatter.
[*Flipping aside his cloak.*]
  Here's our predicament. Take a look for yourselfs.
KORYPHAIOS OF MEN.
  Well, I'll be damned—a regular disaster area.
  Inflamed. I imagine the temperature's rather intense?

---

[43] Main dish.

SPARTAN.
   Hit ain't the heat, hit's the tumidity.
                                          But words
   won't help what ails us. We-uns come after Peace.
   Peace from any person, at any price.

Enter the Athenian delegation from the left, led by KINESIAS. *They are wearing cloaks, but are obviously in as much travail as the Spartans.*

KORYPHAIOS OF MEN.
   Behold our local Sons of the Soil, stretching
   their garments away from their groins, like wrestlers.
   Grappling with their plight. Some sort of athlete's disease, no doubt.
   An outbreak of epic proportions.
                                          Athlete's foot?
   No. Could it be athlete's . . . ?
KINESIAS. [*Breaking in.*]
                                 Who can tell us
   how to get hold of Lysistrata? We've come as delegates
   to the Sexual Congress.
[*Opening his cloak.*]
                                 Here are our credentials.
KORYPHAIOS OF MEN.
[*Ever the scientist, looking from the Athenians to the Spartans and back again.*]
   The words are different, but the malady seems the same.
[*To Kinesias.*]
   Dreadful disease. When the crisis reaches its height,
   what do you take for it?
KINESIAS.
                                 Whatever comes to hand.
   But now we've reached the bitter end. It's Peace
   or we fall back on Kleisthenes.
                                          And he's got a waiting list.
KORYPHAIOS OF MEN. [*To the Spartans.*]
   Take my advice and put your clothes on. If someone
   from that self-appointed Purity League comes by, you
   may be docked. They do it to the statues of Hermes,
   they'll do it to you.[44]
KINESIAS. [*Since he has not yet noticed the Spartans, he interprets the warning as meant for him, and hurriedly pulls his cloak together, as do the other Athenians.*]
             Excellent advice.
SPARTAN.
                                 Hit shorely is.
   Hain't nothing to argue after. Let's git dressed.
[*As they put on their cloaks, the Spartans are finally noticed by Kinesias.*]
KINESIAS.
   Welcome, men of Sparta! This is a shameful
   disgrace to masculine honor.

----

[44] In 415 B.C. the Athenian statues of Hermes, the god of messengers and thieves, were mutilated
   by vandals.

SPARTAN.

Hit could be worser.

Ef them Herm-choppers seed us all fired up,
they'd *really* take us down a peg or two.

KINESIAS.

Gentlemen, let's descend to details. Specifically,
why are you here?

SPARTAN.

Ambassadors. We come to dicker

'bout thet-thur Peace.

KINESIAS.

Perfect! Precisely our purpose.

Let's send for Lysistrata. Only she can reconcile
our differences. There'll be no Peace for us without her.

SPARTAN.

We-uns ain't fussy. Call Lysistratos, too, if you want.

The gates to the Akropolis open, and LYSISTRATA *emerges, accompanied by her handmaid,*
PEACE—*a beautiful girl without a stitch on.* PEACE *remains out of sight by the gates
until summoned.*

KORYPHAIOS OF MEN.

Hail, most virile of women! Summon up all your experience:
Be terrible and tender,

lofty and lowbrow,

severe and demure.

Here stand the Leaders of Greece, enthralled by your charm.
They yield the floor to you and submit their claims for your arbitration.

LYSISTRATA.

Really, it shouldn't be difficult, if I can catch them
all bothered, before they start to solicit each other.
I'll find out soon enough. Where's Peace?

—Come here.

[*Peace moves from her place by the gates to Lysistrata. The delegations goggle at her.*]

Now, dear, first get those Spartans and bring them to me.
Take them by the hand, but don't be pushy about it,
not like our husbands (no savoir-faire[45] at all!).
Be a lady, be proper, do just what you'd do at home:
if hands are refused, conduct them by the handle.

[*Peace leads the Spartans to a position near Lysistrata.*]

And now a hand to the Athenians—it doesn't matter
where; accept any offer—and bring *them* over.

[*Peace conducts the Athenians to a position near Lysistrata, opposite the Spartans.*]

You Spartans move up closer—right *here*—

[*To the Athenians.*]

and *you*

stand over *here*.

—And now attend my speech.

---

[45] Knowledge of the gracious way to do things.

[*This the delegations do with some difficulty, because of the conflicting attractions of Peace, who is standing beside her mistress.*]

I am a woman—but not without some wisdom:
my native wit is not completely negligible,
and I've listened long and hard to the discourse of my
elders—my education is not entirely despicable.
                                                                        Well,
now that I've got you, I intend to give you hell,
and I'm perfectly right. Consider your actions:
                                                              At festivals,
in Pan-Hellenic harmony, like true blood-brothers, you share
the selfsame basin of holy water, and sprinkle
altars all over Greece—Olympia, Delphoi,
Thermopylai . . . (I could go on and on, if length
were my only object.)
                                        But now, when the Persians sit by
and wait, in the very presence of your enemies, you fight
each other, destroy *Greek* men, destroy *Greek* cities!
—Point One of my address is now concluded.
KINESIAS. [*Gazing at Peace.*]
I'm destroyed, if this is drawn out much longer!
LYSISTRATA. [*Serenely unconscious of the interruption.*]
—Men of Sparta, I direct these remarks to you.
Have you forgotten that a Spartan suppliant once came
to beg assistance from Athens? Recall Perikleidas:
Fifty years ago, he clung to our altar,
his face dead-white above his crimson robe, and pleaded
for an army. Messene was pressing you hard in revolt,
and to this upheaval, Poseidon, the Earthshaker, added
another.
                    But Kimon took four thousand troops
from Athens—an army which saved the state of Sparta.
Such treatment have you received at the hands of Athens,
you who devastate the country that came to your aid!
KINESIAS. [*Stoutly; the condemnation of his enemy has made him forget the girl momentarily.*]
You're right, Lysistrata. The Spartans are clearly in the wrong!
SPARTAN. [*Guiltily backing away from Peace, whom he has attempted to pat.*]
Hit's wrong, I reckon, but that's the purtiest behind . . .
LYSISTRATA. [*Turning to the Athenians.*]
—Men of Athens, do you think I'll let *you* off?
Have you forgotten the Tyrant's days,[46] when you wore
the smock of slavery, when the Spartans turned to the
spear, cut down the pride of Thessaly, despatched the
friends of tyranny, and dispossessed your oppressors?
                                                                        Recall:
On that great day, your only allies were Spartans;
your liberty came at their hands, which stripped away
your servile garb and clothed you again in Freedom!

---

[46] "The reign of Hippias, expelled by Athenians in 510 with the aid of Kleomenes and his Spartans, who defeated the tyrant's Thessalian allies." (Translator's note.)

SPARTAN. [*Indicating Lysistrata.*]
 Hain't never seed no higher type of woman.
KINESIAS. [*Indicating Peace.*]
 Never saw one I wanted so much to top.
LYSISTRATA. [*Oblivious to the byplay, addressing both groups.*]
 With such a history of mutual benefits conferred
 and received, why are you fighting? Stop this wickedness!
 Come to terms with each other! What prevents you?
SPARTAN.
 We'd a heap sight druther make Peace, if we was
 indemnified with a plumb strategic location.
[*Pointing at Peace's rear.*]
                                    We'll take thet butte.[47]
LYSISTRATA.
 Butte?
SPARTAN.
     The Promontory of Pylos—Sparta's Back Door.
 We've missed it fer a turrible spell. [*Reaching.*]
                                    Hev to keep our
 hand in.
KINESIAS. [*Pushing him away.*]
         The price is too high—you'll never take that!
LYSISTRATA.
 Oh, let them have it.
KINESIAS.
                 What room will we have left
 for maneuvers?
LYSISTRATA.
             Demand another spot in exchange.
KINESIAS. [*Surveying Peace like a map as he addresses the Spartan.*]
 Then you hand over to us—uh, let me see—
 let's try Thessaly[48] [*Indicating the relevant portions of Peace.*]
                     First of all, Easy Mountain . . .
 then the Maniac Gulf behind it . . .
                             and down to Megara
 for the legs . . .
SPARTAN.
             You cain't take all of thet! Yore plumb
 out of yore mind!
LYSISTRATA. [*To Kinesias.*]
                 Don't argue. Let the legs go.
[*Kinesias nods. A pause. General smiles of agreement.*]
KINESIAS. [*Doffing his cloak.*]
 I feel an urgent desire to plow a few furrows.

[47] In the lines that follow, the discussion of the terms for peace is packed with *double entendre*. "That butte" is both a prominent part of the female anatomy and a reference to the promontory of Pylos, a region in Greece that the Spartans longed to control.
[48] "Puns on proper names, particularly geographical ones, rarely transfer well, as the following bits of sexual cartography will show. "Easy Mountain": an impossible pun on Mt. Oita, replacing the Greek's *Echinous*, a town in Thessaly whose name recalls *echinos* "hedgehog"—slang for the female genitalia. "Maniac Gulf": for Maliac Gulf, with less dimension than the Greek's *Mêlia kolpon*, which puns both on bosom and pudendum. The "legs of Megara" are the walls that connected that city with her seaport, Nisaia." (Translator's note.)

SPARTAN. [*Doffing his cloak.*]
　Hit's time to work a few loads of fertilizer in.
LYSISTRATA.
　Conclude the treaty and the simple life is yours.
　If such is your decision convene your councils,
　and then deliberate the matter with your allies.
KINESIAS.
　Deliberate? Allies?
　　　　　　　　　　We're over-extended already!
　Wouldn't every ally approve our position—
　Union Now?
SPARTAN.
　　　　　　　I know I kin speak for ourn.
KINESIAS.
　And I for ours.
　　　　　　　They're just a bunch of gigolos.
LYSISTRATA.
　I heartily approve.
　　　　　　　　Now first attend to your purification,
　then we, the women, will welcome you to the Citadel
　and treat you to all the delights of a home-cooked
　banquet. Then you'll exchange your oaths and pledge
　your faith, and every man of you will take his wife and
　depart for home. [*Lysistrata and Peace enter the Akropolis.*]
KINESIAS.
　　　　　　　　Let's hurry!
SPARTAN.
　　　　　　　　　Lead on, everwhich
　way's yore pleasure.
KINESIAS.
　　　　　　　　This way, then—and HURRY!
[*The delegations exeunt at a run.*]
CHORUS OF WOMEN.
　　　I'd never stint on anybody.
　　　And now I include, in my boundless bounty,
　　　　　the younger set.
　　　Attention, you parents of teenage girls
　　　about to debut in the social whirl.
　　　　　Here's what you get:
　　　Embroidered linens, lush brocades,
　　　a huge assortment of ready-mades,
　　　　　from mantles to shifts;
　　　plus bracelets and bangles of solid gold—
　　　every item my wardrobe holds—
　　　　　absolute gifts!
　　　Don't miss this offer. Come to my place,
　　　barge right in, and make your choice.
　　　　　You can't refuse.
　　　Everything there must go today.
　　　Finders keepers—cart it away!
　　　　　How can you lose?

Don't spare me. Open all the locks.
Break every seal. Empty every box.
    Keep ferreting—
And your sight's considerably better than mine
if you should possibly chance to find
    a single thing.

CHORUS OF MEN.
Troubles, friend? Too many mouths
to feed, and not a scrap in the house
    to see you through?
Faced with starvation? Don't give it a thought.
Pay attention; I'll tell you what
    I'm gonna do.
I overbought. I'm overstocked.
Every room in my house is clogged
    with flour (best ever),
glutted with luscious loaves whose size
you wouldn't believe. I need the space;
    do me a favor:
Bring gripsacks, knapsacks, duffle bags,
pitchers, cisterns, buckets, and kegs
    around to me.
A courteous servant will see to your needs;
he'll fill them up with A-1 wheat—
    and all for free!
—Oh. Just one final word before
you turn your steps to my front door:
    I happen to own
a dog. Tremendous animal.
Can't stand a leash. And bites like hell—
    better stay home.

[*The united Chorus flocks to the door of the Akropolis.*]

KORYPHAIOS OF MEN. *Banging at the door.*]
  Hey, open up in there!

The door opens, and the COMMISSIONER *appears. He wears a wreath, carries a torch, and is slightly drunk. He addresses the Koryphaios.*

COMMISSIONER.
              You know the Regulations.
Move along!
[*He sees the entire Chorus.*]
        —And why are YOU lounging around?
I'll wield my trusty torch and scorch the lot!
[*The Chorus backs away in mock horror. He stops and looks at his torch.*]
  —This is the bottom of the barrel. A cheap burlesque bit.
I refuse to do it. I have my pride.
[*With a start, he looks at the audience, as though hearing a protest. He shrugs and addresses the audience.*]
           —No choice, eh?
Well, if that's the way it is, we'll take the trouble.
Anything to keep you happy.

[*The Chorus advances eagerly.*]

KORYPHAIOS OF MEN.

Don't forget us!

We're in this too. Your trouble is ours!

COMMISSIONER. [*Resuming his character and jabbing with his torch at the Chorus.*]

Keep moving!

Last man out of the way goes home without hair!

Don't block the exit. Give the Spartans some room.

They've dined in comfort; let them go home in peace.

The CHORUS *shrinks back from the door.* KINESIAS, *wreathed and quite drunk, appears at the door. He speaks his first speech in Spartan.*

KINESIAS.

Hain't never seed sech a spread! Hit were splendiferous!

COMMISSIONER.

I gather the Spartans won friends and influenced people?

KINESIAS.

And *we've* never been so brilliant. It was the wine.

COMMISSIONER.

Precisely.

The reason? A sober Athenian is just

non compos.[49] If I can carry a little proposal

I have in mind, our Foreign Service will flourish,

guided by this rational rule:

No Ambassador

Without a Skinful.

Reflect on our past performance:

Down to a Spartan parley we troop, in a state

of disgusting sobriety, looking for trouble. It muddles

our senses: we read between the lines; we hear,

not what the Spartans say, but what we suspect

they might have been about to be going to say.

We bring back paranoid reports—cheap fiction, the fruit

of temperance. Cold-water diplomacy, pah!

Contrast

this evening's total pleasure, the free-and-easy

give-and-take of friendship: If we were singing,

Just Kleitagora and me,
Alone in Thessaly,

and someone missed his cue and cut in loudly,

Ajax, son of Telamon,
He was one hell of a man—

no one took it amiss, or started a war;

we clapped him on the back and gave three cheers.

[*During this recital, the Chorus has sidled up to the door.*]

—Dammit, are you back here again?

[*Waving his torch.*]

Scatter!

Get out of the road! Gangway, you gallowsbait!

---

[49] *Non compos mentis,* not of sound mind.

KINESIAS.

Yes, everyone out of the way. They're coming out.

Through the door emerge the Spartan delegation, a flutist, the Athenian delegation, LYSIS-TRATA, KLEONIKE, MYRRHINE, and the rest of the women from the citadel, both Athenian and Peloponnesian. The CHORUS splits into its male and female components and draws to the sides to give the procession room.

SPARTAN. [*To the flutist.*]

Friend and kinsman, take up them pipes a yourn.
I'd like fer to shuffle a bit and sing a right sweet
song in honor of Athens and us'uns, too.

COMMISSIONER. [*To the flutist.*]

Marvelous, marvelous—come, take up your pipes!

[*To the Spartan.*]

I certainly love to see you Spartans dance.

[*The flutist plays, and the Spartan begins a slow dance.*]

SPARTAN.

Memory,
send me
your Muse,
who knows
our glory,
knows Athens'—
Tell the story:
At Artemision
like gods, they stampeded
the hulks of the Medes, and
beat them.[50]

And Leonidas
leading us—
the wild boars
whetting their tusks.
And the foam flowered,
flowered and flowed,
down our cheeks
to our knees below.
The Persians there
like the sands of the sea—

Hither, huntress,
virgin, goddess,
tracker, slayer,
to our truce!
Hold us ever
fast together;
bring our pledges

---

[50] Near Artemision in 480 B.C. the Athenian navy defeated the navy of the Persians (or Medes). Meanwhile Leonidas with 300 Spartans held the pass at Thermopylae against the entire Persian army.

love and increase;
wean us from the
fox's wiles—

Hither, huntress!
Virgin, hither!

LYSISTRATA. [*Surveying the assemblage with a proprietary air.*]
   Well, the preliminaries are over—very nicely, too.
   So, Spartans,
[*Indicating the Peloponnesian women who have been hostages.*]
                  take these girls back home. And *you*
[*To the Athenian delegation, indicating the women from the Akropolis.*]
   take *these* girls. Each man stand by his wife, each wife
   by her husband. Dance to the gods' glory, and thank
   them for the happy ending. And, from now on, please be
   careful. Let's not make the same mistakes again.
[*The delegations obey; the men and women of the chorus join again for a rapid ode.*]
CHORUS.[51]
                  Start the chorus dancing,
                  Summon all the Graces,
            Send a shout to Artemis in invocation.
                  Call upon her brother,
                  healer, chorus master,
            Call the blazing Bacchus, with his maddened muster.

                  Call the flashing, fiery Zeus, and
                  call his mighty, blessed spouse, and
                  call the gods, call all the gods,
                  to witness now and not forget
                  our gentle, blissful Peace—the gift,
                     the deed of Aphrodite.
                              Ai!
                     Alalai!   Paion!
                     Leap you!   Paion!
                     Victory!   Alalai!
               Hail!   Hail!   Hail!
LYSISTRATA.
   Spartan, let's have another song from you, a new one.
SPARTAN.[52]

                  Leave darlin' Taygetos,
                  Spartan Muse! Come to us

---

[51] The Athenian chorus concludes with a song invoking many of the Greek gods: Artemis, the
   goddess of chastity; her brother Apollo, the god of medicine and music; Bacchus, the god of
   wine and revelry; Zeus, the leader of the gods; and Hera, the wife of Zeus. Fittingly, the song
   concludes with an appeal to Aphrodite, the goddess of love—for love, as stimulated by the
   sex-strike and the nude figure of Peace, has brought an end to the war.
[52] The Spartan's song celebrates Apollo, worshipped in the Spartan town of Amyklai; Athene,
   whose temple in Sparta was bronze-plated; Kastor and Pollux, the twin sons of Tyndaros, who
   were supposedly born by the Eurotas River in Sparta; and Helen, wife of the Spartan king
   Menelaos and the indirect cause of the Trojan War. Fittingly, the Spartan's song concludes
   with the praises of Athene, the patroness of Athens—thus reaffirming the peace between Sparta
   and Athens.

once more, flyin'
and glorifyin'
Spartan themes:
the god at Amyklai,
bronze-house Athene,
Tyndaros' twins,
the valiant ones,
playin' still by Eurotas' streams.

Up! Advance!
Leap to the dance!

Help us hymn Sparta,
lover of dancin',
lover of foot-pats,
where girls go prancin'
like fillies along Eurotas' banks,
whirlin' the dust, twinklin' their shanks,
shakin' their hair
like Maenads playin'
and jugglin' the thyrsis,
in frenzy obeyin'
Leda's daughter, the fair, the pure
Helen, the mistress of the choir.

Here, Muse, here!
Bind up your hair!

Stamp like a deer! Pound your feet!
Clap your hands! Give us a beat!

Sing the greatest,
sing the mightiest,
sing the conqueror,
sing to honor her—

Athene of the Bronze House!
Sing Athene!
[*Exeunt omnes, dancing and singing.*]

[411 B.C.]

William Shakespeare *1564–1616*

OTHELLO, THE MOOR OF VENICE

DRAMATIS PERSONÆ

DUKE OF VENICE
BRABANTIO, *a senator, Desdemona's father*
OTHER SENATORS
GRATIANO, *brother to Brabantio*
LODOVICO, *kinsman to Brabantio*
OTHELLO, *a noble Moor in the service of the Venetian state*
CASSIO, *his lieutenant*

IAGO, *his ancient*
RODERIGO, *a Venetian gentleman*
MONTANO, *Othello's predecessor in the government of Cyprus*
CLOWN, *servant to Othello*
DESDEMONA, *daughter to Brabantio and wife to Othello*
EMILIA, *wife to Iago*
BIANCA, *mistress to Cassio*

SAILOR, MESSENGER, HERALD, OFFICERS, GENTLEMEN, MUSICIANS, AND ATTENDANTS.

SCENE: *Venice: a seaport in Cyprus.*

ACT I.

SCENE I.
Venice. A street.

Enter RODERIGO *and* IAGO.

ROD. Tush, never tell me; I take it much unkindly
That thou, Iago, who hast had my purse
As if the strings were thine, shouldst know of this.
IAGO. 'Sblood, but you will not hear me:
If ever I did dream of such a matter,
Abhor me.
ROD. Thou told'st me thou didst hold him in thy hate.
IAGO. Despise me, if I do not. Three great ones of the
  city,
In personal suit to make me his lieutenant,
Off-caped° to him: and, by the faith of man,   doffed caps
I know my price, I am worth no worse a place:
But he, as loving his own pride and purposes,
Evades them, with a bombast circumstance°   pompous speech
Horribly stuffed with epithets of war;
And, in conclusion,
Nonsuits° my mediators; for, "Certes," says he,   rejects
"I have already chose my officer."
And what was he?
Forsooth, a great arithmetician,°   theorist
One Michael Cassio, a Florentine,

BRA. What tell'st thou me of robbing? This is Venice;
My house is not a grange.°   *farm*
    ROD.   Most grave Brabantio,
In simple and pure soul I come to you.
    IAGO. 'Zounds, sir, you are one of those that will not
serve God, if the devil bid you. Because we come to do
you service and you think we are ruffians, you'll have your
daughter covered with a Barbary° horse; you'll have your   *North African*
nephews° neigh to you; you'll have coursers° for cousins,   *grandsons / horses*
and gennets° for germans.°   *Spanish horses / kinfolk*
    BRA. What profane wretch art thou?
    IAGO. I am one, sir, that comes to tell you your daughter
and the Moor are now making the beast with two backs.
    BRA. Thou art a villain.
    IAGO.   You are—a senator.
    BRA. This thou shalt answer; I know thee, Roderigo.
    ROD. Sir, I will answer any thing. But, I beseech you,
If't be your pleasure and most wise consent,
As partly I find it is, that your fair daughter,
At this odd-even° and dull watch o' the night,   *wee hour*
Transported with no worse nor better guard
But with a knave of common hire, a gondolier,
To the gross clasps of a lascivious Moor,—
If this be known to you, and your allowance,°   *permission*
We then have done you bold and saucy° wrongs;   *impudent*
But if you know not this, my manners tell me
We have your wrong rebuke. Do not believe
That, from° the sense of all civility,   *contrary to*
I thus would play and trifle with your reverence:
Your daughter, if you have not given her leave,
I say again, hath made a gross revolt,
Tying her duty, beauty, wit and fortunes,
In an extravagant and wheeling° stranger   *roving*
Of here and everywhere. Straight satisfy yourself:
If she be in her chamber or your house,
Let loose on me the justice of the state
For thus deluding you.
    BRA.   Strike on the tinder, ho!
Give me a taper!° call up all my people!   *candle*
This accident is not unlike my dream:
Belief of it oppresses me already.
Light, I say! light! [*Exit above.*]
    IAGO.   Farewell; for I must leave you:
It seems not meet, nor wholesome to my place,
To be produced—as, if I stay, I shall—
Against the Moor: for I do know, the state,
However this may gall him with some check,°   *reprimand*
Cannot with safety cast° him; for he's embarked   *dismiss*
With such loud reason to the Cyprus wars,
Which even now stand in act,° that, for their souls,   *have begun*
Another of his fathom° they have none   *capability*

To lead their business: in which regard,
Though I do hate him as I do hell-pains,
Yet for necessity of present life,
I must show out a flag and sign of love,
Which is indeed but sign. That you shall surely find him,
Lead to the Sagittary° the raised search;   an inn
And there will I be with him. So farewell. [*Exit.*]

    Enter, below, BRABANTIO, *in his night-gown, and* SERVANTS *with torches.*

    BRA. It is too true an evil: gone she is;
And what's to come of my despisèd time
Is nought but bitterness. Now, Roderigo,
Where didst thou see her? O unhappy girl!
With the Moor, say'st thou? Who would be a father!
How didst thou know 'twas she? O, she deceives me
Past thought! What said she to you? Get more tapers.
Raise all my kindred. Are they married, think you?
    ROD. Truly, I think they are.
    BRA. O heaven! How got she out? O treason of the
    blood!
Fathers, from hence trust not your daughters' minds
By what you see them act. Is there not charms
By which the property° of youth and maidhood   true nature
May be abused? Have you not read, Roderigo,
Of some such thing?
    ROD.   Yes, sir, I have indeed.
    BRA. Call up my brother. O, would you had had her!
Some one way, some another. Do you know
Where we may apprehend her and the Moor?
    ROD. I think I can discover him, if you please
To get good guard and go along with me.
    BRA. Pray you, lead on. At every house I'll call;
I may command at most. Get weapons, ho!
And raise some special officers of night.
On, good Roderigo; I'll deserve° your pains. [*Exeunt.*]   reward

SCENE II.
Another street.

    Enter OTHELLO, IAGO, *and* ATTENDANTS *with torches.*

    IAGO. Though in the trade of war I have slain men,
Yet do I hold it very stuff o' the conscience
To do no contrived murder: I lack iniquity
Sometimes to do me service: nine or ten times
I had thought to have yerked° him here under the ribs.   stabbed
    OTH. 'Tis better as it is.
    IAGO.   Nay, but he prated
And spoke such scurvy and provoking terms

Against your honor,
That, with the little godliness I have,
I did full hard forbear him. But I pray you, sir,
Are you fast married? Be assured of this,
That the magnifico° is much beloved,   *nobleman*
And hath in his effect a voice potential
As double° as the duke's: he will divorce you,   *strong*
Or put upon you what restraint and grievance
The law, with all his might to enforce it on,
Will give him cable.°   *scope*
    OTH.   Let him do his spite:
My services, which I have done the signiory,°   *government*
Shall out-tongue his complaints. 'Tis yet to know—
Which, when I know that boasting is an honor,
I shall promulgate—I fetch my life and being
From men of royal siege,° and my demerits°   *rank / merits*
May speak unbonneted° to as proud a fortune   *proudly*
As this that I have reached: for know, Iago,
But that I love the gentle Desdemona,
I would not my unhoused free condition
Put into circumscription and confine°   *i.e., marriage*
For the sea's worth. But, look! what lights come yond?
    IAGO. Those are the raisèd father and his friends:
You were best go in.
    OTH.   Not I; I must be found:
My parts,° my title and my perfect soul,   *qualities*
Shall manifest me rightly. Is it they?
    IAGO. By Janus, I think no.

Enter CASSIO, *and certain* OFFICERS *with torches.*

    OTH. The servants of the duke, and my lieutenant.
The goodness of the night upon you, friends!
What is the news?
    CAS.   The duke does greet you, general,
And he requires your haste-post-haste appearance,
Even on the instant.
    OTH.   What is the matter, think you?
    CAS. Something from Cyprus, as I may divine:°   *speculate*
It is a business of some heat:° the galleys   *urgency*
Have sent a dozen sequent° messengers   *successive*
This very night at one another's heels;
And many of the consuls, raised and met,
Are at the duke's already: you have been hotly called for;
When, being not at your lodging to be found,
The senate hath sent about three several° quests   *separate*
To search you out.
    OTH.   'Tis well I am found by you.
I will but spend a word here in the house,
And go with you. [*Exit.*]
    CAS.   Ancient,° what makes he here?   *Ensign*

IAGO. Faith, he tonight hath boarded a land carack:[2]
If it prove lawful prize, he's made for ever.
   CAS. I do not understand.
   IAGO.   He's married.
   CAS.   To who?

Re-enter OTHELLO.

   IAGO. Marry, to—Come, captain, will you go?
   OTH.   Have with you.
   CAS. Here comes another troop to seek for you.
   IAGO. It is Brabantio: general, be advised;
He comes to bad intent.

Enter BRABANTIO, RODERIGO, and OFFICERS with torches and weapons.

   OTH.   Holla! stand there!
   ROD. Signior, it is the Moor.
   BRA.   Down with him, thief!
[<i>They draw on both sides.</i>]
   IAGO. You, Roderigo! come, sir, I am for you.
   OTH. Keep up your bright swords, for the dew will rust
   them.
Good signior, you shall more command with years
Than with your weapons.
   BRA. O thou foul thief, where hast thou stowed my
   daughter?
Damned as thou art, thou hast enchanted her;
For I'll refer me to all things of sense,°   <i>common sense</i>
If she in chains of magic were not bound,
Whether a maid so tender, fair and happy,
So opposite to marriage that she shunned
The wealthy curled° darlings of our nation,   <i>i.e., coiffured</i>
Would ever have, to incur a general mock,
Run from her guardage° to the sooty bosom   <i>legal home</i>
Of such a thing as thou, to fear, not to delight.
Judge me the world, if 'tis not gross° in sense   <i>obvious</i>
That thou hast practised on her with foul charms,
Abused her delicate youth with drugs or minerals
That weaken motion: I'll have't disputed on;
'Tis probable, and palpable to thinking.
I therefore apprehend and do attach° thee   <i>arrest</i>
For an abuser of the world, a practiser
Of arts inhibited° and out of warrant.°   <i>prohibited / unlawful</i>
Lay hold upon him: if he do resist,
Subdue him at his peril.
   OTH.   Hold your hands,
Both you of my inclining and the rest:
Were it my cue to fight, I should have known it

---

[2] A trading ship with a high stern.

Without a prompter. Where will you that I go
To answer this your charge?
      BRA.   To prison, till fit time
Of law and course of direct session
Call thee to answer.
      OTH.   What if I do obey?
How may the duke be therewith satisfied,
Whose messengers are here about my side,
Upon some present business of the state
To bring me to him?
      FIRST OFF.   'Tis true, most worthy signior;
The duke's in council, and your noble self,
I am sure, is sent for,
      BRA.   How! the duke in council!
In this time of the night! Bring him away:
Mine's not an idle cause: the duke himself,
Or any of my brothers of the state,
Cannot but feel this wrong as 'twere their own;
For if such actions may have passage free,
Bond-slaves and pagans shall our statesmen be. [*Exeunt.*]

SCENE III.
A council-chamber.

The DUKE *and* SENATORS *sitting at a table;* OFFICERS *attending.*

DUKE. There is no composition° in these news   *consistency*
That gives them credit.
      FIRST SEN.   Indeed they are disproportioned;
My letters say a hundred and seven galleys.
      DUKE. And mine, a hundred and forty.
      SEC. SEN.   And mine, two hundred:
But though they jump° not on a just° account,—   *settle / precise*
As in these cases, where the aim° reports,   *trend*
'Tis oft with difference,—yet do they all confirm
A Turkish fleet, and bearing up to Cyprus.
      DUKE. Nay, it is possible enough to judgement:
I do not so secure me in° the error,   *take such assurance from*
But° the main article I do approve°   *But that / believe*
In fearful sense.
      SAILOR. [*Within*] What, ho! what, ho! what, ho!
      FIRST OFF. A messenger from the galleys.

Enter SAILOR.

DUKE.   Now, what's the business?
      SAIL. The Turkish preparation makes for Rhodes;
So was I bid report here to the state
By Signior Angelo.
      DUKE. How say you by this change!

FIRST SEN.   This cannot be,
By no assay° of reason: 'tis a pageant°   *test / ploy*
To keep us in false gaze. When we consider
The importancy of Cyprus to the Turk,
And let ourselves again but understand
That as it more concerns the Turk than Rhodes,
So may he with more facile question° bear° it,   *battle / capture*
For that it stands not in such warlike brace,°   *condition*
But altogether lacks the abilities°   *strengths*
That Rhodes is dressed in: if we make thought of this,
We must not think the Turk is so unskilful
To leave that latest which concerns him first,
Neglecting an attempt of ease and gain,
To wake and wage a danger profitless.
    DUKE. Nay, in all confidence, he's not for Rhodes.
    FIRST OFF. Here is more news.

Enter a MESSENGER

    MESS. The Ottomites,° reverend and gracious,   *Turks*
Steering with due course toward the isle of Rhodes,
Have there injointed° them with an after° fleet.   *combined / following*
    FIRST SEN. Ay, so I thought. How many, as you guess?
    MESS. Of thirty sail: and now they do re-stem°   *turn about to*
Their backward course, bearing with frank appearance
Their purposes toward Cyprus. Signior Montano,
Your trusty and most valiant servitor,
With his free duty recommends° you thus,   *informs*
And prays you to believe him.
    DUKE. 'Tis certain then for Cyprus.
Marcus Luccicos, is not he in town?
    FIRST SEN. He's now in Florence.
    DUKE. Write from us to him; post-post-haste dispatch.
    FIRST SEN. Here comes Brabantio and the valiant Moor.

Enter BRABANTIO, OTHELLO, IAGO, RODERIGO, *and* OFFICERS.

    DUKE. Valiant Othello, we must straight employ you
Against the general enemy Ottoman.
[*To Brabantio*] I did not see you; welcome, gentle signior;
We lacked your counsel and your help tonight.
    BRA. So did I yours. Good your grace, pardon me;
Neither my place nor aught I heard of business
Hath raised me from my bed, nor doth the general care
Take hold on me; for my particular grief
Is of so flood-gate° and o'erbearing nature   *overflowing*
That it engluts° and swallows other sorrows,   *engulfs*
And it is still itself.
    DUKE.   Why, what's the matter?
    BRA. My daughter! O, my daughter!
    ALL.   Dead?

BRA.   Ay, to me;
She is abused, stol'n from me and corrupted
By spells and medicines bought of mountebanks;°   *quacks*
For nature so preposterously to err,
Being not deficient, blind, or lame of sense,
Sans° witchcraft could not.   *without*
        DUKE. Who'er he be that in this foul proceeding
Hath thus beguiled your daughter of herself
And you of her, the bloody book of law
You shall yourself read in the bitter letter
After your own sense, yea, though our proper° son   *own*
Stood in your action.°   *court action*
        BRA.   Humbly I thank your grace.
Here is the man, this Moor; whom now, it seems,
Your special mandate for the state-affairs
Hath hither brought.
        ALL.   We are very sorry for't.
        DUKE. [*To Othello*] What in your own part can you say
        to this?
        BRA. Nothing, but this is so.
        OTH. Most potent, grave, and reverend signiors,
My very noble and approved good masters,
That I have ta'en away this old man's daughter,
It is most true; true, I have married her:
The very head and front of my offending
Hath this extent, no more. Rude am I in my speech,
And little blest with the soft phrase of peace;
For since these arms of mine had seven years' pith,°   *strength*
Till now some nine moons wasted, they have used
Their dearest action in the tented field;
And little of this great world can I speak,
More than pertains to feats of broil and battle;
And therefore little shall I grace my cause
In speaking for myself. Yet, by your gracious patience,
I will a round unvarnished tale deliver
Of my whole course of love; what drugs, what charms,
What conjuration and what mighty magic—
For such proceeding I am charged withal—
I won his daughter.
        BRA.   A maiden never bold;
Of spirit so still and quiet that her motion°   *soul*
Blushed at herself; and she—in spite of nature,
Of years, of country, credit, everything—
To fall in love with what she feared to look on!
It is a judgement maimed and most imperfect
That will confess perfection so could err
Against all rules of nature; and must be driven
To find out practices of cunning hell,
Why this should be. I therefore vouch again,
That with some mixtures powerful o'er the blood,
Or with some dram conjured to this effect,

He wrought upon her.

DUKE.   To vouch° this, is no proof,   *assert*
Without more certain and more overt test
Than these thin habits° and poor likelihoods   *dressings*
Of modern° seeming do prefer against him.   *ordinary*

FIRST SEN. But, Othello, speak:
Did you by indirect and forced courses
Subdue and poison this young maid's affections?
Or came it by request, and such fair question
As soul to soul affordeth?

OTH.   I do beseech you,
Send for the lady to the Sagittary,
And let her speak of me before her father:
If you do find me foul in her report,
The trust, the office I do hold of you,
Not only take away, but let your sentence
Even fall upon my life.

DUKE.   Fetch Desdemona hither.

OTH. Ancient, conduct them; you best know the place.
[*Exeunt Iago and Attendants.*]
And till she come, as truly as to heaven
I do confess the vices of my blood,
So justly to your grave ears I'll present
How I did thrive in this fair lady's love
And she in mine.

DUKE. Say it, Othello.

OTH. Her father loved me, oft invited me,
Still questioned me the story of my life
From year to year, the battles, sieges, fortunes,
That I have passed.
I ran it through, even from my boyish days
To the very moment that he bade me tell it:
Wherein I spake of most diastrous chances,
Of moving accidents by flood and field,
Of hair-breadth 'scapes i' the imminent deadly breach,
Of being taken by the insolent foe,
And sold to slavery, of my redemption thence,
And portance° in my travels' history: *deportment*
Wherein of antres° vast and deserts idle,   *caves*
Rough quarries, rocks, and hills whose heads touch heaven,
It was my hint to speak,—such was the process;
And of the Cannibals that each other eat,
The Anthropophagi°, and men whose heads   *man-eaters*
Do grow beneath their shoulders. This to hear
Would Desdemona seriously incline:
But still the house-affairs would draw her thence;
Which ever as she could with haste dispatch,
She'ld come again, and with a greedy ear
Devour up my discourse: which I observing,
Took once a pliant° hour, and found good means   *convenient*
To draw from her a prayer of earnest heart

That I would all my pilgrimage dilate.°   *relate*
Whereof by parcels she had something heard,
But not intentively:° I did consent,   *attentively*
And often did beguile her of her tears
When I did speak of some distressful stroke
That my youth suffered. My story being done,
She gave me for my pains a world of sighs:
She swore, in faith, 'twas strange, 'twas passing strange;
'Twas pitiful, 'twas wondrous pitiful:
She wished she had not heard it, yet she wished
That heaven had made her such a man: she thanked me,
And bade me, if I had a friend that loved her,
I should but teach him how to tell my story,
And that would woo her. Upon this hint I spake:
She loved me for the dangers I had passed,
And I loved her that she did pity them.
This only is the witchcraft I have used.
Here comes the lady; let her witness it.

Enter DESDEMONA, IAGO, *and* ATTENDANTS.

DUKE. I think this tale would win my daughter too.
Good Brabantio,
Take up this mangled matter at the best:
Men do their broken weapons rather use
Than their bare hands.
     BRA.   I pray you, hear her speak:
If she confess that she was half the wooer,
Destruction on my head, if my bad blame
Light on the man! Come hither, gentle mistress:
Do you perceive in all this noble company
Where most you owe obedience?
     DES.   My noble father,
I do perceive here a divided duty:
To you I am bound for life and education;
My life and education both do learn me
How to respect you; you are the lord of duty,
I am hitherto your daughter: but here's my husband,
And so much duty as my mother showed
To you, preferring you before her father,
So much I challenge° that I may profess   *assert*
Due to the Moor my lord.
     BRA.   God be with you! I have done.
Please it your grace, on to the state-affairs:
I had rather to adopt a child than get° it.   *beget*
Come hither, Moor:
I here do give thee that with all my heart,
Which, but thou hast already, with all my heart
I would keep from thee. For your sake, jewel,
I am glad at soul I have no other child;
For thy escape would teach me tyranny,

To hang clogs° on them. I have done, my lord.   *weights*
   DUKE. Let me speak like yourself, and lay a sentence
Which, as a grise° or step, may help these lovers   *degree*
Into your favor.
When remedies are past, the griefs are ended
By seeing the worst, which late° on hopes depended.   *until lately*
To mourn a mischief that is past and gone
Is the next way to draw new mischief on.
What cannot be preserved when fortune takes,
Patience her injury a mockery makes.
The robbed that smiles steals something from the thief;
He robs himself that spends a bootless° grief.   *useless*
   BRA. So let the Turk of Cyprus us beguile;
We lose it not so long as we can smile.
He bears the sentence well, that nothing bears
But the free comfort which from thence he hears;
But he bears both the sentence and the sorrow,
That, to pay grief, must of poor patience borrow.
These sentences, to sugar or to gall,
Being strong on both sides, are equivocal:
But words are words; I never yet did hear
That the bruised heart was piercèd° through the ear.   *relieved (lanced)*
I humbly beseech you, proceed to the affairs of state.
   DUKE. The Turk with a most mighty preparation makes
for Cyprus. Othello, the fortitude of the place is best known
to you; and though we have there a substitute of most
allowed° sufficiency, yet opinion, a soveriegn mistress of   *acknowledged*
effects, throws a more safer voice on you: you must therefore
be content to slubber° the gloss of your new fortunes with   *sully*
this more stubborn and boisterous expedition.
   OTH. The tyrant custom, most grave senators,
Hath made the flinty and steel couch of war
My thrice-driven° bed of down: I do agnize°   *thrice-sifted / recognize*
A natural and prompt alacrity
I find in hardness; and do undertake
These present wars against the Ottomites.
Most humbly therefore bending to your state,
I crave fit disposition° for my wife,   *provision*
Due reference° of place and exhibition,°   *assignment / funds*
With such accommodation and besort°   *company*
As levels with her breeding.
   DUKE.   If you please,
Be 't at her father's.
   BRA.   I'll not have it so.
   OTH. Nor I.
   DES.   Nor I, I would not there reside,
To put my father in impatient thoughts
By being in his eye. Most gracious duke,
To my unfolding lend your prosperous ear,
And let me find a charter° in your voice   *permission*
To assist my simpleness.

DUKE. What would you, Desdemona?

DES. That I did love the Moor to live with him,
My downright violence and storm of fortunes
May trumpet to the world: my heart's subdued
Even to the very quality° of my lord: *appearance*
I saw Othello's visage in his mind,
And to his honor and his valiant parts
Did I my soul and fortunes consecrate.
So that, dear lords, if I be left behind,
A moth of peace, and he go to the war,
The rites for which I love him are bereft me,
And I a heavy interim shall support
By his dear absence. Let me go with him.

OTH. Let her have your voices.
Vouch with me, heaven, I therefore beg it not,
To please the palate of my appetite;
Nor to comply with heat°—the young affects   *lust*
In me defunct—and proper° satisfaction;   *personal*
But to be free and bounteous to her mind:
And heaven defend° your good souls, that you think   *forbid*
I will your serious and great business scant
For° she is with me. No, when light-winged toys   *Because*
Of feathered Cupid seel° with wanton dullness   *blind*
My speculative and officed instruments,[3]
That my disports° corrupt and taint my business,   *diversions*
Let housewives make a skillet of my helm,°   *helmet*
And all indign° and base adversities   *unworthy*
Make head against my estimation!°   *reputation*

DUKE. Be it as you shall privately determine,
Either for her stay or going: the affair cries haste,
And speed must answer 't; you must hence tonight.

DES. Tonight, my lord?

DUKE.   This night.

OTH.   With all my heart.

DUKE. At nine i' the morning here we'll meet again.
Othello, leave some officer behind,
And he shall our commission bring to you;
With such things else of quality and respect
As doth import° you.   *matter to*

OTH.   So please your grace, my ancient;
A man he is of honesty and trust:
To his conveyance I assign my wife,
With what else needful your good grace shall think
To be sent after me.

DUKE.   Let it be so.
Good night to every one. [*To Brab.*] And, noble signior,
If virtue no delighted° beauty lack,   *delightful*
Your son-in-law is far more fair than black.

FIRST SEN. Adieu, brave Moor; use Desdemona well.

---

[3] My clear-sighted and properly functioning faculties.

BRA. Look to her, Moor, if thou has eyes to see:
She has deceived her father, and may thee.
[*Exeunt Duke, Senators, Officers, &c.*]
    OTH. My life upon her faith! Honest Iago,
My Desdemona must I leave to thee:
I prithee, let thy wife attend on her;
And bring them after in the best advantage.°   *opportunity*
Come, Desdemona; I have but an hour
Of love, of worldly matters and direction,
To spend with thee: we must obey the time.
[*Exeunt Othello and Desdemona.*]
    ROD. Iago!
    IAGO. What say'st thou, noble heart?
    ROD. What will I do, thinkest thou?
    IAGO. Why, go to bed and sleep.
    ROD. I will incontinently° drown myself.   *immediately*
    IAGO. If thou dost, I shall never love thee after. Why,
thou silly gentleman!
    ROD. It is silliness to live when to live is torment; and
then have we a prescription to die when death is our physician.
    IAGO. O villanous! I have looked upon the world for
four times seven years; and since I could distinguish betwixt
a benefit and an injury, I never found man that knew how
to love himself. Ere I would say I would drown myself for
the love of a guinea-hen,° I would change my humanity   *whore*
with a baboon.
    ROD. What should I do? I confess it is my shame to
be so fond; but it is not in my virtue to amend it.
    IAGO. Virtue! a fig! 'tis in ourselves that we are thus
or thus. Our bodies are gardens; to the which our wills
are gardeners: so that if we will plant nettles° or sow lettuce,   *weeds*
set hyssop° and weed up thyme, supply it with one gender   *a mint*
of herbs or distract it with many, either to have it sterile
with idleness or manured with industry, why, the power
and corrigible° authority of this lies in our wills. If the bal-   *corrective*
ance of our lives had not one scale of reason to poise°   *counterweight*
another of sensuality, the blood and baseness of our natures
would conduct us to most preposterous conclusions: but
we have reason to cool our raging motions, our carnal stings,
our unbitted° lusts; whereof I take this, that you call love,   *unbridled*
to be a sect° or scion.°   *cutting / graft*
    ROD. It cannot be.
    IAGO. It is merely a lust of the blood and a permission
of the will. Come, be a man: drown thyself! drown cats
and blind puppies. I have professed me thy friend, and I
confess me knit to thy deserving with cables of perdurable°   *everlasting*
toughness: I could never better stead° thee than now. Put   *assist*
money in thy purse; follow thou the wars; defeat° thy favor°   *disguise / face*
with an usurped° beard; I say, put money in thy purse. It   *false*
cannot be that Desdemona should long continue her love

to the Moor—put money in thy purse—nor he his to her:
it was a violent commencement, and thou shalt see an an-
swerable sequestration;° put but money in thy purse. These   *similar separation*
Moors are changeable in their wills:—fill thy purse with
money. The food that to him now is as luscious as locusts,
shall be to him shortly as bitter as coloquintida.° She must   *bitter apple*
change for youth: when she is sated with his body, she will
find the error of her choice: she must have change, she
must: therefore put money in thy purse. If thou wilt needs
damn thyself, do it a more delicate way than drowning.
Make all the money thou canst: if sanctimony and a frail
vow betwixt an erring barbarian and a supersubtle Venetian
be not too hard for my wits and all the tribe of hell, thou
shalt enjoy her; therefore make money. A pox of drowning
thyself! it is clean out of the way: seek thou rather to be
hanged in compassing° thy joy than to be drowned and   *attaining*
go without her.

    Rod. Wilt thou be fast° to my hopes, if I depend on   *true*
the issue?

    Iago. Thou art sure of me: go, make money: I have
told thee often, and I retell thee again and again, I hate
the Moor: my cause is hearted°; thine hath no less reason.   *heart-felt*
Let us be conjunctive° in our revenge against him: if thou   *joined*
canst cuckold him, thou dost thyself a pleasure, me a sport.
There are many events in the womb of time, which will
be delivered. Traverse; go; provide thy money. We will have
more of this tomorrow. Adieu.

    Rod. Where shall we meet 'i the morning?

    Iago. At my lodging.

    Rod. I'll be with thee betimes.°   *early*

    Iago. Go to; farewell. Do you hear, Roderigo?

    Rod. What say you?

    Iago. No more of drowning, do you hear?

    Rod. I am changed: I'll go sell all my land. [*Exit.*]

    Iago. Thus do I ever make my fool my purse;
For I mine own gained knowledge should profane,
If I would time expend with such a snipe°   *fool*
But for my sport and profit. I hate the Moor;
And it is thought abroad that 'twixt my sheets
He has done my office: I know not if't be true;
But I for mere suspicion in that kind
Will do as if for surety.° He holds me well;   *certainty*
The better shall my purpose work on him.
Cassio's a proper° man: let me see now;   *handsome*
To get his place, and to plume up° my will   *satisfy*
In double knavery—How, how?—Let's see:—
After some time, to abuse Othello's ear
That he is too familiar with his wife.
He hath a person and a smooth dispose°   *disposition*
To be suspected; framed to make women false.
The Moor is of a free and open nature,

That thinks men honest that but seem to be so;
And will as tenderly be led by the nose
As asses are.
I have 't. It is engendered. Hell and night
Must bring this monstrous birth to the world's light. [*Exit.*]

ACT II.

SCENE I.
A sea-port in Cyprus. An open place near the quay.

Enter MONTANO *and two* GENTLEMEN.

MON. What from the cape can you discern at sea?
FIRST GENT. Nothing at all: it is a high-wrought flood;
I cannot, 'twixt the heaven and the main,
Descry° a sail.   *See*
MON. Methinks the wind hath spoke aloud at land;
A fuller blast ne'er shook our battlements:
If it hath ruffianed° so upon the sea,   *raged*
What ribs of oak, when mountains melt on them,
Can hold the mortise?⁴ What shall we hear of this?
SEC. GENT. A segregation° of the Turkish fleet: *dispersal*
For do but stand upon the foaming shore,
The chidden° billow seems to pelt the clouds;   *driven*
The wind-shaked surge, with high and monstrous mane,
Seems to cast water on the burning bear,°   *a constellation*
And quench the guards⁵ of the ever-fixèd pole:
I never did like molestation° view   *disruption*
On the enchafèd flood.°   *raging sea*
MON.   If that the Turkish fleet
Be not ensheltered and embayed, they are drowned;
It is impossible to bear it out.

Enter a third GENTLEMAN.

THIRD GENT. News, lads! Our wars are done.
The desperate tempest hath so banged the Turks,
That their designment° halts: a noble ship of Venice   *plan*
Hath seen a grievous wreck and sufferance°   *suffering*
On most part of their fleet.
MON. How! Is this true?
THIRD GENT.   The ship is here put in,
A Veronesa; Michael Cassio,
Lieutenant to the warlike Moor Othello,
Is come on shore: the Moor himself at sea,
And is in full commission here for Cyprus.

⁴ The slot into which the ribs of the ship are fitted.
⁵ The stars near (or guarding) the North Star.

Mon. I am glad on't; 'tis a worthy governor.

Third Gent. But this same Cassio, though he speak
of comfort
Touching the Turkish loss, yet he looks sadly
And prays the Moor be safe; for they were parted
With foul and violent tempest.

Mon.   Pray heavens he be;
For I have served him, and the man commands
Like a full soldier. Let's to the seaside, ho!
As well to see the vessel that's come in
As to throw out our eyes for brave Othello,
Even till we make the main and the aerial blue
An indistinct regard.°   *view (horizon)*

Third Gent.   Come, let's do so;
For every minute is expectancy
Of more arrivance.

Enter Cassio.

Cas. Thanks, you the valiant of this warlike isle,
That so approve the Moor! O, let the heavens
Give him defence against the elements,
For I have lost him on a dangerous sea.

Mon. Is he well shipped?

Cas. His bark is stoutly timbered, and his pilot
Of very expert and approved allowance°;   *acclaim*
Therefore my hopes, not surfeited to death°,   *not excessive*
Stand in bold cure°. [*A cry within:* "A sail, a sail, a sail!"]   *in good stead*

Enter a fourth Gentleman.

Cas. What noise?

Fourth Gent. The town is empty; on the brow o' the
sea
Stand ranks of people, and they cry "A sail!"

Cas. My hopes do shape him for the governor.
[*Guns heard.*]

Sec. Gent. They do discharge their shot of courtesy:
Our friends at least.

Cas.   I pray you, sir, go forth,
And give us truth who 'tis that is arrived.

Sec. Gent. I shall. [*Exit.*]

Mon. But, good lieutenant, is your general wived?

Cas. Most fortunately: he hath achieved a maid
That paragons° description and wild fame;   *tops*
One that excels the quirks of blazoning° pens,   *praising*
And in the essential vesture° of creation   *clothing*
Does tire the ingener°.   *creator of the praise*

Re-enter second Gentleman.

                   How now! who has put in?
SEC. GENT. 'Tis one Iago, ancient to the general.
  CAS. He has had most favorable and happy speed:
Tempests themselves, high seas, and howling winds,
The guttered° rocks, and congregated sands,   *jagged*
Traitors ensteeped° to clog° the guiltless keel,   *submerged / obstruct*
As having sense of beauty, do omit°   *neglect*
Their mortal° natures, letting go safely by   *deadly*
The divine Desdemona.
  MON.   What is she?
  CAS. She that I spake of, our great captain's captain,
Left in the conduct of the bold Iago;
Whose footing° here anticipates our thoughts   *setting foot*
A se'nnight's° speed. Great Jove, Othello guard,   *week's*
And swell his sail with thine own powerful breath,
That he may bless this bay with his tall ship,
Make love's quick pants in Desdemona's arms,
Give renewed fire to our extincted spirits,
And bring all Cyprus comfort.

          Enter DESDEMONA, EMILIA, IAGO, RODERIGO, *and* ATTENDANTS.

                   O, behold,
The riches of the ship is come on shore!
Ye men of Cyprus, let her have your knees.
Hail to thee, lady! and the grace of heaven,
Before, behind thee, and on every hand,
Enwheel° thee round!   *Encircle*
  DES.   I thank you, valiant Cassio.
What tidings can you tell me of my lord?
  CAS. He is not yet arrived: nor know I aught
But that he's well and will be shortly here.
  DES. O, but I fear—How lost you company?
  CAS. The great contention of the sea and skies
Parted our fellowship—But, hark! a sail.
[*A cry within:* "A sail, a sail!" *Guns heard.*]
  SEC. GENT. They give their greeting to the citadel:
This likewise is a friend.
  CAS.   See for the news.
  [*Exit* GENTLEMAN.]
Good ancient, you are welcome. [*To* EMILIA] Welcome,
  mistress:
Let it not gall your patience, good Iago,
That I extend° my manners; 'tis my breeding   *show*
That gives me this bold show of courtesy. [*Kissing her.*]
  IAGO. Sir, would she give you so much of her lips
As of her tongue she oft bestows on me,
You'd have enough.
  DES.   Alas, she has no speech.
  IAGO. In faith, too much;
I find it still when I have list° to sleep: *desire*

Marry, before your ladyship, I grant,
She puts her tongue a little in her heart
And chides with thinking.
    EMIL. You have little cause to say so.
    IAGO. Come on, come on; you are pictures out of doors,
Bells in your parlors, wild-cats in your kitchens,
Saints in your injuries, devils being offended,
Players in your housewifery, and housewives° in your beds.   *i.e., hard working*
DES. O, fie upon thee, slanderer!
    IAGO. Nay, it is true, or else I am a Turk:
You rise to play, and go to bed to work.
    EMIL. You shall not write my praise.
    IAGO.   No, let me not.
    DES. What wouldst thou write of me, if thou shouldst
praise me?
    IAGO. O gentle lady, do not put me to't;
For I am nothing if not critical.
    DES. Come on, assay°—There's one gone to the harbor?   *try*
    IAGO. Ay, madam.
    DES. I am not merry; but I do beguile°   *divert attention from*
The thing I am by seeming otherwise.
Come, how wouldst thou praise me?
    IAGO. I am about it; but indeed my invention
Comes from my pate as birdlime does from frize[6];
It plucks out brains and all: but my Muse labors,
And thus she is delivered.
If she be fair° and wise, fairness and wit,   *blonde, pretty*
The one's for use, the other useth it.
    DES. Well praised! How if she be black° and witty?   *brunette, ugly*
    IAGO. If she be black, and thereto have a wit,
She'll find a white° that shall her blackness fit.   *fair person*
    DES. Worse and worse.
    EMIL. How if fair and foolish?
    IAGO. She never yet was foolish that was fair;
For even her folly helped her to an heir.
    DES. These are old fond° paradoxes to make fools laugh   *foolish*
i' the alehouse. What miserable praise hast thou for her
that's foul and foolish?
    IAGO. There's none so foul, and foolish thereunto,
But does foul pranks which fair and wise ones do.
    DES. O heavy ignorance! thou praisest the worst best.
But what praise couldst thou bestow on a deserving woman
indeed, one that in the authority of her merit did justly
put on° the vouch° of very malice itself?   *claim / praise*
    IAGO. She that was ever fair and never proud,
Had tongue at will and yet was never loud,
Never lacked gold and yet went never gay°,   *gaily dressed*
Fled from her wish and yet said "Now I may";

---

[6] I.e., but indeed my ideas come from my brain as unwillingly as tar comes unstuck from coarse
cloth.

She that, being angered, her revenge being nigh,
Bade her wrong stay and her displeasure fly;
She that in wisdom never was so frail
To change the cod's head for the salmon's tail;[7]
She that could think and ne'er disclose her mind,
See suitors following and not look behind;
She was a wight,° if ever such wight were,—   *person*
    DES. To do what?
    IAGO. To suckle fools and chronicle small beer.°   *keep trivial accounts*
    DES. O most lame and impotent conclusion! Do not learn
of him, Emilia, though he be thy husband. How say you,
Cassio? Is he not a most profane and liberal° counsellor?   *lewd*
    CAS. He speaks home°, madam: you may relish him more   *pointedly*
in the soldier than in the scholar.
    IAGO. [*Aside*] He takes her by the palm: ay, well said,
whisper: with as little a web as this will I ensnare as great
a fly as Cassio. Ay, smile upon her, do; I will gyve° thee   *fetter*
in thine own courtship. You say true; 'tis so, indeed: if such
tricks as these strip you out of your lieutenantry, it had
been better you had not kissed your three fingers so oft,
which now again you are most apt to play the sir° in. Very   *gentleman*
good; well kissed! an excellent courtesy! 'tis so, indeed.
Yet again your fingers to your lips? Would they were clyster-
pipes° for your sake! [*Trumpet within.*] The Moor! I know   *enema tubes*
his trumpet.
    CAS. 'Tis truly so.
    DES. Let's meet him and receive him.
    CAS. Lo, where he comes!

Enter OTHELLO *and* ATTENDANTS.

    OTH. O my fair warrior!
    DES.   My dear Othello!
    OTH. It gives me wonder great as my content
To see you here before me. O my soul's joy!
If after every tempest come such calms,
May the winds blow till they have wakened death!
And let the laboring bark climb hills of seas
Olympus-high and duck again as low
As hell's from heaven! If it were now to die,
'Twere now to be most happy; for I fear,
My soul hath her content so absolute
That not another comfort like to this
Succeeds in unknown fate.
    DES.   The heavens forbid
But that our loves and comforts should increase,
Even as our days do grow!
    OTH.   Amen to that, sweet powers!

---

[7] The cod, a common edible fish, is often said to be all head. The salmon is a delicacy, but its
    tail would be inedible.

I cannot speak enough of this content;
It stops me here; it is too much of joy:
And this, and this, the greatest discords be [*Kissing her.*]
That e'er our hearts shall make!

      IAGO.   [*Aside*] O, you are well tuned now!
But I'll set down the pegs that make this music
As honest as I am.[8]

      OTH.   Come, let us to the castle.
News, friends; our wars are done, the Turks are drowned.
How does my old acquaintance of this isle?
Honey, you shall be well desired in Cyprus;
I have found great love amongst them. O my sweet,
I prattle out of fashion, and I dote
In mine own comforts. I prithee, good Iago,
Go to the bay, and disembark my coffers:°   *chests*
Bring thou the master to the citadel;
He is a good one, and his worthiness
Does challenge° much respect. Come, Desdemona,   *lay claim to*
Once more well met at Cyprus.
[*Exeunt all but Iago and Roderigo.*]

      IAGO. Do thou meet me presently at the harbor. Come
hither. If thou be'st valiant—as, they say, base men being
in love have then a nobility in their natures more than is
native to them—list° me. The lieutenant tonight watches   *hear*
on the court of guard. First, I must tell thee this: Desdemona
is directly in love with him.

      ROD. With him! why, 'tis not possible.

      IAGO. Lay thy finger thus,° and let thy soul be instructed.   *on your lips*
Mark me with what violence she first loved the Moor, but
for bragging and telling her fantastical lies: and will she
love him still for prating? Let not thy discreet heart think
it. Her eye must be fed; and what delight shall she have
to look on the devil? When the blood is made dull with
the act of sport, there should be, again to inflame it and
to give satiety a fresh appetite, loveliness in favor,° sympathy   *face*
in years, manners and beauties; all which the Moor is defective in: now, for want of these required conveniences, her
delicate tenderness will find itself abused, begin to heave
the gorge°, disrelish and abhor the Moor; very nature will   *vomit*
instruct her in it and compel her to some second choice.
Now, sir, this granted—as it is a most pregnant° and un-   *well conceived*
forced position—who stands so eminently in the degree
of this fortune as Cassio does? A knave very voluble; no
further conscionable than in putting on the mere form of
civil and humane seeming, for the better compassing of
his salt° and most hidden loose affection? Why, none; why,   *salty, lustful*
none: a slipper° and subtle knave; a finder out of occasions;   *slippery*
that has an eye can stamp and counterfeit advantages,

---

[8] I.e., Iago will untune the heartstrings of Othello and Desdemona until their loving music is no
    more honest (harmonious) than he is.

though true advantage never present itself: a devilish knave! Besides, the knave is handsome, young, and hath all those requisites in him that folly and green minds look after: a pestilent complete knave; and the woman hath found him already.

ROD. I cannot believe that in her; she's full of most blest condition.

IAGO. Blest fig's-end! The wine she drinks is made of grapes: if she had been blest, she would never have loved the Moor: blest pudding! Didst thou not see her paddle° *toy* with the palm of his hand? Didst not mark that?

ROD. Yes, that I did; but that was but courtesy.

IAGO. Lechery, by this hand; an index and obscure prologue to the history of lust and foul thoughts. They met so near with their lips that their breaths embraced together. Villanous thoughts, Roderigo! When these mutualities so marshal the way, hard at hand comes the master and main exercise, the incorporate° conclusion: pish! But, sir, be you *carnal* ruled by me: I have brought you from Venice. Watch you tonight; for the command, I'll lay't upon you: Cassio knows you not: I'll not be far from you: do you find some occasion to anger Cassio, either by speaking too loud or tainting° *discrediting* his discipline, or from what other course you please, which the time shall more favorably minister.

ROD. Well.

IAGO. Sir, he is rash and very sudden in choler°, and *anger* haply may strike at you: provoke him, that he may; for even out of that will I cause these of Cyprus to mutiny; whose qualification° shall come into no true taste again but by *equinimity* the displanting of Cassio. So shall you have a shorter journey to your desires by the means I shall then have to prefer° *advance* them, and the impediment most profitably removed, without the which there were no expectation of our prosperity.

ROD. I will do this, if I can bring it to any opportunity.

IAGO. I warrant° thee. Meet me by and by at the citadel: *promise* I must fetch his necessaries ashore. Farewell.

ROD. Adieu. [*Exit.*]

IAGO. That Cassio loves her, I do well believe it;
That she loves him, 'tis apt° and of great credit:° *possible / credibility*
The Moor, howbeit that I endure him not,
Is of a constant, loving, noble nature;
And I dare think he'll prove to Desdemona
A most dear husband. Now, I do love her too,
Not out of absolute lust, though peradventure° *perhaps*
I stand accountant for as great a sin,
But partly led to diet° my revenge, *feed*
For that I do suspect the lusty Moor
Hath leaped into my seat:° the thought whereof *i.e., cuckolded me*
Doth like a poisonous mineral gnaw my inwards;
And nothing can or shall content my soul
Till I am evened with him, wife for wife;

Or failing so, yet that I put the Moor
At least into a jealousy so strong
That judgement cannot cure. Which thing to do,
If this poor trash of Venice, whom I trash°   restrain
For his quick hunting, stand the putting on,°   on (the scent)
I'll have our Michael Cassio on the hip,°   i.e., the ground
Abuse him to the Moor in the rank garb;°   insinuating style
For I fear Cassio with my night-cap° too;   wife
Make the Moor thank me, love me and reward me,
For making him egregiously an ass
And practising upon his peace and quiet
Even to madness. 'Tis here, but yet confused:
Knavery's plain face is never seen till used. [*Exit.*]

SCENE II.
A street.

Enter a HERALD *with a proclamation;* PEOPLE *following.*

HER. It is Othello's pleasure, our noble and valiant general, that upon certain tidings now arrived, importing the
mere perdition° of the Turkish fleet, every man put himself   total loss
into triumph; some to dance, some to make bonfires, each
man to what sport and revels his addiction° leads him: for,   inclination
besides these beneficial news, it is the celebration of his
nuptial. So much was his pleasure should be proclaimed.
All offices° are open, and there is full liberty of feasting   mess-halls
from this present hour of five till the bell have told eleven.
Heaven bless the isle of Cyprus and our noble general
Othello! [*Exeunt.*]

SCENE III.
A hall in the castle.

Enter OTHELLO, DESDEMONA, CASSIO, *and* ATTENDANTS.

OTH. Good Michael, look you to the guard tonight:
Let's teach ourselves that honorable stop,°   self-restraint
Not to outsport discretion.
    CAS. Iago hath direction what to do;
But notwithstanding with my personal eye
Will I look to't.
    OTH.   Iago is most honest.
Michael, good night: tomorrow with your earliest
Let me have speech with you. Come, my dear love,
The purchase made, the fruits are to ensue;
That profit's yet to come 'tween me and you.
Good night. [*Exeunt Othello, Desdemona, and Attendants.*]

Enter IAGO.

Cas. Welcome, Iago; we must to the watch.

Iago. Not this hour, lieutenant; 'tis not yet ten o' the
clock. Our general cast° us thus early for the love of his   *dismissed*
Desdemona; who let us not therefore blame: he hath not
yet made wanton the night with her, and she is sport for
Jove.

Cas. She's a most exquisite lady.

Iago. And, I'll warrant her, full of game.

Cas. Indeed she's a most fresh and delicate creature.

Iago. What an eye she has! Methinks it sounds° a parley°   *signals / conference*
to provocation.°   *sexual excitement*

Cas. An inviting eye; and yet methinks right modest.

Iago. And when she speaks, is it not an alarum° to love?   *call*

Cas. She is indeed perfection.

Iago. Well, happiness to their sheets! Come, lieutenant,
I have a stoup° of wine; and here without are a brace° of   *half-gallon / pair*
Cyprus gallants that would fain have a measure to the health
of black Othello.

Cas. Not tonight, good Iago: I have very poor and unhappy brains for drinking: I could well wish courtesy would
invent some other custom of entertainment.

Iago. O, they are our friends; but one cup: I'll drink
for you.

Cas. I have drunk but one cup tonight, and that was
craftily qualified° too, and behold what innovation° it makes   *diluted / change*
here: I am unfortunate in the infirmity and dare not task
my weakness with any more.

Iago. What, man! 'Tis a night of revels: the gallants
desire it.

Cas. Where are they?

Iago. Here at the door; I pray you, call them in.

Cas. I'll do 't; but it dislikes me. [*Exit.*]

Iago. If I can fasten but one cup upon him,
With that which he hath drunk tonight already,
He'll be as full of quarrel and offence
As my young mistress' dog. Now my sick fool Roderigo,
Whom love hath turned almost the wrong side out,
To Desdemona hath tonight caroused
Potations pottle-deep;° and he's to watch: *by the potful*
Three lads of Cyprus, noble swelling spirits,
That hold their honors in a wary distance,°   *touchily*
The very elements of this warlike isle,
Have I tonight flustered with flowing cups,
And they watch too. Now, 'mongst this flock of drunkards,
Am I to put our Cassio in some action
That may offend the isle. But here they come:
If consequence° do but approve° my dream,   *events / confirm*
My boat sails freely, both with wind and stream.

Re-enter CASSIO; *with him* MONTANO *and* GENTLEMEN;
SERVANTS *following with wine.*

CAS. 'Fore God, they have given me a rouse° already.   *drink*

MON. Good faith, a little one; not past a pint, as I am
a soldier.

IAGO. Some wine, ho!

[*Sings*] And let me the canakin° clink, clink;   *little pot*
          And let me the canakin clink:
              A soldier's a man;
              A life's but a span;
          Why then let a soldier drink.
Some wine, boys!

CAS. 'Fore God, an excellent song.

IAGO. I learned it in England, where indeed they are
most potent in potting°: your Dane, your German, and your   *draining pots*
swag-bellied Hollander,—Drink, ho!—are nothing to your
English.

CAS. Is your Englishman so expert in his drinking?

IAGO. Why, he drinks you with facility your Dane dead
drunk; he sweats not to overthrow your Almain°; he gives   *German*
your Hollander a vomit ere the next pottle° can be filled.   *pot*

CAS. To the health of our general!

MON. I am for it, lieutenant, and I'll do you justice.°   *equal you*

IAGO. O sweet England!

[*Sings*] King Stephen was a worthy peer,
          His breeches cost him but a crown;
          He held them sixpence all too dear,
              With that he called the tailor lown.°   *rascal*

          He was a wight of high renown,
              And thou art but of low degree:
          'Tis pride that pulls the country down;
              Then take thine auld° cloak about thee.   *old*
Some wine, ho!

CAS. Why, this is a more exquisite song than the other.

IAGO. Will you hear't again?

CAS. No; for I hold him to be unworthy of his place
that does those things. Well: God's above all; and there
be souls must be saved, and there be souls must not be
saved.

IAGO. It's true, good lieutenant.

CAS. For mine own part—no offence to the general, nor
any man of quality—I hope to be saved.

IAGO. And so do I too, lieutenant.

CAS. Ay, but, by your leave, not before me; the lieutenant
is to be saved before the ancient. Let's have no more of
this; let's to our affairs. God forgive us our sins! Gentlemen,
let's look to our business. Do not think, gentlemen, I am
drunk: this is my ancient: this is my right hand, and this
is my left. I am not drunk now; I can stand well enough,
and speak well enough.

ALL. Excellent well.

CAS. Why, very well then; you must not think then that
I am drunk. [*Exit.*]
    MON. To the platform, masters; come, let's set the watch.
    IAGO. You see this fellow that is gone before;
He is a soldier fit to stand by Caesar
And give direction: and do but see his vice;
'Tis to his virtue a just equinox,°   *an exact equal*
The one as long as the other: 'tis pity of him.
I fear the trust Othello puts him in
On some odd time of his infirmity
Will shake this island.
    MON.   But is he often thus?
    IAGO. 'Tis evermore the prologue to his sleep:
He'll watch the horologe° a double set,°   *clock / twice around*
If drink rock not his cradle.
    MON.   It were well
The general were put in mind of it.
Perhaps he sees it not, or his good nature
Prizes the virtue that appears in Cassio
And looks not on his evils: is not this true?

Enter RODERIGO.

    IAGO. [*Aside to him*] How now, Roderigo!
I pray you, after the lieutenant; go. [*Exit Roderigo.*]
    MON. And 'tis great pity that the noble Moor
Should hazard such a place as his own second
With one of an ingraft° infirmity: *ingrained*
It were an honest action to say
So to the Moor.
    IAGO.   Not I, for this fair island:
I do love Cassio well, and would do much
To cure him of this evil:—But, hark! what noise?
[*A cry within:* "Help! help!"]

Re-enter CASSIO, *driving in* RODERIGO.

    CAS. 'Zounds! you rogue! you rascal!
    MON. What's the matter, lieutenant?
    CAS. A knave teach me my duty! But I'll beat the knave
into a wicker bottle.
    ROD. Beat me!
    CAS. Dost thou prate, rogue? [*Striking Roderigo.*]
    MON. Nay, good lieutenant; I pray, you, sir, hold your
hand.
    CAS. Let me go, sir, or I'll knock you o'er the mazzard.°   *head*
    MON. Come, come, you're drunk.
    CAS. Drunk! [*They fight.*]
    IAGO. [*Aside to Roderigo*] Away, I say; go out, and cry a
mutiny. [*Exit Roderigo.*]
Nay, good lieutenant! God's will, gentlemen!

Help, ho!—Lieutenant,—sir,—Montano—sir;—
Help, masters!—Here's a goodly watch indeed!
[*A bell rings.*]
Who's that that rings the bell?—Diablo,° ho!   *The devil*
The town will rise: God's will, lieutenant, hold;
You will be shamed forever.

Re-enter OTHELLO *and* ATTENDANTS.

OTH.   What is the matter here?
MON. 'Zounds, I bleed still; I am hurt to the death.
[*Faints.*]
OTH. Hold, for your lives!
IAGO. Hold, ho! Lieutenant,—sir,—Montano,—Gentle-
men,—
Have you forgot all sense of place and duty?
Hold! the general speaks to you; hold, hold, for shame!
OTH. Why, how now, ho! from whence ariseth this?
Are we turned Turks, and to ourselves do that
Which heaven hath forbid the Ottomites?
For Christian shame, put by this barbarous brawl:
He that stirs next to carve for his own rage
Holds his soul light; he dies upon his motion.
Silence that dreadful bell! It frights the isle
From her propriety. What is the matter, masters?
Honest Iago, that look'st dead with grieving,
Speak, who began this? On thy love, I charge thee.
IAGO. I do not know: friends all but now, even now,
In quarter,° and in terms like bride and groom   *on watch*
Devesting° them for bed; and then, but now,   *disrobing*
As if some planet had unwitted men,
Swords out, and tilting one at other's breast,
In opposition bloody. I cannot speak
Any beginning to this peevish odds;°   *fight*
And would in action glorious I had lost
Those legs that brought me to a part of it!
OTH. How comes it, Michael, you are thus forgot?
CAS. I pray you, pardon me; I cannot speak.
OTH. Worthy Montano, you were wont be civil;
The gravity and stillness of your youth
The world hath noted, and your name is great
In mouths of wisest censure°: what's the matter,   *opinion*
That you unlace your reputation thus,
And spend your rich opinion° for the name   *opinion*
Of a night-brawler? Give me answer to it.
MON. Worthy Othello, I am hurt to danger:
Your officer, Iago, can inform you—
While I spare speech, which something now offends° me—   *pains*
Of all that I do know: nor know I aught
By me that's said or done amiss this night;
Unless self-charity be sometimes a vice,

And to defend ourselves it be a sin
When violence assails us.
    OTH.   Now, by heaven,
My blood begins my safer guides to rule,
And passion, having my best judgement collied,°   *blackened*
Assays° to lead the way: if I once stir,   *attempts*
Or do but lift this arm, the best of you
Shall sink in my rebuke. Give me to know
How this foul route began, who set it on,
And he that is approved° in this offence,   *convicted*
Though he had twinned with me, both at a birth,
Shall lose me. What! in a town of war,
Yet wild, the people's hearts brimful of fear,
To manage private and domestic quarrel,
In night, and on the court and guard of safety!
'Tis monstrous. Iago, who began 't?
    MON. If partially affined,° or leagued in office,   *obligated*
Thou dost deliver more or less than truth,
Thou art no soldier.
    IAGO.   Touch me not so near:
I had rather have this tongue cut from my mouth
Than it should do offence to Michael Cassio;
Yet, I persuade myself, to speak the truth
Shall nothing wrong him. Thus it is, general.
Montano and myself being in speech,
There comes a fellow crying out for help,
And Cassio following him with determined sword,
To execute upon him. Sir, this gentleman
Steps in to Cassio and entreats his pause:
Myself the crying fellow did pursue,
Lest by his clamor—as it so fell out—
The town might fall in fright: he, swift of foot,
Outran my purpose; and I returned the rather
For that I heard the clink and fall of swords,
And Cassio high in oath; which till tonight
I ne'er might say before. When I came back—
For this was brief—I found them close together,
At blow and thrust; even as again they were
When you yourself did part them.
More of this matter cannot I report:
But men are men; the best sometimes forget:
Though Cassio did some little wrong to him,
As men in rage strike those that wish them best,
Yet surely Cassio, I believe, received
From him that fled some strange indignity,
Which patience could not pass.
    OTH.   I know, Iago,
Thy honesty and love doth mince this matter,
Making it light to Cassio. Cassio, I love thee;
But never more be officer of mine.

Re-enter DESDEMONA, *attended.*

Look, if my gentle love be not raised up!
I'll make thee an example.
DES.   What's the matter?
OTH. All's well now, sweeting; come away to bed.
Sir, for your hurts, myself will be your surgeon:
Lead him off. [*To Montano, who is led off.*]
Iago, look with care about the town,
And silence those whom this vile brawl distracted.
Come, Desdemona: 'tis the soldiers' life
To have their balmy slumbers waked with strife.
[*Exeunt all but Iago and Cassio.*]

IAGO. What, are you hurt, lieutenant?
CAS. Ay, past all surgery.
IAGO. Marry, heaven forbid!
CAS. Reputation, reputation, reputation! O, I have lost
my reputation! I have lost the immortal part of myself, and
what remains is bestial. My reputation, Iago, my reputation!
IAGO. As I am an honest man, I thought you had received
some bodily wound; there is more sense in that than in
reputation. Reputation is an idle and most false imposition;° *covering*
oft got without merit and lost without deserving: you have
lost no reputation at all, unless you repute yourself such
a loser. What, man! there are ways to recover the general
again: you are but now cast° in his mood°, a punishment *dismissed / anger*
more in policy than in malice; even so as one would beat
his offenceless dog to affright an imperious lion: sue to
him again, and he's yours.
CAS. I will rather sue to be despised than to deceive
so good a commander with so slight, so drunken, and so
indiscreet an officer. Drunk? and speak parrot°? and squab- *i.e., like a parrot*
ble? swagger? swear? and discourse fustian° with one's own *poppycock*
shadow? O thou invisible spirit of wine, if thou hast no
name to be known by, let us call thee devil!
IAGO. What was he that you followed with your sword?
What had he done to you?
CAS. I know not.
IAGO. Is 't possible?
CAS. I remember a mass of things, but nothing distinctly,
a quarrel, but nothing wherefore. O God, that men should
put an enemy in their mouths to steal away their brains!
that we should, with joy, pleasance, revel and applause,
transform ourselves into beasts!
IAGO. Why, but you are now well enough: how came
you thus recovered?
CAS. It hath pleased the devil drunkenness to give place
to the devil wrath: one unperfectness shows me another,
to make me frankly despise myself.
IAGO. Come, you are too severe a moraler: as the time,

the place, and the condition of this country stands, I could
heartily wish this had not befallen; but since it is as it is,
mend it for your own good.

CAS. I will ask him for my place again; he shall tell me
I am a drunkard! Had I as many mouths as Hydra,[9] such
an answer would stop them all. To be now a sensible man,
by and by a fool, and presently a beast! O strange! Every
inordinate cup is unblest, and the ingredient is a devil.

IAGO. Come, come, good wine is a good familiar creature,
if it be well used: exclaim no more against it. And, good
lieutenant, I think you think I love you.

CAS. I have well approved° it, sir. I drunk!   *demonstrated*

IAGO. You or any man living may be drunk at some time,
man. I'll tell you what you shall do. Our general's wife is
now the general. I may say so in this respect, for that he
hath devoted and given up himself to the contemplation,
mark and denotement° of her parts and graces: confess   *notation*
yourself freely to her; importune her help to put you in
your place again: she is of so free,° so kind, so apt, so   *generous*
blessed a disposition, she holds it a vice in her goodness
not to do more than she is requested: this broken joint
between you and her husband entreat her to splinter;° and,   *splint, repair*
my fortunes against any lay° worth naming, this crack of   *wager*
your love shall grow stronger than it was before.

CAS. You advise me well.

IAGO. I protest, in the sincerity of love and honest kindness.

CAS. I think it freely; and betimes° in the morning I   *early*
will beseech the virtuous Desdemona to undertake for me:
I am desperate of my fortunes if they check me here.

IAGO. You are in the right. Good night, lieutenant; I
must to the watch.

CAS. Good night, honest Iago. [*Exit.*]

IAGO. And what's he then that says I play the villain?
When this advice is free I give and honest,
Probal° to thinking, and indeed the course   *probable*
To win the Moor again? For 'tis most easy
The inclining Desdemona to subdue°   *win over*
In any honest suit. She's framed as fruitful
As the free elements. And then for her
To win the Moor—were't to renounce his baptism,
All seals and symbols of redeemèd sin—
His soul is so enfettered to her love,
That she may make, unmake, do what she list,°   *likes*
Even as her appetite shall play the god
With his weak function.° How am I then a villain   *(as commander)*
To counsel Cassio to this parallel course,
Directly to his good? Divinity of hell!
When devils will the blackest sins put on,

---

[9] A mythical monster with nine heads.

They do suggest at first with heavenly shows,
As I do now: for whiles this honest fool
Plies Desdemona to repair his fortunes,
And she for him pleads strongly to the Moor,
I'll pour this pestilence into his ear,
That she repeals° him for her body's lust;   *appeals for*
And by how much she strives to do him good,
She shall undo her credit with the Moor.
So will I turn her virtue into pitch;
And out of her own goodness make the net
That shall enmesh them all.

Enter RODERIGO.

How now, Roderigo!
    ROD. I do follow here in the chase, not like a hound
that hunts, but one that fills up the cry.° My money is almost   *pack*
spent; I have been tonight exceedingly well cudgelled;° and   *beaten*
I think the issue will be, I shall have so much experience
for my pains; and so, with no money at all and a little more
wit, return again to Venice.
    IAGO. How poor are they that have not patience!
What wound did ever heal but by degrees?
Thou know'st we work by wit and not by witchcraft,
And wit depends on dilatory time.
Does't not go well? Cassio hath beaten thee,
And thou by that small hurt hast cashiered Cassio:
Though other things grow fair against the sun,
Yet fruits that blossom first will first be ripe:
Content thyself awhile. By the mass, 'tis morning;
Pleasure and action make the hours seem short.
Retire thee; go where thou art billeted:
Away, I say; thou shalt know more hereafter:
Nay, get thee gone. [*Exit Rod.*] Two things are to be done:
My wife must move° for Cassio to her mistress;   *plead*
I'll set her on;
Myself the while to draw the Moor apart,
And bring him jump° when he may Cassio find   *just*
Soliciting his wife: ay, that's the way;
Dull not device by coldness and delay. [*Exit.*]

ACT III.

SCENE I.
Before the castle.

Enter CASSIO *and some* MUSICIANS.

    CAS. Masters, play here; I will content° your pains; Some-   *reward*
thing that's brief; and bid "Good morrow, general." [*Music.*]

Enter CLOWN.

CLO. Why, masters, have your instruments been in Naples, that they speak i' the nose thus?[10]

FIRST MUS. How, sir, how!

CLO. Are these, I pray you, wind-instruments?

FIRST MUS. Ay, marry, are they, sir.

CLO. O, thereby hangs a tail.

FIRST MUS. Whereby hangs a tale, sir?

CLO. Marry, sir, by many a wind-instrument that I know.
But, masters, here's money for you: and the general so likes
your music, that he desires you, for love's sake, to make
no more noise with it.

FIRST MUS. Well, sir, we will not.

CLO. If you have any music that may not be heard,
to 't again: but, as they say, to hear music the general does
not greatly care.

FIRST MUS. We have none such, sir.

CLO. Then put up your pipes in your bag, for I'll away:
go; vanish into air; away! [*Exeunt Musicians.*]

CAS. Dost thou hear, my honest friend?

CLO. No, I hear not your honest friend; I hear you.

CAS. Prithee, keep up thy quillets.° There's a poor piece   *quibbles*
of gold for thee: if the gentlewoman that attends the general's wife be stirring, tell her there's one Cassio entreats
her a little favor of speech: wilt thou do this?

CLO. She is stirring, sir: if she will stir hither, I shall
seem to notify unto her.

CAS. Do, good my friend. [*Exit Clown.*]

Enter IAGO.

                    In happy time, Iago.

IAGO. You have not been a-bed, then?

CAS. Why, no; the day had broke
Before we parted. I have made bold, Iago.
To send in to your wife: my suit to her
Is, that she will to virtuous Desdemona
Procure me some access.

IAGO.   I'll send her to you presently;
And I'll devise a mean to draw the Moor
Out of the way, that your converse and business
May be more free.

CAS. I humbly thank you for't. [*Exit Iago.*] I never knew
A Florentine more kind and honest.

Enter EMILIA.

---

[10] A reference to the nasal Neapolitan accent but also to the free-wheeling reputation and endemic
syphilis (damaging the nose in advanced stages) of this sailors' town.

Emil. Good morrow, good lieutenant: I am sorry
For your displeasure; but all will sure be well.
The general and his wife are talking of it,
And speaks for you stoutly: the Moor replies,
That he you hurt is of great fame in Cyprus
And great affinity,° and that in wholesome wisdom   *family*
He might not but refuse you; but he protests he loves you,
And needs no other suitor but his likings
To take the safest occasion by the front°   *forelock*
To bring you in again.
    Cas.   Yet, I beseech you,
If you think fit, or that it may be done,
Give me advantage of some brief discourse
With Desdemona alone.
    Emil.   Pray you, come in:
I will bestow you where you shall have time
To speak your bosom freely.
    Cas.   I am much bound to you. [*Exeunt.*]

SCENE II.
A room in the castle.

Enter Othello, Iago *and* Gentlemen.

Oth. These letters give, Iago, to the pilot;
And by him do my duties to the senate:
That done, I will be walking on the works;°   *fortifications*
Repair there to me.
    Iago.   Well, my good lord, I'll do't.
Oth. This fortification, gentlemen, shall we see't?
Gent. We'll wait upon your lordship. [*Exeunt.*]

SCENE III.
The garden of the castle.

Enter Desdemona, Cassio, *and* Emilia.

Des. Be thou assured, good Cassio, I will do
All my abilities in thy behalf.
    Emil. Good madam, do: I warrant it grieves my husband
As if the case were his.
    Des. O, that's an honest fellow. Do not doubt, Cassio,
But I will have my lord and you again
As friendly as you were.
    Cas.   Bounteous madam,
Whatever shall become of Michael Cassio,
He's never any thing but your true servant.
    Des. I know 't: I thank you. You do love my lord:
You have known him long; and be you well assured

He shall in strangeness° stand no farther off   *estrangement*
Than in a politic° distance.   *diplomatic*
   CAS.   Ay, but, lady,
That policy may either last so long,
Or feed upon such nice and waterish diet,
Or breed itself so out of circumstance,
That, I being absent and my place supplied,
My general will forget my love and service.
   DES. Do not doubt° that; before Emilia here   *fear*
I give thee warrant of thy place: assure thee,
If I do vow a friendship, I'll perform it
To the last article: my lord shall never rest;
I'll watch him tame[11] and talk him out of patience;
His bed shall seem a school, his board a shrift;°   *confessional*
I'll intermingle every thing he does
With Cassio's suit: therefore be merry, Cassio;
For thy solicitor shall rather die
Than give thy cause away.

Enter OTHELLO *and* IAGO, *at a distance.*

   EMIL. Madam, here comes my lord.
   CAS. Madam, I'll take my leave.
   DES. Nay, stay and hear me speak.
   CAS. Madam, not now: I am very ill at ease,
Unfit for mine own purposes.
   DES. Well, do your discretion. [*Exit Cassio.*]
   IAGO. Ha! I like not that.
   OTH. What dost thou say?
   IAGO. Nothing, my lord: or if—I know not what.
   OTH. Was not that Cassio parted from my wife?
   IAGO. Cassio, my lord! No, sure, I cannot think it,
That he would steal away so guilty-like,
Seeing you coming.
   OTH.   I do believe 'twas he.
   DES. How now, my lord!
I have been talking with a suitor here,
A man that languishes in your displeasure.
   OTH. Who is't you mean?
   DES. Why, your lieutenant, Cassio. Good my lord,
If I have any grace or power to move you,
His present reconciliation take;
For if he be not one that truly loves you,
That errs in ignorance and not in cunning,
I have no judgement in an honest face:
I prithee, call him back.
   OTH.   Went he hence now?
   DES. Ay, sooth;° so humbled,   *true*

---

[11] Hawks are sometimes kept awake until tamed.

That he hath left part of his grief with me,
To suffer with him. Good love, call him back.
    OTH. Not now, sweet Desdemona; some other time.
    DES. But shall't be shortly?
    OTH.   The sooner, sweet, for you.
    DES. Shall't be tonight at supper?
    OTH.   No, not tonight.
    DES. Tomorrow dinner then?
    OTH.   I shall not dine at home;
I meet the captains at the citadel.
    DES. Why then tomorrow night; or Tuesday morn;
On Tuesday noon, or night; on Wednesday morn:
I prithee, name the time; but let it not
Exceed three days: in faith, he's penitent;
And yet his trespass, in our common reason—
Save that, they say, the wars must make examples
Out of their best—is not almost a fault
To incur a private check.° When shall he come?   *rebuke*
Tell me, Othello: I wonder in my soul,
What you would ask me, that I should deny,
Or stand so mammering° on. What! Michael Cassio,   *hesitant*
That came a-wooing with you, and so many a time
When I have spoke of you dispraisingly
Hath ta'en your part; to have so much to do
To bring him in! Trust me, I could do much—
    OTH. Prithee, no more: let him come when he will;
I will deny thee nothing.
    DES.   Why, this is not a boon;°   *gift*
'Tis as I should entreat you wear your gloves,
Or feed on nourishing dishes, or keep you warm,
Or sue to you to do a peculiar profit
To your own person: nay, when I have a suit
Wherein I mean to touch your love indeed,
It shall be full of poise° and difficult weight,   *matter*
And fearful to be granted.
    OTH.   I will deny thee nothing:
Whereon, I do beseech thee, grant me this,
To leave me but a little to myself.
    DES. Shall I deny you? No: farewell, my lord.
    OTH. Farewell, my Desdemona: I'll come to thee straight.
    DES. Emilia, come. Be as your fancies teach you;
Whate'er you be, I am obedient.
[*Exeunt Desdemona and Emilia.*]
    OTH. Excellent wretch! Perdition catch my soul,
But I do love thee! And when I love thee not,
Chaos is come again.
    IAGO. My noble lord,—
    OTH.   What dost thou say, Iago?
    IAGO. Did Michael Cassio, when you wooed my lady,
Know of your love?

Oth. He did, from first to last: why dost thou ask?

Iago. But for a satisfaction of my thought;
No further harm.

Oth. 　　　　Why of thy thought, Iago?

Iago. I did not think he had been acquainted with her.

Oth. O, yes, and went between us very oft.

Iago. Indeed!

Oth. Indeed! ay, indeed: discern'st thou aught in that?
Is he not honest?

Iago. Honest, my lord!

Oth. Honest! ay, honest.

Iago. My lord, for aught I know.

Oth. What dost thou think?

Iago. Think, my lord!

Oth. Think, my lord! By heaven, he echoes me,
As if there were some monster in his thought
Too hideous to be shown. Thou dost mean something:
I heard thee say even now, thou likedst not that,
When Cassio left my wife: what didst not like?
And when I told thee he was of my counsel
In my whole course of wooing, thou criedst 'Indeed!'
And didst contract and purse thy brow together,
As if thou then hadst shut up in thy brain
Some horrible conceit:° if thou dost love me, 　　　　　*idea*
Show me thy thought.

Iago. My lord, you know I love you.

Oth. 　　　　　　　　　　　　I think thou dost;
And for I know thou'rt full of love and honesty
And weigh'st thy words before thou givest them breath,
Therefore these stops of thine fright me the more:
For such things in a false disloyal knave
Are tricks of custom; but in a man that's just
They're close delations,° working from the heart, 　　　*secret charges*
That passion cannot rule.

Iago. 　　　　　　　For Michael Cassio,
I dare be sworn I think that he is honest.

Oth. I think so too.

Iago. 　　　　　　　Men should be what they seem;
Or those that be not, would they might seem none!

Oth. Certain, men should be what they seem.

Iago. Why then I think Cassio's an honest man.

Oth. Nay, yet there's more in this:
I prithee, speak to me as to thy thinkings,
As thou dost ruminate, and give thy worst of thoughts
The worst of words.

Iago. 　　　　　Good my lord, pardon me:
Though I am bound to every act of duty,
I am not bound to that all slaves are free to.
Utter my thoughts? Why, say they are vile and false;
As where's that palace whereinto foul things
Sometimes intrude not? Who has a breast so pure,

But some uncleanly apprehensions
Keep leets° and law-days, and in session sit   *courts*
With meditations lawful?
    OTH. Thou dost conspire against thy friend, Iago,
If thou but think'st him wronged and makest his ear
A stranger to thy thoughts.
    IAGO.   I do beseech you—
Though I perchance am vicious in my guess,
As, I confess, it is my nature's plague
To spy into abuses, and oft my jealousy
Shapes faults that are not—that your wisdom yet,
From one that so imperfectly conceits,°   *speculates*
Would take no notice, nor build yourself a trouble
Out of his scattering and unsure observance.
It were not for your quiet nor your good,
Nor for my manhood, honesty, or wisdom,
To let you know my thoughts.
    OTH.   What dost thou mean?
    IAGO. Good name in man and woman, dear my lord,
Is the immediate jewel of their souls:
Who steals my purse steals trash; 'tis something, nothing;
'Twas mine, 'tis his, and has been slave to thousands;
But he that filches from me my good name
Robs me of that which not enriches him
And makes me poor indeed.
    OTH. By heaven, I'll know thy thoughts.
    IAGO. You cannot, if my heart were in your hand;
Nor shall not, whilst 'tis in my custody.
    OTH. Ha!
    IAGO.   O, beware, my lord, of jealousy;
It is the green-eyed monster, which doth mock°   *torment*
The meat it feeds on: that cuckold lives in bliss
Who, certain of his fate, loves not his wronger;
But, O, what damnèd minutes tells he o'er
Who dotes, yet doubts, suspects, yet strongly loves!
    OTH. O misery!
    IAGO. Poor and content in rich, and rich enough;
But riches fineless° is as poor as winter   *without end*
To him that ever fears he shall be poor:
Good heaven, the souls of all my tribe defend
From jealousy!
    OTH.   Why, why is this?
Think'st thou I'ld make a life of jealousy,
To follow still the changes of the moon
With fresh suspicions? No; to be once in doubt
Is once to be resolved: exchange me for a goat,
When I shall turn the business of my soul
To such exsufflicate° and blown° surmises,   *puffed up / swollen*
Matching thy inference. 'Tis not to make me jealous
To say my wife is fair, feeds well, loves company,
Is free of speech, sings, plays and dances well;

Where virtue is, these are more virtuous:
Nor from mine own weak merits will I draw
The smallest fear or doubt of her revolt;
For she had eyes, and chose me. No, Iago;
I'll see before I doubt; when I doubt, prove;
And on the proof, there is no more but this,
Away at once with love or jealousy!
    IAGO. I am glad of it; for now I shall have reason
To show the love and duty that I bear you
With franker spirit: therefore, as I am bound,
Receive it from me. I speak not yet of proof.
Look to your wife; observe her well with Cassio;
Wear your eye thus, not jealous nor secure:
I would not have your free and noble nature
Out of self-bounty° be abused; look to 't: *your own kindness*
I know our country disposition well;
In Venice they do let heaven see the pranks
They dare not show their husbands; their best conscience
Is not to leave 't undone, but keep 't unknown.
    OTH. Dost thou say so?
    IAGO. She did deceive her father, marrying you;
And when she seemed to shake and fear your looks,
She loved them most.
    OTH.   And so she did.
    IAGO.   Why, go to° then;   *go on*
She that so young could give out such a seeming,
To seel° her father's eyes up close as oak—   *sew*
He thought 'twas witchcraft—but I am much to blame;
I humbly do beseech you of your pardon
For too much loving you.
    OTH.   I am bound to thee for ever.
    IAGO. I see this hath a little dashed your spirits.
    OTH. Not a jot,° not a jot.   *bit*
    IAGO.   I' faith, I fear it has.
I hope you will consider what is spoke
Comes from my love; but I do see you're moved:
I am to pray you not to strain my speech
To grosser issues nor to larger reach
Than to suspicion.
    OTH. I will not.
    IAGO.   Should you do so, my lord,
My speech should fall into such vile success
As my thoughts aim not at. Cassio's my worthy friend—
My lord, I see you're moved:
    OTH.   No, not much moved:
I do not think but Desdemona's honest.°   *chaste*
    IAGO. Long live she so! and long live you to think so!
    OTH. And yet, how nature erring from itself—
    IAGO. Ay, there's the point: as—to be bold with you—
Not to affect° many proposèd matches   *like*
Of her own clime, complexion and degree,

Whereto we see in all things nature tends—
Foh! one may smell in such a will° most rank,   lust
Foul disproportion, thoughts unnatural.
But pardon me: I do not in position°   hypothesis
Distinctly speak of her; though I may fear
Her will, recoiling to her better judgement,
May fall° to match you with her country forms,°   happen / countrymen
And happily° repent.   perhaps
    OTH.   Farewell, farewell:
If more thou dost perceive, let me know more;
Set on thy wife to observe: leave me, Iago.
    IAGO. [*Going*] My lord, I take my leave.
    OTH. Why did I marry? This honest creature doubtless
Sees and knows more, much more, than he unfolds.
    IAGO. [*Returning*] My lord, I would I might entreat your
    honor
To scan° this thing no further; leave it to time: analyze
Though it be fit that Cassio have his place,
For sure he fills it up with great ability,
Yet, if you please to hold him off awhile,
You shall by that perceive him and his means:
Note if your lady strain° his entertainment°   urge / employment
With any strong or vehement importunity;
Much will be seen in that. In the mean time,
Let me be thought too busy in my fears—
As worthy cause I have to fear I am—
And hold her free,° I do beseech your honor.   guiltless
    OTH. Fear not my government.°   self-control
    IAGO. I once more take my leave. [*Exit.*]
    OTH. This fellow's of exceeding honesty,
And knows all qualities,° with a learnèd spirit,   natures
Of human dealings. If I do prove her haggard,°   a strayed hawk
Though that her jesses° were my dear heart-strings,   restraining straps
I'd whistle her off and let her down° the wind   fly down
To prey° at fortune.° Haply, for I am black   hunt / random
And have not those soft parts of conversation
That chamberers° have, or for I am declined   womanizers
Into the vale of years,—yet that's not much—
She's gone; I am abused, and my relief
Must be to loathe her. O curse of marriage,
That we can call these delicate creatures ours,
And not their appetites! I had rather be a toad,
And live upon the vapor of a dungeon,
Than keep a corner in the thing I love
For others' uses. Yet, 'tis the plague of great ones;
Prerogatived are they less than the base;
'Tis destiny unshunnable, like death:
Even then this forkèd plague° is fated to us   cuckoldry
When we do quicken.° Desdemona comes: are conceived

        Re-enter DESDEMONA *and* EMILIA.

If she be false, O, then heaven mocks itself!
I'll not believe 't.
    DES.   How now, my dear Othello!
Your dinner, and the generous islanders
By you invited, do attend your presence.
    OTH. I am to blame.
    DES.   Why do you speak so faintly?
Are you not well?
    OTH. I have a pain upon my forehead here.
    DES. Faith, that's with watching; 'twill away again:
Let me but bind it hard, within this hour
It will be well.
    OTH.   Your napkin is too little;
[*He puts the handkerchief from him; and she drops it.*]
Let it alone. Come, I'll go in with you.
    DES. I am very sorry that you are not well.
[*Exeunt Othello and Desdemona.*]
    EMIL. I am glad I have found this napkin:
This was her first remembrance from the Moor:
My wayward husband hath a hundred times
Woo'd me to steal it; but she so loves the token,
For he conjured her she should ever keep it,
That she reserves it evermore about her
To kiss and talk to. I'll have the work ta'en out,°   *copied*
And give 't Iago: what he will do with it
Heaven knows, not I;
I nothing but to please his fantasy.°   *whim*

Re-enter IAGO.

    IAGO. How now! What do you here alone?
    EMIL. Do not you chide; I have a thing for you.
    IAGO. A thing for me? It is a common thing—
    EMIL. Ha!
    IAGO. To have a foolish wife.
    EMIL. O, is that all? What will you give me now
For that same handkerchief?
    IAGO.   What handkerchief?
    EMIL. What handkerchief!
Why, that the Moor first gave to Desdemona;
That which so often you did bid me steal.
    IAGO. Hast stol'n it from her?
    EMIL. No, faith; she let it drop by negligence,
And, to the advantage, I being here took 't up.
Look, here it is.
    IAGO.   A good wench; give it me.
    EMIL. What will you do with 't, that you have been so
  earnest
To have me filch it?
    IAGO.   [*Snatching it*] Why, what's that to you?
    EMIL. If't be not for some purpose of import,°   *importance*

Give 't me again: poor lady, she'll run mad
When she shall lack it.
    Iago. Be not acknown on 't;° I have use for it.   *knowledgeable about it*
Go, leave me. [*Exit Emilia.*]
I will in Cassio's lodging lose this napkin,
And let him find it. Trifles light as air
Are to the jealous confirmations strong
As proofs of holy writ: this may do something.
The Moor already changes with my poison:
Dangerous conceits are in their natures poisons,
Which at the first are scarce found to distaste,
But with a little act upon the blood
Burn like the mines of sulphur. I did say so:
Look, where he comes!

Re-enter Othello.

                Not poppy, nor mandragora,°   *a narcotic*
Nor all the drowsy syrups of the world,
Shall ever medicine thee to that sweet sleep
Which thou owedst° yesterday.   *owned*
    Oth.   Ha! ha! false to me?
    Iago. Why, how now, general! no more of that.
    Oth. Avaunt! be gone! thou hast set me on the rack:
I swear 'tis better to be much abused
Than but to know't a little.
    Iago.   How now, my lord!
    Oth. What sense had I of her stol'n hours of lust?
I saw't not, thought it not, it harmed not me:
I slept the next night well, was free and merry;
I found not Cassio's kisses on her lips:
He that is robbed, not wanting what is stol'n,
Let him not know't and he's not robbed at all.
    Iago. I am sorry to hear this.
    Oth. I had been happy, if the general camp,
Pioners° and all, had tasted her sweet body,   *Privates*
So I had nothing known. O, now forever
Farewell the tranquil mind! farewell content!
Farewell the plumèd troop and the big wars
That make ambition virtue! O, farewell,
Farewell the neighing steed and the shrill trump,
The spirit-stirring drum, the ear-piercing fife,
The royal banner and all quality,
Pride, pomp and circumstances° of glorious war!   *pageantry*
And, O you mortal engines,° whose rude throats   *cannons*
The immortal Jove's dread clamors counterfeit,
Farewell! Othello's occupation's gone!
    Iago. Is't possible, my lord?
    Oth. Villain, be sure thou prove my love a whore;
Be sure of it; give me the ocular proof;
Or, by the worth of man's eternal soul,

Thou hadst been better have been born a dog
Than answer my waked wrath!
  Iago.   Is't come to this?
  Oth. Make me to see't; or at the least so prove it,
That the probation° bear no hinge nor loop   *proof*
To hang a doubt on; or woe upon thy life!
  Iago. My noble lord,—
  Oth. If thou dost slander her and torture me,
Never pray more; abandon all remorse;
On horror's head horrors accumulate;
Do deeds to make heaven weep, all earth amazed;
For nothing canst thou to damnation add
Greater than that.
  Iago.   O grace! O heaven defend me!
Are you a man? Have you a soul or sense?
God be wi' you; take mine office. O wretched fool,
That livest to make thine honesty a vice!
O monstrous world! Take note, take note, O world,
To be direct and honest is not safe.
I thank you for this profit,° and from hence   *gain (in wisdom)*
I'll love no friend sith° love breeds such offence.   *since*
  Oth. Nay, stay: thou shouldst be honest.
  Iago. I should be wise; for honesty's a fool,
And loses that it works for.
  Oth.   By the world,
I think my wife be honest, and think she is not;
I think that thou art just, and think thou art not:
I'll have some proof. Her name, that was as fresh
As Dian's° visage, is now begrimed and black   *goddess of chastity*
As mine own face. If there be cords, or knives,
Poison, or fire, or suffocating streams,
I'll not endure it. Would I were satisfied!
  Iago. I see, sir, you are eaten up with passion:
I do repent me that I put it to you.
You would be satisfied?
  Oth.   Would! nay, I will.
  Iago. And may: but, how? How satisfied, my lord?
Would you, the supervisor, grossly gape on?
Behold her topped?
  Oth.   Death and damnation! O!
  Iago. It were a tedious difficulty, I think,
To bring them to that prospect: damn them then,
If ever mortal eyes do see them bolster°   *sleep together*
More than their own! What then? How then?
What shall I say? Where's satisfaction?
It is impossible you should see this,
Were they as prime° as goats, as hot as monkeys,   *lustful*
As salt° as wolves in pride,° and fools as gross   *desirous / heat*
As ignorance made drunk. But yet, I say,
If imputation and strong circumstances,
Which lead directly to the door of truth,

Will give you satisfaction, you may have't.
    OTH. Give me a living reason she's disloyal.
    IAGO. I do not like the office:
But sith I am entered in this cause so far,
Pricked° to 't by foolish honesty and love,   *Driven*
I will go on. I lay with Cassio lately,
And being troubled with a raging tooth,
I could not sleep.
There are a kind of men so loose of soul,
That in their sleeps will mutter their affairs:
One of this kind is Cassio:
In sleep I heard him say "Sweet Desdemona,
Let us be wary, let us hide our loves";
And then, sir, would he gripe° and wring my hand,   *grip*
Cry "O sweet creature!" and then kiss me hard,
As if he plucked up kisses by the roots,
That grew upon my lips: then laid his leg
Over my thigh, and sighed and kissed, and then
Cried "Cursed fate that gave thee to the Moor!"
    OTH. O monstrous! monstrous!
    IAGO.   Nay, this was but his dream.
    OTH. But this denoted a foregone conclusion:
'Tis a shrewd doubt,° though it be but a dream.   *astute suspicion*
    IAGO. And this may help to thicken other proofs
That do demonstrate thinly.
    OTH.   I'll tear her all to pieces.
    IAGO. Nay, but be wise: yet we see nothing done;
She may be honest yet. Tell me but this;
Have you not sometimes seen a handkerchief
Spotted with strawberries in your wife's hand?
    OTH. I gave her such a one; 'twas my first gift.
    IAGO. I know not that: but such a handkerchief—
I am sure it was your wife's—did I today
See Cassio wipe his beard with.
    OTH.   If it be that,—
    IAGO. If it be that, or any that was hers,
It speaks against her with the other proofs.
    OTH. O, that the slave had forty thousand lives!
One is too poor, too weak for my revenge.
Now do I see 'tis true. Look here, Iago;
All my fond love thus do I blow to heaven:
'Tis gone.
Arise, black vengeance, from thy hollow cell!
Yield up, O love, thy crown and hearted throne
To tyrannous hate! Swell, bosom, with thy fraught,°   *freight*
For 'tis of aspics' tongues!
    IAGO.   Yet be content.
    OTH. O, blood, blood, blood!
    IAGO. Patience, I say; your mind perhaps may change.
    OTH. Never, Iago. Like to the Pontic sea,°   *Black Sea*
Whose icy current and compulsive course

Ne'er feels retiring ebb, but keeps due on
To the Propontic and the Hellespont;[12]
Even so my bloody thoughts, with violent pace,
Shall ne'er look back, ne'er ebb to humble love,
Till that a capable° and wide revenge   *capacious*
Swallow them up. Now, by yond marble heaven,
In the due reverence of a sacred vow [*Kneels.*]
I here engage my words.
    IAGO.   Do not rise yet. [*Kneels.*]
Witness, you ever-burning lights above,
You elements that clip° us round about,   *encircle*
Witness that here Iago doth give up
The execution° of his wit, hands, heart,   *action*
To wronged Othello's service! Let him command,
And to obey shall be in me remorse,°   *an act of pity*
What bloody business ever.
    OTH.   I greet thy love,
Not with vain thanks, but with acceptance bounteous,
And will upon the instant put thee to 't:
Within these three days let me hear thee say
That Cassio's not alive.
    IAGO. My friend is dead; 'tis done at your request:
But let her live.
    OTH.   Damn her, lewd minx! O, damn her!
Come, go with me apart; I will withdraw,
To furnish me with some swift means of death
For the fair devil. Now art thou my lieutenant.
    IAGO. I am your own for ever. [*Exeunt.*]

SCENE IV.
Before the castle.

Enter DESDEMONA, EMILIA, *and* CLOWN.

    DES. Do you know, sirrah, where Lieutenant Cassio lies?
    CLO. I dare not say he lies any where.
    DES. Why, man?
    CLO. He's a soldier; and for one to say a soldier lies,
is° stabbing.   *i.e., is cause for*
    DES. Go to: where lodges he?
    CLO. To tell you where he lodges, is to tell you where
I lie.
    DES. Can any thing be made of this?
    CLO. I know not where he lodges; and for me to devise
a lodging, and say he lies here or he lies there, were to
lie in mine own throat.
    DES. Can you inquire him out and be edified by report?

---

[12] The "Propontic" is another name for the Sea of Marmara; the "Hellespont" is an ancient
    name for the Dardanelles through which Sea of Marmara drains into the Mediterranean Sea.

CLO. I will catechize the world for him; that is, make questions and by them answer.

DES. Seek him, bid him come hither: tell him I have moved my lord on his behalf and hope all will be well.

CLO. To do this is within the compass of man's wit, and therefore I will attempt the doing it. [*Exit.*]

DES. Where should I lose that handkerchief, Emilia?

EMIL. I know not, madam.

DES. Believe me, I had rather have lost my purse
Full of crusadoes:° and, but my noble Moor   *gold coins*
Is true of mind and made of no such baseness
As jealous creatures are, it were enough
To put him to ill thinking.

EMIL.   Is he not jealous?

DES. Who, he? I think the sun where he was born
Drew all such humors° from him.   *feelings*

EMIL.   Look, where he comes.

DES. I will not leave him now till Cassio
Be called to him.

Enter OTHELLO.

How is 't with you, my lord?

OTH. Well, my good lady. [*Aside*] O, hardness to dissemble!
How do you, Desdemona?

DES.   Well, my good lord.

OTH. Give me your hand: this hand is moist, my lady.

DES. It yet has felt no age nor known no sorrow.

OTH. This argues fruitfulness and liberal heart:
Hot, hot, and moist: this hand of yours requires
A sequester° from liberty, fasting and prayer,   *separation*
Much castigation, exercise devout;
For here's a young and sweating devil here,
That commonly rebels. 'Tis a good hand,
A frank one.

DES.   You may, indeed, say so;
For 'twas that hand that gave away my heart.

OTH. A liberal hand: the hearts of old gave hands;
But our new heraldry is hands, not hearts.

DES. I cannot speak of this. Come now, your promise.

OTH. What promise, chuck?°   *dear*

DES. I have sent to bid Cassio come speak with you.

OTH. I have a salt and sorry rheum° offends me;   *cold*
Lend me thy handkerchief.

DES. Here, my lord.

OTH. That which I gave you.

DES. I have it not about me.

OTH. Not?

DES. No, indeed, my lord.

OTH. That's a fault. That handerchief

Did an Egyptian to my mother give;
She was a charmer,° and could almost read   *magician*
The thoughts of people: she told her, while she kept it
'Twould make her amiable and subdue my father
Entirely to her love, but if she lost it
Or made a gift of it, my father's eye
Should hold her loathed and his spirits should hunt
After new fancies: she dying gave it me,
And bid me, when my fate would have me wive,
To give it her. I did so: and take heed on 't;
Make it a darling like your precious eye;
To lose 't or give 't away were such perdition
As nothing else could match,
    Des.   Is't possible?
    Oth. 'Tis true: there's magic in the web of it:
A sibyl,° that had numbered in the world   *prophetess*
The sun to course two hundred compasses,
In her prophetic fury sewed the work;
The worms were hallowed that did breed the silk;
And it was dyed in mummy° which the skilful   *fluid from mummies*
Conserved of maidens' hearts.
    Des.   Indeed! is't true?
    Oth. Most veritable; therefore look to 't well.
    Des. Then would to God that I had never seen 't!
    Oth. Ha! wherefore?
    Des. Why do you speak so startingly and rash?
    Oth. Is 't lost? Is 't gone? Speak, is it out o' the way?
    Des. Heaven bless us!
    Oth. Say you?
    Des. It is not lost; but what an if it were?
    Oth. How!
    Des. I say, it is not lost.
    Oth. Fetch 't, let me see it.
    Des. Why, so I can, sir, but I will not now.
This is a trick to put me from my suit:
Pray you, let Cassio be received again.
    Oth. Fetch me the handkerchief: my mind misgives.
    Des. Come, come;
You'll never meet a more sufficient° man.   *able*
    Oth. The handkerchief!
    Des.   I pray, talk me of Cassio.
    Oth. The handkerchief!
    Des.   A man that all his time
Hath founded his good fortunes on your love,
Shared dangers with you,—
    Oth. The handkerchief!
    Des. In sooth, you are to blame.
    Oth. Away! [*Exit.*]
    Emil. Is not this man jealous?
    Des. I ne'er saw this before.
Sure there's some wonder in this handkerchief:

I am most unhappy in the loss of it.

EMIL. 'Tis not a year or two shows us a man:
They are all but stomachs and we all but food;
They eat us hungerly, and when they are full
They belch us. Look you, Cassio and my husband.

Enter CASSIO *and* IAGO.

IAGO. There is no other way; 'tis she must do 't:
And, lo, the happiness!° Go and importune her.   luck
DES. How now, good Cassio! What's the news with you?
CAS. Madam, my former suit: I do beseech you
That by your virtuous means I may again
Exist, and be a member of his love
Whom I with all the office° of my heart   service
Entirely honor: I would not be delayed.
If my offence be of such mortal kind
That nor my service past nor present sorrows
Nor purposed merit in futurity
Can ransom me into his love again,
But to know so must be my benefit;
So shall I clothe me in a forced content
And shut myself up in some other course
To fortune's alms.
DES.   Alas, thrice-gentle Cassio!
My advocation° is not now in tune;   advocacy
And lord is not my lord, nor should I know him
Were he in favor° as in humor altered.   appearance
So help me every spirit sanctified,
As I have spoken for you all my best
And stood within the blank° of his displeasure   center
For my free speech! You must awhile be patient:
What I can do I will; and more I will
Than for myself I dare: let that suffice you.
IAGO. Is my lord angry?
EMIL.   He went hence but now,
And certainly in strange unquietness.
IAGO. Can he be angry? I have seen the cannon,
When it hath blown his ranks into the air,
And, like the devil, from his very arm
Puffed his own brother; and can he be angry?
Something of moment then: I will go meet him:
That's matter in't indeed if he be angry.
DES. I prithee, do so. [*Exit Iago.*]
                      Something sure of state,
Either from Venice or some unhatched practice°   uncovered plot
Made demonstrable here in Cyprus to him,
Hath puddled° his clear spirit; and in such cases   muddied
Men's natures wrangle with inferior things,
Though great ones are their object. 'Tis even so;
For let our finger ache, and it indues°   brings

Our other healthful members even to that sense
Of pain: nay, we must think men are not gods,
Nor of them look for such observancy°   observances
As fits the bridal. Beshrew° me much, Emilia,   Curse
I was, unhandsome° warrior as I am,   unfitting
Arraigning his unkindness with my soul;
But now I find I had suborned° the witness,   induced to perjury
And he's indicted falsely.
    EMIL. Pray heaven it be state-matters, as you think,
And no conception nor no jealous toy
Concerning you.
    DES. Alas the day, I never gave him cause!
    EMIL. But jealous souls will not be answered so;
They are not ever jealous for the cause,
But jealous for they are jealous: 'tis a monster
Begot upon itself, born on itself.
    DES. Heaven keep that monster from Othello's mind!
    EMIL. Lady, amen.
    DES. I will go seek him. Cassio, walk hereabout:
If I do find him fit, I'll move your suit,
And seek to effect it to my uttermost.
    CAS. I humbly thank your ladyship.
[*Exeunt Desdemona and Emilia.*]

Enter BIANCA.

    BIAN. Save you, friend Cassio!
    CAS.   What make you from home?
How is it with you, my most fair Bianca?
I' faith, sweet love, I was coming to your house
    BIAN. And I was going to your lodging, Cassio.
What, keep a week away? Seven days and nights?
Eight score eight hours? And lovers' absent hours,
More tedious than the dial° eight score times?   whole day
O weary reckoning!
    CAS.   Pardon me, Bianca:
I have this while with leaden thoughts been pressed;
But I shall in a more continuate° time   uninterrupted
Strike off this score° of absence. Sweet Bianca,   account
[*Giving her Desdemona's handkerchief.*]
Take me this work out.
    BIAN.   O Cassio, whence came this?
This is some token from a newer friend:
To the felt absence now I feel a cause:
Is 't come to this? Well, well.
    CAS.   Go to, woman!
Throw your vile guesses in the devil's teeth,
From whence you have them. You are jealous now
That this is from some mistress, some remembrance:
No, by my faith, Bianca.
    BIAN.   Why, whose is it?

Cas. I know not, sweet: I found it in my chamber.
I like the work well: ere it be demanded—
As like enough it will—I'ld have it copied:
Take it, and do 't; and leave me for this time.
    Bian. Leave you! Wherefore?
    Cas. I do attend here on the general;
And think it no addition, nor my wish,
To have him see me womaned.°   *with a woman*
    Bian.   Why, I pray you?
    Cas. Not that I love you not.
    Bian.   But that you do not love me.
I pray you, bring me on the way a little;
And say if I shall see you soon at night.
    Cas. 'Tis but a little way that I can bring you;
For I attend here: but I'll see you soon.
    Bian. 'Tis very good; I must be circumstanced.°   *ruled by circumstances*
[*Exeunt.*]

ACT IV.

SCENE I.
Cyprus. Before the castle.

Enter Othello *and* Iago.

Iago. Will you think so?
Oth.   Think so, Iago!
Iago.   What,
To kiss in private?
    Oth.   An unauthorized kiss.
    Iago. Or to be naked with her friend in bed
An hour or more, not meaning any harm?
    Oth. Naked in bed, Iago, and not mean harm!
It is hypocrisy against the devil:
They that mean virtuously and yet do so,
The devil their virtue tempts and they tempt heaven.
    Iago. So they do nothing, 'tis a venial slip:
But if I give my wife a handkerchief—
    Oth. What then?
    Iago. Why, then, 'tis hers, my lord; and being hers,
She may, I think, bestow 't on any man.
    Oth. She is protectress of her honor too:
May she give that?
    Iago. Her honor is an essence that's not seen;
They have it very oft that have it not:
But for the handkerchief—
    Oth. By heaven, I would most gladly have forgot it:
Thou said'st—O, it comes o'er my memory,
As doth the raven° o'er the infected house,   *(emblem of death)*
Boding to all—he had my handkerchief.

IAGO. Ay, what of that?

OTH.   That's not so good now.

IAGO.   What
If I had said I had seen him do you wrong?
Or heard him say—as knaves be such abroad,
Who having, by their own importunate suit
Or voluntary dotage of° some mistress,   doting on
Convincèd° or supplied° them, cannot choose   seduced / met the
But they must blab—   desires of

OTH.   Hath he said anything?

IAGO. He hath, my lord; but be you well assured,
No more than he'll unswear.

OTH.   What hath he said?

IAGO. Faith, that he did—I know not what he did.

OTH. What? What?

IAGO. Lie—

OTH.   With her?

IAGO.   With her, on her; what you will.

OTH. Lie with her! lie on her!—We say lie on her, when
they belie her.—Lie with her! 'Zounds, that's fulsome!°   disgusting
Handkerchief—confessions—handkerchief!—To   confess,
and be hanged for his labor; first, to be hanged, and then
to confess. I tremble at it. Nature would not invest herself
in such shadowing passion without some instruction.[13] It
is not words that shakes me thus. Pish! Noses, ears and
lips. Is 't possible?—Confess?—Handkerchief?—O devil!
[Falls in a trance.]

IAGO. Work on,
My medicine, work! Thus credulous fools are caught;
And many worthy and chaste dames even thus,
All guiltless, meet reproach. What, ho! my lord!
My lord, I say! Othello!

Enter CASSIO.

                              How now, Cassio!

CAS. What's the matter?

IAGO. My lord is fall'n into an epilepsy:
This is his second fit; he had one yesterday.

CAS. Rub him about the temples.

IAGO.   No, forbear;
The lethargy° must have his quiet course: stupor
If not, he foams at mouth, and by and by
Breaks out to savage madness. Look, he stirs:
Do you withdraw yourself a little while,
He will recover straight: when he is gone,
I would on great occasion° speak with you. [Exit Cassio.]   important matters
How is it, general? Have you not hurt your head?

---

[13] I.e., my nature would not be so darkened with passion unless there were some cause.

OTH. Dost thou mock me?

IAGO.   I mock you! No, by heaven.
Would you would bear your fortune like a man!

OTH. A hornèd° man's a monster and a beast.   *cuckolded*

IAGO. There's many a beast then in a populous city,
And many a civil monster.

OTH. Did he confess it?

IAGO.   Good sir, be a man;
Think every bearded fellow that's but yoked°   *married*
May draw with you: there's millions now alive
That nightly lie in those unproper° beds   *unchaste*
Which they dare swear peculiar:° your case is better.   *theirs alone*
O, 'tis the spite of hell, the fiend's arch-mock,
To lip° a wanton in a secure couch,   *kiss*
And to suppose her chaste! No, let me know;
And knowing what I am, I know what she shall be.

OTH. O, thou art wise; 'tis certain.

IAGO.   Stand you awhile apart;
Confine yourself but in a patient list.°   *mood*
Whilst you were here o'erwhelmed with your grief—
A passion most unsuiting such a man—
Cassio came hither: I shifted him away,
And laid good 'scuse upon your ecstasy;°   *trance*
Bade him anon return and here speak with me;
The which he promised. Do but encave° yourself,   *conceal*
And mark the fleers,° the gibes and notable scorns,   *sneers*
That dwell in every region of his face;
For I will make him tell the tale anew,
Where, how, how oft, how long ago and when
He hath and is again to cope° your wife: *cover*
I say, but mark his gesture. Marry,° patience;   *Indeed*
Or I shall say you are all in all in spleen,°   *passion*
And nothing of a man.

OTH.   Dost thou hear, Iago?
I will be found most cunning in my patience;
But—dost thou hear?—most bloody.

IAGO.   That's not amiss;
But yet keep time in all. Will you withdraw?
[*Othello retires.*]
Now will I question Cassio of Bianca,
A housewife that by selling her desires
Buys herself bread and clothes: it is a creature
That dotes on Cassio; as 'tis the strumpet's plague
To beguile many and be beguiled by one.
He, when he hears of her, cannot refrain
From the excess of laughter. Here he comes.

Re-enter CASSIO.

As he shall smile, Othello shall go mad;
And his unbookish° jealousy must construe   *ignorant*

Poor Cassio's smiles, gestures and light behavior,
Quite in the wrong. How do you now, lieutenant?

CAS. The worser that you give me the addition°   *additional title*
Whose want even kills me.

IAGO. Ply Desdemona well, and you are sure on 't.
Now, if this suit lay in Bianca's power,
How quickly should you speed!

CAS.   Alas, poor caitiff!°   *wretch*

OTH. Look, how he laughs already!

IAGO. I never knew a woman love man so.

CAS. Alas, poor rogue! I think, i' faith, she loves me.

OTH. Now he denies it faintly and laughs it out.

IAGO. Do you hear, Cassio?

OTH.   Now he importunes him
To tell it o'er: go to; well said, well said.

IAGO. She gives it out that you shall marry her:
Do you intend it?

CAS. Ha, ha, ha!

OTH. Do you triumph, Roman? Do you triumph?

CAS. I marry her! what, a customer!° I prithee, bear   *prostitute*
some charity to my wit; do not think it so unwholesome.
Ha, ha, ha!

OTH. So, so, so, so: they laugh that win.

IAGO. Faith, the cry goes that you shall marry her.

CAS. Prithee, say true.

IAGO. I am a very villain else.

OTH. Have you scored me?° Well.   *paid me back*

CAS. This is the monkey's own giving out: she is persuaded I will marry her, out of her own love and flattery,
not out of my promise.

OTH. Iago beckons me; now he begins the story.

CAS. She was here even now; she haunts me in every
place. I was the other day talking on the sea-bank with certain Venetians; and thither comes the bauble,° and, by this   *plaything*
hand, she falls me thus about my neck—

OTH. Crying "O dear Cassio!" as it were: his gesture
imports it.

CAS. So hangs and lolls and weeps upon me; so hales°   *drags*
and pulls me: ha, ha, ha!

OTH. Now he tells how she plucked him to my chamber.
O, I see that nose of yours, but not that dog I shall throw
it to.

CAS. Well, I must leave her company.

IAGO. Before me! Look, where she comes.

CAS. 'Tis such another fitchew!° Marry, a perfumed one.   *polecat, harlot*

Enter BIANCA.

What do you mean by this haunting of me?

BIAN. Let the devil and his dam haunt you! What did
you mean by that same handkerchief you gave me even

now? I was a fine fool to take it. I must take out the work?
A likely piece of work, that you should find it in your chamber, and not know who left it there! This is some minx's
token, and I must take out the work? There; give it your
hobby-horse:° wheresoever you had it, I'll take out no work   *rocking horse, whore*
on 't.

CAS. How now, my sweet Bianca! How now! How now!

OTH. By heaven, that should be my handkerchief!

BIAN. An you'll come to supper tonight, you may; an
you will not, come when you are next prepared for. [*Exit.*]

IAGO. After her, after her.

CAS. Faith, I must; she'll rail i' the street else.

IAGO. Will you sup there?

CAS. Faith, I intend so.

IAGO. Well, I may chance to see you; for I would very
fain speak with you.

CAS. Prithee, come; will you?

IAGO. Go to; say no more. [*Exit Cassio.*]

OTH. [*Advancing*] How shall I murder him, Iago?

IAGO. Did you perceive how he laughed at his vice?

OTH. O Iago!

IAGO. And did you see the handkerchief?

OTH. Was that mine?

IAGO. Yours, by this hand: and to see how he prizes
the foolish woman your wife! She gave it him, and he hath
given it his whore.

OTH. I would have him nine years a-killing. A fine
woman! a fair woman! a sweet woman!

IAGO. Nay, you must forget that.

OTH. Ay, let her rot, and perish, and be damned tonight;
for she shall not live: no, my heart is turned to stone; I
strike it, and it hurts my hand. O, the world hath not a
sweeter creature: she might lie by an emperor's side, and
command him tasks.

IAGO. Nay, that's not your way.

OTH. Hang her! I do but say what she is: so delicate
with her needle: an admirable musician: O, she will sing
the savageness out of a bear: of so high and plenteous wit
and invention:—

IAGO. She's the worse for all this.

OTH. O, a thousand thousand times: and then, of so
gentle a condition!°   *nature*

IAGO. Aye, too gentle.°   *generous*

OTH. Nay, that's certain: but yet the pity of it, Iago! O
Iago, the pity of it, Iago!

IAGO. If you are so fond over her iniquity, give her pat-
ent° to offend; for, if it touch not you, it comes near nobody.   *permission*

OTH. I will chop her into messes.° Cuckold me!   *porridge*

IAGO. O, 'tis foul in her.

OTH. With mine officer!

IAGO. That 's fouler.

OTH. Get me some poison, Iago; this night. I'll not ex-
postulate with her, lest her body and beauty unprovide°   *unsettle*
my mind again: this night, Iago.

IAGO. Do it not with poison, strangle her in her bed,
even the bed she hath contaminated.

OTH. Good, good: the justice of it pleases: very good.

IAGO. And for Cassio, let me be his undertaker: you
shall hear more by midnight.

OTH. Excellent good. [*A trumpet within.*] What trumpet
is that same?

IAGO. Something from Venice, sure. 'Tis Lodovico come
from the duke: and, see, your wife is with him.

> *Enter* LODOVICO, DESDEMONA, *and* ATTENDANTS.

LOD. God save the worthy general!

OTH.   With all my heart, sir.

LOD. The duke and senators of Venice greet you.
[*Gives him a letter.*]

OTH. I kiss the instrument of their pleasures.
[*Opens the letter, and reads.*]

DES. And what's the news, good cousin Lodovico?

IAGO. I am very glad to see you, signior;
Welcome to Cyprus.

LOD. I thank you. How does Lieutenant Cassio?

IAGO. Lives, sir,

DES. Cousin, there's fall'n between him and my lord
An unkind breach: but you shall make all well.

OTH. Are you sure of that?

DES. My lord?

OTH. [*Reads*] "This fail you not to do, as you will—"

LOD. He did not call; he's busy in the paper.
Is there division 'twixt my lord and Cassio?

DES. A most unhappy one: I would do much
To atone° them, for the love I bear to Cassio.   *reunite*

OTH. Fire and brimstone!

DES. My lord?

OTH. Are you wise?

DES. What, is he angry?

LOD.   May be the letter moved him;
For, as I think, they do command him home,
Deputing° Cassio in his government.°   *substituting / office*

DES. By my troth, I am glad on 't.

OTH.   Indeed!

DES.   My lord?

OTH. I am glad to see you mad.

DES.   Why, sweet Othello?

OTH. Devil! [*Striking her.*]

DES. I have not deserved this.

LOD. My lord, this would not be believed in Venice,
Though I should swear I saw 't: 'tis very much:

Make her amends; she weeps.

OTH.   O devil, devil!
If that the earth could teem° with woman's tears,   *bear offspring*
Each drop she falls would prove a crocodile.[14]
Out of my sight!

DES.   I will not stay to offend you. [*Going.*]

LOD. Truly, an obedient lady:
I do beseech your lordship, call her back.

OTH. Mistress!

DES. My lord?

OTH. What would you with her, sir?

LOD.   Who, I, my lord?

OTH. Ay; you did wish that I would make her turn:
Sir, she can turn and turn, and yet go on,
And turn again; and she can weep, sir, weep;
And she's obedient, as you say, obedient,
Very obedient. Proceed you in your tears.
Concerning this, sir,—O well-painted passion!—
I am commanded home. Get you away;
I'll send for you anon. Sir, I obey the mandate,
And will return to Venice. Hence, avaunt!°   *be gone*
[*Exit Desdemona.*]
Cassio shall have my place. And, sir, tonight,
I do entreat that we may sup together:
You are welcome, sir, to Cyprus. Goats and monkeys!
[*Exit.*]

LOD. Is this the noble Moor whom our full senate
Call all in all sufficient? This the nature
Whom passion could not shake? whose solid virtue
The shot of accident nor dart of chance
Could neither graze nor pierce?

IAGO.   He is much changed.

LOD. Are his wits safe? Is he not light of brain?

IAGO. He's that he is: I may not breathe my censure°   *adverse opinion*
What he might be: if what he might he is not,
I would to heaven he were!

LOD.   What, strike his wife!

IAGO. Faith, that was not so well; yet would I knew
That stroke would prove the worst!

LOD.   Is it his use?°   *habit*
Or did the letters work upon his blood,
And new create this fault?

IAGO.   Alas, alas!
It is not honesty in me to speak
What I have seen and known. You shall observe him,
And his own courses will denote him so
That I may save my speech: do but go after,
And mark how he continues.

LOD. I am sorry that I am deceived in him. [*Exeunt.*]

---

[14] The crocodile was thought to shed false tears over its victims.

SCENE II.
A room in the castle.

Enter OTHELLO *and* EMILIA.

OTH. You have seen nothing, then?
EMIL. Nor ever heard, nor ever did suspect.
OTH. Yes, you have seen Cassio and she together.
EMIL. But then I saw no harm, and then I heard
Each syllable that breath made up between them.
OTH. What, did they never whisper?
EMIL.   Never, my lord.
OTH. Nor send you out o' the way?
EMIL. Never.
OTH. To fetch her fan, her gloves, her mask, nor
nothing?
EMIL. Never, my lord.
OTH. That's strange.
EMIL. I durst, my lord, to wager she is honest,°   chaste
Lay down my soul at stake:° if you think other,   as wager
Remove your thought; it doth abuse your bosom.
If any wretch have put this in your head,
Let heaven requite it with the serpent's curse!
For if she be not honest, chaste and true,
There's no man happy; the purest of their wives
Is foul as slander.
OTH.   Bid her come hither: go. [*Exit Emilia.*]
She says enough: yet she's a simple bawd
That cannot say as much. This is a subtle whore,
A closet lock and key of villanous secrets:
And yet she'll kneel and pray; I have seen her do 't.

Enter DESDEMONA *with* EMILIA.

DES. My lord, what is your will?
OTH.   Pray, chuck, come hither.
DES. What is your pleasure?
OTH.   Let me see your eyes;
Look in my face.
DES.   What horrible fancy's this?
OTH. [*To Emilia*] Some of your function,[15] mistress;
Leave procreants° alone and shut the door;   fornicators
Cough, or cry hem, if anybody come:
Your mystery,° your mystery: nay, dispatch. [*Exit Emilia.*]   trade
DES. Upon my knees, what doth your speech import?
I understand a fury in your words,
But not the words.
OTH. Why, what art thou?
DES. Your wife, my lord; your true and loyal wife.

---

[15] I.e., perform your function as madam of the brothel.

Отн. Come, swear it, damn thyself;
Lest, being like one of heaven, the devils themselves
Should fear to seize thee: therefore be double-damned;
Swear thou art honest.
Des.   Heaven doth truly know it.
Отн. Heaven truly knows that thou art false as hell.
Des. To whom, my lord? With whom? How am I false?
Отн. O Desdemona! Away! away! away!
Des. Alas the heavy day! Why do you weep?
Am I the motive of these tears, my lord?
If haply° you my father do suspect   *perhaps*
An instrument of this your calling back,
Lay not your blame on me: if you have lost him,
Why, I have lost him too.
Отн.   Had it pleased heaven
To try me with affliction; had they rained
All kinds of sores and shames on my bare head,
Steeped me in poverty to the very lips,
Given to captivity me and my utmost hopes,
I should have found in some place of my soul
A drop of patience: but, alas, to make me
A fixèd figure for the time of scorn
To point his slow unmoving finger at!
Yet could I bear that too; well, very well:
But there, where I have garnered° up my heart,   *stored*
Where either I must live or bear no life,
The fountain from the which my current runs,
Or else dries up; to be discarded thence!
Or keep it as a cistern for foul toads
To knot and gender° in! Turn thy complexion° there,   *mate / Turn pale*
Patience, thou young and rose-lipped cherubin,—
Ay, there, look grim as hell!
Des. I hope my noble lord esteems me honest.
Отн. O, ay; as summer flies are in the shambles,°   *butcher shop*
That quicken even with blowing.[16] O thou weed,
Who art so lovely fair and smell'st so sweet
That the sense aches at thee, would thou hadst ne'er been
   born!
Des. Alas, what ignorant° sin have I committed?   *unwitting*
Отн. Was this fair paper, this most goodly book,
Made to write "whore" upon? What committed!
Committed! O thou public commoner!°   *whore*
I should make very forges of my cheeks,
That would to cinders burn up modesty,
Did I but speak thy deeds. What committed!
Heaven stops the nose at it, and the moon winks;
The bawdy wind, that kisses all it meets,
Is hushed within the hollow mine of earth,

---

[16] That are impregnated even the moment after giving birth.

And will not hear it. What committed!
Impudent strumpet!
    DES.   By heaven, you do me wrong.
    OTH. Are not you a strumpet!
    DES.   No, as I am a Christian:
If to preserve this vessel for my lord
From any other foul unlawful touch
Be not to be a strumpet, I am none.
    OTH. What, not a whore?
    DES.   No, as I shall be saved.
    OTH. Is 't possible?
    DES. O, heaven forgive us!
    OTH.   I cry you mercy then:
I took you for that cunning whore of Venice
That married with Othello. [*Raising his voice*] You, mistress,
That have the office opposite to Saint Peter,
And keep the gate of hell!

Re-enter EMILIA.

                  You, you, ay, you!
We have done our course;° there's money for your pains: *sexual encounter*
I pray you, turn the key, and keep our counsel. [*Exit.*]
    EMIL. Alas, what does this gentleman conceive?
How do you, madam? How do you, my good lady?
    DES. Faith, half asleep.
    EMIL. Good madam, what's the matter with my lord?
    DES. With who?
    EMIL. Why, with my lord, madam.
    DES. Who is thy lord?
    EMIL.   He that is yours, sweet lady.
    DES. I have none: do not talk to me, Emilia;
I cannot weep, nor answer have I none
But what should go by water.° Prithee, tonight   *tears*
Lay on my bed my wedding sheets: remember;
And call thy husband hither.
    EMIL.   Here's a change indeed! [*Exit.*]
    DES. 'Tis meet I should be used so, very meet.
How have I been behaved, that he might stick°   *put*
The small'st opinion° on my least misuse?°   *suspicion / error*

Re-enter EMILIA *with* IAGO.

    IAGO. What is your pleasure, madam? How is 't with you?
    DES. I cannot tell. Those that do teach young babes
Do it with gentle means and easy tasks:
He might have chid me so; for, in good faith,
I am a child to chiding.
    IAGO.   What's the matter, lady?
    EMIL. Alas, Iago, my lord hath so bewhored her,
Thrown such despite° and heavy terms upon her,   *scorn*
As true hearts cannot bear.

DES. Am I that name, Iago?

IAGO.   What name, fair lady?

DES. Such as she says my lord did say I was.

EMIL. He called her whore: a beggar in his drink
Could not have laid such terms upon his callat.°   *slut*

IAGO. Why did he so?

DES. I do not know; I am sure I am none such.

IAGO. Do not weep, do not weep. Alas the day!

EMIL. Hath she forsook so many noble matches,
Her father and her country and her friends,
To be called whore? Would it not make one weep?

DES. It is my wretched fortune.

IAGO.   Beshrew° him for't!   *Evil befall*
How comes this trick° upon him?   *foolishness*

DES.   Nay, heaven doth know.

EMIL. I will be hanged, if some eternal villain,
Some busy and insinuating rogue,
Some cogging,° cozening° slave, to get some office,   *cheating / deceiving*
Have not devised this slander; I'll be hanged else.

IAGO. Fie, there is no such man; it is impossible.

DES. If any such there be, heaven pardon him!

EMIL. A halter pardon him! And hell gnaw his bones!
Why should he call her whore? Who keeps her company?
What place? What time? What form? What likelihood?
The Moor's abused by some most villanous knave,
Some base notorious knave, some scurvy fellow.
O heaven, that such companions thou'ldst unfold,°   *expose*
And put in every honest hand a whip
To lash the rascals naked through the world
Even from the east to the west!

IAGO.   Speak within door.°   *quietly*

EMIL. O, fie upon them! Some such squire he was
That turned your wit the seamy side without,
And made you to suspect me with the Moor.

IAGO. You are a fool; go to.

DES.   O good Iago,
What shall I do to win my lord again?
Good friend, go to him; for, by this light of heaven,
I know not how I lost him. Here I kneel:
If e'er my will did trespass 'gainst his love
Either in discourse of thought or actual deed,
Or that mine eyes, mine ears, or any sense,
Delighted them in any other form,
Or that I do not yet, and ever did,
And ever will, though he do shake me off
To beggarly divorcement, love him dearly,
Comfort forswear° me! Unkindness may do much;   *foresake*
And his unkindness may defeat my life,
But never taint my love. I cannot say "whore":
It doth abhor me now I speak the word;
To do the act that might the addition° earn   *name*
Not the world's mass of vanity could make me.

IAGO. I pray you, be content; 'tis but his humor;
The business of the state does him offense,
And he does chide with you.

DES. If 'twere no other,—

IAGO. 'Tis but so, I warrant. [*Trumpets within.*]
Hark, how these instruments summon to supper!
The messengers of Venice stay° the meat: *await*
Go in, and weep not; all things shall be well.
[*Exeunt Desdemona and Emilia.*]

Enter RODERIGO.

How now, Roderigo!

ROD. I do not find that thou dealest justly with me.

IAGO. What in the contrary.

ROD. Every day thou daffest me° with some device, Iago;   *turn me aside*
and rather, as it seems to me now, keepest from me all
conveniency° than suppliest me with the least advantage   *opportunity*
of hope. I will indeed no longer endure it; nor am I yet
persuaded to put up in peace what already I have foolishly
suffered.

IAGO. Will you hear me, Roderigo?

ROD. Faith, I have heard too much; for your words and
performances are no kin together.

IAGO. You charge me most unjustly.

ROD. With nought but truth. I have wasted myself out
of my means. The jewels you have had from me to deliver
to Desdemona would half have corrupted a votarist:° you   *nun*
have told me she hath received them and returned me expectations and comforts of sudden° respect and acquain-   *immediate*
tance; but I find none.

IAGO. Well; go to; very well.

ROD. Very well! Go to! I cannot go to, man; nor 'tis
not very well: by this hand, I say 'tis very scurvy, and begin
to find myself fopped° in it.   *made foolish*

IAGO. Very well.

ROD. I tell you 'tis not very well. I will make myself
known to Desdemona: if she will return me my jewels, I
will give over my suit and repent my unlawful solicitation;
if not, assure yourself I will seek satisfaction of you.

IAGO. You have said now?

ROD. Ay, and said nothing but what I protest intend-   *intention*
ment° of doing.

IAGO. Why, now I see there's mettle° in thee; and even   *spirit*
from this instant do build on thee a better opinion than
ever before. Give me thy hand, Roderigo: thou hast taken
against me a most just exception; but yet, I protest, I have
dealt most directly in thy affair.

ROD. It hath not appeared.

IAGO. I grant indeed it hath not appeared, and your
suspicion is not without wit and judgement. But, Roderigo,

if thou hast that in thee indeed, which I have greater reason to believe now than ever, I mean purpose, courage and valor, this night show it: if thou the next night following enjoy not Desdemona, take me from this world with treachery and devise engines° for my life. *instruments of torture*

ROD. Well, what is it? Is it within reason and compass?° *reach*

IAGO. Sir, there is especial commission come from Venice to depute Cassio in Othello's place.

ROD. Is that true? Why then Othello and Desdemona return again to Venice.

IAGO. O, no; he goes into Mauritania, and takes away with him the fair Desdemona, unless his abode be lingered here by some accident: wherein none can be so determinate° *convincing* as the removing of Cassio.

ROD. How do you mean, removing of him?

IAGO. Why, by making him uncapable of Othello's place; knocking out his brains.

ROD. And that you would have me to do?

IAGO. Ay, if you dare do yourself a profit and a right. He sups tonight with a harlotry, and thither will I go to him: he knows not yet of his honorable fortune. If you will watch his going thence, which I will fashion to fall out between twelve and one, you may take him at your pleasure: I will be near to second your attempt, and he shall fall between us. Come, stand not amazed at it, but go along with me; I will show you such a necessity in his death that you shall think yourself bound to put it on him. It is now high supper-time, and the night grows to waste: about it.

ROD. I will hear further reason for this.

IAGO. And you shall be satisfied. [*Exeunt.*]

SCENE III.
Another room in the castle.

Enter OTHELLO, LODOVICO, DESDEMONA, EMILIA, *and* ATTENDANTS.

LOD. I do beseech you, sir, trouble yourself no further.

OTH. O, pardon me; 'twill do me good to walk.

LOD. Madam, good night; I humbly thank your ladyship.

DES. Your honor is most welcome.

OTH. Will you walk sir?
O,—Desdemona,—

DES. My lord?

OTH. Get you to bed on the instant; I will be returned forthwith: dismiss your attendant there: look it be done.

DES. I will, my lord.

[*Exeunt Othello, Lodovico, and Attendants.*]

EMIL. How goes it now? He looks gentler than he did.

DES. He says he will return incontinent:° *immediately*

He hath commanded me to go to bed,
And bade me to dismiss you.
    EMIL.   Dismiss me!
    DES. It was his bidding; therefore, good Emilia,
Give me my nightly wearing, and adieu:
We must not now displease him.
    EMIL. I would you had never seen him!
    DES. So would not I: my love doth so approve him,
That even his stubbornness, his checks,° his frowns,—   *rebukes*
Prithee, unpin me,—have grace and favor in them.
    EMIL. I have laid those sheets you bade me on the bed.
    DES. All's one. Good faith, how foolish are our minds!
If I do die before thee, prithee, shroud me
In one of those same sheets.
    EMIL.   Come, come, you talk.
    DES. My mother had a maid called Barbara:
She was in love; and he she loved proved mad
And did forsake her: she had a song of "willow";
An old thing 'twas, but it expressed her fortune,
And she died singing it: that song tonight
Will not go from my mind; I have much to do
But to go hang my head all at one side
And sing it like poor Barbara. Prithee, dispatch.
    EMIL. Shall I go fetch your nightgown.
    DES.   No, unpin me here.
This Lodovico is a proper man.
    EMIL. A very handsome man.
    DES. He speaks well.
    EMIL. I know a lady in Venice would have walked
barefoot to Palestine for a touch of his nether° lip.   *lower*
    DES. [*Singing*] "The poor soul sat sighing by a
sycamore tree,
    Sing all a green willow;
Her hand on her bosom, her head on her knee,
    Sing willow, willow, willow:
The fresh streams ran by her, and murmured her moans;
    Sing willow, willow, willow;
Her salt tears fell from her, and softened the stones"—
Lay by these:—
    [*Singing*] "Sing willow, willow, willow."
Prithee, hie° thee; he'll come anon:°—   *hasten / soon*
    [*Singing*] "Sing all a green willow must be my garland.
    Let nobody blame him; his scorn I approve"—
Nay, that's not next. Hark! who is't that knocks?
    EMIL. It's the wind.
    DES. [*Singing*] "I called my love false love; but what said
he then?
    Sing willow, willow, willow:
If I court moe° women, you'll couch with moe men."   *more*
So get thee gone; good night. Mine eyes do itch;
Doth that bode weeping?

EMIL.   'Tis neither here nor there.

DES. I have heard it said so. O, these men, these men!
Dost thou in conscience think,—tell me, Emilia,—
That there be women do abuse their husbands
In such gross kind?

EMIL.   There be some such, no question.

DES. Wouldst thou do such a deed for all the world?

EMIL. Why, would not you?

DES.   No, by this heavenly light!

EMIL. Nor I neither by this heavenly light; I might do't
as well i' the dark.

DES. Wouldst thou do such a deed for all the world?

EMIL. The world's a huge thing: it is a great price
For a small vice.

DES.   In troth, I think thou wouldst not.

EMIL. In troth, I think I should; and undo 't when I
had done. Marry, I would not do such a thing for a joint-
ring,° nor for measures of lawn,° nor for gowns, petticoats,   *cheap ring / fine linen*
nor caps, nor any petty exhibition; but, for the whole
world,—why, who would not make her husband a cuckold
to make him a monarch? I should venture purgatory
for 't.

DES. Beshrew me, if I would do such a wrong
For the whole world.

EMIL. Why, the wrong is but a wrong i' the world; and
having the world for your labor, 'tis a wrong in your own
world, and you might quickly make it right.

DES. I do not think there is any such woman.

EMIL. Yes, a dozen; and as many to the
Vantage° as would store° the world they played for.   *to boot / people*
But I do think it is their husbands' faults
If wives do fall: say that they slack their duties
And pour our treasures into foreign laps,
Or else break out in peevish jealousies,
Throwing restraint upon us, or say they strike us,
Or scant° our former having° in despite,   *reduce / allowance*
Why, we have galls,° and though we have some grace,   *tempers*
Yet have we some revenge. Let husbands know
Their wives have sense like them: they see and smell
And have their palates both for sweet and sour,
As husbands have. What is it that they do
When they change us for others? Is it sport?
I think it is: and doth affection breed it?
I think it doth: is 't frailty that thus errs?
It is so too: and have not we affections,
Desires for sport, and frailty, as men have?
Then let them use us well: else let them know,
The ills we do, their ills instruct us so.

DES. Good night, good night: heaven me such uses°   *habits*
send,
Not to pick bad from bad, but by bad mend! [*Exeunt.*]

ACT V.

SCENE I.
Cyprus. A street.

Enter IAGO *and* RODERIGO.

IAGO. Here, stand behind this bulk;° straight will he   framework
    come:
Wear thy good rapier bare, and put it home:
Quick, quick; fear nothing; I'll be at thy elbow:
It makes us, or it mars us; think on that,
And fix most firm thy resolution.
    ROD. Be near at hand; I may miscarry in 't.
    IAGO. Here, at thy hand: be bold, and take thy stand.
[*Retires.*]
    ROD. I have no great devotion to the deed;
And yet he hath given me satisfying reasons:
'Tis but a man gone. Forth, my sword: he dies.
    IAGO. I have rubbed this young quat° almost to the
    sense,°   pimple / quick
And he grows angry. Now, whether he kill Cassio,
Or Cassio him, or each do kill the other,
Every way makes my gain: live Roderigo,
He calls me to a restitution large
Of gold and jewels that I bobbed° from him,   filched
As gifts to Desdemona:
It must not be: if Cassio do remain,
He hath a daily beauty in his life
That makes me ugly; and besides, the Moor
May unfold° me to him; there stand I in much peril: expose
No, he must die. Be 't so. I hear him coming.

Enter CASSIO.

    ROD. I know his gait; 'tis he. Villain, thou diest!
[*Makes a pass at Cassio.*]
    CAS. That thrust had been mine enemy indeed,
But that my coat is better than thou know'st:
I will make proof of thine. [*Draws, and wounds Roderigo.*]
    ROD.   O, I am slain!
[*Iago from behind wounds Cassio in the leg, and exit.*]
    CAS. I am maimed forever. Help, ho! murder! murder!
[*Falls.*]

Enter OTHELLO.

    OTH. The voice of Cassio: Iago keeps his word.
    ROD. O, villain that I am!
    OTH.   It is even so.
    CAS. O, help, ho! light! a surgeon!

OTH. 'Tis he. O brave Iago, honest and just,
That hast such noble sense of thy friend's wrong!
Thou teachest me. Minion,° your dear lies dead,   *Mistress*
And your unblest fate hies:° strumpet, I come!   *hastens*
Forth of my heart those charms, thine eyes, are blotted;
Thy bed lust-stained shall with lust's blood be spotted.
[*Exit.*]

Enter LODOVICO and GRATIANO.

CAS. What, ho! No watch?° No passage?° Murder! Mur-   *sentries / passersby*
der!
GRA. 'Tis some mischance;° the cry is very direful.   *mishap*
CAS. O, help!
LOD. Hark!
ROD. O wretched villain!
LOD. Two or three groan: it is a heavy night:
These may be counterfeits: let's think 't unsafe
To come in to the cry without more help.
ROD. Nobody come? Then shall I bleed to death.
LOD. Hark!

Re-enter IAGO, with a light.

GRA. Here's one comes in his shirt, with light and
weapons.
IAGO. Who's there? Whose noise is this that cries on
murder?
LOD. We do not know.
IAGO.   Did not you hear a cry?
CAS. Here, here! For heaven's sake, help me!
IAGO.   What's the matter?
GRA. This is Othello's ancient, as I take it.
LOD. The same indeed; a very valiant fellow.
IAGO. What are you here that cry so grievously?
CAS. Iago? O, I am spoiled, undone by villains!
Give me some help.
IAGO. O me, lieutenant! What villains have done this?
CAS. I think that one of them is hereabout,
And cannot make away.
IAGO.   O treacherous villains!
What are you there? Come in and give some help.
[*To Lodovico and Gratiano.*]
ROD. O, help me here!
CAS. That's one of them.
IAGO.   O murderous slave! O villain!
[*Stabs Roderigo.*]
ROD. O damned Iago! O inhuman dog!
IAGO. Kill men i' the dark! Where be these bloody
thieves?
How silent is this town! Ho! murder! murder!

What may you be? Are you of good or evil?
   Lod. As you shall prove us, praise us.
   Iago. Signior Lodovico?
   Lod. He, sir.
   Iago. I cry you mercy. Here's Cassio hurt by villains.
   Gra. Cassio!
   Iago. How is 't, brother?
   Cas. My leg is cut in two.
   Iago.   Marry, heaven forbid!
Light, gentlemen: I'll bind it with my shirt.

Enter Bianca.

   Bian. What is the matter, ho? Who is't that cried?
   Iago. Who is't that cried!
   Bian. O my dear Cassio! My sweet Cassio! O Cassio,
Cassio, Cassio!
   Iago. O notable strumpet! Cassio, may you suspect
Who they should be that have thus mangled you?
   Cas. No.
   Gra. I am sorry to find you thus: I have been to seek
you.
   Iago. Lend me a garter. So. O, for a chair.
To bear him easily hence!
   Bian. Alas, he faints! O Cassio, Cassio, Cassio!
   Iago. Gentlemen all, I do suspect this trash
To be a party in this injury.
Patience awhile, good Cassio. Come, come;
Lend me a light. Know we this face or no?
Alas, my friend and my dear countryman
Roderigo? No:—yes, sure: O heaven! Roderigo.
   Gra. What, of Venice?
   Iago. Even he sir. Did you know him?
   Gra.   Know him! Ay.
   Iago. Signior Gratiano? I cry you gentle pardon;
These bloody accidents must excuse my manners,
That so neglected you.
   Gra.   I am glad to see you.
   Iago. How do you, Cassio? O, a chair, a chair!
   Gra. Roderigo!
   Iago. He, he, 'tis he. [*A chair brought in.*] O, that's well
said; the chair:
Some good man bear him carefully from hence;
I'll fetch the general's surgeon. [*To Bianca*] For you, mistress,
Save you your labor. He that lies slain here, Cassio,
Was my dear friend. What malice was between you?
   Cas. None in the world; nor do I know the man.
   Iago. [*To Bian.*] What, look you pale? O, bear him out
o' the air.
[*Cassio and Roderigo are borne off.*]
Stay you, good gentlemen. Look you pale, mistress?

Do you perceive the gastness° of her eye?   *ghastliness*
Nay, if you stare, we shall hear more anon.
Behold her well; I pray you, look upon her.
Do you see, gentlemen? Nay, guiltiness will speak,
Though tongues were out of use.

Enter EMILIA.

EMIL. 'Las, what's the matter? What's the matter,
husband?
IAGO. Cassio hath here been set on in the dark
By Roderigo, and fellows that are 'scaped:
He's almost slain, and Roderigo dead.
EMIL. Alas, good gentleman! Alas, good Cassio!
IAGO. This is the fruit of whoring. Prithee, Emilia,
Go know of Cassio where he supped tonight.
What, do you shake at that?
BIAN. He supped at my house: but I therefore shake
not.
IAGO. O, did he so? I charge you, go with me.
EMIL. Fie, fie upon thee, strumpet!
BIAN. I am no strumpet; but of life as honest
As you that thus abuse me.
EMIL.   As I! Foh! Fie upon thee!
IAGO. Kind gentlemen, let's go see poor Cassio dressed.°   *bandaged*
Come, mistress, you must tell's another tale.
Emilia, run you to the citadel,
And tell my lord and lady what hath happed!
Will you go on? I pray. [*Aside*] This is the night
That either makes me or fordoes° me quite. [*Exeunt.*]   *undoes*

SCENE II.
A bedchamber in the castle: DESDEMONA *in bed asleep; a light burning.*

Enter OTHELLO.

OTH. It is the cause, it is the cause, my soul:
Let me not name it to you, you chaste stars!
It is the cause. Yet I'll not shed her blood,
Nor scar that whiter skin of hers than snow
And smooth as monumental alabaster.
Yet she must die, else she'll betray more men.
Put out the light, and then put out the light:
If I quench thee, thou flaming minister,
I can again thy former light restore,
Should I repent me: but once put out thy light,
Thou cunning'st pattern of excelling nature,
I know not where is that Promethean[17] heat

---

[17] In Greek mythology Prometheus stole fire from the gods and gave it to man.

That can thy light relume.° When I have plucked the rose,   *restore*
I cannot give it vital growth again,
It must needs wither. I'll smell it on the tree.
[*Kissing her.*]
Ah, balmy breath, that dost almost persuade
Justice to break her sword! One more, one more:
Be thus when thou art dead, and I will kill thee,
And love thee after. One more, and this the last.
So sweet was ne'er so fatal. I must weep,
But they are cruel tears. This sorrow's heavenly;
It strikes where it doth love. She wakes.

    Des. Who's there? Othello?
    Oth.   Ay, Desdemona.
    Des. Will you come to bed, my lord?
    Oth. Have you prayed tonight, Desdemona?
    Des.   Ay, my lord.
    Oth. If you bethink yourself of any crime
Unreconciled as yet to heaven and grace,
Solicit for it straight.
    Des. Alas, my lord, what may you mean by that?
    Oth. Well, do it, and be brief; I will walk by.
I would not kill thy unpreparèd spirit.
No, heaven forfend!° I would not kill thy soul.   *forbid*
    Des. Talk you of killing?
    Oth. Ay, I do.
    Des. Then heaven have mercy on me!
    Oth. Amen, with all my heart!
    Des. If you say so, I hope you will not kill me.
    Oth. Hum!
    Des. And yet I fear you; for you are fatal then
When your eyes roll so. Why I should fear I know not.
Since guiltiness I know not; but yet I feel I fear.
    Oth. Think on thy sins.
    Des.   They are loves I bear to you.
    Oth. Ay, and for that thou diest.
    Des. That death's unnatural that kills for loving.
Alas, why gnaw you so your nether° lip?   *lower*
Some bloody passion shakes your very frame:
These are portents;° but yet I hope, I hope,   *omens*
They do not point on me.
    Oth.   Peace, and be still!
    Des. I will so. What's the matter?
    Oth. That handkerchief which I so loved and gave thee
Thou gavest to Cassio.
    Des.   No, by my life and soul!
Send for the man, and ask him.
    Oth.   Sweet soul, take heed,
Take heed of perjury; thou art on thy deathbed.
    Des. Ay, but not yet to die.
    Oth.   Yes, presently:
Therefore confess thee freely of thy sin;

For to deny each article with oath
Cannot remove nor choke° the strong conception°   *stifle / belief*
That I do groan withal. Thou art to die.
    Des. Then Lord have mercy on me!
    Oth.   I say, amen.
    Des. And have you mercy too! I never did
Offend you in my life; never loved Cassio
But with such general warranty of heaven
As I might love. I never gave him token.
    Oth. By heaven, I saw my handkerchief in 's hand.
O perjured woman! Thou dost stone° my heart,   *harden*
And makest me call what I intend to do
A murder, which I thought a sacrifice.
I saw the handkerchief.
    Des.   He found it then;
I never gave it him. Send for him hither;
Let him confess a truth.
    Oth.   He hath confessed.
    Des. What, my lord?
    Oth. That he hath used thee.
    Des.   How? Unlawfully?
    Oth. Ay.
    Des. He will not say so.
    Oth.   No, his mouth is stopped;
Honest Iago hath ta'en order for't.
    Des. O, my fear interprets!° What, is he dead?   *explains (itself)*
    Oth. Had all his hairs been lives, my great revenge
Had stomach° for them all.   *appetite*
    Des. Alas, he is betrayed, and I undone!
    Oth. Out, strumpet! Weep'st thou for him to my face?
    Des. O, banish me, my lord, but kill me not!
    Oth. Down, strumpet!
    Des. Kill me tomorrow; let me live tonight!
    Oth. Nay, if you strive,—
    Des. But half an hour!
    Oth.   Being done, there is no pause.
    Des. But while I say one prayer!
    Oth.   It is too late. [*He stifles her.*]
    Emil. [*Within*] My lord, my lord! What, ho! My lord,
my lord!
    Oth. What noise is this? Not dead? Not yet quite dead?
I that am cruel am yet merciful;
I would not have thee linger in thy pain.
So, so.
    Emil. [*Within*] What, ho! My lord, my lord!
    Oth.   Who's there?
    Emil. [*Within*] O, good my lord, I would speak a word
with you!
    Oth. Yes: 'tis Emilia. By and by. She's dead.
'Tis like she comes to speak of Cassio's death.
The noise was here. Ha! No more moving?

Still as the grave. Shall she come in? Were 't good?
I think she stirs again. No. What's best to do?
If she come in, she'll sure speak to my wife:
My wife! My wife! What wife? I have no wife.
O, insupportable! O heavy hour!
Methinks it should be now a huge eclipse
Of sun and moon, and that the affrighted globe
Should yawn° at alteration.   *i.e., in earthquake*
    EMIL.   [*Within*] I do beseech you
That I may speak with you, O, good my lord!
    OTH. I had forgot thee. O, come in, Emilia.
Soft;° by and by. Let me the curtains draw.   *Quietly*
Where art thou? [*Unlocks the door.*]

Enter EMILIA.

                What's the matter with thee now?
    EMIL. O, my good lord, yonder's foul murders done!
    OTH. What, now?
    EMIL. But now, my lord.
    OTH. It is the very error of the moon;
She comes more nearer earth than she was wont
And makes men mad.
    EMIL. Cassio, my lord, hath killed a young Venetian
Called Roderigo.
    OTH.   Roderigo killed!
And Cassio killed!
    EMIL.   No, Cassio is not killed.
    OTH. Not Cassio killed! Then murder's out of tune,
And sweet revenge grows harsh.
    DES. O, falsely, falsely murdered!
    EMIL.   Alas, what cry is that?
    OTH. That! What?
    EMIL. Out; and alas! That was my lady's voice.
Help! Help, ho! Help! O lady, speak again!
Sweet Desdemona! O sweet mistress, speak!
    DES. A guiltless death I die.
    EMIL. O, who hath done this deed?
    DES. Nobody; I myself. Farewell.
Commend me to my kind lord. O, farewell! [*Dies*]
    OTH. Why, how should she be murdered?
    EMIL.   Alas, who knows?
    OTH. You heard her say herself, it was not I.
    EMIL. She said so. I must needs report the truth.
    OTH. She's like a liar gone to burning hell.
'Twas I that killed her.
    EMIL.   O, the more angel she,
And you the blacker devil!
    OTH. She turned to folly and she was a whore.
    EMIL. Thou dost belie her and thou art a devil.
    OTH. She was false as water.

EMIL.   Thou art rash as fire, to say
That she was false. O, she was heavenly true!
    OTH. Cassio did top her; ask thy husband else.
O, I were damned beneath all depth in hell,
But that I did proceed upon just grounds
To this extremity. Thy husband knew it all.
    EMIL. My husband!
    OTH. Thy husband.
    EMIL. That she was false to wedlock?
    OTH. Ay, with Cassio. Nay, had she been true,
If heaven would make me such another world
Of one entire and perfect chrysolite,°   *topaz*
I'ld not have sold her for it.
    EMIL. My husband!
    OTH.   Ay, 'twas he that told me first.
An honest man he is, and hates the slime
That sticks on filthy deeds.
    EMIL.   My husband!
    OTH. What needs this iteration, woman? I say thy
husband.
    EMIL. O mistress, villany hath made mocks with° love!   *a mockery of*
My husband say that she was false!
    OTH.   He, woman;
I say thy husband. Dost understand the word?
My friend, thy husband, honest, honest Iago.
    EMIL. If he say so, may his pernicious soul
Rot half a grain a day! He lies to the heart.
She was too fond of her most filthy bargain.
    OTH. Ha!
    EMIL. Do thy worst:
This deed of thine is no more worthy heaven
Than thou wast worthy her.
    OTH.   Peace, you were best.
    EMIL. Thou hast not half that power to do me harm
As I have to be hurt. O gull!° O dolt!   *simpleton*
As ignorant as dirt! Thou hast done a deed—
I care not for thy sword; I'll make thee known,
Though I lost twenty lives. Help! Help, ho! Help!
The Moor hath killed my mistress! Murder! Murder!

Enter MONTANO, GRATIANO, IAGO, *and others.*

    MON. What is the matter? How now, general!
    EMIL. O, are you come, Iago? You have done well,
That men must lay their murders on your neck.
    GRA. What is the matter?
    EMIL. Disprove this villain, if thou be'st a man.
He says thou told'st him that his wife was false.
I know thou didst not, thou'rt not such a villain.
Speak, for my heart is full.
    IAGO. I told him what I thought, and told no more
Than what he found himself was apt and true.

EMIL. But did you ever tell him she was false?

IAGO. I did.

EMIL. You told a lie, an odious, damnèd lie;
Upon my soul, a lie, a wicked lie!
She false with Cassio! Did you say with Cassio?

IAGO. With Cassio, mistress. Go to, charm° your tongue.   *control*

EMIL. I will not charm my tongue; I am bound to speak:
My mistress here lies murdered in her bed,—

ALL. O heavens forfend!

EMIL. And your reports have set the murder on.

OTH. Nay, stare not, masters. It is true indeed.

GRA. 'Tis a strange truth.

MON. O monstrous act!

EMIL.   Villany, villany, villany!
I think upon't. I think. I smell't. O villany!
I thought so then. I'll kill myself for grief,
O villany, villany!

IAGO. What, are you mad? I charge you, get you home.

EMIL. Good gentlemen, let me have leave to speak.
'Tis proper I obey him, but not now.
Perchance, Iago, I will ne'er go home.

OTH. O! O! O! [*Falling on the bed.*]

EMIL.   Nay, lay thee down and roar;
For thou hast killed the sweetest innocent
That e'er did lift up eye.

OTH. [*Rising*] O, she was foul!
I scarce did know you, uncle. There lies your niece,
Whose breath indeed these hands have newly stopped.
I know this act shows° horrible and grim.   *looks*

GRA. Poor Desdemona! I am glad thy father's dead.
Thy match was mortal to him, and pure grief
Shore his old thread in twain. Did he live now,
This sight would make him do a desperate turn;°   *deed*
Yea, curse his better angel from his side,
And fall to reprobation.°   *damnation*

OTH. 'Tis pitiful; but yet Iago knows
That she with Cassio hath the act of shame
A thousand times committed; Cassio confessed it.
And she did gratify his amorous works
With that recognizance and pledge of love
Which I first gave her; I saw it in his hand.
It was a handkerchief, an antique token
My father gave my mother.

EMIL. O heaven! O heavenly powers!

IAGO. 'Zounds! Hold your peace.

EMIL.   'Twill out, 'twill out. I peace!
No, I will speak as liberal° as the north.°   *freely, coldly / north*
Let heaven and men and devils let them all,   *wind*
All, all, cry shame against me, yet I'll speak.

IAGO. Be wise, and get you home.

EMIL.   I will not.

[*Iago offers to stab Emilia.*]

GRA.   Fie!

Your sword upon a woman!

EMIL. O thou dull Moor! That handkerchief thou speak'st
of

I found by fortune and did give my husband;

For often with a solemn earnestness,

More than indeed belonged to such a trifle,

He begged of me to steal it.

IAGO.   Villanous whore!

EMIL. She give it Cassio! No, alas, I found it,

And I did give't my husband.

IAGO.   Filth, thou liest!

EMIL. By heaven, I do not, I do not, gentlemen.

O murderous coxcomb!° What should such a fool   *dunce*

Do with so good a wife?

OTH.   Are there no stones in heaven

But what serve for the thunder?[18] Precious villain!

[*He runs at Iago. Iago, from behind, stabs Emilia, and exit.*]

GRA. The woman falls; sure, he hath killed his wife.

EMIL. Ay, ay. O, lay me by my mistress' side.

GRA. He's gone, but his wife's killed.

MON. 'Tis a notorious villain. Take you this weapon,

Which I have here recovered from the Moor.

Come, guard the door without; let him not pass,

But kill him rather. I'll after that same villain,

For 'tis a damned slave.

[*Exeunt all but Othello and Emilia.*]

OTH.   I am not valiant neither,

But every puny whipster° gets my sword.   *whipping boy*

But why should honor outlive honesty?

Let it go all.

EMIL.   What did thy song bode, lady?

Hark, canst thou hear me? I will play the swan,

And die in music. [*Singing*] Willow, willow, willow.

Moor, she was chaste; she loved thee, cruel Moor;

So come my soul to bliss, as I speak true;

So speaking as I think, I die, I die. [*Dies.*]

OTH. I have another weapon in this chamber;

It is a sword of Spain, the ice-brook's temper.°—   *i.e., tempered in ice-*

O, here it is. Uncle, I must come forth.   *water*

GRA. [*Within*] If thou attempt it, it will cost thee dear.

Thou hast no weapon, and perforce must suffer.

OTH. Look in upon me then, and speak with me,

Or, naked as I am, I will assault thee.

Re-enter GRATIANO.

---

[18] Thunder was thought by some Elizabethans to be caused by huge boulders falling from the
sky and bouncing along the ground.

GRA. What is the matter?

OTH.   Behold, I have a weapon;
A better never did itself sustain
Upon a soldier's thigh. I have seen the day
That with this little arm and this good sword
I have made my way through more impediments
Than twenty times your stop.° But, O vain boast!   *opposition*
Who can control his fate? 'Tis not so now.
Be not afraid, though you do see me weaponed;
Here is my journey's end, here is my butt°   *target*
And very sea-mark° of my utmost° sail.   *marker / farthest*
Do you go back dismayed? 'Tis a lost fear:
Man but a rush° against Othello's breast,   *reed*
And he retires. Where should Othello go?
Now, how dost thou look now? O ill-starred wench!
Pale as thy smock! When we shall meet at compt,°   *Judgment*
This look of thine will hurl my soul from heaven,
And fiends will snatch at it. Cold, cold, my girl!
Even like thy chastity. O cursed slave!
Whip me, ye devils,
From the possession of this heavenly sight!
Blow me about in winds! Roast me in sulphur!
Wash me in steep-down gulfs of liquid fire!
O Desdemona! Desdemona! Dead!
Oh! Oh! Oh!

Enter LODOVICO, MONTANO, CASSIO *carried in a chair,*
and OFFICERS *with* IAGO, *prisoner.*

LOD. Where is this rash and most unfortunate man?

OTH. That's he that was Othello. Here I am.

LOD. Where is that viper? Bring the villain forth.

OTH. I look down towards his feet; but that's a fable.
If that thou be'st a devil,° I cannot kill thee. [*Wounds Iago.*]   *i.e., with cloven feet*

LOD. Wrench his sword from him.

IAGO.   I bleed, sir, but not killed.

OTH. I am not sorry neither. I'd have thee live;
For, in my sense, 'tis happiness to die.

LOD. O thou Othello, that wert once so good,
Fall'n in the practice° of a damnèd slave,   *scheming*
What shall be said to thee?

OTH.   Why, any thing.
An honorable murderer, if you will;
For nought did I in hate, but all in honor.

LOD. This wretch hath part confessed his villany.
Did you and he consent in Cassio's death?

OTH. Ay.

CAS. Dear general, I never gave you cause.

OTH. I do believe it, and I ask your pardon.
Will you, I pray, demand that demi-devil
Why he hath thus ensnared my soul and body?

IAGO. Demand me nothing; what you know, you know.
From this time forth I never will speak word.
　　LOD. What, not to pray?
　　GRA.　　　　　　　　　　Torments will ope your lips.
　　OTH. Well, thou dost best.
　　LOD. Sir, you shall understand what hath befall'n,
Which, as I think, you know not. Here is a letter
Found in the pocket of the slain Roderigo,
And here another. The one of them imports
The death of Cassio to be undertook
By Roderigo.
　　OTH. O villain!
　　CAS.　　　　　Most heathenish and most gross!
　　LOD. Now here's another discontented paper,
Found in his pocket too; and this, it seems,
Roderigo meant to have sent this damned villain;
But that, belike, Iago in the interim
Came in and satisfied him.
　　OTH.　　　　　　　　　O the pernicious caitiff!°　　　　　*villain*
How came you, Cassio, by that handkerchief
That was my wife's?
　　CAS.　　　　　I found it in my chamber.
And he himself confessed but even now
That there he dropped it for a special purpose
Which wrought to his desire.
　　OTH.　　　　　　　　　O fool! fool! fool!
　　CAS. There is besides in Roderigo's letter,
How he upbraids Iago, that he made him
Brave° me upon the watch; whereon it came　　　　　*Defy*
That I was cast,° and even but now he spake　　　　　*dismissed*
After long seeming dead, Iago hurt him,
Iago set him on.
　　LOD. You must forsake this room, and go with us.
Your power and your command is taken off,
And Cassio rules in Cyprus. For this slave,
If there be any cunning cruelty
That can torment him much and hold him long,
It shall be his. You shall close prisoner rest,
Till that the nature of your fault be known
To the Venetian state. Come, bring away.
　　OTH. Soft you; a word or two before you go.
I have done the state some service, and they know't.
No more of that. I pray you, in your letters,
When you shall these unlucky deeds relate,
Speak of me as I am; nothing extenuate,
Nor set down aught in malice. Then must you speak
Of one that loved not wisely but too well;
Of one not easily jealous but, being wrought,
Perplexed in the extreme; of one whose hand,
Like the base Indian, threw a pearl away
Richer than all his tribe; of one whose subdued eyes,

Albeit unused to the melting mood,
Drop tears as fast as the Arabian trees
Their medicinal gum. Set you down this;
And say besides, that in Aleppo once,
Where a malignant and a turbaned Turk
Beat a Venetian and traduced° the state,   *slandered*
I took by the throat the circumcisèd dog
And smote him, thus. [*Stabs himself.*]
    Lod. O bloody period!
    Gra.   All that's spoke is marred.
    Oth. I kissed thee ere I killed thee. No way but this,
Killing myself, to die upon a kiss.
[*Falls on the bed, and dies.*]
    Cas. This did I fear, but thought he had no weapon;
For he was great of heart.
    Lod.   [*To Iago*] O Spartan[19] dog,
More fell° than anguish, hunger, or the sea!   *cruel*
Look on the tragic loading of this bed;
This is thy work. The object poisons sight;
Let it be hid. Gratiano, keep the house,
And seize upon the fortunes of the Moor,
For they succeed on you. To you, lord governor,
Remains the censure of this hellish villain,
The time, the place, the torture: O, enforce it!
Myself will straight aboard, and to the state
This heavy act with heavy heart relate. [*Exeunt.*]

                        [1604]

---

[19] The Spartans were famous for ferocity.

Molière (Jean-Baptiste Poquelin)   *1622–1673*

TARTUFFE
OR
THE HYPOCRITE
(L'Imposteur)

A Comedy

Translated by A. R. Waller

CHARACTERS

MME. PERNELLE, *Orgon's mother*
ORGON, *Elmire's husband*
ELMIRE, *Orgon's wife*
DAMIS, *Orgon's son, Elmire's stepson*
MARIANE, *Orgon's daughter, Elmire's
  stepdaughter, and Valère's lover*
VALÈRE, *Mariane's lover*

CLÉANTE, *Orgon's brother-in-law*
TARTUFFE, *a hypocrite*
DORINE, *Mariane's maid*
M. LOYAL, *a bailiff*
POLICE OFFICER
FLIPOTE, *Mm. Pernelle's servant*

SCENE
Paris

ACT I

SCENE I
MADAME PERNELLE *and* FLIPOTE, *her servant*, ELMIRE,
MARIANE, DORINE, DAMIS, CLÉANTE

MME. PERNELLE. Come along, Flipote, come along; let me get away from them.
ELMIRE. You walk so fast that I can scarcely keep up with you.
MME. PERNELLE. You need not come any further, child. I can dispense with such ceremony.
ELMIRE. We only give what is due to you. But, mother, why are you in such a hurry to leave us?
MME. PERNELLE. Because I cannot bear to see such goings on and no one takes any pains to meet my wishes. Yes, I leave your house not very well pleased: you ignore all my advice, you do not show any respect for anything, everyone says what he likes, and it is just like the Court of King Pétaud.[1]
DORINE. If . . .
MME. PERNELLE. You are far too free with your tongue for your position, my lass, and too saucy. You offer your advice about everything.
DAMIS. But . . .
MME. PERNELLE. You are a fool thrice over, my boy, though it is your own

---

[1] A court without order where every man is his own master.

grandmother who says it. I have told your father a hundred times that you will become a ne'er-do-well, and will cause him nothing but trouble.

MARIANE. I think . . .

MME. PERNELLE. As for you, his sister, you put on such a demure air that it is difficult to catch you tripping. But, as the saying is, still waters are the most dangerous, and I hate your underhand ways.

ELMIRE. But, mother . . .

MME. PERNELLE. Let me tell you, daughter, that your whole conduct is entirely wrong. You ought to set them a good example: their late mother did much better. You are extravagant: I am shocked to see you decked out like a princess. If a woman wishes to please her husband only, she has no need for so much finery, my child.

CLÉANTE. But, madam, after all . . .

MME. PERNELLE. As for you, sir, who are her brother, I think very highly of you, and I both love and respect you, but, at the same time, if I were my son, her husband, I should request you not to enter our house. You are always laying down rules of conduct which respectable people should not follow. I speak rather frankly to you, but that is my nature: I do not mince matters when I have anything on my mind.

DAMIS. Your Mr. Tartuffe is, no doubt, an excellent person . . .

MME. PERNELLE. He is a very worthy man, one who should be listened to; and it makes me very angry to hear him sneered at by a fool like you.

DAMIS. What! Am I to permit a censorious bigot to exercise a tyrannical influence in the family; and are we not to be allowed any pleasures unless this good gentleman condescends to give his consent?

DORINE. Were we to listen to him and to put faith in his maxims, we should look upon all our acts as criminal, for the zealous critic finds fault with everything.

MME. PERNELLE. And whatever he finds fault with deserves censure. He wants to lead you to Heaven, and it is my son's duty to teach you to value him.

DAMIS. No; look here, grandmother, neither my father nor anyone else shall ever induce me to think well of him: I should be false to myself were I to speak otherwise. His ways irritate me constantly. I can see what the consequence will be: that underbred fellow and I will soon quarrel.

DORINE. Surely it is a scandalous thing to see a stranger exercise such authority in this house: to see a beggar, who, when he came, had not shoes on his feet, and whose whole clothing may have been worth twopence, so far forget himself as to interfere with everything, and play the master.

MME. PERNELLE. Ah! mercy on me! it would be much better if everything were done in accordance with his good rules.

DORINE. He is a saint in your opinion, but, in mine, he is a hypocrite.

MME. PERNELLE. What language!

DORINE. I should not like to trust myself either with him or with his man Laurent, without good security.

MME. PERNELLE. I do not know what the servant may be at heart, but I will swear the master is a worthy man. You all hate and flout him because he tells you unpleasant truths. His anger is directed against sin, and his only desire is to further the cause of Heaven.

DORINE. Yes; but why, especially for some time past, can he not bear any one to come to the house? Why is a polite call so offensive to Heaven that he needs make noise enough about it to split our heads? Between ourselves

I will tell you what I think. Upon my word, I believe that he is jealous of Madame.

Mme. Pernelle. Hold your tongue, and take care what you say. He is not the only person who blames these visits. The whole neighborhood is annoyed by the bustle of the people you receive, their carriages always waiting before the door, and the noisy crowd of servants. I am willing to believe that there is no actual harm done, but people will talk, and it is better not to give them cause.

Cléante. Ah! madam, how can you stop people talking? It would be a sorry thing if in this world we had to give up our best friends, because of idle chatter aimed at us. And even if we could bring ourselves to do so, do you think it would stop people's tongues? There is not any protection against slander. Do not let us pay any attention to foolish gossip, but endeavour to live honestly and leave the scandal-mongers to say what they will.

Dorine. Probably our neighbor Daphné, and her little husband, are at the bottom of all this slander. Those who are the most ridiculous in their own conduct are always the first to libel others. They are quick to get hold of the slightest rumor of a love-affair, to spread it abroad with high glee, giving the story just what twist they like. They paint the actions of others in their own colors, thinking thereby to justify their own conduct to the world; and in the vain hope of a resemblance they try to give their intrigues some show of innocence, or else to shift to other shoulders a part of that blame with which they themselves are overburdened.

Mme. Pernelle. All these arguments have nothing to do with the matter. Everybody knows that Orante leads an exemplary life, and that all her thoughts are towards heaven. Well, I have been told that she strongly disapproves of the company who visit here.

Dorine. The example is admirable, and the lady is beyond reproach! It is true that she lives an austere life, but age is responsible for her fervent zeal, and people know that she is a prude because she cannot help it. She made the most of all her advantages while she had the power of attracting attention. But now that her eyes have lost their luster she renounces the world which renounces her, and hides under the pompous cloak of prudence the decay of her worn-out charms. Such is the last shift of a modern coquette. Mortified to see their lovers fall away from them, their gloomy despair sees nothing for it, when thus forsaken, but the rôle of prudery; and in their strictness these good women censure everything and pardon nothing. They loudly condemn the actions of others, not from principles of charity, but out of envy, since they cannot bear to see another taste those pleasures for which age has taken away their appetite.

Mme. Pernelle. These are idle tales told to please you. I have to be silent in your house, my child, for madam, by gossiping, holds the dice the whole day.[2] Still, I mean to have my say in my turn. I tell you that my son never did a wiser act than when he received this good man into his family; Heaven mercifully sent him into your house to convert your erring thoughts. You ought to hear him for your soul's sake, since he censures nothing but that which deserves censure. All these visits, these balls, these tales, are inventions of the evil one. Not one good word is heard at them, nothing but idle gossip, songs and chatter. Often enough the neighbor comes in for his share, and

---

[2] I.e., she dominates the conversation.

there is scandal right and left. Indeed the heads of sensible people are quite turned by the distraction of these gatherings. A thousand ill-natured stories are spread abroad in no time; and, as a certain doctor very truly said the other day, it is a perfect tower of Babylon, for every one babbles as long as he likes. And to tell the story which brought this up . . . Here is this gentleman giggling already! Go and find the fools who make you laugh, and unless . . . Good-bye, my child. I'll say no more. My regard for your house has fallen by one-half, and it will be a very long time before I set foot in it again. [*Slapping* FLIPOTE'S *face.*] Come along, you, don't stand there dreaming and gaping. Good Lord! I'll warm your ears for you, come on, hussy, come on.

SCENE II
CLÉANTE, DORINE

CLÉANTE. I will not follow her lest she should begin scolding me again. How that old woman . . .

DORINE. Ah! truly it is a pity that she does not hear you use such language. She would soon tell you *your* age, and that *she* is not yet old enough to deserve that title.

CLÉANTE. What a passion she got into with us about nothing, and how infatuated she seems with her Tartuffe!

DORINE. Oh! indeed, her infatuation is nothing in comparison with her sons's, and if you could see him you would say he was far worse! During our civil troubles he gained a reputation for sense, and showed some courage in serving his prince, but he has become an idiot since his head has been full of Tartuffe. He calls him brother, and in his heart loves him a hundred times more than he loves mother, son, daughter, and wife. He makes him the sole confidant of all his secrets, and the sage adviser of all his actions. He caresses him, kisses him, and I do not think he could show more affection to a mistress. He will have him seated at the head of the table, and is delighted to see him eat as much as half-a-dozen other people. All the choice morsels are given to him, and if he chance to hiccup he says to him, "God bless you!" In short, he is crazy about him; he is his all, his hero; he admires him at all points, quotes him on all occasions; he considers that his most trifling actions are miracles, and every word he utters an oracle. Tartuffe, who understands his dupe, and wishes to make the most profit out of him, is clever enough to impose upon him in a hundred different shams. He constantly extorts money from him by his cant, and takes upon himself the right to find fault with us all. Even that puppy of a footboy of his has the cheek to lecture us; he preaches at us with indignant looks, and throws away our ribbons, rouge, and patches.[3] Only the other day the wretch tore a handkerchief to pieces which he found in a 'Flower of the Saints,' saying that it was an abominable sin to put the devil's trappings side by side with holy things.

---

[3] It was the fashion at the time for women to wear small black patches to cover up blemishes (or scars from smallpox) on their faces.

SCENE III
ELMIRE, MARIANE, DAMIS, CLÉANTE, DORINE

ELMIRE. You are very lucky to have missed the sermon she gave us at the door. But I have just seen my husband, and as he did not see me I shall go and wait upstairs for him.

CLÉANTE. I will wait for him here for a little longer, only to bid him "Good-morning."

DAMIS. Sound him a little about my sister's marriage. I suspect that Tartuffe opposes it, because he puts my father up to so many evasions; and you know what a great interest I take in it. If the same passion influences my sister and Valère, his sister is, as you know, dear to me, and if it were necessary . . .

DORINE. Here he is.

SCENE IV
ORGON, CLÉANTE, DORINE

ORGON. Ah! good-morning, brother.

CLÉANTE. I am glad to see you back. I was just going away. The country is not very attractive just now.

ORGON. Dorine . . . Just one moment, brother, I beg. You will, I know, let me relieve my mind by asking how things have gone here. Has all been well during the last two days? What has happened? How are they all?

DORINE. The day before yesterday Madam was feverish from morning to night, with a splitting headache.

ORGON. And Tartuffe?

DORINE. Tartuffe? He is in excellent health, stout and fat, with a fresh complexion and ruddy lips.

ORGON. Poor man!

DORINE. In the evening she felt very sick, and her head ached so violently she could not touch anything at supper.

ORGON. And Tartuffe?

DORINE. He took his supper, in her presence, and very devoutly ate a brace of partridges and half a leg of mutton hashed.

ORGON. Poor man!

DORINE. She passed the whole night without closing her eyes for a moment, kept from sleeping by her feverishness, and we were obliged to sit up with her until morning.

ORGON. And Tartuffe?

DORINE. Comfortably drowsy when he got up from the table, he went to his bedroom and quickly tumbled into his warmed bed, where he slept undisturbed till the morning.

ORGON. Poor man!

DORINE. At length we prevailed upon her to be bled,[4] and immediately she felt relieved.

ORGON. And Tartuffe?

[4] Doctors in Molière's day frequently opened a vein in a patient's arm in an effort to drain off the tainted blood thought to cause illness.

DORINE. He took heart again, as was only right, and to fortify himself against all ills, and to make up for the blood which Madam had lost, he drank four large bumpers of wine at breakfast.

ORGON. Poor man!

DORINE. Both are now well again, and I will go and tell Madam how pleased you are at her recovery.

SCENE V
ORGON, CLÉANTE

CLÉANTE. She is making game of you, brother, to your face, and, without wishing to vex you, I tell you frankly there is good reason for it. Who ever heard of such a whim? How can you be so infatuated with a man at this time of day as to forget everything else for him? And, after having saved him from want by taking him into your own house you should go so far as . . .

ORGON. Stop there, brother, you do not know the man of whom you speak.

CLÉANTE. I do not know him then, if you like; but, after all, to know what sort of a man he is . . .

ORGON. Brother, you would be only too glad to know him, and your astonishment would be boundless. He is a man . . . who . . . ha! . . . a man . . . in fact, a man. He who follows attentively his precepts enjoys a profound peace, and looks upon the rest of the world as so much dross. Yes, I am quite another man since I conversed with him. He teaches me that I must not set my affections upon anything; he detaches my heart from all ties; and I could see my brother, children, mother and wife die without caring as much as a snap of the fingers.

CLÉANTE. Humane feelings these, brother!

ORGON. Oh! had you but seen him as I first saw him, you would have for him the same affection that I have. Every day he would come to church, and with mild looks kneel down in front of me. He drew upon himself the attention of the whole congregation by the fervor of his prayers to Heaven; he sighed deeply in his saintly raptures and kissed the ground humbly every moment, and when I came out he would steal quickly before me to the door to offer me holy water. Having learnt who he was, and that he was poor—through his footboy—who copies everything he does—I gave him presents, but he always modestly wished to return me some part of them. "It is too much, too much by half," he would say, "I do not deserve your pity." And when I refused to take it back he distributed it to the poor before my eyes. At last Heaven moved me to take him into my house, and since then everything has seemed to prosper here. He reproves everything, and, with a view to my honor, he shows an extreme solicitude even towards my wife. He tells me of those who cast sweet looks her way, and he is six times more jealous of her than I am. You would never guess how far he carries his zeal: he accuses himself of sin over the slightest trifle; a mere nothing is enough to shock him; he even accused himself the other day for having killed a flea too angrily which he caught whilst saying his prayers.

CLÉANTE. Really, brother, I think you must be crazy. Are you joking at my expense with this nonsense? How can you pretend that all this foolery . . . ?

ORGON. Brother, your talk savors of free thought: you are somewhat tainted with it; and, as I have repeatedly told you, you will draw down some heavy judgment upon your head.

CLÉANTE. That is the usual style of talking among your set; they want everyone to be as blind as themselves. To be clear-sighted is to be a free-thinker, and he who does not bow down to idle affectations has neither respect for nor faith in sacred things. I tell you none of your sermons frighten me: I know what I say, and Heaven sees my heart. We are not ruled by your formalists. There are pretenders to devotion as to courage; and even as those who are truly brave when honor calls are not those who make the most noise, so the good and truly pious, in whose footsteps we ought to follow, are not those who make so many grimaces. What? will you not make any distinction between hypocrisy and sincerity? Will you speak of them in the same words, and render the same homage to the mask as to the face, put artifice on a level with sincerity, confound the appearance with the reality, value the shadow as much as the substance and false coin as good? Men, truly, are strange beings! They are never seen in their proper nature; reason's boundaries are too limited for them; in every character they over-act the part; and they often mar that which is most noble by too much exaggeration and by wilful extremes. But this, brother, is by the way.

ORGON. Yes, you are doubtless a doctor, revered by all; all the learning of the ages is concentrated in you; you alone are wise, enlightened, an oracle, a Cato[5] for the present age; and compared with you, all men are fools.

CLÉANTE. No, brother, I am not a revered teacher, nor do I possess all wisdom; my learning is simply the knowledge of how to tell the false from the true. And since I do not know any character more admirable than the truly devout, nor anything in the world more noble and more beautiful than the righteous fervor of a sincere piety, neither do I know anything more odious than the whited sepulchre of a specious zeal; than these barefaced hypocrites, these hireling bigots, whose sacrilegious and deceitful mouthings impose on people with impunity, who jest as they please with all that men hold most holy and sacred; these slaves of self-interest who barter religion and make a trade of it, and who would purchase honor and reputation with a false uplifting of the eyes and affected groans. These men, I say, whom we see possessed of such uncommon ardor, make their fortunes in this world by way of the next; themselves asking each day some new favor, they preach solitude in the midst of the Court, burning with zeal and great in prayer. They know how to reconcile their profession with their vices, are passionate, revengeful, faithless, full of deceit, and, in order to ruin a man, insolently cover their fierce resentment with the cloak of Heaven's interests. They are doubly dangerous in their bitter wrath for they use against us the weapons we revere; and their anger, for which they are commended, prompts them to kill us with a consecrated blade. There are too many of these false characters; the truly devout are easily recognised. Our age, brother, has shown us some who should serve us as glorious examples: look at Ariston, look at Périandre, Oronte, Alcidamas, Polydore, Clitandre[6]—no one denies their title. These are not boasters of virtue; unbearable ostentation is not seen in them; their piety is human, is reasonable; they do not condemn all our actions: they

---

[5] Marcus Porcius Cato (234–149 B.C.), a Roman consul renowned for devotion to virtue; or his great-grandson, Marcus Porcius Cato, the Younger (95–46 B.C.), a philosopher.
[6] Fictitious, not historical, persons.

think there is too much arrogance in these censures; and, leaving haughty words to others, they reprove our actions by their own. They do not build upon the appearances of evil, and their minds are inclined to think well of others. No spirit of cabal is found in them; they have no intrigues to scent out; their sole care is to live rightly. They do not persecute a sinner; it is only the sin itself they hate. Neither do they desire to vindicate the interests of Heaven with a keener zeal than Heaven itself shows. These are the people I admire; that is the right way to live; there is, in short, the example to be followed. Your man, to speak truly, is not of this mold: you applaud his piety in good faith, but I believe you are dazzled by a false glitter.

ORGON. Have you said your say, my dear brother?

CLÉANTE. Yes.

ORGON. I am your humble servant. [*going.*]

CLÉANTE. One word, brother, I pray. Let us drop this discussion. You know you promised Valère he should become your son-in-law?

ORGON. Yes.

CLÉANTE. And that you had fixed the happy day.

ORGON. True.

CLÉANTE. Why, then, defer the ceremony?

ORGON. I do not know.

CLÉANTE. Have you another design in view?

ORGON. Perhaps.

CLÉANTE. You will break your word?

ORGON. I do not say that.

CLÉANTE. No obstacle, I believe, can prevent you fulfilling your promises.

ORGON. That depends.

CLÉANTE. Why so much circumspection about a word? Valère sent me to see you on this matter.

ORGON. Heaven be praised!

CLÉANTE. But what shall I tell him?

ORGON. What you please.

CLÉANTE. But it is necessary to know your intentions. What, then, are they?

ORGON. To perform the will of Heaven.

CLÉANTE. Come, speak to the point. Valère has your word. Will you keep it or not?

ORGON. Good-bye.

CLÉANTE. I am afraid his love will not run smooth, and I ought to tell him what is going on.

END OF THE FIRST ACT.

ACT II

SCENE I
ORGON, MARIANE

ORGON. Mariane.

MARIANE. Yes, father.

ORGON. Come here, I have something to say to you privately.

MARIANE. What are you looking for?

ORGON. [*looking into a small side-room.*] I am looking to see whether anyone is there who might overhear us; this is a most likely little place for such a purpose. Now, we are all right. Mariane, I have always found you very good-natured, and you have always been dear to me.

MARIANE. I am very grateful for your fatherly love.

ORGON. That is well said, my child, and in order to deserve it your chief care ought to be to please me.

MARIANE. It is my dearest wish.

ORGON. Very well. What do you think of our guest Tartuffe?

MARIANE. Who, I?

ORGON. You. Think well before you answer.

MARIANE. Oh, dear! I will say anything you like.

ORGON. That is sensibly spoken. Tell me, then, my child, that he is a man whose virtues shine forth, that you love him, and that it would make you very happy were I to choose him for your husband. Eh?

MARIANE. [*draws back, surprised.*] Eh?

ORGON. What is the matter?

MARIANE. What did you say?

ORGON. What?

MARIANE. Am I mistaken?

ORGON. Why?

MARIANE. Whom do you wish me to say I love, father? Whom do I wish you to choose as my husband?

ORGON. Tartuffe.

MARIANE. I don't wish anything of the kind, father, I assure you. Why would you make me tell such a lie?

ORGON. But I wish it to be the truth, and it is enough for you that I have made up my mind on the subject.

MARIANE. What, father, would you . . . ?

ORGON. Yes, my child, I intend to unite Tartuffe to my family by your marriage. I have decided that he shall be your husband, and since you have promised, I . . .

SCENE II
DORINE, ORGON, MARIANE

ORGON. What are you doing here? Your curiosity must be very great, my girl, to urge you to come and listen to us in this way.

DORINE. Indeed, I don't know whether the report is conjecture or simply chance words, but I have just heard some news about this marriage and I treated it as a mere jest.

ORGON. Why? Is the thing incredible?

DORINE. So much so that I could not believe it from your lips, Monsieur.

ORGON. I know how to make you believe it, though.

DORINE. Yes, yes, you tell us a pretty story.

ORGON. I tell you what you will see happen very shortly.

DORINE. Nonsense!

ORGON. I am not jesting, my child.

DORINE. Come, do not believe your father, he is joking.

ORGON. I tell you . . .

DORINE. No, you may say what you like, and no one will believe you.

ORGON. My anger will very soon . . .

DORINE. Very well, we will believe you, but so much the worse for you. What, is it possible, Monsieur, with that air of wisdom and your well-bearded face, that you would be silly enough to want . . .

ORGON. Now listen: you have taken certain liberties in this house, my girl, which I do not like.

DORINE. Let us talk without becoming angry, Monsieur, I beg. Are you making game of everybody by means of this scheme. Your daughter will never do for a bigot: he has other things to think about. Besides, what good will such an alliance be to you? Why, with all your wealth, do you choose a beggar for a son-in-law?

ORGON. Be quiet. If he has nothing he ought to be the more esteemed. His poverty is, without doubt, a noble poverty; it should raise him above all worldly greatness since he has allowed himself to be deprived of his wealth by caring too little for earthly affairs, and by his ardent attachment to things eternal. My help may be the means of getting him out of his troubles and of restoring his property to him: his estates are well known in his native place, but even as he is he is a gentleman.

DORINE. Well, he says he is, but this vanity, Monsieur, does not agree well with his piety. He who embraces the simplicity of a holy life should not boast of his name and lineage: the humble ways of goodness have nothing in common with the glare of ambition. Why such pride? But what I say vexes you: let us speak of himself and leave his quality. Can you have the heart to bestow such a daughter as yours upon a man of his stamp? Ought you not to have some regard for propriety and foresee the consequences of this union? You must know the girl's virtue is not safe when she is married against her inclinations, that her living virtuously depends upon the qualities of the husband who is given to her, and that those who have the finger of scorn pointed at them make their wives what we see they are. It is truly no easy task to be faithful to certain husbands; and he who gives his daughter to a man she hates is responsible to heaven for the sins she commits. Consider, then, to what perils your design exposes you.

ORGON. I see I shall have to learn from her how to live.

DORINE. You could not do better than follow my advice.

ORGON. Do not let us waste time, my child, with this silly talk. I am your father, and I know what is good for you. I had betrothed you to Valère, but I hear he is inclined to gambling, and I also suspect he is a free-thinker, for I never see him at church.

DORINE. Would you like him to go there at stated times like those who go to be seen?

ORGON. I don't ask your advice upon the matter. Tartuffe is on the best possible terms with heaven, and that is a treasure second to none. This union will crown your wishes with every blessing. It will be full of pleasure and joy. You will live together in faithful love like two young children, like turtledoves, there will not be any miserable disputes between you, and you will make anything you like of him.

DORINE. She? Why, I am sure she will never make anything of him but a fool.

ORGON. Good gracious! what language!

DORINE. I tell you he looks it all over, and his destiny, Monsieur, will be stronger than your daughter's virtue.

ORGON. Don't interrupt me. Try to hold your tongue without poking your nose into what does not concern you.

DORINE. I only speak for your good, Monsieur. [*She interrupts him every time he turns to speak to his daughter.*]

ORGON. You are too good! Be quiet, will you?

DORINE. If I did not like you . . .

ORGON. I do not need affection.

DORINE. But I will care for you, Monsieur, in spite of yourself.

ORGON. Ah!

DORINE. Your honor is dear to me, and I cannot bear that you should be jeered at by every one.

ORGON. Will you be silent?

DORINE. It is a shame to let you make such an alliance.

ORGON. Will you hold your peace, you viper, whose brazen face . . .

DORINE. What! you a religious man and you give way to anger?

ORGON. Yes, my choler is roused to fury by your nonsense. I insist upon your holding your tongue.

DORINE. Very well. But if I cannot speak I shall think all the more.

ORGON. Think, if you like, but take care not to tell your thoughts to me, or . . . beware. [*Turning towards his daughter.*] I have deliberately weighed everything as a prudent man should.

DORINE. It makes me furious not to be allowed to speak. [*She is silent when he looks towards her.*]

ORGON. Without being a fop Tartuffe's looks are such . . .

DORINE. Yes, he has a fine mug.

ORGON. That even if you do not appreciate his other qualities . . . [*He turns towards her, and looks at her, his arms folded.*]

DORINE. There's a fine bargain! If I were in her place, depend upon it no man should marry me against my will with impunity. I would soon let him see, after the wedding-day, that a woman has always her vengeance in her own hands.

ORGON. Then you do not mean to take any notice of what I say?

DORINE. What are you complaining about? I was not speaking to you.

ORGON. What were you doing then?

DORINE. I was speaking to myself.

ORGON. All right. I must give her the back of my hand for her unbearable insolence. [*He prepares to slap Dorine's face; and Dorine stands silent and erect each time he looks at her.*] You ought to approve of my plan, my child . . . and have faith in the husband . . . I have chosen for you . . . Why do you not speak to yourself?

DORINE. Because I have no more to say to myself.

ORGON. Only a little word.

DORINE. It does not suit me.

ORGON. I was waiting for you.

DORINE. I am not such a fool.

ORGON. In short, my girl, you must obey, and show all deference to my choice.

DORINE. [*running away.*] I would take care I would not marry such a husband.

ORGON. [*He tries to slap Dorine's face and misses her.*] You have a pestilent hussy there, my child, with whom I cannot live without forgetting myself. I feel I am not fit now to continue the conversation. Such insolent speeches have put me in so great a passion that I must have a breath of air to compose myself.

SCENE III
DORINE, MARIANE

DORINE. Tell me, have you lost your tongue; must I play your part in this matter? To think you allow such an absurd proposal to be made to you without your saying a word against it!

MARIANE. What would you have me do against a tyrannical father?

DORINE. Anything to ward off such a fate.

MARIANE. But what?

DORINE. Tell him a heart cannot love at the bidding of another, that you marry to please yourself not him, that, as the matter concerns you alone it is you, not him, whom the husband must please, and that, since he is so charmed with his Tartuffe, he can marry him himself without any hindrance.

MARIANE. A father has such authority over us that I admit I have not had the courage to say anything.

DORINE. Let us talk it all over. Valère has proposed to you: do you love him, pray, or do you not?

MARIANE. Oh! Dorine, you are very unjust to me. How can you ask me such a question? Have I not opened my heart to you a hundred times on this subject? Do you not know how much I love him?

DORINE. How do I know your lips have spoken what your heart felt and that you really care for this lover?

MARIANE. You wrong me greatly, Dorine, to doubt it. Surely my real feelings have shown themselves only too plainly.

DORINE. Then you love him?

MARIANE. Yes, passionately.

DORINE. And apparently he loves you just as ardently.

MARIANE. I believe so.

DORINE. And you both are eager to be married.

MARIANE. Most certainly.

DORINE. What do you mean to do, then, about this other match?

MARIANE. To kill myself if I am forced into it.

DORINE. Good! I had not thought of that way out of the difficulty; you have but to die to be rid of troubles; what an excellent remedy! It puts me out of all patience to hear such talk.

MARIANE. Good heavens! what a temper you are in, Dorine. You have no sympathy for people in their troubles.

DORINE. I have no pity for those who talk nonsense and give way at the critical moment as you do.

MARIANE. But what can I do? I am afraid.

DORINE. Love asks for courage.

MARIANE. Have I wavered in my love of Valère? Is it not his place to win me from my father?

DORINE. What if your father is a downright lunatic, who has gone clean crazy over his Tartuffe, and who does not keep his promise about this marriage: is your lover to be blamed for that?

MARIANE. But am I, by haughty refusal and contemptuous disdain, to let everyone see my own heart is too deeply smitten? However much I desire Valère, am I to cast aside for him my womanly modesty and my filial duty? And would you have me show my heart to the whole world . . . ?

DORINE. No, no! I won't ask you to do anything. I see you wish to belong to Monsieur Tartuffe; and I should do wrong, now I come to think of it, were I to dissuade you from such a marriage. What excuse have I for opposing your wishes? The match in itself is very advantageous. Monsieur Tartuffe! oh! oh! is it nothing that is proposed? Indeed, Monsieur Tartuffe, to look at the thing in the right light, is not a man to be trifled with by any means, and it is not a piece of bad luck to be his better half. The world has already crowned him with glory; he passes for an aristocrat in his own parish, well set up in person, with his red ears and his florid complexion. How very happy you will be with such a husband!

MARIANE. Oh! dear . . .

DORINE. What delight you will experience when you become the wife of such a bridegroom!

MARIANE. Oh! stop such talk, I beg you, and show me the way to avoid this marriage. Let us make an end of it. I give in, and am ready to do anything.

DORINE. A daughter should obey her father even if he wished her to marry an ape. Yours is an enviable fate; of what do you complain? You will go in the coach to his native town and find yourself rich in uncles and cousins whom it will delight you exceedingly to entertain. You will soon be introduced into the best society; you will begin by visits to the magistrate's wife and the tax-surveyor's lady, who will honor you with a folding-stool. At carnival time you may hope for a ball there, the grand local band, consisting of two bagpipes, in attendance, and possibly the learned ape will be present and marionettes, only, if your husband . . .

MARIANE. Oh! you are enough to kill me. Help me rather with your advice.

DORINE. I am your servant.

MARIANE. Ah! Dorine, for pity's sake . . .

DORINE. This matter ought to go through in order to punish you.

MARIANE. My dear girl!

DORINE. No.

MARIANE. If my declared vows . . .

DORINE. No. Tartuffe is your man, and you must have him.

MARIANE. You know I have always trusted in you. Help me . . .

DORINE. No, upon my word you shall be tartuffed.

MARIANE. Very well, since my fate fails to move you, leave me alone henceforth with my despair: my heart shall borrow help from that, and I know there is one unfailing remedy for my misery. [*She turns to go.*]

DORINE. Here! stop, stop, come back. I won't be angry any longer. It seems I must take pity on you, in spite of everything.

MARIANE. Dorine, you may be sure if they force me to endure this cruel martyrdom I shall surely die.

DORINE. Do not worry yourself. We will be too clever for them, and prevent . . . But here comes your lover Valère.

SCENE IV
VALÈRE, MARIANE, DORINE

VALÈRE. I have just been told a very pretty piece of news which I did not know.

MARIANE. What is it?

VALÈRE. That you are to marry Tartuffe.

MARIANE. It is true my father has this design in his head.

VALÈRE. Your father, Madam . . .

MARIANE. Has changed his mind: he has just proposed this thing to me.

VALÈRE. What, seriously?

MARIANE. Yes, seriously. He has declared himself openly for the match.

VALÈRE. And what is your own decision in the matter, Madam.

MARIANE. I do not know.

VALÈRE. A candid answer. You do not know?

MARIANE. No.

VALÈRE. No?

MARIANE. What do you advise me?

VALÈRE. I? I advise you to accept this husband.

MARIANE. You advise me that?

VALÈRE. Yes.

MARIANE. In earnest?

VALÈRE. Without doubt: the choice is excellent and well worth considering.

MARIANE. Very well, then, sir, I will act on the advice.

VALÈRE. That will not be very disagreeable, I imagine.

MARIANE. Not more painful than for you to give it.

VALÈRE. I? I gave it to please you, Madam.

MARIANE. And I? I shall follow it to please you.

DORINE. Let us see what will come of this.

VALÈRE. This, then, is your affection? And it was deception when you . . .

MARIANE. Pray do not let us talk any more of that. You told me plainly I ought to accept the husband selected for me: and I declare I intend to do so, since you have given me that salutary advice.

VALÈRE. Do not make my advice your excuse. You had already made up your mind, and you seized a frivolous pretext to justify the breaking of your word.

MARIANE. Very true, and well put.

VALÈRE. No doubt; and you never really loved me.

MARIANE. Alas! think so if you please.

VALÈRE. Yes, yes, if I please; but my slighted love may perchance forestall you in a similar design; and I know where to offer both my heart and my hand.

MARIANE. Ah! I do not doubt it. The love which merit can command . . .

VALÈRE. For Heaven's sake, let us leave merit out of the question: there is but little of it in me, no doubt, and you have given proof of it. But I have great hopes of the kindness another woman will have for me, and I know whose heart will not be ashamed to consent to make up for my loss when I am free.

MARIANE. The loss is not great; and you will be consoled easily enough by this exchange.

VALÈRE. I shall do my best, you may depend. To be forgotten wounds self-love; every endeavor must be used to forget also; and if one does not succeed, one must at least pretend to do so; for it is an unpardonable weakness to appear loving when forsaken.

MARIANE. Truly, what noble and praiseworthy sentiments.

VALÈRE. Most certainly; and they should be approved by everyone. What? Would you have me for ever cherish in my heart the warmth of my passion for you? Am I to see you throw yourself into the arms of another before my face, and not elsewhere bestow the heart you no longer want?

MARIANE. On the contrary: I confess that is exactly what I desire. I wish the thing were done already.

VALÈRE. You wish it?

MARIANE. Yes.

VALÈRE. You insult me, Madam. I will go at once to satisfy you. [*He turns to go but keeps on coming back.*]

MARIANE. Very well.

VALÈRE. Recollect at least that it is you yourself who drive me to this extremity.

MARIANE. Yes.

VALÈRE. And that the design I have in my mind is but to follow your example.

MARIANE. My example let it be.

VALÈRE. Be it so: you will be served just as you wish.

MARIANE. I am very glad.

VALÈRE. You see me for the last time in your life.

MARIANE. That is all right.

VALÈRE. Eh? [*He goes; and when he is near the door he returns.*]

MARIANE. What?

VALÈRE. Did you call me?

MARIANE. I? You are dreaming.

VALÈRE. Ah! well, I will go my way then. Farewell, Madam.

MARIANE. Farewell, Monsieur.

DORINE. I think you are mad to talk such nonsense; I have left you to quarrel all this time to see how far you would go. Stop there, seigneur Valère! [*She takes hold of his arm to stop him, and he makes a great show of resistance.*]

VALÈRE. Well, what do you want, Dorine?

DORINE. Come here.

VALÈRE. No, no, I am too indignant. Do not turn me away from doing her will.

DORINE. Stop.

VALÈRE. No, do you not see my mind is made up?

DORINE. Ah!

MARIANE. He cannot bear to see me, my presence drives him away. I had much better give up the place to him.

DORINE. [*She leaves Valère and runs to Mariane.*] Here goes another. Where are you running off to?

MARIANE. Let me go.

DORINE. You must come back.

MARIANE. No, no, Dorine, it is in vain for you to try to keep me.

VALÈRE. I see plainly the sight of me annoys her, and doubtless I had better rid her of my presence.

DORINE. [*She leaves Mariane and runs to Valère.*] Again? Deuce take you if I wish it! Stop this fooling and come here, both of you. [*She seizes hold of them both.*]

VALÈRE. What do you want?

MARIANE. What are you going to do?

DORINE. To bring you together again, and set things straight. Are you mad to wrangle like this?

VALÈRE. Did you not hear how she spoke to me?

DORINE. Are you an idiot to have got into such a passion?

MARIANE. Did you not see how it all happened, and how he treated me?

DORINE. Folly on both sides. She has no other wish than to remain yours; I can vouch for it. He loves you only, and desires nothing else than to be your husband; I will answer for it with my life.

MARIANE. Why, then, did you give me such advice?

VALÈRE. Why did you ask for it on such a subject?

DORINE. What a couple of fools you are. Come, now, give me your hands here.

VALÈRE. [giving his hand to Dorine.] What is the good of my hand?

DORINE. Ah! now, then, yours.

MARIANE. [also giving her hand.] What is the good of my hand?

DORINE. Goodness! be quick, come on. You both are fonder of each other than you think.

VALÈRE. Don't do things with such a bad grace, then, but give a man a civil look. [Mariane turns her eyes on Valère and smiles a little.]

DORINE. What silly creatures lovers are, to be sure!

VALÈRE. But still, have I not cause to complain of you? And, to say the least, were you not unkind to utter such cruel things to me?

MARIANE. But you, are you not also the most ungrateful man . . . ?

DORINE. Let us leave all this talk for another time, and consider how we can avert this wretched marriage.

MARIANE. Tell us, then, what plans we must prepare.

DORINE. We will try every means. Your father is only jesting, and it is mere talk; but as for you, you had better pretend to humor his whim dutifully, so that in case of alarm it would be easier for you to put the wedding off indefinitely. In gaining time, we remedy everything. Sometimes you will give sudden illness as an excuse, and so cause delays; at other times you will bring forward some ill-omen: you had the ill-luck to meet a corpse, broke a mirror, or dreamt of muddy water. But the best of all is that they cannot marry you either to others or to him unless you say "yes." However, the best way to succeed, I think, is for you two not to be seen talking together. [To Valère.] Go away at once, and without delay employ your friends to make her father keep his promise to you. We will enlist the efforts of his brother and the interest of the step-mother on our side. Good-bye.

VALÈRE. [To Mariane.] Whatever efforts we all make my greatest hope is really in you.

MARIANE. [To Valère.] I cannot answer for the will of a father, but I will not belong to any one but Valère.

VALÈRE. Oh! how happy you make me. And whatever they may attempt . . .

DORINE. Ah! lovers never weary of chattering. Be off, I tell you.

VALÈRE. [He goes a step and returns.] In short . . .

DORINE. What a cackle you make! You take yourself off that way; and you, the other. [Pushing each by the shoulder.]

END OF THE SECOND ACT

ACT III

SCENE I
DAMIS, DORINE

DAMIS. May I be struck down by lightning this very moment, may everybody look upon me as the greatest of scamps, if there is any respect or power to stop me from doing something rash!

DORINE. For heaven's sake control your temper: your father merely mentioned the matter. People do not carry out all they propose: there is many a slip 'twixt the cup and the lip.

DAMIS. I must put a stop to this fellow's intrigues and whisper a few words in his ear.

DORINE. Gently, gently, let your stepmother manage him, and your father as well. She has some influence over Tartuffe; he agrees with all she says, and very likely he has a tender feeling for her. Would to heaven it were true! That would be a fine thing! Indeed, she has thought it best to send for him in your interest: she wants to sound him about the marriage which makes you so furious, to find out his feelings, and to let him know what unhappy contentions it would cause were he to entertain the least hope of realising this scheme. His man told me he was at his prayers so I could not see him; but he said he was just coming down; therefore, pray be gone and leave me to wait for him.

DAMIS. I want to be present throughout this interview.

DORINE. Certainly not: they must be alone.

DAMIS. I will not say anything to him.

DORINE. You deceive yourself: we know what rages you get into, and that would be the surest way to spoil everything. Go away.

DAMIS. No; I will look on, without losing my temper.

DORINE. How tiresome you are! Here he comes. Do go away.

SCENE II
TARTUFFE, LAURENT, DORINE

TARTUFFE. [*Perceiving Dorine.*] Laurent, lock up my hairshirt and my scourge, and pray heaven ever to enlighten you. If any one comes to see me, say I have gone to the prisoners to distribute the alms I have received.

DORINE. What affectation and boasting!

TARTUFFE. What do you want?

DORINE. To tell you . . .

TARTUFFE. [*He takes a handkerchief out of his pocket.*] Ah! for the sake of heaven, pray take this handkerchief before you speak to me.

DORINE. What for?

TARTUFFE. To cover that bosom which I cannot bear to see. Such a sight is injurious to the soul and gives birth to sinful thoughts.

DORINE. You are mightily susceptible, then, to temptation, and the flesh seems to make a great impression on your senses. Truly, I do not know why you should take fire so quickly: as for me, my passions are not so easily roused, were I to see you unclothed from top to toe your hide would not tempt me.

TARTUFFE. Be a little more modest in your conversation, or I shall leave you
at once.

DORINE. No, no, I am going to leave you in peace, and I have only two words
to say to you. Madame is coming down into this room, and wishes the favor
of a few moments' talk with you.

TARTUFFE. Alas! most willingly.

DORINE. [*To herself.*] How sweet we are! Upon my word, I still stick to what I
said about it.

TARTUFFE. Will she soon be here?

DORINE. I think I hear her. Yes, here she is. I will leave you together.

SCENE III
ELMIRE, TARTUFFE

TARTUFFE. May a supremely bountiful heaven ever bestow upon you health
of body and of soul, and bless your days as abundantly as the humblest of
its servants can desire.

ELMIRE. I am much obliged for this pious wish. But let us sit down, to be a
little more at our ease.

TARTUFFE. Have you quite recovered from your indisposition?

ELMIRE. Quite: the fever soon left me.

TARTUFFE. My prayers are not worthy to have drawn down such favor from
heaven; but I have not offered up a single pious aspiration which has not
had your recovery for its object.

ELMIRE. You are too solicitous in my behalf.

TARTUFFE. It is impossible to be too anxious concerning your precious health;
I would have sacrificed my own to re-establish yours.

ELMIRE. You carry Christian charity to an extreme; I am much indebted to
you for all this kindness.

TARTUFFE. I do much less for you than you deserve.

ELMIRE. I wished to speak privately to you on a certain matter. I am very
glad no one is watching us.

TARTUFFE. I am equally delighted, and it is indeed very pleasant, Madame,
to find myself quite alone with you. I have often implored heaven to grant
me this favor, but until now it has been denied me.

ELMIRE. I too wish a few words with you; I hope you will speak openly to
me and not hide anything from me.

TARTUFFE. I have but the wish, in return for this singular favor, to lay bare
my whole soul to you, and to swear to you that the reports which I have
spread abroad concerning the visits paid here to your charms do not spring
from any hatred towards you, but rather from a passionate zeal which carries
me away, and from a pure motive . . .

ELMIRE. I quite understand, I feel sure the pains you take are for my welfare.

TARTUFFE. [*He presses the end of her fingers.*] Yes, Madame, you are right, and
such is my devotion . . .

ELMIRE. Oh! you squeeze me too hard.

TARTUFFE. It is from excess of zeal. I never had any intention of doing you
any other ill; I would much sooner . . . [*He places his hand on her knee.*]

ELMIRE. Why do you put your hand there?

TARTUFFE. I am feeling your dress: the stuff is very soft.

ELMIRE. Oh! please, leave off, I am very ticklish. [*She pushes back her chair, and Tartuffe draws his nearer.*]

TARTUFFE. Heavens! how marvellous is the workmanship of this lace! Work nowadays is wonderfully skilful; one could not imagine anything more beautifully made.

ELMIRE. It is true. But let us talk a little about our business. They say my husband wishes to break his word and give you his daughter. Tell me, is it true?

TARTUFFE. He did just mention it; but, Madame, to tell you the truth, that is not the happiness for which I sigh; I see elsewhere the perfect attractions of that bliss which is the end of all my desires.

ELMIRE. That is because you have no love for the things of the earth.

TARTUFFE. My breast does not contain a heart of flint.

ELMIRE. I quite believe all your sighs tend heavenwards, and that nothing here below satisfies your desires.

TARTUFFE. Our love for the beauty which is eternal does not stifle in us the love for things fleeting; our senses can easily be charmed with the perfect works which heaven has created. Its reflected loveliness shines forth in such as are like you; but in you yourself it displays its choicest wonders. It has lavished on your face a beauty which dazzles the eyes and transports the heart, and I am unable to gaze on you, you perfect creature, without adoring in you the author of nature, and without feeling my heart seized with a passionate love for the most beautiful of the portraits in which he has delineated himself. At first I feared lest this secret tenderness might be but an artful assault of the evil one; and my heart even resolved to flee from your eyes, fearing you might be a stumbling-block in the way of my salvation. But at last I learnt, ah! most entrancing beauty, that this passion need not be a guilty one, that I could reconcile it with modesty, and so I have let my heart give way to it. It is, I own, a very great presumption in me to dare to offer you this heart; but my love expects everything from your kindness, and nothing from the vain efforts of my weakness. In you is my hope, my happiness, my peace, on you depends my torment or my bliss; in truth, I shall be happy if you will it, or unhappy if such be your pleasure: you are the sole arbitress.

ELMIRE. The declaration is most gallant, but it is certainly a little surprising. I think you ought to have guarded your heart more carefully, and have reflected a little upon such a design. A pious man like you, whose name is in every one's mouth . . .

TARTUFFE. Ah! I may be pious, but I am none the less a man; and when your heavenly charms are seen the heart surrenders without reasoning. I know such language from me must seem strange; but, after all, Madame, I am not an angel, and, if you condemn my avowal, you must lay the blame on your captivating attractions. You became the queen of my heart the moment your ethereal beauty first shone upon me; the ineffable sweetness of your divine looks broke down the resistance of my obstinate heart; it overcame everything—fasting, prayers, tears, and diverted all my thoughts to the consideration of your charms. My looks and my sighs have declared this to you a thousand times, and to make it still clearer I now add my voice. If it should happen that you would look upon the sufferings of your unworthy slave a little kindly, if you would only of your bounty take compassion upon me and deign to stoop even to my insignificance, I should ever have for you, ah! miracle of grace, a devotion beyond comparison. With me your reputation is not in danger, and you need not fear any disgrace from me. All those court gallants upon whom women dote are noisy in their doings and boastful in their talk, ceaselessly bragging of their successes; they do not receive any favors which they do not divulge, and their indiscreet tongues, in which people believe, dishonor the altar where their hearts worship. But people like ourselves love more discreetly, and our secrets are always safely kept. The care which we take of our reputation is a sufficient safeguard to the woman loved, who finds, in accepting our devotion, love without scandal and pleasure without fear.

ELMIRE. I have listened to what you say, and your eloquence expresses itself to me in sufficiently strong terms. Are you not afraid I may be disposed to tell my husband of this ardent devotion, and that the sudden knowledge of such a feeling may well cause him to change his friendship for you?

TARTUFFE. I know you are too gracious, and that you will forgive my boldness; you will excuse, in consideration of human frailty, the passionate raptures of a love which offends you, and you will consider, when you look in your mirror, that people are not blind, and that a man is of the flesh.

ELMIRE. Others may perhaps take all this in a different way, but I will exercise discretion. I will not speak to my husband about the matter, but I want one thing from you in return: and that is, to forward honestly and openly the union of Valère and Mariane, and to renounce the unjust power which would enrich you with what belongs to another, and . . .

SCENE IV
DAMIS, ELMIRE, TARTUFFE

DAMIS. [*Coming out of the little room in which he had been hiding.*] No, Madame, no; this ought to be made public. I have been in here, where I have overheard everything; and heaven in its goodness seems to have directed me here to confound the pride of a traitor who wrongs me, to point out a way to take vengeance on his hypocrisy and his insolence, to undeceive my father and to show him plainly the heart of the scoundrel who speaks to you of love.

ELMIRE. No, Damis: it is sufficient that he promises to amend and tries to deserve the forgiveness to which I have committed myself. Since I have promised it, do not make me break my word. I have no mind to cause a scandal: a woman laughs at such follies, and never troubles her husband's ears with them.

DAMIS. You have your reasons for acting thus and I have mine also for dealing otherwise. It is a mockery to wish to spare him; the insolent pride of his bigotry has lorded it over my just anger but too often, and he has caused too many troubles in our house. The knave has governed my father too long, and he has thwarted my love as well as Valère's. It is necessary my father should have his eyes opened to this treachery, and Providence has offered me for that an easy opportunity for which I am thankful. It is too favorable to be neglected: and were I not to use it whilst I have it in my hands, I should deserve to have it snatched away from me.

ELMIRE. Damis . . .

DAMIS. No, by your leave, I must take my own counsel. My heart is now overjoyed: it is in vain for you to try to persuade me to give up the pleasure of revenging myself. I shall disclose the affair without delay, and here is just the very opportunity I want.

SCENE V
Orgon, Damis, Tartuffe, Elmire

Damis. Come, father, we will enliven your arrival with an altogether novel and very surprising piece of news. You are well rewarded for all your caresses; this gentleman amply recompenses your kindness. His great zeal for you has just revealed itself: it aims at nothing less than to dishonor you. I have here overheard him make shameful avowal of a guilty passion. She, being too prudent and good-natured, insisted at all hazards upon keeping the matter secret; but I cannot countenance such impudence, and I should wrong you were I to keep silence.

Elmire. Yes, I hold that it is better never to disturb the peace of mind of one's husband by such silly nonsense. Honor does not depend on the confession of attacks upon it, and it is enough for us that we know how to protect ourselves. These are my own sentiments. You would not have said anything, Damis, if I had had more influence over you.

SCENE VI
Orgon, Damis, Tartuffe

Orgon. What do I hear? Good heavens, is it possible?

Tartuffe. Yes, brother, I am a wicked, miserable and guilty sinner, full of iniquity, the greatest wretch who ever lived. Every moment of my life is weighed down with pollution; it is nothing but a mass of crime and corruption, and I see that heaven, for my punishment, intends to mortify me on this occasion. I throw away the pride of self-defence no matter what great crime I may be accused of. Believe what they tell you, let your wrath take up arms and drive me, like a criminal, from your house. I deserve even greater shame than I shall have in being turned away.

Orgon. [*To his son.*] Ah! you villain, how dare you try to sully the purity of his virtue by such falsehoods?

Damis. What? Does the feigned meekness of this hypocrite make you give the lie to . . . ?

Orgon. Be quiet, you accursed plague.

Tartuffe. Oh! let him speak: you chide him wrongfully and you had much better believe his story. Why be favorable to me in the face of such an assertion? Are you aware, after all, of what I am capable? Why trust in my bearing, brother? Why believe me good because of my outward professions? No, no; you suffer yourself to be deceived by appearances, and I am, alas! just what these people think. The world takes me for a worthy man; but the simple truth is that I am worthless. [*Addressing Damis.*] Yes, my dear boy, speak: accuse me of treachery, infamy, theft, murder; overwhelm me with still more despicable names. I do not deny them, I have deserved them; on my knees I will bear the shameful ignominy due to the sins of my life.

Orgon. [*To Tartuffe.*] This is too much, my brother. [*To his son.*] Wretch, does not your heart relent?

DAMIS. What? can his words so far deceive you . . . ?

ORGON. Hold your tongue, rascal. [*To Tartuffe.*] Oh! rise, my brother, I beseech you. [*To his son.*] Infamous scoundrel!

DAMIS. He can . . .

ORGON. Be quiet.

DAMIS. Intolerable! What? I am taken for . . .

ORGON. If you say another word I will break every bone.

TARTUFFE. Control yourself, my brother, in heaven's name. I would rather suffer the greatest injury than that he should receive the slightest hurt on my account.

ORGON. [*To his son.*] Ungrateful wretch!

TARTUFFE. Leave him alone. If I must on my knees ask you to forgive him . . .

ORGON. [*To Tartuffe.*] Oh! you jest? [*To his son.*] Rascal! See how good he is.

DAMIS. Then . . .

ORGON. Cease.

DAMIS. What? I . . .

ORGON. Cease, I say. I know well the motive which makes you accuse him. You all hate him; and I now see my wife, children and servants all incensed against him. You try every impudent trick to drive this saintly person away from me. But the more you strive to send him away, the greater efforts I shall make to keep him here longer, and I will haste my daughter's marriage to him to crush the pride of the whole family.

DAMIS. You mean to force her to take him?

ORGON. Yes, scoundrel, this very night, to confound you all. Ah! I defy the whole household. I will let you know I am the master and must be obeyed. You wretch, come and retract what you have said, and throw yourself instantly at his feet to beg his pardon.

DAMIS. Who, I? Of this villain who, by his impostures . . .

ORGON. Ah! you refuse, you scamp, and abuse him besides? A stick! A stick! [*To Tartuffe.*] Do not prevent me. [*To his son.*] Begone this instant out of my sight, and never have the face to set foot in my house again.

DAMIS. Yes, I will go; but . . .

ORGON. Quick, leave the place. I disinherit you, you hangdog, and curse you, as well.

SCENE VII
ORGON, TARTUFFE

ORGON. To affront a holy person in such a manner!

TARTUFFE. Oh Heaven! forgive him the pain he causes me. [*To Orgon.*] If you only knew with what anguish I see them endeavor to blacken my character in the eyes of my brother . . .

ORGON. Alas!

TARTUFFE. The very thought of such ingratitude is so great a torture to me that . . . . The horror I feel . . . My heart is too full to speak, and I believe I shall die.

ORGON. [*He runs in tears to the door through which he had driven his son.*] Villain! How I regret I held my hand and that I did not instantly make an end of you on the spot. Compose yourself, brother, and do not grieve.

TARTUFFE. Let us put an end to these miserable disputes. I see what great friction I cause in this house, and I feel sure it is needful, my brother, that I should go away.

ORGON. What? You are not in earnest?

TARTUFFE. They hate me, and I see they will seek to rouse suspicions in you as to my integrity.

ORGON. What does it matter? Do you think I pay any attention to what they say?

TARTUFFE. They will not fail to continue, never fear, and the same stories which now you reject you may at another time credit.

ORGON. No, brother, never.

TARTUFFE. Oh! my brother, a wife can very easily influence the mind of her husband.

ORGON. No, no.

TARTUFFE. Let me leave here at once and thus remove all occasion for their attacks.

ORGON. No, you shall stay: my life is at stake.

TARTUFFE. Ah! well, then I must mortify myself. Nevertheless, if you would . . .

ORGON. Ah!

TARTUFFE. Be it so: let us not say anything more about it. But I know how I must act in the future. Honor is a delicate matter, and friendship enjoins me to prevent reports and not to give cause for suspicion. I will shun your wife, and you shall not see me . . .

ORGON. No, You shall see her frequently in spite of everyone. I desire nothing more than to jolt society, and I wish her to be seen in your company at all hours. Nor is this all: the better to defy them all you shall be my sole heir, and I will go forthwith to arrange in due form that the whole of my property shall be made yours. A good and faithful friend, whom I take for son-in-law, is far dearer to me than son, wife, or kindred. Will you not accept my offer?

TARTUFFE. The will of heaven be done in all things!

ORGON. Poor man! Let us go quickly to draw up the deed: then may envy itself burst with spite.

END OF THE THIRD ACT

ACT IV

SCENE I
CLÉANTE, TARTUFFE

CLÉANTE. Indeed, you may believe me, everybody is talking about it. The scandal which this rumor makes is not to your credit. I have met you, Monsieur, very seasonably, and I can tell you plainly my view of the matter, in two words. I do not sift these reports to the bottom; I pass them by and admit the worst view of the case. Let us grant that Damis has not acted wisely, and it may be you have been accused in error: does it not become a Christian to forgive the offence and to extinguish in him every desire for vengeance?

And, because of your quarrel, ought you to suffer a father to drive a son out of his house? I repeat it, and I tell you candidly, high and low are scandalised by it. If you take my advice, you will make peace and not push matters to extremes. Make an offering to God of all your resentment, and restore the son to the father's favor.

TARTUFFE. Alas! So far as I am concerned I would do so with all my heart. I do not bear him any ill-will, Monsieur, I forgive him everything. I do not blame him for anything. I would serve him to the best of my power. But the interests of heaven cannot consent to it; and if he returns home I must go away. After his unparalleled behavior intercourse between us would give rise to scandal. Heaven knows what every one would think of it at once! They would impute it to sheer policy on my part, and it would be said everywhere that, knowing myself to be guilty, I affect a charitable zeal for my accuser; that I am afraid of him; and that I wish to conciliate him in order to bribe him in an underhand manner to silence.

CLÉANTE. You are putting us off, Monsieur, with sham excuses. All your arguments are too far-fetched. Why do you take upon yourself the interests of heaven? Cannot it punish sinners without our help? Leave vengeance to it, leave vengeance to it, and remember only the forgiveness which it directs towards offences. Do not trouble yourself about men's judgments when you follow the sovereign edicts of heaven. What? Shall the paltry fear of men's opinion prevent the accomplishment of a good deed? No, no; let us always do what heaven commands, and not trouble our minds with any other care.

TARTUFFE. I have already told you, Monsieur, that I forgive him as heaven enjoins. But, after the scandal and insult of today, heaven does not ordain that I should live with him.

CLÉANTE. And does it require you, Monsieur, to lend your ears to what a mere whim dictates to his father, and to accept the gift which is made you of a property to which in justice you cannot pretend to have any claim?

TARTUFFE. Those who know me will not think I act from interested motives. All the riches of this world have few attractions for me. I am not dazzled by their false glitter. If I bring myself to take this gift which the father wishes to make to me, it is merely because I fear all this wealth will fall into wicked hands, and that it will be shared only by those who will put it here to bad uses, and not employ it, as I propose to do, for the glory of heaven and the well-being of my fellow-men.

CLÉANTE. Ah! Monsieur, do not entertain these delicate scruples, which may give ground of complaint to a rightful heir. Allow him, without giving yourself any anxiety, to enjoy his rights at his own peril; and consider that it is far better for him to make a bad use of it than that people should accuse you of defrauding him of it. I only wonder you could have suffered unblushingly such a proposal to be made you. For, in truth, do we find among the maxims of true piety one which teaches how to plunder a lawful heir? And, if it is a fact that heaven has put in your heart an invincible obstacle against your living with Damis, would it not be better for you, as a discreet person, honorably to retire from this house, rather than to allow the son of the house to be turned out of it, against all reason, on your account? Believe me, Monsieur, it would give a proof of your probity . . .

TARTUFFE. Monsieur, it is half-past three: a certain religious exercise calls me upstairs; pray excuse me for leaving you so soon.

CLÉANTE. Ah!

SCENE II
ELMIRE, MARIANE, DORINE, CLÉANTE

DORINE. For pity's sake join us in all we do for her, Monsieur. She is suffering great misery, and the agreement which her father has concluded for tonight drives her every moment to despair. Here he comes. Let us unite our efforts, I beseech you, to try, either by force or by skill to frustrate this unhappy design which causes us all this trouble.

SCENE III
ORGON, ELMIRE, MARIANE, CLÉANTE, DORINE

ORGON. Ah! I am delighted to find you all here. [*To Mariane.*] I have something in this document which will please you: you know already what I mean.

MARIANE. [*on her knees.*] Father, in the name of that heaven which knows my grief, in the name of everything that can move your heart, forego a little of a father's rights and do not exact this obedience from me. Do not compel me, by this harsh command, to reproach heaven with my duty to you; do not, oh my father, render most miserable the life which, alas! you gave me. If, contrary to the sweet hopes I had cherished, you forbid me to belong to the one whom I have dared to love, I implore you on my knees at least, of your goodness, to spare me the horror of belonging to one whom I abhor. Do not drive me to despair by exerting all your authority over me.

ORGON. [*feeling himself soften.*] Be firm, my heart; none of this human weakness.

MARIANE. I do not feel aggrieved at your tenderness for him; indulge in it, give him your wealth, and, if that is not enough, add all mine to it: I consent with all my heart and give it to you. But, at least, do not go so far as to include my person, let me wear out in the hardships of a convent the rest of the sad days that heaven has allotted to me.

ORGON. Ah! girls always wish to become nuns when a father crosses their love-sick inclinations. Get up: the more your heart recoils from accepting the offer, the greater will be your merit. Mortify your senses by this marriage, and do not trouble me any further.

DORINE. But what . . . ?

ORGON. You hold your tongue: mind your own business. I absolutely forbid you to dare to say a single word.

CLÉANTE. If you will allow me to speak and advise . . .

ORGON. Brother, your advice is the best in the world, and I value it highly: you will permit me, however, not to take it.

ELMIRE. [*To Orgon.*] In the face of all this I do not know I can say more than that I am astonished at your blindness. You must be quite bewitched with the man and altogether prejudiced in his favor, to deny the truth of what we tell you took place today.

ORGON. I am your humble servant, but I judge by appearances. I know how lenient you are towards my rascal of a son, and you were afraid to disown the trick which he wished to play on the poor fellow. In fact, you took it too calmly to be believed. You should have been a little more disturbed.

ELMIRE. Is it necessary one's honor should take up arms so furiously at a simple declaration of tender feelings? Is it not possible to give a fitting answer without anger in the eyes and invective on the lips? For myself, I simply laugh at such talk; it does not please me to make a noise about it. I prefer to show that prudence can be accompanied by gentleness. I am not at all like the savage prudes who defend their honor with tooth and nail, and who are ready, at the slightest word, to tear a man's eyes out. Heaven preserve me from such discretion! I prefer a virtue that has nothing of the tigress about it, and I believe a quiet and cold rebuff is not less efficient in repelling an advance.

ORGON. Nevertheless, I understand the whole affair and I will not be imposed upon.

ELMIRE. Once more, I wonder at this strange weakness: but what answer would your incredulity give me, if I made you see we have told you the truth?

ORGON. See?

ELMIRE. Yes.

ORGON. Nonsense.

ELMIRE. Never mind! Suppose I found a way of convincing you irresistibly?

ORGON. Moonshine.

ELMIRE. What a man you are! At least, answer me. I do not ask you to believe us, but, look here, suppose we found a place where you could plainly see and hear everything, what would you say then of your good man?

ORGON. In that case I should say . . . I should not say anything, for such a thing could not be.

ELMIRE. Your delusion has lasted too long, and you have taxed us too much with imposture. You must, to satisfy me, and without going any further, be a witness of all that has been told you.

ORGON. Be it so. I take you at your word. We will see your cleverness and how you can carry out this undertaking.

ELMIRE. Make him come here.

DORINE. He is very crafty and perhaps it will be difficult to catch him.

ELMIRE. No; people are easily duped by those whom they love. Self-love leads the way to self-deceit. [*Speaking to Cléante and to Mariane.*] Tell him to come down to me. And you, withdraw.

SCENE IV
ELMIRE, ORGON

ELMIRE. Let us bring this table nearer and you go under it.

ORGON. Why?

ELMIRE. It is necessary you should be well concealed.

ORGON. Why under this table?

ELMIRE. Oh! good heavens, never mind; I have thought out my plan, and you shall judge of it. Go under there, I tell you; and, when you are there, take care you are neither seen nor heard.

ORGON. I must say my complaisance in this matter is great, but I will see you through with your scheme.

ELMIRE. You will not have anything with which to reproach me, that I swear. [*To her husband, under the table.*] Now mind! I am going to speak on a strange subject and you must not be shocked in any way. As I have undertaken to convince you, I must be allowed to say whatever I choose. Since I am compelled to it, I shall flatter this hypocrite until he lets fall his mask: I shall encourage the impudent desires of his love, and give free scope to his audacity. As I am going to pretend to yield to his wishes for your sake alone, and the better to confound him, things need not go any further than you like, and I will cease as soon as you are convinced. I leave it to you to stop his mad passion when you think matters have gone far enough, to spare your wife, and not to expose me longer than is necessary to disabuse you. This is your concern, you must decide, and . . . Here he comes. Keep still, and do not show yourself.

SCENE V
TARTUFFE, ELMIRE, ORGON

TARTUFFE. They tell me you wish to speak to me here.

ELMIRE. Yes. I have some secrets to reveal to you. But shut the door before I begin to tell them to you. Look everywhere, lest we should be surprised. We must certainly not have such an affair here as we had a little while ago. I was never so surprised. Damis put me in a terrible fright on your account. You saw I tried all I could to baffle his design and to calm his anger. In fact I was so confused that the thought of denying what he said never occurred to me; but, nevertheless, thank heaven, it was all for the best and things are on a surer footing. The esteem in which you are held has dispelled the storm, and my husband cannot be offended with you. He wishes us to be together constantly, the better to set at defiance the spiteful remarks which people spread abroad, and that is the reason why I may be shut up here alone with you, without fear of being blamed. This justifies me in opening my heart to you, a little too readily, perhaps, in response to your love.

TARTUFFE. This language, Madam, is a little difficult to comprehend. You spoke but lately in a different strain.

ELMIRE. Ah! if such a refusal has offended you, how very little you know a woman's heart, how little you understand what we mean when we defend ourselves so feebly. At such times our modesty always struggles with any tender sentiments we may feel. Whatever reasons we may find for the love which conquers us, there is always a little shame in the avowal of it. We resist at first, but from our manner it can easily be seen our heart surrenders, that our words oppose our wishes for the sake of honor, and that we refuse in such a way as to promise everything. I am making a very free confession to you, to be sure, and I am not sparing woman's modesty; but, since these words have at last escaped me, should I have been anxious to restrain Damis, should I, I ask you, have listened to you so long and with so much patience, when you offered me your heart, should I have taken the thing as I did, if the offer of your heart had not given me pleasure? What could you infer from such an action when I myself tried to make you renounce the proposed marriage, if it were not that I took an interest in you, and that I should have been grieved if such a marriage had taken place and you had in the least divided that affection which I wanted to be wholly mine?

TARTUFFE. It is certainly, Madam, extremely pleasant to hear such words from the lips one loves. Their honey generously diffuses through all my senses a sweetness which I never before knew. The happiness of pleasing you is my supreme study, and it is the delight of my heart to carry out your wishes, but, with your leave, my heart presumes still to doubt a little of its felicity.

It may be that these words are a plausible stratagem to compel me to break off the approaching marriage; and, if I must speak candidly to you, I shall not trust in these tender words until I am assured they mean what they say by a few of those favors for which I sigh, which will establish in my heart a firm belief in the kindly sentiments you bear towards me.

ELMIRE. [*She coughs to warn her husband.*] What? would you proceed so fast and exhaust the kindness of my heart all at once? I commit myself in making such a tender admission; yet that is not enough for you. Will nothing satisfy you but to push things to their furthest extremity?

TARTUFFE. The less a blessing is merited the less one ventures to hope for it. Our love can hardly be satisfied with words. A condition full-fraught with happiness is difficult to realise and we wish to enjoy it before we believe in it. I so little deserve your favors that I doubt the success of my boldness; and I shall not believe anything, Madam, until you have satisfied my passion by real proofs.

ELMIRE. Good Heavens! How very tyrannical is your love, and into what strange agitation it throws me! What an irresistible power it exercises over the heart, and how violently it clamors for what it desires! What? is there no avoiding your pursuit. Will you not give me time to breathe? Is it decent to be so very exacting, to insist without quarter upon those things which you demand, and, by your pressing ardor, thus to take advantage of the weakness which you see is felt for you?

TARTUFFE. But if you look upon my address with a favorable eye, why refuse me convincing proofs?

ELMIRE. How can I comply with your desires without offending that heaven of which you constantly speak?

TARTUFFE. If heaven is the only thing which opposes my wishes I can easily remove such an obstacle; that need not be any restraint upon your love.

ELMIRE. But the judgments of heaven are terrifying.

TARTUFFE. I can dispel these absurd fears from you, Madam; I know the art of removing scruples. Heaven, it is true, forbids certain gratifications; but there are ways of compounding with it. It is a science to stretch the strings of our conscience according to divers needs and to rectify the immorality of the act with the purity of our intention. I can initiate you into these secrets, Madam; you have only to allow yourself to be led. Satisfy my desire, and do not be afraid: I will be answerable for you in everything, and I will take the sin upon myself. You cough a good deal, Madam.

ELMIRE. Yes, it racks me.

TARTUFFE. Would you please to take a piece of this liquorice?

ELMIRE. It is a troublesome cold, to be sure; and I very much fear all the liquorice in the world will not do it any good now.

TARTUFFE. It is certainly very tiresome.

ELMIRE. Yes, more than I can say.

TARTUFFE. In short your scruple is easily overcome. You may be sure the secret will be well kept here, and no harm is done unless the thing is noised abroad. The scandal of the world is what makes the offence, and to sin in secret is not to sin at all.

ELMIRE. [*After having coughed again.*] Well, I see I must make up my mind to yield: that I must consent to grant you everything: and that with less than this I ought not to expect you should be satisfied, or convinced. It is indeed very hard to come to this, and it is greatly against my will that I venture so far, but, since people persist in driving me to this; since they will not believe anything that is said to them, and since they wish for more convincing testimony, one must even resolve upon it and satisfy them. If this gratification carries any offense in it, so much the worse for those who force me to this violence; the fault, assuredly, is not mine.

TARTUFFE. Yes, Madam, I take it upon myself, and the thing itself . . .

ELMIRE. Open the door a little, and pray, look if my husband is not in that passage.

TARTUFFE. Why need you trouble yourself so much about him? Between ourselves, he is a man to be led by the nose. He is inclined to be proud of our intercourse, and I have brought him so far as to see everything without believing anything.

ELMIRE. Nevertheless, pray, go out for a moment and look carefully everywhere outside.

SCENE VI
ORGON, ELMIRE

ORGON. [*Coming from under the table.*] Well! he is an abominable man, I admit. I cannot get over it, it has stunned me.

ELMIRE. What? you come out so soon? You make fools of people. Go back under the table-cloth, it is not time yet; stay to the end to make sure of things, and do not trust to mere conjectures.

ORGON. No: no one more wicked ever came out of hell.

ELMIRE. Good Heavens! You ought not to believe things too easily: let yourself be fully convinced before you give in, and do not hurry, lest you should be mistaken. [*She pushes her husband behind her.*]

SCENE VII
TARTUFFE, ELMIRE, ORGON

TARTUFFE. Everything conspires, Madam, to my satisfaction. I have looked everywhere, there is no one here; and my ravished soul . . .

ORGON. [*Stopping him.*] Gently, you are too eager in your amorous wishes; you ought not to be so impetuous. Ah! ah! my good man, you want to rob me of my wife. How your soul is led away by temptations! You would marry my daughter and covet my wife. I have very much doubted for a long time whether you were in earnest, and I always thought you would change your tone. But the proof has gone quite far enough: I am satisfied, and for my part I do not want any more.

ELMIRE. [*To Tartuffe.*] The part I have played is contrary to my inclinations, but I was obliged to the necessity of treating you thus.

TARTUFFE. What? Do you believe . . .?

ORGON. Come, pray, no more talk, leave this place, and without ceremony.

TARTUFFE. I intended . . .

ORGON. Your speeches are no longer in season. You must quit this house immediately.

TARTUFFE. It is for you to leave, you who speak as though you were the master of it. The house belongs to me, and I will make you know it. I will show you plainly it is useless to resort to these cowardly tricks in order to pick a quarrel with me. You have made a great mistake in insulting me. I have it in my power to confound and to punish imposture, to avenge an offended heaven, and to make those repent who talk of turning me away.

SCENE VIII
ELMIRE, ORGON

ELMIRE. What talk is this? What does he mean?

ORGON. Alas! I am ashamed; it is no laughing matter.

ELMIRE. Why?

ORGON. I see my fault by what he says, and the deed of gift troubles my mind.

ELMIRE. The deed of gift . . .

ORGON. Yes, the thing is done, but there is still something else which makes me anxious.

ELMIRE. What is that?

ORGON. You shall know all, but let us see first if a particular box is still upstairs.

END OF ACT IV.

ACT V

SCENE I
ORGON, CLÉANTE

CLÉANTE. Where are you going so fast?

ORGON. Indeed, I do not know.

CLÉANTE. It seems to me the first thing to be done is to consult together concerning what steps we can take in this matter.

ORGON. This box troubles me greatly; it distresses me more than anything else.

CLÉANTE. Then it contains an important secret?

ORGON. It is a trust that Argas himself, my unfortunate friend, put secretly into my hands: he selected me for this, when he fled. And, from what he told me, on these papers depend his life and his fortune.

CLÉANTE. Then why did you trust them to any other hands?

ORGON. It was from a conscientious motive. I went straight away to that wretch in utter confidence, and his arguments persuaded me it was better to give him the box to keep, so that, in case of enquiry, I could deny having it. I might have the help of a subterfuge in readiness, by which my conscience might be quite safe in swearing against the truth.

CLÉANTE. If one may judge by appearances, you are in a bad case. The deed of gift and this trust are, to speak frankly, steps taken with little consideration. You may be carried great lengths by such pledges. Since this man has these advantages over you, it is still greater imprudence in you to irritate him: you ought to seek some gentler method.

ORGON. What? To conceal such a false heart and such a wicked soul under so fair an appearance of ardent zeal! And I, who received him as a beggar and penniless . . . It is all over, I renounce all pious people: I shall hold them henceforth in utter abhorrence, and shall become worse to them than the devil.

CLÉANTE. Is not that just like your hasty ways? You never judge anything calmly. Your never keep in due reason. You always rush from one extreme to the other. You see your error, and you realise you have been imposed upon by a false piety. But is it reasonable that, in order to correct one mistake, you should commit a greater, and not make any difference between the heart of a perfidious rascal and that of a good man? What? because a villain has shamelessly imposed upon you, under the pompous mask of austerity, would you have it that all men are like him, and that there is not a sincere worshipper to be found now-a-days? Leave these foolish deductions to unbelievers; distinguish between virtue and the appearance of it; do not bestow your esteem so rashly; and keep in this the rightful middle course. Do not honor imposture, if you can avoid doing so, but at the same time, do not attack true virtue. If you must fall into an extremity, err, rather, on the other side.

SCENE II
DAMIS, ORGON, CLÉANTE

DAMIS. Is it true, father, that this scoundrel threatens you, that he has forgotten every benefit he has received, and that his cowardly and shameless arrogance turns your goodness to him into arms against you?

ORGON. Yes, my son, and it causes me inexpressible grief.

DAMIS. Leave him to me, I will crop his two ears for him: you must not flinch before his insolence. I will rid you of him at a stroke, and, to put an end to the matter, I will put an end to him.

CLÉANTE. That is exactly how a mere boy talks. Try to moderate these violent outbursts. We live under a government, and in an age in which violence only makes matters worse.

SCENE III
MADAME PERNELLE, MARIANE, ELMIRE, DORINE, DAMIS, ORGON, CLÉANTE

MME. PERNELLE. What is the matter? What are these dreadful, mysterious reports I hear?

ORGON. They are of things which I have seen with my own eyes, and you see how I am paid for my kindness. I eagerly take in a man out of charity, I shelter him, and treat him as my own brother. I heap benefits upon him every day, I give him my daughter and everything I possess, and, all the while, the villain, the traitor, harbors the black design of seducing my wife. Not content even with this vile attempt, he dares to threaten me with my own gifts; and, in order to ruin me, he intends to use the advantage he has obtained through my unwise good nature to drive me out of my estate which I made over to him, and to reduce me to the same condition from which I rescued him.

DORINE. Poor man!

MME. PERNELLE. I can never believe, my son, that he would commit so black a deed.

ORGON. Why?

MME. PERNELLE. Good people are always envied.

ORGON. What do you mean by that, mother?

MME. PERNELLE. Why, there are strange goings-on in your house. It is very plain to see the ill-will they bear him.

ORGON. What has this hatred to do with what I have just told you.

MME. PERNELLE. When you were a child I told you a hundred times that in this world virtue is ever persecuted, and that the envious may die, but envy never.

ORGON. But what has this speech to do with what has happened today?

MME. PERNELLE. They have most likely fabricated a hundred idle stories against him for your benefit.

ORGON. I have already told you I have seen everything myself.

MME. PERNELLE. The spite of slanderers is great.

ORGON. You would drive me mad, mother. I tell you I saw with my own eyes this monstrous crime.

MME. PERNELLE. Tongues are always ready to spit venom: nothing here below is proof against them.

ORGON. That remark seems to lack common sense. I have seen it, I tell you, seen it, with my own eyes, seen it, what people call seen it. Must I drum it in your ears a hundred times and shout at the top of my voice?

MME. PERNELLE. Well, appearances deceive more often than not: you must not always judge by what you see.

ORGON. I'm furious.

MME. PERNELLE. We are naturally subject to false suspicions, and a bad construction is often put on a good deed.

ORGON. Must I regard his desire to kiss my wife as charitable?

MME. PERNELLE. You should have just cause before you accuse people. You ought to have waited until you were sure you saw these things.

ORGON. How the devil could I better satisfy myself? Ought I then to have waited, mother, until before my eyes he had . . . You will make me say something obscene.

MME. PERNELLE. Indeed I am sure his soul burns with too pure a zeal; I cannot possibly believe he would attempt the things of which people accuse him.

ORGON. Enough! If you were not my mother I do not know what I might say to you, you make me so angry.

DORINE. Such is the just reward of acts in this world, Monsieur. You would not believe and now you are not believed.

CLÉANTE. We waste time in mere trifles which we ought to use in taking measures. We ought not to sleep when a knave threatens.

DAMIS. What? would his effrontery go to such lengths?

ELMIRE. For my part, I do not believe he can possibly make out a case: his ingratitude would be too glaring.

CLÉANTE. You must not trust to that. He will find means to justify his actions against you: for less than this a powerful party has involved people in sad troubles. I tell you again, armed as he is, you ought never to have driven him thus far.

ORGON. That is true, but what could I do? I was not the master of my feelings when I saw the insolence of this traitor.

CLÉANTE. I wish, with all my heart, we could arrange for even the shadow of peace between you two.

ELMIRE. If I had known he had such weapons in his hands I would not have made so much noise about the matter, and my . . .

ORGON. What does that man want? Go quickly, and see. A nice condition I am in for seeing anybody.

SCENE IV
MONSIEUR LOYAL, MADAM PERNELLE, ORGON, DAMIS,
MARIANE, DORINE, ELMIRE, CLÉANTE

M. LOYAL. Good-morning, my dear sister, pray let me speak to your master.

DORINE. He is engaged with friends, and I doubt whether he can see anyone at present.

M. LOYAL. I do not want to be intrusive in his own house. I do not think my presence concerns anything that will distress him. I have come upon a matter which will please him.

DORINE. What is your name?

M. LOYAL. Simply tell him I come, on behalf of Monsieur Tartuffe, for his good.

DORINE. He is a man who comes with a civil message from Monsieur Tartuffe, concerning a matter which he says will please you.

CLÉANTE. You must see who this man is, and what he can want.

ORGON. Perhaps he comes here to reconcile us. In what way shall I behave to him?

CLÉANTE. You ought not to show your resentment; and if he speaks of an agreement you ought to listen to him?

M. LOYAL. Your servant, Monsieur. May heaven destroy those who wish you harm, and may it be as favorable to you as I wish.

ORGON. This civil beginning bears out my opinion, and augurs already some reconciliation.

M. LOYAL. I was your father's servant, and your whole household has ever been dear to me.

ORGON. I am greatly ashamed, Monsieur, and I beg your pardon in that I do not know you or your name.

M. LOYAL. My name is Loyal, I am a native of Normandy, and, in spite of envious people, a bailiff. Thanks to heaven, I have had, for the last forty years, the happiness of holding this office with much credit. I have come to you, Monsieur, by your leave, to serve a writ of a certain kind . . .

ORGON. What? are you here . . . ?

M. LOYAL. Calm yourself, Sir. It is nothing but a summons, an order to remove you and yours hence, to take your furniture away, and to make way for others, without delay or remission, as hereby decreed.

ORGON. I to leave this house?

M. LOYAL. Yes, Monsieur, if it please you. The house, at present, as you well know, belongs unquestionably to good Monsieur Tartuffe. Henceforth, of all your goods he is lord and master, by virtue of a contract which I have with me. It is in due form and nothing can be said against it.

DAMIS. Truly I admire this impudence: it is colossal.

M. LOYAL. Monsieur, I have not any business with you. It is with this gentleman.

He is both reasonable and civil, and he knows the duty of a sensible man too well to wish to resist what is in any way just.

ORGON. But . . .

M. LOYAL. Yes, Monsieur, I know you would not rebel for a million, and that you will, like a gentleman, allow me to execute here the orders which have been given me.

DAMIS. Monsieur Bailiff, it may happen that you will here get the stick laid across your black gown.

M. LOYAL. Order your son to be silent or withdraw, Monsieur. I should be sorry to have to put your name down in my official report.

DORINE. This Monsieur Loyal has a very disloyal air.

M. LOYAL. I have much sympathy with all worthy people, and I would not have burdened myself, Monsieur, with these documents save to oblige you and to do you service, to take away in this manner the chance of someone else being chosen who, not having for you the esteem I have, would have proceeded in a less gentle manner.

ORGON. What can be worse than to order people out of their own house?

M. LOYAL. Monsieur, you are given time, and I will suspend proceedings under the writ until tomorrow, I will simply come to pass the night here, with ten of my men, without scandal and without noise. For the sake of form, you will be so good as to bring me the keys of your door before you go to bed. I will take care not to disturb your repose, and not to allow anything unseemly. But tomorrow, early in the morning, you must be ready to clear the house even to the smallest utensil. My men will help you. I have chosen strong fellows, so that they can assist you to take everything away. It is not possible to act better than I am acting, I feel sure, and, since I treat you with great consideration, Monsieur, I beg that on your part you will treat me properly and that you will not annoy me in any way in the execution of the duties of my office.

ORGON. With the best heart in the world would I give just now a hundred of the brightest louis d'or[7] that are left me could I have the pleasure of giving one of the soundest clouts possible on his beak.

CLÉANTE. Be quiet, do not make matters worse.

DAMIS. I can hardly contain myself. My hand itches at this monstrous impertinence.

DORINE. Upon my word, Monsieur Loyal, a drubbing with a stick would not sit ill on your broad back.

M. LOYAL. We could easily punish those shameful words, my girl; women, also, are answerable to the law.

CLÉANTE. Let us end all this, Monsieur, there has been enough of it. Give up this paper, for goodness' sake, quickly, and leave us.

M. LOYAL. Good-bye for the present. May Heaven keep you all in happiness!

ORGON. May it confound you and him who sent you!

SCENE V
ORGON, CLÉANTE, MARIANE, ELMIRE, MADAME PERNELLE, DORINE, DAMIS

ORGON. Ah! well. You see now, mother, I was right, and you can judge of the rest by the warrant. Do you acknowledge his treachery at last?

---

[7] Gold coins issued during the reigns of Louis XIII through Louis XVI—that is, from 1610 through 1792.

MME. PERNELLE. I am quite thunderstruck: I feel as though I had dropped from the clouds!

DORINE. You have not any reason to complain, or to blame him. His pious designs are confirmed by this. His virtue reaches its consummation in the love of his neighbor. He knows that riches very often corrupt a man, and, out of pure charity, he would take away from you everything which could become an obstacle in the way of your salvation.

ORGON. Hold your tongue. I am continually telling you to be quiet.

CLÉANTE. Let us see what course we ought to follow.

ELMIRE. Go and expose the ungrateful wretch's audacity. His proceeding destroys the validity of the contract. His disloyalty will appear too black to allow him to gain the success he expects.

SCENE VI
VALÈRE, ORGON, CLÉANTE, ELMIRE, MARIANE, *etc.*

VALÈRE. I am very sorry, Monsieur, that I come to trouble you, but I am forced to it by the urgency of the danger. A friend who is united to me by the closest ties, and who knows the interest I take in you, has, by a hazardous step, violated for my sake the secrecy due to affairs of state and has just sent me some intelligence in consequence of which you will be compelled to make a sudden flight. About an hour ago, the knave, who has imposed upon you for so long, thought proper to accuse you to the king, and, amongst the charges which he brings against you, he has put into his hands the important documents of a state criminal whose guilty secret he says you have kept in contempt of the duty of a subject. I do not know the details of the crime with which you are charged, but a warrant is out against your person, and the better to execute it, he himself is appointed to accompany the person who is to arrest you.

CLÉANTE. His pretensions are now armed, and it is by this means that the traitor seeks to render himself master of your property.

ORGON. I tell you the fellow is a vile brute.

VALÈRE. The least delay may be fatal to you. My coach is at the door to take you away, and I have brought you a thousand louis d'or. Do not let us lose any time; the bolt is shot, and this is one of those blows which must be parried by flight. I myself offer to conduct you to a safe retreat, and I will accompany you even to the end of your flight.

ORGON. Alas! what do I not owe to your thoughtful care? I must thank you another time. I beg that heaven will be propitious enough to enable me to acknowledge some day this generous service. Farewell. The rest of you be careful . . .

CLÉANTE. Go quickly, brother, we will see to everything necessary.

LAST SCENE
A POLICE OFFICER, TARTUFFE, VALÈRE, ORGON, ELMIRE, MARIANE, *etc.*

TARTUFFE. Gently, Monsieur, gently, do not run so fast. You will not have to go very far in order to find your lodging; we take you prisoner in the King's name.

ORGON. Wretch! You have kept this shaft for the last. This is the blow, villain, by which you dispatch me, and it crowns all your evil deeds.

TARTUFFE. Your abuse has no power to disturb me; I am accustomed to endure all things for the sake of heaven.

CLÉANTE. Your moderation is great, to be sure.

DAMIS. How impudently the villain plays with heaven!

TARTUFFE. All your abuse cannot move me. I do not think of anything but of doing my duty.

MARIANE. You may aspire to great glory from *this* duty. And this task is a very proper one for *you* to undertake.

TARTUFFE. A task cannot but be glorious when it proceeds from the power which sends me to this place.

ORGON. Ungrateful wretch, do you remember that it was my charitable hand which raised you from a miserable condition?

TARTUFFE. Yes, I know what assistance I had from you, but the interest of the King is my first duty. The imperative obligation of that sacred duty stifles all gratitude in my heart, and I would sacrifice friend, wife, parents and myself with them to so powerful a bond.

ELMIRE. The hypocrite!

DORINE. How well and artfully he knows how to make himself a fine cloak out of all that men hold sacred.

CLÉANTE. But if this zeal which fills you, and upon which you plume yourself, is as perfect as you say it is, why did it not appear before he happened to surprise you soliciting his wife? Why did you not think to denounce him until his honor obliged him to turn you away? I do not say the gift of all his property he recently made you should have prevented you from doing your duty, but why did you agree to take anything of his when you intended to treat him as a criminal today?

TARTUFFE. [*To the Police Officer.*] Pray, Monsieur, deliver me from this clamor, and be so good as to execute your warrant.

POLICE OFFICER. Certainly. We have delayed the execution too long, without doubt. Your words aptly remind me to fulfil it. My warrant will be executed if you follow me directly to the prison which is assigned you for your dwelling.

TARTUFFE. Who? I, Monsieur.

POLICE OFFICER. Yes, you.

TARTUFFE. Why, then, to prison?

POLICE OFFICER. I have no account to render to you. Compose yourself, Monseiur, after so great an alarm. We live under a king who is an enemy to fraud, a king whose eyes look into the depths of all hearts, and who cannot be deceived by the most artful imposter. Gifted with a fine discernment, his lofty soul at all times sees things in the right light. He is never betrayed into exaggeration, and his sound judgment never falls into any excess. He confers an everlasting glory upon men of worth; but this zeal does not radiate blindly: his esteem for the sincere does not close his heart to the horror aroused by those who are treacherous. Even this person was not the man to overreach him: he has guarded himself against more subtle snares. From the first his quick perception pierced through all the vileness coiled round that man's heart, who, coming to accuse you, betrayed himself, and by a righteous act of divine justice revealed himself to the King as a notorious rogue, of whose deeds, under another name, the King was aware. His life is one long series of utterly black actions, of which volumes might be written. In short, the monarch detested his vile ingratitude and his disloyalty towards you; to his other misdeeds he has added this crime;

and I am placed in this matter under his orders, so that the lengths to which his impudence would carry him might be seen, and in order to make him give you entire satisfaction. Yes, I am instructed to take away from the wretch all your documents of which he declares he is the owner, and to place them in your hands. By his sovereign power he annuls the terms of the contract which made over to that man all your wealth, and, finally, he pardons you the secret offense into which the flight of a friend caused you to fall. This is the reward he bestows for the zeal which he formerly saw you display in the support of his rights, to show that his heart knows, when least suspected, how to recompense a good action, that merit is never ignored by him, and that he remembers good much better than evil.

DORINE. Heaven be praised!

MADAME PERNELLE. Now I breathe again.

ELMIRE. What a happy end to our troubles!

MARIANE. Who would have dared to foretell this?

ORGON. [*To Tartuffe.*] Ah! well, there you go, traitor!

CLÉANTE. Ah! my brother, stay, do not descend to abuse. Leave the wretch to his evil fate, and do not add to the remorse which overwhelms him. Much rather hope his heart may today make a happy return to the bosom of virtue; that he may reform his life in detesting his crime, and thus cause our glorious King to temper justice; whilst you throw yourself on your knees in return for his lenity and render the thanks such mild treatment demands.

ORGON. Yes, it is well said. Let us joyfully throw ourselves at his feet and praise the goodness which his heart has shown to us. Then, having acquitted ourselves a little of this first duty, let us apply ourselves to the pressing claims of another, and by a happy wedding let us crown in Valère the ardor of a generous and sincere lover.

END.

[1664]

Henrik Ibsen   *1828–1906*

HEDDA GABLER

Translated by William Archer and Sir Edmund Gosse

CHARACTERS

GEORGE TESMAN
HEDDA TESMAN   *his wife*
MISS JULIANA TESMAN   *his aunt*
MRS. ELVSTED

JUDGE BRACK
EILERT LÖVBORG
BERTA   *servant at the Tesman's*

SCENE. TESMAN'S *villa, in the west end of Christiania.*

ACT I

A spacious, handsome and tastefully furnished drawing-room, decorated in dark colors. In the back, a wide doorway with curtains drawn back, leading into a smaller room decorated in the same style as the drawing-room. In the right-hand wall of the front room, a folding door leading out to the hall. In the opposite wall, on the left, a glass door, also with curtains drawn back. Through the panes can be seen part of a verandah outside, and trees covered with autumn foliage. An oval table, with a cover on it, and surrounded by chairs, stands well forward. In front, by the wall on the right, a wide stove of dark porcelain, a high-backed arm-chair, a cushioned foot-rest, and two foot-stools. A settee, with a small round table in front of it, fills the upper right-hand corner. In front, on the left, a little way from the wall, a sofa. Farther back than the glass door, a piano. On either side of the doorway at the back a whatnot with terra-cotta and majolica ornaments.[1]*—Against the back wall of the inner room a sofa, with a table, and one or two chairs. Over the sofa hangs the portrait of a handsome elderly man in a General's uniform. Over the table a hanging lamp, with an opal glass shade.—A number of bouquets are arranged about the drawing-room, in vases and glasses. Others lie upon the tables. The floors in both rooms are covered with thick carpets.—Morning light. The sun shines in through the glass door.*

MISS JULIANA TESMAN, with her bonnet on and carrying a parasol, comes in from the hall, followed by BERTA, who carries a bouquet wrapped in paper. MISS TESMAN is a comely and pleasant-looking lady of about sixty-five. She is nicely but simply dressed in a gray walking-costume. BERTA is a middle-aged woman of plain and rather countrified appearance.

MISS TESMAN [*stops close to the door, listens, and says softly*]. Upon my word, I don't believe they are stirring yet!

BERTA [*also softly*]. I told you so, Miss. Remember how late the steamboat got in last night. And then, when they got home!—good Lord, what a lot the young mistress had to unpack before she could get to bed.

MISS TESMAN. Well, well—let them have their sleep out. But let us see that

---

[1] A *whatnot* is a stand with shelves for small decorative articles. *Terra-cotta* is a brownish-red clay used in pottery, and *majolica* is a kind of glazed and richly decorated pottery from Italy.

they get a good breath of the fresh morning air when they do appear. [*She goes to the glass door and throws it open.*]

BERTA [*beside the table, at a loss what to do with the bouquet in her hand*]. I declare there isn't a bit of room left. I think I'll put it down here, Miss. [*She places it on the piano.*]

MISS TESMAN. So you've got a new mistress now, my dear Berta. Heaven knows it was a wrench to me to part with you.

BERTA [*on the point of weeping*]. And do you think it wasn't hard for me too, Miss? After all the blessed years I've been with you and Miss Rina.

MISS TESMAN. We must make the best of it, Berta. There was nothing else to be done. George can't do without you, you see—he absolutely can't. He has had you to look after him ever since he was a little boy.

BERTA. Ah, but, Miss Julia, I can't help thinking of Miss Rina lying helpless at home there, poor thing. And with only that new girl, too! She'll never learn to take proper care of an invalid.

MISS TESMAN. Oh, I shall manage to train her. And of course, you know, I shall take most of it upon myself. You needn't be uneasy about my poor sister, my dear Berta.

BERTA. Well, but there's another thing, Miss. I'm so mortally afraid I shan't be able to suit the young mistress.

MISS TESMAN. Oh, well—just at first there may be one or two things—

BERTA. Most like she'll be terrible grand in her ways.

MISS TESMAN. Well, you can't wonder at that—General Gabler's daughter! Think of the sort of life she was accustomed to in her father's time. Don't you remember how we used to see her riding down the road along with the General? In that long black habit—and with feathers in her hat?

BERTA. Yes, indeed—I remember well enough—! But good Lord, I should never have dreamt in those days that she and Master George would make a match of it.

MISS TESMAN. Nor I.—But, by-the-bye, Berta—while I think of it: in future you musn't say Master George. You must say Dr. Tesman.

BERTA. Yes, the young mistress spoke of that too—last night—the moment they set foot in the house. Is it true, then, Miss?

MISS TESMAN. Yes, indeed it is. Only think, Berta—some foreign university has made him a doctor—while he has been abroad, you understand. I hadn't heard a word about it, until he told me himself upon the pier.

BERTA. Well, well, he's clever enough for anything, he is. But I didn't think he'd have gone in for doctoring people too.

MISS TESMAN. No, no, it's not that sort of doctor he is. [*Nods significantly.*] But let me tell you, we may have to call him something still grander before long.

BERTA. You don't say so! What can that be, Miss?

MISS TESMAN [*smiling*]. H'm—wouldn't you like to know! [*With emotion.*] Ah, dear, dear—if my poor brother could only look up from his grave now, and see what his little boy has grown into! [*Looks around.*] But bless me, Berta—why have you done this? Taken the chintz[2] covers off all the furniture?

BERTA. The mistress told me to. She can't abide covers on the chairs, she says.

MISS TESMAN. Are they going to make this their everyday sitting-room then?

---

[2] A printed cotton fabric.

BERTA. Yes, that's what I understood—from the mistress. Master George—the doctor—he said nothing.

[GEORGE TESMAN *comes from the right into the inner room, humming to himself, and carrying an unstrapped empty portmanteau.*[3] *He is a middle-sized, young-looking man of thirty-three, rather stout, with a round, open, cheerful face, fair hair and beard. He wears spectacles, and is somewhat carelessly dressed in comfortable indoor clothes.*]

MISS TESMAN. Good morning, good morning, George.

TESMAN [*in the doorway between the rooms*]. Aunt Julia! Dear Aunt Julia! [*Goes up to her and shakes hands warmly.*] Come all this way—so early! Eh?

MISS TESMAN. Why of course I had to come and see how you were getting on.

TESMAN. In spite of your having had no proper night's rest?

MISS TESMAN. Oh, that makes no difference to me.

TESMAN. Well, I suppose you got home all right from the pier? Eh?

MISS TESMAN. Yes, quite safely, thank goodness. Judge Brack was good enough to see me right to my door.

TESMAN. We were so sorry we couldn't give you a seat in the carriage. But you saw what a pile of boxes Hedda had to bring with her.

MISS TESMAN. Yes, she had certainly plenty of boxes.

BERTA [*to* TESMAN]. Shall I go in and see if there's anything I can do for the mistress?

TESMAN. No thank you, Berta—you needn't. She said she would ring if she wanted anything.

BERTA [*going towards the right*]. Very well.

TESMAN. But look here—take this portmanteau with you.

BERTA [*taking it*]. I'll put it in the attic.

[*She goes out by the hall door.*]

TESMAN. Fancy, Auntie—I had the whole of that portmanteau chock full of copies of documents. You wouldn't believe how much I have picked up from all the archives I have been examining—curious old details that no one has had any idea of—

MISS TESMAN. Yes, you don't seem to have wasted your time on your wedding trip, George.

TESMAN. No, that I haven't. But do take off your bonnet, Auntie. Look here! Let me untie the strings—eh?

MISS TESMAN [*while he does so*]. Well, well—this is just as if you were still at home with us.

TESMAN [*with the bonnet in his hand, looks at it from all sides*]. Why, what a gorgeous bonnet you've been investing in!

MISS TESMAN. I bought it on Hedda's account.

TESMAN. On Hedda's account? Eh?

MISS TESMAN. Yes, so that Hedda needn't be ashamed of me if we happened to go out together.

TESMAN [*patting her cheek*]. You always think of everything, Aunt Julia. [*Lays the bonnet on a chair beside the table.*] And now, look here—suppose we sit comfortably on the sofa and have a little chat, till Hedda comes.

[*They seat themselves. She places her parasol*[4] *in the corner of the sofa.*]

MISS TESMAN [*takes both his hands and looks at him*]. What a delight it is to have

---

[3] A leather trunk.   [4] A flimsy sun umbrella.

you again, as large as life, before my very eyes, George! My George—my poor brother's own boy!

TESMAN. And it's a delight for me, too, to see you again, Aunt Julia! You, who have been father and mother in one to me.

MISS TESMAN. Oh, yes, I know you will always keep a place in your heart for your old aunts.

TESMAN. And what about Aunt Rina? No improvement—eh?

MISS TESMAN. Oh, no—we can scarcely look for any improvement in her case, poor thing. There she lies, helpless, as she has lain for all these years. But heaven grant I may not lose her yet awhile! For if I did, I don't know what I should make of my life, George—especially now that I haven't you to look after any more.

TESMAN [*patting her back*]. There, there, there—!

MISS TESMAN [*suddenly changing her tone*]. And to think that here you are a married man, George!—And that you should be the one to carry off Hedda Gabler, the beautiful Hedda Gabler! Only think of it—she, that was so beset with admirers!

TESMAN [*hums a little and smiles complacently*]. Yes, I fancy I have several good friends about town who would like to stand in my shoes—eh?

MISS TESMAN. And then this fine long wedding-tour you have had! More than five—nearly six months—

TESMAN. Well, for me it has been a sort of tour of research as well. I have had to do so much grubbing among old records—and to read no end of books too, Auntie.

MISS TESMAN. Oh, yes, I suppose so. [*More confidentially, and lowering her voice a little.*] But listen now, George—have you nothing—nothing special to tell me?

TESMAN. As to our journey?

MISS TESMAN. Yes.

TESMAN. No, I don't know of anything except what I have told you in my letters. I had a doctor's degree conferred on me—but that I told you yesterday.

MISS TESMAN. Yes, yes, you did. But what I mean is—haven't you any—any—expectations—?

TESMAN. Expectations?

MISS TESMAN. Why, you know, George—I'm your old auntie!

TESMAN. Why, of course I have expectations.

MISS TESMAN. Ah!

TESMAN. I have every expectation of being a professor one of these days.

MISS TESMAN. Oh, yes, a professor—

TESMAN. Indeed, I may say I am certain of it. But my dear Auntie—you know all about that already!

MISS TESMAN [*laughing at herself*]. Yes, of course I do. You are quite right there. [*Changing the subject.*] But we were talking about your journey. It must have cost a great deal of money, George?

TESMAN. Well, you see—my handsome traveling-scholarship went a good way.

MISS TESMAN. But I can't understand how you can have made it go far enough for two.

TESMAN. No, that's not so easy to understand—eh?

MISS TESMAN. And especially traveling with a lady—they tell me that makes it ever so much more expensive.

TESMAN. Yes, of course—it makes it a little more expensive. But Hedda had to have this trip, Auntie! She really had to. Nothing else would have done.

MISS TESMAN. No, no, I suppose not. A wedding-tour seems to be quite indispensable nowadays.—But tell me now—have you gone thoroughly over the house yet?

TESMAN. Yes, you may be sure I have. I have been afoot ever since daylight.

MISS TESMAN. And what do you think of it all?

TESMAN. I'm delighted! Quite delighted! Only I can't think what we are to do with the two empty rooms between the inner parlor and Hedda's bedroom.

MISS TESMAN [*laughing*]. Oh, my dear George, I dare say you may find some use for them—in the course of time.

TESMAN. Why of course you are quite right, Aunt Julia! You mean as my library increases—eh?

MISS TESMAN. Yes, quite so, my dear boy. It was your library I was thinking of.

TESMAN. I am specially pleased on Hedda's account. Often and often, before we were engaged, she said that she would never care to live anywhere but in Secretary Falk's villa.

MISS TESMAN. Yes, it was lucky that this very house should come into the market, just after you had started.

TESMAN. Yes, Aunt Julia, the luck was on our side, wasn't it—eh?

MISS TESMAN. But the expense, my dear George! You will find it very expensive, all this.

TESMAN [*looks at her, a little cast down*]. Yes, I suppose I shall, Aunt!

MISS TESMAN. Oh, frightfully!

TESMAN. How much do you think? In round numbers?—Eh?

MISS TESMAN. Oh, I can't even guess until all the accounts come in.

TESMAN. Well, fortunately, Judge Brack has secured the most favorable terms for me,—so he said in a letter to Hedda.

MISS TESMAN. Yes, don't be uneasy, my dear boy.—Besides, I have given security for the furniture and all the carpets.

TESMAN. Security? You? My dear Aunt Julia—what sort of security could you give?

MISS TESMAN. I have given a mortgage on our annuity.

TESMAN [*jumps up*]. What! On your—and Aunt Rina's annuity!

MISS TESMAN. Yes, I knew of no other plan, you see.

TESMAN [*placing himself before her*]. Have you gone out of your senses, Auntie! Your annuity—it's all that you and Aunt Rina have to live upon.

MISS TESMAN. Well, well, don't get so excited about it. It's only a matter of form you know—Judge Brack assured me of that. It was he that was kind enough to arrange the whole affair for me. A mere matter of form, he said.

TESMAN. Yes, that may be all very well. But nevertheless—

MISS TESMAN. You will have your own salary to depend upon now. And, good heavens, even if we did have to pay up a little—! To eke things out a bit at the start—! Why, it would be nothing but a pleasure to us.

TESMAN. Oh, Auntie—will you never be tired of making sacrifices for me!

MISS TESMAN [*rises and lays her hands on his shoulders*]. Have I had any other happiness in this world except to smooth your way for you, my dear boy? You, who have had neither father nor mother to depend on. And now we have reached the goal, George! Things have looked black enough for us, sometimes; but, thank heaven, now you have nothing to fear.

TESMAN. Yes, it is really marvelous how everything has turned out for the best.

MISS TESMAN. And the people who opposed you—who wanted to bar the way for you—now you have them at your feet. They have fallen, George. Your most dangerous rival—his fall was the worst.—And now he has to lie on the bed he has made for himself—poor misguided creature.

TESMAN. Have you heard anything of Eilert? Since I went away, I mean.

MISS TESMAN. Only that he is said to have published a new book.

TESMAN. What! Eilert Lövborg! Recently—eh?

MISS TESMAN. Yes, so they say. Heaven knows whether it can be worth anything! Ah, when your new book appears—that will be another story, George! What is it to be about?

TESMAN. It will deal with the domestic industries of Brabant during the Middle Ages.

MISS TESMAN. Fancy—to be able to write on such a subject as that!

TESMAN. However, it may be some time before the book is ready. I have all these collections to arrange first, you see.

MISS TESMAN. Yes, collecting and arranging—no one can beat you at that. There you are my poor brother's own son.

TESMAN. I am looking forward eagerly to setting to work at it; especially now that I have my own delightful home to work in.

MISS TESMAN. And, most of all, now that you have got the wife of your heart, my dear George.

TESMAN [*embracing her*]. Oh, yes, yes, Aunt Julia. Hedda—she is the best part of all! [*Looks towards the doorway.*] I believe I hear her coming—eh?

[HEDDA *enters from the left through the inner room. She is a woman of nine-and-twenty. Her face and figure show refinement and distinction. Her complexion is pale and opaque. Her steel-gray eyes express a cold, unruffled repose. Her hair is of an agreeable medium brown, but not particularly abundant. She is dressed in a tasteful, somewhat loose-fitting morning-gown.*]

MISS TESMAN [*going to meet* HEDDA]. Good morning, my dear Hedda! Good morning, and a hearty welcome.

HEDDA [*holds out her hand*]. Good morning, dear Miss Tesman! So early a call! This is kind of you.

MISS TESMAN [*with some embarrassment*]. Well—has the bride slept well in her new home?

HEDDA. Oh yes, thanks. Passably.

TESMAN [*laughing*]. Passably! Come, that's good, Hedda! You were sleeping like a stone when I got up.

HEDDA. Fortunately. Of course one has always to accustom one's self to new surroundings, Miss Tesman—little by little. [*Looking towards the left.*] Oh—there the servant has gone and opened the verandah door, and let in a whole flood of sunshine.

MISS TESMAN [*going towards the door*]. Well, then, we will shut it.

HEDDA. No, no, not that! Tesman, please draw the curtains. That will give a softer light.

TESMAN [*at the door*]. All right—all right. There now, Hedda, now you have both shade and fresh air.

HEDDA. Yes, fresh air we certainly must have, with all these stacks of flowers— But—won't you sit down, Miss Tesman?

MISS TESMAN. No, thank you. Now that I have seen that everything is all right

here—thank heaven!—I must be getting home again. My sister is lying longing for me, poor thing.

TESMAN. Give her my very best love, Auntie; and say I shall look in and see
her later in the day.

MISS TESMAN. Yes, yes, I'll be sure to tell her. But by-the-bye, George— [*feeling
in her dress pocket*]—I have almost forgotten—I have something for you here.

TESMAN. What is it, Auntie? Eh?

MISS TESMAN [*produces a flat parcel wrapped in newspaper and hands it to him*].
Look here, my dear boy.

TESMAN [*opening the parcel*]. Well, I declare! Have you really saved them for
me, Aunt Julia! Hedda, isn't this touching—eh?

HEDDA [*beside the whatnot on the right*]. Well, what is it?

TESMAN. My old morning-shoes! My slippers.

HEDDA. Indeed. I remember you often spoke of them while we were abroad.

TESMAN. Yes, I missed them terribly. [*Goes up to her.*] Now you shall see them,
Hedda!

HEDDA [*going towards the stove*]. Thanks I really don't care about it.

TESMAN [*following her*]. Only think—ill as she was, Aunt Rina embroidered these
for me. Oh you can't think how many associations cling to them.

HEDDA [*at the table*]. Scarcely for me.

MISS TESMAN. Of course not for Hedda, George.

TESMAN. Well, but now that she belongs to the family, I thought—

HEDDA [*interrupting*]. We shall never get on with this servant, Tesman.

MISS TESMAN. Not get on with Berta?

TESMAN. Why, dear, what puts that in your head? Eh?

HEDDA [*pointing*]. Look there! She has left her old bonnet lying about on a
chair.

TESMAN [*in consternation, drops the slippers on the floor*]. Why, Hedda—

HEDDA. Just fancy, if any one should come in and see it.

TESMAN. But Hedda—that's Aunt Julia's bonnet.

HEDDA. Is it!

MISS TESMAN [*taking up the bonnet*]. Yes, indeed it's mine. And what's more,
it's not old, Madame Hedda.

HEDDA. I really did not look closely at it, Miss Tesman.

MISS TESMAN [*trying on the bonnet*]. Let me tell you it's the first time I have
worn it—the very first time.

TESMAN. And a very nice bonnet it is too—quite a beauty!

MISS TESMAN. Oh, it's no such great thing, George. [*Looks around her.*] My
parasol—? Ah, here. [*Takes it.*] For this is mine too—[*mutters*]—not Berta's.

TESMAN. A new bonnet and a new parasol! Only think, Hedda!

HEDDA. Very handsome indeed.

TESMAN. Yes, isn't it? But Auntie, take a good look at Hedda before you go!
See how handsome she is!

MISS TESMAN. Oh, my dear boy, there's nothing new in that. Hedda was always
lovely. [*She nods and goes towards the right.*]

TESMAN [*following*]. Yes, but have you noticed what splendid condition she is
in? How she has filled out on the journey?

HEDDA [*crossing the room*]. Oh, do be quiet—?

MISS TESMAN [*who has stopped and turned*]. Filled out?

TESMAN. Of course you don't notice it so much now that she has that dress
on. But I, who can see—

HEDDA [*at the glass door, impatiently*]. Oh, you can't see anything.

TESMAN. It must be the mountain air in the Tyrol—

HEDDA [*curtly, interrupting*]. I am exactly as I was when I started.

TESMAN. So you insist; but I'm quite certain you are not. Don't you agree with me, Auntie?

MISS TESMAN [*who has been gazing at her with folded hands*]. Hedda is lovely— lovely—lovely. [*Goes up to her, takes her head between both hands, draws it downwards, and kisses her hair*]. God bless and preserve Hedda Tesman—for George's sake.

HEDDA [*gently freeing herself*]. Oh—! Let me go.

MISS TESMAN [*in quite emotion*]. I shall not let a day pass without coming to see you.

TESMAN. No you won't, will you, Auntie? Eh?

MISS TESMAN. Good-bye—good-bye!

[*She goes out by the hall door.* TESMAN *accompanies her. The door remains half open.* TESMAN *can be heard repeating his message to Aunt Rina and his thanks for the slippers.*

In the meantime, HEDDA *walks about the room raising her arms and clenching her hands as if in desperation. Then she flings back the curtains from the glass door, and stands there looking out.*

Presently TESMAN *returns and closes the door behind him.*]

TESMAN [*picks up the slippers from the floor*]. What are you looking at, Hedda?

HEDDA [*once more calm and mistress of herself*]. I am only looking at the leaves. They are so yellow—so withered.

TESMAN [*wraps up the slippers and lays them on the table*]. Well you see, we are well into September now.

HEDDA [*again restless*]. Yes, to think of it!—Already in—in September.

TESMAN. Don't you think Aunt Julia's manner was strange, dear? Almost solemn? Can you imagine what was the matter with her? Eh?

HEDDA. I scarcely know her, you see. Is she often like that?

TESMAN. No, not as she was today.

HEDDA [*leaving the glass door*]. Do you think she was annoyed about the bonnet?

TESMAN. Oh, scarcely at all. Perhaps a little, just at the moment—

HEDDA. But what an idea, to pitch her bonnet about in the drawing-room! No one does that sort of thing.

TESMAN. Well you may be sure Aunt Julia won't do it again.

HEDDA. In any case, I shall manage to make my peace with her.

TESMAN. Yes, my dear, good Hedda, if you only would.

HEDDA. When you call this afternoon, you might invite her to spend the evening here.

TESMAN. Yes, that I will. And there's one thing more you could do that would delight her heart.

HEDDA. What is it?

TESMAN. If you could only prevail on yourself to say *du*[5] to her. For my sake, Hedda? Eh?

HEDDA. No, no, Tesman—you really mustn't ask that of me. I have told you so already. I shall try to call her "Aunt"; and you must be satisfied with that.

---

[5] Like the French and the Germans, Norwegians reserve the familiar form of the pronoun "you" (*du*) for conversations between lovers and intimate friends; the more formal *de* is used between strangers and casual acquaintances.

TESMAN. Well, well. Only I think now that you belong to the family, you—

HEDDA. H'm—I can't in the least see why—

[*She goes up towards the middle doorway.*]

TESMAN [*after a pause*]. Is there anything the matter with you, Hedda? Eh?

HEDDA. I'm only looking at my old piano. It doesn't go at all well with all the other things.

TESMAN. The first time I draw my salary, we'll see about exchanging it.

HEDDA. No, no—no exchanging. I don't want to part with it. Suppose we put it there in the inner room, and then get another here in its place. When it's convenient, I mean.

TESMAN [*a little taken aback*]. Yes—of course we could do that.

HEDDA [*takes up the bouquet from the piano*]. These flowers were not here last night when we arrived.

TESMAN. Aunt Julia must have brought them for you.

HEDDA [*examining the bouquet*]. A visiting-card. [*Takes it out and reads.*] "Shall return later in the day." Can you guess whose card it is?

TESMAN. No. Whose? Eh?

HEDDA. The name is "Mrs. Elvsted."

TESMAN. Is it really? Sheriff Elvsted's wife? Miss Rysing that was.

HEDDA. Exactly. The girl with the irritating hair, that she was always showing off. An old flame of yours, I've been told.

TESMAN [*laughing*]. Oh, that didn't last long; and it was before I knew you, Hedda. But fancy her being in town!

HEDDA. It's odd that she should call upon us. I have scarcely seen her since we left school.

TESMAN. I haven't seen her either for—heaven knows how long. I wonder how she can endure to live in such an out-of-the-way hole—eh?

HEDDA [*after a moment's thought says suddenly*]. Tell me, Tesman—isn't it somewhere near there that he—that—Eilert Lövborg is living?

TESMAN. Yes, he is somewhere in that part of the country.

[BERTA *enters by the hall door.*]

BERTA. That lady, ma'am, that brought some flowers a little while ago, is here again. [*Pointing.*] The flowers you have in your hand, ma'am.

HEDDA. Ah, is she? Well, please show her in.

[BERTA *opens the door for* MRS. ELVSTED, *and goes out herself.*—MRS. ELVSTED *is a woman of fragile figure, with pretty, soft features. Her eyes are light blue, large, round, and somewhat prominent, with a startled, inquiring expression. Her hair is remarkably light, almost flaxen, and unusually abundant and wavy. She is a couple of years younger than* HEDDA. *She wears a dark visiting dress, tasteful, but not quite in the latest fashion.*]

HEDDA [*receives her warmly*]. How do you do, my dear Mrs. Elvsted? It's delightful to see you again.

MRS. ELVSTED [*nervously, struggling for self-control*]. Yes, it's a very long time since we met.

TESMAN [*gives her his hand*]. And we too—eh?

HEDDA. Thanks for your lovely flowers—

MRS. ELVSTED. Oh, not at all— I would have come straight here yesterday afternoon; but I heard that you were away—

TESMAN. Have you just come to town? Eh?

MRS. ELVSTED. I arrived yesterday, about midday. Oh, I was quite in despair when I heard that you were not at home.

HEDDA. In despair! How so?

TESMAN. Why, my dear Mrs. Rysing—I mean Mrs. Elvsted—

HEDDA. I hope that you are not in any trouble?

MRS. ELVSTED. Yes, I am. And I don't know another living creature here that I can turn to.

HEDDA [*laying the bouquet on the table*]. Come—let us sit here on the sofa—

MRS. ELVSTED. Oh, I am too restless to sit down.

HEDDA. Oh no, you're not. Come here. [*She draws* MRS. ELVSTED *down upon the sofa and sits at her side.*]

TESMAN. Well? What is it, Mrs. Elvsted?

HEDDA. Has anything particular happened to you at home?

MRS. ELVSTED. Yes—and no. Oh—I am so anxious you should not misunderstand me—

HEDDA. Then your best plan is to tell us the whole story, Mrs. Elvsted.

TESMAN. I suppose that's what you have come for—eh?

MRS. ELVSTED. Yes, yes—of course it is. Well then, I must tell you—if you don't already know—that Eilert Lövborg is in town, too.

HEDDA. Lövborg—!

TESMAN. What! Has Eilert Lövborg come back? Fancy that, Hedda!

HEDDA. Well, well—I hear it.

MRS. ELVSTED. He has been here a week already. Just fancy—a whole week! In this terrible town, alone! With so many temptations on all sides.

HEDDA. But my dear Mrs. Elvsted—how does he concern you so much?

MRS. ELVSTED [*looks at her with a startled air, and says rapidly*]. He was the children's tutor.

HEDDA. Your children's?

MRS. ELVSTED. My husband's. I have none.

HEDDA. Your step-children's, then?

MRS. ELVSTED. Yes.

TESMAN [*somewhat hesitatingly*]. Then was he—I don't know how to express it—was he—regular enough in his habits to be fit for the post? Eh?

MRS. ELVSTED. For the last two years his conduct has been irreproachable.

TESMAN. Has it indeed? Fancy that, Hedda!

HEDDA. I hear it.

MRS. ELVSTED. Perfectly irreproachable, I assure you! In every respect. But all the same—now that I know he is here—in this great town—and with a large sum of money in his hands—I can't help being in mortal fear for him.

TESMAN. Why did he not remain where he was? With you and your husband? Eh?

MRS. ELVSTED. After his book was published he was too restless and unsettled to remain with us.

TESMAN. Yes, by-the-bye, Aunt Julia told me he had published a new book.

MRS. ELVSTED. Yes, a big book, dealing with the march of civilization—in broad outline, as it were. It came out about a fortnight ago. And since it has sold so well, and been so much read—and made such a sensation—

TESMAN. Has it indeed? It must be something he has had lying by since his better days.

MRS. ELVSTED. Long ago, you mean?

TESMAN. Yes.

MRS. ELVSTED. No, he has written it all since he has been with us—within the last year.

TESMAN. Isn't that good news, Hedda? Think of that.

MRS. ELVSTED. Ah, yes, if only it would last!

HEDDA. Have you seen him here in town?

MRS. ELVSTED. No, not yet. I have had the greatest difficulty in finding out his address. But this morning I discovered it at last.

HEDDA [*looks searchingly at her*]. Do you know, it seems to me a little odd of your husband—h'm—

MRS. ELVSTED [*starting nervously*]. Of my husband! What?

HEDDA. That he should send you to town on such an errand—that he does not come himself and look after his friend.

MRS. ELVSTED. Oh, no, no—my husband has no time. And besides, I—I had some shopping to do.

HEDDA [*with a slight smile*]. Ah, that is a different matter.

MRS. ELVSTED [*rising quickly and uneasily*]. And now I beg and implore you, Mr. Tesman—receive Eilert Lövborg kindly if he comes to you! And that he is sure to do. You see you were such great friends in the old days. And then you are interested in the same studies—the same branch of science— so far as I can understand.

TESMAN. We used to be, at any rate.

MRS. ELVSTED. That is why I beg so earnestly that you—you too—will keep a sharp eye upon him. Oh, you will promise me that, Mr. Tesman—won't you?

TESMAN. With the greatest of pleasure, Mrs. Rysing—

HEDDA. Elvsted.

TESMAN. I assure you I shall do all I possibly can for Eilert. You may rely upon me.

MRS. ELVSTED. Oh, how very, very kind of you! [*Presses his hands.*] Thanks, thanks, thanks! [*Frightened.*] You see, my husband is very fond of him!

HEDDA [*rising*]. You ought to write to him, Tesman. Perhaps he may not care to come to you of his own accord.

TESMAN. Well, perhaps it would be the right thing to do, Hedda? Eh?

HEDDA. And the sooner the better. Why not at once?

MRS. ELVSTED [*imploringly*]. Oh, if you only would!

TESMAN. I'll write this moment. Have you his address, Mrs.—Mrs. Elvsted?

MRS. ELVSTED. Yes. [*Takes a slip of paper from her pocket, and hands it to him.*] Here it is.

TESMAN. Good, good. Then I'll go in—[*Looks about him.*] By-the-bye,—my slippers? Oh, here. [*Takes the packet, and is about to go.*]

HEDDA. Be sure you write him a cordial, friendly letter. And a good long one too.

TESMAN. Yes, I will.

MRS. ELVSTED. But please, please don't say a word to show that I have suggested it.

TESMAN. No, how could you think I would? Eh?

[*He goes out to the right, through the inner room.*]

HEDDA [*goes up to* MRS. ELVSTED, *smiles, and says in a low voice*]. There. We have killed two birds with one stone.

MRS. ELVSTED. What do you mean?

HEDDA. Could you not see that I wanted him to go?

MRS. ELVSTED. Yes, to write the letter—

HEDDA. And that I might speak to you alone.

Mrs. Elvsted [*confused*]. About the same thing?

Hedda. Precisely.

Mrs. Elvsted [*apprehensively*]. But there is nothing more, Mrs. Tesman! Absolutely nothing!

Hedda. Oh, yes, but there is. There is a great deal more—I can see that. Sit here—and we'll have a cosy, confidential chat. [*She forces* Mrs. Elvsted *to sit in the easy-chair beside the stove, and seats herself on one of the foot-stools.*]

Mrs. Elvsted [*anxiously, looking at her watch*]. But, my dear Mrs. Tesman—I was really on the point of going.

Hedda. Oh, you can't be in such a hurry.—Well? Now tell me something about your life at home.

Mrs. Elvsted. Oh, that is just what I care least to speak about.

Hedda. But to me, dear—? Why, weren't we school-fellows?

Mrs. Elvsted. Yes, but you were in the class above me. Oh, how dreadfully afraid of you I was then!

Hedda. Afraid of me?

Mrs. Elvsted. *Yes*, dreadfully. For when we met on the stairs you used always to pull my hair.

Hedda. Did I, really?

Mrs. Elvsted. Yes, and once you said you would burn it off my head.

Hedda. Oh, that was all nonsense, of course.

Mrs. Elvsted. Yes, but I was so silly in those days.—And since then, too—we have drifted so far—far apart from each other. Our circles have been so entirely different.

Hedda. Well, then, we must try to drift together again. Now listen! At school we said *du* to each other; and we called each other by our Christian names—

Mrs. Elvsted. No, I am sure you must be mistaken.

Hedda. No, not at all! I can remember quite distinctly. So now we are going to renew our old friendship. [*Draws the foot-stool closer to* Mrs. Elvsted.] There now! [*Kisses her cheek.*] You must say *du* to me and call me Hedda.

Mrs. Elvsted [*presses and pats her hands*]. Oh, how good and kind you are! I am not used to such kindness.

Hedda. There, there, there! And I shall say *du* to you, as in the old days, and call you my dear Thora.

Mrs. Elvsted. My name is Thea.

Hedda. Why, of course! I meant Thea. [*Looks at her compassionately.*] So you are not accustomed to goodness and kindness, Thea? Not in your own home?

Mrs. Elvsted. Oh, if I only had a home! But I haven't any; I have never had a home.

Hedda [*looks at her for a moment*]. I almost suspected as much.

Mrs. Elvsted [*gazing helplessly before her*]. Yes—yes—yes.

Hedda. I don't quite remember—was it not as housekeeper that you first went to Mr. Elvsted's?

Mrs. Elvsted. I really went as governess. But his wife—his late wife—was an invalid,—and rarely left her room. So I had to look after the housekeeping as well.

Hedda. And then—at last—you became mistress of the house.

Mrs. Elvsted [*sadly*]. Yes, I did.

Hedda. Let me see—about how long ago was that?

Mrs. Elvsted. My marriage?

Hedda. Yes.

MRS. ELVSTED. Five years ago.

HEDDA. To be sure; it must be that.

MRS. ELVSTED. Oh, those five years—! Or at all events the last two or three of them! Oh, if you could only imagine—

HEDDA [*giving her a little slap on the hand*]. De?[6] Fie, Thea!

MRS. ELVSTED. Yes, yes, I will try— Well if—you could only imagine and understand—

HEDDA [*lightly*]. Eilert Lövborg has been in your neighborhood about three years, hasn't he?

MRS. ELVSTED [*looks at her doubtfully*]. Eilert Lövborg? Yes—he has.

HEDDA. Had you known him before, in town here?

MRS. ELVSTED. Scarcely at all. I mean—I knew him by name of course.

HEDDA. But you saw a good deal of him in the country?

MRS. ELVSTED. Yes, he came to us every day. You see, he gave the children lessons; for in the long run I couldn't manage it all myself.

HEDDA. No, that's clear.—And your husband—? I suppose he is often away from home?

MRS. ELVSTED. Yes. Being Sheriff, you know, he has to travel about a good deal in his district.

HEDDA [*leaning against the arm of the chair*]. Thea—my poor, sweet Thea—now you must tell me everything—exactly as it stands.

MRS. ELVSTED. Well then, you must question me.

HEDDA. What sort of a man is your husband, Thea? I mean—you know—in everyday life. Is he kind to you?

MRS. ELVSTED [*evasively*]. I am sure he means well in everything.

HEDDA. I should think he must be altogether too old for you. There is at least twenty years' difference between you, is there not?

MRS. ELVSTED [*irritably*]. Yes, that is true, too. Everything about him is repellent to me! We have not a thought in common. We have no single point of sympathy—he and I.

HEDDA. But is he not fond of you all the same? In his own way?

MRS. ELVSTED. Oh, I really don't know. I think he regards me simply as a useful property. And then it doesn't cost much to keep me. I am not expensive.

HEDDA. That is stupid of you.

MRS. ELVSTED [*shakes her head*]. It cannot be otherwise—not with him. I don't think he really cares for any one but himself—and perhaps a little for the children.

HEDDA. And for Eilbert Lövborg, Thea.

MRS. ELVSTED [*looking at her*]. For Eilert Lövborg? What puts that into your head?

HEDDA. Well, my dear—I should say, when he sends you after him all the way to town—[*smiling almost imperceptibly*]. And besides, you said so yourself, to Tesman.

MRS. ELVSTED [*with a little nervous twitch*]. Did I? Yes, I suppose I did. [*Vehemently, but not loudly.*] No—I may just as well make a clean breast of it at once! For it must all come out in any case.

HEDDA. Why, my dear Thea—?

---

[6] *De* is the formal second-person pronoun. Hedda wishes Thea to use the more intimate pronoun *du*.

MRS. ELVSTED. Well, to make a long story short: My husband did not know that I was coming.

HEDDA. What! Your husband didn't know it!

MRS. ELVSTED. No, of course not. For that matter, he was away from home himself—he was traveling. Oh, I could bear it no longer, Hedda! I couldn't indeed—so utterly alone as I should have been in future.

HEDDA. Well? And then?

MRS. ELVSTED. So I put together some of my things—what I needed most—as quietly as possible. And then I left the house.

HEDDA. Without a word?

MRS. ELVSTED. Yes—and took the train straight to town.

HEDDA. Why, my dear, good Thea—to think of you daring to do it!

MRS. ELVSTED [*rises and moves about the room*]. What else could I possibly do?

HEDDA. But what do you think your husband will say when you go home again?

MRS. ELVSTED [*at the table, looks at her*]. Back to him?

HEDDA. Of course.

MRS. ELVSTED. I shall never go back to him again.

HEDDA [*rising and going towards her*]. Then you have left your home—for good and all?

MRS. ELVSTED. Yes. There was nothing else to be done.

HEDDA. But then—to take flight so openly.

MRS. ELVSTED. Oh, it's impossible to keep things of that sort secret.

HEDDA. But what do you think people will say of you, Thea?

MRS. ELVSTED. They may say what they like for aught *I* care. [*Seats herself wearily and sadly on the sofa.*] I have done nothing but what I had to do.

HEDDA [*after a short silence*]. And what are your plans now? What do you think of doing?

MRS. ELVSTED. I don't know yet. I only know this, that I must live here, where Eilert Lövborg is—if I am to live at all.

HEDDA [*takes a chair from the table, seats herself beside her, and strokes her hands*]. My dear Thea—how did this—this friendship—between you and Eilert Lövborg come about?

MRS. ELVSTED. Oh, it grew up gradually. I gained a sort of influence over him.

HEDDA. Indeed?

MRS. ELVSTED. He gave up his old habits. Not because I asked him to, for I never dared do that. But of course he saw how repulsive they were to me; and so he dropped them.

HEDDA [*concealing an involuntary smile of scorn*]. Then you have reclaimed him—as the saying goes—my little Thea.

MRS. ELVSTED. So he says himself, at any rate. And he, on his side, has made a real human being of me—taught me to think, and to understand so many things.

HEDDA. Did he give you lessons too, then?

MRS. ELVSTED. No, not exactly lessons. But he talked to me—talked about such an infinity of things. And then came the lovely, happy time when I began to share in his work—when he allowed me to help him!

HEDDA. Oh, he did, did he?

MRS. ELVSTED. Yes! He never wrote anything without my assistance.

HEDDA. You were two good comrades, in fact?

MRS. ELVSTED [*eagerly*]. Comrades! Yes, fancy, Hedda—that is the very word he used!—Oh, I ought to feel perfectly happy; and yet I cannot; for I don't know how long it will last.

HEDDA. Are you no surer of him than that?

MRS. ELVSTED [*gloomily*]. A woman's shadow stands between Eilert Lövborg and me.

HEDDA [*looks at her anxiously*]. Who can that be?

MRS. ELVSTED. I don't know. Some one he knew in his—in his past. Some one he has never been able wholly to forget.

HEDDA. What has he told you—about this?

MRS. ELVSTED. He has only once—quite vaguely—alluded to it.

HEDDA. Well! And what did he say?

MRS. ELVSTED. He said that when they parted, she threatened to shoot him with a pistol.

HEDDA [*with cold composure*]. Oh, nonsense! No one does that sort of thing here.

MRS. ELVSTED. No. And that is why I think it must have been that red-haired singing woman whom he once—

HEDDA. Yes, very likely.

MRS. ELVSTED. For I remember they used to say of her that she carried loaded firearms.

HEDDA. Oh—then of course it must have been she.

MRS. ELVSTED [*wringing her hands*]. And now just fancy, Hedda—I hear that this singing-woman—that she is in town again! Oh, I don't know what to do—

HEDDA [*glancing towards the inner room*]. Hush! Here comes Tesman. [*Rises and whispers.*] Thea—all this must remain between you and me.

MRS. ELVSTED [*springing up*]. Oh, yes, yes! for heaven's sake—!

[GEORGE TESMAN, *with a letter in his hand, comes from the right through the inner room.*]

TESMAN. There now—the epistle is finished.

HEDDA. That's right. And now Mrs. Elvsted is just going. Wait a moment— I'll go with you to the garden gate.

TESMAN. Do you think Berta could post the letter, Hedda dear?

HEDDA [*takes it*]. I will tell her so.

[BERTA *enters from the hall.*]

BERTA. Judge Brack wishes to know if Mrs. Tesman will receive him.

HEDDA. Yes, ask Judge Brack to come in. And look here—put this letter in the post.

BERTA [*taking the letter*]. Yes, ma'am.

[*She opens the door for* JUDGE BRACK *and goes out herself.* BRACK *is a man of forty-five; thick-set, but well-built and elastic in his movements. His face is roundish with an aristocratic profile. His hair is short, still almost black, and carefully dressed. His eyes are lively and sparkling. His eyebrows thick. His moustaches are also thick, with short-cut ends. He wears a well-cut walking-suit, a little too youthful for his age. He uses an eye-glass, which he now and then lets drop.*]

JUDGE BRACK [*with his hat in his hand, bowing*]. May one venture to call so early in the day?

HEDDA. Of course one may.

TESMAN [*presses his hand*]. You are welcome at any time. [*Introducing him.*] Judge Brack—Miss Rysing—

HEDDA. Oh—!

BRACK [*bowing*]. Ah—delighted—

HEDDA [*looks at him and laughs*]. It's nice to have a look at you by daylight, Judge!

BRACK. Do you find me—altered?

HEDDA. A little younger, I think.

BRACK. Thank you so much.

TESMAN. But what do you think of Hedda—eh? Doesn't she look flourishing? She has actually—

HEDDA. Oh, do leave me alone. You haven't thanked Judge Brack for all the trouble he has taken—

BRACK. Oh, nonsense—it was a pleasure to me—

HEDDA. Yes, you are a friend indeed. But here stands Thea all impatience to be off—so *au revoir,* Judge. I shall be back again presently. [*Mutual salutations. Mrs.* ELVSTED *and* HEDDA *go out by the hall door.*]

BRACK. Well,—is your wife tolerably satisfied—

TESMAN. Yes, we can't thank you sufficiently. Of course she talks of a little re-arrangement here and there; and one or two things are still wanting. We shall have to buy some additional trifles.

BRACK. Indeed!

TESMAN. But we won't trouble you about these things. Hedda says she herself will look after what is wanting.—Shan't we sit down? Eh?

BRACK. Thanks, for a moment. [*Seats himself beside the table.*] There is something I wanted to speak to you about, my dear Tesman.

TESMAN. Indeed? Ah, I understand! [*Seating himself.*] I suppose it's the serious part of the frolic that is coming now. Eh?

BRACK. Oh, the money question is not so very pressing; though, for that matter, I wish we had gone a little more economically to work.

TESMAN. But that would never have done, you know! Think of Hedda, my dear fellow! You, who know her so well—. I couldn't possibly ask her to put up with a shabby style of living!

BRACK. No, no—that is just the difficulty.

TESMAN. And then—fortunately—it can't be long before I receive my appointment.

BRACK. Well, you see—such things are often apt to hang fire for a time.

TESMAN. Have you heard anything definite? Eh?

BRACK. Nothing exactly definite—[*interrupting himself*]. But by-the-bye—I have one piece of news for you.

TESMAN. Well?

BRACK. Your old friend, Eilert Lövborg, has returned to town.

TESMAN. I know that already.

BRACK. Indeed! How did you learn it?

TESMAN. From that lady who went out with Hedda.

BRACK. Really? What was her name? I didn't quite catch it.

TESMAN. Mrs. Elvsted.

BRACK. Aha—Sheriff Elvsted's wife? Of course—he has been living up in their regions.

TESMAN. And fancy—I'm delighted to hear that he is quite a reformed character!

BRACK. So they say.

TESMAN. And then he has published a new book—eh?

BRACK. Yes, indeed he has.

TESMAN. And I hear it has made some sensation!

BRACK. Quite an unusual sensation.

TESMAN. Fancy—isn't that good news! A man of such extraordinary talents—
I felt so grieved to think that he had gone irretrievably to ruin.

BRACK. That was what everybody thought.

TESMAN. But I cannot imagine what he will take to now! How in the world
will he be able to make his living? Eh?

[*During the last words,* HEDDA *has entered by the hall door.*]

HEDDA [*to* BRACK, *laughing with a touch of scorn*]. Tesman is forever worrying
about how people are to make their living.

TESMAN. Well, you see, dear—we were talking about poor Eilert Lövborg.

HEDDA [*glancing at him rapidly*]. Oh, indeed? [*Seats herself in the arm-chair beside
the stove and asks indifferently.*] What is the matter with him?

TESMAN. Well—no doubt he has run through all his property long ago; and
he can scarcely write a new book every year—eh? So I really can't see what
is to become of him.

BRACK. Perhaps I can give you some information on that point.

TESMAN. Indeed!

BRACK. You must remember that his relations have a good deal of influence.

TESMAN. Oh, his relations, unfortunately have entirely washed their hands of
him.

BRACK. At one time they called him the hope of the family.

TESMAN. At one time, yes! But he has put an end to all that.

HEDDA. Who knows? [*With a slight smile.*] I hear they have reclaimed him up
at Sheriff Elvsted's—

BRACK. And then this book that he has published—

TESMAN. Well, well, I hope to goodness they may find something for him to
do. I have just written to him. I asked him to come and see us this evening,
Hedda dear.

BRACK. But, my dear fellow, you are booked for my bachelors' party this evening.
You promised on the pier last night.

HEDDA. Had you forgotten, Tesman?

TESMAN. Yes, I had utterly forgotten.

BRACK. But it doesn't matter, for you may be sure he won't come.

TESMAN. What makes you think that? Eh?

BRACK [*with a little hesitation, rising and resting his hands on the back of his chair*].
My dear Tesman—and you too, Mrs. Tesman—I think I ought not to keep
you in the dark about something that—that—

TESMAN. That concerns Eilert—?

BRACK. Both you and him.

TESMAN. Well, my dear Judge, out with it.

BRACK. You must be prepared to find your appointment deferred longer than
you desired or expected.

TESMAN [*jumping up uneasily*]. Is there some hitch about it? Eh?

BRACK. The nomination may perhaps be made conditional on the result of a
competition—

TESMAN. Competition! Think of that, Hedda!

HEDDA [*leans farther back in the chair*]. Aha—aha!

TESMAN. But who can my competitor be? Surely not—?

BRACK. Yes, precisely—Eilert Lövborg.

TESMAN [*clasping his hands*]. No, no—it's quite inconceivable! Quite impossible!
Eh?

BRACK. H'm—that is what it may come to, all the same.

TESMAN. Well but, Judge Brack—it would show the most incredible lack of consideration for me. [*Gesticulates with his arms.*] For—just think—I'm a married man. We have been married on the strength of these prospects, Hedda and I; and run deep into debt; and borrowed money from Aunt Julia too. Good heavens, they had as good as promised me the appointment. Eh?

BRACK. Well, well, well—no doubt you will get it in the end; only after a contest.

HEDDA [*immovable in her arm-chair*]. Fancy, Tesman, there will be a sort of sporting interest in that.

TESMAN. Why, my dearest Hedda, how can you be so indifferent about it?

HEDDA [*as before*]. I am not at all indifferent. I am most eager to see who wins.

BRACK. In any case, Mrs. Tesman, it is best that you should know how matters stand. I mean—before you set about the little purchases I hear you are threatening.

HEDDA. This can make no difference.

BRACK. Indeed! Then I have no more to say. Good-bye! [*To* TESMAN.] I shall look in on my way back from my afternoon walk, and take you home with me.

TESMAN. Oh yes, yes—your news has quite upset me.

HEDDA [*reclining, holds out her hand*]. Good-bye, Judge; and be sure you call in the afternoon.

BRACK. Many thanks. Good-bye, good-bye!

TESMAN [*accompanying him to the door*]. Good-bye, my dear Judge! You must really excuse me—

[JUDGE BRACK *goes out by the hall door.*]

TESMAN [*crosses the room*]. Oh, Hedda—one should never rush into adventures. Eh?

HEDDA [*looks at him, smiling*]. Do you do that?

TESMAN. Yes, dear—there is no denying—it was adventurous to go and marry and set up house upon mere expectations.

HEDDA. Perhaps you are right there.

TESMAN. Well—at all events, we have our delightful home, Hedda! Fancy, the home we both dreamed of—the home we were in love with, I may almost say. Eh?

HEDDA [*rising slowly and wearily*]. It was part of our compact that we were to go into society—to keep open house.

TESMAN. Yes, if you only knew how I had been looking forward to it! Fancy—to see you as hostess—in a select circle? Eh? Well, well, well—for the present we shall have to get on without society, Hedda—only to invite Aunt Julia now and then.—Oh, I intended you to lead such an utterly different life, dear—!

HEDDA. Of course I cannot have my man in livery just yet.

TESMAN. Oh no, unfortunately. It would be out of the question for us to keep a footman, you know.

HEDDA. And the saddle-horse I was to have had—

TESMAN [*aghast*]. The saddle-horse!

HEDDA.—I suppose I must not think of that now.

TESMAN. Good heavens, no!—that's as clear as daylight.

HEDDA [*goes up the room*]. Well, I shall have one thing at least to kill time with in the meanwhile.

TESMAN [*beaming*]. Oh, thank heaven for that! What is it, Hedda? Eh?

HEDDA [*in the middle doorway, looks at him with covert scorn*]. My pistols, George.

TESMAN [*in alarm*]. Your pistols!

HEDDA [*with cold eyes*]. General Gabler's pistols.

[*She goes out through the inner room, to the left.*]

TESMAN [*rushes up to the middle doorway and calls after her.*] No, for heaven's sake, Hedda darling—don't touch those dangerous things! For my sake, Hedda! Eh?

ACT II

The room at the TESMANS' *as in the first act, except that the piano has been removed, and an elegant little writing-table with bookshelves put in its place. A smaller table stands near the sofa at the left. Most of the bouquets have been taken away.* MRS. ELVSTED'S *bouquet is upon the large table in front.—It is afternoon.*

HEDDA, *dressed to receive callers, is alone in the room. She stands by the open glass door, loading a revolver. The fellow to it lies in an open pistol-case on the writing-table.*

HEDDA [*looks down the garden, and calls*]. So you are here again, Judge!

BRACK [*is heard calling from a distance*]. As you see, Mrs. Tesman!

HEDDA [*raises the pistol and points*]. Now I'll shoot you, Judge Brack!

BRACK [*calling unseen*]. No, no, no! Don't stand aiming at me!

HEDDA. This is what comes of sneaking in by the back way. [*She fires.*]

BRACK [*nearer*]. Are you out of your senses—!

HEDDA. Dear me—did I happen to hit you?

BRACK [*still outside*]. I wish you would let these pranks alone!

HEDDA. Come in then, Judge.

[JUDGE BRACK, *dressed as though for a men's party, enters by the glass door. He carries a light overcoat over his arm.*]

BRACK. What the deuce—haven't you tired of that sport, yet? What are you shooting at?

HEDDA. Oh, I am only firing in the air.

BRACK [*gently takes the pistol out of her hand*]. Allow me, madam! [*Looks at it.*] Ah—I know this pistol well! [*Looks around.*] Where is the case? Ah, here it is. [*Lays the pistol in it, and shuts it.*] Now we won't play at that game any more today.

HEDDA. Then what in heaven's name would you have me do with myself?

BRACK. Have you had no visitors?

HEDDA [*closing the glass door*]. Not one. I suppose all our set are still out of town.

BRACK. And is Tesman not at home either?

HEDDA [*at the writing-table, putting the pistol-case in a drawer which she shuts*]. No. He rushed off to his aunt's directly after lunch; he didn't expect you so early.

BRACK. H'm—how stupid of me not to have thought of that!

HEDDA [*turning her head to look at him*]. Why stupid?

BRACK. Because if I had thought of it I should have come a little—earlier.

HEDDA [*crossing the room*]. Then you would have found no one to receive you; for I have been in my room changing my dress ever since lunch.

BRACK. And is there no sort of little chink that we could hold a parley through?

HEDDA. You have forgotten to arrange one.

BRACK. That was another piece of stupidity.

HEDDA. Well, we must just settle down here—and wait. Tesman is not likely to be back for some time yet.

BRACK. Never mind; I shall not be impatient.

[HEDDA *seats herself in the corner of the sofa.* HEDDA *lays his overcoat over the back of the nearest chair, and sits down, but keeps his hat in his hand. A short silence. They look at each other.*]

HEDDA. Well?

BRACK [*in the same tone*]. Well?

HEDDA. I spoke first.

BRACK [*bending a little forward*]. Come, let us have a cosy little chat, Mrs. Hedda.

HEDDA [*leaning further back in the sofa*]. Does it not seem like a whole eternity since our last talk? Of course I don't count those few words yesterday evening and this morning.

BRACK. You mean since our last confidential talk? Our last *tête-à-tête*?[7]

HEDDA. Well, yes—since you put it so.

BRACK. Not a day has passed but I have wished that you were home again.

HEDDA. And I have done nothing but wish the same thing.

BRACK. You? Really, Mrs. Hedda? And I thought you had been enjoying your tour so much!

HEDDA. Oh, yes, you may be sure of that!

BRACK. But Tesman's letters spoke of nothing but happiness.

HEDDA. Oh, Tesman! You see, he thinks nothing so delightful as grubbing in libraries and making copies of old parchments, or whatever you call them.

BRACK [*with a spice of malice*]. Well, that is his vocation in life—or part of it at any rate.

HEDDA. Yes, of course; and no doubt when it's your vocation—But *I!* Oh, my dear Mr. Brack, how mortally bored I have been.

BRACK [*sympathetically*]. Do you really say so? In downright earnest?

HEDDA. Yes, you can surely understand it—! To go for six whole months without meeting a soul that knew anything of our circle, or could talk about the things we are interested in.

BRACK. Yes, yes—I too should feel that a deprivation.

HEDDA. And then, what I found most intolerable of all—

BRACK. Well?

HEDDA. —was being everlastingly in the company of—one and the same person—

BRACK [*with a nod of assent*]. Morning, noon, and night, yes—at all possible times and seasons.

HEDDA. I said "everlastingly."

BRACK. Just so. But I should have thought, with our excellent Tesman, one could—

HEDDA. Tesman is—a specialist, my dear Judge.

BRACK. Undeniably.

HEDDA. And specialists are not at all amusing to travel with. Not in the long run at any rate.

BRACK. Not even—the specialist one happens to love?

HEDDA. Faugh—don't use that sickening word!

BRACK [*taken aback*]. What do you say, Mrs. Hedda?

---

[7] Private conversation.

HEDDA [*half laughing, half irritated*]. You should just try it! To hear of nothing but the history of civilization, morning, noon, and night—

BRACK. Everlastingly.

HEDDA. Yes, yes, yes! And then all this about the domestic industry of the middle ages—! That's the most disgusting part of it!

BRACK [*looks searchingly at her*]. But tell me—in that case, how am I to understand your—? H'm—

HEDDA. My accepting George Tesman, you mean?

BRACK. Well, let us put it so.

HEDDA. Good heavens, do you see anything so wonderful in that?

BRACK. Yes and no—Mrs. Hedda.

HEDDA. I had positively danced myself tired, my dear Judge. My day was done— [*With a slight shudder.*] Oh no—I won't say that; nor think it either!

BRACK. You have assuredly no reason to.

HEDDA. Oh, reasons— [*Watching him closely.*] And George Tesman—after all, you must admit that he is correctness itself.

BRACK. His correctness and respectability are beyond all question.

HEDDA. And I don't see anything absolutely ridiculous about him.—Do you?

BRACK. Ridiculous? N—no—I shouldn't exactly say so—

HEDDA. Well—and his powers of research, at all events, are untiring.—I see no reason why he should not one day come to the front, after all.

BRACK [*looks at her hesitatingly*]. I thought that you, like every one else, expected him to attain the highest distinction.

HEDDA [*with an expression of fatigue*]. Yes, so I did.—And then, since he was bent, at all hazards, on being allowed to provide for me—I really don't know why I should not have accepted his offer?

BRACK. No—if you look at it in that light—

HEDDA. It was more than my other adorers were prepared to do for me, my dear Judge.

BRACK [*laughing*]. Well, I can't answer for all the rest; but as for myself, you know quite well that I have always entertained a—a certain respect for the marriage tie—for marriage as an institution, Mrs. Hedda.

HEDDA [*jestingly*]. Oh, I assure you I have never cherished any hopes with respect to you.

BRACK. All I require is a pleasant and intimate interior, where I can make myself useful in every way, and am free to come and go as—a trusted friend—

HEDDA. Of the master of the house, do you mean?

BRACK [*bowing*]. Frankly—of the mistress first of all; but of course of the master, too, in the second place. Such a triangular friendhsip—if I may call it so— is really a great convenience for all parties, let me tell you.

HEDDA. Yes, I have many a time longed for some one to make a third on our travels. Oh—those railway-carriage *tête-à-têtes*—!

BRACK. Fortunately your wedding journey is over now.

HEDDA [*shaking her head*]. Not by a long—long way. I have only arrived at a station on the line.

BRACK. Well, then the passengers jump out and move about a little, Mrs. Hedda.

HEDDA. I never jump out.

BRACK. Really?

HEDDA. No—because there is always some one standing by to—

BRACK [*laughing*]. To look at your ankles, do you mean?

HEDDA. Precisely.

BRACK. Well but, dear me—

HEDDA [*with a gesture of repulsion*]. I won't have it. I would rather keep my seat where I happen to be—and continue the *tête-à-tête.*

BRACK. But suppose a third person were to jump in and join the couple.

HEDDA. Ah—that is quite another matter!

BRACK. A trusted, sympathetic friend—

HEDDA. —with a fund of conversation on all sorts of lively topics—

BRACK. —and not the least bit of a specialist!

HEDDA [*with an audible sigh*]. Yes, that would be a relief indeed.

BRACK [*hears the front door open, and glances in that direction*]. The triangle is completed.

HEDDA [*half aloud*]. And on goes the train.

[GEORGE TESMAN, *in a gray walking-suit, with a soft felt hat, enters from the hall. He has a number of unbound books under his arm and in his pockets.*]

TESMAN [*goes up to the table beside the corner settee*]. Ouf—what a load for a warm day—all these books. [*Lays them on the table.*] I'm positively perspiring, Hedda. Hallo—are you there already, my dear Judge? Eh? Berta didn't tell me.

BRACK [*rising*]. I came in through the garden.

HEDDA. What books have you got here?

TESMAN [*stands looking them through*]. Some new books on my special subjects—quite indispensable to me.

HEDDA. Your special subjects?

BRACK. Yes, books on his special subjects, Mrs. Tesman. [BRACK *and* HEDDA *exchange a confidential smile.*]

HEDDA. Do you need still more books on your special subjects?

TESMAN. Yes, my dear Hedda, one can never have too many of them. Of course one must keep up with all that is written and published.

HEDDA. Yes, I suppose one must.

TESMAN [*searching among his books*]. And look here—I have got hold of Eilert Lövborg's new book too. [*Offering it to her.*] Perhaps you would like to glance through it, Hedda? Eh?

HEDDA. No, thank you. Or rather—afterwards perhaps.

TESMAN. I looked into it a little on the way home.

BRACK. Well, what do you think of it—as a specialist?

TESMAN. I think it shows quite remarkable soundness of judgment. He never wrote like that before. [*Putting the books together.*] Now I shall take all these into my study. I'm longing to cut the leaves—! And then I must change my clothes. [*To* BRACK.] I suppose we needn't start just yet? Eh?

BRACK. Oh, dear no—there is not the slightest hurry.

TESMAN. Well then, I will take my time. [*Is going with his books, but stops in the doorway and turns.*] By-the-bye, Hedda—Aunt Julia is not coming this evening.

HEDDA. Not coming? Is it that affair of the bonnet that keeps her away?

TESMAN. Oh, not at all. How could you think such a thing of Aunt Julia? Just fancy—! The fact is, Aunt Rina is very ill.

HEDDA. She always is.

TESMAN. Yes, but today she is much worse than usual, poor dear.

HEDDA. Oh, then it's only natural that her sister should remain with her. I must bear my disappointment.

TESMAN. And you can't imagine, dear, how delighted Aunt Julia seemed to be—because you had come home looking so flourishing!

HEDDA [*half aloud, rising*]. Oh, those everlasting aunts!

TESMAN. What?

HEDDA [*going to the glass door*]. Nothing.

TESMAN. Oh, all right.

[*He goes through the inner room, out to the right.*]

BRACK. What bonnet were you talking about?

HEDDA. Oh, it was a little episode with Miss Tesman this morning. She had laid down her bonnet on the chair there—[*looks at him and smiles*].—And I pretended to think it was the servant's.

BRACK [*shaking his head*]. Now my dear Mrs. Hedda, how could you do such a thing? To that excellent old lady, too!

HEDDA [*nervously crossing the room*]. Well, you see—these impulses come over me all of a sudden; and I cannot resist them. [*Throws herself down in the easy-chair by the stove.*] Oh, I don't know how to explain it.

BRACK [*behind the easy-chair.*] You are not really happy—that is at the bottom of it.

HEDDA [*looking straight before her*]. I know of no reason why I should be—happy. Perhaps you can give me one?

BRACK. Well—amongst other things, because you have got exactly the home you had set your heart on.

HEDDA [*looks up at him and laughs*]. Do you too believe in that legend?

BRACK. Is there nothing in it, then?

HEDDA. Oh, yes, there is something in it.

BRACK. Well?

HEDDA. There is this in it, that I made use of Tesman to see me home from evening parties last summer—

BRACK. I, unfortunately, had to go quite a different way.

HEDDA. That's true. I know you were going a different way last summer.

BRACK [*laughing*]. Oh fie, Mrs. Hedda! Well, then—you and Tesman—?

HEDDA. Well, we happened to pass here one evening; Tesman, poor fellow, was writhing in the agony of having to find conversation; so I took pity on the learned man—

BRACK [*smiles doubtfully*]. You took pity? H'm—

HEDDA. Yes, I really did. And so—to help him out of his torment—I happened to say, in pure thoughtlessness, that I should like to live in this villa.

BRACK. No more than that?

HEDDA. Not that evening.

BRACK. But afterwards?

HEDDA. Yes, my thoughtlessness had consequences, my dear Judge.

BRACK. Unfortunately that too often happens, Mrs. Hedda.

HEDDA. Thanks! So you see it was this enthusiasm for Secretary Falk's villa that first constituted a bond of sympathy between George Tesman and me. From that came our engagement and our marriage, and our wedding journey, and all the rest of it. Well, well, my dear Judge—as you make your bed so you must lie, I could almost say.

BRACK. This is exquisite! And you really cared not a rap about it all the time?

HEDDA. No, heaven knows I didn't.

BRACK. But now? Now that we have made it so homelike for you?

HEDDA. Uh—the rooms all seem to smell of lavender and dried rose-leaves.— But perhaps it's Aunt Julia that has brought that scent with her.

BRACK [*laughing*]. No, I think it must be a legacy from the late Mrs. Secretary Falk.

HEDDA. Yes, there is an odor of mortality about it. It reminds me of a bouquet—the day after the ball. [*Clasps her hands behind her head, leans back in her chair and looks at him.*] Oh, my dear Judge—you cannot imagine how horribly I shall bore myself here.

BRACK. Why should not you, too, find some sort of vocation in life, Mrs. Hedda?

HEDDA. A vocation—that should attract me?

BRACK. If possible, of course.

HEDDA. Heaven knows what sort of a vocation that could be. I often wonder whether—[*breaking off*]. But that would never do either.

BRACK. Who can tell? Let me hear what it is.

HEDDA. Whether I might not get Tesman to go into politics, I mean.

BRACK [*laughing*]. Tesman? No, really now, political life is not the thing for him—not at all in his line.

HEDDA. No, I daresay not.—But if I could get him into it all the same?

BRACK. Why—what satisfaction could you find in that? If he is not fitted for that sort of thing, why should you want to drive him into it?

HEDDA. Because I am bored, I tell you! [*After a pause.*] So you think it quite out of the question that Tesman should ever get into the ministry?

BRACK. H'm—you see, my dear Mrs. Hedda—to get into the ministry, he would have to be a tolerably rich man.

HEDDA [*rising impatiently*]. Yes, there we have it! It is this genteel poverty I have managed to drop into—! [*Crosses the room.*] That is what makes life so pitiable! So utterly ludicrous!—For that's what it is.

BRACK. Now *I* should say the fault lay elsewhere.

HEDDA. Where, then?

BRACK. You have never gone through any really stimulating experience.

HEDDA. Anything serious, you mean?

BRACK. Yes, you may call it so. But now you may perhaps have one in store.

HEDDA [*tossing her head*]. Oh, you're thinking of the annoyances about this wretched professorship! But that must be Tesman's own affair. I assure you I shall not waste a thought upon it.

BRACK. No, no. I daresay not. But suppose now that what people call—in elegant language—a solemn responsibility were to come upon you? [*Smiling.*] A new responsibility, Mrs. Hedda?

HEDDA [*angrily*]. Be quiet! Nothing of that sort will ever happen!

BRACK [*warily*]. We will speak of this again a year hence—at the very outside.

HEDDA [*curtly*]. I have no turn for anything of the sort, Judge Brack. No responsibilities for me!

BRACK. Are you so unlike the generality of women as to have no turn for duties which—?

HEDDA [*beside the glass door*]. Oh, be quiet, I tell you!—I often think there is only one thing in the world I have any turn for.

BRACK [*drawing near to her*]. And what is that, if I may ask?

HEDDA [*stands looking out*]. Boring myself to death. Now you know it. [*Turns, looks towards the inner room, and laughs.*] Yes, as I thought! Here comes the Professor.

BRACK [*softly, in a tone of warning*]. Come, come, come, Mrs. Hedda!

[GEORGE TESMAN, *dressed for the party, with his gloves and hat in his hand, enters from the right through the inner room.*]

TESMAN. Hedda, has no message come from Eilert Lövborg? Eh?

HEDDA. No.

TESMAN. Then you'll see he'll be here presently.

BRACK. Do you really think he will come?

TESMAN. Yes, I am almost sure of it. For what you were telling us this morning must have been a mere floating rumor.

BRACK. You think so?

TESMAN. At any rate, Aunt Julia said she did not believe for a moment that he would ever stand in my way again. Fancy that!

BRACK. Well then, that's all right.

TESMAN [*placing his hat and gloves on a chair on the right*]. Yes, but you must really let me wait for him as long as possible.

BRACK. We have plenty of time yet. None of my guests will arrive before seven or half-past.

TESMAN. Then meanwhile we can keep Hedda company, and see what happens. Eh?

HEDDA [*placing* BRACK*'s hat and overcoat upon the corner settee*]. And at the worst Mr. Lövborg can remain here with me.

BRACK [*offering to take his things*]. Oh, allow me, Mrs. Tesman!—What do you mean by "At the worst"?

HEDDA. If he won't go with you and Tesman.

TESMAN [*looks dubiously at her*]. But, Hedda dear—do you think it would quite do for him to remain with you? Eh? Remember, Aunt Julia can't come.

HEDDA. No, but Mrs. Elvsted is coming. We three can have a cup of tea together.

TESMAN. Oh, yes, that will be all right.

BRACK [*smiling*]. And that would perhaps be the safest plan for him.

HEDDA. Why so?

BRACK. Well, you know, Mrs. Tesman, how you used to gird at my little bachelor parties. You declared they were adapted only for men of the strictest principles.

HEDDA. But no doubt Mr. Lövborg's principles are strict enough now. A converted sinner—

[BERTA *appears at the hall door.*]

BERTA. There's a gentleman asking if you are at home, ma'am—

HEDDA. Well, show him in.

TESMAN [*softly*]. I'm sure it is he! Fancy that!

[EILERT LÖVBORG *enters from the hall. He is slim and lean; of the same age as* TESMAN, *but looks older and somewhat worn-out. His hair and beard are of a blackish brown, his face long and pale, but with patches of color on the cheek-bones. He is dressed in a well-cut black visiting suit, quite new. He has dark gloves and a silk hat. He stops near the door, and makes a rapid bow, seeming somewhat embarrassed.*]

TESMAN [*goes up to him and shakes him warmly by the hand*]. Well, my dear Eilert—so at last we meet again!

EILERT LÖVBORG [*speaks in a subdued voice*]. Thanks for your letter, Tesman. [*Approaching* HEDDA.] Will you too shake hands with me, Mrs. Tesman?

HEDDA [*taking his hand*]. I am glad to see you, Mr. Lövborg. [*With a motion of her hand.*] I don't know whether you two gentlemen—?

LÖVBORG [*bowing slightly*]. Judge Brack, I think.

BRACK [*doing likewise*]. Oh, yes,—in the old days—

TESMAN [*to* LÖVBORG, *with his hands on his shoulders*]. And now you must make yourself entirely at home, Eilert! Mustn't he, Hedda?—For I hear you are going to settle in town again? Eh?

LÖVBORG. Yes, I am.

TESMAN. Quite right, quite right. Let me tell you, I have got hold of your new book; but I haven't had time to read it yet.

LÖVBORG. You may spare yourself the trouble.

TESMAN. Why so?

LÖVBORG. Because there is very little in it.

TESMAN. Just fancy—how can you say so?

BRACK. But it has been very much praised, I hear.

LÖVBORG. That was what I wanted; so I put nothing into the book but what every one would agree with.

BRACK. Very wise of you.

TESMAN. Well but, my dear Eilert—!

LÖVBORG. For now I mean to win myself a position again—to make a fresh start.

TESMAN [*a little embarrassed*]. Ah, that is what you wish to do? Eh?

LÖVBORG [*smiling, lays down his hat, and draws a packet, wrapped in paper, from his coat pocket*]. But when this one appears, George Tesman, you will have to read it. For this is the real book—the book I have put my true self into.

TESMAN. Indeed? And what is it?

LÖVBORG. It is the continuation.

TESMAN. The continuation? Of what?

LÖVBORG. Of the book.

TESMAN. Of the new book?

LÖVBORG. Of course.

TESMAN. Why, my dear Eilert—does it not come down to our own days?

LÖVBORG. Yes, it does; and this one deals with the future.

TESMAN. With the future! But, good heavens, we know nothing of the future!

LÖVBORG. No; but there is a thing or two to be said about it all the same. [*Opens the packet.*] Look here—

TESMAN. Why, that's not your handwriting.

LÖVBORG. I dictated it. [*Turning over the pages.*] It falls into two sections. The first deals with the civilizing forces of the future. And here is the second— [*running through the pages towards the end*]—forecasting the probable line of development.

TESMAN. How odd now! I should never have thought of writing anything of that sort.

HEDDA [*at the glass door, drumming on the pane*]. H'm—I daresay not.

LÖVBORG [*replacing the manuscript in its paper and laying the packet on the table*]. I brought it, thinking I might read you a little of it this evening.

TESMAN. That was very good to you, Eilert. But this evening—? [*Looking at BRACK.*] I don't quite see how we can manage it—

LÖVBORG. Well then, some other time. There is no hurry.

BRACK. I must tell you, Mr. Lövborg—there is a little gathering at my house this evening—mainly in honor of Tesman, you know—

LÖVBORG [*looking for his hat*]. Oh—then I won't detain you—

BRACK. No, but listen—will you not do me the favor of joining us?

LÖVBORG [*curtly and decidedly*]. No, I can't—thank you very much.

BRACK. Oh, nonsense—do! We shall be quite a select little circle. And I assure you we shall have a "lively time," as Mrs. Hed—as Mrs. Tesman says.

LÖVBORG. I have no doubt of it. But nevertheless—

BRACK. And then you might bring your manuscript with you, and read it to Tesman at my house. I could give you a room to yourselves.

TESMAN. Yes, think of that, Eilert,—why shouldn't you? Eh?

HEDDA [*interposing*]. But, Tesman, if Mr. Lövborg would really rather not! I am sure Mr. Lövborg is much more inclined to remain here and have supper with me.

LÖVBORG [*looking at her*]. With you, Mrs. Tesman?

HEDDA. And with Mrs. Elvsted.

LÖVBORG. Ah— [*Lightly.*] I saw her for a moment this morning.

HEDDA. Did you? Well, she is coming this evening. So you see you are almost bound to remain, Mr. Lövborg, or she will have no one to see her home.

LÖVBORG. That's true. Many thanks, Mrs. Tesman—in that case I will remain.

HEDDA. Then I have one or two orders to give the servant—

[*She goes to the hall door and rings.* BERTA *enters.* HEDDA *talks to her in a whisper, and points towards the inner room.* BERTA *nods and goes out again.*]

TESMAN [*at the same time, to* LÖVBORG]. Tell me, Eilert—is it this new subject—the future—that you are going to lecture about?

LÖVBORG. Yes.

TESMAN. They told me at the bookseller's, that you are going to deliver a course of lectures this autumn.

LÖVBORG. That is my intention. I hope you won't take it ill, Tesman.

TESMAN. Oh no, not in the least! But—?

LÖVBORG. I can quite understand that it must be disagreeable to you.

TESMAN [*cast down*]. Oh, I can't expect you, out of consideration for me, to—

LÖVBORG. But I shall wait till you have received your appointment.

TESMAN. Will you wait? Yes, but—yes, but—are you not going to compete with me? Eh?

LÖVBORG. No; it is only the moral victory I care for.

TESMAN. Why, bless me—then Aunt Julia was right after all! Oh yes—I knew it! Hedda! Just fancy—Eilert Lövborg is not going to stand in our way!

HEDDA [*curtly*]. Our way? Pray leave me out of the question.

[*She goes up towards the inner room, where* BERTA *is placing a tray with decanters and glasses on the table.* HEDDA *nods approval, and comes forward again.* BERTA *goes out.*]

TESMAN [*at the same time*]. And you, Judge Brack—what do you say to this? Eh?

BRACK. Well, I say that a moral victory—h'm—may be all very fine—

TESMAN. Yes, certainly. But all the same—

HEDDA [*looking at* TESMAN *with a cold smile*]. You stand there looking as if you were thunderstruck—

TESMAN. Yes—so I am—I almost think—

BRACK. Don't you see, Mrs. Tesman, a thunderstorm has just passed over?

HEDDA [*pointing towards the inner room*]. Will you not take a glass of cold punch, gentlemen?

BRACK [*looking at his watch*]. A stirrup-cup? Yes, it wouldn't come amiss.

TESMAN. A capital idea, Hedda! just the thing! Now that the weight has been taken off my mind—

HEDDA. Will you not join them, Mr. Lövborg?

LÖVBORG [*with a gesture of refusal*]. No, thank you. Nothing for me.

BRACK. Why, bless me—cold punch is surely not poison.

LÖVBORG. Perhaps not for every one.

HEDDA. I will keep Mr. Lövborg company in the meantime.

TESMAN. Yes, yes, Hedda dear, do.

[*He and* BRACK *go into the inner room, seat themselves, drink punch, smoke cigarettes, and carry on a lively conversation during what follows.* EILERT LÖVBORG *remains beside the stove.* HEDDA *goes to the writing-table.*]

HEDDA [*raising her voice a little*]. Do you care to look at some photographs, Mr. Lövborg? You know Tesman and I made a tour in the Tyrol[8] on our way home?

[*She takes up an album, and places it on the table beside the sofa, in the further corner of which she seats herself.* EILERT LÖVBORG *approaches, stops, and looks at her. Then he takes a chair and seats himself at her left, with his back towards the inner room.*]

HEDDA [*opening the album*]. Do you see this range of mountains, Mr. Lövborg? It's the Ortler group. Tesman has written the name underneath. Here it is: "The Ortler group near Meran."

LÖVBORG [*who has never taken his eyes off her, says softly and slowly*]. Hedda—Gabler!

HEDDA [*glancing hastily at him*]. Ah! Hush!

LÖVBORG [*repeats softly*]. Hedda Gabler!

HEDDA [*looking at the album*]. That was my name in the old days—when we two knew each other.

LÖVBORG. And I must teach myself never to say Hedda Gabler again—never, as long as I live.

HEDDA [*still turning over the pages*]. Yes, you must. And I think you ought to practice in time. The sooner the better, I should say.

LÖVBORG [*in a tone of indignation*]. Hedda Gabler married? And married to— George Tesman!

HEDDA. Yes—so the world goes.

LÖVBORG. Oh, Hedda, Hedda—how could you[9] throw yourself away!

HEDDA [*looks sharply at him*]. What? I can't allow this!

LÖVBORG. What do you mean? [TESMAN *comes into the room and goes towards the sofa.*]

HEDDA [*hears him coming and says in an indifferent tone*]. And this is a view from the Val d'Ampezzo, Mr. Lövborg. Just look at these peaks! [*Looks affectionately up at* TESMAN.] What's the name of these curious peaks, dear?

TESMAN. Let me see? Oh, those are the Dolomites.

HEDDA. Yes, that's it—Those are the Dolomites, Mr. Lövborg.

TESMAN. Hedda dear,—I only wanted to ask whether I shouldn't bring you a little punch after all? For yourself at any rate—eh?

HEDDA. Yes, do, please; and perhaps a few biscuits.

TESMAN. No cigarettes?

HEDDA. No.

TESMAN. Very well.

[*He goes into the inner room and out to the right.* BRACK *sits in the inner room, and keeps an eye from time to time on* HEDDA *and* LÖVBORG.]

LÖVBORG [*softly, as before*]. Answer me, Hedda—how could you go and do this?

HEDDA [*apparently absorbed in the album*]. If you continue to say *du* to me I won't talk to you.

LÖVBORG. May I not say *du* when we are alone?

HEDDA. No. You may think it: but you mustn't say it.

---

[8] The Tyrolese mountains discussed in the subsquent exchanges are all in Northern Italy near the Austrian border.

[9] Lövborg uses the intimate pronoun *du*.

Lövborg. Ah, I understand. It is an offense against George Tesman, whom you[10]—love.

Hedda [*glances at him and smiles*]. Love? What an idea!

Lövborg. You don't love him then!

Hedda. But I won't hear of any sort of unfaithfulness! Remember that.

Lövborg. Hedda—answer me one thing—

Hedda. Hush!

[Tesman *enters with a small tray from the inner room.*]

Tesman. Here you are! Isn't this tempting? [*He puts the tray on the table.*]

Hedda. Why do you bring it yourself?

Tesman [*filling the glasses*]. Because I think it's such fun to wait upon you, Hedda.

Hedda. But you have poured out two glasses. Mr. Lövborg said he wouldn't have any—

Tesman. No, but Mrs. Elvsted will soon be here, won't she?

Hedda. Yes, by-the-bye—Mrs. Elvsted—

Tesman. Had you forgotten her? Eh?

Hedda. We were so absorbed in these photographs. [*Shows him a picture.*] Do you remember this little village?

Tesman. Oh, it's that one just below the Brenner Pass. It was there we passed the night—

Hedda. —and met that lively party of tourists.

Tesman. Yes, that was the place. Fancy—if we could only have had you with us, Eilert! Eh? [*He returns to the inner room and sits beside* Brack.]

Lövborg. Answer me this one thing, Hedda—

Hedda. Well?

Lövborg. Was there no love in your friendship for me either? Not a spark—not a tinge of love in it?

Hedda. I wonder if there was? To me it seems as though we were two good comrades—two thoroughly intimate friends. [*Smilingly.*] You especially were frankness itself.

Lövborg. It was you that made me so.

Hedda. As I look back upon it all, I think there was really something beautiful, something fascinating—something daring—in—in that secret intimacy—that comradeship which no living creature so much as dreamed of.

Lövborg. Yes, yes, Hedda! Was there not?—When I used to come to your father's in the afternoon—and the General sat over at the window reading his papers—with his back towards us—

Hedda. And we two on the corner sofa—

Lövborg. Always with the same illustrated paper before us—

Hedda. For want of an album, yes.

Lövborg. Yes, Hedda, and when I made my confessions to you—told you about myself, things that at that time no one else knew! There I would sit and tell you of my escapades—my days and nights of devilment. Oh, Hedda—what was the power in you that forced me to confess these things?

Hedda. Do you think it was any power in me?

Lövborg. How else can I explain it? And all those—those roundabout questions you used to put to me—

Hedda. Which you understood so particularly well—

[10] Here Lövborg begins using the formal pronoun *de*.

LÖVBORG. How could you sit and question me like that? Question me quite frankly—

HEDDA. In roundabout terms, please observe.

LÖVBORG. Yes, but frankly nevertheless. Cross-question me about—all that sort of thing?

HEDDA. And how could you answer, Mr. Lövborg?

LÖVBORG. Yes, that is just what I can't understand—in looking back upon it. But tell me now, Hedda—was there not love at the bottom of our friendship? On your side, did you not feel as though you might purge my stains away if I made you my confessor? Was it not so?

HEDDA. No, not quite.

LÖVBORG. What was your motive, then?

HEDDA. Do you think it quite incomprehensible that a young girl—when it can be done—without any one knowing—

LÖVBORG. Well?

HEDDA. —should be glad to have a peep, now and then, into a world which—

LÖVBORG. Which—?

HEDDA. —which she is forbidden to know anything about?

LÖVBORG. So that was it?

HEDDA. Partly. Partly—I almost think.

LÖVBORG. Comradeship in the thirst for life. But why should not that, at any rate, have continued?

HEDDA. The fault was yours.

LÖVBORG. It was you that broke with me.

HEDDA. Yes, when our friendship threatened to develop into something more serious. Shame upon you, Eilert Lövborg! How could you think of wronging your—your frank comrade?

LÖVBORG [*clenching his hands*]. Oh, why did you not carry out your threat? Why did you not shoot me down?

HEDDA. Because I have such a dread of scandal.

LÖVBORG. Yes, Hedda, you are a coward at heart.

HEDDA. A terrible coward. [*Changing her tone.*] But it was a lucky thing for you. And now you have found ample consolation at the Elvsteds'.

LÖVBORG. I know what Thea has confided to you.

HEDDA. And perhaps you have confided to her something about us?

LÖVBORG. Not a word. She is too stupid to understand anything of that sort.

HEDDA. Stupid?

LÖVBORG. She is stupid about matters of that sort.

HEDDA. And I am cowardly. [*Bends over towards him, without looking him in the face, and says more softly—*] But now I will confide something to you.

LÖVBORG [*eagerly*]. Well?

HEDDA. The fact that I dared not shoot you down—

LÖVBORG. Yes!

HEDDA. —that was not my most arrant cowardice—that evening.

LÖVBORG [*looks at her a moment, understands, and whispers passionately*]. Oh, Hedda! Hedda Gabler! Now I begin to see a hidden reason beneath our comradeship! You and I—! After all, then, it was your craving for life—

HEDDA [*softly, with a sharp glance*]. Take care! Believe nothing of the sort!

[*Twilight has begun to fall. The hall door is opened from without by* BERTA.]

HEDDA [*closes the album with a bang and calls smilingly*]. Ah, at last! My darling Thea,—come along!

[MRS. ELVSTED *enters from the hall. She is in evening dress. The door is closed behind her.*]

HEDDA [*on the sofa, stretches out her arms towards her*]. My sweet Thea—you can't think how I have been longing for you!

[MRS. ELVSTED, *in passing, exchanges slight salutations with the gentlemen in the inner room, then goes up to the table and gives* HEDDA *her hands.* EILERT LÖVBORG *has risen. He and* MRS. ELVSTED *greet each other with a silent nod.*]

MRS. ELVSTED. Ought I to go in and talk to your husband for a moment?

HEDDA. Oh, not at all. Leave those two alone. They will soon be going.

MRS. ELVSTED. Are they going out?

HEDDA. Yes, to a supper-party.

MRS. ELVSTED [*quickly, to* LÖVBORG]. Not you?

LÖVBORG. No.

HEDDA. Mr. Lövborg remains with us.

MRS. ELVSTED [*takes a chair and is about to seat herself at his side*]. Oh, how nice it is here!

HEDDA. No, thank you, my little Thea! Not there! You'll be good enough to come over here to me. I will sit between you.

MRS. ELVSTED. Yes, just as you please.

[*She goes round the table and seats herself on the sofa on* HEDDA'*s right.* LÖVBORG *re-seats himself on his chair.*]

LÖVBORG [*after a short pause, to* HEDDA]. Is not she lovely to look at?

HEDDA [*lightly stroking her hair*]. Only to look at?

LÖVBORG. Yes. For we two—she and I—we are two real comrades. We have absolute faith in each other; so we can sit and talk with perfect frankness—

HEDDA. Not round about, Mr. Lövborg?

LÖVBORG. Well—

MRS. ELVSTED [*softly, clinging close to* HEDDA]. Oh, how happy I am, Hedda; for, only think, he says I have inspired him too.

HEDDA [*looks at her with a smile*]. Ah! Does he say that, dear?

LÖVBORG. And then she is so brave, Mrs. Tesman!

MRS. ELVSTED. Good heavens—am I brave?

LÖVBORG. Exceedingly—where your comrade is concerned.

HEDDA. Ah, yes—courage! If one only had that!

LÖVBORG. What then? What do you mean?

HEDDA. Then life would perhaps be liveable, after all. [*With a sudden change of tone.*] But now, my dearest Thea, you really must have a glass of cold punch.

MRS. ELVSTED. No, thanks—I never take anything of that kind.

HEDDA. Well then, you, Mr. Lövborg.

LÖVBORG. Nor I, thank you.

MRS. ELVSTED. No, he doesn't either.

HEDDA [*looks fixedly at him*]. But if I say you shall?

LÖVBORG. It would be no use.

HEDDA [*laughing*]. Then I, poor creature, have no sort of power over you?

LÖVBORG. Not in that respect.

HEDDA. But seriously, I think you ought to—for your own sake.

MRS. ELVSTED. Why, Hedda—!

LÖVBORG. How so?

HEDDA. Or rather on account of other people.

LÖVBORG. Indeed?

HEDDA. Otherwise people might be apt to suspect that—in your heart of hearts—you did not feel quite secure—quite confident of yourself.

MRS. ELVSTED [*softly*]. Oh please, Hedda—

LÖVBORG. People may suspect what they like—for the present.

MRS. ELVSTED [*joyfully*]. Yes, let them!

HEDDA. I saw it plainly in Judge Brack's face a moment ago.

LÖVBORG. What did you see?

HEDDA. His contemptuous smile, when you dared not go with them into the inner room.

LÖVBORG. Dared not? Of course I preferred to stop here and talk to you.

MRS. ELVSTED. What could be more natural, Hedda?

HEDDA. But the Judge could not guess that. And I saw, too, the way he smiled and glanced at Tesman when you dared not accept his invitation to this wretched little supper-party of his.

LÖVBORG. Dared not! Do you say I dared not?

HEDDA. *I* don't say so. But that was how Judge Brack understood it.

LÖVBORG. Well, let him.

HEDDA. Then you are not going with them?

LÖVBORG. I will stay here with you and Thea.

MRS. ELVSTED. Yes, Hedda—how can you doubt that?

HEDDA [*smiles and nods approvingly to* LÖVBORG]. Firm as a rock! Faithful to your principles, now and forever! Ah, that is how a man should be! [*Turns to* MRS. ELVSTED *and caresses her.*] Well now, what did I tell you, when you came to us this morning in such a state of distraction—

LÖVBORG [*surprised*]. Distraction!

MRS. ELVSTED [*terrified*]. Hedda—oh Hedda—!

HEDDA. You can see for yourself; you haven't the slightest reason to be in such mortal terror—[*interrupting herself*]. There! Now we can all three enjoy ourselves!

LÖVBORG [*who has given a start*]. Ah—what is all this, Mrs. Tesman?

MRS. ELVSTED. Oh my God, Hedda! What are you saying? What are you doing?

HEDDA. Don't get excited! That horrid Judge Brack is sitting watching you.

LÖVBORG. So she was in mortal terror! On my account!

MRS. ELVSTED [*softly and piteously*]. Oh, Hedda—now you have ruined everything!

LÖVBORG [*looks fixedly at her for a moment. His face is distorted*]. So that was my comrade's frank confidence in me?

MRS. ELVSTED [*imploringly*]. Oh, my dearest friend—only let me tell you—

LÖVBORG [*takes one of the glasses of punch, raises it to his lips, and says in a low, husky voice*]. Your health, Thea!

[*He empties the glass, puts it down, and takes the second.*]

MRS. ELVSTED [*softly*]. Oh, Hedda, Hedda—how could you do this?

HEDDA. *I* do it? I? Are you crazy?

LÖVBORG. Here's your health, too, Mrs. Tesman. Thanks for the truth. Hurrah for the truth! [*He empties the glass and is about to re-fill it.*]

HEDDA [*lays her hand on his arm*]. Come, come—no more for the present. Remember you are going out to supper.

MRS. ELVSTED. No, no, no!

HEDDA. Hush! They are sitting watching you.

LÖVBORG [*putting down the glass*]. Now. Thea—tell me the truth—

MRS. ELVSTED. Yes.

LÖVBORG. Did your husband know that you had come after me?

MRS. ELVSTED [*wringing her hands*]. Oh, Hedda—do you hear what he is asking?

LÖVBORG. Was it arranged between you and him that you were to come to town and look after me? Perhaps it was the Sheriff himself that urged you to come? Aha, my dear—no doubt he wanted my help in his office! Or was it at the card-table that he missed me?

MRS. ELVSTED [*softly, in agony*]. Oh, Lövborg, Lövborg—!

LÖVBORG [*seizes a glass and is on the point of filling it*]. Here's a glass for the old Sheriff too!

HEDDA [*preventing him*]. No more just now. Remember, you have to read your manuscript to Tesman.

LÖVBORG [*calmly, putting down the glass*]. It was stupid of me all this, Thea—to take it in this way, I mean. Don't be angry with me, my dear, dear comrade. You shall see—both of you and the others—that if I was fallen once—now I have risen again! Thanks to you, Thea.

MRS. ELVSTED [*radiant with joy*]. Oh, heaven be praised—!

[BRACK *has in the meantime looked at his watch. He and* TESMAN *rise and come into the drawing-room.*]

BRACK [*takes his hat and overcoat*]. Well, Mrs. Tesman, our time has come.

HEDDA. I suppose it has.

LÖVBORG [*rising*]. Mine too, Judge Brack.

MRS. ELVSTED [*softly and imploringly*]. Oh, Lövborg, don't do it!

HEDDA [*pinching her arm*]. They can hear you!

MRS. ELVSTED [*with a suppressed shriek*]. Ow!

LÖVBORG [*to* BRACK]. You were good enough to invite me.

BRACK. Well, are you coming after all?

LÖVBORG. Yes, many thanks.

BRACK. I'm delighted—

LÖVBORG [*to* TESMAN, *putting the parcel of MS. in his pocket*]. I should like to show you one or two things before I send it to the printer's.

TESMAN. Fancy—that will be delightful. But, Hedda dear, how is Mrs. Elvsted to get home? Eh?

HEDDA. Oh, that can be managed somehow.

LÖVBORG [*looking towards the ladies*]. Mrs. Elvsted? Of course, I'll come again and fetch her. [*Approaching.*] At ten or thereabouts, Mrs. Tesman? Will that do?

HEDDA. Certainly. That will do capitally.

TESMAN. Well, then, that's all right. But you must not expect me so early, Hedda.

HEDDA. Oh, you may stop as long—as long as ever you please.

MRS. ELVSTED [*trying to conceal her anxiety*]. Well then, Mr. Lövborg—I shall remain here until you come.

LÖVBORG [*with his hat in his hand*]. Pray do, Mrs. Elvsted.

BRACK. And now off goes the excursion train, gentlemen! I hope we shall have a lively time, as a certain fair lady puts it.

HEDDA. Ah, if only the fair lady could be present unseen—!

BRACK. Why unseen?

HEDDA In order to hear a little of your liveliness at first hand, Judge Brack.

BRACK [*laughing*]. I should not advise the fair lady to try it.

TESMAN [*also laughing*]. Come, you're a nice one, Hedda! Fancy that!

BRACK. Well, good-bye, good-bye, ladies.

Lövborg [*bowing*]. About ten o'clock, then.

[Brack, Lövborg, and Tesman *go out by the hall door. At the same time* Berta *enters from the inner room with a lighted lamp, which she places on the dining-room table; she goes out by the way she came.*]

Mrs. Elvsted [*who has risen and is wandering restlessly about the room*]. Hedda— Hedda—what will come of all this?

Hedda. At ten o'clock—he will be here. I can see him already—with vine-leaves in his hair[11]—flushed and fearless—

Mrs. Elvsted. Oh, I hope he may.

Hedda. And then, you see—then he will have regained control over himself. Then he will be a free man for all his days.

Mrs. Elvsted. Oh God!—if he would only come as you see him now!

Hedda. He will come as I see him—so, and not otherwise! [*Rises and approaches* Thea.] You may doubt him as long as you please; I believe in him. And now we will try—

Mrs. Elvsted. You have some hidden motive in this, Hedda!

Hedda. Yes, I have. I want for once in my life to have power to mold a human destiny.

Mrs. Elvsted. Have you not the power?

Hedda. I have not—and have never had it.

Mrs. Elvsted. Not your husband's?

Hedda. Do you think that is worth the trouble? Oh, if you could only understand how poor I am. And fate has made you so rich! [*Clasps her passionately in her arms.*] I think I must burn your hair off, after all.

Mrs. Elvsted. Let me go! Let me go! I am afraid of you, Hedda!

Berta [*in the middle doorway*]. Tea is laid in the dining-room, ma'am.

Hedda. Very well. We are coming.

Mrs. Elvsted. No, no, no! I would rather go home alone! At once.

Hedda. Nonsense! First you shall have a cup of tea, you little stupid. And then—at ten o'clock—Eilert Lövborg will be here—with vine-leaves in his hair. [*She drags* Mrs. Elvsted *almost by force towards the middle doorway.*]

ACT III

The room at the Tesmans'. *The curtains are drawn over the middle doorway, and also over the glass door. The lamp, half turned down and with a shade over it, is burning on the table. In the stove, the door of which stands open, there has been a fire, which is now nearly burnt out.*

Mrs. Elvsted, *wrapped in a large shawl, and with her feet upon a foot-rest, sits close to the stove, sunk back in the arm-chair.* Hedda, *fully dressed, lies sleeping upon the sofa, with a sofa-blanket over her.*

Mrs. Elvsted [*after a pause, suddenly sits up in her chair, and listens eagerly. Then she sinks back again wearily, moaning to herself*]. Not yet!—Oh God—oh God— not yet!

[Berta *slips in by the hall door. She has a letter in her hand.*]

Mrs. Elvsted [*turns and whispers eagerly*]. Well—has any one come?

[11] Bacchus, the Greek and Roman god of wine and revelry, was often portrayed with vine leaves in his hair.

BERTA [*softly*]. Yes, a girl has brought this letter.

MRS. ELVSTED [*quickly, holding out her hand*]. A letter! Give it to me!

BERTA. No, it's for Dr. Tesman, ma'am.

MRS. ELVSTED. Oh, indeed.

BERTA. It was Miss Tesman's servant that brought it. I'll lay it here on the table.

MRS. ELVSTED. Yes, do.

BERTA [*laying down the letter*]. I think I had better put out the lamp. It's smoking.

MRS. ELVSTED. Yes, put it out. It must soon be daylight now.

BERTA [*putting out the lamp*]. It is daylight already, ma'am.

MRS. ELVSTED. Yes, broad day! And no one come back yet—!

BERTA. Lord bless you, ma'am! I guessed how it would be.

MRS. ELVSTED. You guessed?

BERTA. Yes, when I saw that a certain person had come back to town—and that he went off with them. For we've heard enough about that gentleman before now.

MRS. ELVSTED. Don't speak so loud! You will waken Mrs. Tesman.

BERTA [*looks towards the sofa and sighs*]. No, no—let her sleep, poor thing. Shan't I put some wood on the fire?

MRS. ELVSTED. Thanks, not for me.

BERTA. Oh, very well. [*She goes softly out by the hall door.*]

HEDDA [*is awakened by the shutting of the door, and looks up*]. What's that—?

MRS. ELVSTED. It was only the servant—

HEDDA [*looking about her*]. Oh, we're here—! Yes, now I remember. [*Sits erect upon the sofa, stretches herself, and rubs her eyes.*] What o'clock is it, Thea?

MRS. ELVSTED [*looks at her watch*]. It's past seven.

HEDDA. When did Tesman come home?

MRS. ELVSTED. He has not come.

HEDDA. Not come home yet?

MRS. ELVSTED [*rising*]. No one has come.

HEDDA. Think of our watching and waiting here till four in the morning—

MRS. ELVSTED [*wringing her hands*]. And how I watched and waited for him!

HEDDA [*yawns, and says with her hand before her mouth*]. Well, well—we might have spared ourselves the trouble.

MRS. ELVSTED. Did you get a little sleep?

HEDDA. Oh yes; I believe I have slept pretty well. Have you not?

MRS. ELVSTED. Not for a moment. I couldn't, Hedda!—not to save my life.

HEDDA [*rising and goes towards her*]. There, there, there! There's nothing to be so alarmed about. I understand quite well what has happened.

MRS. ELVSTED. Well, what do you think? Won't you tell me?

HEDDA. Why, of course it has been a very late affair at Judge Brack's—

MRS. ELVSTED. Yes, yes, that is clear enough. But all the same—

HEDDA. And then, you see, Tesman hasn't cared to come home and ring us up in the middle of the night. [*Laughing.*] Perhaps he wasn't inclined to show himself either—immediately after a jollification.

MRS. ELVSTED. But in that case—where can he have gone?

HEDDA. Of course he has gone to his aunts' and slept there. They have his old room ready for him.

MRS. ELVSTED. No, he can't be with them; for a letter has just come for him from Miss Tesman. There it lies.

HEDDA. Indeed? [*Looks at the address.*] Why yes, it's addressed in Aunt Julia's

own hand. Well then, he has remained at Judge Brack's. And as for Eilert
Lövborg—he is sitting, with vine-leaves in his hair, reading his manuscript.

MRS. ELVSTED. Oh Hedda, you are just saying things you don't believe a bit.

HEDDA. You really are a little blockhead, Thea.

MRS. ELVSTED. Oh yes, I suppose I am.

HEDDA. And how mortally tired you look.

MRS. ELVSTED. Yes, I am mortally tired.

HEDDA. Well then, you must do as I tell you. You must go into my room
and lie down for a little while.

MRS. ELVSTED. Oh no, no—I shouldn't be able to sleep.

HEDDA. I am sure you would.

MRS. ELVSTED. Well, but your husband is certain to come soon now; and then
I want to know at once—

HEDDA. I shall take care to let you know when he comes.

MRS. ELVSTED. Do you promise me, Hedda?

HEDDA. Yes, rely upon me. Just you go in and have a sleep in the meantime.

MRS. ELVSTED. Thanks; then I'll try to. [*She goes off through the inner room.*]

[HEDDA *goes up to the glass door and draws back the curtains. The broad daylight
streams into the room. Then she takes a little hand-glass from the writing-table, looks at
herself in it, and arranges her hair. Next she goes to the hall door and presses the bell-
button.* BERTA *presently appears at the hall door.*]

BERTA. Did you want anything, ma'am?

HEDDA. Yes; you must put some more wood in the stove. I am shivering.

BERTA. Bless me—I'll make up the fire at once. [*She rakes the embers together
and lays a piece of wood upon them; then stops and listens.*] That was a ring at
the front door, ma'am.

HEDDA. Then go to the door. I will look after the fire.

BERTA. It'll soon burn up. [*She goes out by the hall door.*]

[HEDDA *kneels on the foot-rest and lays some more pieces of wood in the stove. After
a short pause,* GEORGE TESMAN *enters from the hall. He looks tired and rather serious.
He steals on tiptoe towards the middle doorway and is about to slip through the curtains.*]

HEDDA [*at the stove, without looking up*]. Good morning.

TESMAN [*turns*]. Hedda! [*Approaching her.*] Good heavens—are you up so early?
Eh?

HEDDA. Yes, I am up very early this morning.

TESMAN. And I never doubted you were still sound asleep! Fancy that, Hedda!

HEDDA. Don't speak so loud. Mrs. Elvsted is resting in my room.

TESMAN. Has Mrs. Elvsted been here all night?

HEDDA. Yes, since no one came to fetch her.

TESMAN. Ah, to be sure.

HEDDA [*closes the door of the stove and rises*]. Well, did you enjoy yourself at Judge
Brack's?

TESMAN. Have you been anxious about me? Eh?

HEDDA. No, I should never think of being anxious. But I asked if you had
enjoyed yourself.

TESMAN. Oh, yes,—for once in a way. Especially the beginning of the evening;
for then Eilert read me part of his book. We arrived more than an hour
too early—fancy that! And Brack had all sorts of arrangements to make—
so Eilert read to me.

HEDDA [*seating herself by the table on the right*]. Well? Tell me, then—

TESMAN [*sitting on a foot-stool near the stove*]. Oh Hedda, you can't conceive what a book that is going to be! I believe it is one of the most remarkable things that have ever been written. Fancy that!

HEDDA. Yes, yes; I don't care about that—

TESMAN. I must make a confession to you, Hedda. When he had finished reading—a horrid feeling came over me.

HEDDA. A horrid feeling?

TESMAN. I felt jealous of Eilert for having had it in him to write such a book. Only think, Hedda!

HEDDA. Yes, yes, I am thinking!

TESMAN. And then how pitiful to think that he—with all his gifts—should be irreclaimable after all.

HEDDA. I suppose you mean that he has more courage than the rest?

TESMAN. No, not at all—I mean that he is incapable of taking his pleasures in moderation.

HEDDA. And what came of it all—in the end?

TESMAN. Well, to tell the truth, I think it might best be described as an orgy, Hedda.

HEDDA. Had he vine-leaves in his hair?

TESMAN. Vine-leaves? No, I saw nothing of the sort. But he made a long, rambling speech in honor of the woman who had inspired him in his work— that was the phrase he used.

HEDDA. Did he name her?

TESMAN. No, he didn't; but I can't help thinking he meant Mrs. Elvsted. You may be sure he did.

HEDDA. Well—where did you part from him?

TESMAN. On the way to town. We broke up—the last of us at any rate—all together; and Brack came with us to get a breath of fresh air. And then, you see, we agreed to take Eilert home; for he had had far more than was good for him.

HEDDA. I daresay.

TESMAN. But now comes the strange part of it, Hedda; or, I should rather say, the melancholy part of it. I declare I am almost ashamed—on Eilert's account—to tell you—

HEDDA. Oh, go on—!

TESMAN. Well, as we were getting near town, you see, I happened to drop a little behind the others. Only for a minute or two—fancy that!

HEDDA. Yes, yes, yes, but—?

TESMAN. And then, as I hurried after them—what do you think I found by the wayside? Eh?

HEDDA. Oh, how should I know!

TESMAN. You mustn't speak of it to a soul, Hedda! Do you hear! Promise me, for Eilert's sake. [*Draws a parcel, wrapped in paper, from his coat pocket.*] Fancy, dear—I found this.

HEDDA. Is not that the parcel he had with him yesterday?

TESMAN. Yes, it is the whole of his precious, irreplaceable manuscript! And he had gone and lost it, and knew nothing about it. Only fancy, Hedda! So deplorably—

HEDDA. But why did you not give him back the parcel at once?

TESMAN. I didn't dare to—in the state he was then in—

HEDDA. Did you not tell any of the others that you had found it?

TESMAN. Oh, far from it! You can surely understand that, for Eilert's sake, I wouldn't do that.

HEDDA. So no one knows that Eilert Lövborg's manuscript is in your possession?

TESMAN. No. And no one must know it.

HEDDA. Then what did you say to him afterwards?

TESMAN. I didn't talk to him again at all; for when we got in among the streets, he and two or three of the others gave us the slip and disappeared. Fancy that!

HEDDA. Indeed! They must have taken him home then.

TESMAN. Yes, so it would appear. And Brack, too, left us.

HEDDA. And what have you been doing with yourself since?

TESMAN. Well, I and some of the others went home with one of the party, a jolly fellow, and took our morning coffee with him; or perhaps I should rather call it our night coffee—eh? But now, when I have rested a little, and given Eilert, poor fellow, time to have his sleep out, I must take this back to him.

HEDDA [*holds out her hand for the packet*]. No—don't give it to him! Not in such a hurry, I mean. Let me read it first.

TESMAN. No, my dearest Hedda, I mustn't, I really mustn't.

HEDDA. You must not?

TESMAN. No—for you can imagine what a state of despair he will be in when he awakens and misses the manuscript. He has no copy of it, you must know! He told me so.

HEDDA [*looking searchingly at him*]. Can such a thing not be reproduced? Written over again?

TESMAN. No, I don't think that would be possible. For the inspiration, you see—

HEDDA. Yes, yes—I suppose it depends on that. [*Lightly.*] But, by-the-bye—here is a letter for you.

TESMAN. Fancy—!

HEDDA [*handing it to him*]. It came early this morning.

TESMAN. It's from Aunt Julia! What can it be? [*He lays the packet on the other foot-stool, opens the letter, runs his eye through it, and jumps up*]. Oh, Hedda—she says that poor Aunt Rina is dying!

HEDDA. Well, we were prepared for that.

TESMAN. And that if I want to see her again, I must make haste. I'll run in to them at once.

HEDDA [*suppressing a smile*]. Will you run?

TESMAN. Oh, dearest Hedda—if you could only make up your mind to come with me! Just think!

HEDDA [*rises and says wearily, repelling the idea*]. No, no, don't ask me. I will not look upon sickness and death. I loathe all sorts of ugliness.

TESMAN. Well, well, then—! [*Bustling around.*] My hat—My overcoat—? Oh, in the hall—I do hope I mayn't come too late, Hedda! Eh?

HEDDA. Oh, if you run—

[BERTA *appears at the hall door.*]

BERTA. Judge Brack is at the door, and wishes to know if he may come in.

TESMAN. At this time! No, I can't possibly see him.

HEDDA. But I can. [*To* BERTA.] Ask Judge Brack to come in.

[BERTA *goes out.*]

HEDDA [*quickly whispering*]. The parcel, Tesman! [*She snatches it up from the stool.*]

TESMAN. Yes, give it to me!

HEDDA. No, no, I will keep it till you come back.

[*She goes to the writing-table and places it in the book-case.* TESMAN *stands in a flurry of haste, and cannot get his gloves on.* JUDGE BRACK *enters from the hall.*]

HEDDA [*nodding to him*]. You are an early bird, I must say.

BRACK. Yes, don't you think so? [*To* TESMAN.] Are you on the move, too?

TESMAN. Yes, I must rush off to my aunts'. Fancy—the invalid one is lying at death's door, poor creature.

BRACK. Dear me, is she indeed? Then on no account let me detain you. At such a critical moment—

TESMAN. Yes, I must really rush—Good-bye! Good-bye!

[*He hastens out by the hall door.*]

HEDDA [*approaching*]. You seem to have made a particularly lively night of it at your rooms, Judge Brack.

BRACK. I assure you I have not had my clothes off, Mrs. Hedda.

HEDDA. Not you, either?

BRACK. No, as you may see. But what has Tesman been telling you of the night's adventures?

HEDDA. Oh, some tiresome story. Only that they went and had coffee somewhere or other.

BRACK. I have heard about that coffee-party already. Eilert Lövborg was not with them, I fancy?

HEDDA. No, they had taken him home before that.

BRACK. Tesman, too?

HEDDA. No, but some of the others, he said.

BRACK [*smiling*]. George Tesman is really an ingenuous creature, Mrs. Hedda.

HEDDA. Yes, heaven knows he is. Then is there something behind all this?

BRACK. Yes, perhaps there may be.

HEDDA. Well then, sit down, my dear Judge, and tell your story in comfort.

[*She seats herself to the left of the table.* BRACK *sits near her, at the long side of the table.*]

HEDDA. Now then?

BRACK. I had special reasons for keeping track of my guests—or rather of some of my guests—last night.

HEDDA. Of Eilert Lövborg among the rest, perhaps?

BRACK. Frankly, yes.

HEDDA. Now you make me really curious—

BRACK. Do you know where he and one or two of the others finished the night, Mrs. Hedda?

HEDDA. If it is not quite unmentionable, tell me.

BRACK. Oh no, it's not at all unmentionable. Well, they put in an appearance at a particularly animated soirée.[12]

HEDDA. Of the lively kind?

BRACK. Of the very liveliest—

HEDDA. Tell me more of this, Judge Brack—

BRACK. Lövborg, as well as the others, had been invited in advance. I knew

---

[12] An evening party.

all about it. But he had declined the invitation; for now, as you know, he
has become a new man.

HEDDA. Up at the Elvsteds', yes. But he went after all, then?

BRACK. Well, you see, Mrs. Hedda—unhappily the spirit moved him at my
rooms last evening—

HEDDA. Yes, I hear he found inspiration.

BRACK. Pretty violent inspiration. Well, I fancy, that altered his purpose; for
we men folk are unfortunately not always so firm in our principles as we
ought to be.

HEDDA. Oh, I am sure you are an exception, Judge Brack. But as to Lövborg—?

BRACK. To make a long story short—he landed at last in Mademoiselle Diana's
rooms.

HEDDA. Mademoiselle Diana's?

BRACK. It was Mademoiselle Diana that was giving the soirée to a select circle
of her admirers and her lady friends.

HEDDA. Is she a red-haired woman?

BRACK. Precisely.

HEDDA. A sort of a—singer?

BRACK. Oh yes—in her leisure moments. And moreover a mighty huntress—
of men—Mrs. Hedda. You have no doubt heard of her. Eilert Lövborg was
one of her most enthusiastic protectors—in the days of his glory.

HEDDA. And how did all this end?

BRACK. Far from amicably, it appears. After a most tender meeting, they seem
to have come to blows—

HEDDA. Lövborg and she?

BRACK. Yes. He accused her or her friends of having robbed him. He declared
that his pocket-book had disappeared—and other things as well. In short,
he seems to have made a furious disturbance.

HEDDA. And what came of it all?

BRACK. It came to a general scrimmage, in which the ladies as well as the
gentlemen took part. Fortunately the police at last appeared on the scene.

HEDDA. The police too?

BRACK. Yes. I fancy it will prove a costly frolic for Eilert Lövborg, crazy being
that he is.

HEDDA. How so?

BRACK. He seems to have made a violent resistance—to have hit one of the
constables on the head and torn the coat off his back. So they had to march
him off to the police-station with the rest.

HEDDA. How have you learnt all this?

BRACK. From the police themselves.

HEDDA [*gazing straight before her*]. So that is what happened. Then he had no
vine-leaves in his hair.

BRACK. Vine-leaves, Mrs. Hedda?

HEDDA [*changing her tone*]. But tell me now, Judge—what is your real reason
for tracking out Eilert Lövborg's movements so carefully?

BRACK. In the first place, it could not be entirely indifferent to me if it should
appear in the police-court that he came straight from my house.

HEDDA. Will the matter come into court, then?

BRACK. Of course. However, I should scarcely have troubled so much about
that. But I thought that, as a friend of the family, it was my duty to supply
you and Tesman with a full account of his nocturnal exploits.

HEDDA. Why so, Judge Brack?

BRACK. Why, because I have a shrewd suspicion that he intends to use you as a sort of blind.

HEDDA. Oh, how can you think such a thing!

BRACK. Good heavens, Mrs. Hedda—we have eyes in our head. Mark my words! This Mrs. Elvsted will be in no hurry to leave town again.

HEDDA. Well, even if there should be anything between them, I suppose there are plenty of other places where they could meet.

BRACK. Not a single home. Henceforth, as before, every respectable house will be closed against Eilert Lövborg.

HEDDA. And so ought mine to be, you mean?

BRACK. Yes. I confess it would be more than painful to me if this personage were to be made free of your house. How superfluous, how intrusive, he would be, if he were to force his way into—

HEDDA. —into the triangle?

BRACK. Precisely. It would simply mean that I should find myself homeless.

HEDDA [looks at him with a smile]. So you want to be the one cock in the basket—that is your aim.

BRACK [nods slowly and lowers his voice]. Yes, that is my aim. And for that I will fight—with every weapon I can command.

HEDDA [her smile vanishing]. I see you are a dangerous person—when it comes to the point.

BRACK. Do you think so?

HEDDA. I am beginning to think so. And I am exceedingly glad to think—that you have no sort of hold over me.

BRACK [laughing equivocally]. Well, well, Mrs. Hedda—perhaps you are right there. If I had, who knows what I might be capable of?

HEDDA. Come, come now, Judge Brack. That sounds almost like a threat.

BRACK [rising]. Oh, not at all! The triangle, you know, ought, if possible, to be spontaneously constructed.

HEDDA. There I agree with you.

BRACK. Well, now I have said all I had to say; and I had better be getting back to town. Good-bye, Mrs. Hedda. [He goes towards the glass door.]

HEDDA [rising]. Are you going through the garden?

BRACK. Yes, it's a short cut for me.

HEDDA. And then it is the back way, too.

BRACK. Quite so. I have no objection to back ways. They may be piquant enough at times.

HEDDA. When there is ball practice going on, you mean?

BRACK [in the doorway, laughing to her]. Oh, people don't shoot their tame poultry, I fancy.

HEDDA [also laughing]. Oh no, when there is only one cock in the basket—

[They exchange laughing nods of farewell. He goes. She closes the door behind him. HEDDA, who has become quite serious, stands for a moment looking out. Presently she goes and peeps through the curtain over the middle doorway. Then she goes to the writing-table, takes LÖVBORG's packet out of the book-case, and is on the point of looking through its contents. BERTA is heard speaking loudly in the hall. HEDDA turns and listens. Then she hastily locks up the packet in the drawer, and lays the key on the inkstand. EILERT LÖVBORG, with his great coat on and his hat in his hand, tears open the hall door. He looks somewhat confused and irritated.]

LÖVBORG [looking towards the hall]. And I tell you I must and will come in! There!

[*He closes the door, turns and sees* HEDDA, *at once regains his self-control, and bows.*]

HEDDA [*at the writing-table*]. Well, Mr. Lövborg, this is rather a late hour to call for Thea.

LÖVBORG. You mean rather an early hour to call on you. Pray pardon me.

HEDDA. How do you know that she is still here?

LÖVBORG. They told me at her lodgings that she had been out all night.

HEDDA [*going to the oval table*]. Did you notice anything about the people of the house when they said that?

LÖVBORG [*looks inquiringly at her*]. Notice anything about them?

HEDDA. I mean, did they seem to think it odd?

LÖVBORG [*suddenly understanding*]. Oh yes, of course! I am dragging her down with me! However, I didn't notice anything.—I suppose Tesman is not up yet?

HEDDA. No—I think not—

LÖVBORG. When did he come home?

HEDDA. Very late.

LÖVBORG. Did he tell you anything?

HEDDA. Yes, I gathered that you had had an exceedingly jolly evening at Judge Brack's.

LÖVBORG. Nothing more?

HEDDA. I don't think so. However, I was so dreadfully sleepy—

[MRS. ELVSTED *enters through the curtains of the middle doorway.*]

MRS. ELVSTED [*going towards him*]. Ah, Lövborg! At last—!

LÖVBORG. Yes, at last. And too late!

MRS. ELVSTED [*looks anxiously at him*]. What is too late?

LÖVBORG. Everything is too late now. It is all over with me.

MRS. ELVSTED. Oh no no—don't say that!

LÖVBORG. You will say the same when you hear—

MRS. ELVSTED. I won't hear anything!

HEDDA. Perhaps you would prefer to talk to her alone! If so, I will leave you.

LÖVBORG. No, stay—you too. I beg you to stay.

MRS. ELVSTED. Yes, but I won't hear anything, I tell you.

LÖVBORG. It is not last night's adventures that I want to talk about.

MRS. ELVSTED. What is it then—?

LÖVBORG. I want to say that now our ways must part.

MRS. ELVSTED. Part!

HEDDA [*involuntarily*]. I knew it!

LÖVBORG. You can be of no more service to me, Thea.

MRS. ELVSTED. How can you stand there and say that! No more service to you! Am I not to help you now, as before? Are we not to go on working together?

LÖVBORG. Henceforward I shall do no work.

MRS. ELVSTED [*despairingly*]. Then what am I to do with my life?

LÖVBORG. You must try to live your life as if you had never known me.

MRS. ELVSTED. But you know I cannot do that!

LÖVBORG. Try if you cannot, Thea. You must go home again—

MRS. ELVSTED [*in vehement protest*]. Never in this world! Where you are, there will I be also! I will not let myself be driven away like this! I will remain here! I will be with you when the book appears.

HEDDA [*half aloud, in suspense*]. Ah yes—the book!

LÖVBORG. [*looks at her*]. My book and Thea's; for that is what it is.

MRS. ELVSTED. Yes, I feel that it is. And that is why I have a right to be with you when it appears! I will see with my own eyes how respect and honor pour in upon you afresh. And the happiness—the happiness—oh, I must share it with you!

LÖVBORG. Thea—our book will never appear.

HEDDA. Ah!

MRS. ELVSTED. Never appear!

LÖVBORG. Can never appear.

MRS. ELVSTED [in agonized foreboding]. Lövborg—what have you done with the manuscript?

HEDDA [looks anxiously at him]. Yes, the manuscript—?

MRS. ELVSTED. Where is it?

LÖVBORG. Oh Thea—don't ask me about it!

MRS. ELVSTED. Yes, yes I will know. I demand to be told at once.

LÖVBORG. The manuscript—Well then—I have torn the manuscript into a thousand pieces.

MRS. ELVSTED [shrieks]. Oh no, no—!

HEDDA [involuntarily]. But that's not—

LÖVBORG [looks at her]. Not true, you think?

HEDDA [collecting herself]. Oh well, of course—since you say so. But it sounded so improbable—

LÖVBORG. It is true, all the same.

MRS. ELVSTED [wringing her hands]. Oh God—oh God, Hedda—torn his own work to pieces!

LÖVBORG. I have torn my own life to pieces. So why should I not tear my life-work too—?

MRS. ELVSTED. And you did this last night?

LÖVBORG. Yes, I tell you! Tore it into a thousand pieces and scattered them on the fiord—far out. There there is cool sea-water at any rate—let them drift upon it—drift with the current and the wind. And then presently they will sink—deeper and deeper—as I shall, Thea.

MRS. ELVSTED. Do you know, Lövborg, that what you have done with the book— I shall think of it to my dying day as though you had killed a little child.

LÖVBORG. Yes, you are right. It is a sort of child-murder.

MRS. ELVSTED. How could you, then—! Did not the child belong to me too?

HEDDA [almost inaudibly]. Ah, the child—

MRS. ELVSTED [breathing heavily]. It is all over then. Well, well, now I will go, Hedda.

HEDDA. But you are not going away from town?

MRS. ELVSTED. Oh, I don't know what I shall do. I see nothing but darkness before me. [She goes out by the hall door.]

HEDDA [stands waiting for a moment]. So you are not going to see her home, Mr. Lövborg?

LÖVBORG. I? Through the streets? Would you have people see her walking with me?

HEDDA. Of course I don't know what else may have happened last night. But is it so utterly irretrievable?

LÖVBORG. It will not end with last night—I know that perfectly well. And the thing is that now I have no taste for that sort of life either. I won't begin it anew. She has broken my courage and my power of braving life out.

HEDDA [looking straight before her]. So that pretty little fool has had her fingers in a man's destiny. [Looks at him.] But all the same, how could you treat her so heartlessly?

LÖVBORG. Oh, don't say that it was heartless!

HEDDA. To go and destroy what has filled her whole soul for months and years. You do not call that heartless!

LÖVBORG. To you I can tell the truth, Hedda.

HEDDA. The truth?

LÖVBORG. First promise me—give me your word—that what I now confide to you Thea shall never know.

HEDDA. I give you my word.

LÖVBORG. Good. Then let me tell you that what I said just now was untrue.

HEDDA. About the manuscript?

LÖVBORG. Yes. I have not torn it to pieces—nor thrown it into the fiord.

HEDDA. No, no—But—where is it then?

LÖVBORG. I have destroyed it none the less—utterly destroyed it, Hedda!

HEDDA. I don't understand.

LÖVBORG. Thea said that what I had done seemed to her like a child-murder.

HEDDA. Yes, so she said.

LÖVBORG. But to kill his child—that is not the worst thing a father can do to it.

HEDDA. Not the worst?

LÖVBORG. No. I wanted to spare Thea from hearing the worst.

HEDDA. Then what is the worst?

LÖVBORG. Suppose now, Hedda, that a man—in the small hours of the morning—came home to his child's mother after a night of riot and debauchery, and said: "Listen—I have been here and there—in this place and in that. And I have taken our child with me—to this place and to that. And I have lost the child—utterly lost it. The devil knows into what hands it may have fallen—who may have had their clutches on it."

HEDDA. Well—but when all is said and done, you know—that was only a book—

LÖVBORG. Thea's pure soul was in that book.

HEDDA. Yes, so I understand.

LÖVBORG. And you can understand, too, that for her and me together no future is possible.

HEDDA. What path do you mean to take then?

LÖVBORG. None. I will only try to make an end of it all—the sooner the better.

HEDDA. [*a step nearer to him*]. Eilert Lövborg—listen to me. Will you not try to—to do it beautifully?

LÖVBORG. Beautifully? [*Smiling.*] With vine-leaves in my hair, as you used to dream in the old days—?

HEDDA. No, no. I have lost my faith in the vine-leaves. But beautifully, nevertheless! For once in a way!—Good-bye! You must go now—and do not come here any more.

LÖVBORG. Good-bye, Mrs. Tesman. And give George Tesman my love. [*He is on the point of going.*]

HEDDA. No, wait! I must give you a memento to take with you.

[*She goes to the writing-table and opens the drawer and the pistol-case; then returns to* LÖVBORG *with one of the pistols.*]

LÖVBORG [*looks at her*]. This? Is this the memento?

HEDDA [*nodding slowly*]. Do you recognize it? It was aimed at you once.

LÖVBORG. You should have used it then.

HEDDA. Take it—and do you use it now.

LÖVBORG [*puts the pistol in his breast pocket*]. Thanks!

HEDDA. And beautifully, Eilert Lövborg. Promise me that!

LÖVBORG. Good-bye, Hedda Gabler. [*He goes out by the hall door.*]

[HEDDA *listens for a moment at the door. Then she goes up to the writing-table, takes out the packet of manuscript, peeps under the cover, draws a few of the sheets half out, and looks at them. Next she goes over and seats herself in the arm-chair beside the stove, with the packet in her lap. Presently she opens the stove door, and then the packet.*]

HEDDA [*throws one of the quires into the fire and whispers to herself*]. Now I am burning your child, Thea!—Burning it, curly-locks! [*Throwing one or two more quires into the stove.*] Your child and Eilert Lövborg's. [*Throws the rest in.*] I am burning—I am burning you child.

ACT IV

The same rooms at the TESMANS'. *It is evening. The drawing-room is in darkness. The back room is lighted by the hanging lamp over the table. The curtains over the glass door are drawn close.*

HEDDA, *dressed in black, walks to and fro in the dark room. Then she goes into the back room and disappears for a moment to the left. She is heard to strike a few chords on the piano. Presently she comes in sight again, and returns to the drawing-room.* BERTA *enters from the right, through the inner room, with a lighted lamp, which she places on the table in front of the corner settee in the drawing-room. Her eyes are red with weeping, and she has black ribbons in her cap. She goes quietly and circumspectly out to the right.* HEDDA *goes up to the glass door, lifts the curtain a little aside, and looks out into the darkness. Shortly afterwards,* MISS TESMAN, *in mourning, with a bonnet and veil on, comes in from the hall.* HEDDA *goes towards her and holds out her hand.*

MISS TESMAN. Yes, Hedda, here I am, in mourning and forlorn; for now my poor sister has at last found peace.

HEDDA. I have heard the news already, as you see. Tesman sent me a card.

MISS TESMAN. Yes, he promised me he would. But nevertheless I thought that to Hedda—here in the house of life—I ought myself to bring the tidings of death.

HEDDA. That was very kind of you.

MISS TESMAN. Ah, Rina ought not to have left us just now. This is not the time for Hedda's house to be a house of mourning.

HEDDA [*changing the subject*]. She died quite peacefully, did she not, Miss Tesman?

MISS TESMAN. Oh, her end was so calm, so beautiful. And then she had the unspeakable happiness of seeing George once more—and bidding him good-bye.—Has he come home yet?

HEDDA. No. He wrote that he might be detained. But won't you sit down?

MISS TESMAN. No thank you, my dear, dear Hedda. I should like to, but I have so much to do. I must prepare my dear one for her rest as well as I can. She shall go to her grave looking her best.

HEDDA. Can I not help you in any way?

MISS TESMAN. Oh, you must not think of it! Hedda Tesman must have no hand in such mournful work. Nor let her thoughts dwell on it either—not at this time.

HEDDA. One is not always mistress of one's thoughts—

MISS TESMAN [*continuing*]. Ah yes, it is the way of the world. At home we shall be sewing a shroud; and here there will soon be sewing too, I suppose—but of another sort, thank God!

[GEORGE TESMAN *enters by the hall door.*]

HEDDA. Ah, you have come at last!

TESMAN. You here, Aunt Julia? With Hedda? Fancy that!

MISS TESMAN. I was just going, my dear boy. Well, have you done all you promised?

TESMAN. No; I'm really afraid I have forgotten half of it. I must come to you again tomorrow. Today my brain is all in a whirl. I can't keep my thoughts together.

MISS TESMAN. Why, my dear George, you mustn't take it in this way.

TESMAN. Mustn't—? How do you mean?

MISS TESMAN. Even in your sorrow you must rejoice, as I do—rejoice that she is at rest.

TESMAN. Oh yes, yes—you are thinking of Aunt Rina.

HEDDA. You will feel lonely now, Miss Tesman.

MISS TESMAN. Just at first, yes. But that will not last very long, I hope. I daresay I shall soon find an occupant for poor Rina's little room.

TESMAN. Indeed? Who do you think will take it? Eh?

MISS TESMAN. Oh, there's always some poor invalid or other in want of nursing, unfortunately.

HEDDA. Would you really take such a burden upon you again?

MISS TESMAN. A burden! Heaven forgive you, child—it has been no burden to me.

HEDDA. But suppose you had a total stranger on your hands—

MISS TESMAN. Oh, one soon makes friends with sick folks; and it's such an absolute necessity for me to have some one to live for. Well, heaven be praised, there may soon be something in this house, too, to keep an old aunt busy.

HEDDA. Oh, don't trouble about anything here.

TESMAN. Yes, just fancy what a nice time we three might have together, if—?

HEDDA. If—?

TESMAN [*uneasily*]. Oh, nothing. It will all come right. Let us hope so—eh?

MISS TESMAN. Well, well, I daresay you two want to talk to each other. [*Smiling.*] And perhaps Hedda may have something to tell you too, George. Good-bye! I must go home to Rina. [*Turning at the door.*] How strange it is to think that now Rina is with me and with my poor brother as well!

TESMAN. Yes, fancy that, Aunt Julia! Eh?

[MISS TESMAN *goes out by the hall door.*]

HEDDA [*follows* TESMAN *coldly and searchingly with her eyes*]. I almost believe your Aunt Rina's death affects you more than it does your Aunt Julia.

TESMAN. Oh, it's not that alone. It's Eilert I am so terribly uneasy about.

HEDDA [*quickly*]. Is there anything new about him?

TESMAN. I looked in at his rooms this afternoon, intending to tell him the manuscript was in safe keeping.

HEDDA. Well, did you not find him?

TESMAN. No. He wasn't at home. But afterwards I met Mrs. Elvsted, and she told me he had been here early this morning.

HEDDA. Yes, directly after you had gone.

TESMAN. And he said that he had torn his manuscript to pieces—eh?

HEDDA. Yes, so he declared.

TESMAN. Why, good heavens, he must have been completely out of his mind! And I suppose you thought it best not to give it back to him, Hedda?

HEDDA. No, he did not get it.

TESMAN. But of course you told him that we had it?

HEDDA. No. [*Quickly.*] Did you tell Mrs. Elvsted?

TESMAN. No; I thought I had better not. But you ought to have told him. Fancy, if, in desperation, he should go and do himself some injury! Let me have the manuscript, Hedda! I will take it to him at once. Where is it?

HEDDA [*cold and immovable, leaning on the arm-chair*]. I have not got it.

TESMAN. Have not got it? What in the world do you mean?

HEDDA. I have burnt it—every line of it.

TESMAN [*with a violent movement of terror*]. Burnt! Burnt Eilert's manuscript!

HEDDA. Don't scream so. The servant might hear you.

TESMAN. Burnt! Why, good God—! No, no, no! It's impossible!

HEDDA. It is so, nevertheless.

TESMAN. Do you know what you have done, Hedda? It's unlawful appropriation of lost property. Fancy that! Just ask Judge Brack, and he'll tell you what it is.

HEDDA. I advise you not to speak of it—either to Judge Brack, or to any one else.

TESMAN. But how could you do anything so unheard-of? What put it into your head? What possessed you? Answer me that—eh?

HEDDA [*suppressing an almost imperceptible smile*]. I did it for your sake, George.

TESMAN. For my sake!

HEDDA. This morning, when you told me about what he had read to you—

TESMAN. Yes, yes—what then?

HEDDA. You acknowledged that you envied his work.

TESMAN. Oh, of course I didn't mean that literally.

HEDDA. No matter—I could not bear the idea that any one should throw you into the shade.

TESMAN [*in an outburst of mingled doubt and joy*]. Hedda! Oh, is this true? But—but—I never knew you to show your love like that before. Fancy that!

HEDDA. Well, I may as well tell you that—just at this time—[*impatiently, breaking off*]. No, no; you can ask Aunt Julia. She will tell you, fast enough.

TESMAN. Oh, I almost think I understand you, Hedda! [*Clasps his hands together.*] Great heavens! do you really mean it! Eh?

HEDDA. Don't shout so. The servant might hear.

TESMAN [*laughing in irrepressible glee*]. The servant! Why, how absurd you are, Hedda. It's only my old Berta! Why, I'll tell Berta myself.

HEDDA [*clenching her hands together in desperation*]. Oh, it is killing me,—it is killing me, all this!

TESMAN. What is, Hedda? Eh?

HEDDA [*coldly, controlling herself*]. All this—absurdity—George.

TESMAN. Absurdity! Do you see anything absurd in my being overjoyed at the news! But after all perhaps I had better not say anything to Berta.

HEDDA. Oh—why not that too?

TESMAN. No, no, not yet! But I must certainly tell Aunt Julia. And then that you have begun to call me George too! Fancy that! Oh, Aunt Julia will be so happy—so happy.

HEDDA. When she hears that I have burnt Eilert Lövborg's manuscript—for your sake?

TESMAN. No, by-the-bye—that affair of the manuscript—of course nobody must know about that. But that you love me so much, Hedda—Aunt Julia must really share my joy in that! I wonder, now, whether this sort of thing is usual in young wives? Eh?

HEDDA. I think you had better ask Aunt Julia that question too.

TESMAN. I will indeed, some time or other. [*Looks uneasy and downcast again.*] And yet the manuscript—the manuscript! Good God! it is terrible to think what will become of poor Eilert now.

[MRS. ELVSTED, *dressed as in the first act, with hat and cloak, enters by the hall door.*]

MRS. ELVSTED [*greets them hurriedly, and says in evident agitation*]. Oh, dear Hedda, forgive my coming again.

HEDDA. What is the matter with you, Thea?

TESMAN. Something about Eilert Lövborg again—eh?

MRS. ELVSTED. Yes! I am dreadfully afraid some misfortune has happened to him.

HEDDA [*seizes her arm*]. Ah,—do you think so?

TESMAN. Why, good Lord—what makes you think that, Mrs. Elvsted?

MRS. ELVSTED. I heard them talking of him at my boarding-house—just as I came in. Oh, the most incredible rumors are afloat about him today.

TESMAN. Yes, fancy, so I heard too! And I can bear witness that he went straight home to bed last night. Fancy that!

HEDDA. Well, what did they say at the boarding-house?

MRS. ELVSTED. Oh, I couldn't make out anything clearly. Either they knew nothing definite, or else— They stopped talking when they saw me; and I did not dare to ask.

TESMAN [*moving about uneasily*]. We must hope—we must hope that you misunderstood them, Mrs. Elvsted.

MRS. ELVSTED. No, no; I am sure it was of him they were talking. And I heard something about the hospital or—

TESMAN. The hospital?

HEDDA. No—surely that cannot be!

MRS. ELVSTED. Oh, I was in such mortal terror! I went to his lodgings and asked for him there.

HEDDA. You could make up your mind to that, Thea!

MRS. ELVSTED. What else could I do? I really could bear the suspense no longer.

TESMAN. But you didn't find him either—eh?

MRS. ELVSTED. No. And the people knew nothing about him. He hadn't been home since yesterday afternoon, they said.

TESMAN. Yesterday! Fancy, how could they say that?

MRS. ELVSTED. Oh, I am sure something terrible must have happened to him.

TESMAN. Hedda dear—how would it be if I were to go and make inquiries—?

HEDDA. No, no—don't you mix yourself up in this affair.

[JUDGE BRACK, *with his hat in his hand, enters by the hall door, which* BERTA *opens, and closes behind him. He looks grave and bows in silence.*]

TESMAN. Oh, is that you, my dear Judge? Eh?

BRACK. Yes. It was imperative I should see you this evening.

TESMAN. I can see you have heard the news about Aunt Rina.

BRACK. Yes, that among other things.

TESMAN. Isn't it sad—eh?

BRACK. Well, my dear Tesman, that depends on how you look at it.

TESMAN [*looks doubtfully at him*]. Has anything else happened?

BRACK. Yes.

HEDDA. [*in suspense*]. Anything sad, Judge Brack?

BRACK. That, too, depends on how you look at it, Mrs. Tesman.

MRS. ELVSTED [*unable to restrain her anxiety*]. Oh! it is something about Eilert Lövborg!

BRACK [*with a glance at her*]. What makes you think that, Madam? Perhaps you have already heard something—?

MRS. ELVSTED [*in confusion*]. No, nothing at all, but—

TESMAN. Oh, for heaven's sake, tell us!

BRACK [*shrugging his shoulders*]. Well, I regret to say Eilert Lövborg has been taken to the hospital. He is lying at the point of death.

MRS. ELVSTED [*shrieks*]. Oh God! Oh God—

TESMAN. To the hospital! And at the point of death.

HEDDA [*involuntarily*]. So soon then—

MRS. ELVSTED [*wailing*]. And we parted in anger, Hedda!

HEDDA [*whispers*]. Thea—Thea—be careful!

MRS. ELVSTED [*not heeding her*]. I must go to him! I must see him alive!

BRACK. It is useless, Madam. No one will be admitted.

MRS. ELVSTED. Oh, at least tell me what has happened to him? What is it?

TESMAN. You don't mean to say that he has himself—Eh?

HEDDA. Yes, I am sure he has.

TESMAN. Hedda, how can you—?

BRACK [*keeping his eyes fixed upon her*]. Unfortunately you have guessed quite correctly, Mrs. Tesman.

MRS. ELVSTED. Oh, how horrible!

TESMAN. Himself, then! Fancy that!

HEDDA. Shot himself!

BRACK. Rightly guessed again, Mrs. Tesman.

MRS. ELVSTED [*with an effort at self-control*]. When did it happen, Mr. Brack?

BRACK. This afternoon—between three and four.

TESMAN. But, good Lord, where did he do it? Eh?

BRACK [*with some hesitation*]. Where? Well—I suppose at his lodgings.

MRS. ELVSTED. No, that cannot be; for I was there between six and seven.

BRACK. Well, then, somewhere else. I don't know exactly. I only know that he was found—. He had shot himself—in the breast.

MRS. ELVSTED. Oh, how terrible! That he should die like that!

HEDDA [*to* BRACK]. Was it in the breast?

BRACK. Yes—as I told you.

HEDDA. Not in the temple?

BRACK. In the breast, Mrs. Tesman.

HEDDA. Well, well—the breast is a good place, too.

BRACK. How do you mean, Mrs. Tesman?

HEDDA [*evasively*]. Oh, nothing—nothing.

TESMAN. And the wound is dangerous, you say—eh?

BRACK. Absolutely mortal. The end has probably come by this time.

MRS. ELVSTED. Yes, yes, I feel it. The end! The end! Oh, Hedda—!

TESMAN. But tell me, how have you learnt all this?

BRACK [*curtly*]. Through one of the police. A man I had some business with.

HEDDA [*in a clear voice*]. At last a deed worth doing!

TESMAN [*terrified*]. Good heavens, Hedda! what are you saying?

HEDDA. I say there is beauty in this.

BRACK. H'm, Mrs. Tesman—

TESMAN. Beauty! Fancy that!

MRS. ELVSTED. Oh, Hedda, how can you talk of beauty in such an act!

HEDDA. Eilert Lövborg has himself made up his account with life. He has had the courage to do—the one right thing.

MRS. ELVSTED. No, you must never think that was how it happened! It must have been in delirium that he did it.

TESMAN. In despair!

HEDDA. That he did not. I am certain of that.

MRS. ELVSTED. Yes, yes! In delirium! Just as when he tore up our manuscript.

BRACK [*starting*]. The manuscript? Has he torn that up?

MRS. ELVSTED. Yes, last night.

TESMAN [*whispers softly*]. Oh, Hedda, we shall never get over this.

BRACK. H'm, very extraordinary.

TESMAN [*moving about the room*]. To think of Eilert going out of the world in this way! And not leaving behind him the book that would have immortalized his name—

MRS. ELVSTED. Oh, if only it could be put together again!

TESMAN. Yes, if it only could! I don't know what I would not give—

MRS. ELVSTED. Perhaps it can, Mr. Tesman.

TESMAN. What do you mean?

MRS. ELVSTED [*searches in the pocket of her dress*]. Look here. I have kept all the loose notes he used to dictate from.

HEDDA [*a step forward*]. Ah—!

TESMAN. You have kept them, Mrs. Elvsted! Eh?

MRS. ELVSTED. Yes, I have them here. I put them in my pocket when I left home. Here they still are—

TESMAN. Oh, do let me see them!

MRS. ELVSTED [*hands him a bundle of papers*]. But they are in such disorder—all mixed up.

TESMAN. Fancy, if we could make something out of them, after all! Perhaps if we two put our heads together—

MRS. ELVSTED. Oh, yes, at least let us try—

TESMAN. We will manage it! We must! I will dedicate my life to this task.

HEDDA. You, George? Your life?

TESMAN. Yes, or rather all the time I can spare. My own collections must wait in the meantime. Hedda—you understand, eh? I owe this to Eilert's memory.

HEDDA. Perhaps.

TESMAN. And so, my dear Mrs. Elvsted, we will give our whole minds to it. There is no use in brooding over what can't be undone—eh? We must try to control our grief as much as possible, and—

MRS. ELVSTED. Yes, yes, Mr. Tesman, I will do the best I can.

TESMAN. Well then, come here. I can't rest until we have looked through the notes. Where shall we sit? Here? No, in there, in the back room. Excuse me, my dear Judge. Come with me, Mrs. Elvsted.

MRS. ELVSTED. Oh, if only it were possible!

[TESMAN *and* MRS. ELVSTED *go into the back room. She takes off her hat and cloak. They both sit at the table under the hanging lamp, and are soon deep in an eager examination of the papers.* HEDDA *crosses to the stove and sits in the arm-chair. Presently* BRACK *goes up to her.*]

HEDDA [*in a low voice*]. Oh, what a sense of freedom it gives one, this act of Eilert Lövborg's.

BRACK. Freedom. Mrs. Hedda? Well, of course, it is a release for him—

HEDDA. I mean for me. It gives me a sense of freedom to know that a deed of deliberate courage is still possible in this world,—a deed of spontaneous beauty.

BRACK [*smiling*]. H'm—my dear Mrs. Hedda—

HEDDA. Oh, I know what you are going to say. For you are a kind of a specialist too, like—you know!

BRACK [*looking hard at her*]. Eilert Lövborg was more to you than perhaps you are willing to admit to yourself. Am I wrong?

HEDDA. I don't answer such questions. I only know Eilert Lövborg has had the courage to live his life after his own fashion. And then—the last great act, with its beauty! Ah! that he should have the will and the strength to turn away from the banquet of life—so early.

BRACK. I am sorry, Mrs. Hedda,—but I fear I must dispel an amiable illusion.

HEDDA. Illusion?

BRACK. Which could not have lasted long in any case.

HEDDA. What do you mean?

BRACK. Eilert Lövborg did not shoot himself voluntarily.

HEDDA. Not voluntarily?

BRACK. No. The thing did not happen exactly as I told it.

HEDDA [*in suspense*]. Have you concealed something? What is it?

BRACK. For poor Mrs. Elvsted's sake I idealized the facts a little.

HEDDA. What are the facts?

BRACK. First, that he is already dead.

HEDDA. At the hospital?

BRACK. Yes—without regaining consciousness.

HEDDA. What more have you concealed?

BRACK. This—the event did not happen at his lodgings.

HEDDA. Oh, that can make no difference.

BRACK. Perhaps it may. For I must tell you—Eilert Lövborg was found shot in—in Mademoiselle Diana's boudoir.

HEDDA [*makes a motion as if to rise, but sinks back again*]. That is impossible, Judge Brack! He cannot have been there again today.

BRACK. He was there this afternoon. He went there, he said, to demand the return of something which they had taken from him. Talked wildly about a lost child—

HEDDA. Ah—so that was why—

BRACK. I thought probably he meant his manuscript; but now I hear he destroyed that himself. So I suppose it must have been his pocket-book.

HEDDA. Yes, no doubt. And there—there he was found?

BRACK. Yes, there. With a pistol in his breastpocket, discharged. The ball had lodged in a vital part.

HEDDA. In the breast—yes.

BRACK. No—in the bowels.

HEDDA [*looks up at him with an expression of loathing*]. That too! Oh, what curse is it that makes everything I touch turn ludicrous and mean?

BRACK. There is one point more, Mrs. Hedda—another disagreeable feature in the affair.

HEDDA. And what is that?

BRACK. The pistol he carried—

HEDDA [*breathless*]. Well? What of it?

BRACK. He must have stolen it.

HEDDA [*leaps up*]. Stolen it! That is not true! He did not steal it!

BRACK. No other explanation is possible. He must have stolen it—Hush!

[TESMAN *and* MRS. ELVSTED *have risen from the table in the back room, and come into the drawing-room.*]

TESMAN [*with the papers in both his hands*]. Hedda dear, it is almost impossible to see under that lamp. Think of that!

HEDDA. Yes, I am thinking.

TESMAN. Would you mind our sitting at your writing-table—eh?

HEDDA. If you like. [*Quickly.*] No, wait! Let me clear it first!

TESMAN. Oh, you needn't trouble, Hedda. There is plenty of room.

HEDDA. No, no; let me clear it, I say! I will take these things in and put them on the piano. There! [*She has drawn out an object, covered with sheet music, from under the book-case, places several other pieces of music upon it, and carries the whole into the inner room, to the left.* TESMAN *lays the scraps of paper on the writing-table, and moves the lamp there from the corner table,* HEDDA *returns.*]

HEDDA [*behind* MRS. ELVSTED'S *chair, gently ruffling her hair*]. Well, my sweet Thea,—how goes it with Eilert Lövborg's monument?

MRS. ELVSTED [*looks dispiritedly up at her*]. Oh, it will be terribly hard to put in order.

TESMAN. We must manage it. I am determined. And arranging other people's papers is just the work for me.

[HEDDA *goes over to the stove, and seats herself on one of the foot-stools.* BRACK *stands over her, leaning on the arm-chair.*]

HEDDA [*whispers*]. What did you say about the pistol?

BRACK [*softly*]. That he must have stolen it.

HEDDA. Why stolen it?

BRACK. Because every other explanation ought to be impossible, Mrs. Hedda.

HEDDA. Indeed?

BRACK [*glances at her*]. Of course Eilert Lövborg was here this morning. Was he not?

HEDDA. Yes.

BRACK. Were you alone with him?

HEDDA. Part of the time.

BRACK. Did you not leave the room whilst he was here?

HEDDA. No.

BRACK. Try to recollect. Were you not out of the room a moment?

HEDDA. Yes, perhaps just a moment—out in the hall.

BRACK. And where was your pistol-case during that time?

HEDDA. I had it locked up in—

BRACK. Well, Mrs. Hedda?

HEDDA. The case stood there on the writing-table.

BRACK. Have you looked since, to see whether both the pistols are there?

HEDDA. No.

BRACK. Well, you need not. I saw the pistol found in Lövborg's pocket, and I knew it at once as the one I had seen yesterday—and before, too.

HEDDA. Have you it with you?

BRACK. No; the police have it.

HEDDA. What will the police do with it?

BRACK. Search till they find the owner.

HEDDA. Do you think they will succeed?

BRACK [*bends over her and whispers*]. No, Hedda Gabler—not so long as I say nothing.

HEDDA [*looks frightened at him*]. And if you do not say nothing,—what then?

BRACK [*shrugs his shoulders*]. There is always the possibility that the pistol was stolen.

HEDDA [*firmly*]. Death rather than that.

BRACK [*smiling*]. People say such things—but they don't do them.

HEDDA [*without replying*]. And supposing the pistol was stolen, and the owner is discovered? What then?

BRACK. Well, Hedda—then comes the scandal.

HEDDA. The scandal!

BRACK. Yes, the scandal—of which you are mortally afraid. You will, of course, be brought before the court—both you and Mademoiselle Diana. She will have to explain how the thing happened—whether it was an accidental shot or murder. Did the pistol go off as he was trying to take it out of his pocket, to threaten her with? Or did she tear the pistol out of his hand, shoot him, and push it back into his pocket? That would be quite like her; for she is an able-bodied young person, this same Mademoiselle Diana.

HEDDA. But *I* have nothing to do with all this repulsive business.

BRACK. No. But you will have to answer the question: Why did you give Eilert Lövborg the pistol? And what conclusions will people draw from the fact that you did give it to him?

HEDDA [*lets her head sink*]. That is true. I did not think of that.

BRACK. Well, fortunately, there is no danger, so long as I say nothing.

HEDDA [*looks up at him*]. So I am in your power, Judge Brack. You have me at your beck and call, from this time forward.

BRACK. [*whispers softly*]. Dearest Hedda—believe me—I shall not abuse my advantage.

HEDDA. I am in your power none the less. Subject to your will and your demands. A slave, a slave then! [*Rises impetuously.*] No, I cannot endure the thought of that! Never!

BRACK [*looks half-mockingly at her*]. People generally get used to the inevitable.

HEDDA [*returns his look*]. Yes, perhaps. [*She crosses to the writing-table. Suppressing an involuntary smile, she imitates* TESMAN'S *intonations.*] Well? Are you getting on, George? Eh?

TESMAN. Heaven knows, dear. In any case it will be the work of months.

HEDDA [*as before*]. Fancy that? [*Passes her hands softly through* MRS. ELVSTED'S *hair.*] Doesn't it seem strange to you, Thea? Here are you sitting with Tesman—just as you used to sit with Eilert Lövborg?

MRS. ELVSTED. Ah, if I could only inspire your husband in the same way.

HEDDA. Oh, that will come too—in time.

TESMAN. Yes, do you know, Hedda—I really think I begin to feel something of the sort. But won't you go and sit with Brack again?

HEDDA. Is there nothing I can do to help you two?

TESMAN. No, nothing in the world. [*Turning his head*]. I trust to you to keep Hedda company, my dear Brack.

BRACK [*with a glance at* HEDDA]. With the very greatest of pleasure.

HEDDA. Thanks. But I am tired this evening. I will go in and lie down a little on the sofa.

TESMAN. Yes, do dear—eh?

[HEDDA *goes into the back room and draws the curtains. A short pause. Suddenly she is heard playing a wild dance on the piano.*]

MRS. ELVSTED [*starts from her chair*]. Oh—what is that?

TESMAN [*runs to the doorway*]. Why, my dearest Hedda—don't play dance music tonight! Just think of Aunt Rina! And of Eilert too!

HEDDA [*puts her head out between the curtains*]. And of Aunt Julia. And of all the rest of them.—After this, I will be quiet. [*Closes the curtains again.*]

TESMAN [*at the writing-table*]. It's not good for her to see us at this distressing work. I'll tell you what, Mrs. Elvsted,—you shall take the empty room at Aunt Julia's, and then I will come over in the evenings, and we can sit and work there—eh?

HEDDA [*in the inner room*]. I hear what you are saying, Tesman. But how am *I* to get through the evenings out here?

TESMAN [*turning over the papers*]. Oh, I daresay Judge Brack will be so kind as to look in now and then, even though I am out.

BRACK [*in the arm-chair, calls out gaily*]. Every blessed evening, with all the pleasure in life, Mrs. Tesman! We shall get on capitally together, we two!

HEDDA [*speaking loud and clear*]. Yes, don't you flatter yourself we will, Judge Brack? Now that you are the one cock in the basket—

[*A shot is heard within.* TESMAN, MRS. ELVSTED, *and* BRACK *leap to their feet.*]

TESMAN. Oh, now she is playing with those pistols again.

[*He throws back the curtains and runs in, followed by* MRS. ELVSTED. HEDDA *lies stretched on the sofa, lifeless. Confusion and cries.* BERTA *enters in alarm from the right.*]

TESMAN [*shrieks to* BRACK]. Shot herself! Shot herself in the temple! Fancy that!

BRACK [*half-fainting in the arm-chair*]. Good God!—people don't do such things.

[1890]

George Bernard Shaw *1856–1950*

MRS WARREN'S PROFESSION

ACT I

Summer afternoon in a cottage garden on the eastern slope of a hill a little south of Haslemere[1] in Surrey. Looking up the hill, the cottage is seen in the left hand corner of the garden, with its thatched roof and porch, and a large latticed window to the left of the porch. A paling completely shuts in the garden, except for a gate on the right. The common[2] rises uphill beyond the paling to the sky line. Some folded canvas garden chairs are leaning against the side bench in the porch. A lady's bicycle is propped against the wall, under the window. A little to the right of the porch a hammock is slung from two posts. A big canvas umbrella, stuck in the ground, keeps the sun off the hammock, in which a young lady lies reading and making notes, her head towards the cottage and her feet towards the gate. In front of the hammock, and within reach of her hand, is a common kitchen chair, with a pile of serious-looking books and a supply of writing paper on it.

A gentleman walking on the common comes into sight from behind the cottage. He is hardly past middle age, with something of the artist about him, unconventionally but carefully dressed, and clean-shaven except for a moustache, with an eager susceptible face and very amiable and considerate manners. He has silky black hair, with waves of grey and white in it. His eyebrows are white, his moustache black. He seems not certain of his way. He looks over the palings; takes stock of the place; and sees the young lady.

THE GENTLEMAN [*taking off his hat*] I beg your pardon. Can you direct me to Hindhead View—Mrs Alison's?

THE YOUNG LADY [*glancing up from her book*] This is Mrs Alison's. [*She resumes her work*].

THE GENTLEMAN. Indeed! Perhaps—may I ask are you Miss Vivie Warren?

THE YOUNG LADY [*sharply, as she turns on her elbow to get a good look at him*] Yes.

THE GENTLEMAN [*daunted and conciliatory*] I'm afraid I appear intrusive. My name is Praed. [*Vivie at once throws her books upon the chair, and gets out of the hammock*]. Oh, pray dont[3] let me disturb you.

VIVIE [*striding to the gate and opening it for him*] Come in, Mr Praed. [*He comes in*]. Glad to see you. [*She proffers her hand and takes his with a resolute and hearty grip. She is an attractive specimen of the sensible, able, highly-educated young middle-class Englishwoman. Age 22. Prompt, strong, confident, self-possessed. Plain business-like dress, but not dowdy. She wears a chatelaine[4] at her belt, with a fountain pen and a paper knife among its pendants*].

PRAED. Very kind of you indeed, Miss Warren. [*She shuts the gate with a vigorous*

---

[1] Haslemere is an English town about 40 miles southwest of London. The action in the play takes place near the end of the nineteenth century.

[2] A public field.

[3] Shaw advocated a number of reforms in spelling and typography. Thus, in this play apostrophes are omitted from many contractions ("dont" instead of "don't") and spacing replaces italics for emphasis ("N e v e r!" instead of *"Never!"*).

[4] A decorative clasp or chain.

slam. *He passes in to the middle of the garden, exercising his fingers, which are slightly numbed by her greeting*]. Has your mother arrived?

VIVIE [*quickly, evidently scenting aggression*] Is she coming?

PRAED [*surprised*] Didnt you expect us?

VIVIE. No.

PRAED. Now, goodness me, I hope Ive not mistaken the day. That would be just like me, you know. Your mother arranged that she was to come down from London and that I was to come over from Horsham to be introduced to you.

VIVIE [*not at all pleased*]. Did she? Hm! My mother has rather a trick of taking me by surprise—to see how I behave myself when she's away, I suppose. I fancy I shall take my mother very much by surprise one of these days, if she makes arrangements that concern me without consulting me beforehand. She hasnt come.

PRAED [*embarrassed*] I'm really very sorry.

VIVIE [*throwing off her displeasure*] It's not your fault, Mr Praed, is it? And I'm very glad youve come. You are the only one of my mother's friends I have ever asked her to bring to see me.

PRAED [*relieved and delighted*] Oh, now this is really very good of you, Miss Warren!

VIVIE. Will you come indoors; or would you rather sit out here and talk!

PRAED. It will be nicer out here, dont you think?

VIVIE. Then I'll go and get you a chair. [*She goes to the porch for a garden chair*].

PRAED [*following her*] Oh, pray, pray! Allow me. [*He lays hands on the chair*].

VIVIE [*letting him take it*] Take care of your fingers: theyre rather dodgy things, those chairs. [*She goes across to the chair with the books on it; pitches them into the hammock; and brings the chair forward with one swing*].

PRAED [*who has just unfolded his chair*] Oh, now d o let me take that hard chair. I like hard chairs.

VIVIE. So do I. Sit down, Mr Praed. [*This invitation she gives with genial peremptoriness, his anxiety to please her clearly striking her as a sign of weakness of character on his part. But he does not immediately obey*].

PRAED. By the way, though, hadnt we better go to the station to meet your mother?

VIVIE [*coolly*] Why? She knows the way.

PRAED [*disconcerted*] Er—I suppose she does [*he sits down*].

VIVIE. Do you know, you are just like what I expected. I hope you are disposed to be friends with me.

PRAED [*again beaming*] Thank you, my d e a r Miss Warren: thank you. Dear me! I'm so glad your mother hasnt spoilt you!

VIVIE. How?

PRAED. Well, in making you too conventional. You know, my dear Miss Warren, I am a born anarchist. I hate authority. It spoils the relations between parent and child: even between mother and daughter. Now I was always afraid that your mother would strain her authority to make you very conventional. It's such a relief to find that she hasnt.

VIVIE. Oh! have I been behaving unconventionally?

PRAED. Oh no: oh dear no. At least not conventionally unconventionally, you understand. [*She nods and sits down. He goes on, with a cordial outburst*] But it was so charming of you to say that you were disposed to be friends with me! You modern young ladies are splendid: perfectly splendid!

VIVIE [*dubiously*] Eh? [*watching him with dawning disappointment as to the quality of his brains and character*].

PRAED. When I was your age, young men and women were afraid of each other: there was no good fellowship. Nothing real. Only gallantry copied out of novels, and as vulgar and affected as it could be. Maidenly reserve! gentlemanly chivalry! always saying no when you meant yes! simple purgatory for shy and sincere souls.

VIVIE. Yes, I imagine there must have been a frightful waste of time. Especially women's time.

PRAED. Oh, waste of life, waste of everything. But things are improving. Do you know, I have been in a positive state of excitement about meeting you ever since your magnificent achievements at Cambridge: a thing unheard of in my day. It was perfectly splendid, your tieing with the third wrangler.[5] Just the right place, you know. The first wrangler is always a dreamy, morbid fellow, in whom the thing is pushed to the length of a disease.

VIVIE. It doesnt pay. I wouldnt do it again for the same money.

PRAED [*aghast*] The same money!

VIVIE. I did it for £50.

PRAED. Fifty pounds!

VIVIE. Yes. Fifty pounds. Perhaps you dont know how it was. Mrs Latham, my tutor at Newnham,[6] told my mother that I could distinguish myself in the mathematical tripos[7] if I went in for it in earnest. The papers were full just then of Phillipa Summers beating the senior wrangler. You remember about it, of course.

PRAED [*shakes his head energetically*]!!!

VIVIE. Well anyhow she did; and nothing would please my mother but that I should do the same thing. I said flatly it was not worth my while to face the grind since I was not going in for teaching; but I offered to try for fourth wrangler or thereabouts for £50. She closed with me at that, after a little grumbling; and I was better than my bargain. But I wouldnt do it again for that. £200 would have been nearer the mark.

PRAED [*much damped*] Lord bless me! Thats a very practical way of looking at it.

VIVIE. Did you expect to find me an unpractical person?

PRAED. But surely it's practical to consider not only the work these honors cost, but also the culture they bring.

VIVIE. Culture! My dear Mr Praed: do you know what the mathematical tripos means? It means grind, grind, grind for six to eight hours a day at mathematics, and nothing but mathematics. I'm supposed to know something about science; but I know nothing except the mathematics it involves. I can make calculations for engineers, electricians, insurance companies, and so on; but I know next to nothing about engineering or insurance. I dont even know arithmetic well, Outside mathematics, lawn-tennis, eating, sleeping, cycling, and walking. I'm a more ignorant barbarian than any woman could possibly be who hadnt gone in for the tripos.

PRAED [*revolted*] What a monstrous, wicked, rascally system! I knew it! I felt at once that it meant destroying all that makes womanhood beautiful.

[5] The third wrangler was the Cambridge University student graduating with the third highest mark in mathematics.
[6] A women's college, now part of Cambridge University in England.
[7] An examination for the B.A. with honors in mathematics.

VIVIE. I dont object to it on that score in the least. I shall turn it to very good account, I assure you.

PRAED. Pooh! In what way?

VIVIE. I shall set up in chambers[8] in the City, and work at actuarial calculations and conveyancing. Under cover of that I shall do some law, with one eye on the Stock Exchange all the time. Ive come down here by myself to read law: not for a holiday, as my mother imagines. I hate holidays.

PRAED. You make my blood run cold. Are you to have no romance, no beauty in you life?

VIVIE. I dont care for either, I assure you.

PRAED. You cant mean that.

VIVIE. Oh yes I do. I like working and getting paid for it. When I'm tired of working, I like a comfortable chair, a cigar, a little whisky, and a novel with a good detective story in it.

PRAED [*rising in a frenzy of repudiation*] I dont believe it. I am an artist; and I cant believe it: I refuse to believe it. It's only that you havnt discovered yet what a wonderful world art can open up to you.

VIVIE. Yes I have. Last May I spent six weeks in London with Honoria Fraser. Mamma thought we were doing a round of sightseeing together; but I was really at Honoria's chambers in Chancery Lane[9] every day, working away at actuarial calculations for her, and helping her as well as a greenhorn could. In the evenings we smoked and talked, and never dreamt of going out except for exercise. And I never enjoyed myself more in my life. I cleared all my expenses, and got initiated into the business without a fee into the bargain.

PRAED. But bless my heart and soul, Miss Warren, do you call that discovering art?

VIVIE. Wait a bit. That wasnt the beginning. I went up to town on an invitation from some artistic people in Fitzjohn's Avenue: one of the girls was a Newnham chum. They took me to the National Gallery—

PRAED [*approving*] Ah!! [*He sits down, much relieved*].

VIVIE [*continuing*]—to the Opera—

PRAED [*still more pleased*] Good!

VIVIE.—and to a concert where the band played all the evening: Beethoven and Wagner and so on. I wouldnt go through that experience again for anything you could offer me. I held out for civility's sake until the third day; and then I said, plump out, that I couldnt stand any more of it, and went off to Chancery Lane. N o w you know the sort of perfectly splendid modern young lady I am. How do you think I shall get on with my mother?

PRAED [*startled*] Well, I hope—er—

VIVIE. It's not so much what you hope as what you believe, that I want to know.

PRAED. Well, frankly, I am afraid your mother will be a little disappointed. Not from any shortcoming on your part, you know: I dont mean that. But you are so different from her ideal.

VIVIE. Her what?!

PRAED. Her ideal.

VIVIE. Do you mean her ideal of ME?

PRAED. Yes.

[8] A law office.   [9] A section of London containing law and judicial offices.

VIVIE. What on earth is it like?

PRAED. Well, you must have observed, Miss Warren, that people who are dissatisfied with their own bringing-up generally think that the world would be all right if everybody were to be brought up quite differently. Now your mother's life has been—er—I suppose you know—

VIVIE. Dont suppose anything, Mr Praed. I hardly know my mother. Since I was a child I have lived in England, at school or college, or with people paid to take charge of me. I have been boarded out all my life. My mother has lived in Brussels or Vienna and never let me go to her. I only see her when she visits England for a few days. I dont complain: it's been very pleasant; for people have been very good to me; and there has always been plenty of money to make things smooth. But dont imagine I know anything about my mother. I know far less than you do.

PRAED [*very ill at ease*] In that case—[*He stops, quite at a loss. Then, with a forced attempt at gaiety*] But what nonsense we are talking! Of course you and your mother will get on capitally. [*He rises, and looks abroad at the view*]. What a charming little place you have here!

VIVIE [*unmoved*] Rather a violent change of subject, Mr Praed. Why wont my mother's life bear being talked about?

PRAED. Oh, you really mustnt say that. Isnt it natural that I should have a certain delicacy in talking to my old friend's daughter about her behind her back? You and she will have plenty of opportunity of talking about it when she comes.

VIVIE. No: s h e wont talk about it either. [*Rising*] However, I daresay you have good reasons for telling me nothing. Only, mind this, Mr Praed. I expect there will be a battle royal when my mother hears of my Chancery Lane project.

PRAED [*ruefully*] I'm afraid there will.

VIVIE. Well, I shall win, because I want nothing but my fare to London to start there to-morrow earning my own living by devilling[10] for Honoria. Besides, I have no mysteries to keep up; and it seems she has. I shall use that advantage over her if necessary.

PRAED [*greatly shocked*] Oh no! No, pray. Youd not do such a thing.

VIVIE. Then tell me why not.

PRAED. I really cannot. I appeal to your good feeling. [*She smiles at his sentimentality*]. Besides, you may be too bold. Your mother is not to be trifled with when she's angry.

VIVIE. You cant frighten me, Mr Praed. In that month at Chancery Lane I had opportunities of taking the measure of one or two women v e r y like my mother. You may back me to win. But if I hit harder in my ignorance than I need, remember that it is you who refuse to enlighten me. Now, let us drop the subject. [*She takes her chair and replaces it near the hammock with the same vigorous swing as before*].

PRAED [*taking a desperate resolution*] One word, Miss Warren. I had better tell you. It's very difficult; but—

Mrs Warren and Sir George Crofts arrive at the gate. Mrs Warren is between 40 and 50, formerly pretty, showily dressed in a brilliant hat and a gay blouse fitting tightly over her bust and flanked by fashionable sleeves. Rather spoilt and domineering, and

---

[10] Acting as a legal assistant.

decidedly vulgar, but, on the whole, a genial and fairly presentable old blackguard of a woman.

Crofts is a tall powerfully-built man of about 50, fashionably dressed in the style of a young man. Nasal voice, reedier than might be expected from his strong frame. Clean-shaven bulldog jaws, large flat ears, and thick neck: gentlemanly combination of the most brutal types of city man, sporting man, and man about town.

VIVIE. Here they are. [*Coming to them as they enter the garden*] How do, mater? Mr Praed's been here this half hour, waiting for you.

MRS WARREN. Well, if youve been waiting, Praddy, it's your own fault: I thought youd have had the gumption to know I was coming by the 3.10 train. Vivie: put your hat on, dear: you'll get sunburnt. Oh, I forgot to introduce you. Sir George Crofts: my little Vivie.

Crofts advances to Vivie with his most courtly manner. She nods, but makes no motion to shake hands.

CROFTS. May I shake hands with a young lady whom I have known by reputation very long as the daughter of one of my oldest friends?

VIVIE [*who has been looking him up and down sharply*] If you like. [*She takes his tenderly proffered hand and gives it a squeeze that makes him open his eyes; then turns away, and says to her mother*] Will you come in, or shall I get a couple more chairs? [*She goes into the porch for the chairs*].

MRS WARREN. Well, George, what do you think of her?

CROFTS [*ruefully*] She has a powerful fist. Did you shake hands with her, Praed?

PRAED. Yes: it will pass off presently.

CROFTS. I hope so. [*Vivie reappears with two more chairs. He hurries to her assistance*]. Allow me.

MRS WARREN [*patronizingly*] Let Sir George help you with the chairs, dear.

VIVIE [*pitching them into his arms*] Here you are. [*She dusts her hands and turns to Mrs Warren*]. Youd like some tea, wouldnt you?

MRS WARREN [*sitting in Praed's chair and fanning herself*] I'm dying for a drop to drink.

VIVIE. I'll see about it. [*She goes into the cottage*].

Sir George has by this time managed to unfold a chair and plant it beside Mrs Warren, on her left. He throws the other on the grass and sits down, looking dejected and rather foolish, with the handle of his stick in his mouth. Praed, still very uneasy, fidgets about the garden on their right.

MRS WARREN [*to Praed, looking at Crofts*] Just look at him, Praddy: he looks cheerful, dont he? He's been worrying my life out these three years to have that little girl of mine shewn to him; and now that Ive done it, he's quite out of countenance. [*Briskly*] Come! sit up, George; and take your stick out of your mouth. [*Crofts sulkily obeys*].

PRAED. I think, you know—if you dont mind my saying so—that we had better get out of the habit of thinking of her as a little girl. You see she has really distinguished herself; and I'm not sure, from what I have seen of her, that she is not older than any of us.

MRS WARREN [*greatly amused*] Only listen to him, George! Older than any of us! Well, she h a s been stuffing you nicely with her importance.

PRAED. But young people are particularly sensitive about being treated in that way.

MRS WARREN. Yes; and young people have to get all that nonsense taken out of them, and a good deal more besides. Dont you interfere, Praddy: I know how to treat my own child as well as you do. [*Praed, with a grave shake of his head, walks up the garden with his hands behind his back. Mrs. Warren pretends to laugh, but looks after him with perceptible concern. Then she whispers to Crofts*]. Whats the matter with him? What does he take it like that for?

CROFTS [*morosely*] Youre afraid of Praed.

MRS WARREN. What! Me! Afraid of dear old Praddy! Why, a fly wouldnt be afraid of him.

CROFTS. Y o u r e afraid of him.

MRS WARREN [*angry*] I'll trouble you to mind your own business, and not try any of your sulks on me. I'm not afraid of y o u, anyhow. If you cant make yourself agreeable, youd better go home. [*She gets up, and, turning her back on him, finds herself face to face with Praed*]. Come, Praddy, I know it was only your tender-heartedness. Youre afraid I'll bully her.

PRAED. My dear Kitty: you think I'm offended. Dont imagine that: pray dont. But you know I often notice things that escape you; and though you never take my advice, you sometimes admit afterwards that you ought to have taken it.

MRS WARREN. Well, what do you notice now?

PRAED. Only that Vivie is a grown woman. Pray, Kitty, treat her with every respect.

MRS WARREN [*with genuine amazement*] Respect! Treat my own daughter with respect! What next, pray!

VIVIE [*appearing at the cottage door and calling to Mrs Warren*] Mother: will you come to my room before tea?

MRS WARREN. Yes, dearie. [*She laughs indulgently at Praed's gravity, and pats him on the cheek as she passes him on her way to the proch*]. Dont be cross, Praddy. [*She follows Vivie into the cottage*].

CROFTS [*furtively*] I say, Praed.

PRAED. Yes.

CROFTS. I want to ask you a rather particular question.

PRAED. Certainly. [*He takes Mrs Warren's chair and sits close to Crofts*].

CROFTS. Thats right: they might hear us from the window. Look here: did Kitty ever tell you who that girl's father is?

PRAED. Never.

CROFTS. Have you any suspicion of who it might be?

PRAED. None.

CROFTS [*not believing him*] I know, of course, that you perhaps might feel bound not to tell if she had said anything to you. But it's very awkward to be uncertain about it now that we shall be meeting the girl every day. We dont exactly know how we ought to feel towards her.

PRAED. What difference can that make? We take her on her own merits. What does it matter who her father was?

CROFTS [*suspiciously*] Then you know who he was?

PRAED [*with a touch of temper*] I said no just now. Did you not hear me?

CROFTS. Look here, Praed. I ask you as a particular favor. If you d o know [*movement of protest from Praed*]—I only say, if you know, you might at least set my mind at rest about her. The fact is, I feel attracted.

PRAED [*sternly*] What do you mean?

CROFTS. Oh, dont be alarmed: it's quite an innocent feeling. Thats what puzzles me about it. Why, for all I know, *I* might be her father.

PRAED. You! Impossible!

CROFTS [*catching him up cunningly*] You know for certain that I'm not?

PRAED. I know nothing about it, I tell you, any more than you. But really, Crofts—oh no, it's out of the question. Theres not the least resemblance.

CROFTS. As to that, theres no resemblance between her and her mother that I can see. I suppose she's not y o u r daughter, is she?

PRAED [*rising indignantly*] Really, Crofts—!

CROFTS. No offence, Praed. Quite allowable as between two men of the world.

PRAED [*recovering himself with an effort and speaking gently and gravely*] Now listen to me, my dear Crofts. [*He sits down again*]. I have nothing to do with that side of Mrs Warren's life, and never had. She has never spoken to me about it; and of course I have never spoken to her about it. Your delicacy will tell you that a handsome woman needs s o m e friends who are not—well, not on that footing with her. The effect of her own beauty would become a torment to her if she could not escape from it occasionally. You are probably on much more confidential terms with Kitty than I am. Surely you can ask her the question yourself.

CROFTS. I h a v e asked her, often enough. But she's so determined to keep the child all to herself that she would deny that it ever had a father if she could. [*Rising*] I'm thoroughly uncomfortable about it, Praed.

PRAED [*rising also*] Well, as you are, at all events, old enough to be her father, I dont mind agreeing that we both regard Miss Vivie in a parental way, as a young girl whom we are bound to protect and help. What do you say?

CROFTS [*agressively*] I'm no older than you, if you come to that.

PRAED. Yes you are, my dear fellow: you were born old. I was born a boy: Ive never been able to feel the assurance of a grown-up man in my life. [*He folds his chair and carries it to the porch*].

MRS WARREN [*calling from within the cottage*] Prad-dee! George! Tea-ea-ea-ea!

CROFTS [*hastily*] She's calling us. [*He hurries in*].

Praed shakes his head bodingly, and is following Crofts when he is hailed by a young gentleman who has just appeared on the common, and is making for the gate. He is pleasant, pretty, smartly dressed, cleverly good-for-nothing, not long turned 20, with a charming voice and agreeably disrespectful manners. He carries a light sporting magazine rifle.

THE YOUNG GENTLEMAN. Hallo! Praed!

PRAED. Why, Frank Gardner! [*Frank comes in and shakes hands cordially*]. What on earth are you doing here?

FRANK. Staying with my father.

PRAED. The Roman[11] father?

FRANK. He's rector here. I'm living with my people this autumn for the sake of economy. Things came to a crisis in July: the Roman father had to pay my debts. He's stony broke in consequence; and so am I. What are you up to in these parts? Do you know the people here?

PRAED. Yes: I'm spending the day with a Miss Warren.

FRANK [*enthusiastically*] What! Do you know Vivie? Isn't she a jolly girl? I'm teaching her to shoot with this [*putting down the rifle*]. I'm so glad she knows you: youre just the sort of fellow she ought to know. [*He smiles, and raises the charming voice almost to a singing tone as he exclaims*] It's e v e r so jolly to find you here, Praed.

---

[11] I.e., noble and dutiful—*not* Roman Catholic. Gardner's father is an Anglican clergyman—*rector* (see next line) means "parish priest" or "pastor." Anglican clergymen are often referred to as "priests" and addressed as "Father," but unlike Roman Catholic clergy they are allowed to marry.

PRAED. I'm an old friend of her mother. Mrs Warren brought me over to make her daughter's acquaintance.

FRANK. The mother! Is s h e here?

PRAED. Yes: inside, at tea.

MRS WARREN [*calling from within*] Prad-dee-ee-ee-eee! The tea-cake'll be cold.

PRAED [*calling*] Yes, Mrs Warren. In a moment. Ive just met a friend here.

MRS WARREN. A what?

PRAED [*louder*] A friend.

MRS WARREN. Bring him in.

PRAED. All right. [*To Frank*] Will you accept the invitation?

FRANK [*incredulous, but immensely amused*] Is that Vivie's mother?

PRAED. Yes.

FRANK. By Jove! What a lark! Do you think she'll like me?

PRAED. Ive no doubt youll make yourself popular, as usual. Come in and try [*moving towards the house*].

FRANK. Stop a bit. [*Seriously*] I want to take you into my confidence.

PRAED. Pray dont. It's only some fresh folly, like the barmaid at Redhill.

FRANK. It's ever so much more serious than that. You say youve only just met Vivie for the first time?

PRAED. Yes.

FRANK [*rhapsodically*] Then you can have no idea what a girl she is. Such character! Such sense! And her cleverness! Oh, my eye, Praed, but I can tell you she i s clever! And—need I add?—she loves me.

CROFTS [*putting his head out of the window*] I say, Praed: what are you about? Do come along. [*He disappears*].

FRANK. Hallo! Sort of chap that would take a prize at a dog show, ain't he? Who's he?

PRAED. Sir George Crofts, an old friend of Mrs Warren's. I think we had better come in.

On their way to the porch they are interrupted by a call from the gate. Turning, they see an elderly clergyman looking over it.

THE CLERGYMAN [*calling*] Frank!

FRANK. Hallo! [*To Praed*] The Roman father. [*To the clergyman*] Yes, gov'nor: all right: presently. [*To Praed*] Look here, Praed: youd better go in to tea. I'll join you directly.

PRAED. Very good. [*He goes into the cottage*].

The clergyman remains outside the gate, with his hands on the top of it. The Rev. Samuel Gardner, a beneficed clergyman of the Established Church,[12] is over 50. Externally he is pretentious, booming, noisy, important. Really he is that obsolescent social phenomenon the fool of the family dumped on the Church by his father the patron, clamorously asserting himself as father and clergyman without being able to command respect in either capacity.

REV. S. Well, sir. Who are your friends here, if I may ask?

FRANK. Oh, it's all right, gov'nor! Come in.

REV. S. No, sir; not until I know whose garden I am entering.

FRANK. It's all right. It's Miss Warren's.

REV. S. I have not see her at church since she came.

---

[12] The Church of England or Anglican Church, called the Episcopal Church in the U.S. It is called "Established" because it was founded by King Henry VIII and has been the State religion of England ever since.

FRANK. Of course not: she's a third wrangler. Ever so intellectual. Took a
   higher degree than you did; so why should she go to hear you preach?
REV. S. Dont be disrespectful, sir.
FRANK. Oh, it dont matter: nobody hears us. Come in. [*He opens the gate, unceremo-
   niously pulling his father with it into the garden*]. I want to introduce you to
   her. Do you remember the advice you gave me last July, gov'nor?
REV. S. [*severely*] Yes. I advised you to conquer your idleness and flippancy,
   and to work your way into an honorable profession and live on it and not
   upon me.
FRANK. No: thats what you thought of afterwards. What you actually said was
   that since I had neither brains nor money, I'd better turn my good looks
   to account by marrying somebody with both. Well, look here. Miss Warren
   has brains: you cant deny that.
REV. S. Brains are not everything.
FRANK. No, of course not: theres the money—
REV. S. [*interrupting him austerely*] I was not thinking of money, sir. I was speaking
   of higher things. Social position, for instance.
FRANK. I dont care a rap about that.
REV. S. But I do, sir.
FRANK. Well, nobody wants you to marry her. Anyhow, she has what amounts
   to a high Cambridge degree; and she seems to have as much money as
   she wants.
REV. S. [*sinking into a feeble vein of humor*] I greatly doubt whether she has as
   much money as y o u will want.
FRANK. Oh, come: I havnt been so very extravagant. I live ever so quietly; I
   dont drink; I dont bet much; and I never go regularly on the razzle-dazzle
   as you did when you were my age.
REV. S. [*booming hollowly*] Silence, sir.
FRANK. Well, you told me yourself, when I was making ever such an ass of
   myself about the barmaid at Redhill, that you once offered a woman £50
   for the letters you wrote to her when—
REV. S. [*terrified*] Sh-sh-sh, Frank, for Heaven's sake! [*He looks round apprehensively.
   Seeing no one within earshot he plucks up courage to boom again, but more subduedly*].
   You are taking an ungentlemanly advantage of what I confided to you for
   your own good, to save you from an error you would have repented all
   your life long. Take warning by your father's follies, sir; and dont make
   them an excuse for your own.
FRANK. Did you ever hear the story of the Duke of Wellington[13] and his letters?
REV. S. No, sir; and I dont want to hear it.
FRANK. The old Iron Duke didnt throw away £50: not he. He just wrote: "Dear
   Jenny: publish and be damned! Yours affectionately, Wellington." Thats
   what you should have done.
REV. S. [*piteously*] Frank, my boy: when I wrote those letters I put myself into
   that woman's power. When I told you about them I put myself, to some
   extent, I am sorry to say, in your power. She refused my money with these
   words, which I shall never forget. "Knowledge is power" she said; "and I
   never sell power." Thats more than twenty years ago; and she has never

---

[13] The reference is to Arthur Wellesley (1769–1852), the first Duke of Wellington, who defeated
Napoleon at Waterloo in 1815 and later became prime minister of England (1828–1830).

made use of her power or caused me a moment's uneasiness. You are behaving worse to me than she did, Frank.

FRANK. Oh yes I dare say! Did you ever preach at her the way you preach at me every day?

REV. S. [*wounded almost to tears*] I leave you, sir. You are incorrigible. [*He turns towards the gate*].

FRANK [*utterly unmoved*] Tell them I shant be home to tea, will you, gov'nor, like a good fellow? [*He moves towards the cottage door and is met by Praed and Vivie coming out*].

VIVIE [*to Frank*] Is that your father, Frank? I do so want to meet him.

FRANK. Certainly. [*Calling after his father*] Gov'nor. Youre wanted. [*The parson turns at the gate, fumbling nervously at his hat. Praed crosses the garden to the opposite side, beaming in anticipation of civilities*]. My father: Miss Warren.

VIVIE [*going to the clergyman and shaking his hand*] Very glad to see you here, Mr Gardner. [*Calling to the cottage*] Mother: come along: youre wanted.

Mrs Warren appears on the threshold, and is immediately transfixed, recognizing the clergyman.

VIVIE [*continuing*] Let me introduce—

MRS WARREN [*swooping on the Reverend Samuel*] Why, it's Sam Gardner, gone into the Church! Well, I never! Dont you know us, Sam? This is George Crofts, as large as life and twice as natural. Dont you remember me?

REV. S. [*very red*] I really—er—

MRS WARREN. Of course you do. Why, I have a whole album of your letters still: I came across them only the other day.

REV. S. [*miserably confused*] Miss Vavasour, I believe.

MRS WARREN [*correcting him quickly in a loud whisper*] Tch! Nonsense! Mrs Warren: dont you see my daughter there?

ACT II

Inside the cottage after nightfall. Looking eastward from within instead of westward from without, the latticed window, with its curtains drawn, is now seen in the middle of the front wall of the cottage, with the porch door to the left of it. In the left-hand side wall is the door leading to the kitchen. Farther back against the same wall is a dresser with a candle and matches on it, and FRANK's rifle standing beside them, with the barrel resting in the plate-rack. In the centre a table stands with a lighted lamp on it. VIVIE's books and writing materials are on a table to the right of the window, against the wall. The fireplace is on the right, with a settle: there is no fire. Two of the chairs are set right and left of the table.

The cottage door opens, shewing a fine starlit night without; and MRS WARREN, her shoulders wrapped in a shawl borrowed from VIVIE, enters, followed by FRANK, who throws his cap on the window seat. She has had enough of walking, and gives a gasp of relief as she unpins her hat; takes it off; sticks the pin through the crown; and puts it on the table.

MRS WARREN. O Lord! I dont know which is the worst of the country, the walking or the sitting at home with nothing to do. I could do with a whisky and soda now very well, if only they had such a thing in this place.

FRANK. Perhaps Vivie's got some.

MRS WARREN. Nonsense! What would a young girl like her be doing with

such things! Never mind: it dont matter. I wonder how she passes her time
here! I'd a good deal rather be in Vienna.

Frank. Let me take you there. [*He helps her to take off her shawl, gallantly giving
her shoulders a very perceptible squeeze as he does so*].

Mrs Warren. Ah! would you? I'm beginning to think youre a chip of the
old block.

Frank. Like the gov'nor, eh? [*He hangs the shawl on the nearest chair, and sits
down*].

Mrs Warren. Never you mind. What do you know about such things? Youre
only a boy. [*She goes to the hearth, to be farther from temptation*].

Frank. Do come to Vienna with me? It'd be ever such larks.

Mrs Warren. No, thank you. Vienna is no place for you—at least not until
youre a little older. [*She nods at him to emphasize this piece of advice. He makes
a mock-piteous face, belied by his laughing eyes. She looks at him; then comes back to
him*]. Now, look here, little boy [*taking his face in her hands and turning it up
to her*]: I know you through and through by your likeness to your father,
better than you know yourself. Dont you go taking any silly ideas into your
head about me. Do you hear?

Frank [*gallantly wooing her with his voice*] Cant help it, my dear Mrs Warren: it
runs in the family.

*She pretends to box his ears; then looks at the pretty laughing upturned face for a
moment, tempted. At last she kisses him, and immediately turns away, out of patience
with herself.*

Mrs Warren. There! I shouldnt have done that. I a m wicked. Never you
mind, my dear: it's only a motherly kiss. Go and make love to Vivie.

Frank. So I have.

Mrs Warren [*turning on him with a sharp note of alarm in her voice*] What!

Frank. Vivie and I are ever such chums.

Mrs Warren. What do you mean? Now see here: I wont have any young
scamp tampering with my little girl. Do you hear? I wont have it.

Frank [*quite unabashed*] My dear Mrs Warren: dont you be alarmed. My intentions
are honorable: ever so honorable; and your little girl is jolly well able to
take care of herself. She dont need looking after half so much as her mother.
She aint so handsome, you know.

Mrs Warren [*taken aback by his assurance*] Well, you have got a nice healthy
two inches thick of cheek all over you. I dont know where you got it. Not
from your father, anyhow.

Crofts [*in the garden*] The gipsies, I suppose?

Rev. S. [*replying*] The broomsquires[14] are far worse.

Mrs Warren [*to Frank*] S-sh! Remember! youve had your warning.

Crofts *and the* Reverend Samuel *come in from the garden, the clergyman continuing
his conversation as he enters.*

Rev. S. The perjury at the Winchester assizes[15] is deplorable.

Mrs Warren. Well? what became of you two? And wheres Praddy and Vivie?

Crofts [*putting his hat on the settle and his stick in the chimney corner*] They went
up the hill. We went to the village. I wanted a drink. [*He sits down on the
settle, putting his legs up along the seat*].

Mrs Warren. Well, she oughtnt to go off like that without telling me. [*To

---

[14] Squatters on the English wasteland who live by tying heath into brooms.
[15] Court sessions.

Frank] Get your father a chair, Frank: where are your manners? [*Frank springs up and gracefully offers his father his chair; then takes another from the wall and sits down at the table, in the middle, with his father on his right and Mrs Warren on his left*]. George: where are you going to stay to-night? You cant stay here. And whats Praddy going to do?

CROFTS. Gardner'll put me up.

MRS WARREN. Oh, no doubt youve taken care of yourself! But what about Praddy?

CROFTS. Dont know. I suppose he can sleep at the inn.

MRS WARREN. Havnt you room for him, Sam?

REV. S. Well—er—you see, as rector here, I am not free to do as I like. Er—what is Mr Praed's social position?

MRS WARREN. Oh, he's all right: he's an architect. What an old stick-in-the-mud you are, Sam!

FRANK. Yes, it's all right, gov'nor. He built that place down in Wales for the Duke. Caernarvon Castle[16] they call it. You must have heard of it. [*He winks with lightning smartness at Mrs Warren, and regards his father blandly*].

REV. S. Oh, in that case, of course we shall only be too happy. I suppose he knows the Duke personally.

FRANK. Oh, ever so intimately! We can stick him in Georgina's old room.

MRS WARREN. Well, thats settled. Now if those two would only come in and let us have supper. Theyve no right to stay out after dark like this.

CROFTS [*aggressively*] What harm are they doing you?

MRS WARREN. Well, harm or not, I dont like it.

FRANK. Better not wait for them, Mrs Warren. Praed will stay out as long as possible. He has never known before what it is to stray over the heath on a summer night with my Vivie.

CROFTS [*sitting up in some consternation*] I say, you know! Come!

REV. S. [*rising, startled out of his professional manner into real force and sincerity*] Frank, once for all, it's out of the question. Mrs Warren will tell you that it's not to be thought of.

CROFTS. Of course not.

FRANK [*with enchanting placidity*] Is that so, Mrs Warren?

MRS WARREN [*reflectively*] Well, Sam, I dont know. If the girl wants to get married, no good can come of keeping her unmarried.

REV. S. [*astounded*] But married to him!—your daughter to my son! Only think: it's impossible.

CROFTS. Of course it's impossible. Dont be a fool, Kitty.

MRS WARREN [*nettled*] Why not? Isnt my daughter good enough for your son?

REV. S. But surely, my dear Mrs Warren, you know the reasons—

MRS WARREN [*defiantly*] I know no reasons. If you know any, you can tell them to the lad, or to the girl, or to your congregation, if you like.

REV. S. [*collapsing helplessly into his chair*] You know very well that I couldnt tell anyone the reasons. But my boy will believe me when I tell him there a r e reasons.

FRANK. Quite right, Dad: he will. But has your boy's conduct ever been influenced by your reasons?

---

[16] Caernarvon Castle is one of the most famous tourist attractions in the United Kingdom, but it was built in 1283. Frank is brazenly making fun of his father's ignorance by pretending that Praed designed the castle for the Duke of Wales. There is, however, no *Duke* of Wales; Wales is a *principality* and its lord is the *Prince* of Wales.

CROFTS. You cant marry her; and thats all about it. [*He gets up and stands on the hearth, with his back to the fireplace, frowning determinedly*].

MRS WARREN [*turning on him sharply*] What have you got to do with it, pray?

FRANK [*with his prettiest lyrical cadence*] Precisely what I was going to ask, myself, in my own graceful fashion.

CROFTS [*to Mrs Warren*] I suppose you dont want to marry the girl to a man younger than herself and without either a profession or twopence to keep her on. Ask Sam, if you dont believe me. [*To the parson*] How much more money are you going to give him?

REV. S. Not another penny. He has had his patrimony; and he spent the last of it in July. [*Mrs Warren's face falls*].

CROFTS [*watching her*] There! I told you. [*He resumes his place on the settle and puts up his legs on the seat again, as if the matter were finally disposed of*].

FRANK [*plaintively*] This is ever so mercenary. Do you suppose Miss Warren's going to marry for money? If we love one another—

MRS WARREN. Thank you. Your love's a pretty cheap commodity, my lad. If you have no means of keeping a wife, that settles it: you cant have Vivie.

FRANK [*much amused*] What do y o u say, gov'nor, eh?

REV. S. I agree with Mrs Warren.

FRANK. And good old Crofts has already expressed his opinion.

CROFTS [*turning angrily on his elbow*] Look here: I want none of y o u r cheek.

FRANK [*pointedly*] I'm ever so sorry to surprise you, Crofts; but you allowed yourself the liberty of speaking to me like a father a moment ago. One father is enough, thank you.

CROFTS [*contemptuously*] Yah! [*He turns away again*].

FRANK [*rising*] Mrs Warren: I cannot give my Vivie up, even for your sake.

MRS WARREN [*muttering*] Young scamp!

FRANK [*continuing*] And as you no doubt intend to hold out other prospects to her, I shall lose no time in placing my case before her. [*They stare at him; and he begins to declaim gracefully*]

> He either fears his fate too much,
> Or his deserts are small,
> That dares not put it to the touch
> To gain or lose it all.[17]

The cottage door opens whilst he is reciting; and Vivie and Praed come in. He breaks off. Praed puts his hat on the dresser. There is an immediate improvement in the company's behavior. Crofts takes down his legs from the settle and pulls himself together as Praed joins him at the fireplace. Mrs Warren loses her ease of manner and takes refuge in querulousness.

MRS WARREN. Wherever have you been, Vivie?

VIVIE [*taking off her hat and throwing it carelessly on the table*] On the hill.

MRS WARREN. Well, you shouldnt go off like that without letting me know. How could I tell what had become of you? And night coming on too!

VIVIE [*going to the door of the kitchen and opening it, ignoring her mother*] Now, about supper? [*All rise except Mrs Warren*]. We shall be rather crowded in here, I'm afraid.

MRS WARREN. Did you hear what I said, Vivie?

[17] From "My Dear and Only Love" by the Marquis of Montrose (1612–1650).

VIVIE [*quietly*] Yes, mother. [*Reverting to the supper difficulty*] How many are we? [*Counting*] One, two, three, four, five, six. Well, two will have to wait until the rest are done: Mrs Alison has only plates and knives for four.

PRAED. Oh, it doesnt matter about me. I—

VIVIE. You have had a long walk and are hungry, Mr Praed: you shall have your supper at once. I can wait myself. I want one person to wait with me. Frank: are you hungry?

FRANK. Not the least in the world. Completely off my peck, in fact.

MRS WARREN [*to Crofts*] Neither are you, George. You can wait.

CROFTS. Oh, hang it, Ive eaten nothing since tea-time. Cant Sam do it?

FRANK. Would you starve my poor father?

REV. S. [*testily*] Allow me to speak for myself, sir. I am perfectly willing to wait.

VIVIE [*decisively*] Theres no need. Only two are wanted. [*She opens the door of the kitchen*]. Will you take my mother in, Mr Gardner. [*The parson takes Mrs Warren; and they pass into the kitchen. Praed and Crofts follow. All except Praed clearly disapprove of the arrangement, but do not know how to resist it. Vivie stands at the door looking in at them*]. Can you squeeze past to that corner, Mr Praed: it's rather a tight fit. Take care of your coat against the white-wash: thats right. Now, are you all comfortable?

PRAED [*within*] Quite, thank you.

MRS WARREN [*within*] Leave the door open, dearie. [*Vivie frowns; but Frank checks her with a gesture, and steals to the cottage door, which he softly sets wide open*]. Oh Lor, what a draught! Youd better shut it, dear.

Vivie shuts it with a slam, and then, noting with disgust that her mother's hat and shawl are lying about, takes them tidily to the window seat, whilst Frank noiselessly shuts the cottage door.

FRANK [*exulting*] Aha! Got rid of em. Well, Vivvums: what do you think of my governor?

VIVIE [*preoccupied and serious*] Ive hardly spoken to him. He doesnt strike me as being a particularly able person.

FRANK. Well, you know, the old man is not altogether such a fool as he looks. You see, he was shoved into the Church rather; and in trying to live up to it he makes a much bigger ass of himself than he really is. I dont dislike him as much as you might expect. He means well. How do you think youll get on with him?

VIVIE [*rather grimly*] I dont think my future life will be much concerned with him, or with any of that old circle of my mother's, except perhaps Praed. [*She sits down on the settle*]. What do you think of my mother?

FRANK. Really and truly?

VIVIE. Yes, really and truly.

FRANK. Well, she's ever so jolly. But she's rather a caution, isnt she? And Crofts! Oh, my eye, Crofts! [*He sits beside her*].

VIVIE. What a lot, Frank!

FRANK. What a crew!

VIVIE [*with intense contempt for them*] If I thought that *I* was like that—that I was going to be a waster, shifting along from one meal to another with no purpose, and no character, and no grit in me, I'd open an artery and bleed to death without one moment's hesitation.

FRANK. Oh no, you wouldnt. Why should they take any grind when they can afford not to? I wish I had their luck. No: what I object to is their form. It isnt the thing: it's slovenly, ever so slovenly.

VIVIE. Do you think your form will be any better when youre as old as Crofts, if you dont work?

FRANK. Of course I do. Ever so much better. Vivvums mustnt lecture: her little boy's incorrigible. [*He attempts to take her face caressingly in his hands*].

VIVIE [*striking his hands down sharply*] Off with you: Vivvums is not in a humor for petting her little boy this evening. [*She rises and comes forward to the other side of the room*].

FRANK [*following her*] How unkind!

VIVIE [*stamping at him*] Be serious. I'm serious.

FRANK. Good. Let us talk learnedly. Miss Warren: do you know that all the most advanced thinkers are agreed that half the diseases of modern civilization are due to starvation of the affections in the young. Now, I—

VIVIE [*cutting him short*] You are very tiresome. [*She opens the inner door*]. Have you room for Frank there? He's complaining of starvation.

MRS WARREN [*within*] Of course there is [*clatter of knives and glasses as she moves the things on the table*]. Here! theres room now beside me. Come along, Mr Frank.

FRANK. Her little boy will be ever so even with his Vivvums for this. [*He passes into the kitchen*].

MRS WARREN [*within*] Here, Vivie: come on you too, child. You must be famished. [*She enters, followed by Crofts, who holds the door open for Vivie with marked deference. She goes out without looking at him; and he shuts the door after her*]. Why, George, you cant be done: youve eaten nothing. Is there anything wrong with you?

CROFTS. Oh, all I wanted was a drink. [*He thrusts his hands in his pockets, and begins prowling about the room, restless and sulky*].

MRS WARREN. Well, I like enough to eat. But a little of that cold beef and cheese and lettuce goes a long way. [*With a sigh of only half repletion she sits down lazily on the settle*].

CROFTS. What do you go encouraging that young pup for?

MRS WARREN [*on the alert at once*] Now see here, George: what are you up to about that girl? Ive been watching your way of looking at her. Remember: I know you and what your looks mean.

CROFTS. Theres no harm in looking at her, is there?

MRS WARREN. I'd put you out and pack you back to London pretty soon if I saw any of your nonsense. My girl's little finger is more to me than your whole body and soul. [*Crofts receives this with a sneering grin. Mrs Warren, flushing a little at her failure to impose on him in the character of a theatrically devoted mother, adds in a lower key*] Make your mind easy: the young pup has no more chance than you have.

CROFTS. Maynt a man take an interest in a girl?

MRS WARREN. Not a man like you.

CROFTS. How old is she?

MRS WARREN. Never you mind how old she is.

CROFTS. Why do you make such a secret of it?

MRS WARREN. Because I choose.

CROFTS. Well, I'm not fifty yet; and my property is as good as ever it was—

MRS WARREN [*interrupting him*] Yes; because youre as stingy as youre vicious.

CROFTS [*continuing*] And a baronet isnt to be picked up every day. No other man in my position would put up with you for a mother-in-law. Why shouldnt she marry me?

MRS WARREN. You!

CROFTS. We three could live together quite comfortably. I'd die before her and leave her a bouncing widow with plenty of money. Why not? It's been growing in my mind all the time Ive been walking with that fool inside there.

MRS WARREN [*revolted*] Yes: it's the sort of thing that w o u l d grow in your mind.

He halts in his prowling; and the two look at one another, she steadfastly, with a sort of awe behind her contemptuous disgust: he stealthily, with a carnal gleam in his eye and a loose grin.

CROFTS [*suddenly becoming anxious and urgent as he sees no sign of sympathy in her*] Look here, Kitty: youre a sensible women: you neednt put on any moral airs. I'll ask no more questions; and you need answer none. I'll settle the whole property on her; and if you want a cheque for yourself on the wedding day, you can name any figure you like—in reason.

MRS WARREN. So it's come to that with you, George, like all the other worn-out old creatures!

CROFTS [*savagely*] Damn you!

Before she can retort the door of the kitchen is opened; and the voices of the others are heard returning. Crofts, unable to recover his presence of mind, hurries out of the cottage. The clergyman appears at the kitchen door.

REV. S. [*looking round*] Where is Sir George?

MRS WARREN. Gone out to have a pipe. [*The clergyman takes his hat from the table, and joins Mrs Warren at the fireside. Meanwhile Vivie comes in, followed by Frank, who collapses into the nearest chair with an air of extreme exhaustion. Mrs Warren looks round at Vivie and says, with her affectation of maternal patronage even more forced than usual*] Well, dearie: have you had a good supper?

VIVIE. You know what Mrs Alison's suppers are. [*She turns to Frank and pets him*]. Poor Frank! was all the beef gone? did it get nothing but bread and cheese and ginger beer? [*Seriously, as if she had done quite enough trifling for one evening*] Her butter is really awful. I must get some down from the stores.

FRANK. Do, in Heaven's name!

Vivie goes to the writing-table and makes a memorandum to order the butter. Praed comes in from the kitchen, putting up his handkerchief, which he has been using as a napkin.

REV. S. Frank, my boy: it is time for us to be thinking of home. Your mother does not know yet that we have visitors.

PRAED. I'm afraid we're giving trouble.

FRANK [*rising*] Not the least in the world: my mother will be delighted to see you. She's a genuinely intellectual artistic woman; and she sees nobody here from one year's end to another except the gov'nor; so you can imagine how jolly dull it pans out for her. [*To his father*] Y o u r e not intellectual or artistic: are you, pater? So take Praed home at once; and I'll stay here and entertain Mrs Warren. Youll pick up Crofts in the garden. He'll be excellent company for the bull-pup.

PRAED [*taking his hat from the dresser, and coming close to Frank*] Come with us, Frank. Mrs Warren has not seen Miss Vivie for a long time; and we have prevented them from having a moment together yet.

FRANK [*quite softened, and looking at Praed with romantic admiration*] Of course. I forgot. Ever so thanks for reminding me. Perfect gentleman, Praddy. Always were. My ideal through life. [*He rises to go, but pauses a moment between the two older men, and puts his hand on Praed's shoulder*]. Ah, if you had only been my father instead of this unworthy old man! [*He puts his other hand on his father's shoulder*].

REV. S. [*blustering*] Silence, sir, silence: you are profane.

MRS WARREN [*laughing heartily*] You should keep him in better order, Sam. Good-night. Here: take George his hat and stick with my compliments.

REV. S. [*taking them*] Good-night. [*They shake hands. As he passes Vivie he shakes hands with her also and bids her good-night. Then, in booming command, to Frank*] Come along, sir, at once. [*He goes out*].

MRS WARREN. Byebye, Praddy.

PRAED. Byebye, Kitty.

They shake hands affectionately and go out together, she accompanying him to the garden gate.

FRANK [*to Vivie*] Kissums?

VIVIE [*fiercely*] No. I hate you. [*She takes a couple of books and some paper from the writing-table, and sits down with them at the middle table, at the end next the fireplace*].

FRANK [*grimacing*] Sorry. [*He goes for his cap and rifle. Mrs Warren returns. He takes her hand*] Good-night, dear Mrs Warren. [*He kisses her hand. She snatches it away, her lips tightening, and looks more than half disposed to box his ears. He laughs mischievously and runs off, clapping-to the door behind him*].

MRS WARREN [*resigning herself to an evening of boredom now that the men are gone*] Did you ever in your life hear anyone rattle on so? Isnt he a tease? [*She sits at the table*]. Now that I think of it, dearie, dont you go encouraging him. I'm sure he's a regular good-for-nothing.

VIVIE [*rising to fetch more books*] I'm afraid so. Poor Frank! I shall have to get rid of him; but I shall feel sorry for him, though he's not worth it. That man Crofts does not seem to me to be good for much either: is he? [*She throws the books on the table rather roughly*].

MRS WARREN [*galled by Vivie's indifference*] What do you know of men, child, to talk that way about them? Youll have to make up your mind to see a good deal of Sir George Crofts, as he's a friend of mine.

VIVIE [*quite unmoved*] Why? [*She sits down and opens a book*]. Do you expect that we shall be much together? You and I, I mean?

MRS WARREN [*staring at her*] Of course: until youre married. Youre not going back to college again.

VIVIE. Do you think my way of life would suit you? I doubt it.

MRS WARREN. Y o u r way of life! What do you mean?

VIVIE [*cutting a page of her book with the paper knife on her chatelaine*] Has it really never occurred to you, mother, that I have a way of life like other people?

MRS WARREN. What nonsense is this youre trying to talk? Do you want to shew your independence, now that youre a great little person at school? Dont be a fool, child.

VIVIE [*indulgently*] Thats all you have to say on the subject, is it, mother?

MRS WARREN [*puzzled, then angry*] Dont you keep on asking me questions like that. [*Violently*] Hold your tongue. [*Vivie works on, losing no time, and saying nothing*]. You and your way of life, indeed! What next? [*She looks at Vivie again. No reply*]. Your way of life will be what I please, so it will. [*Another pause*]. Ive been noticing these airs in you ever since you got that tripos or whatever you call it. If you think I'm going to put up with them youre mistaken; and the sooner you find it out, the better. [*Muttering*] All I have to say on the subject, indeed! [*Again raising her voice angrily*] Do you know who youre speaking to, Miss?

VIVIE [*looking across at her without raising her head from her book*] No. Who are you? What are you?

MRS WARREN [*rising breathless*] You young imp!

VIVIE. Everybody knows my reputation, my social standing, and the profession I intend to pursue. I know nothing about you. What is that way of life which you invite me to share with you and Sir George Crofts, pray?

MRS WARREN. Take care. I shall do something I'll be sorry for after, and you too.

VIVIE [*putting aside her books with cool decision*] Well, let us drop the subject until you are better able to face it. [*Looking critically at her mother*] You want some good walks and a little lawn tennis to set you up. You are shockingly out of condition: you were not able to manage twenty yards uphill today without stopping to pant; and your wrists are mere rolls of fat. Look at mine. [*She holds out her wrists*].

MRS WARREN [*after looking at her helplessly, begins to whimper*] Vivie—

VIVIE [*springing up sharply*] Now pray dont begin to cry. Anything but that. I really cannot stand whimpering. I will go out of the room if you do.

MRS WARREN [*piteously*] Oh, my darling, how can you be so hard on me? Have I no rights over you as your mother?

VIVIE. A r e you my mother?

MRS WARREN [*appalled*] A m I your mother! Oh, Vivie!

VIVIE. Then where are our relatives? my father? our family friends? You claim the rights of a mother: the right to call me fool and child; to speak to me as no woman in authority over me at college dare speak to me; to dictate my way of life; and to force on me the acquaintance of a brute whom anyone can see to be the most vicious sort of London man about town. Before I give myself the trouble to resist such claims, I may as well find out whether they have any real existence.

MRS WARREN [*distracted, throwing herself on her knees*] Oh no, no. Stop, stop. I a m your mother: I swear it. Oh, you cant mean to turn on me—my own child! it's not natural. You believe me, dont you? Say you believe me.

VIVIE. Who was my father?

MRS WARREN. You dont know what youre asking. I cant tell you.

VIVIE [*determinedly*] Oh yes you can, if you like. I have a right to know; and you know very well that I have that right. You can refuse to tell me, if you please; but if you do, you will see the last of me tomorrow morning.

MRS WARREN. Oh, it's too horrible to hear you talk like that. You wouldnt— you c o u l d n t leave me.

VIVIE [*ruthlessly*] Yes, without a moment's hesitation, if you trifle with me about this. [*Shivering with disgust*] How can I feel sure that I may not have the contaminated blood of that brutal waster in my veins?

MRS WARREN. No, no. On my oath it's not he, nor any of the rest that you have ever met. I'm certain of that, at least.

Vivie's eyes fasten sternly on her mother as the significance of this flashes on her.

VIVIE [*slowly*] You are certain of that, at l e a s t. Ah! You mean that that is all you are certain of. [*Thoughtfully*] I see. [*Mrs Warren buries her face in her hands*]. Dont do that, mother: you know you dont feel it a bit. [*Mrs Warren takes down her hands and looks up deplorably at Vivie, who takes out her watch and, says*] Well, that is enough for tonight. At what hour would you like breakfast? Is half-past eight too early for you?

MRS WARREN [*wildly*] My God, what sort of woman are you?

VIVIE [*coolly*] The sort the world is mostly made of, I should hope. Otherwise I dont understand how it gets its business done. Come [*taking her mother by the wrist, and pulling her up pretty resolutely*]: pull yourself together. Thats right.

MRS WARREN [*querulously*] Youre very rough with me, Vivie.

VIVIE. Nonsense. What about bed? It's past ten.

MRS WARREN [*passionately*] Whats the use of my going to bed? Do you think I could sleep?

VIVIE. Why not? I shall.

MRS WARREN. You! youve no heart. [*She suddenly breaks out vehemently in her natural tongue—the dialect of a woman of the people—with all her affectations of maternal authority and conventional manners gone, and an overwhelming inspiration of true conviction and scorn in her*] Oh, I wont bear it: I wont put up with the injustice of it. What right have you to set yourself up above me like this? You boast of what you are to me—to m e, who gave you the chance of being what you are. What chance had I? Shame on you for a bad daughter and a stuck-up prude!

VIVIE [*sitting down with a shrug, no longer confident; for her replies, which have sounded sensible and strong to her so far, now begin to ring rather woodenly and even priggishly against the new tone of her mother*] Dont think for a moment I set myself above you in any way. You attacked me with the conventional authority of a mother: I defended myself with the conventional superiority of a respectable woman. Frankly, I am not going to stand any of your nonsense; and when you drop it I shall not expect you to stand any of mine. I shall always respect your right to your own opinions and your own way of life.

MRS WARREN. My own opinions and my own way of life! Listen to her talking! Do you think I was brought up like you? able to pick and choose my own way of life? Do you think I did what I did because I liked it, or thought it right, or wouldnt rather have gone to college and been a lady if I'd had the chance?

VIVIE. Everybody has some choice, mother. The poorest girl alive may not be able to choose between being Queen of England or Principal of Newnham; but she can choose between ragpicking and flowerselling, according to her taste. People are always blaming their circumstances for what they are. I dont believe in circumstances. The people who get on in this world are the people who get up and look for the circumstances they want, and, if they cant find them, make them.

MRS WARREN. Oh, it's easy to talk, very easy, isnt it? Here! would you like to know what m y circumstances were?

VIVIE. Yes: you had better tell me. Wont you sit down?

MRS WARREN. Oh, I'll sit down: dont you be afraid. [*She plants her chair farther forward with brazen energy, and sits down. Vivie is impressed in spite of herself*]. D'you know what your gran'mother was?

VIVIE. No.

MRS WARREN. No you dont. I do. She called herself a widow and had a fried-fish shop down by the Mint, and kept herself and four daughters out of it. Two of us were sisters: that was me and Liz; and we were both good-looking and well made. I suppose our father was a well-fed man: mother pretended he was a gentleman; but I dont know. The other two were only half sisters: undersized, ugly, starved looking, hard working, honest poor creatures: Liz and I would have half-murdered them if mother hadnt half-murdered u s to keep our hands off them. They were the respectable ones. Well, what did they get by their respectability? I'll tell you. One of them worked in a whitelead factory twelve hours a day for nine shillings a week until she died of lead poisoning. She only expected to get her hands a little paralyzed; but she died. The other was always held up to us as a model because she married a Government laborer in the Deptford victualling yard, and kept his room and the three children neat and tidy on eighteen shillings a week— until he took to drink. That was worth being respectable for, wasnt it?

VIVIE [*now thoughtfully attentive*] Did you and your sister think so?

MRS WARREN. Liz didnt, I can tell you: she had more spirit. We both went to a church school—that was part of the ladylike airs we gave ourselves to be superior to the children that knew nothing and went nowhere—and we stayed there until Liz went out one night and never came back. I know the schoolmistress thought I'd soon follow her example; for the clergyman was always warning me that Lizzie'd end by jumping off Waterloo Bridge. Poor fool: that was all he knew about it! But I was more afraid of the whitelead factory than I was of the river; and so would you have been in my place. That clergyman got me a situation as scullery maid in a temperance restaurant where they sent out for anything you liked. Then I was waitress; and then I went to the bar at Waterloo station: fourteen hours a day serving drinks and washing glasses for four shillings a week and my board. That was considered a great promotion for me. Well, one cold, wretched night, when I was so tired I could hardly keep myself awake, who should come up for a half of Scotch but Lizzie, in a long fur cloak, elegant and comfortable, with a lot of sovereigns in her purse.

VIVIE [*grimly*] My aunt Lizzie!

MRS WARREN. Yes; and a very good aunt to have, too. She's living down at Winchester now, close to the cathedral, one of the most respectable ladies there. Chaperones girls at the county ball, if you please. No river for Liz, thank you! You remind me of Liz a little: she was a first-rate business woman— saved money from the beginning—never let herself look too like what she was—never lost her head or threw away a chance. When she saw I'd grown up good-looking she said to me across the bar "What are you doing there, you little fool? wearing out your health and your appearance for other people's profit!" Liz was saving money then to take a house for herself in Brussels; and she thought we two could save faster than one. So she lent me some money and gave me a start; and I saved steadily and first paid her back, and then went into business with her as her partner. Why shouldnt I have done it? The house in Brussels was real high class: a much better place for a woman to be in than the factory where Anne Jane got poisoned. None of our girls were ever treated as I was treated in the scullery of that temperance place, or at the Waterloo bar, or at home. Would you have had me stay in them and become a worn out old drudge before I was forty?

VIVIE [*intensely interested by this time*] No; but why did you choose that business? Saving money and good management will succeed in any business.

MRS WARREN. Yes, saving money. But where can a woman get the money to save in any other business? Could y o u save out of four shillings a week and keep yourself dressed as well? Not you. Of course, if youre a plain woman and cant earn anything more; or if you have a turn for music, or the stage, or newspaper-writing: thats different. But neither Liz nor I had any turn for such things: all we had was our appearance and our turn for pleasing men. Do you think we were such fools as to let other people trade in our good looks by employing us as shopgirls, or barmaids, or waitresses, when we could trade in them ourselves and get all the profits instead of starvation wages? Not likely.

VIVIE. You were certainly quite justified—from the business point of view.

MRS WARREN. Yes; or any other point of view. What is any respectable girl brought up to do but to catch some rich man's fancy and get the benefit of his money by marrying him?—as if a marriage ceremony could make any difference in the right or wrong of the thing! Oh, the hypocrisy of the world makes me sick! Liz and I had to work and save and calculate just like other people; elseways we should be as poor as any good-for-nothing drunken waster of a woman that thinks her luck will last for ever. [*With great energy*] I despise such people: theyve no character; and if theres a thing I hate in a woman, it's want of character.

VIVIE. Come now, mother: frankly! Isnt it part of what you call character in a woman that she should greatly dislike such a way of making money?

MRS WARREN. Why, of course. Everybody dislikes having to work and make money; but they have to do it all the same. I'm sure Ive often pitied a poor girl, tired out and in low spirits, having to try to please some man that she doesnt care two straws for—some half-drunken fool that thinks he's making himself agreeable when he's teasing and worrying and disgusting a woman so that hardly any money could pay her for putting up with it. But she has to bear with disagreeables and take the rough with the smooth, just like a nurse in a hospital or anyone else. It's not work that any woman would do for pleasure, goodness knows; though to hear the pious people talk you would suppose it was a bed of roses.

VIVIE. Still, you consider it worth while. It pays.

MRS WARREN. Of course it's worth while to a poor girl, if she can resist temptation and is good-looking and well conducted and sensible. It's far better than any other employment open to her. I always thought that oughtnt to be. It c a n t be right, Vivie, that there shouldnt be better opportunities for women. I stick to that: it's wrong. But it's so, right or wrong; and a girl must make the best of it. But of course it's not worth while for a lady. If you took to it youd be a fool; but I should have been a fool if I'd taken to anything else.

VIVIE [*more and more deeply moved*] Mother: suppose we were both as poor as you were in those wretched old days, are you quite sure that you wouldnt advise me to try the Waterloo bar, or marry a laborer, or even go into the factory?

MRS WARREN [*indignantly*] Of course not. What sort of mother do you take me for! How could you keep your self-respect in such starvation and slavery? And whats a woman worth? whats life worth? without self-respect! Why am I independent and able to give my daughter a first-rate education, when other women that had just as good opportunities are in the gutter? Because I always knew how to respect myself and control myself. Why is Liz looked up to in a cathedral town? The same reason. Where would we be now if we'd minded the clergyman's foolishness? Scrubbing floors for one and six-pence a day and nothing to look forward to but the workhouse infirmary.

Dont you be led astray by people who dont know the world, my girl. The only way for a woman to provide for herself decently is for her to be good to some man that can afford to be good to her. If she's in his own station of life, let her make him marry her; but if she's far beneath him she cant expect it: why should she? it wouldnt be for her own happiness. Ask any lady in London society that has daughters; and she'll tell you the same, except that I tell you straight and she'll tell you crooked. Thats all the difference.

VIVIE [*fascinated, gazing at her*] My dear mother: you are a wonderful woman: you are stronger than all England. And are you really and truly not one wee bit doubtful—or—or—ashamed?

MRS WARREN. Well, of course, dearie, it's only good manners to be ashamed of it: it's expected from a woman. Women have to pretend to feel a great deal that they dont feel. Liz used to be angry with me for plumping out the truth about it. She used to say that when every woman could learn enough from what was going on in the world before her eyes, there was no need to talk about it to her. But then Liz was such a perfect lady! She had the true instinct of it; while I was always a bit of a vulgarian. I used to be so pleased when you sent me your photos to see that you were growing up like Liz: youve just her ladylike, determined way. But I cant stand saying one thing when everyone knows I mean another. Whats the use in such hypocrisy? If people arrange the world that way for women, theres no good pretending it's arranged the other way. No: I never was a bit ashamed really. I consider I had a right to be proud of how we managed everything so respectably, and never had a word against us, and how the girls were so well taken care of. Some of them did very well: one of them married an ambassador. But of course now I darent talk about such things: whatever would they think of us! [*She yawns*]. Oh dear! I do believe I'm getting sleepy after all. [*She stretches herself lazily, thoroughly relieved by her explosion, and placidly ready for her night's rest*].

VIVIE. I believe it is I who will not be able to sleep now. [*She goes to the dresser and lights the candle. Then she extinguishes the lamp, darkening the room a good deal*]. Better let in some fresh air before locking up. [*She opens the cottage door, and finds that it is broad moonlight*]. What a beautiful night! Look! [*She draws aside the curtains of the window. The landscape is seen bathed in the radiance of the harvest moon rising over Blackdown*].

MRS WARREN [*with a perfunctory glance at the scene*] Yes, dear; but take care you dont catch your death of cold from the night air.

VIVIE [*contemptuously*] Nonsense.

MRS WARREN [*querulously*] Oh yes: everything I say is nonsense, according to you.

VIVIE [*turning to her quickly*] No: really that is not so, mother. You have got completely the better of me tonight, though I intended it to be the other way. Let us be good friends now.

MRS WARREN [*shaking her head a little ruefully*] So it h a s been the other way. But I suppose I must give in to it. I always got the worst of it from Liz; and now I suppose it'll be the same with you.

VIVIE. Well, never mind. Come: good-night, dear old mother. [*She takes her mother in her arms*].

MRS WARREN [*fondly*] I brought you up well, didnt I, dearie?

VIVIE. You did.

Mrs Warren. And youll be good to your poor old mother for it, wont you?

Vivie. I will, dear. [*Kissing her*] Good-night.

Mrs Warren [*with unction*] Blessings on my own dearie darling! a mother's blessing!

She embraces her daughter protectingly, instinctively looking upward for divine sanction.

ACT III

In the Rectory garden next morning, with the sun shining from a cloudless sky. The garden wall has a five-barred wooden gate, wide enough to admit a carriage, in the middle. Beside the gate hangs a bell on a coiled spring, communicating with a pull outside. The carriage drive comes down the middle of the garden and then swerves to its left, where it ends in a little gravelled circus[18] opposite the Rectory porch. Beyond the gate is seen the dusty high road, parallel with the wall, bounded on the farther side by a strip of turf and an unfenced pine wood. On the lawn, between the house and the drive, is a clipped yew tree, with a garden bench in its shade. On the opposite side the garden is shut in by a box hedge; and there is a sundial on the turf, with an iron chair near it. A little path leads off through the box hedge, behind the sundial.

Frank, seated on the chair near the sundial, on which he has placed the morning papers, is reading The Standard. His father comes from the house, red-eyed and shivery, and meets Frank's eye with misgiving.

Frank [*looking at his watch*] Half-past eleven. Nice hour for a rector to come down to breakfast!

Rev. S. Dont mock, Frank: dont mock. I am a little—er—[*Shivering*]—

Frank. Off color?

Rev. S. [*repudiating the expression*] No, sir: u n w e l l this morning. Wheres your mother?

Frank. Dont be alarmed: she's not here. Gone to town by the 11.13 with Bessie. She left several messages for you. Do you feel equal to receiving them now, or shall I wait til youve breakfasted?

Rev. S. I h a v e breakfasted, sir. I am surprised at your mother going to town when we have people staying with us. Theyll think it very strange.

Frank. Possibly she has considered that. At all events, if Crofts is going to stay here, and you are going to sit up every night with him until four, recalling the incidents of your fiery youth, it is clearly my mother's duty, as a prudent housekeeper, to go up to the stores and order a barrel of whisky and a few hundred siphons.

Rev. S. I did not observe that Sir George drank excessively.

Frank. You were not in a condition to, gov'nor.

Rev. S. Do you mean to say that *I*—?

Frank [*calmly*] I never saw a beneficed clergyman less sober. The anecdotes you told about your past career were so awful that I really dont think Praed would have passed the night under your roof if it hadnt been for the way my mother and he took to one another.

Rev. S. Nonsense, sir. I am Sir George Crofts' host. I must talk to him about something; and he has only one subject. Where is Mr Praed now?

Frank. He is driving my mother and Bessie to the station.

---

[18] Circle.

REV. S. Is Crofts up yet?

FRANK. Oh, long ago. He hasnt turned a hair: he's in much better practice than you. Has kept it up ever since, probably. He's taken himself off somewhere to smoke.

Frank resumes his paper. The parson turns disconsolately towards the gate; then comes back irresolutely.

REV. S. Er—Frank.

FRANK. Yes.

REV. S. Do you think the Warrens will expect to be asked here after yesterday afternoon?

FRANK. Theyve been asked already.

REV. S. [*appalled*] What!!!

FRANK. Crofts informed us at breakfast that you told him to bring Mrs Warren and Vivie over here to-day, and to invite them to make this house their home. My mother then found she must go to town by the 11.13 train.

REV. S. [*with despairing vehemence*] I never gave any such invitation. I never thought of such a thing.

FRANK [*compassionately*] How do you know, gov'nor, what you said and thought last night?

PRAED [*coming in through the hedge*] Good morning.

REV. S. Good morning. I must apologize for not having met you at breakfast. I have a touch of—of—

FRANK. Clergyman's sore throat, Praed. Fortunately not chronic.

PRAED [*changing the subject*] Well, I must say your house is in a charming spot here. Really most charming.

REV. S. Yes: it is indeed. Frank will take you for a walk, Mr Praed, if you like. I'll ask you to excuse me: I must take the opportunity to write my sermon while Mrs Gardner is away and you are all amusing yourselves. You wont mind, will you?

PRAED. Certainly not. Dont stand on the slightest ceremony with me.

REV. S. Thank you. I'll—er—er—[*He stammers his way to the porch and vanishes into the house*].

PRAED. Curious thing it must be writing a sermon every week.

FRANK. Ever so curious, if h e did it. He buys em. He's gone for some soda water.

PRAED. My dear boy: I wish you would be more respectful to your father. You know you can be so nice when you like.

FRANK. My dear Praddy: you forget that I have to live with the governor. When two people live together—it dont matter whether theyre father and son or husband and wife or brother and sister—they cant keep up the polite humbug thats so easy for ten minutes on an afternoon call. Now the governor, who unites to many admirable domestic qualities the irresoluteness of a sheep and the pompousness and aggressiveness of a jackass—

PRAED. No, pray, pray, my dear Frank, remember! He is your father.

FRANK. I give him due credit for that. [*Rising and flinging down his paper*] But just imagine his telling Crofts to bring the Warrens over here! He must have been ever so drunk. You know, my dear Praddy, my mother wouldnt stand Mrs Warren for a moment. Vivie mustnt come here until she's gone back to town.

PRAED. But your mother doesnt know anything about Mrs Warren, does she? [*He picks up the paper and sits down to read it*].

FRANK. I dont know. Her journey to town looks as if she did. Not that my mother would mind in the ordinary way: she has stuck like a brick to lots of women who had got into trouble. But they were all nice women. Thats what makes the real difference. Mrs Warren, no doubt, has her merits; but she's ever so rowdy; and my mother simply wouldnt put up with her. So— hallo! [*This exclamation is provoked by the reappearance of the clergyman, who comes out of the house in haste and dismay*].

REV. S. Frank: Mrs Warren and her daughter are coming across the heath with Crofts: I saw them from the study windows. What a m I to say about your mother?

FRANK. Stick on your hat and go out and say how delighted you are to see them; and that Frank's in the garden; and that mother and Bessie have been called to the bedside of a sick relative, and were ever so sorry they couldnt stop; and that you hope Mrs Warren slept well; and—and—say any blessed thing except the truth, and leave the rest to Providence.

REV. S. But how are we to get rid of them afterwards?

FRANK. Theres no time to think of that now. Here! [*He bounds into the house*].

REV. S. He's so impetuous. I dont know what to do with him, Mr Praed.

FRANK [*returning with a clerical felt hat, which he claps on his father's head*]. Now: off with you. [*Rushing him through the gate*]. Praed and I'll wait here, to give the thing an unpremeditated air. [*The clergyman, dazed but obedient, hurries off*].

FRANK. We must get the old girl back to town somehow, Praed. Come! Honestly, dear Praddy, do you like seeing them together?

PRAED. Oh, why not?

FRANK [*his teeth on edge*] Dont it make your flesh creep ever so little? that wicked old devil, up to every villainy under the sun, I'll swear, and Vivie—ugh!

PRAED. Hush, pray. Theyre coming.

The clergyman and Crofts are seen coming along the road, followed by Mrs Warren and Vivie walking affectionately together.

FRANK. Look: she actually has her arm round the old woman's waist. It's her right arm: she began it. She's gone sentimental, by God! Ugh! ugh! Now do you feel the creeps? [*The clergyman opens the gate; and Mrs Warren and Vivie pass him and stand in the middle of the garden looking at the house. Frank, in an ecstasy of dissimulation, turns gaily to Mrs Warren, exclaiming*] Ever so delighted to see you, Mrs Warren. This quiet old rectory garden becomes you perfectly.

MRS WARREN. Well, I never! Did you hear that, George? He says I look well in a quiet old rectory garden.

REV. S. [*still holding the gate for Crofts, who loafs through it, heavily bored*] You look well everywhere, Mrs Warren.

FRANK. Bravo, gov'nor! Now look here: lets have a treat before lunch. First lets see the church. Everyone has to do that. It's a regular old thirteenth century church, you know: the gov'nor's ever so fond of it, because he got up a restoration fund and had it completely rebuilt six years ago. Praed will be able to shew its points.

PRAED [*rising*] Certainly, if the restoration has left any to shew.

REV. S. [*mooning hospitably at them*] I shall be pleased, I'm sure, if Sir George and Mrs Warren really care about it.

MRS WARREN. Oh, come along and get it over.

CROFTS [*turning back towards the gate*] Ive no objection.

REV. S. Not that way. We go through the fields, if you dont mind. Round here. [*He leads the way by the little path through the box hedge*].

CROFTS. Oh, all right. [*He goes with the parson. Praed follows with Mrs Warren. Vivie does not stir: she watches them until they have gone, with all the lines of purpose in her face marking it strongly.*]

FRANK. Aint you coming?

VIVIE. No. I want to give you a warning, Frank. You were making fun of my mother just now when you said that about the rectory garden. That is barred in future. Please treat my mother with as much respect as you treat your own.

FRANK. My dear Viv: she wouldnt appreciate it: the two cases require different treatment. But what on earth has happened to you? Last night we were perfectly agreed as to your mother and her set. This morning I find you attitudinizing sentimentally with your arm round your parent's waist.

VIVIE [*flushing*] Attitudinizing!

FRANK. That was how it struck me. First time I ever saw you do a second-rate thing.

VIVIE [*controlling herself*] Yes, Frank: there has been a change; but I dont think it a change for the worse. Yesterday I was a little prig.

FRANK. And today?

VIVIE [*wincing; then looking at him steadily*] Today I know my mother better than you do.

FRANK. Heaven forbid!

VIVIE. What do you mean?

FRANK. Viv: theres a freemasonry among thoroughly immoral people that you know nothing of. Youve too much character. T h a t s the bond between your mother and me: thats why I know her better than youll ever know her.

VIVIE. You are wrong: you know nothing about her. If you knew the circumstances against which my mother had to struggle—

FRANK [*adroitly finishing the sentence for her*] I should know why she is what she is, shouldnt I? What difference would that make? Circumstances or no circumstances, Viv, you wont be able to stand your mother.

VIVIE [*very angry*] Why not?

FRANK. Because she's an old wretch, Viv. If you ever put your arm round her waist in my presence again, I'll shoot myself there and then as a protest against an exhibition which revolts me.

VIVIE. Must I choose between dropping your acquaintance and dropping my mother's?

FRANK [*gracefully*] That would put the old lady at ever such a disadvantage. No, Viv: your infatuated little boy will have to stick to you in any case. But he's all the more anxious that you shouldnt make mistakes. It's no use, Viv: your mother's impossible. She may be a good sort; but she's a bad lot, a very bad lot.

VIVIE [*hotly*] Frank—! [*He stands his ground. She turns away and sits down on the bench under the yew tree, struggling to recover her self-command. Then she says*] Is she to be deserted by all the world because she's what you call a bad lot? Has she no right to live?

FRANK. No fear of that, Viv: s h e wont ever be deserted. [*He sits on the bench beside her*].

VIVIE. But I am to desert her, I suppose.

FRANK [*babyishly, lulling her and making love to her with his voice*] Musnt go live with her. Little family group of mother and daughter wouldnt be a success. Spoil o u r little group.

VIVIE [*falling under the spell*] What little group?

FRANK. The babes in the wood: Vivie and little Frank. [*He nestles against her like a weary child*]. Lets go and get covered up with leaves.

VIVIE [*rhythmically, rocking him like a nurse*] Fast asleep, hand in hand, under the trees.

FRANK. The wise little girl with her silly little boy.

VIVIE. The dear little boy with his dowdy little girl.

FRANK. Ever so peaceful, and relieved from the imbecility of the little boy's father and the questionableness of the little girl's—

VIVIE [*smothering the word against her breast*] Sh-sh-sh-sh! little girl wants to forget all about her mother. [*They are silent for some moments, rocking one another. Then Vivie wakes up with a shock, exclaiming*] What a pair of fools we are! Come: sit up. Gracious! your hair. [*She smooths it*]. I wonder do all grown up people play in that childish way when nobody is looking. I never did it when I was a child.

FRANK. Neither did I. You are my first playmate. [*He catches her hand to kiss it, but checks himself to look round first. Very unexpectedly, he see Crofts emerging from the box hedge*]. Oh damn!

VIVIE. Why damn, dear?

FRANK [*whispering*] Sh! Here's this brute Crofts. [*He sits farther away from her with an unconcerned air*].

CROFTS. Could I have a few words with you, Miss Vivie?

VIVIE. Certainly.

CROFTS [*to Frank*] Youll excuse me, Gardner. Theyre waiting for you in the church, if you dont mind.

FRANK [*rising*] Anything to oblige you, Crofts—except church. If you should happen to want me, Vivvums, ring the gate bell. [*He goes into the house with unruffled suavity*].

CROFTS [*watching him with a crafty air as he disappears, and speaking to Vivie with an assumption of being on privileged terms with her*] Pleasant young fellow that, Miss Vivie. Pity he has no money, isnt it?

VIVIE. Do you think so?

CROFTS. Well, whats he to do? No profession. No property. Whats he good for?

VIVIE. I realize his disadvantages, Sir George.

CROFTS [*a little taken aback at being so precisely interpreted*] Oh, it's not that. But while we're in this world we're in it; and money's money. [*Vivie does not answer*]. Nice day, isnt it?

VIVIE [*with scarcely veiled contempt for this effort at conversation*] Very.

CROFTS [*with brutal good humor, as if he liked her pluck*] Well, thats not what I came to say. [*Sitting down beside her*] Now listen, Miss Vivie. I'm quite aware that I'm not a young lady's man.

VIVIE. Indeed, Sir George?

CROFTS. No; and to tell you the honest truth I dont want to be either. But when I say a thing I mean it; when I feel a sentiment I feel it in earnest; and what I value I pay hard money for. Thats the sort of man I am.

VIVIE. It does you great credit, I'm sure.

CROFTS. Oh, I dont mean to praise myself. I have my faults, Heaven knows:

no man is more sensible of that than I am. I know I'm not perfect: thats one of the advantages of being a middle-aged man; for I'm not a young man, and I know it. But my code is a simple one, and, I think, a good one. Honor between man and man; fidelity between man and woman; and no cant about this religion or that religion, but an honest belief that things are making for good on the whole.

VIVIE [*with biting irony*] "A power, not ourselves, that makes for righteousness,"[19] eh?

CROFTS [*taking her seriously*] Oh certainly. Not ourselves, of course. You understand what I mean. Well, now as to practical matters. You may have an idea that Ive flung my money about; but I havnt: I'm richer today than when I first came into the property. Ive used my knowledge of the world to invest my money in ways that other men have overlooked; and whatever else I may be, I'm a safe man from the money point of view.

VIVIE. It's very kind of you to tell me all this.

CROFTS. Oh well, come, Miss Vivie: you neednt pretend you dont see what I'm driving at. I want to settle down with a Lady Crofts. I suppose you think me very blunt, eh?

VIVIE. Not at all: I am much obliged to you for being so definite and business-like. I quite appreciate the offer: the money, the position, L a d y C r o f t s, and so on. But I think I will say no, if you dont mind. I'd rather not. [*She rises, and strolls across to the sundial to get out of his immediate neighborhood*].

CROFTS [*not at all discouraged, and taking advantage of the additional room left him on the seat to spread himself comfortably, as if a few preliminary refusals were part of the inevitable routine of courtship*] I'm in no hurry. It was only just to let you know in case young Gardner should try to trap you. Leave the question open.

VIVIE [*sharply*] My no is final. I wont go back from it.

Crofts is not impressed. He grins; leans forward with his elbows on his knees to prod with his stick at some unfortunate insect in the grass; and looks cunningly at her. She turns away impatiently.

CROFTS. I'm a good deal older than you. Twenty-five years: quarter of a century. I shant live for ever; and I'll take care that you shall be well off when I'm gone.

VIVIE. I am proof against even that inducement, Sir George. Dont you think youd better take your answer? There is not the slightest chance of my altering it.

CROFTS [*rising, after a final slash at a daisy, and coming nearer to her*] Well, no matter. I could tell you some things that would change your mind fast enough; but I wont, because I'd rather win you by honest affection. I was a good friend to your mother: ask her whether I wasnt. She'd never have made the money that paid for your education if it hadnt been for my advice and help, not to mention the money I advanced her. There are not many men would have stood by her as I have. I put not less than £40,000 into it, from first to last.

VIVIE [*staring at him*] Do you mean to say you were my mother's business partner?

CROFTS. Yes. Now just think of all the trouble and the explanations it would

---

[19] The quotation is from the first chapter of Matthew Arnold's *Literature and Dogma: An Essay toward a Better Apprehension of the Bible* (1873) in which God is defined as "the enduring power, not ourselves, which makes for righteousness."

save if we were to keep the whole thing in the family, so to speak. Ask your mother whether she'd like to have to explain all her affairs to a perfect stranger.

VIVIE. I see no difficulty, since I understand that the business is wound up, and the money invested.

CROFTS [*stopping short, amazed*] Wound up! Wind up a business thats paying 35 per cent in the worst years! Not likely. Who told you that?

VIVIE [*her color quite gone*] Do you mean that it is still—? [*She stops abruptly, and puts her hand on the sundial to support herself. Then she gets quickly to the iron chair and sits down*]. What business are you talking about?

CROFTS. Well, the fact is it's not what would be considered exactly a high-class business in my set—the county set, you know—o u r set it will be if you think better of my offer. Not that theres any mystery about it: dont think that. Of course you know by your mother's being in it that it's perfectly straight and honest. Ive known her for many years; and I can say of her that she'd cut off her hands sooner than touch anything that was not what it ought to be. I'll tell you all about it if you like. I dont know whether youve found in travelling how hard it is to find a really comfortable private hotel.

VIVIE [*sickened, averting her face*] Yes: go on.

CROFTS. Well, thats all it is. Your mother has a genius for managing such things. We've got two in Brussels, one in Ostend, one in Vienna, and two in Budapest. Of course there are others besides ourselves in it; but we hold most of the capital; and your mother's indispensable as managing director. Youve noticed, I daresay, that she travels a good deal. But you see you cant mention such things in society. Once let out the word hotel and every-body says you keep a public-house.[20] You wouldnt like people to say that of your mother, would you? Thats why we're so reserved about it. By the way, youll keep it to yourself, wont you? Since it's been a secret so long, it had better remain so.

VIVIE. And this is the business you invite me to join you in?

CROFTS. Oh no. My wife shant be troubled with business. Youll not be in it more than youve always been.

VIVIE. *I* always been! What do you mean?

CROFTS. Only that youve always lived on it. It paid for your education and the dress you have on your back. Dont turn up your nose at business, Miss Vivie: where would your Newnhams and Girtons[21] be without it?

VIVIE [*rising, almost beside herself*] Take care. I know what this business is.

CROFTS [*starting, with a suppressed oath*] Who told you?

VIVIE. Your partner. My mother.

CROFTS [*black with rage*] The old—

VIVIE. Just so.

He swallows the epithet and stands for a moment swearing and raging foully to himself. But he knows that his cue is to be sympathetic. He takes refuge in generous indignation.

CROFTS. She ought to have had more consideration for you. *I*'d never have told you.

VIVIE. I think you would probably have told me when we were married: it would have been a convenient weapon to break me in with.

[20] I.e., a house of ill-repute, a brothel.
[21] Newnham and Girton are now women's colleges within Cambridge University.

CROFTS [*quite sincerely*] I never intended that. On my word as a gentleman I didnt.

Vivie wonders at him. Her sense of the irony of his protest cools and braces her. She replies with contemptuous self-possession.

VIVIE. It does not matter. I suppose you understand that when we leave here today our acquaintance ceases.

CROFTS. Why? Is it for helping your mother?

VIVIE. My mother was a very poor woman who had no reasonable choice but to do as she did. You were a rich gentleman; and you did the same for the sake of 35 per cent. You are a pretty common sort of scoundrel, I think. That is my opinion of you.

CROFTS [*after a stare: not at all displeased, and much more at his ease on these frank terms than on their former ceremonious ones*] Ha! ha! ha! ha! Go it, little missie, go it: it doesnt hurt me and it amuses you. Why the devil shouldnt I invest my money that way? I take the interest on my capital like other people: I hope you dont think I dirty my own hands with the work. Come! you wouldnt refuse the acquaintance of my mother's cousin the Duke of Belgravia because some of the rents he gets are earned in queer ways. You wouldnt cut the Archbishop of Canterbury, I suppose, because the Ecclesiastical Commissioners have a few publicans[22] and sinners among their tenants. Do you remember your Crofts scholarship at Newnham? Well, that was founded by my brother the M.P.[23] He gets his 22 per cent out of a factory with 600 girls in it, and not one of them getting wages enough to live on. How d'ye suppose they manage when they have no family to fall back on? Ask your mother. And do you expect me to turn my back on 35 per cent when all the rest are pocketing what they can, like sensible men? No such fool! If youre going to pick and choose your acquaintances on moral principles, youd better clear out of this country, unless you want to cut yourself out of all decent society.

VIVIE [*conscience stricken*] You might go on to point out that I myself never asked where the money I spent came from. I believe I am just as bad as you.

CROFTS [*greatly reassured*] Of course you are; and a very good thing too! What harm does it do after all? [*Rallying her jocularly*] So you dont think me such a scoundrel now you come to think it over. Eh?

VIVIE. I have shared profits with you; and I admitted you just now to the familiarity of knowing what I think of you.

CROFTS [*with serious friendliness*] To be sure you did. You wont find me a bad sort: I dont go in for being superfine intellectually; but Ive plenty of honest human feeling; and the old Crofts breed comes out in a sort of instinctive hatred of anything low, in which I'm sure youll sympathize with me. Believe me, Miss Vivie, the world isnt such a bad place as the croakers[24] make out. As long as you dont fly openly in the face of society, society doesnt ask any inconvenient questions; and it makes precious short work of the cads who do. There are no secrets better than the secrets everybody guesses. In the class of people I can introduce you to, no lady or gentleman would so far forget themselves as to discuss my business affairs or your mother's. No man can offer you a safer position.

[22] Innkeepers.   [23] Member of Parliament.   [24] Chronic complainers.

VIVIE [*studying him curiously*] I suppose you really think youre getting on famously with me.

CROFTS. Well, I hope I may flatter myself that you think better of me than you did at first.

VIVIE [*quietly*] I hardly find you worth thinking about at all now. When I think of the society that tolerates you, and the laws that protect you! when I think of how helpless nine out of ten young girls would be in the hands of you and my mother! the unmentionable woman and her capitalist bully—

CROFTS [*livid*] Damn you!

VIVIE. You need not. I feel among the damned already.

She raises the latch of the gate to open it and go out. He follows her and puts his hand heavily on the top bar to prevent its opening.

CROFTS [*panting with fury*] Do you think I'll put up with this from you, you young devil?

VIVIE [*unmoved*] Be quiet. Some one will answer the bell. [*Without flinching a step she strikes the bell with the back of her hand. It clangs harshly; and he starts back involuntarily. Almost immediately Frank appears at the porch with his rifle*].

FRANK [*with cheerful politeness*] Will you have the rifle, Viv; or shall I operate?

VIVIE. Frank: have you been listening?

FRANK [*coming down into the garden*] Only for the bell, I assure you; so that you shouldnt have to wait. I think I shewed great insight into your character, Crofts.

CROFTS. For two pins I'd take that gun from you and break it across your head.

FRANK [*stalking him cautiously*] Pray dont. I'm ever so careless in handling firearms. Sure to be a fatal accident, with a reprimand from the coroner's jury for my negligence.

VIVIE. Put the rifle away, Frank: it's quite unnecessary.

FRANK. Quite right, Viv. Much more sportsmanlike to catch him in a trap. [*Crofts, understanding the insult, makes a threatening movement*]. Crofts: there are fifteen cartridges in the magazine here; and I am a dead shot at the present distance and at an object of your size.

CROFTS. Oh, you neednt be afraid. I'm not going to touch you.

FRANK. Ever so magnanimous of you under the circumstances! Thank you.

CROFTS. I'll just tell you this before I go. It may interest you, since youre so fond of one another. Allow me, Mister Frank, to introduce you to your half-sister, the eldest daughter of the Reverend Samuel Gardner. Miss Vivie: your half-brother. Good morning. [*He goes out through the gate and along the road*].

FRANK [*after a pause of stupefaction, raising the rifle*] Youll testify before the coroner that it's an accident, Viv. [*He takes aim at the retreating figure of Crofts. Vivie seizes the muzzle and pulls it round against her breast*].

VIVIE. Fire now. You may.

FRANK [*dropping his end of the rifle hastily*] Stop! take care. [*She lets it go. It falls on the turf*]. Oh, youve given your little boy such a turn. Suppose it had gone off! ugh! [*He sinks on the garden seat, overcome*].

VIVIE. Suppose it had: do you think it would not have been a relief to have some sharp physical pain tearing through me?

FRANK [*coaxingly*] Take it ever so easy, dear Viv. Remember: even if the rifle scared that fellow into telling the truth for the first time in his life, that

only makes us the babes in the wood in earnest. [*He holds out his arms to
her*]. Come and be covered up with leaves again.

VIVIE [*with a cry of disgust*] Ah, not that, not that. You make all my flesh creep.

FRANK. Why, whats the matter?

VIVIE. Goodbye. [*She makes for the gate*].

FRANK [*jumping up*] Hallo! Stop! Viv! Viv! [*She turns in the gateway*] Where are
you going to? Where shall we find you?

VIVIE. At Honoria Fraser's chambers, 67 Chancery Lane, for the rest of my
life. [*She goes off quickly in the opposite direction to that taken by Crofts*].

FRANK. But I say—wait—dash it! [*He runs after her*].

ACT IV

*Honoria Fraser's chambers in Chancery Lane. An office at the top of New Stone Buildings,
with a plate-glass window, distempered[25] walls, electric light, and a patent stove. Saturday
afternoon. The chimneys of Lincoln's Inn and the western sky beyond are seen through
the window. There is a double writing table in the middle of the room, with a cigar box,
ash pans, and a portable electric reading lamp almost snowed up in heaps of papers and
books. This table has knee holes and chairs right and left and is very untidy. The clerk's
desk, closed and tidy, with its high stool, is against the wall, near a door communicating
with the inner rooms. In the opposite wall is the door leading to the public corridor. Its
upper panel is of opaque glass, lettered in black on the outside,* FRASER AND WARREN.
A baize screen hides the corner between this door and the window.

FRANK, *in a fashionable light-colored coaching suit, with his stick, gloves, and white
hat in his hands, is pacing up and down the office. Somebody tries the door with a key.*

FRANK [*calling*] Come in. It's not locked.

Vivie comes in, in her hat and jacket. She stops and stares at him.

VIVIE [*sternly*] What are you doing here?

FRANK. Waiting to see you. Ive been here for hours. Is this the way you attend
to your business? [*He puts his hat and stick on the table, and perches himself with
a vault on the clerk's stool, looking at her with every appearance of being in a specially
restless, teasing, flippant mood*].

VIVIE. Ive been away exactly twenty minutes for a cup of tea. [*She takes off her
hat and jacket and hangs them up behind the screen*]. How did you get in?

FRANK. The staff had not left when I arrived. He's gone to play cricket on
Primrose Hill. Why dont you employ a woman, and give your sex a chance?

VIVIE. What have you come for?

FRANK [*springing off the stool and coming close to her*] Viv: lets go and enjoy the
Saturday half-holiday somewhere, like the staff. What do you say to Richmond,[26] and then a music hall, and a jolly supper?

VIVIE. Cant afford it. I shall put in another six hours work before I go to
bed.

FRANK. Cant afford it, cant we? Aha! Look here. [*He takes out a handful of sovereigns
and makes them chink*]. Gold, Viv: gold!

VIVIE. Where did you get it?

FRANK. Gambling, Viv: gambling. Poker.

---

[25] I.e., colored.   [26] A riverside resort on the Thames about ten miles southwest of London.

VIVIE. Pah! It's meaner than stealing it. No: I'm not coming. [*She sits down to work at the table, with her back to the glass door, and begins turning over the papers*].

FRANK [*remonstrating piteously*] But, my dear Viv, I want to talk to you ever so seriously.

VIVIE. Very well: sit down in Honoria's chair and talk here. I like ten minutes chat after tea. [*He murmurs*]. No use groaning: I'm inexorable. [*He takes the opposite seat disconsolately*]. Pass that cigar box, will you?

FRANK [*pushing the cigar box across*] Nasty womanly habit. Nice men dont do it any longer.

VIVIE. Yes: they object to the smell in the office; and weve had to take to cigarets. See! [*She opens the box and takes out a cigaret, which she lights. She offers him one; but he shakes his head with a wry face. She settles herself comfortably in her chair, smoking*]. Go ahead.

FRANK. Well, I want to know what youve done—what arrangements youve made.

VIVIE. Everything was settled twenty minutes after I arrived here. Honoria has found the business too much for her this year; and she was on the point of sending for me and proposing a partnership when I walked in and told her I hadnt a farthing in the world. So I installed myself and packed her off for a fortnight's holiday. What happened at Haslemere when I left?

FRANK. Nothing at all. I said youd gone to town on particular business.

VIVIE. Well?

FRANK. Well, either they were too flabbergasted to say anything, or else Crofts had prepared your mother. Anyhow, she didnt say anything; and Crofts didnt say anything; and Praddy only stared. After tea they got up and went; and Ive not seen them since.

VIVIE [*nodding placidly with one eye on a wreath of smoke*] Thats all right.

FRANK [*looking round disparagingly*] Do you intend to stick in this confounded place?

VIVIE [*blowing the wreath decisively away, and sitting straight up*] Yes. These two days have given me back all my strength and self-possession. I will never take a holiday again as long as I live.

FRANK [*with a very wry face*] Mps! You look quite happy. And as hard as nails.

VIVIE [*grimly*] Well for me that I am!

FRANK [*rising*] Look here, Viv: we must have an explanation. We parted the other day under a complete misunderstanding. [*He sits on the table, close to her*].

VIVIE [*putting away the cigaret*] Well: clear it up.

FRANK. You remember what Crofts said?

VIVIE. Yes.

FRANK. That revelation was supposed to bring about a complete change in the nature of our feeling for one another. It placed us on the footing of brother and sister.

VIVIE. Yes.

FRANK. Have you ever had a brother?

VIVIE. No.

FRANK. Then you dont know what being brother and sister feels like? Now I have lots of sisters; and the fraternal feeling is quite familiar to me. I assure you my feeling for you is not the least in the world like it. The girls will go their way; I will go mine; and we shant care if we never see one another again. Thats brother and sister. But as to you, I cant be easy if I have to pass a week without seeing you. Thats not brother and sister. It's exactly what I felt an hour before Crofts made his revelation. In short, dear Viv, it's love's young dream.

VIVIE [*bitingly*] The same feeling, Frank, that brought your father to my mother's feet. Is that it?

FRANK [*so revolted that he slips off the table for a moment*] I very strongly object, Viv, to have my feelings compared to any which the Reverend Samuel is capable of harboring; and I object still more to a comparison of you to your mother. [*Resuming his perch*]. Besides, I dont believe the story. I have taxed my father with it, and obtained from him what I consider tantamount to a denial.

VIVIE. What did he say?

FRANK. He said he was sure there must be some mistake.

VIVIE. Do you believe him?

FRANK. I am prepared to take his word as against Crofts'.

VIVIE. Does it make any difference? I mean in your imagination or conscience; for of course it makes no real difference.

FRANK [*shaking his head*] None whatever to me.

VIVIE. Nor to me.

FRANK [*staring*] But this is ever so surprising! [*He goes back to his chair*]. I thought our whole relations were altered in your imagination and conscience, as you put it, the moment those words were out of that brute's muzzle.

VIVIE. No: it was not that. I didnt believe him. I only wish I could.

FRANK. Eh?

VIVIE. I think brother and sister would be a very suitable relation for us.

FRANK. You really mean that?

VIVIE. Yes. It's the only relation I care for, even if we could afford any other. I mean that.

FRANK [*raising his eyebrows like one on whom a new light has dawned, and rising with quite an effusion of chivalrous sentiment*] My dear Viv: why didnt you say so before? I am ever so sorry for persecuting you. I understand, of course.

VIVIE [*puzzled*] Understand what?

FRANK. Oh, I'm not a fool in the ordinary sense: only in the Scriptural sense of doing all the things the wise man declared to be folly, after trying them himself on the most extensive scale. I see I am no longer Vivvum's little boy. Dont be alarmed: I shall never call you Vivvums again—at least unless you get tired of your new little boy, whoever he may be.

VIVIE. My new little boy!

FRANK [*with conviction*] Must be a new little boy. Always happens this way. No other way, in fact.

VIVIE. None that you know of, fortunately for you.

Someone knocks at the door.

FRANK. My curse upon yon caller, whoe'er he be!

VIVIE. It's Praed. He's going to Italy and wants to say goodbye. I asked him to call this afternoon. Go and let him in.

FRANK. We can continue our conversation after his departure for Italy. I'll stay him out. [*He goes to the door and opens it*]. How are you, Praddy? Delighted to see you. Come in.

Praed, dressed for travelling, comes in, in high spirits.

PRAED. How do you do, Miss Warren? [*She presses his hand cordially, though a certain sentimentality in his high spirits jars on her*]. I start in an hour from Holborn Viaduct. I wish I could persuade you to try Italy.

VIVIE. What for?

PRAED. Why, to saturate yourself with beauty and romance, of course.

Vivie, with a shudder, turns her chair to the table, as if the work waiting for her there were a support to her. Praed sits opposite to her. Frank places a chair near Vivie, and drops lazily and carelessly into it, talking at her over his shoulder.

FRANK. No use, Praddy. Viv is a little Philistine. She is indifferent to my romance, and insensible to my beauty.

VIVIE. Mr Praed: once for all, there is no beauty and no romance in life for me. Life is what it is; and I am prepared to take it as it is.

PRAED [*enthusiastically*] You will not say that if you come with me to Verona and on to Venice. You will cry with delight at living in such a beautiful world.

FRANK. This is most eloquent, Praddy. Keep it up.

PRAED. Oh, I assure you *I* have cried—I shall cry again, I hope—at fifty! At your age, Miss Warren, you would not need to go so far as Verona. Your spirits would absolutely fly up at the mere sight of Ostend. You would be charmed with the gaiety, the vivacity, the happy air of Brussels.

VIVIE [*springing up with an exclamation of loathing*] Agh!

PRAED [*rising*] Whats the matter?

FRANK [*rising*] Hallo, Viv!

VIVIE [*to Praed, with deep reproach*] Can you find no better example of your beauty and romance than Brussels to talk to me about?

PRAED [*puzzled*] Of course it's very different from Verona. I dont suggest for a moment that—

VIVIE [*bitterly*] Probably the beauty and romance come to much the same in both places.

PRAED [*completely sobered and much concerned*] M y dear Miss Warren: I—[*looking enquiringly at Frank*] Is anything the matter?

FRANK. She thinks your enthusiasm frivolous, Praddy. She's had ever such a serious call.

VIVIE [*sharply*] Hold your tongue, Frank. Dont be silly.

FRANK [*sitting down*] Do you call this good manners, Praed?

PRAED [*anxious and considerate*] Shall I take him away, Miss Warren? I feel sure we have disturbed you at your work.

VIVIE. Sit down: I'm not ready to go back to work yet. [*Praed sits*]. You both think I have an attack of nerves. Not a bit of it. But there are two subjects I want dropped, if you dont mind. One of them [*to Frank*] is love's young dream in any shape or form: the other [*to Praed*] is the romance and beauty of life, especially Ostend and the gaiety of Brussels. You are welcome to any illusions you may have left on these subjects: I have none. If we three are to remain friends, I must be treated as a woman of business, permanently single [*to Frank*] and permanently unromantic [*to Praed*].

FRANK. I also shall remain permanently single until you change your mind. Praddy: change the subject. Be eloquent about something else.

PRAED [*diffidently*] I'm afraid theres nothing else in the world that I c a n talk about. The Gospel of Art is the only one I can preach. I know Miss Warren in a great devotee of the Gospel of Getting On; but we cant discuss that without hurting your feelings, Frank, since you are determined not to get on.

FRANK. Oh, dont mind my feelings. Give me some improving advice by all means: it does me ever so much good. Have another try to make a successful man of me, Viv. Come: lets have it all: energy, thrift, foresight, self-respect, character. Dont you hate people who have no character, Viv?

VIVIE [*wincing*] Oh, stop, stop: let us have no more of that horrible cant. Mr Praed: if there are really only those two gospels in the world, we had better all kill ourselves; for the same taint is in both, through and through.

FRANK [*looking critically at her*] There is a touch of poetry about you today, Viv, which has hitherto been lacking.

PRAED [*remonstrating*] My dear Frank: arnt you a little unsympathetic?

VIVIE [*merciless to herself*] No: it's good for me. It keeps me from being sentimental.

FRANK [*bantering her*] Checks your strong natural propensity that way, dont it?

VIVIE [*almost hysterically*] Oh yes: go on: dont spare me. I was sentimental for one moment in my life—beautifully sentimental—by moonlight; and now—

FRANK [*quickly*] I say, Viv: take care. Dont give yourself away.

VIVIE. Oh, do you think Mr Praed does not know all about my mother? [*Turning on Praed*] You had better have told me that morning, Mr Praed. You are very old fashioned in your delicacies, after all.

PRAED. Surely it is you who are a little old fashioned in your prejudices, Miss Warren. I feel bound to tell you, speaking as an artist, and believing that the most intimate human relationships are far beyond and above the scope of the law, that though I know that your mother is an unmarried woman, I do not respect her the less on that account. I respect her more.

FRANK [*airly*] Hear! hear!

VIVIE [*staring at him*] Is that a l l you know?

PRAED. Certainly that is all.

VIVIE. Then you neither of you know anything. Your guesses are innocence itself compared to the truth.

PRAED [*rising, startled and indignant, and preserving his politeness with an effort*] I hope not. [*More emphatically*] I hope not, Miss Warren.

FRANK [*whistles*] Whew!

VIVIE. You are not making it easy for me to tell you, Mr Praed.

PRAED [*his chivalry drooping before their conviction*] If there i s anything worse— that is, anything else—are you sure you are right to tell us, Miss Warren?

VIVIE. I am sure that if I had the courage I should spend the rest of my life in telling everybody—stamping and branding it into them until they all felt their part in its abomination as I feel mine. There is nothing I despise more than the wicked convention that protects these things by forbidding a woman to mention them. And yet I cant tell you. The two infamous words that describe what my mother is are ringing in my ears and struggling on my tongue; but I cant utter them: the shame of them is too horrible for me. [*She buries her face in her hands. The two men, astonished, stare at one another and then at her. She raises her head again desperately and snatches a sheet of paper and a pen*]. Here; let me draft you a prospectus.

FRANK. Oh, she's mad. Do you hear, Viv? mad. Come! pull yourself together.

VIVIE. You shall see. [*She writes*]. "Paid up capital: not less than £40,000 standing in the name of Sir George Crofts, Baronet, the chief shareholder. Premises at Brussels, Ostend, Vienna and Budapest. Managing director: Mrs Warren"; and now dont let us forget h e r qualifications: the two words. [*She writes the words and pushes the paper to them*]. There! Oh no: dont read it: dont!

She snatches it back and tears it to pieces; then seizes her head in her hands and hides her face on the table.

Frank, who has watched the writing over her shoulder, and opened his eyes very widely at it, takes a card from his pocket; scribbles the two words on it; and silently hands it to Praed, who reads it with amazement, and hides it hastily in his pocket.

FRANK [*whispering tenderly*] Viv, dear: thats all right. I read what you wrote: so did Praddy. We understand. And we remain, as this leaves us at present, yours ever so devotedly.

PRAED. We do indeed, Miss Warren. I declare you are the most splendidly courageous woman I ever met.

This sentimental compliment braces Vivie. She throws it away from her with an impatient shake, and forces herself to stand up, though not without some support from the table.

FRANK. Dont stir, Viv, if you dont want to. Take it easy.

VIVIE. Thank you. You can always depend on me for two things: not to cry and not to faint. [*She moves a few steps towards the door of the inner room, and stops close to Praed to say*] I shall need much more courage than that when I tell my mother that we have come to the parting of the ways. Now I must go into the next room for a moment to make myself neat again, if you dont mind.

PRAED. Shall we go away?

VIVIE. No: I'll be back presently. Only for a moment. [*She goes into the other room, Praed opening the door for her*].

PRAED. What an amazing revelation! I'm extremely disappointed in Crofts: I am indeed.

FRANK. I'm not in the least. I feel he's perfectly accounted for at last. But what a facer for me, Praddy! I cant marry her now.

PRAED [*sternly*] Frank! [*The two look at one another, Frank unruffled, Praed deeply indignant*]. Let me tell you, Gardner, that if you desert her now you will behave very despicably.

FRANK. Good old Praddy! Ever chivalrous! But you mistake: it's not the moral aspect of the case: it's the money aspect. I really cant bring myself to touch the old woman's money now!

PRAED. And was that what you were going to marry on?

FRANK. What else? *I* havnt any money, nor the smallest turn for making it. If I married Viv now she would have to support me; and I should cost her more than I am worth.

PRAED. But surely a clever bright fellow like you can make something by your own brains.

FRANK. Oh yes, a little. [*He takes out his money again*]. I made all that yesterday in an hour and a half. But I made it in a highly speculative business. No, dear Praddy: even if Bessie and Georgina marry millionaires and the governor dies after cutting them off with a shilling, I shall have only four hundred a year. And he wont die until he's three score and ten: he hasnt originality enough. I shall be on short allowance for the next twenty years. No short allowance for Viv, if I can help it. I withdraw gracefully and leave the field to the gilded youth of England. So thats settled. I shant worry her about it: I'll just send her a little note after we're gone. She'll understand.

PRAED [*grasping his hand*] Good fellow, Frank! I heartily beg your pardon. But must you never see her again?

FRANK. Never see her again! Hang it all, be reasonable. I shall come along as often as possible, and be her brother. I can n o t understand the absurd consequences you romantic people expect from the most ordinary transactions. [*A knock at the door*]. I wonder who this is. Would you mind opening the door? If it's a client it will look more respectable than if I appeared.

PRAED. Certainly. [*He goes to the door and opens it. Frank sits down in Vivie's chair to a scribble a note*]. My dear Kitty: come in: come in.

Mrs Warren comes in, looking apprehensively round for Vivie. She has done her best to make herself matronly and dignified. The brilliant hat is replaced by a sober bonnet, and the gay blouse covered by a costly black silk mantle. She is pitiably anxious and ill at ease: evidently panic-stricken.

MRS WARREN [*to Frank*] What! Y o u r e here, are you?

FRANK [*turning in his chair from his writing, but not rising*] Here, and charmed to see you. You come like a breath of spring.

MRS WARREN. Oh, get out with your nonsense. [*In a low voice*] Wheres Vivie?

Frank points expressively to the door of the inner room, but says nothing.

MRS WARREN [*sitting down suddenly and almost beginning to cry*] Praddy: wont she see me, dont you think?

PRAED. My dear Kitty: dont distress yourself. Why should she not?

MRS WARREN. Oh, you never can see why not: youre too innocent. Mr Frank: did she say anything to you?

FRANK [*folding his note*] She m u s t see you, if [*very expressively*] you wait til she comes in.

MRS WARREN [*frightened*] Why shouldnt I wait?

Frank looks quizzically at her; puts his note carefully on the ink-bottle, so that Vivie cannot fail to find it when next she dips her pen; then rises and devotes his attention entirely to her.

FRANK. My dear Mrs Warren: suppose you were a sparrow—ever so tiny and pretty a sparrow hopping in the roadway—and you saw a steam roller coming in your direction, would you wait for it?

MRS WARREN. Oh, dont bother me with your sparrows. What did she run away from Haslemere like that for?

FRANK. I'm afraid she'll tell you if you rashly await her return.

MRS WARREN. Do you want me to go away?

FRANK. No: I always want you to stay. But I a d v i s e you to go away.

MRS WARREN. What! And never see her again!

FRANK. Precisely.

MRS WARREN [*crying again*] Praddy: dont let him be cruel to me. [*She hastily checks her tears and wipes her eyes*]. She'll be so angry if she sees Ive been crying.

FRANK [*with a touch of real compassion in his airy tenderness*] You know that Praddy is the soul of kindness, Mrs Warren. Praddy: what do y o u say? Go or stay?

PRAED [*to Mrs Warren*] I really should be very sorry to cause you unnecessary pain; but I think perhaps you had better not wait. The fact is—[*Vivie is heard at the inner door*].

FRANK. Sh! Too late. She's coming.

MRS WARREN. Dont tell her I was crying. [*Vivie comes in. She stops gravely on seeing Mrs Warren, who greets her with hysterical cheerfulness*]. Well, dearie. So here you are at last.

VIVIE. I am glad you have come: I want to speak to you. You said you were going, Frank, I think.

FRANK. Yes. Will you come with me, Mrs Warren? What do you say to a trip to Richmond, and the theatre in the evening? There is safety in Richmond. No steam roller there.

VIVIE. Nonsense, Frank. My mother will stay here.

MRS WARREN [*scared*] I dont know: perhaps I'd better go. We're disturbing you at your work.

VIVIE [*with quiet decision*] Mr Praed: please take Frank away. Sit down, mother. [*Mrs Warren obeys helplessly*].

PRAED. Come, Frank. Goodbye, Miss Vivie.

VIVIE [*shaking hands*] Goodbye. A pleasant trip.

PRAED. Thank you: thank you. I hope so.

FRANK [*to Mrs Warren*] Goodbye: youd ever so much better have taken my advice. [*He shakes hands with her. Then airily to Vivie*] Byebye, Viv.

VIVIE. Goodbye. [*He goes out gaily without shaking hands with her*].

PRAED [*sadly*] Goodbye, Kitty.

MRS WARREN [*snivelling*]—oobye!

Praed goes. Vivie, composed and extremely grave, sits down in Honoria's chair, and waits for her mother to speak. Mrs Warren, dreading a pause, loses no time in beginning.

MRS WARREN. Well, Vivie, what did you go away like that for without saying a word to me? How could you do such a thing! And what have you done to poor George? I wanted him to come with me; but he shuffled out of it. I could see that he was quite afraid of you. Only fancy: he wanted me not to come. As if [*trembling*] I should be afraid of you, dearie. [*Vivie's gravity deepens*]. But of course I told him it was all settled and comfortable between us, and that we were on the best of terms. [*She breaks down*]. Vivie: whats the meaning of this? [*She produces a commercial envelope, and fumbles at the enclosure with trembling fingers*]. I got it from the bank this morning.

VIVIE. It is my month's allowance. They sent it to me as usual the other day. I simply sent it back to be placed to your credit, and asked them to send you the lodgment receipt.[27] In future I shall support myself.

MRS WARREN [*not daring to understand*] Wasnt it enough? Why didn't you tell me? [*With a cunning gleam in her eye*] I'll double it: I was intending to double it. Only let me know how much you want.

VIVIE. You know very well that that has nothing to do with it. From this time I go my own way in my own business and among my own friends. And you will go yours. [*She rises*]. Goodbye.

MRS WARREN [*rising, appalled*] Goodbye?

VIVIE. Yes: goodbye. Come: dont let us make a useless scene: you understand perfectly well. Sir George Crofts has told me the whole business.

MRS WARREN [*angrily*] Silly old— [*She swallows an epithet, and turns white at the narrowness of her escape from uttering it*].

VIVIE. Just so.

MRS WARREN. He ought to have his tongue cut out. But I thought it was ended: you said you didnt mind.

VIVIE [*steadfastly*] Excuse me: I d o mind.

MRS WARREN. But I explained—

VIVIE. You explained how it came about. You did not tell me that it is still going on [*She sits*].

Mrs Warren, silenced for a moment, looks forlornly at Vivie, who waits, secretly hoping

---

[27] Deposit slip.

that the combat is over. But the cunning expression comes back into Mrs Warren's face; and she bends across the table, sly and urgent, half whispering.

MRS WARREN. Vivie: do you know how rich I am?

VIVIE. I have no doubt you are very rich.

MRS WARREN. But you dont know all that that means: youre too young. It means a new dress every day; it means theatres and balls every night; it means having the pick of all the gentlemen in Europe at your feet; it means a lovely house and plenty of servants; it means the choicest of eating and drinking; it means everything you like, everything you want, everything you can think of. And what are you here? A mere drudge, toiling and moiling early and late for your bare living and two cheap dresses a year. Think over it. [*Soothingly*] Youre shocked, I know. I can enter into your feelings; and I think they do you credit; but trust me, nobody will blame you: you may take my word for that. I know what young girls are; and I know youll think better of it when youve turned it over in your mind.

VIVIE. So that's how it's done, is it? You must have said all that to many a woman, mother, to have it so pat.

MRS WARREN [*passionately*] What harm am I asking you to do? [*Vivie turns away contemptuously. Mrs Warren continues desperately*] Vivie: listen to me: you dont understand: youve been taught wrong on purpose: you dont know what the world is really like.

VIVIE [*arrested*] Taught wrong on purpose! What do you mean?

MRS WARREN. I mean that youre throwing away all your chances for nothing. You think that people are what they pretend to be: that the way you were taught at school and college to think right and proper is the way things really are. But it's not: it's all only a pretence, to keep the cowardly slavish common run of people quiet. Do you want to find that out, like other women, at forty, when youve thrown yourself away and lost your chances; or wont you take it in good time now from your own mother, that loves you and swears to you that it's truth: gospel truth? [*Urgently*] Vivie: the big people, the clever people, the managing people, all know it. They do as I do, and think what I think. I know plenty of them. I know them to speak to, to introduce you to, to make friends of for you. I dont mean anything wrong: thats what you dont understand: your head is full of ignorant ideas about me. What do the people that taught you know about life or about people like me? When did they ever meet me, or speak to me, or let anyone tell them about me? the fools! Would they ever have done anything for you if I hadn't pâid them? Havnt I told you that I want you to be respectable? Havnt I brought you up to be respectable? And how can you keep it up without my money and my influence and Lizzie's friends? Cant you see that youre cutting your own throat as well as breaking my heart in turning your back on me?

VIVIE. I recognize the Crofts philosophy of life, mother. I heard it all from him that day at the Gardners'.

MRS WARREN. You think I want to force that played-out old sot on you! I dont, Vivie: on my oath I dont.

VIVIE. It would not matter if you did: you would not succeed. [*Mrs Warren winces, deeply hurt by the implied indifference towards her affectionate intention. Vivie, neither understanding this nor concerning herself about it, goes on calmly*] Mother: you dont at all know the sort of person I am. I dont object to Crofts more than to any other coarsely built man of his class. To tell you the truth, I rather admire him for being strongminded enough to enjoy himself in his own way and make plenty of money instead of living the usual shooting, hunting, dining-out, tailoring, loafing life of his set merely because all the rest do it. And I'm perfectly aware that if I'd been in the same circumstances as my aunt Liz, I'd have done exactly what she did. I dont think I'm more prejudiced or straitlaced than you: I think I'm less. I'm certain I'm less sentimental. I know very well that fashionable morality is all a pretence, and that if I took your money and devoted the rest of my life to spending it fashionably, I might be as worthless and vicious as the silliest woman could possibly want to be without having a word said to me about it. But I dont want to be worthless. I shouldnt enjoy trotting about the park to advertize my dressmaker and carriage builder, or being bored at the opera to shew off a shopwindowful of diamonds.

MRS WARREN [*bewildered*] But—

VIVIE. Wait a moment: Ive not done. Tell me why you continue your business now that you are independent of it. Your sister, you told me, has left all that behind her. Why dont you do the same?

MRS WARREN. Oh, it's all very easy for Liz: she likes good society, and has the air of being a lady. Imagine m e in a cathedral town! Why, the very rooks in the trees would find me out even if I could stand the dulness of it. I must have work and excitement, or I should go melancholy mad. And what else is there for me to do? The life suits me: I'm fit for it and not for anything else. If I didnt do it somebody else would; so I dont do any real harm by it. And then it brings in money; and I like making money. No: it's no use: I cant give it up—not for anybody. But what need you know about it? I'll never mention it. I'll keep Crofts away. I'll not trouble you much: you see I have to be constantly running about from one place to another. Youll be quit of me altogether when I die.

VIVIE. No: I am my mother's daughter. I am like you: I must have work, and must make more money than I spend. But my work is not your work, and my way not your way. We must part. It will not make much difference to us: instead of meeting one another for perhaps a few moments in twenty years, we shall never meet: thats all.

MRS WARREN [*her voice stifled in tears*] Vivie: I meant to have been more with you: I did indeed.

VIVIE. It's no use, mother: I am not to be changed by a few cheap tears and entreaties any more than you are, I daresay.

MRS WARREN [*wildly*] Oh, you call a mother's tears cheap.

VIVIE. They cost you nothing; and you ask me to give you the peace and quietness of my whole life in exchange for them. What use would my company be to you if you could get it? What have we two in common that could make either of us happy together?

MRS WARREN [*lapsing recklessly into her dialect*] We're mother and daughter. I want my daughter. Ive a right to you. Who is to care for me when I'm old? Plenty of girls have taken to me like daughters and cried at leaving me; but I let them all go because I had you to look forward to. I kept myself lonely for you. Youve no right to turn on me now and refuse to do your duty as a daughter.

VIVIE [*jarred and antagonized by the echo of the slums in her mother's voice*] My duty as a daughter! I thought we should come to that presently. Now once for all, mother, you want a daughter and Frank wants a wife. I dont want a mother; and I dont want a husband. I have spared neither Frank nor myself in sending him about his business. Do you think I will spare y o u?

MRS WARREN [*violently*] Oh, I know the sort you are: no mercy for yourself or anyone else. *I* know. My experience has done that for me anyhow: I can tell the pious, canting, hard, selfish woman when I meet her. Well, keep yourself to yourself: *I* dont want you. But listen to this. Do you know what I would do with you if you were a baby again? aye, as sure as there's a Heaven above us.

VIVIE. Strangle me, perhaps.

MRS WARREN. No: I'd bring you up to be a real daughter to me, and not what you are now, with your pride and your prejudices and the college education you stole from me: yes, stole: deny it if you can: what was it but stealing? I'd bring you up in my own house, I would.

VIVIE [*quietly*] In one of your own houses.

MRS WARREN [*screaming*] Listen to her! listen to how she spits on her mother's grey hairs! Oh, may you live to have your own daughter tear and trample on you as you have trampled on me. And you will: you will. No woman ever had luck with a mother's curse on her.

VIVIE. I wish you wouldn't rant, mother. It only hardens me. Come: I suppose I am the only young woman you ever had in your power that you did good to. Dont spoil it all now.

MRS WARREN. Yes, Heaven forgive me, it's true; and you are the only one that ever turned on me. Oh, the injustice of it! the injustice! the injustice! I always wanted to be a good woman. I tried honest work; and I was slave-driven until I cursed the day I ever heard of honest work. I was a good mother; and because I made my daughter a good woman she turns me out as if I was a leper. Oh, if I only had my life to live over again! I'd talk to that lying clergyman in the school. From this time forth, so help me Heaven in my last hour, I'll do wrong and nothing but wrong. And I'll prosper on it.

VIVIE. Yes: it's better to choose your line and go through with it. If I had been you, mother, I might have done as you did; but I should not have lived one life and believed in another. You are a conventional woman at heart. That is why I am bidding you goodbye now. I am right, am I not?

MRS WARREN [*taken aback*] Right to throw away all my money!

VIVIE. No: right to get rid of you? I should be a fool not to? Isnt that so?

MRS WARREN [*sulkily*] Oh well, yes if you come to that, I suppose you are. But Lord help the world if everybody took to doing the right thing! And now I'd better go than stay where I'm not wanted. [*She turns to the door*].

VIVIE [*kindly*] Wont you shake hands?

MRS WARREN [*after looking at her fiercely for a moment with a savage impulse to strike her*] No, thank you. Goodbye.

VIVIE [*matter-of-factly*] Goodbye. [*Mrs Warren goes out, slamming the door behind her. The strain on Vivie's face relaxes; her grave expression breaks up into one of joyous content; her breath goes out in a half sob, half laugh of intense relief. She goes buoyantly to her place at the writing-table; pushes the electric lamp out of the way; pulls over a great sheaf of papers; and is in the act of dipping her pen in the ink when she finds Frank's note. She opens it unconcernedly and reads it quickly, giving a little laugh at some quaint turn of expression in it*]. And goodbye, Frank. [*She tears the note up and tosses the pieces into the waste-paper basket without a second thought. Then she goes at her work with a plunge, and soon becomes absorbed in its figures*].

[1898]

Anton Pavlovich Chekhov *1860–1904*

THE CHERRY ORCHARD

Translated by Camilla Chapin Daniels and George Rapall Noyes

CHARACTERS

LYUBÓV ANDRÉYEVNA RANÉVSKY, *a landowner*
ANYA, *her daughter, aged seventeen*
VÁRYA, *her adopted daughter, aged twenty-seven*
LEONID ANDRÉYEVICH GÁYEV, *brother of* LYUBOV ANDREYEVNA
YERMOLÁY ALEXÉICH LOPÁKHIN, *a merchant*
PETR* SERGÉICH TROFÍMOV, *a student*
BORÍS BORÍSOVICH SEMEÓNOV-PÍSHCHIK, *a landowner*

SEMÉN† PANTALÉYEVICH EPIKHÓDOV, *a clerk*
DUNYÁSHA, *a maid*
FIRS, *the butler, an old man of eighty-seven*
YÁSHA, *a young footman*
A WAYFARER
THE STATION MASTER
A POST OFFICE OFFICIAL
GUESTS *and* SERVANTS

The action takes place at the country estate of LYUBOV ANDREYEVNA RANEVSKY.

ACT I

Scene I

A room that is still called the nursery. One of the doors leads into ANYA's *room. Day is breaking. The sun will soon rise. It is May, and the cherry trees are in bloom, but it is cold in the orchard, and a light frost lies on the ground. The windows in the room are closed.* DUNYASHA *enters with a candle, and* LOPAKHIN *with a book in his hand.*

LOPAKHIN. The train has come, thank Heaven! What time is it?
DUNYASHA. Almost two o'clock. [*Blows out the candle.*] It's beginning to get light already.
LOPAKHIN. How late was the train, anyway? At least a couple of hours. [*Yawns and stretches.*] I'm a fine one! I surely made a fool of myself. Here I came over on purpose to meet them at the station, and then all at once I fell asleep . . . sitting up! What a nuisance! . . . you might have waked me.
DUNYASHA. I thought you had gone. [*Listens.*] I think they're coming now.
LOPAKHIN [*listens*]. No, they have to collect their baggage and so forth. [*Pause.*] Lyubov Andreyevna has been living abroad now for five years, and I don't know how she may have changed. She's a good soul, a simple, easy-going woman. I remember when I was a young sprout, fifteen years old, my father—he's dead now, but he used to have a little shop in the village then—struck me in the face with his fist one day, and my nose began to bleed. We'd gone out of doors together for some reason or other and he was drunk. I

---

* Pronounced, Pyŏtr (one syllable).   † Pronounced, Se-myŏn′.

remember just as though it were now, how Lyubov Andreyevna—she was still a slim young thing—led me over to the washbasin here in this very room, the nursery. "Come, come, don't cry your eyes away; you'll live to dance on your wedding day, little peasant," says she. [*Pause.*] Little peasant! . . . True, my father was a peasant, and here I am wearing a white waistcoat and yellow shoes. From the sow's ear to the silk purse. . . . I've grown rich, made a lot of money, but when you come to think of it, to figure it out, I'm still a peasant. . . . [*Fingers the pages of the book.*] Here I've been reading this book, and haven't understood a word of it. I fell asleep reading. [*Pause.*]

DUNYASHA. Even the dogs haven't slept all night long. They seem to feel their masters are returning.

LOPAKHIN. What's the matter with you, Dunyasha? You're so . . .

DUNYASHA. My hands are trembling. I'm going to faint.

LOPAKHIN. You're a tender, spoiled little thing, Dunyasha. Why, you even dress like a lady, and comb your hair to match. It's not right. You ought to remember your place.

[EPIKHODOV *enters, carrying a bouquet. He wears a short coat, and highly polished boots, which squeak loudly. As he enters, he drops the bouquet.*]

EPIKHODOV [*picking up the bouquet*]. The gardener sent these, and said to put them in the dining-room. [*Hands the bouquet to* DUNYASHA.]

LOPAKHIN. And bring me some kvass.[1]

DUNYASHA. Yes, sir. [*Goes out.*]

EPIKHODOV. There's a frost this morning. Six degrees below freezing, and the cherry trees all in bloom. I can't praise our climate. [*Sighs.*] No, that I can't. It won't favor us even this once. Just listen to this, Yermolay Alexeich—I bought myself some boots day before yesterday, and I tell you, they squeak so loudly you wouldn't believe it. What shall I grease them with?

LOPAKHIN. Leave me alone. I'm sick of you.

EPIKHODOV. Every day some bad luck or other overtakes me, but I don't grumble. I'm used to it. I just smile.

[DUNYASHA *enters and hands* LOPAKHIN *the kvass.*]

EPIKHODOV. I'm going. [*Stumbles against a chair, knocking it over.*] There! . . . [*With apparent triumph.*] There, if you'll pardon the expression, you see the kind of circumstance that pursues me. This is positively remarkable. [*Goes out.*]

DUNYASHA. Did you know, Yermolay Alexeich, Epikhodov's made me a proposal?

LOPAKHIN. Aha!

DUNYASHA. I don't know how to . . . He's a quiet sort of fellow, only sometimes when he begins talking, you can't make out a word. It's first-rate and full of feeling, only you can't understand it. I half like him, too. He's madly in love with me. An unlucky man. Something goes wrong with him every day. We tease him, and call him two-and-twenty troubles.

LOPAKHIN [*listening*] . I think they're coming now.

DUNYASHA. Coming! What's the matter with me! . . . I'm all goose-flesh!

LOPAKHIN. They're really coming. Let's go out and meet them. Will she recognize me? It's five years since we've seen each other.

---

[1] An alcoholic beverage something like beer.

DUNYASHA [*in agitation*]. I'm going to faint . . . Oh, I'm going to faint!

[*Two carriages are heard drawing up to the house.* LOPAKHIN *and* DUNYASHA *go out quickly. The stage remains empty. There is noise and stir in the adjoining room. Across the stage, leaning on his stick, hastens* FIRS, *who has met* LYUBOV ANDREYEVNA *at the station. He wears an old-fashioned livery and a tall hat. He is muttering to himself, but not a word is distinguishable. The noise behind the scenes continually increases. A voice is heard, saying,* "Come in this way. . . ." LYUBOV ANDREYEVNA, ANYA, *and* CHARLOTTA IVANOVNA, *all wearing traveling clothes, cross the room, accompanied by* VARYA, *clad in a heavy coat and kerchief,* GAYEV, SEMEONOV-PISHCHIK, LOPAKHIN, DUNYASHA, *with a bundle and an umbrella, and a servant carrying the bags.* CHARLOTTA IVANOVNA *is leading a little dog by chain.*]

ANYA. Let's come in here. Do you remember this room, mama?

LYUBOV ANDREYEVNA [*joyfully, through her tears*]. The nursery!

VARYA. It's so cold my hands are numb. [*To* LYUBOV ANDREYEVNA.] Mama, your rooms, the white one and the lavender, have been left just as they were.

LYUBOV ANDREYEVNA. The nursery, my dear, beautiful room! . . . It was here I slept when I was little. . . . [*Weeps.*] And now I feel as though I were a little child again. . . . [*Kisses her brother, then* VARYA, *and then her brother once more.*] And Varya hasn't changed a bit—she's just like a little nun. And if here isn't Dunyasha. [*She kisses* DUNYASHA.]

GAYEV. The train was two hours late. How did it happen? Do you call that punctuality?

CHARLOTTA [*to* PISHCHIK]. My dog even eats nuts.

PISHCHICK [*surprised*]. Just think of that!

[*They all go out, with the exception of* ANYA *and* DUNYASHA.]

DUNYASHA. Here you are at last. . . . [*She takes off* ANYA's *hat and coat.*]

ANYA. I didn't sleep the four nights we were on the road. . . . Now I'm chilled through.

DUNYASHA. You went away during Lent. There was snow on the ground then, there was frost—and now? My darling! [*Laughs and kisses* ANYA.] I've waited for you so long, my joy, my dear one. . . . I must tell you right now; I can't keep it a minuter longer. . . .

ANYA [*listlessly*]. What now? . . .

DUNYASHA. Epikhodov, the clerk, made me a proposal right after Easter.

ANYA. Always harping on the same thing. . . . [*Arranges her hair.*] I've lost all my hairpins. . . . [*She is very tired, can hardly stand.*]

DUNYASHA. I'm all of a flutter. He loves me—he loves me so!

ANYA [*glancing tenderly through the door into her own room*]. My room, my windows—just as though I had never gone away. I'm at home! To-morrow morning I shall get up and run out into the orchard. . . . Oh, if I could only sleep! During the whole journey I couldn't sleep a wink. I was restless.

DUNYASHA. Petr Sergeich arrived day before yesterday.

ANYA [*joyfully*]. Petya!

DUNYASHA. He's sleeping in the bath house, and living there too. He says he's afraid he'll inconvenience us. [*Looks at her watch.*] I'd wake him up, but Varvara Mikhailovna told me not to. "Don't waken him," said she.

[VARYA *comes in with a bunch of keys at her belt.*]

VARYA. Dunyasha, bring us some coffee right away. . . . Mama's asking for it.

DUNYASHA. Right away. [*Goes out.*]

VARYA. Well, thank Heaven, you're here! Once more you are at home. [*Caressing* ANYA.] My darling is here! My pretty one has come home!

ANYA. I was impatient, too.

VARYA. I can just imagine!

ANYA. I left home during Holy Week. It was cold then. Charlotta talked all the way, and did tricks. Why, why did you tie me to Charlotta's apron strings?

VARYA. You couldn't have traveled alone, my dear. Seventeen years old!

ANYA. When we arrived in Paris, it was cold. There was snow on the ground. I speak French horribly. Mamma was living on the fifth floor. I went to find her. There were a few Frenchmen there, and some ladies, and an old priest with a prayer book, and it was full of tobacco smoke and uncomfortable. Suddenly I became sorry for mama, so sorry. I hugged her head, squeezed it tight, and could not let her go. And after that mama kept caressing me and weeping. . . .

VARYA [*through her tears*]. Don't tell me any more, don't! . . .

ANYA. She'd already sold her country house near Mentone. She had nothing left, nothing. And I didn't have a kopek[2] left—we just managed to get there. But mama doesn't realize! We had dinner at the station, and she ordered the most expensive things, and tipped the servants a ruble apiece. Charlotta did too. And Yasha demands his share also: it's just awful! You know mama has a footman—Yasha. We brought him back with us.

VARYA. I saw the good-for-nothing.

ANYA. Well, how are things? Is the interest paid up?

VARYA. Not much!

ANYA. Good heavens, how awful!

VARYA. The estate will be sold in August.

ANYA. God help us!

LOPAKHIN [*looks through the door and moos*]. Moo-oo-oo! [*Withdraws.*]

VARYA [*through her tears*]. I'd like to give him that! . . . [*Shakes her fist.*]

ANYA [*softly, embracing* VARYA]. Varya, has he proposed to you? [VARYA *shakes her head.*] But he does love you. . . . Why don't you both speak out plainly? What are you waiting for?

VARYA. I don't believe anything will come of it. His business takes up so much of his interest—he hasn't time for me. . . . And he doesn't pay any attention to me. Deuce take him anyhow, I'm tired of seeing him. . . . Every one's talking about our marriage, wishing us well—but there's really nothing at all in it. It's like a dream. . . . [*In another tone.*] You have a little brooch shaped like a bee.

ANYA [*sadly*]. Mama bought it for me. [*Goes into her own room and calls back in a happy, childlike voice.*] While I was in Paris I went up in a balloon!

VARYA. My darling has come home! My pretty one is here!

[DUNYASHA *has already returned with the coffee pot, and is making coffee.*]

VARYA. [*standing near the door*]. All day long, my darling, I go to and fro, looking after the housekeeping and daydreaming. We must marry you to a rich man, and then I'd be easier in my mind. I'd go to some hermitage, then to Kiev, then to Moscow. I'd go from one holy shrine to another. . . . I'd wander and wander. . . . How lovely! . . .

ANYA. The birds are singing in the orchard. What time is it now?

[2] A bronze or copper coin worth 1/100 of a ruble. A ruble is close in value to a U.S. dollar.

VARYA. It must be three. It's time for you to sleep, my darling. [*Going into* ANYA's *room.*] How lovely!

[YASHA *comes in with a steamer rug and a traveling bag.*]

YASHA [*tiptoeing across the stage*]. May I come through this way?

DUNYASHA. Why, I wouldn't have recognized you, Yasha. You've changed so while you were abroad.

YASHA. Hm. . . . And who are you?

DUNYASHA. When you went away, I was just so high. . . . [*Holds out her hand.*] I'm Dunyasha, Fedor Kozoyedov's daughter. Don't you remember?

YASHA. Hm. . . . Little cucumber! [*Glances hastily around and embraces her. She screams and drops a saucer.* YASHA *goes out hurriedly.*]

VARYA [*in the doorway, annoyed*]. What's the matter here?

DUNYASHA [*through her tears*]. I broke a saucer.

VARYA. That's good luck.

ANYA [*emerging from her room*]. We must warn mama. Petya is here. . . .

VARYA. I told them not to wake him.

ANYA [*musingly*]. Six years ago father died, and a month later brother Grisha was drowned in the river—such a darling little seven-year-old boy. Mama couldn't stand the shock; she went away, went away without looking behind her. . . . [*Shudders.*] How I understand her, if she only knew it! [*Pause.*] And Petya Trofimov was Grisha's tutor—he may remind her. . . .

[FIRS *comes in. He wears a waiter's jacket and a white waistcoat.*]

FIRS [*going over to the coffeepot with a preoccupied air*]. The Mistress is going to eat in here. [*Puts on his white gloves.*] Is the coffee ready? [*To* DUNYASHA *sternly.*] You there! Where's the cream?

DUNYASHA. Oh, good Lord! [*She goes out hurriedly.*]

FIRS [*bustling around the coffeepot*]. Eh, you're a lummox. . . . [*Mutters to himself.*] So they're back from Paris. . . . The Master visited Paris once too . . . in a coach and four. . . . [*Laughs.*]

VARYA. What are you saying, Firs?

FIRS. Beg pardon? [*Joyfully.*] My Lady's come home! I've lived to see it. I might as well die now. [*Weeps with joy.*]

[LYUBOV ANDREYEVNA, GAYEV, *and* SEMEONOV-PISHCHIK *come in.* SEMEONOV-PISHCHIK *wears a sleeveless coat of light-weight material, and loose trousers.* GAYEV, *as he enters, goes through the motions of a pool player.*]

LYUBOV ANDREYEVNA. How does it go? Let me see if I can remember! Yellow into the corner! Cross the table to the center!

GAYEV. Graze it into the corner! You and I, sister, slept here in this very room once, and now I'm fifty-one, strange though it may seem. . . .

LOPAKHIN. Yes, time flies.

GAYEV. What's that?

LOPAKHIN. I say, time flies.

GAYEV. It smells of patchouli[3] in here.

ANYA. I'm going to bed. Good night, Mama. [*Kisses her mother.*]

LYUBOV ANDREYEVNA. My darling girlie! [*Kisses her hands.*] Are you glad to be home? Somehow I can't calm myself.

ANYA. Good night, uncle.

GAYEV [*kissing her face and hands*]. God bless you! How you resemble your mother! [*To his sister.*] Lyuba, at her age, you were just like her.

---

[3] A plant from the mint family, at that time a popular perfume.

[ANYA *gives her hand to* LOPAKHIN *and* PISHCHIK, *and goes out of the room, closing the door behind her.*]

LYUBOV ANDREYEVNA. She is very tired.

PISHCHIK. It must have been a long journey.

VARYA [*to* LOPAKHIN *and* PISHCHIK]. Well, gentlemen? It's past two o'clock. Time to be decent.

LYUBOV ANDREYEVNA [*laughing*]. You are still the same Varya. [*Draws* VARYA *close and kisses her.*] See, I'll drink my coffee and then we'll all disperse. [FIRS *places a cushion under her feet.*] Thank you, my friend. I've become addicted to coffee. I drink it day and night. Thank you, dear old man. [*Kisses him.*]

VARYA. I'll go and see whether they've brought in all your things. [*Goes out.*]

LYUBOV ANDREYEVNA. Is it really I sitting here? [*Laughs.*] I want to wave my arms and jump for joy. [*Covers her face with her hands.*] And all of a sudden I drop off dozing! God knows, I love my country, I love it dearly. I couldn't look through the train window—I cried all the time. [*Through her tears.*] However, I must drink the coffee. Thank you, Firs. Thank you, dear old man. I am so glad you are still alive.

FIRS. Day before yesterday.

GAYEV. He is hard of hearing.

LOPAKHIN. I must leave shortly, between four and five, for Harkov. What a nuisance! I wanted to have a look at you, and to chat a little. . . . You are just as handsome as ever.

PISHCHIK [*breathing heavily*]. She's even more beautiful. She's dressed Paris style. "This is more than we could hope for, most astonishingly fine."

LOPAKHIN. Your brother there, Leonid Andreich, says I'm a low sort of fellow, a skinflint, but that doesn't bother me. Let him talk. I only want you to have faith in me as before, to see your marvelous, touching eyes look upon me as they used to. God is merciful! My father was the serf of your grandfather and your father, but you, you yourself, once did so much for me that I have forgotten all old wrongs, and love you as though you were my own kin—no, even more.

LYUBOV ANDREYEVNA. I can't sit still—I simply can't. . . . [*She springs up and walks about excitedly.*] I cannot survive this joy. . . . Laugh at me—I'm a silly woman. . . . My darling bookcase! . . . [*Kisses the bookcase.*] My desk! . . .

GAYEV. Nurse died during your absence.

LYUBOV ANDREYEVNA [*sits down and drinks her coffee.*] Yes, God rest her soul! They wrote me about it.

GAYEV. And Anastasy died. Petrushka Kosoy has left me, and is living in the city now at the Police Inspector's house. [*Takes a little box of lozenges out of his pocket and sucks one.*]

PISHCHIK. My daughter Dashenka . . . sends you her regards.

LOPAKHIN. I have something very pleasant and heartening to tell you. [*Looks at his watch.*] I must go at once—there's no time to explain it. . . . Oh, well, here it is in a nutshell. You know already that your cherry orchard is to be sold for debts, and that the auction has been set for the twenty-second of August. But don't you worry, dear lady, put your mind at rest—there's a way out. . . . Here's my proposition: let me have your attention. Your estate is situated only thirteen miles from the city, the railroad runs past it, and if the cherry orchard and the land along the river were divided into plots for cottages and then leased, you would get an annual return of at least twenty-five thousand rubles.

GAYEV. Pardon me, what utter nonsense!

LYUBOV ANDREYEVNA. I don't understand you at all, Yermolay Alexeich.

LOPAKHIN. You'll receive from the cottagers annually at least twenty-five rubles per desyatina,[4] and if you advertise it now, I'll wager anything you please that you won't have a vacant plot left by autumn. They'll all be taken. In short—I congratulate you—you're saved! The site is marvelous, the river deep. Only, of course, you'll have to fix it up a bit, clear it off. . . . Tear down all the old buildings—for instance, this house, which is no use to any one now, cut down the old cherry orchard—

LYUBOV ANDREYEVNA. Cut it down? My dear riend, forgive me, but you don't understand at all. If there is anything interesting—I might say remarkable— in our province it is our cherry orchard.

LOPAKHIN. The orchard is remarkable only for its size. The cherries ripen only every other year, and even then there's no way to dispose of them. Nobody buys them.

GAYEV. Even the Encyclopedia mentions this cherry orchard.

LOPAKHIN [*looking at his watch*]. Unless we devise some plan and arrive at a definite decision, the cherry orchard and the entire estate will be sold at auction on the twenty-second of August. Make up your minds then! I assure you there's no other alternative. There is absolutely none!

FIRS. In times past, forty or fifty years ago, they used to dry the cherries, preserve them, and spice them; they made jam of them, and sometimes—

GAYEV. Be quiet, Firs.

FIRS. And sometimes they sent the dried cherries by cartloads to Moscow and Harkov. Ah, they brought in the money! And the dried cherries were soft, moist, sweet, fragrant. . . . They knew a way then. . . .

LYUBOV ANDREYEVNA. But who has the recipe now?

FIRS. They've forgotten how. No one remembers it.

PISHCHIK [*to* LYUBOV ANDREYEVNA]. What did you do in Paris? Tell us! Did you eat frogs?

LYUBOV ANDREYEVNA. I ate crocodiles.

PISHCHIK. Just think of that! . . .

LOPAKHIN. Only gentry and peasants have lived in the country prior to our time, but now the cottager makes his appearance. Every city—even the smallest—is now surrounded by cottages. And one may safely foretell that within twenty years the number of cottagers will have increased remarkably. Now he only drinks tea on the balcony, but the time may come when he will busy himself with farming on his one desyatina, and then your cherry orchard will become joyous, rich, and luxuriant. . . .

GAYEV [*becoming indignant*]. What nonsense!

[VARYA *and* YASHA *come in.*]

VARYA. There are two telegrams for you here, mama. [*She takes out a key and opens the squeaking lock of the old bookcase.*] Here they are.

LYUBOV ANDREYEVNA. They're from Paris. [*Tears them across without reading them.*] I am through with Paris. . . .

GAYEV. Do you know, Lyuba, how old this bookcase is? A week ago I pulled out the bottom drawer, and there I saw figures burned into the wood. This bookcase was made just a hundred years ago. What do you think of that,

---

[4] A desyatina equals about 2.7 acres.

eh? We ought to celebrate its jubilee. It's an inanimate object, but just the same, say what you will, it's a fine old bookcase.

PISHCHIK [*surprised*]. A hundred years! . . . Just think of that!

GAYEV. Yes. . . . This object. . . . [*Laying his hand on the bookcase.*] Dear, venerated bookcase! I greet thine existence, which for more than a hundred years now has been consecrated to the bright ideals of goodness and justice; thy mute summons to fruitful labor has grown no weaker during the course of these hundred years, as thou hast upheld through generations of our stock [*Tearfully.*] courage, faith in a better future, and hast developed within us ideals of goodness and social conscience. [*Pause.*]

LOPAKHIN. Yes. . . .

LYUBOV ANDREYEVNA. You haven't changed a bit, Lenya.

GAYEV [*somewhat confused*]. Right ball to the corner pocket! Close shot to the center!

LOPAKHIN [*looking at his watch*]. Well, it's time for me to go.

YASHA [*handing* LYUBOV ANDREYEVNA *a vial*]. You must take your pills now. . . .

PISHCHIK. You shouldn't take medicine, my dear. It does you neither harm nor good. . . . Give it to me, most honored lady. [*Takes the pills, pours them out on his palm, blows on them, puts them in his mouth and drinks some kvass.*] There now!

LYUBOV ANDREYEVNA [*frightened*]. Why, you're crazy!

PISHCHIK. I swallowed every pill.

LOPAKHIN. What a glutton! [*They all laugh.*]

FIRS. He was at our house on Easter, and ate half a gallon of cucumbers. . . . [*Mutters.*]

LYUBOV ANDREYEVNA. What is he talking about?

VARYA. He's been mumbling that way for ten years now. We've grown used to it.

YASHA. In his dotage.

[CHARLOTTA IVANOVNA, *a very thin, tightly-laced woman, dressed in white, and with a lorgnette*[5] *at her waist, crosses the stage.*]

LOPAKHIN. Excuse me, Charlotta Ivanovna, I haven't had a chance yet to greet you. [*Tries to kiss her hand.*]

CHARLOTTA [*drawing away her hand*]. If I let you kiss my hand, you'll want to kiss my elbow next, then my shoulder. . . .

LOPAKHIN. I'm out of luck to-day. [*All laugh.*] Charlotta Ivanovna, show us a trick!

LYUBOV ANDREYEVNA. Charlotta, show us a trick!

CHARLOTTA. Not I. I'm too sleepy. [*Goes out.*]

LOPAKHIN. I'll see you again in three weeks. [*Kisses the hand of* LYUBOV ANDREYEVNA.] In the meantime, good-by. [*To* GAYEV.] Time to go. Good-by. [*Exchanges kisses with* PISHCHIK.] Good-by. [*Gives his hand to* VARYA, *then to* FIRS *and* YASHA.] I don't want to leave. [*To* LYUBOV ANDREYEVNA.] If you can come to a decision regarding the subdivision, and make up your mind, let me know. I'll get you a loan of fifty thousand. Think it over seriously.

VARYA [*angrily*]. Do go and be done with it!

LOPAKHIN. I'm going, I'm going. [*He goes out.*]

GAYEV. A low fellow, that. But no—your pardon! . . . Varya's going to marry him. That's Varya's suitor.

---

[5] A pair of eyeglasses with a handle instead of earpieces.

VARYA. Don't talk nonsense, uncle.

LYUBOV ANDREYEVNA. Why, Varya, I should be very glad. He's a good man.

PISHCHIK. A most worthy man, one must admit. . . . Even my Dashenka . . . says also that . . . she says a lot. . . . [*Snores, but rouses himself immediately.*] But still, dear lady, loan me two hundred and forty rubles . . . to pay the interest on our mortgage.

VARYA [*frightened*]. We haven't any, we haven't!

LYUBOV ANDREYEVNA. Really, I haven't any money.

PISHCHIK. You'll find some. [*Laughs.*] I never lose hope. Here I used to think that everything was lost, ruined, and then—the railroad was built across my land, and . . . they paid me. And so, just watch and see—something else will turn up, if not to-day, then to-morrow. . . . Dashenka is going to win two hundred thousand. . . . She has a lottery ticket.

LYUBOV ANDREYEVNA. The coffee's all gone. We can go to bed.

FIRS [*in a lecturing tone, as he brushes off* GAYEV]. You've put on the wrong trousers again. What shall I do with you?

VARYA [*softly*]. Anya's asleep. [*Opens the window gently.*] The sun has risen already. It's not cold any more. Look, mama, what wonderful trees! How glorious the air is! The starlings are singing!

GAYEV [*opening another window*]. The whole orchard is white. Do you remember, Lyuba? There is that long vista; straight, straight as an arrow it shines on moonlight nights. Do you remember? You haven't forgotten?

LYUBOV ANDREYEVNA [*looks out of the window into the orchard*]. Oh, my childhood, those pure and happy years! Here in this nursery I used to sleep; from here I looked out upon the orchard. Gladness awakened with me every morning, and it was just the same then—as now—not a bit changed. [*Laughs joyously.*] White, all white! Oh, my orchard! After the dark, rainy autumns and the cold winters, you are young again, full of gladness. The heavenly angels have not abandoned you. . . . If only I might cast from my shoulders and breast the heavy stone, if only I could forget my past!

GAYEV. Yes, and they'll sell the orchard to pay our debts. How strange it seems! . . .

LYUBOV ANDREYEVNA. Look, the spirit of our mother is walking in the orchard . . . in a white dress! [*Laughs joyously.*] It is she.

GAYEV. Where?

VARYA. Lord help you, mama!

LYUBOV ANDREYEVNA. There's no one there. I only thought it looked so. On the right, at the turn to the summerhouse, a white tree was bent so that it resembled a woman. . . .

[TROFIMOV *comes in. He is dressed in a shabby student's uniform, and wears glasses.*]

LYUBOV ANDREYEVNA. What a wonderful orchard! White masses of flowers, the blue sky! . . .

TROFIMOV. Lyubov Andreyevna! [*She looks at him.*] I shall only pay you my respects, and then go immediately. [*Kissing her hand warmly.*] They told me to wait until morning, but I didn't have the patience. . . .

[LYUBOV ANDREYEVNA *looks at him in bewilderment.*]

VARYA [*through her tears*]. It is Petya Trofimov.

TROFIMOV. Petya Trofimov, who used to be tutor to your Grisha. . . . Can I really have changed so?

[LYUBOV ANDREYEVNA *embraces him and weeps quietly.*]

GAYEV [*embarrassed*]. That's enough, Lyuba, that's enough.

VARYA [*weeping*]. But I told you, Petya, to wait till to-morrow.

LYUBOV ANDREYEVNA. My Grisha . . . my boy . . . Grisha . . . my son! . . .

VARYA. What's the use, mama? It's God's will.

TROFIMOV [*softly, through his tears*]. There . . . there. . . .

LYUBOV ANDREYEVNA [*weeping quietly*]. My little boy is dead, he was drowned.
. . . Why did it happen? Why, my dear? [*More softly.*] Anya is asleep in there
and I am talking in a loud voice . . . disturbing her. . . . What's the matter,
Petya? Why have you lost your good looks? Why have you grown old?

TROFIMOV. On the train a village woman called me "a gentleman gone to
seed."

LYUBOV ANDREYEVNA. You were just a boy then, a dear, young student, but
now your hair is thin, and you're wearing spectacles. Is it possible you're
still a student? [*Going toward the door.*]

TROFIMOV. I suppose I shall be a student forever.

LYUBOV ANDREYEVNA [*kisses her brother, then* VARYA]. Well, let's go to bed. Even
you have grown older, Leonid.

PISHCHIK [*following her*]. So then, we must go to bed. . . . Oh, my gout! I'll
stay the night. . . . Lyubov Andreyevna, my dear friend, if you could just
get me two hundred and forty rubles by to-morrow morning!

GAYEV. That's all he can think of!

PISHCHIK. Two hundred and forty rubles . . . to pay the interest on the mortgage.

LYUBOV ANDREYEVNA. I haven't any money, my dear man.

PISHCHIK. I'll give it back, my dear, it's a trifling sum. . . .

LYUBOV ANDREYEVNA. Well, all right then. Leonid will give it to you. . . . Give
it to him, Leonid.

GAYEV. I'll give it to him—you just watch me!

LYUBOV ANDREYEVNA. What's the use? Give it to him. . . . He needs it. . . .
He'll return it.

[TROFIMOV, LYUBOV ANDREYEVNA, PISHCHIK, *and* FIRS *go out.* GAYEV, VARYA,
and YASHA *remain.*]

GAYEV. My sister has not yet broken herself of the habit of squandering money.
[*To* YASHA.] Get away, my dear fellow. You smell like a chicken.

YASHA [*with a grin*]. And you haven't changed a bit, Leonid Andreyevich.

GAYEV. What's he talking about? [*To* VARYA.] What did he say?

VARYA [*to* YASHA]. Your mother has come in from the village. She's been sitting
in the servants' room since yesterday. She wants to see you.

YASHA. Devil a bit I care!

VARYA. Ah, you're a shameless fellow!

YASHA. Much use her being here. She might have come to-morrow. [*He goes
out.*]

VARYA. Mama is just the same as always. She hasn't changed a bit. If you'd
let her, she'd give away everything she had.

GAYEV. Yes. . . . [*Pause.*] When a great many remedies are suggested for some
ailment, it means that the ailment is incurable. I think, rack my brains, I
find many solutions, very many, which means that in reality there isn't one.
It would be splendid if some one would make us a bequest, splendid if we
could marry our Anya to a very wealthy man, splendid to go to Yaroslavl
and try our luck with our aunt, the Countess. Auntie is very, very rich.

VARYA [*weeping*). If only God would help us!

GAYEV. Don't cry. Auntie is very rich, but she doesn't like us. My sister, in the first place, married an attorney, a man below her class.

[ANYA *appears in the doorway.*]

GAYEV. She not only married below her class, but conducted herself, I must admit, in a manner far from virtuous. She is a kind, admirable, fine woman, I love her very much. But however diligently you may think up extenuating circumstances, you must still admit that she is immoral. One feels it in her slightest movement.

VARYA [*in a whisper*]. Anya is in the doorway.

GAYEV. Who? [*Pause.*] That's strange—I've got something in my right eye—I can't see out of it. And on Thursday, when I was in the district court—

[ANYA *comes in.*]

VARYA. Why aren't you asleep, Anya?

ANYA. I'm not sleepy. I can't go to sleep.

GAYEV. My darling! [*Kisses* ANYA's *face and hands.*] My child! . . . [*Through his tears.*] You're not only my niece—you're my angel—everything in the world to me. Believe in me, believe. . . .

ANYA. I believe in you, uncle. Every one loves you, respects you . . . but, dear uncle, you must keep still—only keep still. What were you just saying about my mother, your sister? Why did you say that?

GAYEV. Yes, yes. . . . [*Covers his face with her hand.*] This is indeed terrible! My God! Save me, God! And just a little while ago I delivered an oration over the bookcase . . . so silly! And it was only when I had finished that I realized it was silly.

VARYA. Yes, uncle dear, you truly must keep still. Just keep still, that's all.

ANYA. You'll be happier yourself if you just keep still.

GAYEV. I'll keep still. [*Kisses their hands.*] I'll keep still. Only here's some news about money matters. I was at the district court on Thursday. Well, people came in, the talk turned from one thing to another, from this to that, and I gathered that we might arrange a loan on a note, to pay the interest at the bank.

VARYA. If only God would help us.

GAYEV. I'll go over on Tuesday and talk it over with them again. [*To* VARYA.] Don't sob so. [*To* ANYA.] Your mama will have a talk with Lopakhin—of course he'll not refuse her. . . . And when you've rested up a bit, you will go to Yaroslavl to see your great-aunt, the Countess. So you see, we'll be working from three points, and the trick is turned already. I'm sure we shall pay off the interest. . . . [*Puts a piece of candy in his mouth.*] On my honor, I swear by whatever pledge you please, the estate shall not be sold! [*Excitedly.*] By my happiness I swear! Here's my hand on it. You may call me a wretched, dishonorable man if I let it be put up at auction. By my whole being I swear it!

ANYA [*cheerfully, her composure restored*]. How good and clever you are, uncle! [*Embraces him.*] I am quite calm now, quite calm and happy.

[FIRS *comes in.*]

FIRS [*reproachfully*]. Leonid Andreich, you're conscienceless! When are you going to bed?

GAYEV. Right away, right away. You may go, Firs. I'll take off my things without your help. Well, children, bye-bye. . . . I'll give you the details to-morrow, but now, go and sleep. [*Kisses* ANYA *and* VARYA.] I'm a man of the eighties.

. . . People don't praise those times much, but just the same, I may say
that I've suffered a lot for my convictions. The peasant loves me with good
reason. One must understand the peasant, one must understand what—

ANYA. There you go again, uncle!

VARYA. You must keep still, uncle dear!

FIRS [*angrily*]. Leonid Andreich!

GAYEV. I'm coming, I'm coming. . . . Go to bed now. Off two cushions into
the center! I'll turn over a new leaf. [*He goes out,* FIRS *shuffling behind him.*]

ANYA. My mind is at peace now. I don't want to go to Yaroslavl, I don't like
auntie; but just the same, I feel calmer, thanks to uncle. [*She sits down.*]

VARYA. We must sleep. I'm going to bed. Things went all to pieces while
you were gone. You know, only the old servants live in the servants' quarters:
Efimyushka, Polya, Evstigney, and Karp, too. They began to let in tramps
to spend the night. I didn't say a word. But then the rumor got around to
me that they were saying I didn't let them have anything but peas to eat.
Out of stinginess—you see? And Evstigney was to blame all the time. Very
well, I thought. If that's so, I thought, you just wait! So I called Evstigney
in. [*Yawns.*] He came. . . . "What's the matter with you, Evstigney? You're
making a fool of yourself!" . . . [*Looks at* ANYA.] Anya darling! [*Pause.*] She's
fallen asleep. [*Takes* ANYA *by the arm.*] Let's go to bed! Come! [*Leading her.*]
My darling has fallen asleep! Come on! [*They start to go.*]

[*In the far distance beyond the orchard a shepherd plays on his pipe.* TROFIMOV *walks
across the stage, and seeing* VARYA *and* ANYA, *stops still.*]

VARYA. Sh . . . sh. She's sleeping . . . sleeping. Come, dear.

ANYA [*softly, and half asleep*]. I am so tired. . . . All the little bells . . . dear
uncle . . . mama and uncle. . . .

VARYA. Come, dear, come on . . . . [*They go into* ANYA'S *room.*]

TROFIMOV [*tenderly*]. My sun! My springtime!

ACT II

*An old, ruined, long-since-abandoned shrine. Near it a well; and a few big stones, evidently
at one time tombstones. An old bench. The road leading to* GAYEV'S *farmhouse can be
seen. At one side poplar trees tower up, dark and tall; beyond them, the cherry orchard
begins. In the distance a row of telegraph poles, and far off along the horizon are dimly
visible the outlines of a great city, which can be seen only during fine, clear weather. It
is nearly sunset.* CHARLOTTA, YASHA, *and* DUNYASHA *are sitting on the bench:* EPIKHO-
DOV *is standing nearby and playing the guitar. They are all thoughtful.* CHARLOTTA *is
wearing a man's old cap; she has lowered a rifle from her shoulder, and is adjusting a
buckle on the strap.*

CHARLOTTA [*thoughtfully*]. I haven't a real passport. I don't know how old I
am, and I always feel I am young. When I was a little girl my father and
mother used to travel from fair to fair and give performances—very good
ones. And I used to do the salto-mortale[6], and other tricks. Then, when
papa and mama died, a German woman took me to live with her and began
to teach me. Well and good. I grew up, and later I became a governess.
But who I am or where I come from—that I don't know. Who my parents

6 Death-leap.

were, I don't know. Perhaps they weren't married. [*Takes a cucumber out of her pocket and begins to eat it.*] I don't know anything. [*Pause.*] I long so to talk, but there's no one to talk to. . . . I haven't anybody at all.

EPIKHODOV [*playing on the guitar and singing*].

> What care I for friends and foes?
> What care I for the noisy world?

How jolly it is to play on the mandolin!

DUNYASHA. That's a guitar, not a mandolin! [*Glances into a little mirror and powders her nose.*]

EPIKHODOV. To the poor idiot who's in love, it's a mandolin. [*Hums.*]

> With the flame of a mutual love
> Would that your heart were burning!

[YASHA *joins in.*]

CHARLOTTA. These men sing horribly. . . . Foh! Like jackals.

DUNYASHA [*to* YASHA]. Just the same, it must be fine to live abroad.

YASHA. Yes, to be sure. I can't contradict you. [*Yawns and lights a cigar.*]

EPIKHODOV. That's easy to understand. Things have been properly established abroad for a long time.

YASHA. Of course.

EPIKHODOV. I'm an educated fellow, I read many remarkable books; but I simply can't understand my own state of mind—what I really want—whether to live, or to shoot myself, so to speak. But just the same, I always carry a revolver around with me. Here it is. . . . [*Produces a revolver.*]

CHARLOTTA. Now I'm through. I'm going. [*Slings the rifle over her shoulder.*] Epikhodov, you are a very clever and very terrifying man. Women must fall madly in love with you. Br-r-r![*Walks away.*] Those smart boys are all so stupid that I haven't a soul to talk to. I'm always alone, alone, no one belongs to me, and . . . and I don't know who I am nor why I was born. [*She goes slowly out.*]

EPIKHODOV. Without mentioning other matters, I should, properly speaking, say of myself among other things that fate has treated me as mercilessly as a storm does a little ship. Supposing you say I am wrong—then tell me why it was that this morning, for instance, I waked up and saw on my chest a spider of terrific size? It was so big. . . . [*Illustrates with both hands.*] And then, when I took up some kvass to have a drink, why there I saw something in the highest degree indecent, in the nature of a cockroach. [*Pause.*] Have you ever read Buckle?[7] [*Pause.*] May I speak a couple of words to you, Avdotya Fedorovna?

DUNYASHA. Speak up.

EPIKHODOV. I should prefer to speak with you alone. [*Sighs.*]

DUNYASHA [*disconcerted*]. Very well. . . . Only bring me my cloak first. . . . It's near the bookcase. . . . It's a little damp here.

EPIKHODOV. Very well. I'll bring it to you. . . . Now I know what to do with my revolver. . . . [*Picks up the guitar and goes out, playing.*]

---

[7] Henry Thomas Buckle (1821–1862), an English historian.

YASHA. Two-and-twenty troubles! Between you and me, he's a stupid fellow. [*Yawns.*]

DUNYASHA. God grant he doesn't shoot himself! [*Pause.*] I'm afraid. I'm all upset. They took me to live with gentlefolk when I was still a little girl, and now I'm not used to humble living. Why, my hands here are snowy white like a lady's. I've grown tender and delicate, and turned into a lady—I'm afraid of everything. It's terrible to be that way. And if you should deceive me, Yasha, then I don't know what would become of my nerves.

YASHA [*kisses her*]. Little cucumber! Of course, every girl should respect herself, and I should be the first to despise one whose conduct was not above reproach.

DUNYASHA. I'm head over heels in love with you; you're well educated, you can discourse on every subject. [*Pause.*]

YASHA [*yawning*]. Oh, yes. . . . To my mind it's this way: if a girl loves some one, that means she's immoral. [*Pause.*] It's nice to smoke a cigar in the open air. . . . [*Listening.*] Some one's coming this way. . . . It's the gentry. . . .

[DUNYASHA *embraces him impulsively.*]

YASHA. Go on home as if you'd been down to the river to bathe. Take that little path, or else they'll meet you and think I've had a rendezvous with you. I couldn't stand that.

DUNYASHA [*coughing softly*]. My head aches a little from the cigar smoke. [*She goes out.*]

[YASHA *remains sitting near the shrine.* LYUBOV ANDREYEVNA, GAYEV, *and* LOPAKHIN *come in.*]

LOPAKHIN. You absolutely must make up your mind—time will not wait. The question is perfectly simple. Are you willing to lease the land for cottages, or not? Answer me in a word: yes or no? One word only!

LYUBOV ANDREYEVNA. Who has been smoking disgusting cigars out here? [*Seats herself.*]

GAYEV: It's convenient since they built the railroad. [*Sits down.*] We rode into town and had lunch. . . . Yellow to the center! I'd like to go into the house first and play just one game. . . .

LYUBOV ANDREYEVNA. You'll have time.

LOPAKHIN. Only one word! [*Beseechingly.*] Please give me an answer!

GAYEV [*yawning*]. What's that?

LYUBOV ANDREYEVNA [*looking into her purse*]. Yesterday I had a lot of money, but to-day there's very little. My poor Varya is scrimping along, feeding every one on milk soup; they're giving the old people in the kitchen nothing but peas to eat, and here I'm squandering money senselessly. . . . [*Drops her purse, scattering gold coins. In vexation.*] Look, they're all scattered. . . .

YASHA. By your leave, I'll pick them up right away. [*Picks up the coins.*]

LYUBOV ANDREYEVNA. Yes, please, Yasha. Why did I go out to lunch anyway! . . . Your vile restaurant with its music, the tablecloths smelling of soap! . . . Why do people drink so much, Lenya? Why do they eat so much? Why do they talk so much? To-day in the restaurant you rambled on and on, and all about nothing. About the seventies, about the decadents.[8] And to whom? Talking to the waiters about the decadents!

---

[8] A name adopted by a group of French and English writers of the late nineteenth century because of their admiration for the decadent period in Roman civilization.

LOPAKHIN. Yes.

GAYEV [*waving his hand*]. I'm incorrigible, that's obvious. . . . [*Exasperatedly to* YASHA.] What's the matter? Why are you always under our noses?

YASHA [*laughing*]. I can't listen to your voice without laughing.

GAYEV [*to his sister*]. Either he or I . . .

LYUBOV ANDREYEVNA. Go away, Yasha, get along with you.

YASHA [*handing* LYUBOV ANDREYEVNA *her purse*]. I'm going right away. [*With difficulty restraining his laughter.*] This very minute. [*He goes out.*]

LOPAKHIN. Deriganov, the rich man, is planning to buy your estate. They say he's coming to the auction himself.

LYUBOV ANDREYEVNA. Where did you hear that?

LOPAKHIN. That's the rumor in town.

GAYEV. Our aunt in Yaroslavl has promised to send some money, but how much she will send, and when, we don't know. . . .

LOPAKHIN. How much will she send? A hundred thousand? Two hundred?

LYUBOV ANDREYEVNA. Well! . . . ten or fifteen thousand, and we'll be grateful for that.

LOPAKHIN. Pardon me for saying so, but I have never yet met such frivolous, unbusinesslike, queer people as you, my friends. People tell you in plain Russian that your estate is to be sold, but you don't take it in.

LYUBOV ANDREYEVNA. What can we do about it? Tell us, what?

LOPAKHIN. Every day I tell you. Every day I repeat the same thing. The cherry orchard, and the land as well, simply must be leased for cottages, and this must be done now, now, without delay! The date of the auction is almost here! You must realize this! Just make up your mind definitely once for all to accept the leasing plan, and people will loan you as much money as you wish. Then you'll be saved.

LYUBOV ANDREYEVNA. Cottages and cottagers—forgive me, that's so vulgar.

GAYEV. I agree with you perfectly.

LOPAKHIN. I shall either sob, or scream, or fall in a faint. I can't stand it! You've worn me out. [*To* GAYEV.] You old woman!

GAYEV. What's that?

LOPAKHIN. Old woman! [*He turns to go.*]

LYUBOV ANDREYEVNA [*frightened*]. No, don't go away. Stay here, my dear friend, I beg you. Perhaps we shall find a way.

LOPAKHIN. What's there to think about?

LYUBOV ANDREYEVNA. Don't go away, I beg of you. It's more cheerful with you here anyway. . . . [*Pause.*] All the time I feel as though I were waiting for something—as though the house were going to fall in ruins above us.

GAYEV [*musing deeply*]. Double into the corner . . . back shot to the center. . . .

LYUBOV ANDREYEVNA. We have committed many sins.

LOPAKHIN. What sins have you committed? . . .

GAYEV [*putting a piece of candy into his mouth*]. They say I've gobbled up all my substance in sugar candy. . . . [*Laughs.*]

LYUBOV ANDREYEVNA. Oh, my sins! . . . I've always squandered my money like a mad woman, and I married a man who only created more debts. My husband died from too much champagne—he drank horribly—and I, to my own misfortune, fell in love with another man, and at the very same time— this was my first punishment, a mortal blow—my little boy was drowned here in the river. I went abroad, broke all ties, planning never to return, never to see that river again. I covered my eyes and fled in desperation, and *he* followed me, with brutal, merciless persistence. I bought a villa near Mentone, for *he* became ill there, and for three years I knew no rest day or night. The sick man exhausted me, my soul shriveled up. And then, last year, when they sold the villa for debts, I went to Paris, and there he plundered me, abandoned me, and took up with another woman. I tried to poison myself. . . . It was so stupid and shameful. . . . And suddenly I was drawn back to Russia, to my native land, to my little girl. . . . [*Wipes away her tears.*] Lord, Lord, be merciful, forgive my sins! Do not punish me any more! [*Takes a telegram out of her pocket.*] I received this to-day from Paris. He asks forgiveness, entreats me to come back. . . . [*Tears up the telegram.*] Don't I hear music somewhere? [*Listens.*]

GAYEV. That's our famous Jewish orchestra. Do you remember? Four violins, a flute, and a double-bass.

LYUBOV ANDREYEVNA. So it's still in existence? We ought to ask them over sometime and have an evening party.

LOPAKHIN [*listening*]. I can't hear. . . . [*Humming softly.*] "Germans, if paid well enough, can make Russians Frenchmen." [*Laughs.*] What a funny thing I saw in the theatre yesterday! It was very amusing.

LYUBOV ANDREYEVNA. I'm sure it wasn't a bit funny. You shouldn't go to plays, but observe yourself more closely. What a drab life you live, how many unnecessary things you say!

LOPAKHIN. That's true enough. One must frankly admit that we lead a fool's life. . . . [*Pause.*] My dad was a peasant and a stupid one, he understood nothing, taught me nothing, but only beat me when he was drunk, and always with a stick. And in reality, I am just the same sort of blockhead and idiot that he was. I never studied anything, my handwriting is wretched. I write like a pig—I feel ashamed of it.

LYUBOV ANDREYEVNA. You ought to get married, my dear man.

LOPAKHIN. Yes, that's true.

LYUBOV ANDREYEVNA. And to our Varya? She's a good girl.

LOPAKHIN. True.

LYUBOV ANDREYEVNA. She's a simple-hearted child, she works the whole day long, and most important of all, she loves you. And you—you've liked her for a long time.

LOPAKHIN. Well? I've no objection. . . . She's a good girl. [*Pause.*]

GAYEV. They've offered me a place in the bank. Six thousand a year. . . . Did you hear about it?

LYUBOV ANDREYEVNA. To a man like you! . . . Just sit still. . . .

[FIRS *comes in, carrying an overcoat.*]

FIRS [*to* GAYEV]. Please put this on, sir, or you'll feel the dampness.

GAYEV [*putting on the coat*]. You're a bother, old man.

FIRS. Never mind. . . . You went off this morning without saying a word to anybody. [*Surveys him.*]

LYUBOV ANDREYEVNA. How old you've grown, Firs!

FIRS. Beg pardon?

LOPAKHIN. She says that you've grown very old.

FIRS. I've lived a long time. They were getting ready to marry me off before your daddy was born. . . . [*Laughs.*] And when the Emancipation[9] came, I was already head valet. I didn't approve of the Emancipation then, I stayed

---

[9] The emancipation of the Russian serfs took place in 1861.

with my masters. . . . [*Pause.*] And I remember, everyone was happy, but *why* they were happy they didn't know themselves.

LOPAKHIN. It was fine before the Emancipation, all right. At least, there used to be flogging.

FIRS [*who has not understood him*]. Yes, indeed. The peasants for the masters, the masters for the peasants, but now they're all split up. You can't make head or tail of it.

GAYEV. Be quiet, Firs. I've got to go to town to-morrow. They promised to introduce me to some general who may loan us some money on a note.

LOPAKHIN. Nothing will come of it. And you'll not pay your interest—you can depend on that.

LYUBOV ANDREYEVNA. He's talking nonsense. There aren't any generals.

[TROFIMOV, ANYA, *and* VARYA *come in.*]

GAYEV. Here come our people.

ANYA. Mama's sitting out here.

LYUBOV ANDREYEVNA [*tenderly*]. Come here, come here, Anya. . . . My dear ones! . . . [*Embracing* ANYA *and* VARYA.] If you only both knew how I love you. Sit down beside me, so. [*They all sit down.*]

LOPAKHIN. Our eternal student is always with the young ladies.

TROFIMOV. That's none of your business.

LOPAKHIN. He'll be fifty pretty soon, but he's still a student.

TROFIMOV. Quit your idiotic jokes.

LOPAKHIN. What are you getting huffy about, you freak?

TROFIMOV. Let me alone.

LOPAKHIN [*laughs*]. Well, what do you think of *me*, anyhow, pray tell?

TROFIMOV. Here's what I think of you, Yermolay Alexeich: You are a wealthy man, you'll be a millionaire soon. And just as a ravenous beast that devours everything crossing his path, is necessary to the transmutation of the elements, even so you are necessary. [*All laugh.*]

VARYA. You'd better talk about the planets, Petya.

LYUBOV ANDREYEVNA. No, please, let's continue our discussion of yesterday.

TROFIMOV. What were we discussing?

GAYEV. The proud man.

TROFIMOV. We talked at length yesterday, but we didn't come to any conclusion. There is, in your opinion, something mystical in a proud man. Possibly from your own point of view you are right, but if you reason it out simply, without evasion, what pride can there be, what grounds for pride can exist if a man's physiological structure is of a poor sort, if in the great majority of cases he is crude, stupid, profoundly unhappy? He must moderate his self-admiration. He must apply himself to work alone.

GAYEV. You'll die just the same.

TROFIMOV. Who knows? And what does it mean—to die? Perhaps a man has a hundred senses, and only the five we know are annihilated by death, while the remaining ninety-five continue to live.

LYUBOV ANDREYEVNA. How clever you are, Petya!

LOPAKHIN [*ironically*]. Awfully!

TROFIMOV. Humanity advances, perfecting its forces. Everything that is unattainable for it now, will sometime become near and comprehensible; only we must work and help to our fullest ability those who are seeking the truth. Only a few are thus far working among us here in Russia. The vast majority of those intellectuals whom I know, are seeking nothing, do nothing, and are as yet incapable of labor. They call themselves intellectuals, but they speak condescendingly to their servants, and treat the peasants like animals. They are wretched students, they don't read anything seriously, they are utterly idle, they only talk about the sciences, and they understand little about art. They are all solemn, they pull long faces and discuss only portentous matters, they philosophize—but in the meantime the enormous majority of us—ninety-nine out of a hundred—are living like wild beasts, wrangling and fighting at the least pretext. We have vile table manners, we sleep in filth, in stifling rooms, there are bedbugs everywhere, stench, dampness, moral impurity. . . . And evidently all our nice conversations have only the purpose of fooling ourselves and others. Show me the day nurseries of which people speak so frequently and at such length, and the reading rooms! Where are they? People only write about them in stories—they really don't exist at all. There's only dirt, vulgarity, Asiatic backwardness. I dislike and fear deeply serious faces, I dread serious conversations. Best to keep silence.

LOPAKHIN. You know, I get up before five o'clock, I work from morning till night. Well, I'm always handling money, my own and other people's, and I observe those around me. You need only start some project of your own to discover how few honorable, decent people there are. Sometimes when I lie in bed awake I think, "Lord, thou hast given us vast forests, boundless fields, remote horizons, and we, living in their midst, should really be giants."

LYUBOV ANDREYEVNA. You want giants? . . . They're only good in fairy tales—they'd frighten you.

[EPIKHODOV *crosses back stage, playing on his guitar.*]

LYUBOV ANDREYEVNA [*thoughtfully*]. Epikhodov is coming.

ANYA [*thoughtfully*]. Epikhodov is coming.

GAYEV. The sun has set, friends.

TROFIMOV. Yes.

GAYEV [*softly, as though declaiming to himself*]. O marvelous Nature, serene and beautiful, thou gleamest with an eternal radiance; thou whom we call our mother unitest within thyself life and death, thou livest and destroyest—

VARYA [*entreatingly*]. Uncle dear!

ANYA. Uncle! At it again!

TROFIMOV. You'd better make it, "Yellow across the table to the center."

GAYEV. I'll keep still, I'll keep still.

[*They all sit pondering. Silence. Only the soft muttering of* FIRS *is audible. Suddenly a distant sound, seemingly from the skies, is heard; a melancholy sound, which dies away like the snapping of a violin string.*]

LYUBOV ANDREYEVNA. What's that?

LOPAKHIN. I don't know. Maybe a cable snapped in a shaft somewhere far off. But it was very far away.

GAYEV. Maybe it's a bird—a heron, perhaps.

TROFIMOV. Or an owl.

LYUBOV ANDREYEVNA [*shudders*]. It depresses me, somehow.

[*Pause.*]

FIRS. It was the same way before the great misfortune. An owl hooted, and the samovar[10] hissed and hissed.

GAYEV. Before what misfortune?

---

[10] A metal urn used in Russia for making tea.

FIRS. Before the Emancipation.

[*Pause.*]

LYUBOV ANDREYEVNA. Come, my friends. It's growing dark already. [*To* ANYA.] There are tears in your eyes. What's troubling you, little girl? [*Embraces her.*]

ANYA. Never mind, mama. Nothing's the matter.

TROFIMOV. Some one is coming.

[*A* WAYFARER *makes his appearance. He has on a long coat and a worn, white cap. He is a little tipsy.*]

WAYFARER. Pray tell me, does this road lead directly to the station?

GAYEV. Yes. Follow the road.

WAYFARER. I'm deeply grateful to you. [*Coughing.*] It's fine weather. . . . [*Dramatically.*] "My brother, my suffering brother!". . . "Go to the Volga, whose groan—?"[11] [*To* VARYA.] Mademoiselle, please give a hungry Russian thirty kopeks. . . .

[VARYA *is frightened, and screams.*]

LOPAKHIN [*angrily*]. There's a limit to every sort of impudence!

LYUBOV ANDREYEVNA [*panic-stricken*]. Take this. . . . Here it is. . . . [*Searches in her purse.*] There's no silver. . . . Oh well, here's a gold piece for you. . . .

WAYFARER. I'm deeply grateful to you! [*Goes out.*]

[*They all laugh.*]

VARYA [*frightened*]. I'm going, I'm going home. Oh, mama dear, there's nothing at home for the servants to eat, and there you gave him a gold piece!

LYUBOV ANDREYEVNA. What's to be done with poor, foolish me? When we get home I'll give you everything I have. Yermolay Alexeich, make me another loan!

LOPAKHIN. Very well.

LYUBOV ANDREYEVNA. Come, friends, it's time to go home. And see here, Varya, we've found a husband for you. I congratulate you!

VARYA [*through her tears*]. Please don't joke about it, mama.

LOPAKHIN. Go to a nunnery, Okhmelia![12]

GAYEV. My hands are trembling. I haven't played pool for a long time.

LOPAKHIN. Okhmelia, nymph, remember me in your prayers!

LYUBOV ANDREYEVNA. Come, every one, we'll have supper soon.

VARYA. He frightened me. My heart's fairly pounding.

LOPAKHIN. Let me remind you, my friends: the cherry orchard will be sold on the twenty-second of August. Think that over! Think that over!

[*They all go out, with the exception of* ANYA *and* TROFIMOV.]

ANYA [*laughing*]. We're alone, now, thanks to the wayfarer who frightened Varya.

TROFIMOV. Varya's afraid that we'll suddenly fall in love with each other; and for days on end she hasn't budged from our side. Her trifling little mind cannot comprehend that we are superior to love. To avoid the petty and deluding things that prevent one from being free and happy—this is the aim and significance of our life. Forward! We shall press on irresistibly toward the bright star that shines beyond in the distance! Forward! Do not fall behind, friends!

---

[11] The quotations are from poems by Syomon Nadson (1862–1887) and by Nikolay Nekrasov (1821–1878).

[12] Here, and below, Lopakhin alludes imprecisely to Hamlet's addresses to Ophelia in act 3, scene 1, lines 89–90 and 121.

Anya [*clapping her hands*]. How splendidly you say it! [*Pause.*] It's marvelous
   here to-day.

Trofimov. Yes, the weather is wonderful.

Anya. What have you done to me, Petya, that I no longer love the cherry
   orchard as I did before? I used to love it so tenderly. It seemed to me
   that there was no place on earth more beautiful than our orchard.

Trofimov. All Russia is our orchard. The land is vast and glorious, there
   are many marvelous places in it. [*Pause.*] Think of it, Anya! Your grandfather,
   your great-grandfather, and all your ancestors were serf-owners, ruling over
   living souls. Don't you hear voices and see human beings looking at you
   from every cherry in the orchard, from every little leaf, from every tree
   trunk? . . . Oh, it is terrible, your orchard is a fearful place, and when one
   walks through it in the evening or at night, the ancient bark is lit then with
   a dull gleam, and the cherry trees seem to be dreaming of things that happened a hundred, two hundred years ago, and grievous visions harass them.
   What's the use of talking! We are at least two hundred years behind the
   times, we have nothing of our own, no definite relationship with the past;
   we do nothing but philosophize, complain of our own unhappiness, or drink
   vodka. But it's all so clear: in order to begin living in the present, we must
   first redeem our past, make an end of it. But we may redeem it only through
   suffering, only through strenuous, constant labor. You must realize this,
   Anya.

Anya. The house in which we are living has for a long time ceased to belong
   to us, and I will go away, I give you my word.

Trofimov. If you have the housekeeper's keys, throw them into the well and
   go away. Be as free as the wind.

Anya [*in ecstasy*]. How well you said that!

Trofimov. Have faith in me, Anya, have faith in me. I am not yet thirty, I
   am young, I am still a student, but how much I have endured already! I'm
   as famished as the winter, sick, distraught, poor as a beggar, and wherever
   fate has driven me, I have gone. But always my soul has been my own; at
   every moment, day and night it has been filled with inexplicable premonitions.
   I feel that happiness is on its way, Anya; I already see it. . . .

Anya [*thoughtfully*]. The moon is rising.

   [Epikhodov *is heard strumming over and over on the guitar the same melancholy
   song. The moon rises slowly.* Varya *is searching for* Anya *somewhere near the poplars,
   and calling* "Anya, *where are you?*"]

Trofimov. Yes, the moon is rising. [*Pause.*] Ah yes, happiness is coming, drawing ever nearer and nearer. Already I hear its footsteps. And if we do not
   see it, do not recognize it, what matter? Others will see it!

Varya's voice. Anya! Where are you?

Trofimov. It's that Varya again! [*Angrily.*] Exasperating!

Anya. Never mind. Let's go down to the river. It's nice there.

Trofimov. All right. [*They go out.*]

Varya's voice. Anya! Anya!

ACT III

*A drawing-room, separated by an arch from the ballroom. A lighted chandelier. The Jewish
orchestra—the same orchestra mentioned in the second act—is heard playing in the hall.*

It is evening. They are dancing the grand rond *in the ballroom. The voice of* SEMEONOV-
PISHCHIK *is heard, calling,* "Promenade à une paire!"[13] PISHCHIK *and* CHARLOTTA
IVANOVNA *are the first couple to enter the drawing-room;* TROFIMOV *and* LYUBOV AN-
DREYEVNA *follows; then* ANYA *and the* POST OFFICE OFFICIAL, *then* VARYA *and the*
STATION MASTER, *and so on.* VARYA *is weeping softly, wiping away her tears as she
dances.* DUNYASHA *and her partner form the last couple. They circle around the drawing-
room.* PISHCHIK *cries out,* "Grand rond, balancez!"[14] *and then,* "Les cavaliers à
genoux, et remerciez vos dames!"[15] FIRS, *wearing a dress coat, is carrying about
a tray with seltzer water.* PISHCHIK *and* TROFIMOV *reënter the drawing-room.*

PISHCHIK. I'm full-blooded, I've had two strokes already, it's hard for me to
dance, but, as the saying goes, "If you join the pack and cannot bay, wag
your tail, anyway!" I have the constitution of a horse. My dear father—may
he rest in peace—was a great joker, and he used to say in speaking of our
ancestry, that the ancient stock of the Semeonov-Pishchiks was descended
from the identical horse appointed senator by Caligula.[16] . . . [*Sits down.*]
But here's the pity of it; I've no money! A hungry dog believes only in
meat. . . . . [*Snores, and suddenly rouses himself.*] And so I, too . . . can think
of nothing but money. . . .
TROFIMOV. True, there really is something about you that reminds one of a
horse.
PISHCHIK. Well . . . a horse is a good beast. . . . You can sell a horse. . . .
[*The click of billiard balls is heard in the next room.* VARYA *appears in the hall under
the archway.*]
TROFIMOV [*teasingly*]. Madam Lopakhin! Madam Lopakhin!
VARYA [*angrily*]. Gentleman-gone-to-seed!
TROFIMOV. Yes, I'm a gentleman gone to seed, and I'm proud of it!
VARYA [*musing bitterly*]. We've hired musicians, but who's going to pay them?
[*Goes out.*]
TROFIMOV [*to* PISHCHIK]. If the energy you've wasted all your life digging up
money to pay interest, had been directed to something else, I believe that
eventually you could have turned the world upside down.
PISHCHIK. Nietzsche,[17] the philosopher . . . most noted . . . most famous . . .
a man of vast intellect, says in his books that one can make counterfeit
money.
TROFIMOV. Have you read Nietzsche then?
PISHCHIK. Bah! Dashenka told me about him. But things have come to such
a pass with me now, that I'd even make counterfeit money. . . . Day after
to-morrow I must pay out three hundred and ten rubles. . . . I've scraped
together a hundred and thirty already. . . . [*Feels through his pockets excitedly.*]
It's gone! I've lost my money! [*In tears.*] Where's my money? . . . [*Joyfully.*]
Here it is, under the lining. . . . Why, that raised a sweat on me! . . .
[LYUBOV ANDREYEVNA *and* CHARLOTTA IVANOVNA *come in.*]
LYUBOV ANDREYEVNA [*humming a Caucasian air*]. Why is Leonid so long in coming? What is he doing in town? [*To* DUNYASHA.] Dunyasha, give the musicians
some tea.

---

[13] "March in pairs!"   [14] "Grand circle, pause!"
[15] "Gentlemen on your knees, and thank your ladies!"
[16] The mad emperor Caligula (12–41 A.D.) appointed a horse to serve in the Roman Senate.
[17] Friedrich Wilhelm Nietzsche (1844–1900), a German philosopher.

TROFIMOV. Most likely the auction wasn't held.

LYUBOV ANDREYEVNA. And so we needn't have asked the musicians to come, and there was no reason for planning a ball. . . . Well, no matter. . . . [*She sits down and hums softly.*]

CHARLOTTA [*handing* PISHCHIK *a pack of cards*]. Here's a pack of cards. Think of a card.

PISHCHIK. I've thought of one.

CHARLOTTA. Now, shuffle the pack. Very good. Give it to me, my dear Mr. Pishchik. *Ein, zwei, drei!*[18] Take a look now—it's in your hip pocket. . . .

PISHCHIK [*takes a card out of his hip pocket*]. The eight of spades. Quite right! [*In astonishment.*] Just think of that!

CHARLOTTA [*holding the pack of cards in her hands and speaking to* TROFIMOV]. Tell me quick! What's the top card?

TROFIMOV. Eh? Why, the queen of spades.

CHARLOTTA. Right! [*To* PISHCHIK.] Well, what's the top card?

PISHCHIK. The ace of hearts.

CHARLOTTA. Right! [*Claps her hands, and the pack of cards disappears.*] But what fine weather we've had to-day! [*A mysterious voice—a woman's—coming as though from beneath the floor, answers her:* "Oh yes, the weather is splendid, madam."] You are charming—my ideal type of person. . . . [*Voice:* "And I likes you fery much too, Madam."]

STATION MASTER [*applauding*]. Bravo, Madam Ventriloquist, bravo!

PISHCHIK [*in amazement*]. Just think of that! Most enchanting Charlotte Ivanovna! . . . I'm fairly in love with you! . . .

CHARLOTTA. In love? [*Shrugging her shoulders.*] Can you really love? *Guter Mensch, aber schlechter Musikant.*[19]

TROFIMOV [*clapping* PISHCHIK *on the shoulder*]. What a horse you are!

CHARLOTTA. Attention, please! Here's another trick. [*Takes a steamer rug from a chair.*] Here's a very good rug, I want to sell it. . . . [*Shakes it.*] Doesn't some one want to buy it?

PISHCHIK [*in amazement*]. Just think of that!

CHARLOTTA. *Ein, zwei, drei!* [*She raises the rug quickly, behind it stands* ANYA. *She makes a low curtsey, runs over to her mother, embraces her, and flies back to the drawing-room amid general delight.*]

LYUBOV ANDREYEVNA [*applauding*]. Bravo, bravo!

CHARLOTTA. Once more now. *Ein, zwei, drei!* [*Raises the rug; behind it stands* VARYA, *bowing.*]

PISHCHIK [*marveling*]. Just think of that!

CHARLOTTA. That's all! [*She throws the rug over* PISHCHIK, *makes a low curtsey, and runs into the ballroom.*]

PISHCHIK [*hurrying after her*]. Rascal! . . . You would then? You would? [*Goes out.*]

LYUBOV ANDREYEVNA. And Leonid's not come yet. What's he doing in the city to keep him so long? I don't understand it. Why, everything must be finished there by now; the estate is sold, or else the sale didn't take place. Why must we be kept so long in ignorance?

VARYA [*trying to console her*]. Uncle has bought it, I'm sure.

TROFIMOV [*mockingly*]. Oh, yes!

[18] "One, two, three!"
[19] "A good man, but a bad musician." A line by Heinrich Heine (1799–1856), a German poet.

VARYA. Auntie gave him authority to buy it in her name and transfer the debt. She did it for Anya. And I'm convinced that with God's help uncle will buy it.

LYUBOV ANDREYEVNA. Our aunt in Yaroslav sent fifteen thousand rubles with which to purchase the estate in her name—she doesn't trust us—but that sum wouldn't be enough even to pay the interest. [*Covers her face with her hands.*] To-day my fate is decided . . . my fate . . .

TROFIMOV [*teasing* VARYA]. Madam Lopakhin!

VARYA [*angrily*]. Eternal student! He's been expelled from the University twice already.

LYUBOV ANDREYEVNA. Why do you lose your temper, Varya? He's teasing you about Lopakhin—well, what of it? Marry Lopakhin if you want to, he's a nice, good man. If you don't want to, don't marry him. No one is forcing you, dear.

VARYA. To be frank, mother dear, I do regard this matter seriously. He's a good man, I like him.

LYUBOV ANDREYEVNA. Well then, marry him. I don't understand what you're waiting for.

VARYA. I surely can't propose to him myself, mama. Every one has been talking to me about him for two years, but he either says nothing or jokes. I understand. He's making money, taken up with business. He hasn't time for me. If I had some money, even a little, even a hundred rubles, I'd give up everything and go far away. I'd enter a convent.

TROFIMOV. Magnificent!

VARYA [*to* TROFIMOV]. A student ought to have some sense! [*Softly, and weeping.*] How old and ugly you've grown, Petya! [*To* LYUBOV ANDREYEVNA, *drying her tears.*] Only I can't stand it to be idle, mama. I must have something to do every minute.

[YASHA *comes in.*]

YASHA [*with difficulty restraining his laughter*]. Epikhodov has broken a billiard cue! . . . [*Goes out.*]

VARYA. And why is Epikhodov in here? Who gave him permission to play pool? I don't understand these people. . . . [*Goes out.*]

LYUBOV ANDREYEVNA. Don't tease her, Petya. You can see she's unhappy enough without it.

TROFIMOV. She takes a lot of pains minding other people's business. All summer she's given Anya and me no peace. She was afraid a romance might spring up between us. What business is it of hers? And moreover, I gave her no occasion—I am beyond such vulgarity. We are superior to love.

LYUBOV ANDREYEVNA. Then I must be inferior to love. [*Deeply agitated.*] Why isn't Leonid here? If only I knew whether the estate had been sold or not! The catastrophe seems so incredible to me that I don't even know what to think. I'm losing my mind. . . . I may cry out or do some idiotic thing. Help me, Petya; say something, do! . . .

TROFIMOV. Isn't it all the same whether or no the estate is sold today? The matter's been settled for a long time; there is no turning back, the path is overgrown. Be calm, my dear friend, no need to deceive yourself. For once in your life at least, you must look truth straight in the eyes.

LYUBOV ANDREYEVNA. What truth? You can see where truth and falsehood lie, but I have quite lost that vision, I see nothing. You settle all important questions boldly, but tell me, my dear boy, is this not because you are young, because you haven't had time to put to painful test a single one of your questions? You look bravely forward—but isn't it because you do not see nor expect any terrible thing, inasmuch as life is still concealed from your young eyes? You are more fearless, more honest, more profound than we, but take thought for a moment, be a tiny bit magnanimous, and have pity on me. You see, I was born here, my father and mother lived here, and my grandfather too. I love this house; without the cherry orchard life is meaningless to me, and if it must be sold now, why then, you must sell me along with the orchard. . . . [*Embraces* TROFIMOV *and kisses him on the forehead.*] You see, my son was drowned here. . . . [*Weeps.*] Pity me, my good, kind friend.

TROFIMOV. You know that I sympathize with all my heart.

LYUBOV ANDREYEVNA. But you must say it differently, differently. [*Takes out her handkerchief and a telegram falls to the floor.*] You cannot imagine how heavy my heart is to-day. Things are so noisy and confusing, my very being shudders at every sound, I quiver all over, but I can't go off by myself—when I'm alone the silence terrifies me. Do not condemn me, Petya. I love you as though you belonged to my own family. I would gladly let Anya marry you, I swear it. Only, my dear boy, you must study, you must finish your course. You aren't doing anything but let fate bear you from place to place, strange as that may seem. . . . Isn't it so? And you simply must do something with your beard to make it grow decently. [*Laughs.*] You're so funny!

TROFIMOV [*picks up the telegram*]. I don't want to be a dandy.

LYUBOV ANDREYEVNA. That's a telegram from Paris. Every day I receive one. That wild man is sick again and in trouble. He asks forgiveness, begs me to come to him; and really, I ought to go to Paris to be near him. Your face is stern, Petya, but what can I do, my dear? What can I do? He is sick, he is alone, unhappy, and who is there to look after him, who will keep him from making mistakes, and give him his medicine at the right time? And why should I keep silence or conceal anything? I love him, that is clear to me. I love him, I love him. . . . This is the stone around my neck, I shall sink with it into the depths, but I love this stone and I cannot live without it. [*Presses* TROFIMOV'S *hand.*] Don't think ill of me, Petya; don't say anything to me, don't say . . .

TROFIMOV [*through his tears*]. Forgive my bluntness, for God's sake—but he robbed you!

LYUBOV ANDREYEVNA. No, no, no, you mustn't say that. . . . [*Covers her ears.*]

TROFIMOV. Why, he's a rascal—you're the only one who doesn't realize it. He's a petty thief, a good-for-nothing . . .

LYUBOV ANDREYEVNA [*restrained, but angry*]. You're twenty-six or seven now, but you're still a high school sophomore!

TROFIMOV. Well?

LYUBOV ANDREYEVNA. You should be a man, at your age you should understand those who love. And you should be in love yourself . . . you must fall in love! [*Angrily.*] Yes, yes! And you're not virtuous, you're only a prude, a sort of freak and monstrosity. . . .

TROFIMOV [*horrified*]. What is she saying?

LYUBOV ANDREYEVNA. "I am superior to love!" You're not superior to love, you're only what our Firs always calls a "lummox." To think of not having a mistress at your age!

TROFIMOV [*horrified*]. This is horrible! What is she saying! [*He walks quickly into the ballroom, clutching his head.*] This is horrible! I can't listen, I'll go away. . . . [*He goes out but returns immediately.*] Everything is over between us! [*Goes out into the hall.*]

LYUBOV ANDREYEVNA [*calling after him*]. Petya, wait! Foolish man, I was joking! Petya!

[*Some one is heard quickly ascending the stairway in the hall, then all of a sudden loudly falling downstairs.* ANYA *and* VARYA *scream, but immediately laughter is heard.*]

LYUBOV ANDREYEVNA. What's the matter out there?

[ANYA *runs in.*]

ANYA [*laughing*]. Petya fell downstairs! [*She runs out.*]

LYUBOV ANDREYEVNA. That Petya's a funny boy.

[*The* STATION MASTER *stops in the middle of the ballroom and begins to recite Alexey Tolstoy's*[20] *"The Magdalen." The others listen to him, but after a few stanzas the strains of a waltz are borne in from the hallway, and the recitation breaks off. They all dance.* TROFIMOV, ANYA, VARYA, *and* LYUBOV ANDREYEVNA *come back from the hallway.*]

LYUBOV ANDREYEVNA. Well, Petya . . . well, pure soul. . . . I beg your forgiveness. . . . Come, let's dance. . . . [*She and* PETYA *dance.*]

[ANYA *and* VARYA *dance together.* FIRS *comes in and leans his stick up near the side door.* YASHA *has also entered from the dining-room and is watching the dancing.*]

YASHA. What's the matter, grandfather?

FIRS. I'm not well. In the old days generals, admirals and barons used to dance at our balls, and now we send for the postal official and the station master, and even they don't come very graciously. I'm not as strong as I used to be. My dead master, their grandfather, used to cure everybody of every disease with sealing wax. I've been taking sealing wax every day for twenty years now, and maybe more; maybe that's what's kept me alive.

YASHA. You make me tired, grandfather. [*Yawns.*] It's time you croaked.

FIRS. Eh, you lummox! . . . [*Mutters.*]

[TROFIMOV *and* LYUBOV ANDREYEVNA *are dancing in the ballroom; then they pass into the drawing-room.*]

LYUBOV ANDREYEVNA. Merci![21] I think I'll sit down. . . . [*Seats herself.*] I'm tired. [ANYA *comes in.*]

ANYA [*excitedly*]. Some man just told them in the kitchen that the cherry orchard was sold to-day.

LYUBOV ANDREYEVNA. Sold to whom?

ANYA. He didn't say to whom. He went away. [*She dances off with* TROFIMOV *into the ballroom.*]

YASHA. Some old fellow was gossiping about it a while ago. A stranger.

ANYA. And Leonid Andreich hasn't come yet. He was wearing a lightweight overcoat. He'd better look out or he'll catch cold. Eh, these green young things!

LYUBOV ANDREYEVNA. I shall die this very minute! Go, Yasha, and find out who's bought it.

YASHA. The old man's been gone a long time. [*Laughs.*]

LYUBOV ANDREYEVNA [*somewhat annoyed*]. Well, what are you laughing at? What are you so happy about?

YASHA. Epikhodov's very amusing. A stupid fellow. Two-and-twenty troubles.

---

[20] Alexey Tolstoy (1817–1875) was a popular Russian poet and playwright. He is not Leo Tolstoy (1828–1910), Russian novelist, author of *War and Peace.*
[21] "Thank you!"

LYUBOV ANDREYEVNA. Firs, if they sell the estate, where will you go?

FIRS. I will go wherever you command.

LYUBOV ANDREYEVNA. Why do you look so strange? Are you sick? You ought to go to bed.

FIRS. Yes. . . . [*With a grimace.*] I'd go to bed, but when I'm gone, who'll hand things around and manage everything? The whole house depends on me.

YASHA [*to* LYUBOV ANDREYEVNA]. Lyubov Andreyevna, permit me to make a request. Be so good! If you go back to Paris, kindly take me with you! It's absolutely impossible for me to remain here. [*In a low voice and looking around him.*] What's the use of talking? You can see for yourself, it's an uncivilized country, the people are immoral, and besides that, it's dull, they give you wretched food in the kitchen, and that Firs is always walking around muttering all kinds of stupidities. Please do take me with you!

[PISHCHIK *comes in.*]

PISHCHIK. May I ask you . . . most lovely lady . . . for a little waltz? . . . [LYUBOV ANDREYEVNA *dances off with him.*] Bewitching one, I'm going to borrow a hundred and eighty little rubles from you, I'm going to borrow . . . [*Dancing.*] a hundred and eighty little rubles. . . . [*They pass out into the ballroom.*]

YASHA [*humming softly*]. "Oh, canst thou comprehend the tumult of my soul?" [*Out in the ballroom a figure in a gray top hat and checkered pantaloons waves its arms and jumps about; cries of* "Bravo, Charlotta Ivanovna!"]

DUNYASHA [*stopping to powder her nose*]. My young mistress told me to come in and dance. There are many gentlemen, and only a few ladies, but my head whirls when I dance, my heart beats, Firs Nikolayevich, and the post office clerk just said something to me that quite took my breath away.

[*The music stops.*]

FIRS. What did he say to you?

DUNYASHA. "You're like a flower," says he.

YASHA [*yawns*]. The bumpkin! . . . [*Goes out.*]

DUNYASHA. Like a little flower. . . . I'm such a delicate girl, I just love tender words.

FIRS. You'll lose your head.

[EPIKHODOV *comes in.*]

EPIKHODOV. You refuse to look at me, Avdotya Fedorovna . . . as if I were a sort of insect. . . . [*Sighing.*] Ah, well, that's life!

DUNYASHA. What do you want?

EPIKHODOV. Of course, you're probably right. [*Sighs.*] But then, if you want to regard it from this point of view, it's you, if you'll pardon my bluntness, who have brought me to such a pass. I know my fate. Every day some misfortune befalls me, and I've long since grown so accustomed to it that I smile at my fate. You gave me your promise, and though I—

DUNYASHA. Please let's talk later and leave me in peace now. I'm musing. [*Plays with her fan.*]

EPIKHODOV. Every day a mishap befalls me, and I—if I may say so—only smile, I even laugh.

[VARYA *comes in from the hall.*]

VARYA. Haven't you gone yet, Semen? What a presuming fellow you are, anyway. [*To* DUNYASHA.] Leave the room, Dunyasha. [*To* EPIKHODOV.] First you play billiards and break a cue, and then you swagger around in the drawing-room as though you were a guest.

EPIKHODOV. You can't expect much of me, if I may say so.

VARYA. I'm not expecting much of you, I'm just telling you the truth. All you know how to do is to walk from place to place, but you don't tend to your business. We keep a clerk, but goodness knows what for!

EPIKHODOV [*offended*]. Only my elders and people who know what they're talking about can pass judgment as to whether I work, or walk, or eat, or play pool.

VARYA. You dare speak to me so? [*Flying into a passion.*] You dare? You mean to imply that I don't know what I'm talking about? Get out of here! This instant!

EPIKHODOV [*cringing*]. Speak more politely, I beg you.

VARYA [*beside herself*]. Get out of here this instant! Out! [*He goes towards the door, she following him.*] Two-and-twenty troubles! Don't let me set eyes on you again! Go away and stay! [EPIKHODOV *goes out. His voice comes back from outside the door:* "I'll call you to account for this."] What, coming back? [*She snatches up the stick* FIRS *has left earlier near the door.*] Come on, then, come on, come on, I'll show you! Well, are you coming? Are you coming? Then take that! . . . [*She deals a blow with the stick just as* LOPAKHIN *enters.*]

LOPAKHIN. I thank you humbly.

VARYA [*angrily and mockingly*]. I beg your pardon.

LOPAKHIN. Don't mention it. I thank you humbly for a pleasant welcome.

VARYA. It deserves no appreciation. [*She moves away, then looks back and asks softly.*] I didn't hurt you, did I?

LOPAKHIN. Oh no, that's all right. All the same, there'll be a big bump.

VOICE [*in the hall*]. Lopakhin's come! Yermolay Alexeyevich!

PISHCHIK. We'll see with our eyes and hear with our ears! [*Exchanges kisses with* LOPAKHIN.] You smell of cognac, my dear fellow. Well, we've been having a jolly time here too.

[LYUBOV ANDREYEVNA *comes in.*]

LYUBOV ANDREYEVNA. So it's you, Yermolay Alexeich? Why were you so long? Where's Leonid?

LOPAKHIN. Leonid Andreich returned with me, he'll be in directly. . . .

LYUBOV ANDREYEVNA [*excitedly*]. Well, what happened? Did the sale take place? Do tell us!

LOPAKHIN [*in confusion and fearing to show his joy*]. The sale was over at four o'clock. . . . We missed the train and had to wait until half past nine. [*Sighing deeply.*] Uh! I'm a little bit dizzy. . . .

[GAYEV *comes in. His right arm is full of bundles; with his left hand he wipes away his tears.*]

LYUBOV ANDREYEVNA. Lenya, what's happened? Come, Lenya? [*Impatiently, through her tears.*] Quickly, for God's sake! . . .

GAYEV [*he does not answer her but only gestures; then to* FIRS, *weeping*]. Come, take these things. . . . Here are anchovies, Crimean herring. . . . I haven't eaten a thing to-day. . . . What I've been through! [*The door into the billiard room is open; one can hear the click of balls and* YASHA's *voice saying,* "Seven and eighteen!" GAYEV's *expression changes, he stops weeping.*] I'm terribly tired. Help me change my clothes, Firs. [*Goes into his own room across the hall,* FIRS *following him.*]

PISHCHIK. What happened? Please tell us.

LYUBOV ANDREYEVNA. Was the cherry orchard sold?

LOPAKHIN. Yes.

LYUBOV ANDREYEVNA. Who bought it?

LOPAKHIN. *I* bought it.

[*Pause.* LYUBOV ANDREYEVNA *is stunned. She would fall were she not leaning against the table and the armchair.* VARYA *takes the bunch of keys from her belt, throws them into the middle of the drawing-room floor, and goes out.*]

LOPAKHIN. *I* bought it! Wait a little, ladies and gentlemen, have patience, my head's swimming, I can't talk. . . . [*Laughs.*] When we arrived at the auction, Deriganov was already there. Leonid Andreich had only fifteen thousand, while Deriganov immediately bid thirty thousand above the amount of the mortgage. I saw I was going to have a tussle with him, and bid forty. He raised to forty-five. I bid fifty-five. So he kept raising me five and I raised him ten. . . . Well, it was over at last. I offered ninety thousand over the mortgage, and it went to me. The cherry orchard's mine now! Mine! [*Roars with laughter.*] O Lord my God, the cherry orchard's mine! Tell me I'm drunk, out of my head, or dreaming. . . . [*Stamps his feet.*] Don't laugh at me! If only my father and grandfather could rise from their graves and see all these things that have come to pass—how their Yermolay, beaten, illiterate little Yermolay, who used to go barefoot in the winter, has bought an estate— the most beautiful one in the world! I have bought the estate where my father and grandfather were slaves, where they weren't allowed even to set foot in the kitchen. I'm asleep, this is only a dream, an hallucination. . . . This is the fruit of my imagination, veiled with the mist of uncertainty. . . . [*Picks up the keys with a caressing smile.*] She threw away the keys, she wants to show that she's no longer housekeeper here. . . . [*Jingles the keys.*] Well, no matter! . . . [*The orchestra is heard tuning up.*] come, musicians, play, I want to hear you! Come, every one, and watch Yermolay Lopakhin swing his ax through the cherry orchard, see the trees fall to the ground! We'll build cottages here, and our grandsons and great-grandsons will see a new life arising here. . . . Let the music play!

[*Music.* LYUBOV ANDREYEVNA *falls into a chair and weeps bitterly.*]

LOPAKHIN [*reproachfully*]. Why, oh, why didn't you listen to me? My poor, dear friend, you cannot return to your home now. [*Weeping.*] Ah, if only this might swiftly pass by, if only we might swiftly change this unhappy, incoherent life of ours!

PISHCHIK [*in a low voice, taking him by the arm*]. She is weeping. Let us go into the ballroom and leave her alone. . . . Come on! . . . [*Takes him by the arm and leads him into the ballroom.*]

LOPAKHIN. What's the matter? Mind your notes, musicians! Let my wishes be obeyed. [*With irony.*] The new proprietor is coming, the lord of the cherry orchard! [*He unexpectedly bumps against a table, almost upsetting the candelabra.*] I can pay for everything! [*He goes out with* PISHCHIK.]

[*The ballroom and the drawing-room are empty save for* LYUBOV ANDREYEVNA, *who is huddled in her chair, weeping bitterly. The music plays softly.* ANYA *and* TROFIMOV *come in quickly.* ANYA *goes over to her mother and kneels before her.* TROFIMOV *remains near the ballroom door.*]

ANYA. Mama! . . . Mama, are you crying? My dear, good, kind mama, my beautiful mama, I love you. . . . I bless you. The cherry orchard is sold, it is gone, that is true, true, but don't cry, mama. Your life to come is left you, your good, pure soul is left you. . . . Come with me, come away with me, darling, come away! . . . We'll plant a new orchard, a more beautiful one; you shall see it, shall understand it; and joy, deep and quiet, shall descend upon your soul like the evening sunlight, and you will smile again, mama. Come, darling, come!

ACT IV

The same as in Act I. There are no curtains at the windows, no pictures; a little furniture remains, which has been piled in one corner, apparently to be sold. There is a feeling of emptiness. Trunks, strapped bundles, etc., are piled near the outside door and back stage. The door to the left is open and, through it may be heard the voices of ANYA *and* VARYA. LOPAKHIN *is standing in the room, waiting.* YASHA *is holding a tray with glasses filled with champagne.* EPIKHODOV *is roping a box in the entry-way. There is a droning behind scenes—the voices of the peasants who have come to say good-by.* GAYEV'S *voice is heard, saying,* "Thank you, my lads, thank you."

YASHA. The peasants have come to say good-bye. It's my opinion, Yermolay Alexeich, that the peasants are a good lot, but unintelligent.
[*The voices die away.* LYUBOV ANDREYEVNA *and* GAYEV *come in through the hall. She is not weeping, but her face is pale and quivering. She cannot speak.*]
GAYEV. You gave them your purse, Lyuba. You mustn't do such things, you must not.
LYUBOV ANDREYEVNA. I couldn't help myself! I couldn't help it! [*They both go out.*]
LOPAKHIN [*calling after them from the doorway*]. Please, I beg of you! Come and have a farewell glass. I forgot to bring any from town, and I could only find one bottle at the station. Please do! [*Pause.*] Don't you really want any? [*Moves away from the door.*] If I'd only known, I wouldn't have bought it. Well, then, I shan't drink any either. [YASHA *places the tray carefully on a chair.*] Yasha, you have a drink anyway!
YASHA. To the departing! Good luck to them! [*Drinks.*] This isn't real champagne, I can tell you that.
LOPAKHIN. It's eight rubles a bottle. [*Pause.*] It's cold as the devil here.
YASHA. We didn't build any fires to-day—it's all the same, we're going away. [*Laughs.*]
LOPAKHIN. Why are you laughing?
YASHA. Because I'm happy.
LOPAKHIN. Here it is October, but it's as quiet and sunny as though it were summer. Good building weather. [*Glances at his watch and calls through the door.*] Well, ladies and gentlemen, remember, it's just forty-seven minutes before train time. That means you must leave for the station in twenty minutes. Hurry up!
[TROFIMOV, *wearing an overcoat, comes in from outside.*]
TROFIMOV. I think it's time to go now. The horses have been brought around. Where the devil are my galoshes? They're lost. . . . [*Calls through the doorway.*] Anya, I can't find my galoshes. They're gone!
LOPAKHIN. I've got to go to Harkov. I'll take the same train you do. I shall spend the whole winter in Harkov. I've been frittering away my time with you people, I'm miserable without work. I can't live without something to do. I don't know what to do with my hands. They fidget around as though they belonged to some one else.
TROFIMOV. We'll be gone soon, and you can turn to your useful labors again.

LOPAKHIN. Have a glass, do.

TROFIMOV. No, thank you.

LOPAKHIN. So you're going on to Moscow now?

TROFIMOV. Yes, I'll accompany them as far as town, and then tomorrow I'll go on to Moscow.

LOPAKHIN. Yes. . . . I suppose the professors are holding up their lectures, every one will wait until you get there!

TROFIMOV. That's none of your business.

LOPAKHIN. How many years have you been studying at the University?

TROFIMOV. Think up a new question. That one's old and worn. [*Looking for his galoshes.*] You know, we probably shan't see each other again, so permit me to give you one parting bit of advice: Don't flourish your hands so! Break yourself of that habit of flourishing. And then too—all this building of cottages and figuring that in time their tenants will become land-owners— that's just another way of flourishing your hands. But for all that, I like you just the same. You have slender, delicate fingers like those of an artist; you have a slender, delicate soul.

LOPAKHIN [*embracing him*]. Good-by, my dear fellow. Thank you for everything. If you need money for your trip, let me lend you some.

TROFIMOV. I don't need any.

LOPAKHIN. But you have none!

TROFIMOV. Oh yes, thank you. I received some for a translation. Here it is, in my pocket. [*Anxiously.*] But I can't find my galoshes!

VARYA [*from the other room*]. Here, take your rubbish! [*Throws a pair of rubber galoshes out on the stage.*]

TROFIMOV. Why are you so angry, Varya? Hm. . . . Those aren't my galoshes.

LOPAKHIN. Last spring I sowed three thousand acres to poppies, and now I've cleared forty thousand on them. And when my poppies were in bloom, what a picture it was! As I was saying, I made forty thousand clear, and I'm offering you a loan because I'm able to. Why turn up your nose at me? I'm a peasant—a plain, blunt fellow.

TROFIMOV. Your father was a peasant, mine an apothecary, and that fact is of no consequence whatever. [LOPAKHIN *takes out his wallet.*] Hold on there, hold on—if you gave me two hundred thousand I wouldn't take it. I am a free man; and everything which you all, rich and poor alike, value so highly and dearly, has not the slightest power over me, even as thistledown borne upon the breeze. I can get along without you, I can pass you by. I am strong and proud. Humanity is moving towards the highest truth, towards the highest happiness attainable on earth; and I am in the front ranks.

LOPAKHIN. Shall you get there?

TROFIMOV. I shall. [*Pause.*] I shall get there, or else I will show others the road whereby they may arrive.

[*The sound of an ax striking against wood is heard in the distance.*]

LOPAKHIN. Well, good-by, my dear fellow. It's time to go. Here we stand chaffing each other, but life goes on just the same. When I work without stopping for a long time, then my thoughts grow clearer somehow, and it seems as though I too knew the reason for my existence. But how many people there are in Russia, brother, who do not know why they are alive! Oh, well—the world wags on just the same. They say Leonid Andreich has taken a position in a bank, six thousand a year. . . . Only you know he won't stay there, he's very lazy.

ANYA [*in the doorway*]. Mama asks you please not to let them cut down the orchard before she goes.

TROFIMOV. Really, haven't you the consideration to . . . [*He goes out through the hall.*]

LOPAKHIN. Right away . . . right away. . . . What people! . . . [*Follows him out.*]

ANYA. Has Firs been taken to the hospital?

YASHA. I told them to this morning. They must have taken him.

ANYA [*to* EPIKHODOV, *who is passing through the hall.*] Semen Panteleich, please find out if Firs has been taken to the hospital.

YASHA [*offended*]. I told Yegor this morning. Why do you have to ask about it a dozen times!

EPIKHODOV. It's my firm opinion that that superannuated Firs isn't worth repairs. It's time he joined his forefathers. I can only envy him. [*Puts a trunk down on top of a hat box and crushes it.*] Well, of course, that had to happen— I knew it! [*Goes out.*]

YASHA [*mockingly*]. Two-and-twenty troubles. . . .

VARYA [*outside the door*]. Have they taken Firs to the hospital?

ANYA. Yes.

VARYA. Why didn't they take the letter to the doctor?

ANYA. We'll have to send it after him. [*Goes out.*]

VARYA [*from the next room*]. Where's Yasha? Tell him that his mother has come and wants to say good-by to him.

YASHA [*waves his hand*]. She bothers me to death!

[*All this time* DUNYASHA *has been bustling about the baggage. Now that* YASHA *is alone on the stage, she approaches him.*]

DUNYASHA. You might look at me just once more, Yasha. You're going away . . . leaving me. . . . [*She bursts into tears and falls on his neck.*]

YASHA. What's the use of crying? [*Drinks champagne.*] In six days I'll be back in Paris again. To-morrow we'll take the express and roll along so fast they can hardly see us flying by. I can scarcely believe it. Veev la France![22] . . . I don't like it here, I can't live here. . . . There's nothing to do. I have looked my fill at ignorance—that's enough for me. [*Drinks champagne.*] What's the use of crying? Act like a lady, then you won't cry.

DUNYASHA [*glancing in the mirror and powdering her nose*]. Write me a letter from Paris. You know I've loved you, Yasha—oh, how I've love you! I'm a tender little creature, Yasha.

YASHA. They're coming. [*Bustles around the trunks, humming softly.*]

[LYUBOV ANDREYEVNA, GAYEV, ANYA, *and* CHARLOTTA IVANOVNA *come in.*]

GAYEV. We ought to be on our way. Time's short. [*Glancing at* YASHA.] Who is it smells of herring around here?

LYUBOV ANDREYEVNA. In ten minutes we shall be sitting in the carriage. . . . [*Surveys the room.*] Good-by, dear house, old grandfather! The winter will pass, spring will return, and then you'll be here no longer, they will tear you down. How many things these walls have seen! [*Kisses her daughter warmly.*] My treasure, you are radiant, your eyes are dancing like two diamonds. Are you happy? Very?

ANYA. Very. A new life is beginning, mama!

GAYEV [*cheerfully*]. Indeed, everything is all right now. Before the cherry orchard

[22] A misspelling of *Vive la France!* ("Long live France!")

was sold, we were all restless, unhappy; but now that the question has been definitely and irrevocably settled, we have all become calm and even cheerful. I'm a bank official now, I'm a financier. . . . Yellow into the middle! While you, Lyuba, somehow look better, no doubt of it.

LYUBOV ANDREYEVNA. Yes, my nerves are quieter, that's true. [*Some one hands her her hat and coat.*] I'm sleeping well. Carry my bags out, Yasha. It's time to go. [*To* ANYA.] My little girl, we shall see each other soon. . . . I am going to Paris, I shall live there on the money your great-aunt from Yaroslavl sent to buy the estate—long life to auntie!—but that money won't last long.

ANYA. You'll come back very, very soon, won't you, mama? I'll study to pass the high school examinations, and then I'll work and help you. We'll read so many books together, mama . . . won't we? [*Kisses her mother's hands.*] We'll read on the autumn evenings, lots of books, and a wonderful new world will open up before us. . . . [*Dreamily.*] Be sure to come, mama.

LYUBOV ANDREYEVNA. I will come back, my treasure. [*Embraces* ANYA.]

[LOPAKHIN *comes in.* CHARLOTTA *is singing softly.*]

GAYEV. Happy Charlotta! She is singing!

CHARLOTTA [*picking up a bundle shaped like a swaddled baby*]. Bye-o-bye, my baby. . . . [*A child's cry is heard:* "Wah! wah!"] Keep quiet, my darling, my nice boy! ["Wah! wah!"] Oh, too bad, too bad! [*Tosses the bundle back to its place.*] Please find a situation for me, I can't manage otherwise.

LOPAKHIN. We'll find one for you, Charlotta Ivanovna, don't you worry.

GAYEV. They're all leaving us. Varya's going away. . . . All of a sudden, nobody needs us.

CHARLOTTA. I've no place to live in town. I'll have to leave you. . . . [*Hums.*] Oh, well! . . .

[PISHCHIK *comes in.*]

LOPAKHIN. Nature's miracle!

PISHCHIK [*panting*]. Oh, let me get my breath! I'm all worn out! Most dear and honored friends—give me some water. . . .

GAYEV. You've come after money, I suppose? Your humble servant! . . . But just the same I'm going to flee temptation. [*Goes out.*]

PISHCHIK. I haven't been to see you for a long time, most lovely lady. . . . [*To* LOPAKHIN.] So you're here. . . . I'm glad to see you . . . man of vast intellect. . . . Here, take this. . . . [*Hands* LOPAKHIN *some money.*] Four hundred rubles. . . . Eight hundred and forty left on my account. . . .

LOPAKHIN [*shrugging his shoulders in bewilderment*]. I'm dreaming. . . . Where did you get it?

PISHCHIK. Wait a minute. . . . I'm too warm. . . . A most unusual circumstance. Some Englishmen came to see me and found some white clay on my land. . . . [*To* LYUBOV ANDREYEVNA.] And four hundred for you . . . most beautiful and marvelous lady. . . . [*Hands her the money.*] I'll have the rest for you later. [*Drinks some water.*] A young man told me on the train just a little while ago how some great philosopher or other told a man how to jump off roofs. . . . "Just jump!" says he, and that's all there is to it. [*In wonderment.*] Just think of that! Water!

LOPAKHIN. But who are these Englishmen?

PISHCHIK. I've leased them the piece of land with the clay for twenty-four years. . . . But excuse me, I haven't time to tell you about it now. . . . I've got to hurry on. . . . I'm going to see Znoykov . . . and Kardamonov.

. . . I'm in debt to every one. . . . [*Drinks.*] Your health! . . . I'll call in on Thursday. . . .

LYUBOV ANDREYEVNA. We're just leaving for the city, and to-morrow I'm going abroad.

PISHCHIK. What? [*In alarm.*] Why are you going to town? Ah, now I see the furniture . . . the trunks. . . . Well, no matter. . . . [*Through his tears.*] No matter. . . . People of great intelligence . . . these Englishmen. . . . No matter. Good luck. . . . God will take care of you. . . . No matter. . . . There's an end to everything on earth. . . . [*Kisses the hand of* LYUBOV ANDREYEVNA.] And should you ever happen to hear that my end has come, remember this old . . . horse, and say, "There used to live upon this earth a certain . . . Semeonov-Pishchik. . . . The heavenly kingdom to him!" . . . It's wonderful weather. . . . Yes. . . . [*He goes out deeply moved, but returns immediately and says from the doorway.*] Dashenka sent her regards! [*Goes out.*]

LYUBOV ANDREYEVNA. Well, we can go now. I'm leaving with two cares on my mind. The first one is poor, sick, old Firs. [*Looks at her watch.*] I have still five minutes to spare. . . .

ANYA. They've sent Firs to the hospital already, mama. Yasha saw to it this morning.

LYUBOV ANDREYEVNA. My second worry is Varya. She is accustomed to early rising and work; and now, with nothing to do, she's like a fish out of water. She's grown thin and pale, and she weeps, poor girl. . . . [*Pause.*] You know very well, Yermolay Alexeich, I have dreamed . . . of giving her to you, for it's quite obvious that you'll marry some one. [*She whispers to* ANYA, *who nods to* CHARLOTTA, *and they both go out.*] She loves you, she's congenial to you, and I really don't know why you avoid each other so. I don't understand it at all!

LOPAKHIN. To tell the truth, I don't understand it myself. It's all strange somehow. . . . If there's still time, why I'm ready now. . . . We'll make an end of it right away and have done with it. But without your help, I feel I shan't propose.

LYUBOV ANDREYEVNA. That's fine now. It'll take only a moment, you know. I'll call her right away.

LOPAKHIN. By the way, there's some champagne. . . . [*Looking at the glasses.*] They're empty. Some one's drained them dry already. [YASHA *coughs.*] That's real guzzling, that is!

LYUBOV ANDREYEVNA [*with animation*]. Splendid! We'll go out. . . . Yasha, *allez!*[23] I'll call her. . . . [*In the doorway.*] Varya, leave everything and come here. Come! [*Goes out with* YASHA.]

LOPAKHIN [*looking at his watch*]. Yes. . . . [*Pause.*]

[*There is a restrained laugh behind the door, and whispering. At last* VARYA *comes in.*]

VARYA [*looking over the baggage carefully*]. That's strange, I can't find it anywhere. . . .

LOPAKHIN. What are you looking for?

VARYA. I packed it myself, and now I'm forgotten where. [*Pause.*]

LOPAKHIN. Where are you going now, Varvara Mikhaylovna?

[23] "Go!"

VARYA. I? To the Ragulins. . . . I've agreed to take over the housekeeping—
something like that. . . .

LOPAKHIN. Don't they live in Yashnevo? That's fifty miles from here. [*Pause.*]
So life in this old house is finished. . . .

VARYA [*surveying the bundles*]. Where can it be? . . . Or perhaps I packed it in
the trunk. . . . Yes, life in this house is over—it will never return.

LOPAKHIN. And I'm off to Harkov now . . . on this same train. I've a lot to
attend to. And I'm going to leave Epikhodov here. . . . I've hired him.

VARYA. You don't say!

LOPAKHIN. Last year at this time, if you remember, snow was already falling,
but now it's quiet and sunny. Only it's cold . . . six degrees below freezing.

VARYA. I haven't looked to see. [*Pause.*] But then, our thermometer is broken
anyway. . . . [*Pause.*]

VOICE [*at the door*]. Yermolay Alexeich!

LOPAKHIN [*as though he had long been waiting that call*]. Right away. [*He goes out
quickly.*]

[VARYA, *sitting on the floor, lays her head on a bundle of wraps and sobs softly. The
door opens and* LYUBOV ANDREYEVNA *tiptoes in.*]

LYUBOV ANDREYEVNA. Well? [*Pause.*] We must be going.

VARYA [*stops crying and wipes her eyes*]. Yes, it's time to go, mama. I'll arrive at
the Ragulins' to-day, if only I don't miss the train.

LYUBOV ANDREYEVNA [*standing in the doorway*]. Anya, put on your things.

[ANYA *comes in;* GAYEV *and* CHARLOTTA IVANOVNA *follow her.* GAYEV *is wearing
a warm overcoat with a cape. The* SERVANTS *and* COACHMEN *assemble.* EPIKHODOV
bustles around the baggage.]

LYUBOV ANDREYEVNA. Now we can start on our way.

ANYA [*joyously*]. On our way!

GAYEV. My friends, my dear, good friends! In leaving this house forever, can
I possibly remain silent, restrain myself, and not express at parting the emotions that now fill my whole being? . . .

ANYA [*beseechingly*]. Uncle!

VARYA. Uncle dear, you mustn't!

GAYEV [*mournfully*]. Yellow across the table into the middle. . . . I'll keep
still. . . .

[TROFIMOV *comes in, after him* LOPAKHIN.]

TROFIMOV. Well, ladies and gentlemen, it's time to go!

LOPAKHIN. Epikhodov, my coat!

LYUBOV ANDREYEVNA. I'll sit here just one moment longer. It's as though I'd
never really seen these walls, these ceilings before, and now I look at them
eagerly, with such tender love. . . .

GAYEV. I remember when I was six years old sitting in this window on Trinity
Sunday, and watching father go to church.

LYUBOV ANDREYEVNA. Has everything been taken out?

LOPAKHIN. I think so. [*To* EPIKHODOV, *who is helping him on with his overcoat.*]
Epikhodov, look and see if everything is all ready.

EPIKHODOV [*in a hoarse voice*]. Put your mind at rest, Yermolay Alexeich.

LOPAKHIN. What's the matter with your voice?

EPIKHODOV. I just drank some water and swallowed it wrong.

YASHA [*contemptuously*]. Bumpkin!

LYUBOV ANDREYEVNA. If we go, there won't be a soul left behind. . . .

LOPAKHIN. Not until spring.

VARYA [*pulls an umbrella out of a bundle and seems about to swing it.* LOPAKHIN *pretends to be frightened*]. What's the matter? What's the matter? . . . I never dreamed of it.

TROFIMOV. Let's climb into the carriages, ladies and gentlemen. It's time to go. It's nearly train time.

VARYA. Petya, there are your galoshes, near that trunk. . . . [*Tearfully.*] And how dirty and old they are! . . .

TROFIMOV [*putting on his galoshes*]. Well, let's be on our way!

GAYEV [*deeply moved, on the verge of unwilling tears*]. The train . . . the station. . . . Back shot to the middle, white across the table to the corner. . . .

LYUBOV ANDREYEVNA. We must go!

LOPAKHIN. Is every one here? No one left? [*He locks the door on the left.*] There are some things stored here, we'll have to lock them up. Come on!

ANYA. Good-bye, old house! Good-by, old life!

TROFIMOV. Welcome, new life! [*He goes out with* ANYA.]

[VARYA *casts a glance around the room and goes slowly out.* YASHA, *and* CHARLOTTA, *her lap dog in her arms, follow.*]

LOPAKHIN. Until spring then! Come on, my friends! Till we meet again! [*Goes out.*]

[LYUBOV ANDREYEVNA *and* GAYEV *are left together. They seem to have been waiting for this moment. They fall into each other's arms and sob softly, restrainedly, as though fearing lest some one hear them.*]

GAYEV [*in despair*]. My sister, my sister! . . .

LYUBOV ANDREYEVNA. Oh, my dear orchard, my tender, beautiful orchard! My life, my youth, my happiness, farewell! Farewell!

ANYA'S VOICE [*joyously, appealingly*]. Mama! . . .

TROFIMOV'S VOICE [*joyously and with ardor*]. Yoo-hoo!

LYUBOV ANDREYEVNA. To look at the walls, at the windows, for the last time! . . . Our dead mother loved to walk to and fro in this room. . . .

GAYEV. My sister, my sister!

ANYA'S VOICE. Mama!

TROFIMOV'S VOICE. Yoo-hoo!

LYUBOV ANDREYEVNA. We're coming! . . . [*They go out.*]

[*The stage is empty. One can hear keys turning in the locks of all the doors, the carriages roll away. Then the sound of an ax striking against wood, a sad and lonely sound, rings out amid the stillness. Footsteps are heard.* FIRS *emerges from the door on the right. He is dressed as usual in a waiter's jacket and white waistcoat, with slippers on his feet. He is ill.*]

FIRS [*going over to the door and pulling at the knob*]. Locked! They've gone away. . . . [*Sits down on the sofa.*] They've forgotten me. . . . No matter. . . . I'll sit here a little while. . . . And I suppose Leonid Andreich didn't put on his fur coat and went off in a light one. . . . [*Sighs anxiously.*] I never looked to see. . . . Young and green! [*Mutters something unintelligible.*] So life has gone by—just as though I'd never lived at all. . . . [*Lies down.*] I'll lie here a little while. . . . You've no strength in you, nothing's left, nothing. . . . Eh, you're a . . . lummox! [*Lies motionless.*]

[*A distant sound is heard, like the melancholy twang of a string, breaking in the heavens. It dies away. Silence, save for the dull sound of an ax chopping, far off in the orchard.*]

[1904]

Eugene O'Neill   1888–1953

DESIRE UNDER THE ELMS

CHARACTERS

EPHRAIM CABOT
SIMEON
PETER } *His sons*
EBEN
ABBIE PUTNAM
Young Girl, Two Farmers, The Fiddler, A Sheriff,
and other folk from the neighboring farms.

The action of the entire play takes place in, and immediately outside of, the Cabot farmhouse in New England, in the year 1850. The south end of the house faces front to a stone wall with a wooden gate at center opening on a country road. The house is in good condition but in need of paint. Its walls are a sickly grayish, the green of the shutters faded. Two enormous elms are on each side of the house. They bend their trailing branches down over the roof. They appear to protect and at the same time subdue. There is a sinister maternity in their aspect, a crushing, jealous absorption. They have developed from their intimate contact with the life of man in the house an appalling humaneness. They brood oppressively over the house. They are like exhausted women resting their sagging breasts and hands and hair on its roof, and when it rains their tears trickle down monotonously and rot on the shingles.
There is a path running from the gate around the right corner of the house to the front door. A narrow porch is on this side. The end wall facing us has two windows in its upper story, two larger ones on the floor below. The two upper are those of the father's bedroom and that of the brothers. On the left, ground floor, is the kitchen—on the right, the parlor, the shades of which are always drawn down.

PART ONE

SCENE ONE

Exterior of the farmhouse. It is sunset of a day at the beginning of summer in the year 1850. There is no wind and everything is still. The sky above the roof is suffused with deep colors, the green of the elms glows, but the house is in shadow, seeming pale and washed out by contrast.
A door opens and EBEN CABOT *comes to the end of the porch and stands looking down the road to the right. He has a large bell in his hand and this he swings mechanically, awakening a deafening clangor. Then he puts his hands on his hips and stares up at the sky. He sighs with a puzzled awe and blurts out with halting appreciation.*

EBEN. God! Purty! [*His eyes fall and he stares about him frowningly. He is twenty-five, tall and sinewy. His face is well-formed, good-looking, but its expression is resentful and defensive. His defiant, dark eyes remind one of a wild animal's in captivity. Each day is a cage in which he finds himself trapped but inwardly unsubdued. There is a fierce repressed vitality about him. He has black hair, mustache, a thin curly trace of beard. He is dressed in rough farm clothes.*

He spits on the ground with intense disgust, turns and goes back into the house.

SIMEON *and* PETER *come in from their work in the fields. They are tall men, much older than their half-brother* [SIMEON *is thirty-nine and* PETER *thirty-seven], built on a squarer, simpler model, fleshier in body, more bovine and homelier in face, shrewder and more practical. Their shoulders stoop a bit from years of farm work. They clump heavily along in their clumsy thick-soled boots caked with earth. Their clothes, their faces, hands, bare arms and throats are earth-stained. They smell of earth. They stand together for a moment in front of the house and, as if with the one impulse, stare dumbly up at the sky, leaning on their hoes. Their faces have a compressed, unresigned expression. As they look upward, this softens.*]

SIMEON. [*grudgingly*] Purty.

PETER. Ay-eh.

SIMEON. [*suddenly*] Eighteen year ago.

PETER. What?

SIMEON. Jenn. My woman. She died.

PETER. I'd fergot.

SIMEON. I rec'lect—now an' agin. Makes it lonesome. She'd hair long's a hoss' tail—an' yaller like gold!

PETER. Waal—she's gone. [*This with indifferent finality—then after a pause*] They's gold in the West, Sim.

SIMEON. [*still under the influence of sunset—vaguely*] In the sky?

PETER. Waal—in a manner o' speakin'—thar's the promise. [*Growing excited*] Gold in the sky—in the West—Golden Gate—Californi-a!—Goldest West!— fields o' gold!

SIMEON. [*excited in his turn*] Fortunes layin' just atop o' the ground waitin' t' be picked! Solomon's mines,[1] they says! [*For a moment they continue looking up at the sky—then their eyes drop.*]

PETER. [*with sardonic bitterness*] Here—it's stones atop o' the ground—stones atop o' stones—makin' stone walls—year atop o' year—him 'n' yew 'n' me 'n' then Eben—makin' stone walls fur him to fence us in!

SIMEON. We've wuked. Give our strength. Give our years. Plowed 'em under in the ground—[*he stamps rebelliously*]—rottin'—makin' soil for his crops! [*A pause*] Waal—the farm pays good for hereabouts.

PETER. If we plowed in Californi-a, they'd be lumps o' gold in the furrow!

SIMEON. Californi-a's t'other side o' earth, a'most. We got t' calc'late—

PETER. [*after a pause*] 'Twould be hard fur me, too, to give up what we've 'arned here by our sweat. [*A pause.* EBEN *sticks his head out of the dining-room window, listening.*]

SIMEON. Ay-eh. [*A pause*] Mebbe—he'll die soon.

PETER. [*doubtfully*] Mebbe.

SIMEON. Mebee—fur all we knows—he's dead now.

PETER. Ye'd need proof.

SIMEON. He's been gone two months—with no word.

PETER. Left us in the fields an evenin' like this. Hitched up an' druv off into the West. That's plum onnateral. He hain't never been off this farm 'ceptin' t' the village in thirty year or more, not since he married Eben's maw. [*A pause. Shrewdly*] I calc'late we might git him declared crazy by the court.

---

[1] According to legend, the fabulous wealth of Solomon (king of Israel in the tenth century B.C.) was extracted from rich gold and silver mines.

SIMEON. He skinned 'em too slick. He got the best o' all on 'em. They'd never b'lieve him crazy. [*A pause*] We got t' wait—till he's under ground.

EBEN. [*with a sardonic chuckle*] Honor thy father! [*They turn, startled, and stare at him. He grins, then scrowls*] I pray he's died. [*They stare at him. He continues matter-of-factly*] Supper's ready.

SIMEON *and* PETER. [*together*] Ayeh.

EBEN. [*gazing up at the sky*] Sun's downin' purty.

SIMEON *and* PETER. [*together*] Ay-eh. They's gold in the West.

EBEN. Ay-eh. [*Pointing*] Yonder atop o' the hill pasture, ye mean?

SIMEON *and* PETER. [*together*] In Californi-a!

EBEN. Hunh? [*Stares at them indifferently for a second, then drawls*] Waal—supper's gittin' cold. [*He turns back into kitchen.*]

SIMEON. [*startled—smacks his lips*] I air hungry!

PETER. [*sniffing*] I smells bacon!

SIMEON. [*with hungry appreciation*] Bacon's good!

PETER. [*in same tone*] Bacon's bacon! [*They turn, shouldering each other, their bodies bumping and rubbing together as they hurry clumsily to their food, like two friendly oxen toward their evening meal. They disappear around the right corner of house and can be heard entering the door.*]

CURTAIN

SCENE TWO

The color fades from the sky. Twilight begins. The interior of the kitchen is now visible. A pine table is at center, a cookstove in the right rear corner, four rough wooden chairs, a tallow candle on the table. In the middle of the rear wall is fastened a big advertising poster with a ship in full sail and the word "California" in big letters. Kitchen utensils hang from nails. Everything is neat and in order but the atmosphere is of a men's camp kitchen rather than that of a home.

Places for three are laid. EBEN takes boiled potatoes and bacon from the stove and puts them on the table, also a loaf of bread and a crock of water. SIMEON and PETER shoulder in, slump down in their chairs without a word. EBEN joins them. The three eat in silence for a moment, the two elder as naturally unrestrained as beasts of the field, EBEN picking at his food without appetite, glancing at them with a tolerant dislike.

SIMEON. [*suddenly turns to* EBEN] Looky here! Ye'd oughtn't t' said that, Eben.

PETER. 'Twa'n't righteous.

EBEN. What?

SIMEON. Ye prayed he'd died.

EBEN. Waal—don't yew pray it? [*A pause.*]

PETER. He's our Paw.

EBEN. [*violently*] Not mine!

SIMEON. [*dryly*] Ye'd not let no one else say that about yer Maw! Ha! [*He gives one abrupt sardonic guffaw.* PETER *grins.*]

EBEN. [*very pale*] I meant—I hain't his'n—I hain't like him—he hain't me!

PETER. [*dryly*] Wait till ye've growed his age!

EBEN. [*intensely*] I'm Maw—every drop o' blood! [*A pause. They stare at him with indifferent curiosity.*]

PETER. [*reminiscently*] She was good t' Sim 'n' me. A good Stepmaw's scurse.

SIMEON. She was good t' everyone.

EBEN. [*greatly moved, gets to his feet and makes an awkward bow to each of them—stammering*] I be thankful t' ye. I'm her—her heir. [*He sits down in confusion.*]

PETER. [*after a pause—judicially*] She was good even t' him.

EBEN. [*fiercely*] An' fur thanks he killed her!

SIMEON. [*after a pause*] No one never kills nobody. It's allus somethin'. That's the murderer.

EBEN. Didn't he slave Maw t' death?

PETER. He's slaved himself t' death. He's slaved Sim 'n' me 'n' yew t' death—on'y none o' us hain't died—yit.

SIMEON. It's somethin'—drivin' him—t' drive us!

EBEN. [*vengefully*] Waal—I hold him t' jedgment! [*Then scornfully*] Somethin'! What's somethin'?

SIMEON. Dunno.

EBEN. [*sardonically*] What's drivin' yew to Californi-a, mebbe? [*They look at him in surprise*] Oh, I've heerd ye! [*Then, after a pause*] But ye'll never go t' the gold fields!

PETER. [*assertively*] Mebbe!

EBEN. Whar'll ye git the money?

PETER. We kin walk. It's an a'mighty ways—Californi-a—but if yew was t' put all the steps we've walked on this farm end t' end we'd be in the moon!

EBEN. The Injuns'll skulp ye on the plains.

SIMEON. [*with grim humor*] We'll mebbe make 'em pay a hair fur a hair!

EBEN. [*decisively*] But t'aint that. Ye won't never go because ye'll wait here fur yer share o' the farm, thinkin' allus he'll die soon. *trapped*

SIMEON. [*after a pause*] We've a right.

PETER. Two-thirds belongs t'us.

EBEN. [*jumping to his feet*] Ye've no right! She wa'n't yewr Maw! It was her farm! Didn't he steal it from her? She's dead. It's my farm.

SIMEON. [*sardonically*] Tell that t'Paw—when he comes! I'll bet ye a dollar he'll laugh—fur once in his life. Ha! [*He laughs himself in one single mirthless bark.*]

PETER. [*amused in turn, echoes his brother*) Ha!

SIMEON. [*after a pause*] What've ye got held agin us, Eben? Year arter year it's skulked in yer eye—somethin'.

PETER. Ay-eh.

EBEN. Ay-eh. They's somethin'. [*Suddenly exploding*] Why didn't ye never stand between him 'n' my Maw when he was slavin' her to her grave—t' pay her back fur the kindness she done t' yew? [*There is a long pause. They stare at him in surprise.*]

SIMEON. Waal—the stock'd got t' be watered.

PETER. 'R they was woodin' t' do.

SIMEON. 'R plowin'.

PETER. 'R hayin'.

SIMEON. 'R spreadin' manure.

PETER. 'R weedin'.

SIMEON. 'R prunin'.

PETER. 'R milkin'.

EBEN. [*breaking in harshly*] An' makin' walls—stone atop o' stone—makin' walls till yer heart's a stone ye heft up out o' growth onto a stone wall t' wall in yer heart!

SIMEON. [*matter-of-factly*] We never had no time t' meddle.

PETER. [*to* EBEN] Yew was fifteen afore yer Maw died—an' big fur yer age. Why didn't ye never do nothin'?

EBEN. [*harshly*] They was chores t' do, wa'n't they? [*A pause—then slowly*] It was on'y arter she died I come to think o' it. Me cookin'—doin' her work— that made me know her, suffer her sufferin'—she'd come back t' help—come back t' bile potatoes—come back t' fry bacon—come back t' bake biscuits— come back all cramped up t' shake the fire, an' carry ashes, her eyes weepin' an' bloody with smoke an' cinders same's they used t' be. She still comes back—stands by the stove thar in the evenin'—she can't find it nateral sleepin' an' restin' in peace. She can't git used t' bein' free—even in her grave.

SIMEON. She never complained none.

EBEN. She'd got too tired. She'd got too used t' bein' too tired. That was what he done. [*With vengeful passion*] An' sooner'r later, I'll meddle. I'll say the thin's I didn't say then t' him! I'll yell 'em at the top o' my lungs. I'll see t' it my Maw gits some rest an' sleep in her grave! [*He sits down again, relapsing into a brooding silence. They look at him with a queer indifferent curiosity.*]

PETER. [*after a pause*] Whar in tarnation d'ye s'pose he went, Sim?

SIMEON. Dunno. He druv off in the buggy, all spick an' span, with the mare all breshed an' shiny, druv off clackin' his tongue an' wavin' his whip. I remember it right well. I was finishin' plowin', it was spring an' May an' sunset, an' gold in the West, an' he druv off into it. I yells "Whar ye goin', Paw?" an' he hauls up by the stone wall a jiffy. His old snake's eyes was glitterin' in the sun like he'd been drinkin' a jugful an' he says with a mule's grin: "Don't ye run away till I come back!"

PETER. Wonder if he knowed we was wantin' fur Californi-a?

SIMEON. Mebbe. I didn't say nothin' and he says, lookin' kinder queer an' sick: "I been hearin' the hens cluckin' an' the roosters crowin' all the durn day. I been listenin' t' the cows lowin' an' everythin' else kickin' up till I can't stand it no more. It's spring an' I'm feelin' damned," he says. "Damned like an old bare hickory tree fit on'y fur burnin'," he says. An' then I calc'late I must've looked a mite hopeful, fur he adds real spry and vicious: "But don't git no fool idee I'm dead. I've sworn t' live a hundred an' I'll do it, if on'y t' spite yer sinful greed! An' now I'm ridin' out t' learn God's message t' me in the spring, like the prophets done. An' yew git back t' yer plowin'," he says. An' he druv off singin' a hymn. I thought he was drunk—'r I'd stopped him goin'.

EBEN. [*scornfully*] No, ye wouldn't! Ye're scared o' him. He's stronger—inside— than both o' ye put together!

PETER. [*sardonically*] An' yew—be yew Samson?[2]

EBEN. I'm gittin' stronger. I kin feel it growin' in me—growin' an' growin'— till it'll bust out—! [*He gets up and puts on his coat and a hat. They watch him, gradually breaking into grins. EBEN avoids their eyes sheepishly*] I'm goin' out fur a spell—up the road.

PETER. T' the village?

SIMEON. T' see Minnie?

EBEN. [*defiantly*] Ay-eh!

PETER. [*jeeringly*] The Scarlet Woman!

SIMEON. Lust—that's what's growin' in ye!

---

[2] An Israelite noted for his great strength. He was ultimately betrayed by his mistress Delilah. See the Bible, Judges, Chapters 13–16.

EBEN. Waal—she's purty!

PETER. She's been purty fur twenty year!

SIMEON. A new coat o' paint'll make a heifer out of forty.

EBEN. She hain't forty!

PETER. If she hain't, she's teeterin' on the edge.

EBEN. [*desperately*] What d'yew know—

PETER. All they is . . . Sim knew her—an' then me arter—

SIMEON. An' Paw kin tell yew somethin' too! He was fust!

EBEN. D'ye mean t' say he . . .?

SIMEON. [*with a grin*] Ay-eh! We air his heirs in everythin'!

EBEN. [*intensely*] That's more to it! That grows on it! It'll bust soon! [*Then violently*] I'll go smash my fist in her face! [*He pulls open the door in rear violently.*]

SIMEON. [*with a wink at* PETER—*drawlingly*] Mebbe—but the night's wa'm—purty—by the time ye git thar mebbe ye'll kiss her instead!

PETER. Sart'n he will! [*They both roar with coarse laughter.* EBEN *rushes out and slams the door—then the outside front door—comes around the corner of the house and stands still by the gate, staring up at the sky.*]

SIMEON. [*looking after him*] Like his Paw.

PETER. Dead spit an' image!

SIMEON. Dog'll eat dog!

PETER. Ay-eh. [*Pause. With yearning*] Mebbe a year from now we'll be in Californi-a.

SIMEON. Ay-eh. [*A pause. Both yawn*] Let's git t'bed. [*He blows out the candle. They go out door in rear.* EBEN *stretches his arms up to the sky—rebelliously.*]

EBEN. Waal—thar's a star, an' somewhar's they's him, an' here's me, an' thar's Min up the road—in the same night. What if I does kiss her? She's like t'night, she's soft 'n' wa'm, her eyes kin wink like a star, her mouth's wa'm, her arms're wa'm, she smells like a wa'm plowed field, she's purty . . . Ay-eh! By God A'mighty she's purty, an' I don't give a damn how many sins she's sinned afore mine or who she's sinned 'em with, my sin's as purty as any one on 'em! [*He strides off down the road to the left.*]

SCENE THREE

It is the pitch darkness just before dawn. EBEN *comes in from the left and goes around to the porch, feeling his way, chuckling bitterly and cursing half-aloud to himself.*

EBEN. The cussed old miser! [*He can be heard going in the front door. There is a pause as he goes upstairs, then a loud knock on the bedroom door of the brothers*] Wake up!

SIMEON. [*startledly*] Who's thar?

EBEN. [*pushing open the door and coming in, a lighted candle in his hand. The bedroom of the brothers is revealed. Its ceiling is the sloping roof. They can stand upright only close to the center dividing wall of the upstairs.* SIMEON *and* PETER *are in a double bed, front.* EBEN'S *cot is to the rear.* EBEN *has a mixture of silly grin and vicious scowl on his face*] I be!

PETER. [*angrily*] What in hell's-fire . . .?

EBEN. I got news fur ye! Ha! [*He gives one abrupt sardonic guffaw.*]

SIMEON. [*angrily*] Couldn't ye hold it 'til we'd got our sleep?

EBEN. It's nigh sunup. [*Then explosively*] He's gone an' married agen!

SIMEON *and* PETER. [*explosively*] Paw!

EBEN. Got himself hitched to a female 'bout thirty-five—an' purty, they says . . .

SIMEON. [*aghast*] It's a durn lie!

PETER. Who says?

SIMEON. They been stringin' ye!

EBEN. Think I'm a dunce, do ye? The hull village says. The preacher from New Dover, he brung the news—told it t' our preacher—New Dover, that's whar the old loon got himself hitched—that's whar the woman lived—

PETER. [*no longer doubting—stunned*] Waal . . . !

SIMEON. [*the same*] Waal . . . !

EBEN. [*sitting down on a bed—with vicious hatred*] Ain't he a devil out o' hell? It's jest t' spite us—the damned old mule!

PETER. [*after a pause*] Everythin'll go t' her now.

SIMEON. Ay-eh. [*A pause—dully*] Waal—if it's done—

PETER. It's done us. [*Pause—then persuasively*] They's gold in the fields o' Californi-a, Sim. No good a-stayin' here now.

SIMEON. Jest what I was a-thinkin'. [*Then with decision*] S'well fust's last! Let's light out and git this mornin'.

PETER. Suits me.

EBEN. Ye must like walkin'.

SIMEON. [*sardonically*] If ye'd grow wings on us we'd fly thar!

EBEN. Ye'd like ridin' better—on a boat, wouldn't ye? [*Fumbles in his pocket and takes out a crumpled sheet of foolscap*] Waal, if ye sign this ye kin ride on a boat. I've had it writ out an' ready in case ye'd ever go. It says fur three hundred dollars t' each ye agree yewr shares o' the farm is sold t' me. [*They look suspiciously at the paper. A pause.*]

SIMEON. [*wonderingly*] But if he's hitched agen—

PETER. An' whar'd yew git that sum o' money, anyways?

EBEN. [*cunningly*] I know whar it's hid. I been waitin'—Maw told me. She knew whar it lay fur years, but she was waitin' . . . It's her'n—the money he hoarded from her farm an' hid from Maw. It's my money by rights now.

PETER. Whar's it hid?

EBEN. [*cunningly*] Whar yew won't never find it without me. Maw spied on him—'r she'd never knowed. [*A pause. They look at him suspiciously, and he at them*] Waal, is is fa'r trade?

SIMEON. Dunno.

PETER. Dunno.

SIMEON. [*looking at window*] Sky's grayin'.

PETER. Ye better start the fire, Eben.

SIMEON. An' fix some vittles.

EBEN. Ay-eh. [*Then with a forced jocular heartiness*] I'll git ye a good one. If ye're startin' t' hoof it t' Californi-a ye'll need somethin' that'll stick t' yer ribs. [*He turns to the door, adding meaningly*] But ye kin ride on a boat if ye'll swap. [*He stops at the door and pauses. They stare at him.*]

SIMEON. [*suspiciously*] Whar was ye all night?

EBEN. [*defiantly*] Up t' Min's. [*Then slowly*] Walkin' thar, fust I felt 's if I'd kiss her; then I got a-thinkin' o' what ye'd said o' him an' her an' I says, I'll bust her nose fur that! Then I got t' the village an' heerd the news an' I got madder'n hell an' run all the way t' Min's not knowin' what I'd do— [*He pauses—then sheepishly but more defiantly*] Waal—when I seen her, I didn't hit her—nor I didn't kiss her nuther—I begun t' beller like a calf an' cuss

at the same time, I was durn mad—an' she got scared—an' I jest grabbed
holt an' tuk her— [*Proudly*] Yes, sirree! I tuk her. She may've been his'n—
an' your'n, too—but she's mine now!

SIMEON. [*dryly*] In love, air yew?

EBEN. [*with lofty scorn*] Love! I don't take no stock in sech slop!

PETER. [*winking at* SIMEON] Mebbe Eben's aimin' t' marry,too.

SIMEON. Min'd make a true faithful he'pmeet! [*They snicker.*]

EBEN. What do I care fur her—'ceptin' she's round an' wa'm? The p'int is
she was his'n—an' now she b'longs t' me! [*He goes to the door—then turns—
rebelliously*] An' Min hain't sech a bad un. They's worse'n Min in the world,
I'll bet ye! Wait'll we see this cow the Old Man's hitched t'! She'll beat
Min, I got a notion! [*He starts to go out.*]

SIMEON. [*suddenly*] Mebbe ye'll try t' make her your'n, too?

PETER. Ha! [*He gives a sardonic laugh of relish at this idea.*]

EBEN. [*spitting with disgust*] Her—here—sleepin' with him—stealin' my Maw's
farm! I'd as soon pet a skunk 'r kiss a snake! [*He goes out. The two stare after
him suspiciously. A pause. They listen to his steps receding.*]

PETER. He's startin' the fire.

SIMEON. I'd like t' ride t' Californi-a—but—

PETER. Min might o' put some scheme in his head.

SIMEON. Mebbe it's all a lie 'bout Paw marryin'. We'd best wait an' see the
bride.

PETER. An' don't sign nothin' till we does!

SIMEON. Nor till we've tested it's good money. [*Then with a grin*] But if Paw's
hitched we'd be sellin' Eben somethin' we'd never git nohow!

PETER. We'll wait an' see. [*Then with sudden vindictive anger*] An' till he comes,
let's yew 'n' me not wuk a lick, let Eben tend to thin's if he's a mind t',
let's us jest sleep an' eat an' drink likker, an' let the hull damned farm go
t' blazes!

SIMEON. [*excitedly*] By God, we've 'arned a rest! We'll play rich fur a change.
I hain't a-going to stir outa bed till breakfast's ready.

PETER. An' on the table!

SIMEON. [*after a pause—thoughtfully*] What d'ye calc'late she'll be like—our new
Maw? Like Eben thinks?

PETER. More'n' likely.

SIMEON. [*vindictively*] Waal—I hope she's a she-devil that'll make him wish he
was dead an' living in the pit o' hell fur comfort!

PETER. [*fervently*] Amen!

SIMEON. [*imitating his father's voice*] "I'm ridin' out t' learn God's message t'
me in the spring like the prophets done," he says. I'll bet right then an'
thar he knew plumb well he was goin' whorin', the stinkin' old hypocrite!

SCENE FOUR

*Same as Scene Two—shows the interior of the kitchen with a lighted candle on table. It
is gray dawn outside.* SIMEON *and* PETER *are just finishing their breakfast.* EBEN *sits
before his plate of untouched food, brooding frowningly.*

PETER. [*glancing at him rather irritably*] Lookin' glum don't help none.

SIMEON. [*sarcastically*] Sorrowin' over his lust o' the flesh!

PETER. [*with a grin*] Was she yer fust?

EBEN. [*angrily*] None o' yer business. [*A pause*] I was thinkin' o' him. I got a notion he's gittin' near—I kin feel him comin' on like yew kin feel malaria chill afore it takes ye.

PETER. It's too early yet.

SIMEON. Dunno. He'd like t' catch us nappin'—jest t' have somthin' t' hoss us 'round over.

PETER. [*mechanically gets to his feet.* SIMEON *does the same*] Waal—let's git t'wuk. [*They both plod mechanically toward the door before they realize. Then they stop short.*]

SIMEON. [*grinning*) Ye're a cussed fool, Peter—and I be wuss! Let him see we hain't wukin'! We don't give a durn!

PETER. [*as they go back to the table*) Not a damned durn! It'll serve t' show him we're done with him. [*They sit down again.* EBEN *stares from one to the other with surprise.*]

SIMEON. [*grins at him*] We're aimin' t' start bein' lilies o' the field.[3]

PETER. Nary a toil 'r spin 'r lick o' wuk do we put in!

SIMEON. Ye're sole owner—till he comes—that's what ye wanted. Waal, ye got t' be sole hand, too.

PETER. The cows air bellerin'. Ye better hustle at the milkin'.

EBEN. [*with excited joy*] Ye mean ye'll sign the paper?

SIMEON. [*dryly*] Mebbe.

PETER. Mebbe.

SIMEON. We're considerin'. [*Peremptorily*] Ye better git t' wuk.

EBEN. [*with queer excitement*] It's Maw's farm agen! It's my farm! Them's my cows! I'll milk my durn fingers off fur cows o' mine! [*He goes out door in rear, they stare after him indifferently.*]

SIMEON. Like his Paw.

PETER. Dead spit 'n' image!

SIMEON. Waal—let dog eat dog! [EBEN *comes out of front door and around the corner of the house. The sky is beginning to grow flushed with sunrise.* EBEN *stops by the gate and stares around him with glowing, possessive eyes. He takes in the whole farm with his embracing glance of desire.*]

EBEN. It's purty! It's damned purty! It's mine! [*He suddenly throws his head back boldly and glares with hard, defiant eyes at the sky*] Mine, d'ye hear? Mine! [*He turns and walks quickly off left, rear, toward the barn. The two brothers light their pipes.*]

SIMEON. [*putting his muddy boots up on the table, tilting back his chair, and puffing defiantly*] Waal—this air solid comfort—fur once.

PETER. Ay-eh. [*He follows suit. A pause. Unconsciously they both sigh.*]

SIMEON. [*suddenly*] He never was much o' a hand at milkin', Eben wa'n't.

PETER. [*with a snort*] His hands air like hoofs! [*A pause.*]

SIMEON. Reach down the jug thar! Let's take a swaller. I'm feelin' kind o' low.

PETER. Good idee! [*He does so—gets two glasses—they pour out drinks of whisky*] Here's t' the gold in Californi-a!

SIMEON. An' luck t' find it! [*They drink—puff resolutely—sigh—take their feet down from the table.*]

PETER. Likker don't pear t' sot right.

SIMEON. We hain't used t' it this early. [*A pause. They become very restless.*]

---

[3] See Matthew 6:34: "Consider the lilies of the field, how they grow; they toil not, neither do they spin."

PETER. Gittin' close in this kitchen.

SIMEON. [*with immense relief*] Let's git a breath o' air. [*They arise briskly and go out rear—appear around house and stop by the gate. They stare up at the sky with a numbed appreciation.*]

PETER. Purty!

SIMEON. Ay-eh. Gold's t' the East now.

PETER. Sun's startin' with us fur the Golden West.

SIMEON. [*staring around the farm, his compressed face tightened, unable to conceal emotion*] Waal—it's our last mornin'—mebbe.

PETER. [*the same*] Ay-eh.

SIMEON. [*stamps his foot on the earth and addresses it desperately*] Waal—ye've thirty year o' me buried in ye—spread out over ye—blood an' bone an' sweat— rotted away—fertilizin' ye—richin' yer soul—prime manure, by God, that's what I been t' ye!

PETER. Ay-eh! An' me!

SIMEON. An' yew, Peter. [*He sighs—then spits*] Waal—no use'n cryin' over spilt milk.

PETER. They's gold in the West—an' freedom, mebbe. We been slaves t' stone walls here.

SIMEON. [*defiantly*] We hain't nobody's slaves from this out—nor nothin's slave nuther. [*A pause—restlessly*] Speaking o' milk, wonder how Eben's managin'?

PETER. I s'pose he's managin'.

SIMEON. Mebbe we'd ought t' help—this once.

PETER. Mebbe. The cows knows us.

SIMEON. An' likes us. They don't know him much.

PETER. An' the hosses, an' pigs, an' chickens. They don't know him much.

SIMEON. They knows us like brothers—an' likes us! [*Proudly.*] Hain't we raised 'em t' be fust-rate, number one prize stock?

PETER. We hain't—not no more.

SIMEON. [*dully*] I was fergittin'. [*Then resignedly*] Waal, let's go help Eben a spell an' git waked up.

PETER. Suits me. [*They are starting off down left, rear, for the barn when* EBEN *appears from there hurrying toward them, his face excited.*]

EBEN. [*breathlessly*] Waal—har they be! The old mule an' the bride! I seen 'em from the barn down below at the turnin'.

PETER. How could ye tell that far?

EBEN. Hain't I as far-sight as he's near-sight? Don't I know the mare 'n' buggy, an' two people settin' in it? Who else . . . ? An' I tell ye I kin feel 'em a- comin', too! [*He squirms as if he had the itch.*]

PETER. [*beginning to be angry*] Waal—let him do his own unhitchin'!

SIMEON. [*angry in his turn*] Let's hustle in an' git our bundles an' be a-goin' as he's a-comin'. I don't want never t' step inside the door agen arter he's back. [*They both start back around the corner of the house.* EBEN *follows them.*]

EBEN. [*anxiously*] Will ye sign it afore ye go?

PETER. Let's see the color o' the old skinflint's money an' we'll sign. [*They disappear left. The two brothers clump upstairs to get their bundles.* EBEN *appears in the kitchen, runs to window, peers out, comes back and pulls up a strip of flooring in under stove, takes out a canvas bag and puts it on table, then sets the floorboard back in place. The two brothers appear a moment after. They carry old carpet bags.*]

EBEN. [*puts his hand on bag guardingly*] Have ye signed?

SIMEON. [*shows paper in his hand*] Ay-eh. [*Greedily*] Be that the money?

EBEN. [*opens bag and pours out pile of twenty-dollar gold pieces*] Twenty-dollar pieces—
thirty on 'em. Count 'em. (*Peter does so, arranging them in stacks of five, biting
one or two to test them.*]

PETER. Six hundred. [*He puts them in bag and puts it inside his shirt carefully.*]

SIMEON. [*handing paper to* EBEN] Har ye be.

EBEN. [*after glance, folds it carefully and hides it under his shirt—gratefully*] Thank
yew.

PETER. Thank yew fur the ride.

SIMEON. We'll send ye a lump o' gold fur Christmas. [*A pause.* EBEN *stares at
them and they at him.*]

PETER. [*awkwardly*] Waal—we're a-goin'.

SIMEON. Comin' out t' the yard?

EBEN. No. I'm waitin' in here a spell. [*Another silence. The brothers edge awkwardly
to door in rear—then turn and stand.*]

SIMEON. Waal—good-by.

PETER. Good-by.

EBEN. Good-by. [*Then go out. He sits down at the table, faces the stove and pulls out
the paper. He looks from it to the stove. His face, lighted up by the shaft of sunlight
from the window, has an expression of trance. His lips move. The two brothers come
out to the gate.*]

PETER. [*looking off toward barn*] Thar he be—unhitchin'.

SIMEON. [*with a chuckle*] I'll bet ye he's riled!

PETER. An' thar she be.

SIMEON. Let's wait 'n' see what our new Maw looks like.

PETER. [*with a grin*] An' give him our partin' cuss!

SIMEON. [*grinning*] I feel like raisin' fun. I feel light in my head an' feet.

PETER. Me, too. I feel like laffin' till I'd split up the middle.

SIMEON. Reckon it's the likker?

PETER. No. My feet feel itchin' t' walk an' walk—an' jump high over thin's—
an'. . . .

SIMEON. Dance? [*A pause.*]

PETER. [*puzzled*] It's plumb onnateral.

SIMEON. [*a light coming over his face*] I calc'late it's 'cause school's out. It's holiday.
Fur once we're free!

PETER. [*dazedly*] Free?

SIMEON. The halter's broke—the harness is busted—the fence bars is down—
the stone walls air crumblin' an' tumblin'! We'll be kickin' up an' tearin'
away down the road!

PETER. [*drawing a deep breath—oratorically*] Anybody that wants this stinkin' old
rock-pile of a farm kin hev it. T'ain't our'n, no sirree!

SIMEON. [*takes the gate off its hinges and puts it under his arm*] We harby 'bolishes
shet gates, an' open gates, an' all gates, by thunder!

PETER. We'll take it with us fur luck an' let 'er sail free down some river.

SIMEON. [*as a sound of voices comes from left, rear*] Har they comes! [*The two brothers
congeal into two stiff, grim-visaged statues.* EPHRAIM CABOT *and* ABBIE PUTNAM
come in. CABOT *is seventy-five, tall and gaunt, with great, wiry, concentrated power,
but stoop-shouldered from toil. His face is as hard as if it were hewn out of a boulder,
yet there is a weakness in it, a petty pride in its own narrow strength. His eyes are
small, close together, and extremely near-sighted, blinking continually in the effort to
focus on objects, their stare having a straining, ingrowing quality. He is dressed in
his dismal black Sunday suit.* ABBIE *is thirty-five, buxom, full of vitality. Her round*

face is pretty but marred by its rather gross sensuality. There is strength and obstinacy in her jaw, a hard determination in her eyes, and about her whole personality the same unsettled, untamed, desperate quality which is so apparent in EBEN.]

CABOT. [*as they enter—a queer strangled emotion in his dry cracking voice*] Har we be t' hum, Abbie.

ABBIE. [*with lust for the word*] Hum! [*Her eyes gloating on the house without seeming to see the two stiff figures at the gate*] It's purty—purty! I can't b'lieve it's r'ally mine.

CABOT. [*sharply*] Yewr'n? Mine! [*He stares at her penetratingly. She stares back. He adds relentingly*] Our'n—mebbe! It was lonesome too long. I was growin' old in the spring. A hum's got t' hev a woman.

ABBIE. [*her voice taking possession*] A woman's got t' hev a hum!

CABOT. [*nodding uncertainly*] Ay-eh. [*Then irritably*] Whar be they? Ain't thar no-body about—'r wukin'—r' nothin'?

ABBIE. [*sees the brothers. She returns their stare of cold apprasing contempt with interest—slowly*] Thar's two men loafin' at the gate an' starin' at me like a couple o' strayed hogs.

CABOT. [*straining his eyes*] I kin see 'em—but I can't make out. . . .

SIMEON. It's Simeon.

PETER. It's Peter.

CABOT. [*exploding*] Why hain't ye wukin'?

SIMEON. [*dryly*] We're waitin' t' welcome ye hum—yew an' the bride!

CABOT. [*confusedly*] Huh? Waal—this be yer new Maw, boys. [*She stares at them and they at her.*]

SIMEON. [*turns away and spits contemptuously*] I see her!

PETER. [*spits also*] An' I see her!

ABBIE. [*with the conqueror's conscious superiority*] I'll go in an' look at *my* house. [*She goes slowly around to porch.*]

SIMEON. [*with a snort*] *Her* house!

PETER. [*calls after her*] Ye'll find Eben inside. Ye better not tell him it's *yewr* house.

ABBIE. [*mouthing the name*] Eben. [*Then quietly*] I'll tell Eben.

CABOT. [*with a contemptuous sneer*] Ye needn't heed Eben. Eben's a dumb fool—like his Maw—soft an' simple!

SIMEON. [*with his sardonic burst of laughter*] Ha! Eben's a chip o' yew—spit 'n' image—hard 'n' bitter's a hickory tree! Dog'll eat dog. He'll eat ye yet, old man!

CABOT. [*commandingly*] Ye git t' wuk!

SIMEON. [*as* ABBIE *disappears in house—winks at* PETER *and says tauntingly*] So that thar's our new Maw, be it? Whar in hell did ye dig her up? [*He and* PETER *laugh.*]

PETER. Ha! Ye'd better turn her in the pen with the other sows. [*They laugh uproariously, slapping their thighs.*]

CABOT. [*so amazed at their effrontery that he stutters in confusion*] Simeon! Peter! What's come over ye? Air ye drunk?

SIMEON. We're free, old man—free o' yew an' the hull damned farm! [*They grow more and more hilarious and excited.*]

PETER. An' we're startin' out fur the gold fields o' Californi-a!

SIMEON. Ye kin take this place an' burn it!

PETER. An' bury it—fur all we cares!

SIMEON. We're free, old man! [*He cuts a caper.*]

PETER. Free! [*He gives a kick in the air.*]

SIMEON. [*in a frenzy*] Whoop!

PETER. Whoop! [*They do an absurd Indian war dance about the old man who is petrified between rage and the fear that they are insane.*]

SIMEON. We're free as Injuns! Lucky we don't skulp ye!

PETER. An' burn yer barn an' kill the stock!

SIMEON. An' rape yer new woman! Whoop! [*He and* PETER *stop their dance, holding their sides, rocking with wild laughter.*]

CABOT. [*edging away*] Lust fur gold—fur the sinful, easy gold o' Californi-a! It's made ye mad!

SIMEON. [*tauntingly*] Wouldn't ye like us to send ye back some sinful gold, ye old sinner?

PETER. They's gold besides what's in Californi-a! [*He retreats back beyond the vision of the old man and takes the bag of money and flaunts it in the air above his head, laughing.*]

SIMEON. And sinfuller, too!

PETER. We'll be voyagin' on the sea! Whoop! [*He leaps up and down.*]

SIMEON. Livin' free! Whoop! [*He leaps in turn.*]

CABOT. [*suddenly roaring with rage*] My cuss on ye!

SIMEON. Take our'n in trade fur it! Whoop!

CABOT. I'll hev ye both chained up in the asylum!

PETER. Ye old skinflint! Good-by!

SIMEON. Ye old blood sucker! Good-by!

CABOT. Go afore I . . . !

PETER. Whoop! [*He picks a stone from the road.* SIMEON *does the same.*]

SIMEON. Maw'll be in the parlor.

PETER. Ay-eh! One! Two!

CABOT. [*frightened*] What air ye . . . ?

PETER. Three! [*They both throw, the stones hitting the parlor window with a crash of glass, tearing the shade.*]

SIMEON. Whoop!

PETER. Whoop!

CABOT. [*in a fury now, rushing toward them*] If I kin lay hands on ye—I'll break yer bones fur ye! [*But they beat a capering retreat before him,* SIMEON *with the gate still under his arm.* CABOT *comes back, panting with impotent rage. Their voices as they go off take up the song of the gold-seekers to the old tune of "Oh, Susannah!"*]

> "I jumped aboard the Liza ship,
> And traveled on the sea,
> And every time I thought of home
> I wished it wasn't me!
> Oh! Californi-a,
> That's the land fur me!
> I'm off to Californi-a!
> With my wash bowl on my knee."

[*In the meantime, the window of the bedroom on right is raised and* ABBIE *sticks her head out. She looks down at* CABOT—*with a sigh of relief.*]

ABBIE. Waal—that's the last o' them two, hain't it? [*He doesn't answer. Then in possessive tones*] This here's a nice bedroom, Ephraim. It's a r'al nice bed. Is it my room, Ephraim?

CABOT. [*grimly—without looking up*] Our'n! [*She cannot control a grimace of aversion and pulls back her head slowly and shuts the window. A sudden horrible thought seems to enter* CABOT'S *head*] They been up to somethin'! Mebbe—mebbe they've pizened the stock—r' somethin'! [*He almost runs off down toward the barn. A moment later the kitchen door is slowly pushed open and* ABBIE *enters. For a moment she stands looking at* EBEN. *He does not notice her at first. Her eyes take him in penetratingly with a calculating appraisal of his strength as against hers. But under this her desire is dimly awakened by his youth and good looks. Suddenly he becomes conscious of her presence and looks up. Their eyes meet. He leaps to his feet, glowering at her speechlessly.*]

ABBIE. [*in her most seductive tones which she uses all through this scene*] Be you— Eben? I'm Abbie— [*She laughs*] I mean, I'm yer new Maw.

EBEN. [*viciously*] No, damn ye!

ABBIE. [*as if she hadn't heard—with a queer smile*] Yer Paw's spoke a lot o' yew. . . .

EBEN. Ha!

ABBIE. Ye mustn't mind him. He's an old man. [*A long pause. They stare at each other*] I don't want t' pretend playin' Maw t' ye, Eben. [*Admiringly*] Ye're too big an' too strong fur that. I want t' be frens with ye. Mebbe with me fur a fren ye'd find ye'd like livin' here better. I kin make it easy fur ye with him, mebbe. [*With a scornful sense of power*] I calc'late I kin git him t' do most anythin' fur me.

EBEN. [*with bitter scorn*] Ha! [*They stare again,* EBEN *obscurely moved, physically attracted to her—in forced stilted tones*] Yew kin go t' the devil!

ABBIE. [*calmly*] If cussin' me does ye good, cuss all ye've a mind t'. I'm all prepared t' have ye agin me—at fust. I don't blame ye nuther. I'd feel the same at any stranger comin' t' take my Maw's place. [*He shudders. She is watching him carefully*] Yew must've cared a lot fur yewr Maw, didn't ye? My Maw died afore I'd growed. I don't remember her none. [*A pause*] But yew won't hate me long, Eben. I'm not the wust in the world—an' yew an' me've got a lot in common. I kin tell that by lookin' at ye. Waal—I've had a hard life, too—oceans o' trouble an' nuthin' but wuk fur reward. I was a orphan early an' had t' wuk fur others in other folks' hums. Then I married an' he turned out a drunken spreer an' so he had to wuk fur others an' me too agen in other folks' hums, an' the baby died, an' my husband got sick an' died too, an' I was glad sayin' now I'm free fur once, on'y I diskivered right away all I was free fur was t' wuk agen in other folks' hums, doin' other folks' wuk till I'd most give up hope o' ever doin' my own wuk in my own hum, an' then your Paw come. . . . [CABOT *appears returning from the barn. He comes to the gate and looks down the road the brothers have gone. A faint strain of their retreating voices is heard:* "Oh, Californi-a! That's the place for me." *He stands glowering, his fist clenched, his face grim with rage.*]

EBEN. [*fighting against his growing attraction and sympathy—harshly*] An' bought yew—like a harlot! [*She is stung and flushes angrily. She has been sincerely moved by the recital of her troubles. He adds furiously*] An' the price he's payin' ye— this farm—was my Maw's, damn ye!—an' mine now!

ABBIE. [*with a cool laugh of confidence*] Yewr'n? We'll see 'bout that! [*Then strongly*] Waal—what if I did need a hum? What else'd I marry an old man like him fur?

EBEN. [*maliciously*] I'll tell him ye said that!

ABBIE. [*smiling*] I'll say ye're lyin' a-purpose—an' he'll drive ye off the place!

EBEN. Ye devil!

ABBIE. [*defying him*] This be my farm—this be my hum—this be my kitchen—!

EBEN. [*furiously, as if he were going to attack her*] Shut up, damn ye!

ABBIE. [*walks up to him—a queer coarse expression of desire in her face and body—slowly*] An' upstairs—that be my bedroom—an' my bed! [*He stares into her eyes, terribly confused and torn. She adds softly*] I hain't bad nor mean—'ceptin' fur an enemy—but I got t' fight fur what's due me out o' life, if I ever 'spect t' git it. [*Then putting her hand on his arm—seductively*] Let's yew 'n' me be frens, Eben.

EBEN. [*stupidly—as if hypnotized*] Ay-eh. [*Then furiously flinging off her arm*] No, ye durned old witch! I hate ye! [*He rushes out the door.*]

ABBIE. [*looks after him smiling satisfiedly—then half to herself, mouthing the word*] Eben's nice. [*She looks at the table, proudly*] I'll wash up *my* dishes now. [EBEN *appears outside, slamming the door behind him. He comes around corner, stops on seeing his father, and stands staring at him with hate.*]

CABOT. [*raising his arms to heaven in the fury he can no longer control*] Lord God o' Hosts, smite the undutiful sons with Thy wust cuss!

EBEN. [*breaking in violently*] Yew 'n' yewr God! Allus cussin' folks—allus naggin' 'em!

CABOT. [*oblivious to him—summoningly*] God o' the old! God o' the lonesome!

EBEN. [*mockingly*] Naggin' His sheep t' sin! T' hell with yewr God! [CABOT *turns. He and* EBEN *glower at each other.*]

CABOT. [*harshly*] So it's yew. I might've knowed it. [*Shaking his finger threateningly at him*] Blasphemin' fool! [*Then quickly*] Why hain't ye t' wuk?

EBEN. Why hain't yew? They've went. I can't wuk it all alone.

CABOT. [*contemptuously*] Nor noways! I'm wuth ten o' ye yit, old's I be! Ye'll never be more'n half a man! [*Then, matter-of-factly*] Waal—let's get t' the barn. [*They go. A last faint note of the "Californi-a" song is heard from the distance.* ABBIE *is washing her dishes.*]

CURTAIN

PART TWO

SCENE ONE

The exterior of the farmhouse, as in Part One—a hot Sunday afternoon two months later. ABBIE, *dressed in her best, is discovered sitting in a rocker at the end of the porch. She rocks listlessly, enervated by the heat, staring in front of her with bored, half-closed eyes.*

EBEN *sticks his head out of his bedroom window. He looks around furtively and tries to see—or hear—if anyone is on the porch, but although he has been careful to make no noise,* ABBIE *has sensed his movement. She stops rocking, her face grows animated and eager, she waits attentively.* EBEN *seems to feel her presence, he scowls back his thoughts of her and spits with exaggerated disdain—then withdraws back into the room.* ABBIE *waits, holding her breath as she listens with passionate eagerness for every sound within the house.*

EBEN *comes out. Their eyes meet; his falter. He is confused, he turns away and slams the door resentfully. At this gesture,* ABBIE *laughs tantalizingly, amused but at the same time piqued and irritated. He scowls, strides off the porch to the path and starts to walk past her to the road with a grand swagger of ignoring her existence. He is dressed in his store suit, spruced up, his face shines from soap and water.* ABBIE *leans forward on her chair, her eyes hard and angry now, and, as he passes her, gives a sneering, taunting chuckle.*

EBEN. [*stung—turns on her furiously*] What air yew cacklin' 'bout?

ABBIE. [*triumphant*] Yew!

EBEN. What about me?

ABBIE. Ye look all slicked up like a prize bull.

EBEN. [*with a sneer*] Waal—ye hain't so durned purty yerself, be ye? [*They stare into each other's eyes, his held by hers in spite of himself, hers glowingly possessive. Their physical attraction becomes a palpable force quivering in the hot air.*]

ABBIE. [*softly*] Ye don't mean that, Eben. Ye may think ye mean it, mebbe, but ye don't. Ye can't. It's agin nature, Eben. Ye been fightin' yer nature ever since the day I come—tryin t' tell yerself I hain't purty t'ye. [*She laughs a low humid laugh without taking her eyes from his. A pause—her body squirms desirously—she murmurs languorously*] Hain't the sun strong an' hot? Ye kin feel it burnin' into the earth—Nature—makin' thin's grow—bigger 'n' bigger— burnin' inside ye—makin' ye want t' grow—into somethin' else—till ye're jined with it—an' it's your'n—but it owns ye, too—an' makes ye grow bigger— like a tree—like them elums— [*She laughs again softly, holding his eyes. He takes a step toward her, compelled against his will*] Nature'll beat ye, Eben. Ye might's well own up t' it fust 's last.

EBEN. [*trying to break from her spell—confusedly*] If Paw'd hear ye goin' on. . . . [*Resentfully*] But ye've made such a damned idjit out o' the old devil. . . ! [ABBIE *laughs.*]

ABBIE. Waal—hain't it easier fur yew with him changed softer?

EBEN. [*defiantly*] No. I'm fightin' him—fightin' yew—fightin' fur Maw's rights t' her hum! [*This breaks her spell for him. He glowers at her*] An' I'm onto ye. Ye hain't foolin' me a mite. Ye're aimin' t' swaller up everythin' an' make it your'n. Waal, you'll find I'm a heap sight bigger hunk nor yew kin chew! [*He turns from her with a sneer.*]

ABBIE. [*trying to regain her ascendancy—seductively*] Eben!

EBEN. Leave me be! [*He starts to walk away.*]

ABBIE. [*more commandingly*] Eben!

EBEN. [*stops—resentfully*] What d'ye want?

ABBIE. [*trying to conceal a growing excitement*] Whar air ye goin'?

EBEN. [*with malicious nonchalance*] Oh—up the road a spell.

ABBIE. T' the village?

EBEN. [*airily*] Mebbe.

ABBIE. [*excitedly*] T' see that Min, I s'pose?

EBEN. Mebbe.

ABBIE. [*weakly*] What d'ye want t' waste time on her fur?

EBEN. [*revenging himself now—grinning at her*] Ye can't beat Nature, didn't ye say? [*He laughs and again starts to walk away.*]

ABBIE. [*bursting out*] An ugly old hake!

EBEN. [*with a tantalizing sneer*] She's purtier'n yew be!

ABBIE. That every wuthless drunk in the country has. . . .

EBEN. [*tauntingly*] Mebbe—but she's better'n yew. She owns up fa'r 'n' squar' t' her doin's.

ABBIE. [*furiously*] Don't ye dare compare. . . .

EBEN. She don't go sneakin' an' stealin'—what's mine.

ABBIE. [*savagely seizing on his weak point*] Your'n? Yew mean—my farm?

EBEN. I mean the farm yew sold yerself fur like any other old whore—my farm!

ABBIE. [*stung—fiercely*] Ye'll never live t' see the day when even a stinkin' weed on it'll belong t' ye! [*Then in a scream*] Git out o' my sight! Go on t' yer slut—disgracin' yer Paw 'n' me! I'll git yer Paw t' horsewhip ye off the place if I want t'! Ye're only livin' here 'cause I tolerate ye! Git along! I hate the sight o' ye! [*She stops, panting and glaring at him.*]

EBEN. [*returning her glance in kind*] An' I hate the sight o' yew! [*He turns and strides off up the road. She follows his retreating figure with concentrated hate. Old* CABOT *appears coming up from the barn. The hard, grim expression of his face has changed. He seems in some queer way softened, mellowed. His eyes have taken on a strange, incongruous dreamy quality. Yet there is no hint of physical weakness about him—rather he looks more robust and younger.* ABBIE *sees him and turns away quickly with unconcealed aversion. He comes slowly up to her.*]

CABOT. [*mildly*] War yew an' Eben quarrelin' agen?

ABBIE. [*shortly*] No.

CABOT. Ye was talkin' a'mighty loud. [*He sits down on the edge of porch.*]

ABBIE. [*snappishly*] If ye heerd us they hain't no need askin' questions.

CABOT. I didn't hear what ye said.

ABBIE. [*relieved*] Waal—it wa'n't nothin' t' speak on.

CABOT. [*after a pause*] Eben's queer.

ABBIE. [*bitterly*] He's the dead spit 'n' image o' yew!

CABOT. [*queerly interested*] D'ye think so, Abbie? [*After a pause, ruminatingly*] Me 'n' Eben's allus fit 'n' fit. I never could b'ar him noways. He's so thunderin' soft—like his Maw.

ABBIE. [*scornfully*] Ay-eh! 'Bout as soft as yew be!

CABOT. [*as if he hadn't heard*] Mebbe I been too hard on him.

ABBIE. [*jeeringly*] Waal—ye're gittin' soft now—soft as slop! That's what Eben was sayin'.

CABOT. [*his face instantly grim and ominous*] Eben was sayin'? Waal, he'd best not do nothin' t' try me 'r he'll soon diskiver. . . . [*A pause. She keeps her face turned away. His gradually softens. He stares up at the sky*] Purty, hain't it?

ABBIE. [*crossly*] I don't see nothin' purty.

CABOT. The sky. Feels like a wa'm field up thar.

ABBIE. [*sarcastically*] Air yew aimin' t' buy up over the farm too? [*She snickers contemptuously.*]

CABOT. [*strangely*] I'd like t' own my place up thar. [*A pause*] I'm gittin' old, Abbie. I'm gittin' ripe on the bough. [*A pause. She stares at him mystified. He goes on*] It's allus lonesome cold in the house—even when it's bilin' hot outside. Hain't yew noticed?

ABBIE. No.

CABOT. It's wa'm down t' the barn—nice smellin' an' warm—with the cows. [*A pause*] Cows is queer.

ABBIE. Like yew?

CABOT. Like Eben. [*A pause*] I'm gittin' t' feel resigned t' Eben—jest as I got t' feel 'bout his Maw. I'm gittin' t' learn to b'ar his softness—jest like her'n I calc'late I c'd a'most take t' him—if he wa'n't sech a dumb fool! [*A pause*] I s'pose it's old age a-creepin' in my bones.

ABBIE. [*indifferently*] Waal—ye hain't dead yet.

CABOT. [*roused*] No, I hain't, yew bet—not by a hell of a sight—I'm sound 'n' tough as hickory! [*Then moodily*] But arter three score and ten the Lord warns ye t' prepare. [*A pause*] That's why Eben's come in my head. Now that his cussed sinful brothers is gone their path t' hell, they's no one left but Eben.

ABBIE. [*resentfully*] They's me, hain't they? [*Agitatedly*] What's all this sudden likin' ye've tuk to Eben? Why don't ye say nothin' 'bout me? Hain't I yer lawful wife?

CABOT. [*simply*] Ay-eh. Ye be. [*A pause—he stares at her desirously—his eyes grow avid—then with a sudden movement he seizes her hands and squeezes them, declaiming in a queer camp meeting preacher's tempo*] Yew air my Rose o' Sharon![4] Behold, yew air fair; yer eyes air doves; yer lips air like scarlet; yer two breasts air like two fawns; yer navel be like a round goblet; yer belly be like a heap o' wheat. . . . [*He covers her hand with kisses. She does not seem to notice. She stares before her with hard angry eyes.*]

ABBIE. [*jerking her hands away—harshly*] So ye're plannin' t' leave the farm t' Eben, air ye?

CABOT. [*dazedly*] Leave . . . ? [*Then with resentful obstinacy*] I hain't a-givin' it t' no one!

ABBIE. [*remorselessly*] Ye can't take it with ye.

CABOT. [*thinks a moment—then reluctantly*] No, I calc'late not. [*After a pause—with a strange passion*] But if I could, I would, by the Eternal! 'R if I could, in my dyin' hour, I'd set it afire an' watch it burn—this house an' every ear o' corn an' every tree down t' the last blade o' hay! I'd sit an' know it was all a'dying with me an' no one else'd ever own what was mine, what I'd made out o' nothin' with my own sweat 'n' blood! [*A pause—then he adds with a queer affection*] 'Ceptin' the cows. Them I'd turn free.

ABBIE. [*harshly*] An' me?

CABOT. [*with a queer smile*] Ye'd be turned free, too.

ABBIE. [*furiously*] So that's the thanks I git fur marryin' ye—t' have ye change kind to Eben who hates ye, an' talk o' turnin' me out in the road.

CABOT. [*hastily*] Abbie! Ye know I wa'n't. . . .

ABBIE. [*vengefully*] Just let me tell ye a thing or two 'bout Eben! Whar's he gone? T' see that harlot, Min! I tried fur t' stop him. Disgracin' yew an' me—on the Sabbath, too!

CABOT. [*rather guiltily*] He's a sinner—nateral-born. It's lust eatin' his heart.

ABBIE. [*enraged beyond endurance—wildly vindictive*] An' his lust fur me! Kin ye find excuses fur that?

CABOT. [*stares at her—after a dead pause*] Lust—fur yew?

ABBIE. [*defiantly*] He was tryin' t' make love t' me—when ye heerd us quarrelin'.

CABOT. [*stares at her—then a terrible expression of rage comes over his face—he springs to his feet shaking all over*] By the A'mighty God—I'll end him!

ABBIE. [*frightened now for* EBEN] No! Don't ye!

CABOT. [*violently*] I'll git the shotgun an' blow his soft brains t' the top o' them elums!

ABBIE. [*throwing her arms around him*] No, Ephraim!

CABOT. [*pushing her away violently*] I will, by God!

ABBIE. [*in a quieting tone*] Listen, Ephraim. 'Twa'n't nothin' bad—on'y a boy's foolin'—'twa'n't meant serious—jest jokin' an' teasin'. . . .

---

[4] Here, and in the following lines, Cabot is echoing the Song of Solomon in the Bible, one of the most impassioned love poems in all of literature.

CABOT. Then why did ye say—lust?

ABBIE. It must hev sounded wusser'n I meant. An' I was mad at thinkin'— ye'd leave him the farm.

CABOT. [*quieter but still grim and cruel*] Waal then, I'll horsewhip him off the place if that much'll content ye.

ABBIE. [*reaching out and taking his hand*] No. Don't think o' me! Ye mustn't drive him off. 'Tain't sensible. Who'll ye get to help ye on the farm? They's no one hereabouts.

CABOT. [*considers this—then nodding his appreciation.*] Ye got a head on ye. [*Then irritably*] Waal, let him stay. [*He sits down on the edge of the porch. She sits beside him. He murmurs contemptuously*] I oughtn't t' git riled so—at that 'ere fool calf. [*A pause*] But har's the p'int. What son o' mine'll keep on here t' the farm—when the Lord does call me? Simeon an' Peter air gone t' hell—an' Eben's follerin' 'em.

ABBIE. They's me.

CABOT. Ye're on'y a woman.

ABBIE. I'm yewr wife.

CABOT. That hain't me. A son is me—my blood—mine. Mine ought t' git mine. An' then it's still mine—even though I be six foot under. D'ye see?

ABBIE. [*giving him a look of hatred*] Ay-eh. I see. [*She becomes very thoughtful, her face growing shrewd, her eyes studying* CABOT *craftily.*]

CABOT. I'm gittin' old—ripe on the bough. [*Then with a sudden forced reassurance*] Not but what I hain't a hard nut t' crack even yet—an' fur many a year t' come! By the Etarnal, I kin break most o' the young fellers' backs at any kind o' work any day o' the year!

ABBIE. [*suddenly*] Mebbe the Lord'll give *us* a son.

CABOT. [*turns and stares at her eagerly*] Ye mean—a son—t' me 'n' yew?

ABBIE. [*with a cajoling smile*] Ye're a strong man yet, hain't ye? 'Tain't noways impossible, be it? We know that. Why d'ye stare so? Hain't ye never thought o' that afore? I been thinkin' o' it all along. Ay-eh—an' I been prayin' it'd happen, too.

CABOT. [*his face growing full of joyous pride and a sort of religious ecstasy*] Ye been prayin', Abbie?—fur a son?—t' us?

ABBIE. Ay-eh. [*With a grim resolution*] I want a son now.

CABOT. [*excitedly clutching both of her hands in his*] It'd be the blessin' o' God Abbie—the blessin' o' God A'mighty on me—in my old age—in my lonesomeness! They hain't nothin' I wouldn't do fur ye then, Abbie. Ye'd hev on'y t' ask it—anythin' ye'd a mind t'!

ABBIE. [*interrupting*] Would ye will the farm t' me then—t' me an' it . . .?

CABOT. [*vehemently*] I'd do anythin' ye axed, I tell ye! I swar it! May I be everlastin' damned t' hell if I wouldn't! [*He sinks to his knees pulling her down with him. He trembles all over with the fervor of his hopes*] Pray t' the Lord agen, Abbie. It's the Sabbath! I'll jine ye! Two prayers air better nor one. "An' God hearkened unto Rachel"![5] An' God hearkened unto Abbie! Pray, Abbie! Pray fur him to hearken! [*He bows his head, mumbling. She pretends to do likewise but gives him a side glance of scorn and triumph.*]

---

[5] The allusion is to Genesis 30:22. Rachel, the wife of Jacob, remained barren for many years until "God hearkened to her" and she bore Jacob a son in his old age.

SCENE TWO

About eight in the evening. The interior of the two bedrooms on the top floor is shown.
EBEN *is sitting on the side of his bed in the room on the left. On account of the heat he
has taken off everything but his undershirt and pants. His feet are bare. He faces front,
brooding moodily, his chin propped on his hands, a desperate expression on his face.*
In the other room CABOT *and* ABBIE *are sitting side by side on the edge of their bed,
an old four-poster with feather mattress. He is in his night shirt, she in her nightdress.
He is still in the queer, excited mood into which the notion of a son has thrown him.
Both rooms are lighted dimly and flickeringly by tallow candles.*

CABOT. The farm needs a son.
ABBIE. I need a son.
CABOT. Ay-eh. Sometimes ye air the farm an' sometimes the farm be yew.
   That's why I clove t' ye in my lonesomeness. [*A pause. He pounds his knee
   with his fist*] Me an' the farm has got t' beget a son!
ABBIE. Ye'd best go t' sleep. Ye're gittin' thin's all mixed.
CABOT. [*with an impatient gesture*] No, I hain't. My mind's clear's a well. Ye
   don't know me, that's it. [*He stares hopelessly at the floor.*]
ABBIE. [*indifferently*] Mebbe. [*In the next room* EBEN *gets up and paces up and down
   distractedly.* ABBIE *hears him. Her eyes fasten on the intervening wall with concentrated
   attention.* EBEN *stops and stares. Their hot glances seem to meet through the wall.
   Unconsciously he stretches out his arms for her and she half rises. Then aware, he
   mutters a curse at himself and flings himself face downward on the bed, his clenched
   fists above his head, his face buried in the pillow.* ABBIE *relaxes with a faint sigh but
   her eyes remain fixed on the wall; she listens with all her attention for some movement
   from* EBEN.]
CABOT. [*suddenly raises his head and looks at her—scornfully*] Will ye ever know
   me—'r will any man 'r woman? [*Shaking his head*] No. I calc'late 't wa'n't t'
   be. [*He turns away.* ABBIE *looks at the wall. Then, evidently unable to keep silent
   about his thoughts, without looking at his wife, he puts out his hand and clutches her
   knee. She starts violently, looks at him, sees he is not watching her, concentrates again
   on the wall and pays no attention to what he says*] Listen, Abbie. When I come
   here fifty odd year ago—I was jest twenty an' the strongest an' hardest ye
   ever seen—ten times as strong an' fifty times as hard as Eben. Waal—this
   place was nothin' but fields o' stones. Folks laughed when I tuk it. They
   couldn't know what I knowed. When ye kin make corn sprout out o' stones,
   God's livin' in yew! They wa'n't strong enuf fur that! They reckoned God
   was easy. They laughed. They don't laugh no more. Some died hereabouts.
   Some went West an' died. They're all under ground—fur follerin' arter an
   easy God. God hain't easy. [*He shakes his head slowly*] An' I growed hard.
   Folks kept allus sayin' he's a hard man like 'twas sinful t' be hard, so's at
   last I said back at 'em: Waal then, by thunder, ye'll git me hard an' see
   how ye like it! [*Then suddenly*] But I give in t' weakness once. 'Twas arter
   I'd been here two year. I got weak—despairful—they was so many stones.
   They was a party leavin', givin' up, goin' West. I jined 'em. We tracked on
   'n' on. We come t' broad medders, plains, whar the soil was black an' rich
   as gold. Nary a stone. Easy. Ye'd on'y to plow an' sow an' then set an'
   smoke yer pipe an' watch thin's grow. I could o' been a rich man—but
   somethin' in me fit me an' fit me—the voice o' God sayin': "This hain't

wuth nothin' t' Me. Git ye back t' hum!" I got afeerd o' that voice an' I lit out back t' hum here, leavin' my claim an' crops t' whoever'd a mind t' take 'em. Ay-eh. I actoolly give up what was rightful mine! God's hard, not easy! God's in the stones! Build my church on a rock—out o' stones an' I'll be in them! That's what He meant t' Peter![6] [*He sighs heavily—a pause*] Stones. I picked 'em up an' piled 'em into walls. Ye kin read the years of my life in them walls, every day a hefted stone, climbin' over the hills up and down, fencin' in the fields that was mine, whar I'd make thin's grow out o' nothin'—like the will o' God, like the servant o' His hand. It wa'n't easy. It was hard an' He made me hard fur it. [*He pauses*] All the time I kept gittin' lonesomer. I tuk a wife. She bore Simeon an' Peter. She was a good woman. She wuked hard. We was married twenty year. She never knowed me. She helped but she never knowed what she was helpin'. I was allus lonesome. She died. After that it wa'n't so lonesome fur a spell. [*A pause*] I lost count o' the years. I had no time t' fool away countin' 'em. Sim an' Peter helped. The farm growed. It was all mine! When I thought o' that I didn't feel lonesome. [*A pause*] But ye can't hitch yer mind t' one thin' day an' night. I tuk another wife—Eben's Maw. Her folks was contestin' me at law over my deeds t' the farm—my farm! That's why Eben keeps a-talkin' his fool talk o' this bein' his Maw's farm. She bore Eben. She was purty—but soft. She tried t' be hard. She couldn't. She never knowed me nor nothin'. It was lonesomer 'n hell with her. After a matter o' sixteen odd years, she died. [*A pause*] I lived with the boys. They hated me 'cause I was hard. I hated them 'cause they was soft. They coveted the farm without knowin' what it meant. It made me bitter 'n wormwood. It aged me—them coveting what I'd made fur mine. Then this spring the call come—the voice o' God cryin' in my wilderness, in my lonesomeness—t' go out an' seek an' find! [*Turning to her with strange passion*] I sought ye an' I found ye! Yew air my Rose o' Sharon! Yer eyes air like. . . . [*She has turned a blank face, resentful eyes to his. He stares at her for a moment—then harshly*] Air ye any the wiser fur all I've told ye?

ABBIE. [*confusedly*] Mebbe.

CABOT. [*pushing her away from him—angrily*] Ye don't know nothin'—nor never will. If ye don't hev a son t' redeem ye. . . . [*This in a tone of cold threat.*]

ABBIE. [*resentfully*] I've prayed, hain't I?

CABOT. [*bitterly*] Pray agen—fur understandin'!

ABBIE. [*a veiled threat in her tone*] Ye'll have a son out o' me, I promise ye.

CABOT. How kin ye promise?

ABBIE. I got second-sight mebbe. I kin foretell. [*She gives a queer smile.*]

CABOT. I believe ye have. Ye give me the chills sometimes. [*He shivers*] It's cold in this house. It's oneasy. They's thin's pokin' about in the dark—in the corners. [*He pulls on his trousers, tucking in his night shirt, and pulls on his boots.*]

ABBIE. [*surprised*] Whar air ye goin'?

CABOT. [*queerly*] Down whar it's restful—whar it's warm—down t' the barn. [*Bitterly*] I kin talk t' the cows. They know. They know the farm an' me. They'll give me peace. [*He turns to go out the door.*]

ABBIE. [*a bit frightenedly*] Air ye ailin' tonight, Ephraim?

---

[6] "Upon this rock I will build my church"—Matthew 16:18.

CABOT. Growin'. Growin' ripe on the bough. [*He turns and goes, his boots clumping down the stairs.* EBEN *sits up with a start, listening.* ABBIE *is conscious of his movement and stares at the wall.* CABOT *comes out of the house around the corner and stands by the gate, blinking at the sky. He stretches up his hands in a tortured gesture*] God A'mighty, call from the dark! [*He listens as if expecting an answer. Then his arms drop, he shakes his head and plods off toward the barn.* EBEN *and* ABBIE *stare at each other through the wall.* EBEN *sighs heavily and* ABBIE *echoes it. Both become terribly nervous, uneasy. Finally* ABBIE *gets up and listens, her ear to the wall. He acts as if he saw every move she was making, he becomes resolutely still. She seems driven into a decision—goes out the door in rear determinedly. His eyes follow her. Then as the door of his room is opened softly, he turns away, waits in an attitude of strained fixity.* ABBIE *stands for a second staring at him, her eyes burning with desire. Then with a little cry she runs over and throws her arms about his neck, she pulls his head back and covers his mouth with kisses. At first, he submits dumbly; then he puts his arms about her neck and returns her kisses, but finally, suddenly aware of his hatred, he hurls her away from him, springing to his feet. They stand speechless and breathless, panting like two animals.*]

ABBIE. [*at last—painfully*] Ye shouldn't, Eben—ye shouldn't—I'd make ye happy!

EBEN. [*harshly*] I don't want t' be happy—from yew!

ABBIE. [*helplessly*] Ye do, Eben! Ye do! Why d'ye lie?

EBEN. [*viciously*] I don't take t'ye, I tell ye! I hate the sight o' ye!

ABBIE. [*with an uncertain troubled laugh*] Waal, I kissed ye anyways—an' ye kissed back—yer lips was burnin'—ye can't lie 'bout that! [*Intensely*] If ye don't care, why did ye kiss me back—why was yer lips burnin'?

EBEN. [*wiping his mouth*] It was like pizen on 'em. [*Then tauntingly*] When I kissed ye back, mebbe I thought 'twas someone else.

ABBIE. [*wildly*] Min?

EBEN. Mebbe.

ABBIE. [*torturedly*] Did ye go t' see her? Did ye r'ally go? I thought ye mightn't. Is that why ye throwed me off jest now?

EBEN. [*sneeringly*] What if it be?

ABBIE. [*raging*] Then ye're a dog, Eben Cabot!

EBEN. [*threateningly*] Ye can't talk that way t' me!

ABBIE. [*with a shrill laugh*] Can't I? Did ye think I was in love with ye—a weak thin' like yew? Not much! I on'y wanted ye fur a purpose o' my own—an' I'll hev ye fur it yet 'cause I'm stronger'n yew be!

EBEN. [*resentfully*] I knowed well it was on'y part o' yer plan t' swaller everythin'!

ABBIE. [*tauntingly*] Mebbe!

EBEN. [*furious*] Git out o' my room!

ABBIE. This air my room an' ye're on'y hired help!

EBEN. [*threateningly*] Git out afore I murder ye!

ABBIE. [*quite confident now*] I hain't a mite afeerd. Ye want me, don't ye? Yes, ye do! An' yer Paw's son'll never kill what he wants! Look at yer eyes! They's lust fur me in 'em, burnin' 'em up! Look at yer lips now! They're tremblin' an' longin' t' kiss me, an' yer teeth t' bite! [*He is watching her now with a horrible fascination. She laughs a crazy triumphant laugh*] I'm a-goin' t' make all o' this hum my hum! They's one room hain't mine yet, but it's a-goin' t' be tonight. I'm a-goin' down now an' light up! [*She makes him a mocking bow*] Won't ye come courtin' me in the best parlor, Mister Cabot?

EBEN. [*staring at her—horribly confused—dully*] Don't ye dare! It hain't been opened since Maw died an' was laid out thar! Don't ye . . . ! [*But her eyes are fixed on his so burningly that his will seems to wither before hers. He stands swaying toward her helplessly.*]

ABBIE. [*holding his eyes and putting all her will into her words as she backs out the door*] I'll expect ye afore long, Eben.

EBEN. [*stares after her for a while, walking toward the door. A light appears in the parlor window. He murmurs*] In the parlor? [*This seems to arouse connotations, for he comes back and puts on his white shirt, collar, half ties the tie mechanically, puts on coat, takes his hat, stands barefooted looking about him in bewilderment, mutters wonderingly*] Maw! Whar air yew? [*Then goes slowly toward the door in rear.*]

SCENE THREE

A few minutes later. The interior of the parlor is shown. A grim, repressed room like a tomb in which the family has been interred alive. ABBIE *sits on the edge of the horsehair sofa. She has lighted all the candles and the room is revealed in all its preserved ugliness. A change has come over the woman. She looks awed and frightened now, ready to run away.*

The door is opened and EBEN *appears. His face wears an expression of obsessed confusion. He stands staring at her, his arms hanging disjointedly from his shoulders, his feet bare, his hat in his hand.*

ABBIE. [*after a pause—with a nervous, formal politeness*] Won't ye set?

EBEN. [*dully*] Ay-eh. [*Mechanically he places his hat carefully on the floor near the door and sits stiffly beside her on the edge of the sofa. A pause. They both remain rigid, looking straight ahead with eyes full of fear.*]

ABBIE. When I fust come in—in the dark—they seemed somethin' here.

EBEN. [*simply*] Maw.

ABBIE. I kin still feel—somethin'. . . .

EBEN. It's Maw.

ABBIE. At fust I was feered o' it. I wanted t' yell an' run. Now—since yew come—seems like it's growin' soft an' kind t' me. [*Addressing the air—queerly*] Thank yew.

EBEN. Maw allus loved me.

ABBIE. Mebbe it knows I love yew, too. Mebbe that makes it kind t' me.

EBEN. [*dully*] I dunno. I should think she'd hate ye.

ABBIE. [*with certainty*] No. I kin feel it don't—not no more.

EBEN. Hate ye fur stealin' her place—here in her hum—settin' in her parlor whar she was laid—[*He suddenly stops, staring stupidly before him.*]

ABBIE. What is it, Eben?

EBEN. [*in a whisper*] Seems like Maw didn't want me t' remind ye.

ABBIE. [*excitedly*] I knowed, Eben! It's kind t' me! It don't b'ar me no grudges fur what I never knowed an' couldn't help!

EBEN. Maw b'ars him a grudge.

ABBIE. Waal, so does all o' us.

EBEN. Ay-eh. [*With passion*] I does, by God!

ABBIE. [*taking one of his hands in hers and patting it*] Thar! Don't git riled thinkin' o' him. Think o' yer Maw who's kind t' us. Tell me about yer Maw, Eben.

EBEN. They hain't nothin' much. She was kind. She was good.

ABBIE. [*putting one arm over his shoulder. He does not seem to notice—passionately*] I'll be kind an' good t' ye!

EBEN. Sometimes she used t' sing fur me.

ABBIE. I'll sing fur ye!

EBEN. This was her hum. This was her farm.

ABBIE. This is my hum! This is my farm!

EBEN. He married her t' steal 'em. She was soft an' easy. He couldn't 'preciate her.

ABBIE. He can't 'preciate me!

EBEN. He murdered her with his hardness.

ABBIE. He's murderin' me!

EBEN. She died. [*A pause*] Sometimes she used to sing fur me. [*He bursts into a fit of sobbing.*]

ABBIE. [*both her arms around him—with wild passion*] I'll sing fur ye! I'll die fur ye! [*In spite of her overwhelming desire for him, there is a sincere maternal love in her manner and voice—a horribly frank mixture of lust and mother love*] Don't cry, Eben! I'll take yer Maw's place! I'll be everythin' she was t' ye! Let me kiss ye, Eben! [*She pulls his head around. He makes a bewildered pretense of resistance. She is tender*] Don't be afeered! I'll kiss ye pure, Eben—same 's if I was a Maw t' ye—an' ye kin kiss me back 's if yew was my son—my boy—sayin' good-night t' me! Kiss me, Eben. [*They kiss in restrained fashion. Then suddenly wild passion overcomes her. She kisses him lustfully again and again and he flings his arms about her and returns her kisses. Suddenly, as in the bedroom, he frees himself from her violently and springs to his feet. He is trembling all over, in a strange state of terror.* ABBIE *strains her arms toward him with fierce pleading*] Don't ye leave me, Eben! Can't ye see it hain't enuf—lovin' ye like a Maw—can't ye see it's got t' be that an' more—much more—a hundred times more—fur me t' be happy—fur yew t' be happy?

EBEN. [*to the presence he feels in the room*] Maw! Maw! What d'ye want? What air ye tellin' me?

ABBIE. She's tellin' ye t' love me. She knows I love ye an' I'll be good t' ye. Can't ye feel it? Don't ye know? She's tellin' ye t' love me, Eben!

EBEN. Ay-eh. I feel—mebbe she—but—I can't figger out—why—when ye've stole her place—here in her hum—in the parlor whar she was—

ABBIE. [*fiercely*] She knows I love ye!

EBEN. [*his face suddenly lighting up with a fierce, triumphant grin*] I see it! I sees why. It's her vengeance on him—so's she kin rest quiet in her grave!

ABBIE. [*wildly*] Vengeance o' God on the hull o' us! What d'we give a durn? I love ye, Eben! God knows I love ye! [*She stretches out her arms for him.*]

EBEN. [*throws himself on his knees beside the sofa and grabs her in his arms—releasing all his pent-up passion*] An' I love ye, Abbie!—now I kin say it! I been dyin' fur want o' ye—every hour since ye come! I love ye! [*Their lips meet in a fierce, bruising kiss.*]

SCENE FOUR

Exterior of the farmhouse. It is just dawn. The front door at right is opened and EBEN *comes out and walks around to the gate. He is dressed in his working clothes. He seems changed. His face wears a bold and confident expression, he is grinning to himself with evident satisfaction. As he gets near the gate, the window of the parlor is heard opening and the shutters are flung back and* ABBIE *sticks her head out. Her hair tumbles over her shoulders in disarray, her face is flushed, she looks at* EBEN *with tender, langourous eyes and calls softly.*]

ABBIE. Eben. [*As he turns—playfully*] Jest one more kiss afore ye go. I'm goin' to miss ye fearful all day.

EBEN. An' me yew, ye kin bet! [*He goes to her. They kiss several times. He draws away, laughingly*] Thar. That's enuf, hain't it? Ye won't hev none left fur next time.

ABBIE. I got a million o' 'em left fur yew! [*Then a bit anxiously*] D'ye r'ally love me, Eben?

EBEN. [*emphatically*] I like ye better'n any gal I ever knowed! That's gospel!

ABBIE. Likin' hain't lovin'.

EBEN. Waal then—I love ye. Now air yew satisfied?

ABBIE. Ay-eh, I be. [*She smiles at him adoringly.*]

EBEN. I better git t' the barn. The old critter's liable t' suspicion an' come sneakin' up.

ABBIE. [*with a confident laugh*] Let him! I kin allus pull the wool over his eyes. I'm goin' t' leave the shutters open and let in the sun 'n' air. This room's been dead long enuf. Now it's goin' t' be my room!

EBEN. [*frowning*] Ay-eh.

ABBIE. [*hastily*] I meant—our room.

EBEN. Ay-eh.

ABBIE. We made it our'n last night, didn't we? We give it life—our lovin' did. [*A pause.*]

EBEN. [*with a strange look*] Maw's gone back t' her grave. She kin sleep now.

ABBIE. May she rest in peace! [*Then tenderly rebuking*] Ye oughtn't t' talk o' sad thin's—this mornin'.

EBEN. It jest come up in my mind o' itself.

ABBIE. Don't let it. [*He doesn't answer. She yawns*] Waal, I'm a-goin' t' steal a wink o' sleep. I'll tell the Old Man I hain't feelin' pert. Let him git his own vittles.

EBEN. I see him comin' from the barn. Ye better look smart an' git upstairs.

ABBIE. Ay-eh. Good-by. Don't ferget me. [*She throws him a kiss. He grins—then squares his shoulders and awaits his father confidently.* CABOT *walks slowly up from the left, staring up at the sky with a vague face.*]

EBEN. [*jovially*] Mornin', Paw. Star-gazin' in daylight?

CABOT. Purty, hain't it?

EBEN. [*looking around him possessively*] It's a durned purty farm.

CABOT. I mean the sky.

EBEN. [*grinning*] How d'ye know? Them eyes o' your'n can't see that fur. [*This tickles his humor and he slaps his thigh and laughs*] Ho-ho! That's a good un!

CABOT. [*grimly sarcastic*] Ye're feelin' right chipper, hain't ye? Whar'd ye steal the likker?

EBEN. [*good-naturedly*] 'Tain't likker. Jest life. [*Suddenly holding out his hand—soberly*] Yew 'n' me is quits. Let's shake hands.

CABOT. [*suspiciously*] What's come over ye?

EBEN. Then don't. Mebbe it's jest as well. [*A moment's pause*] What's come over me? [*Queerly*] Didn't ye feel her passin'—goin' back t' her grave?

CABOT. [*dully*] Who?

EBEN. Maw. She kin rest now an' sleep content. She's quits with ye.

CABOT. [*confusedly*] I rested. I slept good—down with the cows. They know
how t' sleep. They're teachin' me.

EBEN. [*suddenly jovial again*] Good fur the cows! Waal—ye better git t' work.

CABOT. [*grimly amused*] Air yew bossin' me, ye calf?

EBEN. [*beginning to laugh*] Ay-eh! I'm bossin' yew! Ha-ha-ha! See how ye like
it. Ha-ha-ha! I'm the prize rooster o' this roost. Ha-ha-ha! [*He goes off toward
the barn laughing.*]

CABOT. [*looks after him with scornful pity*] Soft-headed. Like his Maw. Dead spit
'n' image. No hope in him! [*He spits with contemptuous disgust*] A born fool!
[*Then matter-of-factly*] Waal—I'm gittin' peckish. [*He goes toward the door.*]

CURTAIN

PART THREE

SCENE ONE

*A night in late spring the following year. The kitchen and the two bedrooms upstairs are
shown. The two bedrooms are dimly lighted by a tallow candle in each.* EBEN *is sitting
on the side of the bed in his room, his chin propped on his fists, his face a study of the
struggle he is making to understand his conflicting emotions. The noisy laughter and music
from below where a kitchen dance is in progress annoy and distract him. He scowls at
the floor.*

In the next room a cradle stands beside the double bed.

*In the kitchen all is festivity. The stove has been taken down to give more room to the
dancers. The chairs, with wooden benches added, have been pushed back against the walls.
On these are seated, squeezed in tight against one another, farmers and their wives and
their young folks of both sexes from the neighboring farms. They are all chattering and
laughing loudly. They evidently have some secret joke in common. There is no end of
winking, of nudging, of meaning nods of the head toward* CABOT *who, in a state of
extreme hilarious excitement increased by the amount he has drunk, is standing near the
rear door where there is a small keg of whisky and serving drinks to all the men. In the
left corner, front, dividing the attention with her husband,* ABBIE *is sitting in a rocking
chair, a shawl wrapped about her shoulders. She is very pale, her face is thin and drawn,
her eyes are fixed anxiously on the open door in rear as if waiting for someone.*

*The musician is tuning up his fiddle, seated in the far right corner. He is a lanky young
fellow with a long, weak face. His pale eyes blink incessantly and he grins about him
slyly with a greedy malice.*

ABBIE. [*suddenly turning to a young girl on her right*] Whar's Eben?

YOUNG GIRL. [*eying her scornfully*] I dunno, Mrs. Cabot. I hain't seen Eben in
ages. [*Meaningly*] Seems like he's spent most o' his time t' hum since yew
come.

ABBIE. [*vaguely*] I tuk his Maw's place.

YOUNG GIRL. Ay-eh. So I've heerd. [*She turns away to retail this bit of gossip to
her mother sitting next to her.* ABBIE *turns to her left to a big stoutish middle-aged
man whose flushed face and starting eyes show the amount of "likker" he has consumed.*]

ABBIE. Ye hain't seen Eben, hev ye?

MAN. No, I hain't. [*Then he adds with a wink*] If yew hain't, who would?

ABBIE. He's the best dancer in the county. He'd ought t' come an' dance.

MAN. [*with a wink*] Mebbe he's doin' the dutiful an' walkin' the kid t' sleep. It's a boy, hain't it?

ABBIE. [*nodding vaguely*] Ay-eh—born two weeks back—purty's a picter.

MAN. They all is—t' their Maws. [*Then in a whisper, with a nudge and a leer*] Listen, Abbie—if ye ever git tired o' Eben, remember me! Don't fergit now! [*He looks at her uncomprehending face for a second—then grunts disgustedly*] Waal— guess I'll likker agin. [*He goes over and joins* CABOT *who is arguing noisily with an old farmer over cows. They all drink.*]

ABBIE. [*This time appealing to nobody in particular*] Wonder what Eben's a-doin'? [*Her remark is repeated down the line with many a guffaw and titter until it reaches the fiddler. He fastens his blinking eyes on* ABBIE.]

FIDDLER. [*raising his voice*] Bet I kin tell ye, Abbie, what Eben's doin'! He's down t' the church offerin' up prayers o' thanksgivin'. [*They all titter expectantly.*]

A MAN. What fur? [*Another titter.*]

FIDDLER. 'Cause unto him a— [*He hesitates just long enough*] brother is born! [*A roar of laughter. They all look from* ABBIE *to* CABOT. *She is oblivious, staring at the door.* CABOT, *although he hasn't heard the words, is irritated by the laughter and steps forward, glaring about him. There is an immediate silence.*]

CABOT. What're ye all bleatin' about—like a flock o' goats? Why don't ye dance, damn ye? I axed ye here t' dance—t' eat, drink an' be merry—an' thar ye set cacklin' like a lot o' wet hens with the pip! Ye've swilled my likker an' guzzled my vittles like hogs, hain't ye? Then dance fur me, can't ye? That's fa'r an' squar', hain't it? [*A grumble of resentment goes around but they are all evidently in too much awe of him to express it openly.*]

FIDDLER. [*slyly*] We're waitin' fur Eben. [*A suppressed laugh.*]

CABOT. [*with a fierce exultation*] T'hell with Eben! Eben's done fur now! I got a new son! [*His mood switching with drunken suddenness*] But ye needn't t' laugh at Eben, none o' ye! He's my blood, if he be a dumb fool. He's better nor any o' yew! He kin do a day's work a'most up t' what I kin—an' that'd put any o' yew pore critters t' shame!

FIDDLER. An' he kin do a good night's work, too! [*A roar of laughter.*]

CABOT. Laugh, ye damn fools! Ye're right jist the same, Fiddler. He kin work day an' night too, like I kin, if need be!

OLD FARMER. [*from behind the keg where he is weaving drunkenly back and forth— with great simplicity*] They hain't many t' touch ye, Ephraim—a son at seventy- six. That's a hard man fur ye! I be on'y sixty-eight an' I couldn't do it. [*A roar of laughter in which* CABOT *joins uproariously.*]

CABOT. [*slapping him on the back*] I'm sorry fur ye, Hi. I'd never suspicion sech weakness from a boy like yew!

OLD FARMER. An' I never reckoned yew had it in ye nuther, Ephraim. [*There is another laugh.*]

CABOT. [*suddenly grim*] I got a lot in me—a hell of a lot—folks don't know on. [*Turning to the fiddler*] Fiddle 'er up, durn ye! Give 'em somethin' t' dance t'! What air ye, an ornament? Hain't this a celebration? Then grease yer elbow an' go it!

FIDDLER. [*seizes a drink which the* OLD FARMER *holds out to him and downs it*] Here goes! [*He starts to fiddle "Lady of the Lake." Four young fellows and four girls form in two lines and dance a square dance. The* FIDDLER *shouts directions for the different movements, keeping his words in the rhythm of the music and interspersing them with jocular personal remarks to the dancers themselves. The people seated along the walls stamp their feet and clap their hands in unison.* CABOT *is especially active in this respect. Only* ABBIE *remains apathetic, staring at the door as if she were alone in a silent room.*]

FIDDLER. Swing your partner t' the right! That's it, Jim! Give her a b'ar hug. Her Maw hain't lookin'. [*Laughter*] Change partners! That suits ye, don't it, Essie, now ye got Reub afore ye? Look at her redden up, will ye? Waal, life is short an' so's love, as the feller says. [*Laughter.*]

CABOT. [*excitedly, stamping his foot*] Go it, boys! Go it, gals!

FIDDLER. [*with a wink at the others*] Ye're the spryest seventy-six ever I sees, Ephraim! Now if ye'd on'y good eye-sight . . . ! [*Suppressed laughter. He gives* CABOT *no chance to retort but roars*] Promenade! Ye're walkin' like a bride down the aisle, Sarah! Waal, while they's life they's allus hope, I've heerd tell. Swing your partner to the left! Gosh A'mighty, look at Johnny Cook high-steppin'! They hain't goin' t' be much strength left fur howin' in the corn lot t'morrow. [*Laughter.*]

CABOT. Go it! Go it! [*Then suddenly, unable to restrain himself any longer, he prances into the midst of the dancers, scattering them, waving his arms about wildly*] Ye're all hoofs! Git out o' my road! Give me room! I'll show ye dancin'. Ye're all too soft! [*He pushes them roughly away. They crowd back toward the walls, muttering, looking at him resentfully.*]

FIDDLER. [*jeeringly*] Go it, Ephraim! Go it! [*He starts "Pop, Goes the Weasel," increasing the tempo with every verse until at the end he is fiddling crazily as fast as he can go.*]

CABOT. [*starts to dance, which he does very well and with tremendous vigor. Then he begins to improvise, cuts incredibly grotesque capers, leaping up and cracking his heels together, prancing around in a circle with body bent in an Indian war dance, then suddenly straightening up and kicking as high as he can with both legs. He is like a monkey on a string. And all the while he intersperses his antics with shouts and derisive comments*] Whoop! Here's dancin' fur ye! Whoop! See that! Seventy-six, if I'm a day! Hard as iron yet! Beatin' the young 'uns like I allus done! Look at me! I'd invite ye t' dance on my hundredth birthday on'y ye'll all be dead by then. Ye're a sickly generation! Yer hearts air pink, not red! Yer veins is full o' mud an' water! I be the on'y man in the county! Whoop! See that! I'm a Injun! I've killed Injuns in the West afore ye was born— an' skulped 'em too! They's a arrer wound on my backside I c'd show ye! The hull tribe chased me. I outrun 'em all—with the arrer stuck in me! An' I tuk vengeance on 'em. Ten eyes fur an eye, that was my motter! Whoop! Look at me! I kin kick the ceilin' off the room! Whoop!

FIDDLER. [*stops playing—exhaustedly*] God A'mighty, I got enuf. Ye got the devil's strength in ye.

CABOT. [*delightedly*] Did I beat yew, too? Waal, ye played smart. Hev a swig. [*He pours whisky for himself and* FIDDLER. *They drink. The others watch* CABOT *silently with cold, hostile eyes. There is a dead pause. The* FIDDLER *rests.* CABOT *leans against the keg, panting, glaring around him confusedly. In the room above,* EBEN *gets to his feet and tiptoes out the door in rear, appearing a moment later in the other bedroom. He moves silently, even frightenedly, toward the cradle and stands there looking down at the baby. His face is as vague as his reactions are confused, but there is a trace of tenderness, of interested discovery. At the same moment that he reaches the cradle* ABBIE *seems to sense something. She gets up weakly and goes to* CABOT]

ABBIE. I'm goin' up t' the baby.

CABOT. [*with real solicitation*] Air ye able fur the stairs? D'ye want me t' help ye, Abbie?

ABBIE. No. I'm able. I'll be down agen soon.

CABOT. Don't ye git wore out! He needs ye, remember—our son does! [*He grins affectionately, patting her on the back. She shrinks from his touch.*]

ABBIE. [*dully*] Don't—tech me. I'm goin'—up. [*She goes.* CABOT *looks after her. A whisper goes around the room.* CABOT *turns. It ceases. He wipes his forehead steaming with sweat. He is breathing pantingly.*]

CABOT. I'm a-goin' out t' git fresh air. I'm feelin' a mite dizzy. Fiddle up thar! Dance, all o' ye! Here's likker fur them as wants it. Enjoy yerselves. I'll be back. [*He goes, closing the door behind him.*]

FIDDLER. [*sarcastically*] Don't hurry none on our account! [*A supressed laugh. He imitates* ABBIE]. Whar's Eben? [*More laughter.*]

A WOMAN. [*loudly*] What's happened in this house is plain as the nose on yer face! [ABBIE *appears in the doorway upstairs and stands looking in surprise and adoration at* EBEN *who does not see her.*]

A MAN. Ssshh! He's li'ble t' be listenin' at the door. That'd be like him. [*Their voices die to an intensive whispering. Their faces are concentrated on this gossip. A noise as of dead leaves in the wind comes from the room.* CABOT *has come out from the porch and stands by the gate, leaning on it, staring at the sky blinkingly.* ABBIE *comes across the room silently.* EBEN *does not notice her until quite near.*]

EBEN. [*starting*] Abbie!

ABBIE. Ssshh! [*She throws her arms around him. They kiss—then bend over the cradle together*] Ain't he purty?—dead spit 'n' image o' yew!

EBEN. [*pleased*] Air he? I can't tell none.

ABBIE. E-zactly like!

EBEN. [*frowningly*] I don't like this. I don't like lettin' on what's mine's his'n. I been doin' that all my life. I'm gittin' t' the end o' b'arin' it!

ABBIE. [*putting her finger on his lips*] We're doin' the best we kin. We got t' wait. Somethin's bound t' happen. [*She puts her arms around him*] I got t' go back.

EBEN. I'm goin' out. I can't b'ar it with the fiddle playin' an the laughin'.

ABBIE. Don't git feelin' low. I love ye, Eben. Kiss me. [*He kisses her. They remain in each other's arms.*]

CABOT. [*at the gate, confusedly*] Even the music can't drive it out—somethin'. Ye kin feel it droppin' off the elums, climbin' up the roof, sneakin' down the chimney, pokin' in the corners! They's no peace in houses, they's no rest livin' with folks. Somethin's always livin' with ye. [*With a deep sigh*] I'll go t' the barn an' rest a spell. [*He goes wearily toward the barn.*]

FIDDLER. [*tuning up*] Let's celebrate the old skunk gittin' fooled! We kin have some fun now he's went. [*He starts to fiddle "Turkey in the Straw." There is real merriment now. The young folks get up to dance.*]

SCENE TWO

*A half hour later—Exterior—*EBEN *is standing by the gate looking up at the sky, an expression of dumb pain bewildered by itself on his face.* CABOT *appears, returning from the barn, walking wearily, his eyes on the ground. He sees* EBEN *and his whole mood immediately changes. He becomes excited, a cruel, triumphant grin comes to his lips, he* *strides up and slaps* EBEN *on the back. From within comes the whining of the fiddle and the noise of stamping feet and laughing voices.*

CABOT. So har ye be!

EBEN. [*startled, stares at him with hatred for a moment—then dully*] Ay-eh.

CABOT. [*surveying him jeeringly*] Why hain't ye been in t' dance? They was all axin' fur ye.

EBEN. Let 'em ax!

CABOT. They's a hull passel o' purty gals.

EBEN. T' hell with 'em!

CABOT. Ye'd ought t' be marryin' one o' 'em soon.

EBEN. I hain't marryin' no one.

CABOT. Ye might 'arn a share o' a farm that way.

EBEN. [*with a sneer*] Like yew did, ye mean? I hain't that kind.

CABOT. [*stung*] Ye lie! 'Twas yer Maw's folks aimed t' steal my farm from me.

EBEN. Other folks don't say so. [*After a pause—defiantly*] An' I got a farm, anyways!

CABOT. [*derisively*] Whar?

EBEN. [*stamps a foot on the ground*] Har!

CABOT. [*throws his head back and laughs coarsely*] Ho-ho! Ye hev, hev ye? Waal, that's a good un!

EBEN. [*controlling himself—grimly*] Ye'll see!

CABOT. [*stares at him suspiciously, trying to make him out—a pause—then with scornful confidence*] Ay-eh. I'll see. So'll ye. It's ye that's blind—blind as a mole underground. [EBEN *suddenly laughs, one short sardonic bark:* "Ha." *A pause.* CABOT *peers at him with renewed suspicion*] What air ye hawin' 'bout? [EBEN *turns away without answering.* CABOT *grows angry*] God A'mighty, yew air a dumb dunce! They's nothin' in that thick skull o' your'n but noise—like a empty keg it be! [EBEN *doesn't seem to hear.* CABOT's *rage grows*] Yewr farm! God A'mighty! If ye wa'n't a born donkey ye'd know ye'll never own stick nor stone on it, specially now arter him bein' born. It's his'n, I tell ye—his'n arter I die—but I'll live a hundred jest t' fool ye all—an' he'll be growed then—yewr age a'most! [EBEN *laughs again his sardonic* "Ha." *This drives* CABOT *into a fury*] Ha? Ye think ye kin git 'round that someways, do ye? Waal, it'll be her'n, too—Abbie's—ye won't git 'round her—she knows yer tricks—she'll be too much fur ye—she wants the farm her'n—she was afeerd o' ye—she told me ye was sneakin' 'round tryin' t' make love t' her t' git her on yer side . . . ye . . . ye mad fool, ye! [*He raises his clenched fists threateningly.*]

EBEN. [*is confronting him, choking with rage*] Ye lie, ye old skunk! Abbie never said no sech thing!

CABOT. [*suddenly triumphant when he sees how shaken* EBEN *is*] She did. An' I says, I'll blow his brains t' the top o' them elums—an' she says no, that hain't sense, who'll ye git t' help ye on the farm in his place—an' then she says yew'n me ought t' have a son—I know we kin, she says—an' I says, if we do, ye kin have anythin' I've got ye've a mind t'. An' she says, I wants Eben cut off so's this farm'll be mine when ye die! [*With terrible gloating*] An' that's what's happened, hain't it? An' the farm's her'n! An' the dust o' the road—that's you'rn! Ha! Now who's hawin'?

EBEN. [*has been listening, petrified with grief and rage—suddenly laughs wildly and brokenly*] Ha-ha-ha! So that's her sneakin' game—all along!—like I suspicioned at fust—t' swaller it all—an' me, too . . . ! [*Madly*] I'll murder her! [*He springs toward the porch but* CABOT *is quicker and gets in between.*]

CABOT. No, ye don't!

EBEN. Git out o' my road! [*He tries to throw* CABOT *aside. They grapple in what becomes immediately a murderous struggle. The old man's concentrated strength is too much for* EBEN. CABOT *gets one hand on his throat and presses him back across the stone wall. At the same moment,* ABBIE *comes out on the porch. With a stifled cry she runs toward them.*]

ABBIE. Eben! Ephraim! [*She tugs at the hand on* EBEN's *throat*] Let go, Ephraim! Ye're chokin' him!

CABOT. [*removes his hand and flings* EBEN *sideways full length on the grass, gasping and choking. With a cry,* ABBIE *kneels beside him trying to take his head on her lap, but he pushes her away.* CABOT *stands looking down with fierce triumph*] Ye needn't t've fret, Abbie, I wa'n't aimin' t' kill him. He hain't wuth hangin' fur—not by a hell of a sight! [*More and more triumphantly*] Seventy-six an' him not thirty yit—an' look whar he be fur thinkin' his Paw was easy! No, by God, I hain't easy! An' him upstairs, I'll raise him t' be like me! [*He turns to leave them*] I'm goin' in an' dance!—sing an' celebrate! [*He walks to the porch— then turns with a great grin*] I don't calc'late it's left in him, but if he gits pesky, Abbie, ye jest sing out. I'll come a-runnin' an' by the Etarnal, I'll put him across my knee an' birch him! Ha-ha-ha! [*He goes into the house laughing. A moment later his loud "whoop" is heard.*]

ABBIE. [*tenderly*] Eben. Air ye hurt? [*She tries to kiss him but he pushes her violently away and struggles to a sitting position.*]

EBEN. [*gaspingly*] T'hell—with ye!

ABBIE. [*not believing her ears*] It's me, Eben—Abbie—don't ye know me?

EBEN. [*glowering at her with hatred*] Ay-eh—I know ye—now! [*He suddenly breaks down, sobbing weakly.*]

ABBIE. [*fearfully*] Eben—what's happened t' ye—why did ye look at me 's if ye hated me?

EBEN. [*violently, between sobs and gasps*] I do hate ye! Ye're a whore—a damn trickin' whore!

ABBIE. [*shrinking back horrified*] Eben! Ye don't know what ye're sayin'!

EBEN. [*scrambling to his feet and following her—accusingly*] Ye're nothin' but a stinkin' passel o' lies! Ye've been lyin' t' me every word ye spoke, day an' night, since we fust—done it. Ye've kept sayin' ye loved me. . . .

ABBIE. [*frantically*] I do love ye! [*She takes his hand but he flings hers away.*]

EBEN. [*unheeding*] Ye've made a fool o' me—a sick, dumb fool—a-purpose! Ye've been on'y playin' yer sneakin', stealin' game all along—gittin' me t' lie with ye so's ye'd hev a son he'd think was his'n, an' makin' him promise he'd give ye the farm and let me eat dust, if ye did git him a son! [*Staring at her with anguished, bewildered eyes*] They must be a devil livin' in ye! T'ain't human t' be as bad as that be!

ABBIE. [*stunned—dully*] He told yew . . . ?

EBEN. Hain't it true? It hain't no good in yew lyin'.

ABBIE. [*pleadingly*] Eben, listen—ye must listen—it was long ago—afore we done nothin'—yew was scornin' me—goin' t' see Min—when I was lovin' ye— an' I said it t' him t' git vengeance on ye!

EBEN. [*unheedingly. With tortured passion*] I wish ye was dead! I wish I was dead along with ye afore this come! [*Ragingly*] But I'll git my vengeance too! I'll pray Maw t' come back t' help me—t' put her cuss on yew an' him!

ABBIE. [*brokenly*] Don't ye, Eben! Don't ye! [*She throws herself on her knees before him, weeping*] I didn't mean t' do bad t' ye! Fergive me, won't ye?

EBEN. [*not seeming to hear her—fiercely*] I'll git squar' with the old skunk—an' yew! I'll tell him the truth 'bout the son he's so proud o'! Then I'll leave ye here t' pizen each other—with Maw comin' out o' her grave at nights—an' I'll go t' the gold fields o' Californi-a whar Sim an' Peter be!

ABBIE. [*terrified*] Ye won't leave me? Ye can't!

EBEN. [*with fierce determination*] I'm a-goin', I tell ye! I'll git rich thar an' come back an' fight him fur the farm he stole—an' I'll kick ye both out in the road—t' beg an' sleep in the woods—an' yer son along with ye—t' starve an' die! [*He is hysterical at the end.*]

ABBIE. [*with a shudder—humbly*] He's yewr son, too, Eben.

EBEN. [*torturedly*] I wish he never was born! I wish he'd die this minit! I wish I'd never sot eyes on him! It's him—yew havin' him—a-purpose t' steal—that's changed everythin'!

ABBIE. [*gently*] Did ye believe I loved ye—afore he come?

EBEN. Ay-eh—like a dumb ox!

ABBIE. An' ye don't believe no more?

EBEN. B'lieve a lyin' thief! Ha!

ABBIE. [*shudders—then humbly*] An' did ye r'ally love me afore?

EBEN. [*brokenly*] Ay-eh—an' ye was trickin' me!

ABBIE. An' ye don't love me now!

EBEN. [*violently*] I hate ye, I tell ye!

ABBIE. An' ye're truly goin' West—goin' t' leave me—all account o' him being born?

EBEN. I'm a-goin' in the mornin'—or may God strike me t' hell!

ABBIE. [*after a pause—with a dreadful cold intensity—slowly*] If that's what his comin's done t' me—killin' yewr love—takin' yew away—my on'y joy—the on'y joy I ever knowed—like heaven t' me—purtier'n heaven—then I hate him, too, even if I be his Maw!

EBEN. [*bitterly*] Lies! Ye love him! He'll steal the farm fur ye! [*Brokenly*] But t'ain't the farm so much—not no more—it's yew foolin' me—gittin' me t' love ye—lyin' yew loved me—jest t' git a son t' steal!

ABBIE. [*distractedly*] He won't steal! I'd kill him fust! I do love ye! I'll prove t' ye . . . !

EBEN. [*harshly*] T'ain't no use lyin' no more. I'm deaf t' ye! [*He turns away*] I hain't seein' ye agen. Good-by!

ABBIE. [*pale with anguish*] Hain't ye even goin' t' kiss me—not once—arter all we loved?

EBEN. [*in a hard voice*] I hain't wantin' t' kiss ye never agen! I'm wantin' t' forgit I ever sot eyes on ye!

ABBIE. Eben!—ye mustn't—wait a spell—I want t' tell ye. . . .

EBEN. I'm a-goin' in t' git drunk. I'm a-goin' t' dance.

ABBIE. [*clinging to his arm—with passionate earnestness*] If I could make it—'s if he'd never come up between us—if I could prove t' ye I wa'n't schemin' t' steal from ye—so's everythin' could be jest the same with us, lovin' each other jest the same, kissin' an' happy the same's we've been happy afore he come—if I could do it—ye'd love me agen, wouldn't ye? Ye'd kiss me agen? Ye wouldn't never leave me, would ye?

EBEN. [*moved*] I calc'late not. [*Then shaking her hand off his arm—with a bitter smile*] But ye hain't God, be ye?

ABBIE. [*exultantly*] Remember ye've promised! [*Then with strange intensity*] Mebbe I kin take back one thin' God does!

EBEN. [*peering at her*] Ye're gittin' cracked, hain't ye? [*Then going towards door*] I'm a-goin' t' dance.

ABBIE. [*calls after him intensely*] I'll prove t' ye! I'll prove I love ye better'n. . . . [*He goes in the door, not seeming to hear. She remains standing where she is looking after him—then she finishes desperately*] Better'n everythin' else in the world!

SCENE THREE

Just before dawn in the morning—shows the kitchen and CABOT's *bedroom. In the kitchen, by the light of a tallow candle on the table,* EBEN *is sitting, his chin propped on his hands, his drawn face blank and expressionless. His carpetbag is on the floor beside him. In the bedroom, dimly lighted by a small whale-oil lamp,* CABOT *lies asleep.* ABBIE *is bending over the cradle, listening, her face full of terror yet with an undercurrent of desperate triumph. Suddenly, she breaks down and sobs, appears about to throw herself on her knees beside the cradle; but the old man turns restlessly, groaning in his sleep, and she controls herself, and, shrinking away from the cradle with a gesture of horror, backs swiftly toward the door in rear and goes out. A moment later she comes into the kitchen and, running to* EBEN, *flings her arms about his neck and kisses him wildly. He hardens himself, he remains unmoved and cold, he keeps his eyes straight ahead.*

ABBIE. [*hysterically*] I done it, Eben! I told ye I'd do it! I've proved I love ye—better'n everythin'—so's ye can't never doubt me no more!

EBEN. [*dully*] Whatever ye done, it hain't no good now.

ABBIE. [*wildly*] Don't ye say that! Kiss me, Eben, won't ye? I need ye t' kiss me arter what I done! I need ye t' say ye love me!

EBEN. [*kisses her without emotion—dully*] That's fur good-by. I'm a-goin' soon.

ABBIE. No! No! Ye won't go—not now!

EBEN. [*going on with his own thoughts*] I been a-thinkin'—an' I hain't goin' t' tell Paw nothin'. I'll leave Maw t' take vengeance on ye. If I told him, the old skunk'd jest be stinkin' mean enuf to take it out on that baby. [*His voice showing emotion in spite of him*] An' I don't want nothin' bad t' happen t' him. He hain't t' blame fur yew. [*He adds with a certain queer pride*] An' he looks like me! An' by God, he's mine! An' some day I'll be a-comin' back an' . . . !

ABBIE. [*too absorbed in her own thoughts to listen to him—pleadingly*] They's no cause fur ye t' go now—they's no sense—it's all the same's it was—they's nothin' come b'tween us now—arter what I done!

EBEN. [*something in her voice arouses him. He stares at her a bit frightenedly*] Ye look mad, Abbie. What did ye do?

ABBIE. I—I killed him, Eben.

EBEN. [*amazed*] Ye killed him?

ABBIE. [*dully*] Ay-eh.

EBEN. [*recovering from his astonishment—savagely*] An' serves him right! But we got t' do somethin' quick t' make it look s'if the old skunk'd killed himself when he was drunk. We kin prove by 'em all how drunk he got.

ABBIE. [*wildly*] No! No! Not him! [*Laughing distractedly*] But that's what I ought t' done, hain't it? I oughter killed him instead! Why didn't ye tell me?

EBEN. [*appalled*] Instead? What d'ye mean?

ABBIE. Not him.

EBEN. [*his face grown ghastly*] Not—not that baby!

ABBIE. [*dully*] Ay-eh!

EBEN. [*falls to his knees as if he'd been struck—his voice trembling with horror*] Oh, God A'mighty! A'mighty God! Maw, whar was ye, why didn't ye stop her?

ABBIE. [*simply*] She went back t' her grave that night we fust done it, remember? I hain't felt her about since. [*A pause.* EBEN *hides his head in his hands, trembling all over as if he had the ague. She goes on dully*] I left the piller over his little face. Then he killed himself. He stopped breathin'. [*She begins to weep softly.*]

EBEN. [*rage beginning to mingle with grief*] He looked like me. He was mine, damn ye!

ABBIE. [*slowly and brokenly*] I didn't want t' do it. I hated myself fur doin' it. I loved him. He was so purty—dead spit 'n' image o' yew. But I loved yew more—an' yew was goin' away—far off whar I'd never see ye agen, never kiss ye, never feel ye pressed agin me agen—an' ye said ye hated me fur havin' him—ye said ye hated him an' wished he was dead—ye said if it hadn't been fur him comin' it'd be the same's afore between us.

EBEN. [*unable to endure this, springs to his feet in a fury, threatening her, his twitching fingers seeming to reach out for her throat*] Ye lie! I never said—I never dreamed ye'd—I'd cut off my head afore I'd hurt his finger!

ABBIE. [*piteously, sinking on her knees*] Eben, don't ye look at me like that—hatin' me—not after what I done fur ye—fur us—so's we could be happy agen—

EBEN. [*furiously now*] Shut up, or I'll kill ye! I see yer game now—the same old sneakin' trick—ye're aimin' t' blame me fur the murder ye done!

ABBIE. [*moaning—putting her hands over her ears*] Don't ye, Eben! Don't ye! [*She grasps his legs.*]

EBEN. [*his mood suddenly changing to horror, shrinks away from her*] Don't ye tech me! Ye're pizen! How could ye—t' murder a pore little critter—Ye must've swapped yer soul t' hell! [*Suddenly raging*] Ha! I kin see why ye done it! Not the lies ye jest told—but 'cause ye wanted t' steal agen—steal the last thin' ye'd left me—my part o' him—no, the hull o' him—ye saw he looked like me—ye knowed he was all mine—an' ye couldn't b'ar it—I know ye! Ye killed him fur bein' mine! [*All this has driven him almost insane. He makes a rush past her for the door—then turns—shaking both fists at her, violently*] But I'll take vengeance now! I'll git the Sheriff! I'll tell him everythin'! Then I'll sing "I'm off to Californi-a!" an' go—gold—Golden Gate—gold sun—fields o' gold in the West! [*This last he half shouts, half croons incoherently, suddenly breaking off passionately*] I'm a-goin' fur the Sheriff t' come an' git ye! I want ye tuk away, locked up from me! I can't stand t' luk at ye! Murderer an' thief 'r not, ye still tempt me! I'll give ye up t' the Sheriff! [*He turns and runs out, around the corner of house, panting and sobbing, and breaks into a swerving sprint down the road.*]

ABBIE. [*struggling to her feet, runs to the door, calling after him*] I love ye, Eben! I love ye! [*She stops at the door weakly, swaying, about to fall*] I don't care what ye do—if ye'll on'y love me agen—[*She falls limply to the floor in a faint.*]

SCENE FOUR

About an hour later. Same as Scene Three. Shows the kitchen and CABOT's *bedroom. It is after dawn. The sky is brilliant with the sunrise. In the kitchen,* ABBIE *sits at the table, her body limp and exhausted, her head bowed down over her arms, her face hidden.*

Upstairs, CABOT *is still asleep but awakens with a start. He looks toward the window and gives a snort of surprise and irritation—throws back the covers and begins hurriedly pulling on his clothes. Without looking behind him, he begins talking to* ABBIE *whom he supposes beside him.*

CABOT. Thunder 'n' lightin', Abbie! I hain't slept this late in fifty year! Looks 's if the sun was full riz a'most. Must've been the dancin' an' likker. Must be gittin' old. I hope Eben's t' wuk. Ye might've tuk the trouble t' rouse me, Abbie. [*He turns—sees no one there—surprised*] Waal—whar air she? Gittin' vittles, I calc'late. [*He tiptoes to the cradle and peers down—proudly*] Mornin', sonny. Purty's a picter! Sleepin' sound. He don't beller all night like most o' 'em. [*He goes quietly out the door in rear—a few moments later enters kitchen—sees* ABBIE*—with satisfaction*] So thar ye be. Ye got any vittles cooked?

ABBIE. [*without moving*] No.

CABOT. [*coming to her, almost sympathetically*] Ye feelin' sick?

ABBIE. No.

CABOT. [*pats her on shoulder. She shudders*] Ye'd best lie down a spell. [*Half jocularly*] Yer son'll be needin' ye soon. He'd ought t' wake up with a gnashin' appetite, the sound way he's sleepin'.

ABBIE. [*shudders—then in a dead voice*] He hain't never goin' t' wake up.

CABOT. [*jokingly*] Takes after me this mornin'. I hain't slept so late in . . .

ABBIE. He's dead.

CABOT. [*stares at her—bewilderedly*] What. . . .

ABBIE. I killed him.

CABOT. [*stepping back from her—aghast*] Air ye drunk—'r crazy—'r . . . !

ABBIE. [*suddenly lifts her head and turns on him—wildly*] I killed him, I tell ye! I smothered him. Go up an' see if ye don't b'lieve me! [CABOT *stares at her a second, then bolts out the rear door, can be heard bounding up the stairs, and rushes into the bedroom and over to the cradle.* ABBIE *has sunk back lifelessly into her former position.* CABOT *puts his hand down on the body in the crib. An expression of fear and horror comes over his face.*]

CABOT. [*shrinking away—tremblingly*] God A'mighty! God A'mighty. [*He stumbles out the door—in a short while returns to the kitchen—comes to* ABBIE, *the stunned expression still on his face—hoarsely*] Why did ye do it? Why? [*As she doesn't answer, he grabs her violently by the shoulder and shakes her*] I ax ye why ye done it! Ye'd better tell me 'r . . . !

ABBIE. [*gives him a furious push which sends him staggering back and springs to her feet—with wild rage and hatred*] Don't ye dare tech me! What right hev ye t' question me 'bout him? He wa'n't yewr son! Think I'd have a son by yew? I'd die fust! I hate the sight o' ye an' allus did! It's yew I should've murdered, if I'd had good sense! I hate ye! I love Eben. I did from the fust. An' he was Eben's son—mine an' Eben's—not your'n!

CABOT. [*stands looking at her dazedly—a pause—finding his words with an effort— dully*] That was it—what I felt—pokin' round the corners—while ye lied— holdin' yerself from me—sayin' ye'd a'ready conceived—[*He lapses into crushed silence—then with a strange emotion*] He's dead, sart'n. I felt his heart. Pore little critter! [*He blinks back one tear, wiping his sleeve across his nose.*]

ABBIE. [*hysterically*] Don't ye! Don't ye! [*She sobs unrestrainedly.*]

CABOT. [*with a concentrated effort that stiffens his body into a rigid line and hardens his face into a stony mask—through his teeth to himself*] I got t' be—like a stone— a rock o' jedgment! [*A pause. He gets complete control over himself—harshly*] If he was Eben's, I be glad he air gone! An' mebbe I suspicioned it all along. I felt they was somethin' onnateral—somewhars—the house got so lonesome—an' cold—drivin' me down t' the barn—t' the beasts o' the field. . . . Ay-eh. I must've suspicioned—somethin'. Ye didn't fool me—not altogether, leastways—I'm too old a bird—growin' ripe on the bough. . . . [*He becomes aware he is wandering, straightens again, looks at* ABBIE *with a cruel grin*] So ye'd liked t' hev murdered me 'stead o' him, would ye? Waal, I'll live to be a hundred! I'll live t' see ye hung! I'll deliver ye up t' the jedgment o' God an' the law! I'll git the Sheriff now. [*Starts for the door.*]

ABBIE. [*dully*] Ye needn't. Eben's gone fur him.

CABOT. [*amazed*] Eben—gone fur the Sheriff?

ABBIE. Ay-eh.

CABOT. T' inform agen ye?

ABBIE. Ay-eh.

CABOT. [*considers this—a pause—then in a hard voice*] Waal, I'm thankful fur him savin' me the trouble. I'll git t' wuk. [*He goes to the door—then turns—in a voice full of strange emotion*] He'd ought t' been my son, Abbie. Ye'd ought t' loved me. I'm a man. If ye'd loved me, I'd never told no Sheriff on ye no matter what ye did, if they was t' brile me alive!

ABBIE. [*defensively*] They's more to it nor yew know, makes him tell.

CABOT. [*dryly*] Fur yewr sake, I hope they be. [*He goes out—comes around to the gate—stares up at the sky. His control relaxes. For a moment he is old and weary. He murmurs despairingly*] God A'mighty, I be lonsomer'n ever! [*He hears running footsteps from the left, immediately is himself again.* EBEN *runs in, panting exhaustedly, wild-eyed and mad looking. He lurches through the gate.* CABOT *grabs him by the shoulder.* EBEN *stares at him dumbly*] Did ye tell the Sheriff?

EBEN. [*nodding stupidly*] Ay-eh.

CABOT. [*gives him a push away that sends him sprawling—laughing with withering contempt*] Good fur ye! A prime chip o' yer Maw ye be! [*He goes toward the barn, laughing harshly.* EBEN *scrambles to his feet. Suddenly* CABOT *turns—grimly threatening*] Git off this farm when the Sheriff takes her—or, by God, he'll have t' come back an' git me fur murder, too! [*He stalks off.* EBEN *does not appear to have heard him. He runs to the door and comes into the kitchen.* ABBIE *looks up with a cry of anguished joy.* EBEN *stumbles over and throws himself on his knees beside her sobbing brokenly.*]

EBEN. Fergive me!

ABBIE. [*happily*] Eben! [*She kisses him and pulls his head over against her breast.*]

EBEN. I love ye! Fergive me!

ABBIE. [*ecstatically*] I'd fergive ye all the sins in hell fur sayin' that! [*She kisses his head, pressing it to her with a fierce passion of possession.*]

EBEN. [*brokenly*] But I told the Sheriff. He's comin' fur ye!

ABBIE. I kin b'ar what happens t' me—now!

EBEN. I woke him up. I told him. He says, wait 'til I git dressed. I was waiting. I got to thinkin' o' yew. I got to thinkin' how I'd loved ye. It hurt like somethin' was bustin' in my chest an' head. I got t' cryin'. I knowed sudden I loved ye yet, an' allus would love ye!

ABBIE. [*caressing his hair—tenderly*] My boy, hain't ye!

EBEN. I begun t' run back. I cut across the fields an' through the woods. I thought ye might have time t' run away—with me—an' . . .

ABBIE. [*shaking her head*] I got t' take my punishment—t' pay fur my sin.

EBEN. Then I want t' share it with ye.

ABBIE. Ye didn't do nothin'.

EBEN. I put it in yer head. I wisht he was dead! I as much as urged ye t' do it!

ABBIE. No. It was me alone!

EBEN. I'm as guilty as yew be! He was the child o' our sin.

ABBIE. [*lifting her head as if defying God*] I don't repent that sin! I hain't askin' God t' fergive that!

EBEN. Nor me—but it led up t' the other—an' the murder ye did, ye did 'count o' me—an' it's my murder, too, I'll tell the Sheriff—an' if ye deny it, I'll say we planned it t'gether—an' they'll all b'lieve me, fur they suspicion everythin' we've done, an' it'll seem likely an' true to 'em. An' it is true—way down. I did help ye—somehow.

ABBIE. [*laying her head on his—sobbing*] No! I don't want yew t' suffer!

EBEN. I got t' pay fur my part o' the sin! An' I'd suffer wuss leavin' ye, goin' West, thinkin' o' ye day an' night, bein' out when yew was in—[*Lowering his voice*] 'r bein' alive when yew was dead. [*A pause*] I want t' share with ye, Abbie—prison 'r death 'r hell 'r anythin'! [*He looks into her eyes and forces a trembling smile*] If I'm sharin' with ye, I won't feel lonesome, leastways.

ABBIE. [*weakly*] Eben! I won't let ye! I can't let ye!

EBEN. [*kissing her—tenderly*] Ye can't he'p yerself. I got ye beat fur once!

ABBIE. [*forcing a smile—adoringly*] I hain't beat—s'long's I got ye!

EBEN. [*hears the sound of feet outside*] Ssshh! Listen! They've come t' take us!

ABBIE. No, it's him. Don't give him no chance to fight ye, Eben. Don't say nothin'—no matter what he says. An' I won't neither. [*It is CABOT. He comes up from the barn in a great state of excitement and strides into the house and then into the kitchen. EBEN is kneeling beside ABBIE, his arm around her, hers around him. They stare straight ahead.*]

CABOT. [*stares at them, his face hard. A long pause—vindictively*] Ye make a slick pair o' murderin' turtle doves! Ye'd ought t' be both hung on the same limb an' left thar t' swing in the breeze an' rot—a warnin' t' old fools like me t' b'ar their lonesomeness alone—an' fur young fools like ye t' hobble their lust. [*A pause. The excitement returns to his face, his eyes snap, he looks a bit crazy*] I couldn't work today. I couldn't take no interest. T' hell with the farm! I'm leavin' it! I've turned the cows an' other stock loose! I've druv 'em into the woods whar they kin be free! By freein' 'em, I'm freein' myself! I'm quittin' here today! I'll set fire t' house an' barn an' watch 'em burn, an' I'll leave yer Maw t' haunt the ashes, an' I'll will the fields back t' God, so that nothin' human kin never touch 'em! I'll be a-goin' to Californi-a— t' jine Simeon an' Peter—true sons o' mine if they be dumb fools—an' the Cabots'll find Solomon's Mines t'gether! [*He suddenly cuts a mad caper*] Whoop! What was the song they sung? "Oh, Californi-a! That's the land fur me." [*He sings this—then gets on his knees by the floor-board under which the money was hid*] An' I'll sail thar on one o' the finest clippers I kin find! I've got the money! Pity ye didn't know whar this was hidden so's ye could steal. . . . [*He has pulled up the board. He stares—feels—stares again. A pause of dead silence. He slowly turns, slumping into a sitting position on the floor, his eyes like those of a dead fish, his face the sickly green of an attack of nausea. He swallows painfully several times—forces a weak smile at last*] So—ye did steal it!

EBEN. [*emotionlessly*] I swapped it t' Sim an' Peter fur their share o' the farm— t' pay their passage t' Californi-a.

CABOT. [*with one sardonic*] Ha! [*He begins to recover. Gets slowly to his feet—strangely*]

I calc'late God give it to 'em—not yew! God's hard, not easy! Mebbe they's easy gold in the West but it hain't God's gold. It hain't fur me. I kin hear His voice warnin' me agen t' be hard an' stay on my farm. I kin see his hand usin' Eben t' steal t' keep me from weakness. I kin feel I be in the palm o' His hand, His fingers guidin' me. [*A pause—then he mutters sadly*] It's a-goin' t' be lonesomer now than ever it war afore—an' I'm gittin' old, Lord—ripe on the bough. . . . [*Then stiffening*] Waal—what d'ye want? God's lonesome, hain't He? God's hard an' lonesome! [*A pause. The* SHERIFF *with two men comes up the road from the left. They move cautiously to the door. The* SHERIFF *knocks on it with the butt of his pistol.*]

SHERIFF. Open in the name o' the law. [*They start.*]

CABOT. They've come fur ye. [*He goes to the rear door*] Come in, Jim! [*The three men enter.* CABOT *meets them in doorway*] Jest a minit, Jim. I got 'em safe here. [*The* SHERIFF *nods. He and his companions remain in the doorway.*]

EBEN. [*suddenly calls*] I lied this mornin', Jim. I helped her to do it. Ye kin take me, too.

ABBIE. [*brokenly*] No!

CABOT. Take 'em both. [*He comes forward—stares at* EBEN *with a trace of grudging admiration*] Purty good—fur yew! Waal, I got t' round up the stock. Good-by.

EBEN. Good-by.

ABBIE. Good-by. [*CABOT turns and strides past the men—comes out and around the corner of the house, his shoulders squared, his face stony, and stalks grimly toward the barn. In the meantime the* SHERIFF *and men have come into the room.*]

SHERIFF. [*embarrassedly*] Waal—we'd best start.

ABBIE. Wait. [*Turns to* ABBIE] I love ye, Eben.

EBEN. I love ye, Abbie. [*They kiss. The three men grin and shuffle embarrassedly.* EBEN *takes* ABBIE's *hand. They go out the door in rear, the men following, and come from the house, walking hand in hand to the gate.* EBEN *stops there and points to the sunrise sky*] Sun's a-rizin'. Purty, hain't it?

ABBIE. Ay-eh. [*They both stand for a moment looking up raptly in attitudes strangely aloof and devout.*]

SHERIFF. [*looking around at the farm enviously—to his companions*] It's a jim-dandy farm, no denyin'. Wished I owned it!

CURTAIN

[1924]

Jean Anouilh   *1910–*

BECKET
or
THE HONOR OF GOD

Translated by Lucienne Hill

CHARACTERS

HENRY II	1ST ENGLISH BARON
THOMAS BECKET	2ND ENGLISH BARON
ARCHBISHOP OF CANTERBURY	3RD ENGLISH BARON
GILBERT FOLLIOT	4TH ENGLISH BARON
BISHOP OF YORK	QUEEN MOTHER
SAXON PEASANT	THE QUEEN
HIS SON	LOUIS, KING OF FRANCE
GWENDOLEN	THE POPE

ACT ONE

An indeterminate set, with pillars. We are in the cathedral. Center stage: BECKET's *tomb; a stone slab with a name carved on it. Two* SENTRIES *come in and take up their position upstage. Then the* KING *enters from the back. He is wearing his crown, and is naked under a big cloak. A* PAGE *follows at a distance. The* KING *hesitates a moment before the tomb; then removes his cloak with a swift movement and the* PAGE *takes it away. He falls to his knees on the stone floor and prays, alone, naked, in the middle of the stage. Behind the pillars, in the shadows, one senses the disquieting presence of unseen lookers-on.*

KING. Well, Thomas Becket, are you satisfied? I am naked at your tomb and your monks are coming to flog me. What an end to our story! You, rotting in this tomb, larded with my barons' dagger thrusts, and I, naked, shivering in the draughts, and waiting like an idiot for those brutes to come and thrash me. Don't you think we'd have done better to understand each other?
   [BECKET *in his Archbishop's robes, just as he was on the day of his death, has appeared on the side of the stage, from behind a pillar. He says softly:*
BECKET. Understand each other? It wasn't possible.
KING. I said, "In all save the honor of the realm." It was you who taught me that slogan, after all.
BECKET. I answered you, "In all save the honor of God." We were like two deaf men talking.
KING. How cold it was on that bare plain at La Ferté-Bernard, the last time we two met! It's funny, it's always been cold, in our story. Save at the beginning, when we were friends. We had a few fine summer evenings together, with the girls . . . [*He says suddenly:*] Did you love Gwendolen, Archbishop? Did you hate me, that night when I said, "I am the King," and took her from you? Perhaps that's what you never could forgive me for?

1374

BECKET. [*Quietly*] I've forgotten.

KING. Yet we were like two brothers, weren't we—you and I? That night it was a childish prank—a lusty lad shouting "I am the King!" . . . I was so young . . . And every thought in my head came from you, you know that.

BECKET. [*Gently, as if to a little boy*] Pray, Henry, and don't talk so much.

KING. [*Irritably*] If you think I'm in the mood for praying at the moment . . . [BECKET *quietly withdraws into the darkness and disappears during the* KING'S *next speech.*] I can see them through my fingers, spying on me from the aisles. Say what you like, they're an oafish lot, those Saxons of yours! To give oneself over naked to those ruffians! With my delicate skin . . . Even you'd be afraid. Besides, I'm ashamed. Ashamed of this whole masquerade. I need them though, that's the trouble. I have to rally them to my cause, against my son, who'll gobble up my kingdom if I let him. So I've come to make my peace with their Saint. You must admit it's funny. You've become a Saint and here am I, the King, desperately in need of that great amorphous mass which could do nothing, up till now, save lie inert beneath its own enormous weight, cowering under blows, and which is all-powerful now. What use are conquests, when you stop to think?[1] They are England now, because of their vast numbers, and the rate at which they breed—like rabbits, to make good the massacres. But one must always pay the price—that's another thing you taught me, Thomas Becket, when you were still advising me . . . You taught me everything . . . [*Dreamily*] Ah, those were happy times . . . At the peep of dawn—well, our dawn that is, around noon, because we always went to bed very late—you'd come into my room, as I was emerging from the bathhouse, rested, smiling, debonair, as fresh as if we'd never spent the entire night drinking and whoring through the town. [*He says a little sourly*] That's another thing you were better at than me . . .

[*The* PAGE *has come in. He wraps a white towel around the* KING *and proceeds to rub him down. Off stage is heard for the first time—we will hear it often—the gay, ironical Scottish marching song which* BECKET *is always whistling.*

The lighting changes. We are still in the empty cathedral. Then, a moment or so later, BECKET *will draw aside a curtain and reveal the* KING'S *room. Their manner, his and the* KING'S, *faraway at first, like a memory relived, will gradually become more real.*

THOMAS BECKET, *dressed as a nobleman, elegant, young, charming, in his short doublet and pointed, upturned shoes, comes in blithely and greets the* KING.]

BECKET. My respects, my Lord!

KING. [*His face brightening*] Oh, Thomas . . . I thought you were still asleep.

BECKET. I've already been for a short gallop to Richmond and back, my Lord. There's a divine nip in the air.

KING. [*His teeth chattering*] To think you actually like the cold! [*To the* PAGE] Rub harder, pig!

Smiling, BECKET *pushes the* PAGE *aside and proceeds to rub the* KING *himself.*

[*To the* PAGE] Throw a log on the fire and get out. Come back and dress me later.

BECKET. My prince, I shall dress you myself. [*The* PAGE *goes.*]

---

[1] King Henry is alluding to the conquest of England by the Normans in 1066 and the subsequent enslavement of the indigenous Saxons. Henry himself is the great-grandson of William the Conqueror while Becket is supposedly a descendant of the displaced Saxon nobility. In actual fact Thomas Becket was a Norman, but Anouilh based his play on the romanticized version of Becket's life in Augustin Thierry's *The Conquest of England by the Normans* (1825).

KING. Nobody rubs me down the way you do. Thomas, what would I do without you? You're a nobleman, why do you play at being my valet? If I asked my barons to do this, they'd start a civil war!

BECKET. [*Smiling*] They'll come round to it in time, when Kings have learnt to play their role. I am your servant, my prince, that's all. Helping you to govern or helping you get warm again is part of the same thing to me. I like helping you.

KING. [*With an affectionate little gesture*] My little Saxon! At the beginning, when I told them I was taking you into my service, do you know what they all said? They said you'd seize the chance to knife me in the back one day.

BECKET. [*Smiling as he dresses him*] Did you believe them, my prince?

KING. N . . . no. I was a bit scared at first. You know I scare easily . . . But you looked so well brought up, beside those brutes. However did you come to speak French without a trace of an English accent?

BECKET. My parents were able to keep their lands by agreeing to "collaborate," as they say, with the King your father. They sent me to France as a boy to acquire a good French accent.

KING. To France? Not to Normandy?

BECKET. [*Still smiling*] That was their one patriotic conceit. They loathed the Norman accent.

KING. [*Distinctly*] Only the accent?

BECKET. [*Lightly and inscrutably*] My father was a very severe man. I would never have taken the liberty of questioning him on his personal convictions while he was alive. And his death shed no light on them, naturally. He managed, by collaborating, to amass a considerable fortune. As he was also a man of rigid principles, I imagine he contrived to do it in accordance with his conscience. That's a little piece of sleight of hand that men of principle are very skillful at in troubled times.

KING. And you?

BECKET. [*Feigning not to understand the question*] I, my Lord?

KING. [*Putting a touch of contempt into his voice, for despite his admiration for Thomas or perhaps because of it, he would like to score a point against him occasionally*] The sleight of hand, were you adept at it too?

BECKET. [*Still smiling*] Mine was a different problem. I was a frivolous man, you'll agree? In fact, it never came up at all. I adore hunting and only the Normans and their protégés had the right to hunt. I adore luxury and luxury was Norman. I adore life and the Saxons' only birthright was slaughter. I'll add that I adore honor.

KING. [*With faint surprise*] And was honor reconciled with collaboration too?

BECKET. [*Lightly*] I had the right to draw my sword against the first Norman nobleman who tried to lay hands on my sister. I killed him in single combat. It's a detail, but it has its points.

KING. [*A little slyly*] You could always have slit his throat and fled into the forest, as so many did.

BECKET. That would have been uncomfortable, and not a lot of use. My sister would immediately have been raped by some other Norman baron, like all the Saxon girls. Today, she is respected. [*Lightly*] My Lord, did I tell you?— My new gold dishes have arrived from Florence. Will my Liege do me the honor of christening them with me at my house?

KING. Gold dishes! You lunatic!

BECKET. I'm setting a new fashion.

KING. I'm your King and I eat off silver!

BECKET. My prince, your expenses are heavy and I have only my pleasures to pay for. The trouble is I'm told they scratch easily. Still, we'll see. I received two forks as well—

KING. Forks?

BECKET. Yes. It's a new instrument, a devilish little thing to look at—and to use too. It's for pronging meat with and carrying it to your mouth. It saves you dirtying your fingers.

KING. But then you dirty the fork?

BECKET. Yes. But it's washable.

KING. So are your fingers. I don't see the point.

BECKET. It hasn't any, practically speaking. But it's refined, it's subtle. It's very un-Norman.

KING. [*With sudden delight*] You must order me a dozen! I want to see my great fat barons' faces, at the first court banquet, when I present them with that! We won't tell them what they're for. We'll have no end of fun with them.

BECKET. [*Laughing*] A dozen! Easy now, my Lord! Forks are very expensive you know! My prince, it's time for the Privy Council.

KING. [*Laughing too*] They won't make head nor tail of them! I bet you they'll think they're a new kind of dagger. We'll have a hilarious time!

[*They go out, laughing, behind the curtain, which draws apart to reveal the same set, with the pillars. The Council Chamber. The Councilors stand waiting. The* KING *and* BECKET *come in, still laughing.*]

KING. [*Sitting in a chair*] Gentlemen, the Council is open. I have summoned you here today to deal with this refusal of the clergy to pay the absentee tax. We really must come to an understanding about who rules this kingdom, the Church—[*The* ARCHBISHOP *tries to speak.*] just a moment, Archbishop!— or me! But before we quarrel, let us take the good news first. I have decided to revive the office of Chancellor of England, keeper of the Triple Lion Seal, and to entrust it to my loyal servant and subject Thomas Becket.

[BECKET *rises in surprise, the color draining from his face.*]

BECKET. My Lord . . . !

KING. [*Roguishly*] What's the matter, Becket? Do you want to go and piss already? True, we both had gallons to drink last night! [*He looks at him with delight.*] Well, that's good! I've managed to surprise you for once, little Saxon.

BECKET. [*Dropping on one knee, says gravely*] My Liege, this is a token of your confidence of which I fear I may not be worthy. I am very young, frivolous perhaps—

KING. I'm young too. And you know more than all of us put together. [*To the others*] He's read books, you know. It's amazing the amount he knows. He'll checkmate the lot of you! Even the Archbishop! As for his frivolity, don't let him fool you! He drinks strong wine, he likes to enjoy himself, but he's a lad who thinks every minute of the time! Sometimes it embarrasses me to feel him thinking away beside me. Get up, Thomas. I never did anything without your advice anyway. Nobody knew it, now everybody will, that's all. [*He bursts out laughing, pulls something out of his pocket and gives it to* BECKET.] There. That's the Seal. Don't lose it. Without the Seal, there's no more England and we'll all have to go back to Normandy. Now, to work!

[*The* ARCHBISHOP *rises, all smiles, now the first shock is over.*]

ARCHBISHOP. May I crave permission to salute, with my Lord's approval, my young and learned archdeacon here? For I was the first—I am weak enough to be proud of pointing it out—to notice him and take him under my wing. The presence at this Council, with the preponderant title of Chancellor of England, of one of our brethren—our spiritual son in a sense—is a guarantee for the Church of this country, that a new era of agreement and mutual understanding is dawning for us all and we must now, in a spirit of confident cooperation—

KING. [*Interrupting*] Etc., etc. . . . Thank you, Archbishop! I knew this nomination would please you. But don't rely too much on Becket to play your game. He is my man. [*He turns to* BECKET, *beaming.*] Come to think of it, I'd forgotten you were a deacon, little Saxon.

BECKET. [*Smiling*] So had I, my prince.

KING. Tell me—I'm not talking about wenching, that's a venial sin—but on the odd occasions when I've seen you fighting, it seems to me you have a mighty powerful sword arm, for a priest! How do you reconcile that with the Church's commandment forbidding a priest to shed blood?

BISHOP OF OXFORD. [*Prudently*] Our young friend is only a deacon, he has not yet taken all his vows, my Lord. The Church in its wisdom knows that youth must have its day and that—under the sacred pretext of a war—a holy war, I mean, of course, young men are permitted to—

KING. [*Interrupting*] All wars are holy wars, Bishop! I defy you to find me a serious belligerent who doesn't have Heaven on his side, in theory. Let's get back to the point.

ARCHBISHOP. By all means, your Highness.

KING. Our customs demand that every landowner with sufficient acreage to maintain one must send a man-at-arms to the quarterly review of troops, fully armed and shield in hand, or pay a tax in silver. Where is my tax?

BISHOP OF OXFORD. *Distingo,*[2] your Highness.

KING. Distinguish as much as you like. I've made up my mind. I want my money. My purse is open, just drop it in. [*He sprawls back in his chair and picks his teeth. To* BECKET.] Thomas, I don't know about you, but I'm starving. Have them bring us something to eat.

[BECKET *makes a sign to the* SENTRY *who goes out. A pause. The* ARCHBISHOP *rises.*]

ARCHBISHOP. A layman who shirks his duty to the State, which is to assist his Prince with arms, should pay the tax. Nobody will question that.

KING. [*Jovially*] Least of all the clergy!

ARCHBISHOP. [*Continuing*] A churchman's duty to the State is to assist his Prince in his prayers, and in his educational and charitable enterprises. He cannot therefore be liable to such a tax unless he neglects those duties.

BISHOP OF OXFORD. Have we refused to pray?

KING. [*Rising in fury*] Gentlemen! Do you seriously think that I am going to let myself be swindled out of more than two thirds of my revenues with arguments of that sort? In the days of the Conquest, when there was booty to be had, our Norman abbots tucked up their robes all right. And lustily too! Sword in fist, hams in the saddle, at cockcrow or earlier! "Let's go to it, Sire! Out with the Saxon scum! It's God's will! It's God's will!" You had to hold them back then! And on the odd occasions when you wanted

---

[2] "I distinguish"—i.e., the Bishop distinguishes on a point of law between ordinary landowners and the clergy.

a little Mass, they never had the time. They'd mislaid their vestments, the churches weren't equipped—any excuse to put it off, for fear they'd miss some of the pickings while their backs were turned!

ARCHBISHOP. Those heroic days are over. It is peacetime now.

KING. Then pay up! I won't budge from that.

[*Turning to* BECKET.]

Come on, Chancellor, say something! Has your new title caught your tongue?

BECKET. May I respectfully draw my Lord Archbishop's attention to one small point?

KING. [*Grunting*] Respectfully, but firmly. You're the Chancellor now.

BECKET. [*Calmly and casually*] England is a ship.

KING. [*Beaming*] Why, that's neat! We must use that, sometime.

BECKET. In the hazards of seafaring, the instinct of self-preservation has always told men that there must be one and only one master on board ship. Mutinous crews who drown their captain always end up, after a short interval of anarchy, by entrusting themselves body and soul to one of their number, who then proceeds to rule over them, more harshly sometimes than their drowned captain.

ARCHBISHOP. My Lord Chancellor—my young friend—there is in fact a saying— the captain is sole master after God. [*He thunders suddenly, with a voice one did not suspect from that frail body.*] After God! [*He crosses himself. All the* BISHOPS *follow suit. The wind of excommunication shivers through the Council. The* KING, *awed, crosses himself too and mumbles, a little cravenly.*]

KING. Nobody's trying to question God's authority, Archbishop.

BECKET. [*Who alone has remained unperturbed*] God steers the ship by inspiring the captain's decisions. But I never heard tell that He gave His instructions directly to the helmsman.

[GILBERT FOLLIOT, *Bishop of London, rises. He is a thin-lipped, venomous man.*]

FOLLIOT. Our young Chancellor is only a deacon—but he is a member of the Church. The few years he has spent out in the tumult of the world cannot have made him forget so soon that it is through His Church Militant and more particularly through the intermediary of our Holy Father the Pope and his Bishops—his qualified representatives—that God dictates His decisions to men!

BECKET. There is a chaplain on board every ship, but he is not required to determine the size of the crew's rations, nor to take the vessel's bearings. My Reverend Lord the Bishop of London—who is the grandson of a sailor they tell me—cannot have forgotten that point either.

FOLLIOT. [*Yelping*] I will not allow personal insinuations to compromise the dignity of a debate of this importance! The integrity and honor of the Church of England are at stake!

KING. [*Cheerfully*] No big words, Bishop. You know as well as I do that all that's at stake is its money. I need money for my wars. Will the Church give me any, yes or no?

ARCHBISHOP. [*Cautiously*] The Church of England has always acknowledged that it was its duty to assist the King, to the best of its ability, in all his needs.

KING. There's a fine speech. But I don't like the past tense, Archbishop. There's something so nostalgic about it. I like the present. And the future. Are you going to pay up?

ARCHBISHOP. Your Highness, I am here to defend the privileges which your illustrious forefather William granted to the Church of England. Would you have the heart to tamper with your forefather's work?

KING. May he rest in peace. His work is inviolable. But where he is now he doesn't need money. I'm still on earth unfortunately, and I do.

FOLLIOT. Your Highness, this is a question of principle!

KING. I'm levying troops, Bishop! I have sent 1,500 German foot soldiers, and three thousand Swiss infantry to help fight the King of France. And nobody has ever paid the Swiss with principles.

BECKET. [*Rises suddenly and says incisively*] I think, your Highness, that it is point-less to pursue a discussion in which neither speaker is listening to the other. The law and custom of the land give us the means of coercion. We will use them.

FOLLIOT. [*Beside himself*] Would you dare—you whom she raised from the obscu-rity of your base origins—to plunge a dagger in the bosom of your Mother Church?

BECKET. My Lord and King has given me his Seal with the Three Lions to guard. My mother is England now.

FOLLIOT. [*Frothing, and slightly ridiculous*] A deacon! A miserable deacon nour-ished in our bosom! Traitor! Little viper! Libertine! Sycophant! Saxon!

KING. My Reverend friend, I suggest you respect my Chancellor, or else I'll call my guards. [*He has raised his voice a little toward the end of this speech. The* GUARDS *come in. Surprised*] Why, here they are! Oh, no, it's my snack. Excuse me, gentlemen, but around noon I need something to peck at or I tend to feel weak. And a King has no right to weaken, I needn't tell you that. I'll have it in my chapel, then I can pray directly afterwards. Come and sit with me, son.

[*He goes out taking* BECKET *with him. The three prelates have risen, deeply offended. They move away, murmuring to one another, with sidelong glances in the direction in which the* KING *went out.*]

FOLLIOT. We must appeal to Rome! We must take a firm line!

YORK. My Lord Archbishop, you are the Primate of England. Your person is inviolate and your decisions on all matters affecting the Church are law in this country. You have a weapon against such intransigence: excommunica-tion.

BISHOP OF OXFORD. We must not use it save with a great deal of prudence, Reverend Bishop. The Church has always triumphed over the centuries, but it has triumphed prudently. Let us bide our time. The King's rages are terrible, but they don't last. They are fires of straw.

FOLLIOT. The little self-seeker he has at his elbow now will make it his business to kindle them. And I think, like the Reverend Bishop, that only the excommu-nication of that young libertine can reduce him to impotence.

[BECKET *comes in.*]

BECKET. My Lords, the King has decided to adjourn his Privy Council. He thinks that a night of meditation will inspire your Lordships with a wise and equitable solution—which he authorizes you to come and submit to him tomorrow.

FOLLIOT. [*With a bitter laugh*] You mean it's time for the hunt.

BECKET. [*Smiling*] Yes, my Lord Bishop, to be perfectly frank with you, it is. Believe me, I am personally most grieved at this difference of opinion and the brutal form it has taken. But I cannot go back on what I said as Chancellor of England. We are all bound, laymen as well as priests, by the same feudal oath we took to the King as our Lord and Sovereign; the oath to preserve his life, limbs, dignity and honor. None of you, I think, has forgotten the words of that oath?

ARCHBISHOP. [*Quietly*] We have not forgotten it, my son. No more than the other oath we took, before that—the oath to God. You are young, and still uncertain of yourself, perhaps. Yet you have, in those few words, taken a resolution the meaning of which has not escaped me. Will you allow an old man, who is very close to death, and who, in this rather sordid argument, was defending more perhaps than you suspect—to hope, as a father, that you will never know the bitterness of realizing, one day, that you made a mistake. [*He holds out his ring and* BECKET *kisses it.*] I give you my blessing, my son.

[BECKET *has knelt. Now he rises and says lightly:*]

BECKET. An unworthy son, Father, alas. But when is one worthy? And worthy of what? [*He pirouettes*[3] *and goes out, insolent and graceful as a young boy.*]

FOLLIOT. [*Violently*] Such insults to your Grace cannot be tolerated! This young rake's impudence must be crushed!

ARCHBISHOP. [*Thoughtfully*] He was with me for a long time. His is a strange, elusive nature. Don't imagine he is the ordinary libertine that outward appearances would suggest. I've had plenty of opportunity to observe him, in the bustle of pleasure and daily living. He is as it were detached. As if seeking his real self.

FOLLIOT. Break him, my Lord, before he finds it! Or the clergy of this country will pay dearly.

ARCHBISHOP. We must be very circumspect. It is our task to see into the hearts of men. And I am not sure that this one will always be our enemy. [*The* ARCHBISHOP *and the three* BISHOPS *go out. The* KING *is heard calling off stage.*]

KING. Well, son, have they gone? Are you coming hunting?

[*Trees come down from the flies. The black velvet curtain at the back opens on a clear sky, transforming the pillars into the leafless trees of a forest in winter. Bugles. The lights have gone down. When they go up again, the* KING *and* BECKET *are on horseback, each with a hawk on his gauntleted wrist. Torrential rain is heard.*]

KING. Here comes the deluge. [*Unexpectedly*] Do you like hunting this way, with hawks?

BECKET. I don't much care to delegate my errands. I prefer to feel a wild boar on the end of my spear. When he turns and charges there's a moment of delicious personal contact when one feels, at last, responsible for oneself.

KING. It's odd, this craving for danger. Why are you all so hell-bent on risking your necks for the most futile reasons?

BECKET. One has to gamble with one's life to feel alive.

KING. Or dead! You make me laugh. [*To his hawk*] Quiet, my pretty, quiet! We'll take your hood off in a minute. You couldn't give much of a performance under all these trees. I'll tell you one creature that loves hawking anyway, and that's a hawk! It seems to me we've rubbed our backsides sore with three hours' riding, just to give them this royal pleasure.

BECKET. [*Smiling*] My Lord, these are Norman hawks. They belong to the master race. They have a right to it.

KING. [*Suddenly, as he reins his horse*] Do you love me, Becket?

BECKET. I am your servant, my prince.

[3] Turns on his toe.

KING. Did you love me when I made you Chancellor? I wonder sometimes if you're capable of love. Do you love Gwendolen?

BECKET. She is my mistress, my prince.

KING. Why do you put labels onto everything to justify your feelings?

BECKET. Because, without labels, the world would have no shape, my prince.

KING. Is it so important for the world to have a shape?

BECKET. It's essential, my prince, otherwise we can't know what we're doing. [*Bugles in the distance.*] The rain is getting heavier, my Lord! Come, let us shelter in that hut over there.

[*He gallops off. After a second of confused indecision, the* KING *gallops after him, holding his hawk high and shouting:*]

KING. Becket! You didn't answer my question!

[*He disappears into the forest. Bugles again. The four* BARONS *cross the stage, galloping after them, and vanish into the forest. Thunder. Lightning. A hut has appeared to one side of the stage.* BECKET *is heard shouting:*]

BECKET. Hey there! You! Fellow! Can we put the horses under cover in your barn? Do you know how to rub down a horse? And have a look at the right forefoot of messire's horse. I think the shoe is loose. We'll sit out the storm under your roof.

[*After a second, the* KING *enters the hut, followed by a hairy Saxon who, cap in hand, bows repeatedly, in terrified silence.*]

KING. [*Shaking himself*] What a soaking! I'll catch my death! [*He sneezes.*] All this just to keep the hawks amused! [*Shouting at the man*] What are you waiting for? Light a fire, dog! It's freezing cold in this shack. [*The* MAN, *terror-stricken, does not move. The* KING *sneezes again. To* BECKET] What is he waiting for?

BECKET. Wood is scarce, my Lord. I don't suppose he has any left.

KING. What—in the middle of the forest?

BECKET. They are entitled to two measures of dead wood. One branch more and they're hanged.

KING. [*Astounded*] Really? And yet people are always complaining about the amount of dead wood in the forests. Still, that's a problem for my intendants, not me. [*Shouting at the* MAN] Run and pick up all the wood you can carry and build us a roaring fire! We won't hang you this time, dog!

[*The peasant, terrified, dares not obey.* BECKET *says gently:*]

BECKET. Go, my son. Your King commands it. You've the right. [*The* MAN *goes out, trembling, bowing to the ground, repeatedly.*]

KING. Why do you call that old man your son?

BECKET. Why not? You call him dog, my prince.

KING. It's a manner of speaking. Saxons are always called "dog." I can't think why, really. One could just as well have called them "Saxon"! But that smelly old ragbag your son! [*Sniffing*] What on earth can they eat to make the place stink so—dung?

BECKET. Turnips.

KING. Turnips—what are they?

BECKET. Roots.

KING. [*Amused*] Do they eat roots?

BECKET. Those who live in the forests can't grow anything else.

KING. Why don't they move out into the open country then?

BECKET. They would be hanged if they left their area.

KING. Oh, I see. Mark you, that must make life a lot simpler, if you know you'll be hanged at the least show of initiative. You must ask yourself far fewer questions. They don't know their luck! But you still haven't told me why you called the fellow your son?

BECKET. [*Lightly*] My prince, he is so poor and so bereft and I am so strong beside him, that he really is my son.

KING. We'd go a long way with that theory!

BECKET. Besides, my prince, you're appreciably younger than I am and you call me "son" sometimes.

KING. That's got nothing to do with it. It's because I love you.

BECKET. You are our King. We are all your sons and in your hands.

KING. What, Saxons too?

BECKET. [*Lightly, as he strips off his gloves*] England will be fully built, my prince, on the day the Saxons are your sons as well.

KING. You are a bore today! I get the feeling that I'm listening to the Archbishop. And I'm dying of thirst. Hunt around and see if you can't find us something to drink. Go on, it's your son's house! [BECKET *starts looking, and leaves the room after a while. The* KING *looks around too, examining the hut with curiosity, touching things with grimaces of distaste. Suddenly he notices a kind of trap door at the foot of a wall. He opens it, thrusts his hand in and pulls out a terrified* GIRL. *He shouts*] Hey, Thomas! Thomas! [BECKET *comes in.*]

BECKET. Have you found something to drink, Lord?

KING. [*Holding the* GIRL *at arm's length*] No. Something to eat. What do you say to that, if it's cleaned up a bit?

BECKET. [*Coldly*] She's pretty.

KING. She stinks a bit, but we could wash her. Look, did you ever see anything so tiny? How old would you say it was—fifteen, sixteen?

BECKET. [*Quietly*] It can talk, my Lord. [*Gently, to the* GIRL] How old are you? [*The* GIRL *looks at them in terror and says nothing.*]

KING. You see? Of course it can't talk! [*The* MAN *has come back with the wood and stops in the doorway, terrified.*] How old is your daughter, dog? [*The* MAN *trembles like a cornered animal and says nothing.*] He's dumb as well, that son of yours. How did you get him—with a deaf girl? It's funny the amount of dumb people I meet the second I set foot out of my palace. I rule over a kingdom of the dumb. Can you tell me why?

BECKET. They're afraid, my prince.

KING. I know that. And a good thing too. The populace must live in fear, it's essential. The moment they stop being afraid they have only one thought in mind—to frighten other people instead. And they adore doing that! Just as much as we do! Give them a chance to do it and they catch up fast, those sons of yours! Did you never see a peasants' revolt? I did once, in my father's reign, when I was a child. It's not a pretty sight. [*He looks at the* MAN, *exasperated.*] Look at it, will you? It's tongue-tied, it's obtuse, it stinks and the country is crawling with them! [*He seizes the* GIRL *who was trying to run away.*] Stay here, you! [*To* BECKET] I ask you, what use is it?

BECKET. [*Smiling*] It scratches the soil, it makes bread.

KING. Pooh, the English eat so little of it . . . At the French Court, yes, I daresay—they fairly stuff it down! But here!

BECKET. [*Smiling*] The troops have to be fed. For a King without troops . . .

KING. [*Struck by this*] True enough! Yes, that makes sense. There must be some sort of reason in all these absurdities. Well well, you little Saxon philosopher, you! I don't know how you do it, but you'll turn me into an intelligent man yet! The odd thing is, it's so ugly and yet it makes such pretty daughters. How do you explain that, you who can explain it all?

BECKET. At twenty, before he lost his teeth and took on that indeterminate age the common people have, that man may have been handsome. He may have had one night of love, one minute when he too was a King, and shed his fear. Afterwards, his pauper's life went on, eternally the same. And he and his wife no doubt forgot it all. But the seed was sown.

KING. [*Dreamily*] You have such a way of telling things . . . [*He looks at the* GIRL.] Do you think she'll grow ugly too?

BECKET. For sure.

KING. If we made her a whore and kept her at the palace, would she stay pretty?

BECKET. Perhaps.

KING. Then we'd be doing her a service, don't you think?

BECKET. [*Coldly*] No doubt.

[*The* MAN *stiffens. The* GIRL *cowers, in terror. The* BROTHER *comes in, somber-faced, silent, threatening.*]

KING. Would you believe it? They understand every word, you know! Who's that one there?

BECKET. [*Taking in the situation at a glance*] The brother.

KING. How do you know?

BECKET. Instinct, my Lord. [*His hand moves to his dagger.*]

KING. [*Bawling suddenly*] Why are they staring at me like that? I've had enough of this! I told you to get something to drink, dog! [*Terrified, the* MAN *scuttles off.*]

BECKET. Their water will be brackish. I have a gourd of juniper juice in my saddlebag. [*To the* BROTHER] Come and give me a hand, you! My horse is restive.

[*He seizes the boy roughly by the arm and hustles him out into the forest, carelessly whistling his little marching song. Then, all of a sudden, he hurls himself onto him. A short silent struggle.* BECKET *gets the boy's knife away; he escapes into the forest.* BECKET *watches him go for a second, holding his wounded hand. Then he walks around the back of the hut. The* KING *has settled himself on a bench, with his feet up on another, whistling to himself. He lifts the* GIRL'S *skirts with his cane and examines her at leisure.*]

KING. [*In a murmur*] All my sons! . . . [*He shakes himself.*] That Becket! He wears me out. He keeps making me think! I'm sure it's bad for the health. [*He gets up,* BECKET *comes in followed by the* MAN.] What about that water? How much longer do I have to wait?

BECKET. Here it is, my Lord. But it's muddy. Have some of this juniper juice instead.

KING. Drink with me. [*He notices* BECKET'S *hand, wrapped in a bloodstained cloth.*] What's the matter? You're wounded!

BECKET. [*Hiding his hand*] No doubt about it, that horse of mine is a nervous brute. He can't bear his saddle touched. He bit me.

KING. [*With a hearty, delighted laugh*] That's funny! Oh, that's very funny! Milord is the best rider in the Kingdom! Milord can never find a stallion with enough spirit for him! Milord makes us all look silly at the jousts, with his fancy horsemanship, and when he goes to open his saddlebags he gets himself bitten! Like a page! [*He is almost savagely gleeful. Then suddenly, his gaze softens.*]

You're white as a sheet, little Saxon . . . Why do I love you? . . . It's funny, I don't like to think of you in pain. Show me that hand. A horse bite can turn nasty. I'll put some of that juniper gin on it.

BECKET. [*Snatching his hand away*] I already have, my Lord, it's nothing.

KING. Then why do you look so pale? Show me your hand.

BECKET. [*With sudden coldness*] It's an ugly wound and you know you hate the sight of blood.

KING. [*Steps back a little, then exclaims with delight*] All this just to fetch me a drink! Wounded in the service of the King! We'll tell the others you defended me against a wild boar and I'll present you with a handsome gift this evening. What would you like?

BECKET. [*Softly*] This girl. [*He adds after a pause*] I fancy her. [*A pause.*]

KING. [*His face clouding over*] That's tiresome of you. I fancy her too. And where that's concerned, friendship goes by the board. [*A pause. His face takes on a cunning look.*] All right, then. But favor for favor. You won't forget, will you?

BECKET. No, my prince.

KING. Favor for favor; do you give me your word as a gentleman?

BECKET. Yes, my prince.

KING. [*Draining his glass, suddenly cheerful*] Done! She's yours. Do we take her with us or shall we have her sent?

BECKET. I'll send two soldiers to fetch her. Listen. The others have caught up. [*A troop of men-at-arms have come riding up behind the shack during the end of the scene.*]

KING. [*To the* MAN] Wash your daughter, dog, and kill her fleas. She's going to the palace. For Milord here, who's a Saxon too. You're pleased about that, I hope? [*To* BECKET *as he goes*] Give him a gold piece. I'm feeling generous this morning. [*He goes out. The* MAN *looks at* BECKET *in terror.*]

BECKET. No one will come and take your daughter away. Keep her better hidden in future. And tell your son to join the others, in the forest, he'll be safer there, now. I think one of the soldiers saw us. Here! [*He throws him a purse and goes out. When he has gone, the* MAN *snatches up the purse, then spits venomously, his face twisted with hate.*]

MAN. God rot your guts! Pig!

GIRL. [*Unexpectedly*] He was handsome, that one. Is it true he's taking me to the palace?

MAN. You whore! You Norman's trollop!

[*He hurls himself onto her and beats her savagely. The* KING, BECKET *and the* BARONS *have galloped off, amid the sound of bugles. The hut and the forest backcloth disappear. We are in* BECKET's *palace.*

FOOTMEN *push on a kind of low bed-couch, with cushions and some stools. Upstage, between two pillars, a curtain behind which can be seen the shadows of banqueting guests. Singing and roars of laughter. Downstage, curled up on the bed,* GWENDOLEN *is playing a string instrument. The curtain is drawn aside.* BECKET *appears. He goes to* GWENDOLEN *while the banqueting and the laughter, punctuated by hoarse incoherent snatches of song, go on upstage.* GWENDOLEN *stops playing.*]

GWENDOLEN. Are they still eating?

BECKET. Yes. They have an unimaginable capacity for absorbing food.

GWENDOLEN. [*Softly, beginning to play again*] How can my Lord spend his days and a large part of his nights with such creatures?

BECKET. [*Crouching at her feet and caressing her*] If he spent his time with learned clerics debating the sex of angels, your Lord would be even more bored, my kitten. They are as far from the true knowledge of things as mindless brutes.

GWENDOLEN. [*Gently, as she plays*] I don't always understand everything my Lord condescends to say to me . . . What I do know is that it is always very late when he comes to see me.

BECKET. [*Caressing her*] The only thing I love is coming to you. Beauty is one of the few things which don't shake one's faith in God.

GWENDOLEN. I am my Lord's war captive and I belong to him body and soul. God has willed it so, since He gave the Normans victory over my people. If the Welsh had won the war I would have married a man of my own race, at my father's castle. God did not will it so.

BECKET. [*Quietly*] That belief will do as well as any, my kitten. But, as I belong to a conquered race myself, I have a feeling that God's system is a little muddled. Go on playing.

[GWENDOLEN *starts to play again. Then she says suddenly:*]

GWENDOLEN. I'm lying. You are my Lord, God or no God. And if the Welsh had been victorious, you could just as easily have stolen me from my father's castle. I should have come with you. [*She says this gravely.* BECKET *rises abruptly and moves away. She looks up at him with anguished eyes and stops playing.*] Did I say something wrong? What is the matter with my Lord?

BECKET. Nothing. I don't like being loved. I told you that.

[*The curtain opens. The* KING *appears.*]

KING. [*A little drunk*] Well, son, have you deserted us? It worked! I told you! They've tumbled to it! They're fighting with your forks! They've at last discovered that they're for poking one another's eyes out. They think it's a most ingenious little invention. You'd better go in, son, they'll break them in a minute. [BECKET *goes behind the curtain to quieten his guests. He can be heard shouting*] Gentlemen, gentlemen! No, no, they aren't little daggers. No, truly— they're for pronging meat . . . Look, let me show you again. [*Huge roars of laughter behind the curtain. The* KING *has moved over to* GWENDOLEN. *He stares at her.*]

KING. Was that you playing, while we were at table?

GWENDOLEN. [*With a deep curtsy*] Yes, my Lord.

KING. You have every kind of accomplishment, haven't you? Get up. [*He lifts her to her feet, caressing her as he does so. She moves away, ill at ease. He says with a wicked smile*] Have I frightened you, my heart? We'll soon put that right. [*He pulls the curtain aside.*] Hey there, Becket! That's enough horseplay, my fat lads! Come and hear a little music. When the belly's full, it's good to elevate the mind a bit. [*To* GWENDOLEN] Play! [*The four* BARONS, *bloated with food and drink, come in with* BECKET. GWENDOLEN *has taken up her instrument again. The* KING *sprawls on the bed, behind her. The* BARONS, *with much sighing and puffing, unclasp their belts and sit down on stools, where they soon fall into a stupor.* BECKET *remains standing.*] Tell her to sing us something sad. I like sad music after dinner, it helps the digestion. [*He hiccups.*] You always feed us far too well, Thomas. Where did you steal that cook of yours?

BECKET. I bought him, Sire. He's a Frenchman.

KING. Really? Aren't you afraid he might poison you? Tell me, how much does one pay for a French cook?

BECKET. A good one, like him, costs almost as much as a horse, my Lord.

KING. [*Genuinely outraged*] It's outrageous! What is the country coming to! No man is worth a horse! If I said "favor for favor"—remember?—and I asked you to give him to me, would you?

BECKET. Of course, my Lord.

KING. [*With a smile, gently caressing* GWENDOLEN] Well, I won't. I don't want to eat too well every day; it lowers a man's morale. Sadder, sadder, my little doe. [*He belches.*] Oh, that venison! Get her to sing that lament they composed for your mother, Becket. It's my favorite song.

BECKET. I don't like anyone to sing that lament, my Lord.

KING. Why not? Are you ashamed of being a Saracen[4] girl's son? That's half your charm, you fool! There must be some reason why you're more civilized than all the rest of us put together! I adore that song. [GWENDOLEN *looks uncertainly at* BECKET. *There is a pause. Then the* KING *says coldly*] That's an order, little Saxon.

BECKET. [*Inscrutably, to* GWENDOLEN] Sing.

[*She strikes a few opening chords, while the* KING *makes himself comfortable beside her, belching contentedly. She begins:*]

GWENDOLEN. [*Singing*]   Handsome Sir Gilbert
Went to the war
One fine morning in May
To deliver the heart
Of Lord Jesus our Saviour,
From the hands of the Saracens.
Woe! Woe! Heavy is my heart
At being without love!
Woe! Woe! Heavy is my heart
All the livelong day!

KING. [*Singing*]   All the livelong day! Go on!

GWENDOLEN.   As the battle raged
He swung his mighty sword
And many a Moor fell dead
But his trusty charger
Stumbled in the fray
And Sir Gilbert fell.
Woe! Woe! Heavy is my heart!
At being without love!
Woe! Woe! Heavy is my heart
All the livelong day.

Wounded in the head
Away Gilbert was led
To the Algiers market
Chained hand and foot
And sold there as a slave.

[4] The Saracens were the Moslems who opposed the efforts of the Christian crusaders to capture and hold Jerusalem from the end of the eleventh to the end of the thirteenth century. The romantic legend that Becket was a Saracen girl's son is, unfortunately, false.

KING. [*Singing, out of tune*]

> All the livelong day!

GWENDOLEN.

> A Saracen's daughter
> Lovely as the night
> Lost her heart to him
> Swore to love him always
> Vowed to be his wife.
>
> Woe! Woe! Heavy is my heart
> At being without love!
> Woe! Woe! Heavy is my heart
> All the livelong day—

KING. [*Interrupting*] It brings tears to my eyes, you know, that story. I look a brute but I'm soft as swansdown really. One can't change one's nature. I can't imagine why you don't like people to sing that song. It's wonderful to be a love child. When I look at my august parents' faces, I shudder to think what must have gone on. It's marvelous to think of your mother helping your father to escape and then coming to join him in London with you inside her. Sing us the end, girl. I adore the end.

GWENDOLEN. [*Softly*]

> Then he asked the holy Father
> For a priest to baptize her
> And he took her as his wife
> To cherish with his life
> Giving her his soul
> To love and keep alway.
>
> Gay! Gay! Easy is my heart
> At being full of love
> Gay! Gay! Easy is my heart
> To be loved alway.

KING. [*Dreamily*] Did he really love her all his life? Isn't it altered a bit in the song?

BECKET. No, my prince.

KING. [*Getting up, quite saddened*] Funny, it's the happy ending that makes me feel sad . . . Tell me, do you believe in love, Thomas?

BECKET. [*Coldly*] For my father's love for my mother, Sire, yes.

> [*The* KING *has moved over to the* BARONS *who are now snoring on their stools. He gives them a kick as he passes.*]

KING. They've fallen asleep, the hogs. That's their way of showing their finer feelings. You know, my little Saxon, sometimes I have the impression that you and I are the only sensitive men in England. We eat with forks and we have infinitely distinguished sentiments, you and I. You've made a different man of me, in a way . . . What you ought to find me now, if you loved me, is a girl to give me a little polish. I've had enough of whores. [*He has come back to* GWENDOLEN. *He caresses her a little and then says suddenly*] Favor for favor—do you remember? [*A pause.*]

BECKET. [*Pale*] I am your servant, my prince, and all I have is yours. But you were also gracious enough to say I was your friend.

KING. That's what I mean! As one friend to another it's the thing to do! [*A short pause. He smiles maliciously, and goes on caressing* GWENDOLEN *who cowers, terrified.*] You care about her then? Can you care for something? Go on, tell me, tell me if you care about her? [BECKET *says nothing. The* KING *smiles.*] You can't tell a lie. I know you. Not because you're afraid of lies—I think you must be the only man I know who isn't afraid of anything—not even Heaven—but because it's distasteful to you. You consider it inelegant. What looks like morality in you is nothing more than esthetics. Is that true or isn't it?

BECKET. [*Meeting his eyes, says softly*] It's true, my Lord.

KING. I'm not cheating if I ask for her, am I? I said "favor for favor" and I asked you for your word of honor.

BECKET. [*Icily*] And I gave it to you.

[*A pause. They stand quite still. The* KING *looks at* BECKET *with a wicked smile.* BECKET *does not look at him. Then the* KING *moves briskly away.*]

KING. Right. I'm off to bed. I feel like an early night tonight. Delightful evening, Becket. You're the only man in England who knows how to give your friends a royal welcome. [*He kicks the slumbering* BARONS.] Call my guards and help me wake these porkers. [*The* BARONS *wake with sighs and belches as the* KING *pushes them about, shouting*] Come on, Barons, home! I know you're connoisseurs of good music, but we can't listen to music all night long. Happy evenings end in bed, eh Becket?

BECKET. [*Stiffly*] May I ask your Highness for a brief moment's grace?

KING. Granted! Granted! I'm not a savage. I'll wait for you both in my litter. You can say good night to me downstairs.

[*He goes out, followed by the* BARONS. BECKET *stands motionless for a while under* GWENDOLEN's *steady gaze. Then he says quietly:*]

BECKET. You will have to go with him, Gwendolen.

GWENDOLEN. [*Composedly*] Did my Lord promise me to him?

BECKET. I gave him my word as a gentleman that I would give him anything he asked for. I never thought it would be you.

GWENDOLEN. If he sends me away tomorrow, will my Lord take me back?

BECKET. No.

GWENDOLEN. Shall I tell the girls to put my dresses in the coffer?

BECKET. He'll send over for it tomorrow. Go down. One doesn't keep the King waiting. Tell him I wish him a respectful good night.

GWENDOLEN. [*Laying her viol on the bed*] I shall leave my Lord my viol. He can almost play it now. [*She asks, quite naturally*] My Lord cares for nothing, in the whole world, does he?

BECKET. No.

GWENDOLEN. [*Moves to him and says gently*] You belong to a conquered race too. But through tasting too much of the honey of life, you've forgotten that even those who have been robbed of everything have one thing left to call their own.

BECKET. [*Inscrutably*] Yes, I daresay I had forgotten. There is a gap in me where honor ought to be. Go now.

[GWENDOLEN *goes out.* BECKET *stands quite still. Then he goes to the bed, picks up the viol, looks at it, then throws it abruptly away. He pulls off the fur coverlet and starts to unbutton his doublet. A* GUARD *comes in, dragging the* SAXON GIRL *from the forest, whom he throws down in the middle of the room. The* KING *appears.*]

KING. [*Hilariously*] Thomas, my son! You'd forgotten her! You see how careless you are! Luckily I think of everything. It seems they had to bully the father and the brother a tiny bit to get her, but anyway, here she is. You see?—I really am a friend to you, and you're wrong not to love me. You told me you fancied her. I hadn't forgotten that, you see. Sleep well, son!

[*He goes out, followed by the* GUARD. *The* GIRL, *still dazed, looks at* BECKET *who has not moved. She recognizes him, gets to her feet and smiles at him. A long pause, then she asks with a kind of sly coquetry:*]

GIRL. Shall I undress, my Lord?

BECKET. [*Who has not moved*] Of course. [*The* GIRL *starts to undress.* BECKET *looks at her coldly, absent-mindedly whistling a few bars of his little march. Suddenly he stops, goes to the* GIRL, *who stands there dazed and half naked, and seizes her by the shoulders.*] I hope you're full of noble feelings and that all this strikes you as pretty shabby?

[*A* SERVANT *runs in wildly and halts in the doorway speechless. Before he can speak, the* KING *comes stumbling in.*]

KING. [*Soberly*] I had no pleasure with her, Thomas. She let me lay her down in the litter, limp as a corpse, and then suddenly she pulled out a little knife from somewhere. There was blood everywhere . . . I feel quite sick. [BECKET *has let go of the* GIRL. *The* KING *adds, haggard*] She could easily have killed me instead! [*A pause. He says abruptly*] Send that girl away. I'm sleeping in your room tonight. I'm frightened. [BECKET *motions to the* SERVANT, *who takes away the half-naked* GIRL. *The* KING *has thrown himself, fully dressed, onto the bed with an animal-like sigh.*] Take half the bed.

BECKET. I'll sleep on the floor, my prince.

KING. No. Lie down beside me. I don't want to be alone tonight. [*He looks at him and murmurs*] You loathe me, I shan't even be able to trust you now . . .

BECKET. You gave me your Seal to keep, my prince. And the Three Lions of England which are engraved on it keep watch over me too. [*He snuffs out the candles, all save one. It is almost dark.*]

KING. [*His voice already thick with sleep*] I shall never know what you're thinking . . .

[BECKET *has thrown a fur coverlet over the* KING. *He lies down beside him and says quietly:*]

BECKET. It will be dawn soon, my prince. You must sleep. Tomorrow we are crossing to the Continent. In a week we will face the King of France's army and there will be simple answers to everything at last.

[*He has lain down beside the* KING. *A pause, during which the* KING's *snoring gradually increases. Suddenly, the* KING *moans and tosses in his sleep.*]

KING. [*Crying out*] They're after me! They're after me! They're armed to the teeth! Stop them! Stop them!

[BECKET *sits up on one elbow. He touches the* KING, *who wakes up with a great animal cry.*]

BECKET. My prince . . . my prince . . . sleep in peace. I'm here.

KING. Oh . . . Thomas, it's you . . . They were after me. [*He turns over and goes back to sleep with a sigh. Gradually he begins to snore again, softly.* BECKET *is still on one elbow. Almost tenderly, he draws the coverlet over the* KING.]

BECKET. My prince . . . If you were my true prince, if you were one of my race, how simple everything would be. How tenderly I would love you, my prince, in an ordered world. Each of us bound in fealty to the other, head, heart and limbs, with no further questions to ask of oneself, ever. [*A pause. The* KING'*s snores grow louder.* BECKET *sighs and says with a little smile*] But I cheated my way, a twofold bastard, into the ranks, and found a place among the conquerors. You can sleep peacefully though, my prince. So long as Becket is obliged to improvise his honor, he will serve you. And if one day, he meets it face to face . . . [*A short pause.*] But where is Becket's honor? [*He lies down with a sigh, beside the* KING. *The* KING'*s snores grow louder still. The candle sputters. The lights grow even dimmer . . .*]

The curtain falls.

END OF ACT I

ACT II

The curtain rises on the same set of arching pillars, which now represents a forest in France. The KING'*s tent, not yet open for the day, is set up among the trees. A* SENTRY *stands some way off.*

It is dawn. Crouched around a campfire, the four BARONS *are having their morning meal, in silence. After a while, one of them says:*

1ST BARON. This Becket then, who is he? [*A pause. All four are fairly slow in their reactions.*]

2ND BARON. [*Surprised at the question*] The Chancellor of England.

1ST BARON. I know that! But who is he, exactly?

2ND BARON. The Chancellor of England, I tell you! The Chancellor of England is the Chancellor of England! I don't see what else there is to inquire into on that score.

1ST BARON. You don't understand. Look, supposing the Chancellor of England were some other man. Me, for instance . . .

2ND BARON. That's plain idiotic.

1ST BARON. I said supposing. Now, I would be Chancellor of England but I wouldn't be the same Chancellor of England as Becket is. You can follow that, can you?

2ND BARON. [*Guardedly*] Yes . . .

1ST BARON. So, I *can* ask myself the question.

2ND BARON. What question?

1ST BARON. Who is this man Becket?

2ND BARON. What do you mean, who is this man Becket? He's the Chancellor of England.

1ST BARON. Yes. But what I'm asking myself is who is he, as a man?

2ND BARON. [*Looks at him and says sorrowfully*] Have you got a pain?

1ST BARON. No, why?

2ND BARON. A Baron who asks himself questions is a sick Baron. Your sword— what's that?

1ST BARON. My sword?

2ND BARON. Yes.

1ST BARON. [*Putting his hand to the hilt*] It's my sword! And anyone who thinks different—

2ND BARON. Right. Answered like a nobleman. We peers aren't here to ask questions. We're here to give answers.

1ST BARON. Right then. Answer me.

2ND BARON. Not to questions! To orders. You aren't asked to think in the army. When you're face to face with a French man-at-arms, do you ask yourself questions?

1ST BARON. No.

2ND BARON. Does he?

1ST BARON. No.

2ND BARON. Does he?

1ST BARON. No.

2ND BARON. You just fall to and fight. If you started asking each other questions like a pair of women, you might as well bring chairs onto the battlefield. If there are any questions to be asked you can be sure they've been asked already, higher up, by cleverer heads than yours.

1ST BARON. [*Vexed*] I meant I didn't like him, that's all.

2ND BARON. Why couldn't you say so then? That we'd have understood. You're entitled not to like him. I don't like him either, come to that. To begin with, he's a Saxon.

1ST BARON. To begin with!

3RD BARON. One thing you can't say though. You can't say he isn't a fighter. Yesterday when the King was in the thick of it, after his squire was killed, he cut his way right through the French, and he seized the King's banner and drew the enemy off and onto himself.

1ST BARON. All right! He's a good fighter!

3RD BARON. [*To* 2ND BARON] Isn't he a good fighter?

2ND BARON. [*Stubbornly*] Yes. But he's a Saxon.

1ST BARON. [*To the* 4TH BARON, *who has so far said nothing*] How about you, Regnault? What do you think of him?

4TH BARON. [*Placidly, swallowing his mouthful of food*] I'm waiting.

1ST BARON. Waiting for what?

4TH BARON. Till he shows himself. Some sorts of game are like that: you follow them all day through the forest, by sounds, or tracks, or smell. But it wouldn't do any good to charge ahead with drawn lance; you'd just spoil everything because you don't know for sure what sort of animal it is you're dealing with. You have to wait.

1ST BARON. What for?

4TH BARON. For whatever beast it is to show itself. And if you're patient it always does in the end. Animals know more than men do, nearly always, but a man has something in him that an animal hasn't got: he knows how to wait. With this man Becket—I'll wait.

1ST BARON. For what?

4TH BARON. For him to show himself. For him to break cover. [*He goes on eating.*] The day he does, we'll know who he is.

[BECKET's *little whistled march is heard off stage.* BECKET *comes in, armed.*]

BECKET. Good morning to you, Gentlemen. [*The four* BARRONS *rise politely, and salute.*] Is the King still asleep?

1ST BARON. [*Stiffly*] He hasn't called yet.

BECKET. Has the camp marshal presented his list of losses?

1ST BARON. No.

BECKET. Why not?

2ND BARON. [*Surlily*] He was part of the losses.

BECKET. Oh?

1ST BARON. I was nearby when it happened. A lance knocked him off his horse. Once on the ground, the foot soldiers dealt with him.

BECKET. Poor Beaumont. He was so proud of his new armor.

2ND BARON. There must have been a chink in it then. They bled him white. On the ground. French swine!

BECKET. [*With a slight shrug*] That's war.

1ST BARON. War is a sport like any other. There are rules. In the old days, they took you for ransom. A Knight for a Knight. That was proper fighting!

BECKET. [*Smiling*] Since one has taken to sending the foot soldiery against the horses with no personal protection save a cutlass, they're a little inclined to seek out the chink in the armor of any Knight unwise enough to fall off his horse. It's repulsive, but I can understand them.

1ST BARON. If we start understanding the common soldiery war will be butchery plain and simple.

BECKET. The world is certainly tending towards butchery, Baron. The lesson of this battle, which has cost us far too much, is that we will have to form platoons of cutthroats too, that's all.

1ST BARON. And a soldier's honor, my Lord Chancellor, what of that?

BECKET. [*Dryly*] A soldier's honor, Baron, is to win victories. Let us not be hypocritical. The Norman nobility lost no time in teaching those they conquered that little point. I'll wake the King. Our entry into the city is timed for eight o'clock and the *Te Deum*[5] in the cathedral for a quarter past nine. It would be bad policy to keep the French Bishop waiting. We want these people to collaborate with a good grace.

1ST BARON. [*Grunting*] In my day, we slaughtered the lot and marched in afterwards.

BECKET. Yes, into a dead city! I want to give the King living cities to increase his wealth. From eight o'clock this morning, I am the French people's dearest friend.

1ST BARON. What about England's honor, then?

BECKET. [*Quietly*] England's honor, Baron, in the final reckoning, has always been to succeed. [*He goes into the* KING'*s tent smiling. The four* BARONS *look at each other, hostile.*]

1ST BARON. [*Muttering*] What a mentality!

4TH BARON. [*Sententiously*] We must wait for him. One day, he'll break cover. [*The four* BARONS *move away.* BECKET *lifts the tent flap and hooks it back. The* KING *is revealed, in bed with a girl.*]

KING. [*Yawning*] Good morning, son. Did you sleep well?

BECKET. A little memento from the French on my left shoulder kept me awake, Sire. I took the opportunity to do some thinking.

KING. [*Worriedly*] You think too much. You'll suffer for it, you know! It's because people think that there are problems. One day, if you go on like this, you'll think yourself into a dilemma, your big head will present you with a solution and you'll jump feet first into a hopeless mess—which you'd have done far better to ignore, like the majority of fools, who know nothing and live to a ripe old age. What do you think of my little French girl? I must say, I adore France.

---

[5] A hymn beginning *Te Deum laudamus* ("We praise you, God.")

BECKET. [*Smiling*] So do I, Sire, like all Englishmen.

KING. The climate's warm, the girls are pretty, the wine is good. I intend to spend at least a month here every winter.

BECKET. The only snag is, it's expensive! Nearly 2,000 casualties yesterday.

KING. Has Beaumont made out his total?

BECKET. Yes. And he added himself to the list.

KING. Wounded? [BECKET *does not answer. The* KING *shivers. He says somberly*] I don't like learning that people I know have died. I've a feeling it may give Death ideas.

BECKET. My prince, shall we get down to work? We haven't dealt with yesterday's dispatches.

KING. Yesterday we were fighting! We can't do everything.

BECKET. That was a holiday! We'll have to work twice as hard today.

KING. Does it amuse you—working for the good of my people? Do you mean to say you love all those folk? To begin with they're too numerous. One can't love them, one doesn't know them. Anyway, you're lying, you don't love anything or anybody.

BECKET. [*Tersely*] There's one thing I do love, my prince, and that I'm sure of. Doing what I have to do and doing it well.

KING. [*Grinning*] Always the es—es . . . What's your word again? I've forgotten it.

BECKET. Esthetics?

KING. Esthetics! Always the esthetic side, eh?

BECKET. Yes, my prince.

KING. [*Slapping the* GIRL's *rump*] And isn't that esthetic too? Some people go into ecstasies over cathedrals. But this is a work of art too! Look at that—round as an apple . . . [*Quite naturally, as if he were offering him a sweetmeat*] Want her?

BECKET. [*Smiling*] Business, my Lord!

KING. [*Pouting like a schoolboy*] All right. Business. I'm listening. Sit down.

[BECKET *sits down on the bed, beside the* KING, *with the* GIRL *like a fascinated rabbit in between them.*]

BECKET. The news is not good, my prince.

KING. [*With a careless wave of the hand*] News never is. That's a known fact. Life is one long web of difficulties. The secret of it—and there is one, brought to perfection by several generations of worldly-wise philosophers—is to give them no importance whatever. In the end one difficulty swallows up the other and you find yourself ten years later still alive with no harm done. Things always work out.

BECKET. Yes. But badly. My prince, when you play tennis, do you simply sit back and let things work out? Do you wait for the ball to hit your racket and say "It's bound to come this way eventually?"

KING. Ah, now just a minute. You're talking about things that matter. A game of tennis is important, it amuses me.

BECKET. And suppose I were to tell you that governing can be as amusing as a game of tennis? Are we going to let the others smash the ball into our court, my prince, or shall we try to score a point, both of us, like two good English sportsmen?

KING. [*Suddenly roused by his sporting instinct*] The point, Begod, the point! You're right! On the court, I sweat and strain, I fall over my feet, I half kill myself, I'll cheat if need be, but I never give up the point!

BECKET. Well then, I'll tell you what the score is, so far. Piecing together all the information I have received from London since we've been on the Continent, one thing strikes me, and that is: that there exists in England a power which has grown until it almost rivals yours, my Lord. It is the power of your clergy.

KING. We did get them to pay the tax. That's something!

BECKET. Yes, it's a small sum of money. And they know that Princes can always be pacified with a little money. But those men are past masters at taking back with one hand what they were forced to give with the other. That's a little conjuring trick they've had centuries of practice in.

KING. [*To the* GIRL] Pay attention, my little sparrow. Now's your chance to educate yourself. The gentleman is saying some very profound things!

BECKET. [*In the same flippant way*] Little French sparrow, suppose you educate us instead. When you're married—if you do marry despite the holes in your virtue—which would you prefer, to be mistress in your own house or to have your village priest laying down the law there?

[*The* KING, *a little peeved, gets up on his knees on the bed and hides the bewildered* GIRL *under an eiderdown.*]

KING. Talk sense, Becket! Priests are always intriguing, I know that. But I also know that I can crush them any time I like.

BECKET. Talk sense, Sire. If you don't do the crushing now, in five years' time there will be two Kings in England, the Archbishop of Canterbury and you. And in ten years' time there will be only one.

KING. [*A bit shamefaced*] And it won't be me?

BECKET. [*Coldly*] I rather fear not.

KING. [*With a sudden shout*] Oh, yes, it will! We Plantagenets[6] hold on to our own! To horse, Becket, to horse! For England's glory! War on the faithful! That will make a change for us!

[*The eiderdown starts to toss. The* GIRL *emerges, disheveled, and red in the face.*]

GIRL. [*Pleadingly*] My Lord! I can't breathe!

[*The* KING *looks at her in surprise. He had clearly forgotten her. He bursts out laughing.*]

KING. What are you doing there? Spying for the clergy? Be off. Put your clothes on and go home. Give her a gold piece, Thomas.

[*The* GIRL *picks up her rags and holds them up in front of her.*]

GIRL. Am I to come back to the camp tonight, my Lord?

KING. [*Exasperated*] Yes. No. I don't know! We're concerned with the Archbishop now, not you! Be off. [*The* GIRL *disappears into the back portion of the tent. The* KING *cries*] To horse, Thomas! For England's greatness! With my big fist and your big brain we'll do some good work, you and I! [*With sudden concern*] Wait a second. You can never be sure of finding another one as good in bed. [*He goes to the rear of the tent and cries*] Come back tonight, my angel! I adore you! You have the prettiest eyes in the world! [*He comes downstage and says confidentially to* BECKET] You always have to tell them that, even when you pay for it, if you want real pleasure with them. That's high politics, too! [*Suddenly anxious, as his childish fear of the clergy returns.*] What will God say to it all, though? After all, they're *His* Bishops!

---

[6] Henry's father was Geoffrey Plantagenet, the Count of Anjou [1112–1151], and his mother was Matilda [1102–1167], the daughter of Henry I of England [1068–1135]. When Henry II [1133–1189] became king of England in 1154, Plantagenet became the name of the ruling family. The Plantagenets ruled England until the death of Richard II [1367–1400].

BECKET. [*With an airy gesture*] We aren't children. You know one can always come to some arrangement with God, on this earth. Make haste and dress, my prince. We're going to be late.

KING. [*Hurrying out*] I'll be ready in a second. Do I have to shave?

BECKET. [*Smiling*] It might be as well, after two days' fighting.

KING. What a fuss for a lot of conquered Frenchmen! I wonder sometimes if you aren't a bit too finicky, Thomas. [*He goes out.* BECKET *closes the tent just as two* SOLDIERS *bring on a* YOUNG MONK, *with his hands tied.*]

BECKET. What is it?

SOLDIER. We've just arrested this young monk, my Lord. He was loitering round the camp. He had a knife under his robe. We're taking him to the Provost.[7]

BECKET. Have you got the knife? [*The* SOLDIER *hands it to him.* BECKET *looks at it, then at the little* MONK.] What use do you have for this in your monastery?

MONK. I cut my bread with it!

BECKET. [*Amused*] Well, well. [*To the* SOLDIERS] Leave him to me. I'll question him.

SOLDIER. He's turbulent, my Lord. He struggled like a very demon. It took four of us to get his knife away and tie him up. He wounded the Sergeant. We'd have finished him there and then, only the Sergeant said there might be some information to be got out of him. That's why we're taking him to the Provost. [*He adds*] That's just to tell you he's a spiteful devil.

BECKET. [*Who has not taken his eyes off the little* MONK] Very well. Stand off. [*The* SOLDIERS *move out of earshot.* BECKET *goes on looking at the boy, and playing with the knife.*] What are you doing in France? You're a Saxon.

MONK. [*Crying out despite himself*] How do you know?

BECKET. I can tell by your accent. I speak Saxon very well, as well as you speak French. Yes, you might almost pass for a Frenchman—to unpracticed ears. But I'd be careful. In your predicament, you'd do as well to be taken for a Frenchman as a Saxon. It's less unpopular. [*A pause.*]

MONK. [*Abruptly*] I'm prepared to die.

BECKET. [*Smiling*] After the deed. But before, you'll agree it's stupid. [*He looks at the knife which he is still holding between two fingers.*] Where are you from?

MONK. [*Venomously*] Hastings!

BECKET. Hastings. And who was this kitchen implement intended for? [*No answer.*] You couldn't hope to kill more than one man with a weapon of this sort. You didn't make the journey for the sake of an ordinary Norman soldier, I imagine. [*The little* MONK *does not answer. Tersely*] Listen to me, my little man. They're going to put you to the torture. Have you ever seen that? I'm obliged to attend professionally from time to time. You think you'll have the necessary strength of spirit, but they're terribly ingenious and they have a knowledge of anatomy that our imbecilic doctors would do well to emulate. One always talks. Believe me, I know. If I can vouch that you've made a full confession, it will go quicker for you. That's worth considering. [*The* MONK *does not answer.*] Besides, there's an amusing detail to this affair. You are directly under my jurisdiction. The King gave me the deeds and livings of all the abbeys in Hastings when he made me Chancellor.

MONK. [*Stepping back*] Are you Becket?

BECKET. Yes. [*He looks at the knife with faint distaste.*] You didn't only use it to

---

[7] The provost marshal in an army is the officer in charge of the military police.

cut your bread. Your knife stinks of onion, like any proper little Saxon's knife. They're good, aren't they, the Hastings onions? [*He looks at the knife again with a strange smile.*] You still haven't told me who it was for. [*The* MONK *says nothing.*] If you meant it for the King, there was no sense in that, my lad. He has three sons. Kings spring up again like weeds! Did you imagine you could liberate your race single-handed?

MONK. No. [*He adds dully*] Not my race. Myself.

BECKET. Liberate yourself from what?

MONK. My shame.

BECKET. [*With sudden gravity*] How old are you?

MONK. Sixteen.

BECKET. [*Quietly*] The Normans have occupied the island for a hundred years. Shame is an old vintage. Your father and your grandfather drank it to the dregs. The cup is empty now.

MONK. [*Shaking his head*] No.

[*A shadow seems to cross* BECKET's *eyes. He goes on, quietly:*]

BECKET. So, one fine morning, you woke in your cell to the bell of the first offices, while it was still dark. And it was the bells that told you, a boy of sixteen, to take the whole burden of shame onto yourself?

MONK. [*With the cry of a cornered animal*] Who told you that?

BECKET. [*Softly*] I told you I was a polyglot.[8] [*Indifferently*] I'm a Saxon too, did you know that?

MONK. [*Stonily*] Yes.

BECKET. [*Smiling*] Go on. Spit. You're dying to.

[*The* MONK *looks at him, a little dazed, and then spits.*]

BECKET. [*Smiling*] That felt good, didn't it? [*Tersely*] The King is waiting. And this conversation could go on indefinitely. But I want to keep you alive, so we can continue it one of these days. [*He adds lightly*] It's pure selfishness, you know. Your life hasn't any sort of importance for me, obviously, but it's very rare for Fate to bring one face to face with one's own ghost, when young. [*Calling*] Soldier! [*The* SOLDIER *comes back and springs clanking to attention.*] Fetch me the Provost. Run! [*The* SOLDIER *runs out.* BECKET *comes back to the silent* YOUNG MONK.] Delightful day, isn't it? This early-morning sun, hot already under this light veil of mist . . . A beautiful place, France. But I'm like you, I prefer the solid mists of the Sussex downs.[9] Sunshine is luxury. And we belong to a race which used to despise luxury, you and I. [*The* PROVOST MARSHAL *of the camp comes in, followed by the* SOLDIER. *He is an important personage, but* BECKET *is inaccessible, even for a* PROVOST MARSHAL, *and the man's behavior shows it.*] Sir Provost, your men have arrested this monk who was loitering round the camp. He is a lay brother from the convent of Hastings and he is directly under my jurisdiction. You will make arrangements to have him sent back to England and taken to the convent, where his Abbot will keep him under supervision until my return. There is no specific charge against him, for the moment. I want him treated without brutality, but very closely watched. I hold you personally responsible for him.

PROVOST. Very good, my Lord.

[*He motions to the* SOLDIERS. *They surround the little* MONK *and take him away*

---

[8] A person who speaks many tongues—probably used figuratively here to suggest Becket's diverse background among both the Saxons and the Normans.

[9] These Downs are a treeless, hilly region in Sussex and Kent in southeastern England.

without a further glance from BECKET. *Left alone,* BECKET *looks at the knife, smiles, wrinkles his nose and murmurs, with faint distaste:*]

BECKET. It's touching, but it stinks, all the same. [*He flings the knife away, and whistling his little march goes toward the tent. He goes in, calling out lightheartedly*] Well, my prince, have you put on your Sunday best? It's time to go. We mustn't keep the Bishop waiting!

[*A sudden joyful peal of bells. The tent disappears as soon as* BECKET *has gone in. The set changes. A backcloth representing a street comes down from the flies. The permanent pillars are there, but the* SOLDIERS *lining the route have decorated them with standards. The* KING *and* BECKET *advance into the city, on horseback, preceded by two* TRUMPET-ERS; *the* KING *slightly ahead of* BECKET *and followed by the four* BARONS. *Acclamations from the crowd. Bells, trumpets throughout the scene.*]

KING. [*Beaming as he waves*] Listen to that! They adore us, these French!

BECKET. It cost me quite a bit. I had money distributed among the populace this morning. The prosperous classes are at home, sulking, of course.

KING. Patriots?

BECKET. No. But they would have cost too much. There are also a certain number of your Highness' soldiers among the crowd, in disguise, to encourage any lukewarm elements.

KING. Why do you always make a game of destroying my illusions? I thought they loved me for myself! You're an amoral man, Becket. [*Anxiously*] Does one say amoral or immoral?

BECKET. [*Smiling*] It depends what one means.

KING. She's pretty, look—the girl on the balcony to the right there. Suppose we stopped a minute . . .

BECKET. Impossible. The Bishop is waiting in the cathedral.

KING. It would be a lot more fun than going to see a Bishop!

BECKET. My Lord, do you remember what you have to say to him?

KING. [*Waving to the crowd*] Yes, yes, yes! As if it mattered what I say to a French Bishop, whose city I've just taken by force!

BECKET. It matters a great deal. For our future policy.

KING. Am I the strongest or am I not?

BECKET. You are, today. But one must never drive one's enemy to despair. It makes him strong. Gentleness is better politics. It saps virility. A good occupational force must not crush, it must corrupt.

KING. [*Waving graciously*] What about my pleasure then? Where does that enter into your scheme of things? Suppose I charged into this heap of frog-eaters now instead of acting the goat at their *Te Deum?* I can indulge in a bit of pleasure, can't I? I'm the conqueror.

BECKET. That would be a fault. Worse, a failing. One can permit oneself anything, Sire, but one must never indulge.

KING. Yes, Papa, right, Papa. What a bore you are today. Look at that little redhead there, standing on the fountain! Give orders for the procession to follow the same route back.

[*He rides on, turning his horse to watch the girl out of sight. They have gone by, the four* BARONS *bringing up the rear. Organ music. The standards disappear, together with the* SOLDIERS. *We are in the cathedral. The stage is empty.*

The organ is heard. Swelling chords. The organist is practicing in the empty cathedral. Then a sort of partition is pushed on, which represents the sacristy.

The KING, *attired for the ceremony, the* BARONS, *an unknown* PRIEST *and a* CHOIR-BOY *come in. They seem to be waiting for something. The* KING *sits impatiently on a stool.*]

KING. Where's Becket? And what are we waiting for?

1ST BARON. He just said to wait, my Lord. It seems there's something not quite in order.

KING. [*Pacing about ill-humoredly*] What a lot of fuss for a French Bishop! What do I look like, I ask you, hanging about in this sacristy like a village bridegroom!

4TH BARON. I quite agree, my Lord! I can't think why we don't march straight in. After all, it's your cathedral now. [*Eagerly*] What do you say, my Lord? Shall we just draw our swords and charge?

KING. [*Going meekly back to his stool with a worried frown*] No. Becket wouldn't like it. And he's better than we are at knowing the right thing to do. If he told us to wait, there must be a good reason. [BECKET *hurries in.*] Well, Becket, what's happening? We're freezing to death in here! What do the French think they're at, keeping us moldering in this sacristy?

BECKET. The order came from me, Sire. A security measure. My police are certain that a French rising was to break out during the ceremony. [*The* KING *has risen. The* 2ND BARON *has drawn his sword. The other three follow suit.*]

2ND BARON. God's Blood!

BECKET. Put up your swords. The King is safe in here. I have put guards on all the doors.

2ND BARON. Have we your permission to go in and deal with it, my Lord? We'll make short work of it!

3RD BARON. Just say the word, Sire! Shall we go?

BECKET. [*Curtly*] I forbid you. There aren't enough of us. I am bringing fresh troops into the city and having the cathedral evacuated. Until that is done, the King's person is in your keeping, gentlemen. But sheathe your swords. No provocation, please. We are at the mercy of a chance incident and I still have no more than the fifty escort men-at-arms in the city.

KING. [*Tugging at* BECKET's *sleeve*] Becket! Is that priest French?

BECKET. Yes. But he is part of the Bishop's immediate entourage. And the Bishop is our man.

KING. You know how reliable English Bishops are! So I leave you to guess how far we can trust a French one! That man has a funny look in his eyes.

BECKET. Who, the Bishop?

KING. No. That priest.

BECKET. [*Glances at the* PRIEST *and laughs*] Of course, my prince, he squints! I assure you that's the only disturbing thing about him! It would be tactless to ask him to leave. Besides, even if he had a dagger, you have your coat of mail and four of your Barons. I must go and supervise the evacuation of the nave. [*He starts to go. The* KING *runs after him.*]

KING. Becket! [BECKET *stops.*] The choirboy?

BECKET. [*Laughing*] He's only so high!

KING. He may be a dwarf. You never know with the French. [*Drawing* BECKET *aside.*] Becket, we talked a little flippantly this morning. Are you sure God isn't taking his revenge?

BECKET. [*Smiling*] Of course not. I'm afraid it's simply my police force taking fright and being a little overzealous. Policemen have a slight tendency to see assassins everywhere. They only do it to make themselves important. Bah, what does it matter? We'll hear the *Te Deum* in a deserted church, that's all.

KING. [*Bitterly*] And there was I thinking those folk adored me. Perhaps you didn't give them enough money.

BECKET. One can only buy those who are for sale, my prince. And those are just the ones who aren't dangerous. With the others, it's wolf against wolf. I'll come back straightaway and set your mind at rest. [*He goes out. The* KING *darts anxious looks on the* PRIEST *as he paces up and down muttering his prayers.*]

KING. Baron!

[*The* 4TH BARON *is nearest the* KING. *He steps forward.*]

4TH BARON. [*Bellowing as usual*] My Lord?

KING. Shush! Keep an eye on that man, all four of you, and at the slightest move, leap on him. [*There follows a little comic dumbshow by the* KING *and the* PRIEST, *who is beginning to feel uneasy too. A sudden violent knocking on the sacristy door. The* KING *starts.*] Who is it?

[*A* SOLDIER *comes in.*]

SOLDIER. A messenger from London, my Lord. They sent him on here from the camp. The message is urgent.

KING. [*Worried*] I don't like it. Regnault, you go and see.

[*The* 4TH BARON *goes out and comes back again, reassured.*]

4TH BARON. It's William of Corbeil, my Lord. He has urgent letters.

KING. You're sure it *is* him? It wouldn't be a Frenchman in disguise? That's an old trick.

4TH BARON. [*Roaring with laughter*] I know him, Sire! I've drained more tankards with him than there are whiskers on his face. And the old goat has plenty!

[*The* KING *makes a sign. The* 4TH BARON *admits the* MESSENGER, *who drops on one knee and presents his letters to the* KING.]

KING. Thank you. Get up. That's a fine beard you have, William of Corbeil. Is it well stuck on?

MESSENGER. [*Rising, bewildered*] My beard, Sire?

[*The* 4TH BARON *guffaws and slaps him on the back.*]

4TH BARON. You old porcupine you!

[*The* KING *has glanced through the letters.*]

KING. Good news, gentlemen! We have one enemy less. [BECKET *comes in. The* KING *cries joyfully*] Becket!

BECKET. Everything is going according to plan, my prince. The troops are on their way. We've only to wait here quietly, until they arrive.

KING. [*Cheerfully*] You're right, Becket, everything is going according to plan. God isn't angry with us. He has just recalled the Archbishop.

BECKET. [*In a murmur*] That little old man . . . How could that feeble body contain so much strength?

KING. Now, now, now! Don't squander your sorrow, my son. I personally consider this an excellent piece of news!

BECKET. He was the first Norman who took an interest in me. He was a true father to me. God rest his soul.

KING. He will! After all the fellow did for Him, he's gone to Heaven, don't worry. Where he'll be definitely more use to God than he was to us. So it's definitely for the best. [*He pulls* BECKET *to him.*] Becket! My little Becket, I think the ball's in our court now! This is the time to score a point. [*He seizes his arm, tense and quite transformed.*] An extraordinary idea is just creeping into my mind, Becket. A master stroke! I can't think what's got into me this morning, but I suddenly feel extremely intelligent. It probably comes of making love with a French girl last night. I am subtle, Becket, I am profound! So profound it's making my head spin. Are you sure it isn't dangerous to think too hard? Thomas, my little Thomas! Are you listening to me?

BECKET. [*Smiling at his excitement*] Yes, my prince.

KING. [*As excited as a little boy*] Are you listening carefully? Listen, Thomas! You told me once that the best ideas are the stupidest ones, but the clever thing is to think of them! Listen, Thomas! Tradition prevents me from touching the privileges of the Primacy. You follow me so far?

BECKET. Yes, my prince . . .

KING. But what if the Primate is my man? If the Archbishop of Canterbury is for the King, how can his power possibly incommodate me?

BECKET. That's an ingenious idea, my prince, but you forget that his election is a free one.

KING. No! You're forgetting the Royal Hand! Do you know what that is? When the candidate is displeasing to the Throne the King sends his Justicer to the Conclave of Bishops and it's the King who has the final say. That's an old custom too, and for once, it's in my favor! It's fully a hundred years since the Conclave of Bishops has voted contrary to the wishes of the King!

BECKET. I don't doubt it, my Lord. But we all know your Bishops. Which one of them could you rely on? Once the Primate's miter is on their heads, they grow dizzy with power.

KING. Are you asking me, Becket? I'll tell you. Someone who doesn't know what dizziness means. Someone who isn't even afraid of God. Thomas, my son, I need your help again and this time it's important. I'm sorry to deprive you of French girls and the fun of battle, my son, but pleasure will come later. You are going over to England.

BECKET. I am at your service, my prince.

KING. Can you guess what your mission will be?

[*A tremor of anguish crosses* BECKET'*s face at what is to come.*]

BECKET. No, my prince.

KING. You are going to deliver a personal letter from me to every Bishop in the land. And do you know what those letters will contain, my Thomas, my little brother? My royal wish to have you elected Primate of England.

[BECKET *has gone deathly white. He says with a forced laugh:*]

BECKET. You're joking, of course, my Lord. Just look at the edifying man, the saintly man whom you would be trusting with these holy functions! [*He has opened his fine coat to display his even finer doublet.*] Why, my prince, you really fooled me for a second! [*The* KING *bursts out laughing.* BECKET *laughs too, rather too loudly in his relief.*] A fine Archbishop I'd have made! Look at my new shoes! They're the latest fashion in Paris. Attractive, that little upturned toe, don't you think? Quite full of unction and compunction, isn't it, Sire?

KING. [*Suddenly stops laughing*] Shut up about your shoes, Thomas! I'm in deadly earnest. I shall write those letters before noon. You will help me.

[BECKET, *deathly pale, stammers:*]

BECKET. But my Lord, I'm not even a priest!

KING. [*Tersely*] You're a deacon. You can take your final vows tomorrow and be ordained in a month.

BECKET. But have you considered what the Pope will say?

KING. [*Brutally*] I'll pay the price!

[BECKET, *after an anguished pause, murmurs:*]

BECKET. My Lord, I see now that you weren't joking. Don't do this.

KING. Why not?

BECKET. It frightens me.

KING. [*His face set and hard*] Becket, this is an order!

[BECKET *stands as if turned to stone. A pause. He murmurs:*]

BECKET. [*Gravely*] If I become Archbishop, I can no longer be your friend.

[*A burst of organ music in the cathedral. Enter an* OFFICER.]

OFFICER. The church is now empty, my Lord. The Bishop and his clergy await your Highness' good pleasure.

KING. [*Roughly to* BECKET] Did you hear that, Becket? Pull yourself together. You have an odd way of taking good news. Wake up! They say we can go in now.

[*The procession forms with the* PRIEST *and the* CHOIRBOY *leading.* BECKET *takes his place, almost reluctantly, a pace or so behind the* KING.]

BECKET. [*In a murmur*] This is madness, my Lord. Don't do it. I could not serve both God and you.

KING. [*Looking straight ahead, says stonily*] You've never disappointed me, Thomas. And you are the only man I trust. You will leave tonight. Come, let's go in. [*He motions to the* PRIEST. *The procession moves off and goes into the empty cathedral, as the organ swells.*

A moment's darkness. The organ continues to play. Then a dim light reveals BECKET*'s room. Open chests into which two* SERVANTS *are piling costly clothes.*]

2ND SERVANT. [*Who is the younger of the two*] The coat with the sable trimming as well?

1ST SERVANT. Everything! You heard what he said!

2ND SERVANT. [*Grumbling*] Sables! To beggars! Who'll give them alms if they beg with that on their backs! They'll starve to death!

1ST SERVANT. [*Cackling*] They'll eat the sables! Can't you understand, you idiot! He's going to sell all this and give them the money!

2ND SERVANT. But what will he wear himself? He's got nothing left at all!

[BECKET *comes in, wearing a plain gray dressing gown.*]

BECKET. Are the chests full? I want them sent over to the Jew before tonight. I want nothing left in this room but the bare walls. Gil, the fur coverlet!

1ST SERVANT. [*Regretfully*] My Lord will be cold at night.

BECKET. Do as I say. [*Regretfully, the* 1ST SERVANT *takes the coverlet and puts it in the chest.*] Has the steward been told about tonight's meal? Supper for forty in the great hall.

1ST SERVANT. He says he won't have enough gold plate, my Lord. Are we to mix it with the silver dishes?

BECKET. Tell him to lay the table with the wooden platters and earthenware bowls from the kitchens. The plate has been sold. The Jew will send over for it late this afternoon.

1ST SERVANT. [*Dazed*] The earthenware bowls and the wooden platters. Yes, my Lord. And the steward says could he have your list of invitations fairly soon, my Lord. He only has three runners and he's afraid there won't be time to—

BECKET. There are no invitations. The great doors will be thrown open and you will go out into the street and tell the poor they are dining with me tonight.

1ST SERVANT. [*Appalled*] Very good, my Lord. [*He is about to go.* BECKET *calls him back.*]

BECKET. I want the service to be impeccable. The dishes presented to each guest first, with full ceremony, just as for princes. Go now. [*The two* SERVANTS *go out.* BECKET, *left alone, casually looks over one or two articles of clothing in the* chests. *He murmurs*] I must say it was all very pretty stuff. [*He drops the lid and bursts out laughing.*] A prick of vanity! The mark of an upstart. A truly saintly man would never have done the whole thing in one day. Nobody will ever believe it's genuine. [*He turns to the jeweled crucifix above the bed and says simply*] I hope You haven't inspired me with all these holy resolutions in order to make me look ridiculous, Lord. It's all so new to me. I'm setting about it a little clumsily perhaps. [*He looks at the crucifix and with a swift gesture takes it off the wall.*] And you're far too sumptuous too. Precious stones around your bleeding Body . . . I shall give you to some poor village church. [*He lays the crucifix on the chest. He looks around the room, happy, lighthearted, and murmurs*] It's like leaving for a holiday. Forgive me, Lord, but I never enjoyed myself so much in my whole life. I don't believe You are a sad God. The joy I feel in shedding all my riches must be part of Your divine intentions. [*He goes behind the curtain into the antechamber where he can be heard gaily whistling an old English marching song. He comes back a second later, his bare feet in sandals, and wearing a monk's coarse woolen robe. He draws the curtain across again and murmurs*] There. Farewell, Becket. I wish there had been something I had regretted parting with, so I could offer it to You. [*He goes to the crucifix and says simply*] Lord, are You sure You are not tempting me? It all seems far too easy.

    [*He drops to his knees and prays.*]

CURTAIN

END OF ACT II

ACT III

A room in the KING'*s palace. The two* QUEENS, *the* QUEEN MOTHER *and the* YOUNG QUEEN, *are on stage, working at their tapestry. The* KING'*s two* SONS, *one considerably older than the other, are playing in a corner, on the floor. The* KING *is in another corner, playing at cup-and-ball. After several unsuccessful attempts to catch the ball in the cup, he throws down the toy and exclaims irritably:*

KING. Forty beggars! He invited forty beggars to dinner!

QUEEN MOTHER. The dramatic gesture, as usual! I always said you had misplaced your confidence, my son.

KING. [*Pacing up and down*] Madam, I am very particular where I place my confidence. I only ever did it once in my whole life and I am still convinced I was right. But there's a great deal we don't understand! Thomas is ten times more intelligent than all of us put together.

QUEEN MOTHER. [*Reprovingly*] You are talking about royalty, my son.

KING. [*Grunting*] What of it? Intelligence has been shared out on a different basis.

YOUNG QUEEN. It seems he has sold his gold plate and all his rich clothes to a Jew. He wears an ordinary homespun habit now.

QUEEN MOTHER. I see that as a sign of ostentation, if nothing worse! One can become a saintly man, certainly, but not in a single day. I've never liked the man. You were insane to make him so powerful.

KING. [*Crying out*] He is my friend!

QUEEN MOTHER. [*Acidly*] More's the pity.

YOUNG QUEEN. He is your friend in debauchery. It was he who lured you
away from your duty towards me. It was he who first took you to the whore-
houses!

KING. [*Furious*] Rubbish, Madam! I didn't need anybody to lure me away from
my duty towards you. I made you three children, very conscientiously. Phew!
My duty is done for a while.

YOUNG QUEEN. [*Stung*] When that libertine loses the evil influence he has on
you, you will come to appreciate the joys of family life again. Pray Heaven
he disobeys you!

KING. The joys of family life are limited, Madam. To be perfectly frank, you
bore me. You and your eternal backbiting, over your everlasting tapestry,
the pair of you! That's no sustenance for a man! [*He trots about the room,
furious, and comes to a halt behind their chairs.*] If at least it had some artistic
merit. My ancestress Mathilda, while she was waiting for her husband to
finish carving out his kingdom, now *she* embroidered a masterpiece—which
they left behind in Bayeux,[11] more's the pity. But that! It's beyond belief
it's so mediocre.

YOUNG QUEEN. [*Nettled*] We can only use the gifts we're born with.

KING. Yes. And yours are meager. [*He glances out of the window once more to
look at the time, and says with a sigh*] I've been bored to tears for a whole
month. Not a soul to talk to. After his nomination, not wanting to seem in
too indecent a hurry, I leave him alone to carry out his pastoral tour. Now,
back he comes at last, I summon him to the palace and he's late. [*He looks
out of the window again and exclaims*] Ah! Someone at the sentry post! [*He
turns away, disappointed.*] No, it's only a monk. [*He wanders about the room, aimlessly. He goes over to join the children, and watches them playing for a while. Sourly*]
Charming babes. Men in the making. Sly and obtuse already. And to think
one is expected to be dewy-eyed over creatures like that, merely because
they aren't yet big enough to be hated or despised. Which is the elder of
you two?

ELDER BOY. [*Rising*] I am, Sir.

KING. What's your name again?

ELDER BOY. Henry III.

KING. [*Sharply*] Not yet, Sir! Number II is in the best of health. [*To the* QUEEN]
You've brought them up well! Do you think of yourself as Regent already?
And you wonder that I shun your bedchamber? I don't care to make love
with my widow.

    [*An* OFFICER *comes in.*]

OFFICER. A messenger from the Archbishop, my Lord.

KING. [*Beside himself with rage*] A messenger! A messenger! I summoned the
Archbishop Primate in person! [*He turns to the women, suddenly uneasy, almost
touching.*] Perhaps he's ill? That would explain everything.

QUEEN MOTHER. [*Bitterly*] That's too much to hope for.

KING. [*Raging*] You'd like to see him dead, wouldn't you, you females—because
he loves me? If he hasn't come, it's because he's dying! Send the man in,
quickly! O my Thomas . . . [*The* OFFICER *goes and admits the* MONK. *The* KING
hurries over to him.] Who are you? Is Becket ill?

---

[11] A city in Normandy in France. The Bayeaux Tapestry is over 200 feet long by 20 inches wide,
and depicts the events of the Normans' conquest of England in 1066. Legend relates that it
was made by Mathilda, the wife of William the Conqueror, late in the eleventh century.

MONK. [*Falling on one knee*] My Lord, I am William son of Etienne, secretary to his Grace the Archbishop.

KING. Is your master seriously ill?

MONK. No, my Lord. His Grace is in good health. He has charged me to deliver this letter with his deepest respects—and to give your Highness this. [*He bows lower and hands something to the* KING.]

KING. [*Stunned*] The Seal? Why has he sent me back the Seal? [*He unrolls the parchment and reads it in silence. His face hardens. He says curtly, without looking at the* MONK] You have carried out your mission. Go.

   [*The* MONK *rises and turns to go.*]

MONK. Is there an answer from your Highness for his Grace the Archbishop?

KING. [*Harshly*] No!

   [*The* MONK *goes out. The* KING *stands still a moment, at a loss, then flings himself onto his throne, glowering. The women exchange a conspiratorial look. The* QUEEN MOTHER *rises and goes to him.*]

QUEEN MOTHER. [*Insidiously*] Well, my son, what does your friend say in his letter?

KING. [*Bawling*] Get out! Get out, both of you! And take your royal vermin with you! I am alone! [*Frightened, the* QUEENS *hurry out with the children. The* KING *stands there a moment, reeling a little, as if stunned by the blow. Then he collapses onto the throne and sobs like a child. Moaning*] O my Thomas! [*He remains a moment prostrate, then collects himself and sits up. He looks at the Seal in his hand and says between clenched teeth*] You've sent me back the Three Lions of England, like a little boy who doesn't want to play with me any more. You think you have God's honor to defend now! I would have gone to war with all England's might behind me, and against England's interests, to defend you, little Saxon. I would have given the honor of the Kingdom laughingly . . . for you . . . Only I loved you and you didn't love me . . . that's the difference. [*His face hardens. He adds between clenched teeth*] Thanks all the same for this last gift as you desert me. I shall learn to be alone. [*He goes out. The lights dim.* SERVANTS *remove the furniture. When the lights go up again, the permanent set, with the pillars, is empty.*

   A bare church; a man half hidden under a dark cloak is waiting behind a pillar. It is the KING. *Closing chords of organ music. Enter* GILBERT FOLLIOT, *Bishop of London, followed by his* CLERGY. *He has just said Mass. The* KING *goes to him.*] Bishop . . .

FOLLIOT. [*Stepping back*] What do you want, fellow? [*His acolytes are about to step between them, when he exclaims*] The King!

KING. Yes.

FOLLIOT. Alone, without an escort, and dressed like a common squire?

KING. The King nevertheless. Bishop, I would like to make a confession.

FOLLIOT. [*With a touch of suspicion*] I am the Bishop of London. The King has his own Confessor. That is an important Court appointment and it has its prerogatives.

KING. The choice of priest for Holy Confession is open, Bishop, even for a King. [FOLLIOT *motions to his* CLERGY, *who draw away.*] Anyway, my confession will be short, and I'm not asking for absolution. I have something much worse than a sin on my conscience, Bishop: a mistake. A foolish mistake. [FOLLIOT *says nothing.*] I ordered you to vote for Thomas Becket at the Council of Clarendon. I repent of it.

FOLLIOT. [*Inscrutably*] We bowed before the Royal Hand.

KING. Reluctantly, I know. It took me thirteen weeks of authority and patience to crush the small uncrushable opposition of which you were the head, Bishop. On the day the Council met you looked green. They told me you fell seriously ill afterwards.

FOLLIOT. [*Impenetrably*] God cured me.

KING. Very good of Him. But He is rather inclined to look after His own, to the exclusion of anyone else. He let me fall ill without lifting a finger! And I must cure myself without divine intervention. I have the Archbishop on my stomach. A big hard lump I shall have to vomit back. What does the Norman clergy think of him?

FOLLIOT. [*Reserved*] His Grace seems to have the reins of the Church of England well in hand. Those who are in close contact with him even say that he behaves like a holy man.

KING. [*With grudging admiration*] It's a bit sudden, but nothing he does ever surprises me. God knows what the brute is capable of, for good or for evil. Bishop, let us be frank with each other. Is the Church very interested in holy men?

FOLLIOT. [*With the ghost of a smile*] The Church has been wise for so long, your Highness, that she could not have failed to realize that the temptation of saintliness is one of the most insidious and fearsome snares the devil can lay for her priests. The administration of the realm of souls, with the temporal difficulties it carries with it, chiefly demands, as in all administrations, competent administrators. The Roman Catholic Church has its Saints, it invokes their benevolent intercession, it prays to them. But it has no need to create others. That is superfluous. And dangerous.

KING. You seem to be a man one can talk to, Bishop. I misjudged you. Friendship blinded me.

FOLLIOT. [*Still impenetrable*] Friendship is a fine thing.

KING. [*Suddenly hoarse*] It's a domestic animal, a living, tender thing. It seems to be all eyes, forever gazing at you, warming you. You don't see its teeth. But it's a beast with one curious characteristic. It is only after death that it bites.

FOLLIOT. [*Prudently*] Is the King's friendship for Thomas Becket dead, your Highness?

KING. Yes, Bishop. It died quite suddenly. A sort of heart failure.

FOLLIOT. A curious phenomenon, your Highness, but quite frequent.

KING. [*Taking his arm suddenly*] I hate Becket now, Bishop. There is nothing more in common between that man and me than this creature tearing at my guts. I can't bear it any more. I shall have to turn it loose on him. But I am the King; what they conventionally call my greatness stands in my way. I need somebody.

FOLLIOT. [*Stiffening*] I do not wish to serve anything but the Church.

KING. Let us talk like grown men, Bishop. We went in hand in hand to conquer, pillage and ransom England. We quarrel, we try to cheat each other of a penny or two, but Heaven and Earth still have one or two common interests. Do you know what I have just obtained from the Pope? His Blessing to go and murder Catholic Ireland, in the name of the Faith. Yes, a sort of crusade to impose Norman barons and clergy on the Irish, with our swords and standards solemnly blessed as if we were off to give the Turks a drubbing. The only condition: a little piece of silver per household per year, for St. Peter's pence, which the native clergy of Ireland is loath to part with and which I have undertaken to make them pay. It's a mere pittance. But at the end of the year it will add up to a pretty sum. Rome knows how to do her accounts.

FOLLIOT. [*Terror-stricken*] There are some things one should never say, your Highness: one should even try not to know about them, so long as one is not directly concerned with them.

KING. [*Smiling*] We are alone, Bishop, and the church is empty.

FOLLIOT. The church is never empty. A little red lamp burns in front of the High Altar.

KING. [*Impatiently*] Bishop, I like playing games, but only with boys of my own age! Do you take me for one of your sheep, holy pastor? The One whom that little red lamp honors read into your innermost heart and mine a long time ago. Of your cupidity and my hatred, He knows all there is to know. [FOLLIOT *withdraws into his shell. The* KING *cries irritably*] If that's the way you feel you must become a monk, Bishop! Wear a hair shirt on your naked back and go and hide yourself in a monastery to pray! The Bishopric of London, for the purehearted son of a Thames waterman, is too much, or too little! [*A pause.*]

FOLLIOT. [*Impassively*] If, as is my duty, I disregard my private feelings, I must admit that his Grace the Archbishop has so far done nothing which has not been in the interests of Mother Church.

KING. [*Eying him, says jovially*] I can see your game, my little friend. You mean to cost me a lot of money. But I'm rich—thanks to Becket, who has succeeded in making you pay the Absentee Tax. And it seems to me eminently ethical that a part of the Church's gold should find its way, via you, back to the Church. Besides, if we want to keep this on a moral basis, Holy Bishop, you can tell yourself that as the greatness of the Church and that of the State are closely linked, in serving me, you will in the long run be working for the consolidation of the Catholic Faith.

FOLLIOT. [*Contemplating him with curiosity*] I had always taken your Highness for a great adolescent lout who cared only for his pleasure.

KING. One can be wrong about people, Bishop. I made the same mistake. [*With a sudden cry*] O my Thomas . . .

FOLLIOT. [*Fiercely*] You love him, your Highness! You still love him! You love that mitered hog, that impostor, that Saxon bastard, that little guttersnipe!

KING. [*Seizing him by the throat*] Yes, I love him! But that's my affair, priest! All I confided to you was my hatred. I'll pay you to rid me of him, but don't ever speak ill of him to me. Or we'll fight it out as man to man!

FOLLIOT. Highness, you're choking me!

KING. [*Abruptly releasing him*] We will meet again tomorrow, my Lord Bishop, and we'll go over the details of our enterprise together. You will be officially summoned to the palace on some pretext or other—my good works in your London Diocese, say—where I am your chief parishioner. But it won't be the poor and needy we'll discuss. My poor can wait. The Kingdom they pin their hopes on is eternal. [*The* KING *goes out.* GILBERT FOLLIOT *remains motionless. His* CLERGY *join him timidly. He takes his crook and goes out with dignity, but not before one of his Canons has discreetly adjusted his miter, which was knocked askew in the recent struggle.*

They have gone out. The lighting changes. Curtains between the pillars. The episcopal palace.

Morning. A PRIEST *enters, leading two* MONKS *and the* YOUNG MONK *from the convent of Hastings.*]

PRIEST. His Grace will receive you here.

[*The two* MONKS *are impressed. They push the* YOUNG MONK *about a little.*]

1ST MONK. Stand up straight. Kiss his Grace's ring and try to answer his questions with humility, or I'll tan your backside for you!

2ND MONK. I suppose you thought he'd forgotten all about you? The great never forget anything. And don't you act proud with him or you'll be sorry.

[*Enter* BECKET, *wearing a coarse monk's robe.*]

BECKET. Well, brothers, is it fine over in Hastings? [*He gives them his ring to kiss.*]

1ST MONK. Foggy, my Lord.

BECKET. [*Smiling*] Then it's fine in Hastings. We always think fondly of our Abbey there and we intend to visit it soon, when our new duties grant us a moment's respite. How has this young man been behaving? Has he given our Abbot much trouble?

2ND MONK. A proper mule, my Lord. Father Abbot tried kindness, as you recommended, but he soon had to have recourse to the dungeon and bread and water, and even to the whip. Nothing has any effect. The stubborn little wretch is just the same; all defiance and insults. He has fallen into the sin of pride. Nothing I know of will pull him out of that!

1ST MONK. Save a good kick in the rump perhaps—if your Grace will pardon the expression. [*To the boy*] Stand up straight.

BECKET. [*To the boy*] Pay attention to your brother. Stand up straight. As a rule the sin of pride stiffens a man's back. Look me in the face. [*The* YOUNG MONK *looks at him.*] Good. [BECKET *looks at the boy for a while, then turns to the* MONKS.] You will be taken to the kitchens where you can refresh yourselves before you leave, brothers. They have orders to treat you well. Don't spurn our hospitality; we relieve you, for today, of your vows of abstinence, and we fondly hope you will do honor to our bill of fare. Greet your father Abbot in Jesus on our behalf.

2ND MONK. [*Hesitantly*] And the lad?

BECKET. We will keep him here.

1ST MONK. Watch out for him, your Grace. He's vicious.

BECKET. [*Smiling*] We are not afraid. [*The* MONKS *go out.* BECKET *and the* YOUNG MONK *remain, facing each other.*] Why do you hold yourself so badly?

YOUNG MONK. I don't want to look people in the face any more.

BECKET. I'll teach you. That will be your first lesson. Look at me. [*The boy gives him a sidelong glance.*] Better than that. [*The boy looks at him.*] Are you still bearing the full weight of England's shame alone? Is it that shame which bends your back like that?

YOUNG MONK. Yes.

BECKET. If I took over half of it, would it weigh less heavy? [*He motions to the* PRIEST.] Show in their Lordships the Bishops. You'll soon see that being alone is not a privilege reserved entirely for you. [*The* BISHOPS *come in.* BECKET *leads the* YOUNG MONK *into a corner.*] You stay here in the corner and hold my tablets. I ask only one thing. Don't leap at their throats; you'd complicate everything. [*He motions to the* BISHOPS *who remain standing.*]

FOLLIOT. Your Grace, I am afraid this meeting may be a pointless one. You insisted—against our advice—on attacking the King openly. Even before the three excommunications which you asked us to sanction could be made public, the King has hit back. His Grand Justicer Richard de Lacy has just arrived in your antechamber and is demanding to see you in the name of the King. He is the bearer of an official order summoning you to appear before his assembled Council within twenty-four hours and there to answer the charges made against you.

BECKET. Of what is the King accusing me?

FOLLIOT. Prevarication. Following the examination of accounts by his Privy Council, his Highness demands a considerable sum still outstanding on your administration of the Treasury.

BECKET. When I resigned the Chancellorship I handed over my ledgers to the Grand Justicer who acquitted me of all subsequent dues and claims. What does the King demand?

OXFORD. Forty thousand marks in fine gold.

BECKET. [*Smiling*] I don't believe there was ever as much money in all the coffers of all England in all the time I was Chancellor. But a clever clerk can soon change that . . . The King has closed his fist and I am like a fly inside it. [*He smiles and looks at him.*] I have the impression, gentlemen, that you must be feeling something very akin to relief.

YORK. We advised you against open opposition.

BECKET. William of Aynsford, incited by the King, struck down the priest I had appointed to the Parish of his Lordship's See, on the pretext that his Highness disapproved of my choice. Am I to look on while my priests are murdered?

FOLLIOT. It is not for you to appoint a priest to a free fief! There is not a Norman, layman or cleric, who will ever concede that. It would mean reviewing the entire legal system of the Conquest. Everything can be called into question in England except the fact that it was conquered in 1066. England is the land of law and of the most scrupulous respect for the law; but the law begins at that date only, or England as such ceases to exist.

BECKET. Bishop, must I remind you that we are men of God and that we have an Honor to defend, which dates from all eternity?

OXFORD. [*Quietly*] This excommunication was bad policy, your Grace. William of Aynsford is a companion of the King.

BECKET. [*Smiling*] I know him very well. He's a charming man. I have drained many a tankard with him.

YORK. [*Yelping*] And his wife is my second cousin!

BECKET. That is a detail I deplore, my Lord Bishop, but he has killed one of my priests. If I do not defend my priests, who will? Gilbert of Clare has indicted before his court of justice a churchman who was under our exclusive jurisdiction.

YORK. An interesting victim I must say! He deserved the rope a hundred times over. The man was accused of rape and murder. Wouldn't it have been cleverer to let the wretch hang—and have peace?

BECKET. "I bring not peace but the sword." Your Lordship must I'm sure have read that somewhere. I am not interested in what this man is guilty of. If I allow my priests to be tried by a secular tribunal; if I let Robert de Vere abduct our tonsured clerics from our monasteries, as he has just done, on the grounds that the man was one of his serfs who had escaped land bondage, I don't give much for our freedom and our chances of survival in five years' time, my Lord. I have excommunicated Gilbert of Clare, Robert de Vere and William of Aynsford. The Kingdom of God must be defended like any other Kingdom. Do you think that Right has only to show it's handsome face for everything to drop in its lap? Without Might, its old enemy, Right counts for nothing.

YORK. What Might? Let us not indulge in empty words. The King is Might and he is the law.

BECKET. He is the written law, but there is another, unwritten law, which always makes Kings bend the neck eventually. [*He looks at them for a moment and smiles.*] I was a profligate, gentlemen, perhaps a libertine, in any case, a worldly man. I loved living and I laughed at all these things. But you passed the burden on to me and now I have to carry it. I have rolled up my sleeves and taken it on my back and nothing will ever make me set it down again. I thank your Lordships. The council is adjourned and I have made my decision. I shall stand by these three excommunications. I shall appear tomorrow before the King's supreme court of Justice. [*The* BISHOPS *look at one another in surprise, then bow and go out.* BECKET *turns to the* YOUNG MONK] Well, does the shame weigh less heavy now?

YOUNG MONK. Yes.

BECKET. [*Leading him off and laughing*] Then stand up straight!

[*The drapes close. Distant trumpets. The* KING *comes out from behind the curtains and turns to peep through them at something. A pause. Then* GILBERT FOLLIOT *comes hurrying in.*]

KING. What's happening? I can't see a thing from up here.

FOLLIOT. Legal procedure is taking its course, your Highness. The third summons has been delivered. He has not appeared. In a moment he will be condemned in absentia.[10] Once prevarication is established, our Dean the Bishop of Chichester will go to see him and communicate according to the terms of the ancient Charter of the Church of England, our corporated repudiation of allegiance, absolving us of obedience to him—and our intention to report him to our Holy Father the Pope. I shall then, as Bishop of London, step forward and publicly accuse Becket of having celebrated, in contempt of the King, a sacrilegious Mass at the instigation of the Evil Spirit.

KING. [*Anxiously*] Isn't that going rather far?

FOLLIOT. Of course. It won't fool anyone, but it always works. The assembly will then go out to vote, in order of precedence, and return a verdict of imprisonment. The sentence is already drawn up.

KING. Unanimously?

FOLLIOT. We are all Normans. The rest is your Highness' concern. It will merely be a matter of carrying out the sentence.

KING. [*Staggering suddenly*] O my Thomas!

FOLLIOT. [*Impassively*] I can still stop the machine, your Highness.

KING. [*Hesitates a second then says*] No. Go.

[FOLLIOT *goes out. The* KING *goes back to his place, behind the curtain.*

The two QUEENS *come into the room, and join the* KING. *All three stand and peer through the curtain. A pause.*]

YOUNG QUEEN. He's doomed, isn't he?

KING. [*Dully*] Yes.

YOUNG QUEEN. At last!

[*The* KING *turns on her, his face twisted with hate.*]

KING. I forbid you to gloat!

YOUNG QUEEN. At seeing your enemy perish—why not?

KING. [*Frothing*] Becket is my enemy, but in the human balance, bastard as he is, and naked as his mother made him, he weighs a hundred times more

---

[10] In his absence.

than you do, Madam, with your crown and all your jewels and your august father the Emperor into the bargain. Becket is attacking me and he has betrayed me. I am forced to fight him and crush him, but at least he gave me, with open hands, everything that is at all good in me. And you have never given me anything but your carping mediocrity, your everlasting obsession with your puny little person and what you thought was due to it. That is why I forbid you to smile as he lies dying!

YOUNG QUEEN. I gave you my youth! I gave you your children!

KING. [*Shouting*] I don't like my children! And as for your youth—that dusty flower pressed in a hymnbook since you were twelve years old, with its watery blood and its insipid scent—you can say farewell to that without a tear. With age, bigotry and malice may perhaps give some spice to your character. Your body was an empty desert, Madam!—which duty forced me to wander in alone. But you have never been a wife to me! And Becket was my friend, red-blooded, generous and full of strength! [*He is shaken by a sob.*] O my Thomas!

[*The* QUEEN MOTHER *moves over to him.*]

QUEEN MOTHER. [*Haughtily*] And I, my son, I gave you nothing either, I suppose?

KING. [*Recovers his composure, glares at her and says dully*] Life. Yes. Thank you. But after that I never saw you save in a passage, dressed for a Ball, or in your crown and ermine mantle, ten minutes before official ceremonies, where you were forced to tolerate my presence. I have always been alone, and no one on this earth has ever loved me except Becket!

QUEEN MOTHER. [*Bitterly*] Well, call him back! Absolve him, since he loves you! Give him supreme power then! But do something!

KING. I am. I'm learning to be alone again, Madam. As usual. [*A* PAGE *comes in, breathless.*] Well? What's happening? How far have they got?

PAGE. My Liege, Thomas Becket appeared just when everyone had given him up; sick, deathly pale, in full pontifical regalia and carrying his own heavy silver cross. He walked the whole length of the hall without anyone daring to stop him, and when Robert Duke of Leicester, who was to read out his sentence, began the consecrated words, he stopped with a gesture and forbade him, in God's name, to pronounce judgment against him, his spiritual Father. Then he walked back through the crowd, which parted for him in silence. He has just left.

KING. [*Unable to hide his delight*] Well played, Thomas! One point to you. [*He checks himself, embarrassed, and then says*] And what about my Barons?

PAGE. Their hands flew to their swords with cries of "Traitor! Perjurer! Arrest him! Miserable wretch! Hear your sentence!" But not one of them dared move, or touch the sacred ornaments.

KING. [*With a roar*] The fools! I am surrounded by fools and the only intelligent man in my Kingdom is against me!

PAGE. [*Continuing his story*] Then, on the threshold, he turned, looked at them coldly as they shouted in their impotence, and he said that not so long ago he could have answered their challenge sword in hand. Now he could no longer do it, but he begged them to remember that there was a time when he met strength with strength.

KING. [*Jubilantly*] He could beat them all! All, I tell you! On horseback, on foot, with a mace, with a lance, with a sword! In the lists they fell to him like ninepins!

PAGE. And his eyes were so cold, and so ironic—even though all he had in his hand was his episcopal crook—that one by one, they fell silent. Only then did he turn and go out. They say he has given orders to invite all the beggars of the city to sup at his house tonight.

KING. [Somberly] And what about the Bishop of London, who was going to reduce him to powder? What about my busy friend Gilbert Folliot?

PAGE. He had a horrible fit of rage trying to incite the crowd, he let out a screech of foul abuse and then he fainted. They are bringing him round now.

[The KING suddenly bursts into a shout of irrepressible laughter, and, watched by the two outraged QUEENS, collapses into the PAGE's arms, breathless and helpless with mirth.]

KING. It's too funny! It's too funny!

QUEEN MOTHER. [Coldly] You will laugh less heartily tomorrow, my son. If you don't stop him, Becket will reach the coast tonight, ask asylum of the King of France and jeer at you, unpunished, from across the Channel. [She sweeps out with the YOUNG QUEEN. Suddenly, the KING stops laughing and runs out.

The light changes. Curtains part. We are at the Court of LOUIS, KING OF FRANCE. He is sitting in the middle of the courtroom, very erect on his throne. He is a burly man with intelligent eyes.]

LOUIS. [To his BARONS] Gentlemen, we are in France and a fart on England's King—as the song goes.

1ST BARON. Your Majesty cannot not receive his Ambassadors Extraordinary!

LOUIS. Ordinary, or extraordinary, I am at home to all ambassadors. It's my job. I shall receive them.

1ST BARON. They have been waiting in your Majesty's anteroom for over an hour, Sire.

LOUIS. Let them wait. That's their job. An ambassador is made for pacing about an antechamber. I know what they are going to ask me.

2ND BARON. The extradition of a felon is a courtesy due from one crowned head to another.

LOUIS. My dear man, crowned heads can play the little game of courtesy but nations owe each other none. My right to play the courteous gentleman stops where France's interests begin. And France's interests consist in making things as difficult as possible for England—a thing England never hesitates to do to us. The Archbishop is a millstone round Henry Plantagenet's neck. Long live the Archbishop! Anyway, I like the fellow.

2ND BARON. My gracious sovereign is master. And so long as our foreign policy permits us to expect nothing of King Henry—

LOUIS. For the time being, it is an excellent thing to stiffen our attitude. Remember the Montmirail affair.[12] We only signed the peace treaty with Henry on condition that he granted to spare the lives of the refugees from Brittany and Poitou whom he asked us to hand over to him. Two months later all of them had lost their heads. That directly touched my personal honor. I was not strong enough at the time, so I had to pretend I hadn't heard of these men's execution. And I continued to lavish smiles on my English cousin. But praise God our affairs have taken a turn for the better. And today he

---

[12] The peace treaty described here was negotiated in January 1169 in Montmirail, a town about seventy miles east of Paris.

needs *us*. So I will now proceed to remember my honor. Show in the ambassadors.

[*Exit* 1ST BARON. *He comes back with* FOLLIOT *and the* DUKE OF ARUNDEL.]

1ST BARON. Permit me to introduce to your Majesty the two envoys extraordinary from his Highness Henry of England; his Grace the Bishop of London and the Duke of Arundel.

LOUIS. [*With a friendly wave to the* DUKE] Greetings to you, Milord. I have not forgotten your amazing exploits at the last tournament at Calais. Do you still wield a lance as mightily as you did, Milord?

ARUNDEL. [*With a gratified bow*] I hope so, Sire.

LOUIS. We hope that our friendly relations with your gracious master will allow us to appreciate your jousting skill again before long, on the occasion of the forthcoming festivities. [FOLLIOT *has unrolled a parchment.*] Bishop, I see you have a letter for us from your master. We are listening.

FOLLIOT. [*Bows again and starts to read*] "To my Lord and friend Louis, King of the French; Henry, King of England, Duke of Normandy, Duke of Aquitaine and Count of Anjou: Learn that Thomas, former Archbishop of Canterbury, after a public trial held at my court by the plenary assembly of the Barons of my realm has been found guilty of fraud, perjury and treason towards me. He has forthwith fled my Kingdom as a traitor, and with evil intent. I therefore entreat you not to allow this criminal, nor any of his adherents, to reside upon your territories, nor to permit any of your vassals to give help, support or counsel to this my greatest enemy. For I solemnly declare that your enemies or those of your Realm would receive none from me or my subjects. I expect you to assist me in the vindication of my honor and the punishment of my enemy, as you would wish me to do for you, should the need arise." [*A pause.* FOLLIOT *bows very low and hands the parchment to the* KING *who rolls it up casually and hands it to one of the* BARONS.]

LOUIS. Gentlemen, we have listened attentively to our gracious cousin's request and we take good note of it. Our chancellery will draft a reply which will be sent to you tomorrow. All we can do at the moment, is express our surprise. No news had reached us of the presence of the Archbishop of Canterbury on our domains.

FOLLIOT. [*Tersely*] Sire, the former Archbishop has taken refuge at the Abbey of St. Martin, near Saint-Omer.

LOUIS. [*Still gracious*] My Lord Bishop, we flatter ourselves that there is some order in our Kingdom. If he were there, we would certainly have been informed. [*He makes a gesture of dismissal. The Ambassadors bow low and go out backwards, ushered out by the* 1ST BARON. *Immediately,* LOUIS *says to the* 2ND BARON] Show in Thomas Becket and leave us. [*The* 2ND BARON *goes out and a second later admits* THOMAS, *dressed in a monk's robe.* THOMAS *drops onto one knee. The* BARON *goes out. Kindly*] Rise, Thomas Becket. And greet us as the Primate of England. The bow is enough—and if I know my etiquette, you are entitled to a slight nod of the head from me. There, that's done. I would even be required to kiss your ring, if your visit were an official one. But I have the impression that it isn't, am I right?

BECKET. [*With a smile*] No, Sire. I am only an exile.

LOUIS. [*Graciously*] That too is an important title, in France.

BECKET. I am afraid it is the only one I have left. My property has been seized and distributed to those who served the King against me; letters have been sent to the Duke of Flanders and all his Barons enjoining them to seize my person. John, Bishop of Poitiers, who was suspected of wanting to grant me asylum, has just been poisoned.

LOUIS. [*Smiling*] In fact you are a very dangerous man.

BECKET. I'm afraid so.

LOUIS. [*Unperturbed*] We like danger, Becket. And if the King of France started being afraid of the King of England, there would be something sadly amiss in Europe. We grant you our royal protection on whichever of our domains it will please you to choose.

BECKET. I humbly thank your Majesty. I must, however, tell you that I cannot buy this protection with any act hostile to my country.

LOUIS. You do us injury. That was understood. You may be sure we are practiced enough in the task of Kingship not to make such gross errors in our choice of spies and traitors. The King of France will ask nothing of you. But . . . There is always a but, as I'm sure you are aware, in politics. [BECKET *looks up. The* KING *rises heavily onto his fat legs, goes to him and says familiarly*] I am only responsible for France's interests, Becket. I really can't afford to shoulder those of Heaven. In a month or a year I can summon you back here and tell you, just as blandly, that my dealings with the King of England have taken a different turn and that I am obliged to banish you. [*He slaps him affably on the back, his eyes sparkling with intelligence and asks, with a smile*] I believe you have dabbled in politics too, Archbishop?

BECKET. [*Smiling*] Yes, Sire. Not so very long ago.

LOUIS. [*Jovially*] I like you very much. Mark you, had you been a French Bishop, I don't say I wouldn't have clapped you in prison myself. But in the present circumstances, you have a right to my royal protection. Do you value candor, Becket?

BECKET. Yes, Sire.

LOUIS. Then we are sure to understand each other. Do you intend to go to see the Holy Father?

BECKET. Yes, Sire, if you give me your safe conduct.

LOUIS. You shall have it. But a word in your ear—as a friend. (Keep this to yourself, won't you?—don't go and stir up trouble for me with Rome.) Beware of the Pope. He'll sell you for thirty pieces of silver. The man needs money.

[*The lights dim. A curtain closes. Two small rostrums, bearing the* POPE *and the* CARDINAL, *are pushed on stage, to a light musical accompaniment.*

The POPE *is a thin, fidgety little man with an atrocious Italian accent. The* CARDINAL *is swarthy, and his accent is even worse. The whole effect is a little grubby, among the gilded splendor.*]

POPE. I don't agree, Zambelli! I don't agree at all! It's a very bad plan altogether. We will forfeit our honor all for 3,000 silver marks.

CARDINAL. Holy Father, there is no question of forfeiting honor, but merely of taking the sum offered by the King of England and thereby gaining time. To lose that sum and give a negative answer right away would solve neither the problems of the Curia,[13] nor those of Thomas Becket—nor even, I am afraid, those of the higher interests of the Church. To accept the money— the sum is meager, I agree, and cannot be viewed as a factor in our decision— is merely to make a gesture of appeasement in the interests of peace in Europe. Which has always been the supreme duty of the Holy See.

---

[13] The Curia Romana, or Holy See, is the papal court, which assists the Pope in governing the Roman Catholic Church.

POPE. [*Concerned*] If we take money from the King, I cannot possibly receive the Archbishop, who has been waiting here in Rome for a whole month for me to grant him an audience.

CARDINAL. Receive the money from the King, Very Holy Father, and receive the Archbishop too. The one will neutralize the other. The money will remove all subversive taint from the audience you will grant the Archbishop and on the other hand, the reception of the Archbishop will efface whatever taint of humiliation there may have been in accepting the money.

POPE. [*Gloomily*] I don't want to receive him at all. I gather he is a sincere man. I am always disconcerted by people of that sort. They leave me with a bad taste in my mouth.

CARDINAL. Sincerity is a form of strategy, just like any other, Holy Father. In certain very difficult negotiations, when matters are not going ahead and the usual tactics cease to work, I have been known to use it myself. The great pitfall, of course, is if your opponent starts being sincere at the same time as you. Then the game becomes horribly confusing.

POPE. You know what they say Becket's been meaning to ask me?—in the month he's spent pacing about my antechamber?

CARDINAL. [*Innocently*] No, Holy Father.

POPE. [*Impatiently*] Zambelli! Don't play the fox with me! It was you who told me!

CARDINAL. [*Caught out*] I beg your pardon, Holy Father, I had forgotten. Or rather, as Your Holiness asked me the question, I thought you had forgotten and so I took a chance and—

POPE. [*Irritably*] Zambelli, if we start outmaneuvering each other to no purpose, we'll be here all night!

CARDINAL. [*In confusion*] Force of habit, your Holiness. Excuse me.

POPE. To ask me to relieve him of his rank and functions as Archbishop of Canterbury—that's the reason Becket is in Rome! And do you know why he wants to ask me that?

CARDINAL. [*Candidly for once*] Yes, Holy Father.

POPE. [*Irritably*] No, you do not know! It was your enemy Rapallo who told me!

CARDINAL. [*Modestly*] Yes, but I knew it just the same, because I have a spy in Rapallo's palace.

POPE. [*With a wink*] Culograti?

CARDINAL. No. Culograti is only my spy in his master's eyes. By the man I have spying on Culograti.

POPE. [*Cutting short the digression*] Becket maintains that the election of Clarendon was not a free one, that he owes his nomination solely to the royal whim and that consequently the honor of God, of which he has now decided he is the champion, does not allow him to bear this usurped title any longer. He wishes to be nothing more than an ordinary priest.

CARDINAL. [*After a moment's thought*] The man is clearly an abyss of ambition.

POPE. And yet he knows that we know that his title and functions are his only safeguard against the King's anger. I don't give much for his skin wherever he is, when he is no longer Archbishop!

CARDINAL. [*Thoughtfully*] He's playing a deep game. But I have a plan. Your Holiness will pretend to believe in his scruples. You will receive him and relieve him of his titles and functions as Primate, then, immediately after, as a reward for his zeal in defending the Church of England, you will reappoint him Archbishop, in right and due form this time. We thus avert the danger, we score a point against him—and at the same time a point against the King.

POPE. That's a dangerous game. The King has a long arm.

CARDINAL. We can cover ourselves. We will send secret letters to the English court explaining that this new nomination is a pure formality and that we herewith rescind the excommunications pronounced by Becket; on the other hand, we will inform Becket of the existence of these secret letters, swearing him to secrecy and begging him to consider them as null and void.

POPE. [*Getting muddled*] In that case, perhaps, there isn't much point in the letters being secret?

CARDINAL. Yes, there is. Because that will allow us to maneuver with each of them as if the other was ignorant of the contents, while taking the precaution of making it known to them both. The main thing is for them not to know that we know they know. It's so simple a child of twelve could grasp it!

POPE. But Archbishop or no, what are we going to do with Becket?

CARDINAL. [*With a lighthearted wave of his hand*] We will send him to a convent. A French convent, since King Louis is protecting him—to the Cistercians say, at Pontigny. The monastic rule is a strict one. It will do that onetime dandy a world of good! Let him learn real poverty! That will teach him to be the comforter of the poor!

POPE. That sounds like good advice, Zambelli. Bread and water and nocturnal prayers are an excellent remedy for sincerity. [*He muses a moment.*] The only thing that puzzles me, Zambelli, is why you should want to give me a piece of good advice . . .

[*The* CARDINAL *looks a little embarrassed. The little rostra go as they came and the curtain opens revealing a small, bare cell, center stage.* BECKET *is praying before a humble wooden crucifix. Crouching in a corner, the* YOUNG MONK *is playing with a knife.*]

BECKET. Yet it would be simple enough. Too simple perhaps. Saintliness is a temptation too. Oh, how difficult it is to get an answer from You, Lord! I was slow in praying to You, but I cannot believe that others, worthier than I, who have spent years asking You questions, have been better than myself at deciphering Your real intentions. I am only a beginner and I must make mistake after mistake, as I did in my Latin translations as a boy, when my riotous imagination made the old priest roar with laughter. But I cannot believe that one learns Your language as one learns any human tongue, by hard studying, with a dictionary, a grammar and a set of idioms. I am sure that to the hardened sinner, who drops to his knees for the first time and murmurs Your name, marveling, You tell him all Your secrets, straight-away, and that he understands. I have served You like a dilettante, surprised that I could still find my pleasure in Your service. And for a long time I was on my guard because of it. I could not believe this pleasure would bring me one step nearer You. I could not believe that the road could be a happy one. Their hair shirts, their fasting, their bells in the small hours summoning one to meet You, on the icy paving stones, in the sick misery of the poor ill-treated human animal—I cannot believe that all these are anything but safeguards for the weak. In power and in luxury, and even in the pleasures of the flesh, I shall not cease to speak to You, I feel this now. You are the God of the rich man and the happy man too, Lord, and therein lies Your profound justice. You do not turn away Your eyes from the man who was given everything from birth. You have not abandoned him, alone in his ensnaring facility. And he may be Your true lost sheep. For Your scheme of things, which we mistakenly call Justice, is secret and profound and You plumb the hidden depths of poor men's puny frames as carefully as those of Kings. And beneath those outward differences, which blind us, but which to You are barely noticeable; beneath the diadem or the grime, You discern the same pride, the same vanity, the same petty, complacent preoccupation with oneself. Lord, I am certain now that You meant to tempt me with this hair shirt, object of so much vapid self-congratulation! this bare cell, this solitude, this absurdly endured winter-cold—and the conveniences of prayer. It would be too easy to buy You like this, at so low a price. I shall leave this convent, where so many precautions hem You round. I shall take up the miter and the golden cope again, and the great silver cross, and I shall go back and fight in the place and with the weapons it has pleased You to give me. It has pleased You to make me Archbishop and to set me, like a solitary pawn, face to face with the King, upon the chessboard. I shall go back to my place, humbly, and let the world accuse me of pride, so that I may do what I believe is my life's work. For the rest, Your will be done. [*He crosses himself.*]

[*The* YOUNG MONK *is still playing with his knife. Suddenly he throws it and watches as it quivers, embedded in the floor.*]

The curtain falls.

END OF ACT III

ACT IV

The King of France's Court.

[KING LOUIS *comes in, holding* BECKET *familiarly by the arm.*]

LOUIS. I tell you, Becket, intrigue is an ugly thing. You keep the smell about you for ages afterwards. There is a return of good understanding between the Kingdom of England and Ourselves. Peace in that direction assures me of a great advantage in the struggle which I will shortly have to undertake against the Emperor. I must protect my rear by a truce with Henry Plantagenet, before I march towards the East. And, needless to say, you are one of the items on the King's bill of charges. I can even tell you, that apart from yourself, his demands are negligible. [*Musingly*] Curious man. England's best policy would have been to take advantage of the Emperor's aggressive intentions and close the other jaw of the trap. He is deliberately sacrificing this opportunity for the pleasure of seeing you driven out. He really hates you, doesn't he?

BECKET. [*Simply*] Sire, we loved each other and I think he cannot forgive me for preferring God to him.

LOUIS. Your King isn't doing his job properly, Archbishop. He is giving way to passion. However! He has chosen to score a point against you, instead of against me. You are on his bill, I have to pay his price and banish you. I do not do so without a certain shame. Where are you thinking of going?

BECKET. I am a shepherd who has remained too long away from his flock. I intend to go back to England. I had already made my decision before this audience with your Majesty.

LOUIS. [*Surprised*] You have a taste for martyrdom? You disappoint me. I thought you more healthy-minded.

BECKET. Would it be healthy-minded to walk the roads of Europe, and beg a refuge where my carcass would be safe? Besides, where would I be safe? I am a Primate of England. That is a rather showy label on my back. The honor of God and common sense, which for once coincide, dictate that instead of risking the knife thrust of some hired assassin, on the highway, I should go and have myself killed—if killed I must be—clad in my golden cope, with my miter on my head and my silver cross in my hand, among my flock in my own cathedral. That place alone befits me. [*A pause.*]

LOUIS. I daresay you're right. [*He sighs*] Ah, what a pity it is to be a King, sometimes, when one has the surprise of meeting a man! You'll tell me, fortunately for me, that men are rare. Why weren't you born on this side of the Channel, Becket? [*He smiles*] True, you would no doubt have been a thorn in *my* side then! The honor of God is a very cumbersome thing. [*He muses for a moment and then says abruptly*] Who cares, I'll risk it! I like you too much. I'll indulge in a moment's humanity. I am going to try something, even if your master does seize on the chance to double his bill. After all, banishing you would merely have cost me a small slice of honor . . . I am meeting Henry in a day or two, at La Ferté-Bernard, to seal our agreement. I shall try to persuade him to make his peace with you. Should he agree, will you be willing to talk with him?

BECKET. Sire, ever since we stopped seeing each other, I have never ceased to talk to him.

[*Blackout. Prolonged blare of trumpets. The set is completely removed. Nothing remains but the cyclorama around the bare stage. A vast, arid plain, lashed by the wind. Trumpets again. Two* SENTRIES *are on stage, watching something in the distance.*]

SENTRY. Open those eyes of yours, lad! And drink it all in. You're new to the job, but you won't see something like this every day! This a historic meeting!

YOUNG SENTRY. I daresay, but it's perishing cold! How long are they going to keep us hanging about?

SENTRY. We're sheltered by the wood here, but you can bet they're even colder than we are, out there in the plain.

YOUNG SENTRY. Look! They've come up to each other! I wonder what they're talking about?

SENTRY. What do you think they're talking about, muttonhead? Inquiring how things are at home? Complaining about their chilblains?[14] The fate of the world, that's what they're arguing about! Things you and I won't ever understand. Even the words those bigwigs use—why, you wouldn't even know what they meant!

[*They go off. The lights go up.* BECKET *and the* KING, *on horseback, are alone in the middle of the plain, facing each other.*

Throughout the scene, the winter blizzard wails like a shrill dirge beneath their words. And during their silences, only the wind is heard.]

KING. You look older, Thomas.

BECKET. You too, Highness. Are you sure you aren't too cold?

---

[14] Swelling or inflamed sores on the hands or feet, caused by cold.

KING. I'm frozen stiff. You love it of course! You're in your element, aren't you? And you're barefooted as well!

BECKET. [*Smiling*] That's my latest affectation.

KING. Even with these fur boots on, my chilblains are killing me. Aren't yours, or don't you have any?

BECKET. [*Gently*] Of course.

KING. [*Cackling*] You're offering them up to God, I hope, holy monk?

BECKET. [*Gravely*] I have better things to offer Him.

KING. [*With a sudden cry*] If we start straightaway, we're sure to quarrel! Let's talk about trivial things. You know my son is fourteen? He's come of age.

BECKET. Has he improved at all?

KING. He's a little idiot and sly like his mother. Becket, don't you ever marry!

BECKET. [*Smiling*] The matter has been taken out of my hands. By you, Highness! It was you who had me ordained!

KING. [*With a cry*] Let's not start yet, I tell you! Talk about something else!

BECKET. [*Lightly*] Has your Highness done much hunting lately?

KING. [*Snarling*] Yes, every day! And it doesn't amuse me any more.

BECKET. Have you any new hawks?

KING. [*Furiously*] The most expensive on the market! But they don't fly straight.

BECKET. And your horses?

KING. The Sultan sent me four superb stallions for the tenth anniversary of my reign. But they throw everyone! Nobody has managed to mount one of them, yet!

BECKET. [*Smiling*] I must see what I can do about that some day.

KING. They'll throw you too! And we'll see your buttocks under your robe! At least, I hope so, or everything would be too dismal.

BECKET. [*After a pause*] Do you know what I miss most, Sire? The horses.

KING. And the women?

BECKET. [*Simply*] I've forgotten.

KING. You hypocrite. You turned into a hypocrite when you became a priest. [*Abruptly*] Did you love Gwendolen?

BECKET. I've forgotten her too.

KING. You did love her! That's the only way I can account for it.

BECKET. [*Gravely*] No, my prince, in my soul and conscience, I did not love her.

KING. Then you never loved anything, that's worse! [*Churlishly*] Why are you calling me your prince, like in the old days?

BECKET. [*Gently*] Because you have remained my prince.

KING. [*Crying out*] Then why are you doing me harm?

BECKET. [*Gently*] Let's talk about something else.

KING. Well, what? I'm cold.

BECKET. I always told you, my prince, that one must fight the cold with the cold's own weapons. Strip naked and splash yourself with cold water every morning.

KING. I used to when you were there to force me into it. I never wash now. I stink. I grew a beard at one time. Did you know?

BECKET. [*Smiling*] Yes. I had a hearty laugh over it.

KING. I cut it off because it itched. [*He cries out suddenly, like a lost child*] Becket, I'm bored!

BECKET. [*Gravely*] My prince. I do so wish I could help you.

KING. Then what are you waiting for? You can see I'm dying for it!

BECKET. [*Quietly*] I'm waiting for the honor of God and the honor of the King to become one.

KING. You'll wait a long time then!

BECKET. Yes. I'm afraid I will. [*A pause. Only the wind is heard.*]

KING. [*Suddenly*] If we've nothing more to say to each other, we might as well go and get warm!

BECKET. We have everything to say to each other, my prince. The opportunity may not occur again.

KING. Make haste, then. Or there'll be two frozen statues on this plain making their peace in a frozen eternity! I am your King, Becket! And so long as we are on this earth you owe me the first move! I'm prepared to forget a lot of things but not the fact that I am King. You yourself taught me that.

BECKET. [*Gravely*] Never forget it, my prince. Even against God. You have a different task to do. You have to steer the ship.

KING. And you—what do you have to do?

BECKET. Resist you with all my might, when you steer against the wind.

KING. Do you expect the wind to be behind me, Becket? No such luck! That's the fairy-tale navigation! God on the King's side? That's never happened yet! Yes, once in a century, at the time of the Crusades, when all Christendom shouts "It's God's will!" And even then! You know as well as I do what private greeds a Crusade covers up, in nine cases out of ten. The rest of the time, it's a head-on wind. And there must be somebody to keep the watch!

BECKET. And somebody else to cope with the absurd, wind—and with God. The tasks have been shared out, once and for all. The pity of it is that it should have been between us two, my prince—who were friends.

KING. [*Crossly*] The King of France—I still don't know what he hopes to gain by it—preached at me for three whole days for me to make my peace with you. What good would it do you to provoke me beyond endurance?

BECKET. None.

KING. You know that I am the King, and that I must act like a King! What do you expect of me? Are you hoping I'll weaken?

BECKET. No. That would prostrate me.

KING. Do you hope to conquer me by force then?

BECKET. You are the strong one.

KING. To win me round?

BECKET. No. Not that either. It is not for me to win you round. I have only to say no to you.

KING. But you must be logical, Becket!

BECKET. No, that isn't necessary, my Liege. We must only do—absurdly—what we have been given to do—right to the end.

KING. Yet I know you well enough, God knows. Ten years we spent together, little Saxon! At the hunt, at the whorehouse, at war; carousing all night long the two of us; in the same girl's bed, sometimes . . . and at work in the Council Chamber too. Absurdly. That word isn't like you.

BECKET. Perhaps. I am no longer like myself.

KING. [*Derisively*] Have you been touched by grace?

BECKET. [*Gravely*] Not by the one you think. I am not worthy of it.

KING. Did you feel the Saxon in you coming out, despite Papa's good collaborator's sentiments?

BECKET. No. Not that either.

KING. What then?

BECKET. I felt for the first time that I was being entrusted with something, that's all—there in that empty cathedral, somewhere in France, that day when you ordered me to take up this burden. I was a man without honor. And suddenly I found it—one I never imagined would ever become mine— the honor of God. A frail, incomprehensible honor, vulnerable as a boy-King fleeing from danger.

KING. [*Roughly*] Suppose we talked a little more precisely, Becket, with words I understand? Otherwise we'll be here all night. I'm cold. And the others are waiting for us on the fringes of this plain.

BECKET. I am being precise.

KING. I'm an idiot then! Talk to me like an idiot! That's an order. Will you lift the excommunication which you pronounced on William of Aynsford and others of my liegeman?

BECKET. No, Sire, because that is the only weapon I have to defend this child, who was given, naked, into my care.

KING. Will you agree to the twelve proposals which my Bishops have accepted in your absence at Northampton, and notably to forego the much-abused protection of Saxon clerics who get themselves tonsured to escape land bondage?

BECKET. No, Sire. My role is to defend my sheep. And they are my sheep. [*A pause.*] Nor will I concede that the Bishops should forego the right to appoint priests in their own dioceses, nor that churchmen should be subject to any but the Church's jurisdiction. These are my duties as a pastor—which it is not for me to relinquish. But I shall agree to the nine other articles in a spirit of peace, and because I know that you must remain King—in all save the honor of God. [*A pause.*]

KING. [*Coldly*] Very well. I will help you defend your God, since that is your new vocation, in memory of the companion you once were to me—in all save the honor of the Realm. You may come back to England, Thomas.

BECKET. Thank you, my prince. I meant to go back in any case and give myself up to your power, for on this earth, you are my King. And in all that concerns this earth, I owe you obedience. [*A pause.*]

KING. [*Ill at ease*] Well, let's go back now. We've finished. I'm cold.

BECKET. [*Dully*] I feel cold too, now. [*Another pause. They look at each other. The wind howls.*]

KING. [*Suddenly*] You never loved me, did you, Becket?

BECKET. In so far as I was capable of love, yes, my prince, I did.

KING. Did you start to love God? [*He cries out*] You mule! Can't you ever answer a simple question?

BECKET. [*Quietly*] I started to love the honor of God.

KING. [*Somberly*] Come back to England. I give you my royal peace. May you find yours. And may you not discover you were wrong about yourself. This is the last time I shall come begging to you. [*He cries out*] I should never have seen you again! It hurts too much. [*His whole body is suddenly shaken by a sob.*]

BECKET. [*Goes nearer to him; moved*] My prince—

KING. [*Yelling*] No! No pity! It's dirty. Stand away from me! Go back to England! It's too cold out here!

[BECKET *turns his horse and moves nearer to the* KING.]

BECKET. [*Gravely*] Farewell, my prince. Will you give me the kiss of peace?

KING. No! I can't bear to come near you! I can't bear to look at you! Later! Later! When it doesn't hurt any more!

BECKET. I shall set sail tomorrow. Farewell, my prince. I know I shall never see you again.

KING. [*His face twisted with hatred*] How dare you say that to me after I gave you my royal word? Do you take me for a traitor?

[BECKET *looks at him gravely for a second longer, with a sort of pity in his eyes. Then he slowly turns his horse and rides away. The wind howls.*]

KING. Thomas!

[*But* BECKET *has not heard. The* KING *does not call a second time. He spurs his horse and gallops off in the other direction. The lights fade. The wind howls.*

The lights change. Red curtains fall. BECKET'*s whistled march is heard off stage during the scene change.*

The curtains open. Royal music. King Henry's palace somewhere in France. The two QUEENS, *the* BARONS *and* HENRY'*s* SON *are standing around the dinner table, waiting. The* KING, *his eyes gleaming maliciously, looks at them and then exclaims:*]

KING. Today, gentlemen, I shall not be the first to sit down! [*To his* SON, *with a comic bow*] You are the King, Sir. The honor belongs to you. Take the high chair. Today I shall wait on *you!*

QUEEN MOTHER. [*With slight irritation*] My son!

KING. I know what I'm doing, Madam! [*With a sudden shout*] Go on, you great loon, look sharp! You're the King, but you're as stupid as ever! [*The boy flinches to avoid the blow he was expecting and goes to sit in the* KING'*s chair, sly and rather ill at ease.*] Take your places, gentlemen! I shall remain standing. Barons of England, here is your second King. For the good of our vast domains, a kingly colleague had become a necessity. Reviving an ancient custom, we have decided to have our successor crowned during our lifetime and to share our responsibilities with him. We ask you now to give him your homage and to honor him with the same title as Ourself. [*He makes a sign. Two* SERVANTS *have brought in a haunch of venison on a silver charger. The* KING *serves his* SON.]

YOUNG QUEEN. [*To her* SON] Sit up straight! And try to eat properly for once, now that you've been raised to glory!

KING. [*Grunting as he serves him*] He hasn't the face for it! He's a little slyboots and dim-witted at that. However, he'll be your King in good earnest one day, so you may as well get used to him. Besides, it's the best I had to offer.

QUEEN MOTHER. [*Indignantly*] Really, my son! This game is unworthy of you and of us. You insisted on it—against my advice—at least play it with dignity!

KING. [*Rounding on her in fury*] I'll play the games that amuse me, Madam, and I'll play them the way I choose! This mummery, gentlemen, which is, incidentally, without any importance at all—(if your new King fidgets, let me know, I'll give him a good kick up his train)—will at the very least have the appreciable result of showing our new friend, the Archbishop, that we can do without him. If there was one ancient privilege the Primacy clung to, tooth and nail, it was its exclusive right to anoint and consecrate the Kings of this realm. Well, it will be that old toad the Archbishop of York— with letters from the Pope authorizing him to do so—I paid the price!— who, tomorrow, will crown our son in the cathedral! What a joke that's going to be! [*He roars with laughter amid the general silence.*] What a tremendous, marvelous joke! I'd give anything to see that Archbishop's face when he has to swallow that! [*To his* SON] Get down from there, you imbecile! Go back to the bottom of the table and take your victuals with you! You aren't officially crowned until tomorrow. [*The boy picks up his plate and goes back to his place, casting a cowed, smoldering look at his father. Watching him, says jovially*] What a look! Filial sentiments are a fine thing to see, gentlemen! You'd like to be the real King, wouldn't you, you young pig! You'd like that number III after your name, eh, with Papa good and stiff under his catafalque![15] You'll have to wait a bit! Papa is well. Papa is very well indeed!

QUEEN MOTHER. My son, God knows I criticized your attempts at reconciliation with that wretch, who has done us nothing but harm . . . God knows I understand your hatred of him! But do not let it drag you into making a gesture you will regret, merely for the sake of wounding his pride. Henry is still a child. But you were not much older when you insisted on reigning by yourself, and in opposition to me. Ambitious self-seekers—and there is never any scarcity of those around Princes—can advise him, raise a faction against you and avail themselves of this hasty coronation to divide the King-dom! Think it over, there is still time.

KING. We are still alive, Madam, and in control! And nothing can equal my pleasure in imagining my proud friend Becket's face when he sees the funda-mental privilege of the Primacy whisked from under his nose! I let him cheat me out of one or two articles the other day, but I had something up my sleeve for him!

QUEEN MOTHER. Henry! I bore the weight of state affairs longer than you ever have. I have been your Queen and I am your mother. You are answerable for the interests of a great Kingdom, not for your moods. You already gave far too much away to the King of France, at La Ferté-Bernard.[16] It is England you must think of, not your hatred—or disappointed love—for that man.

KING. [*In a fury*] Disappointed love—disappointed love? What gives you the right, Madam, to meddle in my loves and hates?

QUEEN MOTHER. You have a rancor against the man which is neither healthy nor manly. The King your father dealt with his enemies faster and more summarily than that. He had them killed and said no more about it. If Thomas Becket were a faithless woman whom you still hankered after, you would act no differently. Sweet Jesu, tear him out of your heart once and for all! [*She bawls suddenly*] Oh, if I were a man!

KING. [*Grinning*] Thanks be to God, Madam, he gave you dugs. Which I never personally benefited from. I suckled a peasant girl.

QUEEN MOTHER. [*Acidly*] That is no doubt why you have remained so lumpish, my son.

YOUNG QUEEN. And haven't I a say in the matter? I tolerated your mistresses, Sir, but do you expect me to tolerate everything? Have you ever stopped to think what kind of woman I am? I am tired of having my life encumbered with this man. Becket! Always Becket! Nobody ever talks about anything else here! He was almost less of a hindrance when you loved him. I am a woman. I am your wife and your Queen. I refuse to be treated like this! I shall complain to my father, the Duke of Aquitaine! I shall complain to my

[15] A catafalque is a temporary, often canopied, structure used to support a coffin during a elaborate funeral.

[16] This meeting on an icy plain in France brought about a temporary peace between France and England and a temporary reconciliation between Becket and Henry II. Anouilh has been exploring the implications of this meeting throughout act 4.

uncle, the Emperor! I shall complain to all the Kings of Europe, my cousins! I shall complain to God!

KING. [*Shouting rather vulgarly*] I should start with God! Be off to your private chapel, Madam, and see if He's at home. [*He turns to his mother, fuming.*] And you, the other Madam, away to your chamber with your secret councilors and go and spin your webs! Get out, both of you! I can't stand the sight of you! I retch with boredom whenever I set eyes on you! And young Henry III too! Go on, get out! [*He chases him out with kicks, yelling*] Here's my royal foot in your royal buttocks! And to the devil with my whole family, if he'll have you! Get out, all of you! Get out! Get out! Get out! [*The* QUEENS *scurry out, with a great rustling of silks. He turns to the* BARONS *who all stand watching him, terror stricken. More calmly*] Let us drink, gentlemen. That's about all one can do in your company. Let us get drunk, like men, all night; until we roll under the table, in vomit and oblivion. [*He fills their glasses and beckons them closer.*] Ah, my four idiots! My faithful hounds! It's warm beside you, like being in a stable. Good sweat! Comfortable nothingness! [*He taps their skulls.*] Not the least little glimmer inside to spoil the fun. And to think that before he came I was like you! A good fat machine for belching after drink, for pissing, for mounting girls and punching heads. What the devil did you put into it, Becket, to stop the wheels from going round? [*Suddenly to the* 2ND BARON] Tell me, do you think sometimes, Baron?

2ND BARON. Never, Sire. Thinking has never agreed with an Englishman. It's unhealthy. Besides, a gentleman has better things to do.

KING. [*Sitting beside them, suddenly quite calm*] Drink up, gentlemen. That's always been considered a healthy thing to do. [*He fills the goblets.*] Has Becket landed? I'm told the sea has been too rough to cross these last few days.

1ST BARON. [*Somberly*] He has landed, Sire, despite the sea.

KING. Where?

1ST BARON. On a deserted stretch of coast, near Sandwich.

KING. So God did not choose to drown him?

1ST BARON. No.

KING. [*He asks in his sly, brutish way*] Was nobody there waiting for him? There must be one or two men in England whom he can't call his friends!

1ST BARON. Yes. Gervase, Duke of Kent, Regnouf de Broc and Regnault de Garenne were waiting for him. Gervase had said that if he dared to land he'd cut off his head with his own hands. But the native Englishmen from all the coastal towns had armed themselves to form an escort for the Archbishop. And the Dean of Oxford went to meet the Barons and charged them not to cause bloodshed and make you look a traitor, seeing that you had given the Archbishop a safe conduct.

KING. [*Soberly*] Yes, I gave him a safe conduct.

1ST BARON. All along the road to Canterbury, the peasants, the artisans and the small shopkeepers came out to meet him, cheering him and escorting him from village to village. Not a single rich man, not a single Norman, showed his face.

KING. Only the Saxons?

1ST BARON. Poor people armed with makeshift shields and rusty lances. Riffraff. Swarms of them though, all camping around Canterbury, to protect him. [*Gloomily*] Who would have thought there were so many people in England!

[*The* KING *has remained prostrate without uttering a word. Now he suddenly jumps up and roars:*]

KING. A miserable wretch who ate my bread! A man I raised up from nothing! A Saxon! A man loved! [*Shouting like a madman*] I loved him! Yes, I loved him! And I believe I still do! Enough, O God! Enough! Stop, stop, O God, I've had enough! [*He flings himself down on the couch, sobbing hysterically; tearing at the horsehair mattress with his teeth, and eating it. The* BARONS, *stupefied, go nearer to him.*]

1ST BARON. [*Timidly*] Your Highness . . .

KING. [*Moaning, with his head buried in the mattress*] I can do nothing! Nothing! I'm as limp and useless as a girl! So long as he's alive, I'll never be able to do a thing. I tremble before him astonished. And I am the King! [*With a sudden cry*] Will no one rid me of him? A priest! A priest who jeers at me and does me injury! Are there none but cowards like myself around me? Are there no men left in England? Oh, my heart! My heart is beating too fast to bear! [*He lies, still as death on the torn mattress. The four* BARONS *stand around speechless. Suddenly, on a percussion instrument, there rises a rhythmic beating, a sort of muffled tom-tom which is at first only the agitated heartbeats of the* KING, *but which swells and grows more insistent. The four* BARONS *look at each other. Then they straighten, buckle their sword belts, pick up their helmets and go slowly out, leaving the* KING *alone with the muffled rhythm of the heartbeats, which will continue until the murder. The* KING *lies there prostrate, among the upturned benches, in the deserted hall. A torch splutters and goes out. He sits up, looks around, sees they have gone and suddenly realizes why. A wild, lost look comes into his eyes. A moment's pause then he collapses on the bed with a long broken moan.*]

KING. O my Thomas!

[*A second torch goes out. Total darkness. Only the steady throb of the heartbeats is heard. A dim light. The forest of pillars again. Canterbury Cathedral. Upstage a small altar, with three steps leading up to it, half screened by a grill. In a corner downstage* BECKET, *and the* YOUNG MONK, *who is helping him on with his vestments. Nearby, on a stool, the Archbishop's miter. The tall silver cross is leaning against a pillar.*]

BECKET. I must look my best today. Make haste.

[*The* MONK *fumbles with the vestments. The muffled tom-tom is heard distantly at first, then closer.*]

MONK. It's difficult with all those little laces. It wants a girl's hands.

BECKET. [*Softly*] A man's hands are better, today. Never mind the laces. The alb, quickly. And the stole. And then the cope.[17]

MONK. [*Conscientiously*] If it's worth doing it's worth doing well.

BECKET. You're quite right. If it's worth doing it's worth doing well. Do up all the little laces, every one of them. God will give us time. [*A pause. The boy struggles manfully on, putting out his tongue in concentration. The throbbing grows louder. Smiling*] Don't pull your tongue out like that! [*He watches the boy as he works away.*]

MONK. [*Sweating but content*] There. That's all done. But I'd rather have cleaned out our pigsty at home! It's not half such hard work!

BECKET. Now the alb. [*A pause.*] Were you fond of your pigs?

MONK. [*His eyes lighting up*] Yes, I was.

BECKET. At my father's house, we had some pigs too, when I was a child.

---

[17] The alb, the stole, and the cope (or chasuble) are vestments worn by Catholic priests in celebrating Mass. The alb is a long white robe; the stole is a decorated strip of cloth that is draped around the back of the neck and crossed over the priest's breast; and the chasuble is a large cloak-like garment decorated on the back with a cross.

[*Smiling*] We're two rough lads from Hastings, you and I! Give me the chasuble. [BECKET *kisses the chasuble and slips it over his head. He looks at the boy and says gently*] Do you miss your knife?

MONK. Yes. [*Pause.*] Will it be today?

BECKET. [*Gravely*] I think so, my son. Are you afraid?

MONK. Oh, no. Not if we have time to fight. All I want is the chance to strike a few blows first; so I shan't have done nothing but receive them all my life. If I can kill one Norman first—just one, I don't want much—one for one, that will seem fair and right enough to me.

BECKET. [*With a kindly smile*] Are you so very set on killing one?

MONK. One for one. After that, I don't much care if I *am* just a little grain of sand in the machine. Because I know that by putting more and more grains of sand in the machine, one day it will come grinding to a stop.

BECKET. [*Gently*] And on that day, what then?

MONK. We'll set a fine, new, well-oiled machine in the place of the old one and this time we'll put the Normans into it instead. [*He asks, quite without irony*] That's what justice means, isn't it?

[BECKET *smiles and does not answer him.*]

BECKET. Fetch me the miter. [*He says quietly, as they boy fetches it*] O Lord, You forbade Peter to strike a blow in the Garden of Olives.[18] But I shall not deprive him of that joy. He has had too few joys in his short span on the earth. [*To the boy*] Now give me my silver cross. I must hold it.

MONK. [*Passing it to him*] Lord, it's heavy! A good swipe with that and they'd feel it! My word, I wish I could have it!

BECKET. [*Stroking his hair*] Lucky little Saxon! This black world will have been in order to the end, for you. [*He straightens, grave once more.*] There. I'm ready, all adorned for Your festivities, Lord. Do not, in this interval of waiting, let one last doubt enter my soul.

[*During this scene, the throbbing has grown louder. Now it mingles with a loud knocking on the door. A* PRIEST *runs in wildly.*]

PRIEST. Your Grace! There are four armed men outside! They say they must see you on behalf of the King. I've barricaded the door but they're breaking it in! They've got hatchets! Quickly! You must go into the back of the church and have the choir gates closed! They're strong enough, they'll hold!

BECKET. [*Calmly*] It is time for Vespers, William. Does one close the choir gates during Vespers? I never heard of such a thing.

PRIEST. [*Nonplused*] I know, but . . .

BECKET. Everything must be the way it should be. The choir gates will remain open. Come, boy, let us go up to the altar. This is no place to be. [*He goes toward the altar, followed by the* YOUNG MONK. *A great crash. The door has given way. The four* BARONS *come in, in their helmets. They fling down their hatchets and draw their swords.* BECKET *turns to face them, grave and calm, at the foot of the altar. They stop a moment, uncertain and disconcerted; four statues, huge and threatening. The tom-tom has stopped. There is nothing now but a heavy silence.* BECKET *says simply*] Here it comes. The supreme folly. This is its hour. [*He holds their eyes. They dare not move. He says coldly*] One does not enter armed into God's house. What do you want?

---

[18] The allusion is to John 18:10. Peter begins to defend Jesus just after Judas has betrayed him to the Roman soldiers; "Then said Jesus unto Peter, Put up thy sword into the sheath: the cup which my Father hath given me, shall I not drink it?"

1st Baron. [*Thickly*] Your death. [*A pause.*]

2nd Baron. [*Thickly*] You bring shame to the King. Flee the country or you're a dead man.

Becket. [*Softly*] It is time for the service. [*He turns to the altar and faces the tall crucifix without paying any further attention to them. The throbbing starts again, muffled. The four men close in like automata. The* Young Monk *suddenly leaps forward brandishing the heavy silver cross in order to protect* Becket, *but one of the* Barons *swings his sword and fells him to the ground.* Becket *murmurs, as if in reproach*] Not even one! It would have given him so much pleasure, Lord. [*With a sudden cry*] Oh how difficult you make it all! And how heavy Your honor is to bear! [*He adds, very quietly*] Poor Henry.

[*The four men hurl themselves onto him. He falls at the first blow. They hack at his body, grunting like woodcutters. The* Priest *has fled with a long scream, which echoes in the empty cathedral. Blackout.*

On the same spot. The King, *naked, on bended knees at* Becket's *tomb, as in the first scene. Four* Monks *are whipping him with ropes, almost duplicating the gestures of the* Barons *as they killed* Becket.]

King. [*Crying out*] Are you satisfied now, Becket? Does this settle our account? Has the honor of God been washed clean? [*The four* Monks *finish beating him, then kneel down and bow their heads. The* King *mutters—one feels it is part of the ceremony*] Thank you. Yes, yes, of course, it was agreed, I forgive you. Many thanks. [*The* Page *comes forward with a vast cloak, which the* King *wraps around himself. The* Barons *surround the* King *and help him to dress, while the* Bishops *and the* Clergy, *forming a procession, move away solemnly upstage to the strains of the organ. The* King *dresses hurriedly, with evident bad temper, aided by his* Barons. *He grimaces ill-humoredly and growls*] The pigs! The Norman Bishops just went through the motions, but those little Saxon monks—my word, they had their money's worth!

[*A* Baron *comes in. A joyful peal of bells is heard.*]

Baron. Sire, the operation has been successful! The Saxon mob is yelling with enthusiasm outside the cathedral, acclaiming your Majesty's name in the same breath as Becket's! If the Saxons are on our side now, Prince Henry's followers look as though they have definitely lost the day.

King. [*With a touch of hypocritical majesty beneath his slightly loutish manner*] The honor of God, gentlemen, is a very good thing, and taken all in all, one gains by having it on one's side. Thomas Becket, who was our friend, used to say so. England will owe her ultimate victory over chaos to him, and it is our wish that, henceforward, he should be honored and prayed to in this Kingdom as a saint. Come, gentlemen. We will determine, tonight, in Council, what posthumous honors to render him and what punishment to deal out to his murderers.

1st Baron. [*Imperturbably*] Sire, they are unknown.

King. [*Impenetrably*] Our justice will seek them out, Baron, and you will be specially entrusted with this inquiry, so that no one will be in any doubt as to our Royal desire to defend the honor of God and the memory of our friend from this day forward.

[*The organ swells triumphantly, mingled with the sound of the bells and the cheering of the crowds as they file out.*]

CURTAIN

[1959]

Tom Stoppard   *1937–*

THE REAL INSPECTOR HOUND

CHARACTERS

Moon	Felicity
Birdboot	Cynthia
Mrs. Drudge	Magnus
Simon	Inspector Hound

The first thing is that the audience appear to be confronted by their own reflection in a huge mirror. Impossible. However, back there in the gloom—not at the footlights—a bank of plush seats and pale smudges of faces. (The total effect having been established, it can be progressively faded out as the play goes on, until the front row remains to remind us of the rest and then, finally, merely two seats in that row—one of which is now occupied by Moon. *Between* Moon *and the auditorium is an acting area which represents, in as realistic an idiom as possible, the drawing-room of Muldoon Manor. French windows at one side. A telephone fairly well upstage (i.e. towards* Moon*). The* Body *of a man lies sprawled face down on the floor in front of a large settee. This settee must be of a size and design to allow it to be wheeled over the body, hiding it completely. Silence. The room. The* Body. Moon.

Moon *stares blankly ahead. He turns his head to one side then the other, then up, then down—waiting. He picks up his program and reads the front cover. He turns over the page and reads.*

He turns over the page and reads.

He turns over the page and reads.

He turns over the page and reads.

He looks at the back cover and reads.

He puts it down and crosses his legs and looks about. He stares front. Behind him and to one side, barely visible, a man enters and sits down: Birdboot.

Pause. Moon *picks up his program, glances at the front cover and puts it down impatiently. Pause. . . . Behind him there is the crackle of a chocolate-box, absurdly loud.* Moon *looks round. He and* Birdboot *see each other. They are clearly known to each other. They acknowledge each other with constrained waves.* Moon *looks straight ahead.* Birdboot *comes down to join him.*

Note: *Almost always,* Moon *and* Birdboot *converse in tones suitable for an auditorium, sometimes a whisper. However good the acoustics might be, they will have to have microphones where they are sitting. The effect must be not of sound picked up, amplified and flung out at the audience, but of sound picked up, carried and gently dispersed around the auditorium.*

Anyway, Birdboot, *with a box of Black Magic,[1] makes his way down to join* Moon *and plumps himself down next to him, plumpish middle-aged* Birdboot *and younger taller, less-relaxed* Moon.

Birdboot [*sitting down; conspiratorially*]. Me and the lads have had a meeting in the bar and decided it's first-class family entertainment but if it goes on beyond half-past ten it's self-indulgent—pass it on . . . [*and laughs jovially*] I'm on my own tonight, don't mind if I join you?

---

[1] A popular English brand of boxed chocolate candies.

MOON. Hello, Birdboot.

BIRDBOOT. Where's Higgs?

MOON. I'm standing in.

MOON AND BIRDBOOT. Where's Higgs?

MOON. Every time.

BIRDBOOT. What?

MOON. It is as if we only existed one at a time, combining to achieve continuity. I keep space warm for Higgs. My presence defines his absence, his absence confirms my presence, his presence precludes mine. . . . When Higgs and I walk down this aisle together to claim our common seat, the oceans will fall into the sky and the trees will hang with fishes.

BIRDBOOT [*he has not been paying attention, looking around vaguely, now catches up*]. Where's Higgs?

MOON. The very sight of me with a complimentary ticket is enough. The streets are impassable tonight, the country is rising and the cry goes up from hill to hill—Where—is—Higgs? [*Small pause.*] Perhaps he's dead at last, or trapped in a lift somewhere, or succumbed to amnesia, wandering the land with his turn-ups[2] stuffed with ticket-stubs.

[BIRDBOOT *regards him doubtfully for a moment.*]

BIRDBOOT. Yes. . . . Yes, well I didn't bring Myrtle tonight—not exactly her cup of tea, I thought, tonight.

MOON. Over her head, you mean?

BIRDBOOT. Well, no—I mean it's a sort of a *thriller*, isn't it?

MOON. Is it?

BIRDBOOT. That's what I heard. Who killed thing?—no one will leave the house.

MOON. I suppose so. Underneath.

BIRDBOOT. *Underneath*? ! ? It's a whodunnit, man!—Look at it! [*They look at it. The room. The* BODY. *Silence.*] Has it started yet?

MOON. Yes. [*Pause. They look at it.*]

BIRDBOOT. Are you sure?

MOON. It's a pause.

BIRDBOOT. You can't start with a *pause!* If you want my opinion there's total panic back there. [*Laughs and subsides.*] Where's Higgs tonight, then?

MOON. It will follow me to the grave and become my epitaph—Here lies Moon the second string: where's Higgs? . . . Sometimes I dream of revolution, a bloody *coup d'état*[3] by the second rank—troupes of actors slaughtered by their understudies, magicians sawn in half by indefatigably smiling glamour girls, cricket[4] teams wiped out by marauding bands of twelfth men—I dream of champions chopped down by rabbit-punching sparring partners while eternal bridesmaids turn and rape the bridegrooms over the sausage rolls and parliamentary private secretaries plant bombs in the Minister's Humber[5]—comedians die on provincial stages, robbed of their feeds[6] by mutely triumphant stooges——and—march—an army of assistants and deputies, the seconds-in-command, the runners-up, the right-hand men—storming the palace gates wherein the second son has already mounted the throne

---

[2] Trouser cuffs.   [3] Overthrow of the government by force.

[4] A popular English game somewhat like baseball, played by teams of eleven men. Twelfth men are, therefore, substitutes.

[5] A British make of automobiles.

[6] I.e., robbed of the feed-lines usually recited by the straight man.

having committed regicide with a croquet-mallet—stand-ins of the world stand up!—[*Beat.*] Sometimes I dream of Higgs.

    [*Pause.* BIRDBOOT *regards him doubtfully. He is at a loss, and grasps reality in the form of his box of chocolates.*]

BIRDBOOT [*Chewing into mike*]. Have a chocolate!

MOON. What kind?

BIRDBOOT [*Chewing into mike*]. Black Magic.

MOON. No thanks.

    [*Chewing stops dead.*]

    [*Of such tiny victories and defeats. . . .*]

BIRDBOOT. I'll give you a tip, then. Watch the girl.

MOON. You think she did it?

BIRDBOOT. No, no—the *girl*, watch her.

MOON. What girl?

BIRDBOOT. You won't know her, I'll give you a nudge.

MOON. *You* know her, do you?

BIRDBOOT [*suspiciously, bridling*]. What's *that* supposed to mean?

MOON. I beg your pardon?

BIRDBOOT. I'm trying to tip you a wink—give you a nudge as good as a tip—for God's sake, Moon, what's the matter with you?—you could do yourself some good, spotting her first time out—she's new, from the provinces, going straight to the top. I don't want to put words into your mouth but a word from us and we could make her.

MOON. I suppose you've made dozens of them, like that.

BIRDBOOT [*instantly outraged*]. I'll have you know I'm a family man devoted to my homely but good-natured wife, and if you're suggesting—

MOON. No, no—

BIRDBOOT. —A man of my scrupulous morality—

MOON. I'm sorry—

BIRDBOOT. —falsely besmirched.

MOON. Is that her? [*For* MRS. DRUDGE *has entered.*]

BIRDBOOT. —don't be absurd, wouldn't be seen dead with the old—ah.

    [MRS. DRUDGE *is the char, middle-aged, turbanned. She heads straight for the radio, dusting on the trot.*]

MOON [*reading his program*]. Mrs. Drudge the Help.

RADIO [*without preamble, having been switched on by* MRS. DRUDGE]. We interrupt our program for a special police message. [MRS. DRUDGE *stops to listen.*] The search still goes on for the escaped madman who is on the run in Essex.[7]

MRS. DRUDGE [*fear and dismay*]. Essex!

RADIO. County police led by Inspector Hound have received a report that the man has been seen in the desolate marshes around Muldoon Manor. [*Fearful gasp from* MRS. DRUDGE.] The man is wearing a darkish suit with a lightish shirt. He is of medium height and build and youngish. Anyone seeing a man answering to this description and acting suspiciously, is advised to phone the nearest police station. [*A man answering this description has appeared behind* MRS. DRUDGE. *He is acting suspiciously. He creeps in. He creeps out.* MRS. DRUDGE *does not see him. He does not see the body.*] That is the end of the police message. [MRS. DRUDGE *turns off the radio and resumes her cleaning. She does*

---

[7] A county on the eastern coast of England.

not see the body. Quite fortuitously, her view of the body is always blocked, and when it isn't she has her back to it. However, she is dusting and polishing her way towards it.]

BIRDBOOT. So that's what they say about me, is it?

MOON. What?

BIRDBOOT. Oh, I know what goes on behind my back—sniggers—slanders— hole-in-corner innuendo—What have you heard?

MOON. Nothing.

BIRDBOOT [*urbanely*]. Tittle tattle. Tittle, my dear fellow, tattle. I take no notice of it—the sly envy of scandal mongers—I can afford to ignore them, I'm a respectable married man—

MOON. Incidentally——

BIRDBOOT. Water off a duck's back, I assure you.

MOON. Who was that lady I saw you with last night?

BIRDBOOT [*unexpectedly stung into fury*]. How dare you! Don't you come here with your slimy insinuations! My wife Myrtle understands perfectly well that a man of my critical standing is obliged occasionally to mingle with the world of the footlights, simply by way of keeping *au fait*[8] with the latest—

MOON. I'm sorry——

BIRDBOOT. That a critic of my scrupulous integrity should be vilified and pilloried in the stocks of common gossip——

MOON. Ssssh——

BIRDBOOT. I have nothing to hide!—why, if this should reach the ears of my beloved Myrtle——

MOON. Can I have a chocolate?

BIRDBOOT. What? Oh——[*Mollified.*] Oh yes—my dear fellow—yes, let's have a chocolate——No point in—yes, good show. [*Pops chocolate into his mouth and chews.*] Which one do you fancy?—Cherry? Strawberry? Coffee cream? Turkish delight?[9]

MOON. I'll have a montelimar.

[*Chewing stops.*]

BIRDBOOT. Ah. Sorry. [*Just missed that one.*]

MOON. Gooseberry fondue?

BIRDBOOT. No.

MOON. Pistachio fudge? Nectarine cluster? Hickory nut praline? Creme de menthe cracknell?

BIRDBOOT. I'm afraid not. . . . Caramel?

MOON. Yes, all right.

BIRDBOOT. Thanks very much. [*He gives* MOON *a chocolate. Pause.*] Incidentally, old chap, I'd be grateful if you didn't mention—I mean, you know how these misunderstandings get about. . . .

MOON. What?

BIRDBOOT. The fact is, Myrtle simply doesn't *like* the theatre. . . . [*He tails off hopelessly.* MRS. DRUDGE, *whose discovery of the body has been imminent, now—by way of tidying the room—slides the couch over the corpse, hiding it completely. She resumes dusting and humming.*]

MOON. By the way, congratulations, Birdboot.

BIRDBOOT. What?

[8] Up to date.
[9] All these are flavors of fillings of chocolate candy. Birdboot is consulting the diagram inside the lid of the candy-box that shows where each flavor is located.

MOON. At the Hippodrome.[10] Your entire review reproduced in neon!

BIRDBOOT [*pleased*]. Oh . . . that old thing.

MOON. You've seen it, of course.

BIRDBOOT [*vaguely*]. Well, I was passing. . . .

MOON. I definitely intend to take a second look when it has settled down.

BIRDBOOT. As a matter of fact I have a few color transparencies—I don't know whether you'd care to?

MOON. Please, please—love to, love to. . . . [BIRDBOOT *hands over a few color slides and a battery-powered viewer which* MOON *holds up to his eyes as he speaks.*] Yes . . . yes . . . lovely . . . awfully sound. It has scale, it has color, it is, in the best sense of the word, electric. Large as it is, it is a small masterpiece— I would go so far as to say—kinetic without being pop, and having said that, I think it must be said that here we have a review that adds a new dimension to the critical scene. I urge you to make haste to the Hippodrome, for this is the stuff of life itself.

BIRDBOOT. Most handsome of you, Moon.

MOON [*viewing*]. A critic who is not afraid to say so when he's had a frankly appalling putrid lousy night in the theater.

BIRDBOOT. 'Appallingly frank but ridiculously right in the theater'—they haven't quite got the hang of the thing——

MOON [*handing back the slides, morosely*]. All I ever got was "Unforgettable" outside. . . . What was it?

[*The phone rings.* MRS. DRUDGE *seems to have been waiting for it to do so and for the last few seconds has been dusting it with an intense concentration. She snatches it up.*]

MRS. DRUDGE [*into phone*]. Hello, the drawing-room of Lady Muldoon's country residence one morning in early spring? . . . He*llo*!—the draw——Who? Who did you wish to speak to? I'm afraid there is no one of that name here, this is all very mysterious and I'm sure it's leading up to something, I hope nothing is amiss for we, that is Lady Muldoon and her houseguests, are here cut off from the world, including Magnus, the wheelchair-ridden half-brother of her ladyship's husband Lord Albert Muldoon who ten years ago went out for a walk on the cliffs and was never seen again—and all alone, for they had no children.

MOON. Derivative, of course.

BIRDBOOT. But quite sound.

MRS. DRUDGE. Should a stranger enter our midst, which I very much doubt, I will tell him you called. Good-bye. [*She puts down the phone and catches sight of the previously seen suspicious character who has now entered again, more suspiciously than ever, through the french windows. He senses her stare, freezes, and straightens up.*]

SIMON. Ah!—hello there! I'm Simon Gascoyne, I hope you don't mind, the door was open so I wandered in. I'm a friend of Lady Muldoon, the lady of the house, having made her acquaintance through a mutual friend, Felicity Cunningham, shortly after moving into this neighborhood just the other day.

MRS. DRUDGE. I'm Mrs. Drudge. I don't live in but I pop in on my bicycle when the weather allows to help in the running of charming though somewhat isolated Muldoon Manor. Judging by the time [*she glances at the clock*] you

---

[10] The name of a theater in London.

did well to get here before high water cut us off for all practical purposes from the outside world.

SIMON. I took the short cut over the cliffs and followed one of the old smugglers' paths through the treacherous swamps that surround this strangely inaccessible house.

MRS. DRUDGE. Yes, many visitors have remarked on the topographical quirk in the local strata whereby there are no roads leading from the Manor, though there *are* ways of getting *to* it, weather allowing.

SIMON. Yes, well I must say it's a lovely day so far.

MRS. DRUDGE. Ah, but now that the cuckoo-beard is in bud there'll be fog before the sun hits Foster's Ridge.

SIMON. I say, it's wonderful how you country people really know weather.

MRS. DRUDGE [*suspiciously*]. Know whether what?

SIMON [*glancing out of the window*]. Yes, it does seem to be coming on a bit foggy.

MRS. DRUDGE. The fog is very treacherous around here—it rolls off the sea without warning, shrouding the cliffs in a deadly mantle of blind man's bluff.

SIMON. Yes, I've heard it said.

MRS. DRUDGE. I've known whole week-ends when Muldoon Manor, as this lovely old Queen Anne House[11] is called, might as well have been floating on the pack ice for all the good it would have done phoning the police. It was on such a week-end as this that Lord Muldoon who had lately brought his beautiful bride back to the home of his ancestors, walked out of this house ten years ago, and his body was never found.

SIMON. Yes, indeed, poor Cynthia.

MRS. DRUDGE. His name was Albert.

SIMON. Yes indeed, poor Albert. But tell me, is Lady Muldoon about?

MRS. DRUDGE. I believe she is playing tennis on the lawn with Felicity Cunningham.

SIMON [*startled*]. Felicity Cunningham?

MRS. DRUDGE. A mutual friend, I believe you said. A happy chance. I will tell them you are here.

SIMON. Well, I can't really stay as a matter of fact—please don't disturb them—I really should be off.

MRS. DRUDGE. They would be very disappointed. It is some time since we have had a four for pontoon bridge at the Manor, and I don't play cards myself.

SIMON. There is another guest, then?

MRS. DRUDGE. Major Magnus, the crippled half-brother of Lord Muldoon who turned up out of the blue from Canada just the other day, completes the house-party. [MRS. DRUDGE *leaves on this,* SIMON *is undecided.*]

MOON [*ruminating quietly*]. I think I must be waiting for Higgs to die.

BIRDBOOT. What?

MOON. Half afraid that I will vanish when he does. [*The phone rings.* SIMON *picks it up.*]

SIMON. Hello?

MOON. I wonder if it's the same for Macafferty?

BIRDBOOT AND SIMON [*together*]. Who?

---

[11] During the reign of Queen Anne (1702–1714), most houses were built of red brick to meet practical needs with only simple and dignified ornamentation.

MOON. Third string.

BIRDBOOT. Your stand-in?

MOON. Does he wait for Higgs and I to write each other's obituary—does he dream——?

SIMON. To whom did you wish to speak?

BIRDBOOT. What's he like?

MOON. Bitter.

SIMON. There is no one of that name here.

BIRDBOOT. No—as a critic, what's Macafferty like as a critic?

MOON [*laughs poisonously*]. Nobody knows——

SIMON. You must have got the wrong number!

MOON. —he's never been called upon to criticise.

[SIMON *replaces the phone and paces nervously. Pause.* BIRDBOOT *consults his program.*]

BIRDBOOT. Simon Gascoyne. It's not him, of course.

MOON. What?

BIRDBOOT. I said it's not him.

MOON. Who is it, then?

BIRDBOOT. My guess is Magnus.

MOON. In disguise, you mean?

BIRDBOOT. What?

MOON. You think he's Magnus in disguise?

BIRDBOOT. I don't think you're concentrating, Moon.

MOON. I thought you said——

BIRDBOOT. You keep chattering on about Higgs and Macafferty—what's the matter with you?

MOON [*thoughtfully*]. I wonder if they talk about me. . . ?

[*A strange impulse makes* SIMON *turn on the radio.*]

RADIO. Here is another police message. Essex county police are still searching in vain for the madman who is at large in the deadly marshes of the coastal region. Inspector Hound who is masterminding the operation, is not available for comment but it is widely believed that he has a secret plan. . . . Meanwhile police and volunteers are combing the swamps with loud-hailers, shouting, "Don't be a madman, give yourself up." That is the end of the police message. [SIMON *turns off the radio. He is clearly nervous.* MOON *and* BIRDBOOT *are on separate tracks.*]

BIRDBOOT [*knowingly*]. Oh yes. . . .

MOON. Yes, I should think my name is seldom off Macafferty's lips . . . sad, really. I mean, it's no life at all, a stand-in's stand-in.

BIRDBOOT. Yes . . . yes. . . .

MOON. Higgs never gives me a second thought. I can tell by the way he nods.

BIRDBOOT. Revenge, of course.

MOON. What?

BIRDBOOT. Jealousy.

MOON. Nonsense—there's nothing *personal* in it——

BIRDBOOT. The paranoid grudge——

MOON [*sharply first, then starting to career . . .*]. It is merely that it is not enough to wax at another's wane, to be held in reserve, to be on hand, on call, to step in or not at all, the substitute—the near offer—the temporary-acting—for I am Moon, continuous Moon, in my own shoes, Moon in June, April, September, and no member of the human race keeps warm my bit of space—yes, I can tell by the way he nods.

BIRDBOOT. Quite mad, of course.

MOON. What?

BIRDBOOT. The answer lies out there in the swamps.

MOON. Oh.

BIRDBOOT. The skeleton in the cupboard is coming home to roost.

MOON. Oh yes. [*He clears his throat . . . for both he and* BIRDBOOT *have a "public" voice, a critic voice which they turn on for sustained pronouncements of opinion.*] Already in the opening stages we note the classic impact of the catalystic figure—the outsider—plunging through to the center of an ordered world and setting up the disruptions—the shock waves—which unless I am much mistaken, will strip these comfortable people—these crustaceans in the rock pool of society—strip them of their shells and leave them exposed as the trembling raw meat which, at heart, is all of us. But there is more to it than that——

BIRDBOOT. I agree—keep your eye on Magnus.

[*A tennis ball bounces through the french windows, closely followed by* FELICITY, *who is in her 20's. She wears a pretty tennis outfit, and carries a racket.*]

FELICITY [*calling behind her*]. Out! [*It takes her a moment to notice* SIMON *who is standing shiftily to one side.* MOON *is stirred by a memory.*]

MOON. I say, Birdboot. . . .

BIRDBOOT. That's the one.

FELICITY [*catching sight of* SIMON]. You! [FELICITY *'s manner at the moment is one of great surprise but some pleasure.*]

SIMON [*nervously*]. Er, yes—hello again.

FELICITY. What are you doing here?

SIMON. Well, I. . . .

MOON. She's——

BIRDBOOT. Ssh. . . .

SIMON. No doubt you're surprised to see me.

FELICITY. Honestly, darling, you really are extraordinary.

SIMON. Yes, well, here I am.

FELICITY. You must have been desperate to see me—I mean, I'm *flattered*, but couldn't it wait till I got back?

SIMON [*bravely*]. There is something you don't know.

FELICITY. What is it?

SIMON. Look, about the things I said—it may be that I got carried away a little—we both did——

FELICITY [*stiffly*]. What are you trying to say?

SIMON. I love another!

FELICITY. I see.

SIMON. I didn't make any promises—I merely——

FELICITY. You don't have to say any more——

SIMON. Oh, I didn't want to hurt you——

FELICITY. Of all the nerve!—to march in here to tell me that!

SIMON. Well, I didn't exactly——

FELICITY. You philandering coward——

SIMON. Let me explain——

FELICITY. This is hardly the time and place—you think you can barge in anywhere, whatever I happen to be doing——

SIMON. But I want you to know that my admiration for you is sincere—I don't want you to think that I didn't mean those things I said——

FELICITY. I'll kill you for this, Simon Gascoyne! [*She leaves in tears, passing* MRS. DRUDGE *who has entered in time to overhear her last remark.*]

MOON. It was her.

BIRDBOOT. I told you—straight to the top——

MOON. No, no——

BIRDBOOT. Sssh. . . .

SIMON [*to* MRS. DRUDGE]. Yes what is it?

MRS. DRUDGE. I have come to set up the card table, sir.

SIMON. I don't think I can stay.

MRS. DRUDGE. Oh, Lady Muldoon *will* be disappointed.

SIMON. Does she know I'm here?

MRS. DRUDGE. Oh yes, sir, I just told her and it put her in quite a tizzy.

SIMON. Really? . . . Well, I suppose now that I've cleared the air. . . . Quite a tizzy, you say . . . really . . . really . . . [*He and* MRS. DRUDGE *start setting up for card game.* MRS. DRUDGE *leaves when this is done.*]

MOON. Felicity!—she's the one.

BIRDBOOT. Nonsense—red herring.

MOON. I mean, it was *her!*

BIRDBOOT [*exasperated*]. *What* was?

MOON. That lady I saw you with last night!

BIRDBOOT [*inhales with fury*]. Are you suggesting that a man of my scrupulous integrity would trade his pen for a mess of potage?! Simply because in the course of my profession I happen to have struck up an acquaintance—to have, that is, a warm regard, if you like, for a fellow toiler in the vineyard of greasepaint—I find it simply intolerable to be pillified and villoried—

MOON. I never implied——

BIRDBOOT. —to find myself the object of uninformed malice, the petty slanders of little men——

MOON. I'm sorry——

BIRDBOOT. —to suggest that my good opinion in a journal of unimpeachable integrity is at the disposal of the first actress who gives me what I want—

MOON. Sssssh——

BIRDBOOT. A ladies' man! . . . Why, Myrtle and I have been together now for——

[*Enter* LADY CYNTHIA MULDOON *through french windows. A beautiful woman in her thirties. She wears a cocktail dress, is formally coiffured, and carries a tennis racket. Her effect on* BIRDBOOT *is also impressive. He half rises and sinks back agape.*]

CYNTHIA [*entering*]. Simon! [*A dramatic freeze between her and* SIMON.]

BIRDBOOT. I *say*—who's that?

MOON. Lady Muldoon.

BIRDBOOT. No, I mean—who *is* she?

SIMON [*coming forward*]. Cynthia!

CYNTHIA. Don't say anything for a moment—just hold me.

[*He seizes her and glues his lips to hers, as they say. While their lips are glued——*]

BIRDBOOT. She's *beautiful*—a vision of eternal grace, a poem. . . .

MOON. I think she's got her mouth open.

[CYNTHIA *breaks away dramatically.*]

CYNTHIA. We can't go on meeting like this!

SIMON. We have nothing to be ashamed of!

CYNTHIA. But darling, this is madness!

SIMON. Yes!—I am mad with love for you!

CYNTHIA. Please—remember where we are!

SIMON. Cynthia, I love you!

CYNTHIA. Don't—I love Albert!

SIMON. He's dead! [*Shaking her.*] Do you understand me—Albert's dead!

CYNTHIA. No—I'll never give up hope! Let me go! We are not free!

SIMON. I don't care, we were meant for each other—had we but met in time.

CYNTHIA. You're a cad, Simon! You will use me and cast me aside as you have cast aside so many others.

SIMON. No, Cynthia!—you can make me a better person!

CYNTHIA. You're ruthless—so strong, so cruel——

    [*Ruthlessly he kisses her.*]

MOON. The son she never had, now projected in this handsome stranger and transformed into lover—youth, vigor, the animal, the athlete as aesthete—breaking down the barriers at the deepest level of desire.

BIRDBOOT. By jove, I think you're right. Her mouth *is* open.

MOON. But an archetypal victim if ever I saw one.

BIRDBOOT. Lucky devil.

    [CYNTHIA *breaks away.* MRS. DRUDGE *has entered.*]

CYNTHIA. Stop—can't you see you're making a fool of yourself!

SIMON. I'll kill anyone who comes between us!

CYNTHIA. Yes, what is it, Mrs. Drudge?

MRS. DRUDGE. Should I close the windows, my lady? The fog is beginning to roll off the sea like a deadly——

CYNTHIA. Yes, you'd better. It looks as if we're in for one of those days. Are the cards ready?

MRS. DRUDGE. Yes, my lady.

CYNTHIA. Would you tell Miss Cunningham we are waiting.

MRS. DRUDGE. Yes, my lady.

CYNTHIA. And fetch the Major down.

MRS. DRUDGE. I think I hear him coming downstairs now [*as she leaves.*]

    [*She does: the sound of a wheelchair approaching down several flights of stairs with landings in between. It arrives bearing* MAGNUS *at about 15 m.p.h., knocking* SIMON *over violently.*]

CYNTHIA. Simon!

MAGNUS [*roaring*]. Never had a chance! Ran under the wheels!

CYNTHIA. Darling, are you all right?

MAGNUS. I have witnesses!

CYNTHIA. Oh, Simon—say something!

SIMON [*sitting up suddenly*]. I'm most frightfully sorry.

MAGNUS [*shouting yet*]. How long have you been a pedestrian?

SIMON. Ever since I could walk.

CYNTHIA. Can you walk now. . . ? [SIMON *rises and walks.*] Thank God! Magnus, this is Simon Gascoyne.

MAGNUS. What's he doing here?

CYNTHIA. He just turned up.

MAGNUS. Really? How do you like it here?

FELICITY [*who has just entered*]. So—you're still here.

CYNTHIA. Of course he's still here. We're going to play cards. Now you two sit there . . . and there . . . Simon you help me with this sofa . . . there— [*The sofa is shoved towards the card table, once more revealing the corpse, though not to the players.*] Right—who starts?

MAGNUS. I do.

    [*A continuous mumble of card talk under the dialogue, dovetailed as follows:*]

CYNTHIA [*as* MAGNUS *rhubarbs*[12]]. Simon just happened to drop by for a game of cards.

FELICITY [*plays, then as* CYNTHIA *plays*]. He's a bit of a cheat you know—aren't you, Simon?

SIMON [*plays*]. Call me what you like, but I hold the cards.

CYNTHIA. Well done, Simon!

[*Cards are thrown down and* MAGNUS *pays* SIMON. CYNTHIA *deals.*]

FELICITY. I hear there's a dangerous madman on the loose. Personally I think he's been hiding out in the deserted cottage on the cliffs.

CYNTHIA. Your opening, Simon.

FELICITY [*as* SIMON *and* CYNTHIA *play*]. I couldn't sleep last night and happening to glance out of the window I saw a strange light shining from that direction. What's the matter Simon, you seem nervous.

[MAGNUS *plays*—SIMON, CYNTHIA, FELICITY, MAGNUS *again and* SIMON *again, who wins.*]

CYNTHIA. No!—Simon your luck's in tonight?

[MAGNUS *pays him again.*]

FELICITY [*getting up and stalking out*]. We shall see—the night is not over yet, Simon Gascoyne!

MAGNUS [*wheeling himself out*]. Well, I think I'll go and oil my gun.

[SIMON *and* CYNTHIA *have stood up.*]

CYNTHIA. I think Felicity suspects something.

SIMON. Let her think what she likes.

CYNTHIA. But she's acting as if—Simon, was there something between you and Felicity?

SIMON. No, no—it's over between her and me, Cynthia—it was a mere passing fleeting thing we had—but now that I have found you——

CYNTHIA. If I find that you have been untrue to me—if I find that you have falsely seduced me from my dear husband Albert—I will kill you, Simon Gascoyne!

[MRS. DRUDGE *has entered silently to witness this. On this tableau, pregnant with significance, the act ends, the body still undiscovered. Perfunctory applause.*

MOON *and* BIRDFOOT *seem to be completely preoccupied, becoming audible, as it were.*]

MOON. Camps it around the Old Vic[13] in his opera cloak and passes me the tat.

BIRDBOOT. Do you believe in love at first sight?

MOON. It's not that I think I'm a better critic——

BIRDBOOT. I feel my whole life changing——

MOON. I am but it's not that.

BIRDBOOT. Oh, the world will laugh at me, I know. . . .

MOON. It is not that they are much in the way of shoes to step into. . . .

BIRDBOOT. . . . call me an infatuated old fool. . . .

MOON. . . . They are not.

BIRDBOOT. . . . condemn me. . . .

MOON. He is standing in my light, that is all.

BIRDBOOT. . . . betrayer of my class . . .

MOON. . . . an almost continuous eclipse, interrupted by the phenomenon of moonlight.

---

[12] Chatters unintelligibly in a low voice (a theatrical term).

[13] A theater in London famous for excellent productions of Shapespeare's plays.

BIRDBOOT. I don't care, I'm a gonner.

MOON. And I dream. . . .

BIRDBOOT. The Blue Angel[14] all over again.

MOON. . . . of the day his temperature climbs through the top of his head. . . .

BIRDBOOT. Ah, the sweet madness of love . . .

MOON. . . . of the spasm on the stairs. . . .

BIRDBOOT. Myrtle, farewell . . .

MOON. . . . dreaming of the stair he'll never reach——

BIRDBOOT. —for I only live but once. . . .

MOON. Sometimes I dream that I've killed him.

BIRDBOOT. What?

MOON. What? [*They pull themselves together.*]

BIRDBOOT. Yes . . . yes. . . . A beautiful performance, a collector's piece. I shall say so.

MOON. A very promising debut. I'll put in a good word.

BIRDBOOT. It would be as hypocritical of me to withhold praise on grounds of personal feelings, as to withhold censure.

MOON. You're right. Courageous.

BIRDBOOT. Oh, I know what people will say—— There goes Birdboot buttering up his latest——

MOON. Ignore them——

BIRDBOOT. But I rise above that—— The fact is I genuinely believe her performance to be one of the summits in the range of contemporary theatre.

MOON. Trim-buttocked, that's the word for her.

BIRDBOOT. —the radiance, the inner sadness——

MOON. Does she actually come across with it?

BIRDBOOT. The part as written is a mere cypher but she manages to make Cynthia a real person——

MOON. *Cynthia?*

BIRDBOOT. And should she, as a result, care to meet me over a drink, simply by way of er—thanking me, as it were——

MOON. Well, you fickle old bastard!

[BIRDBOOT *shudders to a halt and clears his throat.*]

BIRDBOOT. Well now—shaping up quite nicely, wouldn't you say?

MOON. Oh yes, yes. A nice trichotomy of forces. One must reserve judgement of course, until the confrontation, but I think it's pretty clear where we're heading.

BIRDBOOT. I agree. It's Magnus a mile off. [*Small pause.*]

MOON. What's Magnus a mile off?

BIRDBOOT. If we knew that we wouldn't be here.

MOON [*clears throat*]. Let me at once say that it has *élan*[15] while at the same time avoiding *éclat*.[16] Having said that, and I think it must be said, I am bound to ask—does this play know where it is going?

BIRDBOOT. Well, it seems open and shut to me, Moon—Magnus is not what he pretends to be and he's got his next victim marked down——

MOON. Does it, I repeat, declare its affiliations? There are moments, and I would not begrudge it this, when the play, if we can call it that, and I think on balance we can, aligns itself uncompromisingly on the side of life. *Je*

---

[14] A film made in 1930 [remade in 1959] about a slinky performer in a Berlin nightclub who lures a middle-aged English teacher into degeneracy and corruption.
[15] Impetuous ardor.   [16] Showiness.

suis,[17] it seems to be saying, *ergo sum.*[18] But is that enough? I think we are entitled to ask. For what in fact is this play concerned with? It is my belief that here we are concerned with what I have referred to elsewhere as the nature of identity. I think we are entitled to ask—and here one is irresistibly reminded of Voltaire's cry, *"Voilà!"*[19]—I think we are entitled to ask—*Where is God?*

BIRDBOOT [*stunned*]. Who?

MOON. Go-od.

BIRDBOOT [*peeping furtively into his program*]. God?

MOON. I think we are entitled to ask.

   [*The phone rings. The set re-illumines to reveal* CYNTHIA, FELICITY *and* MAGNUS *about to take coffee, which is being taken round by* MRS. DRUDGE. SIMON *is missing. The body lies in position.*]

MRS. DRUDGE [*into phone*]. The same, half an hour later? . . . No, I'm sorry—there's no one of that name here. [*She replaces phone and goes round with coffee. To* CYNTHIA.] Black or white, my lady.

CYNTHIA. White please.

   [MRS. DRUDGE *pours.*]

MRS. DRUDGE [*to* FELICITY]. Black or white, miss?

FELICITY. White please.

   [MRS. DRUDGE *pours.*]

MRS. DRUDGE [*to* MAGNUS]. Black or white, Major?

MAGNUS. White please.

   [*Ditto.*]

MRS. DRUDGE [*to* CYNTHIA]. Sugar, my lady?

CYNTHIA. Yes please.

   [*Puts sugar in.*]

MRS. DRUDGE [*to* FELICITY]. Sugar, miss?

FELICITY. Yes please.

   [*Ditto.*]

MRS. DRUDGE [*to* MAGNUS]. Sugar, Major?

MAGNUS. Yes please.

   [*Ditto.*]

MRS. DRUDGE [*to* CYNTHIA]. Biscuit, my lady?

CYNTHIA. No thank you.

BIRDBOOT [*writing elaborately in his notebook*]. The second act, however, fails to fulfil the promise. . . .

FELICITY. If you ask me, there's something funny going on. [MRS. DRUDGE'S *approach to* FELICITY *makes* FELICITY *jump to her feet in impatience. She goes to the radio while* MAGNUS *declines his biscuit, and* MRS. DRUDGE *leaves.*]

RADIO. We interrupt our program for a special police message. The search for the dangerous madman who is on the loose in Essex has now narrowed to the immediate vicinity of Muldoon Manor. Police are hampered by the deadly swamps and the fog, but believe that the madman spent last night in a deserted cottage on the cliffs. The public is advised to stick together and make sure none of their number is missing.

   [FELICITY *turns off the radio nervously. Pause.*]

CYNTHIA. Where's Simon?

FELICITY. Who?

---

[17] I am.   [18] Therefore I am.   [19] There it is!

CYNTHIA. Simon. Have you seen him?

FELICITY. No.

CYNTHIA. Have you, Magnus?

MAGNUS. No.

CYNTHIA. Oh.

FELICITY. Yes, there's something foreboding in the air, it is as if one of us——

CYNTHIA. Oh, Felicity, the house is locked up tight—no one can get in—and the police are practically on the doorstep.

FELICITY. I don't know—it's just a feeling.

CYNTHIA. It's only the fog.

MAGNUS. Hound will never get through on a day like this.

CYNTHIA [*shouting at him*]. Fog!

FELICITY. He means the Inspector.

CYNTHIA. Is he bringing a dog?

FELICITY. Not that I know of.

MAGNUS. —never get through the swamps. Yes, I'm afraid the madman can show his hand in safety now.

[*A mournful baying hooting is heard in the distance, scary.*]

CYNTHIA. What's that?!

FELICITY [*tensely*]. It sounded like the cry of a gigantic hound!

MAGNUS. Poor devil!

CYNTHIA. Ssssh!

[*They listen.*]

BIRDBOOT. . . . That poise, that profile. . . .

MOON. Has it ever struck you that there are probably hundreds of undiscovered murders every year?

BIRDBOOT. . . . the siren[20] on her sea-washed rock, beckoning, beckoning. . . .

MOON. One tends to assume that the only murders which *happen* are the ones one reads about——

BIRDBOOT. . . . I must go to her . . .

MOON. But of course it's probably quite easy, provided that one's motive is sufficiently obtuse.

BIRDBOOT. . . . I can't stop myself. . . .

MOON. Because if the *motive* defies precedent and understanding, it would never occur to the simple minds of the police or the neighbors to speculate on the possibility, which is the natural thing to do when, for instance, a large legacy or a lover turns up.

BIRDBOOT. —even if I wake and drown.

MOON. Yes, if one wanted to get rid of someone for a perfectly impenetrable reason, one could get away with murder.

[*The baying has been repeated during the above, with exclamations, getting nearer until——*]

FELICITY. There it is again!

CYNTHIA. It's coming this way—it's right outside the house!

[MRS. DRUDGE *enters.*]

MRS. DRUDGE. Inspector Hound!

CYNTHIA. A *police* dog?

[*Enter* INSPECTOR HOUND. *On his head he wears a sort of miner's helmet with a*

---

[20] One of two mythological females in Homer's *Odyssey* whose singing lures seamen to destruction.

flashing light. On his feet are his swamp boots. These are two inflatable—and inflated—
pontoons with flat bottoms about two feet across. He carries a foghorn.]

HOUND. Lady Muldoon?

CYNTHIA. Yes.

HOUND. I came as soon as I could. Where shall I put my foghorn and my
swamp boots?

CYNTHIA. Mrs. Drudge will take them out. How very resourceful.

HOUND [*divesting himself of hat, boots and foghorn*]. It takes more than a bit of
weather to keep a policeman from his duty.
[MRS. DRUDGE *leaves with chattels. A pause.*]

CYNTHIA. Oh—er, Inspector Hound—Felicity Cunningham, Major Magnus Muldoon.

HOUND. Good evening. [*He and* CYNTHIA *continue to look expectantly at each other.*]

CYNTHIA AND HOUND [*together*]. Well?—Sorry——

CYNTHIA. No, do go on.

HOUND. Thank you. Well, tell me about it in your own words—take your time,
begin at the beginning and don't leave anything out.

CYNTHIA. I beg your pardon?

HOUND. Fear nothing. You are in safe hands now. I hope you haven't touched
anything.

CYNTHIA. I'm afraid I don't understand.

HOUND. I'm Inspector Hound.

CYNTHIA. Yes.

HOUND. Well, what's it all about?

CYNTHIA. I really have no idea.

HOUND. How did it begin?

CYNTHIA. What?

HOUND. The . . . thing.

CYNTHIA. What thing?

HOUND [*rapidly losing confidence but exasperated*]. The trouble!

CYNTHIA. There hasn't *been* any trouble!

HOUND. Didn't you phone the police?

CYNTHIA. No.

FELICITY. I didn't.

MAGNUS. What for?

HOUND. I see. [*Pause.*] This puts me in a very difficult position [*A steady pause.*]
Well, I'll be getting along, then. [*He moves towards the door.*]

CYNTHIA. I'm terribly sorry.

HOUND [*stiffly*]. That's perfectly all right.

CYNTHIA. Thank you so much for coming.

HOUND. Not at all. You never know, there might have been a serious matter.

CYNTHIA. Drink?

HOUND. More serious than that, even.

CYNTHIA [*correcting*]. Drink before you go?

HOUND. No thank you. [*Leaves.*]

CYNTHIA [*through the door*]. I do hope you find him.

HOUND [*reappearing at once*]. Find who, Madam?—out with it!

CYNTHIA. I thought you were looking for the lunatic.

HOUND. And what do you know about that?

CYNTHIA. It was on the radio.

HOUND. Was it, indeed? Well, that's what I'm here about, really. I didn't want to mention it because I didn't know how much you knew. No point in causing unnecessary panic, even with a murderer in our midst.

FELICITY. Murderer, did you say?

HOUND. Ah—so that was not on the radio?

CYNTHIA. Whom has he murdered, Inspector?

HOUND. Perhaps no one—yet. Let us hope we are in time.

MAGNUS. You believe he is in our midst, Inspector?

HOUND. I do. If anyone of you have recently encountered a youngish good-looking fellow in a smart suit, white shirt, hatless, well-spoken—someone possibly claiming to have just moved into the neighborhood, someone who on the surface seems as sane as you or I, then now is the time to speak.

FELICITY. Inspector——

CYNTHIA. No, Felicity!

MAGNUS. Is one of us in danger, Inspector?

HOUND. Didn't it strike you as odd that on his escape the madman made a beeline for Muldoon Manor? It is my guess that he bears a deep-seated grudge against someone in this very house! Lady Muldoon—where is your husband?

FELICITY. My husband?—you don't mean——?

HOUND. I don't know—but I have a reason to believe that one of you is the real McCoy!

FELICITY. The real what?

HOUND. William Herbert McCoy who as a young man, meeting the madman in the street and being solicited for sixpence for a cup of tea, replied, "Why don't you do a decent day's work, you shifty old bag of horse manure," in Canada all those many years ago and went on to make his fortune. [*He starts to pace intensely.*] The madman was a mere boy at the time but he never forgot that moment, and thenceforth carried in his heart the promise of revenge! [*At which point he finds himself standing on top of the corpse. He looks down carefully.*]

HOUND. Is there anything you have forgotten to tell me? [*They all see the corpse for the first time.*]

FELICITY. So the madman has struck!

CYNTHIA. Oh—it's horrible—horrible——

HOUND. Yes, just as I feared. Now you see the sort of man you are protecting.

CYNTHIA. I can't believe it!

FELICITY. I'll have to tell him, Cynthia—Inspector, a stranger of that description has indeed appeared in our midst—Simon Gascoyne. Oh, he had charm, I'll give you that, and he took me in completely. I'm afraid I made a fool of myself over him, and so did Cynthia.

HOUND. Where is he now?

MAGNUS. He must be around the house—he couldn't get away in these conditions.

HOUND. You're right. Fear naught, Lady Muldoon—I shall apprehend the man who killed your husband.

CYNTHIA. My husband? I don't understand.

HOUND. Everything points to Gascoyne.

CYNTHIA. But who's that. [*The corpse.*]

HOUND. Your husband.

CYNTHIA. No, it's not.

HOUND. Yes, it is.

CYNTHIA. I tell you it's not.

HOUND. Are you sure?

CYNTHIA. For goodness sake!

HOUND. Then who is it?

CYNTHIA. I don't know.

HOUND. Anybody?

FELICITY. I've never seen him before.

MAGNUS. Quite unlike anybody I've ever met.

HOUND. I seem to have made a dreadful mistake. Lady Muldoon, I do apologize.

CYNTHIA. But what are we going to do?

HOUND [snatching the phone]. I'll phone the police!

CYNTHIA. But you are the police!

HOUND. Thank God I'm here—the lines have been cut!

CYNTHIA. You mean——?

HOUND. Yes!—we're on our own, cut off from the world and in grave danger!

FELICITY. You mean——?

HOUND. Yes!—I think the killer will strike again!

MAGNUS. You mean——?

HOUND. Yes! One of us ordinary mortals thrown together by fate and cut off by the elements, is the murderer! He must be found—search the house!

[All depart speedily in different directions leaving a momentarily empty stage. SIMON strolls on.]

SIMON [entering, calling]. Anyone about?—funny. . . . [He notices the corpse and is surprised. He approaches it and turns it over. He stands up and looks about in alarm. There is a shot. SIMON falls dead. INSPECTOR HOUND runs on and crouches down by SIMON's body. CYNTHIA appears at the french windows. She stops there and stares.]

CYNTHIA. What happened, Inspector?!

[HOUND turns to face her.]

HOUND. He's dead. . . . [He stands up thoughtfully.] So we were all wrong, after all. We assumed that the body could not have been lying here before Simon Gascoyne entered the house . . . but . . . [he slides the sofa over the body] . . . there's your answer. And now—who killed Simon Gascoyne? And why?

["CURTAIN": FREEZE, APPLAUSE, EXEUNT.]

BIRDBOOT. Obviously I wouldn't want to hurt Myrtle. . . .

MOON. I've just had a rather ghastly thought. . . .

BIRDBOOT. But I'm a creative sort of person—artistic you might say . . .

MOON. . . . even if I did, and got away with it, there'd still be Macafferty behind me. . . .

BIRDBOOT. . . . A free spirit, really——

MOON. . . . and if I could, so could he.

BIRDBOOT. Yes, I know of this rather nice hotel, very discreet, run by a man of the world——

MOON. Does Macafferty dream of me?

BIRDBOOT. Breakfast served in one's room and no questions asked—[wakes up]. Hello—what's happened?

MOON. What? Oh yes—what do you make of it, so far?

BIRDBOOT [clears throat]. It is at this point that the play for me comes alive. The groundwork has been well and truly laid, and the author has taken the trouble to learn from the masters of the genre. He has created a real situation, and few will doubt his ability to resolve it with a startling denouement. Certainly that is what it so far lacks, but it has a beginning, a middle and I have no doubt it will prove to have an end. For this let us give thanks, and double thanks for a good clean show without a trace of smut. But perhaps even all this would be for nothing were it not for a performance which I consider to be one of the summits in the range of contemporary theatre. In what is possibly the finest Cynthia since the war——

MOON. If we examine this more closely, and I think close examination is the least tribute that this play deserves, I think we will find that within the austere framework of what is seen to be on one level a country-house week-end, and what a useful symbol that is, the author has given us—yes, I will go so far—he has given us the human condition——

BIRDBOOT. More talent in her little finger——

MOON. An uncanny ear that might have belonged to a Van Gogh[21]——

BIRDBOOT. —a public scandal that the Birthday Honors[22] to date have neglected——

MOON. Faced as we are with such ubiquitous obliquity, it is hard, it is hard indeed, and therefore I will not attempt, to refrain from invoking the names of Kafka, Sartre, Shakespeare, St. Paul, Beckett, Birkett, Pinero, Pirandello, Dante and Dorothy L. Sayers.[23]

BIRDBOOT. A rattling good evening out. I was held.

[*The phone starts to ring on the empty stage.* MOON *tries to ignore it.*]

MOON. Harder still—— Harder still if impossible—— Harder still if it is possible to be—— Neither do I find it easy—— Dante and Dorothy L. Sayers. Harder still——

BIRDBOOT. Others taking part included—*Moon!*

[*For* MOON *has lost patience and is bearing down on the ringing phone. He is frankly irritated.*]

MOON [*picking up phone, barks*]. Hel-lo! [*Pause, turns to* BIRDBOOT, *quietly.*] It's for you. [*Pause.*]

[BIRDBOOT *gets up. He approaches cautiously.* MOON *gives him the phone and moves back to his seat.* BIRDBOOT *watches him go. He looks round and smiles weakly, expiating himself.*]

BIRDBOOT [*into phone*]. Hello. . . . [*Explosion.*] Oh, for God's sake, Myrtle!— I've told you never to phone me at work! [*He is naturally embarrassed, looking about with surreptitious fury.*] What? Last night? Good God, woman, this is hardly the time to—I assure you, Myrtle, there is absolutely nothing going on between me and—that's a complete lie. I took her to dinner simply by way of keeping *au fait* with the world of the paint and the motley[24]—— That's nothing to do with her, I'm here simply doing my job— yes, I promise—— Yes, I do—— Yes, I *said* yes—I *do*—and you are mine too, Myrtle— darling—I can't—[*whispers*] *I'm not alone*—[up.]. No, she's not!—[*he looks around furtively, licks his lips and mumbles.*] All *right!* I love your little pink ears and you are my own fluffy bunny-boo—— Now for God's sake—— Good-bye, Myrtle—[*puts down phone.* BIRDBOOT *mops his brow with his handkerchief. As he turns, a tennis ball bounces in through the french windows, followed by* FELICITY,

---

[21] A Dutch painter [1853–1890] who cut off his own ear in 1888.
[22] The Birthday Honors are titles or other signs of recognition bestowed by the British Sovereign at the ruler's birthday celebration.
[23] This idiosyncratic list of world authors is notable primarily because of the omission of Agatha Christie whose play, *The Mousetrap*, is imitated and parodied throughout *The Real Inspector Hound*.
[24] Grease paint and harlequin (clown-like) costume; i.e., the world of the theater.

as before, in tennis outfit. The lighting is as it was. Everything is as it was. It is, let us say, the same moment of time. The only difference is that FELICITY *must be allowed changes of inflection and emphasis which now also "go with" the fact of a critic appearing in the middle of a play.*]

FELICITY [*calling*]. Out! [*She catches sight of* BIRDBOOT *and is amazed.*] You!

BIRDBOOT. Er, yes—hello again.

FELICITY. What are you doing here?!

BIRDBOOT. Well, I . . .

FELICITY. Honestly, darling, you really are extraordinary——

BIRDBOOT. Yes, well, here I am. [*He looks round sheepishly.*]

FELICITY. You must have been desperate to see me—I mean, I'm flattered, but couldn't it wait till I got back?

BIRDBOOT. No, no, you've got it all wrong——

FELICITY. What is it?

BIRDBOOT. And about last night—perhaps I gave you the wrong impression— got carried away a bit, perhaps——

FELICITY [*stiffly*]. What are you trying to say?

BIRDBOOT. I want to call it off.

FELICITY. I see.

BIRDBOOT. I didn't promise anything—and the fact is, I have my reputation— people do talk——

FELICITY. You don't have to say any more——

BIRDBOOT. And my wife, too—I don't know how she got to hear of it, but——

FELICITY. Of all the nerve! To march in here and——

BIRDBOOT. I'm sorry you had to find out like this—the fact is I didn't mean it this way——

FELICITY. You philandering coward!

BIRDBOOT. I'm sorry—but I want you to know that I meant those things I said—oh yes—shows brilliant promise—I shall say so——

FELICITY. I'll kill you for this, Simon Gascoyne! [*She leaves in tears, passing* MRS. DRUDGE *who has entered in time to overhear her last remark.*]

BIRDBOOT [*wide-eyed*]. Good God. . . .

MRS. DRUDGE. I have come to set up the card table, sir.

BIRDBOOT. [*wildly*]. I can't stay for a game of *cards!*

MRS. DRUDGE. Oh, Lady Muldoon *will* be disappointed.

BIRDBOOT. You mean . . . you mean, she wants to meet me. . . ?

MRS. DRUDGE. Oh yes, sir, I just told her and it put her in quite a tizzy.

BIRDBOOT. Really? Yes, well, a man of my influence is not to be sneezed at— I think I have some small name for the making of reputations—mmm, yes, quite a tizzy, you say?

[MRS. DRUDGE *is busied with the card table.* BIRDBOOT *stands marooned and bemused for a moment.*]

MOON [*from his seat*]. Birdboot!—[*a tense whisper*]. Birdboot!

[BIRDBOOT *looks round vaguely.*]

What the hell are you doing?

BIRDBOOT. Nothing.

MOON. Stop making an ass of yourself. Come back.

BIRDBOOT. Oh, I know what you're thinking—but the fact is I genuinely consider her performance to be one of the summits——

[CYNTHIA *enters as before.* MRS. DRUDGE *has gone.*]

CYNTHIA. Darling!

BIRDBOOT. Ah, good evening—may I say that I genuinely consider——

CYNTHIA. Don't say anything for a moment—just hold me. [*She falls into his arms.*]

BIRDBOOT. All right!—let us throw off the hollow pretences of the gimcrack codes we live by! Dear lady, from the first moment I saw you, I felt my whole life changing——

CYNTHIA [*breaking free*]. We can't go on meeting like this!

BIRDBOOT. I am not ashamed to proclaim nightly my love for you!—but fortunately that will not be necessary—— I know of a very good hotel, discreet—run by a man of the world——

CYNTHIA. But darling, this is madness!

BIRDBOOT. Yes! I am mad with love.

CYNTHIA. Please!—remember where we are!

BIRDBOOT. I don't care! Let them think what they like, I love you!

CYNTHIA. Don't—I love Albert!

BIRDBOOT. He's dead. [*Shaking her.*] Do you understand me—Albert's dead!

CYNTHIA. No—I'll never give up hope! Let me go! We are not free!

BIRDBOOT. You mean Myrtle? She means nothing to me—nothing!—she's all cocoa and blue nylon fur slippers—not a spark of creative genius in her whole slumping knee-length-knickered[25] body——

CYNTHIA. You're a cad, Simon! You will use me and cast me aside as you have cast aside so many others!

BIRDBOOT. No, Cynthia—now that I have found you——

CYNTHIA. You're ruthless—so strong—so cruel——

　　[BIRDBOOT *seizes her in an embrace, during which* MRS. DRUDGE *enters, and* MOON's *fevered voice is heard.*]

MOON. Have you taken leave of your tiny mind?

　　[CYNTHIA *breaks free.*]

CYNTHIA. Stop—can't you see you're making a fool of yourself!

MOON. She's right.

BIRDBOOT [*to* MOON]. You keep out of this.

CYNTHIA. Yes, what is it, Mrs. Drudge?

MRS. DRUDGE. Should I close the windows, my lady? The fog——

CYNTHIA. Yes, you'd better.

MOON. Look, they've got your number——

BIRDBOOT. I'll leave in my own time, thank you very much.

MOON. It's the finish of you, I suppose you know that——

BIRDBOOT. I don't need your twopenny Grubb Street prognostications—I have found something bigger and finer——

MOON [*bemused, to himself*]. If only it were Higgs. . . .

CYNTHIA. . . . And fetch the Major down.

MRS. DRUDGE. I think I hear him coming down stairs now.

　　[*She leaves. The sound of a wheelchair's approach as before.* BIRDBOOT *prudently keeps out of the chair's former path but it enters from the next wing down and knocks him flying. A babble of anguish and protestation.*]

CYNTHIA. Simon—say something!

BIRDBOOT. That reckless bastard [*as he sits up*].

CYNTHIA. Thank God!——

---

[25] *Knickers* in England means women's underdrawers.

MAGNUS. What's *he* doing here?

CYNTHIA. He just turned up.

MAGNUS. Really? How do you like it here?

BIRDBOOT. I couldn't take it night after night.

[BIRDBOOT *limps across towards* MOON.]

BIRDBOOT. Did you see that?! I *told* you it was Magnus. Not that it *is* Magnus.

MOON. What do you mean?

BIRDBOOT. There's more in this than meets the eye, Moon.

MOON. I don't know what you're talking about. For heavens sake sit down—have a chocolate—relax—they've got no right——

BIRDBOOT [*looking over his shoulder*]: They need me to make up a four——

[*The card scene is set-up, the sofa moved, the body visible.* BIRDBOOT *takes his place. The card game of course dovetails into the game on page 1437, the dialogue of which is here reduced to stewed rhubarb, while the former rhubarb becomes as follows:*]

CYNTHIA. Who starts?

MAGNUS. I do. I'll dummy for a no-bid ruff and double my holding on south's queen. [*He does various things with cards.*]

FELICITY. Pay twenty-ones or trump my contract.

CYNTHIA. I'll trump your contract with five dummy's no-trump *there* [*discards*] and I'll move West's rook for the re-bid with a banker ruff on his second trick *there.* [*Discards.*] Simon?

BIRDBOOT [*stupefied*]. Would you mind doing that again?

CYNTHIA [*takes back cards*]. —and I'll ruff your dummy with five no-bid trumps there [*discards*] and I support your rebid with a banker for the solo ruff in dummy trick there. [*Discards.*]

[BIRDBOOT *angrily gets to his feet and throws down his cards.*]

BIRDBOOT. And I'll call your bluff!

CYNTHIA. Well done, Simon! [*As they all inspect his cards.* MAGNUS *pays* SIMON *about £50 in notes, while* CYNTHIA *deals.*] Right, Simon, it's your opening on the minor bid.

[BIRDBOOT *pockets the money warily. After looking carefully at the other players he gingerly extracts a card from his hand and puts it down.*]

CYNTHIA. Hm—hm—Let's see. I think I'll overbid the spade convention with two no-trumps and King's gambit offered there [*discards*] and West's dummy split double to QB4 there! Partner?

[MAGNUS *rolls dice.*]

MAGNUS [*disgusted*]. Snake eyes!

CYNTHIA. Simon?

BIRDBOOT [*triumphantly*]. I call your bluff!

CYNTHIA [*imperturbably*]. I meld.

FELICITY. I huff.

MAGNUS. I ruff.

BIRDBOOT. I bluff.

CYNTHIA. Twist.

FELICITY. I'll see you!

MAGNUS [*dice*]. Double top!

BIRDBOOT [*hysterically*]. Bingo!

CYNTHIA. No!—Simon, your luck's in tonight!

[MAGNUS *counts out another wad of money for* BIRDBOOT, *and finally jiggles around in his trouser pocket for a coin to add to the pile of notes. Meanwhile:*]

FELICITY [*leaving*]. We shall see, the night is not over yet, Simon Gascoyne!

[*But* BIRDBOOT *is staring at* MAGNUS.]

BIRDBOOT. Excuse me, but haven't I seen you somewhere before? There's something about you . . . your voice. . . . [MAGNUS *keeps counting money.*] Where was it?—I must have seen you in something—and yet, I don't think it was quite that——

MAGNUS [*departing*]. Well, I think I'm going to oil my gun.

CYNTHIA. I think Felicity suspects something.

BIRDBOOT [*watching* MAGNUS, *abstracted*]. What?

CYNTHIA. Simon—was there anything between you and Felicity?

BIRDBOOT [*coming round*]. No, no—that's all over now—I merely flattered her a little over a drink, told her she'd go far, that sort of thing—dear me, the fuss that's been made about a little flirtation——

CYNTHIA [*as* MRS. DRUDGE *enters behind*]. If I find you have falsely seduced me from my dear husband Albert, I will kill you, Simon Gascoyne!

[*The* "CURTAIN" *as before.* MRS. DRUDGE *and* CYNTHIA *leave.* BIRDBOOT *starts to follow them.*]

MOON. *Birdboot!*

[BIRDBOOT *stops.*]

MOON. For God's sake pull yourself together.

BIRDBOOT. I can't help it.

MOON. What do you think you're doing? You're turning it into a complete farce!

BIRDBOOT. I know, I know—but I can't live without her. [*He is making erratic neurotic journeys about the stage.*] I shall resign my position, of course. I don't care I'm a gonner, I tell you—— [*He has arrived at the body. He looks at it in surprise, hesitates, bends and turns it over.*]

MOON. Birdboot, think of your family, your friends—your high standing in the world of letters—I say, what are you doing? [BIRDBOOT *is staring at the body's face.*] Birdboot . . . leave it alone. Come and sit down—what's the matter with you?

BIRDBOOT [*dead-voiced*]. It's Higgs.

MOON. What?

BIRDBOOT. It's Higgs. [*Pause.*]

MOON. Don't be silly.

BIRDBOOT. I tell you it's Higgs! [MOON *half rises. Bewildered.*] I don't understand. . . . He's dead.

MOON. Dead?

BIRDBOOT. Who would want to. . . ?

MOON. He must have been lying there all the time. . . .

BIRDBOOT. . . . kill Higgs?

MOON. But what's he doing here? I was standing in tonight. . . .

BIRDBOOT [*turning*]. Moon? . . .

MOON [*faltering*]. But I swear I. . . .

BIRDBOOT. I've got it——

MOON. But I didn't——

BIRDBOOT [*quietly*]. My God . . . so that was it. . . . [*Up.*] Moon—now I see——

MOON. —I swear I didn't——

BIRDBOOT. Now—finally—I see it all——

[*There is a shot and* BIRDBOOT *falls dead.*]

MOON. Birdboot! [*He runs on, to* BIRDBOOT's *body.*]

[CYNTHIA *appears at the french windows. She stops and stares. All as before.*]

CYNTHIA. Oh my God—what happened, Inspector?

[MOON *turns to face her. He stands up and makes swiftly for his seat. Before he gets there he is stopped by the sound of voices.* SIMON *and* HOUND *are occupying the critics' seats.* MOON *freezes.*]

SIMON. To say that it is without pace, point, focus, interest, drama, wit or originality is to say simply that it does not happen to be my cup of tea. One has only to compare this ragbag with the masters of the genre to see that here we have a trifle that is not my cup of tea at all.

HOUND. I'm sorry to be blunt but there is no getting away from it. It lacks pace. A complete ragbag.

SIMON. I will go further. Those of you who were fortunate enough to be at the Comedie Francaise on Wednesday last, will not need to be reminded that hysterics are no substitute for *éclat.*

HOUND. It lacks *élan.*

SIMON. Some of the cast seem to have given up acting altogether, apparently aghast, with every reason, at finding themselves involved in an evening that would, and indeed will, make the angels weep.

HOUND. I am not a prude but I fail to see any reason for the shower of filth and sexual allusion foisted on to an unsuspecting public in the guise of modernity at all costs. . . .

[*Behind* MOON, FELICITY, MAGNUS *and* MRS. DRUDGE *have made their entrances, so that he turns to face their semi-circle.*]

MAGNUS [*pointing to* BIRDBOOT's *body*]. Well, Inspector, is this your man?

MOON [*Warily*]. . . . Yes. . . . Yes. . . .

CYNTHIA. It's Simon . . .

MOON. Yes . . . yes . . . poor. . . . [*Up.*] Is this some kind of a joke?

MAGNUS. If it is, Inspector, it's in very poor taste.

[MOON *pulls himself together and becomes galvanic, a little wild, in grief for* BIRDBOOT.]

MOON. All right! I'm going to find out who did this! I want everyone to go to the positions they occupied when the shot was fired—[*they move; hysterically*]: No one will leave the house! [*They move back.*]

MAGNUS. I think we all had the opportunity to fire the shot, Inspector—but which of us would want to?

MOON. Perhaps you, Major Magnus!

MAGNUS. Why should I want to kill him!

MOON. Because he discovered your secret!

MAGNUS. What secret?

MOON. *I* don't know!—I think that lets me out of it pretty conclusively.

MRS. DRUDGE. Excuse me, sir?

MOON. Yes?

MRS. DRUDGE. Happening to enter this room earlier in the day to set up the card table, I chanced to overhear a remark made by the deceased to her ladyship, viz., "I will kill anyone who comes between us."

MOON. Exactly!—an obvious reference to the first corpse.

CYNTHIA. But he didn't come between us!

MAGNUS. And who, then, killed Simon?

MRS. DRUDGE. Subsequent to that reported remark, I also happened to be in earshot of a remark made by Lady Muldoon to the deceased, to the effect, "I will kill you, Simon Gascoyne!" I hope you don't mind my mentioning it.

MOON. Not at all. I'm glad you did. It is from these chance remarks that we in the force build up our complete picture before moving in to make the arrest. It will not be long now, I fancy, and I must warn you, Lady Muldoon that anything you say——

CYNTHIA. Yes!—I hated Simon Gascoyne, for he had me in his power!—But I didn't kill him!

MRS. DRUDGE. Prior to that, Inspector, I also chanced to overhear a remark made by Miss Cunningham, no doubt in the heat of the moment, but it stuck in my mind as these things do, viz., "I will kill you for this, Simon Gascoyne!"

MOON. Ah! The final piece of the jigsaw! I think I am now in a position to reveal the mystery. This man [*the corpse*] was, of course, McCoy, the Canadian who, as we heard, meeting Gascoyne in the street and being solicited for sixpence for a toffee apple, smacked him across the ear, with the cry, "How's that for a grudge to harbor, you sniffling little workshy!" all those many years ago. Gascoyne bided his time, but in due course tracked McCoy down to this house, having, on the way, met, in the neighborhood, a simple ambitious girl from the provinces. He was charming, persuasive—told her, I have no doubt, that she would go straight to the top—and she, flattered by his sophistication, taken in by his promises to see her all right on the night, gave in to his simple desires. Perhaps she loved him. We shall never know. But in the very hour of her promised triumph, his eye fell on another— yes, I refer to Lady Cynthia Muldoon. From the moment he caught sight of her there was no other woman for him—he was in her spell, willing to sacrifice anything, even you, Felicity Cunningham. It was only today—unexpectedly finding him here—that you learned the truth. There was a bitter argument which ended with your promise to kill him—a promise that you carried out in this very room at your first opportunity! And I must warn you that anything you say——

FELICITY. But it doesn't make sense!

MOON. Not at first glance, *perhaps.*

CYNTHIA. So! So Simon was not the only murderer in our midst.

MAGNUS. If indeed he was a murderer at all. Could not McCoy have been killed by the same person who killed Simon? Suppose Simon, as you surmised, Inspector, discovered the killer's secret.

FELICITY. But why should any of us want to kill a perfect stranger?

MAGNUS. Perhaps he was not a stranger to *one* of us.

MOON [*faltering*]. But Simon was the madman, wasn't he?

MAGNUS. We only have your word for that, Inspector. We only have your word for a lot of things. For instance—McCoy. Who is he? Is his name McCoy? Is there any truth in that fantastic and implausible tale of the insult inflicted in the Canadian streets? Or is there something else, something quite unknown to us, behind all this? Suppose for a moment that the madman, having killed this unknown stranger for private and inscrutable reasons of his own, was disturbed before he could dispose of the body, so having cut the telephone wires he decided to return to the scene of the crime, masquerading as—Police Inspector Hound!

MOON. But . . . I'm not mad . . . I'm almost sure I'm not mad. . . .

MAGNUS. . . . only to discover that in the house was a man, Simon Gascoyne, who happened to be a former inmate of the same asylum, and who, moreover, recognized the corpse as a man against whom you had held a deep-seated grudge——!

MOON. But I didn't kill—I'm almost sure I——

MAGNUS. I put it to you!—are you the real Inspector Hound?!

MOON. You know damn well I'm not! What's it all about?—I didn't kill anyone!

MAGNUS. I'm afraid it all fits.

MOON. I only dreamed . . . sometimes I dreamed——

CYNTHIA. So it was you!

MRS. DRUDGE. The madman!

FELICITY. What made you realize that he was the lunatic, Major?

MAGNUS. It was his funny hat which first put me on to it. But that wasn't all—you see, we had a shrewd suspicion he would turn up here—and he walked into the trap!

MOON. What *trap?*

MAGNUS. I am not the real Magnus Muldoon!—It was a mere subterfuge!—and [*standing up and removing his moustaches*] I now reveal myself as——

MOON [*recoils*]. *Macafferty!*

CYNTHIA. You mean——?

MAGNUS. Yes!—I am the real Inspector Hound!

MOON. Macafferty. . . .

MAGNUS [*with pistol*]. Stand where you are, or I shoot!

MOON [*backing*]. You killed Higgs—and Birdboot tried to tell me——

MAGNUS. Stop in the name of the law! [MOON *turns to run.* MAGNUS *fires.* MOON *drops to his knees.*] He has paid his debt to society.

CYNTHIA. So you are the real Inspector Hound.

MAGNUS. Not only that!—I have been leading a double life—at *least!*

CYNTHIA. You mean——?

MAGNUS. Yes!—It's been ten long years, but don't you know me?

CYNTHIA. You mean——?

MAGNUS. Yes!—it is me, Albert!—who lost his memory and joined the force, rising by merit to the rank of Inspector, his past blotted out—until fate cast him back into the home he left behind, back to the beautiful woman he had brought here as his girlish bride—in short, my darling, my memory has returned and your long wait is over!

CYNTHIA. Oh, Albert!

[*They embrace.*]

MOON [*with a trace of admiration*]. Macafferty! . . . you cunning bastard.

[MOON *dies.*]

THE END

[1968]

Bernard Pomerance 1940–

THE ELEPHANT MAN

1884–1890. London. One scene is in Belgium.

CHARACTERS

FREDERICK TREVES, *a surgeon and teacher*
CARR GOMM, *administrator of the London Hospital*
ROSS, *Manager of the Elephant Man*
JOHN MERRICK, *the Elephant Man*
Three PINHEADS, *three women freaks whose heads are pointed*
BELGIAN POLICEMAN
LONDON POLICEMAN
MAN, *at a fairground in Brussels*

CONDUCTOR, *of Ostend-London boat train*
BISHOP WALSHAM HOW
PORTER, *at the London Hospital*
SNORK, *also a porter*
MRS. KENDAL, *an actress*
DUCHESS
COUNTESS
PRINCESS ALEXANDRA
LORD JOHN
NURSE, MISS SANDWICH

SCENE I
He Will Have 100 Guinea Fees Before He's Forty

The London Hospital, Whitechapel Rd. Enter GOMM, *enter* TREVES.

TREVES. Mr. Carr Gomm? Frederick Treves. Your new lecturer in anatomy.

GOMM. Age thirty-one. Books on Scrofula and Applied Surgical Anatomy— I'm happy to see you rising, Mr. Treves. I like to see merit credited, and your industry, accomplishment, and skill all do you credit. Ignore the squalor of Whitechapel, the general dinginess, neglect and poverty without, and you will find a continual medical richesse in the London Hospital. We study and treat the widest range of diseases and disorders, and are certainly the greatest institution of our kind in the world. The Empire provides unparalleled opportunities for our studies, as places cruel to life are the most revealing scientifically. Add to our reputation by going further, and that'll satisfy. You've bought a house?

TREVES. On Wimpole Street.

GOMM. Good. Keep at it, Treves. You'll have an FRS[1] and 100 guinea[2] fees before you're forty. You'll find it is an excellent consolation prize.

TREVES. Consolation? I don't know what you mean.

GOMM. I know you don't. You will. [*Exits.*]

TREVES. A happy childhood in Dorset. A scientist in an age of science. In an English age, an Englishman. A teacher and a doctor at the London. Two books published by my thirty-first year. A house. A wife who loves me, and my god, 100 guinea fees before I'm forty. Consolation for what? As of the

---

[1] Fellow of the Royal Society, the world's oldest scientific organization, founded in London in 1660 to promote the natural sciences.

[2] A guinea was a former English gold coin, equal to 21 shillings. Thus, a 100 guinea fee would be about £105, worth several hundred dollars in U.S. currency.

year AD 1884, I, Freddie Treves, have excessive blessings. Or so it seems
to me.
[*Blackout.*]

SCENE II
Art Is As Nothing to Nature

*Whitechapel Rd. A storefront. A large advertisement of a creature with an elephant's
head.* Ross, *his manager.*

Ross. Tuppence[3] only, step in and see: This side of the grave, John Merrick
has no hope nor expectation of relief. In every sense his situation is desperate.
His physical agony is exceeded only by his mental anguish, a despised creature
without consolation. Tuppence only, step in and see! To live with his physical
hideousness, incapacitating deformities and unremitting pain is trial enough,
but to be exposed to the cruelly lacerating expressions of horror and disgust
by all who behold him—is even more difficult to bear. Tuppence only, step
in and see! For in order to survive, Merrick forces himself to suffer these
humiliations, I repeat, humiliations, in order to survive, thus he exposes
himself to crowds who pay to gape and yawp at this freak of nature, the
Elephant Man.
[*Enter* TREVES *who looks at advertisement.*]
Ross. See Mother Nature uncorseted and in malignant rage! Tuppence.
TREVES. This sign's absurd. Half-elephant, half-man is not possible. Is he for-
eign?
Ross. Right, from Leicester.[4] But nothing to fear.
TREVES. I'm at the London across the road. I would be curious to see him if
there is some genuine disorder. If he is a mass of papier-maché and paint
however—
Ross. Then pay me nothing. Enter, sir. Merrick, stand up. Ya bloody donkey,
up, up.
[*They go in, then emerge.* TREVES *pays.*]
TREVES. I must examine him further at the hospital. Here is my card. I'm
Treves. I will have a cab pick him up and return him. My card will gain
him admittance.
Ross. Five bob[5] he's yours for the day.
TREVES. I wish to examine him in the interests of science, you see.
Ross. Sir, I'm Ross. I look out for him, get him his living. Found him in
Leicester workhouse. His own ma put him there age of three. Couldn't bear
the sight, well you can see why. We—he and I—are in business. He is our
capital, see. Go to a bank. Go anywhere. Want to borrow capital, you pay
interest. Scientists even. He's good value though. You won't find another
like him.
TREVES. Fair enough. [*He pays.*]
Ross. Right. Out here, Merrick. Ya bloody donkey, out!
[*Lights fade out.*]

---

[3] Two pence (or pennies).   [4] A city in central England, north of London.
[5] Five shillings. There were twenty shillings to the pound and twelve pennies (pence) to the shilling
in the 1880s.

SCENE III
Who Has Seen the Like of This?

TREVES *lectures.* MERRICK *contorts himself to approximate projected slides of the real Merrick.*

TREVES. The most striking feature about him was his enormous head. Its circumference was about that of a man's waist. From the brow there projected a huge bony mass like a loaf, while from the back of his head hung a bag of spongy fungous-looking skin, the surface of which was comparable to brown cauliflower. On the top of the skull were a few long lank hairs. The osseous growth on the forehead, at this stage about the size of a tangerine, almost occluded one eye. From the upper jaw there projected another mass of bone. It protruded from the mouth like a pink stump, turning the upper lip inside out, and making the mouth a wide slobbering aperture. The nose was merely a lump of flesh, only recognizable as a nose from its position. The deformities rendered the face utterly incapable of the expression of any emotion whatsoever. The back was horrible because from it hung, as far down as the middle of the thigh, huge sacklike masses of flesh covered by the same loathsome cauliflower stain. The right arm was of enormous size and shapeless. It suggested but was not elephantiasis, and was overgrown also with pendant masses of the same cauliflower-like skin. The right hand was large and clumsy—a fin or paddle rather than a hand. No distinction existed between the palm and back, the thumb was like a radish, the fingers like thick tuberous roots. As a limb it was useless. The other arm was remarkable by contrast. It was not only normal, but was moreover a delicately shaped limb covered with a fine skin and provided with a beautiful hand which any woman might have envied. From the chest hung a bag of the same repulsive flesh. It was like a dewlap suspended from the neck of a lizard. The lower limbs had the characters of the deformed arm. They were unwieldy, dropsical-looking, and grossly misshapen. There arose from the fungous skin growths a very sickening stench which was hard to tolerate. To add a further burden to his trouble, the wretched man when a boy developed hip disease which left him permanently lame, so that he could only walk with a stick. [*To* MERRICK] Please. [MERRICK *walks.*] He was thus denied all means of escape from his tormentors.

VOICE. Mr. Treves, you have shown a profound and unknown disorder to us. You have said when he leaves here it is for his exhibition again. I do not think it ought to be permitted. It is a disgrace. It is a pity and a disgrace. It is an indecency in fact. It may be a danger in ways we do not know. Something ought to be done about it.

TREVES. I am a doctor. What would you have me do?

VOICE. Well. I know what to do. *I* know.

[*Silence. A policeman enters as lights fade out.*]

SCENE IV
This Indecency May Not Continue

Music. A fair. PINHEADS *huddling together, holding a portrait of Leopold, King of the Congo.*[6] *Enter* MAN.

MAN. Now, my pinheaded darlings, your attention please. Every freak in Brussels Fair is doing something to celebrate Leopold's fifth year as King of the Congo. Him. Our King. Our Empire. [*They begin reciting.*] No, don't recite yet, you morons. I'll say when. And when you do, get it *right*. You don't, it's back to the asylum. Know what that means, don't you? They'll cut your heads. They'll spoon out your little brains, replace 'em in the dachshund they were nicked from. *Cut you.* Yeah. Be back with customers. Come see the Queens of the Congo!
[*Exits.*]
[*Enter* MERRICK, ROSS.]
MERRICK. Cosmos? Cosmos?
ROSS. Congo. Land of darkness. Hoho! [*Sees* PINS.] Look at them, lad. It's freer on the continent. Loads of indecency here, no one minds. You won't get coppers sent round to roust you out like London. Reckon in Brussels here's our fortune. You have a little tête-à-tête[7] with this lot while I see the coppers about our license to exhibit. Be right back. [*Exits.*]
MERRICK. I come from England.
PINS. Allo!
MERRICK. At home they chased us. Out of London. Police. Someone complained. They beat me. You have no trouble? No?
PINS. Allo! Allo!
MERRICK. Hello. In Belgium we make money. I look forward to it. Happiness, I mean. You pay your police? How is it done?
PINS. Allo! Allo!
MERRICK. We do a show together sometime? Yes? I have saved forty-eight pounds. Two shillings. Nine pence. English money. Ross takes care of it.
PINS. Allo! Allo!
MERRICK. Little vocabulary problem, eh? Poor things. Looks like they put your noses to the grindstone and forgot to take them away.
[MAN *enters.*]
MAN. They're coming. [*People enter to see the girls' act.*] Now.
PINS [*dancing and singing*].

> We are the Queens of the Congo,
> The Beautiful Belgian Empire
> Our niggers are bigger
> Our miners are finer
> Empire, Empire, Congo and power
> Civilizuzu's finest hour
> Admire, perspire, desire, acquire
> Or we'll set you on fire!

[6] Leopold II (1835–1909), King of Belgium, founded the Congo Free State (now Zaire) in 1885 and exploited it to his own personal advantage by granting concessions to private companies. See Joseph Conrad's "Heart of Darkness."
[7] Private conversation.

MAN. You cretins! Sorry, they're not ready yet. Out please. [*People exit.*] Get those words right, girls! Or you know what. [MAN *exits.* PINS *weep.*]

MERRICK. Don't cry. You sang nicely. Don't cry. There there.

[*Enter* ROSS *in grip of two* POLICEMEN.]

ROSS. I was promised a permit. I lined a tour up on that!

POLICEMEN. This is a brutal, indecent, and immoral display. It is a public indecency, and it is forbidden here.

ROSS. What about them with their perfect cone heads?

POLICEMEN. They are ours.

ROSS. Competition's good for business. Where's your spirit of competition?

POLICEMEN. Right here. [*Smacks* MERRICK.]

ROSS. Don't do that, you'll kill him!

POLICEMEN. Be better off dead. Indecent bastard.

MERRICK. Don't cry girls. Doesn't hurt.

PINS. Indecent, indecent, indecent, indecent!!

[POLICEMEN *escort* MERRICK *and* ROSS *out, i.e., forward. Blackout except spot on* MERRICK *and* ROSS.]

MERRICK. Ostend[8] will always mean bad memories. Won't it, Ross?

ROSS. I've decided. I'm sending you back, lad. You're a flop. No, you're a liability. You ain't the moneymaker I figured, so that's it.

MERRICK. Alone?

ROSS. Here's a few bob, have a nosh.[9] I'm keeping the rest. For my trouble. I deserve it, I reckon. Invested enough with you. Pick up your stink if I stick around. Stink of failure. Stink of lost years. Just stink, stink, stink, stink, stink.

[*Enter* CONDUCTOR.]

CONDUCTOR. This the one?

ROSS. Just see him to Liverpool St. Station safe, will you? Here's for your trouble.

MERRICK. Robbed.

CONDUCTOR. What's he say?

ROSS. Just makes sounds. Fella's an imbecile.

MERRICK. Robbed.

ROSS. Bon voyage, Johnny. His name is Johnny. He knows his name, that's all, though.

CONDUCTOR. Don't follow him, Johnny. Johnny, come on boat now. Conductor find Johnny place out of sight. Johnny! Johnny! Don't struggle, Johnny. Johnny come on.

MERRICK. Robbed! Robbed!

[*Fadeout on struggle.*]

SCENE V
Police Side with Imbecile Against the Crowd

Darkness. Uproar, shouts.

VOICE. Liverpool St. Station!

[*Enter* MERRICK, CONDUCTOR, POLICEMAN.]

---

[8] A city in northwestern Belgium.   [9] A snack or tidbit.

POLICEMAN. We're safe in here. I barred the door.

CONDUCTOR. They wanted to rip him to pieces. I've never seen anything like it. It was like being Gordon[10] at bleedin' Khartoum.

POLICEMAN. Got somewhere to go in London, lad? Can't stay here.

CONDUCTOR. He's an imbecile. He don't understand. Search him.

POLICEMAN. Got any money?

MERRICK. Robbed.

POLICEMAN. What's that?

CONDUCTOR. He just makes sounds. Frightened sounds is all he makes. Go through his coat.

MERRICK. Je-sus.

POLICEMAN. Don't let me go through your coat, I'll turn you over to that lot! Oh, I was joking, don't upset yourself.

MERRICK. Joke? Joke?

POLICEMAN. Sure, croak, croak, croak, croak.

MERRICK. Je-sus.

POLICEMAN. Got a card here. You Johnny Merrick? What's this old card here, Johnny? Someone give you a card?

CONDUCTOR. What's it say?

POLICEMAN. Says Mr. Frederick Treves, Lecturer in Anatomy, the London Hospital.

CONDUCTOR. I'll go see if I can find him, it's not far. [*Exits.*]

POLICEMAN. What's he do, lecture you on your anatomy? People who think right don't look like that then, do they? Yeah, glung glung, glung, glung.

MERRICK. Jesus. Jesus.

POLICEMAN. Sure, Treves, Treves, Treves, Treves.

[*Blackout, then lights go up as* CONDUCTOR *leads* TREVES *in.*]

TREVES. What is going on here? Look at that mob, have you no sense of decency. I am Frederick Treves. This is my card.

POLICEMAN. This poor wretch here had it. Arrived from Ostend.

TREVES. Good Lord, Merrick? John Merrick? What has happened to you?

MERRICK. Help me!

[*Fadeout.*]

SCENE VI
Even on the Niger and Ceylon, Not This

The London Hospital. MERRICK *in bathtub.* TREVES *outside. Enter* MISS SANDWICH.

TREVES. You are? Miss Sandwich?

SANDWICH. Sandwich. Yes.

TREVES. You have had experience in missionary hospitals in the Niger.[11]

SANDWICH. And Ceylon.[12]

TREVES. I may assume you've seen—

SANDWICH. The tropics. Oh those diseases. The many and the awful scourges our Lord sends, yes, sir.

---

[10] Charles George Gordon (1833–1885), the British general killed in the Sudan in Africa while attempting to defend the city of Khartoum against a Muslim revolt.

[11] An area of what was then French West Africa.   [12] An island off the southeast coast of India.

TREVES. I need the help of an experienced nurse, you see.

SANDWICH. Someone to bring him food, take care of the room. Yes, I understand. But it is somehow difficult.

TREVES. Well, I have been let down so far. He really is—that is, the regular sisters—well, it is not part of their job and they will not do it. Be ordinarily kind to Mr. Merrick. Without—well—panicking. He is quite beyond ugly. You understand that? His appearance has terrified them.

SANDWICH. The photographs show a terrible disease.

TREVES. It is a disorder, not a disease; it is in no way contagious though we don't in fact know what it is. I have found however that there is a deep superstition in those I've tried, they actually believe he somehow brought it on himself, this thing, and of course it is not that at all.

SANDWICH. I am not one who believes it is ourselves who attain grace or bring chatisement to us, sir.

TREVES. Miss Sandwich, I am hoping not.

SANDWICH. Let me put your mind to rest. Care for lepers in the East, and you have cared, Mr. Treves. In Africa, I have seen dreadful scourges quite unknown to our more civilized climes. What at home could be worse than a miserable and afflicted rotting black?

TREVES. I imagine.

SANDWICH. Appearances do not daunt me.

TREVES. It is really that that has sent me outside the confines of the London seeking help.

SANDWICH. "I look unto the hills whence cometh my help."[13] I understand: I think I will be satisfactory.

[*Enter* PORTER *with tray.*]

PORTER. His lunch. [*Exits.*]

TREVES. Perhaps you would be so kind as to accompany me this time. I will introduce you.

SANDWICH. Allow me to carry the tray.

TREVES. I will this time. You are ready.

SANDWICH. I am.

TREVES. He is bathing to be rid of his odor.

[*They enter to* MERRICK.]

John, this is Miss Sandwich. She—

SANDWICH. I—[*unable to control herself*] Oh my good God in heaven. [*Bolts room.*]

TREVES [*puts* MERRICK's *lunch down*]. I am sorry. I thought—

MERRICK. Thank you for saving the lunch this time.

TREVES. Excuse me. [*Exits to* MISS SANDWICH.] You have let me down, you know. I did everything to warn you and still you let me down.

SANDWICH. You didn't say.

TREVES. But I—

SANDWICH. Didn't! You said—just words!

TREVES. But the photographs.

SANDWICH. Just pictures. No one will do this. I am sorry. [*Exits.*]

TREVES. Yes. Well. This is not helping him.

[*Fadeout.*]

---

[13] Psalm 121.

SCENE VII
The English Public Will Pay for Him to Be Like Us

The London Hospital. MERRICK *in a bathtub reading.* TREVES, BISHOP HOW *in foreground.*

BISHOP. With what fortitude he bears his cross! It is remarkable. He has made the acquaintance of religion and knows sections of the Bible by heart. Once I'd grasped his speech, it became clear he'd certainly had religious instruction at one time.

TREVES. I believe it was in the workhouse, Dr. How.

BISHOP. They are awfully good about that sometimes. The psalms he loves, and the book of Job perplexes him, he says, for he cannot see that a just God must cause suffering, as he puts it, merely then to be merciful. Yet that Christ will save him he does not doubt, so he is not resentful.
[*Enter* GOMM.]

GOMM. Christ had better; be damned if we can.

BISHOP. Ahem. In any case Dr. Treves, he has a religious nature, further instruction would uplift him and I'd be pleased to provide it. I plan to speak of him from the pulpit this week.

GOMM. I see our visiting bather has flushed the busy Bishop How from his cruciform[14] lair.

BISHOP. Speak with Merrick, sir. I have spoken to him of Mercy and Justice. There's a true Christian in the rough.

GOMM. This makes my news seem banal, yet yes: Frederick, the response to my letter to the *Times* about Merrick has been staggering. The English public has been so generous that Merrick may be supported for life without a penny spent from Hospital funds.

TREVES. But that is excellent.

BISHOP. God bless the English public.

GOMM. Especially for not dismembering him at Liverpool St. Station. Freddie, the London's no home for incurables, this is quite irregular, but for you I permit it—though god knows what you'll do.

BISHOP. God does know, sir, and Darwin[15] does not.

GOMM. He'd better, sir; he deformed him.

BISHOP. I had apprehensions coming here. I find it most fortunate Merrick is in the hands of Dr. Treves, a Christian, sir.

GOMM. Freddie is a good man and a brilliant doctor, and that is fortunate indeed.

TREVES. I couldn't have raised the funds though, Doctor.

BISHOP. Don't let me keep you longer from your duties, Mr. Treves. Yet, Mr. Gomm, consider: is it science, sir, that motivates us when we transport English rule of law to India or Ireland? When good British churchmen leave hearth and home for missionary hardship in Africa, is it science that bears them away? Sir it is not. It is Christian duty. It is the obligation to bring our light and benefices to benighted man. That motivates us, even as it motivates Treves toward Merrick, sir, to bring salvation where none is. Gordon was a Christian, sir, and died at Khartoum for it. Not for science, sir.

[14] Cross-shaped.
[15] Charles Darwin (1809–1882), the British naturalist whose *Origin of Species* (1859) proposed the theory of evolution.

GOMM. You're telling me, not for science.

BISHOP. Mr. Treves, I'll visit Merrick weekly if I may.

TREVES. You will be welcome, sir, I am certain.

BISHOP. Then good day, sirs. [*Exits.*]

GOMM. Well, Jesus my boy, now we have the money, what do you plan for Merrick?

TREVES. Normality as far as is possible.

GOMM. So he will be like us? Ah. [*Smiles.*]

TREVES. Is something wrong, Mr. Gomm? With us?

    [*Fadeout.*]

SCENE VIII
Mercy and Justice Elude Our Minds and Actions

MERRICK *in bath.* TREVES, GOMM.

MERRICK. How long is as long as I like?

TREVES. You may stay for life. The funds exist.

MERRICK. Been reading this. About homes for the blind. Wouldn't mind going to one when I have to move.

TREVES. But you do not have to move; and you're not blind.

MERRICK. I would prefer it where no one stared at me.

GOMM. No one will bother you here.

TREVES. Certainly not. I've given instructions.

    [PORTER *and* SNORK *peek in.*]

PORTER. What'd I tell you?

SNORK. Gawd almighty. Oh. Mr. Treves. Mr. Gomm.

TREVES. You were told not to do this. I don't understand. You must not lurk about. Surely you have work.

PORTER. Yes, sir.

TREVES. Well, it is infuriating. When you are told a thing, you must listen. I won't have you gaping in on my patients. Kindly remember that.

PORTER. Isn't a patient, sir, is he?

TREVES. Do not let me find you here again.

PORTER. Didn't know you were here, sir. We'll be off now.

GOMM. No, no, Will. Mr. Treves was precisely saying no one would intrude when you intruded.

TREVES. He is warned now. Merrick does not like it.

GOMM. He was warned before. On what penalty, Will?

PORTER. That you'd sack me, sir.

GOMM. You are sacked, Will. You, his friend, you work here?

SNORK. Just started last week, sir.

GOMM. Well, I hope the point is taken now.

PORTER. Mr. Gomm—I ain't truly sacked, am I?

GOMM. Will, yes. Truly sacked. You will never be more truly sacked.

PORTER. It's not me. My wife ain't well. My sister has got to take care of our kids, and of her. Well.

GOMM. Think of them first next time.

PORTER. It ain't as if I interfered with his medicine.

GOMM. That is exactly what it is. You may go.

PORTER. Just keeping him to look at in private. That's all. Isn't it? [SNORK *and* PORTER *exit.*]

GOMM. There are priorities, Frederick. The first is discipline. Smooth is the passage to the tight ship's master. Merrick, you are safe from prying now.

TREVES. Have we nothing to say, John?

MERRICK. If all that'd stared at me'd been sacked—there'd be whole towns out of work.

TREVES. I meant, "Thank you, sir."

MERRICK. "Thank you sir."

TREVES. We always do say please and thank you, don't we?

MERRICK. Yes, sir. Thank you.

TREVES. If we want to properly be like others.

MERRICK. Yes, sir, I want to.

TREVES. Then it is for our own good, is it not?

MERRICK. Yes, sir. Thank you, Mr. Gomm.

GOMM. Sir, you are welcome. [*Exits.*]

TREVES. You are happy here, are you not, John?

MERRICK. Yes.

TREVES. The baths have rid you of the odor, have they not?

MERRICK. First chance I had to bathe regularly.

TREVES. And three meals a day delivered to your room?

MERRICK. Yes, sir.

TREVES. This is your Promised Land, is it not? A roof. Food. Protection. Care. Is it not?

MERRICK. Right, Mr. Treves.

TREVES. I will bet you don't know what to call this.

MERRICK. No, sir, I don't know.

TREVES. You call it, Home.

MERRICK. Never had a home before.

TREVES. You have one now. Say it, John: Home.

MERRICK. Home.

TREVES. No, no really say it. I have a home. This is my home. Go on.

MERRICK. I have a home. This is my home. This is my home. I have a home. As long as I like?

TREVES. That is what home is.

MERRICK. That is what is home.

TREVES. If I abide by the rules, I will be happy.

MERRICK. Yes, sir.

TREVES. Don't be shy.

MERRICK. If I abide by the rules I will be happy.

TREVES. Very good. Why?

MERRICK. Why what?

TREVES. Will you be happy?

MERRICK. Because it is my home?

TREVES. No, no. Why do rules make you happy?

MERRICK. I don't know.

TREVES. Of course you do.

MERRICK. No, I really don't.

TREVES. Why does anything make you happy?

MERRICK. Like what? Like what?

TREVES. Don't be upset. Rules make us happy because they are for our own good.

MERRICK. Okay.

TREVES. Don't be shy, John. You can say it.

MERRICK. This is my home?

TREVES. No. About rules making us happy.

MERRICK. They make us happy because they are for our own good.

TREVES. Excellent. Now: I am submitting a follow-up paper on you to the London Pathological Society. It would help if you told me what you recall about your first years, John. To fill in gaps.

MERRICK. To fill in gaps. The workhouse where they put me. They beat you there like a drum. Boom boom: scrape the floor white. Shine the pan, boom boom. It never ends. The floor is always dirty. The pan is always tarnished. There is nothing you can do about it. You are always attacked anyway. Boom boom. Boom boom. Boom boom. Will the children go to the workhouse?

TREVES. What children?

MERRICK. The children. The man he sacked.

TREVES. Of necessity Will will find other employment. You don't want crowds staring at you, do you?

MERRICK. No.

TREVES. In your own home you do not have to have crowds staring at you. Or anyone. Do you? In your home?

MERRICK. No.

TREVES. Then Mr. Gomm was merciful. You yourself are proof. Is it not so? [*Pause.*] Well? Is it not so?

MERRICK. If your mercy is so cruel, what do you have for justice?

TREVES. I am sorry. It is just the way things are.

MERRICK. Boom boom. Boom boom. Boom boom.

[*Fadeout.*]

SCENE IX
Most Important Are Women

MERRICK *asleep, head on knees.* TREVES, MRS. KENDAL *foreground.*

TREVES. You have seen photographs of John Merrick, Mrs. Kendal. You are acquainted with his appearance.

MRS. KENDAL. He reminds me of an audience I played Cleopatra for in Brighton once. All huge grim head and grimace and utterly unable to clap.

TREVES. Well. My aim's to lead him to as normal a life as possible. His terror of us all comes from having been held at arm's length from society. I am determined that shall end. For example, he loves to meet people and converse. I am determined he shall. For example, he had never seen the inside of any normal home before. I had him to mine, and what a reward, Mrs. Kendal; his astonishment, his joy at the most ordinary things. Most critical I feel, however, are women. I will explain. They have always shown the greatest fear and loathing of him. While he adores them of course.

MRS. KENDAL. Ah. He is intelligent.

TREVES. I am convinced they are the key to retrieving him from his exclusion.

Though, I must warn you, women are not quite real to him—more creatures of his imagination.

MRS. KENDAL. Then he is already like other men, Mr. Treves.

TREVES. So I thought, an actress could help. I mean, unlike most women, you won't give in, you are trained to hide your true feelings and assume others.

MRS. KENDAL. You mean unlike most women I am famous for it, that is really all.

TREVES. Well. In any case. If you could enter the room and smile and wish him good morning. And when you leave, shake his hand, the left one is usable, and really quite beautiful, and say, "I am very pleased to have made your acquaintance, Mr. Merrick."

MRS. KENDAL. Shall we try it? Left hand out please. [*Suddenly radiant*] I am *very* pleased to have made your acquaintance Mr. Merrick. I am very *pleased* to have made your acquaintance Mr. Merrick. I am very pleased to have made your *acquaintance* Mr. Merrick. I *am* very pleased to have made *your* acquaintance Mr. Merrick. Yes. That one.

TREVES. By god, they are all splendid. Merrick will be so pleased. It will be the day he becomes a man like other men.

MRS. KENDAL. Speaking of that, Mr. Treves.

TREVES. Frederick, please.

MRS. KENDAL. Freddie, may I commit an indiscretion?

TREVES. Yes?

MRS. KENDAL. I could not but help noticing from the photographs that—well—of the unafflicted parts—ah, how shall I put it? [*Points to photograph.*]

TREVES. Oh. I see! I quite. Understand. No, no, no, it is quite normal.

MRS. KENDAL. I thought as much.

TREVES. Medically speaking, uhm, you see the papillomatous extrusions which disfigure him, uhm, seem to correspond quite regularly to the osseous deformities, that is, excuse me, there is a link between the bone disorder and the skin growths, though for the life of me I have not discovered what it is or why it is, but in any case this—part—it would be therefore unlikely to be afflicted because well, that is, well, there's no bone in it. None at all. I mean.

MRS. KENDAL. Well. Learn a little every day don't we?

TREVES. I am horribly embarrassed.

MRS. KENDAL. Are you? Then he must be lonely indeed.

[*Fadeout.*]

SCENE X
When the Illusion Ends He Must Kill Himself

MERRICK *sketching. Enter* TREVES, MRS. KENDAL.

TREVES. He is making sketches for a model of St. Phillip's church. He wants someday to make a model, you see. John, my boy, this is Mrs. Kendal. She would very much like to make your acquaintance.

MRS. KENDAL. Good morning Mr. Merrick.

TREVES. I will see to a few matters. I will be back soon. [*Exits.*]

MERRICK. I planned so many things to say. I forget them. You are so beautiful.

MRS. KENDAL. How charming, Mr. Merrick.

MERRICK. Well. Really that was what I planned to say. That I forgot what I planned to say. I couldn't think of anything else I was so excited.

MRS. KENDAL. Real charm is always planned, don't you think?

MERRICK. Well. I do not know why I look like this, Mrs. Kendal. My mother was so beautiful. She was knocked down by an elephant in a circus while she was pregnant. Something must have happened, don't you think?

MRS. KENDAL. It may well have.

MERRICK. It may well have. But sometimes I think my head is so big because it is so full of dreams. Because it is. Do you know what happens when dreams cannot get out?

MRS. KENDAL. Why, no.

MERRICK. I don't either. Something must. [*Silence.*] Well. You are a famous actress.

MRS. KENDAL. I am not unknown.

MERRICK. You must display yourself for your living then. Like I did.

MRS. KENDAL. That is not myself, Mr. Merrick. That is an illusion. This is myself.

MERRICK. This is myself too.

MRS. KENDAL. Frederick says you like to read. So: books.

MERRICK. I am reading *Romeo and Juliet* now.

MRS. KENDAL. Ah. Juliet. What a love story. I adore love stories.

MERRICK. I like love stories best too. If I had been Romeo, guess what.

MRS. KENDAL. What?

MERRICK. I would not have held the mirror to her breath.

MRS. KENDAL. You mean the scene where Juliet appears to be dead and he holds a mirror to her breath and sees—

MERRICK. Nothing. How does it feel when he kills himself because he just sees nothing?

MRS. KENDAL. Well. My experience as Juliet has been—particularly with an actor I will not name—that while I'm laying there dead dead dead, and he is lamenting excessively, I get to thinking that if this slab of ham does not part from the hamhock of his life toute suite,[16] I am going to scream, pop off the tomb, and plunge a dagger into his scene-stealing heart. Romeos are very undependable.

MERRICK. Because he does not care for Juliet.

MRS. KENDAL. Not care?

MERRICK. Does he take her pulse? Does he get a doctor? Does he make sure? No. He kills himself. The illusion fools him because he does not care for her. He only cares about himself. If I had been Romeo, we would have got away.

MRS. KENDAL. But then there would be no play, Mr. Merrick.

MERRICK. If he did not love her, why should there be a play? Looking in a mirror and seeing nothing. That is not love. It was all an illusion. When the illusion ended he had to kill himself.

MRS. KENDAL. Why. That is extraordinary.

MERRICK. Before I spoke with people, I did not think of all these things because there was no one to bother to think them for. Now things just come out of my mouth which are true.

---

16 Right away.

[TREVES *enters.*]

TREVES. You are famous, John. We are in the papers. Look. They have written up my report to the Pathological Society. Look—it is a kind of apotheosis for you.

MRS. KENDAL. Frederick, I feel Mr. Merrick would benefit by even more company than you provide; in fact by being acquainted with the best, and they with him. I shall make it my task if you'll permit. As you know, I am a friend of nearly everyone, and I do pretty well as I please and what pleases me is this task, I think.

TREVES. By god, Mrs. Kendal, you are splendid.

MRS. KENDAL. Mr. Merrick I must go now. I should like to return if I may. And so that we may without delay teach you about society, I would like to bring my good friend Dorothy Lady Neville. She would be most pleased if she could meet you. Let me tell her yes? [MERRICK *nods yes.*] Then until next time. I'm sure your church model will surprise us all. Mr. Merrick, it has been a very great pleasure to make your acquaintance.

TREVES. John. Your hand. She wishes to shake your hand.

MERRICK. Thank you for coming.

MRS. KENDAL. But it was my pleasure. Thank you. [*Exits, accompanied by* TREVES.]

TREVES. What a wonderful success. Do you know he's never shook a woman's hand before?

[*As lights fade* MERRICK *sobs soundlessly, uncontrollably.*]

SCENE XI
He Does It with Just One Hand

Music. MERRICK *working on model of St. Phillip's church. Enter* DUCHESS. *At side* TREVES *ticks off a gift list.*

MERRICK. Your grace.

DUCHESS. How nicely the model is coming along, Mr. Merrick. I've come to say Happy Christmas, and that I hope you will enjoy this ring and remember your friend by it.

MERRICK. Your grace, thank you.

DUCHESS. I am very pleased to have made your acquaintance. [*Exits.*]
[*Enter* COUNTESS.]

COUNTESS. Please accept these silver-backed brushes and comb for Christmas, Mr. Merrick.

MERRICK. With many thanks, Countess.

COUNTESS. I am very pleased to have made your acquaintance. [*Exits.*]
[*Enter* LORD JOHN.]

LORD JOHN. Here's the silver-topped walking stick, Merrick. Make you a regular Piccadilly[17] exquisite. Keep up the good work. Self-help is the best help. Example to us all.

MERRICK. Thank you, Lord John.

LORD JOHN. Very pleased to have made your acquaintance. [*Exits.*]
[*Enter* TREVES *and* PRINCESS ALEXANDRA.[18]]

[17] A fashionable street in London.
[18] Princess Alexandra (1844–1925) of Denmark married Edward, Prince of Wales (1841–1910) in 1863. Edward later became King Edward VII.

TREVES. Her Royal Highness Princess Alexandra.

PRINCESS. The happiest of Christmases, Mr. Merrick.

TREVES. Her Royal Highness has brought you a signed photograph of herself.

MERRICK. I am honored, your Royal Highness. It is the treasure of my possessions. I have written to His Royal Highness the Prince of Wales to thank
him for the pheasants and woodcock he sent.

PRINCESS. You are a credit to Mr. Treves, Mr. Merrick. Mr. Treves, you are
a credit to medicine, to England, and to Christendom. I am so very pleased
to have made your acquaintance.

[PRINCESS, TREVES *exit. Enter* MRS. KENDAL.]

MRS. KENDAL. Good news, John. Bertie says we may use the Royal Box whenever
I like. Mrs. Keppel says it gives a unique perspective. And for Christmas,
ivory-handled razors and toothbrush.

[*Enter* TREVES.]

TREVES. And a cigarette case, my boy, full of cigarettes!

MERRICK. Thank you. Very much.

MRS. KENDAL. Look Freddie, look. The model of St. Phillip's.

TREVES. It is remarkable, I know.

MERRICK. And I do it with just one hand, they all say.

MRS. KENDAL. You are an artist, John Merrick, an artist.

MERRICK. I did not begin to build at first. Not till I saw what St. Phillip's
really was. It is not stone and steel and glass; it is an imitation of grace
flying up and up from the mud. So I make my imitation of an imitation.
But even in that is heaven to me, Mrs. Kendal.

TREVES. That thought's got a good line, John. Plato believed this was all a
world of illusion and that artists made illusions of illusions of heaven.

MERRICK. You mean we are all just copies? Of originals?

TREVES. That's it.

MERRICK. Who made the copies?

TREVES. God. The Demi-urge.

MERRICK [*goes back to work*]: He should have used both hands shouldn't he?

[*Music. Puts another piece on St. Phillip's. Fadeout.*]

SCENE XII
Who Does He Remind You Of?

TREVES, MRS. KENDAL.

TREVES. Why all those toilet articles, tell me? He is much too deformed to
use any of them.

MRS. KENDAL. Props of course. To make himself. As I make me.

TREVES. You? You think of yourself.

MRS. KENDAL. Well. He is gentle, almost feminine. Cheerful, honest within
limits, a serious artist in his way. He is almost like me.

[*Enter* BISHOP HOW.]

BISHOP. He is religious and devout. He knows salvation must radiate to us
or all is lost, which it's certainly not.

[*Enter* GOMM.]

GOMM. He seems practical, like me. He has seen enough of daily evil to be

thankful for small goods that come his way. He knows what side his bread is buttered on, and counts his blessings for it. Like me.
[*Enter* DUCHESS.]

DUCHESS. I can speak with him of anything. For I know he is discreet. Like me.
[*All exit except* TREVES.]

TREVES. How odd. I think him curious, compassionate, concerned about the world, well, rather like myself, Freddie Treves, 1889 A.D.
[*Enter* MRS. KENDAL.]

MRS. KENDAL. Of course he is rather odd. And hurt. And helpless not to show the struggling. And so am I.
[*Enter* GOMM.]

GOMM. He knows I use him to raise money for the London, I am certain. He understands I would be derelict if I didn't. He is wary of any promise, yet he fits in well. Like me.
[*Enter* BISHOP HOW.]

BISHOP. I as a seminarist had many of the same doubts. Struggled as he does. And hope they may be overcome.
[*Enter* PRINCESS ALEXANDRA.]

PRINCESS. When my husband His Royal Highness Edward Prince of Wales asked Dr. Treves to be his personal surgeon, he said, "Dear Freddie, if you can put up with the Elephant bloke, you can surely put up with me."
[*All exit, except* TREVES. *Enter* LORD JOHN.]

LORD JOHN. See him out of fashion, Freddie. As he sees me. Social contacts critical. Oh—by the way—ignore the bloody papers; all lies. [*Exits.*]

TREVES. Merrick visibly worse than 86–87. That, as he rises higher in the consolations of society, he gets visibly more grotesque is proof definitive he is like me. Like his condition, which I make no sense of, I make no sense of mine.
[*Spot on* MERRICK *placing another piece on St. Phillip's. Fadeout.*]

SCENE XIII
Anxieties of the Swamp

MERRICK, *in spot, strains to listen:* TREVES, LORD JOHN *outside.*

TREVES. But the papers are saying you broke the contracts. They are saying you've lost the money.

LORD JOHN. Freddie, if I were such a scoundrel, how would I dare face investors like yourself. Broken contracts! I never considered them actual contracts—just preliminary things, get the old deal under way. An actual contract's something between gentlemen; and this attack on me shows they are no gentlemen. Now I'm only here to say the company remains a terribly attractive proposition. Don't you think? To recapitalize—if you could spare another—ah. [*Enter* GOMM.] Mr. Gomm. How good to see you. Just remarking how splendidly Merrick thrives here, thanks to you and Freddie.

GOMM. Lord John. Allow me: I must take Frederick from you. Keep him at work. It's in his contract. Wouldn't want him breaking it. Sort of thing makes the world fly apart, isn't it?

LORD JOHN. Yes. Well. Of course, mmm.

GOMM. Sorry to hear you're so pressed. Expect we'll see less of you around the London now?

LORD JOHN. Of course, I, actually—ah! Overdue actually. Appointment in the City. Freddie. Mr. Gomm. [*Exits.*]

TREVES. He plain fooled me. He was kind to Merrick.

GOMM. You have risen fast and easily, my boy. You've forgot how to protect yourself. Break now.

TREVES. It does not seem right somehow.

GOMM. The man's a moral swamp. Is that not clear yet? Is he attractive? Deceit often is. Friendly? Swindlers can be. Another loan? Not another cent. It may be your money, Freddie; but I will not tolerate laboring like a navvy[19] that the London should represent honest charitable and compassionate science, and have titled swindlers mucking up the pitch. He has succeeded in destroying himself so rabidly, you ought not doubt an instant it was his real aim all along. He broke the contracts, gambled the money away, lied, and like an infant in his mess, gurgles and wants to do it again. Never mind details, don't want to know. Break and be glad. Don't hesitate. Today. One-man moral swamp. Don't be sucked in.

[*Enter* MRS. KENDAL.]

MRS. KENDAL. Have you seen the papers?

TREVES. Yes.

GOMM. Yes, yes. A great pity. Freddie: today. [*Exits.*]

MRS. KENDAL. Freddie?

TREVES. He has used us. I shall be all right. Come. [MRS. KENDAL, TREVES *enter to* MERRICK.] John: I shall not be able to stay this visit. I must, well, unravel a few things. Nurse Ireland and Snork are—?

MERRICK. Friendly and respectful, Frederick.

TREVES. I'll look in in a few days.

MERRICK. Did I do something wrong?

MRS. KENDAL. No.

TREVES. This is a hospital. Not a marketplace. Don't forget it, ever. Sorry. Not you. Me. [*Exits.*]

MRS. KENDAL. Well. Shall we weave today? Don't you think weaving might be fun? So many things are fun. Most men really can't enjoy them. Their loss, isn't it? I like little activities which engage me; there's something ancient in it, I don't know. Before all this. Would you like to try? John?

MERRICK. Frederick said I may stay here for life.

MRS. KENDAL. And so you shall.

MERRICK. If he is in trouble?

MRS. KENDAL. Frederick is your protector, John.

MERRICK. If he is in trouble? [*He picks up small photograph.*]

MRS. KENDAL. Who is that? Ah, is it not your mother? She is pretty, isn't she?

MERRICK. Will Frederick keep his word with me, his contract, Mrs. Kendal? If he is in trouble.

MRS. KENDAL. What? Contract? Did you say?

MERRICK. And will you?

MRS. KENDAL. I? What? Will I?

[MERRICK *silent. Puts another piece on model. Fadeout.*]

---

[19] A ditch digger.

SCENE XIV
Art Is Permitted but Nature Forbidden

Rain. MERRICK *working.* MRS. KENDAL.

MERRICK. The Prince has a mistress. [*Silence.*] The Irishman had one. Everyone seems to. Or a wife. Some have both. I have concluded I need a mistress. It is bad enough not to sleep like others.

MRS. KENDAL. Sitting up, you mean. Couldn't be very restful.

MERRICK. I have to. Too heavy to lay down. My head. But to sleep alone; that is worst of all.

MRS. KENDAL. The artist expresses his love through his works. That is civilization.

MERRICK. Are you very shocked?

MRS. KENDAL. Why should I be?

MERRICK. Others would be.

MRS. KENDAL. I am not others.

MERRICK. I suppose it is hopeless.

MRS. KENDAL. Nothing is hopeless. However it is unlikely.

MERRICK. I thought you might have a few ideas.

MRS. KENDAL. I can guess who has ideas here.

MERRICK. You don't know something. I have never even seen a naked woman.

MRS. KENDAL. Surely in all the fairs you worked.

MERRICK. I mean a real woman.

MRS. KENDAL. Is one more real than another?

MERRICK. I mean like the ones in the theater. The opera.

MRS. KENDAL. Surely you can't mean they are more real.

MERRICK. In the audience. A woman not worn out early. Not deformed by awful life. A lady. Someone kept up. Respectful of herself. You don't know what fairgrounds are like, Mrs. Kendal.

MRS. KENDAL. You mean someone like Princess Alexandra?

MERRICK. Not so old.

MRS. KENDAL. Ah. Like Dorothy.

MERRICK. She does not look happy. No.

MRS. KENDAL. Lady Ellen?

MERRICK. Too thin.

MRS. KENDAL. Then who?

MERRICK. Certain women. They have a kind of ripeness. They seem to stop at a perfect point.

MRS. KENDAL. My dear she doesn't exist.

MERRICK. That is probably why I never saw her.

MRS. KENDAL. What would your friend Bishop How say of all this I wonder?

MERRICK. He says I should put these things out of my mind.

MRS. KENDAL. Is that the best he can suggest?

MERRICK. I put them out of my mind. They reappeared, snap.

MRS. KENDAL. What about Frederick?

MERRICK. He would be appalled if I told him.

MRS. KENDAL. I am flattered. Too little trust has maimed my life. But that is another story.

MERRICK. What a rain. Are we going to read this afternoon?

MRS. KENDAL. Yes. Some women are lucky to look well, that is all. It is a rather arbitrary gift; it has no really good use, though it has uses, I will say that. Anyway it does not signify very much.

MERRICK. To me it does.

MRS. KENDAL. Well. You are mistaken.

MERRICK. What are we going to read?

MRS. KENDAL. Trust is very important you know. I trust you.

MERRICK. Thank you very much. I have a book of Thomas Hardy's[20] here. He is a friend of Frederick's. Shall we read that?

MRS. KENDAL. Turn around a moment. Don't look.

MERRICK. Is this a game?

MRS. KENDAL. I would not call it a game. A surprise. [*She begins undressing.*]

MERRICK. What kind of surprise?

MRS. KENDAL. I saw photographs of you. Before I met you. You didn't know that, did you?

MERRICK. The ones from the first time, in '84? No, I didn't.

MRS. KENDAL. I felt it was—unjust. I don't know why. I cannot say my sense of justice is my most highly developed characteristic. You may turn around again. Well. A little funny, isn't it?

MERRICK. It is the most beautiful sight I have seen. Ever.

MRS. KENDAL. If you tell anyone, I shall not see you again, we shall not read, we shall not talk, we shall do nothing. Wait. [*Undoes her hair.*] There. No illusions. Now. Well? What is there to say? "I am extremely pleased to have made your acquaintance?"
[*Enter* TREVES.]

TREVES. For God's sakes. What is going on here? What is going on?

MRS. KENDAL. For a moment, Paradise, Freddie. [*She begins dressing.*]

TREVES. But—have you no sense of decency? Woman, dress yourself quickly. [*Silence.* MERRICK *goes to put another piece on St. Phillip's.*] Are you not ashamed? Do you know what you are? Don't you know what is forbidden? [*Fadeout.*]

SCENCE XV
Ingratitude

ROSS *in* MERRICK'*s room.*

ROSS. I come actually to ask your forgiveness.

MERRICK. I found a good home, Ross. I forgave you.

ROSS. I was hoping we could work out a deal. Something new maybe.

MERRICK. No.

ROSS. See, I was counting on it. That you were kindhearted. Like myself. Some things don't change. Got to put your money on the things that don't, I figure. I figure from what I read about you, you don't change. Dukes, Ladies coming to see you. Ask myself why? Figure it's same as always was. Makes 'em feel good about themselves by comparison. Them things don't change. There but for the grace of. So I figure you're selling the same service as always. To better clientele. Difference now is you ain't charging for it.

MERRICK. You make me sound like a whore.

[20] An English novelist and poet (1840–1928).

Ross. You are. I am. They are. Most are. No disgrace, John. Disgrace is to be a stupid whore. Give it for free. Not capitalize on the interest in you. Not to have a manager then is stupid.

Merrick. You see this church. I am building it. The people who visit are friends. Not clients. I am not a dog walking on its hind legs.

Ross. I was thinking. Charge these people. Pleasure of the Elephant Man's company. Something. Right spirit is everything. Do it in the right spirit, they'd pay happily. I'd take ten percent. I'd be okay with ten percent.

Merrick. Bad luck's made you daft.

Ross. I helped you, John. Discovered you. Was that daft? No. Only daftness was being at a goldmine without a shovel. Without proper connections. Like Treves has. What's daft? Ross sows, Treves harvests? It's not fair, is it John? When you think about it. I do think about it. Because I'm old. Got something in my throat. You may have noticed. Something in my lung here too. Something in my belly I guess too. I'm not a heap of health, am I? But I'd do well with ten percent. I don't need more than ten percent. Ten percent'd give me a future slightly better'n a cobblestone. This lot would pay, if you charged in the right spirit. I don't ask much.

Merrick. They're the cream, Ross. They know it. Man like you tries to make them pay, they'll walk away.

Ross. I'm talking about doing it in the right spirit.

Merrick. They are my friends. I'd lose everything. For you. Ross, you lived your life. You robbed me of forty-eight pounds, nine shillings, tuppence. You left me to die. Be satisfied Ross. You've had enough. You kept me like an animal in darkness. You come back and want to rob me again. Will you not be satisfied? Now I am a man like others, you want me to return?

Ross. Had a woman yet?

Merrick. Is that what makes a man?

Ross. In my time it'd do for a start.

Merrick. Not what makes this one. Yet I am like others.

Ross. Then I'm condemned. I got no energy to try nothing new. I may as well go to the dosshouse[21] straight. Die there anyway. Between filthy doss-house rags. Nothing in the belly but acid. I don't like pain, John. The future gives pain sense. Without a future—[*Pauses.*] Five percent? John?

Merrick. I'm sorry, Ross. It's just the way things are.

Ross. By god. Then I am lost.

[*Fadeout.*]

SCENE XVI
No Reliable General Anesthetic Has Appeared Yet

Treves, *reading, making notes.* Merrick *works.*

Merrick. Frederick—do you believe in heaven? Hell? What about Christ? What about God? I believe in heaven. The Bible promises in heaven the crooked shall be made straight.

Treves. So did the rack, my boy. So do we all.

Merrick. You don't believe?

---

[21] A cheap hotel or lodging house, a flophouse.

Treves. I shall settle for a reliable general anesthetic at this point. Actually, though—I had a patient once. A woman. Operated on her for—a woman's thing. Used ether to anesthetize. Tricky stuff. Didn't come out of it. Pulse stopped, no vital signs, absolutely moribund. Just a big white dead mackerel. Five minutes later, she fretted back to existence, like a lost explorer with a great scoop of the undiscovered.

Merrick. She saw heaven?

Treves. Well. I quote her: it was neither heavenly nor hellish. Rather like perambulating in a London fog. People drifted by, but no one spoke. London, mind you. Hell's probably the provinces. She was shocked it wasn't more exotic. But allowed as how had she stayed, and got used to the familiar, so to speak, it did have hints of becoming a kind of bliss. She fled.

Merrick. If you do not believe—why did you send Mrs. Kendal away?

Treves. Don't forget. It saved you once. My interference. You know well enough—it was not proper.

Merrick. How can you tell? If you do not believe?

Treves. There are still standards we abide by.

Merrick. They make us happy because they are for our own good.

Treves. Well. Not always.

Merrick. Oh.

Treves. Look, if you are angry, just say so.

Merrick. Whose standards are they?

Treves. I am not in the mood for this chipping away at the edges, John.

Merrick. That do not always make us happy because they are not always for our own good?

Treves. Everyone's. Well. Mine. Everyone's.

Merrick. That woman's, that Juliet?

Treves. Juliet?

Merrick. Who died, then came back.

Treves. Oh. I see. Yes. Her standards too.

Merrick. So.

Treves. So what?

Merrick. Did you see her? Naked?

Treves. When I was operating. Of course—

Merrick. Oh.

Treves. Oh what?

Merrick. Is it okay to see them naked if you cut them up afterwards?

Treves. Good Lord. I'm a surgeon. That is science.

Merrick. She died. Mrs. Kendal didn't.

Treves. Well, she came back too.

Merrick. And Mrs. Kendal didn't. If you mean that.

Treves. I am trying to read about anesthetics. There is simply no comparison.

Merrick. Oh.

Treves. Science is a different thing. This woman came to me to be. I mean, it is not, well, love, you know.

Merrick. Is that why you're looking for an anesthetic.

Treves. It would be a boon to surgery.

Merrick. Because you don't love them.

Treves. Love's got nothing to do with surgery.

Merrick. Do you lose many patients?

Treves. I—some.

MERRICK. Oh.

TREVES. Oh what? What does it matter? Don't you see? If I love, if any surgeon loves her or any patient or not, what does it matter? And what conceivable difference to you?

MERRICK. Because it is your standards we abide by.

TREVES. For God's sakes. If you are angry, just say it. I won't turn you out. Say it: I am angry. Go on. I am angry. I am angry! I am angry!

MERRICK. I believe in heaven.

TREVES. And it is not okay. If they undress if you cut them up. As you put it. Make me sound like Jack the, Jack the Ripper.[22]

MERRICK. No. You worry about anesthetics.

TREVES. Are you having me on?

MERRICK. You are merciful. I am myself proof. Is it not so? [*Pauses.*] Well? Is it not so?

TREVES. Well. I. About Mrs. Kendal—perhaps I was wrong. I, these days that is, I seem to. Lose my head. Taking too much on perhaps. I do not know— what is in me these days.

MERRICK. Will she come back? Mrs. Kendal?

TREVES. I will talk to her again.

MERRICK. But—will she?

TREVES. No. I don't think so.

MERRICK. Oh.

TREVES. There are other things involved. Very. That is. Other things.

MERRICK. Well. Other things. I want to walk now. Think. Other things. [*Begins to exit. Pauses.*] Why? Why won't she?

[*Silence.* MERRICK *exits.*]

TREVES. Because I don't want her here when you die. [*He slumps in chair.*] [*Fadeout.*]

SCENE XVII
Cruelty Is as Nothing to Kindness

TREVES *asleep in chair dreams the following:* MERRICK *and* GOMM *dressed as* ROSS *in foreground.*

MERRICK. If he is merely papier maché and paint, a swindler and a fake—

GOMM. No, no, a genuine Dorset[23] dreamer in a moral swamp. Look—he has so forgot how to protect himself he's gone to sleep.

MERRICK. I must examine him. I would not keep him for long, Mr. Gomm.

GOMM. It would be an inconvenience, Mr. Merrick. He is a mainstay of our institution.

MERRICK. Exactly that brought him to my attention. I am Merrick. Here is my card. I am with the mutations cross the road.

GOMM. Frederick, stand up. You must understand. He is very very valuable. We have invested a great deal in him. He is personal surgeon to the Prince of Wales.

---

[22] The infamous, unidentified murderer of Englishwomen in 1888.
[23] A county in western England.

MERRICK. But I only wish to examine him. I had not of course dreamed of changing him.

GOMM. But he is a gentleman and a good man.

MERRICK. Therefore exemplary for study as a cruel or deviant one would not be.

GOMM. Oh very well. Have him back for breakfast time or you feed him. Frederick, stand up. Up you bloody donkey, up!

[TREVES, *still asleep, stands up. Fadeout.*]

SCENE XVIII
We Are Dealing With an Epidemic

TREVES *asleep.* MERRICK *at lectern.*

MERRICK. The most striking feature about him, note, is the terrifyingly normal head. This allowed him to lie down normally, and therefore to dream in the exclusive personal manner, without the weight of others' dreams accumulating to break his neck. From the brow projected a normal vision of benevolent enlightenment, what we believe to be a kind of self-mesmerized state. The mouth, deformed by satisfaction at being at the hub of the best of existent worlds, was rendered therefore utterly incapable of self-critical speech, thus of the ability to change. The heart showed signs of worry at this unchanging yet untenable state. The back was horribly stiff from being kept against a wall to face the discontent of a world ordered for his convenience. The surgeon's hands were well-developed and strong, capable of the most delicate carvings-up, for others' own good. Due also to the normal head, the right arm was of enormous power; but, so incapable of the distinction between the assertions of authority and the charitable act of giving, that it was often to be found disgustingly beating others—for their own good. The left arm was slighter and fairer, and may be seen in typical position, hand covering the genitals which were treated as a sullen colony in constant need of restriction, governance, punishment. For their own good. To add a further burden to his trouble, the wretched man when a boy developed a disabling spiritual duality, therefore was unable to feel what others feel, nor reach harmony with them. Please. [TREVES *shrugs.*] He would thus be denied all means of escape from those he had tormented.

[PINS *enter.*]

FIRST PIN. Mr. Merrick. You have shown a profound and unknown disorder to us. You have said when he leaves here, it is for his prior life again. I do not think it ought to be permitted. It is a disgrace. It is a pity and a disgrace. It is an indecency in fact. It may be a danger in ways we do not know. Something ought to be done about it.

MERRICK. We hope in twenty years we will understand enough to put an end to this affliction.

FIRST PIN. Twenty years! Sir, that is unacceptable!

MERRICK. Had we caught it early, it might have been different. But his condition has already spread both East and West. The truth is, I am afraid, we are dealing with an epidemic.

[MERRICK *puts another piece on St. Phillip's.* PINS *exit.* TREVES *starts awake. Fadeout.*]

SCENE XIX
They Cannot Make Out What He Is Saying

MERRICK, BISHOP HOW *in background.* BISHOP *gestures,* MERRICK *on knees.* TREVES *foreground. Enter* GOMM.

GOMM. Still beavering[24] away for Christ?

TREVES. Yes.

GOMM. I got your report. He doesn't know, does he?

TREVES. The Bishop?

GOMM. I meant Merrick.

TREVES. No.

GOMM. I shall be sorry when he dies.

TREVES. It will not be unexpected anyway.

GOMM. He's brought the hospital quite a lot of good repute. Quite a lot of contributions too, for that matter. In fact, I like him; never regretted letting him stay on. Though I didn't imagine he'd last this long.

TREVES. His heart won't sustain him much longer. It may even give out when he gets off his bloody knees with that bloody man.

GOMM. What is it, Freddie? What has gone sour for you?

TREVES. It is just—it is the overarc of things, quite inescapable that as he's achieved greater and greater normality, his condition's edged him closer to the grave. So—a parable of growing up? To become more normal is to die? More accepted to worsen? He—it is just a mockery of everything we live by.

GOMM. Sorry, Freddie. Didn't catch that one.

TREVES. Nothing has gone sour. I do not know.

GOMM. Cheer up, man. You are knighted. Your clients will be kings. Nothing succeeds my boy like success. [*Exits.*]

[BISHOP *comes from* MERRICK'S *room.*]

BISHOP. I find my sessions with him utterly moving, Mr. Treves. He struggles so. I suggested he might like to be confirmed; he leaped at it like a man lost in a desert to an oasis.

TREVES. He is very excited to do what others do if he thinks it is what others do.

BISHOP. Do you cast doubt, sir, on his faith?

TREVES. No, sir, I do not. Yet he makes all of us think he is deeply like ourselves. And yet we're not like each other. I conclude that we have polished him like a mirror, and shout hellelujah when he reflects us to the inch. I have grown sorry for it.

BISHOP. I cannot make out what you're saying. Is something troubling you, Mr. Treves?

TREVES. Corsets. How about corsets? Here is a pamphlet I've written due mostly to the grotesque ailments I've seen caused by corsets. Fashion overrules me, of course. My patients do not unstrap themselves of corsets. Some cannot—you know, I have so little time in the week, I spend Sundays in the poor-wards; to keep up with work. Work being twenty-year-old women who look an abused fifty with worn-outedness; young men with appalling industrial conditions I turn out as soon as possible to return to their labors.

[24] Working.

Happily most of my patients are not poor. They are middle class. They overeat and drink so grossly, they destroy nature in themselves and all around them so fervidly, they will not last. Higher up, sir, above this middle class, I confront these same—deformities—bulged out by unlimited resources and the ruthlessness of privilege into the most scandalous dissipation yoked to the grossest ignorance and constraint. I counsel against it where I can. I am ignored of course. Then, what, sir, could be troubling me? I am an extremely successful Englishman in a successful and respected England which informs me daily by the way it lives that it wants to die. I am in despair in fact. Science, observation, practice, deduction, having led me to these conclusions, can no longer serve as consolation. I apparently see things others don't.

BISHOP. I do wish I understood you better, sir. But as for consolation, there is in Christ's church consolation.

TREVES. I am sure that we were not born for mere consolation.

BISHOP. But look at Mr. Merrick's happy example.

TREVES. Oh yes. You'd like my garden too. My dog, my wife, my daughter, pruned, cropped, pollarded and somewhat stupefied. Very happy examples, all of them. Well. Is it all we know how to finally do with—whatever? Nature? Is it? Rob it? No, not really, not nature I mean. Ourselves really. Myself really. Robbed, that is. You do see of course, can't figure out, really, what else to do with them. Can we? [*Laughs.*]

BISHOP. It is not exactly clear, sir.

TREVES. I am an awfully good gardener. Is that clear? By god I take such good care of anything, anything you, we, are convinced—are you not convinced, him I mean, is not very dangerously human? I mean how could he be? After what we've given him? What you like, sir, is that he is so grateful for patrons, so greedy to be patronized, and no demands, no rights, no hopes; past perverted, present false, future nil. What better could you ask? He puts up with all of it. Of course I do mean taken when I say given, as in what, what, what we have given him, but. You knew that. I'll bet. Because. I. I. I. I—

BISHOP. Do you mean Charity? I cannot tell what you are saying.

TREVES. Help me. [*Weeps.*]

[BISHOP *consoles him.*]

MERRICK [*rises, puts last piece on St. Phillip's*]. It is done.

[*Fadeout.*]

SCENE XX
The Weight of Dreams

MERRICK *alone, looking at model. Enter* SNORK *with lunch.*

SNORK. Lunch, Mr. Merrick. I'll set it up. Maybe you'd like a walk after lunch. April's doing wonders for the gardens. [*A funeral procession passes slowly by.*] My mate Will, his sister died yesterday. Twenty-eight she was. Imagine that. Wife was sick, his sister nursed her. Was a real bloom that girl. Now wife okay, sister just ups and dies. It's all so—what's that word? Forgot it. It means chance-y. Well. Forgot it. Chance-y'll do. Have a good lunch. [*Exits.*]

[MERRICK *eats a little, breathes on model, polishes it, goes to bed, arms on knees, head on arms, the position in which he must sleep.*]

MERRICK. Chancey? [*Sleeps.*]

[*Enter* PINHEADS *singing.*]

PINS. We are the Queens of the Cosmos
    Beautiful darkness' empire
    Darkness darkness, light's true flower,
    Here is eternity's finest hour
    Sleep like others you learn to admire
    Be like your mother, be like your sire.

[*They straighten* MERRICK *out to normal sleep position. His head tilts over too far. His arms fly up clawing the air. He dies. As light fades,* SNORK *enters.*]

SNORK. I remember it, Mr. Merrick. The word is "arbitrary." Arbitrary. It's all so—oh. Hey! Hey! The Elephant Man is dead!

[*Fadeout.*]

SCENE XXI
Final Report to the Investors

GOMM *reading,* TREVES *listening.*

GOMM. "To the Editor of the *Times*. Sir; In November, 1886, you were kind enough to insert in the *Times* a letter from me drawing attention to the case of Joseph Merrick—"

TREVES. John. John Merrick.

GOMM. Well. "—known as the Elephant Man. It was one of singular and exceptional misfortune" et cetera et cetera ". . . debarred from earning his livelihood in any other way than being exhibited to the gaze of the curious. This having been rightly interfered with by the police . . ." et cetera et cetera, "with great difficulty he succeeded somehow or other in getting to the door of the London Hospital where through the kindness of one of our surgeons he was sheltered for a time." And then . . . and then . . . and . . . ah. "While deterred by common humanity from evicting him again into the open street, I wrote to you and from that moment all difficulty vanished; the sympathy of many was aroused, and although no other fitting refuge was offered, a sufficient sum was placed at my disposal, apart from the funds of the hospital, to maintain him for what did not promise to be a prolonged life. As—"

TREVES. I forgot. The coroner said it was death by asphyxiation. The weight of the head crushed the windpipe.

GOMM. Well. I go on to say about how he spent his time here, that all attempted to alleviate his misery, that he was visited by the highest in the land et cetera, et cetera, that in general he joined our lives as best he could, and: "In spite of all this indulgence, he was quiet and unassuming, grateful for all that was done for him, and conformed readily to the restrictions which were necessary." Will that do so far, do you think?

TREVES. Should think it would.

GOMM. Wouldn't add anything else, would you?

TREVES. Well. He was highly intelligent. He had an acute sensibility; and worst for him, a romantic imagination. No, no. Never mind. I am really not certain of any of it. [*Exits.*]

GOMM. "I have given these details thinking that those who sent money to use for his support would like to know how their charity was used. Last Friday afternoon, though apparently in his usual health, he quietly passed away in his sleep. I have left in my hands a small balance of the money for his support, and this I now propose, after paying certain gratuities, to hand over to the general funds of the hospital. This course I believe will be consonant with the wishes of the contributors.

"It was the courtesy of the *Times* in inserting my letter in 1886 that procured for this afflicted man a comfortable protection during the last years of a previously wretched existence, and I desire to take this opportunity of thankfully acknowledging it.

"I am sir, your obedient servant,

F. C. Carr Gomm

"House Committee Room, London Hospital."

15 April 1890.

[TREVES *reenters.*]

TREVES. I did think of one small thing.

GOMM. It's too late, I'm afraid. It is done. [*Smiles.*]

[*Hold before fadeout.*]

[1979]

GLOSSARY

ﷺﷺﷺﷺ

ABSTRACT: The opposite of *concrete;* used to describe a word or group of words representing attitudes, generalities, ideas, or qualities that cannot be apprehended directly through the senses. The language of philosophy and science tends to be abstract.

ABSURD, THEATER OF THE: A type of modern drama (often associated with Edward Albee, Samuel Beckett, Jean Genet, Eugène Ionesco, Arthur Kopit, and Harold Pinter) that attempts to convey the playwright's vision of an absurd, frustrating, illogical, and essentially meaningless human condition by ignoring or distorting the usual conventions of plot, characterization, structure, setting, and dialogue.

ACCENT (pp. 611–613): Used in English poetry to describe the stress or emphasis accorded to certain syllables. When a pronounced syllable receives no stress or emphasis, it is, by contrast, referred to as unaccented. In English poetry, *meter* depends on the pattern of accented and unaccented syllables.

ACROSTIC (p. 646): A poem in which certain letters (ordinarily the first in each line) spell out a word or words.

ACT (p. 959): A major division of a play; sometimes subdivided into a number of separate *scenes.*

ALEXANDRINE (p. 641): A line of poetry consisting of six iambic feet (iambic hexameter).

ALLEGORY (pp. 55–57, 599–601): A type of narrative that attempts to reinforce its thesis by making its characters (and sometimes its events and setting, as well) represent specific abstract ideas or qualities; see also *fable, parable,* and *symbol.*

ALLITERATION (pp. 631–633): The repetition in two or more nearby words of initial consonant sounds. See also *Assonance* and *Consonance.*

ALLITERATIVE VERSE (pp. 622–623): A metrical system in which each line contains a fixed number of accented syllables and a variable number of unaccented ones.

ALLUSION (pp. 574–576): A reference, generally brief, to a person, place, thing, or event with which the reader is presumably familiar.

AMBIGUITY (pp. 579–581): A word, phrase, event, or situation that may be understood or interpreted in two or more ways, each valid in the immediate context.

AMBIVALENCE: The existence of two mutually opposed or contradictory feelings about a given issue, idea, person, or object.

ANACHRONISM: A person or thing that is chronologically out of place.

ANAPEST (ANAPESTIC) (pp. 619–620): A foot of two unaccented syllables followed by an accented one.

ANECDOTE: A brief, unadorned narrative about a particular person or incident. Short stories differ from anecdotes by virtue of their greater length and the deliberate artistic arrangement of their elements.

ANIMISM (pp. 596–597): A poetic figure of speech in which an idea or inanimate object is described as though it were living, without attributing human traits to it; see also *personification*.

ANNOTATION: The explanatory note (or notes) that an author or editor supplies for a given text.

ANTAGONIST (pp. 12, 19–20, 995): The rival or opponent against whom the major character (the *protagonist* or *hero*) is contending.

ANTICLIMAX: A sudden transition from the important (or serious) to the trivial (or ludicrous). We speak of something being anticlimatic when it occurs after the *crisis* (or *climax*) of the plot has been reached.

ANTIHERO: A *protagonist* whose distinctive qualities are directly opposite to, or incompatible with, those associated with the traditional hero. Such an opposition by no means implies that the character is evil or villainous but often tends to reflect the author's belief that modern life no longer tolerates or produces individuals capable of genuine heroism, in its classic sense.

ANTI-NOVEL (ANTI-STORY): A type of experimental novel (or short story), usually associated with the French school of Alain Robbe-Grillet, that attempts to convey to the reader the experience of objective reality without authorial direction by dispensing with the traditional aspects of realistic ("mimetic") fiction, e.g., plot, character, theme, dialogue.

APOSTROPHE (pp. 595–596): A figure of speech in which a person (usually not present) or a personified quality or object is addressed as if present.

ARCHAISM: An obsolete word or phrase.

ARCHETYPE (pp. 52, 599): Used in literary analysis to describe certain basic and recurrent patterns of plot, character, or theme; see also *symbol*.

ARENA STAGE/ARENA THEATER (p. 982): A theater with seating surrounding, or nearly surrounding, the stage.

ARGUMENT: A summary statement of the content or thesis of a literary work.

ASIDE (pp. 974–975): A dramatic convention in which the lines addressed by a character to the audience are presumed to go unheard by the other characters.

ASSONANCE (pp. 631–633): The repetition in two or more nearby words of similar vowel sounds; see also *consonance* and *alliteration*.

ATMOSPHERE (pp. 30–31): The mood or feeling pervading a literary work.

BALLAD (pp. 638–640): A narrative poem consisting of a series of four-line stanzas, originally sung or recited as part of the oral tradition of an unsophisticated rural folk society.

BLANK VERSE (p. 636): Lines of unrhymed iambic pentameter.

BOMBAST: Language that is inflated, extravagant, verbose, and insincere.

BURLESQUE: A form of humor that ridicules persons, attitudes, actions, or things by means of distortion and exaggeration. Burlesque of a particular literary work or style is referred to as *parody*. *Caricature* on the other hand, creates humor by distorting or exaggerating an individual's prominent physical features; see also *satire*.

CACOPHONY: See *euphony*.

CAESURA (pp. 616–617): A pause or break occurring near the middle of a line of poetry.

CANTO: Sections or divisions of a long poem.

CARICATURE: See *burlesque*.

CARPE DIEM: A Latin phrase meaning "seize the day," generally applied to lyric poems that urge the celebration of the fleeting present, e.g., Robert Herrick's "To the Virgins, to Make Much of Time."

CATASTROPHE: A form of *conclusion* (or *dénouement*), usually tragic in its outcome.

CATHARSIS (p. 1001): See *classical tragedy*.

CHANCE AND COINCIDENCE (p. 18): Chance refers to events or "happenings" within a plot that occur without sufficient preparation; coincidence to the accidental occurrence of two (or more) events that have a certain correspondence.

CHARACTER (pp. 18–28, 994–997): An individual within a literary work.

CHARACTERIZATION: The process by which an author creates, develops, and presents a character.

CHAUCERIAN STANZA: See *rhyme royal*.

CHORUS (pp. 970–971): In Greek drama the chorus was a group of singers and dancers who sometimes served as actors to comment on or interpret the significance of the action.

CLASSICAL TRAGEDY (p. 1001): Refers to Greek and Roman tragedies or plays written imitating their subjects or conventions.

CLIMAX: See *crisis*.

CLOSED COUPLET (p. 636): See *couplet*.

CLOSET DRAMA (p. 968): A drama written to be read rather than staged and acted.

COINCIDENCE: See *chance and coincidence*.

COMEDY (pp. 1002–1004): Broadly, any literary work designed primarily to amuse. The term is usually reserved for plays whose tone is lighthearted and humorous, that are amusing, and that have a happy ending.

COMIC RELIEF: A comic scene introduced into an otherwise serious or tragic fictional or dramatic work, usually to relieve, if only momentarily, the tension of the plot; often heightens, by contrast, the emotional intensity of the work.

COMPLICATION (pp. 13–15): That part of the plot in which the conflict is developed and intensified; sometimes referred to as the *rising action*.

CONCEIT (pp. 559–561): Usually refers to a startling, ingenious, perhaps even far-fetched, metaphor establishing an analogy or comparison between two apparently incongruous things.

CONCLUSION: See *resolution*.

CONCRETE: Opposite of *abstract*. Language referring directly to what we see, hear, touch, taste, or smell is concrete. Most literature uses concrete language and expresses even abstract concepts concretely through images and metaphors.

CONFIDANT/CONFIDANTE (pp. 40, 995): The individual, often a minor character, to whom a major character reveals, or "confesses," his or her most private thoughts and feelings. Authors and playwrights use the confidant as a device to communicate necessary information to the reader and audience.

CONFLICT (pp. 12–13): The struggle or encounter within the plot of two opposing forces that serves to create reader or audience interest and suspense.

CONNOTATION (pp. 572–574, 602–603): The meaning suggested or implied by a given word or phrase, as opposed to its literal meaning; see *denotation*.

CONSONANCE (pp. 631–633): The repetition in two or more nearby words of similar consonant sounds preceded by different accented vowels. When it occurs at the end of lines, consonance often serves as a substitute for *end rhyme;* see *alliteration.*

CONTROLLING IMAGE: The image or metaphor that runs throughout a literary work and determines its structure or nature.

CONVENTION: Any literary device, technique, style, or form, or any aspect of subject matter, characterization, or theme that has become recognized and accepted by both authors and audiences through repeated use.

COUPLET (pp. 636–638): A single pair of rhymed lines—when they form a complete thought or statement they are referred to as a *closed couplet.*

CRISIS (pp. 13–15, 991–992): That point during the plot when the action reaches its turning point; also called the climax; see *anticlimax.*

CRITICISM: The description, analysis, interpretation, or evaluation of a literary work of art; see also *historical criticism, new criticism, textual criticism, theoretical criticism, and practical criticism.*

DACTYL (DACTYLIC) (p. 619): A foot of an accented syllable followed by two unaccented ones.

DECORUM: The idea, derived from classical theory and thus at times approaching the status of doctrine, that all the elements of a literary work (i.e., setting, character, action, style) must be appropriately related to one another.

DENOTATION (pp. 570–572, 602): The literal, dictionary meaning of a given word or phrase; see *connotation.*

DÉNOUEMENT: From the French word meaning "unknotting" or "untying." A term sometimes used for the final *resolution* of the conflict or complications of the plot.

DEUS EX MACHINA: "God from the machine." Derived from a practice in Greek drama whereby an impersonation of a god was mechanically lowered onto the stage to intervene in and solve the issues of the play. Commonly used today to describe any apparently contrived or improbable device used by an author to resolve the difficulties of plot.

DIALOGUE (pp. 984–990): The conversation that goes on between or among characters in a literary work.

DICTION (pp. 58–59): The author's choice or selection of words (vocabulary). The artistic arrangement of those words constitutes *style.*

DIDACTIC: Literature designed more to teach a lesson or instruct the reader or audience than to present an experience objectively. In a didactic work *theme* is generally the most important element.

DIMETER: A line of poetry consisting of two metrical feet; see *foot.*

DISSONANCE: See *euphony and cacophony.*

DOGGEREL: A deprecatory term for inferior poetry.

DOMESTIC TRAGEDY: A type of tragedy (originating in the eighteenth century as a reflection of its growing middle-class society) in which an ordinary mid-dle-class (or lower-class) protagonist suffers ordinary (although by no means insignificant) disasters; also called bourgeoise tragedy.

DOUBLE ENTENDRE (pp. 581–582): a form of *pun* in which one of the two meanings is risqué or sexually suggestive.

DOUBLE RHYME: See *masculine and feminine rhyme*.

DOWNSTAGE/UPSTAGE (pp. 974–975): *Downstage* is a stage direction referring to the front half of the stage, the part nearest to the audience; *upstage* refers to the back half of the stage.

DRAMATIC MONOLOGUE (p. 635): A type of poem in which a character, at some specific critical moment, addresses an identifiable but silent audience, thereby unintentionally revealing his or her essential temperament and personality.

DRAMATIS PERSONAE: A play's cast of characters.

ELEGY: In its more modern usage, a poem that laments or solemnly mediates on death, loss, or the passing of things of value.

EMPATHY: The state of entering into and actually participating in the emotional, mental, or physical life of an object, person, or literary character.

END RHYME: Rhyme that occurs at the end of lines of poetry; also called terminal rhyme; see *masculine and femine rhyme*.

END-STOPPED LINE (pp. 616–617): A line of poetry that concludes with a pause.

ENGLISH SONNET: See *sonnet*.

ENJAMBMENT (pp. 616–617): A line of poetry that carries its idea or thought over to the next line without a grammatical pause; also called a *run-on line*.

EPIC: A long narrative poem, elevated and dignified in theme, tone, and style, celebrating heroic deeds and historically (at times cosmically) important events; usually focuses on the adventures of a hero who has qualities that are superhuman or divine and on whose fate very often depends the destiny of a tribe, a nation, or even the whole of the human race.

EPIGRAM (pp. 637–638): A short, pointed, and witty statement, either constituting an entire poem (often in the form of a two-line couplet) or "buried" within a larger one.

EPIGRAPH: A quotation prefacing a literary work, often containing a clue to the writer's intention.

EPILOGUE: The final, concluding section of a literary work, usually a play, offered in summation, to point a lesson or moral, or to thank the audience (reader) for its indulgence; see *prologue*.

EPIPHANY: Applied to literature by James Joyce to describe a sudden revelation, or "showing forth," of the essential truth about a character, situation, or experience.

EPISODE (pp. 20; 274): A single unified incident within a narrative that may or may not advance the plot.

EPISTOLARY NOVEL: A type of novel in which the narrative is carried on by means of a series of letters.

EPITHALAMION/EPITHALAMIUM: A song or poem celebrating a wedding, from the Greek meaning "poem upon or at the bridal chamber."

EUPHONY AND CACOPHONY (pp. 631–633): *Euphony* describes language that is harmonious, smooth, and pleasing to the ear. Harsh, nonharmonious, and discordant language is *cacophony;* cacophony is also referred to as *dissonance*.

EXPOSITION (pp. 13–14, 990–991): The part of a work that provides necessary background information.

FABLE: A story with a moral lesson, often employing animals who talk and act like human beings; see *allegory*.

FALLING ACTION (pp. 13–15; 992–994): The part of a dramatic plot that follows the *crisis* (or *climax*) and precedes the *resolution* (or *dénouement*).

FALSE RHYME (p. 628): Rhyme pairing the sounds of accented and unaccented syllables.

FANTASY: A work of fiction that deliberately sets aside everyday reality.

FARCE: A type of comedy which achieves its effect through ridiculous and exaggerated situations, broad, often crude, verbal humor, and various kinds of buffoonery and physical horseplay.

FEMININE RHYME: See *masculine and feminine rhyme*.

FICTION: A prose narrative that is the product of the imagination.

FIGURATIVE LANGUAGE (p. 604): Language used imaginatively and nonliterally. Figurative language is composed of such figures of speech (or tropes) as *metaphor, simile, personification, metonymy, synecdoche, apostrophe, hyperbole, symbol, irony,* and *paradox*.

FLASHBACK (p. 17): The interruption of a story's narrative in order to present an earlier scene or episode; a method of *exposition*.

FOIL (pp. 40; 995): A character who provides a direct contrast to another character.

FOOT (pp. 611–613; 618–621): The basic metrical or rhythmical unit within a line of poetry. A foot of poetry generally consists of an accented syllable and one or more unaccented syllables arranged in a variety of patterns; see *scansion*.

FORESHADOWING: A device by means of which the author hints at something to follow.

FORM: A term used either as a synonym for literary *genre* or type, or to describe the essential organizing structure of a work of art.

FREE VERSE (pp. 564–565; 624–625): A type of poetry that deliberately seeks to free istself from the restrictions imposed by traditionally fixed conventions of meter, rhyme, and stanza.

GENRE: A *form*, class, or type of literary work—e.g., the short story, novel, poem, play, or essay; often used to denote such literary subclassifications as the detective story, the gothic novel, the pastoral elegy, or the revenge tragedy.

HAIKU (p. 643): A Japanese form of poetry; three lines of five, seven, and five syllables, respectively, present a single concentrated image or emotion.

HEPTAMETER: A line of poetry consisting of seven metrical feet; see *foot*.

HERO/HEROINE (p. 19): The central character in a literary work; also often referred to as the *protagonist*.

HEROIC COUPLET: A pair of rhymed iambic pentameter lines; a stanza composed of two heroic couplets is called a *heroic quatrain*.

HIGH COMEDY AND LOW COMEDY: Any type of highly verbal comedy whose appeal is mainly intellectual and sophisticated, often with a basic seriousness of purpose, is *high comedy* (e.g., a *comedy of manners*). *Low comedy* is nonintellectual and lacks serious purpose (e.g., a *farce*).

HIGH STYLE AND LOW STYLE (pp. 557–558; 988–989): *High style* is a formal and elevated literary style rich in poetic devices. *Low style* is casual and conversational in tone and sometimes ungrammatical and colloquial.

HISTORICAL CRITICISM: Seeks to understand and explain a literary work in terms of the author's life and the historical context and circumstances in which it was written.

HUBRIS: The excessive pride, arrogance, or self-confidence that results in the defeat or downfall of the *hero;* see *tragic flaw.*

HYPERBOLE (p. 586): A figure of speech that achieves emphasis and heightened effect (either serious or comic) through deliberate exaggeration.

IAMB (IAMBIC) (pp. 612–613): A foot of an unaccented syllable followed by an accented one.

IDENTICAL RHYME: Rhyme achieved through the repetition of the same word or two words that have the same sound but are spelled differently and have different meanings.

IMAGERY (pp. 587–591): Most commonly refers to visual pictures produced verbally through literal or *figurative language,* although it is often defined more broadly to include sensory experiences other than the visual.

INCONGRUITY (pp. 583–584): A word, phrase, or idea that is out of keeping, inconsistent, or inappropriate in its context.

INITIATION STORY: Commonly used to describe a narrative focusing on a young person's movement from innocence toward maturity as a result of experience.

IN MEDIAS RES (pp. 15; 990): Latin for a narrative that begins "in the middle of things."

INTERIOR MONOLOGUE: See *monologue.*

INTERNAL RHYME (p. 628): Rhyme within a line of poetry; also called middle rhyme.

INTRIGUE: A scheme that one character devises to entrap another, thus providing impetus for the plot.

IRONY (pp. 584–586): Refers to some contrast or discrepancy between appearance and reality.

ITALIAN SONNET: See *sonnet.*

JUXTAPOSITION (pp. 597–598): A form of implied comparison or contrast created by placing two items side by side.

LIMERICK (p. 643): A light, humorous verse form composed of five anapestic lines, rhyming AABBA; lines one, two, and five contain three feet (trimeter), lines three and four contain two (dimeter).

LITERAL: Accurate, exact, and concrete language, i.e., nonfigurative language; see *figurative language.*

LOCALE: See *setting.*

LOW COMEDY: See *high comedy and low comedy.*

LYRIC (p. 635): A short, songlike poem, by a single speaker on a single subject, expressing a personal thought, mood, or feeling.

MASCULINE AND FEMININE RHYME (p. 628): The two most common kinds of end rhyme. *Masculine end rhyme,* predominant in English poetry, consists of accented words of one syllable or polysyllabic words where the final syllable is accented. *Feminine rhyme* (or *double rhyme*) consists of rhyming words of two syllables in which the accent falls on the first syllable. A variation of feminine rhyme, called *triple rhyme,* occurs when there is a correspondence of sound in the final three syllables, an accented syllable followed by two unaccented ones.

MELODRAMA: In its original Greek sense, a "melodrama" meant a play with music (*melos* means "song"). But by the mid-nineteenth century the term had become synonymous with a highly conventionalized type of sensationalistic play pitting stereotypic hero and villain against one another in a series of suspense-ridden, emotion-charged, and violence-filled scenes. The term *melodramatic* is used generally to describe sensational, emotional, and action-oriented writing, e.g., the cowboy western or the gothic novel.

METAPHOR (pp. 593–594): A figure of speech in which two unlike objects are implicitly compared without the use of *like* or *as;* see also *conceit* and *simile.*

METAPHYSICAL POETRY (pp. 559–561): A kind of realistic, often ironic and witty, verse combining intellectual ingenuity and psychological insight written partly in reaction to the conventions of Elizabethan love poetry by such seventeenth-century poets as John Donne, George Herbert, Richard Crashaw, Thomas Traherne, and Andrew Marvell. One of its hallmarks is the metaphysical *conceit,* a particularly interesting and ingenious type of metaphor.

METER: *See rhythm and meter.*

METONYMY (pp. 594–595): A figure of speech in which the name for an object or idea is applied to another with which it is closely associated or of which it is a part.

MIXED METAPHOR (pp. 605–606): Two or more metaphors combined together in such a way as to be incongruous, illogical, or even ludicrous.

MONOLOGUE: An extended speech delivered by a single speaker, alone or in the presence of others. In a general sense, *asides, dramatic monologues,* and *soliloquies* are all types of monologues. When the monologue serves to reveal a character's internal thoughts and feelings, it is sometimes referred to as an interior monologue.

MONOMETER: A line of poetry consisting of a single metrical foot; see *foot.*

MOOD: See *atmosphere.*

MOTIF: An idea, theme, character, situation, or element that recurs in literature or folklore; see *archetype, convention, stock character, stock situation.*

MOTIVE (p. 27): The cause that moves a character to act.

MYTH: Broadly, any idea or belief to which a number of people subscribe.

NARRATIVE: A series of unified events; see *plot* and *action.*

NARRATIVE POEM: (pp. 634–635): A poem that tells a story.

NARRATIVE TECHNIQUE: The author's methods of presenting or telling a story.

NARRATOR: The character or voice that tells the story; see *point of view* and *persona.*

NATURALISM: A post-Darwinian movement of the late nineteenth century that tried to apply the "laws" of scientific determinism to fiction. The naturalist went beyond the realist's insistence on the objective presentation of the details of everyday life to insist that the materials of literature should be arranged to reflect a deterministic universe in which man is a biological creature controlled by his environment and heredity; see *realism.*

NEW CRITICISM: The New Criticism refers to a type or "school" of criticism that seeks to analyze and study a literary work as autonomous, without reference to the author's intention, the impact or effect on the reader, the historical or cultural period in which the work was written (see *historical criticism*), or the validity of the ideas that may be extrapolated from it. Its method is based on the close reading and analysis of the verbal elements of the text, although its leading exponents and practioners (academic critics such as John Crowe Ransom, I. A. Richards, Cleanth Brooks, Robert Penn Warren, Allen Tate, R. P. Blackmur, Yvor Winters, and Kenneth Burke) often disagree on just how this analysis is to be undertaken. The term originates from the title of John Crowe Ransom's book *The New Criticism* (1941) and is "new" in the sense that it constituted a deliberate break with the older subjective and impressionistic theories of art that allowed extrinsic rather than solely intrinsic considerations to influence the evaluation of art.

NOVEL: The name generally applied to any long fictional prose narrative.

NOVELETTE: A longish prose narrative, not long enough to be regarded as a novel but too long to be a short story.

OBLIGATORY SCENE (pp. 991–992): A scene whose circumstances are so fully anticipated by the audience as the plot develops that the playwright is "obliged" to provide it.

OCCASIONAL VERSE: Poetry written to celebrate or commemorate a particular event or occasion.

OCTAMETER: A line of poetry consisting of eight metrical feet.

OCTAVE: See *sonnet*.

ODE (pp. 642–643): A long lyric poem, serious and dignified in subject, tone, and style, sometimes with an elaborate stanzaic structure, often written to commemorate or celebrate an event or individual.

ONOMATOPOEIA (p. 633): A word (or a group of words) whose sound has the effect of suggesting or reinforcing its denotative meaning.

OTTAVA RIMA (p. 641): A stanza of Italian origin consisting of eight iambic pentameter lines rhyming ABABABCC.

OXYMORON: A figure of speech, used for rhetorical effect, which brings together and combines antithetical, paradoxical, or contradictory terms, e.g., "living death," "wise fool," "sweet sorrow."

PARABLE (p. 599): A story designed to convey or illustrate a moral lesson; see *allegory* and *fable*.

PARADOX (pp. 582–584): A self-contradictory and absurd statement that turns out to be, in some sense at least, actually true and valid.

PARAPHRASE (pp. 604–605): A restatement, using different words, of the essential ideas or argument of a piece or passage of writing. To paraphrase a poem is to restate its ideas in prose.

PARODY: See *burlesque*.

PASTORAL: A literary work dealing with, and often celebrating, a rural world and a way of life lived close to nature. *Pastoral* denotes subject matter rather than form; hence, the terms *pastoral lyric, pastoral ode, pastoral elegy, pastoral drama, pastoral epic,* and *pastoral novel*.

PATHETIC FALLACY: A form of personification, which attributes human qualities or feelings to inanimate objects. Although first used disapprovingly by John Ruskin in *Modern Painters* (1856), the phrase today no longer necessarily carries with it Ruskin's negative connotation; see *personification*.

PATHOS: The quality in a literary work that evokes a feeling of pity, tenderness, and sympathy from the reader or audience. Overdone or misused pathos becomes mere *sentimentality*.

PENTAMETER: A line of poetry consisting of five metrical feet; see *foot*.

PERFECT AND IMPERFECT RHYME (pp. 626; 628): In *perfect rhyme* (also called full rhyme or true rhyme) the vowel and any succeeding consonant sounds are identical and the preceding consonant sounds different. Some poets, particularly modern ones, deliberately alternate perfect rhyme with *imperfect rhyme*, in which the correspondence of sound is inexact, approximate, and "imperfect." Imperfectly rhymed words generally contain identical vowels or identical consonants, but not both. Imperfect rhyme is also referred to as approximate rhyme, half-rhyme, near rhyme, oblique rhyme, off-rhyme or slant rhyme. *Alliteration, assonance,* and *consonance* are types of imperfect rhyme.

PERSONA (PL.: PERSONAE): Applied to the voice or mask the author adopts for the purpose of telling the story or "speaking" the words of a lyric poem. The term *persona* is a way of reminding us that the narrator of the work is not to be confused with the author, and should be regarded as another of the author's creations or fictions.

PERSONIFICATION (pp. 595–596): A figure of speech in which an idea or thing is given human attributes or feelings or is spoken of as if it were alive; see also *pathetic fallacy*.

PETRARCHAN SONNET: See *sonnet*.

PICARESQUE NOVEL: Derived from the Spanish word *picaro* meaning "rogue" or "rascal," the term *picaresque novel* generally refers to a basically realistic and often satiric work of fiction chronicling the career of an engaging, lower-class rogue-hero, who takes to the road for a series of loose, episodic adventures, sometimes in the company of a sidekick. Well-known examples of the type are Miguel de Cervante's *Don Quixote* (1605), Henry Fielding's *Tom Jones* (1749), and Daniel Defoe's *Moll Flanders* (1722).

PICTURE POEM (pp. 645–646): A poem printed in such a way as to create a visual image of the object or idea described.

PLOT (pp. 11–18; 990–994): The patterned arrangement of the events in a narrative or play. See also *exposition, complication, crisis, falling action, anticlimax,* and *resolution*.

POETIC JUSTICE: The doctrine (now generally discredited in theory and practice) that good should be rewarded and evil punished—that characters in the end should reap their just rewards.

POETIC LICENSE: Used to describe (and justify) literary experimentation: a writer's deliberate departure from conventions of form and language—and at times even the departure from logic and fact.

POINT OF VIEW (pp. 33–44): The angle or perspective from which a story is told.

POLEMIC: A work vigorously setting forth the author's point of view, usually on a controversial subject.

PREFACE: The author's or editor's introduction, in which the writer states his or her purposes and assumptions and makes any acknowledgments.

PRELUDE: A short poem introducing a longer one.

PROLOGUE: A prefatory statement or speech beginning a literary work, usually a play, preparing the audience for what is to follow; see *epilogue* and *preface*.

PROSCENIUM (p. 970 n.): In modern stagecraft the proscenium is the forward part of the stage between the curtain and the orchestra. The arch from which the curtain hangs is the *proscenium arch*. The area in front of the proscenium is sometimes also referred to as the apron.

PROSODY: The description and study of the underlying principles of poetry, e.g., its meter, rhyme, and stanzaic form.

PROTAGONIST (pp. 19–20; 995): The chief character of a literary work. Also commonly referred to as the *hero* or *heroine;* see *antagonist*.

PUN (pp. 581–582): A play on words, involving words with similar or identical sounds but with different meanings.

QUANTITATIVE METER (pp. 623–624): A metrical system (used originally in Greek and Latin verse) in which units are measured not by stress but by the length of time it takes to pronounce long and short syllables.

QUATRAIN (pp. 638–640): A four line stanza employing a variety of rhyme schemes.

QUINTET (p. 640): A five line stanza employing a variety of rhyme schemes.

REALISM: The nineteenth-century literary movement that reacted to romanticism by insisting on a faithful, objective presentation of the details of everyday life; see *naturalism.*

RECOGNITION SCENE: The moment in a fictional or dramatic work in which one of the characters makes an important (and often decisive) discovery that determines his or her subsequent course of action.

REFRAIN (pp. 577–579): A line, in whole or in part, or a group of lines that recur, sometimes with slight variation, in a poem or song, at the close of a stanza and help to establish meter, sustain mood, or add emphasis. In a song the refrain is usually called the chorus and listeners are expected to join in.

RESOLUTION (pp. 13–15; 992–994): The final section of the plot in which the major conflict, issue, or problem is resolved; also referred to as the *conclusion* or *dénouement.*

REVENGE TRAGEDY: A type of tragedy (popularized in Elizabethan England by the plays of Thomas Kyd and Christopher Marlowe), that turns on the motive of revenge, revels in violence, horror, and other forms of sensationalism, and typically has a bloody ending.

REVERSAL: The protagonist's change of fortune.

RHETORICAL QUESTION: A question to which no response or reply is expected, because only one answer is possible.

RHYME (pp. 626–630): The repetition at regular intervals in a line or lines of poetry of similar or identical sounds based on a correspondence between the vowels and succeeding consonants of accented syllables; see also *end rhyme, false rhyme, identical rhyme, internal rhyme, masculine and feminine rhyme, perfect and imperfect rhyme,* and *visual rhyme;* also *alliteration, assonance* and *consonance.*

RHYME ROYAL (p. 641): A stanza of seven iambic pentameter lines rhyming ABABBCC.

RHYME SCHEME (p. 630): The pattern of end rhymes within a given stanza of poetry.

RISING ACTION: See *complication.*

RHYTHM AND METER (pp. 609–626): *Rhythm* is the general term given to the measured repetition of accent or beat in units of poetry or prose. In English poetry, rhythm is generally established by manipulating both the pattern of accent and the number of syllables in a given line. *Meter* refers to the predominant rhythmic pattern within any given line (or lines) of poetry.

RUBAIS (p. 638): An iambic pentameter quatrain in which the first two lines rhyme with the last one, AAXA.

RUN-ON LINE: See *enjambment.*

SARCASM (p. 586): A form of verbal irony delivered in a derisive, caustic, and bitter manner to belittle or ridicule its subject.

SATIRE (pp. 585–586): A type of writing that holds up persons, ideas, or things to varying degrees of amusement, ridicule, or contempt in order, presumably, to improve, correct, or bring about some desirable change.

SCANSION (pp. 611–624): The analysis of a poem's metrical pattern.

SCENARIO: The brief outline of the plot of a dramatic or literary work, providing the key details of scenes, situations, and characters.

SCENE (p. 959): A self-contained segment of a work of fiction or drama; also used as a synonym for *setting;* see *act.*

SENSUOUS: In literature, *sensuous* refers to writing that appeals to one or more of the reader's five senses.

SENTIMENTALITY: The presence of emotion or feeling that seems excessive or unjustified in terms of the circumstances; see *pathos*.

SEPTET (p. 641): A seven line stanza employing a variety of rhyme schemes.

SESTET: See *Shakespearean sestet* and *sonnet*.

SETTING (pp. 28–33): The time and place in which the action of a story, poem, or play occurs; physical setting alone is often referred to as the *locale*.

SHAKESPEAREAN SESTET (pp. 640–641): A six-line stanza rhyming ABABCC.

SHAKESPEAREAN SONNET: See *sonnet*.

SHORT STORY: A short work of narrative prose fiction. The distinction between the short story and novel is mainly one of length.

SIMILE (pp. 593–594): A figure of speech in which two essentially dissimilar objects are expressly compared with one another by the use of *like* or *as*; see *metaphor* and *figurative language*.

SOLILOQUY (p. 974): A dramatic convention in which a character, alone on stage *(solus)*, speaks aloud and thus shares his or her thoughts with the audience. See *aside* and *monologue*.

SONNET (pp. 643–644): A poem of 14 iambic pentameter lines expressing a single thought or idea and utilizing one of several established rhyme schemes. The sonnet in English generally follows one of two basic patterns: The *Italian sonnet* (or *Petrarchan sonnet* named after the Italian Renaissance poet) consists of an eight-line *octave*, rhyming ABBAABBA, followed by a six-line *sestet*, rhyming variously CDECDE, CDCCDC, etc.; and the *English sonnet* (or *Shakespearean sonnet*) consists of three four-line *quatrains* and a concluding couplet, rhyming ABAB CDCD EFEF GG. A variant of the English sonnet, the *Spenserian sonnet* (named after English poet Edmund Spenser), links its quatrains by employing the rhyme scheme ABAB BCBC CDCD EE.

SPENSERIAN SONNET: See *sonnet*.

SPENSERIAN STANZA (pp. 641–642): A nine-line stanza consisting of eight lines of iambic pentameter and a concluding line of iambic hexameter, rhyming ABABBCBCC—named after English poet Edmund Spenser.

SPONDEE (SPONDAIC) (p. 620): A foot of two accented syllables.

STANZA (pp. 636–643): A group of lines forming a structural unit or division of a poem. Stanzas may be strictly formal units established and patterned (with possible variation) by the similarity of the number and length of their lines, by their meter and rhyme scheme, or as logical units, determined by their thought or content.

STOCK SITUATION: A situation or incident that occurs so frequently in literature as to become at once familiar: e.g., the family feud, the missing heir, the love triangle, the case of mistaken identity.

STREAM OF CONSCIOUSNESS (pp. 25 n.; 40–41): The narrative method of capturing and representing the inner workings of a character's mind.

STRUCTURE: The overall pattern, design, or organization of a literary work.

STYLE (pp. 57–64): The author's characteristic manner of expression; style includes the author's diction, syntax, sentence patterns, punctuation, and spelling, as well as the use made of such devices as sound, rhythm, imagery, and figurative language.

SUBPLOT (p. 15): The subplot (also called the minor plot or underplot) is a secondary action or complication within a fictional or dramatic work that often serves to reinforce or contrast the main plot.

SUSPENSE: The psychological tension or anxiety resulting from the reader's or audience's uncertainty of just how a situation or conflict is likely to end.

SYLLABIC METER (p. 623): A metrical system (common to Japanese and Romance verse but rare in English) in which units are measured by the number of syllables in a line.

SYMBOL (pp. 50–55; 598–599): Literally, something that stands for something else. In literature, any word, object, action, or character that embodies and evokes a range of additional meaning and significance; see *allegory*.

SYNECHDOCHE (pp. 594–595): A figure of speech in which the part is used to signify the whole *or*, less frequently, the whole is used to signify the part.

SYNOPSIS: A summary or resume of a piece of writing.

TERCET (p. 638): A stanza of three lines.

TERZA RIMA (p. 638): A verse form composed of interlocking three-line stanzas, or *tercets* rhyming ABA BCB CDC, etc.

TETRAMETER: A line of poetry consisting of four metrical feet.

TEXTUAL CRITICISM: The kind of scholarship that attempts to establish through reconstruction the "correct" and authoritative text of a literary work as its author originally wrote it.

THEME (pp. 44–50; 607–608): The controlling idea or meaning of a work of art.

THEORETICAL CRITICISM AND PRACTICAL CRITICISM: *Theoretical criticism* is concerned with identifying and establishing the general, underlying principles of art; *practical criticism* (or *applied criticism*) concerns itself with the study and analysis of specific individual works.

THESIS NOVEL/PLAY: A novel or play that deals with a specific problem and advocates a "thesis" in the form of a solution; also called a problem novel or problem play.

TONE (pp. 64–67; 606–607): The author's attitude toward the subject or audience.

TRAGEDY (pp. 1001–1002): Broadly, any serious literary work in which the protagonist suffers a major reversal of fortune, often leading to his or her downfall, destruction, and/or death; see *classical tragedy, domestic tragedy, revenge tragedy, tragicomedy*.

TRAGICOMEDY: A type of drama (most often associated with Elizabethan and Jacobean drama) that mixes the conventions of tragedy and comedy and in which the protagonist, although subject to a series of crises (often including the threat of death), manages to escape to celebrate a happy (and frequently highly contrived) ending.

TRAGIC FLAW (p. 1001): The principal defeat in character or judgment that leads to the downfall of the *tragic hero*. In Greek tragedy this flaw is often *hubris*, the hero's excessive pride or self-confidence.

TRAGIC HERO (pp. 1001–1002): The name given to the protagonist of a tragedy.

TRIMETER: A line of poetry consisting of three metrical feet; see *foot*.

TRIPLE RHYME: See *masculine and feminine rhyme*.

TRIPLET (p. 638): A stanza of three lines rhyming AAA.

TROCHE (TROCHAIC) (p. 618): A foot composed of an accented syllable followed by an unaccented one.

TROPE: Another name for *figure of speech*.

UNRELIABLE NARRATOR (pp. 37–38; 43–44): A narrator whose knowledge and judgments about characters or events is sufficiently incomplete or flawed to render him an unreliable guide to the author's intentions.

VERISIMILITUDE: The quality of being lifelike or true to actuality.

VERSIFICATION: An all-inclusive term for the art and practice of writing poetry.

VISUAL RHYME (p. 629): Words that rhyme to the eye but not to the ear; their spelling is similar, but they are pronounced differently: "plow" and "blow."

WELL-MADE PLAY (PIÈCE BIEN FAITE) (p. 994): A type of play, written according to formula, characterized by a tightly structured, suspenseful plot that turns on a secret; quickly rising action; and a series of reversals, inevitably leading to a climactic scene that reveals the secret and allows the hero to triumph.

Index to Authors, Titles,
and First Lines

Note: First lines are set in roman type; all titles are italicized except titles of poems listed under authors' names.